Patron: Her Majesty the Queen
Established 2002
Incorporated by Royal Charter 1898

CILIP: the Chartered Institute of Library and Information Professionals

YEARBOOK 2002–2003

Compiled by

Kathryn Beecroft

facet publishing

© CILIP: the Chartered Institute of Library and Information Professionals 2003

Published by Facet Publishing
7 Ridgmount Street, London WC1E 7AE

Facet Publishing is wholly owned by CILIP: the Chartered Institute of Library and Information Professionals. CILIP was formed in April 2002 following the unification of the Institute of Information Scientists and The Library Association.

Except as otherwise permitted under the Copyright Designs and Patents Act 1988 this publication may only be reproduced, stored or transmitted in any form or by any means, with the prior permission of the publisher, or, in the case of reprographic reproduction, in accordance with the terms of a licence issued by The Copyright Licensing Agency. Enquiries concerning reproduction outside those terms should be sent to Facet Publishing, 7 Ridgmount Street, London WC1E 7AE.

British Library Cataloguing in Publication Data

A cataloguing record for this book is available from the British Library.

ISBN 1-85604-451-3
ISSN 0075-9066

Typeset by Facet Publishing.
Printed in Great Britain by MPG Books Ltd, Bodmin, Cornwall.

Contents

President's foreword Sheila Corrall **v**

Introduction Bob McKee **vii**

CILIP's Mission ix

Part 1 THE ORGANISATION 1

CILIP offices 3

Website 5

Structure 6

Part 2   GOVERNANCE   11

Council 13

Committees and Panels   16

CILIP Royal Charter 18

Bye-laws 26

Regulations 2002 48

Part 3   GENERAL INFORMATION   107

Affiliated Members National Committee 109

CILIP Benevolent Fund 110

Branches 111

Special Interest Groups 124

Medals and Awards 149

Organisations in Liaison with CILIP 154

CILIP representatives on other bodies 161

Contents

Retired Members Guild 164

Ridgmount Street facilities 165

Subscriptions 168

Suppliers Network 170

Part 4 LIST OF MEMBERS as at 18 November 2002 171

Part 5 HISTORICAL INFORMATION 401

A short history of the Institute of Information Scientists Elspeth Hyams 403

The Library Association 1877-2002 Ross Shimmon 409

Presidents of the Institute of Information Scientists 418

Presidents of The Library Association 419

Honorary Secretaries of the Institute of Information Scientists 422

Secretaries of The Library Association 423

Library Association honorary awards 424

Institute of Information Scientists Award winners 430

Library Association Medal and Award winners 432

Index 445

President's foreword

I am delighted to launch the first CILIP Yearbook. This compendium is the key to understanding what CILIP does, how it works and who is involved. I hope that it will help Members and others to engage with and benefit from our many activities.

Our new organisation came into being only a few months ago but is now up and running and rapidly making its mark in the library and information world and beyond.

We have a member-led governance structure, with committees, panels and boards supporting the work of an elected council; a refurbished building and a stylish corporate identity conveying a modern professional image; and a corporate plan to guide us through a three-year period of transition from our two predecessor bodies.

We have also taken significant steps towards the transformation of CILIP into a responsive technology-enabled association with the setting up of an email discussion list (LIS-CILIP) and the commissioning of a new interactive website with a design to meet the needs of Members identified through extensive consultation and discussion. In addition CILIP has quickly built up its reputation in the international library arena by masterminding the 68th IFLA General Conference and Council in Glasgow which attracted record levels of attendance and earned universal praise for its organisation.

A great deal has been achieved in a remarkably short time and all the CILIP staff, officers and members involved deserve credit for the parts they have played here. However, there is more hard work ahead if we are to achieve our vision of a truly authoritative professional body, effective in education, in enterprise and in advocacy.

We need to take action on areas flagged in our policy discussions on lifelong learning, national information policy, regionalism, social inclusion and a competitive economy. To do this we need to strengthen our links with government and extend our influence beyond departments traditionally associated with libraries to others (such as the DTI). Another key task is to develop a new framework for qualifications which enables us to widen access to chartered status and build a more inclusive profession that values people for their professional

President's foreword

competence and personal commitment irrespective of their career paths and educational backgrounds. We also need to look at the mix of sectoral and specialist interest groups within CILIP, to ensure that they are fit for purpose and that we eliminate the unhelpful overlaps and gaps that currently exist.

CILIP has a challenging agenda but I am confident that we can rise to meet it if we work together to achieve a shared vision of the future. CILIP's success depends on the engagement and commitment of its Members and so I urge you all to play your part.

Sheila Corrall

Introduction

I join with our President in welcoming you to the very first CILIP *Yearbook*. It is designed to be your chief reference source for CILIP: the Chartered Institute of Library and Information Professionals – a new handbook for a new organisation.

The book is designed to reflect the structure and operation of the Institute, and is divided into the following sections: The organisation, Governance, General information and List of Members. Finally, there is a Historical information section drawing together important facts from the heritage of our two predecessor bodies, the Institute of Information Scientists and The Library Association. I am delighted that Elspeth Hyams, former Director of the Institute, and Ross Shimmon, former Chief Executive of the Association have written succint and informative accounts of the history of the two bodies for this section.

The layout is designed to be as clear and uncluttered as possible, and to this end we have adopted the convention of forename and surname with no postnominal letters for the many personal names that appear in the text. Information on Members' style, honours, degrees and affiliations may of course be found in the List of Members section.

CILIP is still very much an evolving organisation, so change to documents, personnel and other information will be ongoing. In some cases we have indicated information that is likely to change during the lifetime of the *Yearbook*; the CILIP website should be used to complement the information printed here.

I trust that you will find this Yearbook a useful tool in your work as an information professional.

Bob McKee

CILIP's mission

CILIP seeks to work for the public good to promote the highest standards of professional practice and service delivery in the library and information domain. CILIP aims to:

- position the library and information profession at the heart of the information society
- develop and enhance the roles and skills of all its Members, enabling them to achieve and maintain the highest professional standards, both for the professional and the public good
- present and champion those skills, including the new skills that will be acquired through continuing professional development
- set, maintain, monitor and promote standards of excellence in the creation, management, exploitation and sharing of information and knowledge resources
- support the principle of equality of access to information, ideas and works of the imagination, which it affirms is fundamental to a thriving economy, democracy, culture and civilisation.

Part 1
THE ORGANISATION

CILIP offices

CILIP: the Chartered Institute of Library and Information Professionals

7 Ridgmount Street
London WC1E 7AE
Telephone: +44 (0)20 7255 0500
Fax: +44 (0)20 7255 0501
Text phone: +44 (0)20 7255 0505
E-mail: info@cilip.org.uk.
Website: www.cilip.org.uk
Switchboard hours: Monday–Friday 08.30–18.00. An electronic queueing system is in operation: calls are answered in sequence.

CILIP in Scotland

1st floor Building C
Brandon Gate
Leechlee Road
Hamilton ML3 6AU
Telephone: +44 (0)1698 458888
Fax: +44 (0)1698 458899
E-mail: cilips@slainte.org.uk
Website: www.slainte.org.uk/CILIPS/clpshome.htm

CILIP Wales/CILIP Cymru

c/o Department of Information and Library Studies
University of Wales Aberystwyth
Llanbadarn Fawr
Aberystwyth
Ceredigion SY23 3AS
Telephone: +44 (0)1970 622174
Fax: +44 (0)1970 622190
E-mail: hle@aber.ac.uk
Website: http://users.aber.ac.uk/hle/

CILIP offices

CILIP in Ireland

Executive Secretary, CILIP in Ireland
BELB
40 Academy Street
Belfast
Northern Ireland BT1 2NQ
Telephone: +44 (0)28 9056 4011
Fax: +44(0)28 9033 1714
E-mail: elgal@belb.co.uk
Website: www.cilip.org.uk/ireland

Statutory information

Registered Charity Number: 313014
VAT Number: GB 233 1573 87
Solicitors: Bates, Wells and Braithwaite
Bankers: Bank of Scotland
Auditors: Kingston Smith

Website

A new CILIP website is under development. The aim is to transform the current website into an interactive and dynamic tool, which will play a key role in CILIP's communication with its Members and other stakeholders. It will also be key to the effective delivery of up-to-date information, the conduct of the Institute's business, the rolling out of services to Members countrywide, and the sale of products and services.

A wide survey of Member requirements was undertaken under the guidance of specialist consultants, resulting in a Statement of Requirements. The new website will be built during the course of 2003 following a tendering process.

In the interim the current website provides information about CILIP and some services such as the CILIP training directory, an online Buyers' Guide, and a calendar of Branch and Group events. Facet Publishing and Library and Information Appointments have their own searchable websites.

Website address: www.cilip.org.uk
Web Manager: Alan Cooper
    alan.cooper@cilip.org.uk
Web Editor: Juliet Owen
    juliet.owen@cilip.org.uk

Structure

Chief Executive's Directorate

The Chief Executive is responsible for the management of the Institute and leads the Management Board.

Chief Executive: Bob McKee
bob.mckee@cilip.org.uk

External Relations and Marketing

Responsible for internal and external communications, advocacy, public affairs and media relations, promoting the Institute including Awards and PR campaigns.

Head of External Relations: Tim Owen
tim.owen@cilip.org.uk

Finance

Provides financial information, advice and services to staff, committees, Branches and Groups. Responsible for pension scheme and membership benefits.

Head of Finance: Rowena Wells
rowena.wells@cilip.org.uk

ICT

Responsible for the central computing and telecommunications systems.

Acting ICT Manager: Emma Haynes
emma.haynes@cilip.org.uk

Personnel and Administration

Responsible for employment matters, staff recruitment and training, buildings management, health and safety, room bookings and catering.

Head, Personnel and Administration: Teresa Haskins
teresa.haskins@cilip.org.uk

Policy and Advice

The Policy Unit seeks to co-ordinate the development of policy across CILIP and facilitate effective dealing with cross-cutting issues, primarily through the use of Executive Advisory Groups. The Unit liaises closely with other professional adviser staff and retains specific policy responsibility for the public library sector.

Principal Policy Adviser: Guy Daines
guy.daines@cilip.org.uk

Membership Services Directorate

The Directorate of Member Services provides a range of direct and indirect support activities, which focus on Members' needs and promote the profile of the profession to key decision makers.

The Directorate consists of three teams: Membership, Careers & Qualifications (MCQ); International Relations & Information Services (IRIS) and the Advisory team, who work closely with the Director on professional strategy and advocacy matters.

Director: Sue Brown
sue.brown@cilip.org.uk

Advisory team

Youth and School Libraries Adviser: Jonathan Douglas
jonathan.douglas@cilip.org.uk
Post-16 Learning Adviser: Kathy Ennis
kathy.ennis@cilip.org.uk
Information and Knowledge Management Adviser: Mark Field
mark.field@cilip.org.uk
Workplace and Solo Adviser: Lyndsay Rees-Jones
lyndsay.rees-jones@cilip.org.uk

International Relations & Information Services

Head of International Relations & Information Services: Jill Martin
jill.martin@cilip.org.uk

Membership, Careers & Qualifications

Head of Membership, Careers & Qualifications: Marion Huckle
marion.huckle@cilip.org.uk

Structure

CILIP Enterprises

These income-generating activities make up the business portfolio of CILIP. They offer a range of products and services to Members and the wider information community both nationally and internationally, to contribute professionally and financially to CILIP's mission and objectives.

Managing Director: Janet Liebster
janet.liebster@cilip.org.uk

Advertising and *Library and Information Appointments*

Produces the fortnightly recruitment magazine *Appointments*, sent to all Members, and its website www.lisjobnet.org.uk; also responsible for the sale of advertising space in *Library & Information Update*.

Head of Advertising: Andrew Nelson-Cole
andrew.nelson-cole@cilip.org.uk

Conferences

Organiser of conferences, exhibitions and other special events.

Head of Conferences: Rob Palmer [retires March 2003]
rob.palmer@cilip.org.uk
Conferences & Exhibitions Executive: Joan Thompson
joan.thompson@cilip.org.uk

CILIP Consultancy Services

Undertakes a wide range of information-related consultancy and project work, often involving a network of consultants and associates.

Head of CILIP Consultancy Services: David Haynes
david.haynes@cilip.org.uk

Facet Publishing

Leading publisher of books and other materials for the worldwide information profession. To order: contact Bookpoint Ltd, Mail Order Department, 130 Milton Park, Abingdon, Oxon OX14 4SB; Telephone: +44 (0)1235 827794; Fax: +44 (0)1235 400454; Facet@bookpoint.co.uk or visit www.facetpublishing.co.uk.

Publishing Director: Helen Carley
helen.carley@facetpublishing.co.uk

INFOmatch

A recruitment service for library and information staff, offering both permanent and temporary posts at all levels, across all sectors and throughout the UK.

Head of INFOmatch: Susan Baillie
susan.baillie@cilip.org.uk

Library & Information Update

The monthly news-led magazine with features covering events and issues in all sectors. This is sent free to all Members and is also available on subscription.

Editor: Elspeth Hyams
elspeth.hyams@cilip.org.uk

Training and Development

Offers a programme of professional development courses, workshops, seminars, briefings, on-site and tailor-made training and distance learning packages.

Head of Training and Development: Penny Simmonds
penny.simmonds@cilip.org.uk

Structure

CILIP in Scotland

Director of CILIP in Scotland and the Scottish Library and Information Council: Elaine Fulton
1st floor Building C, Brandon Gate
Leechlee Road
Hamilton ML3 6AU
Telephone: +44 (0)1698 458888
Fax: +44 (0)1698 458899
E-mail: cilips@slainte.org.uk
Website: www.slainte.org.uk/CILIPS/clpshome.htm

CILIP Wales/CILIP Cymru

Executive Officer, CILIP Wales/CILIP Cymru: Huw Evans
c/o Department of Information and Library Studies
University of Wales Aberystwyth
Llanbadarn Fawr
Aberystwyth
Ceredigion SY23 3AS
Telephone: +44 (0)1970 622174
Fax: +44 (0)1970 622190
E-mail: hle@aber.ac.uk
Website: http://users.aber.ac.uk/hle/

CILIP in Ireland

Executive Secretary, CILIP in Ireland: Elga Logue
BELB
40 Academy Street
Belfast
Northern Ireland BT1 2NQ
Telephone: +44 (0)28 9056 4011
Fax: +44 (0)28 9033 1714
E-mail: elgal@belb.co.uk
Website: www.cilip.org.uk/ireland

Part 2
GOVERNANCE

Council

Honorary Officers

President
Sheila Corrall (University of Southampton)

President-Elect
Margaret Watson (University of Northumbria at Newcastle)

Immediate Past Presidents
Peter Enser (University of Brighton)
Bernard Naylor

Honorary Treasurer
Keith Webster (School of Oriental & African Studies)

Chair of Council
Sandra Ward (TFPL)

National Councillors
Until March 2003

Suzanne Burge (The Ombudsman's Office)
Liz Dubber (Gloucestershire County Council)
Kate Gardner (Worcester College of Technology)
Shelagh Levett (Bournemouth Council)

Until March 2004

Anne McIlwaine (School of Oriental & African Studies)
Martin Stone (Calderdale Council)
Pearl Valentine (NE Education and Library Board)
Sandra Ward (TFPL)

Until March 2005

Barry Cropper (Corporation of London)
Peter Griffiths (Home Office)
Liz MacLachlan (Department of Trade & Industry)
Debby Shorley (University of Sussex)

Council

Branch Councillors
Until March 2003
CILIP in Ireland: Barry Harrington (Enterprise Ireland)
Eastern: Lesley Noblett (Cambridgeshire County Council)
London & Home Counties: Barry Walkinshaw (London Borough of Bromley)
South Western: Brian Hinton (Julia Margaret Cameron Trust)

Until March 2004
CILIP in Wales: Lloyd Ellis (Neath Port Talbot Borough Council)
East Midlands: Mandy Hicken
Northern: Peter Harbord (University of Durham)
West Midlands: Pat Beech (National Library for the Blind)

Until March 2005
Berks, Bucks & Oxon: Norman Briggs
CILIP in Scotland: Audrey Walker (Signet Library, Edinburgh)
North Western: Fiona Hughes (Manchester Metropolitan University)
Yorkshire & Humberside: Alison Jobey (Sheffield City Council)

Group Councillors
Until March 2003
Affiliated Members: Heather Hedges (Shropshire County Council)
Career Development: Tracy Long (Solihull Metropolitan Borough Council)
Health Libraries: Tony McSeán (British Medical Association)
Local Studies: Elizabeth Melrose (North Yorkshire County Council)
Multimedia & Technology: Catherine Hume (Royal Institute of International Affairs)
Patents & Trademarks: Ann Chapman (Minesoft Ltd)
Prison Libraries: Cathy Evans (Worcestershire County Council)

Until March 2004
Affiliated Members: Karen Newton (Sunderland Metropolitan Borough Council)
Branch and Mobile Libraries: Brian Chapman (Hull City Council)
Colleges of Further & Higher Education: Jacqui Weetman (De Montfort University)
Education Librarians: Diana Rolf (Freman College)

Government Libraries: Sue Westcott (Department of the Environment, Transport and the Regions)
Information Services: Amanda Duffy (retired)
Industrial & Commercial Libraries: Elizabeth Dwiar (Field Fisher Waterhouse)
Personnel, Training and Education: Sheron Burton (Royal Society of Medicine)
Public Libraries: Martin Molloy (Derbyshire County Council)
School Libraries: Gill Purbrick (Eltham Hill School)

Until March 2005

Cataloguing and Indexing: Kayla Tomlinson (Rutherford Appleton Laboratory)
Community Services: Howard Matthew (Sheffield Central Library)
International Library and Information: Barbara Turfan (School of Oriental & African Studies)
Library History: John Crawford (Glasgow Caledonian University)
Publicity and Public Relations: Alasdair MacNaughtan (Plymouth City Council)
Rare Books: George Lilley (University of Wales)
UK Online User Group: Karen Blakeman (RBA Information Services)
University, College & Research Libraries: Andrew McDonald (University of Sunderland)
Youth Libraries: Annie Everall (Derbyshire County Council)

Committees and Panels

Executive Board (XB)
Chair: Barry Cropper

Reporting to XB are:
Equal Opportunities and Diversity Panel
Home Nations Forum
various Executive Advisory Groups

Disciplinary Committee
Chair: Kayla Tomlinson

Enterprise Board (EB)
Chair: Anne McIlwaine

Reporting to EB are
Facet Publishing Advisory Panel
Training and Development Advisory Panel
'Umbrella' 2003 Planning Group
Update Editorial Board

Policy Development Committee (Pol.DC)
Chair: Debby Shorley

Reporting to Pol.DC are
Freedom of Information Panel
International Panel
Post 16 Learning Panel
Preservation and Conservation Panel
Public Libraries Panel
Workplace and Information Services Panel
Youth and Schools Panel

Professional Development Committee (PDC)

Chair: Fiona Hughes

Reporting to PDC are:
Accreditation Board
Chartership Board

Professional Practice Committee (PPC)

Chair: Sue Westcott

Reporting to PPC are
Ethics Panel
JIS Editorial Board
Membership Recruitment and Retention Panel

Further information

Administrator, Chief Executive's Office: Frances Collett
frances.collett@cilip.org.uk

CILIP Royal Charter

ELIZABETH THE SECOND by the Grace of God of the United Kingdom of Great Britain and Northern Ireland and of Our other Realms and Territories Queen, Head of the Commonwealth, Defender of the Faith:

TO ALL TO WHOM THESE PRESENTS SHALL COME, GREETINGS!

WHEREAS Her Majesty Queen Victoria in the year of our Lord One thousand eight hundred and ninety eight by Royal Charter (hereinafter called 'the Original Charter') dated the seventh day of February in the sixty first year of Her Reign constituted a Body Corporate by the name of The Library Association (hereinafter called 'the Association') with perpetual succession and with power to sue and to be sued by this name and to use a Common Seal:

AND WHEREAS the Original Charter was amended by an Order in Council dated the sixteenth day of December One Thousand Nine Hundred and Eighty Six:

AND WHEREAS it has been represented unto Us that the Association seeks with others to unite all persons engaged or interested in library work and information science for the purpose of promoting the development of libraries and information services and the advancement of information science for the public benefit and to that end the Association has resolved to change its name to the Chartered Institute of Library and Information Professionals:

WHEREAS it has been represented unto Us by the Association that it is expedient to revise the objects and powers of the Association and that the provisions of the Original Charter, except in so far as they incorporate the Association, should be replaced:

NOW, THEREFORE, KNOW YE that We, by virtue of Our Prerogative Royal and of all other powers enabling Us so to do, have, of Our especial grace, certain knowledge and mere motion, granted and declared and by these Presents for Us, Our Heirs and Successors, grant and declare as follows:

Interpretation

1. In this Our Charter unless the context otherwise requires:
    i. 'the Institute' shall mean the Chartered Institute of Library and Information Professionals;
    ii. 'the Charter' means the Charter of Incorporation of the Institute;
    iii. 'the Byelaws' shall mean the Byelaws set out in the Schedule below as amended from time to time as provided below;
    iv. 'a Member' means a member of the Institute;
    v. 'a Corporate Member' means a corporate member of the Institute
    vi. 'the Council' means the Council for the time being appointed pursuant to the Charter and the Byelaws;
    vii. 'Council Member' means a member of the Council;
    viii. Words denoting the singular number include the plural and vice versa;
    ix. Words importing the masculine gender include the feminine gender; and
    x. Words importing persons include corporations.

Objects and powers

2. The objects of the Institute shall be to work for the benefit of the public to promote education and knowledge through the establishment and development of libraries and information services and to advance information science (being the science and practice of the collection, collation, evaluation and organised dissemination of information) and for that purpose the Institute shall have power to do all or any of the following things:

    a. **to foster and promote education, training, invention and research in matters connected with information science and libraries and information services and to collect, collate and publish information, ideas, data and research relating thereto;**

    b. **to unite all persons engaged or interested in information science and libraries and information services by holding conferences and meetings for the discussion of questions and matters affecting information science**

and libraries and information services or their regulation or management and any other questions or matters relating to the objects of the Institute;

c. to promote the improvement of the knowledge, skills, position and qualifications of librarians and information personnel;

d. to promote study and research in librarianship and information science and to disseminate the results;

e. to promote and encourage the maintenance of adequate and appropriate provision of library and information services of various kinds throughout the United Kingdom, the Channel Islands and the Isle of Man;

f. to scrutinise any legislation affecting the provision of library and information services and to promote such further legislation as may be considered necessary to that end;

g. to represent and act as the professional body for persons working in or interested in library and information services;

h. to maintain a register of Chartered Members and Certified Affiliates qualified to practise as professional librarians and information personnel;

i. to ensure the effective dissemination of appropriate information of interest to members;

j. to work with similar institutes overseas and with appropriate international bodies to promote the widespread provision of adequate and appropriate library and information services;

k. to provide appropriate services to Members in furtherance of these objectives;

l. to form and promote the formation of branches, sections or groups of the Institute in any part of the world and to dissolve branches, sections or groups so established;

m. to print and publish and to sell, lend and distribute any communications, papers or treatises which are relevant to the objects of the Institute;

n. to raise funds and to invite and receive contributions provided that the Institute shall in raising funds not undertake any substantial trading activities and shall

conform to any relevant statutory regulations;
o. to invest the monies of the Institute not immediately required for the furtherance of its objects in or upon such investments, securities or property as may be thought fit;
p. to purchase, take on lease or in exchange, hire, or otherwise acquire any real or personal property necessary for or conducive to the objects of the Institute and to maintain and equip the same for use in furtherance thereof;
q. to borrow or raise money with or without security for the objects of the Institute provided that no money shall be raised by mortgage of any real or leasehold property of the Institute situate in Our United Kingdom without such consent or approval (if any) as may be by law required;
r. to sell, manage, lease, mortgage or dispose of all or any part of the property of the Institute, provided that no disposition of any real or leasehold property situate in our United Kingdom shall be made without such consent or approval (if any) as may be by law required;
s. to make and give effect to any arrangements for the joint working or co-operation with any other society or body, whether incorporated or not, carrying on work which is within the objects of the Institute;
t. to undertake, execute and perform any trusts or conditions affecting any real or personal property of any description acquired by the Institute;
u. generally to do all other lawful acts whatsoever that are conducive or incidental to the attainment of the objects of the Institute.

Income and property

3. The income and property of the Institute wheresoever derived shall be applied solely towards the promotion of the objects of the Institute as set forth in this Our Charter, and no portion thereof shall be paid or transferred directly or indirectly by way of dividend, bonus or otherwise howsoever by way of profit to any Member of the Institute and save as hereinafter provided no Council Member shall be appointed to any office of the

Institute paid by salary or fees or receive remuneration from the Institute: provided that nothing herein contained shall prevent the payment in good faith by the Institute:

a. (not being a Council Member) in return for services actually rendered or reasonable and proper pensions to former employees of the Institute or their dependants;

b. to any Council Member who possesses specialist skills or knowledge required by the Institute for its proper administration of reasonable fees for work of that nature done by the Council Member when instructed by the Institute to act on its behalf but on condition that:
   i. at no time may a majority of the Council benefit under this provision; and
   ii. a Council Member must withdraw from any meeting whilst his or her appointment or remuneration is being discussed;

c. of reasonable and proper rent for premises demised or let by any Member of the Institute;

d. of reasonable and proper interest on money borrowed by the Institute from a Member for the objects of the Institute;

e. of reasonable and proper out of pocket expenses incurred by any Member or Council Member on behalf of the Institute;

f. of all reasonable and proper premiums in respect of trustees' indemnity insurance effected in accordance with Article 8 of this Our Charter.

Members

4. The members of the Institute shall consist of such persons and shall have such rights and privileges as may be prescribed by the Byelaws of the Institute for the time being to be framed in pursuance of this Our Charter.

5. There shall be such classes of Corporate and non-Corporate members of the Institute as the Byelaws shall prescribe. The qualifications, method and terms of admission, rights, privileges and obligations of each such class of membership and the disciplinary arrangements to which Members shall be subject shall be as the Byelaws and Regulations of the Institute

prescribe. Members may be designated as belonging to the Institute by such abbreviations as the Byelaws shall prescribe. No other abbreviation to indicate a class of membership may be used.

Council

6. The powers of the Institute shall be vested in a Council elected in accordance with the Byelaws and which may in respect of the affairs of the Institute exercise all such powers and do all such things as may lead to the furtherance of the objects of the Institute including all such powers and things as may be exercised or done by the Institute and are not by this Our Charter or the Byelaws expressly directed or required to be exercised or done by the Institute in general meeting.

7. In the execution of their powers under this Our Charter, no Council Member shall be liable for any loss to the property of the Institute arising by reason of any improper investment made in good faith (so long as where appropriate advice shall have been sought before making such investment) or for the negligence or fraud of any other Council Member or by reason of any mistake or omission made in good faith by any Council Member or by reason of any other matter or thing whatsoever except wilful and individual fraud, wrongdoing or wrongful omission on the part of the Council Member.

8. The Council may pay out of the funds of the Institute the cost of any premium in respect of insurance or indemnities to cover any liability of the Council (or any Council Member) which by virtue of any rule of law would otherwise attach to them in respect of any negligence, default, breach of duty or breach of trust of which they may be guilty in relation to the Institute; provided that any such insurance or indemnity shall not extend to any claim arising from criminal or wilful or deliberate neglect or default on the part of the Council (or Council Member).

Committees

9. The Council may delegate any of its powers to an Executive Board or to any standing committee or subcommittee consisting of such Council Members or such Members of the Institute

as it thinks fit provided that the chair of the Executive Board shall be a Council Member. The Executive Board or any other such standing committee or subcommittee so formed shall, in the exercise of the powers so delegated, conform to any regulations or directions that may from time to time be imposed upon it by the Council and shall report back as soon as practicable to the Council.

General meetings

10. Meetings of the Institute shall be convened and the proceedings there regulated in accordance with the Byelaws.

Byelaws

11. The affairs of the Institute shall be managed and regulated in accordance with the Byelaws which shall remain in force until revoked, amended or added to as provided below.

Supplementary provisions

12. The provisions of the Original Charter, except insofar as they incorporate the Institute and confer upon it perpetual succession and a Common Seal, are hereby revoked, but nothing in this revocation shall affect the legality or validity of any act, deed or thing lawfully done or executed under the provisions of the Original Charter.

13. The Byelaws scheduled in the Original Charter as amended from time to time shall be deemed to be and shall continue to be the Byelaws of the Institute. Any of the Byelaws may from time to time be revoked, amended or added to by a resolution passed by a majority of not less than two thirds of the Corporate Members voting in person or by proxy at a duly convened General Meeting of the Institute provided that no new Byelaw and no such revocation, amendment or addition as aforesaid shall have any force or effect if it be repugnant to any of the provisions of this Our Charter or the laws of Our Realm, nor until it shall have been approved by Our Privy Council of which approval a certificate under the hand of the Clerk of Our Privy Council shall be conclusive evidence. This provision shall apply to the Byelaws as revoked, altered or added to in manner aforesaid.

14. The Institute may by resolution in that behalf passed by a majority of not less than two-thirds of the Corporate Members voting in person or by proxy on the question at a duly convened general meeting of the Institute alter, amend or add to any of the provisions of this Our Charter and such alteration, amendment or addition shall, when approved by Us, Our Heirs or Successors in Council become effectual so that this Our Charter shall thenceforward continue and operate as though it had been originally granted and made accordingly. This provision shall apply to this Our Charter as altered, amended or added to in manner aforesaid.

15. The Institute may by resolution passed by a majority of not less than two-thirds of the Corporate Members voting in person or by proxy on the question at a duly convened general meeting of the Institute surrender this Our Charter subject to the sanction of Us, Our Heirs or Successors in Council and upon such terms as We or They may consider fit and wind up or otherwise deal with the affairs of the Institute in such manner as they shall be directed by the special resolution having due regard to the liabilities of the Institute for the time being and if on the winding up or dissolution of the Institute there shall remain after satisfaction of debts and liabilities any properties whatsoever, that property shall not be paid or distributed among the Members of the Institute or any of them but shall subject to any special trust affecting the same be given and transferred to some other charitable Institute or Institutes having objects similar to the objects of the Institute to be determined by the Corporate Members of the Institute at or before the time of dissolution.

IN WITNESS whereof We have caused these Our Letters to be made Patent.

WITNESS Ourself at Westminster the Twenty-first day of May in the Fifty-first Year of Our Reign.

Bye-laws

Made by Council 16 June 1986, as approved by the Annual General Meeting on 10 September 1986 and as allowed by Her Majesty's Privy Council on 15 December 1986. Revised in 1987, 1989 and 1997 and 2001

SECTION 1
Interpretation

1. In the event of any inconsistency between the provisions of the Charter and the provisions of the Bye-laws the provisions of the Charter shall prevail.

2. In these Bye-laws, unless the context otherwise requires: Expressions or words used in the Charter shall have the meanings there defined;

2.1 The expressions "Corporate Member", "non-Corporate Member", "Chartered Fellow", "Chartered Member", "Associate", "Affiliate", "Certified Affiliate", "Supporting Member", "Institutional Member", "Honorary Fellow", "President", "Past President", "President Elect", "Honorary Treasurer", "Chair of Council", "Chair of the Executive Board" and "the Secretary" shall be read and construed as if the words "of the Institute" were inserted thereafter.

2.3 The following expressions have the following meaning:

"The Honorary Officers" means the President, the Past President, the President Elect, the Honorary Treasurer, the Chair of Council and the Chair of the Executive Board.

"Corporate Member" means a Chartered Fellow, an Honorary Fellow, a Chartered Member or an Associate of the Institute.

"non-Corporate Member" means an Affiliate, a Certified Affiliate, a Supporting Member or an Institutional Member.

"Branch" means a body of members within a geographical area as defined from time to time by the Council.

"Special Interest Group" and "Group" means a group established with the approval of the Council to further specialist interests within the Institute.

"General Meeting" means a general meeting in which the Corporate Members assemble.

3. Where these Bye-laws confer any power to make regulations that power shall be construed as including power to rescind, revoke, amend or vary any regulations made in pursuance of that power.

SECTION 2
Membership

4. The categories of membership of the Institute shall be:

4.1 *Corporate Members*
   (a) Chartered Fellows;
   (b) Honorary Fellows;
   (c) Chartered Members;
   (d) Associates: persons who are eligible for election as Chartered Members but are not Chartered Members or Chartered Fellows or Honorary Fellows of the Institute.

4.2 *Non-Corporate Members*
   (a) Affiliates: persons working in libraries or information services not eligible for election as Chartered Fellows, Chartered Members or Associates of the Institute;
   (b) Certified Affiliates;
   (c) Supporting Members: persons interested in the objects of the Institute not eligible for election in any other category;
   (d) Institutional Members: corporate bodies, societies and other organisations which maintain or are interested in libraries or information services;

The decision of Council on the allocation of applicants for membership to the categories set out above shall be final.

Election of Members

5. Members shall be elected by the Council in accordance with the

procedures prescribed in regulations made and published by the Council.

The Council shall have power to reinstate any Member whose membership has been cancelled for any reason, and may cause reinstatement to be subject to previous compliance with such conditions as it may determine, including the payment of subscriptions in arrear.

6. Non-corporate membership shall be subject to the following terms and restrictions:
    (a) Affiliates and Certified Affiliates shall enjoy all the privileges of a Member but shall not be entitled to vote at general meetings nor in the election of members of Council nor to hold office in the Institute save that:
        (i) such Members shall be entitled to vote and to be elected in elections for the two Council Members elected in accordance with Bye-law 51;
        (ii) such Members shall be entitled to vote in elections of Group and Branch Council Members for any Group or Branch of which they are members.
    (b) Institutional Members shall be entitled to appoint one or more representatives being members of their Governing Body or other persons nominated by them and approved by the Council of the Institute. Such representatives shall enjoy all the privileges of a member except that they shall not be entitled to be elected or to remain on the Register of Chartered Members unless they are themselves a Chartered Fellow or Chartered Member and they shall not by virtue of their nomination by an Institutional Member be entitled to vote at general meetings or in the election of members of the Council;
    (c) Supporting Members shall enjoy all the privileges of membership except that they shall not be entitled to vote at general meetings or in the election of members of Council nor to hold any office in the Institute other than the offices of President Elect, President and Past President.

7. All the privileges of membership shall be enjoyed by a Member for his or her own benefit and the Member shall not be entitled to transfer such privileges or any of the benefits derived there-

from to any other person, firm, company or body.

8. The Council shall have power to nominate as Honorary Fellows persons who in the opinion of the Council have rendered distinguished service in promoting the objects of the Institute.

SECTION 3
Professional Qualifications

9. There shall be maintained at the offices of the Institute a Register containing the names of those members who are either Chartered Fellows or Chartered Members of the Institute and a Register containing the names of those Members who are Certified Affiliates of the Institute.

10. Copies of the Register of Chartered Fellows and Chartered Members and the Register of Certified Affiliates shall be published in such manner and at such intervals as the Council shall decide.

11. The Council shall from time to time make regulations for the purpose of testing the proficiency of Members desiring to be elected to the Register of Chartered Fellows and Chartered Members and the proficiency of Affiliates desiring to be elected to the Register of Certified Affiliates and the continuing proficiency of Members and Affiliates so elected.

12. The Council shall have power to grant exemption from the provisions contained in the Regulations or parts thereof to Members who are considered by the Council to have satisfied criteria equivalent to those contained in the Regulations.

13. The Secretary shall cause to be published the names of those elected to the Register of Chartered Fellows and Chartered Members and those elected to the Register of Certified Affiliates.

14. The Council shall issue to each Member who is elected to the Register of Chartered Members a Certificate of Chartered Membership or Chartered Fellowship respectively and to each Member who is elected to be a Certified Affiliate of the

Bye-laws

Institute an Affiliated Membership Certificate.

15. Chartered Members and Chartered Fellows shall have the right to use the letters MCLIP and FCLIP respectively after their names and may describe themselves as "Chartered Member of the CILIP" and "Chartered Fellow of the CILIP" respectively, but only so long as they remain on the Register. Honorary Fellows shall have the right to use the letters HonFCLIP after their names, but may not describe themselves as "Chartered Fellow of the CILIP" or "Chartered Member of CILIP" unless they have been elected to the Register of Chartered Fellows and Chartered Members under the provisions of these Bye-laws.

16. Certified Affiliates of the Institute shall have the right to use the letters CertACLIP after their name and may describe themselves as "Certified Affiliate of the CILIP", but only so long as they remain on the Register.

17. The Council shall have power to cancel the registration of any Chartered Fellow, Chartered Member or Certified Affiliate whose membership is terminated for any reason and to reinstate the registration when such Fellow, Member or Affiliate has been reinstated to membership under Bye-law 5. The Council may specify the conditions under which reinstatement may be made, including the payment of a further registration fee.

Subscriptions

18. The Institute in general meeting shall have power to determine the amount of all subscriptions, entrance, registration, admission and other fees (except for examination fees) payable by the members. The Council, however, shall have the power to make regulations for the payment of subscriptions (including payment by instalment), for suspension and expulsion from the Institute in the case of a Member failing to pay. The Council may also make regulations admitting persons to membership or continuing Members in membership at reduced subscriptions. Members paying reduced subscriptions shall enjoy all the privileges of membership, including voting and the receipt of publications usually distributed to Members, but the Council may provide that they may not hold office. The amount of examination fees shall be determined from time to time by the Council.

SECTION 4
Conduct of Members

19. The Council shall have power to issue a Code of Professional Conduct setting out the standards of professional behaviour expected of Members of the Institute and may from time to time amend the Code or any part or parts thereof.

20. Every Member of the Institute shall observe the provisions of the Charter and the Bye-laws and shall conduct him or herself in such a manner as shall not prejudice his or her professional status or the reputation of the Institute and without prejudice to the generality of the foregoing shall, in particular, comply at all times with any Code of Professional Conduct prescribed and published by the Council under the provisions of the last preceding Bye-law.

21. The Council may make and publish Regulations for the conduct of the disciplinary proceedings in respect of any complaint made against a member of any action contrary to the aims, objects and interests of the Institute or of conduct unbecoming or prejudicial to the profession including power to reprimand a Member or suspend or expel a Member from the Institute and may establish a Disciplinary Committee and such other committees as it sees fit for the conduct of such proceedings.

SECTION 5
General Meetings

22. The Annual General Meeting of the Institute shall be held once in every year at such place and at such time as the Council may determine, provided that no more than sixteen months shall elapse between such meetings.

23. All general meetings other than the Annual General Meeting of the Institute shall be called Extraordinary General Meetings.

24. The Council may whenever it thinks fit convene an Extraordinary General Meeting and the Secretary shall convene an Extraordinary General Meeting within one calendar month of receiving a requisition from any ten Council Members or any one hundred Corporate Members, provided that the pur-

pose for which the meeting is to be called is stated in the requisition.

25. The Council may make and publish Regulations for the submission of motions to Annual General Meetings.

26. One month's notice in writing at the least of every Annual General Meeting and twenty one days notice in writing at the least of every Extraordinary General Meeting (exclusive in every case both of the day on which it is served or deemed to be served and of the day for which it is given) specifying the place, the day and the hour of the meeting and in the case of special business the nature of that business, shall be given to the Members and to the auditors of the Institute.

27. The accidental omission to give notice of a general meeting to any person entitled to receive such notice shall not invalidate anything done at such meeting.

28. The business of the Annual General Meeting shall be to receive and consider the annual report of the Institute, the Honorary Treasurer's report and the balance sheet and accounts of the Institute with the auditor's report thereon to determine the amount of subscriptions and other fees in accordance with Bye-law 18 and any motions of which notice shall have been given in the Notice of the meeting and to consider any questions submitted to the meeting in accordance with regulations made and published by the Council. The Minutes of the preceding Annual General Meeting containing a transcript of all resolutions passed shall be read or submitted to the Annual General Meeting. All other business transacted at any Annual General Meeting and all business transacted at an Extraordinary General Meeting shall be deemed special business.

29. No business shall be transacted at any general meeting unless a quorum is present. Save as herein otherwise provided fifty Corporate Members present in person shall constitute a quorum for an Annual General Meeting and twenty Corporate Members present in person shall constitute a quorum for an Extraordinary General Meeting.

30. If within half an hour from the time appointed for the holding of a general meeting a quorum is not present the meeting, if convened on the requisition of members, shall be dissolved. In any other case it shall stand adjourned to a date, time and place to be determined by the chair of the meeting and notified to Members, and if at such adjourned meeting a quorum is not present within half an hour from the time appointed for holding a meeting the members present shall be a quorum.

31. Every general meeting shall be held at such place as the Council shall appoint. At general meetings the chair shall be taken by the President of the Institute. In the absence of the President the chair shall be taken by the Chair of Council. In the absence of the Chair of Council, the Members present shall choose one of their number to chair the meeting. The President, though present at a general meeting, may if he or she sees fit yield the chair to the Chair of Council or in his or her absence to such other person as the members present may choose.

32. The Chair of any general meeting may, with the consent of the meeting, adjourn the meeting from time to time, and from place to place as the meeting may determine, but no business shall be transacted at any adjourned meeting other than the business left unfinished at the meeting from which the adjournment took place. No notice need be given of any adjourned meeting unless it is so directed in the resolution for adjournment.

33. At every general meeting a resolution put to the vote of the meeting shall be decided on a show of hands, unless a written ballot is, before or upon the declaration of the result of the show of hands, demanded by the Chair or by at least twenty Corporate Members present in person or by proxy, and unless a ballot be so demanded a declaration by the Chair of the meeting that a resolution has been carried or carried by a particular majority, or lost or not carried by a particular majority shall be conclusive, and an entry to that effect in the Minutes of the proceedings of the meeting shall be sufficient evidence of the fact so declared, without proof of the number or proportion of the votes given for or against such resolution.

34. If a ballot is demanded it shall be taken at such time and place and in such manner as the Chair of the meeting shall direct provided always that no ballot shall be taken on the election of the Chair, the appointment of scrutineers or the adjournment of the meeting, and that notwithstanding a demand for a ballot on any resolution, the meeting may continue for the transaction of any other business in respect of which a ballot has not been demanded. The Members or the Chair, as the case may be, demanding a ballot may nominate up to three persons, who need not be Members, to act as scrutineers. If a ballot is demanded it should be taken in such manner as the Chair of the meeting directs, and the result of the ballot shall be deemed the resolution of the general meeting at which the ballot was demanded.

35. In the case of an equality of votes, whether on a show of hands or in a ballot, the Chair of the meeting shall be entitled to a second or casting vote.

36. The persons entitled to vote at general meetings of the Institute are the Corporate Members of the Institute whose subscriptions are not in arrears on 1 May in the year in which the meeting takes place.

37. Every person entitled to vote and present at a general meeting in person or by proxy shall have one vote.

38. The instrument appointing a proxy shall be in writing in the form prescribed by the Council and shall be signed and dated by the Corporate Member appointing the proxy. A proxy must be a Corporate Member of the Institute.

39. The instrument appointing a proxy shall be delivered to the Secretary not less than forty-eight hours before the time appointed for holding the meeting or adjourned meeting at which the person named in the instrument proposes to vote, and in default the instrument of proxy shall not be treated as valid.

40. A vote given in accordance with the terms of an instrument of proxy shall be valid notwithstanding the previous death or

insanity of the principal or revocation of the proxy, provided that no information in writing of the death, insanity or revocation as aforesaid shall have been received by the Secretary of the Institute before the commencement of the meeting or adjourned meeting at which the proxy is used.

41. No objection shall be made to the validity of any vote at a meeting except at the meeting or ballot at which such vote shall be tendered, and every vote not disallowed at such meeting or ballot shall be deemed valid. The chair of the meeting shall be the absolute judge of the validity of every vote tendered at any meeting or ballot.

42. On the demand of one quarter of the Members present in person or by proxy and entitled to vote, rising in their seats after the Members have voted on a motion but before the next business has been taken, the Chair shall rule that the motion be referred to a postal ballot of the Members and that the decision of a postal ballot shall be deemed to be the decision of the meeting. The meeting shall forthwith appoint three persons, who need not be Members, to act as scrutineers. The Chair shall reduce the resolutions or amendments into the form of alternative propositions so as best to take the sense of the Members on the substantial question or questions at issue. The wording of the resolution to appear on the postal ballot paper shall be decided at and agreed by the Members present in person and entitled to vote at the meeting. Voting papers setting forth these propositions shall be issued within fourteen days after the meeting and shall be returnable so as to be receivable within twenty one days after the meeting. The scrutineers shall meet not less than twenty one days nor more than twenty eight days after the meeting and shall draw up a report of the result of the voting, stating what voting papers have been rejected for non-observance of the notes and directions thereon or disqualified by reason of the voter being in arrear or otherwise ineligible to vote. The report of the scrutineers shall be conclusive as to the result of the voting and the result shall take effect from the date of that report. In the event of a tie on a postal ballot conducted under this Byelaw, the resolution shall be declared not carried.

Bye-laws

SECTION 6
The Council

43. The management of the affairs of the Institute shall be vested in the Council, which, in addition to the powers and authority expressly conferred on it by these Bye-laws or otherwise, may in respect of the affairs of the Institute exercise all such powers and do all such things as may lead to the furtherance of the objects of the Institute including all such powers and things as may be exercised or done by the Institute and are not by these Bye-laws expressly directed or required to be exercised or done by the Institute in General Meeting.

Regulations

44. Council shall have power from time to time to make, repeal or alter regulations as to the election of Members, as to the management of the Institute and its affairs, as to the duties of any officers or employees of the Institute, as to the conduct of business of the Institute, the Council or any committee of the Council, any Branch or Group and as to any other matters or things within the powers or under the control of the Council provided that such regulations shall not be inconsistent with the Charter or these Bye-laws.

Composition of the Council

45. The Council shall consist of the following persons:
    (a) The Honorary Officers of the Institute;
    (b) Twelve Councillors elected by the Corporate Members of the Institute in accordance with these Bye-laws (hereinafter referred to as the "National Councillors")
    (c) One Councillor elected by each Branch of the Institute (hereinafter referred to as "Branch Councillors");
    (d) One Councillor elected by each Special Interest Group in accordance with these Bye-laws (hereinafter referred to as "Group Councillors");
    (e) Two Councillors elected by Affiliates of the Institute in accordance with these Bye-laws (hereinafter referred to as "Affiliate Councillors").

46. Except for those Councillors elected by Affiliates, only Corporate Members of the Institute shall be eligible for election

to the Council.

Election of Honorary Officers and Councillors

47. The President Elect and the Honorary Treasurer shall be elected in accordance with Bye-laws 51 and 52. The President Elect shall become the President at the end of his or her year of office as President Elect and the retiring President shall become the Past President and shall hold office until the succeeding President shall retire from office.

48. The Chair of the Council shall be elected by the Council at its first meeting in each year. No person shall occupy the office of Chair of Council for more than three consecutive years.

49. The Chair of the Executive Board shall be elected by the Council at its first meeting in each year and may from time to time be removed by the Council. No person shall occupy the office of Chair of the Executive Board for more than six consecutive years.

50. On the death, resignation or termination of office of an Honorary Officer the Council may fill the vacant place for the remainder of the term.

51.(a) At the annual election to be held each year for the ensuing year commencing 1 April, the Corporate Members of the Institute shall elect a President Elect and an Honorary Treasurer for the ensuing year and four National Councillors to serve for a period of three years, and every third year the members of each Special Interest Group shall elect one of their number to be a Councillor for their Group and the members of each Branch shall elect one of their number to be a Branch Councillor for their Branch and the Affiliates shall elect two Councillors. In the case of Councillors elected by Affiliates, candidates must at the time of nomination and election be Affiliates of the Institute. The National Councillors, Branch Councillors, Group Councillors and Affiliate Councillors shall serve for three years.
(b) The result of the election shall be declared in a list of the candidates in which the names shall be arranged in each division of the Council in order of the number of votes received, the candidates with the highest number of votes to be at the head of the list.

Bye-laws

(c) A retiring Honorary Treasurer shall be eligible for re-election provided that an Honorary Treasurer who has held office for six consecutive years will not be eligible for re-election until the annual election in the following year. A retiring Councillor shall be eligible for re-election provided that a Councillor who has held office for nine consecutive years will not be eligible for re-election until the annual election in the following year.

(d) If the Institute, for any reason, fails to elect any Officer or Councillor who, on election, would serve for a period in excess of one year then the Institute, for the purpose of filling such vacancy or vacancies thereby arising shall elect such Officer or Officers, Councillor or Councillors at the next following annual election and those so appointed shall serve for the remainder of the term.

52. The Council shall make and publish regulations prescribing the requirements and procedures for the nomination of candidates for election.

53. Subject to Bye-law 6 the persons entitled to vote at the Annual General Meeting and elections to fill vacancies shall be Corporate Members of the Institute (or in the case of the Affiliate Councillors, Affiliates of the Institute) whose subscriptions are not in arrears on 1 May in the year of the election. Voting shall be by postal ballot. The Council shall make such regulations as may best enable all qualified voters to record their votes in a secret ballot.

Termination of office and filling of vacancies

54. A Councillor shall vacate office and cease to be a member of the Council if he or she:
    (a) ceases to be a Member of the Institute;
    (b) is suspended from membership of the Institute;
    (c) is absent from meetings of the Council for three consecutive meetings without the consent of the Council and the Council resolves that his or her office be vacated;
    (d) becomes bankrupt or makes any arrangement or composition with his or her creditors;
    (e) becomes incapable by reason of mental disorder;
    (f) becomes prohibited by law from being a Councillor;
    (g) is removed by a resolution passed by a two thirds majori-

ty of the Corporate Members present and voting at a General Meeting.

55. A Councillor may at any time give notice in writing of his or her resignation from the Council with effect from such date as the Councillor indicates.

56. If during his or her term of office a Branch Councillor, a Group Councillor or an Affiliate Councillor ceases to be qualified as a candidate for election in the category in which he or she was elected, the Councillor shall cease to be a member of the Council in that category from 31 March following unless the Council decides otherwise.

57. When the office of a Councillor becomes vacant other than at the end of a term of office and when a contest took place at a previous election for that office, the unsuccessful candidate who received the highest number of votes in the contest shall automatically fill the vacancy. If no contest for the office took place at the previous election, the Council may hold a by-election to fill the vacancy for the remainder of the original term.

Proceedings of the Council

58. The Council may meet together for the despatch of business and adjourn or otherwise regulate their meetings and proceedings as they think fit and may hold meetings in person or by suitable electronic means agreed between the Council in which all participants may communicate simultaneously with all other participants.

59. The President or the Chair of Council may, and shall on the requisition of any ten members of the Council, convene a meeting of the Council.

60. The Chair of Council shall preside at meetings of the Council but in his or her absence the Chair shall be taken by a member of the Council chosen by the Councillors present.

61. The quorum necessary for the transaction of business at Council meetings shall be twelve members or such higher number as the Council may determine.

Bye-laws

62. Every question at meetings of the Council shall be determined by a majority of the votes of the members of the Council personally present and voting and if there is an equality of votes the Chair of the meeting shall have a second or casting vote.

63. The members of the Council may act and exercise all their powers notwithstanding that vacancies for the time being remain unfilled.

64. All acts done by any meeting of the Council or by any committee appointed by the Council under the provisions hereinafter contained shall, notwithstanding that it shall afterwards be discovered that there were defects in the appointment of all or any of the members of the Council or of such committee, be as valid as if every such member had been duly appointed.

65. No member of the Council or of any committee shall vote on any matter in which he or she has a direct financial interest.

SECTION 7
Committees

66. The Council shall appoint Standing Committees or other sub-committees in accordance with the Charter to deal with various departments of the Institute's work with such powers and under such conditions as from time to time shall be determined by the Council. Persons who do not belong to the Institute may be appointed Consultative Members of the Committees, but shall not vote upon any question involving expenditure. The Council shall appoint Standing Committees in each year at the first meeting of the new Council and shall ensure that at least one Council Member is a member of each Standing Committee.

67. The Council shall appoint an Executive Board in accordance with the Charter which shall report to the Council on matters affecting general policy, legal and parliamentary business, on developments proposed in the work of the Institute and on business not assigned to other Standing Committees, and shall act on behalf of the Council, in an executive capacity, in matters of urgency.

68. The Council may delegate any of its powers to any Standing Committee or the Executive Board in accordance with the Charter.

69. The meetings and proceedings of any Committee shall be governed by the Byelaws regulating the meetings and proceedings of the Council so far as the same are applicable and not superseded by any Regulations.

SECTION 8
Advisory Board

70. The Council may appoint an Advisory Board or Boards for the purpose of advising the Council on such matters as are referred to it by the Council. The Council shall appoint the members of any such Advisory Board and shall determine their periods of office.

SECTION 9
Financial Matters

71. Subject to the authority of the Council and of the Executive Board the Honorary Treasurer shall supervise the financial affairs of the Institute and in particular the procedures for dealing with receipts, payments, assets and liabilities. The Honorary Treasurer shall submit a report to the Annual General Meeting of the Institute. In the absence of the Honorary Treasurer the report shall be submitted by the Chair of the Executive Board. The Council may make such regulations as it sees fit as regards the payment of accounts and the signature of cheques and other financial documents.

72. The Council may borrow money for the purposes of the Institute and secure the repayment thereof or the fulfilment of any contract or engagement of the Institute in any manner, upon any security, and issue any debentures to secure the same.

73. The Council may, out of the monies of the Institute, by way of Reserve Fund from time to time reserve or set apart such sums as in its judgement are necessary or expedient to be applied at the discretion of the Council to meet the claims on or liabilities of the Institute, or to be used as a sinking fund to pay off

Bye-laws

debentures or incumbrances of the Institute, or for any other purpose of the Institute.

Investment Management

74. The Council may delegate to one or more investment managers, for such period and upon such terms as it may think fit, power at the discretion of the investment manager to buy and sell investments on behalf of the Institute. Where the Council makes such a delegation it shall ensure that the investment manager is given clear instructions as to investment policy;

75. Except to the extent that the Council has exercised its power of delegation, the Council shall arrange that the investments are kept under review by one or more independent professional advisers, who shall be required to inform the Council promptly about any changes in investments which appear to them to be desirable;

76. Without prejudice to any other of its powers, the Council may if it thinks fit invest in the name of or under the control of any corporation or corporations as nominees of the Council the whole or such part of the investments and income arising from those investments as the Council may determine;

77. The Council may pay reasonable remuneration to the investment managers, independent professional advisers or nominees for services rendered under the above provisions.

Expenses

78. Council Members and members of any committee or subcommittee of the Institute shall be paid out of the funds of the Institute all reasonable out of pocket expenses properly and necessarily incurred by them on behalf of the Institute.

Audit, Accounts and Reports

79. At each Annual General Meeting an auditor or auditors of the Institute shall be appointed by the members present. No person shall be appointed auditor of the Institute who is an officer of the Institute nor unless he or she is qualified for appointment as auditor of a company (other than an exempt private compa-

Bye-laws

ny) under the provisions of the Companies Act 1985 or any statutory re-enactment or modification thereof.

80. The Council shall comply with the requirements of the Charities Act 1993 (or any statutory re-enactment or modification thereof) as to keeping financial records, the audit or examination of accounts and the preparation and submission to the Charity Commission of:
    (a)   Annual Reports;
    (b)   Annual Returns;
    (c)   Annual Statements of Accounts.

SECTION 10
Branches

81. The Council may establish Branches of the Institute for members residing or working in a region and may prescribe regulations for the constitution, functions, financing and procedure of every Branch. The Council may from time to time alter the boundaries of any region served by a Branch.

82. All Members of the Institute residing in the region and whose addresses as registered with the Institute are within the region shall be members of the Branch serving that Region save where the member elects to become a member of the Branch serving the region where he or she works and has notified the Institute accordingly. No member shall be a member of more than one Branch.

83. The Rules of a Branch, which must not conflict with the Byelaws of the Institute, shall be submitted to the Council for approval and no amendment or addition shall be valid until approved by the Council.

84. The Council shall pay to each Branch such part of the annual subscription revenue as it may from time to time determine and no Branch shall levy any subscription charge directly upon members of the Institute.

85. The Honorary Secretary of a Branch shall forward a report on the work of the Branch during each year for the information of

Bye-laws

the Council.

86. The Council may, at its discretion, dissolve a Branch in which case all monies standing to the credit of the Branch after all liabilities have been met shall be returned forthwith to the Institute. The Council shall, however, give at least twelve months' notice of intention to dissolve a Branch.

SECTION 11
Special Interest Groups

87. The Council may establish Special Interest Groups of the Institute and may prescribe regulations for the establishment, constitution, functions, financing and procedures of every Special Interest Group.

88. Members may join Groups on notifying their desire to the Secretary of the Institute.

89. The Council shall determine whether and in what circumstances an additional subscription is levied in respect of membership of Groups and the level of any additional subscription.

90. The Rules of a Group, which must not conflict with the Byelaws of the Institute, shall be submitted to the Council for approval and no amendment or addition shall be valid until approved by the Council.

91. The Council shall pay to each Group such part of the annual subscription revenue as it may from time to time determine and no group shall levy any subscription charge directly upon members of the Institute.

92. The Honorary Secretary of a Special Interest Group shall forward a report on the work of the Group during each year for the information of the Council.

93. The Council may, at its discretion, dissolve a Group in which case all monies standing to the credit of the Group after all liabilities have been met shall be returned to the Secretary of the Institute. The Council shall, however, give at least twelve

months notice of the intention to dissolve a Group.

Organisations in Liaison

94. The Council may from time to time recognise independent organisations which have objects similar to the objects of the Institute and whose membership includes a significant number of members of the Institute as Organisations in Liaison with the Institute and may determine the rights and obligations of such Organisations in Liaison.

SECTION 12
Secretary

95. The Secretary shall be appointed by the Council for such term and upon such conditions by such process as the Council may think fit. The Secretary shall keep a record of all proceedings, shall draft reports, issue notices, and conduct correspondence and shall have charge of all books, papers and other property belonging to the Institute and act generally as the Executive of the Institute. It shall be the duty of the Secretary to supervise the staff of the Institute and to maintain control over its finances, under the supervision of the Honorary Treasurer, the Executive Board and the Council. The Council may authorise the use of such title, additional to that of Secretary, as it thinks fit.

Seal

96. The Seal of the Institute shall only be used by the authority of the Council or of a committee of the Council authorised by the Council. The Council may determine who shall sign any instrument to which this Seal is affixed and unless otherwise so determined it shall be signed by a Council Member and by the Secretary or by a second Council Member.

Notices etc.

97. Unless otherwise provided in these Bye-laws, all notices, voting papers and circulars required by these Bye-laws to be given or sent to Members may be given personally or by sending the same by post to the registered address of the member or by facsimile or electronic means or such other suitable means as the Council may prescribe, provided always that publication of a

notice in the official journal of the Institute shall constitute good service of such notice upon all members.

98. Any such notice, voting paper or circular sent through the post to the registered address of any member shall have been deemed to have been served on the member on the third day after the day it is posted if sent by first class post and on the fifth day after posting if sent by second class post, and in proving such service it shall be sufficient to provide that such notice, voting paper or circular was properly addressed and posted.

99. Any accidental omission to give notice of any meetings to or the non-receipt of such notice by any member or other person entitled to receive the same shall not invalidate the proceedings at any meeting to be held under the provision of these Bye-laws.

Indemnity

100. Every Member and employee of the Institute carrying out the proper business of the Institute shall be indemnified by the Institute against, and it shall be the duty of the Council out of the funds of the Institute to pay, all costs, losses and expenses which any such person may incur or become liable to by reason of any contract entered into, or act or thing done or omitted to be done by him or her as such Council Member or employee or in any other way in the proper discharge of his or her duty, including reasonable travelling expenses.

Transitional arrangements

101. Notwithstanding the foregoing Byelaws, the members of the Council in office on 31 December 2001 shall in consultation with the Council of the Institute of Information Scientists name the persons who shall become Councillors of the Institute on 1 April 2002 in place of the Councillors previously in office, and shall identify the particular office which each person shall hold.

102. The Councillors so named shall be deemed to have been elected to office in accordance with these Byelaws save that:
    (a) All Councillors so named shall hold office initially for the number of years specified at the time they enter into

office. They shall then retire but shall be eligible for re-election in accordance with these Byelaws; and

(b) For one year until 1 April 2003 there shall be two joint Past Presidents of the Institute.

103. Any period in office served by a Councillor as a Councillor of the Institute or as a Council Member of the Institute of Information Scientists prior to 1 April 2002 shall be disregarded for the purpose of calculating eligibility to stand for re-election in accordance with Byelaw 51.

104. Notwithstanding Byelaw 82, a Branch Committee may with the agreement of the Council co-opt into Membership of that Branch any former Member of the Branch whose membership has been terminated as a result of boundary changes. This will apply for two years from the date of those boundary changes.

Regulations 2002

Drawn up under the Provisions of CILIP Bye-law 44.
Adopted by CILIP Council on 3 October 2002.

Index

Under the provisions of Bye-law 44, CILIP Council has the power to make regulations on any matters relevant to CILIP, provided the regulations are not inconsistent with the Charter and Bye-laws. In addition, certain Bye-laws oblige Council to make regulations to give effect to their provisions. As at 3 October 2002, Council has made regulations on the following matters:

General Regulations

1–4	Election of Members
5–8	Honorary Fellows
9–10	Publication of the Register
11	Exemption from Professional Qualifications Regulations
12–13	Subscriptions
14–15	Submission of Motions to the AGM
16–22	Proxy Votes
23	Minutes of Meetings
24–32	Nominations for Elections (of Honorary Officers and Council)
33–57	Voting in Annual Elections
58–87	Regulations for Committees
88–89	Payment of Accounts and Signature of Cheques
90–95	Branches
96–104	Special Interest Groups
105–112	Organisations in Liaison

Appendix A   **Regulations for Professional Qualifications**
Appendix B   **Code of Conduct and Disciplinary Proceedings**
Appendix C   **Regulations for the Retired Members' Guild**
Appendix D   **Regulations for Affiliated Members**
Subject Index for CILIP Charter, Bye-laws and Regulations

General regulations

Election of Members
Bye-law 5

1. Names of individuals or institutions seeking membership of the Institute will be placed before a meeting of the Professional Development Committee of Council.

2. Election will be by the majority vote of those members of the committee present.

3. The decision on the election of any candidate may be deferred if agreed by a majority vote of those members of the committee present.

4. The committee may also reinstate by majority vote members whose memberships have been suspended, including reinstatement to the Register.

Power to Nominate Honorary Fellows
Bye-law 8

5. Nominations for the award of an honorary fellowship may be made by members, branches, groups or committees (and sub-committees) of Council.

6. Nominations may be made for individuals who have made a significant contribution to the profession. Nominees need not be members of CILIP.

7. Nominations for the award of honorary fellowships will be considered in the first instance by the Executive Board, which will propose to Council such of the nominations as it thinks fit.

8. Decisions on the award of honorary fellowships will be made by Council, and Council's decision shall be final.

Regulations 2002: general regulations

Publication of the Register
Bye-law 10

    9.   The current Register of chartered fellows and chartered members will be available through the CILIP website.

    10.   A printed directory of all members will be issued periodically.

Professional Qualifications
Bye-law 11

    The regulations for professional qualifications are given at Appendix A.

Exemption from Provisions of Bye-law 11
Bye-law 12

    11.   The Council will ensure that the terms of reference of the Chartership Board include the responsibility of the Board to draw attention to any need for the use of these powers of exemption, and for any subsequent changes to regulations.

Cancellation of Registration
Bye-law 17

    See regulations 1–4 concerning election of members.

Subscriptions
Bye-law 18

    12.   **Date of Payment**
    12.1   Annual subscriptions shall be due and payable in advance of the first day of January in each year.
    12.2   If by 30th April in any year the subscription due from a member for that year has not been paid, that member's membership will be suspended
    12.3   If the subscription is paid after 30th April and before 1st July the rights of membership will be restored (but see Regulation 13.4 below)
    12.4   If the subscription is not paid by 31st July the member will be deemed to have resigned his/her membership.
    12.5   Any member whose subscription is not paid by 30th April will not be eligible to vote in the annual election of Council or of

Regulations 2002: general regulations

any branch or group committee during the rest of that year.

13. **Payment by Instalment**
13.1 Where any resolution adopted by the annual general meeting of the Institute permits subscriptions, entrance, registration, admission and other fees to be paid by instalments, the provisions of Regulation 12 regarding suspension and termination of membership shall not apply provided each instalment is paid by the date stated in the resolution.
13.2 In the event of an instalment due under such resolution not being paid by the due date, the full subscription or other payment shall fall due immediately and the provisions of Regulation 12 shall apply as if in the case of non-payment.
13.3 The Secretary of the Institute shall have the power to suspend the operation of Regulation 13.2 if a payment is received after the due date as a result of circumstances outside the member's control.
13.4 Where membership is suspended or terminated under Regulation 13.2 no instalment already received shall be refunded to the member.

Code of Conduct
Bye-law 19

The Code of Conduct is given at Appendix B.

Disciplinary Proceedings
Bye-law 21

These regulations are given at Appendix B.

Submissions of Motions to the AGM
Bye-law 25

14. Notices of motion shall be made in writing and shall be served on the Secretary not less than two months before the date of the meeting.

15. Any member who desires to move an amendment to a notice of motion shall serve a notice in writing of such amendment at least one month before the meeting.

Regulations 2002: general regulations

Proxy Votes
Bye-law 38

16. A corporate member who is entitled to be present and to vote at an annual general meeting or extraordinary general meeting, may appoint a proxy to vote on his behalf in a poll. A member present only by proxy shall have no vote on a show of hands. A proxy must be a corporate member.

17. At an annual general meeting or extraordinary general meeting, on a show of hands, every corporate member present in person shall have one vote, but a member present only by proxy shall have no vote.

18. The instrument appointing a proxy shall be in writing under the hands of the appointer or her/his attorney duly authorised in writing.

19. The instrument appointing a proxy and the power of attorney or other authority (if any) under which it is signed (or a notarially certified or office copy thereof) shall be deposited at the registered office not less than forty-eight hours before the time appointed for holding the meeting or adjourned meeting at which the person named in the instrument proposes to vote or, in the case of a poll, not less than twenty-four hours before the time appointed for taking the poll, and in default the instrument of proxy shall not be treated as valid. No instrument appointing a proxy shall be valid after the expiration of twelve months from the date of its execution.

20. A vote given in accordance with the terms of an instrument of proxy shall be valid notwithstanding the previous death or insanity of the principal or revocation of the proxy or of the authority under which the proxy was executed, providing that no intimation in writing of the death, insanity or revocation as aforesaid shall have been received at the registered office before the commencement of the meeting or adjourned meeting at which the proxy is used.

21. Any instrument appointing a proxy shall be in the following form or as near thereto as circumstances will admit:

THE CHARTERED INSTITUTE OF LIBRARY AND INFORMATION PROFESSIONALS
"I ....
"of ....
"a Member of the Chartered Institute of Library and Information Professionals
"hereby appoint ....
"of ....
"and failing her/him ....
"of ....
"to vote for me and on my behalf at the (Annual or Extraordinary or Adjourned, as the case may be) General Meeting of the Institute to be held on the .... day of .... 2... and at every adjournment thereof.
"As witness my hand this .... day of .... 2..."

22. The instrument appointing a proxy shall be deemed to confer authority to demand or join in demanding a poll.

Minutes of Council and Committee Meetings
Council Regulations made under Bye-law 44

23. Proper minutes shall be recorded of all resolutions and proceedings of meetings of the Council and the committees thereof, and every minute signed by the Chair of the meeting to which it relates or by the Chair of a subsequent meeting shall be sufficient evidence of the facts therein stated.

Regulations for the Retired Members' Guild
Council Regulations made under Bye-law 44

The Regulations are given at Appendix C.

Nominations for Election (of Honorary Officers and Council)
Bye-law 52

24. Candidates for the post of President Elect must be nominated by at least 10 members entitled to vote at the annual elections.

25. Candidates for the post of Honorary Treasurer must be nominated by at least two members entitled to vote at annual elections.

Regulations 2002: general regulations

26. A candidate for election to the Council must be nominated by at least two Members entitled to vote for the category for which the candidate seeks election.

27. In the case of branch councillors and group councillors, a candidate must at the time of nomination be a member of the branch or group for which they are candidates and be nominated by two members of the branch or group in question.

28. In the case of councillors elected by affiliated members, candidates must be affiliated members of the Institute at the times of nomination and election.

29. All nominations by members must be signed by the requisite number of members qualified to vote and must be received by the Secretary of the Institute at least three months before the due date of election in each year.

30. On receipt of valid nominations, the Secretary shall send by registered post to all candidates notice that they have been nominated, and shall request them to send their written consent to serve upon Council, if elected.

31. If a nominee declines nomination or fails to reply within 21 days after the last day for receipt of nominations, the nomination shall be invalid and the nominators so informed.

32. In the case of candidates who are nominated for more than one of the following categories, namely national councillor, branch councillor or group councillor, they shall inform the Secretary of the category for which they wish to stand but they may not stand for more than one category and no candidate may stand for election as group councillor for more than one group.

Voting in Annual Elections
Bye-law 53

33. Each nominee shall be invited to send a signed statement of not more than 300 words about himself/herself for the information of voters (hereafter called a manifesto). The nominee shall take

full responsibility for the content of the manifesto but the Secretary shall have discretion to refuse to accept a text which is personally abusive, libellous or otherwise offensive.

34. Not less than two weeks before the issuing of voting papers, the Secretary shall cause a notice to be published in the journal of the Institute, or otherwise despatched to members qualified to vote, stating:
    (i) The date on which voting papers will be issued;
    (ii) That any qualified member failing to receive a voting papers must notify the Secretary of that fact within one week after the date for the issue of voting papers and that no voting paper shall be issued thereafter.

35. Voting papers shall be despatched to members entitled to vote by not later than 15 February and shall be printed in such a way, by means of watermarking and numbering, to make deception by photocopying or reproduction immediately apparent.

36. In issuing voting papers the Secretary shall inform members entitled to vote as to the offices and places on Council for which nominations did not exceed the number of places to be filled and of the names of the persons accordingly to be declared elected without contest.

37. The manifestos of candidates shall be provided to members entitled to vote in a document separate from the ballot paper.

38. The ballot paper shall contain no information about candidates except their names. The names of candidates shall be arranged in sections according to the category of officer or councillor to be elected. Within each section names shall be printed alphabetically.

39. With each ballot paper there shall be sent an envelope. The envelope shall bear no marking by which voters may be identified.

40. The Secretary shall provide instructions on the manner in which the ballot paper is to be completed and general informa-

Regulations 2002: general regulations

tion on the conduct of the election. Such information shall state inter alia:

(i) The section for which different categories of member are entitled to vote

(ii) The fact that failure to adhere to the instructions renders the ballot paper liable to be rejected by the scrutineers

(iii) The latest date for receipt of ballot papers

(iv) The right of members of the Institute to attend the count.

41. The Council at its first meeting each year shall appoint at least six members of the Institute who are not candidates for election to act as scrutineers at the annual election.

42. The scrutineers shall elect a chair either by correspondence with the Secretary before the day of the count or when they assemble on the day of the count.

43. In the event of any dispute on the procedure for the count or on the validity of any ballot paper, the scrutineers shall determine the issue by majority vote. In the event of a tie, the chair shall have a casting vote.

44. It shall be the duty of the Secretary of the Institute to advise the scrutineers on any matter arising at the count.

45. Whenever possible, the counting of the votes shall be completed in a single day. If it is found necessary to continue the count on a second day, the scrutineers and the Secretary shall make arrangements to ensure the security of the ballot papers in the intervening period.

46. The scrutineers and the Secretary of the Institute may make use of such staff of the Institute or other persons as they see fit (whether members of the Institute or not) to assist in the count and may, with the consent of the Honorary Treasurer, make payments for such work.

47. Any envelope which, in the opinion of the scrutineers, does not comply with the instructions sent to voters, may be rejected and any ballot paper contained in it shall be invalid. If, after accept-

ing an envelope, the contents are discovered not to adhere to the instructions sent to voters, any ballot paper contained therein may be declared invalid.

48. The scrutineers shall have discretion to admit ballot papers which have not been completed fully in accordance with the instructions if they are satisfied that the validity of the vote is certain and the secrecy of the vote is not breached. In particular, the scrutineers may accept as valid any votes cast for one or more sections on a ballot paper notwithstanding that votes in another section or sections in that ballot paper are ruled invalid.

49. Ballot papers accepted as valid shall be counted in such manner as the scrutineers shall determine and the candidates receiving the greater number of votes shall be declared elected for the number of places to be filled.

50. If there is a tie between any two or more candidates and the addition of one vote would render one or more of the candidates successful, the scrutineers shall exercise their power under these regulations to decide the result forthwith by lot in such manner as to give each such candidate an equal chance of success.

51. If at any election a vacancy requires to be filled under bye-law 51(a) for a period of less than a full term (in addition to vacancies for a full term) the candidate or candidates with the highest number of votes shall be declared elected for the full terms and the candidate with the next highest number of votes shall be declared elected for the period of less than a full term.

52. The scrutineers shall cause the result of the count to be declared to any members of the Institute attending the count and shall forthwith approve and sign a report stating:
    (i) Which places were filled without contest and the candidates declared elected therefor
    (ii) The number of votes cast for each candidate for contested places and the candidates declared elected
    (iii) The number of ballot papers issued
    (iv) The number of envelopes returned

Regulations 2002: general regulations

(v) The number of returns declared invalid with such analysis of reasons and commentary as the scrutineers think fit.

53. The scrutineers shall declare the result immediately by communicating with the candidates by post. The report of the scrutineers shall be printed in the journal of the Institute and shall be presented to the next following annual general meeting.

54. The Secretary shall inform all existing members of Council of the result of the election.

55. The Secretary shall make arrangements for the ballot papers, together with all envelopes declared unacceptable, to be retained in secure conditions for a period of two months after the date of the count.

56. If, within two weeks of the count, a candidate, supported by the persons who nominated that candidate and at least five other members of the Institute, declares that he/she has reason to believe that errors were made in the counting of the ballots, the scrutineers, in the presence of not more than three persons chosen by the candidate and such other persons as the Executive Board of the Institute may determine, shall conduct a recount of ballot papers and may make such alteration to the result of the count as previously announced as they see fit. Any such alteration shall be without prejudice to the validity of anything done by a person previously declared elected in the intervening period.

57. When a by-election is held to fill a vacancy on Council, the procedure shall follow that prescribed above for annual elections mutatis mutandis.

Regulations for Committees
Bye-laws 66–69

58. **Definitions**
The categories of committees and sub-committees shall be as follows:

58.1 **Standing Committees** shall be established by Council to advise it on policy and other matters. Subject to the need to seek the prior approval of Council for major changes in policy and for decisions which have significant cost and/or staffing implications, each standing committee shall have delegated authority to act on matters within its terms of reference.

58.2 **Boards** may be established by Council on its own initiative or on the advice of a standing committee. Boards shall either report direct to Council or shall be placed under the authority of a standing committee and shall report to that committee. Boards shall be appointed in circumstances where a measure of confidentiality is required and/or in circumstances where executive powers of decision making, within established policy guidelines, are appropriate. The need for each board shall be reviewed from time to time either by Council or by the parent committee as appropriate. Such reviews shall take place at least every three years. These provisions do not apply to boards of directors of any company owned or controlled by the Chartered Institute of Library and Information Professionals.

58.3 **Sub-committees** may be established by standing committees, within authorised expenditure limits and subject to the approval of the Executive Board. Sub-committees shall deal with specific subject areas referred to them by the standing committee and shall to provide specialised advice to the standing committee. The need for each sub-committee shall be reviewed annually by its parent standing committee.

58.4 **Working Parties** may be established, within authorised expenditure limits, by a standing committee, a board or a sub-committee (in the latter case, subject to the approval of the parent committee) in order to carry out a specific task on its behalf. A working party shall not be appointed (or remain in existence) for a period in excess of six months except with the consent of the Executive Board.

58.5 **Panels** may be appointed by Council, standing committees, boards or sub-committees within authorised expenditure and time limits to constitute a source of advice on a specific subject area.

58.6 **Executive Advisory Groups** may be appointed by the Executive Board within authorised expenditure and time limits to advise the Board on topics of strategic interest.

Joint Committees

59.1 Council or any standing committees may, within authorised

Regulations 2002: general regulations

expenditure limits, appoint such members as it sees fit to represent the Chartered Institute of Library and Information Professionals on committees or other bodies established jointly by the Chartered Institute of Library and Information Professionals and other organisations.

59.2 Standing committees may establish joint sub-committees within authorised expenditure limits to ensure co-ordinated consideration of specific issues.

60. Council or any standing committee may appoint such Members as it sees fit to represent the Chartered Institute of Library and Information Professionals on committees or other bodies external to the Institute in which the Institute has an interest. Such appointments shall be for a period of not more than one year but may be continued after review by council or the relevant standing committee. A Member acting as such a representative shall act in accordance with terms of reference set by council or the appointing committee and shall report to council or that committee on a regular basis and at least once per year.

Standing Committees

61. The Executive Board is established under Bye-law 67. In discharging its duties it shall in particular:
    (i) Exercise general oversight over the financial affairs of the Institute
    (ii) Make recommendations to Council on the allocation of funds
    (iii) Submit to Council annual estimates of expenditure and income
    (iv) On the advice of the Honorary Treasurer, make recommendations to Council concerning the subscription rates for members
    (v) Receive reports on the performance of the trading activities of the Institute and make appropriate recommendations to Council
    (vi) Make reports and recommendations to Council on general policy, legal and Parliamentary business and on developments proposed in the work of the Institute
    (vii) Exercise general oversight of the Institute's responsibilities for equal opportunities
    (viii) Consider such policy matters as do not fall within the

Regulations 2002: general regulations

area of responsibility of any other standing committee of Council

(ix) Undertake urgent action on behalf of Council where appropriate.

62. **The Disciplinary Committee** is established under Bye-law 21.

63. **The Professional Practice Committee** has the following terms of reference:
To formulate policies, initiate action and monitor performance in matters pertaining to branches and groups, issues of ethics and standards including the Code of Professional Conduct, membership recruitment and in matters relating directly to personal members, including membership benefits.

64. **The Professional Development Committee** has the following terms of reference:
To formulate policies, initiate action and monitor performance in matters relating to the qualifications framework and structure (including chartered status and all aspects of the scheme for continuing professional development) and to the framework of course accreditation.

65. **The Policy Development Committee** has the following terms of reference:
To formulate and develop an effective programme of library and information service policy at national and international levels and to promote good practice in policy implementation.

66. **The Enterprise Board** shall oversee the affairs of the Institute's enterprises in such a way that professional concerns are supported whilst achieving optimum income generation.

67. The **Update Editorial Board** has the following terms of reference:
To communicate the views of members to the editor in order to ensure that members of CILIP receive a relevant and high quality journal which is in touch with issues of concern and relevance to the profession.

68. **The Facet Advisory Panel** has the following terms of reference:
To consider policy, strategy and business plans for Facet

Regulations 2002: general regulations

Publishing: to provide advice and suggestions; to review and monitor performance; and to assist in promoting Facet as a thriving, profitable and professional imprint.

Chairs of Standing Committees

69. The Chair of the Executive Board and the Chairs of the other standing committees set out in regulations 62 to 68 shall be elected by members of Council from amongst their own number. The Secretary shall conduct the ballot immediately following the annual election of members of Council.

70. Nominations may be made by any member of Council other than the member being nominated. Nominations must be made in writing, including the signature of the nominee indicating his/her willingness to the elected.

71. In the event of more than two candidates being nominated for any one of the chairs, a postal ballot shall be conducted. The votes shall be counted and the person appointed shall be the candidate with the greatest number of votes. In the event of a tie the Council shall decide at its first meeting in the calendar year between the candidates having equal highest votes. In the event of a tie on that occasion, the chair of the meeting shall determine the choice by lot.

72. It shall not be permissible for a person to be a candidate for the chair of more than one committee, save that a person may be a candidate for the chair of the Executive Board and of one other standing committee. In the event of such a candidate being elected to the chair of the Executive Board, the other candidature shall lapse.

73. A chair of a committee may act on behalf of that committee in cases of urgency.

Vice-Chairs of Standing Committees

74. The Executive Board and the other standing committees established under regulations 62–68 shall each appoint a vice-chair, either by postal ballot before the first meeting in each calendar year or at that meeting.

Regulations 2002: general regulations

75. Vice-chairs shall take the chair at meetings of standing committees in the absence of the chair. They may also represent the chair at meetings of the Executive Board.

Composition of the Executive Board

76.1 The Executive Board shall comprise:
The Chair of the Executive Board
The President
The President-Elect
The Immediate Past President
The Chair of Council
The Honorary Treasurer
The Chair of each of the standing committees set out in regulations 62-68 above (except the Disciplinary Committee)
One Councillor elected by Council

76.2 In the absence of the chair of any of the standing committees, the vice-chair (or other member of that committee, with the approval of the chair of the Executive Board) may attend and vote at any meeting of the Executive Board.

76.3 The Executive Board may invite observers to attend its meetings for special purposes. No such observer shall have the right to vote.

Composition of Other Standing Committees

77. Council shall assign each member of Council to be a member of one of the standing committees set out in regulations 62- 68 above and Council's decision on such assignment shall be final. The Honorary Officers of the Institute (President, President-Elect, Immediate Past President, Chair of Council, Chair of Executive Board and the Honorary Treasurer) shall be ex-officio members of each standing committee. No other member of Council shall be a member of more than one standing committee.

78. Council shall exercise its power of appointment in such a manner as to make the number of councillors serving on each committee as equal as possible. The Enterprise Board is an exception to this rule as it has a smaller number of councillors serving on it for reasons of commercial confidentiality.

79. Each standing committee set out in regulations 62–68 may co-

Regulations 2002: general regulations

opt up to three additional members to represent special interests, subject to the approval of the Executive Board. Such co-opted members shall be appointed for periods of no more than one year, but may be re-appointed. They shall have a right to vote at meetings of the committee.

80. Subject to the approval of the Executive Board, which shall not be unreasonably withheld, each standing committee set out in regulations 62-68, shall have power to invite observers to attend their meetings for special purposes, either for a period of up to one year or for particular meetings. Observers shall have no vote.

Composition of Boards

81. Boards (as defined in regulation 58.2) if established by Council on its own initiative, shall comprise such persons as Council shall decide. The chair of such a board shall be appointed by Council from amongst its members and must be a member of the Chartered Institute of Library and Information Professionals.

82. Boards (as defined in regulation 58.2) other than those established by Council on its own initiative, shall comprise such persons as the standing committee under whose authority the board falls shall decide, normally including at least two members of the parent committee. The chair of the parent committee shall be an ex officio member of all boards appointed by that committee.

83. The chair of a board shall be appointed by that board's parent committee. The chair of a board shall be a Member of the Chartered Institute of Library and Information Professionals and, except where authorised by the Executive Board to the contrary, shall be a member of the parent committee.

Composition of Sub-committees and Working Parties

84. Sub-committees and working parties shall comprise such persons as the parent standing committee may appoint. A sub-committee shall normally include two members of its parent committee and a working party shall normally include at least one member of its parent committee. The chair of a standing committee shall be ex

Regulations 2002: general regulations

officio a member of all sub-committees and working parties of that committee. The chair of a sub-committee or a working party shall be a member of the Institute and, except where authorised by the Executive Board to the contrary, shall be a member of the parent committee.

Composition of Panels

85. Panels shall comprise such persons as the Council, committee or sub-committee appointing the panel decides. Panel members do not have to be members of CILIP.

Expenses

86. Reasonable expenses incurred by members, including co-opted members, in attending meetings of committees, boards, sub-committees, working parties and panels shall be reimbursed by the Institute. Expenses incurred by Institute representatives on joint and external committees may also be reimbursed. Expenses incurred by observers shall not normally be reimbursed by the Institute, but the Executive Board may authorise reimbursement if it is satisfied that the interests of the Institute make it appropriate to do so.

Open Meetings

87. Personal members of the Institute and personal members nominated by institutional Members of the Institute under Bye-law 6(b) may attend meetings of standing committees (other than those of the Disciplinary Committee, Executive Board and Enterprise Board) as visitors. Visitors shall be excluded from any part of a meeting at which a standing committee is discussing confidential business.

Payment of Accounts and Signature of Cheques
Bye-law 71

88. **Payment of Accounts**
88.1 Heads of a department shall be responsible for managing their department's budgets and authorising expenditure.
88.2 Invoices and other requests for payments must be signed by the head of the relevant department, or by another member of the department specifically authorised to do so.

Regulations 2002: general regulations

    88.3   In exceptional circumstances, payments may be authorised by the Secretary, a director or the head of finance.

89. **Signature of Cheques**
    89.1   Cheques must be signed by two authorised signatories, at least one of whom must come from the A list.
    89.2   The lists of cheque signatories are:
A List (finance staff): head of finance, senior financial accountant and accounts controller
B List (non-finance staff): Secretary, directors, and two other senior members of staff determined from time to time by the head of finance and notified to the Institute's bankers.

Branches
Bye-law 81

90.   A branch shall appoint a Chair, an Honorary Secretary or Honorary Secretaries, an Honorary Treasurer, and such other members as required to form a committee to manage its affairs. The branch councillor elected in accordance with Bye-law 45(c) shall be an ex-officio member of the branch committee and shall make a report to every meeting of the branch committee and to every annual general meeting of the branch.

91.   A branch shall not take any action, other than by recommendation to Council, which affects other branches, the general conduct of the Institute or the external relations of the Institute.

92.   The funds and facilities of a branch shall not be employed to promote the candidature of any candidate for election to office of the Institute; but this shall not prevent the provision of factual information on a non-discriminatory basis.

93.   Subject to approval by Council, branches may create sub-branches to facilitate provision of services to members.

94.   Members may pay the Institute an additional fee to be a corresponding member of any branch of which they are not a member. A corresponding member is entitled to be placed on the mailing list of the branch and to participate in its meetings and events, but may not vote in branch proceedings or stand for

election within the branch.

95. A member of a branch who retires from employment to an address away from that branch may choose to remain in membership of that branch.

Special Interest Groups
Bye-law 87

96. Upon receipt of a request in writing from not fewer than one per cent of personal members of the Institute, the Council may, at its discretion, issue a certificate creating a Special Interest Group (SIG) of the Institute. The Council shall have power to create a group notwithstanding that no such request has been received.

97. Members may join one or more groups by notice to the Secretary of the Institute. Council shall determine whether and in what circumstances an additional subscription is to be levied in respect of membership of groups and the level of any such additional subscription.

98. A group shall appoint a Chair, and Honorary Secretary or Honorary Secretaries, an Honorary Treasurer, and such other members as required to form a committee to manage its affairs. The group Councillor elected in accordance with Bye-law 45(c) shall be an ex-officio member of the group committee and shall make a report to every meeting of the group committee and to every annual general meeting of the branch.

99. A group shall not take any action, other than by recommendation to Council, which affects other groups, the general conduct of the Institute or the external relations of the Institute.

100. The funds and facilities of a group shall not be employed to promote the candidature of any candidate for election to office of the Institute; but this shall not prevent the provision of factual information on a non-discriminatory basis.

101. Subject to approval by Council, groups may create sub-groups to facilitate provision of services to members.

Regulations 2002: general regulations

Associated members of SIGs

102. The Chartered Institute of Library and Information Professionals recognises that there are people who are interested in the work of one or more of the Institute's special interest groups (SIGs) but who would not wish to become members of the Institute. The Institute wishes to be hospitable to such people and is therefore willing to allow such people to become associated members of a SIG. Associated members are entitled to the advantages of membership of the group, at whatever annual fee the group committee shall decide, but are not Members of the Institute or of the group.

103. Associated members may become members of the group's committee, but not in the office of Chair, Honorary Secretary or Honorary Treasurer, nor may they form the majority of members of the committee.

104. Associated members may not take part in elections for the Group Councillor but they may vote on matters internal to the group.

Regulations for Affiliated Members
Bye-law 87

The regulations for Affiliated Members are given at Appendix D.

Organisations in Liaison
Bye-law 94

105. The rights and obligations arising from liaison agreements are set out below. Liaison may be terminated at any time by notice from either side.

106. The Chartered Institute of Library and Information Professionals shall have the right to appoint an observer to the governing body of each organisation in liaison to effect liaison and to promote partnership activities.

107. An organisation in liaison is entitled to print on its notepaper and reports "In liaison with the Chartered Institute of Library and Information Professionals".

108. The Chartered Institute of Library and Information Professionals, if so requested, will offer the following facilities to an organisa-

Regulations 2002: general regulations

tion in liaison:
(i) To receive a 20% discount on published room hire rates at Ridgmount Street.
(ii) To report news of the organisation's activities in CILIP's journal, at the discretion of the editor.
(iii) To publish notices of organisation meetings in CILIP's journal, subject to space being available.
(iv) To place advertisements in CILIP's journal at the same discount rate as available to CILIP branches and groups
(v) To purchase CILIP publications at the members' discount rate.
(vi) To receive one set of CILIP papers as appropriate.

109. The Chartered Institute of Library and Information Professionals, if so requested, may make a grant to an organisation in liaison in accordance with the following criteria:
(i) That the total amount of grants to all organisations in liaison does not exceed £1,500 in any one year.
(ii) That a grant is made to an organisation in liaison rather than to an individual member of that organisation.
(iii) That the total amount to be allocated to each organisation does not exceed £500 in any one year.
(iv) That an organisation would normally receive support for no more than two consecutive years.

110. Applications for grants must be made during the month of September for consideration early in October each year.

111. Applications will be considered, and grants allocated by, the Executive Board, for one or more of the following purposes:
(i) To provide pump priming or seed corn funding for a new idea or action.
(ii) To underwrite a high risk or capital intensive initiative.
(iii) To subsidise a meeting or event in order to enable more people to attend.

Cognisance will be taken of other sources of funding that are available, particularly grants for travel, CPD, research and international activity.

112. Appropriate acknowledgement must be given to the Chartered Institute of Library and Information Professionals for any financial support.

Appendix A: CILIP Regulations for Professional Qualifications

Bye-laws 11, 12 and 15

Professional qualifications
Bye-law 11

NOTE: These Regulations have been drafted to form part of a Handbook for candidates and supervisors. References to appendices etc. are to additional documents which will form part of that Handbook. The Regulations will apply for the period 1st April 2002–31st December 2004. The Registration Board has drawn up transitional arrangements for candidates preparing for Chartered Membership/Fellowship of the LA or Corporate Membership of the IIS prior to 1st April 2001, designed to ensure that no candidate is disadvantaged by changes to the Regulations.

All candidates for Chartered Membership of CILIP must satisfy certain general requirements, which are set out below. Once you have gained your Chartership you are entitled to use the title Chartered Member and to the post-nominal letters MCLIP. To retain these rights you must remain in membership of CILIP.

Section 1: Gaining Chartered Membership
1) Membership

Candidates for applying for admission to the Register must: -

(1) have been in Membership of CILIP for at least one year
and
(2) be in current membership at the time of making application

Successful candidates must be in Corporate Membership of CILIP before being admitted to the Register

2) Admission qualifications

You must have acceptable qualifications to be considered as a Chartership candidate.
These are:

1. a qualification accredited by CILIP at UK National

Regulations 2002: Regulations for Professional Qualifications

Qualifications Frameworks Levels SCQF 10 or EWNI HE4 or above.

or

2. a qualification from another EU Member State which meets the criteria set down in Directive 89/48/EEC

or

3. a qualification which is accredited by the American Library Association

or

4. a qualification which is accredited by the Australian Library and Information Association for the Associate category of membership

or

5. an information qualification from the UK or any other country which is assessed by the UK National Academic Recognition Information Centre at National Qualifications Frameworks Levels SCQF 9 or EWNI HE3, plus at least 3 years professional experience

For current information about CILIP accredited courses and recognised qualifications you should consult the CILIP website www.cilip.org.uk

3) Registering as a candidate
3.1 CILIP accredited qualifications

Holders of qualifications, which are accredited by CILIP under 2.1 above, may apply to register as candidates under Route A (see next section).

You should normally register as a candidate within one year of gaining your accredited qualification. If you are unable to do so for any reason you should write to the Membership, Careers and Qualifications Department explaining the reasons.

You are also required to inform CILIP when you have completed your training period. This is important as you then have a deadline by which to submit your application for Chartership (see Regulation 5 below).

You will find the forms to register commencement and completion of training at the back of this handbook, or you can find them on the CILIP website at www.cilip.org.uk

Regulations 2002: Regulations for Professional Qualifications

3.2 Recognised qualifications

Holders of qualifications which are recognised by CILIP under 2.2, 2.3, 2.4 or 2.5 above may apply to register as candidates under Route B (see next section). You should apply for recognition of your qualifications in writing, enclosing original documents or certified copies. If your application is successful you will be sent the relevant forms and invited to register as a candidate when you receive notification of recognition of your qualification. You will then be required to comply with the regulations set out for Route B.

4) Practical Experience

To be a candidate for the Register you must have had practical professional experience. Candidates who study full-time must complete this period of practical experience after gaining their accredited qualification. If you are studying part-time and working in an information environment you may register your practical experience training to coincide with the last one or two years of your course. You will not be able to make an application for Chartership until you have gained the award for which you are studying.

Route A

To apply for Chartership under Route A you must have completed at least one year of Supervised Professional Training approved by CILIP before making an application for admission to the Register. You are allowed to change jobs during your training period, as long as your new employer is also able to provide approved training. See Part 3, section 7 for further information.

Route B

To register for Chartership under Route B you submit a Personal Professional Development Plan covering at least two years of professional experience. You must complete this Programme before making application for admission to the Register.

Routes A and B

When calculating how much of the required experience you have completed for your chosen route, you should take note of the following:

(a) Full-time work is deemed to be not less than 30 hours per week. Parttime work of not less than 12 hours per week may be counted, to be calculated pro rata to a full-time week of 30 hours. If

Regulations 2002: Regulations for Professional Qualifications

you work part-time or term-time only it will take you proportionately longer to complete.

(b) temporary posts/short-term contracts – work in a temporary post or on a short-term contract will be counted only if it comprises at least 240 hours overall and lasts for at least 8 weeks.

(c) voluntary practical experience will be acceptable only if the application is accompanied by a statement from a Chartered Member certifying that:-
  (1) the work concerned was not being used as a substitute for that of paid staff
  and
  (2) the work would not otherwise have been undertaken
  and
  (3) the work concerned did not threaten the jobs or earning levels of other paid staff

(d) annual leave included in a contract of employment, or up to 4 weeks unpaid leave per annum, will not be regarded as a break in practical experience

(e) other absences – a period of up to 4 weeks absence per year for other reasons (e.g. illness, industrial disputes, maternity/paternity leave) will not be regarded as a break in practical experience. Any additional periods of absence for such reasons will not normally be acceptable, but CILIP may exercise discretion in special circumstances. You should apply in writing if you want any additional absence to be considered.

5) Date of submission

You should normally submit your application within one year of completion of your Route A or Route B training. Half way through the year you will receive a reminder. If you wish to apply for an extension of the period you should do so before the year is ended.

6) Overseas Qualifications

If you gained your qualification in another country you must still comply with the requirements concerning Membership, Admission Qualifications and Practical Experience as set out above.

You must also provide evidence of your qualifications (original certificates or certified copies). These qualifications must be at a level equivalent to SCQF9 or HE3. CILIP can assist in establishing equivalency.

7) Form of submission

There are two parts to the submission:

(1) a form on which you provide information about the knowledge and skills you have developed since gaining your information studies qualification
(2) a portfolio of evidence of your continuing professional development

7.1 Submission form

The submission form lists the core areas of knowledge and skills for professional practice identified by CILIP. A version of this checklist is also used to assess information studies courses. You will find the submission form at the back of this handbook. It is also available on disk or can be downloaded from the website (www.cilip.org.uk)

7.2 Portfolio of Professional Development

All applicants must submit a personal portfolio of evidence of professional development. This may include existing records of achievement, including the CILIP Framework for Continuing Professional Development, National Vocational Qualifications and the National Record of Vocational Achievement.

Content

The Portfolio must include the following:

(a) evidence gathered over the full period of practical experience required under your chosen route (Route A or Route B)
(b) the titles and job descriptions of the posts you have held
(c) your curriculum vitae, which should include reference(s) to any contributions you have made to the professional literature or to professional organisations
(d) an annotated contents table, indicating the purpose of each section of the portfolio
(e) an evaluative introduction, explaining the choice of material included in the portfolio
(f) material selected to provide evidence of all of the following:
  (1) that you understand the objectives of the organisations and information services/products included in the portfolio, and are able to analyse how effectively these objectives are met

(2) the progress and development of your own personal professional practice
(3) details of training received, with an assessment of its usefulness
(4) work you have produced as part of your professional employment
(5) knowledge of United Kingdom legislation affecting library and information services
(6) understanding of the role of CILIP
(7) information of your own participation in professional activities (this does not have to be in CILIP)
(8) awareness of a range of current issues of general concern to the profession

Presentation

Portfolios should be:

(a) written in the English or Welsh language
(b) the evaluative introduction should be a maximum of 1000 words in length
(c) divided into clearly marked sections as set out in the annotated contents table
(d) word processed
(e) submitted:
  (1) in triplicate in separate binders or other covers, each bearing your name, membership number and current post. The contents must be firmly attached
  or
  (2) in triplicate on separate disks, in Word and ASCII formats. Each disk must be clearly marked with your name, membership number and current post.
  or
  (3) electronically. The first page should contain only your name, membership number and current post
(f) accompanied by the application form for the current year, and the submission fee for that year.

8) Assessment

All applications for Chartered Membership are assessed by the Chartership Board which is appointed by the CILIP Council. The Board appoints Regional Assessors to discuss applications with candidates when necessary. (See Regulation 8.2 below)

8.1 Criteria for assessment

All applications will be assessed against the same criteria. Candidates must demonstrate all of the following:

a. ability to analyse and evaluate the effectiveness of the products/services/organisations referred to in the submission
b. ability to identify and analyse problems encountered in practice
c. competence in a range of management and professional skills developed through professional practice
d. development of a personal professional viewpoint which is constantly reassessed in the light of increasing experience and knowledge
e. critical evaluation of personal performance and development
f. analysis of personal learning outcomes from training received
g. continuing professional development through reading, participation in professional affairs and attendance at courses/conferences
h. understanding of the legal and regulatory framework of information and library provision in the United Kingdom
i. an increased level of understanding of the relationship between theory and practice
j. professional judgement through selection and presentation of material in the application

8.2 Form of Assessment

All applications for admission to the Register of Chartered Members are assessed by the Chartership Board appointed by the CILIP Council.

In reaching its final assessment of your application the Board may ask you to do one or more of the following:

(a) rewrite part or parts of the application
(b) provide additional material
(c) meet with two Regional Assessors to discuss certain aspects of yourapplication.

9) Fees

There is a fee for the submission of an application to the Chartership Board.

Regulations 2002: Regulations for Professional Qualifications

These fees are reviewed annually and may be amended by the Council of CILIP with the approval of the Annual General Meeting. Information on current fees is available from the Membership, Careers and Qualifications Department, and is clearly printed on the relevant forms.

10) Date of Admission to the Register

The date of admission to the Register will normally be that on which the Board accepts your application. If you are not in Corporate Membership of CILIP you will be required to transfer to this category before being admitted to the Register.

If you are not successful you will be given guidance on making a new application. There is no limit to the number of applications you may make.

You have a right of appeal if your application is not accepted. In cases where an appeal is heard, the date of admission to the Register will be the date on which a final decision is made.

11) Appeals Procedure

Candidates whose applications are rejected have a right of Appeal, according to procedures approved by Council. A copy of the Appeals Procedure will be sent to unsuccessful candidates. (See Appendix 1 to these Regulations).

12) Regulations for Route A candidates

In addition to the general requirements for all candidates, there are specific regulations for Route A candidates and their supervisors. If you register under Route A and are subsequently unable to complete the requirements you may transfer to Route B. You will find the notes of guidance on drawing up a Training and Development Plan in Part 3: Section 8. (The proforma is in Appendix 2.)

(a) you must complete twelve months' training approved by CILIP
(b) your approved training must be supervised by a Chartered Member of CILIP
(c) you and your supervisor must be in membership of CILIP throughout the period of training
(d) if you wish to qualify by this route you must register with CILIP at the commencement of the training, and no later than four weeks from the start date of training, using the appropriate

Regulations 2002: Regulations for Professional Qualifications

(e)   form (Form Reg A) of the certificate of professional training). Registration of start of training may not normally be backdated beyond four weeks from your submission of Form Reg A

(e)   training programmes must be compiled and submitted, electronically or on paper in triplicate, by your supervisor within four weeks of the commencement of training

(f)   you must submit Form CPRA of the certificate of professional training at the end of your period of training

(g)   each period of training requires a separate training programme and registration in the timescale stipulated in Regulation 4 above. A change of supervisor constitutes a new period of training and is likewise governed by Regulation 4

(h)   Chartered Members will normally be eligible to act as supervisors of Route A candidates only if they have been at least five years on the Register

(i)   while undertaking supervised training, candidates must have a range of professional experience to enable them to be able to satisfy the criteria for admission to the Register

(j)   external supervision of training may be acceptable, normally only when there is no Chartered Member with a Proficiency Certificate [See Bye-law 11] working for the same employer

(k)   if you have two part-time jobs, supervised approved training may be undertaken in both of them

(l)   you are responsible for submission of appropriate forms within the specified timescale.

13) Regulations for Route B candidates

In addition to the general requirements for all candidates, there are specific regulations for Route B candidates. If you register under Route B and are subsequently able to transfer to Route A you are strongly advised to do so.

To register on Route B you must:

1. draw up a Personal Professional Development Plan which you will follow, covering two years of professional experience. You will find the guidance notes for this in Part 3: Section 9.1. (The template is in Appendix 2)
2. submit this plan during your first six months of employment. Plans will not normally be back-dated for more than this period
3. revise and re-submit the plan if your circumstances change (for example, by changing your job)

There is a Support Scheme for Route B candidates which you are advised to use.
(Further information is in Part 3: Section 9.2)

Appendix 1: Chartered Membership Appeals Procedures

There are two stages in the Chartered Membership procedure at which a candidate may face rejection. The first is at the end of a period of professional training for Route A. A supervisor may indicate to the Chartership Board that some aspect of the candidate's performance has been unacceptable and recommend that the training period should not be accepted. Under such circumstances the candidate would be invited to respond to the comments made by the supervisor. The Board would consider both sides of the case and decide whether or not the training should be accepted. If the Board decided not to accept the period of professional training the candidate would have the right to appeal using the procedure approved by Council.

The other stage at which a rejection may occur is after the final assessment of the candidate's application for Chartered Membership. When the decision is taken not to accept an application the candidate is sent a detailed explanation of the reasons and given any appropriate advice as to how to try to make good the shortcomings identified by the Board. The candidate will also be sent the Appeals Procedure, which sets out the grounds on which the decision of the Board may be challenged.

If it is decided that an appeal should be allowed under either procedure a Panel will be convened to hear the Appeal. This Panel will be drawn from a list of members of Council appointed for the purpose. Any candidate who is invited to appear before an Appeal Panel will be given a clear briefing before the hearing begins, to ensure that the process is fully understood and to try to reduce tension and formality.

APPEALS PROCEDURE: ROUTE A TRAINING

1) An appeal may be made against a decision of the Chartership Board not to accept a candidate's period of professional training under Route A to Chartered Membership.

2) A candidate whose period of professional training is not accepted will be sent the following documents by Recorded Delivery:
   (a) A letter informing the candidate of the decision and the date of the Board meeting at which it was made.
   (b) A summary of the points made at the Board meeting set-

ting out the reasons for rejection.
- (c) A copy of the supervising Chartered Member's comments on the candidate's suitability.
- (d) A copy of this Appeals Procedure.

3) A candidate who wishes to appeal against the decision of the Board must do so within six weeks of the date of receipt of the Recorded Delivery letter referred to in (2). The Appeal must be made in writing to the Chief Executive.

4) The only grounds on which an Appeal may be made are:
- (a) That all or part of the information used by the Board was biased or incorrect due to no fault of the candidate and that the Board did not know this at the time it took its decision
- (b) That the Board failed to follow its own published procedures and that this materially affected its decision.

5) The Chief Executive will decide whether there is a prima facie case for appeal. Where there is not he will inform the candidate of the reason for his ruling. In such cases there will be no further appeal.

6) Where there is a prima facie case for appeal, the Chief Executive will select a panel of three from up to twelve Chartered Members, not members of the Chartership Board, chosen annually by Council from among its membership for this purpose.

7) The Chief Executive will set a date for the hearing of the Appeal to take place within six weeks of the date of receipt of the candidate's written Appeal.

8) The Chief Executive will send to each member appointed to the Appeal Panel a copy of the approved training and development plan or training programme, the papers sent to the candidate referred to in 2 above, and any papers sent by the candidate in support of his/her Appeal.

9) The candidate will be invited to attend the hearing of the Appeal and may be accompanied by a friend. The Chair of the Chartership Board and the Head, Membership, Careers and Qualifications Department (or the nominee of either) should be present to represent the Board and its office based procedures. The Chief Executive should be present at all times to ensure that the Panel only consider matters appropriate to the Appeal and to offer advice.

10) At an Appeal Panel hearing the matters for consideration will

be limited to:

(a) Evidence from the candidate concerning the grounds for the Appeal, and details of how the information and/or procedures were faulty. The candidate should offer the correct information to the Panel. Panel members may question both the candidate and the representative of the Chartership Board.

The Board representative should explain the reasons for any failure to comply with published procedures.

(b) The candidate may ask the "friend" to speak on matters concerning the grounds for the Appeal. The "friend" may not assist (or speak for) the appellant in answering professional questions put by the Panel.

(c) The Panel will be concerned solely to test the candidate's claim that the Board used faulty information, biased statements or failed in its own procedures.

11) Where the Panel finds that the candidate's claim as set out in 10(c) has not been substantiated the Appeal must fail since the Board may not be challenged on other grounds.

12) Where the Panel finds that the candidate has made the case they will instruct the Board to review the matter. The Panel will give precise instructions to the Board as to the evidence which must be considered and what must be discounted. The Chair of the Panel (with assistance from the Chief Executive) will detail the evidence accepted by the Panel. The evidence and decision cannot be challenged by the Board.

13) The Board will review the case at its next meeting after the Appeal Panel hearing. The Board will give written details of its decision to the Chief Executive and the Chair of the Professional Development Committee.

14) The Chief Executive will inform the candidate of the final decision of the Board.

APPEALS PROCEDURE: CHARTERED MEMBERSHIP

1) An appeal may be made against a decision of the Chartership Board not to accept a candidate's Application for Chartered Membership (or Portfolio or Professional Development Report or Proforma and Professional Interview) submitted for the purpose of gaining admission to the Register.

2) A candidate whose submission is not accepted will be sent the following documents

by Recorded Delivery:-
- (a) A letter informing the candidate of the decision and the date of the Board meeting at which it was made.
- (b) A summary of the points made at the Board meeting and in the written reports of Board members, setting out the reasons for rejection.
- (c) Copies of the reports of Regional Assessors if an interview was held.
- (d) A copy of this Appeals Procedure.

3) A candidate who wishes to appeal against the decision of the Board must do so within six weeks of the date of receipt of the Recorded Delivery letter referred to in 2. The Appeal must be made in writing to the Chief Executive.

4) The only grounds on which an Appeal may be made are:
- (a) That all or part of the information used by the Board was biased or incorrect due to no fault of the candidate and that the Board did not know this at the time it took its decision.
- (b) That the Board failed to follow its own published procedures and that this materially affected its decision.

5) The Chief Executive will decide whether there is a prima facie case for appeal. Where there is not he will inform the candidate of the reason for his ruling. In such cases there will be no further appeal.

6) Where there is a prima facie case for appeal, the Chief Executive will select a panel of three from up to twelve Chartered Members, not members of the Chartership Board, chosen annually by Council from among its membership for this purpose.

7) The Chief Executive will set a date for the hearing of the Appeal to take place within six weeks of the date of receipt of the candidate's written Appeal.

8) The Chief Executive will send to each member appointed to the Appeal Panel a copy of the candidate's submission on his/her professional development, the papers sent to the candidate referred to in 2 above, and any papers sent by the candidate in support of his/her Appeal.

9) The candidate will be invited to attend the hearing of the Appeal and may be accompanied by a friend. The Chair of the Chartership Board and the Head, Membership, Careers and Qualifications Department (or the nominee of either) should

be present to represent the Board and its office based procedures. The Chief Executive should be present at all times to ensure that the Panel only consider matters appropriate to the Appeal and to offer advice.

10) At an Appeal Panel hearing the matters for consideration will be limited to:
   (a) Evidence from the candidate concerning the grounds for the Appeal and details of how the information and/or procedures were faulty. The candidate should offer the correct information to the Panel. Panel members may question both the candidate and the representative of the Chartership Board.
   The Board representative should explain the reasons for any failure to comply with published procedures.
   (b) The candidate may ask the "friend" to speak on matters concerning the grounds for the Appeal. The "friend" may not assist (or speak for) the appellant in answering professional questions put by the Panel.
   (c) The Panel will be concerned solely to test the candidate's claim that the Board used faulty information, biased statements or failed in its own procedures.

11) Where the Panel finds that the candidate's claim as set out in 10(c) has not been substantiated the Appeal must fail since the Board may not be challenged on other grounds.

12) Where the Panel finds that the candidate has made the case they will instruct the Board to review the matter. The Panel will give precise instructions to the Board as to the evidence which must be considered and what must be discounted. The Chair of the Panel (with assistance from the Chief Executive) will detail the evidence accepted by the Panel. The evidence and decision cannot be challenged by the Board.

13) The Board will review the case at its next meeting after the Appeal Panel hearing. The Board will give written details of its decision to the Chief Executive and the Chair of the Professional Development Committee.

14) The Chief Executive will inform the candidate of the final decision of the Board.

Regulations 2002: Regulations for Professional Qualifications

Section 2: Chartered Fellow

Note: the following are transitional arrangements, which will be reviewed during the period 1st April 2002-31st December 2004 as part of the consideration of future regulations for a Continuing Professional Development scheme for CILIP Members.

1) Membership

All candidates for Chartered Fellowship must be in current membership of CILIP.

2) Chartered Members applying for Fellowship

Candidates cannot normally submit applications for Fellowship until they have completed a period of not less than 5 years on the Register of Chartered Members of CILIP.

To qualify to transfer from Chartered Member to Chartered Fellow you must provide evidence that you:
a) have the ability to carry out demanding work
b) have the ability to handle complex professional issues
c) are contributing to the profession in general or in a specific context
d) are developing your professional knowledge
e) are maintaining and enhancing your professional competencies.

3) Associate Members applying for Fellowship

Associate Members who are not Chartered may apply for Fellowship provided that evidence is produced of having reached a level of professional development commensurate with that required for the award of Chartered Membership, followed by a period of subsequent professional practice and development comparable in duration and quality with the minima required of Chartered Members admitted to Fellowship.

4) Form of application

Application may be made by submission of documentary or other evidence of any appropriate kind (see page 6 of this handbook for further guidance).

5) Presentation

    a) Candidates should submit a statement of not more than 500 words, setting out the grounds on which the application is based.

    b) A curriculum vitae must be provided.

    c) One copy of each document or other evidence must be provided.

    d) Applications may be submitted in the English or Welsh languages. (See pages 5/6 of this handbook for further guidance).

6) Criteria for assessment

Assessment will be on the basis of the following criteria:

    a) the ability of the candidate to carry out demanding tasks and handle complex professional issues

    b) the contribution made by the candidate to all or part of the profession*.

The activities that support this criteria may either reflect the candidate's contribution to a broad area of professional work or to work in a very specific and specialised context.

Appeals Procedure – Fellowship

1. An Appeal may be made against a decision of the Chartership Board not to accept a candidate's application for the award of Fellowship.

2. A candidate whose application is not accepted will be sent the following documents by Recorded Delivery:-

    (a) a letter informing the candidate of the decision and the date of the Board meeting at which it was made

    (b) a summary of the points made at the Board meeting and in the written reports of Board members, setting out the reasons for rejection

    (c) copies of the reports of Regional Assessors (if applicable)

    (d) a copy of this Appeals Procedure.

3. A candidate who wishes to appeal against the decision of the Board must do so within six weeks of the date of receipt of the Recorded Delivery letter referred to in 2. The Appeal must be made in writing to the Chief Executive.

4. The only grounds on which an Appeal may be made are:

    (1) that all or part of the information used by the Board was biased or incorrect due to no fault of the candidate and that the Board did not know this at the time it took its

decision
- (2) that the Board failed to follow its own published procedures and that this materially affected its decision.
5. The Chief Executive will decide whether there is a prima facie case for appeal. Where there is not he will inform the candidate of the reason for his ruling. In such cases there will be no further appeal.
6. Where there is a prima facie case for appeal, the Chief Executive will select a panel of three from up to 12 Chartered members, not members of the Chartership Board, chosen annually by Council from among its membership for this purpose.
7. The Chief Executive will set a date for the hearing of the Appeal to take place within six weeks of the date of receipt of the candidate's written Appeal.
8. The Chief Executive will send to each member appointed to the Appeal Panel a copy of the candidate's application and supporting documents, the papers sent to the candidate referred to in 2 above, and any papers sent by the candidate in support of his/her Appeal.
9. The candidate will be invited to attend the hearing of the Appeal and may be accompanied by a friend. The Chair of the Chartership Board and the Head, Membership, Careers and Qualifications Department (or the nominee of either) should be present to represent the Board and its office based procedures. The Chief Executive should be present at all times to ensure that the Panel only consider matters appropriate to the Appeal, and to offer advice.
10. At an Appeal Panel hearing the matters for consideration will be limited to:
   - (1) evidence from the candidate concerning the grounds for the appeal, and details of how the information and/or procedures were faulty. The candidate should offer the correct information to the Panel. Panel members may question both the candidate and the representative of the Chartership Board. The Board representative should explain the reasons for any failure to comply with published procedures
   - (2) the candidate may ask the "friend" to speak on matters concerning the grounds for the Appeal. The "friend" may not assist (or speak for) the appellant in answering professional questions put by the Panel.

Regulations 2002: Regulations for Professional Qualifications

      (3)   the Panel will be concerned solely to test the candidate's claim that the Board used faulty information, biased statements or failed in its own procedures.

11   Where the Panel finds that the candidate's claim as set out in 10 (3) has not been substantiated the Appeal must fail since the Board may not be challenged on other grounds.

12   Where the Panel finds that the candidate has made the case they will instruct the Board to review the matter. The Panel will give precise instructions to the Board as to the evidence which must be considered, and what must be discounted. The Chair of the Panel (with assistance from the Chief Executive) will detail the evidence accepted by the Panel. The evidence and decision cannot be challenged by the Board.

13   The Board will review the case at its next meeting after the Appeal Panel hearing. The Board will give written details of its decision to the Chief Executive and the Chair of the Professional Development Committee.

14   The Chief Executive will inform the candidate of the final decision of the Board.

Appendix B: Code of Conduct and Disciplinary Proceedings

Bye-law 19 Code of Conduct
Note: The following is the current text of the LA Code of Conduct. This is under review, in consultation with the IIS. This text will be replaced with the new Code when it has been approved.

The purpose of this Code of Conduct is to set out the standards of professional conduct expected of members of the Association and to indicate what matters may be regarded by the Disciplinary Committee as being contrary to the aims, objects and interests of the Association or to the profession of librarianship. This code shall apply to all classes of individual members of the Association.

The essential principle which lies behind the Code is that the professional librarian's prime duty is to facilitate access to materials and information in order to meet the requirement of the client, irrespective of the librarian's personal interests and views on the content of the material and the client's requirement.

1. Members of the Association must conduct themselves in such a way that their conduct would not be reasonably regarded by their professional colleagues within the field of librarianship (including provision of information services) as serious professional misconduct or professional misconduct. It is by this test that the conduct overall will be judged.

2. a) Members must comply with the Charter and Bye-laws of the Association and the provisions of this Code of Conduct

    b) Members must not engage in conduct which may seriously prejudice the standing of the profession or of the Library Association

    c) Members must be competent in their professional activities including the requirement
    i.   to keep abreast with developments in librarianship in those branches of professional practice in which qualifications and experience entitle them to engage;
    ii. in respect of those members of the Association responsible for supervising the training or duties of another

Regulations 2002: Code of Conduct and Disciplinary Proceedings

librarian, to ensure that those whom they supervise are trained to carry out their duties in a competent manner.

d) Members' primary duty when acting in the capacity of librarian is to their clients, i.e. the persons or groups of persons for whose requirements and use are intended the resources and services which the members are engaged to provide. In all professional considerations the interests of the clients within their prescribed or legitimate requirements take precedence over all other interests. It is recognised that the persons or groups of persons to whom this duty is owed will vary according to the nature of the employment which members undertake. In particular it is recognised that different considerations will apply where members are working at a place to which the public has right of access from those where they are working in an environment where the public is excluded or given only limited access.

e) In places to which the public has right of access, save where the flow of information must be restricted by reason of confidentiality, members have an obligation to facilitate the flow of information and ideas and to protect and promote the rights of every individual to have free and equal access to sources of information without discrimination and within the limits of the law.

f) Members must fulfil to the best of their ability the contractual obligations owed to their employer. However circumstances may arise when the public interest or the reputation of the profession itself may be at variance with the narrower interests of an employer. If it is found to be impossible to reconcile such differences then the public interest and the maintenance of professional standards must be the primary considerations.

g) Members shall not knowingly promote material the prime purpose of which is to encourage discrimination on the grounds of race, colour, creed, gender or sexual orientation. It shall not be regarded as promoting such material to divulge it for the purpose of studying the subject of that discrimination.

h) i   Members must not divulge or permit to be divulged any

Regulations 2002: Code of Conduct and Disciplinary Proceedings

            materials, information or administrative record (in manual or electronic form) which has been entrusted to them in confidence, to any third party nor use such information without the prior consent of the client for any purpose other than that for which it was first obtained. This duty to the client continues after the relationship of librarian and client ceases.

      ii   Members are absolved from the duty set out in sub-paragraph (i) above in so far as is required by law and in so far as it is necessary to answer accusations before the Disciplinary Committee.

i) Members actions and decisions should be determined solely by their professional judgement and they should not profit from their position otherwise than by normal remuneration or fee for professional services.

j) Members must report the facts to the Secretary of the Institute if convicted of any offence involving dishonesty or one which brings the profession into disrepute.

k) Members must:
    i.   respond to any requirements from the Disciplinary Committee for comments or information on a complaint;
    ii. attend the committee proceedings when required to do so, with such representation as is provided for in the Byelaws;
    iii. attend upon a nominated person for the purpose of receiving guidance as to future conduct if required to do so.

3 a) Failure to comply with the requirements set out in paragraph 2, including the requirements relating to competence, may if proved before the Disciplinary Committee be regarded as serious professional misconduct and if so shall render the member concerned liable to be expelled or suspended (either unconditionally or subject to conditions), to be ordered to repay or forego fees and expenses as appropriate, or to be reprimanded and/or to be ordered to pay the costs of the hearing.

b) Failure to comply with the requirements set out in paragraph 2, which, in the opinion of the Disciplinary Committee, falls short of serious professional misconduct may, if proved, render the member liable to be admonished or to be given appropriate guidance as to his or her future conduct.

c) The provisions of Bye-law 21 shall apply.

Bye-law 21 Disciplinary proceedings
Interim draft prepared by legal advisers pending revised Code of Conduct

1. At its first meeting in each calendar year, the Council shall appoint a Disciplinary Committee which shall consist of the Chair of the Executive Board, the Honorary Treasurer and at least ten other members of the Council. Any Disciplinary Committee in the process of hearing a complaint shall continue as the Disciplinary Committee for that complaint for all purposes until the decision of the Council has been given on it. The Council may fill any vacancy arising in the Disciplinary Committee during the year, but no person appointed to fill a vacancy may participate in a hearing begun before his or her appointment. (A meeting of the Disciplinary Committee to decide whether a complaint is to be dismissed or further investigated shall not be deemed to be the hearing of a complaint for the purpose of this paragraph.)

2. The Disciplinary Committee shall consider all complaints laid before it in accordance with these Regulations and may from time to time make such recommendations to the Council on disciplinary matters of the Institute as it thinks fit.

3. The quorum for a meeting of the Disciplinary Committee shall be eight members. Subject thereto the Disciplinary Committee may make such regulations for the conduct of its affairs as it thinks fit and may have a legal representative or legal representatives including Counsel present on its behalf at any meeting of the Disciplinary Committee or at any meeting of the Council considering a report of the Disciplinary Committee.

4. It is the duty of the Secretary on the request of any three or more persons (whether or not Members of the Institute) or of

Regulations 2002: Code of Conduct and Disciplinary Proceedings

the Committee of any branch or group of the Institute to lay before the Disciplinary Committee any complaint against a Member of any action contrary to the aims, objects and interests of the Institute or of conduct unbecoming or prejudicial to the profession. Where any such complaint has been received by the Institute, the Council or the Secretary, the complaint shall be laid as soon as may be practicable before the Disciplinary Committee. Where any person makes a written complaint to the Secretary against a Member of action or conduct as aforesaid but the conditions of this paragraph as to the persons complaining are not satisfied, the Secretary has no duty to lay the said complaint before the Disciplinary Committee. The Secretary must nonetheless consider the complaint and lay the complaint before the Disciplinary Committee if the Secretary in his or her absolute discretion thinks fit.

5. The Secretary may lay a complaint before the Disciplinary Committee either at a meeting of the Committee or by correspondence to members of the Committee.

6. The Disciplinary Committee and the Council, in exercising their functions under these Regulations to consider complaints against members, shall have regard to the Code of Conduct issued by the Council in accordance with Byelaw 19.

7. The Disciplinary Committee shall consider any complaint laid before it and shall either dismiss the complaint or rule that the complaint requires further investigation. Members of the Committee may express their decision by correspondence, but if a meeting of the Committee is called, only, those members present at the meeting shall participate in the decision. There is no right of appeal against a decision of the Disciplinary Committee to dismiss a complaint.

8. When the Disciplinary Committee rules that a complaint requires further investigation it must give at least 28 days' written notice to the Member concerned of its intention to consider the complaint. The notice may be served personally on the Member but must otherwise be sent by registered post to the Member at his or her registered address. The notice must state the day, the time and the place of the proposed meeting, details

of the complaint and be accompanied by a copy of these Regulations made under Byelaw 21.

9. If the Disciplinary Committee rules that a complaint requires further investigation, the Committee may at the same time temporarily suspend the Member against whom the complaint has been made from the Institute. The Member shall be notified of their suspension in the notice referred to in paragraph 8 above and shall remain suspended until the Council has given its decision on the complaint. Any decision to temporarily suspend a Member requires a two thirds majority of those present at the meeting of the Disciplinary Committee.

10. The Disciplinary Committee must give the Member an opportunity of being heard before it and must, if the Member so desires, permit the Member to be represented before it by Counsel or by a solicitor or by a Member of the Institute or by a friend. The Member is entitled to call witnesses on his or her own behalf and to cross examine any witnesses called against the Member. If the Member concerned fails to reply to the notice or fails, without reasonable cause, to appear before the Committee, the Disciplinary Committee may make its recommendations in respect of the complaint without further reference to the Member concerned.

11. At the meeting of the Disciplinary Committee to consider the complaint, the Committee may resolve either to dismiss the complaint against the Member or to report the result of its inquiry to the Council together with its recommendation. Any recommendation that the Member be reprimanded, suspended or expelled from the Institute requires a two thirds majority of those present at the meeting of the Disciplinary Committee. Notice of whether the complaint is dismissed or a report has been submitted to the Council shall be given as soon as may be practicable to the Member and to the Council.

12. Every report on the result of an inquiry into a complaint and every recommendation of the Disciplinary Committee thereon shall be considered at a meeting of the Council at which the Member shall have the same rights as are provided in paragraphs 10 and 11 above, provided always that if the Member has

not replied to the notice of the resolution of the Disciplinary Committee or fails, without reasonable cause, to appear before the Council, the Council may nonetheless proceed with its consideration of the matter. Members of the Disciplinary Committee who heard the complaint concerning a Member may be present at the meeting of the Council at which the Disciplinary Committee's report concerning the Member is considered and may take part in the proceedings and deliberations of the Council meeting, but may not vote.

13. The Council may accept the findings of the Disciplinary Committee on all questions of fact but shall have discretion if it appears that there are special grounds so to do to rehear any witness who gave evidence before the Disciplinary Committee or to receive fresh evidence and hear new witnesses, in which event the Member shall be entitled to cross examine any witness called against him or her and the Council may make findings of fact from such evidence in addition to or in substitution for the facts found by the Disciplinary Committee. The Council may draw inferences from facts found and may affirm, vary or reverse the recommendation of the Disciplinary Committee. Any decision of the Council to reprimand, suspend or expel a Member requires a two thirds majority of all those present at the Council meeting and entitled to vote.

14. The Disciplinary Committee and the Council meeting to consider a report on the result of the inquiry into the complaint may have a legal assessor, being a barrister or solicitor of not less than seven years standing, to assist them on questions of law, evidence and procedure. Such assessor, if appointed, shall be present during the proceedings and deliberations of the Disciplinary Committee and the Council and shall advise upon any question of law, procedure or the admission of evidence in the proceedings as may be required.

15. Notice of the findings and decision of the Council shall be given as soon as practicable to the Member concerned, and the decision shall thereupon take effect at the time the Notice is deemed to have been served. The decision of the Council shall be final and binding on the Member. The Council may, in its absolute discretion, decide to publish its decision or any deci-

Regulations 2002: Code of Conduct and Disciplinary Proceedings

sion of the Disciplinary Committee to dismiss a complaint in such newspapers and journals, including branch journals, as it shall think desirable. No branch or group may publish any report of any decision on disciplinary matters in any journal or otherwise except with the prior consent of the Secretary.

16. The Notice of the finding and decision of the Council shall be given in accordance with Byelaw 97.

17. The Disciplinary Committee of the Council may resolve that any member of the Disciplinary Committee or the Council (as the case may be) be excluded from any meeting of the Disciplinary Committee or the Council concerned with hearing a disciplinary complaint on the grounds that the just hearing of the complaint appears to require that such member be excluded.

Appendix C: Regulations for the Retired Members' Guild

Bye-law 44

Objects

1. The objects of the Retired Members' Guild are to encourage Members of the Chartered Institute of Library and Information Professionals to remain in membership after retirement, to foster their social interaction, and to afford them the opportunity of making a positive contribution to librarianship and information science.

Activities

1. To support the efforts of the Chartered Institute of Library and Information Professionals for the improvement of libraries of all types.
2. To keep Members in touch with one another by arranging meetings and conferences and by the publication of a newsletter.
3. To seek out and make known, further benefits available for retired members.
4. To assist in the work of appropriate voluntary organizations by publicizing their activities and maintaining a register of expertise.
5. To undertake historical research and the conservation of records relating to the history of the Institute and its Branches and Groups.

Membership

Membership of the Guild is open to all personal Members of the Chartered Institute of Library and Information Professionals and to representatives of institutional members appointed in accordance with the bye-laws of the Institute. Persons and institutions shall become members of the Guild on notifying a desire to do so to the Secretary of the Guild and on of payment of the additional subscription.

The Guild shall be able to admit, at the discretion of the National Committee, persons who cannot be Fellows or Members of the Chartered Institute of Library and Information Professionals, as Personal Affiliates. Such members will not have the right to vote and will not be entitled to hold office. They will pay such annual subscriptions as may be determined by the National Committee.

Subordinate Bodies

The Guild Committee shall have authority to establish subordinate bodies on a regional or subject basis. The Committee shall require the Chair or Secretary of any such subordinate body to report regularly on its activities. The National Committee shall lay down such provisions for the conduct of business of subordinate bodies as it sees fit.

Officers

The Officers of the Guild shall be:

Chair
Secretary
Treasurer
Editor

Guild Committee

The affairs of the Guild shall be governed by a committee comprising the officers of the Guild and six elected members of the Guild. In addition the committee may co-opt up to three members of the Guild to the committee.

The Guild Year

The Year for all Guild activities, including terms of office and accounts shall be the calendar year.

Terms of Office

Officers of the Guild shall hold office for two years. Other committee members shall hold office for two years. In both cases terms shall commence on 1 January following election.

Elections

The election of officers and committee members shall be conducted in accordance with the regulations set out in Annex A (available upon application).

Committee Procedure

The Guild Committee shall meet not less frequently than twice a year. Meetings shall be called by the Chair or the Secretary. The Chair or Secretary shall call a meeting whenever required to do so by one third of the members of the committee and at other times at their discretion.

Each member of the committee, including co-opted members, shall exercise one vote. Observers invited to attend committee meetings shall have no vote. In the event of a tie, the chair shall have a casting vote irrespective of whether he/she has exercised his/her initial vote on the same issue. No decisions shall be taken by the committee if fewer than one quarter of the members are present but the committee may continue to sit despite the lack of that quorum.

The committee shall have authority to establish sub-committees and working parties as appropriate to deal with matters within the responsibilities of the Guild.

Accounts and Treasurer

The Treasurer of the Guild shall be responsible for the receipt of all monies due to the Guild and shall make such payments as the committee shall direct and shall maintain accounts of all receipts, payments, assets and liabilities of the Guild. In discharging his/her duties the Treasurer of the Guild shall adhere to the requirements of the byelaws of the Chartered Institute of Library and Information Professionals and shall abide by such guidance as the Chartered Institute of Library and Information Professionals issues with regard to the keeping of accounts.

Two honorary auditors shall be appointed at the annual general meeting of the Guild. The honorary auditors shall not be members of the Guild committee and need not be members of the Guild. They shall be required to sign a certificate in respect of the adequacy of the accuracy of the accounts as presented to the annual general meeting.

The audited accounts, in addition to being presented to the annual general meeting, shall be communicated to members of the Guild either in the Guild's newsletter or otherwise.

Secretary

The Secretary of the Guild shall maintain a record of all proceedings and shall be responsible for preparing reports, issuing notices, conducting correspondence, giving notice of impending elections, circulating ballot papers in accordance with the election regulations in Annex A, and the safe keeping of ballot papers. She/he shall forward to the Secretary of the Chartered Institute of Library and Information Professionals any reports and records required under the bye-laws of the Institute and shall submit regularly to the Institute copies of the minutes of the Guild Committee meetings and general meetings of the Guild.

Annual General Meeting

A general meeting of the members of the Guild shall be held each year before 30 June. Preliminary notice of the date of the meeting and the business to be considered shall be given to all members of the Guild not less than five weeks before the date of the meeting. Notice of further business proposed by the members shall be given to all members of the Guild not less than three weeks before the date of the meeting. Notice of the dates of meetings and of the business to be transacted shall be provided to members either by notice in the Chartered Institute of Library and Information Professionals *Update* or in the Guild newsletter or by other direct postal communication to members of the Guild.

At the annual general meeting there shall be distributed to every member present a copy of the audited accounts and the annual report of the Guild committee for the previous year. The texts of the annual report and accounts shall be communicated to all members of the Guild either in the Guild's newsletter or otherwise.

Special General Meeting

The Secretary of the Guild shall convene a special general meeting of the Guild when required to do so either by the Guild committee or by any 20 members of the Guild. Any demand for a special meeting shall state the business proposed to be conducted at the meeting. A special general meeting shall be held not later than 10 weeks after the receipt of the demand. A notice of the meeting and of the business to be conducted shall be given to all members of the Guild not less than three weeks before the date fixed for the meeting. It shall contain the words of any motion which has been submitted for the meeting. All members of the Guild shall be entitled to vote on any such motion whether present at the special meeting or not and for this purpose ballot papers shall be circulated with the notice of the meeting. The notice shall specify that ballot papers are to be returned not later than the day before the date of the special meeting.

No business shall be conducted at a special meeting unless 30 members of the Guild are present, irrespective of the number of ballot papers which have been returned by post.

Votes at general meetings shall be by show of hands unless the meeting decides otherwise by simple majority. Only those persons entitled to vote in elections of the Guild as detailed above shall be entitled to vote. In the event of a tie the chair of the meeting shall exercise a casting vote irrespective of whether he/she has exercised an initial vote on the issue.

Procedure at General Meetings

The chair of a general meeting shall conduct its business as far as possible in accordance with the rules of procedure adopted by the Chartered Institute of Library and Information Professionals for its general meetings mutatis mutandis.

Accidental Omissions

Any accidental omission to give notice to or the non-receipt of notice by any member of the Guild shall not invalidate any resolution passed or proceedings held at any meeting.

Amendment of these rules

These rules may be amended only by decision of a general meeting of the Guild. No amendment shall be adopted unless it has been approved by two-thirds of the members voting in person or by postal ballot as detailed above. No amendment shall take effect until it has been approved by the Council of the Chartered Institute of Library and Information Professionals.

Appendix D: Regulations for Affiliated Members

1) Affiliated Membership of the Chartered Institute of Library and Information Professionals is available to all persons working in library and information services other than those entitled to be Chartered, Associate or Supporting Members of the Institute.

2) The purpose of the Affiliated Membership category is to encourage contact between members, to offer opportunity to such members to participate fully in the affairs of the Institute and to contribute to discussion of all matters relevant to the provision of library and information services.

3) There shall be an Affiliated Members' National Committee elected by Affiliated Members.

4) The Committee shall comprise:
   i. Six members elected by Affiliated Members of whom two shall retire each year. Retiring members of the Committee shall be eligible for re-election.
   ii. The two Affiliated Members' Councillors elected under Bye-law 45(e) of the Chartered Institute of Library and Information Professionals.
   iii. Up to three Affiliated Members of the Institute co-opted by the Committee.

5) A postal ballot shall be held annually for the election of the six Members referred to in Regulation 4(i) above. No postal ballot shall be required if the requisite number of nominations shall be made in writing, signed by two Affiliated Members and countersigned by the candidate who must also be an Affiliated Member. Nominations shall be made in writing, signed by two Affiliated Members and countersigned by candidate who must also be an Affiliated Member. Nominations must reach the Secretary of the National Committee by the date specified in the notice of election. All Affiliated Members who have not been suspended under the Institute's Bye-law 18 shall be eligible to vote. Notice of the election shall be published in the Chartered Institute of Information Professionals *Update* in the month preceding the election and the National Committee

Regulations 2002: Regulations for Affiliated Members

shall take such other steps as it deems appropriate to advertise the election to its Members. In the first elections held under this regulation two places shall be for a term of three years. The terms for each elected Member shall be established by lot.

6) The Officers of the Affiliated Membership category shall be:
A Chair
An Honorary Secretary
An Honorary Treasurer
chosen each year by the members of the Committee from among their own number.

7) Any vacancy occurring in the National Committee (apart from that of the two Affiliated Members' Councillors) shall be filled for the remainder of its term by the unsuccessful candidate at the preceding election who scored the largest number of votes. If there is no such candidate the Committee shall fill the vacancy by co-option.

8) The Committee shall meet at least three times a year. The quorum for a meeting of the National Committee shall be one third of the members of the Committee subject to a minimum of three.

9) The Committee may authorize the establishment of Affiliated Members' Branches to serve as a vehicle for bringing together Affiliated Members in particular areas and shall make such arrangements for the governance of such branches as it sees fit, subject to approval by the Council of the Chartered Institute of Library and Information Professionals.

10) The Committee will have the authority to establish special subject sub-committees, when appropriate, to deal with matters which are the concern of Affiliated Members and may nominate to serve upon such sub-committees persons who are not members of the Affiliated Members' Committee.

(11) The Honorary Secretary of the Affiliated Membership category shall call all meetings of the National Committee and shall prepare and circulate to other members agendas, minutes and other appropriate papers and shall liaise with Chartered Institute of

Regulations 2002: Regulations for Affiliated Members

Library and Information Professionals Headquarters.

12) The Treasurer shall be responsible for all receipts and payments of funds of the Committee.

13) The Committee shall make an annual report to the Chartered Institute of Library and Information Professionals' on the affairs of the Committee and the Treasurer shall provide to Chartered Institute of Library and Information Professionals Headquarters income and expenditure accounts for each calendar year and a balance sheet as at the end of that year before 28 February in the next following year.

14) An Annual General Meeting of the Affiliated Members category shall be called each year on a date between 1 January and 30 April. The Annual General Meeting shall receive the accounts and a report on the activities of the category during the previous year.

15) Notice of the date and place of the Annual General Meeting shall be given to all Affiliated Members at least five weeks before the date of the meeting together with information on the matters to be discussed at the meeting. Any Affiliated Members may submit a motion of consideration at the meeting on giving at least two weeks' notice to the Secretary before the date of the meeting.

16) Any 20 Affiliated Members may require the Honorary Secretary to call a Special General Meeting of Affiliated Members upon serving a written notice requesting the meeting and stating its purpose. Such a meeting shall be held within eight weeks of the notice being served upon the Honorary Secretary of the National Committee. A notice of the meeting and the business to be considered shall be given to all Affiliated Members not less than three weeks before the date fixed for the meeting. Such notification shall contain the words of any motion which the member requiring the meeting intends to introduce.

17) The quorum for a meeting of an Annual or Special General Meeting shall be 20 members.

Regulations 2002: Regulations for Affiliated Members

18) At any Annual or Special General Meeting on the demand of one-quarter of the Members present, rising in their seats after the Members have voted upon a motion but before the next business has been taken the Chairman shall rule that the motion be referred to a postal ballot of the Members and that the decision of the postal ballot shall be deemed to be the decision of the Meeting.

19) In the event of a tie an any vote at an Annual General Meeting, Special General Meeting or at a meeting of the National Committee, the Chair of the meeting shall have a casting vote additional to his/her other original vote.

Subject index for CILIP Charter, Bye-Laws and Regulations

	Charter	Bye-laws	Regulations
Affiliated Members		4, 6	Appendix D
Audit and Accounts		79-80	88-89
Branches	2(l)	81-86, 104	90-95
Bye-laws	11-12		
Charter, amendments to	13		
Code of Conduct	19-20		Appendix B
Committees	9	66-70	58-87
Council	6-8	43-65, 101-103	
Council composition		45-46	
Councillors - Elections		47-53	24-57
Councillors - Terminations		54-57	
Disciplinary Proceedings		21	Appendix B
Executive Board		67-69	58, 61, 69, 74, 76
Expenses	3(e)	78	86
Financial Matters		71-80	
General Meetings	10	22-42	
Groups	2(l)	87-93	96-104
Honorary Fellows		4, 8	5-8
Honorary Officers		2, 47-53	24-57
Income and Property	3	71-78	
Indemnity	3(f), 7-8	100	
Interpretation	1	2	
Investments	2(o), 7	74-77	
Members	4-5	4-8, 19-21	1-4
Minutes			23
Notices		97-99	
Objects and Powers	2		
Organisations in Liaison		94	105-112
Postal Ballot		42	
Professional Qualifications		9-17	11, Appendix A
Proxy Votes		37-40	16-22
Register	2(h)	9-17	9-10
Remuneration	3(a)(b)		
Retired Members' Guild			Appendix C
Seal		96	
Secretary		95	
Special Interest Groups	2(l)	87-93	96-104

Subject index for CILIP Charter, Bye-laws and Regulations

Subscriptions	2(n)	18	12–13
Votes of Members		33–42	
Winding-up	14		

Part 3
GENERAL INFORMATION

Affiliated Members National Committee

Special category of CILIP Membership for paraprofessionals, library assistants, and those who hold clerical or administrative posts within a library and information service. The National Committee runs special events and publishes a newsletter.

Chair

Jim Jackson
c/o The Law Library
University of Exeter
Rennes Drive
Exeter EX4 4RJ
Telephone: +44 (0)1392 263356
Fax: +44 (0)1392 263196 or +44 (0)1392 263871
E-mail: j.j.jackson@exeter.co.uk

Secretary

Gerdette Doyle
c/o Antrim Group Library Headquarters
Ballycraigy School
Bracken Avenue
Antrim
Northern Ireland BT41 1PU
Telephone: +44 (0)28 9446 8125
E-mail: gerdettedoyle@hotmail.com

CILIP Liaison Officer

Judith Howells
judith.howells@cilip.org.uks

Website

www.cilip.org.uk/groups/amnc/amnc.html

CILIP Benevolent Fund

The Benevolent Fund was established by The Library Association in the last century and became a registered charity in 1964. With the formation of CILIP in 2002, it changed its name to the CILIP Benevolent Fund and its Trust Deed was amended to enable it to provide help to all Members of CILIP and former members of The Library Association and The Institute of Information Scientists, together with their dependents.

The Fund is able to provide emergency assistance by means of either a grant or an interest free loan, to help in meeting any unusual or unexpected expenses that are causing anxiety and hardship. Its income derives principally from CILIP Members' donations, plus interest on that part of its capital that has been invested. The Fund is a separate registered charity from CILIP and its finances do not form part of those of CILIP. It is administered by seven Trustees appointed by CILIP Council, who meet at least three times a year. However, between meetings most requests for help can be promptly met as the Chair is authorised to take action provided that is in accordance with agreed policy.

A leaflet – *The Benevolent Fund: what it is and what it does* – is readily available from the Secretary of the Fund. All enquiries should be addressed to the Secretary in the first instance.

Trustees

Godfrey Thompson (Chair), Terence Bell, Graham Cornish, Bernard Naylor, Lorna Paulin, Gillian Pentelow, Jean Plaister

Secretary

Eric Winter
CILIP Benevolent Fund
7 Ridgmount Street
London WC1E 7AE
Telephone: +44 (0)20 7255 0648
Fax: +44 (0)20 7255 0501
E-mail: eric.winter@cilip.org.uk

Registered Charity number

237352

Branches

In the developing regional and devolution agenda, CILIP's Branches are an influential voice for the profession, as well as providing important opportunities for the personal professional development of Members. CILIP is redrawing the boundaries of its Branches in England to match the Regional Development Agencies (RDAs).

The information that follows reflects the current geographical coverage, which will be subject to change in England during 2003.

Branches

Berkshire, Buckinghamshire and Oxfordshire Branch (BBOB)

Covers Berkshire, Buckinghamshire and Oxfordshire.

Chair

Vicky Hibberd
OXERA
Blue Boar Court
Alfred Street
Oxford OX1 4EH
Telephone: +44 (0)1865 253000
Fax: +44 (0)1865 251172
E-mail: vicky_hibberd@oxera.co.uk

Hon. Secretary

Catherine Lidbetter
Bulmershe Library
The University of Reading
Bulmershe Court
Woodlands Avenue
Earley
Reading RG6 1HY
Telephone: +44 (0)118 931 8652
Fax: +44 (0)118 931 8651
E-mail: c.s.lidbetter@rdg.ac.uk

CILIP Liaison Officer

Marion Huckle
marion.huckle@cilip.org.uk

Website

www.cilip.org.uk/bbob

CILIP in Scotland

Chair

Derek Law
Librarian and Director of Information Strategy
Andersonian Library
University of Strathclyde
Curran Building
101 St James Road
Glasgow G4 0NS

Director CILIP in Scotland

Elaine Fulton
1st floor Building C
Brandon Gate
Leechlee Road
Hamilton ML3 6AU
Telephone: +44 (0)1698 458888
Fax: +44 (0)1698 458899
E-mail: cilips@slainte.org.uk

CILIP Liaison Officer

Bob McKee
bob.mckee@cilip.org.uk

Website

www.slainte.org.uk/CILIPS/clpshome.htm *or* www.cilip.org.uk/scotland

Branches

CILIP Wales/CILIP Cymru

Chair

Rhidian Griffiths
The National Library of Wales
Aberystwyth
Ceredigion SY23 3BU
Telephone: +44 (0)1970 632801
Fax: +44 (0)1970 632882
E-mail: wrg@wlgc.org.uk

Executive Officer CILIP Wales/CILIP Cymru

Huw Evans
c/o Department of Information and Library Studies
University of Wales Aberystwyth
Llanbadarn Fawr
Aberystwyth
Ceredigion SY23 3AS
Telephone: +44 (0)1970 622174
Fax: +44 (0)1970 622190
E-mail: hle@aber.ac.uk

CILIP Liaison Officer

Sue Brown
   sue.brown@cilip.org.uk

Website

http://users.aber.ac.uk/hle/ *or* www.cilip.org.uk/wales

CILIP in Ireland

Chair

Madeleine Coyle
North West Institute of F & H Education Library
Strand Road
Derry
Northern Ireland BT48 7BY
Telephone: +44 (0)28 7127 6127
Fax: +44 (0)28 7126 7054
E-mail: memc@nwifhe.ac.uk

Executive Secretary

Elga Logue
BELB
40 Academy Street
Belfast
Northern Ireland BT1 2NQ
Telephone: +44 (0)28 9056 4011
Fax: +44 (0)28 9033 1714
E-mail: elgal@belb.co.uk

CILIP Liaison Officer

Bob McKee
bob.mckee@cilip.org.uk

Branches

East Midlands Branch

Covers Derbyshire, Leicestershire, Lincolnshire, Northamptonshire and Nottinghamshire.

President

Kath Owen
26 Manor Close
Costock
Loughborough
Leics LE12 6XH
Telephone:
Fax: +44 (0)1623 629276
E-mail: kath.owen@nottscc.gov.uk

Hon. Secretary

Rob McInroy
(Lincolnshire Libraries)
Lincolnshire County Council
Brayford House
Lucy Tower Street
Lincoln LN1 1YL
Telephone: +44 (0)1522 552851
Fax: +44 (0)1522 552858
E-mail: rob.mcinroy@lincolnshire.gov.uk

CILIP Liaison Officer

Michael Martin
michael.martin@cilip.org.uk

Website

www.cilip.org.uk/em

Eastern Branch

Covers Cambridgeshire, Norfolk and Suffolk.

Chair

Jenny Salisbury
Customer Services Manager (Cambridge City)
Cambridgeshire Libraries and Information Services
Central Library
7 Lion Yard,
Cambridge CB2 3QD
Telephone: +44 (0)1223 712003
Fax: +44 (0)1223 712019
E-mail: jenny.salisbury@cambridgeshire.gov.uk

Secretary

Jacky Offord
Sure Start Community Librarian
Central Library,
Clapham Road South
Lowestoft
Suffolk NR32 1DR
Telephone: +44 (0)1502 405335
Fax: +44 (0)1502 405350
E-mail: jacky.offord@libher.suffolkcc.gov.uk

CILIP Liaison Officer

Barbara Stratton
barbara.stratton@cilip.org.uk

Website

www.elipp.org.uk/

Branches

London and Home Counties Branch

Covers Bedfordshire, Essex, Hertfordshire, Kent, London, Surrey, East Sussex and West Sussex.

Joint Chair

Keith Stevens
21 Meridian Way
Amwell Lane
Great Amwell
Herts. SG12 9SS
Telephone: +44 (0)1920 877043
Fax: +44 (0)1920 877043
E-mail: keithrstevens@compuserve.com

Joint Chair

Diana Grimwood-Jones
Artemis Consulting
19 Kynaston Road
London N16 0EA
Telephone: +44 (0)20 7249 3181
Fax: +44 (0)20 7249 3181
E-mail: diana@artemisconsult.demon.co.uk

Executive Secretary

Eric Winter
CILIP
7 Ridgmount Street
London WC1E 7AE
Telephone: +44 (0)20 7255 0648
Fax: +44 (0)20 7255 0501
E-mail: eric.winter@cilip.org.uk

CILIP Liaison Officer

Bob McKee
bob.mckee@cilip.org.uk

Website

www.cilip.org.uk/lhc

North West Branch

Covers Cumbria, Lancashire, Cheshire, Merseyside, Manchester, and the Isle of Man.

Chair

Peter Brophy
CERLIM
Department of Information and Communications
The Manchester Metropolitan University
Geoffrey Manton Building
Rosamond Street West
Manchester M15 6LL
Telephone: +44 (0)161 247 6153
Fax: +44 (0)161 247 6351
E-mail: p.brophy@mmu.ac.uk

Hon. Secretary

Albert Hartley
2 Solway Close
Cinnamon Brow
Warrington
Cheshire WA2 0UP
Telephone: +44 (0)1925 810788
E-mail: albert_hartley@hotmail.com/albert_hartley@ntlworld.com

CILIP Liaison Officer

Lyndsay Rees-Jones
lyndsay.rees-jones@cilip.org.uk

Website

www.cilip.org.uk/nw

Branches

Northern Branch

Covers Durham, Northumberland, those parts of Yorkshire lying within Darlington and Teesside postal districts, Newcastle upon Tyne, Gateshead, Hartlepool, Middlesborough, Redcar and Stockton-on-Tees.

Chair

Jane Hall
City Library and Arts Centre
Fawcett Street
Sunderland SR1 1RE
Telephone: +44 (0)191 514 8404
Fax: +44 (0)191 514 8428
E-mail: jane.fhall@edcom.sunderland.gov.uk

Hon. Secretary

Pamela Dodds
Robinson Library
University of Newcastle upon Tyne
Newcastle upon Tyne NE2 4HQ
Telephone: +44 (0)191 222 5143
Fax: +44 (0)191 222 6235
E-mail: pamela.dodds@ncl.ac.uk

CILIP Liaison Officer

Kathy Ennis
kathy.ennis@cilip.org.uk

Website

www.cilip.org.uk/northern

South Western Branch

Covers Bath, North East Somerset, Bournemouth, Bristol, Cornwall, Devon, Isle of Wight, North Somerset, Poole, Portsmouth, South Gloucestershire, Somerset, Southampton, Swindon, Torbay, Wiltshire, Channel Islands.

President

Sarah Dobson
King Sturge
40 Berkeley Square
Bristol BS8 1HV
Telephone: +44 (0)117 930 5690
Fax: +44 (0)117 929 9669
E-mail: sarahdobson@kingsturge.co.uk

Hon. Secretary

Andrew Davey
Exeter Central Library
Castle Street
Exeter EX4 3PQ
Telephone: +44 (0)1392 384225
Fax: +44 (0)1392 384228
E-mail: Ajdavey@devon.gov.uk

CILIP Liaison Officer

Jill Martin
jill.martin@cilip.org.uk

Website

www.cilip.org.uk/sw

Branches

West Midland Branch

Covers Herefordshire, Worcestershire, Shropshire, Staffordshire, Warwickshire and West Midlands.

Chair

Kate Millin
Dudley Central Library
St James's Street
Dudley DY1 1HR
Telephone: +44 (0)1384 814745
Fax: +44 (0)1384 815543
E-mail: kate.millin@dudley.gov.uk

Hon. Secretary

Brian Hall
School of Information Studies
University of Central England
Perry Barr
Birmingham B42 2SU
Telephone: +44 (0)121 331 5688
Fax: +44 (0)121 331 5675
E-mail: brianhall@msn.com

CILIP Liaison Officer

Susan Kay
susan.kay@cilip.org.uk

Website

www.cilip.org.uk/wm

Yorkshire and Humberside Branch

Covers Barnsley, Bradford, Calderdale, Doncaster, East Riding of Yorkshire, Huddersfield, Kingston upon Hull, Kirklees, Leeds, North East Lincolnshire, North Lincolnshire, North Yorkshire (except those parts lying within the postal districts of Darlington and Teesside), Rotherham, Sheffield, Wakefield, York.

Chair

Ronan O'Beirne
Shipley Library
2 Wellcroft
Shipley
West Yorkshire BD18 3QH
Telephone: +44 (0)1274 757155
Fax: +44 (0)1274 530247
E-mail: ronan@openline.go-legend.net

Hon. Secretary

Alison Jobey
The Sheep Pen
161 Manchester Road
Deepcar
Sheffield S36 2QY
Telephone: +44 (0)114 203 7121
Fax: +44 (0)114 203 7000
E-mail: a.jobey@talk21.com

CILIP Liaison Officer

Judith Howells
judith.howells@cilip.org.uk

Website

www.cilip.org.uk/yh

Special Interest Groups

CILIP's Groups enable Members to share their professional concerns and interests. Membership of two Groups is included in the CILIP subscription but Members may join as many others as they wish on payment of a nominal charge for each. CILIP directly supports its Groups by providing funding for events and activities, as well as helping to cover the costs of production of regular newsletters.

Branch and Mobile Libraries Group (BAMLG)

For all staff working in public libraries, with special reference to staff managing branches and mobiles.

Chair

Michael Brook
West Berkshire Libraries
Avonbank House
West Street
Newbury
Berks RG14 1BZ
Telephone: +44 (0)1635 519580
Fax: +44 (0)1635 519936
E-mail: mbrook@westberks.gov.uk

Hon. Secretary

Vivien Warren
145 Queens Park Road
Brighton
East Sussex BN2 0GH
Telephone: +44 (0)1273 697224
E-mail: vivw@aol.com

CILIP Liaison Officer

Judith Howells
judith.howells@cilip.org.uk

Website

www.cilip.org.uk/groups/bmlg/index.html

Special Interest Groups

Career Development Group (CDG)

Encourages Members to involve themselves in all aspects of professional activity and is committed to giving a voice to newer Members of the library and information profession.

President

Tracy Long
6 Goulds Hill Close
Upwey
Weymouth DT3 4LG
Telephone: +44 (0)1305 762401
Fax: +44 (0)1305 762409
E-mail: t.long@dorset-cc.gov.uk

Hon. Secretary

Joanna Ball
Trinity College Library
Cambridge
CB2 1TQ
Telephone: +44 (0)1223 338568
Fax: +44 (0)1223 338532
E-mail: jeb30@cam.ac.uk

CILIP Liaison Officer

Marion Huckle
marion.huckle@cilip.org.uk

Website

www.careerdevelopmentgroup.org.uk

Cataloguing and Indexing Group (CIG)

Unites Members engaged or interested in the organisation and retrieval of information and in the planning, production, maintenance and exploitation of library catalogues, bibliographies and indexes.

Chair

Alan Danskin
British Library
Scholarship and Collections
Boston Spa
Wetherby
W. Yorks LS23 7BQ
Telephone: +44 (0)1937 546669
Fax: +44 (0)1937 546979
E-mail: alan.danskin@bl.uk

Hon. Secretary

Emma Bull
Team Leader: Information Resources Management
Central Library
Imperial College of Science, Technology and Medicine
Exhibition Road
London SW7 2AZ
Telephone: +44 (0)20 7594 8883
Fax: +44 (0)20 7594 8876
E-mail: e.bull@ic.ac.uk

CILIP Liaison Officer

Mark Field
mark.field@cilip.org.uk

Website

www.cilip.org.uk/cig

Special Interest Groups

Colleges of Further and Higher Education Group (CoFHE)

Promotes the role of library and information services, and of the profession, in further education, higher education and sixth form colleges.

Chair

Vacancy

Vice-Chair

Chris Kelland
Implementation Manager
NLM-MDIT
Becta
Milburn Hill Road
Coventry CV4 7JJ
Telephone: +44 (0)24 7641 6994
Fax: +44 (0)24 7641 1418
E-mail: Chris_Kelland@becta.org.uk

Hon. Secretary

Helen Ashton
Librarian
Bishop Auckland College
Woodhouse Lane
Bishop Auckland
Co. Durham DL14 6JR
Telephone: +44 (0)1388 443018
Fax: +44 (0)1388 609294
E-mail: helen.ashton@bacoll.ac.uk

CILIP Liaison Officer

Kathy Ennis
kathy.ennis@cilip.org.uk

Website

www.cilip.org.uk/cofhe

Community Services Group (CSG)

Under the banner 'information, equality, opportunity', the Group promotes equal access for all communities to library and information services, and combats social exclusion.

Acting Chair

Philip Wark
Library HQ
Midlothian Council
2 Clerk Street
Loanhead
Midlothian EH20 9DR
Telephone: +44 (0)131 271 3971
Fax: +44 (0)131 440 4635
E-mail: philip.wark@midlothian.gov.uk

Hon. Secretary

Nick Coe
County Community Services Librarian
County Library HQ
81 North Walls
Winchester SO23 8BY
Telephone: +44 (0)1962 826629
Fax: +44 (0)1962 856615
E-mail: nick.coe@hants.gov.uk

CILIP Liaison Officer

Jonathan Douglas
jonathan.douglas@cilip.org.uk

Website

www.cilip.org.uk/csg

Special Interest Groups

Education Librarians Group (ELG)

Concerned with the provision of library and information services to all involved in education as a profession, or the study of education.

Chair

Judy Reading
Department of Educational Studies
Oxford University
15 Norham Gardens
Oxford OX2 6PY
Telephone: +44 (0)1865 274 024
Fax: +44 (0)1865 274 027
E-mail: judy.reading@educational-studies.oxford.ac.uk

Hon. Secretary

Clare Swanson
General Teaching Council for England
344–354 Gray's Inn Road
London WC1X 8BP
Telephone: +44 (0)20 7841 2921
Fax: +44 (0)20 7841 2909
E-mail: clare.swanson@gtc.org.uk

CILIP Liaison Officer

Michael Martin
michael.martin@cilip.org.uk

Website

www.cilip.org.uk/elg

Government Libraries Group (GLG)

Represents the professional interests of library and information workers in Government Departments, Agencies, Parliamentary and National library and information services.

Chair

Suzanne Burge
Library and Information Service
Ombudsman's Office
15th Floor
Millbank Tower
Millbank
London SW1P 4QP
Telephone: +44 (0)20 7217 4102
Fax: +44 (0)20 7217 4295
E-mail: suzanne.burge@ombudsman.gsi.gov.uk

Hon. Secretary

David Taylor
Intranet Content Team
Information Services
Department for Work and Pensions
Room 2/E22
Quarry House
Quarry Hill
Leeds LS2 7UA
Telephone: +44 (0)113 232 4237
Fax: +44 (0)113 232 4209
E-mail: david.taylor2@dwp.gsi.gov.uk

CILIP Liaison Officer

Mark Field
mark.field@cilip.org.uk

Website

www.cilip.org.uk/glg

Special Interest Groups

Health Libraries Group (HLG)

Unites all those working or interested in library and information services for medical, nursing and allied health professions, for people with disabilities and health problems, the housebound and those in residential care, and for carers and patients in hospital.

Chair

Jackie Lord
Head of Library and Information Services
Royal College of Nursing
20 Cavendish Square
London W1G 0RN
Telephone: +44 (0)20 7647 3616
Fax: +44 (0)20 7647 3420
E-mail: jackie.lord@rcn.org.uk

Hon. Secretary

James Beaton
Librarian
Royal College of Physicians and Surgeons of Glasgow
232-242 St Vincent Street
Glasgow G2 5RJ
Telephone: +44 (0)141 227 3204
Fax: +44 (0)141 221 1804
E-mail: james.beaton@rcpsglasg.ac.uk

CILIP Liaison Officer

Guy Daines
guy.daines@cilip.org.uk

Website

www.cilip.org.uk/hlg

Industrial and Commercial Libraries Group (ICLG)

Represents library and information workers in a wide range of commercial and industrial workplaces, and those acting as independent consultants. Also includes an Aerospace and Defence Librarians Sub-Group.

Chair

Simon Jones (until December 2002)
Pemberton Greenish
45 Pont Street
London SW1X 0BX
Telephone: +44 (0)20 7591 3373
Fax: +44 (0)20 7591 3300
E-mail: s.jones@pglaw.co.uk

Vice-Chair

Jill Halford
Charles Taylor and Co. Ltd
International House
1 St Katharine's Way
London E1 9UN
Telephone: +44 (0)20 7522 6457
Fax: +44 (0)20 7522 7527
E-mail: jill.halford@ctcplc.com

Secretary

Dawn Taylor-Williams
Olswang
90 High Holborn
London WC1V 6XX
Telephone: +44 (0)20 7067 3000
Fax: +44 (0)20 7067 3999
E-mail: dawn.taylor-williams@olswang.com

CILIP Liaison Officer

Lyndsay Rees-Jones
lyndsay.rees-jones@cilip.org.uk

Website

www.iclg.org.uk

Special Interest Groups

Information Services Group (ISG)

Supports Members' interests in the provision of information services by promoting activities that improve the effectiveness of information provision to all sectors of society.

Chair

Valerie Nurcombe
42 Moors Lane
Darnhall
Winsford
Cheshire CW7 1JX
Telephone: +44 (0)1606 558242
Fax: +44 (0)1606 558242
E-mail: nurcombe@cix.co.uk

Hon. Secretary

Diana Herman
Main Library
University College London
Gower Street
London WC1E 6BT
Telephone: +44 (0)20 7679 2612
Fax: +44 (0)20 7679 7373
E-mail: d.herman@ucl.ac.uk

CILIP Liaison Officer

Jill Martin
jill.martin@cilip.org.uk

Website

www.cilip.org.uk/isg

International Library and Information Group (ILIG)

Unites Members worldwide who have a strong interest in international work, fostering good international relations, encouraging closer understanding and contributing to the development of library and information services overseas.

Chair

Paul Sturges
Department of Information Science
Loughborough University
Loughborough LE11 3TU
Telephone: +44 (0)1509 223069
Fax: +44 (0)1509 223053
E-mail: r.p.sturges@lboro.ac.uk

Secretary

Diana Rosenberg
The Secretary, ILIG
Roadways
The Ridge
Bussage
Stroud
Glos. GL6 8BB
Telephone: +44 (0)1453 887214
Fax: +44 (0)1453 887214
E-mail: drosenberg@gn.apc.org

CILIP Liaison Officer

Jill Martin
jill.martin@cilip.org.uk

Website

www.cilip.org.uk/ilig

Special Interest Groups

Library History Group (LHG)

Aims to raise awareness of library and information heritage within and beyond the profession, frequently through activities with an international flavour.

Chair

John Crawford
Library Research Officer
Glasgow Caledonian University
Cowcaddens Road
Glasgow G4 0BA
Telephone: +44 (0)141 331 3847
Fax: +44 (0)141 331 3005
E-mail: jcr@gcal.ac.uk

Hon. Secretary

Jean Everitt
Broncastell
Devil's Bridge
Aberystwyth SY23 4QU
Telephone: +44 (0)1970 890615

CILIP Liaison Officer

Rosy Corrigan
rosy.corrigan@cilip.org.uk

Website

www.cilip.org.uk/lhg

Local Studies Group (LSG)

Improves public and professional awareness of local studies library and information services and the valuable role they play within their community.

Chair

Ian Maxted
County Local Studies Librarian
Exeter Central Library
Castle Street
Exeter EX4 3PQ
Telephone:
Fax: +44 (0)1392 384228
E-mail: imaxted@devon.gov.uk

Hon. Secretary

Diana Dixon
11 Cautley Road
Southwold
Suffolk IP18 6DD
Telephone: +44 (0)116 271 3796
E-mail: diana.dixon@cilip.org.uk

CILIP Liaison Officer

Damien McManus
damien.mcmanus@cilip.org.uk

Website

www.cilip.org.uk/lsg

Special Interest Groups

Multimedia Information and Technology Group (MmIT)

Aims to unite Members engaged or interested in multimedia information and technology developments within the profession, enabling communication and promotion of professional interests.

Chair

Tina Theis
Library Consultant
1 Highfield Park
Heaton Mersey
Stockport
SK4 3HD
Telephone: +44 (0)161 442 0657
E-mail: tina@tinatheis.com

Hon. Secretary

Antony Brewerton
Subject Team Leader (Arts, Social Sciences & Health Care)
Oxford Brookes University Library
Headington Campus
Headington
Oxford OX3 0BP
Telephone: +44 (0)1865 483139
Fax: +44 (0)1865 483998
E-mail: awbrewerton@brookes.ac.uk

CILIP Liaison Officer

Barbara Stratton
barbara.stratton@cilip.org.uk

Website

www.mmit.org.uk

Special Interest Groups

Patent and Trademark Group

Acts as a collective voice for Members involved in patent and trademark searching and other related information matters in dealing with Government and other official bodies, both nationally and internationally.

Chair

Ann Chapman
Minesoft Ltd
100 South Worple Way
London SW14 8ND
Telephone: +44 (0)20 8404 0651
Fax: +44 (0)20 8404 0681
E-mail: achapman@minesoft.com

Secretary

Liz Hearle
Institute of Physics Publishing
Dirac House
Temple Back
Bristol BS1 6BE
Telephone: +44 (0)117 930 1109
Fax: +44 (0)117 930 1202
E-mail: liz.hearle@iop.org

CILIP Liaison Officer

Mark Field
mark.field@cilip.org.uk

Website

www.patmg.org.uk

Special Interest Groups

Personnel, Training and Education Group (PTEG)

Provides a focal point for study and discussion of every aspect of personnel work (including training) relating to staff in library and information services and to professional education.

Chair

Tony Durcan
Head of Libraries and Information
City Library
Princess Square
Newcastle upon Tyne NE99 1DX
Telephone: +44 (0)191 277 4152
Fax: +44 (0)191 277 4137
E-mail: tony.durcan@newcastle.gov.uk

Hon. Secretary

Anne McIlwaine
Library Manager
School of Oriental and African Studies
Thornhaugh Street
London WC1H 0XG
Telephone: +44 (0)20 7898 4161
Fax: +44 (0)20 7898 4159
E-mail: am90@soas.ac.uk

CILIP Liaison Officer

Susan Kay
susan.kay@cilip.org.uk

Website

www.cilip.org.uk/pteg

Prison Libraries Group (PRLG)

Unites Members concerned with the provision of library and information services to penal establishments and serves as a focus for staff who could otherwise feel isolated owing to the nature of their working environment.

Chair

Cathy Evans
Library Services Manager
Worcestershire County Libraries and Information Services
County Hall
Spetchley Road
Worcester WR5 2NP
Telephone: +44 (0)1905 766232
Fax: +44 (0)1905 766244
E-mail: cevans@worcestershire.gov.uk

Secretary

Carole Bowe
Prison Librarian
Gloucester County Libraries
HMP Gloucester
Barrack Square
Gloucester GL1 2JN
Telephone: +44 (0)1452 529551 ext. 361
Fax: +44 (0)1452 310302
E-mail: cbowe@gloscc.gov.uk

CILIP Liaison Officer

Caroline Nolan
caroline.nolan@cilip.org.uk

Website

www.cilip.org.uk/prlg

Special Interest Groups

Public Libraries Group (PLG)

Concerned with all aspects of public librarianship, including standards, staffing, service delivery and promotion, with Membership open to all interested in the work of public libraries.

Chair

Jacquie Campbell
34 Wingrave Road
Tring
Herts HP23 5HE
Telephone: +44 (0)1442 826637
E-mail: js.campbell@audit-commission.gov.uk

Secretary

Anne Kelsall
Senior Librarian
Morecambe Library
Central Drive
Morecambe
Lancs LA4 5DL
Telephone: +44 (0)1524 402100
Fax: +44 (0)1524 415008
E-mail: anne.kelsall@lcl.lancscc.gov.uk

CILIP Liaison Officer

Guy Daines
guy.daines@cilip.org.uk

Website

www.cilip.org.uk/plg

Publicity and Public Relations Group (PPRG)

Demonstrates to the library and information profession that continuous and planned public relations is essential in every type of library and information service.

Chair

> Linda Smith
> Nottingham Trent University
> Dryden Street
> Nottingham NG1 4FZ
> Telephone: +44 (0)115 848 2256
> Fax: +44 (0)115 848 4230
> E-mail: linda.smith@ntu.ac.uk

Secretary

> Vacancy

CILIP Liaison Officer

> Louisa Myatt
> louisa.myatt@cilip.org.uk

Website

> www.cilip.org.uk/pprg

Special Interest Groups

Rare Books Group (RBG)

Unites library and information workers responsible for collections of rare books, manuscripts and special materials with other interested individuals.

Vice Chair and current Acting Chair (until April 2003)

Timothy Hobbs
Chief Executive
East Midlands Museums, Libraries and Archives Council
56 King Street
Leicester LE1 6RL
Telephone: +44 (0)116 285 1350
Fax: +44 (0)116 285 1351

Hon. Secretary

Yvonne Lewis
1 Earle Croft
Warfield
Berkshire RG42 2QY
Telephone: +44 (0)1344 304459
Fax: +44 (0)1344 304459
E-mail: yvonnel@easynet.co.uk

CILIP Liaison Officer

Caroline Nolan
caroline.nolan@cilip.org.uk

Website

www.cilip.org.uk/rbg

Special Interest Groups

School Libraries Group (SLG)

Promotes school libraries and school library services as being essential to all areas of the curriculum, to enable the exploitation of a wide range of resources, develop pupils' information skills, encourage the reading habit and support equal opportunities and multi-cultural education.

Chair

Glenys Willars
Library Services for Education for Leicestershire and Leicester City
929/931 Loughborough Road
Rothley
Leicester LE7 7NH
Telephone: +44 (0)116 267 8008
Fax: +44 (0)116 267 8039
E-mail: gwillars@leics.gov.uk

Secretary

Anne-Marie Tarter
Ripon Grammar School
Clotherholme Road
Ripon
North Yorkshire HG4 2DG
Telephone: +44 (0)1765 602647
Fax: +44 (0)1765 606388
E-mail: tarters@globalnet.co.uk

CILIP Liaison Officer

Jonathan Douglas
jonathan.douglas@cilip.org.uk

Website

www.cilip.org.uk/slg

Special Interest Groups

UKOLUG: the UK Online User Group

Advancing the effective use of electronic information resources. The national user group for online, CD-ROM and internet searchers, aiming to act as a user forum, and also as a consumer group to represent users' interests within the information industry.

Chair

Chris Armstrong
Information Automation Ltd
Penbryn
Bronant
Aberystwyth SY23 4TJ
Telephone: +44 (0)1974 251 302
Fax: +44 (0)1974 251 441
E-mail: lisqual@cix.co.uk

Hon. Secretary

Karen Blakeman
RBA Information Services
88 Star Road
Caversham
Berkshire RG4 5BE
Telephone: +44 (0)118 947 2256
Fax: +44 (0)870 056 8547
E-mail: Karen.Blakeman@rba.co.uk

CILIP Liaison Officer

Lyndsay Rees-Jones
lyndsay.rees-jones@cilip.org.uk

Website

www.ukolug.org.uk

University, College and Research Group (UCRG)

Concerned with the interests of library and information specialists in national, research, university and other higher education libraries, including playing a significant part in continuing professional development.

Chair

Andrew Martin
Deputy Librarian
University College Northampton
Park Campus
Boughton Green Road
Northampton NN2 7AL
Telephone: +44 (0)1604 735500
Fax: +44 (0)1604 718819
E-mail: andrew.martin@northampton.ac.uk

Hon. Secretary

Jo Webb
Academic Librarian (Business, Law & Humanities Team Leader)
Kimberlin Library
De Montfort University
The Gateway
Leicester LE1 9BH
Telephone: +44 (0)116 207 8046
Fax: +44 (0)116 257 7046
E-mail: jwebb@dmu.ac.uk

CILIP Liaison Officer

Kathy Ennis
kathy.ennis@cilip.org.uk

Website

www.ucrg.org.uk

Special Interest Groups

Youth Libraries Group (YLG)

Works independently and with other professional organisations to preserve and influence the provision of quality literature, library and information services for children and young people in public libraries and school library services.

Chair

Anne Marley
Children's and Schools Library Service
Hampshire Libraries and Information
County Library HQ
81 North Walls
Winchester
Hants. SO23 8BY
Telephone: +44 (0)1962 826658
Fax: +44 (0)1962 856615
E-mail: anne@marleyhcl.freeserve.co.uk

Secretary

Sue Roe
Bebington Central Library
Civic Way
Bebington
Wirral CH63 7PN
Telephone: +44 (0)151 643 7223
Fax: +44 (0)151 643 7231
E-mail: susanroe4@aol.com

CILIP Liaison Officer

Jonathan Douglas
jonathan.douglas@cilip.org.uk

Website

www.cilip.org.uk/ylg

Medals and Awards

The CILIP Carnegie and Kate Greenaway Medals

The CILIP Carnegie and Kate Greenaway Medals are the UK's most prestigious children's book awards. The Carnegie Medal is awarded for outstanding writing and The Kate Greenaway Medal is awarded for outstanding illustration, in a book for children and young people.

Nominations are invited from all Members of CILIP via a nomination form, which is published in the February edition of *Library & Information Update*. Eligible titles must be written in English; be published originally for children and young people and have received their first publication in the United Kingdom during the preceding year or have had co-publication elsewhere within a three month time lapse.

The selection process is organised by CILIP's Youth Libraries Group (YLG), who appoint 12 regional judges who are experienced children's librarians.

A shortlist for each medal is announced at the end of April each year and the winners are announced and presented at a London ceremony in July. The winning author and illustrator receive a golden medal, a certificate and £500 worth of books to donate to a library of their choice. Since 2000 the winner of the Kate Greenaway Medal has also received the Colin Mears Award, which is a cash prize of £5,000.

The accompanying shadowing scheme for children and young people has over 1,000 registered reading groups in schools and public libraries. An estimated 25,000 children 'shadowed' the judging process in 2002, reading the shortlisted titles and posting their book reviews on a specially created award website.

For further information on the Carnegie and Kate Greenaway Medals including past winners, criteria and information on the shadowing scheme visit www.carnegiegreenaway.org.uk or contact CILIP Marketing on +44 (0)20 7255 0650.

Carnegie Medal winners

2001   Terry Pratchett, *The Amazing Maurice and His Educated Rodents*, Transworld

Kate Greenaway Medal winners

2001   Chris Riddell, *Pirate Diary*, Walker Books

Medals and Awards

The CILIP Jason Farradane Award

The Award is made to an individual or a group of people for outstanding work in the information field. It was first awarded to Jason Farradane, founder of the Institute of Information Scientists, in 1979. Previous Awards have been made for: development of a major database; reorganisation of an information service; important research in an aspect of information retrieval theory, establishing a significant new information service.

It is an international award, open to all, although nominations must be made by a CILIP Member. The winner receives a commemorative plaque which will be presented at the CILIP Awards Gala Presentation Day in November.

For further information see the CILIP website www.cilip.org.uk/awards or contact CILIP Marketing, telephone: +44 (0)20 7255 0650.

Winners

2002   William Hann for Free Pint

The CILIP / Library + information Show Libraries Change Lives Award

The Libraries Change Lives Award promotes good practice, recognises innovation and celebrates the achievements of grass roots projects and frontline staff, particularly those working with socially excluded groups. The Award is run by CILIP and its Community Services Group (CSG) and is sponsored by the Library + information Show.

A trophy, a certificate and £4000 are presented to the winning project and two finalists receive £1000 and a certificate. The Award ceremony takes place during the Library + information Show at the ExCel Events Centre in London in June.

The winning project should be a partnership between a library or information service and one or more community agencies. It should be an example of good practice, have started in the past three years and be ongoing. Applications are invited from any type of library or information service throughout the UK. An entry form is published in the November edition of *Library & Information Update* and further information and an electronic entry form is available on the CILIP website www.cilip.org.uk/awards. Entries close at the end of January.

The 2002 Award was won by The Big Bookshare, Nottingham – a partnership between LaunchPad, Nottingham City Libraries and HMP Nottingham. A 10th anniversary booklet featuring all the past winners of the Award is available from CILIP Marketing, telephone: +44 (0)20 7255 0650.

Winners

2002   The Big Bookshare Nottingham

The CILIP/Emerald Public Relations and Publicity Awards

The Awards recognise innovation and excellence in the promotion of library and information services in all sectors. They are administered by CILIP and its Publicity and Public Relations Group (PPRG) and sponsored by Emerald.

Awards are made in five categories: promotional campaign with a budget under £500; promotional campaign with a budget over £500, printed publicity, multimedia and web based publicity and sponsorship and partnership. Winners and commended projects are presented with a plaque and a free period of access to Emerald's fulltext database of electronic journals.

The Awards are presented at the CILIP Awards Gala Presentation Day in November along with the Tom Farries Award for Personal PR Achievement, in memory of Tom Farries, a founder of the original Awards. Farries International Booksellers donate a glass trophy.

For further information see the CILIP website www.cilip.org.uk/awards or contact CILIP Marketing, telephone: +44 (0)20 7255 0650.

Winners

2002   Julie Spencer, Senior Children's and Schools Librarian, Bolton Libraries

The CILIP Robinson Medal for Innovation in Library Administration

The Robinson Medal is awarded to recognise innovation and excellence in library administration. It is aimed specifically at people working at para-professional levels in the library and information field. Entrants are judged for innovation, practical application, adaptability, improved efficiency to working conditions or systems and how well the project met the original need.

It is administered by the CILIP Affiliated Members National Committee with support from CILIP Marketing. It is presented at the CILIP Awards Gala Presentation Day in November. For further infor-

Medals and Awards

mation see the CILIP website www.cilip.org.uk/awards or contact CILIP Marketing, telephone: +44 (0)20 7255 0650.

Winners

2002 Christine Stevenson, University of Sunderland, for a Library Support Service for Distance Learners.

The CILIP/Nielsen BookData Reference Awards

These annual Awards are sponsored by Nielsen BookData and comprise the Besterman/McColvin Medals for an outstanding work of reference (print and electronic categories), the Wheatley Medal for indexing (awarded jointly with the Society of Indexers) and the Walford Award for an individual who has made a longstanding contribution to bibliography.

The judges represent CILIP's Information Services Group, Multimedia and Information Technology Group and Cataloguing and Indexing Group, together with the Society of Indexers.

Nominations for the Awards are invited from CILIP Members, publishers and other interested individuals. As well as a golden medal, winners of the Besterman/McColvin and Wheatley Medals also receive a certificate and a cash prize of £500. The winner of the Walford Award receives a certificate and £500. The Awards are presented at the CILIP Awards Gala Presentation Ceremony in November.

For further information see the CILIP website www.cilip.org.uk/awards or contact CILIP Marketing, telephone: +44 (0)20 7255 0650.

Besterman/McColvin Medal winners
Electronic category

2002 *The Visual Culture of Wales: Imaging the Nation* by Peter Lord. University of Wales Press (CD-ROM)

Printed category

2002 *20th Century Ceramic Designers in Britain* by Andrew Casey. Antique Collectors' Club

Walford Award winners

2002 Robin Alston

Wheatley Medal winners

2002 *Encyclopaedia Britannica 2002 Revision* edited by Dale H. Hoiberg. Encyclopaedia Britannica Inc.

Tony Kent Strix Award

The Award is given in recognition of an outstanding practical innovation or achievement in the field of information retrieval. This could take the form of an application or service, or an overall appreciation of past achievements from which significant advantages have emanated. The Award is open to individuals or groups from anywhere in the world.

The Award is in memory of Dr Tony Kent, a past fellow of the Institute of Information Scientists, who died in 1997. The winner receives a statuette of an owl which is presented at the CILIP Awards Gala Presentation Day in November.

For further information see the CILIP web site www.cilip.org.uk/awards or contact CILIP Marketing: telephone: +44 (0)20 7255 0650.

Winners

2002 Malcom Jones

Organisations in Liaison with CILIP

Even though CILIP's Groups comprehensively cover its Members' interests, the opportunities for specialist professional activities go still further.

Other organisations have formal links with CILIP as well, under the Organisations in Liaison (OiL) scheme. The scheme offers two-way communication and, where appropriate, mutual support to organisations that are concerned in some way with promotion of objectives similar to those of CILIP.

There are over 20 OiLs including several for minority groups, as well as others covering topics as diverse as the arts, construction, consumer health, music, maps and much more. Although independent of CILIP in their policy and administration, OiLs receive a number of benefits similar to those enjoyed by Branches and Groups, including discounts on a range of CILIP services, and they can also qualify for grant aid in certain circumstances.

African Caribbean Library Association (ACLA)

ACLA Project Office
c/o 52 Burgundy House
9 Bedale Road
Enfield
Middlesex EN2 0NZ
Telephone: 01992 620 239
Fax: 01992 620 239
E-mail: acla_uk@yahoo.co.uk

Agency Information Group (AIG)

Membership Officer: Heather Hulse
Librarian, Veterinary Laboratories Agency
New Haw, Addlestone
Surrey KT15 3NB
Telephone: +44 (0)1932 341111
Fax: +44 (0)1932 347046

Arts Libraries Society of the United Kingdom and Ireland (ARLIS/UK and Ireland)

Sonia French
18 College Road
Bromsgrove
Worcs B60 2NE
Telephone: +44 (0)1527 579298
Fax: +44 (0)1527 579298
E-mail: sfrench@arlis.demon.co.uk
Website: www.cilip.org.uk/arlis

Asian Librarians and Advisors Group (ALAG)

Kalyan Dutt
Southall Library
Osterley Park Road
Southall
Middlesex UB2 4BL
Telephone: +44 (0)20 8574 3412
www.cilip.org.uk/alag

Association for the Education and Training of Library Technicians and Assistants

Christopher Smith
45 Surrey Road
Seaford
Sussex BN25 2NR
Telephone: +44 (0)1323 895212

Association of British Theological and Philosophical Libraries

Colin Clarke
Head of Reader Services
Dr Williams's Library
14 Gordon Square
London WC1H 0AR
Telephone: +44 (0)20 7387 3727
E-mail: colin.clarke@dwlib.co.uk
Website: www.abtapl.org.uk

Organisations in Liaison with CILIP

Association of Land-based Librarians in Colleges and Universities (ALLCU)

Stella Vain
The Library
Wiltshire College Lackham
Lacock
Chippenham
Wiltshire SN15 2NY
Telephone: +44 (0)1249 466814
E-mail: viansm@wiltscoll.ac.uk

Bliss Classification Association

Heather Lane
The Library
Sidney Sussex College
University of Cambridge
Cambridge CB2 3HU
Telephone: +44 (0)1223 338852
Fax: +44 (0)1223 338884

Children's Books History Society

Pat Garrett
25 Field Way
Hoddesdon
Herts EN11 0QN
Telephone: +44 (0)1922 464885
Fax: +44 (0)1922 464885
E-mail: cbhs@abcgarrett.demon.co.uk

Community Care Network

Linda Butler (Chair)
Birmingham Central Library
Chamberlain Square
Birmingham B3 3HQ
Telephone: +44 (0)121 303 4402
Fax: +44 (0)121 233 9702

Construction Industry Information Group

Malcolm Weston

c/o URS Corporation
St George's House
5 St George's Road
London SW19 4DR
Website: www.ciig.org.uk

Consumer Health Information Consortium (CHIC)

Diane Finlayson
St Thomas' Hospital
Patients Library
North Wing
Lambeth Palace Road
London SE1 7EH
Telephone: +44 (0)20 7928 9292 ext: 2507

Council for Learning Resources in Colleges (CoLRiC)

Jeffrey Cooper
122 Preston New Road
Blackburn
Lancashire BB2 6BU
Telephone: +44 (0)1254 662923
Fax: +44 (0)1254 610979

HE Colleges Learning Resources Group

Mary Davies
Head of Learning Support Services
University of East London
Longbridge Road
Dagenham
Essex RM8 2AS
Telephone: +44 (0)20 8223 2620
Fax: +44 (0)20 8223 3612

Historic Libraries Forum

Peter Hoare
21 Oundle Drive
Nottingham NG8 1BN
Telephone: +44 (0)115 978 5297
Fax: +44 (0)115 978 5297

Information Focus for Allied Health

Clare Burnham
Information Officer
Royal College of Speech and Language Therapists
2 White Hart Yard
London SE1 1NX
Telephone: +44 (0)20 7378 1200
Fax: +44 (0)20 7403 7254

Information for Social Change

John Pateman
32 Petten Grove
Orpington
Kent BN5 4DU
Telephone: +44 (0)1689 872586

International Association of Music Libraries, Archives and Documentation Centres (United Kingdom Branch) (IAML UK)

Peter Baxter
General Secretary (IAML UK)
Edinburgh City Libraries
9 George IV Bridge
Edinburgh EH1 1EG
Telephone: +44 (0)131 242 8050
Fax: +44 (0)131 225 8783

Librarians' Christian Fellowship

Graham Hedges
34 Thurlestone Avenue
Seven Kings
Ilford
Essex IG3 9DU
Telephone (mobile): +44 (0)7947 063293

Library and Information Research Group (LIRG)

Biddy Fisher
Head of Academic Services & Devt Learning Centre
Sheffield Hallam University
Howard Street

Sheffield S1 1WB
Telephone: 0114 225 2104
Fax: 0114 225 3859
E-mail: b.m.fisher@shu.ac.uk
Website: www.cilip.org.uk/lirg

LINK: a Network for North-South Library Development

John Pateman
c/o 64 Ennersdale Road
London SE13 5JD
E-mail: link-up@talk21.com

Map Curators Group of the British Cartographic Society

Ann Sutherland
Map Library
Edinburgh University Library
43 George Square
Edinburgh EHG8 9LJ
Telephone: +44 (0)131 650 3969
Fax: +44 (0)131 667 9780

Private Libraries Association

Hon. Secretary: James Brown
49 Hamilton Park West
London N5 1AE
Telephone: +44 (0)20 7503 9827

Sexuality Issues in Libraries Group (SILG)

Mark Norman
Library IT Manager
Regent's College
Inner Circle
Regent's Park
London NW1 4NS
Telephone: +44 (0)20 7487 7567
Fax: +44 (0)20 7487 7667

Society of Indexers

Liza Furnival

Blades Enterprise Centre
John Street
Sheffield S2 4SU
Telephone: +44 (0)114 292 2350
Fax: +44 (0)114 292 2351

SPRIG

Martin Scarrott
SPRIG Chair
IRC
St Mary's College
Waldegrave Road
Twickenham TW1 4SX
Tel: 0208 240 2304
E-mail: chair@sprig.org.uk
Website: www.sprig.org.uk

Trade Union Information Group

Ursula Coxhead
Policy and Research Department
UNISON
1 Mabledon Place
London WC1H
Telephone: +44 (0)20 7551 1528
E-mail: u.coxhead@unison.co.uk

CILIP representatives on other bodies

AACR Committee of Principals – Sue Brown
AACR Fund Trustees – Janet Liebster
AACR Publishers – Janet Liebster
ACE Council (The Association for Conferences and Events) – Rob Palmer (member)
Advisory Council on the Export of Works of Art – Robin Price
AELTA (The Association for the Education and Training of Library Technicians and Assistants) – Marion Huckle
Arts Council Steering Committee for Children's Literature Policy – Jonathan Douglas
Association of Learned & Professional Society Publishers – Alan Gilchrist
Association of Senior Children's and Education Librarian's National Committee – Jonathan Douglas
AUT Libraries Committee – Kathy Ennis
BAILER Heads of Department Committee (British Association for Information & Library Education and Research) – Marion Huckle
Book Aid International – Sue Brown
Book Industry Communication – Mark Field (representative for Onix)
Book Industry Communication Board of Directors – Sue Brown, Jenny Varney
Bookstart Steering Committee – Jonathan Douglas
British and Irish Association of Law Librarians (BIALL) – Mark Field (Council member)
British Committee for Map Information & Cataloguing Systems – Ian Maxted
British Council Knowledge and Information Advisory Committee – Bob McKee
British Library Advisory Committee – Una Byrne, Bob McKee
British Library Advisory Council – Barry Cropper, Bob McKee
British Records Association – M. V. Roberts
British Standards Institution: IDT/2/2 – Ken Bakewell
British Standards Institution: IDT/2/15 – Guy Daines
British Standards Institution: IST/2/17 – David Haynes, Julie McLeod
British Standards Institution: IDT/3 – Vincent Roper
British Standards Institution: IDT/7 – Verina Horsnell
BSI Records Management Standards Committee – David Haynes

CILIP representatives on other bodies

Cathedrals as Partners in Lifelong Learning – Kathy Ennis
Chartered Institute of Public Finance & Accountancy: Public Libraries Working Party – Guy Daines
CILIP/British Library Committee on AACR2 – Sue Brown, Stuart Hunt, Jane Savidge, Rodney Brunt
CILIP/CILIPS bi-annual meetings – Chair, Executive Board; Chair, Council; Hon. Treasurer; Chief Executive
City Information Group – Lyndsay Rees-Jones
CoLRiC: Council for Learning Resources in Colleges – Kathy Ennis
Construction Industry Information Group (OiL) – Mark Field (liaison)
Dewey Decimal Classification Editorial Policy Committee – Lucy Evans
DfES School Library Working Group – Jonathan Douglas
English Speaking Union Library Committee – Sue Brown/Jill Martin
European Bureau for Library, Information & Documentation Associations (EBLIDA) – Sue Brown
Forum For Interlending (FIL) – Alan Cooper
Health Library Confederation (HELICON) – Susan Howard
Information for Development Co-ordinating Committee – Jill Martin
IFLA (voting member) – Barry Cropper
IFLA Committee on Copyright and other Legal Matters – Sandy Norman
IFLA Committee on Freedom of Access to Information and Freedom of Expression – Bob McKee
IM and WiM – Lyndsay Rees-Jones
Information Asset Register Policy Group – Tim Owen
Institute of Management – Lyndsay Rees-Jones
International Association of Music Librarians – Susi Woodhouse
IPMS/CILIP Liaison Committee (IPMS now known as Prospect) – Sue Westcott
Joint Steering Committee for the Revision of AACR – Robert Atkinson
LACA (Libraries and Archives Copyright Alliance) – Tamara Eisenschitz, Sandy Norman, Philip Plumb, Barbara Stratton
Learned Information Online Conference Committee 2002 – Tim Owen
Learning Place Consortium – Mark Field
LIBER – Debby Shorley
Library & Information Statistics Unit (LISU) – Sue Brown
Library and Information Research Group (LIRG) – Alan Cooper

CILIP representatives on other bodies

Library Campaign – Guy Daines
Library Services Trust – Hon Treasurer; Gillian Pentelow
MEG: Mixed Economy Group – Kathy Ennis
NAEGA: National Association for Educational Guidance for Adults – Kathy Ennis
NAG (National Acquisitions Group) – Lyndsay Rees-Jones
National Book Committee – Bob McKee
National Literacy Trust Advisory Committee – Jonathan Douglas
National Reading Alliance – Jonathan Douglas
Networked Services Policy Task Group – Judith Howells
Public Libraries Research Group – Guy Daines
Re:source Learning and Access Standard Think Tank – Jonathan Douglas
Re:source Need to Read basic skills working party – Jonathan Douglas
Reading is Fundamental (RIF) ABC project–Steering Committee – Jonathan Douglas
School Library Forum – Chair, YLG; Chair, Schools Libraries Group; Youth & School Libraries Adviser
Society of Archivists Education, Training & Development Committee. – Marion Huckle
Society of Chief Librarians (SCL) – Guy Daines
Special Libraries Association – Lyndsay Rees-Jones
Standing Committee on Official Publications – Lyndsay Rees-Jones
Statistics Users' Council – Alastair Allan
The Reading Agency – Sue Brown
Ufi Libraries Cluster – Kathy Ennis
UK Inter-Professional Group – Sue Brown
UKSG (United Kingdom Serials Group) – Lyndsay Rees-Jones
Unesco – UK Communications Committee – Bob McKee
University of Sheffield Department of Information Studies Advisory Committee. – Martin Stone
Women in Management (SIG of IM) – Lyndsay Rees-Jones
World Book Day Executive Committee – Jonathan Douglas
Women Connect – Lyndsay Rees-Jones

Retired Members Guild

Enables retired library and information workers to keep in touch with each other, participate in activities and assist CILIP in promoting library and information services.

Chair

Tom Featherstone
6 The Moorings
Hollinwood Road
Disley
Stockport SK12 2DU
E-mail: tm.featherstone@which.net

Hon. Secretary

Jean Plaister
3 St Regis Close
London N10 2DE
Telephone: +44 (0)20-8444-8860
Fax: +44 (0)20-8444-8860
E-mail: plaister@dircon.co.uk

Ridgmount Street facilities

Ridgmount Street offers Members a range of facilities in London's West End. The building is conveniently located near to several tube stations, and within 10 minutes of King's Cross and Euston main line stations.

Ewart Room

Monday–Friday 9 am–6 pm
Members are welcome to use the Ewart Room, situated on the ground floor, as a meeting point. A vending machine is available.

Rooms for hire

All our rooms offer natural light and are fully equipped with audio-visual and presentation equipment. Induction loops are available in all rooms. Furniture can be adapted for a range of room layouts. Our friendly staff will ensure that you have an anxiety free meeting or event.

The Charter Suite

A double-glazed, air-conditioned room which seats up to 100 people and can be divided into two smaller areas (Charter East and West)

The Lorna Paulin Room

A double-glazed, air-conditioned room which seats up to 40 people. Most CILIP Training and Development Events are held in this room.

The Farradane Room

A new fully-equipped meeting room, which seats up to 36 people

Catering facilities

CILIP provides a wide range of high quality catering services for meetings, courses and seminars held at Ridgmount Street.

Disabled access

There is full disabled access to all areas of the building.

Ridgmount Street facilities

Further information and bookings

Please contact Margaret Poole, Administrative Assistant for further information and bookings. Telephone +44 (0)207 255 0518; e-mail: margaret.poole@cilip.org.uk

Information and advice

CILIP offers a range of information and advice services to Members and non-Members, including journalists and researchers. Expert staff are available to deal with simple or complex enquiries on issues such as knowledge management, library building projects, copyright and employment, supporting Members in the workplace, with their professional development and with their own professional interests.

The Information Centre

A new Information Centre is now available on the fourth floor at CILIP Ridgmount Street, with space to study, internet access and a special Members' lounge.

The Centre contains a reference collection of current books and journals and access to databases and e-journals focusing on the library and information sector and the needs of those working in it. As well as reports, consultation documents, directories and statistics, the Centre also holds a complete set of CILIP guidelines, publications and leaflets, all Branch and Group journals and key professional journals. The Information Services team currently provide a remote search service for Members from online services *LISAnet*, *Bookfind Online* and *Information Research Watch International*. A photocopier and computer printer are provided for fair dealing copies from both hard copy and electronic material and one of the computer workstations is dedicated to meeting DDA requirements.

The Members' lounge provides a relaxed and comfortable environment for all Members, whether working locally or who are in London for a meeting or training course. Daily broadsheet newspapers and refreshments are available.

The Centre is open Monday to Friday from 9 am to 5pm and the Information Services team are on hand to answer any enquiries.

The CILIP Archives

The CILIP archives incorporate the archives of The Library Association and the Institute of Information Scientists.

Ridgmount Street facilities

Information Services contacts

Telephone: +44 (0)20 7255 0620
Fax: +44 (0)20 7255 0501
Textphone: +44 (0)20 7255 0505
E-mail: info@cilip.org.uk
In person: between 9 am and 5 pm, Monday to Friday
Website: www.cilip.org.uk

Subscriptions

Personal Members

Band	Members earning:	Full	Reduced rate
U	in excess of £57,000 p.a.	£259	£252
A	£52,001 to £57,000 p.a.	£246	£240
B	£47,001 to £52,000 p.a.	£232	£226
C	£42,001 to £47,000 p.a.	£215	£209
D	£37,001 to £42,000 p.a.	£200	£194
E	£32,001 to £37,000 p.a.	£184	£178
F	£27,001 to £32,000 p.a.	£173	£167
G	£22,001 to £27,000 p.a.	£151	£145
H	£17,001 to £22,000 p.a.	£140	£134
I	£14,001 to £17,000 p.a.	£120	£114
J	£12,001 to £14,000 p.a.	£97	£93
K	£10,001 to £12,000 p.a.	£78	£74
L	£8,001 to £10,000 p.a.	£57	£53
M	£5,001 to £8,000 p.a.	£36	£34
N	Less than £5,001 p.a.	£25	£23
O	Student Members	£24	£22
Q	Unemployed Members	£24	£22
R	Retired Members	£33	£31
P	All Affiliated Members	£30	£28
S	All Supporting Members	£68	
	Life membership	£152	

Overseas members

V	UK Expatriates, wherever resident	£42
W	Countries coded W	£42
X	Countries coded X	£35
Y	Countries coded Y	£26

Institutional members

Budget in excess of:

£2m p.a.	£538
£1m to £2m p.a.	£426
£0.5m to £1m p.a.	£326
£0.1m to £0.5m p.a.	£214
£0.05m to £0.1m p.a.	£113
Budget less than £0.05m p.a.	£76
Additional subscriptions under Bye-law 4	£65

Suppliers Network

Suppliers Network continues to flourish. In the past year we have seen membership increase to 20 companies. CILIP works across the whole library and information domain and recognises the importance of partnerships with the vendor community. Suppliers Network offers companies that sell to the library and information sector the opportunity to have a closer association with CILIP, the only chartered body for library and information professionals. This involvement generates better awareness of both sides' needs and expectations for the future and lends a louder voice for our lobbying activities.

Suppliers Network Executive: Joan Thompson
joan.thompson@cilip.org.uk

Companies in membership

3M UK Plc
ADLIB Information Systems Ltd
Book Data
Cedric Chivers Ltd
Community Media
Cypher
D S Limited
EMOS Information Systems Limited
Innovative Interfaces
IS Oxford
Keytools Ltd
OCLC
Ovid Technologies Ltd
Pearson Education
Riley Dunn & Wilson Ltd
Severn House Publishers Ltd
SPI Technologies Ltd
Talis Information Ltd
Ulverscroft Large Print Books
Whitaker Information Services

Part 4
CILIP MEMBERS

List of Members of CILIP

Professional Register
Personal Members
Institutional Members
Overseas Institutional Members

Note: This list of members reflect the membership of CILIP at 18 November 2002.

Personal Members

The date shown in italics indicates when a member joined the Institute.

The date following the letters AS (Associate) is the year of election to the professional register as a Chartered Member; that following FE (Fellow) is the year of election to Fellowship.

Affiliated Members are indicated by the letters AF and Supporting Members by the letters SP.

Lists of members by country are held at CILIP Ridgmount Street and are available to members on request.

Members' personal addresses are confidential and are in no circumstances sold to outside agencies. However, if members wish to contact one another and the information provided here is insufficient for that purpose, Membership may be able to provide assistance.

Further information

Membership Executive: Angela Norman
angela.norman@cilip.org.uk
Telephone: +44 (0)20 7255 0602

Abbreviations

The following abbreviations in designations and addresses have been adopted in the Personal Members section. P.L. (Public Library(ies)) is used to indicate all types of urban Public Libraries. Co.L. (County Library(ies)) is used to indicate all County Libraries. Within Greater London 'L.B. of . . .' is used.

Abbreviations used in the Membership list

Admin.	Administration or Administrative	Lab.	Laboratory
Arch.	Archives or Archivist	Lect.	Lecturer
Asst.	Assistant	Lend.	Lending
Assoc.	Associate or Association	Lib.	Librarian or Librarianship
Auth.	Authority		
		Mgmnt.	Management
Bibl.	Bibliographer or Bibliography	Mgr.	Manager
Bor.	Borough	Med.	Medical
Br.	Branch	Met.	Metropolitan
Brit.	British	Min.	Ministry
		Mob.	Mobile
C.A.E.	College of Advanced Education	Mus.	Museum
Catg/Catr.	Cataloguing/Cataloguer		
Cent.	Central or Centre	N.	North
Ch.	Chief	Nat.	National
Child.	Children or Children's		
Circ.	Circulation	Off.	Office
Co.	Company or County	Offr.	Officer
Co.L.	County Library(ies)		
Coll.	College	Poly.	Polytechnic
Comm.	Commerce or Commercial	Postgrad.	Postgraduate
Comp.	Comprehensive	P.L.	Public Library(ies)
		Prof.	Professor
Dep.	Deputy	p./t.	Part time
Dept.	Department		
Devel.	Development	Ref.	Reference
Dir.	Director	Reg.	Region or Regional
Dist.	District	Rep.	Representative
Div.	Division or Divisional	Res.	Research
E.	East	S.	South
Educ.	Education	Sch.	School or Schools
Elect.	Electrical	Sci.	Science or Scientific
Eng.	Engineering	Sec.	Secretary
Estab.	Establishment	Sect.	Section
Exec.	Executive	Sen.	Senior
		Serv.	Service or Services
F.E.	Further Education	Soc.	Society
Fed.	Federation	Stud.	Student
Form.	Formerly	Super.	Supervisor
		Supt.	Superintendent
Grp.	Group		
		Tech.	Technical or Technology(ical)
H.E.	Higher Education	Temp.	Temporary
Hist.	Historical or History	Trav.	Travelling
Hon.	Honorary		
Hosp.	Hospital	Univ.	University
H.Q.	Headquarters		
		W.	West
i/c.	In charge of		
Ind.	Industry or Industries	Y.	Youth
Inf.	Information		
Inst.	Institute or Institution		
Internat.	International		
L.	Library(ies)		
L.B.	London Borough		

Personal Members — Addison

Aanonson Mr AJ, BSc MSc MCLIP, Lib., Brunel Univ.L., Uxbridge. [0025199] 15/01/1976
Abaza Miss NH, BA MA, Dir.LIS-Alexandria, The Brit.Council, Alexandria, Egypt. [0049228] 14/10/1993
Abbas Miss T, MSc MCLIP, Child.Co-ordinator, Clifton L., Nottingham City Council. [0043390] 18/10/1989
Abbas Mr Z, MA, Unemployed, [0059907] 01/11/2001
Abbay Miss OJ, BA FCLIP, Retired, 15 Vincent St., Sandringham, Victoria, Australia 3191. [0016487] 20/01/1951 **FE 07/04/1980**
Abbott Mrs AA, (was Foster), MCLIP, Sch.Lib., West Park Community Sch., Derbys. [0000002] 01/01/1970
Abbott Miss CL, BA(Hons), grad.Trainee, Taylor Institution L., Oxford. [0059846] 16/10/2001
Abbott Mr DN, MCLIP, Retired. [0000005] 01/01/1968
Abbott Sister EM, SRN BA, Sch.Lib., St.Anthony's Sch., Winsted, CT 06098, USA. [0042541] 09/12/1988
Abbott Mrs G, (was Collins), Inf.Asst., Lazard Bros.& Co.Ltd., London. [0045424] 28/01/1991 **AF**
Abbott Mr JB, DipEuroHum BA(Hons)Hum(Open), Acting Dep.Lib., Bishopsgate Institute, London. [0054588] 06/02/1997
Abbott Ms KJ, BSc DipLib MCLIP, Subject Lib., Queen Mary Coll., Univ.of London. [0023406] 06/01/1975
Abbott Mrs L, MCLIP, Child.Lib., Bracknell Forest, Bracknell L. [0000009] 21/02/1964
Abbott Mr PAB, BA DipLib MCLIP, Lib., Royal Armouries, Leeds [0009268] 12/01/1986
Abbott Mr PHR, BA HDipLIS, Unemployed. [0047418] 05/08/1992
Abbott Mr R, MA BSc MCLIP, Position unknown, Boots Healthcare Internat., Nottingham. [0060125] 10/12/2001
Abbott Mrs R, (was Maltby), MCLIP, Lib., Shropshire Co.L., Shrewsbury. [0009667] 13/01/1970
Abbott Miss SJ, BA(Hons), Corp.Inf.Serv.Lib., Public Record Off., Kew. [0038097] 08/01/1985
Abbott Miss SKM, BA DipLib, Electronic Serv.Support Mgr., Univ.of Glamorgan. [0053666] 27/08/1996
Abbott Mr WR, BA DipLib MCLIP, Lib., Local Studies & Hist.Serv., Birmingham Cent.L. [0021107] 05/10/1973
Abbs Mr CR, BA(Hons) MA MCLIP, Lib., L.B.of Brent. [0055551] 20/10/1997
Abbs Mrs EA, (was Brown), BA DipIM, Lib., Reg.Training Unit, Belfast. [0047871] 22/10/1992
Abdallah Mrs DM, Teacher, Cairo Univ., Giza, Egypt. [0061217] 16/04/2002
Abdirahman Mr AM, BA MLIS MA, Asst.Lib., American Intercontinental Univ., London. [0059632] 05/07/2001
Abdy Mrs C, BA (Hons), Stud., Manchester Metropoliton, [0060981] 23/01/2002
Abel Mr FY, BA, Life Member, 90 Glandon Dr., Cheadle Hulme, Cheshire, SK8 7EY,Tel.061 485 1439. [0000015] 01/01/1947
Abel Mr P, BSc MSc, Stud., Manchester Met. Univ. [0059208] 08/01/2001
Abel Mrs YC, (was Codling), BTech MCLIP, Resident in U.S.A. [0060077] 07/12/2001
Abell Mrs AG, BA FCLIP, Dir., TFPL Ltd., London. [0000017] 01/01/1959 **FE 01/04/2002**
Abell Ms JST, BA(Hons) FA DipHons LA, L.Asst., City Univ. [0059484] 09/04/2001 **AF**
Abercrombie Mr WJ, BSc MCLIP, Employment not known. [0060126] 10/12/2001
Abernethy Mrs BA, (was Hunter), MCLIP, Sen.Lib., Renfrewshire. [0007489] 01/01/1966
Abernethy Miss SH, BA DipLib MCLIP, Lib., Wansbeck Hosp., Northumberland. [0037791] 26/10/1984
Abiola Miss O, BSc, Stud., Univ.of N.London. [0060007] 21/11/2001
Abit Miss D, BA(Hons) DipLib MCLIP, Self-Employed, Freelance Lib. [0046615] 25/11/1991
Abrahaley Mebrahtu Mrs MT, (was Truneh), MSc, Cust.Serv.Asst., Barham Pk.L. [0046079] 01/10/1991
Abraham Miss AC, BA(Hons) MA MCLIP, [0049168] 08/10/1993
Abraham Mr JM, BLib MCLIP, Operations Mgr., Cent.L., Newport L. [0030576] 03/02/1979
Abraham Mrs MT, (was Stoddart), Unemployed, 2 Oakshawhead, Paisley, PA1 2DS. [0000024] 28/08/1967
Abson Miss C, BA(Hons) MA MCLIP, Inf.Specialist, Sheffield Hallam Univ. [0048356] 02/12/1992
Aburadwan Mrs A, BA DipLib, Unemployed. [0053395] 04/06/1996
Aburrow-Jones Mrs NC, (was Aburrow), BA(Hons), Stud., Aberystwyth Univ. [0059613] 03/07/2001
Acham Ms K, BSc DipInfSc MCLIP, Employment not known. [0060701] 12/12/2001
Acharya Miss D, MSC IS, Lib., L.B. of Sutton, Sutton Cent.L. [0041994] 14/07/1988
Acharyya-Choudhury Mrs S, BA BEd DipLib, Ethnic Communities Lib., Palmers Green L., L.B.of Enfield. [0039281] 11/01/1986
Achen-Owor Ms F, BA(Hons) MA, Asst.Lib., Greenwich Comm.Coll., London. [0057561] 26/04/1999
Achour Ms CG, BA(Hons), p./t.Stud./Inf.Offr., Univ.of N.London/Univ.of Herts., St Albans [0055033] 01/07/1997
Ackerman Miss GS, BA MCLIP, Position Unknown, Univ.of Westminster, London. [0034255] 09/10/1981
Ackland Ms RA, Res.Lib., Credit Lyonnais Securities, London. [0049792] 07/12/1993
Acreman Mrs P, (was Crocker), MCLIP, Learning Res.Offr.(Bibl.), W.Herts.Coll., Watford. [0000030] 06/12/1966
Adair Ms HW, BA DipLib MCLIP, Princ.Lib., Young People's Serv., The Moray Council, Elgin, Moray. [0032836] 09/10/1980
Adair Miss RK, BSc(Hons) DipIM MCLIP, Sen.L.Asst., Univ.of Nottingham. [0047516] 22/09/1992
Adal Miss S, Stud., Loughborough Univ. [0056920] 04/11/1998

Adam Miss JE, MA DipLib MCLIP, Grp.Mgr., Sheffield L.Arch.& Inf., Cent.L. [0021744] 25/04/1974
Adam Miss JM, BA MCLIP, Serv.Devel.Lib., Curriculum Res.& Inf.Serv., Aberdeen. [0030593] 26/02/1979
Adam Mr R, BSc MA MCLIP, Employment not known. [0060127] 10/12/2001
Adams Mr AF, MCLIP, Systems Admin., Barnsley Cent.L., S.Yorks. [0000034] 01/01/1970
Adams Mrs AF, (was Barnes), BA MCLIP, Sch.Lib.(Job Share), E.Renfrewshire Council. [0031182] 08/10/1979
Adams Mr AJ, BA(Hons), Inf.Specialist, HM Customs & Excise, London. [0050177] 01/01/1969
Adams Mrs AM, (was Craig), MA DipLib MCLIP, Asst.Editor, Journal of Documentation, Queens Univ.,Belfast. [0000035] 10/10/1967
Adams Mr AS, MA MPHIL DipLib MCLIP, Sen.Lib., Middle Temple, London. [0022923] 02/10/1974
Adams Mrs B, MA, Lib., Inst.of Orthopaedics, Univ.Coll.London. [0052005] 07/09/1995
Adams Mr BPF, MBE FCLIP, Life Member. [0000036] 01/01/1949 **FE 01/01/1953**
Adams Miss C, BA PGCE DipIM MCLIP, LRC Mgr., Brent Council - Educ., Willesden High Sch. [0052261] 19/10/1995
Adams Mrs C, (was Bennett), BA DipLib MCLIP, Unemployed. [0038054] 17/01/1985
Adams Mrs C, (was Mcinally), MCLIP, Unemployed. [0009417] 07/01/1965
Adams Ms C, BA(Hons), Sen.L.Asst./p./t.Stud. [0061520] 04/09/2002
Adams Ms DM, (was Dean), BA MCLIP, ITC Consultant, Auckland City Council, New Zealand. [0019991] 08/01/1973
Adams Mrs ES, BA MCLIP DMS, Dist.Mgr., Essex C.C. [0027865] 15/10/1983
Adams Mrs H, (was Taylor), Database Lib., Stockport MBC. [0049897] 07/01/1994
Adams Mrs J, (was Green), BA MCLIP, Sen.Lib., (Lifelong Learning), Norfolk C.C., Norwich Millennium L. [0025288] 07/01/1976
Adams Ms JE, BA DipLib MCLIP AssocCIPD, Area Serv./Training & Devel.Mgr., & Health & Safety Co-ordinator, Lincoln Cent.L. [0028468] 30/12/1977
Adams Ms JP, BA(Hons) PGDipILM, Learning Res.Base Mgr., Prenton High Sch.for Girls, Birkenhead. [0055492] 15/10/1997
Adams Mr JR, BA MSc MCLIP, Retired. [0040697] 01/01/1962
Adams Mr KW, BA(Hons) MA, Grad.Trainee/Admin.Offr., Brit.L.Newspaper L., London. [0059509] 18/04/2001
Adams Miss MF, BA MA MCLIP, Unemployed. [0000052] 01/01/1964
Adams Miss PA, Life Member. [0018468] 24/08/1962
Adams Mr PM, BA MCLIP, Comm.Lib., St.John's L., Worcs C.C. [0000054] 01/01/1971
Adams Mr PM, MA MCLIP, Employment not known. [0060128] 10/12/2001
Adams Mrs POM, (was Pardy), MA MCLIP, Life Member. [0020029] 08/01/1973
Adams Mrs PW, (was Hick), BA MCLIP, Operations Mgr., Northants.L.& Inf.Serv., Northampton. [0018087] 03/10/1972
Adams Mrs RA, (was Patrick), BA DipLib MCLIP, Asst.Ch.Lib.-Support Serv., W.Educ.& Lib.Board. [0011354] 01/01/1968
Adams Mr RE, BA MCLIP, Life Member. [0000058] 06/10/1960
Adams Mr RH, MCLIP, Life Member, Delfan, North Road, Whitland, Dyfed, SA34 0BA. [0000059] 01/01/1949
Adams Mr RS, MCLIP, Vol.Lib., Terence Higgins Trust L. [0000061] 01/01/1950
Adams Mrs S, BA, L.Asst., Norton Radstock Coll., Bath. [0057890] 23/09/1999 **AF**
Adams Miss SJ, BA MCLIP, Level I Mgr., Central L., L.B.of Croydon. [0018338] 10/10/1972
Adams Ms SJ, BA MCLIP, Sales Account Mgr., Talis Inf.Ltd. [0026669] 14/10/1976
Adams Mr SR, BSc MSc CChem MRSC MCLIP, Employment not known. [0060141] 10/12/2001
Adams Mrs SU, (was Eden), BSc MCLIP, Mgr.Regulatory Assessment Serv., Law Soc., Redditch,Worcs. [0027505] 21/02/1977
Adams Ms TL, BA(Hons) MCLIP, Co.Lib., Powys C.C., Llandrindod Wells. [0025780] 16/03/1976
Adams Mrs TM, (was Walford), Retired, 72 Bateman Rd., E.Leake, Loughborough, Leics. [0000063] 01/01/1963
Adamson Dr GW, BSc MBCS PhD MCLIP, Retired. [0060516] 11/12/2001
Adamson Mr GW, Asst.Lib., Allen & Overy, London. [0051023] 09/11/1994
Adamson Mrs J, (was Frazier), BA MCLIP, p./t.Heritage Offr., Shepway,Folkestone L., Kent C.C.Educ.& Ls. [0005204] 12/01/1965
Adamson Mrs ME, (was Brown), BA MCLIP, Unemployed. [0000067] 12/03/1963
Adamson Mr P, BA(Hons) DipLib, Cataloguer, Cardiff Univ. [0051602] 06/04/1995
Adamson Mr RD, PGDipILS, Document Supply Asst., Scottish Parliament H.Q., Edinburgh. [0055261] 04/05/1995
Adamson Miss S, L.Asst., DMBS, Doncaster. [0054969] 03/06/1997
Adaran Mrs OM, (was Fambegbe), BSc(Hons), Lib., London Underground Ltd., L.& Inf.Serv. [0054703] 07/03/1997
Adcock Mrs LB, L.Mgr., Chelmsley Wood L., Solihull. [0047896] 22/10/1992 **AF**
Adcock Miss LM, BA(Hons) MSc(Econ) MCLIP, Asst.Lib.(Catr.), Royal Nat.Inst.for the Blind, Peterborough. [0055988] 13/01/1998
Adcock Miss SJ, BA DipLib MCLIP, Lib., Beckenham L., W.Area, L.B.of Bromley. [0038651] 30/08/1985
Adcock Mrs SJ, L.Asst., Leicester Univ. [0058079] 25/10/1999 **AF**
Adderley Miss CA, MCLIP, Asst.Lib., Solihull Cent.L. [0000070] 01/01/1968
Addis Mrs FE, (was Brown), MCLIP, Retired. [0000073] 01/01/1956
Addison Mrs CM, (was Booth), MCLIP, Unemployed. [0001477] 31/01/1967
Addison Ms JF, BA DipLib MCLIP, Resident in Hungary. [0011390] 10/05/1968

Addison Mrs JM, (was Deacon), MA(Hons) PgDipInf MCLIP, Position Unknown, Aberdeen City Council, [0027414] 01/01/1969
Addison Mrs LA, (was Higham), BA MCLIP, Media Res.Mgr., Aberdeenshire L.& Inf.Serv., Oldmeldrum. [0044861] 01/01/1991
Addison Mr PJ, BA(Hons), Lib., C.M.H.T., Manchester. [0055661] 04/11/1997
Addison Mr R, MCLIP, Life Member, 24 Walsgrave Dr., Solihull, W.Midlands, B92 9PN. [0000074] 01/01/1950
Addy Miss CE, BSc(Hons), Grp.Leader, L.Serv., BAE Systems, Preston. [0058091] 27/10/1999
Addy Mrs MAS, (was Brown), BA MCLIP, Unemployed. [0001907] 01/01/1970
Adelberg Miss AAC, BA MCLIP, Life Member. [0000076] 01/01/1949
Adeloye Mr A, MA MPhil MSc MCLIP, Ch.Lib., Nigeria High Commission, London. [0045491] 16/01/1991
Adewale Ms AS, BA(Hons), p./t.Stud./Lib., Univ.of N.London, Tate L., Brixton. [0059904] 31/10/2001
Adey Miss C, Administrator, Aston Univ. [0059506] 18/04/2001 **AF**
Adey Mr FC, FCLIP, Life Member, Tel.01242 523960. [0000077] 01/01/2029 **FE 01/01/2029**
Adey Mrs H, (was Wheelhouse), BA MSc MCLIP, Collection Devel.Mgr., Nottingham Trent Univ., L.& Inf.Serv. [0039602] 17/03/1986
Adey Ms LA, BA(Hons), p./t.Stud., N.London Univ., Politics L., Oxford. [0056798] 19/10/1998
Adlem Mrs AM, (was Johncock), BA DipLib MCLIP, Asst.Catr., Dorset Co.L.Serv., Dorset Co.Council. [0036324] 06/10/1983
Adleman Mrs S, (was Gable), BA MCLIP, Teacher/Lib., Ilford Ursuline High Sch., Essex. [0000082] 01/01/1969
Adler Mrs E, MCLIP, Retired. [0000084] 01/01/1969
Adnams Mrs JL, (was Webb), BA MA MCLIP, Sch.Lib., Norwich High Sch. [0018189] 11/10/1972
Adnum Mrs VB, (was Hutt), BA MCLIP, Life Member. [0016499] 01/01/1941
Adodoadji Mr LN, BA(Hons) DipLIS, Learning Resources Asst., Coll.of NW London, Kilburn. [0044333] 18/09/1990
Adomi Mr EE, BEd MLS, Head of Catg.operations, Delta State Univ., Nigeria. [0059563] 30/05/2001
Adu Mr JM, MLS MCLIP, Med.Lib., Univ.of Sci.& Tech., Kumasi, Ghana. [0028749] 01/01/1955
Afshari Miss F, BA MSc MCLIP, IT Serv.Lib., Imperial Coll.Sch.of Med., Hammersmith Campus, London. [0044468] 10/10/1990
Agacy Miss TG, Learning Adviser, RNIB. Redhill Coll., Surrey. [0040076] 16/10/1986
Agaja Mr JA, BLs MBA, Dep.Lib., Ramat L., Nigeria. [0059826] 10/10/2001
Agar Ms BK, Lib., Birmingham LEA, W.Midlands. [0045833] 21/06/1991
Agar Mrs CS, Learning Support Lib., Leeds City Council, W.Yorks. [0051964] 21/08/1995 **AF**
Agar Mrs SN, (was Clarke), MCLIP, p./t.Sch.L.Asst., W.Bridgford Sch., Notts. [0002792] 01/01/1969
Agate Miss C, BA MCLIP, Sen.Lib., Norfolk L.& Inf.Serv., Norfolk & Norwich Millennium L. [0024930] 27/10/1975
Agboola Mrs T, BSc MSc ARCH PgDip, Unemployed. [0053528] 09/07/1996
Ager Mrs CR, BA(Hons) PGCE MCLIP, Lib., Taunton Sch., Somerset. [0053013] 24/01/1996
Agnew Mrs AL, BA(Hons) PGCE PGDip, Inf.Editor, N.Lanarkshire Council. [0059411] 08/03/2001
Agus Mrs J, (was Whyatt), BA BMus MCLIP, Lib., Welsh Coll.of Music & Drama, Cardiff. [0000093] 19/09/1967
Agyare Mrs J, BSc DipInf, Lib., Sos Hermann Gmeiner Internat.Coll., Tema, Ghana. [0046264] 21/10/1991
Ah Fat Miss PF, B LIB MCLIP, Lib., Mauritius Coll. of the Air, Reduit, Mauritius. [0028469] 19/01/1978
Ahern Mrs C, (was Spinetto), BA, Lib., Gilbert Inter., Manchester [0042092] 01/10/1988
Ahern Ms JV, BA(Hons) DipInfLMgmt, Lib., Halton Lea L., Runcorn. [0052463] 02/11/1992
Aherne Mrs IB, (was Fleck), MA MSc, Knowledge Content Theatre Leader, Price Waterhouse Coopers, London. [0045392] 21/11/1990
Aherne Mrs MGM, BA MCLIP, Sch.Res.Lib., N.Lanarkshire Council. [0038490] 30/04/1985
Ahluwalia Mr H, MA MCLIP, Life Member. [0000096] 01/01/1964
Ahmad Mrs LS, (was Baldwin), MCLIP, Unemployed. [0000664] 13/01/1968
Ahmad Dr N, PhD MPhil DipLib MCLIP, Researcher-Freelance. [0010687] 01/01/1970
Ahmad Mrs RM, MA, L.& Serv.Mgr., L.B.of Merton. [0041060] 09/10/1987
Ahmed Mr HSS, BA, Stud.(Research-PhD), Univ.of London, Inst.of Educ., (Hon.Treasurer-ISG(SE)Sect.). [0052341] 30/10/1995
Ahmed Ms S, BSc PGCE DipLIS MA, Subject.Lib., Univ.of N.London, London. [0047577] 22/10/1992
Aiken Mrs JD, (was Lenton), BA MCLIP, Infotech Mgr., Hartlepool Coll.of F.E. [0033680] 03/02/1981
Aiken Mrs WA, (was Wilkes), MCLIP, Neighbourhood Lib., Staffs.Co.L. [0015841] 09/02/1968
Aikens Mrs JA, (was Skinner), BA, Employment not known. [0044326] 03/09/1990
Ainger Ms J, Resource Lib., King James's Sch., Huddersfield. [0059657] 16/07/2001
Ainley Mrs JM, (was Stevens), BA(Hons) DipIM, Sen.Asst.Lib., Manchester Metro.Uni. [0051354] 27/01/1995
Ainscough Mr PJ, MA DMS FCLIP, Retired. [0000104] 01/01/1954 **FE 21/07/1989**
Ainsley Mrs C, (was Buglass), BA MA MCLIP, Lib., St.Johns Coll., Nottingham. [0026943] 11/01/1976
Ainsley Mrs TA, L.Asst., Newcastle Univ., Robinson L. [0058064] 22/10/1999
Ainsworth Mrs A, (was Mchardy), BA MCLIP, Dist.Lib., Chesterfield L., Derbys.C.C. [0022034] 16/01/1974

Ainsworth Mr DJ, BA MCLIP, Database Editor/Local Hist., Local Hist.L., Battersea L. [0000107] 01/01/1970
Ainsworth Mrs ES, BSc, P./t.Stud./Gateway Advisor, Univ.Aberystwyth, Brunswick Learning Cent.Gloucester. [0059678] 26/07/2001
Ainsworth Mrs FHS, (was Speight), BA(Hons) DipLib, Lib.& Inf.Offr., Royal Botanical Gardens Kew, Haywards Heath. [0046184] 14/10/1991
Ainsworth Mr JW, BA MCLIP, Mgr.(Res.), Avril Robarts LRC., Liverpool John Moores Univ. [0000108] 01/01/1968
Ainsworth Mr M, MA DipLib MCLIP, Position unknown, Hawkpoint Partners, London. [0060823] 12/12/2001
Ainsworth Mrs M, (was Killick), BA MCLIP, Unemployed. [0021051] 24/09/1973
Airaksinen Miss KS, Stud., Edinburgh, [0061834] 15/11/2002
Aird Mrs CD, MA MCLIP, Life Member, Tel.0141 637 4758, 66 Ormonde Ave., Glasgow, G44 3QZ. [0000109] 01/01/1963
Aird Mrs LP, BA DipLib MCLIP, Sch.Lib., St.Christopher Sch., Letchworth, Herts. [0036906] 13/01/1984
Aird Miss ME, MCLIP, Lib., Croydon P.L. [0000113] 01/01/1963
Airey Miss VE, BA BBibl, L.Asst., Univ.of Nottingham, Hallward L. [0058603] 11/04/2000
Aitchison Mrs J, (was Binns), BA FCLIP, Consultant, 12 Sollershott W., Letchworth, Herts., SG6 3PX. [0000118] 01/01/1948 **FE 01/01/1953**
Aitchison Miss MJ, MPhil MCLIP, Employee, Radiocommunications Agency, London. [0000119] 01/01/1963
Aitchison Mr TM, OBE BSc HonFCLIP, Retired. [0000120] 01/01/1950 **FE 01/04/2002**
Aither Mrs SF, Stud., Northumbria at Newcastle Univ. [0060020] 26/11/2001
Aitken Ms AJ, BA(Hons) PGDip, Lib., National Mentoring Network, Manchester. [0052677] 21/11/1995
Aitken Mrs C, BA DipLS, Libr., British Med.Ass.L., London. [0059791] 03/10/2001
Aitken Mrs J, (was Sweeney), MA(Hons) MCLIP, Asst.Lib., Mitchell L., Glasgow. [0032706] 04/07/1980
Aitken Mrs JL, BA(Hons), Stud., Manchester Metro.Univ. [0061732] 30/10/2002
Aitken Miss K, BSc(Hons), L.Asst., Strathclyde Univ. [0059071] 07/11/2000
Aitken Miss KV, MA(Hons) DipILS, Temp.L.Asst., Dundee Univ. [0058093] 27/10/1999
Aitken Mrs PA, MA DipLib MCLIP, Sch.Lib., Glasgow City Council. [0034092] 01/10/1981
Aitkins Mrs JU, (was Goodley), BA MSc DMS MCLIP, Public Serv.Lib., Univ.of Leicester. [0031622] 08/10/1979
Aiton Mrs A, (was Goodwin), MA DipLib MCLIP, Campus Lib., Univ.of Dundee, Fife Campus. [0038993] 18/10/1985
Ajai-Ajagbe Ms KFB, BA(Hons), Unemployed. [0057800] 02/08/1999
Ajala Mr EB, BSc MLS, System Lib., Kenneth Dike L., Univ.of Ibadan, Nigeria. [0061223] 16/04/2002
Ajayi Mrs A, (was Awoyinfa), BSc, Unemployed. [0051425] 14/02/1995
Ajibade Miss AOA, BSc(Hons) MSc, Stud./p./t.L.Asst., City Univ./Grays Inn L., London. [0056379] 01/07/1998
Ajibade Miss BAIA, BA(Hons) MSc MCLIP, Inf.Researcher, Dept.of Trade & Ind., London. [0050843] 21/10/1994
Akande Mr SB, MLS DipLib MCLIP, Sen.Ref.Lib., Cent.Ref.L., Bromley Cent.L. [0034767] 10/02/1982
Akene Mr Z, Unemployed. [0061341] 30/05/2002
Akeroyd Mrs CM, (was White), MCLIP, Inf.Offr., Manches Solicitors, London. [0019937] 09/01/1973
Akeroyd Mr J, BSc MCLIP, Head of Learning & Inf.Sci., Southbank Univ., London. [0031533] 20/10/1979
Akhtar Mr M, BSc Dip IS&T MCLIP, Employment not known. [0060811] 12/12/2001
Akhtar Mr S, PGDipHuman Resource Man., Stud., Strathclyde Univ. [0061655] 14/10/2002
Akinbola Miss SO, Stud., Thames Valley Univ. [0058176] 11/11/1999
Akinlade Mrs RO, (was Banjo), BA, Admin.Asst., Benefits Agency, Stoke Newington. [0049981] 02/02/1994
Akintunde Dr SA, BSc(Hons) DipLib MSc PhD, Dep.Univ.Lib.(Systems), Univ.of Jos L., Jos, Plateau State, Nigeria. [0051134] 21/11/1994
Akowe Mr SP, BLS MA, Unemployed. [0061327] 23/05/2002
Akroyd Mrs SK, (was North), BA(Hons) MA, Lib., Nottingham City Council. [0051791] 07/10/1994
Al-Jumah Mr AO, MA, Dir.of Sch.L.Dept., Kuwait. [0046816] 06/02/1992
Al-Shabibi Mrs AMR, BA DipLib MCLIP, Unemployed. [0033970] 01/07/1981
Al-Shorbaji Dr NMA, BA DipDOC MLib PhD, Reg.Advisor, World Health Org., Cairo, Egypt. [0034941] 14/05/1982
Al-Talal Miss GR, BSc (Hons), Inf.Offr., British Cement Association. [0059183] 08/12/2000
Alabaster Miss C, BA MCLIP, Area Mgr., Bromley P.L., Beckenham Area. [0000128] 01/01/1970
Alafiatayo Mr BO, BSc(Hons) MLS MPhil, Doctoral Research Stud., Univ.of Cent.England, Birmingham. [0056470] 21/07/1998
Alan Miss S, Sen.L.Asst.-Inf.& Local Studies, Solihull L.& Arts, Solihull Cent.L. [0057790] 06/08/1999 **AF**
Alberici Mr SU, Med.L.Mgr., States of Jersey Health Dept., St.Helier. [0056312] 01/05/1998
Albin Mrs LE, (was Smallbone), BA(Hons) DipLib MCLIP, Lib.Tutor, The Arts Inst.at Bournemouth, Poole. [0047035] 06/04/1992
Albon Mrs RG, MCLIP, Life Member. [0000013] 01/01/1939
Albrow Mr AJ, BA MCLIP, L.& Inf.Mgr., Med.Protection Soc., Leeds. [0026925] 11/01/1977
Albu Miss KM, BA, Retired. [0016517] 01/01/1953
Alcock Mr D, MA MCLIP, Depute Lib., Jordanhill L., Univ.of Strathclyde. [0021400] 19/10/1973
Alcock Mrs JMD, (was Paterson), MA MCLIP, Self-employed. [0011343] 01/01/1970

Personal Members   Allen

Alcock Ms L, MCLIP, Sen.Lib.:Prison L.Serv., Staffs.L.& Inf.Serv. [0000135] 01/01/1970
Alcock Ms RJ, BA MCLIP, Asset Inf.Offr., Ballakermeen High Sch., Isle of Man. [0038080] 08/01/1985
Alder Mrs EDA, (was Elliott), BA MCLIP, Asst.Sch.Res.Offr.(Job Share), Redcar & Cleveland Sch.Res.Serv., Middlesbrough. [0033846] 01/04/1981
Alder Mr J, BA DipLib MCLIP, Princ.Lib., (Resources), Middlesbrough Council, Cent.L. [0033617] 14/01/1981
Alder Miss JK, BA(Hons), Inf.Asst., Kings Coll.London. [0061301] 16/05/2002
Alderman Mrs LA, (was Adamthwaite), BA(Hons) DipLIS MCLIP, Med.Lib., Queens Hosp., Burton Hosp.NHS, Trust, Burton-on-Trent. [0047959] 28/10/1992
Aldersley Mr SAJ, Organisational Devel.Mgr., Essex Libraries. [0045220] 15/08/1990 **AF**
Alderson Ms EM, MCLIP, Freelance Stage Mgr. [0026670] 27/10/1976
Alderson Miss KM, MCLIP, Asst.Lib., N.Yorkshire Co.L., Northallerton. [0000141] 01/01/1972
Alderson-Rice Ms J, Clerical Offr., Bridge Warden's Coll., Univ.ofKent. [0058465] 24/02/2000
Alderton Miss SM, BA MCLIP, Life Member. [0000142] 28/09/1950
Aldrich Mrs E, (was Jones), MLib MCLIP, Co.Bib.& Arch., Conwy Co.Bor.Council. [0007998] 16/01/1969
Aldrich Mrs EJ, (was Graveling), BA(Hons) MA MCLIP, Asst.Lib., Maidstone & Turnbridge Wells NHS T. [0055991] 12/01/1998
Aldrich Mr MJ, BA FBCS CIMgt HonFCLIP, Hon Fellow. [0060718] 12/12/2001 **FE 01/04/2002**
Aldridge Mr LF, BSc MCLIP, Performance Mgr., Leeds City Council. [0020027] 08/01/1973
Aldridge Ms LM, BA(Hons) MA MCLIP, Sen.Lib.-Child.Serv., Cambs.L. [0047923] 26/10/1992
Aldridge Mr PJ, BA MCLIP, Young Peoples Serv.Lib., Peterborough Cent.L., Peterborough City Council. [0038935] 22/10/1985
Aldridge-Morris Ms WV, BA MCLIP, Learning Cent.Co-ordinator, Poplar Cent., Tower Hamlets Coll. [0000150] 01/01/1963
Alexander Mrs AV, BA, p./t.Asst.Lib., Brit.Mus., London. [0040322] 01/01/1967
Alexander Ms C, MA(Hons), Distance Learn.Stud. [0053335] 07/05/1996
Alexander Mrs DG, (was Bungay), MCLIP, L.& Res.Cent.Mgr., King Edward VI Sch., Southampton. [0002056] 01/01/1967
Alexander Miss FH, BA(Hons), L.Asst., Leeds Uni., Brotherton L. [0059749] 10/09/2001
Alexander Mrs IA, (was Aitken), MCLIP, Area Lib., E.Dunbartonshire Council, Glasgow. [0000154] 01/01/1961
Alexander Mrs L, Inf.Asst., DSTL., Salisbury. [0061463] 06/08/2002 **AF**
Alexander Mrs LM, (was Henderson), MCLIP, Joint Lib.i/c., Denny L., Falkirk. [0026408] 04/10/1976
Alexander Mr MF, MCLIP, Princ.Lib.(Community Pro.Serv.), Surrey Co.L., Co.L.H.Q.Dorking. [0021818] 01/01/1974
Alexander Mr MG, BA DipLib, Unemployed. [0039559] 19/02/1986
Alexander Mr RJ, ICT Offr., L.and lifelong learning, Berkshire. [0061379] 05/07/2002
Alexander Mrs RW, MA MCLIP MSc, Learning Tech.Offr., Univ.of Edinburgh. [0027674] 04/07/1977
Alexander Mr WE, MA DipLib MCLIP, Dep.Lib., Med.L.,Salisbury Health Care Trust, Salisbury, Wilts.Auth. [0035170] 06/10/1982
Alferovs Mr A, BA(Hons) DipLibInf, Sales & Marketing Dir., Coutts Inf.Services Ltd. [0033875] 09/04/1981
Alford Mrs M, BA(Hons), Cent.Serv.Mgr., Hull Cent.L. [0061334] 28/05/2002
Ali Mrs K, BA, Br.Lib., Linlithgow L., W.Lothian Council. [0048728] 28/04/1993
Ali Mrs TJ, BA(Hons), Stud., Univ.of N.London. [0058947] 09/10/2000
Alimi Mr DA, BTech, Employment unknown. [0060323] 10/12/2001
Alison Mr WAG, FCLIP, Life Member. [0000161] 01/01/1935 **FE 01/01/1950**
Alkhalaf Mrs E, (was Righton), MCLIP, Lib., Kings High Sch.for Girls, Warwick. [0023421] 10/01/1975
Allan Mr A, BLS MCLIP, Unemployed. [0031778] 07/05/1980
Allan Mrs AI, (was Slaven), BA Dip Lib MCLIP, Career Break. [0038864] 15/10/1985
Allan Mr AJ, BLib MCLIP, Liaison Lib., Sheffield Univ.L., S.Yorks. [0000164] 01/01/1968
Allan Miss BA, BA MCLIP DMS, Coll.Lib., Clifton Coll., Bristol. [0018310] 12/10/1972
Allan Ms BC, (was Carr), MSc MCLIP MA PGCE, Independent Trainer & Author. [0026671] 11/11/1976
Allan Ms CM, BSc(Hons) MSc MCLIP, Sci.Inf.Offr., Univ.of Stirling. [0049534] 09/11/1993
Allan Mrs G, (was Macfarlane), BA MCLIP, Sen.Lib., Thamesmead Cent., L.B.of Bexley, Kent. [0009363] 25/06/1973
Allan Mrs J, (was Whalley), BA(Hons), Sch.L.Adviser, Leeds City Council. [0028207] 11/10/1977
Allan Ms J, BA(Hons) MA MCLIP, Liaison Lib., City Coll., Norwich. [0054397] 03/12/1996
Allan Mr JG, MCLIP, Lib., Falkirk Council. [0022273] 21/03/1974
Allan Mrs JM, (was Kruger), BA(Hon), Asst.Inf.Offr., Univ.of Reading, Berks. [0049778] 06/12/1993
Allan Mrs JR, (was Bowcott), BA DipLib MCLIP, H.of Bibl.Servs., Univ.of London L. [0034578] 15/01/1982
Allan Ms LD, (was McKiernan), BSc MCLIP, Inf.Offr., Scottish Environment Protection, Agency, E.Kilbride. [0000174] 01/01/1964
Allan Ms NE, Unemployed. [0035471] 10/07/1990 **AF**
Allan Ms ME, MA(Hons) DipLIS MCLIP, Asst.Ref.& Local Studies Lib., Aberdeen Cent.L. [0049647] 18/11/1993
Allan Mrs MM, (was Rees), MA MCLIP, Life Member. [0012248] 01/01/1950

Allan Dr NMW, MA PhD MCLIP, Curator of Oriental Books &, Manuscripts, Wellcome Inst.for Hist.of Med. [0023016] 17/10/1974
Allan Mr RV, BA MCLIP, Faculty Lib., Birmingham Conservatoire, Univ.of Cent.England in Birmingham. [0021915] 05/02/1974
Allan Miss SL, MA(Hons) DipLIS, Sch.Lib., Preston Lodge High Sch., Prestonpans. [0058725] 01/07/2000
Allanach Mr DR, MCLIP, Serv.Mgr.-Dist., Cambs.C.C. [0000176] 01/01/1966
Allard Ms M, MA DipLib MCLIP, L.Resource Cent.Mgr., Aberdeen Grammar Sch. [0039865] 01/10/1986
Allardice Ms CM, BA HDipLIB BA(Hons) MA, Agent for the Copyright L's., Copyright Libraries Agency, London. [0044598] 02/11/1990
Allason Miss EA, FCLIP, Life Member. [0000181] 01/01/1936 **FE 01/01/1952**
Allatt Mrs G, (was Ryan), BA(Hons) MSc MA MCLIP, Unemployed. [0046981] 16/03/1992
Allauddin Mrs S, BSc MCLIP, Princ.L.Offr.-Ethnic Serv., Edinburgh City L. [0031779] 19/01/1980
Allaway Mrs SM, (was Cheetham), BA MCLIP, Site Lib., L.B.of Camden. [0019957] 10/01/1973
Allberry Mr ES, DipLib MCLIP, Support Serv.Mgr., L.B.of Hackney, Homerton L. [0028475] 12/01/1978
Allbrooke Ms JC, (was Sargison), BA MCLIP, Newspaper Serv.Mgr., The Brit.L., London. [0022095] 29/01/1974
Allcock Mrs JV, (was Qualter), BA MCLIP, L.Asst., Knowsley M.B.C., Prescot, Merseyside. [0042750] 16/02/1989
Allcock Mrs KJ, BA(Hons) MA MCLIP, Special Collections Lib., Nottingham Univ.L. [0050621] 01/10/1994
Allcock Mrs LW, (was Blackburn), BA(Hons), Tax Lib., Ernst & Young, London. [0041862] 27/04/1988
Allcock Ms SJ, BA(Hons) MCLIP, Digital Asset Mgr., Reed Educ.& Prof.Publishing, Oxford. [0032250] 28/02/1980
Allcorn Mr RT, BSc MCLIP, Employment not known. [0060132] 10/12/2001
Allden Ms A, BA MSc MBCS MCLIP, Position unknown, Univ.of Warwick. [0060778] 12/12/2001
Allely Ms M, MCLIP, Local Studies P./t., Nat.City P.L., Nat.City CA 91950, USA. [0016951] 01/01/1959
Allen Mrs AC, BA(Hons), Unemployed. [0029066] 03/05/1978
Allen Ms AJ, BA DipLIS, Prison Lib., HMP Hollesley Bay, Woodbridge. [0050778] 01/01/1994
Allen Ms AJ, BA MCLIP, Sen.Spec.Lib.:Child.& Young People, Wigston Magna L., Leics. [0025945] 06/05/1976
Allen Mrs BD, (was Karoubas), BA(Hons) DipLIS MCLIP, Unemployed, [0044527] 22/10/1990
Allen Mrs BJ, (was Parkes), MBE MCLIP, Life Member. [0000192] 01/01/1937
Allen Ms DJ, BA DipLib MCLIP, Head of L.,Mus.& Arts, L.B.of Wandsworth. [0000194] 01/01/1969
Allen Mr DK, BA MSc PhD MCLIP, Employment not known. [0060223] 10/12/2001
Allen Mr DL, BA MCLIP, Life Member, 3 The Range, Langham, Oakham, Leics., LE15 7EB. [0000195] 01/01/1953
Allen Mr DM, MCLIP, L.Serv.Mgr., Swindon Bor.Council. [0000196] 01/01/1968
Allen Mr DW, BScSoc MCLIP, Lib., Horniman Mus.& Gardens, Forest Hill, London. [0000197] 01/01/1968
Allen Mrs EM, (was Williams), BSc MCLIP, Unemployed. [0015921] 11/01/1972
Allen Ms G, (was Allen Goves), BA(Hons), Learning Res.Cent.Mgr., Blue Coat Sch., Oldham. [0044344] 01/10/1990
Allen Mr GC, MCLIP, Position Unknown, CIP, Treaty Cent., Hounslow. [0025711] 23/02/1976
Allen Mrs GP, (was Harraway), BA MCLIP, Lib., Foreign & Commonwealth Off., London. [0038692] 01/10/1985
Allen Mr GR, BSc CChem MRSC MCLIP, Retired. [0060129] 10/12/2001
Allen Mr IC, BA, Asst.Inf.Offr., Slaughter and May, London. [0034457] 04/11/1981
Allen Mrs J, (was Russell), BA(Hons), System Lib., Christie Hosp.NHS Trust, Kostoris Med.L., Manchester. [0049682] 22/03/1993
Allen Mrs JC, (was Ward), MCLIP, Child.Serv.Mgr., L.B.of Sutton. [0034667] 01/02/1982
Allen Mr JER, BA DipLib, Catg.Team Leader, City Univ., London. [0041877] 07/05/1988
Allen Mr JN, BA FCLIP, Life Member. [0000207] 01/01/1952 **FE 01/01/1964**
Allen Mrs JW, (was Green), MCLIP, Unemployed. [0000208] 20/01/1964
Allen Miss K, BA(Hons) MA, L.Asst., Nottingham City C. [0057256] 03/02/1999
Allen Mrs K, (was Johnson), BA MCLIP, Inf.Consultant, Univ.of Herts, Watford. [0040025] 08/10/1986
Allen Mrs KL, BA(Hons) MScEcon, Asst.Lib-Cataloguer, Nat.Assembly for Wales. [0059658] 16/07/2001
Allen Ms KM, BA(Hons), Director, Learned Information, London. [0059676] 25/07/2001 **SP**
Allen Mr L, BA DipLib MCLIP, Inf.Mgr.(Recreation), L.B.of Sutton. [0034834] 15/03/1982
Allen Miss LA, BA(Hons), L.Mgr., Heartlands Educ.Cent., Birmingham Heartlands Hosp. [0037038] 31/01/1984
Allen Mrs LJ, (was Watling), BSc(Hons) MCLIP, Unemployed. [0046907] 24/02/1992
Allen Mr N, BA, Faculty Inf.Consultant, Univ.of Herts., Watford. [0036957] 19/01/1984
Allen Mr N, BSc MSc MCLIP, Position unknown, GlaxoSmithKline, Ware. [0060740] 12/12/2001
Allen Mr NE, BSc MCLIP, Unemployed. [0018464] 01/01/1969
Allen Mr P, Head of Business Inf., John Lewis plc., London. [0051446] 14/02/1995
Allen Mr P, BA(Hons), Unemployed. [0047580] 05/10/1992

177

Allen Mr PN, MCLIP, Retired. [0000219]   01/01/1961
Allen Miss R, BA(Hons) MA MCLIP, Writer/Hist.& Secondhand Bkseller, Bufo Books-01794-517149, Romsey, Hants, S051 5AJ. [0011527] 01/01/1968
Allen Mr R, Stud., Univ.Brighton. [0059107]   16/11/2000
Allen Ms S, BA(Hons), Inf.Offr., Drugscope, London. [0056433]   13/07/1998
Allen-Smith Ms PJ, (was Farrell), BA MA DipLib MCLIP, Unemployed. [0037488]   04/10/1984
Allery Miss JC, BA DipLib, Lend.Serv.Mgr., De Montfort Univ. [0038348] 11/03/1985
Allhouse Mr LM, BA(Hons), p./t.Stud./Audio-visual Lib., Univ.of Bradford. [0050808]   19/10/1994
Alliez Miss SJ, MCLIP, Database Lib., Beds.C.C. [0000226]   01/01/1966
Allison Miss AG, BA(Hons), Catr., Brit.L., Boston Spa. [0056358]   16/06/1998
Allison Mrs AS, (was Calton), MA DipLib MCLIP, L.Mgr., Falkirk Council. [0002288]   01/01/1971
Allison Mr C, MSc, Unemployed. [0048092]   06/11/1992
Allison Mrs C, BSc(Hons) MA DipLS MCLIP, Asst.Lib.(p./t.), De Montfort Univ., Leicester. [0039684]   21/05/1986
Allison Miss FI, BA MCLIP, Asst.Lib., W.Sussex C.C., Haywards Heath L. [0034684]   28/01/1982
Allison Mrs J, L.Mgr., Surrey C.C., Surrey. [0057533]   22/04/1999
AF
Allison Miss L, BA MCLIP, Sales Consultant, Epixtech, Chesham. [0053057] 04/03/1996
Allison Mr NG, LLB(Hons), Employment not known. [0058543]   01/04/2000
Allison Mr RD, Inf.Researcher, UBS Warburg, London. [0057036] 27/11/1998
Allonby Mrs S, B.Ed(Hons), Stud., Manchester Met.Univ. [0059790] 03/10/2000
Allott Ms HC, BA MCLIP, Lib., Berks.Shared Serv.Organisation, Berks.Health Auth. [0000236]   01/01/1972
Allred Mr JR, FCLIP MPhil, Retired. [0000237]   01/01/1953
FE 01/01/1964
Allsop Miss HE, MCLIP, L.Mgr., Green Street L., L.B.of Newham. [0027104] 01/01/1974
Allsop Mrs J, (was Hughes), BA DipLib MCLIP, P./t.Night Clerk, Short Loans, Lancaster Univ.L., Lancs. [0032799]   10/09/1980
Allsopp Dr D, BSc PhD CBiol FIBiol MCLIP, Retired. [0060130]   10/12/2001
Allum Mr DN, BA MCLIP, Ch.Lib., Nat.Assembly for Wales, Cardiff. [0019462]   01/01/1966
Allwood Mrs CM, (was Woolf), MA MCLIP, Training Exec., Prof.Devel., CILIP. [0029236]   08/04/1978
Alman Mrs M, BA BCom MCLIP, Life Member, Flat B, 31 Winchester Rd., London, NW3 3NR. [0000242]   01/01/1937
Alman Ms SB, BA, Unemployed. [0044302]   22/08/1990
Almeida Mr DJ, MSc MCLIP, Employment not known. [0060833]   12/12/2001
Almond Mr CD, MCLIP, Team Coordinator, W.Area, Southwark P.L. [0000242]   01/01/1971
Almond Mrs CW, BA DipLIS DMS MCLIP, Learning Support Lib., Bury M.B.C.- Lancs. [0048270]   21/11/1994
Almond Ms MP, (was Gregg), BA DipHE DipLib MCLIP, Team Lib., Bracknell Forest Bor.Council. [0042304]   17/10/1988
Aloba Mrs YM, (was Cameron), BA MCLIP, Retired. [0016530]   14/01/1965
Alper Mrs HAC, (was Turner), MA MHSM MCLIP, NHS Liaison Lib., St.Georges Hosp.Med.Sch., London. [0014951]   23/08/1970
Alsac Ms PA, Inf.Mgr., UK Unesco, The British Council. [0059207] 08/01/2001   **AF**
Alshaya Mr AM, MLS, Stud., Univ.of Wales, Aberystwyth. [0057355] 17/02/1999
Alsmeyer Mr DH, BA MSc MCLIP, Employment not known. [0060133] 10/12/2001
Alsop Miss G, Stud., Manchester Metro.Univ. [0061820]   12/11/2002
Alston Prof RC, OBE MA PhD HonFCLIP, Retired. [0039809]   10/09/1986
FE 10/09/1986
Alston Mr SJ, BA(Hons) MSc(Econ) MCLIP, Inf.Lib., Univ.of Bath. [0050830] 20/10/1994
Altaner Mrs A, BA MLS, Unemployed. [0061022]   01/02/2002
Althorpe Mrs P, (was Wilson), BA(Hons) DipLIS MCLIP, Med.Lib., Ipswich Hosp.NHS Trust. [0040125]   13/10/1986
Alvarez Mrs NB, (was Bissicks), BA MCLIP, Retired. [0001317]   27/09/1967
Alvey Mrs KJ, BA(Hons) MCLIP, Stock Mgr., Bath Cent.L., Bath & N.E.Somerset. [0039445]   28/01/1986
Amaeshi Prof BO, BA MA MCLIP, Prof.of L.Science, Abia State Univ., Nigeria. [0042309]   07/02/1967
Amarakoon Mr LR, FLA(SL) FCLIP, Co.Inf.Offr., Save the Children UK, Sri Lanka. [0060098]   07/12/2001   **FE 01/04/2002**
Amatt Mr LK, FCLIP, Retired. [0000251]   01/01/1963   **FE 05/11/1973**
Ambler Mrs AJ, BA, Stud.,L.Asst.p./t., Leeds Metro.Uni., Dewsbury L. [0061650]   14/10/2002
Ambler Mrs AJ, (was North), MCLIP, Team Lib., Oxfordshire Co.Council, Abingdon Br.L. [0000252]   01/01/1962
Ambrosi Mrs LA, BA MA, Inf.Offr., BECTA, Coventry. [0059055] 02/11/2000
Amery Miss JE, BSc(Hons) DipILM MCLIP, Learning Resources Mgr., Askham Bryan Coll., York. [0046521]   15/11/1991
Ames Mrs DE, BA(Hons), Stud., Univ.of Wales, Aberystwyth. [0061592] 02/10/2002
Amesbury Ms S, BA(Hons) PGDip, Lib., S.Birmingham Mental Hlth.NHS Trust, QEPH L. [0046894]   28/02/1992
Amies Mr PS, BA(Hons) DipLIS MCLIP, Asst.Lib., Bibl.Serv.Section, Corp.of London L. [0050659]   05/10/1994
Amoah Ms L, BA(Hons) DipEd MLIS MCLIP, L.& Learning Res.Asst., Handsworth Coll., Birmingham. [0053714]   20/09/1996
Amos Mr AR, MCLIP, Lib., Mulberry Girls Sch., London. [0018467] 01/01/1967
Amos Miss J, Stud., Univ.of Central England. [0060871]   18/12/2001
Amos Mrs MJ, Sen.L.Asst., Doncaster MBC. [0000257]   05/10/1971

Amy Mrs LG, MCLIP, Team Lib.(Sch.Lib.Serv.), Western Area, E.Sussex. [0026879]   11/10/1976
Anagnostelis Ms DM, BSc MSC, Lib., Med.L., Royal Free & Univ.Coll.Med.Sch., London. [0040416]   02/02/1987
Anandasivam Mrs GK, (was Anandaswam), BA DipLib MCLIP, Lib., Overseas Sch.of Colombo, Sri Lanka. [0050077]   05/04/1994
Anderhub Dr AF, H.of Univ.L., Johannes Gutenberg Univ., Mainz, Germany. [0055097]   09/07/1997
Anderson Miss A, BA(Hons), P./t.Stud./Admin.Asst., Inland Revenue, Newcastle, Univ.Northumbria. [0059878]   29/10/2001
Anderson Mrs A, BEd DipAIM, L.Asst., Health Promotion L.Scotland, Edinburgh. [0052780]   12/12/1995   **AF**
Anderson Ms A, p./t.Stud./Inf.Centre Mgr., Univ.Averystwyth, Interfleet Tech.Derby. [0059617]   03/07/2001
Anderson Mr AC, BA DMS MCLIP, Dep.Div.Lib., N.Div., Hants.C.C. [0021817]   01/01/1974
Anderson Mrs AM, (was Gale), MCLIP, Community Inf.Lib., Wilts.L.& Heritage, Trowbridge. [0005297]   18/05/1970
Anderson Miss CA, L.Asst., St.Loyes Sch.of Health Studies, Exeter. [0061347] 07/06/2002   **AF**
Anderson Mrs CA, BA MCLIP, Subject Lib.-Philosophy & Latin, American Stud., Univ.of London L. [0029038]   09/03/1978
Anderson Ms CJ, BA(Hons) MCLIP, Inf.Offr., Linklaters & Alliance, London. [0048073]   04/11/1992
Anderson Mrs D, MA DipLib HonFCLIP, Dir., I.F.L.A.Office for U.B.C. [0000267]   01/01/1953   **FE 12/06/1984**
Anderson Mrs EH, (was Maund), Sen.Asst.Lib., Northern Coll., Stainborough. [0041786]   06/04/1988
Anderson Mrs FE, (was Macdonald), BA MCLIP, Ref.& Inf.Lib., S.Lanarkshire Council, E.Kilbride. [0029733]   18/10/1978
Anderson Mr G, BA MCLIP, Inf.Serv.Mgr., The Mitchell L., Glasgow C.C. [0037434]   14/09/1984
Anderson Ms GC, (was Cramond), BA MCLIP, Desk Serv.Mgr., Univ.of Wales, Bangor, Inf.Serv., Main L. [0027867]   03/10/1977
Anderson Miss GM, MA(Hons) DipILS, L.Asst., Univ.of Strathclyde, Glasgow. [0058455]   22/02/2000
Anderson Miss J, BA(Hons) MA, Lib., S.Tyneside NHS Trust, Training & Devel.Cent., S.Shields. [0058316]   10/01/2000
Anderson Miss J, MA MCLIP, Campus Lib., Bell Coll., Dumfries Campus. [0032771]   25/08/1980
Anderson Mrs JC, (was Walker), MA MCLIP, Community Lib., Nottingham City Council. [0000275]   01/01/1963
Anderson Mr JE, BA MLib MCLIP, Enquiry Serv.Mgr., Cambridgeshire C.C., Cambridge Cent.L. [0043050]   03/07/1989
Anderson Mrs JE, (was Barker), BA DipLib MCLIP, Unemployed. [0000759] 01/01/1970
Anderson Miss LE, BA(Hons), Asst.Lib., Stockport NHS Trust. [0058431] 11/02/2000
Anderson Miss LR, BA(Hons), Quality Assurance Offr., Liverpool John Moores Univ. [0057303]   05/02/1999
Anderson Miss M, BA MCLIP, Life Member. [0000283]   01/01/1953
Anderson Mr M, BSc MSc MCLIP, Employment unknown. [0060265] 10/12/2001
Anderson Ms ME, (was Millar), BA MCLIP, Inf.Serv.Advisor, Napier Univ., Edinburgh. [0030082]   06/12/1978
Anderson Miss ML, BSc(Hons), Systems Lib., Charles Russell, London. [0050832]   20/10/1994
Anderson Mr P, BA(Hons) MCLIP, L.Liaison Offr., Scottish Parliament, Edinburgh. [0039952]   09/10/1986
Anderson Mrs P, (was Ridler), MCLIP, Lib.i/c., Teignmouth L., Devon. [0024795]   09/10/1975
Anderson Mrs PA, (was Sutherland), MA MCLIP, Unemployed. [0021087] 05/10/1973
Anderson Mrs PK, LLB DipLib MCLIP, Sen.Lib., The Law Soc., London. [0038189]   02/02/1985
Anderson Ms RR, BSocSc BA MCLIP, Coll.Lib., Richmond Adult Comm.Coll., Twickenham. [0042397]   27/10/1988
Anderson Mrs SA, (was Gillbe), MCLIP, Child.Lib., L.B.of Barnet. [0000289] 26/09/1964
Anderson Mrs T, (was Gannon), DipILS, Temp.Lib., Aberdeen C.C., Aberdeen City Music Sch. [0050094] 21/03/1994
Anderson Mr TJB, BA MCLIP, Retired. [0016539]   01/01/1948
Anderson Mr W, BSc(Econ) FCLIP, Life Member. [0000292]   01/01/1959
FE 01/01/1964
Anderson Mr WA, BA MCLIP MILAM, Lib., Off.for Nat.Statistics, Titchfield Site. [0018468]   01/01/1964
Anderson Mrs WA, (was Loates), Stud., Loughborough Univ. [0057075] 07/12/1998
Anderson-Smith Mrs M, (was Matthew), MA DipLib, Sen.Curator, Special L's.& Arch., Univ.of Aberdeen. [0009930]   01/01/1965
Anderton Ms CF, MA(Hons), Lib. [0057831]   27/08/1999
Anderton Mrs E, (was Chaffin), MCLIP, Life Member. [0000294]   28/03/1944
Anderton Miss M, BSc MSc FCLIP, Employment not known. [0060517] 11/12/2001   **FE 01/04/2002**
Andrew Miss C, MA(Hons) DipILS MCLIP, L.Offr., Edinburgh City Council. [0055795]   24/11/1997
Andrew Mrs LM, BA MCLIP, Inf.Offr., Building Design Partnership, Belfast. [0021222]   04/11/1973
Andrew Miss SM, BA PGCE DipLib MCLIP, L.Offr., Merton Local Studies Cent., L.B. of Merton. [0038600]   25/07/1985
Andrew Ms SM, (was Nayee), BA MSc MCLIP, Head of L.Inf.Cent., NHS Exec., London & S.E.Regions. [0010678]   21/09/1967
Andrews Mr A, BA FCLIP, Life Member. [0000301]   01/01/1932
FE 01/01/1955
Andrews Mrs AM, (was Cutting), BA(Hons) MPhil, Stud., Univ.Aberystwyth. [0059969]   14/11/2001

Andrews Ms BE, MA, Research Collections Co-ordinator, Reading Univ.L. [0054109] 28/10/1996
Andrews Mrs C, (was Mann), MA MCLIP, Head of International Affairs &, Defence Section, House of Commons L. [0009682] 07/10/1967
Andrews Mr CC, MCLIP, Retired. [0000302] 01/01/1966
Andrews Miss CE, BA(Hons) MSc, Position Unknown, Nat.Foundation for Educ.Res., Slough. [0058362] 25/01/2000
Andrews Miss CJ, BA(Hons) MSc MCLIP, Head Lib., Masons, London. [0050352] 04/07/1994
Andrews Mr DJ, BA MCLIP, Mgr., Bransty Comm.Devel.Cent., Cumbria C.C. [0000304] 01/01/1964
Andrews Ms G, L.Asst., Chester L., Cheshire. [0059144] 28/11/2000
AF
Andrews Mrs GE, (was Stockwell), FRSA MCLIP, Life Member, 01223 834827. [0000308] 01/01/1951
Andrews Miss J, MA DipLib MCLIP, Dir.of L.Serv., Univ.of Cent.England in Birmingham. [0032009] 29/01/1980
Andrews Mr JM, BA DipLibInf AIL DipTrans, Professional Lib., Birmingham Uni. [0042624] 24/01/1989
Andrews Dr JS, MA PhD MCLIP, Life Member. [0016540] 01/01/1951
Andrews Ms KJ, BMUS, Stud., London Metro. [0061581] 02/10/2002
Andrews Mrs LM, (was Appleton), MA, Life Asst., Royal & Sun Alliance Insurance, Bristol. [0035445] 15/10/1982
Andrews Mrs M, (was Mcwhirter), BA MCLIP, Lib., Dalkeith High Sch., Midlothian. [0009585] 18/05/1968
Andrews Mr MJ, BA(Hons) MSc(Econ), Sen.L.Asst., Upper Camera, Bodleian L., Oxford. [0051232] 01/12/1994
Andrews Mr PD, BD MINSTAM MCLIP, Indexer,Copy Editor, Proof Reader, Freelance. [0000310] 01/01/1967
Andrews Miss PM, MCLIP, Br.Lib., Penn L., Wolverhampton. [0026929] 11/12/1976
Andrews Miss RE, BSc(Hons) MSc, L.Asst., UCE Birmingham. [0059214] 09/01/2001
Andrews Mrs SE, BA(Hons) MLS MCLIP, Learning Res.Lib., Leicester Coll., Freemans Pk.Campus. [0053207] 22/04/1996
Angel Ms JE, BA(Hons) DipInf, Career Break. [0053041] 19/02/1996
Angrave Mr NJ, BA MCLIP, Mgr., Sch.L.Serv., L.B.of Barnet. [0023309] 21/11/1974
Angus Mrs KJ, (was Dark), BA(Hons) MA, Child.& Young Peoples Lib. [0057522] 21/04/1999
Angus Mrs S, MA(Hons) MCLIP, p./t.L.Asst., Newcastle Upon Tyne Univ. [0021853] 10/02/1974
Aning Mr TK, Arch., Univ.of Ghana, Accra. [0049161] 08/10/1993
Anley Ms CM, BSc MCLIP MSc, Audit Comm.Inspector, The Audit Commission. [0036834] 03/01/1984
Annable Mrs JA, (was Capstick), BA MCLIP, Asst.Bibl.Serv.Lib., Tameside Leisure Serv., Ashton under Lyne. [0028746] 06/01/1978
Annetts Mrs EA, (was Chaloner), BA MCLIP, Learning Res.Mgr., Milton Keynes Coll. [0023331] 03/12/1974
Annis Mr CH, MA DipLib MCLIP, Lib., Inst.of Classical Studies, London. [0024586] 02/10/1975
Annis Mr M, BSc(Hons) DipLib MCLIP, Asst.Lib., Blyth L., Northumberland C.C. [0034108] 01/10/1981
Annis Ms SE, BA MPhil MCLIP, Lib., S.Lancs.Health Auth., Eccleston. [0030891] 11/05/1979
Ansari Mrs JF, BA(Hons), Lib., Islamic Foundation, Markfield. [0042215] 19/10/1988
Anscombe Mrs RA, BA MCLIP, Child.Lib., W.Grp., L.B.of Bromley. [0021060] 01/10/1973
Ansell Mrs E, (was Jones), BA MA MCLIP, Sen.Lect., Bus.Sch., Liverpool John Moores Univ. [0007997] 12/01/1970
Ansell Mrs J, (was Watton), MCLIP, Retired. [0000321] 01/01/1958
Ansell Mr R, MCLIP, Team Lib.(Inf.), Yeovil L.Inf., Somerset L.Arts & Inf. [0025204] 16/12/1975
Ansley Ms WJ, BA(Hons) MA, Researcher, Enterprise Oil plc., London. [0056477] 23/07/1998
Anson Mrs JM, (was Wilkinson), BA DipLib MCLIP, [0033365] 04/11/1980
Ansorge Mrs CA, (was Broadbelt), MA MCLIP, Lib., Faculty of Oriental Studies, Univ.of Cambridge. [0001760] 01/01/1969
Anstead Mrs AH, (was Pytlik), BSc(Hons) DipLib DipTrans, Asst.Lib., The Wellcome Trust, London. [0037400] 09/08/1984
Anstead Mr NJ, MIM MCLIP, Employment not known. [0060134] 10/12/2001
Anstey Mrs KA, MCLIP, Area Lib., Peckham L., L.B.of Southwark. [0022153] 21/02/1974
Anstey Mr LM, (was Hart), MCLIP, Sch.Lib., All Saints Catholic High Sch., Huddersfield. [0006471] 08/10/1971
Anstis Ms PL, Learning Resources Asst., Partnership for Theological Ed., Manchester. [0056924] 06/11/1998
Antell Mrs LC, BA MCLIP, Lib., Gillingham, Dorset C.C. [0037338] 02/07/1984
Antenbring Mrs SM, (was Warrington), RGN RM BA(Hons) MA MCLIP, Inf.Offr., Clifford Chance, London. [0052034] 02/10/1995
Anthony Mr JG, BA, L.Asst., Warburg Inst., London. [0059295] 31/01/2001
Anthony Mr LJ, BA HonFCLIP FCLIP, Life Member. [0000326] 01/01/1936
FE 01/01/1950
Anthony Mr RL, BA DipLib, Sen.Asst.Lib., House of Lords L., London. [0045494] 20/02/1991
Anthony Ms SG, BSc PGDipLib, Lib., Cwmbran L., Torfaen C.B.C., Gwent. [0039409] 27/01/1986
Antill Mr JK, FCLIP, Life Member, Tel:0534 33082. [0016544] 01/01/1953
FE 01/01/1968
Antill Mrs MA, (was Sweet), BA, p./t.Stud., Bristol, L.Asst., Cranfield Univ., Shrivenham. [0057706] 05/07/1999
Anuar Mrs H, (was Aroozoo), BA HonFCLIP FCLIP, Resident in Singapore. [0016545] 01/01/1952 FE 01/01/1958

Ap Emlyn Mr H, BA DipLib MCLIP, Llyfrgellydd Gwybodaeth. [0026673] 09/11/1976
Ap Thomas Miss SJ, BA(Hons), Subject & Learning Support Lib., Staffs.Univ., Sch.of Health, Royal Shrewsbury Hosp(N.). [0044798] 06/12/1990
Apaki Miss K, Dir.Med.Lib., Athens Gen.Hosp., G Gennimatas, Greece. [0036813] 01/01/1984
Apfel Mrs M, L.Asst., Sidcot School L., N.Somerset. [0059664] 24/07/2001
AF
Appleby Mrs F, (was Burrows), MA MCLIP, p./t.Arch.Asst., St.Helens M.B.C. [0031754] 11/12/1979
Appleby Mrs H, (was Amphlett), MCLIP, Retired. [0000259] 01/01/1955
Appleby Mr JM, BA MCLIP, Client IT Offr.(L.), Cent.L., L.B.Hillingdon. [0023231] 12/11/1974
Appleby Mrs S, MA, Stud./Asst.Lib., Inverness Royal Academy, Inverness. [0061101] 25/02/2002
Appleby Mr TB, BA(Hons), p./t.Stud., Manchester Met.Univ., Nantwich L. [0061028] 07/02/2002
Appleton Mr CE, MCLIP, Lib., Latymer Upper Sch. [0000339] 01/01/1970
Appleton Ms CM, BA DipLib MCLIP, Comm.Devel.Lib., City of York L., York. [0040608] 01/04/1987
Appleton Ms J, DipLib MCLIP, Young Peoples Lib., L.B.of Newham, Stratford. [0037005] 30/01/1984
Appleton Mr L, BA(Hons) MA, Learning Support Advisor, Edge Hill Coll., Aintree Campus. [0059163] 04/12/2000
Appleton Miss LJ, MCLIP, Freelance Lib., Bristol/Glos./Bath. [0021892] 01/01/1974
Appleton Mrs M, (was Kerfoot), MCLIP, Life Member. [0000340] 10/03/1960
Appleyard Sir R, HonFCLIP, Hon.Fellow. [0060135] 10/12/2001
FE 01/04/2002
Aquilina Mr JB, MCLIP, Support Serv.Mgr., L.B.of Hammersmith & Fulham. [0000344] 01/01/1970
Arai Mrs R, (was Scudder), MCLIP, Sch.Lib., Wheldon Sch., Nottingham. [0019182] 09/08/1972
Araniello Mrs JE, (was Byott), L.Mgr., Hoddesdon L., Herts.C.C. [0045483] 14/02/1991 AF
Arathoon Ms AE, BSc MCLIP, Div.Lib., Mereside L., I.C.I Pharmaceuticals. [0034876] 01/04/1982
Arathoon Mrs PM, BA MCLIP, Mgr., Westminster Ref.L. [0022436] 30/04/1974
Arch Mrs M, (was Hines), BA(Hons), L.Mgr., Silsoe Research Inst., Beds. [0038070] 15/01/1985
Archdeacon Mrs JME, (was King), MCLIP, Team Lib, Local Studies, Norfolk C.C. [0000349] 01/01/1967
Archer Ms BA, BA, Heritage Project Mgr., Nat.Art L., Victoria & Albert Mus., London. [0043382] 16/10/1989
Archer Mr GG, BLib MCLIP, Sen.Lib., Inf.Servs., Warks.Co.L. [0029503] 05/09/1978
Archer Mrs JM, (was Howell-Davies), MCLIP, Retired, Chester. [0007303] 01/01/1965
Archer Mrs JP, BSc, L.Asst., L.B.of Harrow. [0036245] 01/01/1958
Archer Mr MK, BSc BA MCLIP, Employment not known. [0060608] 11/12/2001
Archibald Ms G, Inf.Team Leader, Home Off.Crime Reduction Unit., Easingwold, York. [0038806] 08/10/1985
Archibald Mrs PV, DipEd, Learning Res.Cent.Asst., Scottish Police Coll., Kincardine. [0061265] 13/05/2002 AF
Archibald Mrs R, L.Asst., Jewel & Esk Valley Coll., L.Learning Cent. [0054147] 07/11/1996
Arden Miss KE, BA(Hons) MSc(Econ) MCLIP, Public L.Lib., Cheshire C.C. [0052500] 02/11/1995
Ardener Mrs M, (was Morris), MCLIP, Retired. [0000357] 01/01/1949
Ardern Mr RJ, BSc MA MCLIP, Retired. [0000360] 01/01/1971
Ardizzone Ms JT, MA MCLIP, Lib., Deutsch-Franzosisches Inst., Ludwigsburg, Germany. [0044083] 25/04/1990
Argust Mrs JE, (was Pope), MSC DIP LIB MCLIP, Retired. [0038418] 11/03/1985
Aries Miss PJ, MCLIP, Retired. [0000364] 01/01/1960
Arlotte Mrs EM, BA MCLIP, Asst.Lib., Corp.of London, St.Bride Printing L. [0000367] 01/01/1971
Armitage Mrs J, (was White), BSc MCLIP, Subject Lib.-Catg., (Job Share), Faculty of Health & Exercise Sci., Univ.Coll.Worcester. [0032358] 03/03/1980
Armitage Ms LH, BA(Hons), P./t.Visiting Lect., Univ.of Brighton, Sch.of Inf.Mgmt. [0047588] 06/10/1992
Armitage Mr TR, BA MCLIP, L.Mgr., Confederate Investments, Weapons Div., Leeds. [0029364] 01/07/1978
Armour Miss A, MA DIP LIB MCLIP, Sch.Lib., Carrongrange Sch., Falkirk. [0032389] 01/04/1980
Armour Mr AJ, FCLIP, Life Member. [0000374] 01/01/1952
FE 01/01/1959
Armsby Mr AF, BA MCLIP, Retired. [0000377] 01/01/1962
Armsby Mrs J, (was Sanderson), MCLIP, [0000378] 09/02/1965
Armson Miss M, BSc MA, System Consultant, ExLibris UK Ltd., Hayes. [0057168] 07/01/1999
Armson Mr P, MCLIP, Life Member. [0000380] 01/01/1947
Armstrong Miss A, BA(Hons) DipILM MCLIP, Pub.Serv.Lib., Univ.of Durham. [0049738] 29/11/1993
Armstrong Mr AJT, BA DipLib MBA MCLIP, Equality & Human Rights Offr., N.E.E.L.B., Antrim. [0023227] 12/11/1974
Armstrong Mr ANL, MCLIP, Retired. [0033482] 01/01/1964
Armstrong Mrs CA, (was Parsons), BA MCLIP, Asst., N.Warwickshire & Hinckley Coll. [0000383] 29/09/1965
Armstrong Mr CJ, BLib FIAP FCLIP, Dir., Inf.Automation Ltd., Bronant, Aberystwyth. [0048480] 21/01/1993 FE 01/04/2002
Armstrong Miss DM, BA MLib MCLIP, Irish & Local Studies Lib., SEELB L.H.Q., Ballynahinch, N.Ireland. [0031177] 03/10/1979

Armstrong Mrs DM, (was Pearl), MCLIP, Child.Lib., Essex C.C., Harlow. [0000384] 06/03/1963
Armstrong Ms E, BA(Hons) MA, Comparative Parliamentary Enq.Offr., Scottish Parliament Inf.Cent., Edinburgh. [0050623] 01/10/1994
Armstrong Ms E, BA(Hons) DipILM MCLIP, Learning Res.Mgr., Cramlington Community High Sch., Northumberland. [0047702] 19/10/1992
Armstrong Ms EJ, BA MCLIP, L.Mgr., Hull Coll. [0048268] 19/11/1992
Armstrong Miss EK, Unemployed. [0049757] 02/12/1993
Armstrong Ms FA, BA MA DipLIS, Asst.Lib., N.Glamorgan NHS Trust L., Merthyr Tydfil. [0061306] 20/05/2002
Armstrong Ms FM, (was Pack), MA MCLIP, Retired. [0000387] 12/02/1952
Armstrong Ms H, MA(Hons) DipLib MCLIP, Sen.Readers Advisor, c/o Current Affairs Room, House of Commons L. [0031742] 25/11/1979
Armstrong Miss HD, MCLIP, Asst.Lib., Corp.of London, City Business L. [0028776] 11/02/1978
Armstrong Miss J, BA(Hons) MCLIP, Sen.Lib., L.B.of Enfield, Palmers Green L. [0041818] 21/04/1988
Armstrong Mrs J, (was Aspden), MCLIP, Sen.Lib., Northumberland Co.L. [0000468] 01/01/1969
Armstrong Mrs J, (was Clough), MCLIP, Sch.Lib., Valley Comp., Worksop, Notts. [0002867] 01/01/1967
Armstrong Mrs JL, (was Young), MCLIP, Unemployed. [0016462] 17/03/1967
Armstrong Miss KF, BA(Hons), Stud., Thames Valley Univ. [0058956] 10/10/2000
Armstrong Miss LE, BA (Hons) MCLIP, Accessions Lib., S.Ayrshire Educ.Serv., L.H.Q.,26 GreenSt., Ayr. [0041575] 25/01/1988
Armstrong Miss LM, Lib., BBC Inf.& Arch., London. [0046729] 09/01/1992
Armstrong Mrs MCS, (was Brown), MCLIP, L.Mgr.(Job Share), W.Lothian Council, Bathgate L. [0001909] 14/09/1962
Armstrong Ms NL, BSc MSc MCLIP, Employment unknown. [0060342] 10/12/2001
Armstrong Miss RJ, MCLIP, Life Member. [0000395] 01/01/1951
Armstrong Ms S, Unemployed. [0042419] 07/11/1988
Armstrong Mrs T, BA(Hons) MCLIP, Asst.Lib., News Internat., London. [0052553] 07/11/1995
Arnison Mrs VT, BA(Hons) MCLIP, p./t.Child.Lib., Farnborough P.L., Hants.C.C. [0033688] 28/01/1981
Arnison-Newgass Mrs OR, MCLIP, Inf.Serv.Mgr., Mishcon de Reya, London. [0040737] 22/05/1987
Arnold Mr BC, BA MCLIP, Unemployed. [0000398] 01/01/1952
Arnold Miss BW, MCLIP, Life Member. [0000399] 01/01/1950
Arnold Mrs E, Stud., Univ.of Cent.England &, L.Mgr., Alcester Grammar Sch. [0056880] 04/11/1998
Arnold Miss EM, MA, Asst. Lib., Greenwich Sch. of Mgmnt, London. [0057977] 07/10/1999
Arnold Mr KJ, (was Bond), BA DipLib MCLIP, H.of L.Serv., De Montfort Univ., Leicester. [0032872] 12/10/1980
Arnold Ms KL, BA(Hons) MSc, Content Mgr., BECTA, Coventry. [0039858] 29/08/1986
Arnold Ms M, BSc, Lib., Dept.of Health, London. [0044299] 21/08/1990
Arnold Miss ME, MCLIP, Subject Specialist Lib., Northants.L. [0000403] 01/01/1965
Arnold Mr RJ, MA BA MCLIP ALAA, City Lib., Applecross, W.Australia. [0016553] 01/01/1948
Arnold Ms SL, BA, Sen.Lib.:Inf.Serv., Gloucestershire County L., Gloucester. [0051449] 15/02/1995
Arnot Ms J, MA(Hons) PhD, Stud., Strathclyde Univ. [0061784] 05/11/2002
Arnott Mrs FR, BA(Hons), L.Asst., W.Cheshire Coll., Chester. [0057517] 16/04/1999 **AF**
Arnott Miss MF, (was Brydon), BA DipLib MCLIP, Sch.Lib., Musselburgh Grammar Sch., E.Lothian. [0043917] 20/02/1990
Arroway Ms LH, BA(Hons), Stud., Univ.Aberystwyth. [0059777] 02/10/2001
Arrowsmith Ms AJE, MA MBA FIMt, Retired. [0039916] 01/10/1986
Arrowsmith Ms J, Learning Resource Cent.Co-ord., Cheadle High Sch. [0061481] 16/08/2002 **AF**
Arrowsmith Mrs J, BA(Hons) MA, Unemployed. [0059028] 24/10/2000
Arrowsmith Miss L, BA(Hons), p./t.Stud./Asst.P/Way Engineer, London Underground Ltd., UNL. [0059908] 01/11/2001
Artherton Mrs JCJ, (was Dolan), BA DipLIS, Team Lib.-Culture & Learning, S.E.E.L.B., Dairy Farm L., Belfast. [0039498] 30/01/1986
Arthur Mrs EM, (was Wylie), BA MCLIP DMS, Sen.L.Offr., S., Bournemouth L.Serv., Landsdowne L. [0040995] 02/10/1987
Arthur Mr HHG, FRSA FIMgt FCLIP, Life Member, Tel.0151 652 7723, 20 Christchurch Rd., Oxton, Wirral, Merseyside, CH43 5SF. [0000421] 01/01/1942 **FE 01/01/1948**
Arthur Miss J, BA MA MCLIP, Asst.Dir.(Inf.Res.Mgmt.), Univ.of Herts. [0036418] 12/10/1983
Arthur Mrs M, MA, Sch.Lib., Rawlins Comm.Coll., Quorn, Leics. [0057674] 01/07/1999
Arthur Miss ME, BA MCLIP, Managing Dir., Peters Bookselling Serv., Birmingham. [0018473] 01/01/1972
Arthur Mrs RE, (was Allen), BA FCLIP, Asst.Dir., Chartered Inst.of L.& Inf.Prof.in, Scotland. [0029559] 01/01/1978 **FE 21/11/2001**
Arton Mrs ME, (was Jackson), BA MCLIP, Unemployed. [0023049] 24/10/1974
Arts Mrs I, p./t.Stud./Sen.L.Asst., Aberystwyth, Kensington Cent.L. [0061406] 09/07/2002
Arunachalam Mr S, FCLIP, Hon Fellow. [0060105] 07/12/2001 **FE 01/04/2002**
Asgarali Mrs LMM, (was Mural), MCLIP, Sen.Asst., Council of Legal Educ.L., Trinidad. [0016558] 01/01/1968
Ash Mrs LP, BSc(Hons) DipLib, Tuition Mgr., Belle Assoc., Coventry. [0036382] 03/10/1983
Ashbey Mrs K, (was Vanns), MCLIP, Unemployed. [0015067] 29/12/1970
Ashburner Mrs SM, (was Walker), BA MCLIP, p./t.Adult Educ.Tutor, Derby City Council. [0015259] 22/02/1971

Ashby Miss DA, Stud., Liverpool John Moores Univ. [0061812] 12/11/2002
Ashby Mrs JC, BSc MCLIP, Sch.Lib., Knowsley M.B.C., Merseyside. [0000430] 13/01/1970
Ashby Ms KE, BA(Hons), Unemployed. [0041331] 02/11/1987
Ashby Miss MM, MA DipEdTech MCLIP, Retired. [0000431] 01/01/1959
Ashby Mr RF, MCLIP, Retired. [0000434] 01/01/1965
Ashby Mr RF, FCLIP, Life Member. [0000433] 01/01/1934 **FE 01/01/1949**
Ashby Mr SJ, BLib MCLIP, Br.Lib., L.B.of Enfield, Southgate Library. [0025845] 02/04/1976
Ashcroft Ms DM, BA(Hons) MCLIP, Sen.Lib., Altrincham L., Trafford L. [0043643] 15/11/1989
Ashcroft Mrs LS, BA DipLib MA MCLIP, Reader, Inf.Mgmt., Liverpool John Moores Univ. [0040339] 21/01/1987
Ashcroft Mrs MA, (was Ward), BA DipLib MCLIP, Project Dir., St.Ivo Sch., St.Ives. [0015357] 01/01/1971
Ashcroft Mrs SK, MCLIP, Asst.Lib., Surrey Archaeological Soc., Guildford. [0001015] 01/01/1963
Ashdown Miss K, DipLib ALIA, Lib., St.Pauls Special Sch., Kew, Australia. [0059377] 23/02/2001
Ashdown Mrs LB, MA, Inf.Serv.Offr., Business Link Milton Keynes & N., Bucks, Milton Keynes. [0058448] 16/02/2000
Ashfield Mr ND, BA MCLIP, Built Environ.Faculty Lib., Kenrick L., Univ.of Cent.England in Birmingham. [0000438] 01/01/1965
Ashford Mrs CJ, (was Witchell), MCLIP, Unemployed. [0025685] 02/02/1976
Ashford Mrs M, DipLib MCLIP, Learning Support Lib., Leeds City Council. [0037411] 01/01/1985
Ashford Mrs SM, BA(Hons) DipLib MCLIP, Head of Serv., Birmingham L.Serv., Sci.Tech.& Mgmt.Serv. [0041174] 19/10/1987
Ashill Mr CG, BA MLib, L.Asst., Univ.of London L. [0049271] 20/10/1993
Ashley Mr BL, BA DipLib MCLIP, Asst.Dir.-(L.Inf.& Museums), Nottingham City Council. [0029564] 04/10/1978
Ashley Mrs E, (was Jordan), BA MCLIP, Unemployed. [0035297] 06/10/1982
Ashley Miss FJ, B.Lib MCLIP, Reading & Youth Mgr., Monmouthshire C.C., Chepstow. [0038543] 23/06/1985
Ashley Mrs J, BA(Hons), L.Asst., Univ.of the W.of England, Frenchay Campus, Bristol. [0057376] 17/02/1999
Ashley Mrs K, (was Edwards), BA(Hons) MCLIP, Unemployed. [0045390] 23/11/1990
Ashley Ms L, BA(Hons) MA, Inf.Specialist, TDA Transitions, Brentford. [0057039] 27/11/1998
Ashley Miss SE, BA(Hons) DipILS MCLIP, Ref.Lib., Inverclyde Council, Greenock. [0053976] 15/10/1996
Ashman Mrs R, (was Andrew), BA(Hons) MCLIP, Asst.Sch.Lib., Southampton Sch.L.Serv. [0030577] 27/01/1979
Ashman Mr RA, BA MCLIP DMS, Princ.Lend.Lib., Southampton Cent.L. [0032729] 13/08/1980
Ashmore Ms JH, (was Alvey), BA DipLib MCLIP, Princ.Lib., Planning & Devel., Wokingham Dist.Council. [0043768] 08/01/1990
Ashmore Mr WSH, BA FCLIP, Life Member. [0000444] 01/01/1941 **FE 01/01/1954**
Ashraf Mr SA, MA DipLib MCLIP, Lib., Cent.L., Peterborough. [0034207] 12/10/1981
Ashton Mrs C, BSc(Econ), L.Super., Med.L., Doncaster Royal Infirmary. [0055404] 09/10/1997
Ashton Mr CA, BA BSc PGCE MCLIP, Prof.Reg., Leicestershire Co.Council. [0037999] 01/01/1985
Ashton Mrs E, (was Walsh), MCLIP, Asst.i/c., Rhu L., Argyll & Bute. [0031167] 01/01/1961
Ashton Mrs HC, (was Wood), BSc, Learning Resources Mgr., Bishop Auckland Coll., Bishop Auckland. [0040393] 28/01/1987
Ashton Ms JL, BLib MCLIP, Customer Serv.Mgr., Bibliomondo UK Ltd., Stevenage. [0023291] 18/11/1974
Ashton Mrs MM, (was Hamilton), BA(Hons), Lib.i/c., S.Hornchurch L., L.B.of Havering. [0045468] 14/02/1991
Ashton Mr PA, BA(Hon), Voluntary L.Asst., Lancs.Devel.Educ.Cent., Preston. [0049796] 30/11/1993
Ashton Ms SJ, MA, Internet Lib., Industrial Soc., London. [0049828] 24/11/1993
Ashton Ms SV, BA MSc MCLIP, Employment not known. [0060136] 10/12/2001
Ashton-Griffiths Miss ZL, BSc(Hons), Stud., Univ.of Wales, Aberystwyth. [0058912] 03/10/2000
Ashwell Mr SJ, Web Developer, S.E.P.H.Observatory, Oxford. [0042269] 13/01/1988
Ashwood Mrs BA, (was Bricker), MCLIP, Sen.Lib., Stock Team, Cent.Stock Unit, Cambridge. [0000457] 01/01/1964
Ashwood Mrs CJ, (was Skelton-Foord), BA(Hons) MA MCLIP, Inf.Offr., Computing Serv., Staffs.Univ. [0039938] 05/10/1986
Ashworth Mrs G, (was Fairbrother), MCLIP, Support Serv.Lib., L.Serv.for Sch., Carlisle. [0000463] 12/02/1968
Ashworth Mrs L, (was Murray), BA DipLib MCLIP, Community Child.Lib., City of Salford. [0033087] 08/10/1980
Ashworth Mr M, MA BSc MCLIP, Language & EDC Support Lib., George Edwards L., Univ.of Surrey. [0019881] 01/01/1973
Ashworth Mrs R, (was Wood), Inf.Research Offr., N.W.Employers, Manchester. [0051766] 01/07/1995
Ashworth Miss S, BA(Hons), Lib., Manchester P.L. [0057352] 17/02/1999
Ashworth Prof W, BSc FCLIP ARPS, Life Member, The Princess Alexandra Home, Rm175, Newland Hse.,Common Rd., HA7 3JE. [0000464] 01/01/1935 **FE 01/01/1938**
Ashworth Mrs WM, MCLIP, Life Member. [0000466] 01/01/1932
Aske Ms PA, BA(Hons) DipLib MA, Sub.Lib., Butler L., Corpus Christi Coll.Cambs. [0059933] 06/11/2001
Askew Mrs DV, (was Bush), BA(Hons) MCLIP, Lib., Priory Sch., Lewes, E.Sussex. [0043804] 17/01/1990

Askew Miss EA, BA(Hons) PGCE MA MCLIP, Sci.Inf.Asst., Warwick Univ.L., Coventry. [0054155] 07/11/1996
Askey Mrs J, (was Woodward), MCLIP, Lib., Brereton L., Staffs.L.H.Q. [0023446] 10/12/1974
Askin Ms S, (was Bates), BA(Hons) MCLIP, Sen.Learning Cent.Asst., Wolverhampton Coll. [0000461] 21/07/1967
Askira Mrs AB, DipLibSc BLS, Lib., Nat.Maritime Auth., Lagos, Nigeria. [0059188] 11/12/2000
Aslam Miss H, BA(Hons) MA, Lib., Slough L. [0053985] 15/10/1996
Aslett Mrs AM, (was Ryder), BA MCLIP, Lib., St Paul's Sch., Barnes, London. [0002116] 09/05/1972
Asnaghi Ms L, Lib., BAP., London. [0045952] 23/07/1991
Aspey Mr R, BSc FCMA MCLIP, Employment not known. [0060197] 10/12/2001
Aspinall Mr PN, BA MCLIP, Project Offf., Wirral Bor.Council. [0038912] 17/10/1985
Aspinall Dr Y, PhD, Inf.Offr., Cambs.Antibody Tech, Cambridge. [0061479] 14/08/2002
Asprogeraka Miss T, MBA, Stud., Loughborough. [0061388] 02/07/2002
Asquith Mrs SJ, (was Heath), BA(Hons), Learning Res.Cent.Mgr., Myrtle Springs Sch., Sheffield. [0046463] 07/11/1991
Asser Mrs EJ, (was Wilson), BA MCLIP, Inspector, Audit Commission, Leicester. [0028977] 16/01/1978
Assinder Mrs DS, (was Hopwood), BA DipLib MCLIP, Lib., Business Insight, Cent.L.Birmingham. [0035832] 28/01/1983
Astall Mr HR, FCLIP, Life Member. [0000476] 01/01/1953
FE 18/05/1973
Astbury Miss CA, Unemployed. [0054525] 14/01/1997
Astbury Mr RG, FCLIP, Life Member. [0000477] 01/01/1949
FE 01/01/1958
Astin Ms MP, BSc MSc, P,.t,Stud., U.W.A., Aberystwyth, &, Med.Lab.Sci.Offr., Dir.of, Biochemical Med., Dundee. [0055488] 15/10/1997
Astin Mrs SJ, (was Davis), P/t.Asst.Lib., Thames Valley Univ., Royal Berks.Hosp., Reading. [0041479] 12/01/1988
Astle Mr PJ, Quality & Standards Mgr., Interfleet Tech.Ltd., Derby. [0058335] 17/01/2000
Astley Miss EM, MCLIP, Life Member. [0000480] 01/01/1968
Aston Mrs JEF, BA MSc MCLIP, Resident in Ireland. [0060111] 07/12/2001
Aston . MT, BSc(Hons) MCLIP, Lib.(Local Studies), Holborn L., L.B.of Camden. [0046212] 01/01/1991
Atherton Ms LH, BA(Hons) MA MCLIP, Team Lib.- Inf.Serv., Medway Council, Strood L. [0046355] 30/10/1991
Atherton Miss LM, Trainee Asst.Lib., Wrexham P.L. [0057132] 18/12/1998
Atherton Mr NE, BSc(Hons), Ref.Lib., Harold Cohen L., Univ.of Liverpool. [0053179] 01/04/1996
Atiogbe Miss PK, BSc(Hons) MSc(Dist), Stud., City Univ. [0059529] 26/04/2001
Atkin Miss JM, BLS MCLIP, Lib., Derby Cent.L. [0033461] 08/01/1981
Atkin Mr S, MCLIP, Life Member, Tel.01322 225913, 1 Lodge Ave., Dartford, Kent, DA1 3DX. [0000486] 01/01/1935
Atkins Ms CJ, (was Ryder), BA DipLib, Lib., Eversheds, Norwich. [0040758] 26/05/1987
Atkins Mr CP, BA(Hons) MCLIP, Lib., Adult Lending, Maidenhead P.L. [0044854] 01/01/1991
Atkins Mr LC, BA(Hons) DipILS MCLIP, Asst.Lib., Bournemouth L., Dorset. [0050958] 03/11/1994
Atkins Mrs PK, BSc DipLib MCLIP, p./t.Lunchtime Super., St.George's Sch., Herts. [0034776] 11/02/1982
Atkinson Mrs AC, (was Burnett), BSc DipLib MA MCLIP, Position Unknown, EMAP, London. [0042574] 04/01/1989
Atkinson Mrs AL, (was Lukehurst), BA(Hons) MCLIP, Co.Local Stud.Lib./Asst.Mgr., Cent.for Kentish Stud., Kent C.C. [0026767] 23/11/1976
Atkinson Mrs B, (was Olive), MCLIP, Relief Enq.Offr., Suffolk C.C., Ipswich. [0000494] 04/01/1968
Atkinson Ms C, MPhil, Head of Conservation Train.&Devel., The British L., London. [0061644] 10/10/2002 **AF**
Atkinson Mrs E, (was Milner), BA MCLIP, Management & Training Consultant, Milner Atkinson Assoc., Beds. [0037247] 09/05/1984
Atkinson Mrs J, (was Kirby), BSc BA MCLIP, Tech.Lib., Sci.Dept.,Nat.Gallery, London. [0008425] 17/01/1967
Atkinson Ms JCE, BA(Hons) PGDipILS MA, Asst.Lib., Univ.of Ulster at Coleraine, Co.Londonderry. [0044588] 31/10/1990
Atkinson Ms JD, BA MA DipLib MCLIP, Operations Mgr.-L.& Inf.Serv., Royal Coll.of Nursing, London. [0027875] 12/10/1977
Atkinson Mr JH, BSc DipLib MCLIP, Inf.Serv.Mgr., Ministry of Defence, Wareham, Dorset. [0024876] 01/11/1975
Atkinson Mrs JM, BA(Hons) DipILM, Child.& Young Persons Lib. [0056679] 01/10/1998
Atkinson Miss K, BA(Hons), Stud., Univ.of Northumbria. [0058928] 05/10/2000
Atkinson Mrs KA, (was Bancroft), BA(Hons) MSc MCLIP, Lib., Manchester Health Auth. [0044747] 15/11/1990
Atkinson Mrs L, MSc BA AKC MCLIP, Team Lib., Swiss Cottage L., L.B.of Camden. [0020501] 24/01/1973
Atkinson Mrs LA, MA, Catr., Wokingham Dist.Council, Woodley L. [0051909] 04/08/1995
Atkinson Mrs LS, BSc MSc MCLIP, Lib., Sch.of Geography, Oxford Univ. [0026080] 16/07/1976
Atkinson Ms MA, BA(Hons), Inf.Analyst/Researcher, Lucent Tech., Swindon. [0053573] 25/07/1996
Atkinson Miss NP, MCLIP, Retired, Hunters Tryst, Wych Hill Way, Woking, Surrey, GU22 0AE. [0000509] 01/01/1957
Atkinson Mr PJ, BSc MPhil MCLIP, Head of Learning Res., Univ.of Glamorgan. [0020485] 01/01/1973

Atkinson Mr RG, BA(Hons) MA MCLIP, H.of Catg., Univ.Coll.London. [0043670] 22/11/1989
Atkinson Mr S, BSc DipLib MCLIP, Dep.Lib., Camborne Sch.of Mines, Redruth, Cornwall. [0039973] 07/10/1986
Atkinson Mrs S, (was O'Connor), BA MCLIP, Asst.Lib., Staveley L., Derbys.C.C. [0028873] 20/01/1978
Atkinson Mrs S, (was Allenby), BA MCLIP DipRSA, Borough Lib., Hartlepool Bor.Council, Cent.L. [0023609] 17/01/1975
Atkinson Mr SCR, L.Asst., Hants.C.C., Winchester. [0057429] 01/04/1999
Atlass Mrs HJ, (was Jacobson), MCLIP, Lib., Royal Coll.of Nursing, London. [0007698] 01/11/1970
Atlee Mr IHN, MCLIP, Retired, 9 St.Johns Terrace, Pendeen, Penzance, Cornwall, TR19 7DP. [0000512] 01/01/1962
Atta Mrs EE, P./t.Stud.,L.Asst., Univ.Central London, Dulwich L. [0059857] 17/10/2001
Attar Dr K, BA PhD MA, Rare Books & Special Coll.Catr., Univ.of London L. [0056653] 01/10/1998
Attenborough Mr GC, BA MCLIP, Consultant - self employed. [0000514] 24/09/1958
Attenborough Mr RL, MCLIP, Stock Lib., Co.L., Ipswich. [0000515] 01/01/1970
Atter Mr LJ, BA DipLib MCLIP, Grp.Lib., Formby/ Coll.Rd.L., Sefton M.B.C. [0020260] 02/02/1973
Attewell Mrs CA, (was Fish), MA MCLIP, Grp.Lib., Consett L., Durham. [0021463] 17/10/1973
Attree Mrs CM, (was Lederer), PGDipLib BA(Hons), L.Asst., Comm.Serv., Hants.C.C., Winchester. [0030459] 22/01/1979
Attwood Mrs CJ, MCLIP, County Specialist Y.& Media, Staffs.C.C., Tamworth L. [0025480] 26/01/1976
Attwood Mr CR, BA(Hons), Dep.Grp.Lib., Dudley Metro.Borough. [0045175] 31/07/1990
Attwood Mr P, BA(Hons) MA, L.Mgr., KAE Marketing Intelligence, London. [0052035] 02/10/1995
Au Mr PKK, BSc DipIS, Sen.L.Asst.(Special Serv.), Plumstead L., London. [0048889] 12/07/1993
Aubertin-Potter Miss NAR, BA PhD MCLIP, Lib.i./c., Codrington L., All Souls Coll., Oxford. [0043664] 21/11/1989
Aubrey Mrs SJ, p./t.Stud./Admin.Offr., Liverpool City Council, Liv.John Moores Univ. [0059357] 07/11/2001
Aubrey-Petrie Mrs CM, BA DipLIS MCLIP, Asst.Lib.(Acquisitions & Catg.), Queen Margaret Univ.Coll., Edinburgh. [0056025] 28/01/1998
Auchinvole Miss R, BA MCLIP, Res.Lib., Turnbull High Sch., Bishopbriggs. [0038988] 22/10/1985
Auckland Ms MJ, OBE BSc MSc MCLIP HonFCLIP, Dir.of L.& Learning Res., The London Inst., London. [0000522] 01/01/1969
FE 24/10/2002
Aucock Miss J, MA DipLib, System Mgr.& Head of Catg., (Asst.Lib.), Univ.of St Andrews, Fife. [0036265] 12/09/1983
Audouard Mrs EM, Inf.Sci., BPB Gypsum, E.Leake, Leics. [0048797] 28/05/1993
Audsley Miss EM, MCLIP, Inf.Lib., Surrey Co.L. [0000523] 01/01/1971
Auger Mr CP, FCLIP, Life Member. [0000525] 01/01/1949
FE 01/01/1965
Auld Miss J, MCLIP, Retired. [0000527] 01/01/1960
Aungle Miss AM, BA MCLIP, Site L. Mgr., Univ.of N.London, London. [0000525] 01/01/1965
Auro Mrs A, BSc, Nat.Inf.Offr., Leonard Cheshire, London. [0059691] 08/08/2001 **AF**
Aust Mrs AF, (was Kay), BA DipLib MCLIP, Comm.Serv.Lib.(Job Share), Portsmouth City Council. [0027179] 29/01/1977
Austerfield Ms VA, BA DipLib MCLIP, J.H.L.S.Lib., Wakefield M.D.C. [0035104] 06/09/1982
Austin Mrs GM, (was Davies), BA(Hons) MA, Asst.Lib., MOD, Sch.of Logistics, Camberley. [0047085] 21/04/1992
Austin Miss IS, BA(Hons), Stud., Brighton Univ. [0059396] 28/02/2001
Austin Mrs J, (was Small), MCLIP, Res.Unit Mgr., Stoke on Trent Unitary Auth., Hanley L. [0000530] 06/01/1968
Austin Mrs J, BA MCLIP, Lib., Hazelwick Sch., Crawley, W.Sussex. [0008541] 01/01/1961
Austin Mrs JE, BA DipLib MCLIP, Inf.& Knowledge Serv.Mgr., Inf.Res.Cent., Environ.Serv., Essex C.C. [0038079] 17/01/1985
Austin Mrs JY, (was McKnight), BA MCLIP, Grp.Lib., N.E.E.& L.Board, Carrickfergus. [0020347] 12/03/1973
Austin Miss N, BA(Hons), p./t.Stud./Learning Res.Asst., Foreign & Commonwealth Off., Metro.Univ., N.London. [0059217] 09/01/2001
Austin Ms PA, MCLIP, IRC Super., St. Mary's Univ.Coll., Twickenham. [0000532] 04/02/1971
Austin Mr RHL, BSc LRSC MCLIP, Resident in Germany. [0060069] 07/12/2001
Austin Mrs SM, (was Bloomfield), BA(Hons) MAAT DipILM MCLIP, Health Inf.Mgr., Gateshead & S.Tyneside Health Auth. [0047771] 14/10/1992
Austin Mrs Y, (was Simpson), MCLIP, Unemployed. [0022567] 01/07/1974
Auty Miss CC, BA(Hons) MSc MCLIP, Asst.Lib., House of Lords L., London. [0056267] 23/04/1998
Avafia Mr KE, FCLIP, Retired. [0022518] 15/03/1962 **FE 29/01/1992**
Avent-Gibson Ms DJ, BScEcon(Hons), Subject Lib./SDC, Univ.of Bristol. [0048824] 16/06/1993
Averill Mr MJ, (was Averill), BSC DPSE, Tech., St.John Wall Sch., Birmingham. [0050295] 07/06/1994
Avery Mrs CM, Sen.Supervisor, Ely L.& Learning Centre. [0060011] 22/11/2001 **AF**
Avery Ms N, BA DipLib MCLIP, Princ.Lib., Inf.Serv., Bedford Cent.L., Beds. [0042129] 04/10/1988
Awogbami Dr PA, BSc(Hons) DipLib MSc MLS PhD, Employment not known. [0057772] 02/08/1999

181

Awoniyi Mrs RO, PGDip, Systems & Resources Co-ordinator, E.Berks.Coll., Slough. [0049557] 12/11/1993
Awosanya Mrs CE, (was Okunriniboye), MCLIP DipLib, Retired. [0016564] 01/01/1959
Awre Mr CL, BSc MSc, Employment not known. [0060821] 12/12/2001
Axford Mrs WA, (was Camps), MA MCLIP, Retired. [0000544] 01/01/1955
Axon Ms CL, BA (Hons) MCLIP, L.,Learning and Print Serv.Mgr., Tameside Coll. [0045650] 15/04/1991
Ayiku Miss LT, BA(Hons), Stud., Univ.of Sheffield. [0061143] 08/03/2002
Ayley Mr FE, MCLIP, Retired. [0000549] 01/01/1950
Ayling Ms BA, (was Collins), BSc(Hons) MCLIP MA PGCE, Team Leader, Med.Health & Life Sci., Univ.of Birmingham. [0047073] 13/04/1992
Ayling Ms SM, BA DipLib MCLIP, p./t.Lib., Linslade Lower Sch., Beds.C.C. [0030306] 19/01/1979
Ayo Mrs TA, (was Amosu), BLS, Asst.Ch.Lib., Nat.L.of Nigeria. [0044221] 13/07/1990
Ayoola Mrs BBE, (was Tologbonshe), MSc, Learning Cent Super., Westminster Kingsway Coll., London. [0049093] 01/10/1993
Ayre Mr A, BA MCLIP, Unemployed. [0033260] 12/11/1980
Ayre Mr SM, BA MA(Dist), Project Offr., Collection Devel.Policy, Leicester Univ.L. [0057487] 06/04/1999
Ayres Miss CA, BSc DipLib MCLIP, Head of Systems, Univ.of Reading L. [0036003] 11/04/1983
Ayres Mr FH, BA FCLIP, Life Member. [0000551] 01/01/1947
FE 01/01/1958
Ayres Mrs IMH, (was Grove), BA(Hons) MA, Sen.Inf.Offr., Research L., Gtr.London Auth. [0051880] 24/07/1995
Ayres Mr JE, MA DipLib MCLIP, Tech.Lib., TWI, Cambridge. [0000552] 01/01/1971
Ayres Miss S, BA(Hons), Res.Lib., Coll.of St.Mark & St.John, Plymouth. [0052771] 11/12/1995
Ayris Mr DA, BA MCLIP, Life Member. [0000553] 01/01/1956
Azmey Dr HM, BA MA PhD, Asst.Prof., Qatar Univ., Faculty of Humanties. [0037824] 02/11/1984
Azubike Mrs MT, (was De Gannes), BA MCLIP, Sen.Subject Lib., Hammersmith & W.London Coll. [0032915] 03/10/1980
Azzi Miss L, Asst.Lib., Slaughter and May, London. [0040956] 01/01/1987
Baah Mr KA, BA(Hons) MA MCLIP DipJour, Team Lib., L.B.of Enfield. [0043482] 27/10/1989
Baah Miss MS, DipLib BLS, L.Asst., Nottingham Univ. [0059581] 05/06/2001
Baalham Mrs GR, (was Hunter), BSc MCLIP, Asst.Play Leader, Brookside Preschool, Ipswich. [0035478] 25/10/1982
Babcock Mr CJ, BA DipLib MCLIP, Inf.Serv.Team Leader, Croydon Coll.L. [0050244] 13/05/1994
Babcock Ms MJ, BA MLitt MILS, Sen.Asst.Ed.(L.Research), Oxford Univ.Press. [0042844] 28/03/1989
Bacchus Miss J, BA DipLib MCLIP, EDC Lib., Univ.of N.London. [0046016] 16/08/1991
Bach Miss HLG, BA, Stud., Univ.Coll.London. [0059784] 02/10/2001
Bache Mrs JA, MA BA(Hons) MCLIP, Child.Lib., Bexley Council. [0053766] 01/10/1996
Bache Mrs JE, (was Cameron), MA DipLib MCLIP, Lib., The Glasgow Academy. [0002303] 01/01/1970
Bachelor Miss NA, MA, Asst.Lib., Park Lane Coll. [0053991] 14/10/1996
Back Miss AC, p./t.L.Asst., Taunton. [0061601] 03/10/2002
AF
Backham Mr D, MCLIP, Asst.Lib., Univ.of Liverpool L. [0021444] 01/11/1973
Backler Ms C, BA CertEd MSc MCLIP, Acq.& Academic Liaison Lib., Univ.of Dundee. [0057241] 25/01/1999
Bacon Mrs AMR, (was Hay), MA MCLIP, Lib., St.Brendans 6th Form Coll., Bristol. [0024694] 06/10/1975
Bacon Ms AR, MCLIP, Unemployed. [0031555] 18/10/1979
Bacon Mrs CM, (was Green), MCLIP, Retired. [0000560] 01/01/1951
Bacon Mrs DE, MA MCLIP, Asst.Lib., Amersham L., Bucks.C.C. [0027880] 11/10/1977
Bacon Mrs HA, (was Riordan), BA MCLIP, Asst.Lib., Surrey Inst.of Art & Design, Farnham. [0026650] 30/09/1976
Bacon Miss JV, MSc MCLIP, Lib., Countryside Agency, John Dower House, Cheltenham. [0000561] 27/11/1972
Bacon Mr M, BA MCLIP, L.Mgr., Edgware L., L.B.of Barnet. [0041026] 01/10/1987
Bacon Mr N, BEd DipLib MCLIP, Res.Cent.Mgr., W.Lancs.Council for Voluntary Serv. [0046882] 21/02/1992
Baddock Mr C, DMS MIPD MCLIP, Training Consultant-Life Member, Yorkstone, Birches Walk, off Margaretting Rd., Galleywood. [0000563] 16/03/1956
Bader Mrs HM, BA DipLib, p./t.Lib.-Ref., Newport Co.Bor.Council. [0038137] 21/01/1985
Badhams Mrs AP, (was Yates), MCLIP, Asst.Lib., Buckinghamshire Chilterns Univ., Coll., Chalfont St.Giles, Bucks. [0016409] 23/09/1969
Badhe Mrs M, BSc PG DipIS, Unemployed. [0050887] 26/10/1994
Badman Mrs DO, (was Lowe), MCLIP, p./t.Team Lib., Somerset C.C. [0000565] 18/05/1965
Badman Mr SW, BA MCLIP, Regional Inf.Offr., Sports Council, E.Region. [0041016] 01/10/1987
Badyan Miss AK, (was Badjan), BA(Hons) DipLib MCLIP, Data & Copyright Co-ordinator, The Wellcome Trust, London. [0044384] 03/10/1990
Baeuml Mrs L, Res.Base Mgr., Bellerive FCJ & Bellerive 6th Form, Liverpool. [0046865] 19/02/1992
Baffour-Awuah Mrs M, BA PGLib MLIS, Princ.Lib., Botswana Nat.L.Serv., Gaborone. [0034371] 23/10/1981
Bagaglia Miss F, Stud., Loughborough Univ. [0061220] 16/04/2002
Baggott Mrs GM, (was Harnor), Asst.Lib., King Alfreds Coll., Winchester. [0041962] 04/07/1988

Baggs Dr CM, BA MA PhD DipLib MCLIP, Lect., Univ.of Wales, Dept.of Inf.L.Studies, Aberystwyth. [0000568] 03/01/1972
Baggs Mrs H, Asst.Lib., Off.for Nat.Statisics, S.Wales. [0057557] 01/04/1999
Bagley Mr DE, MA FCLIP, Life Member. [0000571] 25/09/1948
FE 01/01/1966
Bagley Mrs E, Sen.Res.Asst., Sutton Coldfield Coll. [0052527] 03/11/1995
Bagley Mr SP, BA(Hons) MCLIP, Catg.Mgr., Brit.L., Boston Spa. [0048861] 05/07/1993
Bagnall Ms CS, MA MCLIP, p./t.Lib., Univ.Dundee, Faculty of Educ.& Social Work. [0000573] 08/07/1970
Bagnall Mr J, MA DipLib MCLIP, Position unknown, Univ.of Dundee. [0060225] 10/12/2001
Bagshaw Mrs JA, BA MCLIP, Child.Lib., Essex L., Rayleigh. [0038551] 02/07/1985
Bagshaw Ms K, BA(Hons) DipLIS, Sen.Asst.Lib., Brit.Architectural L., RIBA., London. [0043381] 16/10/1989
Baguley Mrs G, (was Walmesley), MA MCLIP, Life Member. [0000576] 26/09/1950
Bahl Mr J, BA(Hons), L.Communications Team Leader, Allen & Overy, London. [0056173] 01/04/1998
Baig Mrs QA, BSc MCLIP, Unemployed. [0000577] 17/10/1971
Baigent Ms HL, BA(Hons) MA, Network Adviser, Resource, London. [0052909] 15/01/1996
Baildam Mrs LJ, BEd(Hons) MA, Asst.Lib., Newbold Coll.L., Bracknell, Berks. [0057234] 14/01/1999
Bailes Mr WR, (was Baines), Stud., Manchester Metro.Univ. [0061747] 01/11/2002
Bailes-Collins Mrs RA, (was Elliott), BLib MCLIP, Career Break. [0042151] 10/10/1988
Bailey Mr AEJ, BA MCLIP, Asst.Lib., Lewisham P.L. [0023382] 01/01/1975
Bailey Mrs AJ, (was Smith), BA(Hons) MA, Inf.Offr., Derbys.C.C., Matlock. [0053007] 14/02/1996
Bailey Ms AJ, BA MA, Curator in Humanities Ref.Serv., Brit.L., London. [0035221] 07/10/1982
Bailey Mrs AM, BA, Learning Res.Adviser, Thomas Danby Coll., Leeds. [0039806] 29/07/1986
Bailey Mr ARG, BA, Learning Serv.Mgr., Halesowen Coll., W.Mids. [0061413] 11/07/2002 AF
Bailey Mrs CA, MA MCLIP, Acting Dir.L.Serv., Glasgow Univ.L. [0026271] 13/10/1976
Bailey Mrs DA, p./t.Stud./Learning Res.Cent.Asst., Manchester Met.Univ., The Sheffield Coll. [0061205] 08/04/2002
Bailey Mrs E, (was Knowles), BA FCLIP, Life Member. [0008508] 04/04/1932
FE 01/01/1939
Bailey Mrs FF, (was Wickenden), BA MCLIP, County Child.Specialist., Staffs.C.C. [0038345] 28/03/1985
Bailey Miss FM, BLib MCLIP, Sen.Br.Lib., Cardiff C.C. [0032854] 06/10/1980
Bailey Mr GJ, PGDipLib, Tax Lib., Deloitte & Touche, London. [0036172] 01/07/1983
Bailey Miss HL, (was Sharrock), MLib MCLIP, User Serv.Lib., Univ.Arts & Soc.Sci.L., Bristol. [0001307] 23/08/1967
Bailey Mr I, BSc MSC MCLIP, Administrator (Technical), gLafarge Cement UK, Greenhithe. [0048965] 16/06/1989
Bailey Ms JC, BA(Hons) PGCEA MCLIP, Sen.Learning Res.Offr., Hackney Community Coll., London. [0048965] 06/08/1993
Bailey Mr JG, BSc, Sen.Business Analyst, BSI, Chiswick. [0048086] 05/11/1992
Bailey Mr JL, BA MCLIP, Partner, Cajohns Inf.Serv., Canberra, Australia. [0018476] 01/01/1965
Bailey Miss LK, BA(Hons) MLib MCLIP, Coll.Lib., Selwyn Coll., Cambridge. [0049281] 20/10/1993
Bailey Miss LM, Lib., Maps & Geographical Inf., Foreign & Commonwealth Off. [0034380] 26/10/1981
Bailey Mrs LN, (was Wingrave), BA MA MCLIP, Out Reach Lib., Univ.of Bournemouth. [0028250] 26/10/1977
Bailey Mr M, DipLib MCLIP, Br.Lib., Cardiff C.C. [0034320] 20/10/1981
Bailey Mrs M, (was Ritchie), MCLIP, Asst.Lib.-Local Hist., Bath & N.E.Somerset Council, Bath Cent.L. [0012437] 09/07/1968
Bailey Ms MB, (was Jones), MCLIP, Retired. [0000591] 18/01/1946
Bailey Ms MD, (was Ellis), BA(Hons) MCLIP, Inf.Asst., RSPB. [0021714] 04/01/1974
Bailey Mrs PM, (was Fransella), MA FCLIP, Life Member. [0000594] 28/02/1944 FE 01/01/1956
Bailey Mrs PM, (was Woodruff), BA MCLIP, Inf.Specialist, Univ.of Northumbria, Newcastle upon Tyne. [0018372] 17/10/1972
Bailey Mrs R, (was Crowe), BA MCLIP, p./t.L.Asst., Southampton City Coll. [0026917] 15/12/1976
Bailey Mr RA, BA(Hons) MCLIP, Asst.Lib., John Spalding L., Wrexham Med.Inst., Maelor Hosp. [0049290] 20/10/1993
Bailey Mr RJ, BA(Hons), Inf.Systems Administrator, Theodore Goddard, London. [0051888] 31/07/1995
Bailey Mrs RJ, (was Champion), MCLIP, Comm.L.Mgr., W.Bromwich N., Sandwell M.B.C. [0002568] 01/01/1969
Bailey Mrs S, (was Roberts), BEd(Hons) DipLIS MCLIP, Lib., HMP Downview, Surrey C.C. [0048245] 11/02/1964
Bailey Miss SM, BA MCLIP, Freelance Film Researcher. [0033486] 15/01/1981
Baillie Mr IM, MCLIP, Sen.Offr.-L., W.Dunbartonshire Council. [0000601] 01/10/1968
Baillie Mrs L, MCLIP, Unemployed. [0011347] 01/01/1966
Bain Mr JR, BA MCLIP, L.Consultant, Nat.L.Board, Singapore. [0028259] 02/11/1977
Bain Mrs LJ, Unemployed. [0054325] 20/11/1996
Bain Mrs LM, (was Stott), BA MCLIP, Inf.Offr., N.H.S.Grampian Bd., Aberdeen. [0021875] 05/02/1974
Bainbridge Miss EL, BA(Hons) MA, L.Executive, House of Commons, London. [0050635] 01/10/1994
Bainbridge Ms LC, MA MCLIP, Stud., Univ.of Exeter. [0034479] 13/11/1981

Personal Members — Balmforth

Baines Miss LM, BA MCLIP, Asst.Inf.Specialist, Nottingham Trent Univ. [0000610]   29/09/1970
Baines Miss PJ, BLitt MA, Lib., House of Commons L., London. [0058328]   11/01/2000
Bains Miss A, BA(Hons), Inf.Offr., CIPFA, London. [0055963]   02/01/1998
Bains Miss J, BA(Hons) PgDip, Ass.Inf.Offr., CMS Cameron McKenna, London. [0055165]   28/07/1997
Bains Mr MS, BA(Hons), Research Stud., Univ.of Cent., England, Birmingham, & Community, Lib., Coventry City Ls. [0042710]   10/02/1989
Bainton Mr AJC, MA MCLIP, Sec., SCONUL, London. [0000614]   01/10/1971
Baird Mrs D, (was Noble), MA(Hons) DipLIS, Lib., St.Ninian's High Sch., Renfrewshire. [0049472]   05/11/1993
Baird Mr IS, MA DipLib FSAS MCLIP, Subject Inf.Team Leader(Health), Univ.of Teesside, Middlesbrugh. [0036259]   04/09/1983
Baird Mrs JSM, (was Lawrie), MCLIP, Life Member, 139 Old Ancaster Rd., Dundas, Ontario, Canada, L9H 3R3. [0016569]   06/02/1959
Baird Ms KA, BA MLib GradIPD MCLIP, Head of Learning Res., London Coll.of Fashion, London Inst. [0000618]   17/01/1966
Baird Mr TH, MA(Hons) MLitt, Unemployed. [0059492]   09/04/2001
Bairstow Mrs M, (was Butler), BA MCLIP, Lib., Health & Safety Exec., Sheffield, & Inf.Advisor, Sheffield, Hallam Univ., S.Yorks. [0025498]   25/01/1976
Baker Mrs AE, (was Dimmick), BA MCLIP, Interloans Lib., Weston L., N.Somerset Council. [0000622]   25/09/1968
Baker Mrs AF, (was Whyte), MCLIP, Unemployed. [0015792]   26/12/1971
Baker Miss AJ, BA(Hons) MCLIP, Asst.Lib., Univ of the W.of England, Hartpury Campus. [0048661]   02/04/1993
Baker Mr AJ, BA(Hons) MCLIP, Subject Specialist-Music & Arts, Staffs.C.C. [0026837]   01/01/1976
Baker Mrs AL, (was Rolph), BLib MCLIP, Sch.Lib., Stoke High Sch., Ipswich. [0036835]   04/01/1984
Baker Mr AR, BA MCLIP, Princ.Lib., Blackpool Bor.Council. [0000624]   01/04/1969
Baker Mr ASJ, BA DipLib MCLIP, Lib., Haddon L.of Arch.& Anthropology, Cambridge Univ. [0034411]   05/11/1981
Baker Mrs B, (was Marshall), BA(Hons) MCLIP, Asst.Lib., Solihull Coll., W.Midlands. [0018357]   05/10/1972
Baker Miss C, BA, Stud., Univ.Cent.London. [0059709]   28/08/2001
Baker Mrs CA, Sch.Lib., Alderman White Sch., Bramcote, Nottingham. [0056383]   01/07/1998   **AF**
Baker Ms CA, HonFCLIP, Hon.Fellow. [0061176]   26/03/2002   **FE 26/03/2002**
Baker Mrs CJ, (was Helliwell), BSc DipLib, Inf.Researcher, Inst.of Mgmt., Corby. [0039969]   08/10/1986
Baker Miss CM, MA, Asst.Lib., Trade Partners UK., London. [0058251]   25/11/1999
Baker Mr CR, MCLIP, Princ.L.& Arch.Offr., Co.L.H.Q., Northumberland C.C. [0000627]   11/10/1965
Baker Mr DL, (was Richardson), MA MCLIP, Unemployed. [0038898]   18/10/1985
Baker Dr DM, MA MMus MLS PhD FIMgt FCLIP FRCO FRSA, Pro-Vice Chancellor, Inf.Serv.Dir., Univ.of E.Anglia, Norwich. [0022964]   31/08/1974   **FE 15/03/1983**
Baker Ms G, BSc MSc, Sen.Lib., D.F.E.S., London. [0043839]   29/01/1990
Baker Mrs GR, MCLIP, Careers Inf.Asst., CASCAID Ltd., Loughborough Univ.Company, Leics. [0000632]   01/01/1958
Baker Miss H, BA(Hons), Reg.L.& Inf.Serv.Offr., The Environment Agency, Peterborough. [0054643]   06/02/1997
Baker Miss J, BSc(Hons), Trainee Lib., States of Jersey L., Jersey. [0059729]   10/09/2001
Baker Mr J, MA MCLIP, Lib., E.Kent Hospitals NHS Trust, Margate. [0044610]   06/11/1990
Baker Mrs JE, (was Rimmer), BA MCLIP, Lib., Grp.4 Prison Serv.Ltd., HMP Altcourse, Liverpool. [0042691]   09/02/1989
Baker Miss JK, BA MCLIP, Princ.Asst.Lib., Univ.of Leicester. [0000633]   16/10/1966
Baker Mrs JK, (was Cooper), BLib MCLIP, p./t.Lib., Telford L. [0032410]   01/04/1980
Baker Mr JL, BSocSc MSocSc PhD DipLib MCLIP, Learning Res.Cent.Mgr., Abingdon & Witney Coll., Oxon. [0046414]   04/11/1991
Baker Mrs JM, (was Richardson), MLS MCLIP, Inf.Scientist, BASF Plc., Birkenhead. [0012366]   08/10/1969
Baker Mrs KL, BA, Stud., Sheffield Univ. [0059985]   15/11/2001
Baker Miss L, BA(Hons) MCLIP, Training & Resource Dev.Lib., Hereford Hosp.NHS Trust, Primary Care Trust. [0054615]   04/02/1997
Baker Mr LW, FCLIP, Life Member, Tel.01323 505565. [0000637] 15/03/1948   **FE 01/01/1958**
Baker Mrs M, (was Lewis), MCLIP, Lib., Park Mains High Sch., Erskine. [0025065]   21/11/1975
Baker Mrs MC, (was Abbott), BA(Hons) PGDip, Music Lib., Nat.L.for the Blind, Stockport. [0053916]   10/10/1996
Baker Mrs NJ, (was Wood), BA MCLIP MBA, District Mgr., Essex C.C. [0032475]   15/04/1980
Baker Mr OA, MCLIP, Retired. [0000641]   01/01/1963
Baker Miss P, MCLIP, Life Member. [0000642]   01/01/1934
Baker Mrs PD, BEd BSc, L.Asst., John Rylands Univ.L.Manchester. [0052714]   24/11/1995
Baker Ms RJ, BA DipLib MCLIP, Unemployed. [0044035]   01/04/1990
Baker Mr RP, MA, L.Mgr., The Royal Soc.L., London. [0053831]   03/10/1996
Baker Mrs SE, (was Pitches), BA(Hons) MCLIP, Unemployed. [0035238]   07/10/1982
Baker Mr SJ, BA MCLIP, Area Co-ordinator, Retford L., Notts.C.C. [0039271]   01/01/1986
Baker Ms TA, BA DipLib MCLIP, Lib., Warwickshire C.C., Leamington Spa. [0038622]   12/08/1985

Baker Dr W, BA MPhil PhD MLS, Prof., Northern Illinois Univ., Dekalb, U.S.A. [0042960]   02/05/1989
Bakewell Mrs A, (was Lawson), BA FCLIP, Life Member. [0000650]   06/09/1949   **FE 01/01/1955**
Bakewell Miss GM, MEd MCLIP, Retired. [0000651]   19/08/1964
Bakewell Prof KGB, MA FCLIP MCMI, Life Member, Tel.0151 486 4137, 9 Greenacre Rd., Liverpool, L25 0LD. [0000652]   28/08/1948   **FE 01/01/1958**
Bakhshi Mrs L, p./t.Stud./Multimedia Advisor, City Univ., Hendon L. [0059558]   22/05/2001
Bakker Mrs S, MSc MSLS, Lib./Inf.Specialist, Cent.Cancer L., The Netherlands Cancer Inst. [0047003]   27/03/1992
Balaam Miss AJ, BSc(Hons) MCLIP, Sch.Lib., Copleston High Sch., Ipswich. [0049432]   27/10/1993
Balaam Miss DJ, BSc DipLib MCLIP, Asst.Tech.Serv.Lib., Univ.Coll.Chichester. [0029365]   01/07/1978
Balasubramaniam Mr S, (was Sabanayakam), BSc DipLib, Employment not known. [0037649]   15/10/1984
Balbinski Mrs J, (was Castle), BSc DipLib MCLIP, Unemployed. [0034544]   22/12/1981
Balchin Ms JM, BA(Hons) MA MCLIP, Site Lib., Bournemouth & Poole Coll.of F.E. [0050956]   10/11/1994
Baldock Mrs IE, Inf.& Comms Offr., Voluntary Service Council., Medway. [0060908]   10/01/2002   **AF**
Baldwin Ms AK, BA(Hons) MCLIP, Head of Marketing, Trade & Ref., Oxford Univ.Press, Oxford. [0047851]   21/10/1992
Baldwin Mrs BW, (was Abbott), BA MCLIP, Retired. [0000656]   02/10/1960
Baldwin Mr DR, MCLIP, Asst.City Lib., Southampton City L. [0023504]   02/01/1975
Baldwin Mr HFJ, BA(Hons) DipLib, Catr., Hants.Co.L., Winchester. [0039884]   06/01/1986
Baldwin Mrs J, (was Richardson), MCLIP, L.Mgr.-Community Ls., L.& Heritage Serv., L.B.of Sutton. [0000660]   20/01/1969
Baldwin Mr LR, BA DipLib MCLIP, Site Sub-librarian, City University, London. [0000663]   20/10/1969
Baldwin Mrs RJ, BA DipHE DipLib, L.Asst., Winchester Sch.of Art, Southampton Univ. [0037472]   01/10/1984
Baldwin Miss S, Info.Specialist, Glaxosmithkline, Greenford, Middx. [0045428]   04/02/1991   **AF**
Bale Mrs DK, (was Black), BA(Hons) DipLib, Asst.Lib., Cent.Ref.L., Plymouth City Council. [0001325]   29/10/1969
Bale Mrs MA, (was Hook), MCLIP, Unemployed. [0007150]   01/10/1971
Balfe Miss SP, BA(Hons) MA, Inf.Offr., Wellington Underwriting Plc. [0057806]   09/08/1999
Balke Mrs MN, (was Schoales), BA MCLIP, Box 27, Sea Dog, Nanoose Bay, B.C., Canada, V0R 2R0. [0016577]   01/01/1940
Ball Mr AJ, BA(Hons), Stud., Univ.of Wales, Aberystwyth. [0061771]   05/11/2002
Ball Mr AW, BA FCLIP FSA FRHistS FRSA, Life Member, Tel.01923 228882, 71 Cassiobury Park Ave., Watford, WD18 7LD. [0000670]   01/01/1954   **FE 01/01/1958**
Ball Mrs CA, MA MCLIP, PhD Stud. [0019582]   16/11/1972
Ball . CF, Esq BA MCLIP, Life Member. [0000672]   29/08/1958
Ball Mr DJT, MA DipLib MLITT FCLIP, Inf.Mgr., Geo.Outram & Co.Ltd., Glasgow. [0026222]   06/09/1976   **FE 01/04/2002**
Ball Mrs GM, BA DipLib MCLIP, Lib., Royal Ordnance, Summerfield,Kidderminster. [0028489]   17/01/1978
Ball Mr GR, BA FCLIP, Retired. [0000675]   01/02/1951   **FE 01/01/1965**
Ball Ms H, Sch.Lib., E.Barnet Sch., L.B.of Barnet. [0054398]   08/11/1996   **AF**
Ball Mrs HC, (was Stokes), BA MCLIP, [0034690]   26/01/1982
Ball Mrs J, BA(Hons), L.Asst., Ashcroft, Bridgewater. [0058650]   04/05/2000   **AF**
Ball Ms JE, BA(Hons) MA MCLIP, Sub-Lib., Trinity Coll., Cambridge. [0051150]   24/11/1994
Ball Mrs JES, (was Stratford), BLib MCLIP, Child.Lib., Bath & N.E.Somerset, Bath Cent.L. [0039532]   18/02/1986
Ball Mrs LD, (was Parkes), BA MCLIP, Br.Mgr., Lostock Hall, Lancs.Co.L. [0011258]   11/10/1971
Ball Mrs MJ, (was Winspear), MA DipLib MCLIP, Career Break (Childcare). [0031724]   12/11/1979
Ball Mrs NE, (was Cripps), MCLIP, Retired. [0000680]   01/01/1956
Ball Ms RG, BA(Hons) PGDip, Visual Res.Lib., Falmouth Coll.of Arts, Cornwall. [0046850] 13/02/1992
Ball Miss SE, BBibl, Sen.Inf.Asst., Kings Coll.London. [0057741]   19/07/1999
Ball Miss SJ, BA, Asst.Lib., Govt.Communications H.Q., L., Cheltenham. [0035916]   24/01/1983
Ball Miss SK, BA(Hons), Inf.Offr., Inst.of Petroleum, London. [0059345]   12/02/2001
Ballantyne Mr JJ, BA DipLib MCLIP, Retired. [0000686]   01/01/1969
Ballantyne Miss MMW, MCLIP, Life Member. [0000687]   26/09/1951
Ballantyne Mr PG, BA MCLIP, Mgr., Int.Inst.Communication & Dev. [0030961]   01/07/1979
Ballard Ms H, BLib MCLIP, Adult Lend.Serv.Lib., Chatham L., Medway Council. [0037641]   10/10/1984
Ballard Mrs J, (was Glover), BLS MCLIP, Unemployed. [0027983]   03/10/1977
Ballard Mrs SA, (was Simons), BA(Hons) MCLIP, Sch.Lib., Stratford Upon Avon Grammar Sch., for Girls, Warks. [0023642]   09/11/1975
Ballouz Mrs MA, MA DipLib BSc AAS, P./t.Asst.Lib., Univ.of N.London. [0038735]   01/11/1985
Balmforth Mr CJ, MSc, p./t.Stud.,Leeds Met.Univ., Learning Cent.Asst., Barnsley Coll. [0059244]   15/01/2001
Balmforth Mr CK, MA FCLIP, Life Member. [0000692]   26/02/1956   **FE 01/01/1963**
Balmforth Mrs LD, (was Davies), BA(Hons) MCLIP, Unemployed. [0003718]   13/01/1971

Balnaves Dr FJ, PhD MA MLitt BA FLAA MCLIP, Life Member. [0016579] 27/08/1951
Bamber Mr AL, BA FCLIP, Life Member. [0000694] 22/01/1954 FE 11/12/1989
Bamber Mrs BE, (was Spicer), BA LLB MCLIP, Unemployed. [0013819] 15/03/1972
Bamber Mrs N, BA, Asst.Lib., Kidderminster Coll.of F.E. [0041246] 19/10/1987
Bamber Mr RN, MA MCLIP, Life Member, Tel.01995 604812, 64 Lancaster Rd., Garstang, Preston, Lancs., PR3 1JA. [0000696] 09/10/1947
Bamborough Miss SC, BA MCLIP, L.Sales Mgr., GMTV, London. [0029921] 01/11/1978
Bamford Mrs GS, (was Archer), BA(Hons) DipLib MCLIP, p./t.Reader Serv.Lib., Farnborough Coll.of Tech., Hants. [0032238] 26/02/1980
Bamford Mrs MM, (was Sweetmore), MA, Sch.Lib., Stoke-on-Trent City Council. [0049334] 25/10/1993
Bamford Mr P, BA MCLIP, Local Studies Lib., Cheshire C.C., Record Off., Chester. [0000697] 01/01/1972
Bamidele Mr JA, BSc MSc MPhil, L.Asst.(Serials/Acquisitions), Serial & Acquisitions Office, Univ.of London, SOAS. [0059477] 04/04/2001
Bampton Mrs BM, (was Cull), BA FCLIP, Retired. [0018482] 16/10/1943 FE 01/01/1953
Bamunusinghe Mrs JCK, DipLib, Admin.Asst., Charles Edward Brooke School. [0040610] 01/04/1987
Band Mrs BC, BSc(Econ), Sch.Lib., Hants.C.C. [0054582] 30/01/1997
Bandara Mr SB, BA(Hons) MCLIP, Acting Deputy Lib., Univ.of W.Indies L., Mona, Kingston 7, Jamaica. [0021895] 11/02/1974
Bandari Mrs KL, (was Robb), BSc DipLib MCLIP, Teacher/Lib., Bishop Wand Secondary Sch., Surrey C.C. [0042108] 03/10/1988
Bandeh-Robinson Mrs F, (was Robinson), BA, Stud., Univ.of N.London. [0058823] 15/08/2000
Bandy Mrs HF, (was Patrick), MA MCLIP, Sch.Lib., Beal High Sch., Ilford, Essex. [0011351] 28/10/1970
Banerjee Mrs A, BA(Hons) DipLib MCLIP, Assoc.Lib., Med.L., Mayday Healthcare Trust, Croydon Health Auth. [0038247] 12/02/1985
Banerjee Mrs B, BA MA DipLib MCLIP, Trust Lib., Cent.Manchester Hosp.NHS Trust. [0040446] 06/02/1987
Banfield-Potter Mrs JR, LIS Admin.Asst., The Chartered Inst.of Building, Berkshire. [0061445] 25/07/2002 AF
Bangar Ms K, BA(Hons) MA, Area Committee Lib., Nottingham City Council. [0048149] 11/11/1992
Banham Miss CR, MCLIP, P./t.Asst.Mgr., Sue Ryder Foundation, Wells, Norfolk. [0022243] 18/03/1974
Banister Mrs KJ, (was Hart), BA(Hons) MCLIP, Sen.L.Asst., Lancs.Co.L., Harris Cent.L. [0042258] 13/10/1988
Bankes Mrs L, (was Thain), BA MCLIP, Head of L.Services, HM Customs and Excise, Salford. [0043434] 26/10/1989
Bankier Mrs K, BA MCLIP, L.Asst., Preston Acute Hosp.NHS Trust, Lancs. [0000710] 01/01/1968
Banks Miss CA, BA(Hons), Inf.Offr., St Mungos, London. [0057410] 10/03/1999
Banks Mrs CA, BSc MA MCLIP, Unemployed. [0021681] 01/01/1974
Banks Miss CH, BA(Hons) MA MCLIP, Inf.Offr., Dickinson Dees Law Firm, Newcastle upon Tyne. [0055949] 23/12/1997
Banks Mrs GM, L.Mgr., Colton Hills Community Sch., Wolverhampton. [0057691] 02/07/1999
Banks Mrs J, MA(Hons), Stud./Asst.Lib., Robert Gordon Univ., Aberdeen, George Watson's Coll., Edinburgh. [0058656] 08/05/2000
Banks Mrs JFT, (was Yates), MCLIP, Retired. [0000711] 01/01/1941
Banks Mrs JN, (was Bellis), BA(Hons) MCLIP PGCE, Unemployed. [0036903] 01/02/1984
Banks Mr ML, Employment unknown. [0060322] 10/12/2001
Banks Mrs MM, BSc MCLIP, Off.Admin., Buchan Agric.Consultants Ltd., Peterhead. [0000712] 01/01/1970
Banks Mr PD, BA(Hons) DipLib MCLIP, Asst.Lib., Law Soc., London. [0048656] 02/04/1992
Banks Mr PJ, MCLIP, Retired. [0000714] 01/01/1950
Banks Mr PR, MA MCLIP, Resource Advisor, Policy Studies Directorate, Cabinet Office, London. [0041193] 15/10/1987
Banks Miss PS, MCLIP, Child.Lib., Kingston upon Thames P.L. [0000716] 15/10/1971
Banks Mr RER, MCLIP, Retired. [0000717] 04/03/1961
Banner Ms L, BA MA(Hons), Subject Lib.-Gen.& Adult Educ., Grove L., Bradford Coll. [0058178] 18/11/1999
Banner Mrs LS, (was Town), MCLIP, Assoc.Dir.-Mktg., Watts Publishing Grp.Ltd., London. [0000718] 07/10/1968
Bannister Mrs BC, BA MA DipLib MCLIP, Learning Cent.Coordinator, Tower Hamlets Coll., London. [0032390] 16/04/1980
Bannister Dr D, BA MSc PhD MCLIP, Retired. [0060518] 11/12/2001
Bannister Mrs GC, (was Wilson), BA(Hons) DMS MCLIP, Inspector, Audit Commission, Norfolk. [0020611] 07/05/1973
Bannister Mrs HM, (was Chapman), MCLIP, Tech.Asst., Jardine Lloyd Thompson, Crawley. [0002595] 23/11/1971
Banting Miss VA, DipLib MCLIP, Br.Lib., Wolverton L., Milton Keynes Council. [0032010] 28/01/1980
Banwell Dr LM, (was Hayes), MA PhD MCLIP, Acting Dir.-Inf.Mgmt.Res.Inst., Sch.of Inf.Studies, Univ.of Northumbria at Newcastle. [0006597] 13/10/1971
Baptie Mr DG, BA(Hons), Unemployed. [0059223] 09/01/2001
Bapty Mr RJ, MA MA, Subject Lib., Univ.of Glasgow. [0042993] 30/05/1989
Bar Mrs EAL, (was Arthur), MA MCLIP, Asst.Lib., Zentralbibliothek, Zurich. [0022498] 28/05/1974
Bara Mrs GM, (was Tanner), BA MCLIP, Mother/Home Educator. [0030552] 23/01/1979
Barbarino Mrs P, MA MA MCLIP, Special Appeals Mgr., The Brit.L., London. [0048409] 05/01/1993

Barber Mr AC, BSc DipLib MCLIP, Princ.Community Lib., Rhyl L., Denbighshire C.C. [0029575] 04/10/1978
Barber Mrs BM, (was Searle), MCLIP, Life Member, [0000726] 04/07/1949
Barber Mrs C, Bookstart Co-ord./Learn.Supp.Lib., Leeds L.& Inf.Serv. [0051508] 13/03/1995 AF
Barber Ms C, (was Snowdon), BA MCLIP, Sen.Inf.Offr., Univ.of Teesside, Middlesbrough. [0043856] 02/02/1990
Barber Mrs CE, (was Davies), MCLIP, Community Lib., Holywell L. [0023121] 05/11/1974
Barber Mr D, BSc MCLIP, Employment not known. [0060461] 11/12/2001
Barber Ms JC, MA MCLIP, Mgr., Learning Res.Cent., St.Francis Xavier Coll. [0041177] 20/10/1987
Barber Miss JM, (was Dawes), BA DipLib MCLIP, Co.Dir.(IT Bureau), Self-employed. [0032857] 03/10/1980
Barber Mrs JN, (was Massie), MCLIP, Head of Donation Unit, Nat.L.of Scotland, Edinburgh. [0026774] 03/11/1976
Barber Mr KE, BA MCLIP, Malvern L.Mgr., Cultural Serv., Worcs.C.C. [0000731] 01/01/1967
Barber Miss LJ, BA(Hons) MCLIP, Specialist Lib., Adult Serv., Coalville Grp. [0035299] 11/10/1982
Barber Mrs MC, (was Goold), BA DipLib MCLIP, Br.Lib., Coll.of Law, Chester. [0031840] 07/01/1980
Barber Mr PD, BA(Hons), Stud. [0054062] 24/10/1996
Barber Mrs S, (was Walls), BA DipLib MCLIP, Lib.Mgr., L.B.of Barnet, N.Finchley L. [0036534] 20/10/1983
Barber Mrs SM, (was Nicholas), MCLIP, Inf.Offr., Brit.L.-STB. [0000735] 27/09/1967
Barbet Ms MJ, BA, Sen.L.Asst., Uni.of London L. [0060861] 13/12/2001 AF
Barbour Ms A, BA MCLIP, Team Lib., Glasgow City Council, Mitchell L. [0030357] 16/01/1979
Barbour Miss DE, BA MCLIP, Sen.Lib., W.Educ.& L.Board, Omagh. [0021476] 17/10/1973
Barcena Ms L, Grad.Trainee, Department of Health, London. [0060025] 26/11/2001
Barclay Mrs CA, (was Homewood), MLib MCLIP, Learning Resource Mgr., Elmwood Coll., Cupar,Fife. [0025052] 01/11/1975
Barclay Miss CM, BA DipLib MCLIP, Stud. [0042347] 18/10/1988
Barclay Mrs J, (was Dolley), GDipMan MCLIP, Lib.:Database Mgmt., N.Yorks.Co.L. [0004051] 07/07/1969
Barclay Mrs JM, BA MA MCLIP, Employment not known. [0060844] 12/12/2001
Barclay Mrs P, BSc DipLib MCLIP, Digital Resources Lib., Univ.of Westminster. [0031257] 01/10/1979
Barclay Mrs PA, MCLIP, Life Member, Tel.0181 399 8314. [0000737] 01/01/1945
Barclay Miss PM, BA MCLIP, Lib., The City Lit.Inst., London. [0000738] 07/07/1967
Barclay Mr T, BA MCLIP, Inf./Local History Serv.Lib., S.Ayrshire Council, Ayr. [0020430] 15/03/1973
Barcroft Ms SE, BA PGDip, Learning Cent.Mgr., Napier Univ., Edinburgh. [0047114] 08/05/1992 AF
Bardi Mr L, Direttore del Centro, di Atend per le Biblioteche, Universita di Padova. [0058849] 04/09/2000
Bardolia Miss R, MCLIP, Catr., Univ.of Zimbabwe, Med.Sch.L., Harare. [0028490] 10/01/1978
Bardwell Rev JE, MA MCLIP, Lib.(p/t.), St.Stephen's House, Oxford. [0026272] 05/10/1976
Barefoot Ms A, BA(Hons) DipLib MCLIP, Volunteer L.Asst., Scope, London. [0026273] 01/10/1976
Barefoot Mrs SJ, (was Davies), BA MCLIP, Asst.Lib., Med.L., Univ.of Bristol. [0030747] 04/04/1979
Bareham Mr RE, BA DipLib MCLIP, Dep.Div.Lib., Hants.C.C., Fareham. [0034288] 21/10/1981
Barette Mrs HM, (was Le Maistre), BA MCLIP, Sen.Lib.-Catg., States of Jersey L.Serv. [0039199] 04/01/1986
Barfield Mrs PJ, (was Edenborough), BA MCLIP, Asst.Lib., Worcs.C.C., Evesham L. [0026355] 01/10/1976
Barfield Mrs PL, (was Gath), MCLIP, Lib., Keighley Ref.L., Bradford City L. [0005400] 24/01/1964
Barford Mrs S, (was Laflin), MCLIP, Area L.Mgr., L.B.of Enfield. [0008552] 07/01/1970
Barham Mrs MMT, (was Middleton), BA MCLIP, Asst.Lib., Christ Church Univ.Coll., Canterbury. [0000747] 04/10/1966
Barham Mrs PB, (was Brady), MA MCLIP, Unwaged. [0043325] 19/10/1989
Barker Mrs A, (was Hand), MCLIP, Asst.Dir.(Cultural Serv.), Stockton on Tees Bor.Council, Stockton. [0020256] 12/02/1973
Barker Mr AC, BA(Hons) DipILM MCLIP, Liaison Lib., City Coll.Norwich, Norwich. [0054189] 30/10/1996
Barker Mr AJ, MA, Asst.Lib., Home Off., London. [0045166] 27/07/1990
Barker Dr AL, BSc MSc PhD MCLIP, Documentation Mgr, Support Ops., Mercy Ships, Texas, USA. [0025152] 08/12/1975
Barker Miss AR, BA(Hons), p./t.Stud, L.Asst., St.George's L., Univ.N.London. [0059835] 16/10/2001
Barker Mrs CA, (was Jackson), BA(Hons) CertEd MSc MCLIP, Co.Specialist, Inf.& Knowl.Mgmt., Staffs.C.C. [0050350] 04/07/1994
Barker Mrs CB, BA MLS MCLIP, Asst.Sch.Lib., St.Joseph's R.C.Sch., Swindon, Wilts. [0025209] 15/01/1976
Barker Mrs CE, (was Lucas), MSc MCLIP, Asst.Mgr.(Project Mgmt.), KPMG, London. [0051649] 09/11/1994
Barker Mrs CK, (was Lewis-Lavender), BA(Hons) DipILM MCLIP, Lib., Howes Percival, Norwich. [0052007] 07/09/1995
Barker Mr DC, BA MCLIP, Mgr., N.E.Wales S.L.S., Flintshire C.C. [0000751] 23/10/1967

Personal Members — Barratt

Barker Ms DM, BA(Hons) Dip, Intranet Content Quality Devel., Freshfields Bruckhaus Deringer, London. [0061081]   01/03/2002 **AF**
Barker Mrs ED, (was Hutchinson), BA(Hons), Lib.-Child.& Young Peoples Serv., Warwickshire C.C., Leamington Spa. [0037989]   01/01/1985
Barker Mrs EJ, (was Winwood), BSc(Hons) MSc(Econ), Learning Resources Asst., Southampton Inst., Southampton. [0055708]   06/11/1997
Barker Mrs GD, BA DipLib MCLIP, Princ.Lib.:Reader Serv., Glos.Co.L. [0035530]   26/10/1982
Barker Mrs J, (was Lewis), BA DipLib MCLIP, L.Mgr., Cinderford L., Glos.C.C. [0008878] 29/09/1969
Barker Mrs J, (was Mcnally), MCLIP, Dir.of Comm.Serv., Hartlepool Bor.Council. [0009543]   05/02/1968
Barker Mrs J, MCLIP, Employment unknown. [0060357]   10/12/2001
Barker Mrs JB, Inf.Mgr., Bank of England, London. [0061475]   06/08/2002
Barker Mr JD, BA DipLib MCLIP, Princ.Literature Offr./Dep.Dir., Lit.Dept., Brit.Council, London. [0035680]   01/01/1983
Barker Miss JM, BA DipLib MCLIP, Sen.Lib.(Adult Serv.), Luton Area, Luton Bor.Council. [0038026]   14/01/1985
Barker Miss KE, MA MSc, Asst.Lib.(Systems), Salisbury Dist.Hosp.L. [0059611]   28/06/2001
Barker Mrs KS, BA(Hons) MSc DipIT DipSocAdmin PGCE, Head of L.& Politics, Clifton High Sch., Bristol. [0060005]   21/11/2001
Barker Ms L, BSc, Admin.Projects Lib., Imperial Coll., London. [0057563]   04/05/1999
Barker Mr LA, BA PGCE DipLib MCLIP DMS, Learning Res.Cent.Mgr., Thurrock Coll., Essex. [0040976]   02/10/1987
Barker Miss MA, (Hons) MCLIP, Sen.Learning Res.Offr., Thomas Rotherham Coll., S.Yorks. [0044570] 29/10/1990
Barker Mrs NJ, BA DipLib MCLIP, Unemployed. [0021142]   07/10/1973
Barker Mrs PA, (was Evans), Support Analyst II, Sagebrush Corp., Edmonton, Canada. [0047179]   21/05/1992
Barker Mr PH, BA MCLIP, Retired., 2 Brooklands Ave., Burnley, BB11 3PS. [0000764]   16/02/1964
Barker Mrs RD, (was Brown), BA HNC, Lib., Viewforth High Sch., Kirkcaldy. [0058190]   16/11/1999
Barker Mrs S, (was Horner), B LIB MCLIP, Sch.Lib., Cheshire C.C., Chester. [0021468]   18/10/1973
Barker Mrs S, (was Young), BA DipLib MCLIP, Sen.Inf.Offr., Northants.C.C. L.E.A., Northampton. [0028491]   02/01/1978
Barker Miss SE, BA, Counter Asst., Herts.C.C., Letchworth L. [0058814]   07/08/2000
Barker Miss VK, BA(Hons) MLib, p./t.Admin.Asst., Willis, Ipswich, Suffolk. [0047857]   21/10/1992
Barkess Mrs PM, BA PGCE, Inf.Asst., The Brit.Council, Mozambique. [0057896]   01/10/1999
Barkway Mrs JA, BA DipLib MCLIP, Team Lib., Wirral Bor.Council, W.Kirby L. [0040110]   16/10/1986
Barlow Mrs D, (was Davis), MCLIP, Child.Serv.Co-ordinator, Notts.L., E.Grp. [0000773]   02/07/1963
Barlow Mrs EA, (was Heath), BA MA MCLIP, Sen.Sch.Lib., Staffs.Sch.L.Serv., Stafford. [0028313]   15/11/1977
Barlow Mrs HC, BSc MCLIP, Freelance Inf.Sci., 36 Durler Ave., Kempston, Bedford. [0044295]   20/08/1990
Barlow Mrs JB, (was Broadribb), MA DipLib MCLIP, Career Break. [0044399]   04/10/1990
Barlow Miss LC, BA(Hons) MA, child.Lib., Upper Norwood L., London. [0056667]   01/10/1998
Barlow Mrs MT, (was D'Souza), BA MCLIP, p./t.Asst.Inf.Adviser, Univ.of Brighton, Eastbourne, E.Sussex. [0000775]   28/10/1966
Barlow Mr R, BA MA PhD MCLIP, Community Librn.Mgr., Leicester City Librn., Leicester. [0025211] 02/01/1976
Barlow Ms R, BA DipLib, Asst.Lib., Reynolds Porter Chamberlain, London. [0049497]   05/11/1993
Barlow Mr SH, FCLIP, Life Member, 4 Arden Rd., Nuneaton, CV11 6PT. [0000777]   09/10/1930   **FE 01/01/1938**
Barlow Mrs SM, (was Jeays), MCLIP, p./t.Lib., Leics.L.& Inf.Serv. [0019801] 23/11/1972
Barltrop Mrs E, FCLIP, Life Member, Tel.0308 424705. [0000778] 13/03/1935   **FE 01/01/1948**
Barnabas Mrs SM, (was Chell), MCLIP, Life Member. [0000779]   06/03/1961
Barnard Mrs FEK, LLB MCLIP, Sch.Lib., Bishops Hatfield Girls Sch., Herts. [0000781]   04/02/1972
Barnard Miss FH, BA(Hons) MA, Asst.Curator, Nat.Art L., Victoria & Albert Mus. [0057773]   02/08/1999
Barnard Ms GM, MCLIP, Retired. [0000782]   13/02/1961
Barnard Mrs GR, (was Long), BMus DipLib MCLIP, Unemployed. [0034437] 23/10/1981
Barnard Mr I, BSc PGCE, Stud. [0061503]   02/09/2002
Barnard Mr NE, BA DipLIS MCLIP, Sub-Lib., Oxford Brookes Univ. [0046484]   12/11/1991
Barnard Mr SJ, BA MCLIP, Systems Lib., Doncaster M.B.C., Cent.L. [0000784]   13/02/1971
Barnard-Foulds Dr SL, (was Foulds), Project Consultant, Esprit Soutron Partnership. [0038697]   01/10/1985
Barnes Ms AJ, BA MA DIP ENG ST MCLIP, Head of L.Serv., Min.of Defence, Bulford, Wilts. [0000787]   09/01/1970
Barnes Mr CI, CEng MCLIP MBCS, Inf.Tech.Offr., Food & Agric.Organization, Rome, Italy. [0031035]   01/01/1966
Barnes Mr CJ, BA MCLIP, Princ.Child.Lib., Southampton City Council. [0019579]   26/10/1972
Barnes Mrs DJ, BA DipLib MSc, Inf.Systems Mgr., Abbeywood L.& Inf.Serv., MOD, Bristol. [0038370]   01/04/1985
Barnes Mrs DL, (was Moore), BSc(Hons) MSc MCLIP, IT Systems Mgr., S.Dartmoor Community Coll., Ashburton, Devon. [0053362]   20/05/1996

Barnes Miss EL, BSc(Hons) MSc(Econ), Child.Lib., Chichester L. [0057521]   15/04/1999
Barnes Mrs G, (was Kings), MCLIP, Spec.Needs Asst., Warwickshire C.C., Rugby. [0008412]   22/09/1970
Barnes Mrs GM, (was Bell), BSc(Hons) DipILM, Learning Advisor (Maternity Leave), Learndirect, Leicester. [0056726]   07/10/1998
Barnes Miss HM, MSc, Inf.Cent.Mgr., King Sturge, Bristol. [0057474]   01/04/1999
Barnes Mrs HV, (was Young), Dist.Super., W.C.C.Educ.& L., Amesbury. [0045075]   05/07/1990   **AF**
Barnes Miss J, MCLIP, Special Serv.Lib., Wilts.Educ.& L.Dept., Salisbury L. [0000802]   19/11/1968
Barnes Mrs J, BA(Hons), Sch.Lib., Hirst High Sch., Northumberland. [0054363]   25/11/1996
Barnes Ms J, BSc(Hons), Sen.L.Asst., Anglo-Euro.Coll.of Chiropractic, Bournemouth. [0061312]   17/05/2002   **AF**
Barnes Mrs JA, (was Leicester), MCLIP, Unemployed. [0000799]   01/01/1960
Barnes Mrs JAM, BA DipLib MCLIP, Lib., Min.of Defence, Tech.L.Sch.of Signals,Dorset. [0039284]   07/01/1986
Barnes Mrs JE, (was Ward), MCLIP, Retired. [0000800]   27/01/1964
Barnes Mr JJ, BA Dip MSc MCLIP, Employment not known. [0061171]   26/03/2002
Barnes Mrs KM, (was Davey), BA DipLib MCLIP, L.& Arts Asst., Ashford L., Kent C.C. [0030585] 22/02/1979
Barnes Miss MJ, BA(Hons) MCLIP, Catg.& Acquisitions Lib., Fire Serv.Coll., Moreton-in-Marsh, Glos. [0043678]   22/11/1989
Barnes Mr MPK, OBE DMA FIMgt FRSA MCLIP, Guildhall Lib., Dir.of L.& Art Galleries, City of London. [0000805] 01/01/1960
Barnes Ms SJ, BA(Hons), Stud./Pre course training, Kings Coll.London. [0059817]   10/10/2001
Barnes Miss WIL, BA MCLIP, Lib., Cultural Serv., Oxon.C.C. [0038414]   17/04/1985
Barnes-Downing Mrs EA, BA(Hons) FRGS, Inf.Centre Mgr., Bovis Lend Lease Ltd., Middlesex. [0059466]   03/04/2001
Barnet Ms S, BA MCLIP, Lib., S.Univ., Alabama, U.S.A. [0000809] 03/10/1971
Barnett Mr C, MA MInstAM MCLIP, Research Offr., E.Riding of Yorks.Council, Beverley. [0000810]   01/01/1966
Barnett Mrs EM, (was Mullins), MCLIP, Unemployed. [0010562]   18/01/1963
Barnett Mr G, FCLIP, Head, Media Visits & Inf.Training, Internat.Press Section, Foreign & Commonwealth Off. [0000811]   11/12/1963   **FE 21/02/1974**
Barnett Mrs JA, (was Cholerton), BA MCLIP, Lib., Broomfield Coll., Derbys. [0020047]   18/01/1973
Barnett Mrs K, (was White), DF ASTROL S MCLIP, Liaison Offr, Study Advice Serv., Univ.of Hull. [0000814] 28/09/1967
Barnett Miss KL, MSc(Econ), Asst.Lib., Educ.L.& Res.Serv., Port Talbot. [0053397]   03/06/1996
Barnett Mrs P, B Lib MCLIP, Resources Mgr., Eckington Sch., Sheffield. [0000818]   30/06/1968
Barnett Mrs PM, BA(Hons) MCLIP, Inf.Offr., Scottish Envir.Protection Agency, Aberdeen. [0048068]   04/11/1992
Barnett Miss R, BA(Hons) DipLib MCLIP, Resident Overseas. [0045652]   15/04/1991
Barney Miss DJ, BA(Hons) MA, Asst.Lib., Foreign & Commonwealth Off., London. [0049563]   11/11/1993
Barney Mr TH, MA PhD, Research Fellow, Dept.of Linguistics, Univ.of Lancaster. [0040500]   25/02/1987
Barnsley Mrs CE, (was Parker), BA MCLIP, p./t.Community Team Lib., Tewkesbury, Glos.Co.L. [0011226]   27/09/1966
Barnsley Miss S, MCLIP, Div.Lib., Rugby L., Warwicks Co.L. [0000823]   02/05/1965
Baron Ms CL, BSc, Stud., Univ.Coll.London. [0061633]   09/10/2002
Baron Mr D, BA(Hons) MBA, Record Creation Mgr., Brit.L., Boston Spa. [0042797]   07/03/1989
Baron Mrs JR, (was Cooke), BA MCLIP, Lib., Area Serv., Bradford M.D.C. Bradford. [0040211] 13/11/1986
Baron Miss L, BA(Hons), Inf.Offr.& Webmaster, Brit.Cement Assoc., Crowthorne. [0055526]   20/10/1997
Baron Mrs LM, (was Dearnaley), BA DipLib MCLIP, Sch.Lib., Sutton High Sch., Surrey. [0029951]   12/11/1978
Barontini Ms C, MA, Subject Lib., Drama Cent.London Inst., London. [0047557]   01/10/1992
Barr Mr CBL, MA FSA MCLIP, Life Member. [0000826]   02/05/1958
Barr Ms DJ, BA MIMgt MCLIP, L.& Comm.Learning Mgr., S.Lanarkshire Council. [0018428]   17/10/1972
Barr Mrs F, (was Forbes), MA DipEd RISI MCLIP, Self-employed-Freelance Indexer, Aberdeenshire. [0000828]   01/11/1969
Barr Mr GR, MCLIP, Life Member. [0000829]   12/03/1942
Barr Mr JD, BA MCLIP, L.Devel.Offr., S.Lanarkshire Council, Hamilton. [0019670]   07/11/1972
Barr Mrs W, BSc, Position unknown, Armadale Academy. [0061263]   13/05/2002
Barraclough Miss CE, BA MCLIP, Dist.Lib., Herts.C.C.Comm.Inf.:L.s., Hemel. [0038753]   04/10/1985
Barratt Miss J, BA, L.Asst., Somerset C.C. [0056390]   01/07/1998   **AF**
Barratt Miss J, MA FCLIP, Life Member. [0000835]   18/10/1956   **FE 01/01/1961**
Barratt Miss JA, BA(Hons) DipLIS MCLIP, H.of Serv.-Soc.Sci., Central L., Birmingham. [0050024]   21/02/1994
Barratt Ms MM, BA MCLIP DipLaw, Branch Lib., Fullwell Cross Lib., Barkingside. [0028778]   19/01/1978
Barratt Miss PF, Asst.Inf.Consultant, The Boots Co.plc, Nottingham. [0061513]   29/08/2002   **AF**
Barratt Miss PM, MCLIP, Life Member. [0000839]   02/03/1943

185

Barrett Mr BJ, BTh DipLib MCLIP, Lib., S.E.Health Board, Kilkenny, Ireland. [0041115] 08/10/1987
Barrett Mr DA, BA, Lib., Kent C.C., County Cent.L. [0041048] 05/10/1987
Barrett Miss E, MA BA(Hons), p./t.Stud./Inf.Mgr., Univ.of Wales, Aberystwyth, Ketchum, London. [0061199] 08/04/2002
Barrett Mrs E, MCLIP, Princ.Lib., Inf.Serv., Hants.Co.L. [0018319]13/10/1972
Barrett Miss EA, BA(Hons) MSc, Sen.Inf.Researcher, BBC Inf.& Arch., London. [0042589] 13/01/1989
Barrett Miss EM, BA(Hons), Stud., N.London. [0060870] 18/12/2001
Barrett Mrs HC, (was Willis), BA MCLIP, Local Studs.Lib., Lancs.Co.L., Hyndburn District. [0018487] 28/03/1962
Barrett Miss IMR, BA, Lib.Asst., Thames Valley Univ., Slough. [0033265] 27/10/1980
Barrett Mrs JP, (was Davies), L.Asst., Cardiff City Council. [0038032] 10/01/1985
Barrett Mrs LM, (was Melcher), BA MLS MCLIP, Inf.Serv.Mgr., Dixons City Tech.Coll., Bradford, W.Yorks. [0044405] 05/10/1990
Barrett Miss MA, Grad.Trainee, Inst.of Advanced Legal Studies, London. [0061829] 14/11/2002
Barrett Mr R, BA MA MCLIP, Asst.Lib., Dublin Inst.of Tech. [0040985] 01/10/1987
Barrett Mrs SE, (was Crabb), BA(Hons), L.Br.Super., Wokingham Dist.Council, Lower Earley L. Reading. [0057794] 11/08/1999
Barrett Mrs SJ, (was Chapman), DipLib MCLIP, p./t.L.Asst., Univ.of Huddersfield. [0002611] 01/01/1971
Barringer Miss TA, MA DipLib MCLIP, Freelance Bibl.& Editor. [0030100] 10/01/1979
Barrington Mr JW, BA MCLIP, Indexer/Catr. [0018488] 20/09/1972
Barriskill Mrs KR, (was Dodds), BSc(Hons) DipLIS MCLIP, Sen.Asst.Lib., Guildhall L., Corporation of London. [0037497] 01/10/1984
Barron Ms E, BA(Hons) MA MCLIP, Literature/Reading Devel.Offr., Cheshire C.C., Cheshire Arts Serv. [0052171] 10/10/1995
Barron Mrs FM, (was Edwards), BSc(Hons) MCLIP, Site Sales Negotiator. [0004428] 20/01/1970
Barron Mrs LE, (was Conti), MA DipLib MCLIP, Lib., Gordonstoun Sch., Elgin. [0037868] 01/11/1984
Barron Mrs SA, BA DipLib MCLIP, Retired. [0032862] 11/10/1980
Barrow Mr A, BSc MCLIP MIBiol MLib CBiol FRSA, Employment not known. [0023630] 12/01/1975
Barrow Mrs BM, (was Wakeling), MCLIP, Life Member, 93 Westway, London, SW20 9LT. [0000858] 09/01/1951
Barrow Mrs GS, (was Wallace), BA MCLIP, Resource Cent.Mgr., Village High Sch., Derby. [0021219] 08/10/1973
Barrow Ms JH, BA(Hons) DipIS, Prof.Support Lawyer, Baker & McKenzie, London. [0050820] 20/10/1994
Barrow Mrs JW, (was Burton), MCLIP, Serv.Devel.Mgr., Surrey C.C. [0002157] 19/01/1969
Barrow Dr M, (was Ryder), BA MA PhD FCLIP, Asst.Lib., Joule L., U.M.I.S.T. [0000860] 13/03/1964 FE 08/08/1977
Barrow Mr PA, BA DipLib MCLIP, Sen.Lib., L.B.of Haringey. [0035081] 02/08/1982
Barrowcliffe Mrs DJ, p./t.Stud./L.Asst., Univ.of Wales, Bolton Public L. [0059630] 05/07/2001
Barry Mrs AM, (was Brown), BA MCLIP, Lib., Merchant Taylors Sch.for Girls, Liverpool. [0039272]14/01/1986
Barry Mrs FJ, (was Williamson), BA DipLib MCLIP, Field Operations Mgr., Warrington L., Warrington Bor.Council. [0031983] 06/01/1980
Barry Mrs GR, (was Sheard), BA MSc MCLIP, Dep.Lib., Manchester Metro.Univ. [0024964] 24/10/1975
Barry Mr J, MCLIP, User Serv.Lib., Learn Res., Univ.of Brighton. [0000865] 06/02/1968
Barry Ms JA, (was Chalmers), BA(Hons) MCLIP, Lib., Bishopbriggs High Sch. [0045301] 04/10/1990
Barry Mr JM, Resident in Japan. [0038539] 10/06/1985
Barry Ms MS, BA DipLib, Employment not known. [0038330] 06/03/1985
Barry Mrs RW, (was Wilson), MOD BA, Asst.Lib., Royal Belfast Academical Inst., Belfast. [0042298] 01/10/1988
Barson Miss AJ, BSc, Stud., Sheffield Univ. [0061234] 17/04/2002
Barson Mrs JM, (was Claridge), BA FCLIP, Retired. [0002720] 04/02/1960 FE 01/01/1963
Barter Mrs EK, (was Foord), Unemployed. [0005695] 11/11/1992
Barthel-Rosa Mrs J, Head Lib., WTO L., Geneva, Switzerland. [0051754] 21/06/1995
Bartholomew Mrs FM, MCLIP, Lib., Fulham L., L.B.of Hammersmith & Fulham. [0022166] 20/02/1974
Bartholomew Mr J, BSc BA(Hons) PGDip, Team Lib., Norfolk L.& Inf.Serv., Costessey L. [0058466] 24/02/2000
Bartholomew Mr J, MCLIP, Unemployed. [0030879] 01/01/1964
Bartholomew Mrs JM, MA DipLib MCLIP, Unemployed. [0034914] 19/04/1982
Bartle Mr DG, BA DipLib MCLIP, Mgr.of Marine Inf.Cent., Inst.of Marine Engineer.Sci.&Tech., London. [0036302] 01/10/1983
Bartle Mr R, MA B LITT FCLIP, Life Member. [0000870] 10/03/1953 FE 01/01/1960
Bartleman Ms CA, CertEd, L.Asst., Westminster Kingsway Coll., London. [0047940] 27/10/1992 AF
Bartlett Mr DA, Unemployed. [0059498] 11/04/2001
Bartlett Mrs FL, BA(Hons) MCLIP, Inf.Sci., Det Norske Veritas, Aberdeen. [0048065] 04/11/1993
Bartlett Mrs LM, (was McAllen), L.Supervisor, Shirley L., Southampton. [0037035] 01/02/1984
Bartlett Mrs R, BA MCLIP, Life Member. [0000876] 11/09/1956
Bartlett Mrs SJV, (was Rose), BA DipLib MCLIP, Coll.Lib., Otley Coll., Ipswich. [0026865] 28/12/1976
Bartlett Mrs SM, (was Hewell), BA Adv DipEdTech MCLIP, Sch.Lib., Berkhamsted Collegiate Sch., Herts. [0023556] 20/01/1975

Bartlett Mrs WM, BA(Hons), p./t.Lib., Univ.of Wolverhampton. [0052315] 25/10/1995
Bartley Mrs VJ, BSc DipLib MCLIP, Mgr.of Content Devel., The Dialog Corporation, London. [0031557] 03/11/1979
Barton Mrs C, BSc MA, p./t.Asst.Subject Advisor, Distance Learning, Univ.of Derby. [0059276] 25/01/2001
Barton Mrs E, (was Lee), BSc MCLIP, Bibl.Serv.Lib., Middx.Univ. [0008776] 01/02/1972
Barton Mrs HEB, (was Biggs Barton), BSc(Hons) MSc MCLIP, Inf.Sci., BPB plc., Loughborough. [0047730] 15/10/1992
Barton Mrs J, Relief Lib.Asst., Moray Council. [0053506] 10/07/1996 AF
Barton Mrs JA, (was Dustin), BA MCLIP, Retired. [0004309] 21/03/1959
Barton Mrs RL, (was Fortnam), BAMA, Outreach Lib., Hastings & Rother NHS Trust, E.Sussex. [0056095] 12/02/1998
Barton Miss SE, BA MCLIP, Head of Inf., McCann Erickson, London. [0034773] 09/02/1982
Barua Mr A, MA MPhil, Stud., SOAS Univ. [0060892] 20/12/2001
Barwell Ms CA, BA(Hons) MCLIP, Unemployed. [0035302] 06/10/1982
Barwell Miss ER, Stud., Loughborough Univ. [0059901] 26/10/2001
Bashforth Mr S, BA MCLIP, Ch.L.Offr., Barnsley M.B.C., S.Yorks. [0000886] 29/05/1970
Basinger Mrs DR, (was Short), MCLIP, Sch.Lib., Cowley High Sch., Merseyside. [0013322] 01/10/1970
Basinger Mrs EC, (was Bloom), MCLIP, Inf.Devel.Mgr., CSU Ltd., Manchester. [0020238] 13/02/1973
Basker Mr AJ, BSc MA MIMgt MCLIP FRSA, MD, Basker Research, Southsea. [0033668] 01/01/1968
Basra Mrs CM, (was Watson), MLS MCLIP, Resident in Canada. [0031974] 02/01/1980
Bass Miss J, MCLIP, Retired. [0000891] 02/01/1960
Bass Miss KM, BA, Stud., UCL London. [0059805] 03/10/2001
Bass Mrs P, BA MCLIP, Retired. [0000892] 12/10/1960
Bassant Mr R, Lib., Carnegie Free L., Trinidad, West Indies. [0058422] 07/02/2000
Bassett Mrs CD, MCLIP, Retired. [0015127] 01/01/1963
Bassett Mrs H, BA(Hons) DipLib, Lib., St.Augustine of Canterbury, Uppr.Sch., Oxford. [0055308] 24/09/1997
Bassett Mr P, FCLIP, Retired. [0000895] 14/03/1955 FE 01/01/1968
Bassington Miss SJ, MLS MCLIP, Lib., Francis Holland Sch., London. [0036073] 25/04/1983
Bassnett Mr PJ, FCLIP, Life Member. [0016595] 02/06/1958 FE 01/01/1971
Bastable Mrs LM, (was Warrick), MCLIP, Unemployed. [0015400] 06/11/1971
Bastiampillai Miss MA, BA MA MCLIP, Head of L.Serv., Commonwealth Inst., Commonwealth Res.Cent., London. [0039299] 15/01/1986
Bastone Mrs SC, (was Pegg), Sch.Lib., Ryeish Green Sch., Wokingham Dist.Council. [0051099] 15/11/1994 AF
Batchelor Miss EJ, BA DipILS MCLIP, Ch.L.& Inf.Asst., Univ.of Cambridge. [0047024] 02/04/1992
Batchelor Mr K, MCLIP, Princ.Lib.(N.), L.B.of Brent. [0000901] 14/01/1969
Batchelor Mrs KM, (was Brookes), BA DipLib MCLIP, Sen.Lib., Oxon.Co.L., Cowley L. [0032242] 11/02/1980
Batchelor Mr NS, MA MCLIP, Lect., Cent.Coll.of Comm., Glasgow. [0026277] 20/10/1976
Batchelor Mrs SC, (was Pickup), BA DipLib MCLIP, Lib., Cambs.C.C., St Neots, Cambs. [0035810] 24/01/1983
Batcock Miss C, MCLIP, Retired. [0000902] 10/02/1959
Bate Mr D, FCLIP, Retired, 144 Colville Rd., Lowestoft,Suffolk,NR33 9QZ. [0000904] 23/04/1952 FE 01/01/1961
Bate Mrs DM, DipLIS MCLIP, Learning Support Lib., Staffs.Univ. [0055098] 08/07/1997
Bate Miss GM, BA PGCE DipLib, L.Supply Offr., The Brit.Council, (Inf.Serv.Mgmt.), Manchester. [0044644] 13/11/1990
Bate Mr JL, MBE MA DipEd FCLIP, Retired. [0000906] 04/10/1937 FE 01/01/1953
Bate Mrs MA, BA MCLIP, Employment not known. [0060511] 11/12/2001
Bate Mrs VJ, BA MCLIP, Princ.L.Asst., Bodleian Law L., Oxford. [0027200] 03/02/1977
Bateman Miss D, BA MCLIP, Head of Customer Servs., Univ.Coll., Cork. [0000909] 19/09/1967
Bateman Mrs P, (was Johnson), BA MSc, Lib., Inf.Mgmnt., Dept.of Health, London. [0044677] 23/11/1990
Bateman Mrs VE, (was Ryall), Sen.L.Asst., Bracknell L., Berks. [0050332] 03/06/1994 AF
Bateman-Wang Mrs MJ, Stud., Somerset Coll. of Arts & Tech. [0052955] 31/01/1996
Bater Miss P, BA MCLIP, Head of Bus.Serv., Inst.of Directors, London. [0000915] 21/09/1966
Bater Mr RJ, MCLIP, Unemployed. [0019858] 01/01/1973
Bates Miss AJ, Unemployed. [0056347] 02/06/1998 AF
Bates Mr AT, MCMI MCLIP, Retired, 33 Bradwell Rd., Peterborough, PE3 9PY, Tel:(01733) 263536. [0000916] 21/01/1947
Bates Miss CA, BA(Hons), Asst.Lib., L.B.of Barnet. [0056657] 11/10/1998
Bates Ms CA, BA(Hons), Lib., Nottingham City Council. [0052352] 26/10/1995
Bates Mrs E, BA PG DipLib MCLIP, L.Res.Cent.Mgr., Cent.Tech.Coll., Glos. [0046568] 12/11/1991
Bates Mrs EJ, BA(Hons) MCLIP, Readers Serv.Lib., Trafford M.B.C., Sale. [0048326] 25/11/1992
Bates Mrs EM, BSc(Hons), Asst. Lib., Dept.Ed.skills., London. [0053660] 27/08/1996
Bates Mrs HM, (was Mackay), MCLIP, Learning Res.Cent.Mgr., Totton Coll., Southampton. [0027449] 01/04/1977
Bates Miss J, MCLIP, Lib., Warwickshire Co.L. [0000920] 08/08/1964

Bates Ms J, BSocSc MA, Resident in Ireland. [0060123] 10/12/2001
Bates Mrs JH, MSc, Grad.Trainee, Glengormley L., Co.Antrim. [0059773] 02/10/2001
Bates Mr P, MA MSc MRS MCLIP, Employment not known. [0060623] 11/12/2001
Bates Mrs P, BA(Hons) MA, Unemployed. [0056733] 07/10/1998
Bates Miss SE, BSc MSc MCLIP, Marketing Exec., PFDS Online, London. [0044211] 09/07/1990
Bates Mrs VK, (was Hough), BSc(Hons) DipLib MCLIP, Lib., St Helens Coll., Town Cent.Campus. [0051170] 23/11/1994
Bates-Hird Mrs SB, (was Bates), FCLIP, Info Mgr., Sandwell Met.Board, W.Bromwich. [0006828] 27/01/1969 FE 17/11/1999
Bateson Mrs VC, BA DipLib MCLIP, Dep.Br.Lib.(Job Share), Woodford Green L., L.B.of Redbridge. [0026278] 06/10/1976
Bathgate Ms WCP, (was Aprilchild), BA MA MCLIP, Learning Res.Cent.Co-ordinator, Bannockburn High Sch., Stirling. [0043302] 17/10/1989
Batho Mrs VA, (was Lightfoot), MA DipLib MCLIP, Unemployed. [0032113] 16/01/1980
Batley Miss P, MA MCLIP, Head of Learning Res., London Coll.of Printing, The London Inst. [0000929] 05/02/1958
Batt Mr C, OBE BA FCLIP HonFCLIP, Dir.of Learn.& Inf.Soc.Team, Resource: The Council for Museums, Arch.& Ls., London. [0000930] 17/03/1966 FE 21/12/1988
Batten Mrs AM, (was Thomas), BSc DipLib MCLIP, Lib., Herts.C.C., Nobel Sch. [0014523] 17/01/1968
Batten Mr MK, BSc MCLIP, Stock Team Lib., Westminster City L., Victoria L. [0021622] 28/11/1973
Batten Miss ML, MCLIP, Employment not known. [0060435] 11/12/2001
Batterbury Mrs JA, BA DipIM, Asst.Super., Fareham L., Hants.C.C. [0056672] 01/10/1998
Battersby Mrs A, (was Stevens), BA, Inf.Serv.Mgr., Eversheds, Nottingham. [0042919] 21/04/1989
Battersby Mrs M, BA MCLIP, P./t.Lib., Young People's Serv., N.Watford L., Herts. [0037796] 28/10/1984
Battersby Mr R, BA DipLib MCLIP, Faculty Grp.Lib.,-Sci.& Eng., Univ.of Edinburgh, Darwin L. [0032630] 30/06/1980
Battison Mrs V, Sen.Lib.-Yth.& Comm., Blackpool Bor.Council. [0000932] 01/01/1965
Battistini Miss A, BA, Postgrad.in Inf.Serv.Mgr., Univ.of N.London., London. [0058888] 01/10/2000
Battle Mrs LA, (was Evans), BSc MSc MCLIP, Employment not known. [0060139] 10/12/2001
Battley Miss KC, MA, Grad.Trainee, Manchester Metro.Univ. [0061013] 01/02/2002
Batton Miss C, Sch.Secretary, Leics.C.C., Old Dalby. [0046256] 21/10/1991
Batty Mr CD, FCLIP, President, CDB Enterprises Inc., Silver Spring, MD20902, USA. [0026218] 07/02/1955 FE 01/01/1963
Battye Ms JE, BA MCLIP, Head of L.& Inf.Serv., L.B.Ealing, London. [0032392] 31/03/1980
Baud Mrs A, (was Cramond), MA MCLIP, Head of Bibl.Serv., Univ.of Bath. [0036540] 19/10/1983
Bauer Mrs JL, Lib., Novartis Horsham Research Cent., W.Sussex. [0054773] 01/04/1997
Bauld Mrs A, MCLIP, Special Needs Asst., Surrey C.C., Bagshot. [0000938] 01/01/1966
Baum Mrs BI, (was Butler), BA MLIS MCLIP DipLib HDipEd, Inf.Offr., The Planning Exchange, Scotland. [0029607] 17/10/1978
Baumfield Mr BH, MA FRSA FCLIP, Life Member. [0000939] 25/02/1946 FE 01/01/1958
Baumfield Mr NJ, BA MLITT MLS MCLIP, Cultural Serv.Mgr., Wansbeck Dist.Council. [0032864] 01/10/1980
Baverstock Mr JAG, BA PhD, Temp., TFPL Ltd., London. [0057173] 08/01/1999
Baveystock Mrs GY, (was Williams), BA DipLib MCLIP, Mobile & Home Serv.Lib., Slough Bor.Council, Berks. [0041214] 16/10/1987
Bax Mrs KJ, (was Skinner), B LIB MCLIP, Sch.Lib., Doon Academy, E.Ayrshire Council. [0022207] 25/01/1974
Baxendale Mrs M, (was Cheetham), BA MCLIP, Life Member. [0000941] 14/04/1952
Baxter Miss AR, BSc(Hons) DCG, p./t.Stud./Careers Adviser(Inf.), Univ.of Cent.England, Birmingham. [0059016] 02/10/2000
Baxter Ms BJ, (was Thompson), BA(Hons) MCLIP, Arch., World Images, Bristol. [0054666] 17/02/1997
Baxter Mr D, MCLIP, Life Member. [0000943] 20/06/1956
Baxter Mr G, Research Asst., The Robert Gordon Univ., Aberdeen. [0046031] 05/09/1991
Baxter Mr J, BA DipLib MCLIP, Area Lib., Met.Bor.of Wirral, Cent.L. [0000945] 01/01/1970
Baxter Mrs JR, Sch.Lib., Bedford Sch., Bedford. [0054355] 26/11/1996
Baxter Miss K, MA DipLib MCLIP, Sub-Lib., Univ.of Dundee. [0000947] 19/10/1971
Baxter Mr PB, B MUS DipLib MCLIP, Music L.Offr., Edinburgh City L. [0033477] 05/01/1981
Baxter Mr PJ, FRSC CChem MCLIP, Employment not known. [0060796] 12/12/2001
Baxter Mrs R, p./t.Clerical Offr.Asst./Stud., Kirklees Cultural Serv., Huddersfield. [0055624] 27/10/1997
Baxter Miss VJ, BA DipLib MCLIP, Local Studies Lib., L.B.of Richmond upon Thames. [0030596] 06/03/1979
Bayir Miss D, MA, Asst.Dir., Documentation & Inf.Serv., KOC Univ.L., Istanbul. [0047372] 27/07/1992
Bayley Miss A, BA MCLIP, L.Tech., Dawson Coll.L., Quebec, Canada. [0000953] 01/07/1972
Bayley Miss DJ, MBE BA DipLib MCLIP, Life Member. [0000954] 01/01/1949
Bayley Mrs P, (was Barrett), MCLIP, P./t.Lib., Telford & Wrekin Council, Shropshire. [0000957] 01/03/1965

Baylis Miss AC, BA MA DipLib MIMgt MCLIP, Local Studies & Archives Mgr., R.B.of Kensington & Chelsea, Kensington Cent.L. [0044114] 18/05/1990
Baylis Ms JI, (was Long), BA DipLib MCLIP, Collection Mgr., Inst.of Chart.Accountants, London. [0031359] 11/10/1979
Bayliss Mr G, BA MCLIP, Lib., Preston Manor High Sch., Brent Council. [0000959] 14/10/1969
Bayliss Mrs JA, (was Goldsmith), BLib MCLIP, Regional Lib., Suffolk C.C., Coounty L. [0037922] 22/11/1984
Bayliss Mrs SE, (was Dakin), BA MCLIP, Info.Specialist, Univ of Birmingham. [0029495] 25/10/1978
Bayman Mr AJ, MA, Lib., Foreign & Commonwealth Off., Milton Keynes. [0045672] 19/04/1991
Baynes Mr D, MCLIP, Partner, Vacation Enhancement, Old Portsmouth. [0000965] 01/04/1965
Baynham Miss L, BA(Hons) MCLIP MA, Catg.Lib., Univ.of London, Inst.of Educ. [0000966] 19/10/1976
Bazell Ms C, MCLIP, Sch.Lib., The King Alfred Sch., London. [0000967] 09/08/1965
Bazely Mrs JH, (was Gershon), BA DipLib MCLIP, Lib., Southend-on-Sea Cent.L., Southend-on-Sea Bor.Council. [0031594] 24/01/1981
Beach Mrs AE, BSc(Hons) PGDipLib, Asst.Lib., English Nature, Peterborough. [0035312] 07/10/1982
Beach Mrs D, (was Hawes), BA MCLIP, p./t.Inf.Specialist, QinetiQ, Farnborough. [0024996] 02/09/1975
Beach Mr MC, BA(Hons), Community Lib., Firth Pk.L., Sheffield. [0021287] 11/10/1973
Beadle Miss RV, B ED DipLib MCLIP, Comm.Lib., Theale L., W.Berks.Council. [0040023] 07/10/1986
Beadnell Mrs GE, (was Prew), BA(Hons) MA, Sen.L.Asst., Corpus Christi Coll.Oxford. [0055832] 20/11/1997
Beagan Mr J, FCLIP, Comm.Lib., Prestatyn L., Denbighshire. [0000971] 27/10/1967 FE 30/11/1984
Beagan Mrs LM, (was Davies), BSc MCLIP, Position Unknown, [0023903] 06/02/1975
Beaglehole Ms M, BA(Hons) MA, Asst.Lib., Gonville & Caius Coll.L., Cambridge. [0052749] 22/02/1999
Beagrie Mrs G, (was Little), MCLIP, Lib., Largs Academy, N.Ayrshire Council, Irvine. [0008980] 21/03/1963
Beal Mr G, BLib DMS MCLIP, System Mgr., Guildhall L., Corp.of London. [0030817] 14/05/1979
Beale Mr C, BA MCLIP, Unemployed. [0000973] 05/02/1969
Beale Mrs HE, (was Thomas), BA MCLIP, Lib., Morgan Cole Solicitors, Swansea. [0034548] 06/01/1982
Beale Ms PA, Sen.i/c., Solihull M.B.C., Solihull. [0046947] 28/02/1992
AF
Beall Ms J, BA PhD MLS, Asst.Editor,DDC, Lib.of Congress, USA. [0034921] 21/04/1982
Beaman Miss HL, Stud., Manchester Met.Univ. [0059847] 16/10/2001
Beamish Mrs D, (was Balchin), MCLIP, Unemployed. [0000978] 04/03/1968
Beamond Miss C, MCLIP, Ref.Lib., Sutton Coldfield L., W.Midlands. [0000979] 08/07/1968
Bean Mr AR, BTh DipTh (Disc) DipTh(Min) MTh, Stud., Manchester Met.Univ. [0055565]21/10/1997
Bean Mr C, BA(Hons) MA MCLIP, Inf.Mgr., Mercer Mgmt.Consulting, London. [0035506] 07/10/1982
Beard Mr A, BA DipLib MCLIP, Princ.Lect., Sch.of Law, Governance & Inf.Mgmt., Univ.of N.London. [0000983] 17/01/1972
Beard Mr D, MCLIP, Retired. [0000984] 17/08/1954
Beard Ms JL, BA(Hons) DipILM MCLIP, Comm.Lib., Stoke-on-Trent City Council. [0055843] 21/11/1997
Beard Mrs LC, (was Pinnell), MCLIP, L.Asst., Univ.Wales Coll.Newport, Caerleon. [0032373] 24/03/1980
Beard Mrs M, (was Beech), MCLIP, Local Studies Lib., Stoke-on-Trent City Arch., Hanley L. [0024601] 01/01/1978
Beard Mr RJ, Evidence Based/Knowledge Mgmnt.Lib, Brighton & Sussex Univ. [0059174] 05/12/2000
Beard Mr SL, MA MCLIP, Learning Res.Mgr., Thurrock & Basildon Coll., Essex. [0031562] 28/10/1979
Beardmore Miss SH, LLB(Hons)DipILS, p./t.Sch.Lib.(Job Share), Merrill Coll., Derby. [0055964] 02/01/1998
Beards Mr SPR, BA MCLIP, Team Lib., Ealing L.Serv., L.B.of Ealing. [0029880] 17/10/1978
Beardshall Ms KA, BLib MCLIP, Subject Lib., The Peirson L., Univ.Coll.Worcester. [0031187] 01/10/1975
Beardsley Ms HR, MA(Hons) MLib MCLIP, Arts Inf.Offr., Stirling Univ.L. [0049287] 20/10/1993
Beardsmore Mr SJ, BA(Hons) MA, Employee, Wolverhampton Cent.L. [0054626] 09/12/1996
Bearne Miss V, MCLIP, Dep.Grp.Lib., Bath & N.E.Somerset. [0000993] 20/08/1969
Beary Mrs CD, PGCE DipLib MCLIP, Sch.Lib., Parmiters Sch., N.Watford. [0032393] 11/04/1980
Beasley Ms A, (was Ruszkowska), MA, Humanities Team Leader, The Univ.of Reading, Berks. [0047842] 20/10/1992
Beasley Miss CL, BA(Hons), Stud., City Univ., London. [0050842] 21/10/1994
Beasley Mr DA, BA MCLIP, Lib., Worshipful Company of Goldsmiths, London. [0032253] 17/03/1980
Beasley Mr DR, BSc DMS MCLIP, Employment not known. [0060828] 12/12/2001
Beasley Miss PA, BA DipTEFL, Site Lib., Chemical Eng.& Electronic &, Electrical, Univ.of Birmingham. [0037343] 02/07/1984
Beasley Mrs VA, BA MCLIP, Unemployed. [0024877] 01/10/1975
Beaton Miss AM, MA(Hons) DipILS MCLIP, Film Catr., Scottish Screen Arch., Glasgow. [0055230] 05/09/1997
Beaton Mrs AM, BA DipLib MCLIP, Lib./L.Asst., Univ.of Glasgow. [0036570] 09/10/1983

Beaton Mr JJ, MA DipLib MCLIP FSA(Scot), Lib., Royal Coll.of Physicians& Surgeons, Glasgow. [0040878] 22/07/1987
Beaton Miss M, BA MCLIP, Access Serv.Co-ordinator, Glasgow City L., Inf.&Arch., Mitchell L. [0000995] 03/11/1971
Beattie Miss AC, BA MCLIP, Learning Serv.Lib. [0050042] 22/02/1994
Beattie Mr AGJ, BEng(Hons) MSc MCLIP, Sen.Cataloguer., British Film Institute. [0055955] 24/12/1997
Beattie Mr H, BA MCLIP, Lib., HMP Kilmarnock, Kilmarnock. [0027654] 04/07/1977
Beattie Miss J, MCLIP, Child.Serv.Lib., Inverclyde L. [0000998] 22/01/1972
Beattie Miss JA, BA(Hons) MSc, Cent.Document Mgr., Instant L.Ltd., Loughborough. [0052326] 30/10/1995
Beattie Mrs N, BSc, Employment unknown. [0060303] 10/12/2001
Beattie Mr WS, BA MCLIP, Retired. [0001001] 04/08/1951
Beatty Mrs LF, (was Reay), MLib MCLIP, Self-employed, Re_Inform, Australia. [0001003] 04/03/1963
Beauchamp Mrs J, (was Charlton), BA(Hons), Mgr.-Learning Serv., Salisbury Coll., Wilts. [0058798] 31/07/2000
Beauchamp Mr PJ, MCLIP, Ch.L.Adviser, Dept.for Cult., Media & Sport, London. [0001004] 15/02/1967
Beaufoy Mrs ME, (was Harrison), FCLIP, Life Member. [0001005] 06/10/1938 FE 01/01/1958
Beaulieu Prof MM, (was Hancock), BA PhD FCLIP, Head of Dept.of Inf.Sci., City Univ. [0041491]08/01/1988 FE 01/04/2002
Beaumond Mrs CM, (was Rogers), MCLIP, Retired. [0001006] 18/03/1964
Beaumont Mrs AJ, (was Miller), BA DipLib MCLIP, Unemployed. [0023734] 12/02/1975
Beaumont Mrs AM, (was Kelly), BA, Lib., Preston Acute Hosp.NHS Trust, Preston. [0046780] 22/01/1992
Beaumont Mrs FA, BA DipLib, Lending & Inf.Serv.Lib., Leominster L. [0026113] 01/01/1976
Beaumont Mr GC, MCLIP, Life Member. [0001010] 19/09/1950
Beaumont Mrs GM, (was Peace), BA MCLIP, Employment not known. [0011400] 14/02/1967
Beaumont Mrs J, MCLIP, LRC Co-ordinator, Swindon Coll., Wilts. [0001011] 01/01/1967
Beaumont Mrs J, (was Lee), BA(Hons) MCLIP, Councillor, Stockton-on-Tees. [0001012] 10/03/1962
Beaumont Mr JS, BA MA MCLIP, Facilities & Planning Lib., Univ.of Adelaide. [0001013] 21/10/1964
Beaumont Ms MJ, (was Boyes), MCLIP, Consultant. [0016599] 12/02/1964
Beavan Dr IM, BA PhD FCLIP, Sen.Curator, Historic Collections, Dir.of Inf.Systems & Serv., Univ.of Aberdeen. [0001018] 01/01/1970 FE 23/03/1994
Beaven Mr AR, BSc MCLIP, Employment not known. [0060793] 12/12/2001
Beaven Mrs OJ, (was Jones), BSc(Hons) MSc, Inf.Specialist, BMJ Publ.Grp., London. [0047709] 19/10/1992
Beaver Miss WJ, BA MCLIP, Comm.Lib., Devizes L., Wilts.C.C. [0041207] 19/10/1987
Beavis Mrs J, (was Morse), BA MCLIP, Div.Child.Lib., Hants.Co.L. [0033433] 31/10/1980
Beazleigh Mrs DH, BSc(Hons) MSc, Metadata Project Offr., Open Univ., Milton Keynes. [0056891] 02/11/1998
Beber Mr J, BA, L.Asst., Aberdeen City L. [0046696] 13/12/1991
Beck Mrs AL, (was Broom), BA(Lib) MCLIP, Dep.Cent.Area Mgr.(Job Share), Solihull M.B.C. [0046225] 31/10/1966
Beck Mrs IJ, (was Scott), BA DipLib MCLIP, Sch.Lib., John F.Kennedy Sch., Hemel Hempstead. [0040293] 14/07/1987
Beck Mrs JA, (was West), MCLIP, Housewife. [0001025] 25/08/1966
Beck Miss SL, BA(Hons) MCLIP, Stud. [0043924] 22/02/1990
Beck Mr TJ, MSc MBCS MCLIP, Independent Consultant. [0001028] 07/12/1967
Becker Mrs HC, BA MCLIP, Bookstart Offr., Lancs.C.C. [0021269] 03/10/1973
Beckett Mrs A, BA(Hons), Sch.L./Res.Asst., Sefton Bor.Council, Merseyside. [0054438] 06/12/1996
Beckett Mrs DM, (was Job), MA DipLIS, Sub.Lib.(Acting), St.Bartholomews Sch.of Nursing & Midwifery, City Univ. [0051905] 03/08/1995
Beckett Miss ES, BSc(Hons) DipLib MCLIP, Stock Mgmnt., N.Bristol NHS Trust, Bristol. [0044323] 06/09/1990
Beckett Mrs HL, (was Simms), BA(Hons), Team Lib., Bracknell Forest Bor.Council. [0038208] 27/01/1985
Beckett Miss IC, BA(Hons) MA MCLIP, LTSN Inf.Offr., Inf.Sci.Cent., Loughborough Univ. [0055191] 07/08/1997
Beckett Mrs PM, (was Hufton), Unemployed (Career Break). [0055379] 06/10/1997
Beckett Mrs SJ, (was Bloxham), BA MCLIP, Comm.Lib.(Job Share), Caerphilly Co.Bor.Council, Risca L. [0042410] 26/10/1988
Beckley Mrs SG, BA DAA MCLIP, Co.Arch., City & Co.of Swansea & Co.Bor.of, Neath Port Talbot. [0001032] 16/02/1970
Beckton Mr JE, DipLib MCLIP, Learning & Teaching Co-ordinator, Univ.of Lincs.& Humberside, Hull. [0034203] 05/10/1981
Beckwith Mrs JA, (was Allum), BA MCLIP MSc, Collections Lib., Royal Coll.of Physicians of London. [0038046] 09/07/1979
Bedbrook Mr JD, BA MCLIP, Retired, 19 Roundway Park, Devizes, SN10 2ED. [0020802] 05/07/1973
Beddard Miss AFM, MCLIP, User Serv.Mgr., Arup, London. [0018077] 02/10/1972
Beddard Miss VL, BA(Hons), Stud., Univ.of Central Eng., Birmingham. [0060865] 13/12/2001
Beddows Mrs EA, (was Thacker), BA, Sch.L.Serv.Lib., Staffs.C.C., Stafford. [0048190] 16/11/1992
Beddows Mrs SP, BA DipLib, Unemployed. [0041227] 19/10/1987
Bedford Mr MA, BA DipLib MCLIP, Child.Lib., New Addington L. [0038047] 17/01/1985

Bedi Mrs K, MA BA MCLIP, Sen.L.Mgr., L.B.of Greenwich, London. [0028495] 06/01/1978
Bednall Mr PJ, BA MCLIP, Asst.Inf.Lib., L.B.of Sutton Pub.L., Surrey. [0023320] 19/11/1974
Bedri Ms A, BA, Asst.Lib., Home Off., London. [0040448] 31/01/1987
Bee Miss EA, BEd DipLib MCLIP, Inf.Mgr., Funderfinder, Leeds. [0032015] 12/02/1980
Bee Mrs V, BA, Inf.Asst., TFPL Ltd., London. [0061414] 17/07/2002
Beeby Miss LA, BSc(Hons), Biome Project Asst., The Natural History Mus., London. [0058113] 01/11/1999
Beech Mrs M, MCLIP, Life Member. [0001037] 01/01/1944
Beech Mrs PM, (was Holmes), MCLIP, Consultant, Shropshire. [0001039] 16/01/1969
Beedle Mrs FJ, Lib., Univ.of Cambridge, Local Exam., Syndicate, Cambridge. [0057273] 29/01/1999
Beedle Mr JA, BA MCLIP, Area Lib., Scottish Borders L.Serv., Hawick. [0001042] 04/01/1968
Beegan Mrs J, (was Mignogna), B LIB MCLIP, Med.Inf.Exec., Solvay Healthcare Ltd., Southampton SO18 3JD. [0030653] 09/03/1979
Beeley Mrs C, (was Ball), MCLIP, Inf.Lib., Kingston Univ. [0000671] 01/04/1967
Beeley Mrs JE, (was Powell), MCLIP, Lib., Mid-Kent Coll.of H.& F.E., Chatham, Kent. [0011869] 29/08/1969
Beer Mrs DM, (was Love), MA BA MCLIP, Internet Inf.Systems Mgr., Inst.of Devel.Stud., Brighton. [0031360] 05/10/1979
Beer Mr RN, FCLIP FInstPet, Life Member. [0001044] 23/09/1952 FE 01/04/2002
Beer Mrs SF, BSc(Hons) PGDip MSc, Stud., Robert Gordon Univ. [0053785] 01/10/1996
Beesley Mr MHG, MCLIP, Retired. [0001048] 01/09/1961
Beeson Mr ML, BA(Hons) DipIS MCLIP, Subject Lib., Middlesex Univ. [0050561] 16/09/1994
Beeston Mrs M, (was Smith), MCLIP, Retired. [0001052] 23/03/1943
Beever Mrs SJ, (was Robson), MCLIP, Retired. [0001054] 29/02/1968
Beevers Mr CJ, BSc(Hons) PGDipLIM, Stud., Manchester Met.Univ., &, Document Delivery Super., Univ.of Huddersfield. [0058357]19/01/2000
Beevers Mr KA, BA MCLIP, Area Lib., Bolton Metro.Bor. [0019044] 23/09/1969
Begg Mr JA, BA DipLib MCLIP, Sch.Lib., Winston Churchill Sch., Woking. [0029580] 16/01/1978
Begg Mrs KE, BSc(Econ) PGDip, p./t.Stud./L.Asst., Univ.of Wales, Aberystwyth, Sidney Sussex Coll., Cambridge. [0057309] 08/02/1999
Begley Miss RME, B LIB MCLIP, Team Lib.,Lend., L.B.of Kingston, Surrey. [0023566] 01/01/1975
Beglin Mr PA, BA(Hons), Grad.Trainee, L.Dept.for Ed.and Skills, London. [0059979] 15/11/2001
Begum Miss S, BSc MSc, Lib., Royal Bor.of Kensington & Chelsea, London. [0061636] 07/10/2002
Behr Ms AF, BA MCLIP, Acquisitions & Inf.Tech.Offr., L.B.of Hammersmith & Fulham., London. [0027889] 04/10/1977
Beighton-Delille Mrs E, MCLIP, Dep.Head of L.Serv., W.Kent Coll. [0059235] 11/01/2001
Beilby Mrs RJ, BA(Hons) MCLIP, Lib., King Sturge, Bristol. [0056105] 17/02/1998
Beisty Ms BM, BA(Hons) MA PgD, Asst.Lib., Manchester Metro.Univ. [0046225] 16/10/1991
Beken Mrs LR, BA(Hons), Stud., Univ.of Strathclyde, Glasgow. [0061212] 08/04/2002
Belcher Miss JS, Employment not known. [0019889] 01/01/1973
Bell Mrs A, (was Mccaw), BA MScEd DipLib MCLIP, (Primary)Educ.Lib., N.E.Educ.& L.Serv., Ballymena. [0022789] 17/10/1974
Bell Mrs A, (was Johnston), BA DipLib MCLIP, Univ.of Edinburgh, Faculty of Sci.& Engineering. [0029988] 21/11/1978
Bell Mrs AH, (was Laing), BA DipLib MCLIP, L.Offr., Edinburgh City L. [0028851] 26/01/1978
Bell Mrs AM, BA MCLIP, Adult Educ.Tutor, Suffolk Basic Skills, Ipswich. [0035459] 19/10/1982
Bell Mr AP, BSc MCLIP, Employment unknown. [0060334] 10/12/2001
Bell Mrs AR, (was Cuthbertson), BA DipLib MCLIP, Br.L.Mgr., S.E.E.& L.B., Moira L. [0023354] 26/11/1974
Bell Mr AW, MCLIP, Mgr.of Public L.Operations, Cheshire L.& Culture, Crewe L. [0001060] 24/09/1965
Bell Mrs CS, BA MCLIP, Unemployed. [0027511] 26/04/1977
Bell Ms D, Bsc(Hon) DipInf DMA, Inf.Devel.Offr., Charity, London. [0050043] 23/02/1994
Bell Mr DAH, MCLIP, Strategy & Support Mgr., N.E.Lincs.Council. [0001066] 01/01/1968
Bell Mr DG, MCLIP, Team Lib., N.W.Area, Norfolk C.C. [0001067] 20/03/1967
Bell Mr DJ, MCLIP, Bus.Intelligence Adviser, Business Link Surrey, Woking. [0019619] 24/10/1972
Bell Ms DL, BA(Hons) MA MCLIP, Asst.Lib., H.M.Treasury & Cabinet Off., London. [0052074] 02/10/1995
Bell Mrs EF, (was Walters), MCLIP, Sch.Lib., Christchurch Middle Sch., Stone, Staffs. [0018073] 04/10/1972
Bell Mrs EJ, MA MCLIP, Sen.Lib.(Job-Share), N.Ayrshire Dist.L. [0001070] 08/05/1972
Bell Mrs EL, (was Walters), BA(Hons) DipIS MCLIP, Career Break. [0053165] 20/03/1996
Bell Mrs EM, (was Blackwood), BA(Hons) MA MCLIP, Lib., RNIB. [0055393] 09/10/1997
Bell Mrs F, (was Hague), BA(Hons) PGCE DipIM, Supply Teacher, Bracknell Forest. [0053806] 02/10/1996 SP
Bell Mrs HC, (was Jurkowski), BA DipLib MCLIP, Not Currently Employed. [0035733] 17/01/1983

Bell Miss HL, MA, Inf.Offr., The Ruskin High Sch., Crewe. [0058697] 30/05/2000
Bell Mrs HM, ThB DipLib, Lib., Nazarene Theological Coll., Manchester. [0038205] 14/01/1985
Bell Mrs J, (was Livesey), MCLIP, Asst.Div.Lib., Lancs.Co.L., Preston. [0030774] 04/04/1979
Bell Mrs JA, (was Scott), MCLIP, Sch.Lib., St.Brendan`s High Sch., Linwood, Paisley. [0001076] 08/09/1966
Bell Mrs JA, (was Patterson), BA(Hons) DipLIS MCLIP, Educ.Lib.(Special Serv.), N.E.Educ.& L.Board, Co.Antrim. [0029787] 01/10/1978
Bell Miss JC, BA(Hons) MA, Inf.Researcher, Dept.of Trade & Ind., London. [0055512] 16/10/1997
Bell Ms JC, BEd DipLIS MCLIP, Dir.of L.& Learning Support, Newman Coll.of H.E., Birmingham. [0049372] 29/10/1993
Bell Miss JD, MCLIP, Asst.Ref.Lib., Burnley P.L., Lancs.C.C. [0001077] 09/10/1967
Bell Mrs JHM, (was Davie), MCLIP, Unemployed. [0020933] 10/09/1973
Bell Mr K, MA, Employment not known. [0060447] 11/12/2001
Bell Mr KE, BA M Phil DipLib MCLIP, Retired. [0001081] 03/02/1970
Bell Mrs KE, BSc(Hons) MA, Head of L.& Learning Res., King Edward VI Coll., Stourbridge. [0055977] 07/01/1998
Bell Mr KF, BA MCLIP, Area Lib.(Cent.), Bolton L. [0018498] 15/03/1963
Bell Mr KW, MBE MInstE MCLIP, Retired. [0060519] 11/12/2001
Bell Mrs LAJ, (was Johnson), MA(Oxon) MSc MCLIP, Census Reg.Serv.Co-ordinator, UK Data Arch., Univ.of Essex. [0050847] 21/10/1994
Bell Mr M, MCLIP, Retired. [0001083] 01/01/1972
Bell Mrs M, (was Millar), BA DIP LIB MCLIP, Inf.Mgr., Scottish Enterprise, Glasgow. [0035236] 04/10/1982
Bell Ms M, BA DipLib, Asst.Lib., Brit.L.of Political & Econ.Sci., London Sch.of Economics. [0046611] 25/11/1991
Bell Miss MA, BA(Hons) MA MCLIP, User Support Offr., MIMAS, Univ.of Manchester. [0056159] 01/04/1998
Bell Mrs MA, (was Watkins), BA DipLib MCLIP, Sci.Lib., Univ.of Wales., Coll.of Cardiff. [0021716] 31/12/1973
Bell Miss MC, MCLIP, Young Peoples Serv.Lib., N.Lanarkshire Council, Coatbridge. [0021286] 01/10/1973
Bell Miss MD, MA MCLIP, Life Member. [0001084] 13/10/1948
Bell Mrs MH, (was Liposits), BA MSc, p./t.Lib., Crewe P.L., Cheshire C.C. [0042327] 20/10/1988
Bell Mrs MS, BLS MCLIP, Grp.L.Mgr., S.E.Educ.& L.Board, Lisburn. [0040524] 05/02/1987
Bell Mr P, BSc(Econ) MLib, Lib., Dept.of the Environ., Trans., & the Regions, Hove. [0050825] 19/10/1994
Bell Mrs RA, BA(Hons) MA MCLIP, Lib., Doncaster Coll. [0058249] 25/11/1999
Bell Mr RD, MA MCLIP, Head of Reader Serv., (Princ.Asst.Lib.), Bodleian L., Oxford. [0001093] 26/07/1967
Bell Mrs S, BA MCLIP, Ref./Local Studies Lib., Aberdeen Cent.L. [0022990] 07/10/1974
Bell Mr TI, FCLIP, Life Member, Tel.01730 821381. [0001098] 15/08/1949 **FE 01/01/1958**
Bell Mrs VN, (was Hoftijzer), BSc(Hons), Systems Lib., UHB Trust L., Queen Elizabeth Hosp., Birmingham. [0048426] 04/01/1993
Bell Miss WJ, DipLib MCLIP, Lib., Oak Hill Coll., London. [0031511] 18/10/1979
Bell Mr WN, BA MCLIP, Retired, 20 Church Rd., Giffnock, Glasgow, G46 6JR. [0001099] 15/09/1964
Bellamy Miss D, Stud., Robert Gordon Univ. [0056654] 01/03/1998
Bellamy Miss LM, BA(Hons), Grad.Trainee, Cable & Wireless, London. [0058301] 22/12/1999
Bellamy Ms M, DMS MBA MCLIP, Asst.Ch.Lib., Leics.C.C. [0002052] 20/01/1970
Bellamy Mr PD, BA MCLIP, Lib., Falkirk Council. [0030597] 01/03/1979
Bellamy Mr PR, BA DipLib MCLIP, Faculty Lib., Applied Soc.Sci.& Humanities, Bucks.Chilterns Univ.Coll. [0038044] 10/01/1985
Belles Ms AM, Off.Mgr., Wrexham Co.Bor.Council. [0056710] 07/10/1998
Bellinger Mr RP, BLib MCLIP, Resources Lib., Bridgend Co.Bor.Council. [0046314] 28/10/1991
Bellingham Mrs RA, (was Jones), MCLIP, P/t.Lib., Bentleys Stokes & Lowless, Solicitors, London. [0024716] 07/10/1975
Bellingham Mrs ST, MA DipLib, Career Break. [0046396] 31/10/1991
Bellis Mr GOHP, BA(Hons), Stud., Univ.of Sheffield. [0061815] 11/11/2002
Belsham Mrs CT, (was Berry), N.W.Kent Coll., Dartford. [0047504] 14/09/1992
Belsham Ms JK, (was Atkinson), BA DipLib MCLIP, Lib., Kingston Univ., Kingston. [0037422] 30/08/1984
Belsham Mrs SR, (was Izzard), MCLIP, Asst.Lib., Thomas Plume L., Maldon. [0001108] 08/11/1967
Belton Mrs MC, BSc PGCE, Grad.Trainee, Lochinvar Sch., Cumbria. [0059802] 03/10/2001
Bembridge Mrs AM, (was Newberry), BA MCLIP, Electronic Res.Devel.Offr., Birmingham P.L. [0001111] 25/09/1968
Ben-Tahir Mr I, BA MS MCASI MCLIP, Resident in Canada. [0060082] 07/12/2001
Benaim Mr JR, BA(Hons), Asst.Lib., Manchester Inc.Law L. [0061244] 22/04/2002 **AF**
Bendall Dr AS, MA MCLIP, Fellow & Devel.Dir., Emmanuel Coll., Cambridge. [0035661] 23/11/1972
Bending Mr SJ, BA(Hons) DipILM MCLIP, Lib., Cambridgeshire C.C. [0049945] 27/01/1994
Benefield Mrs PM, (was Tuitt), BA DipLib, Dep.Lib., Nat.Foundation for Educ.Res., Slough. [0014914] 01/10/1971
Beney Mr A, BSc(Hons) MA, Lib./Catr., BBC Inf.& Arch. [0055486] 15/10/1997
Beney Mr CM, MCLIP, Asst.Lib., Queen Mary & Westfield Coll., London. [0029366] 08/07/1978

Benfield Miss JC, BA DipInf, Lib., Cultural Services Dept., Norwich. [0045538] 04/03/1991
Benge Mrs ME, (was Thompson), BA MCLIP, Unemployed. [0001120] 01/01/1965
Benge Prof RC, MC MM MA HonFCLIP FCLIP, Resident Overseas, Life Member. [0001121] 24/03/1936 **FE 02/06/1950**
Benham Mrs GM, (was Platt), DipLib MCLIP, Tourist Inf.Asst., Derby Tourist Inf.Cent., Derby City Council. [0029209] 04/04/1978
Benjamin Mr MS, MCLIP, Asst.Lib., S.Grp., Northumberland C.C. [0026279] 12/10/1976
Benjamin Mrs PJ, (was Groves), BA(Hons) MCLIP, Lib., Backwell Sch., Bristol. [0006030] 06/05/1971
Benjamin Mr SA, BA(Hons) MSc MCLIP, Site Lib., Univ.of Bath in Swindon. [0054260] 11/11/1996
Benjamin Miss VC, BA DipLib, Mgr.-Inf.Serv., Wedlake Bell, London. [0036368] 07/10/1983
Benjamin-Coker Mr P, BA(Hons), Asst.Comm.Lib., Hall Green L., Birmingham. [0056542] 13/08/1998
Benjamin-Fast Ms SF, L.Mgr., Liskeard L., Cornwall. [0057255] 02/02/1999 **AF**
Bennell Ms A, BSc(Hons) MSc, Asst.Data Mgr., Freshfields Bruckhaus Deringer, London. [0057295] 21/08/1996
Bennet Miss MJ, BSc(Econ), L.Asst., Jewel & Esk Valley Coll., Dalkeith. [0045381] 01/07/1982
Bennett Mr A, MA MLitt, Lib., Pendlebury L.of Music, Univ.Music Sch., Cambridge. [0039646] 01/04/1986
Bennett Miss ALC, BA(Hons) MA MCLIP, Customer Serv.Lib., Guille-Alles L., St Peter Port, Guernsey. [0052312] 23/10/1995
Bennett Mr C, BA(Hons), Inf.Serv.Mgr., N.Lanarkshire Council, Motherwell. [0030734] 10/04/1979
Bennett Miss CE, BScEcon(Hons), Med.Collections Catg., Univ. of Exeter, Devon. [0058517] 20/07/2000
Bennett Mr CJ, BA MCLIP, Lib., Bank for International Settlements, Switzerland. [0020386] 17/02/1973
Bennett Mrs DA, (was Lowther), MCLIP, Asst.Lib., Nottingham High Sch., Nottingham. [0001129] 11/01/1965
Bennett Miss DE, BA(Hons) MSc, Learning & Teaching Advisor, Faculty of Med.Computing Cent., Newcastle. [0060215] 10/12/2001
Bennett Ms EC, BSc MA, Asst.Lib., Natural Hist.Mus., London. [0054272] 11/11/1996
Bennett Ms EC, BA(Hons) PGDipLib, Spec.Lib.(Child.), Kingston upon Hull City L., Cent.L., Hull. [0035781] 24/01/1983
Bennett Miss FJ, MA DipLib, Employment not known. [0040715] 06/05/1987
Bennett Mrs J, (was Stewart), BA MCLIP, Unemployed. [0036757] 09/11/1983
Bennett Mrs J, BA(Hons) MCLIP, Head of Inf.Serv., Engineering Employers Fed., London. [0037622] 16/10/1984
Bennett Ms JA, (was Johns), MPhil FGS MCLIP, Stud. [0007858] 12/01/1971
Bennett Mr JD, MCLIP, Retired. [0001133] 14/01/1955
Bennett Miss JER, BA(Hons) MA MCLIP, Learning Support Lib., Staffordshire Univ. [0049621] 19/11/1991
Bennett Mr JF, FCLIP, Mgr., Inf.Servs.Unit., E.Sussex C.C., Lewes. [0001135] 28/04/1968 **FE 16/09/1976**
Bennett Miss JJ, Stud., Univ.of Cent.England, Birmingham. [0059595] 26/06/2001
Bennett Mrs JM, (was Newton), Grp.Inf.Support Lib..(job share), Leeds City Council. [0043247] 16/01/1990
Bennett Mrs KG, (was Roberts), Asst.Lib., Darlington L., Darlington Bor.Council. [0042856] 01/04/1989
Bennett Miss LJ, BA(Hons) MCLIP, Cent.L.Mgr., Peterborough City Council, Cent.L. [0045954] 30/07/1991
Bennett Miss MA, BA MCLIP, Asst.Lib., Church End L., L.B.of Barnet. [0039816] 24/07/1986
Bennett Miss MA, BA(Hons), Learning Cent.Mgr., City of Bristol Coll. [0049307] 20/10/1993
Bennett Mrs ME, (was Downward), BA MCLIP, Life Member. [0001139] 17/01/1956
Bennett Mr MR, MCLIP, Retired. [0001141] 25/04/1963
Bennett Mrs MR, (was Grevett), MCLIP, Lib., Stroud Coll.of F.E., Glos. [0005956] 01/01/1970
Bennett Miss MS, BSc, Sen.Lib., L.B.Enfield Leisure Serv., L.Res.Unit. [0056552] 18/08/1998
Bennett Mr MS, BA MA MCLIP, Electronic Publ.Mgr., D.E.F.R.A., Leighton Buzzard. [0043234] 10/10/1989
Bennett Mr MW, BA MCLIP, Lib., Lady Margaret Sch., Hammersmith & Fulham. [0028780] 26/01/1978
Bennett Mr N, BSc DMS MCLIP, H.of Inf.& Cultural Serv., Pembrokeshire Co.Council. [0021935] 29/01/1974
Bennett Miss PA, p./t.Admin.Asst., Academi - The Welsh Academy, Cardiff. [0035212] 06/10/1982
Bennett Mrs PH, (was Reed), BA MCLIP, Unemployed. [0033339] 05/11/1980
Bennett Mr RPW, MCMI MCLIP, Position unknown, Bennett Associates, Chester. [0060520] 11/12/2001
Bennett Mrs S, BA(Hons) DipLib, p./t.Asst.Lib., Stratford upon Avon Coll., Warwickshire. [0051986] 31/08/1995
Bennett Ms S, BA(Hons) MA MCLIP, Lib., Chinese L., Oxford Univ. [0056754] 08/10/1998
Bennett Mr S, Retired. [0060428] 11/12/2001
Bennett Mr SE, BA, L.Asst., Kirklees Cultural Serv., Huddersfield. [0040496] 10/02/1987
Bennett Miss SJ, BA(Hons), Asst.Lib., Chethams Sch.of Music, Manchester. [0061181] 03/04/2002
Bennett Mrs SM, BA MCLIP, Lib., E.Riding of Yourshire Council., York. [0024603] 11/10/1975

Bennett Mrs W, (was Robertson), BA MCLIP, Lend.Serv.Mgr., N.Lanarkshire Council, Cumbernauld. [0029474] 29/07/1978
Bennetts Mr DC, MCLIP, Sen.Lib., Hampshire C.C., Hants. [0019911] 12/01/1973
Bennington Mrs RS, (was May), BA(Hons)DipLib MCLIP, Lib., Prince Henry's High Sch., Evesham. [0026472] 07/10/1976
Bennion Mr WM, FCLIP, Retired. [0001146] 01/01/1950 FE 01/01/1963
Benoy Mrs K, BA MCLIP, p./t.L.Asst., Collenswood Sch., Stevenage. [0034982] 25/05/1982
Benson Mr AS, BA, Unemployed. [0032241] 20/02/1980
Benson Miss JE, B Lib MCLIP, Lib., Brit.Geological Survey, Keyworth, Notts. [0001156] 24/10/1968
Benson Miss JM, BA MCLIP, Retired. [0001157] 28/09/1965
Benson Miss MA, BSc(Hons) MSc MCLIP, Inf.Sci.Mgr., Diabetes UK, London. [0050356] 04/07/1994
Benson Mrs P, Prof.Lib., Off.of the Prime Minister L.Div., Trinidad. [0055721] 11/11/1997
Benson Mr RM, L.& Inf.Asst., Gt.Homer St.Comm.L., Liverpool L.& Inf.Serv. [0026253] 31/08/1965
Benstead Miss K, BA(Hons), Grad.Trainee, The London L. [0059845] 16/10/2001
Benstead Mrs P, (was Marshall), BA MCLIP, Learning Res.Asst., Worcester Coll.Tchnology. [0023479] 01/01/1975
Bent Mrs MJ, (was Gilliland), MA BSc PGDip MCLIP, Sci.Lib., Univ.of Newcastle. [0029170] 29/03/1978
Bentkowski Mr AL, MA, Photo Lib., Royal Anthropological Inst., London. [0058851] 06/09/2000
Bentley Mrs EA, BA MCLIP, Head of Learning Res., Northbrook C.E.Sch., L.B.of Lewisham. [0029008] 08/03/1978
Bentley Mrs JV, BA MA MCLIP, Asst.Lib., Charles Frears Campus, De Montfort Univ., Leicester. [0040672] 13/04/1987
Bentley Mrs M, (was Wolfe), MCLIP, L.Asst., L.B.of Croydon. [0025947] 18/05/1976
Bentley Miss MR, MCLIP, Retired. [0001166] 18/02/1959
Bentley Ms MR, BA(Hons), Stud., Dept.of Inf.Studies, Univ.of Sheffield. [0059013] 25/10/2000
Benton Mr E, MA(Hons), Databases Asst., London Coll.of Fashion L. [0059054] 06/11/2000
Benton Mr TF, BA PG DipLib MCLIP, Bibl.Database Mgr., Wilts.C.C., Dept.of Educ.& L. [0020929] 05/09/1973
Beresford Miss BH, BA(Hons), Asst.Lib., Univ.of Brighton, Aldrich L. [0040087] 24/10/1986
Beresford Mrs LM, Unemployed. [0051603] 06/04/1995
Bergen Ms CL, MA MCLIP DipRSA CertEd, Head of NGFL Contnet, Brit.Educ.Comm.& Tech.Agency, (BECTA). [0026034] 01/07/1976
Bergendorff-Evans Mrs IMC, BA DipLib, Asst.Lib., Univ.of East London. [0041097] 09/10/1987
Berger Mrs RJG, (was Greenwood), Unemployed. [0045829] 21/06/1991
Bergh-Apton Ms EL, (was Robertson Jeffs), MA PgDip HRM MIPD MCLIP, Employment not known. [0060422] 11/12/2001
Bergin Ms CJ, BSc PGDip, Asst.Lib., Wellcome L.for the Hist.&, Understanding of Med., London [0049496] 05/11/1993
Bergin Ms S, BA(Hons), Stud., Univ.of N.London. [0057970] 08/10/1999
Bergna Mrs J, (was Morrell), MCLIP, Life Member. [0001172] 18/04/1943
Bergstrom Miss TJ, BLib MCLIP, Lib., N.Warwicks.& Hinckley Coll., Nuneaton. [0037998] 01/01/1985
Berkeley Mrs J, BA(Hons), Child.Lib., Southampton City Council, Portswood/Shirley Areas. [0054009] 16/10/1996
Berkeley Miss VA, MLS MBIM MCLIP FRSA, Retired. [0001173] 05/07/1961
Berkmen Mrs M, (was Beeley), MCLIP, Asst.Lib., Robert Coll., Istanbul, Turkey. [0017039] 30/01/1960
Bernard Miss MA, BA DipLib MCLIP, L.Offr.:Cent.Serv., Bournemouth Bor.Council. [0032254] 22/02/1980
Bernard Mrs S, (was Mayall), MCLIP, Employer [0009988] 01/01/1971
Bernstein Mrs AJ, MA, Sen.L.Asst., Univ.of Sheffield, Main L. [0058654] 04/05/2000
Berridge Mrs JJ, (was Dobson), BA MCLIP, p./t.L.Asst., Nailsea Grp., N.Somerset. [0027154] 03/02/1977
Berridge Ms PJ, BSc(Hons) MSc MCLIP, LRC Mgr., Warwickshire Coll., Leamington Spa. [0048360] 14/01/1993
Berrieman Mrs S, p./t.Lib., HM Prison Hull, Kingston-upon-Hull City Council. [0059102] 15/11/2000
Berringer Mr RA, BA(Hons) DipILM, Unemployed. [0058857] 07/09/2000
Berry Ms BL, BA, Lib., Royal Coll.of G.P.'s., London. [0046311] 28/10/1991
Berry Ms EH, BA MA, p./t.Stud./Inf.Offr., Univ.of N.London, Hendon Ref.L., Barnet L. [0051526] 21/03/1995
Berry Mrs EJC, MA DipLib MCLIP, Learning Serv.Mgr., Yeovil College. [0019731] 30/10/1970
Berry Miss HE, BA DipLib MCLIP MCIT MILT, Employment Unknown. [0039288] 09/01/1986
Berry Mrs HM, (was Charity), BA PGCE MSc MCLIP, Learning Support Lib., Leeds City L. [0042412] 30/10/1988
Berry Miss IA, MCLIP, Acquisitions Lib., Renfrew Dist. [0031787] 12/12/1979
Berry Mrs J, BA MCLIP, Sen.Lib., Lancs.C.C., S.Lancs.Skelmersdale. [0040192] 04/11/1986
Berry Mrs J, Support Staff, Learning Res., Univ.Coll.Northampton. [0055896] 15/12/1997 AF
Berry Mr JA, BA(Hons) MA MA MCLIP, Inf.Specialist, Cardiff Univ. [0053246] 19/04/1996
Berry Mrs JL, DipLib MCLIP, Adult Stock Lib., Leics.L., Merton L. [0031193] 11/10/1979
Berry Miss JP, BA(Hons) MCLIP, Inf.Mgr., Linklaters & Alliance, London. [0022833] 12/10/1974
Berry Ms K, BA DMS MCLIP, Sen.Team Lib., City of Coventry. [0030539] 13/03/1979

Berry Mrs LS, (was Foster), BA MCLIP, Academic Team Leader, Eagle L.S.& D., Bolton Inst. [0023168] 30/10/1974
Berry Mrs M, (was Sykes), MCLIP, Lib., Brighton & Hove Council, Brighton L. [0026573] 01/10/1976
Berry Mrs NJ, BA(Hons), p./t.Stud./L.Asst., Univ.of Bristol., L.& Learning Cent. [0059260] 23/01/2001
Berry Miss SJ, BA DipLib MCLIP, Cent.Res.Mgr., Clifford Chance LLP, London. [0034235] 15/10/1981
Berry Mr TJ, MCLIP, Special Serv.Lib., Hounslow. [0001188] 01/10/1971
Berry Ms TJ, (was Kent), MA BLib MCLIP, Local Stud.Offr., Oldham Metro.Bor. [0024724] 07/10/1975
Berryman Mr B, BA MCLIP, Inf.Lib., N.Yorks.Co.L., Scarborough. [0001189] 14/09/1960
Berryman Ms GJ, BA DipLib, Unemployed. [0044098] 17/05/1990
Berryman Mrs K, Inf.Cent.Asst., DSTL Porton Down, Salisbury, Wilts. [0058645] 28/04/2000 AF
Bersekowski Miss AK, Bibliotheks-Amtmaennin, Universitaet Hannover, Germany. [0039479] 31/01/1986
Bertoni Mr A, Dir.of L.Serv., Universita Ca'Foscari Di Venezia, Venezia,Italy. [0032785] 17/08/1980
Bertram Mrs CA, (was Spode), BA(Hons) DipTP MCLIP, Retired. [0013833] 01/01/1969
Bertulis Ms RB, BA MCLIP, Sch.Lib., Chiswick Comm.Sch., London. [0037103] 21/02/1984
Berube Ms L, MLS, Co-E.Plus Project Offr., L.& Inf.Serv., Cambridge. [0057383] 24/02/1999
Berwick Mrs J, BA MCLIP, L.Serv.Mgr., CMS Cameron McKenna, London. [0032634] 01/01/1980
Berwick-Sayers Mrs SJ, (was Sargeant), FCLIP, Life Member. [0001193] 01/01/1939 FE 01/01/1948
Besford Mrs D, (was Baker), BA MCLIP, Local Govt.Lib., Knowsley M.B.C., Huyton. [0001194] 13/01/1962
Besson Dr A, PhD DipLib MCLIP, Med.Systems Lib., St.Bartholomews & Royal London Sch., of Med.& Dentistry, London. [0026280] 08/10/1976
Best Mrs AC, (was Foskett), MCLIP, Inf.Offr., BECTA, Coventry. [0005088] 28/09/1971
Best Mr AJ, MCLIP, Life Member. [0001196] 31/01/1949
Best Mr KR, BA MSc, Library Offr., Lincoln Central L., Lincoln. [0057671] 01/07/1999
Best Mr KW, MBE FCLIP, Life Member, Tel.01403 242537. [0001198] 17/01/1949 FE 01/01/1959
Best Miss NL, Sen.L.Asst., Royal Soc.of Chemistry L., London. [0044878] 07/01/1991
Best Miss RM, BA (Hons), Stud./L. Asst., Robert Gordon Univ./Brunel Univ. [0060882] 18/12/2001
Best Mr SJ, MCLIP, Retired, 23 Trentdale Rd., Carlton,Nottingham,NG4 1BU. [0001200] 18/03/1957
Bestel Mrs JS, BA(Hons), p./t.Stud., Brighton Univ. [0059963] 12/11/2001
Beswick Mrs JC, BSc MSc MCLIP, Employment not known. [0060757] 12/12/2001
Beswick Mrs S, BA(Hons) MCLIP, Sen.Lib., Wokingham Dist.Council, Berks. [0049784] 06/12/1993
Betaneur Ms A, Lib., Dept Culture & L., Columbia. [0061573] 02/10/2002
Bethel Ms AC, BSc DipLib, Inf.Cent.Mgr., Environment Agency, Bristol. [0045962] 29/07/1991
Bethel Mrs J, (was Beautement), MCLIP, L.Serv.Mgr., S.Tees Acute Hosp.NHS Trust, Middlesbrough. [0001017] 30/09/1965
Beton Miss H, BA(Hons) MA MCLIP, L.Computing Asst., Canterbury Christ Church Univ.Coll. [0056651] 01/10/1998
Bett Miss NK, BA(Hons) MSc, Learning Resource Co-ord., Breadalbane Academy, Aberfeldy, Perthshire. [0054066] 22/10/1996
Betteridge Mrs JM, MCLIP, Sen.L.Asst.(Job-share), Business & Tech.L., Cent.L., Liverpool. [0025217] 22/12/1975
Bettinson Mrs HR, BSc DipInfSci MCLIP, Sch.Lib., Surrey C.C. [0032704] 08/07/1980
Bettinson Mrs JM, (was Besterfield), BSc, Unemployed. [0049639] 16/11/1993
Bettles Miss ME, BA MCLIP, Systems Lib., Leics Univ.L. [0018072] 02/10/1972
Bettley Dr J, MA PhD MCLIP, Unemployed. [0046892] 28/02/1992
Betts Mr A, BA(Hons) DipLib, Project Offr., St.Bartholomews Hosp. [0048303] 25/11/1992
Betts Mr DA, BA FCLIP, Retired, 5 New Rd., Forest Green, Dorking, Surrey, RH5 5SA. [0001208] 26/02/1958 FE 01/01/1970
Betts Mr N, BA(Hons) MCLIP, Sen.Asst.Lib., Birmingham Coll.of Food L. [0043710] 05/12/1989
Betts Ms S, BSc MSc, Employment unknown. [0060300] 10/12/2000
Betts-Gray Mrs MJF, (was Dunnett), MA MCLIP, Bus.Inf.Specialist, Cranfield Univ., Beds. [0033285] 28/10/1980
Bevan Mr A, MCLIP, Res.& Inf.Offr., An Chomhairle Leabharlanna, L.Council, Dublin. [0001210] 23/01/1967
Bevan Mrs EA, (was Payne), MCLIP, Stock Mgr., Bath, Bath & North E. Somerset. [0011386] 12/01/1971
Bevan Mrs EM, MA, Sen.Asst.Lib., Lytham L., Lancs.Co.L., N.Div. [0058858] 08/09/2000
Bevan Mr NP, BSc MSc DipLib MCLIP, Dep.Lib., Birkbeck Coll., London. [0027891] 01/10/1977
Bevan Mr SJ, BSc(Econ) MA MCLIP, Inf.Systems Mgr., Cranfield Univ. [0040294] 17/11/1986
Beveridge Ms K, DipLIS, Lib., Univ.of Dundee. [0048327] 26/11/1992
Beveridge Mrs PDR, (was Bell), MA MCLIP, Retired. [0023657] 28/01/1975
Beveridge Mr RM, BA(Hons) MCLIP, Sales Training Mgr., The Dialog Corp., London. [0048425] 04/01/1993
Beverley Miss CA, BSc MSc MCLIP, Inf.Offr., Scharr, Univ.of Sheffield. [0055662] 04/11/1997

Personal Members

Beverton Mrs MCI, (was Needes), MSc BA DipLib MCLIP, Retired. [0010702] *11/10/1971*
Bevin Mr DJ, BA(Hons) MA MCLIP, Head Lib., Univ.Cent., Cesar Ritz, Switzerland. [0053773] *01/10/1996*
Bevin Mrs PJ, (was Rye), MA MCLIP, Retired. [0001213] *13/09/1951*
Bevis Mrs CE, BA DipLib, Asst.Lib.-Acquisitions, Royal Coll.of Nursing, London. [0036089] *20/05/1983*
Bevis Mrs J, BA(Hons) MSc MCLIP, Requests Lib.(Inter-L.Loans), Portsmouth City Council, Portsmouth, Hants. [0049582] *19/11/1993*
Bevis Mrs JM, (was Hill), MCLIP, P/t.Team Lib., Somerset C.oL. [0001214] *26/02/1957*
Bevis Mrs SA, (was Hart), Devel.& Inf., Notts.C.C. [0044359] *01/10/1990*
Bewick Miss EN, MCLIP, Life Member. [0001215] *22/03/1937*
Bexon Miss NS, BSc MA, Inf.Serv.Mgr., Inst.of Health Sci., Univ.of Oxford. [0055730] *10/11/1997*
Bhadhal Miss I, BA DipLib MCLIP, Customer Serv.Mgr., Hounslow Cult.& Comm.Serv. [0040074] *25/10/1986*
Bharier Mrs M, MA, Study Researcher, Univ. of London, Inst.of Educ. [0033271] *04/11/1980*
Bharj Mrs JK, DipMgmt, p./t.Stud./Sen.L.Asst., Univ.of N.London, London Guildhall. [0061070] *12/02/2002*
Bhatt Ms AL, MSc BA(Hons), Digital Lib.Offr., Univ.of Cent.England, Birmingham. [0056751] *08/10/1998*
Bhimani Ms N, (was Bhimans), MA MLS, Operational Support Mgr., Univ.of Herts., Hatfield Campus. [0039120] *20/11/1985*
Bhimji Miss AB, Stud. [0048433] *06/01/1993*
Bibb Mrs A, (was Baggott), BA MCLIP, Unemployed. [0000567] *06/01/1964*
Bibby Mrs JM, (was Higgins), MA FCLIP, Life Member. [0001218] *23/03/1943* FE *01/01/1966*
Bickel Mrs RJ, BLib MCLIP BLS, Lib., Hucknall L., Notts.C.C. [0030105] *07/12/1978*
Bickerstaff Mr K, MCLIP, Unemployed. [0044417] *09/10/1990*
Bickerton Mrs DN, (was Watson), BA MCLIP, Life Member. [0028204] *27/08/1977*
Bickerton Mr KTR, BA(Hons), Lib., Instant L., Loughborough. [0052739] *30/11/1995*
Bickerton Mrs M, (was Robertson), BA(Hons), Asst.Lib., Robert Gordon Univ., Aberdeen. [0052695] *23/11/1995*
Bickley Miss AL, BA(Hons) MA MCLIP, Dep.Lib., L., Peter Symonds Coll., Winchester. [0056794] *16/10/1998*
Bicknell Mr DJ, BA MCLIP, Inf.& Heritage Mgr., Barnet. [0001226] *19/05/1967*
Bicknell Mr TA, MCLIP, Life Member. [0001227] *01/01/1951*
Biczysko Ms A, (was Benson), BA MA, Child.Lib., Southampton City Council. [0053617] *12/08/1996*
Biddiscombe Mr R, BA MCLIP, Team Leader, Arts Soc.Sci.& Law, Univ.of Birmingham, Main L. [0001228] *06/01/1966*
Biddle Mrs HE, Stud., Univ. of Cent. England. [0060984] *24/01/2002*
Biddulph-Davies Mrs SK, (was Biddulph), BA MA MSc, Unemployed. [0054787] *01/04/1997*
Bide Mrs RAC, Learning Resources Mgr., Teddington Sch., Middlesex. [0054985] *03/06/1997* **AF**
Bidgood Mrs AM, (was McGregor), BA MCLIP, Lib., Coll.of St.Mark & St.John, Plymouth. [0024028] *02/09/1959*
Bidston Mrs PJ, (was Harvey), BA MCLIP, Sen.Team Lib., Glos.C.C. [0021833] *12/02/1974*
Bidwell Mr MR, MA, Researcher, Lowestoft Heritage Cent., Suffolk. [0044307] *23/08/1990*
Bienek Ms J, BA MCLIP, Sen.Lib.,Ref.& Inf., Shropshire C.C. [0024878] *25/10/1975*
Bierman Mrs V, (was Hargreaves), Book Consultant, Self-Employed, Edinburgh. [0023886] *01/01/1957*
Bigford Mrs VR, (was Bristow), MSc BA MCLIP, Learning Resources Mgr., Wolverhampton Coll., W.Midlands. [0027751] *04/08/1977*
Bigger Mr CJ, BSc MCLIP, Inf.Offr., Inst.of Electrical Engineers, London. [0023245] *08/11/1974*
Biggins Mr A, BSc MCLIP, Lib., Inst.of Latin American Studies, Univ.of London. [0001233] *18/01/1972*
Biggins Mrs J, (was Mccaig), BA MCLIP, Area L.& Inf.Mgr.(E.), Newcastle L.& Inf.Serv., Newcastle-Upon-Tyne. [0018502] *08/03/1966*
Biggs Miss HC, BA(Hons) MCLIP, Lib., NIACE, Nat.Inst.of Adult Cont.Educ. [0049890] *12/01/1994*
Biggs Miss PE, BSc DipLib MCLIP, Dep.Lib., Nat.Inst.Med.Res., London. [0036331] *05/10/1983*
Biggs Mrs PT, (was Torr), FCLIP, Life Member, Tel.01865 556481, 35 Ritchie Crt., 380 Banbury Rd., Oxford, OX1 7PW. [0001240] *01/01/1959* FE *18/06/1986*
Biggs Ms SM, BA DipLib MCLIP, Sen.Inf.Offr., Greater London Auth. [0026937] *12/01/1977*
Biggs Mrs SP, Sch.Lib., W.Derby Comp.Sch., Liverpool City Co. [0057863] *14/09/1999*
Biglou Ms LSJ, MA DipLib MCLIP, Dir., Brit.Council, Kiev, Ukraine. [0039453] *31/01/1986*
Bignell Mr AP, BA DipLib MCLIP, L.Inf.Serv.Mgr., Herts.C.C. [0031564] *20/11/1979*
Bignold Mrs HDN, (was Craig), BLib MCLIP, Prof.Relief Lib./Sch.Lib., Dorset Co.L.Serv.& Poole B.C., Clayesmore Prep.Sch., Blandford. [0038331] *08/03/1985*
Bignold Mrs J, BA, Sch.Lib., New Hall Sch., Essex. [0054586] *04/02/1997* **AF**
Biles Mrs KA, BA MCLIP, Unemployed. [0022891] *08/08/1974*
Bilkhu Mrs PK, (was Phull), BA MCLIP, Self-employed. [0029528] *28/07/1978*
Billett Mrs EM, MCLIP, Child.& Young Peoples Lib., Kettering L., Northants. [0021253] *15/10/1973*
Billing Mrs C, (was Hall), MCLIP, Prison Lib., H.M.P.Haverigg, Cumbria. [0006127] *01/01/1972*

Billingham Miss JA, MCLIP, Retired. [0001246] *14/03/1963*
Billingham Ms LK, (was Hutchinson), BSc MCLIP, L.System Mgr., L.Sch.of Economics, London. [0041042] *01/10/1987*
Billings Ms KA, (was Billings Phillips), BSc MCLIP Mild, Educ.Offr., Brit.Educ.Comms.& Tech.Agency, Sci.Park, Milburn Hill, Coventry. [0034685] *26/01/1982*
Billings Mr RD, L.Asst., The Brit.L., London. [0046209] *10/10/1991* **AF**
Billington Mr AR, MCLIP, Life Member. [0001248] *10/03/1948*
Billington Mr MB, BA(Hons) DipILS MCLIP, Bibl.Asst., John Rylands Univ.L., Univ.of Manchester. [0048005] *02/11/1992*
Billot Miss MM, BA, Retired. [0001251] *01/01/1966*
Bilson Mrs J, (was Ashenden), BA MCLIP, Literature Res.Assoc., Merck Sharp Dohme Res.Labs., Neuroscience Res.Cent., Harlow. [0035673] *01/01/1983*
Bilton Mrs H, (was Pickup), MA, Stud., City Univ., & Inf.Offr., St Mungo's London. [0056417] *06/07/1998*
Bilton Miss RA, BLib MCLIP, Stock Devel.Lib., Herts.L.Serv., Welwyn Garden City. [0039422] *24/01/1986*
Bilton-Roos Mrs C, (was Roos), BA, L.Clerk., Lovells, London. [0059064] *07/11/2000*
Binding Miss SL, H.of Inf., Eversheds, London. [0036942] *18/01/1984*
Bing Ms PA, BA(Hons), Stud., Univ.Sheffield. [0059928] *06/11/2001*
Bingham Miss HE, BSc MSc MCLIP, L.Serv.Mgr., Portsmouth Hosp.NHS Trust. [0039256] *12/01/1986*
Bingley Mr CH, MA HonFCLIP, Publisher. [0031194] *30/09/1971* FE *10/09/1986*
Binnie Mrs JG, (was Blakebell), MA(Hons) DipLib, Univ.Lib., Univ.of Wollongong, Dubai. [0035583] *03/11/1982*
Binns Mrs CA, MCLIP, Lib.:Child.Serv.& Xchange, Bradford Cent.L. [0032232] *01/01/1963*
Binns Mr NE, FCLIP, Life Member. [0001261] *19/10/1933* FE *01/01/1949*
Birbeck Mr VP, BA(Hons) MPhil MCLIP, Nat.L.& Inf.Serv.Mgr., Environment Agency, Solihull. [0034645] *21/01/1982*
Birch Mr JL, B LIB MCLIP, Ch.Lib., Off.for Nat.Statistics, London. [0033209] *22/10/1980*
Birch Mrs M, (was Bayliss), BA MCLIP, Head of Tech.Serv., Inst.of Advanced Legal Studies. [0000962] *10/10/1968*
Birch Mrs PA, MCLIP, Lib., Cambs.C.C., Cambridge. [0015968] *10/08/1970*
Birch Mrs S, (was Lancaster), MCLIP, P./t.Filing Clerk, High St.Med.Partners, Hythe, Kent. [0008608] *10/01/1972*
Birch Mrs S, (was Martin), MCLIP, Life Member. [0001270] *17/10/1944*
Birch Mrs VH, (was Morrell), BLib MCLIP, Lib., Herts.C.C. [0034934] *29/04/1982*
Birch Ms ZE, BA(Hons) MA, Asst.Lib., English Nature, Peterborough. [0058929] *06/10/2000*
Birchall Miss AG, MCLIP, Business Analyst, Foster Wheeler Energy Ltd., Reading. [0001272] *27/01/1970*
Birchenall Mr DJ, MA(Hons) MSc, Lib., The Internat.Sch.of the Regents, Thailand. [0054101] *28/10/1996*
Birchenough Mrs J, (was Lamb), BA MCLIP, Retired. [0008577] *17/02/1959*
Birchmore Mrs J, BA MCLIP, Area Co-ordinator, Notts.C.C. [0028261] *18/10/1977*
Bird Mrs A, p./t.Stud./Br.Lib., Univ.of Wales, Aberystwyth, Treorchy L., Rhondda. [0059379] *23/02/2001*
Bird Mrs B, (was Lee), BEd DipLIS MCLIP, Career Break. [0049392] *21/10/1993*
Bird Mrs CA, (was Brunt), Lib.Mgr., Parkside Community Coll., Cambridge. [0045519] *28/02/1991* **AF**
Bird Miss EA, MA MCLIP, Retired. [0001281] *13/01/1970*
Bird Mrs EM, (was Jones), MCLIP, Life Member, 8 Langham Dr., Burton Joyce, Nottingham,NG14 5EJ, 0115 931 2316. [0001282] *27/09/1944*
Bird Mrs EM, (was Tappenden), BSc(Hons), L.& Inf.Cent.Mgr., Bristows, London. [0050069] *21/01/1994*
Bird Ms HA, BA MCLIP, Lib., Memery Crystal, London. [0036839] *10/01/1984*
Bird Ms JJ, MA DipLib MCLIP, Res.Matters Mgr., Sandwell M.B.C., Oldbury. [0041565] *28/01/1988*
Bird Miss JV, BSc DipLib MCLIP, Reading Room Serv.Lib., NERC-Brit.Geological Survey, Nottingham. [0031728] *05/11/1979*
Bird Mrs MP, (was Martin), MCLIP, LRC Mgr., Wolstanton High Sch., Newcastle. [0024903] *17/10/1975*
Bird Mrs S, BSc MCLIP, Asst.Lib., St.John Fisher R.C.High Sch., Harrogate. [0027800] *05/08/1977*
Bird Ms SM, BA MSc MCLIP, L.& Learning Cent.Mgr., Brookesby Melton Coll. [0042681] *09/02/1989*
Birdsall Mrs D, (was Chalk), BA (Hons) MCLIP, Law Subject Lib., London Guildhall Univ. [0029017] *13/03/1978*
Birk Mrs CE, (was Warnett), BA MCLIP, Unemployed. [0015389] *14/01/1969*
Birkby Mrs AE, (was Rowley), BA FCLIP, Life Member. [0001292] *03/10/1957* FE *01/01/1962*
Birkenhead Mr G, BA(Hons) MSc MCLIP, Policy & Res.Offr., SCOPE, Nottingham. [0048950] *03/08/1993*
Birkinshaw Miss AD, BA DipLib MCLIP, Acting Princ.L.Offr., Wester Hailes L., Edinburgh City L. [0039147] *12/11/1985*
Birks Ms JA, BA MCLIP, Academic Liaison Lib., Anglia Polytechnic Univ., Cambridge. [0024933] *01/10/1975*
Birley Mr RJ, BA(Hons), Stud., Univ.of Cent.England, Birmingham. [0061103] *22/02/2002*
Birnie Miss SE, Stud., Queen Margaret Univ.Coll. [0059502] *24/04/2001*
Birse Ms SD, (was Tagi), BSc(Hons) MLIM MCLIP, Res.Cent.Co-ordinator, Baldragon Academy. [0053478] *01/07/1996*
Birtle Mrs A, (was Costello), MCLIP, Learning Resources Offr., Durham Constabulary, Durham. [0003188] *15/01/1971*
Birtwhistle Mrs JM, BA(Hons) MA DipIM MCLIP, Registrar & H.of I.T., Royal Naval Museum, Portsmouth, Hants. [0055664] *07/11/1997*

Birtwistle Mrs JL, (was Austin), BA MCLIP, Asst.Lib., Bucks.C.C. [0027876] 12/10/1977
Bishop Mrs AR, (was Hicks), BA MCLIP, p./t.Sch.Lib., Chatham House Grammar Sch., Ramsgate. [0006836] 02/01/1969
Bishop Mr BE, BA MCLIP, Retired. [0018504] 25/09/1950
Bishop Mr GBA, MCLIP, Lib., Lambeth P.L. [0001305] 08/11/1966
Bishop Miss J, BA(Hons), Customer Serv.Consultant, Sirsi Ltd., Potters Bar. [0050790] 18/10/1994
Bishop Miss J, BA MCLIP, Lib., Essex C.C., Braintree. [0029583] 12/10/1978
Bishop Ms JA, BA(Hons), Duty Editor, BBC Monitoring Customer Serv.Unit, Reading. [0061089] 04/03/2002 **SP**
Bishop Mr JD, BSc MCLIP, Sen.Sci.Off., Building Res.Establishment, Garston. [0001306] 28/10/1971
Bishop Mrs JE, (was Dickinson), Lib., Kingston-upon-Hull City Council. [0047134] 06/05/1992
Bishop Mr PJ, BSc(Hons) MCLIP, Catr., Brit.L., Boston Spa. [0049429] 27/10/1993
Bishop Mrs RA, BA DipLib, Sen.Lib., Home Off., London. [0043216] 05/10/1989
Bishop Ms S, MCLIP, Employment not known. [0060193] 10/12/2001
Bishop Mr TAJ, BA MA, Sen.Lib.(Inf.Serv.), Royal Coll.of Surgeons L., London. [0049230] 14/10/1993
Bishop Mr TD, BA DMS MCLIP, Sen.Asst.Lib., Doncaster Coll. [0001313] 06/01/1972
Bisiker Miss PE, MCLIP, Retired. [0001315] 27/01/1957
Bisnath Mrs VE, (was Brown), MCLIP, Sen.Lib., Carmarthen & Dist.NHS Trust, Derwen NHS Trust, W.Wales. [0001937] 19/09/1963
Bissels Mr GJ, MA MA, Lib./Inf.Specialist, Richmond American Internat.Univ., London. [0057310] 12/02/1999
Bisset Mr DW, MCLIP FSA, Unemployed. [0001316] 05/02/1957
Bisson Mrs A, (was Higginbottom), MCLIP, Lib., Townsend C.of E.Sch., Herts. [0001318] 27/03/1957
Bithell Miss CJ, BSc MSc(Econ) MCLIP, Unemployed. [0054630] 12/02/1997
Bithell Mrs CM, (was Illingworth), MCLIP, Team Lib., Leics.L. [0007584] 06/01/1972
Bitner Mrs IK, (was Mcconnachie), MA MCLIP, Life Member. [0016617] 15/01/1953
Black Mr ADL, LLB DipLib MCLIP, Branch Lib., L.B.of Redbridge. [0040398] 22/01/1987
Black Miss AJ, BA MCLIP, Corp.Finance Inf.Off.Mgr., Clifford Chance, London. [0036146] 02/07/1983
Black Dr AM, BA MA DipLib PhD, Prof.of L.&Inf.History, Sch.of Inf.Mgmnt.,Leeds Metro.Univ., Beckett Park. [0035918] 25/02/1983
Black Mrs BHR, BA(Hons) PGCE MCLIP MA, Bus.Mgr., Tech.Support Serv., Renny's Lane Indust.Est., Durham. [0041446] 01/01/1988
Black Ms EP, MA, Team Lib.(Job Share), Aberdeen City Council. [0052971] 06/02/1996
Black Dr FA, BEd MLIS PhD, Asst.Prof., Dalhousie Univ., Nova Scotia. [0061294] 14/05/2002
Black Mrs FJ, (was Steven), BA DipEdTech DipCG(HE) MCLIP, Careers Adviser, Univ.of Glasgow. [0032779] 23/08/1980
Black Miss FM, (was Gibbs), BA(Hons) MCLIP, p./t.Systems Engineer, EDS Defence Ltd., Hook, Hants. [0035665] 01/01/1983
Black Mr GH, BA(Hons), Sen.L.Asst., Jordanhill L., Univ.of Strathclyde. [0058055] 21/10/1999
Black Mrs JA, (was Jackson), BA, Sch.Lib., Intake High Sch.& Arts Coll., Leeds. [0042828] 10/03/1989
Black Miss JM, Learning Res.Mgr., IBM UK Ltd., Greenock. [0044533] 23/10/1990
Black Miss JM, BA MCLIP, Team Lib., Coventry City L. [0001330] 12/01/1972
Black Miss KJ, BA(Hons), L.Asst., Glasgow Univ., St.Andrews Campus L. [0059467] 03/04/2001
Black Ms L, (was Burton), BA MCLIP, Lend.Serv.Mgr., Bristol City Council. [0026693] 17/11/1974
Black Ms M, PGDipLib, Lib., Islington L.& Inf.Serv. [0034795] 08/02/1982
Black Ms MA, MLib MCLIP, Faculty Lib., Univ.of the W.of England, Bristol. [0001331] 18/02/1966
Black Ms MP, (was Leo), BLib DipLib MCLIP, Freelance. [0040971] 01/10/1987
Black Dr MW, BA(Hons) PhD, p./t.ICT Advisory Serv., Web Designer, Stockport Educ.Auth. [0054753] 01/04/1997
Black Miss S, BSc DipLIS MCLIP, Asst.Lib., L.B.of Redbridge, Ilford. [0044460] 10/10/1990
Blackbourn Mrs SE, (was Parrott), BLib MCLIP, Unwaged. [0039504] 11/02/1986
Blackburn Miss A, MCLIP, Asst.Lib., Barnsley Cent.L., Barnsley Bor.Council. [0001336] 05/01/1970
Blackburn Mr D, MCLIP, Retired. [0060145] 10/12/2001
Blackburn Mrs HM, BA(Hons) MCLIP, Head Lib., Alder Hey Hosp., Liverpool. [0052755] 06/12/1995
Blackburn Ms JA, BA PGCE DipLib, Knowledge Mgr.-Clinical Support, Maidstone & Tunbridge Wells NHS T., Tunbridge Wells, Kent. [0041476] 01/01/1988
Blackburn Mrs JY, (was Wicks), MCLIP, Sch.Lib., Penwortham Girls High Sch., Preston, Lancs. [0001339] 01/01/1961
Blackburn Mrs M, (was Young), BA MCLIP, Retired. [0016467] 01/01/1970
Blackburn Mrs ME, Stud., Manchester Met.Univ. [0059136] 22/11/2000
Blackburn Mrs NA, MA BA MCLIP, L.Services Mgr., Blackpool Victoria Hospital, NHS Trust. [0028502] 11/01/1978
Blackett Mr DJ, BA MCLIP, Bibl.Serv.Mgr., Lancs.Co.L. [0018507] 28/08/1972
Blackett Mrs S, (was Parker), BA(Hons) MCLIP, Trust Lib., N.Durham Health Care NHS Trust, Durham. [0050847] 07/06/1993
Blackett Mrs SD, (was Taylor), MCLIP, Sch.Lib., Perth & Kinross Council, Blairgowrie, Perthshire. [0014463] 18/11/1968
Blackhurst Miss A, LLB(Hons) MPhil, Inf.& Marketing Asst., Connexions Cheshire & Warrington, Northwich, Cheshire. [0059203] 08/01/2001

Blackhurst Mrs JK, (was Holden), MA(Hons) MA MCLIP, Asst.Lib., Girton Coll., Univ.of Cambridge. [0053983] 15/10/1996
Blackley Mrs IJ, (was Chambers), MCLIP, Team Lib., Surrey C.C., Redhill, Surrey. [0022099] 29/01/1974
Blacklock Miss LS, BA(Hons), Stud., Northumbria Univ. [0061695] 21/10/2002
Blackman Mrs AJ, (was Coker), BA(Hons) MCLIP, Campus Co-Ordinator, Seale Haynes, Univ.Plymouth. [0001345] 16/01/1970
Blackman Mr MJR, BSc CChem MRSC MCLIP, Retired. [0060791] 12/12/2001
Blackmoor Mrs CE, BA(HOns) CertEd, Sch.Lib., Kingsmead High Sch., Cannock. [0058878] 28/09/2000
Blackmore Ms AM, L.Mgr., Dorchester, Dorset C.C. [0045136] 18/07/1990 **AF**
Blackmore Mr TC, MCLIP, Head of L's., Isle of Wight Council, Newport. [0001349] 28/07/1970
Blackshaw Mrs GM, MCLIP, Parish Clerk, Chalgrove Parish Council, Oxon. [0003458] 01/01/1967
Blackshaw Mr LR, Resources & Inf.Serv.Offr., N.Notts.Health Promotion, Kirkby in Ashfield. [0043900] 15/02/1990
Blackwell Mrs F, (was Hoddinott), MCLIP, Life Member. [0001352] 01/01/1933
Blackwell Ms K, BA(Hons), p./t.Stud./Issue Desk Super., Univ.of N.London, St.Georges Med.Sch., London. [0061408] 10/07/2002
Blackwell Mrs ML, (was Moore), BA MCLIP, General L.Asst., L.B.of Ealing, Cent.L. [0024767] 07/10/1975
Blackwood Ms RI, BSc(Econ)(Hons) MCLIP, Asst.Lib., Davis, Langdon & Everest, London. [0051181] 23/11/1994
Bladen Mr R, BA MCLIP, Lib., Manchester P.L. [0001356] 18/09/1965
Blagbrough Mrs HP, (was Briggs), BSc DipLib MCLIP, Princ.Offr.(Job-Share), N.Dist.L., Manchester L.& Theatres. [0030367] 26/01/1979
Blagbrough Miss S, BA(Hons) DipILS MCLIP, p./t.Asst.Lib., Liverpool Hope Univ.Coll. [0044535] 23/10/1990
Blagden Mr JF, MA MCLIP, Retired. [0001359] 28/02/1955
Blagden Mrs PE, (was Halsall), BA MA DipLib CertEd MCLIP, L.Devel.Facilitator, St.Mary's Hosp., Portsmouth. [0026970] 10/01/1977
Blagg Ms EJ, MSc, Enquiry Desk Mgr., DFES, London. [0052354] 26/10/1995
Blain Mr PJC, BA CPE, Inf.Offr., Freshfields, London. [0056140] 05/03/1998
Blaine Mrs J, (was Walker), MCLIP, Sch.Lib., Wolverhampton M.B.C., W.Midlands. [0015227] 21/01/1969
Blair Mrs CL, (was Powell), BA(Hons) MA MCLIP, Asst.Lib., Prince Consort's L., Hants. [0044868] 02/01/1991
Blair Miss CM, MCLIP, Lib., Glasgow P.L. [0001363] 04/01/1967
Blair Ms CM, BA DipLib MCLIP, L.Exec., Ref.& Reader Serv., House of Commons L. [0038952] 21/10/1985
Blair Miss EH, MA(Hons) MSc MCLIP, Mailbase User Grp.Support Offr., Univ.of Newcastle. [0048083] 03/11/1992
Blair Miss J, DipLib MCLIP, Div.Lib., S.Educ.& L.Board, N.Ireland. [0001367] 01/01/1969
Blair Mrs KM, BA(Hons), Unemployed. [0053978] 15/10/1996
Blair Miss TM, BSc DipLib MCLIP, L.Offr., Stockbridge L., City of Edinburgh Council. [0048100] 09/11/1992
Blair Kavanagh Ms JM, (was Blair), MCLIP, Team Lib., Glasgow City Council, Mitchell L. [0030601] 12/03/1979
Blair Rains Mrs HK, MCLIP, Life Member. [0001369] 01/01/1942
Blaisdale Miss JM, BA MCLIP, Head of L.& Arts, N.Yorks.C.C., L.H.Q. [0031568] 24/10/1979
Blake Miss BR, BA MA, Stud., City University London. [0061797] 13/11/2002
Blake Mr DS, BA MSc DipLib MCLIP, Lib., Commonwealth Secretariat. [0030108] 15/01/1979
Blake Mrs FM, (was Smith), BEd DipLib MCLIP, Housewife. [0033348] 11/11/1980
Blake Mr JA, BSc DipLib DipEdTech MCLIP, Team Leader(Comm.L.Serv.), Clackmannanshire L., Alloa. [0032870] 06/10/1980
Blake Mrs JE, (was Bayly), BA MCLIP, Operations Mgr.(Job Share), S.Somerset. [0029144] 20/04/1978
Blake Mr JM, BLib MCLIP, Dep.LIS Mgr., Barking Coll., Romford. [0031198] 08/10/1979
Blake Mrs MA, (was Whitney), BA MCLIP, Lect., Knowsley Comm.Coll., Kirkby. [0015774] 17/01/1972
Blake Mrs ME, (was Cutting), BA MCLIP, Unemployed. [0028284] 07/11/1977
Blake Ms MM, BA DipInfSc FCLIP MA, Information Consultant, Self-employed. [0057480] 06/04/1999 **FE 01/04/2002**
Blake Ms P, Temp.Worker. [0050128] 06/04/1994
Blake Mr PG, BA, Stud., Loughborough Univ. [0059982] 15/11/2001
Blake Mr PSP, BLib MCLIP, Sen.Lib., New Milton L., Hants.Co.L. [0031744] 09/12/1979
Blake Mrs SA, (was Clarke), MCLIP, Prison Lib., HMP Ford, W.Sussex C.C. [0018042] 08/10/1972
Blakeley Mrs AE, (was Armitage), BA MCLIP DMS, Area Lib.-Batley/Cleckheaton, Kirklees Cult.Serv., Huddersfield. [0026035] 07/06/1976
Blakeman Miss KH, BSc DipInfSc FCLIP, Position unknown, RBA Inf.Serv., Caversham. [0060146] 10/12/2001 **FE 01/04/2002**
Blaker Mrs CJ, MCLIP, Res.Cent.Mgr., Spen Valley High Sch., Kirklees M.C. [0012963] 01/01/1976
Blakeway Ms AJ, BA(Hons) DipLib, Inf.Asst., Local Stud.L., Hants.Co.L. [0025221] 05/01/1976
Blakeway Miss J, BA MCLIP, Data Support Offr., S.Lanarkshire Council, Hamilton. [0021397] 01/11/1973
Blakey Mrs NRM, BA MCLIP, Research Mgr., Acquisitions Monthly, Tunbridge Wells. [0001376] 29/09/1971
Blakey-Lodge Ms PP, BA(Hons), Unemployed. [0049956] 02/02/1994
Blanch Miss SL, BA(Hons) DipILM, Inf.Offr., Halliwell Landau, Manchester. [0055341] 01/10/1997
Blanco Ms CP, BSc(Hons), Analyst/Abstractor, Edmerk. [0059471] 04/04/2001

Personal Members

Bland Mr JA, MLS MCLIP, Life Member. [0001382] 21/03/1957
Blandford Miss FM, BA MCLIP, Life Member. [0001383] 07/10/1948
Blandford Miss SL, MCLIP, Retired. [0001384] 14/09/1949
Blanks Ms JD, BA(Hons) DipLIS MCLIP, Med.Lib., Barking, Havering & Redbridge NHS. [0046799] 30/01/1992
Blankson-Hemans Ms EA, BA(Hons) DipLib MCLIP, Mgr.,Inf.Professional Devel., Dialog Corp., London. [0042324] 20/10/1988
Blanshard Miss AC, BA MCLIP, Ch.Lib., Leeds L.& Inf.Serv. [0025489] 20/01/1976
Blaxter Mrs EA, (was Wood), BA(Hons) MA MCLIP, Sen.Lib., Univ.of Strathclyde, Glasgow. [0041096] 06/10/1987
Blaylock Ms J, MSc(Econ), Unemployed. [0054092] 25/10/1996
Bleakley Mrs C, (was Luff), MCLIP, Catg.Asst., Gloucestershire Records Off. [0020551] 02/04/1973
Bleasdale Dr CH, MA AIRT MCLIP, Retired. [0001387] 03/09/1950
Bleasdale Mrs F, (was O'Brien), BA MCLIP, Learning Resources Mgr., Aquinas Sixth Form Coll., Stockport. [0039701] 20/05/1986
Bleathman Mrs KM, (was Runciman), BA(Hons) MCLIP, Asst.Lib., UWE, Bristol. [0031476] 29/09/1979
Blewett Mrs CA, (was Pater), DipLib MCLIP, Career Break. [0032147] 16/01/1980
Blewitt Mr RM, L.Asst., Birkbeck Coll., Univ.of London. [0059218] 09/01/2001
Bley Mr RS, BA DipLib MCLIP, Sales Mgr.-E-Access Solutions, Swets Blackwell, Abingdon. [0041447] 01/01/1988
Blinko Mr BB, MA MCLIP, Asst.Lib., Univ.of Westminster. [0048387] 17/12/1992
Blishen Ms SJ, Educ. Projects Mgr., The Paul Hamlyn Foundation, London. [0060996] 28/01/2002
Bliss Miss AM, MA MCLIP, Retired. [0016622] 07/10/1963
Bliss Mrs MM, (was Proctor), MCLIP, Life Member, Tel.01223 843601, 4 Spinney Dr., Gt.Shelford, Cambridge, CB2 5LY. [0001392] 11/02/1948
Blizzard Mr A, BA MCLIP CertEd, Head of L.& Inf.Serv., Cowes High Sch., I.O.W. [0028504] 16/01/1978
Blockwell Miss HA, MA, Stud. [0059675] 25/07/2001
Blood Mrs C, (was Mallender), BA DipLib MCLIP, Learning Res.Mgr., Longslade Comm.Coll., Leicester. [0024194] 01/05/1975
Bloom Mr N, BA(Hons), Sen.Inf.Offr., Learning & Skills Devel.Agency, London. [0047561] 01/10/1992
Bloomfield Mrs GMN, (was Pinho), BA, Asst. Mgr., Westminster Kingsway Coll., London. [0041689] 08/02/1988
Bloomfield Mr MA, BA MCLIP, Life Member. [0001400] 03/10/1968
Bloomfield Mrs SA, BSc Dip Lib MCLIP, Info.Lib., St.Albans Cent.L., Herts.C.C. [0022272] 01/03/1974
Bloor Mr PN, BA(Hons), Rec.Mgr., Brit.C., Manchester. [0055576] 21/10/1997
Blott Mrs JS, (was Westcott), MCLIP, Unemployed. [0030292] 05/12/1978
Blount Miss MN, MA DipLib FCLIP, Life Member, 58,St Pancras Rd., Lewes, E.Sussex. [0001402] 11/01/1952 FE 01/01/1965
Blow Miss JA, BA MCLIP, Life Member. [0001404] 20/09/1954
Blower Mr AV, BA(Hons) DipHE MCLIP, ILC Serv.Mgr., Ministry of Defence HQ L., London. [0039212] 01/01/1986
Blower Mrs ME, MCLIP, Sch. Lib., St.Albans High Sch. [0001406] 01/01/1965
Blows Ms S, DipIS MCLIP, L.Mgr., Suffolk C.C. [0046210] 10/10/1991
Bloxham Ms HA, MCLIP, L.Mgr., UKAEA, Fusion L., Oxon. [0021861] 04/02/1974
Bluck Mrs S, (was Knight), BA MCLIP, Unemployed (Housewife). [0031650] 12/11/1979
Blue Mr CH, BA(Hons), Asst.Lib., Barlow Lyde & Gilbert, London. [0059327] 07/02/2001
Bluhm Mr RK, FCLIP, Life Member. [0001410] 31/03/1955 FE 01/01/1968
Blundell Miss C, MCLIP, Retired. [0001411] 26/10/1970
Blundell Mrs L, (was Rounsevell), BA MCLIP, Asst.Dir.-L.& Arch., Corp.of London. [0012723] 23/03/1967
Blundell Mrs PM, (was Hopkins), Housewife. [0051528] 28/03/1995
Blundell Mr SRA, BA DipLib MCLIP, Lib., The Reform Club, London. [0039785] 12/07/1986
Blundell Mr TE, L.Asst., Midlothian Council, L.H.Q.-Loanhead. [0046772] 22/01/1992 **AF**
Blunden Mr AJ, BSc MCLIP, Employment not known. [0060144] 10/12/2001
Blunden Mr D, BA(Hons), Stud., Univ.of Sheffield. [0061814] 11/11/2002
Blunt Mrs A, (was Howlett), BA(Hons), Asst.Lib., Univ.of the W.of England. [0057717] 06/07/1999
Blunt Mr P, MSc HonFCLIP, Princ.Educ.Offr.-Prison Serv., Home Off., HMP Leyhill, CEO Br.Area Off., Glos. [0050581] 22/09/1994 FE 22/09/1994
Blysniuk Mrs JA, (was Taylor), BA MCLIP, Sen.Lib., Lancs.C.C. [0032195] 25/01/1980
Blyth Mr JGW, BA MCLIP, Unemployed. [0001416] 04/07/1972
Blyth Mr JM, BA(Hons) MCLIP, Lib., Hackney Comm.Coll., London. [0022242] 05/03/1974
Blyth Mrs KA, (was Ellis), BA(Hons) MA MCLIP, Sen.Team Leader, Warwickshire C.C., Stratford L. [0055685] 04/11/1997
Blyth Ms SJ, BA MSc MCLIP, System Admin./Helpdesk Coordinator, BAR Systems (Avionic Systems), Edinburgh. [0020222] 06/02/1973
Blythe Mrs C, (was Williams), MCLIP, Retired. [0001420] 13/02/1958
Boadi Dr BY, PhD MLS MCLIP, Sen.Lect., Dept.of L.& Inf.Studies, Univ.of Botswana, Gaborone. [0025193] 02/01/1978
Boagey Mr PW, MSc MCLIP, Asst.Lib., Hartley L., Univ.of Southampton. [0001421] 14/01/1971
Boal Mrs C, (was Clark), BA MCLIP, Res.Cent.Mgr., City of Edinburgh Council. [0034605] 19/01/1982
Boal Miss HM, BSc(Hons) DipLIS MCLIP, Neighbourhood Lib., Bristol City Council, Horfield L. [0043375] 16/10/1989

Boanas Mrs AE, (was Hendler), BA MCLIP, Lib.(Bibl.Serv.), Carcroft L.H.Q., Doncaster M.B.C. [0038475] 26/04/1985
Boardman Mrs F, (was Glass), BA(Hons) MA, Unemployed. [0050785] 18/10/1994
Boateng Miss AK, BA, Graduate Trainee, Employment Unknown. [0061482] 14/08/2002
Boateng Mrs RM, (was Robinson), BA FCLIP, Life Member. [0016625] 01/01/1961 FE 04/09/1978
Bobby Ms JL, Br.L.Mgr., Earlsdon L., Coventry. [0053425] 07/05/1996 **AF**
Bock Mrs JP, (was Smith), MCLIP, Prison L.Serv.Asst., Durham C.C. [0016626] 23/09/1962
Bocking Miss M, BSc(Econ) MCLIP, Life Member. [0001427] 15/03/1955
Boddington Miss SK, BA MCLIP, Comm.Lib., Wilts.L.& Heritage. [0001428] 01/01/1968
Boden Mrs C, (was Evans), MCLIP, Welsh Materials Lib., City & Co.of Cardiff. [0022803] 09/10/1974
Boden Mrs DJ, BA(Hons) DipLIS MA MCLIP ILT, Health Studies Serv.Mgr., Univ.of Luton. [0055272] 11/09/1997
Boden Ms SM, (was Parker), BA MCLIP, Head of Policy & Planning, Cultural Serv., Norfolk C.C. [0036664] 31/10/1983
Bodey Mrs GM, BEd AALIA MCLIP, Area Mgr.(W.), W.Lothian Council. [0056545] 18/08/1998
Bodian Mrs MT, (was Murphy), BSc MCLIP, Postion unknown, Building Research Estab.L., Watford. [0060561] 11/12/2001
Boeg Mr NP, BA MA MCLIP, Resident in U.S.A. [0046581] 20/11/1991
Boehme Miss AM, DipLib MA, Head of Music, Nat.L.of Scotland, Edinburgh. [0049710] 25/11/1993
Boffa Mr JM, FCLIP, Lib., Nat.L.of Malta. [0021759] 07/01/1974 FE 15/12/1981
Boggust Mrs CJ, (was Thomsen), BA(Hons) MCLIP, Self-employed. [0042261] 13/10/1988
Bogle Mrs AR, (was Clapham), MA DipLib MCLIP, Asst.Lib., Scottish Health Serv.Cent., Edinburgh. [0040112] 18/10/1986
Bogle Dr KR, MA MCLIP PhD, Res.Off., City of Edinburgh Council, Edinburgh. [0041244] 11/10/1987
Bolam Miss FJ, BA(Hons) MLib, Sch.Lib., Sheffield City Council. [0058188] 15/11/1999
Boland Miss J, BA(Hons), Asst.Subject Advisor, Univ.of Derby. [0051678] 09/05/1995
Boler Mrs JS, BA(Hons) MA MCLIP, Subject & Learning Support Lib., Staffs.Univ., Stoke on Trent. [0046056] 13/09/1991
Boler Mrs KB, (was Dudley), BA MCLIP, Team Lib., S.Area, Norfolk. [0035580] 07/11/1982
Bolton Mrs BA, (was Ellson), BA PGD MSc MCLIP, Trust Clinical Librarian, Dudley Grp.of Hosp.NHS.Trust, W.Midlands. [0001439] 01/03/1962
Bolton Mr DC, BA(Hons) MA MCLIP, Sen.Inf.Advisor, Electronic Res., Univ.of Gloucestershire. [0052331] 30/10/1995
Bolton Mrs EM, (was Smith), BA MCLIP MBA, Grp.Lib.-Access Serv., Birmingham L.Serv. [0033632] 10/01/1981
Bolton Mrs M, (was Wilson), FCLIP, Life Member. [0001443] 03/02/1933 FE 01/01/1939
Bolton Mrs R, (was Pearce), BA(Hons) MLib MCLIP, Lib., Swindon Bor.L's., W.Swindon L. [0048099] 09/11/1992
Bolton Mrs RP, (was Forbes), BA MCLIP, Unemployed. [0024417] 18/08/1975
Bolton Mrs SE, (was Stock), BA MCLIP, Lib., Gravesend Grammar Sch.for Boys, Gravesend, Kent. [0038027] 08/01/1985
Bomford Mrs HB, (was Stevens), BA MCLIP, Sch.Lib., N.Somerset Council, Weston-super-Mare. [0040184] 18/10/1986
Bonansea-Ryan Mrs S, (was Peniston), BA MCLIP, Global Ptnr.Publishing Specialist, Ovid Tech.Ltd., London. [0021904] 24/01/1974
Bonar Mr I, BSc MCLIP, Univ.Lib., Univ.of Portsmouth, Hants. [0001448] 01/07/1970
Bond Mr A, BA(Hons) MA, Lib., Royal Bor.of Kensington & Chelsea. [0056537] 12/08/1998
Bond Mrs C, (was Kettle), B LIB MCLIP, L.Asst., Trafford Healthcare NHS Trust, Manchester. [0025172] 09/12/1975
Bond Mrs C, (was Nield), BA MCLIP, Sch.Lib., Rainhill High Sch., Rainhill. [0010835] 01/01/1971
Bond Mr CE, FCLIP, Life Member. [0001450] 01/01/1944 FE 01/01/1954
Bond Mr DR, MCLIP, Retired. [0001452] 29/03/1952
Bond Mrs GS, BA MA MCLIP, Lib., Internat.Christian Coll., Glasgow. [0048145] 11/11/1992
Bond Mr H, BA MCLIP, Sen.Asst.Lib., Lancs.Co.L.H.Q. [0001453] 05/02/1964
Bond Mrs HM, Sen.L.Asst., P.G.Med.L., Horizon NHS Trust, Harperbury Hosp., Herts. [0051722] 26/05/1995 **AF**
Bond Miss J, BA(Hons), L.& Publications Offr., Essex C.C., Learn.Serv., Chelmsford. [0057385] 24/02/1999
Bond Mrs JL, BA(Hons) MCLIP, Volunteer Lib., Taunton Deane Council for Vol.Serv., Somerset. [0040596] 01/04/1987
Bond Mr NJ, MCLIP, Retired. [0001459] 01/01/1961
Bond Mrs S, (was Jones), MCLIP, Lib., Australian Inst.of Steel Const., N.S.W. [0008104] 22/08/1965
Bond Mrs WM, (was Downie), BA MCLIP, Comm.Lib.-Young People, Lincs.C.C., Nettleham L. [0038055] 08/01/1985
Bone Miss C, BA(Hons) MA MCLIP, Child.Lib., Harrow L. [0054144] 01/01/1996
Bone Miss M, Stud., Manchester Met.Univ. [0060013] 23/11/2001
Bone Mrs M, (was Nutter), MCLIP, Asst.Area. Sch.Lib., Hampshire County L., Waterlooville, Hants. [0023053] 01/10/1974
Bone Mrs MA, (was Henderson), MCLIP, Sen.Lib., Fleet L., Hants.Co.L. [0001463] 07/03/1962
Bone Mr PW, BA MCLIP, City Sch.Lib., Portsmouth City L. [0021180] 29/09/1973

Boney, Mr AJV, BSc, Industrial Policy Offr., Scottish Exec., Glasgow. [0037898] 17/10/1984
Bonham Mrs AO, (was Smith), BA MCLIP, Lib., Southend-on-Sea L., Essex. [0035593] 15/11/1982
Bonner Mr AR, MA MCLIP, Life Member. [0001467] 29/10/1951
Bonnett Mrs P, (was Mcloughlin), BA FCLIP, Asst.Editor, Health Inf.& L.Journal. [0009518] 20/02/1962 **FE 17/11/1999**
Boney Miss NJ, BA(Hons), Lib., St.Helens Coll., St.Helens. [0050725] 14/10/1994
Bonnici Mrs ME, BA(Hons), Stud., Univ.of Brighton &, L.Asst., George Edwards L., Univ.of Surrey, Guildford. [0058410] 10/02/2000
Bonnici Mr N, BA MLS MCLIP AInstAM, Sch.Lib., London. [0023736] 27/01/1975
Bonnick Ms NJ, BA(Hons) DipIS, Inf.Lib., Kingston Univ., Surrey. [0052067] 02/10/1995
Bonnin Mr JF, Head Lib., Vive de Macon, Bibl.Municipale, Macon, France. [0051990] 01/09/1995
Bonsall Mrs SM, (was Reford), BA(Hons) DipLIS MCLIP, Asst.Lib., Catg., Oxfordshire C.C. [0044603] 05/11/1990
Bonser Mrs CA, (was Charnley), BA MBA, Mgr., Product & Programme Support, OCLC PICA, Birmingham. [0040418] 13/01/1987
Bonser Mr DE, BA MCLIP, Div.Dir.of L,Arts & Heritage, Northumberland Co.L., Morpeth. [0021743] 10/01/1994
Bonthron Mrs KA, BSc(Hons), Stud., Univ.of Wales, Aberystwyth. [0057888] 01/10/1999
Booker Miss CV, BA, Grad.L.Asst., The Templeman L., Univ.of Kent at Canterbury. [0061213] 16/04/2002
Booler Miss VJ, (was Dobbie), MCLIP, Lib., Droitwich L., Worcs.Co.L. [0003995] 04/09/1965
Boon Mrs J, Health Inf.Offr., NHS Direct Online., Stevenage. [0052843] 04/01/1996
Boon Ms KL, BA(Hons), Stud., Univ.Coll.London. [0059210] 08/01/2001
Booth Mr A, BA DipLib MSc MCLIP, Dir.of Inf.Res., Sch.of Health & Related Research, Univ.of Sheffield. [0035227] 01/10/1982
Booth Dr BKW, MA MIFA MBCS PhD FM MCLIP, Employment not known. [0060805] 12/12/2001
Booth Mrs CM, (was Myles), MA MCLIP, p./t.Sci.Curator, Nat.L.of Scotland. [0022706] 17/09/1974
Booth Mrs ERR, (was Drakes), BA(Hons), Lib., Cheshire C.C., Crewe. [0049843] 21/12/1993
Booth Miss JA, MCLIP, Child.Lib.I/c., Fulham L., L.B.of Hammersmith. [0001482] 25/07/1967
Booth Ms JA, (was Booth-Clarke), BA(Hons) DipILS, Unemployed. [0046448] 07/11/1991
Booth Miss JI, Subject Lib.Maths & Physics, Betty & Gordon Moore L., Cambridge. [0057917] 01/10/1999
Booth Ms P, (was Ford), MED BA MCLIP, Indexer/Trainer in Indexing, Self-employed. [0001485] 12/09/1955
Booth Mr RD, BSc DipLib MCLIP, Grp.Lib., Cheshire C.C., Ellesmere Port. [0018511] 20/09/1972
Booth Mr S, LLB, p./t.Stud./Inf.Offr., Bristol Univ./Veale Wasbrough. [0059997] 19/11/2001
Booth Mr SG, BA, Unemployed. [0050733] 13/10/1994 **AF**
Boothby Mrs J, (was Hassall), MCLIP, Unemployed. [0006536] 11/01/1963
Boothroyd Mrs HR, (was Ward), BA MCLIP, Sch.L.Serv.Mgr., Suffolk. [0025923] 01/04/1976
Boothroyd Mrs KM, (was Fenn), BA(Hons) MCLIP, Sen.Lib., Harris L., Preston Lancs.C.C. [0047867] 22/10/1992
Boothroyd Miss MJ, MIL MCLIP, Life Member. [0001487] 15/03/1948
Bootle Mr WE, MCLIP, Retired. [0001489] 05/03/1947
Booton Mr PH, BA, Collection Devel.Offr., Brit.Council, Manchester. [0045595] 04/04/1991
Boraston Ms JA, MA AdvDipEd BA(Hons), Tutor/Advisor(Res.), Coll.of Cont.Educ., Walsall. [0029588] 24/10/1978
Borchgrevink Mrs H, (was Woo), BA(Hons) DipLib MCLIP, P./t.Sch.Lib., Oslo Internat.Sch., Norway. [0026066] 20/05/1976
Bord Mrs RI, (was Gerson), Housebound Serv.Lib., Sefton, Liverpool, Merseyside. [0044713] 13/11/1990
Borda Ms AE, BA MA MLS, P.G.Res.Stud., Sch.of L.Arch.& Inf.Studies, Univ.Coll.London. [0048000] 30/10/1992
Bordiss Mr PJ, BSc MCLIP, Employment not known. [0060149] 10/12/2001
Boreham Mr GB, MCLIP, Life Member, Tel.01303 257263, 45 Walton Gdns., Folkestone, CT19 5PR. [0001492] 16/02/1950
Boreham Mrs GM, (was Hickling), BA(Hons) MCLIP, Life Member, Oleander, Westwood Ave., Woodham, KT15 3QF, Tel.01932 343127. [0001493] 12/02/1949
Boreham Mrs M, (was Mclean), MCLIP, Lib., West Hatch Sch., Chigwell. [0009503] 11/01/1973
Boreland-Testa Mrs H, BA, Stud., London Metro.Univ. [0061753] 31/10/2002
Borland Miss MC, MCLIP, Life Member. [0001494] 12/01/1943
Borman Miss DJ, BA(Hons), Stud., Leeds Met.Univ. [0059656] 07/11/2001
Bornet Mr CP, MA DipLIP MCLIP, Ref.Lib., Royal Coll.of Music, London. [0030738] 23/04/1979
Borrows Mr G, BA DipLib MCLIP, Assoc.Dir., L.& Inf.Serv., Staffs.Univ., Stoke on Trent. [0027426] 01/04/1977
Borst-Boyd Mrs RR, (was Boyd), BA DipLib MCLIP, Inf.Asst., Oakville P.L., Oakville. [0030818] 08/05/1979
Borthwick Mrs AL, (was Brisbane), BA MCLIP, Asst.Dir., Gateshead M.B.C. [0027134] 01/02/1977
Borthwick Mrs HE, (was Goodman), BSc, Asst.Lib., General Register Off., for Scotland, Edinburgh. [0043257] 13/10/1989
Borutan Mrs JA, (was Crocker), BA MCLIP, Unemployed. [0018588] 01/01/1972
Borwick Ms CF, BA, Stud.,L.Asst., Univ.of Bristol. [0061680] 18/10/2002

Bosanko Ms S, BSc DipLib MCLIP, Freelance Consult., Self-employed. [0038705] 01/10/1985
Bosch Ms AS, BSc PGDipLIS, Asst.Public Serv.Mgr., City Univ.L.Inf.Serv., London. [0054759] 01/04/1997
Boscoe Mrs M, (was Leader), BA MCLIP, p./t.Serials Catr., Middx.Univ. [0018874] 02/10/1972
Bosher Mrs C, (was Rowe), BA FCLIP, Retired. [0020246] 01/01/1940 **FE 01/01/1951**
Boshnakova Mrs A, MLS, Unemployed. [0061355] 20/06/2002
Boss Miss CE, MCLIP, Lib.-Sen.Team Leader, Stock-Reader Devel., Nuneaton L., Warks.Co.L. [0001500] 04/02/1971
Boss Ms LC, MA(Hons) DipLIS, Study Cent.Adviser(Circulation), S.E.Essex Coll., Southend on Sea. [0051344] 24/01/1995
Bossom Mrs AK, (was Leach), BA DipLib MCLIP, Lib., Monkton Combe Sch., Bath. [0027695] 01/07/1977
Bostle Mr CAR, DMA FCLIP, Retired. [0001501] 10/03/1961 **FE 12/08/1975**
Bostle Mrs CM, (was Snape), BA DipLib MCLIP, Sales Asst., Phoenix Bookshop, Evesham. [0026243] 22/09/1976
Bostle Mrs E, (was Perolz), MCLIP, Patients Lib., Northwick Park Hosp., Harrow, Middx. [0001502] 10/01/1966
Bostock Mr AC, MCLIP, Employment not known. [0060147] 10/12/2001
Bostock Mrs EM, (was Kelly), MCLIP, Lib., Paton Lib., Manchester Grammar Sch. [0001503] 15/02/1967
Bostock Mrs G, (was Tomlinson), BA(Hons) MA, Lib.(Job Share), Derbys.L.Serv./Leics.C.C., Matlock/Dept.Planning & Trans. [0050189] 27/04/1994
Bostock Mr NA, BA(Hons), English Teacher, Cambridge House, Spain. [0049959] 01/02/1994
Boston Mr JA, BA DipLib MCLIP, Bibl.Serv.Mgr., Liverpool Univ. [0018412] 18/10/1972
Bostrom Ms T, BA, Stud., London Met. [0061631] 08/10/2002
Bosworth Mrs S, BA MCLIP, p./t.Sch.Lib., Manning Sch., Nottingham. [0025222] 19/01/1976
Bott Mr M, LLB, Princ.Lib., Marcus Garvey L., L.B.of Haringey. [0047813] 19/10/1992
Botten Ms PC, (was Nelson), BA(Hons) MCLIP, Lib., Libraries, Heritage & Trading, Standards. [0025617] 26/01/1976
Botterill Mrs CA, BA(Hons) MCLIP, Unemployed. [0035792] 25/01/1983
Bottomley Miss CN, MCLIP, Lib., Co.Heritage Dept., Cumbria C.C. [0001514] 30/03/1914
Bottrill Mr PJ, BA MCLIP, H.of L.Serv., Torbay Council. [0001515] 01/01/1971
Bouault Miss NJ, BA(Hons) MA, L.Asst., Broomfield Coll., Derby. [0052337] 30/10/1995
Boucher Mrs CM, BA MPhil MA, Dep.Health Sci.Lib., L.I.C.Univ.of Wales Swansea. [0056758] 09/10/1998
Boucher Miss HC, MLS MCLIP, H.of L.Serv., Birmingham Law Soc. [0001517] 09/01/1967
Boughey Mr A, BA DipLib MCLIP DipMgmt, Area Lib., Rochdale Ls. [0038138] 17/01/1985
Boughton Mr JE, MCLIP, Life Member. [0001520] 07/01/1947
Boughton Ms LCW, BA DipLib MCLIP, Investor Devel.Mgr., One Northeast, Newcastle upon Tyne. [0030364] 29/01/1979
Boughton Ms S, BA(Hons) MSc, Inf.Offr., MIDIRS, Bristol. [0056070] 06/02/1998
Bould Ms CM, DipLIS, Sen.Learning Resources Asst., S.Bank Univ., Perry L. [0041430] 04/12/1987
Boulding Mrs AD, Retired. [0024249] 02/10/1961
Boulter Miss H, Sen.L.Asst., Bucks.C.C., Chesham. [0053402] 10/06/1996 **AF**
Boulton Mrs A, BA MCLIP, Asst.Lib., Birmingham L.Serv. [0001523] 01/10/1971
Boulton Mr GH, BA MCLIP, Princ.Lib., Thamesmead Cent., L.B.of Bexley. [0029928] 27/10/1978
Boulton Mr KG, MA MCLIP, Asst.Lib., Univ.Of York. [0019792] 22/11/1972
Boulton Miss MC, BA DipLib MCLIP, Lib., London Coll.of Fashion. [0045629] 08/04/1991
Boundy Mrs NJ, BA(Hons) MSc MCLIP, P./t.Sen.L.Asst., Kirklees Met.Council, Huddersfield. [0055868] 02/12/1997
Bourguignon Mrs GV, (was Goldsworthy), MCLIP, L.Offr.:Inf., Cornwall C.C., Falmouth Br.L. [0005651] 10/09/1966
Bourne Mrs EM, (was Hewitt), MCLIP, Lib./Local History Secretary, Redcliffe Coll./Glos.Rural Comm.C., Gloucester. [0006794] 15/01/1961
Bourne Miss MGM, BA(Hons), p./t.Stud., Telford Coll., Edinburgh. [0060003] 21/11/2001
Bourne Mr RM, BA FCLIP, Retired. [0001527] 01/08/1961 **FE 18/11/1993**
Bourne Ms RM, BA(Hons) DipIM MCLIP, Lib.& Asst.Lib., S.& W.Devon Health Auth., Dartington/Derriford Hosp. [0047850] 21/10/1992
Bourner Mr BV, MA MA DipEdTech MCLIP, Lib., Scottish Exec., Edinburgh. [0026209] 24/08/1976
Bourouba Mrs VA, Sch.Lib., Minehead Middle Sch., Somerset. [0061709] 23/10/2002 **AF**
Bourton Mrs CM, (was Dixon), MCLIP, Lib., L.B.of Bromley, Kent. [0032648] 19/07/1980
Boutland Mr MT, Stud., Loughborough Univ. [0059939] 08/11/2001
Bouttell Mr NE, BA MCLIP, Retired. [0001529] 10/02/1966
Bowden Mr CW, L.Co-ordinator, St.Edmund of Canterbury High Sch., Merseyside. [0055938] 19/12/1997
Bowden Ms MJ, BA(Hons) MA, Stud., Univ.N.London. [0056239] 15/04/1998
Bowden Prof RG, MLS FCLIP HonFCLIP, Life Member. [0016634] 03/07/1961 **FE 15/09/1993**
Bowe Mrs CB, (was Howgill), BA MCLIP, Prison Lib., HMP Gloucester, Glos.Co.L. [0030321] 10/01/1979

Personal Members — Bradford

Bowe Mrs EC, (was Watson), Sen.L.Mgr., Penrith, Cumbria C.C. [0032354] 25/03/1980
Bowell Mrs LM, BA MCLIP, Grp.Lib., Leics.L.Inf.Serv. [0032636] 18/07/1980
Bowen Mr DK, BA MCLIP, Asst.Lib., Carmarthen Area L. [0026686] 08/11/1976
Bowen Mr DM, BA(Hons) DipInf, L.Asst., Carmarthen Public L. [0056413] 06/07/1998
Bowen Mr GJ, BSc(Hons) DipLIB MCLIP, ICT Systems Lib., Portsmouth Cent.L., Portsmouth City Council L.Serv. [0048721] 26/04/1993
Bowen Mr GP, MCLIP, Life Member. [0001540] 15/09/1950
Bowen Ms JA, (was Green), MCLIP, Stock Mgr., L.B.of Newham. [0005879] 18/01/1971
Bowen Mrs K, MCLIP, Employment not known. [0060460] 11/12/2001
Bowen Miss L, BA DipLib MCLIP, Lib., Univ.of Westminster. [0026286] 01/10/1976
Bowen Mr M, BA DipLib, Inf.Lib., Nat.Mus.of Sci.& Ind., (Sci.Mus.), London. [0040053] 15/10/1986
Bowen Mrs MA, (was Nicholas), BA MCLIP, Lend.Lib., Carmarthenshire C.C., Carmarthenshire P.L. [0030225] 02/01/1970
Bowen Mrs PA, (was Balmer), MCLIP, Med.& Health Lib., W.Middlesex Univ.Hosp. [0001542] 01/01/1961
Bowen Miss SL, L.Asst., The Hon.Soc.of The Inner Temple, London. [0054115] 01/01/1996
Bowen Ms SV, BA DipLib MCLIP, Grp.Lib., Leics.L., Ashby de la Zouch. [0035268] 03/10/1982
Bowen Mrs VA, MCLIP, Young Peoples Serv.Devel.Lib., Comm.Inf.:L., Herts.W.Area. [0001543] 01/01/1966
Bower Mrs C, (was Taylor), BA DipLib MCLIP, Lib., N.Yorks.C.C. [0030334] 22/01/1979
Bower Mrs PL, (was Chan), BA(Hons) DipLib MCLIP, Head of L.& Inf.Serv., Dept.of Health. [0021523] 18/10/1973
Bowers Mrs FE, (was Cowie), BA MCLIP, Safety Eng.Lib., Halliburton KBR, Aberdeen. [0049548] 09/11/1993
Bowers Ms GE, BA(Hons), Team Lib., Leighton Buzzard L. [0061599] 03/10/2002
Bowers Mrs ZD, (was Turner), Self-Employed. [0037539] 03/10/1984
Bowers Sharpe Ms K, BA MA, Ref.Lib., Western Illinois Univ.L., USA. [0056009] 16/01/1998
Bowes Mr ATH, BSc(Hons), p./t.Help Desk Asst., Univ.of Bristol. [0058861] 13/09/2000
Bowie Miss JE, BA MCLIP, Area Serv.Mgr.-E.Kent, Kent C.C. [0025223] 05/01/1976
Bowie Mrs LM, (was Stewart), BA, L.Serv.Co-ordinator, BAE Systems Electronics Ltd., Hants. [0048196] 16/11/1992
Bowker Mrs CJ, (was Dobson), BA(Hons) MA, Not employed. [0035466] 09/10/1982
Bowl Miss CL, BA MCLIP, Inf.Off., Travers Smith Braithwaite, London. [0039767] 01/07/1986
Bowler Mrs M, JP BA MCLIP, Careers Instructor, Garendon High Sch., Loughborough. [0036747] 14/11/1983
Bowles Mr DH, BA(Hons) MA DipLIS MCLIP, Asst.Lib., Cent.L., Bexleyheath. [0046234] 18/10/1991
Bowles Mrs JM, BA(Hons) DipIM MCLIP, P./t.Ref.Lib., Chandlers Ford L., Hants. [0052661] 16/11/1995
Bowles Mr JR, BA MCLIP, Sen.Res.Asst., Nat.L.of Scotland. [0001550] 06/10/1970
Bowles Mrs SF, MCLIP, Lib., Wellington Br.L., Somerset C.C. [0005119] 01/01/1969
Bowling Mr RG, BA MCLIP, Inf.Serv.Lib.-Ref., City of York Council, York Cent.L. [0001553] 26/09/1968
Bowlt Ms H, BA(Hons) MCLIP, Ref.& Inf.Lib., MiltonKeynes Ls. [0041788] 08/04/1988
Bowman Dr JH, MA MCLIP, Lect., Sch.of L.Arch.& Inf.Studies, Univ.Coll.London. [0024476] 08/09/1975
Bowman Miss S, Intranet Content Builder, Foseco Internat.Ltd., Tamworth. [0054514] 15/01/1997
Bowman Mr SA, BA MCLIP, L.& LR Mgr., Park Coll., Eastbourne. [0042457] 16/11/1990
Bownes Mrs K, MCLIP, Retired. [0016635] 02/08/1950
Bowrage Mr TG, BA DipLib MSc MCLIP, p./t.Lecturer. [0043935] 26/02/1990
Bowring Mr JR, BA MCLIP, Lib., Douglas Bor.L., Isle of Man. [0001559] 16/03/1965
Bowtell Ms SM, (was Hyde), MCLIP, Sch.Lib., Forest Comp.Sch., Wokingham. [0001561] 07/09/1964
Bowyer Ms HM, BA(Hons) DipLIS, Learning Resources Mgr., N.Area Coll., Stockport. [0049669] 25/11/1993
Bowyer Mrs KL, (was Shorthouse), BA MCLIP, Regional Co-Ordinator, Inst.of Chartered Accountants, Cambridge. [0035488] 22/10/1982
Bowyer Ms SE, BA(Hons) DipLib, Asst.Arch., Nat.L.of Wales, Aberystwyth. [0045427] 19/02/1991
Bowyer Mr TH, BSc FCLIP, Life Member. [0001563] 16/12/1949 FE 01/01/1955
Boxall Ms JD, BSc(Hons) MA MCLIP, Unemployed. [0027514] 01/05/1977
Boxford Miss AJ, BA(Hons) MA, Community Lib., Lincolnshire C.C. [0053942] 11/10/1996
Boyce Mr LE, BA DipLib MCLIP, Learning Resources Mgr., E.Devon Coll., Tiverton. [0024403] 08/08/1975
Boyd Mrs AS, (was Buchanan), MCLIP MIPD MBA, Select Committee Research Offr., W.Sussex C.C., Worthing. [0018532] 07/08/1972
Boyd Mr DF, MA MCLIP, Lib., Mitchell L., Glasgow P.L. [0018269] 11/10/1972
Boyd Mr DH, MCLIP, Retired. [0001569] 09/10/1965
Boyd Ms F, BA (Hons), Mgr.Database/Website. [0048056] 03/11/1992
Boyd Mr G, BA(Hons), Stud., Univ.of Strathclyde. [0061648] 15/10/2002
Boyd Ms MA, MA MCLIP, Sen.Specialist(Job Share), Child.& Young Peoples Serv., Hinckley, Leics. [0038068] 10/01/1985
Boyd Mrs MB, (was Williams), BA MA MCLIP, Sch.Lib., Cleveden Secondary, Glasgow. [0042112] 01/10/1988
Boyd Mr N, BA(Hons) MCLIP, Systems Lib., Barking Coll., Romford. [0049296] 20/10/1993
Boyd Mrs PC, BA(Hons) DipLIS MCLIP, Asst.Lib., Surrey Inst.of Art & Design, Farnham,Surrey. [0046091] 01/10/1991
Boyd Miss R, BA MCLIP, Asst.Co.Lib., Policy & Devel., Somerset C.C. [0001575] 01/01/1971
Boyd-Moss Miss SAL, BSc(Hons) MA, Grad.Trainee, Sci.& Environ.Sect., House of Commons L. [0059486] 09/04/2001
Boyde Miss SJ, MA DipLib MCLIP, p./t.Consultancy. [0001577] 14/10/1971
Boydell Ms L, BA(Hons) MA MCLIP, Inf.Offr., Clifford Chance, LLP, London. [0049163] 08/10/1993
Boyer Mrs B, (was Hazell), MCLIP, Life Member. [0001578] 03/10/1941
Boyes Mrs A, (was Rothery), MCLIP, Life Member, 12 Linver Rd.,London,SW6 3RB. [0014339] 01/01/1950
Boyes Mrs D, (was Harper), BA DipLib MCLIP, L.& Res.Cent.Mgr., Bedford Coll. [0035811] 17/01/1983
Boyes Mrs J, Stud., Univ.of Wales, Aberystwyth, & Sen.Asst., Cent.L., Barnsley. [0058728] 01/07/2000
Boylan Mr B, MCLIP, Lib.i/c., Mobile L., Edinburgh City L. [0001579] 06/01/1970
Boyle Miss AM, BA DipLib, Cataloguing Asst., Marx Memorial L., London. [0043061] 01/07/1989
Boyle Mr DN, BA(Hons) MSc, Asst.Lib., Caledonian Univ., Univ.of Strathclyde. [0055073] 07/07/1997
Boyle Ms GA, L.Asst., Univ.of Cent.England, Birmingham. [0056900] 02/11/1998
Boyle Mrs J, PGDip, Data Inventory Offr., Scottish Natural Heritage, Lenzie. [0057473] 01/04/1999
Boyle Miss S, MCLIP, Retired. [0029117] 01/01/1954
Boyle Mrs VA, BA PGCE, p./t.Stud./Lib., Univ.Northumbria, Ryton Comp.Sch. Tyne & Wear. [0059909] 01/11/2001
Boynton Miss J, BA(Hons), Health Inf.Mgr., Health Tech.Board for Scotland, Glasgow. [0048650] 01/04/1993
Boys Mrs GJ, BA, Stud., Manchester Metropolitan Univ. [0059096] 14/11/2000
Bozic Ms AC, BSc DipISM, Asst.Lib.(Acquisitions), HM Treasury & Cabinet Off.L., London. [0051107] 16/11/1994
Brabazon Mr CR, BA DipLib MCLIP, Sen.Lib., Young Peoples Serv., Scunthorpe Cent.L. [0038683] 01/10/1985
Brabban Mr N, MCLIP, Asst.Lib., Newcastle Univ.L. [0001584] 29/01/1968
Brabban Mr PJ, BA(Hons) MA CertEd, Asst.Lib., Durham Univ.L. [0055968] 02/01/1998
Brabner Mrs BP, (was Ashby), MCLIP, Sch.Lib., Cedars Upper Sch., Leighton Buzzard. [0001585] 29/03/1962
Brace-Jones Miss WE, BA, [0047547] 01/10/1992
Bracegirdle Mrs AAS, (was Cruickshank), MA MSc MCLIP, Temp.Sch.Lib., Radyr Comp.Sch., Cardiff C.C. [0022718] 29/08/1974
Bracegirdle Ms SJ, BA DipInf, Head of Catg., John Rylands Univ.L.of Manchester. [0043003] 05/06/1989
Bracher Mrs DM, (was Payne), BA DipLib MCLIP, Careers L.Asst., Wakefield Dist.Guidance Serv., W.Yorks. [0030229] 17/12/1978
Bracher Mrs J, (was Davies), BA(Hons) DipLib MCLIP, Team Lib.-Access, Northants.E. [0042558] 04/01/1989
Bracher Mr TN, BA MSc DipLIB MCLIP, Subject Specialist, Local Studies, Northants.Cent.L. [0046167] 07/10/1991
Bracken Mrs ER, (was Hadingham), BA MCLIP, Unemployed. [0021527] 04/10/1973
Bracken-Kemish Mr SH, BA(Hons), Business Intelligence Researcher, Business Link Surrey, Woking. [0051676] 10/05/1995
Brackenbury Mr SC, BA(Hons), BOPCRIS Project Mgr.& BOPCAS, Content Developer, Hartley L., Univ.of Southampton. [0056157] 10/03/1998 AF
Bradberry Mrs H, L.Asst., Off.for Nat.Stat., Fareham, Hants. [0056292] 28/04/1998 AF
Bradbrook Ms SL, BA(Hons) DipILM, Photographic Lib., Countryside Agency, Cheltenham. [0052994] 13/02/1996
Bradburn Mrs J, (was Goss), MCLIP, Ref.& Inf.Offr., Halton Bor.Council. [0020134] 01/01/1967
Bradbury Mrs AGM, BA(Hons), Team Lib., Windsor P.L., Royal Bor.of Windsor & Maidenhead. [0036041] 19/04/1983
Bradbury Mr DAG, MA MCLIP, Dir.of Ls.& Guildhall Art Gallery, Corporation fo London, London. [0021747] 10/01/1974
Bradbury Mrs L, (was Jones), BA MCLIP, Catr.Mgr., Devon L.Serv., Exeter. [0008043] 22/07/1969
Bradbury Mrs MR, (was Smith), BA MCLIP, L.Asst., Stockport MBC., Marple Br.L. [0018518] 02/10/1968
Bradbury Mrs R, (was Radcliff), MCLIP, Lib.Asst., Alsop High Sch., Liverpool. [0012103] 01/07/1971
Bradbury Mrs SL, (was Frearson), BA MCLIP, L.Mgr.(Job-share), Glos.C.C., Cinderford, Glos. [0019683] 22/10/1972
Braddick Mrs AC, (was Williams), BA(Hons) MSc, Employment not known. [0043963] 08/03/1990
Braddick Mrs JE, (was Fincham), BLib DipEd MCLIP, Resident in Australia. [0031276] 02/10/1979
Braddock Mrs CH, (was Turner), BLIB MCLIP, Town Lib., Staffs.L.&Inf, Leek L., Leek, Staffs. [0037287] 01/06/1984
Bradfield Miss JM, MSc RGNRM MCLIP, Employment unknown. [0060356] 10/12/2001
Bradford Miss C, MA MCLIP, Education Lib., Univ.of Warwick. [0042607] 18/01/1989
Bradford Mrs JI, (was Powell), BA MA DipLIB MSc(Econ) MCLIP, Asst.Lib., Univ.of Bristol L. [0021031] 01/10/1973
Bradford Ms SE, DipLib, Inf.& Learning Mgr., Chepstow L., Monmouthshire C.C. [0038223] 12/02/1985

Bradford Miss SJ, BA(Hons) MA, Asst.Lib., Oxford Union Society, Oxford. [0056875] 29/10/1998
Bradford Mrs SP, BSc(Econ) MCLIP, Lib./Learning Res.Mgr., Chislehurst & Sidcup Gramm.Sch., Kent. [0051542]01/04/1995
Bradley Miss A, BA MCLIP, Life Member. [0001594] 21/03/1950
Bradley Mrs A, (was Stannard), BA(Hons) MA DipLib MCLIP, Sen.Lib., Foreign & Commonwealth Off., London. [0035172] 06/12/1982
Bradley Mrs BE, MCLIP, Stock Lib.-Wealden, E.Sussex C.C., Uckfield. [0023994] 01/03/1975
Bradley Mr CD, MA(Hons) DipIS, Inf.Adviser, Watson, Wyatt & Partners, Reigate. [0051417] 10/02/1995
Bradley Mrs CJ, (was Atkinson), BA(Hons) PGCE, Lib., Chelmsford Cent.L., Essex. [0057468] 29/03/1999
Bradley Miss DJ, BA(Hons) MA, Inf.Specialist, Basildon & Thurrock NHS Trust, Basildon Hosp. [0054986] 03/06/1997
Bradley Mr G, FCLIP, Life Member, Tel:0785 662237. [0001600] 17/02/1948 FE 01/01/1963
Bradley Miss GF, BA(Hons) DipILS, Sch.Lib., St Joseph's Academy, Kilmarnock. [0055769] 14/11/1997
Bradley Mr I, Stud., Univ.Northumbria. [0059528] 26/04/2001
Bradley Mr IG, MCLIP, Life Member, Tel.020 8669 4073. [0001602] 09/01/1962
Bradley Ms JH, MLS BA, Retired. [0044018] 01/04/1990
Bradley Miss KL, BSc, Inf.Sci., MRC Inst.for Environ.&Health, Univ.of Leicester. [0057736] 14/07/1999
Bradley Miss LF, Asst.Lib., Hammond Suddards Edge, Leeds. [0059956] 09/11/2001
Bradley Miss M, BA DipLib MCLIP, Team Lib.-Inf., S.E.Educ.& L.Board, Holywood L. [0024327] 23/07/1975
Bradley Mrs M, BA(Hons), Businessline Lib., Wrexham Co.Borough Council. [0058003] 12/10/1999
Bradley Mr P, MA M Phil FCLIP, Retired. [0001607] 21/01/1949 FE 01/01/1967
Bradley Mrs PG, BA MA, Inf.Asst., newton Pk.L., Bath Spa Univ.Coll. [0058242] 24/11/1999
Bradley Mrs SE, BA (Hons), Lib., Joseph Rowntree Foundation, York. [0059095] 14/11/2000
Bradley Miss SJ, BSc MCLIP, Employment not known. [0044957] 23/01/1991
Bradley Miss T, BA MCLIP, Unemployed. [0029149] 22/04/1978
Bradley-Cox Mrs MJ, (was Powrie), JP BA DipLib, Asst.Lib., Bournemouth Univ. [0041632] 05/02/1988
Bradly Mrs JE, (was Drakard), BA MCLIP, Teaching Resources Mgr., Marling Sch., Stroud. [0004160] 02/02/1969
Bradnock Mrs AM, (was Orrock), BA DipLib MCLIP, Head of L's., Dulwich Coll., London. [0049886] 07/01/1994
Bradshaw Mrs AE, (was Fletcher), BA DipLib, Career Break. [0037676] 12/10/1984
Bradshaw Mrs CM, MSc MCLIP, Lib., Ashworth Hosp., Liverpool. [0001612] 01/07/1967
Bradshaw Mrs EC, (was Miller), BA DipLib MCLIP, Lib., Reading L. [0025786] 02/03/1976
Bradshaw Miss J, Stud./Sen Bus Inf.Advisor, Liverpool John Moores Univ., St Helens Chamber Ltd. [0061826] 14/11/2002
Bradshaw Mrs JN, Lib./Copyright Offrr., Assessment & Quals.Alliance, Univ.of Surrey. [0056562] 20/08/1998
Bradshaw Mrs K, (was Dhillon), BSc(Hons) DipLIS MCLIP, Inf.Serv.Lib., Univ.of Hull, Brynmor Jones L. [0047057] 08/04/1992
Bradshaw Mrs SE, L.Asst., Cambs.C.C. [0048891] 12/07/1993 AF
Bradshaw Ms WA, BA MA, Unemployed. [0061557] 01/10/2002
Bradtke Dr E, Research Asst., NATCET/Univ.of Sheffield. [0055267] 15/09/1997
Bradwell Mr A, BA CertEd DipLib MCLIP, Academic Liaison Lib., Anglia Poly.Univ., Chelmsford, Essex. [0043606] 09/11/1989
Brady Ms AE, (was Williams), BA(Hons) MCLIP, Asst.Subject Lib., Oxford Brookes Univ. [0030298] 17/01/1979
Brady Mrs AP, (was Lawrence), BA DipLib MCLIP, Lib., M.O.D., London. [0028050] 04/01/1977
Brady Ms D, (was Butler), BA BSocSc MCLIP, Lib., St.Christophers Hospice, Sydenham. [0028270] 31/10/1977
Brady Mrs FI, (was Southward), BSc(Hons), Lib., Harrogate Ladies Coll. [0046067] 23/09/1991
Brady Mr MR, BSc, Crown Servant, HMS Nelson, Portsmouth. [0056197] 01/04/1998 SP
Brady Mr SJ, Serv.Mgr., Rayleigh L., Essex. [0061017] 01/02/2002 AF
Bragg Mr JHR, MSC MCLIP, Life Member. [0016640] 28/01/1965
Bragg Mrs JM, BA, Stud., Manchester Met.Univ. [0059934] 07/11/2001
Bragg Lord M, HonFCLIP, Hon.Fellow. [0050582] 22/09/1994 FE 22/09/1994
Bragg Mr MJ, BA(Hons) MSc, Group Lib., Calderdale L., W.Yorkshire. [0050200] 28/04/1994
Brahmbhatt Mrs SG, BA MA MCLIP, Learning Res.Lib., Leicester Coll. [0043677] 22/11/1989
Brailsford Mrs CEA, (was Vickers), MA, Unwaged. [0039049] 31/10/1985
Brailsford Mrs CJ, p./t.Stud./Learning Cent.Co-ord., Univ.of Wales, Aberystwyth, S.Kent.Coll., Ashford. [0058063] 21/10/1999
Brain Miss CA, MTheol(Hons), Stud., Northumbria Univ. [0061698] 21/10/2002
Brain Mrs EA, BA(Hons), Stock Mgr., & Project Mgr., Suffolk C.C., Ls.& Heritage. [0057886] 01/10/1999
Brain Mrs ME, BA MCLIP, Lib., Dr.J.H.Burgoyne & Ptnrs., Ilkley, W.Yorks. [0001622] 19/10/1974
Brain Miss SJ, BA(Hons) DipLib PGCE MCLIP, Lib., NHS Direct Hants.& Isle of Wight. [0035279] 05/10/1982
Brainard Mr A, BSc, Employment not known. [0060505] 11/12/2001

Braithwaite Mrs CI, (was Ross), BA MCLIP, Sch.Lib., Albyn Sch.for Girls, Aberdeen. [0001625] 14/10/1968
Braithwaite Mrs MW, (was Hodgson), MCLIP, Tech.Lib., Environment & Tech.Serv.Dept., Durham C.C. [0007029] 03/10/1971
Bralant Mr AP, BA MCLIP, Music Lib., Hendon Music L., L.B.of Barnet. [0001626] 18/01/1971
Brall Mr RJ, BA DipLib MCLIP, Lib., Crown Prosecution Serv., London. [0033559] 16/01/1981
Brall Mrs SJ, (was Hallbery), BA MCLIP, Snr.Asst.Lib., L.Services., L.B.of Harrow. [0031627] 29/10/1979
Bramall Mrs HD, (was Bridges), BEd DipLib, Shelver, Univ.of Wolverhampton. [0034421] 05/11/1981
Bramble Miss SA, MCLIP, Br.Lib., Somerset Co.L. [0001628] 21/01/1966
Bramley Mrs AW, (was Hurley), MCLIP, Advisor to PG Dean, Dept.for NHS Postgrad.Med.Educ., Univ.of Leeds. [0007269] 06/01/1965
Bramley Mrs CL, (was See), BA(Hons) MSc MCLIP, Inf.Offr., Royal Inst.of Chartered Surveyors, London. [0055484] 17/10/1997
Brammer Mr MG, MA, Sen.Inf.Offr., Cent.for Inf.& Knowledge Mgmt., Essex C.C. [0038477] 09/05/1985
Bramwell Mrs JF, (was Sage), BA(Hons) DipLib MCLIP, Community Lib., Liniclate L., Western Isles, Scotland. [0012854] 21/01/1972
Bramwell Mr KM, BEM BA MCLIP, Life Member. [0001634] 28/06/1937
Branaghan Mr SA, BSc(Hons) DipIM MCLIP, Asst.Inf.Lib., L.B.of Barnet, Mill Hill L. [0056338] 26/05/1998
Brand Mrs E, (was Avery), BA DipLib MCLIP, Schs.Lib., Sch.L.Serv., Bletchley L., Milton Keynes. [0021997] 10/01/1974
Brand Dr HM, BA(Hons) MA DipLib PhD, Sch.Lib., Queen Annes Sch., Caversham, Reading. [0053357] 23/05/1996
Brand Miss SH, BA MSc MCLIP, Employment not known. [0060155] 10/12/2001
Brandon Mrs AS, BA(Hons) DipLib MCLIP, p./t.L.Asst., Rugeley L., Staffs.C.C. [0037717] 17/10/1984
Brandon Mr D, AIMLS, Lib., Lilly Research Cent., Windlesham. [0060973] 22/01/2002
Brandreth Mr E, FCLIP, Life Member. [0001640] 27/02/1948 FE 01/01/1967
Branford Mrs LM, (was Duncan), BA, Full-time mother, 80 Mulgrave Rd., Sutton,Surrey,SM2 6LZ. [0036728] 10/11/1983
Branford Mr ME, BA DipLib PGCE MCLIP, Lect./Head of L., Bridgend Coll.of F.& H.E., Mid Glamorgan. [0060180] 05/10/1972
Brangwyn Mr DC, MA MCLIP, Sen.Lib., L.B.of Waltham Forest. [0001642] 14/02/1969
Branigan Ms J, BA(Hons DipLib MCLIP, Nat.Inf.Mgr., Berrymans Lace Mawer, Manchester. [0043177] 14/09/1989
Branney Mrs CM, BA(Hons) MSc MCLIP, Asst.Lib., Foreign & Commonwealth Off., London. [0035836] 21/01/1983
Branson Mrs ME, (was O'Neill), BA DipLib MCLIP, Mother. [0030020] 30/10/1978
Branston Mrs EM, (was Wakefield), MCLIP, Sch.Lib.(p/t.), Copthill Sch.(Private Sch.), Stamford,Lincs. [0001645] 01/01/1968
Brant Miss L, BMus(Hons) MA, Peripatetic Music Teacher. [0057879] 14/11/1999
Brasch Mr S, PG dipInf, Volunteer Lib., Fostering Network, London. [0059710] 28/08/2001
Brasier Mrs ME, (was Cranna), MA DipLib MCLIP, Partner, Melchior Telematics, Educ.Web Publish.& Research. [0034056] 21/08/1981
Brassington Mrs JC, (was Smith), MCLIP, L.Operations Mgr., Bath & N.E.Somerset. [0022716] 12/09/1974
Brassington Mrs M, (was Grimwood), BA MCLIP, p./t.Enquiry Serv.Lib., Peterborough City Council. [0001648] 17/01/1966
Brathwaite Ms AW, BA DipM, Head of Marketing, Walker Books, London. [0058816] 07/08/2000
Bratman Mrs M, (was Williams), BA MCLIP, Retired. [0015953] 01/01/1969
Braun Mrs HL, (was Cross), BA MCLIP, Unemployed through Ill Health. [0034042] 29/07/1981
Braune Mrs JV, MA LLB, L.Asst., Muswell Hill L., London. [0056873] 27/10/1998
Bravin Mrs KB, (was Burton), BA MCLIP, Lib./Teacher, Brit.Sch.of Brussels, Tervuren, Belgium. [0026302] 01/10/1976
Bray Miss AM, BA MCLIP, Life Member. [0001654] 29/01/1955
Bray Mr CM, BLib MCLIP, Principal Lib.Child.& Young Serv., Slough Ls., Slough. [0052273] 20/10/1995
Bray Mrs JG, (was Walters), BA MCLIP, Customer Serv.Mgr., Nottingham City Council, Cent.L. [0001655] 19/12/1966
Bray Ms M, BA MCLIP, L.Projects Offrr., Cent.L., L.B.of Bromley. [0023244] 14/11/1974
Bray Miss RE, BA(Hons), Trainee Lib., Horsham L. [0058084] 25/10/1999
Bray Mrs SB, (was Fopp), BA, L.Mgr., Guildford L., Surrey. [0047432] 12/08/1992
Brayner Mrs ARA, MA, Trainee L.Asst., Univ.of London L., Senate House, London. [0059911] 02/11/2001
Brazendale Mrs EH, MA MCLIP, Lib., Robert Gordons Coll., Aberdeen. [0029315] 26/05/1978
Brazier Mrs C, (was Mitchell), MA DipLib MA, Employment not known. [0034131] 08/10/1981
Brazier Ms H, MA MCLIP, Ch.Exec., Nat.L.for the Blind, Stockport. [0032881] 06/10/1980
Brazier Ms JM, (was Harrold), BA MCLIP, Head of L.Serv., L.H.Q., MOD, Germany. [0025549]21/01/1976
Breaden Ms D, BA HDipEd DipLIS, Coll.Lib., St.Catherines Coll.of Educ., Dublin. [0041814] 11/04/1988
Bream Mrs CA, (was Wright), MA MCLIP, Civil Servant(L.), Commission of the E.U., Belgium. [0018223] 01/10/1972
Bream Mr PJ, BA(Hons) MCLIP, E.Area L.Mgr., N.Tyneside Cent.L., N.Shields. [0001664]01/07/1968

Personal Members   Briscoe

Breasley Mrs HM, (was Cater), MA MCLIP, Lib., MWH., High Wycombe. [0050689]   10/10/1994
Brebner Mrs J, (was Wall), Market Inf.Mgr., W.H.Smith plc., Swindon. [0049368]   29/10/1993
Brecknell Ms SM, (was Newton), BA(Hons) DipLib MCLIP, Lib., Univ.Mus.of Nat.Hist., Oxford. [0039431]   23/01/1986
Breckon Mr GJ, DipLib, Asst.Lib., Wirral Bor.Council, Birkenhead. [0057787] 05/08/1999
Breed Mr A, BA(Hons), Telecoms Inf. Specialist, N.M.Rothschild & Sons, London. [0058196]   16/11/1999
Breeden Miss SB, MCLIP, Life Member. [0001667]   01/10/1953
Breen Mr DF, BA(Hons)LIS, Unemployed. [0037969]   01/01/1985
Bremer Mrs RAP, (was Stephens), MCLIP, Retired. [0011495]   31/08/1963
Bremer Mr RJ, MCLIP, Employment not known. [0060784]   12/12/2001
Bremner Miss A, BSc(Hons) DipILM MCLIP, Asst.Lib.-Learner Support, Open Univ., Milton Keynes. [0050809]   19/10/1994
Bremner Mr IC, BSc MCLIP, Employment not known. [0060150] 10/12/2001
Bremner Ms JM, (was Jordan), BA DipLib MCLIP, Lend.Serv.Mgr.-Job Share, Bristol Cent.L. [0032882]   06/10/1980
Brenchley Miss SE, BA MCLIP, Community Serv.Lib., W.D.H.Q., Hants. [0025226]   08/01/1976
Brennan Miss EC, Lib./Head of Res., Beacon Comm.Coll., Crowborough. [0055510]   20/10/1997
Brennan Miss MM, BA MCLIP, Life Member. [0001673]   18/09/1951
Breslin Ms CL, MSc BSc, Systems Analyst/Developer, Univ.of Strathclyde, Glasgow. [0061184] 03/04/2002
Breslin Mrs TR, (was Green), MCLIP, Self employed writer. [0001675] 13/10/1967
Bretney Miss N, BA MLS MCLIP, Lib.II, Univ.of the W.Indies, Barbados. [0016642]   08/09/1958
Brett Mr CW, BSc MCLIP, Lib.-Serv.Provision, L.Serv.for Educ., Leics.L. [0041562]   21/01/1988
Brett Ms IJ, BA(Hons), Inf.Offr., Linklaters & Alliance, London. [0049407] 21/10/1993
Brett Miss J, BLib MCLIP, Mgr., Inf.Cent., Leeds Metro.Univ. [0037234] 08/05/1984
Brett Mr SJ, FCLIP, Life Member. [0001681]   12/10/1936
FE 01/01/1954
Brettle Mrs AJ, (was Warburton), BA(Hons) MSc, Research Fellow (Inf.), Salford Univ., Salford, Greater Manchester. [0046485]   12/11/1991
Brettle Mrs M, (was Davies), BA MCLIP MA, p./t.Lect./EFL Teacher/Examiner, Shrewsbury Coll.of Art & Tech., Trinity Coll. [0003724]   15/01/1972
Brevitt Mrs B, (was Mee), BA(Hons) MSc MCLIP, Sen.L.Clerk, House of Commons L., Westminster. [0048658]   02/04/1993
Brevitt Mr J, BA MCLIP, Employment not known. [0060851]   12/12/2001
Brew Ms A, Asst.Lib., British Med.Assoc., London. [0058457]   22/02/2000
Brew Mrs I, Stud., Loughborough Univ. [0058250]   25/11/1999
Brewer Mrs AM, BSc DipInfSci MCLIP, Employment not known. [0060433] 11/12/2001
Brewer Mrs HK, (was Grant), Hatrics Mgr., Hants.C.C. [0038432] 26/04/1985
Brewer Miss JA, (was Butt), MCLIP, Retired. [0002216]   20/07/1962
Brewer Mr JG, MCLIP, Lib., Univ.of Derby. [0001683]   01/01/1966
Brewer Mrs MJ, (was Wensley), BA DipLib MCLIP, p./t.L.Asst., Royal Devon & Exeter Healthcare, NHS Trust, Exeter Med.L. [0031975] 10/01/1980
Brewer Miss MK, Temp.Worker. [0057552]   28/04/1999
Brewer Miss PMSJ, MBIM MCLIP, Life Member, Clifton Lodge, 70 Epsom Rd., Guildford, Surrey, GU1 3PB. [0001684]   03/09/1946
Brewer Mr SA, MA FIMgt FRSA MCLIP, Freelance, 37 Moor Court, Westfield, Newcastle upon Tyne, NE3 4YD. [0001686]   02/10/1963
Brewer Mrs SG, (was Jones), BA, Unemployed. [0046436]   06/11/1991
Brewerton Mr AW, MA DipLib FCLIP, Subject Team Leader, Oxford Brookes Univ., Oxford. [0042415]   21/10/1988   **FE 20/05/1998**
Brewin Mr HBG, MCLIP, Strategy & Commissioning Offr., Merton Civic Centre. [0001688]   03/02/1969
Brewin Mr PMR, MA MCLIP, Project Coordinator, European Patent Off., Rijswijk, Netherlands. [0001689]   12/03/1969
Brewis Miss MM, BA DIP ED TECH MCLIP, Course Resources Off.& Slide Lib., Faculty of Art & Design L., Univ.of Brighton. [0021255] 11/10/1973
Brewster Mrs A, (was Clarkson), BA MCLIP, Asst.Young People's Lib., Tameside MBC. [0002797]   16/01/1972
Brewster Mrs E, MCLIP, Retired. [0019888]   01/01/1973
Brewster Mrs JB, (was Greaves), MCLIP, Lib., Hertfordshire Ls., Hertford, Herts. [0001689]   06/11/1964
Brewster Mr JH, BA(Hons) MA MCLIP, Lend.Lib., Hants.C.C. [0051660] 02/05/1995
Brewty Miss CA, BA MCLIP, L.Res.Mgr., Christ Church C.of E.Sch., N.Finchley. [0038693]   01/10/1985
Brice Mrs A, (was Power), BA(Hons) DipLib MCLIP, Asst.Dir., Health Care L.Unit., Univ.of Oxford, John Radcliffe Hosp., Oxford. [0035248] 05/10/1982
Brice Mrs RE, (was Fredericks), BSc(Hons) MA MCLIP, Inf.Devel.Offr., Herts.C.C. [0054225]   08/11/1996
Brick Miss LJ, BA(Hons) MSc, Inf.Researcher, CSFB, London. [0053772] 01/10/1996
Briddock Miss RM, MA MA C TEFLA MCLIP, Lib./Teacher, Uskudar American Sch., Istanbul, Turkey. [0031208]   16/10/1979
Briddon Mr JM, BSc PGCE MA, Faculty Lib., Health & Social Care, Univ.of the W.of England. [0053190]   25/03/1996
Bridge Ms JJ, BA(Hons) DipEd DipLIS MCLIP, Unemployed. [0056925] 10/11/1998
Bridge Mrs LE, (was Barker), MCLIP, Sen.L.Asst./Readers Adviser, Bolton M.B.C. [0021773]   10/01/1974
Bridge Mrs MA, (was Robertson), OBE MA MCLIP, Asst.Dir./IMPE, Dept.of Trade & Industry, London. [0012544]   30/10/1971
Bridge Miss ME, MCLIP, Life Member. [0001702]   25/06/1952

Bridge Mrs PM, L.Mgr., Great Baddow L., Chelmsford. [0057625] 25/05/1999 **AF**
Bridgeman Mrs G, BSc(Hons) PG DipLib, L.Asst., Oxford Brookes Univ., Oxford. [0035783]   12/01/1983
Bridgen Mr MS, BA(Hons), Unemployed. [0055309]   24/09/1997
Bridger Mrs JS, Employment not known. [0060835]   12/12/2001
Bridges Mrs BM, (was Evenett), MCLIP, L.Inf.Offr., Chartered Inst.of Personnel & Dev., London SW19. [0026229]   30/08/1976
Bridges Ms HM, BA, Grad.Trainee, Inst.of Classical Studies L. [0061743] 31/10/2002
Bridges Mrs L, (was Iveson), MCLIP, Grp.Lib., Metro.Bor.of Sefton. [0001708]   18/02/1970
Bridgman Mrs J, (was Hawksley), MCLIP, Temp./p./t.Housebound Lib., Newport L. [0006574]   07/03/1972
Bridgwater Mrs SM, (was Jenkins), BA MPhil MCLIP, L.Mgr.(Devel.), Tower Hamlets L., London. [0007803]   01/01/1972
Bridson Mrs PA, (was Cox), MCLIP, Res.Cent.Mgr., Maricourt High Sch., Sefton M.B.C. [0003285]   06/10/1969
Brien Miss A, BA MCLIP, Lib., Health & Safety Exec., Sheffield. [0026225] 31/08/1976
Brierley Mrs GL, (was Richards), BA MCLIP, Unemployed. [0021923] 25/01/1974
Brierley Miss J, DipLib MCLIP, Lib.-Leisure L., Cent.L., Nottingham Cent.L. [0037995]   01/01/1985
Brierley Mrs L, (was Forrester), BA(Hons) MCLIP, Multimedia Learning Cent.Mgr., Deeside Coll., Flintshire. [0046019]   28/08/1991
Brierley Mr RJ, BA MA, Lib., Derby City Council. [0045444]   06/02/1991
Briers Mrs KL, (was Brown), BSc(Econ) MCLIP, L.Asst., Univ.of Wales, Aberystwyth. [0051171]   23/11/1994
Briers Mrs SC, (was Randolph), BA MCLIP, Lib., SOG Ltd., The L., Runcorn. [0030516]   29/01/1979
Briggs Mrs A, (was Walton), BA MCLIP, Resident in Dubai. [0001715] 13/01/1965
Briggs Mrs BP, MCLIP, BA MCLIP, Lib., Holy Family Sch., W.Yorks. [0001716] 08/10/1969
Briggs Mr CA, BA DipLib MCLIP, Curator F, Brit.L., Boston Spa,W.Yorks. [0037455]   01/01/1984
Briggs Miss CP, BA MCLIP, Career Break. [0026292]   16/10/1976
Briggs Ms G, BA MCLIP, Career Break. [0036684]   03/11/1983
Briggs Mrs GM, MA FCLIP, Life Member. [0001719]   15/10/1937
FE 01/01/1941
Briggs Mrs H, (was Broad), BA DMS MIMgt MCLIP, Sen.Lib., Music & Drama, Glos.C.C. [0001720] 15/02/1967
Briggs Miss HJC, BA MCLIP, Lib., International Sch of Berne. [0047100] 30/04/1992
Briggs Mr JR, BA, L.Asst., Hallward L., Univ.of Nottingham. [0040977] 01/10/1987
Briggs Mr JW, BSc MCLIP, H.of Catr., Defence Evaluation & Res.Agency, Farnborough, Hants. [0029592]   19/10/1978
Briggs Mr NW, BSc MA MCLIP, Employment not known. [0060157] 10/12/2001
Briggs Mrs SF, (was Wood), L.Asst., Main L., Univ.of Birmingham. [0046756] 16/01/1992   **AF**
Briggs Miss TJ, BA(Hons) MCLIP, Inf.Arch., Syngenta, Bracknell. [0049011] 27/08/1993
Briggs Miss V, BSc, Stud., Univ.of Wales, Aberystwyth, & Learning Cent.Asst.-Learning, Cent., S.Thames Coll., London. [0057898]   01/10/1999
Bright Mr DJ, Life Member. [0001724]   10/09/1948
Bright Miss E, BA(Hons), L.Asst., Ely L., Cambs. [0059674]   25/07/2001 **AF**
Bright Miss H, BA(Hons) MCLIP, Team Lib., Northants.C.C. Northants.L.Serv. [0055615]   27/10/1997
Bright Mr KM, BA DipLib MCLIP, Business Analyst Financial Serv., Egon Zehnder Int. [0033612]   29/01/1981
Bright Mrs M, (was Foster), Lib., Essex C.C., Chelmsford L. [0005111]   05/10/1971
Bright Mrs S, BA(Hons) FAETC, p./t.Sen.L.Asst., Univ.of Northumbria at Newcastle. [0052543]   06/11/1995
Brighting Mrs L, (was Thorpe), MCLIP, L.Mgr., Bethlehem Inst.of Educ., Tauranga, New Zealand. [0014693]   01/01/1966
Brill Ms KT, MSc, Media Spec./Lib., USA. [0056521]   03/08/1998
Brimlow Miss AE, MA DipLib MCLIP, Access Serv.Mgr., Essex C.C.L., Chelmsford. [0027901]   01/01/1977
Brindle Mrs J, (was Coates), MA MCLIP, Head of Strategy,Performance & Dev., Arts & Leisure, Leicester City Council. [0036531]   13/10/1983
Brindley Mr GD, BA(Hons), Stud., Loughborough Univ. [0059975] 14/11/2001
Brindley Ms LJ, MA FCLIP, Ch.Exec., Brit.L. [0022909]   03/10/1974
FE 18/04/1990
Brine Mr AC, BA MSc MCLIP, LTSN Cent.Mgr., Loughborough Univ., Dept.Inf.Science. [0040215]   17/11/1986
Brine Mrs AM, (was Kenny), BA DipLib MCLIP, Grp.Lib.(Acting), Leics.C.C., Syston. [0043195]   02/10/1989
Brine Dr JJ, BA PhD MCLIP, Freelance Bibl. [0001729]   03/01/1972
Brinkman Miss RC, BA(Hons) PGCE, Stud., Univ.Brighton. [0059927] 06/11/2001
Brinkworth Miss SC, MCLIP, Retired. [0001736]   03/03/1958
Brinkworth Ms SK, Asst.Lib., Univ.of W.of England, Bristol. [0054498] 02/01/1997
Brinson Mr CM, MCLIP, Lib.(Access), Essex C.C., Loughton, Essex. [0001737]   01/01/1971
Brisbourne Mrs JD, (was Ward), MCLIP, Lib., Essex L.Serv., Chelmsford L. [0001739]   07/11/1966
Briscoe Miss JH, JP MCLIP, OFSTED Inspector, Sch.& Child.Offr., Sefton Leisure Serv., Crosby L. [0001740]   25/09/1959
Briscoe Mrs WM, (was Smith), MCLIP, Life Member. [0001741]   19/01/1940

Brisland Mrs JE, (was Summerson), BLS(Hons) MCLIP, Community Lib., Frankley L., Frankley Comm.High Sch.,Birmingham. [0034734] 22/01/1982
Brisley Mr AJ, BLib MCLIP, L.Area Mgr.-N., N.Somerset Dist.Council. [0023614] 17/01/1975
Bristow Mrs PA, (was Kerswell), MCLIP, L.& Inf.Mgr., Herts.Health Auth., St.Albans. [0001746]01/02/1961
Bristow Mr RK, MCLIP, Employment not known. [0001747] 16/10/1970
Britchford Mrs HC, (was Foster), MCLIP, Unemployed. [0005100] 05/09/1963
Britland Miss I, MCLIP, Life Member. [0001749] 17/07/1961
Britt Mrs ME, (was Green), DipLib DipEd MCLIP, p./t.Law Lib., Russell Jones & Walker, London. [0042130] 04/10/1988
Britt Mr R, BSc MIL MITI MCLIP, Employment not known. [0060158] 10/12/2001
Brittain Mrs GM, (was Bird), LLB DipLib, Inf.Offr., BCD Underwriting Agency Ltd., London. [0045715] 01/05/1991
Brittain Ms JA, BA MA MCLIP, Reg.Inf.Co-ordinator, E.& Cent.Africa, Brit.Council, London. [0053137] 01/04/1996
Brittain Mrs JM, (was Brown), BA(Hons), Princ.Lib.(Operations), Middlesbrough Council. [0037298] 08/06/1984
Brittain Mrs RH, (was Cooper), MA DipLib MCLIP, Unemployed. [0003136] 01/01/1970
Brittain Mrs RJ, Inf.Serv.Offr., Canbridge Consultants. [0060911] 10/01/2002
Brittan Ms C, (was Huntley), MA MCLIP, Princ.Lib., Notts.C.C. [0007504] 12/02/1969
Brittan Miss SO, DipIM, Lib., Clyde & Co., London. [0055203] 13/08/1997
Brittin Mrs ME, (was Irving), BA MCLIP, L.& Inf.Consultant, 31 Solihull Rd., Shirley, Solihull, B90 3HB. [0001752]02/01/1970
Britton Miss J, BD AKC DipLib MCLIP, Unemployed. [0035875] 21/01/1983
Britton Ms J, (was Wilson), BA DipLib MCLIP, Sen.Lib.(Devel.), Wakefield M.D.C. [0039522] 13/02/1986
Britton Mrs JC, Sen.Lib.Asst., Beaconsfield L., Bucks. [0059200] 19/12/2000 **AF**
Britton Mrs RP, BA MA DipLib MCLIP, Sen.Comm.Lib., Bolton M.B.C., Westhoughton L. [0025493] 26/01/1976
Broad Mrs EB, (was Ritchie), MA MCLIP, Inf.Cent.Mgr., DLA, Solicitors, Glasgow. [0018132] 03/10/1972
Broad Mrs JM, (was Dempsey), BEd DipLib MCLIP, Site Operations Mgr., Staffs.Univ., Stoke on Trent. [0046530] 18/11/1991
Broadbent Miss AY, BA MCLIP, Tech.Serv.Lib., Oxon.C.C. [0027903] 17/10/1977
Broadbent Mrs EB, (was Hollier), BA FCLIP, Life Member. [0001761] 01/01/1931 **FE 01/01/1966**
Broadbent Miss HA, MCLIP, Bibl.Lib., Cornwall C.C. [0001762] 21/03/1971
Broadbent Mrs KJ, (was Doidge), BA(Hons), p./t.Asst.Lib., The Henley Coll., Henley-on-Thames, Oxon. [0044981] 24/01/1991
Broadbent Mrs LR, (was Stephen), BA FCLIP, Life Member. [0013945] 01/01/1957 **FE 01/01/1962**
Broadbent Mrs VM, (was Woodhouse), BSc MCLIP, L.Mgr., Hawke's Bay Dist.Health Board L., Hastings, New Zealand. [0016645] 13/10/1964
Broadhead Mrs JE, BA DipLib, L.Asst., Laban Cent., London. [0053130] 01/03/1996
Broadhurst Miss EJ, BA MCLIP, Retired. [0001763] 14/10/1968
Broadis Mr GJ, MA FCLIP, Retired. [0001765] 08/10/1958 **FE 01/01/1963**
Broadley Ms LC, BA(Hons), EI Guidance Mgr., QinetiQ, Farnborough. [0050796] 18/10/1994
Broady-Preston Dr JE, BA MA PhD AIMgt MCLIP ILTM, Dir.of Learning & Teaching, Dept.of Inf.& L.Studies, Univ.of Wales, Aberystwyth. [0035476] 13/10/1982
Brock Miss AJ, MA(Hons) DipILS MCLIP, Sch.Lib., W.Dunbartonshire Council, Clydebank. [0051600] 06/04/1995
Brock Miss EJ, BLS MCLIP, Team Lib., Norfolk L.& Inf.Serv. [0027904] 07/10/1977
Brock Dr JR, BSc PhD MCLIP, Employment not known. [0043785] 11/01/1990
Brock Ms L, BA MA, Retired. [0044242] 23/07/1990
Brock Miss SA, BA DipLib MA MCLIP, Site Mgr., S.Bank Univ., Elephant & Castle. [0046135] 07/10/1991
Brock Dr SL, BA(Hons) PhD DAA, Head L. & Inf.Resources., Shakespeare Centre L. [0059211] 08/01/2001
Brockett Mrs RA, (was Campion), Sen.Inf.Offr., Eversheds, Nottingham. [0052224] 16/01/1995
Brockhill Mr K, BA MCLIP, Sen.Asst.Lib., Kirklees P.L., W.Yorks. [0018308] 13/10/1972
Brockie Miss JK, BSc(Hons) MSc(Econ), Inf.Sci., DSTL, Glasgow. [0055466] 13/10/1997
Brocklebank Mrs J, BA DipLib MIL MCLIP, Team Leader- Bus.Lang.& Euro.Stud., Aston Univ., LIS., Birmingham. [0037822] 01/10/1984
Brocklebank Mrs PM, (was Hulbert), BA MCLIP, Lib., Writhlington Sch., Radstock. [0007427]05/10/1971
Brocklehurst Mrs ML, (was Gardiner), BSc(Hons) MA, Inf.Serv.Co-ordinator, Wellcome Trust. [0050047] 21/02/1994
Broderick Mrs SA, (was Beales), BA(Hons) MCLIP, Lib., Child.& Sch.Section, L.HQ., Winchester, Hants. [0018423] 23/10/1972
Brodie Mr A, BA DipLib, Stud., Dept.of Vision Sci., Glasgow Caledonian Univ. [0044891] 09/01/1991
Brodie Miss AE, BA DipLib MCLIP, Unemployed. [0032481] 23/04/1980
Brodie Mrs AH, (was Higges), MCLIP, Life Member. [0001772] 19/04/1944
Brodie Mr CJ, BA PgDip, Asst.Lib., Royal Soc.of Medicine, London. [0050106] 28/03/1994
Brodie Mrs MCD, BA MCLIP, Asst.Lib., Grangemouth L. [0028416] 07/12/1977

Brodie Mrs MD, BA ANZLA FCLIP, Resident in New Zealand. [0006958] 21/10/1970 **FE 24/09/1997**
Brodie Ms MR, MCLIP, Retired. [0001774] 15/08/1966
Broekmann Mrs EP, BA, Lib.:Child.&Young Peoples Serv., Slough L. [0061522] 04/09/2002
Brogarth Ms DJ, LLB (Hons) LLM DipInfoSc, L. Mgr., Freshfields Bruckhaus Deringer, London. [0061001] 29/01/2002
Brolly Mrs AM, (was Kiely), BA MCLIP, Asst.Lib., L.B.of Redbridge. [0032104] 28/01/1980
Bromley Mr DW, JP MA FCLIP, Life Member. [0001780] 03/03/1953 **FE 01/01/1960**
Bromley Mrs GM, (was Batt), MCLIP, Area Serv.Mgr., Kent C.C. Arts & L., Ashford L. [0025484] 20/01/1976
Brommeland Mrs RR, (was Ritland), MCLIP, Lib., Univ.L.of Bergen, Norway. [0016647] 03/06/1961
Bromwich Mr D, MA MCLIP, Somerset Studies Lib., Somerset Co.L. [0001783] 31/08/1965
Bromwich Mr SD, BA(Hons), Lib./Res.Mgr., Harvey Grammar Sch., Folkestone. [0047881] 23/10/1992
Brook Ms AEJ, BA DipLib MCLIP, Sch.Lib., Highbury Grove Sch., Islington. [0025494] 20/01/1976
Brook Mrs DM, BA RGN, Inf.Servs.Mgr., Hewlett Packard Ltd., Bristol. [0041890] 11/05/1988
Brook Mr GW, MCLIP, Retired. [0001785] 16/08/1960
Brook Miss KJ, BA MCLIP, Unemployed. [0038056] 08/01/1985
Brook Mrs LFC, (was Hale), BA MCLIP, Asst.Lib., Home Off., London. [0011475] 01/01/1972
Brook Mr M, MA MCLIP, Life Member, Tel.0115 969 2350, 18 Whittingham Rd., Mapperley, Nottingham, NG3 6BL. [0001789] 27/03/1949
Brook Mr MJ, BA DipLib MCLIP, Comm.Serv.Mgr., W.Berks.Council, Newbury. [0030369] 13/01/1979
Brook Mr NJ, BA(Hons) PGDip, Inf.Lib., Asst.Lib., Glenfield Med.L., Leicester. [0055232] 05/09/1997
Brook Mr RA, BA(Hons) PGDip, Inf. Support Lib., Worcestershire Acute Hosp., Worcs. [0046279] 22/10/1991
Brooke Miss ES, MCLIP, Retired. [0001795] 02/02/1956
Brooke Mr JD, BA, Lib./Inf.Offr., G.M.Drugs Ref.L., Trafford Substance Misuse Serv. [0042408] 21/10/1988
Brooke Miss PEMO, MCLIP, Life Member. [0001797] 08/03/1949
Brooke Mrs VA, BA MCLIP, Bibl.Serv.Lib., Royal Horticultural Soc., Wisley, Surrey. [0026626] 14/10/1976
Brooke Miss WM, BLib MCLIP, Ch.L.Asst., Mgmt.Cent.L., Univ.of Bradford. [0023807] 27/01/1975
Brooker Miss DJ, BA MCLIP, Systems Mgr., Devon L.Serv.L.H.Q., Exeter. [0032883] 06/10/1980
Brooker Mr J, Special Collections Asst., Univ.of Bradford, J.B.Priestley L. [0046773] 22/01/1992 **AF**
Brooker Mrs J, MA BLS MCLIP, Not in paid employment, 20 East Avenue,Parkgate, Frankfield, Cork, Ireland. [0030096] 08/12/1978
Brooker Mrs JC, (was Mitchell), MCLIP, Lib., Maidstone Girls Grammar Sch., Kent. [0022933] 01/10/1974
Brooker Ms MM, BSc, p./t.L.Asst., Sittingbourne P.L., Kent. [0045294] 02/10/1990 **AF**
Brookes Miss EJ, BLib AdvDipEd MCLIP, H.of Court L., The Court Serv. [0037606] 10/10/1984
Brookes Mrs JJA, (was Hopper), FCLIP, Life Member. [0001803] 13/09/1948 **FE 01/01/1963**
Brookes Mrs JM, MA MCLIP, Sen.Lib.-Inf.& ICT, Retford L., Notts.C.C. [0037661] 15/10/1984
Brookes Ms LJ, MSc MCLIP, Employment not known. [0060159] 10/12/2001
Brookes Miss SJ, BA(Hons) MLib MCLIP, Database Offr., Careers Advisory Serv., Univ.of Warwick. [0049283] 20/10/1993
Brooking Mrs AJ, (was Fleming), BA MCLIP, Full-time Mum. [0037548] 10/10/1984
Brooking Mr CD, RIBA, Pre-Lib.Student, Camberwell Coll. of Arts. [0059751] 17/09/2001
Brookman Mrs AJ, (was Reynolds), BA DipLIS PGCE MCLIP, Lib., King Edward VII Hosp., Midhurst, W.Sussex GU29 0BL. [0035785] 12/01/1983
Brooks Mr DJ, MA MCLIP, Asst.Div.Lib., S.Lancs.Div.L.(Chorley), Lancs.Co.L. [0024477] 29/08/1975
Brooks Ms IM, BA(Hons) MA DipLIS, Stud., Royal Holloway, Univ.of London. [0047551] 01/10/1992
Brooks Mrs J, (was Riding), BA MCLIP, Learning Resources Mgr., Milton Cross Sch., Portsmouth. [0025404] 06/01/1976
Brooks Mrs JM, (was Pindard), BA MCLIP, Br.Lib., Poulton L., Lancs.C.C. [0027619] 21/06/1977
Brooks Mrs JS, BA(Hons) MCLIP, Asst.Educ.Serv.Lib., Trafford Met.Bor.Council, Manchester. [0050948] 31/10/1994
Brooks Mrs LG, (was Frost), BA DipLib MCLIP, Asst.Lib., Bibl.Serv.Section, Guildhall L., London. [0026962] 19/01/1977
Brooks Mrs M, (was Yoxall), BA MCLIP, Asst.IT Mgr., Oxon.C.C. [0026041] 27/05/1976
Brooks Mrs M, (was Kearsley), BA MCLIP, Lib.ICT, Bolton Cent.L. [0047068] 21/04/1992
Brooks Mr PC, BA(Hons) PGCE MA MCLIP, Sen.Asst.Lib., The Royal Agric.Coll. [0051873] 21/07/1995
Brooks Miss PR, BSc MCLIP, Retired. [0060522] 11/12/2001
Brooks Miss RD, BA(Hons) DipLIS MCLIP, Asst.Lib., Univ.of the West of England, Bristol. [0048018] 03/11/1992
Brooks Ms S, BA, L.Asst., New Coll., Durham. [0053758] 01/10/1996
Brooks Ms SA, MA MCLIP, L.Offr., Mus.of London. [0050681] 10/10/1994
Brooks Mrs SL, BA, Lib., Gifford & Partners, (Eng.Consultants), Southampton. [0035231] 07/10/1982
Brooks Miss SL, (was Poyner), BA(Hons) MCLIP, Sch.Lib., Ackworth Sch., W.Yorks. [0046459] 07/11/1991

Brooks Mrs SM, Unemployed. [0057964] 07/10/1999 AF
Broome Miss AM, BA(Hons), Lib., Royal Inst.of Cornwall, Truro. [0046858] 19/02/1992
Broome Mr EM, OBE FCLIP HonFCLIP, Life Member, Fig Tree Cottage, 14 Market St., Bottlesford, NG13. [0001822] 27/09/1943 FE 01/01/1957
Brophy Mrs JA, (was Harvey), MCLIP, Self Employed. [0006512] 27/02/1969
Brophy Prof P, BSc HonFCLIP FCLIP FRSA, Prof.of Inf.Mgmt., Manchester Metro.Univ. [0024063] 14/04/1975 FE 15/02/1989
Broster Mr TA, FCLIP, Life Member. [0019469] 08/01/1954 FE 01/01/1966
Brotchie Mr NGT, MA DipLib MCLIP, Lib., Scottish Law Commission, Edinburgh. [0023247] 12/11/1974
Broughton Miss CE, BA DipLib MCLIP, Grp.Lib.-Glenfield Grp., Leics.L.& Inf.Serv., Leics. [0001829] 01/01/1972
Broughton Mrs DV, BA DipLib MA MCLIP, Learning Resource Lib., Bradford Educ. Auth., Bradford, West Yorkshire. [0043865] 05/02/1990
Broughton Miss SC, BA DipLib MCLIP AILAM MCLIP, Inf.Mgr., Inst.of Leisure & Amenity Mgmt., Reading. [0030118] 11/01/1979
Broughton Ms VD, MA DipLib, Lect., Univ.Coll.London. [0044471] 11/10/1990
Brown Mrs A, (was Butler), BA MCLIP, Not Employed. [0032640] 10/07/1980
Brown Ms A, BSc MSC, Subject Lib.,Health, Univ.of Plymouth, Redruth. [0043614] 09/11/1989
Brown Mr AA, MA(Hons) FCLIP, Retired. [0001935] 01/01/1958 FE 09/11/1973
Brown Miss AC, BEcon DipLib MCLIP, Lib.-State L.Serv., State L.of Victoria, Australia. [0025010] 01/11/1975
Brown Mr AD, BSc(Hons) MA MCLIP, L.Systems Liaison Offr., Bury M.B.C., Lancs. [0049932] 25/01/1994
Brown Mr AE, FCLIP, Life Member. [0001836] 26/02/1934 FE 01/01/1953
Brown Mrs AF, p./t.Sen.L.Asst., Leeds Univ. [0052286] 23/10/1995
Brown Mr AG, MA DipEd FCLIP, Life Member, 47 Bryce Rd., Currie, Midlothian, EH14 5LP. [0018527] 19/01/1951 FE 01/01/1960
Brown Ms AI, BA(Hons), Inf.Admin., Yorkshire Arts, W.Yorkshire. [0061620] 04/10/2002 AF
Brown Miss AJ, BA, Unemployed. [0059599] 26/06/2001
Brown Mrs AJ, (was Mcharg), MCLIP, Retired. [0016653] 01/01/1960
Brown Mr AT, BA(Hons) MSc(Econ) MCLIP, Inf.Systems Lib., Univ.of Wales Swansea. [0052957] 26/01/1996
Brown Rev BE, MCLIP, Retired. [0001840] 01/01/1955
Brown Mrs BI, (was Cole), MCLIP, Sen.Lib., S.Lanarkshire L.Dept. [0002946] 22/01/1970
Brown Mrs BM, (was Prince), MA MSc MCLIP, Lib.-(Job Share), Fine Art Dept., Edinburgh City L. [0039195] 05/01/1986
Brown Dr BW, BSc PhD, Employment not known. [0060500] 11/12/2001
Brown Mr C, MCLIP, Princ.Asst.City Lib., Portsmouth City Council. [0001845] 01/01/1969
Brown Mrs C, (was Shaw), MA MCLIP, Lib., Cent.L., Manchester [0001843] 14/01/1968
Brown Ms C, BA MCLIP MLib, Area Lib., L.B.of Southwark. [0024196] 19/05/1975
Brown Miss CA, BA MCLIP, Lib., Salans Hertzfeld Heilbronn, London. [0049656] 23/11/1993
Brown Mrs CE, BA(Hons) MA, Lib., Ollerton L., New Ollerton, Newark. [0042640] 30/01/1989
Brown Miss CJ, BA(Hons) MSc, Inf.Res.Co-ordinator, Construction Ind.Training Board, Kings Lynn. [0057148] 22/12/1998
Brown Mrs CJ, (was Freeland), BA MCLIP, Lib., Essex C.C., Colchester. [0001849] 06/01/1967
Brown Miss CW, BA MCLIP, Asst.Lib., Rhondda Cynon Taff C.B.C., Aberdare. [0023503] 01/01/1975
Brown Ms D, BA(Hons) MPhil MA MCLIP, Lib./Teacher, Goethe Institut, Manchester. [0050097] 28/03/1994
Brown Mr DJ, BA MA MCLIP, Lib., St.Martins Coll., Lancaster. [0001854] 26/02/1965
Brown Mr DJ, MA(Hons) DipEd DipLib, Warden Support Offr., Historic Scotland, Edinburgh. [0061722] 29/10/2002
Brown Mr DL, FCLIP, Life Member, No.of 1242 522307, 34,Westbury Rd., Leckhampton, Cheltenham. [0001855] 07/04/1937 FE 01/01/1969
Brown Miss EA, BA PGDipLib MCLIP, Lib., Montrose L. [0045716] 02/05/1991
Brown Miss EC, (was Sinclair), MCLIP, Life Member. [0001862] 08/03/1941
Brown Ms ES, MA DipLib MCLIP, Inf.& Life Long Learning Mgr., E.Dunbartonshire Council, Kirkintilloch. [0031729] 19/11/1979
Brown Ms FJ, MA(Hons) DipLIS CGLI MCLIP, p./t.I.T.Instructor/Lib./Stud., Clinterty Cent., Aberdeen Coll. [0053439] 01/07/1996
Brown Mr FJL, MA(Hons), (was Laird), MA(Hons), p./t.Stud./Sen.L.Asst., Cent.for Tropical Vet.Med.L., Univ.of Edinburgh., Roslin. [0049134] 01/07/1993
Brown Mr G, BA(Hons), p./t.Stud./Lib.Asst., University of Brighton., Poole Ref.L. [0059128] 21/11/2000
Brown Mrs G, BA MCLIP, Team Lib., Bibl.Serv., Glos.Co.L.Serv. [0027135] 19/01/1977
Brown Mrs G, (was Whittingham), BSc DipInfSc, Lib., Nycomed Amersham Plc., Amersham, Bucks. [0033794] 05/03/1981
Brown Mrs G, BA(Hons), L.Super./ Asst.i./c., Broadway L., Worcs. [0057201] 14/01/1999 AF
Brown Miss GA, MCLIP, Team Lib., Norfolk L.& Inf.Serv., Diss L. [0001868] 29/09/1964
Brown Miss HF, BA(Hons) MCLIP, Learning Res.Cent.Mgr., Reading Coll., & Sch.of Art & Design. [0052355] 26/10/1995
Brown Miss HI, stud., Loughborough University, Loughborough. [0061435] 29/07/2002

Brown Mrs HJ, (was Metcalfe), MCLIP CertEd PGCPD ILTHE, Lib./Tutor, Shrewsbury Coll.of Art & Tech., Shrewsbury. [0029522] 27/06/1978
Brown Mrs HJ, (was Cadman), Asst.Lib.& Inf.Serv.Offr., Off.of Water Serv., Birmingham. [0044696] 28/11/1990
Brown Miss HL, B SOC SC LGSM MCLIP, L.Asst., Allen & Overy, London. [0030119] 11/12/1978
Brown Mr IH, LLB, Legal Research Offr./Lib., Grampian Police, Strategic Devel.Dept. [0058032] 18/10/1999
Brown Mrs IS, (was Crawford), MCLIP, Housewife & Mother. [0001875] 14/10/1964
Brown Miss J, BA(Hons) MCLIP, Res.Lib., Herts.C.C., Sch.L.Serv. [0044829] 10/12/1990
Brown Mrs J, L.Mgr., Peterborough City Council, Cent.L. [0056616] 18/09/1998 AF
Brown Ms J, (was Pickup), BA(Hons) MCLIP, Lib.& Inf.Mgr., Bilborough Coll., Nottingham. [0047714] 19/10/1992
Brown Mrs JA, (was Owen), BLib MCLIP, p./t.Site Lib., Worcs.Acute Hosp.NHS Trust, Kidderminster Hosp. [0028110] 22/09/1977
Brown Mrs JAW, (was Watson), BA MCLIP, Area L.Offr., Highland Council, Caithness. [0032355] 13/02/1980
Brown Mrs JC, BSc MSc(Hons), Med.Lib.& P.G.Administrator, Vale of Leven D.G.Hosp., Argyll & Clyde Acute Trust. [0058103] 29/10/1999
Brown Miss JE, BA MCLIP, Local & Naval Studies Lib., Plymouth City Council. [0025011] 05/11/1975
Brown Mrs JE, (was Plank), MCLIP, Business/Mgmt.Lib., Chester Coll.of H.E. [0022904] 02/10/1974
Brown Mrs JL, (was Galaway), Asst. Librarian, B.E.L.B.,Central L., Belfast. [0046481] 12/11/1991
Brown Mrs JL, (was Duffy), BSc(Hons) MCLIP, Sen.Lib.HMP Manchester, Manchester City Ls., Manchester. [0004240] 12/01/1971
Brown Mrs JL, (was Kelvin), Unemployed. [0040577] 01/04/1987
Brown Miss JM, MA DipLib MCLIP, Sen.Lib., Robert Gordon Univ., Aberdeen. [0036477] 14/10/1983
Brown Mrs JM, (was Wareham), MCLIP, Retired. [0001888] 04/09/1952
Brown Miss JO, FCLIP, Life Member. [0001889] 11/10/1946 FE 01/01/1960
Brown Mrs JT, (was Broadhurst), BA, Asst.Lib., Univ.of Wales Inst., Cardiff, Cyncoed Site. [0044580] 30/10/1990
Brown Mr JW, BA DipILM MCLIP, LRC Mgr., Heaton Manor Sch., Newcastle upon Tyne. [0048906] 15/07/1993
Brown Mrs K, BA(Hons), Lib., The Royal Sch., Haslemere. [0056187] 01/04/1998
Brown Mrs KG, (was Evans), BA MCLIP, Unemployed. [0022629] 04/07/1974
Brown Mrs KH, (was Neave), BA DipLib MCLIP, Dep.Br.Lib., Fullwell Cross L., L.B.of Redbridge, Ilford, Essex. [0043970] 16/03/1990
Brown Miss KI, BA(Hons) MCLIP, Sen.Asst.Lib., Denton Wilde Sapte, London. [0049833] 16/12/1993
Brown Mrs L, (was Williamson), BA MCLIP, Primary Sch.Lib./Vol.Teacher, 86 Hole Lane, Northfield, Birmingham, B31 2DF. [0026882] 16/12/1976
Brown Ms L, DipLIS MCLIP, Dist.Lib., Western Educ.& L.Bd., Limavady, N.Ireland. [0021529]16/11/1973
Brown Mrs LM, BA(Hons) DipLIS MCLIP, P./t.Asst Lib.(Learning Support), Holy Cross Coll., Bury, Lancs. [0022413] 04/05/1974
Brown Miss LP, MCLIP, Unemployed. [0001896] 04/01/1968
Brown Mr LS, MRSC FInstPet FRSH GrIMFMgt MICorr MCLIY, Employment not known. [0060160] 12/01/2001
Brown Miss M, MCLIP, Ed., BNFVC., Brit.Film Inst., London. [0001900] 09/01/1968
Brown Mrs M, Lib., Faculty of Arch.& Hist.of Art L., Univ.of Cambridge. [0051287] 21/11/1996
Brown Susan M, BA(Hons) DipInfMgt MCLIP, L.Exec., House of Commons L., London. [0046101] 02/10/1991
Brown Miss MA, FCLIP, Life Member. [0001906] 28/03/1957 FE 01/01/1963
Brown Ms ME, BSc MCLIP, Sen.Lib., Lancs.C.C. E., Burnley Cent.L. [0023166] 07/10/1974
Brown Mr ML, MA PhD DipLib DipMgmt MCLIP, Univ.Lib., Univ.of Southampton, Hartley L. [0025229] 05/01/1976
Brown Mr MP, BA(Hons), Asst.Lib., Lazard & Co., London. [0057082] 04/12/1998
Brown Mrs MS, BA(Hons), Sen.L.Asst., Egglescliffe L., Stockton on Tees. [0058323] 10/01/2000 AF
Brown Miss NC, BA(Hons) MSc(Econ) MCLIP, Training & Devel.Co-ordinator, Oxfordshire Health Auth., NHS Trust, Oxfordshire. [0051199] 23/11/1994
Brown Mr PJT, BA MCLIP, Area L.Mgr., L.B.of Enfield, Edmonton Green L. [0019555] 21/11/1972
Brown Ms PWK, BA MA MCLIP, Asst.Youth Serv.Mgr., Durham Learning Res., Arts L.& Mus.Dept. [0036926] 16/01/1984
Brown Miss R, Grad.Trainee, Exeter Univ. [0059925] 10/09/2001
Brown Mr R, FCLIP, Life Member. [0001922] 01/01/1938 FE 01/01/1953
Brown Miss RA, B.lib MCLIP FSA Scot, Stud., Southampton Inst. [0031212] 19/10/1979
Brown Mr RD, BSc MCLIP, Sen.Lib., Smithkline Beecham Pharmaceuticals, Harlow, Essex. [0025231] 05/01/1976
Brown Mr RW, BA(Hons) MCLIP, Sen.Team Lib., N.Lanarkshire Educ.Res.Serv., Coatbridge. [0043658] 16/11/1989
Brown Miss S, BA(Hons) MA, Subject Lib., Kent.Inst.of Art & Design, Canterbury. [0058156] 09/11/1999
Brown Mrs S, (was Walmsley), Stud., Leeds Met.Univ. &, Employee, Brit.L., Wetherby. [0057555] 26/04/1999
Brown Miss SA, MCLIP, Search Admin.Asst., Heidrick & Struggles Exec.Search, London. [0056228] 07/04/1998
Brown Mrs SA, (was Calvert), BA MCLIP, Sen.Lib.Devl.Team, Huntingdon L., Cambridge. [0024619] 07/10/1975

Brown Mrs SJ, BSc(Econ), Res.Cent.Mgr., Portsmouth City Council, Springfield Sch. [0055157] 24/07/1997
Brown Ms SJ, BA(Hons) DipLib MCLIP, Coll.Lib., Archbishop Michael Ramsey Tech., Coll., London. [0030308] 17/01/1979
Brown Ms SJ, (was Walkden), BA(Hons) DipLib, Lib., Child.Serv., Chelmsford Cent.L. [0046372] 30/10/1991
Brown Ms SJ, BSc(Hons) MSc MCLIP, L.Serv.Mgr., Plymouth Hosp.NHS Trust, Derriford Hosp., Staff L. [0052258] 19/10/1995
Brown Miss SK, MCLIP, Team Lib.--Ref.& Local Stud., Kent Educ.& Ls., Tunbridge Wells. [0001931] 23/01/1968
Brown Miss SL, BSc(Hons), Inf.Specialist., Towers Perrin, London. [0049569] 19/11/1993
Brown Miss SL, BA, Lib., Trinity Coll., Bristol. [0035719] 21/01/1983
Brown Miss SL, BA(Hons) DipLIS MCLIP, Co.Inf.Offr., L.B.of Camden, London. [0047641] 09/10/1992
Brown Miss SLR, p./t.Stud., Inf.Asst., Univ.Central England, Hammond Suddards Edge. [0059552] 16/05/2001
Brown Ms SM, (was Jeffs), MCLIP, Dir.of Member Serv., CILIP., London. [0022349] 09/04/1976
Brown Mrs SME, (was Escott), MCLIP, p./t.Law Lib., Chambers of Michael Crystal QC, London. [0004614] 26/03/1970
Brown Ms SR, BA(Hons), Lib., BBC Inf.& Arch. [0051437] 14/02/1995
Brown Mr T, Res.Cent.Mgr., N.Chadderton Sch., Oldham. [0061033] 01/02/2002
Brown Miss TM, BLIB MCLIP, Tech.Lib., Benoy Ltd., London. [0029601] 23/10/1978
Brown Mr TWB, BSc DipLib MCLIP, Sen.Lib., Bell Coll.of Tech., Hamilton. [0028265] 24/10/1977
Brown Mr TY, BA, Community Lib., Gainsborough L., Lincs.C.C. [0058170] 09/11/1999
Brown Mrs V, (was Keene), MCLIP, Asst.Lib., Worcs.Co.L., Worcester. [0008209] 14/10/1963
Brown Mrs V, (was Smith), BA DipLib MCLIP, Children & Sch. Lib., Bolton L. [0044007] 05/04/1990
Brown Mrs V, (was Reed), MCLIP, Asst.Lib., L.B.of Bromley. [0001938] 01/01/1968
Brown Ms VC, BA(Hons), Inf.& Lifelong Learn.Lib., Inf.Desk, Bolton Cent.L. [0045958] 31/07/1991
Brown Mrs VFG, (was Hart), MCLIP, Lib., Lewis & Hickey, Edinburgh. [0006476] 21/03/1963
Brown Mr WH, ERD MSc FCLIP, Life Member. [0001942] 25/03/1949 FE 01/01/1963
Brown Mr Y, Asst.Lib., Cont.Educ.L., Birkbeck L. [0046663] 03/12/1991 AF
Brownbridge Ms SJ, BA(Hons) MScEcon, Local Studies Lib., Bath Cent.L. [0058886] 01/10/2000
Browne Mrs JH, BA, Unemployed. [0061723] 29/10/2002
Browne Mrs LM, BSc MCLIP, Employment unknown. [0060317] 10/12/2001
Browne Mr M, BA(Hons), Sen.L.Asst., Mus.& Drama, Carlisle L., Cumbria. [0056116] 20/02/1998
Browne Miss MA, MCLIP, Life Member. [0001950] 01/01/1937
Browne Mr MI, MA DipLib MCLIP ACIS, Ch.Operating Offr., Intelligent Exhibitions Ltd., Edinburgh. [0037600] 09/10/1984
Browne Mrs MP, (was Gilliland), MBE BA DipEd LGSM MCLIP, Sch.Lib., Friends Sch., Lisburn, Co.Antrim. [0047376] 29/07/1992
Browne Mr PJ, BA DMS MCLIP, Client Mgr., Kent C.C., Arts & L.Dept. [0022872] 08/10/1974
Browne Mr RJ, MCLIP, Inf.Offr., BP Exploration L., Iron Mountain UK Ltd., London. [0001952] 13/01/1968
Browne Mr RK, MA FCLIP, Life Member. [0001953] 17/09/1955 FE 01/01/1962
Browne Mrs SA, BA DipLib, Employment not known. [0034619] 05/01/1982
Browne Ms SC, BA(Hons) DipIS MA MCLIP, Inf.Lib.-Soc.Sci., Southampton Inst. [0046587] 20/11/1991
Brownhill Mr DW, Stud., Dept.of Lib., Univ.of Cent.England in Birmingham. [0030122] 02/01/1979
Brownhill Mrs HK, (was Herdsman), BA(Hons) DipIM MCLIP, Lib., York Dist.Hosp. [0052241] 18/10/1974
Browning Mrs DA, (was Phipps), BA DipLib MCLIP, L.Mktg.Mgr., Bath & N.E.Somerset Auth., Bath. [0038008] 04/01/1985
Browning Ms GM, BA MCLIP, Dep.L.Mgr., Univ.of Westminster, New Cavendish St.L. [0031580] 08/10/1979
Browning Mrs JW, SRN RMN DipLib, Asst.Lib., Guildford Coll.F.& H.E., Surrey. [0045404] 01/04/1990
Browning Mr TS, BA DipLib MCLIP, Business Lib., Bristol Cent L., Bristol. [0007359] 16/07/1984
Brownlee Mrs AC, (was Livingstone), BA MCLIP, Lib., Wester Hailes Educ.Cent., Edinburgh. [0028622] 09/01/1978
Brownlee Mr SC, BA DipLib MCLIP, Unemployed. [0024329] 07/07/1975
Brownlow Mr WG, BA DipLib MCLIP, Self-employed. [0033276] 17/10/1980
Broxis Mr PF, FCLIP, Retired/Inf.Consultancy. [0001961] 24/08/1958 FE 01/01/1967
Bruce Mrs AM, (was Lennie), BA MCLIP, Asst.Lib., Robert Gordon Univ., Aberdeen. [0034229] 14/10/1981
Bruce Mr B, BA(Hons) MPhil, Unemployed. [0055899] 15/12/1997
Bruce Mr CJ, MA DipLib MCLIP, Curator(Maps), Imperial War Mus., London. [0035118] 19/08/1982
Bruce Mr DJ, BSc, Grad.Trainee, Univ.of Kent at Canterbury, Templeman L. [0061532] 16/09/2002
Bruce Mr DJL, BA MLIS, Unemployed. [0061806] 11/11/2002
Bruce Miss J, BA(Hons) MCLIP, Lib., Environment Agency, Worthing, Sussex. [0050147] 12/04/1994
Bruce Ms J, Northwick Park & Marks Hosp., Middx. [0047882] 23/10/1992
Bruce Mrs LJ, (was Sterritt), BA MCLIP, Site Lib., Ambleside, St.Martins Coll. [0039203] 02/01/1986

Bruce Mr NM, MA DipLib MCLIP LLM, Princ.Offr.(L.& Inf.Serv.), Aberdeen City Council. [0029370] 26/06/1978
Bruce Mr RA, BA(Hons), Unemployed. [0053866] 07/10/1996
Bruce Mr RJ, BA(Hons), L.Asst.,p./t.Stud., Barbican Library, Aberystwyth Univ. [0059543] 01/05/2001
Bruce Mrs RM, (was Archibald), BA MCLIP, Child.Lib., Alloa L. [0041134] 06/10/1987
Bruce Mr RS, MA BD DipLib, Lib., All Nations Christian Coll., Ware, Herts. [0034609] 01/01/1982
Bruce Ms S, Stud., Northumbria at Newcastle Univ. [0061738] 30/10/2002
Bruce-Cudjoe Miss EE, BLS DipLib, Stud., Univ.Coll. London. [0060922] 10/01/2002
Bruch Miss SJ, Asst.Lib., Carmarthenshire NHS Trust, Prince Philip Hosp.L. [0058415] 04/02/2000
Brumhead Mrs JM, (was Lawler), BA(Hons) MCLIP, Pershore Lib., Worcs.C.C., Worcester. [0018326] 07/10/1972
Brummitt Ms P, (was Warburton), BA MCLIP, Lib., Burton L., Staffs.C.C. [0040379] 23/01/1987
Brumwell Ms JA, MCLIP, Dep.Dir., L.& Heritage, Derbys.C.C., Matlock. [0021778] 09/01/1974
Brun Mr J, BSc MCLIP, Retired. [0060161] 10/12/2001
Brunel Cohen Mr RS, BA DCC DipLib, Bookseller, D.M.Jeffers, London. [0041524] 15/01/1988
Brunt Mr D, LLB Dip Lib, Midland & Oxford Circuit Lib., Birmingham Crown Court. [0033640] 29/01/1981
Brunt Mr RM, BA DipLib FCLIP, Principal Lecturer, Inf.& L.Studies, Leeds Metro.Univ., Beckett Park. [0018037] 20/10/1972 FE 15/10/2002
Brussee Mr ES, BScEcon, Unemployed. [0061699] 21/10/2002
Brutus Mrs L, Documentation Offr., Min.of Health, Seychelles. [0050935] 07/11/1994
Bruveris Miss LA, BA(Hons), Asst.Lib., Ashurst Morris Crisp, London. [0056359] 12/06/1998
Bruwer Mrs GS, (was Mountjoy), BA MCLIP, Catr., Melbourne Bus.Sch., Melbourne, Victoria, Australia. [0023414] 28/01/1975
Bryan Ms A, p./t.Lib., Group 4 Prison Serv., HMP Altcourse, Liverpool. [0046389] 31/10/1991
Bryan Ms CA, MCLIP, Sen.Asst.Lib.(Community Serv.), City & Co.of Swansea, Swansea. [0001976] 13/07/1971
Bryan Mr FJ, MCLIP, Life Member. [0001977] 06/11/1947
Bryan Mrs GJ, (was Dingley), MCLIP, p./t.L.Asst., Langley Br.L., Sandwell P.L. [0003963] 06/10/1965
Bryan Mrs GM, (was Oxley), BA MCLIP, Team Lib., Glos.C.C. [0024038] 09/03/1975
Bryan Miss MA, BA(Hons), Stud., Univ.of Central England. [0060040] 03/12/2001
Bryan Mr TDB, BA MCLIP, Sen.Lend.Lib., L.B.of Harrow. [0040980] 01/10/1987
Bryant Mr DJ, FIMgt FCLIP FILAM FRSA, Life Member, (Devel.Advisor). [0001981] 23/09/1948 FE 01/01/1958
Bryant Mrs HM, BA(Hons) MCLIP, Sen.Lib., Waterlooville L., Hants.C.C. [0043306] 17/10/1989
Bryant Mrs JE, (was Marfleet), BA, Head of L.& Inf.Serv., Osborne Clarke, Bristol. [0050005] 18/02/1994
Bryant Mr LC, BA(Hons) MA MCLIP, Learning Res.Cent.Mgr., City of Bristol Coll., Learning Res.Cent. [0054274] 12/11/1996
Bryant Miss M, BSc(Hons), Trials Search Co-ordinator, Cochrane Cystic Fibrosis & Genetic, Disorders Group, Liverpool. [0061316] 17/05/2002 AF
Bryant Miss MC, BA MA MCLIP, Catr., Middx.Univ. [0043860] 05/02/1990
Bryant Mr MEN, BA FCLIP BA MCLIP, Resource Devl.Lib., Aylesbury Vale & Chiltern Dist., Bucks.C.C. [0029316] 10/05/1978
Bryant Mr P, HonFCLIP, Sen.Research Fellow, Centre for Bibl.Management, Univ.of Bath. [0001986] 01/02/1950 FE 01/01/1992
Bryce Mr AF, FSA SCOT FCLIP, Life Member., Tel.01738 552288, 17 Pinedale Terrace, Scone, Perth, PH2 6PH. [0001988] 16/02/1949 FE 01/01/1969
Bryce Mrs KB, (was Burton), MCLIP, President, Andornot Consulting Inc., Vancouver, Canada. [0002158] 19/01/1970
Bryce Miss LA, BA(Hons) MA, Social & Environ.Studies Lib., Univ.of Liverpool, Sydney Jones L. [0048864]05/07/1993
Bryceland Mrs PMM, MCLIP, Multicultural Lib., Leicester City Council, Educ.Dept. [0022197] 27/02/1974
Bryceland Miss S, BA(Hons), Research Stud., Sch.of Inf.& Media Studies, Robert Gordon Univ., Aberdeen. [0049545] 09/11/1993
Bryder Ms J, BA(Hons) DipILM, Sen.L.Asst., Imperial Coll., London. [0046646] 02/12/1991
Bryn Jones Mrs LK, (was Evans), BSc MCLIP, Health Inf.Advisor, NHS Direct Wales, Swansea. [0004680] 26/03/1969
Bryn-Jones Mr DS, MCLIP, Unemployed. [0001991] 01/01/1966
Bryon Mrs J, (was Clegg), BA MCLIP, Special Needs Adviser, Exeter Univ., Guild of Students. [0001992] 17/03/1961
Bryon Mr JFW, FCLIP, Life Member. [0001993] 04/10/1937 FE 01/01/1950
Bryson Mrs AV, (was Henderson), BA DipLib MCLIP, Asst.Ch.Lib.(Pub.Serv.), N.E.E.L.B., Ballymena. [0032526] 16/05/1980
Bryson Mr P, BSc MCLIP, Employment unknown. [0060259] 10/12/2001
Bubb Mr AC, MA FCLIP, Life Member. [0001994] 02/04/1951 FE 01/01/1957
Buchan Mrs EM, (was Richardson), BA(Hons), Lib., Scottish Agricultural Coll., Aberdeen. [0044862] 01/01/1991
Buchan Miss MLT, MA DipLib MCLIP, Lib., Hilton L., The Robert Gordon Univ., Aberdeen. [0038549] 01/07/1985
Buchan Mrs PM, (was Adkins), BLib MCLIP, Sen.Lib.-Open Access, Kent Arts & L., Kent C.C. [0000081] 01/01/1969

Personal Members — Burgess

Buchanan Miss A, MA(Hons) MPhil, L.& Inf.Asst., Nat.Maritime Mus., Greenwich. [0055810] 19/11/1997
Buchanan Mrs CM, MCLIP, Prof.Serv.Mgr., Co.L.H.Q., Cornwall. [0021263] 03/10/1973
Buchanan Mr DS, MA MCLIP, Life Member. [0001997] 14/10/1955
Buchanan Ms HV, BA, Asst.to Head of Acq., Imperial Coll., Univ.of London. [0044666] 21/11/1990
Buchanan Mr MS, BA MCLIP, Princ.Asst.Lib., S.E.Educ.& L.Serv., Co.Down. [0002002] 26/10/1971
Buchanan Ms N, BA DipLib BBibl(Hons) MBibl, Dep.Univ.Lib., EG Malherbe L., Univ.of Natal, Durban, S.Africa. [0058993] 17/10/2000
Buchanan Mr R, HonFCLIP, Retired. [0031109] 29/06/1979 FE 29/06/1979
Buchanan Mrs S, (was Horrocks), MCLIP, Learning Res.Cent.Mgr., Chessington Community Coll., Surrey. [0007212] 30/07/1970
Buck Mrs AM, BA(Hons) PGDip, Stud., Univ.of Brighton. [0059973] 14/11/2001
Buck Mr MW, MSC DipLib MCLIP, Lib., Scottish Churches Open Coll., Edinburgh. [0039929] 01/10/1986
Buck Mrs RG, (was Wallace), BA(Hons) DipIM, Lib., Oxfam, Oxford. [0048885] 12/07/1993
Bucke Miss J, BA MCLIP, Sub Lib., Main L., Queens Univ.Belfast. [0002010] 16/09/1967
Buckham Mrs CH, (was Neville), BSc DipLib MCLIP, Sch.Lib., Peebles High Sch. [0036725] 10/11/1983
Buckingham Miss RE, BA(Hons), Learning Res.Cent.Mgr., Wellington Sch., Altrincham. [0056890] 02/11/1998
Buckle Mr DGR, BA, Retired. [0031116] 17/08/1979
Buckle Ms EA, BA MCLIP, Head of Nat.L.& Inf.Serv., The Environment Agency, Bristol. [0027788] 01/08/1977
Buckle Mrs EW, BA MCLIP, Asst.Dir.(Cranfield Univ.), Royal Military Coll.of Sci., Shrivenham. [0023029] 01/10/1974
Buckle Mrs JA, (was Yeates), BSc DipLib MCLIP, p./t.Inf.Offr., Drug Scope, London. [0042858] 05/04/1989
Buckle Mrs LK, (was Batt), BA MCLIP, Freelance Indexer. [0032629] 06/07/1980
Buckle Mrs P, (was Beer), MSc MCLIP, Inf.Devel.Mgr., Interfleet Tech.Ltd., Derby. [0045601] 01/04/1991
Buckles Mr DF, MCLIP, Retired. [0002017] 10/10/1966
Buckley Miss BJ, CertEd BLS FRSA MCLIP, Sec.to the Commission, Statistics Commission, London. [0027516] 17/05/1977
Buckley Mrs C, (was Richards), BA(Hons) MSc(Econ) MCLIP, Lib., Shropshire C.C., Shrewsbury L. [0055459] 01/08/1977
Buckley Ms J, BA(Hons), Asst.Lib., S.Tyneside Coll., S.Shields. [0055677] 04/11/1997
Buckman Mrs EA, (was Plimsaul), MCLIP, Life Member. [0011750] 03/09/1959
Bucknall Mrs JA, (was Williams), BA MCLIP, p./t.Lib., Bullingdon Prison, Oxon.C.C. [0021863] 08/02/1974
Bucknall Miss RJ, BSc(Hons), Unemployed. [0061186] 03/04/2002
Bucknell Mr TD, BSc MSc MA, Electronic Res.Mgr., Univ.of Liverpool L. [0050320] 22/06/1994
Buckner Ms K, BA MBCS MCLIP, Position unknown, Queen Margaret Univ.Coll. [0060243] 10/12/2001
Buckroyd Mrs M, BA MCLIP, Retired. [0034248] 15/10/1981
Budd Mrs AM, (was Cervi), BD DipLib MCLIP, Sen.Asst.Lib.(Casual), L.B.of Harrow P.L. [0040037] 07/10/1986
Budd Mr UB, FIL KAND DipLib MCLIP, Unemployed. [0029931] 09/11/1978
Buddell Mr KJ, Unemployed. [0035091] 30/07/1982
Buddle Mrs JMM, BSc DipInf, Unemployed. [0052228] 16/10/1995
Buddle Mrs KE, (was Brown), BA MCLIP, Head of L.& Lifelong Learning, Wigan Cent.L. [0030603] 21/03/1979
Budge Mrs PM, (was Long), BA MA MCLIP, P/t.Prof.Lib., Univ.of Birmingham. [0028329] 15/11/1977
Budiarsa Ms TR, (was Dharmawidjaya), DA MLS, Head of L., Naval Dental Inst., Jakarta, Indonesia. [0034728] 03/02/1982
Buettner Mrs M, BA, Unemployed. [0046152] 07/01/1991
Bugden Ms RJ, BEd DipLIS MCLIP PGDipEd(SEN), Lib., Bromsgrove Sch., Bromsgrove. [0043190] 01/10/1989
Bugden Mrs S, Visiting Lect., Univ.of Brighton. [0057470] 01/04/1999
Bugg Miss A, BSc, p./t.Stud./Asst.Lib., Brighton Univ., L.B.Islington, Cent.L. [0059541] 01/05/2001
Buick Mrs L, (was McFetridge), BLib MCLIP, Inf.Devel.Offr., N.E.E.L.B.-L.Serv., Area L.H.Q., Ballymena, Co.Antrim. [0030856] 23/05/1979
Bukumunhe Ms LPR, BSc, Team Administrator, Barnet Link Scheme, London. [0061350] 13/06/2002
Bukunola Mrs CA, (was Adepoju), MCLIP, Learning Cent.Facilitator, Southwark Coll., London. [0002031] 01/01/1970
Buley Mr CG, Unemployed, 22 Hyde Terrace, Gosforth, Newcastle-u-Tyne, NE3 1AT. [0042784] 08/03/1989
Buliciri Ms F, LLB, Stud., London. [0061835] 15/11/2002
Bull Mr CR, BA MCLIP, Team Leader, Local Serv., Kent Arts & L., Gravesend. [0028520] 03/01/1978
Bull Mrs EJ, (was Baker), BA(Hons) DipInf MCLIP, Head of Tech.Serv., Imperial Coll., Cent.L., London. [0048010] 02/11/1992
Bull Miss KR, BSc(Hons) MSc MCLIP, Inf.Sci., KIR Div., Imperial Coll., Hammersmith. [0047479] 01/09/1992
Bull Mrs PA, (was Ellison), MCLIP, Liaison Lib.(Job Share), Norwich City Coll. [0002037] 28/03/1967
Bull Ms SJ, BA DipLib MCLIP, L.Mgr., Hammersmith & W.London Coll. [0021289] 08/10/1973
Bullas Mrs FM, (was Long), BA MCLIP, Lib.(Special Serv.), Derbyshire L.Serv., Belper L. [0021494] 23/10/1973
Bullen Mr AS, MCLIP, Life Member. [0002038] 27/08/1951
Bullen Mr GC, BA MCLIP, Head of Business Serv., Gas Systems & Plants, Shell Expro. [0037093] 17/02/1984

Bullen Mrs JM, (was King), MCLIP, Life Member, 50 Brean Down Ave., Bristol, BS9 4JF. [0002039] 16/03/1942
Bullen Mr SP, MSc, Unemployed. [0051211] 23/11/1994
Bullimore Ms A, BA MA, Stud./p./t.L.Asst., City Univ. [0061534] 16/09/2002
Bullimore Mr AM, BA DipLib MCLIP, Asst.Lib., Univ.of Luton. [0041823] 19/04/1988
Bullimore Mrs RA, (was Curtis), MCLIP, Northallerton Grp.Lib., N.Yorks.C.C. [0002043] 29/08/1963
Bullivant Mrs EM, (was Flynn), MCLIP, Life Member. [0002044] 10/02/1944
Bullivant Mrs KI, BA(Hons), p./t. Stud./L.Asst., Robert Gordon Univ., English Nature, Northminster. [0059202] 22/03/2001
Bullivent Mr CJ, BA MCLIP, Unemployed. [0018401] 18/10/1972
Bulloch Miss J, BSc DipLib, Sch.Lib., Hutchesons Grammar Sch., Glasgow. [0048118] 19/11/1992
Bulloch Dr PA, MA PhD MCLIP, Lib., The L., Balliol Coll., Oxford. [0033522] 08/01/1981
Bullock Mrs JA, (was Humble), MCLIP, L.Asst.(p./t.), Cheshire C.C., Bollington L. [0024896] 20/10/1975
Bullock Miss JP, MA FCLIP, Life Member. [0002047] 31/10/1940 FE 01/01/1966
Bullock Miss KS, BA(Hons) MCLIP, Asst.Lib., Harrogate L. [0047847] 20/10/1992
Bulman Mrs MJ, (was Wiltshire), MA MCLIP, Lib., Med.Res.Council, Harwell, Didcot. [0016109] 10/11/1971
Bulmer Mrs VM, (was Ellis), MCLIP, p./t.Asst.Br.Lib., L.B.of Croydon, S.Norwood L. [0021166] 01/01/1973
Bulpitt Mr G, MA CertEd MCLIP, Dir, Learning Cent./Univ.Lib., Sheffield Hallam Univ. [0002051] 01/08/1967
Bulson Miss SJ, MA, Lib., Inst.of Heraldic & Genealogical, Studies, Canterbury. [0051638] 21/04/1995
Bunch Miss AJ, OBE MA FCLIP FSA(Scot), Retired. [0002053] 01/10/1953 FE 06/06/1973
Bunch Mr AJ, BA(Hons) DMS MCLIP, Retired. [0002054] 25/03/1957
Bunch Miss MR, MA DipLib MCLIP, Unemployed. [0028267] 07/11/1977
Bundhoo Mr J, BSc MSc MCLIP, Resident in Mauritius. [0060095] 11/03/2001
Bundy Ms CM, BSc(Econ) MSc MCLIP, Team Lib., Norfolk Sch.L.Serv. [0056614] 18/09/1998
Bundy Mr DE, BA MCLIP, Quality Serv.Mgr., L.B.of Sutton, Cent.L. [0002055] 14/09/1970
Bunn Ms LC, BA(Hons), Inf.Offr., Sandwell Inf.Serv., W.Bromwich L. [0046731] 16/01/1992
Bunn Miss RM, ISO, Life Member. [0002058] 29/07/1960
Bunn Mrs S, (was Woolerton), CertEd BA DipLib MCLIP, Sch.Res.Lib., King Alfreds Coll., Winchester. [0044362] 01/10/1990
Bunn Mrs V, (was Jones), MCLIP, Lib., Loughborough Grammar Sch., Leics. [0008108] 30/01/1970
Bunney Ms AJ, BSc MSc, Med.Inf.Offr., Takeda UK, High Wycombe. [0052721] 27/11/1995
Bunt Mrs MA, Off.Mgr., CH Bunt, Indep.Financial Adviser, Leigh Woods, N.Somerset. [0038088] 08/01/1985
Bunten Miss L, BA, Stud., Robert Gordon Univ. [0061124] 19/02/2002
Bunting Miss CA, BA(Hons) DipLib, Catr., Brit.L. [0039939] 02/10/1986
Bunting Miss KM, B Lib MCLIP, Catr., Univ.of Derby. [0002059] 26/10/1971
Bunting Mrs PA, MCLIP, Lib./Arch., Assoc.of Police Surgeons. [0032378] 01/01/1957
Bunton Ms L, MA MSc, Unemployed. [0061419] 15/07/2002
Bunyan Mrs JB, BA(Hons) MA MCLIP, Asst.Lib., Database Team, Kimberlin L., De Montfort Univ., Leicester. [0052356] 26/01/1995
Burbage Mr BE, LRSC MCLIP AALIA, Retired. [0019884] 01/01/1973
Burbidge Mrs BA, (was Tookey), MA MCLIP, Retired. [0014794] 01/01/1967
Burbridge Miss JM, BSc MSc, Team Lib., Leics.City L.& Inf.Serv., Leicester. [0002063] 17/02/1969
Burch Mr B, OBE MA MCLIP, Retired. [0002064] 01/01/1959
Burch Mrs GE, (was Fairclift), BA MCLIP, Employment not known. [0032941] 01/10/1980
Burch Mr MP, BA(Hons) MLib MA, H.of L., Inf.& Communication, W.Berks.Council, Newbury. [0040645] 28/04/1987
Burcher Miss KE, (was Susilovic), BA, L.Exec., House of Commons Commission, London. [0043725] 07/12/1989
Burden Ms C, (was Hall), MA MCLIP, Manager - Electronic Services, The British Library, London. [0024613] 06/10/1975
Burden Mr JS, FCLIP, Life Member, Tel.01536 514803, 70 Bowhill, Kettering, Northants., NN16 8TW. [0002066] 01/01/1934 FE 01/01/1945
Burden Miss L, BA, L.Mgr., Herbert Smith (Solicitors), London. [0037517] 06/03/1984
Burge Ms SM, (was Smiddy), BA(Hons) FCLIP, Inf.Mgr., Ombudsman's Off., London. [0021247] 08/10/1973 FE 23/09/1998
Burgess Miss AF, BA MLib DipLib MCLIP, Sch.L.Serv.Mgr., Dorset Sch.L.Serv., Blandford. [0026944] 19/01/1977
Burgess Mrs DH, (was Carter), p./t.L.Asst., N.Somerset Dist.Council. [0002431] 15/04/1970
Burgess Miss GM, MSc MCLIP, Employment unknown. [0060524] 11/12/2001
Burgess Mrs HM, (was Langford), MCLIP, Life Member. [0002078] 03/03/1942
Burgess Ms K, Learning Resources Adviser, Barnet Coll., Indep.Learning, Resources Cent., Barnet, Herts. [0057231] 26/01/1999 AF
Burgess Mrs RP, BLib MCLIP, Head of L.Arts & Inf., Bracknell Forest Bor.Council, Berks. [0027910] 04/10/1977
Burgess Mrs S, BA(Hons), Sen.L.Asst., Chadderton L., Oldham. [0055740] 11/11/1997
Burgess Ms S, BA MCLIP, Lib., Kajima Europe UK Holdings Ltd., London. [0032400] 23/04/1980
Burgess Miss SC, BA(Hons) MCLIP, Site L.Mgr., Morecambe Bay NHS, Westmorland Gen.Hosp. [0052357] 26/10/1995

201

Burgess Mr SP, BA(Hons) MSc, Lib., W.Yorks.Probation Board, Wakefield. [0057364] 17/02/1999
Burgess Mrs VF, (was Mosley), BSc DipLib MLS MCLIP, Unemployed. [0010506] 24/01/1967
Burgess Miss VJ, BA MA MCLIP, Reg.Inf.Mgr., Sport England, N.E., Aykley Heads, Durham. [0039731] 04/06/1986
Burgess Mrs VM, (was Griffiths), MCLIP, Sen.Asst., Dudley Ref.L., Met.Bor.of Dudley. [0005997] 01/01/1969
Burgess Mr VW, MCLIP, Unemployed. [0002088] 06/03/1967
Burgum Miss SJ, BA DipLib MCLIP, Sch.Lib., Erith Sch., Kent. [0034233] 15/10/1981
Buri Mrs RE, (was Dodge), BA MCLIP, Self-employed, Abstracting Journals. [0031253] 04/10/1979
Burioni Mr L, Managing Director, Italy. [0059990] 16/11/2001
Burke Mr J, LLB MCLIP, Asst.Lib., Univ.of Glasgow. [0023220] 12/11/1974
Burke Mr J, MA DipLib MCLIP, Dep.Lib., Bell Coll.of Tech., Hamilton. [0032639] 01/07/1980
Burke Miss JL, BA, Evening Issue Desk Super.p.t., Univ.Coll.London. [0061647] 11/10/2002
Burke Mrs L, (was Morton), BA MCLIP, Lib.(Job-share), Mitchell L., Glasgow. [0025081] 18/10/1975
Burke Miss LM, DipEurHum BA(Hons), Stud., Leeds Met.Univ. [0061279] 08/05/2002
Burke Ms MA, MA DLIS, Assoc.Lib., Univ.Coll.Dublin, Ireland. [0050292] 31/05/1994
Burke Mr PT, MCLIP, Retired. [0002093] 18/10/1968
Burkett Miss R, BA(Hons) MCLIP, Project Mgr., Epixtech, Chesham. [0030373] 09/01/1979
Burkitt Mr JK, MCLIP, Retired. [0002099] 01/01/1962
Burley Mrs AB, MLS, Unemployed. [0044529] 22/10/1990
Burley Mr IP, BA(Hons) MCLIP, Comm.Lib., Tamworth P.L., Staffs. [0046927] 28/02/1992
Burley Dr RA, (was Heritage), MA MSc PhD MCLIP, Employment not known. [0060771] 12/12/2001
Burlton Mrs V, (was Humphreys), Life Member. [0002102] 01/01/1938
Burmajster Mrs A, MA MCLIP, Acquisitions Mgr., Inst.of Financial Serv., London. [0051803] 04/07/1995
Burmajster Mrs M, BA MCLIP, Life Member. [0002103] 01/01/1956
Burman Mr RT, Stud. [0057013] 23/11/1998
Burn Mrs PS, (was Dunlop), BA MCLIP, Upper Sch.Lib., Internat.Sch.of Luxembourg. [0025028] 27/10/1975
Burn Ms SM, BA(Hons) MA, Sen.L.Asst.-Catg., Birkbeck Coll.L., Univ.of London. [0055444] 13/10/1997
Burne Mr JH, MCLIP, Operations Mgr., Operation Mobilisation, London. [0002108] 01/01/1952
Burnett Mr AD, MA FIAP MCLIP, Retired. [0002109] 15/08/1959
Burnett Ms CF, (was Payne), BA MPhil MCLIP, Asst.Princ.Inf.Lib., Bethnal Green Ref.L., L.B.of Tower Hamlets. [0037318] 02/07/1984
Burnett Mr GE, MA DipLib MCLIP, Systems Lib., Norwich City Coll. [0033507] 16/01/1981
Burnett Mrs JC, (was Davies), BA MCLIP, Inf.& Lifelong Learning lib., Herts.C.C., Bishops Stortford L. [0028286] 06/11/1977
Burnham Mrs MA, MCLIP, Retired. [0002114] 01/01/1951
Burnham Mr TG, MA MSc MCLIP, Employment not known. [0060772] 12/12/2001
Burningham Miss ES, MSc BA, Records & Arch.Admin.Asst., TFPL, London. [0059730] 10/09/2001
Burns Mr DJ, BA(Hons) DipILS, Asst.Lib., Gartnavel Royal Hosp., Gtr.Glasgow Prim.Care NHS Trust. [0053960] 16/10/1996
Burns Mr JE, BA(Hons) MSc(Econ) MCLIP, Dep.Area Lib., Worthing Grp., W.Sussex C.C. [0052799] 15/12/1979
Burns Mrs JM, (was Proudlock), MA DipLib MCLIP, L.Asst., Newton Stewart L., Dumfries & Galloway Council. [0037466] 01/10/1984
Burns Miss JRM, MCLIP, Team Lib., Slough Cent.L. [0002124] 28/07/1992
Burns Mr P, MCLIP, Yth.Serv.Mgr., Arts,L.& Mus.Dept., Durham C.C. [0002125] 28/01/1967
Burns Miss PA, BA, Admin., Walker Safety Cabinets Ltd., Derbyshire. [0040139] 16/10/1986
Burns Ms RA, BA DipLib MCLIP, Lib., Australian Tax Off., Canberra. [0026909] 10/01/1977
Burns Mr RO, (was Hilke), Resources Lib., Univ.of Wolverhampton, Wolverhampton. [0044216] 11/07/1990
Burns Miss RT, BSocSc DipILM, Unemployed. [0050848] 24/10/1994
Burns Mrs S, BA(Hons) MCLIP, Asst.Div.Lib., Accrington L., Lancs.C.C. [0039749] 08/06/1986
Burns Ms SJ, BSc, Asst.L.& Learning Res.Cent.Mgr., Barnfield Coll., Luton. [0053699] 10/09/1996
Burnside Mr DW, MA DipLib MCLIP, Cent.Ref.& Inf.Lib., Oxford Cent.L. [0027912] 20/10/1977
Burr Mr JF, BA MCLIP, Sen.Lib., Sanofi-Synthelabo Research, Alnwick, Northumberland. [0030741] 16/04/1979
Burr Ms MA, BSc DipLib MCLIP, Cent.Co-ordinator, Humanities Educ.Cent., Tower Hamlets. [0025232] 01/01/1976
Burr Mrs SA, (was Smithson), Sen.L.Asst., Univ.of Northumbria at Newcastle. [0048760] 30/04/1993 AF
Burr Miss T, BA MCLIP, Stock Spec., Halton Bor.Council. [0042707] 10/02/1989
Burrell Mrs JW, (was Wilde), BA DipLib MCLIP, Sen.Inf.Offr., Liverpool John Moores Univ. [0040900] 16/08/1987
Burrell Mrs KA, MCLIP, Retired. [0023980] 01/01/1958
Burrell Mrs RMM, (was Lingard), BA DipLib MCLIP, Teaching Asst.& Midday Super.Asst., E.Sussex C.C. [0034908] 13/04/1982
Burridge Miss E, BA MCLIP, Ref.Lib., Inverness P.L., Highland Council. [0026300] 18/10/1976
Burridge Mrs GM, (was Allen), MCLIP, P/t Child.Lib., L.B.of Bexley, Directorate of Educ. [0002135] 01/01/1965

Burridge Mrs VM, (was Blackden), MCLIP, Unemployed. [0021272] 12/10/1973
Burrington Dr GA, (was Marshall), OBE MA FCLIP, Training Consultant, 33 Green Courts, Bowdon, Altrincham, Cheshire, WA14 2SR. [0002139] 01/01/1962 FE 01/01/1965
Burrough Mrs PJ, (was Haydon), MCLIP, Life Member, Tel.01458 448265, 1 Wilton Close, Street, Somerset. [0006591] 15/08/1949
Burroughs Miss LH, BSc(Hons) MSc(Econ) MCLIP, Faculty Liaison Lib., Canterbury Christchurch Univ.Coll. [0054364] 25/11/1996
Burrowes Mrs LR, (was Shuttler), MCLIP, Sen.Lib., Basingstoke. [0002141] 01/01/1966
Burrows Mrs C, (was Hopkinson), MCLIP, Mgr., S.P.C.K. Bookshop, Durham Cathedral. [0004897] 09/01/1967
Burrows Ms ELJ, BA MCLIP, Teacher of English, Elysees Langues, Paris, France. [0044946] 23/01/1991
Burrows Mr JBS, L.Asst., Bible Soc.L., Cambridge Univ.L. [0042878] 06/04/1989
Burrows Mr K, BA DipLib MCLIP, Ref.Lib., Lancs.C.C., Accrington, Lancs. [0037967] 01/01/1985
Burry Mrs KM, (was Callen), BA MCLIP, Career Break. [0038356] 25/03/1985
Bursey Mrs RLL, BA CertEd DipLib, Asst.Lib., Bournemouth Univ. [0047412] 11/08/1992
Burslem Mrs JK, (was Sinclair), BA MCLIP, Lib.for Visually impaired people, Bury Soc.for the Blind, Bury M.B.C. [0024378] 18/07/1975
Burslem Ms MR, BA(Hons) DipLIS MCLIP, Asst.Lib., London Inst., Camberwell Coll.of Arts. [0047712] 19/10/1992
Burnsell Miss RL, MA, Intranet Content Mgr., NSPCC, [0052235] 16/10/1995
Burt Mrs AC, (was Tweedlie), MA DipLib MCLIP, Editorial Asst., Univ.of Newcastle upon Tyne. [0029485] 31/07/1978
Burt Mr AJ, Employment not known. [0059087] 13/11/2000
Burt Mrs E, (was Kelly), MCLIP, Area Lib.& Inf.Mgr.(Outer W.), Newcastle L.& Inf.Serv. [0008231] 27/01/1972
Burt Miss JH, Life Member. [0002150] 16/12/1946
Burt Mrs JM, (was Board), BA DMS MCLIP, Reg.Strategy Mgr., Open Univ., Milton Keynes. [0001422] 04/04/1968
Burton Mr A, BA MCLIP, Automation/Admin.Offr., Bridgend L.& Inf.Serv. [0027239] 09/02/1977
Burton Ms AJ, (was Hewitt), BLib MCLIP, Locality Mgr., Suffolk C.C. [0028829] 30/01/1978
Burton Mrs B, MA FCLIP, Life Member. [0002152] 19/02/1954 FE 01/01/1961
Burton Mr BL, BA AALIA MCLIP MIIM MCMI FHKLA, Univ.lib., The Hong Kong Poly.Univ., Kowloon. [0016671] 26/04/1972
Burton Sir CA, Kt OBE BA MSc MCLIP FRSA JP, Life Member, Tel.809 429 3724, Pine Gardens, St.Michael, Barbados. [0016672] 18/01/1951
Burton Mr GR, BSc MCLIP, Employment not known. [0060163] 10/12/2001
Burton Mrs JE, (was Merritt), BA MCLIP, Educ.Care Offr., The Curzon (C.of E.) Prim.Sch., Quarndon. [0023483] 01/01/1975
Burton Mr JJ, BA, Stud.m, Manchester Met.Univ. [0058624] 18/04/2000
Burton Miss JM, BLib MCLIP, Grp.Lib., Bath & N.E.Somerset, Bath. [0034175] 07/10/1981
Burton Mrs LM, (was Crawford), BA MCLIP, Res.Lib., Kilsyth Academy, Glasgow. [0002160] 23/01/1968
Burton Mr ME, BA(Hons) MSc, Asst.Team Leader, Cranfield Univ., Royal Military Coll.of Sci. [0056711] 05/10/1998
Burton Mrs ME, BA DipLib MCLIP, Head of L.& Inf.Serv., S.Glos.Council. [0034744] 16/02/1982
Burton Mrs MI, (was Glossop), MCLIP, Lib., L.B.of Bromley. [0012102] 17/03/1966
Burton Mrs PA, BA(Hons) MSc, Sch.Lib., King James's Sch., Knaresborough. [0056373] 01/07/1998
Burton Mr PF, MPhil MA FCLIP, Sen.Lect., Dept.of Comp.& Inf.Sci., Univ.of Strathclyde, Glasgow. [0002163] 21/09/1966 FE 01/04/2002
Burton Miss RJ, BSc(Hons), Inf.Cent.Mgr., Environment Agency. [0057268] 02/02/1999
Burton Ms S, (was Pilecki), BA(Hons) MA MCLIP, Head of Customer Serv., Dept.of Inf.Serv., Royal Soc.of Med., London. [0027519] 29/04/1977
Burtonshaw Miss BE, MCLIP, Life Member. [0002169] 01/02/1948
Burtrand Mrs DC, (was Brown), MCLIP, Sch.Lib., Honywood Sch., Coggeshall, Essex. [0001851] 12/10/1970
Bury Miss AE, BA(Hons), p.t/Sen.L.Asst., Warwickshire C.C., Leamington Spa, Warwickshire. [0059143] 28/11/2000
Bury Mrs CM, (was Fitzpatrick), MCLIP, Tax Lib., KPMG., Birmingham. [0023322] 05/12/1974
Bury Mr NJ, BA MCLIP, Sen.Lib., Rawtenstall L., Lancs. [0031795] 02/01/1980
Bury Mrs RM, Stud./Enquiry Asst., Cent.Lend.L., Norwich. [0054872] 24/04/1997
Bury Mr RS, MA MCLIP, Employment not known. [0039098] 05/11/1985
Bury Dr SJ, MA MA PhD FCLIP, Head of Modern English Collections, Brit.L., London. [0024407] 30/07/1975 FE 18/04/1989
Busby Mrs AJ, (was Mayo), BA(Hons), Res.Cent.Mgr., Kings Norton High Sch., Birmingham. [0047884] 23/10/1992
Busby Mrs JA, (was Hepplewhite), BA DipLib MCLIP, Prison Lib., HMP Usk, Monmouthshire L. [0028010] 11/10/1977
Busby Mr RJ, FCLIP FSA, Retired. [0002174] 30/01/1962 FE 29/07/1974
Busby Miss S, BA MCLIP, Bibl.Serv.Lib., E.Dunbartonshire Council. [0002175] 01/01/1972
Bush Mr EAR, BA FCLIP, Life Member. [0002178] 01/01/1954 FE 06/11/1977
Bush Mrs ML, (was Edwards), MCLIP MSc, Unemployed. [0024881] 13/10/1975
Bushell Ms AJ, LLB(Hons) MSc, Corp./Finance Inf.Offr., Freshfields Bruckhaus Deringer, London. [0053077] 28/02/1996
Bushell Mr JM, BA(Hons) MA, Asst.Lib.(IT Support), Inst.of Chartered Accountants L., London. [0050207] 04/05/1994

Bushnell Mrs GH, (was Barnes), BA MCLIP, Team Lib.(Inf.), L.B.of Hillingdon, Cent.L. [0000795]   12/03/1971
Bushnell Mr IW, BA MCLIP, Dep.Ch.Lib., Off.for Nat.Stats., Newport. [0002182]   01/01/1971
Bussey Mrs SJM, Lib., Derby High Sch. [0056317]   13/05/1998
Bussey Mrs SM, (was Pritchard), BA MCLIP, Princ.Lib.-Young People's Serv., Harrow P.L. [0002183]   07/02/1963
But Ms YCK, Ref.Lib., Nat.L.Board, Nat.Ref.L., Singapore. [0052816] 19/12/1995
Butchart Mr GF, MA(Hons) DipLib MCLIP, Asst.Lib., Highland Council, L.Support Unit. [0043002]   05/06/1989
Butchart Mr IC, BA MSc MCLIP PGCE, Dir.of L.& Inf.Serv., Teesside Univ., Middlesbrough. [0002185]   01/01/1969
Butcher Miss AL, Music Catr., BBC Inf.& Arch., London. [0038936] 17/10/1985
Butcher Mr AS, BSc MLib MCLIP, Employment unknown. [0060234] 10/12/2001
Butcher Mrs D, (was Bedford), MCLIP, Freelance Registered Indexer. [0001035]   21/07/1969
Butcher Mrs DPE, (was Tennant), MCLIP, Retired. [0002186]   01/01/1936
Butcher Mr DR, BA MCLIP, Lect., Sch. of Inf.Stud., Univ.of Cent.England in Birmingham. [0002187]   15/10/1965
Butcher Miss FD, BA MCLIP, Lib., Renfrew Div.Sch.L.Serv. [0029606] 15/10/1978
Butcher Mr GE, MCLIP, Retired. [0002189]   18/08/1950
Butcher Mr JR, BSc(Hons) MCLIP(Econ) MCLIP, Res.Lib., (Catg.& Acquisitions), Plymouth Cent.L. [0056098]   12/02/1998
Butcher Mrs JW, (was Hall), MCLIP, Asst.Lib.(p/t.), Huddersfield, Kirklees M.B.C. [0021259]   15/10/1973
Butcher Ms R, L.Asst., British Standards Inst., London. [0054972]   05/06/1997
Butcher Miss SE, Sen.Inf.Offr., CB Hillier Parker, London. [0049867] 17/01/1994
Butcher Mrs SK, (was Yeoh), MCLIP, Sch.Lib., St.Martin`s Sch., Solihull. [0025461]   15/12/1975
Butchers Miss TA, BA(Hons) MA MCLIP, Comm.Lib., Winton L., Bournemouth Bor.Council. [0050588]   26/09/1994
Butler Miss A, MA MCLIP, Lib., Manches Solicitors, Oxford. [0002194] 14/02/1964
Butler Mrs A, (was Holmes), MCLIP, p./t.Lib., Telford L., Telford & Wrekin. [0007105]   27/01/1971
Butler Mrs A, (was Boreham), BA(Hons) DipILM MCLIP, Adult Lend.Lib., Newbury L., W.Berks.Dist.Council. [0052457]   22/11/1995
Butler Mr AJ, BA DipLIS, Inf.Researcher, Dept.of Transp.Local Gov.& Regions, London. [0057734]   06/07/1999
Butler Mrs CE, (was Macmillan), MCLIP, Retired. [0032233]   01/01/1960
Butler Mr DA, BA MCLIP, Area L.Mgr., Doncaster M.B.C. [0002195] 10/07/1971
Butler Miss E, BA, Lib.Masters Stud., Sheffield. [0059194]   13/12/2000
Butler Mrs EJ, (was Taylor), BA(Hons) DipLib., Special Support Asst., Poverest Primary Sch., Orpington, Kent. [0032708]   15/07/1980
Butler Mrs HS, BA MCLIP, Lib., Gloucestershire C.C., St.Peter's High Sch. [0002198]   11/01/1971
Butler Ms JC, BA DipLIB MCLIP, Database Design Mgr., Unilever plc, London. [0035197]   01/10/1982
Butler Mrs JJ, (was Pinnock), MCLIP, Sen.Asst., L.& Records Unit, Sussex Police H.Q., Lewes. [0011714]   01/03/1969
Butler Mrs JM, (was Wells), MCLIP, Level 3 Mgr., Cent.L., L.B.of Croydon. [0015589]   10/01/1966
Butler Prof KW, MA MCLIP, Life Member. [0002203]   07/03/1941
Butler Mrs LA, (was Featherstone), BSc(Hons), Asst.Lib., Dudley Coll.of Technology, West Mids. [0027967]   11/10/1977
Butler Mrs LL, (was Fielding), BA MBA MCLIP, Head of Best Value, Birmingham City Council, Cent.L. [0024667]   18/10/1975
Butler Ms M, BEd MEd, Head of L.Serv., Joseph Chamberlain Coll., Birmingham. [0045603]   02/04/1991
Butler Mr MJ, BA MCLIP, Grp.Lib., Birmingham L.Serv. [0029608] 01/10/1978
Butler Miss ML, BA FCLIP, Retired. [0002206]   08/03/1935
FE 01/01/1946
Butler Mr P, Sch.Lib., The Coopers Co.& Coborn Sch., Upminster, Essex. [0058300]   20/12/1999
Butler Ms PI, MCLIP, L.Mgr., L.B.of Camden. [0019600]   08/11/1972
Butler Miss PJ, MCLIP, Bibl.Serv.Mgr., L.B.of Barnet. [0002208]   01/01/1969
Butler Mr R, MSc MCLIP, Lib., Univ.of Essex. [0002210]   22/10/1971
Butler Mrs RA, (was Rueffer), MCLIP, P./t.Retail Asst., Public Record Off., London. [0023836]   01/01/1970
Butler Miss SC, BA(Hons) MA MCLIP, Subject Lib., Oxford Brookes Univ., Harcourt Hill Campus. [0049188]   11/10/1993
Butler Mr T, BA(Hons), Acquisitions Lib., W.Thames Coll., Isleworth. [0056028]   28/01/1998
Butler Miss WF, MA DipLIB MCLIP, Lib., Newcastle under Lyme Ind.Sch. [0027308]   01/03/1977
Butt Mrs HM, (was Dowdell), BA MCLIP, Asst.Lib.(p./t.), Haileybury, Hertford. [0004121] 18/01/1971
Butt Miss J, Asst. Aga & Conf.Co-ordinator, European Foundation Cent., Belgium. [0059180]   07/12/2000
Butt Mrs L, BA MA MCLIP, Sen.Inf.Asst.(Periodicals), De Montfort Univ., Leicester. [0051531] 01/04/1995
Butt Mr RD, BA MA MCLIP, P/t.Asst.Catr., L.B.of Waltham Forest. [0031215] 19/10/1979
Butterfield Mr D, BA FCLIP, Retired. [0002218]   29/07/1952
FE 01/01/1957
Butteriss Miss M, MCLIP, L.Mgr., Inverness Coll. [0002219]   19/03/1965
Butters Mrs AJ, (was Apted), BA MSc, Comm.Lib., Cambs.C.C. [0046580] 20/11/1991
Butterwick Mr NB, BSc MSc MLS MCLIP, Asst.Dir.of Inf.Serv., Queen's Univ.of Belfast, Main L. [0028271]   31/10/1977

Butterworth Mr AK, BA(Hons) MSc, Inf.& Res.Advisor, Kensington & Chelsea & Westminster, Health Auth., London. [0061011]   08/02/2002
Butterworth Mr JC, BA(Hons), Scounl Trainee, Plant Scineces L., Oxford Univ.L.Serv. [0059786]   02/10/2001
Butterworth Mrs JM, (was Sissons), BA MCLIP, ICT Lib., Bolton M.B.C., Cent.L. [0020508]   14/01/1973
Butterworth Mrs S, (was Whitelegg), BA MCLIP, Freelance Indexer. [0015752]   21/01/1969
Buttery Mrs AA, (was Lowes), JP MCLIP, Retired, Aruncroft,137 Doncaster Rd., Thrybergh,Rotherham,S65 4BE. [0002225]   05/04/1950
Buttolph Miss ME, MCLIP, Sen.Lib., Notts.Co.L., Ravenshead L. [0019634] 25/10/1972
Button Mrs A, BA(Hons), L.Mgr.(Job Share), Birmingham Bible Inst.and, Solihull Hosp., Staff L. [0049389]   21/10/1993
Button Mr AJ, BA MCLIP, Div.Lib.(N.Warks.), Warwickshire Co.L. [0040275] 09/12/1986
Button Mrs EP, BA MCLIP, Local Studies Lib., Suffolk Record Office, Bury St Edmunds. [0022782] 03/10/1974
Button Miss HJ, DipLib MCLIP, Lib., N.Westminster Sch., London. [0033556] 19/01/1981
Button Miss J, BA MLIS, Asst. Lib., Conde Nast Publications, London. [0060966]   10/01/2002
Button Miss JI, BLib MCLIP, Comm.Lib., Special Needs, Lincs.C.C. [0034097] 01/10/1981
Button Miss LK, CertEd BA ADV DipEd, L.Asst., Sandwell MBC, W.Bromwich. [0059780]   AF
Button Miss SM, BA(Hons), Postal Worker, Royal Mail. [0052496] 02/11/1995
Butts Miss SC, MA DipLib MCLIP, Lib., N.Berwick L., E.Lothian Council. [0033836]   24/03/1981
Buxton Dr AB, MA PhD FCLIP, Position unknown, Inst.of Devel.Studies, Univ.of Brighton. [0060164]   10/12/2001   FE 01/04/2002
Buxton Miss AM, BA(Hons) PGDipILM, Sch.Lib., Northampton High Sch. [0046814]   05/02/1992
Buxton Ms B, LLB PGDip, Sen. Inf. Mgr., Eversheds, Nottingham. [0060940] 10/01/2002
Buxton Mrs CN, (was Bowen), Sch.Lib., Highland Council, Grantown Grammar Sch. [0036437]   12/10/1983
Buxton Mrs E, (was Richards), BA DipLib MCLIP, Unemployed. [0035688] 24/01/1983
Buxton Miss EM, MA FCLIP, Life Member, Tel.01865 554790. [0002229] 25/02/1954   FE 01/01/1966
Buxton Mr RN, MA MCLIP, Acad.Lib.-Humanities, Univ.of Huddersfield, Mus.Lib. [0002231]   10/03/1970
Bwye Mrs SA, (was Lucas), BA MCLIP, Inf.Offr., Volunteer Devel.Scotland, Stirling. [0028850]   31/01/1978
Bye Mr DJ, Inf.Adviser, Sheffield Hallam Univ. [0043415]   18/10/1989
Byers Mrs LJ, (was Page), MCLIP, Cent.Ref.Lib., Torbay Council, Cent.L. [0011143]   13/10/1970
Byers Miss VMJ, MA MCLIP, Retired. [0002233]   21/10/1952
Byfield Mr PA, LLB(Hons) MA, Legal Inf.Specialist, EBRD, London. [0056448] 06/07/1998
Byford Mr AJ, BA MCLIP, Head, Legal Deposit Strategy, Brit.L., London. [0002234]   19/10/1970
Byford Mrs EM, Retired. [0016675]   08/02/1958
Byford Miss KJ, BA MCLIP, Ref.Lib., Suffolk C.C., Ipswich. [0026695] 27/10/1976
Byford Mrs RL, (was Fletcher), BLS MCLIP, Inf.Offr., Essex C.C.L., Chelmsford. [0033463]   01/12/1980
Byng Mr MB, MCLIP, Asst.Head of Inf.& L.Serv., Dept.of Trade & Ind., London. [0038729]   01/10/1985
Byrd Mrs LA, MCLIP, Grp.Lib., Bath & N.E.Somerset, Keynsham L. [0025724]   02/03/1976
Byrne Ms A, BA(Hons) MA DipLib, L.Asst., Greasby Pub.L., Wirral, Merseyside. [0051485]   08/03/1995
Byrne Mrs BM, BA DipEd DipLib MCLIP, Mgr., Inf.Resources, Australian Securities & Investments, Commission, Perth, Australia. [0023356] 09/12/1974
Byrne Mr DF, BA MLib MCLIP, Inf.Serv.Mgr., BT Corp.Comm.Serv., London. [0034202]   10/10/1981
Byrne Mrs HM, (was Corran), BA MCLIP, Devel.Lib:ICT, Herts.Sch.L.Serv., Hatfield. [0028535]   10/01/1978
Byrne Mr M, BA DipLib MCLIP, Community Lib., Birmingham L.Serv. [0027141]   27/01/1977
Byrne Ms U, BA FCLIP, Employment not known. [0060436]   11/12/2001
FE 01/04/2002
Byron Mrs AHE, (was Warry), MCLIP, Unemployed. [0021541]   29/10/1973
Bytheway Miss SJ, Stud./Counter Support Asst., Univ.of Cent.England, Birmingham. [0061167]   15/03/2002
Bytheway Mrs RG, (was Rawlings), BA(Hons) MSc, Internet/Intranet Asst., Durham C.Council. [0055222] 20/08/1997
Cable Mr PJ, BA, Stud., Sheffield Univ. [0061157]   15/03/2002
Cadby Mrs SE, (was Clarke), MCLIP, Learning Res.Mgr., Stourbridge Coll., W.Midlands. [0002248]   14/03/1967
Cade Ms CE, (was Johnson), BA(Hons) DipLIS MCLIP, L.& Inf.Serv.Mgr., N.Hants.Hosp., Basingstoke. [0046980]   16/03/1992
Cadell Mrs EM, (was Cleworth), MCLIP, Retired. [0002252]   04/07/1955
Cadge Mr NL, BA MCLIP, London Sch.of Economics L. [0002252] 04/01/1964
Cadman Mrs EA, (was Hayhurst), BA(Hons) MCLIP, Sch.Lib., Blackfen Sch.for Girls, Sidcup. [0021624]   22/11/1973
Cadman-Goode Mrs FA, (was Cadman), Health Lib./Career Break. [0050170]   20/04/1994
Cadney Mr DLJ, BA FCLIP, Retired. [0002254]   21/01/1953
FE 01/01/1968
Cadney Miss JW, BA MCLIP, Asst.Lib., Norwich P.L. [0002255]   01/10/1971
Cadwalader Mrs E, (was Saville), MCLIP, L.Asst., Doncaster M.B.C. [0012982]   01/01/1972

203

Cadwell Mrs M, (was Buckley), MCLIP, Life Member. [0002020]   31/03/1933
Caffell Mr SCG, BA MCLIP, Inf.Tech.Co-ordinator, Isle of Anglesey C.C. [0002256]   10/10/1970
Caffell Mrs T, (was Lees), MCLIP, Unemployed. [0008802]   23/02/1967
Caffin Miss L, BSc(Hons), Sen.L.Asst., Inst.of Advanced Legal Studies, London. [0048087]   05/11/1992
Caffrey Mrs UL, (was McMullan), BA MCLIP, Freelance Indexer. [0009538]   27/10/1970
Cage Mrs SA, MSc MCLIP, Employment not known. [0060165]   10/12/2001
Cahill Ms AT, BSc DipLib MCLIP, Serv.Devel.Mgr - Young People, Royal Bor.of Kensington & Chelsea, Kensington Cent.L. [0044045]   17/04/1990
Cahill Miss KJ, Sen.L.Asst., Chelsea Ref.L., R.B.of Kensington & Chelsea L. [0059167]   04/12/2000
Cai Mrs KF, (was Wynter), Recon.Asst., Tate Gallery, London. [0050538]   09/09/1994
Cain Ms CF, MA MSc, L.& Learning Cent.Mgr., Sabhal Mor Ostaig, Isle of Skye. [0041906]   16/05/1988
Caine Mrs BM, (was Milne), BA MCLIP, L.Offr.(Job Share), Edinburgh City L. [0038670]   01/01/1963
Caine Mrs SJ, BSc MCLIP, Lib., Ordnance Survey L., Southampton. [0056609]   14/09/1998
Caird Ms SM, BSc MA, Sen.Asst.Lib., Ashurst Morris Crisp, London. [0055417]   10/10/1997
Cairney Ms GA, MA PGDip, Stud., Strathclyde Univ. [0061231]   18/04/2002
Cairns Miss AM, BA DipLib MCLIP, Inf.Serv.Mgr., Thurrock L., Grays. [0030123]   04/01/1979
Cairns Ms C, BA MCLIP Lib, Lib., The Civil Aviation Auth., Gatwick Airport. [0038306]   01/03/1985
Cairns Miss EM, MA DipLib FCLIP, Life Member. [0002262]   19/10/1938
FE 01/01/1943
Cairns Mr GA, BA DMS DipLib MCLIP, L.Registration & Inf.Serv.Mgr., E.Ayrshire Council. [0028521]   25/01/1978
Cairns Miss HB, Stud./L.Adminstrator, Telford Coll./Perth Coll. [0060888]   20/12/2001
Cairns Miss J, BA(Hons), Stud., Univ.Coll.London. [0061646]   11/10/2002
Cairns Mrs J, (was Gregory), BA MCLIP, Bookstart Offr., Bolton Met.Bor.Council, Bolton, Lancs. [0039864]   01/10/1986
Caisley Ms JD, BA(Hons) DipLIS MCLIP, Asst.Lib., Univ.of Southampton. [0045469]   14/02/1991
Calcraft Mrs P, BA MSc, Inf.Spec.(p./t.), Sch.of Mgmt., Cranfield Univ., Cranfield, Beds. [0034919]   20/04/1982
Caldarone Ms EA, BA(Hons) DipLIS, Unemployed. [0049526]   12/11/1993
Caldicott Mrs SC, Sen.L.Asst., Clinical L., Sandwell Healthcare N.H.S.Trust. [0061499]   02/09/2002
Caldwell Miss A, Inf.Asst., Naitional Probation Services, Merseyside. [0059828]   11/10/2001   AF
Caldwell Ms A, (was Fitzgerald), BA MCLIP, Lib., Brit.Sch., Riyadh. [0031218]   05/10/1979
Caldwell Miss LM, BSc(Hons), Unemployed. [0058158]   09/11/1999
Caldwell Mrs MA, MA MCLIP, Sch.Lib., St.Andrews High Sch., Kirkcaldy. [0029318]   03/04/1978
Caldwell Mr W, FCLIP, Life Member. [0002274]   09/03/1939
FE 01/01/1950
Cale Mrs GA, (was Arnill), Inf.Offr., Inf.Direct, Birmingham Cent.L. [0039237]   01/01/1986
Caley Mrs CM, (was Quayle), MCLIP, Life Member, Kilmuir, Ballure Promenade, Ramsey, IM8 1NN, Tel.01624 812215. [0002275]   12/11/1940
Caley Mrs JP, (was Share), BSc DipLib MCLIP, Dept.Lib., Dept.of Planning & Transport, Leics.C.C. [0047897]   22/10/1992
Caley Mr RJ, BA DipLib, Asst.Lib., Liverpool John Moores Univ. [0033624]   29/01/1981
Calixto Mr JA, Chief Lib., Biblioteca Publica Municipal, de Setubal, Portugal. [0050372]   07/07/1994
Callaghan Mrs S, L.& Inf.Asst., NHS Inf.Auth., Birmingham. [0058753]   05/07/2000   AF
Callaghan Miss TM, L.Asst., Tavistock Clinic, London. [0046017]   16/08/1991   AF
Callanan Mrs ED, (was Briggs), BA MCLIP, Lib., Ulverston Victoria High Sch., Cumbria. [0002279]   24/03/1955
Callegari Mr L, BA(Hons) MA MSc, Inf.Offr. [0054475]   20/12/1996
Callen Mr ALA, BA DipLIS MCLIP, Inf.Offr., (Music & Media Prod.), Academic Inf.Serv.L., Univ.of Salford, Adelphi Campus. [0037092]   21/02/1984
Callen Mrs CA, (was Goddard), MA(Oxon) MSc, Sen.Researcher, KPMG, Manchester. [0052638]   05/11/1995
Callow Mrs E, BA(Hons), Grad.Trainee, Inst.of Health Sci.L., Univ.of Oxford. [0057998]   07/10/1999
Callow Mr MJ, BA MCLIP, Team Leader, Web Serv.Team, Home Off., London. [0019594]   07/11/1972
Calonge Miss M, BA(Hons) MA, Stud., Univ.Coll.London, &, L.Asst., Imperial Coll., Cent.L., London. [0058320]   23/12/1999
Calver Mrs M, (was Stephenson), MCLIP, Deputy L.Serv.Mgr., Worthing & Southlands Hosp.NHS, PG Med.Cent., Worthing Hosp. [0023336]   31/10/1974
Camacho Mrs BJ, (was Radford), BA MCLIP, Lib.(p./t.), Epping Forest Coll. [0033120]   06/10/1980
Cambrook Mrs FV, BA(Hons) MA, Res.Fellow, Bournemouth Univ., Dorset. [0050891]   27/10/1994
Cameron Mr AB, BA MCLIP, Life Member. [0029296]   05/01/1970
Cameron Mrs C, MSc MCLIP, Employment not known. [0060347]   10/12/2001
Cameron Mrs DA, (was Bruce), MCLIP, Area Mgr.-W., Gateshead L.& Arts. [0001964]   23/01/1970
Cameron Mrs DJ, Sen.L.Asst., The L., Guernsey Coll. of F.E., St Peter Port, Guernsey. [0058546]   04/04/2000   AF

Cameron Mrs HM, (was Edmondson), BA MCLIP, Unemployed. [0023236]   16/11/1974
Cameron Miss IMM, MA MCLIP, Lib., BMI Health Serv., London. [0002301]   18/09/1968
Cameron Miss L, MA BA(Hons), Lib., Mills & Reeve, Norwich. [0047823]   14/10/1992
Cameron Miss SHM, MA MLitt MA MCLIP, Asst.Under Lib., Cambridge Univ.L. [0002313]   01/01/1970
Cameron Mrs SI, (was Davidson), BSc DipLib MCLIP, Lib., Falkirk Coll.of F.& H.E. [0003653]   14/10/1969
Cameron Mr SR, Learning Res.Asst., City of Bristol Coll. [0061264]   13/05/2002   AF
Camm-Jones Mrs PA, (was Hollidge), BSc MCLIP, Bibl.Serv.Lib., London Business Sch.L. [0002314]   24/10/1966
Camosso-Stefinovic Mrs J, BA MA, Stud., Loughborough Univ. [0059938]   08/11/2001
Camp Mrs AP, (was Purves), MCLIP, Retired. [0002316]   11/02/1942
Camp Mrs SA, MA BSc, Unemployed (Career Break). [0056337]   26/05/1998
Campbell Mr C, MBA MCLIP, Head of L.Serv., Glos.C.C. [0002320]   25/03/1971
Campbell Ms C, BA, Lib., Special Resp.for Serv.to Child. [0059049]   06/11/2000
Campbell Miss CA, L.Asst., Nat.L.of Scotland. [0061822]   13/11/2002   AF
Campbell Mrs CJ, (was Markham), BA MCLIP, Asst.Lib.(Counter Serv.), Oxford Brookes Univ. [0033045]   16/10/1980
Campbell Ms E, Inf.Offr., N.Ireland Council for Vol. Action., Belfast. [0059331]   09/02/2001   AF
Campbell Mrs ES, BA, Network Lib., Aberdeenshire Council. [0034543]   15/12/1981
Campbell Mrs FC, MA(Hons) DipLib MCLIP, Res.Asst., Napier Univ., Edinburgh. [0025959]   24/05/1976
Campbell Mr G, BA(Hons) MPhil MSc, Unemployed. [0056738]   12/10/1998
Campbell Mr GA, MA B COM MCLIP, Lib. & Mus. Mgr., The Moray Council, [0025499]   09/02/1976
Campbell Mr GM, MCLIP, Asst.Lib., OFTEL., London. [0038482]   30/04/1985
Campbell Ms HI, BA DipIM, Unemployed. [0059770]   01/10/2001
Campbell Dr I, MA DipLib MCLIP, Head of Customer Serv., W.Sussex C.C., Chichester. [0030125]   16/01/1979
Campbell Miss JM, MA(Hons), Stud., Univ.of Strathclyde. [0061099]   01/03/2002
Campbell Ms JS, (was Cowlan), BA MCLIP, Head of L.Arts & Arch., Bath & N.E.Somerset Council. [0031513]   22/10/1979
Campbell Mrs K, Lib., Buro Happold, Bath. [0057574]   10/05/1999   AF
Campbell Mrs KP, BA, Sen.Asst., Nursing L., Lovelock-Jones Educ.Cent., Bucks. [0056553]   18/08/1998   AF
Campbell Ms L, MCLIP, Team Lib.(Inf.), Thetford L., Norfolk L.& Inf.Serv. [0002326]   28/01/1970
Campbell Mrs LR, (was Collins), Career Break. [0045011]   25/05/1990
Campbell Mrs M, (was Mcgrath), MCLIP, Sch.Lib., Oaklands Sch., Tower Hamlets. [0009394]   13/01/1968
Campbell Ms M, BA MCLIP, Br.Lib., Hornchurch L., L.B.of Havering. [0036298]   01/10/1983
Campbell Ms M, Stud., Drumragh Coll. [0059636]   09/07/2001   AF
Campbell Mr MJ, MBE MA MCLIP, Retired. [0002332]   01/01/1947
Campbell Mr MM, MA MCLIP, Dist.Lib., Watford, Herts.C.C. [0024408]   31/07/1975
Campbell Mrs OL, DipLib FCLIP, Lib., Council of Legal Educ., Freetown, Sierra Leone. [0019039]   01/01/1965   FE 27/11/1996
Campbell Miss PM, Sen.Lib., NSW,Govt., Australia. [0057300]   04/02/1999
Campbell Mr R, MCLIP, Adult Serv.Co-ordinator, The Mitchell L., Glasgow. [0002336]   07/01/1971
Campbell Mr RM, BA MA MCLIP, Retired. [0002337]   18/09/1970
Campbell Miss RS, BA(Hons), Stud. [0058839]   29/08/2000
Campbell Mrs SA, (was Dawson), MCLIP, Princ.Lib.(Cent.Servs.), Moray Council. [0003833]   18/03/1972
Campbell Mrs SCC, (was Malcolm), MCLIP, Lib., Falkirk Council. [0040246]   18/11/1986
Campbell Miss SE, BA DipLib MCLIP, Asst.Customer Serv.Lib., Fife Council L. [0026629]   26/10/1976
Campbell Mr WA, MA MCLIP MA(LIB), Systems Lib., The Robert Gordon Univ.L., Aberdeen. [0020459]   21/03/1973
Campbell-Blair Mrs R, (was Mundy), BA MCLIP, Business Devel.Mgr., Leeds Univ. [0025370]   14/01/1976
Campbell-Hayes Mrs CM, (was Campbell), BA MCLIP, Area Co-ordinator (L.), Ollerton Area L., Notts.Comm.Serv. [0027143]   31/01/1977
Campion Ms KS, (was Bumfrey), BSc MSc, Inf.Sci., Diabetes UK, London. [0055764]   17/11/1997
Campion Mr PR, MA DipLib MCLIP, L.& Serv.Mgr., L.B.of Merton, Donald Hope L. [0002342]   03/01/1972
Campling Ms JMA, BA(Hons), Asst.Lib., Dept.of Health, London. [0045977]   14/02/1985
Camps Mrs PM, (was Brown), MCLIP, Retired. [0001920]   13/02/1960
Camroux Miss JA, MSc MCLIP, Dep.H.of Learning Resources, London Inst., London Coll.of Printing. [0019613]   26/10/1972
Canavan Mrs JJ, (was Fauvel), MCLIP, Lib.(Job-share), Arts L., Manchester Cent.L. [0004820]   13/05/1965
Canaway Mr NS, MBA MCLIP, Asst.Dir., Durham Co.L., Arts L.& Mus. [0021824]   07/02/1974
Candeland Ms SC, BSc MCLIP, Dep.L.Serv.Mgr., Manchester Metro.Univ., All Saints L. [0039694]   13/05/1986
Candler Mrs FT, (was Langridge), BA MCLIP, Lend.Lib., Hants.Co.L. [0021502]   24/09/1973
Canham Mrs SE, (was Scott), MCLIP, Retired. [0002349]   09/01/1956

Cann Mrs J, BA(Hons) MA, Sen.L.Asst., New Garswick/York Ref.L., York. [0059258] 23/01/2001 **AF**
Cann Miss JC, BSc DipLib MCLIP, Lib., Radiocommunications Agency, London. [0039332] 13/01/1986
Cann Mr JC, Inf.Specialist, NBS Serv., Newcastle upon Tyne. [0049859] 11/01/1994
Cannan Mrs E, MA MCLIP, Lib., DCE Consultants, The Netherlands. [0023131] 06/11/1974
Cannell Mrs SE, (was Best), MA MCLIP, Dep.Lib., Univ.of Edinburgh. [0023170] 02/11/1974
Canner Mr CJ, BA(Hons) DipLib, Asst.Lib., John Rylands Univ.L., Univ.of Manchester. [0002351] 12/11/1968
Canning Mr JP, MA BA MCLIP, Retired. [0019998] 11/01/1973
Canning Ms JS, Unemployed. [0041852] 28/04/1988
Canning Mrs W, (was Devenney), BA(Hons), L.Asst., Coleraine High Sch., Coleraine. [0037525] 08/10/1984
Cannon Ms CJ, BA MPhil MA MCLIP, Tech.Serv.Mgr., London Inst., London Coll.of Printing. [0050616] 01/10/1994
Cannon Mrs CS, (was Mobbs), BA DipLib AKC MCLIP, Unemployed. [0040169] 06/11/1986
Cannon Mrs IL, (was Clack), MCLIP, Retired. [0002354] 15/03/1947
Cant Miss EM, BA DipLib MCLIP, Clerical Offr., Soc.Serv.Dept., Sefton M.B.C. [0026697] 25/11/1976
Cant Mrs SL, (was Attle), BA(Hons) MCLIP, ESG Lib., Environmental Serv., L.B.of Enfield. [0044770] 14/11/1990
Cantrell Ms J, (was Picken), BA DipLib MCLIP, Sen.lib.-Proposals, Epixtech Ltd., Chesham. [0040337] 12/01/1987
Cantwell Miss IA, MCLIP, L.Mgr., Homerton Univ.NHS Trust, London. [0021920] 01/02/1974
Cantwell Mrs R, Asst.Lib., Morgan Cole, Cardiff. [0055925] 10/12/1997
Canty Mrs SA, (was Holland), MCLIP, P/t.Sch.Lib., Isleworth & Syon Sch.for Boys, Middx. [0018196] 04/10/1972
Cape Mr BEM, BA(Hons), Stud., Northumbria Univ. [0059475] 04/04/2001
Capel Mr GA, MCLIP, Inf.Lib., N.Yorks.Co.L., Harrogate. [0002357] 10/08/1962
Capel Ms SE, Inf.for Public Offr., Eden Valley PCT., Carlisle. [0049717] 25/11/1993
Capitanchik Mrs REJ, MA (Hons), Stud., Robert Gordon Univ. [0061567] 02/10/2002
Caporn Ms SL, BA(Hons) PGCE DipLIS MCLIP, LRC Mgr., City of Bristol Coll., Bristol. [0036355] 05/10/1983
Carbines Ms V, BA(Hons), Systems Lib., RCVS L.& Inf.Serv., London. [0040181] 29/10/1986
Carbonell Mr MH, BA DipLib MA, L.Asst.,Reader Serv., Birkbeck Coll., London. [0049788] 03/12/1993
Card Robert M, BA MA, Asst.Lib., Woodbrooke Quaker Study Cent., Birmingham. [0058200] 16/11/1999
Carden Mrs KJ, (was Sherwood), Inf.Offr.& Stud., Robert Gordon Univ. [0058623] 19/04/2000 **AF**
Cardnell Mrs JA, (was Cottam), BA DipLib MCLIP, Sch.Lib., Colfe's Sch., London. [0026623] 26/10/1976
Cardy Ms L, BSc MSc, Unemployed. [0053026] 15/02/1996
Cardy Mr TS, FCLIP, Life Member, Tel.01207 543399, 16 Norman Rd., Rowlands Gill, ME39 1JS. [0002365] 08/05/1937 **FE 01/01/1945**
Caregnato Mrs SE, BSc MSc, Lect., Univ.Fed.do Rio Grande do Sul, Porto Alegre, Brazil. [0046453] 06/11/1991
Careless Mr GC, MA MCLIP, Lib., Collingwood Coll., Camberley. [0032404] 01/04/1980
Caren Ms V, BA(Hons) MCLIP, ICT Classroom Tech., Childwall Comp.Sch., Liverpool. [0052142] 06/10/1995
Carey Mrs AJ, (was Storos), BSc MCLIP, L.& Inf.Mgr., Bond Pearce, Plymouth. [0060444] 11/12/2001
Carey Mrs GG, MA MCLIP, Unemployed. [0034634] 14/10/1981
Carey Mrs J, (was Little), MCLIP, Retired. [0008981] 29/01/1960
Carey Mr P, BA(Hons), Stud., Manchester Met.Univ. [0057320] 09/02/1999
Carey Ms SL, (was Becconsall), BA MCLIP, Head of L.& Inf.Serv., Hammond Suddards Edge, Leeds. [0028523] 10/01/1978
Cargill Mrs J, (was Reed), MCLIP, Unemployed. [0002369] 01/01/1964
Cargill Thompson Dr HEC, BSc PhD FSA MCLIP, Retired. [0002370] 01/01/1966
Cargill-Thompson Mrs KCP, (was Sargent), BA(Hons), Stud., UCL., London. [0059037] 31/10/2000
Carle Miss CA, MCLIP, Life Member. [0002371] 09/09/1951
Carless Miss BH, BA(Hons), Stud., Northumbria Univ. [0061684] 21/10/2002
Carleton Mrs J, (was Davies), MCLIP, P/t.L.Asst., Univ.of Ulster. [0021710] 10/01/1974
Carley Mrs WJ, (was Sherrington), BA MA MCLIP, Acad.Liaison Mgr., Bolton Inst.of H.E., Bolton, Lancs. [0029823] 02/10/1978
Carlile Mrs SJ, (was Jarvis), BA(Hons) MCLIP, Lib., Nottingham Univ., Sch.of Nursing, Mansfield. [0040411] 03/02/1987
Carline Mr F, B LIB MCIIP, Retired. [0002372] 31/05/1978
Carling Mrs AS, Unemployed. [0052068] 02/10/1995
Carlisle Mrs CA, (was Smith), BA MCLIP, Unemployed/Housewife. [0032178] 25/01/1980
Carlisle Mrs FM, (was Windass), MA DipLib MCLIP, APS5, Nat.L.of Australia, Canberra. [0042319] 07/10/1988
Carlson Miss R, BA(Hons) MSc(Econ), Intranet Mgr., Bridgend Coll., S Wales. [0057514] 14/04/1999
Carlton Mrs J, (was Milne), MCLIP, Asst.Lib., N.Yorkshire C.C., Filey, N.Yorks. [0018377] 18/10/1972
Carlton Ms JE, (was Mee), BA, Inf.Spec., Leeds Health Promotion Serv., St.Mary's Hosp. [0038404] 17/04/1985
Carlyle Mrs ER, (was Whittaker), MA(Cantab) MA MCLIP, Dir.of Educ.& Inf., Nat.Eczema Soc., London. [0042046] 18/08/1988
Carlyle Ms JS, (was Jeeves), Sen.Asst., Witney L., Cult.Serv. [0056469] 21/07/1998 **AF**

Carman Ms B, (was Reynolds), BA PGDipLib MCLIP, Retired. [0012304] 15/09/1975
Carmel Mr MJ, BA MSc FCLIP, Dir., S.Thames L.& Inf.Serv., (NHS), Guildford. [0018545] 01/01/1966 **FE 16/10/1989**
Carmichael Ms E, BA MCLIP, Educ.Offr., Glasgow L.,Inf.& Learning. [0022027] 10/01/1974
Carmichael Mrs HP, (was Jones), BA DipLib, Arch.Asst., Conwy Co.Bor.Council, Llandudno. [0036571] 18/10/1983
Carmichael Mrs JG, (was Henderson), MA MCLIP, Inf.Offr., Motherwell L., N.Lanarkshire Council. [0024684] 07/10/1975
Carnaby Ms PE, BA DipEd MCLIP, Univ.Lib., Macquarie Univ., Sydney, Australia. [0021246] 24/09/1973
Carne Mrs SJ, (was Ryan), MA MCLIP, p./t.Sch.Lib., The Rodney Sch., Kirklington, Notts. [0033138] 06/10/1980
Carnes Mrs LK, (was Hawley), MCLIP, Publicity & Promotions Lib., Rugby L., Warwickshire. [0002383] 07/02/1963
Carney Miss L, BA(Hons) PGDipILM, Inf.Asst., Liverpool John Moores Univ. [0056065] 06/02/1998
Carnson Miss SF, (was Majury), BA DipLib MIIS MCLIP, Mgr.-Comm.& People, QinetiQ, Farnborough. [0026468] 05/10/1976
Carpenter Miss AM, MSc MCLIP, Employment not known. [0060166] 10/12/2001
Carpenter Mr B, Inf.Offr., L.B.of Camden. [0057835] 03/09/1999
Carpenter Mrs CD, (was Eaton-Taylor), MCLIP, Unemployed. [0002388] 02/10/1967
Carpenter Mr DL, BA DipLib MCLIP, Unemployed. [0030375] 11/01/1979
Carpenter Mrs EJ, (was Warner), MCLIP, L.Mgr., Pictons, Hemel Hempstead. [0034936] 27/04/1982
Carpenter Mrs FC, BA MCLIP, Teacher of English, James Hornsby High Sch., Laindon, Essex. [0024630] 08/10/1975
Carpenter Mrs J, (was Lamb), BA DipLib DipBIT MCLIP, Lib., DEFRA, London. [0008580] 01/01/1969
Carpenter Mr KP, MCLIP, Retired. [0002389] 05/07/1948
Carpenter Mr RA, BA(Hons) DipLib MCLIP, Freelance Researcher. [0002391] 01/01/1971
Carpenter Mr SBD, BA MCLIP, Inf.Offr., Brit.Energy plc., Gloucester. [0032405] 04/04/1980
Carpmael Ms CM, (was Ford), BSc MCLIP MANL, Dep.Lib., Univ.of the W.of England at Bristol, . [0025532] 02/02/1976
Carr Mr AM, MA, Sen.Lib., Records & Res.Cent., Shropshire C.C. [0023841] 19/09/1967
Carr Mrs AR, BSc MCLIP, Mgr., Mgmt.Servs, Queen Mother L., Univ.of Aberdeen. [0022659] 27/07/1974
Carr Mrs CA, (was Johnson), BA(Hons) CertEd, Learning Centre Mgr., Tyneside Training & Enterprise C. [0048830] 15/06/1993
Carr Mrs CAR, (was Kay), MA DipLib MCLIP, Salary Clerk/Asst.Lib., County Hall, Worcester. [0028485] 16/01/1978
Carr Mrs CH, (was Followell), BSc MCLIP, Inf.Off., Alcan Internat.Ltd., Banbury. [0042021] 20/07/1988
Carr Mrs CM, (was Perkins), MCLIP, Learning Cent.Mgr., Abbot Beyne Endowed Sch., Burton upon Trent. [0018388] 19/10/1972
Carr Miss EC, BA(Hons) PGDip, Asst.Lib., Gateshead Cent.L., Gateshead. [0054404] 04/12/1996
Carr Mrs H, (was Manns), BA MCLIP, Learning Res.Cent.Mgr., Peter Symonds Coll., Winchester. [0009699] 06/10/1965
Carr Mrs KJ, (was Campbell), BSc(Hons) MSc, Sen.L.Asst., City Univ., London. [0054011] 17/10/1996
Carr Mrs MA, BA MCLIP, Princ.Lib., N.Lincs.Council. [0002398] 10/02/1970
Carr Mr MG, MBiochem(Hons), Stud., Univ.Coll.London, London. [0058943] 05/10/2000
Carr Mrs MH, (was Flood), Life Member, Tel:020 8679 1277. [0002399] 22/01/1942
Carr Mrs MS, (was Chater), MCLIP, Sch.Lib., Dir.of Educ., L.B.of Newham. [0025725] 23/09/1975
Carr Mr RB, BA DipLib MCLIP, Unemployed. [0034330] 22/10/1981
Carr Mr RP, MA, Dir.of Univ.L.Serv., Univ.of Oxford. [0025960] 24/05/1976
Carr Mr SJ, BA(Hons) MCLIP, Asst.Lib., Health & Safety Exec., Bootle. [0043475] 06/01/1989
Carr Miss SM, BSc(Hons), Asst.Lib., Royal Soc.of Med.Support Serv., London, W1. [0047802] 19/10/1992
Carradice Mrs CH, (was Stansfield), BA DipILS MCLIP, Sen.L.Asst., Lancs.C.C., Nelson L. [0049503] 08/11/1993
Carragher Ms BA, (was Coward), MCLIP, Young Peoples Serv.Lib., Cheshunt L., Herts. [0036341] 05/10/1983
Carragher Mrs SA, MA MA MCLIP, Mgr.-Lifelong Learning, W.Dunbartonshire Council. [0023280] 12/11/1974
Carrick Mrs EJ, (was Buckley), BA MCLIP, Child.Lib., Milton Keynes Council. [0040296] 20/01/1987
Carrick Mr G, MA MCLIP, Customer Support Offr., ICT Devel.Team, Marylebone L., Westminster L. [0040190] 03/11/1986
Carrick Ms P, BA(Hons) DipLib MCLIP, Lib., Nottinghamshire C.C. [0026086] 05/07/1976
Carrick Mr RM, BA DipILS, Inf.Asst., St.Martins Coll., Carlisle. [0056139] 05/03/1998
Carrington Mrs A, (was Kennedy), BSc MCLIP, p./t.Freelance Law Lib. [0008268] 04/01/1971
Carrington Mrs H, BA DipLib MCLIP, Retired. [0036065] 07/05/1983
Carrington Mr MN, MSc MCLIP, Employment not known. [0060528] 11/12/2001
Carrington Ms RJ, BSc(Hons), Stud., Loughborough Univ. [0058864] 18/09/2000
Carrington Mrs SJ, (was Brooke), BLib MCLIP, Prof.Relief Lib., Bournemouth Bor.Council. [0040750] 01/06/1987
Carritt Ms AS, (was Smith), BA(Hons) MA MCLIP, Inf.Offr., The Univ.of Reading. [0050627] 01/10/1994
Carroll Miss C, BA, Unemployed. [0041747] 10/03/1988

205

Carroll Dr DM, BSc PhD MSc MCLIP, Biological Sci.Lib., The Darwin L., Edinburgh Univ.L. [0047061] 09/04/1992
Carroll Mrs FL, (was Allsopp), MCLIP, Career Break. [0000239] 01/01/1970
Carroll Mrs LK, BA(Hons), Stud., Strathclyde Univ. [0060023] 26/11/2001
Carroll Mrs M, (was Monaghan), MCLIP, Prison Serv.Lib.(Job Share), ALM Dept., Durham C.C. [0010289] 26/04/1972
Carroll Mrs MM, (was Kennedy), BA MCLIP, p./t.Inf.Lib., Kingston Univ., Learning Res.Cent. [0033015] 12/10/1980
Carroll Miss P, BA MCLIP, Policy Offr., Leeds L.& Inf.Servs., Leeds City Council. [0024409] 12/08/1975
Carroll Mr RA, BA FCLIP FRGS, Life Member. [0016736] 12/02/1948 **FE 01/01/1963**
Carroll Mrs SM, (was Collinge), BA(Hons) MCLIP, Lib., St.Francis of Assisi RC Sch., Aldridge. [0046379] 30/10/1991
Carroll Ms T, MCLIP, Learning & Skills Lib., Milton Keynes Council L.Serv., Milton Keynes. [0008407] 01/01/1967
Carron . HC, BA MA MPhil PhD MCLIP, Employment not known. [0025961] 19/05/1976
Carruthers Miss VM, BA FCLIP, Retired. [0002421] 01/01/1934 **FE 01/01/1934**
Carse Mrs SA, BSc, Asst.Lib., BPP Law Sch., London. [0057657] 22/06/1999
Carson Mr CJ, BA MCLIP, Snr.Lib., City of Salford. [0020850] 02/08/1973
Carson Mrs CJ, MCLIP, Ref.Lib.(Spec.Resp.Local Studies), Wokingham Dist.Council, Berks. [0004958] 29/11/1966
Carson Mrs CM, Stud.,L.Asst., Aberystwyth Univ.,St.Ives L. [0061682] 21/10/2002
Carson Mr WRH, FLAI HonFCLIP FCLIP, Life Member, 10 Woodford Dr., Armagh, BT60 2AY. [0002425] 01/01/1949 **FE 01/01/1968**
Carson Mrs ZA, (was Chodanowicz), BA(Hons), Legal Administrator, Brit.Gas Trading Ltd., Staines. [0050890] 27/10/1994
Carter Mr A, MA FCLIP FSAS, Life Member. [0002426] 24/03/1949 **FE 01/01/1968**
Carter Mrs A, (was Taylor), BA DipLib MCLIP, Unemployed. [0030047] 04/11/1978
Carter Mrs AC, MA MSc, p./t.Stud./Learning Res.Asst., Univ.of Wales, Aberystwyth, Chester Coll.of H.E. [0061122] 19/02/2002
Carter Miss B, BA(Hons), p./t.Stud./L.Asst., Univ.of Cent.England, Birmingham Child.Hosp., Med.L. [0061200] 08/04/2002
Carter Mrs BA, (was Bristow), Position unknown, The Nat.Trust. [0042948] 28/04/1989
Carter Mrs CJ, BLS MCLIP, IT Consultant, Self-employed. [0033460] 01/01/1980
Carter Miss D, BLib MCLIP, Resident in Switzerland. [0039682] 06/05/1986
Carter Mrs E, (was Kidman), MCLIP, Lib., HMP Sudbury, Derbys. [0008350] 23/03/1971
Carter Miss EH, BA (Hons) MCLIP, Sen.Inf.Offr., Notts.Chamber of Comm. [0045703] 29/04/1991
Carter Mr ER, BSc MCLIP, Employment not known. [0060525] 11/12/2001
Carter Mrs ER, (was Smith), MCLIP, Life Member, Tel.013722 78826, 5 Broadmead, The Marld, Ashtead, Surrey, KT21 1RT. [0002433] 29/01/1932
Carter Miss HF, BA(Hons) MCLIP, Clinical Lib., Cairns L., John Radcliffe Hosp. [0054008] 16/10/1996
Carter Mrs HM, (was Blowey), BA MCLIP, Research/Inf.Offr., N.Derbys.Chamber of Comm.& Ind.&, Business Link, Derbyshire. [0032871] 07/10/1980
Carter Mr IED, BSc DipLib MCLIP, Head, Specialist Serv., Sci.Mus.L., London. [0023457] 05/01/1975
Carter Mr J, DMS MIMgt MCLIP, Cult.Serv.Mgr., Metro.Bor.of Bury, Gtr.Manchester. [0002438] 01/01/1970
Carter Mrs J, (was Hill), BA MCLIP, Comm.Lib., Bolton M.B.C. [0006885] 02/07/1971
Carter Mrs J, (was Porter), BA MCLIP, p./t.Adult Educ.Tutor, Birmingham Educ.Dept. [0002441] 29/07/1964
Carter Mrs JM, BA(Hons) MCLIP, Asst.Lib., Kirklees Cult.Serv., Dewsbury, nr Huddersfield. [0054829] 08/04/1997
Carter Ms JM, BA, Catr., The London L. [0043033] 13/07/1989
Carter Miss LA, BA(Hons) MCLIP, Lib., H.M.Customs & Excise. [0050452] 03/08/1994
Carter Mr LJ, BSc MSc PhD MCLIP, Retired. [0048288] 24/11/1992
Carter Mrs M, BA MCLIP, Asst.Lib., Bolton Community Coll. [0000254] 08/06/1971
Carter Mrs M, (was Robertson), MA DipLib MCLIP, Research Stud., Queen Margaret Univ.Coll. [0038691] 01/10/1985
Carter Mrs M, MCLIP, Lib. [0060927] 10/01/2002
Carter Mrs ME, (was Street), BA FCLIP, Life Member. [0002448] 01/01/1940 **FE 01/01/1946**
Carter Miss MF, BA DipLib MCLIP, Health Sci.Lib., (Oswestry), Robert Jones & Agnes Hunt, Orthopaedic & Dist.Hosp.NHS Trust. [0002449] 15/10/1971
Carter Mr NB, BA(Hons), p./t.Catr., Leeds Metro.Univ. [0047848] 20/10/1992
Carter Miss P, BD MA MSc MCLIP, Lib., Nat.Gallery of Scotland, Edinburgh. [0043579] 09/11/1989
Carter Mrs PM, (was Day), MCLIP, Head of L.& Inf.Serv., Defence Logistics Organisation, Chertsey. [0003844] 03/08/1964
Carter Mrs PR, BSc(Hons) BSc(Econ) MCLIP, Lib., Brentwood L., Essex. [0053225] 04/04/1996
Carter Mr R, BA MCLIP, Admin.Mgr., L.B.of Barnet. [0024271] 20/05/1975
Carter Mr RD, MCLIP, Life Member. [0002454] 01/01/1947
Carter Mr RO, BSc, Employment not known. [0060526] 11/12/2001
Carter Mr S, BA(Hons) MA, Analyst Programmer, Xansa plc., Manchester. [0038932] 21/10/1985
Carter Mrs S, (was Mcpherson), MA MCLIP, Asst.Lib., Univ.of Bristol. [0009565] 01/12/1969

Carter Mrs SA, (was Clarke), BSc MSc MBA MCMI HonFCLIP, Hon Fellow. [0060527] 11/12/2001 **FE 01/04/2002**
Carter Ms SE, BA(Hons) MA MCLIP, Lib., Home Off., London. [0046893] 28/02/1992
Carter Mrs SL, L.Mgr., Cefas, Lowestoft. [0059508] 18/04/2001
Carter Ms UP, BEd(Hons) DipLIS MCLIP, Asst.Lib., City Business L., London. [0049994] 08/02/1994
Carter Mrs VI, Sen.L.Asst., Princess Alexandra Hosp., Harlow. [0061211] 16/04/2002 **AF**
Carter Ms VI, BSc(Hons), Asst.Lib., Learn.Cent., South Thames Coll. [0058980] 16/10/2000
Cartlidge Mrs CA, (was Breakwell), MCLIP, Princ.Lib., Shropshire C.C. [0001662] 02/10/1971
Cartwright Miss AL, BA(Hons), Asst.Lib., Bedfont L., Hounslow, Middlesex. [0040457] 10/02/1987
Cartwright Mrs D, BA, Unemployed. [0039590] 04/03/1986
Cartwright Miss HF, BA(Hons) MA MCLIP, Inf.Offr., Berrymans Lace Mawer, London. [0055380] 06/10/1997
Cartwright Miss HJ, BA(Hons) MA, Secretarial temp., Univ.of York. [0059404] 05/03/2001
Cartwright Mrs JA, BA MCLIP, Campus Co-ordinator(IIs), Univ.of Plymouth, Exeter Campus. [0002466] 21/10/1971
Cartwright Miss LC, BA(Hons), Stud., UCE Birmingham. [0059600] 26/06/2001
Cartwright Mrs PM, Inf.Offr., Cancer Support, Dudley, W.Midlands. [0055477] 17/10/1997
Cartwright Mr RA, Catr., Instant L., Reading. [0031799] 14/01/1980
Cartwright Mrs S, Lib., Woodbridge Sch., Woodbridge, Suffolk. [0045884] 08/07/1991 **AF**
Carty Ms CJ, BA(Hons) MPhil MA, Employment not known. [0056985] 18/11/1998
Carvell Mrs PA, (was Marshall), BA MCLIP, Head of Tech.Serv., Bermuda Nat.L., Hamilton. [0026772] 26/11/1976
Carver Mrs CB, (was Dow), BA MA(Hons) MPhil DipLIS MCLIP, p./t.Home Worker Lib., Home Off., London. [0036473] 13/10/1983
Carver Mrs CE, MA MCLIP, Fac.Lib., Glasgow Caledonian Univ. [0024621] 01/10/1975
Cascoe Mr G, AIMgt BSc(Hons), Head of Learning Res.Cent., Burlington Danes CofE Sch., London. [0057531] 23/04/1999
Case Mrs A, (was Liversuch), MCLIP, Child.& Yth.Serv.Mgr., Caerphilly Co.Bor.Council, Blackwood. [0008999] 21/03/1972
Case Miss H, L.Super., Sidcup L., Sidcup, Kent. [0052967] 31/01/1996 **AF**
Case Mr JC, BSc(Econ), Inf.Serv.Mgr., Surrey C.C., Woking. [0046676] 06/12/1991
Case Mr ML, BSc PGDipIM, Subject Lib.,(DACS), Anglia Poly.Univ., Chelmsford, Essex. [0052243] 18/10/1995
Casey Miss BA, BA MCLIP, Comm.Serv.Mgr., Bristol L.Serv. [0020781] 01/07/1973
Casey Mr BM, BA Diplib MIInfoSc, Univ.Librarian, City Univ.London. [0044612] 06/11/1990
Casey Mrs JO, (was Porter), BA(Hons) MCLIP, Head of English(Res.), Cartmel Priory Sch., Cumbria. [0002473] 09/02/1968
Casey Prof M, MSC PhD, Jean Monnet Prof., Dept.of L.& Inf.Studies, Univ.Coll.Dublin. [0032890] 01/10/1980
Cash Mrs CKM, (was Southworth), BLib MCLIP, Learning Cent.Mgr., S.Nottingham Coll., W.Bridgford. [0032703] 01/07/1980
Cashman Mr DJ, BA(Econ) DipLib, Temp.L.Asst., Middlesbrough. [0057245] 14/01/1999
Cashman Dr HA, MA PhD DipLib MCLIP, Lib., Stockton L., H.M.Prison, Holme House. [0032025] 28/01/1980
Cashman Mr JM, BA DipLib MCLIP, Lib./Arch., Foreign Exchange Co., Killorglin, Co.Kerry. [0041120] 07/10/1987
Cashmore Ms L, Lib., L.B.of Camden, Kentish Town L. [0057151] 22/12/1998
Casimir Mrs HS, (was Dobinson), MCLIP, Life Member. [0002478] 02/09/1947
Cass Miss EJ, BA(Hons) MSc MCLIP, Project Mgr., Vrisko Ltd., London. [0052453] 02/11/1995
Cass Miss L, MA, Inf.Asst., Wellington Underwriting, London. [0059722] 05/09/2001
Casselden Ms B, (was Casseldon), BA(Hons) PGCE MA MCLIP, Lect., Univ.of Northumbria, Sch of Inf.Studies. [0049768] 06/12/1993
Casselden Mrs L, (was Asbury), BA MA MCLIP, Adult Serv.Mgr.,(Acting), Leicester City Council, Leicester Cent.L. [0044692] 27/11/1990
Cassells Mrs ATS, (was Smith), MA MCLIP, Sch.Lib.(Job Share), Boclair Academy, E.Dunbartonshire. [0028167] 06/10/1977
Cassels Mrs AF, (was Garden), BA MCLIP, Dep.Lib., Basingstoke L., Hants. [0032519] 20/04/1980
Cassels Mr AM, MA MSc MCLIP, Inf.Cent.Mgr., Cent.Sci.Lab., York. [0038099] 17/01/1985
Casserley Miss LD, BA MCLIP, L.Learning Cent.Mgr., Speedwell Tech.Coll., Bristol. [0028789] 24/01/1978
Cassettari Ms G, MA MCLIP, Lib., Met.Police, London. [0052975] 07/02/1996
Cassidy Mrs AEB, (was Baker), BA MSc DipInfSc MCLIP, Employment not known. [0060137] 10/12/2001
Cassidy Mrs AM, (was Seatter), MCLIP, Learning Res.Asst., York Coll. [0021145] 04/10/1973
Cassidy Mrs J, (was Culver), BA DipLib, Inf.Offr., Univ.of Salford. [0049972] 31/01/1994
Cassidy Ms J, BA DipLIS, L.& Inf.Offr., Combat Poverty Agency, Ireland. [0057497] 06/11/1998
Cassidy Mrs R, (was Doyle), BA (Hons) DipLis, Lib., Nursery & Midwifery Educ., Ulster Hosp. [0042178] 04/10/1988
Cassidy Mrs TC, Inf. Devel. Worker, Wolverhampton Childrens Inf. Serv. [0060971] 21/01/2002
Casson Mr PS, BA MCLIP, Unemployed. [0034419] 29/10/1981

Personal Members

Casteleyn Mrs MT, (was Aylward), FCLIP, Life Member. [0002483] 18/10/1963 **FE 27/11/1984**
Castell Mrs HS, (was Argent), BSC, Not working in library, Employment Agency, Cornwall. [0036102] 27/05/1983
Castens Mrs LD, LLB(Hons) PGDip, p./t.Stud./Inf.Cent.Mgr., Univ.of Bristol. [0056278] 20/04/1998
Castens Ms ME, BSc MA DMS MCLIP, Dir.of Acad.Servs., London Guildhall Univ. [0002484] 18/06/1969
Castens Mr S, BSc, Stud./Sen.L.Asst., Bristol Univ. [0061791] 07/11/2002
Castle Ms CM, BA(Hons) MCLIP, Lib.i/c., Dept.of Zoology, Univ.of Cambridge. [0052425] 25/10/1995
Castle Mrs EM, BA MCLIP, Sch.Lib., Perse Prep.Sch., Cambridge. [0023323] 27/11/1974
Castle Mrs J, (was McManus), MA(Hons) DipILS MCLIP, Carnegie Lib., S.Ayrshire Council, Carnegie L. [0038902] 14/10/1985
Castle Mr JD, BA(Hons) MA, Inf.Offr., Rouse & Co.Internat., London. [0056844] 26/10/1998
Castle Mrs JM, (was Ranson), MCLIP, Dep.Learning Cent.Mgr., S.Thames Coll., London. [0012150] 19/10/1971
Castle Ms S, Pub.Enquiries Lib., The Children's Society, London. [0060034] 29/11/2001
Castle-Smith Mr D, BA(Hons) MCLIP, Comm.Lib., Fife Council, Cupar. [0054377] 29/11/1996
Castro Mr A, MCLIP, Leisure Serv.IS/IT Mgr., L.B.of Enfield, Leisure Serv. [0022075] 16/01/1974
Caswell Miss PJ, MCLIP, Comm.Lib., Birmingham L.Serv. [0002486] 05/01/1964
Catcheside Mr PR, BA MCLIP, Retired. [0002489] 01/01/1964
Catchpole Mrs A-DE, (was Mason), BA MCLIP, Relief Lib., R.B.of Windsor & Maidenhead. [0009884] 04/01/1972
Cater Mr M, BA(Hons), Asst.Lib., Birmingham Cent.L. [0049400] 21/10/1993
Cathcart Mrs JM, (was Campbell), PGDipLIS, p./t.L.Asst.(relief), N.E.E.L.B., Ballymena. [0039580] 10/03/1986
Cather Miss C, (was Mellis), BA MCLIP, Evening Serv.Mgr., Glasgow Univ.L. [0031225] 05/10/1979
Catherall Mr P, BA MA(Dist) MCLIP, Web Developer., N.E.Wales Inst.Higher Ed. [0057815] 20/08/1999
Catley Mrs SA, Sch.Lib. [0056329] 20/05/1998 **AF**
Catt Mrs BA, (was Harding), BA MCLIP, Coll.Lib., Bell Coll., Hamilton. [0006297] 06/05/1971
Catteau Mr N, BA MA MCLIP, Lib., L.B.of Croydon, Croydon Cent.L. [0050311] 15/06/1994
Cattermole Ms J, (was Langtree), BA(Hons) DipLib MCLIP, Asst.Head of ILRS (Admin.), Middx.Univ. [0008639] 03/01/1972
Cattle Mrs AJ, (was Dangerfield), BA(Hons) MCLIP, Career Break. [0039274] 06/01/1986
Cattle Mrs J, (was Hambly), MCLIP, Asst.Lib., Northallerton & Thirsk L., N.Yorks. [0006186] 02/10/1969
Catto Mr PM, MA DipLib MCLIP, Database Mgr., L.B.of Islington. [0024622] 10/10/1975
Catton Ms CM, BA MCLIP, Arch.Admin., The Documentation Cent., Amnesty Internat. [0037585] 01/10/1984
Caudwell Mr JW, BA(Hons) MA, Rare Books/Special Coll.Catr., Univ.of London L. [0053872] 15/10/1996
Caul Mrs S, (was Malins), BA DipLib MCLIP, P./t.Asst.Lib., Univ. of Ulster. [0002504] 18/10/1966
Caulfield Mrs AT, (was Prendergast), BA MCLIP, Asst.Inf.Advisor, Univ.of Surrey Roehampton, London. [0011910] 16/03/1967
Caulton Miss JA, BA(Hons) MA MCLIP, Team Lib., Northants.C.C. [0054259] 11/11/1996
Cavanagh Mrs MS, (was Calderwood), MA DipLib MCLIP, Head of Local Studies, W.Lothian Council. [0026696] 27/10/1976
Cave Mr RJ, MA FCLIP, Employment not known. [0060168] 10/12/2001 **FE 01/04/2002**
Cave Mrs ZT, (was Ahamed), MLib BA MCLIP, Unemployed. [0026922] 13/12/1976
Caven Mrs AJ, BA(Hons) MSc, System Support Offr., Warks.C.C.L.& Heritage, Warwick. [0057248] 25/01/1999
Caveney Mrs V, BA MCLIP, Head of Inf.Serv., Woolgate Exchanges, London. [0060411] 11/02/2001
Cavill Mrs CP, (was Thomas), MCLIP, Co.Councillor, Pembrokeshire. [0002514] 06/02/1962
Cavill Ms M, BA(Hons) MA, Asst.Lib., Dept.for Educ.and Skills, London. [0056365] 17/06/1998
Cawkell Mr AE, CEng FIERE MIEEE FCLIP, Position unknown, CITECH, Iver. [0060169] 10/12/2001 **FE 01/04/2002**
Cawley Mrs CE, Sen.Lib., Cheltenham Coll., Glos. [0057697] 01/07/1999
Cawood Mrs AL, (was Partridge), BA(Hons) DipLIS MCLIP, Inf.Specialist, Aston Univ., Birmingham. [0048917] 21/07/1993
Cawood Ms D, BA(Hons), Inf.Asst., Portsmouth Cent.L. [0045412] 14/01/1991 **AF**
Caws Mrs SM, (was Swift), BA DipLib MCLIP, Co.Ref.Lib., Isle of Wight Council, Newport. [0030277] 09/01/1979
Cawsey Mrs PM, Lib., Internat.Sch.of Lausanne, Switzerland. [0060905] 09/01/2002
Cawthorne Mr DJ, BA MCLIP, Asst.Co.Lib., Somerset Co.L.Serv., Taunton L. [0002518] 24/09/1970
Cawthorne Ms L, BA(Hons) DipLIS, Child.& Young Peoples Lib., Nottingham Cent.L. [0048843] 01/07/1993
Cawthorne Ms WA, BSc(Hons) DipLib MCLIP, Asst.Lib., Geological Soc.L., London. [0026310] 30/09/1976
Cawthra Miss LA, MA DipLib MCLIP, Inf.& L.Serv.Mgr., King's Fund, London. [0036863] 09/01/1984
Cefai Mrs JA, (was Smith), MCLIP, Academic Liaison Lib., Anglia Poly.Univ., Cambridge. [0018069] 21/09/1972

Celik Mrs MARF, (was Freeman), BA MCLIP, Lib., Middleton Potts, London. [0033293] 12/11/1980
Ceresa Mr MA, BA DipLib DMS MCLIP, Prin.Bibl.Lib., Southampton Cent.L., Southampton C.C. [0021201] 29/09/1973
Cerroti Mrs H, (was Pemberton), BA(Hons) MCLIP, Princ.Lib., Child.Serv., Calderdale M.B.C. [0044573] 29/10/1990
Chaberska Miss KBL, Unemployed. [0021129] 01/10/1973
Chachu Mrs EN, Dir.-Kumasi, The Brit.Council, Kumasi, Ghana. [0030581] 12/12/1978
Chad Mr KS, MCLIP, Position Unknown, Tails Inf.Ltd., Birmingham. [0021601] 30/11/1973
Chadder Miss JE, BA MCLIP, Life Member. [0002522] 01/01/1954
Chadwick Mr A, Cert.of Merit. [0048816] 08/06/1993
Chadwick Mrs CA, (was Davis), BA(Hons) MCLIP, Sch.Lib., Clitheroe Royal Grammar Sch., Lancs. [0003764] 01/10/1967
Chadwick Mrs KA, (was King), MCLIP, Mob.& Comm.Serv.Offr., L.& Inf.Serv., Skirlaugh, E.Riding of Yorks.Council. [0008389] 01/01/1971
Chadwick Miss LS, BA(Hons), Researcher, Lehman Brothers, London. [0056811] 23/10/1998
Chadwick Mrs M, BSc DipLib MCLIP, Lib., Kingston Maurward Coll., Dorchester. [0041488] 01/01/1988
Chadwick Ms M, MCLIP, Temp.Catr., Birkbeck Univ., London. [0032895] 01/10/1980
Chadwick Miss SJ, BA(Hons), Comm.Child.Lib., Salford Educ.& Leisure Dir.(L.), Salford. [0059014] 25/10/2000
Chadwick Mr SJ, BEng(Hons) MSc, Asst.Lib., BDGH Trust, Barnsley. [0053841] 16/01/1997
Chadwyck-Healey Sir CE, BART, Retired. [0036031] 27/01/1983
Chafey Mr KG, MCLIP, Retired. [0002532] 01/01/1959
Chai Miss CYJ, BSc MLIS, Ch.Lib., Sandakan Reg.L., Sabah, Malaysia. [0050344] 01/07/1994
Chakrabarty Mrs E, (was Chattopadhyay), BA MCLIP, 7 Monkhams Lane, Woodford Green, Essex, IG8. [0012187] 17/10/1967
Chakraborty Mrs J, BSc BLS MCLIP, Sen.Lib., L.B.of Haringey, Hornsey L. [0002535] 02/07/1972
Chalcraft Mr AJA, BA MA MCLIP, Coll.Lib., York St.John Coll., York. [0033393] 08/10/1980
Chalk Dr AJ, BSc PhD MCLIP, Employment not known. [0060191] 10/12/2001
Chalkley Mrs LC, (was Greenaway), MCLIP, Housewife. [0005910] 26/09/1963
Challen Mr M, BSc DipLib, Team Lib.,Music & AV Serv., L.B.Southwark, London. [0044066] 24/04/1990
Challinor Miss HL, BA(Hons), Inf.Serv.Lib., Dept.for Educ.& Skills, Sheffield. [0042638] 20/01/1989
Chalmers Dr AM, BSc PhD MCLIP, Position unknown, GlaxoSmithKline, Regulatory, Policy & Inf. [0060170] 10/12/2001
Chalmers Mrs ICL, (was Ludlow), BA MCLIP, Trust/Dist.Lib., Kingston Hosp., The Stenhouse L., Surrey. [0042162] 12/10/1988
Chalmers Miss JES, MCLIP, Retired. [0002541] 01/01/1958
Chalmers Mrs KM, (was Wilcox), BA(Hons), Career Break. [0039250] 01/01/1986
Chalmers Ms L, MA(Hons), Inf.Cent.Asst./Stud., Scottish Parliament & Inf.Cent., Edinburgh Telford Coll. [0061292] 16/05/2002
Chalmers Mrs ME, (was Chamlers), BA MCLIP, Lib., Bootham Sch., York. [0002542] 15/10/1971
Chalmers Miss S, BSc, Asst.Lib., Middlesex Univ. [0059008] 23/10/2000
Chaloner Mrs H, (was Sharp), MCLIP, Dep.Area Lib., Calderdale L., Sowerby Bridge Br. [0013182] 01/01/1972
Chamberlain Ms A, (was Thompson), MCLIP, Lib., H.M.Y.O.I.,Onley, Northamptonshire. [0014590] 22/01/1972
Chamberlain Mr CJ, Self-Employed. [0053194] 01/04/1996
Chamberlain Mr DC, BA(Hons) DipLIM MCLIP, Asst.Lib., Worcester Comm& Menai Health NHS, Redditch. [0057101] 14/12/1998
Chamberlain Mrs EA, (was Bradley), MCLIP, Br.Lib., Rumney Br., S.Glamorgan C.C. [0032365] 25/03/1980
Chamberlain Mrs EJ, (was Ellis), MA MCLIP, Sen.IT Offr.(L.), Bucks.Chilterns Univ.Coll., High Wycombe, Bucks. [0037048] 02/02/1984
Chamberlain Mr EM, BA(Hons), Stud. [0059134] 22/11/2000
Chamberlain Mrs H, (was Dunkley), BA DipLib MCLIP, Dep.Lib., Brooklands Coll., Weybridge, Surrey. [0002547] 24/07/1969
Chamberlain Mrs JA, BA MCLIP, Unemployed. [0002548] 24/01/1968
Chamberlain Ms PM, MCLIP, Stock Mgr., Westminster L. [0023901] 01/02/1975
Chamberlain Mr RJ, MCLIP, Sub-Lib., Univ.of Nottingham, Notts. [0025016] 04/11/1975
Chamberlayne Miss NJ, BA MCLIP, Retired. [0002549] 17/03/1946
Chambers Miss A, BA MA MCLIP, Employment not known. [0060502] 11/12/2001
Chambers Mr APM, BA(Hons), Stud., Thames Valley Univ. [0061537] 16/09/2002
Chambers Miss C, BA(Hons) MA, Sch.Lib., St.Davids RC High Sch., Midlothian. [0058599] 11/04/2000
Chambers Mrs JA, (was Marshall), BA DipLib MCLIP, Sen.Lib., Merck,Sharp & Dohme, Neuro-Sci.Research Cent., Harlow. [0042656] 31/01/1989
Chambers Miss JH, MA BA, Asst.Lib., London Undergroung Eng.L. [0058065] 22/10/1999
Chambers Mrs K, (was Houghton), BA MCLIP, L.& Inf.Mgr., Bracknell Forest Bor.Council, Berks. [0030435] 23/01/1979
Chambers Mrs L, (was Hamilton), BA MSc MCLIP, Self-employed, Freelance Researcher, Fact Checker, Copy Editor. [0031848] 08/01/1980
Chambers Mr MW, MA MA DipLib, Curator, German Sect., Brit.L., London. [0036406] 05/10/1983
Chambers Mrs NE, (was Mattley), BA MCLIP, Sch.Lib., Evesham High Sch., Evesham, Worcs. [0028743] 23/01/1978
Chambers Ms SE, BA(Hons) MA, Electronic L.Proj.Co-ordinator, Univ.of London L., London. [0054796] 02/04/1997

Chambers Mrs WM, BA, Stud., Univ.of Wales, Aberystwyth, & Duty Lib., Univ.of Edinburgh. [0057897] *01/10/1999*
Chambers-Huggins Mrs CR, BA, Lib., St.Vincent Community Coll., St.Vincent & The Grenadines. [0057560] *28/04/1999*
Chambre Mr TR, BA MCLIP, Lib.,Catg., Southampton City L. [0002562] *01/01/1971*
Champion Mr KJ, BA(Hons) MA MCLIP, Knowledge Mgr., Accenture, London. [0052826] *01/01/1996*
Champion Mrs M, (was Evans), MA MCLIP, Unemployed. [0004682] *02/01/1965*
Champion Mrs MM, (was Ewels), MCLIP, Life Member. [0002566] *04/07/1950*
Champion Mrs PM, (was Blake), MCLIP, p./t.Admin.Asst., Prestwood Jnr.Sch., Great Missenden. [0023392] *11/01/1975*
Champion Mrs SP, (was Brown), MA, Inf.Offr., Becta, (Brit.Educ.Comm.& Tech.Ag.), Coventry. [0051045] *09/11/1994*
Champion Mrs Y, (was Emerson), BA DipLib MCLIP, Unemployed. [0031607] *15/11/1979*
Chan Miss BYC, Asst.Lib., The Open Univ.of Hong Kong, Kowloon. [0054226] *08/11/1996*
Chan Miss CKN, BA MCLIP, Retired. [0031512] *09/10/1979*
Chan Mrs GC, (was Doody), MCLIP, p./t.L.Asst., U.W.I.C., Cardiff. [0022200] *22/02/1974*
Chan Mr GKL, MSc MCLIP, Learning Res.Mgr., John Moores Univ., Liverpool. [0002569] *30/08/1969*
Chan Mrs GM, (was Grant), MCLIP, Unemployed. [0022343] *02/04/1974*
Chan Miss K, Asst.Lib., Hong Kong. [0057572] *05/05/1999*
Chan Miss LC, BA MCLIP, Resident in Indonesia. [0029612] *01/10/1978*
Chan Mr SF, LLB MCLIP, Partner, Chan & Chuk Solicitors, Hong Kong. [0016743] *01/01/1969*
Chan Ms WSM, Inf.Offr., Linklaters, Hong Kong. [0061484] *19/08/2002*
Chan Miss YL, MA, L.Asst., Open Univ.of HK. [0059707] *16/08/2001*
Chan Kam Lon Mr Y, DipLib MSc MCLIP, Dir., Nat.L., Mauritius. [0027922] *01/10/1977*
Chanay Mr J, Employment not known. [0060858] *12/12/2001*
Chandler Miss A, Stud., U.C.L. [0056797] *08/10/1998*
Chandler Mrs A, (was Sutton), MCLIP, Lib., Blenheim High Sch., Epsom. Surrey. [0002570] *19/03/1957*
Chandler Mr DJ, MCLIP, Retired. [0002572] *02/02/1953*
Chandler Mrs HE, MA MCLIP, Retired/p./t.Lib., Cheshire C.C., Ellesmere Port. [0021062] *03/10/1973*
Chandler Mrs JM, (was Watson), Lib.& Intranet Mgr., D.F.I.D. [0042198] *10/01/1988*
Chandler Miss M, BA(Hons), Academic Liaison Lib.Asst., Univ.of Liverpool. [0046390]*31/10/1991*
Chandler Mr MA, MCLIP, Dist.Lib.Kennet, Wilts.L.Arts & Arch., Devizes, Wilts. [0002577] *01/01/1966*
Chandler Mrs MR, (was Mackinnon), MA MCLIP, Sch.Lib., Harrogate Grammar Sch., N.Yorks. [0009476] *06/10/1971*
Chandler Ms MR, BA MSc MCLIP, Asst.Lib., Queen's L., Univ.of Bristol. [0031229] *07/10/1979*
Chandler Mr PJ, Asst.Lib., Royal Coll.of Defence Studies, London. [0051294] *04/01/1995*
Chandler Mr PN, BA MCLIP, Princ.Devel.Lib., Knowsley Metro.Bor.L.Serv. [0018117] *02/10/1972*
Chandler Ms PS, BLS MA PGCE MCLIP, Periodicals Dept., Univ.of York. [0030129] *05/12/1978*
Chandler Mrs SH, (was Cox), BA MCLIP, Stock Lib., Knowsley M.B.C., Merseyside. [0020013] *09/01/1973*
Chandler-Benjamin Mrs SJ, (was Chandler), BA(Hons) MSc, Asst.Lib., Swindon Coll., Wilts. [0054993] *13/06/1997*
Chaney Mrs AEP, BA MCLIP, Asst.Lib., H.M.Customs & Excise L., London. [0029783] *01/10/1978*
Chaney Mrs KV, (was Lyons), MCLIP, L.Asst.-Salomans, Canterbury Christ Church Univ.Coll., Southborough, Kent. [0002579] *07/02/1972*
Chaney Mr MA BA MCLIP, Asst.Lib., Loughborough Univ.of Tech. [0018359] *13/10/1972*
Chantavaridou Miss E, Stud., Univ.of Strathclyde, Glasgow. [0059999] *19/11/2001*
Chaplin Miss EL, BA(Hons), Stud., Univ.of Sheffield. [0061092] *27/02/2002*
Chaplin Ms NJ, MCLIP, Learning Resources Asst., The Coll.of W.Anglia, Kings Lynn, Norfolk. [0019804] *01/01/1972*
Chaplin Miss T, BA, (Hons), Stud., City Univ. [0060958] *21/01/2002*
Chapman Ms A, BA, Position unknown, Minesoft Ltd., London. [0060829] *12/12/2001*
Chapman Mrs AD, (was Batt), Unemployed. [0031560] *01/11/1979*
Chapman Mrs AD, (was Loker), MA FCLIP, p./t.Research Offr., UKOLN, The Off.for L.& Inf., Networking, Univ.of Bath L. [0002589] *08/09/1967* **FE 09/07/1981**
Chapman Mrs AV, (was Greenwood), BA(Open) MCLIP, Unemployed. [0002590] *04/02/1959*
Chapman Miss BJ, BA DipLib MCLIP, L.& Inf.Mgr., Archway Healthcare L., Middx.Univ. [0029263] *26/04/1978*
Chapman Mrs BJ, (was Pegg), MCLIP, Child.Lib., L.B.of Redbridge. [0002591] *24/09/1964*
Chapman Mr BM, MCLIP, Head of Comm.Learning, Hull City Council, Cent.L. [0018237] *01/10/1972*
Chapman Miss CE, BA(Hons), L.Asst., Music & Drama L., Wakefield L.H.Q., W.Yorks. [0055065] *03/07/1997*
Chapman Ms EA, BA MA DipLib FCLIP, Lib., Taylor Inst.L., Univ.of Oxford. [0018409] *30/09/1972* **FE 18/01/1989**
Chapman Mr EJ, MA MILAM FRSA MCLIP, Retired. [0019471] *19/10/1954*
Chapman Mrs JB, (was Hird), BA MCLIP, Life Member. [0002597] *01/01/1944*
Chapman Mr JH, MSc MCLIP, Records Serv.Mgr., Dept.of Trans.Local Govt.and the, Regions, London. [0027311] *28/02/1977*

Chapman Miss JL, MA BA(Hons), Inf.Cent., Bus.Link York & N.York., Huntington, York. [0056618] *18/09/1998*
Chapman Mr JL, MA MCLIP, Faculty Inf.Consultant, Univ.of Herts., Art & Design. [0029375] *19/07/1978*
Chapman Mrs KV, (was Coulson), BSocSc(Hons), Finance Inf.Offr., Clifford Chance, London. [0057992] *11/10/1999*
Chapman Mrs LH, (was Frenchman), BA MCLIP, Housewife. [0005228] *01/01/1971*
Chapman Mrs M, (was Lewis), MCLIP, Retired. [0008884] *01/01/1956*
Chapman Ms M, (was Lowe), MCLIP, Team Lib., Surrey C.C., Ewell L. [0025896] *01/04/1976*
Chapman Ms M, MA CertEd FCLIP, Mgr.of Coll.L.Serv., Bradford Coll., Grove L. [0002604] *01/01/1971* **FE 21/11/2001**
Chapman Miss ME, MA MCLIP, Br.Lib., Egglescliffe Br.L., Stockton Bor.Council. [0026312] *30/09/1976*
Chapman Miss MG, BA CertHSC MCLIP, Inf.Offr., Bell Coll., Hamilton. [0032641] *01/07/1980*
Chapman Mr MM, MA MCLIP, Head of Customer Serv., Min.of Defence, Whitehall L. [0002609] *16/10/1970*
Chapman Ms NC, BA(Hons) DipIS MCLIP, Sch.Lib., St.Albans High Sch., Ipswich. [0050230] *11/05/1994*
Chapman Mr NG, BA MCLIP, Self-Employed, Antiquarian Bookde. [0018553] *30/09/1972*
Chapman Ms NJ, BA(Hons), Sen.Reseracher, Lovells, London. [0055398] *09/10/1997*
Chapman Mr PA, BSc DipILM MCLIP, Learning Res.& I.L.T. Mgr., Cambridge Reg.Coll. [0047241] *19/06/1992*
Chapman Ms PAM, (was Gaskin), BA DipLib MCLIP, Unemployed. [0039974] *08/10/1986*
Chapman Mr PJD, MCLIP, Freelance Web Consultant. [0028526] *13/01/1978*
Chapman Mr RE, BSc MCLIP, Employment not known. [0060171]*10/12/2001*
Chapman Mrs S, (was McCluskey), MCLIP, Life Member. [0002610] *01/01/1957*
Chapman Mrs SM, (was Caldwell), MA MLib MCLIP, Unemployed. [0022584] *04/07/1974*
Chapman Mrs SM, (was Womack), B LIB MCLIP, Employment not known. [0022428] *30/04/1974*
Chapman Mrs VJ, (was Roberts), MCLIP, Sen.Mgr.(N.), Dorset C.C. [0012521] *05/10/1967*
Chapman Mr VS, BLib(Hons) MCLIP, Br.Lib., Wandsworth Bor.Council, Southfields L. [0031586] *01/01/1979*
Chappell Mr DL, BA(Hons), Stud., Univ.Stratchclyde. [0056513] *04/08/1998* **AF**
Chappell Ms FM, BSc MA, Inf.Offr., SIGN, Edinburgh. [0055320] *01/10/1997*
Chappell Miss SE, BSc MCLIP, Employment not known. [0060156] *10/12/2001*
Chappelle Mrs CA, (was Bayliss), BA MCLIP, Unemployed. [0002614] *10/09/1970*
Chard Mrs CM, (was Harrison), p./t.L.Asst., Kingswood L., Bristol. [0045698] *24/04/1991* **AF**
Chard Mrs J, (was Bayley), MCLIP, p./t.Sen.Asst., Thornton L., Lancs. [0000955] *26/09/1969*
Charles Mrs AR, L.Serv.Mgr., Treasury Solicitors, London. [0059463] *03/04/2001* **AF**
Charles Mrs BJ, (was Ball), BSc DipLib MCLIP, Asst.Lib., Scottish Exec., Edinburgh. [0028488] *20/01/1978*
Charles Ms EE, BA MSc MCLI, Lib., FCE, Birkbeck, London. [0037713] *17/10/1984*
Charles Ms JC, BA(Hons) DipLIS, Career Break. [0043441] *26/10/1989*
Charles Mrs JY, BA, BA(Hons) MSc MRQA, Sen.QA Offr., Astra Zeneca, Loughborough. [0051040] *09/11/1994*
Charles Mrs S, (was Methven), MA MSc(Econ), Sen.L.Asst., Univ.L., Univ.of Dundee. [0046163] *07/10/1991*
Charlesworth Miss AD, BA(Hons) MA, Sen.Inf.Asst., Kings Coll.London. [0056799] *19/10/1998*
Charlesworth Mrs FM, (was Sherwood), MCLIP, Life Member. [0008730] *01/01/1941*
Charlton Miss D, BSc(Hons) PGCertILS, L.& Inf.Asst., Denton Park L., Newcastle City Council. [0058759] *10/07/2000*
Charlton Mr D, BA DipLIS, Sen.Inf.Asst., Univ.of Leicester. [0056259] *20/04/1998*
Charlton Mrs HM, (was Shield), BA MCLIP, Dept.Lib.(Art/Design), (Jobshare), Newcastle Coll., Newcastle upon Tyne. [0036883] *13/01/1984*
Charlton Mr JA, HND BEd MSc, LIAZE Project Offr., Hetton L., Hetton-Le-Hole. [0061062] *15/02/2002* **AF**
Charman Mr D, BA, Records Management Consultant, Derek Charman Associates, Holcot. [0060843] *12/12/2001*
Charnley Ms C, BA MSc MCLIP, L.& Inf.Serv.Offr., Shropshire Comm.& Mental Hlth.Serv., NHS Trust. [0046457] *07/11/1991*
Charnock Ms RMC, MA(Hons) DipILS MCLIP, Lib., DJ Freeman, London. [0049439] *27/10/1993*
Charteris Mr BA, ILT & New Devel.Mgr., Barnet Coll., London. [0058764] *10/07/2000*
Chase Mr BJ, FCLIP, Retired. [0002626] *01/01/1959* **FE 01/01/1964**
Chase Miss MI, BA MCLIP, Sen.Lib., Lafarge Roofing Tech.Cents., Crawley, W.Sussex. [0019975] *18/12/1972*
Chase Ms SA, BA(Hons) DipInf, Dep.Inf.Mgr., Weil, Gotshal & Manges, London. [0049506] *08/11/1993*
Chatfield Mrs SJ, (was Beales), BLS MCLIP, Unemployed. [0039209] *01/01/1986*
Chatten Mr RM, BA, Associate Postperson, Employer Unknown. [0040283] *12/01/1987*
Chatten Miss ZJ, BA(Hons) MA, Asst.Lib., Royal Automobile Club, London. [0057975] *07/10/1999*

Personal Members — Chudasama

Chatterjee Mr A, Prof.& Head, Dept.of L.& Inf.Sci., Jadavpur Univ., Calcutta 700032. [0046168] 07/10/1991
Chatterjee Mrs FJ, (was Coffey), BA MCLIP, Corporate Administrator, Appleby, Spurling & Kempe, Hamilton, Bermuda. [0027522] 30/04/1977
Chau Miss CWC, MLib MCLIP, Asst.Lib., Hong Kong Poly.L. [0042202] 13/10/1988
Chau Miss M, MSc, L.Asst., City of Westminster. [0048085] 04/11/1992
Chaudhary Dr MA, MBA MSc, Unemployed. [0061502] 02/09/2002
Chaudhary Mr MY, MLS, Ch.Lib., Univ.of Azad Jammu & Kashmir, Pakistan. [0061556] 01/10/2002
Chaudhry Ms RY, (was Rehman), BA(Hons) MCLIP, Casual Relief, Birmingham City Council. [0037656] 13/10/1984
Chauhan Mr BP, BSc MLS LLB MBA, Head, .Dept.of L.& Inf.Serv., Thapar Cent.for Ind.R.& D., Patiala,India. [0056468] 20/07/1998
Chave-Cox Mrs J, (was Kelly), BA(Hons) MA MCLIP, [0022645] 04/08/1974
Chawdhuri Ms RJ, Graduate Trainee., Univ. Coll. Lon. [0060917] 10/01/2002
Cheal Mr BS, BA MCLIP, Lib., Army L.Serv., M.O.D.,Woolwich. [0002639] 26/10/1970
Checkland Mrs M, BA(Hons), Sch.Lib., Leics.C.C., King Edward VII Community Coll. [0051898] 02/08/1995
Checkley Miss CR, LLB(Hons) MA MDip, Asst. L., Univ. of Essex, Colchester. [0054271] 12/11/1996
Chedgzoy Mr JN, BA(Hons) DipLis MCLIP, Sen.Lib., Shropshire C.C., Bridgnorth L. [0046986] 20/03/1992
Chedgzoy Mrs SL, (was Appleyard), BA(Hons) DipLib MCLIP, Lib., The Herefordshire Council. [0046593] 21/11/1991
Cheesbrough Mrs GM, BA, Lib., N.Yorks.Co.L., HMYOI Remand Cent. [0024272] 10/06/1975
Cheese Mrs JL, (was Lewis), MCLIP, Retired. [0002642] 29/02/1964
Cheeseman Miss FJ, BA(Hons) MCLIP, Inf.Offr., Norton Rose, London. [0055509] 16/10/1997
Cheesman Mr B, MA MCLIP, Life Member, 6 Pimlico, Durham, DH1 4QW. [0002643] 01/10/1956
Cheesman Miss DA, BA DipLib MCLIP, Implementation Lib., Ex Libris USA, Chicago. [0043572] 09/11/1989
Cheetham Mrs LM, (was Jones), BA MCLIP, Sch.Lib., Hitchin Girls Sch., Herts. [0030196] 08/01/1979
Chelin Ms JA, BA DipLib MCLIP, IT Devel.Lib., Univ.of the W.of England, Bristol. [0039406] 29/01/1986
Chemorei Mr PC, BSc, Chief Lib., Kenya Utalii Coll. [0061758] 05/11/2002
Chen Ms G, Employment not known. [0047228] 02/06/1992 AF
Chen Dr KC, MBA MSc FInstBA FBSC MCLIP PhD, Management Consultant, Inf.Tech., Singapore. [0016750] 22/06/1969
Chen Miss R, BA DipIM MA, L.Asst., Imperial Coll., London. [0056703] 01/10/1998
Chen Mr YK, BSc MCLIP, Mgr.-Business Inf.Cent., Dept.of State Devel., Hobart. [0002651] 05/02/1968
Cheney Ms CR, BA MCLIP, Asst.Lib., Univ.Coll.London. [0036530] 17/10/1983
Cheong Mrs MMS, (was Li), MSc BSc MIInfSc MCLIP, p./t.Asst.Lib., NUS Med.L., Singapore. [0025857] 15/04/1976
Cherpeau Mrs CM, (was Jaeger), Res.Offr., Knowsley M.B.C., Page Moss L. [0045304] 04/10/1990
Cherry Mr IH, BSc MCLIP, Inf.Specialist, Univ.of Northumbria at Newcastle. [0002654] 31/10/1969
Cheshire Miss MM, BA MCLIP, Retired. [0002658] 18/05/1966
Chesmond Mrs B, (was Walker), BA ALAA MCLIP, Life Member, Resident Australia. [0016757] 27/09/1956
Chesney Mrs AR, (was Whitall), BA MCLIP, Sch.Lib., Sandy Upper Sch., Beds.C.C. [0034617] 19/01/1982
Chesney Mr BJ, MA MCLIP, Unemployed. [0002659] 06/10/1967
Chester Miss J, BA(Hons) DipLib MCLIP, Head: L.& Inf.Serv., Imperial Cancer Research Fund, London. [0024182] 01/04/1975
Chester Ms KA, BA, Stud., Birkbeck Coll. [0052308] 23/10/1995
Chester Ms SA, BSc(Hons) DipLib MCLIP, Inf.Offr.(P./t.), Univ.of Salford. [0042014] 21/07/1988
Chesters Mrs HA, (was Toolin), BA(Hons) MA MCLIP, Sen.L.Asst., Imperial Coll., Computing Collection, Cent.L. [0054423] 09/12/1996
Chestnutt Miss MA, BA DipLib MCLIP, Sch.Lib., Down High Sch., S.E.Educ.& L.Board. [0027145] 25/12/1976
Cheung Mrs EYL, BA MCLIP, Unemployed. [0043682] 24/11/1989
Cheung Mrs HM, BA DipLib MCLIP MEd, Learning Res.Cent.Mgr., Longbenton Comm.Coll., N.Tyneside. [0041261] 21/10/1987
Cheung Mr ST, BA MSc MEd MBA DipB MCLIP, I.T.Operations Mgr., Hutchison-Priceline Ltd., Hong Kong. [0060090] 07/12/2001
Cheung Mr WF, BEd DipEd(EdAdmin) DipLIM MA, Systems Lib., High Court, Judiciary, Hong Kong. [0050353] 04/07/1994
Cheung Miss YK, Lib., P.L., Hong Kong Govt. [0050140] 28/03/1994
Chew Mr JK, FCLIP, Life Member, 6 Glenview Crt., Ribbleton, Preston, PR2 6EG, Tel.01772 655543. [0002664] 26/03/1950 FE 01/01/1960
Chew Miss P, MCLIP, Lib., The Perse Sch.for Girls, Cambridge. [0019716] 19/07/1968
Cheyne Mrs TA, (was Jenkins), MCLIP, Sch.Lib., Langley Park Sch.for Girls, L.B.of Bromley. [0028437] 30/11/1977
Cheyney Mr KG, MCLIP, Life Member. [0002666] 13/03/1951
Chia Mrs GCK, (was Tseng), MCLIP, Resident Overseas. [0016759] 01/01/1963
Chibnall Miss MI, BA MCLIP, Asst.Lib., Royal Astronomical Society, London. [0018422] 21/10/1972
Chilcott Miss CH, BA MCLIP, Lib.i/c., Newton Abbot L., Devon C.C. [0042477] 23/11/1988
Child Mrs AM, (was Love), BSc MCLIP, Temp.Sen.Community Lib.-Sch., Lincs.C.C. [0002673] 24/02/1966
Child Mrs CA, BSc DMS, Sen.Inf.Offr., Greater London Authority, London. [0059291] 29/01/2001

Child Mr SC, BA, Room Bookings Asst., Univ.of Southampton. [0051172] 23/11/1994
Child . VJ, MA MPhil DPhil DipIM MCLIP, Asst.Lib., Nuffield Coll.L., Oxford. [0049887] 07/01/1994
Childs Mr AD, BA FCLIP, Life Member, 7 Haye Close, Lyme Regis, Dorset, DT7 3NT. [0002677] 04/03/1948 FE 01/01/1960
Childs Ms SM, BSc MSc MCLIP, Research Assoc., Inf.Mgmt.Research Inst., Univ.of Northumbria. [0033392] 24/11/1980
Childs Smith Ms KE, (was Childs), BA MCLIP, Head of L.& Inf.Serv.(Job Share), NSPCC. [0030895] 05/05/1979
Chillingworth Mr PC, Unemployed. [0041229] 10/10/1987
Chillman Mrs S, (was Ellis), BA MCLIP, Lib., George Ward Sch., Wilts.C.C. [0022873] 09/10/1974
Chilmaid Mrs DJ, (was Pickles), MBA DipLib MCLIP, Access Serv.Mgr., Kent Arts & L. [0032148] 21/01/1980
Chilvers Dr AH, (was Lomas), BA(Hons) DipLib MA PhD MCLIP, Child.& Sch.Lib., Bolton Metro. [0043982] 20/03/1990
Chin Miss CS, BA ED M MCLIP, Life Member. [0002681] 17/01/1966
Chinenyanga Miss M, DipLib, Stud./L.Asst., Dublin City Univ. [0061794] 08/11/2002
Chiner Arias Mr A, MA(Hons), Pre-Post Grad Trainee, Taylor Institution L., Univ.of Oxford. [0059697] 08/08/2001
Chinn Ms M, MCLIP, Lib.(Job-share), Age Concern England, London. [0021810] 15/01/1974
Chinnery Miss C, BLib MCLIP, Learning Resources & L.Cent.Mgr., Peterborough Reg.Coll. [0021992] 18/01/1974
Chinnock Mrs SJ, p./t.Stud./Sen.L.Asst., Univ.of Cent.England, Birmingham, Erdington L. [0061093] 27/02/2002
Chirgwin Mr FJ, BA MSc FCLIP, Life Member. [0002685] 21/05/1959 FE 01/01/1965
Chirgwin Mrs TMdW, MA(Oxon) MMus DipLIM MCLIP, Resources Lib., Cheshire C.C., L.H.Q., Chester. [0055321] 01/10/1997
Chirnside Ms RE, MA(Hons) DipLIS MCLIP, Asst.Lib., Chichester P.L., W.Sussex. [0054353] 26/11/1996
Chisholm Mrs AI, (was Bainbridge), MCLIP, Retired. [0002686] 20/01/1961
Chivas Mrs G, (was Ball), BA MCLIP, Sch.Lib., Cox Green Sch., Maidenhead. [0023816] 31/01/1975
Chivers Mrs B, (was Law), MA MCLIP, Sen.L.Asst., Univ.of Cent.England in Birmingham. [0008666] 29/03/1946
Chivers Miss I, BA(Hons) DipLib, Dep.Lib.(Systems), English Nature, Peterborough. [0035964] 14/02/1983
Chng Miss CN, BA MCLIP, Asst.Lib., Nanyang Tech.Univ.L., Singapore. [0022267] 19/10/1973
Chong Mr CM, Careers Devel.Offr., Halton Bor.Council, Widnes. [0054045] 22/10/1996
Chopra Mr P, BA MCLIP, Campus Lib., Univ.of E.London, Stratford Campus. [0037124] 28/02/1984
Chorley Miss S, MA MSc, Lib., Shearman & Sterling, London. [0051812] 06/07/1995
Choudhury Miss B, BA MCLIP, Asst.Lib., Allen & Overy, London. [0040375] 22/01/1987
Choudhury Mr S, BSc, Lib., Haringey L., London. [0061002] 29/01/2002
Chouglay Mrs LA, (was Durkin), BSc(Hons) DipLib MCLIP, Unemployed - Full-time Mother. [0039216] 01/01/1986
Choules Miss JE, BA(Hons) MA MCLIP, L.Mgr., Cent.L., R.B.of Kensington & Chelsea. [0049237] 14/10/1993
Chowdhury Mr GG, BSc(Hons) DipLib MLib PhD FCLIP, Sen.Lect., Univ.of Strathclyde, Glasgow. [0056835] 26/10/1998 FE 22/09/1999
Chowdhury Mr MT, Stud., Manchester Metro.Univ. [0061748] 01/11/2002
Choying T Mr JC, Unemployed. [0047626] 08/10/1992
Chrimes Mr MM, BA MLS MCLIP, Lib., Inst.of Civil Engineers, London. [0026211] 29/09/1977
Christian Mr WD, Relief L.Asst., Lincs.C.C. [0042549] 07/12/1988
Christie Miss EV, BA DipLib MCLIP, Team Lib.-Yth., S.E.Educ.& L.Board. [0040905] 17/08/1987
Christie Mr GF, MA MSc, Digital L.Offr., Edinburgh Univ. [0055796] 24/11/1997
Christie Mr JAF, BA(Hons) DipLIS MCLIP, p./t.Lib., Scott-Moncrieff, Glasgow. [0046657] 21/10/1987
Christie Mrs KM, (was Melville), MA(Hons), Learning Resources Co-Ord.(Is.), Borders Coll. [0047177] 21/05/1992
Christie Miss PM, BA MCLIP, Head of Learning Res., London Inst., Cent.St.Martins Coll.of Art & Des. [0025018] 02/11/1975
Christine Miss R, MA MCLIP, Lib., Mary Erskine Sch. [0053834] 03/10/1996
Christison Mr A, MA(Hons), Training Co-Ordinator, Epixtech Ltd., Bucks. [0055901] 15/12/1997
Christison Mrs A, (was Shah), BSc(Hons) MSc MCLIP, Comm.Inf.Lib., Slough L. [0054523] 14/01/1997
Christmas Miss JA, Unemployed. [0051182] 23/11/1994
Christopher Miss JM, BA(Hons), Unemployed. [0056610] 14/09/1998
Christopher Mrs LP, (was Domine), MBA DMS BLib MCLIP, Assoc.Dir.:Learn.&Inf.Resources, The Isle of Wight Coll. [0004060] 30/10/1918
Christopher Mr RJ, MCLIP, Inf.Mgr., Ricardo Consulting Eng., Shoreham-by-sea. [0002699] 14/02/1958
Christophers Mr RA, MA PhD FCLIP, p./t.L.Consultant. [0002700] 14/02/1958 FE 01/01/1963
Chu Mrs SF, PGDipILM, Inf.Skills Training Lib., Croydon Health Sci.L., Mayday Univ.Hosp., Surrey. [0061344] 07/06/2002
Chu Miss SY, BA(Hons) MCLIP, Lib., UCL, London. [0034294] 14/10/1981
Chuah Miss M, BA MCLIP, Lib., Univ.of Malaya L., Kuala Lumpur. [0024410] 29/07/1975
Chubb Mrs C, (was Hattell), Sen.L.Asst., Plymouth Coll.of Art & Design. [0045520] 28/02/1991 AF
Chudasama Mr AK, BSc MCLIP, Stud., Dept.of Inf.Studies, Univ.of Sheffield. [0045685] 25/04/1991

209

Church, Ms AM, MA DipInf MCLIP, Asst.Lib., Cent.St.Martins Coll.of Art &, Design, London. [0047812] 19/10/1992
Church Mr JW, BA, L.Asst., English Faculty L., Cambridge. [0061346] 07/06/2002 **AF**
Churches Mr KJ, MCLIP, Life Member. [0002705] 30/09/1947
Churchward Mrs M, (was Edwards), MCLIP, Inf.Res.Cent.Mgr., Bognor Regis Community Coll. [0002709] 11/10/1966
Churchward Mr SM, MCLIP, Customer Serv.Mgr., WSCC L.Serv., L.Admin Cent., Chichester. [0002710] 01/01/1966
Chute Mrs M, BA MCLIP, Community Lib., Birmingham L.Servs. [0009306] 01/01/1972
Cieciura Mrs EK, (was Coleman), BA MLib MCLIP, p./t.Asst.Lib., Bournemouth Univ., Poole. [0039291] 07/01/1986
Cimals Mrs AD, (was Zuicens), BA DipLib, Employment not known. [0036429] 13/10/1983
Cini Mr L, Asst.Lib., Nat.L.of Malta. [0049896] 07/01/1994
Cinnamond Mrs J, (was Thurgood), MCLIP, Life Member. [0002712] 03/03/1960
Cipkin Mr CB, BA(Hons) MA ARCO MCLIP, Liaison Lib., Univ.of Reading, Music L. [0051805] 04/07/1995
Cirtina Ms OS, BA MCLIP, Careers Inf.& Guidance Advisor, Gloscat, Cheltenham. [0032020] 12/02/1980
Citroen Dr CL, FCLIP, Resident in the Netherlands. [0060051] 07/12/2001 **FE 01/04/2002**
Clackson Mrs AM, (was Waterson), BMus(Hons) DipLib, L.Asst., Univ.of Strathclyde. [0034247] 13/10/1981
Clague Mr P, BA FCLIP, Life Member. [0002713] 29/03/1955 **FE 01/01/1967**
Claiden Mrs J, (was Lewis), BA MCLIP, Nat.Meteorological L.& Arch.Mgr., Met.Off., Bracknell. [0027537] 18/05/1977
Clanchy Miss J, B Lib MCLIP, Lib., G.C.H.Q., Cheltenham. [0002714] 11/10/1970
Clanchy Dr MT, HonFCLIP, Hon.Fellow. [0059434] 15/03/2001 **FE 15/03/2001**
Clapham Ms L, (was Johnstone), BA MCLIP, Mother. [0036716] 11/11/1983
Clapp Mrs FC, (was Popkin), MCLIP, Casual Employment. [0026516] 13/10/1976
Clapp Mrs MA, BA(Hons), L.Asst., Burges Salmon, Bristol. [0053401] 10/06/1996 **AF**
Clare Mrs C, (was Gregory), MA, Unemployed. [0045263] 28/01/1991
Clare Mr CJC, MCLIP, Lib., Essex County L. [0021636] 24/11/1973
Clare Mr DW, MA MCLIP, Learning Cent.Mgr., Univ.of Wolverhampton, Telford Campus. [0023183] 05/11/1974
Clare Mrs JB, (was Stephens), BA(Hons) MCLIP, Lib./interlending Manager(J.Share), The Billericay School, Essex Libraries. [0026807] 07/11/1976
Clare Mrs SA, MA MCLIP, Unemployed. [0027924] 12/10/1977
Clare-Grant Miss CH, BA BSc(Hons) MCLIP, Sen.Asst.Lib., Perth & Kinross Dist.L., A.K.Bell L.,Perth. [0002718] 01/01/1964
Clargo Mrs LM, (was Gadbury), BA(Hons) MCLIP, Catr., LSE L., London. [0002719] 16/10/1968
Claridge Miss C, MA(Hons), Stud. [0058129] 04/11/1999
Clark Ms A, Area Mgr., London Bor. Newham, East Ham. [0061380] 05/07/2002
Clark Miss AH, BA(Hons), Stud., Liverpool John Moores Univ. [0058786] 20/07/2000
Clark Mr AJ, BSocSci MCLIP, Site Lib., Thomas Parry L., Univ.of Wales, Aberystwyth. [0022092] 09/01/1974
Clark Mrs AM, (was Martin), BA DipLib MCLIP, Asst.Lib., Minster Sch., Southwell. [0025834] 02/10/1971
Clark Miss BC, FCLIP, Life Member. [0002723] 26/10/1938 **FE 01/01/1952**
Clark Mr BF, BLib MCLIP, Principal Lib.Offr., Business Support, Sandwell L.& Inf.Serv. [0029937] 09/11/1978
Clark Ms BL, BA(Hons) DipIM MCLIP, Princ.L.Asst., Sch.of Oriental & African Studies, London. [0049355] 28/10/1993
Clark Mrs C, BA MCLIP, Advisory Lib., Met.Bradford Council, W.Yorks. [0034039] 06/08/1981
Clark Ms CJ, BEd MLib MCLIP, Upper Sch.Lib., American Internat.Sch.of Budapest, Hungary. [0026389] 21/07/1976
Clark Mrs CL, (was Dunne), MCLIP, L.Asst., Woodhall L., Herts.C.C. [0004283] 01/01/1967
Clark Miss CR, MA, Asst.Lib., Bexley Council, Thamesmead. [0056820] 23/10/1998
Clark Mr D, MCLIP, Sci.& Tech.Lib., Univ.of Derby. [0029019] 21/03/1977
Clark Mr DA, BA DipLib MCLIP, Sch.Lib., Tarbert/Argyll, Argyll & Bute Council. [0036722] 10/11/1983
Clark Mr DH, MCLIP, Life Member. [0002725] 12/10/1944
Clark Mrs DW, (was Barnard), MCLIP, H.L.Res.Sect., House of Commons L., London. [0000780] 23/09/1968
Clark Mrs E, (was Wienke), BA PGLib MCLIP, Retired. [0042538] 28/11/1988
Clark Mr EJ, BA B COM FCLIP, Retired. [0002727] 29/07/1931 **FE 01/01/1931**
Clark Mrs EP, BSc(Econ) MCLIP, L.Res.Asst., Lauder Coll., Dunfermline. [0051087] 14/11/1994
Clark Mrs F, (was Karaman), BLib, Unemployed. [0053138] 01/04/1996
Clark Mrs FH, (was Dempster), BA MCLIP, Multi-Media Lib., Cent.L., Aberdeen City L. [0030394] 07/02/1979
Clark Mrs GS, (was Graham), BLib, Lib., Beachcroft Wansbroughs, London. [0037078] 06/02/1984
Clark Mr HG, MCLIP, Retired. [0002728] 11/10/1941
Clark Miss HJ, BA(Hons), Stud., Northumbria Univ. [0061697] 21/10/2002
Clark Mr HM, Catr., Wadham Coll., Oxford. [0049269] 20/10/1993
Clark Mr HM, (was Keates), BA MCLIP, Voluntary Advice Worker, Bangor Citizens Advice Bureau. [0021873] 18/01/1974

Clark Mrs HR, (was Le Seelleur), BA DipLib MCLIP, L.& Inf.Mgr., Sligo Gen.Hosp., N.Western Health Bd., Republic of Ireland. [0037979] 01/01/1985
Clark Mrs IJ, (was Dunn), BA(Hons), Team Lib., Aberdeen City Libraries. [0048620] 15/03/1993
Clark Miss J, BA AIL MCLIP, Life Member, 18 Ashdene Cres., Crofton, Wakefield, WF4 1PN. [0002733] 09/02/1955
Clark Mrs J, (was Lawrenson), MA MCLIP, Deutsch Catr., Hamlyn L., British Museum, London. [0008717] 02/01/1969
Clark Mrs JA, (was Brook), BA MCLIP, Grp.Mgr., Leeds City Council. [0027860] 28/09/1977
Clark Miss JE, MSc BA MCLIP, Picture Lib., Friends House L., London. [0002737] 13/10/1970
Clark Mrs JM, (was Crewe), MCLIP, Local Stud.Asst., Oldham M.B.C. [0028988] 20/02/1978
Clark Mr JR, BA MBA CertEd MCLIP, Tutor/Lib., Rampton Hosp., Notts. [0002738] 05/08/1971
Clark Mrs JS, BA(Hons) DipILM, Sen.L.Asst., Univ.of Newcastle. [0052474] 02/11/1995
Clark Mrs JS, (was Brown), Sen.L.Asst., Anglia Poly.Univ., Chelmsford. [0047582] 02/10/1992 **AF**
Clark Mrs K, (was Salvage), B LIB MCLIP, Inf.Serv.Lib., Royal Coll.of Nursing, London. [0022511] 13/05/1974
Clark Mrs KM, (was Boyle), BA MCLIP, Educ.Offr., BECTA, Coventry. [0019945] 12/01/1973
Clark Mrs LH, (was Robinson), BA(Hons), Section Head, Inter-L.Loans, Univ.of Leicester L. [0045115] 12/07/1990 **AF**
Clark Mrs LJ, BA MCLIP, Lib., Scottish Agric.Sci.Agency, Edinburgh. [0023075] 31/10/1974
Clark Mrs LM, (was Wilkinson), BA MCLIP, Lib. User Serv., Stockport Coll.of F.& H.E., Stockport. [0040421] 22/01/1987
Clark Mrs LMM, (was Hughes), MCLIP, Asst.Princ.Lib., Dudley MBC, Stourbridge L. [0002740] 21/02/1970
Clark Miss M, BA MCLIP, Sch.Lib., Angus Council, Carnoustie. [0045643] 08/04/1991
Clark Mrs M, (was Williams), MCLIP, Sch.Lib., Nottingham High Sch. [0026824] 01/01/1966
Clark Mrs ME, (was Birchwood), MCLIP, Asst.Lend.Lib.-Cent.L., Bristol City Council. [0001276] 03/09/1968
Clark Mrs ME, (was Taylor), MCLIP, Life Member. [0002741] 01/01/1957
Clark Mrs ME, MCLIP, Unemployed. [0028943] 15/02/1978
Clark Mrs MJ, (was Goodsell), Lib., Mott Macdonald Grp., Croydon. [0047121] 05/05/1992
Clark Mrs PE, (was Nettlefold), BA FCLIP FRSA, Worldwide Contracts Mgr., American Internat.Companies, New York & London. [0022019] 19/01/1974 **FE 01/04/2002**
Clark Mr PJ, BSc DipLib, Team Lib., L.B.of Enfield, Palmers Green L. [0044084] 25/04/1990
Clark Mr RM, BA DipLib MCLIP, Asst.Lib., Slaughter & May, London. [0037702] 19/10/1984
Clark Mr RSC, BA MCLIP, Stock Lib., Motherwell L., N.Lanarkshire Council. [0019601] 08/11/1972
Clark Mrs S, (was Hepburn), BA MCLIP, L.Mgr., Thornton Heath, L.B.of Croydon. [0026740] 18/10/1976
Clark Ms S, Inf.Offr., Nat.Energy Action, Newcastle upon Tyne. [0050836] 21/10/1994
Clark Mrs SA, BA(Hons) PGDip, Comm.L.Offr., Newton-Le-Willows L. [0059868] 18/10/2001
Clark Mrs SE, (was Kingsley), BA(Hons) MCLIP, Res.Asst., Univ.of Brighton, St.Peters House L. [0002751] 16/07/1968
Clark Miss VK, MCLIP, Asst.Lib., Glasgow City Ls.& Arch., Mitchell L. [0027926] 01/10/1977
Clark Ms VM, MA MCLIP, N.Mersey L.Alliance Co-ordinator, Liverpool Health Auth. [0023162] 08/11/1974
Clark Miss W, BA(Hons) MCLIP, Lib.-Child.Serv., Essex C.C., Brentwood L. [0049119] 06/10/1993
Clarke Mrs A, (was Coote), MCLIP, Unemployed. [0002752] 08/02/1962
Clarke Mrs A, Staff Devel.& Training Offr., City L.& Arts Cent., Sunderland. [0060898] 21/12/2001 **AF**
Clarke Mrs A, BSc, Sen.Learning Resource Asst., Wiltshire Coll., Trowbridge. [0055046] 01/07/1997 **AF**
Clarke Mrs AM, (was Meadowcroft), BA MCLIP, Head of Knowledge & L.Serv., N.E.Lincs.PCT, Brigg. [0024361] 18/07/1975
Clarke Mrs BA, (was Waling), BA(Hons) MA, Team Leader, Whitaker Inf.Serv., Stevenage. [0051343] 24/01/1995
Clarke Mrs C, BA MA MCLIP, Literacy/Numeracy Asst., Warwickshire C.C., Thomas Tolyffe Primary Sch. [0041274] 22/10/1987
Clarke Mrs CA, BA MCLIP, Br.Lib., (Job-share), Fullwell Cross L., L.B.of Redbridge. [0034295] 23/10/1981
Clarke Mrs CMS, (was Williams), Learning Res.Offr., Coleg Powys, Llandrindod Wells. [0054810] 08/04/1997 **AF**
Clarke Mr DA, MA FRSA MCLIP, Life Member, Tel:01404 812130. [0020689] 19/03/1948
Clarke Mr DE, MLS MCLIP, Retired. [0002759] 01/01/1956
Clarke Mrs ECL, (was Picken), Career Break (to Jan 2004), [0043016] 16/06/1989
Clarke Miss EJ, B SC MCLIP, Stock Lib., Area L.H.Q., N.E.Educ.& L.Board, Co.Antrim. [0022722] 30/08/1974
Clarke Miss EM, BA MCLIP, Lib.-Learning Literacy & Child., E.Sussex L.Inf.& Arts, Hastings [0035605] 10/11/1982
Clarke Ms EM, BA(Hons), Asst.Lib. [0056053] 20/01/1998
Clarke Mr FA, DMS MIMgt PGDipTheol MCLIP, Retired. [0002765] 20/01/1964
Clarke Mr FR, BA MCLIP, Team Lib.(Ref.& Inf.), Somerset Co.L., Taunton. [0023874] 13/10/1975
Clarke Mrs GJ, (was Piercey), BA, Unemployed. [0037056] 12/01/1984

Clarke Mrs IA, (was Budd), MCLIP, Unemployed. [0002768] 25/01/1964
Clarke Mr IJ, BA MCLIP, Princ.Lib.-W., Daventry L., Northants.L.& Inf.Serv. [0002769] 28/02/1970
Clarke Miss J, BA DMS MCLIP, Self-employed, 19 Alvern Ave., Fulwood, Preston, PR2 3QR. [0025021] 01/11/1975
Clarke Ms J, Stud., Univ.of Brighton. [0061593] 02/10/2002
Clarke Mrs JL, (was Cunnew), MCLIP, Head of L.& Inf.Serv., Holman,Fenwick & Willan, London. [0023042] 23/10/1974
Clarke Miss JM, BA MCLIP, Lib., King Edward VII Sch., Lytham St.Annes. [0002773] 31/01/1968
Clarke Mr JM, MA DipLib, Inst.Lib., Inst.of Child Health L., London. [0035188] 03/10/1982
Clarke Mrs JM, Sch.Lib., Werneth Sch., Stockport. [0052726] 28/11/1995
Clarke Mrs JM, (was Cox), MBE MCLIP, Life Member. [0002774] 11/10/1945
Clarke Mr JP, BA(Hons) DipLib, Unemployed, [0058710] 01/07/2000
Clarke Mrs KA, (was Sneddon), BA(Hons), Lib.(Job Share), Bradford L., Keighley & W.Area. [0042604] 18/01/1989
Clarke Miss L, BSc(Hons) PGDip, Comm.L.Offr., Eccleston L., St.Helens M.B.C. [0057488] 07/04/1999
Clarke Ms L, BA (Hons), Knowledge Administrator, BTG International. [0060899] 21/12/2001 **AF**
Clarke Mrs LA, BA(Hons) PGCE MCLIP, Bank Lib., Reg.L.Unit, Univ.of Birmingham. [0042268] 13/10/1988
Clarke Mrs LJ, BA MA MCLIP, Dep.Lib., Social Studies L., Univ.of Oxford. [0054171] 04/11/1996
Clarke Miss ME, BA(Hons) MCLIP, Catr., Derbyshire C.C., L.& Heritage. [0056916] 04/11/1998
Clarke Mr ME, BA MCLIP, Dir.of Inf., Arts Council of England, London. [0039336] 17/01/1986
Clarke Ms NH, BA(Hons), Stud., Univ.Northumbria @ Newcastle. [0059240] 15/01/2001
Clarke Ms PM, BA MCLIP, Grp.Child.Lib., Redcar Cent.L., Redcar & Cleveland Bor.Council. [0019882] 01/01/1973
Clarke Mr PR, BSc MCLIP, Consultant. [0002788] 12/08/1968
Clarke Mr PRT, MCLIP, Grp.L.Mgr., L.B.Greenwich. [0023612] 16/01/1975
Clarke Miss RE, BA DipLib MCLIP, Inf.Specialist, Kings Coll., Univ.of London. [0024625] 14/10/1975
Clarke Mrs RM, (was Chirnside), BA(Hons) MCLIP, Career Break. [0038199] 28/01/1985
Clarke Mrs SB, (was Lynn), MA DipLib MCLIP, Sch.Lib., George Abbot Sch., Guildford. [0035411] 03/10/1982
Clarke Mrs SC, (was Chuter), MCLIP, Casual Relief Lib., Hampshire County L. [0002790] 30/01/1963
Clarke Mrs SD, BSc(Hons), P./t.Stud.,Business Researcher, Manchester Met.Univ., CMC, Cheshire. [0059852] 17/10/2001
Clarke Mrs SH, (was Wright), MCLIP, Retired. [0021809] 29/12/1966
Clarke Mr SJ, BA MCLIP, L.Mgr.(Customer Serv.), L.B.of Tower Hamlets. [0034296] 20/10/1981
Clarke Ms SJ, BSc(Hons) MSc MCLIP, Inf.Sci., Hollinger Telegraph New Media, London. [0053895] 09/10/1996
Clarke Miss SK, BSc(Hons), Stud., Manchester Met.Univ., L.Asst., Kirkham L., Preston. [0056940] 09/11/1998
Clarke Ms SM, BA MCLIP, Admin.Offr., Land Registers N.I., Belfast. [0023018] 15/10/1974
Clarke Mrs SP, (was Booth), BA FCLIP, Retired. [0002793] 03/10/1949 **FE 20/01/1999**
Clarke Mrs TM, (was Crowley), BSc MCLIP, Lib., Hertford.Partnership NHS Trust, St.Albans. [0003429] 01/01/1970
Clarke Ms U, BA (Hons), Asst. Mgr., Goldman.Sachs. [0060954] 18/01/2002
Clarke Ms ZA, BA MA MCLIP, Res.Fellow, Manchester Met.Univ. [0040320] 10/01/1987
Clarkson Mrs CB, (was Wilcox), BA(Hons) DipILM MCLIP, Lib., Cheshire C.C., Sandbach L. [0052170] 12/10/1995
Clarkson Mrs EM, (was Wilson), MCLIP, Lib., Whitby Br.L., N.Yorks. [0002798] 26/01/1966
Clarkson Mrs HJ, (was Moore), BSc MCLIP, Lib., The Godolphin Sch., Salisbury. [0010340] 23/11/1971
Clarkson Mr JAJ, BA MCLIP, Sch.Lib., Trinity Academy, Edinburgh. [0039761] 01/07/1986
Clarkson Mr MA, (was Smith), BA MCLIP, Sch.Lib., Salford C.C. [0039789] 04/07/1986
Clarkson Mrs MA, (was Orrell), MCLIP, Unemployed. [0011043] 17/02/1969
Clarkson Miss R, MSc BA MCLIP, L.& Inf.Serv.Mgr., Gillette Mgmt.Inc., Reading, Berks. [0035648] 25/11/1982
Clarkstone Mrs CE, (was Bayes), BA DipLib MCLIP, Comm.Lib.(Job Share), Kent C.C., Faversham L. [0032258] 27/02/1980
Clasen Ms CF, (was Milburn), MA MA, Career Break. [0043549] 06/11/1989
Claughton Ms D, MCLIP, Ref.Lib., Ocean Springs P.L., MS, U.S.A. [0055961] 01/01/1964
Clausen Mr H, PhD MA MLibSc FCLIP, Sen.Research Fellow, State & Univ.L, Aarhus, Denmark. [0046818] 05/02/1992 **FE 21/07/1993**
Clausen Mrs JH, (was Alexander), MCLIP, Retired. [0002800] 09/10/1944
Clavel-Merrin Ms GM, (was Merrin), M LIB MCLIP, L.Consultant, Swiss Nat.L., Bern, Switzerland. [0027544] 28/04/1977
Claxton Mr MD, Lib., Inst.of Mechanical Engineers, London. [0050095] 24/03/1994
Claxton Miss MT, MA MCLIP, Life Member. [0002801] 05/09/1960
Claxton Miss P, BA MCLIP, Retired, [0002802] 17/03/1965
Claxton Ms S, Lib., Inst.of Structural Engineers, London. [0049760] 03/12/1993
Clay Mrs AJ, (was Birchall), BA(Hons) MCLIP, Bibl.Serv.Offr., Warrington Bor.Council Ls., Warrington,Cheshire. [0048955] 02/08/1993
Clay Mr AM, FCLIP, Retired, [0002805] 07/01/1941 **FE 01/01/1958**
Claydon-Park Mr R, Employment not known. [0060218] 10/12/2001
Clays Ms LE, MA, Nursing & Allied Health Lib., Imperial Coll., Charing Cross Hosp, London. [0059378] 23/02/2001

Clayton Mr CJ, BA DMS MCLIP, Dir., SINTO, Sheffield. [0002812] 01/01/1972
Clayton Ms GM, (was Fergus), BA DipLib MCLIP, Lib.(Jobshare), Kingswood, S.Glos.Council. [0030310] 16/01/1979
Clayton Miss JE, BA MCLIP, Ch.Lib., HM Treasury & Cabinet Off., L.& Inf.Serv., London. [0018169] 04/10/1972
Clayton Miss JM, BA DLIS MCLIP, Employment not known. [0025242] 03/01/1976
Clayton Miss L, BA MCLIP, Ref.& Inf.Asst., John Rylands Univ.L.of Manchester. [0040637] 01/04/1987
Clayton Miss LA, BA(Hons) MA MCLIP, Ref.Lib., Southampton Cent.Ref.L. [0055219] 20/08/1997
Clayton Mrs LS, (was Jacobs), BA MCLIP, Currently not working due to, health reasons. [0035417] 01/10/1982
Clayton Dr M, MA MCLIP, Independent Consultant. [0002816] 19/04/1971
Clayton Mr PA, FSA FRNS FCLIP DipArch, Lect.in Archaeology/Author, Self-employed. [0002817] 14/03/1955 **FE 01/01/1964**
Clayton Mr RE, BA(Hons) MA MCLIP, L.Serv.Mgr., Rutland C.C., Oakham. [0048366] 08/12/1992
Clayton Mrs SK, (was Millen), BA MCLIP, Inf./Gen.Lib., Derbys.C.C. [0020114] 23/01/1973
Clayton Mrs SM, (was Hawksworth), BA MCLIP, Lib., Buxton L., Derby. [0034061] 02/09/1981
Claythorn Mrs SP, (was Roberts), BA(Hons) MCLIP, Tech.Serv.Co-ordinator, Coutts L.Serv.UK, Hants. [0030522] 08/01/1979
Clayton Mrs VA, (was Wilson), BA(Hons) MCLIP, Sch.Lib., Sherborne Sch., Dorset. [0041294] 30/10/1987
Clear Mrs FC, BA DipLib MCLIP, Sen.Inf.Worker, Family Inf.Link, Stockport. [0034575] 12/10/1981
Cleary Miss A, BA DipLIS MCLIP, Lib., MIS L.Project, Inst.of Tech., Dublin, Ireland. [0045842] 24/06/1991
Cleary Mrs RL, (was Rontynen), MA MCLIP, Lib., Language Cent., Univ.of Cambridge. [0042032] 27/07/1988
Cleaver Mrs AV, (was Moores), MSC MCLIP, Inf.Mgr., Watson Wyatt Partners, Reigate, Surrey. [0026991] 05/01/1977
Clee Mrs AS, (was State), BA(Hons) MCLIP, Head Lib., Bromsgrove Sch. [0050085] 16/03/1994
Cleeve Mrs ML, BA MCLIP, Inf.Consultant. [0002825] 01/01/1965
Clegg Mrs A, (was Turner), MA FCLIP, p./t., Univ.of Portsmouth. [0002827] 10/03/1960 **FE 01/01/1968**
Clegg Mrs DJE, (was Pethick), BTech MSc FCLIP, Position unknown, Sheffield S.W. PCT. [0060531] 11/12/2001 **FE 01/04/2002**
Clegg Mr DW, BA MCLIP, Life Member. [0002829] 01/01/1962
Clegg Miss H, BA(Hons) MSc MCLIP, Market Analyst, R.R.Donnelley Europe, Netherlands. [0041558] 28/01/1988
Clegg Mrs MA, BA(Hons), Stud.(from 10/2000). [0058412] 04/02/2000
Clegg Ms SJ, BA MCLIP, General Serv. Co-ordinator, Glasgow City Council, Mitchell L. [0033964] 15/08/1981
Clegg Miss SM, BA MBA MCLIP, Dir.of Inf.Serv., Univ.of Surrey Roehampton, Learning Res.Cent. [0002834] 01/01/1970
Cleghorn Ms FA, MSc, Inf.Offr., NERA, London. [0021971] 17/01/1974
Clement Ms AL, (was Dunn), BA MA MCLIP, Lib., Chaucer Coll., Canterbury,Kent. [0044281] 09/08/1990
Clement Ms E, BA MA MCLIP, Subject Lib., Bradford Coll. [0056935] 06/11/1998
Clement Mrs GEG, (was Barton), FCLIP, Life Member. [0002835] 11/10/1942 **FE 01/01/1957**
Clement-Stoneham Mrs GM, (was Clement), MA, Inf.Offr., Linklaters, London. [0053751] 01/01/1996
Clements Mrs CT, BLib MCLIP, Princ.L.Offr.(Young People), Cornwall C.C. [0028275] 01/11/1977
Clements Mrs ER, (was Jackson), MCLIP, Retired. [0007670] 15/07/1955
Clements Mr FA, FCLIP, Dir.of Inf.Serv., Coll.of St.Mark & St.John, Plymouth. [0002838] 15/07/1965 **FE 27/10/1975**
Clements Mrs FR, BA(Hons) MA, Unemployed. [0055357] 03/10/1997
Clements Mrs GF, (was Hopwood), BA, Inf.& Lifelong Learning Lib., (Job Share), Stevenage L. [0044071] 09/02/1987
Clements Mrs GJ, (was Woods), BA Dip MCLIP, Unemployed, [0039383] 21/01/1986
Clements Mrs JJ, (was Bell), MBE BA MCLIP, Retired. [0001079] 06/10/1970
Clements Mrs M, (was McLean), BA MCLIP, p./t.L.Asst., Heriot-Watt Univ.L., Edinburgh. [0009504] 21/09/1970
Clements Mrs SA, (was Smith), BA MCLIP, Neighbourhood Lib., Coventry City L., Jubilee Crescent L. [0037050] 04/02/1984
Clemetson Miss S, BA MCLIP, L.Asst., Oxford Co.L. [0036098] 31/05/1983
Clemow Mrs HL, (was Gutteridge), BA(Hons) DipLib MCLIP, Bus.Lib., Southampton City Council. [0046083] 01/10/1991
Clemson Mrs TK, (was Garvey), BA MCLIP, Housewife. [0033294] 19/11/1980
Clennett Ms MA, BA MCLIP, Ch.Lib., Pub.Health Lab.Serv., Cent.Pub.Health Lab., London. [0003266] 02/10/1965
Cleverley Mrs PE, (was Grafton), MCLIP, Grp.Lib., Birmingham. [0005769] 02/10/1970
Clibbens Mrs A, Stud., Univ.of Wales Aberystwyth. [0061562] 02/10/2002
Cliffe Mrs CM, (was White), MCLIP, Sen.Team Lib.-Learning & Literacy, Glos.C.C. [0005631] 01/01/1971
Cliffe Mr DE, BA MCLIP, Sen.Ref.Lib., Cent.L., Reading Bor.Council. [0002849] 27/01/1969
Clifford Tony, BA MCLIP, Princ.Lib.(Inf.& Res.), L.B.of Barking & Dagenham. [0002850] 09/09/1971
Clifford Mr BE, BA MA HonFCLIP, Head of Learning & Research Support, The Library, Univ.Leeds. [0002852] 12/04/1976 **FE 01/04/2002**
Clifford Mrs CA, BA MCLIP, Local Studies Lib., Huntingdon L., Cambs.C.C. [0035880] 01/11/1983
Clifford Mrs EML, (was McCallum), MCLIP, Community Lib.(Job-share), E.Dunbartonshire Council, Bishopbriggs. [0036332] 03/10/1983

211

Clifford Mr JN, BA DipLib MCLIP, Br.Lib., Bob Lawrence & Hatch End L., L.B.of Harrow,. [0035795]   12/01/1983
Clifford Mrs KJ, p./t.Stud./ Team Lib., Univ.Aberystwyth, Gravesend L. [0059725]   05/09/2001
Clifford Mrs SF, Stud., Brighton Univ. [0061818]   11/11/2002
Clifford Miss SK, MCLIP, Retired. [0002854]   25/08/1948
Clifford Ms SL, MCLIP, Asst.Lib., U.W.E., Bristol. [0028530]   12/01/1978
Clifford-Winters Mr A, BSc MCLIP, Employment not known. [0060678]   12/12/2001
Clift Mrs C, (was Stevens), BA(Hons) MA MCLIP, Lib., Rutlish Sch., Merton. [0002855]   14/02/1964
Clift Mrs MA, (was Howard), BA PGDipLib MCLIP, Mob.Serv.Lib., Reading L., Reading Bor.Council. [0045187]   03/08/1990
Cliftlands Mr AD, BA(Hons) DipLib, Lib., Off.for Nat.Statistics, London. [0043241]   13/10/1989
Clifton Ms BA, (was Twigg), BA(Hons) MCLIP, Knowledge Analyst, Min.of Res.Sci.& Tech., Wellington, New Zealand. [0033179]   23/10/1980
Clifton Mr BJ, BA MSc FCLIP, Retired. [0002856]   10/08/1970 **FE 15/11/1988**
Clifton Mrs SD, BA (Hons) MCLIP, L.Mgr., Small Heath GM Sch., Small Heath, Birmingham. [0046289]   23/10/1991
Climpson Mr DG, MA MCLIP, Sen.Lib., E.Lancs.Div., Lancs.Co.L. [0002857]   01/10/1968
Clinch Mr PC, BA MA MPhil PhD MCLIP, Employment unknown. [0060172]   10/12/2001
Clipsham Mrs G, BA MCLIP, Br.Lib., Wendover L., Bucks. [0027488]   25/02/1977
Clisby Mrs CS, Doc.Mgr./Inf.& Advisory Serv., TNO Bibra Internat.Ltd., Carshalton. [0061258]   30/04/2002   **AF**
Clitheroe Mr FR, BA MCLIP, Literary Editor, The Lymes Press, Staffs. [0002862]   07/06/1963
Clogg Mrs MJ, BSc DipLib MCLIP, Retired. [0031587]   01/11/1979
Cloke Miss JE, MBE FCLIP, Life Member. [0002865]   04/03/1940 **FE 01/01/1945**
Cloke Mrs MA, L.Asst., Gilbert Inglefield Middle Sch. [0059559]   23/05/2001 **AF**
Close Ms S, (was Broadmeadow), BLib MCLIP, Tech.Lib., BT Exact Technologies, Ipswich. [0027929]   01/10/1977
Clough Mr CR, FCLIP, Employment unknown. [0060580]   11/12/2001 **FE 01/04/2002**
Clough Miss HA, BSc(Hons), Stud., Univ.of Oxford. [0059843]   16/10/2001
Clough Mrs SD, (was Goodridge), MCLIP, Retired. [0002868]   28/04/1968
Cloughley Miss KM, MA, Stud., Univ.of Strathclyde. [0061628]   07/10/2002
Clouston Mrs PA, (was Forbes), MCLIP, Public Serv.Mgr., Edinburgh Univ.L. [0021067]   01/10/1973
Clouston Mr RW, BSc MCLIP, Inf.Specialist, Business & Management, Aston Univ., Birmingham. [0002870]   03/11/1967
Cloutman Ms EA, L.Asst., Woodbridge High Sch., Woodford Green, Essex. [0056247]   17/04/1998   **AF**
Clover Mr DC, BCom DipLib, Circulation Lib., Inst.of Educ., London. [0057646]   14/06/1999
Clower Mrs MJ, (was Hall), BA DIPLIB MCLIP, Lib., Royal Russell Sch., Croydon. [0024692]   06/10/1975
Clowes Miss E, MCLIP, Lib.-Acquisitions, Torfaen L.H.Q., Cwmbran, Torfaen. [0025732]   25/03/1976
Clowes Ms HM, BSc MSc MCLIP, Inf.Offr., Arjo Wiggins Ltd., Beaconsfield, Bucks. [0042985]   24/05/1989
Cloynes Mrs VJ, (was Byrne), MBA DMS MIMgt MCLIP, UFI Hub Mgr., Bury Coll. [0023137]   17/04/1975
Clucas Mrs MG, (was Trent), BA DipLib MCLIP, Legal Lib., DEFRA, London. [0002873]   27/02/1970
Clyde Dr LA, MA PhD ALAA FCLIP, Prof., Faculty of Soc.Sci., Univ.of Iceland. [0034012]   16/01/1981   **FE 21/01/1998**
Clyne Mrs NM, (was Snell), BA(Hons) DipLib MCLIP, p./t.Stud./Unemployed. [0030044]   04/10/1978
Coane Dr S, MA DPhil, Grad.L.Trainee, Warburg Inst., London. [0061615]   03/10/2002
Coast-Smith Miss CT, BA MCLIP, Mgr., Pub.Enquiry Unit, H.M.Treasury, London. [0038630]   19/08/1985
Coates Ms A, BA(Hons) MA MCLIP, Sen.Asst.Lib., Manchester Metro.Univ., L.Support Serv. [0055951]   23/12/1997
Coates Mr AE, MA DPhil DipLib MCLIP, Asst.Lib.-Rare Bks., Univ.of Oxford, Bodleian L. [0037575]   08/10/1984
Coates Mrs AE, BA, Stud., John Moores Univ., Liverpool. [0061665]   16/10/2002
Coates Mrs CM, BA MCLIP, Inf.Mgr., Clifton Campus L., Nottingham Trent Univ. [0018267]   01/10/1972
Coates Ms CM, MA MCLIP, Lib., (TUC Collections), Univ.of N.London. [0002884]   28/01/1969
Coates Mr EJ, HonFCLIP FCLIP, Retired. [0002885]   14/05/1934 **FE 01/01/1943**
Coates Mrs G, Learning Res.Offr., Vale of Ancholme Sch., N.Lincs. [0061367]   01/07/2002   **AF**
Coates Mrs S, (was Radcliffe), BA, Asset Inf.Offr., Ballakermeen High Sch., Douglas, Isle of Man. [0042722]   13/02/1989
Coates Mrs S, (was Kordys), Lib., Brighton & Hove City Council, Brighton L. [0050639]   04/10/1994
Coates Ms SJ, Sen. L. Asst. (acting), Wanstead L., London. [0060950]   15/01/2002
Coates-Smith Mr M, MA MCLIP, Sen.L.Asst.p/t., L.B.of Barnet. [0002894]   01/11/1965
Cobb Mrs A, (was Davis), BA MCLIP, Standby Lib., Middx.Univ., London. [0039897]   06/10/1986
Cobb Miss AJ, BA(Hons) MCLIP, Reader Serv.Co-ordinator, Univ.of Leeds. [0046828]   15/01/1985
Cobb Ms JL, BA DipLib MCLIP, Temp.Contract. [0031770]   02/01/1980

Cobb Ms M, BA DipLIS, Asst.Lib., Worcester Sixth Form Coll., Worcester. [0049266]   20/10/1993
Cobb Mr WPC, MCLIP, Life Member. [0002899]   29/03/1948
Coburn Mr AA, BA MCLIP, Acquisitions & Catg.Mgr., Essex C.C. [0022640]   27/07/1974
Coburn Mrs HM, (was Cufflin), BSc DipLib MCLIP, Coll.Lib.,s Lib., Farnborough Coll.of Tech., Hants. [0027523]   12/04/1977
Cochrane Mr AC, BA MPhil DipEd FCLIP, Lect., Queen's Univ.Belfast. [0002901]   20/07/1972   **FE 14/11/1989**
Cochrane Mr F, ISO DGA FCLIP, Life Member. [0002903]   19/02/1948 **FE 01/01/1956**
Cochrane Miss FJ, BA(Hons) MSc, Inf.Offr., Weil, Gotshal & Manges, London. [0057756]   23/07/1999
Cochrane Mr JA, FCLIP, Life Member, 15 Pope Lane, Penwortham, Preston, PR1 9JN. [0002905]   01/01/1934   **FE 01/01/1949**
Cochrane Mrs JS, L.Supervisor, Crosby Road North, Liverpool. [0061396]   24/06/2002   **AF**
Cockarill Miss NA, BA(Hons) MA MCLIP, Dep.LRC Mgr., Brockenhurst Coll. [0051834]   11/07/1995
Cockayne Ms J, BA, Sen.Lib., Home Off., London. [0039000]   28/10/1985
Cockburn Ms SE, (was Cowe), BA DipHE DipLib MCLIP, Head of Catg., Oxford Brookes Univ.L. [0042332]   19/10/1988
Cockcroft Miss DM, Retired. [0002914]   01/11/1948
Cockin Mrs ML, (was Cartwright), MCLIP, Child.& Young People's Serv.Mgr., Wolverhampton Cent.L. [0002921]   01/01/1970
Cocking Mrs YM, (was Foy), MCLIP, Life Member. [0005158]   31/01/1963
Cockrill Mrs CA, (was Middleton), BA DipLib MCLIP, Representative/Sales Exec., Roger Bayliss Prof.Representation. [0022767]   01/01/1974
Cockrill Mr IW, BA MCLIP, Dep.Learning Cent.Mgr., Swansea Coll., Swansea. [0044802]   05/12/1990
Cocks Ms F, L.Asst., The Stenhouse L., Kingston Hosp.NHS Trust, Surrey. [0058986]   13/10/2000   **AF**
Codd Mr FM, BA(Hons) MSc(Econ)ILS, L.Exec., House of Commons L. [0054387]   02/12/1996
Codd Mrs JE, (was Horlock), BA MCLIP, p./t.Inf.Offr., Birmingham City Cent.CAB. [0007195]   01/10/1971
Codd Mr RGW, BA MCLIP, Unemployed. [0002924]   21/04/1967
Codington Mr SH, BA MSc MA MBCS MCLIP, Retired. [0060782]   12/12/2001
Codlin Mrs EM, (was Humphreys), FCLIP, Life Member. [0002925]   13/03/1930   **FE 01/01/1969**
Codrington Mrs AJ, (was Atkinson), JP MCLIP, Life Member. [0000492]   02/08/1951
Coe Mr N, BA MLS MCLIP, Comm.Serv.Lib., Hants.Co.L. [0034307]   19/10/1981
Coe Ms SL, BA(Hons), Dep.Lib., Leatherhead Food Research Assoc. [0038800]   09/10/1985
Coffer Mr JP, BSc(Hons) PGDipIS, Inf.Specialist, Tobacco Documentation Cent., Brentford. [0048418]   04/01/1993
Coffey Mr CM, BSc, Stud., City Univ.London. [0061739]   01/11/2002
Coffin Mrs JES, MCLIP, Freelance Writer & Novelist. [0002932]   21/01/1954
Cogar Mrs AV, (was Warner), BA MCLIP, Support Serv.Mgr., Southend on Sea Bor.L. [0035387]   20/10/1982
Cogdell Mrs CR, (was Morton), MCLIP, Retired. [0002933]   04/09/1952
Coggan Mrs SK, (was Brown), MCLIP, Unemployed. [0018247]   04/10/1972
Cogger Mrs DJ, (was Bird), MCLIP, Lib., Chineham Br., Hants.Co.L. [0001278]   19/09/1968
Coggins Mr AJ, BA MCLIP, Retired, 40 Woodbank Drive, Nottingham, NG8 2QU. [0002934]   23/01/1960
Coggins Mr AM, MA MA(Lib) MCLIP, Co.Lib., Cult.Serv., Oxon.C.C. [0002941]   07/01/1969
Coghlan Ms VE, MSc(Econ) FLAI FCLIP, Lib., Church of Ireland Coll.of Educ., Dublin 6. [0037263]   09/05/1984   **FE 17/03/1999**
Cohen Mr B, Publisher, The Haworth Press. [0041676]   11/02/1988
Cohen Mrs CJ, BA(Hons), Learning Res.Mgr., Oldham 6th Form Coll., Oldham. [0052954]   31/01/1996
Cohen Mrs CJ, (was Shad), BA DipLib MCLIP, Lib., Portsmouth City Council. [0033249]   14/10/1980
Cohen Mr DJL, MCLIP, Unemployed. [0002936]   17/08/1966
Cohen Ms JE, BA (Hons) MSc MCLIP, Lib., Serv.Cent.L., Royal Military Acad., London. [0043884]   08/02/1990
Cohen Dr M, BA MLS PhD, Modern Languages Bibl., McGill Univ.L., Montreal, Canada. [0025509]   01/02/1976
Cohen Mr MJ, BA(Hons) MSc, Asst.Lib., Barlow, Lyde & Gilbert, London. [0057018]   25/11/1998
Cohen Dr PM, BA PhD DipLib MCLIP, Head of Tech.Serv., Univ.of Liverpool L. [0034668]   21/01/1982
Cohen Mr R, BA, Unemployed. [0060919]   10/01/2002
Cohen Ms S, BSc(Hons) MSc, Asst.Lib., Staff L., Derriford Hosp., Plymouth. [0058477]   25/02/2000
Coker Ms C, BA MA MCLIP, Employment not known. [0060465]   11/12/2001
Coker Mrs G, BA(Hons) MA, Lib., Business L., Nottingham City L. [0051120]   16/10/1985
Colaianni Ms LA, HonFCLIP, Assoc.Dir., L.Ops., Nat.L.of Medicine, Bethesda, U.S.A. [0053196]   01/01/1996   **FE 01/01/1996**
Colbeck Miss CJ, BA(Hons) MSc, w/e Sen.Inf.Offr., Leeds Met.Univ., Learning Cent. [0061345]   07/06/2002
Colborne Miss EJ, BA, Stud., Univ. of Cent.England. [0061674]   17/10/2002
Colborne Mr MB, BLib MCLIP, User Serv.Coordinator, NS Provincial L., Canada. [0021485]   05/10/1973
Colborne Ms T, (was Newman), BA(Hons) MA MCLIP, Team Lib., Oxfordshire C.C. [0046131]   07/10/1991
Colbourn Dr P, BSc PhD MSc(Econ), L.Asst., Thomas Parry L., Univ.of Wales Aberystwyth. [0051195]   23/11/1994
Colbourne Mrs GM, BA, Stud.& L. Asst., Univ.of Cent. Eng./Rugby L. [0060903]   09/01/2002

Personal Members   *Collins*

Colbourne Mr M, BA(Hons) MSc(Econ), Inf.Asst., PJB Publications Ltd., Richmond, Surrey. [0055755]   *17/11/1997*
Colclough Ms JA, BA MA MCLIP, Asst.Lib., J.B.Morrell L., Univ.of York. [0039908]   *03/10/1986*
Colcomb Miss CA, BA MA DipLib MCLIP, Unemployed. [0034509]   *19/11/1998*
Coldwell Mrs J, (was Batty), MCLIP, p./t.Asst.Lib., Kirklees Cultural Serv., Huddersfield. [0000934]   *19/03/1969*
Coldwell Mrs J, (was Spencer), BA MCLIP, Request Lib./Readers Advisor, Barnsley M.B.C. [0013804]   *21/02/1972*
Coldwell Mr JD, MCLIP BA, Br.Lib., Goldthorpe L., Barnsley M.B.C. [0021893]   *23/01/1974*
Cole Mrs BJ, (was Barrett), BA MCLIP, Lib., Sir Thomas Browne L., Norfolk & Norwich Univ.Hosp.NHS. [0025001]   *20/11/1975*
Cole Mrs CA, (was Wood), MA MCLIP, Maternity Leave. [0036420]   *05/10/1983*
Cole Ms CE, (was Parrott), BA MCLIP, Subject Specialist, Cent.L., Northants.C.C. [0032409]   *27/03/1980*
Cole Mr FD, FCLIP, Life Member, 16 Thornton Dene, Beckenham, Kent, BR3 3ND. [0002949]   *01/01/1938*   **FE 01/01/1951**
Cole Mr GP, BA MCLIP, Faculty Lib.(Art, Media & Design), Univ.of the W.of England, Bristol. [0028277]   *09/11/1977*
Cole Miss JL, BSc MSC, Employment not known. [0037250]   *10/05/1984*
Cole Ms KML, BA MCLIP, Business Systems Mgr., Bristol C.C. [0033804]   *02/03/1981*
Cole Miss L, BA(Hons) MCLIP, Electronic Resourcer Co-Ordinator, Collection Mgmt.Div., Brotherton L., Univ.of Leeds. [0044842]   *13/12/1990*
Cole Ms NA, BA(Hons) MA PhD, Asst.Dir., California Cent.for the Book, Los Angeles. [0049256]   *18/10/1993*
Cole Miss PVM, BA DipLib MCLIP, Reaearch Offr., Pub.& Comm.Serv.Union, London. [0029616]   *16/10/1978*
Cole Mr REJ, BA DipLib MCLIP, Sen.Lend.Lib., Cent.L., Southampton City Council. [0035544]   *18/10/1982*
Cole Mr S, BA, L.Asst., Cardiff City Council. [0055131]   *16/07/1997*
Cole Mr SL, BA DipLib MCLIP, Head of Fin.& Support, ISD., The Court Serv., London. [0026327]   *05/10/1976*
Cole Miss WE, BA(Hons) MCLIP, Asst.Lib., Rhondda-Cynon-Taff Co.Bor.Council. [0045456]   *11/02/1991*
Colehan Mr P, FCLIP, Life Member, 82 Vine Lane, Hillingdon, Middx., UB10 0BE, TEL.01895 238473. [0002956]   *01/01/1941*   **FE 01/01/1950**
Coleman Miss AH, BA(Hons) MCLIP, Asst.Lib., Richards Butler, London. [0053973]   *15/10/1996*
Coleman Mrs C, (was Greenland), BA MA, Asst.Lib.(Career Break), Cricklade Coll., Andover. [0043528]   *01/12/1989*
Coleman Mr CDG, MLS MCLIP, Ref.L., Univ.of California, Los Angeles. [0002957]   *01/01/1963*
Coleman Mr D, BA(Hons) DMS MIMgt MCLIP, Head of Inf., English Sports, London. [0034566]   *13/01/1982*
Coleman Mr DO, BA MCLIP, Consultant, DOC Information, Aberdeen. [0002959]   *07/02/1957*
Coleman Mrs IA, (was Brown), MA MCLIP, Area Lib., S.& E., Stirling Dist.L. [0029353]   *03/09/1969*
Coleman Mr J, BSc MCLIP, Retired. [0060174]   *10/12/2001*
Coleman Mrs MM, (was Murphy), MCLIP, Area Child Lib., N.Somerset Dist.L. [0022237]   *22/03/1974*
Coleman Mrs MT, (was Reidy), BA MCLIP, Content Strategy Mgr., GlaxoSmithKline, Middlesex. [0026528]   *11/10/1976*
Coleman Miss P, BA(Hons), Asst.Lib., Univ.of Bristol. [0043499]   *31/10/1989*
Coleman Ms PM, Catg.Mgr., Brit.L., Boston Spa., W.Yorks. [0057443]   *01/04/1999*
Coleman Mrs SE, (was Pywell), BA MA MCLIP, Housewife. [0042105]   *03/10/1988*
Coleman Mrs SE, (was Hockaday), BA MCLIP, Sch.Lib., Bedford High Sch. [0026743]   *04/11/1976*
Coleman Mr SM, BA(Hons) MSc, Unemployed. [0057817]   *18/08/1999*
Coles Mrs AM, BA(Hons) DipHE MPhil MCLIP, Tech. Lib., Plymouth Coll. Further Educ. [0025243]   *02/01/1976*
Coles Mrs BM, MSc MCLIP, Employment not known. [0060419]   *11/12/2001*
Coles Mrs OR, (was Wearn), MCLIP, Learning Resource Mgr., L.B.of Tower Hamlets, London. [0015497]   *23/09/1967*
Coleshaw Ms VG, BA, L.Mgr., Sharples Sch., Bolton. [0058555]   *01/04/2000* **AF**
Coley Mrs AN, (was Milford), BA DipLib MCLIP, p./t.Lib., Royal S.Hants.Hosp., Southampton Univ.Hosp.NHS Trust. [0040058]   *20/10/1986*
Coley Mrs C, (was Owen), MLib MCLIP, Gen.Mgr.:L.Serv., Basildon & Thurrock NHS Trust, Essex. [0018435]   *16/10/1972*
Coley Mrs JA, (was Dawson), BA(Hons) MCLIP, Sch.Lib., Claydon High Sch., Ipswich, Suffolk. [0003822]   *02/06/1968*
Colgan Mr J, FCLIP, Retired. [0002975]   *30/09/1937*   **FE 01/01/1952**
Colgrave Ms KM, BSc(Hons), Retired. [0050067]   *04/03/1994*
Colinese Mr PE, BSc AKC FCIS FCLIP, Retired. [0060175]   *10/12/2001* **FE 01/04/2002**
Coll Mr JP, BA DipLib, H.of the Scottish Sci.L., Nat.L.of Scotland, Edinburgh. [0039004]   *28/10/1985*
Coll Miss L, BA PGCE, L.Tech., Dubai Women's Coll., U.A.E. [0059454]   *30/03/2001*
Collacott Mrs SM, (was Osband), B LIB MCLIP, Unemployed. [0030503]   *14/02/1979*
Collas Mr SA, BSc DipLib MCLIP, Lib., Guille-Alles L., St.Peter Port,Guernsey. [0027267]   *15/01/1977*
Colledge Mrs DAH, (was Greenall), BA MCLIP, Faculty Group Lib., Univ.of Edinburgh. [0005907]   *01/01/1969*
Collett Miss CP, MCLIP, Inf.Specialist, Qinetiq, Dorchester. [0002977]   *01/01/1970*

Collett Mr PJ, BA DipLib MCLIP, L.Serv.Mgr., Cent.Sch.of Speech & Drama, London. [0038700]   *01/10/1985*
Collett Mrs PR, (was Godding), MCLIP, Lib., Easter Ross, Highland L., Invergordon. [0018568]   *01/01/1961*
Colley Miss B, BA(Hons), Inf.Offr., Osborne Clarke, Bristol. [0056155]   *10/03/1998*
Colley Mr RPG, BA(Hons) DipLIS MCLIP, Team Leader, L.B.of Enfield, Enfield Cent. [0042559]   *04/01/1989*
Colleypriest Mrs PJ, MCLIP, Med.Lib., Gwent Healthcare NHS Trust. [0024032]   *08/11/1974*
Collicutt Mrs AJ, (was Satterthwaite), MLib MCLIP, Tech.Lib.-L.& Inf.Serv., Dept.Planning,Trans.& Econ.Strat., Warks.C.C. [0024918]   *13/10/1975*
Collier Ms AH, BA MCLIP, Life Member. [0002985]   *25/03/1954*
Collier Ms CJ, BA(Hons) MA, L.& Inf.Serv.Mgr., Chartered Institute of Building, Ascot, Berkshire. [0059123]   *21/11/2000*
Collier Ms DV, BA(Hons), Welfare Secretary, Brit.Polio Fellowship, S.Ruislip. [0042029]   *07/08/1988*
Collier Mrs E, (was Davis), BSc DipLib MCLIP, Asst.Dist.Lib., Bucks C.C., High Wycombe L. [0030392]   *25/01/1979*
Collier Mrs EA, (was Carrick), MCLIP, Learning Resources Cent.Mgr., Arden Cent., City Coll.Manchester. [0002405]   *13/01/1967*
Collier Mrs G, (was MacWhannell), BA(Hons) MCLIP, Lib., Wilmslow L., Cheshire CC. [0025068]   *20/11/1975*
Collier Mrs JL, (was Bussey), BA MCLIP, Lib., Sinan Comm.Sch., Derby City Council. [0033451]   *09/01/1981*
Collier Mrs MA, (was Loten), MCLIP, Coll.Lib., Portsmouth Coll., Hants. [0029520]   *31/08/1978*
Collier Mr MC, MCLIP, Team Lib., Southall L. [0023133]   *01/11/1974*
Collier Prof MW, MA DipLib MCLIP, L.Dir., Tilburg Univ., Netherlands. [0030606]   *19/03/1979*
Collier-Wilson Ms RM, (was Wilson), BA(Hons) DipIS MCLIP, Inf.Adviser, Sheffield Hallam Univ., Sheffield. [0049657]   *23/11/1993*
Collieson Ms JM, BA(Hons) DipLib MCLIP, L.& Inf.Serv.Mgr., NCH, London. [0041969]   *08/07/1988*
Collin Dr MYC, (was Fitzsimmons), BA PhD MCLIP, Employment not known. [0004970]   *01/01/1989*
Collin Miss RDM, BA mclip, Princ.Lib.-Yth.Serv., Scottish Borders L.Serv. [0031804]   *01/01/1980*
Collinge Mrs FH, (was Howitt), MCLIP, [0023031]   *01/10/1974*
Collinge Mrs M, (was Allen), MCLIP, Specialist Lib., Leics.L.& Inf.Serv., Market Harborough. [0000211]   *01/01/1968*
Collinge Mr WH, BA(Hons) DiplnfMA, Business Lib., City Univ.L., Bratislave, Slovak Republic. [0052250]   *19/10/1995*
Collingham Miss B, MBE DipLib FCLIP BA(Open), Life Member. [0002988]   *22/10/1935*   **FE 01/01/1941**
Collings Mr Nd, BA, Dep.Lib., Allen & Overy, Solicitors, London. [0037431]   *11/09/1984*
Collingsworth Ms J, BA DipLib MCLIP, Sen.Lect., London Guildhall Univ. [0026705]   *31/10/1976*
Collingwood Ms L, BA DipLib MCLIP, L/Res.Cent.Mgr., Finham Park Sch., Coventry. [0048945] *02/08/1993*
Collins Mrs A, (was Harrington), BA MCLIP, Asst.Lib., Cambridge Univ. [0018272]   *18/09/1972*
Collins Mr B, BA MCLIP, Team Lib., Cent.Lend.L., L.B.of Ealing. [0002992]   *23/09/1976*
Collins Miss BJ, MCLIP, Retired. [0002994] *29/10/1943*
Collins Mrs CW, (was Bradshaw), BSc DipLib MCLIP, Learning Support Offr., Univ.of Nottingham Inf.Serv.Div. [0026289]   *12/10/1976*
Collins Ms DJ, Lib., Inst.for Animal Health, Nr.Newbury, Berks. [0018236]   *04/10/1972*
Collins Miss EA, Asst.Health Lib., Herefordshire NHS. [0058981]   *16/10/2000*
Collins Mr G, BA MCLIP, Retired. [0002999]   *12/02/1963*
Collins Mrs HJ, (was Tomlinson), BA MCLIP, Outreach Co-ordinator, Child.& Yth.Serv., L.B.of Hillingdon. [0014777]   *15/09/1969*
Collins Mrs IJ, (was Lewis), Stud., Univ.of Cent.England, &, Lib., Highways Agency, Birmingham. [0058167]   *08/11/1999*
Collins Mr IS, BA MLIS, Position unknown, L.Serv., Univ.of the W.of England. [0058704]   *09/06/2000*
Collins Mrs J, MA BA MCLIP, Semi-Retired. [0026329]   *04/10/1976*
Collins Mrs JC, BSc(Hons) PGDip, Asst.Lib., Acton L., London. [0047052]   *01/04/1992*
Collins Mrs JP, Head of Marketing, Swets Blackwell Ltd., Abingdon,Oxon. [0037337]   *09/07/1984*
Collins Miss K, DipLib MCLIP, Mus.& Drama Lib., Co.L.H.Q., Warwick. [0034659]   *10/01/1982*
Collins Mrs LA, L.Asst., Wellington L., Wellington, Telford, Shropshire. [0054930]   *14/05/1997*   **AF**
Collins Mrs LD, (was Jackson), BA DipLib MCLIP, Asst.City Sch.Lib., Portsmouth City Council. [0030190] *16/12/1978*
Collins Miss LM, Inf.Offrs., Eversheds, Leeds. [0058203]   *17/11/1999*
Collins Mrs MT, (was Fearon), BSc MSc MCLIP, Head Librarian, Regents College London. [0027107]   *01/01/1955*
Collins Mrs NC, (was Clifton), BA(Hons), p./t.L.C.Asst.& Weekend Super., Univ.of Derby. [0047878]   *23/10/1992*
Collins Mrs NM, (was Holdsworth), BSc FCLIP, Life Member. [0016782]   *07/10/1933*   **FE 01/01/1934**
Collins Mr P, BA(Hons) MA, Lib., Notts.C.C., Worksop P.L. [0058940]   *09/10/2000*
Collins Mrs P, (was Davis), Learning Cent.Mgr., Univ.of Wolverhampton, Wolverhampton. [0047120]   *08/05/1992*
Collins Mrs PA, BA DipLib MCLIP, Arts Lib.(Job Share), Cent.L., Arts L., Manchester City Council. [0034606] *14/01/1982*
Collins Mrs PD, (was Mardon), MCLIP, Housewife. [0003003]   *01/02/1968*
Collins Mr PJ, MCLIP, Lib.:Arts, Ref.L., Westminster. [0032267]   *04/03/1980*
Collins Mrs PL, (was Dickinson), BA MCLIP, Systems Lib., Dept.for Educ.& Skills, London. [0042913]   *19/04/1989*

Collins Mr SC, BA DipLib MCLIP, Area Lib., L.B.of Southwark. [0035687] 17/01/1983
Collins Mr SN, BA(Hons) MA MCLIP, Inf.Lib., Kingston Univ. [0052702] 22/11/1995
Collins Ms T, (was Newland), BA(Hons) MSc(Econ), Lib., Marx Memorial L., London. [0057765] 29/07/1999
Collinson Miss J, BA(Hons), Grad.Trainee, Barnfield Coll., Luton, Beds. [0058160] 09/11/1999
Collinson Mr T, BA(Hons) FRGS MCLIP, Inf.Lib.(Tech.), Southampton Inst., Hants. [0039496] 07/02/1986
Collis Mr C, BA(Hons), Stud., Univ.of Cent.England. [0061676] 17/10/2002
Collis Mr GP, BA(Hons), Data Editor, Univ.of Manchester. [0052561] 06/11/1995
Collis Mr J, BA DipLib ARCM MCLIP, Coll.Lib., Rose Bruford Coll., Sidcup. [0042300] 11/10/1988
Collis Mr RJ, DL DMA HonFCLIP, Retired. [0003009] 06/03/1963
FE 01/01/1999
Collis Miss SM, BA MCLIP, L.Asst., L.B.of Sutton. [0003010] 01/01/1971
Collison Mrs AM, (was Merrifield), DipLib MCLIP, Learning Resources Adviser, Greenwich Comm.Coll. [0035774] 24/01/1983
Collison Mrs E, (was Czirok), BA MCLIP, Unemployed. [0036614] 27/10/1983
Collman Miss E, (was Bach), MA BLib MCLIP, Team Leader, City Coll., Birmingham. [0000556] 08/10/1968
Collop Miss JH, BA(Hons) MA MCLIP, Asst.Lib., Open Univ., Milton Keynes. [0055508] 16/10/1997
Collyer-Strutt Mrs Z, Sen.Inf.& Stud.Serv.Asst., N.E.Wales Inst., Wrexham. [0058838] 29/08/2000 **AF**
Colombo Mrs J, BSc DipLib MCLIP, Dist.Lib., Derbys.C.C., Ilkeston, Derbys. [0030384] 28/01/1979
Colquhoun Mr HA, FCLIP, Life Member. [0003015] 24/09/1954
FE 01/01/1967
Colquhoun Ms JM, MA(Hons) DipIM, Sch.Lib., Cumnock Academy, Ayrshire. [0054345] 27/11/1996
Colquhoun Mr JW, LLB MSc, Employment not known. [0060239] 10/12/2001
Coltart Mrs IC, MCLIP, Life Member. [0003016] 01/01/1969
Coltart Miss KM, LLB(Hons), Lib., Stobhill Hosp., N.Glasgow Univ.Hosp.NHS Trust. [0056870] 29/10/1998
Colver Ms R, (was Pierce), MCLIP, Lib., Cambs.C.C., Cambs. [0011679] 01/10/1971
Colville Mrs SE, (was Smith), BA(Hons) DipIM MCLIP, Career Team Lib., Shevington L., Wigan Council. [0044574] 29/10/1990
Combe Mr GA, BA MCLIP, Area Mgr., Community Serv., Surrey C.C., Kingston upon Thames. [0003021] 01/01/1971
Comben Mrs CA, BSc DipLib MCLIP, Lib., Time Trax Ltd., Guildford, Surrey. [0029155] 17/03/1978
Combes Mrs AJ, (was Moore), Mother. [0038308] 08/03/1985
Combley Mr R, BA, Stud., Univ.N.London. [0059840] 16/10/2001
Comer Miss CM, (was Spencer), BA MCLIP, Community Lib., Stockton Heath L., Warmington. [0022288] 01/04/1974
Comfort Miss S, BEd, Stud., Manchester Metro.Univ. [0061706] 22/10/2002
Comissing Miss BLW, BA DipLib MCLIP, Life Member. [0016785] 01/01/1950
Comley Mr WR, BA DipLib MCLIP, Inf.Serv.Mgr., S.Thames Coll., Wandsworth, London. [0031054] 06/08/1979
Common Miss DJ, BSc MCLIP, Retired. [0003024] 20/03/1964
Compston Mrs JL, (was Brown), BA(Hons), Br.L.Mgr., Richhill Br.L., Co.Armagh. [0050410] 19/07/1994
Compton Mrs FD, (was Dawson), BA MCLIP, Lib., London Studio Cent., London. [0038846] 14/10/1985
Compton Miss PJ, BA MCLIP, Retired. [0003025] 25/09/1963
Conboy Ms CM, B ED MCLIP, Inf.Serv.Lib., Beds.L.Serv. [0040297] 19/01/1987
Concannon Mr JG, BA(Hon), Lib.Asst., Thames Valley Univ., London. [0050188] 27/04/1994
Condell Mrs MI, (was Robinson), MCLIP, Classroom Asst., Brighton & Hove Council. [0012577] 04/10/1971
Conder Mrs AM, BSc DipLib MCLIP, Comm.Team Lib., Glostershire Co.L., Hucclecote L. [0023050] 16/10/1974
Conder Miss KAE, BA(Hons), Stud., Sheffield Univ. [0061246] 22/04/2002
Condon Mrs JE, (was Pache), BA MCLIP, Tech.Lib., Barnardos Property Serv. [0029203] 01/04/1978
Condon Mrs JI, (was Burden), BA MCLIP, L.& Learning Resources Mgr., Solihull VI Form Coll., Solihull, W.Midlands. [0003027] 26/09/1969
Condon Mr P, BA MCLIP, Sen.Asst.Lib., Luton Sixth Form Coll., Beds. [0041792] 08/04/1988
Condon Miss SE, Exec.Offr., Privy Council, London. [0056293] 28/04/1998 **AF**
Conlon Ms L, BA PG DipLib, Lib., N.Lincs.C., Lincolnshire. [0044623] 08/11/1990
Conn Mrs BA, MA MCLIP, Lib., Harlaw Academy L., Aberdeen. [0003034] 15/01/1971
Connally Miss MT, BA(Hons) DipLib, Sen.L.Asst., Kings Coll.London. [0047041] 06/04/1992
Connell Mr MG, MA(Hons) MSc MCLIP, Faculty Team Mgr., Univ.of Reading, Berks. [0046296] 24/10/1991
Connell Mr PHL, Asst.Dist.Mgr., Braintree L., Essex. [0059728] 10/09/2001 **AF**
Connell Mr R, BA(Hons) MA PGDip, Inf.Asst.-Law, Univ.of Warwick L. [0059006] 20/10/2000
Connell Miss S, BA MCLIP, Authority Records Offr., UKAEA, Harwell. [0029157] 05/04/1978
Connell Ms SE, (was Rench), BA DipLib MCLIP, p./t.Lib., Withers Solicitors, London. [0037684] 19/10/1984
Connellan Mrs JM, (was Baker), MCLIP, Learning L., Medway Council. [0003037] 14/01/1957

Connelly Mr J, MA, Inf.Res.Consultant, New Zealand Dairy Res.Inst. [0036130] 16/06/1983
Connolly Mrs AF, (was Wray), BLib MCLIP, Comm.Inf.Lib., Southampton Ref.L. [0000749] 22/09/1970
Connolly Mrs C, BA MCLIP, Employment not known. [0060854] 12/12/2001
Connolly Ms CL, BA(Hons) MA, Asst.Lib., Dept.of Health, London. [0061788] 07/11/2002
Connolly Mrs SK, DipIM, Asst.Lib., L.B.of Hammersmith & Fulham. [0052657] 16/11/1995
Connor Mrs CA, (was Marsland), BA MCLIP, Indexing Analyst(p./t.), LexisNexis Butterworths Tolley, London. [0027618] 01/06/1977
Connor Ms CM, BA(Hons) DipLIS MCLIP, Dir., L.N.W., Chester Coll., Chester. [0046430] 04/11/1991
Connor Mrs D, BA DipLib MCLIP, Princ.Offr.-Business & Tech., Manchester Cent.L. [0039716] 19/05/1986
Connor Mrs ES, (was Lilley Chatt), BSc DipInfSc MCLIP, CAB International, Oxon. [0060734] 12/12/2001
Connor Mrs ET, (was Salaheddin), BA MA DipLib, Unemployed. [0046265] 21/10/1991
Connor Mr JV, MCLIP, Retired. [0003040] 01/01/1933
Connor Ms M, BA PGCE, Stud., City Univ., London. [0057472] 01/04/1999
Connors Miss E, p./t.Stud./Inf.& Learning Asst., Univ.of Aberyswyth/Camberley L., Surrey. [0056080] 12/02/1998
Conroy Mrs D, (was Hougham), BA(Hons) MCLIP, Lib., Wythenshawe P.L., Manchester Council. [0048210] 16/11/1992
Conroy Ms HC, (was Coulson), BA(Hons) MSc MCLIP, Trainer., Netskills, Univ.of Newcastle. [0048135] 11/11/1992
Conroy Mr JP, MCLIP, Special Serv.Lib., L.B.of Greenwich. [0020146] 09/02/1973
Considine Miss JMG, MCLIP, Dep.Business Lib., City Business L., London. [0018294] 11/10/1972
Constable Ms AH, BA DipLib MCLIP, Head of Inf.Serv.& Learning Res., London Guildhall Univ. [0027936] 06/10/1977
Constable Mrs BI, (was Pierce), MCLIP, L.Operations Mgr., Cent.L., L.B.of Croydon. [0011678] 23/01/1964
Constable Mrs CL, (was Wells), MA BA(Hons), Inf.Specialist, Royal Coll.of Nursing L., London. [0056815] 20/10/1998 **AF**
Constable Mrs LC, (was Adams), MCLIP, I.T.Offr.-L., Arts, L.& Mus., Bournemouth Bor.Council. [0018116] 02/10/1972
Constance Miss HM, BA MLib MCLIP, Asst.Lib., Fareham Coll. [0043448] 26/10/1989
Constantinou Ms S, BA, Learning Res.Mgr., L.B.of Haringey, London. [0037207] 05/04/1984
Conti Ms MJ, BA(Hons), Stud., Univ.of Brighton. [0058972] 13/10/2000
Conway Mr DJJ, DipLib MCLIP, Head of Knowledge Res., Nottingham Health Inf.Serv., Nottingham City PCT. [0034517] 19/11/1981
Conway Miss J, MA MCLIP, Talis System Team, The London Inst., London. [0031590] 02/11/1979
Conway Mrs KJ, (was Mortimer), BA MA MCLIP, Sen.Inf.Adviser, Sheffield Hallam Univ. [0042963] 10/05/1989
Conway Miss LA, PGDipIS, Inf.Offr., Linklaters Business Serv., London. [0061047] 11/02/2002
Conway Ms M, BSocSci, Inf.Offr., Drugscope, London. [0047106] 01/05/1992
Conway Mrs MA, (was MacCalman), BA MCLIP, Sen.Customer Serv.Super., Glasgow City Council, Stirlings L. [0035262] 07/10/1982
Conway Mrs PJ, (was Holman), BA MCLIP, Employment not known. [0003047] 24/02/1968
Conway Mr PS, BA MIMgt MILAM FCLIP, Dir.of Arts, L.& Mus., Durham Co.L. [0003048] 02/05/1968 **FE 21/11/2001**
Conyers Dr AD, MA MCLIP, Dir.of L.Serv., Canterbury Christ Church Univ.Coll., Kent. [0003049] 11/10/1965
Cooban Mrs JE, (was Smith), BA(Hons) DipLib MCLIP, p./t.Asst.Lib., Univ.Coll.London. [0036430] 01/01/1984
Cooch Mr CR, BA MCLIP, Grp.Lib., Halcrow Grp.Ltd, Swindon. [0023427] 13/01/1975
Cook Mr AC, Inf.Analyst, Cent.for Health Serv.Studies, Tunbridge Wells. [0048230] 16/11/1992
Cook Mr AJ, BA ALCM MCLIP, Princ.L.Offr., Pub.Serv.Operations & Quality, Notts.C.C. [0030511] 01/01/1961
Cook Miss BA, BA MCLIP, L.& Inf.Worker, Dundee City Council. [0025861] 01/04/1976
Cook Mrs CC, (was Ewing), BA MCLIP, Lib., Cent.for Ecology & Hydrology (CEH), Grange-over-Sands. [0018230] 04/10/1972
Cook Mrs CM, BA DipLib MLib MCLIP, Unemployed. [0030385] 24/01/1979
Cook Mr D, BA DipLib MCLIP, Inf.Sci., Tioxide Grp.Ltd., Cleveland. [0034787] 11/02/1982
Cook Mrs DA, (was Jennings), BA(Hons) MA DipArch RMSA, Arch., Soc.of Apothecaries, London. [0049162] 08/10/1993
Cook Mr DGF, MCLIP, Lib.i/c.Media Team, Cent.Lend.L., L.B.of Bromley. [0021542] 22/10/1973
Cook Mr DM, BA(Hons) MA DipILS MCLIP, Sen.Lib., Merchant Taylors' Sch., Northwood, Middlesex. [0048224] 16/11/1992
Cook Mr DS, BA(Hons) MCLIP, Retired. [0003055] 25/08/1969
Cook Miss E, BSc MLS MCLIP, Application Consultant, Montgomery Watson, High Wycombe. [0048860] 05/07/1993
Cook Miss E, BA(Hons), Stud., Univ.of Sheffield. [0061653] 15/10/2002
Cook Mrs E, (was Mcclymont), BSc MCLIP, Freelance Indexer. [0003056] 15/10/1964
Cook Mrs FS, MCLIP, Lib., , Cheney Sch., Oxford. [0030899] 12/06/1979
Cook Mrs H, (was Maltby), MCLIP, Sen.Asst., Royal Bor.of Kensington, Dir.of L.& Arts. [0009664] 21/02/1965
Cook Mrs HJ, (was Walker), BA MCLIP, p./t.Asst.Lib., Angus Dist.Council, Arbroath. [0029860] 08/10/1978
Cook Mr IN, MCLIP, Inf.Mgr., Communication Workers Union, London. [0003058] 01/01/1972

Personal Members

Cook Mrs JA, (was Lee), Inf.Offr./IT Co-ordinator, Davies Arnold Cooper, London. [0044758] *15/11/1990*
Cook Miss JC, BA (Hons), Stud./p./t.L.Asst., Surrey Inst.of Art & Design. [0061489] *19/08/2002*
Cook Miss JE, MPhil MCLIP, Tutor Lib., Univ.of Cent.England in Birmingham. [0003059] *26/09/1966*
Cook Mrs JK, (was Slater), MCLIP, L.Asst., Falmough Coll.of Arts. [0003060] *01/05/1968*
Cook Mrs KJ, (was Wilks), BA MCLIP, Unemployed. [0033446] *02/01/1981*
Cook Mrs KSM, BSc, Dep.Lib., Homerton Coll., Sch.of Hlth.Studies, Cambridge. [0050152] *01/04/1994*
Cook Mrs LJ, (was Chapman), L.Asst., TRL Ltd., Crowthorne. [0045328] *10/10/1990* **AF**
Cook Mrs MM, BA, Caseworker(Job-Share), Dept.of Training, Leeds C.C. [0053211] *02/04/1996*
Cook Mrs PE, MBE BA, Retired. [0032735] *20/08/1980*
Cook Mr R, BA(Hons) DipInf, Lib., Mayer Brown & Platt, London. [0052617] *13/11/1995*
Cook Mr RG, BA MA, Stud., Univ.of Sheffield. [0060904] *09/01/2002*
Cook Mrs RL, (was Davis), BA(Hons) MLib MCLIP, Acquisitions Team Leader, Environment Agency, Bristol. [0049375] *01/11/1993*
Cook Mr S, BA(Hons) MA, Asst. Lib., Royal College of, Obstetricians & Gynaecologists. [0057867] *01/10/1999*
Cook Mrs S, (was Featherstone), MCLIP, Agency Serv.Mgr., Leeds City Council. [0018577] *23/09/1968*
Cook Mrs SL, MCLIP, Retired. [0003071] *01/01/1966*
Cook Miss VC, BA(Hons), L.Serv.Consultant, OCLC Europe, Middle E.& Africa, Birmingham. [0038156] *24/01/1985*
Cook Miss WJ, BA MCLIP, Sen.Lib.-Bibl.Serv., Cent.Div., Lancs.C.C. [0003073] *10/01/1967*
Cook-McAnoy Mrs PM, (was Cook), BA MLib DMS MIMgt MCLIP, Budget Mgr./Resource Offr., G.C.H.Q.Cheltenham. [0028280] *01/01/1977*
Cooke Mr A, BA(Hons) DipHE PGDipIS, Unemployed. [0048904] *16/07/1993*
Cooke Dr AL, BA Phd, Res.Cent.Co-ordinator, Zambia HIV/AIDS Business Sect.Proj., Lusaka. [0057818] *31/10/1991*
Cooke Miss AM, BA, Stud., Manchester Met.Univ. [0059820] *10/10/2001*
Cooke Mr BA, BA MCLIP, Dist.Lib., Leics.C.C., Wigston. [0025735] *15/01/1976*
Cooke Miss BJ, BScEcon, Unemployed. [0059853] *17/10/2001*
Cooke Miss CD, MCLIP, Retired. [0003075] *26/03/1960*
Cooke Miss CM, MA ALCM MCLIP, Projects & Devel.Co-ordinator, Marylebone L., Westminster City Council. [0029617] *02/10/1978*
Cooke Ms CP, BA(Hons) Dip, Stud., Univ.of Strathclyde. [0061189] *08/04/2002*
Cooke Mrs DM, (was Johnson), BA MCLIP, Retired. [0003077] *26/02/1959*
Cooke Mrs GA, (was Cotterill), MCLIP, Sch.Lib., Carlton Le Willows Sch., Nottingham. [0022464] *21/05/1974*
Cooke Mr HG, MA MCLIP, Retired. [0003080] *10/01/1967*
Cooke Mr IC, BA(Hons) MA, Resources Devel.Lib., Inst.of Commonwealth Studies, Univ.of London. [0055515] *16/10/1997*
Cooke Miss J, BA(Hons), p./t.Stud./Asst.Lib., Univ.Central Eng., Sandwell Clinical L., West Brom. [0059758] *19/09/2001*
Cooke Ms J, BA(Hons) MCLIP, Bibl.Serv.Mgr., City Univ.L. [0048444] *11/01/1993*
Cooke Miss JR, BA(Hons) DipIS MCLIP, Asst.Lib., Goldsmiths Univ.of London, SE14. [0051493] *03/03/1995*
Cooke Mrs JS, (was Wade), BA(Hons), L.Asst., Lord Louis L., Newport, Isle of Wight. [0058535] *24/03/2000*
Cooke Ms L, (was Voakes), MA MCLIP, Sen.Lect., Bucks.Chilterns Univ.Coll., High Wycombe. [0028533] *19/01/1978*
Cooke Ms PA, BA MCLIP, Translator/Abstractor, 6 The Alley,Stetchworth, Newmarket,Suffolk,CB8 9TL. [0021131] *04/01/1973*
Cooke Mr PN, BA(Hons) MA, Systems Offr., Halton L., Runcorn, Cheshire. [0051036] *09/11/1994*
Cooke Miss PV, MCLIP, Life Member, Tel.01903 717053., 4 Humber Close, Littlehampton, W.Sussex, BN17 6RB. [0003082] *01/01/1942*
Cooke Mr R, FCLIP FRSA, Employment not known. [0060178] *10/12/2001* **FE 01/04/2002**
Cooke Mrs RD, Sen.Doc.Offr., Nat.Devel.Bank, Sri Lanka. [0059533] *27/04/2001*
Cooke Mrs RJ, (was Piggott), BA MLib MCLIP, Asst.Dir., S.Thames L.& Inf.Serv., Surrey. [0039151] *07/11/1985*
Cooke Ms SM, (was Uppadine), MA MCLIP, Retired (Ill health). [0003086] *06/10/1964*
Cooke Mr TJ, MCLIP, Retired. [0003087] *17/03/1967*
Cookes Mrs VL, (was Fennell), Life Member. [0003090] *06/07/1931*
Cookhorn Miss S, p./t.Stud./I.T.Offr., Univ.of Cent.England, Birmingham, Sandwell Council. [0059073] *08/11/2000*
Cookman Mrs NW, (was Schenk), BA HDipLib, Consultant, David Haynes Assoc., London. [0046109] *01/01/1991*
Cooksey Ms J, BA(Hons) DipILS MCLIP, Subject Lib.:Languages, Oxford Brookes Univ. [0048655] *02/04/1993*
Coomber Miss C, Lib., Assoc.for the Brit.Pharm.Ind., London. [0049587] *19/11/1993*
Coomber Mrs JC, (was Ablett), MLib MCLIP, Unemployed. [0022332] *01/01/1974*
Coombes Mrs LM, (was Rhodes), Sch.Lib., Burton Bor.Sch., Newport, Shropshire. [0047201] *20/05/1992* **AF**
Coombes Ms R, BA(Hons) MSc, Lib., L.& Museum of Freemasonry, London. [0044631] *12/11/1990*
Coombes Miss T, BSc MCLIP, Prison Lib., Wormwood Scrubs, L.B.of Hammersmith & Fulham. [0032506] *07/05/1980*
Coombs Miss MA, MPhil BA MCLIP, Lib., N.Yorks.Co.L., Richmond. [0003101] *18/02/1961*
Cooper Dr A, (was Winterbottom), BA PhD FRSA MCLIP, Lib., Aylesbury Young Offenders Inst., Bucks.Co.L. [0003104] *07/01/1970*

Cooper Mr AB, MLS MCLIP, Retired. [0003106] *05/02/1962*
Cooper Mrs AL, (was Barker), BA MCLIP, Child.Serv.Adviser, Essex L., Co.L.H.Q. [0037327] *02/07/1984*
Cooper Mr AP, MA BLS MCLIP, p./t.Asst.Lib., De Montfort Univ., Leicester. [0033452] *01/01/1981*
Cooper Mr B, BSc(Econ) GradCertEd AdvDipBFM MCLIP, Life Member. [0003108] *25/08/1964*
Cooper Mrs C, BA MCLIP, Learning Res.Mgr., Poynton High Sch., Cheshire. [0038770] *01/10/1985*
Cooper Mrs C, BA DipLib MCLIP, Employment not known. [0036589] *18/10/1983*
Cooper Miss D, Customer Serv.Mgr., Clacton L., Essex. [0059412] *06/03/2001*
Cooper Mr E, BEd(Hons), Sen.L.Asst., Bradford Univ.L., W.Yorkshire. [0050827] *20/10/1994* **AF**
Cooper Mr E, FCLIP, Retired. [0018578] *01/01/1954* **FE 06/11/1975**
Cooper Mrs E, MCLIP, Life Member. [0003113] *07/10/1959*
Cooper Mrs EP, BA(Hons) MCLIP, Dep.Cent.Area Mgr., Solihull MBC., Solihull Cent,L. [0055903] *15/12/1997*
Cooper Mrs GJ, Lib., Abingdon Sch. [0054587] *04/02/1997*
Cooper Ms GS, PGDipLib MCLIP, Catr., Brit.L., Boston Spa. [0033600] *22/01/1976*
Cooper Mr HF, MCLIP, Retired. [0003118] *26/02/1934*
Cooper Mrs HM, (was Hope), MA MCLIP, Life Member. [0007164] *08/03/1953*
Cooper Mr J, MA FCLIP, Independent Consultant. [0003120] *01/01/1968* **FE 21/03/1985**
Cooper Mr JB, MA MCLIP, Retired. [0003121] *01/01/1949*
Cooper Mrs JC, (was Caley), BA(Hons) PGCE PGDipIS, Tech.Lib., TNT Aircraft Maintenance Serv., Stansted Airport. [0047794] *19/10/1992*
Cooper Mr JJ, MCLIP, Br.Lib., Wandsworth P.L. [0003123] *27/09/1966*
Cooper Mrs JM, (was Goodall), BA MA MCLIP, Lib., Park House Sch., Newbury. [0031300] *11/10/1979*
Cooper Mrs JM, (was Nabbs), BA MCLIP, Lib., Colchester Cent.L., Essex. [0033816] *11/03/1981*
Cooper Mr K, HonFCLIP, Hon Fellow. [0060774] *12/12/2001* **FE 01/04/2002**
Cooper Mrs K, (was Springhall), BA MCLIP, Lib., Cornish Studies L., Cornwall C.C. [0040276] *29/11/1986*
Cooper Miss KJ, MSc BA(Hons), Inf.Offr., Leeds Met.Univ. [0057019] *25/11/1998*
Cooper Mrs KJ, (was Hepworth), BA PGDipLib MCLIP, Asst.Lib., Cripps L., Northampton Gen.Hosp. [0036362] *03/10/1983*
Cooper Miss LA, MCLIP, Sen.Lib., Home Office, London. [0003125] *08/11/1969*
Cooper Mrs LC, (was Cousins), BA DipLib MCLIP, L.Serv.Mgr., Sandwell Gen.Hosp., W.Bromwich. [0034162] *08/10/1981*
Cooper Mrs LD, (was Smith), MPhil MCLIP, L.& Learning Res.Mgr., N.Lincs.Coll., Lincoln. [0003126] *10/01/1968*
Cooper Mrs LI, (was Hansford), MCLIP, Lib., Crofton Sch., Educ.Dept., L.B.of Lewisham. [0006278] *01/01/1970*
Cooper Miss LM, Sen.L.Asst., IWC, Freshwater L. [0045076] *05/07/1990* **AF**
Cooper Mrs M, Sen.L.Asst., Swanley L., Kent. [0058297] *20/12/1999* **AF**
Cooper Ms MH, BA, Unemployed. [0040936] *07/09/1987*
Cooper Miss MI, BA FCLIP MBA, Life Member. [0003128] *26/09/1949* **FE 01/01/1961**
Cooper Mr MP, BA MCLIP, Lib./EU Specialist, Reading Ref.L. [0040785] *08/06/1987*
Cooper Mrs NA, (was Rawlinson), BA(Hons) DipLib MCLIP, Asst.Lib., GCHQ, Cheltenham. [0049298] *20/10/1993*
Cooper Miss OF, MCLIP, Life Member. [0003129] *29/03/1946*
Cooper Mrs PAM, (was Moore), BLS PGD(A&LS) MCLIP, Grp.L.Mgr., S.E.Educ.& L.Board, Down Group. [0028635] *06/01/1978*
Cooper Miss PI, MCLIP, Life Member. [0003131] *16/02/1949*
Cooper Mrs RJ, BA, p./t.Stud./ Inf.Advisor, Univ.of Gloucestershire, Univ.Cent.England. [0059497] *11/04/2001*
Cooper Mr RR, BBS MLIS MCLIP, Employment Unknown. [0060112] *07/12/2001*
Cooper Mrs SJ, (was Davidson), BA(Hons) DipLib MCLIP, Res.Cent.Lib., Brighouse High Sch. [0032269] *12/01/1980*
Cooper Mr SL, Inf.& Knowledge Serv.Mgr., Chelmsford L., Essex C.C. [0043118] *03/08/1989*
Cooper Mrs SM, BA(Hons) MCLIP, Team Leader, L.Serv., AstraZeneca R&D Charnwood, Loughborough. [0042677] *01/02/1989*
Cooper Mrs TM, (was Walker), BA(Hons) DipLIS MCLIP, Lib., Univ.of Birmingham, Orchard Learning Res.Cent. [0049397] *21/10/1993*
Cooper Miss V, BA, Retired. [0044317] *30/08/1990*
Coopland Ms HL, BA PGSE MCLIP, Lib., Holland Park Sch., London. [0028534] *19/01/1978*
Cope Mr BE, MCLIP DMS, Retired. [0020187] *01/02/1973*
Cope Miss EJ, BA(Hons) DipILS MCLIP, Inf.Specialist, Nokia UK Ltd., Hants. [0053980] *15/10/1996*
Cope Miss ES, BA(Hons), Stud., Brighton Univ. [0059686] *07/11/2001*
Cope Mrs YM, (was Othen), MCMI MCLIP, Head of L.& Inf., Slough Bor.Council. [0018382] *18/10/1972*
Copeland Mrs C, (was Mason), MCLIP, Ref.& Inf.Serv.Lib., Darlington Bor.Council. [0009885] *08/01/1963*
Copeland Dr SM, MA MPhil PhD DipLib MCLIP, Sen.Lib., The Robert Gordon Univ., The Georgina Scott Sutherland L. [0034167] *08/10/1981*
Copestake Ms EG, (was Walsh), MA DipLib MCLIP, Employment not known. [0036951] *21/01/1984*
Copland Ms C, (was Noble), BA, Project Document Controller, Coflexip Stena Offshore Ltd., Aberdeen. [0049953] *27/01/1994*
Copland Mr IC, MCLIP, Retired. [0003145] *26/09/1963*

Copleston Mrs NJ, (was Smith), BA MCLIP, Princ.Lib., Stock Serv., L.B.of Harrow. [0013663] *05/10/1971*
Copling Mrs JM, (was North), BLib MCLIP, Systems Lib., Solihull P.L. [0018197] *05/10/1972*
Copnall Mr ME, BSc DipLib MCLIP, Asst.Lib., Bexley Council, L.B.of Bexley. [0030309] *19/01/1979*
Coppack Miss MA, BA DipLib MCLIP, Retired. [0022039]   *17/01/1974*
Coppen Miss JM, MCLIP, Life Member. [0003147]   *24/02/1934*
Coppendale Ms LM, (was Johnson), BA(Hons) DipIS MCLIP, Sch.Lib., Danum Sch., Doncaster. [0052131]   *05/10/1995*
Coppins Mr M, L.Asst., London Trans.Museum. [0050155]   *13/04/1994*
Copsey Mr DJ, MA DipLib MCLIP, L.& Inf.Serv.Mgr., Maidstone & Tunbridge Wells NHS. [0003149]   *05/10/1971*
Copus Mrs AM, (was O'Donnell), MCLIP, Stock Serv.Mgr., Civic Cent., L.B.of Harrow L.Serv. [0020309]   *10/01/1973*
Corall Mrs KIH, MA MCLIP, p./t.Site Services Mgr., Univ.of Aberdeen, Education L. [0003150]   *02/10/1969*
Corben Miss LM, BA MCLIP, Sen.Lib., Business Sci.& Tech.L., Nottingham City L. [0024411]   *07/08/1975*
Corbett Mrs EM, (was Metherell), BA(Hons) MCLIP, Lib., Dept.of Chemical Engineering, Imperial Coll., London. [0029196]   *04/04/1978*
Corbett Mr EV, MA FCLIP FRSA, Retired. [0003151]   *06/03/1930* **FE 01/01/1932**
Corbett Miss HL, BLib MCLIP, Lib., Dept. of Health & Soc.Servs.&, Public Safety, Belfast. [0038512]   *07/05/1985*
Corbett Miss K, BD Dip Lib MCLIP, Sen.Team Lib., St.Helens Metro.Council. [0044524]   *22/10/1990*
Corbett Mr L, HonMA FCLIP, Life Member/ Univ.of Stirling. [0003152]   *20/03/1941* **FE 01/04/2002**
Corbett Mrs PC, (was Wilson), MLib MCLIP, Community Lib., Buckley L., Flintshire C.C. [0023607]   *20/01/1975*
Corbett Mr SJ, BA DipLib MCLIP, L.& Inf.Offr., Chartered Inst.of Personnel & Devel, London. [0030140]   *15/01/1979*
Corby Mrs RJ, (was Arrowsmith), BA MCLIP, Br.Lib., Torbay L.Serv., Churston L., Devon. [0036199]   *04/07/1983*
Corcoran Miss AP, BA DipLib, Sen.Asst.Lib., Baker & McKenzie, London. [0042803]   *01/03/1989*
Cordeiro Mrs MIDC, PGLib, Stud., Univ.Coll.London. [0057955]   *05/10/1999*
Cordell Miss H, BA MA MSc MCLIP, Special Projects Dir., Sch.of Oriental & African Studies, Univ.of London. [0003154]   *11/10/1971*
Cordes Mr C, MCLIP, Grp.L.Mgr., Walsall M.B.C. [0003156]   *01/01/1971*
Cordiner Miss M, BSc MCLIP, Head, Enquiries, L.& Pub., UNEP - WCMC, Cambridge. [0024332]   *12/07/1976*
Cording Mr I, MCLIP, Employment unknown. [0060362]   *10/12/2001*
Cordingley Mrs J, (was Cook), BA, Ref.Lib., Oldham M.B.C. P.L. [0041970]   *04/07/1988*
Cordwell Mr GAW, BA MCLIP, Lib.Mgr., New Addington L., L.B. of Croydon. [0029158]   *18/04/1978*
Cordwell Mrs JM, BA DipLib, Team Lib.-Ref.Inf.& Local Studs., Kent C.C.Educ.& L., Maidstone, Kent. [0045812]   *10/06/1991*
Core Prof JK, BA MLib MCLIP, Asst.Head of Inf.Serv., Univ.of Abertay Dundee. [0027939]   *01/10/1977*
Corea Mrs I, BA MCLIP, Retired. [0018925]   *12/08/1950*
Corey Miss IJ, BSc DipLib MCLIP, Special Serv.Lib., Blaenau Gwent Co.Bor. [0030386]   *07/01/1979*
Corfield Mrs L, (was Bushell), MCLIP, Retired. [0010406]   *01/01/1964*
Corin Mrs AM, (was Rabjohns), BA MCLIP, Princ.Bibl.Offr., Support Serv., Notts.Co.L. [0021999]   *17/01/1974*
Corkill Mrs AJ, (was Hemming), BA MA MCLIP, Inf.Mgr., Abercrombie & Kent Europe, Oxon. [0050613]   *01/10/1994*
Cormack Miss JE, BA MCLIP, Community Lib., Edinburgh City L., Cent.L. [0029020]   *14/02/1978*
Cormie Ms VH, MSc MCLIP, Site Lib., Queen Margaret Univ.Coll., Leith Campus L., Edinburgh. [0043578]   *09/11/1989*
Cornelius Mr EH, MA MCLIP, Retired. [0003166]   *09/10/1947*
Cornelius Mrs GA, BSc MCLIP, Bibl.Serv.Lib., The Natural Hist.Mus., London. [0049082]   *01/10/1993*
Cornelius Dr IV, BA MLitt PhD MCLIP, Lect., Dept.of L.& Inf.Studies, Univ.Coll.Dublin. [0003167]   *18/10/1967*
Cornell Mrs BA, (was Thompson), MCLIP, Unemployed. [0043968]   *01/01/1963*
Cornell Ms E, BEd DipLib MCLIP, Inf.Lib.(Humanities), Univ.of Leicester. [0038415]   *15/04/1985*
Corner Mrs C, (was Phillips), Asst.Local Studies Lib., L.B.of Croydon. [0037977]   *01/01/1985*
Cornick Mrs ME, (was Kilpatrick), MCLIP, Lib., Norton Radstock Coll., Radstock, Bath. [0023683]   *10/01/1975*
Cornick Mrs R, (was Harding), BA(Hons) DipLib, Grad.Lib., B.R.I.T., Croydon, Surrey. [0048246]   *17/11/1992*
Cornish Mr AL, BA(Hons) DipLib MCLIP, Lib., Westminster Ref.L., London. [0030900]   *01/06/1979*
Cornish Rev GP, BA FCLIP, Consultant, Copyright Circle, Harrogate. [0003174]   *24/05/1968* **FE 27/07/1994**
Cornish Mrs SR, (was Croxford), BA DipLib MCLIP, Serv.Devel.Mgr.-Social Inclusion, Royal Bor.of Kensington & Chelsea. [0036306]   *01/10/1983*
Cornmell Mrs S, BA(Hons) PGDipLib LLB(Hons), Inf.Specialist, Health & Safety Exec., Bootle. [0035444]   *11/10/1982*
Corns Mr IJ, BSc MA MCLIP, Business Analyst, Talis Info.Ltd., Birmingham. [0051058]   *09/11/1994*
Cornwall Ms JL, BA MA DipLib MCLIP, Sen.Lib., Essex L., Chelmsford. [0050064]   *22/03/1994*
Cornwell Mrs GM, BSc(Econ) MCLIP, Sen.L.Asst., Anglia Polytechnic Univ., Cambridge. [0053144]   *01/04/1996*
Cornwell-Long Mrs A, BLib CertEd MCLIP, Life Member. [0023346]   *29/11/1974*

Corp Miss FAN, BA MCLIP, Unemployed, Tel:01747-870301. [0003176]   *14/03/1963*
Corr Ms DA, BA MCLIP, Inf.Scientist, Dept.of Environment L., St Martins House, E.P.A. [0003178]   *12/02/1960*
Corr Ms M, BA DipLib MCLIP, Strategic L.Serv.Mgr., Edinburgh City L. [0027146]   *20/01/1977*
Corradini Miss E, Ch.Lib., Comune Di Ala, Ala, Italy. [0056668]   *29/09/1998*
Corragio Ms F, Learning Support Lib., Paddington L. [0060043]   *03/12/2001*
Corrall Ms SM, MA MBA FCLIP FRSA MIMgt, Dir.Academic Supp.Serv., Univ.Southampton. [0024068]   *19/04/1975* **FE 16/11/1994**
Correia Prof AMR, PhD HonFCLIP, Prof., ISEGI, Lisbon. [0053437]   *01/07/1996* **FE 01/04/2002**
Correia Mr MF, BSc(Hons), Stud., Univ.of N.London. [0058908]   *03/10/2000*
Corrick Miss VA, BA MA MCLIP, Asst.Lib., Reader Serv., Bodleian L., Oxford. [0041291]   *30/10/1987*
Corrigall Mrs K, BA, RSLP Catr.,Whipple L., Univ of Cambs. [0054984]   *03/06/1997*
Corrigan Ms L, BSc DipLib MCLIP, Intranet Mgr., Napier Univ., Edinburgh. [0039944]   *06/10/1986*
Corrigan Mrs LM, (was Gill), BA MA MCLIP, Reader Advice Mgr., Nat.L.for the Blind, Bredbury, Stockport. [0003182]   *02/09/1970*
Corrigan Mrs M, (was O'Reilly), LLCM(TD) MCLIP, Ch.Lib., States of Jersey, Jersey L. [0003183]   *19/01/1967*
Corrigan Mrs M, (was Wilcock), BA(Hons) MA MCLIP, Lib., Northern Ireland Assembly, Belfast. [0050687]   *10/10/1994*
Corrigan Miss P, DipLib BA, Dep.Lib., Univ.Coll.Dublin, Main L. [0031807]   *07/12/1979*
Corrigan Prof PRD, PhD FRHisS FCLIP, Professor - Retired. [0003184]   *27/09/1960* **FE 01/01/1967**
Corrigan Ms RP, BA, Internat.Offr., CILIP, London. [0058946]   *06/10/2000*
Corti Mrs SA, MCLIP, Lib., Thames Valley Probation Serv., Reading. [0003185]   *01/01/1959*
Cosart Mrs B, BA(Hons) MLIS MCLIP, Engineering Lib., Coventry Univ. [0059447]   *04/04/2001*
Cosens Mrs SJ, (was Allison), BA, Bibl.Offr., Cumbria C.C., Mgmnt.& Inf.Unit. [0036014]   *07/04/1983*
Cosgrove Miss A, BA DipLib MCLIP, Council of Europe, Strasbourg. [0040463]   *12/02/1987*
Cosgrove Mrs CM, (was Ainley), BSc(Hons) BA MCLIP FInstPet, Head of L./Inf.Serv., Inst.of Petroleum, London. [0028471]   *09/12/1977*
Cosnett Miss JE, BA(Hons) MCLIP, Knowledge Agent, Qinetiq, Malvern, Worcs. [0052591]   *10/11/1995*
Cossins Mrs L, BSc MSc MCLIP, Stud., Liverpool Poly. [0045571]   *05/10/1987*
Costa Mrs S, (was Bhave), BA(Hong) MSc, Business Inf.Offr., Inst.of Directors, London. [0054212]   *04/11/1996*
Costa Dr SMDS, PhD MSc, Sen.Lect., Univ.de Brasilia. [0061402]   *09/07/2002*
Costain Mrs C, Mgr.L.& Inf.Serv., Brit.Council L., Cairo. [0033734]   *09/02/1981*
Costanzo Ms B, BA(Hons) MSc DipLib MCLIP, Br.Lib., L.B.Wandsworth, Earlsfield L. [0023073]   *01/11/1974*
Costas Miss V, BA(Hons), Stud., Univ.N.London. [0059696]   *08/08/2001*
Costello Mr AS, Stud., Manchester Met.Univ. [0055368]   *06/10/1997*
Costello Mrs B, BA DipLib MCLIP, Asst.Lib., Univ.of Bristol, Dept.of Biological Sci. [0034363]   *23/10/1981*
Costello Mrs D, BA(Hons), P./t.Stud./L.Asst., Bedford Central L., Univ.Coll.London. [0059449]   *30/03/2001*
Costello Mrs M, BA(Hons) MCLIP, Sch.Lib., Coatbridge High Sch., N.Lanarkshire Council. [0056986]   *18/11/1998*
Costello Miss TK, BA MCLIP, Asst.Lib., Bucks.C.C., Hazlemere P.L. [0044119]   *22/05/1990*
Costelloe Mrs CM, (was Humphreys), BSc MCLIP, Unwaged. [0024427]   *31/07/1975*
Costelloe Mrs SJ, (was Beardsley), BSc(Hons) MCLIP, Dep.L.& Learning Cent.Mgr., E.Surrey Coll., Redhill. [0047146]   *11/05/1992*
Coster Mr JH, MCLIP, Life Member. [0003189]   *22/02/1937*
Cotera Miss M, BA MCLIP, Sen.L.Asst., Retroconversion Project, U.C.L. [0056698]   *05/10/1998*
Cotes Mrs AAB, BA MCLIP, Lib., HMP Wayland, Norfolk. [0005731]   *01/01/1972*
Cothey Mr V, BSc MSc FCII, Stud., Univ.of Bristol. [0052995]   *13/02/1996*
Coton Mrs NC, (was Condillac), BA MA, Thesaurus Mgr., Home Off., London. [0050742]   *13/10/1994*
Coton Miss RL, BA(Hons) MA, Asst.Lib., BMA, London. [0051960] *21/08/1995*
Cotsell Miss AR, BA(Hons), Childrens Libr., Bexley L Serv., Thamesmead. [0047772]   *14/10/1992*
Cotterell Mrs ME, Lib., Napp Pharm.Ltd., Cambridge. [0047408]   *03/08/1992*
Cotterill Miss A, BA MA MCLIP, Head of Inf.& L.Serv., D.T.I., London. [0027941]   *02/10/1977*
Cotterill Mrs LP, (was Shaw), BA MCLIP, Lib., Congleton L., Cheshire C.C. [0028155]   *12/10/1977*
Cotterill Mr R, MCLIP, Resident in New Zealand. [0003194]   *30/04/1970*
Cotton Miss MT, BA(Hons), Asst.Lib., Coll.of Law, London. [0055506]   *16/10/1997*
Cotton Ms RIM, BA DipLib MCLIP, Employment not known. [0027140]   *24/01/1977*
Cotton Miss SC, BA MCLIP, Sen.Asst.Lib., S.Molton L., Devon. [0024184]   *21/04/1975*
Cotton Miss YE, BA(Hons), Sen.Inf.Offr., Univ.of Teesside, Middlesbrough. [0046659]   *03/12/1991*
Cottrell Mrs JAS, (was Raworth), L.Asst., Theodore Goddard, London. [0057239]   *19/01/1999* **AF**
Cottrell Mr JCS, MA(Cantab) MCLIP, Life Member. [0003200]   *21/04/1947*
Couch Miss DE, BA MCLIP, Lib., Essex C.C., Colchester. [0003202]   *15/09/1961*
Coughlan Miss RM, BA(Hons), Position Unknown, Dept for Envir.Food &Rural Affairs., London. [0057308]   *05/02/1999*

Personal Members

Coulbeck Mrs SM, (was Douglas), BA MCLIP, Unemployed. [0024977] 01/01/1971
Coules Mr SB, DipILS, Unemployed. [0061343] 07/06/2002
Couling Mrs SM, (was Sturdey), BSc MCLIP, Clerical Work/Word Processing. [0030332] 17/01/1979
Coulling Ms KR, BA(Hons) DipLib MIQA MCLIP, Section Head, Circulation Serv., Univ.of Cent.Lancs., L.& Learning Res.Serv., Preston. [0041915] 18/05/1988
Coulshed Mr NJ, BA DipLib, Lib., Mental Health Serv.of Salford NHS, Trust. [0039499] 10/02/1986
Coulson Mrs A, (was Mellor), MCLIP, Sen.Lib., Manchester P.L. [0020046] 19/01/1973
Coulson Miss SJ, BA(Hons) MSc, Unemployed. [0056664] 01/10/1998
Coulter Miss SA, Unemployed. [0055912] 11/12/1997
Coulthard Mrs P, BA, L.& Learning Res.Mgr., Framwellgate Moor Sch., Durham. [0058500] 14/03/2000
Coupe Ms A, (was Easterbee), MCLIP, L.Mgr., Scottish Natural Heritage, Edinburgh. [0003213] 01/01/1971
Coupe Ms MT, (was Caldwell), MCLIP, Self-employed, Glos. [0024635] 01/10/1975
Coupe Mrs P, (was Agnew), MCLIP, Res.& Inf. Mgr., Morton Fraser Solicitors, Edinburgh. [0003214] 21/03/1962
Coupland Mr JW, BA MCLIP, Inf.Off., Inst.of Elec.Engineers, London. [0023039] 17/10/1974
Courage Mrs FP, (was Arthur), BA, Stud., Univ.of Brighton, &, L.Asst., Main L., Univ.of Sussex, Brighton. [0057707] 05/07/1999
Court Ms AJJ, BA PGDipSSRM, Sen.L.Asst./Stud., Ystrad Mynuch L./Robert Gordon Uni, Caerphilly County Bor.Council. [0061637] 07/10/2002
Court Mrs JE, BA DipLib, Sen.Sch.Lib., Coventry City L., Sch.L.Serv. [0030141] 17/01/1979
Court Mrs T, (was Mellor), BA MCLIP, Lib., Worcs.C.C., Cult.Serv., Sch.L.Serv. [0010063] 15/01/1971
Courtenay Smith Miss DM, MCLIP, Retired. [0003218] 01/01/1955
Courtney Mrs EM, (was Povey), BA DipLib MCLIP, p./t.Lib., Richmond American Internat.Univ.in, London, Richmond. [0032151] 01/02/1980
Courtney Mr OJ, BA(Hons) PGDipILS, Unemployed, 75 Moorfield Rd., Salford, Manchester, M6 7GD. [0057826] 26/08/1999
Cousens Mrs H, BA(Hons) DipLIS MCLIP, Asst.Lib., Univ.of W.of England, Bristol. [0052334] 30/10/1995
Cousins Mrs A, (was Banks), MCLIP, Sen.Inf.Adviser, S.Bank Univ., London. [0008839] 12/01/1967
Cousins Mrs JD, (was Phillips), MCLIP, I.T.Lib.-S.L.S., Essex C.C., Chelmsford, Essex. [0020042] 09/01/1973
Cousins Miss MF, BA(Hons), Child.Lib., I.O.M.Govt., Douglas, Isle of Man. [0056579] 01/09/1998 **AF**
Cousins Mr PC, BA MCLIP, Systems & Devel.Mgr., S.Bank Univ., London. [0003224] 10/10/1968
Cousins Dr SA, BSc MLib PhD MCLIP, Stud., Coll.of Lib.Wales. [0040003] 14/10/1986
Cousins Mrs SM, BSc PGCE, Sch.Lib., Looe Community Sch., East Looe, Cornwall. [0058438] 14/02/2000 **AF**
Coussins Mrs SN, BA(Hons), Stud., Univ.of Strathclyde. [0061783] 05/11/2002
Coutts Mrs A, (was Craven), MCLIP, Inf.Mgr., Leeds City Council. [0003226] 06/10/1969
Coutts Miss MM, MA MA MCLIP, Dir.of Inf.Serv.& Lib., Templeman L., Univ.of Kent, Canterbury. [0029941] 24/10/1978
Coveney Miss CA, BA(Hons) DipLib MA, Curriculum Res.Offr., W.Herts.Coll., Watford. [0053271] 12/04/1996
Coventry Miss LKS, BA(Hons), Asst.Lib., Camden & Islington NHS Trust, St.Pancras Hosp. [0049291] 01/10/1993
Coverdale Mrs JD, (was Langley), BA DipLib MCLIP, Employment not known. [0028616] 09/01/1978
Coverdale Mrs KM, (was Willshere), BA DipLib MCLIP, Learning Support Lib., Staffs.Univ.L. [0041530] 11/01/1988
Coverdale Miss PA, MCLIP, Asst.Inf.Advisor, Aldrich L., Univ.Brighton. [0028282] 02/11/1977
Coverson Mrs CR, BSc(Hons) MSc, Asst.Lib., Wexham Park Hosp., John Jamison L., Slough. [0056909] 04/11/1998
Covington Mrs CR, (was Wharton), BA, L.Mgr., Shakespeares Solicitors, Birmingham. [0044374] 02/10/1990
Cowan Miss CM, MA MCLIP, Sen.L.Asst., Univ.L., Newcastle-upon-Tyne. [0003233] 06/02/1967
Cowan Miss MA, MCLIP, Literacy Devel.Co-ordinator, S.Lanarkshire Council, Cent.L. [0018080] 01/10/1972
Cowan Mr PF, BEd DipLib MCLIP, Area Offr., N.Ayrshire Council. [0037685] 19/10/1984
Coward Ms JM, BA(Hons) DipLib MCLIP, Lib. [0027942] 01/10/1977
Cowburn Miss L, BA(Hons) MA, Head of L.Res., Royal Masonic Sch., Rickmansworth. [0058813] 04/08/2000
Cowell Miss A, Learning Res.Mgr., Churchill Community Coll., Wallsend. [0040114] 16/10/1986
Cowell Mr J, BA(Hons) MA MCLIP, Dep.Cent.Mgr., Durham C.C. [0003244] 01/01/1968
Cowell Mrs M, (was Gill), MCLIP, Lib., Bus.& Tech.L., Cent.L., Hull. [0003245] 12/03/1963
Cowen Miss A, BA(Hons) MSc, Asst.Inf.Offr., Slaughter & May, London. [0055449] 13/10/1997
Cowie Miss AE, BSC DIP LIB MCLIP, Readers Serv.Lib., Wills L., Guy'S Hosp.Med.Sch. [0030142] 11/01/1979
Cowie Mr CF, BA MCLIP, Employment not known. [0060180] 10/12/2001
Cowie Miss EL, MA MSc MCLIP, Employment not known. [0060181] 10/12/2001
Cowie Mrs J, (was Lowery), BA(Hons) DipLib MCLIP, Sch.Lib., Balderstone High Sch., Rochdale. [0025739] 20/02/1976

Cowin Miss P, BA MA MCLIP, Asst.Lib., BBC.Film & Videotape L. [0042243] 17/10/1988
Cowley Mr J, BA FCLIP, Life Member. [0003254] 10/10/1947 **FE 01/01/1959**
Cowley Mr RJ, MCLIP, Content Devel.Mgr., Ovid Tech., London. [0003257] 10/01/1969
Cowley Miss RM, BA MSc MCLIP, Associate, Financial Serv.Auth., London. [0023193] 03/11/1974
Cowling Mrs A, (was Steele), MCLIP, Lib., Cumbria C.C., Whitehaven, Cumbria. [0020217] 26/01/1973
Cowling Mrs IL, (was Lutzhoft), MCLIP, Life Member. [0003258] 16/07/1957
Cowling Miss N, Sen.Sch.Lib., Devon C.C., Exeter. [0039503] 12/02/1986
Cowlishaw Mrs JM, (was Taylor), BA MCLIP, Retired. [0003261] 01/01/1956
Cowlishaw Mrs SA, (was Webb), MCLIP, Child.Lib., Cent.L., Oxford. [0003262] 03/09/1956
Cowper Miss AS, BA(Hons) FCLIP FSA Scot, Life Member, Tel.0131 337 6703, 32 Balgreen Ave., Edinburgh, EH12 5SU. [0003264] 15/06/1935 **FE 01/01/1939**
Cowper Mrs JC, BA(Hons), Website & Intranet Offr.(Inf.Mgmnt), E.Sussex C.C., Lewes. [0053610] 12/08/1996
Cowperthwaite-Price Ms KA, (was Price), BLib MCLIP, Stud., Coll.of Lib.Wales. [0041162] 14/10/1987
Cox Mr A, BA(Hons) MSc, Lib., Greenwich L.Support Serv., Plumstead. [0057843] 09/09/1999
Cox Dr AM, BA PhD, L.Asst., Beachcroft Wansbroughs, London. [0058228] 19/11/1999
Cox Mr AM, MSc MA, Stud., Loughborough Univ. [0061657] 15/10/2002
Cox Mrs C, (was Brinkworth), Career Break. [0039413] 22/01/1986
Cox Miss CM, BA, Unemployed. [0039485] 02/02/1986
Cox Mr CR, BA DipLib MCLIP, Faculty Inf.Consultant, Univ.of Herts.Learning Resource, Cent., Hatfield. [0003271] 31/01/1969
Cox Mr D, BA MCLIP, Life Member. [0003273] 01/01/1937
Cox Mrs H, (was Graham), Stud.,Univ.of Wales,Aberystwyth, & L.Asst., Churchill Coll.L., Cambridge. [0055971] 02/01/1998
Cox Mrs HC, (was Whittaker), BA DipLib MCLIP, p./t.Team Lib., Sch.L.Serv., Norfolk. [0033227] 01/10/1980
Cox Miss J, BLib MCLIP, Cent.L.Mgr., Northants.L.& Inf.Serv. [0034953] 14/05/1982
Cox Mrs J, (was Dufton), MCLIP, Disadvantaged Serv. L., Penistone L., Barnsley. [0004243] 28/06/1968
Cox Mrs JA, (was Knowles), MCLIP, Sen.L.Asst., Leominster L., Herefordshire L.& Inf.Serv. [0003279] 01/01/1966
Cox Miss JC, BA, Asst.Lib., Bromsgrove L., Worcs.C.C. [0047981] 29/10/1992
Cox Mr JG, BA MCLIP, p./t.Sen.L.Asst., Univ.of Reading. [0003280] 16/02/1962
Cox Mr JGE, MCLIP, Sch.Lib., Stanborough Sch., Herts.C.C.,Welwyn Garden City. [0003281] 18/01/1979
Cox Mrs JL, (was Wallace), BSc(Econ) MCLIP, Database Mgmnt., Bromley P.L., Kent. [0045357] 25/10/1990
Cox Miss JM, BA MCLIP, Team Lib., Brighton L., Brighton & Hove Council. [0040360] 12/01/1987
Cox Mrs KA, (was Barney), BA(Hons) MSc, Asst.Lib., Univ.of Bristol. [0055729] 10/11/1997
Cox Mrs KL, BA(Hons) DipMS MCLIP, Lib., Monmouthshire Sch.L.Serv., Cwmbran. [0046589] 20/11/1991
Cox Ms KL, BA(Hons) MA, Sen.L.Asst., Baker & Mckenzie, London. [0059369] 06/02/2001
Cox Mrs L, (was Jerram), BA(Hons) DipLib, Lib., Northumbria Healthcare Trust/, Northumberland Health Auth. [0039349] 14/01/1986
Cox Ms LA, BA DipLib MCLIP, Inf.Cent.Mgr., Consumers Assoc., London. [0040941] 02/02/1987
Cox Mrs LAC, MSc MCLIP, Lib., ARRB Transport Research Ltd., Australia. [0023190] 05/11/1974
Cox Ms M, BA MCLIP, Med.Lib., King's Mill Cent., Mansfield, Notts. [0024250] 01/01/1971
Cox Mrs MA, (was Applegate), BA MCLIP, Sen.Asst., Moreton in Marsh L., Glos.C.C. [0038781] 04/10/1985
Cox Mr PJ, FCLIP, Life Member, Tel.01509 212667, 41 Fairmount Dr., Loughborough, Leics., LE11 3JR. [0003288] 01/01/1932 **FE 01/01/1948**
Cox Mrs R, (was Hughes), BSc DipLib MCLIP, Knowledge Serv.Mgr., E.Kent Hosp.Trust L., Kent & Canterbury Hosp. [0020011] 06/01/1973
Cox Mr RDJ, MCLIP, Head of Media & Inf.Res.Cent., Laban Cent.London, London. [0031810] 02/01/1980
Cox Miss S, Stud., Univ.of Wales, Aberystwyth. [0061185] 01/04/2002
Cox Miss S, BA(Hons), Stud., Strathclyde Univ. [0061715] 25/10/2002
Cox Ms SA, (was Hemingray), BPharm, Position unknown, Covance Clinical & Periapproval, Serv.Ltd., Maidenhead. [0060313] 10/12/2001
Cox Miss SJ, BA(Hons) DipILS MCLIP, Lib., Freshfields, Bruckhaus, Deringer, London. [0049438] 27/10/1993
Cox Mr T, MCLIP, Carer. [0003289] 17/01/1971
Cox Miss TJ, BA(Hons) MSc MCLIP, Unemployed. [0055934] 19/12/1997
Cox Mrs Y, BA(Hons), Literacy Administrator, Luton Educ.Auth. [0058264] 29/11/1999 **AF**
Coxall Mr SF, BSc MCLIP, Employment not known. [0060777] 12/12/2001
Coxon Mrs P, (was Barton), BA MCLIP, Housewife. [0003293] 04/01/1965
Coy Mrs TM, (was Stribling), MCLIP, Grp.Lib., Dumfries & Galloway Council, Newton Stewart. [0014146] 01/01/1969
Coyle Ms J, MA, Stud. [0061471] 05/08/2002
Coyle Ms MA, BA(Hons), Info.Serv.Mgr., Bus.Link, Durham. [0049876] 21/01/1994
Coyle Mrs MEM, (was Cunning), MCLIP, Lib., N.W.Inst.of F.& H.E., Londonderry. [0003470] 01/01/1971
Coyle Mrs MM, Research & Inf.Offr., Oldham Educ.Guidance & Bus.Serv. [0046684] 10/12/1991

Coyle Mrs RJ, (was Hooper), MCLIP, Sch.Lib., Wootton Upper Sch., Beds. [0007157] 07/10/1967
Coyne Miss AM, BA(Hons), Asst.Lib., S.Manchester Univ.,Hosp.NHS Trust, Manchester. [0048233] 16/11/1992
Coyne Mrs D, (was Watson), MCLIP, Inf.Lib., Herts.C.C. [0015444] 14/02/1969
Coyne Mrs JF, (was Cole), First Asst., Sherborne L., Dorset C.C. [0045744] 09/05/1991 **AF**
Coyne Miss SE, BA(Hons), Grad.Trainee/L.Asst., Manchester Met.Univ., Manchester. [0059690] 08/08/2001
Coysh Ms LJ, BSc(Econ), Asst.Lib., Derriford Hosp., Devon. [0061660] 14/10/2002
Coyte Miss J, BA MCLIP, L.Serv.Mgr., Lewisham Hosp., Lewisham Hosp.NHS Trust. [0025740] 03/03/1976
Cozens Ms TA, MCLIP, Dist.Lib., Buxton L., Derbys.C.C. [0022878] 01/10/1974
Crabb Mrs JM, (was Nicholson), FCLIP, Life Member. [0029118] 23/01/1950 **FE 01/01/1958**
Crabb Mrs SM, (was Bird), MLS MCLIP, Dist.Lib., Dronfield L., Derbys. [0003296] 22/01/1969
Crabtree Mrs CA, (was Bell), MCLIP, Self-employed Consultant. [0003297] 01/01/1964
Crabtree Mr RJ, LLB MCLIP, Sen.L.Asst., Univ.of London L. [0003299] 05/10/1971
Crabtree Mrs SA, (was Marshall), BSc(Hons) CPhys MCLIP, Resident in Australia. [0018324] 10/09/1972
Craddock Ms CE, BA MA, Inf.Specialist, Inf.Cent., Unilever R.& D.Colworth. [0055592] 22/10/1997
Craddock Mr PR, FCLIP HonFCLIP, Retired. [0003301] 09/07/1950 **FE 01/01/1968**
Craddock Mr PW, MBA, Stud., Univ.of Wales, Aberystwyth,&, Cent.Mgr., Sch.L.Serv., Guille-Alles L., Guernsey. [0058914] 03/10/2000
Craddock Mr SM, BA Lib MCLIP, Stock Lib., Kirklees M.C. [0039222] 01/01/1986
Cradock Mrs B, Sch.Lib.Mgr., Denefield Sch., Reading. [0059769] 01/10/2001 **AF**
Craggs Mrs VJ, (was Gibson), MCLIP, Asst.Ch.Lib., City of Sunderland. [0003303] 03/04/1965
Crago Ms EA, BA DipInfMgt, Med.Secretary, Brighton Health Care Trust. [0049143] 08/10/1993 **SP**
Craig Mrs A, (was Wilson), B LIB MCLIP, Faculty Lib., Univ.Coll.Worcester, Worcester. [0023673] 23/01/1975
Craig Mr AN, DipInfMan, Systems Lib., Educ.& Research Cent.L., Greater Manchester. [0061645] 11/10/2002
Craig Miss C, BA (Hons), Graduate Trainee., Dept.of Educ.& Skills., Sheffield. [0060930] 10/01/2002
Craig Mrs CM, (was Connor), BSc DipLib MCLIP, L.Offr.-Access Serv., Edinburgh City L.& Inf.Serv. [0025511] 22/01/1976
Craig Ms CM, BA DipLib, Dep.Lib., R.C.S of England L. [0039226] 01/01/1986
Craig Mrs Ell, (was Stanton), BA MCLIP, Promotions Lib., Knowsley M.B.C. [0013896] 21/10/1971
Craig Ms EM, (was Hiesley), BA MCLIP, Inf.Offr., Academic Inf.Serv., Univ.of Salford. [0050916] 31/10/1994
Craig Mrs FM, (was Eusebio), MCLIP, Comm.Lib. Young People's Serv., Fife Co.,Carnegie L., Dunfermline. [0025692] 01/01/1971
Craig Mrs IC, (was Bell), DipEdTech MCLIP, Sch.Lib., Dumfries & Galloway Council, Castle Douglas High Sch. [0018353] 01/10/1972
Craig Miss ISH, MA DipLib MCLIP, Faculty Lib., Heriot-Watt Univ.L., Edinburgh. [0028537] 13/01/1978
Craig Miss J, BA(Hons), p./t.Stud./Intelligence Offr., Univ.of Sheffield, Sheffield First for Investment. [0061034] 05/02/2002
Craig Mrs JB, (was Buchanan), BA MCLIP, Book Publisher, Self Employed. [0002000] 12/01/1971
Craig Mr JL, BA MCLIP, Retired. [0003305] 24/09/1963
Craig Ms LM, BSc, Employment not known. [0060619] 11/12/2001
Craig Miss MR, BA DipLib, Lib., A.T.Kearney, London. [0038778] 08/10/1985
Craig Mr R, OBE BA MA MCLIP HonFCLIP, Dir., CILIP Scotland. [0018587] 06/05/1966 **FE 24/10/2002**
Craig Miss S, MCLIP, Dept.Lib., Computing Sci., Newcastle Univ. [0003307] 29/01/1968
Craig Mrs S, L.Asst., Stirling Council, ERIS, Educ.Dept. [0045286] 01/10/1990 **AF**
Craig Miss VE, BA(Hons) MA, Unemployed. [0058987] 16/10/2000
Craigs Mrs L, (was Parkin), MCLIP, Educ.Res.Lib. [0025443] 07/01/1976
Craine Mrs AM, (was Stanley), BA Cert Ed MCLIP DMS, Inf.Consultant, Univ.of Herts., Hatfield. [0022998] 01/10/1975
Cramp Miss MA, BA(Hons) DipLib MA, Orchestral Lib., Guildhall Sch. of Music & Drama, London. [0050003] 10/02/1994
Crampton Mr JM, BSc DipLib MCLIP, L.Serv.Mgr., RNIB, Peterborough. [0003315] 14/10/1969
Crane Mrs A, (was Baxter), BLS MCLIP, Team Lib.-Child.& Young People, Glengormley L., Newtownabbey. [0032257] 20/02/1980
Crane Mrs JM, (was Brown), MCLIP, Sch.Lib., Leicester Grammar Sch. [0003316] 01/11/1965
Crane Mrs LD, (was Stanmore), BA(Hons) MCLIP, Asst.Lib., Liverpool Med.Inst. [0045604] 02/04/1991
Crane Mrs SP, (was Davies), Sen.L.Asst., Stirchley Library, Telford. [0045352] 22/10/1990 **AF**
Crane Miss VD, BA MCLIP, H.of L.& Learning Resources, Kent Inst.of Art & Design, Maidstone. [0024639] 01/10/1975
Cranfield Mr LSG, MCLIP, Team Lib., L.& Arts, L.B.of Richmond upon Thames. [0003317] 27/01/1967
Cranfield Mrs REG, (was Bole), MA FCLIP, Life Member. [0003318] 09/10/1946 **FE 01/01/1951**
Cranmer Mr CIA, MCLIP, Sen.Asst.Lib., Cent.L., Dundee City Council. [0003320] 17/02/1968

Cranmer Mrs IM, (was Finlayson), Sen.L.Asst., Univ.L., Univ. of Dundee. [0045191] 03/08/1990 **AF**
Cranmer Mrs JSJ, (was Weeks), BSc MLS MCLIP, Dep.Lib., Off.of Water Serv., Birmingham. [0028205] 12/10/1977
Cranmer Miss S, BSc MCLIP, Asst.Lib., Cranfield Univ.at Silsoe, Beds. [0031591] 26/10/1979
Crate Ms M, BSc(Hons) MSc(Econ), Asst.Lib., Brit.Med.Assoc., London. [0053043] 19/02/1996
Craven Mr AB, FCLIP, Retired. [0003326] 01/03/1933 **FE 01/01/1948**
Craven Miss AE, Project Admin.Mgr., ISNTO, [0059755] 13/09/2001 **AF**
Craven Mrs EA, BA MCLIP, Catr., Literary & Philosophical Soc., Newcastle upon Tyne. [0020755] 26/06/1973
Craven Miss G, MCLIP, Lib., Penistone Br., Barnsley Met.Dist.L. [0019894] 14/12/1972
Craven Mrs JE, (was Crabbe), BA(Hons) MCLIP, Research Fellow, Manchester Met.Univ. [0048521] 02/02/1993
Craven Mr N, MA FSA(SCOT) FCLIP, Retired. [0003331] 30/06/1950 **FE 01/01/1972**
Crawford Mrs A, (was McAuley), Princ.L.Asst., Greystone L., Antrim. [0045291] 02/10/1990 **AF**
Crawford Mr D, MA DipLib MCLIP, Sch.Lib., Notre Dame H.Sch., Greenock. [0029159] 13/03/1978
Crawford Mr DS, BA DipLib FCLIP, Dir., Health Sci.L., McGill Univ., Canada. [0016802] 23/10/1966 **FE 26/11/1997**
Crawford Miss IC, MCLIP, Retired. [0003335] 07/09/1962
Crawford Dr JC, BA MA PhD FCLIP FSA(Scot), L.Research Offr., Glasgow Caledonian Univ. [0003337] 02/10/1963 **FE 21/12/1988**
Crawford Mrs JD, (was Jones), BA MCLIP, Learning Cent.Mgr., Queensbury Sch., Bradford. [0029896] 06/01/1967
Crawford Miss LE, MA, Stud., Northumbria Univ. [0061693] 21/10/2002
Crawford Mr MJ, BA MLS MCLIP, Retired. [0060190] 10/12/2001
Crawford-Di Natale Mrs RMC, (was Di Natale), BA(Hons), L.Asst., Brit.L., London. [0054448] 16/12/1996 **AF**
Crawley Mrs L, (was West), MCLIP, L.Technician, Mill Hill Co.High Sch., London. [0021672] 01/01/1974
Crawley Mrs SA, MSc, p./t.Bibl.Co-ordinator, Thomas Parry L., Univ.of Wales, Aberystwyth. [0061536] 16/09/2002
Crawshaw Mr K, BA DLIS MCLIP, Head of Leisure Serv., Sheffield City Council. [0019644] 30/10/1972
Crawshaw Ms LA, BA DipLib MCLIP, Faculty Inf.Consultant(Nat.Sci.), Univ.of Herts., Learning & Inf.Serv. [0037899] 18/11/1984
Crawshaw Mrs NJ, PGCE BA(Hons), Lib. & Inf. Offr., CIPD, Wimbledon. [0059393] 27/02/2001 **AF**
Creamer Mr DM, Dip, Learning Res.Asst., Sion Manning R.C.Girls'Sch., London. [0061110] 22/02/2002 **AF**
Creamer Mrs LR, MA DipLib MCLIP, Projects Mgr., BDS Ltd., Dumfries. [0024642] 01/10/1975
Creamer Ms RME, MSSC MCLIP, Lib., Nat.L.Board, Nat.Ref.L., Singapore. [0029942] 13/11/1978
Creasey Ms J, BA(Hons), Lib., BABTIE Grp.Ltd., London. [0051183] 23/11/1994
Creasey Mr JC, MA DipLib MCLIP, Life Member. [0003351] 06/10/1961
Creasey Mr JO, MA MCLIP, Retired. [0003352] 03/10/1956
Creber Mr JK, BA MCLIP, Consultant, Libraries Unlimited UK, Norfolk. [0003354] 28/10/1970
Creek Mrs GM, (was Keeble), MSc BSc(Hons), Unemployed. [0048261] 18/11/1992
Crees Mrs JC, (was Penniall), BA MCLIP, Employment not known. [0003358] 07/02/1961
Creese Ms PB, BA MSC MCLIP, Inf.Mgr., World Health Organisation, Geneva, Switzerland. [0032905] 15/10/1980
Cregg Ms CL, BA(Hons), MCLIP, Communications Offr., BNFL, Romney Marsh. [0045589] 02/04/1991
Creissen Ms SA, BA MSc MCLIP, Unemployed. [0036984] 25/01/1984
Crellin Ms CJ, (was Ellison), BA MA MCLIP, Asst.Lib., Foreign & Commonwealth Off., London. [0043430] 26/10/1989
Cresswell Ms LA, BA DipLib MCLIP, Self-employed, Administrator. [0036363] 01/10/1983
Creswick Miss HM, MCLIP, Unemployed, 19 Askew Rd., Moor Park, Northwood, Middx., HA6 2JE. [0028797] 07/02/1978
Crew Mr JHE, BSc(Hons) BA DipLIS MCLIP, Comm.Lib.& Register Lib., Leics.C.C. [0021632] 24/11/1973
Crewe Mrs LF, (was Franzoni), BA(Hons) DipILS MCLIP, Site Lib., Warrington Collegiate Inst., Cheshire. [0048329] 26/11/1992
Crichton Mrs HB, (was Male), BA MCLIP, Employment not known. [0019320] 22/08/1972
Crick Mrs LM, (was Bolam), BA MCLIP, Coll.Lib., Easton Coll., Norfolk. [0001433] 01/01/1971
Crick Mrs MP, (was Murphy), MCLIP, Lib., L.B.of Croydon, Cultural Serv. [0010605] 20/02/1960
Crighton Mrs JM, (was Brooks), MA DipLib MCLIP, Unemployed. [0003374] 14/10/1970
Crill Mrs CA, (was Riches), MCLIP, Retired. [0012379] 02/10/1970
Crilly Ms JF, (was Underhill), BA(Hons) MSc MCLIP, Electronic Inf.Mgr., London Inst. [0032473] 21/04/1980
Crimes Mr SM, BA(Hons), Inf.Offr., Bolton Inst.of H.E., Bolton. [0052081] 22/09/1995
Cripps Mrs AE, (was Abercromby), MA DipLib MCLIP, Sch.Lib., Charleston Academy, Kinmylies, Inverness. [0027864] 30/09/1977
Crisp Mrs JM, (was Brookfield), MCLIP, Life Member. [0003379] 01/01/1933
Critchley Miss AS, BSc MA MCLIP, Research & Devel.Offr., Blackburn with Darwen Bor.Council, Blackburn Cent.L. [0058009] 12/10/1999
Critchley Mr DA, BA MCLIP, Mgr.-Inf.Mgmnt.Team, Home Off., London. [0039035] 29/10/1985

Personal Members — Cryer

Critchley Mr SM, BA(Hons) MA MCLIP, p./t.Stud./Inf.Worker, Liverpool John Moores Univ., Merseyside Innovation Cent. [0046439] 06/11/1991
Croall Mrs SM, (was Keogh), BSc DipLib MCLIP, Team Lib., City of Glasgow Ls.& Arch. [0030202] 09/10/1978
Crockford Mr GN, BA DipTrans FCII FIRM MCLIP, Employment not known. [0060183] 10/12/2001
Croft Mr DJ, FCLIP, Asst.Area Lib., Eccleshill L., Bradford. [0003390] 09/02/1966 FE 18/03/1985
Croft Miss JL, BA(Hons) DipLib MCLIP, Learning Res.Co-ordinator, Cambridge Reg.Coll. [0045597] 01/04/1991
Croft Mrs KP, (was McElvogue), BLib MCLIP, Learning Adviser (Law), Leeds Metro.Univ. [0038522] 15/05/1985
Croft Miss TL, L.Asst., Hertford Reg.Coll., Broxbourne Cent.L. [0051622] 18/04/1995 AF
Crofts Mrs AJ, MA PGCE, L.Asst., St.Edmund Hall. [0060012] 23/11/2001 AF
Crofts Miss SJ, BA DipLib MA MCLIP, Law Lib., Univ.of Greenwich, Greenwich. [0044185] 02/07/1990
Crofts Mrs SMQ, (was Rogers), BA(Hons) PGCE MCLIP, Lib.-Sen.L., Pates Grammar Sch., Cheltenham. [0020875] 27/08/1973
Croghan Mr A, MA FCLIP, Life Member, Tel.0181 767 1028, 8 Beechcroft Road, London, SW17 7BY. [0003392] 01/01/1951 FE 01/01/1966
Croghan Miss MFJ, MA(Oxon) MA MSc MCLIP, Lib., St Hilda's Coll., Oxford. [0028538] 01/01/1978
Croll Mr HM, MA MCLIP, Sen.Asst.Lib., Edinburgh Univ.L. [0003396] 19/09/1966
Croll Miss KJ, BA(Hons) MSc MCLIP, Educ.Lib., Greenwich L. [0051292] 06/01/1995
Cromar Ms S, DipCom DipLIS MCLIP, Lib., Shetland Coll.of F.E., Lerwick, Shetland. [0050130] 06/04/1994
Cromey Miss S, MA MA DipLib MCLIP, Lib., English Faculty L., Univ.of Cambridge. [0031238] 02/10/1979
Cromie Mrs EV, (was Coulter), Sen.L.Asst., E.Tyrone Coll.of F.& H.E., Dungannon. [0045147] 24/07/1990 AF
Crompton Mr C, BA MA MPhil MCLIP, Asst.Lib., Moulton Coll., Northants. [0056888] 30/10/1998
Crompton Miss JH, BA MCLIP, Inf.Off., G.L.C.Res.L., County Hall. [0032509] 28/04/1980
Crone Mrs C, BA MCLIP, p./t.Sch.Lib., The Nelson Thomlinson Sch., Wigton, Cumbria. [0036101] 18/05/1983
Cronin Prof B, PhD FCLIP FIIS FIMgt, Dean & Prof., Indiana Univ., Sch.of L.& Inf.Sci., U.S.A. [0024487] 15/09/1975 FE 19/12/1984
Cronin Mrs H, (was Martin), BA DipLIS MCLIP, Unemployed. [0044531] 22/10/1990
Crook Revd C, JP BSc DMS FCLIP, Retired. [0003400] 03/09/1964 FE 18/11/1993
Crook Miss CM, BA MCLIP, Customer Serv.Lib., Herts.C.C., Hoddesdon L. [0033549] 20/01/1981
Crook Mr DA, BA MA MCLIP, Account Mgr., Copyright Licensing Agency, London. [0031240] 08/10/1979
Crook Mr DM, MCLIP, Retired. [0003402] 07/03/1955
Crook Mrs JSK, (was Jednorog), MCLIP, Unemployed. [0003403] 01/01/1963
Crook Miss K, BA(Hons) MA, Stud., Manchester Met.Univ. [0057642] 09/06/1999
Crook Mrs KE, (was Bishop), BA MCLIP, Asst.Lib., Dept.for Educ.& Skills, London. [0039662] 03/03/1986
Crook Mr KQ, MCLIP, Lib.I/c., Exmouth L., Devon. [0003404] 05/06/1969
Crook Mrs LG, (was Bowen), BMus DLIS MCLIP FIST(MCC), Unemployed. [0026287] 15/10/1976
Crook Miss LH, BA(Hons), Stud., Manchester Met.Univ. [0058879] 29/09/2000
Crook Mr RV, BSc(Hons) MCLIP, Inf.& Knowledge Mgr., GCHQ, Cheltenham. [0044104] 11/05/1990
Crook Mr T, FCLIP, Retired. [0003406] 13/09/1949 FE 01/01/1965
Crookes Mr RK, BA(Hons) MA MCLIP, Lib., E.Anglias Child.Hosp.L., Cambridge. [0052382] 26/10/1995
Crooks Miss C, MA (Hons), Stud., Loughborough Univ. [0061571] 02/10/2002
Crooks Mrs JM, (was Hamilton), BLS MSc MCLIP, p./t. Teaching Associate, Queens Univ.Belfast. [0030836] 09/05/1979
Crooks Mrs V, Res.Mgr./Lib., Torells School, Essex. [0059464] 03/04/2001
Crooks Mrs VM, (was Bishop), MCLIP, L.Asst., Cripps L., Northampton Gen.Hosp. [0001314] 07/09/1967
Croot Mr JF, BA MCLIP, Unemployed. [0037268] 11/05/1984
Cropley Mrs JG, (was Tabberer), BA(Hons) DipLib MCLIP, Consultant, London. [0018100] 30/09/1972
Cropley Mr JMA, Chairman, Askews L.Serv., Preston. [0058673] 16/05/2000 SP
Cropp Mrs VY, (was George), MA BA MCLIP, Head of Inf.Res., Woodrofee Sch., Lyme Regis. [0029270] 03/05/1978
Cropper Mr B, MA DipLib MCLIP MIMgt, Asst.Dir., Art Galleries & Support Serv., Corporation of London. [0018442] 19/10/1972
Cropper Miss JL, MCLIP, Asst.Lib., Worthing L., W.Sussex Co.L. [0003410] 01/01/1971
Cropper Mr ST, BA(Hons) MCLIP, Sen.Inf.Res.Offr., Wirral Metro.Coll., Internat.Business & Mgmt.Cent. [0038293] 20/02/1985
Crosbie Miss HA, BA(Hons) MCLIP, Nat.Sales Mgr., Rowecom Australia Pty Ltd., Queensland. [0031241] 09/10/1979
Crosby Ms GS, BA(Hons) MCLIP, Dep.Dir., Cent.for Policy on Ageing, London. [0027948] 21/10/1977
Crosier Miss PA, BSc(Hons) DipIS MCLIP, Princ.L.Asst., Essex Univ. [0048333] 27/11/1992
Cross Mrs A, (was Mitchell), BLib PGCE MCLIP, Inf.Serv.Mgr., Learning Resources Cent., Univ.of Glamorgan. [0033689] 04/02/1981
Cross Mrs CA, DipHE BA(Hons), Learning Res.Asst., Wilts.Coll., Trowbridge. [0061342] 07/06/2002 AF
Cross Mr CDJ, BA(Hons) PGDip, p./t.Stud./Child.& Yth.Lib., Univ.of Cent.England, Rugby L. [0058388] 31/01/2000
Cross Ms E, BA(Hons) MA, Asst.Lib., Univ.of W.England. [0054143] 31/10/1996
Cross Miss JA, Inf.Serv.Advisor, GlaxoSmithKline UK Pharma, Middlesex. [0056960] 13/11/1998
Cross Mrs JV, (was Smith), MCLIP, Unemployed. [0013621] 29/06/1970
Cross Mrs LA, (was Prust), BLIB MCLIP, Ref.& Inf.Serv.Lib., R.B.of Kensington & Chelsea. [0030787] 18/04/1979
Cross Mrs ME, (was Price), MCLIP, Employment not known. [0011950] 04/03/1969
Cross Miss MS, MA(Hons) DipILS, L.Asst., Edinburgh Univ.L. [0052604] 13/11/1995
Cross Miss SA, BA(Hons) MCLIP, Sen.Asst.Lib., Northumberland Co.L.Serv. [0034116] 01/10/1981
Crossey Mr LP, BA MCLIP, Asst.Ch.Lib.(Operational Serv.), W.Educ.& L.Board, N.Ireland. [0018592] 28/09/1963
Crossland Mr ID, BA DipLib MCLIP, Inf.Serv.Advisor (Job Share), Napier Univ., Edinburgh. [0023366] 04/11/1974
Crossland Ms P, BA MA MCLIP, Employment not known. [0060815] 12/12/2001
Crossland Miss SL, BA(Hons), Asst.Lib., Doncaster Coll., Learning Res.Cent. [0059921] 02/11/2001
Crossland Mrs T, (was Jameson), BA(Hons) DipILM MCLIP, L.Asst., Woodcroft Coll., Adelaide, S.Australia. [0044617] 25/11/1991
Crossley Mrs JL, (was Coutts), BA(Hons) DipLIS MCLIP, Asst.Lib., Univ.of the W.of England, Bristol. [0049154] 08/10/1993
Crossman Mrs JA, (was Edisbury), MCLIP, Stock Purchasing Mgr., Knowsley M.B.C., Huyton, Merseyside. [0020066] 22/01/1973
Crosthwaite Mrs JE, BScEcon., P./t.Stud./Sen.L.Asst., Univ.Aberystwyth, Ed.Res.& Inf.Services, Stirling. [0059654] 13/07/2001
Croston Mrs DP, (was Stockill), BA MCLIP, Employment not known. [0014069] 26/04/1971
Croton Mrs DA, (was Lamprey), MA MSc MCLIP, Leader, L.& Inf., Brit.Gas plc., London Research Station. [0033993] 01/07/1981
Crotty Ms L, MCLIP, Retired. [0003421] 07/11/1969
Crouch Miss AL, BA(Hons) MCLIP, Bibl.Asst., John Rylands Univ.L.of Manchester. [0049752] 01/12/1993
Crouch Mrs KE, (was Appelbe), BA(Hons) MSc MCLIP, Inf.Offr., Linklaters & Alliance, London. [0048986] 17/08/1993
Crouch Mr SE, BA(Hons) DipIM, Volunteer Disability Advice Worker, Disability Inf.Advice Lines, Gravesend. [0052278] 23/10/1995
Croucher Dr BC, BA(Hons) DipIS, Deputy Site Lib., St.Peters L., Univ.of Sunderland. [0050650] 06/10/1994
Croucher Miss MM, BA DipEd MCLIP, Research Programme Mgr., Res:Council for Mus., Arch.& Ls. [0003423] 17/02/1972
Croughton Mrs J, BA MCLIP, Training Offr., Camden Leisure Serv., London. [0021028] 01/10/1973
Crow Ms U, BA(Hons), Stud./Inf.Asst., Univ.of Cent.England, Univ.of Birmingham. [0058193] 16/11/1999
Crow Mr WJ, MBE BA, formerly Hon.Lib., Sussex Arch.Soc. [0032793] 27/08/1980
Crowe Ms CM, BA(Hons), Unemployed. [0061490] 19/08/2002
Crowe Miss JA, BSc MCLIP, Lib./Inf.Offr., Inst.of Alcohol Studies, London. [0003427] 01/01/1970
Crowe Mrs NJ, (was Clarkson), BA MCLIP, p./t.Local Stud.Lib., Medway Arch.& Local Studies Cent., Medway Council. [0034402] 29/10/1981
Crowe Miss SM, MA, Inf.Asst., CILIP., London. [0059634] 09/07/2001
Crowe Mr TR, MCLIP, Retired. [0027108] 26/06/1967
Crowhurst Mr JD, BA, Stu./L.Trainee, Norton Rose, London. [0061518] 04/09/2002
Crowley Mrs SA, (was Apperley), B LIB MCLIP, Principal Lib., Somerset Ls.,Arts & Inf.Serv., Somerset. [0029562] 01/01/1978
Crown Miss S, BSc(Hons), Employment unknown. [0060355] 10/12/2001
Crowther Miss AL, Employment not known. [0037237] 07/05/1984
Crowther Mrs CA, (was Avards), MCLIP, Sen.Asst.Lib., Wealdstone L., L.B.of Harrow. [0027878] 01/10/1977
Crowther Ms JM, (was Cockshott), MCLIP, Sch.Lib., St.Bedes Grammar Sch., Bradford. [0003433] 19/11/1971
Crowther Mrs M, (was Hadlow), MLib DMS MCLIP, p./t.Enquiry Desk Lib., Canterbury Christ Church Univ.Coll. [0049270] 20/10/1993
Croxford Mrs AC, (was Chapman), Lib., Tony Chapman Electronics., Epping. [0049998] 13/12/1993 AF
Crozier Mr DJ, BA MSc(Econ), Dep.Mgr., Coleg Glan Hafren, Cardiff. [0054322] 20/11/1996
Crozier Ms J, BA DipLib MCLIP, Unemployed. [0027663] 18/02/1977
Cruddace Mrs J, (was Green), BA(Hons), Prison Serv.Lib., Durham C.C. [0049860] 12/01/1994
Crudge Mr RJ, MCLIP, Retired. [0003439] 25/01/1949
Crudge Ms SE, BSc(Hons) MSc, Stud., Manchester Metro.Univ. [0057862] 14/09/1999
Cruickshank Ms DG, p./t.Stud./Desk Serv.Asst., Univ.of Wales, Aberystwyth, Wolfson L., U.W.B., Bangor. [0045883] 08/07/1991
Cruickshank Mrs E, (was Haddon), BSc PGDipLib MCLIP, Lib.-Stock Serv., Rugby L., Warwickshire. [0037639] 12/10/1984
Cruickshank Mrs M, Sch.Lib., Sen.L., George Heriot's Sch., Edinburgh. [0058122] 02/11/1999
Crum Mrs SED, Self-employed. [0055349] 02/10/1997
Crumplin Mr JD, MA MLitt, Stud., Univ.Coll.London. [0059299] 31/01/2001
Cruse Mrs E, (was Dugdale), BA MCLIP, Retired. [0016115] 15/01/1962
Cruse Ms JE, BA Dip Lib MCLIP, Stock Serv.Lib., Bracknell L., Bracknell Forest Bor.Council. [0037581] 09/12/1984
Crutchfield Miss P, MCLIP, Asst.Lib., Hounslow P.L. [0003443] 16/03/1964
Crute Mr D, MCLIP, Lib., Mansfield L., Notts. [0003444] 15/03/1967
Cryer Ms JE, (was Handley), BA(Hons) MCLIP, Grp.Mgr., Leeds L.& Inf.Serv., W.Yorkshire. [0039161] 26/11/1985

Csoka Mrs SE, BA(Hons) DipLIS MCLIP, Acad.Liaison Lib., Univ.of Luton. [0056196]   01/04/1998
Cudworth Mrs FM, (was Pocock), BSc MCLIP, Unemployed. [0042812]   06/03/1989
Cuff Mr RH, Brit.Aerospace(Dynamics)Ltd., Filton, Bristol. [0003450]   05/05/1966
Culbertson Mrs KB, MA DipLib MCLIP, Learning Cent.Coordinator, N.E.Inst.of Further & H.E., Magherafelt, Co.Londonderry. [0036356]   03/10/1983
Culkin Mrs GE, Stud., Manchester University, Manchester. [0061438]   19/07/2002
Cull Mr AM, BA(Hons) MCLIP, Catr., Courtauld Inst.of Art, London. [0041010]   01/10/1987
Cull Ms SE, BA MA, Acquisitions Lib.,Serials, Royal Coll.of Nursing, London. [0037753]   13/10/1984
Cullen Mrs C, BA DipLib MLIS, Resident in Ireland. [0033926]   22/05/1981
Cullen Mr D, Grad.Trainee, The Inst.of Petroleum, London. [0060029]   28/11/2001
Cullen Mrs JR, Sch.Lib., The Oratory Sch., Reading. [0061843]   18/11/2002 AF
Cullen Ms PB, (was Hutchinson), BA FCLIP, Dir.of Learning & Teaching, Univ.Coll.of Ripon & York, York. [0007545]   01/01/1971 FE 14/03/1990
Culley Mrs MB, (was Clark), BA MCLIP, Lib., Leicester City L., Ref.& Inf.L. [0022993]   01/01/1974
Cullimore Mr SJ, ILT & New Devel.Co-ordinator, Barnet Coll.of F.E., Colindale, London. [0043897]   13/02/1990
Cullingford Ms A, BA MA MCLIP, Special Collections Lib., Univ.of Bradford, J.B.Priestley L. [0046475]   11/11/1991
Cullington Miss HE, Sen.L.Asst., Colchester Cent.L., Essex. [0061462]   12/08/2002 AF
Cullis Miss DD, BA, Learning Cent.Asst., Wolverhampton Coll., Bilston Learning Cent. [0058205]   18/11/1999 AF
Cullis Mr TP, BA MA DipLib MCLIP, p./t.Subject Lib., Middx.Univ. [0044203]   05/07/1990
Cumberpatch Ms SR, BA MSc MCLIP, Electronic Serv.Lib., Univ.of York. [0022553]   01/07/1974
Cumbers Ms BJ, BA MCLIP, L.Mgr., Cent.Middlesex Hosp., London. [0003459]   28/11/1969
Cumbers Mr GF, BSc MCLIP, Principal Lib.(Inf.Serv.), Hants.C.C., L.H.Q.Winchester. [0003460]   14/08/1969
Cumbridge Ms M, BA(Hons), p./t.Stud.,L.Asst., Univ.North London, The London L. [0059887]   29/10/2001
Cumming Dr DA, BSc MLib PhD MCLIP, Research Support Advisor/Lect., Napier Univ., Edinburgh. [0020714]   27/04/1973
Cumming Mrs LJ, (was Mitchell), BA MCLIP, Asst.Lib., Tonbridge Sch., Kent. [0023544]   03/01/1975
Cummings Miss AJ, MA, Learning Res.Cent.Asst., Derwentside Coll., Co.Durham. [0055709]   10/11/1997
Cummings Mrs AM, (was Hawker), BA(Hons), Lib., Wycliffe Coll., Glos. [0056014]   19/01/1998
Cummings Mr GK, MLS MCLIP, Reader Serv.Lib., Co.of Los Angeles. [0030609]   27/02/1979
Cummings Mrs MEM, (was Ervine Cummings), DipLIS MCLIP, Asst.Div.Lib., L.H.Q., , Omagh, N.Ireland. [0024209]   08/05/1975
Cummins Ms S, BEd MCLIP, Lib./L.Advisor, L.B.Tower Hamlets, Sch.L.Serv. [0035982]   03/03/1983
Cundall Ms AP, BA, Stud., Univ.Brighton. [0059823]   10/10/2001
Cuningname Mrs JL, BA MA MCLIP, Head of Dept.of Learning Support, Westminster & Kingsway Coll., London. [0037457]   03/10/1984
Cunnea Mr PA, MA(Hons) PGDipLis, Bibl.Serv.Mgr., Napier Univ., Edinburgh. [0044929]   18/01/1991
Cunnew Mr RL, BA FCLIP, Lib., Chartered Insurance Inst., London. [0021666]   01/01/1974 FE 14/02/1990
Cunningham Mrs AJ, Stud., Lincoln Univ. [0061147]   13/03/2002
Cunningham Ms B, BA MA DipLib, Dep.Lib., Royal Irish Acad. [0039549]   21/02/1986
Cunningham Mrs EA, (was Kinsler), FCLIP, Retired - Life Member. [0003472]   05/03/1954 FE 01/01/1968
Cunningham Mr G, BA BSc(Econ) HonFCLIP, Hon.Fellow. [0047152]   01/01/1992 FE 01/01/1992
Cunningham Miss HA, BSc(Hons) DipILM MCLIP, Unemployed. [0048857]   02/07/1993
Cunningham Miss HJ, BA(Hons) DipLIM MCLIP, Child.Serv.Co-ordinator, Notts.C.C. [0048573]   23/02/1993
Cunningham Mrs IJ, (was Graham), MCLIP, Life Member. [0003474]   17/10/1969
Cunningham Mr JP, BA MCLIP, Systems Admin., N.Lanarkshire Council, Motherwell. [0029626]   05/10/1978
Cunningham Ms K, (was Murray), MA DipLib MCLIP, Serv.Devel.Mgr., Cult.& Leisure Serv., Glasgow. [0031089]   20/08/1979
Cunningham Mrs KAA, (was Middleton), MA DipLib, Sub Lib., Andersonian L., Univ.of Strathclyde. [0041589]   25/01/1988
Cunningham Mrs LA, BA(Hons) DipLIS, Lib., Manchester City Council, Crumpsall L. [0057748]   20/07/1999
Cunningham Mr M, BA FRSSA FSA MCLIP, Retired. [0003476]   01/01/1961
Cunningham Mrs MK, Stud., Brighton Univ. [0059756]   08/11/2001
Cunningham Mr P, BA MCLIP, Sen.Lib., Sch.L.Serv., Norfolk C.C. [0037491]   01/10/1984
Cunningham Mrs RM, (was Templeman), MCLIP, Lib., Bridgnorth Coll., Shropshire. [0014488]   16/06/1961
Cunningsworth Mrs BM, BA DipLib MCLIP, Prison Lib., H.M.P.Canterbury, Kent Arts & L. [0041194]   10/10/1987
Cupik Mr R, BA DipLIS MCLIP, ICT Learning Facilitator, Manchester Cent.L. [0039833]   20/08/1986

Curbbun Mrs CMB, (was Lamb), BA MCLIP, Unemployed. [0036142]   01/07/1983
Curell Mr VE, MLS BA MCLIP, Lib., Terrace P.L., B.C.,Canada. [0022491]   29/05/1974
Currall Mr HFJ, FCLIP, Life Member, Tel.01273 415984. [0003485]   10/10/1930 FE 01/01/1950
Currall Ms MA, MCLIP, Sen.Lib., Co.L., Chandlers Ford,Hants. [0003486]   09/03/1967
Curran Mrs ERM, (was Williams), BA DipLib MCLIP, p./t.Lib., N.London Collegiate Sch., Edgware. [0037342]   06/07/1984
Curran Mr HS, MA DipLib, Sch.Lib., Kirkwall Grammar Sch., Orkney Islands Council. [0038411]   24/04/1985
Curran Mr KT, BA(Hons) DipIS MCLIP, Lib., T.W.I., Chiswick. [0049640]   16/11/1993
Curran Mr S, BA(Hons) MA, Lib.(Temp.), Cheshire C.C. [0057923]   05/10/1999
Currant Miss SE, BA(Hons), Stud., Univ.of Sheffield. [0059965]   13/11/2001
Currie Ms E, BA MCLIP, Inf.Lib., Norfolk L.& Inf.Serv. [0044062]   23/04/1990
Currie Miss IJ, MCLIP, Retired. [0003492]   08/08/1969
Currie Mrs JS, BA(Hons), Community Lib., Torquay L., Devon. [0057566]   05/05/1999
Currie Mrs KR, (was Gommon), MA DipLib MCLIP, Site Librarian, City & Islington College, London. [0031299]   11/10/1979
Currie Mrs PA, (was Bennett), MCLIP, L.Asst.(Job Share), Edinburgh City L., City of Edinburgh Council. [0001142]   15/01/1970
Currie Ms S, BA MCLIP, Prin.Lib.;Cust.& Professional Serv, Barking Cent.L. [0003497]   01/01/1969
Currier Mrs SJ, Res.Fellow, Dept.of Computing & Inf.Sci., Univ.of Strathclyde. [0054864]   24/04/1997
Currington Mrs HM, (was Horsburgh), MCLIP, Sch.Lib., Tanbridge House Sch., Horsham. [0007216]   02/09/1970
Curry Miss D, FCLIP, Retired. [0003499]   19/03/1942 FE 01/01/1966
Curry Miss MET, BA MCLIP, Princ.L.Offr., Edinburgh City.L. [0003502]   13/01/1969
Curry Mrs SG, (was Douglas), Heron Project Mgr., Univ.of Stirling. [0003503]   03/07/1969
Curry Mr ST, BA MCLIP, Team Lib., L.Serv.Devel.Team(S.W.), Surrey Co.L. [0003504]   19/08/1969
Curtis Miss AD, BSc(Hons) MSc, Inf.Advisor, De Montfort Univ., Leicester. [0056482]   22/07/1998
Curtis Mr C, BA MCLIP, Retired. [0003506]   01/01/1967
Curtis Mrs DJ, (was Daniel), BA MCLIP DipRSA, L.Serv.Mgr., Glos.Hosp.NHS Trust. [0022588]   05/07/1974
Curtis Miss EJ, Knowledge Co-ordinator, Chesterton PLC., Milton Keynes. [0050212]   04/05/1994
Curtis Miss GA, BA MCLIP, Sen.Lib.-Inf., Gloucester L., Glos.C.C. [0029160]   07/04/1978
Curtis Ms JA, BA, Br.Lib., Barnsley L. [0041507]   11/01/1988
Curtis Ms JE, MCLIP, Records Offr., Faculty of Med., Univ.of Manchester. [0003510]   26/08/1968
Curtis Mr JP, BSc(Hons) DipIM, Electronic Inf.Lib., N.W.London Hosp.NHS Trust, Harrow. [0050389]   13/07/1994
Curtis Mr JS, MA MCLIP, Lib., Davenport Lyons, London. [0003512]   01/01/1971
Curtis Ms LA, BA DipLib MCLIP, Asst.Dir.of L.Serv., Imperial Coll.of Sci.Tech.& Med., London. [0003513]   14/09/1970
Curtis Mr M, MA MCLIP, Retired. [0003514]   15/10/1970
Curtis Mrs PM, MCLIP, Sen.Lib.:Ref.& Inf., R.B.of Windsor & Maidenhead, Berks. [0014579]   01/01/1965
Curtis Mr R, Learning Cent.Asst., New Coll.Nottingham. [0059807]   04/10/2001 AF
Curtis Mrs R, (was Haynes), BA(Hons) MCLIP, Sen.L.Asst., Univ.of Nottingham, George Green L. [0041386]   17/11/1987
Curtis Mrs R, (was Black), MA MCLIP, Acquisitions Lib., Renfrew Dist.L.Serv., Paisley. [0026281]   13/10/1976
Curtis Miss RA, (was Wintringham), BA(Hons) DipLIP MCLIP, P./t.Inf.Lib., Waterlooville L., Hants. [0021572]   09/10/1973
Curtis Mrs SA, (was Fraser), BA(Hons) MCLIP, Unemployed. [0037522]   01/10/1984
Curtis Miss VM, BA FCLIP, Life Member, Formerly Tutor-Lib., Halton Coll.of F.E., Widnes. [0003516]   05/09/1950 FE 01/01/1957
Curtis-Brown Miss LA, BA(Hons) MA, Subject Lib.(Soc.Sci.), Middx.Univ. [0052201]   12/10/1995
Curwen Mr AG, MA FCLIP, Lect.(Retired), p./t.Consultant. [0003517]   09/02/1951 FE 01/01/1959
Cusack Ms JA, BA(Hons), Sen.L., W.E.L.B., Sch.L.Serv., Derry. [0043122]   04/08/1989
Cusack Mrs KJ, (was Barclay), DipLIS MCLIP, Unemployed. [0053047]   19/02/1996
Cushworth Mrs EM, (was Sharp), MCLIP, L.Asst., St.Peters Lutheran Coll., Queensland, Australia. [0003522]   24/08/1967
Cusk Ms S, BA MA PhD, Unemployed. [0055917]   11/12/1997
Custance Mr MJ, BA(Hons) PGDipLS MCLIP, Unemployed. [0035956]   03/03/1983
Cusworth Mrs MR, (was Wood), FCLIP, Quality & Performance Mgr., Herts.Community Inf.Directorate, Herts.C.C. [0003525]   02/08/1967 FE 26/01/1994
Cuthbert Miss DL, BBibl, Resident in S.Africa. [0054264]   14/11/1996
Cuthbert Mrs TE, (was Wade), MCLIP, Asst.Dist.Lib.(Job Share), Beaconsfield L., Bucks.C.C. [0018177]   07/10/1972
Cuthbertson Miss JC, MCLIP, Life Member. [0003530]   20/09/1948
Cuthbertson Ms SA, BA MCLIP, L.Servs.Mgr., Ayrshire & Arran Acute Hosp.NHS, Kilmarnock. [0029627]   18/10/1978
Cuthell Miss H, MCLIP, Retired. [0003531]   23/01/1946
Cutler Miss EJ, BA(Hons), Temp.Asst.Lib., Dudley Coll. [0058288]   14/12/1999

Personal Members   Darlington

Cutler Mr N, BSc(Hons) MA MCLIP, Catr., Inst.of Astronomy, Univ.of Cambridge. [0053434] 25/06/1996
Cutler-Spencer Mrs JA, BSc MLIS MA, Retired. [0057529] 14/04/1999
Cutmore Mrs RA, (was Jell), MCLIP, Life Member. [0003534] 27/09/1951
Cuttine Mr GJ, BA(Hons), Stud., London Metro. [0061725] 29/10/2002
Cutts Ms AL, BA DipLib MCLIP, Lib., Univ.of Cambridge, Faculty of Educ. [0037991] 01/01/1985
Cutts Mrs EA, (was Linton), MCLIP, Sen.Lib.-Bibl.Serv.(Job-share), Hounslow Cult.& Comm.Serv. [0023357] 10/12/1974
Cutts Mr ID, Inf.Lib.(Job Share), L.B.of Barnet, Chipping Barnet L. [0038946] 23/10/1985
Cuzner Mr GD, BA MCLIP, Sen.Lib., N.Manchester L. [0003537] 29/05/1969
Cybulska Miss G, BSc MSc, Inf.Scientist. [0052371] 26/10/1995
Cyphus Ms RA, (was Woodall), BMus DipLib, Asst.Lib., Royal Academy of Music, London. [0040988] 05/10/1987
Czajkowskyj Mrs J, BA DipLib MCLIP, Inf.& Support Serv.Mgr., Oldham L. [0033560] 06/01/1981
Czerepowicz Mrs AP, P./t.Stud., L./Res.Cent.Asst., Univ.Aberystwyth, [0059819] 10/10/2001
D'Aguiar Mrs H, (was Campbell), BA(Hons), Inf.Asst., Tech.Advisory Serv., CIMA, London. [0059915] 16/10/2001
D'Eye Ms AA, BA DipLib MCLIP, Techn.Support, L.B.of Croydon, Central L., Croydon. [0021303] 02/10/1973
da Costa Mrs H, (was Setterfield), BA(Hons), Community Lib., Kent Arts & L., Kent C.C. [0047487] 02/09/1992
Da Silva Mr LR, BSc DipLIS MCLIP, Systems & Electronic Serv.Lib. [0047692] 15/10/1992
Dabbs Mrs BM, BA, Resource Cent. Lib., Durham C.C., Newton Ayrcliffe. [0052733] 29/11/1995
Dabbs Mrs J, (was Shore), BA(Hons) MCLIP, Community Lib.-Sleaford, Sleaford L., Lincs. [0021347] 02/10/1973
Dabor Mr AA, Employment not known. [0061173] 26/03/2002
Dace Mr JM, MCLIP, Retired. [0018602] 30/09/1948
Dade Mrs P, (was Watt), BA DipLib MCLIP, Learning Res.Mgr., Middlesex Univ., Barnet. [0021430] 29/10/1973
Dagger Mr JR, BA(Hons), Unemployed. [0060862] 13/12/2001
Daghagheleh Ms Z, MLS BA, Snoklokkeveien 4, 4100 Jorpeland, Norway. [0042634] 27/01/1989
Daglish Mrs SE, (was Ancrum), BSc DipLib DipBDP MCLIP, Contract Lib., New Zealand. [0003541] 01/01/1968
Dagnall Mrs A, BA, Stud., Manchester Met.Univ., &, Lib.,Ellsmere Port Catholic High. [0058002] 12/10/1999
Dagnall Mrs JM, (was Jackson), BA MCLIP, Unemployed. [0007674] 01/11/1969
Dagpunar Miss AS, BA DipLib MCLIP, Princ.L.Asst., Sch.of Oriental & African Studies, London. [0030610] 05/03/1979
Dai Mrs L, BA, Lib., Newland Sch.for Girls, Hull. [0058096] 29/10/1999
Dai Miss ZF, Sen.L.Asst.(Job Share), Surrey Univ.L., George Edwards L. [0056261] 27/04/1998
Dailey Miss AF, BSc(Hons) MA, Stud. [0060887] 20/12/2001
Daines Mr GF, BA DipLib MCLIP FRSA, Princ.Policy Adviser, CILIP., London. [0023173] 05/11/1974
Dainton Mr M, BSc MSc, Stud., Liverpool John Moores Univ. [0061552] 18/09/2002
Dakers Ms FJG, BA GDipLM, Lib., High Sch., Dundee. [0061074] 01/03/2002
Dakers Mrs HP, MA MSc FCLIP FRSA, Project Mgr., Electronic Records Mgmt., Brit.L., London. [0024645] 12/10/1975 FE 27/11/1996
Dakin Miss AE, MCLIP, Res.Lib., Sch.Effectiveness, Bexley Council. [0003548] 09/10/1968
Dalby Mrs PL, (was Messer), MA(Ed) MCLIP, Sch.Lib., L.B.of Havering. [0010092] 02/02/1970
Dale Mr AR, MA FCLIP, Employment not known. [0060485] 11/12/2001 FE 01/04/2002
Dale Mrs G, L.Mgr., Mossley Hollins High Sch., Tameside. [0055570] 21/10/1997
Dale Mrs KK, Ethnic Serv. Mgr., Wolverhamton City L. [0057415] 03/03/1999
Dale Mrs PG, (was Heath), BA MCLIP, Subject Lib., Bournemouth Univ., Poole. [0003553] 07/10/1968
Dale Miss PS, MCLIP, Lib., Bradford Met.Dist.L. [0003554] 17/01/1967
Dale Mrs R, (was Currid), MCLIP, L.Acquisitions Mgr., De Montfort Univ., Leicester. [0041283] 25/10/1987
Dale Mrs R, MCLIP, Lib., Scarborough Sixth Form Coll., Scarborough, N.Yorkshire. [0031245] 15/10/1979
Dale Mr RJ, MCLIP, Sen.Mgr.E., Dorset Co.L. [0003555] 16/06/1969
Dale Miss SM, BA DipTransIoL AIL MCLIP, Retired. [0003557] 06/04/1963
Daley Ms GC, BA MA MCLIP, Project Mgr., Bank of Scotland, Edinburgh. [0030976] 13/07/1979
Daley Mrs K, (was Redmond), BA(Hons), Operations Mgr., Liverpool Community Coll., Liverpool. [0043694] 30/11/1989
Daley Mrs MR, BSc DipLib MCLIP, Asst.Lib., Liverpool City L. [0040762] 02/06/1987
Dalgleish Dr AJ, MA DipLib MCLIP, L.Serv.Mgr., Univ.of Glamorgan, Pontypridd. [0042827] 09/03/1989
Dalley Mr NM, BA(Hons) DipInfSc, Doc.Delivery Coordinator, The L., Univ.of Reading. [0051817] 06/07/1991
Dalley Mrs PM, (was Ladbrook), BA DipLib MCLIP, Retired. [0032533] 30/04/1980
Dalling Mr GC, MA MCLIP, Local History Off., Southgate Town Hall., L.B.OF Enfield L. [0003561] 28/05/1968
Dalling Mrs V, Learning Cent.Asst., City & Islington Coll., London. [0045415] 14/01/1991 AF
Dallman Mrs SJ, (was Cole), MA DipLib MCLIP, Asst.Lib., Nat.Mus.of Scotland, Edinburgh. [0034151] 10/10/1981
Dalmau Mrs A, Facilities Mgr., Ascot. [0061044] 05/02/2002 SP

Dalrymple Mr IR, Asst.Lib., Network Monitor, The Highland Council, Inverness. [0056378] 01/07/1998
Dalton Miss AJ, BA DipLib MCLIP MA, Dir., John Russell Associates Ltd., Bagshot, Surrey. [0026338] 04/10/1976
Dalton Mr AM, MA HDipEd MCLIP, Life Member. [0016692] 29/03/1962
Dalton Miss HE, B SC MCLIP, Learning Res.Mgr., London Guildhall Univ., Calcutta House L. [0021019] 17/09/1973
Daly Mrs AC, p./t.Stud., Sen.L.Asst., Birmingham Heartlands Hosp. [0059268] 23/01/2001
Daly Mrs CD, (was Keen), BA MCLIP, Housewife. [0018313] 12/10/1972
Daly Mrs MA, (was Nimmo), MCLIP, Lib.i/c.(Job-share), Haddington Br.L., E.Lothian. [0018386] 20/10/1972
Dalziel Mr AF, MA MCLIP, Sen.Lib.-Acquisitions, Hants.Co.L. [0025970] 03/05/1976
Dalziel Miss K, BA(Hons) MCLIP, Asst.Lib., Univ.of Paisley. [0046081] 01/10/1991
Dalziel Miss KL, BA(Hons) MA, Asst.Lib., King Alfreds Coll., Winchester. [0053706] 10/09/1996
Damiani Mr M, Br.Lib., N.Lincs.Council, Scunthorpe. [0053634] 19/08/1996
Damon Ms J, BA(Hons), LRC Mgr., Waltham Forest C.C. [0056882] 09/10/1998
Dance Miss JK, BSc MCLIP, Trainer, Endeavor. [0032908] 06/10/1980
Dancey Mrs AR, (was Wilson), MCLIP, Comm.Lib., Leisure & Culture, Birmingham C.C. [0003571] 23/08/1964
Dancy Mr DJ, C Phys MInstP MCLIP, [0003572] 04/01/1972
Dando Ms CJ, MLib MCLIP, Learning Res.Cent.Mgr., Featherstone High Sch., L.B.of Ealing. [0038531] 31/05/1985
Dando Mrs KM, (was McCombe), BA, Tech.Lib., British Standards Inst., London. [0054566] 23/01/1997
Dandy Miss J, BA(Hons), Grad.Trainee/L.Asst., Birkbeck Coll, Westminster Univ.L., Marylebone Campus. [0059450] 30/03/2001
Dane Mrs KE, (was Baxter), BA MCLIP, Sys.Lib., Royal Nat.Inst.for the Blind, Peterborough. [0037367] 27/07/1984
Danels Miss JL, BD DipLib, Unemployed. [0040127] 17/10/1986
Danes Mrs NE, (was Morrison), BLIB MCLIP, Unemployed. [0028637] 11/01/1978
Daniel Ms C, BA MA MCLIP, Lib., Cumbria Coll.of Art & Design, Carlisle. [0043763] 01/01/1990
Daniel Mrs JHM, (was Orme), BLIB MCLIP, Child.Lib., Wilts.C.C., Chippenham. [0029780] 04/10/1978
Daniel Mrs KA, (was Moore), MCLIP, Unemployed. [0003580] 29/09/1965
Daniel Miss LR, BA(Hons), L.Asst./Catr., Courtauld Inst.of Art, Book L., London. [0058305] 04/01/2000
Daniel Mr F, BA(Hons) DipLib MCLIP, Sen.Music.Lib., Balham Mus.L., Wandsworth Ls., London. [0023440] 01/01/1975
Daniels Mr K, BA MCLIP, Academic Liaison Lib.-Sci., Univ.of Luton. [0040863] 20/07/1987
Daniels Mrs K, BSc(Hons), Resident in France. [0053424] 05/06/1996
Daniels Mrs M, R.& I.Offr., N.W.Lancs.Health Promotion, Kirkham. [0061201] 08/04/2002 AF
Daniels Mrs MJ, (was Rowland), Automation Supp.Lib., L.Headquarters, Powys. [0003588] 01/01/1984
Daniels Mr PG, BA MSc Dip Lib MCLIP, Electronic Serv.Lib., Coventry Univ. [0037845] 01/11/1984
Daniels Mr PJ, BA DipLib MA, p./t.Asst.Lib., Soc.of Friends, London. [0033510] 13/01/1981
Daniels Mrs TJ, (was Kirtland), BLIB MCLIP, Asst Catr., Torfaen CBC., Cwmbran. [0034315] 20/10/1981
Dankyi Ms D, BSc(Hons), Cent.Mgr. [0057380] 26/02/1999
Dann Mrs JM, (was Stockdale), BA DipLib MCLIP, Lib., Rickmansworth Sch., Herts. [0042206] 09/10/1988
Dann Miss LA, PGDipILM, Lib., HM Prison, Forest Bank, Manchester. [0052136] 05/10/1995
Dann Mr MJ, BA(Hons), Bibl.Serv.Lib., Univ.of Northumbria. [0052584] 09/11/1995
Danquah Miss MA, BSc(Hons) MA, Careers Adviser, Thames Valley Univ. [0052117] 05/10/1995
Dansey Mr P, BSc MCLIP, Employment not known. [0060185] 10/12/2001
Dansie Miss JV, MCLIP, Retired. [0003593] 27/03/1961
Danskin Mr AR, MA(Hons) DipLib, Catg.Mgr., The Brit.L., Boston Spa. [0039355] 19/01/1986
Danton Miss SJ, Sen.L.Asst., Medway Council, Rochester, Kent. [0055489] 15/10/1997 AF
Daodu Mrs T, BLS(Hons) MA, Deputy Coll.Lib., Federal Govt.of Nigeria. [0050063] 03/03/1994
Darby Mrs JA, (was Wright), MCLIP, p./t.post, Education L.Serv., Nottingham. [0003597] 04/03/1963
Darbyshire Mr JB, FCLIP, Retired. [0003598] 06/02/1952 FE 01/01/1967
Darbyshire Ms VFJ, (was Wincott), BA(Hons) MCLIP, Asst.Lib.(Job Share), N.Yorks.Co.L., Knaresborough L. [0022056] 07/01/1974
Dare Mrs JE, BA(Hons) MA, p./t.Stud., Loughborough Univ. [0056124] 03/03/1998
Darling Mrs A, (was Green), MCLIP, Hosp.Lib., Pilgrim Hosp., Boston. [0005858] 01/10/1968
Darling Miss HO, BA(Hons) MCLIP, Lib.:Arch./Local Hist./Ref., Scottish Borders Council, Selkirk. [0035854] 31/01/1983
Darling Sister MP, MCLIP, Unemployed. [0020814] 13/07/1973
Darling Ms SL, (was Butler), BA MA MCLIP, Self Employed. [0045436] 04/02/1991
Darlington Mrs MF, BA(Hons) MCLIP, Retired. [0044754] 15/11/1990
Darlington Mrs NJ, (was Robinson), BA(Hons) MCLIP, Sen.L.Asst., Univ.of Nottingham. [0051173] 23/11/1994
Darlington Mr PM, MCLIP, L.Helpdesk Support Analyst, D S Ltd., Nottingham. [0052578] 08/11/1995

Darnbrook   **CILIP**

Darnbrook Mrs T, (was Michaelson), MCLIP, Unemployed. [0000533] 15/02/1972
Dart Mr GAC, FCLIP, Life Member. [0003609] 25/10/1935 **FE 01/01/1947**
Darter Ms PE, BA MCLIP, Retired. [0003610] 03/10/1963
Dase Ms A, MA, Stud., Loughborough Univ. [0059138] 23/11/2000
Dash Miss DL, BA MCLIP, Asst.Lib., Croydon Coll. [0023188] 16/10/1974
Dash Mr GP, MCLIP, IT Bus.Systems Mgr., Cent.L., L.B.of Sutton. [0003614] 03/05/1971
Date Mrs CLE, (was Monks), MIPD MCLIP, Princeial Area Serv.Mgr., Bournemouth L. [0010299] 09/08/1967
Date Mr WJS, MA MCLIP, Music Lib., Bournemouth L. [0003617] 18/04/1967
Dattili Ms M, BA DipLib MCLIP, Lib., N.Lanarkshire Council, Bellshill. [0037463] 01/10/1984
Davenport Mrs AS, (was Jones), BA PGCE MCLIP, Teacher, Biggin Hill Infant Sch., Kent. [0007958] 23/03/1971
Davenport Dr ER, PhD MLitt MSc MA FCLIP, Prof.of Inf.Mgmt., Napier Univ.Sch.of Computing, Edinburgh. [0037138] 25/02/1984 **FE 01/04/2002**
Davenport Ms KP, MA MCLIP, Head of L., Bristol City Council. [0032909] 30/09/1980
Davey Mr AJ, BSc MCLIP, L.Mgr., Devon C.C., Exeter. [0033283] 27/10/1980
Davey Mr AT, FCLIP, Retired. [0003626] 02/01/1933 **FE 01/01/1936**
Davey Ms EM, BA, Unemployed. [0046298] 24/10/1991
Davey Mrs JM, (was Akers), BA(Hons) DipLib, Lib., Falmouth Coll.of Arts, Cornwall. [0047886] 23/10/1992
Davey Mr JS, FCLIP, Life Member. [0003629] 01/01/1939 **FE 01/01/1950**
Davey Mr M, MSc BA HDipEd DLIS, L.Co-Ordinator, Saudi Aramco, Dhahran, Saudi Arabia. [0040554] 04/03/1987
Davey Mrs M, (was Souter), MCLIP, Retired. [0003630] 31/12/1965
Davey Mrs P, BSc DipLib MCLIP, Equal Access Offr., Kent C.C., Arts & L., Kings Hill, W.Malling. [0021699] 07/01/1974
Davey Mrs PA, (was Miles), BA MCLIP, Knowledge Cent.Mgr., Higher Ed.Funding C.for England. [0028858] 16/01/1978
Davey Mr PL, BA MCLIP, Sen.Asst.Lib., Wellcome Trust, London. [0027953] 12/10/1977
Davey Mr RL, BA DipLib, Sen.L.Asst., Univ.of London L. [0043150] 23/08/1989
David Bar'ss, Hon.Vice President. [0046049] 11/09/1991
David Mrs SJ, (was Dudley), BA MA MCLIP, Educ.& Training Co-ordinator, St.Georges Hosp.Med.Sch., London. [0047964] 28/10/1992
David Mr WT, MA MSc DipLib MCLIP, Asst.Lib., The London L., London. [0042310] 21/10/1988
Davidson Mrs A, (was Pateman), BA MCLIP, Asst.Lib., Thamesmead Cent., L.B.of Bexley. [0039604] 19/03/1986
Davidson Mr AJ, BA DipLIS MCLIP, Asst.Lib., Foreign & Commonwealth Off., London. [0049512] 09/11/1993
Davidson Ms BT, (was Pumphrey), BSc DipLib MCLIP, Asst.Lib., Capel Manor Coll., Enfield, Middx. [0041653] 05/02/1988
Davidson Miss CM, MCLIP, Unemployed. [0003636] 23/02/1965
Davidson Mrs DJ, L.Asst., Basingstoke L., Hants. [0061090] 04/03/2002 **AF**
Davidson Mr FJ, Inf.Offr., Toxteth Health Forum, Liverpool. [0048748] 05/05/1993
Davidson Miss JA, BA(Hons) MA, Asst.Lib., Coventry Sch.L.Serv. [0057833] 03/09/1999
Davidson Mrs JE, (was Kinsella), MA, Tech.Author, Fretwell-Downing Informatics Ltd., Sheffield. [0034438] 27/10/1981
Davidson Mrs JE, (was Alcock), MCLIP, Sch.Lib., Ilford Ursuline High Sch., Ilford. [0000134] 01/01/1971
Davidson Mr JM, MCLIP, Comm.Lib., E.Renfrewshire Council. [0028541] 14/12/1977
Davidson Miss KB, MCLIP, Retired. [0003643] 15/09/1952
Davidson Mrs KJ, (was Goonan), BA MCLIP, Lib., Fyfe Ireland W.S., Edinburgh. [0003644] 05/01/1966
Davidson Mrs M, (was Hanlin), MCLIP, p./t.L.Asst., Perth & Kinross Council, Blairgowrie, Perthshire. [0003645] 06/09/1962
Davidson Mrs MW, (was Hooker), BA DipLib MCLIP, Employment not known. [0028592] 11/01/1978
Davidson Mrs P, (was Green), MCLIP, Sch.Lib.(Job Share), Renfrewshire Council, Renfrewshire. [0018106] 01/10/1972
Davidson Ms P, Stud., Robert Gordon Univ., Aberdeen. [0051588] 05/04/1995
Davidson Mrs PB, (was Farquharson), MA MCLIP, Network Lib., Banchory Acad., Banchory, Kincardineshire. [0026368] 11/10/1976
Davidson Mrs SA, (was Wing), MCLIP, Housewife. [0003651] 22/03/1965
Davidson Mrs SA, (was Ellis), BA(Hons) DipLIS MA, Academic Res.Lib., Univ.of Wolverhampton, Walsall. [0047676] 14/10/1992
Davie Mrs DE, (was Cook), BA DipLib MCLIP, Mgr, Learning Resource Cent., W.Nottinghamshire Coll., Notts. [0041256] 26/10/1987
Davie Mrs ME, (was Yule), MA DipLIS MCLIP, Lib., Falkirk Council, Comm.Serv., L.Support for Sch. [0046288] 23/10/1991
Davies Mrs A, (was Kaye), BA(Hons), Lib., Univ.Coll.Sch.(J.B.), London. [0047010] 01/04/1992
Davies Mrs A, (was Pye), MCLIP, Asst.Lib., Cent.L., Bury Metro.Bor. [0019268] 15/08/1972
Davies Ms A, (was Candlish), MA MCLIP, L.Offr., Edinburgh City L. [0040224] 11/11/1986
Davies Miss AC, Asst.Lib., Herefordshire Council, Leominster L. [0049773] 06/12/1993
Davies Ms AC, (was Driver), MCLIP, Head of Research L., Greater London Auth. [0022690] 15/08/1974
Davies Mrs AJ, BA BA(Hons), Planning Offr., Staffs.C.C., Educ.Dept., Stafford. [0046709] 06/01/1992

Davies Ms AL, BA PGDip/MA MCLIP, Performance Imp.Mgr., Surrey C.C., Kingston-upon-Thames. [0046951] 10/03/1992
Davies Miss AM, BA(Hons), Tech.Serv.Mgr., Social Studies L., Oxford. [0055187] 05/08/1997
Davies Ms AM, L.& Inf.Serv.Mgr., Hammond Suddards Edge, Birmingham. [0046949] 09/03/1992
Davies Mr AN, BSc MCLIP, Inf.& User Educ.Lib., Tameside Coll., Ashton-under-Lyne. [0026340] 01/01/1976
Davies Mr APK, BSc ARCS MCLIP, Ref.Lib., Enfield P.L. [0003661] 22/01/1968
Davies Mr AR, BA PgD ILM, Inf.Offr.(L.), Princess Royal Hosp., Telford. [0057123] 14/12/1998
Davies Mr BT, BA DMS MCLIP, Sen.Lect., Sch.of Management, City Coll., Norwich. [0033216] 29/10/1980
Davies Mrs C, BA(Hons) DipILM, Asst.Lib.(Ref.& Comm.), Sefton Council, Southport L. [0059588] 11/06/2001
Davies Mrs C, (was Evans), MCLIP, Asst., Lib., Dudley Coll. of Tech., Dudley, Worcs. [0046643] 12/01/1972
Davies Ms C, BA MLS MCLIP, Resident in Switzerland. [0060067] 07/12/2001
Davies Mr CB, BA MCLIP, Team Leader (Inf.Serv.), L.B.of Enfield, Palmers Green L. [0031127] 30/08/1979
Davies Miss CH, BA(Hons) MSc, L.Exec., House of Commons L., Westminster. [0057532] 23/04/1999
Davies Miss DMW, L.Asst., Victoria Univ.of Wellington, New Zealand. [0003671] 02/01/1970
Davies Mrs DO, (was Burton), MCLIP, p./t.Lib., Theological Book Review, Feed The Minds, Guildford. [0030881] 09/03/1963
Davies Mr DT, MA BA MCLIP, L.Serv.Mgr., Sci.& Engineering, All Saints L., Manchester Met.Univ. [0021690] 09/01/1974
Davies Mrs DV, BA MCLIP, Sen.L.Asst., Lincs.C.C., Woodhall Spa. [0003673] 01/10/1971
Davies Miss EC, MA FCLIP, Life Member, Tel.01865 510201, 3 Eaton Crt., Water Eaton Rd., Oxford, OX2 7QT. [0003676] 13/10/1949 **FE 01/01/1968**
Davies Ms EC, BA MA DipLib, Head Inf.Serv., Charterhouse Devel.Capital, London. [0046292] 23/10/1991
Davies Mrs EI, (was Garrett), MCLIP, Housewife & Mother. [0021306] 10/10/1973
Davies Mr EJ, BA MA DipLib MCLIP, Employment not known. [0060850] 12/12/2001
Davies Mrs EJ, BA MCLIP, Unemployed. [0031249] 03/10/1979
Davies Mr F, (was Matthews), MCLIP, Ref.Lib., Newbury L., Berks. [0009937] 04/01/1970
Davies Mrs F, (was Lloyd-Williams), MCLIP, Stand-by Lib., Harrow P.L., & Middx.Univ. [0009025] 25/09/1957
Davies Miss G, MCLIP, Retired. [0003682] 18/10/1945
Davies Mr G, FRSA FCLIP, Retired. [0003681] 01/01/1936 **FE 01/01/1950**
Davies Mr G, Learning Cent.Asst., City of Wolverhampton Coll. [0045966] 29/07/1991 **AF**
Davies Mr GA, MCLIP, Team Lib., Serv.to Older People, Coventry City L. [0003686] 11/01/1968
Davies Mr GB, BSc, Asst. Lib., Tile Hill Coll., Coventry. [0060969] 21/01/2002
Davies Mrs GC, (was Dewey), BA MCLIP, Team Lib., Sch.L.Serv., Hillingdon L. [0038992] 22/10/1985
Davies Mr GE, MCLIP, Inf.Serv.Mgr., Dept.of Trade & Industry, London. [0003687] 31/10/1966
Davies Miss GM, BA MCLIP, Retired. [0003690] 08/01/1968
Davies Mr GR, OBE FCLIP, Retired., Crotchets, Rotherfield Lane. [0003691] 01/10/1946 **FE 01/01/1949**
Davies Mr H, (was Lloyd), BA MCLIP, P/t.Sch.Lib., Adams Grammar Sch., Newport. [0009014] 27/10/1971
Davies Ms HE, BA(Hons) DipILM MCLIP, Learning Res.Adviser, Liverpool Inst.for Performing Arts. [0054261] 11/11/1996
Davies Mrs HG, (was Carr), BA MCLIP, Retired. [0003698] 24/04/1966
Davies Mrs HJ, (was Neve), MCLIP, IS Project Mgr., Kent C.C., Maidstone. [0010740] 21/07/1969
Davies Mrs HJ, (was Farries), BA(Hons) MCLIP, Lib., Esher Coll., Surrey. [0042668] 06/02/1989
Davies Ms HJ, BA MSc MCLIP, Lib., Enfield Borough Council. [0043427] 26/10/1989
Davies Ms HJ, (was Briggs), BA(Hons) MSc MCLIP, Inf.Cent.Mgr., Qualifications & Curriculum Auth., London. [0047991] 30/10/1992
Davies Ms HM, BA MLib MCLIP, Employed outside LIS. [0033992] 17/06/1981
Davies Mrs IJ, BA DipLib, Lib., Essex Sch.L.Serv., Chelmsford. [0036990] 27/01/1984
Davies Mrs J, BA MCLIP, H.Learning Res.Cent., Worcester 6th Form Coll., Worcester. [0060611] 01/01/1972
Davies Ms J, BPharm MRPharmS MCLIP, Dir.of Med.Serv., Bristol-Myers Squibb Pharm.Ltd., Hounslow. [0060834] 12/12/2001
Davies Mrs JA, (was Cole), BA MCLIP, Career Break. [0034549] 15/01/1982
Davies Dr JE, MA PhD FinstAM MIMgt FCLIP, Dir., L.I.S.U., Loughborough Univ., Leics. [0003705] 25/01/1961 **FE 21/10/1974**
Davies Miss JE, BA(Hons) MCLIP DipLib, Lib., Blaenau Gwent Bor.Council. [0046394] 31/10/1991
Davies Mrs JE, (was Birtwistle), BA MCLIP, Young Peoples Lib., Sevenoaks Grp., Kent. [0033375] 27/11/1980
Davies Ms JE, BSc MCLIP, Employment not known. [0060196] 10/12/2001
Davies Ms JE, (was Quick), BA MA MCLIP, Retired. [0003706] 25/01/1966
Davies Ms JE, BA, Grad.Trainee, St.Johns Coll.L., Cambridge. [0059831] 15/10/2001
Davies Mr JI, FCLIP, Life Member. [0003709] 27/02/1958 **FE 29/01/1976**
Davies Miss JM, BSc DipLib MCLIP, Readers Devel.Lib., W.Area, Northants. C.C. [0026341] 12/10/1976

Davies Miss JM, BSc DipLib MCLIP, Head of L.& Manuscripts, Nat.Maritime Museum, London. [0041649] 01/02/1988
Davies Mr JM, Stud., Univ.of Wales, Aberystwyth. [0057142] 21/12/1998
Davies Mr JRM, MA MCLIP, Retired. [0018608] 10/04/1965
Davies Miss KL, BSc(Hons), Stud., Univ.Coll.London. [0059050] 06/11/2000
Davies Ms KL, MCLIP, Legal Sec., Ealing, London. [0003666] 01/01/1970
Davies Ms KM, (was Bateman), BA MCLIP, The Lib., The Warwick Sch., Redhill. [0003716] 01/01/1970
Davies Mrs L, BA DipLib MCLIP, Community Lib., Denbighshire C.C., Ruthin L. [0043446] 26/10/1989
Davies Mrs LA, (was Stutely), BA MCLIP, Biomedical Sci.Lib., Univ.of Wales, Cardiff. [0035019] 22/06/1982
Davies Miss LC, BA FCLIP, Life Member. [0003717] 01/01/1956 FE 01/01/1961
Davies Mrs LC, (was Jones), MCLIP, Lib., St.Margaret Ward R.C.High Sch., Tunstall. [0025573] 11/02/1976
Davies Mr LE, MCLIP, Retired. [0003719] 26/03/1934
Davies Ms LM, BA PGCE DipLib MCLIP, Reading Devel.Lib.(Adult)Job Share, L.B.of Richmond Upon Thames. [0040626] 01/04/1987
Davies Mrs LY, (was Borne), BLib MPhil, Resource Cent.Mgr., Storminster Newton High Sch., Dorset. [0043902] 15/02/1990
Davies Dr M, BA DipLib MCLIP, Head of Learning Support Serv., Univ.of E.London. [0021317] 04/10/1973
Davies Miss M, BA MCLIP, Life Member. [0003720] 19/02/1959
Davies Mrs M, (was Heaslip), MCLIP, Life Member. [0003722] 23/06/1954
Davies Mrs M, MCLIP, Div.Lib., S.Div., Hants.C.C. [0003723] 16/02/1949
Davies Mrs M, (was Bunce), MA BLib MCLIP, Head of L.& Inf.Serv., Norton Rose, London. [0035176] 04/10/1982
Davies Mrs M, (was Case), MCLIP, Area Mgr., Risca L., Caerphilly Co.Bor.Council. [0002470] 21/01/1971
Davies Mrs MA, (was Jackson), MCLIP, Head of Inf.& Learning, Suffolk C.C. [0003725] 21/03/1962
Davies Ms ME, (was Evans), Saturday Asst., Monmouthshire L., Abergavenny. [0004685] 01/01/1966
Davies Mr MH, DipInf, Unemployed. [0049350] 27/10/1993
Davies Mr MJ, BA(Hons) DipLib, L.Asst., Univ.of Wales,Aberystwyth. [0044837] 11/12/1990
Davies Mr MO, BSc MA MCLIP, Asst.Lib., Charles Mussal Solicitors, London. [0054795] 02/04/1997
Davies Miss N, BA(Hons) MPhil MScEcon, Asst.Lib., Caredigion C.C., Llanbadarn Fawr. [0059577] 05/06/2001
Davies Mrs N, Stud., Liverpool John Moores Univ. [0059998] 19/11/2001
Davies Miss NH, BSc, Stud., Univ.of Brighton. [0061045] 05/02/2002
Davies Mr NP, BSc(Econ) DipILM, Asst.Lib.(Serials/Doc.Units), Durham Univ.L. [0056434] 13/07/1998
Davies Mrs PA, (was Clarke), Res.Cent.Mgr., SLS L.& Heritage, Suffolk C.C. [0045208] 13/08/1990 AF
Davies Mrs PH, (was Mears), BA MCLIP, Lib., Kings Langley Sch., Herts. [0010053] 06/11/1971
Davies Mrs PJ, (was Bailey), M.Ed BA MCLIP DipLib, p./t.Music Teacher, L.B.of Hackney. [0031050] 28/07/1979
Davies Mrs PJ, (was Shail), BLib AI, Freelance Indexer. [0026007] 11/05/1976
Davies Mrs PM, (was Bratherton), BSc MSc MCLIP, Sen.Asst.Lib., Leeds Univ.L., Brotherton L. [0022793] 08/10/1974
Davies Mr R, BSc MCLIP, Asst.Lib., Univ.of Exeter., Devon. [0003737] 01/01/1972
Davies Ms R, MA, L.& Inf.Offr., Lovells, London. [0051855] 14/07/1995
Davies Ms R, BLib(Hons), Health Sci.Lib., Univ.of Wales, Swansea. [0049016] 06/09/1993
Davies Miss RE, BSc(Hons) DipLib, Business Inf.Specialist, Hermes Pensions Mgmt.Ltd., London. [0048043] 05/11/1992
Davies Mrs RE, (was Kimber), BA(Hons), Unemployed. [0059424] 12/03/2001
Davies Mr RL, LRSC MCLIP, Position unknown, Corus Research, Devel.& Tech., Port Talbot. [0060271] 10/12/2001
Davies Miss RM, MLS MCLIP, L.Asst., Univ.of Cambridge, Sch.of Educ. [0003743] 13/03/1972
Davies Mr RN, BA DipLib MCLIP, Stock Devel.Mgr., L.B.of Newham. [0040477] 16/02/1987
Davies Mr RR, BA(Hons), Stud., Univ.Aberystwyth, [0059809] 04/10/2001
Davies Mrs RS, BA, Stud./Grad.Trainee, Westminster Univ. [0061678] 17/10/2002
Davies Mrs SA, (was Brown), BA MCLIP, p./t.Ref.Lib., Stockport M.B.C. [0024611] 01/10/1975
Davies Mrs SI, (was Wilo), MCLIP, Retired. [0003751] 28/09/1950
Davies Miss SM, BA MCLIP DMS, Br.Lib., N.Harrow/Wealdstone L., L.B.of Harrow. [0020179] 01/02/1973
Davies Miss SS, MA, Project Mgr., Greater Glasgow NHS Board, Glasgow. [0051219] 28/11/1994
Davies Mrs T, (was French), MCLIP, Lib., Elan Drug Delivery, Nottingham. [0005226] 05/01/1970
Davies Mr TH, BA MSc MCLIP, Dep.Lib., Courtauld Inst. of Art., London. [0038994] 21/10/1985
Davies Mrs VHS, (was Beresford), MCLIP, Admin.Offr., Min.of Defence, Winchester. [0001170] 22/02/1965
Davies Mrs VM, (was Browning), MCLIP, Lib., Bournemouth Sch.for Girls, Dorset. [0003756] 11/10/1965
Davies Mr W, FCLIP, Retired. [0003758] 06/01/1948 FE 01/01/1970
Davies Mrs WM, BA MCLIP, Housewife. [0018398] 02/10/1972
Davies Terry Ms HM, (was Davies), BA DipLib MCLIP, Child.Serv.Lib., W.Sussex C.C. [0035175] 01/10/1982
Davis Mrs A, (was Allan), MCLIP, Unemployed. [0000162] 01/01/1971
Davis Mrs AEC, PGDipInf Man, Resource & Devel.Lib., Hillingdon L., Middx. [0061587] 02/10/2002
Davis Ms AK, BA(Hons) PGDipILMgmt, Sen.L.Asst., The English Faculty L., Oxford Univ. [0057203] 14/01/1999

Davis Miss AM, BA MCLIP, Life Member, 6 Clayton Drive, Burgess Hill, Sussex, RH15 9HH. [0003763] 01/03/1952
Davis Mrs AMT, (was Britt), MCLIP, Lib., Greater Glasgow Health Board, Glasgow. [0001750] 01/01/1969
Davis Miss CA, BA(Hons) MA MCLIP, Lib., Shrewsbury L., Shropshire. [0056589] 04/09/1998
Davis Ms CA, BSc MSc MCLIP, Asst.Subject Lib.Computing & Maths, Oxford Brookes Univ. [0050265] 25/05/1994
Davis Ms DER, BA(Hons), Retired. [0050585] 26/09/1994
Davis Miss E, BA(Hons) MCLIP, Bus.Lib., City of York L. [0050429] 28/07/1994
Davis Miss E, Inf.Offr., Eversheds, Nottingham. [0058259] 30/11/1999
Davis Mrs EA, BSc MCLIP, Lib., Imperial Coll.Sch.of Med., Hammersmith Campus. [0028542] 21/01/1978
Davis Miss GP, MCLIP, Retired. [0003773] 08/03/1959
Davis Mrs H, (was Whitham), MCLIP, P./t.L.Asst., Univ.of Bradford. [0015760] 23/09/1968
Davis Mr HJ, BSc FBIS MCLIP, Employment unknown. [0060272] 10/12/2001
Davis Mrs J, (was Absalom), MCLIP, Retired. [0003776] 01/01/1940
Davis Miss JE, B LIB MCLIP, Dist.Lib., Wilts.Co.L.& Heritage, Chippenham. [0026180] 02/08/1976
Davis Mr JG, MA FCLIP, Catr., John Smith & Son, Glasgow. [0003777] 01/01/1970 FE 13/12/1979
Davis Mrs JM, (was Evans), BA MCLIP, Asst.Lib., Nat.Police L., Basingstoke. [0033598] 21/04/1982
Davis Ms JM, (was Treacher), BLib MCLIP, Position Unknown, Sarum Coll.L., Salisbury, Wilts. [0031475] 15/10/1979
Davis Mrs KA, BSc MCLIP, Sch.Lib., Sheringham High Sch., Norfolk. [0003778] 02/07/1969
Davis Mr KM, MA DipLis, F./t.Lib., Hasmonean High Sch., Hendon, NW4. [0045982] 30/07/1991
Davis Miss L, Document Controller, Maritime House, Bath. [0061331] 28/05/2002 AF
Davis Ms L, MA, Unemployed. [0061673] 17/10/2002
Davis Miss M, MCLIP, Retired. [0018613] 28/09/1949
Davis Miss M, BSc MSc, Med.Inf.Offr., Norton Health Care Ltd., London. [0060434] 11/12/2001
Davis Mr MC, MA DipLip MCLIP, Asst.Lib., Brotherton L., Univ.of Leeds. [0003783] 03/10/1970
Davis Ms MV, Sen.Asst.Lib., Wandsworth Bor.Council, Battersea L. BA GradDipLib. [0047110] 21/04/1992
Davis Miss P, MCLIP, Retired. [0018614] 20/11/1949
Davis Mr P, MCLIP, Life Member, Tel.01295 259 671. [0003788] 14/03/1951
Davis Mrs PE, (was O'Reilly), MCLIP, L.& Heritage Mgr., Telford & Wrekin Council. [0011028] 01/01/1972
Davis Mr PJ, MCLIP, Asst.Lib., Redditch P.L. [0003790] 12/05/1964
Davis Ms S, BA DipLIS MCLIP, Freelance Web Designer &, Inf.Architect. [0047280] 01/07/1992
Davis Ms SC, BA MCLIP, Sen.Young Person's Lib.(Job Share), Reading Cent.L. [0031594] 21/11/1979
Davis Mrs SD, BA CertEd, Stud., Univ.of Wales, Aberystwyth. [0055957] 22/12/1997
Davis Mrs SJ, (was Ward), Unemployed. [0038087] 14/01/1985
Davis Mrs V, (was Wise), BSc MCLIP, Employment not known. [0060680] 12/12/2001
Davison Ms AM, BA(Hons) MCLIP, Lib.i/c., Dorchester L. [0045180] 02/08/1990
Davison Mrs C, Asst. Lib., Rhodesway School, Bradford. [0061377] 05/07/2002
Davison Mrs CP, MCLIP, Catr., Cambs.L. [0003796] 24/07/1972
Davison Mrs E, (was Raine), BA MCLIP, Head of Learning Res., London Inst. [0003797] 12/01/1965
Davison Mrs KM, (was Jones), BA(Hons) MA MCLIP, Sch.Lib., Nottingham City Council. [0051033] 09/11/1994
Davison Miss LE, BA, Stud., Univ.Coll.London. [0059255] 19/01/2001
Davison Mr RA, BA DipLib, Lib., Med.L., General Hosp., Hartlepool. [0036965] 26/01/1984
Davy Miss AF, MCLIP, Democratic Serv.Offr., Tameside M.B.C., Ashton under Lyne. [0038801] 20/09/1969
Davy Miss I, MA MCLIP, Lib., New Hall Prison, Wakefield. [0003803] 06/02/1963
Davy Miss J, BA(Hons), Grad.Trainee, Univ.of Westminster, Harrow Learning Res.Cent. [0059991] 16/11/2001
Davy Mr MR, Collection Offr., Inland Revenue, Newcastle upon Tyne. [0038581] 01/07/1985
Davy Mrs PM, (was Meikle), MCLIP, Retired. [0003804] 25/02/1964
Davy Ms SM, (was Pilling), MCLIP, Academic Inf.Serv.Mgr., Univ.of N.London. [0002564] 01/01/1967
Davys Miss RC, BA(Hons) MA, Asst.Lib., Solihull Cent.L. [0056549] 10/08/1998
Dawe Mrs CL, (was Finney), BLib MCLIP, Career Break. [0042694] 07/02/1989
Dawe Miss MI, MCLIP, Retired. [0003808] 15/09/1958
Dawe Mr RNE, MCLIP, Life Member. [0003809] 01/01/1939
Dawes Ms LJ, BA MCLIP, Princ.Offr.:Humanities, Manchester Cent.L., Manchester City Council. [0034979] 24/05/1982
Dawes Mrs MI, (was Crocker), MCLIP, Prof.Serv.Mgr., Swindon Bor., Wilts. [0003386] 24/03/1971
Dawes Mr PEV, BA MCLP, Team Lib., Norfolk L.& Inf.Serv. [0027954] 01/01/1977
Dawes Miss PJ, BA MCLIP, Systems Lib., Univ.of Bradford. [0033998] 08/07/1981
Dawes Mrs S, BA MA DipLib MCLIP, Sen.Inf.Offr.-London, Building Design Ptnrshp., London. [0035410] 18/10/1982
Dawes Mrs S, (was Allen), BLib MCLIP, Not seeking Employment. [0033725] 09/02/1981

Dawkins Mrs JE, (was Adams), BLib MCLIP, Inf.Specialist, Qinetiq, Farnborough, Hants. [0026836]   01/01/1976
Daws Mr AL, BA MCLIP, Media Lib., Inst.of Educ.L., Univ. of London. [0003813]   01/04/1967
Dawson Mr AD, BA MCLIP, MSc Programme Dir., Sch.of L.Arch.& Inf.Studies, Univ.Coll.London. [0032647]   01/07/1980
Dawson Mrs AE, (was Baker), MCLIP, L.Asst., Preston Coll. [0000621]   15/10/1970
Dawson Mrs AE, (was Brookes), MCLIP, Jnr.Sch.Lib., Dulwich Coll., London. [0001800]   04/05/1970
Dawson Miss AH, BA DipLib, L.Asst.(evenings), Univ.of Ulster, & Catr., Linen Hall L., Belfast. [0035533]   29/10/1982
Dawson Mrs AJ, BA CertEd MCLIP, Lib., Watts & Partners, London. [0032385]   01/01/1972
Dawson Dr BK, MLib PhD MCLIP, Electronic Serv.Proj.Mgr., Test Valley B.C., Andover. [0003816]   12/07/1971
Dawson Mrs CM, (was Lamb), BA MA, Freelance Data Manipulator, Somerset Computing, Chipping Norton. [0041099]   14/10/1987
Dawson Mrs DM, (was Short), BA MCLIP, Faculty Liaison Offr., Nottingham Trent Univ.L., Nottingham. [0039034]   29/10/1985
Dawson Mrs FN, p./t.Asst.Lib., Bath Univ.L. [0030393]   09/02/1979
Dawson Miss HS, BA MA DipLib MCLIP, Asst.Lib., Brit.L.of Political & Econ.Sci. [0046102]   02/10/1991
Dawson Miss JA, BA(Hons) MCLIP, Team Lib.-Educ.Dept., Educ.Res.Serv., Coatbridge, N.Lanarks. [0039923]   02/10/1986
Dawson Mr JA, MA DipLib MCLIP, p./t.Site Lib., Univ.of Sheffield. [0039911]   01/10/1986
Dawson Mr JD, BLIB MCLIP, Sen.Lib., Arup, London. [0039426]   24/01/1986
Dawson Mrs JE, (was Pratt), BA MCLIP, Lib., Warwicks.C.C., Stratford upon Avon L. [0011900]   01/01/1976
Dawson Mrs JE, L.Asst., Cromer High Sch., Norfolk. [0061332]   28/05/2002 AF
Dawson Miss JM, MCLIP, Retired. [0003823]   08/01/1951
Dawson Mrs L, (was Ashworth), BA(Hons) MCLIP, Outreach & Inclusion Mgr., Oldham M.B.C. [0043960]   05/03/1990
Dawson Miss LM, MCLIP, Res.Cent.Mgr., Educ.Res.Serv., Renfrewshire Council. [0003827]   01/01/1968
Dawson Ms MM, BA(Hons), Lib., Airedale NHS Trust, Airedale General Hosp. [0058271]   01/12/1999
Dawson Miss NJ, BA MCLIP, Lib., Shrewsbury L., Shropshire C.C. [0042295]   18/10/1988
Dawson Ms PJ, (was Round), BSc DipLib CertEd MCLIP, Learning Cent.Mgr., Swansea Coll., City & County of Swansea. [0021187]   27/09/1973
Dawson Mrs VJ, BA, Princ.Lib.(C.& S.S.), Cent.L., L.B.of Islington. [0003836]   08/01/1968
Day Mrs A, (was Mcrobie), BA MCLIP, Lib., Archway Sch., Stroud. [0021454]   18/10/1973
Day Mrs AA, (was Gill), BA(Hons) MA MCLIP, Unemployed. [0047482]   01/09/1992
Day Dr AE, MA PhD FRGS FCLIP, Author. [0003837]   30/01/1958 FE 01/01/1961
Day Mrs AF, (was Sahay), BLib MCLIP, Lib., B.B.C.Research & Devel.Dept., Surrey. [0027212]   24/01/1977
Day Miss AL, BA, L.Asst., Kent C.C., Ashford L. [0054547]   15/01/1997
Day Mrs AM, (was Swan), BA MCLIP, P./t.Inf.Asst., Chesterton plc, Bracknell, Berks. [0032193]   25/01/1980
Day Mrs AM, (was Firbank), BA(Hons) MCLIP, Yorkshire L.Devel.Offr., Yorkshire Museums Council. [0047005]   01/04/1992
Day Mrs BE, (was Harris), MCLIP, Bibl.Serv.Lib., Solihull M.B.C. [0006398]   05/09/1967
Day Miss CA, MSc MCLIP, Systems Mgr., L.B.of Ealing L.Serv. [0027955]   01/10/1977
Day Mrs CJ, (was Downes), BA MCLIP, Comm.Inf.Network Offr., Essex C.C. [0025971]   29/04/1976
Day Mrs EA, BA(Hons) MA MCLIP, Early Years Lib., L.B.of Lewisham. [0051761]   01/07/1995
Day Mrs EV, (was Pitman), MCLIP, Inf.Offr./Lib., Powergen, Nottingham. [0011726]   26/04/1971
Day Mrs HJ, BSc MMRS MCLIP, Position unknown, Boots, Nottingham. [0060425]   11/12/2001
Day Miss JICA, MA, Unemployed. [0032912]   02/10/1980
Day Mr JS, BA, L.Asst.,Stud., Univ.Aberystwyth. [0058881]   29/09/2000
Day Mrs M, BSc, Stud., City Univ. [0061735]   30/10/2002
Day Mrs MA, (was Bradshaw), MCLIP, Sch.Lib., The Highfield Sch., Letchworth, Herts. [0003840]   23/10/1967
Day Mrs MM, (was Kelsall), BSc(Hons), Unemployed. [0050222]   09/05/1994 AF
Day Mr NJ, MCLIP, Life Member, 88A Cranston Ave., Bexhill-on-sea, E.Sussex, TN39 3NL. [0003842]   27/09/1951
Day Mrs S, BA, Unemployed. [0032043]   05/02/1980
Day Mr SR, BA MLib MCLIP, Sen.Product Specialist, OCLC PICA, Birmingham. [0041393]   27/09/1987
Day Mr TG, BA(Hons), Sen.Asst.Lib.(Media), L.B.Wandsworth, Putney L. [0048243]   17/11/1992
Day Dr VLE, MA PHD MCLIP, Sch.Lib., Sir John Lawes Sch., Herts.C.C. [0023019]   01/10/1974
Dayasena Mr PJU, BSc AMIEE MCLIP, Position unknown, Business Link Hertfordshire, St.Albans. [0060721]   12/12/2001
De Abaitua Ms CA, (was Wheeler), MSc, Unemployed. [0055394]07/10/1997
De Andrade Ms P, Marketing Database Super./Stud., Harcourt Brace & Co./City Univ., London. [0050007]   18/02/1994
de Blieck Mrs L, MA(Hons) MSc, Inf.Offr., The Planning Exchange, Glasgow. [0059360]   15/02/2001
De Carvalho Ms AM, BA DipLIS, Project Worker, Age Concern England. [0044360]   01/10/1990

de Chazal Mrs PM, (was Felton), MA MCLIP, Research Stud., Loughborough Univ. [0048195]   16/11/1992
De Cruz Ms CL, BA(Hons) DipLib, Inf.Offr.(tax), Linklaters & Alliance, London. [0053113]   14/03/1996
De Fleury Mr AM, BA(Hons) MCLIP, p./t.Asst.Lib., Avon Health Auth., Bristol. [0046249]   18/10/1991
De Fonblanque Mrs FE, (was Keene), p./t.L.Asst., Somerset Coll.of Art & Tech., Taunton. [0050088]   17/03/1994 AF
De Freitas Mrs PA, (was Phillip-Smith), BA MCLIP, Sen.Lib.(N.Area), Oxon.Co.L. [0011603]   21/09/1970
de Heer-Graham Mrs C, MCLIP, Ch.L.Asst., Univ.of Ghana. [0005796]   01/01/1968
De Kauwe Ms KF, (was Hudson), MA MCLIP, Lib., Internat.Accounting Standards Board, London. [0028594] 16/01/1978
De Klerk Mr ME, BSc(Econ), Res.Cent.Co-ordinator, Dundee City Council. [0057590]   13/05/1999
De Kock Ms SAM, BLS, Sen.Inf.Asst., Kings Coll.London, Foyles Special Collections. [0061178]   03/04/2002
de Koning Ms SM, Resident in Germany, [0059070]   07/11/2000
De La Haye Mrs FA, (was Heys), BA MCLIP, Know-How Offr., Mourant, du Feu, & Jeune, St.Helier, Jersey. [0031324]   07/10/1979
De Motte Mrs M, (was Webster), BA MCLIP, Lib., Local Stud.Unit, Manchester P.L. [0015547]   23/10/1971
de Paris Mr PM, FCLIP, Life Member, 5 Gold St., Stalbridge, Sturminster Newton, 01963 362075. [0003900] 22/10/1937 FE 01/01/1947
de Rochefort Mrs JE, BA MCLIP, Lib., Electricity Council, London. [0027753]   17/08/1977
De Silva Mrs MJ, (was Stenhouse), BLS MCLIP, Freelance Lib., Various locations. [0030271]   07/12/1978
De Silva Mr WRG, FCLIP, Lib., Univ.of Rajatata, Mihintale. [0023141]   18/08/1970   FE 15/11/1988
de Silva Mr R, BA MEd DipLib DipEdTech MBA MCLIP, Client Serv.Lib., Aberdeenshire L.& Inf.Serv., Aberdeen. [0026715]   21/11/1976
De Sousa E Andrade Ms SLC, BA BSc, p./t. Accountant, The Surgery, Maida Vale, London. [0059944]   08/11/2001
De Souza Mrs Y, BA DipLib MCLIP, Lib., Bedford Hosp. [0042629]   23/01/1989
De Tommaso Mr O, PGCE ARCM, L. Asst., London Sch.of Economics. [0060889]   20/12/2001
De Weirdt Miss NA, BA DipInf MCLIP, Lib., Essex C.C., Rayleigh Pub.L. [0046378]   30/10/1991
De'Ath Miss AF, BA DipLib MCLIP, Lib., Eastwood High Sch., Glasgow. [0043164]   04/09/1989
Deacon Mrs DA, (was Painting), MCLIP, Lib., RIO Tinto Mining & Exploration, Ltd,. Newbury, Berks. [0022384]   01/04/1974
Deacon Miss H, BScEcon(Hons) MCLIP, Group Lib., S.Group, N.End L., Portsmouth City Council. [0045019] 04/06/1990
Deacon Mr MJ, BSc DLIS MCLIP, Employment not known. [0060469]   11/12/2001
Deadman Mrs PM, BA MCLIP, Lib., Wilmslow, Cheshire C.C. [0003849]   01/01/1991
Deadman Mrs S, (was Wilkinson), BA, p./t.L.Catr., Macmillan Cancer Relief. [0035599]   26/10/1982
Deady Mr ES, BSc(Econ) DMA MCLIP, Retired. [0018620]   29/04/1966
Deakin Miss KJE, BSc(Hons) DipIM MCLIP, Asst.Lib.- User Serv., Nat.Oceanographic L., Univ.of Southampton. [0052656]   16/11/1995
Deakin Ms P, BSc, Lib., American Univ.of Sharjah, UAE. [0057017]25/11/1998
Deakin Mrs PJ, (was Males), BA DipLib MCLIP, Child.Serv.Mgr.(Job Share), L.B.of Sutton. [0038246]   12/02/1985
Deakin Mr S, BA DipLib MCLIP, L.Network Mgr., L.B.of Enfield. [0037820]   22/10/1984
Deakin Mrs SW, (was Wagstaff), MCLIP, Life Member, Whitecroft, Vale Rd., Ashvale, Nr.Aldershot, GU12. [0003850]   03/02/1949
Dean Mrs A, (was Oliver), MA MCLIP, [0020733]   01/07/1973
Dean Mr AJE, MA MCLIP, Prof.of L.& Inf.Studies, Univ.Coll.Dublin, Eire. [0016707]   21/01/1952
Dean Mrs C, Stud., Sheffield Univ. [0059091]   14/11/2000
Dean Mrs EJ, (was Stockwell), BA(Hons) MA MCLIP, Lib., Wyke Manor Sch., Bradford. [0051743] 12/06/1995
Dean Mrs EJ, (was Stevens), BA MCLIP, Unemployed. [0033352]   15/10/1980
Dean Ms H, Best Value Inspector, Stockton Bor.Council. [0048160]   11/11/1992
Dean Mrs HL, (was Ninnim), MCLIP, Bus.Inf.Lib., N.Lincs.Council, Scunthorpe. [0010844]   01/11/1966
Dean Mr JA, BA DipLib MCLIP, Lib., Technology Innovation Cent., Birmingham. [0041057]   05/10/1987
Dean Ms JE, (was Offley), BA MCLIP, Audio Visual Tech., St.Helen's Sch., Middlesex. [0022778]   17/10/1974
Dean Mrs L, (was Brown), MCLIP, Sch.Lib., Verdin High Sch., Cheshire. [0019847]   02/01/1973
Dean Ms MI, MA, Asst.Lib.(Jnr.Specialist), Derbys.C.C., Matlock. [0038213]   16/01/1985
Dean Mr SC, FCLIP, Life Member. [0003859]   31/01/1950 FE 01/01/1961
Dean Ms SM, BA(Hons), p./t.Stud./Systems Lib., City Univ., Luton Sixth Form Coll. [0061204]   08/04/2002
Deans Miss IM, FSA Scot MCLIP, Life Member. [0003863]   24/07/1957
Dearden Mr A, FCLIP, Retired. [0003864] 03/10/1946   FE 01/01/1957
Dearden Mr S, BA DipLib MCLIP, Acting Team Leader-Stock Devel., Liverpool City L. [0032914]   12/10/1980
Dearie Ms SJ, BA (Hons) DipLib MCLIP, Lib.,p./t., Rotherhithe Primary Sch., London. [0034664]   08/01/1982
Dearness Ms KL, BSc LLS, Knowledge Offr., Univ.Oxford., Warneford Hosp. [0059156]   30/11/2000
Deas Ms AJ, (was Osborne), BA MCLIP, Sch.Lib., Dalkeith High Sch. [0035915]   10/01/1983

Deas Mr C, MCLIP, Ls.& Galleries Mgr., S.Ayrshire Council, Ayr. [0003869] 23/01/1966
Deas Miss SJ, MA DipLib MCLIP, Childcare Inf.Offr., Sandhell MBC, W.Midlands. [0040707] 01/05/1987
Deasy Miss PA, Asst.Lib., Dr.J.H.Burgoyne & Partners, London. [0049317] 21/10/1993
Deaville Mrs AM, (was Southgate), BA, Unemployed. [0038455] 03/05/1985
Debenham Mr BRJ, BSc MCLIP, Employment not known. [0060184] 10/12/2001
Debenham Mrs ZA, (was Griffith), BA MA, E-Learning Lib., Royal Shrewsbury Hosp., NHS Trust. [0056910] 04/11/1998
Debnam Ms A, MCLIP, Retired. [0015687] 30/08/1964
Deboys Mrs JM, (was Fletcher), MA MSc MCLIP, Managing Dir., Quisitor Ltd., Cambridge. [0060766] 12/12/2001
Deegan-Spragg Ms CM, BA MA, Child.Co-ordinator, Knowsley M.B.C. [0038780] 09/10/1985
Deen Miss FA, MSc, Lib., OPEC, Vienna, Austria. [0037607] 03/10/1984
Deering Dr CM, BA PhD MCLIP, Lib., Liverpool Sch.of Tropical Med. [0037245] 04/05/1984
Deering-Punshon Ms SE, (was Deering), BLib MCLIP, Child.Lib., Newbury P.L., W.Berks.Dist.Council. [0021506] 27/10/1973
Defriez Mr PE, MA MCLIP, Database Lib., Dept.of Health L., London. [0026713] 19/10/1976
Del Bono Miss MRS, MA DipIS MCLIP, Lib., R.B.of Kensington & Chelsea, Cent.L., London. [0052643] 15/11/1995
Del-Pizzo Ms JE, MSc(Econ), Lib., 6th Form Cent. [0053343] 14/05/1996
Delahunty Miss S, BA(Hons) MCLIP, Child.Lib., Portsmouth City Council, Cosham L. [0049740] 29/11/1993
Delaney Mrs EA, (was Murphy), MCLIP, Sen.Lib.-Adult Lend., Reading Bor.Council. [0021296] 16/10/1973
Delaney Miss EL, (was Dolman), BA(Hons) MCLIP, Mgr., Document Delivery, GlaxoSmithkline, Herts. [0050908] 31/10/1994
Delaney Mrs H, (was Barkett), BSc HDipEd DLIS, Lib., Rotunda Hosp., Dublin. [0051503] 13/03/1995
Delfolie Miss SC, BA, Resident in Switzerland. [0058189] 15/11/1999
Deliot Ms CA, MA DipILM, Catr., The Brit.L. [0056714] 07/10/1998
Dellar Mr G, MCLIP, Retired. [0016715] 28/09/1948
Dellar Mr MG, MA MCLIP, Learning Res.Adviser, Coll.of N.W.London. [0039669] 30/04/1986
Dellow Miss CJ, BA MCLIP DipInfSc, Unemployed/Career Break. [0028546] 16/01/1978
Delve Mr B, MCLIP, Head of Learning & Inf.Serv., Tameside M.B.C. [0003881] 12/09/1961
Dempsey Mr N, BA DLIS ALAI MCLIP, Vice President, Research, OCLC. [0041053] 06/10/1987
Dempster Miss FM, (was Wellburn), MCLIP, Employment not known. [0017941] 20/11/1963
Dempster Dr JAH, MA PhD MCLIP, Sen.Lib.-Systems Support, Highland Council, Cultural & Leisure Serv. [0020774] 01/07/1973
Dempster Mr SD, Unemployed. [0033808] 06/03/1981
Dendy Revd JW, FCLIP, Retired. [0003885] 01/01/1950 FE 01/01/1967
Dendy Mrs SA, (was Beard), BSc MCLIP, Asst.Lib., The L., European Sch.of Osteopathy, Kent. [0046934] 01/01/1965
Denham Ms DA, (was Bowler), BLib MCLIP, Sen.Lect., Univ.of Cent.England in Birmingham, Sch.of Inf.Studies. [0033724] 09/02/1981
Denham Miss HI, p./t. Inf.Offr./Stud., Cent.L.Walsall, Univ.Central England. [0059490] 09/04/2001
Denham Mrs ME, (was McGovern), MA DipLib MCLIP, Unemployed. [0035161] 23/09/1982
Denham Mrs MF, (was Stanway), BA MCLIP, Sen.Lib., Manchester City Council. [0019280] 01/07/1971
Denholm Miss FM, MA DipLib MCLIP, L.Offr.Yth.Serv., Edinburgh City L. [0043425] 26/10/1989
Denholm Mrs V, MA, p./t.Duty Lib., Univ.of Edinburgh. [0056727] 07/10/1998
Dening Mrs J, BA(Hons), Sch.Lib., St.Aidans C.of E.High Sch., Harrogate. [0057345] 18/02/1999
Denley Ms CA, DipLib, Lib., Askham Bryan Coll., York. [0036595] 25/10/1983
Dennehy Miss MM, BA DipLib MCLIP, Learning Cent.Adviser, Richmond Adult & Comm.Coll, Surrey. [0033995] 30/06/1981
Denner Mr MJ, BA(Hons) DipILS, Document Researcher, UBS Warburg, London. [0053192] 01/04/1996
Denning Mr RTW, BA FCLIP, Retired. [0003888] 08/01/1945 FE 01/01/1959
Dennis Miss AJ, BA MCLIP, Dep.Lib., Inst.of Chartered Accountants, London. [0023882] 11/02/1975
Dennis Mrs F, (was Ali), BLib MCLIP, Unemployed. [0028474] 16/01/1978
Dennis Miss JM, BA MCLIP, Stud., Leeds Metro.Uni. [0025449] 12/01/1976
Dennis Miss N, BSc(Hons) MA MCLIP, Asst.Lib., Faculty of Mgmt.& Business, Univ.Coll.Northampton. [0053740] 18/09/1996
Dennis Ms S, LLB(Hons), Employment not known. [0054282] 15/11/1996
Dennis Ms SE, BA DipLib MCLIP, Head of L.& Inf.Serv., Charles Russell, London. [0033720] 02/01/1981
Dennison Mr PJ, BA(Hons) MSc, L.Systems Admin., Birkbeck Coll.,Univ.of London, London. [0049467] 03/11/1993
Denniss Mr RC, BA FCLIP, Retired. [0003893] 17/02/1947 FE 01/01/1953
Denny Mrs EA, (was Hart), BA(Hons) DipIM MCLIP, Career Break. [0047468] 25/08/1992
Denny Mr GE, BA(Hons) DipInfMgmt, Inf.Mgr., Cadwalader Wickersham & Taft, London. [0051085] 14/11/1994
Denoon Ms CM, MA DipLib MCLIP, L.Serv.Mgr., Greater Glasgow Primary Care NHS, Maria Henderson L. [0043561] 08/11/1989
Dent Mrs AC, LLB DipLIS MCLIP, Sch.Lib., The Heathcote Sch., Stevenage. [0046835] 14/02/1992

Dent Ms CAR, BA(Hons) MLib, Bus.Lib., Bradford Business & Comm.L., W.Yorks. [0038020] 17/01/1985
Dent Miss LM, MA(Hons), Music Lib., BBC Scotland, Glasgow. [0058669] 12/05/2000
Denton Mr D, BSc MCLIP, Employment not known. [0060456] 11/12/2001
Denton Mr JF, MCLIP, Retired. [0003897] 06/07/1966
Denyer Miss J, BA DipLib MCLIP, Hants.Naval Collection Lib., Hants.Co.L.Serv., Gosport. [0038245] 06/02/1985
Deoraj Mrs S, BBIBL, Lib., Durban Metro.L., South Africa. [0061474] 08/08/2002
Depledge Miss AJ, BA(Hons) DPS MA MCLIP, Short Loans & Processing T.Leader, University of Leeds. [0044670] 22/11/1990
Derbyshire Mrs JD, (was Gale), BA PGCE DipLib MCLIP, Sch.Lib., Chichester High Sch.for, Boys, W.Sussex C.C. [0032954] 01/10/1980
Deregowska Mrs EL, BA MCLIP, Unemployed. [0003901] 12/11/1963
Derrett Mrs JA, (was Haigh), BA(Hons) MCLIP, Supply Learning Res.Asst., Thames Valley Univ., Reading. [0025292] 10/11/1975
Deschamps Mrs JA, MCLIP, Retired. [0023158] 28/10/1974
Desimone Mrs AL, BA(Hons), Inf.Asst./p./t.Stud., Univ.Central England. [0059252] 17/01/2001
Detraz Dr M-P, PhD, Executive Sec., C.U.R.L., Univ of Birmingham. [0051125] 17/11/1994
Deunette Miss J, CChem MRIC MCLIP, Employment unknown. [0060269] 10/12/2001
Dev-Modak Mrs R, BA(Hons) MA, Asst.Lib., Dept of Health, London. [0055735] 10/11/1997
Devane Miss PM, BA MCLIP, Asst.Lib.(Ref.& Inf.), Blackburn Cent.L. [0037176] 13/03/1984
Devaney Miss KR, BA DipLib, Acquisitions Team Leader, The Library, Univ.of Reading. [0059890] 29/10/2001
Devas Mrs A, BSc(Hons), Sch.Lib., Wallasey Sch., Moreton. [0054176] 08/11/1996
Devine Ms DM, MA DipLib MCLIP, Dep.Lib., Robert Gordon Univ., Aberdeen. [0034385] 30/10/1981
Devine Mrs FS, BA DipLib MCLIP, Sen.Lib., Longsight L., Manchester Cent.Dist.L. [0021148] 01/10/1973
Devine Mr JG, BA(Hons) MLIS, Inf.Offr., Eversheds, Newcastle upon Tyne. [0061225] 15/04/2002
Devitt Ms B, BSc(Hons), Asst.Inf.Offr., Slaughter and May, London. [0055383] 07/10/1997
Devlalapalli Mrs UM, MSc B.Li.Sc M.Li.Sc, L. Asst., Maria Henderson L., Gartnavel Royal Hosp. [0060891] 20/12/2001
Devlin Ms DI, BA MCLIP, Retired. [0032739] 09/08/1980
Devlin Mrs LM, (was Musgrove), DMS MCLIP, Retired. [0010625] 16/01/1968
Devnally Mr DK, BA DipLib HonFCLIP, Resident Bombay. [0039728] 06/07/1956 FE 13/09/1984
Devonald Ms JA, BA(Hons) MA, p./t.Project Offr., Race Relations Arch., Manchester. [0056889] 02/11/1998
Devonish Miss HE, MA, Lib., Cable & Wireless, Barbados. [0038123] 16/01/1985
Devoy Mrs F, MA DipLib MCLIP, Lib., St Mungos High Sch., Falkirk. [0036236] 15/08/1983
Dewar Miss DR, BA MCLIP, L.& Inf.Offr., Chartered Inst.of Personnel Dev., London. [0020594] 03/05/1973
Dewar Mrs HW, (was Hutchison), MA MCLIP, Client Serv.Lib., Aberdeenshire L.& Inf.Serv., Oldmeldrum. [0021294] 11/10/1973
Dewar Mrs N, (was Perry), BA MCLIP, Lib.,Spec.Serv., N.Yorks.C.C., Skipton. [0041934] 24/05/1988
Dewdney Mrs J, Position unknown, Filton/Downend L., Glos. [0059025] 19/10/2000
Dewe Mrs AJ, BSc FNZLA AALIA MCLIP, Resident in New Zealand. [0060070] 07/12/2001
Dewe Dr MD, MA PhD FCLIP, Retired. [0003918] 28/03/1958 FE 01/01/1968
Dewhirst Mr I, MBE DLitt BA MCLIP, Retired, 14 Raglan Ave., Keighley,W.Yorks,BD22 6BJ. [0003919] 26/01/1959
Dewhurst Mr JA, Stud., John Moores Univ. [0061757] 04/11/2002
Dewhurst Mr SE, (was King), MCLIP, L.Asst., Warrington Bor.Council. [0003920] 01/01/1965
Dewick Mrs GA, BSc(Hons), L.Mgr., Cornwall C.C., Penryn L. [0057387] 26/02/1999 AF
Dews Mrs E, (was Hammond), BA FCLIP, Retired. [0003921] 26/02/1951 FE 01/01/1961
Dextre Clarke Mrs SG, MSc FCLIP, Employment unknown. [0060275] 10/12/2001 FE 01/04/2002
Dhaliwal Mrs BK, (was Dhanda), MCLIP, Lib.(Job Share), Leicester City Council. [0023156] 27/10/1974
Dhamecha Miss GD, BA (Hons), Lib., Kilmarnock Coll., Ayrshire. [0043705] 08/12/1989
Dhawan Ms K, Unemployed. [0051983] 31/08/1995
Dhillon Mrs M, BA(Hons), Stud. [0058395] 01/02/2000
Dholiwar Miss V, MCLIP, Asst.Lib.(Catr.), L.Support Cent., Greenford. [0031814] 15/12/1979
Di Biasio Mr PA, BA, P./t.Stud./L/Asst., Civic Centre, Enfield, Univ.N.London. [0059877] 29/10/2001
Di Gesso Mrs C, (was Winward), MCLIP, Housewife. [0016143] 09/01/1965
Di Tillio Mr C, Funzionario, Biblioteca Provinciale, A.C.De Meis, Chieti, Italy. [0058734] 01/07/2000
Diaper Mrs PH, (was Clark), BLib MCLIP, L.Asst., Fowey L., Cornwall C.C. [0019874] 01/01/1973
Dibben Mr PA, BSc(Hons) MSc MCLIP, Asst.Lib., Croydon Coll. [0048482] 21/01/1993
Dibble Mrs SL, (was Hurford), BLib MCLIP, Learning Res.Cent.Mgr., Churchill Comm.Sch., N.Somerset. [0044629] 12/11/1990
Dibnah Mr ST, FCLIP, Retired. [0003928] 01/01/1936 FE 01/01/1949

225

Dick Miss AM, Inf.Offr., Scottish Envir.Protection Agency, Heriot Watt Res.Park, Edinburgh. [0045620] 04/04/1991
Dick Miss BAM, MA DipLib MCLIP, Local Studies Lib., Whitehaven Record Off.& Local Stud., L., Cumbria Comm.Econ.& Environ. [0027153] 24/01/1977
Dick Mr KT, BA(Hons) DipIS MCLIP, Acting Lib., Norwich Research Park, Norwich. [0054356] 26/11/1996
Dick Miss L, MA, Learning Cent.Co-ordinator, Harrow Coll. [0053966] 16/10/1996
Dick Dr LA, BA(Hons) MA MA PhD, Super., Learning Cent., Sharjah Mens Coll., United Arab Emirates. [0028291] 03/11/1977
Dick Mr M, BA(Hons), Stud., City Univ.London. [0061742] 31/10/2002
Dick Miss MH, MCLIP, Retired. [0003931] 05/02/1952
Dickens Ms ZM, BA(Hons) MA MCLIP, Lib.-Young Peoples Team, R.B.of Windsor & Maidenhead, Maidenhead L. [0053692] 06/09/1996
Dickenson Mrs LJ, Shop Asst., Dornoch Bookshop., Dornoch, Sutherland. [0058693] 02/06/2000
Dicker Mrs C, (was Rawlinson), Lib./Administrator, Lincoln Theological Inst.for the, Study of Religion & Soc.,Sheffield. [0037761] 22/10/1984
Dickerson Ms YB, BA(Hons) DipLib MCLIP, User Serv.Lib., Middlesex Univ., London. [0050767] 17/10/1994
Dickey Miss MT, MCLIP, Sen.Asst.Lib., Battersea Ref.L. [0030614] 19/02/1979
Dickie Mrs KS, (was Milne), MA DipLib MCLIP, Sen.L.Asst., Heriot-Watt Univ.L., Edinburgh. [0010196] 12/01/1968
Dickins Ms JK, BA, Lib.:Records & Research Cent., Shropshire C.C., Shrewsbury. [0038394] 16/04/1985
Dickins Mr LGE, BA MCLIP, Princ.Lib.,Young People & Access, Shropshire Co.L. [0003938] 01/02/1972
Dickinson Mrs A, (was Bacon), MCLIP, Lib., Netherhall Sch., Cambridge. [0000559] 01/01/1971
Dickinson Miss E, BA MCLIP, Retired. [0013246] 01/01/1961
Dickinson Mrs FA, (was English), MCLIP, Lib., Stud., Open Univ., (Law). [0021805] 01/01/1963
Dickinson Mrs J, MA DipLRCM, LRC Mgr., George Stephenson High Sch., Newcastle upon Tyne. [0053465] 01/07/1996
Dickinson Mr PJ, MCLIP, Employment not known. [0060276] 10/12/2001
Dickinson Mr T, OBE HonFCLIP, Hon.Fellow. [0046052] 11/09/1991 FE 11/09/1991
Dickinson Mrs TA, (was West), BA MCLIP, Young Peoples Serv.Lib., Torbay L.Serv., Torquay Cent.L. [0046877] 20/02/1992
Dickinson Miss TJ, L.Asst., E.Cheshire NHS Trust, Macclesfield Dist.Gen.Hosp. [0055579] 21/10/1997
Dicks Mrs KC, (was Jaquest), MCLIP, Prison Lib., H.M.P.Wellingborough, Northants. [0003942] 04/01/1967
Dicks Mrs KL, (was Giles), BA DipLib MCLIP, Full-time Mother, 66 The Lanes, Over, Cambridge, CB4 5NQ. [0042893] 04/04/1989
Dicks Mrs SM, (was Lizius), BSc MCLIP, Inf.Offr., NHS Direct E.Mids., Nottingham. [0041918] 20/05/1988
Dickson Mrs AE, Sen.L.Asst., Queen Margaret Univ.Coll., Edinburgh. [0058360] 24/01/2000 **AF**
Dickson Miss CD, MCLIP, Inf.Serv.Advisor, Napier Univ., Edinburgh. [0032414] 02/04/1980
Dickson Miss DM, FCLIP, Life Member. [0003944] 17/02/1951 FE 01/01/1964
Dickson Mrs E, (was Clarke), BA DipLib MCLIP, Asst.Lib., S.E.L.B., Armagh, N.Ireland. [0033650] 01/02/1981
Dickson Miss EM, BSc MCLIP, Asst.Lib., Univ.of Ulster, Jordanstown. [0003946] 07/10/1970
Dickson Miss IA, MA MCLIP, Comm.Lib., Fife Council, Cent.Area Ls. [0021275] 10/10/1973
Dickson Mr J, MA DipLib MCLIP, Lib., Falkirk Council L.Serv., L.Support, Falkirk. [0024651] 30/09/1975
Dickson Mr JCM, MCLIP, Asst.Document Mgr., World Trade Organisation (WTO), Geneva, Switzerland. [0029634] 10/10/1978
Dickson Miss JJ, BSc(Hons) MCLIP, Asst.Lib., Herbert Smith, London. [0051690] 15/05/1995
Dickson Mrs M, MA MCLIP, Asst.Lib., Aberdeen City L., Business & Tech.Dept. [0024652] 06/10/1975
Dickson Miss MG, MA MCLIP, Life Member. [0003949] 12/10/1964
Dickson Mrs MG, (was MacAngus), MA MCLIP, Sch.Lib.(Job-Share)., Edinburgh Dist.Council. [0003947] 01/01/1969
Dickson Mrs SMT, BA DipLib MCLIP, Lib., Craigroyston Comm.High Sch., City of Edinburgh Council. [0056198] 01/04/1998
Dienelt Mr O, DipLib MCLIP, Lib., Inst.fuer Baustoffe, Tech.Univ.of, Braunschweig, Germany. [0042897] 18/04/1989
Dieneman Mrs ML, (was Oka), MA DipLib HDipEd MCLIP, L.Asst., Univ.of Wales Aberystwyth. [0021386] 01/11/1973
Digby Mr AR, MA, Lib., Dept.of Soc.Security. [0059436] 23/03/2001
Diggins Ms CA, Acquisitions Asst., L.Support Cent., Perivale. [0045288] 01/10/1990 **AF**
Diggle Mr AH, BSc MBA MCLIP, Consultant, Self-employed, London. [0023176] 02/11/1974
Digney Mr JF, BA DipILS, Stud. [0044795] 21/11/1990
Dike Mrs MC, (was Elton), MCLIP, Child.& Y.Serv.Lib., Bor.of Poole, Dorset. [0024207] 12/05/1975
Dillingham Ms SL, DipIS, Inf.Offr., Freshfields Bruckhaus Deringer, London. [0052868] 01/01/2001
Dillon Mr C, BA, Inf.Asst., Investec, London. [0049524] 10/11/1993
Dillon Miss KMW, BA(Hons), Unemployed. [0049468] 03/11/1993
Dillon Miss LJ, BA PGDip, Inf.Offr., Linklaters, London. [0048388] 18/12/1992
Dillon Mrs M, BA DipLib MCLIP, Inf.Offr., Standard Bank London Ltd., London. [0035902] 02/02/1983
Dimelow Mr MG, BA DipLib MCLIP, Princ.L.Offr., Cent.L., Northumberland. [0018633] 01/01/1972
Dimmock Ms E, MCLIP, Employment not known. [0060839] 12/12/2001

Dimond Ms AL, LLB ACA MA, Position Unknown, Univ.of Bristol. [0058467] 23/02/2000
Dimond Mrs AM, DipLib MCLIP, Sen.Subject Lib.for Health, Middlesex Univ., Enfield Campus. [0036060] 02/04/1983
Dina Mrs OA, BA MA LLB MLS, Law Lib., Coll.of the Bahamas Law L., Nassau. [0053464] 01/07/1996
Dine Mr DG, MCLIP, Retired. [0003962] 24/08/1951
Dines Miss AM, BSc MA, Inf.Offr., Nat.Poisons Inf.Serv., London. [0049758] 02/12/1993
Dingle Mrs SJ, MLitt, Unemployed. [0039539] 18/02/1986
Dingley Mrs PO, BA MCLIP, Head of L., Sci.Mus., London. [0003964] 31/10/1971
Dinsdale Mrs DIM, (was Burroughs), MCLIP, Life Member. [0002140] 31/12/1932
Dionisi Mrs AM, (was MacNair), MA, [0058640] 25/04/2000
Distin Ms JA, BSc(Hons), L.Mgr., Saltash L., Cornwall. [0057542] 28/04/1999
Ditchburn Mrs R, (was Moore), BA MCLIP, Sch.Lib., Colonel Frank Seely Sch., Notts. [0003973] 01/01/1966
Ditri Miss MC, Career Break. [0036120] 07/02/1983
Divers Mrs M, (was Stein), MCLIP, Life Member. [0003975] 01/01/1950
Dix Mr PA, BA MCLIP, Div.Lib., Cent.Div., Hants Co.L. [0003977] 04/02/1960
Dix Ms PE, BA MCLIP, Head, Educ.L.Serv., L.B.Islington. [0024338] 01/07/1975
Dixon Mrs AL, (was Wilson), BA(Hons) MA MCLIP, Sen.L.Asst., Nottingham Univ., Jubilee Campus. [0056642] 01/10/1998
Dixon Mrs AP, (was Rowlands), MCLIP, Sen.Lect., Univ.of Northumbria at Newcastle. [0027717] 01/01/1967
Dixon Mr AT, MA LLM, Inf.Mgr., TLT Solicitors, Bristol. [0043395] 19/10/1989
Dixon Mrs AW, (was Cheesley), BA MCLIP, Asst.Lib., Batley L., Kirklees M.B.C. [0041189] 19/10/1987
Dixon Miss BA, BA MCLIP, Sen.L.Asst.(Catg.), Univ.of Sheffield. [0003979] 06/01/1970
Dixon Ms CA, BA(Hons), Copyright Lib., Inst.of Educ., Newsam L., London. [0056955] 13/11/1998
Dixon Ms D, BA MPhil DipLib MCLIP, Stud., Univ.Coll.London. [0018636] 18/10/1969
Dixon Mrs DA, (was Hume), BA MCLIP, p./t.Lib., Newcastle City L., Newcastle upon Tyne. [0024090] 13/03/1975
Dixon Miss ED, Super., Templeman L., Univ.of Kent, Canterbury. [0047216] 08/06/1992 **AF**
Dixon Mr G, BA(Hons) MCLIP, Life Member, 93 Carcluie Cres., Ayr, KA7 4SZ, Tel:01292 441547. [0003980] 27/06/1950
Dixon Miss IL, MCLIP, Retired. [0003981] 30/03/1944
Dixon Miss J, Asst. Lib., Kennedys, London. [0060938] 10/01/2002
Dixon Mr J, BA MCLIP, Area Mgr., Barnet P.L. [0022421] 17/04/1974
Dixon Mrs JE, (was Preece), MCLIP, Planning Devel.Mgr., Customer Serv.L.& Inf., Bath & N.E.Somerset. [0021768] 09/01/1974
Dixon Mrs JS, BA(Hons) MA PhD PGCE, Asst.Lib., Food Standards Agency, London. [0056136] 05/03/1998
Dixon Mr KA, MA MA MCLIP, Sci.Inf.Offr., IOM., Edinburgh. [0038193] 30/01/1985
Dixon Mrs MLR, (was Banks), MCLIP, Retired. [0003987] 01/10/1945
Dixon Miss MW, BA MCLIP, Trainee Lib., L.B.of Sutton L. [0022165] 18/02/1974
Dixon Mr NJ, BA(Hons), Stud., Manchester Met.Univ. [0061016] 01/02/2002
Dixon Mr P, BSc MSc FIMgt MCLIP, Employment unknown. [0060274] 10/12/2001
Dixon Mrs R, BA, p./t.Stud./Learn Direct Admin., Univ.Central Eng., Gloscat, Gloucestershhire. [0057626] 07/06/1999
Dixon Mrs R, MA DipLib MCLIP, L.Mgr., Eastern Counties Newspapers, Norwich. [0039531] 13/02/1986
Dixon Miss RP, MCLIP, Retired. [0003989] 01/01/1964
Dixon Mr SM, BA(Hons) MA MCLIP, Head of Web & Learning Tech., Newman Coll., Birmingham. [0051659] 01/05/1995
Dixon Mrs SM, (was Patterson), BA MCLIP, Mgr.(Job Share), African-Caribbean Serv., Walsall L.Serv. [0047885] 23/10/1992
Dlugoszewska Mrs LJ, (was Twomlow), BA MCLIP, L.Asst., Northants.C.C. [0029290] 15/05/1978
Dmytriw Mr D, MSc BSc(Hons), Stud., Univ.of Northumbria at Newcastle. [0061617] 03/10/2002
Dobb Mr CR, BA MCLIP, L.Serv.Devel.Mgr., Putney L., Wandsworth Bor.Council. [0029636] 05/10/1978
Dobbing Mr RM, MA BA MCLIP, Lib.:Inf.& I.T.Serv., Doncaster L.& Inf.Serv., Cent.L. [0019983] 09/01/1973
Dobbins Mrs DA, (was Kirk), BA(Hons) MCLIP, Database Indexer/Ed., Business Database Production, Sidcup. [0041645] 02/08/1988
Dobbins Ms SL, BA(Hons) MCLIP, Alliance Co-ordinator, Durham & Teesside Workforce Devel., Stockton on Tees. [0036631] 18/10/1983
Dobby Mrs PA, (was Mulvanny), MCLIP, Sen.Lib.:Young People, Maidenhead L., Royal Bor.of Windsor & Maidenhead. [0004000] 22/01/1968
Dobby Miss PC, BA MCLIP, Lib., Royal Town Planning Inst., London. [0004001] 01/01/1967
Dobie Mrs HD, (was Paterson), MA DipLib MCLIP, Not library-related. [0028116] 04/10/1977
Dobson Ms A, Learning Res.Mgr., East Norfolk Sixth Form Coll. [0059895] 30/10/2001 **AF**
Dobson Mrs AB, (was Maule), BA MCLIP, Lib., Clifton High Jun.Sch. [0020172] 30/10/1978
Dobson Mrs CM, (was Sparkes), BA PGCE MCLIP, Sen.Lib., N.Yorks.Sch.L.Serv. [0022444] 10/05/1974
Dobson Miss E, MA FCLIP, Life Member. [0004005] 02/02/1954 FE 01/01/1968
Dobson Miss G, BA(Hons) MCLIP, Childcare Inf.Adviser, Bolton Metro., Cent.L. [0042050] 19/08/1988

Dobson Mrs KL, BSc(Hons) DipLIS MCLIP, Sen.Asst.Lib.-Lend.Serv., Harris L., Preston, Lancs. [0058581]   05/04/2000
Dobson Mrs L, BSc(Hons), Sen.Lib.Asst., Durham C.C. [0058662]   09/05/2000
Dobson Miss LN, MA, Grad.Trainee, St.Deiniols L., Flintshire. [0059849]   16/10/2001
Dobson Mrs M, (was Wilkinson), MCLIP, Sch.L.Asst., St.Anthonys Girls School, Sunderland. [0037229]   18/03/1962
Dobson Mr NF, BA DipLib MCLIP, Lib., Essex C.C., Loughton. [0041429]   09/12/1987
Dobson Mrs P, (was Coverdale), BA(Hons) MCLIP, Resident in Germany. [0039354]   13/01/1986
Dobson Ms PJ, BA(Hons) DipLib MCLIP, H.of Inf.Serv., Leeds L.& Inf.Serv. [0035144]   27/08/1982
Dobson Mrs R, (was Gray), MCLIP, Retired. [0005841]   07/02/1961
Dobson Mrs R, (was Dempsey), MA, Asst.Lib., the Brit.Museum, Cent.L.,London. [0054327]   15/11/1996
Dobson Miss SE, BA MCLIP, Intranet Mgr., King Sturge, Bristol. [0038296]   22/02/1995
Docherty Mrs J, (was Brooks), MA BA MCLIP, Lib., Eccles Coll., Manchester. [0001810]   07/06/1971
Docherty Mr MJ, BA(Hons) MCLIP, Catr., Brit.L., Boston Spa, W.Yorkshire. [0043573]   09/11/1989
Dockeray Mrs LJ, (was Hex), BA, Housewife. [0031044]   24/07/1979
Dockerty Ms C, BSc, Dep.Head of Bibl.Serv., Everetts, London. [0044093]   10/05/1990
Dodd Mr DC, BSc(Hons) MCLIP, Unemployed. [0004018]   01/01/1967
Dodd Miss J, BA(Hons) MA, Unemployed. [0056232]   14/04/1998
Dodd Miss KJ, BMus MSc, Lib., Grays L., Thurrock Council. [0058162]   10/11/1999
Dodd Mrs M, (was Lyons), Site Learning Res.Co-ordinator, Barnet Coll., London. [0004024]   15/01/1966
Dodd Miss S, BSc MA, Website Mgr., Trade Partners UK, London. [0059101]   15/11/2000
Dodd Mr TC, BA DipLib MCLIP, Lib., Brit.Council L., Milano, Italy. [0032920]   10/10/1980
Dodds Mr D, BA(Hons) DipLib MCLIP FRSA, H.of Collection Mgmt., Nat.Art L., Victoria & Albert Museum, London. [0032246]   21/02/1980
Dodds Mr IM, BSc(Hons) MA DipIS MCLIP, Reading Re-mix Project Mgr., L.B.Bromley, Cent.L. [0051464]   24/02/1995
Dodds Mr JC, FCLIP, Life Member. [0004030]   24/09/1951
FE 18/11/1998
Dodds Mrs P, (was Cunningham), BA(Hons), Head of Tech.Serv., Univ.of Newcastle. [0049951]   28/01/1994
Dodds Mr SC, IT & L.Mgr., Shepherd Design, York. [0059782]   02/10/2001
Dodge Miss ER, BA, Inf.Asst./Asst.Ed., Paperbase, PIRA Internat., Leatherhead. [0052601]   13/11/1995
Dodgson Mrs CE, (was Drinkall), Unemployed. [0048966]   05/08/1993
Dodgson Mrs J, (was Turner), MCLIP, Life Member. [0004032]   28/01/1946
Dodgson Sarah J, MA MCLIP, Lib., The Athenaeum, London. [0039548]   26/02/1986
Dodhia Miss H, L.Asst., NCH, London. [0057143]   21/12/1998
AF
Dodshon Miss JA, BA(Hons) DipLib, Site Lib., Univ.of Sunderland, Ashburne L. [0045517]   28/02/1991
Dodson Mrs ER, BA DipLib MCLIP, Head of L./Resources p./t., Myton Sch., Warwick, Warks. [0030152]   17/01/1979
Dodsworth Mrs JH, (was Coad), BA MCLIP, Sch.Secretary, Rotherham M.B.C. [0004033]   11/10/1972
Doe Ms SE, DipLib MCLIP, L.Mgr., Sidley Austin, Brown & Wood, London. [0044288]   15/08/1990
Doel Mrs JD, (was Boynton), BSc MSc MBIRA MCLIP, Employment not known. [0060746]   12/12/2001
Dogar Mrs SA, Stud., Oxford Coll.of F.E. [0061111]   21/02/2002
Doggett Ms J, (was Green), BA(Hons) MCLIP, Sen.Team Lib., Sch.L.Serv., Gloucester. [0004037]   14/01/1969
Doggrell Miss CJ, Sen.Asst.Lib., Wellcome Trust, London. [0037363]   15/07/1984
Dogterom Miss ME, Lib., Westeinde Hosp., The Hague. [0046198]   10/10/1991
Doherty Mr A, MA PgDipILS, Learning Res.Asst., S.Bank Univ., London. [0056502]   28/07/1998
Doherty Mr AF, MCLIP, Academic Co-ordinator, Health Studies, Univ.of Plymouth. [0022740]   02/09/1974
Doherty Ms CE, BA MCLIP, Dep.Lib., Stranmillis Univ.Coll., Belfast. [0004040]   08/07/1971
Doherty Mrs HJ, (was Sunderland), BA MCLIP, Dist.Lib., D.C.C., Derbys. [0004041]   01/01/1972
Doherty Mrs HS, (was Sidney), BA, Inf.Offr., Scottish Mus.Council, Edinburgh. [0043410]   01/01/1969
Doherty Mr J, BSc MCLIP, L.& Inf.Serv.Mgr., Angus Council Cult.Serv., Forfar. [0021691]   09/01/1974
Doherty Mrs K, (was O'Grady), MCLIP, Unemployed. [0020202]   20/02/1973
Doherty Mrs MP, (was Booth), MCLIP, Coll.Lib., St Bede's Col., Manchester. [0004042]   29/09/1969
Doherty Miss S, BA(Hons) MSc MA, Customer Serv.Lib., Medicines Control Agency, London. [0053970]   16/10/1996
Doherty Allan Ms R, (was Doherty), BA MA, Lib., Thornhill Coll., Co.Londonderry. [0054702]   06/03/1997
Doig Miss C, MA(Hons) DipILS MCLIP, Lib., Bell Baxter High Sch., Fife. [0054391]   02/12/1996
Doig Mr C, BA(Hons) PGDipLIS MCLIP, Child.Lib., Reading Bor.C. [0055485]   15/10/1997
Doig Mrs FL, (was Mitchell), MA DipLib MCLIP, p./t. Lib. (User Serv.), Univ.of Dundee. [0026290]   01/10/1983
Doig Mrs MR, (was Tucker), MCLIP, Serials & Inter-Lend.Lib., Univ.of Derby, L.& Res.Cent. [0004044]   19/01/1967

Dolamore Mrs SM, BA(Hons) MA MCLIP, Catr., Brit.L., Boston Spa. [0004046]   01/01/1969
Dolan Mr J, OBE BA MCLIP, Asst.Dir.L.& Inf.Serv., Leisure & Community Servs., Birmingham. [0023907]   21/01/1975
Dolan Miss K, BA(Hons) DipILM MCLIP, Lib., Reading Cent.L. [0055487]   15/10/1997
Dolan Revd MJ, MA FCLIP, Retired. [0004047]   20/01/1956
FE 01/01/1965
Dolben Ms L, BA DipLib MCLIP, Unwaged. [0037097]   14/02/1984
Dolby Mr KW, BSc(Hons) DipILM, Inf.Offr., Wellcome Trust, London. [0050702]   12/10/1994
Dolby Mrs SM, (was Keane), BA(Hons) MA MCLIP, Unemployed. [0046797]   28/01/1992
Dolitzscher Mrs A, MA FCLIP, Retired. [0004050]   25/09/1951
FE 01/01/1959
Dollamore Ms JE, BLIB MCLIP, Sen.Asst.Lib., Univ.of Westminster, Harrow. [0037595]   10/10/1984
Dolman Mr PK, BA(Hons) MCLIP, Head of L.& Learning Cent., Matthew Bolton Coll.of F.& H.E., Birmingham. [0048877]   08/07/1993
Dolman Mr SJ, BA(Hons) MCLIP, Serv.Devel.Lib., Stirling Council, L.H.Q. [0028803]   18/01/1978
Dolphin Ms PM, MA DipLib MCLIP, Lib., Birkbeck Coll. [0004057]   30/07/1970
Dolton Mrs GG, MCLIP, Retired. [0004058]   19/02/1955
Domaniewska-Sobczak Mrs K, MA MCLIP, Retired. [0004059]   01/01/1952
Dominy Mrs R, (was Peacock), BSc MSc MCLIP, Unemployed(Career Break). [0046665]   05/12/1991
Don Miss K, MA DipLib MCLIP, Sch.Lib., Greenfaulds High Sch., Cumbernauld,Glasgow. [0045917]   17/07/1991
Donaghy Mr G, BTech BA(Hons), Stud., Strathclyde Univ. [0061068]   12/02/2002
Donaghy Mrs MD, (was Lewnes), BA MCLIP, Lib., (Maternity Leave), ICL, Birmingham. [0038006]   01/01/1985
Donald Mrs A, MA MCLIP, Lib.,Elgin Academy, The Moray Council, Elgin, Moray. [0024653]   03/10/1975
Donald Mrs AE, (was Green), MCLIP, Br.Lib., Highland Council, Inverness. [0005861]   01/01/1968
Donald Mrs MS, (was Simpson), MA DipLib MCLIP, Sch.Lib., Greenock High Sch., Inverclyde. [0036575]   18/10/1983
Donald Mr P, BLS MCLIP, Inf.Spec., Nottingham Trent Univ., L.& Inf.Servs. [0053507]   10/07/1996
Donaldson Miss A, BA MA, Inf.Specialist, The Nottingham Trent Univ. [0053228]   09/04/1996
Donaldson Ms D, BSc MSc MCLIP, Employment not known. [0060232]   10/12/2001
Donaldson Ms F, MA(Hons) DipLIS MCLIP, Asst.Lib., Univ.of Westminster. [0052727]   28/11/1995
Donaldson Mrs JL, (was Reece), MA DipLib MCLIP, Sch.Lib., Jordanhill Sch., Glasgow. [0037694]   16/10/1984
Donaldson Dr R, MA PhD, Life Member, Tel.0131 667 5954, 18B Mortonhall Rd., Edinburgh, EH9 2HW. [0004070]   23/04/1956
Donaldson Mrs SA, (was Fraser), BSc, L.& Inf.Worker (Yth.), Cent.L., Dundee. [0035600]   10/11/1982
Donegan Mrs CM, (was Smith), MCLIP, Lib., Sacred Heart RC High Sch., Crosby, Merseyside. [0013550]   22/02/1967
Donegani Ms KL, (was Cheetham), BA DipLib MCLIP, Records Mgmt.Consultant, Loughborough. [0032028]   29/01/1980
Doney Ms EJ, BA(Econ) MSc MCLIP, Primary Care Knowledge Mgr., Nottingham City PCT, Res.Cent. [0054268]   12/11/1996
Donkersley Mr ST, L.Asst., GlaxoSmithKline, Dartford, Kent. [0054023]   18/10/1996   **AF**
Donkin Mrs E, BA(Hons) MCLIP, Sch.Lib., Biddick Sch. Tyne & Wear. [0059198]   21/10/2002
Donnan Miss CE, BA, Stud., Northumbria Univ. [0061692]   21/10/2002
Donnelly Mrs A, BA(Hons) MCLIP, Asst.Res.Mgr., Essex L., Chelmsford. [0004075]   21/01/1972
Donnelly Mr AA, BSc MA DipLib MCLIP, Lib.i/c., Glasgow Coll.of Food Tech. [0036879]   01/01/1984
Donnelly Ms AC, BA(Hons) MSc, Sen.L.Asst., Edinburgh Univ., Med.L. [0052217]   15/09/1995
Donnelly Mrs AJ, (was Whitcutt), BA(Hons), Inf.Spec.- Educ.& Training, Unilever Research, Bebington. [0050553]   15/09/1994
Donnelly Mr JE, MA DLIS, Resident in Ireland. [0060117]   10/12/2001
Donnelly Miss KA, BA(Hons) DipILM MCLIP, Asst.Lib., Manchester Met.Univ. [0053383]   03/06/1996
Donnelly Ms KM, BA(Hons) MCLIP, Sen.Lib.Bus.Inf.(Job-share), Bus.Inf.Dept., The Mitchell L., Glasgow. [0037163]   07/03/1984
Donnelly Miss MR, BA DipLib MCLIP, Retired, (020)7229 4439. [0004080]   06/10/1969
Donnelly Miss SJ, MSc MCLIP, Employment unknown. [0060270]   10/12/2001
Donnison Ms M, BA(Hons), Prof.Lib.-Inf.Points, Univ.of Birmingham, Main L. [0057864]   14/09/1999
Donoghue Ms A, BA(Hons) MCLIP, Inf.Adviser, Learning Cent.(City), Sheffield Hallam Univ. [0057739]   15/07/1999
Donoghue Mr SP, BA, Lib. in Charge, London Borough Havering, Harold Wood Library. [0042834]   14/03/1989
Donovan Mrs M, (was Sweeney), MCLIP, Unemployed. [0004085]   30/08/1967
Donovan Mrs M, MBA BA DipLib MCLIP, Policy Offr., Kent C.C., Maidstone. [0037912]   15/11/1984
Doody Mrs AL, (was Johnson), BLS(Hons) MCLIP, L.Adviser, Reading, Berks. [0033533]   01/01/1981
Doody Ms MC, BA MCLIP, p./t.Lib., Inf.Mgmt., Dept.of Health, London. [0028292]   01/11/1977
Doolan Miss LF, BA MA, Inf.Offr., Investec, London. [0048619]   15/03/1993

Dooley Mrs MEA, (was Enser), MCLIP, Lib., Tettenhall Coll., Wolverhampton. [0004088] 06/10/1967
Dorabjee Miss S, BSc MCLIP, Employment unknown. [0060278] 10/12/2001
Doran Miss BM, BA MBA DipLib ALAI, Lib., Royal Coll.of Surgeons in Ireland, The Mercer L. [0022381] 01/04/1974
Doran Ms E, BA MCLIP, Life Member. [0024204] 18/04/1975
Doran Ms JD, BA(Hons) MA, Document Delivery Lib., London Inst.of Fashion. [0058214] 18/11/1999
Doran Miss L, PgD LIS, Inf.Offr., CBI, London. [0055788] 19/11/1997
Doran Mr M, MSc MCLIP, Grp.Lib.:Newry, SELB, Armagh. [0029162] 01/01/1978
Doran Mrs N, LLB MSc(Econ), Asst.Lib., The Bar L., Royal Courts of Justice, Belfast. [0057565] 05/05/1999
Doran Mr PM, BA MCLIP, Retired. [0004091] 05/03/1954
Dorantt Mrs VT, BSc(Hons) MA, Learning Res.Co-ordinator, Barnet Coll. [0053825] 03/10/1996
Dore Mrs JD, (was Tiller), MCLIP, Inf.Lib., Worthing L., W.Sussex C.C. [0022783] 15/10/1974
Dorey Mrs SJ, BA(Hons) DipLib MCLIP, Indexer, B.N.I., Poole, Dorset. [0037047] 01/02/1984
Dorme Mrs KE, BA MCLIP, Retired. [0005357] 01/01/1968
Dorney Mr CG, BA(Hons), p./t.Stud., Loughborough Univ., Rushden L., Northants.C.C. [0061025] 03/02/2002
Dorney Mr PA, BA(Hons) MCLIP, Asst.Lib., Milton Keynes Council. [0052358] 26/10/1995
Dorricott Ms H, BA(Hons) MA MCLIP, Team Lib., Glos.C.C. [0047901] 22/10/1992
Dorrington Miss LF, MCLIP, Life Sci.& Med.Lib., Life Sci.& Med., Imperial Coll., London. [0004096] 04/10/1968
Dory Mr K, BA, Asst.Lib., Internat.Coll., Beirut. [0061323] 22/05/2002
Dossett Ms A, BSc(Hons), Stud., Univ.of Wales, Aberystwyth & L.Asst., Herefordshire Coll.of. Tech., Hereford. [0058391] 28/01/2000
Doubleday Miss PA, BA MCLIP, Retired. [0004099] 22/09/1956
Douch Mrs CE, L.Asst., Sherborne Sch., Macnaghten L., Dorset. [0061528] 13/09/2002 AF
Douch Mr P, BA MCLIP, Stock Serv.Offr., Maidenhead, R.B.of Windsor & Maidenhead. [0032922] 25/10/1980
Dougan Mr DJ, MA(Hons) DipILS, Inf.Serv.Mgr., Scottish Cent.for Infection &, Environ.Hlth., Glasgow. [0046563] 13/11/1991
Doughan Mr DTJ, MBE BA DipEd MIL MCLIP, Retired. [0030153] 11/01/1979
Doughty Mr KA, FCLIP, Retired. [0004103] 27/01/1948 FE 01/01/1957
Doughty Miss SJ, BA(Hons), p./t.Stud./Inf.Asst., Robert Gordon Univ., Aberdeen, Napier Univ., Edinburgh. [0061097] 28/02/2002
Douglas Miss AM, MA FCLIP, Life Member. [0004107] 13/01/1948 FE 01/01/1960
Douglas Ms AM, H.of L.Serv., Tavistock & Portman NHS Trust, London. [0018644] 25/09/1972
Douglas Mrs CAM, (was Decker), BA MCLIP, Unemployed. [0026631] 04/10/1976
Douglas Mr JD, BA(Hons) DipIS MCLIP, Prof.Adviser-Yth.& Sch.L., CILIP. [0051334] 16/01/1995
Douglas Mrs MJ, (was Lower), BA(Hons) MCLIP, Mother. [0031888] 02/01/1980
Douglass Miss RZ, BA(Hons) MSc, Lib., Swindom Bor. Council., Swindon Cent.L. [0057506] 14/04/1979
Doust Mr RW, FCLIP, Lib./Secy., Bulawayo P.L., Zimbabwe. [0018645] 01/03/1962 FE 23/06/1982
Douthwaite Mrs L, (was Hand), BA MCLIP, Asst.Mgr., Clayton L.for Genealogical Res., Houston P.L., U.S.A. [0004115] 23/09/1970
Dovey Mrs BC, BA(Hons), Asst.Lib., Evesham L., Worcs.C.C. [0047218] 08/06/1992
Dovey Mr MJ, BA MSc MCLIP, Employment not known. [0060464] 11/12/2001
Dowd Mr J, BA(Hons), Reg.L.Serv.Consultant, OCLC PICA, Birmingham. [0042737] 24/02/1989
Dowdall Mrs DJ, (was Girling), MCLIP, Unemployed. [0024682] 09/10/1975
Dowdell Mr MT, MCLIP, Retired. [0004122] 27/09/1950
Dowers Mrs LM, MA DipLib MCLIP, Bibl.Serv.Lib., W.Dunbartonshire Council, Dumbarton. [0035340] 08/10/1982
Dowey Mrs EM, (was Thompson), BA(Hons) MCLIP, Lib., PG Med.Cent., Leighton Hosp., Crewe. [0047849] 21/10/1992
Dowie Mrs CL, (was Woodsford), BSc MA, Lib., Lovells, London. [0051309] 12/01/1995
Dowie Mrs KJ, (was Mathieson), MA DipLib MCLIP, Head of L.Serv., Cent.Coll.of Comm., Glasgow. [0035718] 10/01/1983
Dowle Mr TE, BA(Hons) MA, Sen.Learning Res.Asst., S.Bank Univ., London. [0055345] 02/10/1997
Dowley Miss E, BA MCLIP, Sch.Lib., Sch.L.Serv., Sunderland. [0022731] 28/08/1974
Dowling Mr A, BA PhD FCLIP, Life Member. [0004124] 07/03/1957 FE 23/03/1976
Dowling Mrs CA, (was Wotherspoon), MCLIP, Community Lib.(Job Share), Birmingham City Council. [0019695] 19/01/1971
Dowling Ms CA, (was Chandler), BA(Hons) DipLib MCLIP, L.Res.Mgr., Age Concern England, London. [0037015] 30/01/1984
Dowling Mrs HM, (was Tunley), BA MCLIP, Customer Serv.Mgr., L.B.of Islington L.Serv., London. [0038182] 24/01/1985
Dowling Mr IJ, MCLIP, Local Stud.Lib., Cent.L., L.B.of Redbridge. [0004125] 14/05/1972
Dowling Mr JA, BA(Hons), Inf.Offr., CBI, London. [0055628] 28/10/1997
Dowling Mr JH, MCLIP, Asst.Lib., Crosby Ref.L., Sefton M.B.C. [0004126] 18/01/1962
Dowling Ms ME, BA MCLIP, Sen.Asst.Lib., Edinburgh Univ.L. [0004127] 31/07/1965

Dowling Miss SD, BA MCLIP, Retired, Tel:01772 744069. [0004129] 14/03/1962
Dowling Ms TL, BA(Hons) DipIM MCLIP, Lib., Swindon Bor.Council, W.Swindon L. [0055797] 24/11/1997
Down Mrs HJ, (was Borrett), MCLIP, Prison Lib., HMP Channings Wood, Newton Abbot, Devon. [0001495] 15/10/1968
Down Mrs JP, (was Casbolt), BLib MCLIP, Retired. [0032889] 10/10/1980
Downard Mrs KJ, (was Gunter), BA DipILS MCLIP, Lib., Terra Nova Sch., Holmes Chapel, Cheshire. [0043659] 20/11/1989
Downer Mrs DS, (was Harding), MCLIP, Ch.Catr., Waltham Forest P.L. [0020909] 21/08/1973
Downer Miss H, BA MA MCLIP, Asst.Lib., Royal Naval Museum L., Hampshire. [0058104] 27/10/1999
Downes Miss D, BA DipLib MCLIP, Lib., Southwark Coll., London. [0035936] 14/02/1983
Downes Mrs HJ, (was Podlesney), MA MCLIP, Trainee Teacher, Univ.of Northumbria. [0034246] 12/10/1981
Downes Mrs L, (was Hicks), MCLIP, Evesham Comm.Lib., Worcestershire C.C., Evesham. [0004132] 11/01/1968
Downey Mrs LD, (was Thurgur), MCLIP, Lib.-Learning Res., Kent Arts & L., Kings Hill. [0022792] 10/10/1974
Downey Mrs RA, (was Barnett), BA(Hons) MCLIP, Lib., Brentwood Ursuline Convent High, Sch., Essex. [0032255] 05/03/1980
Downham Ms GJ, BA DipLib MCLIP, Princ.L.Asst., Univ.of Surrey, George Edwards L. [0034261] 08/10/1981
Downie Ms CM, BA, Lib., L.B.of Ealing. [0044584] 30/10/1990
Downie Miss GM, BA MCLIP, Br.Lib./Registrar, Lanthorn & E.Calder, W.Lothian Council. [0026095] 06/07/1976
Downie Mrs H, (was O'Hare), BSc MCLIP, Retired. [0004140] 10/02/1965
Downie Mrs LP, (was Christie), BA(Hons), Lib., Angus Council, Brechin High Sch. [0050317] 17/06/1994
Downie Mr P, Unemployed. [0050509] 26/08/1994 AF
Downie Miss PM, MA FCLIP, Retired. [0004141] 01/01/2029 FE 01/01/1948
Downing Miss EAJ, BA MCLIP, Retired. [0016813] 31/08/1945
Downing Ms EM, BA(Hons) MA MCLIP, Sch.Lib., Fortrose Academy, Highland Council. [0048684] 13/04/1993
Downing Miss NB, BSc, Stud., Univ of Wales Aberystwyth. [0061832] 14/11/2002
Downing Mr RC, BA MSc FCLIP, Sen.Inf.Offr., Nat.Foundation for Educ.Research, Slough. [0004145] 05/04/1968 FE 15/02/1989
Downing Miss S, BA(Hons) MA, Internal Comm.Adviser, S.W.of England Reg.Devel.Agency. [0054089] 25/10/1996
Downs Mrs MR, (was Oliver), BSc MCLIP, Unemployed. [0011003] 10/10/1969
Downs Mr S, BA(Hons), Learning Res.Co-ordinator, Academy of Live & Recorded Arts. [0058590] 07/04/2000
Downsborough Mrs JR, (was Fisher), BA MCLIP, Child.Lib., Dronfield L., Derbys.C.C. [0004946] 26/04/1971
Dowson Miss N, BSc(Hons) DipIS MCLIP, Asst.Lib., Surrey Inst.of Art & Design, Epsom Campus. [0052539] 06/11/1995
Doxey Miss SK, BA, Inf.Asst., Lawrence Graham, London. [0059765] 27/09/2001
Doyle Mr A, MCLIP, Life Member. [0004152] 24/08/1953
Doyle Mrs A, (was Besson), BA MCLIP, P./t.Lib., Bromley. [0031788] 14/01/1980
Doyle Dr AI, MA PhD, Retired. [0004153] 01/01/1964
Doyle Mrs GCA, (was Cooper), MCLIP, Lib./Inf.Res.Mgr., King Charles I Sch., Kidderminster. [0021493] 09/10/1973
Doyle Mrs KM, (was Watson), BA MCLIP, Sen.Asst.Lib., L.B.of Havering. [0030059] 17/10/1978
Doyle Mrs L, (was Brock), MCLIP, Unemployed. [0021353] 17/11/1973
Doyle Mrs MG, BA, Princ.L.Asst., Antrim Grp., N.E.E.L.B., Ballymena. [0053320] 09/05/1996 AF
Doyle Ms RA, DMS MCLIP, Scrutiny Mgr., L.B.Merton, Morden. [0025730] 11/03/1976
Doyle Ms SM, BA MCLIP, Retired. [0004157] 09/10/1969
Doyle Ms SP, MCLIP, Devel.Mgr., Social Inclusion, Lambeth L. [0026717] 07/10/1976
Dozier Mrs MF, MA DipILS, Asst.Lib., Univ.of Edinburgh. [0052184] 12/10/1995
Dracup Miss JB, BSc MCLIP, Lib., Hartland Sch., Notts. [0028806] 25/01/1978
Draffin Ms AM, BA DipLib MCLIP, Lib., The Coll.of Law, Guildford, Surrey. [0029638] 03/10/1978
Drage Mrs JM, (was Seaman), BSc MCLIP, Research Lib., Univ.of Luton. [0004159] 04/10/1966
Drake Miss C, BA(Hons) MSc(Econ) MCLIP, Database Lib., News Internat., London. [0054366] 25/11/1996
Drake Mr LS, MA MCLIP, Res.Mgmt.Lib., Univ.of Ulster, Antrim. [0004163] 17/10/1966
Drake Mrs PMB, (was Smith), MCLIP, Team Lib.-Job Share, Metro.Bor.of Wirral, Upton Br.L. [0004165] 02/03/1964
Draper Mr D, Employment unknown. [0060327] 10/12/2001
Drayton Mrs AC, L. Asst., Marsh Jackson Educ. Cent. [0060992] 28/01/2002
Drayton Mrs CE, (was Parr), MCLIP, p./t.Asst.Lib., Sch.L.Serv., Northants.L.& Inf.Serv. [0004172] 01/01/1966
Drazin Mrs CA, (was Freeman), MCLIP, Resident in U.S.A. [0024491] 11/08/1975
Dredge Rev DJ, BA MCLIP, Life Member. [0004173] 01/09/1967
Dredge Mrs M, MA DipLIS MCLIP, Lib., Arbroath High Sch., Angus. [0036606] 17/10/1983
Dreher Mrs RM, BA MCLIP, Purbeck Lib., Wareham L., Dorset Co.L. [0027546] 16/05/1977
Drever Ms RM, MA DipLib MCLIP, Mgr., Sch.L.Serv., E.Sussex. [0037531] 01/10/1984

Personal Members

Drew Miss GM, BA MCLIP, Inf.Offr., Bovis Lendlease Pharmaceutical Ltd, Elstead. [0004178]   25/07/1967
Drew Mrs HP, (was Moore), BSc MCLIP MA, Asst.Lib., New Coll.Durham. [0025080]   11/11/1975
Drew Dr JA, BA MSc MCLIP PhD, Employment not known. [0036497]   13/10/1983
Drew Mrs PA, (was Hayman), MCLIP, Lib., Coppenhall High Sch., Crewe, Cheshire. [0004180]   15/12/1965
Drew Mr PNH, BA(Hons) DipLib MLib MCLIP, H.of Acad.L.Serv., Bath Spa Univ.Coll. [0004181] 01/01/1971
Drew Mrs SG, (was Noble), BLib MCLIP, Comm.L.Mgr., Langley L., Sandwell M.B.C. [0019783]   30/10/1972
Drewett Mrs AJ, (was Lucas), MCLIP, Head of Profession.Support, Min.of Defence, London. [0021912]   04/02/1974
Drewett Mr FPH, MCLIP, Off.Mgr., Staywarm Heating, Exeter. [0018046] 11/10/1972
Drewett Mrs WM, FCLIP, Life Member, 5 Portway, N.Marston, Buckingham, MK18 3PL. [0004184]   11/01/1951   FE 07/01/1982
Drewitt Mrs BL, (was Baker), MCLIP, Lib.-Inf.& Lending Servs., Worcs.C.C., Evesham L. [0004185]   27/01/1965
Drewitt Mr DJ, BA MCLIP, Princ.Lib.-Inf.Serv., Worcs.C.C. [0004186] 27/02/1961
Drewry Mrs EM, (was Stebbing-Allen), MCLIP, Retired, USA. [0016815] 13/03/1963
Drewry Mr N, Clerical Asst., L.B.of Bromley. [0051630]   20/04/1995 AF
Drewry Mrs TI, BA MCLIP, Lib., Doha Coll., Qatar. [0036802]   01/01/1984
Driels Ms J, (was Andrews), BA MCLIP, Team Leader-Inf.Policy, Highways Agency, London. [0004187]   01/01/1967
Driffield Mrs EM, (was Read), BA(Hons), L.Asst., Trinity & All Saints, Horsforth., Leeds. [0034940]   14/05/1982
Dring Mrs AM, (was Brett), MCLIP, Lib., Wymondham High Sch., Norfolk. [0001680]   06/01/1971
Drinkwater Miss CE, MA MCLIP, Asst.Lib., Inst.of Educ.L., London. [0025521]   10/02/1976
Drinkwater Mrs M, MA MCLIP, Sch.L.Serv.Mgr., Leeds Sch.L.Serv. [0004190]   16/09/1971
Driscoll Ms MC, BA DipLib MCLIP, Early Years/Child.Inf.Co-ordinator, Colwyn Bay L., Conwy Co.Bor.Council. [0034188]   15/10/1981
Driskell Mr AMB, BA MCLIP, Resident Overseas. [0004192]   09/06/1969
Driver Mr EHC, MSc FCLIP, Life Member, 18 Warwick Dr., Houghton-Le-Spring, Tyne & Wear, DH5 8JR, Tel.0191 584 5449. [0004194] 05/01/1937   FE 01/01/1956
Driver Miss KA, BA, Sen.L.Asst., Kings Coll.London, Univ.of London. [0040464]   03/02/1987
Driver Ms T, BA DipLib MCLIP, Asst.Lib., Religious Soc.of Friends, London. [0034263]   20/10/1981
Drodge Mrs CA, (was Baker), BA MCLIP, Grp.Lib.p/t., Leics.C.C. [0021423] 17/09/1973
Droogmans Ms LS, (was Murray), BA MCLIP PGDipHRM, Site Lib., De Montfort Univ., DMU Bedford L. [0038877]   15/10/1985
Drozdziak Miss KA, BA(Hons), Stud., Northumbria Univ. [0061686] 21/10/2002
Druce Ms I, BSc(Hons) MLInf MCLIP, L.Mgr., Golders Green L., London. [0042286]   12/10/1988
Drumm Mr PS, BA(Hons) MSc(Econ) MCLIP, Asst.Lib., Norfolk Studies, Norfolk C.C. [0054378]   25/11/1996
Drummond Mrs BA, Temp.Asst.Lib., Catterbridge Cent.for Oncology, Wirral, Merseyside. [0054609]   31/01/1997
Drummond Mr GN, MBE MCLIP, Retired. [0004199]   01/01/1957
Drummond Mr H, BA MCLIP, Project Mgr., Univ.of Wolverhampton. [0004200]   05/02/1974
Drummond Mrs JD, BA MCLIP, Freelance. [0004202]   01/01/1970
Drummond Mrs M, (was Shaw), BA(Hons) MCLIP, Co-ordinator Customer Serv., Floreat L., W.Australia. [0022467]   20/05/1974
Drummond Miss OF, MCLIP, Retired. [0004204]   25/09/1967
Drummond Ms SE, BA (Hons), Sch.Lib., Royal Blind Sch., Edinburgh. [0057028]   26/11/1998
Drury Miss JC, BA(Hons) MA MCLIP, Asst.Lib., Univ.of Nottingham. [0052279]   23/10/1995
Drury Mrs ME, (was Shawe), BA MCLIP, Child.Reading Devel.Lib., Kirklees Cult.Serv., Huddersfield. [0004207]   29/09/1969
Drury Mrs MH, (was Pearson), MCLIP, Inf.Lib., Trafford M.B.C. [0004206] 01/01/1969
Drury Mrs MI, (was Selby), BA MCLIP, Lib., Rotherham P.L. [0004208] 01/01/1969
Drury Mr RA, BA MCLIP, L.Offr., W.Div., Edinburgh City L. [0032927] 24/10/1990
Drury Ms S, MEd BA MCLIP, L.& Learning Res.Mgr., Southgate Coll. [0004211]   30/01/1961
Drury Ms SM, (was Palliser), BA MPhil MCLIP, Business Researcher & Analyst, Self-Employed. [0011163]   19/07/1972
Drust Mrs WV, (was Beer), BA MCLIP, Princ.Lib., Bibl.Serv., Co.L., W.Sussex. [0032633]   04/06/1980
Dryburgh Mrs RF, (was Sutherland), MA DipLib MCLIP, Asst.Lib., L.H.Q., Midlothian Council. [0030550]   05/02/1979
Du Miss MA, BSc (Hons), Asst.Lib./Stud., City of London Sch.L. [0059433] 15/03/2001
Dua Mr ED, MCLIP, Life Member. [0004215]   25/02/1958
Dubber Mrs EHS, BA MCLIP, Asst.Co.Lib., Glos.Co.L.Arts & Mus.Serv. [0004216]   18/11/1971
Dubber Dr MJ, (was Williams), BA MLS PhD MCLIP, L.Asst./Helper Lunch Time, Wood Green Sch. [0031501]   01/10/1979
Dubois Mr P, MA MBCS FCLIP, Position unknown, Internat.Coffee Organisation, London. [0060279]   10/12/2001   FE 01/04/2002
Duce Mrs MP, (was Robertson), MA MCLIP, Retired. [0012545]   15/09/1967

Duck Mrs MA, (was Rowson), MCLIP, Life Member. [0004221]   21/02/1938
Ducker Mrs AJ, Learning Res.Co-ordinator., Knowsley Comm.Coll. [0056706]   01/10/1998
Ducker Mr JM, MA MBCS FCLIP, Employment not known. [0060767] 12/12/2001   FE 01/04/2002
Duckett Mrs PN, (was Evans), BSc MA MSc MCLIP, Coll.Lib., Leeds Coll.of Building. [0004223]   13/10/1966
Duckett Mr RJ, MA MCLIP, Ref.Lib., Bradford L. [0004224]   03/10/1963 FE 27/05/1992
Duckworth Mrs A, (was McBride), BA MCLIP, Acad.Serv.Mgr., Liverpool Hope Univ.Coll. [0035829]   17/01/1983
Duckworth Mrs C, (was Mansley), BA MCLIP, p./t.Local Studies Lib., Lancs.Co.L., Accrington L. [0019325]   10/10/1972
Duckworth Mrs CI, (was Duddy), BA DipLib MCLIP, Asst.Lib., Bexley London Bor. [0043938]   27/02/1990
Duckworth Mr JC, BA(Hons), Sales Asst., Tesco Stores. [0060883] 18/12/2001
Duckworth Mrs SJ, (was Ramsden), BA(Hons) MCLIP, Comm.Lib., Ashford L., Kent C.C. [0049189]   12/10/1993
Dudek Mrs JL, (was Pettigrew), BLib MCLIP, P./t.Bookseller, Ottakars plc., Kendal, Cumbria. [0011585]   06/03/1969
Dudley Mr EP, HonFCLIP FCLIP, Editorial Consultant. [0004228]   16/02/1937 FE 01/01/1953
Dudley Ms JS, MCLIP, Learning Resources Asst., Southampton Inst., Southampton. [0004229]   14/01/1971
Dudley Ms K, BSc(Hons), Stud., City Univ., London & , L.Asst., L., John Innes Cent., Norwich Research Cent., Norwich. [0056977]   17/11/1998
Dudley Miss LA, Modern Apprentice/L.Asst., Harborne L., Birmingham. [0058016]   01/10/1999
Dudley Mr PE, BEd(Hons) MA MCLIP, Teacher, Leys Primary Sch., Dagenham. [0056938]   06/11/1998
Dudman Miss JA, BSc MSc, L.Researcher, Self-emp., London. [0046159] 03/10/1991
Dudman Mr PV, BA(Hons) MSc(Econ) MCLIP, Sen.Catg.& Arch.Asst., St.Georges Med.Sch., London. [0055112]   15/07/1997
Duerden Miss MG, MCLIP, Retired. [0004231]   27/09/1955
Duff Mr HAM, MA M LITT MCLIP, Lib., Gleniffer High Sch., Paisley. [0028426]   01/12/1977
Duffield Dr RJ, BSc PhD CChem MRSC MCLIP, Employment not known. [0060252]   12/12/2001
Duffin Mrs GM, MCLIP BA DMS, Princ.Asst.Lib., S.E.Educ.& L.Board H.Q., N.Ireland. [0018044] 16/01/1972
Duffin Ms JK, (was Gunn), MCLIP, Internal Knowledge Offr., The Industrial Soc., London. [0026874]   20/12/1976
Duffus Miss J, BA(Hons), Lib., S.Birmingham Coll. [0052010]   08/09/1995
Duffy Mrs AJ, (was Garner), BA MCLIP, Inf.Serv.Mgr., Westminster L. [0004236]   03/01/1965
Duffy Mr DA, BA MCLIP, Head of Cent.& Support Serv., Met.Bor.of Calderdale, Leisure Serv., L.Div., Halifax. [0034514]   02/10/1981
Duffy Mrs DG, (was Hirst), BA MCLIP, Electronic Inf.Lib., Bradford Coll. [0031639]   18/10/1979
Duffy Mrs EP, (was Barlow), MCLIP, Retired. [0045592]   01/01/1957
Duffy Mr JO, BA MSc, Asst.Lib., Oireachtas Eireann, Dublin. [0058081] 25/10/1999
Duffy Miss K, PGDipILS, Inf.Offr., Univ.of Abertay, Dundee. [0061260] 10/05/2002
Duffy Mr M, MCLIP, L.Team Mgr.-S., Comm.Serv.Dept., S.Glos.Council. [0023301]   19/11/1974
Duffy Mr M, MA PgDip ILS, Asst.Lib./Website Administrator, Dept.for Work & Pensions, London. [0059437]   23/03/2001
Duffy Mrs M, (was Watson), BA MCLIP, Lib., PG.Med.Cent.L., S.Tyneside Dist.Hosp. [0004240]   06/01/1966
Duffy Miss MF, BA (hons) MA, Lib., Army and Navy Club., London. [0060914] 10/01/2002   AS 19/09/2002
Duffy Mrs PA, MA DipLib MCLIP, Team Lib., Glasgow C.C. [0033506] 14/01/1981
Duffy Mr PJ, BA(Hons), Lib., Hammond Suddards Edge, Manchester. [0051561]   01/04/1995
Duffy Mr RA, BA FCLIP, Retired. [0004242]   24/10/1938 FE 01/01/1953
Duffy Miss SM, MA(Hons) CertEd, Inf.& Res.Mgr., ASH Scotland, Edinburgh. [0054903]   06/05/1997   AF
Duffy Ms SM, (was Morris), BA MCLIP, Asst.Tech.Servs.Lib., King's Fund, London. [0022114]   11/03/1974
Dufty Miss ED, BA(Hons) DipLIS MCLIP, Inf.Cent.Mgr., Wilsons, Salisbury. [0048114]   09/11/1992
Dugan Mrs JE, (was Lovell), BSc MCLIP, Unemployed. [0019485]   21/01/1969
Dugdale Mrs C, BA DipLIS MA MCLIP, Unemployed. [0051752]   20/06/1995
Dugdale Mr CE, BA MA, Nursing & Allied Health Lib., Imperial Coll.of Sci.Tech.& Med., London. [0061423] 08/07/2002
Duggan Mrs CA, (was Coen), MA DipLib MCLIP, Sessional Tutor, Comm.Educ., Glasgow. [0043527]   03/11/1989
Duggan Ms KA, BA MCLIP, Offr., Univ.of Northumbria at Newcastle. [0040753]   29/05/1997
Duggan Mr MI, B.Ed(Hons), Stud., Somerset Coll.Arts & Tech. [0059880] 29/10/2001
Duguid Mrs AM, (was Grieve), BA DipLib MCLIP, Lib., Mott MacDonald, Croydon. [0029387]   29/06/1978
Duke Mr CA, BA DipLib MCLIP, Team Lib., Staines L., Surrey C.C. [0042508] 22/11/1988
Duke Mrs SM, (was Preston), BA MCLIP, Retired. [0011928]   26/09/1955
Duke Mr WL, MCLIP, Team Lib., E.Sussex Co.L. [0004251]   14/10/1971
Duke-Cox Mrs PE, (was Duke), BSc MCLIP, Lib., Lincoln Co.Hosp. [0004252]   04/09/1969
Dukes Ms AJ, BA(Hons), Comm.Lib., Caerphilly C.B.C., Bargoed L. [0056418]   07/07/1998

Dukic Dr Z, PhD, Resident in Hong Kong. [0058248] 25/11/1999
Duley Mrs MC, (was Davis), Asst.Lib.(Child.Team), Hounslow L., Comm.Initiative Partnerships. [0049855] 10/01/1994
Dumbell Ms J, MCSP, L.& Inf.Offr., Newcastle L.& Inf.Serv., Newcastle-upon-Tyne. [0052473] 02/11/1995
Dumble Ms M, BA(Hons) MA, Employment not known. [0053694] 11/09/1996
Dumont Mrs AJ, (was Hoare), BA, Employment not known. [0039953] 06/10/1986
Dumper Miss LJ, BA DipLib MCLIP, Mgr., Inf.Serv., TWI Ltd., Cambridge. [0026955] 19/01/1977
Dunbar Mrs C, (was Whalley), MA MCLIP, Unemployed. [0015648] 25/10/1971
Dunbar Mr GGW, BA MCLIP MAPM ASOCITM, [0004255] 22/02/1965
Dunbar Mr JA, BA(Hons), Asst.Lib., Comm.Initiative Partnership, Chiswick L. [0041658] 08/02/1988
Dunbar Miss K, BSc(Hons), p./t.Stud./Inf.Serv.Asst., Robert Gordon Univ., Aberdeen, McGrigor Donald, Glasgow. [0061053] 19/02/2002
Dunbar Mrs PM, (was Andrews), MCLIP, Audio Visual Lib., Solihull M.B.C. [0004257] 16/03/1962
Duncan Mrs A, Sen.L.Asst., Univ.of Dundee. [0057267] 04/02/1999 **AF**
Duncan Miss AJ, MA(Hons), Stud., The Robert Gordon Univ. [0059961] 12/11/2001
Duncan Mrs AS, (was Brown), BA(Hons), Asst.Lib., Worcs.C.C. [0045890] 10/07/1991
Duncan Mrs CL, (was Ward), BA MCLIP, Head of Dept.Learning Serv., N.E.Worcs.Coll., Bromsgrove, Worcs. [0027713] 06/07/1977
Duncan Mrs CL, BA(Hons) DipLIS MCLIP, Sch.Lib., Balerno Comm.High Sch., Edinburgh. [0048084] 03/11/1992
Duncan Mr CM, MA DipLib, Res.Co-ordinator, Inverclyde L., Greenock. [0040106] 21/10/1986
Duncan Mr DA, BA MCLIP, Sen.Lib.:Stock & Promotion, Doncaster L.& Inf., Mexburough L. [0004259] 23/04/1972
Duncan Miss HM, BA MCLIP, Br.Serv.Lib., Aberdeen City Council. [0033905] 03/05/1981
Duncan Mr J, MA MCLIP, Retired. [0004260] 04/02/1960
Duncan Mrs JJA, (was Merriman), MCLIP, Project Offr., Caribbean Community Secretariat, Bank of Guyana, Georgetown. [0020919] 06/01/1970
Duncan Mrs JM, (was Peacock), BA MCLIP, Asst.Lib.p/t., Med.L.,Royal Berks.Hosp., Reading. [0011407] 27/01/1972
Duncan Mrs JS, BA, Unemployed. [0037549] 01/10/1984
Duncan Mrs PH, (was Walmsley), BSc DipLib MCLIP, Subj.Lib., Anglia Poly.Univ., Essex. [0033185] 01/10/1980
Duncan Mr PL, BSc DipInfSc MCLIP, Mgr.-Research & Graphics, IBM UK Ltd., Croydon. [0045480] 14/02/1991
Duncan Mrs PS, (was Cooper), BA DipLib MCLIP, Asst.Lend.Lib., Farnborough L., Hants.C.C. [0029379] 27/06/1978
Duncan Mrs S, (was Jenaway), BA(Hons) MCLIP, Princ.L.Adviser, Sch.L.Serv., Essex C.C. [0029050] 06/02/1978
Duncan Mrs SF, (was Ginn), BA MCLIP, Lib.-SIHV, Gaskell House Psychotherapy Cent., Manchester. [0025286] 13/01/1976
Duncan Ms SJ, BA DipLib MCLIP, Sen.Inf.Offr., The Brit.L., London. [0036397] 04/10/1983
Duncanson Mrs EA, (was Watkins), BA(Hons) MCLIP, Child.Serv.Co-ordinator, Notts.C.C., Eastwood. [0028975] 07/02/1978
Duncombe Mrs C, (was Preece), BA MA MCLIP, Bibl.Lib. (Sales), Peters Bookselling Serv., Birmingham. [0042282] 05/10/1988
Dundas Mrs KM, (was Bateman), MA MCLIP, Life Member. [0020509] 14/03/1973
Dundas Mrs PJ, (was Hallam), BA MCLIP, Readers Adviser, Liverpool City L. [0028820] 09/02/1978
Dundon Mrs JL, (was Grey-Lloyd), L.Serv.Mgr., Gwent Healthcare NHS Trust, Newport. [0043711] 05/12/1989
Dungworth Mrs NM, (was Adlington), BA(Hons) MA MCLIP, Career Break, 3 Benscliffe Drive, Loughborough, LE11 3JP. [0048450] 12/01/1993
Dunham Miss JE, Sen.Asst.Lib., Univ.of Leicester, Clinical Sci.L. [0042673] 02/02/1989
Dunigan Mr JW, BA MCLIP, Lib.(Requests), Cent.L., Bradford L.s. [0036526] 18/10/1983
Dunkerley Mrs LM, (was Armstrong), BA MCLIP, Retired. [0004267] 27/06/1964
Dunkin Ms S, BA MA, Lib., Maricopa County L.District., USA. [0058876] 01/10/2000
Dunlea Ms AJ, BA MA, L.Asst., Cork Inst.of Tech., Ireland. [0058687] 06/06/2000
Dunlop Ms CA, BA(Hons) MA MCLIP, Asst.Lib., Northern Ireland Assembly L., Belfast. [0054409] 05/12/1996
Dunlop Miss CJS, Stud., Univ.of Strathclyde. [0061429] 26/07/2002
Dunmore Mr TG, BA(Hons), Clubhouse Lib., Royal Automobile Club, London. [0053958] 16/10/1996
Dunmow Mrs JM, (was Hunt), BA(Hons) DipIM MCLIP, Comm.Lib., Corsham & Box L., Wiltshire Co.Co. [0055367] 03/10/1997
Dunn Mr A, MA, Stud., Brighton Univ. [0059118] 20/11/2000
Dunn Mrs A, (was Evans), BA(Hons), Dist.Super., Cent.L., Walsall M.B.C. [0058349] 14/01/2000
Dunn Miss C, BLib MCLIP, Secretarial Asst.(Temp.), York Careers Cent. [0032050] 28/01/1980
Dunn Mrs CFH, (was Morris), BA MSc MCLIP, Employment unknown. [0060277] 10/12/2001
Dunn Miss CI, DIP LOC HIST MCLIP, Retired. [0004275] 09/02/1961
Dunn Miss DV, BSc(Hons), F.T.L.Asst., Birmingham Coll.of Feed, Birmingham. [0059732] 10/09/2001 **AF**
Dunn Dr H, BA MDiv PhD MSc MCLIP, Project Mgr./Knowledge Serv., Univ.Hosp.Coventry & Warwickshire, Coventry. [0049318] 22/10/1993

Dunn Ms HM, BA DipLib MCLIP, Lib., Higgs & Sons, Solicitors, Brierley Hill. [0031605] 25/10/1979
Dunn Mrs J, (was Mcnee), BA MCLIP, P./t.Lib., Royal Nat.Coll.for the Blind, Hereford. [0029195] 11/04/1978
Dunn Mrs J, (was Allanson), MSc MCLIP, Dir.of Ed.Serv., News Internat.Newspapers Ltd., London. [0026672] 15/11/1976
Dunn Miss JM, BA(Hons) DipIM, Stock Lib., L.B.of Barnet, London. [0056563] 25/08/1998
Dunn Mrs L, (was Thompson), Yth.Team Lib., Down Grp.L., S.E.E.L.B. [0044105] 15/05/1990
Dunn Mrs PJ, (was Calvert), MCLIP, Unemployed. [0004281] 15/10/1957
Dunn Mrs RJ, (was Winthorpe), BA(Hons), L.Asst., Sanderson Townend & Gilbert, Newcastle upon Tyne. [0047696] 16/10/1992
Dunn Miss T, Res.Cent.Asst., City of Leeds Sch., Yorks. [0055855] 02/12/1997
Dunnachie Ms T, BA(Hons), Sen.L.Asst., Northbrook Coll.Sussex, Goring-by-Sea. [0056505] 04/08/1998
Dunne Mr EJ, BA(Hons) DipLib, L.Asst., Humanities Grp., Manchester Cent.L. [0043542] 01/11/1989
Dunne Mr JFA, BA MCLIP, Asst.Co.Lib., Hants.Co.L., Winchester. [0004285] 05/02/1968
Dunne Mr MB, BA MCLIP, Acqu.Lib., Univ.of Luton. [0041153] 16/10/1987
Dunne Ms P, p./t.Stud./Lib., London Met./Brixton L., London. [0061594] 02/10/2002
Dunnett Mr JW, MCLIP, Life Member. [0004289] 01/01/1946
Dunnicliff Miss J, L.Asst., Leamington L., Leamington Spa. [0059612] 28/06/2001 **AF**
Dunning Mr AJ, BSc MCLIP, Inf.Res.Mgr., Euro.Comm., Dir.Gen.Inf.Soc., Luxembourg. [0060058] 07/12/2001
Dunning Miss P, BTECH MLib MCLIP, Sen.Subject Lib., Staffs.Univ. [0027962] 05/10/1977
Dunphy Mrs EM, MA MCLIP, Ch.Lib., The Robert Gordon Univ., Aberdeen. [0021214] 01/10/1973
Dunsford Mrs JBI, (was Fountain), MCLIP, Life Member, 183 Sheen Lane, London, SW14 8LE. [0004291] 04/03/1944
Dunsford Mr SF, FCLIP, Life Member. [0004292] 19/01/1950 **FE 01/01/1957**
Dunsire Mr GJ, BSc MCLIP, Research & Projects Mgr., Napier Univ.of Edinburgh. [0029551] 26/09/1978
Dunsire Mr R, DipMus MCLIP, Social Care Offr. (p./t.), Partnership, Aberdeen. [0004293] 29/01/1968
Dunstan Mrs RM, (was Ensell), BA MCLIP, p./t.Casual Relief Lib., Wokingham Dist.Council. [0025525] 20/01/1976
Dunstan Miss S, MCLIP, Lib., Marine Sci.L., Univ.of Puerto Rico. [0032621] 02/03/1917
Dunster Mrs JM, (was Unwin), BA DMS MCLIP, Stock & Client Mgr.(E.), Dorset Co.L. [0025676] 14/01/1976
Durber Mr DM, BA, Volunteer Asst.Lib.(Catg.), Victim Support, London. [0049902] 01/01/1994
Durbidge Mrs DM, (was Armstrong), MCLIP, Retired. [0004297] 01/01/1947
Durbidge Mr LG, MA FCLIP, Life Member. [0004299] 14/01/1942 **FE 01/01/1955**
Durcan Mr AJ, BA MCLIP, Head of L.&Inf.Serv., Newcastle City L. [0026956] 14/01/1977
Durcan Mrs J, (was Brown), MCLIP, Sch.Lib., Durham High Sch. [0026690] 25/10/1976
Durham Mr BJ, BA MCLIP, Systems Lib., Trafford Pub.L., Manchester. [0032051] 01/02/1980
Durham Mrs FPR, (was Lynn), BA DipLib MCLIP, Asst.Lib., Open Univ.L., Milton Keynes. [0033504] 13/01/1981
Durham Mrs SR, BA DipLib MCLIP, Community Lib., Croxley Green L., Herts.Co.Council. [0039408] 24/01/1986
Durkan Miss C, L.Asst., Health Science L., The Princess Royal Hosp. [0059699] 08/08/2001
Durkan Mrs SK, (was Cooper), BA MCLIP, p./t.Lib., Derbys.C.C., Swadlincote. [0030607] 16/02/1979
Durndell Ms HM, (was Mackie), BA DipLib, Sub-Lib., Glasgow Univ.L. [0027344] 08/03/1977
Durrani Mrs C, (was Kellas), BA MCLIP, Lib., Our Lady & St.Patricks High Sch., Dumbarton. [0008220] 21/08/1964
Durrani Mr S, BA DipLib FCLIP, Strategy & Comm.Offr., L.B.Merton. [0039636] 14/04/1986 **FE 19/03/1997**
Durrans Miss K, BA DipLib MCLIP, Lib., Hants.Co.L., Winchester. [0034392] 28/10/1981
Durrant Miss CL, BA(Hons), Retrospective Catr., Trinity Coll., Cambridge. [0059017] 26/10/2000
Durrant Ms FM, MA DipLib, Research Serv.Super., Baker & McKenzie, London. [0049099] 01/10/1993
Dury Mrs SC, Sen.L.Asst., Weston Ref.L., Weston Super Mare, Somerset. [0058754] 10/07/2000 **AF**
Dutch Mr MR, BA(Hons) DipLib MCLIP, Grp.Mgr., Sheffield City Council, Ls., Arch.& Inf., Highfield L. [0032052] 12/02/1980
Duthie Miss CJ, Administrator, Scottish Provident, Edinburgh. [0055438] 13/10/1997
Duthie Ms CN, MSc, Employment Unknown. [0061492] 06/08/2002
Duthie Mr P, MA(Hons), Unemployed. [0046549] 13/11/1991
Dutt Mr KK, MA MCLIP, Ethnic Serv.Lib., Ealing Bor. [0043111] 23/01/1967
Dutton Dr AM, BA(Hons) MA DPhil, Catr., Univ.of Oxford. [0053756] 01/10/1996
Dutton Dr BG, BSc PhD CChem FRSC FCLIP, Retired. [0060581] 11/12/2001 **FE 01/04/2002**
Dutton Mrs CM, (was Morgan), A INST AM MCLIP, Customer Serv.Mgr., Cambs C.C. [0004313] 03/02/1958
Dutton Mrs GDM, (was Clarke), MCLIP, Asst.Subj.Lib.p/t., Univ.of Wolverhampton. [0025241] 02/01/1976
Dutton Ms SH, (was Mkanda), MA, Knowledge Mgr., S.Norfolk P.C.T. [0043089] 21/07/1989

Personal Members

Duxbury Mr A, MA FCLIP, Life Member, Tel.0161 762 9405, 22 Newington Dr., Bury, Lancs., OL15 9BB. [0004318] 25/02/1949 **FE 01/01/1965**
Duxbury Mrs PJ, BSc(Hons) DipAppSocSc, p./t.Stud./Learning Advisor, Pontypridd Coll. [0061285] 08/05/2002
Duxbury Mrs R, (was Plant), MCLIP, Lib., Walford & N Shropshire Coll., Baschurch, Shrewsbury. [0011739] 01/10/1969
Dwiar Miss E, MA PGCE DipIS, Lib., Field Fisher Waterhouse, London. [0043218] 02/10/1989
Dwiar Miss P, BA MSc CertEd DipLib MCLIP, p./t.L.Asst./Asst.Lib p./t., L.B.of Redbridge/Farrer & Co. [0032931] 07/10/1980
Dwyer Mr BA, BA DPA MCLIP, Retired, Myrtle Cottage, Mill St., Westleton, Suffolk. [0018652] 03/02/1953
Dwyer Miss HM, BA(Hons) MA, Official Publications Co-ordinator, Inf.& L.Serv., Dept.of Trade & Industry. [0056100] 08/02/1998
Dwyer Mrs JM, (was Scarborough), BA DipLib MCLIP, Sen.L.Asst., Sheffield Univ.L. [0033141] 05/10/1980
Dwyer Ms MM, BA(Hons) MA, Lib., Royal Coll.of Nursing, Belfast. [0050424] 27/07/1994
Dyce Mr J, MCLIP, Retired. [0029297] 30/09/1970
Dyce Mrs SE, (was Milne), MA DipLib MCLIP, Asst.Cent.Lending Lib., Aberdeen C.C., Aberdeen. [0031384] 01/10/1979
Dye Mrs A, (was Green), BA, Unemployed-Career Break. [0043265] 12/10/1989
Dye Mrs MA, (was Yarnall), BSc, Sen.Inf.Analyst, Brit.Standards Inst., Chiswick, London. [0044349] 01/10/1990
Dyer Miss A, BA MCLIP, Sen.L.Asst., Univ.of E.Anglia. [0042598] 20/01/1989
Dyer Mrs BS, (was Fidler), BA MCLIP, Lib., Aylesbury High Sch., Bucks. [0025529] 14/01/1976
Dyer Mrs CH, (was Sharman), BA MCLIP, Serv.Mgr.:Child.& Comm., Nottingham City Council. [0031445] 15/10/1979
Dyer Miss CML, BA MCLIP, Team Leader-Database Team, De Montfort Univ. [0030399] 29/01/1979
Dyer Miss D, BSc(Hons), Lib., Llewelyn-Davies, London. [0046291] 23/10/1991
Dyer Mr GE, MCLIP, Mgr.-GIST/IMP, Pera Internat., Melton Mowbray. [0060730] 12/12/2001
Dyer Miss JS, MA MCLIP, Dep.Lib., St.Martins Coll., Lancaster. [0004324] 16/11/1970
Dyer Miss MH, Operations Support Analyst, Telewest Communications, Liverpool. [0049452] 27/10/1993
Dyer Miss S, BA(Hons) MA, Inf.Specialist, LEK Consulting, London. [0052828] 17/10/1997
Dyke Mrs S, Stud., City Univ. [0059886] 29/10/2001
Dykes Mrs E, (was Dawson), BA MCLIP, Child.Serv.Lib.(Job Share), Nottingham City Council. [0022063] 22/01/1974
Dymond Mr GR, LLB MSc MCLIP, Research Serv.& Legal Inf.Lib., House of Lords, London. [0036375] 01/10/1983
Dymott Mr EAE, BSc MA MSc MRTPI MCLIP, Lib., 114 Himley Green, Linslade, Leighton Buzzard, Beds., LU7 7QA. [0038595] 01/08/1985
Dyne Mrs EA, (was Crooks), Inf.Serv.Asst., Kirkland & Ellis, London. [0059511] 18/04/2001 **AF**
Dyson Ms CJ, BA(Hons) MSc MCLIP, Inf.Res.Mgr., Zurich Re(UK)Ltd., London. [0039007] 21/10/1986
Dyson Mrs CL, (was Wagner), BA MCLIP, Sen.Lib., Bradford L., Cent.L. [0030055] 01/11/1978
Dyson Mrs HM, (was Barnes), BA MCLIP, Princ.Lib.-Stock Res., Wokingham Dist.Council. [0033587] 21/01/1981
Dyson Mrs JE, (was Peacock), BA MCLIP, Coll.Lib., Bradfield Coll., Reading. [0020154] 25/01/1973
Dyson Mrs L, L.Asst., Dickinson Dees, Newcastle upon Tyne. [0057287] 02/02/1999
Dyson Mrs P, (was Jones), BA MSc PGCE MCLIP ILTM, Supporting Mgr.-Learning Res., Univ.of Lincoln. [0022663] 01/08/1974
Dzielski Mrs BM, (was West), FCLIP, Life Member, 99 Berwick Crescent, Sidcup, Kent, DA15 8HV, Tel:0181 300 2822. [0018656] 09/02/1942 **FE 01/01/1952**
Eades Ms AB, BSc PGDip MBA, Inf.& Communications Mgr., European Commissiion, Brussels, Belgium. [0059114] 17/11/2000
Eadon Mrs JM, (was Lee), BA(Hons), Sen.L.Asst., Coventry Univ. [0043565] 24/07/1996
Eagle Ms HM, BA LIAC, L.Asst., St Neots L., Cambridgeshire. [0059746] 12/09/2001
Eagle Mr RS, MA DPA FCLIP, Life Member, Tel.0181 959 1230, 47 Flower Lane, London, NW7 2JN. [0004339] 04/02/1950 **FE 01/01/1959**
Eagle Mrs SE, BSc, Sch.Lib., Whitesmore Sch., Solihull. [0040494] 11/02/1987
Eagles Mrs J, (was Taylor), MSc MCLIP, Statistician, Unilever Res., Port Sunlight Lab., Merseyside. [0025121] 04/11/1975
Eales Mrs SM, Coll.Mgr.-Learning Materials, JISC - London. [0053696] 11/09/1996
Eales Mr SW, LRAM ABSM MCLIP, Lib., H.M.Prison Gartree, Leics. [0044896] 01/01/1958
Eamon Ms MEM, BA MLS, Sen.Asst.Lib., L.B.of Harrow. [0051546] 01/04/1995
Eardley Mr DM, MA FCLIP, Retired. [0004342] 11/10/1951 **FE 01/01/1965**
Eardley Mr N, BA, Inf.Offr., Hanley L., Stoke on Trent City Council. [0043120] 03/08/1989
Earl Miss AT, BA(Hons), Grad.Trainee, H.M.Treasury & Cabinet Office L., London. [0061821] 12/11/2002
Earl Mr C, BSc HonFCLIP, Retired. [0004343] 11/01/1960 **FE 01/01/1999**
Earney Miss SL, BA(Hons) MA MCLIP, Mgr., Aberconway L.Services, Cardiff Univ. [0050694] 12/10/1994
Earnshaw Mrs D, (was Singhal), BA MCLIP, Child.& Lifelong Learning Lib., Solihull M.B.C. [0040819] 01/07/1987

Earnshaw Mrs LC, Stud., Manchester Met.Univ. [0060036] 30/11/2001
Easson Ms K, MA DipLib MCLIP, Lib., Literary & Philosophical Soc., Newcastle. [0043278] 12/10/1989
East Mr GG, MCLIP, Ref.Lib., Suffolk L.s.& Heritage, Ipswich. [0023859] 12/02/1975
East Miss J, MCLIP, Life Member. [0004353] 12/02/1952
East Miss JL, MCLIP, P./t.Lib., Doncaster Coll., Doncaster, S.Yorks. [0024169] 24/02/1965
East Mrs PA, (was Ryan), MCLIP, Med.Lib., Med.L., Tolworth Hosp., Surrey. [0019172] 01/10/1972
East Mrs SE, (was Fountain), BA MCLIP, Advisory Lib., Sch.L.Serv., E.Sussex Co.Council. [0021806] 16/01/1974
Eastell Ms C, BA(Hons) MA MCLIP, Serv.& Financial Planning Mgr., Cambs.L. [0049267] 20/10/1993
Eastell Mrs RA, (was Lambie), Unemployed. [0045106] 11/07/1990 **AF**
Easter Mr DP, BSc, L. Asst., Bournemouth Univ. [0060916] 10/01/2002 **AF**
Easter Miss M, MCLIP, Retired. [0004358] 04/03/1957
Easter Miss RA, BA, p./t.Stud./Asst.Lib., Freshfields Bruckhaus Deringer, London. [0061023] 07/02/2002
Easterbrook Miss CB, MLib BA MCLIP, Retired. [0016827] 06/09/1960
Easton Mr FMJ, FCLIP, Retired. [0004362] 16/02/1955 **FE 01/01/1965**
Easton Ms L, MA(Hons) DipLIS MCLIP, Lib., Argyll & Clyde NHS Board, Paisley. [0048348] 01/12/1992
Eastwell Mr MH, BA MCLIP, Knowledge Mgmt.Strategy Coordinator, Environment Agency, Bristol. [0042883] 04/04/1989
Eastwood Mr CR, FCLIP, Life Member. [0004366] 27/08/1938 **FE 01/01/1951**
Eastwood Miss EJ, BA(Hons) MLIS MCLIP, Inf.Mgr., Arthritis Care, London. [0045721] 07/05/1991
Eastwood Ms H, Stud., Manchester Met.Univ. [0059129] 21/11/2000
Eastwood Miss LA, Unemployed. [0059250] 17/01/2001
Eathorne Ms V, Disability Advisor, St Lawrences Hosp., Cornwall. [0061470] 01/07/2002
Eato Mrs KA, (was Gascoigne Ward), BA(Hons) DipLib MCLIP, Dukinfield L., Tameside. [0038201] 09/01/1985
Eaton Miss C, (was Gammage), BA(Hons) PGCE MCLIP, Inf.Offr., Policy Planning & Performance Rev., Doncaster Soc.Serv.Dept. [0047014] 01/04/1992
Eaton Mrs CL, (was Royce), MA MCLIP, Sen.Lib., Guildhall Sch.of Music & Drama, London. [0040055] 20/10/1986
Eaton Miss DH, BA MA, Lib., St.Edmund Hall, Oxford. [0045073] 04/07/1990
Eaton Mr JJ, MA, Employment not known. [0040228] 07/11/1986
Eaton Ms MM, BA(Hons), Cent.Mgr., L.Bor.of Lambeth, W.Norwood L. [0039593] 10/03/1986
Eaton Mr RC, MCLIP, Life Member. [0004371] 01/01/1932
Eaton Mrs SM, (was Ryan), MCLIP, p./t.Pub.Sch.Lib., Licensed Victuallers Sch., Ascot, Berks. [0004372] 11/01/1964
Eatough Miss EL, L.Asst., Burton L., Staffs. [0061321] 22/05/2002 **AF**
Eats Mrs HM, Lib., Aldro Sch., Godalming. [0055846] 21/11/1997
Eatwell Mr RF, MA FCLIP, Retired. [0004374] 17/01/1947 **FE 01/01/1962**
Eatwell Mrs SJ, MA, Lib., Hastings Coll.of Art., St.Leonards on sea. [0058427] 16/02/2000
Eaves Mrs JK, BA(Hons) MA, Comm.Lib., Middleton L., Rochdale Metro.Council. [0052509] 09/01/1995
Eaves Miss KE, MA(Oxon) DipILS MCLIP, Sen.Lib., Southampon City Ls. [0054132] 30/10/1996
Eaves Mr RM, BA DIP ED MCLIP, Ch.Lib., Western Isles L., Stornoway. [0026353] 01/10/1976
Eavis Mrs AMH, (was Brown), MCLIP, P.t.Catr., L.Support Unit, Bor.of Swindon. [0001838] 01/01/1960
Ebden Mr EAM, Law Lib., Payne Hicks Beach, London WC2. [0038703] 01/10/1985
Ebenezer Ms CM, MA STM AKC MCLIP, Trust Lib., S.London & Maudsley NHS Trust, London. [0047544] 01/10/1992
Eccleston Miss CJ, BA(Hons) MA, Inf.Cent.Mgr., Nokia (UK) Ltd., Farnborough. [0054329] 17/12/1996
Eccleston Mrs H, (was Barclay), BA(Hons) LLB(Hons) MCLIP, Asst.Regional Lib., The Court Service, Newastle Upon Tyne. [0041348] 06/11/1987
Eccleston Mrs TL, (was Montague), BLib MCLIP, Sen.Lib., N.Shropshire Shropshire C.C. [0035199] 01/10/1982
Ecclestone Ms BM, MCLIP, Retired. [0032417] 24/03/1980
Ecclestone Ms KF, MLib, Devel.Mgr., Cornwall Coll., Cornwall. [0041757] 10/03/1988
Ecclestone Mrs MJ, BA DipLib MCLIP, Lib., Alpine Club L., London. [0031129] 24/09/1979
Eckersley Miss SL, BSc(Econ), Sen.L.Asst., Univ.of Oxford, Hist.Faculty Lib. [0054446] 13/12/1996
Eckford Miss K, BA(Hons) MSc(Econ), Sen.L.Asst.-Catg., Univ.of Nottingham. [0052697] 23/11/1995
Eckley Mrs DM, (was Lewis), BA DipLib MCLIP, Comm.Lib., Gwynedd L.& Inf.Serv. [0045450] 11/02/1991
Eddie Dr GD, DipEd MA MLitt PhD DipLib MCLIP, Asst.Lib., Univ.of Edinburgh. [0049766] 07/12/1993
Eddison Mrs SM, (was Hayes), MA MCLIP, Div.Ref.& Inf.Specialist(Job Share), Cheshire C.C., Crewe L. [0037669] 17/10/1984
Eddleston Miss JE, MA MCLIP, Employment not known. [0047173] 21/05/1992
Ede Mrs J, BSc(Hons), Inf.Consultant. [0059076] 08/11/2000
Eden Mr R, MCLIP, Operational Support Lib., Devon L.Serv., Admin.Cent., Exeter. [0004390] 01/01/1968
Edenborough Mrs A, (was Morgan), BA(Hons), NPSS Inf.Offr., Pricewaterhousecoopers. [0057322] 09/02/1999

231

Edgar Prof JR, MA FCLIP, Retired. [0004392]   23/05/1947
FE 01/01/1964
Edgar Mrs RJ, BA(Hons) MCLIP, Sen.Lib., Bridlington L., E.Riding of Yorks.Council. [0004391]   01/01/1964
Edgar Miss SC, BA MCLIP, Dir.Knowledge Mgmt.& Inf.Serv., Europe & Middle E., Booz Allen & Hamilton, London. [0029954]   28/10/1978
Edge Mr F, MCLIP, Community Lib.:Inf.Lead, Stoke on Trent L.,Arts & Arch. [0004394]   19/05/1966
Edge Mrs JM, (was Mason), BA(Hons) MCLIP, Principal L. Offr., Kingston Upon Hull L. [0020258]   16/02/1973
Edgson Mrs CA, BA MCLIP, Lib., Rugby L., Warwickshire C.C. [0004399]   11/03/1971
Edis Miss SE, BA MCLIP, Sen.Ref.Lib., Civic Cent.Ref.L., L.B.of Harrow. [0004400]   14/09/1971
Edlin Mrs DE, (was Hedley), BA DIP LIB MCLIP, p./t.Res.Lib., Sandwell Educ.L.Serv. [0034561]   11/01/1982
Edmond Mrs L, L.& Inf.Offr., C.I.P.D., London. [0058516]   14/03/2000
Edmonds Mrs DJ, (was Tuxford), BA FCLIP, Managing Dir., Instant L.Ltd., Loughborough. [0014993]   01/01/1971   FE 01/04/2002
Edmonds Mrs JC, (was Wisdom), BA MCLIP, Learn.Cent.Lib., Nab Wood Sch., Bingley,W.Yorks. [0025455]   19/12/1975
Edmonds Mrs L, (was Stokes), BA MCLIP, Clinical Lib.Mgr., Papworth Hosp. [0004402]   04/07/1971
Edmonds Miss MJ, BA(Hons) DipIS MCLIP, Coll.Lib., Northwood Coll., Middx. [0050395]   15/07/1994
Edmonds Mr RE, MCLIP, Retired. [0004404]   12/02/1969
Edmondson Mrs V, FCLIP, Housewife. [0004406]   02/02/1971
FE 08/03/1979
Edmondston Miss ME, BA FCLIP, Life Member. [0004408]   18/10/1938
FE 01/01/1944
Edmunds Ms A, BA(Hons) MCLIP, Youthboot Project Co-ordinator, Nat.Yth.Agency, Leicester. [0052111]   04/10/1995
Edmunds Ms A, BA CertEd MCLIP, Unemployed. [0004409]   03/10/1968
Edmunds Mr GL, BSc(Econ) DipLib MCLIP, Dep.Area Lib., Arun, W.Sussex C.C. [0040358]   22/01/1987
Edmunds Mrs HB, General Mgr., Adset, Northants. [0050151]   14/12/1993
AF
Edmunds Otter Mrs ML, (was Edmunds), BA, Clinical Effectiveness Inf.Lib., Univ.of Leicester. [0036651]   23/10/1983
Edmundson Mrs JA, (was Riley), BA MCLIP, [0032555]   23/05/1980
Edney Miss CPL, FCLIP, Retired. [0004411]   01/01/1939
FE 01/01/1964
Edser Ms RM, BA(Hons) MCLIP, Area Lib.-Worthing, W.Sussex C.C. [0022434]   29/04/1974
Edward Miss EM, BA MCLIP, Inf.Offr., Age Concern, Rugby. [0004413]   26/03/1964
Edward Mr RC, MLib, Unemployed. [0047863]   22/10/1992
Edwardes Miss GE, BA (Hons), Sen.Learning Res.Advisor, Barnet Coll., London. [0046675]   06/12/1991
Edwards Ms AC, MA, Asst.Lib., Warburg Inst., London. [0052109] 04/10/1995
Edwards Mr AJ, BA MCLIP, Retired. [0004415]   09/01/1953
Edwards Mr AS, BLib(Hons) MCLIP, Dep.Reading Room Mgr., Early Printed Coll., Brit.L., London. [0038488]   17/05/1985
Edwards Miss CA, MA MIL MCLIP DipTrans, Head of Ref.L., Victoria Univ., Wellington. [0039067]   14/10/1985
Edwards Mr CD, BA(Hons) DipLib MCLIP, Princ.Lib., Vale of Glamorgan Council, Barry. [0035127]   01/08/1982
Edwards Mrs CE, MA, Retired. [0040267]   18/11/1984
Edwards Mrs CE, BA DipLib MCLIP, Public Enquiries Point Offr., Dept.for International Devel., East Kilbride. [0029643]   11/10/1978
Edwards Mrs CM, (was Lewis), BA DipLib MCLIP, Asst.Lib., Nat.L.of Wales, Aberystwyth. [0040006]   15/10/1986
Edwards Mrs E, BA(Hons) DipILM, Inf.& Stud.Serv.Asst., NENI, Wrexham. [0057424]   15/03/1999
Edwards Mr EA, MCLIP, Retired. [0060731]   12/12/2001
Edwards Ms EC, BA DipLib MCLIP, Art Lib./NVQ Co-ordinator, Carmarthenshire Coll., Coleg Sir Gar, Carmarthen. [0030156]   17/01/1979
Edwards Mrs EM, (was Clifford), BA PGDipLis, Catr. [0043704]   04/12/1989
Edwards Mr FCF, MCLIP, Retired. [0004427]   11/01/1967
Edwards Miss G, BA(Hons) MCLIP, Lib., Greenwich Council, Woolwich Ref.L. [0036040]   20/04/1983
Edwards Mr G, BA(Hons) MCLIP, Asst.Lib., Lifelong Learning, Flintshire L.& Inf.Serv., Mold. [0040242]   11/11/1986
Edwards Mrs GB, BA(Hons) MSc(Econ) MCLIP, Sch.Lib., Co.L., Haverfordwest. [0055494]   15/10/1997
Edwards Mrs GF, Sch.Lib., Llantarnam Sch., Cwmbran. [0055895] 16/12/1997
AF
Edwards Dr HA, BA MA PhD FRSM MCLIP, Employment not known. [0060775]   12/12/2001
Edwards Mrs HC, (was Hughes), BA DipLib MCLIP, Head of Inf.Serv., London Business Sch.L. [0028596]   12/01/1978
Edwards Ms HEA, (was Sunter), B LIB MCLIP, Princ.Lib.(Field Serv.), Powys C.C., Llandrindod Wells. [0014229]   14/05/1970
Edwards Mr HJ, MCLIP, Life Member. [0004429]   15/03/1951
Edwards Mrs HM, BSc MA MCLIP, Comm.L.Mgr., Leicester City L., St.Barnabas L. [0002886]   01/01/1971
Edwards Mrs J, (was Salkeld), BA MCLIP, Retired. [0004432]   04/03/1959
Edwards Mrs J, (was Cooper), MCLIP, Lib., Dudley Coll.of Tech. [0004433]   01/01/1971
Edwards Mrs J, (was Orton), BSc MCLIP, Housewife. [0004431]   16/10/1967
Edwards Mr JA, BA MSc MCLIP, H.of Learning and Inf.Serv., Cent.Sch.of Speech & Drama, London. [0036527]   19/10/1983
Edwards Mrs JA, (was Goodlet), BSc MA MCLIP, Systems Administrator, QinetiQ, Hants. [0004436]   14/02/1968

Edwards Mrs JA, (was Grainger), FCLIP, Learning Resources Mgr., Kidderminster Coll. [0005799]   16/01/1969   FE 14/06/1978
Edwards Ms JE, BA MCLIP, Lib., Maclay, Murray & Spens, Edinburgh. [0026358]   14/10/1976
Edwards Mrs JG, (was Freeman), MCLIP, Freelance L.Serv.to Architects., Glasgow. [0004439]   01/01/1963
Edwards Mrs JL, (was Hogg), MCLIP CTEFLA, Unemployed. [0021261]   17/10/1973
Edwards Miss JM, MA MLib MCLIP, Bibl.Serv.Lib., Lincs.C.C. [0039983]   08/10/1986
Edwards Mr JN, BSc MCLIP, Employment unknown. [0060315]   10/12/2001
Edwards Miss K, BSc(Hons) MSc, Lib., Dept.of Health, London. [0051580]   03/04/1995
Edwards Miss KL, BA(Hons) MSc(Econ), L.Asst., Univ.of Wales, Aberystwyth. [0056901]   02/11/1998
Edwards Mrs L, (was Summers), BA MCLIP, Unemployed. [0030686]   13/03/1979
Edwards Mrs LA, (was Wyld), BA MCLIP, Neighbourhood Lib., Bedminster Grp., Bristol City Council. [0038831] 14/10/1985
Edwards Miss LI, MBE MCLIP, Life Member. [0004444]   10/03/1931
Edwards Mrs LM, BA(Hons) DipLib MCLIP, Head, Mgmt.Inf.& Res.Cent., Cranfield Sch.of Mgmt., Bedford. [0034837]   15/03/1982
Edwards Mrs MB, (was Punchard), MCLIP, Asst.Lib., The Ravensbourne Sch., Bromley. [0012042] 03/10/1970
Edwards Mrs MB, (was Marsh), MCLIP, p./t.Inf.Lib./Catr., Kingston Univ., Surrey. [0004447]   15/10/1966
Edwards Mrs ML, MCLIP, Comm.Lib., Denbigh, Denbighshire. [0004450]   01/01/1966
Edwards Mrs MME, (was Arundel), MCLIP, Team Lib., Glos.C.C. [0000423]   22/02/1968
Edwards Mrs MY, (was Taylor), MCLIP, Housewife. [0004451]   14/01/1963
Edwards Miss NC, BA(Hons) DipIS MA, Media Lib., London Guildhall Univ., London. [0050593]   27/09/1994
Edwards Mr PCG, BA MCLIP, Lib., Salisbury Dist., Wilts.C.C. [0023264]   20/11/1974
Edwards Mr RI, BA MIMgt MCLIP FRSA, Retired. [0018662]   30/10/1964
Edwards Mrs RJ, (was Hansell), BA MCLIP, Sen.Lib., Manchester L., Cent.L. [0026106]   01/07/1976
Edwards Mrs RJB, MA MSc, p./t.Stud., Inf.Asst., Univ.Northumbria, Univ.Teeside. [0059836]   16/10/2001
Edwards Ms RS, (was Hutchings), MA DipLib, Lib.-Lend., Herts.C.C., Cheshunt. [0036492]   14/10/1983
Edwards Mrs S, (was Ghio), BA MA DipLib MCLIP, Unemployed. [0042379]   16/10/1988
Edwards Ms S, Position unknown, Smith & Williamson, London. [0060418]   11/12/2001
Edwards Miss SC, MA MCLIP, Campus Lib., Glenside L., Univ.of the W.of England at Bristol. [0034187]   15/10/1981
Edwards Mrs SD, L.Asst., Maelor Sch., Penley, Wrexham. [0050862]   24/10/1994
Edwards Mr SM, BA(Hons) MCLIP, Project Mgr.-Peoples Network, W.Sussex Ls., Worthing. [0049122]   06/10/1993
Edwards Mr SP, Child.Lib., L.B.of Barnet. [0038739]   03/10/1985
Edwards Mrs SP, (was McGillicuddy), BA MLS DipLib MCLIP, Lib., Kennet Dist., Wilts.C.C. [0030806]   11/06/1979
Edwards Mrs SV, (was Cavey), MCLIP, Periodicals SLA, Kings Coll.London. [0021489]   12/07/1973
Edwards Mr SW, BA DipLib MCLIP, Princ.Lib.-Bibl.Serv., Hants.Co.L., Winchester. [0029510]   11/09/1978
Edwards Mr SW, BA(Hons) MA, Temp. Asst. L., The Home Office, London. [0054257]   11/11/1996
Edwards Mrs V, (was Thakkar), BA MA MCLIP, Career Break. [0044222]   13/07/1990
Edwards Miss VA, BA(Hons), Inf.Offr., Berrymans Lace Mawer, Manchester. [0053638]   19/08/1996
Edwards Mrs VL, (was Smith), BA MCLIP, Unemployed. [0025421]   10/01/1976
Edwards Mrs WE, BA(Hons) MA, Unemployed. [0058997]   18/10/2000
Edwards Mrs YP, BSc MCLIP, Employment not known. [0060346] 10/12/2001
Edwin Ms JE, BA(Hons) MCLIP, Career Break. [0039316]   07/01/1986
Ee Mrs SC, (was Lee), BA MCLIP, Resident in Switzerland. [0022352]   09/04/1974
Egan Mrs BA, BA DipLib MCLIP, Classroom Asst., W.Sussex C.C., E.Grinstead. [0032247]   19/01/1980
Egan Mr D, BA(Hons), R.& D.Offr., Nat.L.for the Blind, Stockport. [0058695]   02/06/2000
Egan Mr P, Asst.Lib., Univ.of Portsmouth. [0040126]   17/10/1986
Egan Mr RT, MCLIP, [0027719]   16/01/1964
Egarr Mrs HE, (was Frankcom), MCLIP, Lib.i/c., S.Glos.Council. [0021039]   01/10/1973
Egerton Mrs JE, (was Cadge), BA MCLIP, Lib./Inf.Mgr., Res.Unit, Inst.for Soc.& Econ.Res., Univ.of Essex. [0027659]   04/07/1977
Eggington Miss CE, MA MSc MCLIP, Employment not known. [0060776]   12/12/2001
Eggleston Miss KJ, MA MEd MCLIP, Life Member. [0004469]   25/09/1956
Egleton Miss SL, BA(Hons) MA MCLIP, Learning Support Co-Ordinator, Reading Univ. [0055158]   24/07/1997
Ehibor Mr AO, BA MSc MCLIP, Lib., Ras Al Khaimah Men's Coll., Higher Coll.of Tech., U.A.E. [0048364]   04/12/1992
Ehlers Dr H, DrPhil MCLIP, Resident in Germany. [0060060]   07/12/2001
Eichhorn Mrs R, BA(Hons) DipILM, Learning Resources Tutor, Luther King House L., Partnership for Theological Educ. [0058785]   20/07/2000
Eisenschitz Dr TS, BSc MSc PhD MCLIP, Lect., Cent.For Info.Sci., City Univ. [0031267]   05/10/1979

Personal Members

Ekberg Mrs MA, (was Piper), MCLIP, Life Member, Tel.0372 464551, Beaver Lodge, 2 Acorns Way, Esher Park Ave., Surrey, KT10 9NX. [0004472] 01/01/1949
Ekin Mrs SM, BA DipLib, Lib., L., N.B.N.I., Belfast. [0058336] 17/01/2000
Ekmekcioglu Dr FC, (was Ekmekcioglu-Hatton), BSc(Hons) MSc MCLIP, Stud., Univ.of Sheffield. [0051669] 05/05/1995
Ekue Miss RA, BSc MSc MCLIP, Position unknown, Chugai Pharma UK Ltd., London. [0060358] 10/12/2001
Ekundayo Mrs O, BSc(Hons) MLS LLB LLM, Lect., Univ.of Ibadan, Nigeria. [0061256] 30/04/2002
El Rayah Mrs SB, BA PGDipLIS MCLIP, African Caribbean Comm.Lib., L.B.of Wandsworth, African Caribbean Comm.L. [0040564] 19/03/1987
El-Sukhon Mrs ANS, DipLib MCLIP, Unemployed. [0026359] 05/10/1976
Elcock Miss Y, Stud., Manchester Met.Univ. [0059988] 16/11/2001
Elder Mr DB, BA MLib MCLIP, Head of Inf.Serv., G.C.H.Q., Cheltenham, Glos. [0036547] 10/10/1983
Elder Mr GC, Learning Cent.Offr., City of Sunderland Coll., Sunderland. [0043895] 13/02/1990
Elder Mr MA, BA(Hons) DipILS, IT Lib., Dunstable Coll., Beds. [0055522] 20/10/1997
Elder Mr MR, MA DipLib MCLIP, Sen.Lib.Bibl.Serv., N.Yorks.Co.L. [0004478] 10/11/1969
Elder Mrs V, (was Thangarasu), BA(Hons), Asst.Lib., Northumberland Health Auth., Morpeth. [0041295] 30/10/1987
Elderton Mrs DL, BA DipEd MCLIP, Lib., Ibstock Place Sch., Roehampton, London. [0053647] 13/08/1996
Eldridge Mrs KM, (was Atkinson), BMus(Hons) MA, Stud., Univ.Central England. [0060016] 26/11/2001
Elengorn Mrs MH, BA(Hons), Inf.Lib., Kingston Univ. [0052660] 16/11/1995
Eley Mr SR, MA MCLIP, Sen.Lib., Cent.L., L.B.of Enfield. [0020283] 17/02/1973
Elgar Mr PG, Retired. [0004488] 29/10/1946
Eling Mr NT, BA(Hons), Stud., Univ.of Sheffield, &, L.Asst., DeMontfort Univ. Leics. [0056896] 04/11/1998
Elkes Mr MH, BA MCLIP, Comm.Lib.(Inf.), Staffs.Co.L., Cult.& Corp.Serv. [0004490] 25/07/1968
Elkin Prof JC, (was Atkin), BA PhD Sc FCLIP ACSS, Dean, Computing Studies, Univ.of Cent.England in Birmingham. [0004491] 13/03/1962
FE 27/03/1991
Ell Mrs AE, BA(Hons) MCLIP, Community Lib., Tamworth L., Staffs. [0055093] 17/07/1997
Ellarby Mrs CF, (was Jones), BA MCLIP, Lib., Telford & Wrekin L., Newport. [0007976] 20/07/1972
Ellard Mrs GM, (was Springett), MCLIP, Sch.Lib., Canon Slade Sch., Bolton. [0015857] 01/01/1966
Ellard Mr KR, BA MA DMS MCLIP, Head of L.& Learning Res.Serv., Univ.of Cent.Lancs. [0004492] 09/11/1971
Ellen Miss CL, BA(Hons) MCLIP, Inf.Offr., Veale Wasbrough, Bristol. [0049853] 07/01/1994
Ellen Mrs M, (was Grose), MCLIP, Sen.Learning Res.Offr., Sheppey Coll., Kent. [0006025] 01/01/1963
Ellery Ms J, BSc(Hons) MA MCLIP, Dir.of Knowledge Mgmnt., Univ.Hosp.Lewisham L. [0046836] 14/02/1992
Ellingham Mrs S, MA Dip MCLIP, Lib., Northumbria Healthcare NHS Trust, Hexham. [0054940] 21/05/1997
Elliot Mrs J, (was Winstanley), BA DipLib, Sch.Lib., Oswestry Sch. [0047680] 14/10/1992
Elliott Miss AM, Employment not known, [0037080] 22/01/1984
Elliott Miss C, BSc(Hons) MA, Unemployed. [0059057] 01/11/2000
Elliott Ms C, BA MSc MCLIP, Asst.Lib.,p./t., London Sch.of Econ., London. [0050806] 19/01/1994
Elliott Mrs CA, (was Mcvittie), BA MCLIP, Lib., Cent.Newcastle High Sch., Newcastle Upon Tyne. [0022589] 02/07/1974
Elliott Mrs DA, (was Thomson), MA(Hons) MCLIP, Branch Lib., East Lothian Council, [0022589] 01/10/1992
Elliott Mrs DDE, BEd(Hons) PGDipILM MA, p./t.L.Asst., Univ.of Durham. [0053046] 19/02/1996
Elliott Mr DJ, MCLIP, Lib.Inf.Serv., Norfolk L.& Inf.Serv. [0027157] 26/01/1977
Elliott Mr DT, BA MLS FCLIP MIMgt, Retired. [0004501] 25/11/1968
FE 16/09/1976
Elliott Mrs E, (was Platt), MCLIP, Retired. [0004505] 01/01/1939
Elliott Miss EM, BA MCLIP, Retired. [0004507] 05/10/1961
Elliott Mrs ES, (was Curtis), BA MCLIP, Office Mgr., Tyne & Wear Museums. [0021937] 23/01/1974
Elliott Mr GD, BA MSc PGCHE MCLIP, Employment not known. [0060799] 12/12/2001
Elliott Mrs HL, First Asst., Lending L., Exeter Cent.L., Devon. [0054853] 15/04/1997 AF
Elliott Mrs HP, BA DipLib MCLIP, Unemployed. [0026362] 01/10/1976
Elliott Mr JC, Employment not known. [0060213] 10/12/2001
Elliott Mr JP, BA(Hons) DipILM, Parliamentary Documentation Offr., Scottish Parliament Inf.Cent., Edinburgh. [0047345] 17/07/1992
Elliott Mr JS, BA MCLIP, Life Member. [0004512] 17/08/1938
Elliott Miss K, BEd(Hons) DipILS MCLIP, Sch.Lib., Angus Council, Arbroath. [0055888] 16/12/1997
Elliott Mrs L, (was Dodd), MA FCLIP, Head of Tech.Serv./Joint Dep., Manchester Metro.Univ. [0004513] 20/01/1965 FE 22/05/1991
Elliott Mrs LP, BA MCLIP, City Child.Lib., Portsmouth Cent.L., Portsmouth City Council. [0031268] 02/10/1979
Elliott Mr M, MLib(Hons) MCLIP, Asst.City Lib. [0039510] 10/02/1986
Elliott Miss P, BA CertEd MCLIP, Lib., Wesminster Sch.L., London. [0028948] 07/02/1978
Elliott Mrs PE, M Phil BA MCLIP, Inf.Consultant. [0004519] 03/01/1972
Elliott Mr PJV, BSc MCLIP, Position unknown, Royal Air Force Mus., London. [0060282] 10/12/2001

Elliott Ms PM, (was Close), MCLIP, p./t.Asst.Lib., Rochdale M.B.C., Middleton L. [0004520] 01/01/1970
Elliott Mrs RJ, (was Mitchell), MCLIP, Asst.Lib., W.Educ.L.Board, N.Ireland. [0023241] 17/11/1974
Elliott Mrs SM, (was Arnold), MCLIP, Lib., Truro Coll., Cornwall. [0000405] 01/01/1971
Ellis Mrs A, BA MA, Inf.Project Mgr., Cambridge Univ., Devel.Off. [0058308] 06/01/2000
Ellis Dr ACO, MA PhD FCLIP, Life Member. [0004525] 19/01/1950
FE 01/01/1964
Ellis Mrs AJ, (was Toase), BA MCLIP, Principal Lib.Customer Serv., Blackpool Borough Council. [0022973] 02/10/1974
Ellis Mrs AR, (was Tradewell), BLib MCLIP, Careers Inf.Lib., Guidance Enterprises Ltd., Scarborough. [0026813] 02/11/1976
Ellis Mrs AW, (was Struthers), MCLIP, Retired. [0004527] 22/01/1950
Ellis Ms CE, BA(Hons), Inf.Offr., Chester City Council. [0059344] 12/02/2001
Ellis Ms CM, BA AKC DipLib MCLIP, Dep.Lib., CCLRC Rutherford Appleton Lab., Didcot. [0031262] 15/10/1979
Ellis Mr D, BA(Hons) DipLib MCLIP, Inf.Res.Mgr., Ashton, Leigh & Wigan PCT., Wigan. [0004530] 01/10/1971
Ellis Mrs D, Dist. L.Mgr., Borehamwood L. [0058556] 01/04/2000
AF
Ellis Prof. D, BA MA PhD MCLIP, Lect., Dept.of Inf.Studies, Univ.of Sheffield. [0032933] 01/10/1980
Ellis Mrs FA, (was Ashworth), MSc MCLIP, Retired. [0000462] 25/10/1966
Ellis Miss FM, BA MCLIP, Inf.Serv.Co-ordinator/Web Mgr., Brit.Council Paris. [0041646] 05/02/1988
Ellis Mr JL, BLib MCLIP, Co.Bor.Lib., Neath Port Talbot Co.Bor.Council, Neath Port Talbot. [0004536] 01/01/1968
Ellis Miss KE, Relief L.Asst., Leeds L.& Inf.Serv., L.H.Q. [0047936] 26/10/1992
Ellis Mrs M, (was Martin), BA DipLib MCLIP, Sch.Lib., Chepstow Comp.Sch., Monmouthshire Educ.Dept. [0009852] 01/01/1971
Ellis Mrs MJ, (was Thompson), BA(Hons) DipInfSci MCLIP, Sen.Inf.Asst., Roffry Pk.Inst., W.Sussex. [0034375] 26/10/1981
Ellis Mr P, MSc MCLIP BSc, Dept.Inf.Serv., Kodak Ltd., Harrow. [0025866] 01/04/1976
Ellis Mrs P, (was King), BA MCLIP, Sen.Subject Lib.(Business), Univ.of Plymouth. [0008399] 12/10/1971
Ellis Mr PM, Unemployed. [0046678] 09/12/1991
Ellis Mr RJ, MCLIP, Asst., Ceredigion C.C. [0021326] 17/10/1973
Ellis Ms RR, Elec.Resources Lib., State & Univ.L.Bremen, Germany. [0052397] 31/10/1995
Ellis Ms RS, BA(Hons) DipInfMan, Unemployed. [0049171] 08/10/1993
Ellis Ms S, BA(Hons), Mgr., Serv.Devel.& Delivery, Qinetiq, Dorchester. [0046229] 17/10/1991
Ellis Mrs TA, BA MA, Asst. Lib., Office Nat.Stats., London. [0056778] 14/10/1998
Ellis Miss VA, BA(Hons) DipILM, Unemployed. [0053123] 07/03/1996
Ellis-Barrett Mrs LGA, (was Ellis), BA(Hons) MSc, Dep.Librarian, St.Charles Catholic VI Form Coll., London. [0056262] 17/04/1998
Ellison Mrs A, MA, Stud., Liverpool John Moores. [0061729] 29/10/2002
Ellison Mrs M, BA(Hons) MSc, Acquisitions Lib., Freshfields bruckhaus Deringer, London. [0057413] 04/03/1999
Ellison Miss WL, BA(Hons) DipILM MCLIP, Subject Lib., Univ.Coll.Chichester. [0048699] 01/04/1993
Elliston Mrs D, (was Matthews), MCLIP, Coll.Res.Lib., Cambridge C.C. [0009936] 20/01/1970
Ellwood Miss CV, (was Lewis), BSc DipLib, Head of Subject Serv.& Systems, York Univ. [0033028] 07/10/1980
Ellwood Mrs F, (was Crawford), BA MCLIP, Bookseller, Ottakars plc., Loughborough. [0027489] 26/04/1977
Ellwood Mr MP, BA MCLIP, Project Offr., ASK, Lowestoft. [0026363] 04/10/1976
Ellyard Mrs JM, (was Whittaker), BA MCLIP, Sch.Lib., Glossopdale Comm.Coll. [0031490] 18/10/1979
Elmes Mrs SD, BA(Hons) PGDipInfMgmt, P./t.Sch.Lib., Sch.L.Serv., Dorset C.C. [0049774] 06/12/1993
Elmes Mrs TA, BA(Hons) MA, Inf.Exec., Brit.Film Comm., London. [0050805] 18/10/1994
Else-Jack Mrs J, (was Else), BLib MCLIP, Unemployed. [0040782] 08/06/1987
Elsegood Ms SA, BSc(Hons) MCLIP, Head of User Serv., Univ.of London L. [0043563] 08/11/1989
Elsmere Mrs HN, (was Phillips), MCLIP, Sen.Lib.-Resources, Croydon Coll., Croydon. [0018668] 11/02/1957
Elsmore Miss BM, MCLIP, Life Member. [0004550] 19/10/1942
Elson Mrs D, BA(Hons), p./t.Stud./Sen.Sec., Leeds Met.Univ. [0061314] 17/05/2002
Elson Miss SA, BA MCLIP, Dep.Ref.& Inf.Lib., Milton Keynes Council, Bucks. [0039225] 01/01/1986
Elstob Miss K, BA(Hons), Asst.Lib., City of Sunderland. [0050476] 15/08/1994
Elstob Ms SJ, BA(Hons) MA, Learning Resource Asst., Sussex Downs Coll. [0058261] 25/11/1999
Elston Mr LH, MCLIP, Retired. [0004554] 04/08/1941
Elton Mrs EA, (was Dutch), BA(Hons), Asst.Lib., Huddersfield Univ. [0047148] 11/05/1992
Elves Mr RJ, BSc(Hons) MSc MCLIP, Campus Lib., Brunel Univ., Isleworth. [0047361] 23/07/1992
Elwall Mr RF, MA DipLib MCLIP, Photographs Curator, Brit.Architectural L., R.I.B.A., London. [0023910] 23/01/1975
Elwell Ms H, (was Lewis), BA(Hons) MSc, Asst.Lib., Brit.Med.Assoc., London. [0047353] 21/07/1992
Ely Mrs HJ, (was Masters), MA MCLIP, L.Serv.Mgr.-(E.Surrey), Surrey C.C. Comm.Serv., Reigate. [0021457] 12/10/1973
Emberson Mrs JE, (was Isaac), MCLIP, Lib., L.B.of Sutton P.L. [0004568] 05/02/1959

Embling Mrs S, BA DipIM MCLIP, P./t.Child.Lib., Hants.C.C., Alton, Hants. [0053967] 16/10/1996
Emeniru Mr CE, HND, Unemployed. [0059548] 10/05/2001
Emerson Mr SD, BA MCLIP, Sen.Asst.Lib., L.B.of Harrow. [0004571] 16/01/1972
Emery Mr CD, BA MPhil MCLIP, Life Member. [0016845] 12/03/1958
Emery Miss EA, BA DipLib MCLIP, Asst.Lib., W.Kirklees Br., Kirklees. [0040363] 24/01/1987
Emery Mrs JM, (was Veasey), MCLIP, Unemployed. [0028384] 28/10/1977
Emery Mrs L, (was Reid), MA MCLIP, Sub-Lib., Univ.of Strathclyde, Glasgow. [0026526] 17/10/1976
Emery Mrs VA, p./t.work, Spring, Stoke-on-Trent. [0058294] 17/12/1999
Emery Mrs VM, (was Smith), MCLIP, Asst.Area Sch.Lib., Hants.Co.L., Winchester. [0021886] 20/01/1974
Emery-Wallis Cllr F, CBE HonFCLIP, Hon.Fellow. [0053197] 01/01/1996 FE 01/01/1996
Emly Mr MA, MA MCLIP, Sen.Asst.Lib.(Systems), Univ.of Leeds L. [0028427] 01/12/1974
Emmerson Mrs GJ, (was Johnson), MSc MCLIP, Employment not known. [0060052] 07/12/2001
Emmett Miss LE, BA MCLIP, Inf.Mgr., Chartered Inst.of Personnel & Dev., Wimbledon. [0038018] 01/01/1985
Emmett Mr MS, BSc MCLIP, Support Serv.Mgr., Brunel Univ., Uxbridge. [0020069] 12/01/1973
Emmott Mrs AJ, (was Mccann), BSc MCLIP, Sen.Lib., Wandsworth Prison L.Serv., L.B.of Wandsworth. [0004581] 01/01/1968
Emmott Mrs SJ, (was Goldsmith), BA, Lib., Heckmondwike Gram.Sch. [0043698] 28/11/1989
Empl Mrs W, P./t.L.Asst., Solihull M.B.C. [0052555] 07/11/1995
Emslie Mrs PA, (was Lee), BA MCLIP, p./t. L. Asst. - Sch. L., Essex C.C., Chelmsford, Essex. [0027074] 04/01/1977
Endicott Mrs AJ, (was Longdon), BA(Hons) PGDip, Asst.Lib., Learning Res.Cent., Univ.of Glamorgan. [0056167] 01/04/1998
Engel Mr CD, BA DipLib MCLIP, L.Serv.Mgr., Swansea NHS Trust, Swansea. [0033491] 10/01/1981
England Mrs AJ, (was Luke), BA MLS MCLIP, Lib., Cambridgeshire C.C., Wisbech (Base L.). [0033036] 08/10/1990
England Miss KJ, MA, Sch.Lib., Tiree High Sch., Isle of Tiree. [0055342] 01/10/1997
England Mrs P, (was Burbidge), MCLIP, Lib., St Laurence Sch., Bradford on Avon. [0004588] 18/02/1964
England Ms PM, MA BA MCLIP, L.& Inf.Serv.Mgr., Marie Curie Cancer Care, London. [0029165] 05/04/1978
England Ms SA, BA MA, Asst.Lib., English Heritage, London. [0061524] 05/09/2002
Englert Ms G, (was Jones), MCLIP, Asst.Grp.Lib., Wavelengths L., L.B.of Lewisham. [0008021] 08/10/1970
English Mr D, MCLIP, Dev.Mgr., Durham C.C. [0004595] 12/03/1963
English Mr DJ, BA MCLIP, Retired. [0004596] 07/10/1963
English Miss HE, BA(Hons) MA, Unemployed. [0059462] 03/04/2001
English Mr JS, MCLIP, Retired. [0004598] 23/08/1950
English Mr L, BA HDipEd PGDipLib, Inf.Researcher, SBC Warburg Dillon Read, London. [0039061] 29/10/1985
English Mrs LH, (was Scrogham), BA(Hons) DipILM MCLIP, Lib., Barrow Cent.L., Cumbria. [0052195] 12/10/1995
Ennion Mrs C, BA DipEdTech MCLIP, Sch.Lib., Scottish Borders Council, Hawick High Sch. [0023560] 20/01/1975
Ennis Mrs AP, (was Bartlett), BSc MCLIP, Sen.Marketing Offr.STN Agency UK, Royal Soc.of Chemistry, Cambridge. [0019994] 11/01/1973
Ennis Miss KA, BA(Hons) DipLib MCLIP, Prof.Adviser, Academic & Research L., CILIP. [0035972] 10/03/1983
Enright Ms S, BA DipLib MCLIP, Dir.ISLS, Univ.of Westminster, London. [0030831] 17/05/1979
Enser Prof PGB, BA(Econ) MTech PhD MBCS FCLIP HonFCLIP, Head of Sch., Sch.of Computing, Math.& Inf.Sci., Univ.of Brighton. [0060283] 10/12/2001 FE 01/04/2002
Ensing Miss RJ, FCLIP, Life Member, 103 Engadine St., London, SW18 5DU. [0004606] 08/03/1940 FE 01/01/1951
Ensor Mrs TK, (was James), BA(Hons) MA MCLIP, Lib., Slaughter & May, London. [0055718] 05/11/1997
Entwisle Mrs J, (was Bullifant), BA MCLIP, Community Lib.(Job-share), Sheffield L.& Inf.Serv., Broomhill L. [0002042] 01/01/1967
Entwisle Miss PM, MCLIP, Retired. [0004609] 09/03/1950
Entwistle Miss GA, BA PGDipLib MCLIP, Asst.Div.Lib., Lancs.C.C.L. [0041073] 06/10/1987
Entwistle Mr MA, BA(Hons) MCLIP, Lib., Warrington Bor.Council. [0048319] 25/11/1992
Entwistle Mr NW, MA MCLIP, Main L.Mgr., Queen Mary, Univ.of London. [0018345] 13/10/1972
Envy Mrs D, Employee, Gateshead M.B.C. [0052302] 24/10/1995
Epps Mrs AT, (was Bourdon), BSc MCLIP, Employment not known. [0060151] 10/12/2001
Erbach Ms GME, MPhil DipLib, Sen.Editorial Serv.Mgr., News Internat.Newpapers Ltd., London. [0040160] 30/10/1986
Erentz Ms JD, (was McWilliam), BA MCLIP, Sch.Lib., St.Andrews Secondary Sch., Glasgow City Council. [0044393] 05/10/1990
Erlanger Miss S, Student (non-LIS), Kingston Maurward Coll., Dorchester, Dorset. [0058629] 18/04/2000
Ernesta Mrs LGE, MCLIP, Tech.Adviser, Min.of Culture & Inf., Seychelles. [0029381] 01/07/1978
Ernestus Mr H, FCLIP, Retired, Am Eckbusch 41/82, D-42113 Wuppertal. [0016853] 30/01/1956 FE 15/09/1993
Erskine Mr JGW, BA DIP ED MCLIP, Asst.Lib., Stranmillis Univ.Coll., Belfast. [0023911] 22/02/1975
Erskine Mrs KJ, (was Dennis), BA(Hons) MA DipLS MCLIP, Book Rep., Roger Bayliss Prof.Rep., Maidstone, Kent. [0041059] 09/10/1987

Erskine Mr SCB, MA MCLIP, Company Lib., Nat.Air Traffic Serv.Ltd. [0023120] 06/11/1974
Escott Ms A, MA MCLIP, Retired. [0004613] 28/01/1967
Escott-Allen Mrs CS, (was Escott), BA(Hons), Admin.Asst., Self Employed. [0038440] 24/04/1985
Escreet Mr PK, MA MCLIP, Life Member, 29 Southview Drive, Bearsden, Glasgow, G61 4HQ, Tel:0141 9424356. [0004615] 15/08/1951
Eskriett Ms CJ, BA(Hons), p./t.Stud./Asst.Lib., Media Res., Univ.of Brighton. [0058843] 29/08/2000
Espitalier-Noel Mrs C, (was Jones), BA MCLIP, Career Break. [0036693] 03/11/1983
Essakhi Ms RA, (was Collins), BA DipLib, Lib.(Job Share), Hertfordshire C.C. [0034343] 26/10/1981
Essex Mrs A, (was Allen), BEd(Hons) DipLIS MCLIP, Sen.Team Leader, Warwickshire C.C., Nuneaton L. [0047454] 19/08/1992
Essex Mrs SE, (was Dalton), MCLIP, Asst.Lib., High Peak Dist., Derbys.C.C. [0026880] 16/12/1976
Esslemont Mr JL, MA MSc MCLIP, Position unknown, DTC Research Cent., Maidenhead. [0060284] 10/12/2001
Esson Mrs AC, (was Heron), BA DipLib MCLIP, Freelance Law Lib., Beachcroft Wansbroughs, Manchester. [0018765] 07/08/1972
Esson Ms KA, (was Berry), BA MCLIP, Audit Commission Inspector, Inspection Serv., S.Reg., Bristol. [0030736] 10/04/1979
Esteve-Coll Dame EAL, DBE BA MCLIP, Vice-Chancellor, Univ.of E.Anglia. [0032580] 20/09/1969
Ethell Ms E, ALAA MCLIP, Unemployed. [0016859] 01/02/1967
Etheridge Mr M, BA(Hons) MSc MIIA, p./t.Stud.,Head of Inf.& Records, Univ.North London, Transport for London. [0059783] 02/10/2001
Etherton Mrs JJ, BSc DipInfSc, Inf.Consultant,Jean Etherton Assoc, 3 Little Common, Stanmore, Middx., HA7 3BZ. [0051859] 17/07/1995
Etkind Mrs A, (was Kahan), BA DipLib MCLIP, p./t.Inf.Consultant, Univ.of Herts., Hatfield. [0026876] 28/12/1976
Eu Ahara Mrs SIT, MCLIP, Retired. [0004624] 01/01/1965
Euden Mr WBE, BA FKC MCLIP, Life Member. [0004625] 12/02/1934
Euesden Mr MA, MSc DipInfSc MCLIP, Asst.Lib., Dept.of Trade & Ind.H.Q.L., I.R.S.Dialtec. [0035440] 01/10/1982
Eunson Miss BG, BA FCLIP, Life Member. [0004626] 03/01/1947 FE 01/01/1959
Evans Mr A, BA, Reg.L.Serv.Consultant, OCLC PICA, Birmingham. [0039947] 06/10/1986
Evans Mrs A, BScMSc, Research Asst., KPMG, London. [0061801] 13/11/2002
Evans Mr AC, MCLIP, Mgr., Informatics, UBQT Media Plc, Berkshire. [0028754] 06/01/1971
Evans Ms AJ, BA(Hons) DipLib MCLIP, p./t.Asst.Lib., Univ.of W.of England, Bristol. [0042330] 20/10/1988
Evans Prof AJ, BPharm PhD HonFCLIP FCLIP, Life Member, Tel.01636 700174, The Moorings, Mackleys Lane, N.Muskaham, Newark, NG23 6EY. [0004634] 16/04/1958 FE 01/01/1969
Evans Mrs AKL, (was Norton), BA MCLIP, Asst.Lib., Swansea Inst.of H.E., City & County of Swansea. [0004635] 08/10/1967
Evans Miss AM, MCLIP, Lib., Herschel Grammar Sch., Slough. [0029645] 02/10/1978
Evans Ms AM, BSc(Hons) MA, SR Comm.Lib., Leicester City Council. [0038960] 15/10/1985
Evans Mrs AP, (was Thompson), BA(Hons) DipLib, Prof.Lib.-p./t., Birmingham Univ. [0043379] 16/10/1989
Evans Mr BD, BA MCLIP, Retired. [0004641] 10/09/1956
Evans Mrs BT, BSc DipLib MCLIP, Sch.Lib./Res.Mgr., Agnes Stewart C.of E.High Sch., Leeds City Council. [0025748] 16/02/1976
Evans Miss CA, MA MLib MCLIP, Lib., Child.Serv., Billericay L. [0049301] 20/10/1993
Evans Mrs CA, (was Helman), BA MALS, Ref.Lib., L.B.of Lewisham. [0042116] 03/10/1988
Evans Mr CH, MLS MCLIP, Dep.Lib., Univ.of Wolverhampton, Wolverhampton. [0004645] 17/01/1972
Evans Mrs CH, (was Edwards), BA(Hons) PGCE, p./t.L.Asst., Univ.Coll.of N.Wales, Bangor. [0047276] 01/07/1992 AF
Evans Mr CJ, BA MCLIP, Unemployed. [0004646] 05/10/1971
Evans Mr CJ, BSc, Inf.Offr., Rhodia Chirex Ltd., Cramlington. [0060472] 11/12/2001
Evans Mrs CK, (was Cox), MCLIP, L.Serv.Mgr., Worcestershire C.C. [0020120] 23/01/1973
Evans Miss CL, BA(Hons), p./t.Stud./Sen.L.Asst., Univ.of Cent.England, Birmingham, Univ.Coll.Worcester. [0059088] 13/11/2000
Evans Miss CM, BA(Hons), Stud., Univ.N.London. [0059761] 20/09/2001
Evans Miss CR, BA MSc, Asst.Inf.Offr., Help the Hospices, London. [0057771] 02/09/1999
Evans Mr D, BMus(Hons) ALCM DipLIS, Stud., Thames Valley Univ., p./t.L.Asst., Sevenoaks Sch., Kent. [0058686] 05/08/1999
Evans Mr DE, BMus DipLib MCLIP, I.L.T./Dep.Coll.Lib., Hammersmith & W.London Coll., London. [0027964] 21/09/1977
Evans Mr DH, BA DipLib MCLIP, Inf.& Local Studies Lib., Isle of Anglesey C.C., Llangefni. [0024274] 22/05/1975
Evans Mrs E, BA PGDip, Stud., Loughborough Univ. [0058686] 30/05/2000
Evans Miss EA, MCLIP, Retired. [0004655] 01/01/1955
Evans Miss EE, BA MCLIP, Retired. [0004657] 09/02/1960
Evans Mrs EE, (was Hills), MCLIP, Life Member. [0004658] 10/10/1966
Evans Miss EJ, BA(Hons), Distance Learn.Stud., Univ.of Waled, Aberystwyth. [0061762] 06/11/2002
Evans Miss EJA, CBE HonFCLIP FCLIP, Life Member. [0004660] 08/04/1930 FE 01/01/1953
Evans Mrs FM, (was Brown), BLib MCLIP, Unemployed. 0029508] 18/09/1978
Evans Ms G, BA(Hons) MSc, Lib., Berwin Leighton, London. [0052202] 12/10/1995
Evans Mr GH, BLib MCLIP, Systems Lib., Torfaen C.C. [0043980] 23/03/1990

Evans Ms GM, BA DipLib MCLIP, Inf.Serv.Devel.Lib., Rhondda Cynon Taff Council, Treorchy. [0024663] 07/10/1975
Evans Miss GR, BA(Hons) MCLIP, Asst.Subject Lib.(Music), Lanchester L., Coventry Univ. [0046323] 28/10/1991
Evans Mr HB, MA, Retired. [0004666] 09/09/1936
Evans Mrs HJ, (was Bray), BA MCLIP, Career Break. [0039476] 31/01/1986
Evans Mr HL, BSc DipLib MCLIP, Welsh L.A.Exec.Offr., D.I.L.S., Univ.of Wales, Aberystwyth. [0032940] 23/10/1980
Evans Ms HP, Asst.Lib., Queen Elizabeth Grammar Sch., Horncastle, Lincs. [0054934] 16/05/1997
Evans Mr I, BSc(Hons), Unemployed. [0061372] 04/07/2002
Evans Mrs IH, MA MCLIP, Retired. [0004669] 01/01/1952
Evans Miss J, BA MCLIP, Policy Offr., DTI, State Aid Policy Unit, London. [0037825] 17/11/1984
Evans Miss J, BA (Hons) DipMus DipLib, Lib.i/c.of Inter-L.Loans, Edinburgh Univ.L. [0055159] 25/07/1997 AF
Evans Mrs J, MCLIP, Unemployed. [0023379] 01/01/1968
Evans Mrs J, BA DipLib MCLIP, Coll. Lib., Brighton Coll.of Tech., E.Sussex. [0022855] 07/10/1974
Evans Dr JA, MSC PhD BSc MCLIP ALAA, Unemployed. [0020259] 18/02/1973
Evans Mr JA, BSc MSc MCLIP, Inf.Serv.Asst., Nat.Inst.Biological Standards Ctrl., S.Mimms, Herts. [0051970] 24/08/1995
Evans Mrs JB, (was Ruane), BA(Hons) MA MCLIP, Document & Electronic Res.Mgr., The Coll.of Law, Birmingham. [0053687] 05/09/1996
Evans Mr JC, MA(Oxon) PGCE MSc(Econ), Sch.Lib., Warwickshire C.C., Kenilworth Sch. [0054187] 06/11/1996
Evans Mr JE, MCLIP, Area Lib., Gwynedd L., Gwynedd Council. [0004673] 20/10/1969
Evans Mrs JE, BA MCLIP, Inf.Systems Mgr., Imperial Coll., London. [0018450] 15/10/1972
Evans Ms JE, BSc(Hons) DipInf, Dep.Dir., Australian Sci.& Tech.Heritage, Cent., Carlton, Australia. [0054493] 02/01/1997
Evans Mrs JFG, (was Gunson), BA DipHE MCLIP, L.Mgr.-E., Stockport M.B.C. [0025754] 12/02/1976
Evans Mr JH, BSc, p./t.L.Asst., Eastman Dental Inst., London. [0047604] 05/10/1992
Evans Mr JK, BA MCLIP, Retired. [0004675] 19/10/1966
Evans Miss JL, BA(Hons) MA, Sen.Exec.to the Dir., Univ.of Oxford. [0049048] 15/09/1993
Evans Ms K, BA(Hons), Retrospective Conversion Catr., Natural History Museum, London. [0058584] 04/04/2000
Evans Miss KL, BA(Hons) MCLIP, Project Offr., Univ.of Southampton. [0055414] 08/10/1997
Evans Mr KM, BA(Hons) MA MCLIP, Lib., E.Riding of Yorkshire Council. [0055519] 16/10/1997
Evans Mrs LA, (was Bostock), MCLIP, L.Tech., Thomas Aveling Sch., Kent. [0021049] 27/09/1973
Evans Mr LD, BA(Hons) MCLIP PGCE DipLib, Sen.Educ.Lib., N.E.Wales SLS, Flintshire. [0050313] 17/06/1994
Evans Miss LR, BSc(Hons) DipILM, Asst.Lib., Manchester Metro.Uni. [0056276] 17/04/1998
Evans Mrs LS, (was Cockrill), MCLIP, Child.Lib.(p/t), Basingstoke L., Hants.C.C. [0031803] 18/01/1990
Evans Mr LSE, BA(Hons) MA, Lib., Taylor Joynson Garrett, London. [0054596] 29/01/1997
Evans Lord M, of Temple Guiting CBE HonFCLIP, Hon.Fellow. [0057252] 04/02/1999 FE 01/01/1999
Evans Mr M, BA MCLIP, Lib., William Hulmes Grammar Sch., Manchester. [0009309] 01/01/1970
Evans Mrs M, (was Mackendrick), DipLIS, Lib., Land Rover, Gaydon, Warks. [0049879] 07/01/1994
Evans Ms M, BD(Hons) MSc DipCG, Unemployed. [0050893] 27/10/1994
Evans Mrs MA, (was Lomax), MA MCLIP, Retired. [0016862] 04/04/1951
Evans Mrs ME, MCLIP, Princ.L.Mgr.:Med.& Healthcare Serv., Doncaster M.B.C., Head & Prof.L., Doncaster Royal Inf. [0004687] 04/01/1970
Evans Mrs ME, (was Johns), BA MCLIP, Asst.Lib.(Saturdays), Worcs.C.C., Kidderminster. [0027821] 06/09/1977
Evans Mr MP, Lib., MOD, Royal Artillery, James Clavell L., Woolwich. [0059304] 31/01/2001
Evans Mrs N, Retired. [0004691] 01/01/1952
Evans Miss NA, BEd(Hons) DipLIS MCLIP, Art & Design Lib., Univ.of Wales Coll., Newport. [0047553] 01/01/1994
Evans Miss NL, BA (Hons), E-Lib., Henley Mgmnt Coll. [0060957] 18/01/2002
Evans Mrs NN, BA MSc, Dep.Mgr., Learning Res., N.Herts.Coll., Stevenage. [0054437] 09/12/1996
Evans Miss OP, MCLIP, Life Member. [0004693] 24/02/1945
Evans Mrs PE, DipInfSc MCLIP, Employment unknown. [0060316] 17/10/1979
Evans Mr PJ, BA MCLIP, Ref.Lib., Educ.& Leisure Dept., L.B.of Southwark. [0036855] 11/01/1984
Evans Mrs PM, (was Jervis), BA MCLIP (PGCE)FE, LC Devel.Mgr., Coleg Glan Hafren, Cardiff. [0024078] 20/03/1975
Evans Mr PW, BA MCLIP, Dir., Biblio Tech Ltd., Bristol. [0004696] 09/01/1968
Evans Miss RA, Stud., Univ. of Wales Aberystwyth. [0059389] 27/02/2001
Evans Ms RA, BA(Hons) MA, Position Unknown, Court Serv., London. [0058014] 12/01/1999
Evans Miss RM, MCLIP, Retired. [0004699] 01/01/1962
Evans Mr RS, BA MCLIP, Princ.Lib., Luton Cent.L., Luton Bor.Council. [0023617] 01/01/1975
Evans Mrs RS, (was Howells), BA MA, Consultant, London. [0049166] 08/10/1993
Evans Mrs S, (was Barton), MCLIP, Unemployed. [0000885] 26/04/1971
Evans Mrs SA, BA(Hons) MA MCLIP, Asst.Lib., Colwyn Bay L., Conwy Co.Council, N.Wales. [0051893] 31/07/1995

Evans Miss SJ, BA MCLIP, Lib., Nat.Assembly for Wales, Cardiff. [0033976] 05/06/1981
Evans Mr SJ, BA MSc, Inf.Mgr., Eversheds, London. [0054520] 14/01/1997
Evans Mrs SJ, (was Young), BA (Hons) PG DIP LIS, Unemployed, [0050051] 02/03/1994
Evans Mrs SM, (was Bigland), MCLIP, Sch.Lib., Wells Cathedral Sch., Somerset. [0004704] 27/01/1966
Evans Mrs TN, (was Legge), BSc(Hons) MA MCLIP, Unemployed. [0052888] 19/01/1996
Evans Mrs VS, MCLIP, Lib., Nottingham City Council. [0004495] 12/08/1968
Evans Mr WE, MCLIP, Resident Germany. [0004707] 25/02/1968
Evans Mrs WJ, (was Townsend), BA(Hons), Asst.Lib.-I.T., Coll.of St Mark & St John, Plymouth. [0040407] 02/02/1987
Evans Mr WR, BA(Hons), Stud., Oxford Univ. [0061825] 11/11/2002
Evans Mrs YE, (was Denly), MCLIP, Life Member. [0004709] 05/01/1949
Evason Miss M, MA MCLIP, Retired. [0004710] 01/01/1939
Eve Mr CRT, Stud. [0044320] 07/09/1990
Eveleigh Mr FH, BA DipLib MCLIP, Lib., Westminster Sch., London. [0029648] 10/10/1978
Evenson Ms SE, BA, Inf.Cent.Mgr., Nabarro Nathanson, London. [0047798] 19/10/1992
Everall Mrs AM, OBE BA MCLIP, Serv.Mgr., Derbyshire L.& Heritage, Young People & Policy Devel. [0026365] 12/10/1976
Everall Mr IR, BA MCLIP, Pub.L.Serv.Mgr., Walsall M.B.C., Lib.& Inf.Serv.Div., Cent.L. [0026366] 12/10/1976
Everall Mrs SA, (was Sams), MCLIP, Lib., Herts.L.Serv., Cunningham, St Albans. [0026540] 01/10/1976
Everatt Mrs J, (was Smith), MCLIP, As & When Lib., L.B.of Harrow, Middx. [0019818] 01/10/1972
Everest Miss GH, MCLIP, Comm.Lib., Tonbridge, Kent C.C. [0025032] 23/11/1975
Everett Mrs C, (was Farquhar), BA MCLIP, p./t.Asst.Lib., Chester/Neston, Cheshire C.C. [0032943] 13/10/1980
Everett Mrs JE, (was Fish), BA DipLib MCLIP, Trust Fundraiser, Motor Neurone Disease Assoc., Northampton. [0036996] 16/01/1984
Everett Mrs JS, (was Sutherland), MCLIP, Sen.Asst.Lib., Leamington Spa Br., Warwickshire Co.L. [0014253] 11/03/1971
Everett Mrs LCA, (was Charnock), MCLIP, Relief Lib., R.B.Windsor & Maidenhead, Windsor. [0002624] 23/02/1971
Everhard Ms CJ, MA DipLib MCLIP, Resident Overseas. [0018329] 12/10/1972
Everiss Ms E, BSc(Hons), Lib./Resources Mgr., I.C.I.T., Heriot-Watt Univ., Stromness, Orkney. [0058372] 31/01/2000 AF
Everist Mrs J, Sch.Lib., Holmewood House Sch., Tunbridge Wells. [0057067] 07/12/1998
Everist Mrs LA, (was Latham), BA(Hons) PGDip, Child.L.Mgr., Walsall M.B.C. [0054056] 15/01/1996
Everitt Ms CE, BA(Hons) CertEd DipLIS MCLIP, Asst.Lib., Southampton City Coll. [0052330] 30/10/1995
Everitt Mrs EA, (was Sutherland), BSc MSc MCLIP, p./t.Acquisitions Lib., Royal Coll.of Nursing, London. [0028374] 17/11/1977
Everitt Mrs FI, Super., Droitwich L., Worcs. [0061187] 01/04/2002 AF
Everitt Dr J, (was Timmins), B.Lib PhD, Project Mgr., Univ.of Wales, Aberystwyth. [0042496] 23/11/1988
Everitt Mrs L, (was Pajcin), L.Asst., Missionary Inst.London. [0045383] 20/11/1990
Everitt Mr P, BA(Hons) MCLIP, Lib., Cheshire C.C. [0053003] 14/02/1996
Everitt Mrs R, MSc, Snr.L.Asst., Imperial Coll., Cent.L.,London. [0059628] 04/07/2001
Everitt Mrs SM, (was Partridge), BSc DipLib MCLIP, Relief L.Asst., Wolverhampton P.L. [0030024] 13/11/1978
Everson Mr AD, MA Med MA MCLIP, Asst.Lib., Inst.of Electrical Engr., London. [0044034] 01/04/1990
Everson Mr ME, BA MCLIP, Knowledge Mgr., The Thomas Saunders Partnership, London. [0037454] 02/10/1984
Everton Miss LC, BA, Stud., Loughborough Univ. [0061570] 02/10/2002
Eves Mr AJ, MCLIP, Inf.Lib., L.B.of Enfield, Edmonton Green L. [0004718] 24/02/1969
Eves Mr BJ, B LIB MCLIP, Inf.Offr., Limra, Watford. [0023355] 27/11/1974
Evetts Mrs L, (was Price), BA(Hons) MA MCLIP, Asst.Lib., Nat.Police L., Bramshill. [0054445] 10/12/1996
Ewan Mr AI, MCLIP, Princ.L.& Inf.Serv.Offr., Argyll & Bute L.Serv. [0004721] 01/01/1966
Ewart Mrs KUH, (was Drummond), MCLIP, Res.Lib., Univ.of Wolverhampton. [0004723] 22/03/1965
Ewen Miss SM, BA MCLIP, Sch.Lib., Rosehall High Sch., Coatbridge. [0031270] 17/10/1979
Ewins Mrs KB, (was Whittard), MCLIP, Operation Mgr., Bridgend L.& Inf.Serv., Bridgend. [0019702] 06/02/1973
Exall Mr SD, BA MCLIP, Asst. Lib., Redbridge Cent. L. [0023177] 23/10/1974
Exon RevdDr FCA, BA DipLib FCLIP FALIA, Priest-in-Charge, Anglican Church of Australia, Shelley, Perth. [0025273] 01/10/1967 FE 01/04/2002
Exton Miss LS, BSc MSc MCLIP, Employment not known. [0060756] 12/12/2001
Eyeons Mrs MC, (was Closier), BTh, L.Asst., Oxford Brookes Univ.L. [0056222] 07/04/1998 AF
Eynon Mr AD, BA(Hons) DipLIS MCLIP, L.Resource Mgr., Llandrillo Coll., Colwyn Bay. [0045745] 15/05/1991
Eyre Mrs F, (was Rutherford), MCLIP, Unemployed. [0019986] 11/01/1973
Eyre Mrs GD, (was White), BA PhD MCLIP AALIA, Lect./Dir., Sch.of Inf.Studies/Cent.for Inf.Std, Charles Sturt Univ., Australia. [0015702] 28/09/1970
Eyre Mr JB, MCLIP, Retired. [0004731] 06/02/1951

Eyre Mr RJ, BA(Hons), Asst.Lib., Health & Safety Exec., Sheffield. [0057825] 25/08/1999
Eyres Mrs AG, (was Theakstone), BA MCLIP, Retired. [0004733] 01/01/1955
Eyres Mrs RJ, (was Shore), BA(Hons) DipLIS MCLIP, Asst.Lib., Manchester Met.Univ., Alsager, Staffs. [0050864] 24/10/1994
Eze Miss AOA, BA (Hons), Grad.Trainee Lib., Trinity Coll., Cambridge. [0061464] 08/08/2002
Fabling Miss JL, BA MCLIP, Lib., Totton L., Hants.C.C. [0037284] 31/05/1984
Fadele Mr AO, BSc, Ch.Exec., African Books & Arts, Nigeria. [0061030] 07/02/2002
Faden Mrs AC, (was Banks), BA DipLib MCLIP, Unemployed. [0038717] 01/10/1985
Fagan Mr LA, BA(Hons) MCLIP, Asst.Lib., Coll.of Occupational Therapists, London. [0054605] 27/01/1997
Fagg Mrs AR, (was Bexon), MCLIP, Housewife. [0004742] 20/10/1965
Fagg Miss BEM, MCLIP, Retired. [0004743] 27/03/1956
Faherty Miss MT, B.LIB MCLIP, Lib./IT Offr., Internat.Cocoa Organization, London. [0032796] 12/09/1980
Fahy Mr E, Sen.Mgr., PricewaterhouseCoopers, Tax Inf.Cent., London. [0038795] 04/10/1985
Fairall Mrs JB, (was Barnes), MCLIP, Employment not known. [0032011] 01/02/1980
Fairall Mrs SAC, (was Stevens), Retired. [0027759] 01/08/1977
Fairbrass Ms VJ, (was Coles), MCLIP, Learning Res.Co-ordinator, Brit.Sch., Croydon. [0011919] 01/01/1970
Fairbrother Mr JV, MCLIP, Life Member. [0004747] 20/01/1961
Fairbrother Mr P, BA(Hons) MSc MCLIP, Knowledge Mgr., Mental Welfare Communion for Scot., Edinburgh. [0050426] 27/07/1994
Fairburn Ms J, BA MCLIP, Pub.Serv.Mgr., L.B.of Hillingdon, Cent.L. [0035716] 18/01/1983
Fairclough Mr DT, BA, Stud., Loughborough Univ. [0060024] 26/11/2001
Fairclough Mrs MR, BA(Hons), Br.Lib., Brighton NHS Healthcare Trust, Rosaz House Br.L. [0051930] 09/08/1995
Fairfax Mrs WA, Stud., Univ.of Wales, Aberystwyth, & Employee, Readers Serv., Robinson L., Newcastle Univ. [0058746] 03/07/2000
Fairhurst Mrs DJ, (was Ward), MCLIP, Dep.Area/Lend.Lib., Birkenhead Cent.L., Wirral Bor.Council. [0004751] 22/01/1970
Fairhurst Miss SL, MCLIP, Team Co-ordinator (Job Share), L.B.of Southwark. [0027060] 14/01/1977
Fairless Mrs OJ, (was Barton), BA DipLIS MCLIP, Reader Dev.Offr.-Sure Start, Blackburn with Darwen B.C. [0048037] 04/11/1992
Fairman Mr RB, BSc DipLib MCLIP, Learning & Inf.Systems Mgr., Univ.Coll.Worcester, Worcester. [0033288] 07/11/1980
Fairweather Mrs JM, (was Green), MCLIP, Sch.Lib., Heritage Community Sch., Derbys.C.C. [0019494] 01/01/1969
Fairweather Mrs KJ, BA(Hons), L.Asst., Ellon Academy. [0057610] 24/05/1999
Fairweather Miss N, DipLib MCLIP, County Stock Mgr., Cambs. [0032942] 09/10/1990
Fairweather Mrs PJ, (was Wing), MCLIP, [0029111] 27/02/1978
Fairweather Ms SK, BA PGDip MA, Asst.Lib., House of Lords, London. [0055326] 01/10/1997
Faisal Mrs FM, BSc, Learning Facilitator., Westminster Kingsway Coll. [0058782] 20/07/2000
Faithfull Miss AC, BA(Hons) DipInf, Inf.Offr., Freshfields,Bruckhaus Deringer, London. [0053020] 31/01/1996
Fajemisin Mr MO, BEd MLS, Unemployed. [0061701] 22/10/2002
Falconer Mrs L, (was Lockley), MCLIP, Inf.Devel.Mgr., Leeds City Council. [0009040] 23/11/1971
Falconer Mrs TA, Sch.L.Mgr., St.Margaret's Sch. [0061398] 07/07/2002
Falla Mrs J, (was Dale), BA DipLib MCLIP, Head of Serv.to Educ.& Young People, Guille-Alles L., Guernsey. [0036629] 24/10/1983
Falla Miss MJ, BA MA MLib MCLIP, Ch.Lib., Guille-Alles L., Guernsey. [0035477] 06/10/1982
Fallis Mr CA, BA(Hons) MA, Sports Lib., B.B.C., Sports L., London. [0055270] 11/09/1997
Fallon Mrs SA, BA(Hons), Sen.Editor, Sweet & Maxwell, W.Yorks. [0052770] 11/12/1995
Fallon Miss SM, (was Opie), MCLIP, Nat.Maritime Museum, Cornwall. [0011023] 13/12/1971
Fallone Mrs E, (was Boak), BA MCLIP, Unemployed. [0031200] 02/10/1979
Falzon Mrs AL, (was Hutchinson), BA DipInf MCLIP, Sen.Inf.Offr., Sch.Health & Related Research, Univ.Sheffield. [0045290] 01/10/1990
Fancy Mrs JM, (was Goodridge), MCLIP, Unemployed. [0005697] 03/03/1964
Fanning Mrs JL, (was Singleton), BA(Hons) MA, Inf.Offr., Consumers Assoc., London. [0055542] 17/10/1997
Fanshawe Mrs GJ, (was Bryce), MCLIP, p./t.Lib., Archbishop Tenison Sch., Croydon. [0004758] 14/02/1962
Faragher Mrs HF, (was Crimmins), BA MA PGCE MCLIP, Knowledge Mgmt.Co-ordinator, N.Cheshire Health Auth. [0007009] 28/03/1960
Farbey Mr RA, BA DipLib MCLIP, Mgr.-Inf.Cent., Brit.Dental Assoc., London. [0027965] 13/10/1977
Fardon Mr C, BA(Hons) DMS DipLib MCLIP, Grp.Mgr., L.B.of Waltham Forest, Cent.L. [0029958] 20/11/1978
Farley Mr D, BA MCLIP, Lib., King Alfred's Coll., Winchester. [0026367] 07/10/1976
Farley Mrs J, (was Kendall), MCLIP, Enquiry Offr., Sudbury L., Suffolk. [0008260] 01/01/1971
Farley Mrs LM, L.& Learning Res.Offrr., Stephenson Coll., Coalville. [0052790] 14/12/1995
Farley Miss LS, BA MCLIP, Trust Lib., N.Middlesex Univ.Hosp NHS Trust, London. [0004763] 01/01/1971
Farley Mrs MA, (was Williams), BA MCLIP, Unemployed. [0027381] 16/03/1977
Farley Mr MJ, BSc MSc, Inf.Offr., Linklaters & Alliance, London. [0059170] 05/12/2000

Farley Mrs S, Learning Cent.Advisor, Knowsley Comm.Coll., Huyton. [0055671] 07/11/1997
Farline Mrs DJ, Stud., Manchester Met.Univ. [0061359] 24/06/2002
Farlow Mrs EM, (was Williams), MCLIP, Non LIS. [0015922] 02/10/1967
Farmer Mrs CM, (was Jupp), BA DipLib MCLIP, Lib., Essex C.C. [0030444] 29/01/1979
Farmer Mrs JGS, (was McAvoy), BA MSc MCLIP, Lib.,Sch.Resource Cent., Ballerup High Sch., S.Lanarkshire Council. [0042405] 15/10/1988
Farmer Miss JK, Document Control Asst.(Temp.), Office Angels, Woking. [0047135] 06/05/1992
Farmer Ms KE, BA(Hons) DipInf, Lib., L.B.Bromley. [0048011] 02/11/1992
Farmer Miss M, MA DipLib MCLIP, Sen.L.Asst., Univ.of St.Andrews, Fife. [0035694] 14/01/1983
Farmer Miss RS, BA MA MCLIP, Inf.Offr., Linklaters, London. [0052603] 13/11/1995
Farmer Miss VG, MA(Hons), Stud., Strathclyde Univ. [0059768] 01/10/2001
Farmilo Miss VL, BA(Hons), L.Asst., L., Oxford Brookes Univ. [0058329] 12/01/2000 AF
Farn Mrs HM, (was Mortimore), BA MA MCLIP, p./t.Sen.L.Asst., Univ.L., Newcastle-upon-Tyne. [0024529] 01/09/1975
Farncombe Mrs JC, (was Greenberg), BA(Hons) MCLIP, Self employed Website Designer. [0036843] 11/01/1984
Farndale Mrs LC, (was Banham), Sen.Super., Local Govt.Inf.Serv., Cambs.C.C. [0045429] 01/02/1991 AF
Farndell Mrs M, (was Burton), BA(Hons) MCLIP, Employment Unknown. [0048933] 26/07/1993
Farndon Mrs AJ, (was White), MCLIP, Sen.Lib.-Educ., Sch.L.Serv., W.Sussex C.C. [0004770] 15/11/1965
Farnham Mr DG, MCLIP, Sen.Lib., Petersfield, Hants Co.L. [0004772] 08/03/1967
Farnsworth Mr MR, MA MCLIP, Retired. [0004774] 19/01/1961
Farnsworth Mrs MR, (was Powell), BA MCLIP, Career Break. [0022143] 21/02/1974
Farnworth Miss CM, MA, Sch.Lib., St.Thomas More RC High Sch., N.Shields. [0061073] 26/02/2002
Farnworth Mrs LM, (was Butler), BA DMS MCLIP, Div.Lib., Cent.Div., Preston. [0002205] 13/07/1970
Farquhar Mr JD, MCLIP, Retired, 26 Yewlands Avenue, Fulwood, Preston, PR2 9QR. [0004777] 21/09/1955
Farquhar Miss SC, MA DipLib, Help-desk Serv.Mgr., Aberdeen Univ.L. [0027966] 20/09/1977
Farquharson Mrs H, BA(Hons), Reader Serv.Lib., UHB Trust L., Birmingham. [0057159] 05/01/1999
Farquharson Miss VR, MA DipLib MCLIP, Community Lib., S.Lanarkshire Council. [0031062] 01/08/1979
Farr Mr DJ, BA(Hons) MCLIP, Asst.Lib., Staffs.C.C., Stafford, Staffs. [0048764] 12/05/1993
Farr Miss EMJ, BA MCLIP, Area Lib., Stirling Council. [0004779] 08/05/1970
Farr Mrs HE, (was Bracey), BA(Hons) MSc(Econ) MCLIP, Customer Serv.Team Leader, Staffs.C.C. [0051179] 23/11/1994
Farr Miss JM, BA MCLIP, Asst.Lib., Aberdeen City.L., Scotland. [0032721] 24/07/1980
Farr Mrs MF, BA DipLib, Local Stud.Lib., Surrey Hist.Cent., Woking. [0033289] 16/11/1980
Farr Mr RC, BA MCLIP, Subject Lib., London Guildhall Univ. [0004780] 06/11/1966
Farr Mrs S, (was Hill), BA(Hons) DipILS, Gallery Asst., 20-21 Visual Arts Cent., Scunthorpe. [0047485] 02/09/1992
Farrall Mrs HJ, (was Shail), BA MLib MCLIP, Learning Adviser, Univ.of Lincs., Hull. [0039277] 01/01/1986
Farrar Mrs AF, (Greenaway), MCLIP, Lib., Patrick McGrath L., Broadmoor Hosp.Auth., Crowthorne, Berks. [0005908] 01/09/1968
Farrar Mrs CC, (was Molloy-Morley), MA MCLIP, Sen.L.Asst., Trinity Coll.of Music, London. [0004783] 02/08/1967
Farrar Mr DP, BA(Hons) DipILS MCLIP, Information Researcher, Inst.of Electrical Engineers. [0050258] 27/05/1994
Farrar Mrs HM, (was Arnold), BLS MCLIP, L.Mgr., L.B.of Ealing, W.Ealing L. [0027871] 04/10/1977
Farrell Miss A, Admin.Asst., RehabCare, Dublin 4, Ireland. [0053863] 07/10/1996
Farrell Mrs CE, (was Brown), MCLIP, p./t.Subject Lib., Nursing & Midwifery, Chester Coll.of H.E. [0004784] 19/03/1962
Farrell Ms EJ, BA(Hons) MCLIP, Lib.Serv.Mgr., Salford PCT., Salford, Manchester. [0027670] 01/04/1977
Farrell Mrs HE, (was Puckette), BA MCLIP, Unemployed. [0012024] 04/04/1967
Farrell Miss HP, BA(Hons) DipILS MCLIP, Lib., Oxfordshire C.C. [0042786] 01/03/1989
Farrell Mrs I, (was Harper), MA DipILS MCLIP, Asst.Lib., W.Sussex C.C., Crawley P.L. [0042747] 16/02/1989
Farrell Mr JP, MA DipLib MCLIP, Inf.Lib., Kingston Univ., Surrey. [0037516] 04/10/1984
Farrell Mrs JP, (was Grindrod), MCLIP, Div.Lib., Lancs.C.C., S.E.Div. [0006010] 09/07/1968
Farrell Miss KE, BA(Hons), Stud. [0059382] 23/02/2001
Farrell Mrs PP, (was Parsons), BA MCLIP, Asst.Ref.&Inf.Serv.Lib., Bury M.B.C., Bury, Lancs. [0021838] 08/02/1974
Farrell Mrs SM, MSc MCLIP, Employment not known. [0060673] 11/12/2001
Farrelly Ms CA, BA MCLIP, Sen.L.Asst., Chatsworth L., Lancs.C.C. [0030833] 28/04/1979
Farrer Ms EC, (was Gibbs), Research Lib., B.B.C., Manchester. [0056152] 11/03/1998
Farrimond Mrs AE, (was Hayward), BA(Hons) MCLIP, Operations Super., Worcs.C.C., Bibl.Serv.Unit. [0026738] 07/11/1976
Farrington Mrs A, BA MCLIP, Princ.Lib.:Inf.Serv., Wakefield M.D.C. [0020953] 03/09/1973

Farrington Mrs AJ, (was McKinnon), BSc, Stud., Liverpool John Moores Univ. [0049436] 27/10/1993
Farrington Mrs GM, (was Fenn), BA MCLIP, Comm.Serv.Lib., Beds.C.C., Biggleswade L. [0004788] 01/11/1963
Farrington Mrs SI, BA MCLIP, Sch.Lib., The Sele Sch., Hertford. [0004790] 01/01/1963
Farrow Mrs AE, (was Picksley), BA MA MCLIP, Issue Desk Super., Univ.of Durham, Palace Green L. [0028121] 04/10/1977
Farrow Mrs AJ, (was Bardsley), MA BA MCLIP, Sen.Lect., Liverpool John Moores Univ., Business Sch. [0000741] 13/10/1970
Farrow Miss EC, BA(Hons) MA MCLIP, Lib. [0049849] 22/12/1993
Farrow Mr JF, BA MEd MCLIP, Retired. [0004791] 27/05/1963
Farrow Mr RTA, BA ALAI FRSA MCLIP, Retired. [0004792] 06/03/1964
Farthing Mr A, BA (Hons) MCLIP, Local Hist.Lib.-N., Sefton M.B.C., Merseyside. [0046712] 02/01/1992
Farthing Miss T, BA(Hons), Inf.Offr., Inst.of Chemical Engineers, Rugby, Warwickshire. [0048423] 14/05/1993
Fasanya Dr JO, BA(Hons) DipLib MLS PhD, Self-employed, Fasal Inf., Nigeria. [0046874] 17/02/1992
Fasciato Mr E, Stud., Manchester, [0061837] 15/11/2002
Faseyi Mr JAO, MCLIP, Retired, Agags Propriety Ltd., Nigeria. [0016872] 01/01/1962
Fatoki Mrs OC, BSc(Hons) MA, Systems Lib./Lib., Kenneth Dike L., Univ.of Ibadan, Nigeria. [0061222] 16/04/2002
Faughey Mr J, FCLIP DAES, Life Member. [0004793] 30/01/1948
FE 01/01/1958
Faughey Mrs LC, (was Likeman), MCLIP, Retired. [0008923] 17/01/1962
Faul Mrs JM, (was Pakenham-Walsh), BA DipLib MCLIP, Lib., Slough Bor.Council, Slough L. [0044341] 01/10/1990
Faulknall-Mills Ms JS, (was Faulknall), BLS MCLIP, Asst.Lib., Atherstone L., Warwickshire C.C. [0039227] 01/01/1986
Faulkner Mrs DA, (was Cook), BA MA DipLib MCLIP, Dir.-Academic Serv., Dartington Coll.of Arts, Nr Totnes,Devon. [0034340] 01/01/1962
Faulkner Ms K, (was Roud), BA(Hons) MSc MCLIP, Serials Lib., Baker & Mckenzie, London. [0054755] 01/04/1997
Faulkner Mr M, BA(Hons), Asst.Lib., Dept.of Trans.Local Govt.and the, Regions, London. [0051982] 30/08/1995
Faulkner Mrs M, BA(Hons) MCLIP AITI, p./t.Lib. [0031608] 09/11/1979
Faulkner Ms S, DipLib MCLIP, Lib., Sister of Charity of Jesus & Mary, Moore Abbey, Kildare. [0040931] 27/08/1987
Faulkner Miss SA, BA(Hons) MSc(Econ), Asst.Inf.Specialist., Cardiff Univ. [0055223] 18/08/1997
Faulkner Mrs SF, (was East), BA MCLIP, Asst.Lib., Univ.of N.London. [0022235] 18/03/1974
Faulkner Mr TWA, MCLIP, Retired. [0004799] 29/01/1948
Faulkner-Brown Mr H, OBE MC RIBA HonFCLIP, Hon.Fellow. [0035168] 01/06/1982 FE 01/06/1982
Faulks Ms KM, MCLIP, Co-ordinator, Rochdale Domestic Violence Forum, Council for Vol.Serv. [0023515] 21/11/1975
Faux Mrs JM, BSc(Hons), Stud., Univ.of Central England, Birmingham. [0059233] 11/01/2001
Favarato Ms G, BSc MSc, Asst.Librarian, LSE Library. [0053117] 15/03/1996
Favell Mrs VA, (was Hurley), MA PGCE MCLIP, Res.Lib., Yth.Serv., Herts.C.C. [0007509] 23/08/1969
Favret Mr LF, BA MIMgt FRSA MCLIP, L.Operations Mgr., Bromley P.L. [0004801] 06/04/1970
Fawcett Mrs AB, (was Harrison), BA MCLIP, Unemployed. [0004802] 25/02/1959
Fawcett Mr DJ, FInstPet DipTh MCLIP, Life Member. [0004804] 20/08/1948
Fawcett Mrs EA, P./t.Stud./L.Asst., Manchester Met.Univ., Lancaster Univ.L. [0059648] 11/07/2001
Fawcett Mrs GM, (was Knight), BA MLS MCLIP, Team Leader, Talis Inf.Ltd., Inst.of Res.& Devel.,Univ.of Birm. [0009715] 01/10/1978
Fawcett Mrs H, (was Purcell), MCLIP, Unemployed. [0012047] 01/01/1978
Fawcett Mrs H, BA, Sen.Lib., N.Westminster Sch., London. [0029269] 13/04/1978
Fawcett Miss LA, Inf.Mgr., Entec UK Ltd., Newcastle upon Tyne. [0056461] 16/07/1998
Fay Mr D, BA MCLIP, Grp.Lib., Scarborough, N.Yorks.C.C. [0032275] 29/02/1980
Fay Miss J, BA(Hons), Lib., Transport Research Lab.Ltd., Crowthorne, Berks. [0037987] 03/01/1985
Fazackerley Miss A, BA(Hons), Asst.-Local Studies, Cumbria C.C. [0058717] 01/07/2000
Fazackerley Miss ME, BA(Hons) MCLIP, Life Member. [0004808] 04/10/1945
Fazackerley Miss VJ, BA(Hons), Bookstart Plus Offr., Hattersley. [0049282] 20/10/1993
Fazal Mrs HM, BA PGCE MA MCLIP, Lib., High Sch.for Girls, Gloucester. [0041537] 16/01/1988
Fea Miss VA, MBE MCLIP, Retired. [0004809] 02/09/1956
Fealdman Ms M, (was Perkins), CertED MCLIP, Area Child.Lib., Church End L., London. [0011546] 24/01/1972
Fearn Mrs SB, (was Potter), BA MCLIP, Sch.Lib., Eltham Coll., Mottingham. [0020198] 07/02/1973
Feather Prof JP, MA BLitt PhD FCLIP, Prof., Dept.of Inf.Sci., Loughborough Univ. [0022488] 20/04/1974 FE 14/03/1986
Featherstone Mrs A, (was Armstrong), BA MCLIP, Retired. [0040673] 01/01/1952
Featherstone Ms AW, MCLIP, Princ.Lib.Adult & Community Serv., Beds. [0004814] 01/10/1971
Featherstone Mr JR, BA DipLib MCLIP, Lib., Dept.of Trans.Local Govt.and the, Regions, London. [0039918] 01/10/1986
Featherstone Mr TM, BA FCLIP, Life Member, Tel:01663 765508. [0004815] 03/05/1949 FE 01/01/1961
Febry Miss JH, BA(Hons) DipIS MCLIP, Inf.Offr., Olswang, London. [0051004] 08/11/1994

Feeley Ms AC, BA(Hons), Stud./Unemployed, Loughborough Univ. [0058774] 17/07/2000
Feely Mrs J, Stud. [0058497] 15/03/2000
Feeney Mr SG, BA(Hons) MA DipLib, Unemployed. [0051825] 07/07/1995
Feetham Miss MG, BA(Hons) DipLib ILTM MCLIP, Inf.Lib., Southampton Inst.of H.E. [0039072] 28/10/1985
Fei Ms F, BA, L.Asst.(p./t.), Sheffield Coll. [0058919] 06/10/2000
Felgate Miss CW, BA(Hons), Inf.Offr., Norton Rose, London. [0055497] 16/10/1997
Fell Miss C, BA DipLib, Lib., Prison Serv.Coll., Rugby. [0037160] 16/02/1984
Fellerman Miss JB, BA MCLIP, Sen.Lib,Comm.Devel., L.B.of Barking & Dagenham. [0028559] 27/12/1977
Fellowes Mr RC, L.Asst./Publicity Co-ordinator, Carlton Int.Media Ltd. [0056525] 10/08/1998 AF
Fellows Miss CR, MCLIP, Community Lib., Quinton, Birmingham L.s. [0023444] 01/01/1975
Fellows Miss SC, MCLIP, Campus L.& Inf.Mgr., Middlesex Univ. [0019930] 01/01/1973
Felmingham Mr EM, BA(Hons) DipILM, Stud., Liverpool John Moores Univ. [0057786] 05/08/1999
Felstead Ms AP, BA PG DipLib MCLIP, Asst.Lib., Bodleian L., Oxford. [0038730] 01/10/1985
Feltham Mrs V, MA MCLIP, Research Offr., Knowsley L.Serv., Merseyside. [0042636] 25/01/1989
Felton Miss AE, BA MA(Ed) MCLIP, Lib., Aylwin Sch., London. [0024943] 22/10/1975
Fender-Brown Mrs AJ, (was Brown), BA MCLIP, Mgr., Brent/Harrow Work Experience Cons., Middx. [0004828] 22/10/1964
Fenerty Mrs VJ, (was Smith), BSc(Hons) MA MCLIP, Unemployed. [0043515] 06/11/1989
Fenn Miss JM, BA DipLib MCLIP, Asst.Lib., Min.of Defence, London. [0038949] 23/10/1985
Fenn Miss KL, BA, Stud., Loughborough Univ. [0059395] 28/02/2001
Fensom Mr RJ, L.Asst., Cambridge Univ.L. [0004835] 13/10/1967 AF
Fenton Ms AC, BA(Hons) MSc MCLIP, Inf.Offr., Building Design Partnership, Glasgow. [0051420] 10/02/1995
Fenton Miss CR, BA(Hons), Stud./Community Info.Dev.Worker, Manchester Meto.Uni. [0057840] 06/09/1999
Fenton Mrs DE, (was Smith), BA MCLIP, Unemployed - not actively seeking, work. [0033157] 10/10/1980
Fenton Mrs I, (was Belfield), MCLIP, L.& Inf.Serv.Mgr., N.Staffs.Hosp.Trust, Stoke-on-Trent. [0004836] 17/02/1961
Fenton Mrs J, BA MCLIP, Acq.lib., Trinity & All Saints, Leeds. [0027158] 09/02/1977
Fenton Mrs L, (was Greenway), BA MCLIP, Sch.L.Serv.Mgr., Lancs.C.C., Sch.L.Serv., Preston. [0022426] 29/04/1974
Fenwick Mrs A, (was Kitching), Super./Sen.Asst.(Job Share), Cent.Ref.L., Doncaster M.B.C. [0045146] 24/07/1990 AF
Ferber Mrs LA, (was Morris), BSc MCLIP, Unemployed. [0004839] 13/07/1968
Fereance Ms JT, BSc LLB DLIS, Employment not known. [0043419] 26/10/1989
Fereday Miss HJ, MCLIP, Sen.Lib., L.B.of Waltham Forest, Young Peoples Stock Team. [0033218] 16/10/1980
Fergus Mrs J, MCLIP, Sen.Lib., Midlothian Council. [0031063] 03/08/1979
Ferguson Mrs B, BA BA(Hons)ILM, Asst.Inf.Lib., Northumberland Co.L.H.Q., Morpeth. [0056091] 16/02/1998
Ferguson Miss CM, MA MCLIP, Unit Leader, Lend.Serv., Dundee City Council. [0028429] 29/11/1977
Ferguson Mr DJ, MA DipLib MCLIP, Retired. [0027159] 31/01/1977
Ferguson Mrs HO, MA DipLib MCLIP, Temp.Employment. [0023377] 15/12/1974
Ferguson Mr IS, PG Dip MSc, Stud., Strathclyde Univ. [0060896] 21/12/2001
Ferguson Mr JB, MBE MA FCLIP, Retired. [0004850] 10/09/1937
FE 01/01/1949
Ferguson Mrs J, MCLIP, Retired. [0004851] 11/10/1966
Ferguson Miss JPS, MBE MA FRCP Edin MCLIP, Retired, 21 Howard Place, Edinburgh, EH3 5JY. [0004852] 18/02/1953
Ferguson Mrs KM, (was James), BA MCLIP, Unemployed. [0007714] 02/10/1969
Ferguson Mrs LJ, (was Donald), MA DipLib MCLIP, Unemployed. [0035901] 11/02/1983
Ferguson Mrs LS, (was Horn), MA MCLIP, Dep.Dir.of Health L., Warrington Hosp., Health Care L.Unit. [0031643] 25/10/1979
Ferguson Mrs M, (was Devlin), BLib MCLIP, Team Lib., Culture & Learning, Castlereagh Grp., Tullycarnet L. [0046928] 28/02/1992
Ferguson Mrs MM, (was Macrae), MA MCLIP, Sen.Lib.Youth Services., Western Isles Libraries. [0009572] 22/10/1971
Ferguson Miss RA, BA(Hons) MCLIP, Sen.Asst.Lib., Manchester Met.Univ. [0052393] 31/10/1995
Ferguson Mrs S, (was Robertson), BA MCLIP, Library & Inf.Worker, Dundee Dist.Council. [0033130] 01/10/1980
Ferguson Mrs S, BA(Hons) ACII MCLIP, L. Mgr., Northumbria Water. [0050750] 17/01/1994
Ferguson Mrs SM, MCLIP, Inf.Lib., Ewell L., Surrey Co.L. [0004861] 23/02/1968
Ferguson Mrs SR, (was Edwards), MA DipLib MCLIP, Resident in U.S.A. [0038967] 22/10/1985
Ferguson Mrs VA, (was Martin), BA FCLIP, Retired. [0004862] 03/10/1957
FE 20/12/1976
Fergusson Mrs AD, (was Mackie), MA MCLIP, Comm.Lib., E.Dunbartonshire Council, Kirkintilloch. [0021327] 15/10/1973
Fergusson Mr JJ, BA DRLP MCLIP, Outreach Lib., E.Dunbartonshire Council. [0004863] 01/01/1963
Fern Mr RF, BA MCLIP, Retired. [0023223] 30/10/1974

237

Fernandes Mr DC, MCLIP, Peoples Network Proj.Co-ordinator, L.Borough Richmond Upon Thames. [0022025] 21/02/1974
Fernandez Ms B, Inf.Mgr., NHS Direct - S.E.London, Beckenham, Kent. [0051822] 07/07/1995
Fernando Mrs A, BSc(Hons), Asst.Lib., Dept.for Educ.& Skills, London. [0046645] 02/12/1991
Ferrabee Mrs JAG, (was Jones), BA, p./t.Asst.Lib., Surbiton High Sch., Kingston, Surrey. [0037698] 17/10/1984
Ferrand Ms HC, MA(Hons) MCLIP, Retired. [0058494] 01/01/1958
Ferrar Mrs L, (was Provan), DipEdTech MCLIP, Educ.Res.Offr., Educ.Res.Serv., E.Dunbartonshire. [0022005] 11/01/1974
Ferrie Ms JM, MA DipLib MCLIP, Librarian, St.Leonards Library, East Kilbride. [0035348] 08/10/1982
Ferris Mr DJ, MCLIP, Retired. [0004868] 01/01/1968
Ferris Mrs HC, (was Henson), BA(Hons) MSc MCLIP, Maternity leave. [0056599] 09/09/1998
Ferris Miss JA, BA(Hons) DipLIS MCLIP, Asst.Lib., Allen & Overy, London. [0054018] 18/10/1996
Ferris Mrs M, (was Guest), MCLIP, Asst.Lib.(Job Share), Stourbridge L., Dudley M.B.C. [0004869] 13/09/1965
Ferro Mr DP, BA MA MCLIP, Sub-Lib., Liaison, Edinburgh Univ.L. [0004870] 27/08/1966
Ferro Mrs EA, (was Adam), MCLIP, Fine Art Dept., Univ.of Edinburgh, Old Coll. [0000031] 15/02/1967
Fessey Mr MC, CB MSc FSS HonFCLIP, Retired. [0037823] 02/11/1984
FE 02/11/1984
Few Mrs DRE, (was Brown), BSc MCLIP, Lib., Leics.L.& Inf.Serv. [0004873] 01/01/1968
Fewings Mrs L, (was Marsh), MCLIP, Asst.Lib., Univ.of the W.of England,., Bristol. [0009782] 04/04/1972
Fiander Ms L, BSc(Hons), Stud., Univ.of Sheffield. [0061298] 16/05/2002
Fiander Mrs WJ, (was Archer), BSc MA MCLIP, Asst.Dir., Learning Res.(Nursing & Midwifery), Chester Coll.of H.E. [0028394] 20/11/1977
Ficken Miss EJ, BSc(Hons) DipILS MCLIP, Unemployed. [0048211] 16/11/1992
Fiddes Mr AJC, BSc(Hons) PhD, Admin.Support Offr., Comm.Health Sheffield. [0053444] 01/07/1996
Fiddes Mrs DJ, BA(Hons), L.Asst.& Stud., Edinburgh Univ.L. [0061565] 02/10/2002
Fidelle Mr CP, BA(Hons), L.& Inf.Asst., BHP Billiton, London. [0059271] 24/01/2001 AF
Field Mrs A, (was Buxton), BA MCLIP, Child.Lib., Barnsley Cent.L. [0035577] 25/10/1982
Field Mr B, FCLIP, Life Member, Tel.01775 725006, 35 Grange Dr., Spalding, Lincs., PE11 2DX. [0004878] 21/10/1940 FE 01/01/1956
Field Mrs C, (was Edwards), BA(Hons) MA MCLIP, Unemployed. [0049332] 22/10/1993
Field Mr CR, FAMS MIMgt FCLIP, Retired. [0004881] 12/02/1959
FE 01/01/1965
Field Mrs KL, (was Davis), BA(Hons) DipIM MCLIP, Inf.Lib.-Chemistry & Earth Sci.L., Kingston Univ., Surrey. [0049260] 19/10/1993
Field Mr M, BA PGDip DipLib MCLIP, Inf.& Knowledge Mgmt Adviser, CILIP., London. [0034495] 17/11/1981
Field Mr R, Stud., Univ.of Brighton. [0058831] 22/08/2000
Field Mrs SK, (was Jones), BA(Hons) MA, Comm.Lib., Resp.for Peoples Network, Nottingham City Council. [0055861] 04/12/1997
Field Mr TJ, BSc MCLIP MISTC, Employment not known. [0060610] 11/12/2001
Field Ms WE, BA MCLIP, Lib., Bacon's Coll., London. [0037700] 11/10/1984
Field Mrs WM, (was Bailey), BA MCLIP, Life Member. [0004884] 02/07/1953
Field-Taylor Mrs AJ, (was Taylor), BA(Hons) MSc MCLIP, R&D Lib., Instant L.Ltd., Hull. [0024230] 12/05/1975
Fielden Miss E, MA MA, Sen.L.Asst., Fitzwilliam Museum, Cambridge. [0058853] 05/09/2000
Fielder Mrs CA, (was Scratcherd), BA MCLIP, p./t.Asst.Lib., Hinchingbrooke Sch., Huntingdon. [0021235] 11/10/1973
Fielder Mrs EM, (was Herron), MCLIP, Retired. [0004888] 12/03/1938
Fielding Miss D, MCLIP, Cent.Dir., American Embassy, The Hague, The Netherlands. [0023117] 05/11/1974
Fielding Mr DJ, BSc(Hons) PGDip, Asst.Lib., Soc.Inclusion, Bury Met.L., Bury. [0057469] 29/03/1999
Fielding Mrs MHL, (was Chapman), BA(Hons) DipILM MCLIP, Career Break. [0047768] 14/10/1992
Fielding Ms VK, (was Moore), BA(Hons) MCLIP, Sen.Inf.Offr., Osborne Clarke, Bristol. [0044685] 26/11/1990
Fieldsend Mrs VC, (was Mcard), BA MCLIP, Retired. [0004893] 11/01/1956
Fileman Mrs J, (was Grundy), BA MCLIP, Systems Lib., Brit.Geological Survey, Nottingham. [0026394] 10/10/1976
Filer Mr RB, BA MCLIP, Lib., Thornbury L., S.Glos. [0004896] 14/03/1971
Files Mr RB, MCLIP, Self-employed, 81 Merrie Gardens, Sandown, IOW, PO36 9QS. [0004898] 10/03/1966
Finch Miss AM, BA(Hons) MSc(Econ) MCLIP, L.Mgr., UKDS., Middx. [0052053] 02/10/1995
Finch Mr JR, BA(Hons) MSc(Econ) CIPD MCLIP, L.& Inf.Offr., Chartered Inst.of Personnel & Dev., London. [0054537] 20/01/1997
Finch Ms K, BA(Hons), Coll.Lib., Fakenham Coll. [0059246] 15/01/2001
Finch Mr RJA, MA DipLib MCLIP, Deputy Head-L.& Learning Res., Univ.of Derby. [0021422] 22/10/1973
Finch Mr SKW, BA MCLIP, Sen.Lib., Local Studies, Bromley Cent.L. [0029650] 19/10/1978
Finch Mr TW, MCLIP, Mgr., Doncaster L.& Inf.Serv. [0004905] 23/01/1966
Fincham Ms LK, BA(Hons) DipLib, Inf.Mgr., RMJM Ltd., London. [0036300] 01/10/1983
Fincher Mrs PJ, (was Hudson), BA DipLib MCLIP, Team Lib., Young Peoples Serv., Kent C.C.Educ.& Ls., Ashford, Kent. [0028595] 29/12/1977

Findlay Miss DH, Position unknown, Birmingham Coll.of Food, Tourism, and Creative Studies. [0056219] 07/04/1998
Findlay Mrs J, (was Holliday), BA MCLIP, Dep.Lib.:Reader Serv., Univ.of Luton. [0018093] 01/10/1992
Findlay Miss JA, BSc PGDip, Asst.Lib., SSC L. Edinburgh. [0060944] 14/01/2002
Findlay Ms M, CertEd MA MCLIP, H.of Learning Resources, Lambeth Coll., London. [0018681] 26/01/1968
Fineberg Mrs LME, (was Lewis), MCLIP, [0008883] 16/01/1968
Finerty Mr AH, MCLIP, Special Serv.Lib., Richmond Cent.L., L.B.of Richmond-upon-Thames. [0004911] 21/09/1970
Finerty Mr ET, FCLIP, Life Member, Tel.01923 263907, 9 Gable Close, Abbots Langley, Herts., WD5 0LD. [0004912] 26/08/1935
FE 01/01/1957
Finlay Ms A, BA DipLib MCLIP, Sen.L.Asst., Univ.of Edinburgh. [0044940] 23/01/1991
Finlay Mrs E, (was McGraw), BA DipLib MCLIP, Music & Media Lib., Renfrewshire L.H.Q., Paisley. [0038675] 19/09/1985
Finlay Ms HJ, (was Loughran), BA(Hons) MCLIP, Learning Advisor, Leeds Met.Univ. [0044556] 26/10/1990
Finlay Mrs JE, Asst.Lib., Northern Ireland Civil Serv., Dept.of Agriculture & Rural Devel. [0053791] 01/10/1996
Finlayson Ms DM, BA MCLIP, Health Inf.Mgr., NHS Direct, Kent Surrey & Sussex, Kent. [0021324] 13/10/1973
Finlayson Mrs G, Dir., John Mackintosh Hall, Gibraltar. [0055037] 01/07/1997
Finlayson Mrs HO, (was Wilson), MA DipLib MCLIP, Training & Stock Circulation Lib., L., Alloa. [0016069] 01/01/1970
Finn Mrs AJ, (was van der Linden), BA MCLIP, Administrator, Dept.of the Environment, Transport, & the Regions, London. [0025440] 13/01/1976
Finn Ms N, BA(Hons) DipIS MCLIP, Grp.Mgr., E.Sussex C.C., Bexhill L. [0047797] 19/10/1992
Finnemore Mr BG, BA DIP MCLIP, Asst.Lib., Keele Univ.L., Staffs. [0004916] 01/01/1968
Finnen Mr JR, BA(Hons) MSc MCLIP, Business Planning Offr., City of Westminster. [0050421] 17/07/1996
Finnerty Miss RM, BA(Hons), Deputy Curator, Ruskin L., Lancaster Univ. [0053513] 10/07/1996
Finnesey Mrs SA, (was Landers), BSc DLIS MCLIP, Team Leader-Stock Supply, Liverpool L.& Inf.Serv. [0022949] 01/10/1974
Finnett Miss CEA, BLIB MCLIP, Sen.Asst.Lib., Mobiles & Housebound Serv., L.B.of Barnet. [0030162] 27/12/1978
Finney Ms EP, BA(Hons), Info.Adviser, Adsetts Cent., Sheffield. [0058276] 06/12/1999
Finnie Mr SP, BA MCLIP, Area Co-ordinator, N.E.Area Off., Dennistoun L., Glasgow City Council. [0034955] 14/05/1982
Finnigan Mrs LJ, (was Wadge), L.Asst., Northwick Park Hosp., Harrow. [0040216] 04/11/1986
Finnis Mrs A, (was Holgate), Sen.Asst.Lib., Denton Wilde Sapte, London. [0048928] 26/07/1993
Finnis Miss ML, FCLIP, Retired. [0004919] 11/03/2029 FE 01/01/1933
Firbank Miss HR, BA(Hons) MA, Temp.Sen.Inf.Asst., Bibliographic Services. [0057494] 06/04/1999
Firby Miss NK, BA M Phil FCLIP, Retired. [0004920] 12/03/1935
FE 01/01/1946
Firebrace Ms C, Inf.Offr., London. [0055401] 09/10/1997
Firmin-Cooper Mrs KA, BA(Hons), Records Mgr p./t., Nat.Audit Off., London. [0039069] 24/10/1985
Firth Miss A, BA(Hons), Stud., Univ.Northumbria @ Newcastle. [0059804] 03/10/2001
Firth Mrs C, (was Grice), BA MCLIP, Non Resident Tutor, St.John's Coll., Univ.of Durham. [0005960] 19/10/1970
Firth Mr FJ, MA MCLIP, Subject Lib., Univ.Cent.England, Birmingham. [0035180] 05/10/1982
Firth Mr GW, BA MCLIP, Liaison Lib., Royal Holloway & Bedford New Coll., Egham. [0025441] 22/09/1966
Firth Mrs N, (was Bhatia), BSc MCLIP, Resident in U.S.A. [0060071] 07/12/2001
Firth Mrs PM, (was Vine), BA MCLIP, Inf.Resources Cent.Mgr., The Emmbrook Sch., L., Wokingham, Berks. [0030898] 25/01/1979
Firth Miss S, BA (Hons), L.Asst., Harpenden L. [0060881] 18/12/2001 AF
Firth Mr TC, DipLIP MCLIP, Div.Ref.Lib., Hants.Co.L.Serv., Winchester Ref.L. [0034064] 08/09/1981
Fish Ms WS, BA(Hons)PG DipLib, H.of Public Servs., Wellcome Inst.for the Hist.of Med., L., London. [0039885] 06/10/1986
Fishburn Mrs RK, (was Stickley), MCLIP, Chief Catr., Harrow P.L. [0014047] 09/01/1970
Fisher Mrs A, (was Tossell), BA(Hons) DipLIS MA MCLIP, Weekend LRC Mgr., Univ.of London. [0050116] 05/04/1994
Fisher Ms A, (was Kropholler), MA MCLIP, Asst.Ch.Exec., Herts.C.C. [0034281] 21/10/1981
Fisher Miss B, BA(Hons), Stud., Strathclyde Univ. [0059977] 14/11/2001
Fisher Mrs BA, (was Dick), MCLIP, Inf.Cent.Asst., Philips Research Labs., Redhill. [0004937] 30/01/1967
Fisher Ms BM, MLib FCLIP, Head of Academic Serv.& Devel., Learning Cent., Sheffield Hallam Univ. [0004938] 11/07/1971 FE 17/11/1999
Fisher Miss CM, MA(Hons) DipILS, Lib., James Watt Coll.of F.& H.E., N.Ayrshire Campus. [0058812] 07/08/2000
Fisher Ms CR, (was Humby), BA(Hons), Trust Lib., City Hosp.Sunderland, Sunderland Royal Hosp. [0038302] 11/03/1985
Fisher Ms DC, (was Dickinson), MA DipLib MCLIP, Unemployed. [0029633] 10/10/1978
Fisher Mrs DJG, (was Collinson), BA MCLIP, Inf.Adviser(Health), S.Bank Univ., London. [0024485] 01/10/1975
Fisher Mrs E, (was Wagstaff), MCLIP, Lib.:Learning Res.Mgr., Truro Coll.(Tertiary), Cornwall. [0015169] 02/10/1971

Personal Members

Fisher Mrs ERK, (was Taylor), DipLib MCLIP, Mgr.-Community & E-L.Serv., Cent.L., Rotherham. [0031470] 26/09/1979
Fisher Mrs HS, (was Burt), MCLIP, Team Lib.p/t.Cent.L., P/t HMYOI Huntercombe, Oxon.C.C. [0033771] 18/03/1961
Fisher Mrs J, (was Edmond), MCLIP, Asst.Lib., Bucks.C.C., Burnham L. [0004940] 25/02/1959
Fisher Mrs JC, (was Thorpe), MSc MCLIP, Child.Serv., W.Sussex Co.L., Reading Is Fundamental U.K. [0004944] 01/01/1961
Fisher Mr JH, BA(Hons) MSc, Inf.Offr., The Learning Cent., Leeds Met.Univ. [0061272] 09/05/2002
Fisher Mr JK, MA MCLIP, Lib., Guildhall L., London. [0023561] 12/01/1975
Fisher Miss JW, BSc MCLIP, Lib., Off.of Water Serv., Birmingham. [0021250] 08/10/1973
Fisher Miss L, BA(Hons), p./t.Stud/Trainee Lib., Bristol Univ., TLT Solicitors. [0059309] 02/02/2001
Fisher Miss LC, BA(Hons), Site L.Inf.Offr., Irwin Mitchell Solicitors, Birmingham. [0058974] 13/10/2000
Fisher Miss LJ, MA MCLIP, Inf.Cent.Mgr., Competition Commission, London. [0031277] 08/10/1979
Fisher Mr M, BA MCLIP, Retired. [0004947] 07/10/1961
Fisher Mrs M, (was Nettleton), MCLIP, Unemployed. [0020926] 19/09/1973
Fisher Mrs MID, (was Wood), MCLIP, Asst.Lib., Kirklees Metro.Council, Dewsbury, W.Yorks. [0021682] 01/01/1974
Fisher Mrs MJ, (was Herridge), MCLIP, Head of L.Serv., Hadlow Coll., Tonbridge. [0021097] 02/10/1973
Fisher Mr R, BA MCLIP, Br.Lib., W.Lothian Council. [0021138] 04/10/1973
Fisher Mr RK, M LITT MA FCLIP, Retired. [0004950] 02/01/1961
FE 16/07/1986
Fisher Miss RM, BA MCLIP, Life Member. [0004951] 24/06/1948
Fisher Mrs SA, Lib./Resources Offr., Wilmington Grammar School for Boys, Dartford. [0052154] 09/10/1995 **AF**
Fisher Mrs SJ, (was Richardson), BLib MCLIP, Requests Lib., Hants.Co.L., Winchester. [0025403] 19/01/1976
Fisher Mrs SJ, MA, L.Asst., Univ.of London, Inst.of Classical Studies. [0050620] 01/10/1994
Fisher Ms VL, BSc(Econ) MCLIP, Lib.(Special Resp.for Child.Serv.), Winchester Lend.L., Hants.L.Serv. [0050746] 11/10/1994
Fisher Mr WE, BA MEd DipLib MCLIP, Lect., Chiba Inst.of Tech., Japan. [0029187] 03/04/1978
Fishleigh Miss JF, BA MA MCLIP, Inf.Serv.Mgr., Norton Rose, London. [0040966] 01/01/1987
Fishwick Mrs HP, BA(Hons) MCLIP, Asst.Lib., City Coll.Manchester. [0020037] 16/01/1973
Fisken Mrs SL, MA(Hons) PGCE, Lib., Royal Hosp.for Sick Child., Edinburgh. [0057648] 16/06/1999
Fitch Mr AC, MCLIP, Librarian, Colchester Central L. [0004956] 21/11/1970
Fitch Miss JM, MCLIP, Retired. [0004957] 30/09/1950
Fitch Ms KA, BA(Hons) MA MCLIP, Higher L.Exec., House of Commons, London. [0052232] 16/10/1995
Fitt Mrs CA, (was Greenhalgh), BA MCLIP, Area Lib.:Child.& Young People, Mexborough L., Doncaster M.B.C. [0025541] 25/01/1976
Fittall Miss PS, BA DipLib MCLIP, Records Administrator, Norman Disney & Young, Australia. [0042672] 08/07/1977
Fitter Miss MS, BA DipLib MCLIP, Multicultural Lib., Coventry City Council. [0031278] 02/10/1979
Fitton Mr JA, BA DipLib MCLIP, Unemployed. [0028811] 05/02/1978
Fitton Ms M, (was Griffiths), MA M LITT MCLIP, p./t.Off.Mgr., Hadfield Med.Cent. [0026393] 01/10/1976
Fitton Ms ML, BA MCLIP, Asst.Lib., GCHQ, Cheltenham. [0036914] 16/01/1984
Fitz Gerald Mrs J, MA, Coll.Lib., Queen's Coll., London. [0042931] 24/04/1989
FitzGerald Miss SMD, BA(Hons) FLS MCLIP, Retired. [0004963] 12/08/1958
Fitzgerald Mr JA, BA DipLIS MPhil, Univ.Lib., Univ.Coll.Cork, Ireland. [0051699] 16/05/1995
Fitzgerald Ms K, BA(Hons), Asst.Lib., Northumberland C.C., Alnwick L. [0047181] 26/05/1992
Fitzgerald Miss MCL, BA(Hons) MA, Team Lib., Lend., L.B.of Enfield, Edmonton Green L. [0057950] 04/10/1999
Fitzgerald Mrs MT, (was Wardman), B LIB MCLIP, Project Offr., Hartley L., Univ.of Southampton. [0024152] 10/03/1975
Fitzgerald Mr P, MA, Lib., Southern Health Board, Tralee Gen.Hosp. [0050231] 11/05/1994
Fitzgerald Mrs PA, (was Shannon), BA CERT ED MCLIP, Sch.Lib., Gosforth High Sch., Newcastle upon Tyne. [0013165] 02/03/1969
Fitzmaurice Mrs AM, (was Haines), BA MCLIP, Head of L.R.C., St.Marks R.C. Sch., Hounslow. [0031308] 01/10/1979
Fitzpatrick Mr DJ, BA MCLIP, Sen.Lib.(Stock), Altrincham L., Trafford Bor.Council. [0024668] 01/01/1975
Fitzpatrick Mrs GM, (was Collingwood), BA MCLIP, Sen.Lib.(Res.), Stretford L., Trafford Bor.Council. [0002989] 20/01/1972
Fitzpatrick Mrs MO, BA DipLib MCLIP, Lib.-Humanities, Univ.Coll., Cork, Ireland. [0033768] 24/02/1981
Fitzsimons Mr J, MA MSSC MCLIP, Sub-Lib.(Eng.& Built Enf.& Inf.), Univ.of Ulster, Jordanstown. [0022410] 30/04/1974
Fitzsimons Ms J, BA(Hons) MCLIP, Lib./Asst.Media Offr., Police Ombudsmans Off., Belfast. [0044207] 10/07/1990
Fitzsimons Miss KM, BA(Hons), Inf.Offr., Aldham Robarts Learning Res.Cent., Liverpool John Moores Univ. [0051353] 25/01/1995
Flach Miss CM, BA MCLIP, Unemployed. [0036340] 28/01/1985
Flack Mr HJD, BA MCLIP, Marketing Mgr., S.E.Educ.& L.Board, Ballynahinch. [0021561] 22/10/1973
Flagner Ms KE, BA, Lib., Halton Bor.Council, Widnes, Cheshire. [0045882] 08/07/1991
Flain Mrs RM, MCLIP, Consultant Lib., Envirotox-International, Herts. [0051278] 16/12/1994

Flanagan Mr JP, MCLIP, Lib., Royal Botanic Gdns., Kew, Surrey. [0020482] 04/01/1966
Flanagan Ms L, Employment not known. [0053140] 01/04/1996
Flatman Miss ML, BA(Hons), Evening Asst., Trade Partners UK, London. [0059012] 24/10/2000
Flatten Ms K, BSc MSc PED mclip, Community L.Mgr., Monmouthshire C.C. [0046713] 03/01/1992
Fleck Miss GL, BSc(Hons) MA, Sales Asst., Easons Bookshop, Belfast. [0058071] 22/10/1999
Fleet Mr C, BA, Stud. [0059364] 22/02/2001
Fleet Mrs CJ, (was Baker), BA(Hons) MCLIP, Career Break. [0049187] 11/10/1993
Fleet Mrs D, (was Laybourne), Special Clients Offr., Middlesbrough Bor.Council. [0040303] 20/01/1987
Fleet Mr GE, BA MSc CertEd MCLIP, Employment unknown. [0060285] 10/12/2001
Fleetwood Mrs PR, (was Emmott), M Phil BA MCLIP, Unemployed. [0004583] 06/01/1970
Fleetwood Mr R, BA FCLIP, Retired. [0004981] 06/10/1959
FE 01/01/1966
Fleetwood Miss SJ, BA MCLIP, Lib., Chamber of Commerce, Birmingham. [0004982] 04/03/1960
Fleming Mr AED, DMS MIMgt MCLIP, Retired, Tel./Fax.:(0151)7245149, Email:edwinfleming@clara.net. [0004984] 28/02/1961
Fleming Miss B, DipLib MCLIP, Asst.Lib., Belfast Educ.& L.Board. [0004986] 02/01/1969
Fleming Ms CA, BSc, Sci.Faculty Lib., Heriot-Watt Univ., Edinburgh. EH14 4AS. [0038159] 15/01/1985
Fleming Mrs FJ, (was Lambert), MCLIP, Reader Devel.& Stock Lib., Warwick Lib. [0008588] 01/01/1971
Fleming Mrs GR, (was Gardner), BA MCLIP, Lib., Sch.L.Serv., Herefordshire Council. [0004988] 21/09/1964
Fleming Mrs I, Data Entry Asst., Nat.Maritime Mus., Greenwich. [0051733] 01/06/1995
Fleming Mr JG, MCLIP, 130 Corve St., Ludlow, Shropshire. [0004990] 03/05/1965
Fleming Ms JL, (was Welsh), BA(Hons) PGDipILS, Learning Res.Asst., Exeter Coll.of F.E. [0054288] 15/11/1996 **AF**
Fleming Mrs JM, (was Williams), MA MCLIP, Tech.Lib., Environ.Dept., Surrey C.C. [0004992] 04/01/1971
Fleming Mrs KEL, (was Lane), BA(Hons) MCLIP, Electronic L.Inf.Offr., S.Humber Health Auth., N.Lincs. [0054614] 04/02/1997
Fleming Miss LC, BSc(Hons) MSc, Inf.Asst., PJB Publications, Richmond. [0057106] 14/12/1998
Fleming Miss LJ, BA(Hons) DipIM, Asst.Lib., Instant L.Ltd., London. [0056021] 28/01/1998
Fleming Mrs SJ, BA(Hons), Employment unknown. [0060255] 10/12/2001
Fleming Mr W, BA MCLIP, Princ.Lib.(Inf.), Warks.L.& Heritage. [0004995] 29/10/1969
Flemington Mrs J, BSc MSc, Eng.& Informatics Lib., Edinburgh Univ.L. [0041984] 01/07/1988
Fletcher Miss BJ, BA DipLib MCLIP, L.Serv.Mgr., Western Mail & Echo Ltd., Cardiff. [0034460] 04/11/1981
Fletcher Mrs EG, (was Cox), MA MCLIP, NHS Lib., Queen's Med.Cent., Nottingham. [0018688] 02/04/1963
Fletcher Mrs HA, (was Knox), BA AKC DipLib MCLIP, Sch.Lib., Bishop's Stortford High Sch., Herts. [0035773] 20/01/1983
Fletcher Ms JE, BA(Hons) MA, Child.Lib., Royal Bor.of Kensington & Chelsea. [0055346] 29/09/1997
Fletcher Mrs JM, (was Whalley), BA MCLIP, Bookstart Offr., Tameside M.B.C. [0005003] 01/10/1966
Fletcher Mr JR, MCLIP, Community L.Mgr., Leicester City Ls. [0018690] 27/07/1967
Fletcher Mrs L, BA, Lib., Halliwell Landau, Manchester. [0055563] 21/10/1997
Fletcher Mrs MA, BA(Hons) MCLIP, Content Mgmt.Lib., Chartered Inst.of Personnel & Dev., London. [0026370] 13/10/1976
Fletcher Ms MA, MA MIL MCLIP, Sen.Asst., Cent.Lend.L., L.B.Harrow. [0005005] 25/10/1964
Fletcher Mr NS, MCLIP, Unemployed. [0034016] 11/07/1981
Fletcher Mr PJ, BA(Hons) DipILM MCLIP, Asst.Lib.& Arch., Dulwich Coll. [0047770] 14/10/1992
Fletcher Mrs SA, (was Miller), BLib, Primary Age Lib., Essex L.H.Q. [0027198] 31/01/1977
Fletcher Miss SK, BA MA MCLIP, Asst.Lib., Guille-Alles L., Guernsey, C.I. [0044875] 04/01/1991
Fletcher Ms SM, MA MCLIP, Proposals Specialist, Sirsi Ltd., Potters Bar. [0018692] 07/09/1969
Fletcher Mr TH, BA MCLIP, L.Systems Mgr., Birkbeck Coll, Univ.of London. [0023484] 01/01/1975
Fletcher Miss VC, BA MCLIP, Asst.Lib., Univ.Coll.Cork, Eire. [0005008] 16/10/1959
Flett Mrs ED, (was Jackson), BSc MCLIP, Mgr.,The-SRDA, Serco Assurance, Warrington, Cheshire. [0005010] 10/03/1966
Flett Miss MI, BA MA MCLIP, Trainee Liaison Lib., Reading Univ.L. [0055798] 26/11/1997
Flint Mrs JR, (was Chapman), MLS DMS MCLIP, Grp.Lib., Leics.C.C. [0002600] 01/10/1969
Flint Mr RF, MCLIP, Life Member. [0005018] 20/09/1948
Flintham Mrs CHG, (was Nott), MCLIP, p./t.Admin.Asst., Diocese of Lincoln. [0010921] 08/01/1964
Flintoff Mrs HF, BA(Hons), p./t.Stud./L.Super., Bristol Univ./Queen Mary's Coll., Basingstoke. [0058706] 06/09/2000
Flitcroft Mr AP, Stud., Manchester Met.Univ. [0059995] 16/11/2001
Flitton Mrs HJ, (was Ashley), MA, Unemployed. [0048893] 12/07/1993
Floate Miss RC, BA DipLib MCLIP, Stud., Trinity Coll., Bristol. [0034214] 08/10/1981

Flood Mrs A, (was Matthews), BA MCLIP, Staff Lib., Amersham Hosp., S.Bucks.NHS Trust. [0009932] 26/04/1968
Flood Mrs D, (was Lewis), BA(Hons) DMS MCLIP, Devel.& Strategy Mgr., Slough Bor.Council, Berks.C.C. [0034597] 07/01/1982
Flor Mrs PA, (was Idenden), MCLIP, Sen.Lib., Telemark Univ.Coll., Skien, Norway. [0005023] 20/09/1967
Florence Miss GM, MCLIP, Lib., Havant Br., Hants.Co.L. [0005025] 27/01/1970
Florence Miss J, BA MCLIP, Lib., Speyside High Sch., Aberlour. [0039433] 26/01/1986
Florey Mr CC, ALAA FCLIP, Life Member, 503 St.Francis Crt., 34 Robinson St, Inglewood, WA6052, Australia. [0016888] 30/10/1948 FE 01/01/1957
Florin Ms J, BA(Hons) DipInf, Asst.Lib., Financial Serv.Auth., London. [0047077] 15/04/1992
Flower Ms CS, BA(Hons) Lib., Gensler, London. [0047805] 19/10/1992
Flowers Mrs D, BA MA, Sch.Lib., The Heathland Sch., Hounslow. [0052750] 04/12/1979
Flowers Miss GM, MCLIP, Community Lib., L.B.of Barking P.L. [0005026] 31/01/1970
Floyd Ms EK, MA MCLIP, Lib., Paul Mellon Cent.for Stud.in Brit., Art, London. [0044408] 05/10/1990
Floyd Mrs FM, (was Bird), MCLIP, Inf.Mgr., Bath Spa Univ.Coll. [0005027] 02/10/1963
Floyd Mrs HA, BA DipLib MCLIP, Sen.Lib., Church End.L., L.B.of Barnet. [0027673] 04/07/1977
Floyd Ms JM, BA(Hons) DipLib MCLIP, p./t.Lib., Hammersmith & W.London Coll. [0030318] 10/01/1979
Flude Mrs EM, (was Foster), MCLIP, Retired. [0005028] 17/03/1944
Flynn Ms CM, MA DipLib CNAA, Lib., B.B.C. [0034652] 25/01/1982
Flynn Mrs HJ, (was Matcham), BA MCLIP, Unemployed. [0022218] 06/03/1974
Flynn Miss J, BA MSc MCLIP, Tutor, Cardinal Newman Coll., Preston. [0044592] 01/11/1990
Flynn Miss JA, MA(Hons) DipILS, Sch.Lib., Angus Council, Arbroath High Sch. [0058030] 19/10/1994
Flynn Mrs JE, (was Worsnip), BSc MSc, Unemployed. [0041469] 01/01/1988
Flynn Mr JM, BA MCLIP, Cent.L.Mgr., Birmingham L.& Inf.Serv., Cent.L. [0028739] 24/01/1978
Flynn Mrs M, MA, Inf.Asst., Clifford Chance, LLP, London. [0057711] 09/07/1999
Flynn Mrs MJ, Inf.Offr., Sight Savers Internat., Haywards Heath. [0055243] 01/09/1997 AF
Flynn Miss O, BEd MA, Lib., Notts.C.C. [0046832] 14/02/1992
Flynn Ms PA, BA MCLIP, Area Lib., Argyl & Bute L.Serv., Dunoon Br.L. [0029961] 07/11/1978
Foard Mrs C, BA, Unemployed. [0035467] 05/10/1982
Fodder Mr HGW, MA FCLIP DipFE, Life Member, 10 Boston Vale, Hanwell, London, W7 2AP, Tel:0181 567 5683. [0005030] 25/02/1947 FE 01/01/1955
Foden Miss S, BA(Hons), Inf.Mgr., Cadbury Trebor Bassett, Birmingham. [0040338] 20/01/1987
Foden-Lenahan Ms EL, BA(Hons) MA, Head of Readers' Serv., Tate L.& Arch., London. [0055307] 24/09/1997
Fodey Mr WJ, MA DipLib MCLIP, Asst.Lib., Glasgow Caledonian Univ. [0043580] 09/11/1989
Foe Mr LS, BA(Hons) DipLib, Learning Support Lib., Paddington L., Westminster City Council. [0046266] 21/10/1991
Fogg Miss HS, BA, Asst.Lib., DJ Freeman, London. [0055333] 01/10/1997
Fogg Mr NJ, DRSAM BA, L.Asst., The Soc.of Genealogists, London. [0040791] 15/06/1987
Foggo Miss L, BD(Hons), Stud., City Univ. [0058268] 03/12/1999
Foglieni Mrs O, Head of Beni Librari, Biblioteche, Sistem Documentari. [0052916] 02/01/1996
Folan Mr TJ, BA(Hons) MCLIP, Schroder Salomon Smith Barney, London. [0032065] 13/01/1980
Foley Miss JA, BA(Hons) DipILM DipComp MCLIP, Web-based Inf.Mgr., Univ.of Liverpool. [0052069] 02/10/1995
Foley Mrs JM, Inf.Offr., Environment Agency, Reading, Berks. [0048623] 18/03/1993
Foley Mr M, MA BEd MSc DipLib MIInfSc MCLIP, Lib., Salvation Army, London. [0035008] 15/06/1982
Foley Mr RN, BA(Hons), Unemployed. [0049369] 29/10/1993
Folkes Mrs R, (was Moran), BSc(Hons) MSc(Econ) MCLIP, Site Lib., City Coll.Manchester. [0053868] 07/10/1996
Follett Sir BK, HonFCLIP, Chairman/Chair, Arts & Humanities Research Board, Strategy Grp.on Res.L's. [0054736] 19/03/1997 FE 19/03/1997
Folorunso Ms I, L.Asst., Univ.of Edinburgh. [0057200] 14/01/1999
Folwell Ms IM, MA, Inf.Resources Mgr., Freshfields Bruckhaus Deringer, London. [0045682] 22/04/1991
Fomo Mrs AEG, (was Strain), MCLIP, Life Member. [0016893] 20/03/1961
Fone Mrs CH, (was Lowther), MA MCLIP, p./t.Asst.Lib., Bassetlaw Dist.Gen.Hosp., Worksop, Notts. [0030081] 29/11/1978
Fonseca Ms M-J, (was Eddo), BFA MLS, Resident in U.S.A. [0049793] 06/12/1993
Font Mrs JA, (was Wallace), BA(Hons) DipILM MCLIP, Maternity Leave. [0050685] 10/10/1994
Foo Mr KW, BA MCLIP, Life Member. [0016894] 12/03/1962
Foord Mr PW, BSc MA, Research Researcher, Inst.of Electrical Engineers, London. [0056444] 09/07/1998
Foot Mrs CE, (was Nickels), BA MCLIP, Asst.Lib., Southampton Univ.L. [0010827] 28/09/1959
Foot Mrs HC, L.Asst., Sherborne Sch., Dorset. [0061564] 02/10/2002 AF

Foot Dr MM, MA DLitt, Prof.L.Arch.& Studies, Univ.Coll.London. [0059237] 22/03/2001
Foote Ms J, BSc MA MCLIP, CSM Lib., Camborne Sch.of Mines, Univ.of Exeter,Redruth,Cornwall. [0035247] 06/10/1982
Foote Mrs L, (was Lawrence), MCLIP, Asst.Lib., E.Somerset NHS Trust L., Yeovil. [0008707] 21/11/1969
Footitt Mrs AC, (was Gent), BSc MSc MCLIP, Mgr., Barclays Univ.L., Barclays Bank plc., Godalming. [0041271] 23/10/1987
Foran Mr JJ, BA MA DipLib, Lib., Inst.of Tech., Sligo, Ireland. [0036675] 13/10/1983
Forbes Mr GS, BA MA MBA MCLIP, Sub.-Lib., Napier Univ., Edinburgh. [0030906] 13/05/1979
Forbes Miss LE, (was Harding), BA MCLIP, Keeper of Oriental Collections, Bodleian L., Oxford. [0005040] 01/01/1965
Forbes Ms R, MA DipILS, Stud., Univ.of Dundee. [0053881] 08/10/1996
Forbes Mrs RC, BEd DipLIS, Unemployed. [0058501] 13/03/2000
Forbes-Buckingham Mrs LG, BSc, P./t.L.Asst., Bridgwater Coll. [0057057] 26/11/1998
Forcella Ms V, BA(Hons) MA, Unemployed (F./time Parent). [0049463] 03/11/1993
Ford Ms A, BA DipLib MCLIP, Lib., Canterbury Christ Church Univ.Coll., Hayloft L., Kent. [0040828] 03/07/1987
Ford Miss AM, BLib MCLIP, Inf.Offr., Careers Advisory Serv., Univ.of Wales, Aberystwyth. [0032518] 29/04/1980
Ford Mrs C, (was Bedell), MA MCLIP, Unemployed. [0025214] 13/01/1976
Ford Mrs CEM, (was Muller), MA Dip Lib MCLIP, Vol.L.Asst., Doncaster&Bassetlaw Hosp.NHS Trust, Worksop. [0040907] 11/08/1987
Ford Mr GA, BSc MA, Catr., The Brit.L.,err., Chapel Allerton, W.Yorkshire. [0057079] 04/12/1998
Ford Mrs J, L.Asst., Beaulieu Convent Sch., St Helier, Jersey. [0056188] 01/04/1998 AF
Ford Mrs JM, (was McCann), BA DipLib MCLIP, Position Unknown, Royal Bor.of Windsor & Maidenhead, Windsor L. [0019752] 13/03/1971
Ford Ms JM, BA MCLIP, Career Break. [0037612] 12/10/1984
Ford Mr JP, BA MCLIP, Learning Support Lib., Westminster City Council. [0045045] 07/10/1970
Ford Mrs KM, MA DipLib MCLIP, Sen.Lib., S.Ham, Hants.C.C. [0005047] 16/10/1967
Ford Mrs LJ, BA(Hons) MA, Asst.Lib., Park Lane Coll., Horsforth, Leeds. [0052532] 06/11/1995
Ford Mr MG, MSc BSc MCLIP, Dir.of Inf.Serv., Univ.of Bristol. [0005049] 14/01/1965
Ford Miss MJ, BA(Hons) MCLIP, Lib., Notts.C.C., Stapleford L. [0047921] 26/10/1992
Ford Mrs MT, L.& Inf.Offr., St.Helens & Knowsley Health Auth. [0054771] 01/04/1997
Ford Mrs P, MA DipLib MCLIP, Sen.Asst.Lib., Univ.of Bradford, J.B.Priestley L. [0005054] 05/03/1967
Ford Mr P, BA MCLIP, Retired, 41 Grosvenor Av., Carshalton, Surrey, SM5 3EJ. [0005053] 13/07/1967
Ford Miss RJ, BA(Hons), Resident in Ireland. [0049564] 11/11/1993
Ford Ms SJ, BA MSc MCLIP, Position unknown, Victoria & Albert Mus., London. [0060713] 12/12/2001
Ford Miss SM, Lib., St.Helens & Knowsley Hosp.Trust, Whiston, Merseyside. [0046644] 02/12/1991
Ford Mrs V, BA(Hons), p./t.Lib., Mace & Jones (Solicitors). [0037023] 10/02/1984
Ford Miss VL, BA(Hons) DipLib, Lib. [0053909] 10/10/1996
Ford-Smith Ms AM, BA(Hons) MA, Asst.Lib., The Wellcome Trust. [0056939] 09/11/1998
Forde Ms AM, BA DipLib MCLIP, p./t.Asst.Lib., Univ.of Strathclyde, Glasgow. [0043784] 11/01/1990
Forde Mrs JR, BA PGCE MCLIP, Retired. [0005060] 01/01/1965
Forde Mrs LL, BA DipLib MCLIP, Head Lib., Cardonald Coll., Glasgow. [0043478] 27/10/1989
Forder Blakeman Mr K, BA MCLIP, Life Member. [0001373] 01/01/1953
Fordham Mr G, MCLIP, Life Member. [0018697] 12/10/1942
Fordham Mrs HF, (was Chinnery), MCLIP, Asst.Lib., Hudson L., Trustees Hudson Memorial L., Herts. [0026701] 16/11/1976
Fordyce Mr DW, BSc MSc, Res.L.Offr., Cent.for Inf.on Beverage Alcohol, London. [0056083] 13/02/1998
Foreman Mrs AJ, (was Pilcher), BA MCLIP, Retired. [0005064] 29/03/1962
Foreman Miss JM, BA(Hons), p./t.Stud./L.Asst., Univ.of N.London, Redbridge Cent.L., Ilford. [0061333] 28/05/2002
Foreman Ms JM, MA DipLib, Asst.Lib., Scottish Exec.L., Edinburgh. [0037781] 17/10/1984
Foreman Mr P, L.Asst., Broadstairs L. [0061051] 18/02/2002 AF
Foreman Mr RLE, M Lib FCLIP, Retired. [0005065] 01/01/1961 FE 13/06/1972
Foreman Mrs SE, (was Kremer), MA MCLIP, Retired. [0012902] 09/09/1964
Forester Mrs SE, (was Allam), M.Ed MCLIP, Princ.Offr.(Ref.& Inf.), Co.Ref.& Inf.L., Truro, Cornwall. [0005066] 01/01/1966
Forrest Mrs A, Stud., R.G.Univ., &, p./t.Knowledge Mgr., McClure Naismith, Glasgow. [0058175] 11/11/1999
Forrest Mrs AJ, (was Davies), BA DipLib MCLIP, Child.Team Leader, CIP, Hounslow L. [0049340] 26/10/1993
Forrest Mrs AY, (was Hunter), BA MCLIP, Sutherland Area L.Offr., Highland Reg.L.Serv. [0030842] 20/05/1979
Forrest Ms C, BA(Hons) PgDIP, Stud.p./t./Document controller, Robert Gordons Univ., Woodgroup Eng., Aberdeen. [0058778] 19/07/2000
Forrest Ms EL, (was Wardrope), BA MCLIP, Asst.Lib.(Yth.Serv.), Edinburgh Cent.L., City of Edinburgh Council. [0041028] 05/10/1987
Forrest Ms K, BA(Hons) MA, p./t.Sen.L.Asst., Univ.of Newcastle, Robinson L. [0058074] 26/10/1999

Personal Members — Foxcroft

Forrest Mrs MEM, MA MCLIP, Inf.Offr., Res.Cent.for Soc.Sci., Univ.of Edinburgh. [0005071] 02/10/1971
Forrest Mrs MES, MA MSc DipLib FCLIP FSA(Scot), Lib., Health Educ.Board for Scotland, Edinburgh. [0036541] 19/10/1983 FE 19/05/1999
Forrest Mrs MV, (was Salter), MCLIP, Life Member. [0005072] 01/01/1955
Forrest Mr PI, BA(Hons) DipIS MCLIP, Asst.Lib., L.B.of Hounslow. [0048681] 13/04/1993
Forrest Miss R, BSc(Hons) MCLIP, Lib., Surrey C.C., Kingston-upon-Thames. [0046634] 29/11/1991
Forrest Mrs SA, (was Fretwell), BA DipLib MCLIP, Unemployed. [0039569] 04/03/1986
Forrester Miss WG, MCLIP, Life Member. [0005074] 10/03/1949
Forsey Mrs S, (was Waldron), BSc MSc MCLIP, Lib., Univ.of Southmpton, Princess Anne Hosp. [0015195] 05/01/1972
Forster Mr G, BA MA MCLIP, Lib., The Leeds L. [0032948] 07/10/1980
Forster Mrs MA, (was Adey), BA MCLIP, Lib.Asst., Bretton Woods Sch., Peterborough. [0026267] 04/10/1976
Forster Miss TDA, MSc, Resident in Uruguay. [0060084] 07/12/2001
Forsyth Miss EM, BSc MCLIP, Lib., RCN Scottish Board, Edinburgh. [0028951] 10/02/1978
Forsyth Miss JM, BSc MCLIP, Retired. [0005082] 17/09/1951
Forsyth Ms ME, MA(Hons) DipILS MCLIP, Sch.L.Res.Cent.Co-ordinator, Northfield Academy, Aberdeen. [0054320] 18/11/1996
Forsyth Miss PM, BA(Hons), Stud., Starthclyde Univ. [0061702] 22/10/2002
Forsyth Miss S, BSc, Reg.LIS Offr., Environment Agency, Worthing. [0055539] 20/10/1997
Forsythe Mrs FM, (was McMurray), BA MCLIP, Head of L.Serv., Newcastle Coll. [0038078] 17/01/1985
Forsythe Mrs JE, (was Hodgson), BA MCLIP, Lib., Havering Coll.of F.& H.E., Hornchurch,Essex. [0007025] 01/10/1970
Fortnam Mrs BL, (was Thomas), MCLIP, Head of L.Res., Exeter Coll. [0014528] 24/02/1971
Fortune Mrs SC, (was Kendrew), DipLib MCLIP, Area Lib., Campbeltown L., Argyll & Bute L.Serv. [0008263] 16/09/1970
Forward Ms RH, Researcher, Oliver, Wyman & Co. [0052325] 30/10/1995
Fosker Mrs RE, MCLIP, Communication & Marketing Mgr., L.& Inf.Devel.Unit, London. [0005084] 08/01/1974
Foskett Prof. AC, MA FCLIP AALIA, Life Member, 11 Haseldene Drive, Christie Downs, South Australia 5164. [0005087] 09/09/1952 FE 01/01/1958
Foskett Mr DJ, OBE MA HonFCLIP FCLIP, Retired. [0005089] 23/02/1940 FE 01/01/1949
Fossey Miss L, BA(Hons) MA, Asst.Lib., Circulation Serv., Exeter Univ. [0049165] 08/10/1993
Foster Mr AJ, BA FCLIP, Dir.of Inf.Serv., Keele Univ. [0005094] 21/02/1966 FE 01/04/2002
Foster Mrs C, MCLIP, Lib.Bibl.Support/Catg.A/V., N.Yorks.Co.L., Northallerton. [0005096] 01/01/1965
Foster Mrs C, (was Searl), BSc MSc MLib MCLIP, Maths Lect., Vosper Thornycroft Serv., Arborfield, Berks. [0045975] 19/07/1991
Foster Mrs CA, (was Feather), BA DipLib, Career Break. [0036371] 07/10/1983
Foster Mr CM, BA DipLib, Res.Lib., Wolverhampton Univ., Compton Learning Cent. [0056243] 07/04/1998
Foster Mrs EM, (was Haward), B LIB MCLIP, Lib./Sen.Arch., Lodders, Stratford-upon-Avon. [0021874] 07/02/1974
Foster Mrs EMM, MBE, Lib., Garrick Club, London. [0037933] 25/11/1984
Foster Mrs FE, (was Thompson), DipPhysEd MCLIP, Life Member, Overseas. [0016897] 01/01/1963
Foster Miss FM, (was Marsh), DMS MA MCLIP, Unit Leader - L.& Inf.Serv., Dundee City Council. [0022054] 16/01/1974
Foster Mrs G, (was Harris), BA MSc MCLIP, p./t.Lib., NHS Direct (N.E.), Newcastle upon Tyne. [0038171] 23/01/1985
Foster Mrs GA, (was Rushton), DipLib, Tech.Lib., Filtronic, Shipley. [0049092] 01/10/1993
Foster Mrs H, BA MCLIP, Asst.Lib., Astrazeneca UK Ltd., Mereside L., Macclesfield. [0033681] 03/02/1981
Foster Mrs J, (was Garber), BA MCLIP, Freelance Inf.Offr.& Indexer, London/Herts. [0041181] 16/10/1987
Foster Mrs J, (was Thompson), BA MCLIP, Lib., Equal Opportunities Commission, Manchester. [0005102] 08/02/1968
Foster Mrs JC, BSc PhD DipILS MCLIP, Inf.Specialist, GCHQ, Cheltenham. [0051108] 16/11/1994
Foster Mrs JE, (was Mills), MCLIP, Inf.Lib., Surrey C.C., Guildford. [0005104] 01/01/1968
Foster Ms JM, Stud., Univ.of Cent.England, & L.Asst., Univ.of the W.of England, Frank Parkinson LRC. [0058380] 20/01/2000
Foster Mrs KM, (was Sullivan), BA MCLIP, Asst.Lib., Manchester Metro.Univ. [0014209] 20/10/1967
Foster Mrs KM, (was Hodgson), BA MCLIP, Sen.Lib., Cent.Lend.L., Sheffield P.L. [0005109] 28/09/1960
Foster Mr L, MCLIP, Retired. [0005110] 04/03/1940
Foster Mrs L, MA(Hons) MSc, Grad.Trainee, Inst.of Chartered Accountants, London. [0057317] 09/02/1999
Foster Mrs L, (was Haines), BA MSc MCLIP MIHM, L.Serv.Mgr., N.Glamorgan NHS Trust, Merthyr Tydfil. [0043064] 10/07/1989
Foster Ms LM, BA DipLib MCLIP, Ref.Lib., Bexley L.Serv., Ref.& Inf. [0040348] 21/01/1987
Foster Mr MJ, FCLIP, Life Member, Tel:01760 755 019. [0005113] 28/03/1972 FE 01/01/1968
Foster Mrs RE, (was Cooper), MCLIP, L.Mgr., Worcester L., Worcs.C.C. [0041533] 12/01/1988
Foster Mrs RL, BA DipIM, Counter Serv.Team Leader, St.Thomas's Med.Sch.L. [0050807] 19/10/1994
Foster Miss SL, (was Pooley), MLS, Team Lib., Enfield Public L., Middlesex. [0058614] 18/04/2000

Foster Mrs SM, (was McBain), BLib MCLIP, H.of Inf.Servs., Limra Europe Ltd., Watford, Herts. [0037102] 13/02/1984
Foster Miss VJ, BA(Hons), Nat.Inf.Mgr., Pinsent Curtis Biddle, Birmingham. [0053821] 02/10/1996
Foster Mrs W, (was Kinsella), BA DipLib MCLIP, Sch.Lib., Renfrewshire Council. [0034487] 09/11/1981
Foster Ms WFA, BA(Hons) MCLIP, Lib., R.B.Kensington & Chelsea. [0042950] 04/05/1989
Foster Mrs WJ, (was Dyos), BA MCLIP, Unemployed. [0028737] 27/01/1978
Foster Mr WT, BSc DipLib MCLIP, H.of Teaching Learning & Quality, Sch.of Inf.Studies, Univ.of Cent.England in Birmingham. [0026960] 10/01/1977
Foster-Jones Mrs JJ, (was Broadhurst), BA(Hons) MCLIP, Multi-media Serv.Devel.Offr., Interactive Open Learn.Cent.&, Media Arch., Open Univ.L. [0052590] 09/11/1995
Fothergill Ms EJ, BA(Hons)ILS, Asst.Lib., Swansea Inst.of H.E. [0050403] 18/07/1994
Fothergill Mrs J, (was Rowe), MCLIP, Unemployed. [0012734] 01/01/1963
Fothergill Mrs JA, (was Francis), BA MCLIP, Not Seeking Work. [0005173] 30/10/1966
Foulkes Mr JH, BBA(Hons) DipLib MCLIP, Asst.Lib., Nat.L.of Wales, Aberystwyth. [0047705] 19/10/1992
Foulkes Mr RM, MCLIP, Br.Lib., Welshpool, Powys C.C. [0005126] 06/05/1972
Foulkes Miss SJ, BM MRCPath, Catr., Brit.L., Boston Spa. [0046146] 07/10/1991
Fountain Mrs B, (was Mcconnell), MCLIP, Unemployed. [0009286] 23/09/1969
Fountain Mrs KM, MSc(Econ) MCLIP, p./t.Sch.Lib., L.B.of Hounslow. [0022777] 09/10/1974
Fourie Dr I, BBibl MBilb MCLIP, Resident in S.Africa. [0060102] 07/12/2001
Fovargue Miss M, BA MCLIP, Retired. [0005127] 08/10/1948
Foweraker Miss DM, B Lib MCLIP, Unemployed. [0005128] 01/01/1969
Fowke Mrs AS, (was Walker), BA MCLIP, Asst.Lib., Royal Pharmaceutical Soc., London. [0045803] 04/06/1991
Fowkes Mr R, MCLIP, Retired. [0005129] 15/08/1938
Fowler Miss AMR, BA MCLIP, Child.& Sch.Lib., L.B.Redbridge. [0032653] 23/07/1980
Fowler Ms CA, (was Chandler), MA BSc MCLIP, Head of LIS, Healthcare Serv.Div., Univ.of Southampton, Gen.Hosp. [0031228] 08/10/1979
Fowler Ms CB, BSc(Hons), Grad.Trainee, Oxford Brookes Univ.L. [0056739] 12/10/1998
Fowler Mr DJ, MCLIP, Sen.Lib.-Adult Serv., Western Isles L., P.L., Stornoway. [0005131] 01/01/1968
Fowler Mr G, Retired. [0005132] 20/10/1947
Fowler Mrs JB, (was Stebbing), MCLIP, Inf.Offr., Baker Tilly, London. [0005133] 03/10/1963
Fowler Miss MK, BA(Hons) MLib(Dist) MCLIP, Special Serv.Offr., Redcar & Cleveland B.C. [0047987] 30/10/1992
Fowler Mr PD, BA MCLIP, Grp.Lib., Metro.Boro.of Sefton, Merseyside. [0005137] 28/10/1969
Fowler Mrs SA, BA MA, Local Studies Lib., Medway Council, Strood. [0057504] 14/04/1999
Fowler Miss SF, MCLIP, Retired. [0005139] 04/06/1952
Fox Mr AJ, FCLIP, Life Member. [0005141] 27/02/1952 FE 01/01/1959
Fox Mrs BM, (was Cotterill), BSc DipLib MCLIP DMS, Unemployed. [0026901] 03/12/1976
Fox Ms DA, (was Mitchell), BA DipLib MCLIP, Unemployed. [0037256] 14/05/1984
Fox Mr DJ, MA, Inf.Mgr., Cable & Wireless PLC. [0056699] 05/10/1998
Fox Mr ES, MSc M Phil FCLIP, Life Member. [0005144] 01/01/1943 FE 01/01/1952
Fox Mr J, DMS MCLIP, L.& Inf.Mgr., N.Lanarkshire Council. [0005146] 10/02/1965
Fox Mrs J, (was Goodall), BA MCLIP, Team Leader-Inf.Cent., Rolls Royce plc., Derby. [0034622] 19/01/1982
Fox Mrs JA, (was Ellis), Asst.Lib., Univ of Cent.England, Birmingham. [0045625] 05/04/1991
Fox Ms JA, BSc, Asst.Map Curator, Univ.of Reading, Geography Dept., Berks. [0035409] 08/10/1982
Fox Miss JE, MA, Lib., Mansfield L., Notts.C.C. [0045892] 01/07/1991
Fox Mrs JM, (was Freeman), MRCS MIM MCLIP, Position unknown, Dyson Industries Ltd., Sheffield. [0060582] 11/12/2001
Fox Mrs MB, (was Boyden), BSc DLIS MCLIP, Lib., Duke of Kent Sch., Ewhurst. [0027427] 01/04/1977
Fox Mrs MJ, (was Lambert), BA MCLIP, Med.Records Mgr., Clatterbridge Cent.for Oncology, Wirral. [0016899] 01/01/1965
Fox Mr NJ, BA MCLIP, Inf.Offr., Linklaters & Paines, London. [0027972] 06/10/1977
Fox Mr NJ, BA(Hons), Lib., Lenkiewicz Foundation, Plymouth. [0059942] 08/11/2001
Fox Mr NR, BA FCLIP FRSA, Asst.Co.Lib., Hants.Co.L., Winchester. [0005149] 01/01/1967 FE 27/01/1993
Fox Mr PK, MA AKC MCLIP, Univ.Lib., Univ.of Cambridge. [0018257] 01/10/1972
Fox Mr RV, M Phil MCLIP, Retired. [0005150] 01/01/1947
Fox Mr SM, BA, Graduate Trainee., DFES L., London. [0060931] 10/01/2002
Fox Ms V, (was Cook), MCLIP, Sen.Lib., (Youth Serv.), Leighton Buzzard L., Beds. [0026634] 19/10/1976
Fox Mrs VJ, (was Glover), MCLIP, Housewife. [0005602] 18/01/1966
Foxall Mrs AM, (was Davies), Stock Lib.(Rother Grp.), Bexhill P.L., E.Sussex C.C. [0045051] 01/07/1990
Foxall Mrs HK, (was Payne), BA MA MCLIP, Mgr., Inf.Servs., Instant L.Ltd., Loughborough. [0042500] 23/11/1988
Foxcroft Mr PR, BSc DIS MCLIP, Lib./Inf.Sci., Yorks.Water Serv.Ltd., Bradford. [0005155] 23/02/1971

241

Foxley Mrs DK, (was Goulty), BLib MCLIP, Lib., CPM Environ.Planning & Design, Gloucestershire. [0026100] 24/06/1976
Foy Mr M, BA(Hons) DiplM, SLA./ Asst.Lib., Bournemouth Univ. [0058627] 19/04/2000
France Mrs C, (was Bates), BA MCLIP, Employment not known. [0000917] 12/01/1967
France Mrs RF, (was Mortimore), MTh(Hons) DipLib MCLIP, Lib., The Girls Grammar Sch., Bradford. [0037310] 22/06/1984
Francis Mrs AEB, MA MCLIP, Retired. [0021321] 08/10/1973
Francis Mrs C, (was Bentley), MCLIP, L.Offr., Lincs.C.C., Cent.L. [0025003] 27/10/1975
Francis Ms C, BA(Hons), Trainee Lib., W.Sussex C.Council. [0056728] 07/10/1998
Francis Mrs CP, (was Bunn), BA MCLIP, Facilitator, Kent Inst.of Art & Design, Rochester. [0041085] 07/10/1987
Francis Miss EC, Stud., Sheffield Uni. [0061366] 01/07/2002
Francis Miss HS, BA(Hons), Child.Lib., Leigh Park L., Hants. [0047210] 04/06/1992
Francis Mr JPE, BA FCLIP, Life Member. [0005175] 16/10/1948 FE 01/01/1961
Francis Mr L, BA(Hons), Lib., L.B.of Haringey. [0048557] 15/02/1993
Francis Ms M, (was Young), MCLIP, Learning Support Lib., Leeds L.& Inf.Serv., W.Group. [0016465] 15/09/1966
Francis Mrs MA, MCLIP, Unwaged. [0020776] 09/07/1973
Francis Miss NE, BA MSc(Econ), Asst.Lib., Morgan Cole Solicitors, Cardiff. [0052059] 02/11/1995
Francis Mrs NE, (was Browning), MCLIP, Inf.Specialist., QinetiQ, Fareham, Hants. [0005177] 01/03/1963
Francis Mrs P, p./t.Stud./Lib., Univ.of Wales, Aberystwyth, Med.L., Royal Bolton Hosp. [0057836] 03/09/1999
Francis Mrs PA, (was Ware), MCLIP, Gen.Asst.(L.), Hastingbury Upper Sch., Beds.C.C. [0005178] 19/09/1967
Francis Mrs PA, BA MA MCLIP, Writer. [0044419] 08/10/1990
Francis Mrs PA, (was Gent), BSc, Unemployed. [0039647] 08/04/1986
Francis Mr RK, BSc(Hons) MA MCLIP, Head of Arch.& L., Nat.Portrait Gallery. [0034065] 22/08/1981
Francis Mr S, MA FCLIP, Life Member. [0005180] 24/03/1958 FE 02/03/1965
Francis Mrs SM, (was Oliver), BA CertMgmt MCLIP, Lib., Royston L., Herts.L.Serv. [0025551] 20/01/1976
Frangeskou Dr V, BA PhD MA, Asst.Lib., Bristol Univ. [0042217] 03/10/1988
Franklin Mr AG, MA MCLIP, Asst.Lib., Manx Nat.Heritage, Douglas, Isle of Man. [0021952] 29/01/1974
Franklin Miss AM, BA MCLIP, Sch.Lib., Canons High Sch., Middx. [0033596] 21/01/1981
Franklin Miss C, Position Unknown, Right Mgmnt.Consultants, London. [0059045] 07/11/2000
Franklin Miss CE, BA(Hons) MA, Research Asst., Bird & Bird, London. [0051441] 14/02/1995
Franklin Mr CW, FCLIP, Life Member, Willow Corner, 51 Southwick Road, N.Bradley, Trowbridge, Wilts. [0005186] 15/02/1941 FE 01/01/1950
Franklin Mrs FS, (was Maltby), BA MCLIP, Child.Lib.(Job Share), Derby City Council. [0025597] 27/01/1976
Franklin Mrs K, (was Anderson), MCLIP, Sen.Team Lib.-Reader Serv., Cirencester L., Glos. [0019370] 19/01/1965
Franklin Mrs LE, (was Jales), BA(Hons) DipLib MCLIP, Sen.L.Asst., Uckfield L., E.Sussex C.C. [0018256] 02/10/1972
Franklin Mrs M, (was Meeres), BA MCLIP, Learning Resources Mgr., St Peter's Catholic Comp.Sch., Guildford, Surrey. [0010044] 13/12/1968
Franklin Miss MJ, MA MCLIP, Div.Lib., W., Hants.C.C. [0023010] 17/10/1974
Franklin Mrs MJ, (was Hutchison), MSC MCLIP, Asst.Lib., (p./t.), Ninewells Med.L., Univ.of Dundee. [0022848] 11/10/1974
Franklin Mrs V, (was Bennett), BA MA MCLIP, Academic Lib., Loughborough Univ. [0043332] 20/10/1989
Franks Ms AY, (was Yarrow), MA DipLib PGCE MCLIP, Sch.Lib., Rushcliffe Comp.Sch., Nottingham. [0030067] 17/11/1978
Franks Mrs C, BA MCLIP, Retired. [0019491] 01/10/1970
Franks Mrs D, (was Walker), BSc MCLIP, Lib., CCLRC, Warrington. [0037756] 23/10/1974
Frankum Ms J, BA MCLIP, Inf.Mgr., Saffery Champness, London. [0033987] 03/07/1981
Franses Mrs CM, (was Lewis), BSc(Hons) PGCE, Self Employed. [0022596] 03/07/1974
Franssen Mr J, BA(Hons) MA, Inf.Offr., Davies Arnold Cooper, London. [0057628] 02/06/1999
Franz Miss G, Columbia Internat.Univ., Extension Site Korntal L., Germany. [0052421] 27/10/1995
Franzen Mrs GL, BA DipLib MSc, Ref.Lib., IAEA, Vienna. [0052099] 03/10/1995
Frascina Ms JM, p./t.L.Asst., Concord Coll., Shrewsbury. [0061320] 17/05/2002
Fraser Mr A, MCLIP, Retired. [0005189] 10/01/1936
Fraser Mrs BA, (was O'Rourke), Unemployed. [0038918] 21/10/1985
Fraser Dr DM, BA(Hons) MCLIP, Sen.Lib.:Young People's Serv.(Pub.), Norfolk C.C. [0019893] 19/12/1972
Fraser Mrs EL, MCLIP, Retired. [0005193] 01/04/1970
Fraser Mrs EM, (was Singer), BA MCLIP, [0025109] 08/10/1975
Fraser Ms F, BA MCLIP, Community Lib.(Job-share), Bannockburn L., Stirling Dist.Ls. [0030618] 19/02/1979
Fraser Mrs G, (was Doodson), MA MCLIP, Comm.Serv.Mgr.& Area Serv.Mgr., (N.) Lincs.C.C., Louth L. [0033759] 12/02/1981
Fraser Mrs GR, (was Phillips), BA MCLIP, Sen.Inf.Lib., Flintshire C.C., Mold. [0028652] 07/01/1978
Fraser Mrs IB, (was Rutherford), BA MCLIP, Retired. [0005195] 26/09/1962

Fraser Ms JM, BSc MA DipLib MCLIP, Lib., Grampian Univ.Hosp.NHS Trust, Elgin. [0039182] 24/11/1985
Fraser Mr JR, BA DipLib MCLIP, Support Serv.Lib., Angus Council, Cultural Servs., Forfar. [0031065] 22/08/1979
Fraser Mr KC, MA BSc MCLIP, Retired. [0005197] 19/10/1966
Fraser Mr KG, BA DMS MCLIP, Lib., The Robert Gordon Univ., Aberdeen. [0033932] 22/05/1981
Fraser Mrs L, (was Gildersleeve), BA(Hons) MCLIP, Res.Lib., B.B.C. Newcastle, Newcastle upon Tyne. [0043707] 08/12/1989
Fraser Mrs LM, BA MCLIP, Lib., Davis Langdon & Everest, London. [0015949] 01/01/1971
Fraser Ms MA, MA MCLIP, Sen.Lib., Dept.for Internat.Devel.L., E.Kilbride. [0023251] 15/10/1974
Fraser Mrs MS, (was Long), MA MCLIP, Child.Serv.Mgr., L.B.of Croydon, Cent.L. [0031759] 30/11/1979
Fraser Mr PS, BA MCLIP, Unemployed. [0024670] 17/09/1975
Fraser Mrs S, (was Taylor), BA(Hons) MCLIP, Inf.Mgr., The Learning Shop, Hull. [0020103] 25/01/1973
Fraser Mrs SM, MCLIP, Learning Cent.Mgr., Cornwall Coll., Falmouth. [0031131] 30/08/1979
Fraser Miss VL, BA(Hons), Asst.Lib., Sch.L.Serv., Powys. [0051026] 09/11/1994
Frater Mr GS, MA MCLIP, Sen.Lib., Alton Co.Br.L., Hampshire Co.L. [0005203] 14/10/1969
Fredricks Mr RL, BA(Hons) MCLIP, Inf.Lib., W.Sussex C.C., Horsham L. [0053784] 01/10/1996
Freebury Mr R, BA DipLib MCLIP, Higher Lib.Exex., L.Dept.House of Commons. [0040817] 01/07/1987
Freedman Miss E, MSc BA(Hons), VT Lib., GMTV. [0059420] 07/03/2001
Freedman Mrs HH, (was Woolfson), BA DipLib MCLIP, Lib., Jewish Free Sch., London. [0031504] 08/10/1979
Freedman Ms JD, BA(Hons), p./t.Lib., World Wide Group, London. [0038091] 08/01/1985
Freedman Dr MJ, BA MLS PhD, Dir., Westchester L.System, USA. [0061497] 02/09/2002
Freedman Ms SB, (was Peries), Lib., Seven Kings High Sch., L.B.of Redbridge. [0049898] 07/01/1994
Freeman Mrs CA, (was Jones), MCLIP, Freelance, 51 Leatherhead Road, Ashtead, Surrey, KT21 2TP. [0022937] 01/10/1974
Freeman Mrs JH, (was Cashmore), BA MCLIP, [0028788] 26/01/1978
Freeman Mrs KE, (was Mowle), MCLIP, Unemployed. [0027284] 14/02/1977
Freeman Mrs LA, (was Fallows), BA MCLIP, Unemployed. [0041511] 11/01/1988
Freeman Ms LJ, (was Wilkinson), BSc(Hons) DipLIS MCLIP, Elec.Resources Lib., UMIST, Manchester. [0049841] 20/12/1993
Freeman Mr MCE, BA MCLIP, L.Mgr., S.Tyneside Metro.Bor. [0031288] 08/10/1979
Freeman Dr MJ, BA MEd PhD FCLIP, Retired. [0005216] 30/09/1959 FE 18/04/1989
Freeman Mrs NA, (was Hardy), BLS MCLIP, Team Lib.:Eastern Area, Norfolk L.& Inf.Serv., Sprowston L. [0028432] 04/12/1977
Freeman Miss OJ, MLS MCLIP, Self Employed. [0005217] 27/09/1967
Freeman Ms P, BA(Hons) DipLIS MCLIP, Project Leader, Shropshire C.C., Shrewsbury. [0047829] 12/10/1992
Freeman Mrs SD, (was Young), MCLIP, Br.Lib., Stockton Bor.Council. [0023217] 15/11/1974
Freeman Miss SE, MA DipLib MCLIP, Lib., Winchester Ref.L., Hants.C.C. [0029656] 03/10/1978
Freemantle Mr DJ, BA DipLib MCLIP, Inf.Analyst, BG Grp.plc., Reading. [0036404] 08/10/1983
French Mr JM, BA MCLIP, Asst.Lib., U.M.I.S.T. [0005223] 19/01/1971
French Mrs LM, (was Wedge), BSc, Asst.Lib., Bexley Central L. [0050131] 06/04/1994
French Miss MJ, BA(Hons) DipLIS, Dep.Lib., Vet.Labs.Agency, Addlestone. [0050591] 26/09/1994
French Mrs RJ, (was Raynham), MCLIP, Retired, New Zealand. [0005224] 29/09/1967
French Mr T, MA DipLib MCLIP, Head, Modern Brit.Collections, Brit.L. [0005225] 01/01/1966
French Mr WE, FCLIP, Life Member, Tel.01252 332209. [0005227] 01/01/1935 FE 01/01/1951
Freshwater Mrs M, BA(Hons), p./t.Stud./Asst.Lib., Univ.Cent.England, St.Clare's Coll., Oxford. [0059321] 07/02/2001
Freshwater Mr PB, MA MCLIP, Retired. [0005230] 16/03/1966
Fretten Miss CE, MCLIP, Sen.L.Exec., House of Commons L. [0005231] 02/10/1968
Freund Ms A, BSc FCLIP, Head of Customer Serv., Lloyds TSB Grp., Bristol. [0001710] 01/01/1971 FE 01/04/2002
Frew Mrs LM, (was Harrison), BA MCLIP, Sch.Lib., Bolton Sch.(Girls' Div.), Lancs. [0024495] 29/08/1975
Frew Mrs SA, (was Biggin), BA DipLib MCLIP, Sch.Lib., Keswick Sch., Cumbria. [0027512] 09/05/1977
Frias Montoya Mr JA, Prof., Univ.de Salamanca, Facultad de Traduccion y Docum. [0047536] 01/10/1992
Fricker Mr A, BSc MSc, Lib., N.W.London NHS Trust, Cent.Middx.Hosp. [0055376] 06/10/1997
Fricker Mr J, MCLIP, Life Member. [0005235] 12/10/1945
Fricker Mrs R, (was Rees), BA MA, Inf.Offr., Norton Rose, London. [0055369] 06/10/1997
Friedlander Ms JR, BA MCLIP, Inf.Offr., Nat.Union of Teachers. [0032654] 15/07/1980
Friedman Miss JE, MA MCLIP, Retired. [0005238] 23/06/1948
Friggens Miss GL, BA(Hons) MSc(Econ) MCLIP, Sen.Asst.Lib., De Montfort Univ., Leicester. [0052529] 06/11/1995
Fripp Mr AJ, BA MCLIP, Team Lib.-Under 8's Serv., Glos.L.Arts & Mus.Serv. [0038508] 28/05/1985

Friswell Mrs M, BA(Hons), L.Asst., Blackpool Cent.L., Lancs. [0056305] 06/05/1998 **AF**
Frith Mrs JA, (was Bieniek), BA MIMgt MCLIP, Stock Operations Mgr., Nat.L.for the Blind, Stockport. [0044509] 16/10/1990
Frodin Mrs A, BA, Website Inf.Mgr., Glos.C.C. [0045269] 01/10/1990
Froggatt Ms SJ, Lib., Reynolds Porter Chamberlain, London. [0039167] 01/10/1985
Frood Miss EK, DipLib MCLIP, Devel.Offr.:Best Value, Leeds L.& Inf.Serv. [0029657] 03/10/1978
Frossman-Finney Mrs M, BSc MCLIP, Sen.L.Asst., Univ.of Strathclyde, Glasgow. [0053174] 01/04/1996
Frost Miss AJ, BLS MCLIP, Reader Serv.Lib., Norfolk L.& Inf.Serv. [0029324] 23/05/1978
Frost Mrs CL, (was Steel), BA MCLIP, Lib.(Accessions) Job Share, Cent.L., Oldham. [0013938] 01/03/1967
Frost Mr DW, MCLIP, Sen.L.Mgr., L.B.of Greenwich. [0018708] 27/03/1963
Frost Mrs LM, (was Holloway), MCLIP, Retired. [0005245] 27/09/1965
Frost Mr RA, BSc(Hons), Lib., Tower Hamlets Sch. L. Serv. [0061371] 05/07/2002
Frost Mrs S, (was Broad), BA MCLIP, p./t.Administrator, Brit.& Irish Assoc.of Law Lib., Warwick. [0024609] 01/10/1975
Frost Ms SA, BA MCLIP, Lib., M.O.D. Whitehall L., London. [0024672] 02/10/1975
Frost Mr SH, BA(Hons) MA, L.Asst., Marshall L.Economics., Univ.of Cambridge. [0047304] 08/07/1992
Frost Mr SK, BA(Hons) DipInf, L.Asst., Fullwell Cross L., Essex. [0053010] 14/02/1996
Frost Miss SM, BA MCLIP, Learning Centre Mgr., Learning Res.Cent., Carlisle Coll. [0031826] 18/01/1980
Froud Miss L, Unemployed. [0054631] 12/02/1997
Froud Mr RN, BLib DMS MIMgt FCLIP, Co.Lib., Somerset Co.L., Bridgwater. [0021900] 21/01/1974 **FE 23/07/1997**
Frow Mrs R, Cert.of Merit. [0048817] 08/06/1993
Froy Mr SG, BA MCLIP, Website Mgr., Wakefield M.D.C.L.& Inf. [0026378] 01/10/1976
Fry Ms CAM, BA MCLIP, Lib., Varndean Coll., Brighton. [0021899] 24/01/1974
Fry Mrs EM, (was Waugh), BLib(Hons), Res.Mgr., Oxford Economic Research Assoc., Oxford. [0043550] 06/11/1990
Fry-Smith Mr JCH, BA(Hons)DipLib, Faculty Lib., Univ.of Cent.England, Birmingham. [0032953] 09/10/1980
Fryer Miss H, BSc(Hons), Asst.Lib., Royal Agricultural Coll., Cirencester. [0055975] 07/01/1998
Fryer Mrs MR, (was Plank), MCLIP, Retired. [0005255] 01/01/1960
Fuchs Dr H, PhD, Sen.Asst.Lib., Univ. of Gottingen, Germany. [0039726] 23/05/1986
Fuchs Ms I, MA, Grad.Trainee, Royal Holloway. [0061154] 15/03/2002
Fudakowska Miss E, BA MCLIP, Retired. [0005257] 01/01/1953
Fuegi Mr DF, MA MCLIP, Partner, MDR Partners. [0005258] 04/12/1967
Fujiwara Mr Y, MLS, Lect.of Lib., Chubu Gakuin Coll., Seki City, Japan. [0057740] 20/07/1999
Fulcher Mrs AM, BA MCLIP, Reader Serv.Lib., Univ.of Greenwich, Dartford, Kent. [0024674] 10/10/1975
Fulcher Miss P, MA MCLIP, Retired. [0018709] 24/03/1959
Fulker Mrs AJ, (was Bexley), L.Mgr., Binnie Black & Veatch, Redhill. [0045528] 21/02/1991 **AF**
Fuller Mrs DA, Retired. [0005260] 06/02/1947
Fuller Miss MA, BA MIMgt MCLIP, Lib., Fire Serv.Coll. [0005262] 20/07/1970
Fuller Mrs MA, (was Preston), FCLIP, Life Member. [0005259] 01/01/1935 **FE 01/01/1939**
Fuller Mr NR, BA(Hons) DipLIS MCLIP, Mgr., Westminster Sch.L.Serv., London. [0043637] 13/11/1989
Fuller Mr RJ, BA DipLib MCLIP, Learning Support Lib., Leeds L.& Inf.Serv. [0005263] 28/01/1972
Fuller Mrs SJ, BA(Hons)DipLIS mclip, Team Lib., Northants.L.& Inf.Serv. [0053294] 29/04/1996
Fullick Ms LJ, (was Eves), BA DipLib MCLIP, Career Break. [0028567] 09/01/1978
Fulljames Mr DR, MSc MCLIP, Retired. [0005264] 16/10/1970
Fullwood Mrs J, (was Morgan), MCLIP, p./t.Asst.Lend.Lib., Newport Cent.L. [0032372] 25/03/1980
Fulton Mr AR, MCLIP, Asst.Dir.-L.& Cult.Serv., Aberdeen City Council. [0005265] 26/02/1968
Fulton Mrs BL, (was Holmes), BA MCLIP, Unemployed. [0027492] 22/04/1977
Fulton Mrs E, (was Robertson), BA MCLIP, Asst.Dir., Scottish L.& Inf.Council, Scottish L.Assoc., Hamilton. [0031430] 12/10/1979
Fulton Mrs JA, MCLIP, Sen.Lib., Havant L., Hants. [0005266] 13/11/1972
Fulton Mrs JL, (was Skinner), BA MSc(Econ), Asst.Lib., Internat.Christian Coll., Glasgow. [0055382] 06/10/1997
Fulton Mrs MA, (was Kennedy), BA, Asst.Central Lending Lib., Aberdeen Central L. [0059609] 01/01/1970
Fulwell Ms S, MCLIP, Tutor (p./t.), S.E.Essex Coll., Southend, Essex. [0018710] 19/02/1968
Fung Miss SMA, BSc MEd DipLib MLib MCLIP, Asst.Lib., Univ.of Westminster. [0046366] 30/10/1991
Furber Mrs ACB, (was Varney), BA DipLib MCLIP, Housing Advice Co-ordinator, Bromley C.A.B. [0027675] 01/07/1977
Furber Mrs MC, BA MA PGCE, P./t.Asst.Lib., Wellcome L.for the Hist.&, Understanding of Med. [0053961] 16/10/1996
Furlong Mrs CMM, (was Monk), BA(Hons) MLib, Inf.Offr., Chamber of Commerce, Milton Keynes. [0047737] 16/10/1992
Furlong Mrs JC, (was Miller), Resident in Oman. [0044999] 04/02/1991
Furner Dr J, MA MSc PhD MCLIP, Resident in U.S.A. [0060094] 07/12/2001
Furness Ms A, BSc, Reader Serv.Lib., H.M.Treasury & Cabinet Off.L., London. [0040580] 07/04/1987

Furness Miss EL, Stud., Manchester Met.Univ. [0059302] 31/01/2001
Furness Mr M, Stud., Manchester Met.Univ. [0061311] 17/05/2002
Furphy Mr DK, BA DipEd GradDipLS AALIA AIMM, City Lib., City of Cockburn L., Bibra Lake, Australia. [0057092] 07/12/1998
Furphy Miss P, BA(Hons), Stud., Univ.of Brighton. [0061326] 22/05/2002
Fussell Mrs J, Stud., Brighton Univ. [0059415] 06/03/2001
Futter Mr DW, BA CertEd MCLIP, Learning Res.Mgr., Sussex Downs Coll.:Eastbourne, E.Sussex. [0005274] 02/04/1969
Fynes-Clinton Mrs AB, (was McGuire), BA DipLib MCLIP, Sch.Lib., Haberdashers' Aske's Sch.for Girls. [0040152] 09/10/1986
Gabbatt Miss JM, B LIB MCLIP, Sen.Lib.-Child./Sch.Serv., Blackburn with Darwen B.C. [0025535] 29/01/1976
Gabbitas Mrs EM, (was Ray), BA MCLIP, Lib., Sen.Sch., Kings Sch., Rochester, Kent. [0012189] 05/10/1971
Gabe Ms NBM, PGDip, Lib.(Electronic Resouces), Anglo-Euro.Coll.of Chiropractic, Dorset. [0054686] 25/02/1997
Gabler Mrs C, (was Bridden), MCLIP, Inf.Lib., The Library, Paul Street,Somerset. [0001699] 01/01/1970
Gabr Mrs RA, BA, Learning Cent.Co-ordinator, S.Kent Coll., Dover. [0056284] 28/04/1998
Gabriel Ms CL, BA(Hons) MA, Lib., Kings Coll.London, Multidisciplinary L. [0053178] 01/04/1996 **AF**
Gadd Mr DWJ, DipLib MCLIP, Retired. [0035879] 07/02/1983
Gadsby Mr DE, AssocIPD MCLIP, Unemployed. [0005281] 11/03/1958
Gadsden Mr SR, MLS MCLIP, Life Member, Tel.01934 742405, Old Forge Hse., Lower N.St., Cheddar, Somerset, BS27 3HA. [0005282] 08/11/1947
Gaffney Ms P, BA, Sen.Lib., Birmingham Cent.Lend.L. [0033561] 21/01/1981
Gage Mrs HMW, (was Walley), MA(Oxon) MA MCLIP, p./t.Asst.Lib., Manchester Metro.Univ., Crewe Campus. [0039032] 30/10/1985
Gahan Mr PN, MA, Lib., Swindon Cent.L. [0050364] 01/07/1994
Gailani Miss J, (was Al-Gailani), MA(Hons) DipLIS MCLIP, L.Asst., Edinburgh Univ. [0009457] 29/10/1971
Gain Mrs M, (was Copeland), MCLIP, Consultant, Practica, Warks. [0005289] 14/01/1969
Gaine Mr F, Lib.Asst., Southampton. [0061590] 02/10/2002
Gair Miss J, BA MCLIP, Staff Devel.Worker, Dundee City Council, Dundee. [0036019] 04/04/1983
Gaj Mrs LAT, (was Hobday), BA MCLIP, Learning Cent.Mgr., Westminster Kingsway Coll. [0035914] 07/02/1983
Gajadhar Mr R, Stud., Univ.of N.London. [0058990] 17/10/2000
Gajewski Mrs W, DipLIS, L.Volunteer, Macmillan Cancer Relief, London. [0061296] 16/05/2002
Galambos Mrs EF, (was Bartos), MCLIP, Life Member. [0005293] 25/10/1945
Galber Mrs KD, BA DipLib, Sen.Asst./Child.Lib., L.B.of Harrow. [0056949] 13/11/1998
Galbraith Mr J, MCLIP, Vice-President, Blackwell N.A., London, Ontario, Canada. [0005295] 21/07/1961
Gale Mrs CA, (was Harding), BA(Hons) MA, Subject Support Lib., Exeter Univ.L. [0056661] 01/01/1998
Gale Mrs CA, (was Rees), BA(Hons) MCLIP, Asst.Lib., Brooklands Coll., Weybridge. [0031426] 11/10/1979
Gale Mrs CJ, (was Hersey), MCLIP, Unemployed. [0006778] 01/01/1970
Gale Miss EF, BA MCLIP, Young People's Lib., Tonbridge L., Kent. [0030834] 30/04/1979
Gale Miss KA, BA(Hons) MA, Careers Inf.Mgr., Univ.of Luton. [0053865] 07/10/1996
Gale Mr MJM, BA(Hons) MLib MCLIP, Prof.Lib., Univ.of Birmingham. [0044858] 01/01/1991
Gale Mrs MTC, (was Smith), DipLib MCLIP, L.Mgr., Suffolk C.C., Rosehill L. [0033917] 14/05/1981
Gale Mrs P, (was Rorison), MCLIP, Retired. [0005302] 01/01/1958
Gale Mrs SA, (was Whitehead), BA MCLIP, Temp.Asst.Lib., Hutt Valley High Sch., New Zealand. [0024561] 20/08/1975
Gallacher Mrs A, BA(Hons), Lib., Royal Bor.of Windsor & Maidenhead. [0061114] 21/02/2002
Gallacher Ms CA, MLS, Asst.Dir.of Inf., Univ.of Bristol. [0040388] 21/01/1987
Gallacher Miss F, BA(Hons) MCLIP, Customer Serv.Consultant, SIRSI Ltd., Potters Bar, Herts. [0054330] 21/11/1996
Gallacher Mr JA, BDS DipILM, Asst.Inf.Spec. [0057631] 04/06/1999
Gallacher Mrs M, (was Spence), BSc MSc, Lib., Cardonald Coll., Glasgow. [0048081] 03/11/1992
Gallagher Mr CC, BA(Hons) DipIM, Asst.Lib., The Home Off., London. [0056533] 10/08/1998
Gallagher Mrs CF, BA(Hons) MA, Lib., Nottingham C.C., Beeston L. [0059348] 13/02/2001
Gallagher Miss HM, BA(Hons) MSc, Catr., Leeds Met.Univ. [0059705] 15/08/2001
Gallagher Mr JA, MA(Hons), Stud., Manchester Met.Univ. &, Team Leader - Altrincham L., Trafford Bor.Council, Manchester. [0058152] 10/11/1999
Gallagher Mr P, MA, Sch.Lib.(Job Share), Whitehill Secondary, Glasgow. [0043688] 30/10/1989
Gallagher Miss T, L.Asst., E.Sheen L. [0061542] 10/09/2002 **AF**
Gallagher Miss T, (was Aitken), BA(Hons), Sch.Lib., Boston High Sch., Lincs. [0044759] 15/11/1990
Gallart Marsillas Ms N, Project Mgr., Univ.Autonoma de Barcelona, L.Serv., Bellaterra,Spain. [0037396] 16/08/1984
Gallehawk Miss RK, BA(Hons) MCLIP, Lib., Essex C.C., Brentwood. [0041744] 10/03/1988
Gallen Mr G, BA, Retired. [0023342] 18/11/1974
Galletly Mrs CA, BA DipLib MCLIP, Company Secretary, Employment Unknown. [0036981] 17/01/1984
Gallimore Mr A, B SC MCLIP, Cent.L.Mgr., Manchester City C. [0022801] 11/10/1974

243

Galloway Mr BJ, MCLIP, Lib., E.Bridgwater Community Sch., Somerset. [0005314] 04/05/1962
Galloway Mrs J, (was Liversedge), MCLIP, Mobile L.Asst., North Area, Clevedon L., N.Somerset. [0005317] 11/01/1964
Galloway Mr JS, MCLIP, Unemployed. [0024081] 18/03/1975
Gallwey Mr JB, BA MIIS DipLib MCLIP, Tech.Serv.& Outreach Lib., Inst.of Transportation Stud., Univ.of California, Berkeley. [0027763] 09/08/1977
Galsworthy Ms JG, FCLIP, Life Member. [0005322] 20/09/1956 **FE 01/01/1965**
Galt Ms CO, BA(Hons) DipILM, Child.Lib., S.Tyneside Comm.Serv.Dept., S.Shields. [0054247] 14/11/1996
Galt Ms E, BA MCLIP, Team Lib., Educ.Resource Serv., Glasgow. [0035568] 18/10/1982
Galvin Mrs VS, (was Pearce), BA PDIM MCLIP, Asst.Lib., Secunda P.L., Highveld E.Municipal L.Serv. [0011430] 22/05/1969
Galway Miss L, BSc MSc DipILM MCLIP, Sch.Lib., S.Lanarkshire Council. [0050729] 14/10/1994
Gamble Mrs D, (was Hamel), MA MCLIP, Freelance Editor. [0006188] 01/01/1971
Gamble Mrs P, (was Foster), MCLIP, Lib.-Support Serv., City L.& Arts Cent., Sunderland. [0005324] 08/03/1966
Gamble Mrs PR, (was Ely), MCLIP, Bibl.Serv.& Support Mgr., Leeds Metro.Univ. [0005328] 09/02/1968
Gambles Mr BR, MA DipLib MCLIP, Acting Head of Cent.L., Birmingham L.Serv. [0027976] 02/10/1977
Games Mr GJ, BA(Hons) MSc(Econ) PGDip, Ref.Lib., Reading Cent.L. [0057008] 19/11/1998
Gammie Mrs J, (was Brownlee), MSc(Econ) MCLIP, Stud., U.W.A., Aberystwyth, &, Lib., Selkirk Pub.L., Selkirkshire. [0045313] 08/10/1990
Gander Mr N, BA(Hons) MSc, ICT & Inf.Mgr., Yorkshire Mus.Council. [0050717] 13/10/1994
Gandon Ms A, (was Pearson), MCLIP, Coll.Lib., Plymouth Coll.of F.E., Devon. [0020882] 10/08/1973
Gandy Ms F, MA MCLIP, Fellow Lib., Girton Coll., Univ.of Cambridge. [0009054] 01/10/1966
Gandy Mr JE, BA(Hons) DipILS, Rare Bks.Catr., Chetham's L., Manchester. [0051419] 10/02/1995
Ganeser Miss M, MLS MCLIP, L.Asst., Inst.of Advanced Legal Studies, Univ.of London. [0020726] 26/06/1973
Gann Mr PD, FCLIP, Life member, 11 Honeybourne Way, Petts Wood, Orpington, Kent, BR5 1EZ. [0005333] 26/02/1949 **FE 01/01/1957**
Gannaway Mrs K, B.Ed(Hons), Stud., Thames Valley Univ. [0059879] 29/10/2001
Gannaway Mr NM, MCLIP, Retired. [0005334] 07/01/1953
Gannon Mrs J, (was Ingham), MCLIP, Asst.Lib.(Job-share), Heywood L., Heywood, Lancs. [0007600] 01/01/1972
Gannon Miss VJ, MA BA MCLIP, Catr., Stoke-on-Trent Coll. [0005335] 07/11/1967
Gant Mrs DM, (was Livingstone), BA(Hons) MCLIP, Sen.Inf.Asst., City Coll. E.Birmingham. [0009002] 09/10/1969
Garbacz Ms SJ, BA(Hons) MA MCLIP, Asst.Lib., N.Yorks.C.C., Scarborough. [0052338] 30/10/1995
Garbett Miss P, BA MCLIP, Customer Support &Data Mgr., Birmingham L.Serv. [0005337] 01/01/1971
Garcia Mr M, BA, Employment not known. [0060512] 11/12/2001
Garcia-Ontiveros Ms DM, BA MA, Asst.Lib., College of Law, London. [0058112] 01/11/1999
Garden Mrs AH, (was Grounds), B LIB MCLIP, Organiser., Osborne Books At Home. [0034879] 29/03/1982
Garden Mr DLW, MA MCLIP, Asst.Ch.Lib., Shetland L. [0026230] 15/09/1976
Garden Mrs E, (was Russell), MA MCLIP, L.Resource Cent.Co-ordinator, Bridge of Don Academy, Aberdeen. [0029475] 17/08/1978
Garden Mr L, MA DipLib MCLIP, Clerical Asst., Highland Council, Dingwall. [0023866] 17/02/1975
Gardham Mr MP, MA MCLIP, Diocesan Secretary, Anglican Church of Papua New Guinea, Mt.Hagen. [0021357] 15/11/1973
Gardiner Mrs CJ, (was Mitchell), BA MCLIP, Unemployed. [0038148] 22/01/1985
Gardiner Mrs E, (was Matthews), MCLIP, Retired. [0024047] 08/03/1941
Gardiner Ms G, MCLIP, Lib., Rotherham P.L., S.Yorks. [0005341] 03/04/1972
Gardiner Mrs JA, (was Greeney), BA DipLib MCLIP, p./t.Lib.Asst., Taunton & Somerset NHS Trust, Saunton & somerset Hospital. [0026101] 30/06/1976
Gardiner Miss JM, BA(Hons), Stud. [0058019] 13/10/1999
Gardiner Mr K, BSc BA MCLIP, Resident in France. [0060066] 07/12/2001
Gardiner Miss LC, BA(Hons) MSc, Peoples Network Project Offr., Inverclyde Council, Cent.L., Greenock. [0058105] 27/10/1999
Gardner Miss CA, BA(Hons) MSc, Inf.Offr., Bank of England, London. [0049201] 12/10/1993
Gardner Miss CL, BA, Stud., Univ.of Sheffield [0059421] 22/03/2001
Gardner Miss H, BA(Hons), Stud., Univ.of Cent.England, Birmingham. [0059323] 07/02/2001
Gardner Mrs HC, (was Sparkman), BSc MCLIP, Knowledge Mgr.,Primary Care, Babington Hosp., Derby. [0031456] 18/10/1979
Gardner Mrs JE, (was Macdonald), BA DipILS MCLIP, Sch.Lib., W.Dunbartonshire Council, Clydebank. [0046560] 14/11/1991
Gardner Mrs JK, IT Facilitator, Royal Cornwall Hosp.NHS Trust, Cornwall. [0061420] 25/07/2002 **AF**
Gardner Mrs JM, BA MCLIP, Learning Cent.Mgr., Thomas Danby Coll., Leeds. [0033625] 29/01/1981
Gardner Miss JR, BA MCLIP, Head of Tech.Serv., The L., Univ.of Warwick. [0005355] 20/01/1970
Gardner Mrs KM, (was Fish), BA MLib MCLIP, L.& Learning Res.Cent.Mgr., Worcester Coll.of Tech., Worcester. [0004931] 28/08/1968

Gardner Mrs ML, (was Hammond), MCLIP, Housewife. [0005360] 15/01/1964
Gardner Miss MV, Retired. [0020727] 20/06/1973
Gardner Mr S, Unemployed. [0059193] 13/12/2000
Gardner Mrs SJ, (was Bawcutt), MCLIP, Life Member, Tel.01865 246783, 5 Haynes Rd., Old Marston, Oxford, OX3 0SE. [0005361] 19/01/1946
Garfield Mrs DM, BA MCLIP, Academic Liaison Lib., Anglia Poly.Univ., Chelmsford, Essex. [0053391] 05/06/1996
Garfield Dr E, BSc MS PhD MIEEE HonFCLIP, Hon Fellow. [0060072] 07/12/2001 **FE 01/04/2002**
Gargett Miss C, MCLIP, Life Member. [0005364] 10/01/1944
Garibyan Mrs M, BA DMS, Stud., Middlesex Univ. [0060968] 21/01/2002
Garland Mr JR, BA(Hons), Lib., Brighton & Hove L. [0049980] 02/02/1994
Garland Mrs KE, MA, Serv.Co-ordinator, Univ.of Leicester L. [0051606] 07/04/1995
Garman Mrs EA, BA MA, L.Asst., Harrogate Library. [0056979] 17/11/1998
Garmendia Galbete Ms JM, BA MA MCLIP, Employment not known. [0060451] 11/12/2001
Garner Miss AJ, Asst.Lib., Aquinas Coll., Stockport. [0055580] 21/10/1997
Garner Mrs EJS, MCLIP, Asst.Area Sch.Lib., Hants.C.C. [0013567] 04/01/1972
Garner Ms FA, PGDip, L.Mgr., Welsh Coll.of Horticulture, Mold, Flintshire. [0057354] 17/02/1999
Garner Ms H, BA(Hons) DipLib, L.Mgr., Freshfields Bruckhaus Deringer, London. [0044523] 22/10/1990
Garner Miss HJ, BA(Hons) DipILM MCLIP, Inf.Adviser, Sheffield Hallam Univ. [0045851] 03/07/1991
Garner Ms JE, Inf.Mgr., Dept.of Trade & Industry, London. [0039317] 10/01/1986
Garner Mrs JS, BA(Hons), Recruitment Cons., TFPL Ltd., London. [0055781] 17/11/1997
Garner Mr MS, BA DipLib MCLIP, Devel.Mgr.for Lifelong Learning, Lambeth L. [0037699] 11/10/1984
Garner Mr PA, BSc MCLIP, Employment not known. [0060440] 11/12/2001
Garner Ms SA, Stud., Univ.of Wales, Aberystwyth. [0061378] 05/07/2002
Garnham Miss VL, BA(Hons) MA MCLIP, Sch.Lib./Learning Res.Cent.Mgr., Wolsingham Sch.& Comm.Coll., Bishop Auckland. [0055774] 18/11/1997
Garratt Mr CC, BA, L.Electronic App.Mgr., Hammond Suddards Edge, Birmingham. [0042952] 02/05/1989
Garratt Mr M, BA MA MCLIP, Retired, 59 Malmesbury Rd., Cheadle Hulme, Cheshire SK8 7QL. [0005378] 16/12/1955
Garrett Miss ED, BSc(Hons) MSc MCLIP, Reader Serv.Lib., Royal Coll.of Obstetricians &, Gynaecologists, London. [0049211] 12/10/1993
Garrett Mrs MEP, MCLIP, Sch.Lib., Bishops Stortford Coll., Herts. [0027061] 20/01/1977
Garrett Miss PL, BSc(Hons), p./t.Stud./Bibl.Asst., Brighton Univ., Portsmouth Cent.L. [0061132] 07/03/2002
Garrigan Mrs MRC, MCLIP, Employment unknown. [0060266] 10/12/2001
Garriock Dr JB, (was Wood), MA PhD FCLIP FRSA, Life Member. [0016195] 01/01/1951 **FE 01/01/1963**
Garrity Miss G, BA(Hons) PGDipIS, Inf.Mgr./Lib., Home Off., London. [0061149] 21/03/2002
Garrod Mr JE, MA MCLIP, 51 Avenue Hector Otto, MC 98000, Monaco. [0016918] 06/09/1955
Garrod Mrs PA, (was Perkins), BA(Hons) MA MCLIP, Public L.Networking Focus, UKOLN, Univ.of Bath. [0046001] 15/08/1991
Garrote Miss VL, Lib., Hospital Italiano de Buenos Aires, Biblioteca Central, Argentina. [0058267] 03/12/1999
Garside Miss KL, (was Denman), BSc(Econ), Inf.Lib., Southampton Inst.of Higher Educ., Southampton. [0053797] 01/10/1996
Gartland Mrs J, (was Whitfield), MCLIP, Asst.Lib., Durham C.C., Arts & L.& Mus.Dept. [0005388] 16/03/1965
Gartland Ms LM, BA(Hons) MA, Lib.Asst., Newcastle, [0061444] 27/08/2002
Gartside Ms EJ, BA(Hons) MCLIP, Research Mgr., TDA Transitions Ltd., Brentford. [0042354] 25/10/1988
Gas Mr Z, BA MA MCLIP AIL, Digital Res.Support Lib., Inf.Serv., Univ.of Birmingham L. [0037568] 09/10/1984
Gascoigne Mrs J, (was Stoker), MCLIP, Retired. [0018716] 11/09/1967
Gascoigne Miss JE, BA(Hons), Asst.Inf.Offr., Slaughter & May, London. [0054278] 13/12/1996
Gascoyne Ms HM, (was Foster), MLS CertEd MCLIP, Learning Cent.Mgr., S.E.Derbyshire Coll. [0005391] 09/09/1969
Gaskell Miss AL, BA(Hons), Asst.Lib., Dept.of Health, Leeds. [0059375] 01/02/2001
Gasson Mr SM, BA(Hons), Web Inf.Mgr., L.B.of Merton. [0049127] 06/10/1993
Gaster Mrs KR, (was Wedderspoon), MCLIP, Learning Res.Mgr., Linden Lodge Sch., London. [0005395] 26/03/1957
Gaston Mr RS, BA(Hons) MA, Researcher, Lehman Brothers, London. [0057874] 22/09/1999
Gate Mr J, BA MCLIP, Advisory Serv.Lib., Bristol City Council. [0005396] 03/10/1968
Gatenby Miss K, BA MCLIP, Site Lib., Ridge Danyers Coll., Stockport, Cheshire. [0005397] 02/10/1967
Gater Miss L, BA(Hons), Lib., St.Thomas More Catholic Coll., Stoke on Trent. [0046812] 02/04/1992
Gates Miss S, MCLIP, Lib.,-Tennyson Research Cent., Lincs.C.C., Lincoln. [0005398] 10/01/1966
Gauci Miss ML, BA MSc MCLIP, Cent.Serv.Lib., Court Serv.L.& Inf.Serv., London. [0026183] 19/08/1976
Gauld Ms MA, MA DipEdTECH MCLIP, Doc.Delivery Lib., Univ.of Queensland, Australia. [0005402] 23/09/1970
Gault Mrs CRM, (was Hanson), BA PGCE DipLib MCLIP, Asst.Lib., Barbican L., London. [0036582] 12/10/1983
Gaunt Miss JJ, BA(Hons), Grad.Trainee, Open Univ.L. [0061121] 20/02/2002

Personal Members — Gibbs

Gaunt Ms LM, BA MCLIP, Asst.Lib.-Catg., Univ.of Greenwich, Woolwich. [0005403] 18/02/1969
Gauss Mr JH, BSc DipLib MCLIP AMinstP, Team Lib.,(Ref.Dept.), Ealing Cent.L., L.B.of Ealing. [0021183] 01/10/1973
Gavaghan Miss SH, BA(Hons) DMS, Sen.Stock Devle.Lib., Middlesborough L.& Inf., Cent.L. [0049705] 25/11/1993
Gavan Mrs AK, (was Hansen-Just), MCLIP, Br.Lib.-Job Share, Haddington P.L., E.Lothian. [0026400] 12/10/1976
Gavars Mrs RC, (was Reynolds), Law L.Consultant. [0041112] 11/10/1987
Gavigan Mrs J, BA DipLib MCLIP, Special Serv.Lib., Norton L., N.Yorks.C.C. [0023637] 16/01/1975
Gavin Mrs JM, (was Page), BA MCLIP, Sch.Lib., Trinity Sch., Belvedere, Kent. [0011142] 24/09/1965
Gavin Mrs JS, BA(Hons) DiplM MCLIP, Career Break. [0052715] 24/11/1995
Gaw Mrs AJ, (was Goodall), BEd MSc MCLIP, Sch.Lib.(Volunteer), Cedars Sch., Greenock. [0044704] 30/11/1990
Gaw Ms E, MA MCLIP, Princ.L.Offr., City of Edinburgh Council. [0043167] 06/09/1989
Gaw Mr MD, BA DipLib MCLIP, Serv.Mgr.-L., Trafford M.B.C. [0031831] 10/01/1980
Gaw Mr PW, BA MCLIP, Princ.Lib., Inf.Serv., Glos.C.C. [0043645] 15/11/1989
Gawley Ms EM, (was Hutchinson), BSc MCLIP, Employment not known. [0007541] 13/02/1968
Gay Mrs AC, (was Welson), MCLIP, Team Lib.(P./t.), Bracknell L., Berks.C.C. [0005407] 01/01/1967
Gay Ms ME, MCLIP, Unemployed. [0019743] 02/02/1970
Gaylard Mr R, BA, Stock Lib., Ipswich Co.L., Suffolk C.C. [0005409] 01/01/1972
Gaymard Ms SFS, BLS Dip, Head Lib., Greenwich Sch.of Mgmt., London. [0061194] 08/04/2002
Gaywood Miss GM, BSc, p./t.Stud./Princ.Lib., Univ.Aberystwyth, Geoff Bolton L, Bexleyheath. [0059824] 10/10/2001
Gaze Miss PH, MSc MCLIP, Retired. [0005412] 07/11/1964
Gazey Mrs TL, (was Mans), BA(Hons) DipLIS MA, Sen.Res.Advisor, City Coll., Birmingham. [0051305] 18/01/1995
Geaney Ms DF, BA MA, Sen.L.Asst., Newham, [0061399] 07/07/2002
Gear Mr SJ, MCLIP, Life Member. [0005413] 27/01/1950
Gear Mrs SJ, (was Pett), MCLIP, Retired. [0033788] 01/01/1953
Gearey Mr MJ, Tech.Lib., BAE Systems, Tabuk, Saudi Arabia. [0058826] 17/08/2000
Geary Miss K, BA(Hons) MA, Learning Resources Asst., Diplomatic Serv.Language Cent., London. [0059215] 09/01/2001 **AF**
Geater Mr DD, BA MSc MCLIP, Inf.Mgr., Home Off., London. [0052283] 24/11/1995
Gedalovitch Mrs RC, (was Norton), BA(Hons) MCLIP, Lib., L.B.of Havering, Romford, Essex. [0047326] 13/07/1992
Geddes Mrs A, (was Shanks), MCLIP, Comm.Lib.(Heritage), E.Ayrshire Council. [0018074] 01/10/1972
Geddes Mr GT, MA DipLib MCLIP, Systems Lib., Jordanhill L., Univ.of Strathclyde. [0005415] 21/10/1968
Geddes Miss HM, (was Screen), BA DipLib MCLIP, L.Mgr., Glos.Co.L.Arts & Mus.Serv. [0045947] 23/07/1991
Geddes Mrs M, (was Knight), MCLIP, Retired. [0005416] 04/03/1930
Geddes Ms SJ, (was Ranson), BLib MCLIP, Lib., Hertswood Sch., Borehamwood. [0058622] 10/01/1978
Gee Mr AP, BA DipLib MCLIP, L.Systems Support, N.Yorks.C.C., L.H.Q. [0025036] 10/11/1975
Gee Mr CP, MA BA(Hons), Business Inf.Offr., Armstrong Craven Ltd., Manchester. [0056603] 10/09/1998
Gee Mr DR, BA MA DipLib MCLIP, Sen.DipLib MCLIP, Inst.Advanced Legal Studies, Univ.of London. [0040939] 07/09/1987
Gee Mrs J, (was Cubitt), BA MCLIP, Asst.Lib.p./t., Northallerton Health Serv.NHS Trst, N.Yorks. [0023645] 26/01/1975
Gee Mrs MD, (was Jennings), MA MSc, Stud., Dept.of Inf.Studies, Univ.of Sheffield, Western Bank, Sheffield. [0051993] 01/09/1995
Gee Miss R, BSc(Hons) MA, Inf.Mgr., David Lock Associates, Milton Keynes, Bucks. [0053924] 10/10/1976
Geekie Mrs J, (was Mair), BA(Hons) MCLIP, Staff Devel.& Mob.Serv.Lib., ALIS, Oldmeldrum. [0044706] 30/11/1990
Geeson Mr AR, BA MCLIP, Retired. [0005424] 25/08/1960
Geeson Miss RE, BA MA, User Serv.Mgr., Bournemouth Univ., Bournemouth House L. [0056351] 05/06/1998
Geh Dr H, FCLIP, Hon.Vice President. [0046050] 11/09/1991 **FE 11/09/1991**
Gellatly Mrs CJ, (was Altmann), BA MLS MCLIP, Team Lib., Frome L., Somerset C.C. [0034144] 08/10/1981
Gem Mr MGDM, BA MSc MCLIP, Employment not known. [0060287] 10/12/2001
Gent Mr ASA, Systems Administrator, Tate Gallery, London. [0040198] 28/10/1986
Gent Mr RP, BA DMS MIMgt MCLIP, Asst.Dir.of L.& Heritage, Derbyshire C.C. [0005434] 13/04/1970
Gent Mrs S, (was Russell), BSc(Hons) MCLIP, Team Lib., Redhill Inf.Cent., Surrey. [0012804] 04/10/1971
Geoffroy Ms JA, BA(Hons) MSc, Unemployed. [0052574] 08/11/1995 **SP**
George Mr BS, MCLIP, Head of Ls., Beds.C.C. [0005436] 08/12/1961
George Mrs C, (was Longworth), BA DipLib MCLIP, Lib.-Lend., Torfaen Co.Bor.Council, Cwmbran. [0028330] 01/11/1977
George Mrs ERL, BA(Hons), Sen.Learning Res.Asst., Stoke-on-Trent Coll., Cauldon Campus. [0057960] 05/10/1999
George Mr G, (was Washington), Learning & Educ.Res.Administrator, PricewaterhouseCoopers, London. [0057837] 03/09/1999 **AF**
George Mrs J, BA DipLib MCLIP, Sen.Asst.Lib., Univ.of Bristol L. [0032959] 06/10/1980
George Miss JA, BA(Hons) PGDipIS, Stud., Univ.of Brighton. [0059582] 06/06/2001
George Mr JM, BA(Hon), Litigation Paralegal, Charles Russell, London. [0050186] 26/04/1994
George Mrs K, (was Goldstraw), BA (Hons) MCLIP, Lib., Shropshire C.C., Shrewsbury. [0036946] 18/01/1984
George Miss KR, BA, Sen.Lib., Inf.Serv.Unit, Home Off., London. [0043181] 19/09/1989
George Ms LJ, (was Bray), BA MCLIP, L.Mgr., Luton Borough Council. [0001656] 28/01/1972
George Mrs LK, (was Berry), BA MCLIP, Sch. Lib., Dover Grammar Sch. for Boys, Dover, Kent. [0026936] 17/01/1977
George Mr RH, BA/MCLIP, Support Serv.Lib., Caerphilly, Educ.Leisure & L., Blackwood. [0045471] 14/02/1991
George Ms SJ, BA(Hons), L.Asst., Bridgend County Borough Council, Ref.& Local Studies L. [0058433] 11/02/2000
George Miss SM, BA MCLIP, Lib., Bro Morgannwg NHS Trust, Neath Gen.Hosp. [0040752] 01/06/1987
George Mr WH, BA DipLib FGS MCLIP, Sen.Lib., L.B.of Barking & Dagenham. [0027980] 03/10/1977
Georgiou Mr M, BA(Hons), Stud., Thames Valley Univ. [0058917] 03/10/2000
Germain Miss ND, BA(Hons), Asst.Lib., Dechert, London. [0057089] 03/12/1998
Germany Mr A, MCLIP, Life Member. [0005446] 27/02/1940
Gerrard Mr AD, BA(Hons) MSc(Econ), Sen.L.Asst., Univ.of Nottingham. [0054299] 20/11/1996
Gerrard Mrs AJ, BA MCLIP, Coordinator of L.Serv.to, Young People, L.& Inf.Serv., Plymouth Cent.L.Serv. [0049549] 09/11/1993
Gerrard Mr JC, BA DipLib MCLIP, Sub-Lib., Univ.of Kent, Canterbury. [0022337] 01/04/1974
Gerrard Mrs KS, (was Hankinson), BA(Hons) MSC(Econ), Unemployed. [0053471] 01/01/1995
Gerrard Ms SE, (was Lucas), BA DipLib MCLIP, Lib.& Dep.Dir.of Inf.Serv., Royal Holloway, Univ.of London. [0026458] 30/09/1976
Gerrish Mrs A, (was Coutts), BA CNAA DipLib MCLIP, Catr., Oxford Univ., Cairns L. [0024883] 06/10/1975
Gerrish Mr SH, MSc MCLIP, Position unknown, Brit.Potato Council L., Oxford. [0060288] 10/12/2001
Gerry Miss N, BA(Hons), Journal Sales Mgr., Blackwell Publishing Ltd., Oxford. [0054222] 07/11/1996
Gervin Mr JP, BA DLIS MCLIP, Lib., S.E.L.B., Tyrone. [0029271] 12/05/1978
Gething Mrs SA, (was Blundred), BA MCLIP, Employment not known. [0021073] 01/10/1973
Ghansah Miss CJ, BA(Hons) MSc, Inf.Specialist, [0055965] 02/01/1998
Ghiggino Mrs R, (was Hern), BA MCLIP, Housewife. [0035552] 01/11/1982
Ghilchik Mr TC, BSc BA, Unemployed. [0054913] 13/05/1997
Ghiotto Miss A, BA PGDipILS, Catr., SEDOC srl, Italy. [0057600] 19/05/1999
Ghosal Mrs CR, (was Adkins), BSc MCLIP, Retired. [0038392] 25/01/1965
Ghosal Mr N, BA MCLIP, Life Member. [0005450] 01/09/1961
Ghose Mrs V, MCLIP, Asst.Lib., Dorset C.C. [0005451] 24/09/1968
Ghosh Mrs JE, (was Harris), BA MCLIP, Lib., Colstons Collegiate Sch., Bristol. [0023724] 14/01/1975
Ghosh Mrs ME, BA MLS MBA, Manuscript Studies Devel.Lib., Univ.of London L. [0058421] 09/02/2000
Ghosley Miss VK, MCLIP, Retired. [0020631] 28/02/1958
Ghumra Ms I, BA(Hons) MCLIP, Dep.Lib., Q.E.Hosp.NHS Trust, London. [0044778] 19/11/1990
Gibb Mrs CE, (was Walker), MA DipLib MCLIP, Asst.Lib., Univ.of the W.of England, Hartpury Campus. [0033887] 10/04/1981
Gibb Mr F, BA DipLib FCLIP, H.of Dept., Dept.of Inf.Sci., Univ.of Strathclyde, Glasgow. [0025752] 19/02/1976 **FE 01/04/2002**
Gibb Mr IP, BA MCLIP, Life Member, Tel.01442 256352, The Old Cottage, 16 Tile Kiln Lane, Leverstock Grn., Hemel Hempstead. [0005453] 05/10/1950
Gibb Mrs TH, (was Svenson), MCLIP, Lib., Young Peoples Serv., Hertfordshire C.C., Ware. [0023687] 23/01/1975
Gibbins Miss EM, BA DipLib MCLIP, Lib.-S.Area, Oxfordshire C.C. [0030417] 16/01/1979
Gibbins Mrs KJ, (was Grint), BA MCLIP, Sen.Asst.Lib., Neath & Port Talbot L & Inf. Serv. [0041544] 12/01/1988
Gibbins Ms MCA, BA MCLIP, Tutor Lib., Plater Coll., Oxford. [0005457] 05/01/1967
Gibbons Mrs A, MCLIP, Retired. [0032715] 29/09/1958
Gibbons Mrs CJ, (was Bower-Smith), BA(Hons) DipLib, Local Serv.Team Lib., Canterbury L., Kent. [0037087] 04/02/1984
Gibbons Mrs DJ, (was Harris), BLib DipEd MCLIP, Learning Support Worker, Glos.C.C. [0026403] 04/10/1976
Gibbons Miss DM, MCLIP, Retired. [0005460] 12/01/1937
Gibbons Dr F, MA FCLIP, Retired. [0019492] 27/07/1949 **FE 01/01/1960**
Gibbons Mr M, PGDipILM, Lib., Halton Lea L., Cheshire. [0061451] 31/07/2002
Gibbons Mrs SI, (was Davis), BA MCLIP, Lib., Soc.of Genealogists, London. [0022333] 26/03/1974
Gibbons Ms SJ, BA MCLIP, Lib., Southfields L., Leicester City L. [0036842] 01/01/1984
Gibbons Miss SL, BA(Hons), Team Lib., Oxon.C.C., Banbury. [0049405] 21/10/1993
Gibbons Mrs W, (was Green), MCLIP, p./t.Asst.Lib., Worcs.C.C. [0005905] 20/01/1970
Gibbs Mrs D, BA MCLIP, Retired. [0005461] 05/08/1950
Gibbs Mr DW, BA MCLIP, Res.Mgr., Lincs.C.C., Sleaford. [0035764] 17/01/1983

Gibbs Mr JC, BA(Hons) MCLIP, Asst.Lib., Barbican L., London. [0041020] 01/10/1987
Gibbs Miss JM, BA MCLIP, Life Member. [0005462] 01/01/1948
Gibbs Miss JS, MA DipLib MCLIP, Lib., L.B.of Grenwich. [0027981] 17/10/1977
Gibbs Mr PRR, BA MLib MCLIP, Unemployed. [0005465] 31/01/1967
Gibbs Mr PW, BSc MCLIP, Employment unknown. [0060289] 10/12/2001
Gibbs Dr SE, BA DipLib FCLIP MA DipCounselling, Princ.Lect., Sch.of Inf.Mgmt., Leeds Metro.Univ. [0018402] 19/10/1972 **FE 15/11/2000**
Gibbs Miss TA, BA, p./t.Stud./Learning Serv.Co-ordr., Univ.of Bristol, Yeovil Coll. [0060008] 21/11/2001
Giblin Mrs L, (was Siddall), BA DipLib, Mgr., PricewaterhouseCoopers, Leeds. [0034191] 12/10/1981
Gibson Ms AR, BA DipLib MCLIP, Learning Res.Cent.Asst., Churchill Comm.Sch., N.Somerset. [0036562] 19/10/1983
Gibson Ms CA, BA MCLIP, Independent Consultant, Web-Site Provider., www.buildline.net; www.ciig.org.uk [0005471] 07/09/1971
Gibson Ms CR, BA MA, Sen.Lib., Dept.of Trans.Local Govt.and the Regions, London. [0038300] 21/02/1989
Gibson Mr DB, FCLIP, Life Member. [0005473] 19/03/1945 **FE 01/01/1955**
Gibson Mrs EA, (was Challenger), MCLIP, p./t.Res.Cent.Mgr., Third Age Trust, London. [0002538] 25/09/1969
Gibson Mr I, BA MCLIP, Lib., E.Dunbartonshire Council. [0005476] 01/01/1967
Gibson Ms J, BA MA MCLIP, L.Resources & Devel.Mgr., L.B.of Enfield. [0035720] 01/01/1983
Gibson Dr JA, MD FLS FSA, Hon.Lib., Scot.Nat.Hist.L., Renfrewshire. [0029887] 14/10/1978
Gibson Mr KL, BA DipLib FCLIP, Life Member. [0005478] 01/01/1947 **FE 01/01/1958**
Gibson Miss LC, MA MCLIP, Unemployed, [0021459] 05/10/1973
Gibson Mrs M, BA, Sch.Lib., Derby City Council. [0028299] 31/10/1977
Gibson Mrs M, MCLIP, Team Lib., N.W.Area, Glasgow City L.Inf.& Arch. [0028300] 10/11/1977
Gibson Miss ME, MLS MCLIP, Retired. [0005483] 11/03/1960
Gibson Ms ME, (was Johnson), MA MCLIP, Research Stud., Univ.of Sunderland. [0035745] 16/01/1983
Gibson Ms MH, MA(Hons) LLB(Hons), Legal Inf.Mgr., HSBC Holdings plc., London. [0057942] 01/10/1999
Gibson Mr MK, BA MCLIP, Pub.Serv.Lib., N.Yorks Co.L. [0021162] 03/10/1973
Gibson Ms MM, BA(Hon), Asst.Lib., Northern Ireland Housing Exec., Belfast. [0050273] 25/05/1994
Gibson Ms R, MA DipLib, Bus.Analyst (Maternity Leave), DTI, London. [0038892] 18/10/1985
Gibson Miss RE, MTheol DipLib MCLIP, Catr., Birmingham Univ.L. [0032960] 09/10/1980
Gibson Miss RJ, MA(Hons), Inf.Asst., Gtr.Glasgow & Clyde Valley, Tourist Board, Paisley. [0057330] 12/02/1999
Gibson Mrs S, (was Moult), MCLIP, Housewife. [0005486] 27/08/1962
Gibson Mrs SK, (was Croker), MCLIP, Unemployed. [0003394] 14/01/1971
Gibson Mr SP, Asst.Lib., Falmouth Coll.of Arts, Cornwall. [0034942] 14/05/1982
Gibson-Saxty Miss KL, Sen.Asst.Lib., L.B.of Harrow, Harrow. [0056266] 23/04/1998
Giddings Mrs M, (was Dobby), MCLIP, Unemployed. [0005488] 22/01/1968
Gidziewicz Mrs CA, BA(Hons), Learning Adviser/Lib., Tamworth & Lichfield Coll., Staffs. [0052554] 07/11/1995
Giesbrecht Mrs BM, (was Ask), MCLIP, Life Member, Box 230, Canoe BC, V0E 1K0, Canada. [0017387] 30/01/1951
Giffen Miss SA, BA MCLIP, Reader Serv.Lib., Univ.of Greenwich. London. [0005491] 01/10/1968
Giggey Ms SE, MLS MCLIP, Consultant, 995 15th St., W.Vancouver, B.C., V7T 2T3, Canada. [0036539] 23/10/1983
Gijsen Ms S, L.Asst., Blue Anchor L., Southwark Ls. [0057152] 13/01/1999
Gilbane Ms M, BSc(Hons) DipLib, Asst.Lib., Christain Aid, London. [0049653] 22/11/1993
Gilbart Mrs JEP, (was Hann), MSc MCLIP, Employment unknown. [0060374] 11/12/2001
Gilbert Mrs DM, (was Morgan), BA MCLIP, Life Member. [0010391] 03/09/1946
Gilbert Mrs FH, (was Tipping), BA MCLIP, Unemployed. [0024552] 02/09/1975
Gilbert Dr GH, PhD FRPharmS WS PhC MCLIP, Retired. [0060290] 10/12/2001
Gilbert Miss HE, BA MA MCLIP, Lib.:Child.Serv., Worcester City L. [0032961] 08/10/1980
Gilbert Mr J, BA MCLIP, Retired. [0005496] 17/03/1963
Gilbert Mrs JA, (was Gameson), MCLIP, p./t.Lib., Kelsey park Sch., Beckenham. [0005329] 14/01/1971
Gilbert Miss JAM, BA(Hons), Stud./L.Asst., Robert Gordon Univ. [0061589] 02/10/2002
Gilbert Mr LA, MSC HonFCLIP, Retired. [0036768] 19/09/1983 **FE 19/09/1983**
Gilbert Mr MN, BA MCLIP, Lib., Prison Serv.HQ., London. [0021443] 01/11/1973
Gilbert Ms N, BSc DipInfMan, Project Mgr., Queen Margarets Univ.Coll., Edinburgh. [0061810] 11/11/2002
Gilbert Ms SE, MSC MCLIP, Electronic Res.Lib., St.Georges Hosp.Med.Sch., London. [0023577] 13/01/1975
Gilberthorpe Dr EC, BA PhD FCLIP, Life Member. [0005502] 01/01/1948 **FE 01/01/1967**
Gilchrist Mrs A, (was Robertson), MCLIP, Sen.Lib., Glasgow City L. [0022416] 08/05/1974

Gilchrist Mr ADB, CMC MIMC HonFCLIP, Sen.Partner, Alan Gilchrist & Partners, Brighton. [0005506] 21/04/1961 **FE 01/04/2002**
Gilchrist Mrs IM, (was Craig), MA(Hons) DipLib MCLIP, Educ.Resouce Serv.Lib., Educ.Serv.Dept., Inverclyde Council, Greenock. [0034482] 11/11/1981
Gilchrist Mrs JM, (was Robertshaw), BA MCLIP, Child.Specialist Lib., Leics.C.C. [0019798] 28/11/1972
Gilchrist Mrs JR, (was White), MA DipLib MCLIP, Outside Serv.Lib., N.Lanarkshire Council, Coatbridge. [0031106] 25/07/1979
Gilchrist Mr NM, MA DipILS, Lib., Glenfield L., Leics. [0059044] 07/11/2000
Gilchrist Mrs PM, (was Bell), BA FCLIP, Retired. [0001090] 07/09/1960 **FE 01/01/1965**
Gilder Mrs LP, BA MCLIP, Position unknown, Hartley L., Univ.of Southampton. [0060693] 12/12/2001
Gildersleeves Mrs ELP, MA M LIB MCLIP, p./t.Lect., Univ.Coll.London. [0037489] 01/01/1984
Giles Ms AS, BA(Hons) MCLIP, Trust Lib., Somerset Partnership NHS & Social, Care Trust, Taunton. [0050498] 22/08/1994
Giles Miss CA, BA(Hons), Stud., Strathclyde Univ. [0061721] 29/10/2002
Giles Mrs DJ, (was Price), MCLIP, Learning Res.Asst., N.Herts.Coll., Hitchin. [0011937] 09/10/1969
Giles Mrs GH, (was Lindsay), MLib BA MCLIP, Trust L.Serv.Mgr., Good Hope Hosp., Sutton Coldfield,W.Midlands. [0025349] 05/01/1976
Giles Mrs H, (was Cherry), MA BA MCLIP, Sen.Lib.(Job Share), Ringwood L., Hants.C.C. [0027804] 02/09/1977
Giles Mrs JB, (was Laurie), MA DipLib MCLIP, Curator, Nat.L.of Scotland, Edinburgh. [0035463] 15/10/1982
Gilham Miss JL, MA MCLIP, Life Member. [0005521] 27/08/1954
Gilham Mrs LA, (was Bebbington), Asst.Lib., Royal Berkshire Hosp. [0044920] 16/01/1991
Gilham-Skinner Mrs WJ, MA(Hons), p./t.Stud./Sen.L.Asst., Univ.of Wales, Aberystwyth, Univ.of Dundee, Main L. [0061091] 04/03/2002
Gilheany Mr MF, BSSc MSSc PhD DipLib, Unemployed. [0041255] 19/10/1987
Gilkerson Mrs EA, (was Pace), MCLIP, Life Member. [0005524] 07/03/1949
Gilkes Mr AR, BA DipLib, Asst.Lib., Thames Valley Univ., Slough Campus. [0038769] 01/10/1985
Gilkes Miss SM, BA(Hons) MA, Sen.L.Asst., Inst.of Historical Res., Univ.of London. [0055360] 03/10/1997
Gill Mrs A, (was Mowat), BA(Hons), p./t.Stud./Sen.L.Asst.i/c., Milton Keynes L., Olney. [0050603] 30/09/1994
Gill Miss AK, BA(Hons) MCLIP, Ref.Lib., Hants.C.C., Gosport. [0046325] 28/10/1991
Gill Miss CJ, p./t.Learning Res.Asst., ADT Coll., London. [0054836] 14/04/1997 **AF**
Gill Miss CJ, BA(Hons), Grad.Trainee, [0059850] 16/10/2001
Gill Mrs D, (was Wells), BA DipLib MCLIP, Showroom Mgr., Peters Bookselling Serv., Birmingham. [0039494] 10/02/1986
Gill Mr DA, BLib MCLIP, Head of Inf.& Local Studies, Solihull MBC, Solihull. [0034475] 16/11/1981
Gill Mrs FM, BMus(Hons) DipTheol, Sen.Asst.Lib., Performing Arts L., Cent.L., Exeter. [0053732] 02/09/1996
Gill Mrs J, MA(Hons) MSc, Marketing Inf.Analyst, Target Direct Marketing, Cheltenham. [0058370] 31/01/2000
Gill Mrs J, (was Halford), BA MCLIP, Sch.Lib., Galashiels Academy, Scottish Borders Council. [0026102] 30/06/1976
Gill Mr JB, BSc MCLIP, Princ.Lib., Poole Hosp.NHS Trust., Dorset. [0005531] 26/04/1971
Gill Mrs JE, BA MCLIP, Sen.Ref.Lib., Taunton L., Somerset C.C. [0005532] 01/01/1970
Gill Mrs JR, (was Lax), Inf.& Reference Supervisor (p./t.), Beds.County Council. [0025342] 09/01/1976
Gill Mrs KL, (was Rennison), BA MCLIP, Learning Res.Asst., Lymm High Sch., Cheshire. [0030520] 08/01/1979
Gill Mrs L, BA(Hons) DipIM MCLIP, Unemployed. [0049466] 03/11/1993
Gill Mr M, BA PGCE, Asst.Lib., Dept.of Health, London. [0041088] 07/10/1987
Gill Mrs MA, BA DipLib MCLIP, Lend.Serv.Lib., St.Martins Coll., Lancaster. [0025538] 05/01/1976
Gill Miss ME, BA(Hons) MA, Unemployed. [0043964] 09/03/1990
Gill Mrs ME, BA MCLIP, Campus L.Mgr., Napier Univ., Edinburgh. [0005533] 14/01/1970
Gill Mrs MH, (was Valentine), BA(Hons) MCLIP, Lib., Wallsend L., Tyne & Wear. [0033643] 01/02/1981
Gill Mr MR, BA(Hons), Faculty Team Lib., Health Sci.L., Leeds Univ. [0046613] 25/11/1991
Gill Mr PG, FCLIP, Life Member. [0005534] 16/01/1957 **FE 21/08/1974**
Gill Ms SV, Administrator, Primary Care Knowledge Mgmt., Nottingham City Primary Care Trst. [0061529] 16/09/2002 **AF**
Gill-Martin Mr PJ, MA CMA Grad(IPM) MCLIP, Retired. [0005535] 01/01/1967
Gill-Martin Mrs YV, (was Conkleton), BA DMS MCLIP, Head of Ls.& Arch., Bolton M.B.C., Cent.L. [0003031] 19/12/1970
Gillam Mr LA, BD DipSocAdmin MCLIP, Retired. [0005537] 08/01/1968
Gillan Mr JC, MCLIP, Employement not known. [0022725] 29/08/1974
Gillan Mrs LE, (was McElroy), MCLIP, Comm.Lib., Glasgow City L., Inf&Arch. [0020635] 18/05/1973
Gillanders Miss J, MCLIP, Team Lib., Medway Council, Gillingham, Kent. [0005539] 11/02/1963
Gillard Mrs SG, (was Billingham), BA DipLib MCLIP, Child.Lib., Fareham. [0038916] 17/10/1985
Gilleard Mrs J, MSc BA CertTEFL MCLIP, Training Consultant, Hong Kong. [0005542] 16/01/1971
Giller Mrs PA, BA(Hons) PGCE PGDipIS, Site Lib., L.B.of Camden. [0052070] 02/10/1995

Personal Members — Goddard

Gillespie Mrs DB, BA DipLib PGCE PGDipEd MCLIP, Principal, St.Mary's Primary Sch., Strabane, Co.Tyrone. [0034300] 20/10/1981
Gillespie Miss GC, BA(Hons), Asst.Customer Service Lib., Dunfermline L. [0054386] 02/12/1996
Gillespie Ms H, BSc, Freelance Med.Inf.Offr. [0041758] 10/03/1988
Gillespie Mrs KJ, (was Kyle), BLS MCLIP, p./t.Asst.Lib., Northern Ireland Assembly, Belfast. [0033018] 17/10/1980
Gillespie Mrs MA, (was McConville), BA DipLib MCLIP, Area & Campus Lib., Univ.of Stirling, Inverness. [0027189] 06/12/1976
Gillespie Mr RA, FCLIP, Life Member, Tel 0141 641 2555. [0005547] 27/09/1949 FE 01/01/1968
Gillespie Mrs SM, MCLIP, Life Member, Tel.0141 641 2555. [0005548] 01/01/1950
Gillespie Mr TS, FCLIP, Retired. [0005549] 10/09/1948 FE 01/01/1957
Gillham Dr MH, BSc PhD MBCS MCLIP, Employment unknown. [0060245] 10/12/2001
Gillies Mrs FF, (was Bruce), BA MCLIP, Network Lib.(Job-share), Turriff Acad., Aberdeenshire. [0035608] 19/10/1982
Gillies Mr GA, MCLIP, Head of L.Heritage & Culture, Stirling Council. [0005555] 01/01/1967
Gillies Mrs HH, (was Gordon), DipILS MCLIP, Unemployed. [0042740] 23/02/1989
Gillies Miss M, BA MA, Stud., City Univ. [0061718] 29/10/2002
Gillies Mr S, MA, Inf.Serv.Mgr., The Brit.L., London. [0041770] 25/03/1988
Gillies Mrs VJ, MCLIP, Learning Res.Cent.Co-ordinator, Stirling Council., McLaren High Sch. [0005556] 21/03/1966
Gilliland Ms GM, (was Davies), BA PGCE DipLIS, Asst.Comm.Lib., Sutton Coldfield Lend.L., Birmingham L.Serv. [0044661] 20/11/1990
Gilling Mrs JM, (was Iveson), MA, Learner Serv.Mgr., E.Durham & Houghall Comm.Coll., Co.Durham. [0045531] 26/02/1991 AF
Gillings-Grant Ms FLA, BSc(Hons) DipLib, Comm.Lib., Birmingham City Council, Sheldon L. [0058855] 07/09/2000
Gillis Ms HR, Stud. [0061469] 12/08/2002
Gillis Mr IR, BSc MCLIP, Recs.Administrator, Financial Serv.Auth., London E14. [0005557] 05/10/1968
Gillman Mr PL, MSc FCLIP FRSA, Proprietor, The Inf. Partnership, 40 Coulsdon Rise, Coulsdon, CR5 2SB. [0005559] 11/10/1966 FE 01/04/2002
Gillott Miss EL, BA(Hons) MSc, Lib., Instant L.Ltd., Loughborough. [0056097] 12/02/1998
Gilman Miss AHE, BA MCLIP, Lib., Derbyshire C.C., Derbyshire. [0025037] 14/11/1975
Gilman Ms HM, BA MA, Unemployed. [0054096] 28/10/1996
Gilman Ms V, Inf.Offr., Pinsent Curtis Biddle, London. [0053119] 11/03/1996 AF
Gilmore Mr J, BA(Hons) PGCE DipLib MCLIP, Retired Teacher. [0031067] 17/08/1979
Gilmore Miss S, BA, Stud./Presentation Lib., Thames Valley Univ./BBC, London. [0061828] 14/11/2002
Gilmour Miss A, BA MCLIP, Lib., Cent.L., Dunfermline. [0035780] 24/01/1983
Gilmour Ms AE, BA DipIT MCLIP, Employment unknown. [0060258] 10/12/2001
Gilmour Mrs ER, (was Mcgoldrick), MA MCLIP, Area Co-ord., E.Renfrewshire Council, Barrhead. [0025375] 07/01/1976
Gilmour Mrs FM, MA(Hons) DipLib MCLIP, Lib., English Heritage (NMR), Swindon, Wilts. [0027982] 01/01/1978
Gilmour Mrs HB, (was Chadwick), BA MCLIP, Asst.Lib., Charing Cross Hosp.Med.Sch.L., London. [0019638] 31/10/1972
Gilmour Mrs SM, (was Dunsmure), MA MCLIP, Asst.Lib., Falkirk Coll. [0049542] 09/11/1993
Gilmurray Mrs SM, (was Tuck), MA PGCE DipIS MCLIP, Subject Lib., Arts & Letters, The L., Anglia Poly.Univ., Cambridge. [0047090] 28/04/1992
Gilroy Mr DP, BA(Hons) MA, Lib. (Cookridge), Leeds Teaching Hospitals., NHS Trust. [0055282] 15/09/1997
Gilroy Mrs J, (was Higginson), MCLIP, Project Offr., Univ.of Leeds, Sch.of Healthcare S. [0006859] 01/01/1968
Ginger Ms TA, BA MCLIP, H.of Inf.& Personnel, RHM Tech.Ltd., High Wycombe, Bucks. [0047022] 06/04/1992
Ginn Mr JW, BSc LCGI MA, Asst.Lib., Medical Devices Agency, London. [0059491] 09/04/2001
Girdharry Mr AK, BSc MSc, Inf.Spec., Unilever Research Port Sunlight, Lab., Bebington, Wirral. [0048834] 01/07/1993
Girdher Mr RK, MA FCLIP, Retired. [0005570] 04/10/1962 FE 01/01/1967
Girdlestone Ms M, BA(Hons) MSc, Unemployed. [0055194] 07/08/1997
Girdwood Ms PG, DipLib MCLIP, L.Adviser, L.B.of Southwark, Educ.L.Serv. [0031836] 08/01/1980
Girling Miss KE, BA Lib MCLIP, Retired. [0032067] 10/02/1980
Gitlin Ms NR, BSc DipLib, Career Break. [0044487] 12/10/1990
Gitsham Mr CL, BA(Hons) DipLib, Inf.Lib., Middlesbrough Bor.Council. [0054923] 13/05/1997
Gittins Mrs L, (was Burwell), Cert Ed Lib., Bradford Met.Council. [0044023] 02/04/1990
Giurlando Ms L, BA MCLIP, Asst.Lib., Oundle Sch., Oundle. [0053452] 01/07/1996
Givan Mr AM, MA(Hons) MSc MCLIP, Asst.Lib., Johnstone Comm.L., Renfrewshire Council. [0051084] 14/11/1994
Glacki Miss AS, BA MCLIP, Inf.Mgr., Knowles Holdings plc., Cheshire. [0021962] 14/01/1974
Gladden Mr G, MA DipLib MCLIP, Lib., Bewdley L., Worcs.Co.Council. [0033434] 13/01/1981
Gladden Mr NJ, PGDip, Acq.& Catg.Asst., N.W.Film Arch., Manchester Met.Univ. [0058906] 23/10/2000
Gladstone Ms CL, BA, Lib., Birmingham L.Serv., Arts Languages & Literature Sect. [0039599] 18/03/1986

Gladstone Mr TM, LLB(Hons), Employment not known. [0051740] 12/06/1995
Gladwin Ms AR, BA, Researcher, Financial Times, London. [0047078] 15/04/1992
Glancy Mr A, MA(Hons), Asst.Lib., Bexley Council, Thamesmead Cent. [0059171] 05/12/2000
Glancy Mr MJ, BA MCLIP, Flexible Learning Serv.Mgr., Edinburgh's Telford Coll., Edinburgh. [0032520] 21/05/1980
Glancy Mr PC, MA(Hons), Asst.Inf.Specialist, Nottingham Trent Univ., Dryden Cent. [0042375] 18/10/1988
Glanville Mrs DM, BA MCLIP, Sch.Lib., Fearnhill Sch., Letchworth, Herts. [0005578] 13/09/1969
Glanville Ms JM, BA PGDipLib MSc MCLIP, Inf.Serv.Mgr.,Cent.for Health Econ, Cent.for Reviews & Dissemination, Univ.of York. [0035198] 05/10/1982
Glasby Mrs JB, (was Hutchison), BA MCLIP, L.Mgr., Leeds Coll.of Music. [0027817] 28/08/1977
Glaser Mrs J, (was Drozynska), BA MCLIP, Catr., Min.of Defence, London. [0005580] 18/03/1971
Glass Mrs HF, (was Keaveny), BA(Hons) DipHist MSc, Lib., Foreign & Commonwealth Off., London. [0034719] 27/01/1982
Glasspool Mrs SH, (was Giles), MCLIP, Serv.Mgr., Essex Co., Chelmsford. [0005584] 01/11/1964
Glavey Miss JE, BA MCLIP, Community Lib.-Child.Lead, Tamworth, Staffs.C.C. [0034591] 01/01/1982
Glayzer Ms JA, (was Reid), MCLIP, Strategic Mgr.:Serv.Delivery, Ls.,Inf., Heritage & Cult.Serv., Essex. [0005586] 06/10/1964
Gleadhill Mrs D, (was Howitt), BA DipLib MCLIP, Systems Lib., Univ.of Newcastle upon Tyne. [0020687] 04/06/1973
Gleave Miss SE, MA BA(Ed) MCLIP, Sen.Inf.Asst., Kings Coll.London. [0057010] 24/11/1998
Gledhill Dr J, BSc PhD Dip MCLIP, Head of Group Inf.Serv., Smith & Nephew Group, York. [0060204] 10/12/2001
Gledhill Mr PF, BA(Hons) DipLIS MCLIP, Inf.Adviser, Sheffield Hallam Univ. [0053102] 15/11/1991
Gledhill Ms SE, BA DipLib MCLIP, Devel.Lib., Herts.C.C. [0039264] 15/01/1986
Gledhill Mrs VC, (was Deas), MA DipLib MCLIP, W/E.Lib./Lib., Westminster Coll., Chandlings Manor Sch., Oxford. [0038704] 01/10/1985
Glen Dr IG, MA PhD DIP ED, Asst.Lib.(Arts), Univ.Coll., Swansea. [0041090] 05/10/1987
Glen Mrs S, (was Mann), FCSD DipLib MCLIP, Coll.Lib., Brasenose Coll., Oxford. [0044403] 04/10/1990
Glen Mrs SM, (was Fish), BA, Dep.Subject Lib., Univ.of Wales, Swansea. [0044058] 20/04/1990
Glenn Miss ES, B Lib MCLIP, Learning Res.Mgr., Castlereagh Coll., Belfast. [0034450] 10/11/1981
Glenn Mrs HB, (was Nesbitt), DipLib MCLIP, Princ.Asst.Lib., S.E.Educ.& L.Board L.H.Q., Ballynahinch. [0025378] 31/12/1975
Glenn Mr JW, BA MA DipLib MCLIP, Princ.Asst.Lib., S.E.Educ.& L.Board L.H.Q., Co.Down. [0028430] 05/12/1977
Glover Mrs C, BA(Hons) DipILM, p./t.L.Asst.Lib., Lancs.C.C. [0057999] 08/10/1999
Glover Mrs FE, Stud., Moray Coll. [0059586] 11/06/2001
Glover Mrs GA, (was Page), BA(Hons) MA MCLIP, Unemployed. [0043695] 30/11/1989
Glover Ms HL, Stud., Brighton Univ. [0057199] 14/01/1999
Glover Mrs KB, (was Slater), BA(Hons) MA MCLIP, Career Break. [0050196] 04/05/1994
Glover Mrs L, (was Jones), MCLIP, p./t.L.Asst., Walsall Cent.L. [0008050] 26/02/1970
Glover Ms M, B ED, Asst.Lib., Bibl.Dept., L.B.of Hounslow, London. [0042359] 01/10/1988
Glover Mrs SA, (was Foote), BA MCLIP, Lib., Notts.C.C.Educ.L.Serv. [0019627] 01/07/1999
Glover Mr SJ, BA(Hons), L.Asst.-Distance Learning Unit, Univ.of Leicester L. [0057698] 01/07/1999
Glover Mr SW, BSc(Hons), Med.Lib., Christie Hosp.NHS Trust, Manchester. [0054233] 28/10/1996
Glowczewska Ms JA, BA DipLib, Catr., Brit.L., Boston Spa,W.Yorks. [0042853] 01/04/1989
Glyde Mrs HM, (was Wootten), MCLIP, Comm.Lib., Wilton L., Wilts. [0021781] 14/01/1974
Goacher Mrs WC, (was Austin), MCLIP, Lib., Brinsbury Coll. [0005606] 04/10/1965
Gobey Mr PF, BA DipLib MCLIP, Sen.Lib., Beaumont Leys L., Leicester City L. [0032576] 08/05/1980
Gobin Mr CF, BSc MSc, Business Devel., SofTec, Florida, USA. [0050296] 08/06/1994
Goda Miss M, MCLIP, Asst.Lib., Bury M.B.C. [0005608] 16/01/1964
Godbolt Mrs LS, (was Spanner), BA FCLIP, Head, L.& Inf.Devel.Unit, NHS Exec., Dir.Educ.& Training, Univ.of London. [0013786] 01/10/1965 FE 23/05/1975
Goddard Mrs AG, (was Howard), MCLIP, Sch.Lib., Queens Coll., Taunton. [0005610] 17/09/1963
Goddard Miss BM, MCLIP, L.& Inf.Serv.Mgr., Winchester & Eastleigh Healthcare, NHS Trust, Hants. [0005611] 01/02/1966
Goddard Mr C, B MUS DipLib MCLIP, Inf.Mgr., Plymouth L.Serv. [0031838] 01/01/1980
Goddard Miss CW, BA(Hons) PGCE, P./t.Stud./Inf.Asst., Kings Coll.London. [0052521] 03/11/1995
Goddard Mr M, MSc BSc(Hons), Inf.Sci., Medicines Control Agency, London. [0046714] 03/01/1992
Goddard Mr NR, MCLIP, Operations Mgr., DERA Inf.Res. [0026729] 24/11/1976

Goddard Mrs PC, (was Hogg), MCLIP, Inf.Specialist., D.S.T.L., Salisbury. [0028017] 04/10/1977
Goddard Ms S, BA, Asst.Lib., Univ.Coll.London, London. [0058274] 06/12/1999
Goddard Mr SC, BSc MCLIP, Retired. [0005619] 07/07/1947
Godden Ms GC, Stud., Manchester Met.Univ. [0055771] 25/11/1997
Godfree Mrs JCJ, (was Robertson), MA DipLib MCLIP, Sch.Lib., Bohunt Sch., Liphook. [0026533] 06/10/1976
Godfrey Mrs AJ, (was Woodman), MCLIP, Lib.(Sunday), Balham L., London. [0026617] 19/10/1976
Godfrey Ms H, BA(Hons) MA, Confederation Outreach Lib., Chesterfield & N.Derbys.Hosp., Univ.of Sheffield. [0054255] 11/11/1996
Godfrey Miss JC, BA, Unemployed. [0057395] 03/03/1999
Godfrey Mrs JE, (was Price), Stud., Univ.of Northumbria at Newcastle. [0048026] 04/11/1992
Godfrey Mrs JV, (was Weston), MCLIP, Princ.L.Asst., Univ.of Oxford, Acquisitions Serv., Bodleian L. [0015634] 29/05/1969
Godfrey Mrs KJ, (was Behan), BA MA(Ed) ILTM MCLIP, Lib., Kent Inst.of Art & Design, Canterbury. [0005624] 02/10/1970
Godfrey Ms MA, (was Allen), MA ARMIT ALAA MCLIP, Life Member. [0005625] 03/03/1970
Godleman Mrs C, Stud.p./t., Univ.of N.London. [0061630] 08/10/2002
Godliman Miss L, Stud., Thames Valley Univ. [0059841] 16/10/2001
Godman Ms JME, MCLIP, L.ICT Mgr., Bath Cent.L., Bath & N.E.Somerset. [0005629] 23/03/1964
Godman Mrs PA, (was Bell), BA MCLIP, Local Studies Offr., Rochdale M.B.C. [0046784] 22/01/1992
Godrich Mrs DA, BA(Hons) DipIM MCLIP, Career Break. [0052437] 31/10/1995
Godsalve Miss SJ, BSc MCLIP, Lib., Wilmer, Cutler & Pickering, London. [0044441] 08/10/1990
Godsell Mr AR, BSc BA MSc, Learning Res.Asst., Worcester Coll.of Tech. [0054956] 28/05/1997
Godsell Miss K, MCLIP, Asst.Br.Mgr., Lancs.Co.L., Cent.Div. [0040847] 14/07/1987
Godsell Mrs S, BSc MCLIP, Employment not known. [0060830] 12/12/2001
Godsmark Mrs RJ, (was Marlow), BA DipLib MCLIP, Employment not known. [0026986] 10/01/1977
Godwin Mrs J, (was Hunter), BA(Hons) MCLIP, Coll.Lib., Bishop Burton Coll., Beverley. [0033944] 04/06/1981
Godwin Mr P, BA MCLIP, Academic Serv.Mgr., South Bank Univ. [0005632] 03/01/1972
Godwin Ms P, BA(Hons) PGCE, Sch.Lib., Leiston High Sch., Suffolk. [0059920] 29/10/2001 **AF**
Goh Beng Neo Miss M, MCLIP, Dep.Lib., Singapore Poly.L. [0016932] 01/01/1969
Going Mrs G, (was Chipman), MCLIP, Sen.Asst.Lib., Imperial Coll.Sch.of Medicine, London. [0002684] 16/09/1970
Going Miss ME, MBE HonFCLIP FCLIP, Retired. [0005634] 01/05/1933 **FE 01/01/1948**
Gokce Mrs CM, (was Breadmore), BSc MSc, Natural Hist.Lib., Gen.L., Natural Hist.Mus., London. [0035950] 23/03/1983
Gold Miss RJ, LLB(Hons) MA, Unemployed. [0058070] 22/10/1999
Gold Miss SE, BA DipLib, Reader Serv.Mgr., Wellcome L.for the Hist.&, Understanding of Med., Lodnon. [0040306] 05/01/1987
Golden Mrs SM, (was Sullivan), BSc(Hons) PGCE, Young Peoples Serv.Team Leader, (Mid Kent), Kent C.C., Educ.& L. [0046158] 03/10/1991
Goldfinch Mr JE, BA(Hons) MA MCLIP, Rare Books Reading Room Mgr., British L., London. [0027813] 20/09/1977
Goldfinch Mr RG, MSc MCLIP, Unemployed. [0033755] 31/01/1981
Goldie Dr AM, MB ChB MScEcon, Unemployed. [0049983] 25/02/1994
Goldie Mr FJ, BA(Hons) MCLIP, Retired. [0005640] 01/01/1953
Goldie Mr IM, BA MCLIP, Sen.Lib., Eastleigh Co.L., Hants. [0005641] 01/01/1972
Goldie Mrs J, (was Shipley), MCLIP, Area Sch.Lib., Hants.C.C. [0023956] 04/02/1975
Goldie Miss JH, BA DipLib MCLIP, L.Business & Devel.Mgr., Dumfries & Galloway L.Inf.& Arch., Dumfries. [0035504] 20/10/1982
Goldie Mrs VS, BA DipIS, Relief Lib., Bournemouth Bor.Council. [0030908] 08/06/1979
Golding Mrs S, (was Beech), BA(Hons) MA, Asst.Lib., Evesham Coll., Worcs. [0045929] 15/07/1991
Golding Mrs V, MCLIP, Adult Lend.Serv.Lib., Medway Council, Kent. [0019918] 08/01/1973
Golditch-Williams Mrs OR, (was Golditch), BSc(Hons) DipLib MCLIP, Lib.i/c., Grangemouth L., Grangemouth. [0027441] 14/04/1977
Goldrick Miss ME, FCLIP, Life Member. [0005644] 05/03/1942 **FE 01/01/1954**
Goldschmidt Mrs MKS, (was Studer), MCLIP, 285 Riverside Drive, New York, U.S.A. [0016933] 13/01/1936
Goldschmidt Mrs T, (was Lowy), BA, Catr., The Stationery Off., London. [0043845] 31/01/1990
Goldsmith Mrs J, BA PGDIP, Inf.Serv.Mgr., Henley Mgmnt.Coll., Henley-on-Thames. [0061523] 04/09/2002
Goldsmith Mrs MB, (was Balchin), MCLIP, Lib., Burgess Hill Sch., W.Sussex. [0005647] 03/04/1963
Goldsmith Mrs R, BA MCLIP, Staff Devel.Mgr., Cambs.L.& Inf.Serv. [0029300] 01/01/1973
Goldstone Mr J, BSc DipLib MCLIP, Music Lib., L.B.of Barking & Dagenham. [0026967] 11/01/1977
Goldstone Mrs PA, (was Carter), Bibl.& Systems Offr., Bracknell Forest Bor.Council. [0005649] 03/01/1962 **AF**
Goldwater Mr SJ, BA MCLIP, Inf.Offr., Montagu Evans, London. [0024492] 21/08/1975
Golinski Ms PM, BA DipLib MSc MCLIP, Inf.Res.Mgr., Shaw Trust, Trowbridge. [0036447] 12/10/1983

Golland Mr ARL, BA DipLib MCLIP, Keeper, Printed Books, Imperial War Museum, London. [0019839] 10/01/1973
Golland Mr D, BA DipLib MCLIP, Comm.Lib.-Child., L.B.of Barking & Dagenham. [0037480] 01/10/1984
Golland Mrs FK, (was Price), MA MCLIP, Family Reading Lib., L.B.of Barking & Dagenham, Cent.L. [0035512] 22/10/1982
Golledge Mrs CM, (was Allen), MCLIP, Lib., St.Philips Chambers, Birmingham. [0005653] 01/01/1964
Gomersall Mr A, BSc(Eng) MPhil FCLIP, Employment unknown. [0060291] 10/12/2001 **FE 01/04/2002**
Gomersall Mrs B, BA, Lib., E.Sussex Co.L., Sch.L.Serv., Eastbourne. [0047496] 04/09/1992
Gomersall Mrs RF, (was Gregory), BSc(Econ) MCLIP, L.Mgr., Cheshire C.C., Crewe L. [0047402] 10/08/1992
Gomez Ms MM, PGDip, p./t.Market Research Interviewer, BMRB Internat., Birmingham. [0054920] 15/05/1997
Gomm Miss B, MCLIP, Life Member. [0005657] 16/09/1956
Gomm Miss SI, MCLIP, Retired. [0005658] 06/03/1945
Gommersall Miss K, BA MCLIP, Employment not known. [0041566] 28/01/1988
Goncalves Ms KL, BA(Hons), L. Asst., Univ. of York. [0060999] 28/01/2002
Goncalves Mrs TH, (was Fagg), BA(Hons) MCLIP, Inf.Offr., Consumers Assoc. [0050781] 18/10/1994
Gooch Mrs PM, BSc MCLIP, L.Serv.Mgr., Acad.Dept., Glasgow Homoeopathic Hosp. [0045993] 13/08/1991
Gooch Mr PSL, BSc MCLIP, Retired. [0060292] 10/12/2001
Good Mrs AM, (was Bremner), BA MCLIP, Unemployed. [0029590] 23/10/1978
Good Mr D, BA MCLIP, Retired. [0005662] 14/01/1958
Good Mrs GR, (was Carver), L.Asst., L.& Inf.Cent., Cotham Sch., Bristol. [0050358] 01/07/1994 **AF**
Goodacre Mrs I, MA MSc, Asst.Lib., Kenilworth Sch., Warks. [0058210] 17/11/1999
Goodair Mrs CM, (was Allen), BA MCLIP, Unemployed. [0026883] 24/11/1976
Goodall Mrs C, (was Sillett), MCLIP, p./t.Lib., Bishops Waltham, Hants.C.C. [0023027] 24/10/1974
Goodall Dr DL, MPhil BA PhD MCLIP, Lib.(Job-share), N.Tyneside L. [0038792] 07/10/1985
Goodall Miss ES, MA MCLIP, Lib., N.Lanarkshire Dist.Council. [0005668] 20/10/1968
Goodall Miss H, BA(Hons) MA MCLIP, Lib., Chester C.C., Chester L. [0056186] 01/04/1998
Goodall Ms L, BA(Hons) MA, Catr., Leicester Univ., Leics.L.& Inf.Serv. [0054306] 20/11/1996
Goodall Mr N, MA FCLIP, Retired. [0005669] 03/08/1948 **FE 01/01/1964**
Goodall Miss WF, Casual L.Asst., Sch.L.Serv., Hatfield, Herts. [0056396] 01/07/1998 **AF**
Gooday Miss BJ, MCLIP, Admin.Mgr., E.Surrey Health Auth., Epsom. [0005670] 16/09/1968
Gooday Mrs EMM, (was Wright), BA MCLIP, Lib., Willis Group Ltd., London. [0036897] 13/01/1984
Goodchild Miss AM, BA(Hons), Stud., Univ.Coll.L. [0058962] 10/10/2000
Goodchild Miss G, BA DipLib MCLIP, Coll.Lib., Colchester Sixth Form Coll., Essex. [0033810] 01/10/1979
Goodchild Ms GE, BSc, Comm.Liaison & Inf.Co-ordinator, Whitefield Sch.& Cent., The Turner L., London. [0055700] 04/11/1997
Goode Miss M, BLib, Lib., Arthur Terry Sch., Sutton Coldfield. [0039848] 09/09/1986
Gooderham Mr A, MA MCLIP, Catr., Brit.L., Boston Spa, W.Yorks. [0023065] 26/10/1974
Gooderham Ms JG, (was Chapman), BA PGCE MCLIP, Sch.Lib., Sir John Leman High Sch., Suffolk. [0005676] 17/07/1971
Goodey Miss JB, MCLIP, Playgroup Super., New Milton. [0005679] 02/10/1968
Goodey Mr KC, BA(Hons), Inf.Specialist, HM Treasury, London. [0056168] 01/04/1998
Goodey Mrs LF, (was Fowler), BA(Hons) MA, Asst.Lib., Allen & Overy. [0057023] 26/11/1998
Goodey Miss LJ, BA(Hons), Knowledge Network Mgr., DEFRA, London. [0040650] 30/04/1987
Goodfellow Miss CA, MA MCLIP, Area L.Offr.(Inverness), Inverness Br.L., Highland Council. [0005681] 15/08/1969
Goodfellow Mrs JA, (was Haigh), MA(Hons) MA MCLIP, Lib., Dept.of Health, Leeds. [0053934] 11/10/1996
Goodfellow Mrs JMV, (was Moss), MCLIP, Unemployed. [0003237] 25/10/1967
Goodfellow Mr NJ, BA MA MCLIP, Campus LIS Mgr.& Faculty Inf.Con., Univ.of Herts. [0042070] 03/10/1988
Goodger Ms GR, BA DipLib, Lib., Herbert Smith, London. [0037372] 25/07/1984
Goodhand Mr N, BEng, Unemployed. [0056707] 05/10/1998
Goodhew Ms L, BA(Hons), Grad.Trainee, Freshfields Bruckhaus Deringer, London. [0061302] 16/05/2002
Goodier Mr JC, BSc MSc MCLIP, Employment not known. [0060690] 12/12/2001
Gooding Mrs B, (was Kearns), BA, Career Break. [0037667] 17/10/1984
Gooding Mrs LA, (was McAvoy), BSc MSc MCLIP, Asst.Lib.(p./t.), Univ.of Southampton. [0052754] 05/12/1995
Gooding Miss MIE, BA MCLIP, Retired. [0005686] 24/09/1964
Gooding Mrs R, (was Linnett), BA DipLib MCLIP, Sen.L.Asst., Catg.Dept., Univ.of Reading L. [0043494] 30/10/1989
Gooding Miss SL, BA(Hons), Dep.Lib., Clerk of Tynwald, Douglas/Isle of Man. [0056071] 06/02/1998
Goodlet Mr AH, MCLIP, Retired. [0005687] 15/03/1938

Personal Members

Goodliffe Mr EC, BA(Hons) MCLIP, Head of L.Admin., Res.L., Gtr.London Auth. [0005688]   04/10/1963
Goodman Mrs A, BMedSci, P./t.Stud., Univ.Coll.London. [0057672]   01/07/1999
Goodman Mr AD, BA MCLIP, Dep.Area Lib., Chichester L., W.Sussex C.C. [0035924]   28/02/1983
Goodman Ms E, (was Spain), BSc MSc MCLIP, Employment not known. [0060711]   12/12/2001
Goodman Mrs G, (was Laycock), BA DipLib MCLIP, Lib., Ref.L., Doncaster L.& Inf.Serv. [0034384]   23/10/1981
Goodman Miss HL, BA DipInfSc MCLIP, Project Lib., London L.& Inf.Devel.Unit, London Deanery. [0045873]   03/07/1991
Goodman Mrs M, BA MCLIP, Lib.(p/t.), Cheshire C.C., Poynton. [0019980]   15/12/1972
Goodman Miss TJ, MCLIP, Life Member. [0005695]   17/02/1964
Goodman Mrs TS, (was Amos), BA(Hons) MCLIP, Inf.Offr., Allen & Overy, London. [0054552]   20/01/1997
Goodrich Mrs IA, (was Tokarski), BA MCLIP, Raising Children. [0031025]   09/07/1979
Goodson Mrs J, (was Lock), MCLIP, Head of Operations: West, Staffs.C.C. [0009031]   12/01/1971
Goodwill Miss GM, BA MCLIP, Unemployed. [0005701]   01/01/1969
Goodwill Mrs LM, (was Gaunt), MCLIP, Head of Operations, W.Sussex Co.L.Serv., Chichester. [0000587]   01/01/1970
Goodwillie Mr JS, MCLIP BA DLS, Official Publications Lib., Trinity Coll.L.Dublin. [0016940]   05/10/1967
Goodwin Ms AJ, MA DipLib, Inf.Serv.Mgr., Crichton Univ.Campus, Dumfries. [0036485]   18/10/1983
Goodwin Miss CH, Learning Res.Cent.Asst., Bridgwater Coll., Somerset. [0053787]   01/10/1996   **AF**
Goodwin Mr CJ, BA(Hons), Asst.Lib. [0051200]   23/11/1994
Goodwin Mrs JR, (was Barker), BA MCLIP, Unemployed. [0038038]   09/01/1985
Goodwin Mrs KA, (was Eggleton), BA(Hons) MA MCLIP, Team Lib., Kent C.C., Sittingbourne. [0050619]   01/10/1994
Goodwin Miss KE, BA(Hons), Grad.Trainee. [0059723]   05/09/2001
Goodwin Mrs S, (was Cooper), MCLIP, Head of Resources/Sen.Lib., Ken Stimpson Comm.Sch./Werrington, Dist.L.,Peterborough,Cambs. [0026916]   17/12/1976
Goody Mrs MJ, (was Wright), DipLib FCLIP, H.of KM Operations, KPMG, London. [0028217]   03/10/1977   **FE 01/04/2002**
Goom Miss N, FCLIP, Retired. [0005706]   30/09/1935   **FE 01/01/1946**
Goonawardena Mrs M, Sch.Lib., St.Thomas the Apostle Coll., London. [0059371]   21/02/2001   **AF**
Goonetileke Mr HAI, BA DLitt FCLIP, Life Member, 36D Mahajana Mawatha, Oruwela, Athuruguiriya, Sri Lanka. [0016942]   01/01/1955   **FE 01/01/1967**
Goostrey Mrs SC, (was Iden), BA(Hons) MSc, Lib., St.Austell Coll.L., Cornwall. [0056965] 11/11/1998
Gordon Miss A, L.Asst., Blackburn Bor.Council. [0045644]   11/04/1991
Gordon Mr A, MA(Hons) DipLib MCLIP, Lib., Hillpark Secondary, Glasgow. [0046787]   23/01/1992
Gordon Mrs AM, (was Whyte), MA MCLIP, Inf.Specialist, Univ.of Abertay Dundee. [0020041]   15/01/1973
Gordon Mrs CE, (was Jackson), BA MCLIP, Asst.Lib., Sch.of Earth Sci., Leeds Univ. [0038811]   09/10/1985
Gordon Mrs EA, BSc DipLib MCLIP, [0034253]   13/10/1981
Gordon Miss GL, BA PhD MCLIP, Asst.Lib., Newcastle Univ. [0005715]   27/12/1968
Gordon Mrs IS, (was Simpson), MA MCLIP, Unemployed. [0028160]   11/10/1977
Gordon Miss JP, MCLIP, Inf.Offr., Regional Coll., Cambridge. [0005716]   16/01/1969
Gordon Mrs JT, (was Green), BA DipLib MCLIP, Area Res.Mgr., Mid Surrey L., Ewell L. [0038245]   13/10/1989
Gordon Ms KE, BA HDipLIS, Lib., Lovells, London. [0047602]   05/10/1992
Gordon Mrs LA, (was Armour), BA(Hons) DipLib MCLIP, Lib., Paisley Grammar, Strathclyde Region. [0045780]   28/05/1991
Gordon Ms MD, (was Reed), MA MCLIP, Br.Lib., Crieff Br.L., Perth. [0035233]   07/10/1982
Gordon Mrs MP, Serv. Mgr., Braintree L. [0060989]   25/01/2002
Gordon Mrs RA, (was Poirrette), BA MCLIP, Local Studs.Lib., Derbys.C.C., Matlock, Derbys. [0022697]   15/08/1974
Gordon Mrs S, MA(Hons), p./t.Inf.Asst., ENABLE, Family Advice Serv., Glasgow. [0059414] 06/03/2001
Gordon Mrs SE, (was Gellman), BA(Hons) DipLis, Unemployed. [0043015]   14/06/1989
Gordon-Till Mr JWG, BSc FCLIP, Inf.Mgr.(Research), Aon Ltd., Harrow. [0049730]   25/11/1993   **FE 01/04/2002**
Gore Ms JM, MA DipLib MCLIP, Lib., Dept.of Trans.Local Govt.and the, Regions, London. [0028572]   17/01/1978
Goreham Miss AL, BLib MCLIP, Sen.Lib., R.B.Kensington & Chelsea, Cent.Ref.L. [0035200]   01/10/1982
Goreham Miss HD, B LIB MCLIP, Asst.Dist.Lib., Bucks Co.L. [0032068]   24/01/1980
Gorgon Mrs Y, BA(Hons), ICT Devel.Offr., S.Tyneside M.B.C., Cent.L. [0055756]   17/11/1997
Gormal Mrs CA, (was Galt), BA MCLIP, Ref.& Inf.Lib., Renfrewshire Council, Paisley. [0005323]   17/09/1970
Gorman Dr GE, MA DipLib ALAA FCLIP, Prof., Victoria Univ.of Wellington. [0023125]   06/11/1974   **FE 07/04/1986**
Gorman Ms SJ, (was Grant), BA MCLIP, Lib., Castlebrae Community High Sch., Edinburgh, EH16 4DP. [0025146]   14/10/1975
Gormley Ms J, BA(Hons), Stud., Brighton Univ. [0059080]   10/11/2000
Gorring Ms HM, BA(Hons) DipLib, Inf.Offr., Birmingham Soc.Serv. [0058244]   24/11/1999

Gorton Miss CL, BA(Hons) MA, Sen.Inf.Asst., Liverpool John Moores Univ. [0052044]   02/10/1995
Gorton Mrs JE, BSc(Hons) MCLIP, Resource Centre Mgr., Nunthorpe Comm.School, Middlesbrough. [0033090]   02/10/1980
Gorton Mrs MJ, (was Walker), BA MCLIP, Retired. [0005728]   08/10/1946
Gorton Mrs P, (was James), BA MCLIP, Asst.Lib., Sinclair Roche & Temperley, London. [0030192]   10/01/1979
Gosby Mrs EJ, BSc MSc MCLIP, Unemployed. [0037950]   25/11/1984
Gosden Mrs C, BSc MSc, Lib., Writtle Coll., Chelmsford. [0051397]   03/02/1995
Gosland Miss EM, BSc, Life Member. [0005730]   07/01/1948
Gosling Miss JR, DipLib MCLIP, Head of Learning & Research, Support Serv., Univ.of Plymouth. [0024947]   23/10/1975
Gosling Miss PL, MCLIP, Retired. [0005733]   11/09/1953
Goss Mrs KN, (was Ordish), BLib, Music Teacher - self-employed. [0039770]   01/07/1986
Goss Miss LJ, BSc MCLIP, Inf.Res.Mgr., Univ.of Herts. [0005735]   05/05/1969
Goss Miss P, MCLIP, Life Member, 7 Belle Vue Terrace, Lincoln, LN1 1HQ. [0005736]   01/01/1942
Gossler Ms AM, Lib., Cirencester Kingshill Sch., Glos. [0051479]   27/02/1995
Gotts Mr ST, BA DipLib MCLIP, Inf.Lib., Flintshire L.& Inf.Serv., Mold. [0033530]   01/01/1981
Goudie Mrs S, (was Enion), MCLIP, Asst.Inf.Mgr., Marks & Clerk, Manchester. [0004603]   26/03/1966
Gouffe Ms C, DipLib MCLIP, Team Lib., Univ.of Northumbria at Newcastle. [0055027]   01/07/1997
Gough Ms A, BA(Hons), Dep.Inf.Serv.Mgr., McGrigor Donald, Glasgow. [0055858]   04/12/1997
Gough Miss AA, MBE BA FCLIP, Retired. [0005741]   06/11/1946   **FE 01/01/1948**
Gough Mrs E, (was Mcluckie), MCLIP, Unemployed. [0009519]   14/03/1971
Gough Mrs HC, (was Francis), BA MA MCLIP, Sen.L.Asst., Univ.of Warwick. [0039243]   01/01/1986
Gough Mrs JV, (was Wilson), MCLIP, Life Member, 56 Kingfisher Way, Bournville, Birmingham, B30 1TG. [0005743]   10/03/1942
Goulborn Mrs AM, MCLIP, Reader Serv.Lib.(Job Share), Plymouth Coll.of F.E. [0005747]   01/01/1966
Gould Mrs A, Lib./Stud., Manchester Met.Univ. [0059500]   05/04/2001
Gould Mrs AM, (was Hall), BA(Hons) MSc MCLIP, Res.Lib., Herts.Sch Improvement & Advisory, Serv., Wheathampsted. [0044068]   09/04/1990
Gould Ms GM, Comm.Lib., Newcastle Lib., Newcastle Under Lyme. [0059181]   08/12/2000
Gould Miss IA, BA MCLIP, Retired. [0005750]   09/01/1943
Gould Mrs JA, Br.Super., Winton L., Bournemouth Bor.Co. [0050010]   16/02/1994   **AF**
Gould Ms PE, (was Miles-Swatton), BA(Hons) DipLIS, Sen.Comm.Lib., Westcotes L., Leicester City L. [0041520]   20/01/1988
Gould Miss PM, MCLIP, Asst.Lend.Lib., Swindon Bor.Council. [0005753]   13/02/1967
Gould Mrs SM, (was Harris), BA, Research Offr., I.F.L.A., Off.for, U.A.P./Internat.Lend., c/o Brit.L., Boston Spa, W.Yorks. [0037726]   12/10/1984
Goulding Dr A, BA MA, Reader, Loughborough Univ., Leics. [0042698]   07/02/1989
Goulding Miss LV, BA DipLib, Inf.Lib., Simmons & Simmons, London. [0035464]   19/10/1982
Goulding Mrs SP, Lib., Girls'Day Sch.Trust, Bromley. [0057579]   27/04/1999   **AF**
Goult Mrs AE, (was Rogers), Asst.Lib., N.Yorkshire County Lib. [0037451]   01/10/1984
Goult Mr R, MCLIP, Acquisitions Team Leader, Instant L., Loughborough. [0005757]
Goult Mrs SC, Team Lib.(Cyps & SP Serv.), Loughborough L., Leics.L.& Inf.Serv. [0039230]   01/01/1986
Goundry Mrs P, MCLIP, Retired. [0029171]   01/04/1978
Gourdie Mrs E, (was Daniel), BA MCLIP, Retired. [0003577]   07/02/1954
Gourlay Mrs JA, (was Grier), BA MCLIP, Comm.Lib., Renfrew Dist.L., Paisley. [0026845]   07/12/1976
Gourley Mrs H, BA(Hons), Inf.-Learning Offr., Learning & Skills Council, Gateshead. [0053342]   14/05/1996
Govan Mrs CA, (was Hasler), BA CertEd MCLIP, Learning Res.Mgr., Dartford Grammar Sch., Kent. [0005759]   05/03/1968
Govan Mrs JB, (was Orr), BA MCLIP, Lib., N.Lanarkshire Council, Motherwell. [0029781]   20/10/1978
Gover Miss SA, BA MCLIP, Customer Serv.Lib., Herts C.C. [0021750]   11/01/1974
Gow Ms F, Inf.& Admin.Co-ordinator, Univ.of E.London. [0057733]   13/07/1999   **AF**
Gow Mrs HM, (was Daman), BA DipLib, Project Worker Inf.and L., Sure Start (Bournemouth). [0051145]   23/11/1994
Gower Mrs EP, MA MCLIP, Stud., Hornsby Internat.Dyslexia Cent., London. [0026387]   18/10/1976
Gower Mrs FM, (was Maguire), MCLIP, Sen.Asst.Lib., Cambridge Univ. [0005763]   01/01/1967
Gower Mrs SC, BA, p./t.Stud., Lib., Aberystwyth Univ., Chigwell High Sch. [0059117]   17/11/2000
Gowers Miss EJ, CertEd BA MCLIP, Learning Cent.Mgr., Strode Coll., Street,Somerset. [0040973]   01/10/1987
Gowland Miss AS, BA(Hons) MA, Asst.Lib., Barlow, Lyde & Gilbert, London. [0057115]   09/12/1998
Gowlett Mrs JE, Mgr., Billericay L., Essex. [0055032]   01/07/1997
Goy Miss J, BSc, Inf.Asst., Clifford Chance, LLP. [0059403]   05/03/2001
Goy Mr JR, BA MCLIP, Deputy Lib., Univ.of Kent, Canterbury. [0005766]   01/10/1961

249

Graaf Miss M, BA, p./t.Stud./Sen.L.Asst., Bolton Inst.of H.E., Eagle Campus. [0059339] 09/02/2001
Grace Ms CE, (was Baker), BA MSc MCLIP, Electronic Resources Mgr., The Open Univ., Milton Keynes. [0038895] 07/10/1985
Grace Mrs DJ, BSc MCLIP, Employment unknown. [0060365] 10/12/2001
Gracey Ms SM, BA DMS MCLIP, Bibl.& Support Servs.Lib., Educ.& Arts, Bolton M.B.C. [0038346] 26/03/1985
Graddon Mrs PH, BA MIBiol MCLIP, Employment not known. [0060716] 12/12/2001
Grady Ms HJ, BA MA MSc MCLIP, Inf.Offr., N.W.Arts Board, Manchester. [0037477] 01/10/1996
Grady Ms J, BA(Hons), Unemployed. [0056712] 07/10/1998
Graf Miss JE, MA, Unemployed. [0037414] 22/08/1984
Graffy Mr N, BA(Hons)DipLib MCLIP, Asst.Lib.-Arts, Univ.of Southampton. [0033237] 27/01/1980
Grafton Mrs PR, (was Madden), MA MCLIP, Unwaged. [0029734] 03/10/1978
Graham Mrs A, (was Hodgkiess), BA(Hons) MSc MCLIP, Inf.Spec., Government Comm.H.Q., Cheltenham. [0052189] 12/10/1995
Graham Mrs AE, (was Duffy), BSc MSc, Unemployed. [0043718] 04/12/1989
Graham Mrs CDR, BA(Hons) MCLIP, Asst.Lib., N.H.S.Exec.Northern & Yorkshire, Durham. [0046567] 12/11/1991
Graham Miss CI, MSc BA MCLIP, Sen.Lib., Isle of Man Coll., Douglas. [0005776] 01/01/1972
Graham Ms CM, BSc DipLib DipEd MCLIP, Lib., N.I.Council for the Curriculum, Examinations & Assess., Belfast. [0032522] 22/04/1980
Graham Miss E, MA, Acting Inf.Serv.Mgr., Wellcome Trust, London. [0042831] 16/03/1989
Graham Mrs JA, (was Tattersall), MCLIP, Princ.Lib.-Young People, States of Jersey P.L., St.Helier. [0016946] 17/01/1963
Graham Mr JH, BA MCLIP, Asst.Mgr.-Bibl.Serv., S.Lanarkshire Council, E.Kilbride. [0005782] 08/02/1972
Graham Mr JP, MCLIP, Training Lib., S.E.L.B., N.Ireland. [0025540] 29/01/1976
Graham Mrs KA, (was Norton), BA(Hons) DipIS MCLIP, GCHQ Webmaster, GCHQ, Cheltenham. [0049001] 24/08/1993
Graham Miss L, BA MA, Inf.Offr., The Learning Place, Sunderland. [0056772] 12/10/1998
Graham Mrs LJ, (was Stewart), MCLIP, Team Lib., Glasgow City L. [0021098] 04/10/1973
Graham Dr M, MA PhD FSA MCLIP, Head of Oxfordshire Studies, Oxfordshire C.C., Cent.L. [0005787] 03/10/1968
Graham Mrs ME, (was Dickson), MA BEd DipLib MIMgt MCLIP, Principal Lecturer, Univ.of Northumbria, Sch. of Computing & Maths. [0003948] 01/01/1972
Graham Ms N, BA(Hons), L.Asst., Univ.Westminster. [0056471] 23/07/1998 AF
Graham Miss PA, BA MCLIP, Asst.Lib., W.Dorset Gen.Hosp.NHS Trust, Dorchester. [0026388] 01/01/1976
Graham Mrs PM, (was Carson), BA(Hons) MCLIP, Inf.Offr., Harrogate Coll.Faculty, Leeds Met.Univ. [0018252] 03/10/1972
Graham Mrs S, L.Mgr., Sunderland Health Auth. [0057223] 20/01/1999
Graham Mrs S, (was Dancer), BA DipLib MCLIP, p./t.Asst.Lib., Thames Valley Univ. [0031813] 17/12/1979
Graham Mrs SA, (was Heslop), BA(Hons) DipInfMan MCLIP, Inf.Offr., St.Albans & Hemel Hempstead NHS, Herts. [0048677] 08/04/1993
Graham Mrs SC, BSc, Stud., City Univ., London. [0052585] 09/11/1995
Graham Mr SJ, MCLIP, Catr., Rhondda Cynon Taff Co.Bor.Council, Treorchy L. [0023545] 10/01/1975
Graham Mrs SJ, BA(Hons), p./t.Lib./Stud., Aberystwyth Univ., Perins Comm.Sch. [0059517] 18/04/2001
Graham Mr SP, BSc(Hons) DipLib MCLIP, Knowledge Mgr., Vantico Ltd., Duxford, Cambs. [0034511] 19/11/1981
Graham Mr TW, MCLIP, Life Member. [0005794] 01/01/1939
Graham Mrs TY, (was Rice), MA(Hons) DipILS, Sch.Lib., Montrose Acad., Montrose, Angus, Scotland. [0053221] 04/04/1996
Graham Mrs V, Coll.Lib., Manchester Coll.of Arts & Tech., Manchester. [0039417] 27/01/1986
Grainge Mrs V, Stud., Loughborough Univ., &, Inf.Resources Mgr., City Hosp., Nottingham. [0058454] 22/02/2000
Grainger Dr F, BSc PhD MCLIP, Lib., Kennedy Inst., London. [0031302] 04/10/1979
Grainger Miss H, BA(Hons), Stud., Loughborough Univ. [0061675] 17/10/2002
Grainger Mr P, BA(Hons) DipLIS, Asst.Lib.(Bibl.Serv.), Middx.Univ. [0043357] 25/10/1989
Grainger Mrs SB, (was Woodhead), MCLIP, Acting Serv.Mgr., L.Learning & Arch., Walsall Cent.L. [0016239] 29/11/1971
Grainger-Jarvis Miss E, BSc, L.Mgr.,Child.Serv., Walsall MBC. [0043259] 13/10/1989
Grajcarek Mrs JL, (was Harrington), MCLIP, Employed outside LIS. [0031851] 07/01/1980
Granger Mrs AM, (was Wilkinson), BLib MCLIP, Unemployed. [0027853] 12/09/1977
Grant Mrs A, (was Edgington), MA, Retired. [0044043] 17/04/1990
Grant Miss DM, MCLIP, Lib., L.Support, Falkirk Council. [0021956] 12/01/1974
Grant Mrs E, MCLIP, Retired. [0009110] 01/01/1938
Grant Mr EA, MA(Hons), Stud., Robert Gordon Univ., Aberdeen. [0061309] 20/05/2002
Grant Miss EJ, BPharm MSc MRPharmS MCLIP, Employment unknown. [0060293] 10/12/2001
Grant Mrs FGT, BA(Hons) MA, Team Lib., Chatham L. [0056455] 13/07/1998
Grant Mrs HL, (was Gray), BA(Hons) MA, Unemployed. [0049232] 14/10/1993
Grant Mr J, BSc DipLib MCLIP, Head Inf.Serv., Quintiles Scotland Ltd., Heriot-Watt Research Pk.,Edinburgh. [0028304] 03/11/1977

Grant Ms J, BSc(Hons), Asst.Lib., Law Soc., London. [0059406] 05/03/2001
Grant Mr JD, BA MCLIP, Public Serv.Lib.-Lend., Aberdeen City Council, Cent.L. [0039922] 01/10/1986
Grant Ms JE, BA(Hons) DipIM MCLIP, Asst.Inf.Lib., London Transport Mus., London. [0048505] 27/01/1993
Grant Miss JL, MCLIP, Freelance Law Lib. [0005808] 26/01/1970
Grant Mrs JL, (was Gray), MA DipLib BA MCLIP, Lib., Ayr Hosp. [0019621] 20/10/1972
Grant Mrs JL, BA(Hons), Self-employed Administrator. [0050929] 22/01/1991 SP
Grant Mrs JM, (was Bright), BA MCLIP, Inf.& Learning Res.Co-ordinator, St.Robert of Newminster Sch., Tyne & Wear. [0046161] 08/10/1991
Grant Mrs KA, (was Bingley), BA, Asst.Lib., Health & Safety Exec., Inf.& Advisory Serv., Sheffield. [0040594] 01/04/1987
Grant Miss M, BA DipLib MCLIP, Community Lib., S.Lanarkshire Council. [0032070] 07/01/1980
Grant Mrs ME, (was Mchardy), MCLIP, Asst.Lib., The Robert Gordon Univ., Aberdeen. [0009404] 13/10/1969
Grant Ms MIM, BScEcon(Hons), Lib., Orkney Coll., Kirkwall. [0051267] 13/12/1994
Grant Ms MJ, Research Fellow, Health Care Practice R&D Unit, Salford Univ. [0044872] 03/01/1991
Grant Ms MP, MA DipLib MCLIP, Cultural Diversity Offr., Glasgow City Council, Cultural & Leisure Serv. [0034491] 17/11/1981
Grant Miss N, Inf.Offr., Hammond Suddards Edge, Birmingham. [0054678] 20/02/1997
Grant Mrs P, (was Broughton), MCLIP, Asst.Lib., City Literary Inst., London. [0005814] 09/09/1964
Grant Mrs PP, (was Johnson), Retired. [0050433] 29/07/1994
Grant Ms RH, MA(Hons), Inf.Mgr.(Acting), Sport Scotland, Edinburgh. [0054570] 28/01/1997
Grant Mrs S, MA(Hons) MSc, Term-time Lib., Univ.of St.Andrews, Sch.of Greek, Latin & Ancient Hist. [0058076] 25/10/1999
Grant Mr SJ, MA PGCE MCLIP, Coll.Lib., Reid Kerr Coll., Paisley. [0040979] 01/10/1987
Grant Mr SNL, BA(Hons) MCLIP, Asst.Dist.Lib., Buckingham L., Bucks.C.C. [0027324] 20/02/1977
Grant Mrs WM, BA MCLIP, Unemployed. [0032014] 29/01/1980
Graph Ms F, BA DipLib MCLIP, Head, Inf.Team, Gtr.London Auth.Research L. [0043547] 06/11/1989
Gratsea Mrs A, BA, Stud., Univ.of Wales, Aberystwyth. [0061123] 19/02/2002
Gratton Mr PD, MBE BA DPA FCLIP FRSA, Life Member. [0005817] 14/09/1950 FE 01/01/1959
Grattoni Ms S, L.Asst., Paddington L., London. [0059365] 22/02/2001 AF
Grau Mrs M, BA, Sen.L.Asst., Univ.of London L. [0055051] 02/07/1997 AF
Graveling Mrs RK, Customer Liaison Offr., Boston L., Lincs. [0058434] 11/02/2000 AF
Graver MS JF, BSc DipLib MIIS MCLIP, [0021055] 19/09/1973
Graves Mrs JA, (was Taylor), Unemployed. [0037992] 01/01/1985
Graves Mrs JL, (was French), BA MCLIP, L.& Serv.Mgr.-Staff Train.& Devel., L.B.of Merton, Surrey. [0005222] 01/07/1970
Graves Mrs L, (was Stevenson), BA MCLIP, Asst.Lib., Univ.of Glamorgan, Pontypridd. [0014008] 01/03/1972
Gravestock Miss JD, MSc MCLIP, I.T.Projects Offr., The Open Univ., Milton Keynes. [0046424] 05/11/1991
Gray Dr ACG, MA PhD MCLIP, Retired. [0060336] 10/12/2001
Gray Mrs AP, (was Sharp), MCLIP, Asst.Lib.,p/t, De Montfort Univ., Leicester. [0005825] 26/01/1963
Gray Mrs BE, (was Willmott), BA MCLIP, Lib., King Edward VI Grammar Sch., Chelmsford. [0016017] 14/04/1970
Gray Miss CM, MA MPhil DipLib MCLIP, Learning Res.Serv.Mgr., Dundee Coll. [0037743] 16/10/1984
Gray Miss EL, BA (Hons) MCLIP, Sch.Lib., Bishop Thomas Grant Sch., London. [0045475] 14/02/1991
Gray Mrs EWM, (was Malkin), MA MCLIP, Sen.Lib., E.Ayrshire Council. [0021477] 21/10/1973
Gray Mrs GJ, (was Watchorn), BA MCLIP, Lib., Family Inf.Cent., QMC, Nottingham. [0052569] 15/01/1976
Gray Mrs H, BA(Hons) PGDipLibMgm, Knowledge & Inf.Asst., Radical Dept.& Res.Cent., N.Mersey Comm.NHS Trust. [0056678] 01/10/1998
Gray Mrs H, (was Swan), MA DLIS MCLIP, Web Content Mgr., Shell IT International., London. [0026571] 01/10/1976
Gray Mrs J, MA MCLIP, Life Member. [0005830] 15/09/1954
Gray Mrs JA, (was Crawford), MCLIP. [0037677] 04/10/1984
Gray Mr JC, BA DLIS, Lib., Linen Hall L., Belfast. [0034490] 17/11/1981
Gray Mr JC, MA HonFCLIP, Hon Fellow. [0060294] 10/12/2001 FE 01/04/2002
Gray Mrs JM, MCLIP, Retired. [0005834] 17/01/1947
Gray Miss KA, BA MCLIP, Employment unknown. [0060295] 10/12/2001
Gray Mrs KA, BSc(Hons), L.Asst., Sch.of St.Helen & St.Katharine, Oxon. [0059478] 05/04/2001 AF
Gray Ms KJ, BA DipLib MCLIP, Inf.Unit Mgr., Lawrence Graham, London. [0044155] 06/06/1990
Gray Ms LM, BA(Hons) DipILM MCLIP, Asst.Lib.(Ref.& Inf.Serv.), Huddersfield L., Kirklees. [0055561] 21/10/1997
Gray Ms LS, BA(Hons) MCLIP, Unemployed. [0035352] 15/10/1982
Gray Mrs ME, (was Taylor), BA DipEdTech MCLIP, Young People's Serv.Lib., Educ.L.Serv., Fife. [0035423] 01/10/1982
Gray Mrs MJ, (was Woods), MCLIP, Inf.Offr., Newcastle Council for Voluntary, Serv. [0018002] 01/01/1963
Gray Miss NJ, BA(Hons) MA, Lib./Inf.Prof., Dept.of Trade & Industry ILS, London. [0056932] 06/11/1998
Gray Mr PA, BA, L.Asst., Southampton Inst.of H.E. [0039835] 16/08/1986

Personal Members   Greenwood

Gray Mr PK, L.Asst., Health Promotion L.Scotland, Edinburgh. [0051853] *13/07/1995*
Gray Mrs PL, (was Hurd), MCLIP, Prison Lib., Warrington Bor., Risley. [0021096] *04/10/1973*
Gray Miss RL, BA(Hons), Stud., Aberystwyth, [0061436] *18/07/2002*
Gray Mrs S, (was Blackburn), BA CertEd MCLIP, Resource & Inf.Offr., Priory Res.Cent., Barnsley Metro.Bor.Council. [0026224] *15/09/1976*
Gray Mrs SAL, BSc(Econ) MCLIP, Consultant/Asst.Lib., Univ.of Wales, Aberystwyth, Canterbury Cathedral L., Kent. [0051570] *01/04/1995*
Gray Mr SM, MA, Man.Dir., Talis Information Ltd. [0059116] *17/11/2000* **SP**
Gray Mr TM, DPA FCLIP, Life member, Tel:01349 861 232. [0005843] *01/03/1941* **FE 01/01/1967**
Gray Mrs VC, MSc MA BA DipEd MPhil, p./t.L.Asst., Univ.of Reading. [0045693] *24/04/1991*
Gray Miss Z, B LIB MCLIP, Ref.Inf.& Local Stud.(RILS), Team Lib., Gravesend L., Kent C.C. [0021887] *21/01/1974*
Grayson Mrs HE, (was Griffiths), BA(Hons) DipLib MCLIP, Sen.Asst.Lib., Nat.Foundation for Educ.Research, Slough. [0045515] *28/02/1991*
Grayson Mr J, BA(Hons) MA, Asst.Lib., Scarborough L., N.Yorks.C.C.(Educ.& Ls.). [0055560] *21/10/1997*
Grayson Mr SD, BSc DipLib, Inf.Mgr., BNSC, DTI, London. [0044727] *27/11/1990*
Grayson Mrs SW, (was Ives), BA(Hons), Sen.L.Asst.-Reader Serv., Univ.of Leeds. [0044989] *30/01/1991* **AF**
Greatorex Miss MA, BA MCLIP, Retired. [0005848] *05/09/1955*
Greaves Mr CE, FCLIP, Life Member. [0005851] *21/08/1933* **FE 01/01/1958**
Greaves Mr DJ, MA DMS MCLIP, Lib., Lifelong Learning, Cent.Lend.Serv., Rotherham M.B.C. [0005853] *01/01/1969*
Greaves Miss KR, BLib MCLIP, L.Serv.Mgr., Harper Adams Univ.Coll. [0038545] *17/06/1985*
Greaves Miss MA, BA MA FCLIP AI, Retired, 307 Sprowston Rd., Norwich, NR3 4HY. [0016954] *08/03/1954* **FE 01/01/1966**
Greaves Ms P, BSc MCLIP, Employment not known. [0060504] *11/12/2001*
Greaves Mrs RM, (was Bush), BA DipLib MCLIP, p./t. Lib., Tunbridge Wells Grammar Sch. [0035254] *04/10/1982*
Gredley Mrs EJ, BA MSc DipLib MCLIP, MCLIP. [0005856] *01/01/1966*
Green Mrs A, (was Wilkinson), MCLIP, Retired. [0005857] *12/03/1956*
Green Mrs AC, (was Pyrah), BA MA MCLIP, Asst.Lib., Horniman Mus., London. [0029799] *10/10/1978*
Green Mrs AE, (was Halliwell), BA DLIS MCLIP, Learning Cent.Coordinator, E.Berks.Coll., Maidenhead. [0018744] *07/08/1972*
Green Mrs AJ, (was Watson), Asst.Lib., FCO., London. [0056640] *01/10/1998*
Green Miss AM, MCLIP, Admin.Asst., N.Devon Coll., Barnstaple. [0005864] *13/05/1971*
Green Mr AMW, MA MCLIP, Lib., Nat.L.of Wales. [0023294] *06/11/1974*
Green Mrs BG, (was Vile), MCLIP, Lib., Federation of Master Builders, London. [0005867] *22/03/1961*
Green Mr BS, MCLIP, Retired. [0005868] *12/01/1965*
Green Miss C, BA MA, Asst.Lib., Wellcome Trust. [0058083] *25/10/1999*
Green Mrs CM, (was Tomlinson), BSc MCLIP, p./t.Sch.Lib., Ellesmere Port Catholic High Sch., Cheshire C.C. [0014775] *01/01/1969*
Green Mrs CR, BEd(Hons), L.Asst../p./t.Stud., L.& Learning Cent., Univ.of Bath. [0061501] *30/08/2002*
Green Mrs CS, MA(Hons), Learning Resource Asst., Kinross High Sch. [0058184] *15/11/1999*
Green Mr DC, BA(Hons) DipILS MCLIP, Bus.Inf.Broker, Armstrong Craven Assoc., Manchester. [0048518] *02/02/1993*
Green Mr DJ, BA MCLIP, Stock Mgr., Wilts.L.& Heritage. [0005874] *09/02/1965*
Green Mrs DJ, BA DipLib MCLIP, Unemployed. [0038383] *03/04/1985*
Green Mrs DT, Unemployed. [0054694] *27/02/1997*
Green Mrs EC, (was Hurd), BA(Hons) MCLIP, Temp.Trainee Lib., W.Sussex C.C., Worthing Public L. [0049727] *25/11/1993*
Green Ms EJ, BA(Hons), Stud., Univ.Central Lancashire. [0060032] *28/11/2001*
Green Miss EV, BA DipLib MCLIP, Lib., Southampton Ref.L., Southampton City L. [0030172] *10/01/1979*
Green Ms FJ, BSc(Hons) MA, Higher L.Exec., House of Commons, London. [0054227] *06/11/1996*
Green Mrs G, (was Vidler), BA MCLIP, p./t.L.Asst., Lancs.C.C. [0030563] *15/01/1979*
Green Miss GE, MCLIP, Life Member. [0005876] *17/08/1955*
Green Miss GM, BA MCLIP, Asst.Dist.Lib., Aylesbury, Bucks.C.C. [0024892] *08/10/1975*
Green Mrs H, (was Littlewood), DMA MCLIP, Head of L.& Inf.Serv., Barlow Lyde & Gilbert, London. [0008994] *01/01/1965*
Green Mrs HC, (was Howarth), BA DipLib MCLIP, Sch.Lib.(Job Share), Holy Cross High Sch., Hamilton. [0030588] *14/02/1979*
Green Mrs J, (was Desaleux), BA MCLIP, Sen.Lib., N.Tyneside Council, Wallsend L. [0005878] *25/04/1965*
Green Mrs J, (was Marks), BA MCLIP, Asst.Lib., Cheshunt P.L., Herts. [0035640] *23/11/1982*
Green Mrs J, BSc, Sen.L.Asst., R.B.of Kensington & Chelsea. [0047013] *01/04/1992*
Green Mr JA, Lib., S.Birmingham Coll., St.Philips Sixth Form Cent. [0057306] *05/02/1999* **AF**
Green Mrs JE, MSc MCLIP, Employment unknown. [0060192] *11/12/2001*
Green Mrs JE, (was Moss), BA MCLIP, Inf.Manager, Covington & Burling, London. [0024771] *29/09/1975*
Green Mr K, BSc MA MCLIP, Employment unknown. [0060583] *11/12/2001*
Green Ms K, BA(Hons) MSc(Econ) MCLIP, Asst.Lib., W.Sussex C.C., W.Sussex. [0055015] *25/06/1997*
Green Mrs KA, BA, Systems Lib., N.W.Kent Coll., Gravesend. [0053839] *04/10/1996*

Green Mrs KA, (was Marsland), BA MCLIP, Lend.Serv.Offr., Barnsley M.B.C. [0031895] *17/01/1980*
Green Mrs KS, (was Minnis), BSc PGDip MCLIP, Acad.Liaison Lib., Univ.of Surrey L., Guildford. [0028086] *24/09/1977*
Green Mrs L, (was Bontoft), MCLIP, Serv.Lib., Lincs.Educ.& Cultural Serv.Dir. [0018726] *04/10/1963*
Green Miss LW, BSc MCLIP, Asst.Lib., Queens Univ.Belfast, Main L. [0022696] *02/08/1974*
Green Mrs M, (was Mallon), MCLIP, Catr., Leics.Co.L. [0009659] *10/03/1965*
Green Mr ME, MCLIP, Asst.Lib., Building Design Partnership, London. [0005891] *07/10/1961*
Green Mrs MH, BSc MSc, Career Break. [0054094] *25/10/1996*
Green Mrs MJ, (was Woods), BA MCLIP, Lib., Boodle Hatfield, London. [0028979] *18/01/1978*
Green Mrs MJ, (was Clark), BA MLS MCLIP, Head of L.Inf.& Arch., Stoke-on-Trent City Council. [0029443] *08/08/1978*
Green Mrs MM, (was Carr), MCLIP, Lib.,Lend.Serv., Redditch.L., Worcestershire L.Dept. [0005892] *30/09/1964*
Green Mrs NA, (was Tegetmeier), BA DipLib, Full Time Mother. [0044212] *09/07/1990*
Green Mr PR, BA MA DipLib MCLIP, H.of Inf.Serv., Univ.of Warwick L., Coventry. [0030909]*31/05/1979*
Green Mrs PR, BA(Hons) MCLIP, Learning Resources Coordinator, Knowsley M.B.C., Huyton. [0050037] *21/02/1994*
Green Miss RAM, FCLIP, Life Member. [0005896] *20/10/1949* **FE 01/01/1971**
Green Mrs RJ, (was Fyfield), BA MCLIP, L.Mgr., Glenmoor Sch., Bournemouth, Dorset. [0034632] *16/01/1982*
Green Mr RS, MA MLib MCLIP, Inf.Researcher, Dept.of Trade & Ind., London. [0028305] *15/10/1977*
Green Mrs RS, (was Andrews), MCLIP, Sen.Lib.-Young Peoples Serv., L.B.of Richmond, Leisure Serv.Dept. [0019954] *15/01/1973*
Green Mr S, MA MCLIP, Lib., Cent.Ref.L., Hull City Council. [0018258] *03/10/1972*
Green Ms SA, BA(Hons) MCLIP, Sen.Inf.Offr., St.Martins Coll., Carlisle. [0035551] *01/10/1982*
Green Mrs SAM, (was Poynton), MA MCLIP, Lib., Brighton & Hove Council, E.Sussex. [0039542] *01/01/1967*
Green Ms SI, (was Allen), MCLIP, Co.Records Mgr., Surrey C.C., Kingston upon Thames. [0005900] *10/01/1966*
Green Mr SJ, BA DipSoc FCLIP, Life Member, Tel:(020)8428 4386. [0005901] *05/10/1934* **FE 01/01/1950**
Green Ms SJ, BA(Hons) DipLis MCLIP, Sen.Asst.Lib., Univ.of Westminster. [0043484] *30/10/1989*
Green Mrs SM, (was Wood), MCLIP, L.Asst., Herts.C.C. [0016219] *02/02/1970*
Green Mr SP, MA MCLIP, Retired. [0024083] *09/04/1975*
Green Miss SV, DipLib MCLIP, Sch.Lib., Camden Sch.for Girls, London. [0034756] *17/02/1982*
Green Mr VAM, BSc BA MCLIP, Dir., Victor Green & Co., London. [0060296] *10/12/2001*
Green Mr WS, FCLIP, Retired. [0005906] *17/01/1940* **FE 01/01/1948**
Greenacre Ms S, MCLIP, Sch.Lib., Westbourne High Sch., Ipswich. [0001311] *01/01/1972*
Greenall Mr J, MCLIP, Retired. [0019744] *01/01/1966*
Greenaway Mr KW, BA(Hons), Stud., UCL., London. [0058893] *02/10/2000*
Greenfield Mrs FE, (was Ling), MCLIP, Lib., Parsons Brinckerhoff Ltd., Bristol. [0005914] *08/01/1965*
Greenfield Mrs KF, (was Stockley), BA MCLIP, Learning Resource Cent Mgr., Farnborough Coll.of Tech., Hants. [0025116] *21/10/1975*
Greenfield Mr L, BA MCLIP, Asst.Lib., Nat.Univ.of Ireland, Galway. [0005915] *01/01/1967*
Greenfield Miss SJ, BA MIMgt MCLIP, Div.Lib.-N., Hants.Co.L. [0024685] *21/10/1975*
Greenhalgh Mrs MC, BSc MCLIP, Employment unknown. [0060368] *11/12/2001*
Greenhalgh Mr SJ, Stud., Manchester Met.Univ. [0054896] *02/05/1997*
Greenhill Mr RA, FCLIP, Life Member. [0005921] *24/03/1938* **FE 01/01/1951**
Greening Mrs PM, (was Archer), L.Asst., Royal Coll.of Veterinary Surgeons, Wellcome L. [0045010] *24/05/1990* **AF**
Greenley Mr JP, BA(Hons) MPhil DipILS MCLIP, p./t.Asst.Lib., Manchester Met.Univ. [0054111]*28/10/1996*
Greenley Ms SL, BA(Hons) DipIS, Inf.Specialist, Clinical Evidence, BMJPG, London. [0055757] *17/11/1997*
Greenshields Mrs MS, MA DipLib MCLIP, Sen.Lib., Glasgow L.&Inf.& Learning. [0032658] *11/07/1980*
Greenslade Mr RJ, CChem MRSC MCLIP, Employment not known. [0060817] *12/12/2001*
Greenslade Mrs SA, BA(Hons), Stud., Liverpool John Moores Univ. [0058441] *15/02/2000*
Greensmith Mrs M, (was Curley), BA DipLib, Inf.Mgr., Sport England, London. [0041002] *01/05/1987*
Greenway Mrs J, (was Cotterell), MCLIP, Comm.L.Mgr., Monmouthshire L.& Inf.Serv. [0025862] *25/01/1976*
Greenwood Miss AM, Knowledge Harvester, Diamondcluster International, Barcelona, Spain. [0057003] *19/11/1998*
Greenwood Mrs AS, BA(Hons) MA, Inf.Mgr., Arnold & Porter, London. [0047315] *10/07/1992*
Greenwood Mrs C, (was Watson), MCLIP, Local Stud.Lib., Bradford Cent.Ref.L. [0019906] *01/01/1961*
Greenwood Mrs C, (was Smyth), BA MCLIP, Unemployed. [0034589] *01/01/1982*
Greenwood Miss CM, BA MCLIP, Learning & Inf.Facilitator, Hopwood Hall Tertiary Coll., Lancs. [0005928] *21/10/1969*

251

Greenwood Ms E, BA(Hons) MA, Child.Lib., Cent.L., L.B.of Croydon. [0056968] *11/11/1998*
Greenwood Mrs ER, (was Shaw), p./t.Research & Data Mgr., King Sturge, Birmingham. [0047467] *25/08/1992*
Greenwood Ms HM, (was Roach), BA, Project Mgr., Midcheshire Hosp Trust, Leighton Hosp., Cheshire. [0012446] *09/01/1972*
Greenwood Mrs HN, (was Struthers), B Tech DipLib MCLIP, Asst.Lib.(Ref.), Bucks.C.C., High Wycombe Ref.L. [0043104] *27/07/1989*
Greenwood Mr JB, BA FCLIP, Retired. [0005931] *05/10/1961* **FE 27/03/1991**
Greenwood Mrs LS, BA DipLib MCLIP, Sen.L.Mgr., Belfast Educ.& L.Board., Belast. [0031751] *01/12/1979*
Greenwood Mrs MC, (was Young), MA(Hons) DipLib, p./t.Asst., Canterbury Christ Church Univ.Coll., Turnbridge Wells. [0048537] *08/02/1993*
Greer Mr AE, Inf.Mgr., Barclays Bank plc, Coventry. [0061277] *08/05/2002* **AF**
Greer Ms MJ, BA MLS MCLIP, Employment unknown. [0060369] *11/12/2001*
Greeve Mr NA, PGDip GDip BEd ALIA MAppSc, M.D./Consultant, Inform Consultants, Perth, Australia. [0050438] *29/07/1994*
Gregory Mrs AM, (was Edwards), MA MCLIP, Resident in U.S.A. [0037737] *23/10/1984*
Gregory Ms C, BSc(Hons) DipILM MCLIP, Asst.Lib.(Multimedia), L.& Learning Resources Cent., Surrey Inst.of Art & Design. [0058771] *17/07/2000*
Gregory Mrs CMB, (was O'Gorman), BA MA, Legal Editor, European Legal News, Paris. [0041326] *02/11/1987*
Gregory Mrs CV, (was Barker), BA MCLIP, Team Lib., Melton L., Leics.C.C. [0005940] *24/09/1960*
Gregory Mrs E, BA(Hons), Stud., Virtual L.Devel.Mgr., Beds.C.C., Beds. [0055428] *09/10/1997*
Gregory Mrs EA, BA(Hons), Stud., Exeter Univ. [0061831] *14/11/2002*
Gregory Miss J, BA MCLIP, Web Site Mgr., Health & Safety Exec., Inf.Serv., Sheffield. [0032524] *01/05/1980*
Gregory Mr JDP, Employment not known. [0049739] *29/11/1993*
Gregory Miss JR, MCLIP, Retired. [0005943] *05/10/1965*
Gregory Mrs K, BA MCLIP, Asst.Child.Lib., Child.& Sch.L.Serv., Halifax Cent.L. [0005945] *01/01/1968*
Gregory Mrs KE, (was Baker), BA MCLIP, Lib., Queen Elizabeth's Sch., Ashbourne, Derbys. [0000634] *11/03/1971*
Gregory Miss LM, BA(Hons) MCLIP, Lib., Portchester Grp., Hants.Co.L. [0030984] *15/06/1979*
Gregory Miss MGG, JP LLB FCLIP, Retired. [0005946] *30/09/1938* **FE 01/01/1949**
Gregory Mrs RS, (was Brewster), BA MCLIP, Sch.Lib.(Job Share), Sinfin Comm.Sch., Derby. [0029591] *29/07/1978*
Gregory Mr S, BA MA FCLIP, Lib., Union Theological Coll., Belfast. [0016960] *01/01/1969* **FE 15/03/1983**
Gregory Mrs S, DipLib MCLIP, ESL Instructor, Paradise Valley Coll., Phoenix, U.S.A. [0034580] *01/01/1982*
Gregory Mr SF, BSc MA MCLIP, Campus Lib.-Cyncoed, Univ.of Wales Inst., Cardiff. [0043628] *14/11/1989*
Gregory Miss SJ, BA(Hons), Picture Lib., The Kennel Club, London. [0059335] *09/02/2001*
Gregory Miss SM, BA(Hons) MA, Sen.Inf.Offr., Educ.Mgmt.Inf.Exchange, Nat.Foundation for Educ.Research. [0057405] *11/03/1999*
Gregson Mrs CA, (was Williams), BA(Hons) MCLIP, Unemployed. [0036622] *25/10/1983*
Greig Miss F, BA MCLIP, L.& Inf.Cent.Mgr., D.T.L.R., London. [0043862] *05/02/1990*
Greig Mrs LR, (was Muncer), MCLIP, Southmead L.Mgr., N.Bristol NHS Trust, Bristol. [0005953] *07/09/1966*
Greig Mrs RD, (was Evans), BA MCLIP, Multi-Media Lib., Aberdeenshire L.& Inf.Serv., Oldmeldrum. [0004697] *28/11/1971*
Greliak Mrs RM, (was Klodzinska), BA MCLIP, Sen.Lib., Swiss Cottage Cent.L., L.B.of Camden. [0022008] *09/01/1974*
Gresty Miss HG, BA MCLIP, Co-ordinator, J.P.Morgan Fleming Asset Mgmt., Luxembourg. [0030423] *10/01/1979*
Greville Mrs SE, BSc(Econ), p./t.Stud., Liverpool John Moores Univ., Wrexham Co.Bor.Council. [0061160] *20/03/2002*
Grey Mr ML, MA, Hon.Affiliate Scholar, Harvard Business Sch. [0041587] *12/01/1988*
Gridley Mrs EP, (was Force), MCLIP, Teaching Asst., L.B.of Lewisham, Torridon Infants Sch. [0027270] *20/02/1977*
Grier Mrs VC, (was Ward), BA MCLIP, Health Inf.Lib., Poole Bor.Council, Dorset. [0005961] *01/01/1967*
Grieser Ms S, L.Asst.,Stud., Goethe-Institut London. [0061746] *01/11/2002* **AF**
Grieve Mrs CM, (was Kevan), MCLIP, Sen.Lib., Wokingham Dist.L., Woodley, Reading. [0005964] *05/01/1970*
Grieve Mrs EJ, MA PGCE, Employment unknown. [0060306] *10/12/2001*
Grieve Mr S, MCIBS, Open Learning Stud., Telford Coll., Edinburgh. [0049040] *13/09/1993*
Grieves Miss K, Asst.Lib., Univ.of Sunderland, St.Peters L. [0056145] *05/03/1998*
Grieves Miss M, MCLIP, Employment unknown. [0060370] *11/12/2001*
Griffin Mrs A, BA DipLib PGCE, Retired. [0040856] *10/07/1987*
Griffin Miss AEM, Stud., Loughborough Univ. [0058150] *08/11/1999*
Griffin Ms BJ, BA MCLIP, Lib., Abbotsholme Sch., Rocester, Staffs. [0037897] *13/11/1984*
Griffin Miss CA, L.Asst., Birmingham City Council, Sutton Coldfield Ref.L. [0045104] *11/07/1990* **AF**
Griffin Mrs D, (was Sloan), MA MCLIP DMS, Head of L.Serv., L., Suffolk Coll., Ipswich. [0020582] *22/04/1973*
Griffin Ms EM, BSc MSc MCLIP, Employment not known. [0060262] *10/12/2001*
Griffin Miss FR, BSc(Hons) MA, Lib., Devel.Planning Partnership. [0044867] *02/01/1991*

Griffin Mrs GE, (was Pascall), MCLIP, Asst.Dist.Lib., Bucks.Co.L. [0011323] *01/01/1968*
Griffin Mrs MA, L.Mgr.-Cent.L., Herts.C.C, Watford. [0053288] *01/05/1996* **AF**
Griffin Ms MAV, BA, Inf.Specialist, HM Customs & Excise, Salford. [0040834] *22/07/1987*
Griffin Ms MF, BSc MSc MCLIP, Employment unknown. [0060584] *11/12/2001*
Griffin Mrs R, (was Moore), BA(Hons) DipLib MCLIP, Retired. [0010357] *09/09/1971*
Griffin Mrs S, (was Barnes), Team Lib., Surrey C.C., Guildford P.L. [0050107] *05/04/1994*
Griffin Ms SJ, BSc, Planning Inf.Offr., Wokingham Dist.Council. [0038019] *16/01/1985*
Griffin Mrs SM, (was Bryden), BA(Hons) DipLIS, Lib., Hertford Coll., Oxford. [0051083] *14/11/1994*
Griffin Mrs VC, (was Groom), BA(Hons) MCLIP, Sen.L.Exec., House of Commons L., London. [0054034] *18/10/1996*
Griffin Mrs W, (was Starks), BA MCLIP, p./t.Lib., Surrey C.C., Weybridge L. [0028306] *03/11/1977*
Griffith Mrs JF, BSc MCLIP, Employment not known. [0060710] *12/12/2001*
Griffith Miss MA, BA MCLIP, Comm.Outreach Asst., Home Serv., L.B.of Newham. [0005972] *22/03/1971*
Griffith Ms MT, BA MSc, Sen.L.Asst., Queen's Univ.of Belfast. [0045292] *02/01/1990*
Griffith Miss MW, BA MCLIP, Sen.Asst.Lib., De Montfort Univ., Bedford. [0005973] *14/01/1968*
Griffith Mrs SV, (was Kabos), BA DipLib MCLIP, Resident Australia. [0025574] *02/02/1976*
Griffiths Mrs AA, BA(Hons) MCLIP, Asst.Lib., Liverpool Hope Univ.Coll., Liverpool. [0056605] *15/09/1998*
Griffiths Miss AF, BA BSc, L.Asst., Bolton Cent.L., Lancs. [0045183] *03/08/1990* **AF**
Griffiths Mrs AJ, (was Cake), BA(Hons) MSc(Econ) MCLIP, Team Lib., Child.& Young People, Luton B.C. [0051167] *23/11/1994*
Griffiths Mrs AL, BA(Hons) MA MSc(Econ) MCLIP, Inf.Researcher, Mgmt.Inf.Cent., Inst.of Mgmt., Corby, Northants. [0055857] *02/12/1997*
Griffiths Mr DC, BA MCLIP, Inf.Offr., Stoke on Trent City Council, Hanley L. [0029968] *02/11/1978*
Griffiths Mr DJ, BA MA MCLIP, Lib., Brit.Maritime Tech.Ltd., Teddington, Middx. [0025878] *01/01/1976*
Griffiths Mr DJ, BSc MCLIP, Retired. [0030911] *25/05/1979*
Griffiths Mrs DVM, (was Bertram), B SC MCLIP, Self-Employed. [0022893] *01/10/1974*
Griffiths Mrs GE, (was Davies), BA DipLib MCLIP, Asst.Lib., Powys C.C., Newtown. [0045451] *11/02/1991*
Griffiths Mr GR, BA DipLib MCLIP, Community Lib., Lincs.C.C., Stamford. [0045861] *07/01/1991*
Griffiths Mrs H, (was Banyard), BA(Hons) MLib, Asst.Lib., Welsh Coll.of Music & Drama, Cardiff. [0047750] *16/10/1992*
Griffiths Mrs J, (was Alderson), BSc MCLIP, Area Lib., Workington Grp., Cumbria Co.L., Workington. [0021508] *23/10/1973*
Griffiths Mr JM, MCLIP, Life Member. [0005985] *05/09/1959*
Griffiths Mrs JM, (was Richardson), MA MCLIP, p./t.L.Asst., Denbighshire C.C. [0026649] *12/10/1976*
Griffiths Miss JPW, JP BA MCLIP, Life Member, Tel.(020)8472 4158. [0005987] *19/02/1948*
Griffiths Mr JW, BSc(Hons) MSc, Intranet Mgr., British Trade Intl., London. [0056289] *28/04/1998*
Griffiths Miss KJ, BA(Hons) MA, Sch.L.Serv.Team Lib., Norfolk C.C. [0056700] *05/10/1998*
Griffiths Miss LM, MLS BA MCLIP, Unemployed. [0027678] *13/07/1977*
Griffiths Miss LS, BEng(Hons), Stud., Thames Valley Univ. [0061069] *12/02/2002*
Griffiths Miss LS, MA(Hons), Stud., Strathclyde Univ. [0061218] *16/04/2002*
Griffiths Mrs MA, (was Thomas), BLib MCLIP, Child./Promotions Lib., Bridgend L.& Inf.Serv. [0014566] *04/10/1971*
Griffiths Mr MJ, BA(Hons), P./t.L.Asst., Lancashire C.C. [0057690] *02/07/1999*
Griffiths Mr PD, BA FCLIP, Head of Inf.Serv.Unit, Comm.Directorate, Home Off., London SW1. [0005990] *01/01/1970* **FE 01/04/2002**
Griffiths Miss PE, MCLIP, Life Member. [0005991] *01/01/1957*
Griffiths Mr RD, BA MCLIP, Lib./Hosp.Lib., Swindon Bor.Council, Swindon Hosp. [0025164] *03/12/1975*
Griffiths Mrs RJ, p./t.Stud./L.Asst., Manchester Met.Univ., Dept.of Inf.& Comm. [0061221] *16/04/2002*
Griffiths Miss S, BA(Hons), Stud., Sheffield Univ. [0058967] *11/10/2000*
Griffiths Mrs SNT, BA MA DipLib MCLIP, Asst.Lib., St.Catharine's Coll., Cambridge. [0030757] *11/04/1979*
Griffiths Mr TE, BA MCLIP, Retired. [0005996] *14/10/1948*
Griffiths Mrs VM, BA MCLIP, Retired. [0005998] *15/06/1971*
Griffiths Miss WR, BA MCLIP, Sen.Lib., E.Area L.& Inf.serv., Stockport M.B.C. [0032074] *01/01/1980*
Griffiths Dr WRM, MA MLitt DipLib MCLIP, Dir.of Pub.Serv., Nat.L.of Wales, Aberystwyth. [0024688] *02/10/1975*
Griffiths-Jones Mrs RS, (was Griffiths), BA(Hons), Asst.Lib., Llandrillo Coll., Rhos-on-sea, Colwyn Bay. [0049990] *10/04/1994*
Griggs Ms AJ, (was Cooper), BA MCLIP, Lib., Gouldens, London. [0033935] *28/05/1981*
Griggs Mr JE, BA (Hons) MA MCLIP, Inf.Offr., Drivers Jonas, London. [0043622] *06/10/1989*
Grigson Ms AC, BA(Hons) MA MCLIP, Sen.L.Asst., Kings Coll.London. [0049022] *01/09/1993*
Grigson Mrs GM, MA MCLIP, P/t.Lib., Cheshire C.C., Congleton. [0040307] *01/01/1987*
Grima Mr JR, BA MCLIP, Mgr., Inf.Serv.Dept., Central Bank of Malta, Valetta. [0028818] *02/01/1978*

Grimley Mrs AE, (was Bingham), BA(Hons) MSc(Econ) MCLIP, L.&Inf.Cent.Mgr., Hampshire County Council, Brune Pk.Community Sch. [0050175] 25/04/1994

Grimmond Mrs MAG, (was Chisholm), BA(Hons) MCLIP, Sch.Lib., The High Sch.of Glasgow, Anniesland, Glasgow. [0024483] 16/09/1975

Grimshaw Miss JM, BA, Head-Soc.Policy Inf.Serv., Brit.L., London. [0018218] 01/10/1972

Grimshaw Mr RE, FCLIP, Retired. [0006007] 26/04/1940 FE 01/01/1951

Grimstone Miss PG, MA, Asst.Lib., Eton Coll.L., Eton. [0052156] 09/01/1995

Grimwood-Jones Miss D, MA DipLib MCLIP, Unemployed. [0032075] 01/02/1980

Grindlay Dr DJC, BSc Phd, Stud., Loughborough Univ. [0059195] 14/12/2000

Grindle Mrs JM, (was Thompson), BA MCLIP, Sen Team Leader (Jobshare), Warwickshire C.C. [0029849] 09/10/1978

Grindrod Ms KJ, BA MIL MCLIP, Employment not known. [0060237] 10/12/2001

Grinnell Miss AL, BSc, Unemployed, [0060970] 21/01/2002

Grisdale Mrs M, (was Dodds), MCLIP, Life Member. [0006012] 05/03/1953

Grist Ms AP, (was Hockings), BA(Hons) MA, Sch.Lib., Henbury Sch., Bristol. [0054757] 01/04/1997

Gristwood Mrs H, (was Agutter), MCLIP, p./t.Sch.Lib., Cable House Sch., Woking. [0000094] 01/01/1947

Groark Mr DM, BA MCLIP, Retired. [0006013] 13/01/1968

Grocott Mrs JL, (was Watson), BA MCLIP, Serv.Advisor: Stock Mgmnt.& Promo., Staffs.L.& Inf.Serv. [0021230] 10/10/1973

Grogan Miss JC, BTEC HND BLib MCLIP, Asst.Lib., Government L. [0041510] 18/01/1988

Gronland Miss JLS, BScEcon (DILS), Stud., Univ.Aberystwyth. [0059620] 03/07/2001

Grooby Ms DJ, BAppSc, Unemployed. [0061496] 22/08/2002

Groom Miss A, BA(Hons) PGDipLIS, Lib./Inf.Mgr., Home Off., London. [0056238] 14/04/1998

Groom Mrs AM, (was Harding), MA MCLIP, Inf.Specialist, Cardiff Univ. [0047466] 24/08/1992

Groom Mrs JEC, (was Tattersall), MCLIP, Legal Inf.Consultant & Lib., Self-Employed. [0006021] 27/09/1967

Groombridge Mrs SEA, (was Cave), BA DipLib MCLIP, Lib., TRL Ltd., Crowthorne, Berks. [0031226] 11/10/1979

Groome Mrs CR, (was Newby), Career Break / Borough Councillor, [0034782] 22/01/1982

Gros Miss AB, Asst.Lib., H.H.Aga Khan, France. [0058572] 03/04/2000

Grose Mr MW, BA MCLIP, Retired. [0006026] 04/10/1962

Gross Ms SL, BA MA MLIS, Lib.(Ref.), Hedi Steiberg L., Stern Coll.for Women, Yeshiva Uni., NY, NY, USA. [0055966] 13/01/1998

Grosvenor Mrs JD, BA DipIS MCLIP, Subject Lib., Learning Res.Cent., Nescot Coll., Surrey. [0051227] 30/11/1994

Grosvenor Mr JRH, DipLib DipMgmt(Open) MCLIP, Lib., L.B.of Bexley, Thamesmead. [0031364] 01/10/1979

Grosvenor Mr R, BSc MSc, L.Systems Mgr., Univ.of Oxford, Economics L. [0051176] 23/11/1994

Grounds Mrs G, (was Adam), MA(Hons) DipInf MCLIP, Sen.Asst.Lib., Nat.Foundation for Educ.Research, Slough. [0047355] 21/07/1992

Grout Mr PN, BA DipLib MCLIP, Ref.Lib., Thames Valley Univ., London. [0019648] 30/10/1972

Grove Mrs EJ, (was Stocks), MCLIP, Locate Project Leader, Gloucester L., Glos.Co.L. [0014070] 07/02/1969

Grove-Jones Ms PM, (was Jones), BSc AdvDipCrim DAppSocSci MCLIP, Tutor-Lib., H.M.P. Blundeston, Lowestoft. [0000485] 11/03/1963

Grove-Smith Miss P, BA MCLIP, Lib., Stadtbuechereien Frankfurt, Zweigstelle Schwanheim. [0006029] 08/10/1971

Grover Ms C, Law Lib., BPP Law Sch., London. [0049568] 19/11/1993

Grover Ms SM, BA MA DipLib MCLIP, Lib., Inst.of Actuaries, Oxford. [0027325] 10/03/1977

Groves Mrs JA, (was Huish), BA MCLIP, Unemployed. [0031337] 08/10/1979

Gruffudd Mr C, BA MCLIP, Asst.Lib., Llyfrgell Genedlaethol Cymru, Aberystwyth. [0020076] 01/01/1973

Gruffydd Ms NV, BA MLib MCLIP, Child.& Young Peoples Lib., Cyngor Gwynedd Co., Gwynedd. [0040205] 06/11/1986

Grundy Mrs JE, (was Credland), BA MCLIP, p./t.Casual, Univ.of Warwick, Coventry. [0028795] 25/01/1978

Guard Mrs O, BSc(Econ) MCLIP, Asst.Area Mgr.-W., Truro, Cornwall. [0051507] 13/03/1995

Gubbels Miss W, BA(Hons), Team Leader, Qinetiq. [0050792] 18/10/1994

Guest Mr DA, Nursing & Midwifery Lib., Coventry Univ., Lanchester L. [0038098] 17/01/1985

Guest Mrs MR, (was Bloom), BA(Hons) DipLib MLS MCLIP, Lib.& Inf.Offr., Camden & Islington Health Auth., London. [0031199] 15/10/1979

Guest Mr PJ, Employee, Brian Dryden Domestic, Appliances, Wimborne Minster, Dorset. [0054090] 25/10/1996

Guest Mrs RS, Bookseller, Paperback Exchange, Dorset. [0061426] 25/07/2002 SP

Guha Mr MAB, BA MCLIP, Lib., Univ.of London Inst.of Psychiatry, Kings Coll.London. [0006039] 25/01/1969

Guild Mrs FR, (was Crosby), BA MCLIP, Lib., Catg., Edinburgh City L. [0020832] 24/07/1973

Guinevan Mrs FM, (was Woodward), BA MCLIP, Lib., Aircraft Res.Assoc.Ltd., Bedford & Lib. [0006042] 11/01/1969

Guiney Mrs P, BA MCLIP, Learning Res.Mgr., St.Clement Danes Sch., Chorleywood. [0030758] 17/04/1979

Guite Miss CJE, (was Scott), MA LTCL MCLIP, Sub-Lib., Christs Coll., Cambridge. [0030174] 17/01/1979

Guiver Mrs KM, BA MCLIP, Asst.Lib., Norwich Sch.of Art & Design, Norfolk. [0038805] 08/10/1985

Gulamali Miss S, BA(Hons) MA, Lend.Lib., L.B.of Enfield, Cent.L. [0056029] 28/01/1998

Gulland Mrs D, (was Griffiths), MCLIP, Retired. [0006043] 18/01/1957

Gulliver Mrs LK, (was Edmunds), BA MCLIP, Retired. [0035611] 12/11/1982

Gummerson Mrs SM, BA MCLIP, p./t.Asst.Lib., Coll.of W.Anglia, Kings Lynn. [0027992] 27/09/1977

Gundelund Andersen Mrs A, Unemployed. [0054699] 03/03/1997

Gunderson Mrs AE, (was Hawkey), BA DipLib MCLIP, ICT Training Co-ordinator, Cornwall C.C., Penzance L. [0026735] 03/11/1976

Gunn Mrs AA, (was Hampton), MCLIP, Inf.Serv.Cent.Mgr., King's Coll.London, Med.L., St.Thomas'Hosp. [0025881] 10/04/1976

Gunn Mrs CS, (was Macadie), BSc DipLib MCLIP, Sch.Lib., St.Mungo's High Sch., Falkirk Council. [0034558] 13/01/1982

Gunn Mr DR, MCLIP, Special IT Project Offr., Newcastle City Council. [0006051] 01/01/1969

Gunn Miss MF, BA (Hons), Reader Serv.Lib., Advocates L. [0050924] 01/11/1994

Gunn Mrs PJ, MCLIP, Employment not known. [0060694] 12/12/2001

Gunning Mr SJ, BA(Hons) DipLIS MCLIP, Asst.Lib., Imperial Coll.of Sci.Tech.& Med., London. [0044205] 06/07/1990

Gunter Mrs FR, BA(Hons), p./t.Stud./L.Asst., Univ.of Sheffield, J.B.Morrell L., Univ.of York. [0061280] 08/05/2002

Gunton Mr DH, OBE MA FCLIP, Life Member, Drayton Farm Cottages,Wendens Ambo, Saffron Walden, CB11 4JX. [0016970] 07/01/1947 FE 05/03/1973

Gupta Mrs I, MA MPHIL PhD, Unemployed & Stud., Southgate College, London. [0060975] 22/01/2002

Gura Mrs E, (was Hughes), MCLIP, Life Member, Tel.020 8681 7910. [0006054] 28/01/1953

Gurajena Miss CR, LLB(Hons) MSc, Asst.Lib., Macfarlanes, London. [0056964] 13/11/1998

Gurnsey Mr J, FCLIP, Retired. [0006057] 09/07/1966 FE 26/09/1977

Guthrie Mrs AI, BSc(Econ)(Hons) MA(Hons), Learning Resource Mgr., Dumfries & Galloway Coll., Dumfries. [0052959] 05/02/1996

Guthrie Miss DH, MCLIP, Asst.Lib., Inst.of Educ.L., London Univ. [0006058] 09/11/1969

Guthrie Miss KE, MA(Hons), Stud., Univ.Coll.London. [0058969] 12/10/2000

Gutridge Mrs JN, (was Harding), MCLIP, Acquisitions Lib., Portsmouth City L. [0006308] 15/01/1971

Gutteridge Mr PJ, BA MSC MCLIP, Lib., The Stationery Off., London. [0034886] 27/03/1982

Gutteridge Mr SR, BA MCLIP, Asst.Lib., Biggleswade L., Beds.C.C. [0038602] 18/07/1985

Guttuso Mr F, Direttore, Biblioteca Comunale, Palermo, Italy. [0047154] 13/05/1992

Guy Ms HAC, (was Knight), MCLIP, Learning Opportunities Mgr., Tresham Inst.of F.& H.E., Northants. [0006064] 07/06/1966

Guy Mrs JE, (was Bullard), MCLIP, Asst.Lib./Catr.(P./t.), Salisbury Healthcare NHS Trust, Salisbury. [0020768] 02/07/1973

Guy Ms MI, (was Napier), BA, QA Focus/NOF & Digitise, UKOLN, Univ.of Bath. [0056015] 19/01/1998

Guy Miss MM, BA DipLib MCLIP, Coll.Lib.& Arch., RAF Coll., Cranwell. [0039877] 01/10/1986

Guy Mr NG, MA MCLIP, Employment unknown. [0060372] 11/12/2001

Guy Mr RF, BA MA MCLIP, Dir.of I.C.T. [0006070] 01/07/1971

Guyatt Miss EJ, BA FCLIP, Life Member. [0006071] 04/01/1950 FE 01/01/1954

Gwilliam Mr AB, MA MCLIP, Life Member. [0006073] 10/09/1955

Gwilliam Mrs SM, (was Lewis), BLS MCLIP, Lib., Lancing Coll., W.Sussex. [0030209] 05/12/1978

Gwilt Ms RV, BA MA p./t., Chaucer Bookshop, Canterbury. [0042924] 20/04/1989

Gwinn Mrs HE, (was Wilson), B LIB MCLIP, Inf.Offr., White & Bowker, Winchester. [0040757] 29/05/1987

Gwyer Ms R, (was Lound), BLib MSc MCLIP PGCert MILT, Assoc.Univ.Lib., Frewen L., Univ.of Portsmouth. [0027187] 12/01/1977

Gwynn-Jones Ms PA, BA DipLib MCLIP, Issue Desk Super., Imperial Coll., London. [0043765] 09/01/1990

Gwynne-Smith Miss DE, BA MCLIP, Unemployed. [0024691] 01/10/1975

Gyebi-Ababio Mr O, Dep.Lib., Wandsworth Prison. [0058944] 06/10/2000

Gynane Mrs CD, BA MCLIP, Coll.Lib., Hills Rd.Sixth Form Coll., Cambridge. [0021461] 18/10/1973

H Clark Miss RN, (was Hart), MA(Hons) DipILS, Sch.Lib., Hillpark Sec.Sch., Glasgow. [0058827] 18/08/2000

Haberer Miss IJ, MA FCLIP, Life Member, Flat 24E Four Limes, Garrard Way, Wheathampstead, Herts., AL4 8JN. [0016972] 26/02/1951 FE 01/01/1965

Habibi Ms K, BA(Hons) MA MCLIP, p./t.Lib., Croydon Cent.L., Surrey. [0053781] 01/10/1996

Hackett Mrs H, (was Murphy), BA(Hons) MSc MCLIP, Stud. [0041297] 28/10/1987

Hackett Miss JL, BA(Hons), Stud., UCE. [0059598] 26/06/2001

Hackett Mrs L, MSc MCLIP, Lib.(Child.& Sch.L.Serv.), Calderdale Leisure Serv., Cent.L.,Halifax. [0009895] 01/01/1970

Hacking Mrs E, (was Jones), MCLIP, Housewife. [0008005] 30/01/1969

Hadcroft Mr MM, MA MCLIP, Retired. [0006080] 01/01/1963

Hadden Miss MM, BA MCLIP, Young People's Serv.Lib., N.Ayrshire Council, Ayrshire. [0049661] 23/11/1993

Hadder Miss E, MCLIP, Retired. [0018738] 21/07/1941

Haddow Mrs L, BSc MSc MCLIP, p./t.Faculty Lib.-Natural Sci., Univ.of Stirling, Scotland. [0044217] 11/07/1990

Haddrell Ms R, BA(Hons) MSc, Stud., Leeds Met.Univ. [0055244] 08/09/1997

Hadley Mrs J, BEd(Hons) DipILM, Inf.Consultant, HM Customs & Excise. [0055689] 04/11/1997

Hadley Mrs JEM, (was Crawforth), FCLIP BSc, Life Member. [0006084] 17/09/1956 FE 01/01/1966

Hadlum Mrs P, BA(Hons), Stud./L.Asst., Univ.of Central Eng./, Warwickshire County Council. [0060863] 13/12/2001

Hadwick Mrs KE, (was Wiltshire), BA DipLib, Lib., HMP Highdown, Surrey C.C. [0034688] 25/01/1982
Hagan Mrs E, (was Lear), BA DipLib MCLIP, Head of L.Serv., Freshfields Bruckhaus Deringer, London. [0021894] 24/01/1974
Hagart Mr JM, MCLIP, Sen.Asst.Lib., York St. John Coll., York. [0006086] 25/08/1969
Hagberg Miss S, HNC HND, P./t.Stud.,Information Asst., CBI, Centre Point, London, Edinburgh Telford Coll. [0059673] 25/07/2001
Hagger Street Mrs EM, (was Hagger), BA(Hons) MCLIP, p./t.Learning Advisor, Southgate Coll., London. [0026023] 25/09/1967
Haggerty Ms MH, BA MCLIP, LRC Co-ordinator, Kincorth Acad., Aberdeen. [0020713] 29/05/1973
Hague Mr HR, MA MCLIP, Asst.Lib., Imperial Coll., Univ.of London. [0016974] 02/10/1969
Hague Miss MG, BA MCLIP, Youth Team Lib., S.E.Educ.& L.Board, Co.Down. [0030759] 18/04/1979
Haider Miss J, MAG PHil, Stud., City Univ. [0061717] 29/10/2002
Haigh Mr B, MLS MCLIP, Asst.City Lib., Derby City Council. [0006090] 02/01/1972
Haigh Mrs JI, BSc(Hons), L.Asst., Norfolk Health Auth.L., Norwich. [0057551] 26/04/1999 **AF**
Haigh Ms VA, BA(Hons), L.Asst., Univ.of Leeds, Brotherton L. [0055763] 17/11/1997
Haigh Mrs VC, (was Pittam), BA MCLIP, Ch.Lib., Salford Royal Hosp.NHS Trust, Hope Hosp. [0041451] 01/01/1988
Haines Miss CMC, MA BA BSc CBiol, Writer/Researcher/Abstractor. [0033238] 30/10/1980
Haines Mrs JM, (was Taylor), BLib DipM ACIM MCLIP, Head of Academic L.Serv., Academic Serv., Oxford Brookes Univ. [0024143] 24/03/1975
Haines Mr MJ, BSc MSc MCLIP, Asst.Law Lib., Barlow Lyde & Gilbert, London. [0052740] 30/11/1995
Haines Ms MPJ, (was Haines-Taylor), BA MLS, Acting Dir.of Knowledge Mgmt., NHS Modernisation Agency, London. [0043248] 09/10/1989
Haines Mrs N, MA(Hons), Inf.Prof., Rouse & Co.Internat., London. [0061138] 06/03/2002
Haines Mrs PG, (was Long), MCLIP, Hon.Lib., Sussex Archaeological Soc., Lewes. [0006103] 01/01/1950
Hair Mrs F, (was Kitchen), BA MA MCLIP, Sen.Asst.Catr., S.Tyneside Pub.L., Tyne & Wear. [0020292] 26/01/1973
Hair Ms FM, BA DipILM MCLIP, Asst.Lib., Sheppard-Worlock L., Liverpool Hope Univ.Coll. [0055160] 28/07/1997
Haiselden Mr GC, MCLIP, Area Res.Mgr., Surrey Co.L., N.W.Area Off. [0023339] 26/10/1974
Halcrow Mrs J, (was Wyatt), BA MCLIP, Retired. [0016392] 01/01/1963
Haldane Mr GC, BD MSc MCLIP, Health Studies Lib., Homerton Coll., Sch.of Health, Stud., Fulbourn, Cambs. [0034230] 12/10/1981
Haldane Mr JD, MA PhD MCLIP, H.Lib., Inst.of Ismaili Stud., London. [0038768] 01/01/1985
Halden-Pratt Mrs AJ, (was Halden), BA DipLIS, Lib., Essex L.Serv. [0046630] 28/11/1991
Haldon Mrs EM, (was Foote), BA MCLIP, Princ.Lib.-Reader Serv., Glos.C.C., Co.L.Arts & Mus.Serv. [0020930] 23/08/1973
Hale Mr A, BA MA DipLIS, Asst.Lib., Bodleian L., Univ.of Oxford. [0043078] 14/07/1989
Hale Mrs CJ, (was Michie), BA MCLIP, Resident in U.S.A. [0027545] 16/05/1977
Hale Mrs GP, (was Clapp), MEd MCLIP, Unemployed. [0006113] 22/09/1969
Hale Mrs HR, (was Barlow), BA MCLIP, Lib., Melbourn Village Coll., Cambs. [0024597] 01/10/1975
Hale Miss JM, BEd, Lib., Westminster C.C., Queens Park L. [0058141] 08/11/1999
Hale Mrs N, (was Walsh), BA(Hons), Subject Lib., Univ.of E.London, Barking. [0044925] 16/01/1991
Hale Mrs PC, BA DipLib MCLIP, Unemployed. [0024343] 05/06/1975
Hale Mr WA, MA, Early Printed Book Lib., Christ Church, Oxford. [0050339] 01/07/1994
Hale-Martin Ms HS, BA(Hons) BSc(Hons) PGDip MA, Inf.Asst., King's Coll., London. [0057795] 10/08/1999
Haley Miss MJ, BA MCLIP, Asst.Community Lib., E.Grp.Sheffield City L. [0006117] 01/01/1972
Halford Mrs EJ, (was Maybin), BSc DipLib MCLIP, Inf.Offr., Charles Taylor & Co.Ltd., London. [0027195] 28/01/1977
Halford Ms JA, (was Callagham), BA MCLIP, Retired. [0023664] 18/01/1975
Halfpenny Mrs K, (was Wisedale), BA(Hons), Unemployed. [0040132] 17/10/1986
Hall Mr ACL, MA MCLIP, Life Member. [0006118] 21/01/1959
Hall Mrs AJ, BSc, Stud., Univ.of Northumbria. [0058910] 03/02/2000
Hall Miss AJB, BA B MUS FCLIP, Head of Catg., Carleton Univ.L., Ottawa, Canada. [0016977] 07/03/1961 **FE 26/11/1997**
Hall Mrs AM, (was Mitchell), BA MCLIP, Unemployed. [0041789] 08/04/1988
Hall Mrs AM, BA Hons PGCE DipLIB MCLIP, Readers Adviser, Bolton Cent. L. [0038599] 28/07/1985
Hall Mrs AM, BA MCLIP, Unemployed. [0031310] 01/10/1979
Hall Mr AR, MA MCLIP, Dir., Book Industry Communication, Birmingham. [0006120] 01/09/1967
Hall Mr BM, MLS MCLIP, Sen.Lect., Sch.of Inf.Studies, Univ.of Cent.England in Birmingham. [0006124] 15/03/1960
Hall Miss BP, MCLIP, Team Lib., Southwark Bor.Council. [0006125] 16/01/1961
Hall Mr CA, MA MCLIP, Bibl.Serv.Lib., City of London L., Guildhall L. [0026398] 08/10/1976
Hall Mrs CA, (was Roberts), BA MCLIP, Young Peoples & Comm.Serv.Mgr., Herts. [0026797] 11/11/1976
Hall Mr CJD, BA DipLib MCLIP, Team Lib.(Ref.,Inf.& Local Stud.), Canterbury, Kent Arts & Ls. [0036347] 03/10/1983

Hall Mr CM, BA DipLib MCLIP, LRC Administrator, City Coll., Manchester. [0034081] 23/09/1981
Hall Ms D, BSc(Hons) DipIS MCLIP, Bus.Inf.Offr., Armstrong Craven, Manchester. [0050162] 18/04/1994
Hall Ms DM, BA DipLib MCLIP, Bibl.Serv.Lib., Powys L.Serv.H.Q., Llandrindod Wells. [0033219] 10/10/1980
Hall Ms DM, BA MBA MCLIP, Campus Learning Resources Mgr., Middx.Univ. [0006130] 13/09/1971
Hall Miss EA, Admin.Team Leader, Independent Combined Inf.Serv., Littlehampton. [0058504] 08/03/2000
Hall Miss EJ, DipLib MCLIP, Inf.Devel.Offr., Herts.C.C. [0037978] 01/01/1985
Hall Ms FE, BA(Hons) MA(Dist), Inf.Specialist, Aston Univ., Birmingham. [0058005] 12/10/1999
Hall Ms GE, (was Hooley), MCLIP, Learning Res.Offr., Oaklands Coll., St.Albans City Campus. [0006133] 01/01/1972
Hall Mr GL, MCLIP DipM MCIM, Acct.Dir., Prolog UK, Sudbury. [0006134] 20/09/1968
Hall Mr GW, BA DipLib MCLIP, Asst.Lib., Eastwood L., Notts.C.C. [0037813] 22/10/1984
Hall Ms HJR, BA(Hons) MA FCLIP, Sen.Lect., Napier Univ., Edinburgh. [0041231] 19/10/1987 **FE 01/04/2002**
Hall Miss J, BA DipLib MCLIP DMS, Cent.Ref.Lib., L.B.Richmond upon Thames. [0031311] 10/10/1979
Hall Mr J, BA MCLIP, Sen.Lect., Leeds Metro.Univ. [0006137] 11/10/1966
Hall Mr J, MCLIP, Catr., Hants.Co.L., Winchester. [0018347] 12/10/1972
Hall Mrs J, (was Wilkinson), MCLIP, Priority Serv.Mgr., Byker Br.L., Newcastle upon Tyne. [0022409] 06/05/1974
Hall Miss JB, MA MCLIP, Higher L.Exec., House of Commons L., London. [0016978] 01/01/1972
Hall Miss JC, BA DipLib MCLIP, Team Lib., Liverpool City Council. [0037068] 15/01/1984
Hall Mrs JC, (was Simpson), BA DipLib, p./t.Legal Practice Lib., John Collins & Partners, Swansea. [0041667] 11/02/1988
Hall Mrs JC, (was Smith), BA DipLIS, Unemployed. [0047072] 13/04/1992
Hall Ms JF, (was Elsey), BA MCLIP, H.of Ls.Arts & Inf., City of Sunderland, Sunderland. [0035208] 04/10/1982
Hall Miss JM, BLib MCLIP, Sen.Community Lib.(N.), Tameside Met.Bor. [0006141] 01/07/1971
Hall Mr JM, BA(Hons), Sen.Researcher, Warburg Dillon Read, London. [0038218] 02/02/1985
Hall Mr JTD, MA PhD, Univ.Lib., Univ.of Durham. [0042811] 02/03/1989
Hall Miss K, BA MCLIP, Sch.Lib., Chuter EDE Educ.Cent., S.Tyneside. [0026103] 12/07/1976
Hall Miss KM, BA MA, Asst.Lib., Dorset County Council. [0058028] 19/10/1999
Hall Dr L, BA PhD, Employment not known. [0060468] 11/12/2001
Hall Mrs LK, (was Woolgrove), BA DipLib MCLIP, Faculty Inf.Consultant, Univ.of Herts., Hatfield. [0043487] 30/10/1989
Hall Miss MA, BA MCLIP, Sen.Team Leader, (Stock & Reader Devel.), Warks.C.C., Rugby L. [0025039] 28/10/1975
Hall Miss ME, MCLIP, Retired. [0006148] 11/01/1944
Hall Dr MJL, BA(Mus) FCLIP PhD, Retired. [0006150] 01/01/1963 **FE 01/10/1975**
Hall Mrs ML, (was Iles), MCLIP, Learning Resource Asst., The Coll.of W.Anglia, Kings Lynn. [0007579] 05/09/1968
Hall Mr MR, BA MSc MCLIP, Employment unknown. [0060585] 11/12/2001
Hall Miss N, BSc(Hons), Media Mgr., Inf.& Arch.Dept., B.B.C. Manchester. [0056886] 12/10/1998
Hall Mr NTA, BEng, Stud., Univ.of Sheffield. [0058945] 06/10/2000
Hall Mr PF, BA(Hons) PGDipLIS, L.Serv.Mgr., E.Kent Hosp.NHS Trust, William Harvey Hosp., Ashford. [0053641] 16/08/1996
Hall Miss R, Sen.L.Asst., Bucks.C.C., Winslow L. [0018741] 18/09/1959
Hall Miss R, BA, p./t.Stud./Grad.Trainee-Catg., Loughborough Univ., Univ.of Nottingham. [0055800] 26/11/1997
Hall Mr R, BLib MCLIP, Inf.Mgr., Linklaters & Alliance, London. [0030953] 22/06/1979
Hall Mrs RA, MCLIP, Asst.Ref.Lib., Southport L., Sefton M.B.C. [0006155] 22/10/1970
Hall Mr RB, BA MA MCLIP, Mgr., Leeds Med.Inf., Leeds. [0041036] 01/10/1987
Hall Mr RE, LLB, Asst.Lib., City of Sunderland, City L.& Arts Cent., Sunderland. [0059004] 20/10/2000
Hall Ms RH, BA DipLIS, Mgr.ofInf.Resources & Marketing, Morrison & Foerster, London. [0050764] 17/10/1994
Hall Mr RJ, BA MCLIP, L.Serv.Devel.Mgr., L.B.of Wandsworth, W.Hill L. [0020518] 20/03/1973
Hall Ms RJ, BA(Hons), Sch.Lib., New Mills Sch.& 6th Form, High Peak. [0061411] 10/07/2002
Hall Miss RS, BA MA MCLIP, Subject Lib., Business Stud., Coventry Univ. [0028740] 16/01/1978
Hall Miss S, BA MCLIP, Sen.Inf.Mgr., Sport England, London. [0026105] 23/06/1976
Hall Mrs S, (was Chatwin), BA MCLIP, Subject & Learning Support Lib., Staffs.Univ., Beaconside, Stafford. [0031125] 09/09/1979
Hall Miss SA, BA(Hons) DipILS MCLIP, Asst.Lib., Manchester Met.Univ. [0053769] 18/05/1977
Hall Mrs SA, (was Wright), BLib BA MA PGCE MCLIP, [0027579] 18/05/1977
Hall Ms SA, BA, Inf.Mgr., Poulter Partners, [0044365] 10/10/1990
Hall Ms TM, BA MCLIP, Inf.Mgr., Nat.Family & Parenting Inst., London. [0035306] 12/10/1999
Hall Miss WM, BA(Hons) PGDipILM, Navigation Co-ordinator, Nat.L.for the Blind, Stockport. [0054871] 24/04/1997
Hallam Miss CM, BA MCLIP, Professional Asst., Music L., Nottingham P.L. [0006161] 01/10/1968
Hallam Ms PA, BSc DipLib MCLIP, Adult Serv.Lib., Northumberland C.C. [0035469] 14/10/1982

Personal Members — Handley

Hallam Miss RC, Grad.Trainee, Royal Holloway Univ.of London. [0061134] 07/03/2002
Hallam Ms SM, BA MSC, Employment not known. [0060173] 10/12/2001
Hallaways Mrs K, (was Goodman), BA MCLIP, Housewife. [0018185] 10/10/1972
Hallett Miss ANE, BA(Hons) MSc, Researcher, London. [0052213] 10/10/1995
Hallett Miss LA, BSc MSc MCLIP, Lib., Basildon L., Essex. [0044337] 20/09/1990
Hallett Mrs PA, MCLIP, Lib., Lord's Hill L., Southampton. [0006166] 11/01/1971
Hallewell Prof L, BA PhD FCLIP, Life Member. [0006167] 10/01/1950 FE 01/01/1959
Halliday Mrs A, (was Llewellyn), BA DipLIS MCLIP, Resources Mgr., Thurrock Council, Essex. [0046214] 16/01/1991
Halliday Ms HJ, (was Hussey), BA MCLIP, Support Serv.Mgr., Solihull M.B.C., Cent.L. [0028758] 27/01/1976
Halliday Ms L, MA MPhil, Employment unknown. [0060298] 10/12/2001
Halliday Mrs LE, (was Kendall), BA MCLIP, Promotions Lib., L.B.of Camden. [0027181] 02/02/1977
Halliday Mr MR, BA MCLIP, Life Member. [0006169] 23/08/1957
Halliday Ms S, BA(Hons) DipILM MCLIP, Asst.Lib., Herts.L. [0054120] 30/10/1996
Halligan Mr CF, MA DipLIP MCLIP, Lib., St.Lukes H.S., Barrhead. [0043489] 30/10/1989
Halligan Mr F, BA (Hons), Sen.Inf.Asst., Liverpool John Moores Univ., Liverpool. [0048347] 01/12/1992
Hallinan Mrs PS, (was Summers), MCLIP, Retired. [0023618] 16/01/1975
Hallissey Mrs AJ, (was Thomson-Graham), BA MA, Inf.Offr., Chartered Inst.of Marketing, Cookham, Berks. [0052237] 17/10/1995
Hallissey Mr MH, BA(Hons) DipLIS MCLIP, Asst.Lib., Law Comm.L., London. [0046623] 28/11/1991
Halliwell Mrs H, (was Allen), MCLIP, Database Mgr., Cambs.L. [0006171] 01/01/1962
Halliwell Mr PJ, MCLIP, Locality Mgr., Suffolk C.C. [0006173] 06/05/1964
Halls Mrs SJ, (was Blackburn), BA MCLIP, Lib., Legal L., Foreign & Commonwealth Off., London. [0001340] 15/03/1964
Hallworth Mrs A, (was Richardson), MCLIP, p./t.Asst.Lib., N.Yorks.Co.L. [0006176] 27/01/1967
Hallworth Mrs B, (was Dooley), BA MCLIP, p./t.Anciliary L.Asst., Priory Sch., Shrewsbury. [0004087] 18/01/1971
Halper Mrs SD, BA(Hons) PGDip, Intranet Editor, Ealing Council. [0058140] 08/11/1999
Halpern Miss JS, BA(Hons) DipLIS, Lib., Crumpsall L., Manchester City Council. [0055207] 12/08/1997
Halpin Mrs BM, Stud., Manchester Met.Univ. [0058325] 05/01/2000
Halpin Mr EF, MA MCLIP, Sen.Research Fellow, Cent.for Research in L.& Inf., Mgmt.., (CERLIM), MMU. [0055140] 23/07/1997
Halsall Ms JL, MSc MCLIP, Employment unknown. [0060373] 11/12/2001
Halse Mrs HA, (was Hughes), MA MCLIP, [0025315] 12/01/1976
Halsey Mr LA, FCLIP, Retired. [0006180] 11/03/1935 FE 01/01/1950
Halsey Mrs M, (was McBride), BA MCLIP, Career Break. [0031372] 15/10/1979
Halstead Mr JC, BSc MSc, Asst.Lib., Royal Soc.of Med., London. [0057141] 21/12/1998
Halstead Mrs MA, (was Rugman), BA(Hons) DipLib MCLIP, Lib., W.Cumberland Hosp., Whitehaven, Cumbria. [0019007] 01/10/1971
Halstead Ms SA, BA MCLIP, Sen.Lib.:Ref., Lancs.C.C., Burnley. [0025756] 22/02/1976
Halstead Mrs SJ, BA DipLib CertEd MCLIP DMS, Head of Learning Serv., Cornwall Coll., Camborne Pool Redruth Coll. [0034662] 22/01/1982
Halton Mrs VM, MCLIP, L.Inf.Serv.Mgr., N.Ireland Housing Executive, Belfast. [0034184] 15/10/1981
Hambidge Mrs FAM, (was Riddell), BA MCLIP, Business Inf.Specialist, Univ.of Bath in Swindon. [0035561] 25/10/1982
Hambleton Mrs JA, Sch.Lib.& Res.Mgr., Beverley Grammar Sch., E.Yorks. [0054879] 05/06/1997
Hamblett Miss E, MCLIP, Bibl.Serv.Lib., City of York. [0018251] 04/10/1972
Hamblin Mrs M, MCLIP, Lib., Castle Douglas L., Scotland. [0061395] 26/06/2002
Hamblin Mrs YC, BA(Hons) MA MCLIP, p./t.Lib., Notts.C.C. [0052402] 30/10/1995
Hambling Mrs LJ, BA(Hons), Asst.Lib., Haileybury Coll., Herts. [0054479] 24/12/1996 AF
Hambrook Ms KMP, BA DipLib MCLIP, A.V.Lib., Oxford Brookes Univ. [0037110] 09/02/1984
Hamer Miss EJ, MCLIP, Sch.L.Mgr., Bury P.L. [0006190] 07/09/1966
Hamer Ms KL, (was King), BA(Hons) MCLIP, Inf.& Learning Resources Mgr., Oakbank Sch., W.Yorkshire. [0046028] 06/09/1991
Hamer Mrs LS, (was Jones), MCLIP, Child.Lib., Bath Child.L., Bath & N.E.Somerset. [0021300] 16/10/1973
Hamerton Miss DM, BA MCLIP, Life Member. [0006192] 02/01/1946
Hamidah Mrs A, MCLIP, Lib., Nat.L.Board, Singapore. [0022754] 05/09/1974
Hamidah Arifin Mrs, MCLIP, Sen.Exec., Servs.Dept., Amanah Saham Nasional Berhad, Kuala Lumpur, West Malaysia. [0016550] 25/08/1971
Hamill-Stewart Ms NC, BA DipLib MCLIP, Relief L.Asst., Cambridgeshire Ls. [0042485] 23/11/1988
Hamilton Miss A, BA(Hons) MA MSc MCLIP, Legal Inf.Serv.Mgr., Inst.of Advanced Legal Studies, London. [0055717] 05/11/1997
Hamilton Miss AE, BA(Hons), Inf.Asst., Merighouse Learning Cent., Napier Univ. [0057726] 08/07/1999
Hamilton Mrs AF, (was Mccormick), MA MCLIP, Sen.L.Asst., City of York Council, Clifton L. [0026475] 08/10/1976
Hamilton Mrs AM, (was Cheyne), MCLIP, Freelance Editor. [0023129] 24/10/1974
Hamilton Miss CA, BA(Hons), L.Asst., Glasgow Univ.L. [0058161] 09/11/1999

Hamilton Mr CJ, MCLIP, Head of L.& Lifelong Learning, Wokingham Dist.Council, Berks. [0018746] 20/09/1972
Hamilton Miss D, MTH BA MCLIP, Life Member. [0016985] 27/09/1951
Hamilton Mr DRL, MCLIP, Higher Sci.Off.(Tech.Enquiries), Defence Research Inf.Cent., Glasgow. [0033723] 01/01/1967
Hamilton Mr GE, FCLIP, Life Member. [0006200] 14/09/1955 FE 01/04/1960
Hamilton Miss GW, BA MCLIP, Nat.L.of Scotland, Edinburgh. [0035235] 05/10/1982
Hamilton Mrs HL, (was Roskill), BA(Hons) MA MCLIP, f/t.Parent. [0052226] 16/01/1995
Hamilton Mr JA, MA PGDip, Unemployed. [0061626] 03/10/2002
Hamilton Mr JE, FCLIP, Retired. [0006203] 05/03/1963 FE 18/06/1976
Hamilton Miss KM, BA, Grad.Trainee, Univ.Coll.London. [0061337] 30/05/2002
Hamilton Miss MA, Retired. [0006208] 04/03/1947
Hamilton Ms MC, Sen.L.Asst., St.Charles Catholic Sixth Form Coll, London. [0059917] 02/11/2001 AF
Hamilton Miss MC, MA(Hons) DipLib MCLIP, Inf.Support Mgr., N.Lanarkshire Council, Motherwell. [0025040] 10/10/1975
Hamilton Mr PCW, BA(Hons) DipLib MCLIP, Asst.Lib., Off.of Fair Trading, London. [0032076] 11/02/1980
Hamilton Mrs VAM, PGDipLIS, Asst.Lib., The Godolphin & Latymer Sch., London. [0056574] 01/09/1998
Hamley Miss J, BA DipLib MCLIP, Law Lib., Univ.of the W.of England, Bristol. [0039582] 07/03/1986
Hamlyn Mr DH, MCLIP, Retired. [0006220] 11/10/1961
Hammersley Mr RN, BA(Hons), Customer Support Lib., Epixtech. [0040705] 01/05/1987
Hammerton Ms SL, MCLIP, P./t.Hosp.Lib., Nottingham City Council. [0006224] 05/04/1969
Hammett Mrs AM, BA(Hons) MA MCLIP, Lib., Essex L., Chelmsford. [0056781] 15/10/1998
Hammill Mrs SL, (was Dodd), BA MCLIP, Team Lib., L.Serv.for Educ., Gloucs. [0006226] 15/07/1967
Hammond Ms CA, BSc MSc, Asst.Lib., Coll.of Law, Guildford. [0046590] 20/11/1991
Hammond Mrs DC, (was Mitchell), BA MCLIP, Asst.Lib., Milton Keynes Council, Milton Keynes L. [0037450] 01/10/1984
Hammond Mr HI, OBE MIMgt FCLIP FRSA, Cultural Consultant, h2c2, Norfolk. [0006229] 15/02/1962 FE 16/04/1973
Hammond Mrs J, (was Inwood), MCLIP, Administrator, h2c2, Norfolk. [0006230] 11/06/1969
Hammond Miss KA, Stud., Brighton Univ. [0061048] 05/02/2002
Hammond Mrs KM, BSc MSc DipLib MCLIP, Life Member. [0006232] 30/01/1964
Hammond Miss LA, BA(Hons), Stud., Northumbria Univ. [0061681] 21/10/2002
Hammond Mrs MA, (was Holden), BA(Hons) PGCE MCLIP, Project Lib., Dudley Priority Health NHS Trust, W.Midlands. [0020227] 12/02/1973
Hammond Mr MP, BA MCLIP, Asst.Lib., Cent.for Inf.on Language Teaching, & Research (CILT), London. [0006236] 03/10/1964
Hammond Ms PM, BA(Hons) MA, Unemployed. [0052101] 02/10/1995
Hammond Mr PW, BA BSc MCLIP, Retired. [0028308] 10/11/1977
Hamner Mr PH, BA MCLIP, Sen.Lib.-Music & Arts, Hanley L., Stoke on Trent L's. [0020801] 05/07/1973
Hampson Mrs AM, (was Bradshaw), MCLIP, Unemployed. [0001611] 21/02/1968
Hampson Mrs EP, (was Steel), MA MCLIP, Unemployed. [0021283] 12/10/1973
Hampson Mrs H, (was Wragg), BSc(Hons) MA, Inf.Offr., Business Link Tyne & Wear, Sunderland. [0049986] 11/02/1994
Hampson Mr JP, BSc MSc MRPharmS MCLIP, Employment not known. [0060443] 11/12/2001
Hampson Mrs MJ, (was Garton), MCLIP, Head of Bibl.Serv., Co.L., W.Sussex C.C. [0005389] 01/07/1965
Hampton Mrs CE, Lib., BP Internat., Sunbury on Thames. [0042804] 20/02/1989 AF
Hampton Miss JA, MA BSc PGCE, p./t.Stud./IT Programme Mgr., Inland Revenue, Telford. [0061616] 03/10/2002
Hamza Mr D, BA MCLIP, Lib., Brit.Council L., Kano, Nigeria. [0055574] 21/10/1997
Hanafin Mrs S, BSc MCLIP, Inf.Offr., Action for Blind People, London. [0006244] 26/10/1971
Hanbidge Miss A, MA MCLIP, Retired. [0006245] 19/10/1969
Hanby Miss PM, BA MCLIP, Sub-Lib./Acquisitions Mgr., Reading Univ.L. [0006246] 15/09/1965
Hancock Mr DC, MCLIP, Coordinator, L.Res., London Bor.of Tower Hamlets, Limehouse L. [0016989] 02/02/1970
Hancock Mrs E, BA(Hons), p./t.Stud./L.Asst., Univ.North London, Harlesden L. [0059872] 29/10/2001
Hancock Mr EJ, BSc(Hons) MSc(Econ), Acquisitions Lib., Farnborough Coll.of Tech. [0058899] 02/10/2000
Hancock Miss FH, BA(Hons) Dip.Inf., Bus.Inf.Offr., Armstrong Craven Ltd. [0055327] 01/10/1997
Hancock Miss KM, MCLIP, Retired. [0006249] 01/09/1941
Hancock Miss RJ, BA, Employment not known. [0060494] 11/12/2001
Hancox Mr DG, BA, Sen.Lib., Educ.& Young People, Doncaster M.B.C. [0043798] 17/01/1990
Hancox Miss RL, Unemployed. [0058800] 01/08/2000
Hand Mrs JF, (was Richardson), BA(Hons) DipLib MCLIP, N.Area Mgr., Solihull P.L. [0039323] 14/01/1986
Handley Mr GD, BSc(Hons) MSc MCLIP, IT Adviser, Univ.of Derby. [0046350] 30/10/1991
Handley Mr J, BA MCLIP, Asst.Lib., Buckingham L. [0006256] 04/10/1971

255

Handley Mrs SL, (was North), BA MCLIP, Life Member, Tel.01323 720281, 42 Glendale Avenue, Eastbourne, E.Sussex, BN21 1UU. [0006259] 15/02/1950

Hands Miss CA, Sen.L.Asst.-Inf.Serv., Kenrick L., Univ.of Cent.England in Birmingham. [0045161] 31/07/1990 **AF**

Hands Miss SM, MCLIP, Retired. [0006260] 19/09/1955

Handy Mrs JA, (was Sinclair), MCLIP, L.Asst., Telford & Wrekin Council, Newport. [0021092] 03/10/1973

Handy Mrs SD, (was Rooke), BA DipLIS MCLIP, Systems Lib., Crawley Coll., W.Sussex. [0042771] 23/02/1989

Hanes Mrs SC, BA(Hons), Team Lib., Univ.of Northumbria, Newcastle. [0054251] 13/11/1996

Hanford Mrs A, (was Roberts), MCLIP, Life Member. [0006263] 09/09/1954

Hanford Miss J, BA(Hons) MSc MCLIP, LRC Mgr., Itchen Coll., Southampton. [0052000] 05/09/1995

Hania Miss HM, MA MEd MCLIP, Subject Lib., Glasgow Univ.L., Glasgow. [0026971] 14/01/1977

Hankin Mr A, BA DipLib MCLIP, Lib., Reading Bor.Ls., Reading Ref.L. [0041094] 09/01/1987

Hanlon Ms C, BA(Hons) MA(Econ) MCLIP, L.& Res.Mgr., HMP Whitemoor, Cambs. [0054642] 05/02/1997

Hanlon Mrs R, (was Warren), MCLIP, Retired. [0006268] 28/10/1965

Hanlon Mrs SM, (was Dean), BComm PGCE MA, Lect., Northumbria Univ. [0048119] 09/11/1992

Hann Mr W, BSc(Hons) MCLIP, Managing Editor, Free Pint Ltd., Ashford. [0061410] 10/07/2002

Hanna Mrs EE, (was Haire), BA, Sen.L.Asst., SELB. [0041155] 14/10/1987

Hannabuss Dr CS, PhD FCLIP ACIS, Lect., Sch.of Inf.& Media, The Robert Gordon Univ., Aberdeen. [0021311] 11/10/1973 **FE 18/01/1989**

Hannaford Mrs LE, (was Clark), BA(Hons) DipLib MCLIP, Subject Lib., Kent Inst.of Art & Design, Rochester. [0045785] 28/05/1991

Hannah Miss I, MCLIP, Retired. [0006272] 29/03/1970

Hannah Mrs J, (was Kelly), BA(Hons) DipILM MCLIP, Lib., Frodsham High Sch., Cheshire. [0050499] 22/08/1994

Hannah Mrs KA, MA (ILM), Website Administrator, Durham C.C. [0054188] 30/10/1996

Hannah Mrs PA, (was Lines), MCLIP, Community Lib., Fife Council. [0020993] 25/09/1973

Hannah Mr T, BA(Hons), Learning Cent.Facilitator, Swansea Coll.Learning Cent. [0061126] 19/02/2002

Hannahs Mrs SL, BS MA, Stud., Univ.of Northumbria at Newcastle. [0061168] 21/03/2002

Hannam Mr H, BA MCLIP, Retired, 35 Queens Avenue, Dorchester, Dorset, DT1 2EP. [0006272] 19/02/1949

Hanney Mrs JB, BSc MSc DIC MCLIP, Employment unknown. [0060375] 11/12/2001

Hanney Ms PG, BA(Hons) MA, Learning Support Lib., Staffordshire Univ. [0050117] 05/04/1994

Hannington Miss GP, MCLIP, Asst.Youth Serv.Mgr., Durham Learning Res., Durham C.C. [0023044] 14/10/1974

Hannington Mrs PE, (was Jackson), MCLIP, Law & Legal Inf.Lib.(Freelance), 64 Park House Gardens, E.Twickenham, Middx., TW1 2DE. [0017098] 28/09/1967

Hannon Mr MSM, MA DipLSc FRSA MCLIP, Dir.of L.Serv., Univ.of Sheffield. [0006277] 02/10/1969

Hannuell Mr DT, L.Asst./Driver, Bullsmoor L., Enfield Leisure Serv., Middx. [0047257] 26/06/1992 **AF**

Hanos Dr S, BA, Teacher of English - PhD Sch.Lib., Greek Ministry of Educ., Macedonia, Greece. [0043870] 02/02/1990

Hanrahan Miss FM, DipLib MCLIP, Co.Lib., Wexford C.C. [0025296] 14/01/1976

Hanrahan Mrs JBG, (was Dixon), MA MCLIP, Lib., H.M.P.Lincoln, Lincs.C.C. [0022918] 07/10/1974

Hans Mrs KA, (was Holloway), BSc(Hons) MA MCLIP, Sch.Lib., St.Martin-in-the-Fields High Sch., For Girls, London. [0051849] 13/07/1995

Hansell Mrs P, (was Hastings), MBA BA MCLIP, H.of Lifelong Learning, Blackpool Bor.Council. [0016216] 15/01/1966

Hansen M/s ME, (was Farmer), MA MLib MCLIP, Mgr.-Circulation & Customer Serv., Univ.of N.London. [0016993] 13/10/1965

Hansen Mr P, BA MA DipLib, Admin.Offr., Dept.for Work & Pensions, Newcastle Upon Tyne. [0053432] 13/06/1996

Hansford Ms R, BA(Hons) PGCE, p./t.Stud., City Univ., London. [0050881] 25/10/1994

Hansford Mr RJ, MCLIP, Inf.Lib., Hythe Br.L., Hants. [0027392] 05/02/1963

Hanson Mr DT, BA DipLib MCLIP, Lib., Bethnal Green Tech.Cent., London. [0022681] 11/08/1974

Hanson Miss KL, BA(Hons) PG Cert MCLIP, Sen.Lib., Dept.of Health, Leeds. [0040409] 04/02/1987

Hanson Mrs VAR, (was Sharman), MA MCLIP, [0019189] 17/08/1967

Haque Mr RS, BA(Hons) MA, Associate Dir., Bangladesh Friendship Educ.Society, Bangladesh. [0061525] 05/09/2002

Haque Mrs SW, BA(Hons), Asst.Lib., Denton Wilde Sapte, London. [0054845] 13/03/1997

Harahan Mrs JM, (was Boyce), MCLIP, Learning Res.Mgr., Mortimer Wilson Sch., Alfreton. [0001565] 19/03/1972

Haran Mr RA, BSc MPhil, Knowledge Agent, QinetiQ, Hants. [0061785] 07/11/2002

Harave Mr N, DipIM, Br.Lib., Wandsworth Bor.Council. [0055390] 09/10/1997

Harbin Mr DJ, BA LLB DipILM, Tech.Lib., Logica UK Ltd., Clifton, Nottingham. [0055211] 20/08/1997

Harbord Mrs EA, MA MCLIP, Sub-Lib., Univ.of York, J.B.Morrell L. [0026185] 09/08/1976

Harbord Mr PJ, MA MCLIP, H.of Inf.Serv., Stockton Campus, Univ.of Durham. [0024345] 13/07/1975

Harbour Mrs CM, (was Stevens), MCLIP, Employment not known. [0013981] 01/03/1968

Harbour Mrs GP, (was Hartley), BA MCLIP, Asst.Lib., Lancashire C.C., Lancs. [0026734] 19/11/1976

Harbour Mr RT, BSc(Hons) MCLIP, Sign Inf.Mgr., Royal Coll.of Physicians, of Edinburgh. [0018749] 01/01/1965

Harcup Mrs SE, (was Morgan), BA MCLIP, Retired. [0006290] 20/02/1962

Hardarson Mr HA, FCLIP, Chief Lib., Skyrrhf, Kopagovur P.L., Reykiavik. [0016896] 05/01/1970 **FE 27/07/1994**

Harden Mr RA, BA MCLIP, Retired. [0006293] 12/10/1967

Harden Mrs SK, BA MCLIP, Asst.Ch.Lib., (Lend.Serv.& Promotions), Richmond upon Thames L. [0020766] 23/06/1973

Hardenberg Mrs IH, (was Davies), MCLIP, Enquiries Mgr., Min.of Defence, Abbey Wood, Bristol. [0006294] 31/01/1916

Hardie Mrs K, BScEcon, P./t.Stud./Lib., Aberystyth Univ., Arbroath Pub.L. [0059740] 10/09/2001

Harding Mrs A, (was Rixon), BA(Hons), Lib., Brit.Sch.in the Netherlands, The Netherlands. [0040455] 09/02/1987

Harding Ms A, MA DipLib MCLIP, Self-Employed, Trainer & Lect., Supporting Child.& Young Peoples, Reading Devel.& L. [0030176] 15/01/1979

Harding Mrs AC, (was Moore), MA MSc MCLIP, Asst.Librarian, Ornithology & Rothschild L., Nat.Hist.Mus., Tring. [0035815] 11/01/1983

Harding Ms AR, BA(Hons) MLib MCLIP, Educ.Lib., Univ.of Wales Coll., Newport. [0048278] 20/11/1992

Harding Mr GL, MCLIP, Life Member, Tel:01892 870353. [0006304] 14/02/1947

Harding Ms J, MCLIP, Unemployed. [0006312] 12/02/1972

Harding Mrs JA, Position Unknown., Lackham Coll., Wilts. [0051625] 18/04/1995

Harding Miss L, BA MA MCLIP, Lib., Plymouth Coll.of Art & Design, Devon. [0026039] 01/07/1976

Harding Mrs MA, (was Fletcher), BA(Hons) MA(Dist), Sen.L.Asst., Univ.of Northumbria at Newcastle. [0047957] 28/10/1992

Harding Ms MJ, (was Grieve), MA(Hons) DipLib MCLIP, L.Asst., Open Univ., Milton Keynes. [0040238] 10/11/1986

Harding Mr R, (was Matthews), BA(Hons), Stud., Univ.Coll.London. [0058616] 13/04/2000

Harding Mrs R, (was Joughin), BA ALAA, Head of L.& Learning Res., Catholic Archdiocese of Birmingham. [0045906] 12/07/1991

Hardisty Mr JK, BA(Hons) DipIM, Electronic Gateways Offr., Nat.L.for the Blind, Stockport. [0056548] 17/08/1998

Hardman Miss LC, MSc MCLIP, Sen.Lib., ., L.B.of Hammersmith & Fulham, London. [0006316] 19/04/1971

Hardman Mr D, BSc(Econ), Inf.Offr., Blaenau Gwent L. [0059488] 09/04/2001

Hardwick Mr DH, MCLIP, Self Employed Consultant. [0006319] 27/01/1969

Hardwick Mr JR, BSc MCLIP, Position unknown, GlaxoSmithKline. [0060723] 12/12/2001

Hardwick Miss SE, BA DipLib MCLIP, Inf.Advisor, Univ.of Brighton, Eastbourne Dist.Gen.Hosp. [0034902] 01/04/1982

Hardy Mrs AD, (was Simon), MCLIP, Retired. [0025694] 12/02/1959

Hardy Mr AR, MA, Unemployed, [0059213] 25/09/2001

Hardy Mrs EA, BSc(Econ) DipLib MCLIP, Classroom Asst., Wigan M.B.C.-Educ.Dept. [0021025] 04/10/1973

Hardy Mr G, BA(Hons) PGDip, Asst.Lib., Royal Botanic Garden, Edinburgh. [0055867] 03/12/1997

Hardy Miss JE, MSc MCLIP, Life Member. [0006326] 28/09/1959

Hardy Miss JM, MCLIP, Unemployed. [0032368] 24/03/1980

Hardy Miss SJ, MBE FCLIP, Life Member. [0006331] 04/10/1935 **FE 01/01/1948**

Hardy Mrs SL, BA(Hons), Sen.Inf.Asst., Baker Tilly, London. [0061012] 08/02/2002

Hare Mrs CE, BA PGCE MCLIP, Sen.Lect., Univ.of Northumbria at Newcastle, Sch.of Inf.Studies. [0006333] 01/10/1971

Hare Mr G, OBE MCLIP, Retired. [0006335] 31/08/1954

Hare Mrs MM, (was Newman), MCLIP, Lib., St.Helena Hospice, Colchester, Essex. [0006336] 21/03/1958

Haresign Mrs C, BSc MSc, Sci.Lib., Chester Coll. [0054628] 06/02/1997

Hargest Mr GW, CertEd DipEd DipIS, p./t.Sch.Lib.-Inf.Mgmt. [0044431] 08/10/1990

Hargest Mrs S, Stud., Manchester Metro.Univ. [0061639] 07/10/2002

Hargis Mrs JM, (was Pickering), Coll.Mgr.-Flexible Learning, Newark & Sherwood Coll., Newark. [0043646] 17/11/1989

Hargrave Mrs IR, (was Podmore), MCLIP, Sch.Welfare Asst., Weymouth L. [0031687] 03/08/1978

Hargreave Ms D, (was Wilson), DIP AD DipLib MCLIP, p./t.Sch.Lib., Glyn Derw High Sch., Cardiff. [0028249] 17/10/1977

Hargreaves Ms CW, (was Davies), BA(Hons), Document Supply Lib., Coventry Univ. [0046737] 16/01/1992

Hargreaves Mr JA, BA FCLIP, Life Member, Tel.01234 356708. [0006347] 17/05/1941 **FE 01/01/1958**

Hargreaves Mrs SM, MA DipILS, L.Asst., Aberdeenshire L.I.S. [0057113] 09/12/1998

Harhoff Mrs W, (was Lucas), BA MCLIP, Lib.-Healthcare, Doncaster M.B.C., Patients L., Doncaster Royal Inf. [0009162] 01/04/1972

Hariff Miss S, BA(Hons) PGDip MCLIP, Comm.Lib., Bolton M.B.C. [0058273] 06/12/1999

Harker Mr ATL, BA(Hons) DipLib, Inf.Cent.Mgr., Defence Research Agency, Dunfermline. [0039097] 22/10/1985

Harket Mrs EJ, L.Asst., Orpington Coll.of F.E., The Walnuts, Kent. [0047079] 15/04/1992 **AF**

Harkett Mrs PJ, (was Burkett), BA MA MCLIP, Coll.Lib., Grantham Coll., Lincs.C.C. [0043927] 22/02/1990

Harkins Miss PC, BA(Hons) DipLis, Asst.Lib., Wellcome Trust, London. [0045395] 26/11/1990

Harkison Mrs JA, (was Gilbert), BSc DipLib MCLIP, Inf.Offr., RNID, Manchester. [0026964] 17/01/1977
Harland Mrs CM, (was Sutherland), MCLIP, Learning Res.Mgr.(S.), City & Islington Coll., London. [0006355] 08/01/1970
Harland Miss EA, BA MA DipLib MCLIP, Unemployed. [0032291] 06/03/1980
Harland Mrs HF, DipLib, Asst.Lib., Herefordshire L. [0018159] 10/10/1972
Harley Mrs CJ, (was Warne), MCLIP, No longer working in a L., At present working in an office. [0006359] 29/03/1961
Harley Mrs WB, (was Bryce), BA MCLIP, Retired. [0024312] 01/01/1952
Harling Mrs AM, LLB(Hons) MSc, Resource Based Learning Instructor, Calderdale Coll.of F.E., Halifax. [0048481] 21/01/1993
Harling Mr BSC, CertEd MCLIP, Life Member. [0006362] 05/03/1958
Harling Mr CS, BA MCLIP, Dist.Lib., Wilts.C.C., Salisbury. [0029570] 26/10/1978
Harling Miss PJ, BA MSc MCLIP, Temp., C.E.G.B., London. [0029971] 08/11/1978
Harman Mrs C, BSc(Econ) MCLIP, Floor Mgr., Univ.of Portsmouth. [0051590] 04/04/1995
Harman Mr CK, BA DipLib MCLIP, Asst.Lib., St.Annes Cent.L., Lancs.Co.L. [0039040] 27/10/1985
Harman Ms CL, BA(Hons) DipIM MCLIP, Position Unknown, Gloucester Royal NHS Trust. [0055782] 17/11/1997
Harman Ms CM, BSc MSc, Asst.Lib., Alsager Site L., Manchester Met.Univ. [0058900] 02/10/2000
Harman Lady EJ, (was Bridgeman), MA, Life Member. [0006363] 13/10/1959
Harman Miss PA, MA, Retired. [0047791] 19/10/1992
Harmer Mr HRH, MCLIP, Retired. [0006367] 26/03/1946
Harmer Miss NA, BA, Stud., London Metro. [0061790] 07/11/2002
Harnden Miss MJ, BA(Hons), Sen.Consultant, CAP Gemini UK plc., Woking. [0056407] 01/07/1998 **AF**
Harper Mr AC, BSc MBA DipLib MCLIP, Head of Reader Serv., Cambridge Univ.L. [0021802] 01/01/1974
Harper Mr ALS, BA MCLIP, Deputy Ref.Lib., Guildhall L., London. [0024949] 21/10/1975
Harper Ms AM, BA (Hons), L. Asst., Morecambe L. [0060884] 18/12/2001 **AF**
Harper Miss BE, BA MCLIP, Retired. [0006372] 01/01/1971
Harper Mr DM, BA MCLIP, Academic Inf.Co-ordinator, S.Devon Coll., Torquay. [0023498] 01/01/1975
Harper Mrs J, (was Trotter), BA Learning Resources Mgr., Barton Peveril Coll., Eastleigh, Hants. [0044352] 01/10/1990
Harper Mrs J, DipILS, Dept.Lib., Architecture & Bldg.Sci., Univ.of Strathclyde. [0054335] 21/11/1996
Harper Mr JL, BA MSc, Employment not known. [0060439] 11/12/2001
Harper Mrs P, (was Court), BA(Hons) MCLIP, Lending L., Hampshire C.C., Winchester Lending L. [0035609] 08/11/1982
Harper Mr WM, BA MA DipTEFLA PGCE, Reg.Inf.Co-ordinator, The Brit.Council, Rome, Italy. [0049333] 25/10/1993
Harridge Mrs JM, (was Harvey), BLib MCLIP, Local Studies Lib., Warwickshire Co.L., Leamington Spa. [0033758] 20/02/1981
Harries Ms FHE, BA L.& Learning Cent.Mgr., E.Surrey Coll., Redhill. [0041159] 09/10/1987
Harries Miss JM, BA FCLIP FSA, Life Member, Tel.01252 852762, 6 Orchard Ct., Church St., Goudall, Farnham, GU10 5QP. [0006386] 04/06/1935 **FE 01/01/1939**
Harries Mr K, BA MCLIP, Cent.Lend.L.Mgr., Blackpool with Darwen Council. [0006387] 24/02/1964
Harries Miss SM, BA MA DipLib MCLIP, Sch.Lib., Sch.of St.Helen & St.Katharine, Abingdon. [0037986] 01/01/1985
Harries Mr SP, BA DipLib MSC, Consultant, Inf.Architectures, E.Sussex. [0028825] 27/01/1978
Harrigan Mr PM, BD MTh PGCE(FE), Stud. [0052082] 26/09/1995
Harrington Mrs AB, (was Arguile), MCLIP, Retired. [0006390] 22/11/1940
Harrington Mrs BM, (was Doherty), BA MCLIP, Lib., The Latymer Sch., L.B.of Enfield. [0006393] 23/01/1968
Harrington Ms C, BA(Hons) DipLIS MCLIP, Comm.Support Worker p./t., Colchester Inst., Essex. [0054307] 20/11/1996
Harrington Dr CF, BSc MSc PhD FCLIP, Inf.Offr., Enterprise Ireland. [0060116] 07/12/2001 **FE 07/12/2001**
Harrington Ms EJ, BA MLib MCLIP, L.Mgr., Univ.of Westminster. [0006394] 01/01/1971
Harrington Mr JD, BA MA DipLib MCLIP, Inf.Serv.Mgr., Cranfield Univ., Bedford. [0035289] 08/10/1982
Harrington Mrs KA, (was Fowler), Res.Lib., Film & Video L., Dorset Co.Council. [0054134] 08/11/1985
Harris Mrs A, (was Vinson), BA(Hons) DipISM, Asst.lib., D.T.I., London. [0050512] 30/08/1994
Harris Miss AM, Sen.L.Asst., Univ.of Strathclyde, Ref.& Inf.Div., Andersonian L. [0049550] 09/11/1993
Harris Mrs AM, (was Luddy), BLib, Asst.Learning Cent.Mgr., Uxbridge Coll., Middx. [0033582] 21/01/1981
Harris Mrs B, (was Woolf), BSc(Hons) MSc, Self-employed, 22 The Birches, Bushey, Herts, WD23 4TW, (020)84204361. [0049204] 12/10/1993
Harris Miss C, BA MCLIP, Stud., Loughborough Univ. [0059766] 08/11/2001
Harris Miss CLJ, BA(Hons) MA, Temp., TFPL, London. [0059540] 01/05/2001
Harris Miss CR, BA MCLIP, Asst.Lib.(Music & Drama), Chesterfield L., Derbys. [0040558] 20/03/1987
Harris Mr CWJ, MCLIP, Stock Circulation Mgr., Bromley L. [0006400] 24/01/1967
Harris Mrs D, BA MSc MCLIP, Employment not known. [0061228] 18/04/2002
Harris Miss ED, BA(Hons) MCLIP, Head of Operations, City Univ.L., London. [0031317] 10/10/1979
Harris Mrs EJ, (was Patterson), BA MCLIP, P/t.L.Asst., Carryduff L., S.E.Educ.& L.Serv. [0018344] 10/10/1972

Harris Miss EL, BA MCLIP, Town Lib., Staffordshire C.C. [0030429] 25/01/1979
Harris Mrs EL, (was Sturips), Learning Resources Adviser p./t., Trinity Coll., Carmarthen. [0036925] 18/01/1984
Harris Mrs EM, BA LTCL DipILS MCLIP, Local Studies Lib., Argyll & Bute Council, L.H.Q., Dunoon. [0036706] 03/11/1983
Harris Mrs F, (was Waumsley), MCLIP, Sch.Lib., Ditcham Park Sch., Petersfield, Hants. [0006403] 07/02/1968
Harris Mr GA, BSocSci MPhil FCLIP, Consultant. [0006404] 25/06/1970 **FE 26/07/1995**
Harris Ms GR, MA MCLIP, Head of Sch.L.Serv., L.B.of Tower Hamlets. [0026404] 12/10/1976
Harris Mrs IF, (was Jones), MCLIP, Sch.Lib., Thurso High.Sch., Caithness. [0006406] 10/08/1964
Harris Mrs IM, MA DipLib MCLIP, Unemployed. [0033521] 16/01/1981
Harris Mrs JA, BA DipLib MCLIP, Site Lib., Bournemouth Univ. [0030838] 02/05/1979
Harris Mrs JBA, (was Mitchell), BSc DipLib MCLIP, Inf.Offr., The Moray Council, Elgin. [0029197] 29/03/1978
Harris Mr JK, MSc MCLIP, Inf.Specialist, PricewaterhouseCoopers, London. [0051418] 10/02/1995
Harris Miss JM, BA DipLib MCLIP, Reader Serv.Lib., Royal Coll.of Veterinary Surgeons, London. [0030178] 06/01/1979
Harris Mr JN, FCLIP, Life Member, Tel:01243 528704. [0006407] 01/01/1934 **FE 01/01/1946**
Harris Mrs JS, (was Gibson), MCLIP, Unemployed. [0006408] 01/01/1966
Harris Mrs JS, BA, L.& Inf.Asst., Nat.Maritime Mus., Greenwich. [0057875] 20/09/1999
Harris Mrs JS, (was Walls), MCLIP, Admin.Asst./Lib., Kent C.C., Maidstone. [0020093] 15/01/1973
Harris Mrs KJ, (was Stephens), Unemployed. [0056555] 18/08/1998
Harris Mrs KM, MCLIP, Lib., Shrewsbury L., Shropshire C.C. [0006410] 30/01/1970
Harris Mrs KR, MLS, Unemployed. [0061668] 16/10/2002
Harris Ms L, (was Jones), MCLIP, Comm.Lib.(Job-share), Bow L., L.B.of Tower Hamlets. [0051280] 19/12/1994
Harris Mrs LIP, (was Lea), MA DipILS MCLIP, Lib.-Bibl.Serv., Faculty of Advocates, Advocates L., Edinburgh. [0051280] 19/12/1994
Harris Mrs LK, MA DipLib ALAA, L.Mgr., The Queen Elizabeth Hosp.Campus, Woodville, Australia. [0040255] 16/11/1986
Harris Miss LM, MA MLib MCLIP, RSLP Project Co-ordinator:, Mapping the World, Map Room, Bodleian L., Univ.of Oxford. [0040291] 15/01/1987
Harris Mrs LM, BA(Hons) DipLIS, Lib., King Edward VI Sch.Handsworth, Birmingham, W.Midlands. [0050782] 18/10/1994
Harris Ms M, BA DipLib MCLIP, Sen.Lib., Dept.of Soc.Security, London. [0033536] 19/01/1981
Harris Mrs MA, (was Kilgallen), MCLIP, Unemployed. [0031876] 01/01/1980
Harris Mrs MA, (was Chambers), MCLIP, Inf.Lib., SLAIS., Somerset. [0033377] 01/11/1980
Harris Mrs ME, (was Tibbles), BA MCLIP, Asst.Lib., L.B.of Havering, Romford. [0014713] 04/02/1970
Harris Miss N, BA(Hons) MSc, Unemployed. [0055433] 13/10/1997
Harris Mr P, BSc CChem MRSC FCLIP, Employment unknown. [0060380] 11/12/2001 **FE 01/04/2002**
Harris Mrs PA, BA(Hons) MSc, Lib.& Head of Inf.Studies, Leeds Girls'High Sch. [0052403] 30/10/1995
Harris Mr R, MA DipLib MCLIP, Asst.Co.Lib.(Collections), Oxfordshire C.C., L.Support Serv., Holton. [0018095] 01/10/1972
Harris Miss RIC, MA(Hons) MSc, Dep.Lib., Theology Faculty L., Oxford. [0058690] 30/05/2000
Harris Miss RM, BA MCLIP, Life Member. [0006415] 07/02/1965
Harris Mr RS, BA(Hons) DipLib DMS MCLIP, Learning Co-ordinator, Bexley Coll., St.Joseph's Academy. [0043951] 06/03/1990
Harris Miss S, BA MCLIP, Self Employed as Inf.Broker/, Consultant, Herts. [0028311] 07/11/1977
Harris Mr S, MA(Hons) MSc MCLIP, Br.Mgr., W.Lothian Council, Livingstone, W.Lothian. [0051281] 19/12/1994
Harris Ms S, BA MA MCLIP, Employed outside LIS. [0039052] 30/10/1985
Harris Mrs SE, (was Turner), BLib MCLIP, Lib., Simon Balle Sch., Hertford. [0038909] 15/10/1985
Harris Mrs SJ, BA DSW PGCE, p./t.Stud./Learning Support Worker, Moray Coll., Elgin. [0061104] 22/02/2002
Harris Miss SM, MCLIP, Head of Learning Res., Highlands Coll., Jersey. [0020487] 13/03/1973
Harris Miss VJ, BA(Hons), L.Asst., Thanet Coll.L., Broadstairs, Kent. [0058750] 05/07/2000 **AF**
Harris Mr WN, BA(Hons), Asst.Lib., Sch.of Oriental & African Studies, London. [0050243] 12/05/1994
Harris Mrs Y, (was Lott), MCLIP, Area Mgr., Caerphilly Co.Bor.Council, Caerphilly L. [0009095] 28/09/1967
Harrison Dr A, PhD MA MCLIP, Retired. [0017002] 01/09/1953
Harrison Mrs AAM, (was Gilchrist), MCLIP, Cent.Support Serv.Mgr., Aberdeenshire L.& Inf.Serv., Oldmeldrum. [0005505] 06/10/1969
Harrison Mrs AC, (was Lavin), MCLIP, Life Member. [0006419] 08/03/1950
Harrison Mrs AE, BSc, Retired. [0041335] 03/11/1987
Harrison Mrs AJ, (was Barry), BA MCLIP, Curator-Hum.Ref.Serv., Brit.L., Reader Serv.& Coll.Dev., London. [0019576] 16/11/1972
Harrison Mr AP, BSc MCLIP, Employment not known. [0060212] 10/12/2001
Harrison Mrs AP, (was Sanders), BSc MSc MCLIP, Career Break. [0037875] 05/11/1984
Harrison Ms C, BA(Hons) MCLIP, Lend.Lib., Newport Cent.L. [0046857] 19/02/1992
Harrison Mrs CJ, BSc(Econ), Stud., Univ.of Wales, Aberystwyth, & Mobil L.Co-ordinator, Derbys.L.& Heritage, Matlock. [0058628] 18/04/2000
Harrison Mrs CJ, (was Andrews), BA MCLIP, Freelance Researcher. [0038582] 15/07/1985

257

Harrison Prof CT, FRSA MIMgt MCLIP, Life Member. [0006424] 01/09/1958
Harrison Mr D, MCLIP, Lib., N.Tyneside Cent.L. [0006426] 24/01/1972
Harrison Mr D, MA HonFCLIP FCLIP, Hon.Fellow, 3 Tower Gdns., Bearsted, Maidstone, ME14 4JG. [0006425] 07/01/1950 **FE 01/01/1954**
Harrison Mr DG, DipLib MCLIP, Lib., Essex C.C., Braintree. [0036596] 11/10/1983
Harrison Mrs EA, (was Ure), MA MCLIP, Locality Mgr., Suffolk L.& Heritage, St.Edmunds. [0015045] 09/10/1967
Harrison Ms EC, BA(Hons) MSc(Econ) MCLIP, L.Inf.Mgr., Barking & Havering Health Auth., Barking. [0055480] 17/10/1997
Harrison Mrs EJ, MCLIP, L.Network Mgr.-Staffing, Hounslow L.Network. [0029893] 01/01/1965
Harrison Mrs EN, (was Newton), MA(Lond), Peoples Network ICT Training Offr., Cheshire C.C., Macclesfield L. [0050622] 01/10/1994
Harrison Mrs FA, (was Bray), BA(Hons) MPhil, Comm.Serv.Lib., W.Berks.Council, Thatcham L. [0038090] 08/01/1985
Harrison Ms FC, BA MA, Retired. [0036176] 03/07/1983
Harrison Mr GVC, BSc MSC MCLIP, Coordinator Child.L.Serv., Whitechapel L., L.B.of Tower Hamlets. [0032292]03/03/1980
Harrison Mr I, Stud., Liverpool John Moores Univ. [0061724] 29/10/2002
Harrison Miss ID, (was Priestley), MA DipEd MCLIP, Acad.Liaison Lib., Univ.of Sheffield. [0024085] 01/04/1975
Harrison Miss J, MCLIP, Br.Lib., Whalley L., Lancashire Co.Council. [0006434] 02/01/1968
Harrison Mrs J, (was Howe), BA MCLIP, Inf.Consultant, Univ.of Herts., Hertford. [0007294] 01/01/1972
Harrison Ms J, L.Asst., Egerton Park Arts Coll. [0059305] 31/01/2001 **AF**
Harrison Mrs JA, (was Walker), BA MCLIP, p./t.L.Asst., Josiah Mason Coll., Birmingham. [0033454] 09/01/1981
Harrison Miss JE, BA DipLib MCLIP, Faculty Inf.Offr., Roehampton Univ.of Surrey. [0032743] 01/08/1980
Harrison Miss JE, BA(Hons), Stud., Univ.of Bristol. [0061733] 30/10/2002
Harrison Ms JK, BA DipLib MCLIP, Unemployed. [0006437] 06/01/1967
Harrison Mrs JM, L.Asst., Hants.C.C., Stubbington L. [0054186] 06/11/1996 **AF**
Harrison Miss K, BA(Hons), p./t.Stud./L.Administrator, Robert Gordon Univ., Aberdeen, Irwin Mitchell, Sheffield. [0059372] 21/02/2001
Harrison Mrs K, (was Ackroyd), BA DipLib MCLIP, Sen.Lib.-Ref.& Inf., Wakefield M.D.C., Balne Lane Ref.& Inf.L. [0039198] 06/01/1986
Harrison Mr KC, OBE FCLIP, Life Member, 01323 726 747. [0006440] 09/03/1932 **FE 01/01/1938**
Harrison Miss KJ, BA(Hons) MCLIP, Team Lib., Luton Bor.Council. [0051091] 14/11/1994
Harrison Mrs KJ, (was Meclurg), MA MCLIP, Lib., Tayside Primary Care NHS Trust, Carseview Cent., Dundee. [0006443] 01/01/1971
Harrison Miss LJ, BA(Hons) DipLib MCLIP, Unemployed. [0030760] 03/04/1979
Harrison Mrs MB, (was Tomkins), MCLIP, Deputy Area Lib., Wealden Grp., W.Sussex C.C. [0006447] 15/10/1962
Harrison Mrs MC, (was Fraser), MCLIP, Retired. [0006448] 01/05/1962
Harrison Mrs MM, (was Nicoll), MA MCLIP, Lib., Univ.of Strathclyde, Jordanhill Campus. [0010834] 03/04/1965
Harrison Dr NA, (was Hall), BSc PhD DipLib MCLIP, Inf.Sci., Atos Origin, Middlesbrough. [0041657] 09/02/1988
Harrison Miss PA, BA MCLIP, Lib., Wimbledon Sch.of Art. [0006452] 28/09/1962
Harrison Mr PA, BSc MSc, Electronic Serv.Mgr., Norfolk L.&Inf.Serv. [0045736] 09/05/1991
Harrison Mrs PH, (was Hilton), MCLIP, Life Member, Corbiere, Telham Lane, Battle, E.Sussex, TN33 0SN. [0006453] 11/03/1948
Harrison Mrs PM, MA BSc(Hons) PGCE MCLIP, Inf.Offr., Dementia N., Newcastle upon Tyne. [0051749] 16/06/1995
Harrison Miss REJ, BA(Hons), Sen.L.Asst., Imperial Coll.of Sci., Tech.& Med., London. [0055953] 19/12/1997
Harrison Mr RJ, BA MCLIP, Ref.& Inf.Serv.Mgr., Bristol City Council, Leisure Serv. [0028581] 20/01/1978
Harrison Mr S, MA MCLIP, Systems Mgr., Holmesglen Inst. of T.A.F.E., Australia. [0022724] 02/09/1974
Harrison Mrs S, Stud., Manchester Met.Univ., &, Med.Lib., Tameside & Glossop NHS, Trust, Ashton-U-Lyne. [0058450] 15/02/2000
Harrison Miss SA, BA(Hons) MSc(Econ) MCLIP, Inf.Researcher, Dept.of Trade & Industry., London. [0055424] 13/10/1997
Harrison Mrs SJ, (was Batters), BA DipLib MCLIP, Unemployed. [0040077] 17/10/1986
Harrison Miss SM, BA MCLIP, Sen.L.& Inf.Offr.-Cent.Grp., Newcastle L.& Inf.Serv. [0026405] 01/10/1976
Harrison Mrs SM, (was Pardoe), Lib., Postgrad.Cent., Warrington Hosp.NHS Trust. [0011207] 13/01/1968
Harriss Mr PD, BA DipLib MCLIP, Asst.Lib., City Business L. [0027679] 12/07/1977
Harrison Ms R, BA DipLib MCLIP, Unemployed. [0036853] 01/01/1984
Harrisson Ms WJ, BMUS(Hons)MA, Music Catr., BBC, London. [0057393] 03/03/1999
Harrity Mrs S, MBE BA BPhil, Cert.of Merit. [0050583] 22/09/1994
Harrop Mr P, BA DipLib MCLIP, Temp Catr., TUC L., London. [0035861] 03/02/1983
Harrop Ms S, BA(Hons) MSc, Asst. Subject Lib., Univ.Bristol, Inf.Services. [0051565] 01/04/1995
Harrow Mr AJ, MA DipLib MCLIP, Seeking paid emp. [0006461] 10/03/1958
Harry Miss K, BA DipLib MCLIP, Bibl.Serv.Lib., Coventry Univ. [0021130] 15/10/1973
Harry Mrs SA, BA, Stud., Thames Valley Univ. [0059788] 03/10/2001
Harston Miss KS, BA, Comm.Lib., Beverley L., E.Yorks. [0048122] 08/11/1992

Hart Miss AJ, BA DipLIS, Territory Mgr., ISI Thomson Scientific, Uxbridge. [0045334] 11/10/1990
Hart Mrs AM, (was Steward), BA MCLIP, Lib., The Philip Morant Sch., Colchester. [0024922] 07/10/1975
Hart Mr B, MCLIP, Life Member. [0006463] 21/03/1948
Hart Dr BA, BA PhD MA, L.Catr., Theatre Mus., London. [0054812] 08/04/1997
Hart Mrs CR, (was Macdonald), BA(Hons) DipLIS MCLIP, Lib., Airdrie Academy, N.Lanarkshire Council. [0045790] 31/05/1991
Hart Mr DR, MA MCLIP, Law Lib., The Univ.L., Dundee. [0028582] 28/12/1979
Hart Mrs EA, (was Wilson), BA DipLib FCLIP, Dir.of L.& Learning Res., Staffordshire Univ. [0024320] 02/01/1974 **FE 13/06/1990**
Hart Miss EM, BA MCLIP, Audio Visual Serv.Lib., Enfield P.L. [0006465] 26/09/1966
Hart Ms J, BA(Hons) DipILM, Asst.Lib., Manchester Met.Univ. [0056846] 26/10/1998
Hart Mrs JE, BA DipLib MCLIP, Unemployed. [0028312] 31/10/1977
Hart Mr RE, BA DipLib MCLIP, Asst.Lib., Lewisham L., L.B.of Lewisham. [0006472] 02/01/1969
Hart Ms S, BA(Hons) MA, Services Lib., Middlesex Univ. [0050375] 07/07/1994
Hart Mrs SM, (was Bevan), MCLIP, Relief L.Asst., Cumbria C.C., Maryport L. [0006475] 02/04/1965
Harte Mrs H, Stud., Manchester Metro.Univ. [0061802] 13/11/2002
Hartell Mrs RE, (was Narborough), BSc(Econ)(Hons), Asst.Lib., Home Office, London. [0053929] 11/10/1996
Hartland Mrs D, (was Taylor), BA(Hons) PGCE DipLib MCLIP MTh, p./t.Stud., Union Coll., Queens Univ.Belfast. [0042563] 05/01/1989
Hartland Miss HR, FCLIP, Retired. [0006481] 17/02/1931 **FE 01/01/1934**
Hartley Mr A, MA MCLIP, Retired. [0006483] 16/01/1968
Hartley Mrs BC, (was Gover), MA DipLib MCLIP, Lib., Gordonstoun Sch., Elgin. [0024584] 01/10/1975
Hartley Mrs BP, BA DIPLIS MCLIP, Retired. [0039628] 04/04/1986
Hartley Mr CD, BA(Hons) DipLIS MCLIP, L., Hull Grammar Sch. [0049395] 21/10/1993
Hartley Mr CM, MA FCLIP, Life Member. [0006486] 10/10/1946 **FE 01/01/1958**
Hartley Mrs DK, (was Stone), M LIB BA MCLIP, Bibl.Serv.Team Leader, Univ.of Wales, Aberystwyth, Aberystwyth. [0014086] 19/05/1971
Hartley Miss HM, Admin.Offr., Benefits Agency, Leeds. [0044769] 14/11/1990
Hartley Mrs JE, BScEcon(Hons) DipLib MCLIP, Div.Ref.Lib.(Job Share), Crewe L., Cheshire C.C. [0023106] 01/01/1974
Hartley Mr KJ, BSc MCLIP, Employment not known. [0060379] 11/12/2001
Hartley Mr RJ, BSc MLib FCLIP, Head, Dept.of Inf.& Communications, Manchester Metro.Univ. [0006495] 11/01/1972 **FE 01/04/2002**
Hartman Mr AMN, BA(Hons) DipLIS, Asst.Lib., City & Islington Coll., London. [0050011] 14/02/1994
Hartnall Mrs AM, (was Ryan), BLib DMS MCLIP, Unemployed. [0029087] 28/02/1978
Hartnoll Ms GA, MBE FCLIP, Life Member. [0006499] 14/01/1957 **FE 01/01/1963**
Hartridge Mrs AJ, (was Capon), MCLIP, L.Team Mgr.-N., S.Glos.Council. [0016732] 02/09/1964
Hartshorne Mr DI, BA DipLib MCLIP, H.of L., Yorkshire Post Newspapers, Leeds. [0039055] 31/10/1985
Hartshorne Mr S, BA(Hons) MA, Inf.& Lifelong Learning Lib., Bolton Met.Bor.Council, Cent.L. [0054464] 18/12/1996
Hartt Miss EM, MCLIP, Team Lib., Wokingham L., Wokingham Dist.Council. [0006500] 01/01/1971
Hartwell Miss J, BA(Hons) MSc, Sen.L.Asst., Coll.of Law, Birmingham. [0056829] 20/10/1998
Harty Mrs T, BSc MSc MCLIP, Sch.Lib., N.Lanarkshire Council, Clyde Valley High Sch. [0055882] 09/12/1997
Harvell Ms JL, BA(Hons) PGDipLib, Head of Inf./Playback Serv., Nat.Sound Arch., Brit.L., London. [0043729] 11/12/1989
Harvey Miss A, LLB, Lib., Swansea Inst.of H.E. [0037634] 14/10/1984
Harvey Mrs A, BA, Position unknown, St.Pauls Sch., London. [0061339] 30/05/2002 **AF**
Harvey Mrs AM, (was Izmidlian), BA(Hons), p./t.Med.L.Asst., Eastbourne Hosp.NHS Trust, E.Sussex. [0049407] 20/10/1993
Harvey Mr AP, MCLIP, Retired. [0020873] 07/08/1973
Harvey Mrs C, (was Brownhill), BA(Hons) MCLIP, Sen.Leader - Community, Warks.C.C., Dept.L.& Heritage, Rugby. [0049409] 14/10/1993
Harvey Mrs CHR, (was Simpson), MCLIP, Sen.Lib.-Business & Commerce, Cent.L., Bradford L. [0027121] 08/06/1970
Harvey Ms EMM, MA DipLib MCLIP, Unemployed. [0030181] 02/01/1979
Harvey Mrs G, (was Shepherd), MCLIP, Principal Lib., L.B.of Haringey, Cent.L., Wood Green. [0026550] 01/10/1976
Harvey Dr J, Chair, Sheffield Inf.Org.(SINTO). [0059435] 15/03/2001
Harvey Ms J, Lib.,Reader Devel., Brighton & Hove Council, Hove. [0055926] 10/12/1997
Harvey Mrs JA, (was Adam), MA DipLib MCLIP, Support Serv.Lib., E.Ayrshire Council. [0029897] 10/10/1978
Harvey Mrs JDM, (was Matthews), BSc(Hons) MCLIP, L.Asst., Foxhills Junior Sch., Southampton. [0022126] 21/02/1974
Harvey Dr JF, AB BSLS PhD MCLIP, Resident in Cyprus. [0060053] 07/12/2001
Harvey Miss JM, MA FCLIP, Life Member. [0006514] 24/02/1953 **FE 01/01/1965**
Harvey Mrs LA, (was Manley), BA(Hons) MCLIP, LRC Mgr., Stoke on Trent Coll., Staffs. [0046785] 23/01/1992
Harvey Miss MJ, B ED DLIS DMS MCLIP, Inf.Serv.Lib., City Univ., London. [0022889] 01/10/1974

Personal Members — Hayes

Harvey Mr N, BA(Hons) MCLIP, Acting Sen.Lib., L.B.of Haringey. [0059408] 05/03/2001
Harvey Miss PK, MCLIP, Cent.Ref.Lib., Plymouth City Council. [0006517] 02/03/1962
Harvey Mr PM, BA(Hons) MCLIP, Asst.Inf.Offr., Comm.Practitioners'&Hlth.Visitors, Assoc., London. [0055271] 11/09/1997
Harvey Mr RAM, MA MCLIP, Asst.Lib., Guildhall L., London. [0006518] 10/07/1967
Harvey Mrs RD, (was Hawke), MA MCLIP, Retired. [0006519] 29/08/1960
Harvey Miss SC, MA, Learning Cent.Co-ordinator, E.Berks.Coll., Langley. [0044327] 03/09/1990
Harvey Miss SL, BA(Hons), Stud., Loughborough Univ. [0059811] 10/10/2001
Harvey Mrs SM, (was Mccarthy), BA MCLIP, Lib., The Landscape Inst., London. [0006521] 22/01/1958
Harvey Mr TN, BA DipLib MCLIP, Inf.Offr., Clifford Chance LLP, London. [0028826] 16/01/1978
Harvey Mr WJ, (was Stephens), MCLIP, Community Lib.(Sch.), Lincs.C.C. [0013961] 15/08/1965
Harvey-Brown Mrs J, (was Snowden), MA MCLIP, Team Lib., Bracknell Forest. [0033349] 07/11/1980
Harvie Ms AJ, MCLIP, Lib., Business and Tech.Grp., Cent.L., Manchester. [0024278] 10/06/1975
Harwood Mrs CA, (was Jones), PGDipLib, Team Lib., Oxon.C.C., Cent.L. [0033006] 01/10/1980
Harwood Mrs J, P./t.Stud./Lib., Univ.Aberystwyth, Longridge High Sch., Preston. [0059641] 09/07/2001
Harwood Mr PR, BA DipLib MCLIP, Dir., Swets Blackwell Ltd., Abingdon. [0036889] 09/01/1984
Harwood Miss S, BLib(Hons) MLib MCLIP, Lib.& Inf.Offr., CancerBacup, London. [0043866] 30/01/1990
Has Mrs A, (was Dorman), DipLib MCLIP, Unemployed. [0030749] 03/04/1979
Hasan Ms B, MA(Hons), Asst.Lib., Instant Library, London. [0059254] 18/01/2001
Haselton Ms AE, BA DipLib MCLIP, Dep.Lib., Tavistock & Portman Library, London. [0036148] 04/07/1983
Hasker Mr LF, FCLIP, Retired. [0006528] 06/08/1931 FE 01/01/1946
Hasker Mr NA, LLB MCLIP, Lib., Legal L., Dept.of Trade & Ind. [0006529] 17/02/1969
Haskins Mr WT, BSc, Stud. [0059384] 27/02/2001
Haslam Miss A, BA DMS MCLIP, Lib., Devon C.C., Exeter. [0021985] 01/01/1974
Haslam Mrs SC, (was Adams), BA, p./t.Inf.Advisor, S.Bank Univ., London. [0042928] 24/04/1989
Haslem Mr J, MCLIP, Life Member, Oakwood Books, 37 Church St., Newent, Glos., GL18 1AA, 0531 821040. [0006535] 02/02/1950
Haslett Miss S, BA(Hons), Stud., Manchester Met.Univ. [0061206] 08/04/2002
Hassall Mr I, BA(Econ), Learning Support Offr., Staffs.Univ., Stoke on Trent. [0044636] 13/11/1990
Hassall Mrs S, (was Messenger), BA(Hons) Asst.Lib., Martineau Johnson Solicitors. [0055426] 13/10/1997
Hassan Ms S, BA(Hons) MA MCLIP, Area Lib., Attleborough Library. [0035717] 13/01/1983
Hasson Mr ARC, MA DipLib MBA MCLIP, Head of Cult.Serv., Scottish Borders Council, By Melrose. [0033950] 06/03/1981
Hastie Mr GA, Tech.Serv.Asst., Coutts L.Serv.UK, Ringwood. [0061407] 08/07/2002 SP
Hastie Mrs ME, (was Forsyth), MCLIP, Lib., Horndean Community Sch., Hants. [0005083] 18/01/1971
Hastie Mr PS, MCLIP, Lib., Ref.& Inf.Serv., Herts. [0019680] 15/10/1972
Hastings Mrs MR, BA(Hons) MCLIP, Dir., Infomasters Assoc., Sheffield. [0034237] 14/10/1981
Hatch Ms PJ, Lib., Physics L., Blackett Lab., Imperial Coll.of Sci.Tech.& Med. [0050425] 27/07/1994
Hatcher Mr DW, BSc DipLib MCLIP DMS, Area Lib., Kirklees M.C. [0030624] 05/03/1979
Hatcher Ms MEF, BA DipLib MCLIP, Asst.Area Lib., Bradford Met., Bradford. [0023745] 08/01/1975
Hateley Miss DM, BSc(Econ), Lib.(Generic), Warwickshire C.C. [0057732] 13/07/1999
Hatfield Mr IJ, BA MCLIP, Lib., Shropshire L. [0025832] 23/09/1968
Hathaway Ms HM, MA DipLib ILTM, Faculty Team Mgr., Sci., Univ.of Reading L. [0006542] 01/01/1972
Hatherley Mrs RCE, (was Starr), BEd(Hons) MLib MCLIP, Career Break. [0047743] 16/10/1992
Hatto Mrs SM, (was Hawker), BA MA MCLIP, Unemployed/Career Break. [0040149] 21/10/1986
Hatton Mrs JD, BA(Hons), P./t.Inf.Offr., Stretford L., Stretford, Manchester. [0056634] 25/09/1998
Hatton Mrs L, MCLIP, Sch.Lib., Maghull High Sch., Maghull, Merseyside. [0017009] 01/01/1964
Hatton Dr PHS, PhD MA DipLib MCLIP, Retired. [0024693] 07/10/1975
Haugh Miss JM, GRSM DipLib MCLIP, Retired. [0031319] 03/10/1979
Haugh Mr WS, BA DPA HonFCLIP FCLIP, Retired. [0006549] 10/03/1931 FE 01/01/1931
Haughney Ms K, MLS DLIS, Lib., Saudi Aramco, Exploration & Producing Inf.Cent. [0040553] 04/03/1987
Hauke Mrs ER, BA MCLIP, Inf.Devel.Offr., Herts.C.C. [0026912] 06/02/1976
Haule Mr LL, Sen.Lib., Bank of Tanzania, Dar Es Salaam. [0049261] 19/10/1993
Hauw Mrs SK, BA MCLIP MBA, Mgr., Competitive Intelligence Res.Cent., Kent Ridge Digital Labs.,Singapore. [0020950] 07/09/1973
Havard Miss EA, BA(Hons) MSc, Asst.Team Leader, Royal Military Coll.of Sci., Cranfield Univ. [0056075] 05/02/1998

Havard Mrs L, (was Bozarth), MLS, Employment not known. [0059808] 14/05/2001
Havergal Mrs VR, BA(Hons) MSc, Learning Cent.Mgr., Wilts.Coll., Trowbridge. [0051383] 01/02/1995
Haw Miss Z, BA(Hons) PGCE, p./t.Stud., Loughborough Univ., Ashby Gramm.Sch., Leics. [0060002] 20/11/2001
Haward Mrs J, (was Venables), MCLIP, Teacher - English, Teacher Training Coll., Czech Republic. [0006554] 29/01/1970
Hawes Mrs BM, BA, Curator, Brit.L., Scandinavian Dept. [0041123] 06/10/1987
Hawes Mrs BM, (was Norton), MCLIP, Life Member, Tel:01923 225086. [0006555] 12/05/1948
Hawes Mr DFW, MA FCLIP FRSA, Retired. [0006556] 03/03/1941 FE 01/01/1965
Hawes Mr JE, BA MCLIP, p./t.Lib., (Prison), Rochester/Cookham Wood/Maidstone, Medway Council. [0025982] 13/05/1976
Hawes Mr RA, BA DipLIS MCLIP, Team Lib., Housebound Readers, L.B.of Ealing. [0044138] 29/05/1990
Hawker Miss S, BSc(Hons) MSc, Inf.Advisor, Uni.of Wales (UWIC), Cardiff. [0055453] 13/10/1997
Hawkes Miss CEA, BA MCLIP, Retired. [0006563] 02/10/1946
Hawkes Mrs EA, (was Nicholson), MA MCLIP, Dep.Lib., Field Fisher Waterhouse, London. [0024778] 03/10/1975
Hawkin Mrs KE, (was Ainsworth), BA(Hons) MA PgD, Asst.Lib., Northumberland C.C., Hexham L. [0046427] 04/11/1991
Hawkins Mrs AC, (was Tolworthy), MCLIP CertEd, Life Member. [0014763] 01/01/1949
Hawkins Mrs AM, (was Hurley), BA DipLib MCLIP, Unemployed. [0033239] 29/10/1980
Hawkins Mr BJ, BA MCLIP, Comm.Serv.Lib., Isle of Wight Council. [0028434] 08/11/1977
Hawkins Ms E, BA MCLIP, Resident in Italy. [0060061] 07/12/2001
Hawkins Miss EJ, BA(Hons) Dip.Inf., Asst.Lib., Denton Wilde Sapte, London. [0056571] 01/09/1998
Hawkins Mrs JM, (was Barker), BA DipLib MCLIP, L.Asst., Winstanley Coll., Billinge, Lancs. [0035808] 17/01/1983
Hawkins Miss M, BLib MSc MCLIP, Project Mgr., Instant L.Ltd., Loughborough. [0026109] 01/07/1976
Hawkins Mrs RE, (was Evans), MCLIP, Lib., Alton L., Hants.Co.L. [0006572] 16/02/1967
Hawkins Mrs SK, (was Robinson), BLib MCLIP, L.Super., Brynmill Primary Sch., Swansea. [0012589] 14/06/1972
Hawkridge Mrs KM, (was Storr), MCLIP, Life Member. [0006573] 08/03/1941
Hawksworth Mr DM, BA DipLib MCLIP, Academic Serv.Lib., Bradford Coll. [0042192] 11/10/1988
Hawksworth Mrs V, Stud., Univ.of N.London. [0054086] 24/10/1996
Hawkyard Mrs LA, Asst.Lib., Walker Morris, Leeds. [0056126] 03/03/1998
Hawley Mr GJ, MSc PgDipInf., Temp., Reed Recruitment, Edinburgh. [0059448] 30/03/2001
Hawley Mrs GM, BA MA MCLIP, Lib. [0026110] 24/05/1976
Haworth Mr AL, BA(Hons) MSc, L.& Inf.Mgr., Skanska Construction Grp., Maple Cross. [0056656] 01/10/1998
Haworth Ms J, BA(Hons), Stud., Univ.Coll.Northampton. [0061208] 08/04/2002
Haworth Mr JH, MA MCLIP, Asst.Site Lib., L.B.of Hackney. [0032974] 01/10/1980
Haworth Ms SC, BSc MA MCLIP, Lib., Paint Res.Assoc., Middx. [0006580] 01/01/1972
Hawthorne Mrs C, (was Headley), BA, Learndirect Product Devel.Offr., City of Sunderland Coll., Tyne & Wear. [0056079] 12/02/1998
Hay Ms KJ, DipLib MCLIP, Unemployed. [0039267] 14/01/1986
Hay Mr L, BA(Hons), Employment unknown. [0060304] 10/12/2001
Hay Miss SJ, BA(Hons), Asst.Lib., Allen & Overy, London. [0056697] 05/10/1998
Hayball Miss SR, BA MCLIP, Inf.Lib., (Nuneaton L.), Warwickshire C.C. [0020613] 30/04/1973
Haycraft Miss AC, BA(Hons) DASP MA, Lib., Surrey Performing Arts L., Dorking. [0052387] 26/10/1995
Haydock Mr I, MCLIP, Electronic Inf.Systems Mgr., Staffs.Univ., Stoke on Trent. [0040488] 12/02/1987
Haydock Mrs S, (was Glover), MCLIP, Coll.Lib., Southport Coll., Merseyside. [0006590] 21/02/1966
Haydon Ms SV, BA, 'Health Shop' Mgr., Lambeth,Southwark & Lewisham Hlth., Auth., London. [0052387] 26/05/1998
Hayes Ms A, BA(Hons) PGDip MCLIP, Subject Lib.(Art & Design), Coventry Univ., Lanchester L. [0031856] 10/01/1980
Hayes Ms B, BA(Hons) MSc DipILM MCLIP, Clinical Studies Facilitator, Warrington Comm.Health Care Trust, Cheshire. [0054004] 17/10/1996
Hayes Miss BE, BA MCLIP, Sch.Lib., English Speaking Sch., Dubai, U.A.E. [0028827] 03/02/1978
Hayes Mrs CA, BA MCLIP, Unemployed. [0006593] 01/01/1970
Hayes Mr DA, BA DipLib MCLIP, Princ.Systems Lib., L.B.of Camden, Holborn L. [0006594] 03/10/1971
Hayes Mr DC, BA(Hons) DipLib, Assoc.Lib., Mayday Healthcare NHS Trust, Thornton Heath, Surrey. [0036143] 01/07/1983
Hayes Mr DP, MA PhD, Lib., The Library, Canada House, Trafalgar Square. [0059754] 17/09/2001
Hayes Ms J, (was Bullock), MCLIP, Stock Mgr., L.Support Unit, Swindon Bor.Council. [0023514] 01/01/1975
Hayes Mrs JA, p./t.L.Asst., Shirebrook L., Derbys. [0061245] 22/04/2002 AF
Hayes Mr JR, BSc(Hons), Ref.I.C.A., SPICE, Scottish Parliament. [0054781] 01/04/1997
Hayes Miss KV, BA(Hons), Stud., Sheffield Univ. [0061786] 07/11/2002

Hayes Mr MA, DipLib MCLIP, Princ.Lib. (Local Stud.), W.Sussex Co.Council, Chichester. [0033299]   27/10/1980
Hayes Mrs MA, (was Hewitt), MCLIP, Lib., Wilts.NHS Consortium, Devizes. [0018758]   15/01/1967
Hayes Mrs RE, (was Gait), BA MCLIP, Lib., Centre for Policy on Ageing. [0005292]   05/10/1971
Hayet MS M, MCLIP, Employment not known. [0060148]   10/12/2001
Haygarth-Jackson Miss A, OBE MSc CChem FRSC HonFCLIP, Hon Fellow. [0060589]   11/12/2001   **FE 01/04/2002**
Hayhurst Mr GL, BA FCLIP, Life Member. [0006600]   05/01/1954 **FE 01/01/1960**
Hayler Mr DG, MCLIP, Inf.Lib., Chichester, W.Sussex C.C. [0027239] 17/03/1965
Hayler Mr WEF, MCLIP, Retired. [0006604]   01/01/1950
Hayles Miss JM, BA MCLIP, Asst.L.Mgr., Queen Mary, Univ.of London. [0025302]   13/01/1976
Hayley Mrs C, (was Renwick), BLib MCLIP, p./t.Inf.Offr., BECTa, Coventry. [0033695]   04/02/1981
Haylock Mr JR, BA MCLIP, Asst.Co.Lib., Hants.Co.L. [0023255]   01/01/1967
Haylock Mrs L, (was Mycock), BA(Hons) MSc, Unemployed. [0036845] 08/01/1984
Hayne Mr JM, BA, Teacher, Via Gola 16/4, 20143 Milano. [0038991] 25/10/1985
Haynes Mr D, MSc FCLIP, Head of Consultancy, CILIP, London. [0033404] 24/11/1980   **FE 01/04/2002**
Haynes Ms EC, BA DipLib, Lib., Metro.Police Serv., London. [0044464] 10/10/1990
Haynes Miss EM, BSc MCLIP, Asst.Lib., U.K.A.E.R.E., Harwell. [0006606] 13/09/1969
Haynes Mrs G, (was Widdowson), MCLIP, Lib.-Corp.Serv., Cultural Serv., Worcs.C.C. [0015802]   01/04/1966
Haynes Mrs HM, MCLIP, Ref.Lib.(Job Share), Rochdale M.B.C. [0035005] 01/01/1959
Haynes Mrs NJC, (was Hunt), BA(Hons) MCLIP, Unemployed. [0046324] 28/10/1991
Haysman Miss WF, MSc BH MCLIP, Mgr.Resources, Southend on sea Bor.Ls. [0006607]   26/08/1969
Haysom Mrs D, (was McGerty), BA MCLIP, Academic Liaison Lib., Univ.of Luton. [0033869]   07/04/1981
Hayter Mrs SA, BA(Hons) MA, Stud., Univ.of Northumbria, Newcastle upon Tyne. [0055884]   09/12/1997
Haythornthwaite Prof JA, BA PhD FCLIP, Retired, Flat 2, 59 Queensborough Gdns., Hyndland, G12 9TT. [0006608]   01/01/1957 **FE 01/01/1964**
Hayton Mrs AC, (was Jackson), BA MCLIP, Team Lib.(Young peoples Serv.), Kent Arts & L., Sevenoaks, Kent. [0037839]   31/10/1984
Hayton Miss JA, BA MCLIP, Music Lib., Lancaster L., Preston. [0023485] 01/01/1975
Hayward Mrs CJ, p./t.Stud./L.Asst., Univ.of Wales, Aberystwyth, Strood L., Kent. [0061679]   17/10/2002
Hayward Mrs D, BSc(Hons) MCLIP, Asst.Lib., De Montfort Univ., Leicester. [0045464]   14/02/1991
Hayward Mr DL, BA MCLIP, Team Lib., Coventry City Council. [0036203] 16/07/1983
Hayward Ms EJ, BA(Hons) DipInf, Lib., Nottingham Evening Post. [0050643] 06/10/1994
Hayward Mrs GEM, (was Magee), MCLIP, Adult Lend.Lib., W.Berks.Council, Newbury L. [0006605]   14/04/1967
Hayward Mr K, BA MCLIP, Lib., Cent.Ref.L., Hants.C.C. [0006614] 24/01/1965
Hayward Mr PG, MCLIP, Life Member. [0006618]   17/09/1952
Hayward Mr TE, BA(Hons) MA MLib, Stud., Dept.of Inf.& L.Studies, Univ.Coll.Wales. [0048895]   13/07/1993
Hayward Ms VA, BA(Hons) MCLIP, Keeper of The L., The Hon.Soc.of The Middle Temple, London. [0040747]   29/05/1987
Haywood Mr EJ, MCLIP, Life Member. [0006621]   28/03/1941
Haywood Miss G, BA MCLIP, Lib., Thames Water, Reading. [0030764] 23/04/1979
Haywood Mr GC, MCLIP, Lib., Tynwald L., Isle of Man Govt. [0021854] 14/02/1974
Haywood Mrs KJS, (was Allen), Unemployed. [0045928]   15/07/1991 **AF**
Haywood Mrs RJ, (was Barker), BA MCLIP, Sch.Lib., Henry Mellish Sch., Nottingham. [0024596]   08/10/1975
Hayworth Mr PH, MCLIP, Retired. [0006628]   01/01/1952
Hayworth Mr RA, MA MPhil DipILS MCLIP, Asst.Lib., The Robert Gordon Univ., Aberdeen. [0055985]   08/01/1998
Hazel Ms JC, BA(Hons) MA LIS, p./t.L.Asst., Birkbeck, London. [0056647] 01/10/1998
Hazeldine Miss AE, Data/Inf.Processor, Northern Connectors Ltd.,., St.Helens. [0056989]18/11/1998
Hazelgrove Mr RA, BSc(Hons), Researcher/Classifier, Bardour Index, Berks. [0054119]   30/10/1996
Hazell Miss JL, CertEd BEd MSc MCLIP, Comm.Inf.Mgr., Kirkless Cult.Servs., Huddersfield. [0052309]   23/10/1995
Hazell Ms K, LLB(Hons) MSc, Inf.Offr., Clifford Chance. [0054976] 09/06/1997
Hazell Mr R, BSc MCLIP, Sen.Lib.(Business), Peterborough Cent.L., Peterborough City Council. [0006629]   01/07/1972
Hazell Mrs VA, (was Sharp), DipLib MCLIP, Sch.Lib., St Michael's R.C.Sch., Bermondsey. [0037140]   08/08/1961
Hazlehurst Mrs J, (was Saunders), MCLIP, Unemployed. [0017012] 15/02/1962
Hazlewood Mrs CA, (was Field), BA(Hons) DipLib MCLIP, Lib., Haybridge High Sch.& Sixth Form, Hagley, Worcs. [0029168]   11/03/1978

Hazlewood Mrs M, (was Clarke), BA(Hons) MA, Lansdowne Site Lib., Bournemouth & Poole Coll.of F.E., Bournemouth. [0051456] 27/02/1995
Hazzard Ms C, (was Townley), BSc(Hons) MA, Resident in Canada. [0055164]   28/07/1997
Hazzelby Mr GW, BA(Hons) MLib, L.Mgr., Home Off., London. [0049285] 20/10/1993
He Miss C, MSc, Stud., Grad.Sch.of Educ., Univ.of Bristol. [0061535] 16/09/2002
Head Mrs AD, (was Sadler), DipLib MCLIP, Sch.Lib., Thurleston High Sch., Ipswich. [0032170]   06/01/1980
Head Mrs AL, (was Pearl), MCLIP, Trust Lib., Newham Healthcare NHS Trust, Newham Dist.Gen.Hosp. [0006631]   13/03/1967
Head Mr MC, BA MA MCLIP, Retired. [0006633]   05/03/1965
Head Mr PA, FRSA MCLIP, Unemployed, 4 Grange Ave., Manchester, M19 2GD. [0006634]   01/01/1963
Head Mrs SR, (was Wyatt), MCLIP, Life Member. [0006636]   06/03/1950
Headden Ms GM, BA DipLib MCLIP PGDipAIM, p./t.Inf.Asst., Napier Univ., Edinburgh. [0035075]   30/06/1982
Headford Mrs JE, MA BA MCLIP, Life Member. [0021048]   30/09/1973
Heads Mrs LM, (was Ledger), BA MCLIP, Asst.Lib., Hull Coll. [0031540] 24/10/1979
Heal Miss D, BA(Hons), Asst.Lib., Barnet Council, Hendon L. [0057729] 13/07/1999
Heald Miss J, BSc(Hons) MSc, Database Mgr., Univ.of Reading, Berks. [0053738]   20/09/1996
Heald Mrs MD, (was Smart), MA DipLib MCLIP, Unemployed. [0031702] 01/11/1979
Heale Mrs SP, (was Lawler), BSc MA MCLIP, Faculty Inf.Consultant, Univ.of Herts., Hatfield. [0047579]   02/10/1992
Healey Miss AE, BA MCLIP, Retired. [0006641]   07/10/1954
Healey Ms JM, BA DPS, Stud. [0061506]   30/08/2002
Healey Miss NFL, BA(Hons), Stud., Univ.of Wales, Aberystwyth. [0059578] 05/06/2001
Healey Miss S, MCLIP, Comm.Serv.Lib., N.Area, Atherstone L., Warks.C.C. [0006643]   18/09/1963
Healy Mrs EM, (was Brown), BA MCLIP, Housebound/Mob.Co-ordinator, Glasgow City L. [0029598]   01/10/1978
Healy Mrs RA, (was Hardwick), BA(Hons) DipIM, Asst.Lib., House of Lords L., London. [0050560]   16/09/1994
Heane Mr CC, BA MCLIP, Electronic Serv.Mgr., Northumberland Co.L., Hexham. [0023793]   04/02/1975
Heaney Ms DJ, BA(Hons) MA MCLIP, Knowledge Mgmnt.Programme Offr., Offr., WWF-UK., Godalming, Surrey. [0044482]   12/10/1990
Heaney Mr M, MA FCLIP, Head of Serv.Assessment & Planning, Planning & Provision, Univ.L.Serv., Univ.of Oxford. [0022383]   08/04/1974 **FE 15/03/2000**
Heaney Mrs ME, BA DipLib FRSA MCLIP, Manager,L.Serv., B.B.C.Scotland, Glasgow. [0029174]   17/04/1978
Heap Ms AM, BA MCLIP, Internet Copyright Res. [0036380]   03/10/1983
Heap Miss BJ, BA MCLIP, Sen.Lib., Res.& Serv.Devel., Bradford L. [0026407] 01/10/1976
Heap Mrs PA, (was Daunt), BA MCLIP, Head of Child.Yth.& Educ.Serv., Birmingham L.Serv., Cent.L. [0020319]   01/03/1973
Heaps Mr DJ, BA(Hons)DipLib MCLIP, Princ.Lib.- Community, Warwickshire C.C., Warwick. [0026111]   01/07/1976
Hearn Mrs AA, BA DipILS, Legal Lib., Instant L., TotalFina Elf, Aberdeen. [0057520]   16/04/1999
Hearn Mr C, Stud., Univ.of Wales, Aberystwyth. [0058921]   04/10/2000
Hearn Mrs CE, BA(Hons) DipInf MCLIP, Head of L.Serv., Irwin Mitchell Solicitors, Sheffield. [0054411]   09/01/1991
Hearn Mr NJ, MA MLib MCLIP DipTrans, Asst.Lib., Taylor Inst.L., Univ.of Oxford. [0058156]   01/04/1995
Hearne Mrs Z, (was Laxton), BA(Hons) MCLIP, Retired. [0006658] 01/01/1963
Heaster Miss SC, MA MCLIP, Asst.Lib., Univ.of Nottingham. [0024497] 28/08/1975
Heath Mr AJ, BA MCLIP, Retired. [0006660]   29/01/1955
Heath Mrs CS, (was Sheavyn), BA MCLIP, Asst.Lib., Croydon Coll. [0028678] 14/12/1977
Heath Mrs GM, (was Short), BA MCLIP, Inf.Offr., Help the Aged. [0029824] 17/10/1978
Heath Ms JP, BA DipLib, Market Research Asst., Bain Clarkson Ltd., London. [0031070]   26/07/1979
Heath Miss M, MCLIP, Retired. [0006663]   04/01/1954
Heath Mrs MS, (was Hayes), PGCE BA MCLIP, Accredited Indexer, Soc.of Indexers. [0006658]   01/01/1972
Heath Mr NFH, BA, Catr., Kingsway Coll., London. [0041149]   14/10/1987
Heath Mrs NL, (was Strickland), BA(Hons), Sch.Lib., Marple Hall Sch., Marple, Stockport, Cheshire. [0057503]   12/04/1999
Heath Ms RB, MCLIP, Life Member. [0006664]   20/03/1952
Heath Ms SP, BA(Hons), Lib., S.E.E.R.A.D., Marine Lab.L.-Aberdeen. [0040345]   23/01/1987
Heathcote Mrs A, BSc(Hons) MCLIP, Learning Res.Lib., Leicester Coll. [0049892]   07/01/1994
Heathcote Mr DA, BA MCLIP, Univ.Lib., Univ.of Greenwich, London. [0006668]   01/01/1963
Heathcote Miss HA, BSc, Asst.Lib., Food Standards Agency, London. [0046507]   14/11/1991
Heather Mrs RM, (was Verrall), BA(Hons) MA, p./t.Asst.Lib., CIP, Centrespace, Hounslow. [0050490]   29/07/1994
Heatley Miss NL, BA DipLib MCLIP, Sunday Serv.Offr., Hartlepool Borough Council, Cent.L. [0041497]   12/01/1988
Heatlie Miss DC, BA, Lib., Univ.Coll.London, Moorfields Eye Hosp. [0041166]   13/10/1987

Heaton Mrs BC, (was Hatton-Gore), BA(Hons) MCLIP, Lib., Malbank Sch.& 6th Form Cent., Nantwich, Cheshire. [0028721]   11/01/1978
Heaton Mr CM, MA MCLIP, Asst.Head of Serv.(Res.), Cambs.L.& Inf.Serv. [0018763]   30/08/1972
Heaton Mrs CP, (was Medland), MA MCLIP, Princ.Lib.-Ref.& Inf., Calderdale M.B.C., Halifax. [0031144]   29/08/1979
Heaton Miss E, MA FIL DHMSA MCLIP, Retired. [0006673]   26/09/1953
Heaton Mrs JA, (was Harbord), MCLIP, Child.Lib., Sutton L., Birmingham C.C. [0028002]   05/10/1977
Heaton Mrs JD, (was Moor), BA MCLIP, p./t.Lib., Knutsford P.L., Cheshire C.C. [0035342]   14/10/1982
Heaton Mr JM, BA DipLib MCLIP, Principal Off. e-L.Serv., Rotherham M.B.C. [0028236]   12/10/1977
Heaton Mr MG, BA, Stud., Manchester Met.Univ. [0058856]   08/09/2000
Heaton Miss W, BA(Hons) MCLIP, Operations Mgr., Wigan Council. [0028957]   16/01/1978
Heaven Ms S, BA(Hons), Stud. [0057857]   10/09/1999
Heawood Ms KE, BA(Hons), L.Asst., St.Johns Coll.L. [0059750]   17/09/2001   **AF**
Heaword Mr RA, BA MSc MCLIP, Employment unknown. [0060381]   11/12/2001
Hebblethwaite Mrs R, (was Elliott), MCLIP, Unemployed. [0006677]   30/09/1964
Hebden Miss MJ, MCLIP, Retired. [0006676]   06/10/1941
Hebden Mrs S, MCLIP, Unemployed. [0030626]   12/03/1979
Hebditch Ms P, BA(Hons) DipILM MCLIP, Asst.Lib., Manchester Metro.Univ. [0055940]   22/12/1997
Hebdon Mr PR, BA MCLIP, Lib., Wallsend Area L., N.Tyneside L. [0034766]   24/01/1982
Heckford Mr IJ, BA MLS, Dep.CEO/ Systems Mgr., Oshawa Pub.L., Ontario, Canada. [0043773]   05/01/1990
Hector Miss EJ, MA MCLIP, Head of L.& Arch., Trustees of the Nat.Gallery. [0024695]   01/10/1975
Hedges Mr G, MCLIP, Sen.Asst.Lib., L.B.Wandsworth, Battersea Ref.L. [0022662]   02/08/1974
Hedges Mrs GE, (was Parker), MCLIP, Sch.Lib., Thomas Alleyne's High Sch., Uttoxeter. [0006682]   29/02/1964
Hedges Mrs HM, (was Beardall), L.Asst., Sch.L.Serv., Shropshire Ls., Shrewsbury. [0045570]   06/03/1991   **AF**
Hedges Miss J, BA(Hons), Liaison Lib., Univ.of London, [0058890]   08/09/1999
Hedley Mrs AR, (was Hughes), BA MCLIP, p./t.Yth.Serv.Lib., Gateshead M.B.C., L.& Arts Dept. [0026415]   12/10/1976
Hee Houng Mrs M, (was Pantin), MCLIP, Freelance Consultant. [0017544]   10/10/1961
Heeks Dr PE, (was Lawless), MA FCLIP, Retired. [0006685]   31/01/1941   **FE 01/01/1959**
Heery Mr MJ, MA FCLIP, Retired., . [0024951]   24/10/1975   **FE 22/07/1998**
Heery Mrs S, BA DipLib MCLIP, Inf.Res.Mgr., Christian Aid, London. [0043360]   20/10/1989
Heffer Mr CM, BA DipLib MCLIP, Lib.-W.Grp., Cent.L., L.B.of Bromley. [0031857]   16/01/1980
Heffernan Mr RC, BA MCLIP, Asst.Lib., The Inst.of Civil Eng., London. [0028586]   16/01/1978
Heftman Mrs Y, (was Bennett), MCLIP, Unemployed. [0006687]   20/10/1963
Hegenbarth Mrs JA, (was Powell), BA(Hons) MA MCLIP, Liaison Lib., Univ.of Birmingham, Barnes L. [0051951]   17/08/1995
Heid Ms U, Resident in Germany. [0060068]   07/12/2001
Heinecke Mr PM, BA MCLIP, Retired. [0024697]   06/10/1975
Heissig Mr HN, BA FCLIP, Life Member. [0018764]   15/03/1955   **FE 01/01/1965**
Heiton Mrs KM, (was Miller), MCLIP, Unemployed. [0010157]   06/03/1963
Helgesen Ms JC, BA(Hons), Stud., Univ.of N.London, & Inf.Asst., The Industrial Soc., London. [0058859]   12/09/2000
Hellen Mrs R, (was Knightley), MCLIP, L.Res.Unit Mgr., L.B.of Enfield. [0008495]   04/04/1972
Hellen Mr RJ, MCLIP, Research & Devel.Mgr., Barnet P.L., London. [0006692]   12/01/1971
Heller Ms Z, MITI MCLIP, Retired. [0060382]   11/12/2001
Helliwell Mrs AP, (was Barnes), MA FCLIP, Life Member. [0000788]   09/10/1946   **FE 01/01/1952**
Helliwell Miss CS, MCLIP BSc, Retired. [0021754]   12/01/1974
Helliwell Miss J, MCLIP, Local Hist.Lib., Local Studies & Archives Dept, Local Hist.L., Kirklees Cult.Serv. [0006695]   28/03/1969
Helliwell Mrs JF, (was Hind), L.Mgr., Kedington L., Suffolk C.C. [0045903]   01/07/1991   **AF**
Helliwell Mrs MR, (was Bowker), DMS MCLIP, Team Leader, Market Weighton, E.Riding. [0028395]   19/11/1977
Helliwell Mrs S, BA(Hons), Grad.Inf.Asst., The Ind.Soc., London. [0059902]   25/10/2001
Hellon Mrs C, (was Beasant), BLS MCLIP, Career Break. [0033458]   01/01/1981
Hellon Mrs SJ, (was Kellett), BA DipLib MCLIP, Lib., Alfreton L., Derbys.C.C. [0036323]   10/10/1972
Helm Miss CN, BA MA, Inf.Offr., Lloyd's of London. [0058095]   29/10/1999
Helm Miss SV, BA MCLIP DipMS, Mgmt.Support & Staff Devel.Lib., Dudley P.L. [0029039]   13/03/1978
Helsby Mrs K, BS, Lib., Crewe L., Cheshire. [0061621]   04/10/2002
Helyar Mr LEJ, MCLIP, Curator in Graphics, Univ. of Kansas L., U.S.A. [0017021]   15/01/1948
Helyar Mrs ME, (was Garratt), BA MCLIP, Retired. [0006699]   01/01/1958
Hemans Ms N, BSc(Hons), Stud., 61 Moray Rd.,London N4 3LD. [0055461]   13/10/1997
Hemings Miss SA, BA(Hons) MSc MCLIP, Inf.Lib., Univ.of Bath, L.& Learning Cent. [0051296]   04/01/1995

Hemming Mrs AC, (was Mcdonald), BA(Hons) PGDipLib, Inf.Serv.Mgr., Hugh James Solicitors, Cardiff. [0030484]   03/01/1979
Hemming Miss AE, BA(Hons) MSc, Website Asst., Coll.of Occupational Therapists, London. [0059296]   31/01/2001
Hemming Mrs HE, (was Knight), BA(Hons), Sen.Lib., Nat.Air Traffic Serv., Southampton. [0049404]   21/10/1993
Hemming Ms RJ, BA BMus(Hons) MSc, Head of L., Univ.Coll.Sch., Hampstead. [0055544]   17/10/1997
Hemmings Miss C, BA(Hons), Asst.Lib., Portsmouth Cent.L. [0055921]   10/12/1997
Hemmings Mr PM, BLib MCLIP, Cent.L.Mgr., Birmingham City Council, Cent.L. [0028314]   07/10/1977
Hemmings Mr RJ, BA MCLIP DMS MIMgt DipM MCIM, Customer Serv.Mgr., Peterborough City Council, Cent.L. [0022407]   03/05/1974
Hemmings Mrs VJ, (was Wright), MCLIP, Team Leader,-Child.Serv., Edmonton Green L., L.B.of Enfield. [0026621]   01/10/1976
Hempshall Mrs MCS, Unemployed. [0052688]   17/11/1995
Hemsley Mr MA, BA MCLIP, p./t.Learning Cent.Asst., Sussex Downs Coll., Eastbourne. [0006709]   12/10/1970
Hemsoll Mrs DS, (was George), BA DipLib MCLIP, Professional Lib., Univ.of Birmingham. [0034647]   25/01/1982
Hemus Ms E, PGDip, Inf.Offr., Linklaters, London. [0055559]   21/10/1997
Hendel Dr GE, PhD, Grad.Trainee, The London L. [0059659]   19/07/2001
Henderson Mr A, BSc, Stud., Sheffield Univ. [0061842]   18/11/2002
Henderson Mr AC, BSc(Hons) PGDip, Research Exec. [0057987]   08/10/1999
Henderson Miss B, MCLIP, Life Member. [0006715]   13/03/1943
Henderson Mrs CH, (was Wilson), BA MCLIP, Team Lib., Arch. & Spec.Collect., Glasgow City L. [0023732]   01/02/1975
Henderson Ms EF, BA DipLib MCLIP, Knowledge Mgr., HM Treasury, Pub.Serv.Dir., London. [0027737]   21/07/1977
Henderson Mrs HL, (was Grierson), BSc FCLIP, Consultant, Self-employed. [0005963]   01/01/1971   **FE 01/04/2002**
Henderson Miss J, BA(Hons), L.Asst., Northumberland C.C. [0056022]   28/01/1998
Henderson Miss J, (was Howie), BA(Hons) MA, Asst.Curator Early Printed Books, Wellcome L., London. [0044407]   04/10/1990
Henderson Mrs J, BA(Hons) MCLIP, Community Lib., Birmingham L.Serv., Handsworth L. [0032978]   04/10/1980
Henderson Ms JA, BSc DipLib MCLIP MSc, Resident in Namibia [0040377]   23/01/1987
Henderson Mrs JAF, (was Scott), MA MCLIP, Asst.Lib., Crawley L., W.Sussex C.C. [0006720]   01/01/1968
Henderson Mr JD, BA(Hons), Stud. [0056592]   07/09/1998
Henderson Miss JM, BA MCLIP, Learning Cent.Devel.Offr., Scottish F.E.Unit, Stirling. [0029040]   22/03/1978
Henderson Mrs JM, (was Martin), BA(Hons), Sen.Lib., Wesley Coll., Bristol. [0048502]   28/01/1993
Henderson Mrs JP, (was Barnes), BA DipLib MCLIP, Inf.Team Lib., Wimbledon Ref.L., L.B.of Merton. [0036315]   02/10/1983
Henderson Mr JT, BSc, Customer Serv.Asst., Lambeth L.& Arch. [0039089]   01/11/1985
Henderson Miss K, MCLIP, Retired. [0006724]   28/03/1948
Henderson Miss LW, MCLIP, Comm.Lib., Renfrew Dist.L., Renfrewshire L. [0031859]   11/01/1980
Henderson Mrs ME, (was Gladhill), BA DipLib MCLIP, Lib., Somerset C.C. [0029265]   02/05/1978
Henderson Mrs MM, (was Wilkie), BA FCLIP, Retired, 11 Holmhead Place, Aberdeen. [0015844]   17/02/1951   **FE 01/01/1968**
Henderson Mr N, MSc BA(Hons), Stud., Queen Margaret univ.Coll. [0059873]   29/10/2001
Henderson Miss R, BA DipLib MCLIP, Unemployed. [0024423]   22/07/1975
Henderson Miss RS, BA(Hons), Learning Res.Asst., Exeter Coll. [0059330]   08/02/2001
Henderson Mrs S, MCLIP, Inf.Mgr., Brewing Research Internat., Redhill. [0027645]   01/01/1966
Henderson Mrs SG, (was Bryce), MCLIP, P/t.Lib., Dundee City Council, Architectural Serv. [0001989]   20/10/1969
Henderson Mrs SG, (was Jack), BA MCLIP, Unemployed. [0007658]   02/11/1967
Henderson Mrs SJ, (was Bradley), BA MLib MCLIP, p./t.Acquisitions Lib., St.Martins Coll., Lancaster. [0036395]   05/10/1983
Henderson Mrs SM, (was Lindley), MCLIP, Lib.i/c., Mob.L., Dept.of Educ., Isle of Man. [0028621]   11/01/1978
Henderson Mrs SR, MCLIP, P/t.L.Asst., S.E.Educ.& L.Board, N.Ireland. [0029180]   19/04/1978
Hendley Mrs JC, (was Goff), BA(Hons), p./t.Stud, Music Asst., Bristol Univ., Central L. Oxford. [0059671]   25/01/2001
Hendricks Miss JA, Subject Lib., Univ.of N.London. [0055835]   20/11/1997
Hendrix Ms GF, (was Sewell), JP BA MBA FCLIP MInstD, Retired. [0006728]   13/02/1963   **FE 18/11/1998**
Hendron Miss E, BA(Hons), Inf.Offr., Nottingham City PCT. [0051037]   09/11/1994
Hendry Mrs CM, (was Cooper), BA MCLIP, Unemployed. [0019643]   31/01/1972
Hendry Ms JA, BA(Hons) DipLib MA, Unemployed. [0048377]   10/12/1992
Hendry Prof JD, MA FCLIP FSA, Retired. [0006731]   02/12/1963   **FE 17/07/1972**
Hendry Miss JM, BA(Hons) MCLIP, Network Lib., Aberdeenshire L.& Inf.Serv. [0051027]   11/11/1994
Hendry Mrs MM, (was Brownridge), MA MBA DipLib FCLIP, Admin.Mgr., Cartmell Shepherd, Solicitors. [0026178]   04/08/1976   **FE 21/07/1993**
Henesey Mrs AJ, (was Beecham), BA MCLIP, Lib., Nat.Coal Mining Mus., Wakefield. [0024402]   01/08/1975
Henley Miss C, BA(Hons), Stud., Univ.of Strathclyde. [0061764]   05/11/2002

Henley Ms J, BSc(Econ), Project Offr.(Mapping), Hugh Owen L., Ceredigion. [0059542] 01/05/2001
Henley Mrs JM, (was Spooner), BSc DipLib MCLIP, Proprietor, Locator Inf.Serv., Milton Keynes. [0026564] 01/10/1976
Henley Ms JS, MA MCLIP, Self-employed. [0042944] 26/04/1989
Henley Ms TM, (was Sedgewick), BA MSc MCLIP, Mgmt.Inf.Offr.(Job Share), Darlington Bor.Council, Soc.Serv. [0037692] 17/10/1984
Henn Ms SM, BSc DipLib MCLIP, P/t.Teacher-Lib., Claremont Coll.I.L., Tasmania. [0032979] 07/10/1980
Hennessy Mrs VC, BA MA DipLib MCLIP, Unemployed. [0006737] 01/01/1972
Hennin Miss GM, FCLIP, Retired. [0006739] 11/03/1940 **FE 01/01/1949**
Henning Mrs HME, (was Agnew), BA, L.Asst., S.Educ.& L.Board, Rathfriland Br.L. [0048036] 26/10/1992 **AF**
Henry Ms AK, MA(Hons) DipILS MCLIP, Acting Asst.Lib., Shetland L. [0057365] 26/02/1999
Henry Dr EC, BSc(Hons) DipILS MCLIP, Lib., NHS Tayside, Dundee. [0057247] 20/01/1999
Henry Miss J, BSc(Hons) MSc, Inf.Offr., DTZ Pieda Consulting, Edinburgh. [0057986] 08/10/1997
Henry Mr M, MA MSc MIMgt DMS MCLIP FRSA MILAM, Retired. [0022966] 01/10/1974
Henry Miss S, BA(Hons) DipILM, Lib., Halton Bor.Council, Runcorn. [0056775] 12/10/1998
Henry Miss SA, DipILS, Catr., Bibl.Data Serv.Ltd., Dumfries. [0057956] 05/10/1999
Henshaw Miss DA, BA (Hons), Stud., Manchester Metropolitan Univ. [0059093] 14/11/2000
Henshaw Miss J, BMus(Hons) MA, Learning Res.Mgr., Music & Performing Arts, Colchester Inst., Essex. [0057021] 25/11/1998
Henshaw Miss SA, MA DipLib MCLIP, Unemployed. [0037299] 10/06/1984
Henson Miss JB, Unemployed. [0059767] 01/10/2001
Henton Miss AE, BA, Duty Mgr., The Peach Tree Restaurant, Shropshire. [0061602] 03/10/2001
Hepburn Mrs M, BLIS, Research Lib., Agilent Tech., W.Lothian. [0061009] 30/01/2002
Heppinstall Mr DM, MCLIP, Lib.(Voluntary), N.S.F.(Rotherham). [0006748] 06/11/1968
Hepworth Mrs J, BA, Sch.Lib., City of York Council, Canon Lee Sch. [0057899] 01/01/1999
Hepworth Miss JS, BA(Hons) DipIS MCLIP, Grp.Support Lib., Leeds City L., Morley, Leeds. [0052276] 23/10/1995
Hepworth Mr M, MA BSc MCLIP, Local Studies Lib., Barnsley Met.Dist.L., S.Yorks. [0006752] 01/01/1968
Hepworth Mr M, BA MSc MCLIP, Employment not known. [0060476] 11/12/2001
Herbert Mrs AJ, (was Anderson), BA MCLIP, Prison Lib., Young Offenders Inst., Durham C.C. [0040835] 07/07/1987
Herbert Mrs CM, BA MCLIP, Unemployed. [0022883] 01/10/1974
Herbert Mrs DA, BA(Hons) MLS MCLIP, Princ.Lib.-Pub.Serv., L.B.of Hammersmith & Fulham. [0029678] 02/10/1978
Herbert Mrs DJ, (was Lynham), BSc(Hons) MCLIP, Unemployed. [0046782] 22/01/1992
Herbert Mrs E, (was Sporne), BA DMS MCLIP, Cent.Serv.Mgr., E.Riding of Yorkshire Council, L.H.Q. [0023962] 24/02/1975
Herbert Mrs JS, (was Howarth), MCLIP, Life Member, Tel.(020)8953 2999, 12 W.View Gardens, Elstree, Herts., WD6 3DD. [0006758] 26/05/1950
Herbert Mrs KE, (was Howard), BA(Hons) DipILS MCLIP, L.Inf.Serv.Mgr., Hinchingbrooke NHS Healthcare Tru., Huntingdon. [0049462] 02/11/1993
Herbert Mrs KM, BA, Bus.Inf.Exec., Small Business Gateway, Aberdeen. [0051021] 09/11/1994
Herbert Mrs OT, (was Smith), FCLIP, Life Member, 4 Wyncote Way, Selsdon, S.Croydon, CR2 8NH. [0006759] 07/10/1942 **FE 01/01/1969**
Herbert Miss PA, MCLIP, Retired. [0006760] 30/01/1960
Hercod Miss CE, BA, Stud./Admin., LJMU./Liverpool Excel.Partnership. [0061808] 11/11/2002
Herd Mrs HK, BA(Hons) MCLIP, Asst.Subject Lib., Coventry Univ. [0048508] 01/02/1993
Herdan Mr N, Corporate Finance, USB Warburg, New York. [0035498] 19/10/1982
Heritage Mr ID, BA MCLIP, Inf.Offr., Nai Gooch Webster, London. [0034458] 06/11/1981
Herman Ms D, BSc MSc MCLIP MIBiol CIBiol, Lib., Middlesex Univ., Tottenham Campus. [0043149] 22/08/1989
Herman Ms IL, MA BA, Project Offr.-Electronic L., Nottingham Trent Univ., Boots L. [0042338] 17/10/1988
Hermiston Mr BN, BSc BA MPhil MCLIP, Employment unknown. [0060383] 11/12/2001
Hermon Mrs FD, (was Harris), MSc MCLIP, Employment unknown. [0060377] 11/12/2001
Hernando Mrs SA, BA DipLib MCLIP, Head of Div.:Inf.& L.Serv.Devel., NHS Exec., S.W.NHS.Region. [0033539] 19/01/1981
Herne Mr IM, BA MA FAETC MCLIP, Lib., S.Bank Internat.Sch., London. [0021256] 05/10/1973
Herniman Miss J, MCLIP, Unemployed. [0024390] 15/02/1964
Heron Miss C, BA(Hons) DipILS MCLIP, Local Stud.Lib., Rotherham Metro.Bor.Council, Cent.L. [0052385] 30/10/1995
Heron Mr IMW, BSc, Employment not known. [0060479] 11/12/2001
Herriman Mrs MC, (was Hale), BA DipLib MCLIP, Child.Lib., Milton Keynes L. [0033757] 25/01/1981
Herring Mrs J, BA DipLib MCLIP, Lib., Foreign & Commonwealth Office L. [0026409] 07/10/1976

Herring Mr JE, MA MA(Lib) MCLIP, Head of the Dept.of Inf.Mgmt., Queen Margaret Univ.Coll., Edinburgh. [0006774] 18/10/1971
Herring Miss KE, BA DipLib MCLIP, Lib.-Reader Devel., N.Warks.Div., Warwickshire Co.L.Serv. [0036532] 17/10/1983
Herring Ms PS, (was Hicks), BA MLS MCLIP, Lib., Queen Elizabeth Sch., Atherstone, Coventry. [0021323] 07/10/1973
Herring Mrs RV, (was Warren), BA MA DipLib MCLIP, Temping/Contract Work. [0050519] 31/08/1994
Herrington Mrs AP, BA MCLIP, Housewife. [0025050] 30/10/1975
Herriott Miss NF, BSc(Hons) MA MCLIP, Systems Lib.& Catr., Hertford Reg.Coll. [0050036] 21/02/1994
Herrmann Ms C, MSc BA MCLIP, Devel.Offr., Enfield Cent.L., L.B.of Enfield. [0021753] 01/01/1974
Herron Miss A, MA DipLib MCLIP, Employment not known. [0036616] 24/10/1983
Hersom Mr DH, FCLIP, Retired-formerly Durham Co.L. [0006779] 01/07/1934 **FE 01/01/1937**
Hesketh Mrs C, (was Thomas), BA DipLib MCLIP, Community Lib.(Jobshare), Conwy Co.Bor.Council, Abergele L. [0042242] 12/10/1988
Hesketh Mrs JE, (was Darbyshire), BA MCLIP, Inf.Resources Spec., Swiss RE Life & Health Ltd., London. [0027664] 04/07/1977
Hesketh Mrs M, (was Stewart), MA DipLib MCLIP, Sen.Asst.Lib.(Requests), Lancs.Co.L. [0026568] 08/10/1976
Hesmondhalgh Ms J, Faculty Co-ordinator, Inf.Serv., Univ.of Salford. [0041290] 24/10/1987
Hess Mrs CC, (was Dawe), MCLIP, Lib., Educ.L.Serv., Notts. [0026344] 13/10/1976
Hester Mrs PI, (was Casemore), MCLIP, Life Member. [0006785] 01/01/1951
Hetherington Miss J, BA MCLIP, Asst.Lib./Reader Serv.Lib., Univ.of Sunderland. [0036691] 09/11/1983
Hetherington Mrs NC, (was Henwood), BLS MCLIP, Sch.Lib., Lady Manners Sch., Bakewell. [0033457] 01/01/1981
Hetherington-Field Miss JA, BA(Hons), Inf.Offr., Linklaters & Alliance, London. [0058977] 13/10/2000
Hettiaratchi Mrs W, MCLIP, Life Member. [0006786] 02/01/1968
Heusinkveld Mrs LA, MLS, Weekend Lib., Horniman Museum & Gardens, Forest Hill. [0050979] 04/11/1994
Hevey Mrs MM, (was Mckinlay), MCLIP, Life Member, 01227 771916, Trebor House, Clifton Road, Whitstable, Kent, CT5 1DQ. [0018766] 15/03/1947
Hewerdine Mrs V, BSc(Hons), Unemployed. [0057799] 02/08/1999
Hewett Ms AM, BA DipLib MCLIP, Unemployed. [0028435] 05/12/1977
Hewett Mr SJR, BA, Lib., Sports Docum.Cent., Univ. of Birmingham. [0018148] 09/10/1972
Hewings Mrs RM, (was Young), BSc DipLib MCLIP DMS ILT, H.of Learning Inf.Servs., Writtle Coll., Chelmsford. [0030575] 29/01/1979
Hewins Mrs JM, (was Watson), BA MCLIP, p./t.Site Lib., Bournemouth Univ., Dorset. [0031485] 16/10/1979
Hewison Mrs H, (was Nicholson), BA MCLIP, Lib., Oxford Inst.of Legal Practice. [0027286] 14/02/1977
Hewitt Mr AR, FCLIP, Life Member. [0006793] 24/03/1930 **FE 01/01/1964**
Hewitt Mr AW, BA MCLIP, Retired. [0018767] 12/09/1972
Hewitt Miss CE, BA MCLIP, Asst.Lib., Harrogate L., N.Yorks.C.C. [0031637] 22/10/1979
Hewitt Miss G, BA(Hons) MCLIP, Mgr., SHSC Health Mgmt.L., Common Serv.Agency, Edinburgh. [0047522] 25/09/1992
Hewitt Mr M, Inf.Spec., Kings Coll.London. [0045504] 26/02/1991
Hewitt Miss MJ, DipLib MCLIP, Asst.Dir., N.W.Film.Arch., Manchester Metro.Univ. [0028830] 07/02/1978
Hewitt Miss PM, BA DipLib MCLIP, Lib., Univ.of E.Anglia, Robert Sainsbury L., Norwich. [0029679] 04/10/1978
Hewitt Ms R, BA, Stud., Farnborough Ed.Cent., Kent. [0061421] 15/07/2002
Hewitt Ms S, MCLIP, Retired, Resident South Africa. [0018943] 27/05/1943
Hewitt Mrs SM, (was Hoskins), MCLIP, Br.Lib., Okehampton L., Devon Co.C. [0006798] 08/10/1964
Hewitt Mrs VJ, (was Etherington), MLS MCLIP, Retired. [0006799] 01/01/1956
Hewlett Mrs J, (was Goodwin), MCLIP, Unemployed. [0006800] 12/04/1966
Hewlett Mr JF, MSc(InfSc) MCLIP, Dir., Northern & Yorks.Reg.L.Advisory, Serv., NHS. [0006801] 11/03/1967
Hewlett Miss MA, MA MCLIP, Retired & Unemployed, on health grounds. [0006802] 07/03/1966
Hewson Mrs A, (was Wright), BA MCLIP, L.Asst., Kings Coll., Guildford. [0023055] 16/10/1974
Hewson Miss CA, BA, Unemployed. [0042089] 04/10/1988
Hextall Mrs JM, (was Burgess), MCLIP, p./t.L.Asst., Cheltenham Ref. [0002081] 30/01/1965
Hey Mrs JMN, MA MCLIP, Researcher, Digital Ls.Research, Cent., Univ.of Southampton, Southampton, Hants. [0023655] 22/01/1975
Heyda Miss B, BSc DipLib MCLIP, Employment not known. [0060733] 12/12/2001
Heydon Mrs JR, (was Perfect), CertEd BEd BA DipLIS MCLIP, Lib., Beaconsfield High Sch., Bucks. [0044649] 14/11/1990
Heyes Mrs DJ, (was Bastable), DipLib MCLIP, Retired. [0000896] 26/01/1967
Heyes Mrs JL, (was Spice), BA(Hons) MCLIP, Sen.Project Support Offr., Comm.Serv., Kent C.C. [0039739] 10/06/1986
Heyes Mr JT, FCLIP, p./t.Inf.& Lifelong Learning Lib., Bolton M.B.C. [0006807] 24/03/1965 **FE 31/03/1980**
Heyes Mrs RK, (was Hammersley), MCLIP, Sch.Lib., Moseley Park Sch., Wolverhampton. [0025295] 10/01/1976
Heyes Miss SA, BA(Hons) CertEd MCLIP, Head of Sch.L.Serv., W.Sussex C.C., Chichester. [0035400] 15/10/1982
Heyes Ms VM, (was Oglethorpe), BA MCLIP, Self Employed-Educ.Consultant. [0006808] 17/10/1966

Personal Members

Heynes Ms P, Customer Support Lib., Univ.of Bath L. [0045036]   09/06/1988   AF
Heywood Mrs JM, (was Stocks), BA MCLIP, Unemployed. [0018293]   11/10/1972
Heywood Mrs K, L.Asst., The Harris L., Preston. [0053150]   01/04/1996
Heywood Mr RW, BA MCLIP, Lib., Huddersfield Royal Infirmary, Calderdale & Huddersfield NHS Trst. [0006814]   12/10/1967
Heywood Mrs S, BA MCLIP, Lib., Educ.L.Serv., Berks. [0006815]   16/01/1972
Heyworth Mrs BM, FIL KAND MCLIP, Devel.Offr., Leeds City Council-Leisure., Leeds. [0006816]   05/01/1970
Hiatt Mr GR, BA MCLIP, Grp.Lib.,N.Glos., Glos.Co.L.Arts & Mus.Serv. [0006817]   01/02/1962
Hibbard Mrs JM, (was Phillips), MCLIP, Retired. [0011624]   18/01/1961
Hibberd Miss RA, BA(Hons) PGDip, p./t.Stud., U.C.E., Birmingham. [0056544]   17/08/1998
Hibberson Mr SR, Stud. [0061422]   17/07/2002
Hibbert Miss FL, BA(Hons) MSc(Econ), L.Systems Offr., The Wellcome L.for the Hist.&, Understanding of Med. [0052120]   05/10/1995
Hibbert Miss L, BA(Hons) DipILM, Inf.Devel.Offr., N.E.Mus.L.& Arch.Council, Newcastle upon Tyne. [0058985]   18/10/2000
Hibbert Mr O, MSc CChemMRSC Cert MCLIP, Employment unknown. [0060588]   11/12/2001
Hibbert Ms PC, L.Asst., Kensington Cent.L., London. [0056147]   05/03/1998   AF
Hibbert Mrs SHM, (was Woodley), MA MCLIP, Freelance Ed. [0032223]   05/02/1980
Hibbert Mrs VF, BA(Hons) MCLIP, Inf.Devel.Offr., N.E.Mus.L.& Arch.Council, Newcastle-upon-Tyne. [0039186]   02/12/1985
Hibbs Miss EJ, BA DipLib MCLIP, L.Mgr., Royal Borough Kensington & Chelsea. [0034422]   28/10/1981
Hibbs Mr FA, MCLIP, Lib.-Inf.Servs., E.Sussex L.Inf.& Arts. [0006824]   30/01/1962
Hick Miss JM, BA MCLIP, Retired. [0006825]   01/01/1965
Hicken Miss A, BA(Hons) DipIM MCLIP, Reader Devel.L., Portsmouth Cent.L., Hants. [0058381]   20/01/2000
Hicken Mrs ME, (was Holland), MLS MCLIP, Retired. [0006827]   24/01/1951
Hickey Mr JA, L.Asst., Brit.Med.Assoc., London. [0056495]   28/07/1998
Hickford Mrs BGS, MA DipLib MCLIP, Lib., Our Lady's Convent Sen.Sch., Abingdon. [0029680]   09/10/1978
Hickford Miss MB, BA, Stud., Univ.of Sheffield. [0061638]   07/10/2002
Hicklin Miss PN, BSc, Customer Serv.Mgr., Hyprotech UK Ltd., Harwell,Oxon. [0037540]   06/10/1984
Hickling Mr CD, Asst.Lib.-Catr., The Nottingham Trent Univ. [0057402]   05/03/1999
Hickman Mrs L, (was James), MCLIP, Senior Resource Asst., Univ.of Wolverhampton. [0023048]   20/10/1974
Hickman Mrs MA, (was Hurt), BA(Hons), L.Serv.Mgr., Royal Berks.& Battle Hosp.NHS, Trust, Reading, Berks. [0047136]   06/05/1992
Hickman-Ashby Mrs GIJ, (was Smart), MLib MCLIP, Asst.Systems Mgr., Corp.of London. [0006835]   05/10/1970
Hicks Miss AC, BA(Hons) MA, Asst.Lib., Nat.Assembly Wales, Cardiff. [0057510]   14/04/1999
Hicks Mrs AC, L.Support Asst., Co.L.H.Q., Wilts.C.C. [0058317]   06/01/2000   AF
Hicks Mr DSSC, MCLIP, Asst.Lib., Lewisham P.L. [0006838]   14/01/1968
Hicks Mrs JH, (was Simpson), BA MCLIP, Unemployed. [0022253]   01/01/1950
Hicks Ms LMS, BA MCLIP, Freelance Editor/Indexer, 5 Winters Close, Portesham, Weymouth, Dorset, DT3 4HP. [0006841]   24/04/1961
Hicks Ms S, L.Asst., Univ.of Cambridge, Judge Inst.of Mgmt.Studies. [0056298]   07/05/1998
Hicks Mr TJ, BA(Hons) MCLIP MA, Academic Res.Lib.-Art & Design, Univ.of Wolverhampton. [0051443]   10/02/1995
Hickton Ms JM, BA(Hons) DipInf MCLIP, L.& Inf.Offr., Canning House, London. [0050656]   04/10/1994
Hider Mr PM, BSc(Hons) MLib MCLIP, Manager, Singapore Int.L.Automation Serv., Singapore. [0049277]   20/10/1993
Hidson Mr R, DIP ARCH FCLIP, Retired. [0006844]   01/01/1961   FE 17/10/1990
Hierons Miss JA, MCLIP, L.Mgr., Shirley L., Croydon. [0006845]   01/01/1970
Higgens Mr GL, FCLIP, Life Member, Tel.01929 427200, 3 Beach Gdns., Swanage, Dorset, BH19 1PG. [0006848]   01/01/1947   FE 01/01/1953
Higgin Mrs JM, (was Unsworth), BA DipLib MCLIP, Lib., Warrington Bor.Council, Warrington L. [0042972]   11/05/1989
Higgins Mrs A, (was Bolton), BA, Relief Lib., Doncaster M.B.C. [0055212]   13/11/1978
Higgins Miss BA, MCLIP, Team.Lib., Liverpool L.& Inf.Serv. [0006852]   13/09/1968
Higgins Mrs EM, (was Joy), BA DipLib, Lib., Madras Coll., Fife Reg.Council Educ.Dept. [0028843]   30/01/1978
Higgins Ms FA, (was Claridge), MCLIP, Lib., Wilts.C.C., Chippenham L. [0006853]   01/01/1965
Higgins Mrs HW, (was Ashcroft), BA MCLIP, Sen.Inf.Offr., Univ.of Cent.Lancs. [0000435]   27/10/1971
Higgins Mrs J, (was McEwan), MCLIP, Asst.Lib.(Job Share), Renfrewshire L., Paisley. [0035723]   20/01/1983
Higgins Mr MJW, MA MCLIP, Retired. [0006856]   10/10/1957
Higgins Mrs MM, BA(Hons), Lib., English Martyrs Sch., Leicester. [0059429]   13/03/2001
Higgins Mrs PL, (was Edgar), Support Consultant, Fretwell-Downing Inf.Ltd., Sheffield. [0039189]   09/01/1986
Higgins Mrs RJB, (was Bavin), MLib MCLIP, Bookseller, Med.Health & Prof.Texts, Inverness. [0021442]   30/10/1973
Higginson Miss J, BA(Hons) DipLIS MCLIP, Ref.Lib., Hants.C.C., Basingstoke. [0049708]   25/11/1993
Higgison Ms MS, (was Gold), Asst.Lib., Scottish Exec. [0043916]   19/02/1990

Higgs Mrs GM, (was Forster), BA MCLIP, Unemployed. [0025533]   28/01/1976
Higgs Mr GP, BSc(Hons) DipILS, Lib., Higher Coll.of Tech., Ras Al-Khaimah Womens Coll., UAE. [0048519]   02/02/1993
Higgs Mrs LA, Chamber's Lib., Fountain Court, Birmingham. [0058591]   07/04/2000
High Mr B, BA(Hons) MA MCLIP, Sen.Inf.Asst.-Special Colletions, Kings Coll., London. [0045781]   28/05/1991
Higham Ms C, BA(Hons), L.Asst., Bolton Central L. [0050730]   14/10/1994
Higham Miss JW, MCLIP, Retired. [0006863]   25/09/1950
Higham Dr N, OBE MA DLitt MCLIP, Retired. [0006864]   01/01/1952
Higham Ms SP, BA(Hons) DipLIS, Dep.Lib., N.Warwickshire & Hinckley Coll., Nuneaton, Warwickshire. [0056831]   23/10/1998
Highley Ms S, MA DIP NZLS MCLIP, Ref.Lib., L.B.of Southwark. [0029681]   03/10/1978
Higley Mr G, BSc MCLIP, IT Dir., Quantum Partnership Ltd. [0030183]   09/01/1979
Higson Miss JL, BA MSc(Econ), Sch.Lib., Penglais Sch., Aberystwyth. [0058733]   01/07/2000
Higson Mrs MD, (was Soden), MA MCLIP, Sen.Lib., Telford & Wrekin Council, Telford. [0013753]   01/01/1967
Hikins Mr HR, FCLIP, Life Member, Tel.051 733 7728, 25 Alverstone Rd., Liverpool, L18 1HB. [0006867]   01/01/1936   FE 01/01/1959
Hikmany Mr SR, DipLib, Stud., Univ.of Wales, Aberystwyth. [0059460]   30/03/2001
Hilbourne Mrs RA, Employment not known. [0060486]   11/12/2001
Hildred Miss E, BA(Hons), Stud., Univ.of Brighton & Employee, East Surrey Coll., Redhill, Surrey. [0058935]   07/10/2000
Hilfi Mrs DF, (was Jones), BA MCLIP, Retired. [0017029]   14/01/1960
Hill Ms A, (was Sherlock), MA MCLIP, Head of Learning Res., Doncaster Coll. [0018231]   03/10/1972
Hill Mr AJ, MCLIP, Retired. [0006871]   20/03/1955
Hill Ms C, MLS, Mgr.,Sun L., Sun Microsystems, Inc., California, USA. [0061425]   29/07/2002
Hill Mrs CA, (was Harris), MCLIP, Local Hist.Lib., Cent.L., Doncaster M.B.C. [0028756]   01/01/1965
Hill Mrs CC, (was Stewart), BSc(Hons) PGILM, Assoc.Dir., UBS Warburg, London. [0050696]   12/10/1994
Hill Mr CJ, p./t.Stud./ICT Devel.Offr., Manchester Met.Univ., Bolton Cent.L. [0061141]   03/03/2002
Hill Mrs CJ, (was Frost), BA MCLIP, Dist.Lib., Herts.C.C., Hoddesdon L.,Herts. [0036586]   24/10/1983
Hill Mrs CJ, (was Hughes), BA MCLIP DMS, Comm.Lib., Kent C.C., Gravesend. [0033907]   02/05/1981
Hill Mrs CL, (was Vining), BA MCLIP, p./t.L.Asst., L.B.of Enfield. [0032207]   15/02/1980
Hill Miss CM, MCLIP, Adult Serv.Lib., Rutland Co.L. [0006874]   29/10/1965
Hill Mr D, BA(Hons) MCLIP, [0042942]   28/04/1989
Hill Miss DE, BA MCLIP, L.Mgr., Cheshire C.C., Ellesmere Port L. [0040386]   26/01/1987
Hill Miss EJ, BA(Hons) MCLIP, Learning Res.Cent.Asst., Shrewsbury Coll.of Arts & Tech., Shropshire. [0052686]   21/11/1995
Hill Mrs FA, BA(Hons), Inf.Offr., Parenting Educ.& Support Forum, London. [0056783]   15/10/1998   AF
Hill Mr FJ, MA FCLIP, Retired. [0006877]   20/09/1946   FE 01/01/1953
Hill Mrs G, (was Urmston), Princ.L.Asst., Bolton M.B.C., Bolton Cent.Child.L. [0046203]   07/10/1991   AF
Hill Mrs HI, BA MCLIP, Res.Cent.Mgr., E.Sussex C.C., St.Leonards on sea. [0006879]   01/01/1969
Hill Mr IW, BSC MSC MI BIOL MCLIP, Tech.Inf.Off., British Gypsum, Loughborough. [0031073]   07/08/1979
Hill Miss J, MCLIP, Retired. [0006882]   30/03/1933
Hill Mr J, BSc LLM MCLIP, Retired. [0060226]   10/12/2001
Hill Mrs J, (was Duffy), MCLIP, Lib., E.Somerset NHS Trust L., Yeovil Dist.Hosp. [0042733]   01/01/1962
Hill Mrs JK, (was White), MCLIP, Sch.Lib., Sch.L.Cent., Exeter. [0015709]   14/04/1970
Hill Mrs JM, BA(Hons), Stud., p./t.L.Asst., Bath Cent.L., Univ.Aberystwyth. [0055057]   01/01/1997
Hill Mrs JMA, (was Lee), BA MCLIP, Reader Devel.Lib., Herts C.C., Hemel Hempstead. [0025344]   21/01/1976
Hill Mr JR, BA(Hons), Grad.Trainee, Univ.of Gloucestershire. [0059794]   03/10/2001
Hill Mrs KA, MCLIP, Team Leader(Job Share), Scunthorpe Br., N.Lincs.Council. [0023303]   30/10/1974
Hill Ms M, BA MCLIP AdvDipEd, Med.Lib., Royal Bournemouth Hosp., Dorset. [0044025]   02/04/1990
Hill Mrs MA, Asst.Lib., Lincoln Cent.L., Lincs.C.C. [0056568]   26/08/1998   AF
Hill Miss ME, BA MCLIP, L.Mgr., Camden., London. [0024700]   01/10/1975
Hill Mrs ME, (was Lusk), BA MCLIP, Sch.Lib., W.Dunbartonshire Council. [0023666]   25/01/1975
Hill Mrs MEA, BSc DipLib MCLIP, Unemployed. [0028741]   14/01/1978
Hill Mrs ML, BSc MPhil DipIM, Learning Res.Mgr., Xaverian Coll., Manchester. [0059297]   13/01/2001
Hill Mrs MM, (was Warne), MCLIP, Princ.Lib.-Comm.Serv., L.B.of Enfield. [0018171]   16/09/1966
Hill Mr MW, MA MSc MRSC CChem FCLIP, Life Member. [0006893]   15/02/1976   FE 01/04/2002
Hill Mrs P, Lib., Bermuda Aquarium, Natural Hist.Mus.& Zoo, Flatts. [0045702]   29/04/1991
Hill Mrs PE, (was Niemeyer), BA MCLIP, Circulation Offr., Univ of Lincoln. [0019216]   14/09/1972
Hill Mrs PM, (was Taylor), BSc MCLIP, Lib./Records Mgr., Historic Scotland, Edinburgh. [0024827]   10/10/1975

Hill Ms PM, BA(Hons) DIP LIB MCLIP, Ditrict Lib., Matlck L., Derbyshire. [0026636] 26/10/1976
Hill Mrs RC, (was Sturgess), BSc MSC MCLIP, Unemployed. [0039108] 29/10/1985
Hill Mr RJH, BA MCLIP, Sen.Lib., Herefordshire L.& Inf.Serv. [0006898] 06/06/1968
Hill Mrs RM, MCLIP, Inf.Lib., Woking Inf.Cent., Woking, Surrey. [0005029] 01/01/1971
Hill Mr RW, BA(Hons) DipLIS MA MCLIP, Res.Offr., Brit.L., Bibl.Serv., Boston Spa. [0020715] 23/05/1973
Hill Mrs S, (was Robertson), BA(Hons) MCLIP, L.Mgr., Middlesex Univ., Chase Farm Hosp. [0039391] 22/01/1986
Hill Ms S, BA, Employment not known. [0060483] 11/12/2001
Hill Mrs SA, (was Mason), BA(Hons) MCLIP, p./t.Lib., Harper Adams Univ.Coll. [0006899] 01/01/1971
Hill Mrs SA, (was Ross), BA MCLIP, Joint Lib.i./c., Falkirk Council. [0030247] 30/12/1978
Hill Mrs SE, (was Pringle), MCLIP BA, Asst.Lib., Bell Coll.of Tech., Hamilton. [0019536] 26/03/1965
Hill Miss SJ, HonFCLIP, Dir., Sue Hill Recruitment, London. [0040725] 19/05/1987 FE 01/04/2002
Hill Ms V, BA(Hons) DipLIS MCLIP MA, Sen.Asst.Lib., L.B.of Havering, Romford. [0050783] 18/10/1994
Hill Miss VE, BA MCLIP, Sen.Subject Lib., Middx.Univ., Barnet. [0042724] 13/02/1989
Hill Mr WR, MCLIP, Life Member. [0006902] 22/11/1932
Hilliard Miss NM, BA MCLIP, Head of L.& Inf., Nat.Child.Bureau, London. [0026410] 08/10/1976
Hilliard Mr RP, BSc(Econ) FCA HonFCLIP, Form.L.A.Sec. [0031110] 29/06/1979 FE 29/06/1979
Hillier Miss DM, BA DipLib MCLIP, Lib., Min.of Defence, Royal Sch.of Military Survey. [0040040] 07/10/1986
Hillier Miss GR, BD DipLib MCLIP, Music Lib., L.B.of Ealing, L.Support Cent. [0033302] 30/10/1980
Hillier Mrs J, (was Mossey), BA MCLIP, Learning Resources Mgr., New Coll., Swindon. [0010518] 28/06/1970
Hillier Mr RWE, BA MCLIP, Lib.(Local Studies), Cent.L., Peterborough. [0024701] 01/01/1975
Hillier Miss SL, BA PGCE MCLIP, Co.Child.Lib., Westbury L., Wilts. [0037292] 07/06/1984
Hillman Mrs G, (was Staples), MCLIP, Res.Mgr., Bell Educational Trust, Cambs. [0006905] 16/01/1968
Hillmann Mrs LP, BSc(Econ), p./t.Sen.Lib.Asst., Univ.of Northumbria, Carlisle Campus. [0051946] 15/08/1995 AF
Hills Mr DS, BA DipLib MCLIP, p./t.Memorial Lib., Norfolk C.C., Norwich. [0020775] 12/07/1973
Hills Miss GP, MCLIP, Life Member. [0006911] 25/03/1959
Hills Ms J, BA DipLib MCLIP, Inf.Lib., Univ.of Leicester, Clinical Sci.L. [0029393] 06/07/1978
Hills Ms SB, BSc MSc FCLIP, Employment not known. [0060712] 12/12/2001 FE 01/04/2002
Hills Mr SJ, MA MCLIP, Under-Lib., Univ.of Cambridge L. [0006912] 30/10/1971
Hillyer Ms SJ, (was Smith), BA(Hons) MSc MCLIP, Unemployed. [0048176] 11/11/1992
Hilton Mrs BE, BA(Hons), Child.& Yth.Lib., Cent.L., Birmingham City Council. [0053712] 13/09/1996
Hilton Mr J, MCLIP, Head of L.& Inf.Serv., Sefton M.B.C. [0006914] 07/02/1962
Hilton Mrs JA, (was Taylor), BA MSc(Econ) MCLIP, Section H.,-Distributed Serv., Univ.of Cent.Lancs., Preston. [0019109] 02/10/1972
Hilton Mr JJ, BA(Hons) MA, L.Asst., Univ.of Liverpool. [0059159] 04/12/2000
Hilton Mrs JJ, (was Webster), L.& Learning Res.Mgr., Mackworth Coll., Derby. [0047261] 29/06/1992
Hilton Mrs R, (was Ashton), MCLIP, Unemployed. [0000452] 01/01/1962
Hilton Mr RD, BA MCLIP, Mgr., -Business Inf.Unit, C.W.S.Ltd., Manchester. [0006916] 05/04/1967
Hilton Mrs W, (was Richardson), MCLIP, Community Lib., Salford, Gtr.Manchester. [0020542] 05/04/1973
Hincapie Miss LM, Independent Consultant, Medellin-Colombia. [0053100] 27/02/1996
Hinchcliffe Mr P, MCLIP, Life Member, Tel.0116 278 2240, 10 Cardigan Dr., Wigston, Leics., LE18 4XE. [0006921] 23/02/1951
Hinchley Mrs JM, (was Degg), MCLIP, Retired. [0003874] 24/02/1953
Hinchliffe Mrs AL, BSc MCLIP, Employment not known. [0060384] 11/12/2001
Hind Miss BC, Employment not known. [0052646] 15/11/1995
Hind Ms SJ, Senior Stock Asst., Slough Cent.L., Slough. [0059698] 08/08/2001 AF
Hind Mrs VF, MA MSc MCLIP, Employment not known. [0060620] 11/12/2001
Hindell Mrs CM, (was Pikesley), MCLIP, Retired. [0006924] 30/01/1957
Hinder Mrs HP, (was Cole), BA PG DipLib MCLIP, Sch.Lib., Greenfield Sch., Woking, Surrey. [0027931] 11/10/1977
Hindmarch Mr D, BA MCLIP, Sen.Local Studies Lib., Sheffield L.Arch.& Inf., Cent.L. [0006929] 14/01/1971
Hindmarch Mrs K, (was Procter), MCLIP, Lib., Sheffield Occupational Health Advis, Sheffield. [0012006] 11/03/1970
Hinds Mr M, BA MCLIP, Bibl.& Support Serv.Mgr., City of Edinburgh C. [0021113] 04/10/1973
Hindson Miss A, BA(Hons) DipIM MCLIP, Lend.Lib.(Requests), Southampton City Ls.& Arch., Hants. [0057743] 15/07/1999
Hindson Mrs EM, (was Thornton), DipLib MA(Hons) MCLIP, Housewife. [0039972] 10/10/1986
Hine Miss LK, BA(Hons), Grad.Traniee/p./t.Stud., Manchester Metro. [0061584] 02/10/2002

Hines Mr WD, MA M LIB MCLIP, Asst.Dir.-Inf.Serv., Univ.of Wales, Aberystwyth. [0023350] 05/11/1974
Hingley Mrs SM, (was Strongman), MA MCLIP, Cathedral Lib.-Canterbury, Dean & Chapter of Canterbury. [0014159] 01/10/1971
Hinkley Miss RD, MCLIP, Inf.Serv.Mgr., Coutts Career Consultants, London. [0027276] 24/01/1977
Hinks Mr J, MA MLS MIPD MCLIP, Retired. [0006934] 06/12/1964
Hinshalwood Mr KW, MA MCLIP, Life Member. [0006935] 07/03/1961
Hinton Miss BG, MCLIP, L.Asst., Inst.of Educ., Univ.of London. [0033847] 30/01/1981
Hinton Dr BJC, MA MA(OXON) PhD MCLIP, Hon.Lib., Julia Margaret Cameron Trust, Freshwater Bay, I.O.W. [0028344] 08/11/1977
Hinton Mrs GH, (was Alexander), BA MCLIP, NOF Training Project Co-ordinator, Herts.C.C., Hatfield. [0027600] 01/06/1977
Hinton Mr JR, BA MCLIP, Inf.Off., Sports Council for Wales, Cardiff. [0021603] 30/11/1973
Hinton Mrs ML, (was Parry), MCLIP, Asst.Lib., Oxford Brookes Univ.L. [0011300] 01/01/1966
Hinton Mrs SE, (was Beard), BA(Hons) MCLIP, Inmf.Mgr., Scientific Generics Ltd., Cambridge. [0043878] 07/02/1990
Hipkin Mrs AL, (was Hardy), BA DipLib MCLIP, Freelance Indexer. [0026401] 11/10/1976
Hipperson Mrs CM, (was Simkins), MCLIP, Br.Lib., Elm Park L., L.B.of Havering. [0006942] 23/02/1966
Hipperson Mr LG, FCLIP, Life Member. [0006943] 03/11/1952 FE 01/01/1964
Hipperson Mr MJ, MCLIP, Retired, 104 Warren Dr., Hornchurch, Essex, RM12 4QX. [0006944] 19/08/1966
Hirano Mr A, Catg.Asst., SOAS, Univ.of London. [0058892] 02/10/2000
Hird Mrs DL, (was Firth), MCLIP, Child.Lib., Kirklees Met.Council. [0019961] 10/01/1973
Hird Mr NW, BA MCLIP, Retired. [0006948] 01/01/1965
Hird Mr SJ, BA MCLIP, Sen.Lib., Educ.& Young Peoples Serv., Sch.L.Serv., Maltby L.H.Q. [0006949] 12/02/1969
Hird Mrs WD, (was Simkin), MCLIP, Lib., Tadcaster Grammar Sch., N.Yorks. [0006951] 01/01/1958
Hirons Mrs CM, (was England), BSc MSc, L.Res.Mgr., N.Oxfordshire Coll., Banbury. [0047320] 10/07/1992
Hirons Ms K, Statistics & Surveys Admin., Herts.Comm.Inf. [0059551] 11/05/2001 AF
Hirsh Mr R, BA(Hons), Lib., Freshfields Bruckhaus Deringer, Berlin. [0050993] 07/11/1994
Hirst Mrs AJ, (was Marwood), BA MA MCLIP, Asst.Lib., Arnold L., Notts. [0036456] 01/10/1983
Hirst Mrs GM, (was D'Coster), MCLIP, Retired. [0003847] 31/01/1962
Hirst Mrs H, (was Charlton), MCLIP, Sch.Lib., National Sch., Notts. [0002619] 25/01/1968
Hirst Mrs LM, (was Hynes), BA(Hons) MSc, Career Break. [0041116] 09/10/1987
Hirst Ms Y, BEd DipLib MCLIP, Local Studies Devel.Offr., N.E.E.L.B., Ballymena. [0044075] 30/04/1990
Hiscock Mrs G, (was Woodward), Flexible Learning Cent.Mgr., Derby Moor Community Sch., Derby City Council. [0038658] 19/09/1985
Hiscoe Ms AM, (was Le Breton), BSc DipLib, Self Employed, Consultant. [0036319] 03/10/1983
Hissett Mrs AM, (was Waters), BA(Hons) MCLIP, Med.Lib., Ayrshire & Arran Prim.Care NHS, Ayr. [0022717] 12/09/1974
Hitchcock Mrs NK, (was Cox), BA(Hons) DipILS MCLIP, Learning Res.Mgr., The Kings Sch., Wolverhampton. [0052340] 30/10/1995
Hitchen Mrs E, MCLIP, Retired. [0023985] 01/01/1956
Hitchen Miss J, BA(Hons) DipLIS MCLIP, Inf.Offr., Univ.of Cent.Lancs., Preston. [0045634] 08/04/1991
Hitchen Mrs SE, BA(Hons) MCLIP, Sch.Lib., St.Margarets High Sch., Airdrie. [0049702] 25/11/1993
Hitchin Miss J, BA(Hons), Mgr.of L.Serv., Universal Music, London. [0045614] 01/04/1991
Hitchings Mrs DE, (was Endersby), MCLIP, Br.Lib., L.B.of Havering, Essex. [0006967] 16/02/1962
Hitchmough Mrs SL, BSc(Hons), Learning Cent.Mgr., W.Cheshire Coll., Chester. [0054323] 21/11/1996
Hives Mrs JP, (was Wilkes), BA MCLIP, Sen.Lib., Co.Stock Team, Cambs.L.& Inf.Serv. [0015837] 25/10/1971
Hixon Ms BC, BA MA MCLIP, Asst.Subject.Lib., Oxford Brookes Univ. [0028317] 20/11/1977
Hjelmqvist Mr B, Hon.Vice-President. [0048844] 02/07/1993
Ho Ms EM, (was Goh), MSc MCLIP, Resident in Australia. [0027739] 15/07/1977
Ho Miss LYC, BA(Hons), Lib., Baker & Mckenzie, Hong Kong. [0054310] 18/11/1996
Ho Miss P, BA MLib, Exec.Offr., Pao Yue-kong L., The Hong Kong Polytechnic Univ. [0058429] 21/02/2000
Ho Mr WPA, MCLIP, Resident in Hong Kong. [0049219] 14/10/1993
Hoar Mrs KJ, (was Marsh), MCLIP, Lib., The Kings Sch., Canterbury, Kent. [0006974] 07/01/1961
Hoare Mr EP, MLS MCLIP ALAA, Communications Mgr., Food & Agric.Res.Mgmt.(Farm)Africa, London. [0019826] 01/01/1963
Hoare Mrs GM, (was Williams), B LIB MCLIP, Admin.Asst., L.B.of Richmond, The Russell Sch. [0015933] 20/01/1970
Hoare Mrs J, (was Ingham), BA DipLib MCLIP, Individual Tutor, Wakefield M.D.C., W.Yorks. [0006975] 09/10/1967
Hoare Ms JE, BA(Hons) DipLIS, Collection Devel.American History, Cambridge Univ.L. [0054175] 08/11/1996
Hoare Mr PA, MA FSA HonFCLIP, Retired., 21 Oundle Dr., Nottingham NG8 1BN. [0006979] 01/01/1960 FE 10/10/1995
Hoare Temple Miss KB, BA DipLib, Unemployed. [0033478] 01/01/1981
Hoban Ms R, BA(Hons), Sen.L.Asst., Durham C.C. [0058238] 24/11/1999

Hobart Miss AEL, BA MCLIP, Life Member. [0006983]   25/08/1954
Hobart Mrs JL, (was Ingrey), BA MCLIP, Lib., Greenwich L., London. [0031338]   01/10/1979
Hobbis Mrs MA, (was Middleton), BA MCLIP, L.Mgr., Neithrop L., Banbury, Oxfordshire C.C. [0028634]   18/01/1978
Hobbs Mrs CE, (was Edwards), MCLIP, Med.Lib., Defence Med.Serv., Train.Cent. [0023181]   05/11/1974
Hobbs Miss DK, MCLIP, Sen.Asst.Lib., Cent.Lend.L., Birmingham P.L. [0022328]   01/01/1974
Hobbs Mrs DM, L.Mgr., Ixworth L., Bury St.Edmunds. [0046943]   21/02/1992 **AF**
Hobbs Mr GP, BA(Hons), Stud., Univ.of Strathclyde, Glasgow. [0061268]   09/05/2002
Hobbs Miss ME, MCLIP, Lib., Bibl.Serv.Dept., Birmingham L.Serv. [0022295]   01/04/1974
Hobbs Mrs MS, (was Maggs), MCLIP, p./t.Asst.Lib., Worcs.Co.L., Stourport. [0021061]   01/10/1973
Hobbs Mr NR, BA MA MCLIP, Co-Ordinator of Educ.Tech., The Henley Coll., Henley on Thames. [0042179]   10/10/1988
Hobbs Dr TD, MA PhD MCLIP, Ch.Exec., E.Midlands Mus.L.& Arch.Council. [0032982]   16/10/1980
Hobby Mr PA, BA DipLib MCLIP, Music Collections Mgr., Brit.L., London. [0037501]   01/10/1984
Hoblyn Mrs KM, (was Hohne), BSc MCLIP, Career break. [0033405]   10/10/1980
Hobson Mrs AMR, (was Godfrey), BA DipLib MCLIP, L.Asst., London Guildhall Univ. [0005621]   28/04/1972
Hobson Ms CR, BA, Stud., Univ.Coll.London. [0059084]   10/11/2000
Hobson Mr EM, BA MCLIP, Area Lib., Dewsbury/Mirfield, Kirklees Met.Council. [0017345]   07/03/1966
Hobson Mr JA, MBE BA DipLib MCLIP, Self Employed. [0006994]   01/01/1970
Hobson Miss LC, BA(Hons) PgDipLIM, Bookseller, Waterstones Booksellers, Southport. [0059918]   23/10/2001
Hobson Mr MP, BA(Hons) MA, Coll.Lib., Evangelical Theological Coll., of Wales. [0055081]   09/07/1997
Hockey Mrs J, (was Barlow), MCLIP, Sen.Asst.Lib., Lancs.Co.L., Thornton-Cleveleys. [0019881]   10/01/1973
Hockey Ms RM, BA(Hons) DipLIS MCLIP, Community Lib., Denton L., Tameside L.& Heritage. [0042635]   26/01/1989
Hockey Mr SW, OBE HonFCLIP FCLIP, Hon.Fellow. [0018775]   04/01/1938 **FE 01/01/1942**
Hocking Mrs EJ, (was Westerby), L.Asst., Newcastle upon Tyne City Council. [0050745]   17/10/1994   **AF**
Hocking Miss KM, MCLIP, Unemployed. [0027647]   08/01/1964
Hocking Miss M, BSc MCLIP, Retired. [0060385]   11/12/2001
Hocking Mrs SM, (was Catt), BA(Hons) MA MCLIP, Coll.Lib., Kent Inst.of Art & Design, Maidstone. [0037426]   07/09/1984
Hockley Mrs PE, Sen.L.Asst., Princess Alexandra Hosp.NHS Trust, Harlow. [0061251]   29/04/2002   **AF**
Hodd Miss E, BA(Hons), Grad.Trainee, Reading Univ.L. [0061805]   11/11/2002
Hodder Mrs DK, MA MCLIP, Lib., Newnham Coll., Cambridge. [0035182]   06/10/1982
Hodds Mr J, BA(Hons), Info. Librarian, University of Bath, Bath. [0056645]   01/10/1998
Hodge Mr G, BLIP MCLIP, L.Serv.Mgr., N.E.Surrey Coll.of Tech., Ewell. [0037425]   15/09/1984
Hodge Mrs HM, (was Scurry), MCLIP, Lib., Glyn Tech.Sch., Epsom, Surrey. [0022700]   22/08/1974
Hodge Mrs JM, (was Crossley), MCLIP, Relief Asst.Lib., Kirklees M.C., Dewsbury. [0007010]   01/01/1961
Hodgens Mrs S, (was Hutchinson), MCLIP, Unemployed. [0025321]   05/01/1976
Hodgeon Mrs A, (was Leathem), BA DipLib MCLIP, Unemployed. [0039387]   22/01/1986
Hodges Mrs HA, (was Chappell), BLIB MCLIP, Unemployed. [0032026]   07/02/1980
Hodges Mr MT, BA(Hons) Dip Eur Hum. Dip Inf Sci, Sen.L.Asst., Univ.of Southampton. [0058716]   01/07/2000
Hodges Mrs PA, (was Prosser), MCLIP, L.Asst., Maesteg L., Bridgend Co.Bor.Council. [0020186]   04/02/1973
Hodges Mrs SA, BA MA MCLIP, Tech.Serv.Mgr., Liverpool John Moores Univ. [0027740]   19/07/1977
Hodges Mr TM, FCLIP, Life Member, Townhouse 3B, 5025 Hillsboro Road, Nashville, TN 37215-3796, USA. [0017038]   18/09/1954 **FE 18/07/1990**
Hodgetts Miss R, BA(Hons) PGDipLIMgt, Inf.Offr., Southport Coll., Merseyside. [0058010]   12/10/1999
Hodgkin Mr JC, BA, Stud. [0061472]   05/08/2002
Hodgkins Ms L, (was Brody), MLS MCLIP, Lib., Conde Nast Publications, London. [0050976]   04/11/1994
Hodgkins Mrs LK, BA MCLIP, Sen.L.Mgr: Reader Devel., Nottingham City L.& Inf.Serv. [0029328]   26/05/1978
Hodgkinson Ms CD, BA(Hons) DipLIB, Inf.Policy Devel., HM Customs & Excise, Salford. [0040364]   23/01/1987
Hodgkinson Mr DP, MA, Unemployed. [0061286]   07/05/2002
Hodgkinson Mrs HM, (was Birt), BA CertEd MCLIP, Sch.Lib.(p./t.), Portwey Comm.Sch., Bristol. [0021479]   20/01/1973
Hodgson Dr AM, MA DipAdEd PhD, Stud., Loughborough Univ. [0059955]   09/11/2001
Hodgson Ms C, BSc(Hons) PGCE MCLIP, Res.Mgr.,(Mat.Leave), Holloway Sch., L.B.of Islington. [0050868]   24/10/1994
Hodgson Mrs CE, (was Hard), BA MCLIP, Mgr.Reader Devel.Serv., Leicester City Council. [0006291]   14/08/1971
Hodgson Mrs DJ, BA MA MCLIP, Academic Liaison Lib., Univ.of Sheffield L. [0031138]   31/08/1979

Hodgson Ms J, BA(Hons) MA, Local Govt.Ombudsmans Investigator, York. [0059916]   02/11/2001
Hodgson Ms JA, (was Holt), BA(Hons), L.Serv.Super., Univ.of Durham L., Stockton Campus Sect. [0043602]   09/11/1989
Hodgson Miss KB, BSc MCLIP, Head of Knowledge & Inf.Mgmnt., CMS Cameron McKenna, London. [0038646]   26/08/1985
Hodgson Mrs KE, (was O'Flynn), BA(Hons), Inf.Offr., Linklaters, London. [0050432]   29/07/1994
Hodgson Mrs LM, MCLIP, Sen.Asst.Lib., Huddersfield Cent.L., Kirklees M.C. [0025308]   14/01/1976
Hodgson Mr M, BA(Hons) DipLIS MA MCLIP, Inf.Spec.(Humanities), King's Coll., London. [0047351]   20/07/1992
Hodgson Mrs PE, (was Brennand), MCLIP, Sch.Lib., Loughborough High Sch., Leics. [0007032]   01/09/1966
Hodgson Miss PL, BA(Hons), Customer Serv.Asst., Cheltenham & Gloucester, Harrogate. [0061087]   04/02/2002   **SP**
Hodgson Mrs RN, (was Hough), BA(Hons) DipILM, Sch.Lib., Altrincham Grammar Sch.for Boys, Cheshire. [0052135]   05/10/1995
Hodgson Mr SR, BSc(Hons) DipILS, Unemployed. [0050551]   15/09/1994
Hodkinson Miss CE, BA(Hons) MSc(Econ) MCLIP, Asst.Lib., Manchester Univ.L. [0051169]   23/11/1994
Hodsoll Miss VM, MCLIP, Life Member. [0007036]   01/06/1950
Hodson Mrs AA, (was Underwood), BA(Hons) MCLIP, Stud., Cranfield Univ. [0037084]   08/02/1984
Hodson Mrs MK, DipLib, Inf.Offr., Help the Hospices, London. [0048129]   11/11/1992
Hoenig Mrs CS, (was Stiff), BLib MCLIP, Bibliotheksangestellte VB Bat, Bochum Univ.Lib., Germany. [0028370]   25/10/1977
Hoey Mr PO, BSc MBCS FCLIP, Retired. [0060387]   11/12/2001 **FE 01/04/2002**
Hoffman Dr C, BA MLS PhD, Lect., Hebrew Univ.of Jerusalem., Israel. [0035826]   30/01/1983
Hoffman Ms M, HonFCLIP, Hon.Fellow, Writer. [0056142]   11/03/1998 **FE 11/03/1998**
Hogan Miss HJ, Grad.Trainee, Macfarlanes, London. [0061156]   15/03/2002
Hogarth Ms AJ, (was Perry), BA DipLib MCLIP, Stock Mgr., Cent.L., Middlesbrough L.& Inf. [0032087]   25/01/1980
Hogarth Miss J, BA MSc, Sen.Research Fellow, Sch.of L.Arch.& Inf.Studies, Univ.Coll.London. [0007042]   04/10/1960   **SP**
Hogben Mr BM, MA MCLIP, Retired. [0020606]   08/05/1973
Hogg Miss A, BA(Hons) MCLIP, L/LRC Asst. [0048071]   04/11/1992
Hogg Mr A, MSc BLibSc MCLIP, Dir.of L.Learning, Arts Inst., Bournemouth. [0007043]   02/04/1970
Hogg Mrs AL, (was Reid), BA, Primary Sch.Lib., Aberdeenshire L.& Inf.Serv. [0044708]   30/11/1990
Hogg Ms CG, BA MCLIP, Campus L.& Inf.Serv.Mgr., Univ.of Greenwich, Avery Hill Campus. [0007044]   02/02/1970
Hogg Mr D, BA MCLIP, Sch.Lib., Glasgow City Council, Glasgow. [0036707]   11/11/1983
Hogg Ms K, BMus(Hons) MusM MA, Music Ls.Consultant, Self-employed. [0041098]   08/10/1987
Hogg Mrs L, (was Steven), BA MCLIP, Team Lib., Glasgow City Council. [0034370]   27/10/1981
Hogg Mrs MA, (was Jackson), BA(Hons) BLibSc MCLIP, Health Inf.Offr., Poole Hosp.NHS Trust, Dorset. [0007679] 27/04/1970
Hogg Ms MF, MA(Cantab) MA, Lib., Trinity Coll.of Music, London. [0049589]   19/11/1993
Hogg Mr QE, BA(Hons) MSc, Inf.Offr., PCS L., London. [0042994] 30/05/1989
Hogg Mrs RJ, (was Powderley), BA MSc MCLIP, Sen.L.Asst., The Coll.of Law, York. [0054953]   28/05/1997
Hogg Mrs SG, (was Stapleton), BA MCLIP, Self-employed. [0013905]   21/09/1969
Hoggarth Mr R, MA MCLIP, L.Mgr., Kidderminster L., Worcs.C.C. [0007049]   06/09/1969
Hoggarth Mrs SB, (was Walker), MCLIP, Subject Lib., Univ.of Gloucestershire. [0015257]   02/10/1970
Hoggett Mr P, MCLIP, Retired. [0007050] 26/01/1951
Holah Ms JC, MCLIP, Sch.Lib., Marlborough Sch., Woodstock, Oxon. [0002678]   01/01/1972
Holborn Mr GF, MA LLB MCLIP, Lib., Lincolns Inn L., London. [0028590]   13/01/1978
Holbourn Mrs CJ, (was Jones), MCLIP, Teaching Asst., John Warner Sch., Hoddesdon, Herts. [0077977]   05/11/1972
Holbrook Mrs AM, (was Thompson), BA MCLIP, Retired. [0007054]   22/02/1950
Holbrook Miss G, (was Tremble), MCLIP, Outreach Serv.Lib., Bristol City Council. [0010136]   26/01/1967
Holcombe Mrs SJ, (was Robinson), BA MCLIP, Unemployed (Career Break). [0043709]   07/12/1989
Holdcroft Mrs LS, BA, Sen.L.Asst., Croydon Coll.Library. [0059092]   14/11/2000
Holden Mrs DM, BEd DipILS MCLIP, Lib., Sandbach & Wilmslow, Cheshire C.C. [0051872]   20/07/1995
Holden Mr DR, BSc(Hons) MSc MCLIP, Inf.Serv.Lib., Queens Univ., Belfast. [0052246]   18/10/1995
Holden Mrs GM, (was Mills), BA M PHIL DipLib MCLIP, Comm.Lib, Oldham MBC, Crompton, Royton & Mobile. [0031865]   11/01/1980
Holden Mrs HV, BA MSc MCLIP, Parliamentary Ref.Specialist, House of Commons L., London. [0007059]   02/10/1968
Holden Mrs LE, BA, Housewife & Mother. [0058253]   29/11/1999
Holden Miss MR, MCLIP, Life Member, Tel:01282 68679. [0007061]   01/01/1951
Holden Mr P, L.& Inf.Specialist, Astrazeneca, Loughborough. [0053917]   10/10/1996
Holden Ms PA, BSc MCLIP, Employment not known. [0060386]   11/12/2001

Holden Mrs SH, (was Bolton), MCLIP, Ref.Lib., Clitheroe L., Lancs. [0020296]   01/02/1973
Holder Ms AJ, BA(Hons) DipILM, Inf.Devel.Lib., Marylebone Inf.Serv., London. [0053522]   08/07/1996
Holder Mr B, Sen.Br.Mgr., Reading Bor.Council, Cent.L. [0061059] 14/02/2002   **AF**
Holder Mrs BE, (was Howarth), MLS MCLIP, Lib., Forintek Canada Corp., Vancouver, B.C., Canada. [0007282]   23/08/1971
Holder Miss CE, BA(Hons), Head of Inf.Serv., Kvaerner E&C UK Ltd., Whiteley, Hants. [0034256]   12/10/1981
Holdstock Miss ME, MCLIP, Retired. [0007065]   20/03/1943
Holdsworth Miss ME, MCLIP, Asst.Lib., Bexley P.L. [0007068]   21/08/1966
Hole Ms J, MA MCLIP, Asst.Lib.-Catr., Newbold Coll., Binfield, Berks. [0051701]   22/05/1995
Holgate Ms CM, BA DipLib MCLIP, Asst.Lib., N.Yorks.C.C., Ripon L. [0043651]   16/11/1989
Holland Mrs AE, BSc MSc MCLIP, IT Support Asst., Malmesbury Sch., Wilts. [0025885]   23/04/1976
Holland Mr CJ, BA MCLIP, Lib.& Head of Inf.Serv., The Law Society, London. [0025309]   05/01/1976
Holland Miss DB, BA(Hons), Metadata Project Offr., Open Univ., Milton Keynes. [0057074]   07/12/1998
Holland Mrs J, (was Giles), BA MCLIP, Head of L.& Inf.Serv., Norfolk C.C. [0030419]   08/01/1979
Holland Mrs JA, BA DipLib MCLIP, Asst.Co.Lib., Field Serv., Glos.Co.L.Arts & Mus.Serv. [0024953]   16/01/1975
Holland Miss JE, BA(Hons) MCLIP, College Retrain. [0023198]   01/11/1974
Holland Mrs KJ, (was Carter), BA(Hons) MCLIP, Inf.Lib., Norfolk County Council. [0032243]   15/02/1980
Holland Mrs M, (was Coffey), BA MA MCLIP, Inf.Desk Co-ordinator, Univ.of Surrey. [0042088]   03/01/1988
Holland Mr MJ, BA DipLib MCLIP, Employment not known. [0038280] 14/02/1985
Holland Mrs MS, BLib MLib MCLIP, Sen.Asst.Lib., Hertford Reg.Coll., Broxbourne. [0044481]   03/10/1990
Holland Miss PC, BA DipLib MCLIP, Head of Customer Serv., Inf.& Learning Serv., Univ.of Plymouth. [0025310]   06/01/1976
Holland Miss PJS, MCLIP, Team Lib., Blue Anchor L., L.B.of Southwark. [0007078]   01/08/1967
Holland Miss S, BA, L.Exec., House of Commons L. [0036227]   08/08/1983
Holland Mrs SA, Unemployed. [0053922]   10/10/1996
Holland-Bright Mrs DL, (was Holland), BA, Unemployed (Career break). [0037037]   31/01/1984
Hollands Mrs AM, (was Newley), BSc MCLIP, Relief Lib., Royal Bor.of Windsor & Maidenhead. [0038825]   14/10/1985
Hollerton Mr EJ, MCLIP, Sen.Asst.Lib., Cent.L., Tyne & Wear. [0007081] 19/02/1969
Holley Ms A, MA, De Montfort Univ., Leicester. [0048416]   01/01/1997
Holley Miss RC, BA(Hons), Unemployed. [0058021]   13/10/1999
Holley Ms RJL, BA MCLIP, Digital Projects Lib., Univ.of Auckland, New Zealand. [0040372]   21/01/1987
Holliday Ms AK, BA(Hons), Stud., City Univ.London. [0059227]   09/01/2001
Holliday Mr GW, MA MCLIP, Inf.Mgr., Clyde & Co., London. [0022836] 14/10/1974
Holliday Mrs J, (was Theobald), Unemployed. [0044773]   14/11/1990
Holliday Mr PJ, BA(Hons) DipEd DipLib MCLIP, Grp.Lib., Leominster L., Herefordshire Council. [0029394]   01/07/1978
Holliday Mrs S, MSc AdDipEd(OU), Head of L.Services, Birmingham Coll.Food & Tourism, Birmingham. [0057045]   30/11/1998
Holliday Mr TP, BA(Hons) DipInf MCLIP, Asst.District Mgr., Chelmsford, Maldon & Rochford, Essex C.C. [0043993]   03/04/1990
Holliday Miss V, MCLIP, Reg.Sch.Lib., Hants.Co.L. [0007088]   10/10/1963
Holling Miss LM, BA DipLib MCLIP, Princ.Inf.Asst., Univ.of Salford, The L. [0027171]   11/01/1977
Hollingdale Miss EA, MCLIP, Retired. [0007090]   07/03/1956
Hollingsworth Mr BP, BA(Hons) MA MCLIP, Evening/Weekend L.Super., UMIST, Manchester. [0052611]   13/11/1995
Hollingworth Mrs PL, (was Lake), MCLIP, Lib., HMP Ranby, Notts.C.C., Retford. [0007099]
Hollins Mrs AB, (was Noltingk), BA DIP LIB MCLIP, Inf.Offr., Roke Manor Research (Siemens), Romsey, Hants. [0033496]   14/01/1981
Hollins Mrs JH, (was Irving), MA DipLib MCLIP, Librarian, Bibliographical Services, Worcester County Council. [0029984]   25/10/1978
Hollinshead Mr RJN, MA MCLIP, Retired. [0007092]   24/03/1964
Hollis Miss AE, MA BA MCLIP, H.of Acquisitions Serv., Bodleian L., Oxford. [0037633]   16/10/1984
Hollis Mrs BME, (was Bostock), MCLIP, Retired. [0007093]   21/03/1941
Hollis Mrs E, (was Stone), BA(Hons) MA, Asst.Lib., Dixons City Technology Centre. [0055612]   24/10/1997
Hollis Mrs HE, L.Serv.Mgr., Girdlestone Memorial L., Oxford. [0061433] 22/07/2002
Hollis Mrs ME, (was Tizzard), MCLIP, Life Member. [0007094]   19/02/1951
Hollis Mr NG, BA DipLib BA MCLIP, Circ.Serv.Mgr., Reading Uni.L. [0036488]   11/10/1983
Holloway Mrs CM, (was Norton), MCLIP, Currently not working. [0010913] 11/01/1965
Holloway Mr MF, BA MCLIP, Retired. [0007100]   11/10/1951
Holloway Mr ND, BA DipLib, Asst.Lib.Ref.& European Docu.Cent., Queen Mary & Westfield Coll., Univ.of London. [0030187]   04/01/1979
Holloway Ms TJ, BA MA MCLIP, Unemployed. [0043758]   01/01/1990
Hollowell Ms AF, BA(Hons), Unpaid Volunteer, Bristol Naturalists Soc., Bristol. [0053698]   01/09/1996
Hollwey Mrs O, (was Zdravkovic), BA, Sen.L.Asst., Guille-Alles L., St.Peter Port, Guernsey. [0048476]   22/01/1993
Holly Ms C, Publns.Unit Mgr., Dept.of Trade & Industry, London. [0047529] 01/10/1992

Holly Mrs CS, (was Bagshaw), BSc(Hons) PGDipInf, Asst.Lib., Chester Coll., Cheshire. [0044522]   22/10/1990
Holman Miss AP, MCLIP, Life Member. [0007102]   22/05/1950
Holman Miss MR, BA(Hons) PGDipLib, Unemployed. [0057779]   02/08/1999
Holman Mrs R, (was Jackson), MCLIP, Team Lib., Bridgwater L., Somerset Co.L. [0022286]   29/01/1965
Holmes Ms A, Employment Unknown. [0044762]   14/11/1990
Holmes Ms AL, BA(Hons), L.Asst., Sir John Deane's 6th Form Coll., Northwich, Cheshire. [0032662]   06/07/1980
Holmes Ms BA, BA DipLib, Lib., Patients & Staff L., St.Bartholomews Hosp. [0040935]   01/09/1987
Holmes Miss C, MCLIP, Unemployed. [0007107]   23/09/1969
Holmes Ms C, BA(Hons) DipLIM, Sen.Learning Serv.Advisor., Liverpool Inst.Performing Arts. [0056663]   01/10/1998
Holmes Mrs EM, (was Shearer), BA(Hons) MA MCLIP, Ch.Lib., Sidcot Sch., Winscombe, N.Somerset. [0047833]   19/10/1992
Holmes Mrs F, (was Cooke), BA MCLIP, Unemployed. [0043266]   12/10/1989
Holmes Miss FM, MCLIP, Asst.Lib., Confed.of Brit.Industry, London. [0042556]   16/12/1988
Holmes Ms J, BA MCLIP DMS, Dist.Lib.-E., Herts.C.C., Bishops Stortford L. [0021328]   15/10/1973
Holmes Mrs JC, MA MCLIP, Retired. [0028318]   05/11/1977
Holmes Mrs JR, (was Hunt), BA MCLIP, Retired. [0007477]   20/10/1966
Holmes Mrs K, (was Skaife), BA MA MCLIP, Dep.Head of L., Suffolk Coll., Ipswich. [0036295]   01/10/1983
Holmes Miss KR, BA(Hons), L.Offr., Lincoln Cent.L. [0053045]   19/02/1996
Holmes Mr M, MA DipLib, Asst.Lib., Catg.Support Serv., Bodleian L., Oxford. [0037490]   04/10/1984
Holmes Mrs M, BA(Hons), Stud., Northumbria Univ. [0061685]   21/10/2002
Holmes Mrs M, (was Pigg), BA MLib MCLIP, Marketing Offr., Foreign & Commonwealth Off., London. [0007119]   01/01/1965
Holmes Mr MJ, BA MCLIP, Bor.Arch., Holborn L., Local Studies L., L.B.of Camden. [0007121]   05/02/1962
Holmes Mrs MM, BA(Hons) DipIS MCLIP, Sen.Lib., L.B.of Enfield. [0045127] 17/07/1990
Holmes Ms NM, MA MCLIP, Asst.Lib., Arts L., Nottingham Cent.L. [0035356]   13/10/1982
Holmes Ms P, BA(Hons) MSc MCLIP, Project Lib., L.B.of Croydon, Cent.L. [0026115]   23/07/1976
Holmes Dr PL, PhD FCLIP, Ch.Publishing & Inf.Offr., The Open Group, Reading, Berks. [0030765]   01/04/1979   **FE 14/02/1990**
Holmes Mr RK, BA MA, L.Clerk, BBC Research & Devel., Tadworth. [0057995]   08/10/1999
Holmes Miss SE, BA(Hons) MA MCLIP, Serv.Devel.Mgr., Dorset C.C. [0051587]   04/04/1995
Holmes Mrs SJ, (was Whiteman), BSc(Hons) MCLIP, Sen.L.Asst., Southampton City Coll. [0015757]   01/10/1971
Holmes Mrs SJ, (was Raybould), BA MCLIP, L.Asst., Ecclesbourne Sch., Duffield. [0024445]   10/08/1975
Holmes Mr TC, Higher L.Exec., House of Commons L. [0038808]   10/10/1985
Holmes Miss VA, BA MCLIP, Retired. [0007125]   30/06/1969
Holroyd Ms G, BA MSc AcDipEd FCLIP, Life Member. [0007127]   04/01/1957 **FE 01/01/1965**
Holt Miss A, MA, Electronic Serv.Lib., NESCOT, Surrey. [0058663] 09/05/2000
Holt Mr BP, BA MCLIP, Retired. [0007132]   15/10/1963
Holt Ms GA, (was Walker), DipLib BA MCLIP, Sen.Inf.Offr., N.F.E.R., Slough. [0034433]   30/10/1981
Holt Mrs L, (was Cherry), BA MCLIP, Sch.Lib., Upton High Sch., Cheshire C.C. [0002655]   04/02/1971
Holt Miss M, MCLIP, 8 Mentone Road, Stockport, SK4 4HF. [0007136] 16/12/1946
Holt Mrs MB, (was Park), MA DipLib MCLIP, Unemployed (Career Break). [0036467]   08/10/1983
Holt Mrs SK, (was Shaw), MCLIP, Lib./Team Leader, S.Area, Norfolk L.& Inf.Serv., Watton L. [0013226]   17/01/1972
Holt Mrs SL, Inf.Offr., BP Amoco Plc., Hemel Hempstead, Herts. [0053172] 01/04/1996   **AF**
Holt Mr WA, MA ACP MCLIP, Retired. [0007138]   15/01/1953
Holton Mr GS, BA DipLib MCLIP, Asst.Lib./Catg., Jordanhill L., Univ.of Strathclyde. [0024500]   27/08/1975
Holvey Mrs LD, (was Brewster), BLib MCLIP, Advisory Lib., LRE, Northants.L.I.S. [0027428]   01/04/1977
Holyoak Mrs H, (was Medlock), BSc MCLIP, Sen.Lib., The Kings Sch., Chester. [0010039]   16/06/1968
Homan-Russell Mrs BA, (was Hodgson), BA MCLIP, Child.Lib.(Job-Share), Birkenhead Cent.L., Wirral Bor.Council. [0030587]   10/02/1979
Homden Ms MM, MA MA, Asst.Lib., Univ.of London. [0055749]   13/11/1997
Home Miss ME, BA DipLib MCLIP, Inf.Specialist, Northumbria Univ., Newcastle upon Tyne. [0032986]   02/10/1980
Homer Miss M, MCLIP, Life Member. [0007141]   29/03/1951
Homer Mr SD, BA(Hons) DipLib MCLIP, Co-ordinator, Cent.Processing Unit, Univ.of Wolverhampton. [0035885]   07/02/1983
Homer-Brine Mrs CL, (was Homer), BA(Hons) MA MCLIP, Unemployed. [0047725]   15/10/1992
Homewood Mrs JEC, BSc(Hons), Grad.Trainee. [0059428]   13/03/2001
Hone Mrs G, (was Broomhall), MCLIP, Life Member, 27 Station Cres., Wembley, HA0 2LB. [0020796]   21/10/1947
Honeyball Mrs VM, (was Tobin), MCLIP, Sch.Lib., Sacred Heart of Mary Sch., L.B.of Havering. [0018342]   29/09/1972
Honeybourne Ms CJ, BSc(Hons) MSc MCLIP, Lib., Educ.Cent.L., Leicester Gen.Hosp.NHS Trust. [0054297]   20/11/1996
Honeybun Mrs N, (was Brace), BA DipLib MCLIP, Inf.Advisor, Univ.of Wales Inst.Cardiff. [0036422]   05/10/1983
Honohan Ms JT, (was Sognen), BA DipLib MCLIP, Knowledge Mgr., Accenture., Oslo.Norway. [0027173]   01/01/1977

Hood Mrs EM, BA MSc MCLIP, Official Pub.Lib., Hertfordshire L., Hatfield. [0036537] 04/10/1983
Hood Mr G, BA(Hons), p./t.Stud./L.Asst., Univ.of N.London, Ashurst Morris Crisp, London. [0059439] 28/03/2001
Hood Mrs GT, (was White), BA MCLIP, Lib., S.Hampstead High Sch., London. [0023118] 05/11/1974
Hood Miss IY, BA(Hons) MCLIP, Legal Lib., Semple Fraser, W.S., Glasgow. [0051957] 21/08/1995
Hood Mrs J, MA(Hons), I.T.Instructor & Lib., Aberdeen Coll. [0055675] 07/11/1997
Hood Mr JP, BA(Hons) DipLib MCLIP, Records Mgr., Crestco Ltd., London. [0043616] 09/11/1989
Hood Mr JR, BA(Hons) DipIS MCLIP, p./t.Asst.Inf.Offr., NCTEPO, Strathclyde Univ., Glasgow. [0047059] 09/04/1992
Hood Mrs MA, (was Bennett), BSc DipLib MCLIP, Educ.Res.Lib., Angus Cultural Serv. [0031192] 04/10/1979
Hook Mrs RS, (was Daniell), BA DPSE DMS MCLIP, Lib., Beds.C.C., Dunstable. [0034634] 18/01/1982
Hooker Miss DJV, BA DipLib MCLIP, Lib., Harbottle & Lewis (Solicitors), London. [0034147] 09/10/1981
Hooker Mrs SM, (was Simmonds), MCLIP, Lib., The Amersham Sch., Bucks. [0013368] 05/03/1968
Hookway Mrs C, (was Bennett), BA(Hons) PGDipLib, Freelance Indexer, [0053811] 02/10/1996
Hookway Sir HT, LLD FCLIP HonFCLIP, Retired. [0024219] 28/04/1975 **FE 15/06/1982**
Hoolboom-Kuah Mrs SP, (was Kuah), BA(Hons) DipLib MCLIP, Consultant, Australia. [0029717] 04/10/1978
Hooper Ms A, BA(Hons), Lib., S.Glos.Council, Winterbourne L. [0052811] 18/12/1995
Hooper Miss BJ, BA DIP ED MCLIP, p./t.Asst.Lib., Bibl.Serv., Somerset L.Admin. [0018343] 02/10/1972
Hooper Mrs BR, (was Carter), MCLIP, Princ.Lib.SLS, N.Yorks.Co.L. [0002428] 22/04/1971
Hooper Mrs CEM, BA(Hons) MA, Unemployed. [0056572] 01/09/1998
Hooper Mrs CM, (was Gauntlett), BA MCLIP, Lib./AV Technician, Stokesley Sch., N.Yorks C.C. [0005405] 20/01/1968
Hooper Ms DJ, (was Hole), BA MCLIP, Career Break. [0031537] 22/10/1979
Hooper Miss DM, BA(Hons), Inf.Offr., ROSPA., Birmingham. [0040419] 26/01/1987
Hooper Mrs FJ, (was Henderson), BA MCLIP, H.Lib., George Watson's Coll., Edinburgh. [0023471] 07/01/1975
Hooper Ms HB, MSc DipLIS MCLIP, Literacy Tutor, L.B.Waltham Forest. [0046111] 01/10/1991
Hooper Mrs JM, (was Jones), BA(Hons) MA MCLIP, Lib., Royal Glamorgan Hosp. [0048870] 07/07/1993
Hooper Mr LH, MCLIP, Retired. [0007155] 01/01/1964
Hooper Mrs RMF, (was Verran), BA MCLIP, Inf.Lib., Derby City Council. [0029210] 01/01/1974
Hoover Mrs MR, (was Jay), MCLIP, Unemployed. [0017048] 20/10/1965
Hope Mrs CM, (was Mayne), BEd CertLib MCLIP, Unemployed. [0033051] 06/10/1980
Hope Miss CU, BA MCLIP, Consultant Lib., Royal Academy of Dramatic Art, London. [0028020] 05/10/1977
Hope Mr J, BA(Hons) MA, Clerical Offr., Lancs.Educ.Off., Lancaster. [0061210] 16/04/2002 **AF**
Hope Mrs JG, (was Brasnett), NFF MCLIP, Life Member. [0007166] 13/10/1965
Hope Mrs LH, BSc MSc MCLIP, Employment not known. [0060389] 11/12/2001
Hope Ms PA, BA MA MSc DipLib MCLIP, Lib., Bank of England, London. [0025561] 05/02/1976
Hope Mrs PN, MCLIP, Dep.Lib., The L., Ambleside Campus, St.Martin Coll. [0030992] 22/07/1979
Hope Mrs RJ, (was Wootton), MCLIP, p./t.Asst.Lib., Derby C.C., Derby Cent.L. [0016296] 07/11/1969
Hopkins Ms AB, BA MSc, Unemployed. [0043814] 24/01/1990
Hopkins Mrs BL, BA MCLIP, Lib., Parmiters Foundation Sch., Watford. [0038517] 09/05/1985
Hopkins Mrs G, MCLIP, Team Lib., John Harvard L., L.B.of Southwark. [0007171] 28/01/1966
Hopkins Mrs JA, (was Cooper), MCLIP, Inf.Adviser (User Serv.), Univ.of Gloucestershire. [0007174] 17/05/1967
Hopkins Ms L, MCLIP, Self-employed Consultant. [0007173] 30/09/1965
Hopkins Miss LA, BA MPhil, Employment not known. [0056894] 02/11/1998
Hopkins Mr M, BA PhD MCLIP, Dir.of Inf.Serv., Univ.of Wales Aberystwyth. [0007178] 06/02/1968
Hopkins Mrs SM, (was Smith), MCLIP, Retired. [0007180] 13/01/1964
Hopkinson Mr A, MA DipLib MBCS FCLIP, Head of L.Systems, Middlesex Univ., London. [0018783] 05/09/1972 **FE 14/02/1990**
Hopkinson Mr IT, BA(Hons) DipLIM MCLIP, Lib., Longsight L., Longsight, Manchester. [0057869] 01/10/1999
Hopkinson Ms JM, (was Dodd), DipLib MCLIP, Grp.Lib., Birstall L., Leics.C.C. [0034242] 10/10/1981
Hopley Miss EJ, BA(Hons) MCLIP, Asst.L.Serv.Mgr., The Cent.Sch.of Speech & Drama. [0050744] 17/10/1994
Hopner Mr GN, BA MCLIP AIL PgDip.Ed, Inf.Serv.Lib., W.Dunbartonshire Council, Dumbarton. [0020025] 23/12/1965
Hopson Mrs I, (was Hewitt), MCLIP, ICT Serv.Co-ordinator, George Abbot Sch., Guildford. [0006795] 27/10/1971
Hopton Mrs JM, BA MA MCLIP, Asst.Lib.(Job Share), Blackpool Bor.Council. [0038963] 23/10/1985
Hopwood Mrs H, (was Outram), BA PGCE DipLib MCLIP, Asst.Lib., Univ.of the W.of England, Bristol. [0043915] 19/02/1990
Horan Ms A, BA MA MCLIP, Employment not known. [0060477] 11/12/2001

Horan Mrs C, (was Stanley), BA(Hons) MCLIP, Sch.& Community Lib., Lostock Sch.& Community L., Stretford, Manchester. [0048220] 16/11/1992
Horbacka Mrs MP, (was Rew), MCLIP, Literacy Co-ordinator, Greenwich Ls. [0007192] 05/04/1967
Horder Miss B, BA MCLIP, Retired. [0007193] 11/10/1960
Hordon Mrs FM, (was Aglen), MA DipLib MCLIP, Child.Lib., Alvering L., Wandsworth Bor.Council. [0000090]01/01/1971
Hordon Mrs K, (was Wright), BA(Hons) MA MCLIP, Sen.Offr., Enquiry Serv., Univ.of Northumbria at Newcastle. [0042366] 24/10/1988
Hore Mrs EJ, BA MCLIP, Mgr., Namara Ltd., Dulwich Books Ltd.,London. [0020149] 08/02/1973
Hore Miss MI, MCLIP, Asst.Lib., Glasgow P.L. [0018785] 20/01/1957
Horley Mr NGB, BA(Hons) MSc(Econ), Learning Res.Advisor, Abingdon & Witney Coll., Witney. [0051225] 30/11/1994
Horn Mrs FN, (was Seccombe), BA MCLIP, Unemployed. [0007196] 01/01/1966
Horn Mrs KR, (was Maff), BA DipLib, Unemployed. [0044898] 10/01/1991
Horn Mr V, BA MCLIP, Retired. [0007198] 01/01/1965
Hornbrook Mrs HC, (was Moyse), BA MCLIP, Unemployed. [0026850] 08/12/1976
Horne Mrs A, (was McIntosh), BA DipMgmt MCLIP, Lib., The Robert Gordon Univ., Hilton L., Aberdeen. [0009420] 12/10/1971
Horne Mr AK, BA(Hons) MA, Inf.Offr., Eversheds, London. [0052095] 03/10/1995
Horne Mr IA, BSc DipLib, Systems Lib., Calderdale M.B.C., Halifax. [0038384] 03/04/1985
Horne Dr MD, BSc MA MSc PhD, Stud., Univ.of Cent.England in Birmingham. [0061649] 14/10/2002
Horne Mr PA, LLB DipLib, Lib., Lothian Health NHS Board, Edinburgh. [0045593] 04/04/1991
Horne Mr PAE, MA, Lib.& Printroom Mgr., Fairham Community Coll., Clifton, Nottingham. [0052990] 13/02/1996
Horner Mrs H, (was Milby), MCLIP, p./t.Lib., N.W.Evening Mail, Cumbria. [0010127] 01/01/1970
Horner Mr PM, MA(Oxon) MSc, Inf.Offr., Bradford CVS. [0055900] 15/12/1997
Hornung Ms E, DipBibl MLIS, Lib./Inf.Mgr., Curriculum Devel.Unit, Dublin. [0061527] 13/09/2002
Horrell Mrs JF, (was Venn), BA MCLIP, Inf.Serv.Mgr., Plymouth City Council. [0037182] 21/03/1984
Horrex Mr DB, BEng(Hons), Stud., Univ.of Sheffield. [0061105] 26/02/2002
Horrigan Miss M, BA(Hons), Asst.Lib., Liverpool H.A. [0059519] 21/06/2001
Horrocks Mrs ACM, BA MSc DipLib MCLIP, Faculty Lib., The L., Kingston Univ., Surrey. [0022794] 12/10/1974
Horrocks Mr GJ, BA MSc, Sen.L.Asst.-Periodicals, King's Coll.Sch.of Med.& Dentistry, London. [0046008] 22/08/1991
Horrocks Dr N, HonFCLIP BA MLS PhD ALAA FCLIP, Sch.of L.& Inf.Studies, Dalhousie Univ., Canada. [0017055] 20/01/1945 **FE 01/01/1952**
Horsburgh Mrs AM, (was Shearer), B LIB MCLIP, Community Lib., Johnstone, Renfrewshire L. [0028246] 11/10/1977
Horsfield Mrs K, BEd, Stud., Bristol Univ. [0061710] 23/10/2002
Horslen Ms JC, (was Blyth), BA MCLIP, Reader Serv.Mgr., Law Soc. [0028533] 03/01/1978
Horsley Miss JE, MCLIP, Lib., Camden P.L. [0007220] 24/09/1968
Horsnell Ms PJ, DipEdTech MCLIP, Inf.Adviser, South Bank Univ., London. [0007223] 01/10/1970
Horsnell Ms V, BSc MSc FCLIP, Euro.Standards Mgr., Sun Microsystems Ltd., Bracknell. [0031077]27/08/1979 **FE 01/04/2002**
Horton Mr APJ, MA BA, p./t.Stud./Inf.Asst., London Met., Inns of Court Sch.of Law. [0061604] 03/10/2002
Horton Mrs E, (was Johns), MCLIP, Employment not known. [0060438] 11/12/2001
Horton Mr H, MA MCLIP, Life Member. [0007224] 18/03/1949
Horton Mrs JA, MA DipLib MCLIP, Unemployed. [0030841] 08/05/1979
Horton Dr PB, MA DipLib MCLIP, Ref.Lib./Research Co-ord., Royal Coll.of Music, London. [0034321] 21/10/1981
Horton Mrs SJ, BA(Hons) MCLIP, Inf.Super., Lovells, London. [0024281] 06/06/1975
Horwood Miss LK, BA MCLIP, Devel.Consultant &, Special Advisor in K.M., PTS Consortium (PTSC). [0038803] 11/05/1985
Horwood Mrs M, (was Port), BA MCLIP, Retired. [0008120] 09/10/1947
Hosie Mrs J, BA(Hons), Stud., Robert Gordon Univ. [0059535] 01/05/2001
Hosier Mrs C, (was Benton), MCLIP, Unemployed. [0007236] 12/04/1965
Hoskin Mrs CE, BA(Hons) DipLIS MCLIP, Sen.L.Asst., Rawtenstall L., Lancs.C.C. [0046122] 02/10/1991
Hoskin Ms R, BA(Hons), Community Resources Offr., Community Action Hampshire. [0061792] 08/11/2002 **AF**
Hosking Miss EM, MCLIP, Life Member. [0007238] 03/10/1947
Hosking Mr MG, MCLIP, Head of L.& Inf.Servs., Cambs.Co.L., Cambridge. [0007239] 19/09/1968
Hoskins Mrs JA, (was Graham), Freelance Film/VT Lib. [0039980] 08/10/1986
Hou Mrs SG, (was Pooley), BA MCLIP, Career Break. [0037120] 30/01/1984
Hough Mrs LJ, (was Say), BA(Hons) MSc, Mother. [0046650] 02/12/1991
Hough Mr MJ, BA MCLIP, Retired. [0007248] 22/02/1968
Houghton Mrs AC, (was Rashleigh), MA MCLIP, Retired. [0022646] 05/08/1974
Houghton Mrs CM, (was Gibson), MA, Med.Lib., S.Durham Health Care NHS Trust, Darlington. [0032741] 02/07/1980
Houghton Mrs DA, (was Plumpton), BA MCLIP, Unemployed. [0011759] 15/01/1970
Houghton Mr DJ, BA MCLIP, Life Member, Merrowdown, Porthallow, St Keverne, Cornwall, TR12 6PN. [0007250] 25/09/1955
Houghton Mrs EA, (was Hardie), MCLIP, Playleader, Longdon Leapfrogs, Glos. [0021835] 31/01/1974

Houghton Mrs IM, (was Howard), MCLIP, Life Member. [0012860] 20/01/1959
Houghton Miss JEM, MCLIP, Inf.Serv., Bor.of Poole, Poole Cent.L. [0023860] 03/02/1975
Houghton Ms M, BA MCLIP, Lib., Herts.C.C., Central Resources Lib, Hatfield. [0007253] 17/02/1972
Houghton Ms MC, B LIB MCLIP, Head of Business Devel., Amey IT Serv. [0035428] 01/10/1982
Houghton Ms SI, (was Hampson), BA(Hons) MCLIP FRSA, Dep.Co.Lib., W.Sussex C.C., Chichester. [0033834] 25/03/1981
Houghton Mr T, BSc DipLib DPA MCLIP MBA, Business Devel.& Contracts Mgr., Contracts Mgr., St.Martins Coll., Lancaster. [0021360] 20/11/1973
Houlston Mrs LR, BA MSC MED MCLIP, Retired. [0031329] 15/10/1979
Hounsell Mr NO, BA MCLIP, Inspector, Audit Commission, London. [0031045] 24/07/1979
Hounsome Mrs LM, (was Firth), BA MCLIP, Unemployed, [0004926] 18/01/1971
House Mr DE, BA MCLIP, Dep.Vice-Chancellor, Univ.of Brighton. [0007266] 20/11/1968
House Mrs FL, (was Auger), BA(Hons) DipLIS MCLIP, Career Break. [0050950] 31/10/1994
House Mrs MEA, (was Goldmann), MA DipLib MCLIP, Unemployed. [0034179] 12/10/1981
House Ms S, BA(Hons) MSc, Inf.Lib., Law & Computing, Univ.of Glamorgan, Pontypridd. [0047026] 02/04/1992
Housley Mrs AM, (was Foster), BA(Hons) DipLib MCLIP, Lib., N.Devon Healthcare NHS Trust, Devon Dist.Hosp. [0030619] 23/02/1979
Housley Mrs BJ, (was Rookes), B Lib MCLIP, Inf.& Lifelong Learning Lib., Cent.L., St Albans. [0012675] 15/06/1972
Housley Miss CL, BSc(Hons) MA, Inf.Offr., Davies Wallis Foyster, Liverpool. [0055980] 06/01/1998
Housley Mrs VA, (was McGarvey), BA(Hons) DipLib MCLIP, Accommodation & Planning Offr., Inf.Serv., Univ.of Nottingham. [0023096] 29/10/1974
Houston Miss F, MCLIP, Sen.L.Asst., Royal Vet.Coll., London. [0007268] 23/03/1971
Houston Mrs LY, (was Crozier), BLS MBA MCLIP, Ch.Lib., Belfast Educ.& L.Bd., Belfast. [0027148] 03/02/1977
Houston Miss M, BA MCLIP, Lifelong Learning Lib., Dennistoun L., Glasgow City Council. [0032747] 26/08/1980
Houston Mrs SJ, (was Ellis), BA MCLIP, Asst.Lib.(Readers'Serv.), Goldsmiths Coll.L., London. [0032055] 12/02/1980
Hovish Mr JJ, BA DipLib MLib MCLIP, Lib.& Curator, The American Legion, Indianapolis, U.S.A. [0021338] 17/10/1973
Howard Mr AG, MA FCLIP, Retired. [0007270] 06/10/1960
FE 01/01/1970
Howard Mrs AG, (was Culpeck), BA MCLIP, Ref.& Inf.Lib., Torbay Council, Torquay, Devon. [0027951] 04/10/1977
Howard Miss AS, BA MCLIP, Inf.Offr., Royal Inst.of Chartered Surveyors, London. [0033303] 20/11/1980
Howard Mrs BA, (was Parnell), BA MA MCLIP, P/t.L.Asst., Trinity & All Saints Coll., Horsforth,Leeds. [0022808] 01/01/1972
Howard Mrs C, BA(Hons), Sch.Lib., St Edwards Coll., Liverpool. [0059748] 12/09/2001
Howard Ms CE, BA(Hons), Stud., Univ.of Sheffield. [0059011] 24/10/2000
Howard Miss EC, BA DipLib MCLIP, Lib., St.Helens Sch., Northwood, Middx. [0034283] 20/10/1981
Howard Mrs EM, BA(Hons) MA, Asst.Lib., Vet.Lab.Agency, Surrey. [0056135] 05/03/1998
Howard Mr G, BA DipIS, Papers Clerk, House of Commons L., London. [0047127] 05/05/1992
Howard Mrs HE, (was Davies), BA(Hons) MSc MCLIP, Faculty Team Leader, Univ.of Leeds, Brotherton L. [0050819] 19/10/1994
Howard Miss IC, BA DipLib MCLIP, Sen.Lib., Particle Physics & Astonomy, Research Council, Swindon. [0032989] 16/10/1980
Howard Mrs J, BA(Hons) MA, L.Inf.Serv.Mgr., Marie Curie Cancer Care, Newcastle upon Tyne. [0052779] 12/12/1995
Howard Ms J, BA(Hons) MA, Employment not known. [0052784] 13/12/1995
Howard Miss JE, BA BD PGDipLIS, Retired. [0044334] 19/09/1990
Howard Ms JE, BA MCLIP, Sch.Lib., Samuel Whitbread Community Coll., Shefford, Beds. [0025762] 10/03/1976
Howard Mr JV, MA FCLIP, Life Member. [0007276] 17/09/1952
FE 01/01/1958
Howard Mr L, BSc MCLIP, Resident in Australia. [0060106] 07/12/2001
Howard Mr M, MSc BSc Cert Adult Ed, Editor, L.Solutions, Banbury. [0061656] 14/10/2002 AF
Howard Mr PR, BA MCLIP, Learning Res.Cent.Mgr., Blessed John Roche Catholic Sch., London. [0024954] 28/10/1975
Howard Miss PJ, BSc MA MCLIP, Temp.Bibl.Asst., The John Rylands Univ.L., Univ.of Manchester. [0055787] 19/11/1997
Howard Ms SV, BA MSc DipLib MCLIP, Asst.Dir., Imperial Coll.of Sci.Tech.& Med., S.Kensington Campus. [0029689] 09/10/1978
Howard Mr TW, FCLIP, Retired. [0007281] 04/03/1947
FE 01/01/1960
Howarth Mrs A, BSc(Hons) MSc MCLIP, Unemployed. [0023875] 01/02/1975
Howarth Mr C, BA MCLIP, Mgr., Inf.& I.T.Serv., Doncaster M.B.C. [0007283] 29/01/1965
Howarth Ms C, BA MLS MBA, Br.Lib., Wednesfield L., Wolverhampton. [0007332] 07/02/1980
Howarth Ms CA, MA MCLIP, L.& Inf.Worker (Job-share), Commerce & Tech.Dept., Dundee City Council, Dundee L. [0037513] 05/10/1984
Howarth Mr JA, BA MA, Stud., Univ.Coll.London. [0061606] 03/10/2002
Howarth Mrs KJ, (was Madden), BA(Hons) DipInf MCLIP, Lib., Cheshire C.C., Macclesfield L. [0046766] 14/01/1992
Howat Mrs MM, (was White), BA MCLIP, Retired. [0007289] 11/02/1957
Howcroft Mr B, FCLIP, Life Member. [0007290] 27/01/1955
FE 01/01/1965

Howcroft Mrs GRI, (was Pardon), MCLIP, Retired. [0011208] 01/01/1941
Howcroft Mrs ME, BSc, Position unknown, HBG Construction Ltd., London. [0061273] 09/05/2002 AF
Howden Ms JS, MA DipLib MCLIP MPhil, Sen.Lib., Glasgow Caledonian Univ. [0035541] 04/10/1982
Howe Mrs AE, (was Nicolaides), BA MCLIP, Lib., Church Sch.Company, Kingston upon Thames. [0013010] 01/01/1969
Howe Mrs C, (was Baty), BA MCLIP, Special Serv.Lib., Carlisle L. [0000936] 27/06/1972
Howe Miss CEA, BLS MCLIP, [0028022] 02/10/1977
Howe Mrs G, (was Johnson), MCLIP, Sch.Lib., Baston Sch., Bromley, Kent. [0007884] 24/09/1964
Howe Mr JA, FCLIP, Life Member, Tel.0131 337 3598. [0007295] 06/01/1949
FE 01/01/1957
Howe Mr MP, BA, Administrator, Corp.& Legal Serv., Durham C.C. [0035096] 10/08/1982
Howe Mr MWF, MA, Lib./Inf.Offr., Cruising Assoc. [0055777] 17/11/1997
Howe Miss PJ, BEd, Unemployed. [0055752] 12/11/1997
Howe Mr RW, BA DMS, Locality Mgr., Suffolk C.C. [0045374] 08/11/1990
Howell Miss ES, BA MCLIP, H.ofInf., Investec, London. [0041005] 01/10/1987
Howell Mr IN, Mgr., Inf.Systems, Tobacco Manufacturers Assoc., London. [0047322] 13/07/1992
Howell Mrs JLM, (was Williamson), BA(Hons) MCLIP, Website Editor, Royal Nat.Inst.for the Blind, London. [0046025] 22/08/1991
Howell Mrs M.R., (was Adams), BA PGDipLib MCLIP, Asst.Lib., Corp.of London, City Business L. [0045777] 22/05/1991
Howell Mrs MF, BA(Hons) MA, L.R.C.Cent.Mgr., Nottingham City Council. [0055077] 09/07/1997
Howell Mrs P, (was Bevan), MA MCLIP, Unemployed. [0007301] 10/01/1958
Howell Mrs PA, (was Teasdale), BA DipLib MCLIP, Lib., Leicester City Council. [0024728] 01/10/1975
Howell Miss SL, MSc, P./t.Stud./L.Asst., Swansea Cent.L., Univ.Aberystwyth. [0059772] 01/10/2001
Howell-Badham Mr MG, Inf.& L.Resource Mgr., King Edward VII Sch., Sheffield. [0039310] 10/01/1986
Howells Miss EA, BA MCLIP, Unemployed. [0007304] 24/04/1972
Howells Mrs EW, (was Evans), BA, Collection Devel.Mgr., Hugh Owen L., Univ.of Wales Aberystwyth. [0039153] 18/11/1985
Howells Mrs GI, (was Fulton), MCLIP MLib, Self Employed. [0007305] 12/03/1970
Howells Miss JA, BA DipLib MCLIP, Asst.Prof.Adviser, CILIP, London. [0031867] 08/01/1980
Howells Miss MA, MA PGCE MCLIP, Teacher of English, Rodillian Sch., Leeds. [0041983] 01/07/1988
Howells Mr MD, BA DipLib MCLIP, Sen.Lib.-Res., County L.H.Q., Essex C.C. [0035961] 16/03/1983
Howells Mr ND, MCLIP, Career Break. [0020985] 03/09/1973
Howells Mrs PA, (was Lawrence), MCLIP, Life Member. [0007309] 06/10/1944
Howells Mr WH, BA MLib MCLIP, Swyddog Llyfrgell y Sir, Ceredigion. [0023138] 01/11/1974
Howes Mr MG, FCLIP, Employment not known. [0060388] 11/12/2001
FE 01/04/2002
Howes Mr RC, FCLIP, Life Member. [0007314] 07/08/1948
FE 01/01/1961
Howes Mr RW, MA PhD MCLIP, Sub-Lib.(Collections), Univ.of Sussex L., Brighton. [0025169] 01/12/1975
Howes Mrs SM, (was Draper), Sen.L.Asst., Lincs.C.C., Bourne, Lincs. [0052943] 26/01/1996 AF
Howey Miss H, BA(Hons) MCLIP, Deputy Area Lib., W.Sussex C.C., Horsham L. [0043662] 20/11/1989
Howie Mrs AS, (was Perrins), BBibl, Tech.Researcher/Classifier, Barbour Index plc., Windsor. [0048886] 12/07/1993
Howie Mrs IB, MCLIP, Team Lib., Glasgow L., Inf.& Learning. [0011912] 01/01/1968
Howie Miss JC, BA(Hons) MSc, Inf.Serv.Mgr., Tite & Lewis, London. [0048027] 04/11/1992
Howie Mrs S, BA MPhil DipLib MCLIP, Lib., Royal Agricultural Coll., Cirencester. [0034021] 12/07/1981
Howkins Miss HM, Inf.Asst., De Montfort Univ., Kimberlin L., Leicester. [0055682] 04/11/1997
Howkins Mr SJ, BA MCLIP, Dep.Ref.& Inf.Serv.Lib., Exeter Cent.L., Devon C.C. [0026902] 07/01/1977
Howland Mrs VR, (was Bates), BA DipLib MCLIP, Sch.Lib., Prospect Tech.Coll., Reading. [0042294] 19/10/1988
Howley Mr PR, BSc PGCE PGDip, Temp. [0047492] 04/09/1992
Howley Mrs SM, (was Evans), BA MA MCLIP, Sen.Policy Adviser, Resource, London. [0004703] 01/01/1969
Howman Mr REJ, MA MCLIP, Unemployed. [0022502] 28/05/1974
Howsam Miss DC, BA DipLib MCLIP, Principal Lib.(Inf.Direct), Northants.C.C. [0038004] 01/01/1985
Howson Mr AH, MCLIP, Retired. [0007330] 11/03/1957
Howson Ms NJ, BA(Hons) MCLIP, Lib., Royal Soc.of Med., London. [0050955] 31/10/1994
Hoyal Ms AC, (was Cadogan), BA DipLib MCLIP, P./t.Stockroom Asst., Edinburgh Woollen Mill, Bath. [0032990] 13/10/1980
Hoyes Mrs ME, BA DipLib, Lib.(Bibl.Serv.), Royal Soc.of Med., London. [0007332] 01/01/1961
Hoyet Miss S, Asst.Lib., Morgan COle, London. [0059827] 11/10/2001
Hoyle Mrs B, (was Croop), MCLIP, Retired. [0003409] 01/01/1961
Hoyle Mr JN, BA(Hons) DipLib, ICT Lib., Wandsworth Bor.C., London. [0044395] 04/10/1990
Hoyle Miss SE, MA MCLIP, Princ.Sch.Lib., The Highland Council, Educ.Cent., Dingwall. [0007340] 19/07/1971
Hoyles Miss JL, Sen.Inter-Lend.Asst., L.B.Richmond-upon-Thames, Surrey. [0059662] 23/07/2001 AF

Personal Members   Hughes

Hoysted Mrs HJ, (was Wright), BA(Hons) MA MCLIP, Resident in USA. [0042499]   23/11/1988
Huang Ms Z, MSc MCLIP, Sen.L.Asst., Imperial Coll.of Sci.Tech.& Med., London. [0054624]   27/01/1997
Hubbard Miss JT, MA MCLIP, Retired. [0007345]   11/10/1948
Hubbard Ms KC, BA, Team Lib.-Inf., L.B.of Enfield, Cent.L. [0044036]   06/04/1990
Hubbard Mrs LD, (was Wyatt), BLib MCLIP, Self-Employed Proof-Reader. [0027233]   21/01/1977
Hubbard Miss LM, BA DipLib MCLIP, Dep.Br.Lib., Wanstead L., L.B.of Redbridge. [0028023]   11/10/1977
Hubbard Mr WJI, BSc, Stud., Loughborough Univ. [0061361]   26/06/2002
Hubble Mrs MM, (was Gill), MCLIP, Life Member. [0007346]   01/01/1951
Huber Miss SV, BA(Hons) DipHE, p./t.Stud./L.Asst., Univ.of N.London/Univ.of Greenwich. [0053036]   16/02/1996
Hubschmann Ms K, MA MA, Accessions Lib., Wiener L., London. [0053688]   05/09/1996
Hucbourg-Muller Mrs L, MA, Inf.Offr., Linklaters & Alliance, London. [0056141]   05/03/1998
Huckfield Mrs CJ, BA MCLIP, Acquisitions Mgr., Herefordshire Council. [0030402]   06/02/1979
Huckin Mrs DV, (was Farmer), B LIB MCLIP, Principal Inf.Offr - IT Dept., N.E.Lincs.Council, Cleethorpes. [0022397]   13/05/1974
Huckle Mrs FM, (was Burrell), BA MCLIP, Business Inf.Specialist, Univ.of Bath in Swindon. [0024616]   29/09/1975
Huckle Ms MJ, (was Ford), BSc(Hons) MCLIP, Head, Membership Careers & Qualifications, CILIP. [0021069]   21/10/1973
Huckstep Miss IJ, MCLIP, Team Lib., Local Serv., Kent C.C., Margate. [0007347]   28/09/1961
Huddart Mr DJ, MA MSc MCLIP, Employment not known. [0060390]   11/12/2001
Huddy Mr EJ, BA DipLib FCLIP, Retired. [0007349]   14/07/1954   **FE 01/01/1964**
Hudson Mr A, BSc MCLIP, Sen.Lib., L.B.of Waltham Forest. [0021226]   10/10/1973
Hudson Miss B, MCLIP, Team Lib., Southwark P.L. [0007353]   17/02/1966
Hudson Mr BP, MA MCLIP, Life Member, Tel.01280 703508, 32 Church Lane, Evenley, Brackley, Northants., NN13 5SG. [0007354]   29/02/1948
Hudson Mrs C, (was Harris), BA MCLIP, Head Of Inf.& Collections Mgmnt., Theatre Mus., London. [0022433]   23/04/1974
Hudson Mrs CS, (was Geary), MCLIP, Team Lib.-Under 5's, Glos.C.C., Cirencester. [0007356]   31/01/1969
Hudson Ms DR, BA(Hons), Subject Lib., Univ.of Cent.England, Birmingham, Birmingham Coll.of Food, Tourism. [0059036]   31/10/2000
Hudson Mrs GL, MA MPhil MIL MCLIP, Sen.Asst.Lib., Univ.of Bradford. [0018630]   01/01/1972
Hudson Mr J, MISTC BA MCLIP, Unemployed. [0038011]   01/01/1985
Hudson Mrs J, BA(Hons), Sch.Lib., Milford Haven Sch., Milford Haven, Pembs. [0053504]   10/07/1996
Hudson Mrs JA, (was Mutter), BA MCLIP, Lib., Faringdon Comm.Coll., Oxon. [0022578]   01/07/1972
Hudson Ms JA, BA DipLib MCLIP, Subject Analyst, BDS Ltd., Dumfries. [0035074]   01/07/1982
Hudson Mrs K, MSc BSc MCLIP, Asst.Lib., Duncan McMillan House, Nottingham. [0007362]   18/08/1971
Hudson Mr KJ, BSC MSC, C.A.B.Internat., L.Serv.Cent. [0035834]   24/01/1983
Hudson Miss MC, BA DipLib MCLIP, Retired. [0021740]   06/01/1974
Hudson Mr ML, BA MCLIP, Asst.Lib., Dept.for Educ.& Skills L., Sheffield. [0007364]   03/09/1971
Hudson Mrs MP, BA MCLIP, Inf.Lib., Southampton Inst. [0040658]   23/04/1987
Hudson Mr NA, BA DipLib MCLIP, Lib., Meat & Livestock Commission, Milton Keynes. [0025888]   01/04/1976
Hudson Mr P, BA(Hons) DipLib, L.Offr., Blackhall L., City of Edinburgh Council. [0047244]   22/06/1992
Hudson Mrs PA, BA(Hons) MSc(Econ) MCLIP, Local Studies Lib., Derby City L. [0054415]   05/12/1996
Hudson Mr RE, BA DipLib MCLIP, Inf.Offr., Royal Soc.of Chemistry, London. [0042343]   21/10/1988
Hudson Miss SE, BA DipLib MCLIP, Lend.Lib., Bournemouth Bor.Council, Lansdowne L. [0042222]   14/10/1988
Hudson Mrs SJ, (was Huston), BA MCLIP, Research Offr., Royal Bor.of Windsor & Maidenhead. [0037014]   27/01/1984
Hudson Mrs SJ, (was Saunders), BA(Hons) DipLIS MCLIP, Sen.Subject Lib., Middlesex Univ. [0050743]   14/10/1994
Hudson Mr TJ, MCLIP, Unemployed. [0007368]   04/10/1971
Hudson Mrs WE, (was Robertson), BA MCLIP, Learning & Inf.Strategies Lib., Sheffield L.Arch.& Inf. [0034138]   01/01/1981
Huffer Mrs J, (was Mills), BA DipLib MCLIP, Princ.Lib.,Educ.L.Serv., Notts.C.C., Nottingham. [0025788]   04/07/1990
Hugall Mrs JA, (was Game), BA MCLIP, Operational Resources Mgr., Brighton & Hove L. [0031619]   05/11/1979
Huggan Miss AM, BA(Hons) MA MCLIP, Unemployed. [0054249]   14/11/1996
Huggett Mr JM, BA(Hons) MSc(Econ), Catr., The London L., London. [0057929]   05/10/1999
Huggins Mrs JM, (was Towson), MCLIP, Sch.Resources Lib., The Queen`s Sch., Wisbech, Cambs. [0007373]   10/01/1966
Huggins Mr P, BA(Hons), L.Mgr., Inst.Logistics & Transport, Northants. [0046983]   25/03/1992
Huggins Miss SL, BA(Hons), Child.Lib., The Royal Bor.of Windsor &, Maidenhead. [0058747]   03/07/2000
Hugh-Jones Miss GE, BLib, Lib., Cornerstone Cent.for Intercultural, Studies, The Netherlands. [0043238]   12/10/1989
Hughes Miss A, BA(Hons) MLIS, Mgr.-Enquiry Serv., Trade Partners UK, London. [0056580]   28/08/1998

Hughes Mrs A, (was Mcaulay), BA MCLIP DMS MBA PGCE, Head of Learner Serv., Sandwell Coll.of F.& H.E., Wednesbury. [0025067]   28/10/1975
Hughes Mrs A, BA(Hons) PGDipLIS MCLIP, Mgr., Gatesbield Quaker Housing Assoc.Ltd, Windermere. [0054502]   02/01/1997
Hughes Mrs AC, BA(Hons) MA, Forbes Mellon Lib., Clare Coll., Cambridge. [0051644]   25/04/1995
Hughes Ms AL, MA MCLIP, Community Lib., Rhos, Wrexham Co.Bor.Council. [0025054]   14/11/1975
Hughes Mrs AM, L.Asst., Yale Coll., Wrexham. [0059650]   12/07/2001
Hughes Mrs AP, (was Cahill), Retired. [0007375]   01/01/1954
Hughes Mr B, (was Williams), MCLIP, p./t.Br.Lib., Burryport Br., Carmarthenshire C.C. [0007376]   01/01/1966
Hughes Mrs BJ, (was Swain), MCLIP, Retired. [0007377]   02/03/1941
Hughes Miss BM, BA DipLib MCLIP, L.Adviser, Child.& Young People & Welsh Serv., Denbighshire C.C.L.& Inf.Serv. [0041198]   18/10/1987
Hughes Miss BS, BA, Asst.Lib.(Collection Devel.), Univ.of Exeter. [0044540]   23/10/1990
Hughes Mrs C, BA(Hons) MCLIP, Tech.Serv.Mgr., Liverpool Hope, The Sheppard-Worlock L. [0052297]   23/10/1995
Hughes Mrs CA, (was Crane), MCLIP, Housewife. [0022732]   27/08/1974
Hughes Miss CH, BSc MA, Sen.Inf.Offr., Business Link Lincs.& Rutland, Lincoln. [0061549]   11/09/2002
Hughes Mr CJ, BA MCLIP, Grp.Lib.(W.), Gloucester L., Glos.C.C. [0007380]   06/03/1961
Hughes Mrs CL, (was Hall), BA(Hons) DipILS MA, Inf.& Local Studies Lib., Warwickshire C.C., Atherstone L. [0051890]   31/07/1995
Hughes Miss CM, Receptionist/L.Asst., Twickenham Pk.Surgery, East Twickenham. [0045398]   27/11/1990   **AF**
Hughes Ms CM, (was Perring), MCLIP, Sch.L.Serv.Mgr., Essex Sch.L.Serv. [0007381]   15/10/1968
Hughes Ms CW, BSc(Hons), Retired. [0045399]   26/11/1990
Hughes Mr DM, BA FCLIP, Retired. [0007385]   03/01/1950   **FE 01/01/1959**
Hughes Mr DR, BSc DipEd MCLIP, Retired. [0007386]   07/02/1972
Hughes Mrs FCM, (was Morris), BA(Hons) MLib MCLIP, L.Site Mgr., Crewe L., Manchester Metro.Univ. [0044594]   01/11/1990
Hughes Mrs G, (was Bonas), B LIB MCLIP, Learning Cent.Mgr., Walsall Campus, Univ.of Wolverhampton. [0019733]   10/01/1972
Hughes Mr GH, BA MA DipLib MCLIP, Serv.& Operational Support Lib., Devon L.& Inf.Serv., Exeter. [0034312]   21/10/1981
Hughes Ms GM, MCLIP, Unemployed. [0011419]   01/01/1969
Hughes Mr GO, BA MSc MCLIP, Employment not known. [0040969]   01/10/1987
Hughes Mr GW, BA MCLIP, Retired. [0007393]   28/04/1965
Hughes Mrs HEM, MA BA MCLIP, Campus Lib., Cent.Queensland Univ., Brisbane, Australia. [0028399]   07/11/1977
Hughes Dr HGA, MA DPhil CSc FCLIP FRAI, Life Member. [0007394]   06/09/1954   **FE 01/01/1960**
Hughes Ms J, BA MCLIP, Community Lib., Birmingham L.Serv., Sparkhill & Balsall Heath L. [0007396]   01/01/1969
Hughes Mrs JA, (was Harding), MCLIP, Asst.City Lib., N.End Br., Portsmouth City Council. [0006305]   15/01/1971
Hughes Mrs JA, BA MLib MCLIP, Career Break. [0044678]   23/11/1990
Hughes Mrs JB, (was Bingham), BSc(Hons) MCLIP, Employment not known. [0001257]   17/01/1968
Hughes Mr JE, MCLIP, Retired. [0007402]   28/09/1965
Hughes Mrs JE, (was Clee), BA(Hons) MCLIP, Div.Comm.Serv.Lib., Winchester DHQ., Hants.C.C. [0046833]   14/02/1992
Hughes Mrs JE, (was Morgan), BA DipLib MCLIP, Unemployed. [0035425]   01/01/1982
Hughes Mrs JE, BA(Hons), Lib., Sutton High Sch., Ellesmere Port. [0057312]   08/02/1999
Hughes Mrs JL, (was Gibson), BSc MCLIP, Career Break, Home Off. [0041236]   20/10/1987
Hughes Mr JM, (was Groome), MCLIP, Unemployed. [0007403]   05/10/1966
Hughes Mr JS, MCLIP, Sen.Lib., Harlesden L., L.B.of Brent. [0043712]   05/12/1989
Hughes Miss L, Sen.Asst.in Charge, Somerset C.C., The L., Street. [0054770]   01/04/1997
Hughes Miss LJ, BSc(Hons) MCLIP, Lib., Telford & Wrekin Council. [0054349]   14/11/1996
Hughes Mrs LM, (was Reid), BA DipLib MCLIP, L.Advisory Offr., Wilts.& Swindon Learning Res., Trowbridge. [0022070]   07/01/1974
Hughes Mr M, FCLIP DMS, Life Member. [0007411]   22/09/1954   **FE 01/01/1962**
Hughes Mr M, BA(Hons), Inf.Asst., Spencer Stuart, London. [0061634]   09/10/2002   **AF**
Hughes Mrs M, BA(Hons) MA MCLIP, Inf.Serv.Trainer, Dibb Lupton Alsop, Birmingham. [0049733]   08/12/1993
Hughes Mrs M, (was Waylen), Inf.Asst., Cent.L., Portsmouth. [0045132]   19/07/1990   **AF**
Hughes Mrs M, (was Day), BA(Hons) DipLib MCLIP, Retired. [0029025]   19/02/1978
Hughes Mr MJ, p./t.Stud./L.Asst., Coventry Univ.L., UCE Birmingham. [0059615]   03/07/2001
Hughes Mrs NJ, BA MCLIP, Web & InfT.Mgr., Cheshire C.C. [0043604]   09/11/1989
Hughes Mrs PA, (was Mcevan), DipIT MCLIP, Life Member. [0007418]   16/08/1955
Hughes Ms PM, BA(Hons), Asst.Lib., Nat.Police L., Hook. [0058119]   03/11/1999
Hughes Mr R, MCLIP, Employment Unknown. [0018794]   11/03/1960
Hughes Mr R, BA(Hons) MA MCLIP, Catr., Bibl.Serv.Cent., Chipping Barnet L. [0022473]   24/05/1965
Hughes Mr RA, MA BA DipLib MCLIP, Bus.Inf.Serv.Mgr., Bolton M.B.C. [0042705]   07/02/1989

Hughes Mr RD, BA DipLib MCLIP, Ls.Offr., Wrexham L.& Inf.Serv. [0034469] 16/11/1981
Hughes Mr RI, BLib MCLIP, Head, Nat.L.of Wales, Nat.Screen & Sound Arch.of Wales. [0025565] 30/01/1976
Hughes Ms S, (was Raghavan), BA(Hons) DipLib, Swyddog Datblygu Cymuned, Cyngor Sir Powys, Llanfyllin. [0033850] 01/04/1981
Hughes Ms S, OBE HonFCLIP, Hon.Fellow. [0054737] 01/01/1997 **FE 01/01/1997**
Hughes Miss SJ, BA(Hons) MA MCLIP, Learning Resources Mgr., Sheffield City Council, The City Sch. [0057392] 01/03/1999
Hughes Mrs SJ, (was Alvarez), MCLIP, Inf.Mgr., Bus.Link Herts., St.Albans. [0000249] 28/05/1968
Hughes Miss SM, BA(Hons), Inf.Administrator, UNISON, Unison. [0059247] 16/01/2001
Hughes Mrs SM, MA, LIS Consultant. [0051372] 01/02/1995
Hughes Mr SP, BA(Hons) DipILS, Learning Res.Lib., Worcester Coll.of Tech. [0048017] 03/11/1992
Hughes Mrs SP, (was Hind), BA MCLIP, Freelance Copy-Editor &, Proofreader. [0006923] 08/09/1965
Hughes Ms SR, (was Hughes-Dimascio), Admin.Offr., Norfolk C.C. [0045295] 02/10/1990 **AF**
Hughesdon Mrs RF, (was Cryer), BA MCLIP, Lib., Surrey Co.L., Woking L. [0021153] 06/10/1973
Hughson Miss CM, BA(Hons), P./t.Stud./Inf./Search Dept.Asst., Aberystwyth Univ. [0059771] 01/10/2001
Hugo Mrs M, (was Macphail), MCLIP, Lib., Dumfries & Galloway Coll., Dumfries. [0009557] 19/03/1971
Huish Mr AW, BA MA FCLIP, Life Member, 34 Kenwood Gdns., Gants Hill, Ilford, Essex, IG2 6YQ. [0007425] 21/01/1947 **FE 01/01/1967**
Hukins Mrs CE, (was Weatherill), BA MCLIP, Mgr., Small Business Gateway Inf.Cent., Aberdeen. [0017072] 01/10/1987
Hukins Mrs F, (was Anning), MA, Asst.Inf.Offr., Brit.L., Bus.Inf.Serv., London. [0053693] 09/09/1996
Hulance Mrs WP, (was Nicolson), BLib MCLIP, Y.Lib.p./t., Beds.C.C., Dunstable L. [0027622] 24/05/1977
Hull Mr RC, MA MCLIP, Research Offr., Liverpool Record Off. [0007429] 17/01/1972
Hullin Mrs PM, (was Collino), MCLIP, Life Member. [0002990] 22/09/1948
Hulme Mrs JM, (was Hardwick), MCLIP, Unemployed. [0032289] 19/03/1980
Hulse Mrs HJ, (was Lamb), BSc, Veterinary Lab.Agency, Addlestone, Surrey. [0039416] 23/01/1986
Hulyer Mrs MC, (was Cawthorne), BA MCLIP, Lib., Cambridge Cent.L. [0022800] 14/10/1974
Humber Miss ALJ, BA(Hons) MA MCLIP, Asst.Lib., Dept.for Culture, Media & Sport, London. [0052359] 26/10/1995
Humbert Miss SI, LLB MA, Temp.Lib., Chartered Insurance Inst. [0059402] 05/03/2001
Hume Mrs CL, (was Thompson), BA MSc MCLIP, Lib., Royal Inst.of Internat.Affairs, London. [0032469] 22/04/1980
Hume Mrs EM, CertEd DipILM MA MCLIP, Local Studies & Arch.Lib., Huyton L., Knowsley M.B.C. [0049442] 27/10/1993
Hume Mr FW, MCLIP, Life Member. [0007439] 24/03/1948
Hume Ms K, BA(Hons), p./t.Stud./L.Asst., Robert Gordon Univ., Wirral Bor.Council. [0061075] 04/03/2002
Hume Mrs S, (was Flooks), BA(Hons), L.Inf.& Knowledge Skills Trainer, Worcester Community NHS Trust, Worcs. [0047970] 29/10/1992
Hume Mr WE, BA DipEd MCLIP, Retired. [0007441] 24/01/1950
Humfrey Mr JR, MA BA(Hons) DipLib DipEdMan MCLIP, Coll.Lib., Myerscough Coll., Bilsborrow, Preston, Lancs. [0046420] 05/11/1991
Humm Miss D, MCLIP, Freelance. [0017074] 01/01/1963
Humm Mrs JS, (was Hair), MCLIP, Princ.Lib.- Child.& Young People, & S.L.S.,Luton Bor.Council. [0021292] 16/10/1973
Humm Miss YM, BLib MCLIP, Sales Asst., Hever Castle Ltd., Kent. [0025317] 21/01/1976
Humphrey Mrs LA, (was Mason), MCLIP, Unemployed, 2 Hill Grove, Romford, Essex, RM1 4JP. [0007447] 15/01/1964
Humphrey Mr M, MCLIP, Life Member. [0007448] 10/01/1961
Humphrey Mr NJ, B LIB MA MCLIP, Area Lib., Somerset C.C., Frome. [0032300] 24/02/1980
Humphrey Mrs PA, (was Tremblett), BLIB MCLIP, Team Lib., Somerset L.Serv. [0032202] 30/01/1980
Humphrey Miss SJ, BA DipLib, Inf.Specialist, Min.of Transport, Netherlands. [0040839] 18/07/1987
Humphreys Miss CD, BA(Hons), Lib.Asst., St.Albans L. [0059142] 28/11/2000 **AF**
Humphreys Mrs DE, (was Davies), Book Club Offr., Welsh Books Council, Aberystwyth. [0007450] 23/02/1970
Humphreys Mrs DS, (was Surridge), BA, Unemployed. [0020739] 01/01/1973
Humphreys Miss EA, MCLIP, Stock Serv.Dept., Wolverhampton P.L. [0007451] 22/09/1960
Humphreys Ms EJ, BSc(Econ), Intranet Ed., Home Off., London. [0043928] 23/02/1990
Humphreys Mr GP, FRSA MCLIP, Business Lib., Corporation of London. [0007454] 29/03/1966
Humphreys Mr JF, MSc MCLIP, System Mgr., London Inst. [0007455] 01/05/1972
Humphreys Mrs JP, (was Ferguson), MCLIP, Asst.Lib., Falkirk Council, Falkirk. [0004853] 26/01/1969
Humphreys Miss R, BA DipLib MCLIP, Asst.Lib., Dept.for Educ.& Skills, Sheffield. [0034161] 05/10/1981
Humphreys Mrs R, Stud., Aberystwyth Univ.of Wales. [0061651] 14/10/2002
Humphreys Mrs S, (was Moore), BA, Asst.Lib., Further Educ.Funding Council, Coventry. [0007459] 14/01/1950
Humphreys Ms SJ, BA(Hons) PGDip LIS, Sch.Lib., Solihull M.B.C., Alderbrook Sch., W.Mids. [0049091] 01/10/1993

Humphries Mrs AE, (was Brookes), B Lib MCLIP, Educ.Admin., Hereford & Worcester C.C. [0001801] 18/10/1971
Humphries Miss BA, BA, Asst.Lib., Brit.L. of Pol.& Econ.Sci., L.S.E., London. [0027331] 22/02/1977
Humphries Mrs CM, BA DipLib MCLIP, Asst.Lib., Queen Margaret Univ.Coll., Edinburgh. [0044736] 21/11/1990
Humphries Dr CR, BSc MSc PhD, Stud., Leeds Met.Univ. [0061324] 22/05/2002
Humphries Ms JK, BA(Hons) MA MSc, Asst.Learning Res.Cent.Mgr., Bristol Univ.& Hereford 6th Form. [0057166] 04/01/1999
Humphries Mrs LC, (was Woodall), MCLIP, Comm.Lib., Cannock P.L., Staffs.C.C. [0032222] 07/01/1980
Humphries Mr ND, FCLIP, Life Member. [0007463] 08/12/1945 **FE 01/01/1957**
Humphries Miss PK, BA MCLIP, Life Member. [0007464] 04/10/1946
Humphries Mrs SJ, (was Dickenson), MCLIP, P/t.Lib., Waterlooville L., Hants. [0003933] 05/11/1967
Humphris Mrs J, (was Dix), BA MSc, Unemployed. [0037734] 16/10/1984
Hundertmark Mr IR, BA(Hons) DipIM MCLIP, Asst.Lib., Dept.for Educ.& Skills, London. [0053819] 02/10/1996
Hundsberger Ms S, BA(Hons), Stud., Manchester Met.Univ. [0048238] 16/11/1992
Hundu Mr JT, BLS, Coll.Lib., Sch.of Biblical Studies, Nigeria. [0059132] 21/11/2000
Hung Miss MY, BSc MA, Lib., Tower Hamlets Sch.L.Serv., London. [0056561] 20/08/1998
Hunn Miss RA, BSc(Hons), Asst.Team Leader, Cranfield Univ., Swindon. [0058230] 22/11/1999
Hunnings Ms C, BA, Inf.Offr., AIG Europe, London. [0058347] 19/01/2000
Hunt Ms A, MA DipLib MCLIP, Area Mgr., W.Lothian C. [0026419] 18/10/1976
Hunt Mrs AM, (was Small), BA MCLIP, p./t.Asst.Lib., Trinity Hall, Cambridge. [0038225] 03/02/1985
Hunt Miss CA, BSc, Lib., Dechert, London. [0052640] 15/11/1995
Hunt Mr CJ, BA MLitt FSA MCLIP, Dir.& Univ.Lib., Univ.of Manchester. [0018798] 14/09/1959
Hunt Mrs D, (was Abby), BA MCLIP, Sen.Learning Resources Asst., Leeds Met.Univ., Leeds, W.Yorks. [0000012] 01/01/1961
Hunt Mrs EA, (was Shaw), MCLIP, Unemployed. [0013210] 04/02/1968
Hunt Mr G, BA DipLib MCLIP, Lib., Cent.L., L.B.of Croydon. [0034786] 02/02/1982
Hunt Mrs G.M., (was McMahon), BA(Hons) MCLIP, Lib., Coatbridge L., N.Lanarkshire Council. [0049688] 25/11/1993
Hunt Mrs JA, BA MIPD MCLIP, Employment not known. [0060696] 12/12/2001
Hunt Mr JB, BA CertEd MCLIP, Business Devel. Mgr., DS Ltd, Nottingham. [0033220] 28/10/1980
Hunt Mrs JD, CertEd, Lecturer, IT., Runshaw Coll.L., Lancs. [0057844] 09/09/1999 **AF**
Hunt Miss JL, BA(Hons) CertEd MA, Learning Res.Mgr., Herne Bay High Sch., Kent. [0053755] 01/10/1996
Hunt Miss JM, BA MPHIL, Lead Consultant, Brit.L., London. [0037911] 15/11/1984
Hunt Mr JM, BA(Hons), Inf.Specialist, Kings Coll., London. [0050378] 08/07/1994
Hunt Mr JM, MCLIP, County Records & Local Stud.Mgr., County Hall, Bucks. [0007476] 09/01/1970
Hunt Mr JW, BA MCLIP, Life member, 1 Dynevor Terr., Fairford, Glos., GL7 4JD, Tel:01285 712577. [0007478] 05/01/1946
Hunt Mr K, FCLIP, Retired. [0007479] 01/04/1938 **FE 01/01/1959**
Hunt Miss L, Stud., Aberystwyth, Univ.of Wales. [0061661] 15/10/2002
Hunt Mrs L, (was Whitlam), MCLIP, Lib., Sutton P.L. [0015768] 01/10/1971
Hunt Ms L, BA(Hons) DipLib, Res.Lib., Childcare Inf.Devel.Serv., Wolverhampton. [0048618] 15/03/1993
Hunt Mr M, BSc(Hons) DipInfSc, Corp.Inf.Mgr., Royal Nat.Inst.Blind, London. [0048836] 01/07/1993
Hunt Mrs MC, (was Williams), BA DipLib MCLIP, Unemployed. [0036656] 31/10/1983
Hunt Mrs ME, (was Humpage), MCLIP, L.Mgr.(Building Project), Open Univ., Milton Keynes. [0007444] 03/01/1972
Hunt Mrs MM, (was Houston), BA MCLIP, Child.Lib.(Job Share), Sutton Coldfield L., Birmingham P.L. [0032988] 10/10/1980
Hunt Ms NJ, BA MA MCLIP, Catg.Mgr., (Retro.Catg.Conversion), London Sch.of Economics L. [0038575] 12/07/1985
Hunt Mrs PA, (was Fenbow), BA MCLIP, Business Research Exec., 31 PLC., W.Midlands. [0004827] 21/01/1972
Hunt Mr RA, FCLIP, Retired. [0007484] 02/09/1954 **FE 01/01/1967**
Hunt Mrs RAH, (was Matthews), BA DipLib MCLIP, Unemployed. [0041384] 17/11/1987
Hunt Mrs S, Sch.Lib., Richard Hale Sch.L., Hertford. [0060000] 19/11/2001 **AF**
Hunt Ms S, BA DipLib MCLIP, Child.Lib., Stratford upon Avon L., Warwickshire C.C. [0033407] 10/11/1980
Hunt Mr SW, BA MA DipLib MA MCLIP, Sen.Product Specialist, OCLC Europe, The Middle E.& Africa. [0045898] 09/07/1991
Hunt Miss TM, BA MCLIP, Sen.Lib., Shropshire C.C., Shrewsbury L. [0043342] 24/10/1989
Hunter Mrs AM, (was Murray), BA DipLib MCLIP, Sen.Lib.Young Peoples Serv., E.Lothian Council. [0033413] 19/11/1980
Hunter Ms C, BA(Hons), Stud., Univ.of Strathclyde. [0061226] 15/04/2002
Hunter Mrs CM, (was Wilkinson), MLib MA MCLIP, Head of Pub.Serv.Unit, Dept.of Trade & Ind., London. [0024970] 24/10/1975
Hunter Mr DJ, Unemployed. [0060932] 11/01/2002
Hunter Mrs EG, (was McIntosh), MCLIP, Lib.Mgr., Armadale L., West Lothian. [0007493] 28/04/1970

Hunter Prof EJ, MA AMIET FCLIP, Life Member. [0007494]   16/12/1948 FE 01/01/1966
Hunter Mrs GH, MA(Hons) DipILS, Subject Lib., Bolton Inst., Lancs. [0052487]   02/11/1995
Hunter Mr GJ, MA MA MCLIP, Lib., Angus Council, Brechin L. [0044335]   19/09/1990
Hunter Mrs HD, (was Wright), BA MSc MCLIP, Inf.Mgr., Comm.Justice NTO. [0042527]   28/11/1988
Hunter Mr IJ, BA(Hons) MSc MCLIP, Asst.Inf.Offr., Slaughter and May, London. [0046741]   14/01/1992
Hunter Miss J, MA(Hons) MA, Asst.Lib., Cairns L., Oxford Radcliffe Hosp. [0052024]   15/09/1995
Hunter Mrs JA, MA(Hons) DipILS MCLIP, Unemployed. [0053948]   15/10/1996
Hunter Mr JG, MCLIP, Retired. [0007496]   17/01/1969
Hunter Mrs JL, (was Bromley), MCLIP, Asst.Lib., Balne Lane L., Wakefield M.D.C. [0007497]   10/11/1967
Hunter Mrs LGY, (was Caulker), MPhil BA FCLIP, Unemployed, 224 Aldermoor Rd., Southampton, Hants., SO16 5NT. [0017076]   01/01/1965   FE 18/11/1998
Hunter Ms M, Off.Mgr., Scottish Parliament Inf.Cent., Edinburgh. [0058405]   07/02/2000
Hunter Mrs MP, (was Connolly), MCLIP, Retired. [0007499]   17/09/1950
Hunter Mrs NR, (was Howell), BA MCLIP, Members Inf.Serv., Cumbria C.C., Carlisle. [0007300]   24/10/1967
Hunter Mr PS, MSc CChem MRSC MCLIP, Retired. [0060392]   11/12/2001
Hunter Ms SM, (was Dick), MA MCLIP, Lib., Database Mgmt., Edinburgh City L. [0003932]   22/10/1969
Hunter Mrs T, (was Greaves), BA(Hons) MSc MCLIP, Learning Resources Advisor -, Health & Social Studies, Colchester Inst. [0053912]   10/10/1996
Hunwick Ms ER, BA(Hons) MA, p./t.Stud./L.Asst., UCL, Anglia Poly.Univ., Chelmsford. [0057042]   30/11/1998
Hurcombe Mrs M, (was Sutherland), BA MCLIP, Project Mgr., Family Advice & Inf.Resource, Edinburgh. [0031465]   15/10/1979
Hurd Mrs SM, MCLIP, Res.Lib., (P./t.), Univ.of Wolverhampton. [0037360]   01/01/1996
Hurford Mr G, MA MCLIP, Catr., EBRD, London. [0007506]   04/10/1971
Hurley Ms KA, BA(Hons) DipLIS, Lib., Stockport Coll.of F.& H.E. [0048228]   16/11/1992
Hurn Mr MD, MA MCLIP, Dept.Lib., Inst.of Astronomy, Univ.of Cambridge. [0040975]   28/09/1987
Hurry Miss P, MA MCLIP, Unemployed. [0007512]   25/05/1970
Hursey Mrs RA, (was Limbert), Researcher, William M Mercer Ltd., London. [0046474]   11/11/1991
Hurst Miss A, BA MCLIP, Life Member. [0007513]   29/01/1972
Hurst Mrs A, (was Newton), BA MCLIP, Sch.Lib., Royal Grammar Sch., Guildford. [0020662]   15/05/1973
Hurst Miss J, BA(OU) MCLIP, Lib., Brit.Geological Survey, Nottingham. [0019976]   01/01/1973
Hurst Mr J, BA DipLIP MCLIP, L.Consultant & Trainer, Freelance. [0029691]   01/10/1978
Hurst Mrs JM, (was Gallop), BA MCLIP, Dep.H.of L.Serv., Maidstone & Tunbridge Wells NHS, Kent. [0007519]   24/08/1961
Husband Miss DG, MA DipLIP MCLIP, L.Inf.Serv.Mgr., Peterborough Hosp.NHS Trust, Cambs. [0037438]   10/09/1984
Husband Ms KR, (was MacCallum), BSc DipLib MCLIP, p./t.Research Lib., Glasgow Univ., Dept.of Accounting, & Finance. [0042232]   13/10/1988
Husbands Mrs ES, (was Houghton), BA DipLib MCLIP, Subject Classifier, Whitaker Inf.Serv., Herts. [0019776]   26/11/1972
Husbands Mrs SD, (was Hanson), MCLIP, Life Member. [0006284]   30/09/1952
Huse Mr RJ, FCLIP, Life Member, Tel.01243 826393. [0007524]   01/10/1946 FE 01/01/1959
Huss Mrs LM, (was Carson), BA(Hons) MSc(Econ) MCLIP, Asst.Clinical Lib., Birmingham Spec.Comm.Hlth.Trust, Smallwood Clinical L. [0048988]   20/08/1993
Hussey Mrs NM, (was Smith), MCLIP, Lib., Peacehaven Comm.Sch., E.Sussex. [0013665]   04/09/1971
Hutchens Mrs EG, BA(Hons) MA MCLIP, Inf.Offr., ERA Tech.Ltd, Surrey. [0026421]   14/10/1976
Hutcheon Mrs HJ, (was Telfer), BSc MCLIP, Ch.Lib., Royal Botanic Garden, Edinburgh. [0024144]   26/02/1975
Hutcheon Mr JR, BA MCLIP, Retired. [0007529]   09/02/1968
Hutchings Miss SM, BA MCLIP, Retired. [0007535]   08/08/1960
Hutchins Mr JVP, MA DipLib MCLIP, L.Serv.Mgr., Royal Surrey Co.Hosp., Guildford. [0032993]   03/10/1980
Hutchinson Mr AJ, BA(Hons), Head of L.Serv. [0039465]   31/01/1986
Hutchinson Mr C, BA, Unemployed. [0032992]   14/10/1980
Hutchinson Miss CA, BMUS MCLIP, Lib.Music L., Birmingham P.L. [0007539]   07/01/1972
Hutchinson Mrs E, BSc, Stud., Aberystwyth Univ. [0059191]   12/12/2000
Hutchinson Mrs KTV, (was Murphy), BA MCLIP, Unwaged. [0032324]   12/02/1980
Hutchinson Mrs P, BA MCLIP, Lib., Astley Comm.High Sch., Northumberland. [0043608]   09/11/1989
Hutchinson Miss SV, BA(Hons), Asst.Lib.Catr., Scottish Exec., Edinburgh. [0049305]   20/10/1993
Hutchison Ms DME, BA DipLib MCLIP, Unemployed, 9 Montague Road, Cambridge,CB4 1BU. [0041001]   01/10/1987
Hutchison Mrs EM, (was Rae), BSc(Econ)(Hons), Inf.Offr., Bell Coll.of Tech.L., Hamilton. [0047162]   18/05/1992
Hutchison Miss HM, Unemployed. [0038234]   11/02/1985
Hutchison Miss SA, BA MCLIP, Retired. [0007549]   02/10/1967
Hutt Ms J, Inf.Knowledge Mgr., Salisbury Health Care NHS Trust, Salisbury, Wilts. [0039343]   15/01/1986

Hutton Mrs AG, (was Tarquini), BA(Hons), Project Mgr., Sch.of Inf.Studies, Univ.of Northumbria at Newcastle. [0049711]   25/11/1993
Hutton Mrs C, (was Prentice), BA MCLIP, Retired. [0026517]   22/10/1976
Hutton Mrs DE, Sen.L.Asst., Rosyth L.(Br.), Dunfermline. [0051645]   25/04/1995   AF
Hutton Mr I, BA MA, L.Asst., J.B.Priestley L., Univ.of Bradford. [0039891]   01/10/1986
Hutton Mrs JIF, (was Sparshott), MCLIP, Retired. [0007553]   01/01/1951
Hutton Mrs JS, MA DipLIS, Inf.Offr., Univ.of Abertay Dundee. [0051399]   06/02/1995
Hutton Miss MA, BSc(Hons) MCLIP, L.Mgr., Royal Bromp.& Harefield NHS Trust, Harefield Hosp. [0053305]   25/04/1996
Huws Mrs DP, (was Williams), BA(Hons) DipLib MCLIP, Asst.Lib., Nat.L.of Wales, Aberystwyth. [0045441]   06/02/1991
Huws Mr G, BA MCLIP, Head of Dept., Dept.of Inf.& L.Stud., Univ.of Wales, Aberystwyth. [0007554]   11/10/1966
Huws Mr RE, MLib FCLIP, Head of Serv., Dept.of Public Serv., Nat.L.of Wales. [0007555]   01/01/1968   FE 07/01/1982
Hwang Mrs JR, (was Dunn), BA MCLIP, Team Leader - Bibl.Serv., Inf.Serv., Univ.of Birmingham. [0004279]   02/01/1969
Hyams Ms E, HonFCLIP, Editor, CILIP. [0059133]   21/11/2000 FE 01/04/2002
Hyams Mr M, FRSC HonFCLIP, Hon Fellow. [0060393]   11/12/2001 FE 01/04/2002
Hyatt Mrs FS, (was Topping), BA(Hons) DipLib MCLIP, Inf.Offr.:Acquisitions, Univ.of Salford. [0045662]   17/04/1991
Hyde Mrs AM, (was Roaf), FCLIP, Position Unknown, Manches Solicitors, London. [0012448]   14/01/1970   FE 26/07/1995
Hyde Ms D, BA(Hons) DipIM, Sen.L.Asst., L.B.of Merton, Wimbledon L. [0051286]   20/12/1994
Hyde Mrs J, (was Payne), MCLIP, Sch.Lib., Devon C.C. [0023620]   13/01/1975
Hyde Mrs J, (was Andrew), BA(Hns) DipLib MCLIP, P./t.Lib., Slough Cent.L. [0032848]   01/09/1980
Hyde Mr JA, FCLIP, Retired. [0007558]   02/03/1962   FE 01/04/2002
Hyde Ms JC, (was Paxton), BA DipLib MCLIP, Unemployed. [0041285]   28/10/1987
Hyde Mrs MP, BA DipILS, Position unknown, Scottish Agricultural Coll., Bucksburn. [0058666]   11/05/2000
Hyde Miss N, BA MCLIP, Life Member. [0007559]   21/03/1952
Hyde Mrs NL, (was Bowers), L.Asst., Derby C.C. [0057171]   17/10/1996
Hyde Mrs NM, Sch.L., Wirral Educ. [0054625]   04/02/1997
Hyde Mr RW, MCLIP, Retired. [0007562]   06/01/1971
Hyde Ms SF, MA PGCE, Staffing & Serv.Dev.Mgr., Sheffield Hallam Univ. [0059461]   03/04/2001
Hyde Ms SG, BSc(Hons) DipLib MCLIP, p./t.Tech.Lib., Thales Research Ltd., Reading, Berks. [0032601]   30/05/1980
Hyde Mrs VA, BA MEd MCLIP, Lib., Blessed Robert Johnson Catholic, Coll., Telford. [0007563]   01/01/1963
Hyde Mr VG, MCLIP, Retired. [0018800]   01/05/1964
Hyder Ms G, MCLIP, Stock Serv.Mgr., L.B.of Croydon Cent.L. [0007564]   13/07/1966
Hyett Mr DJ, BSc DipLib MCLIP, Lib., Cent.for Environment, Fisheries &, Aquaculture Sci., Lowestoft. [0037170]   14/03/1984
Hyland Mrs D, BA, Sen.Learning Res.Cent.Mgr., Belfast Inst.F.& H.E. [0059572]   04/06/2001
Hyland Mrs JJ, BBA MBA, Lib., S.Hampstead High Sch., London. [0057718]   06/07/1999
Hyland Mrs JW, (was Gray), MCLIP, Sen.Asst., Ellon L., Aberdeenshire. [0007565]   09/10/1975
Hyland Miss SA, BA MCLIP, Ch.Youth Serv.Lib., Bucks.C.C. [0024707]   09/10/1975
Hylton Ms BJ, (was Harding), BA(Hons) DipIM MCLIP, L.Mgr., Bucks.Health Auth., Aylesbury. [0052208]   13/10/1995
Hyman Mrs B, BA(Hons) DipIM, L.Asst., UMIST, Manchester. [0057014]   24/11/1998
Hynd Mr DA, MCLIP, L.Serv.Mgr., Clackmannanshire Council. [0007567]   25/03/1965
Hynes Mr AR, BA MCLIP, Coll.Lib., Longsands Coll., St.Neots, Cambs. [0033813]   18/02/1981
Ibbetson Mrs G, (was Willetts), MCLIP, Prison Lib., Cheshire C.C.(Ls.), Chester. [0007570]   09/08/1955
Ibbotson Mrs KJ, (was Eastaugh), BA MCLIP, Sch.Lib., Glos.C.C. [0004355]   14/02/1968
Ibrahim Mr AA, BLIS, Princ.Lib., Standards Org.of Nigeria, Lagos. [0061254]   29/04/2002
Ibrahim Mr AY, Resident in Nigeria. [0061237]   01/04/2002
Ifidon Miss N, BA, p./t.stud., Acquisitions Offr., Univ.North London, Food Standards Agency, London. [0059865]   18/10/2001
Iga Miss MG, DipLib BLS, Registry Super., PTA Bank, Bujumbura, Burundi. [0047190]
Ihediwa Miss GO, NCE BLS MLS PhD, Position Unknown, Delta State Univ., Nigeria. [0061519]   04/09/2002
Ike Prof AO, MA DipLib, Life Member. [0017084]   14/03/1964
Ikeogu Mrs CE, BA DMS MCLIP, Lib., L.B.of Brent, Kilburn L. [0030633]   26/02/1979
Iles Miss CE, ALCM MCLIP, H.of L.Serv., IFPI Secretariat, London. [0007578]   20/04/1966
Ilett Ms RC, BA(Hons) DipLib MSc(Econ) MIMgt, Assoc.Dir., NHS Greater Glasgow, Glasgow. [0041883]   09/05/1988
Illes Mr AJ, MA MCLIP, Life Member, 8 Roman Hill, Barton, Cambs., CB3 7AX. [0007582]   24/01/1953
Illingworth Mr MET, BSc(Hons) DipLib MCLIP, Learning Serv.Mgr., Gt.Yarmouth Coll., Norfolk. [0045618]   04/04/1991
Illsley Mr RW, FCLIP, Life Member. [0007591]   11/02/1955 FE 01/01/1962

271

Imi Mr N, BA DipLib MCLIP, Professional & Collections Mgr., Brighton L., Brighton & Hove Council. [0032996] 02/10/1980
Imison Ms NM, BA(Hons), Inf.Asst., Chancery Lane L., Kings Coll.London. [0059257] 22/03/2001
Imlah Mr GB, BSc MSc MCLIP, Employment not known. [0060391] 11/12/2001
Ince Ms C, BA(Hons), Stud., Robert Gordon Univ., Aberdeen. [0061214] 16/04/2002
Ince-Vize Dr AC, (was Ince), BA MA DPhil MCLIP, Unemployed. [0039724] 22/05/1986
Inchmore Miss CRS, BA MSc, Lib., Schutz American Sch., Alexandria, Egypt. [0050141] 11/03/1994
Indran Mrs N, BA(Hons) PGDip, Saturday L.Asst., London Bor.of Barnet. [0054516] 15/01/1997
Infield Mr NJ, BA DipLib MCLIP, BIS Mgr., Hermes Pensions Management, London. [0040621] 01/04/1987
Ingham Miss A, BA(Hons), Grad.Trainee, Bodleian L., Oxford. [0059926] 06/11/2001
Ingham Ms EA, BA(Hons), Employed(p./t.), Ysgol Gyfun Penweddig, Ceredigion. [0057404] 11/03/1999
Ingham Miss JK, Stud., City Univ., London. [0055343] 02/10/1997
Ingham Mr JL, FCLIP, Retired. [0007601] 12/06/1931 **FE 01/01/1948**
Ingham Ms KL, BSc, Learnig Resources Administrator, Sheffield. [0060900] 21/12/2001 **AF**
Ingham Mr RA, BA, Sen.L.Asst., Lancaster Univ.(Resources). [0050720] 13/10/1994
Inglehearn Miss AM, BA(Hons) MSc MCLIP, Subject Lib., Middlesex Univ. [0051627] 19/04/1995
Inglis Mrs A, (was O'Neill), MA DipLib MCLIP, Sch.Lib., James Gillespies High Sch., Edinburgh. [0020558] 18/04/1973
Inglis Mrs MS, (was Watt), MA, Resource Cent.Co-ordinator, Heriot Watt Univ., Sch of the Build Enviro.,Edinburgh. [0046403] 30/10/1991 **AF**
Inglis Ms SJ, BSc, Stud., Univ.of Strathclyde. [0059949] 09/11/2001
Ingman Mrs H, (was Naisbitt), BA(Hons) MCLIP, Inf.Adviser, De Montfort Univ., Leicester. [0054078] 24/10/1996
Ingram Mrs D, BA(Hons) DipLIS MCLIP, Weekend L.Super., Univ.of Reading. [0054269] 12/11/1996
Ingram Mrs GA, (was Freeman), BA MIMgt MCLIP, Learning Res.Mgr., W.Cumbria Coll., Workington. [0007611] 26/08/1964
Ingram Mr KEN, BA M PHIL FCLIP, Retired. [0017087] 12/01/1945 **FE 01/01/1955**
Ingram Ms M, (was Hoolachan), MSc MCLIP, Lib./Inf.Offr., ARC Epidemiology Unit, Univ.of Manchester. [0007611] 11/01/1974
Ingrey Miss HM, BA(Hons), Grad.Trainee, Reader Serv.Dept., Bodleian L., Oxford. [0059922] 02/11/2001
Ingwersen Mr PER, DipLIS FCLIP PhD, Prof., Royal Sch.of LiS, Denmark. [0041751] 04/03/1988 **FE 15/08/1990**
Inman Mrs J, BA(Hons) DipLib MCLIP, Lib., Birmingham Sch.L.Serv., Birmingham. [0053054] 14/02/1996
Inman Mrs JL, (was Pilkington), MCLIP, Tech.Lib., Dept of Planning,Trans., & Economic Strategy, Warwickshire, County Council. [0011692] 04/09/1971
Innes Miss CH, BSc, Stud., Robert Gordon Univ. [0058802] 01/08/2000
Inness Mrs JE, (was Clunie), MA DipLib MCLIP, Enterprise Offr., Educ.Serv., S.Ayrshire Council. [0029444] 31/07/1978
Innis Mrs J, (was Dubas), MCLIP, Sch.Lib., Kingsland Sch., London. [0023210] 08/11/1974
Innocent Ms NM, BA(Hons) DipLib, Princ.Lib.Reader Devel.(Job-share), Camden L.Serv., L.B.of Camden. [0035418] 01/10/1982
Inns Mrs CMR, (was Chambers), Higher L.Exec., House of Commons L. [0039452] 08/02/1986
Inoue Ms Y, MLIS, Assoc.Prof., Dokkyo Univ., Dept.of Economics., Japan. [0047428] 13/08/1992
Inskip Mr AA, BSc(Hons), Stud., Northumbria Univ. [0061696] 21/10/2002
Ip Mrs KY, Stud., Liverpool John Moores Univ. [0061707] 23/10/2002
Iqbal Mrs GA, (was Zaidi), BA DipLib, Ethnic Comm.Lib./Team Leader, Hounslow L., L.B.of Hounslow. [0036837] 09/01/1984
Iqbal Mr M, MSc(Hons), Stud., Leeds Met.Univ., &, Trainee L.& Inf.Offr., Kirklees Met.Council. [0058352] 19/01/2000
Iqbal-Gillani Ms N, (was Gillani), BA MCLIP, Lib., London Sch.of Commerce. [0029047] 27/02/1978
Ireland Mrs EJ, BEd(Hons) DipILM MCLIP, L.Mgr., Ferndown Middle Sch., Dorset. [0048241] 17/11/1992
Ireland Mrs H, (was Charnock), MA MCLIP, Science Lib., Univ.of Warwick L. [0002623] 31/10/1971
Ireland Mr IB, MCLIP, Team Leader, S.Yorkshire Key Fund. [0007622] 12/02/1968
Ireland Miss J, BA MCLIP, Unemployed. [0036857] 11/01/1984
Ireland Mr PDE, BSc MSc MCLIP, Employment not known. [0060202] 10/12/2001
Ireland Mrs SM, (was Mitchell), MCLIP, Area Lib.-Inf.& Inf.Tech., Doncaster P.L. [0007625] 24/01/1968
Irish Mrs GEM, BSc MCLIP, Unwaged. [0027766] 16/08/1977
Irish Mrs RC, L.Asst., Osborne Clarke, Bristol. [0057238] 18/01/1999 **AF**
Irons Mr PS, BA MCLIP, Area Lib.North (Wirral), Wallasey Cent.L., Wallasey, Wirral. [0028836] 07/02/1978
Ironside Mrs C, (was Atkinson), MA MCLIP, Lib., Stratton Upper Sch., Biggleswade. [0018350] 01/01/1974
Ironside Ms JC, BA MCLIP, Unemployed. [0052444] 01/11/1995
Irvine Mrs GC, (was Bassett), MCLIP, Retired. [0007629] 08/09/1958
Irvine Mr K, BA BSc CEng MBCS MCLIP, Employment not known. [0060397] 11/12/2001
Irving Dr A, (was Waters), MLS Dip AdEd PhD MCLIP, Freelance Consultant. [0007632] 23/08/1961

Irving Ms CM, Unemployed. [0057124] 14/12/1998
Irving Miss DC, BA(Hons) MCLIP, Faculty Team Lib., Univ.of Leeds, Brotherton L. [0053385] 03/06/1996
Irving Miss KE, Inf.Team Lib., Medway Council, Chatham P.L. [0039786] 11/07/1996
Irving Mrs LR, (was Hayward), MCLIP, Catr., City of York L., York. [0006615] 01/02/1964
Irving Mr PJ, BSc DipLib DMS MCLIP, Retired. [0007636] 01/04/1970
Irwin Mrs CM, BA, Coll.Lib., Yeovil Coll., Somerset. [0046269] 21/10/1991
Irwin Mr DP, BA DipLib, Asst.Lib., Inst.of Contemporary History &, Wiener L., London. [0043641] 15/11/1989
Irwin Mrs H, (was Noble), DipLIS MCLIP, P./t.Stud.& p./t.L.Asst., De Montfort Univ., Bedford. [0010862] 12/01/1971
Irwin Miss JM, ALAA Retired, 10/23 Rose St., Armadale, Victoria 3143, Australia. [0007637] 01/01/1947
Irwin Miss R, BLib MCLIP, Sen.Lib., Ferndown L., Dorset. [0038466] 02/05/1985
Irwin Mrs SE, (was Hart), BA MSc MCLIP, Chemistry Lib., Chemistry Dept.L., Imperial Coll., London. [0027442] 04/04/1977
Irwin Tazzar Mrs JL, (was Irwin), BA(Hons) MCLIP, Sen.Asst.Lib./Systems Admin., Coll.of St.Mark & St.John, Plymouth. [0047205] 03/06/1992
Isaac Ms A, BA(Hons) DipLib, L.Asst., N.Devon Coll., Barnstaple, Devon. [0049046] 14/09/1993
Isaac Ms CM, DipLib MCLIP, Comm.Lib., Wilts.C.C. [0041727] 15/02/1988
Isaac Mr DG, BA DipLib MCLIP DMS, Area Mgr., Stockport L. [0007640] 01/10/1971
Isaac Miss K, MCLIP, Inf.Lib., L.B.of Sutton. [0026747] 02/11/1976
Isaac Mrs MO, (was Lewis), BA MCLIP, Asst.Young Peoples Lib., Tameside M.B.C., Ashton under Lyne. [0021159] 09/10/1973
Isaac Ms S, Sen.L.Asst., King's Coll.London. [0045276] 01/10/1990 **AF**
Isaacs Mr JM, MA FCLIP, Life Member. [0007642] 21/06/1957 **FE 01/01/1966**
Isaacs Ms L, BA MA, Ref.& Inf. Mgr., East Sussex Co. Council. [0060897] 21/12/2001
Isaksen Miss KG, BA(Hons) DipLib, Special Catr., The Congregational L., London. [0007644] 13/07/1971
Isanski Mr V, MCLIP, Branch Lib., Rhydypennau Library, Cardiff. [0007645] 20/03/1972
Isetta Mr M, DipIM MCLIP, Projects & Devel.Lib., Epsom & St.Helier NHS Trust, Carshalton. [0051948] 15/08/1995
Isherwood Mrs GM, (was Wright), MCLIP, Sen.Lib., Notts.Cent.L. [0021772] 10/01/1974
Isles Miss L, BA(Hons), Stud., Univ.of Bristol, &, Inf.Asst., Osborne Clarke, Bristol. [0058953] 10/10/2000
Ismail Mr IB, MA FCLIP, Lib., Asia-Europe Inst., Univ.of Malaya, Kuala Lumpur. [0017093] 19/10/1970 **FE 14/07/1986**
Ison Mrs UJ, BSc DipLib MCLIP, Trust Lib., Birmingham Child.Hosp. [0028599] 16/01/1978
Issler Mr A, BA MCLIP, Community & Devel.Mgr., Brighton & Hove City L, Brighton. [0022816] 08/01/1974
Itani Ms N, Inf.Systems Co-ordinator, Alhayat Publishing Co.Ltd., Lebanon. [0041150] 13/10/1987
Itayem Mr MA, MA FCLIP, Life Member. [0017094] 20/09/1963 **FE 26/02/1992**
Ivanova-Coelho Ms D, BA MA MCLIP, Sub Lib., BMA. [0043824] 17/01/1990
Ivatts Mr B, Unemployed. [0061107] 25/02/2002
Ives Mrs TM, (was Goffin), MCLIP, Unemployed. [0026968] 20/01/1977
Iwabuchi Mr Y, Prof.of L.Sci., Faculty of Sociology, Toyo Univ., Japan. [0026117] 05/05/1976
Iwugo Miss II, BSc, Unemployed, [0044267] 31/07/1990
Izatt Mr RJ, BA MCLIP, Operations Lib., Fife Council, Dunfermline. [0032663] 10/01/1980
Izzard Mr DF, BA(Hons) DipIS MCLIP, Asst.Lib., L.B.of Barnet, Edgware L. [0046742] 15/01/1992
Izzard Miss DP, MCLIP, Retired. [0007654] 28/02/1959
Jabbari Mrs SE, (was Collison), BLS MCLIP, Sen.Asst.Lib., S.E.Lancs. [0027933] 03/10/1977
Jablkowska Miss HM, MCLIP, Asst.Lib., R.B.of Kensington & Chelsea. [0021800] 15/01/1974
Jackson Miss A, Inf.Asst., C.B.Hillier Parker, London. [0058845] 30/08/2000
Jackson Mr A, BA MCLIP, Sch.Lib., Univ.of Dundee. [0039713] 24/05/1986
Jackson Mrs A, MA MCLIP, Sen.L.Asst., Univ.of Sheffield. [0007661] 04/04/1972
Jackson Ms AB, (was Goldie), BA MCLIP, Career Break. [0029667] 05/10/1978
Jackson Mrs AC, BA MCLIP, Grp.Lib., Elland L., Calderdale M.B.C. [0047023] 02/04/1992
Jackson Miss AJ, BA MCLIP, Br.Lib., Tring L., Herts. [0007663] 14/01/1971
Jackson Mr AM, BA, Sch.Lib., Clyde Valley High Sch., Wishaw. [0040277] 20/11/1986
Jackson Mrs B, (was Torlot), BA(Hons), Unemployed. [0048172] 11/11/1992
Jackson Mrs C, (was Barker), B LIB MCLIP, Unwaged. [0032859] 13/10/1980
Jackson Mrs CB, (was Moores), MCLIP, Sen.Comm.Lib., Coventry City Council. [0007665] 22/03/1963
Jackson Miss CJ, MA DipArchStud MCLIP, Employment unknown. [0060353] 10/12/2001
Jackson Mrs CJ, (was Blackman), BA MCLIP, Lib., Alderman Peel High Sch, Norfolk. [0018505] 25/09/1972
Jackson Mrs CM, (was Cope), BSc(Econ) MSc PGCE(FE), Inf.Specialist-Law, Law L., Cardiff Univ. [0044722] 29/11/1990
Jackson Mrs CM, (was Turner), BA MCLIP, Med.Retired/Unemployed. [0018361] 01/01/1972
Jackson Mrs CS, (was Gilman), BA DipLib MCLIP MSc, Lib.(Job Share), Calderdale Healthcare NHS Trust, Halifax. [0030169] 01/01/1979
Jackson Mrs DM, DipLib MCLIP, Retired. [0031382] 17/10/1979

Personal Members

Jackson Mrs DY, BA MA, Res.Centre Mgr., Stroud High School, Gloucestershire. [0055217] 20/08/1997
Jackson Mr E, LLB MCLIP, Lib., Kingston upon Hull City L. [0007669] 03/10/1969
Jackson Mrs E, (was Richardson), MA DipLib MCLIP, Home Educator & Voluntary, Breastfeeding Counsellor, (La Leche League). [0031429] 01/10/1979
Jackson Mrs E, (was Barker), BA DipLib MA MCLIP, Lib., Joseph Rowntree Foundation, York. [0018806] 01/01/1965
Jackson Mrs EK, (was Edward), BA(Hons) DipLIS MCLIP, Asst.Young Peoples Serv.Lib., Lord Louis L., Newport, I.O.W. [0050038] 24/02/1994
Jackson Miss G, Employment not known. [0060216] 10/12/2001
Jackson Mrs GE, (was Faichney), MCLIP, Inf.Offr./Catg., The Royal Soc., London. [0040745] 15/01/1969
Jackson Mr GP, MCLIP, Retired. [0007671] 21/11/1931
Jackson Ms HA, BSc MCLIP, Knowledge Mgr., Cambs.Health Auth., Anglia Support Partnership. [0020254] 26/01/1973
Jackson Mrs HF, (was Peet), B LIB MCLIP, Lead Offr.-Best Value, Staffs.C.C., Stafford. [0023737] 31/01/1975
Jackson Mr IB, BA MCLIP, Head of User Serv., Univ.of Liverpool, Sydney Jones L. [0022543] 01/07/1974
Jackson Miss J, Unemployed. [0053160] 19/03/1996
Jackson Mrs J, (was Jones), BA DipLib MCLIP, p./t.Sch.Lib., Oxstalls Comm.Sch., Gloucester. [0008030] 01/10/1971
Jackson Miss JD, BA(Hons) BSc, Asst.Lib., S.Birmingham Mental Health NHS Tr., Edgbaston, Birmingham. [0050961] 03/11/1994
Jackson Mr JG, Princ.L.Asst., The Law L., Univ.of Exeter. [0052778] 12/12/1995 AF
Jackson Mrs JM, (was Tyler), BA MCLIP, Community Lib., Bournemouth Borough Council. [0027250] 01/01/1971
Jackson Mr K, BSc MCLIP, Sen.Lib., DEFRA, London. [0032094] 28/02/1980
Jackson Ms L, Inf.& Research Specialist, Univ.of London, Careers Serv. [0037209] 02/04/1984
Jackson Miss LE, BA(Hons) MSc, L.Asst., Leeds Coll.of Music. [0056790] 15/10/1998
Jackson Miss LM, FCLIP, Freelance. [0007676] 08/10/1968 FE 19/09/1989
Jackson Mr M, BA DipILS, L.Asst., Highland Counci. [0049635] 16/11/1993
Jackson Mrs M, BPhilEd MEd, PhD Stud., Univ.of Northumbria at Newcastle. [0050709] 12/10/1994
Jackson Mr MC, MCLIP, Bibl.Offr., R.B.of Kensington & Chelsea P.L. [0007680] 05/10/1969
Jackson Ms MF, MA, Catg., Scottish Parliment Inf.Cent., Edinburgh. [0040056] 10/10/1986
Jackson Mrs MM, (was Ally), BA(Hons) MCLIP, Sch.Lib., Suffolk C.C., Northgate High Sch. [0049665] 25/11/1993
Jackson Mr N, Sales Exec., Intrpid Security Sols.Ltd., Middx. [0061827] 15/11/2002 SP
Jackson Mrs NV, MSc BA(Hons), Dep.Coll.L.& Inf.Mgr., Bilborough Coll., Nottingham. [0061153] 15/03/2002
Jackson Mr P, MA, Lib., 1 King's Bench Walk Chambers, Temple, London. EC4Y 7EQ. [0050328] 05/05/1994 AF
Jackson Mr PF, MCLIP, Retired. [0007689] 21/02/1955
Jackson Mr PL, MA DipLib MCLIP, Dep.Lib., Inst.of Classical Studies L., London. [0042690] 06/02/1989
Jackson Mr PM, (was Cripps), MCLIP, Retired. [0003377] 20/02/1956
Jackson Ms PS, BA DipEd BEd Grad DipIfs, Research Asst., Cambridge Univ.L. [0059196] 14/12/2000
Jackson Mrs RA, MA DipLib MCLIP, Bibl.Serv.Offr., Leicestershire L., Leics. [0036016] 06/04/1983
Jackson Miss SB, BEd AdvDipEd, Teacher/Lib., Ripley St.Thomas C.E.High Sch., Lancaster. [0048774] 24/05/1993 SP
Jackson Mrs SK, MSc ARCS MCLIP, Employment not known. [0060396] 11/12/2001
Jackson Miss SL, Unemployed. [0041424] 09/12/1987
Jackson Mrs SM, (was Hoare), BA MCLIP, Asst.Reader-Serv.Lib., Anglia Poly.Univ., Rivermead L., Chelmsford. [0022168] 16/02/1974
Jackson Mr TP, (was Monk), Sen.L.Asst., Herts.Comm.Inf.L. [0045031] 25/06/1990 AF
Jackson Mrs W, (was Kingsley), MCLIP, Lib.:Literacy, Learning & Child., E.Sussex C.C. [0008414] 03/05/1971
Jackson Mrs W, (was Wright), MCLIP, P/t.L.Asst., Culcheth L., Cheshire. [0019616] 22/10/1972
Jackson-Morris Mrs KA, (was Jackson), BSc(Hons) MA, Team Leader, Business Support, MOD, Glasgow. [0048284] 24/11/1992
Jacob Miss FS, BSc DipInf, Unemployed. [0055144] 23/07/1997
Jacob Ms K, BA(Hons), Researcher, HSBC Investment Bank. [0046171] 08/10/1991
Jacob Mrs L, (was Thomson), BLib, Asst.Lib., Slaughter & May, London. [0041247] 21/10/1987
Jacob Mr TJ, MA MCLIP, Sen.L.Asst., Nottingham Univ.L. [0046348] 29/10/1991
Jacobs Mrs J, (was Cohen), BA(Hons), Knowledge Mgr., Brent & Harrow Health Auth., Harrow. [0043277] 01/10/1989
Jacobs Miss S, MCLIP, Outreach Serv.Lib., Bancroft L., Tower Hamlets. [0029397] 01/07/1978
Jacobson Mr L, BA, p./t.Stud., Bolton Comm.Coll. [0061155] 15/03/2002
Jacques Mrs C, (was March), DipInf, Lib., Home Office, London. [0056536] 31/07/1998
Jacques Mr MO, BA DipLib MCLIP, Documentation Tech., DSP Design Ltd., Chesterfield, Derbys. [0041041] 06/10/1987
Jacques Mr RM, (was Howells), MCLIP, L.Asst.i/c.(Llanberi's), Gwynedd L.Serv. [0007310] 23/01/1968
Jacques Miss SE, Asst.Lib., N.E.Wales Sch.L.Serv., Mold. [0051328] 12/01/1995

Jaffray Mrs EM, Lib., Falkland Islands Community L., Stanley, Falkland Islands. [0057693] 05/07/1999
Jaffray Mrs KC, (was Spears), BA MCLIP, Lib.i./c., Bonnybridge, Falkirk Council. [0035453] 17/10/1982
Jaffray Miss ME, MA DipLib MCLIP, Unemployed. [0030844] 15/05/1979
Jago Mrs AJ, DipPM MCLIP, Recruitment Serv.Mgr., Instant L.Recruitment, London. [0007701] 29/11/1971
Jailani Ms HB, BA PGDipLib, Stud., Serv.Devel.Mgr., Univ.of Central England, Nat.L. Board of Singapore. [0060044] 04/12/2001
Jain Mrs P, MSc MLIS, Lib., Gov.Autonomous Sci.Coll., Jabalpur, India. [0061216] 16/04/2002
Jain Mrs P, MLIS, Asst.Lib., Botswana Coll.of Agriculture L., Gaborone, Botswana. [0058547] 01/04/2000
Jaiteh Mrs SM, (was Pinnell), BA(Hons), Sen.Implementation Consultant, Esprit Soutron Partnership, Derby. [0033444] 07/01/1981
Jakes Mr CR, MCLIP, Sen.Lib.(Local Studies), Cambs.C.C. [0021715] 02/01/1974
Jalie Ms BM, BA(Hons) DipInf, P.t/.Voluntary Work./Training, Throssel Hole Buddhist Abbey, Northumberland. [0045203] 10/08/1990
Jalil Ms ZK, BA MA, Devel.& Projects Offr., L.B.Newham. [0056842] 26/10/1998
James Mr AC, BA MCLIP, Asst.Lib., Society of Antiquaries, London. [0032602] 06/06/1980
James Miss AE, BA(Hons)(Open) MCLIP, Retired. [0007706] 29/01/1962
James Miss AM, BA DipLib MCLIP, Sch.Lib., Pembrokeshire C.C., Tenby. [0049062] 28/09/1993
James Mrs B, BSc DipInf, Sch.Lib., The Knights Templar Sch. [0059239] 15/01/2001
James Ms BE, Learning Resources Asst., South Bank Univ., London. [0050448] 02/01/1995 AF
James Mrs BR, (was Couper), BA MCLIP, Life Member. [0003215] 07/09/1955
James Mrs BS, MCLIP, Asst.Lib., Wellington Sch., Somerset. [0055034] 01/07/1997
James Mrs C, (was Gillatt), BA(Hons) MCLIP, Asst.Lib., Univ.of Nottingham, Sch.of Nursing, Derby. [0035149] 01/10/1982
James Mrs CV, MCLIP, Inf.Lib., Warks L.& Heritage, Stratford-Upon-Avon. [0007709] 15/03/1971
James Mr DS, Unemployed. [0061010] 08/02/2002
James Mrs E, (was Ellerton), MCLIP, Sen.L.Asst., Bath Cent.L., Bath & N.E.Somerset. [0004494] 07/02/1963
James Miss EC, MSc BA(Hons), Inf.Offr., Enable, Glasgow. [0059280] 25/01/2001
James Miss G, (was Thomas), BA MCLIP, Systems Lib., City & Co.of Swansea L., Swansea. [0014549] 08/10/1970
James Mr GH, BA DipLib MCLIP, Head of L., Merthyr.Cent.L., Mid-Glam. [0030191] 28/12/1978
James Miss H, MCLIP, Asst.Lib.-Ref.& Inf.(Job Share), Bridgend Co.Bor.Council, L.& Inf.Serv.H.Q., Bridgend. [0007713] 17/07/1972
James Mr H, BA DipLib MCLIP, Ch.Lib.& Literature Offr., Gwynedd Council, Caernarfon. [0029985] 31/10/1978
James Mr HI, BA(Hons), Asst.Lib., The London L., London. [0050234] 11/05/1994
James Ms JG, BA DipLib AALIA, Retired. [0036427] 01/01/1968
James Mrs JH, (was Lewis), BA Dip Lib MCLIP, Grp.Leader, City & Co.of Swansea. [0038853] 15/10/1985
James Mrs JM, (was Dix), BA MCLIP, Housewife. [0026924] 11/12/1976
James Miss JT, BA(Hons) MSc(Econ) MCLIP, Sch.Lib., Elliot Sch., London. [0052840] 02/01/1996
James Miss KT, BA MCLIP, Dep.Lib., Barlow Lyde & Gilbert, London. [0036769] 03/01/1984
James Mrs L, BA MCLIP, Employment unknown. [0060363] 10/12/2001
James Mr MC, MSc BA MCLIP, Knowledge Mgr., Occupational Psychology Div., Employment Serv., Sheffield. [0032603] 16/06/1980
James Mrs MM, BA DLS MCLIP, p./t.L.Asst., Univ.of Kent at Canterbury, Templeman L. [0007717] 01/01/1965
James Miss N, BA, Grad.Trainee/Sen.L.Asst., The Law Society, London. [0059407] 05/03/2001
James Ms N, PGDip, Unemployed. [0059945] 09/11/2001
James Miss PJ, (was Homer), MCLIP, Lib., St.Edwards Sch., Oxon. [0021973] 17/01/1974
James Mr PM, MSc MIIS CertEd MCLIP, L.Media Specialist, Daniel Hand High Sch., Madison, Connecticut, USA. [0007719] 01/11/1969
James Mr RD, MA MPhil MCLIP, Retired. [0007721] 01/01/1968
James Mr S, BA FCLIP, Univ.Lib., Univ.of Paisley. [0007723] 26/10/1965 FE 22/07/1992
James Mr SM, BA(Hons), Mgr.Inf.Mgmt., Kerr-McGee N.Sea (UK) Ltd., Aberdeen. [0059031] 27/10/2000
James Mr SP, (was Demery), BLib MCLIP, Dep. Inf. Co-ordinator, Ryegate Children's Cent. [0033988] 05/06/1981
James Mrs SRM, BSc MCLIP, Employment not known. [0060707] 12/12/2001
James Mr W, FCLIP, Retired. [0007727] 05/03/1940 FE 01/01/1954
Jameson Ms RC, (was Foster), MCLIP, Area Co-ordinator, Nottinghamshire C.C. [0005117] 21/01/1966
Jameson Mr SM, Tech.Lib., EDS, Basingstoke. [0038317] 28/02/1985
Jamieson Miss AK, BSc(Hons) MA, Grad.Trainee, Manchester Metro.Uni. [0061585] 02/10/2002
Jamieson Ms EF, BSc MSc, Inf.Asst., Nat.Hist.Mus., London. [0053360] 21/05/1996
Jamieson Mrs ES, (was Gunn), FCLIP, Retired. [0007731] 26/01/1959 FE 01/01/1970
Jamieson Mrs HM, Lib.Asst., Carisbrooke High Sch., Newport. [0059178] 06/12/2000 AF
Jamieson Mr IM, FCLIP CertEdFE, Retired. [0019503] 27/09/1955 FE 01/01/1961
Jamieson Mr IR, Stud., Queen Margaret Univ.Coll. [0059910] 01/11/2001

Jamieson Mrs J, Lib., Univ.Hosp.Lewisham. [0040054] 16/10/1986
Jamieson Mrs J, MA DipLib MCLIP, Lib., Dept.of Educ., Glasgow City Council. [0041606] 20/01/1988
Jamieson Mrs S, BA(Hons) MSc DipLIS MCLIP, Asst.Lib., Royal Inst.of Chartered Surveyors, Edinburgh. [0055447] 13/10/1997
Jamieson Mrs SL, (was Allan), BA MCLIP, System Support Lib., A.L.I.S. [0037663] 15/10/1984
Jamieson Mrs SV, (was Land), MCLIP, Life Member, Rocky Bank, Stotfield Rd., Lossiemouth, IV31 6QS. [0008613] 23/11/1967
Jamnezhad Miss B, BA(Hons) MA, Asst.Inf.Offr., Slaughter and May, London. [0051882] 24/07/1995
Jane Mrs E, (was Williams), MCLIP, Life Member. [0007737] 01/01/1953
Janering Mrs TM, Asst.Lib., Highgate Sch., London. [0054750] 01/04/1997 AF
Janes Mr AC, BA DipLib MCLIP, Sen.Asst.Lib., L.B.of Havering, Cent.Ref.L., Romford. [0038136] 21/01/1985
Janes Miss CL, Arch.Researcher, ITN, London. [0052501] 02/11/1995
Janes Ms FE, (was Lamb), BA MSc(Econ) MCLIP, Principal Asst.Lib., L.B.of Havering. [0038847] 14/10/1985
Jannetta Ms VK, BA, L.& Inf.Mgr., Landwell, London. [0040425] 30/01/1987
Janota Miss H, BA(Hons) MA, Inf.Adviser, Connexions Nottinghamshire. [0056822] 23/10/1998
Jansen Ms L, p./t.Lib., Leics.Inf.L.Serv. [0055505] 16/10/1997
Jansen Miss RJP, MCLIP, Life Member. [0007738] 04/02/1960
Janta-Lipinski Mrs PM, (was Cotterell), MCLIP, p./t.Sch.Lib., St.Gregorys Sch., Cheltenham. [0024333] 01/07/1975
Jap Miss YS, Stud., Univ.of Sheffield. [0061813] 13/11/2002
Jaques Ms LJ, BA(Hons) MA, Unemployed. [0058884] 01/10/2000
Jara de Sumar Mrs J, (was Jara-Holliday), Ref.Lib., McGill Univ., Montreal, Canada. [0022781] 19/10/1974
Jardine Mrs AL, (was Carlisle), BA MCLIP, Child.Lib., Ewart L., Dumfries. [0039444] 29/01/1986
Jardine Mrs HM, (was Cox), BA MCLIP, Dep.Bibl.Serv.Lib., Corp.of London L. [0024636] 07/10/1975
Jardine Miss K, BA PGDipILS, Inf.Offr., Brit.Med.Assoc., Edinburgh. [0061365] 26/06/2002
Jardine Miss S, Catr., Bibl.Data Serv., Dumfries. [0052569] 06/11/1995
Jarman Mr DJ, MA MCLIP, Co-ordinator, Serv.for Disabled, People, Liverpool L.& Inf., Merseyside. [0007741] 20/08/1969
Jarratt Mr D, MCLIP, Life Member. [0007742] 29/03/1942
Jarratt Ms KM, BSc DipILS MCLIP, Sen.Inf.Researcher, Citigroup, London. [0054237] 12/11/1996
Jarrett Mrs AJM, BA, Health Records Offr., Oxford Radcliffe Hosp.NHS Trust, Banbury. [0036075] 14/03/1983
Jarrett Mrs G, (was Senior), Mgr.of the L.& Inf.Serv., Strayside Educ.Cent., Harrogate Dist.Hosp. [0035857] 10/01/1983
Jarritt Mr GR, BA(Hons), ICT/Special Projects Mgr., Hartlepool Bor.L., Hartlepool. [0048428] 06/01/1993
Jarvis Miss AE, BA MCLIP, Housebound L.& Literacy Lib., Newport Co.Bor.L., S.Wales. [0032095] 25/01/1980
Jarvis Mrs AL, MSC MCLIP, Scientific Inf.Offr., Silsoe Research Inst., Beds. [0025325] 29/12/1975
Jarvis Miss BC, BA MCLIP, Team Lib., Somerset L.,Arts & Info., Bridgwater L. [0007748] 15/09/1971
Jarvis Miss CL, MA(Hons), Stud., Univ.Coll.London. [0057512] 14/04/1999
Jarvis Mr K, DMS MIMgt MCLIP, Bibl.Serv.Mgr., Kent Arts & L., Kings Hill, W.Malling. [0007749] 01/01/1972
Jarvis Mr KA, MA FCLIP, Retired. [0017110] 14/03/1955 FE 29/05/1974
Jarvis Mrs LR, Stud., Univ.of Wales, Aberystwyth. [0055247] 08/09/1997
Jarvis Miss S, BA(Hons), p./t.Stud./L.Asst., Univ.Central England, Kidderminster L. [0060027] 27/11/2001
Jarvis Ms S, BA MCLIP, Principal L.Serv., Beachcroft Wansbroughs, Bristol. [0044775] 14/11/1990
Jasinski Mr JJ, MCLIP, Principal Info.Lib., L.B.of Tower Hamlets, Bethnal Green L. [0007751] 09/03/1972
Jay Mr KN, BSc, Sen.Analyst, Patents Admin.Dept., Derwent Inf.Ltd., London. [0061183] 03/04/2002
Jay Miss ME, B LIB MCLIP, Sen.Lib./Business & Euro.Inf., Derby Cent.L., Derby City L. [0026749] 11/01/1976
Jayatillake Mrs ES, BA ASLLA, Asst.Dir., Sri Lanka Export Devel.Board, Colombo, Sri Lanka. [0043772] 01/01/1990
Jayawardene Mrs MJ, (was Braithwaite), BLS MCLIP, Lib., Bushey Hall Sch., Herts.C.C. [0027801] 26/08/1977
Jaysmith Mrs S, (was Delaney), BMus DipMusEd MLIS, Intranet Application Developer, Environment Agency, Bristol. [0056285] 28/04/1998
Jeal Mrs YA, (was Tilson), MA DipInfLib MCLIP, Sen.Lib., Manchester L., Wythenshawe L. [0044388] 03/01/1990
Jeans Mrs SM, (was Hargreaves), BA(Hons) DipLib, Lib., French Internat.Sch., Hong Kong. [0033719] 06/01/1981
Jebson Mr JR, MCLIP, Head of Community Libs., Calderdale L., Central L., Halifax. [0007761] 12/07/1965
Jeeves Mr J, BA MCLIP, Sen.Asst.Lib., L.B.of Harrow. [0031871] 03/01/1980
Jefcoate Mr GP, MA FRSA MCLIP, Dir.General, Berlin State Library, Germany. [0022556] 30/06/1974
Jeffers Mrs JB, (was Bendy), MCLIP, Sch.Lib., Governors of Christs Hosp., Horsham, W.Sussex. [0007763] 25/01/1965
Jefferson Mrs CF, (was Harris), BA MCLIP, Inf.Asst., Guideline Careers Serv., Nottingham. [0023046] 10/01/1974
Jefferson Dr G, BSc MA PhD FCLIP PGCE, Life Member. [0007764] 30/04/1948 FE 01/01/1953
Jefferson Mr JA, B MUS DipLib MCLIP, Comm.Lib., Stirling Dist.Council, Dunblane. [0042227] 14/10/1988
Jefferson Miss JK, MCLIP, Retired. [0007766] 18/02/1955
Jeffery Miss AC, BSc(Hons), Electronic Inf.Systems Mgr., Univ.of Herts. [0058169] 08/11/1999

Jeffery Mrs CI, (was Preston), BA MCLIP, Inf.Cent.Mgr., Dibb Lupton Alsop, London. [0011922] 01/01/1970
Jeffery Ms CM, BSc MCLIP, Head of Learning Resources, Oxford Brookes Univ.L., Harcourt Hill, Oxford. [0022721] 30/08/1974
Jeffery Mrs H, (was Guilford), BA DipLib MCLIP, P./t.Lib.:Ref.Asst., Hants C.C., Petersfield L. [0031306] 17/10/1979
Jeffery Mrs J, (was Tabraham), MCLIP, Sch.Lib., Langley Sch.(1960) Ltd., Norwich. [0007768] 19/09/1959
Jeffery Miss JB, MCLIP, Life Member. [0007769] 22/01/1942
Jeffery Mrs MA, (was Christie), BA DipLib MCLIP, Inf.Offr.-Human Sci., Univ.of Stirling. [0036555] 15/10/1983
Jeffery Mrs ME, (was Thurston), MCLIP, Retired. [0007772] 12/02/1957
Jefford Miss LE, Mgr.Contract Rec., TFPL Ltd., London. [0059742] 08/11/2001 AF
Jefford Ms MJ, BA MCLIP, Cent.Mgr., MERC, S.Ayrshire Council, Troon. [0039762] 01/07/1986
Jeffrey Mr AA, MCLIP, Retired. [0019504] 01/05/1954
Jeffries Mr J, BA FRSA FCLIP, Freelance. [0007781] 01/10/1969 FE 21/12/1988
Jeffries Mrs SL, BSc(Hons) MSc MCLIP, Asst.Lib., Further Educ.Funding Council, Coventry. [0051444] 10/02/1995
Jeffs Mr HR, MCLIP, Life Member, 0737 823277. [0007782] 10/03/1939
Jefkins Miss AC, MA(Hons) MA MCLIP, Sen.L.Asst., Imperial Coll., Wellcome L., London. [0056018] 05/01/1998
Jefkins Mrs HJ, (was Painter), MCLIP, Unemployed. [0028646] 12/01/1978
Jelleyman Miss S, BA MCLIP PGCE, Unemployed. [0023419] 13/01/1975
Jellis Miss S, FCLIP, Life Member. [0007786] 21/09/1944 FE 01/01/1971
Jemna Mrs SC, (was Brier), MCLIP, Lib., Nicholson Graham & Jones, London. [0018143] 19/01/1972
Jenkerson Ms E, (was Rodriguez), MLS, Unemployed. [0022069] 22/01/1974
Jenkin Mrs A, (was Cadwallender), MCLIP, Sch.Lib., Honley High Sch., Huddersfield. [0007787] 02/02/1966
Jenkings Mrs ME, (was Barclay), BA MCLIP, Leisure Lib., Nottingham Cent.L. [0029143] 05/04/1978
Jenkins Mr AL, BA MA DipLib MCLIP, Dep.Dir.& H.of Customer Serv., Cardiff Univ.Inf.Serv. [0007790] 06/10/1971
Jenkins Mr BM, BA DipLib MCLIP, Sen.L.Asst., Inst.of Cancer Res., Sutton. [0039943] 03/10/1986
Jenkins Mrs C, MCLIP, Employment unknown. [0060264] 10/12/2001
Jenkins Mrs CE, (was Caughlin), BSc(Econ)DipLib MCLIP, Lib., Minton,Treharne & Davies Ltd., Pentwyn, Cardiff. [0002502] 01/10/1971
Jenkins Mrs CF, BA DipLib MCLIP, Dir.of L.Serv., Imperial Coll., London. [0007791] 04/11/1971
Jenkins Miss EW, BA(Hons) DipLib, Asst.Lib., Gwynedd Council, Dolgellau, Gwynedd. [0042483] 23/11/1988
Jenkins Mrs G, (was Brinnand), BA DipLib MCLIP, Lib., Covington & Burling, London. [0038139] 18/01/1985
Jenkins Ms GM, MCLIP, Waveney Locality Mgr., Suffolk C.C., Suffolk. [0018814] 25/10/1967
Jenkins Mrs K, (was Grayling), MCLIP, Customer Adviser, Essex C.C., S.L.S., L.H.Q. [0030811] 03/01/1970
Jenkins Mrs KA, (was Greenwood), MCLIP, Dep.Coll.Lib., Sparsholt Coll., Hants. [0013441] 03/01/1966
Jenkins Elin LL, BA(Hons) DipLib, Stills Lib., S4C., Cardiff. [0049883] 13/01/1994
Jenkins Miss M, MA(Hons), Stud. [0057138] 21/12/1998
Jenkins Mr M, BSc MCLIP ILTM MEd, Team Leader-Learning Tech.& Skills, Support Team, Univ.of Glos. [0038160] 24/01/1985
Jenkins Mrs MW, (was Jones), MCLIP, Self Employed. [0026164] 11/01/1965
Jenkins Miss N, BA FCLIP, Unemployed. [0007800] 01/02/1964 FE 11/04/1973
Jenkins Mrs NG, (was Davies), BA DipLib MCLIP, Dep.Lib.Mgr., Llandrillo Coll.of F.E., Colwyn Bay. [0046084] 18/09/1991
Jenkins Ms R, (was Greenwood), BA(Hons) MCLIP, Inf.Serv.Lib., Slough Bor.Council, Slough L. [0031640] 26/09/1962
Jenkins Mrs RM, (was Hitchings), BA MCLIP, p./t.L.Asst., Maesteg Br.L. [0033733] 11/02/1981
Jenkins Ms SA, BA, Unemployed. [0038283] 22/02/1985
Jenkins Mrs SE, BA(Hons), Sen.Lib., Wolverhampton L. [0047890] 22/10/1992
Jenkins Ms SE, BA MA MCLIP, Team Lib., Daventry L., Northants. [0049574] 19/11/1993
Jenkinson Mrs AJ, (was Staples), BA, Freelance Lib., 29 Hartlebury Way, Cheltenham,GL52 6YB. [0046423] 05/11/1991
Jenkinson Miss CM, MCLIP, Catr.& Subject Lib.for Euro.Lang., Goldsmith Coll., Univ.of London. [0007805] 15/09/1970
Jenkinson Mrs EM, (was Worster), MCLIP, Life Member. [0007806] 01/01/1956
Jenkinson Mr M, BA MCLIP, Chartered Sen.L.Asst., Lancs.C.C., Preston. [0041351] 15/08/1987
Jenkinson Miss RM, MSc BA DipLib MCLIP, Dean of Learning Support & Devel., Bolton Inst.of H.E., Lancs. [0026750] 29/10/1976
Jenkinson Ms S, BSc DipLib MCLIP, Local Access Offr., Surrey Hist.Serv., Woking,Surrey. [0043074] 11/07/1989
Jenkinson Mr TS, BA DipLib MCLIP, Sen.Lib., Harrogate L., N.Yorks.C.C. [0043383] 17/10/1989
Jennings Ms BJ, BA DipLib MCLIP, Unemployed. [0031872] 13/11/1979
Jennings Mrs D, (was Martin), DipPM DipLib MA MCLIP, p./t.Lib.(Temp.), Cheshire C.C., Macclesfield L. [0042002] 17/07/1988
Jennings Ms DM, (was Stuart), BA MSC DipLib MCLIP, Unemployed. [0026145] 12/07/1976
Jennings Mr G, Mgr.-Data Quality (Europe), Spencer Stuart & Assoc.Ltd., London. [0045757] 15/05/1991
Jennings Mr I, BA(Hons) DipLib, Electronic Resources Co-Ordinator, Univ.of Huddersfield L. [0044994] 04/02/1991

Personal Members Johnson

Jennings Mrs J, BA(Hons) DipLib MCLIP, Inf.& Publications Mgr., Essex C.C., Learning Serv., Chelmsford. [0035870] 02/02/1983
Jennings Mrs VJ, (was Mills), MCLIP, Hosp.Lib., Queen Mary's Hosp., Bexley Council. [0007819] 22/10/1966
Jennings-Wardle Miss D, BA(Hons), Stud., Northumbria Univ. [0061683] 21/10/2002
Jenno Ms MM, MCLIP, Self-Employed, Gardener. [0007820] 07/02/1968
Jenrick Miss RA, BSc Econ, Asst.Inf.Offr., Slaughter & May, London. [0051266] 13/12/1994
Jensen Mrs KM, (was Bird), MCLIP, Clerk to the Governors, High Hurstwood Sch., E.Sussex. [0007821] 16/04/1964
Jensen Miss S, LLB (Hons), Stud., John Moores Univ. [0060964] 18/01/2002
Jeorrett Mr PW, BA MCLIP, User Serv.Mgr., N.E.Wales Inst., Wrexham. [0026825] 19/11/1976
Jepson Ms A, (was Plant), MLS MCLIP, Town Lib., Staffs. [0011734] 20/10/1969
Jepson Miss DM, MCLIP, Retired. [0007822] 10/10/1938
Jepson Mrs PFM, MA MCLIP, Retired. [0007823] 23/02/1962
Jeraj Mrs MJF, (was Thompson), MA MCLIP, Sch.Lib.(Job Share), Manshead Sch., Beds.C.C. [0014625] 01/01/1968
Jerred Mrs KL, (was Dewar), BEd(Hons) DipLib MCLIP, Lib., Cent.L., Croydon. [0046252] 22/10/1991
Jervis Mrs B, BSc(Hons) MA MCLIP, Sch.& Res.Team Lib., L.B.of Hillingdon. [0055410] 10/10/1997
Jervis Mrs JM, (was Phillips), BA MCLIP, p./t.Asst.Co.Reserve Stock, W.Sussex C.C., Worthing. [0022087] 28/01/1974
Jeskins Miss LJ, BA(Hons) MSc MCLIP, Asst.Lib., Manchester Met.Univ. [0058732] 01/07/2000
Jesmont Mrs CJ, (was Bell), MA DIP LIB MCLIP, Sch.Lib., St.Aidans High Sch., Wishaw. [0033445] 01/01/1981
Jesper Mrs ME, (was Cresswell), FCLIP, Retired. [0007828] 21/03/1942 FE 09/02/1965
Jess Mr D, BA MLS MCLIP CDipAF, Asst.Ch.Lib., Belfast P.L., Cent.L. [0021554] 22/10/1973
Jesson Revd AF, MA MLS FCLIP, Rector of Outwell;, Rector of Upwell. [0007830] 26/01/1966 FE 27/03/1991
Jessop Miss SE, MCLIP, Princ.Lib., L.B.of Camden. [0007835] 17/10/1971
Jessup Mrs J, (was Marshall), BLib MCLIP, Lib., Dunraven Sch.Foundation, London. [0009796] 15/06/1970
Jewell Mr EE, MA MCLIP, Sch.L.Liaison Offr., Sch.L.Cent., Guernsey. [0056510] 30/07/1998
Jewell Mr PD, BSc(Hons) MCLIP, Lib., Sch.L.Serv., Hammersmith & Fulham. [0049139] 07/10/1993
Jewitt Miss DW, BA, Lib., Wakefield Metro.Dist.Co. [0036970] 23/01/1984
Jewitt Miss V, Child.Lib., Redcar & Cleveland B.C. [0055493] 15/10/1997
Jhavary Mr AC, BA DipLib, p./t.Lib., Dept.of Radiology, Nat.Hosp.for Neurology & Neurosurg. [0041754] 11/03/1988
Jiggens Miss J, Stud., Manchester Met.Univ. [0061297] 16/05/2002
Jillings Mrs LM, BA DipLib MCLIP, Tech.Inf.Mgr., Soc.of Motor Manufacturers & Trad., London. [0054823] 14/04/1997
Jinks Miss TA, Unemployed. [0054420] 10/12/1996
Job Mr DEV, MCLIP, Life Member. [0007841] 01/01/1950
Jobes Mr IM, BA, Ref.Lib., Sydney Jones L., Univ.of Liverpool. [0040188] 31/10/1986
Jobey Ms A, BA MCLIP, Grp.Mgr.N./Coll.Mgmt., Sheffield City Council. [0031078] 01/06/1977
Jobling Mr MW, BA MCLIP, Inf.Lib.(Erewash), Derbys.L. [0027582] 06/01/1970
Jobson Mrs JA, (was Longhurst), MCLIP, Retired. [0027597] 01/01/1959
Joel Ms B, BA MA, Asst.Lib., Royal Coll.of Nursing, London. [0061198] 08/04/2002
Jogi Mrs M, (was Shah), BSc(Hons) MCLIP, ESL Teacher/Lib., Internat.Sch.of Beijing, China. [0034989] 03/06/1982
Joglekar Mr PL, BSc DipLib MISTC MCLIP, Retired. [0026118] 15/07/1976
John Mrs A, BSc BLibSc PGDipLib, Job Seeker. [0031758] 30/11/1979
John Ms AC, (was Marsden), BA DipLib MCLIP, Health Inf.Offr., Hants.Ambulance Trust. [0035905] 25/10/1983
John Mrs G, (was Locke), MBA MCLIP, Borough Lib., Support Serv., Newport L.& Inf.Serv. [0024009] 04/03/1975
John Miss JM, BA(Hons) DipLib MCLIP, Training Instructor, GEAC Computers, Almondsbury. [0033002] 17/10/1980
John Mr KR, BA, L.Asst., Batley L., Batley. [0058582] 04/04/2000 AF
John Mrs LJ, (was Ibram), BLib MCLIP, Learning Res.Lib., Leicester Coll. [0030917] 28/06/1979
John Mrs MC, (was Stout), MCLIP, Semi-Retired. [0029359] 01/01/1965
John Mrs SM, (was Northrop), MA MCLIP, IT Cent.Mgr., Flintshire Enterprise Ltd., Holywell. [0021649] 18/12/1973
Johns Mrs AA, BA DipLib MCLIP, Lib., Hants.Co.L., Winchester. [0039780] 01/07/1976
Johns Miss JA, BA FCLIP, Sen.Lib., Ref.& Inf.Serv., L.B.of Havering P.L. [0025569] 26/01/1976 FE 09/08/1988
Johns Mrs JM, BSc(Econ) MCLIP, Lib., Ely, Cambs.C.C. [0007859] 26/05/1971
Johns Miss LM, (was Page), BA(Hons) MSc(Econ) MCLIP, Asst.Tax Lib. [0052495] 02/11/1995
Johnsen Mrs J, (was Lennon), MCLIP, Retired. [0007860] 19/02/1960
Johnson Miss AL, BA(Hons) MSc(Econ), Asst.Team Leader., Cranfield Univ., RMCS. [0057081] 04/12/1998
Johnson Dr AR, MA MLib MCLIP, Administrator, St.Michaels Church, Aberystwyth. [0044508] 17/10/1990
Johnson Mr ARI, BA (Hons) ECDL, L.Asst., Donald Mason L., Liverpool Sch.of Tropical Med. [0061493] 22/08/2002
Johnson Mr BG, DipInf, Unemployed. [0053312] 02/05/1996
Johnson Mr BK, BSc MCLIP, Employment not known. [0060789] 12/12/2001
Johnson Miss BL, Unemployed. [0054336] 20/11/1996 AF

Johnson Mrs CM, (was Gilroy), MA DipLib MCLIP, Employment not known. [0028816] 03/02/1978
Johnson Mr D, BA DipLib MCLIP, Catr., Brit.L., Boston Spa, W.Yorks. [0037948] 28/11/1974
Johnson Mr DP, BA(Hons) MA DPhil, Lib.i./c., Oxford Union Soc., Oxford. [0056042] 22/01/1998
Johnson Mrs E, (was Webb), MCLIP, Life Member. [0007876] 01/01/1934
Johnson Mrs EE, (was Hall), FCLIP, Life Member. [0007879] 15/10/1937 FE 01/01/1950
Johnson Dr FC, BA MSc PhD MCLIP, [0035258] 04/10/1982
Johnson Mr FV, LLB DMS MILAM MCLIP, H.of L.& Cultural Serv., L.B.of Bexley. [0007883] 05/07/1972
Johnson Mr G, BSc MSc, Sci.Lib., J.B.Morrell L., Univ.of York. [0053304] 25/04/1996
Johnson Mrs G, (was Atkinson), MA MCLIP, Head of L.& Inf.Serv., Doncaster M.B.C. [0007885] 04/02/1964
Johnson Miss H, Lib., Tobago House of Assembly, L.Serv.Dept., W.Indies. [0061035] 16/05/2002
Johnson Miss HF, BA MA MSc MCLIP, Trust Lib., Worcs.Comm.& Mental Health Trust. [0053530] 09/07/1996
Johnson Ms HF, BA(Hons) PgDip, Product Support Analyst, Whitaker. [0045727] 02/05/1991
Johnson Ms HJ, BA MCLIP, Ch.Lib., Univ.Coll., Northampton. [0020614] 05/05/1973
Johnson Mr IM, BA FCLIP MIMgt, Head, Sch.of Inf.& Media, Robert Gordon Univ., Aberdeen. [0007889] 06/03/1963 FE 26/01/1994
Johnson Mrs J, (was Davies), MCLIP, Cashier, Sainsburys Supermarkets Ltd., Nantwich. [0003700] 22/01/1970
Johnson Mrs JE, (was Armstrong), BA DBA MCLIP, Lib.(p./t.), Cheshire L.& Culture, Congleton L. [0038093] 14/01/1985
Johnson Miss JM, BA DipLib MCLIP, Unemployed. [0024428] 04/08/1975
Johnson Ms JM, BA DipLib MCLIP, Employment Unknown. [0026426] 23/10/1976
Johnson Miss KF, BA, Stud., City Univ., London. [0058075] 25/10/1999
Johnson Miss KHB, BA(Hons), L.Secretary, The Hon.Soc.of the Middle Temple, The L., London. [0052745] 01/12/1995 AF
Johnson Mr KM, MCLIP, Stock Mgr., L.B.of Richmond upon Thames. [0007895] 22/02/1972
Johnson Ms L, BA, Child.Outreach Lib., L.B.Haringey., Central L. [0057934] 04/10/1999
Johnson Miss LC, MLS MCLIP, Area Lib., Mid-Sussex, W.Sussex Co.L.Serv. [0025326] 15/01/1976
Johnson Mrs LG, (was Bratt), MCLIP, Inf.Lib., L.B.of Sutton. [0001649] 01/10/1971
Johnson Mrs LJ, BA DipLib MCLIP, Lib., Great Barr Sch., Birmingham. [0026427] 11/10/1976
Johnson Miss LM, BA(Hons) MSc, Inf.Offr., Environment Agency, Exeter. [0054484] 07/01/1997
Johnson Miss M, MA FCLIP, Life Member, Tel.0191 386 4098. [0007899] 01/01/1939 FE 16/09/1952
Johnson Mrs M, MCLIP, Comm.Lib., Warrington B.C., Warrington Library. [0046716] 02/01/1992
Johnson Ms M, BA(Hons) DipLib LLA, LRC Mgr., Treloar Coll., Alton. [0034089] 06/10/1981
Johnson Ms M, MA, Shop Stewards Asst.(p./t.), Amnesty Int. [0051683] 28/04/1995
Johnson Mrs MAC, (was Thorpe), BA FCLIP, Sen.Lib., Management Devel.Inst., The Gambia, W.Africa. [0038009] 01/01/1985 FE 21/07/1999
Johnson Mrs MC, (was Pritchard), BA MCLIP, Lib., Neston High Sch., Cheshire. [0020569] 18/04/1973
Johnson Mrs MD, (was Reynolds), Unemployed. [0012310] 10/11/1971
Johnson Miss ME, BA(Hons), Management Inf.Offr., Suffolk C.C., L.& Heritage Dept., Ipswich. [0051985] 31/08/1995
Johnson Miss MM, Life Member. [0007902] 03/10/1935
Johnson Mrs MT, (was Potts), MCLIP, Sen.Lib., Bibl.Serv, S.Div.Lancashire Co.L. [0007903] 04/09/1968
Johnson Mr P, BA MCLIP, p./t.Arch.Asst., York City Arch. [0043280] 02/02/1964
Johnson Mrs P, (was Barrett), MCLIP, p./t.Inf.Offr., Cambridge Consult., Cambridge. [0000846] 01/01/1966
Johnson Mrs PA, (was Gilroy), MCLIP, Learning Cent.Mgr., Univ.of Derby. [0020298] 29/01/1973
Johnson Mr PB, BA, Grad.Trainee., Oxford. [0061839] 15/11/2002
Johnson Mrs PC, BA MCLIP, Scholarship and Collections, Brit.L., Pub.Serv.Dir., Boston Spa. [0007908] 11/10/1970
Johnson Mr PJ, BA MCLIP, Arch., Herefordshire Records Off., Hereford. [0036474] 15/10/1983
Johnson Mrs PJ, (was Ibbotson), BA MCLIP, Sen.Subject Lib., Univ.of Plymouth, Devon. [0007909] 12/10/1967
Johnson Mrs PJ, (was Trevena), MA MCLIP, Lib./Archivist (p./T.), Akerkvaerner MMO UK, Aberdeen. [0022628] 15/07/1974
Johnson Mr PNW, MA MAS BLib MCLIP, City Archivist, City of Surrey, B.Columbia, Canada. [0007910] 10/11/1970
Johnson Mr R, Inf.Systems Lib., Wolverhampton Bor.Council. [0047081] 21/04/1992
Johnson Mrs R, BSC(Econ), L.Operations Mgr., Somerset L.Arts & Inf., Taunton, Somerset. [0056996] 19/11/1998
Johnson Ms R, BA MSc, p./t.Learning Res.Cent.Mgr., p./t.Res.& Inf.Worker, Sheffield Coll., Football Unites. [0051700] 22/05/1995
Johnson Miss RA, Stud., Brighton Univ. [0060979] 22/01/2002
Johnson Mrs RDA, (was Bennett), BA MCLIP, Child.Specialist Bookseller, The Word, Market Harborough. [0026223] 12/08/1976
Johnson Mrs RE, (was Brown), MCLIP, Sub.Lib.-Catg., Univ.Coll.Worcester, Peirson L. [0023689] 23/01/1975

275

Johnson

Johnson Mrs RL, (was Isaacson), MCLIP, p./t.Lib.Team, Norfolk C.C.Cultural Serv., Norwich. [0007643] 01/01/1971
Johnson Ms RN, BA MA MCLIP, Freelance. [0043199] 03/10/1989
Johnson Miss S, MCLIP, Cult.Serv.Mgr., Torfaen L., Pontypool. [0020513] 21/03/1973
Johnson Mrs SA, (was Jones), MA BA(Hons) DipLib MCLIP, Asst.Lib., Univ.of Nottingham. [0047905] 22/10/1992
Johnson Mrs SA, BEd MLS, Public Serv.Lib., Queens Univ., Kingston, Ontario, Canada. [0054452] 13/12/1996
Johnson Mrs SA, (was Ball), BA, L.Asst.(Sch.), Staffs.C.C., Stafford. [0038942] 22/10/1985
Johnson Ms SA, BSc Cert Ed MSc, Sales (Temp). [0053562] 22/07/1996
Johnson Mrs SE, BA(Hons), L.Asst., Middlesex Univ., Enfield. [0058836] 25/08/2000
Johnson Mrs SFE, (was Coumbe), BSc MSc MCLIP, Stud., Dept.of Inf.Sc. [0039666] 29/04/1986
Johnson Mr SJ, BA DipLib MCLIP, Unemployed. [0036186] 13/07/1983
Johnson Mrs SJ, (was Gibson), BA MCLIP, Lib., Health L., Hull Univ. [0035920] 24/02/1983
Johnson Miss TJ, MA, Comm.L.Mgr., Sandwell M.B.C., Oldbury, Warley,W.Midlands. [0043432] 26/10/1989
Johnson Mrs VJ, (was Brearley), Princ.L.Asst., Univ.of Essex, Inter-L.Loans, Albert Sloman L., Colchester. [0055745] 12/11/1997
Johnson Mr WD, BA DipLib MCLIP, Med.Lib., Luton & Dunstable Hosp., Beds. [0025327] 10/04/1978
Johnson Mrs YK, (was Bowers), BEd MCLIP, Freelance Law Lib. [0039632] 07/04/1986
Johnston Miss A, BA MCLIP, Unemployed. [0026978] 03/10/1976
Johnston Miss AG, BA MCLIP, Sch.Lib., Dunbar Grammar Sch., E.Lothian. [0022631] 03/07/1974
Johnston Miss AM, BA DipLib MCLIP, Lib., Herts.Arch.& Local Studies. [0043034] 13/07/1989
Johnston Mr AR, BA FSA SCOT MCLIP, L.Inf.& Arch.Mgr., Dumfries & Galloway Council. [0007922] 01/04/1970
Johnston Miss C, BA(Hons) MA, Acquisitions Co-ordinator, Lehman Brothers, London. [0055750] 13/11/1997
Johnston Miss CC, (was Mackenzie), MA DipLib MCLIP MSc, Inf.Serv.Mgr., The Planning Exchange,., Glasgow. [0028253] 01/01/1970
Johnston Miss CE, BA(Hons) DipLib MCLIP, Half-Time Inf.Offr., Cent.for Educ.& Ind., Univ.of Warwick. [0046616] 25/11/1991
Johnston Ms CJ, BA(Hons) MA MCLIP, Sen.Lib., N.Yorks.C.C., Sherburn L.Grp.H.Q. [0047592] 05/10/1992
Johnston Miss E, MA(Hons), Sen.L.Asst., Crewe Site L., Manchester Met.Univ. [0059867] 18/10/2001 **AF**
Johnston Mrs FE, (was Swann), BLS MCLIP, Sch.Lib., E.Dunbartonshire Council, Kirkintilloch High Sch. [0039429] 19/01/1986
Johnston Mr GP, BSc, Employment not known. [0060495] 11/12/2001
Johnston Dr JOD, DipMgmt(OU) BSc MSc MCLIP, Employment not known. [0060401] 11/12/2001
Johnston Miss K, BA(Hons) MA, Tech.Asst., Matra Bae Dynamics (UK) Ltd., Stevenage. [0056817] 23/10/1998
Johnston Miss KF, MA(Hons) MA MCLIP, Asst.Lib., Queens Univ.of Belfast. [0051979] 29/08/1995
Johnston Mrs KJ, (was Edwards), BA(Hons) DipLib MCLIP, Asst.Lib., ELCHA, Romford. [0046492] 13/11/1991
Johnston Mrs M, (was McDonald), BA MCLIP, Learning Resources Offr., Clackmannan Coll.of F.E., Alloa. [0028337] 27/10/1977
Johnston Miss MA, MCLIP, Retired. [0007936] 01/01/1966
Johnston Ms ME, BA DipLib MCLIP, Online Inf.Asst., Inst.of Arable Crop Research, (Rothamsted), Harpenden, Herts. [0027447] 01/04/1977
Johnston Mr NE, BA PGDip, Parlim Exec.Offr., House of Commons L., London. [0061036] 01/02/2002
Johnston Mrs RA, (was Willatt), BA MA MCLIP, Unemployed. [0037399] 09/08/1984
Johnston Mrs SE, MA MLS, p./t.L.Asst., Wandsworth Council. [0029454] 18/08/1978
Johnston Miss SEF, BA MCLIP, Lib.(Job Share), Age Concern England, London. [0007937] 26/02/1964
Johnston Mrs SM, BSc MSc FCLIP, Employment not known. [0060402] 11/12/2001 **FE 01/04/2002**
Johnston Mr WCP, BA, L.Asst., Leicester City L., Southfields L. [0041846] 17/03/1988
Johnstone Mr GT, BA(Hons), Catg.Asst.(Legal Deposit), Nat.L.of Scotland, Edinburgh. [0061401] 09/07/2002
Johnstone Mrs JA, BA, Stud./Volunteer, Robert Gordon Univ., Scottish Poetry L. [0061144] 11/03/2002
Johnstone Miss JC, MA MCLIP, L.Consultant for schools, Sel-employed-freelance, Ardrossan, Ayrshire. [0031339] 01/10/1979
Johnstone Miss RMJ, BA(Hons) CertMgt CertO&DE, Learning Res.Mgr., Communities Scotland, Edinburgh. [0035751] 13/01/1983
Johnstone Mr T, BA(Hons) MA MCLIP, Lib., N.E.Lincs.Council, Grimsby Cent.L. [0050376] 08/07/1994
Joice Mrs SM, (was Pearson), BA, Support Serv.Lib. - Acquisitions, Dunfermline Carnegie L. [0022116] 28/02/1974
Joint Mr NC, BA MA, Head of Ref.& Inf., Univ.of Strathclyde, Andersonian L., Glasgow. [0038275] 15/02/1985
Jolly Ms EC, BA(Hons) DiplLS MCLIP, Dep.Head of Learning Support Serv., Univ.East London, Essex. [0043745] 14/12/1989
Jolly Miss J, MCLIP, Retired. [0007945] 01/01/1961
Jones Mr A, MCLIP, Life Member. [0007947] 26/02/1947
Jones Mrs A, (was Coombes), MLib MCLIP, Princ.Lib., Monmouthshire C.C. [0027315] 03/03/1977
Jones Mrs A, (was Brown), BA, I.T.Tutor, Powys Training, Ystradgyn Lais L. [0058520] 14/03/2000
Jones Mrs A, (was Poole), BLib MCLIP, Unemployed. [0028123] 23/09/1977

Jones Mrs A, (was Davidson), BA DipLib MCLIP, Unemployed. [0037100] 21/02/1984
Jones Mrs A, (was Lindley), FCLIP, Life Member. [0007950] 22/01/1952 **FE 05/05/1980**
Jones Mrs A, BLib MCLIP, Sen.Lib., Ysbyty Gwynedd Bangor. [0007949] 01/01/1969
Jones Mr AC, MCLIP, Position unknown, GEC Marconi Res.Cent.L., Gt.Baddow. [0061240] 01/04/2002
Jones Mr AC, DMA HonFCLIP FCLIP, Life Member. [0007951] 14/09/1944 **FE 01/01/1951**
Jones Mr AD, BSc MSc MCLIP, Employment not known. [0060399] 11/12/2001
Jones Mr AD, MA LesL FCLIP, Life Member, Tel.0280 847907. [0007952] 18/03/1949 **FE 01/01/1956**
Jones Miss AE, BA Hons, Stud., Univ.of Brighton. [0060945] 14/01/2002
Jones Miss AE, Stud., Loughborough Univ. [0061021] 01/02/2002
Jones Mrs AE, (was Horrocks), BLIB MCLIP, Inf.Serv.Lib., L.B.of Hillingdon, [0029688] 10/10/1978
Jones Mrs AE, (was Swire), BA DipLib MCLIP, Team Lib., Inf., Cheltenham Ref.L., Glos.Co.L.Arts & Mus. [0031710] 01/11/1979
Jones Mrs AH, (was Rees), Stud., Cambridge Univ., MA MPhil BA(Hons). [0054024] 23/10/1996
Jones Mrs AH, BSc(Econ) MCLIP, Lib., Manor High Sch.(Foundation), Wednesbury. [0050113] 05/04/1994
Jones Mrs AJ, (was Trigg), BA MSc MCLIP, Unemployed. [0040904] 18/08/1987
Jones Mrs AJ, (was Moore), Semi Retired/Unemployed. [0007953] 14/09/1967
Jones Mrs AJ, (was Guppy), BA, Career Break. [0043023] 21/06/1989
Jones Mrs AJ, (was Pendry), BLib MSc MCLIP, Mgr.-Operational Serv., Cardiff Univ.L. [0021126] 12/10/1973
Jones Mr AJH, BA MCLIP, Bibl.Serv.Lib., TalNet Caernarfon. [0021535] 17/10/1973
Jones Miss AM, BSc, Stud., Loughborough Univ. [0061229] 18/04/2002
Jones Mrs AM, (was Walker), MCLIP, Site Lib., Mid Kent Coll.of H.& F.E., Rochester. [0007955] 10/10/1967
Jones Mrs AM, Retired. [0053191] 01/04/1996
Jones Mrs AM, (was Graham), MA MCLIP, Life Member, 7 Howecroft Gdns., Stoke Bishop, Bristol, BS9 1HN. [0007954] 24/02/1955
Jones Mrs AM, (was Gasston), MCLIP, Sch.Lib., Queens Sch., Bushey, Herts. [0005394] 04/10/1969
Jones Mrs AM, (was Swann), BA MCLIP, P/t.Inf.Lib., Kingston Univ., Kingston upon Thames. [0028694] 13/01/1978
Jones Mr AR, BA MCLIP, Lib., Northants Libraries. [0007956] 24/03/1963
Jones Mr AR, BA MCLIP, Learning Res.Adviser, Thomas Danby Coll. [0043513] 01/11/1989
Jones Ms AR, BA(Hons) DipInf, Sen.Lib., City of York Council. [0037057] 21/01/1984
Jones Mr AT, BSc MCLIP, Retired. [0060400] 11/12/2001
Jones Mr B, BA MCLIP, Head of Inf.& L.Serv., St.Helens Coll., Merseyside. [0007964] 01/01/1972
Jones Mrs BC, (was Denbury), BA DipLib MCLIP, Health Sci.Lib., Trinity Coll., Carmarthen. [0033703] 12/02/1981
Jones Mr BP, BA DipLib FCLIP, Life Member, Tel.0117 9683870, 7 Howecroft Gdns., Bristol, BS9 1HN. [0007966] 01/01/1960 **FE 01/01/1968**
Jones Mrs BW, (was Wynne), BA DipLib MCLIP, Subject Lib., Univ.of Wales, Bangor. [0041763] 11/03/1988
Jones Miss C, BA(Hons) MCLIP, Position unknown, ICC Inf.Ltd., London. [0047240] 18/06/1992
Jones Mr C, BA FCLIP, Retired. [0007968] 11/10/1951 **FE 01/01/1961**
Jones Mrs C, BA MCLIP, F./t.Sen.Asst.Lib., Met.Bor.of Wirral, Dept.of Educ.& Cult.Serv. [0007972] 12/04/1970
Jones Mrs C, DipLib, Lib.Offr., L.B.of Merton, Morden L. [0042800] 01/03/1999
Jones Mr CB, BSc MCLIP, Co.Sch.Lib., Sch.L.Serv.Res.Cent., Somerset Co.Council. [0018335] 02/10/1972
Jones Miss CE, MCLIP, L.& Inf.Offr., Bristol Cancer Help Cent., Clifton. [0023508] 01/01/1975
Jones Miss CG, Systems Lib., Glan Clwyd Hosp., Bodelwyddan. [0037682] 08/10/1984
Jones Miss CL, MA(Hons) DipILS MCLIP, Princ.Offr., Sch.L.Serv., Edinburgh. [0041748] 03/03/1988
Jones Miss CL, BSc(Hons) MSc MA, p./t.Inf.Offr., Univ.of Plymouth Business Sch., Plymouth. [0058619] 14/04/2000
Jones Mrs CM, (was Grose), BSc DiplM, Systems Lib., Council for the Cent.Lab.of the, Research Councils, Didcot. [0052932] 25/01/1996
Jones Mrs CM, (was Clutterbuck), BA MCLIP, Life Member, Flat 6,10 Ashcombe Park Rd., Weston-super-Mare,Avon,BS23 2YE. [0007979] 07/01/1964
Jones Mrs CP, (was Deeley), BA MCLIP, First Asst., Solihull Met.Bor.Council, Cent.L. [0003872] 05/01/1971
Jones Miss CR, Sen.L.Offr., Kingston L., Surrey. [0045216] 08/08/1989 **AF**
Jones Miss CW, BA, Asst.Lib., Beachcroft Wansbroughs, London. [0041337] 06/11/1987
Jones Mr D, OBE MA HonFCLIP FCLIP, Retired, Mulberry Cottage, 30 Ratton Drive, Eastbourne, Email: djmulberrry@compuserve.com. [0007981] 01/01/1951 **FE 01/01/1961**
Jones Mrs D, (was Mitchell), MCLIP, Princ.Lib., Educ.Sch.& Child.Serv., Powys Co.L. [0010237] 09/10/1967
Jones Ms DA, BA(Hons) DiplLM, Cont.Educ.Lib., Univ.of Liverpool. [0055828] 01/12/1997
Jones Mrs DC, (was Hannigan), BA(Hons) DipLib MCLIP, Community Lib., Liverpool L.& Inf.Serv. [0046972] 11/03/1992
Jones Mr DE, MA DipMgmt MCLIP, Princ.Support Lib., Knowsley L.Serv., Merseyside. [0007987] 01/01/1968

Personal Members — Jones

Jones Mr DE, BA MA MCLIP, Asst.Dir., Sheffield Univ. [0007986] 11/10/1967
Jones Mrs DE, (was Waldegrave), MCLIP, Life Member. [0007985] 01/01/1941
Jones Mr DL, MA FSA MCLIP, Lib., House of Lords L., Westminster. [0007990] 01/01/1968
Jones Mr DL, BSc MCLIP, Project Leader, BG Tech., Gas Research & Tech.Cent., Leics. [0022507] 31/05/1974
Jones Mr DM, B LIB MCLIP, Group L.Mgr., Swindon L.Services. [0029699] 05/10/1978
Jones Mr DM, BA(Hons) MSc, Careers Inf.Offr., Univ.of Sussex, Career Devel.Unit. [0056084] 06/02/1998
Jones Dr DY, PhD MLS, L.Asst., Chalfont St.Peter P.L., Buckinghamshire. [0058679] 18/05/2000
Jones Miss E, BA(Hons) MA, Asst.Lib., Manchester Metro.Univ. [0058586] 05/04/2000
Jones Miss E, BA MCLIP, Bibl.Serv.Mgr., Denbighshire L.& Inf.Serv., Mold. [0007996] 15/01/1970
Jones Mr E, MCLIP, Lib., Coleg Meirion-Dwyfor, Dolgellau, Gwynedd. [0040772] 02/06/1987
Jones Miss EA, BSc MSc, Unemployed. [0061796] 08/11/2002
Jones Miss EL, MCLIP, Asst.Bibl.Serv.Lib., Bibl.Network for N.W.Wales, Caernarfon. [0031341] 13/10/1979
Jones Miss EL, BA(Hons) PGDipMSc, Unemployed. [0058111] 01/11/1999
Jones Mrs EL, (was James), BA(Hons) MCLIP, Cent.Mgr., Swansea Psychiatric Educ.Cent., Cefn Coed Hosp. [0049578] 19/11/1993
Jones Miss EM, MCLIP, Retired. [0008010] 01/01/1970
Jones Mrs EP, Research & Devel.Off., Cornwall L. [0057567] 05/05/1999 AF
Jones Mrs F, BA MCLIP, p./t.Sen.L.Asst., Sparsholt Coll., Hants. [0008013] 01/01/1972
Jones Mrs F, BA MA MCLIP, Retired. [0060152] 10/12/2001
Jones Ms FA, BA DipLib, Asst.Lib., St Mary's Univ.Coll., Belfast. [0025171] 31/10/1975
Jones Ms FJ, (was Bradley), BA(Hons), Mother. [0040380] 23/01/1987
Jones Dr G, FCLIP, 190/4 S.Gyle Mains, Edinburgh, EH12 9ER. [0008015] 26/02/1947 FE 01/01/1952
Jones Miss G, Retired. [0008018] 04/01/1933
Jones Mrs GA, (was Clarke), BA(Hons) MCLIP, Lib., Lending, Calderdale M.B.C., Halifax, W.Yorks. [0030743] 04/04/1979
Jones Mrs GA, (was Morton), BA(Hons), Full-time Mother. [0045951] 23/07/1991
Jones Mrs GD, (was Morris), BA MA MCLIP, Lib., E.& N.Herts.NHS Trust, QEII Learning Res.Cent. [0029762] 05/10/1978
Jones Mr GE, BA(Hons), Inf.& Knowledge Mgr., Foreign & Commonwealth Off. [0049121] 06/10/1993
Jones Mrs GH, (was Parry), BLib MCLIP, Sch.Lib.Asst., Dinas Bran Sch.,Denbighshire C.C. [0027088] 19/01/1979
Jones Mr GL, FCLIP, Retired. [0008020] 04/01/1955 FE 01/01/1967
Jones Mr GT, BA MSc, Employment not known. [0060403] 11/12/2001
Jones Mr GW, BA(Hons) DipILS MCLIP, Sch.Lib., Islay High Sch., Isle of Islay. [0052450] 02/11/1995
Jones Mr GW, BLIB MCLIP, Asst.Lib., Ammanford L., Dyfed C.C. [0040799] 26/06/1987
Jones Mr H, MCLIP, Sen.Asst.Lib., Nat.L.of Wales. [0008023] 26/02/1945
Jones Mrs H, PGDipLis, Project Mgr., UWA, DILS, Aberystwyth. [0058565] 01/04/2000
Jones Mrs HA, (was Evans), MA MCLIP, Unemployed. [0004665] 09/01/1970
Jones Mrs HC, (was Johns), MCLIP, Team Lib.(Youth), Beds.C.C., Bedford Cent.L. [0024092] 19/04/1975
Jones Ms HC, MCLIP, Lib., Macclesfield L., Cheshire C.C. [0043097] 17/07/1989
Jones Miss HE, Classifier, Stevenage, Herts. [0056915] 04/11/1998
Jones Mr HE, BA(Hons) DipLIS, Asst.Lib., Gonville & Caius Coll., Cambridge. [0057431] 01/04/1999
Jones Mrs HE, BSc(Hons), Stud., Sheffield Univ. [0057877] 20/09/1999
Jones Mrs HJ, (was Bromilow), BLib MCLIP, Lib., Siemens plc, Automation & Drives L., Manchester. [0030767] 04/04/1979
Jones Mrs HL, BA(Hons) MCLIP, Asst.Lib., St.Martins Coll., Lancaster. [0040383] 21/01/1987
Jones Ms HL, BA MCLIP, Sen.Lib., City of Stoke on Trent. [0039613] 01/04/1986
Jones Mrs HM, BSc(Hons)MSc DipEd MCLIP, Life Member., Spring Gr.Farm,Woodend,Ashperton, Ledbury,HR8 2RS,Tel:01432-890279. [0019870] 01/01/1973
Jones Mrs HN, BA DipLib MCLIP, Cyfieithydd, Undeb Myfyrwyr Prifysgol Cymru, Llanbedr Pont Steffan. [0028324] 25/11/1977
Jones Mrs HR, BA DipLib MCLIP, Sen.Lib.(Bibl.Serv.)Job Share, Hanworth L., Hounslow. [0008024] 01/01/1970
Jones Mr I, Stud., Univ.of Wales, Aberystwyth. [0056998] 19/11/1998
Jones Mrs I, (was Wilkinson), Unemployed. [0048812] 01/06/1993 AF
Jones Mr IA, Research & Inf.Asst., Financial Ombudsman Serv., London. [0053884] 08/10/1996
Jones Ms IJ, DipILM, Housewife. [0049815] 15/12/1993
Jones Mrs J, (was Phillips), BA MCLIP, Asst.Lib.p./t., Reading Remand Cent., Oxford Brookes Univ. [0011621] 30/09/1971
Jones Mrs J, (was Carter), MCLIP, Lib., Coleg Gwent, Ebbw Vale Campus. [0002439] 02/04/1965
Jones Mrs J, (was Southcott), BA MCLIP, Dep.Grp.Lib., Neath & Port Talbot L.& Inf.Serv., Neath L. [0024302] 07/06/1975
Jones Mrs JA, Inf.Specialist, Irwin Mitchell Solicitors. [0059325] 07/02/2001 AF
Jones Mrs JA, (was Dunn), BSc(Econ)(Hons), Learning Cent.Mgr./Lib., Harlow L., Essex C.C. [0051196] 23/11/1994
Jones Mrs JA, (was Brooks), BLib MCLIP, Tech.Serv.Mgr., W.Berks.Council, Newbury. [0026688] 15/11/1976

Jones Mrs JA, BA MCLIP, Co.Bor.Lib., Rhondda-Cynon-Taff. [0018060] 01/10/1972
Jones Mr JH, MCLIP, Retired. [0019507] 01/11/1951
Jones Miss JM, BA DipLib MA MCLIP, Lib., Tonbridge Grammar Sch.for Girls, Kent. [0045360] 26/10/1990
Jones Mrs JS, (was Stevens), B LIB MCLIP, Asst.Lib., Worcester Sixth Form Coll. [0027219] 11/01/1977
Jones Mrs JSH, (was Robinson), MCLIP, Team Lib.,Inf.Serv., Kempston Lib., Beds.C.C. [0012570] 01/01/1970
Jones Mrs K, BA MCLIP, p./t.Sch.Lib., Manor Sch., Abingdon. [0009501] 01/01/1971
Jones Mrs K, (was Marchant), BA DipLib MCLIP, Lib., Wimbledon High Sch., London. [0024754] 01/10/1975
Jones Mrs K, (was Sweeney), BA DipLib, L.Asst., Coleg Sir Gar, Pibwrlwyd Campus. [0040485] 19/02/1987
Jones Mrs KD, (was Burke), LL B MCLIP, Lib., Cuff Roberts, Solicitors, Liverpool. [0002092] 28/06/1965
Jones Mrs KH, BA DipLib, Prof.Lib.(P./t./Casual/Term-time), Univ.of Birmingham. [0042256] 13/10/1988
Jones Mr KL, BA(Hons), Stud., Univ.of Wales, Aberystwyth. [0058107] 27/10/1999
Jones Mrs KM, (was McCormack), BA MA MCLIP, Sen.L.Asst., Univ.of Wales Swansea. [0043596] 09/11/1989
Jones Mrs KS, BA MCLIP, Mgr.-Res., SLS, Warks.C.C. [0026752] 07/11/1976
Jones Mrs L, (was Dunlop), MSc MCLIP, Employment not known. [0060281] 10/12/2001
Jones Ms L, (was Daywood), BA MCLIP, Inf.Offr., Colon Cancer Concern, London. [0031874] 03/01/1980
Jones Ms L, BA MA DipLib MCLIP, Clinical Sci.Lib., Univ.of Leicester. [0042177] 03/10/1988
Jones Miss LA, MA, Electronic Res.Specialist, London Business Sch. [0054002] 17/10/1996
Jones Mrs LA, (was Roe), BA MCLIP, Princ.Lib.-Inf.Serv., Stoke-on-Trent L., Inf.& Arch. [0012623] 12/02/1972
Jones Mrs LF, (was Price), MCLIP, Tech.Lib., Environment & Property Dept., Somerset C.C. [0020055] 18/01/1973
Jones Ms LH, (was Cornelissen), MCLIP, Br.Lib.(job share), Pontypridd L., Rhondda Cynon Taff. [0031640] 01/01/1969
Jones Mrs LI, (was Beard), BA DipLib MCLIP, Tutor Lib., Highbury Coll., Portsmouth. [0026935] 10/01/1977
Jones Miss LSH, BSc(Hons), Sch.Lib., John Ogilvie High Sch., Hamilton. [0058341] 14/01/2000
Jones Mrs LU, MSc MCLIP, Ret. [0028838] 30/01/1978
Jones Miss M, MCLIP, Asst.Head of L., L.B.of Wandsworth. [0008058] 13/10/1970
Jones Mr M, MCLIP, Br.Lib., Redcar & Cleveland Bor.Council, Marske Br.L. [0008051] 01/01/1965
Jones Mr M, BA DipTh MCLIP, Self-employed Consultant. [0008080] 20/04/1967
Jones Mrs M, BA DipLib MCLIP DipEcon(Open), Retired. [0032100] 08/02/1980
Jones Mrs M, (was Thomas), MLib MCLIP, Co.Bor.Lib., Co.Bor.of Blaenau Gwent. [0008055] 28/01/1967
Jones Mrs M, (was Fletcher), MCLIP, Self-employed. [0029545] 01/01/1954
Jones Miss MA, Lib.-Ref.& Inf.Serv., E.Sussex C.C., Eastbourne. [0048821] 09/06/1993
Jones Mr MA, BA(Hons) DipILS, Marketing Intelligence Exec., Scottish Power, Glasgow. [0054545] 17/01/1997
Jones Mr MA, BA, Unemployed. [0059510] 18/04/2001
Jones Miss MF, Learning Res.Offr., MANCAT, Moston Campus, Manchester. [0056539] 14/08/1998
Jones Mrs MF, BA(Hons) MCLIP, Life Member. [0030322] 23/01/1979
Jones Dr MG, MSc, Position unknown, Univ.of Liverpool. [0060590] 11/12/2001
Jones Mrs MG, BA, Dep.Lib., Hon.Soc.of Gray's Inn, London WC1. [0035057] 15/06/1982
Jones Mrs MH, (was Rawlinson), MCLIP, Requests Lib./p./t.Lib.-Catg.Dept., W.Berks.L., Newbury/Hants.Co.L. [0021704] 02/01/1974
Jones Ms ML, BLib(Hons) MCLIP, Community Lib., Llandudno L. [0033456] 01/01/1981
Jones Mr MP, BA(Hons) DipLib MCLIP, Head of Inf.Serv., Napier Univ., Edinburgh. [0037088] 04/02/1984
Jones Mr MR, BA(Hons), Unemployed. [0056464] 16/07/1998
Jones Ms MT, BA(Hons) PGDipLIS, Lib., B.B.C.T.V.Arch., Brentford. [0041126] 13/10/1987
Jones Mrs N, MSc MCLIP MIMgt, Princ.Lib., Rhondda Cynon Taff C.B.C., Aberdare. [0008069] 01/01/1966
Jones Mrs NJ, (was Dobson), BA, Unemployed. [0039302] 10/01/1986
Jones Mrs NM, (was Shephard), BA MCLIP, Complex Mgr. (Job Share), Heswall L., Wirral. [0023206] 04/11/1974
Jones Miss NW, BLib MCLIP, Community Lib., Mold L., Flintshire C.C. [0033943] 14/11/1981
Jones Mrs O, Web Asst., The Isle of Anglesey C.C. [0061491] 21/08/2002
Jones Miss P, JP MCLIP, Life Member. [0008074] 11/06/1952
Jones Ms P, BA MCLIP, Learning Resource Mgr., Knowsley M.B.C., Page Moss L. [0027688] 01/07/1977
Jones Miss PA, BA(Hons) DipLib MCLIP, Asst.Lib., MDT Unit L., Bangor. [0046886] 27/02/1992
Jones Miss PA, DipLib MCLIP, Sch.Lib., Dudley M.B.C. [0037085] 31/01/1984
Jones Mrs PA, BSc DipLib MCLIP, Freelance Inf.Sci./Journalist. [0028606] 19/01/1978
Jones Mr PE, MCLIP, Retired. [0008076] 06/03/1957
Jones Mr PF, BA MCLIP, Inf.Serv.Lib., Tameside M.B.C. [0008077] 06/10/1970
Jones Mr PH, MA FCLIP, Retired. [0008078] 02/01/1968 FE 16/08/1977

Jones Mr PH, MPhil MLib MCLIP, Retired, Menai Bridge, Anglesey. [0041347] 05/11/1987
Jones Mr PHW, MBE BA(Hons) MA, Asst.Dir., Min.of Defence, Tolworth. [0057332] 10/02/1999
Jones Mrs PJ, (was Tilley), MCLIP, Housewife. [0014723] 26/08/1963
Jones Mrs PJ, BA ACIB, L.Asst., Merchant Taylors'Sch., Northwood. [0061266] 13/05/2002
Jones Mrs PL, MA, Childrens Lib., Eccles Salford. [0057232] 15/01/1999
Jones Mrs PM, BSc Econ, LRC Mgr. [0059763] 25/09/2001
Jones Mr PRJ, BA(Hons) DipLib, Sen.L.Asst./Periodicals Mgr., Cent.Ref.L., Richmond. [0046143] 07/10/1991
Jones Miss R, BA DipLib, Child.Serv.Mgr., Thurrock Council, Grays L. [0034488] 16/11/1981
Jones Miss R, BA(Hons) DipIM MCLIP, Asst.Lib., Applied Sciences., De Montfort Univ. Leics. [0054032] 21/10/1996
Jones Mr R, BA MCLIP, Princ.Lib.-Cent.Grp., Co.L.Serv.Community Servs., Nottingham. [0008091] 09/01/1966
Jones Mrs R, MCLIP, Sch.Lib., Ysgol David Hughes, Isle of Anglesey. [0008085] 01/01/1970
Jones Ms R, BA MCLIP, Sch.Lib., Malvern Girls Coll., Worcs. [0047525] 01/10/1992
Jones Mr RA, DipLib MCLIP, Princ.Lib., Denbighshire C.C. [0033009] 20/10/1980
Jones Mrs RA, (was Douglas), MCLIP, Lib., Notts.Co.L., Nottingham. [0004111] 09/09/1970
Jones Mrs RA, (was Barton), MCLIP, Housewife. [0000883] 27/09/1971
Jones Mr RB, BA MCLIP, Mgmt.Inf.Offr., L.& Heritage Dept., Derbys.C.C. [0028438] 07/12/1977
Jones Mr RB, BA DipLib MCLIP, Prif Swyddog LLyfrgelloedd, Cyngor Sir Ynys Mon. [0035436] 01/10/1982
Jones Miss RCM, MA DipLib MCLIP, Asst.Lib., The Countryside Agency, Cheltenham. [0043450] 26/10/1989
Jones Miss RE, BA MCLIP, Lib., Cheshire L.& Mus. [0024187] 26/04/1975
Jones Mrs RE, (was Pack), MCLIP, Community Lib.-Child.Serv., Coventry City L., Coventry. [0011127] 01/10/1971
Jones Mr RG, MCLIP, Local Studies Lib., Uxbridge Cent.L., L.B.of Hillingdon. [0018351] 11/10/1972
Jones Mrs RJH, BA(Hons), Stud., Manchester Metro.Univ. [0061726] 29/10/2002
Jones Miss RL, BA MCLIP, Lib.(Europen Comm.), Middle Temple L., London. [0008088] 20/04/1972
Jones Mr RL, GradDipMus DipLib MCLIP, Asst.Lib., The Barbican Music L., London. [0045567] 15/03/1991
Jones Mr RM, BA MLS MCLIP, Head of Reader Serv., Brit.Med.Assoc.L., London. [0034413] 05/11/1981
Jones Mrs RM, BMus CertEd MA, Sen.Asst.Lib., Royal N.Coll.of Music, Manchester. [0044297] 21/08/1990
Jones Mr RP, BA, p./t.Stud., City Univ., Financial Serv.Auth., London. [0056962] 17/11/1998
Jones Miss RS, BA(Hons), Stud., Univ.Newcastle @ Northumbria. [0059796] 03/10/2001
Jones Miss S, BA MA Diplib MCLIP, Stud. [0037807] 25/10/1984
Jones Ms S, (was Vodden), MA, Comm.Lib., Rochdale Metro.Bor.Council. [0038017] 07/01/1985
Jones Mrs S, (was Knowles), MCLIP, Child.Lib., Carmarthenshire C.C., Llanelli. [0008105] 11/02/1965
Jones Mrs S, (was Richards), BA DipLib MCLIP, Princ.Lib.-Inf., Serv.& Ref., Jersey L. [0041405] 25/11/1987
Jones Mrs S, MCLIP, Retied. [0008103] 01/01/1955
Jones Mrs S, (was Swan), MCLIP, Inf.Resources Offr., Wirral M.B.C., Birkenhead. [0029420] 18/07/1978
Jones Miss SA, BSc DipLib MCLIP, Inf.Offr.- Law & Applied Soc.Stud., Liverpool John Moores Univ. [0037909] 15/11/1984
Jones Miss SA, BA DipLib MCLIP, Project Mgr., Claudine, Univ.of Bristol. [0036561] 18/10/1983
Jones Mrs SA, BSc, p./t.Stud., U.W.A., Aberystwyth, Team Lib., Local Sevs., Kent C.C., Broadstairs, Kent. [0053701] 09/09/1996
Jones Mrs SA, Sch.Lib., Hainault Forest High Sch., Essex. [0061754] 21/10/2002 **AF**
Jones Mrs SA, (was Buckle), BSc MA, Lib., MRC Human Nutrition Res., Elsie Widdowson Lab., Cambridge. [0049217] 13/10/1993
Jones Mr SAH, BA(Hons) DipLib, Lib., Pemberton Greenish, London. [0041620] 02/02/1988
Jones Mrs SC, MA(Hons) DipILS, Asst.Lib., Angus Council, Educ.Res.Serv., Arbroath. [0054658] 12/02/1997
Jones Miss SD, BA DipLib MCLIP, Team Lib., Sunderland. [0039221] 01/01/1986
Jones Mr SE, Stud., Loughborough Univ. [0057894] 01/10/1999
Jones Mrs SE, (was Ison), BA MCLIP, H.of Serv., Herts.Sch.L.Serv. [0041305] 01/01/1962
Jones Mrs SE, BScEcon MScEcon MCLIP, Ch.Lib., Vale of Glamorgan Council, Barry. [0023596] 16/01/1975
Jones Mrs SJ, (was Goodey), B SOC SC MCLIP, Lib.Music L., Birmingham L.Serv., Birmingham. [0018054] 18/10/1972
Jones Ms SL, Lib., Acland Burghley Sch., London. [0056765] 03/04/1998
Jones Mrs SM, (was Dukes), BA MCLIP, Sch.Lib., (p./t.), Newbold Community Sch., Derbys.C.C. [0026096] 20/06/1976
Jones Mrs SW, BA DipLib MCLIP, Llyfrgellydd Bro Arfon, Bangor (Cyngor Gwynedd). [0035328] 08/10/1982
Jones Miss T, L.Asst., Stirchley L., Shropshire. [0059854] 17/10/2001 **AF**
Jones Mr T, BA MCLIP, Retired. [0008106] 14/09/1954
Jones Mrs TA, BA DipLib MCLIP, Team Asst., Kent C.C., Canterbury L. [0027069] 11/01/1977
Jones Mr TH, (was Hughes Jones), BA(Hons) MCLIP, Asst.Lib., Bangor P.L., Gwynedd Council. [0037347] 12/07/1984

Jones Mrs TH, BSc, Researcher, Brunel Univ., Uxbridge, Middx. [0054295] 15/11/1996
Jones Miss TM, MCLIP, Sen.Lib., Sch.L.Serv., Shropshire C.C. [0026753] 20/11/1976
Jones Mr TR, BA(Hons) DipIA MCLIP, Lib., Emanuel Sch.L., London. [0045560] 06/03/1991
Jones Mrs V, (was Rastin), BSc(Econ), Lib., Bridgend Coll., Mid Glam. [0045571] 06/03/1991
Jones Ms VL, Stud., Univ.of Cent.England, &, L.Asst., Oxford Brookes Univ., Westminster Campus. [0058842] 25/08/2000
Jones Mrs WA, (was Powney), BScEcon(Hons) MCLIP, Asst.Lib.(Catg.), Oxford Brookes Univ. [0045229] 21/08/1990
Jones Mr WO, BSc DipLib MCLIP, Asst.Lib.-Health, Univ.of E.Anglia, Norwich. [0037732] 10/10/1984
Jones Mrs YB, (was Noble), BA MCLIP, Clerical Offr., Liverpool Victoria, Exeter. [0031914] 10/01/1980
Jones-Butler Ms SA, BA, L.Asst., DJ Freeman. [0057766] 29/07/1999
Jones-Evans Mrs AM, (was Sullivan), BLib(Hons) PGCED PhD MCLIP, Inf.Support Grp.Mgr., Univ.of Wales Bangor. [0039175] 04/12/1985
Jope Miss J, MCLIP, Life Member. [0008115] 11/02/1946
Jordan Mrs AA, (was Poat), MCLIP, Self Access Language Cent.Mgr., Univ.of Bath, Somerset. [0011767] 01/09/1970
Jordan Mr AC, BSc MCLIP, Retired. [0060404] 11/12/2001
Jordan Mrs AM, (was Collins), BA MCLIP, L.Operations Mgr., Swindon Bor.C. [0024627] 03/10/1975
Jordan Dr AT, (was Warner), BA MCLIP ARCM MLS DLS(Col.), Life Member, Resident Trinidad. [0017134] 01/01/1951
Jordan Mrs CJ, (was Ganczakowski), BA(Hons) MA, Research Assoc., Egon Zehnder Internat., London. [0052475] 02/11/1995
Jordan Mr HJ, BA(Hons) MA, L.Asst., Shepherds Bush L., London. [0059380] 23/02/2001
Jordan Mr HV, FCLIP, Life Member, Tel.01460 53353, 24 Springfield, Ilminster, TA19 0ET. [0008118] 13/10/1930 **FE 01/01/1956**
Jordan Mrs JL, (was Webb), BSc(Hons) MSc MA, Res. Assoc., Staffordshire Univ. [0057513] 14/04/1999
Jordan Ms L, BLib MCLIP, Serv.Devel.Mgr., Dorset C.C., Dorset. [0024719] 09/10/1975
Jordan Mr M, BSc(Hons) MA MCLIP, Content Manager, NHS Direct Online, Winchester. [0051094] 15/11/1994
Jordan Ms M, (was Cox), BA(Hons) DipLib, Acq.& Catr.Lib.(Maternity Leave), The Scottish Parliament Inf.Cent., Edinburgh. [0058424] 26/01/2000
Jordan Mr NP, BA DipLib MCLIP, Lib., Cent.L., Manchester. [0038537] 03/06/1985
Jordan Mr P, MPhil BSc FCLIP, Retired, Tel:061-973-1950. [0008122] 16/03/1954 **FE 01/01/1961**
Jordan Mrs PM, BA(Hons) MSc MCLIP, L.Mgr., Whitley Bay High Sch., Whitley Bay. [0047765] 14/10/1992
Jordan Miss SE, BA(Hons) MSc, p./t.L.Asst., Malvern L., Worcs. [0057325] 09/02/1999
Jordin Mr AV, MLib MCLIP, Tech.Consultant, Empolis UK Ltd., Swindon. [0028036] 01/10/1977
Jorgensen Mr A, BA PGDip IM, Stud., Thames Valley Univ., London. [0056005] 20/01/1998
Joslin Mrs KL, BA PGDip, Stud., City Univ., Team Leader, Braintree Coll. [0058514] 10/03/2000
Jowett Ms AP, BSc MSc MCLIP, Lib.Serv.Mgr., Royal Oldham Hosp., Oldham,Lancs. [0054865] 28/04/1997
Jowett Mr D, BA MCLIP, Retired. [0008120] 12/10/1971
Jowett Mr T, BA MA MCLIP, Asst.Princ.Lib., Bury Cent.L. [0021569] 26/10/1973
Joy Miss AJ, BA(Hons) MA, Employment not known. [0056941] 06/11/1998
Joyce Mrs EM, (was Ryan), BA DipLib MCLIP, Unemployed. [0041376] 16/11/1987
Joyce Miss L, Child.Lib., Croydon Co., Shirley L., Croydon. [0047825] 14/10/1992
Joyce Mrs L, BEd MSc MCLIP, Dep.Learning Cent.Mgr., Harrogate Coll. [0049851] 07/01/1994
Joyce Mrs P, (was Wells), BA(Hons) MCLIP, Asst.Lib.-Bibl.Serv., Somerset C.C., Bridgwater. [0018425] 23/10/1972
Joye Mrs GF, (was Finch), BSc(Econ) MCLIP, Lib., Cripps Harries Hall, Tunbridge Wells. [0049869] 19/01/1994
Joyner Ms DK, (was Garnett), Child.Lib., Southampton Cent.L. [0052698] 22/11/1995
Judd Mr PM, MA MCLIP, Sen.Inf.Offr., Univ.of Northumbria at Newcastle. [0025767] 03/08/1976
Judge Ms A, BAgrSc DipLIS ALAI, Stud.Inf.Unit Mgr., Univ.of Glamorgan, Pontypridd. [0046379] 16/03/1992 **SP**
Judge Mrs JMF, (was Goodfellow), BA(Hons) MCLIP, L.Mgr., Nantwich L., Cheshire. [0023422] 28/01/1975
Judge Mrs YA, (was Holder), BA(Hons) DipLib MCLIP, Sch.Lib., Jumeirah English Speaking Sch., Dubai, United Arab Emirates. [0032995] 04/10/1980
Judson Mrs JE, (was Grundy), MCLIP, Inf.Offr., Broxtowe & Hucknell PCT, Nottingham. [0018103] 01/10/1972
Julian Miss L, BA MA MCLIP DMS, Learning Cent.Mgr., Oaklands Coll.Learning Res., St.Albans. [0036508] 18/10/1983
Juliusdottir Mrs S, MS, Stud., Finland. [0041494] 14/01/1988
Jung Miss I, DipL, p./t. Stud., Inf.Asst., OLRC, Univ.Birmingham. [0059267] 23/01/2001
Juniper Mrs SJ, (was Lawrence), BSc DipLib MCLIP, Teaching Asst., S.Glos.Council. [0027186] 10/01/1977
Junnor Miss M, BA MCLIP, Learning Res.Cent.Mgr., Woodhouse Coll., London. [0038469] 06/05/1985
Juric Mrs TL, (was Smith), BLS MCLIP, Area Mgr.-Lifelong Learning, Hendon Area, Barnet L.Arts & Mus. [0034733] 22/01/1982

Personal Members

Jury Ms CL, BA DipLib MCLIP, Area Coordinator, Kirkby in Ashfield L., Notts.C.C. [0029704] 02/10/1978
Jury Mrs MK, (was Green), MCLIP, Life Member. [0008148] 24/09/1952
Juttke Miss JJ, BA MSc MCLIP, Sen.Researcher, KPMG UK Ltd., London. [0022510] 23/05/1974
Kafetzaki Mrs JE, CertEd BA, Learning Resource Cent.Mgr., William Morris Academy. [0043261] 13/10/1989
Kahan Mr AH, BA MCLIP, Keeper/Lib., Working Class Movement L., City of Salford Educ.& Leisure. [0022001] 02/01/1974
Kahn Miss AMC, MBE BA FCLIP, Life Member. [0008154] 09/10/1946 FE 01/01/1958
Kakinuma Mr T, BA, P./T. Lect., Daito Bunka Univ., Tokyo, Japan. [0039233] 01/01/1986
Kakoullis Mrs J, (was Martin), BA MCLIP, Res.& Inf.Off., Capital Intelligence Ltd., Limassol, Cyprus. [0009848] 09/04/1972
Kale Ms A, BA(Hons), L.Asst., Scarborough P.L., N.Yorks. [0058315] 10/01/2000
Kale Mrs E, (was Nkweta), Ref. Lib., Zayed Univ., Abu Dhabi, UAE. [0041113] 12/10/1987
Kalsi Miss BK, (was Deerhe), Stud. [0021227] 08/10/1973
Kamen Mrs RH, BA MAT MSLS FCLIP FRSA HonFRIBA, Dir.& Sir Banister Fletcher Lib., Brit.Architectural L., R.I.B.A.,London. [0023454] 01/01/1975 FE 15/09/1993
Kan Dr LB, BSc MA MLS PhD ALAA MCLIP, Resident in Hong Kong. [0060073] 07/12/2001
Kandan Goode Mrs R, BA(Hons), Counter Asst., St.Albans Cent.L., Herts. [0061120] 21/02/2002
Kane Mrs AD, (was Wilton), DipLib MCLIP, Study Cent.Mgr., Wood Green Sch., Oxon. [0036452] 02/10/1983
Kane Mr DJ, Stud., Univ.of Central England, Birmingham [0052333] 30/10/1995
Kane Mrs GA, (was Williams), BA MCLIP, Lib., Widnes L., Halton Bor.Council, Widnes, Cheshire. [0033547] 08/01/1981
Kane Miss PA, MA, Resident in New Zealand. [0044021] 02/04/1990
Kane Mrs PM, MCLIP, Asst.Dist.Lib., Glasgow P.L. [0018305] 02/10/1972
Kane Miss SM, MCLIP, Grp.Lib., Cheshire L.& Arch., Congleton Grp. [0008161] 28/09/1968
Kang Ms H, DipLIS MCLIP, Lib., Westminster L., London. [0050877] 25/10/1994
Kaplan Mr L, BA(Hons) MSc, Resources & Inf.Offr., Rotherham Health Auth., Rotherham, S.Yorks. [0058181] 11/11/1999
Kaplish Ms L, BEng MSc MCLIP, Asst.Lib., London Inst., Chelsea Coll.of Art & Design. [0048875] 08/07/1993
Kargianioti Mrs E, BA MA, Lib./Arch., Black Sea Trade & Devel.Bank. [0053876] 07/10/1996
Karn Miss JC, BA MCLIP, Lib., Blaenau Gwent Co.Bor., Tredegar. [0037617] 15/10/1984
Karunanithy Mr DS, BA MA, Unemployed. [0048491] 26/01/1993
Karwat Miss A, BA(Hons) MCLIP, Reader Devel.Offr.-Child.Serv., Blackburn with Darwen P.Ls., Lancs. [0039673] 07/05/1986
Kassir Miss L, BA, Sen.L.Asst., London Sch.of Economics, London. [0061416] 12/07/2002 AF
Kathoria Mrs A, MA MCLIP, Sch.Lib., Berks.C.C., Reading. [0040401] 02/02/1987
Katny Mrs M, (was Pleskot), DipIS MA MCLIP, Inf.Asst., BBC World Serv., London WC2. [0046330] 28/10/1991
Katsina Mr MN, BLS MLS, Univ. Lib., Nigeria, [0060926] 10/01/2002
Kattan Mrs LB, (was Ennab), MCLIP, Housewife. [0021531] 24/10/1973
Katts Mrs MS, PGDipLIS BA, Position Unknown, Bucks.C.C., Marlow. [0061136] 07/03/2002
Kattuman Mrs MP, BA MA DipLIS, Catr., Cambridge Univ.L. [0046313] 28/10/1991
Kaufman Mrs KL, (was Crowle), MCLIP, p./t.Comm.Liaison Offr., Jewish Deaf Assoc., London. [0021333] 01/01/1971
Kaung Mr T, BA ALIA HonFCLIP, Lib., Univ.Cent.L., Rangoon, Burma. [0017154] 01/01/1960 FE 12/06/1984
Kaur Mrs M, BA(Hons) MCLIP, Community L.Mgr., Rowley Town, Sandwell M.B.C. [0049411] 21/10/1993
Kavanagh Mr AS, MCLIP, Retired. [0008167] 23/01/1967
Kavanagh Mrs CH, (was Bradney), BA MA, Sen.Inf.Offr., Nabarro Nathanson, London. [0053752] 01/10/1996
Kavanagh Ms JM, MA, Research Offr., Inst.of Educ., London. [0050176] 25/04/1994
Kay Mrs A, BA MCLIP, Unemployed. [0008169] 23/09/1968
Kay Mrs CA, (was Freeman), LLB MA MCLIP, P/t.Lib., Lee,Bolton & Lee, London. [0031615] 29/10/1979
Kay Mr CH, BA MCLIP, Inf.Lib., Crawley L., W.Sussex Co.Council. [0024722] 01/10/1975
Kay Ms EA, Asst.Lib., Brasenose Coll.L. [0059288] 29/01/2001 AF
Kay Mrs FJ, BSc(Hons), Learning Res.Cent.Advisor, W.Notts.Coll., Mansfield. [0061050] 05/02/2002
Kay Mrs JC, (was Hill), BA DipLib MCLIP, Sen.Lib., Colchester Cent.L., Essex Co.L. [0031632] 12/11/1979
Kay Miss KI, BA DipLib MCLIP, Comm.Lib., N.Lanarkshire Council, Cumbernauld. [0027533] 05/05/1977
Kay Mrs L, (was Jones), MCLIP, Div.Mgr., Warwickshire C.C., Leamington Spa. [0028605] 20/01/1978
Kay Mrs PM, MCLIP, Employment not known. [0060591] 11/12/2001
Kay Mrs S, (was Deitch), BA(Hons) DipIM MCLIP, Prof.Adviser, Membership, Careers & Qualification, CILIP. [0048469] 18/01/1993
Kay Mrs VE, (was Peters), MA MCLIP, Area Coordinator, Notts.C.C., Mansfield L. [0008177] 05/01/1970
Kaye Mr D, BA MSc FCLIP, Life Member. [0008179] 07/01/1954 FE 01/01/1969
Kaye Miss I, BA FCLIP, Retired. [0008180] 24/01/1949 FE 01/01/1954

Kaye Miss J, BA(Hons), P./t.Learning Resource Asst., Bury Coll. [0049360] 28/10/1993
Kaye Mrs M, Lib.Asst., Univ.Edinburgh. [0057185] 17/12/1998 AF
Kaye Miss R, BA MCLIP, Sen.Lib.-Chesterfield Dist., Derbys.C.C. [0018374] 22/10/1972
Kayumba Mr F, BA, Unemployed. [0060048] 04/12/2001
Kazmierczak Mr P, BSc PGCE, Stud., Brighton, [0061437] 19/07/2002
Keable Mrs C, (was Honour), BA MCLIP, Asst.Lib., Ruskin Coll., Oxford. [0008186] 22/08/1964
Keady Miss EM, CertEd BPhilEd MSc MCLIP, Systems Lib., Colchester Inst.L., Essex. [0051039] 09/11/1994
Kean Mrs KF, MCLIP, Unemployed. [0020982] 03/09/1973
Kean Miss M, BA MCLIP, Inf.Mgr., Renfrewshire Council. [0008188] 17/02/1972
Keane Mr J, MSc Econ FCLIP, Retired. [0008189] 08/02/1944 FE 01/01/1958
Keane Ms MP, BA DipLib MCLIP, Special Serv.Lib., Bolton L.& Arts, Bolton. [0035405] 13/10/1982
Keane Mrs P, (was Gransby), MCLIP, Inf.Mgr., SETNET., London. [0008190] 12/04/1962
Keane Mrs RM, B PHIL MA MCLIP, Academic Serv.Mgr., Liverpool Hope Univ.Coll. [0040195] 27/10/1986
Kearl Mr DH, BA MCLIP, Team Lib., Local Serv., Deal L., Kent Arts & L. [0040000] 14/10/1986
Kearney Ms C, (was Gillespie), BA MEd DipLib DipEdTech MCLIP, Dir.of L.& Learning Serv., Glasgow Coll.of Building & Print, Glasgow. [0037871] 09/11/1984
Kearns Mrs DL, (was Chamberlain), MCLIP, Subject Specialist, Univ.of Bradford. [0002546] 16/01/1971
Kearns Mrs HR, (was Smith), BA DipLib MCLIP, Teacher, Piano. [0039681] 07/05/1986
Kearns Mr TG, BA DipLib MCLIP, Asst.Music Lib., L.B.of Harrow. [0043841] 06/02/1990
Keary Mrs M, (was Scott), MPhil FCLIP, Inf.Mgr.Consultant, 6 Ashgrove House, Bessborough Gdns., London, SW1V 2HW. [0008195] 12/03/1962 FE 31/07/1974
Keating Mrs C, (was Lewthwaite), BA DipLib MCLIP, Career Break. [0030465] 29/01/1979
Keating Mrs CJ, p./t.Stud./Sen.L.Asst.Super., Univ.of Wales, Aberystwyth, Milton Keynes P.L. [0061253] 29/04/2002
Keating Miss JM, BA(Hons) MA, Asst.Lib., Macfarlanes, London. [0061082] 01/03/2002
Keating Mrs LJ, (was Luce), BA DipLib MCLIP, Resident in Ireland. [0033035] 08/10/1980
Keay Mrs JM, (was Gold), BA MCLIP, Asst.Mgr.-IT & Systems, S.Lanarkshire Council. [0029665] 13/10/1978
Keay Mrs MA, (was Simpson), MCLIP, Team Lib., Aberdeen City L. [0013402] 28/02/1972
Keddie Mrs A, BA(Hons) MCLIP, Asst.Lib., Bolton Inst.of H.E., Chadwick L. [0039741] 10/06/1986
Keddie Ms CA, BA(Hons) MA MCLIP, Asst.Lib., De Montfort Univ., Leicester. [0054462] 16/12/1996
Keddie Mrs J, (was Lyall), BA MCLIP, Sen.L.Exec.(Res.serv.), House of Commons L., London. [0041652] 06/02/1988
Kedge Ms KM, BA (Hons), L. Asst., Camden Local Studies & Arch. Cent., Holborn L. [0060972] 22/01/2002
Kee Mr S, BA(Hons) MPhil PGCE PGDipILM, Subject Lib.:Theology, Oxford Brookes Univ. [0052481] 02/11/1995
Keeble Miss HP, Employment not known. [0060407] 11/12/2001
Keech Mr DJ, BSc DipLib MCLIP, Dep.Lib., Cent.Public Health Lab., London. [0039882] 01/10/1986
Keedle Mr VP, BA GradIPD MCLIP, Systems Lib., Corp.of London, Barbican L. [0037464] 01/10/1984
Keefe Mrs JH, (was Wolstenholme), BA MCLIP, Asst.Mgr.-Humanities Dept., Calgary P.L., Alberta, Canada. [0034716] 30/01/1982
Keefe Mr S, BSc(Hons), Stud., Manchester Metro.Univ. [0061654] 14/10/2002
Keelan Mr PJ, BSc DipLib MCLIP, Salisbury Lib., Univ.of Wales Cardiff L. [0029708] 04/10/1978
Keeley Mr MG, BA MCLIP, Lib.-Arts L., Manchester Cent.L. [0028609] 22/12/1977
Keeling Mr D, FCLIP, Retired. [0008204] 12/03/1956 FE 01/01/1964
Keeling Dr DM, (was Buxton), BA(Hons) MA PhD MCLIP, Head of L., Essex C.C., Inf.Heritage - Cultural Service. [0008205] 19/03/1957
Keen Miss CL, BA MSc MCLIP, Team Lib., Leicester City L., Leicester. [0037980] 01/01/1985
Keen Mrs E, (was Jennings), MCLIP, Sen.Asst.Lib., L.B.of Harrow, Rayners Lang L., Harrow. [0018396] 08/10/1972
Keen Mrs P, (was Dutton), BSc MCLIP, Inf.Offr., Liverpool L.& Inf. [0004316] 21/11/1968
Keenan Mrs D, (was Bell), BA MCLIP, Lib., W.Pennine Health Auth., Oldham. [0025718] 29/02/1976
Keenan Ms MS, BA(Hons) MSc, NHS/HE Link Lib., W.Mids.NHS Reg.L.Unit., Birmingham. [0056771] 12/10/1998
Keenan Mr S, MPhil FCLIP, Retired. [0018956] 12/03/1951 FE 01/04/2002
Keene Dr JA, (was Dayton), BSc DipLib MCLIP, Faculty Lib.(Job-Share), Univ.Coll.Worcester. [0042259] 13/10/1988
Keene Mrs NM, BSc(Hons) PGCE, Stud., Manchester Met.Univ. [0061125] 19/02/2002
Keeping Mrs MM, (was Nicholson), Inf.Offr., Nestec York Ltd., York. [0053116] 15/03/1996
Keepins Mr ID, BA(Hons) MSc PG DipInf, Project Lib., N.Warwickshire NHS Trust, Brian Oliver Cent.L. [0058182] 12/11/1999
Kees Mr SJ, FCLIP, Lib., Niagara Coll.of Appl.Arts & Tech., Ontario, Canada. [0017156] 12/10/1937 FE 01/01/1948

279

Keeves Mrs D, (was Carr), Asst.Lib., Univ.of Cent.England, Birmingham, Cent.for the Child, Cent.L. [0059030] 26/10/2000
Keevil Mr D, MCLIP, Lib./Inf.Mgr., Aluminium Fed., Birmingham. [0008213] 09/09/1958
Kehoe Miss A, ALAI MCLIP, Retired. [0008215] 01/01/1949
Kehoe Mrs MCF, Clerical Asst.(L.Acq.), Bromley Cent.L., Kent. [0057426] 15/03/1999 **AF**
Keighley Miss ACL, Grad.Trainee, Leeds Met.Univ. [0059338] 09/02/2001
Keightley Mr PM, BA DipLib MCLIP, Systems Lib., Barnet Coll.L., Barnet, Herts. [0030200] 09/01/1979
Keiller Mrs HC, BA(Hons) MA, L.& Inf.Asst., Emmanuel Coll., Gateshead. [0055680] 04/11/1997
Keir Mrs K, BA(Hons) PGDipLIS MCLIP, p./t.Team Lib., Gloucester Ref.L. [0053717] 19/09/1996
Keith Mrs E, (was Barr), MCLIP, Sen.L.Asst., Royal Veterinary Coll., Univ.of London. [0008218] 17/03/1959
Keith Mrs SD, BA DipEd MA DipILS MCLIP, Sch.Lib., Whitehill Sec.Sch., Glasgow. [0055804] 24/11/1997
Kelby Mrs SE, (was Furniss), BA MCLIP, Unemployed. [0020299] 02/02/1973
Keld Mrs LM, (was Kelsey), Community Serv.Lib., Portsmouth City Council, Carnegie L. [0015948] 01/01/1963
Kelk Mrs RE, (was Child), MCLIP, Lib.Interlending, Essex Co.L.H.Q., Chelmsford. [0002675] 16/11/1969
Kelland Mr CR, BA(Hons) DipLib MCLIP, Educ.Offr., Becta, Coventry. [0036937] 23/01/1984
Kelland Mr NE, BSc(Econ), Asst.Lib.(Ref), Treorchy L., Rhondda-Cynon-Taff C.B.C. [0058626] 18/04/2000
Kellas Mr SD, MA(Hons), Project Offr., Newsplan 2000 Project, Brit.L.Newspaper L., London. [0054729] 12/03/1997
Kelleher Mrs CG, BA(Hons) DipIM, Subject Lib., Kent Inst.of Art & Design, Canterbury. [0056863] 29/10/1998
Kelleher Miss JA, DipLib, Cent.Inf.Offr., Clifford Chance, London. [0050766] 17/10/1994
Kelleher Mr MD, BA(Hons) MSc, Sen.L.Asst., Univ.of Liverpool. [0056474] 23/07/1998
Kellet Mrs K, BSc(Hons) MSc, p./t.Stud./Principle Inf.Offr., Manchester Met.Univ., Univ.Of Salford. [0059913] 02/11/2001
Kelley Mrs LM, (was Stanbury), BA(Hons) DipIM MCLIP MSc, LRC Mgr., L.B.Kingston upon Thames, Coombe Girls Sch. [0050911] 31/10/1994
Kellie Mrs AP, (was Henderson), MA MCLIP, Unemployed. [0033710] 14/01/1981
Kelly Mrs A, (was Durant), MCLIP, Unemployed. [0008225] 04/03/1967
Kelly Miss AAM, BSc MLIS MCLIP, Position Unknown, L.B.of Lewisham, London. [0049510] 09/11/1993
Kelly Mrs AF, (was Blackwell), BLS MCLIP, Life Member. [0030350] 30/01/1958
Kelly Miss AP, BA(Hons) MSc, Unemployed. [0051933] 10/08/1995
Kelly Mrs C, (was Barnes), MA(Hons) MSc MCLIP, Res.Cent.Co-ordinator, Dundee City Council, Lawside R.C.Academy. [0057088] 08/12/1998
Kelly Mrs C, (was Wilkinson), MCLIP, Dept.Lib., Sch.of Hosp.Leisure & Tourism, Newcastle Coll. [0015850] 29/08/1968
Kelly Mr DG, MSc MCLIP, Sci.Inf.Specialist, BBC Data, London. [0036557] 19/10/1983
Kelly Mrs EM, (was Thomas), MA DipLib MCLIP, Med.Lib., Univ.of Wales Coll.of Med., Cardiff. [0031471] 12/10/1979
Kelly Mrs EM, (was Mulhall), BSc MCLIP, Unemployed/Career Break. [0037152] 16/02/1984
Kelly Mr GI, BA MCLIP, Hist.Res.Consultant, Buxton Rd., Frettenham, Norwich. [0008233] 01/06/1964
Kelly Mrs I, Life Member. [0008235] 07/01/1962
Kelly Mr IP, MCLIP, Lib., Brent L.Servs. [0020248] 28/03/1963
Kelly Mrs JF, (was Wood), BSc MCLIP, Sch.Lib., Longdean Sch., Hemel Hempstead. [0041973] 04/07/1988
Kelly Mrs L, (was Williamson), BA MCLIP, Asst.Lib., Newcastle-upon-Tyne Univ.L., Tyne & Wear. [0015998] 15/01/1972
Kelly Ms LC, BA(Hons) PGDip DipLIS, Lib., Cramlington L., Northumberland. [0036692] 07/11/1983
Kelly Mrs LV, (was Lewis), BA MCLIP, Inf.Servs., Cardiff Univ. [0008239] 12/01/1961
Kelly Miss M, MA MCLIP, Asst.Lib., Queen'S Univ., Belfast. [0008241] 10/05/1965
Kelly Mr MJ, MCLIP, Life Member, 24 Avon Park, Bath, Somerset, BA1 3JP. [0018846] 01/01/1956
Kelly Mr N, BA DMS MIMgt MCLIP, Area L.Mgr., N.Somerset L. [0008242] 16/10/1968
Kelly Mr P, MA MCLIP, Internet Mgr., Leeds L.& Inf.Serv. [0008243] 22/01/1969
Kelly Mrs SA, (was Negus), MCLIP, Unemployed. [0010717] 21/02/1972
Kelly Mrs SJ, (was Hartland), MCLIP, Res.Cent.Mgr., Salvatorian Coll., Harrow Weald. [0006482] 13/03/1962
Kelly Mrs SL, BA DipLib MA MCLIP DipMgmt, Asst.Princ.Lib., Bury Metro., Radcliffe L. [0037139] 15/02/1984
Kelly Miss SM, MCLIP, Br.Lib., Roehampton L., Wandsworth. [0026256] 01/01/1965
Kelly Mr TE, MCLIP, Resident in Ireland. [0060113] 07/12/2001
Kelly Mr TJ, BA(Hons) MA MCLIP, Sen.Comm.Lib., Salford L., Manchester. [0048447] 12/01/1993
Kelly Mrs UW, DIP INF STUD MCLIP, Unemployed. [0030846] 09/05/1979
Kelly Dr W, MA MA PhD FCLIP, Hon.Research Fellow, Scottish Cent.for the Book, Napier Univ. [0008246] 19/10/1966 **FE 15/03/1983**
Kelly Mrs ZC, BA(Hons) MSc, Asst.Lib., Burges Salmon, Bristol. [0056010] 28/01/1999
Kelly-Keightley Mrs J, (was Yaeger), MA, Lib., Pershore Group of Colleges. [0043207] 04/10/1989
Kelman Mrs EA, (was Ford), MA(Hons) MSc MCLIP, Sch.Lib., Hermitage Acad., Helensburgh. [0049538] 09/11/1993

Kelman Harrison Mrs MM, (was Kelman), BA MLS MA MCLIP, Res.Support Lib., All Saints L., Manchester Metro.Univ. [0041692] 18/02/1988
Kelsall Mrs A, BA MCLIP, Sen.Lib., Lancs.Co.Ls., Morecambe. [0040428] 27/01/1987
Kelsall Mrs MD, BA DipLib MCLIP, Life Member. [0027690] 08/07/1977
Kelsey Mrs J, (was Millington), MSc MCLIP, Records Mgr., Pfizer Global R & D., Sandwich, Kent. [0008248] 12/07/1962
Kelsey Mrs ML, (was Watson), BA MCLIP, On Career Break. [0042230] 17/10/1988
Kelson Ms JS, L.Serv.Mgr., Stoke Mandeville Hosp., Aylesbury, Bucks. [0051953] 18/08/1995
Kelt Mr PR, BA PGDip MCLIP, Sch.Lib., Eastbank Academy, Glasgow. [0036241] 08/08/1983
Kelter Miss C, BA MA DipLib MCLIP, Lib., L.B.of Hillingdon. [0023852] 12/02/1975
Kemp Ms AJ, BA(Hons) MSc MCLIP, Asst.Lib., Dept.for Work and Pensions, Leeds. [0044572] 29/10/1990
Kemp Ms CJ, MA DipLib MCLIP, Asst.Lib., Queen Margaret Univ.Coll., Edinburgh. [0044571] 29/10/1990
Kemp Mr DA, MSc MBCS MCLIP, Retired. [0060405] 11/12/2001
Kemp Mrs HJ, (was Still), BA MCLIP, Lib., Angmering Sch., W.Sussex. [0038925] 21/10/1985
Kemp Ms L, BA MA, L.Asst., The Univ.of Hull. [0061578] 02/10/2002
Kemp Mrs LM, (was Glover), MCLIP, Inf.Mgr., City Tech.Coll., Birmingham. [0021709] 07/01/1974
Kemp Dr NM, BSc PhD MCLIP, Employment not known. [0060467] 11/12/2001
Kemp Mr PJ, Stud., Univ.of Wales, Aberystwyth. [0056630] 23/09/1998
Kempling Mr HK, (was Rose), DipLib MCLIP, Admin.Asst., Norwich C.C. [0030668] 10/03/1979
Kempshall Mrs JR, (was Hines), BA MCLIP, Faculty Lib., Lang.& Euro.Studs., Bolland L., Univ.of the W.of England, Bristol. [0006933] 28/09/1970
Kempster Mrs GD, (was Hutchins), OBE BA MLIS MCLIP, Dir.of Inf.Serv.Mgmt., The British Council. [0027333] 21/02/1977
Kempthorne Mr B, MA MCLIP, Asst.Co.Lib.(Bibl.& Lend.Serv.), Hants.Co.L., Winchester. [0008257] 20/10/1969
Kendall Mrs AJ, (was Hannell), BSc(Hons) MSc(Hons), Inf.& Database Administrator, The Child.Soc., Winchester. [0057854] 10/09/1999
Kendall Mr E, MCLIP, Sen.Lib., Hampshire Co.L., Andover. [0008259] 01/01/1971
Kendall Miss EM, MA, Prof.Support Lawyer, Bircham Dyson Bell, London. [0058368] 28/01/2000
Kendall Mrs H, (was Bulmer), BSc DipLib MCLIP, Lib., Hepworth Lawrence Bryer & Bizley, Epping. [0032732] 12/08/1980
Kendall Miss M, MA MCLIP, Lib., Churchill Coll., Cambridge. [0008262] 02/04/1972
Kendall Mr M, BSc MSc GradCerEd MCLIP, Position unknown, Univ.of Birmingham. [0060533] 11/12/2001
Kendall Mrs M, M Theol MCLIP, Placement Liaison/Client Offr., Scottish Council for Vol.Org., Inverness. [0026872] 01/01/1977
Kendall Mrs M, (was Barr), FCLIP, Life Member. [0008261] 12/03/1936 **FE 01/01/1944**
Kendall Ms MA, MA MPhil MCLIP, Princ.Lect., Manchester Metro.Univ. [0029993] 02/10/1978
Kendall Mrs PJ, BA MSc, Team Lib., (P./t.), Cent.L., Oxon.C.C. [0056701] 05/10/1998
Kendall Ms PMN, BLS, Acquisitions Lib., Instant L.Ltd., Loughborough. [0036118] 07/02/1983
Kendall Ms S, BA DipLib MCLIP, Lib., Mills & Reeve (Solicitors), Birmingham. [0040901] 14/08/1987
Kendlin Ms V, BA DipPR MA, Lib.& Inf.Mgr., Scott Tallon Walker Architects, Dublin. [0061219] 16/04/2002
Kendrick Mr E, BA DipLib MCLIP, Asst.Bibl.Off., Bucks.Co.L., Aylesbury. [0008264] 30/10/1969
Kendrick Miss L, BA(Hons), Sen.L.Asst./Stud., Heartlands Educ.Cent., Birmingham Heartlands Hosp. [0061618] 03/10/2002
Kendrick Mrs M, CertEd BEd(Hons) MA MCLIP, Sch.Lib., Leic.C.C., Ashby de la zouch. [0054258] 11/11/1996
Kenley Miss M, (was Wallace), p./t.Stud., Manchester Met.Univ. [0059993] 16/11/2001
Kenna Miss H, BSc DipILM, P./t.Stud./Learning Inf.Asst., Manchester Met.Univ., Thompson L., Staffs. [0059875] 29/10/2001
Kenna Mrs S, (was Hamilton), MA MCLIP, Co-operation & Partnership Prog., The British L., London. [0020786] 02/07/1973
Kennan Ms NJ, BSc(Hons) MLitt, Unemployed. [0059139] 23/11/2000 **AF**
Kennard Mrs VR, BSocSci DipInf MCLIP, Employment not known. [0060684] 12/12/2001
Kennaway Mrs M, (was Swallow), FCLIP FSA Scot, Life Member, 49 Falcon Av., Edinburgh, EH10 4AN. [0008266] 31/03/1939 **FE 13/02/1975**
Kennedy Mr AJ, BA(Hons) DMS MCLIP, H.of Mus.Arch.& L., Reading Council, Reading L. [0035448] 18/10/1982
Kennedy Ms C, BA DipLIS, Inf.Serv.Offr., Ravensbourne Coll.of Design & Comm. [0061635] 09/10/2002
Kennedy Mrs CM, (was Ogiluy), BA MCLIP, P./t.Lib., Wilts.C.C., Malmesbury L. [0032689] 16/06/1980
Kennedy Ms CM, (was Ni Chinneide), BA DipLIS, Unemployed. [0038834] 14/10/1985
Kennedy Dr J, BA DIP A PhD DipLib, Lect.,Sch.of Inf.Stud., Charles Sturt Univ., Riverina,NSW,Australia. [0040563] 18/03/1987
Kennedy Mr J, MA FCLIP, General Mgr., Age Concern Wigston. [0008273] 01/01/1962 **FE 29/04/1975**
Kennedy Miss JL, MA MCLIP, Asst.Dept.Records Offr., Dept.for Educ.& Skills, London. [0039018] 28/10/1985

Personal Members

Kennedy Mrs ML, (was Paton), MA(Hons), Inf.Offr., Lothian Primary Care NHS Trust, Astley Ainslie Hosp. [0048769] 17/05/1993 **AF**
Kennedy Mrs RL, (was Hawkes), BA MCLIP, Asst.Lib., S.Woodford L. [0030432] 29/01/1979
Kennedy Miss RM, BA(Hons), Inf.Serv.Mgr., Walsall M.B.C. [0033592] 22/01/1981
Kennedy Mrs S, (was Walton), BSc DipLib MCLIP, Site Ops.Lib., Staffs.Uni., Sch.of Health L. Swrewsbury. [0033604] 22/01/1981
Kennedy Mrs SA, (was Skerry), BA DipLib MCLIP, Faculty Lib.-Educ.& Psychology, Univ.Coll.Worcester. [0013447] 08/06/1971
Kennedy Mrs TM, BA DipLIS MCLIP, Community Serv.Lib., Hants.C.C., S.Div. [0047585] 06/10/1992
Kennedy Miss YM, MCLIP, Lib., Edinburgh Cent.L. [0026430] 05/10/1976
Kennell Mrs JM, (was Rollinson), MCLIP, Unemployed. [0018848] 02/12/1968
Kennell Mr R, MCLIP, Coll.Lib., Britannia Royal Naval Coll., Dartmouth. [0008283] 15/03/1969
Kennerley Mr FC, FCLIP, Life Member, Tel.0181 856 5451. [0008284] 24/04/1935 **FE 01/01/1949**
Kennington Mr D, FCLIP, Retired. [0008287] 14/10/1947 **FE 01/01/1969**
Kennouche Mrs ME, (was Cruickshank), BA MCLIP, Unemployed. [0029624] 12/10/1978
Kenny Miss AGM, MCIArb, Admin.Asst., Chartered Inst.of Arbitrators, London. [0058615] 13/04/2000 **AF**
Kenny Mrs LE, (was Davies), BA MA MCLIP, Asst.Lib.(P./T.), Bournemouth Univ., Dorset House L., Talbot Campus. [0044324] 04/09/1990
Kenny Mr MJC, BA(Hons), p./t.Stud./Asst.Arch., Univ.of Northumbria at Newcastle. [0061603] 03/10/2002
Kenny Mrs S, BA(Hons), Lib., Brit.Internat.Sch., Cairo, Egypt. [0058001] 12/10/1999
Kensall Ms SW, BA(Hons) DipLIM MCLIP, Child.Lib., Wrexham Pub.L. [0054156] 07/11/1996
Kensett Mrs C, (was Francis), MCLIP, Lib.:Child., L.B.of Hammersmith & Fulham. [0005165] 15/01/1968
Kensler Ms EA, BA(Hons) DipLib MCLIP, Project Mgr., Univ.of Leeds. [0050168] 20/04/1994
Kent Mrs A, Sch.Lib., Croham Hurst Sch., Croydon. [0057663] 01/07/1999
Kent Miss EG, BSc MCLIP, Res.& Tech.Serv.Lib., Torquay L., Devon. [0039427] 20/01/1986
Kent Ms EJ, [0022915] 07/10/1974
Kent Miss H, BA(Hons), Asst.Lib., HM Treasury, London. [0056780] 14/10/1998
Kent Mrs H, (was Leigh), BA DipLib MCLIP, Learning Res.Mgr., Hillcroft Coll., Surbiton. [0008820] 05/10/1970
Kent Ms J, (was Uhlar), MA MCLIP, Asst.Lib., Royal Inst.of Brit.Architects. [0038667] 09/09/1985
Kent Mrs JM, (was Robson), MCLIP, Unemployed. [0012598] 23/09/1968
Kent Mrs LC, BA MLS, Mgr.of L.Serv., City of Kawartha Lakes, Ontario, Canada. [0057801] 30/07/1999
Kent Miss S, BA MCLIP, Retired. [0008297] 13/09/1953
Kent Ms W, (was Steeper), BA(Hons) MCLIP, Learning Lib., Leeds City Council. [0036415] 11/10/1983
Kenvyn Mr DB, BA MCLIP, Asst.Mgr.Adult Lending & Support, E.Dunbartonshire, William Patrick L. [0030323] 17/01/1979
Kenward Mrs C, (was May), MCLIP, Age Concern, East Sussex. [0008298] 14/01/1970
Kenyon Miss A, BSc GradIPM, Stud., Liverpool John Moores Univ., & Research Asst., Public Health, Univ.of Liverpool. [0058931] 06/10/2000
Kenyon Ms JE, BA(Hons) DipLib MCLIP, Sen.Inf.Offr., The Muscular Dystrophy Campaign, London. [0037240] 01/05/1984
Kenyon Mr JR, BA FSA FR HIST MCLIP, Lib., Nat.Museum of Wales. [0008300] 29/09/1970
Kenyon Mr R, BA MCLIP, Data Serv.Mgr., Univ.of Salford. [0035923] 26/02/1983
Kenyon Miss RH, BA(Hons) MCLIP, Learning Serv.Coordinator, City of Westminster Coll., London. [0042593] 12/01/1989
Keogh Mr M, BA(Hons) DipIM, Asst.Lib., Ealing Hosp.MHS Trust, Southall, Middlesex. [0055690] 04/11/1997
Ker Miss CS, BA FCLIP, Life Member. [0008302] 08/10/1947 **FE 01/01/1952**
Kerameos Ms A, Collections Devel.Lib., Brit.Film Inst., London. [0041019] 02/10/1987
Kerby Ms S, (was Townsend), MCLIP, Inf.Lib., Bognor Regis, W.Sussex C.C. [0014827] 14/01/1972
Kerney Mrs JL, BA DipIS, Learning Res.Cent.Mgr., Newham Coll.of F.E., Stratford. [0057077] 04/12/1998
Kerr Mrs C, (was Henderson), BA MCLIP, Lib., Tynecastle High Sch., Edinburgh. [0032798] 24/09/1980
Kerr Dr CL, BSc DipLib PhD MCLIP, Med.Inf.Worker, 8 Rosebery Grove, Dalgety Bay, Fife. [0043022] 15/06/1989
Kerr Miss DS, MA DipLib MCLIP, Princ.L.Offr., Comm.Inf.& CapInfo, City of Edinburgh Council. [0038209] 08/01/1985
Kerr Mr GD, BA MCLIP, Customer Serv.Mgr., W.Lothian Council. [0018850] 01/01/1962
Kerr Ms GL, MA DipLib FAETC MCLIP, Head of Learning Res., Croydon Coll., Surrey. [0033619] 28/01/1981
Kerr Miss I, Retired. [0008305] 28/08/1958
Kerr Mr IR, MSc, Sen.Researcher, Enterprise Oil, London. [0050233] 11/05/1994
Kerr Miss J, BSc(Hons), Stud., Strathclyde Univ. [0060001] 20/11/2001
Kerr Ms L, MA DipLib MCLIP, Sen.Lib., Glasgow Dist.L. [0026233] 01/09/1976
Kerr Mrs LH, (was Warnock), BA DipBITS MCLIP, Inf.Mgr., Enable, Glasgow. [0023773] 22/01/1975
Kerr Mrs MG, (was Boner), BA(Hons) MCLIP, Inf.Mgr., Aberdeen City Council, Aberdeen. [0022296] 01/04/1974

Kerr Mrs SP, L.Super., W.Sussex C.C., E.Grinstead. [0056214] 07/04/1998 **AF**
Kerr Ms SV, BA(Hons) DipILM, Temp.Asst.Lib.(Job Share), N.Yorks.C.C. [0053596] 01/08/1996
Kerr Miss V, BA MIMgt MSc MCLIP, Princ.Lib., Renfrewshire L., Paisley, Renfrewshire. [0008313] 01/07/1971
Kerr Mr WAL, MCLIP, Ref.Lib./Head Collections Devel., Univ.of New Brunswick, Saint John, New Brunswick, Canada. [0019773] 08/01/1968
Kerridge Mrs EJ, (was Avis), BA, Asst.Subject Lib., Lanchester L., Coventry Univ. [0035657] 06/12/1982
Kerridge Mr P, BA MCLIP, Area Mgr., Cornwall C.C. [0021606] 26/11/1973
Kerrison Dr GD, BSc PhD MCLIP, Employment not known. [0060455] 11/12/2001
Kerrison Mr RJ, MLS MCLIP, Man.Dir., Botsalo Books (Pty) Ltd., Botswana. [0020136] 06/09/1966
Kerrod Mr N, MA MCLIP, Life Member. [0008315] 31/08/1949
Kerry Mr DA, MA DipInf, Lib., Near East Sch.of Theology, Beirut. [0048700] 07/04/1993
Kerry Mrs JC, (was Bates), BSc MCLIP, p./t.Child.Serv.Coordinator, Beeston L., Notts.C.C. [0038049] 10/01/1985
Kersey Mrs M, (was Beeden), MCLIP, Retired. [0008316] 23/09/1955
Kersey Mrs S, (was Higginson), MCLIP, Relief Lib., Bournemouth L. [0021370] 13/11/1973
Kershaw Mrs C, (was Holland), BA MCLIP, Comm.Lib., Tameside Leisure Serv., Stalybridge L. [0046939] 04/03/1992
Kershaw Mrs H, (was Starkey), BA DipLib MCLIP, [0033769] 16/02/1981
Kershaw Miss NJ, BA CERT ED MCLIP, Univ.Lib., Anglia Poly.Univ., Chelmsford. [0024353] 28/06/1975
Kerslake Mrs SE, (was Crundwell), BA(Hons) MA MCLIP, Asst.Lib., Forest Healthcare Trust, Whipps Cross Hosp., Leytonstone. [0048292] 01/01/1993
Kesson Mrs J, (was Scott), BSc MCLIP, Sch.Lib., Drumchapel High Sch., Glasgow, Glasgow City Council. [0008320] 01/01/1961
Kestell Mrs CM, (was Walker), BA(Hons) DipLib, Inf.Mgr., The Devel.Planning Partnership, Bedford. [0024842] 01/01/1975
Kett Mr D, MCLIP, L.& Inf.Offr., Dundee City Council. [0008325] 01/01/1972
Kettle Mrs BW, MCLIP, Serv.Advisor Child.Serv., Staffs.C.C., Cannock L. [0019748] 01/01/1971
Kettle Mr SJ, BA DipLib MCLIP GDipMan, Dist.Lib., Leics.L.& Inf.Stud., Leicester. [0034531] 02/12/1981
Kettlewell Ms AM, BA(Hons), Advocacy Mgr., Age Concern Cheshire, Northwich. [0055648] 31/10/1997 **AF**
Kettlewell Mr P, MCLIP, Documentalist/Webmaster, UNICE, Bruxelles, Belgium. [0008329] 08/03/1961
Kew Mrs AL, (was Lloyd), Retired. [0045250] 20/08/1990
Kewley Mr P, BA CertEd MCLIP, Tutor Lib., Barnfield Coll.of F.E., Luton. [0008331] 18/01/1966
Key Mrs A, (was Brown), BA MCLIP, Life Member. [0008332] 23/08/1955
Key Mrs J, (was Waterman), BA MCLIP, Literature Searcher, Royal Coll.of Nursing, London. [0034722] 19/01/1982
Key Mr M, BA MCLIP, Lib.(Camomile St.), Corp.of London. [0019791] 23/11/1972
Key Mr MH, BA DipLib MCLIP, Unemployed. [0024898] 13/10/1975
Keyes Ms AM, BSc DpbA MLS, Director of L.Serv., Yavapai Coll., USA. [0061642] 07/10/2002
Keys Ms J, BSc, Employment not known. [0060432] 11/12/2001
Keysell Mrs M, (was Barber), BA MCLIP, Sch.Lib., The Campion Sch., Hornchurch, Essex. [0000732] 28/10/1971
Keyte Miss ME, MCLIP, Lib., Dept.L., Hertford C.C. [0021295] 09/10/1973
Kgosiemang Ms RT, MSc, Coordinator, Humanities, Subject Lib., Univ.Botswana. [0051436] 14/02/1995
Khan Miss A, Reading Room Lib., Brit.Film Inst., London. [0049834] 16/12/1993
Khan Mr A, BA(Hons), Principal Project Offr., Birmingham City Council. [0044888] 08/01/1991
Khan Mr AS, MA BA, Unemployed. [0059912] 02/11/2001
Khan Mrs GM, (was Holmes), MCLIP, Asst.Lib., Peterborough City Council. [0007111] 01/10/1970
Khan Mr N, Inf.Asst., British Red Cross, London. [0061509] 27/08/2002 **AF**
Khan Mrs PM, L.Asst., Richmond upon Thames Coll.L., Twickenham. [0047164] 07/05/1992 **AF**
Khan Miss R, BSc(Hons) MSc MCLIP, Assoc., Financial Serv.Auth., London. [0050526] 01/09/1994
Khan Ms RS, MLS MEd MCLIP, Freelance Consultant, 13 Newnham Way, Kenton, Harrow, HA3 9NU. [0008343] 24/09/1970
Khoo Miss GS, BA MCLIP, Inf.& L.Serv.Mgr., Brit Co., Kuala Lumpur. [0017172] 24/06/1972
Khoo Mrs SM, MCLIP, Ch.Lib., Sunway Coll., Malaysia. [0019899] 14/10/1971
Khoo Miss SP, BA MCLIP, Parliament Lib., Parliament of Singapore. [0020547] 16/03/1973
Khoo Miss YLL, (was Wong), BA MCLIP, Sen.Asst.Lib., Harrow. [0016169] 02/10/1969
Khorshidian Mrs M, (was Duncan), BA DipLIS MCLIP, Asst.Lib., The L., Univ.of Ulster at Belfast. [0045066] 03/07/1990
Kia Mr D, BSc, Stud./Supply Teacher, Thames Valley Univ./Ealing. [0060874] 18/12/2001
Kidane Mr RS, MA, Unemployed. [0057829] 27/08/1999
Kidd Mr AJ, MA MCLIP, Head of Serials/Doc.Del., Glasgow Univ.L. [0023153] 08/10/1974
Kidd Ms E, (was Halake), MA(Hons) DipLIS MCLIP, Comm.Lib., W.Berks.Dist.Council, Thatcham. [0046174] 09/10/1991
Kidd Miss VMA, BA(Hons), Inf.Specialist, GCHQ, Cheltenham. [0058101] 29/10/1999
Kidds Mr MD, BA(Hons) DipILM MCLIP, Asst.Lib., Nat.Meteorological L., London. [0051620] 13/04/1995

Kidwell Miss C, BA(Hons), Stud., Univ.Coll.London. [0059263] 23/01/2001
Kiehl Dr CA, (was Buchanan), MA MCLIP PhD, Assoc.Univ.Lib.for Tech.Serv., Univ.of California-Irvine, California, USA. [0024559] 19/08/1975
Kiely Mrs CM, (was Atkinson), BA(Hons) DipILS, Housewife. [0040822] 01/07/1987
Kiely Ms MA, BA MA, Inf.Offr., BECTA., Coventry. [0049608] 19/11/1993
Kift Ms SML, BA MCLIP, Young Peoples Serv.Mgr., Leeds City Council. [0037032] 30/01/1984
Kilbourn Mrs MI, (was Parker), FCLIP, Life Member. [0008353] 25/03/1931 FE 01/01/1936
Kilbride Mrs S, (was McManus), MA(Hons) DipILS PGCE MCLIP, Early Intervention Team Lib., N.Lanarkshire Council. [0046839] 13/02/1992
Kilburn Ms KJ, BA DipLib MCLIP, Sen.Lib.w/e(Job Share), Univ.of Huddersfield. [0032105] 26/01/1980
Kilburn Ms PA, BA(Hons), Dep.Learning Res.Mgr., Middlesbrough Coll. [0043173] 05/09/1989
Kilburn-Easlea Mr A, Computer Super., Phoenix Tech.Serv., Wandsworth. [0047966] 28/10/1992 AF
Kiley Mr RJ, BA MSc MCLIP, H.of Systems Strategy, Wellcome Trust L., London. [0041662] 07/02/1988
Kilgallon Mrs IJ, (was Spence), MCLIP, Inf.Specialist, Faculty of the Environment, Univ.of Portsmouth. [0013794] 01/10/1971
Kilgannon Ms JS, BA(Hons) MA, Serials Lib., Courtauld Inst.of Art, London. [0053993] 14/10/1996
Kilgour Miss AE, BA(Hons) DipLib MCLIP, Faculty Lib.(Arts), Queen Margaret Univ.Coll., Edinburgh. [0046120] 02/10/1991
Kill Mrs A, MCLIP, Bibl.Serv.Lib., Hampshire Co.L., S.Division. [0026433] 01/10/1976
Killah Mr D, MCLIP, Sen.Lib., Falkirk Council. [0008355] 13/01/1970
Killean Mrs EJ, (was Berwick), BA MCLIP, Unemployed. [0041092] 07/10/1997
Killiard Ms P, MA DipLib MCLIP, Head of IT Serv., Cambridge Univ.L. [0032531] 24/04/1980
Killick Miss BH, FCLIP, Head of Planning & Research, Calgary P.L., Canada. [0017178] 26/02/1958 FE 02/12/1974
Killick Mr J, BA(Hons) DipLIS MCLIP, Lib.Mgr., L.B.of Barnet, Mill Hill L. [0046066] 18/09/1991
Killoran Mrs PA, Coll. Lib. [0061603] 29/01/2002
Killoran Ms SA, (was Corns), BA DipLib MCLIP, Coll.Lib., Univ.of Oxford., Harris Manchester Coll. [0034965] 18/05/1982
Kilminster Mr GJ, BA(Hons) FMA, Ls.Mus.& Arts Mgr., Rotherham M.B.C. [0059187] 11/12/2000 SP
Kilmurray Miss L, MCLIP, Retired. [0008358] 17/03/1960
Kilmurry Miss EM, BA MCLIP, Princ.L.Offr., City of Edinburgh Council. [0037874] 06/11/1984
Kilner Mrs A, BA(Hons) MA MCLIP, Admin.Offr., Learning Res., Univ.of Northumbria L. [0051529] 01/04/1970
Kilvington Mrs LM, (was Cox), BA MCLIP, Housewife. [0024335] 08/07/1975
Kim Mr Y, MA, Stud., Sheffield Univ. [0059455] 30/03/2001
Kim Prof YW, Prof., Faculty of Cult.Inf.Res., Surugadai Univ., Japan. [0048793] 26/05/1993
Kimber Mrs CE, BA(Hons) MA, Asst.Lib.:Collection Devel., Rutherford Appleton Lab., Oxon. [0057580] 12/05/1999
Kimber Mr JM, Electronic Inf.Supp., QinetiQ Ltd., Worcs. [0059864] 18/10/2001
Kimberlee Mrs SL, (was Tinson), BA(Hons) MCLIP, Community Lib., Plymouth City Council, Eggbuckland Coll. [0049420] 21/10/1993
Kimberley Mr RM, BA MSc MCLIP, Employment not known. [0060534] 11/12/2001
Kimmins Mrs O, BA (Hons), Unemployed. [0061483] 15/08/2002
Kincaid Mrs IC, (was Mcdonald), BA MCLIP, L.Asst., Stirling Univ.L., Stirling. [0026125] 14/07/1976
Kindness Mrs F, (was Sanders), BA MCLIP, Lib., S.Lanarkshire L., E.Kilbride Cent.L. [0040103] 21/10/1986
King Dr A, CMB DBE DSc LID HonFCLIP, Hon Fellow. [0060408] 11/12/2001 FE 01/04/2002
King Miss A, BA MCLIP, Lib., Dame Alice Harpur Sch., Bedford. [0008366] 16/07/1971
King Mrs A, (was Vale), MCLIP, Child.Lib., Southampton City Council. [0002129] 01/01/1970
King Mrs A, BA MCLIP, Lib., Challney High Sch., Luton Bor.C. [0008368] 01/01/1969
King Mr ALB, MCLIP, Application Support Mgr., DS Grp., Ferndown, Dorset. [0020932] 19/09/1973
King Mrs AM, (was Slaymaker), BA MLib, Sch.Lib., The Perse Sch., Cambridge. [0044645] 14/11/1990
King Mr AP, BA DipLib MCLIP AIL, Hist.Collections Lib., Portsmouth City Council. [0018430] 01/10/1975
King Mr BMA, BA MCLIP, Team Lib.(Inf.), Bury St.Edmunds L., Suffolk C.C. [0035056] 21/07/1982
King Ms C, MA DipLib FSAS MCLIP, Sen.Catr.,Tech.Serv., Dorset Co.L.Serv., Dorchester. [0029713] 07/10/1978
King Miss CL, Learning Res.Instructor, Newham Coll.of F.E. [0058034] 18/10/1999
King Mrs CM, (was Mcgrane), BA MSc MCLIP, L.Serv.Mgr., Manchester Sch.of Physiotherapy, Cent.& Manchester Child.Univ.Hosp. [0027833] 24/08/1977
King Mr D, MA MCLIP, Acquisitions Lib., Dept.of Trans., Local Govt., & the Regions L., London. [0023923] 26/02/1975
King Mrs DL, (was Marshall), BA(Hons) MCLIP, Health Sci.Lib.Mgr., Univ.Hospitals Coventry & Warks. [0049418] 21/10/1993
King Miss DR, BA(Hons) MSc MCLIP, Lib., Herbert Smith, London. [0047160] 20/05/1992
King Miss EJ, BA(Hons) MSc MCLIP, Researcher, KPMG, Birmingham. [0056279] 20/04/1998

King Mrs FE, (was Lawler), BA MCLIP, Learning Support Asst., The Grange CP Sch., Banbury. [0029455] 03/08/1978
King Miss G, MCLIP, Team Lib., Glos.C.C. [0008381] 25/02/1963
King Ms G, BSc(Econ) MCLIP, LRC Mgr., Westminster City School, London. [0054540] 20/01/1997
King Ms G, (was Varley), BA MCLIP, Br.Lib., Calderdale L.Serv., Cent.L., Halifax. [0041976] 05/07/1988
King Miss HLA, MA MSc MCLIP, Inf.Mgr., GCHQ, Cheltenham. [0049471] 05/11/1993
King Mr IPG, BA MCLIP, Sen.Lib., Bradford Hosp.NHS Trust, Med.L., Bradford Royal Infirmary. [0019513] 12/10/1966
King Mrs J, (was Fearis), BA MCLIP, Unemployed. [0040514] 27/02/1987
King Mrs J, (was Murphy), Unemployed. [0039721] 22/05/1986
King Mrs J, (was Marshall), MCLIP, Unemployed. [0009798] 16/02/1970
King Mrs JA, (was Phillips), BA(Hons) MCLIP, Retired. [0006016] 08/09/1954
King Mrs JC, (was Maughan), BA MA MCLIP, Inf.Advisor, Sheffield Hallam Univ. [0043834] 25/01/1990
King Mrs JJ, (was Cheeseman), BLib MCLIP, Se.Lib., Court Serv., London. [0037261] 14/05/1984
King Mrs JL, (was Danson), BA MCLIP, Comm.Lib., Top Valley L., Nottingham. [0019862] 01/01/1973
King Ms JM, BA MCLIP, Self-Employed. [0017181] 25/09/1968
King Mr KD, MA MCLIP, Life Member, 3,Waldon Ave., Cheadle. [0008390] 30/07/1946
King Mrs LA, BA(Hons), L.& Inf.Serv.Mgr., Stockton Borough L. [0051866] 18/07/1995
King Mr LJ, BA MCLIP, Lib., Shoe Lane L., City of London. [0029995] 23/10/1978
King Mrs M, (was Ellis), MCLIP, Sch.Lib., Herts.C.C. [0008391] 24/01/1963
King Mr MB, MCLIP FIMgt, Retired. [0008393] 03/02/1961
King Ms MC, MLS MCLIP, Sen.Lib.-Access & Promotions, Derby City L., Derbys. [0008394] 10/01/1967
King Mrs ML, BA DipLib, Lib., HMP & YOI Ashfield, Bristol. [0058173] 08/11/1999
King Ms ML, (was Smith), BA, Sen.L.Asst., N.Ayrshire Council. [0043367] 26/10/1989
King Miss NCS, BA(Hons) MA(Hons) PGCE, Unemployed. [0057041] 27/11/1998
King Ms P, (was Halasovski), BA FCLIP, Head of Sch.for Inf.& Learning Dev., Cambridge Reg.Coll. [0008398] 06/10/1970 FE 21/03/2001
King Ms PA, BLS DipHE MCLIP, Inf.Offr., The Fostering Network, London. [0028040] 13/10/1977
King Mrs PAM, (was Hillier), MA MCLIP, Lib., Reading Coll., Sch.of Arts & Design. [0041567] 28/01/1988
King Mr PM, MA DipLib, Dep.Inf.Serv.Mgr., Holman, Fenwick & Willan, London. [0035670] 10/01/1983
King Mrs R, (was Philp), MCLIP, Comm.Serv.Lib.(Job Share), Neath, Port Talbot L. [0008402] 19/01/1966
King Mrs RH, (was Steff), BSc(Econ) MCLIP, The Lib., The Dragon Sch., Oxford. [0008401] 12/10/1965
King Mrs RJ, MCLIP, Child.Lib., Worcs.C.C., Redditch. [0002634] 01/01/1971
King Mrs S, (was Lowe), MCLIP, Ch.Lib., Nat.Police L., Hook, Hants. [0009130] 05/01/1970
King Mrs S, MA MCLIP, Learning Res.Mgr., Harrow Coll. [0008403] 01/01/1969
King Miss SD, Lib., Northern Sch.of Contemporary Dance, Leeds. [0048676] 08/04/1993
King Mrs SH, (was Brown), BA(Hons) DipILS MCLIP, Asst.Lib., MOD, London. [0049034] 07/09/1993
King Mr SJ, BSc MCLIP, Bibl.Serv.Lib., Robert Gordon Univ., Aberdeen. [0020526] 08/04/1973
King Mrs SJ, DipLib MCLIP, Sch.Lib., Aylesford Sch., Warwick. [0033240] 27/10/1980
King Mrs XW, (was Li), BA MA, Chinese Comm.Lib., Charing Cross L. [0058714] 01/07/2000
Kingham Mr JJ, BMus LTCL ALCM MCLIP, Sen.Asst., Essex Co.L. [0008410] 21/02/1965
Kings Miss PA, BA MCLIP, Freelance:Training, Project & Dev., Child.L.Serv.& Literacy Activities. [0032309] 05/03/1980
Kingsbury-Barker Mrs TC, (was Cornelius), BA MCLIP, Child.Lib.(Job Share), Bexley L.Serv. [0041964] 04/07/1988
Kingsley Mr BJK, BA (CNAA) MCLIP, Sch.Lib., Immanuel CE Comm.Coll., Bradford. [0027115] 16/05/2001
Kingsley Mrs SM, (was Summerhayes), MA PGCE MCLIP, Community Team Lib., Glos.Co.L.Arts & Mus. [0028907] 08/02/1978
Kingston Mr CE, Business Inf.Offr., Inst.of Directors. [0051575] 03/04/1995
Kingston Miss MD, BA(Hons) MSc(Econ), PhD Stud., DILS, Univ.of Wales, Aberystwyth. [0052893] 17/01/1996
Kingston Ms PJ, BA DipLib PGCE MCLIP, Confed.Lib., W.Midland S.Workforce, Devel.Confed., Worcester. [0040794] 01/06/1987
Kingston Mrs S, (was Wallbank), BA DipLib MCLIP, Sch.Lib., Suffolk C.C., Ipswich, Suffolk. [0031717] 25/10/1979
Kinnear Mrs CA, BSc MSc, L.Inf.Systems Mgr., The Law Society Library, London. [0046808] 30/01/1992
Kinnear Miss JMM, MA DipLib MCLIP, Asst.Lib., Northumberland C.C., Hexham L. [0034317] 29/09/1981
Kinnersley Ms DM, BA(Hons) DipIS, Business Lib., London Guildhall Univ. [0045385] 28/01/1991
Kintner Mrs MP, (was Mcgonnell), BA DipLib MSSc MCLIP, Team Lib.-Inf., N.E.E.L.B., Rathcoole. [0023268] 25/11/1974
Kipling Mr G, BA MCLIP, L.Mgr., Cheshire L.& Culture, Macclesfield. [0008419] 13/09/1963
Kirby Miss AJ, BA(Hons) MCLIP, Lend.Lib., City Council, Southampton. [0048613] 09/03/1993
Kirby Mr C, MCLIP, Inf.Offr., Iron Mountain, BP Exploration. [0008424] 15/01/1963

Personal Members

Kirby Mrs CE, BA PGDipLib MCLIP, L.Asst., Bridgwater Coll., Somerset. [0033016] 01/10/1980
Kirby Mrs HG, BA, Ref./Inf.Serv.Mgr., Croydon L., L.B.of Croydon. [0020595] 01/04/1973
Kirby Miss KM, MA DipLib MCLIP, Acting L., Manchester Business Sch. [0030448] 31/01/1979
Kirby Miss MH, BA MCLIP, Life Member. [0008429] 06/01/1958
Kirby Mrs ML, BA, Content Devel.Mgr., City of Westminster, London. [0028326] 11/11/1977
Kirby Mr RC, Retired. [0038428] 02/05/1985
Kirby Mr S, BA MCLIP, Catr., Bibl.Serv.,Stationery Off.Ltd., London. [0008430] 01/01/1969
Kirby Mrs SM, MCLIP, Princ.Lib., Community L.& Arts, Flintshire C.C. [0012519] 12/01/1972
Kirk Mr A, BA(Hons) MA, Team Lib.(Ref.Inf.& Local Stud.), Canterbury L., Kent C.C. [0058834] 23/08/2000
Kirk Mrs CG, (was McCracken), BA MLib MCLIP, Lib., Bucks.C.C., Aylesbury. [0044956] 23/01/1991
Kirk Prof J, BA MLitt MA DipEd AALI MCLIP, Resident in Australia. [0060091] 07/12/2001
Kirk Mr R, BA MCLIP, Head of E-Govt.& Co.Lib., W.Sussex C.C., Chichester. [0008433] 15/01/1968
Kirk Mr RW, BA MCLIP HonFCLIP, Educ.Lib., Univ.of Leicester. [0008434] 21/03/1966 FE 24/10/2002
Kirk Miss W, BA(Hons), Stud., Strathclyde Univ. [0061767] 05/11/2002
Kirkby Mrs E, BA MCLIP, Retired. [0008436] 01/01/1966
Kirkegaard Dr P, HonFCLIP, Retired. [0027611] 08/06/1977 FE 08/06/1977
Kirkham Miss BD, BA(Hons) DipLIS MCLIP, Asst.Lib., Rhyl L., Clwyd. [0046441] 06/11/1991
Kirkham Mrs CG, (was Laing), BA DipLib MCLIP, Field Offr./Lib., City of Edinburgh Council. [0029719] 18/10/1978
Kirkham Miss HL, BA(Hons) MA, Ass.Inf.Offr., De Montfort Univ., Bucks. [0059833] 16/10/2001
Kirkham Ms SV, BA(Hons) DipIS MCLIP, Arts Lib., Suffolk Coll., Ipswich,Suffolk. [0048088] 02/11/1992
Kirkham Mrs VE, BA DipLib MCLIP, Career Break. [0038106] 15/01/1985
Kirkland Miss LC, BA(Hons) MCLIP, Asst.Lib., Milton Keynes City Council. [0048672] 07/04/1993
Kirkness Ms MF, MCLIP, Bibl.Serv.Lib., Bucks.Chilterns Univ.Coll., High Wycombe. [0035146] 10/01/1982
Kirkpatrick Mrs AS, (was Griffin), BA, Midday Super., St.Botolph's C of E Primary Sch., Peterborough. [0037707] 10/10/1984
Kirkpatrick Miss BJ, MBE FCLIP, Life Member. [0008441] 12/06/1941 FE 01/01/1950
Kirkpatrick Mrs J, (was Fletcher), BA DipILS MCLIP, Electronic L.Project Offr., Worc.Health Informatics, Kidderminster Hospital. [0047870] 22/10/1992
Kirkpatrick Mrs K, (was Laurie), MA DipLib MCLIP, Career Break. [0043505] 31/10/1989
Kirkpatrick Mrs SD, (was Park), BLS MCLIP, Asst.Chief Lib., L.B.of Richmond upon Thames., Young Peoples & Sch.L.& Resource. [0032327] 03/03/1980
Kirkpatrick Mrs WH, MA DipLib MCLIP, Asst.Lib., Kings Coll.L., Cambridge. [0044458] 10/10/1990
Kirkwood Mrs LJ, (was Cowan), MCLIP, Sen.Local Studies Lib., Warwickshire Co.L. [0003240] 30/01/1972
Kirkwood Miss ML, MA(Hons) MSc, Lib.Nursing & Midwifery, Glasgow Royal Infirmary. [0055830] 20/11/1997
Kirkwood Mr R, OBE BSc MCLIP, Retired. [0008443] 14/10/1966
Kirkwood Ms RJ, BA(Hons) MSc DipTrans, Dep.Lib., Goethe-Institut, London. [0051247] 07/12/1994
Kirschner Mrs HG, L.Asst./Staff Devel.Offr., Sleaford L., Lincs. [0059781] 02/10/2001 AF
Kirtan Mrs M, (was Howard), MCLIP, Retired. [0008444] 07/02/1963
Kirton Miss AD, BA DipLib MCLIP, Sen.Educ.Lib., Sch.L.Serv., Northumberland C., Morpeth. [0030204] 29/12/1978
Kirton Miss MH, BA MA MCLIP, Inf.Serv.Advisor, Napier Univ., Edinburgh. [0036484] 18/10/1983
Kirui Mr JK, Head of L.Serv., Kenya Broadcasting Corp., Nairobi. [0044158] 13/06/1990
Kirven Ms S, BA MLS, Ref.Lib., Congressman Frank J Guerini L., New Jersey City Univ., U.S.A. [0061076] 04/03/2002
Kirwan Ms EM, BA MA, Asst.Keeper, Dept.Manuscripts, The Nat.L.of Ireland, Dublin. [0048705] 23/04/1993
Kirwan Mr P, MA FCLIP, Life Member, Tel.020 8299 0761. [0008449] 23/09/1958 FE 01/01/1963
Kirwan Mrs P, (was Lucas), MCLIP DipPsych, Retired. [0009158] 01/01/1967
Kisiedu Mrs CO, Assoc.Professor, Univ.of Ghana, Legon, Accra. [0020906] 28/08/1973
Kisner Mrs E, (was Hazeldine), MCLIP, Retired, 3 Erith Grove, Norbreck, Blackpool, FY2 9AR. [0008451] 10/03/1948
Kisz Miss JM, BSc MIHort, Lib., Inf.Serv., Hampshire C.C., L.H.Q. [0059381] 23/02/2001
Kitani Ms M, Resident in Japan. [0059001] 20/10/2000
Kitch Mrs PW, MLib MCLIP, L.Serv.Mgr., Royal Cornwall Hosp.Trust, Truro. [0034104] 01/01/1960
Kitchen Miss JA, BA MCLIP, Unemployed. [0028613] 04/01/1978
Kitcher Mrs H, BA(Hons) MSc MCLIP, PG Cent.Lib., PG Cent.L., PG Med.Cent., Whitchurch Hosp., Cardiff. [0056457] 10/07/1998
Kitchin Mrs E, (was Mattocks), MCLIP, Life Member. [0008453] 27/02/1947
Kitson Ms M, (was Gladston), BLIB MCLIP, Yth.Team Lib., Beds.C.C. [0036672] 03/11/1983
Kitto Mr N, BA, Stud., Univ. of Brighton. [0060902] 09/01/2002
Kitwood Miss JA, BA DipLib MCLIP, Area Lib., Shipley L., W.Yorks. [0037357] 12/07/1984

Kjaernested Mrs R, MSc, Head of Dept., FSA Univ.Hosp., Med.L., Iceland. [0049893] 07/01/1994
Klak Mrs JM, (was Fraser), BA MCLIP, Inf.Serv.Lib., Fife Council, Kirkcaldy. [0005196] 01/01/1971
Klausen Miss KM, Lib., Engineering Coll.of Aarhus, Denmark. [0054168] 04/11/1996
Kloska Miss BZ, BSc(Hons) MSc MCLIP, Asst.Lib.(Search Serv.), Royal Soc.of Med., London. [0043736] 13/12/1989
Kneebone Mrs C, (was Jefferis), MCLIP, Retired. [0008468] 09/02/1960
Kneebone Mr WJR, BSc MCLIP, Retired. [0008469] 23/01/1961
Knibb Mr RJ, BA DipLib MCLIP, Asst.Lib., W.Sussex C.C., Worthing L. [0032107] 28/01/1980
Knight Ms AJ, (was Delany), BSc(Hons), Editor, ASSIA, C.S.A., W.Sussex. [0044152] 07/06/1990
Knight Mrs CA, BA MCLIP, Unemployed. [0039458] 22/01/1986
Knight Mrs D, MCLIP, Dist.Lib., Hertsmere, Herts.C.C. [0008475] 01/07/1967
Knight Mrs F, (was Williams), MCLIP, Dep.Lib.& Inf.Serv.Mgr., Surrey & Sussex NHS Trust, Redhill. [0008478] 22/02/1956
Knight Dr GA, PhD FIL FIAP MCLIP AMBCS, Employment not known. [0060535] 11/12/2001
Knight Ms HB, BA(Hons) MCLIP, Inf.Specialist, Cardiff Univ., Aberconway Guest Res.Cent. [0041343] 06/11/1987
Knight Mr HJ, BLib MLib, Ch.Inf.Offr., Lloyd's Bus.Intelligence Cent., London. [0043665] 21/11/1989
Knight Mrs J, (was Pickup), MCLIP, Area Child.Spec.-Market Harborough, Leics.C.C., Leics. [0008481] 11/03/1966
Knight Mrs JE, L.Mgr., Colchester L. [0059453] 30/03/2001 AF
Knight Miss JL, BSc(Econ) MCLIP, Lib.Designate, Inst.of Health Studies, Princess Elizabeth Hosp., Guernsey. [0056524] 10/08/1998
Knight Mrs JS, (was Ware), BA MCLIP, Coll.Lib., Evesham Coll., Worcs. [0026600] 23/09/1976
Knight Mrs KM, (was Antill), BA(Hons) MA, Sen.L.Asst., Imperial Coll., London. [0046964] 06/03/1992
Knight Ms LE, (was Goodrich), BA DipLib, Mgr., Waterstones Booksellers, London. [0042131] 06/10/1988
Knight Miss LS, BA MCLIP DMS, Sen.Lib., Cheltenham Ref.L., Glos.Co.L. [0032803] 16/09/1980
Knight Mrs MB, BA, Lib.Asst., John Rylands Univ.L.of Manchester, Univ of Manchester. [0058789] 24/07/2000
Knight Mrs ME, (was Stevens), MCLIP, MLib., Vaughan L., Harrow Sch., Middx. [0013989] 23/12/1964
Knight Mrs PA, (was Moy), MCLIP, Unemployed. [0010540] 19/01/1968
Knight Ms PC, BA(Hons) MA MCLIP, Bibl.Serv.Lib., Farnborough Coll.of Tech., Hants. [0046338] 29/10/1991
Knight Mr PJ, Lib., B.B.C. [0055540] 20/10/1997 AF
Knight Mr R, BA MCLIP, H.of Cultural Serv., Rutland C.C., Oakham. [0008487] 05/03/1966
Knight Mr R, Retired. [0008489] 10/01/1950
Knight Mr RFE, MA FRSA FCLIP, Life Member. [0008488] 14/03/1952 FE 01/01/1969
Knight Mr RG, BA MCLIP, Princ.Offr., Local Studies & Arch., L.B.of Camden. [0023804] 31/01/1975
Knight Miss SC, BA DipLib MCLIP, Operations Mgr.(W.Div.), Dorset. [0035728] 01/01/1982
Knight Mrs ST, (was Pettengell), JP FCLIP MPhil MIMgt, Lib./Contract Mgr., N.Herts NHS Trust, Health Inf.First. [0008490] 01/01/1965 FE 12/09/1990
Knight Mr T, MLib FCLIP, Exec.Head of L., Heritage & Registration Serv., L.B.Sutton. [0008492] 11/10/1976 FE 17/12/1982
Knight Mrs T, MA MA MCLIP, Lib., Royal Coll.of Surgeons of England. [0029054] 01/03/1978
Knight Mrs ZM, (was Court), BA MCLIP, Retired. [0003217] 03/01/1962
Knock Mr LD, BA(Hons), L.Asst., Wellcome L., London. [0058830] 22/08/2000
Knott Mrs JF, (was Harris), BA(Hons) DipLib MCLIP, Casual L.Asst., Ashford L., Kent. [0035252] 01/10/1982
Knowles Miss C, MCLIP, Asst.Lib., Univ.of Manchester. [0008505] 11/03/1961
Knowles Mrs D, BA(Hons), p./t.Stud., Lib.Asst., Liverpool John Moores., Lib.St Helens College. [0059147] 28/11/2000
Knowles Mrs EJB, (was Mcphail), MA MCLIP, Serv.Mgr.(QDD), Perth & Kinross Council, Perth. [0023215] 10/11/1974
Knowles Mrs GA, (was Rickaby), BA MA MCLIP, Employment not known. [0043607] 09/11/1989
Knowles Ms H, (was Mayou), BA MCLIP, Advisory Lib., L.Serv.for Educ., Leics.L.& Inf.Serv. [0023740] 22/01/1975
Knowles Miss J, BSc MSc(Econ) MCLIP, Electronic Res.Lib., Univ.of Durham. [0054263] 14/11/1996
Knowles Mr JA, BA(Hons), L.Asst., Univ.Coll.London. [0057438] 01/04/1999
Knowles Miss MD, MCLIP, Lib., Alleyn's Sch., Dulwich. [0008510] 16/01/1968
Knowling Ms LS, BA(Hons) DipILM, Asst.Inf.Lib., Warrington Ls., Cheshire. [0054370] 25/11/1996
Knowlson Mrs A, (was Butler), BA MCLIP, Sen.Learning Cent.Offr.(Operations), City of Sunderland Coll. [0032886] 06/10/1980
Knox Miss A, BA MCLIP, Dep.Lib., Middle Temple, London. [0008513] 30/10/1969
Knox Mrs A, BA, Stud., Robert Gordon Univ., Aberdeen. [0057375] 26/02/1999
Knox Ms AMF, BA(Hons) MCLIP, Weekend Servs.Lib., Woolwich Campus L., Univ.of Greenwich, London. [0030637] 01/03/1979
Knox Ms EB, (was Hamer), BA MCLIP, Lib., Forfar Acad., Angus Council. [0039540] 19/02/1986
Knox Miss J, MA MCLIP, p./t.Asst.Lib., Univ.of Ulster at Jordanstown, Newtownabbey. [0033421] 23/11/1980
Knox Mr P, BA(Hons) MA, Res.Support Lib., Kingston Univ. [0053695] 11/09/1996

Knox ms SJ, BA(Hons) DipILM MCLIP, L.Mgr., L.B.of Croydon, Croydon. [0049156] 08/10/1993
Knutson Mrs B, (was Chambers), BA(Hons), Sen.L.Asst., N.Somerset Council, Nailsea L. [0045355] 24/10/1990
Koch Ms L, BA(Hons), Learning Res.Devel.Offr., Eccles Coll., Manchester. [0057293] 03/02/1999
Kocienski Ms A, BA PGCE, Cent.Asst., Peter Symonds Coll., Winchester. [0057433] 01/04/1999 **AF**
Kock Mr MM, BA(Hons), Inf.Mgr., Eicon Networks, Copenhagen, Denmark. [0054112] 30/10/1996
Koeper-Saul Mrs VE, MLIS, Temp.Webpage Designer &, Language Teacher/L.Asst., Univ.of Liverpool. [0057381] 26/02/1999
Kohli Mr G, BA BSc DipLib MCLIP, Retired. [0008517] 02/02/1966
Kohli Mrs JK, MA B.Ed PG Dip Lib, Multicultural Lib., Warwickshire C.C., Leamington Spa. [0036679] 01/11/1983
Kohli Miss N, BA MCLIP, Child.Lib., S.Norwood L., Croydon Council. [0024958] 28/10/1975
Kohlwagen Ms J, DipLib MCLIP, Sen.Asst.Lib., Univ.of Westminster, London. [0052148] 06/10/1995
Kolsky Miss R, BA, Mgr.-Desk Research, AIG (Europe), London. [0035223] 04/10/1982
Komiliades Mrs SS, BA(Hons) DipLIS, Asst.L.& Inf.Serv.Mgr., Health Sciences L., Ashford & St Peters Hosp.NHS Trust. [0037493] 03/10/1984
Kondopoulou Ms Y, BA(Hons) MA, Social Inclusion Lib., Cent.L., London. [0061521] 04/09/2002
Kong Mr PY, MCLIP AALIA, Resident in Australia. [0018394] 19/10/1972
Konn Ms TF, BA MA MCLIP, Princ.Asst.Lib., Glasgow Univ.L. [0033824] 16/03/1981
Konviser Mrs LD, (was Hammar), BA BSocSci H DipLib, P/t.Sch.Lib., Orley Farm Boys Sch., Harrow,Middx. [0043887] 07/02/1990
Kopecky Mrs BJ, (was Squires), MCLIP, Sch.Lib., St.John the Baptist lower Sch., Northamptonshire C.C. [0030267] 09/01/1979
Korale Mrs SR, BA FCLIP, Lib., Open Univ.of Sri Lanka, Nawala. [0020505] 25/03/1973 **FE 29/06/1981**
Kordmahini Ms HA, MA BA, Lib., The Brit.Inst.of Persian Studies, Tehran. [0061112] 19/02/2002
Korjonen-Close Mrs HM, BSc(Hons), Stud., Univ.Coll.London, &, Med.Inf.Offr.& Co.Lib., Merck Pharm., W.Drayton. [0058950] 10/10/2000
Korolewicz Mr T, MCLIP, Employment not known. [0008522] 16/10/1971
Kosinski Mrs ZE, (was Bzdega), BA CNAA Dip MCLIP, Lib., Adams Grammar Sch., Telford & Wrekin C.C. [0023762] 10/01/1974
Koster Mr C, BA FRSA MCLIP, Life Member. [0008524] 17/02/1959
Kotake Ms E, Inf.Mgr., Brit.Council Inf.Cent., Tokyo. [0046303] 15/10/1991
Koumi Ms PA, (was Clarke), BA MCLIP, Curator, Brit.L., London. [0023849] 13/02/1975
Kousseff Mrs GE, (was Fernie), MA(Oxon) FCLIP, Life Member, Tel.0181 883 8987, 17 The Chine, Muswell Hill, London, N10 3PX. [0008525] 14/10/1938 **FE 01/01/1943**
Koutsomichali Ms K, BA MEd, Res.Mgr., Bell-London, London. [0061232] 18/04/2002
Kowalczuk Mr F, BA(Hons) DipILM, Asst.Lib., Veterinary Lab.Agency, Addlestone. [0052480] 02/11/1995
Kowalczuk Mrs SRL, (was Williams), BA DipLib MCLIP, Digital L.Devel.Mgr., Univ.of Luton. [0034980] 24/05/1992
Kowalski Mrs DM, BA(Hons), Inf.Offr., Registered Nursing Home Assoc., Birmingham. [0048632] 26/03/1993
Koyama Mr N, DipLib MCLIP, Under-Lib., Cambridge Univ.L. [0032671] 03/07/1980
Krabhuis Dr J, MCLIP, Position unknown, Highland Data, Tarbert. [0060238] 10/12/2001
Krajnyk Mrs VC, (was Robinson), BA MCLIP, L.Asst., Buckingham L., Bucks.C.C. [0028890] 19/01/1978
Kramskoy Mrs CS, (was Williams), BEd(Hons) SpEd MEd MCLIP, Statement Offr., Bristol City Council (DELL). [0015901] 07/01/1966
Krawszik Miss AH, B ED MCLIP, Local Studies Lib., Chesterfield L., Derbys.C.C. [0026437] 18/10/1976
Krethlow Shaw Mrs MET, (was Krethlow), BA MCLIP, Asst.Dist.Mgr., Essex County L.Services., Basildon L. [0034627] 13/01/1982
Kriki Miss I, BA, Stud., Univ.Coll.London. [0061574] 02/10/2002
Kroebel Ms C, (was Paulos), BA MSc, Hon.Lib.& Arch., Whitby Lit.& Phil.Soc., Whitby Mus., N.Yorks. [0044227] 17/07/1990
Ku Mrs JB, (was Ong), Dir., Sabah State L., Malaysia. [0022693] 25/07/1974
Kueh Mr KSJ, B SOC SCI MCLIP, Ch.Lib., L.Div., Ministry of Environment & Pub., Health, Malaysia. [0017201] 01/01/1970
Kukoyi Miss M, BA(Hons), p./t.Stud./Inf.Asst., Univ.N.London. [0059822] 10/10/2001
Kulas Miss M, RGN BSc MCLIP, Learning Adviser, Skills for Learning, Leeds Met.Univ. [0043591]09/11/1989
Kumiega Miss LU, (was Kelly), BA DipLib MCLIP, Extended Hours Team Co-ordinator, Oxford Brookes Univ.L. [0028999] 10/02/1978
Kunkler Mr PA, MA DipLib, Self-employed. [0037073] 05/01/1984
Kuphal Mrs VA, (was Sweeney), BA MCLIP, Sen.Lib:Music, Colchester Cent.L., Essex Co.Music L. [0029841] 02/10/1978
Kurkal Dr R, MBBS, Stud., Queen Margaret Univ. Coll. [0060907] 10/01/2002
Kuruppu Mr C, Asst.Lib., Parliament of Sri Lanka. [0059688] 06/08/2001
Kvebekk Mrs MD, (was Robarts), BA MCLIP, Retired. [0017207] 07/02/1956
Kwabla-Oklikah Mrs G, (was Denning), BA MCLIP, Retired. [0008535] 01/01/1955
Kwafo-Akoto Mrs KC, (was Woode), MA DipLib FCLIP, Lib./Inf.Cent.Mgr., Overseas Devel.Inst., London. [0036558] 18/10/1983 **FE 31/01/1996**
Kwan Miss CL, DipLib MLib MCLIP, Sen.Asst.Lib., Univ.of Westminster, London. [0044725] 27/11/1990
Kwok Mr CYK, MCLIP, Sen.Lib., Vocational Training Council, Hong Kong. [0017211] 02/01/1970

Kyawt Mrs DK, BA DipEd FCLIP, Hon.Advisor, Univ.Cent.L., Yangon, Myanmar. [0021696]08/01/1974 **FE 22/07/1992**
Kybird Mrs CL, (was Beatty), MCLIP, Sch.Lib., St.Marys Coll., Crosby. [0001002] 18/01/1970
Kyffin Ms E, BA(Hons) MA DipIS MCLIP, Asst.Lib., Univ.of Westminster, Harrow. [0052244] 18/10/1995
Kyle Mrs M, MA DipLib MCLIP, Princ.L.Offr., Ref.L., Edinburgh City L. [0031651] 29/10/1979
Kyriakides Mrs C, BA MCLIP, P./t.Inf.Offr., Child.Aid to Ukraine, London. [0008539] 01/01/1966
Lacey Dr AE, MSc PhD, Inf.Mgr., Cussons International Ltd., Stockport. [0056349] 04/06/1998
Lacey Mr BK, BA DipLib MCLIP, Sales Consultant, 3M U.K., Bracknell,Berks. [0027341] 20/02/1977
Lacey Mr CS, L.Mgr., F.C.O., London. [0048259] 18/11/1992
Lacey Mrs FK, BA MCLIP CIPD MiM, Employee Devel.Adviser, Shropshire C.C., Shrewsbury. [0031881] 01/01/1980
Lacey Mrs PM, (was Don), MA DipLib MCLIP, Lib., Marlborough Coll., Wilts. [0004062] 03/09/1971
Lacey Mr R, MCLIP, Br.Lib., Fairfield Br.L., Stockton on Tees Bor.L. [0008543] 15/09/1967
Lacey Mr T, BA(Hons), Grad.Trainee, Univ.of Surrey, Guildford. [0061227] 15/04/2002
Lacey Bryant Mrs SMJ, (was Lacey), BA DipLib MSc MCLIP, Knowledge Mgr., Vale of Aylesbury PCT &, Independent Inf.Specialist. [0028615] 16/01/1978
Lack Mr NJ, BSc MCLIP, Employment unknown. [0060301] 10/12/2001
Lack Mr SJ, BA(Hons) DipLib MCLIP, Training Offr., Holborn L., London. [0037932] 16/11/1984
Lackajis Miss I, BA MCLIP, Chelsea Area Lib., R.B.of Kensington & Chelsea, London. [0022582] 10/04/1974
Lackey Ms A, BA(Hons) DipLib, Lib., E.Sussex,Brighton & Hove Health, Auth., Lewes, E.Sussex. [0037619] 09/10/1984
Lacy Miss CP, BSc MCLIP, Unemployed. [0028047] 05/10/1977
Ladd Miss H, MCLIP, Sen.Lib., Worcs.C.C. [0008547] 13/01/1966
Ladd Miss LD, MCLIP, Life Member. [0008548] 13/01/1948
Ladizesky Mrs KA, (was Owens), BA FCLIP, Retired. [0028745] 22/01/1978 **FE 22/07/1998**
Ladoux Mrs PM, BA(Hons), Unemployed. [0058286] 10/12/1999
Ladyman Miss SEL, DipHE BA MCLIP, Dir., Cramer Music Ltd., London. [0026896] 06/01/1977
Lafferty Miss IM, MA(Hons), Sen.L.Asst., Courtauld Inst.of Art, London. [0054219] 05/11/1996
Lafferty Ms J, BA(Hons) MA MCLIP, Learning Res.Cent.Mgr., Firth Park Comm.Coll., Sheffield. [0043769] 09/01/1990
Lafferty Mrs S, (was Hunt), BA DipILS MCLIP, Comm.Access Lib., L.B.of Enfield, Ordnance Road L. [0043820] 17/01/1990
Lafferty Mr STH, BA MSc, Business Inf.Offr., Armstrong Craven, Manchester. [0057050] 01/12/1998
Lahav Mrs KM, (was Southwell), MA BA MCLIP, Unemployed. [0013775] 27/10/1964
Lai Miss SF, PGDip, Stud., Northumbria Univ. [0061689] 21/10/2002
Laidlaw Mrs C, (was Hamilton), MA DipLib MCLIP, Research Administrator, Univ.of Gloucestershire, Cheltenham. [0008555] 26/10/1970
Laidlaw Mrs J, (was Legerton), MCLIP, Sch.Lib., The King's Sch.in Macclesfield, Cheshire. [0008810] 13/10/1969
Laidlaw Mr JO, BSc MCLIP, Life Member, Tel.01728 746728, 9 Churchill Cres., Wickham Market, Woodbridge, Suffolk, IP13 0RW. [0008557] 19/03/1959
Laidlaw Ms LC, Inf.Serv.Mgr., McGrigor Donald,Solicitors, Glasgow. [0038066] 10/01/1985
Laidlaw-Farmer Mrs AW, (was Laidlaw), MLS BA MCLIP, Cent.Lib., Acton Cent., Ealing Tertiary Coll. [0016868] 23/05/1966
Lain Mr MIJ, MPhil BA MCLIP, Retired. [0018864] 27/04/1966
Laing Mr CJ, BA(Hons), Asst.Lib., De Montfort Univ., Leicester. [0052476] 02/11/1995
Laing Mrs D, (was Easson), Asst.(Shelving), Stirling Univ. [0038976] 22/10/1985
Laird Mrs A, (was Potts), MA MCLIP, P./t.L.Asst., Educ.Dept., Dundee City Council, Dundee. [0008563] 22/10/1965
Laird Ms A, BA PGDipLib, Product Trainer, ICC Inf., London. [0044498] 16/10/1990
Laird Mr D, MA DipLib MCLIP, LIS Mgr., Instant L.Ltd., Cardiff. [0032109] 27/01/1980
Laird Miss EMC, MA MCLIP, Outside Serv.Mgr., N.Lanarkshire Council, Coatbridge. [0026438] 14/01/1976
Laird Mr R, BA MA PGCE, Dir., Rod Laird Organisation. [0056123] 03/03/1998 **AF**
Lake Ms CJ, MA, L.System Mgr., Environment Agency, Bristol. [0040422] 29/01/1987
Lake Mr FH, FCLIP, Life Member. [0018090] 03/10/1972 **FE 04/12/1985**
Lake Mr JB, BA MCLIP, Lib., Barbican L., Corporation of London. [0022774] 11/10/1974
Lake Miss NJ, BA(Hons) MA MCLIP, Academic Liaison Lib., Anglia Poly.Univ., Cambridge Campus. [0055748] 13/11/1997
Lake Ms SM, (was Palfrey), MCLIP, Cent.Serv.Mgr., L.B.Hillingdon L.Serv., Uxbridge. [0022814] 10/10/1974
Laker Mr K, MCLIP, Area Lib., W.Sussex L.Serv., Storrington L. [0008572] 01/05/1969
Laker Miss SC, BA DipLib MCLIP, Lib., Guille-Alles L., Guernsey. [0037861] 14/10/1984
Lakie Mrs MH, MBA MRPharmS MCLIP, Life Member. [0026120] 01/07/1976
Lakin Mrs DE, (was Waterhouse), BA DipLib MCLIP, Family Learning Cent.Mgr., The Clarendon Sch., Trowbridge. [0034103] 30/09/1981
Lal Mr D, BSc MSc MCLIP, Employment not known. [0060536] 11/12/2001

Personal Members

Lalani Mrs N, (was Teja), BA MCLIP, Inf.Serv.Lib., Royal Coll.of Nursing, London. [0029201] 01/04/1978
Lally Mr C, MCLIP, ICT Devel.Mgr., Westminster L., Charing Cross L. [0008574] 25/09/1970
Lally Mrs P, (was Keeble), MCLIP, Lib., HMP Coldingley, Surrey. [0008199] 01/04/1971
Lalwan Mr R, Local Hist.& Arch.Asst., City of Westminster Arch.Cent., London. [0048783] 20/05/1993 **AF**
Lamb Mrs B, (was Strong), MCLIP, Life Member. [0008575] 09/02/1955
Lamb Mr J, BA MCLIP, Head of L.& Learning Support, Swansea Inst.of H.E., Swansea. [0008579] 07/10/1968
Lamb Mrs J, (was Tabern), BA MCLIP, p./t.Subject Lib., Writtle Coll., Chelmsford. [0023853] 13/02/1975
Lamb Mrs JO, BA DipLib MCLIP, Lending Serv.Mgr., Oldham M.B.C., Educ.& Cultural Serv. [0028048] 01/10/1977
Lamb Mr KDI, BA(Hons) DipLib,MA, Library Serv.Mgr., Liverpool Health Authority. [0044406]05/10/1990
Lamb Mrs M, (was Brodie), MCLIP, Support Serv.Lib., Weston L., Weston-super-Mare, N.Somerset Dist.Council. [0023195] 25/10/1974
Lamb Mrs R, (was Hodkin), MA MCLIP, Retired. [0020896] 01/10/1958
Lamb Mrs SA, (was Straker), BA, Catr., Tameside M.B.C., Ashton-under-Lyne. [0039172] 28/11/1985
Lambden Miss G, MCLIP, Retired. [0008582] 17/03/1938
Lambe Mr AJ, BA(Hons) MSc, Knowledge Integrator, Andersen Consulting. [0051234] 01/12/1994
Lambe Mrs G, (was Franks), MCLIP, Sch.Lib., Putney High Sch., London. [0020381] 22/02/1973
Lambe Mrs K, (was McManus), BA(Hons) MA, JISC Inf.Offr., Leeds Univ. [0049259] 18/10/1993
Lambe Ms M, BA DipLIS MA, Lib., Marino Inst.of Educ., Dublin. [0058596] 07/04/2000
Lambert Mrs A, (was Dalby), MCLIP, Sen.Asst.Lib., Sheffield City L. [0008585] 26/01/1963
Lambert Ms C, BA MA, Sen.L.Asst., Univ.of Leicester L. [0044614] 06/11/1990
Lambert Ms C, MA, Resources Lib., Shropshire Campus Learn.Cent., Univ.of Wolverhampton, Telford. [0049061] 01/10/1993
Lambert Mrs CL, (was Ticehurst), BA(Hons) MCLIP, Unemployed. [0040579] 02/04/1987
Lambert Mr J, MCLIP, Learning Res.Cent.Mgr., The Sheffield Coll., Sheffield. [0008591] 27/06/1966
Lambert Mrs J, (was Rollinson), BSc MA MCLIP, Team Leader & H.of Pub.Serv., Aston Univ., Birmingham. [0012665] 01/01/1970
Lambert Mrs JJ, (was Oakley), BA DipLib MCLIP, Asst.Inf.Lib., L.B.of Sutton, Cent.L. [0035794] 20/01/1983
Lambert Ms JS, MSc BSc(Hons) MCLIP, Sen.Lect., Dept.Inf.& Communications, Manchester Metro.Univ. [0046248] 18/10/1991
Lambert Ms M, BA MCLIP, Lib., L.B.of Ealing. [0035952] 07/03/1983
Lambert Mr RA, Unemployed. [0053141] 01/04/1996
Lambert Mr RJ, BA MA MCLIP, Head of L.,Inf.& Archives, Oldham M.B.C. [0019970] 04/01/1973
Lambert Miss SV, BA(Hons) DipLIS MPhil, Reader Serv.Lib., The Betty, Cambridge. [0038465] 03/05/1985
Lambie Miss A, BA(Hons), Stud., Strathclyde Univ. [0061804] 12/11/2002
Lambie Ms LT, MA DipLib MCLIP, Economic Devel.Offr., Inverclyde Council. [0039936] 10/10/1986
Lamble Mr WH, RFD BA ALAA MCLIP, Retired. [0017225] 21/02/1949
Lambon Mrs AR, (was Eves), BLib MCLIP MA, Lend.Serv.Lib.(Job-share), Univ.of Cent.England, Birmingham. [0036129] 02/06/1983
Lambourne Mrs AR, (was Sansom), MCLIP, Team Lib., Medway Council, Strood. [0012936] 01/01/1968
Lamin Mr RG, BA(Hons) DipLib MCLIP, Lib.(Branches Team), Hessle L., E.Riding of Yorks.Ls. [0037678] 14/10/1984
Lamming Mr JD, BA DipLib MCLIP, Asst.Lib., Inst.of Chartered Accountants, London. [0031346] 30/09/1979
Lamond Mrs JW, (was Tanton), BA DipLib, Knowledge Agent, Qinetiq, Farnborough. [0038105] 18/10/1985
Lamond Mrs SM, (was Walker), BA(Hons), Sen.Inf.Offr., CMS Cameron McKenna, London. [0041896] 15/05/1988
Lamont Mr D, BSc(Hons) BA DipLib MCLIP, Educ.Lib.-Post Primary Sch., N.E.Educ.& L.Board. [0034143] 01/01/1981
Lampard Miss EM, BA DipLib MCLIP, Solicitors L., HM Customs & Excise, London. [0033663] 12/01/1981
Lamusse Mrs FM, BA DipLib, Sen.Learning Res.Offr., Highbury College, Portsmouth. [0058966] 10/10/2000
Lamyman Miss JE, MCLIP, Life Member. [0024959] 28/10/1975
Lancashire Mrs LR, (was Priestley), BA DipLib MCLIP, Lib., Queens Gate Sch., London SW7. [0021751] 07/01/1974
Lancaster Mr FW, FCLIP, Retired, Resident U.S.A. [0027649] 13/01/1950 **FE 01/01/1969**
Lancaster Prof JM, MPhil MCLIP, Dir.of L.& Inf.Serv., Univ.of Limerick, Ireland. [0020085] 04/12/1967
Lancaster Miss KH, BA(Hons), Stud., Leeds Met.Univ. [0060022] 26/11/2001
Lancaster Mr KR, BA MCLIP, Unemployed. [0028847] 31/01/1978
Lancaster Miss MKC, (was Nicholas Owen), BSc M PSYCH MCLIP, Clin./Forensic Psychologist, Private Practice, Melbourne, Victoria, Australia. [0019720] 07/06/1966
Lancaster Mrs P, BA(Hons) MSc, Asst.Lib.(Ref.& Inf.), Calderdale M.B.C., Halifax Cent.L. [0056386] 01/07/1998
Lancaster Miss R, BA(Hons) MA, Asst.Lib., Open Univ., Milton Keynes, Bucks. [0058099] 29/10/1999
Lancaster Mr SJ, Inf.Consultant, Self Employed. [0059000] 19/10/2000
Lancaster Mrs SJ, (was Wallinger), BLS MCLIP, Sen.Community Lib., (South), Plymouth L.Serv. [0030288] 08/12/1978
Lancaster Ms SM, BSc(Hons) MA MCLIP, Lib., Camborne Pool Redruth Coll., Redruth. [0056660] 01/10/1998

Lancey Mrs AK, (was Cochrane), BNurs DPS(m) MA, Outreach Lib., Winchester & Eastleigh Healthcare, NHS Trust. [0049075] 01/10/1993
Land Mr AJ, BA PGDipIM MCLIP, Employment not known. [0060493] 11/12/2001
Land Mrs EM, BA DipLib MCLIP, Bibl.Serv.Libr., Winchester, [0033537] 16/01/1981
Landa Mr MH, BA MSc DPSE LTCL, [0052291] 23/10/1995
Landau Mrs DM, (was Viner), MCLIP, Self-employed. [0015134] 05/01/1971
Landau Mrs MJ, BSc MCLIP, Retired. [0026440] 05/10/1976
Landau Mr T, MCLIP, Life Member, 139 Chevening Road, London NW6 6DZ, Tel:0181 969 2862. [0008614] 17/09/1948
Lander Ms FH, BA MA DipLib MCLIP, Faculty Inf.Offr., Univ.of Surrey, Roehampton, London. [0024730] 10/10/1975
Lander Miss KN, BA MCLIP, VSO Volunteer, CPC Bali, Cameroon. [0048074] 04/11/1992
Lander Mrs KT, (was Waller), Indexer, Dept.of the Parliamentary L., Canberra, Australia. [0017229] 30/09/1968
Lander Miss SK, BA(Hons) MCLIP, Team Lib., Somerset C.C. [0049584] 19/11/1993
Landgraeber Ms A, DipLib, Inf.Mgr., British Council, HA, Berlin. [0059150] 28/11/2000
Landmann Mrs T, (was Byrne), Unemployed. [0046942] 04/03/1992
Landsburgh Park Mrs GD, (was Landsburgh), MA MCLIP, Sch.Lib., Woodlea Primary Sch., Caterham. [0033023] 16/10/1980
Lane Miss AKE, BA(Hons), Inf.Specialist, British Med.Journal Pub.Group. [0046619] 26/11/1991
Lane Mrs C, (was Poulter), MCLIP, Lib., Literacy Learning & Child., E.Sussex Co.L., Rother Grp. [0011849] 03/11/1967
Lane Miss CM, BA, Employment not known. [0035054] 09/07/1982
Lane Mrs E, (was Haynes), BA MCLIP, Learning Cent.Lib.:Cust.Serv., Warwickshire Coll., Leamington Spa & Moreton Morrell. [0008617] 19/10/1965
Lane Ms EA, (was Lenton), BA(Hons), Sen.Inf.Offr., Irwin Mitchell Solicitors, Sheffield. [0054943] 21/05/1997
Lane Mrs GK, (was Moss), BA DipLib MCLIP, Sen.Adviser, Resource, London. [0022895] 01/10/1974
Lane Mrs HE, (was Owen), MA DipLib MCLIP, Lib., Sidney Sussex Coll., Cambridge. [0035148] 01/10/1982
Lane Mr JSM, MCLIP, Res.Mgr.-Cultural Serv., Bor.of Poole. [0023142] 06/11/1974
Lane Mrs LG, (was Pope), BA MLS MCLIP, Customer Serv.Mgr., Talis Inf.Ltd. [0030786] 01/04/1979
Lane Mrs MI, BA(Hons) MCLIP, Lib., Bristol Grammar Sch., Bristol. [0052952] 26/01/1996
Lane Mrs MJ, (was Heard), MCLIP, Team Lib., Glos.C.C., Cheltenham L. [0022812] 08/10/1974
Lane Mr PG, MA DipLib MCLIP, Princ.Lib.(Ref.& Inf.Serv.), L.B.of Harrow. [0024732] 01/10/1975
Lane Miss R, Clerical/Admin.Offr., Wirral Soc.Serv., Merseyside. [0055050] 03/07/1997
Lane Mrs RA, (was Hayward), BA(Hons), Child.Lib., Hants.Co.Ls., Fleet. [0034826] 15/03/1982
Lane-Clarke Ms RL, BA(Hons) MA, Asst.Lib., Denton Wilde Sapte, London. [0056104] 17/02/1998
Lane-Gilbert Mrs P, (was Lane), MCLIP, Head of L.& Inf.Serv., R.I.C.S., London. [0008625] 02/05/1969
Laney Mrs IM, (was Harrison), MCLIP, Retired. [0006433] 18/03/1952
Lang Mrs A, (was Tweddle), MCLIP, Local Studies Lib., Gateshead L.Arts & Inf., Cent.L. [0020742] 15/06/1973
Lang Mr BA, MA PhD HonFCLIP, Chief Exec., The Briish L., London. [0053387] 01/01/1996 **FE 01/01/1997**
Lang Miss CM, MA(Hons) MSc, Inf.Offr., Leeds Met.Univ. [0059035] 31/10/2000
Lang Mr GA, BEd DipLib MA, Unemployed. [0042139] 07/10/1988
Lang Mrs JC, (was Ward), BA DipLib MCLIP, Head Lib., Salisbury Healthcare NHS Trust, Dist.Hosp. [0034159] 01/10/1981
Lang Mr K, BSc(Eng) PGCE DipHE, p./t.Stud./L.IT Offr., Univ.of Wales, Aberystwyth, Richmond upon Thames Coll. [0058218] 18/11/1999
Langdon Ms CA, BA DipLib MCLIP, Br.Lib., Rhondda Cynon Taff, Aberdare L. [0039060] 31/10/1985
Langdon Mrs K, BA, (Hons), Branch Asst., Ipswich Cent.L. [0060140] 10/12/2001 **AF**
Langdon Ms K, BSc, Unemployed. [0059545] 02/05/2001
Langerman Mrs S, MLS, Chairperson of ASMI, Israel. [0060994] 28/01/2002
Langford Mrs B, BA, Sen.Learning Res.Offr., Milton Keynes Coll. [0057810] 13/08/1999 **AF**
Langford Mrs JC, (was Brown), BA MA MCLIP, Inf.Specialist, (Languages & European Studies), Aston Univ., Birmingham. [0038244] 04/02/1985
Langford Miss NR, BA(Hons), Stud., Univ.Sheffield. [0059893] 30/10/2001
Langham Mr M, BA DipLib MCLIP, Dep.Br.Lib., Cheshire C.C. [0027692] 06/07/1977
Langley Mrs KM, (was Rees), BA MCLIP, Stock Supplies Lib., Rhondda Cynon Taff Co.Bor.L. [0012244] 05/01/1972
Langley Mr MA, MSc, Intellectual Property Lib., Queen Mary, Univ.of London. [0056903] 02/11/1998
Langley Miss S, Stud., Univ.of Brighton. [0060037] 03/12/2001
Langridge Mr GM, MA MLS MCLIP, Prof.Serv.Lib., Torbay L.Serv., Devon. [0036885] 01/01/1984
Langrish Mr TM, BA DipLib AIL MCLIP, L.Asst., Bodleian Law L., Oxford Univ. [0034045] 01/08/1981
Langstaff Miss H, Unemployed. [0061235] 16/04/2002
Langton Mr B, MCLIP, Retired. [0022619] 11/09/1950
Langworthy Mrs V, (was Thorpe), MCLIP, Retired. [0008641] 24/03/1944
Lanham Mrs J, (was Davis), MCLIP, Clerk, Clifton Parish Council, Beds. [0008642] 04/03/1960

285

Lankshear Miss A, MCLIP, Asst.Lib., Lancs.Co.L., S.E.Lancs.Div. [0008643] 26/01/1968
Lannon Mrs AP, (was Mullan), MA DipLib MCLIP, Res.Lib., Dept.for Work & Pensions, London. [0042161] 10/10/1988
Lannon Mrs IJ, (was Dunnett), MA MCLIP, Retired. [0004288] 16/10/1964
Lansley Mrs G, Inf.Offr., Stephen Lansley & Co., Colchester. [0058825] 16/08/2000 **AF**
Lantry Ms M, MA HDipEd MA MCLIP, Resident in Ireland. [0043675] 22/11/1989
Lantz Ms MA, (was Dainty), BA DipLib MCLIP, IT Consultant, Ise Valley Inf.Serv. [0033215] 27/10/1980
Lanza Mrs DL, (was Evans), BA(Hons) MCLIP, Career Break. [0044676] 23/11/1990
Lapa Ms ALS, Asst.Lec., Faculade de Letras., Universidade de Coimbra. [0050471] 12/08/1994
Lapworth Mr AL, BA MCLIP, Head, P.Websites Team, Trade Partners UK, London. [0026439] 13/10/1976
Lara Miss EJ, BA MA DipLib, Lib., Univ.Ls., St.Augustine, Trinidad. [0036373] 07/10/1983
Larbey Mrs MA, (was Brown), BA MCLIP, p./t.Asst.Lib., TWI, Granta Pk., Cambridge. [0029600] 01/10/1978
Larbi Mr K, MA MSc MCLIP, Employment not known. [0008646] 07/07/1971
Larby Mrs P, (was Fiddes), MA FCLIP, Life Member. [0008647] 08/09/1952 **FE 01/01/1962**
Larcombe Miss Y, Stud., Univ.of Brighton. [0059005] 20/10/2000
Lardent Mrs SMD, BA MCLIP, Inf.Lib., W.Sussex C.C. [0038514] 20/05/1985
Lardner Mrs L, (was Wilson), Res.Cent.Mgr., Blackheath High Sch., London. [0039461] 10/01/1986
Lardner Mrs M, (was Galloway), MCLIP, Sch.Lib., Harris Academy, Dundee. [0005318] 23/09/1969
Lardner Mr MD, BA MCLIP, Head, New Media & Customer Support, The Teacher Support Network, London. [0038005] 01/01/1985
Large Mrs N, BA(Hons) MCLIP, Life Member. [0008652] 31/08/1954
Larkham Mrs EA, BA(Hons) MA MCLIP, Business Res.Exec., 3i plc., W.Midlands. [0050797] 18/10/1994
Larkin Ms FE, BA, Trainee Prof.Lib., Halton Bor.Council. [0061731] 29/10/2002
Larkin Ms JJ, Strategic Inf.Offr., Highlands & Islands Ent., Inverness. [0052655] 16/11/1995
Larkin Mr JRW, BA DipLib MCLIP, Inf.Offr., NCH L.& Inf.Serv., London. [0031539] 16/10/1979
Larkin Ms KA, BA MSc, L.Asst.(Ref.Serv.& Inter-L.Loans), Prince Rupert P.L., Brit.Columbia, Canada. [0061038] 11/02/2002
Larkin Miss MT, BA(Hons) MSc, Team Lib.,(Inf.), N.E.Educ.& L.Board, Antrim Grp.L.H.Q. [0046900] 25/02/1992
Larkin Mr MT, DipLIS, Position Unknown, Univ.Coll.London Hosp., London. [0042239] 10/10/1988
Larkin Miss P, L.Asst., Liverpool City L. [0039660] 26/04/1986
Larkin Mrs VS, (was Mahoney), BA DipLib MCLIP, Child.Lib., L.B.of Bexley, Bexley L.& Mus. [0032441] 17/04/1980
Larkins Miss A, BA DiplS, Periodicals & Elect.Texts Lib., p./t.Catr., Univ.of Huddersfield. [0048506] 01/02/1993
Larkins Mrs PEM, (was Ward), BA MA MCLIP, Unemployed. [0015362] 01/10/1964
Larkinson Mrs KML, (was Kirton), MCLIP, P./t.Curriculum Res.Offr., W.Herts.Coll., Leggatts Campus, Watford. [0030205] 04/12/1978
Lascelles Mr DG, PGDiplS, Asst.Mgr., Universal Music (UK), Tape Facility. [0051505] 13/03/1995
Laskey Miss AE, Inf.Lib., L.B.of Newham, London. [0045162] 31/07/1990 **AF**
Laslett Mrs CJ, (was Briars), BA MCLIP, Bibl.Serv.Co-ordinator (Job Share), Yate L., S.Glos. [0025339] 01/01/1974
Lass Mr DM, MA DipLib MCLIP ALAI, Asst.Lib./Catr.for Eng.& Classics, Trinity Coll., Dublin L., Eire. [0024514] 01/10/1975
Lass Ms DM, BA(Hons) MSc MCLIP, Asst.Lib., GCHQ, Cheltenham. [0051054] 09/11/1994
Lassam Miss C, MCLIP, M.W.Sch.Lib., Hampshire Co.L. [0008663] 04/01/1957
Last Miss AJ, BA(Hons) MA, L.Asst., Suffolk Coll., Ipswich. [0058020] 13/10/1999
Last Ms NJ, (was Dominy), Systems Lib., H.M.Treasury, London. [0042453] 14/11/1988
Last Mrs RA, (was Barrett), MLS MCLIP, Consultant for L.in Sch.& Educ., Rosemary Last L.Serv. [0000847] 09/02/1960
Latham Mrs EA, BA(Hons), p./t.Asst.Lib., Dr.Challoner's Gramm.Sch., Amersham. [0056671] 01/10/1998
Latham Mrs G, MA, Acting Curriculum Res.Offr., W.Herts.Coll., Watford. [0058134] 05/11/1999
Latham Mr SJ, BA MA MPhil MSc MCLIP, Head, LIS, Foreign & Commonwealth Off.L., London. [0043719] 04/12/1989
Lathbury Mrs MG, (was Thomson), BA MLS MCLIP, L.& Knowledge Serv.Mgr., S.Derbys.Acute Hosp.NHS Trust, Derbys.Royal Infirmary. [0029850] 01/10/1978
Lathrope Mr D, BSc MCLIP DMS, Asst.Dir.(Ls., Arch.& Inf.), Notts.C.C., Community Servs. [0021996] 15/01/1974
Latif-Shaikh Ms N, (was Latif), BA(Hons), Liaison Lib.-Ethnic Health, Kings Fund, London. [0051396] 03/02/1995
Latimer Miss C, BA MCLIP, Homework Cent.Lib., Notts.C.C. [0030849] 23/04/1979
Latimer Mrs CM, (was Roberts), Unemployed. [0039001] 23/10/1985
Latimer Mrs K, (was MacKnight), MA DipLib, Agriculture & Food Sci.Lib., The Queens Univ.of Belfast, Sci.L. [0009482] 01/01/1970
Latko Mrs N, MCLIP, Retired. [0008674] 10/01/1966
Lattimer Ms BI, BA(Hons) MCLIP, Coll.Lib., St.Charles Catholic 6th Form Coll., London. [0019844] 01/01/1973
Lattimore Dr M, MA FCLIP, Retired, 3 The Priory, Abbotskerswell, Newton Abbot, TQ12 5PP. [0008675] 14/07/1958 **FE 01/01/1965**

Latto Mrs JM, p./t.L.Asst./Stud., Dundee Coll./Univ.of Wales, Dundee/Aberystwyth. [0057076] 04/12/1998
Lau Mr FK, BBA MSc DipEd DMS, Teacher Lib., Po Leung Kuk Centenary Li Shiu, Chung Mem.Coll., Hong Kong. [0061551] 11/09/2002
Lau Miss JS, MSc MCLIP, Lib., Trinity Theological Coll., Singapore. [0021015] 02/10/1973
Lau Ms R, BSc(Hons), Sen.Inf.Sci., Ribotargets, Cambridge. [0061405] 09/07/2002
Lauchlan Miss EA, Inf.Sci., Diageo Brand Tech.Cent., Clacks. [0049846] 07/12/1993
Lauder Mrs H, (was Fox), BA MCLIP, Comm.Lib., N.Lanarkshire Council. [0034218] 13/10/1981
Lauder Mr JE, BA MCLIP, Project Dir., The Newsplan 2000 Project, Brit.L.& Newspaper L., London. [0038986] 22/10/1985
Laugesen Mrs D, BA(Hons), Lib., Wigan & Leigh Coll., Lancs. [0043467] 26/10/1989
Laughlan Miss GA, Grad.Trainee, The Boots L., Nottingham. [0061098] 28/02/2002
Laughlin Ms PA, BSc MSc MCLIP, Employment not known. [0060617] 11/12/2001
Laughton Mrs DJ, (was Fox), BA(Hons), Asst.Lib., Trinity & All Saints Coll., Leeds. [0049072] 01/10/1993
Laughton Mr GE, FCLIP, Retired. [0008678] 23/07/1938 **FE 01/01/1949**
Laughton Mrs GM, MCLIP, Piano/Keyboard/Theory Teacher. [0008679] 25/01/1970
Laughton Mr PF, MBA MCLIP, Unemployed. [0021960] 21/01/1974
Launder Mr C, BA(Hons) MA MCLIP, Asst.Lib., Reader Serv., Courtauld Inst.of Art. [0056791] 23/10/1998
Laundy Mr PAC, FCLIP, Clerk Asst., House of Commons, Canada. [0017236] 22/03/1948 **FE 27/09/1976**
Laundy Parri Ms K, (was Laundy Parry), BA(Hons) MLS, Ed. Lib., Llangefni L., Anglesey. [0059333] 09/02/2001
Laurence Mrs MT, (was Ratcliffe), MCLIP, Playgroup Worker/Creche Worker. [0012164] 06/10/1967
Laurence Mrs S, (was Halfpenny), BA(Hons) DipLib MCLIP, Sen.Lib., Glos.Sch.L.Serv. [0058481] 31/10/1991
Laurenson Mr JCM, BSc(Hons) DipLib MCLIP, Sen.Lib., Dick.Inst., E.Ayrshire L., Kilmarnock, Ayrshire. [0030208] 19/01/1979
Laurie Mrs E, (was Smith), MCLIP, Casual Lib., W.Berks.Dist.Council, Newbury. [0008682] 06/05/1967
Laurie Mr R, BA DipLib, Curator, Map L., Brit.L., St.Pancras. [0034279] 21/10/1981
Lauriol Miss C, BA MA, Stud., Univ.of Wales, Aberystwyth, & Sen.L.Asst., Inst.for Chinese, Stud.L., Oxford. [0058933] 06/10/2000
Lausen Mrs PA, BA DipLib MCLIP, Career Break. [0035612] 10/11/1982
Lavelle Mrs ME, (was Turner), DipLib MCLIP, Sen.Lib., B.B.C. News V.T. L., London. [0031028] 06/07/1979
Lavelle Mrs T, Campus L.Mgr., Craighouse L., Napier Univ., Edinburgh. [0052865] 05/01/1996 **AF**
Laverick Mr D, FCLIP, Life Member. [0008688] 13/03/1948 **FE 01/01/1961**
Laverick Ms SJ, (was Glew), BA MCLIP, Employment Unknown. [0036681] 04/11/1983
Laverty Miss D, BA(Hons) MCLIP, Inf.& L.Serv.Mgr., Dickinson Dees Law Firm, Newcastle upon Tyne. [0045225] 31/07/1990
Lavery Ms JA, Inf.Offr., The Stroke Assoc., London. [0044820] 03/12/1990
Lavery Mrs SM, (was Filippi), MA MCLIP, Lib.Technician, Carlsbad Unified Sch.Dist., Carlsbad, California, USA. [0027405] 22/03/1977
Lavigueur Ms JD, BA(Hons) BSc MCLIP, Asst.Lib., Trinity & All Saints Coll., Leeds. [0026961] 13/01/1977
Lavis Mrs CE, (was Davies), BLib MCLIP, Literature Devel.Offr., Bath & N.E.Somerset L., Bath. [0029322] 09/05/1978
Lavis Ms PD, BA(Hons) DipInf, p./t.Inf.Offr./Inf.Asst., Young Minds/Royal Coll.of Nursing, London. [0050610] 01/10/1994
Law Miss AW, BA(Hons), Asst. Learning C.Mgr., Uxbridge College, Middlesex. [0039756] 20/06/1986
Law Prof D, MA FCLIP FKC, Lib.& Dir.of Inf.Strategy, Univ.of Strathclyde, Glasgow. [0008690] 21/10/1969 **FE 18/01/1989**
Law Mr DI, BA(Hons), Health Intelligence Lib., Dudley Health Auth. [0052396] 31/10/1995
Law Mrs J, BA(Hons) MA, P./t.Passport Offr., UKPA., Peterborough. [0052693] 20/11/1995
Law Miss M, BA FCLIP, Life Member. [0017237] 05/06/1951 **FE 22/09/1975**
Law Mrs M, (was Felton), MA BMus MCLIP, p./t.Music Teacher, MA Lowe, Sheffield. [0008692] 08/11/1968
Law Mrs S, (was Bousfield), MCLIP, L.& Inf.Serv.Mgr., Blackburn w/ Darwen. [0024461] 01/01/1963
Law Mrs V, (was Hobson), MA DipLib, Adult Lending Lib., Maidenhead L. [0050710] 12/10/1994
Law Ms WA, BA(Hons), L.Asst., Willingham L., Cambridge. [0061614] 03/10/2002 **AF**
Law Ms YL, BA MSc MCLIP, Serials Lib., Hong Kong Inst. of Educ., Hong Kong. [0041525] 13/01/1988
Lawal Dr OO, BA MA PhD FCLIP, Univ.Lib., Univ.of Calabar, Nigeria. [0017238] 19/09/1971 **FE 21/11/2001**
Lawer Mrs DW, (was Maynard), BA(Hons) MACertEd MCLIP, Lib., Saltash Coll., Cornwall. [0041360] 20/03/1961
Lawes Dr MJ, BSc(Hons) MSc MCLIP, Asst.Lib., Earth Sci.L., Natural Hist.Mus. [0047968] 28/10/1992
Lawler Ms URE, MLS MCLIP, Unemployed. [0008107] 18/08/1967
Lawrence Mrs A, (was Vincent), BA MCLIP, Dep.Lib., Univ.of the W.of England, Bristol. [0008696] 03/09/1963
Lawrence Miss AR, BA(Hons), Stud, Univ.Cent.England. [0059858] 17/10/2001

Lawrence Mrs CS, MA MSc MCLIP, Retired. [0021665] 24/12/1973
Lawrence Mrs DM, (was McNamara), BA MCLIP, Unemployed. [0036211] 27/05/1983
Lawrence Mrs ER, BSc, Knowledge Mgr.Offr., Pricewaterhouse Coopers, London. [0059113] 17/11/2000
Lawrence Ms G, MLib BA MCLIP, Sch.Lib., Kent Educ.& Ls., W.Malling, Kent. [0008702] 01/01/1969
Lawrence Ms KE, BA(Hons), Bus.Enquiry Researcher, HSBC Bank, London. [0052941] 29/01/1996
Lawrence Mrs L, (was Robinson), L.Asst., Bracknell Forest Bor.Council. [0008706] 15/09/1964 **AF**
Lawrence Mrs L, (was Thompson), BA(Hons) DipILM MCLIP, Asst.Subject Lib., Univ.of Coventry. [0046529] 18/11/1991
Lawrence Miss LL, BA, Child.Lib., Norbury L., Croydon. [0052930] 25/01/1996
Lawrence Miss LS, BA, Resident in Canada. [0056559] 20/08/1998
Lawrence Mrs MF, (was Rowland), FCLIP, Life Member, 0181 657 7462, Flat 1, Sanderstead Crt., Addington Rd., S.Croydon, CR2 8RA. [0008710] 11/10/1935 **FE 01/01/1950**
Lawrence Mr MR, BA(Hons) DipInf, MS/HS Lib., Internat.Sch.of Stuttgart, Germany. [0046223] 15/10/1974
Lawrence Mr MW, BSc MCLIP, Sen.Lib., Cent.for Oxfordshire Studies, Cent.L., Oxon.C.C. [0037985] 03/01/1985
Lawrence Mr N, MCLIP, Ref.Lib., Dorset C.C. [0008711] 05/02/1961
Lawrence Miss NR, BA(Hons), ICT Project Worker/Lib., Wrexham Co.Bor.Council. [0058198] 16/11/1999
Lawrence Mrs PA, BA(Hons), Asst.Lib., Sandwell Healthcare NHS Trust, London. [0044835] 11/12/1990
Lawrence Mr R, BA MCLIP, Retired. [0008713] 01/01/1964
Lawrence Mr S, BSc MSc MCLIP, Retired. [0060537] 11/12/2001
Lawrence Mrs SJT, (was Townsend), DipLib ALAA MCLIP, Lib., St Catherine's Sch., Guildford, Surrey. [0029484] 20/07/1978
Lawrence Miss VJ, BA DipLib MCLIP, Dep.Lib., History Faculty L., Oxford. [0029997] 04/11/1978
Lawrence Mrs YT, MLS MCLIP, Lib., Council of Legal Educ., Kingston,Jamaica. [0025194] 23/03/1962
Lawrie Mrs RF, BA(Hons) MCLIP, Dep.Learning Res.Mgr., Luton Sixth Form Coll., Luton, Beds. [0019635] 30/10/1972
Laws Ms ELE, BA(Hons) MSc(Econ) MA MCLIP, Catr.-Child.Literature Collection, Victoria & Albert Mus., Nat.Art L. [0053419] 20/06/1996
Lawson Miss AV, MCLIP, Map Lib., Queen Mary, Univ.of London, Main L. [0019664] 09/10/1972
Lawson Mrs CA, (was Wood), BSc MCLIP, Asst.Area Sch.Lib.(p./t.), Hants.Co.Ls., Winchester. [0023467] 07/01/1975
Lawson Mrs D, (was Thompson), BA DipLib MCLIP, p./t.Res.Lib., Wolverhampton Univ. [0040850] 08/07/1987
Lawson Mrs EJ, (was Turner), MA(Hons) DipLib CertTESOL MCLIP, Unemployed. [0029289] 17/05/1978
Lawson Mrs JB, L.Asst., Open Learning Resource Cent., Thanet Coll. [0056211] 01/04/1998 **AF**
Lawson Miss K, BSc MSc MBA MCLIP, Employment not known. [0060720] 12/12/2001
Lawson Mrs L, BA MCLIP, Unemployed. [0008721] 02/10/1969
Lawson Mrs LJ, (was Kirwan), BSocSc MA, Sen.Inf.Offr., Royal Soc.for the Prevention of, Accidents (ROSPA), Birmingham. [0052413] 30/10/1995
Lawson Miss M, MA DipLib MCLIP, Dept.Lib., Hist.of Art Dept., Univ.of Glasgow. [0031351] 15/10/1979
Lawson Mr MG, MA, Inf.Sci., Brit.Nuclear Fuels, Preston. [0051335] 16/01/1995
Lawson Mr MJ, BA(Hons) MA MCLIP, Site Mgr., E.London Campus L., S.Bank Univ., Whipps Cross Hosp. [0056588] 04/09/1998
Lawson Mr RR, FCLIP, Life Member, Matson Baring Rd., St.Giles Hill, Winchester, Hants., SO23 0JN. [0008723] 01/01/1935 **FE 01/01/1946**
Lawson Miss S, BSc(Hons) DipILM MCLIP, L.Mgr., Tower Hamlets PCT, Health Inf.E.London. [0050715] 12/10/1994
Lawson Mrs SH, (was Scattergood), BSc MCLIP, Inf.Mgmnt.Offr., British Med.Assoc., Edinburgh. [0024134] 18/04/1975
Lawson Mrs SM, (was Brown), MA DipLib MCLIP, Unemployed. [0034530] 02/12/1981
Lawton Miss AP, BSc MSc MCLIP, Knowledge Serv.Mgr., BRE Ltd., Watford. [0039678] 06/05/1986
Lawton Ms SL, (was Brock), P./t.Stud., Manchester Met.Univ., & Princ.Inf.Asst., Univ.of Salford. [0049064] 01/10/1993
Laxton Miss R, MCLIP, Inf.& Community Devel.Mgr., Durham C.C. [0008726] 16/01/1970
Lay Mr SJ, GTCL LTCL DipLib MCLIP, Employment Unknown. [0045941] 26/07/1991
Laybourn Mrs CE, (was Harris), BA(Hons) PGCE MA MCLIP, Classroom Asst./Child.Auth., Moss Hey Primary Sch., Bramhall, Stockport. [0032969] 06/10/1980
Laycock Mrs HL, (was Clarke), BA(Hons) PGDipIS, Serv.Cent.Mgr.(flex.), Newham Coll.of F.E., London. [0050649] 06/10/1994
Laycock Mrs PEH, MCLIP, Lib., Rastrick High Sch., W.Yorks. [0008729] 01/01/1966
Layton Mrs AR, (was Rouault), p./t.Sen.Lib., Dept.of Trans.Local Govt.and the, Regions, London. [0022347] 01/04/1974
Layton Ms C, Stud., Univ.of Wales, Aberystwyth, & L.Asst., Ordnance Survey, Southampton. [0057394] 03/03/1999
Layzell Ward Prof P, MA PhD FCLIP FIM, Life Member. [0008732] 01/01/1954 **FE 01/01/1963**
Lazenbatt Mrs K, (was Mellor), MA DipLib, p./t.Catr., Royal Horticultural Soc., London. [0034128] 08/10/1981
Lazim Mrs A, (was Cooper), BA MCLIP, Lib., L.B.of Southwark, Cent.for Language in Primary Educ. [0021862] 08/02/1974

Le Bailly Mrs M, BA(Hons) PGDip DipILM MCLIP, Coll.Res.Lib., Impington Village Coll., Cambs. [0051684] 11/05/1995
Le Bourdon Ms E, BA DipLib, Learning & Inf.Resourses Mgr., Trinity Coll., Carmarthen. [0041433] 02/12/1987
Le Boutillier Miss F, MCLIP, Life Member. [0017243] 12/09/1959
Le Chat Mrs SA, BA DipLib MCLIP, Learning Res.Cent.Mgr., Daventry William Parker Sch., Northants. [0033831] 24/03/1981
Le Cheminant Mrs M, MCLIP, Educ.Lib., Southfields Community Coll., London. [0012409] 08/09/1971
Le Couteur Mrs EM, (was Domville), MCLIP, Life Member. [0017244] 01/01/1943
Le Gassick Mrs P, MCLIP, Indexer/Consultant, 1C Calton Avenue, Dulwich, SE21 7DE. [0008809] 21/02/1957
Le Grice Miss JB, MA MCLIP, Ch.Catg., Kingston Univ.L. [0018416] 19/10/1972
Le Huquet Mrs D, (was Grundy), JP MCLIP, Retired. [0008819] 18/09/1951
Lea Mrs C, (was Pietka), BSc MCLIP, L.Asst., Chesterfield Law Cent., Derbys. [0008734] 02/11/1995
Lea Miss E, BA(Hons) MSc(Econ), Asst.Lib., New Coll., Swindon. [0052451] 02/11/1995
Lea Mrs ERM, (was Dennis), BA(Hons) MA MCLIP, Process Worker, Harwell Drying & Restoration Serv., Didcot, Oxon. [0036628] 26/10/1983
Lea Mrs ES, BSc DipLIS MCLIP, Team Lib., Reading Bor.Council. [0043333] 20/10/1989
Lea Mr P, MLS MCLIP, Snr.Lect., Manchester Metro.Univ. [0008741] 15/09/1958
Lea Mrs R, (was Ross), MCLIP, E.Sussex L.I.A., Lewes. [0008742] 21/11/1965
Lea Mr RA, BSc, Inf.Sci., Glaxo Grp.Res.Ltd., Greenford. [0037990] 01/01/1985
Lea Mrs V, MCLIP, Lib., Leicester City Council. [0008744] 04/02/1959
Lea Mrs YA, BA MA MCLIP, Team Leader, Lend.Serv., Scunthorpe Cent.L., N.Lincs. [0024736] 07/10/1975
Leach Mr A, BA DPA FCLIP, Life Member. [0008745] 08/03/1948 **FE 01/01/1959**
Leach Mrs B, (was Gadsby), BA MCLIP, Life Member. [0008746] 18/09/1949
Leach Mr C, BA MA DipLib MCLIP, Sen.Learning Adviser(Arch.), Univ.of Lincs.& Humberside. [0029722] 05/10/1978
Leach Mrs C, BSc(Hons) PGCE,p./t.Stud./L.Asst., Univ.of Wales, Aberystwyth, Univ.of Edinburgh. [0059066] 06/11/2000
Leach Mrs CL, BA(Hons) MSc(Econ), Community Lib., Lincolnshire C.C., Boston. [0056212] 01/04/1998
Leach Miss DS, MA MA MA, Inf.Offr., L., Royal Coll.of Physicians, London. [0043205] 04/10/1989
Leach Miss E, FCLIP, Retired. [0008747] 12/02/1937 **FE 04/04/1946**
Leach Mrs GE, (was Brice), BSc DipLib MCLIP, Asst.Lib., Trinity & All Saints Coll., Leeds. [0045474] 14/02/1991
Leach Mrs MD, BA MCLIP MBA, Lend.Serv.Lib., Wolverhampton Bor.Council. [0028617] 09/01/1978
Leach Mrs MW, BA, Sen.L.Asst., Albrighton L., Shropshire C.C. [0057597] 17/05/1999 **AF**
Leach Mrs P, (was Chapman), Asst.Lend.Lib.(Job Share), Accrington L., Lancs.C.C. [0042504] 21/11/1988
Leach Miss PR, Publications Lib., Goldman Sachs International, London. [0038758] 06/10/1985
Leach Mrs SE, (was Kenney), BA MCLIP, Career Break. [0035553] 24/10/1982
Leach Ms SP, BA MCLIP, Div.Child.Lib.-S., Hants.L.Serv. [0026444] 30/09/1976
Leadbeater Mrs J, BLib, Sch.Lib., Quarrydale Sch., Sutton in Ashfield. [0050083] 18/03/1994
Leadbeater Mrs JG, (was Medley), MCLIP, Sen.L.Asst., City of York Council. [0022131] 12/02/1974
Leader Mrs LM, (was Sharma), BA MCLIP, Faculty Serv.Mgr., Univ.of Salford. [0031927] 17/12/1979
Leahy Mrs J, (was Naisby), MCLIP, Unemployed. [0026995] 06/01/1977
Leahy Miss SM, BA MCLIP, [0020942] 13/09/1973
Leak Miss AR, BA(Hons) MA, Lib.& Study Room Mgr., Heinz Arch.& L., Nat.Portrait Gallery, London. [0046011] 22/08/1991
Leak Mrs KA, (was Rawlinson), BA DipLib MCLIP, Inf.Asst., Middx.Univ. [0029212] 30/03/1978
Leake Ms JM, BA(Hons) CertEd MA, Asst.Lib.-DH Lawrence Project, Univ.of Nottingham. [0052152] 09/10/1995
Leakey Mrs D, BPharm MRPharmS MCLIP, Employment not known. [0060853] 12/12/2001
Leaman Miss AJ, MSc, Inf.Mgmt.Consultant. [0058808] 03/08/2000
Lean Mrs L, (was Wright), MCLIP, Sch.Lib., Balcarras Sch., Cheltenham. [0016353] 01/01/1968
Lear Mrs AM, (was Sensier), BA DipLib MCLIP, Head of L.& Inf.Serv., Oakham Sch., Rutland. [0033595] 12/01/1981
Lear Mrs HF, (was Smith), MCLIP, Teaching Asst., W.Sussex C.C., Chichester. [0013589] 12/01/1969
Lear Ms JD, BA(Hons), Lib., Cheshire C.C. [0049919] 19/01/1994
Learmonth Mrs SL, (was De Santos), BLib MCLIP, Playgroup Leader. [0003905] 01/11/1971
Leary Mrs JA, (was Burling), BSc(Hons) DipIS MCLIP, Lib.Mgr., Princess Alexandra Hosp.NHS Trust, Harlow. [0048189] 13/11/1992
Leason Mrs AW, (was Chamberlain), BA MCLIP, P/t.Asst.Lib., Warwickshire L. [0018070] 01/04/1974
Leather Mrs C, Sen.L.Offr., Reading. [0061566] 02/10/2002 **AF**
Leatherdale Mrs DE, (was Perry), MBA MCLIP, Campus Lib., Univ.of Wales Coll., Newport. [0011559] 14/01/1971
Leckey Ms E, BA(Hons) DipLib MCLIP, Publications Asst., UNICEF Innocenti Research Cent., Florence, Italy. [0030458] 29/01/1979
Leckie Mrs RL, Web Site Administrator, Scunthorpe General Hospital. [0050219] 06/05/1994 **AF**

Leckie Mrs SE, (was Tweedie), BA MCLIP, P./t.L.Asst., Queen Margaret Univ.Coll., Edinburgh. [0028195] *14/10/1977*
Lecky-Thompson Mrs JE, (was Kolousek), BA(Hons) MA, Resources Lib., Wolverhampton Univ. [0055504] *16/10/1997*
Leddy Mrs DM, BSc BA MPhil CBiol MIBi MCLIP, Employment not known. [0060538] *11/12/2001*
Ledgard Mrs D, (was Wells), MCLIP, Retired. [0008766] *22/03/1954*
Ledger Mrs DM, BA, Head of Learning Res., All Saints R.C. Sch., L.B.of Barking & Dagenham. [0042291] *03/10/1988*
Ledger Mrs HF, (was Platt), MCLIP, Sen.Lib., Yateley L., Hants.C.C. [0025394] *02/12/1975*
Ledger Mr P, MCLIP, Cent.L.Mgr., L.B.of Redbridge, Ilford, Essex. [0008768] *25/03/1963*
Ledsom Miss J, BA(Hons), Lib., Cheshire C.C. [0058961] *10/10/2000*
Ledson Mrs JE, BA MCLIP, Retired. [0017245] *01/01/1967*
Lee Mrs AS, BA(Hons), Learn.Cent.Resources Facilitator, Rother Valley Coll., Sheffield. [0058512] *06/03/2000*
Lee Miss B, BA MCLIP, Head of L.Serv., Royal Bor.Kingston on Thames, Kingston L. [0008773] *18/09/1969*
Lee Mrs B, (was Craddock), MCLIP, Retired. [0008772] *31/01/1947*
Lee Mrs CE, (was Wilkinson), BA MCLIP, Lib.-Serv.to Young People, Derby City L., Derby. [0032216] *17/01/1980*
Lee Mr CL, MCLIP, Sub-Lib., Chinese Univ.of Hong Kong. [0024284] *04/06/1975*
Lee Miss CR, MA, Product Mgr., Oxford Univ.Press, Oxford. [0058528] *28/03/2000*
Lee Mrs DE, (was Leinster), BA MCLIP, Strategic L.Mgr., Hounslow Cultural & Community Serv. [0025346] *13/01/1976*
Lee Mrs DT, BA, Stud., Univ.of Oxford. [0060876] *18/12/2001*
Lee Mr DY, (was Li), MLS, Systems/IT Offr., Mid Kent Coll.of H.E. & F.E., Chatham, Kent. ME5 9UQ. [0041941] *10/05/1988*
Lee Miss E, BA, L.Asst.Super./Stud., Portsmouth L.Serv. [0059176] *05/12/2000*
Lee Mrs ECP, (was Jacobs), MCLIP, Retired. [0030343] *01/01/1953*
Lee Mrs ER, Lib., Hemel Hempstead Sch., Herts. [0051576] *03/04/1995 AF*
Lee Miss FM, MA MSc(Econ) MCLIP, Inf.Professional, Dept.of Trade & Industry, London. [0053591] *29/07/1996*
Lee Mrs FMM, (was Laing), MA MLIS LLB LLM, Curator, Nat.L.of Scotland, Edinburgh. [0050418] *25/07/1994*
Lee Miss G, MCLIP, Retired. [0008777] *01/01/1966*
Lee Miss GJ, BA(Hons), Grad.Trainee, St.Deiniols L., Flintshire. [0059842] *16/10/2001*
Lee Mrs GM, (was Davies), BA MLS DipLib MCLIP, Health Inf.Specialist, Instant L.Ltd., Loughborough. [0034199] *12/10/1981*
Lee Ms HJ, BA(Hons) MA, Lib., Brit.Red Cross, London. [0052671] *20/11/1995*
Lee Mrs J, (was Luton), BA MCLIP, Learning & Inf.Serv.Offr., Barnsley M.B.C., Cent.L. [0028065] *13/10/1977*
Lee Mrs J, (was Thomas), MCLIP, Manager Operations, Caerphilly Co.Bor.Council. [0022826] *08/10/1974*
Lee Mr JD, FCLIP, Retired, 1 Borrage Green Lane, Ripon, N.Yorks., HG4 2JH. [0008781] *05/09/1955* **FE 01/01/1960**
Lee Miss JM, MLS BA DipLib MCLIP, Princ.Systems Developer, Inf.Systems Unit., Leics.C.C. [0029185] *19/04/1978*
Lee Mrs LA, BA(Hons) MCLIP, Head Lib., Harrow Internat.Sch., Bangkok. [0033208] *01/01/1973*
Lee Miss LCY, BA MCLIP JCL, Resident in Hong Kong. [0017248] *01/01/1969*
Lee Mr MI, BA(Hons) MSc, Lib., 10 Downing St., London. [0052346] *26/10/1995*
Lee Miss MNJ, MAppSc BSc MCLIP, Resident in Hong Kong. [0060103] *07/12/2001*
Lee Mr NE, BLib, Volunteer L.Asst., Gloucester Law Cent. [0044992] *31/01/1991*
Lee Mrs P, (was Tolmie), MCLIP, Asst.Lib., Liverpool City L. [0020440] *09/01/1973*
Lee . PJ, BA MA PhD, Stud., Univ.Coll.London. [0058866] *15/09/2000*
Lee Miss RA, MA DipILS MCLIP, Comm.Lib., Lincs.C.C., Spalding Grp.-S.Area. [0050686] *10/10/1994*
Lee Mr RA, MA MIPD MCLIP, Retired. [0008786] *01/01/1962*
Lee Miss S, Sen.L.Asst., Edinburgh City L., Cent.Lend.Dept. [0045338] *15/10/1990 AF*
Lee Mrs S, Clerical Offr., West Sussex C.C. [0059160] *04/12/2000 AF*
Lee Mr SJ, BA MCLIP, p./t.Sen.Inf.Lib., Tower Hamlets, London. [0038856] *17/10/1985*
Lee Mrs SM, (was Booth), BA MCLIP, Saturday Lib., Rayners Lane & Roxeth L., L.B.of Harrow. [0031203] *14/10/1979*
Lee Mr SNS, BA(Hons) MCLIP, Dep.Website Mgr., Website Team. [0054007] *16/10/1996*
Lee Mr SRV, BA MLib PGCE FCLIP, Applied Sci.Lib., Univ.of Glamorgan, Mid Glamorgan. [0044506] *17/10/1990* **FE 18/03/1998**
Lee Mr WL, MLib MCLIP, Resident in Hong Kong. [0050570] *03/10/1994*
Lee-Hart Mr AE, (was Hart), BA(Hons) DipILS MCLIP, Local Hist.Asst.Lib., Sefton L. [0049559] *11/11/1993*
Leech Ms H, BA MA DipLIS MCLIP, Mgr., Medway Council. [0042770] *23/02/1991*
Leech O'Neale Ms CAS, (was Leech), BSc MCLIP, Asst.Lib., C.E.R.N., Geneva, Switzerland. [0017254] *26/02/1968*
Leedham Miss A, BA MCLIP, Lib.Offr., Stock Serv.Team, L.B.of Merton L. [0028618] *24/01/1978*
Leeds Mrs ML, (was Berkley), MCLIP, Retired. [0017255] *04/03/1955*
Leek Mrs W, (was Garner), MA BA CertEd MCLIP, Retired. [0008795] *09/03/1980*
Leeks Mrs SL, (was Elkington), BA(Hons), Lib., Amersham plc., Bucks. [0050606] *01/10/1994*
Leeming Mrs A, (was Steel), MCLIP, Sen.Devel.Offr., Cambs.Sch.L.Serv., Whittlesey. [0013924] *01/01/1969*

Lees Ms A, DipLib MCLIP, Project Offr., Kings Coll.London L. [0031352] *15/10/1979*
Lees Miss CH, BA MCLIP, Asst.Lib.(Lending Serv.), Malvern L., Worcs. [0030462] *06/02/1979*
Lees Mrs FA, (was Willingham), DipLib MCLIP, Learning Cent.Mgr., Newbury Coll., Berks. [0037385] *04/08/1984*
Lees Mrs J, (was Nutter), MCLIP, L.Asst., Univ.of Sheffield. [0022494] *10/06/1974*
Lees Ms JS, (was Mitchell), MA MCLIP, Dir., OCLC PICA, Birmingham. [0010245] *01/01/1971*
Lees Mr NG, MSc MCLIP, Employment not known. [0060540] *11/12/2001*
Lees Ms SH, Lib., Partnerships in Care, Kneesworth House Hosp., Royston. [0055128] *14/07/1997*
Leese Mrs AK, (was Butterworth), Self-Employed(Inf.Serv.), AIMS, 3 Ballards Row, Coll.Rd., Aston Clinton, Bucks. [0042465] *27/10/1988*
Leese Mr P, BA MCLIP, Unemployed. [0008803] *03/02/1964*
Leeson Mrs BD, MCLIP, Life Member, Tel.020 8868 9185, 50 The Sigers, Pinner, Middx., HA5 2QH. [0008804] *01/09/1967*
Leeson Miss DC, BA MCLIP, Head of Catg., Brynmor Jones L., Univ.of Hull. [0035598] *11/11/1982*
Leet Mrs JH, (was Arnold), BA(Hons) MA MCLIP, p./t.Specialist Lib., Market harborough L., Leics.C.C. [0048177] *11/11/1992*
Leeuwerke Mrs A, MCLIP, Employment not known. [0060364] *10/12/2001*
Leeves Miss A, BSc(Hons), Stud., Brighton Univ. [0058551] *01/04/2000*
Leeves Ms J, BA MCLIP, L.Systems Consultant, Farnham, Surrey. [0008807] *22/06/1971*
Lefebvre Mrs CJ, Inf.Specialist, The U.K.Cochrane Cent., NHS R&D Programme, Oxford. [0037226] *01/04/1984*
Lefebvre Ms MJ, (was Huck), MA MLS MA AALIA, Univ.Lib.,Chief Admin., St.Marys Univ., Halifax, Canada. [0018790] *30/09/1972*
Leftley Mr CP, BA BSc MCLIP, Lib./IT Co-ordinator, Wycliffe Hall, Univ.of Oxford. [0030463] *27/01/1979*
Legard Mrs P, Inf.Mgr., Northgate & Prudhoe NHS Trust. [0049865] *14/01/1994*
Legg Mr CA, LLB(Hons), Stud., Loughborough Univ. [0059319] *22/03/2001*
Legg Mrs EA, BA DipLib MCLIP, Sch.Lib., Beaulieu Convent Sch., St.Helier, Jersey. [0033026] *10/10/1980*
Legg Mrs JC, (was Young), BA(Hons) MCLIP, Self Employed. [0041328] *03/11/1987*
Legg Miss JM, MCLIP, Life Member. [0008811] *01/01/1942*
Legg Mr JR, MA, Lib., Sackler L., Oxford. [0039869] *01/10/1986*
Legg Miss R, Grad.Trainee Lib., Clyde & Co., London. [0060895] *21/12/2001 AF*
Legg Mrs RJ, (was Stout), BA(Hons) MCLIP, Resources Lib., Flexible Learning. [0025669] *21/01/1976*
Legg Mr TJ, BSc DipLib MCLIP, Lifelong Learning Lib., Essex.C.C., Clacton L. [0042340] *11/10/1988*
Leggat Miss IK, MA, L.& Inf.Support Offr., Perth Coll., Study Cent., Perth, Tayside. [0047681] *14/10/1992*
Leggate Dr P, MA DPhil FCLIP, Employment not known. [0060539] *11/12/2001* **FE 01/04/2002**
Legge Mrs KE, (was Thomas), BLib MCLIP, Sch.Lib., Hants.C.C., Cove. [0029847] *06/10/1978*
Leggett Mrs D, (was Hollis), BA(Hons) MCLIP, Child.Lib., North Tyneside Council., Tyne & Wear. [0049992] *08/02/1994*
Leggett Mrs MJ, (was Joiner), MCLIP, Sch.Lib., Brighton & Hove High Sch. [0013878] *25/03/1963*
Legon Ms KE, BA(Hons), Inf.Offr., Osborne Clarke, London. [0061209] *08/04/2002*
Lehmann Mrs J, (was Selbourne), BA MCLIP, Head of L.Serv., Brighton & Sussex Univ.Hosp.NHS Tst, Sussex P.G.Med.Cent., The L. [0008817] *23/04/1967*
Lehva Mrs MA, (was Robinson), MCLIP, Lib., Havering Sch.L.Serv., Romford. [0010248] *16/01/1971*
Leibowitz Miss Y, BA(Hons), Asst.Lib., American Intercontinental Univ., London. [0059631] *05/07/2001*
Leifer Mrs JE, (was King), BA DipLib MA MCLIP, Sch.Lib., Immanuel Coll., Bushey. [0042809] *19/07/1988*
Leigh Miss JR, BA(Hons) MCLIP, Floor Mgr., Ottakars, Lincoln. [0050370] *07/07/1994*
Leigh Mrs MEM, (was Eves), MCLIP, Res.Mgr., The Royal Wolverhampton Sch. [0004719] *01/01/1969*
Leigh Miss P, BA(Hons) MCLIP, Research Mgr./Web Designer. [0053560] *22/07/1996*
Leigh Mrs R, MCLIP, Unemployed. [0005947] *01/01/1968*
Leighton Mrs SJ, MA MCLIP, Principal Lib., L.B.of Barking & Dagenham., Learning & Devel. [0020417] *28/02/1973*
Leitch Mr A, BA(Hons) DipILM, ICT Support Offr., Hanley Ref.L., Stoke on Trent. [0059270] *23/01/2001*
Leitch Mr A, MCLIP, Lib.Arch.& Bus.Rec.Cent., Univ.of Glasgow. [0008825] *16/01/1966*
Leitch Mrs C, (was Massey), MCLIP, Br.Lib., Saltburn L., Redcar & Cleveland Bor.Council. [0017258] *01/01/1960*
Leitch Mrs EM, MA MCLIP, Bibl., CSCNWW Himalayan Arch.Project, Edinburgh. [0024431] *31/07/1975*
Leitch Ms S, BA DipLib MCLIP, Site Lib., City Univ., London. [0044943] *22/01/1991*
Leitch Mr SP, BA DipILS, Unemployed. [0059547] *04/05/2001*
Leith Mrs A, (was Kretsis), BA DipLib MSc MCLIP, Knowledge Mgmt.Project Developer, Freshfields Bruckhaus Deringer, London. [0032108] *06/02/1980*
Leivers Mr P, BA MBA MCLIP, Customer Serv.Mgr., E.Sussex C.C., Lewes. [0033410] *02/12/1980*
Lemaire Ms KA, BA DipLib MCLIP FRSA, Ch.Exec., Sch.L.Assoc. [0042825] *09/03/1989*

Personal Members — Lewis

Lemans Mr JM, BA(Hons) MCLIP, ICT Administrator, Brent L.,Mus.& Arch., Wembley. [0044870] 03/01/1991
Lembanaka Ms H, MA, Unemployed, [0060955] 18/01/2002
Lemonidou Ms M, BA MA MCLIP, Unemployed. [0049173] 08/10/1993
Lendon Mr JW, FCLIP FRSA, Life Member, Tel.0121 707 2950, 51 Victoria Rd., Acocks Grn., Birmingham, B27 7YB. [0008830] 01/01/1951 **FE 01/01/1968**
Lenferna De La Motte Mrs JA, (was Askey), BLS FCLIP, Unemployed. [0030094] 25/12/1978 **FE 19/05/1999**
Leng-Ward Mr GD, BSc MA, Sen.Asst.Lib., Univ.of Warwick, Coventry. [0050399] 13/07/1994
Lennon Mrs JS, (was Sanderson), BA MCLIP, Div.Child.Lib., Lancs.Co.L., S.Lancs.Div. [0038588] 08/07/1985
Lennon Miss S, BSc(Hons) PGDip, Production Asst., Blackwell Publishers, Edinburgh. [0058509] 06/03/2000
Lennox Mrs S, (was Young), BA MCLIP, Unemployed. [0032230] 09/02/1980
Leonard Mrs D, (was Wingrove), MCLIP, Life Member. [0008835] 01/01/1949
Leonard Mrs LE, BSc(Econ), Lib., Univ.of Cambridge. [0052231] 16/10/1995
Leonard Miss MB, BA DipLib MCLIP, Inf.Off., Slaughter and May, London. [0028328] 24/10/1977
Leonard Mr P, BA MCLIP, Sen.Asst.Lib., Manchester Metro.Univ. [0008838] 09/09/1994
Leonard Mr PAL, BA, Grad.Trainee Lib., Univ.Coll.of London. [0061480] 16/08/2002 **AF**
Leonetti Miss C, BA, Lib., Golders Green L., London. [0055248] 08/09/1997
Leong Mrs M, BA DipLib MLib FCLIP FHKLA, Retired. [0019715] 08/04/1970 **FE 19/01/2000**
Lepley Mrs DJ, (was Freezer), BA(Hons) MCLIP, Electronic Inf.Training Lib., Mid Essex Hosp.Trust, Chelmsford. [0044816] 03/12/1990
Leppard Miss AM, BSc(Hons) MA, Asst.Lib., The Natural Hist.Mus., London. [0058186] 15/11/1999
Lepper Mrs AM, (was Greenwood), BSc MCLIP, Enquiries Offr., Nat.Assoc.of Toy & Leisure L., London. [0041809] 07/04/1988
Leppington Mr CE, BA(Hons) MA MCLIP, Delivery Team Leader, HM Customs & Excise, London. [0053947] 15/10/1996
LeSadd Mr CW, L.Asst., Dept.of Trade & Ind., London. [0052870] 02/01/1996
Leslie Miss AE, BA, Catg.Asst., Nat.L.of Scotland, Edinburgh. [0056902] 02/11/1998
Leslie Ms AFV, LLB MScInfSc, Conflicts Mgr., Freshfields, London. [0049326] 22/10/1993
Leslie Mrs AH, MA DipLib MCLIP, Res.Devel.Offr., Educ.Devel.Serv., Dundee. [0031243] 15/10/1979
Leslie Miss GI, LLB(Hons) DipLIS, Stud., Univ.Strathclyde. [0059287] 29/01/2001
Leslie Mr R, MCLIP, Ch.Lib., Orkney Islands Council, Orkney. [0008843] 12/09/1967
Lesser Mrs N, (was Bolsom), MCLIP, Retired. [0008847] 09/07/1953
Lester Mrs M, MCLIP, Lib., Ewell L., Surrey. [0008849] 02/01/1967
Lester Dr RG, BSc PhD FCLIP FLS, Head, L.& Inf.Serv., The Nat.Hist.Mus., London. [0033852] 01/04/1981 **FE 01/04/2002**
Leszczynska Miss MA, BA MCLIP, Business Systems Admin., L.B.of Merton, Educ.Leisure & Ls.Dept. [0032672] 15/07/1980
Letendrie Mrs FE, (was Darling), BA(Hons), Asst.Training & Devel.Co-ordinator, London L.& inf.Devel.Unit. [0044210] 09/07/1990
Letford Mr JC, BSc DipILS MCLIP, Sch.Lib., Castlemilk High Sch., Glasgow. [0055847] 19/11/1997
Letterborough Miss C, Stud., Manchester Met.Univ. [0060021] 26/11/2001
Letton Miss CR, MA FSA SCOT MCLIP, Area Lib.-Cent.Area, Galashiels L., Scottish Borders Council. [0019623] 10/10/1972
Letton Mr S, MCLIP, Retired. [0008852] 12/03/1945
Letton Mr VE, MCLIP, Life Member. [0008853] 09/01/1939
Leung Mr CK, MLIS, Asst. Lib., Chinese Univ. Hong Kong, Hong Kong. [0061374] 03/07/2002
Leung Mrs EYH, (was Kam), MCLIP, Lib., STD/AIDS Resource Cent., BC Cent.for Disease Control, Vancouver, Canada. [0017146] 26/10/1971
Leung Mr K, MCLIP, Mgr.(L.Operations), Hosp.Auth., Hong Kong. [0021669] 01/01/1974
Leung Ms SYR, BPhil DipLIS MA, Lib., St.Mary's Canossian Coll., Hong Kong. [0050030] 24/02/1994
Levay Mr P, BA(Hons) MA, Asst.Lib., Nat.Police L., Hook, Hants. [0058185] 15/11/1999
Levene Mrs A, (was Minchom), BA MCLIP, Lib., Rowe & Maw, London. [0010217] 20/04/1969
Levenson Mrs J, L.Asst., N.London Collegiate Jnr.Sch., Edgware. [0057811] 16/08/1999 **AF**
Leventhall Mr AM, BA(Hons) DipLib MCLIP, Team Lib., Fakenham L., Norfolk C.C. [0035762] 01/11/1982
Lever Mrs HL, (was McIntyre), BSc PGDip, Principal Inf.Offr.p./t., Salford Univ. [0052588] 09/11/1995
Lever Mrs J, (was Standen), MCLIP, Retired. [0008856] 25/09/1954
Leverton Miss J, MCLIP, Asst.Health Inf.Adviser, NHS Direct, Nottingham. [0008858] 03/02/1970
Levett Mr JA, MCLIP, L.Stock Mgr., L.B.of Bromley. [0019989] 12/01/1973
Levett Mr PR, BA(Hons), Stud., Univ.of Sheffield. [0058709] 01/07/2000
Levett Miss SE, BA CertED MCLIP, Head of Arts L.& Mus., Bournemouth Bor.Council. [0029518] 23/09/1978
Levey Ms CA, MCLIP, Asst.Lib.-Systems, Univ.of London, Goldsmiths Coll.L., New Cross. [0032674] 20/06/1980
Levick Mrs JE, (was Morgan), BA(LIB) MCLIP, Lib.-EYP, Doncaster M.B.C. [0010402] 24/02/1968
Levin Mrs AJT, (was Macbride), FCLIP, Life member. [0008859] 11/10/1933 **FE 01/01/1948**
Levin Mrs CL, (was Sladen), BA(Hons) MA MCLIP, Web Mgr., Dept.for Transport, London. [0052157] 09/10/1995
Levine Mrs KM, (was Wallen), MSc MCLIP, Inf.Offr., MIDIRS, Bristol. [0015279] 01/01/1968

Levitt Mrs CM, (was Tarplee), BA, Asst.Lib., Worcestershire C.C. [0041880] 09/05/1988
Levy Mrs J, MLS, Managing Dir., CINAHL Inf.Systems, Glendale, California. [0050511] 19/08/1994
Levy Ms R, BA(Hons), Stud., Univ.of Brighton, Moulscombe Campus. [0061543] 10/09/2002
Lewent Mrs JA, (was Clague), BSc DipLib MCLIP, Casual Lib./p./t.Sch.Lib., Sch.L.Serv./Sandringham Sch., Herts. [0033815] 26/02/1981
Lewin Mrs HL, (was Bridgeman), BSc, Res.Mgr., Stanley Tee, Bishops Stortford. [0053182] 28/03/1996
Lewin Mrs M, BSc MCLIP, Reader Serv.Lib., Park Lane Coll., Leeds. [0023391] 12/01/1975
Lewin Mrs SC, BA, Stud. [0059855] 17/10/2001
Lewington Dr RJ, BSc PhD MCLIP, Employment not known. [0060541] 11/12/2001
Lewis Miss A, L.Asst., Univ.Coll.Oxford.L. [0058642] 01/05/2000
Lewis Mr AI, BSc DipLib MCLIP, Lib., Moore Stephens, London. [0031887] 14/01/1980
Lewis Miss AJ, Stud., Loughborough Univ. [0059512] 18/04/2001
Lewis Miss AJ, BSc, Child.Lib., Surrey C.C., Guildford L. [0056983] 18/11/1998
Lewis Mr AJ, BSc, E-Services Offr., Royal Bor.of Windsor & Maidenhead, Maidenhead. [0059310] 02/02/2001 **AF**
Lewis Mr AM, BSc(Hons) DipIM MCLIP, Catg.Supervisor, Westminster L., London. [0048973] 10/08/1993
Lewis Ms AN, BA(Hons) DipILS MCLIP, Researcher/Comm.Offr., BBC Wales. [0049923] 24/01/1994
Lewis Mrs CL, (was Watson), BA DipLib MCLIP, Lib., Torfaen Co.Bor.Council, Pontypool. [0035237] 06/10/1982
Lewis Mrs CM, (was Prince), BA MCLIP, Researcher, Budde Comm., Australia. [0020650] 01/01/1973
Lewis Mrs CM, (was Smith), BA MCLIP, Dep.Learning Res.Mgr., Loughborough Coll. [0008867] 01/01/1968
Lewis Ms CV, BA MSc MCLIP, Asst.Dir.-L.& Culture, L.B.Enfield, Civic Cent. [0026450] 30/09/1976
Lewis Mr D, PhD MA MCLIP, Catg.Mgr., Pilkington L., Loughborough Univ. [0008869] 03/03/1965
Lewis Mrs DA, (was Nightingale), BA MCLIP, Lib./Inf.Offr., Royal Inst.of Chartered Surveyors, Edinburgh. [0010837] 01/08/1969
Lewis Mr DF, BSc CBiol MCLIP, Retired. [0060725] 12/12/2001
Lewis Mr DG, MA BA DipLib MCLIP, Unemployed. [0021316] 06/10/1973
Lewis Mr DG, MA MCLIP, Asst.Dir.of Educ., Aberystwyth L., Ceredigion C.C. [0008870] 23/11/1967
Lewis Miss DJ, BSc(Hons) MSc(Econ), Asst.Lib., Dudley Coll.of Tech., W.Midlands. [0054536] 20/01/1997
Lewis Mrs E, (was Panchen), FCLIP, Retired. [0008872] 27/08/1935 **FE 01/01/1935**
Lewis Ms EA, BA MA, Res.Cent.Guide, BBC, London. [0053269] 15/04/1996
Lewis Miss EC, L.&Inf.Asst., Norfolk L.& Inf.Serv., Norwich. [0054050] 22/10/1996
Lewis Mrs EM, BSc(Econ) DipLib, Lib., Nevill Hall Hosp., Rowland Isaac L., Abergavenny. [0055445] 13/10/1997
Lewis Mr GJ, BA(Hons) MSc, Sen.L.Asst., Warwick Univ.L. [0058059] 21/10/1999
Lewis Ms GR, (was Swain), MCLIP, Lib., HM Prison, Nottingham. [0008874] 29/03/1968
Lewis Miss HM, BA(Hons) MSc, Intranet Editor, HM Treasury, London. [0058670] 10/05/2000
Lewis Mr HM, BA(Hons), Lib. [0058187] 15/11/1999
Lewis Mrs HM, (was Sayer), MCLIP, Inf.Co-ordinator, CFBT Advice & Guidance, Beds. [0008875] 17/11/1969
Lewis Miss I, BA, Arch.Asst., City of Westminster Arch. [0059451] 30/03/2001 **AF**
Lewis Miss IA, MLib BA DipLib MCLIP, FE Acct.Mgr., UKERNA, Didcot. [0024900] 14/10/1975
Lewis Miss IJ, BA MCLIP, Head of Ls.& Arts, Dorset C.C., Dorchester. [0008876] 01/01/1964
Lewis Miss J, MCLIP, Sen.Lib., Cent.L., L.B.of Bromley. [0008879] 06/07/1972
Lewis Mr J, FCLIP, Retired. [0008880] 24/01/1952 **FE 01/01/1962**
Lewis Mrs JA, (was Fellows), BA DipLib MCLIP, Lib., Hants.Co.L. [0027671] 01/07/1977
Lewis Mrs JA, (was Whiley), BLib MCLIP, p./t.Med.Sec., James Paget Hosp., Gt.Yarmouth, Norfolk. [0027714] 01/07/1977
Lewis Mrss JM, (was Grives), BA(Hons) MA, Intranet Content Mgr., Dept.of Work & Pensions, London. [0043639] 15/11/1989
Lewis Ms KA, BA(Hons)DipLib, Prin.Res.Advisor, CMPS Cabinet Off., London. [0035871] 26/01/1983
Lewis Mrs L, (was Bird), BA MCLIP, Lib., Essex C.C. [0024605] 18/09/1975
Lewis Ms LC, BA(Hons), L.Asst., The Chartered Insurance Inst., London. [0061095] 28/02/2002 **AF**
Lewis Ms LJ, (was Dukes), BA(Hons) DipLIS, Asst.Lib., Bevan Ashford, Bristol. [0052229] 16/10/1995
Lewis Miss LM, RSA CPC, P./T.Stud., Lib., Univ.Aberystwyth., Nokia Networks. [0059204] 08/01/2001
Lewis Miss MJ, MBE FCLIP, Life Member. [0008888] 03/01/1948 **FE 25/04/1974**
Lewis Mr MJ, MA DipLib MCLIP, Dep.Dir.of L.Serv., The Univ.of Sheffield. [0028619] 01/01/1978
Lewis Mr MR, MCLIP, Sen.Lib.: Music & Multimedia, Nottingham City L. [0008892] 20/02/1968
Lewis Mr N, BA(Hons) MA MCLIP, Electronic Res.Lib., Univ.of E.Anglia, Norwich. [0054721] 17/03/1997
Lewis Mr PR, MA HonFCLIP FCLIP, Life Member, Wyvern Blackheath Rd., Wenhaston, Suffolk, IP19 9HD. [0008894] 23/03/1949 **FE 01/01/1955**

289

Lewis Mrs PT, (was Goldstein), MCLIP, Lib., Highways Agency, London. [0005648] 01/10/1968
Lewis Miss RC, BA(Hons) MSc(Econ), Asst.Lib., Sandwell Healthcare NHS Trust, W.Bromwich. [0049414] 22/10/1992
Lewis Mrs RJ, MCLIP, Systems Lib., Canterbury Christ Church Coll., Kent. [0029059] 14/03/1978
Lewis Mr RW, BA DipLib MLS MBA MCLIP, Head Bus.Efficiency Unit, Health & Safety Exec., Bootle. [0034581] 01/01/1982
Lewis Mrs SE, (was Double), MCLIP, Sch.Lib., Homewood Sch., Tenterden, Kent. [0026482] 16/10/1976
Lewis Ms SJ, BEd MLIS, Sch.Lib., Biggar High Sch. [0041468] 01/01/1988
Lewis Miss SJE, BA(Hons) MCLIP, Learning Res.Lib., Llysfasi Coll., Ruthin. [0045991] 12/08/1991
Lewis Ms SJI, (was Chitranukroh), MCLIP, P./t.Lib., Hampstead Sch., London. [0008900] 09/07/1969
Lewis Ms SM, BA(Hons) MA MCLIP, Lib., Berkshire Shared Serv.Organisation, Cholsey, Oxon. [0053737] 20/09/1996
Lewis Miss VP, BA(Hons), External Content Co-Ordinator, KPMG., London. [0050917] 31/10/1994
Lewis Miss Y, BA MA, Asst.L.Adviser, The Nat.Trust, London. [0042181] 05/10/1988
Lewis Mrs YM, Unemployed. [0025473] 02/03/1970
Lewsey Miss SW, MCLIP, Life Member. [0017264] 11/06/1950
Leydon Mrs MT, (was Collins), BSc DipLib, Sen.Asst.Lib./Team Leader(Jobshare), Bibl.Serv., Birmingham L.Serv., Cent.L. [0040316] 08/01/1987
Leyland Mrs M, (was Boughey), MCLIP, Lib.(Ref.), Reading Bor.Council. [0008908] 22/10/1969
Leyland-Green Ms VM, (was Leyland), BA DipLib MCLIP, TUUS Consultancy, Church Stretton, Shropshire. [0035899] 01/02/1983
Li Mr HC, MA MCLIP, Sen.Asst.Lib., Hong Kong Poly.Univ. [0018966] 08/09/1972
Li Miss KH, BA MLib MCLIP, Asst.Lib., City Univ.of Hong Kong. [0043890] 13/02/1990
Li Miss ML, BA(Hons) MA, Lib., Nottinghamshire C.C., Keyworth L. [0054618] 04/02/1997
Li Ms PL, BA(Hons) MSc(Econ) MCLIP, Asst.Lib., Bircham Dyson Bell, London. [0051161] 23/11/1994
Liang Ms M, BA ALAA, Lib., Futures American Sch., Cairo, Egypt. [0042469] 18/11/1988
Libbey Miss JP, BA, Stud., Univ.of Wales Aberystwyth. [0061776] 04/11/2002
Lichfield Mrs LM, (was Thomas), BA MCLIP, Learning Resources Mgr., Oaklands Coll., Welwyn Garden City Campus. [0037896] 15/11/1984
Lickley Mr D, BA DipLib, Br.Lib., Coll.of Law, London. [0044453] 09/10/1990
Lidbetter Mrs CS, (was Wilson), BA(Hons) MA MCLIP, Trainee Liaison Lib., Reading Univ. [0052173] 10/10/1995
Liddle Mrs DL, Sen.Lib., Inf.Serv., Cent.L., Walsall. [0052629] 13/11/1995
Liddle Mrs M, (was Hill), BA MCLIP, Dist.Lib., W.Wilts., L.& Heritage, Wilts.Co.Council, Towbridge. [0008913] 28/02/1965
Liddle Miss MO, MCLIP, Life Member, Tel.091 236 4658. [0008912] 02/03/1950
Lievesley Mr G, BSc MSc FRSS MCLIP, Employment not known. [0060761] 12/12/2001
Lifford Ms HM, (was Reynolds), BSc, Freelance Abstractor, Self-Employed. [0040852] 13/07/1987
Lightfoot Mr D, MA DMS MCLIP, Co.L.Mgr., Lancs.Co.L., Preston. [0008921] 08/01/1969
Lightwood Miss EG, MCLIP, Life Member. [0008922] 09/11/1931
Lile Mrs J, (was Hildreth), MCLIP, Lend.Serv.Lib., Univ.of Wales, Aberystwyth. [0008925] 15/02/1963
Liley Mrs J, (was Mortimer), MCLIP, Sch.Lib., Luton Bor.Council. [0008926] 20/02/1967
Lill Ms FS, Reading Room Co-ordinator, Brit.L. [0041035] 06/10/1987
Lilley Mr G, MA DipLib FCLIP, Life Member &, Sen.Research Fellow in Bibl., Dept.of English, Univ.of Wales. [0008927] 06/10/1961 FE 01/01/1970
Lilley Mrs M, (was North), BA LTCL MCLIP, Music Teacher, Self-employed. [0008930] 03/02/1960
Lilley Mr MI, BLib MCLIP, Sch.Lib., Leicester High Sch.for Girls. [0043947] 02/03/1990
Lillie Miss AVN, Stud., Univ.of Brighton. [0061094] 27/02/2002
Lilliman Mr RM, BA MCLIP, Br.Lib., West Hill L., Wandsworth P.L. [0020854] 02/08/1973
Lillis Mr M, BTech MCLIP, Employment not known. [0061239] 12/12/2001
Lim Mrs KL, (was Chan), MCLIP, Employment not known. [0018914] 27/09/1972
Lim . SH, BSocSc MCLIP, Lib., Univ.of Malaya L., Kuala Lumpur. [0022989] 08/10/1974
Limper Ms K, MA, Grad.Trainee, The Brit.L. [0059481] 09/04/2001
Linacre Miss CE, BA DipLib MCLIP, Systems Mgr.L., Royal Inst.of Chartered Surveyors, London. [0037597] 09/10/1984
Lincoln Mrs JM, (was Walker), BA MCLIP, No present position. [0019685] 30/10/1972
Linden Prof R, MA PhD FCLIP, Retired. [0008935] 28/03/1945 FE 01/01/1955
Lindley Mrs J, (was Latto), MCLIP, Unemployed. [0008676] 01/01/1969
Lindley Mrs JM, (was Simpson), BA(Hons) MCLIP, Lib., Milton Keynes Council. [0048164] 11/11/1992
Lindley Mr P, MCLIP, Lib.:Hinckley, Leics.L.& Inf.Serv. [0008939] 04/05/1967
Lindsay Ms AE, (was Brent), LLB MCLIP, [0026452] 04/10/1976
Lindsay Mrs C, (was Jackson), MCLIP, Reader Serv.Lib., Farnborough Coll.of Tech., Hants. [0008940] 21/01/1972
Lindsay Mrs CA, (was Dean), BLib MCLIP DMS, Sen.Lib., Hants.Co.L., Ringwood L. [0032913] 01/10/1980
Lindsay Miss D, MA DipLib MCLIP, Sen.Lib., Strathclyde Univ., Glasgow. [0028058] 01/10/1977

Lindsay Mr DG, BA DipLib MCLIP, Knowledge & Inf.Mgr., The Motor Neurone Disease Assoc., Northampton. [0028442] 28/11/1977
Lindsay Mrs EYL, (was Smith), BA MCLIP, Local Hist.Offr., Stirling Council L. [0030592] 01/01/1964
Lindsay Ms GM, BEd, H.of Learning Resources, Warden Pk.Sch., Haywards Heath, East Sussex. [0057911] 01/10/1999
Lindsay Miss JA, BA DipLib MCLIP, Coll.Res.Lib., Sixth Form Coll., Cambridge. [0031655] 07/11/1979
Lindsay Mr JW, BA MCLIP, Stock & Admin.Mgr., N.Lanarkshire Council, Motherwell. [0025589] 02/02/1976
Lindsay Ms M, BA MPhil RGN MCLIP, Inf.Offr., London Cent., Dementia Care, Univ.Coll.London. [0008942] 19/07/1971
Lindsay Mrs S, (was Norquay), BSc MSc, Asst.Lib., SIRCC, Univ of Strathclyde, Glasgow. [0058073] 25/10/1999
Lindsey Mr C, MCLIP, Researcher. [0008944] 18/03/1965
Lindsey Mrs P, (was Longrigg), MCLIP, Life Member, Tel:01753 642775. [0008945] 25/10/1945
Line Mrs CE, (was Hodgkinson), Sen.L.Asst., L.B.of Havering L. [0045089] 10/07/1990 **AF**
Line Mrs J, MA MCLIP, Retired. [0023747] 09/01/1975
Line Mrs JM, (was Ramsey), BA(Hons) DipLIS MCLIP, Unemployed. [0044863] 01/01/1991
Line Prof MB, MA FCLIP CCMI HonDLitt HonDSc, Life Member, Tel.01423 872984, 10 Blackthorn Lane, Burn Bridge, Harrogate, HG3 1NZ,Fax.879849. [0008947] 10/04/1951 **FE 01/01/1955**
Linehan Ms CD, BA(Hons) DipLib, Inf.& Research Offr., Optima Comm.Assoc., Birmingham. [0044108] 15/05/1990
Linehan Mrs MT, BA MLIS, Asst.Lib., Dept.of Health, Social Serv., Stormont, N.Ireland. [0058726]01/07/2000
Linfield Mr AM, BA DipLib MCLIP, Coll. Lib., London Bible Coll., Northwood. [0029729] 04/10/1978
Linford Ms RES, MA(Hons) DipILS(Dist), Univ.Web.Admin, Univ. Dundee, Dundee. [0052649] 15/11/1995
Lingard Miss C, MCLIP, Lib.[Lang.& Lit.L.], Manchester P.L. [0008952] 02/03/1967
Lingard Miss KE, BA (Hons), Inf.Researcher, Inst.of Mgmt., Corby, Northants. [0044772] 14/11/1990
Lingard Mrs L, (was Wills), BA DipLib MCLIP, Unemployed. [0035778] 10/01/1983
Lingham Mrs AM, (was Pryde), BA, Sen.Team Lib., Learning & Literacy, Gloucester & W., Glos.C.C. [0019652] 31/10/1972
Lingwood Mrs J, (was Waterhouse), BA(Hons) MSc, Learning Cent.Mgr., Wakefield Coll., Thornes Pk Cent. [0054267] 11/11/1996
Linin Mrs SA, Young People's Serv.Team Asst., Kent C.C., Educ.& L., Swanley, Kent. [0056401] 01/07/1998 **AF**
Linnard Mrs D, (was Joiner), MCLIP, Principal L.Asst., Gloucestershire C.C., Glos. [0025329] 29/12/1975
Linneman Mrs AV, (was Campbell), BA L-es-L MCLIP, Retired. [0002319] 01/01/1970
Linton Mrs AM, (was Hutchison), BA(Hons) DipLib MCLIP, Asst.Lib.-Bibl.Serv., Univ.of Ulster, Newtownabbey. [0042238] 06/10/1988
Linton Mr DH, MCLIP, Area L.Offr., Skye & Lochalsh, Highland L. [0008963] 22/02/1969
Linton Mr WD, BSc BLS CBiol MIBiol ALAI FCLIP HonFCLIP, Life Member, Cloona, 25 Newcastle Road, Castlewellan, Co Down, N.Ireland. [0008965] 23/09/1965 **FE 27/05/1992**
Lipscombe Mrs M, Lib., St.Nicholas House Sch., Hemel Hempstead. [0051671] 05/05/1995
Liptrot Mrs SM, (was Browning), BLib MCLIP, p./t.Team Lib., Cheltenham L., Glos. [0001958] 21/01/1959
Lipworth Mrs EL, (was Lipschitz), BA HDLIS HDE, L.& Records Offr.p./t., CPRE, London. [0048499] 29/01/1993
Liquorice Miss ME, FCLIP, 5 Grange Avenue, Dogsthorpe, Peterborough, Cambs., PE1 4HH. [0008969] 01/01/1942 **FE 01/01/1955**
Lisgarten Mrs L, (was Knight), BA MCLIP, Head of L.& Inf.Dept., Sch.of Pharmacy, Univ.of London. [0008970] 06/09/1968
Lisle Mr PE, BA MSc MCLIP, Dir.of Educ.Res., Newbold Coll.L., Bracknell. [0046718] 08/01/1992
Lison Mrs B, Dir., Stadt bibliothek Bremen, Friedrich-Ebert-Strasse 101/105, 28199 Bremen, Germany. [0051911]07/08/1995
List Mr D, Consultant, Self-employed, London. [0039181] 11/12/1985
List Ms JA, BSC, Resident Heidelberg. [0039998] 16/10/1986
Lister Mr A, MA PGCE DipLib MCLIP, Team Lib., Kent C.C., Sevenoaks L. [0039514] 14/02/1986
Lister Mrs CA, Acquisitions Lib., Isle of Wight Coll., Newport. [0057530] 14/04/1999 **AF**
Lister Mrs E, (was Lee), BA FCLIP, Life Member. [0008974] 07/01/1958 **FE 26/10/1962**
Lister Mrs J, BA(Hons), Sen.Asst., Lord Louis L., Isle of Wight. [0024571] 22/09/1959
Lister Ms M, BA MSc MIMgt MILAM MCLIP, Audit Commission, [0008975] 28/02/1969
Lister Mr MJ, BA MCLIP, L.Operational Mgr., Isle of Wight Council, Newport. [0024520] 03/09/1975
Litchfield Mrs M, (was Clark), MCLIP, P/t.Sch.Lib., L.B.of Havering. [0008978] 01/01/1966
Little Mr B, MPhil FCLIP, Princ.Lib., Wilts.C.C.Educ.& L., Trowbridge. [0008979] 18/02/1963 **FE 02/11/1973**
Little Mr BJ, BA MCLIP, Snr.Lib., Hornsey L., London. [0026765] 01/10/1976
Little Miss CE, BA, Sen.Bus.Inf.Offr., Inst.of Directors, London. [0054170] 04/11/1996
Little Mr DJ, BA(Hons) MA MCLIP, Inf.Offr.(History of Med.Gateway), The Wellcome Trust, London. [0052911] 16/01/1996
Little Mr DRT, MCLIP, Mgr.Inf. & L.Serv., DERA, Malvern. [0050718] 13/10/1994

Little Mrs FM, (was Pimley), MCLIP, Comm.Lib., W.Hampshire Primary Care Trust, Moorgreen Hosp., Southampton. [0026791] 18/11/1976
Little Miss J, MA PgDip, Stud. [0061508] 28/08/2002
Little Mrs J, (was Liddle), BA MCLIP, Child.Lib., Salisbury, Wilts.C.C., Educ.& L. [0008982] 01/01/1966
Little Miss JH, BA MBA MCLIP, Head of the L.& Inf.Serv., Liverpool City Council. [0008984] 30/06/1970
Little Mr MC, MA(Hons) MSc MCLIP, Systems & Catg.Lib., Public Records Off., Richmond. [0051466] 22/01/1995
Little Ms PA, (was Lawrence), BA MCLIP, Dep.Head of Cultural Serv., L.B.of Barnet. [0021825] 29/01/1974
Little Mrs PM, (was Lowry), Volunteer, Scott Polar Research Inst., Univ.of Cambridge. [0045259] 18/09/1990 **AF**
Little Ms RM, (was Jones), BA(Hons) MSc(Econ) MCLIP, Funding Devel.Offr., Bridgend Assoc.of Voluntary org. [0053767] 01/10/1996
Littleboy Miss C, BA(Hons) MCLIP, Sen.Asst.Lib., W.Sussex L.Serv., Worthing L. [0046774] 22/01/1992
Littledale Mrs FJ, MA(Hons), Asst.Lib., Richmond Coll. [0057353] 17/02/1999
Littlefair Ms EE, MA(Hons) DipLIB MCLIP, L.& Inf.Worker, Dundee City Council. [0039931] 01/10/1986
Littlefield Ms RM, BSc PGCE MSc, Learning Strategies Coordinator, Joseph Priestley Coll., Leeds. [0044278] 20/02/1979
Littlehales Mrs R, (was Doughty), BA DipEd MCLIP, Retired. [0008989] 07/01/1969
Littler Ms AR, (was Witten), BA(Hons) MLS MCLIP, Lib., Inst.of Gas Engineers, London. [0031503] 19/10/1979
Littler Miss J, MCLIP, Retired. [0008992] 11/02/1963
Littlewood Miss A, BA(Hons) MA, Bibl.Asst., John Rylands Univ., L.of Manchester. [0057215] 19/01/1999
Litton Miss J, BA(Hons), Computing Advisor, Univ.of Wales, Aberystwyth,. [0057596] 12/05/1999
Litwin-Roberts Mrs ML, BA, Stud., Univ.of Wales, Aberystwyth. [0053146] 01/04/1996
Liu Mr D, MA, Med.Educ.Res.Mgr., Royal Coll.of Physicians, London. [0050626] 01/10/1994
Liu Mrs H, BA MA, Asst.Lib., S.Thames Coll. [0056823] 23/10/1998
Liu Miss LMC, BEng(Hons) MSc, Asst.Lib., N.W.London Hosp.Trust, Cent.Middlesex Hosp. [0057868] 23/09/1999
Liversidge Miss E, MBE FCLIP, Retired. [0008997] 27/10/1932 **FE 01/01/1943**
Livesey Mrs J, (was Hoare), MCLIP, Lib., S.E.Wakefield, Wakefield Met.Dist.C. [0006976] 03/09/1969
Livesey Mrs JA, BSc(Hons), Stud., Manchester Met.Univ. [0059859] 18/10/2001
Livesey Mrs JA, (was Downham), MA MCLIP, Sen.Lib., Lancs C.C., Preston. [0004136] 17/01/1970
Livesey Dr JB, BSc PhD CEng MIInstE FCLIP, Employment not known. [0060592] 11/12/2001 **FE 01/04/2002**
Livesey Mrs L, (was Mapp), BA(Hons) DipILS, Subject Lib.(Liaison), Univ.Coll.Worcester, Peirson L. [0055026] 01/07/1997
Livesey Revd LJ, FCLIP, Life Member. [0009000] 19/03/1951 **FE 01/01/1957**
Livingstone Mrs CM, (was Wyver), BSc(Hons), p./t.Inf.Offr., Aberdeen City Council, Social Work Dept. [0058894] 02/10/2000
Livingstone Mr RG, MCLIP, Asst.Lib., Aberdeen City L. [0020351] 22/02/1973
Llewellyn Mr G, FCLIP, Life Member. [0009006] 20/02/1941 **FE 01/01/1967**
Llewellyn-Jones Ms FDW, (was Willis Byatt), BA MCLIP, p./t.Lect./Tutor, F.E./Comm.Educ., Suffolk C.C., Lowestoft. [0016015] 01/01/1971
Lloyd Mrs CE, (was Bonnaud), BA MCLIP, Community Lib., Faversham L., Kent. [0037643] 12/10/1984
Lloyd Mr CJ, BLib MCLIP, Loc.Hist.Lib., L.B.of Tower Hamlets. [0009009] 01/10/1971
Lloyd Mrs CL, (was Etherington), BLib MCLIP, Unemployed. [0004622] 01/01/1972
Lloyd Mrs CL, (was McNicoll), MSc, Employment not known. [0058168] 08/11/1999
Lloyd Miss CMH, BA(Hons), Stud./L.Trainee, Taylor Inst.L., Oxford. [0059962] 12/11/2001
Lloyd Ms CS, BA MA MCLIP, Reader Serv.Lib., Birkbeck Coll., London. [0047638] 09/10/1992
Lloyd Mr CT, BA(Hons) MCLIP, Asst.Area Mgr., L.B.of Barnet, Church End L. [0038135] 15/01/1985
Lloyd Ms D, BA DipLib MCLIP, Lib., Countryside Council for Wales, Bangor. [0033312] 06/10/1980
Lloyd Mr DR, BA, Neighbourhood Lib., Coventry City Council, The Hill L. [0054068] 22/10/1996
Lloyd Mrs E, (was Main), BA MEd MCLIP, Network Lib., Westhill Academy, Aberdeenshire L.Inf.Serv. [0031002] 01/07/1979
Lloyd Ms EV, BLib MCLIP, Stud. [0041546] 20/01/1988
Lloyd Mrs GE, (was Wilkinson), BA(Hons) MCLIP, Reg.L.Mgr., Instant L.Ltd., Wrexham. [0048500] 27/01/1993
Lloyd Mr GK, MCLIP MA, Life Member. [0018888] 21/10/1968
Lloyd Mr HG, MSc BSc HND, Project Cataloguer, Univ.of Wales. [0060901] 21/12/2001
Lloyd Mrs JM, (was Hanson), BA(Hons) MCLIP, p./t.Child.Lib./Area Child.Lib., L.B.of Barnet. [0019496] 01/01/1969
Lloyd Mrs JO, BA DipLib MIM, Head Lib., Avondale Coll., NSW, Australia. [0061476] 12/08/2002
Lloyd Mrs ME, BA(Hons) MPhil MSc(Econ) MCLIP, Lib., Stamford High Sch., Lincs. [0056002] 01/01/1998
Lloyd Mr P, MCLIP, Outreach Lib., L.B.of Newham. [0009021] 23/09/1969
Lloyd Miss S, BA(Hons) MCLIP, Clinical Lib., Worcs.Acute Hosp.NHS Trust, Alexandra Hosp., Redditch. [0048979] 11/08/1993

Lloyd Mrs S, (was Curry), DipLib MCLIP, Resident in Australia. [0022597] 02/07/1974
Lloyd Mrs S, L.Asst., Motor Neurone Disease Assoc., Northampton. [0061108] 22/02/2002 **AF**
Lloyd Mrs V, (was Jeffers), BA MCLIP, Asst.Lib., Worcs.C.C. [0024509] 01/09/1975
Lloyd Jones Ms K, BSc(Hons), Lifesign Project Offr., Learning Res.Cent., Univ.of Glamorgan. [0055102] 14/07/1997
Lloyd-Evans Miss B, BA(Hons) DipLIS MCLIP, Asst.Lib.(Catg.), The Wellcome Trust, London. [0044889] 09/01/1991
Lloyd-Jones Mr RA, BA DipLib MCLIP, Asst.Lib., Bor.of Hammersmith & Fulham, Fulham L. [0041722] 18/02/1988
Lloyd-Wiggins Mrs A, (was Toase), BA MCLIP, Consultant. [0030559] 08/01/1979
Llwyd Mr R, MA DipEd DipLib MCLIP, Univ.Lect., Dept.of Inf.& L.Studies, Univ.Coll.of Wales. [0009026] 20/01/1969
Llwyd Ms SS, (was England), BLib LLA, Mother. [0034687] 20/01/1982
Llywelyn Mr G, BA DipLib MCLIP, Llyfrgellyd Ysgolion/Sch.Lib., Cyngor Sir Caerfyrddin. [0040046] 12/10/1986
Loarridge Mrs C, (was Clark), BA MCLIP, Unemployed. [0002724] 01/01/1972
Loat Ms SM, BA MCLIP, Lib., Horticulture Research Internat., W.Malling. [0036881] 11/01/1984
Lobban Miss M, MA DipLib MCLIP, Dep.Dir.of LIS, Napier Univ.of Edinburgh. [0028060] 08/10/1977
Lobban Mrs MA, (was Philip), MA DipLib MCLIP, Sen.L.Asst., Univ.of Edinburgh, Erskine Med.L. [0028356] 28/10/1977
Lobban Miss R, BA MCLIP, Retired. [0009030] 03/01/1963
Lochhead Mrs A, (was Somerville), BA MCLIP, Bibl.Serv.Asst., Napier Univ., Edinburgh. [0022542] 22/06/1974
Lochhead Ms IR, BA DipLib MCLIP, Liaison Lib., Norwich City Coll. [0036351] 04/10/1983
Lock Mrs DA, BA(Hons) DipIM MCLIP MA, Projects Mgr., UMis Direct, Univ.of Surrey. [0051350] 25/01/1995
Lock Mrs EL, BSc, Unemployed. [0052123] 05/10/1995
Lock Mrs G, BA(Hons) DipLib, Housemistress/Sch.Lib., Queenswood Sch., Hatfield. [0034608] 07/07/1981
Lock Ms MA, BA MPhil MCLIP, Lo.Hist.Lib., Tameside P.L., Gt.Manchester. [0024434] 25/07/1975
Locke Mr DW, BA MSc MCLIP, Consultant, BBC, London. [0020050] 15/01/1973
Locke Mrs MC, (was Desmond), BA MCLIP, Support & Operations Mgr., L.B.of Lambeth. [0030613] 19/02/1979
Locke Miss S, BSc(Hons) MA MCLIP, L.Serv.Mgr., Bury Health Care NHS Trust, Bury Gen.Hosp. [0049346] 26/10/1993
Locker Miss GP, LLB PGDipLib, Local Govt.Offr., Derby City Council. [0038261] 19/02/1985
Locker Ms JE, BSc MSc MCLIP, Princ.Inf.Offr., Bowthorpe plc., Crawley. [0026642] 20/10/1976
Lockett Mrs J, (was Stevens), BA MCLIP, Mob.& Home L.Serv.Lib., Solihull M.B.C. [0032184] 13/02/1980
Lockett Miss KJ, BA, (Hons), Trainee Lib., Corpus Christi College, Oxford. [0060963] 18/01/2002
Lockley Mrs C, (was Porter), MCLIP, L.Asst., Inst.of Cancer Res., London. [0009039] 01/11/1964
Lockley Mrs RA, (was Evans), MCLIP, Unemployed. [0013676] 07/09/1962
Lockley Mrs UK, (was Rooke), BSc MSc(Econ) MCLIP, Head of L.& Inf.Serv., Rutherford Appleton Lab., Didcot. [0027809] 06/10/1978
Lockwood Miss AT, MA, Sch.Lib., Ian Rausey CE Sch., Stockton-on-Tees. [0052318] 26/10/1995
Lockwood Miss J, MCLIP, Sen.Lib.:Bibl.& Support Serv., City of York Council, Cent.L. [0009045] 13/02/1967
Lockwood Mrs JM, MCLIP, Infomatch. [0059579] 05/06/2001
Lockwood Mrs JR, (was Fuller), BA MCLIP, Lib., Millfield Prep Sch., Glastonbury. [0005261] 06/10/1971
Lockyer Mrs D, (was Pridmore), FCLIP, Life Member. [0009049] 09/09/1955 **FE 30/01/1978**
Loder Miss EP, FCLIP, Life Member. [0009051] 01/01/1948 **FE 18/08/1975**
Lodge Ms A, BA MCLIP, Sen.Lib., Comm.Serv., Wakefield Met.Dist.L. [0009053] 01/01/1971
Lodge Mrs AJ, (was Elston), BA(Hons) DipInf MCLIP, p./t.Lib., Herts.Cent.Res.L., Comm.Inf.L. [0044371] 02/10/1990
Lodge Miss EE, BLib MCLIP, Lib., Serious Fraud Off., London. [0039568] 06/03/1986
Lodge Mrs F, (was Watt), MA Msc, Reader Serv.Lib., Laban Cent.London, New Cross. [0049064] 01/01/1971
Lodge Ms G, MCLIP, Educ.& Training Coordinator for, Clinical Effectiveness, Salisbury NHS., Wilts. [0018761] 29/09/1964
Lodge Mr GA, MCLIP, Inf.Exec., Business Link Herts., St.Albans. [0050340] 01/01/1994
Lodge Ms H, MSc MCLIP, Position unknown, Wessex Water, Bath. [0060741] 12/12/2001
Lodge Mrs HA, BLib MCLIP MSc, Lib., Eastman Dental Inst., London. [0035272] 01/10/1982
Lodge Mrs V, (was Wagstaff), MA MCLIP, Lib., Arts Inst.at Bournemouth, Dorset. [0038897] 14/10/1985
Loewenstein Mr P, BA MSc FCLIP, Devel.Offr., Nat.Yth.Agency, Leicester. [0037007] 19/01/1984 **FE 23/09/1998**
Lofthouse Mrs A, (was Bowman), MA DipEd MCLIP, p./t.English Tutor, Northumberland C.C., Newcastle C.C. [0001554] 23/09/1970
Lofthouse Miss B, MCLIP, Outreach Serv.Mgr.(p./t.), Peterborough L., Cent.L.,Peterborough. [0009056] 01/10/1971
Loftus Mrs CJ, BA MCLIP, Inf.Team Leader, TPAS Ltd., Salford. [0030775] 08/03/1979

Logan Miss C, BA MCLIP, Br.Lib., Redcar & Cleveland Bor.Council, Skelton L. [0033913] 14/05/1981
Logan Miss ER, BA MSc MCLIP, Asst.Lib., Univ.of Ulster, Cent.L., Serials Management Div. [0025592] 29/01/1976
Logan Mr HJ, BA DipLib MCLIP, Learning Res.Co-ordinator, Perth & Kinross Council, Kinross High Sch. [0035372] 18/10/1982
Logan Mr MD, Stud., Queen Margaret Univ.Coll. [0058691] 30/05/2000
Logan Mr R, LLB FCLIP, Deputy Lib., Bodleian Law L. [0009062] 05/08/1969 FE 28/09/1978
Logue Mrs LET, (was Haan), BLS MCLIP, Exec.Offr., L.Assoc.N.Ireland Br., Belfast Educ.& L.Board. [0036207] 20/07/1983
Loi Miss SB, DipLib MCLIP, Sen.Asst.Lib., Nat.Inst.of Educ., Singapore. [0032678] 30/06/1980
Lomas Mr DB, MCLIP, Life Member. [0009065] 02/02/1949
Lomas Miss FA, BSc(Hons) MSc, I.T.Lib., Barrow Grp.Ls., Cumbria Co.Council. [0055649] 31/10/1997
Lomas Ms JA, BA DipLIS MCLIP, Inf.& Website Coordinator, The Market Research Soc., London. [0046347] 29/01/2001
Lomas Ms JM, BA MCLIP, Lib., Queen Elizabeth II Hosp., E.& N.Hertfordshire NHS Trust. [0041151] 12/10/1987
Lomas Mrs RA, (was Wilson), BA(Hons) MCLIP, Community Lib., Tameside Educ.& Cultural Serv., Learning & Info.Serv. [0041003] 01/10/1987
Lomas Mrs SC, BA MCLIP, Helpline Inf.Mgr., R.N.I.B., London. [0027432] 01/04/1977
Lomas Mr TC, BA MSc MCLIP, Lib., Stoke Heath HMYOI, Shropshire. [0021516] 01/01/1969
Lomax Mrs SM, BA MCLIP, Unemployed. [0025904] 01/04/1976
London Mrs HF, BA MA, Head, Readers Serv.Div., Univ.of Guyana L., Georgetown. [0046349] 30/10/1991
London Mr NJ, BA(Hons) MA MCLIP, Princ.Systems Offr., Notts.C.C., Nottingham. [0036968] 09/01/1984
Lonergan Mrs GF, (was Edwards), BA MCLIP, Arch., Co-Operative Coll. Leics. [0030401] 15/01/1979
Long Mr CA, BA DipLIS, L.Mgr., Eversheds, London. [0053109] 01/02/1996
Long Mr CJ, FCLIP, Life Member, 01344 623693, Portland, 27 Llanvair Dr.,S.Ascot, Berks., SL5 9HS. [0009069] 01/02/1937 FE 01/01/1955
Long Miss DS, BA MCLIP, Project Mgr., County L.H.Q., Lancs County L., Preston, Lancs. [0024102] 17/04/1975
Long Miss EJ, BA MSc, Sen.L.Asst., Imperial Coll., London. [0058469] 28/02/2000
Long Mrs JM, Inf.Sci., Glaxosmith Kline. [0050447] 15/08/1994 AF
Long Mrs JP, (was Schaap), MCLIP, H.of Mobile L., PBC Noord-Brabant, Tilburg. [0020531] 10/04/1973
Long Ms KMK, BA(Hons), L.Asst./Stud., Norfolk & Norwich Millennium L., Univ.Coll.London. [0059487] 09/04/2001
Long Miss NJ, BA(Hons), Inf.Offr., Univ.of Herts., Hertford Campus. [0057846] 09/09/1999 AF
Long Mr NW, BLib MBA MCLIP, Resident in Canada. [0029731] 20/10/1978
Long Miss P, BA MCLIP, L.Mgr., Norbury, Croydon Leisure Serv. [0009076] 24/07/1969
Long Mrs SE, (was Brooks), MCLIP, Sch.Lib., Nicholas Breakspear Sch., St.Albans. [0028264] 26/10/1977
Long Ms SL, BA(Hons) MSc, Asst.Lib., Dept.of Health L., Leeds. [0058094] 29/10/1999
Long Mrs T, (was Osborne), BA MCLIP, Sen.Mgr., W.Div., Weymouth L., Dorset C.C. [0037983] 01/01/1985
Long Mr TN, BA DipLib MCLIP CertNatSci, Inf.Offr., Clifford Chance, LLP. [0036312] 02/10/1983
Longbottom Mr PR, BSc(Hons) MCLIP DipLIS, Lib., PG Med.Cent., Lancaster Royal Infirmary. [0043251] 11/10/1989
Longden Mrs C, MLS MCLIP, Retired. [0009079] 27/01/1965
Longden Mr PR, MCLIP, Res.Mgr., Acquisitions Sect., Bucks.Co.L.H.Q. [0018242] 05/10/1972
Longden Ms R, Language Cent.Res.Lib., Univ.of Leeds. [0051525] 22/03/1995
Longhorn Mr RA, BSc MSc MCLIP, Employment not known. [0060857] 12/12/2001
Longman Mrs E, Unemployed. [0061215] 16/04/2002
Longmuir Ms SJ, BA(Hons), Inf.Specialist, NBS Serv., Newcastle. [0054266] 11/11/1996
Longstaff Mrs J, (was Mcgrath), MCLIP, Bibl.Serv.Lib., Darlington Bor.Council. [0009392] 01/01/1966
Lonsdale Mr D, MA(Hons) MSc MCLIP, Asst.Lib., Coatbridge Coll., Lanarkshire. [0048079] 03/11/1992
Lonsdale Miss JM, BLib MCLIP, Prim.Sch.Teacher, Eastfield Sch., Leics. [0028331] 01/11/1977
Looney Ms LC, MA MSc Econ., Lib., Berwin Leighton Paisner, London. [0061486] 19/08/2002
Lord Miss J, BA MCLIP, Head of L.& Inf.Serv., Royal Coll.of Nursing, London. [0033034] 17/10/1980
Lord Miss KD, BA(Hons), Grad.Trainee, Exeter. [0060004] 21/11/2001
Lord Mr P, BA MA MCLIP, Acting Employment & Train.Mgr., Sheffield Futures, Sheffield. [0033629] 28/01/1981
Lord Mrs P, (was Tatton), BSc DipLib MCLIP, Stock Mgmt.& Requests Lib., Bolton M.B.C., ` . [0039764] 01/07/1986
Lord Mr PW, BSc MSc AFIMA MCLIP, Employment not known. [0060724] 12/12/2001
Lord Mrs SI, (was Holmes), MCLIP, Retired. [0007123] 23/09/1957
Lorimer Mr CR, BA MCLIP, Asst.Lib.:Stock & Circulation, S.Lanarkshire Ls., E.Kilbride. [0042078] 03/10/1988
Lorimer Miss HK, BA DipLib MCLIP, Unemployed. [0038731] 04/10/1983
Lorimer Mrs JE, DipILS, Asst.Lib.(Job Share), Angus Council, Arbroath. [0054298] 20/11/1996
Loring Miss A, BA(Hons) DipLib MA MCLIP, Inf.& Knowledge Mgr., S.W.of England Reg.Devel.Agency. [0054003] 17/10/1996

Lornie Miss MA, BA DipLIS, Sen.Inf.Offr., Communities Scotland, Glasgow. [0054313] 18/11/1996
Lorusso Mrs H, (was King), MCLIP, Stock Systems Mgr., L.B.of Hillingdon, Cent.L., Uxbridge. [0008383] 26/03/1970
Loth-Hill Mrs JM, MA, Learning Res.Lib., William Howard Sch., Brampton, Cumbria. [0038082] 11/01/1985
Lott Ms M, BA(Hons) MA, Gateway Mgr., Nat.Maritime Mus. [0054952] 28/05/1997
Loud Mrs S, Membership Inf.Offr., Assoc.of Brit.Credit Unions, Manchester. [0055667] 07/11/1997
Louden Mr M, BA(Hons), Educ.Lib., S.E.E.L.B., L.H.Q., Ballynahinch. [0042034] 08/08/1988
Louden Mrs NE, (was John), BA(Hons), Inf.Offr., Eversheds Solicitors, Cardiff. [0050013] 16/03/1994
Loughborough Mrs TJ, BSc MCLIP, Employment not known. [0060501] 11/12/2001
Loughlin Mrs AL, (was Howarth), BA(Hons) MCLIP, Sch.Lib., Leyland St.Mary's R.C.(GM)Tech.Coll, Preston. [0046823] 11/02/1992
Loughran Miss A, MA MLitt DipLib MCLIP, Self-employed Consultant in, Librarianship., Tel&Fax:(028) 90729353. [0041371] 15/11/1987
Loughridge Mr FB, MA FCLIP, Lect., L.& Inf.Sci., Sheffield Univ. [0030468] 16/02/1979 FE 01/04/2002
Loughridge Mrs JI, (was Hamilton), BA MCLIP, Sen.L.Asst., Univ.of Sheffield. [0006204] 25/10/1966
Louison Miss P, BA MCLIP DMS, Subject Lib., Thames Valley Univ., London. [0034703] 11/02/1982
Loutit Ms NH, MA DipILS, L.Offr., City of Edinburgh Council. [0057334] 15/02/1999
Lovatt Mrs CA, (was Barker), BA MCLIP, Princ.Lib.-Child.& Y.P.Serv., Hanley L., Stoke on Trent. [0042578] 10/01/1989
Lovatt Mr D, BA MCLIP, Grp.Lib., Birmingham L.Serv. [0009099] 07/03/1969
Love Miss A, BA(Hons) MCLIP, Sen.Consultant, Records Systems Australia pty Ltd., Sydney. [0046242] 07/10/1991
Love Mr AG, MSc MCLIP, Employment not known. [0028623] 01/01/1978
Love Miss AME, PGDipILS, Unemployed. [0061360] 21/06/2002
Love Miss H, BA MCLIP, Lib., N.Area, Northumberland C.C. [0018894] 02/10/1972
Love Mr JG, BA DipLib MCLIP, Learning Res.Cent.Mgr., Coll.of N.E.London, Muswell Hill Cent. [0033313] 23/10/1980
Love Mrs JH, (was Miller), MA DipLib MCLIP, Project Offr.(L.& Inf.), N.Lanarkshire Council. [0037049] 07/02/1984
Love Miss JI, MCLIP, Life Member. [0009102] 16/04/1943
Love Mrs LR, (was Wineberg), BA DipLib MCLIP, Princ.Lib.-Children & Educ., L.B.of Enfield., London. [0027043] 10/01/1977
Love Ms SM, LLB BA DipEd CertInfSc MCLIP, NLIS - Mgr.,Anglian, Environment Agency, Peterborough. [0043198] 02/10/1989
Love Mr WM, BA MCLIP, Comm.Lib., N.Lanarkshire Council. [0026766] 26/10/1976
Love Rodgers Mrs CR, (was Love), MA MA MCLIP ILTA, Asst.Lib., Learner Support (Arts & IET), Open Univ. [0053151] 01/04/1996
Lovecy Dr IC, MA PhD HonFCLIP FCLIP, L.Consultant, Univ.of Wales,Bangor, Gwynedd. [0020617] 01/05/1973 FE 18/11/1993
Loveday Miss CL, BA(Hons), Stud., Univ.Coll.London. [0061605] 03/10/2002
Loveday Mrs EM, Business Inf.Offr., Irwin Mitchell, Sheffield. [0058461] 25/02/2000 AF
Loveland Mr A, BA(Hons) MA, Sen.L.Asst., Univ.of London L. [0055837] 21/11/1997
Lovell Mrs JR, (was Prowse), BA FCLIP, Life Member. [0009106] 04/10/1945 FE 01/01/1965
Lovell Mr LG, FCLIP, Life Member. [0009107] 03/10/1943 FE 01/01/1946
Lovell Mrs SL, L.Asst., Stourbridge L., Dudley M.B.C. [0057592] 13/05/1999
Lovelock Mr W, MCLIP, Retired. [0009105] 07/02/1949
Loveluck Ms RC, BA MCLIP, Open Learning Mgr., G.C.H.Q., Cheltenham. [0033499] 05/11/1981
Loveridge Mrs G, (was Smith), MBA BA MCLIP, Sen.Grp.Lib., Coalville Grp., Leics.L.& Inf.Serv. [0013574] 05/11/1971
Loveridge Mrs J, (was Clarkson), MCLIP, Ref.Lib., Lancs.L., Lancaster. [0009112] 19/09/1962
Loveridge Mrs MA, (was Taylor), BA MCLIP, Lib., Cardinal Newman Catholic Sch., Hove. [0017295] 22/03/1963
Lovett Mr JH, FCLIP, Life Member. [0009116] 06/02/1951 FE 01/01/1959
Lovibond Mrs R, MCLIP, Sch.Lib.(Job Share), Ashcroft High Sch., Luton,Beds. [0014452] 01/01/1969
Low Mrs H, (was Corris), BA MCLIP, Lib., Clevedon L., N.Somerset L.& Inf.Serv. [0028281] 01/01/1985
Low Miss J, BSc, Project Editor-Indexing, The HW Wilson Co., Dublin. [0043363] 26/10/1989
Low Miss YM, MSc MCLIP, Employment not known. [0050341] 01/07/1994
Lowden Mrs M, (was Mckerlie), MCLIP, L.& Inf.Worker, Dundee City Council. [0020210] 01/01/1971
Lowe Mr A, FCLIP, Retired. [0009121] 13/10/1947 FE 01/01/1969
Lowe Mrs AH, (was Boyd), BA MCLIP, Area Co-ordinator, Notts.C.C./Comm., W.Bridgford. [0033128] 10/10/1980
Lowe Mrs CE, (was Hosker), MCLIP, Unemployed. [0025053] 04/11/1975
Lowe Mrs HM, BA(Hons), stud., Manchester, [0061838] 15/11/2002
Lowe Mrs I, (was Condon), MCLIP, Retired. [0009125] 28/03/1947
Lowe Miss J, Head of Inf.Serv., Eversheds, Newcastle upon Tyne. [0036927] 12/01/1984
Lowe Mrs K, BSc MCLIP, Lib., Cheshire C.C., Macclesfield L. [0023570] 14/01/1975
Lowe Ms P, Asst.Lib., Bldg.Design Ptnrshp., Manchester. [0046624] 27/11/1991
Lowe Mr R, BSc MCLIP, Inf.Analyst, Brit.Standards Inst. [0009128] 14/01/1972

Lowe Miss SM, BA(Hons) MA, Asst.Lib., Univ.of Brighton, E.Sussex. [0050615] 01/10/1994
Lowen Ms TB, (was Sykes), BLib(Hons) MCLIP, Lib., N.Derbys.Tertiary Coll., Chesterfield. [0037324] 02/07/1984
Lower Mrs SB, (was Harris), DipLib MCLIP, Learning Resources Mgr., Penwith Coll., Penzance, Cornwall. [0034486] 12/11/1981
Lowes Mrs M, (was Rowley), BA(Hons), Inf.& Learning Res.Mgr., Kenton Sch., Newcastle-upon-Tyne. [0047852] 21/10/1992
Lowing Mr AC, BA(Hons) MA, Corp.& Bibl.Asst., London Business Sch.L. [0058541] 01/04/2000
Lowis Mr DR, BA MCLIP, Serv.Advisor, Univ.of Lincs.& Humberside. [0020986] 03/09/1973
Lowis Mrs J, BA MCLIP, Retired. [0009136]16/09/1940
Lowley Ms S, BA(Hons) MSc, Intranet Team Leader, Environment Agency. [0057714] 09/07/1999
Lowndes Mrs M, (was Atkin), MCLIP, L.Mgr.-Res., Carcroft L.H.Q., Doncaster M.B.C. [0028982] 01/01/1959
Lowry Mr FT, MCLIP, Support & Devel.Lib., Plymouth L.& Inf.Serv., Cent.L. [0009142] 19/09/1963
Lowry Mr J, BA MCLIP, Life Member. [0009143] 25/03/1958
Lowther Mr CG, BA(Hons) DipILM, Comm.Inf.Offr., Seaforth Inf.Network Group, Liverpool. [0054324] 21/11/1996
Lowther Mr SR, BA DipLib, Asst.Lib.-Catg., Wellcome Trust, London. [0038111] 20/01/1985
Loy Mr JA, BA MA, [0053918] 10/10/1996
Loyd Mr S, MCLIP, Lib., Building Serv.Res.& Inf.Assoc. [0009147] 07/10/1969
Lubarr Ms K, BA, p./t.L.Asst., Maitland Robinson L., Downing Coll.,Cambridge. [0059328] 07/02/2001
Lubega Miss G, Acq.Lib., Norwegian Inst.of Public Health, Norway. [0058240] 22/11/1999
Luc Ms DL, (was Wyness), BA MSc MCLIP, Lib., Craigholme Sch., Glasgow. [0042723] 13/02/1989
Lucas Ms C, BSc MSc MCLIP, Position unknown, Girton Inf.Serv., Cambridge. [0060860] 12/12/2001
Lucas Mrs E, (was Garland), BSc MCLIP, Head of Kempe Cent.& Lib., Imperial Coll.of Sci.Tech.& Med., Ashford. [0009152] 07/10/1966
Lucas Mrs L, (was Broome), MCLIP, Lib., Warwick Sch. [0009154]18/10/1966
Lucas Mrs N, (was Norman), MCLIP, Life Member. [0009157] 30/03/1954
Lucas Mrs P, (was Jeavons), BA MCLIP, P/t.Abstractor, L.& Inf.Sci.Abstracts, Bowker-Saur, Abstracts & Indexers. [0009159] 12/09/1960
Lucas Mrs RMA, (was Phillips), MCLIP, Area Lib., Crawley L., W.Sussex C.C.L.Serv. [0020095] 21/01/1973
Lucas Mrs S, BA(Hons), Asst.Lib., TFPL. [0056762] 08/10/1998
Lucas Mr ST, MA FRSA FCLIP JP, Life Member, 3 Welham Rd., Retford,Notts.,DN22 6TN. [0009161] 01/10/1953 FE 01/01/1965
Luccock Mr GR, BA MCLIP, Head of Serv.-Recreation & Culture, Trafford Lifelong Learning Dir., Trafford M.B.C. [0009163] 05/11/1967
Lucking Mrs JM, (was Sellwood), BA DipLib MCLIP, Stud. [0035725] 19/01/1983
Lucy Mrs CM, (was Barran), BA MCLIP, Design Support Asst., Dulwich Coll., London. [0034579] 01/01/1982
Luddington Mr RW, BSc MIQA MCLIP, Database Mgr., Northants.LIS. [0026460] 18/10/1976
Luddington Ms SC, BA DipLib MCLIP, Inf.Research Mgr., Logica plc, London. [0034170] 05/10/1981
Ludford Miss J, MCLIP, Life Member. [0009166] 30/01/1958
Luke Miss BM, Stud., Univ.Aberystwyth. [0059936] 08/11/2001
Luke Mr ER, DPA FRSA FCLIP, Retired. [0009174] 12/01/1932 FE 01/01/1935
Luke Mr JRG, BA DipLib MCLIP, Serv.Devel.Lib., Minehead Area, Somerset C.C. [0035295] 01/10/1982
Lukhele Dr LNM, BA DipLib&Info MPhil DPhil, Mgr., VJR Estate Agents, Swaziland. [0061487] 20/08/2002
Luland Mrs C, (was Machin), MCLIP, Lib.-Team Leader, Norfolk L.& Inf.Serv. [0004553] 25/09/1969
Lum Ms A, BSc DipLib MCLIP, The Earth Sci.Lib., The Natural Hist.Mus., London. [0021179] 01/10/1973
Lum Mr MCN, BA(Hons) DipILM MScILM, Comm.Lib., (Job Share), Coventry City L., Cent.L. [0058124] 04/11/1999
Lumbard Mrs M, (was Sweeney), BA MCLIP, Retired. [0009177] 01/09/1949
Lumsden Miss D, MCLIP, Asst.Lib., Univ.L., Osnabrueck. [0009179] 14/01/1969
Lumsden Mr J, MCLIP, Asst., Durham Univ. L. [0009180] 12/10/1967
Lund Miss MS, MA, Unemployed. [0056635] 24/09/1998
Lund Mr OP, BSc MSc DipLib MCLIP, Academic Serv.Mgr.(Sci.), Loughborough Univ., Pilkington L. [0036442] 11/10/1983
Lundbaek Miss AE, MLIS, Web Content Super., Matchwork World Wide, Denmark. [0061191]08/04/2002
Lundbeck Mrs V, (was Haslam), MCLIP, p./t.Sen.Selection Support Lib., Askews L.Supply, Preston. [0006533] 05/04/1965
Lunn Miss C, Learning Support Super., Leeds Met. L. [0060893] 20/12/2001
Lunn Mr M, BSc, Employment not known. [0060201] 10/12/2001
Lunn Mrs RJ, (was Nazareth), BLib(Hons) MCLIP, L.Adviser, Sch.L.Serv., Co.L.H.Q., Chelmsford, Essex. [0024625] 22/06/1976
Lunn Ms SD, (was Evans), MA(Hons) DipLib MCLIP, Inf.Lib., Waterlooville L., Hants. [0009189] 15/10/1971
Lunnon Mrs JS, (was Wells), BA(Hons) CertEd MSc, Inf.Lib., Blackburn Coll., Lancs. [0044915] 14/01/1991
Lunny Miss CH, BLib, Lib., St.Albans L., Herts. [0038325] 19/03/1985
Lunt Mrs C, (was Martin), MCLIP, Dep.Head of Learning Resources, Mid Cheshire Coll., Northwich, Cheshire. [0030199] 05/06/1965
Lunt Mr MW, FCLIP, Life Member,Tel: 020 8399 8090. [0009191]04/09/1955 FE 01/01/1962
Lunt Mr R, BA MCLIP, Missionary Soc.Employee, S.American Mission Soc., Tunbridge Wells. [0009192] 13/10/1970

Lunt Mrs TL, (was Coombe), BA(Hons) MSc, Inf.Offr., Building Design Partnership, Sheffield. [0049521] 10/11/1993
Lupton Miss M, MCLIP, Dep.Lib., Barbican L., City of London. [0009195] 14/01/1963
Luscombe Mr RA, BA MLS MCLIP, Sen.Lib., Sch.L.Serv., Luton. [0034819] 12/03/1982
Lusher Miss AH, Inf.Specialist, UK Cochrane Cent., Cochrane Methodology Register. [0039399] 28/01/1986
Lusted Ms CA, BA(Hons) MA MCLIP, Child.Lib., L.B.of Barnet, Mill Hill L. [0057635] 07/06/1999
Lutman Mrs CA, (was Hope), MCLIP, Sch.Lib., Highworth Warneford Sch., Wilts. [0007160] 17/10/1966
Luton Mrs JL, BA DipIMLib, Unemployed. [0052522] 03/11/1995
Luxford Mr IW, BA MCLIP, Employment not known. [0060798] 12/12/2001
Luxmoore-Peake Ms F, BA(Hons) MA, Stud., Univ.of Brighton. [0058973] 13/10/2000
Luxton Mrs JE, BEd, p./t.Stud./Subject Lib., Univ.of Wales, Aberystwyth, Univ.of Plymouth. [0057856] 10/09/1999
Luxton Mr TJ, BA MCLIP, Lib., L.B.of Hackney. [0021551] 23/10/1973
Luyken Miss J, MCLIP, Retired. [0009204] 25/03/1955
Luzeckyj Ms AM, BA DipLib MCLIP, Campus Lib., Univ.of S.Australia, Adelaide. [0048610] 12/03/1993
Luzzi Ms AB, Stud., Oxford, Christ Church Coll. [0061669] 16/10/2002
Lyall Mrs SA, (was Young), BScEcon(Hons) MA, Inf.Asst., BPP Law School, London. [0057932] 04/10/1999
Lyden Mrs M, Acting Lib., Clydebank Coll., Clydebank. [0054909] 13/05/1997
Lydiatt Mrs AE, BEd DipLib MCLIP, Lend.Serv.Mgr.(Yth.), Sandwell M.B.C., W.Bromwich. [0035676] 01/01/1983
Lyle Mr RM, MCLIP, Life Member. [0009208] 01/01/1945
Lynam Miss M, Employee, The L., Dept.of Soc.Welfare, Dublin, Ireland. [0054388] 02/12/1996
Lynas Mrs HM, (was Dilworth), MCLIP, Retired. [0009210] 14/08/1954
Lynch Miss AE, BA(Hons), Stud. [0061512] 29/08/2002
Lynch Miss CA, BA(Hons) MA MCLIP, Asst.Lib., Royal Coll.of Nursing, London. [0047296] 06/07/1992
Lynch Mr CJ, BA DipILM MCLIP, Lib., Rotherham Gen.Hosp. [0049765] 06/12/1993
Lynch Mr J, MA DipLib MCLIP, Retired. [0024741] 04/10/1975
Lynch Prof MF, BSc PhD CChem HonFCLIP, Hon Fellow. [0060593] 11/12/2001 FE 01/04/2002
Lynch Ms RC, BA(Hons) MA MCLIP, Learning Resources Mgr., Surrey Inst.of Art & Design, Univ.Coll. [0038327] 19/03/1985
Lynch Mrs RJ, (was Gailey), BSc, Devel.Team Lib., Surrey C.C. [0046267] 21/10/1991
Lynch Miss SJ, BA, p./t/Stud./L.Asst., Univ.North London, Barbican L.London. [0059881] 29/10/2001
Lyndhurst Mrs MI, MCLIP, Employment not known. [0060416] 11/12/2001
Lyndon Mrs R, MA MA, Inf.Offr., Faulkner Browns, Newcastle upon Tyne. [0058708] 01/07/2000
Lynn Miss ITP, BA MLitt DipLib MCLIP, Lib., The London L. [0042658] 31/01/1989
Lynn Mr M, BA(Hons) DipIM MCLIP, Child.Lib., Larne N., N.E.E.L.B. [0057635] 16/03/1999
Lynn Mrs SV, (was Haigh), MCLIP, Learning Res.Cent.Mgr., Bridgwater Coll., Somerset. [0009213] 10/02/1968
Lynott Miss H, BA(Hons) DipInf, Inf.Adviser, Univ. of Surrey, Inf.Services, oehampton. [0058437] 11/02/2000
Lynwood Miss WJ, BA(Hons) MA MCLIP, Subject Lib.(Law), Middlesex Univ. [0055249] 09/09/1997
Lyon Dr EJ, BSc PhD MCLIP, Head of Res.& Multimedia Dept., Univ.of Surrey, George Edwards L. [0040109] 20/10/1986
Lyon Mrs LVA, (was Crighton), L.Co-ordinator, Eng.Lang.L., Lycee International, France. [0053408] 18/01/1996
Lyon Mrs PG, (was White), MA MCLIP, Lib.& Inf.Resources Mgr., Girls Day Sch.Trust, , London. [0017311] 27/11/1967
Lyon Mrs RM, BA MA MCLIP, Freelancing as Editor. [0037733] 23/10/1984
Lyon Ms WG, BA MSc(Econ) MCLIP, Sch.Lib., Fettes Coll., Edinburgh. [0051544] 01/04/1995
Lyons Miss CJ, Human Res.Offr., The Brit.Mus., London. [0056931] 10/11/1998
Lyons Miss D, MCLIP, Requests Lib., L.B.of Ealing. [0019294] 26/08/1972
Lyons Ms JA, BA DipLib, Inf.Mgr., SG London Branch. [0037121] 11/02/1984
Lyons Mrs SE, Learning Res.Asst., St.Brendan's Sixth Form Coll., Bristol. [0061281] 08/05/2002 AF
Lyth Miss M, BA MCLIP, Retired. [0009221] 22/01/1962
Lythall Mrs JM, (was Kyte), MCLIP, p./t.Lib., Worcs.Co.L., Stourport on Severn. [0018369] 12/10/1972
Lythgoe Mrs K, BA DipLIS MCLIP, Community Lib., Tameside M.B.C. [0039691] 05/03/1986
Lythgoe Mrs MW, (was Winchester), MCLIP, Retired. [0016113] 01/01/1954
Ma Ms LK, BA PGCE MLib MCLIP, Hosp.Lib., Caritas Med.Cent., Hong Kong. [0042512] 22/11/1988
Mabey Mr G, MA MCLIP, Open Learning Lib., L.B.of Lewisham. [0009225] 18/03/1971
Macari Mrs AE, BA, P./t.L.Asst., Rosyth Br.L., Fife Council. [0059553] 16/05/2001
MacArthur Mrs CE, (was Waite), BA(Hons) DipLib MCLIP, Lib., Wester Ross, c/o Ullapool Comm.L., Ullapool, Wester Ross. [0015176] 01/01/1972
MacArthur Mrs F, MA(Hons), Serv.Point Offf., Highland Council, Inverness. [0058889] 01/10/2000
MacArthur Mrs FM, (was McQuillan), MA DipLib MCLIP, Young Peoples Serv.Lib., E.Dunbartonshire Council. [0035562] 01/11/1982
Macarthur Mr CM, BA MSc MCLIP, Systems Lib., Southampton Inst., Southampton. [0019821] 20/11/1972

Macarthur Mr NJS, BSc(Hons) MSc, Temp.Periodicals Cat.Correction, Imperial War Museum, London. [0051222]   29/11/1994
Macartney Mr NS, MA DipLib MCLIP, Dir.-Inf.Serv., Univ.of Ulster, N.Ireland. [0009230] 21/08/1968
MacColl Mr JA, MA MEd DipLib MCLIP, Sellic Dir., Univ.of Edinburgh. [0036218]   01/08/1983
MacCormack Mr JAD, BSc IEng MIAgrE MCLIP, Retired. [0060228]   10/12/2001
MacCorquodale Ms MA, MA(Hons) DipLib MCLIP, Systems Mgr., DNM, Hants. [0046698]   16/12/1991
MacDermott Miss GE, BA(Hons), Learning Res.Mgr., Seaford Head Comm.Coll., E.Sussex. [0055969]   02/01/1998
MacDermott Mr PD, BA DipLib MCLIP, Div.Lib., Warwickshire Co.L., Leamington Spa. [0034090]   08/09/1981
MacDiarmaid-Gordon Mrs J, (was Quayle), FCLIP, Life Member. [0009311]   28/10/1935   FE 01/01/1943
MacDonald Mr AJ, MA, Asst.Ed. [0057943]   01/10/1999
MacDonald Ms AM, BA MCLIP, Clerk, Aldershot Police Station. [0009314]   01/01/1971
MacDonald Mr BI, MBE MA MCLIP, Retired. [0009317]   12/03/1962
MacDonald Mr CJ, BA MBA DipLib MCLIP, L.& Inf.Serv.Mgr., Wakefield L.& Inf.Serv. [0024435]   21/07/1975
MacDonald Mr CN, MA DipLib, Record Clerk, N.Devon Record Office, Barnstaple. [0035537]   28/10/1982
MacDonald Mr DN, BA DipLIS, Unemployed. [0055206]   08/08/1997
MacDonald Miss E, MA(Hons) DipILS, Doc.Supply Mgr., The Scottish Parliament, Edinburgh. [0056114]   23/02/1998
MacDonald Mrs EMT, (was Wylie), MA DLIS, Sen.Asst.Lib., Nat.L.of Scotland. [0039210]   01/01/1986
MacDonald Ms HC, BA(Hons), Asst.Mgr.Inf., Arts & Business, London. [0058303]   23/12/1999
MacDonald Mr IA, BA MCLIP, Lib., Mott MacDonald Ltd., Brighton. [0037128]   12/02/1984
MacDonald Mr JC, BA(Hons) MCLIP, Web Site Mgr., Inf.Serv.Unit, E.Sussex C.C., Lewes. [0053511]   10/07/1996
MacDonald Miss L, MA(Hons) MSc, Inf.Offr., IPA, London. [0058087]   26/10/1999
MacDonald Mr LT, BA(Hons), L.Asst., Lubricants UK Ltd, Reading. [0061800]   13/11/2002
Macdonald Miss A, MCLIP, Retired. [0009313]   07/09/1949
Macdonald Mrs CG, MCLIP, Tech.Lib., Harley Haddow Partnership, Edinburgh. [0032440]   01/04/1980
Macdonald Miss EM, BA MCLIP, Lib., Scottish Exec., Edinburgh. [0021619]   27/11/1973
Macdonald Miss FV, MA DipLib MCLIP, Sen.Offr., L., W.Dunbartonshire Council, Dumbarton. [0030474]   12/02/1979
Macdonald Miss MIB, MA MCLIP, Life Member. [0009330]   26/09/1950
Macdonald Miss NE, BA(Hons), Stud., Univ.Sheffield. [0059885]   29/10/2001
MacDougall Mrs FA, BA MCLIP, Lib., Denny High Sch. [0041369] 12/11/1987
MacDougall Dr JJ, (was Roddick), PhD BA MCLIP, Inf.Research Consultant. [0012606]   22/02/1972
Macdougall Miss S, MA MCLIP, Asst.Princ.Offr., Inverclyde L. [0026462]   02/10/1976
Mace Mrs J, (was Burke), MCLIP, Sch.Lib., Godstone Prep.Sch., High Wycombe. [0009350]   13/08/1964
Mace Mrs SJ, (was Berry), BA MCLIP DMS MIMgt, Inf.Editor, Univ.of Wales, Swansea. [0023531] 01/01/1975
MacEachen Mr AJ, BA MCLIP, Team Lib., Cultural & Leisure Services, Glasgow City Council. [0024436]   07/08/1975
MacEachern Mrs E, (was Duthie), LLB, Researcher, 39 Deanston Gdns., Doune, FK16 6AZ, Tel:(01786) 841144. [0045979]   05/08/1991
Macey Mr IR, MCLIP, Lib., Halcrow Grp.Ltd., Swindon, Wilts. [0023261]   20/11/1974
Macfadyen Mrs JL, (was Mackie), MA(Hons) DipLib, Sch.Lib., Our Lady's High Sch., Motherwell. [0048188]   13/11/1992
MacFarlane Mrs H, BA MCLIP, Med.Lib., Univ.of Newcastle upon Tyne. [0023071]   30/10/1974
Macfarlane Mr JM, MA(Hons), Stud., Robert Gordon Univ. [0056389]   01/07/1998
Macfarlane Miss MAC, FCLIP, Life Member, 15A Normanton Rd., S.Croydon, Surrey, CR2 7AE. [0009366]   01/01/1931   FE 01/01/1933
Macfarlane Ms SE, BA, Lib., Support Serv.-Database Maintenance, Notts. [0046029]   06/09/1991
MacGillivray Mrs MD, (was Anthony), Life Member. [0024056]   01/04/1975
MacGrath Miss JB, MCLIP, Lib., La Retraite High Sch., London. [0009393]   07/09/1966
MacGregor Miss A, BA(Hons) MA, Stud., Univ.Coll.London. [0058924]   04/10/2000
MacGregor Mrs EM, (was Paine), BA MCLIP, Asst.Lib., The Scottish Poetry L., Edinburgh. [0011155]   01/05/1971
MacGregor Mrs G, BA(Hons), Stud., Strathclyde Univ. [0061780]   05/11/2002
MacGregor Mr GRW, BA(Hons), Stud., Univ.of Strathclyde. [0059946]   09/11/2001
MacGregor Mr IG, BA BSc MPhil CBiol MIBi FCLIP, Retired. [0060227]   10/12/2001   FE 01/04/2002
MacGregor Ms JC, MA(Hons) MSc(Econ) MCLIP, Lib., GCHQ, Cheltenham. [0053761]   01/10/1996
Macgregor Mr AN, MA MCLIP, Life Member. [0009397]   01/01/1963
MacGuigan Ms DM, BA(Hons) MLIS, Knowledge Development Co-Ordinator, Bucks Shared Serv. [0061795]   08/11/2002
MacHale Mrs E, BSc DipLib MCLIP, Coll.Lib., The Henley Coll., Oxon. [0019562]   08/11/1972
Machell Mrs J, (was Tinmouth), MBE MCLIP, Retired, 20 Kenton Close, Hartburn, Stockton-on-Tees, TS18 5EX. [0009405]   21/03/1955

Machin Mrs EA, (was Agar), BA, Sen.L.Asst., Radcliffe Sci.L., Oxford. [0038252]   12/02/1985
Machinnes Mr NC, Serv.Devel.Offr., Glasgow City Council. [0061494]   19/08/2002   **AF**
Macho Mr J, BSc(Hons) MA, L.Asst., Camomile Street L. [0056942]   09/11/1998
Macindoe Mrs JH, BA, Lib., Birkenhead 6th Form Coll. [0058018]   13/10/1999
MacInnes Mr A, MA MSc, Bookseller, Waterstones, Renfrew. [0061553]   18/09/2002
MacInnis Mrs JS, (was Causer), Sen.L.Asst.-Child.Serv., Barbican L., Corporation of London. [0047063]   09/04/1992   **AF**
Macintosh Mrs JJ, (was Saunders), BSc DipLIS MCLIP, Retired. [0045913]   18/07/1991
MacIntyre Miss CM, BA MCLIP, L.Offr., Edinburgh City L. [0031892]   08/01/1980
MacIver Mr D, BSc BD DipILM, Asst.Lib., Nazarene Theological Coll., Manchester. [0056296]   08/05/1998
Mack Ms CS, BA(Hons), Asst.Lib., Foreign & Commonwealth Off., London. [0049966]   01/02/1994
MacKay Ms I, BSc MCLIP, Employment unknown. [0060345]   10/12/2001
MacKay Miss JI, BA(Hons), Stud., Robert Gordon Univ. [0061744] 31/10/2002
MacKay Ms AJE, BA MA MCLIP, Ch.Lib.& Head of L.Serv., The Bishopsgate Inst., London. [0021147]   06/10/1973
Mackay Mr DM, MA(Hons) MA MCLIP, Enquiry Serv.Mgr., Univ.of Oxford, Cairns L. [0048410]   05/01/1993
Mackay Mr DNB, BA DipLib MCLIP, Ref.& Inf.Lib., Doncaster M.B.C. [0023345]   19/11/1974
Mackay Ms ES, BA MCLIP MSc MIMgt, Support & Devel.Mgr., Renfrewshire Council, Dept.Educ.& Leisure Serv. [0024748]   07/10/1975
Mackay Mr H, BA MCLIP, Retired. [0009433]   20/03/1958
Mackay Mr I, BA MCLIP, Lib./Copyright Licensing Offr., Highland Council, Culloden Academy, Inverness. [0009434]   24/10/1966
Mackay Mrs IA, (was Horne), MA MCLIP, p./t.Lect., Edinburgh's Telford Coll., Dept.of L.& Inf.Sci. [0023093]   24/10/1974
Mackay Miss J, BA(Hons) MCLIP, Inf.Serv.Lib., Aberdeenshire L.& Inf.Serv., Oldmeldrum. [0048566]   17/02/1993
Mackay Mrs JEA, (was Boyers), BA DipLib MCLIP, Peak Relief, Essex C.C., Witham. [0032875]   07/10/1980
Mackay Ms MA, DipLib BEd(Hons) MCLIP, Asst.Lib., H.M.Treasury, London. [0026463]   01/10/1976
Mackay Ms MS, BA, Unemployed. [0053056]   04/03/1996
Mackay Ms RA, (was Dukes), MA(Hons) MA MCLIP, Lib., Marathon Oil UK Ltd., Aberdeen. [0044840]   12/12/1990
Mackay Mrs RC, (was Cross), MA MCLIP, Sch.Lib., St.Mary's High Sch., Herts. [0021036]   06/10/1973
Mackay Mr RR, BSc MIMgt MIPD MCLIP, Research Fellow, Edinburgh Business Sch. [0033040]   11/10/1980
Mackay Mr S, BA MCLIP, Cultural Serv.Lib., Fife Council L.(East), Cupar. [0025897]   21/04/1976
Mackay Mrs ST, (was Hague Mackenzie), Retired. [0026168]   06/10/1948
Mackechnie Mr JW, MA MCLIP, p./t.Lib., Learning & Teaching Scotland, Glasgow. [0019523]   16/10/1970
Mackender Ms EM, BSc MPhil DipLib DipMa MCLIP, Employment not known. [0060108]   07/12/2001
Mackenna Mr RO, MA MCLIP, Life Member. [0009448]   19/02/1937
MacKenzie Mrs CL, BA(Hons), Lib., Workington L., Cumbria C.C. [0055655]   24/10/1997
MacKenzie Mrs FM, (was Watson), MA DipLib DipEdTech MCLIP, Dir.of L.& Inf.Cent., Giggleswick Sch., Settle. [0039321]   13/01/1986
Mackenzie Mrs AA, (was Brown), MBE FCLIP, Retired. [0001835]   29/01/1953   FE 01/01/1967
Mackenzie Mr AG, MA MCLIP, Life Member. [0009450]   12/02/1951
Mackenzie Mrs AM, (was Steele), BA DipLib DipEdTech MCLIP, Tutor Lib., Moray Coll., Elgin. [0032889]   02/04/1981
Mackenzie Mr D, MA(Hons) DipILS, Sen.L.Asst., Kings Coll.London. [0052838]   02/01/1996
Mackenzie Mrs JC, BA MCLIP, Lib., Bibl.D.Inst.Am.Engl.Garten., Univ.Munich. [0019309]   16/08/1972
Mackenzie Ms JM, BA MA MCLIP, Ch.Lib., Scottish Exec., Edinburgh. [0031365]   15/10/1979
Mackenzie Miss MF, DHMSA MCLIP, Inf.Sci., PIRA Internat., Leatherhead. [0021242]   04/10/1973
Mackenzie Miss R, BSc MSc MCLIP, Asst.Lib., Chartered Insurance Inst., London. [0051695]   19/05/1995
Mackey Ms AL, BA MCLIP, Princ.Lib.-Child.Serv., Stoke on Trent City Council, Hanley L. [0030475]   13/02/1979
Mackie Mr AR, MA(Hons), Inf.Asst., Univ.of Aberdeen. [0055250] 28/08/1997
Mackie Ms C, (was Bennett), MCLIP, Sen.Lib., Warwickshire C.C., Leamington L. [0009467]   01/01/1971
Mackie Mrs EH, (was Jones), BSc PhD, Stud., City Univ. [0043946]   01/03/1990
Mackie Miss MM, MA(Hons) MSc, Subject Lib.(Modern Lang.& Music), Glasgow Univ.L. [0053768]   01/11/1996
Mackie Mrs S, BA DipLib MCLIP, Lib., Brit.Museum Dept.of Ethnography L., London. [0040449]   09/02/1987
Mackin Mrs HD, (was Roberts), BA DipLib MCLIP, Dep.Lib., Barnardos L., Ilford, Essex. [0029415]   01/07/1978
Mackinnon Miss AM, BA(Hons) MCLIP, Inf.Scientist., Scottish Environ.Protection Agency, Stirling. [0028627]   12/01/1978
Mackinnon Mr NA, MA DipLib MCLIP, Business Serv.Mgr., Epixtech Ltd. [0021646]   18/12/1973
Mackness Mrs L, (was Rumble), MCLIP, Unemployed. [0049480]   21/09/1966
Mackown Miss SE, BSc MSc MCLIP, Inf.Mgr., Lupton Fawcett, Leeds. [0043327]   19/10/1989
Mackwell Miss C, MA B LITT MCLIP, Sen.Asst.Lib., Lambeth P.L. [0009483]   09/10/1970

MacLachlan Ms EA, MA FCLIP, Dir.Elect.Record & Document Mgmnt., DTI, London. [0024749]   08/10/1975   FE 01/04/2002
Maclachlan Miss EC, BA DipLib, Unemployed. [0044193]   04/07/1990
Maclachlan Mr HC, MA FCLIP, Life Member, 3 Cedar Grove, Cardross, G82 5JW, Tel.0389 841748. [0009486]   15/02/1956   FE 01/01/1967
Maclaine Mrs J, (was Williams), BA DipLib MCLIP MSc, Campus L.Mgr., Napier Univ., Edinburgh. [0043585]   09/11/1989
MacLaren Mrs C, (was Davies), BA(Hons), Lib., Kent Coll., Canterbury. [0009490]   01/01/1965
MacLean Ms CJ, MA MEd DipLib MCLIP, Mgr., Sch.Ethos Network, Univ.of Edinburgh. [0037727]   18/10/1984
MacLean Mrs CM, (was Scarfe), BA, Lib., Rugby L., Warks. [0025650]   13/01/1976
MacLean Mr D, MA(Hons) DipILS MCLIP, Learning Resource Co-ordinator, Auchterarder High Sch., Perth & Kinross. [0055476]   17/10/1997
MacLean Mr H, MA DipLib MCLIP, Area Lib., E.Ayrshire. [0044924]   16/01/1991
MacLean Mrs S, (was Marshall), MA MCLIP, Retired. [0009507]   17/02/1957
Maclean Mrs AD, (was Blair), BA DipEurHum MCLIP AssociateCIPD, L.Administrator, Univ.of Strathclyde, Andersonian L. [0028503]   23/11/1977
Maclean Mrs GM, BA MEd MCLIP, Lib., State Hosp., Carstairs. [0041894]   27/04/1988
Maclean Miss LJO, BA, Sch.Lib., Perth & Kinross Council, Perth High Sch. [0041164]   10/07/1987
MacLeavy Mrs VA, BA DipEd DipLib MCLIP, Moravian Manse, 51 South Street, Leominster, Herefordshire, Tel.01568-613754. [0017333]   02/10/1969
MacLellan Miss F, Stud., Loughborough Univ. [0061799]   13/11/2002
Maclellan Mrs IM, (was Lees), BA MCLIP, Sen.Lib., Glasgow City L.& Arch. [0034961]   14/05/1982
MacLennan Mr A, MA MSc, Lect., Robert Gordon Univ., Aberdeen. [0046744]   14/01/1992
MacLeod Mr AD, B LIB MCLIP, Sen.Lib., Lancs.Co.L., Preston. [0029999]   31/10/1978
MacLeod Ms CME, BSc MSc MCLIP, Sunday Lib., Queen Mary & Westfield Coll., Univ.of London. [0040465]   02/02/1987
MacLeod Mrs J, (was Brannan), BA(Hons) MA, Lib., Weymouth L., Dorset C.C. [0044828]   10/12/1990
MacLeod Mr JC, Contract Super., Hays Inf.Management. [0053446]   01/07/1996
MacLeod Miss LM, BA DipLib MCLIP, Lib., N.Tyneside M.B.C., Wallsend L. [0035435]   01/10/1982
MacLeod Mr NG, BA DipIT MCLIP, Res.Cent.Coordinator, Dundee City Council. [0042546]   06/12/1988
MacLeod Mr RA, MA DipLib MCLIP, Sen.Faculty Lib., Heriot-Watt Univ., Edinburgh. [0025377]   07/01/1976
Macleod Mrs A, MA, Stud., Strathclyde Univ. [0061008]   30/01/2002
Macleod Mrs CJ, (was Lonie), MA MCLIP, Inf.Specialist, Agilent Tech., S.Queensferry. [0038434]   25/04/1985
Macleod Mrs DH, (was Mansley), BLib MCLIP, Asst.Lib., Lancs.Co.L., Preston. [0029736]   04/10/1978
Macleod Mrs EJ, (was Devine), MCLIP, A-V Lib., W.Dunbartonshire Council, Clydebank. [0003914]   04/11/1970
Macleod Mrs EK, MCLIP, Retired. [0027416]   10/02/1958
Macleod Mr M, BA, Lib., Instant L., Loughborough. [0061538]   17/09/2002
Macleod Ms M, MA(Hons) MLitt MSc, IT Adviser (Special Needs), Glasgow Univ. [0044664]   21/11/1990
Macleod Miss S, MA(Hons) PGDipILS, Asst.Lib., N.Glasgow Univ., Hosp.NHS Trust. [0059058]   01/11/2000
MacMahon Mr TM, BA DipLib, Lib., Herbert Smith, London. [0045516]   28/02/1991
Macmahon Ms BBP, BA(Hons) DipLib, Membership Admin//Asst.Accountant., The London L. [0048766]   12/05/1993
MacManus Miss C, BA(Hons) MSc(Econ), Lib., Winckworth Sherwood, Wesminster. [0054833]   21/04/1997
MacMaster Mr T, MA(Hons) DipILS MCLIP, Lib.Res.Mgr., Lauder Coll., Dunfermline. [0047740]   21/11/1990
Macmillan Miss AL, MA(Hons), Stud., Strathclyde Univ. [0059937]   08/11/2001
Macmurray Miss L, BSc, Stud., Stratclyde Univ. [0060985]   25/01/2002
MacNab Ms LM, MA(Hons) MA MCLIP, Asst.Lib., Guildhall L., London. [0044567]   29/10/1990
Macnair Miss MA, BA MCLIP, Recruitment Consultant, Hays IT, Bristol. [0044618]   07/11/1990
MacNamara Miss F, BA DIP LIB MCLIP, Lib., Southall L. [0030326]   12/01/1979
MacNaughtan Mr A, BA DMS MIMgt MCLIP, City Lib., Plymouth City Council. [0009544]   16/10/1969
MacNeil Miss JK, BSc MA MCLIP, Coll.Lib., Barony Coll., Dumfries. [0051220]   29/11/1994
MacNeill Mrs DMA, BA(Hons) CertEd, L.Mgr., St.Gregory's Middle Sch., Bedford. [0057607]   26/05/1999
MacNeill Mr N, BA DipLib, Unemployed. [0036416]   12/10/1983
Macneill Mr M, MCLIP, Sen.Lib., Young Peoples Serv., Renfrewshire Council. [0020308]   20/01/1973
Macoustra Mrs JE, Asia Aacific Reg.Lib.& Inf.Offr., Credit Suisse First Boston(HK)Ltd., Hong Kong. [0057609]   26/05/1999
Macphail Miss AC, MA(Hons) DipILS MCLIP, Sch.Lib., James Hamilton Academy, E.Ayrshire Council. [0056872]   01/10/1998
MacPherson Miss MA, Stud., Univ.of Wales, Aberystwyth, & L.Asst., Bournemouth Univ., Poole, Dorset. [0052725]   27/11/1995
Macpherson Mrs C, (was Smeall), MA MCLIP, Lib.,Inf.Serv., Edinburgh City L. [0009558]   06/03/1962
Macpherson Mr EA, BA(Hons), Res.Worker, Mitchell St.Comm.Educ.Cent., Dundee. [0041252]   21/10/1987

Macpherson Miss F, MA DipLib MCLIP, Sen.Adult L.& Inf.Worker, Dundee City Council. [0034124]   01/10/1981
Macpherson Ms K, BSc(Hons) DipILS MCLIP, Health Inf.Sci., Health Tech Board of Scotland, Glasgow. [0052620]   13/11/1995
Macpherson Miss L, MCLIP, Sen.Lib.N.E.Area, Cultural & Leisure Serv.L., Mitchell L.Glasgow. [0021236]   04/10/1973
Macpherson Mrs T, BSc, Stud., Univ.of Northumbria at Newcastle. [0058414]   04/02/2000
Macquarrie Mr AD, DipLib MCLIP, L.& Inf.Offr., Scottish Inst.for Residential Child, Care, Univ.of Strathclyde. [0049555]   09/11/1993
MacRae Mr I, BA MCLIP, Princ.Lib., Perth & Kinross L., AK Bell L., Perth. [0009569]   02/10/1968
Macrae Miss J, BA DipEdTech MCLIP, Retired. [0009570]   17/02/1959
Macrae Mr JB, MA MCLIP, Dist.Lib., Comm.Inf., Welwyn Garden City L., Herts.C.C. [0023347]   22/11/1974
Macrae-Gibson Miss RK, BA(Hons) MA MCLIP, Subject Liaison Lib., Brunel Univ. [0047062]   09/04/1992
Macready Miss AL, BSc(Hons) MCLIP, Housewife. [0047253]   24/06/1992
Macready Mrs HM, (was Coe), BA MCLIP, p./t.Sch.Lib., Penketh High Sch., Warrington. [0002928]   01/10/1970
MacRitchie Mr DJ, BA MCLIP, Lib., Hurstville P.L., Sydney, Australia. [0028333]   04/11/1977
Macrow Mrs FC, (was Garwood), BA(Hons) DipLib MCLIP, Bibl.Serv.Mgr., L.B.of Enfield. [0035864]   31/01/1983
Madden Dr JL, CBE HonFCLIP MA, Hon.Fellow. [0009590]   04/10/1962   FE 01/01/1964
Madders Mr A, MCLIP, Grp.Lib., Cheshire C.C., Chester L. [0009593]   21/09/1966
Maddison Ms CM, BSc DipLib MCLIP, Br.Lib., Norton Br.L., Stockton. [0027192]   27/01/1977
Maddison Mr JR, BSc MSc CEng, Employment not known. [0060489]   11/12/2001
Maddison Mrs S, L.Clerk, Marden High Sch., N.Shields, Tyne & Wear. [0054727]   13/03/1997
Maddock Mr G, BA MCLIP, Retired. [0009599]   28/03/1963
Maddock Miss JR, BA DipLib MCLIP, Lib., The Babrahham Inst., Cambridge. [0028070]   11/10/1977
Maddock Mrs LL, (was Campsall), BA MCLIP, Site Lib., Doncaster Coll., Waterdale L. [0028522]   05/01/1978
Maddock Mrs SC, (was Mackenzie), MA MCLIP, Lib., Ashton 6th Form Coll. [0020578]   30/04/1973
Maddock Ms SN, MA MCLIP, Freelance Inf.Spec. [0030000]   24/10/1978
Maddock Mrs SR, BA(Hons) MA, Sen.L.Asst., Beds.Health, Bedford. [0061109]   22/02/2002   AF
Maddox Ms JI, BA MA, Mgr., Inf.Devel., Pfizer Inc., New York, U.S.A. [0044583]   30/10/1990
Madelin Miss L, MCLIP, Ref.Lib., Exmouth L., Devon C.C. [0009604]   14/01/1965
Madge Mr BE, DHSMA MCLIP, Head of Healthcare Inf.Serv., The Brit.L., London. [0027193]   27/01/1977
Madge Mrs CL, (was Fowler), BA MA, Researcher, Financial Times, London. [0055916]   12/12/1997
Madgwick Mrs AC, (was Bassett), BA MCLIP, Career Break. [0033267]   05/11/1980
Madhavan Mrs DM, (was Payne), MCLIP, Area Mgr., Caerphilly Co.Borough L., Blackwood L. [0020378]   27/02/1973
Madle Mrs G, BSc, Stud., City Univ., London. [0061119]   21/02/2002
Madni Mr SNI, BSc, Unemployed. [0042872]   02/01/1997
Magba Dr EA, (was Parker), MA MCLIP, Lib., U.C.C.F., Tyndale Hse., Cambridge. [0011230]   30/07/1968
Magee Mrs B, (was Phillips), BA MA MCLIP, p./t.Lib., Newbury L., W.Berks.Council. [0041438]   09/12/1987
Magee Ms JG, BA(Hons) DipIS MCLIP, Asst.Lib., Nat.Hist.Museum, London. [0046331]   28/10/1991
Magee Mrs M, Stud., Univ.of Wales, Aberystwyth. [0053729]   18/09/1996
Magee Mrs SE, p./t.Sen.L.Asst., Bell Coll., Dumfries Campus. [0052817]   19/12/1995   AF
Magen Ms D, (was Hurwitz), BSc DIP LIS, Lib., Inst.of Earth Sci., Hebrew Univ., Jerusalem. [0042898]   18/04/1989
Maggs Mrs DT, BA(Hons) MA, Subject Lib., Hendon Campus, Middlesex Univ. [0054205]   04/11/1996
Maggs Miss M, MEd MCLIP, Retired. [0009610]   22/10/1962
Maggs Mr PR, BA MA MCLIP, Asst.Lib., Univ.of Southampton. [0047538]   01/10/1992
Magrill Dr DS, PhD MCLIP, Retired. [0060544]   11/12/2001
Maguire Miss CB, PSAILIS MCLIP, Life Member. [0017345]   29/09/1948
Maguire Mrs GV, (was Akerman), BA MCLIP, Lib., Foundation for Conductive Educ., Birmingham. [0019317]   01/01/1967
Maguire Mr IM, BA MA MTh MSc PGCE, Careers Inf.Mgr., Middlesex Univ. [0057449]   01/04/1999
Maguire Mrs LR, (was Stewart), MA DipLib MCLIP, L.Serv.Mgr., Milton Keynes Gen.NHS Trust. [0034329]   20/10/1981
Maguire Miss RE, Lib., Hants C.C.L.Serv., New Milton. [0046745]   14/01/1992
Maguire Ms SC, BA(Hons), Sen.L.Asst.-Super., Milton Keynes L. [0058209]   11/11/1999
Maguire Mrs V, (was Daft), MCLIP, Sen.Subject Lib., Inf. & Learning Services, Univ. of Plymouth. [0003540]   01/01/1970
Mahal Mrs SK, Race Equality Lib., Sandwell M.B.C., Langley. [0058913]   03/10/2000
Maher Miss P, MCLIP, Slide Lib., Faculty of Art & Design, Univ.of Northumbria at Newcastle. [0057449]   23/07/1969
Mahon Ms CL, Res.Asst., Univ.of Wolverhampton, Telford. [0056999]   19/11/1998
Mahoney Mrs DK, (was Nunn), MCLIP, Br.Lib., L.B.of Havering, Cent.L. [0010931]   01/12/1971

295

Mahoney Mrs JA, (was Denyer), BA MCLIP, Sen.Inf.Asst., Cambridge Consultants. [0034297] 23/10/1981
Mahoney Mr JR, MSc MCLIP, Systems Project Leader, Inspec Systems, Hitchin. [0026466] 01/10/1976
Mahurter Miss SJA, BA(Hons) MA MCLIP, RSLP Project Mgr. [0043260] 13/10/1989
Maiden Mr CI, BA MSc MIMgt MCLIP, Resident in Bermuda. [0061259] 02/05/2002
Maidment Mrs JR, (was Hibbs), BLib MCLIP, Learning Res.Mgr., W.Herts.Coll., Watford. [0042921] 20/04/1989
Maidment Mr M, DipLib MCLIP, [0031658] 12/11/1979
Maier Ms E, Resident in Austria. [0050902] 28/10/1994
Mailer Mrs ME, (was Hartley), BA MA DipLib MCLIP, Asst.Lib., St.Martins Coll., Lancaster. [0028005] 11/10/1977
Main Mrs BA, (was Martin), BA DipLib, Area Manager, Connolly House, L.HQ, West Lothian. [0034177] 02/10/1981
Main Mrs JR, (was Davis), BA DipLib MCLIP, Career Break/Saturday Asst., Ongar L., Essex L. [0036206] 18/07/1983
Main Mrs K, (was Yates), MA MCLIP, Retired. [0017347] 01/01/1965
Main Mrs LV, (was Quine), MCLIP, P/t.Sch.Lib., The Mall Sch., Twickenham. [0026794] 26/10/1976
Main Mr S, BA(Phil) MTheol DipCG DipLib MCLIP, Promoted Lib., Lanark L., S.Lanarks.Council. [0044962] 28/01/1991
Mainds Mr GR, MA MCLIP, L.Offr., Cent.L., City of Edinburgh Council. [0053422] 17/06/1996
Mainwaring Ms J, MCLIP, Acting Co.Ref.& Inf.Lib., Aylesbury Lend.L., Bucks. [0009631] 27/01/1970
Mainzer Mr HC, MA DPhil, Retired. [0039830] 20/08/1986
Mair Miss AE, BA MCLIP, Record Mgr., Aberdeen City L. [0018129] 02/10/1972
Mair Miss LA, LLB DipLP DipLib MA MCLIP, Asst.Lib., The Robert Gordon Univ., Aberdeen. [0046306] 25/10/1991
Maisey Mr AS, BA, Stud., UCL SLAIS, London. [0059465] 03/04/2001
Maisey Mrs EM, (was Rolfe), BA MCLIP, Lib., Royal Engineers, Chatham. [0012662] 01/01/1968
Maisey Ms VT, BA(Hons) PGCE DipLib, Lib., Nanuet L., New York, U.S.A. [0027076] 01/01/1977
Maisokwadzo Mrs LT, Unemployed. [0061511] 23/08/2002
Maitland Mrs CA, MA, Lending Serv.Lib., City of York Council, York L. [0039352] 17/01/1986
Maitland Mrs K, (was Brooks), MA MCLIP, p./t.Asst.Lib., Preston Prison, Lancs. [0001814] 15/01/1970
Maitland Miss S, BA(Hons), Stud., Univ.Coll.London. [0061627] 04/10/2002
Maitland-Cullen Mr PS, BD PhD DipLIS MCLIP, Sen.Project Mgr., HMC Scotland Ltd., Edinburgh. [0045992] 12/08/1991
Majithia Mrs K, Child.Inf.Offr., Royal Bor.of Windsor & Maidenhead. [0055384] 09/10/1997
Major Miss G, Sen.L.Asst., Cent.L., Lincoln. [0059353] 13/02/2001 **AF**
Major Miss MA, BA(Hons) DipIS, Web Serv.Lib., St.Marys Coll., Twickenham. [0047796] 15/10/1992
Major Mr R, BA MCLIP, Systems Lib., Univ.of Cent.England, Kenrick L., Birmingham. [0038715] 01/01/1985
Major Mr RM, BA MA MCLIP, Retired. [0009637] 28/10/1965
Mak Mrs J, BSc MCLIP, Employment not known. [0060546] 11/12/2001
Mak Mr KL, BSc MCLIP, Asst.Dir., Leisure & Cult.Serv.Dept., Hong Kong. [0024523] 05/09/1975
Mak-Van Strijthem Mrs SAL, (was Van Strijthem), MA DipLIS MCLIP, Inf.Offr., Consulate General of Belgium, Hong Kong. [0048039] 04/11/1992
Makeham Miss JC, BSc(Hons) MSc, Asst.Lib., E.Barnet L. [0056855] 27/10/1998
Makepeace Mr C, BA FSA MCLIP, Loc.Hist.L.& Inf.Consultant, 5,Hilton Rd., Disley, Cheshire. [0009640] 15/10/1965
Makepeace Mr SJ, BA MCLIP, Asst.Multi-media Lib., Aberdeen. [0040324] 15/01/1987
Makin Mrs A, (was Walton), MCLIP, Freelance Tech.Lib., Working with Construction Ind.Prof. [0009642] 01/01/1956
Makin Miss H, FCLIP, Retired. [0009643] 28/10/1943 **FE 01/01/1954**
Makin Mr JL, BA MLS CertEd, Faculty Liaison Offr., Nottingham Trent Univ., LIS. [0021473] 16/10/1973
Makin Mrs JM, (was Wright), MCLIP, Learning Support Offr., Learning Support Serv., Univ.of Nottingham. [0011945] 01/01/1965
Makin Miss L, BA(Hons) DipILM MCLIP, Asst.Lib., Crewe & Alsager Faculty, Manchester Met.Univ. [0056093] 12/02/1998
Makin Mr P, BA(Hons) PGCE DipHE, Grad.Trainee. [0060006] 21/11/2001
Makin Mrs PJ, (was Ions), MCLIP, p./t.Lib., Havant L., Hants.Co.L. [0007619] 05/03/1967
Makinta Mrs LY, DipLSc, Lib., Ramat L., Univ.of Maiduguri, Nigeria. [0061066] 13/02/2002
Makulski Mr ME, BA LLM, p./t.Stud., Univ.North London., TFPL. [0060030] 28/11/2001
Malbon Mr R, MA FCLIP, Retired. [0009644] 18/03/1936 **FE 01/01/1951**
Malcolm Mrs C, (was Barber), BA MCLIP, Lib., Sir William Perkins's Sch., Chertsey. [0025716] 23/02/1976
Malcolm Miss F, BA MLIS, Asst.Lib., Law Soc.of N.Ireland, Belfast. [0057311] 10/02/1999
Malcolm Miss PA, MCLIP, Inf.Serv.Lib., W.Dunbartonshire Council, Clydebank. [0023296] 20/11/1974
Malcomber Mrs B, Intellectual Prop.Asst., Lafarge Roofing, W.Sussex. [0061389] 02/07/2002 **AF**
Malde Mrs N, (was Shah), BSc MCLIP, Inf., Corp.Intellectual Property, GlaxoSmithKline, Brentford. [0048325] 25/11/1992
Male Ms J, MCLIP, Inf.Serv Unit:Special Projects, Home Off., London. [0009647] 01/01/1970

Male Mrs LM, (was Harris), MCLIP, Unemployed. [0018253] 04/10/1972
Males Mrs B, (was Perry), BA MCLIP, Lib., Lord Wandsworth Coll., Hook. [0009648] 01/10/1968
Malin Mrs J, (was Bariffi), DMS MCLIP, As & When Lib., L.B.of Harrow. [0029505] 21/09/1978
Malin Ms MA, BA, Self-employed, Agent, Editor & Consultant. [0026235] 25/03/1991 **SP**
Malinowski Miss RJ, BA(Hons) PGDipLIS, Lib., Oxfordshire C.C. [0048030] 04/11/1992
Maliphant Miss M, MCLIP, Retired. [0009650] 16/05/1951
Mallach Mr RC, MCLIP, Research Analyst, Ernst & Young, London. [0026984] 10/12/1976
Mallam Mr J, MCLIP, Div.Lib., Durham Co.L. [0009654] 01/10/1964
Mallen Miss SL, BSc(Hons) DipILS MCLIP, Dep.Inf.Mgr., Careers Serv., Univ.of Manchester & UMIST. [0052484] 02/11/1995
Mallett Mr CJ, MA MCLIP, Coll.Lib., Civil Serv.Coll., Ascot. [0043250] 06/10/1989
Mallett Ms DL, BSc(Hons) MA MCLIP, Liaison Lib.(Sci.), Univ.of Birmingham, [0055502] 16/10/1997
Mallett Mrs EA, (was Farrell), BA MCLIP, Mgr.-IOLCMA, Open Univ.L., Milton Keynes. [0041634] 02/02/1988
Mallett Mrs S, (was Dallison), MCLIP, Retired. [0009657] 11/01/1953
Mallinder Ms AT, (was Shah), MA(Hons) DipLIS, L.& Inf.Worker, Art & Music Dept., Dundee City L. [0055791] 24/11/1997
Mallon Mrs SM, (was Reid), BA MCLIP, Asst.Lib., N.Ayrshire L.H.Q., Ardrossan. [0031427] 15/10/1979
Mallows Miss K, BA BMus FinalDipLib MCLIP, Resident in Germany. [0029402] 01/07/1978
Malloy Ms A, BA LLB MCMI MCLIP MILAM FSA Scot, Dir.of Customer & Advice Serv., L.B.of Hackney. [0009660] 06/01/1972
Malone Mrs EA, (was Jones), BA DipLib MCLIP, Sci.Faculty Lib., Kingston Univ.L., Surrey. [0009200] 01/01/1986
Malone Mrs EM, (was Woodhouse), LLB DipLIS MCLIP, Comm.Lib., Stoke L., Coventry. [0049390] 21/10/1993
Malone Miss HM, BSc(Hons) MSc, Mgr., GlaxoSmithKline, Greenford, Middx. [0048478] 20/01/1993
Maloney Mrs CA, (was Reading), BLib MCLIP, Inf.Lib., Warwick L., Warks.C.C. [0032553] 21/05/1980
Maloney Mrs FM, BA(Hons) MA, Lib., Brighton & Hove City Council, Brighton L. [0056812] 23/10/1998
Maloney Miss MJ, BA MCLIP, Learning Res.Mgr., Basingstoke Coll.of Tech. [0038827] 14/10/1985
Maloney Ms PST, BA(Hons) DipIM, Unemployed. [0059764] 25/09/2001
Maloney Mr T, BA MCLIP, Lib., Doughty Street Chambers. [0023694] 07/01/1975
Malsher Ms CA, BD DipIS, Asst.Lib., Lincolns Inn L., London. [0057737] 05/07/1999
Malton Mr R, BSc LRSC DipCG MCLIP, Employment unknown. [0060236] 10/12/2001
Maluty Miss S, BSc MCLIP, Lib., Glasgow City L. [0018292] 08/10/1972
Malyon Mrs L, (was Broadhurst), BA MCLIP, Acad. Cit. Lib., Teesside Tertiary Coll., Middlesbrough. [0034847] 16/03/1982
Mamtora Ms J, BLib MCLIP AALIA, Palmerston Campus Lib., Northern Territory Univ., Australia. [0026469] 05/10/1976
Mancino Miss MJ, BA(Hons), Sen.Inf.Offr., Eversheds, Cardiff. [0051153] 23/11/1994
Mandelstam Mr C, BA MCLIP, Retired. [0009668] 07/10/1948
Mander Mr SG, BA(Hons) PGDipLib, Team Leader, Birmingham City Council, Cent.L., Birmingham. [0048523] 05/02/1993
Mandley Mrs PJ, (was Scriven), BA(Hons) MSc, Unemployed. [0046855] 14/02/1992
Mandt Mr C, Stud., Univ.of Strathclyde. [0061250] 24/04/2002
Mangat Mrs GK, (was Chakal), MCLIP, Lib., Lampton Sch., L.B.of Hounslow. [0002631] 01/01/1960
Manghani Mr P, BA(Hons) DipILS, Learning Cent.Lib., Westminster Kinsgway Coll., London. [0052012] 11/09/1995
Mangold Miss EM, BLib MLib, Mgr., Inf.Cent., Dow Europe S.A., Horgen, Switzerland. [0033043] 01/10/1980
Manise Mrs C, BA(Hons), Sch.Resource Mgr., Shipston High Sch., Warks. [0061600] 03/10/2002
Manisty Dr D, BA PhD, Unemployed. [0059580] 05/06/2001
Manku Mr KS, PhD, p./t.Stud./L.Asst., Univ.of Cent.England, Birmingham, Coventry City L., Tile Hill L. [0059019] 26/10/2000
Manley Mrs DA, BA(Hons) PGDipLib MCLIP, Literacy Asst./Lib., St.Pauls Catholic Sch., Milton Keynes. [0032807] 23/09/1980
Manley Dr K, DPhil FRSA MCLIP, Asst.Lib., Inst.of Historical Res., Univ.of London. [0009677] 30/09/1969
Manley Mrs PM, (was Brown), BA MLS DipLib MCLIP MA(Educ), Sen.Lib.(Child.& Young People), Salford M.B.C. [0022869] 09/10/1974
Mann Mrs C, (was Davies), BA DipLib, AV Serv.Lib., Audio Visual Serv., L.B.of Enfield. [0038206] 25/01/1985
Mann Mrs C, (was Heskett), BA MCLIP, Sen.Community Lib.(Job-share), Staffs.C.C., Tamworth L. [0039430] 22/01/1986
Mann Miss CL, BA DipLib MCLIP, Know How Mgr., Dickinson Dees, Newcastle upon Tyne. [0042091] 01/10/1988
Mann Mrs E, (was Bence), BA MCLIP, Proprietor, Forest Books of Cheshire, Manchester. [0009684] 10/02/1971
Mann Mrs JA, BSc(Hons), Stud., Univ.of Wales, Aberystwyth. [0058304] 04/01/2000
Mann Mrs JM, MSc MIDM MCLIP, Unemployed. [0055647] 31/10/1997
Mann Mrs JM, (was Holland), BA MCLIP, Asst.Lib., The Cheltenham Ladies Coll., Glos. [0007074] 01/01/1976
Mann Miss K, BA(Hons) MA, Inf.Offr., Royal Inst.of Chartered Surveyors, London. [0055529] 20/10/1997
Mann Mrs MK, MCLIP, Employment not known. [0060466] 11/12/2001

Mann Mr MR, BEd MCLIP, Lib., European Parliament, Luxembourg. [0022316] 01/04/1974
Mann Dr PH, MA PhD HonFCLIP, Hon.Fellow. [0046053] 11/09/1991 FE 11/09/1991
Mann Ms RY, BA MPhil DipIS, Journals Mgr., Inst.of Chartered Accountants, in England & Wales, London. [0044188] 25/10/1990
Mann Mrs SA, (was Prince), MCLIP, Sch.Lib., Beckfoot Grammar Sch., Bradford, W.Yorkshire. [0023794] 04/02/1975
Mann . SG, BA MCLIP, Lifelong Learning Lib., Mitchell L., Glasgow Ls.& Arch.Serv. [0034112] 01/10/1981
Mann Mrs W, (was Toplis), BSc MCLIP, Multimedia & Learning Cent.Mgr., Barnsley M.B.C., Cent.L. [0033425] 17/12/1980
Manners Mrs J, (was Nelson), DipLib MCLIP, Princ.Lib.-Special Serv., W.Sussex C.C., Worthing L. [0038113] 18/01/1985
Manners Miss LC, BA MA DipLib MCLIP, Inf.& Database Offr., Cent.for Inf.on Beverage Alcohol, London. [0038765] 04/10/1985
Manning Miss HM, BA MA MCLIP, L.Serv.Devel.Mgr., Child.& Young People, L.B.Wandsworth, Battersea L. [0034078] 23/09/1981
Manning Miss Y, MA DipLib MCLIP, Princ.Lib., L.Support, Falkirk Council. [0036463] 11/10/1983
Manning Mrs YA, BSc(Hons) MSc, Sen.L.Asst., Warwickshire Coll., Moreton Morrell Cent. [0053919] 10/10/1996
Manoharan Mr P, BSc(Hons), L.Mgr., L.B.of Merton, Wimbledon L. [0055007] 20/06/1997
Manoli Miss T, BA(Hons) MA, L.Asst., The Royal Agricultural Coll., Cirencester. [0055001] 19/06/1997
Mansbridge Mrs D, (was Prewett), MA DipLib MCLIP, Ch.Lib., London Coll.of Fashion. [0022896] 01/10/1974
Mansbridge Mrs EB, (was Craven), MCLIP, Retired. [0003328] 28/12/1968
Mansell Mrs BA, (was Silcock), BA ARICS MCLIP, Retired. [0043110] 31/07/1989
Mansfield Ms JD, MA MA(Hons) DipLIS MCLIP, Inf.Worker, Manchester Council, Cent.L. [0046747] 09/01/1992
Mansfield Mrs M, BA DipLib MCLIP, Employment not known. [0036431] 04/10/1983
Mansfield Mrs SJ, MA MCLIP, Sen.Inf.Adviser, Univ.of Surrey Roehampton, London. [0021024] 02/10/1978
Mansi Mr D, L.Asst., Queens Crescent L., L.B.of Camden. [0056841] 26/10/1998 AF
Manson Mrs CE, (was Carpenter), BA(Hons) DipLib MCLIP, Roxeth/Rayners Lane L., L.B.Harrow. [0025015] 01/10/1975
Manson Ms H, MA(Hons) DipILS, L.Offr., Oxgangs L., Edinburgh. [0056788] 15/10/1998
Manson Mrs HE, (was Woodward), BA MCLIP, Unemployed. [0038353] 01/04/1985
Manson Miss KA, MA(Hons) MSc, Asst.Lib., Modern & Medieval Lang.L., Univ.of Cambridge. [0057978] 07/10/1999
Manson Ms PM, MA DipLib MCLIP, Princ.Administrator, European Commission,DG INFSO/D2, Luxembourg. [0023854] 05/02/1975
Manson Mr RAH, BA(Hons), Stud., Univ.of Stathclyde. [0060131] 10/12/2001
Manson Mrs SL, (was Halpern), BA(Hons) MSc MCLIP, Lib., Highgate Jnr.Sch., London. [0050400] 18/07/1994
Mantell Mr J, BA MCLIP, Bibl.Data Mgr., Warwickshire Co.L. [0009709] 11/01/1967
Mantell Mrs JB, (was Saunders), BA(Hons) MCLIP, Lib., Warwickshire Co.L., Kenilworth L. [0009710] 01/01/1966
Mantell Mr KH, MA MCLIP, Life Member. [0009711] 10/07/1946
Mantle Mr DK, BSc(Hons), Asst.Inf.Offr., Serv.Mgr., CMS Cameron McKenna, London. [0059363] 14/02/2001
Mantle Mrs SJ, (was Brown), MCLIP, Outreach Lib., Bancroft L., Tower Hamlets. [0021675] 03/01/1974
Mao Mr CC, Assoc.Prof., Dept.of L.& Inf.Sci., Fu-Jen Catholic Univ., Taiwan. [0033495] 05/12/1981
Mapasure Mr S, HND, L.Asst., NHS London Reg.Off. [0060041] 03/12/2001
Maplesden Miss CA, MCLIP, p./t.Div.Young Peoples Specialist, Cheshire C.C., Chester/Ellesmere Port. [0023123] 05/11/1974
Mapleson Mrs D, (was Wood), MCLIP, Retired. [0009717] 06/03/1940
Maratheftis Mr A, MLIS, L.Dir., Cyprus L., Nicosia. [0051579] 03/04/1995
Marcella Prof RC, (was Lawrie), MA(Hons) DipLib DipEd FCLIP PhD, Head of Sch./Prof.Inf.Studies, Univ.of Northumbria at Newcastle. [0035650] 21/11/1982 FE 19/01/2000
March Miss H, BSc, Asst.Learning Resource Mgr., UBHT, Bristol. [0055313] 01/10/1997
March Mrs K, (was Porter), BA MCLIP, Unemployed. [0033114] 06/10/1980
March Ms M, BA MA MCLIP, Campus L.Mgr., Anglia Poly.Univ., Rivermead Campus. [0040395] 30/01/1987
Marchant Mr AS, BA MCLIP, Lib., Orwell High Sch., Felixstowe. [0038395] 16/04/1985
Marchant Mr PC, BH(Hons) MA DipLib DM MCLIP, Head of L.Serv., Knowsley M.B.C. [0036294] 03/10/1983
Marchant Mrs SD, (was Bishop), BA MCLIP, Lib., The Weald Sch., Billingshurst, W.Sussex. [0027131] 01/02/1977
Marchant Mrs SM, (was Jupp), MCLIP, Sch.Lib., Tunbridge Wells Grammar Sch.for Boys, Tunbridge Wells, Kent. [0012060] 27/09/1966
Marchbank Dr AM, MA PhD, Dir.,Pub.Serv., Nat.L.of Scotland, Edinburgh. [0042042] 10/08/1988
Mardo Mrs PE, BA(Hons) PGCE DipLS MCLIP, Child.Lib., Devon L.& Inf.Serv. [0050784] 18/10/1994
Margerison Mr MA, BA(Hons), Stud., Manchester Met.Univ. [0061139] 12/03/2002
Marin Ms A, MSc(Econ) BA DipLIS CIM MCLIP, Ref.Lib., Cent.Ref.L., L.B.of Bromley. [0040755] 01/06/1987
Marin Ms JM, Employment not known. [0061174] 26/03/2002
Mariner Miss L, BA(Hons) MA MCLIP, Catr., Tate Gallery, London. [0052972] 06/02/1996

Mark Miss RJ, BSc MSc, Lib., HSBC Broking Serv.(Asia) Ltd., Hong Kong. [0049198] 12/10/1993
Marker Mrs BCB, (was Butters), BA PGDipLIS, P/t.Resource Lib., Ealing Tertiary Coll.,Acton Cent., London. [0046048] 01/01/1963
Markham Mr CB, Team Lib., Sevenoaks L., Kent Arts & L. [0033044] 01/10/1980 AF
Markham Mrs JA, (was Dunn), MA DipLib MCLIP, Lib., Meridian TV., Berks. [0032929] 08/10/1980
Markham Mrs R, (was Bennett), BA DipLib MCLIP, Asst.Inf.Lib., Morpeth L., Northumberland C.C. [0028225] 12/10/1977
Markmann Mrs L, Stud., Univ.of Brighton. [0061541] 10/09/2002
Marks Mr HD, BA MCLIP, Res.Mgr., Northants L.& Inf.Serv., Northampton. [0021488] 16/10/1973
Marks Mrs R, (was Spratley), MA MCLIP, Retired. [0009746] 26/05/1966
Markus Ms A, (was Bawcutt), MCLIP, Retired. [0000940] 30/07/1959
Marland Mr PD, BA MA MCLIP, Sen.Lib., Keith L., Moray Council. [0037885] 07/11/1984
Marley Miss EA, BA MCLIP, Princ.Lib., Child.& Sch.Serv., Hampshire. [0009749] 26/05/1972
Marley Mrs EA, (was Harvey), MSc, Sen.Ed., Proquest Inf. & Learning, Cambridge. [0048173] 11/11/1992
Marley Mr PR, BA MCLIP, Lib., Blaenau Gwent Co.Bor.Council. [0027617] 01/06/1977
Marlow Mr J, MCLIP, Retired, Ground Floor Flat, 284 Pitsmoor Rd, Sheffield, S3 9AW. [0009751] 04/04/1972
Marmoy Mr CFA, FCLIP FSA, Life Member. [0009753] 03/02/1931 FE 01/01/1935
Marney Miss RM, BA MCLIP, Dep.Lib., Inst.of Civil Engineers, London. [0033047] 11/10/1979
Marpole Mr B, MCLIP, Asst.L.Serv.Mgr., Royal Bor.of Windsor & Maidenhead. [0020435] 07/02/1973
Marr Ms CF, BA DipLib MCLIP, Inf.Asst., City of Edinburgh Social Work Dept. [0041054] 06/10/1987
Marr Mrs Y, (was Watson), Curator, Nat.L.of Scotland, Edinburgh. [0049634] 16/11/1993
Marrable Dr DM, BSc PhD MCLIP, Employment not known. [0060820] 12/12/2001
Marriage Miss J, MCLIP, Retired. [0009756] 13/02/1961
Marriott Ms A, BA MCLIP, Data Mgr., Freshfields Bruckhaus Deringer, London. [0025354] 15/01/1976
Marriott Ms EJ, Employment not known. [0046021] 24/08/1991
Marriott Mrs G, (was McMullen), MA DipLib MCLIP, f./t.Mother. [0042147] 10/10/1988
Marriott Miss H, MCLIP, Life Member. [0009758] 01/01/1951
Marriott Mr JR, BA(Hons) MA MCLIP, Asst.Lib.,, Horniman Mus.& Gardens, London. [0057980] 08/10/1999
Marriott Mr P, MCLIP, Lib., Cent.L., Cambs.C.C. [0009759] 15/10/1971
Marriott Mr R, BA(Hons) MA MCLIP, Lib.Devel.Mgr., Southern Derbys.Health Auth., Derby. [0046872] 17/02/1992
Marsden Ms CJ, BA MA PGDipLib MCLIP, Sen.Lib., Totton L., Hants.L.Serv. [0030218] 11/01/1979
Marsden Miss LC, BA(Hons) MSc, Asst.Lib., Thomas Eggar Church Adams, Solicitors, Chichester. [0053878] 17/10/1996
Marsden Mrs S, (was Kellett), MCLIP, p./t.Lib., Oundle Sch., Cripps L., Peterborough. [0009711] 01/01/1966
Marsden Mr TS, BA(Hons) MA MCLIP, Acting Dep.Tech.L.Serv.Offr., City of Sunderland Coll., Sunderland. [0056237] 14/04/1998
Marsden Mrs VF, BA DipLib MCLIP, Asst.Stock Lib., L.B.of Barnet, Cultural Serv. [0043092] 20/07/1989
Marsh Mrs AC, (was Mitchell), MA MCLIP, Reader Serv.Lib., Jordanhill L., Univ.of Strathclyde. [0029755] 09/10/1978
Marsh Mr AL, MCLIP, Retired. [0009773] 21/03/1941
Marsh Mrs AM, (was Highley), BLIB MCLIP, Sen.Lib., Bibl.& Support Serv., S.E.Div., Lancs.C.C. [0030628] 05/03/1979
Marsh Ms AM, BA MA, Sen.Learning Resources Offr., Hackney Community Coll., London. [0053571] 26/07/1996
Marsh Miss AS, BA FCLIP, Life Member. [0009774] 04/10/1951 FE 01/01/1956
Marsh Mr AT, (was Corbett), BEd(Hons), L.Asst., Royal Coll.of Veterinary Surgeons, London. [0044170] 01/07/1990 AF
Marsh Mrs BL, (was Wild), BA DipLib MCLIP, Unemployed. [0024854] 21/10/1975
Marsh Mrs C, MCLIP, Retired. [0009775] 11/02/1968
Marsh Mrs CE, BMus MSc, Lib., Leeds Coll.of Music. [0058507] 18/03/2000
Marsh Mrs CG, (was Steptowe), BA MA MCLIP, Lib., Essex Ls., Clacton. [0040311] 01/01/1987
Marsh Miss EA, BA MCLIP, P./t.Lib.-Home Servs., Westminster, London. [0025355] 14/01/1976
Marsh Dr FS, BSc PhD CPhys MIInstP MCLIP, Employment not known. [0060748] 12/12/2001
Marsh Miss J, BA(Hons), Asst.Ref.L., Lansdowne L., Bournemouth. [0045281] 01/10/1990
Marsh Mrs JD, Inf.Offr., Allen & Overy, london. [0051071] 10/11/1994
Marsh Miss S, BA(Hons), Dep.Site Lib., Univ.of Sunderland. [0045043] 01/07/1990
Marsh Mrs S, (was Ditchfield), BA MSc MCLIP, L.& Inf.Serv.Mgr., Surrey & Sussex Hlthcare NHS Trust, E.Surrey Hosp., Redhill. [0037012] 28/01/1984
Marsh Miss SA, BA(Hons) DipLib, Retired. [0056357] 16/06/1998
Marsh Mrs SA, (was Brakell), MA MCLIP, Sch.Lib.(Job-share), Moray Council (from 01/04/96), Buckie, Moray. [0024404] 30/07/1975
Marsh Miss SJA, BA DipLib MCLIP, [0038387] 10/04/1985
Marsh Miss SL, BA MA MCLIP, Dep.Dir., L.& Inf.Serv., Univ.of Wales Swansea. [0041489] 08/01/1988
Marsh Mrs WM, (was Mears), BA(Hons) DipLIS MCLIP, Lib., Suffolk Health Auth., Ipswich. [0049687] 25/11/1993

297

Marshall Mr A, BA DipLib MCLIP, Asst.Lib., Univ.of Portsmouth. [0009787] 07/01/1970
Marshall Mr A, BA MCLIP, Asst.Lib., Milton Keynes L.Serv., Milton Keynes L. [0021367] 12/11/1973
Marshall Mrs AB, (was Paton), MA MCLIP, Sch.Lib., Elgin High Sch., Moray. [0044839] 19/11/1990
Marshall Mrs AB, MA MSc MCLIP, Employment not known. [0060845] 12/12/2001
Marshall Mr AD, BSc(Hons) MSc DipInf, Asst.Lib., Newcomb L., Homerton Univ.Hosp.NHS Trust. [0055747] 12/11/1997
Marshall Mrs AF, (was Bickham), MCLIP, Learning Res.Cent.Asst., The L.R.C., W.Oxon.Coll., Witney. [0001224] 15/03/1972
Marshall Mrs AJ, BA DipLib MCLIP, Lib.(Local Studies), Comm.Initiatives Partnership, L.B.of Hounslow. [0038230] 07/02/1985
Marshall Ms AM, (was Anderson), MA DipLib MCLIP, Research Offr., Univ.of Brighton, Sch.of Inf.Mgmnt. [0025476] 05/02/1976
Marshall Mr AP, BA MCLIP, Princ.L.Offr., Notts.C.C. [0021441] 30/10/1973
Marshall Mrs C, BSc MCLIP, Sen.Lib., Hants.Co.L.Serv., Winchester. [0044646] 14/11/1990
Marshall Mrs CJ, (was Hodge), BA DipLib MCLIP, Lib.(Job Share), St.Georges Sch., Herts. [0040930] 01/09/1987
Marshall Mrs CM, (was Godfrey), BA MBA MCLIP, Sch.Lib., Lodge Park Tech.Coll., Corby, Northants. [0005622] 01/10/1971
Marshall Mrs D, (was Machen), BA MCLIP, Asst.Tech.Lib., Portakabin Ltd., York. [0044640] 13/11/1990
Marshall Mr DG, BSc DipLib MCLIP, Sunject Team Leader, (Sci.Tech.& Built Environment), Oxford Brookes Univ. [0030001] 24/10/1978
Marshall Miss DL, MCLIP, Col.Lib., Guildford Coll.of F.& H.E., Guildford,Surrey. [0021604] 21/11/1973
Marshall Miss DM, Stud., Univ.of Wales, Aberystwyth. [0058896] 02/10/2000
Marshall Mr DN, Professor Emeritus, Univ.of Bombay L., India. [0017357] 20/05/1953
Marshall Ms EJ, BA(Hons) DipLib MCLIP, Inf.Offr., Manchester Business Sch. [0046545] 11/11/1991
Marshall Miss FL, Stud., Manchester Met.Univ. [0060014] 23/11/2001
Marshall Mrs GP, (was Lyon), MA DipLib MCLIP, L.Res.Cent.Co-ordinator, Aberdeen City Council, Educ.Dept. [0031362] 16/10/1979
Marshall Mr GTC, BA MCLIP, Bromsgrove Comm.Lib., Worcs.C.C. [0009794] 01/04/1967
Marshall Miss HE, BA(Hons), Stud., Manchester Met.Univ. [0059848] 16/10/2001
Marshall Miss HI, BA, Inf.Offr., Berrymans Lace Mawer, London. [0052294] 23/10/1995
Marshall Miss HL, BA(Hons), Unemployed. [0059930] 06/11/2001
Marshall Mrs HM, (was Bell), BA MCLIP, Child.Lib.(Job Share), Derby City L. [0023145] 06/11/1974
Marshall Mr J, MCLIP, Retired. [0009797] 19/03/1957
Marshall Mrs JA, (was Forrest), MCLIP, Unemployed. [0005070] 23/02/1966
Marshall Mrs JA, (was Brining), BA, Unemployed-Career Break. [0039486] 04/02/1986
Marshall Dr JD, PhD, Rare Books Curator, Nat.L.of Scotland. [0059792] 03/10/2001
Marshall Miss JK, BLib MCLIP, Head of Serv., Birmingham City Council. [0034324] 10/10/1981
Marshall Mrs L, (was Mortimer), MCLIP, Asst.Lib., Worcester City L., Worcester C.C. [0020667] 20/04/1963
Marshall Mrs LA, (was Hudson), BA(Hons), Stud., Robert Gordon Univ., Aberdeen. [0057508] 14/04/1999
Marshall Mrs LT, BA(Hons), Lib., Staffs.C.C. [0053285] 24/04/1996
Marshall Miss M, Records Offr., Royal Oldham Hosp., Oldham. [0055678] 04/11/1997
Marshall Mr P, MCLIP, Project Devel.Lib., Bexley Council. [0009805] 23/01/1963
Marshall Mrs PM, (was Rowarth), MCLIP, Asst.Lib., Milton Keynes Council, Milton Keynes L. [0021115] 09/10/1973
Marshall Mrs RC, (was Palin), BA MA MCLIP, p./t.Lib., Chilwell Comp.Sch., Notts.C.C. [0038861] 17/10/1985
Marshall Mr RL, BA(Hons) MA, Inf.Offr., Imperial Coll., London. [0055658] 30/10/1997
Marshall Dr SE, (was Brown), MB BS MSc, Resident in USA. [0044294] 20/08/1990
Marshall Mr SN, FCLIP, Life Member, 103 Lee Rd., London, SE3 9DZ, Tel.(020)8852 1658. [0009806] 17/09/1949 **FE 01/01/1963**
Marshall Mrs TM, (was Linton), BA MA, Sen.L.Asst., Loughborough Univ., Leics. [0052401] 30/10/1995
Marshall Mrs V, (was Bolton), BA MA, Full-time Mother. [0044817] 03/12/1990
Marshall Miss VL, BA(Hons), Stud., Loughborough Univ. [0059957] 12/11/2001
Marshall Mr W, BA(Hons), Sch.Lib., John Willmott Sch., Sutton Coldfield. [0051253] 08/12/1994
Marshall McDonald Mrs M, (was Seals), FCLIP, Retired. [0009803] 01/01/1950 **FE 01/01/1970**
Marshman Mr M, MCLIP, Trowbridge Ref.& Co.Local Studies Lib., Wilts.C.C. [0009811] 12/03/1967
Marshman Mrs RV, (was Burton), BSc MCLIP, Unemployed. [0024330] 01/07/1975
Marsland Miss GH, MA MCLIP, Sen.Lib., Blackpool Bor.Council. [0025357] 11/01/1976
Marson Mrs VA, (was Snell), BA(Hons), Sch.Lib., Oakwood High Sch., Manchester. [0044082] 25/04/1990
Marsterson Mrs KM, (was Gallagher), BSc(Hons), Inf.Offr., The Brit.L., London. [0057016] 24/11/1998
Marsterson Mr W, MA MCLIP, Head of Inf.& Learn.Resource Serv., Middx.Univ. [0009812] 23/10/1967

Martch Ms H, BA MA, Business Inf. Offr., Institute of Directors, London. [0057953] 01/10/1999
Martell Miss H, MA BA MCLIP, Author. [0009814] 28/09/1967
Martens Mrs A, Stud., Moray Coll., Elgin. [0061180] 03/04/2002
Martin Mrs AA, MA PGCE, p./t. Stud./L.Asst., Saffron Walden L., Univ.Coll.London. [0059536] 01/05/2001
Martin Miss AE, BA(Hons) MA MCLIP, Team Lib., Co.Cent.L., Maidstone. [0055298] 19/09/1997
Martin Miss AF, MA MCLIP, Inf.,Intelligence & Knowledge Mgr., London Devel.Agency, London. [0041131] 14/10/1987
Martin Mr AH, BA MCLIP, Lib., Southend Dist, Southend Bor.Council. [0023249] 14/11/1974
Martin Mrs AJ, MSc(Econ), Inf.Offr., Simmons & Simmons, London. [0052447] 02/11/1995
Martin Mr AJ, BSc MA MCLIP, Deputy Lib., Univ.Coll.Northampton. [0023929] 24/02/1975
Martin Ms AM, BA(Hons) DipLIS MCLIP, Asst.Lib., Corp.of London. [0046294] 24/10/1991
Martin Mr AV, MA MCLIP, Business Serv.Sen.Admin., Nat.Care Standards Commission, Devon C.C. [0025600] 27/01/1976
Martin Mr B, BA(Hons), Grad.Trainee, Univ.Coll.London. [0061727] 29/10/2002 **AS 29/10/2002**
Martin Mrs BJ, (was Catherall), MCLIP, Team Lib., Yeovil P.L., Somerset C.C. [0009818] 07/10/1968
Martin Mrs BM, BA(Hons) PGDip DipLIS MCLIP, Subject & Learning Support Lib., Nelson L., Staffs.Univ., Stafford. [0030778] 04/04/1979
Martin Mrs C, BA AKC DipLib MCLIP, Asst.Community Serv.Mgr., Bristol City Council Ls. [0009819] 24/05/1971
Martin Miss CA, Stud., Brighton Univ. [0061777] 04/11/2002
Martin Mr CA, Br.Asst., Suffolk C.C., &, Stud., Dist.Learning, Univ.of Wales. [0057373] 01/03/1999
Martin Mr CJ, BA MCLIP, Asst.Lib., Univ.of Portsmouth, Eldon L. [0020214] 01/02/1973
Martin Mrs CMC, (was Smith), BSc DipLib, L.& Learning Resources Mgr., W.Cheshire Coll., Chester. [0040268] 01/01/1968
Martin Mr D, FCLIP, Ref.& Inf.Lib., E.Dunbartonshire Council, Kirkintilloch. [0009823] 28/03/1960 **FE 18/03/1985**
Martin Mr D, MIPD MCLIP, Ref.& Inf.Devel.Lib.(Job Share), Rochdale M.B.C. [0009822] 14/01/1967
Martin Ms D, BA MCLIP, Employment not known. [0060221] 10/12/2001
Martin Mrs E, (was Dewar), MCLIP, Sch.Lib., Torry Academy, Aberdeen City Council. [0009827] 16/02/1961
Martin Ms E, (was Andrews), MA MCLIP, Lib., Nuffield Coll., Oxford. [0028074] 02/10/1977
Martin Mrs EA, (was Evans), BLib MCLIP, Community Lib., Flintshire C.C., Mold. [0004656] 02/01/1969
Martin Ms FC, MA BA DipLib MCLIP, Asst.Lib., BLPES, London Sch.of Economics. [0034755] 17/02/1982
Martin Mrs FS, (was Carter), BA DipLib MCLIP, p./t.Lib.Asst., Sanger Cent.,Wellcome Tr.Genome C., Cambs. [0031745] 21/11/1979
Martin Miss GM, BA MCLIP, Head Lib., Johns Hopkins Univ., S.A.I.S. Bologna, Italy. [0031367] 08/10/1979
Martin Mrs GM, (was Pritchard), MCLIP, Sen.Learning Res.Asst., Stoke on Trent Coll., Staffs. [0019327] 13/03/1964
Martin Dr H, BSc BA MCLIP PhD, Biopharmation Consulting, Denmark. [0036724] 03/11/1983
Martin Mrs HM, (was Miller), MA DipLib MCLIP, Sch.Lib., E.Dunbartonshire Council. [0029753] 09/10/1978
Martin Miss J, MA MCLIP, Princ.Offr.(L.Ops.), N.Ayrshire Council, Irvine. [0009842] 20/04/1970
Martin Miss J, Retired. [0009844] 01/01/1934
Martin Mrs J, Project Co-ordinator, Stoke On Trent College. [0061005] 30/01/2002
Martin Mrs J, (was Cambridge), MCLIP, H.of Internat.Off., CILIP., London. [0046606] 01/01/1968
Martin Mrs J, (was Hanlon), MCLIP, Advisory Lib., Sch.L.Serv., Suffolk C.C. [0009836] 24/02/1965
Martin Ms J, BA MSc MCLIP, Lib., NERC, POL, Bidston Observatory. [0033622] 07/10/1997
Martin Mrs JE, BA(Hons) DipLib, Resources Manager, Samuel Ward Upper School &, Technology Coll. [0035886] 27/01/1983
Martin Mrs JF, (was Imrie), Filing Clerk, Streets & Co., Lincoln. [0042672] 07/02/1989
Martin Mrs JJ, BA MCLIP, Comm.Lib., N.Lanarkshire Council. [0034010] 01/07/1981
Martin Miss JM, BA MCLIP, Unemployed. [0033971] 01/07/1981
Martin Mr JR, MA BA MCLIP, Sen.Lib., Hinckley L., Leics.L.& Inf.Serv. [0035092] 02/08/1982
Martin Mr K, MCLIP, Catr./L.Support Serv., Liverpool Leisure Serv. [0020703] 11/06/1973
Martin Mrs KD, BA(Hons), Records Mgmnt.Lib., Southampton Inst. [0059367] 19/02/2001
Martin Mrs L, BA, Learning Projects Co-ordinator, Learning Support Adviser, Edge Hill Coll.of H.E., Ormskirk. [0055432] 13/10/1997
Martin Mrs LG, (was Scott), MA MCLIP, Lib., Culford Sch., Bury St.Edmunds. [0038883] 18/10/1985
Martin Mrs LM, (was Hunt), MCLIP, Partnership & Devel.Mgr., Cambs.C.C. [0007481] 02/01/1969
Martin Mrs MA, (was Doggett), BA MCLIP, Freelance Book Indexer, & Bibl.Researcher. [0044038] 14/01/1969
Martin Mr MG, BA DipLIS MCLIP, Inf.Mgr., CILIP., London. [0048833] 28/06/1993
Martin Mrs NS, BA DipLib MCLIP, Academic Liaison Lib., Business & Law, Anglia Poly.Univ. [0042321] 08/10/1988
Martin Mr P, BA(Hons) MSc MCLIP, Employment Inf.Offr., Linklaters, London. [0009855] 07/04/1972

Martin Mrs P, (was Jones), BA DipLib MCLIP, Corporate Web Mgr., Isle of Anglesey C.C. [0033008] 22/10/1980
Martin Mr PD, BA(Hons) MA, Lib., Eastbourne Coll. [0055323] 01/10/1997
Martin Mrs PI, (was Chinery), MCLIP, Unemployed. [0002683] 01/01/1962
Martin Miss PJ, BA MCLIP, Sen.Lib.-Ref.& Local Studies, E.Riding of Yorkshire Council, Beverley Ref.L. [0009854] 04/11/1963
Martin Ms PK, (was Kincaid), BA(Hons) MA MCLIP, Br.Lib., Jarrow/E.Boldon L., S.Tyneside. [0041989] 12/07/1988
Martin Mr RA, BSc PGDipLIS, Asst.Lib., Dept.for Internat.Devel., E.Kilbride. [0046201] 11/10/1991
Martin Mrs RA, (was Peters), BA MCLIP, Sen.Specialist Lib.-Adult Serv., Loughborough L., Leics.C.C. [0009858] 04/01/1970
Martin Mrs RH, (was Lewis), BA(Hons) DipILM MCLIP, Lib., Bristol Law Soc. [0052105] 03/10/1995
Martin Ms S, BA(Hons) DipIS MCLIP, Med.Liaison Lib., St.Georges Med.Sch., London. [0051303] 12/01/1995
Martin Miss SE, BSc DipLib MCLIP, Trust Lib., S.Devon Healthcare (NHS) Trust, Torbay, Devon. [0041829] 22/04/1988
Martin Mrs SE, (was Coleman), BA MCLIP, Position Unknown, De Montfort Univ. [0028532] 05/01/1978
Martin Mrs SI, (was Johnson), BA MCLIP, Managing Dir., L.Supply (Int.) Ltd., Warwicks. [0021355] 19/11/1973
Martin Miss W, BA FCLIP, Retired. [0009868] 01/04/1943
FE 01/01/1957
Martin Mrs W, (was Gulliver), BSc MCLIP, Catr., Welsh Coll.of Music & Drama, Cardiff. [0009867] 20/09/1968
Martin-Jones Mrs S, (was Clarke), BA MCLIP, Sen.Community Lib., Leics.City Council. [0009871] 26/08/1966
Martin-Rueda Mr J, General Postal Asst., Watford General Hosp. [0059456] 30/03/2001
Martindale Mr CR, BA DipLIS, Subject Advisor, Derbys.Sch.of Business & Tourism, Learn.Cent., Univ.of Derby. [0033505] 13/01/1981
Martindale Miss P, (was Cartwright), BA DipLib MCLIP, Area Mgr.(W.), Redruth L. [0032888] 21/10/1980
Martinelli Mrs F, Stud. [0060877] 18/12/2001
Martland Miss DF, BA(Hons), Inf.Offr., Linklaters, London. [0058060] 21/10/1999
Martland Ms KW, BA MCLIP, Life Member. [0009874] 08/03/1955
Martlew Mrs RE, BA Dip Lib MCLIP, p./t.Asst.Lend.Lib., Lancs.C.C. [0034426] 26/10/1981
Martnes Ms B, BA, Lib., Norwegian Dir. Immigration, Norway. [0061373] 03/07/2002
Martyn Mrs LA, L.Serv.Mgr., S.Bucks.NHS Trust, Wycombe Hosp., Bucks. [0019921] 09/01/1973
Martyres Mrs S, Sen.L.Asst., Lewisham NHS Trust Hosp. [0045179] 02/08/1990 **AF**
Martzoukou Miss K, MA MSc, Stud., Robert Gordon Univ. [0060890] 20/12/2001
Maryon Mr AW, BSc DipLib MCLIP, Ref.& Inf., Greenwich L., L.B.of Greenwich. [0030648] 18/02/1979
Masini Mrs G, (was Musson), MCLIP, Customer Serv.Lib., Fife Council - W.Area, Dunfermline. [0010632] 27/01/1961
Maskell Ms L, (was Richardson), BA MCLIP, I.T.Trainer, Univ.of Bath. [0042493] 23/11/1988
Maskelyne Mrs RH, BA(Hons) MA, Team Lib., Woking L., Surrey C.C. [0058282] 12/12/1999
Mason Miss AH, BA DipLib MCLIP, Comm.Lib.(Res.), Lincs.Co.L.Serv. [0029738] 03/10/1978
Mason Miss AM, BA MCLIP, Lib., Coll.of Occupational Therapists, London. [0025075] 28/10/1975
Mason Miss AP, Sen.L.Asst., Univ.of Birmingham, Mechanical & Manufacturing Eng. [0053068] 23/02/1996 **AF**
Mason Ms BC, BA(Hons) MCLIP, L.& Learning Resources Mgr., Wiltshire Coll., Chippenham. [0041543] 17/01/1988
Mason Mrs D, MCLIP, Grp.Lib., Durham Co.L. [0009888] 30/05/1968
Mason Mr D, BSc(Econ), Asst.Lib.,., Royal W.Sussex NHS Trust., Chichester. [0057000] 24/11/1998
Mason Mrs ET, (was North), BA MCLIP, Special Sch.Asst., Hants C.C. [0010906] 01/01/1972
Mason Mrs F, (was Coxall), BA MCLIP, Yth.Serv.Lib., L.B.of Bexley., Bexley. [0027755] 01/08/1977
Mason Ms J, MBA BA(Hons) DipM, p./t.Stud./Consultant. [0061403] 09/07/2002
Mason Miss JE, BA MA, Inf.Offr./Intranet Co-ordinator, E.Sussex C.C., East Sussex. [0058681] 18/05/2000
Mason Ms JIA, (was Apps), BLib MCLIP, Child.& Yth.Lib.(Job Share), Birmingham L. [0022898] 01/10/1974
Mason Miss JV, BA(Hons) DipLIS MCLIP, Team Lib., Westgate L., Oxon.C.C. [0047509] 16/09/1992
Mason Miss KL, BA(Hons), Dep.Learning Resources Mgr., Peoples Coll.Nottingham. [0053718] 19/09/1996
Mason Mrs LA, (was Martin), BA MCLIP, Sch.Lib., Belmont Sch., London. [0009849] 07/01/1969
Mason Miss LH, LLB(Hons) DipILM DipLP, Inf.Offr., Stoke-on-Trent City Council, Hanley Ref.L. [0058125] 04/11/1999
Mason Miss M, BCL LLM MSc, Intranet Developer, Freshfields Bruckhaus Deringer, London. [0061080] 01/03/2002
Mason Mr M, MCLIP, Retired. [0009897] 20/09/1971
Mason Mr MA, MCLIP, Trust L.Serv.Mgr., Southport &Ormskirk Hosp.NHS Trust. [0009896] 18/10/1967
Mason Mrs MA, Sen.L.Asst., Anglia Poly.Univ. [0059503] 18/04/2001 **AF**
Mason Mrs MR, (was Clay), BLib MCLIP, Unemployed. [0002809] 27/01/1969
Mason Mr P, ICT Advisor, Lincoln Cent.L. [0059272] 24/01/2001 **AF**

Mason Mrs RW, (was Walker), BA MCLIP MLib, Lib., The N.Highland Coll., Thurso. [0026597] 18/10/1976
Mason Miss VE, BA(Hons), Research Asst., Univ.of Lincolnshire & Humberside. [0059627] 04/07/2001
Massam Ms DE, BA(Hons) DipInf MCLIP, L.Serv.Mgr., Manchester Metro.Univ. [0046432] 04/11/1991
Massey Mrs AE, (was Christie), MA(Hons) DipLIS MCLIP, Proj.Mgr., (SECF), E.Lothian Mus.Serv., L.& Mus.HQ. [0049633] 16/11/1993
Massey Mr JL, BA MCLIP, Lib., Stockport Cent.Inf.L., Cheshire. [0044675] 23/11/1990
Massey Mr OG, Catr., Royal Coll.of Surgeons of England, London. [0056885] 03/11/1998
Massey Mrs SJE, (was Watkins), BLib MCLIP, Lib., Illingworth L., Sheffield Child.NHS Hosp.Trust. [0034245] 10/10/1981
Massil Mr SW, BA DipLib FCLIP, Lib., Huguenot L., c/o Univ.Coll.London. [0009906] 12/01/1970 **FE 13/06/1990**
Masson Mrs J, (was Waters), BA MCLIP, Retired. [0009908] 07/02/1941
Masson Mrs LM, (was Paterson), BA MCLIP, Adult Fiction Lib., Aberdeenshire L.& Inf.Serv. [0034071] 02/09/1981
Masson Ms S, BA DipLib MCLIP, p./t.Catr./Classifier, Univ.of N.London. [0031898] 08/01/1980
Masterman Miss C, BA(Hons), P.G.Cent.Lib., S.Durham Healthcare Trust, Memorial Hosp., Darlington. [0051130] 23/11/1994
Masters Ms MA, BSc DipLib MCLIP, Comm.Devel.Lib.(Job Share), City of York Council, York. [0028498] 19/01/1978
Masters Ms SL, BSc MCLIP, Res.Lib., John Mansfield Sch., Peterborough. [0044880] 08/01/1991
Masters Mr T, MCLIP, Retired, 63 Hillside Ave., Canterbury,Kent,CT2 8HA. [0009913] 17/03/1958
Mastoris Mrs L, (was Martin), BLib MCLIP, Learning Cent.Mgr., Henley Coll.Coventry, Coventry. [0022004] 16/01/1974
Matchett Mrs SL, BA(Hons) MA, Lib., Bingham Area, Notts.C.C. [0054185] 04/11/1996
Mateer Miss HE, BA(Hons) MA MCLIP, Catalogue Mgr., Birkbeck Coll., London. [0054408] 04/12/1996
Mather Miss EC, BA(Hons) MSc(Econ) MCLIP, Inf.Offr., NHS Cent.for Reviews & Dissem., Cent.for Health Econ., York. [0051168] 23/11/1994
Mather Mr IM, BA MCLIP, Lib., Southend Hosp.NHS Trust, Westcliff-on-Sea,Essex. [0029907] 26/10/1978
Mathers Ms BH, Sen.L.Asst., The Univ.of Reading. [0057195] 12/01/1999 **AF**
Matheson Ms CM, (was Crockett), BSc MCLIP, Lib., Glen Urquhart High Sch., Drumnadrochit. [0025076] 19/01/1975
Matheson Mrs DM, (was Tiffin), FCLIP, Life Member. [0009918] 06/03/1942 **FE 01/01/1946**
Matheson Miss FM, MA, Co-ordinating Lib., W.Dunbartonshire Council, Clydebank. [0044525] 22/10/1990
Matheson Miss JI, BA MCLIP, Research & Inf.Res.Coordinator, Tower Hamlets L.B.C. [0033049] 08/10/1980
Matheson Ms LA, BA(Hons) DipLib, Lib., Birmingham Sch.L. [0050029] 23/02/1994
Matheson Miss V, MSc, Asst.Lib., BBC Film & TV L., London. [0044934] 21/01/1991
Mathew Mr MV, BA MA DLSC FCLIP, Life Member. [0009921] 03/01/1958 **FE 18/04/1989**
Mathews Mrs SEB, (was Hovell), BSc(Hons) MSc MCLIP, Inf.Mgr.-Knowledge Sharing, Dept.for Internat.Devel., London. [0051954] 18/08/1995
Mathewson Mrs JM, (was Glanville), BA MCLIP, Lib., Reading Bor.Council. [0027112] 11/10/1973
Mathias Miss BR, BA(Hons) DipLIM, Dep.Lib., Univ.of Wales, Swansea. [0053905] 09/10/1996
Mathias Ms GM, MCMI MLib DipLib CertEd, p./t.Lib., Kingfisher plc., London. [0025990] 05/05/1976
Mathias Miss J, MCLIP, Retired. [0009925] 01/02/1967
Mathias Mrs NJ, (was Wilks), BEd(Hons) MSc, Job-share Child.Lib.& Temp., Cent.L., Bristol. [0052984] 1/12/1995
Mathie Ms AE, MCLIP, Head of Learning Cent., Univ.of Gloucestershire. [0017364] 15/09/1967
Mathieson Miss A, MCLIP, Life Member. [0009927] 22/09/1951
Mathieson Mrs JE, (was Higham), MA BA MCLIP, Princ.Offr.Arts.Grp., Manchester Cent.L., Manchester. [0021464] 16/10/1973
Mathieson Ms K, BA(hons) MA MSc, Stud., City Univ. [0060928] 10/01/2002
Maton Mrs RJA, (was Magloire), Stud., Univ.of Wales, Aberystwyth & Prendergast Sch., London. [0057369] 26/02/1999
Matsuki Ms M, BA, Lib., The United Nations Univ., Tokyo, Japan. [0042394] 17/10/1988
Matsumura Miss T, MA, Prof., Sugiyama Jogakuen Univ., Japan. [0027280] 01/02/1977
Matsuya Mrs R, BA MA DipILM MCLIP, Tech.Serv.Lib., Richmond-upon-Thames Coll.L., Surrey. [0055352] 03/10/1997
Matthew Mr JH, BA MA MCLIP, Grp.Mgr.(Community Inf.)Bibl.Serv., Cent.L., Sheffield. [0009929] 05/01/1971
Matthews Mrs A, (was Hetherington), BA(Hons) DipLib MCLIP, Sch.Lib., Benton Park Sch., Leeds. [0035896] 18/02/1983
Matthews Mrs BS, (was Smale), MCLIP, Sen.Lib., Tonbridge Sch., Kent. [0013503] 13/09/1969
Matthews Mr D, BA FCLIP, Retired. [0009934] 03/03/1952 **FE 01/01/1954**
Matthews Mrs EA, (was Walton), BA MCLIP, Area Sch.Lib., Hants.C.C. Sch.L.Serv. [0026248] 21/09/1976
Matthews Mr G, BA DipLib PhD MCLIP, Faculty Dir.of Research, Sch.of Inf.Studies, Univ.of Cent.England in Birmingham. [0025077] 10/11/1975
Matthews Mr GL, MCLIP, Health Care L.Mgr., Rotherham P.L., S.Yorks. [0009938] 19/02/1964
Matthews Mr IJ, MCLIP, Retired. [0019331] 24/01/1957

299

Matthews Mrs J, BSc PGCE, L.Asst., Henley Pub.L., Oxon. [0056646] 01/10/1998 **AF**
Matthews Mrs JE, (was Moore), BLib MCLIP, Child.Serv.Offr., Barnsley Cent.L., Barnsley M.B.C. [0033355] 07/11/1980
Matthews Mr JS, BA DipLib MCLIP, Tutor-Lib., Highbury Coll., Portsmouth. [0029739] 02/10/1978
Matthews Mrs KM, (was Everett), BA MCLIP, Subject Specialist Lib., Northants.L. [0004714] 18/05/1970
Matthews Ms LM, BA MA DipLib MCLIP, Ref.Lib., Wilts.C.C.L.& Heritage, Trowbridge. [0042095] 01/10/1988
Matthews Mr N, BA(Hons), Princ.L.& Inf.Offr., Northants.C.C. [0009948] 15/09/1970
Matthews Mrs N, (was Corcoran), MA MCLIP, Lib., Cains Advocates, Douglas, I.O.M. [0040050] 13/10/1986
Matthews Mrs NC, BA(Hons) DipInf, Lib., Addleshaw Booth & Co., Manchester. [0048653] 01/04/1993
Matthews Mrs PA, (was Richardson), MCLIP, Standards Offr., Consumers.Assn.Research-Test.Cent., Milton Keynes. [0012373] 01/07/1971
Matthews Mr PF, BA(Hons), Temp. [0054664] 13/02/1997 **AF**
Matthews Mrs PV, (was Scattergood), MCLIP, Childcare Co-ordinator, Wrexham Co.Bor.Council. [0018847] 13/07/1966
Matthews Mrs R, (was Wilkins), MCLIP, Lib., Wokingham Dist.Council. [0009951] 01/10/1963
Matthews Miss SA, BA MCLIP, Lib., Worcs.C.C., Tenbury Wells. [0027699] 04/07/1977
Matthews Mr SA, BEd MSc MCLIP, Lower Sch.Lib., The American Sch.in London, London. [0040776] 04/06/1987
Matthews Mrs SC, (was Dowell), BA BSc MCLIP, Lib., Northumberland C.C. [0019332] 01/10/1972
Matthews Miss SE, BSc(Hons) MA, Online Catr., Environment Agency, Bristol. [0057855] 10/09/1999
Matthews Mrs SE, (was Harris), BA(Hons) DipLib, Lib., HMP Askham Grange, York, & Asst.Lib., York & Co.Press. [0042524] 30/11/1988
Matthews Mrs SJ, (was Cathcart), BSc DipLib MCLIP, Sch.Lib., Pinewood Sch., Shivenham, Wilts. [0035619] 16/10/1982
Matthews Mrs SM, (was Smart), MCLIP, Grp.Lib.Cent.Serv., Haverfordwest L., Pembrokeshire C.C. [0013510] 01/01/1965
Matthews Mrs TJ, (was Barnard), BA(Hons) MCLIP, Lib.:Cent.Lend.Serv., Doncaster M.B.C., Cent.L. [0048414] 04/01/1993
Matthews Dr VC, BSc(Econ) MA MA PhD MCLIP, Grp.Mgr.for Reader Serv., UCL L.Serv. [0051840] 12/07/1995
Mattison Miss DP, MA(Hons), Research Offr., Historic Scotland, Edinburgh. [0055439] 13/10/1997
Maud Mr GP, BA(Hons) MCIPS LicIPD MCLIP, Unemployed. [0009955] 03/07/1967
Mauger Ms AJ, (was Le Moignan), MCLIP, Head of L.Serv., City of York. [0037571] 03/10/1984
Maughan Mr G, MCLIP, Life Member. [0009957] 24/04/1947
Maughan Mrs JD, CertEd MSc MCLIP, Lib., Univ.of Lincoln. [0054816] 11/04/1997
Maunder Ms FM, MCLIP, Lib., Castrol Internat.Tech.Cent., Berks. [0041827] 15/04/1988
Maunder Mrs M, (was West), BA DipLib, Unemployed. [0040760] 31/05/1987
Maurice Miss SJ, Sen.Inf.Offr., Hertford L.R.C., Univ.of Herts. [0061530] 16/09/2002 **AF**
Maville Mr AJ, BA MCLIP, Employment not known. [0060210] 10/12/2001
Maw Mrs CJ, (was Hamblin), MSc, Unemployed. [0036959] 18/01/1984
Mawby Mrs B, (was Tooth), MCLIP, Admin.Offr., N.Staffs.C.H.C., Stoke on Trent. [0009962] 16/08/1960
Mawby Mrs E, (was Dobson), BA MCLIP, Retired. [0009964] 27/08/1956
Mawby Miss J, BSc MCLIP, Retired. [0009965] 20/03/1969
Mawer Mr KP, MCLIP, Lib., Selby Coll., N.Yorks. [0039170] 26/11/1985
Mawhinney Ms JV, BA MCLIP, Employment not known. [0024106] 01/04/1979
Mawson Ms MB, (was Taylor), BA MA MCLIP, Academic Liaison Lib., Univ.of Sheffield, Crookesmoor L. [0035462] 20/10/1982
Maxim Mrs AJ, (was Bamford), CertEd MCLIP, Life Member. [0009970] 22/03/1950
Maxim Mr GE, MA FCLIP, Life Member. [0009971] 01/01/1959 **FE 01/01/1965**
Maxted Mr I, MA MCLIP, Co.Local Studies Lib., Devon L.Serv., Exeter. [0009972] 01/01/1967
Maxwell Mrs CM, BSc MCLIP, Employment not known. [0060670] 11/12/2001
Maxwell Ms D, MA(Hons) DipLIS MCLIP, Asst.Lib., Arch.& Colour Ref.Collection, Royal Coll.of Art, London. [0046550] 14/11/1991
Maxwell Mrs EA, (was Dunn), BA, P/T Lib./P/T Lib. Asst., Sportscotland/Edinburgh City L. [0037951] 27/11/1984
Maxwell Mrs H, (was Connacher), PGDipLIS, p./t.Lib., Pattison/Sim, Paisley. [0048061] 03/11/1992
Maxwell Mrs LJ, (was Gray), MA MCLIP, Unemployed. [0005835] 08/10/1970
Maxwell Mr M, BA DMS MCLIP, Cent.L.Mgr., Leicester City L. [0009975] 02/01/1970
Maxwell Mr N, FCLIP, Life Member. [0009977] 29/02/1960 **FE 01/01/1967**
Maxwell Mrs N, p./t.Stud, Asst.Lib., Univ.Wales., St Pauls Sch.Sao Paolo Brazil. [0058748] 04/07/2000
Maxwell Mrs P, BSc, Employment not known. [0060846] 12/12/2001
Maxwell Mrs S, (was Haffenden), BA(Hons) DipIS, Unemployed. [0052133] 05/10/1993
May Ms C, BA (Hons), Stud./Acting Lib.in charge., Univ. N.London./Middlesex Univ. [0060875] 18/12/2001
May Mr HMH, MA MCLIP, Retired. [0017368] 24/09/1953

May Ms JA, BA(Hons) MA MCLIP, Lib., Ewell Publishing, Ewell, Surrey. [0054405] 03/12/1996
May Mrs L, Records Lib., AstraZeneca (R.& D.), Loughborough. [0048146] 11/11/1992
May Mrs LC, (was Watson), BA DipLib MCLIP, Dep.Head, L.Learning Res./Campus L., Univ.of Wales Coll., Newport. [0027377] 28/02/1977
May Mrs M, BSc MSc MCLIP, Position unknown, Britvic Soft Drinks. [0060783] 12/12/2001
May Mr NW, BSc MCLIP, Inf.& Learning Serv.Co-ordinator, Univ.of Plymouth. [0023751] 16/01/1975
May Mr RE, BSc PGDipLIB MCLIP, LIS Faculty Liaison Offr.-Sci., Clifton Campus L., Nottingham Trent Univ. [0028854] 05/02/1978
May Mr SD, BSc MSc MCLIP, H.of Operations, Southend on Sea Bor.L. [0040712] 05/05/1987
May Ms TG, BScEcon(Hons) MSc MCLIP, Subj.Lib., A.P.U., Cambridge. [0047531] 01/10/1992
May Miss TK, Distribution & Devel.Co-ordinator, Med.Records, Royal United Hosp. [0061135] 07/03/2002
May-Bowles Mrs J, (was May), BA(Hons), Head of L.& Inf.Serv., NFER, Slough. [0009984] 30/11/1967
Maybury Mrs JE, BA(Hons) PGCE, Stud., Manchester Met.Univ. [0059474] 04/04/2001
Mayer Mr KEA, BA(Hons) DipIM, Asst.Lib., L.B.of Barnet, Mill Hill L. [0053804] 02/10/1996
Mayers Mrs A, Stud., Liverpoool John Moores Univ. [0055890] 16/12/1997
Mayers Mr RO, MCLIP, Life Member, 55 Brereton Dr., Nantwich, CW5 6HE. [0019335] 01/01/1955
Mayes Miss FE, FCLIP, Life Member. [0009993] 02/10/1934 **FE 01/01/1950**
Mayes Mrs GD, BA(Hons) MSc, Lib., St.Michaels Coll., Co.Fermanagh, N.Ireland. [0059316] 02/02/2001
Maynard Ms C, MCLIP, Unemployed. [0009999] 03/01/1972
Maynard Ms IM, BA MCLIP, Grp.Lib., Harrogate, N.Yorks.Co.L. [0025359] 12/01/1976
Maynard Ms LH, (was Wontner-Smith), LLB DipLib MCLIP, Inf.Serv.Mgr., McDermott, Will & Emery, London. [0042176] 08/10/1988
Mayo Mrs L, (was Adcock), BA MCLIP, Lib., Essex County L., Clacton L. [0028772] 23/01/1978
Mayor Mrs FE, (was Bull), BA MCLIP, Lib., Ormskirk L. [0022403] 07/05/1974
Mayston Mr AJ, MA MCLIP, Retired. [0010010] 24/10/1964
Mayston Mrs SA, BSc(Hons) MSc, Inf.Mgr., Cambridge Antibody Tech., Royston, Cambs. [0057798] 02/08/1999
Maythorne Mrs I, (was Julian), MCLIP, Unemployed. [0008141] 06/02/1967
Maywood Mrs DM, MA AMA FSA(Scot) DipILM, Grad.Trainee, L.Resource Cent., Coleg Llandrillo, Colwyn Bay, Conwy. [0057186] 05/01/1999
Mazumdar Mr P, BSc MSc MCLIP, Employment not known. [0060790] 12/12/2001
Mbye Mr AW, MA DipLib, Ch.Lib., Gambia Nat.L., The Gambia. [0043996] 01/04/1990
McAbery Mrs K, (was Russell), BSc(Hons), Unemployed. [0057441] 01/04/1999
McAdam Mrs J, BA(Hons) PGCE, Market Inf.Co-ordinator, Traidcraft Exchange, Gateshead. [0061269] 10/05/2002 **AF**
McAdam Mrs VP, (was Sayers), BSc(Hons) MCLIP, Lib., N.Staffs.Heatlh, Stoke-on-Trent. [0041706] 23/02/1988
McAdams Mr AC, LLB DipAcc, Lib., MacRoberts, Glasgow. [0049989] 10/02/1994
McAdoo Miss WL, BLS, Exec.Offr.-Res., Holy Trinity Coll., SEELB., Co.Tyrone. [0038606] 22/07/1985
McAinsh Mrs CM, (was Hendry), MA(Hons) DipLib MCLIP, Asst.Lib., East Kilbride Cent.L., Glasgow. [0031631] 15/10/1979
McAllister Mrs AM, (was Fairlie), BA(Hons) MCLIP, Primary Educ.Resource Co-ordinator, N.Ayrshire Council, Greenwood Teachers Cent. [0038389] 15/04/1985
McAlpin Mrs A, (was Lister), MA MCLIP, Classification & Catg.Proj.Mgr., Edinburgh Univ.L. [0008973] 11/11/1969
McAlpine Mr IK, MA, Unemployed. [0049641] 16/11/1993
McAra Mrs YM, (was Cockett), BA MCLIP, L.Offr.(Job Share), City of Edinburgh Council. [0029938] 02/11/1978
McArdle Mrs C, (was Robinson), BA DipLib MCLIP, Dep.Lib., Lincoln's Inn L., London. [0038131] 19/01/1985
McArthur Ms CA, Learning & Inf.Serv.Asst., Cent.Sch.of Speech & Drama. [0059289] 29/01/2001 **AF**
McAulay Miss AMN, BA FCLIP, Life Member. [0009237] 24/08/1950 **FE 01/01/1957**
McAulay Mrs KE, (was Manley), BA MA LTCL DipLib MCLIP, Music & Academic Serv.Lib., Royal Scottish Academy of Music &, Drama, Glasgow. [0036433] 11/10/1983
McAuley Mrs DE, BA, Stud., Univ.of N.London. [0058026] 14/10/1999
McAuley Mrs G, MCLIP, L.Asst., Tamworth Coll., Staffs. [0009238] 01/01/1963
McAuliffe Mr SJ, BA DipLib MCLIP, Asst.Lib., Lincoln Coll.L., Oxford. [0029740] 01/10/1978
McAvoy Mrs FCM, BA(Hons) CertEd MSc MCLIP, Acquisitions Lib., Univ.of Bath, L.& Learning Cent. [0051496] 16/03/1995
McBride Miss F, BA(Hons), Stud., UCL., Sch of L.,Inf.& Archive Stud. [0059007] 23/10/2000
McBride Mrs KE, BA, Asst.Lib., Bishop Grosseteste Coll., Lincoln. [0052586] 09/11/1995
McBride Mrs M, (was Reid), MA MCLIP, P./t.Lib., G.Practice, Aberfeldy. [0009245] 14/10/1968
McBride Mrs VJ, BA MCLIP, Admin.Lib.Circulation, Univ.of Northumbria at Newcastle. [0035800] 25/01/1983
McBryde-Wilding Mrs HA, (was McBryde), BA(Hons) MA MCLIP, Faculty Lib., Univ.Coll.Northampton, Northampton. [0046046] 10/09/1991

McCabe Miss J, BSc(Hons) DipIS MCLIP, Lib.(Acq.), Hants.C.C., Winchester, Hants. [0052263]   19/10/1995
McCaig Ms GA, DipLib MCLIP, Comm.L.Serv.Mgr., City L.& Inf.Serv., Edinburgh. [0020468]   30/09/1968
McCaig Miss L, BSc(Hons) DipILS, Inf.Analyst, DSTL, Glasgow. [0052191]   12/10/1995
McCall Mrs HM, (was Callander), MA DipLib MCLIP, Inf.Offr., Grampian CareData, Old Meldrum,Aberdeenshire. [0044860]   01/01/1991
McCall Mrs MR, MCLIP, Life Member. [0017315]   01/01/1951
McCallum Ms AJ, Admin.Offr., Lib, Countryside Council for Wales. [0059290]   29/01/2001
McCallum Mr D, MCLIP, Retired, Cllr., N.Lanarkshire Council. [0009250]   19/09/1964
McCallum Mr J, BA(Hons), Info.Offr., Glasgow City Council. [0061700]   14/10/2002
McCallum Mrs SEJ, (was Hemes), MCLIP, Sen.Lib., Redditch L., Worcs.C.C. [0006701]   15/02/1971
McCance Miss C, BA(Hons) MCLIP, Team Lib., N.Lanarkshire Council, Educ.Res.Serv. [0053066]   09/02/1996
McCann Mrs BM, BA(Hons) DipEurHum, Sen.L.Asst., SELB, Banbridge L., Armagh. [0058984]   13/10/2000
McCann Miss JE, BA MCLIP, Princ.Offr., ICT & Systems Mgmt., City of Sunderland Council. [0031660]   05/11/1979
McCann Mr PJ, BA MCLIP, Area Lib.& IT Devel.Mgr., Argyll & Bute Council, Helensburgh L. [0039653]   08/04/1986
McCann Miss SA, BA, Mgmnt. Support, Thomson Pettie Group, Carluke. [0060997]   28/01/2002
McCappin Miss J, BA MCLIP, p./t.Inf.Offr., Manchester Comm.Health Councils. [0022897]   02/10/1974
McCarren Ms JF, BA PGDip MCLIP ILT, Academic Liaison Lib., Anglia Poly.Univ., Cambridge. [0046880]   20/02/1992
McCarrick Mrs CV, (was Gee), BA(Hons), Unemployed. [0050757]   17/10/1994
McCarroll Miss R, MCLIP, Asst.Lib., Inverclyde L. [0009260]   30/09/1968
McCarron Mrs L, BA(Hons), p./t.Stud./Ref.Serv.Mgr., Nat.L.of Scotland. [0057233]   15/01/1999
McCarron Mrs SM, (was O'Hare), BA DipLib, P./t.Lib., High Sch.of Glasgow (Jnr.Sch.), Glasgow. [0038359]   25/03/1985
McCarthy Mrs A, (was Bowman), MCLIP MA, Retired. [0024984]   12/01/1960
McCarthy Mrs AP, (was Glover), BA DipLib MCLIP, L.& Inf.Co-ordinator, Somerset Learning & Skills Council, Taunton. [0028301]   15/11/1977
McCarthy Mrs BE, BSc(Econ), Visual Res.Curator, Slide L., Tate Gallery, London. [0053242]   19/04/1974
McCarthy Mrs CJ, Asst.Arch., British Railways Board, London. [0053907]   09/10/1996
McCarthy Dr CM, PhD MLS BA MCLIP, Asst.Prof., Sch.of L.& Inf.Sci., Louisiana State Univ., U.S.A. [0029245]   01/01/1965
McCarthy Mr CR, L.Asst., Univ.of Surrey. [0056666]   30/09/1998   **AF**
McCarthy Mr DF, BA, Unemployed. [0061417]   12/07/2002
McCarthy Mrs J, (was Palmer), BA(Hons) DipLIS, Lib., Rapra Tech.Ltd., Shropshire. [0052376]   30/10/1995
McCarthy Ms JI, MA MA PGCE, Trainee Liaison Lib., Reading Univ.L. [0057031]   13/11/1999
McCarthy Mr PJ, BA MCLIP, Resources Lib., L.B.of Barking & Dagenham, Barking. [0034803]   26/01/1982
McCartney Ms FM, BA(Hons) PGCE, Res.Mgr., BELL, Cambridge. [0057372]   26/02/1999
McCartney Mrs KM, PhilCand MEd MCLIP, Head of L., Hampton Sch., Middx. [0028962]   15/02/1978
McCaskie Ms L, BA, Grad.Trainee, Newnham College L., Cambridge. [0061596]   02/10/2002
McCaskill Ms K, BA(Hons) MA MCLIP, Community Lib., Northants.Cent.L. [0058068]   22/10/1999
McCausland Miss JD, BLib MCLIP, L.Devel.Mgr., Swindon Bor.L. [0037344]   04/07/1984
McChesney Mrs P, (was Wyness), BA MCLIP, Careers Adviser, Univ.of Northumbria at Newcastle. [0009270]   01/01/1965
McClarnon Miss MJ, BA(Hons), Deputy Lib., Inf.Centre & L., Irish Management Inst. [0059892]   29/10/2001
McClean Mrs H, (was Sture), BA(Hons) DipILS MCLIP, Lend.Lib., Dover. [0054564]   28/01/1997
McClean Miss M, BA DipLib MCLIP, Educ.Resources Lib., Sch.L.Serv., Belfast P.L. [0009273]   14/02/1972
McClean Mr NM, BA(Hons) MA MSc(Econ), Subject Lib., Educ.& Language, Kent C.C. [0055996]02/01/1998
McClean Mrs PM, (was Sproull), BA DipLib MCLIP, Young Peoples Serv.Co-ordinator, Mitchell L., Glasgow. [0035406]   05/10/1982
McClean Mrs SAC, (was Dean), BA DipLib MCLIP, p./t.Team Lib., Stockport M.B.C. [0026712]   12/10/1976
McClellan Mrs JA, (was Green), MCLIP, Employment not known. [0029062]   13/03/1978
McClelland Ms PM, BA DipILM, Lib.(Acquisitions), Oxford Brookes Univ., Gypsy Lane Campus. [0050191]   28/04/1994
McClelland Mr W, FCLIP, Retired. [0009276]   17/03/1934   **FE 01/01/1946**
McClen Mrs RL, (was Grey), BA(Hons) DipILM, Sen.Inf.Offr., Eversheds, Newcastle upon Tyne. [0052472]   02/11/1995
McCloskey Mr PCM, MCLIP, BA DipLib MCLIP, Unemployed. [0034906]   27/03/1982
McCloskey Mrs T, BSc, L.Asst./Stud., Suffolk Br.L., Belfast. [0061459]   02/08/2002
McClure Mrs CB, BA MCLIP, Acquisitions Lib., Bournemouth & Poole Coll., Poole. [0029741]   03/10/1978

McClure Mr CJ, MA MLib MCLIP, Princ.Asst.Lib., Havering L.Serv., L.B.of Havering. [0039814]   28/07/1986
McClure Mrs SM, (was Gullick), MA MCLIP, Sec.to Trustees, Nat.Mus.of Scotland, Edinburgh. [0006044]   01/10/1971
McClure Mrs VB, MA(Hons) MScILS, Asst.Lib., R.C.P.S.of Glasgow. [0058413]   04/02/2000
McCluskey Miss CJ, BA(Hons), Stud., Leeds Metro.Univ. [0061782]   06/11/2002
McCluskey Mrs E, (was Farrell), MCLIP, Tutor Lib., Braidhurst High Sch., Motherwell. [0004785]   06/10/1969
McCluskey Miss FJ, MCLIP, Lib., Support Servs., Notts.C.C. [0018318]   16/10/1972
McCluskey Mrs M, (was Duff), BA MCLIP, Sch.Lib.(Job Share), Bellarmine Secondary Sch., Glasgow. [0034962]   14/05/1982
McCluskey Mrs S, BA(Hons), Lib., St.Louis Grammar Sch., Ballymena, Co Antrim. [0057760]   26/07/1999   **AF**
McClymont Mr T, MCLIP, Retired. [0027831]   07/09/1977
McColl Mrs G, BSc MSc MCLIP, Employment not known. [0060704]   12/12/2001
McColl Ms S, L.Asst., Dunfermline Carnegie L., Fife Council. [0050357]   01/07/1994   **AF**
McComb Mr D, BA MCLIP, p./t.Asst.Lib., Ref.L., Richmond upon Thames P.L. [0009283]   11/01/1965
McCombe Mrs C, (was Cousins), MCLIP, L.Asst., Surrey C.C. [0009285]   14/01/1965
McCombs Mrs GM, (was Clive), BA MPA, Dir.of L's., Southern Methodist Univ., Dallas, Texas, U.S.A. [0034865]   01/01/1968
McConchie Mrs TA, (was Bailey), BA MCLIP, Learning Support Asst., The Leys Primary Sch., Stevenage. [0034671]   27/01/1982
McConnachie Mrs SLE, (was Macduff), BA MCLIP, Lib., Douglas Academy, E.Dunbartonshire. [0032116]   28/01/1980
McConnell Mr GA, BA(Hons), Unemployed. [0053962]   16/01/1996
McConnell Mr MRA, MA MSc PgDip MCLIP, Employment unknown. [0060249]   10/12/2001
McConnell Mrs SL, (was Hull), BdEd(Hons) DipIM MCLIP, Unemployed. [0049094]   01/10/1993
McConville Mrs OP, (was Rooney), BA DIP, Team Lib.-Child.& Young People, S.E.L.B., Warrenpoint, Co.Down. [0031006]   28/06/1979
McCormick Mr EA, MA DipLib MCLIP, Team Leader, Edinburgh City Ls. [0045473]   14/02/1991
McCormick Mrs N, (was Adamson), CEd MCLIP, Learning Res.Advisor, Bedford Coll. [0009292]   01/01/1965
McCorry Miss MCI, DipLib MCLIP, Asst.Lib., Dublin P.L.H.Q., Eire. [0027498]   26/04/1977
McCosh Mrs L, (was Pennington), BA DipLib, Ch.L.Asst., Univ.of Bradford, W.Yorks. [0033699]   05/02/1981
McCoskery Mrs WR, (was Huish), BA MCLIP, Asst.Lib., L.B.of Redbridge. [0027067]   24/01/1977
McCracken Mrs H, (was Johnston), BSc MCLIP, Mother. [0040062]   16/01/1986
McCracken Mr IG, BA MCLIP, Lib.i/c, Govan High Sch., Glasgow City Council. [0026776]   26/01/1976
McCrae Mr G, MPhil BA MCLIP, Employment unknown. [0060240]   10/12/2001
McCraw Mrs EH, BA(Hons), Sch.Lib., Milnes High Sch., Moray Council. [0041795]   01/04/1988
McCrea Mrs PA, (was Metson), L.Mgr., Glos.C.L., Hucclecote L. [0045204]   10/08/1990   **AF**
McCrea Mr R, MA(Hons), Stud., Strathclyde Univ. [0061765]   05/11/2002
McCready Mrs A, (was Hunter), BA MCLIP, Lib., Cheshire Co.L. [0026420]   01/10/1976
McCready Mr R, Bibl.Serv.Lib., Univ.of Liverpool. [0057048]   30/11/1998
McCree Mr M, BSc(Hons) MA MCLIP, Lib., Earl Shilton L., Leics.C.C. [0055135]   16/07/1997
McCreedy Miss KS, BA(Hons) MCLIP, Intranet Lib., H.M.Treasury, London. [0030483]   08/01/1979
McCrisken Mrs HMB, (was O'Kelly), BA(Hons) DipLib, Inf.Offr. [0034265]   19/10/1981
McCrohan Ms MG, BA(Hons), Legal Inf.Mgr., Coudert Bros., London. [0048463]   15/01/1993
McCrudden Mrs PA, (was Gray), MCLIP, Inf.& L.Serv.Mgr., Essex Soc.Serv., Chelmsford. [0032657]   02/07/1980
McCubbin Mr ED, BSc DipILS MCLIP, Liaison Offr., HERON Project, Univ.of Stirling. [0052730]   29/11/1995
McCullagh Mrs SGC, (was Brown), BA(Hons) MCLIP, Networked Inf.Lib., Cent.L., Bristol. [0039257]   13/01/1986
McCulloch Mr DA, BA MCLIP, Policy & Research Offr., UNISON, London. [0025372]   31/12/1975
McCulloch Mr E, MA(Hons) MSc, p./t.L.Asst., William Patrick L., E.Dunbartonshire Council. [0055820]   26/11/1997
McCulloch Mrs S, (was Clark), BA MCLIP, Head of Learning Res., Wilts.C.C., Trowbridge. [0009308]   01/01/1968
McCulloch Mrs S, (was Mercer), BA MCLIP, Area Co-ordinator, Comm.Serv., Notts.Co.L. [0008312]   01/01/1970
McCullough Miss JE, BA(Hons)(Oxon) MA(QUB), Stud., Strathclyde Univ. [0059708]   28/08/2001
McCullough Ms SM, BSc(Hons) DipLib MCLIP MIPD, Training & L.Consultant. [0019787]   14/10/1972
McCutcheon Miss A, MA(Hons), Stud., Strathclyde Univ. [0061179]   03/04/2002
McDaid Mrs MG, MCLIP, Retired. [0029461]   17/08/1978
McDermid Mrs K, (was Schouten), BSc(Hons), Stud., Univ.of Northumbria, Newcastle. [0057849]   09/09/1999
McDermott Ms N, BA DLIS DipSocStud, Dir., L.Council, Dublin, Ireland. [0049322]   22/10/1993

301

McDevitt Mrs A, AIL, Learning Res.Cent.Mgr., Cardiff High Sch., Cardiff. [0054801] 04/04/1997
McDonagh Mr BJ, Head of Inf.Serv., The Industrial Soc., London. [0040539] 23/02/1987
McDonagh Miss C, BA(Hons) MA, Team Leader Content, Royal Inst.of Chartered Surveyors, London. [0056528] 10/08/1998
McDonagh Mrs J, (was Mcintosh), MCLIP, Housebound Serv.Lib., Edinburgh City L. [0009421] 04/04/1968
McDonagh Mr MJM, BLS(Hons), Br.Lib., Southern Educ.& L.Board, Brownlow. [0033055] 01/10/1980
McDonald Prof AC, BSc FCLIP, Dir.of Inf.Serv., Univ.of Sunderland, Tyne & Wear. [0018403] 18/09/1972 **FE 19/07/2000**
McDonald Mr AG, BA(Hons) MA, Unemployed. [0058634] 25/04/2000
McDonald Mr AH, MA, Unemployed. [0058676] 15/05/2000
McDonald Ms B, BA MA DipLib ALAI, Asst.Lib., Trinity Coll., Dublin, Ireland. [0057249] 25/01/1999
McDonald Miss C, MA(Hons), Stud., Strathclyde Univ. [0059418] 07/03/2001
McDonald Mrs CS, (was Robins), BA DipLib MCLIP, Housewife & Mother. [0042326] 24/10/1988
McDonald Miss CT, MCLIP, Retired. [0009321] 16/04/1948
McDonald Mrs DP, (was Fordham), BA MCLIP, Unemployed. [0018696] 01/10/1972
McDonald Ms EA, BA MCLIP, Systems Lib., Peterhouse, Cambridge. [0022139] 07/01/1974
McDonald Mrs EE, (was Orrock), MA(Hons), Sch.Lib., Chancellor's Sch., Hatfield. [0044976] 28/01/1991
McDonald Miss EF, BA, Asst.Lib., Burleigh Comm.Coll. [0058133] 04/11/1999
McDonald Miss F, BA DipLib MCLIP, Community Servs.Devel.Lib., Comm.Inf.:L., Herts. [0037613] 09/10/1984
McDonald Mrs FC, (was Campbell), BA MCLIP, Comm.Lib., N.Lanarkshire Council, Bellshill. [0034513] 20/11/1981
McDonald Mrs GA, MA MCLIP MBA, Reader Serv.Mgr., Heriot-Watt Univ., Edinburgh. [0031373] 16/10/1979
McDonald Ms L, (was Lake), BLib MCLIP, Lib., Brockenhurst Coll., Hants. [0008569] 01/10/1968
McDonald Ms MJ, BA PGDip, Asst.Lib., DEFRA, London. [0056674] 01/10/1998
McDonald Ms P, (was Paine), BA MCLIP, Dep.Coll.Lib., City Coll.Brighton & Hove. [0009332] 13/03/1967
McDonald Mr V, BA MCLIP, Business Mgr., L.& Heritage, Suffolk C.C., Ipswich. [0009336] 01/01/1971
McDonald Mrs YM, (was Wilson), BA DMS DipLib MCLIP, Asst.Co.Lib., Oxon.Co.L. [0030572] 22/01/1979
McDonnell Miss G, BA BA MCLIP, Catg.Lib., Staffs.Univ., Stoke-on-Trent. [0009339] 04/10/1967
McDonough Mrs CM, (was Booth), BSc DipLIB MCLIP, Princ.Lib., Cent.L., L.B.of Sutton. [0031791] 14/01/1980
McDougall Mr GI, BA(Hons) DipIT MCLIP, L.Systems Mgr., Univ.of the Highlands & Islands, Elgin. [0044905] 11/01/1991
McDougall Mrs S, MCLIP, Lib., Deans Community High Sch., Livingston. [0028865] 30/01/1978
McDougle Miss AEE, MBE FCLIP, Retired. [0009345] 19/01/1938 **FE 01/01/1954**
McDowell Mrs AD, (was Donaghy), BA DipLib MCLIP, L.Res.Cent.Co-ordinator, The Moray Council, Forres Academy, Moray. [0031059] 08/08/1979
McDowell Mrs BA, Secretary, St.Albans City & Dist.Council. [0056380] 01/07/1998 **SP**
McDowell Mrs H, (was Henry), BA MCLIP, Unemployed. [0009347] 18/10/1965
McEachen Mr J, BSc MCLIP, Head of L.& Arts, Royal Bor.of Kensington & Chelsea, London. [0019304] 03/03/1970
McEachen Ms S, BSc DipIM MCLIP, Inf.Offr., Clifford Chance LLP, London. [0049129] 06/10/1993
McEachern Miss KL, BA MCLIP, Lib., Mearns Castle High Sch. [0042380] 28/10/1988
McEachran Mrs C, (was Revell), MCLIP, Relief L.Asst., Dumfries & Galloway L. [0012267] 01/01/1968
McEachran Mr MA, BA MCLIP, Faculty Lib., Univ.of the W.of England, Bristol. [0024745] 02/10/1975
McElligott Mrs ME, BA DipLib, L.Res.Asst., Southgate Coll., London. [0034210] 12/08/1981
McElroy Prof R, MA MBA DipLib FCLIP, Retired, Marfield View, Kitley Knowe, Carlops, Midlothian, EH26 9NJ. [0009352] 12/10/1967 **FE 18/04/1989**
McElwain Mrs SE, BA DipLib MCLIP, Unemployed. [0024527] 01/09/1975
McElwee Ms G, BA(Hons) DipLib MCLIP, Child.Serv.Mgr.(Job-share), L.B.of Croydon, Cent.L. [0034661] 21/01/1982
McEnaney Miss C, BA(Hons), Asst.Lib., Hammond Suddards Edge, Leeds. [0056911] 04/11/1998
McEnroe Mrs SM, (was Finn), MCLIP, Trust Lib., Taunton & Somerset NHS Trust, Taunton, Somerset. [0039491] 20/01/1960
McEntegart Miss CFM, BSc MSc, Self Employed. [0054333] 21/11/1996
McEvoy Miss EM, BA(Hons), Stud., (distance learn.), RGU., & Montgomery Watson, High Wycombe. [0058269] 17/08/2000
McEvoy Ms H, BA(Hons) DipILM, Ref.& Info.Asst., John Rylands Univ L., Manchester. [0058661] 09/05/2000
McEvoy Mrs P, (was Madden), MCLIP, Asst.Lib.,[Cent.Reader Serv.], City L.& Arts Cent., City of Sunderland. [0009353] 16/03/1965
McEwan Mrs AEK, BA (Hons), Stud., Univ.of Strathclyde. [0060879] 18/12/2001
McEwan Mr K, MCLIP, Retired, 34 Rutland Gdns., London,N4 1JP. [0009359] 01/01/1957
McFadden Mrs K, (was Boyden), Unemployed. [0031206] 17/10/1979
McFadyen Mrs L, BA(Hons) MSc, Catr., Greater Glasgow NHS Board. [0058246] 24/11/1999

McFadzien Mrs BWC, (was Samman), FCLIP, Retired. [0012897] 01/01/1932 **FE 01/01/1938**
McFarland Miss J, MCLIP, Project Mgr.(Computerisation), Educ.& Leisure Dept., City of Salford. [0009361] 11/09/1970
McFarland Mrs MP, (was Norton), BA MCLIP, L.Asst., E.Tyrone Coll.of F.E., Dungannon. [0025084] 29/10/1975
McFarlane Ms CJ, DipEd DipLib MCLIP, Sch.Lib., Devon C.C., Exeter. [0043871] 02/02/1990
McFarlane Ms EG, MA MCLIP, Asst.Lib., Univ.of Southampton New Coll. [0022930] 23/09/1974
McFarlane Mrs J, BA MCLIP, P./t.Asst.Lib., W.Herts Hosp.Trust, Mount Vernon Hosp. [0009365] 25/05/1971
McFarlane Ms J, BA MCLIP, Head of Ref.Serv., Nat.L.of Scotland. [0030890] 21/05/1979
McFarlane Mrs JA, (was Brown), BA MCLIP, Sen Lib., Inf.Serv., Renfrewshire L. [0023408] 09/01/1975
McFarlane Ms KA, (was Sage), BA MLib MCLIP, Head of Corp.Inf.Knowledge Serv., Government Communications H.Q., Cheltenham. [0028245] 10/10/1977
McFarlane Mrs ME, (was Honess), MCLIP, Lib., Noel-Baker Community Sch., Alvaston, Derbys. [0007144] 03/02/1966
McFaul Mr MJ, MBA(Hons) DipM MCLIP, Asst.Ch.Lib., N.E.E.L.B., Ballymena. [0018383] 10/10/1972
McFetridge Mrs D, (was Patterson), BA(Hons), Inf.Offr., Law Soc.of N.Ireland, Belfast. [0052844] 01/09/1996
McGaffney Ms J, Inf.Asst., Hammond Suddards Edge, London. [0061457] 02/08/2002
McGarrigle Mrs HP, (was Hunter), MCLIP, Lib., Rutland C.C. [0025319] 05/01/1976
McGarrity Mr J, BA MCLIP, Inf.Serv.Co-ordinator, S.Lanarkshire Council, Hamilton Cent.L. [0026476] 01/10/1976
McGarrity Mrs M, (was Fay), MCLIP, Retired. [0009370] 20/01/1948
McGarry Ms D, MLS, Retired. [0044630] 12/11/1990
McGarry Dr K, PhD FCLIP, Retired. [0009372] 28/01/1956 **FE 01/01/1967**
McGarry Ms M, MA DipLib MCLIP, Lib., N.Lanarkshire Council. [0035253] 01/10/1982
McGeachin Mrs S, (was Chippendale), BA MCLIP, Lib.& Learning Res.Cent.Mgr., Culcheth Co.High Sch., Warrington. [0009377] 12/01/1967
McGeachy Mrs AMS, (was Scott), BSc DipLib MCLIP, Process Mgr., Defence Sci.Tech.Lab., Glasgow. [0020125] 21/01/1973
McGee Mrs KM, BA, Stud., Northumbria Univ. [0061694] 21/10/2002
McGeown Mr BJ, BA(Hons) MBA MCLIP, Grp.Lib., Lurgan Grp.L.H.Q., Co.Armagh. [0024528] 20/08/1975
McGettigan Mrs A, Asst.Lib., St Aidens's Co.High Sch., Carlisle, Cumbria. [0057695] 01/07/1999 **AF**
McGibben Ms JM, (was Howlett), BA MCLIP, Sen.Lib., S.Div., Hants.Co.L. [0007326] 08/02/1972
McGibbon Mrs B, (was Donnelly), BLS DMS DipCompSci MCLIP, Inf.Offr., L.E.D.U., Belfast. [0040809] 01/07/1977
McGill Mr I, BA MCLIP, Sen.Asst.Lib., Liverpool City L. [0009379] 02/11/1971
McGill Miss J, BSc, Grad.Trainee, St.Hughs Coll. Oxford. [0059935] 07/11/2001
McGill Miss JC, BA(Hons) DipILS, Lib., Auchinleck Acad., Auchinleck, Ayrshire. [0052845] 01/01/1996
McGilloway Mrs M, (was Poulain), MSc(Econ) MCLIP, Lib., Clevedon Comm.Sch. [0053850] 04/10/1996
McGinley Ms D, (was Allan), BSc MCLIP, Lib., Fife Acute NHS Trust, Kirkcaldy. [0026219] 14/08/1976
McGivern Miss KL, MA DipILS MCLIP, Sch.Lib., St.Patrick's High Sch., Coatbridge. [0058086] 26/10/1999
McGlen Miss HE, BSc MCLIP, Inf.Advisor, Shell U.K.Exploration, Aberdeen. [0033058] 20/10/1980
McGlew Ms CK, MA(Hons) MSc, Asst.Lib., Health Educ.Board for Scotland, Edinburgh. [0053956] 16/10/1996
McGlynn Mrs SP, (was Fraser), BA MCLIP, Retired. [0017329] 04/12/1962
McGough Mrs KE, (was Dove), BA(Hons) MSc MCLIP, Open Learning Centre Co-ordinator, Essex C.C., Chelmsford. [0049200] 12/10/1993
McGowan Mr B, MCLIP, Retired, [0009386] 26/02/1969
McGowan Mr ID, BA, Lib., Nat.L.of Scotland, Edinburgh. [0044953] 22/01/1991
McGowan Mr J, BA MA, Unemployed. [0061100] 01/03/2002
McGowan Mr S, BA(Hons) DipLIS, ICT Systems Lib., S.Ayrshire C. [0055121] 16/07/1997
McGrain Mrs CL, BSc(Hons) PGCE, Stud., London Metro. [0061625] 03/10/2002
McGrath Mrs AJ, (was Warburton), MSc, Lib., Withers Solicitors, London. [0049756] 02/12/1993
McGrath Mrs AM, (was Glegg), BSc MSc MCLIP, Inf.Specialist, Kings Coll.London. [0045681] 22/04/1991
McGrath Mrs CM, (was Mackintosh), BA MCLIP, Sch.Lib., Bankhead, Aberdeen. [0046402] 01/11/1991
McGrath Ms FM, (was McGarth), BA, Ref.Serv.Mgr., Scottish Parliament Inf.Cent., Edinburgh. [0038875] 16/10/1985
McGrath Ms HM, BSc(Hons) MA MCLIP, Indexer, Chartered Inst.of Marketing, Cookham. [0051434] 14/02/1995
McGrath Miss PM, BA(Hons) DipILM MCLIP, Asst.Lib., Liverpool Hope Univ.Coll. [0053988] 14/10/1996
McGrath Mr WG, Tutor-Lib., Amersham & Wycombe Coll., Bucks. [0036231] 09/08/1983
McGrave Mrs AJ, (was Whitter), BA MCLIP, Lib.,Mus.& Drama, Hants.Co.L. [0015782] 10/02/1965
McGrave Mr M, MA MCLIP, Retired. [0009395] 11/01/1962
McGreevy Mr T, BA(Hons), Sen.L.Asst., Bell Coll.of Tech., Hamilton. [0056764] 08/10/1998

McGregor Mr C, BA MCLIP, Lib., Grangemouth L. [0028867] 13/02/1978
McGregor Mr I, BA MCLIP AALIA, Quality & Training Mgr., Yarra Plenty Reg.L.Serv., Victoria, Australia. [0009398] 22/09/1968
McGregor Mr R, BA(Hons) MLITT, p./t.Stud./L.Asst., Robert Gordon Univ., Univ.of Strathclyde. [0061313] 17/05/2002
McGrimmond Miss J, BA MCLIP, Asst.Lib., Aberdeen City L. [0028080] 11/10/1977
McGrory Mrs C, p./t.Stud./Lib., Univ.of Aberystwyth, The Deans High Sch., Lowestoft. [0053370] 24/05/1996
McGugan Miss CJ, MA(Hons) MSc, Trainee Lib., Glasgow City Council. [0059716] 05/09/2001
McGuigan Ms AC, BA DipInf MCLIP, Mgr.-Tech.Forecasting & Inf., Oxford. [0055053] 03/07/1997
McGuigan Mr JD, BA PGDip, Unemployed. [0059376] 23/02/2001
McGuiggan Mr JM, BA DipLib MCLIP, Dist.Lib., WELB., Co.Tyrone. [0027347] 09/03/1977
McGuinness Mr D, MCLIP, Lend.Serv.Mgr., N.Lanarks.Council, Motherwell. [0009401] 22/04/1971
McGuinness Mrs JA, (was Brown), BLib MCLIP, Asst.Lib., Macaulay Land Use Research Inst., Aberdeen. [0036128] 27/05/1983
McGuire Ms J, (was Gray), BA(Hons) DipLIS MCLIP, Team Lib., Univ.of Northumbria, Newcastle. [0044545] 24/10/1990
McGuire Miss LE, MA(Hons) DipILS, Higher L.Executive, House of Commons L., London. [0055821] 26/11/1997
McGurk Miss GR, MCLIP, Asst.Arch., USPG- United Soc.for Prop.Gospel, London. [0019753] 23/09/1967
McHale Ms A, Local Enquiry Offr., Business Link for Tees Valley, Middlesbrough. [0061041] 11/02/2002
McHale Miss GA, BSc(Hons) MSc MCLIP, Lib., LSL HA, London. [0047270] 01/07/1992
Mcharazo Dr AAS, BA MA PhD FCLIP, Lib./Head of Dept., Univ.Coll.of Lands & Arch.Studies, Dar es Salaam, Tanzania. [0047548] 01/10/1992 FE 21/11/2001
McHardy Miss FS, MA(Hons), I.T.Admin., Aker Kvaerner Oil & Gas, Aberdeen. [0057164] 05/01/1999
McHugh Ms EA, MA(Hons) DipILS MCLIP, Coll.Lib., Wigston Coll.of F.E., Wigston, Leicester. [0052836] 02/01/1996
McHugh Mrs M, (was Chanter), MCLIP, L.Mgr., Laing Tech.Grp., London. [0019968] 04/01/1973
McHugo Ms PME, BA(Hons) MA Msc, Educ.Offr., Westminster City Council. [0059727] 05/09/2001
McIlraith Mr B, BSc MCLIP, Retired. [0009411] 20/09/1952
McIlroy Miss AJ, MLIS, Sch.L.Asst., Belfast Educ.& L.Board, Wellington Coll. [0058222] 12/11/1999
McIlwaine Prof IC, (was Thorold), BA PhD FCLIP, Prof.& Sen.Research Fellow, Sch.of Lib., Univ.Coll.London. [0009414] 01/01/1958 FE 01/01/1962
McIlwaine Prof J, BA MCLIP, Prof.of the Bibl.of Asia & Africa, Sch.of Lib., Univ.Coll.London. [0009415] 05/10/1961
McIlwaine Miss KA, BA(Hons) MPhil MA, Asst.Lib.-Staff Devel., Univ.Coll.London, L.Serv. [0051467] 22/02/1995
McInnes Ms ALM, MA(Hons) DipILS MCLIP, Inf.Specialist, Scottish Prison Serv., Falkirk. [0052186] 12/10/1995
McInnes Mrs AM, (was Lang), BA DipLib MCLIP, Young Peoples Serv.Lib., E.Ayrshire Council, Kilmarnock,Ayrshire. [0034745] 05/02/1982
McInroy Mr RW, BA MCLIP, Operations Mgr., Lincs.C.C., Lincoln. [0035786] 21/01/1983
McIntosh Mrs AR, (was Grant), MLib MCLIP, Sch.Lib., Angus Council, Webster High Sch.,, Kirriemuir. [0045342] 15/10/1990
McIntosh Mrs J, MA(Hons) DipLIS MCLIP, Sch.LRCC., (Job Share), Hazlehead Academy, Aberdeen City Council. [0055402] 09/10/1997
McIntosh Mrs JM, (was Chettle), BEd DipLib MCLIP, Housewife. [0027923] 07/10/1977
McIntosh Mrs S, BA MSc MCLIP, Learning Res.Mgr., Heanor Gate Sch. [0057524] 20/04/1999
McIntyre Mr A, BSc DipLib MCLIP, Tutor Lib., James Watt Coll., Greenock. [0009423] 30/03/1966
McIntyre Mrs AH, BA MCLIP, MA, Unemployed. [0056767] 08/10/1998
McIntyre Mrs I, (was Whittaker), MCLIP, Lib.i/c., L.Support, Falkirk Council L.Serv. [0009425] 03/02/1969
McIntyre Mrs JI, DipHE MCLIP, Comm.L., Renfrew Council. [0026477] 14/10/1976
McIntyre Mrs MA, MCLIP, Area Lib., Cent.L., Stirling. [0028632] 28/10/1977
McIntyre Mrs S, CertEd BA(Hons) CDip MCLIP, Lib., Leicester City L.& Inf.Serv. [0051060] 09/11/1994
McIver Mrs HF, Life Member. [0021134] 12/10/1973
McIver Mrs S, (was Young), BA MCLIP, Asst.Lib., Renfrewshire L., Paisley. [0043308] 03/10/1989
McIvor Miss EMC, BA MSSc MCLIP, Lib., W.Educ.& L.Board, Cent.for Migration Studies. [0024286] 04/06/1975
McIvor Mrs IM, (was Schumacher), BA H DipLib, Unemployed. [0031096] 08/08/1979
McKay Mrs C, BA MLitt MCLIP AIL, Freelance Writer/Translator. [0024188] 15/04/1975
McKay Mr DJ, FCLIP, Inf.Serv.Specialist, Conoco (UK) Ltd., Aberdeen. [0022838] 04/10/1974 FE 01/04/2002
McKay Mr JF, MA DipLib MCLIP, H.ofInf.Serv., Glasgow Sch.of Art. [0023713] 06/01/1975
McKay Mrs MC, (was Macleod), DipLib MCLIP, Unemployed. [0039875] 01/10/1986
McKay Mr PN, BA DipLib DMS MCLIP, Asst.Div.Lib., Accrington L. [0009439] 15/10/1970
McKay Mrs SHC, (was Paterson), BA MCLIP, L.Asst., Aberdeenshire Council. [0033417] 29/09/1980

McKay Miss VSM, BEd DipLib MCLIP, Lib., Strathallan Sch. [0036464] 11/10/1983
McKean Miss L, BA MCLIP, Community Lib., Northwood Hills L., Hillingdon L.Serv. [0038250] 13/02/1985
McKean Mrs PE, (was Weir), MCLIP, Lib., Glasgow. [0027378] 01/03/1977
McKean Mr WJ, MA MCLIP, Asst.Lib.Catr.Dept.(Ref), The Mitchell L., Glasgow. [0024036] 07/03/1975
McKeating Mrs SF, (was Pilkington), MSc MCLIP, Acad.Lib.(Sci.), Loughborough Univ., Pilkington L. [0042588] 13/01/1989
McKee Mrs J, MCLIP, Sen.Lib.-Bibl.Serv.Unit, Renfrewshire L., Paisley. [0027348] 10/03/1977
McKee Mrs KJ, (was Mathias), BA MSc MCLIP, Sub-Lib., St.John's Coll., Cambridge. [0042110] 01/10/1988
McKee Mrs OR, BA(Hons), Team Lib./Inf., N.E.E.L.B., Co.Antrim. [0051922] 07/08/1995
McKee Dr RA, PhD MCLIP FRSA, Ch.Exec., CILIP, London. [0026870] 18/12/1976
McKeegan Mr JM, Br.L.Mgr., Ballycastle L. [0061164] 15/03/2002 AF
McKeeman Mrs RL, (was King), BA(Hons) MLib MCLIP, Unemployed/Housewife. [0043766] 05/01/1990
McKeen Mr MS, MCLIP, Lib./Inf/Offr., Roslin Inst.(Edinburgh), Midlothian. [0031086] 08/08/1979
McKeever Miss LM, BA(Hons) MCLIP, Netskills Trainer., Univ. of Newcastle Upon Tyne, Univ. Computing Serv. [0049044] 13/09/1993
McKellar Ms AE, (was Gill), BSc DipLib MCLIP, Princ.Lib., Warwickshire C.C. [0036920] 02/02/1984
McKellar Miss R, MA(Hons), Stud., Univ.of Strathclyde, Glasgow. [0061096] 28/02/2002
McKellen Ms C, BSc FCLIP, Employment not known. [0060543] 11/12/2001 FE 11/12/2001
McKelvey Mrs C, BEd DipLIB MCLIP, L.Asst.,(Sch.L.), Lancs.C.C., Lytham St.Annes High Tec.Coll. [0046929] 29/02/1992
McKenna Mr G, MA MCLIP, Ch.Lib., Brit.Geological Survey, Nottingham. [0009445] 13/09/1966
McKenna Mrs G, BA(Hons), Sch.Lib., Morton Sch., Carlisle, Cumbria. [0058490] 25/02/2000
McKenna Mr JG, BA DipLib MCLIP, Asst.Lib., Western Educ.& L.Board., N.Ireland. [0031518] 23/10/1979
McKenna Ms T, MSc, Stud., Univ.of Wales, Aberystwyth. [0061559] 02/10/2002
McKennall Mrs GM, (was Lavelle), MCLIP, Position unknown, Mermaid Cent.RCH., Truro, Cornwall. [0020880] 20/08/1973
McKenzie Ms AK, LLB(Hons), Inf.Serv.Mgr., Olswang, London. [0056449] 06/07/1998
McKenzie Mrs HEM, BSc MLS, Lib., Cardinal Wiseman High Sch., Greenford. [0055278] 12/09/1997
McKenzie Mr IM, BSc MCLIP, Dir., Knowledge Mgmt.Directorate, Brit.Trade Internat., London. [0036874] 15/01/1984
McKenzie Mr J, MA DipLIB MCLIP, Sch.Lib.(Job Share), Lothian Reg. [0032444] 14/04/1980
McKenzie Mr JM, LLB(Hons) DipLIS, Lib., Glasgow City Council. [0054013] 17/10/1996
McKenzie Miss LE, BA(Hons) MCLIP, Asst.Lib., Instant L.Ltd., Leics. [0048040] 04/11/1992
McKenzie Miss P, BA MBBO MCLIP, Head-Inter-L.Serv., Nat.L.of Scotland, Edinburgh. [0009460] 04/10/1993
McKenzie Mrs S, BA, Unemployed. [0059830] 15/10/2001
McKenzie Ms YW, BA(Hons), Acquisitions Lib., Univ.Dundee., Sch.of Nursing L. [0048531] 09/02/1993
McKeown Mrs DR, BA(Hons), Inf.Communication Tech.Coordinator, New Coll.Nottingham, Notts. [0054576] 21/01/1997
McKeown Miss S, BA(Hons), Stud., Univ.Northumbria. [0059876] 29/10/2001
McKeown Mrs S, (was Penfare), MCLIP, Asst.Lib., Norfolk Co.L.& Inf., Norwich. [0011489] 09/05/1972
McKerchar Mr K, BA(Hons), p./t.Stud./Learn.Res.Asst., Manchester Met.Univ., S.Trafford Coll., Altrincham. [0053745] 25/09/1996
McKernan Mr S, MEd BA(Hons), MCLIP, Lib., Northern Coll., Barnsley. [0042908] 12/04/1989
McKernan Ms VM, BA MLIS, Systems Lib., Univ.Coll.Dublin, Main L. [0035045] 15/07/1982
Mckie Mrs A, (was Dudley), BA(Hons) MA MCLIP, Lib., Kent Inst.of Art& Design, Maidstone Campus. [0048120] 09/11/1992
McKiernan Mrs P, (was Green), MCLIP, Sch.Lib., Argyll & Bute Council, Oban. [0009471] 03/02/1962
McKinlay Miss IMC, MCLIP, Life Member, Tel.01333 425872, 11 Laburnum Rd., Methil, Fife, KY8 2HA. [0009472] 22/09/1942
McKinlay Mr KW, MA(Hons) PGDipLib MCLIP, Head of Cultural Serv., E.Renfrewshire Council. [0024439] 30/07/1975
McKinlay Mrs L, (was Pentney), BA(Hons), Literacy Lib., Gateshead L.& Arts. [0046574] 12/11/1991
McKinley Ms MG, MA DipLibStud MCLIP, Principal Lib.-Support Serv., Western Educ.& L.Board, Omagh, Co.Tyrone. [0029404] 06/07/1978
McKinney Miss D, MCLIP, Life Member. [0009474] 09/05/1956
McKinstery Miss SJ, BA(Hons), Stud., Queen Margaret Univ., Edinburgh. [0060864] 13/12/2001
McKrell Dr L, BA MSc PGDip PhD MCLIP, Comm.Lib., Cent.L., Stirling. [0043521] 01/11/1989
McLachlan Mrs AM, (was Nisbet), MA DipLib MCLIP, L.Inf.Serv.Coordinator, Fife Council L., E.Area, Fife. [0028349] 06/10/1977
McLachlan Mrs CM, (was Hodges), MCLIP, Unemployed. [0009484] 31/01/1958
McLachlan Mr DE, BSc(Econ), Inf.Serv.Lib./Lect., Edinburgh's Telford Coll., Edinburgh. [0053268] 15/04/1996

McLachlan Mrs LM, (was Morgan), BA MCLIP, Sch.Lib., Beath High Sch., Cowdenbeath. [0010407] 06/01/1969
McLaney Mr J, BA MCLIP, Life Member. [0009489] 02/04/1953
McLaughlin Miss KA, Stud., Univ.of Cent.England, Birmingham. [0058515] 15/03/2000
McLaughlin Ms ME, BA DipLib MCLIP, Sen.Sch.Lib., Fermanagh, Div.L., W.Educ.& L.Board, Co.Tyrone. [0033793] 05/03/1981
McLaven Miss TJ, BA(Hons) MA, Asst.Lib., Ipswich Hosp NHS Trust. [0047792] 27/02/1997
McLean Ms A, BA, Stud. [0052511] 02/11/1995
McLean Ms F, BSc MSc, Healthcare Inf.Offr., Brit.L., Health Care Inf.Serv., London. [0055412] 08/10/1997
McLean Mr ID, BA MCLIP, Community Lib., Bridge of Allan L., Stirling Dist.Council. [0025784] 19/01/1976
McLean Miss J, MCLIP, Health Promotion Lib., Croydon & Surrey Downs Comm.NHS, Surrey. [0009499] 05/01/1966
McLean Mrs JBB, (was Carmichael), BA MCLIP, Asst.Lib.(job share), Renfrewshire Council. [0002378] 18/09/1970
McLean Ms M, BA(Hons), Data Mgmt.Asst., Freshfields Bruckhaus Deringer, London. [0052797] 15/12/1995
McLean Prof N, BA DipEd DipLib MCLIP, Univ.Lib., Macquarie Univ., Australia. [0009505] 03/01/1972
McLean Miss R, Stud., Queen Margaret Univ.Coll., Edinburgh. [0055674] 07/11/1997
McLean Mr R, BA MCLIP, Retired. [0009506] 18/09/1948
McLean Mr RJ, MCLIP, Records Mgr., Wellcome Trust, London. [0060420] 11/12/2001
McLean Mrs S, (was Cameron), BA MCLIP, Sch.Lib., Buckie High Sch., Moray Council. [0036448] 14/10/1983
McLean Mrs SL, BSc DipLib MCLIP, Career Break. [0034287] 23/10/1981
McLeish Mr J, MA DipLib MCLIP, Asst.Lib.(Ref./Inf.), Cent.L., E.Kilbride. [0030006] 27/10/1978
McLellan Mr K, DipLib MCLIP, Sen.Lib.-Inf., Edmonton Green L., London. [0024751] 01/10/1975
McLellan Miss LA, BA, L.Asst., L.H.Q., Stirling. [0048635] 26/03/1993
McLelland Mrs DH, (was White), MA DIP ED TECH FCLIP, Life Member. [0015695] 01/01/1956 **FE 01/01/1966**
McLennan Mrs DA, MA(Hons) MCLIP, Yth.Serv.Lib., L.H.Q., Argyll & Bute Council. [0009511] 12/01/1968
McLeod Ms A, (was Eveleigh), BSc(Hons) MCLIP, Assoc.Lib., United Nations Inf.Cent., New York. [0036210] 11/07/1983
McLeod Ms FG, MA DipLib MCLIP, Shadow Deputy Minister for, Transport & Environment, Scottish Parliament. [0033475] 15/01/1981
McLeod Ms HG, (was Borys), MA DipLib MCLIP, p./t.Sch.Lib., St Columbas Prep.Sch., Herts. [0026285] 08/10/1976
McLeod Dr J, (was Scoltock), BSc MSc PhD MCLIP, Position unknown, Univ.of Northumbria. [0060167] 10/12/2001
McLeod Mr M, IT Instructor/Lib., Aberdeen Coll. [0040541] 06/03/1987
McLeod Miss SE, BSc, Stud., Univ.of Wales. [0009863] 18/10/2001
McLoughlin Mrs A, (was Waters), BA MCLIP, Br.Lib., Wirral B.C. [0039805] 29/07/1986
McLoughlin Miss CN, BSc, Stud., Loughborough Univ. [0060873] 18/12/2001
McLoughlin Mrs UM, BA(Hons) PGDip MA, Asst.Lib., NNC Ltd., Knutsford, Cheshire. [0058963] 10/10/2000
McLullich Mrs JJ, BA MCLIP, Career Break. [0034507] 19/11/1981
McMahon Mrs E, (was Welsh), MCLIP, Principal Lib., Northamptonshire C.C., Young People Child.& Learning. [0021948] 29/01/1974
McMahon Ms EA, Learning Res.Co-ordinator, N.E.Worcs.Coll., Bromsgrove Campus. [0046327] 28/10/1991
McMahon Mr S, MA(Hons) DipILS MCLIP, Learning Resource Co-ordinator, Perth & Kinross Council. [0057117] 15/12/1998
McMahon Mrs SJ, (was Homer), MCLIP, Asst.Lib., Worthing L., W.Sussex C.C. [0022790] 21/10/1974
McMahon Ms STA, BA DipLib MCLIP, Head of L.& ICT, Royal Pavilion, Brighton. [0031731] 23/11/1979
McMahon-Bates Mrs J, (was Bates), BA(Hons), Asst.Learning Support Lib., Unsworth L., Bury, Lancs. [0055602] 24/10/1997
McManus Mrs C, (was Curlet), MA MCLIP, Unemployed. [0009524] 18/10/1971
McManus Mrs CS, (was Wagstaff), BA(Hons) MA, Asst.Lib., HM Treasury & Cabinet Off., London. [0056006] 20/01/1998
McManus Mr DJ, BA(Hons) MA, Asst.Inf.Mgr., CILIP, London. [0056763] 08/10/1998
McManus Mr J, BA(Hons), Stud., Manchester Metro.Univ. [0061711] 23/10/2002
McMaster Mrs AR, BA MA MCLIP, H.of L.Serv., L.B.of Newham. [0026988] 10/01/1977
McMaster Mrs C, (was Brittain), BLib MCLIP, Subject Lib.: Education, Anglia Poly.Univ., Essex. [0023265] 18/11/1974
McMaster Ms L, (was Dickinson), BSc(Hons), Support Mgr., Trafford M.B.C., Manchester. [0055566] 21/10/1997
McMath Mrs PC, (was Coulter), BA MCLIP, Unemployed. [0018410] 16/10/1972
McMeekan Mr I, MA FCLIP, Life Member. [0009526] 07/02/1956 **FE 15/02/1989**
McMenemy Mr D, BA(Hons) MSc MCLIP, Lect., Dept.of Computer & Inf.Sci., Univ.of Strathclyde. [0053830] 03/10/1996
McMichael Mrs S, (was McConville), BA, Sch.Lib., N.Lanarkshire Council. [0056747] 12/10/1998
McMillan Mrs BM, BA MCLIP, Lib., Gt.Cornard L., Sudbury, Suffolk. [0018371] 21/10/1972
McMillan Mr DH, BA(Hons) MSc(Econ), Inf.Offr., Glasgow Chamber of Comm., Glasgow, Lanarkshire. [0054610] 31/01/1997
McMillan Miss E, BA MCLIP, Outreach Mgr., Central L., London Bor.of Hillingdon. [0035133] 31/08/1982

McMillan Ms JE, BA(Hons) MCLIP, Sch.Lib., Tain Royal Academy, Highland Council. [0052507] 02/11/1995
McMillan Mrs S, (was Izard), BA MCLIP, Asst.Lib., Hampton Sch., Hampton,Middx. [0009534] 14/01/1969
McMorran Mr RL, MA MCLIP, Catg.Mgr., Univ.of Aberdeen, Queen Mother L. [0020305] 01/02/1973
McMullan Mrs EA, (was McMillan), BA, Br.L.Mgr., Dairy Farm L., Dairy Farm Cent., Belfast. [0032317] 22/02/1980
McMullan Mr G, BA MBA MPhil DipLib MCLIP, Head of IT Strategy Grp., Birmingham City Council. [0023238] 05/11/1974
McMullan Miss SA, BA, Campus Lib.Mgr., Univ.of Ulster Magee L. [0034725] 05/02/1982
McMullan Mrs VV, (was Newell), BA, Br.L.Mgr., Downpatrick Br.L., S.E.E.L.B. [0044990] 01/01/1991 **AF**
McMullen Mrs PA, (was Sloan), BA MCLIP, Asst.Lib., PHLRC, Thames Valley Univ., Slough. [0022750] 02/09/1974
McMullin Ms AJ, BA MCLIP, Stud. [0048274] 20/11/1992
McMullin Mrs JE, BA DipLib MCLIP, Asst.Lib., Christ Church L., Oxford. [0039909] 01/10/1986
McMurray Mr N, BSc DipHIST ART MCLIP, Lib.i/c., Mob.L. & H/B Reader Serv., Barnet P.L. [0009539] 09/01/1969
McNab Ms AS, MA(Hons) MSc MCLIP, Collections Mgr., Joint Inf.Systems Committee(JISC), London. [0037630] 08/10/1984
McNab Mrs I, BSc(Econ), Comm.Lib., Glenwood L., Fife. [0059432] 14/03/2001
McNabb Mrs HM, (was Carter), BLib MCLIP, Bibl.Servs., Vale of Glamorgan Ls., Barry. [0002437] 19/01/1972
McNabola Mr PG, BA(Hons) MCLIP, Inf.Lib., Morpeth L., Northumberland C.C. [0033322] 27/10/1980
McNae Miss HM, BA(Hons) DipILS MCLIP, Asst.Lib., The Robert Gordon Univ., St.Andrews St.L. [0057842] 09/09/1999
McNally Mrs AM, (was Roberts), MCLIP, Unemployed. [0019754] 18/08/1964
McNally Mrs RC, (was Adshead), BSocSci DipLIS MCLIP, L.& Inf.Offr., Nat.Primary Care Res.& Devel.Cent., Univ.of Manchester. [0044060] 20/04/1990
McNamee Miss D, BEng, L.Asst., Glos.C.C., Cheltenham. [0057808] 11/08/1999
McNaught Mrs G, Web Tech.Co-ordinator, McGrigor Donald Solicitors, Glasgow. [0057378] 01/03/1999 **AF**
McNay Mrs P, (was Price), MA MCLIP, Comm.& Operations Lib., Scottish Borders Council. [0009547] 01/10/1964
McNee Ms NJ, BLS MCLIP, Team Lib.(Inf.), Maghera L. [0034480] 13/11/1981
McNeely Miss A, MCLIP, Sch.Lib., Cathkin High Sch., Cambuslang. [0009549] 28/02/1972
McNeff Mr KG, BA MSc MCLIP, Lib., Newburn Ellis, Bristol. [0028083] 04/10/1977
McNeil Miss FJ, BA MCLIP, Dep.Lib., Inst.of Actuaries, Oxford. [0041586] 21/01/1988
McNeill Mr AJJ, BA(Hons) MCLIP FSA SCOT, [0019312] 07/09/1972
McNeill Miss E, BA DLS ATCL MCLIP, Life Member, 42 Chelsea Towers, Chelsea Manor, Gardens, London, SW3 5PN. [0009554] 07/03/1957
McNichol Mrs KA, (was Lowe), MA DipLib MCLIP, Lib., Health & Safety Executive, Merseyside. [0034183] 09/10/1981
McNicol Miss FE, Systems Lib., Scottish Exec., Edinburgh. [0053021] 31/01/1996
McOwat Mrs HM, (was Pickett), BSc DipInfSc MCLIP, Lib., Eng.Dept., Cambridge Univ. [0024538] 27/08/1975
McPartlin Ms EC, BSc(Econ) MCLIP, Comm.Access Lib., Stirling Libraries. [0049315] 18/10/1993
McPhail Mrs RJ, (was Turner), BA(Hons) MCLIP, Inf.Offr., Update, Edinburgh. [0044600] 05/11/1990
McPhee Mr AD, BSc MCLIP, Employment not known. [0060545] 11/12/2001
McPherson Mrs EA, (was Mcdaid), MA MCLIP, Sen.Lib., Glasgow City C.L.,Inf,& Learning. [0025373] 07/01/1976
McPherson Mrs M, BA MCLIP, Comm.Lib., S.Lanarkshire Council, Strathaven L. [0029463] 14/08/1978
McQuade DJ, BA MCLIP, Lib.:Stock & Promotion, Doncaster M.B.C. [0021490] 12/10/1973
McQueen Mr GJ, BA(Hons) DipIM MCLIP, Lib.,(Child.), Hounslow Cultural & Comm.Serv. [0053276] 12/04/1996
McQueen Miss K, BA, L. Asst., Ashurst Morris Crisp. [0060974] 21/01/2002
McQuilkin Miss JM, BA(Hons) MSc(Econ), p./t.Sen.L.Asst./Asst.Lib., Univ.of Ulster, Magee Coll., Londonderry. [0051402] 06/02/1995
McQuillan Miss D, MA(Hons), Stud., Univ.of Strathclyde. [0061770] 05/11/2002
McQuistan Miss SE, BSc(Hons) MSc, Div.Lib., N.Glasgow Hosp.NHS Trust. [0054778] 01/04/1997
McReynolds Mrs MH, BSc(Hons) MCLIP MSc(Econ), p./t.Asst.Lib./P/T Lib., Univ.of Ulster/Causeway Institute, Coleraine/Ballymoney. [0027357] 01/03/1977
McRoy Mrs CA, (was Bashford), BA(Hons) MCLIP, I/lnf.Mgr., Inst.of Occupational Health, Univ.of Birmingham. [0031184] 03/10/1979
McSean Mr T, BA DipLib FCLIP, Lib., Brit.Med.Assoc., London. [0030884] 04/10/1973 **FE 15/09/1993**
McShane Mrs NH, BA(Hons), Asst.Lib., Proudman Ocenographic Lab., Bidston Observatory, Prenton. [0049338] 25/10/1993
McShane Mr PC, BA MCLIP, Ch.Lib., DEFRA, London. [0022396] 30/04/1974
McSorley Ms JB, (was Hanlon), BA MCLIP, Sen.Subject Lib.(Psychology), Middlesex Univ.L., Enfield Campus. [0020096] 01/01/1973
McTavish Miss SM, MCLIP, Inf.& L.Manager, Beaumont & Son, London. [0042752] 16/02/1994
McTeer Miss SA, BA(Hons), Currently Unemployed. [0048706] 23/04/1993
McTeigue Mr B, BA(Hons) MCLIP, Guidance Worker, Leeds City Council. [0027543] 10/05/1977
McTernan Mr DJ, BA(Hons) DipLib, Curator, B.L., Early Printed Coll., London. [0031001] 15/07/1979

Personal Members — Menon

McTiffin Mrs HA, (was Irving), BA MCLIP, Housewife, 15 Dean Lane, Winchester,Hants.,SO22 5LH. [0021169] 09/10/1973
McVeigh Ms GF, (was Hourican), BA MCLIP, Stock Mgr., L.B.of Ealing, L. Support Cent. [0029122] 01/01/1962
McVeigh Mr KJ, MA MCLIP, The Official Publications Dept., Cambridge Univ.L. [0025073] 22/10/1975
McVey Mrs A, BA DipLib MCLIP, Grp.L.Mgr., S.E.E.L.B., Tullycarnet L. [0037236] 04/05/1984
McVey Mr DM, BSc(Hons) MSc MCLIP, Inf.Offr., Motor Industry Research Assoc., Nuneaton, Warwickshire. [0051213] 25/11/1994
McVicar Mr N, BA MCLIP, Asst.Lib., Glasgow Caledonian Univ. [0024359] 01/07/1975
McVittie Ms JAK, (was King), MA BA(Hons), Unemployed. [0042775] 22/02/1989
McWatt Mr CW, BA DipLib MCLIP, Retired. [0009582] 23/09/1966
McWilliam Mrs CJW, (was Park), BA MLS MCLIP, Inf.Mgr., Clarks, Solicitors, Reading. [0011218] 08/10/1969
McWilliam Mrs R, BA(Hons) MCLIP, Ref.Lib., Lancashire C.C. [0052128] 05/10/1976
McWilliams Mrs FS, (was King), BA(Hon) MCLIP, Inf.Researcher, Inst.of Management, Corby. [0050264] 25/05/1994
Meachem Mrs LVM, (was Harris), MA MCLIP, Analyst, Corp.Relations Dept., Unilever, London. [0032079] 28/01/1980
Mead Mrs AF, (was Davison), BA MCLIP, Team Lib., Young Peoples Serv., Kent Educ.& L., Dartford. [0034562] 13/01/1982
Mead Mrs BJ, BA, p./t.Stud./Dep.Intranet Mgr., Freshfields Bruckhaus Deringer, London. [0061079] 01/03/2002
Mead Mrs CA, (was Birch), BA MCLIP, Career Break. [0036973] 22/01/1984
Mead Mr DK, BA MCLIP, L.Serv.Mgr., Medway Council, Kent. [0035513] 26/10/1982
Mead Mrs GF, MA DipLib MCLIP, Res.Cent.Mgr., Chesterton Comm.Coll., Cambridge. [0002179] 07/01/1974
Mead Mr WD, Asst.Lib., Home Off., London. [0050755] 17/10/1994
Meade Mrs PA, (was Kane), BA(Hon), Inf.Offr., AEA Tech., Warrington. [0050133] 08/04/1994
Meaden Miss K, BA(Hons), Network Inf.Specialist, Cranfield Univ. [0056102] 17/02/1998
Meadows Prof AJ, MA MSc DPhil FCLIP, Prof.of L.& Inf.Studs., Loughborough Univ. [0038903] 18/10/1985 **FE 13/06/1989**
Meadows Ms L, BA MSc MCLIP, Employment not known. [0060840] 12/12/2001
Meadows Mr P, BA MCLIP, Asst., Beds.Co.L. [0010018] 01/10/1968
Meadows Mrs SK, (was Shaw), BA(Hons) MCLIP, Career Break. [0041828] 12/04/1988
Meadows Mr W, MCLIP, Retired. [0010020] 03/12/1930
Meads Miss V, BA(Hons), Sen.Learning Res.Asst., Walsall Coll.of Arts & Tech., W.Midlands. [0049742] 29/11/1993
Meakin Miss C, BA(Hons) MA, Inf.Offr., Norton Rose, London. [0058204] 17/11/1999
Mealey Mr MA, BA(Hons), Stud., Manchester Met.Univ. [0059470] 04/04/2001
Mealor Mr JK, FCLIP, Retired. [0010029] 05/02/1932 **FE 01/01/1936**
Meaney Mr HP, BA(Hons) DipLib MA, Unemployed. [0048267] 19/11/1992
Meardon Mrs RE, Sen.L.Asst.-Local Studies, Milton Keynes Council. [0050392] 15/07/1994 **AF**
Meares Mrs BM, (was Parker), BA MCLIP, MCLIP. [0019820] 18/12/1972
Mears Miss AM, Project cataloguer, Univ.of Wales. [0054113] 30/10/1996
Mears Miss SJ, MA BSc DipLib MCLIP, Study Support Mgr., Essex C.C.L.H.Q., Chelmsford. [0041050] 08/10/1987
Mears Ms WE, BA(Hons) MA, Devel.Offr., Rockingham L., UCN., Northampton. [0044824] 07/12/1990
Medcalf Miss HD, BA DipLib MCLIP ILTM, Liaison Lib.(Med.& Health Sci.), Univ.of Birmingham, Barnes L. [0038788] 09/10/1985
Medcalf Miss HJ, BA MCLIP, Retired. [0010036]
Medcalf Mr JP, BA(Hons) DipLib MCLIP, Lib.Sound & Vision, Halifax Cent.L. [0038035] 15/01/1985
Medd Miss KS, BLib MCLIP, Research Exec.-Retail, Estates Gazette Interactive, London. [0041132] 07/10/1987
Medd Mrs SH, BA DipLib MCLIP, Support Offr., ILS NVQ Cent., Lincs.C.C. [0025162] 19/11/1975
Medin Ms S, Research Dir., Self Employed. [0059234] 11/01/2001 **SP**
Medlen Miss P, BA(Hons), Lib., Royal Bor.of Kensington & Chelsea., Cent.L. [0040627] 13/04/1987
Medley Miss L, MCLIP, Sen.Asst.Lib., Burnley Div., Lancs.Co.L. [0010038] 16/01/1968
Medlock Miss J, BSc MSc MCLIP, Employment not known. [0060859] 12/12/2001
Medlock Miss L, BEd MCLIP, Head of Devon Sch.L.Serv., Devon L.Serv. [0010040] 18/01/1968
Medway Mr A, BLib MCLIP, Portal Lib., Staffordshire C.C., Tamworth L. [0031379] 20/10/1979
Mee Mrs LJ, (was Christie), BA MCLIP, Lib., Dick Inst., E.Ayrshire Dist.Council. [0033574] 21/01/1981
Meechan Mr TMD, BA, Serials Team Leader, Dept.of Trade & Industry, Inf.System Unit. [0041773] 22/03/1988
Meehan Mr BW, BA(Hons) MMus MSc(Econ) MCLIP, Lib., Hampshire C.C., Basingstoke L. [0054776] 01/04/1997
Meeson Mrs PL, (was Roberts), BA(Hons) MCLIP, Med.Lib., Hosp.of St.Cross, Rugby. [0033812] 18/02/1981
Meeuwissen Mrs I, (was Hindle), MCLIP ACTT, Life Member, 4 Mount Pleasant Drive, Mt.Waverley, Victoria, Australia. [0017473] 01/01/1948
Meharg Mrs J, BA, Stud., Robert Gordon Univ. [0061568] 02/10/2002
Meheux Dr KL, BA(Hons) PhD, Issue Desk Head, Inst.of Archaeology L., Univ.Coll.London. [0058508] 06/03/2000

Mehew Mrs EK, BSc(Hons), Inf.Specialist, Health and Safety Executive, Liverpool. [0055550] 20/10/1997
Mehrer Ms S, BA(Hons) MA DipILS MCLIP, Asst.Lib., BLPES, London Sch.of Econ.& Political Sci. [0052167] 11/10/1995
Mehta Mrs LP, BA MCLIP, Teacher, Warwickshire C.C. [0031830] 07/01/1980
Meikle Mrs JR, (was Lacey), BA(Hons) MCLIP, Learning Res.Cent.Mgr., Allertonshire Sch., N.Yorks. [0034388] 26/10/1981
Meineck Mrs J, Asst.Lib., Glyn Tech.Sch., Surrey. [0061449] 31/07/2002 **AF**
Melgosa Mrs AAD, BSc MA, Assoc.Lib., AIIAS, Cavite, Philippines. [0052220] 16/10/1995
Melia Ms KM, BA(Hons) DipIS MCLIP, Asst.Lib., Dept.of Health, London. [0047810] 19/10/1992
Meliniotis Mrs B, (was Laidlaw), Sch.Lib., Meridian Sch., Royston. [0050329] 07/02/1994 **AF**
Mellard Mr OM, BA(Hons) MSc, Document Researcher, Inf.Cent., Warburg Dillon Read, London. [0055430] 13/10/1997
Mellenchip Mrs S, (was Norman), BA(Hons) DipLIS MCLIP, Team Leader Knowledge/ICT, Staffs.C.C., Shire Hall L. [0048313] 25/11/1992
Meller Ms FC, MCLIP, Freelance Lib. [0010050] 15/02/1966
Mellers Ms J, (was Parsons), BA MCLIP, Career Break. [0032813] 17/09/1980
Melling Mrs DJ, (was Stephenson), BA MCLIP, Sch.Lib., Formby High School., Merseyside. [0027783] 29/07/1977
Melling Mrs EC, (was Walton), MCLIP, p./t. Co. Dir., Checkwell Ltd. [0010051] 25/03/1964
Melling Ms M, BA(Hons) MLib MCLIP, Dir.of Learning & Inf.Serv., Liverpool John Moores Univ., Liverpool. [0032753] 07/08/1980
Melling Miss MA, MCLIP, Asst.Community Lib., Sheffield City L. [0010052] 21/08/1966
Melling Miss P, BA MCLIP, Asst.Lib., Guildhall L., Corporation of London. [0010053] 03/10/1968
Melling Miss RH, BA MCLIP, Life Member. [0010054] 08/11/1957
Mellis Mrs MJH, MA MCLIP, Asst.Lib., The Robert Gordon Univ., Aberdeen. [0010055] 23/09/1969
Mellmann Ms LS, BSc, Stud./Employee, City Univ./Price Waterhouse, London. [0054223] 31/10/1996
Mellody Miss B, BA(Hons) DipILS MCLIP, Dep.L.Serv.Mgr.(Acquisitions)/, Serials Lib., Manchester Met.Univ. [0052597] 10/11/1995
Mellon Mrs R, (was Bromley), BA MCLIP, Branch Mgr., Darwen L., Blackburn with Darwen L.& Inf.Serv. [0010058] 22/10/1963
Mellor Mrs A, MA(Hons), Operations Mgr., BDS, Dumfries. [0061086] 04/03/2002
Mellor Miss C, BSc DipLib MCLIP, Heritage Serv.Mgr., Cumbria C.C., Barrow-in-Furness. [0035403] 01/10/1982
Mellor Ms D, BA(Hons) DipILM, p./t.Asst.Lib., Manchester Met.Univ., Crewe. [0048434] 06/01/1993
Mellor Mr DJL, MCLIP, Mgr.:Special Serv., Cent.L., Doncaster M.B.C. [0010061] 05/10/1967
Mellor Mrs EM, (was McCourt), BA MCLIP, Ref.& Loc.Studies Lib., Weston Cent.L., N.Somerset Dist.Co. [0036486] 18/10/1983
Mellor Mr KA, BA DipLib MCLIP, Devel.Mgr.:Learning Res., W.Notts.Coll., Mansfield. [0027350] 15/02/1977
Mellor Mrs M, (was Ainsworth), BA MCLIP, Unemployed. [0010062] 01/01/1968
Mellor Mrs TR, (was Harper), BA MCLIP, Learning Cent.Mgr./Subject Adviser, Univ.of Derry, Buxton Site. [0029036] 25/02/1978
Mellors Mrs AR, (was Buckingham), BA MCLIP, Special Serv.Lib.(Job Share), Derbys.C.C., Belper. [0020012] 12/10/1970
Mellors Mr DC, MCLIP, Sen.Lib., Cent.L., Derby. [0010064] 26/10/1963
Mellors Mrs JJ, MLib, Inf.Serv.Mgr., Environment Agency, Reading, Berks. [0053339] 13/05/1996
Mellors Mrs MJ, (was Gulson), DipLib MCLIP, Unemployed. [0037605] 10/10/1984
Melluish Mr DW, FCII, Retired. [0051265] 13/12/1994
Melmoth Mrs A, (was McNamara), BA MCLIP MBA, Sen.Lib., ICT, Bolton Cent.L. [0040015] 09/10/1986
Melone Miss HA, BA(Hons) Dip MCLIP, Sch.Lib., Duncanrig Secondary Sch., S.Lanarkshire. [0056251] 17/04/1998
Melrose Ms EA, MA DipLib MCLIP, Inf.Serv.Adviser, N.Yorks.Co.L. [0010065] 11/11/1964
Melton Ms MR, BA(Hons) MLitt, Stud., Leeds Met.Univ. [0057163] 05/11/1999
Melville Mrs A, BA(Hons) MCLIP, Retired/Self-employed. [0010066] 01/01/1958
Melville Mrs AJ, (was Campbell), BA DipLib MCLIP, Curriculum Adviser, International Sch.of Choueifat, Abu Dhabi. [0027919] 03/10/1977
Melville Mrs DEF, (was Robertson), BA MCLIP, P./t.Asst.Lib., Univ.of Dundee, Sch.of Nursing & Midwifery. [0021679] 01/01/1974
Memery Mrs J, (was Ratcliffe), BA(Hons) DipLib, Arts Adminstrator, Bleddfa Cent.for the Arts, Powys. [0038899] 16/01/1985
Mendham Mrs CM, (was Towndrow), BA DipLib MCLIP, Resident in Germany. [0030284] 04/01/1979
Mends Ms SJ, BA(Hons) MSc(Econ), Devel.Offr., Univ.of Wales, Aberystwyth. [0054395] 03/12/1996
Mengu Mr MD, BSc MSc MGIP MCLIP, Resident in Denmark. [0060054] 07/12/2001
Menhinick Miss MJ, BA MCLIP, Acq.Lib., McIntosh L., M.O.D.Abbeywood. [0034006] 10/07/1981
Mennie Mr HJ, BA MCLIP DMS, Operations Mgr.,S.Area, Beds.C.C. [0019890] 01/01/1973
Menniss Mrs J, (was Dawson), BA(Hons) DipIM MCLIP, Sen.Lib., Slough Bor.C. [0050614] 01/10/1994
Menon Mrs CT, BSc, Devel.Mgr., New Learning Tech., W.Herts Coll., Watford. [0058174] 10/11/1999

Menor Ms V, MLIS, Child.Lib.Employed, Stanislaus County L., USA. [0061498] 30/08/2002
Menzies Miss MD, BA MLib MCLIP, L.& Inf.Serv.Mgr., Scottish Borders Council, L.H.Q., Selkirk. [0029749] 09/10/1978
Menzies Mrs PM, (was Davis), MA MCLIP, Unemployed. [0010072] 21/10/1966
Menzies Mrs VA, (was Haynes), MA DipLib MCLIP, Community Lib., Edinburgh City L., Blackhall. [0029676] 12/10/1978
Mercer Miss A, MCHEM, Graduate Trainee, Nuffield College, Oxford. [0060978] 22/01/2002
Mercer Ms AI, (was Probert), BLS MCLIP, Princ.Lib., N.Area, Northants.C.C. [0033110] 17/10/1980
Mercer Miss EK, BSc(Econ) MCLIP, Team Lib., Somerset Co.Council, Wincanton, Somerset. [0051304] 16/01/1995
Mercer Mrs PA, (was Hellyer), MCLIP, Retired. [0010077] 30/03/1954
Mercer Watkins Ms C, (was Watkins), MCLIP, Unemployed. [0010074] 29/09/1965
Merchant Mr AJ, BSc MA, Sen.Asst.Lib., Inst.of Ismaili Stud., London. [0057012] 20/11/1998
Merchant Mrs BA, BSc MCLIP, Head of L.& Inf.Serv., SPRU, Univ.of Sussex, Brighton. [0028963] 10/02/1978
Merchant Miss LR, BA(Hons), Asst.Lib., Oakham Sch. [0058280] 07/12/1999
Merchant Mrs SE, BA DipLib, Unemployed. [0058511] 06/03/2000
Meredith Ms C, BA(Hons) MA, Asst.Lib., BMA L., London. [0055860] 04/12/1997
Meredith Ms R, (was MacMillan), BA DipIM, Asst.Lib., Redbridge Bor.Council, Ilford Cent.L. [0061249] 24/04/2002
Merison Mrs SF, (was Schofield), BSc MLib MCLIP, Lib., Herts.C.C., Cheshunt L. [0043961] 05/03/1990
Meriton Mr JC, BA(Hons) MA DipLib, Deputy Keeper, Prints, Drawings, Nat.Art L., Victoria & Albert, Museum, London. [0055956] 22/12/1997
Merner Miss S, BLib MCLIP, Lib., Poole Hosp., Poole,Dorset. [0037094] 02/02/1984
Merola Miss B, BA(Hons) DipLib MCLIP, Br.Lib., Cardiff Co.Ls., Cardiff Cent.L. [0037510] 03/10/1984
Merrett Mr CE, BA MA, Univ.Lib., Univ.of Natal, Pietermaritzburg, S.Africa. [0023934] 18/02/1975
Merrett Ms GE, BLib MCLIP MSc, Head of Staff Devel., Oxford Univ.L.Serv., Oxford. [0041486] 13/01/1988
Merrett Miss SJ, BA MA, p./t.Stud./Learning Res.Mgr., Univ.of Wales, Aberystwyth, The Test Valley Sch., Hants. [0061278] 08/05/2002
Merricks Mrs HJ, (was Hammond), MCLIP, Staff Devel.Lib., Northants.L.& Inf.Serv. [0020370] 13/02/1973
Merrifield Mrs BA, (was Collier), BA DipLib MCLIP, Asst.Princ.Lib., Milton Keynes L., Milton Keynes Council. [0030897] 23/05/1979
Merrill Miss RC, BA MCLIP, Med.L., Barnsley Dist.Gen.Hosp. [0032607] 21/05/1980
Merriman Mrs AM, (was Crichton), M Lib MCLIP, Head of Monitoring & Devel., Worthing, W.Sussex Co.L. [0003368] 14/01/1971
Merriman Miss C, BA MCLIP, Mgr., Warwickshire Sch.L.Serv., Warwickshire. [0038407] 21/04/1985
Merriman Mrs HA, (was Taylor), MCLIP, P/t.Lib., N.Grp., Portsmouth City Council. [0014404] 17/08/1971
Merriman Mr JB, MCLIP, Life Member, 1 Thames Gdns., Charlbury, Chipping Norton, Tel.01608 810375. [0010086] 23/02/1951
Merrington Mr OJ, BSc(Hons) MSc MCLIP, p./t.Website Mgr., Scott Polar Res.Inst., Univ.of Cambridge. [0043577] 09/11/1989
Merriott Mrs DM, (was Mcneelance), BA DipLib MCLIP, Primary Sch.Teacher, St.Andrews C.of E.Primary Sch., Weeley, Essex. [0033324] 29/10/1980
Merritt Mrs EJG, (was Montague), MCLIP, Team Lib., Norfolk Co.L.& Inf.Serv., Norfolk & Norwich Millennium L. [0010302] 09/09/1968
Merritt Ms LA, BA(Hons), P./t.Learning Res.Offr., N.Tyneside Coll., Wallsend. [0053476] 01/07/1996
Merritt Mrs MA, (was Bagguley), BEd MCLIP, Teacher/Lib., Bournville Sch., Birmingham. [0048820] 07/06/1993
Merryweather Miss MHH, p./t.Stud., Univ.of Westminster. [0048716] 21/04/1993
Merryweather Ms TA, DipLRCM MCLIP, Med.Lib., PGMC Bishop Auckland Hosp. [0056146] 01/03/1998
Merskey Mrs SJ, (was Chann), MA MCLIP, Housewife & Freelance Editor. [0010088] 14/09/1963
Meshack Mr G, Florist. [0057963] 06/10/1999
Mesquita Mr MCJ, BSc, Employment not known. [0060352] 10/12/2001
Messenger Mrs GS, (was Clarke), MA MCLIP, Asst.Lib., Inst.Chartered Accountants, London. [0035502] 12/10/1982
Messenger Mr MF, OBE FCLIP, Life Member. [0010091] 13/09/1954 FE 01/01/1964
Messer Mrs SJ, (was Mckerrigan), MCLIP, Sch.Lib.(Job Share), Williamwood High Sch., Glasgow. [0009466] 02/04/1970
Messere Mrs AP, (was Breen), BA, Sen.Lib., Hendon L., London Borough Barnet. [0043299] 16/10/1989
Messum Mrs AP, (was Baber), BA(Hons) DipLib, p./t.Lib., Clarke, Willmott & Clarke, Taunton. [0044502] 16/10/1990
Metcalf Mr A, BSc DipLib MCLIP, Lib.-Support Servs., Liverpool City Council, Liverpool. [0038454] 30/04/1985
Metcalf Mrs D, BSc, Inf.Mgr., CIMA, London. [0052398] 27/10/1995
Metcalf Ms SM, BA MCLIP, Advisory Lib., Comm.Inf.:SLS, Herts. [0023723] 14/01/1975
Metcalf Mrs V, (was Burdon), BA MCLIP, Catr., S.Tyneside Corp., Cent.L., S.Shields. [0010094] 09/02/1961
Metcalfe Miss CF, BA(Hons) MA, Asst.Lib., House of Lords, London. [0056200] 19/10/1998
Metcalfe Miss F, BA DipLIS MCLIP, Music Lib., Kent Arts & L. [0044410] 05/10/1990

Metcalfe Mrs PA, (was Webster), MCLIP, Lib., Health Servs.Mgmt.Cent., Univ.of Birmingham. [0015551] 14/02/1961
Metcalfe Mrs SJ, L.Asst., Cumbria C.C., Penrith L. [0055852] 02/12/1997 AF
Metcalfe Ms SL, BA(Hons), Reg.Inf.Co-ordinator-S.Africa, Brit Council, Johannesburg. [0040777] 04/06/1987
Methold Mrs DM, (was Rawlings), MCLIP, Learning Res.Cent.Mgr., Woking Coll. [0018166] 01/10/1972
Methven Mrs M, (was MacGowan), MCLIP, Neighbourhood Resources Mgr., City of Dundee Council, Dundee, Angus. [0009388] 08/09/1969
Metzger Mr AJB, MLS FCLIP, Sen.Lect., Univ.of Botswana, Gaborone. [0024462] 01/10/1964 FE 16/05/2001
Mews Miss JE, MCLIP, Asst.Lib., Birchfield Br., Birmingham P.L. [0010106] 22/02/1970
Mexi-Jones Ms D, (was Mexi), BSc MSc MCLIP, Self-employed. [0051032] 09/11/1994
Meyer Mrs R, (was Meyer-Klugel), BA(Hons) MSc MCLIP, Lib.f/t., Wilts.C.C., Trowbridge. [0048810] 02/06/1993
Miao Mr P, MA MCLIP, Comp.Servs.Lib., Atkinson L., Southport. [0037030] 01/02/1984
Micallef Mrs DE, (was Connolly), BA(Hons) DipLib, Subject Lib., Thames Valley Univ., Slough. [0036891] 09/01/1984
Michael Mr DA, BSc DipLib MCLIP, Lib.Dir., Ransom L., Plainwell, Michigan, USA. [0032320] 12/02/1980
Michael Miss E, MCLIP, Area L.& Inf.Mgr., Newcastle City Council. [0010110] 04/01/1971
Middlemist Miss FE, BA MCLIP, Coll.Lib., Northumberland Coll., Ashington. [0021088] 10/10/1973
Middleton Ms A, BSc(Hons) DipILS, p./t.Team Lib., Univ.of Northumbria at Newcastle. [0055195] 28/10/1996
Middleton Miss C, BA(Hons), Document Controller, Stolt Offshore Ltd., Aberdeen. [0061310] 17/05/2002
Middleton Mrs C, (was Thornley), BSc(Hons) MSc MIMechE MIEE MCLIP, Engineering Lib., Univ.of Nottingham. [0049561] 12/11/1993
Middleton Mr DP, BA(Hons), Child.Lib., Salford City Council, Salford. [0052956] 26/01/1996
Middleton Ms FSC, MA DipLib MCLIP, Subject Lib., Birkbeck Coll., Univ.of London. [0039038] 24/10/1985
Middleton Mr I, BSc MSc PGDip MCLIP, Employment unknown. [0060267] 10/12/2001
Middleton Ms JC, BSc(Hons) MA, Trainee Lib., W.Sussex C.C. [0058911] 03/10/2000
Middleton Mrs JM, (was Coleman), MA MCLIP, Bookstart Coordinator, Sandwell MBC., W.Midlands. [0024484] 12/08/1975
Middleton Ms JM, MCLIP, Head of L.Serv., Maurice Bishop House, L.B.of Hackney. [0027081] 11/01/1977
Middleton Miss KP, BSc(Econ), Asst.Lib., Owen L., Swansea. [0059779] 02/10/2001
Middleton Mrs LM, (was Pringle), BA(Hons) MCLIP, Sch.Lib., Alloa Academy, Clackmannanshire. [0048218] 16/11/1992
Middleton Ms M, MA DipLib MCLIP, Unemployed. [0044113] 18/05/1990
Middleton Mrs MA, (was Metcalf), BA(Hons) MCLIP, Lib., St.Andrew's Sch., Leatherhead. [0033064] 07/10/1980
Middleton Mrs PE, (was Coe), BLib MCLIP, Sen.Lib.(Support Serv.), Notts.C.C. [0039324] 16/01/1986
Middleton Mrs PJ, (was York), MCLIP, Retired. [0010121] 12/03/1959
Midgley Ms CM, BA MA MCLIP, Head of Inf., Council for Environmental Educ., Reading. [0035354] 08/10/1982
Midgley Mrs EA, BA(Hons) DMS PGCM MCLIP MCMI MInstLM, Cent.L.Mgr., Blackpool Bor.Council. [0038701] 01/10/1985
Midgley Mrs L, (was Wilson), BSc DipLib MCLIP, Career Break. [0038852] 14/10/1985
Midgley Mrs MJ, (was Chappellow), MCLIP, Sch.Lib., Thornton Grammar Sch., Bradford. [0017379] 23/03/1963
Midlane Mrs JC, BA(Hons) CertEd DipCG, Sch.Lib., Health Promotion Serv., Univ.of Aberystwyth. [0059787] 03/10/2001
Mieczkowska Miss SM, BA(Hons) MA, Research Asst., Open Univ., Business Sch., Milton Keynes. [0058053] 21/10/1999
Miehe Ms D, MA MLib MCLIP, Curator, The British L., London. [0048332] 27/11/1992
Miers Mrs SM, Sch.Lib., Brentwood Co.High Sch., Essex. [0055415] 08/10/1997
Migliavacca Ms AM, Lib./Inf.Mgr., Inst.of Internat.Visual Arts, London. [0050407] 18/07/1994
Milam Miss T, BA(Hons), Grad.Trainee, The London L. [0059724] 05/09/2001
Milburn Miss SJ, BA(Hons) MA MCLIP, Lib., Judge Inst.of Management, Univ.of Cambridge. [0047701] 19/10/1992
Milby Ms CL, BA DipLib MCLIP, Inf.& Learning Mgr., Monmoughshire C.C., Chepston L. [0034828] 15/03/1982
Milby Mrs Y, BSc(Hons) MCLIP, Learning Res.Co-ordinator, Stirling High Sch. [0053654] 21/08/1996
Mildren Mr KW, BSc MCLIP, Academic Serv.Lib., Univ.of Portsmouth. [0010128] 29/08/1968
Miles Mr JLS, BA DipEd FCLIP, Life Member. [0010129] 07/08/1958 FE 01/01/1963
Miles Mr PG, BA MCLIP, Retired. [0010131] 25/10/1967
Miles Miss R, BA(Hons), L.& Inf.Offr., C.I.P.D., London. [0057558] 06/04/1999
Miles Mrs R, L.Asst., W.Berks.Dist.Council, Newbury. [0058846] 31/08/2000 AF
Miles Mrs SA, BA(Hons) DipRSA, L.Asst., Bath Cent.L. [0061597] 03/10/2002 AF
Miles Mrs SJ, BA MCLIP, Database Designer, Ovid Tech.Ltd., Chiswick. [0035346] 12/10/1982
Miles Mrs SJ, (was Baker), MA MCLIP, Head of Catalogue Mgmt., Bodleian L., Univ.of Oxford. [0000647] 14/10/1971

Personal Members

Milford Miss H, BA(Hons), Grad.Trainee, Lincoln's Inn Library, London. [0059692] 08/08/2001
Milford Miss SN, BA, Career Break. [0046268] 21/10/1991
Mill Ms FF, MA DipLib, Asst.Dir.of Learning Cent., Univ.of Wolverhampton. [0034506] 19/11/1981
Millar Ms DR, BSc DipLib, Inf.Serv.Advisor, Napier Univ., Edinburgh. [0031761] 29/11/1979
Millar Ms K, MA MSc, Career Break. [0043346] 24/10/1989
Millar Mrs LMM, (was Hendry), BA MCLIP, Housewife. [0021382] 13/11/1973
Millar Ms MS, BSc DipLib MCLIP, Inf.Mgr., Univ.of Abertay Dundee. [0037144] 01/03/1984
Millar Mrs N, (was Brownlee), BA(Hons) DipLib MCLIP, Grp.L.Mgr., S.E.E.L.B., N.Down & Ards. [0030009] 23/10/1978
Millar Mrs PM, BSc DipLib MCLIP, Sub-Lib., Univ.of Paisley L. [0029751] 11/10/1978
Millar Ms SM, BA MCLIP, Local Studies Offr.(Job Share), Midlothian Council, Loanhead. [0026739] 01/01/1976
Millar Mr WJ, MCLIP, Stock & Collections Mgr., Dumfries & Galloway L.Inf.& Arch., Ewart L. [0021650] 07/12/1973
Millard Mr RE, BA(Hons) DipLib MCLIP, Dep.Inf.Systems Mgr., M.O.D., Bristol. [0029752] 04/10/1978
Millard Mrs SJ, (was Hearne), BA(Hons) DipIM MCLIP, Child.Lib., Hants.Co.L., Andover. [0054697] 27/02/1997
Millen Mrs CP, (was Parker), MCLIP, Team Lib., Arts & L.Dept., Kent C.C. [0010139] 12/01/1965
Miller Mr A, MA FCLIP, Retired. [0010140] 03/10/1955 **FE 01/01/1967**
Miller Mrs A, (was Winton), BA (Hons) MCLIP, Life Member. [0010141] 20/10/1953
Miller Ms AE, (was Black), BA DipLib MCLIP, Lib.(Job Share), Database Management, Edinburgh Cent.L. [0033066] 19/09/1980
Miller Ms B, LDipLib MA, Unemployed. [0061043] 05/02/2002
Miller Mrs BL, BA(Hons) AALIA, Learning Resources Cent.Mgr., Aylesbury Coll., Bucks. [0021629] 01/01/1973
Miller Miss CA, BA MCLIP, Special Projects Mgr., , L.Serv., Queen Mother L., Univ.of Aberdeen. [0010146] 27/02/1969
Miller Ms CA, BA(Hons) MA, Employment not known. [0052097] 03/10/1995
Miller Ms CL, (was Muir), BA DipLib MCLIP, Housewife. [0027743] 05/07/1977
Miller Mrs CL, (was Clapham), BA DipLib MCLIP, Dep.Lib., Theodore Goddard, London. [0044538] 23/10/1990
Miller Mrs CM, BA DipLib MCLIP, Inf.& Local Studies Lib., William Patrick L., E.Dunbartonshire L. [0035752] 10/01/1983
Miller Ms CM, BA(Hons) MA MCLIP, Sen.Offr., The Chartered Soc.of Physiotherapy, London. [0051731] 31/05/1995
Miller Miss D, BA(Hons) MA (DUNELM) MA, Sen.Inf.Offr., Lawrence Graham, Solicitors, London. [0056088] 02/02/1998
Miller Mrs DA, (was Cairns), MBA MA MCLIP, L.Policy & Learn.Serv.Coordinator, Dunfermline L., Dunfermline. [0032262] 03/03/1980
Miller Ms DE, BA DipLib, Care Asst., Lincs.Assoc.for Care of the Elderly, Lincoln. [0034686] 29/01/1982
Miller Mrs FAM, (was Walter), MCLIP, Term-Time Sch.Lib., Perth & Kinross Council. [0015319] 14/01/1972
Miller Miss J, MA(Hons) PGDipILS, L.Asst., Andersonian L., Univ.of Strathclyde. [0061270] 09/05/2002
Miller Mr J, Stud., Strathclyde Univ. [0059932] 06/11/2001
Miller Mr J, Life Member. [0026778] 04/11/1976
Miller Mr JP, BA MCLIP, L.Dir., Coll.of Europe, Bruges, Belgium. [0020790] 06/07/1973
Miller Mrs KC, BSc(Econ) PGAG MCLIP, Asst.Lib., Orkney L., Orkney Islands Council. [0052731] 29/11/1995
Miller Mrs KK, DipLib MCLIP, Asst.Lib.(Mob.& Home L.Serv.), N.Ayrshire Council, Ardrossan, Ayrshire. [0040094] 20/10/1986
Miller Ms LM, , Lib., Daventry Tertiary Coll., Northants. [0058233] 19/11/1999
Miller Mrs MA, (was Nightingale), BA MCLIP, Inf.Specialist Statistics, Nottingham Trent Univ. [0010841] 27/02/1970
Miller Mr MD, (was Gozzett), MCLIP, Life Member, Tel.01359-242221. [0010162] 28/09/1946
Miller Miss MH, MA FCLIP LRAM, Retired. [0040738] 07/03/1956 **FE 01/01/1969**
Miller Ms ML, (was Gray), BA MCLIP, Acad.Liaison Lib., Glasgow Caledonian Univ. [0026907] 10/01/1977
Miller Mrs NM, BSc(Hons), Asst.Lib., Nat.Audit Off.L., London. [0059397] 28/03/2001
Miller Mrs S, BA, Tech.Inf.Controller, Virgin Atlantic Airways, Crawley. [0057417] 03/03/1999
Miller Mrs SJ, (was Chapman), MCLIP, Babies Need BooksProject Offr., Warks.C.C. [0025239] 05/12/1975
Miller Ms SM, (was Mackenzie), MCLIP, Asst.Operations Lib., Stirling Council. [0022733] 22/08/1974
Millerchip Mr JJG, BLib MA FCLIP MIMgt, Head of Dept.of Educ.Resources, Northbrook Coll., Worthing, W.Sussex. [0018392] 16/10/1972 **FE 18/11/1998**
Millgate Mr S, BSc MSc, Lib., GlaxoSmithKline, Dartford. [0043787] 11/01/1990
Millican Miss SE, L.Asst., Gorleston L., Norfolk. [0045040] 01/07/1990 **AF**
Millican Mr TJ, BA FCLIP, Life Member. [0010169] 23/10/1935 **FE 01/01/1940**
Milligan Ms DE, MA(Hons), Stud., Univ.of Strathclyde. [0061322] 22/05/2002
Milligan Mr EH, BA MCLIP, Life Member, Tel.01734 871851, 4 Lancaster Close, Reading, RG1 5HB. [0010171] 08/03/1940
Milligan Miss JC, BA, L.Asst., Inst.of Classical Studies, London. [0054895] 22/04/1997

Milligan Miss LB, (was Ponsford), BEd MSc(Econ) DipLib MCLIP, Dep.Ch.Lib., Guille-Alles L., Guernsey. [0031904] 16/01/1980
Milligan Ms MAT, (was Stewart), MA DipLib MCLIP, Support Offr.-Educ.Res., Falkirk Council. [0023221] 08/11/1974
Milligan Miss TJ, MA(Hons) DipILS MCLIP, Lib., Falkirk Council, Larbert L. [0053851] 04/10/1996
Milliken Miss RJ, Unemployed. [0020572] 28/04/1973
Millin Mrs KJ, (was Holder), BLib MCLIP, Asst.Head of Lib., Dudley M.B.C., Dudley L. [0029516] 18/09/1978
Millington Ms KJ, BSc MSc, L.I.T.Trainer, Croydon Coll., Surrey. [0051319] 10/01/1995
Millington Mr PT, BSc MCLIP, Unemployed. [0026779] 17/11/1976
Million Miss AR, BA MCLIP, Freelance Law Lib. [0044197] 04/07/1990
Millis Mrs AJ, BSc(Hons), Stud., W.Kent Coll. & P./t.Sch.Lib., Bedgebury Sch., Goudhurst, Kent. [0057056] 30/11/1998
Millman Mrs SM, (was Bugler), MCLIP, Retired. [0002029] 04/03/1954
Mills Mr BD, MCLIP, Local Studies Lib., Bolton Metropolitan Bor. [0027483] 01/01/1972
Mills Mr C, BA MA DipLib MCLIP, Dep.Head of L.& Inf.Serv., The Natural Hist.Mus., London. [0031664] 05/11/1979
Mills Mr CDJ, BA BSc DipLIS DipIS CertMS AI, Freelance Indexer/Lib. [0043256] 13/10/1989
Mills Miss E, MCLIP, Life Member. [0010176] 23/09/1965
Mills Mr GJ, MSc BA DipLib MCLIP, Head of Comm.L.Serv., Birmingham. [0020191] 06/02/1973
Mills Miss HE, BA(Hons) DipLib, Asst.Lib., Homerton Univ.NHS Trust, London. [0047129] 05/05/1992
Mills Mr HP, (was Rogers), BLib MCLIP, Grp.L.Mgr.(Job Share), S.E.Educ.L.Board. [0036175] 02/06/1983
Mills Mr J, FCLIP, Retired. [0018034] 04/03/1937 **FE 01/01/1950**
Mills Mrs JA, Unemployed. [0059518] 18/04/2001
Mills Mrs JA, (was Simpson), BA DipLib MCLIP, Sen.Inf.Advisor, Univ.of Surrey Roehampton, London. [0031701] 25/10/1979
Mills Mrs JS, (was Robinson), BA MCLIP, Retired. [0010179] 12/09/1957
Mills Miss K, MCLIP, Community Lib., Bryntec, Wrexham Co.Bor., Wrexham. [0044964] 28/01/1991
Mills Mrs KJ, BA DipLib MCLIP, p./t.Sch.Lib., Surrey C.C., Horley. [0038249] 14/02/1985
Mills Mrs KM, (was Ashworth), MCLIP, Sen.L.Asst., Lancs.L., Preston, Lancs. [0023787] 08/01/1975
Mills Mrs MAR, (was Gibbs), MCLIP, Sen.Asst.Catr.(Job-share), Univ.of Bath. [0010180] 01/01/1961
Mills Mr RA, MA MCLIP, Lib.& Inf.Serv.Mgr., Oxford Univ.L.Serv., Plant Sci.L. [0010185] 02/04/1970
Mills Mr RJR, BSc DMS MCLIP, L.Serv.Mgr., Harrow P.L. [0010186] 28/08/1969
Mills Mrs SJ, (was Pedley), MA MCLIP, Lib./Arch., Regents Park Coll., Oxford. [0011466] 13/07/1970
Mills Mr SP, (was Farquhar), BA MCLIP, Sch.Lib., Boston Spa Comp.Sch., W.Yorks. [0045514] 26/02/1991
Mills Mrs VA, (was Hibberd), BA DipLib MCLIP, Researcher, Oxford Economic Research Assoc., Oxford. [0044101] 17/05/1990
Mills Mr WJ, MA DipLib MCLIP, Lib. & Keeper, Univ.of Cambridge, Scott Polar Research Inst. [0034193] 15/10/1981
Millum Ms CS, Personnel & Devel.Offr., E.Sussex C.C., Lewes. [0052808] 01/12/1995 **AF**
Millward Miss S, MA, ETD Co-ordinator, Brent&Harrow Health Auth. [0060925] 10/01/2002
Milne Mr C, BA(Hons) DipIA MCLIP, Inf.Specialist, Univ.of Abertay, Dundee. [0048063] 04/11/1992
Milne Mrs CJ, (was Gormley), BA MA DipLIS, Trainee Liaison Lib., Univ.of Reading. [0055279] 12/09/1997
Milne Miss DC, Life Member, Tel.01506 655137. [0010190] 09/03/1938
Milne Mr DC, BA(Hons) DipLib PGDip, Taxonomy Coordinator, 186K Ltd., Reading. [0049262] 19/10/1993
Milne Ms DE, MCLIP, Lib., Angus Council. [0018123] 02/10/1972
Milne Ms FE, (was Hutchison), BA(Hons) MCLIP, Lect., The Robert Gordon Univ., Aberdeen. [0040992] 01/10/1986
Milne Miss HM, BA(Hons) MA, Subject Support Lib., Univ.of York. [0057976] 07/10/1999
Milne Mr IA, MLib MCLIP, Lib., Royal Coll.of Physicians, Edinburgh. [0032446] 11/04/1980
Milne Miss J, BA MCLIP, Sen.L.& Inf.Worker, Cent.L., Dundee. [0033067] 01/10/1980
Milne Mr J, MA FCLIP, Life Member, Tel.0706 41698, 167 Wardle Rd., Rochdale, Lancs., OL12 9JA. [0010194] 25/08/1947 **FE 01/01/1966**
Milne Miss JR, MA(Hons) DipILS MCLIP, Accessions Lib., E.Lothian Council, Haddington. [0056878] 29/10/1998
Milne Mr JR, BA MCLIP, Asst.Lib., The Robert Gordon Univ., Aberdeen. [0044814] 04/12/1990
Milne Mrs LA, BA MCLIP, Br.Lib., Porthcawl L., Bridgend Co.Bor.Council. [0010197] 04/10/1971
Milne Mr RR, MA FCLIP FRSA, Dir.of the Res.Support L.Programme, Joint H.E.Funding Council. [0034100] 02/10/1981 **FE 21/03/2001**
Milne Mrs S, (was Pott), BA MCLIP, Life Member. [0010201] 16/09/1960
Milne Mrs SA, (was Shaw), MA DipLib MCLIP, Inf.Serv.Lib., Scottish Borders Council, L.Serv. [0044777] 21/11/1990
Milne Mr SD, MSc MCLIP, Commercial Mgr., N.E.Wales Inst.of H.E., Business Devel.Unit, Wrexham. [0028085] 12/10/1977
Milner Mrs JA, (was Bulleyment), BA MCLIP, Asst.Lib.-Catg., Univ.Coll., Northampton. [0024480] 01/09/1975
Milner Miss JK, BA DipLib MCLIP, Stock Offr., Wigan Council. [0037104] 08/02/1984
Milner Miss S, MA MCLIP, Retired. [0010204] 12/02/1966

Milner Mr WJ, BA(Hons), p./t.Stud., Lib., Robert Gordon Univ., Swiss Hotel Mgmt.Sch.Switzerland. [0059968] 13/11/2001
Milnes Miss BAM, MCLIP, Retired. [0010206] 01/01/1956
Milnes Mrs VJ, (was Crees), BA MCLIP, Res.Cent.Lib., Dept.Arts Policy, City Univ. [0003359] 01/10/1971
Milnes Gaskell Mrs WA, BA(hons) PGCE, Lib., Tunbridge Wells High Sch. [0060920] 10/01/2002
Milns Ms AVL, BSc(Hons) MCLIP, Asst.Lib., Home Off., London. [0054058] 24/10/1996
Milot Miss VC, BA DipLIB MCLIP, Team Lib.-Young Peoples Team, Kent C.C., Arts & L.Dept. [0036767] 16/12/1983
Milroy Miss JC, BA, Unemployed. [0057575] 10/05/1999
Milsom Miss CHL, BSc MA MCLIP, Inf.Mgr., Pinsent Curtis Biddle, Leeds. [0041216] 19/10/1987
Milsted Miss RS, Lib., Leics.C.C. [0058712] 01/07/2000
Milton Mrs AM, (was Queen), MCLIP, Tutor Lib., HMYO1/RC Feltham, L.B.of Hounslow. [0019271] 09/09/1972
Milton Mrs CM, (was Holbrook), BA MCLIP, Life Member. [0010212] 05/09/1953
Milton Mr HR, BA DipLib MCLIP, Sen.Lib., Min.of Defence H.Q.L.Serv., London. [0010213] 29/01/1969
Milton Mr IS, BA DipLib MCLIP, L.& Lifelong Learning Mgr., S.W.Surrey, Surrey C.C. [0019928] 12/01/1973
Milton Miss J, BA, Implementation Consultant, FDI, Sheffield. [0039263] 14/01/1986
Milton Mr LE, MA MCLIP, Life Member. [0010214] 18/07/1954
Milton Mrs MB, BA(Hons) DipLIS MCLIP, Inf.Mgr., BHP Billiton plc., London. [0050631] 01/10/1994
Milton-Worssell Mrs AE, (was Heathcote), MA MCLIP, Subject Leader, History Sch.of Educ.Studies, Univ.of Surrey. [0019498] 02/10/1969
Mina Mrs JG, (was Logan), MCLIP, Asst.Reader Serv.Lib., Carnegie L., Dunfermline. [0009061] 28/03/1971
Minamoto Mr S, Prof., Shukutoku Univ., Japan. [0031088] 21/08/1979
Minde Mrs D, (was Lee), Inf.Offr.-Docu Delivery &Copyright, Liverpool John Moores Univ. [0043904] 14/02/1990
Minett Ms AE, (was Quinton), BA MCLIP, Sch.Lib., St Saviours & St Olaves Sch., L.B.of Southwark. [0022798] 16/10/1974
Ming Miss LHR, BEd(Hons), Sen.L.Asst., Sch.L.Serv., Cent.L., Londonderry, & Star Project Offr., Limavady L., Limavady. [0051245] 05/12/1994
AF
Minkova Miss EE, MA DipLIS, Sen.Resource Cent.Asst., Anniesland Coll. [0058608] 12/04/2000
Minns Mrs A, (was Hunt), BA(Hons) MCLIP, Resource Cent.Coordinator, St John's High Sch., Dundee. [0048461] 14/01/1993
Minns Mrs AE, (was Tott), BA DipLib FCLIP, Inf.Adviser, St.Peter's House L., Univ.of Brighton. [0018419] 17/10/1972 **FE 20/03/1996**
Minshull Mrs LR, (was Woods), MCLIP, Learning Res.Mgr., Ernulf Comm.Sch., Cambs. [0010224] 22/10/1966
Minter Ms CA, MCLIP, Inf.Specialist, QinetiQ, Malvern. [0010227] 01/01/1968
Minter Mrs EC, (was Wheadon), BA(Hons) DipIS MCLIP, Inf.Offr., Clifford Chance, LLP, London. [0054818] 11/04/1977
Minter Mr P, Unemployed. [0058179] 11/11/1999
Minter Mrs SM, (was Stanyon), BA(Hons) DipLIS MCLIP, Lib., Child.& Young Peoples Serv., Oxhey L., Herts.C.C. [0048465] 19/01/1993
Minton Mrs C, (was Lobb), BA MCLIP, Reg.Inf.Mgr., Sport England, Reading. [0009029] 16/07/1967
Mintowt-Czyz Mrs EJ, (was Fielding), MCLIP, Sch.Lib., Rougemont Sch., Newport, S.Wales. [0018307] 05/10/1972
Minty Mr MJ, MA MCLIP, Asst.Lib., Oriental Inst., Univ.of Oxford. [0010229] 20/07/1972
Minty Mrs WLF, M THEOL MA, Head of Acquisitions Mgmt., Bodleian L., Univ.of Oxford. [0042023] 25/07/1988
Mircic Ms AA, BA DipLib MCLIP, Sen.Lib.(Maternity Leave), N.Yorks.C.C. [0045013] 02/03/1987
Mires Miss E, BA(Hons), Grad.Trainee, Univ.Westminster. [0059874] 29/10/2001
Mishra Mr D, BLib BSc, Lib.-Catg., Dept.of Forest Res.& Survey, Kathmandu. [0061169] 20/03/2002
Misir Ms PD, BEng(Hons) MA, Network Planning & Devel.Engineer, Government Communications Bureau, London. [0054069] 21/10/1996
Miskin Mrs CE, (was Mithinson), LLB MCLIP, Inf.Consultant. [0020807] 01/01/1969
Miskin Mr CRD, BA MA MCLIP, Team Lib., Slough Bor.Unitary Auth. [0043708] 08/12/1989
Misra Mr D, BA MA, Learning Serv.Mgr., City of Westminster Coll., London. [0049819] 15/12/1993
Missen Mr RS, MCLIP, Sen.Lib., Haringey P.L. [0010232] 24/07/1970
Misso Ms KV, BSc MCLIP, p./t.Stud./Inf.Offr., Leeds Metro.Univ., NHS Cent., York Univ. [0054117] 31/10/1996
Mistry Mr P, BSc(Hons), Stud., Manchester. [0061836] 15/11/2002
Mistry Mrs SS, (was Davda), MCLIP, Ethnic Communities Coordinator, L.B.of Hillingdon, Uxbridge Cent.L. [0032039] 14/01/1980
Mitchell Mrs AB, (was Stourton), MCLIP, L.Asst., Worcester C.C. [0014119] 01/01/1970
Mitchell Miss ATA, BA(Hons), Unemployed. [0041399] 20/11/1987
Mitchell Mr BR, BA (Hons) MA, Inf.Offr. [0060880] 18/12/2001
Mitchell Mrs C, (was Hemsworth), BSc(Hons) MCLIP, Learning Cent.Res.Lib., Arthur Mee Learning Cent. [0048359] 07/12/1992
Mitchell Mrs C, (was Harrison-Osborne), BSc MCLIP, Foster Lib., Lincs.Arch., Lincs.C.C. [0033443] 08/01/1981
Mitchell Miss CL, BA(Hons) DipILM, I.T.& Learning Cent.Facilitator, Denbigh Comm.Coll. [0058146] 08/11/1999
Mitchell Mrs CM, (was Pearson), BA MCLIP, Unemployed. [0029205] 07/04/1978
Mitchell Ms CM, (was Switzer), BA MCLIP, p./t.Asst.Lib., Davenent Foundation Sch., Loughton. [0033441] 08/01/1981

Mitchell Mr D, BA MLib, Unemployed. [0057339] 10/02/1999
Mitchell Mr DJD, BA MA FCLIP, LRC Mgr., Pontypridd Coll. [0032129] 28/01/1980 **FE 26/11/1997**
Mitchell Mrs DM, (was Wilcox), MCLIP, Retired, 2 Moana Road, Plimmerton, New Zealand. [0017388] 01/01/1952
Mitchell Mrs DM, BA(Hons) MA, Helpline Mgr., DEFRA, London. [0056308] 05/05/1998
Mitchell Mrs DM, (was Jackson), BA(Hons) PGCE MCLIP, Team Lib., Greasby L., Wirral. [0038185] 24/01/1985
Mitchell Mrs DMJ, (was Brown), BA DipLib MCLIP, Asst.Lib., Univ.of Sussex L. [0020184] 05/02/1973
Mitchell Ms DN, BA DipLib, Asst.Inf.Mgr., Off.Parliamentary Commissioner, London. [0060942] 10/01/2002
Mitchell Mr G, Assembler, NCR, Dundee. [0041171] 12/10/1987
Mitchell Mrs GA, BA DipLib MCLIP, Learning Resource Cent. Mgr., Inst.of Further and Higher Educ., Belfast. [0031665] 12/11/1979
Mitchell Mr GD, BA MCLIP, Sen.Lib., Bletchley L., Milton Keynes Council. [0028859] 31/01/1978
Mitchell Mr GPCR, BA DipIS, Dep.Dir.of L.& Inf.Serv., BPP Law Sch., London. [0056331] 18/05/1998
Mitchell Mrs HF, (was Davies), BA MCLIP, Exec.Offr., Nat.Assembly for Wales, Carmarthen. [0003697] 04/10/1967
Mitchell Ms J, Stud., Univ.of Wales, Aberystwyth, & Sen.L.Asst., Shoe Lane Pub.L., Corporation of London. [0045901] 01/07/1991
AF
Mitchell Mrs JA, (was Duckham), MCLIP, Head of P.Serv., L.B.of Hillingdon, Cent.L., Uxbridge. [0010242] 05/01/1967
Mitchell Mr JB, BA, Patent Watch Specialist, RWS Group Inf.Div., London. [0035143] 19/08/1982 **SP**
Mitchell Mrs JE, FIBMS, P./t.Stud./Lib., Univ.of Cent.England. [0059593] 26/06/2001
Mitchell Mr JL, BMus MMus Dip MLIS, Rare Books Curator, Nat.L.of Scotland, Edinburgh. [0055728] 10/11/1997
Mitchell Mrs KJ, (was Hicks), BLib MCLIP, Sen.Lib.:Ref., L.& Inf., Wokingham Dist.Council. [0026112] 16/07/1976
Mitchell Miss L, BSc(Hons) DipLib MCLIP, Asst.Lib.(Natural Sci.), Queen Mary & Westfield Coll. [0048453] 13/01/1993
Mitchell Miss LA, MA DipLib MCLIP, Sch.Lib., Stewarton Academy, Kilmarnock. [0035932] 20/02/1983
Mitchell Mrs LJ, (was Greer), BA MCLIP, p./t.L.Asst., Belfast Educ.& L.Board. [0031515] 15/10/1979
Mitchell Ms LM, MA MAppSc DipLib MCLIP, Human Sci.Inf.Offr., Univ.of Stirling. [0039652] 08/04/1986
Mitchell Mrs M, (was Livingstone), MA DipLib MCLIP, Subject Lib., Melrose Campus L., Napier Univ., Borders Gen.Hosp. [0037838] 22/10/1984
Mitchell Mrs MA, (was Elstob), BA MCLIP, Admin.Offr.for Serv.Sen.Lib., Army L.Serv. [0038785] 08/10/1985
Mitchell Miss MB, BA MCLIP, Learning Res.Offr., Kingston L., Surrey. [0010249] 07/10/1970
Mitchell Mrs MJ, (was Jackson), MCLIP, Unemployed. [0022512] 26/05/1974
Mitchell Mrs MJ, (was Etchells), MCLIP, Lend.Lib., L.B.of Enfield. [0004618] 03/07/1969
Mitchell Mrs MM, Mob.Serv.Super., Herts.C.C., Hatfield. [0045154] 26/07/1990 **AF**
Mitchell Mrs MR, BA MA, L.Asst., Soc.of Antiquaries of London. [0057952] 01/10/1999
Mitchell Miss MS, BA MCLIP, Retired. [0010244] 26/07/1971
Mitchell Ms OC, BA(Hons) MSc, Inf.Offr., Linklaters, London. [0049780] 22/12/1993
Mitchell Mr RE, MCLIP, Self-employed, Brownhills,Walsall,W.Midlands. [0010240] 01/01/1956
Mitchell Mr RG, BA MCLIP, Southern Area Mgr., LFC/Gresswell Projects, London. [0010256] 17/01/1966
Mitchell Mrs RM, BA MCLIP, Asst.Lib., George Edwards L., Univ.of Surrey. [0035969] 08/03/1983
Mitchell Ms S, BSc PGDip, Asst.Lib., Dept.for Work & Pensions, London. [0050235] 12/05/1994
Mitchell Mrs SA, MCLIP, Ref.& Inf.serv.Mgr., Leics.City Council, Ref.& Inf.L. [0026484] 01/01/1977
Mitchell Mrs SM, (was Phillips), BA DipIS MCLIP, Inf.Devel.Offr., Herts.C.C., St.Albans. [0049145] 08/01/1993
Mitchell Mrs T, (was Morait), BA MCLIP, Unemployed. [0042237] 13/10/1988
Mitchell Mrs TD, (was Schaverien), Lib., L.B.of Greenwich. [0038656] 01/01/1968
Mitchell Mrs VJLW, (was Coles), BA(Hons) DipLIB MCLIP, Area Lib.,S., Treharris L., Merthyr Tydfil Co.Bor.Council. [0037075] 06/02/1984
Mitchell Ms VM, L.Services Mgr., S.Warwicks General Hosp., Warwick. [0052619] 13/11/1995
Mitchelmore Ms RA, BA MA, Lib., Archbishop King Middle Sch., Newport, I.O.W. [0051347] 25/01/1995
Mitcheson Mrs EA, BA DipLib MCLIP, Retired. [0026131] 30/07/1976
Mitford Miss J, BSc(Hons), Admin., North MLSK Trust., Gateshead. [0061824] 13/11/2002 **AF**
Mizuno Miss VY, Resident overseas. [0061712] 24/10/2002
Mjamtu-Sie Mrs LN, (was Barlatt), MLib FCLIP, Med.Lib., Univ.of Sierra Leone, Coll.of Med.& Allied Health Sci. [0019343] 01/01/1963 **FE 20/01/1999**
Mobbs Mr EA, MCLIP, Unemployed. [0010264] 20/02/1968
Mochrie Mrs D, (was Hinks), MCLIP, Life Member. [0010265] 19/03/1955
Mochrie Mr GSN, MCLIP, Life Member. [0010266] 15/02/1958
Mockert Miss B, BA MCLIP, H.of Acq.& Binding, London L. [0010267] 01/01/1969
Mocroft Mrs SK, (was Wilkinson), MCLIP, Lifelong Learning Lib., Sandwell M.B.C. [0030297] 01/01/1979
Moffat Miss SA, BA(Hons), p./t.Stud./Admin.Offr., Univ.of Wales, Aberystwyth, The Benefits Agency, Dundee. [0059052] 06/11/2000

Moffat Ms SH, BSc MSc DMS MCLIP, Faculty Inf.Serv.Advisor, Napier Univ., Edinburgh. [0036551] 21/10/1983
Moffatt Mrs SA, (was Armitage), MCLIP, Retired. [0016552] 01/01/1965
Moffett Mr GR, BA(Hons), Lib., Essex L., Chelmsford. [0049993] 08/02/1994
Moger Mr D, BA DipLib MCLIP, L.Inf.Serv.Mgr., Bath & N.E.Somerset, Bath Cent.L. [0038399] 17/04/1985
Mogford Mrs FM, (was Taylor), MCLIP, P/t.L.Asst., Reading Univ. [0019344] 08/10/1970
Mogg Miss RJ, BA(Hons), Stud., Univ. of Sheffield. [0058885] 01/10/2000
Mohamed Ms M, DipLS, Stud., Univ.of Central England. [0060046] 04/12/2001
Mohamed Ibrahim Ms H, DipLS, Stud., Univ.of Central England. [0060045] 04/12/2001
Mohamedali Mr ON, BA MA MLS, Sen.Lect./Head, Dept.of L.& Inf.Studies, Univ.of W.Indies, Mona, Jamaica. [0043169] 05/09/1989
Mohammed Lani Ms R, DipLS, Stud., Univ.of Central England. [0060047] 04/12/2001
Mohan Mr DJ, BA(Hons) MA PGCE, Communication Offr./Web-Editor, The Methodist Church UK, London. [0058359] 24/01/2000
Moir Mrs G, (was Marchant), MCLIP, Retired. [0010274] 12/10/1966
Moir Mr MCG, H.of L.& Arch., Perth & Kinross Council, Educ.& Child.Serv. [0010275] 07/03/1968
Moldon Mr D, FCLIP, Asst.Lib., E.Finchley L., L.B.of Barnet. [0010277] 08/01/1964 **FE 06/08/1973**
Mole Mrs KIM, (was Tunnicliffe), MA DipInfSc, Self-employed, Editorial Work & Club Lib. [0032351] 21/02/1980
Moll Mr C, Acquistions Lib., Brynmor Jones L., Univ.of Hull. [0030011] 30/10/1978
Moll Mrs E, (was Lord), BLib MCLIP, Unemployed. [0028063] 04/10/1977
Moll Mr PA, BA MCLIP, Lib., Harney, Westwood & Riegels, Brit.Virgin Islands. [0010280] 17/02/1961
Mollard Mr TW, MCLIP, Life Member, Tel.01263 761638. [0019526] 01/10/1948
Mollins Mrs L, (was Douglas), DipIM MCLIP, Lib., Dunoon Grammar Sch., Argyll. [0045258] 14/09/1990
Mollison Mrs JF, (was Tyler), MCLIP, Unemployed. [0019669] 04/11/1972
Molloy Mrs BL, MCLIP, Inf.Mgr., Bath Spa Univ.Coll. [0024791] 01/10/1975
Molloy Miss CAL, BA(Hons) PGDipILS, Asst.Lib., Northern Coll., Aberdeen. [0055687] 04/11/1997
Molloy Mrs H, (was Jones), BA MA MAPM MCLIP MISTC, Dir.& Company Sec., MCMS Ltd. [0046093] 01/10/1991
Molloy Ms J, BA MPhil DipInfSci, Employment not known. [0060445] 11/12/2001
Molloy Mr MJ, BA DipLib MCLIP, Dir.of L.& Heritage, Derbys.L.Serv., Derbys. [0029465] 28/07/1978
Molloy Mr SP, BA(Hons) DipILM, Asst.Lib., Alder Hey Child.Hosp., Liverpool. [0055606] 24/10/1997
Molnar Mrs ME, BA, L.Asst., Dr.J.H.Burgoyne & Partners, London. [0061077] 04/03/2002
Moloney Ms AM, BA MSc MCLIP, L. Systems Team Leader, Cardiff Univ. [0010287] 01/01/1971
Moloney Mrs EJL, (was Jones), BA MA, Maternity Leave, Hill Taylor Dickinson, London. [0054070] 21/10/1996
Monaghan Miss AM, L.Asst., Zoological Soc.of London. [0051421] 10/02/1975
Monaghan Miss MA, MA DipLib MCLIP, Asst.Lib., Queen Margaret Univ.Coll., Edinburgh. [0028465] 20/12/1977
Monaghan Miss V, BA MCLIP, L.Devel. Mgr., Inf. & L. Devel. Serv., Derby. [0033073] 29/09/1980
Moneta Ms C, (was Monetta), L.& Inf.Mgr., Veale Wasbrough, Bristol. [0040800] 26/06/1997
Money Mrs EP, MCLIP DipBUSSc ANZLA, Dir., Pat Money Inf.Serv., Havelock N., New Zealand. [0017401] 15/10/1947
Moniati Ms G, BA, [0054083] 24/10/1996
Monie Mr IC, MSc FCLIP, Life Member. [0010295] 12/01/1957 **FE 01/01/1967**
Monk Mrs A, MA DipLib MCLIP, Mgr.Learning Res.Cent., Car Hill High Sch., Kirkham. [0033042] 03/10/1980
Monk Mr GC, BA MCLIP, Head of Inf.Services, Dept.of Soc.Security, London. [0026780] 25/10/1976
Monk Mrs H, Tech.L.Mgr., Williams Fl., Oxon. [0057774] 02/08/1999 **AF**
Monk Mrs LA, (was Lancaster), L.Serv.Mgr., Walsall M.B.C. [0042248] 13/10/1988
Monk Miss LK, BSc(Hons) MCLIP, Asst.Lib., Univ.Coll.London, DMS Watson Sci.L. [0051100] 15/11/1994
Monk Miss TK, Inf.Offr., Building Soc.Assoc., London. [0058139] 08/11/1999
Monkcom Miss AE, MCLIP, Sen.L.Asst., Kings Coll.London L. [0010298] 26/03/1970
Monks Mrs CC, (was Green), MCLIP, Resource Lib., Bury Coll., Manchester. [0005870] 28/01/1969
Monks Mr GF, BSc MCLIP, Lib., Southgate Sch., Cockfosters, Herts. [0030072] 27/11/1978
Monks Ms LCS, BSc, Temp.Office Worker. [0059793] 03/10/2001
Monks Mrs NL, (was Hodgkinson), MCLIP, Asst Dir.Culture Leisure & Sport, Blackburn w/ Darwen Bor.Council, Blackburn. [0016479] 16/03/1964
Monkton Mrs RC, MCLIP, Inf.Offr., Mouchel Property Serv., Bedford. [0048794] 26/05/1993
Monopoli Miss M, BSc MSc, Resident in Greece. [0057367] 26/02/1999
Monserrate Mr E, Unemployed. [0043816] 15/01/1990
Montague Mrs CJ, (was Kelner), Sen.Researcher, Arthur Andersen, London. [0050293] 02/06/1994
Montague Miss MB, BEd(Hons) DipLib MCLIP, Site Lib., Queen Mary & Westfield Coll., Med.Sch.L., London. [0031385] 03/10/1979
Monteith Miss IJ, BA MCLIP, Retired. [0010303] 01/10/1968

Montgomery Mrs A, (was Lawley), BA DipLib MCLIP, p./t.Asst.Lib., Bury Grammar Sch.(Boys), Bury. [0032777] 25/08/1980
Montgomery Mr AC, MSc FCLIP, Systems Mgr., Bristol L.Serv., Cent.L. [0010304] 11/01/1965 **FE 24/05/1979**
Montgomery Miss FG, BED DipLib MCLIP, Inf.Cent.Mgr., Dept.for Culture, Media & Sport, London. [0031667] 02/11/1979
Montgomery Mr JN, MCLIP, Retired. [0010305] 01/01/1958
Montgomery Mrs PD, (was Jones), MCLIP, Lib., Crossways Jun.Sch., S.Glos. [0010307] 01/01/1966
Moodie Mrs ATL, (was Carr), MCLIP, Application Support Offr., Newcastle L.& Inf.Serv., Ed.& L.IT Support. [0002393] 25/09/1967
Moodie Miss EB, BA(Hons) MCLIP, Retired. [0025079] 11/11/1975
Moody Mr CA, BA MCLIP, Lib., Essex C.C., Harlow. [0010309] 29/01/1969
Moody Mrs DA, (was Porter), BA, Sen.Lib., Manchester P.L. [0036164] 06/07/1983
Moody Mr DM, MCLIP, Princ.L.Offr., E.Lothian Council L.Serv., Haddington. [0024171] 20/01/1971
Moody Mrs JM, BA(Hons) PGCE DipTrans MIL, p./t.Stud./Temp.Inf.Asst., Robert Gordon Univ., Univ.of Plymouth. [0059953] 09/11/2001
Moody Mrs KB, (was Vollertzen), BLib MCLIP, Employment not known. [0020442] 05/12/1972
Moody Mrs PH, (was Arrand), MCLIP, Res.Cent.Super., John Taylor High Sch., Barton-under-Needwood, Staffs. [0024999] 18/11/1975
Moody Miss R, BA(Hons), Stud., Univ.of Northumbria at, Newcastle, & Secretary, NCFS., Univ.of Newcastle. [0058772] 17/07/2000
Moohan Mrs G, Lib., Goethe Inst.Inter Nationes e.v., Glasgow. [0040602] 02/04/1987
Moon Miss BE, MA MPhil FCLIP FRSE, Retired. [0010313] 17/03/1954 **FE 01/01/1958**
Moon Mr C, BA, Unemployed. [0060960] 21/01/2002
Moon Miss CE, BA MCLIP, Registrar & Sec., Univ.of Brighton. [0010314] 13/09/1963
Moon Mr EE, HonFCLIP FCLIP, Resident in U.S.A. [0017404] 01/01/1939 **FE 01/01/1950**
Moorbath Mr P, BSc MSc MA MCLIP, Lib., Chaucer Coll.Canterbury, Kent. [0037534] 05/10/1984
Moore Mrs AE, Sen.L.Asst., Univ.of Sussex L., Brighton. [0060009] 21/11/2001 **AF**
Moore Mrs AMB, (was Sale), MA DipLib PGCE MCLIP, Inf.Offr, Nat.Assoc.of Citizens Advice, Bureaux (NACAB), London. [0021758] 15/01/1974
Moore Miss CA, BSc MA MCLIP, L.Inf.Offr., CIPD, London. [0030223] 10/01/1979
Moore Mr CA, BA, Stud., Univ.of Strathclyde. [0061816] 11/11/2002
Moore Mrs CA, (was Edwards), BA DipLib MCLIP, Site Lib., Leicester S.Fields Coll. [0027403] 01/03/1977
Moore Mrs CA, BSc, Stud., Univ.N.London. [0059812] 10/10/2001
Moore Mr CC, BA DipLib MCLIP, Lib.Mgr., Royal Bor.of Kensington & Chelsea, London. [0031906] 20/12/1979
Moore Mr CJK, BA(Hons) MSc MCLIP, Comm.Lib., Wilts.C.C., Wootton Bassett L. [0055501] 16/01/1997
Moore Miss DM, MBE BA FCLIP, Retired. [0010329] 29/05/1935 **FE 01/01/1939**
Moore Mr DR, BA, Unemployed. [0058795] 31/07/2000
Moore Mrs E, (was Middleton), BSc, Inf.Asst., Yorkshire Dales Nat.Pk.Auth. [0010330] 07/01/1970
Moore Ms E, BA(Hons) DipIS MCLIP, [0047275] 01/07/1992
Moore Mrs EA, (was Dickie), MCLIP, Learning Resources Offr.(Bibl.), W.Herts.Coll., Watford Campus. [0003936] 05/02/1970
Moore Ms EJ, MCLIP, Lib.(Job Share), Glos.C.C. [0010332] 14/09/1970
Moore Mrs F, BSc PGCE MCLIP, Employment not known. [0061236] 01/04/2002
Moore Mr G, BA MCLIP, Princ.Lib., Aberdeenshire Council. [0010335] 20/09/1967
Moore Mrs GM, (was Tarpey), BA DipLib MCLIP, Administrator, Moving Image Studio, Cambridge Univ. [0038179] 22/01/1985
Moore Mr GR, BA DipLib, Employment not known. [0060177] 10/12/2001
Moore Miss HM, BA PGDipIM, Inf.Specialist, CDC Grp.plc., London. [0052969] 24/01/1996
Moore Mrs JC, (was Cave), BA MCLIP, Area Lib., Southampton City Co., Shirley L. [0002511] 19/01/1966
Moore Miss JE, BSc, Sen.Asst.Lib., De Montfort Univ., Bedford. [0041858] 29/04/1988
Moore Mr JM, BA, Stud., Loughborough Univ. [0061809] 11/11/2002
Moore Mrs JM, (was Follett), BA MCLIP, Freelance Hist.Researcher/, Genealogist, Self-employed, 21 Shawe Hall Av, Manchester. [0024341] 12/07/1975
Moore Mr JM, LLB BA DipLib MCLIP, Cathedral Lib., Dean & Chapter of Wells Cathedral, Wells, Somerset. [0029339] 17/06/1978
Moore Mrs JP, (was Cox), BA MCLIP, p./t.Classroom Asst. [0031809] 30/12/1979
Moore Mrs JR, BA MSLS MBA PhD, Retired, Resident USA. [0017405] 26/07/1961
Moore Mrs KM, BA(Hons) DipLib MCLIP, Inf.Spec., Learning Cent., Sheffield Hallam Univ. [0033080] 06/10/1980
Moore Mrs LM, Stud., Univ.of Wales, Aberystwyth. [0050227] 10/05/1994
Moore Ms LR, BA DipLib MCLIP, Inf.Co-ordinator, Denbighshire C.C., Ruthin. [0038643] 21/08/1985
Moore Ms MJ, DipLIS, Client Management Inf.Mgr., Insignia Richard Ellis, London. [0053764] 01/11/1996
Moore Mr NF, FCLIP, Retired. [0010353] 30/03/1960 **FE 01/01/1969**
Moore Mr NL, BTech MCLIP, Editor, L.& Inf.Sci.Abstracts. [0010351] 01/10/1968
Moore Dr PJF, BA BA(Hons) MA(Cantab) PhD, Stud. [0057440] 01/04/1999 **SP**

Moore Ms PT, (was Perry), BA DipIS MCLIP, Inf.& Ref.Lib., L.B.of Sutton, Surrey. [0048255] 18/11/1992
Moore Mr RJ, BA MCLIP, Head of L., Southampton Inst. [0010360] 16/01/1968
Moore Mr RJ, BA MI BIOL MCLIP, Retired. [0010359] 01/01/1957
Moore Mrs SE, (was Macormac), MCLIP, Child.Lib., Lordshill L., Southampton City L. [0009289] 29/01/1970
Moore Mr SJ, MPhil MLib MCLIP, Area L.Offr., Highland Council. [0045447] 06/02/1991
Moore Mrs SJ, (was Lovell), BA MCLIP, Inf.Direct ICT Learning Offr., Northants C.C., Weston Farell L. [0037601] 10/10/1984
Moore Ms SP, BA MCLIP, H.of L.& Inf.Serv., Inst.of Chartered Accountants, London. [0018141] 09/10/1972
Moore Mr SR, BA MCLIP, Head of Inf.Resources, Civil Aviation Auth., Safety Regulation Grp., Gatwick. [0019527] 07/10/1968
Moore Ms W, (was Bergman), MCLIP, Area Co-ordinator, Glasgow L.Inf.& Arch. [0027259] 17/02/1977
Moore Mr WA, MCLIP, Retired. [0010366] 14/10/1947
Moore Fitzgerald Ms LJ, BSc MSc, Datastar Database Mgr., Dialog, London. [0052758] 07/12/1995
Moorhouse Ms P, BA(Hons) MCLIP, Lib., Cent.L., Manchester. [0028862] 30/01/1978
Moorman Miss BC, BA MCLIP, Knowledge Mgr., Palamon Capital Partners, London. [0024907] 05/01/1970
Moors Mrs RM, BSc DipLib MCLIP, Coll.Lib., Greenhead Coll., Huddersfield. [0030328] 19/01/1979
Mootyen Miss CS, MCLIP, P./t.Sch.Lib., Chichester High Sch.for Boys, W.Sussex C.C. [0053273] 11/04/1996
Moran Ms A, (was Lennon), BA(Hons) PGDip PGCET, Sch.Lib., S.E.E.L.B., Castlewellan. [0040475] 16/02/1987
Moran Mr CK, BA(Hons) PGDipLIS, Lib., RSM Robson Rhodes, London. [0061356] 24/06/2002
Moran Miss DM, BA(Hons) MLib MCLIP, Regional Inf.Mgr., Sport England, Birmingham. [0044650] 15/11/1990
Moran Mrs E, (was Keating), Sch.Lib., Our Lady's High Sch., N.Lanark Council. [0008196] 13/06/1967
Moran Miss EA, BA, L.& Inf.Worker, Dundee City Council. [0047011] 01/04/1992
Moran Mrs J, BEd(Hons), Relief Work, Perth & Kinross Council, Auchterarder Br.L. [0058739] 03/07/2000
Moran Ms KS, MA PgDip, Lib., PPARC, Royal Observatory, Edinburgh. [0059539] 01/05/2001
Moran Miss S, BA MCLIP, Stud., Greenwich Univ., London. [0020824] 19/10/1973
Morar Mrs KS, BSc BLibSc DMS, L.- Consutltant, Sonex Marketing, Harrow. [0031008] 01/07/1979
Morbey Mrs AE, (was Richards), BA DipLib, Unemployed. [0035036] 24/06/1982
Morden Mrs CE, BA MCLIP, Team Lib., Norfolk & Norwich Millennium L. [0010375] 01/01/1967
Mordi Mrs L, DipEd MEd, Dep.Head of Catg., Univ.of St.Andrews L. [0051865] 19/07/1995
Morel Ms CS, BA MPhil, Deputy Lib., Institut Francais du R.U., London. [0053184] 01/04/1996
Morel Miss VH, BA(Hons), Unemployed. [0061662] 14/10/2002
Moreland Mrs DA, (was Lynas), BA DipLib MCLIP, Team Lib., Child.& Young People, N.E.E.L.B., Kilrea. [0022942] 01/10/1974
Moreland Mrs MC, (was Conlon), BA MCLIP, Asst.Dir.-Learning Serv., Univ.of Northumbria at Newcastle. [0003033] 01/03/1971
Moreton Miss AL, Sen.Lib.Asst., Leeds City Council. [0046583] 20/11/1991
Morey Mrs C, (was Sladen), BA(Hons) DipLib MCLIP, Playgroup Supervisor, Lake St.Comm.Centre, Oxford. [0037758] 16/10/1984
Morgan Miss AM, MCLIP, Life Member. [0010385] 01/01/1938
Morgan Mr BA, MLS MCLIP, Retired. [0010386] 23/05/1955
Morgan Mr BM, BSc DipLib MCLIP, Sen.Team Lib., Cent.L., Coventry City L. [0010387] 11/07/1972
Morgan Mrs CA, (was Parry), BA DipLib MCLIP, Br.Lib., Pontypridd, Rhondda Cynon Taff Co.Bor.Council. [0037142] 29/02/1984
Morgan Ms CE, (was Ladley), BEd(Hons) DipIIS MCLIP, Reader Serv.Libr., Univ.of Sussex, Brighton. [0053474] 01/07/1996
Morgan Mrs CL, (was Cook), BA(Hons), Asst.Lib., Learning Resource Cent., Ashridge, Berkhamsted, Herts. [0056113] 23/02/1998
Morgan Ms CL, BA DipLib MCLIP, Lib., Faculty of Actuaries, Edinburgh. [0036682] 04/11/1993
Morgan Mrs CW, Grad.Trainee., Cat.Asst., National L. of Wales. [0059355] 13/02/2001
Morgan Mrs DJ, (was McLeavy), BA(Hon) MCLIP, Lib.Asst., Lakes Coll.W.Cumbria, Workington. [0021797] 01/01/1974
Morgan Mrs EF, (was Sandy), MCLIP, Sch.Lib., Northfields Upper Sch., Dunstable. [0012929] 23/09/1969
Morgan Mr EG, BMus DipLib MCLIP, Inf.Advisor, UWIC, Cardiff. [0035288] 01/10/1982
Morgan Mrs FM, BSc(Econ) BA, Asst.Dir.-Reg.Med.Comm., GlaxoSmithKline, Brentford. [0061274] 09/05/2002
Morgan Mr G, MCLIP, Managing Dir., Ferret Inf.Systems, Cardiff. [0060753] 12/12/2001
Morgan Ms G, BA MLib MCLIP, Inf.Consultant, Hebden Consultants, Hebden Bridge. [0028636] 13/12/1977
Morgan Ns SJ, BA MA, P./T.Stud./L.Asst., Univ.of Wales, Aberystwyth. [0057691] 04/06/2001
Morgan Mr GJA, BSc(Hons) MSc Econ, L.Asst., Middx.Univ., London. [0059576] 04/06/2001
Morgan Mrs GM, MCLIP, Retired. [0010396] 01/01/1962
Morgan Ms GM, BA DipLib MCLIP, Adult Community Educ. Co-ordinator, Cyngor Sir Ceredigion, Aberystwyth. [0024769] 07/10/1975
Morgan Mr GR, BSc MCLIP, Employment not known. [0060551] 11/12/2001
Morgan Mr GS, BA MSc, Unemployed, 79A Westgate, Hunstanton, Norfolk. [0049525] 10/11/1993

Morgan Miss HL, Asst. Lib., Dept.of Health, Leeds. [0058397] 01/02/2000
Morgan Mrs I, MCLIP, Retired. [0022453] 01/01/1939
Morgan Mr J, BA(Hons), L.Asst., New Coll.L., Oxford. [0061055] 19/02/2002 **AF**
Morgan Mrs JA, (was Huxtable), BA MCLIP, Classroom Asst., Kingswood Pri.Sch., Gloucestershire. [0035313] 12/10/1982
Morgan Ms JG, BA(Hons) MA, Asst.Lib., All Souls Coll., Oxford. [0049170] 08/10/1993
Morgan Mr JHD, BA MLib(Wales) MCLIP, Asst.Lib., Univ.of Cent.England, L.Serv., Birmingham. [0041838] 18/04/1988
Morgan Mr JL, BA MCLIP, Life Member. [0010403] 21/10/1950
Morgan Ms JL, BA, Grad.Trainee, Manchester Metro.Univ. [0061579] 02/10/2002
Morgan Miss JRR, BA MCLIP, Life Member. [0010404] 20/09/1948
Morgan Mr JS, DMS MCLIP, Sen.L.Mgr., Greenwich Council L. [0010405] 03/01/1970
Morgan Mrs JS, (was Embleton), MCLIP, Lib., Brecon High Sch., Powys. [0051338] 01/01/1960
Morgan Miss K, MA BA(Hons) DipLIS MCLIP, Learning Support Lib., Staffs.Univ. [0053578] 02/08/1996
Morgan Ms K, BA(Hons) MA MCLIP, Project Finance Inf.Offr., Linklaters & Alliance, London. [0051044] 09/11/1994
Morgan Mrs KB, (was Rowlands), BA MCLIP, Sen.Lib./Arch., N.London Collegiate Sch., Edgware. [0018379] 09/10/1972
Morgan Mrs KL, (was Patch), BSc(Hons) MSc MCLIP, Lib., Medical Devices Agency, London. [0049597] 19/11/1993
Morgan Mrs KS, (was Finch), MCLIP, Sen.Area Child.& Sch.Lib., Bolton Metro.Bor. [0004902] 09/01/1970
Morgan Miss LP, BA MCLIP, Stock Specialist, Cheshire L., Crewe. [0024910] 16/01/1975
Morgan Mrs MA, MA DipLib, Sen. L. Asst., Univ. of Liverpool. [0060995] 28/01/2002
Morgan Mr MG, BA DipLib MCLIP, Dep.Lib., Heythrop Coll., Univ.of London. [0039631] 03/04/1986
Morgan Ms MJ, BA MA, Asst.Lib., Leeds Univ. [0040329] 22/01/1987
Morgan Mrs N, (was Forryan), BA MCLIP, Quality & Devel.Mgr., Leics.City C., Leicester. [0027590] 24/05/1977
Morgan Mr NJ, BA(Hons) DipLib MCLIP ILTM, Inf.Specialist, Cardiff Univ. [0043457] 26/10/1989
Morgan Mr PB, MA MCLIP, Lib., Med.L., Cambridge Univ. [0019640] 18/10/1972
Morgan Mr PH, MCLIP, Inf.Lib., Redhill L., Surrey Co.L. [0010414] 28/09/1967
Morgan Mrs PM, (was Thomson), MCLIP, [0000329] 31/10/1955
Morgan Mr RL, Lib., Regents Theol.Coll., Nantwich, Cheshire. [0049930] 25/01/1994
Morgan Mrs RP, (was Darlington), BA DipLib MCLIP, p./t.Asst.Lib., Manchester Metro.Univ. [0025256] 15/01/1976
Morgan Mr RS, MA FBCS FCLIP, Employment not known. [0060552] 11/12/2001 **FE 01/04/2002**
Morgan Mr SA, Stud., Manchester Met.Univ. [0059684] 31/07/2001
Morgan Mr SE, BA MEd MBA FCLIP, Dep.Head of Learning Res.Cent., Univ.of Glamorgan. [0024113] 07/03/1975 **FE 20/01/1999**
Morgan Mrs SJ, (was Payton), BLib MCLIP, Lib., Cwmbran L., Gwent. [0041402] 24/11/1987
Morgan Mrs SL, (was Rees), BA(Hons) DipLIS MCLIP, Comm.Lib., Conwy L., Conwy Co.Bor.Council. [0049949] 28/01/1994
Morgan Mrs T, (was Lindfield), MCLIP, Acq.Lib.(Job-share), Portsmouth City Council, Portsmouth. [0008936] 06/01/1969
Morgan Mrs UM, (was Clough), MCLIP, Life Member. [0002869] 03/09/1948
Morgan Mrs URM, (was Stone), BA MCLIP, Unemployed. [0015593] 04/10/1965
Morgan Ms VE, MLS MA MCLIP, Resident in France. [0020032] 19/01/1973
Morgan James Mrs J, (was Morgan), BA (Hons), Learning Service.Mgr., Crawley Coll., W.Sussex. [0044892] 09/01/1991
Morgan-James Miss KA, (was James), Sch.Lib., Hagley R.C.High Sch. [0039232] 01/01/1986
Morgan-Jones Mrs CCM, (was Jones), MA MCLIP, Casual Asst., UCW, Aberystwyth. [0033848] 14/01/1981
Morgans Mr SG, MCLIP, Retired, 2 The Brough Hall, 56 Oakshaw St.W., Paisley, PA1 2DE. [0010422] 16/01/1968
Morgante Dr L, PhD DipLib MCLIP, p./t.Lib., The Pilgrims Sch., Winchester, Hants. [0049051] 20/09/1993
Moriarty Mrs DJ, (was Stanley), MCLIP, p./t.Child.Lib., Hants.Co.L., Hythe. [0010423] 25/03/1965
Moriarty Mr MA, BA MPhil, L.Asst., Guildhall L., London. [0061385] 04/07/2002 **AF**
Moriarty Mrs SE, (was Haworth), BA MCLIP, Asst.Lib.(Job Share), Young People, Lancs.C.C., Rossendale. [0038782] 04/10/1985
Morley Ms A, MA BA(Hons) MCLIP, Head Lib., Benenden Sch., Kent. [0045635] 08/04/1991
Morley Mrs C, (was Uffindell), MCLIP, Childminder. [0005299] 05/04/1967
Morley Mrs JE, (was Houston), MA DipLib MCLIP, Lib.(Job share), Hyndland Sec.Sch., Glasgow. [0040196] 27/10/1986
Morley Mrs MD, (was Danes), BA DipLib MCLIP, Univ.Lib., Loughborough Univ. [0003575] 01/01/1972
Morley Miss SA, Stud., Univ.of Wales, Aberystwyth. [0061282] 08/05/2002
Morley Ns SJ, BA MA, P./T.Stud./L.Asst., Univ.of Wales, Aberystwyth, Babraham Inst., Cambridge. [0059905] 31/10/2001
Morley Miss TL, Stud. [0059931] 06/11/2001
Morley Miss ZB, BA(Hons) MA, Stud., Univ.Newcastle @ Northumbria. [0059797] 03/10/2001
Moroney Ms MS, MA MSc MCLIP, Knowledge Mgr., Community Inf., Herts.C.C. [0041538] 14/01/1988
Morrell Mrs LM, Asst.Lib.(Audiovisual/Choral), Royal Coll.of Music, London. [0052789] 14/12/1995 **AF**

Morrell Mr P, BA MCLIP, Asst.Lib., ICSM., London. [0010431] 29/12/1963
Morrell Mrs S, BSc MA MCLIP, Tech.Abstractor, Paint Research Assoc., Teddington,Middx. [0018213] 06/10/1972
Morris Mrs AM, L.Inf.Serv.Co-ordinator., Chartered Inst.of Building. [0059242] 15/01/2001 **AF**
Morris Miss BA, BA MCLIP, Faculty Team Mgr., Univ.of Reading L. [0010434] 22/03/1967
Morris Ms BA, MPhil MSc MCLIP, Dir.(Tel:020)85059453), Hudson Rivers Mgmt.& Training, Consultants, London. [0020151] 16/01/1973
Morris Mrs BG, BA(Hons), p./t.L.Asst., Liverpool Univ.Hosp. [0058036] 18/10/1999
Morris Ms CA, (was Redfern), BA DLIS MCLIP DMS, Princ.L.Mgr., Kirklees Cultural Serv., Huddersfield. [0026525] 13/10/1976
Morris Ms CR, BA(Hons) MA, Learning Resources Adviser p./t., Trinity Coll, Carmarthen. [0061468] 07/08/2002
Morris Mrs D, (was Lewis), BA MCLIP, Lib., Slaughter and May, London. [0029519] 12/09/1978
Morris Mrs DA, BA MA MCLIP, Lib., Ashlyns Sch., Berkhamsted. [0030224] 02/01/1979
Morris Mr DJ, BA MCLIP, Asst.Dist.Lib., High Wycombe L., Bucks.C.C. [0038442] 01/05/1985
Morris Ms DJ, MA BA MLib MCLIP, Health Serv.L.Mgr., Univ.of Southampton. [0039026] 28/10/1985
Morris Mrs EL, BA DipLib MCLIP, Asst.Lib., E.Dunbartonshire Council, Kirkintilloch. [0033083] 03/10/1980
Morris Mr G, BA DipLib MCLIP, Employment unknown. [0060321] 10/12/2001
Morris Mrs GA, (was Williams), BLib MCLIP, Child.Lib., Brighton & Hove, Brighton L. [0015929] 28/01/1970
Morris Mrs GL, (was White), BA(Hons) DipILS MCLIP, Asst.Lib., L.& Inf.Serv., Univ.of Wales, Swansea. [0051175] 23/11/1994
Morris Mrs HC, BA MCLIP, Head of L.& Inf., Council for the Protection of, Rural England, London. [0029198] 17/04/1978
Morris Miss HJ, BA(Hons), Position unknown, Shropshire Social Serv., Ludlow. [0057619] 18/05/1999
Morris Mrs I, BSc, Inf.Officer, Lib.Serv., Carlisle. [0051270] 14/12/1994
Morris Mrs JA, (was Pacey), MCLIP, p./t.Sen.L.Asst., Univ.of Warwick. [0010448] 28/01/1966
Morris Mrs JC, BA DipLib MCLIP, Asst.Lib./Br.Mgr., Bucks.Co.L., Princes Risborough L. [0037027] 30/01/1984
Morris Mr JD, Employment not known. [0032755] 06/08/1980
Morris Miss JM, BA DipLib MCLIP, Euro.Inf.Offr., Manchester Cent.L. [0030490] 29/01/1979
Morris Mrs JM, (was Marks), FSALA MCLIP, Life Member. [0017408] 03/02/1947
Morris Mrs JM, (was Laver), BA DipLib MCLIP, [0032437] 07/04/1980
Morris Mr JT, Stud., Univ.of Wales, Aberystwyth. [0057002] 19/11/1998
Morris Miss KA, BA MCLIP, Community Lib., Broughton L., Flintshire C.C. [0023078] 14/10/1974
Morris Mrs KJ, (was Bossons), BA(Hons) MCLIP, Sen.L.& Inf.Offr., (Outer W.Area), Newcastle City L., Denton Pk.L. [0038764] 04/05/1993
Morris Mrs L, Head of Learning Cent., Quarry Bay Sch., Hong Kong. [0059034] 31/10/2000
Morris Mrs LA, BA AKC MCLIP, Unemployed. [0018156] 01/01/1972
Morris Ms LA, DipLib, Sen.Lib., Business Inf.Serv. [0031391] 04/10/1979
Morris Mrs LM, (was Spurgeon), BA MCLIP, Area Lib.(S.), Rhondda-Cynon-Taff, Pontypridd L. [0013844] 04/10/1970
Morris Mrs M, Sen.Inf.Offr., Osborne Clarke, Bristol. [0046982] 25/03/1992 **AF**
Morris Mr MA, MA MA DipLib MCLIP, Asst.Lib., Inst.of Soc.& Cultural Anthropology, Univ.of Oxford. [0043370] 17/10/1989
Morris Ms ME, MCLIP, Sen.Lib.(Mob.& Special Serv.), Rhondda Cynon Taff Unitary Auth., Aberdare. [0020208] 29/01/1973
Morris Mr MI, MA, Resources Adviser, Kingston Coll., Kingston upon Thames. [0050103] 29/03/1994
Morris Mrs ML, (was Woffenden), MCLIP, Retired. [0010455] 01/01/1941
Morris Miss N, BA(Hons) DipLib MCLIP, Lib., Glan Clwyd Hosp.NHS Trust, Bodelwyddan, Denbighshire. [0039057] 28/10/1985
Morris Mrs P, (was Comery), MCLIP, Unemployed. [0018573] 01/01/1964
Morris Mr PE, HonFCLIP FCLIP, Life Member. [0010457] 15/03/1937 **FE 01/01/1956**
Morris Mrs PM, (was Jones), MCLIP, Sen.Sch.Lib.(Job Share), Staffs.C.C. [0010459] 20/03/1967
Morris Mrs RA, (was Ademokun-Jones), BA(Hons), Lib.H.of Lib.Serv., Food Standards Agency, London. [0042360] 27/10/1988
Morris Ms RC, MA MCLIP, Unemployed. [0038170] 25/01/1985
Morris Mrs RM, (was Hewitt), MCLIP, Asst.i./c., E.Sussex C.C., Crowborough L. [0001175] 01/10/1971
Morris Miss S, BSc (Hons), p./t/Stud/Inf.Offr., City Univ., Royal Soc.L.London. [0059126] 21/11/2000
Morris Mrs S, (was Welbourn), MCLIP, p./t.Subject Lib., Buckinghamshire Chilterns Univ.Coll, Chalfont St.Giles. [0010462] 22/01/1959
Morris Miss SE, (was Broughton), BA DipLib MCLIP, Sch.L.Liason Offr., Sch.L.Serv., Guernsey. [0044474] 11/10/1990
Morris Mrs SJ, (was Edgar), BSc(Hons), Inf.Offr., LGC, Middx. [0055553] 21/10/1997
Morris Mrs SM, (was Tompkins), BA DipLib MCLIP, Dep.Head of L.& RSC Lib., Shakespeare Birthplace Trust, Stratford-upon-Avon. [0028191] 22/10/1977
Morris Mrs SR, (was Tarlton), BA MCLIP, Unemployed. [0010463] 21/10/1969
Morris Mrs UM, (was Spridgeon), MCLIP, Not employed. [0010465] 09/02/1966
Morris Mr W, BSc DipLib, Databases Mgr., Learning Resources Cent., Univ.of Glamorgan, Pontypridd. [0046362] 30/10/1991

Morris Mrs WD, (was Todd), BSc MCLIP, Inf.Lib.(p/t.), Kingston Univ. [0028704] 12/01/1978
Morris-Newton Ms DL, (was Morris), BA(Hons) MCLIP, Sen.Inf.Offr., Leeds Metro.Univ. [0048454] 13/01/1993
Morrison Mrs AE, (was Seddon), BA DipLib MCLIP, Res.Asst., Edinburgh Room, Edinburgh City L. [0033248] 28/10/1980
Morrison Mr AJ, BLib MCLIP, Adult Stock Mgr., Southwark L., L.B.of Southwark. [0029405] 01/07/1978
Morrison Mr AJ, LLB LLM MA, p./t.Stud., University of Strathclyde. [0051500] 05/03/1995
Morrison Mr AM, Retired. [0024262] 20/05/1975
Morrison Mrs AM, MCLIP, Inf.Offr., Educ.L., Liverpool John Moores Univ. [0010469] 17/03/1967
Morrison Mr CJ, MA DipLib MCLIP, Sch.Lib., Linlithgow Academy, W.Lothian. [0033328] 08/10/1980
Morrison Mrs D, (was Clements), MCLIP, Temp.Dep.Child.& Sch.Lib., Ilford Cent.L., L.B.of Redbridge. [0001669] 01/02/1968
Morrison Mr DA, BA(Hons) BSc(Hons) DipLib MCLIP, Lib., Glasgow City Council, Educ.Res.Serv. [0038708] 01/10/1985
Morrison Mrs DA, (was Wood), MA DipLib MCLIP, Inf.Offr., Univ.of Edinburgh Mgmt.Sch. [0026067] 10/06/1976
Morrison Dr DJ, BA MA PhD, Lib./Arch., Worcester Cathedral L., Worcester. [0061448] 22/07/2002
Morrison Mrs EA, (was Jackson), BA, Lib., Stranmillis Univ.Coll., Belfast. [0039892] 01/10/1986
Morrison Mrs ER, (was Cohen), BA(MUS) DipLib MCLIP, Unemployed. [0027053] 07/12/1976
Morrison Miss JC, MCLIP, Retired. [0010476] 09/03/1962
Morrison Mrs JH, (was Taylor), MCLIP, Sch.Lib., Glasgow City Council. [0014416] 06/06/1972
Morrison Mrs M, (was Davidson), BA MCLIP, Sch.Lib., Graeme High Sch., Falkirk. [0003646] 14/01/1972
Morrison Mrs MF, (was McPhail), MA DipLib MCLIP, Asst.Lib., Epsom Health Care, Sally Howell L., Epsom Hosp. [0010480] 24/01/1966
Morrison Mrs NJ, BA DipLib MCLIP, Res., Self Employed. [0026835] 23/11/1976
Morrison Miss PD, Lib., Clacton L., Essex. [0059960] 12/11/2001 **AF**
Morrison Mrs PS, (was Cardno), BA(Hons), Local Studies Sen.L.Asst.p./t., Aberdeenshire L.& Inf.Serv., Oldmeldrum. [0052633] 16/11/1995
Morrison Mrs RAL, (was Brogan), MCLIP, Lib., Highland Theological Coll., Dingwall. [0001778] 08/02/1962
Morrison Mrs SE, (was Hay), MPhil DipEd FCLIP, Lib., High Sch.of Dundee. [0010482] 01/01/1964 **FE 24/09/1997**
Morrison Mr VR, MCLIP, Retired. [0060555] 11/12/2001
Morrisroe Miss S, BSc DipLib MLib, Corp.Lib., WRc Plc, Swindon. [0038920] 16/10/1985
Morrissey Mrs JM, (was Perkes), L.Exec., (Career Break), Ref.Serv.Sect., House of Commons L. [0037126] 31/01/1984
Morrow Mr A, MCLIP, Ch.Lib., S.Educ.& L.Board, Armagh. [0010485] 16/03/1964
Morrow Mr JM, BA(Hons) DipLib MCLIP, Sub-Lib., Univ.L., Univ.of Newcastle-upon-Tyne. [0031392] 01/10/1979
Morse Mrs GM, (was Dennis), MCLIP, Lib., Hereford.Council. [0003890] 24/01/1972
Morse Ms HR, BA(Hons) PGDipLib MCLIP, p./t.Lib., Lymington L., Hants. [0028345] 08/11/1977
Mort Mr G, FCLIP, Retired., Sedgemoor, 2 Beech Ave., Whitchurch, Shropshire, SY13 1UE. [0010489] 06/09/1952 **FE 01/01/1959**
Morten Mr M, BA MCLIP, Lib., City of Westminster, London. [0042200] 14/10/1988
Morter Mr GMB, BA(Hons), Stud., Univ.of Bristol, Acquisitions Asst., Environment Agency, Bristol. [0058738] 01/07/2000
Mortifee Mr AVW, CChem FRSC MCLIP, Retired. [0060558] 11/12/2001
Mortimer Mrs AE, (was Osborn), MCLIP, Sch.Lib., Holmwood House Prep.Sch., Colchester. [0011047] 22/11/1967
Mortimer Mrs CA, (was Hawes), L.Mgr., Horton Hosp., Banbury. [0050178] 25/04/1994
Mortimer Miss DL, MCLIP, Retired. [0010491] 04/03/1954
Mortimer Mrs DM, (was Park), BA(Hons) MA DipLib MCLIP, Lib., York Minster L., Dean & Chapter of York. [0031411] 22/10/1979
Mortimer Mrs FM, BA(Hons) DipIS, p./t.Lib., Hornsey Sch., London. [0050937] 01/11/1994
Mortimer Mrs GC, (was Turner), MCLIP, Sen.Lib., Shropshire C.C., Ludlow L. [0010492] 05/11/1965
Mortimer Ms JR, BA DMS DipLib MCLIP, Academic Lib.Stud.Support, De Montfort Univ., Leicester. [0039400] 22/01/1986
Mortimer Mr RS, MA FCLIP, Life Member. [0010493] 04/08/1938 **FE 01/01/1945**
Mortimer Mr W, PGCE, L.Asst., Cranfield Univ.L., Bedfordshire. [0061450] 31/07/2002
Mortimer Mrs ZC, CertEd, Lib.(Sch.), Bryanston Sch., Blandford, Dorset. [0053135] 01/04/1996 **AF**
Mortimore Mr AD, MA FCLIP, Life member, 72 Friary Grange Park,Winterbourne, Bristol, BS17 1NB. [0010495] 18/10/1952 **FE 01/01/1956**
Morton Ms EA, BA(Hons) MCLIP, Lib., Falkirk P.L. [0039960] 04/10/1986
Morton Miss HJ, BLib MCLIP, Sen.Lib., Ref.& Local Hist., Jersey L.Serv. [0010499] 27/10/1971
Morton Mr I, BA MCLIP, Inf.Worker, L.B.of Hillingdon. [0042329] 20/10/1988
Morton Mrs J, (was Beardshall), BA MA MCLIP, Faculty Lib., Leeds Univ., Brotherton L. [0025485] 27/01/1976
Morton Mrs J, BA (Hons), Asst.Lib., N.Yorks.C.C., Knaresborough L. [0055607] 24/10/1997
Morton Mrs JA, (was Milne), BA MCLIP, Unemployed. [0034793] 15/02/1982

Morton Miss JJ, MA(Hons) DipILS, Sen.Inf.Asst., Univ.of Abertay, Dundee. [0057448] 01/04/1999
Morton Mr JR, BA DipLib MCLIP, Sen.Inf.Adviser, Sheffield Hallam Univ. [0030492] 03/02/1979
Morton Mr LT, FCLIP, Retired. [0010501] 01/12/1932 **FE 01/01/1964**
Morton Dr M, BSc MLib MCLIP PhD, Broadcast Arch., Nat.Assembly for Wales, Cardiff. [0039958] 06/10/1986
Morton Ms M, BA(Hons), Inf.Asst., Sheffield Hallam Univ. [0061203] 08/04/2002 **AF**
Morton Miss MM, BLib MCLIP, Stock Serv.Lib., Met.Bor.of Sefton. [0028744] 23/01/1978
Morton Mr NJ, BA PGDipILM, Sch.Lib., Parklands High Sch., Manchester. [0057446] 01/04/1999
Morton-High Mrs AE, BA MCLIP, Sch.Lib., Holy Trinity Coll., Kent. [0019592] 10/11/1972
Mosley Miss CM, Freelance, Legal Inf.Support & Advice. [0035447] 01/10/1982
Mosley Mr MS, Loan Lc.Co-ordinator, WMY Learning, Warrington. [0058805] 02/08/2000
Moss Mr A, BA MCLIP, Retired. [0017411] 25/09/1961
Moss Ms J, Employment not known. [0061241] 01/04/2002
Moss Miss JE, MCLIP, Principal Librarian, Shropshire C.Library, Shropshire. [0023365] 05/11/1974
Moss Mrs JE, MCLIP, Res.Cent.Mgr., St.Joseph's Catholic Comp.Sch., Swindon. [0001275] 28/08/1969
Moss Mrs JM, (was Kearsley), BA(Hons) MA MBCS MCLIP, Head of Inf.Systems, Brit.Council, Manchester. [0022390] 22/04/1974
Moss Ms ME, MSc(Econ), Web Development Offr., Hull & E.Yorks.Hosp.NHS Trust, Hull Royal Infirmary. [0054639] 07/02/1997
Moss Mrs SE, (was Dunwoody), MSc(Econ) MCLIP, Community Inf.Lib., L.B.of Croydon. [0010515] 27/08/1964
Moss Mrs SG, (was Rogers), BA LLB FCLIP, Retired. [0017413] 01/01/1958 **FE 01/07/1969**
Moss Miss TC, MCLIP, Sen.Asst.Lib., Hertford Reg.Coll., Ware. [0029199] 01/04/1978
Moss Mr W, BA MCLIP, Retired. [0010516] 11/01/1976
Moss-Gibbons Ms CA, (was Moss), BLib(Hons) PGCE, H.of L.& Inf.Serv., Royal Coll.of Physicians, London. [0032131] 21/01/1980
Mosson Mrs E, (was Marlow), BA MCLIP, Retired. [0010519] 16/09/1958
Mostajir Mrs N, Stud., Thames Valley Univ. [0060912] 10/01/2002
Mostyn Miss LB, BA MA Indept.Consult.v. Inf.Res., 01865 739482. [0046192] 14/10/1991
Motegi Miss M, Ref.Lib., Meisei Univ.L., Tokyo. [0055189] 04/08/1997
Moth Ms S, BA DipLib MCLIP, Career Break - to raise family. [0043380] 16/10/1989
Mothersole Mrs P, (was Mcinerney), MCLIP, Position unknown, Augusta-Margaret-River Shire, Australia. [0009418] 21/01/1969
Mottahedeh Miss LP, MA DipILS, Catr., HM Customs & Excise. [0053726] 18/09/1996
Mottram Ms SJ, BA(Hons) MCLIP, Faculty Team Lib., Leeds Univ.L. [0023867] 12/02/1975
Moughton Mrs CB, MA DipLib MCLIP, Asst.Lib., Oxford Brookes Univ.L. [0035246] 06/10/1982
Mould Miss SM, MLitt MA MCLIP, Retired. [0029340] 06/06/1978
Moulden Miss J, BA FCLIP, Life Member. [0010528] 21/01/1950 **FE 01/01/1958**
Moulder Mr DS, BSc MCLIP, Lib., World Maritime Univ., Sweden. [0060055] 07/12/2001
Moule Mrs P, (was Newson), Support Serv.Offr., Bracknell Forest Bor.Counil, Berks. [0045380] 01/04/2001 **AF**
Moulson Mrs J, (was Renshaw), MCLIP, Serv.Lib., Inf.Serv.Grp., Cent.L. Sheffield. [0010532] 11/01/1968
Moulton Ms J, BA DipIM MCLIP, Child.Lib., R.B.of Kensington & Chelsea. [0053873] 07/10/1996
Mount Ms RJ, BA(Hons) PhD DipIS MCLIP, Unemployed. [0051118] 16/11/1994
Mountain Miss W, BA(Hons), Lib., HTV W., Bristol. [0055500] 16/10/1997
Mountford Mrs A, BA(Hons), Clerical Asst., Nether Stowe High Sch., Staffs.LEA. [0055970] 02/01/1998
Mountford Ms BA, BA DipLib MCLIP, Coll.Lib., Ras Al Khaimah Womens Coll., Utd.Arab Emirates. [0038248] 10/02/1985
Mountjoy Mr PR, BA MLitt MCLIP FRSA, Retired. [0029406] 02/07/1978
Mousavi-Zadeh Miss MS, BA(Hons) MA, Stud., Brighton Univ. [0059173] 05/12/2000
Mousley Mr SP, BSc MCLIP, Head Lib., London Internat.Coll. [0020859] 20/07/1971
Mowat Miss MW, BA MLib MCLIP, Lib./Inf.Sci., Rowett Res.Inst., Aberdeen. [0029077] 25/03/1978
Mowbray Mr AH, BA MCLIP, Learning Res.Mgr., Lewes Tertiary Coll., Sussex Downs Coll. [0037635] 08/10/1984
Mowbray Ms SJ, (was Binfield), MCLIP, Employment not known. [0060669] 11/12/2001
Moxham Mrs HE, (was Day), BA MCLIP, Grp.Lib., Bath & N.E.Somerset Council. [0036133] 14/06/1983
Moy Mrs LM, (was Dorward), BA MCLIP, Sen.Yth.L.& Inf.Worker, Devel.& Quality Assurance Team, Arthurstone Neighbourhood L.,Dundee. [0048863] 05/07/1993
Moye Mrs BF, (was Dixon), BSc MSc, Inf.Mgr., Thames Valley Chamber of Comm., Slough. [0049632] 15/11/1993
Moyes Mrs KA, (was Brocklebank), BA MCLIP, Resident in USA - Homemaker. [0039388] 24/01/1986
Moyes Miss LE, MA DipILS, Asst.Lib., Gen.Serv., Faculty of Advocates L., Edinburgh. [0056161] 01/04/1998
Moyle Mr AM, BA MSc DipLib MCLIP, Asst.Lib., The L., Univ.Coll.London. [0053306] 25/04/1996
Moyo Mr WG, Lib., Bishop Mackenzie Sch., Malawi. [0048854] 02/07/1993

Moyse Mrs WJE, (was Jarman), MCLIP, Lunchtime Super., Waverly Abbey Sch., Tilford. [0023043] 21/10/1974
Moyses Mrs V, BA MCLIP, Lib./Inf.Mgr., CCH, Banbury. [0017115] 01/01/1967
Msiska Mr AWC, BSocSc MA DipLib FCLIP, Coll.Lib., Univ.of Malawi, Zomba., Malawi. [0020676] 16/05/1973 **FE 27/12/1984**
Mudd Miss CL, BA(Hons) MCLIP, Local Enquiry Serv.Mgr., Business Link Tees Valley, Middlesbrough. [0047713] 19/10/1992
Muddiman Mr DJ, MSc BA DipLib MCLIP, Princ.Lect., Leeds Metro.Univ., Beckett Park. [0033450] 01/01/1981
Muddyman Mrs CE, BA(Hons), p./t.Stud./L.Asst., Univ.of Wales/Goethe-Inst.L., Aberystwyth/London. [0056271] 27/04/1998
Mudford Miss JL, BA DipLib MCLIP, Asst.Lib., Cardiff Co., Cent.L., Cardiff. [0029765] 06/10/1978
Mugliston Miss PSM, MA, Retired. [0010550] 04/02/1960
Muir Miss A, MA MSc MCLIP, Res.Offr., Policy Studs.Inst., 100 Park Village East. [0045606] 02/04/1991
Muir Mr D, MCLIP, Arch., Penguin Books Ltd., Harmondsworth,Middx. [0010552] 01/07/1967
Muir Ms EP, MA MCLIP, Sen.Lib., SAC, Auchincruive, Ayr. [0038420] 24/04/1985
Muir Mrs HA, (was Czeschel), BA(Hons) MCLIP, Sch.Lib., St.Pauls Way Comm.Sch., London. [0047950] 27/10/1992
Muir Mrs NJ, (was Middleton), BA(Hons), Book-keeper, M&S Dental, Fort William. [0050768] 18/01/1999
Muirhead Mr ATN, MA MLitt MCLIP, Operations Lib., Stirling Council, L.H.Q. [0022289] 04/04/1974
Mukoro Miss MO, BSc PGDip, Stud., City Univ. [0061142] 08/03/2002
Mulcahy Miss BM, BA FCLIP, Retired. [0010557] 24/09/1948 **FE 01/01/1953**
Mulchrone Mrs JB, (was Henderson), BSc DipLIS MCLIP, Head Lib., Haberdashers'Aske's Boys Sch., Elstree,Herts. [0044237] 20/07/1990
Mulhern Mr NP, MA MA DipLIS, Lib., ACU, London. [0050174] 22/04/1994
Mullan Mr JP, BA(Hons) MCLIP, Inf.Offr., CMS Cameron Mckenna. [0049852] 07/01/1994
Mullarkey Mrs TA, (was Kidd), BA(Hons) MCLIP, Lib., Wyke Coll., Hull. [0042477] 18/11/1988
Mullen Miss JL, BA(Hons), Asst.Lib., Newcastle Hosp.NHS Trust, Newcastle upon Tyne. [0057366] 26/02/1999
Mullen Mrs SE, Stud., Univ.of Aberystwyth. [0059643] 10/07/2001
Muller Miss BB, BA(Hons) MCLIP, Res.Cent.Administrator, Excellence in Liverpool, King David High Sch. [0043461] 26/10/1989
Muller Mrs CS, (was Brookes), BA(Hons) MCLIP, Dep.H.-L.& Inf.Serv., South Bank Univ., London. [0002147] 16/10/1968
Muller Mrs N, (was Williams), BA, Asst.Lib., Sch.L.Serv., Worcs.C.C. [0035002] 09/06/1982
Muller Ms NJ, BA DipLib, Ch.Lib., Technikon Natal, Durban. [0057793] 10/08/1999
Muller Mrs RN, BA DipLib, Lib.Mgr., Univ.of Cape Town -grad.Sch.of Bus., Cape town, RSA. [0037077] 31/01/1984
Mullett Miss CM, BA MCLIP, Sen.Lib., Fingal Co.C., Ireland. [0017419] 31/01/1968
Mullinger Mrs JK, (was Bonnington), BA MCLIP, p./t.Asst.Lib., W.Sussex Co.L., Horsham. [0025952] 06/05/1976
Mullins Miss AV, BA(Hons) MA, Asst.Lib., Dept.of Health, Leeds. [0057103] 14/12/1998
Mullins Mrs CA, (was Robinson), BA MCLIP, Sch.Lib., Birmingham C.C. [0024301] 30/05/1975
Mullins Mrs F, (was Williams), BA DipLIS MCLIP, Inf.Lib., Petersfield Br.L., Hants.C.C. [0044873] 04/01/1991
Mullins Ms M, BSc, Lib., Institut Hotelier 'Cesar Ritz', Switzerland. [0060949] 15/01/2002
Mullins Mrs PR, BSc MCLIP, Retired. [0060557] 11/12/2001
Mullis Mr AA, MCLIP, Retired. [0028924] 21/01/1953
Mullner Mr K, MCLIP, Ch.Catr., Kensington & Chelsea P.L. [0010563] 23/10/1963
Mulvaney Ms SS, BA, Stud., City Uni. [0060952] 18/01/2002
Mumford Mrs HA, BSc(Hons) PGDipLib MCLIP, Sen.Inf.Offr., ERA Tech., Leatherhead. [0033085] 03/10/1980
Munasinghe Mrs AI, (was Gunawardena), BA MCLIP, Inf.Res.Offr., CPHVA, 40 Bermondsey St., London, SE1. [0020148] 25/01/1973
Muncy Mr GB, MCLIP, Sen.Lib., Performing Arts, Surrey Arts, Dorking. [0010567] 01/01/1969
Muncy Mrs VC, (was Houlston), BA DipLib MCLIP, Music & Drama Lib., Reading Bor.Council. [0031330] 01/10/1979
Mundell Mrs CA, (was Hewitt), P./t.Admin.Asst. [0026741] 24/10/1976
Mundell Miss SI, BA MA MCLIP, Head of L., Brighton Coll. [0050698] 12/10/1994
Mundill Mrs E, (was Strugnell), MA DipLib MCLIP, P./t.Sch.Lib., Glenalmond Coll., Perth. [0033775] 23/02/1981
Munford Mrs LM, (was Hurst), MCLIP, Sen.Lib., Rotherham M.B.C., Cent.L.Serv. [0007520] 01/01/1968
Munford Mrs M, (was Elderton), BA BSc(Econ) MCLIP, Team Lib., Norfolk & Norwich Millennium L., Norwich. [0045242] 29/08/1990
Munford Dr WA, MBE BSc(Econ) PhD HonFCLIP FCLIP, Life Member, Tel.01223 62962, 11 Manor Ct., Pinehurst, Grange Rd.,Cambridge. [0010571] 14/01/1932 **FE 01/01/1933**
Munks Miss EJ, BA(Hons) DipLib MCLIP, Faculty/User Serv.Lib.(York), Coll.of Ripon & York St.John, York. [0042244] 13/10/1988
Munks Miss SL, BA, P./t.Stud./L.Asst., University of Huddersfield, Manchester Met.Univ. [0059680] 31/07/2001
Munn Mrs GJ, (was Groocock), MCLIP, Housewife. [0006017] 21/01/1972
Munns Mrs KC, (was Oliver), BLib MCLIP, Relief Lib., Reading Bor.Council. [0034975] 24/05/1982
Munns Mrs PR, (was Wyatt), MCLIP, Retired. [0010573] 03/10/1946

Munro Ms CI, (was Finlayson), BA MCLIP, Team Lib., Surrey Co.L. [0029652] 03/10/1978
Munro Mr DR, BA DipLib MCLIP, Dir.of Cult.Serv., Oxon.C.C., Cent.L. [0027499] 21/04/1977
Munro Ms GM, MA DipLIS, Asst.Lib., Scottish Exec., Edinburgh. [0052852] 11/01/1996
Munro Mr JAJ, MCLIP, Retired. [0010576] 22/05/1950
Munro Mrs JH, MSc MBA ARCS MCLIP, Position unknown, Univ.of Reading. [0060556] 11/12/2001
Munro Mrs JM, (was Hamilton), BA MCLIP, Retired. [0010577] 17/07/1956
Munro Mrs KA, (was Gwyther), BA(Hons) DipLib, Asst.Lib., Inst.of Opthalmology. [0051269] 14/12/1994
Munro Mrs RE, (was Pratt), MCLIP, p./t.Inf.Asst., Napier Univ., Edinburgh. [0011901] 07/11/1970
Munro Mrs RJ, (was Mee), MCLIP, Life Member. [0010581] 12/02/1943
Munro Miss SF, BA MCLIP, Lib./Computer Inf.Off., Univ.of Huddersfield. [0010582] 22/02/1966
Munro Ms TP, BSc DipLib MCLIP, Inf.Lib., Andover, Hants.County L. [0048847] 01/07/1993
Munslow Miss AM, MCLIP, Unemployed. [0010586] 20/01/1965
Munton Mrs S, (was Moss), MCLIP, Sen.L.Asst., City.Univ. London. [0010514] 01/01/1971
Murad Mrs R, DipLib MCLIP, Sch.Lib., King Fahad Academy, London. [0036401] 07/10/1983
Murchie Mrs E, (was Hanks), MCLIP, p./t.L.Asst., Educ.Cent.L., Royal Oldham Hosp. [0010588] 14/09/1967
Murchison Mr AP, MCLIP, Retired. [0010589] 23/11/1965
Murchison Mrs VM, Lib., Argyll & Clyde Acute Hosp., NHS Trust, Oban. [0040667] 06/04/1987
Murcoch Mr CE, BSc, Stud., The Robert Gordon Univ. [0061775] 04/11/2002
Murcutt Miss SJ, Exec.Asst., CILIP, Member Serv.Dir., London. [0061454] 01/08/2002
Murden Mrs JP, (was Dodd), MCLIP, Learning Cent.Mgr., New Coll., Nottingham. [0010590] 12/01/1967
Murdie Miss J, BA DipLib, L.Shelver, City Campus L., Univ.Northumbria at Newcastle. [0046610] 25/11/1991
Murdoch Mrs JA, MA MCLIP, Coll.Lib., Bromley Coll.of F.E.& H.E., Kent. [0002961] 01/01/1966
Murdoch Mrs JF, (was Paton), MA MCLIP, Self Employed. [0036505] 11/10/1983
Murdoch Mrs JM, (was Cruickshank), BA MCLIP, Asst.Lib., Nairn Academy, Highland Council. [0039562] 04/03/1986
Murdoch Mr JW, MCLIP, Asst.Lib., Shettleston L., Glasgow Dist.L. [0026832] 22/03/1965
Murdoch Miss MAS, BA DipLib MCLIP, Retired. [0026487] 13/11/1976
Murdoch Miss PA, Sen.Document Mgmt.Asst., CDM Dept., Ernst & Young, Birmingham. [0059952] 09/11/2001 AF
Murdoch Mrs SBM, (was Dick), MCMI MCLIP, Retired. [0010591] 14/03/1953
Murdoch Mrs SE, DipIT BA BSc, Employment unknown. [0060250] 10/12/2001
Murdoch Mr SG, BSc(Hons) MCLIP, Community Lib., Bloomsbury L., Birmingham City Council. [0025179] 04/12/1975
Murdock Ms KP, BA(Hons) PGDip, Inf.Offr., Beds.& Luton CCTE, Luton. [0058396] 01/02/2000
Murfitt Mr SG, Stud., Univ.of Wales, Aberystwyth. [0055657] 28/10/1997
Murgatroyd Miss DC, BA MCLIP, Inf.Mgr., Foreign & Commonwealth Off., London. [0035465] 22/10/1982
Murgatroyd Mrs DM, (was Wright), BSc MCLIP, p./t.Child.Lib., Bracknell Forest Bor.Council, Bracknell L. [0022023] 07/01/1974
Murgatroyd Miss G, MSc MCLIP, L.Asst., Univ.of York. [0046118] 02/10/1991
Murgatroyd Mrs SM, (was Gardner), MCLIP, Unemployed. [0005362] 29/07/1971
Muris Mr C, MA FCLIP, Retired. [0010594] 21/01/1952 FE 01/01/1957
Murphy Miss AC, MCLIP, Sch.Lib., John Paul II Sch., London SW19. [0010599] 17/09/1968
Murphy Mr B, BA MCLIP, Dir.of Academic Inf.Serv., Queen Mary, Univ.of London. [0010601] 08/04/1970
Murphy Mr BP, BA MA MCLIP, Princ.Lib., Lend.Serv., Calderdale M.B.C. [0035141] 30/09/1982
Murphy Mrs C, (was Goodchild), MCLIP, Head of Coll.L.Resource Cent., W.Sussex C.C., Bognor Regis. [0010602] 15/03/1957
Murphy Mrs C, (was Pollard), BA(Hons) MCLIP, Knowledge Mgr., Cabinet Off., Strategy Unit, London. [0044218] 12/07/1990
Murphy Miss CA, MCLIP, Lib., Leicester City L. [0028863] 16/01/1978
Murphy Mrs CJ, (was Brown), BA(Hons) DipILM, Lib., Cheshire C.C., Wilmslow L. [0055375] 06/10/1997
Murphy Mr DH, BA DIP LIS, Dir.of L., Walsh Coll., Michigan, U.S.A. [0040889] 04/08/1987
Murphy Mrs EJ, MCLIP, Project Mgr., L.B.of Camden, Swiss Cottage L. [0019361] 17/09/1963
Murphy Mr EJ, BA PGDip, Res. Exec. Offr., House of Commons L., London. [0060998] 28/01/2002
Murphy Mrs EJ, BSocSC MCLIP, Lib., Trinity & All Saints Coll., Leeds. [0021566] 05/10/1973
Murphy Ms EJ, BA DipLIS, Asst.Lib.-Reader Serv., Nat.Univ.of Ireland, Maynooth, Maynooth,Co.Kildare,Ireland. [0048746] 05/05/1993
Murphy Mrs GR, MCLIP DipLib, Lib., King William's Coll., Isle of Man. [0026994] 12/01/1977
Murphy Mrs J, MCLIP, Br.Lib., Valence/Markyate, L.B.of Barking & Dagenham. [0020634] 16/05/1973
Murphy Mr JJ, MCLIP, Reg.Lib., The Court Serv., Liverpool. [0019673] 30/10/1972
Murphy Ms JV, MA, Unemployed. [0058674] 15/05/2000
Murphy Miss LA, BSc(Econ) MCLIP, Sch.Lib., Firrhill High Sch., Edinburgh. [0054504] 02/01/1997

Murphy Mrs MK, (was Lawrence), MCLIP, Retired. [0010604] 19/03/1956
Murphy Miss PC, BA(Hons) MA DipLib PGCE MCLIP, Inf.Offr., Nat.Child.Bureau, London. [0037920] 17/10/1984
Murphy Mr PC, BA(Hons), Stud., Thames Valley Univ. [0058183] 12/11/1999
Murphy Ms R, MA, Stud., Univ.of Strathclyde. [0061623] 04/10/2002
Murphy Mrs R, BA DipLib MCLIP, Lib., Camden & Islington Comm.Health Serv., NHS Trust. [0032756] 04/08/1980
Murphy Miss S, BA(Hons), Stud., Univ.Coll.London. [0059964] 12/11/2001
Murphy Miss TA, Coll.Lib., Huddersfield New Coll.(FE). [0038580] 01/07/1985
Murphy Ms Y, MSSc BA DipEd, Lib., N.Ireland Political Collection, Linen-Hall L., Belfast. [0042128] 05/10/1988
Murr Mrs SL, (was Mitchell), MCLIP, Sen.Asst.Lib., Paignton L., Devon. [0025364] 07/01/1976
Murray Mrs AFA, BEd DipInf, Sch.Lib., Oxfordshire C.C. [0050500] 22/08/1994
Murray Miss AM, BLib MCLIP, Asst.Lib., Rochdale Cent.Ref.L. [0031910] 21/01/1980
Murray Mrs BM, (was Hills), MCLIP, Asst.Lib., N.Bristol Trust. [0021889] 23/01/1974
Murray Ms C, MA DipLib, Grp.Lib., Dumfries & Galloway L., Dalbeattie & Kirkcudbright. [0036736] 18/11/1983
Murray Miss CA, MA DipLib MCLIP DipEdTech, Learning Resources Super., Kilmarnock Coll., Holehouse Rd., KA3 7AT. [0037574] 10/10/1984
Murray Mrs CL, BA(Hons) MSc, Lib., Yorks.Martyrs Collegiate Sch., Bradford. [0054583] 31/01/1997
Murray Mr D, BLib MCLIP, Dir., London L.Devel.Agency, London. [0041960] 02/07/1988
Murray Ms E, BA DipInf MCLIP, Asst.Lib., Dept.for Work & Pensions, London. [0047155] 13/05/1992
Murray Mrs EJ, (was Cuthill), BA(Hons) MCLIP, Housewife. [0049875] 20/01/1994
Murray Ms EM, BA MCLIP, Sen.Lib., Renfrewshire Council. [0010609] 09/10/1970
Murray Mrs HL, (was Tyrer), BSc(Hons) MA, Unemployed. [0056734] 12/10/1998
Murray Mr ID, MA DipLib MCLIP DAA, Inf.Lib.& Arch., Clackmannanshire L., Alloa, Clackmannanshire. [0031395] 01/10/1979
Murray Mrs IS, (was Cox), MCLIP, Lib., Wards Solicitors, Bristol. [0003278] 10/01/1972
Murray Ms JA, (was Gould), BA DipLib, Catr., Brit.L., Boston Spa. [0038639] 25/08/1985
Murray Ms JA, MCLIP, Community Lib., Glasgow City C. [0019907] 11/01/1973
Murray Mrs JC, (was MacLeod), MA MCLIP, Lib., Lews Castle Coll., Stornoway. [0009515] 01/01/1969
Murray Mrs JFE, MA DipLib, p./t.L.Asst., N.London Collegiate Sch., Edgward, Middx. [0038363] 01/04/1985
Murray Dr JR, MCLIP, Dir., Murray Consulting & Training, Australia. [0005017] 19/09/1969
Murray Mrs K, (was Saynor), BA MCLIP, Br.Lib., Brecon L. [0040226] 07/11/1986
Murray Mrs KJ, (was Harries), BA(Hons) DipLib MCLIP, Asst.Lib., Manchester Metro.Univ. [0041372] 16/11/1987
Murray Miss L, BA(Hons) MCLIP, Inf.Mgr., E.of Scotland Water, Edinburgh. [0054374] 28/11/1996
Murray Mrs MEJ, (was Chambers), BA MCLIP, Princ.Lib., Stirling Council, E.R.I.S., Stirling. [0002556] 06/11/1970
Murray Mr MF, MA MSc MCLIP, Resident in Ireland. [0060114] 07/12/2001
Murray Mr NF, MA(Hons), Lib., Parliamentary Doc.Cent., European Parliament, Brussels. [0050309] 14/06/1994
Murray Miss P, BSc, Stud., Univ.of N.London. [0055451] 13/10/1997
Murray Mrs RA, (was Illingworth), MA MBA MCLIP, Stud., Queens Univ., Belfast. [0007590] 07/01/1957
Murray Mr RAC, MCLIP, Lib., Bo'ness L. [0010617] 07/09/1971
Murray Ms S, BSc DipLib MCLIP MA, Dep.Mgr.-Learning Res., Liverpool Hope Univ.Coll. [0042305] 17/10/1988
Murray Miss SA, MCLIP, Press Offr., C.B.I., London. [0010618] 10/02/1964
Murray Mrs SJ, P.G.Research Stud., Queen Margaret Univ.Coll., Edinburgh. [0054681] 19/02/1997
Murray Miss SMJ, BA MCLIP DMS, Comm.Lib., Cubitt Town L., London. [0010619] 01/10/1965
Murray Mrs VA, (was Harry), MA MSc, Subject Lib., Paisley Univ. [0047212] 05/06/1992
Murray Miss VL, BA(Hons), p./t.stud., Lo-Res.Cataloguer., Univ.Coll.London, Dorling Kindersley, London. [0059980] 15/11/2001
Murray Miss VSY, MA MCLIP, Asst.Lib., Dept.of Educ.Studies, Univ.of Oxford. [0054612] 31/01/1997
Murray-Rust Ms CL, BA MCLIP, Assoc.Univ.Lib., Oregon St.Univ., U.S.A. [0021954] 21/01/1974
Murrell Mr JF, BA(Hons), Sen.Inf.Offr., SJ Berwin & Co., London. [0038175] 03/02/1985
Murrell Mrs JM, (was Bacon), MCLIP, Lib.(p./t.), YMCA George Williams Coll., London. [0010621] 29/09/1962
Murtagh Miss EH, MCLIP, Retired. [0010622] 03/01/1969
Murtagh Mr JPP, MCLIP, Mgr.LRC, Barnet Coll., Grahame Park Site. [0020868] 20/03/1967
Murtagh Mr TM, BA DLIS MCLIP, Asst.Lib., Mayo Co.L., Ireland. [0039839] 23/08/1986
Murton Mrs CA, (was Broom), MCLIP, Catr., Suffolk Co.L., Ipswich. [0010623] 17/10/1966
Musa Ms N, MA, Stud./Inf.Asst., Robert Gordon Univ., Cent.L., Dundee. [0057047] 30/11/1998
Mushakoji Mr N, MA, Teacher (Univ.), Dept.of Literature, Daito Bunka Univ., Tokyo. [0047499] 09/09/1992

313

Musoke Mrs LO, BLIS DipLib, Lib., EFMPII, Ministry of Fin.Plan.&, Economic Devel.Uganda. [0061465] 08/08/2002
Mussell Miss J, BA DipLib MCLIP, Dep.Ch.Lib., Nat.Police Training, Bramshill, Hants. [0044433] 08/10/1990
Mussett Mr PK, MCLIP, Asst County Lib., Bucks C.C. [0010631] 01/03/1971
Mustapha Ms S, MA (Hons), Stud., Strathclyde Univ. [0061338] 30/05/2002
Mustard Miss CA, BEd, Stud., Robert Gordon Univ. [0059516] 18/04/2001
Muston Miss A, BLib MCLIP, Sen.Lib., Fareham L., Hants.Co.L. [0034173] 07/10/1981
Mutch Mrs FM, (was Buchanan), MA MCLIP, p./t.Asst.Lib., Shrewsbury 6th Form Coll. [0027906] 04/10/1977
Mutch Mrs LK, L.Asst., Moray Coll., Elgin. [0058220] 16/11/1999 AF
Muthama Mrs SL, BA, Child.Lib., Alfreton L. [0059715] 28/08/2001
Mutti Mrs L, (was Angus), BA(Hons) MA DipLib, Freelance, 01442 252755, Inf.& Research (Lexikos). [0048266] 19/11/1992
Muyawala Ms CT, BA, Lib., Zambia Privatisation Agency, Lusaka, Zambia. [0051829] 10/07/1995
Muzzu Mr FS, BA MA MSc(Econ), Sen.Consultant, Sue Hill Recruitment & Serv., London. [0056215] 07/04/1998
Mwenda Miss LLK, BLS DipLib MCLIP, Employment Unknown. [0051074] 14/11/1994
Mwesigme Birakawte Mr R, Employment not known. [0061172] 26/03/2002
Mwiyeriwa Mr SS, MA MLS FCLIP, Univ.Lib., Univ.of Malawi L., Zomba. [0017429] 01/09/1967 **FE 01/06/1979**
Myall Mrs NJ, p./t.Stud./Inf.Specialist, Univ.of Brighton/Qinetiq, Sevenoaks. [0058377] 26/01/2000
Myall Mr R, BA MA MCLIP, Lib., W.Sussex C.C., Haywards Heath L. [0043233] 10/10/1989
Myatt Mrs EJ, (was Arrow), BA MCLIP, Unemployed. [0028777] 23/01/1978
Myatt Mrs KF, (was Highet), BA DipLib MCLIP, Learning Resources Mgr., Hugh Baird Coll., Bootle. [0032981] 08/10/1980
Mydrau Mr NF, BA MCLIP, Asst., Inst.of Psychiatry L., London. [0010641] 29/02/1972
Myears Mr MC, BA MCLIP, Ref.Lib., Valence L., L.B.of Barking & Dagenham. [0025083] 20/10/1975
Myers Mr A, BSc DipLib FCLIP, Inf.Scientist, Heriot Watt Univ., Edinburgh. [0010642] 01/01/1972 **FE 01/04/2002**
Myers Miss AC, BA MCLIP, Sen.Advisory Lib., Sch.L.Serv., L.& Heritage Dept., Suffolk C.C. [0036696] 31/10/1983
Myers Ms JA, Unemployed. [0037724] 19/10/1984
Myers Ms LA, BSc(Hons) DipILS MCLIP, Inf.Offr., Social Policy Res.Unit, Univ.of York. [0047526] 01/10/1992
Myers Rev PH, MPhil MCLIP, Retired. [0010644] 02/10/1970
Myhill Mrs JL, (was York), BA(Hons) DipLIS MCLIP, Asst.Faculty Lib., Univ.Coll.Northampton, Avenue Campus. [0047888] 22/10/1992
Myhill Mrs LF, (was Parnell), BA DipLib MCLIP, Child.Lib., Self-employed. [0041910] 17/05/1988
Myles Mrs F, (was McIntosh), BA DipLib MCLIP, Princ.L.Offr., Scottish Dept., Edinburgh City L. [0037915] 20/11/1984
Myles Miss MF, MA MCLIP, Retired. [0010646] 14/02/1959
Mylett Miss EL, Lib., Byng Kenrick Cent.Sch., Birmingham. [0055181] 01/08/1997
Mylles Mr M, MCLIP, Inf.Consultant - p./t., Univ.of Herts., Hertford. [0038928] 17/10/1985
Mynott Ms GJ, BA(Hons) MCLIP, L.Mgr., Stockport NHS Trust. [0050239] 12/05/1994
Mynott Mrs J, BA(Hons) DipLib MCLIP, Maternity Career Break. [0037703] 15/10/1984
N'Jie Miss I, Unemployed. [0058373] 28/01/2000
Nagata Mr H, MA, Prof., Univ.of L.& Inf.Sci., Japan. [0028094] 10/10/1977
Nahal Mrs HC, (was Brooks), BLib MCLIP, Sen.Lib., Telford L. [0035097] 09/08/1982
Nail Mr M, MA DipLib MCLIP, Research Programme Mgr., Resource, London. [0019985] 08/01/1973
Nair Mrs R, BA MCLIP, L.Project Mgr., Wigan & Bolton Health Auth. [0012837] 01/01/1966
Naish Mr PJ, BA MLib MCLIP, Asst.Learning Res.Cent.Mgr., Univ.of Luton. [0039630] 11/04/1988
Naismith Mrs RS, (was Hayter), BLib MCLIP, Unemployed. [0040601] 05/04/1987
Najib Mrs G, BSc, Learning Cent. Facilitator., Swansea Coll. [0060910] 10/01/2002
Nakane Mr K, Sen.Lib., Nat.Diet L., Tokyo, Japan. [0051661] 01/01/1995
Nambiar Miss V, BA (Hons) MA mclip, Coordinator, Document Deliv.Serv., Nat.Univ.of Singapore. [0023469] 01/01/1975
Nancarrow Mrs CR, (was Morgan), BA MCLIP, Tutor, Univ.of Hong Kong, Dept.of Linguistics. [0025836] 02/10/1963
Nangia Mr SK, BSc MCLIP, Employment not known. [0060450] 11/12/2001
Nankivell Mr B, BSc(Hons) DipILS MCLIP, Inf.Res.Offr., Envolve, Bath, Partnerships for Sustainability. [0053875] 07/10/1996
Nankivell Miss MC, BA DipLIS, Dir., Univ.of Cent.England in Birmingham, Cent.for Inf.Research. [0042265] 13/10/1988
Nankivell-Hall Ms JS, (was Nankivell), BA MCLIP, L.Mgr., Radio Telefis Eireann, Dublin. [0010657] 17/01/1970
Nannestad Miss EE, BA MCLIP, Comm.Lib.-Inf., Lincs.C.C. [0024532] 22/09/1975
Nanu Mrs D, MSc BSc MCLIP, Employment not known. [0060841] 12/12/2001
Napier Ms AM, BA ALAA MCLIP, Resident in Australia. [0043559] 08/11/1989
Napier Mrs PEN, BA MCLIP, Retired. [0030017] 30/10/1978
Napper Mr CJ, BA DipLib MCLIP, Lib., Silsoe Campus, Cranfield Univ. [0030857] 10/05/1979
Napper Mrs J, (was Andrews), BA MCLIP, Sch.Lib., John Bunyan Upper Sch., Bedford. [0030091] 05/01/1979

Napper Ms MJ, (was Beattie), BA DipLib MCLIP, Inf.Offr., Health Economics Research Unit, Univ.of Aberdeen. [0043538] 06/11/1989
Narasimham Mrs J, (was Cox), FCLIP BA, Retired. [0010659] 09/10/1935 **FE 01/01/1939**
Narayanaswami Dr S, MSc PhD, Employment unknown. [0060337] 10/12/2001
Nash Miss M, MCLIP, Retired. [0022003] 15/01/1974
Nash Mr PW, Curator of Rare Books, Brit.Architectural L., Royal Inst.of Brit.Architects. [0052881] 15/01/1996
Nash Mrs R, (was Amson), BA FCLIP, Retired. [0010666] 20/09/1951 **FE 01/01/1964**
Nash Mrs VR, (was Bing), BA MCLIP, Retired. [0017435] 17/01/1966
Nassar Miss HT, BA MCLIP, Dir.-Med.L., American Univ.of Beirut, Saab Med.L., Lebanon. [0029768] 18/10/1978
Nassimbeni Ms MC, BA PhD, Assoc.Prof., Dept.Inf.& L.Studies., Univ.of Cape Town. [0044277] 07/08/1990
Nathan-Marsh Ms E, LLB BL DipLib, Health Inf.Offr., NHS Direct S.E.London, Beckenham. [0055299] 19/09/1997
Nattrass Mr GR, MA MCLIP, Head of Germanic Collections, Brit.L. [0026671] 26/04/1971
Nattriss Mr JB, BA FCLIP, Life Member. [0010672] 15/03/1953 **FE 01/01/1958**
Naughton-Davidson Mrs M, (was Naughton), BA MCLIP, Lib., Bablake School, Coventry. [0041444] 06/01/1988
Nauta Mr MF, FCLIP, Asst.Dir.-Cult.Serv., Lincs.C.C. [0010675] 14/01/1967 **FE 21/09/1972**
Navarrete Mrs MJ, BA(Hons) MA, Sch.Lib., Archbishop Tenisons Sch., London. [0059950] 09/11/2001
Navascues Moraga Ms L, BA(Hons), Unemployed. [0045737] 09/05/1991
Nawe Miss J, BA MA PhD, Dir. UDSM L. Serv., Univ.of Dar es Salaam, Tanzania. [0034651] 01/01/1982
Nayler Mrs PK, (was Duggan), MCLIP, Retired. [0010679] 27/03/1954
Naylor Mrs A, (was Craven), BA MCLIP, Inf.Team Mgr., L.& Inf.Serv., Nottingham Trent Univ. [0019369] 22/09/1961
Naylor Mr B, MA DipLib FRSA MCLIP, Retired. [0010680] 23/10/1963
Naylor Mrs CA, (was Jones), MCLIP, Asst.Lib., Cent.Lend.Lib., Bor.of S.Tyneside. [0023582] 13/01/1975
Naylor Mrs E, (was Elliott), MCLIP, Housewife. [0004502] 09/01/1963
Naylor Ms EJ, MCLIP, Community Lib., City of Sunderland. [0024395] 18/03/1966
Naylor Mr F, BA BEd MCLIP, Life Member. [0010683] 09/03/1942
Naylor Mr JA, BSc MCLIP, Asst.Lib., Univ.of Warwick L. [0010684] 12/09/1963
Naylor Mrs JA, (was Donaldson), BLIB MCLIP, Unemployed. [0028804] 01/02/1978
Naylor Mr K, MCLIP, Team Lib., St.Helens M.B.C. [0010685] 22/05/1967
Naylor Mrs SJ, (was Yarwood), BA MCLIP, N.E.Circuit Lib., The Court Serv., Sheffield. [0027638] 29/04/1977
Nazir Mr S, BSc(Hons) DipIS MCLIP, Inf.Offr., Bank of England, London. [0049824] 24/01/1994
Neal Miss CL, BA(Hons) MCLIP, Tech.Inf.Mgr., Virgin Atlantic Airways, Crawley, W.Sussex. [0039818] 05/08/1986
Neal Mr GP, Employment not known. [0038445] 03/05/1985
Neal Dr T, PhD BSc(Hons), Chemical Inf.Sci., Eli Lilly & Co.Ltd., Windlesham. [0061555] 08/09/2002
Neale Mrs H, (was McAuley), BLib MCLIP, Lib., Queens Univ.Belfast. [0038480] 09/05/1985
Neale Mr IM, BSc MSc MIMgt MCLIP, Employment not known. [0060768] 12/12/2001
Nealon Ms LA, DipLib MCLIP, Lib., St.Thomas of Aquins High Sch., Edinburgh. [0037657] 15/10/1984
Neary Mrs BJ, BSc(Hons), Sen.L.Asst., Bath & N.E.Somerset, Bath Cent.L. [0057214] 19/01/1999
Neath Mrs CY, BA(Hons), Grad.Trainee, West Bridgford L., Nottingham. [0059967] 13/11/2001
Neathey Mrs BM, (was McMichael), FCLIP, Retired. [0010701] 01/01/1951 **FE 08/03/1988**
Needham Miss H, FCLIP, Life Member. [0010705] 01/01/1934 **FE 01/01/1955**
Needham Miss J, MCLIP, Div.Inf.Lib., Basingstoke L., Hants.Co.L. [0010706] 23/07/1968
Needham Mrs JA, (was Adey), BA MCLIP, ICT Support Lib., Staffs.Cultural & Corp.Serv., Burton L. [0044974] 28/01/1991
Needham Mrs LL, (was Knox), BA(Hons) DipLIS, Clinical Support Outreach Lib., Medway NHS Trust, Medway Maritime Hosp. [0048472] 18/01/1993
Needham Mrs S, (was Loveridge), MCLIP, Mgr., Sch.L.Serv., Birmingham City Council. [0009113] 25/01/1967
Needle Mrs BM, (was Palmer), BA MCLIP, Life Member. [0010709] 15/01/1951
Needles Mrs LG, (was Jones), MCLIP, Retired. [0027118] 28/08/1959
Needles Miss M, BA MCLIP, L.Serv.Mgr.(Fin.& Acquisitions), Manchester Metro.Univ. [0010711] 02/10/1967
Neel Ms LJ, BA(Hons), Lib., Metropolitan Police, London. [0053328] 07/05/1996
Neesam Mr MG, MPhil FCLIP, 16 E.Park Road, Harrogate, Yorks., HG1 5QT. [0010713] 07/09/1964 **FE 18/07/1991**
Neeve Mrs MP, (was Cavanagh), B Lib MCLIP, Teaching Asst., Essex C.C. [0002507] 17/03/1970
Negin Mr M, Retired. [0019953] 17/01/1973
Negus Mr AE, MA FCLIP, Inf.Systems Consultant, 14 Carr Gate, Wirral. [0010714] 20/07/1964
Negus Mrs Y, (was Hughes), BA MCLIP, Local Area Mgr., South, Solihull Educ., Ls.& Arts, Knowle L. [0018311] 03/10/1972
Neifer Mr RS, BA, L.Asst., Vancouver Comm.Coll., Canada. [0061305] 21/05/2002

Neil Mr IK, MA MCLIP, Lib., Angus Council Cultural Serv. [0010720] 20/10/1970
Neil Mrs V, BA MLS, Lib., Milton P.L., Ontario, Canada. [0059919] 23/10/2001
Neild Mr GCA, BSc MCLIP, Area Mgr.N., Liverpool L.& Inf.Serv., Liverpool. [0026783] 26/10/1976
Neilly Miss E, BA(Hons), Stud., Leeds Univ., Leeds. [0061443] 29/07/2002
Neilson Miss CL, MA(Hons), Faculty Administrator/p.t.Stud., Napier Univ., Queen Margaret Univ. [0059544] 02/05/2001
Neilson Mr DT, DipLib MCLIP, Self-employed:, Brighton. [0028097] 30/09/1977
Neilson Dr J, BA PhD MCLIIP, Sch.Lib., E.Ayshire Council, Kilmarnock. [0010724] 15/09/1969
Neilson Ms JR, BA MPhil DipLib, Inf.Offr., Clifford Chance, LLP, London. [0044806] 05/12/1990
Neilson Mrs KG, BSc MCLIP, Employment not known. [0039169] 01/12/1985
Neilson Mrs LS, (was Nicholas), BSc(Hons) PGDipILM, Reader Devel.Offr.-Child.Serv., Blackburn with Darwen L.& Inf.Serv., Blackburn Cent.L. [0058012] 12/10/1999
Neilson Mr RP, BA, Market Research Mgr., Sheffield Hallam Univ. [0038367] 01/04/1985
Neilson Miss TE, Stud., Queen Margaret Univ.Coll. [0059899] 30/10/2001
Neligan Miss MA, BA HDE MCLIP, Lib., NUI, Maynooth, Co.Kildare. [0017441] 16/10/1970
Neller Miss RM, BA DipLib MCLIP, Comm.Lib., Mablethorpe, Lincs.Co.L. [0025180] 23/11/1975
Nellis Mrs AJ, (was Suscens), MCLIP, Special Serv.Lib., N.Yorks.C.C., Scalby. [0014234] 28/01/1972
Nelmes Mrs ML, BSc(Hons), Stud./Lib., Univ.of Wales Aberystwyth, County Central L.,Kent. [0061705] 22/10/2002
Nelson Mrs CA, (was Bell), BA DipLIS MCLIP, Asst.Dist.Lib., Bucks.C.C., Marlow L. [0046020] 24/08/1991
Nelson Mrs CJ, BSc, Lib., L.B.of Haringey, Hornsey L. [0049654] 22/11/1993
Nelson Ms DG, BSc MPhil DipLib MSc IT, Faculty Lib., Computing, Eng., & Maths, Univ.West of England. [0039907] 05/10/1986
Nelson Mrs GJ, (was Gaskin), BA DipLib MCLIP, p./t.Sch.Lib., Dorset County. [0035420] 01/10/1982
Nelson Mrs ME, (was Gautry), MCLIP, p./t.Child.Lib., Portsmouth City Council, North End, Portsmouth, Hants. [0023184] 05/11/1974
Nelson Mrs PE, BA MCLIP, Inf.Mgr., FPD Savills, London. [0025587] 29/01/1976
Nelson Mr SA, BA DipLib, Heritage Project Catr., Nat.Art L., Victoria & Albert Mus. [0040808] 22/06/1987
Nelson Mrs SE, (was Haycock), MCLIP, Inf.Offr., Sheffield Educ.Dept., S.Yorks. [0023420] 07/01/1975
Nelson Mrs SJ, BA(Hons) PGDipILM, Inf.Asst., Liverpool John Moores Univ. [0057406] 15/03/1999
Nelson Mrs ST, BA MCLIP, Asst.Lib., Trinity Coll., Cambridge. [0020658] 01/01/1974
Nelson Ms T, (was Green), BSc MSc MCLIP, Unemployed. [0042027] 01/08/1988
Nephin Miss EL, BA(Hons), Stud., Leeds Metro.Univ. [0061807] 11/11/2002
Nesaratnam Mrs JA, (was Duffy), BA MCLIP, Unemployed. [0035021] 09/06/1982
Nestor Ms BA, Retired. [0021607] 01/01/1973
Nettlefold Mrs MB, (was Dalton), MCLIP, Dir., Cawdor Book Serv., Glasgow, Scotland. [0010736] 11/01/1966
Nettleton Mrs SJ, (was Hallam), BA(Hons), Lib.,- Moreton Morrell Cent., Warwicks.Coll., Warwick. [0033653] 19/01/1981
Neves Mr RM, BA DipLIS, Head Lib., Biblioteca Municipio Montijo, Montijo, Portugal. [0053081] 04/03/1996
Neville Miss KE, BA DipLib MCLIP, Mob.L.Serv.Coordinator/Trans.Offr., Derbys.C.C. [0036374] 04/10/1983
Neville Ms LSC, BA(Hons), L.Asst., Royal Coll.of Art, London. [0046113] 01/10/1991
Nevin Mrs L, BEd, Research & Inf.Mgr., Financial Ombudsman Serv., London. [0053931] 11/10/1996
New Mr PJ, MCLIP, Lib., N.Somerset Council, Nailsea. [0019371] 29/04/1967
Newall Mrs GM, (was Bateman), Mgr., P.G.Med.Cent., Leighton Hosp.,Crewe. [0045257] 13/09/1990 AF
Newall Ms LA, BA(Hons), Unemployed. [0053255] 17/04/1996
Newbould Mrs S, (was Wadsworth), MCLIP, Asst.Ref.Lib.(Job Share), Cent.L., Calderdale M.B.C. [0015167] 31/01/1966
Newbury Mrs JI, (was Fothergill), MCLIP, Unemployed. [0010745] 13/10/1964
Newbury Mr KMG, FCLIP, Life Member, Tel.01243 788567, 70 Cambrai Ave., Chichester, W.Sussex, PO19 2JU. [0010746] 23/03/1932 FE 01/01/1948
Newbury Mrs TM, MA DipLib MCLIP, Sch.Lib., All Saints Secondary Sch., Glasgow. [0040754] 22/05/1987
Newby Mr CP, BA(Hons) DipILM MCLIP, Comm.Lib., Lincs.C.C. [0050714] 12/10/1994
Newell Mrs AR, (was Jones), Unemployed. [0010751] 24/01/1967
Newell Mrs E, BA(Hons), Sch.Lib., St Peters Sch., Huntingdon, Cambs. [0051510] 13/03/1995
Newell Mr GG, BA, L.Exec., House of Commons Commission L., London. [0041158] 09/10/1987
Newey Mr NWO, BA(Hons) MA, Unemployed. [0052820] 20/12/1995
Newham Ms H, (was Wilmer), MCLIP, Mgmt.Consultant, HNA., Windrush, The Ridgeway, Enfield, EN2 8AN. [0016036] 25/08/1964
Newiss Miss J, MA MCLIP, Life Member. [0010755] 23/01/1960
Newland Mrs BJM, (was Donlin), BA(Hons), Lib., English Nature, Peterborough. [0046160] 03/10/1991
Newlands Miss KS, MA(Hons), Inf.Offr., McGrigor Donald, Glasgow. [0057925] 05/10/1999
Newlove Mrs CM, (was James), BA MCLIP, p./t.Lib., Taylor Vinters Solicitors, Cambridge. [0032999] 01/10/1980

Newman Ms A, MSc BA CertEd, Clerical. [0044378] 03/10/1990
Newman Ms A, BA(Hons), Inf.Exec., BTG Internat.Ltd., London. [0054998] 19/06/1997
Newman Mrs B, (was Harlock), BA MCLIP, Sch.L.Serv.Mgr., Bristol City Council. [0006648] 21/02/1969
Newman Miss BR, BA(Hons) MA(Hons), Readers Serv.Lib., The Child.Soc., London. [0054765] 01/04/1997
Newman Mrs C, BA MCLIP, Sen.L.Mgr., Greenwich Council, Clackheath L. [0041824] 17/04/1988
Newman Mrs C, (was Howarth), BA(Hons) DipLIS, Sen.L.Asst., Lancs County L., Harris Cent.L.Preston. [0049458] 02/11/1993
Newman Mr CJ, BA DipLib MCLIP, Asst.Lib., Corporation of London L., Bibl.Serv.Section-Guildhall L. [0037923] 19/11/1984
Newman Mrs HM, (was Faiers), BA PGCE MLib MCLIP, Sen.L.Serv., W.Sussex C.C. [0042371] 27/10/1988
Newman Mr IA, Unemployed. [0058779] 20/07/2000
Newman Mr JC, BA, Stud., Manchester Met.Univ. [0061190] 08/04/2002
Newman Mrs LE, FCLIP, Employment not known. [0060564] 11/12/2001 FE 01/04/2002
Newman Mrs LM, BA PhD MCLIP, Retired. [0010765] 06/01/1964
Newman Mrs M, (was Norquay), MA MCLIP, Coll.Lib., Fareham Coll., Hants. [0010766] 07/01/1971
Newman Mrs NB, (was Herman), BA(Hons) DipInf MCLIP, Head Lib., St.Andrews Hosp., Northampton. [0047690] 15/10/1992
Newman Mrs OH, (was Obuchiwskyj), BA CertEd DipLIS, Lib., Congleton L., Cheshire C.C. [0041636] 03/02/1988
Newman Miss OS, MA FCLIP, Retired., Form.Co.Lib.,Shropshire. [0010767] 04/01/1935 FE 01/01/1951
Newman Miss RM, BA, Stud., Thames Valley Univ. [0059747] 12/09/2001
Newman Mrs S, (was Wrigglesworth), BA DipLib MCLIP, [0037786] 26/10/1984
Newman Mr WG, MCLIP, Devel.Mgr., Derbys.C.C., Alfreton L. [0010772] 12/05/1971
Newman Spaul Ms DM, (was Newman), BA M Phil MCLIP, Saturday Lib., Anglia Poly.Univ., Chelmsford. [0040849] 12/07/1987
Newnham Mr P, BA(Hons), Sen.Asst.Lib., Birmingham Cent.L. [0055076] 07/07/1997
Newsam Mrs AM, (was Hurley), BA(Hons) DipLIS MCLIP, Community Lib., Abergavenny L., Monmouthshire. [0046473] 11/11/1991
Newsam Mr BA, BSc FRSC MCLIP, Retired. [0060595] 11/12/2001
Newsome Miss J, L.Asst., Univ of Leeds, Bretton Hall L. [0056439] 13/07/1998
Newson Mr BAR, MCLIP, Retired. [0010775] 17/04/1956
Newton Miss AJ, BA(Hons) MA MCLIP, Sen.L.Asst., Univ.of Leeds L. [0055772] 18/11/1997
Newton Mr AJ, BLib MCLIP, Lib., Trowbridge P.L., Wilts. [0028640] 04/01/1978
Newton Mrs C, (was Bailey), Dep.Area Lib.(N.Area), Wallasey Cent.L., Wirral Bor.Council. [0038177] 24/01/1985
Newton Mrs CE, BA(Hons) MA DipLib MSc MCLIP, Inf.Res.Worker, Harrogate & Area Council for, Vol.Serv. [0024776] 16/10/1975
Newton Mrs CJ, (was Beck), BA MA, Dir.of General Collections, Nat.L.of Scotland, Edinburgh. [0021288] 14/10/1973
Newton Mr D, MA, Stud., JMU. [0061841] 15/11/2002
Newton Dr DC, BSc PhD MCLIP, Position unknown, Brit.L., London. [0060560] 11/12/2001
Newton Mrs DM, (was Gore), BLib MCLIP, Catr./Performing Arts Lib., Trowbridge/Devizes P.L., Wilts.C.C. [0028431] 06/12/1977
Newton Mrs J, Database Serv.Lib., Leeds City Council H.Q. [0050726] 14/10/1994
Newton Mrs JL, (was Lerpiniere), MCLIP, Unemployed. [0025347] 14/01/1976
Newton Mrs JM, (was Campbell), MCLIP, H.of Ls.& Inf., Educ.& Culture, L.B.of Lewisham. [0053993] 22/06/1970
Newton Mrs JRD, BA(Hons) BSc MCLIP, Homework Club Support Lib.(Temp.), Torfaen Co.Bor.Council, Pontypool. [0054239] 13/11/1996
Newton Mrs K, (was Galley), Sen.L.Asst., City of Sunderland, Hetton L. [0045188] 06/08/1990 AF
Newton Mrs M, (was Greening), BSc DipLib MCLIP, Br.Lib., Cardiff C.C. [0031132] 14/08/1979
Newton Mrs M, (was Farrell), BA MCLIP, Sen.Lib., Child.& Young Peoples Serv., Rotherham M.B.C. [0044913] 14/01/1991
Newton Mrs ME, (was Masson), MCLIP, Lib., Soc.of Solicitors & Procurators, for the E.Dist.of Fife, Cupar. [0010784] 09/01/1962
Newton Mr NS, BA MA PGDipLib MCLIP, Sen.Lib.-Inf.Coordinator, Highland L., L.Support Unit, Inverness. [0010785] 01/01/1975
Newton Mrs SH, (was Morley), BA(Hons) MA MCLIP, Marketing Inf.Exec., AXA Sun Life, Bristol. [0048806] 02/06/1993
Newton Miss VB, BSc DipLib MCLIP, Lib., Univ.of Exeter. [0026996] 19/01/1977
Newton Sen VE, SCM MA FCLIP LLB, Law Lib., Univ.of the W.Indies, Cane Hill Campus, Barbados. [0022535] 17/07/1974 FE 02/07/1984
Newton Miss VV, MCLIP, Retired. [0010788] 23/09/1995
Ng Ms DBE, MBIT BAppSc MCLIP, Offr.-i/c.-Classification, Singapore Prisons Dept. [0017451] 01/01/1970
Ng Miss LH, MCLIP, Sen.Reg.Program Offr.,Inf.Sci.Div., Internat.Devel.Research Cent., Republic of Singapore. [0017453] 02/02/1968
Ng Mrs RE, (was Neilson), BA(Hons) MScEcon MCLIP, Inf.Offr., Norton Rose, London. [0055431] 13/10/1997
Ng Kee Kwong Mrs RSY, (was Hip-Hoi-Yen), MSc MCLIP, Resident in Mauritius. [0060081] 07/12/2001
Ngwira Ms M, (was Gunn), MSc BA MCLIP, Snr.Asst.Libr., Bunda Coll. Agriculture, Malawi. [0010790] 01/01/1964

Niblett Mrs BS, (was Johns), MSc BSc(Econ) DipLib MCLIP, Training Instructor, GEAC Software Solutions Ltd., Bristol. [0019574] 17/11/1972
Nichol Mrs S, (was Honor), BSC MCLIP, Sch.L.Consultant. [0018380] 19/10/1972
Nicholas Mr CJ, BA(Hons), Stud., Aberystwyth Univ. [0059457] 30/03/2001
Nicholas Mr JR, BA MCLIP, Retired. [0010794] 18/09/1963
Nicholas Dr RO, MA PhD, Stud., City Univ. [0059127] 21/11/2000
Nicholls Miss D, LLB(Hons) LPC PgDip, P./t.Stud., Univ.Aberystwyth. [0059775] 02/10/2001
Nicholls Miss E, MCLIP, Life Member. [0010799] 02/10/1940
Nicholls Mrs G, (was Scarr), BA MCLIP, Unwaged. [0033142] 03/10/1980
Nicholls Ms HBZ, Sen.L.Asst., Westminster L. [0046961] 12/03/1992 **AF**
Nicholls Mrs HT, (was Troy), BA DipLib MCLIP, Lib./Copyright Offr., Assessment & Qualifications Allia., Manchester. [0023605] 16/01/1975
Nicholls Mr JE, Retired. [0010801] 15/08/1949
Nicholls Mrs LJ, Sen.L.Asst., Univ.of Sussex L., Brighton. [0061317] 17/05/2002 **AF**
Nicholls Miss MJ, Stud., Univ.of Brighton. [0058569] 01/04/2000
Nicholls Miss ML, Learning Res.Asst., Univ.of Wolverhampton. [0051794] 01/07/1995 **AF**
Nicholls Mr NAG, BA GradDipBus MCLIP, Adviser, European Union, Papua New Guinea. [0010802] 21/11/1966
Nicholls Miss PJ, BA DipLib MCLIP, Dep.Lib., Richmond upon Thames Coll., Twickenham. [0037371] 16/07/1984
Nicholls Miss PS, Lib., Mascalls Sch., Paddock Wood. [0010803] 16/01/1966
Nicholls Mrs S, (was Kew), MCLIP, Lib., Calthorpe Park Sch., Fleet. [0008330] 22/04/1971
Nicholls Dr SE, BSc MSc PhD MCLIP, Retired. [0060594] 11/12/2001
Nicholls Mrs SM, (was Howarth), MCLIP, Housebound Serv.Lib., Harrow. [0010804] 01/01/1963
Nicholls Mrs WG, (was Gibbs), MCLIP, Child.& Young Peoples Lib., S.Glos.Council, Downend L. [0005467] 05/02/1972
Nichols Miss AJ, BSc(Hons) DipIM, Stud., Manchester Met.Univ. [0057809] 11/01/1999
Nichols Mrs FM, (was Williams), BA(Hons) MCLIP, Subject Lib., Univ.of Southampton. [0038187] 29/01/1985
Nichols Mr H, MA FCLIP, Life Member, 44 Main St., Cherry Burton, Beverley, N.Humberside, HU17 7RF. [0010807] 29/03/1938 **FE 01/01/1952**
Nichols Ms JL, BA DipLib MBA MCLIP, Faculty Lib., UWE L.Services, Hartpury Coll. [0030782] 02/04/1979
Nichols Mrs LL, BA DipLib MA, Readers Adviser, L.& Mus.Dept., L.B.of Bexley. [0043546] 06/11/1989
Nichols Mrs ME, (was Cooley), MCLIP, Asst.L.Mgr., Holborn L., L.B.of Camden. [0003095] 12/01/1970
Nichols Mr NJ, BA(Hons), Dep.Mgr -Inf.Resources, Trade Partners UK, London. [0057958] 05/10/1999
Nichols Mr PE, BA MCLIP, Asst.Co.Lib.(Operations), Somerset Co.L. [0019214] 04/09/1972
Nichols Mr PWL, BSc MCLIP, Position unknown, Hampden Data Serv.Ltd., New Barnet. [0060562] 11/12/2001
Nichols Mr RM, MCLIP, Team Lib.(Lend.), Edmonton Green L., L.B.of Enfield. [0010812] 12/01/1969
Nichols Mrs SE, (was Lee), MCLIP, Dep.Learning Res.Cent.Mgr., St.Francis Xavier 6th Form Coll., London. [0025345] 10/01/1976
Nichols Ms SJ, Lib., Bircham Dyson Bell, London. [0035042] 05/07/1982
Nicholson Mr AP, BA MSC, Employment not known. [0060186] 10/12/2001
Nicholson Ms B, (was Solomon), Lib., Babtie Group Ltd., Glasgow. [0041624] 02/02/1988
Nicholson Ms CL, BA MCLIP, Sen.Lib.Farnham, Surrey C.C. [0031762] 03/12/1979
Nicholson Ms CM, (was Benson), MA DipLib MCLIP, p./t., Devel.Dir., Caledonian L.Info.Cent., Glasgow Caledonian Univ. [0021505] 22/10/1973
Nicholson Mrs CT, (was Dubois), BA MCLIP, Sen.Lib.:Stock & Reader Devel., Glos.Co.L.Arts & Mus.Serv. [0029640] 09/10/1978
Nicholson Mr DM, BSC DIP LIB MCLIP, Sub-Lib., Andersonian L., Strathclyde Univ. [0024912] 11/10/1975
Nicholson Mrs H, (was Johnson), BSc(Econ), L.Asst.(p./t.), Cornwall Coll., Learning Res.Cent. [0048614] 11/03/1993 **AF**
Nicholson Miss HC, MA DipLib MCLIP, Head of Inf.& Research, Cent.Lobby Consultants, London. [0036525] 05/10/1983
Nicholson Mr HD, MA MCLIP, Univ.Lib., Univ.of Bath, Bath, BA2 7AY. [0025379] 05/01/1976
Nicholson Mr J, BA(Hons) DipILS, Staff Devel.& Mobile Serv.Lib., Aberdeenshire L.& Inf.Serv. [0059427] 12/03/2001
Nicholson Ms J, BA MA, Child.Lib., Derbys.C.C., Long Eaton. [0040138] 17/10/1986
Nicholson Mrs JD, (was Hayton), MCLIP, Prison Lib., Portland Y.O.I., Dorset C.C. [0019972] 01/01/1973
Nicholson Miss JE, BSc DipLib MCLIP, Asst.Lib., W.Hants.NHS Trust, Hants. [0021178] 30/09/1973
Nicholson Ms KE, Retired. [0010821] 12/10/1946
Nicholson Miss M, BA MCLIP, Asst.Lib., Hull Univ.L. [0010822] 01/01/1961
Nicholson Miss MS, BA(Hons) MA, Learning Adviser:Soc.Policy, Univ.of Lincoln, Lincoln. [0051877] 24/07/1995
Nicholson Mrs MV, (was West), MCLIP, Press Cuttings Res., Tellex Monitors, Peterborough. [0017461] 01/01/1969
Nicholson Miss NM, MA FCLIP, Life Member, Tel.0181 567 2083, 13 Disraeli Rd., Ealing, London, W5 5HS. [0010823] 28/05/1949 **FE 01/01/1968**
Nicholson Mr NT, MA DipLib MCLIP, Non-Book Materials Catr., Univ.of Oxford. [0031519] 15/10/1979

Nicholson Mrs PM, (was Olive), MCLIP, Comm.Lib., Bolton L. [0010824] 28/02/1965
Nicholson Mr RP, BA(Hons) MMus, L.Asst., Royal Coll.of Music L., London. [0057493] 01/04/1999 **AF**
Nicholson Mrs VV, (was Dukelow), BLS, Team Lib.(Job Share), N.E.Educ.& L.Board, Co.Antrim. [0048689] 15/04/1993
Nicholson Mrs YM, (was Tyrell), MCLIP, Unemployed. [0019132] 01/01/1972
Nicklen Mrs AE, (was Clement), BA MCLIP, Team Lib., Burnham on Sea, Somerset. [0040657] 30/04/1987
Nicklen Mr JE, BA(Hons) DipLib MCLIP, Head of Serials Unit, Nat.L.of Scotland, Edinburgh. [0028348] 31/10/1977
Nicklin Mr BM, BA(Hons), p./t.Stud./L.Asst., Univ.of Wales, Aberystwyth, N.E.Wales Sch.L.Serv. [0061067] 12/02/2002
Nicol Miss AL, MA MCLIP, Ls.Offr., Highland Council, Ross & Cromarty. [0024013] 03/03/1975
Nicol Mrs EH, (was Milne), MA DipLib MCLIP, L.Resource Cent.Coordinator, Aberdeen City Council, Aberdeen. [0045705] 29/04/1991
Nicol Miss KE, LIS Mgr., Environment Agency, Bristol. [0048312] 25/11/1992
Nicolaides Ms E, BA DipLib MCLIP, Employment not known. [0035760] 24/01/1983
Nicolaides Mr F, BA MA MLib MSc MCLIP, Project Offr., M25 Consortium. [0042036] 06/08/1948
Nicoll Miss FL, MA DipLIS MCLIP, Sen.L.Asst., Andersonian L., Univ.of Strathclyde. [0041639] 05/02/1988
Nicolson Ms B, Unemployed. [0059731] 10/09/2001
Nicolson Mrs MAS, (was Graham), BA DipLib MCLIP, Sch.Lib., Shetland Islands Council, Lerwick. [0027986] 03/10/1977
Nicolson Mr MS, BA MA, Media & I.T.Lib., Bournemouth & Poole Coll.of F.E. [0054253] 11/11/1996
Nief Miss R, BA, Lib., Wiener L., London. [0041702] 22/02/1988
Nield Mrs L, (was Sams), BA DipLib MCLIP, Area Lib.-W., Dumfries & Galloway Council, Stranraer. [0035910] 12/02/1983
Nield-Dumper Mrs M, BScEcon, p./t.Stud./L.Asst., Univ.Aberystwyth, King Alfreds Coll.London. [0057691] 03/07/2001
Nielsen Ms J, Asst.Lib., The Wellcome Trust, London. [0057860] 13/09/1999
Nielsen Mrs ME, BA MLib MCLIP, Res.Collections Devel.Mgr., Univ.of Birmingham. [0034625] 19/01/1982
Nieminen Miss SM, MA DipILM MSc MCLIP, Sen.L.Asst., Imperial Coll., London. [0057066] 07/12/1998
Nieuwold Ms L, BA MA MCLIP, Unemployed. [0039003] 28/10/1985
Nightingale Mrs F, (was Boulton), DipLib MCLIP, Res.Lib., Bury Coll., Lancs. [0001524] 29/02/1972
Nightingale Mrs LK, (was Musson), MCLIP, L.Mgr., L.B.of Croydon, London. [0010633] 25/09/1969
Nikitina Ms M, BA MA, Unemployed. [0059085] 10/11/2000
Nikolich Miss PM, MCLIP, p./t.Comm.Lib., Stoke-on-Trent City Co., Hanley L., Staffs. [0022130] 17/02/1974
Nilan Mr RG, BSc, Unemployed. [0038178] 15/01/1985
Nimmo Mrs JS, L.Asst., Hele Rd.L., Exeter Coll. [0061032] 06/02/2002 **AF**
Nisbet Mrs JA, (was Brown), MCLIP, Catr., Edinburgh City L., Cent.L. [0001881] 26/05/1968
Nisbet Ms MJ, BSc DipLib MCLIP, Unemployed. [0035691] 19/01/1983
Nisbet Mr PW, MA MCLIP, Asst.Lib., N.Lanarkshire Council, Motherwell. [0024118] 01/04/1975
Niven Ms AS, MA(Hons) DipLib MCLIP, Sen.Lib.(Acq.), Mitchell L., Glasgow. [0032137] 10/01/1980
Niven Ms ES, (was Waheed), MA(Hons) DipLib MCLIP, Sch.Lib., Dingwall Academy, Highland Council. [0032811] 29/09/1980
Niven Miss EW, MCLIP, Lib., Inveresk Res., E.Lothian. [0028872] 06/02/1978
Nix Mrs A, (was Landers), BA DipLib MCLIP, Princ.L.Offr., Edinburgh Room, Edinburgh Cent.L. [0027495] 27/04/1977
Nixon Mrs A, (was Cracknell), MCLIP, Sch.Lib., Chepstow Comprehensive, Gwent C.C. [0008367] 01/01/1971
Nixon Mrs AW, (was McCrea), MCLIP, Retired. [0010849] 23/03/1959
Nixon Mrs CM, (was Brown), BA(Hons) MSc, Inf.Asst., Napier Univ., Borders Gen.Hosp.NHS Trust. [0061353] 29/05/2002
Nixon Mrs LA, (was Jessop), BLib MCLIP, Inf.Offr., Child.Cent., City Hosp., Nottingham. [0036247] 15/01/1975
Nixon Miss MC, BA MA DipLib MCLIP, Researcher [0021110] 08/10/1973
Noah Mrs JA, BA(Hons) MA PGCE, Stud., Univ.Cent.England. [0059273] 22/03/2001
Noaks Miss PE, MCLIP, Life Member. [0010856] 10/02/1949
Noall Miss CAF, MCLIP, Branch Lib., Cardiff L.Services. [0010857] 03/03/1972
Nobbs Mrs JE, (was George), MCLIP, Life Member, 3 Priors Gate, Werrington, Peterborough, Cambs., PE4 6LZ. [0005438] 30/09/1963
Noble Ms A, BA DipLib MCLIP, Princ.Lib., Sch.L.Serv., Monmouthshire C.C. [0038241] 12/02/1985
Noble Miss AD, MA FCLIP, Retired. [0010858] 27/09/1943 **FE 01/01/1965**
Noble Mrs AH, (was Dickson), BA MCLIP, Sch.Lib., Marr Coll., Troon. [0032271] 24/01/1980
Noble Mrs J, BA MCLIP. [0032500] 13/05/1980
Noble Miss JA, BA(Hons), Community Lib., Bournemouth Bor.Council, Kinson L. [0056045] 30/11/1998
Noble Miss L, BSc MCLIP, Employment not known. [0060752] 12/12/2001
Noble Miss M, MBE FCLIP, Life Member. [0017466] 01/01/1931 **FE 01/01/1937**
Noble Mrs RA, (was Seddon), MCLIP, Unemployed. [0013101] 02/10/1968
Noble Mrs RJ, (was Pearson), MCLIP, Dir.of Learning Res., Coll.of Richard Collyer, Horsham, W.Sussex. [0010869] 02/01/1968
Noble Mrs SM, (was Clair), BA CertEd, Sch.Lib., Great Sankey High Sch., Warrington. [0036701] 18/11/1983
Noblett Miss J, MA MCLIP, Lend.Serv.Lib., Hallward L., Univ.of Nottingham. [0026785] 26/10/1976

Personal Members — Nye

Noblett Mrs LP, (was Bullivant), MA MCLIP, Asst.H.of Serv., Cambs.L.& Inf.Serv. [0021610] *19/11/1973*
Noblett Mr WA, MA MCLIP, Head Official Publications, Cambridge Univ.L. [0021517] *11/10/1973*
Nockels Mr KH, MA(Hons) DipLib MCLIP, Site Services Mgr., Med.Sch.L., Univ.Aberdeen. [0039975] *08/10/1986*
Nocker Ms CP, MCLIP, Lifelong Learning Lib., Glasgow City Ls. [0010874] *24/07/1969*
Nodder Mrs M, (was Bradley), MCLIP, Asst.Catr., Bucks.Co.Council. [0001605] *12/01/1966*
Noden Miss BE, MCLIP, Asst.Lib., Ellesmere Port Br., Cheshire Co.L. [0010877] *07/05/1963*
Noel Ms LC, BA(Hons) PGDip MBA, p./t.Stud/Site Serv.Mgr., Manchester Met.Univ., Learning Cent.Univ.Huddersfield. [0059313] *02/02/2001*
Nokes Miss EM, MA FRGS MCLIP, RIBA Enterprises, London. [0010878] *14/01/1969*
Nolan Mrs CA, BA(Hons) MA MCLIP, Inf.Exec., CILIP. [0056356] *11/06/1998*
Nolan Miss S, BA(Hons) DipLIS, Unemployed. [0055139] *23/07/1997*
Norbury Mrs L, (was Pickavance), BSc MPhil, Liaison Lib., Univ.of Birmingham. [0043001] *02/06/1989*
Norcliffe Ms H, MA, Learning Res.Cent.Mgr., St.Damians R.C.High Sch., Ashton-under-Lyne. [0056773] *12/10/1998*
Norcott Miss CV, MA CertEd, Learning Resources Offr., Tiffin Girls Sch., Kingston upon Thames. [0044079] *26/04/1990*
Nordon Mrs JA, MSc MCLIP, Academic Serv.Mgr/Dep.Head L.Serv., Univ.Surrey. [0019531] *01/01/1961*
Noren Ms JA, MLS, Asst.Lib., Pub.Hlth.Lab.Serv., London. [0058587] *05/04/2000*
Norfolk Mr AJ, Asst.Lib.(Tech.Support), Salford Royal Hosp.NHS Trust. [0044855] *01/01/1991*
Norfolk Mrs EJW, Inf.Asst., Nat.Union of Teachers, London. [0054794] *02/04/1997*
Norfolk Ms SE, BSc DipLib MCLIP, Inf.Cent.Mgr., IHS Energy Grp., Tetbury, Glos. [0035043] *01/07/1982*
Norgrove Miss H, BA(Hons), Stud., Univ.Central England. [0060017] *26/11/2001*
Norkett Mr TJ, BA MA, Researcher, PricewaterhouseCoopers, London. [0049157] *08/10/1993*
Norledge Mrs DA, BA(Hons), Sen.L.Asst., Pendeford High Sch., Wolverhampton. [0056143] *06/03/1998*
Norman Ms AE, Asst.L.Mgr., Queens Crescent L. [0059317] *02/02/2001* **AF**
Norman Mrs CA, (was Lukes), BLib MCLIP, Sen.L.Mgr., Eltham L., Greenwich Council. [0022071] *16/01/1974*
Norman Miss CL, BEd(Hons) MA MCLIP, Team Leader, Ref., Reading L. [0050287] *01/06/1994*
Norman Miss EEA, MA MLib ARCM LRAM, Asst.Lib./p./t.Lib., St.Paul's Cathedral, London, American Internat.Univ.in London. [0046365] *30/10/1991*
Norman Mrs G, (was Wellings), BA MCLIP, Stock Mgr., Bracknell Forest Bor.Council, Bracknell, Berks. [0027573] *18/05/1977*
Norman Mrs J, BLib MCLIP, Learning Res.Mgr., Richard Huish Coll., Taunton. [0038140] *11/01/1985*
Norman Mr JF, BSc DipLib MCLIP, Lib., Nat.Inst.for Med.Res., London. [0032138] *29/01/1980*
Norman Mrs KF, BSc MSc, Employment not known. [0060359] *10/12/2001*
Norman Mrs LHM, (was St John), MCLIP, Lib., Neath & Port Talbot Coll., Neath Campus. [0012346] *01/01/1968*
Norman Miss MA, MCLIP, P./t.Sch.Lib., Addey & Stanhope Sch., London. [0019219] *18/01/1969*
Norman Mr MA, BA(Hons) MCLIP, Head of Res., Orton L., Peterborough C.C. [0052365] *26/10/1995*
Norman Mr MP, L.Mgr., Harwich. [0059413] *06/03/2001* **AF**
Norman Mr MW, BA(Hons), Dep.Lib., Regents Coll., London. [0055319] *01/10/1997*
Norman Mr N, BA MA DipInfSc MCLIP, Retired. [0030498] *09/02/1979*
Norman Mr N, BA MCLIP, Lib. (Support Serv.), L.B.of Greenwich, Plumstead L. [0029525] *18/09/1978*
Norman Mr P, MA MCLIP, Sen.Asst.Lib., Inst.of Advanced Legal Studies, London. [0010894] *21/01/1970*
Norman Mr PL, MCLIP, Unwaged. [0010895] *23/01/1961*
Norman Ms R, (was Filler), DipLib MCLIP, Pool Lib., Hammersmith & Fulham. [0033481] *05/01/1970*
Norman Miss SA, Lib., Inst.of Oriental Philosophy, Taplow. [0024037] *12/03/1975*
Norman Ms SA, BA DipLib FCLIP, Copyright Consultant, St.Albans. [0032451] *01/04/1980* **FE 27/07/1994**
Normaschild Ms J, BA(Hons) MSc, Client Serv.Exec., Dialog Corp., London. [0056970] *13/11/1998*
Normington Mr J, FCLIP, Retired. [0019220] *03/04/1945* **FE 01/01/1962**
Nornable Mrs J, (was Froggett), MCLIP, Unemployed. [0005241] *28/02/1965*
Noronha Miss AP, B Bus MCLIP, Faculty Lib., Edith Cowan Univ., Western Australia. [0017468] *06/01/1969*
Norris Mrs AM, LL B MCLIP, Asst.Lib., L.B.of Redbridge, L.Serv., Ilford, Essex. [0010898] *09/01/1971*
Norris Mr CF, BA DPA MCLIP, Retired. [0010899] *01/01/1961*
Norris Mr DJ, BA(Hons), Asst.Lib., Imperial Coll., Cent.L. [0052266] *20/10/1995*
Norris Mrs HE, (was Chapman), MA DipLib MCLIP, Lib., St.Gabriels Sch., Newbury. [0032894] *02/10/1980*
Norris Mrs M, (was Avery), MA DipLib MCLIP, Unemployed, 19 Meeks Rd., Arnold, Nottingham. [0000539] *14/10/1969*
Norris Mrs M, Inf.Mgr., Street Management, London. [0059829] *11/10/2001* **AF**

Norris Ms SD, BA MISM MCLIP, Unemployed, 65 Park Rise, Leicester LE3 6SG. [0025903] *01/04/1976*
Norry Miss JP, BA MA DipLib MCLIP, Dep.Learning Cent.Mgr., Leeds Met.Univ. [0039205] *01/01/1986*
North Ms A, MCLIP, Employment not known. [0060729] *12/12/2001*
North Miss AM, BA MCLIP, Asst.Lib., Ealing Cent.P.L. [0033916] *02/05/1981*
North Mr CR, BA(Hons) DipIM MCLIP, Ref.Lib., Fareham L., Hants.C.C. [0050737] *13/10/1994*
North Miss DL, L.Asst., Univ.of Greenwich, Avery Hill Campus. [0054938] *21/05/1997* **AF**
North Ms LP, BA DipLib MCLIP, L's.Mgr., Carlton W.Country, Plymouth. [0027772] *26/07/1977*
North Mr PM, BA MCLIP, Coll.Lib., S.Kent Coll. [0019222] *11/08/1972*
Northall Miss DM, MSC MCLIP, Asst.Lib., Univ.of Nottingham, George Green L. [0027000] *19/01/1977*
Northall Miss H, DipLib MCLIP, Lib., Mott Macdonald, Cambridge. [0033093] *20/10/1980*
Northam Miss J, BA(Hons) MA, Asst.Lib., Child.Serv., Barnsley M.B.C. [0056689] *05/10/1998*
Northey Mr DWA, BLib MCLIP, Lib.-Bibl.Support, E.Sussex Co.L., Lewes. [0028103] *01/10/1977*
Norton Mrs C, BA(Hons), Subject Lib., Bolton Inst.H.Ed., Chadwick L., Bolton. [0059866] *18/10/2001*
Norton Mr IC, BLIB MCLIP, Cent.Support Lib., Univ.of Plymouth. [0021585] *29/10/1973*
Norton Mr JCW, MA MCLIP, Honorary Research Associate, Liverpool Hope. [0010914] *26/06/1968*
Norton Mr P, BSc MCLIP, Retired. [0060773] *12/12/2001*
Norwell Miss M, MA MCLIP, Retired. [0026498] *04/10/1976*
Norwood Miss MR, BA(Hons) MCLIP, Grp.Lib., Birmingham L.Serv. [0020264] *23/02/1973*
Norwood Mr R, BA MCLIP, Adult Lend.Serv.Lib., Medway Council, Stroud L. [0010919] *09/10/1969*
Nother Miss M, BA MCLIP, Sen.Lib., Hazel Grove L., Stockport. [0042361] *25/10/1988*
Notman Ms M, (was Bailey), MTh(Hons) DipLIS MCLIP, Career Break. [0042125] *04/10/1988*
Nott Miss SA, BA(Hons) MSc MCLIP, Subject Lib., PCFE, Plymouth. [0055669] *07/11/1997*
Nottage Mr BL, BA MA PGCE MCLIP, Temp.p./t.Lect., Univ.of Huddersfield. [0027841] *16/09/1977*
Nowacki-Chmielowiec Mrs CM, (was Nowacki), BA(Hons) DipLib MCLIP, Retired. [0033095] *06/10/1980*
Nowakowska Mrs KE, (was Hill), BSc MA MCLIP, Res.Lib., N.Ayrshire Council, Irvine. [0024425] *04/08/1975*
Nowell Mr GFH, BA FCLIP, Life Member, Tel.0274 573000. [0010925] *03/10/1950* **FE 01/01/1955**
Nowell Ms TC, MCLIP, Subject Spec.-Inf.Resources Cent., St Mary's Coll., Twickenham. [0033494] *15/01/1981*
Nowocin Ms MJ, BA(Hons), Stud. [0043530] *03/11/1989*
Nuawanda Miss P, BSc, Stud. [0061473] *05/08/2002*
Nugent Mrs DM, p./t.Stud./Princ.L.Mgr., Omagh L., Local Studies Dept. [0061130] *19/02/2002*
Nugent Mr GT, BA(Hons) DipILM MCLIP, Resources Mgr., N.E.Lincs.Council, Grimsby Cent.L. [0047781] *14/10/1992*
Nugent Miss MCR, MCLIP, Retired. [0010930] *09/09/1957*
Nundy Mrs DJ, (was Smith), BA(Hons), P./t.Stud.,L.Asst., Hertford Regional Coll., Robert Gordon Univ. [0059670] *25/07/2001*
Nunn Mrs HM, (was Barnes), BSc MSc MCLIP, Project Mgr., Open Univ., Milton Keynes. [0027885] *04/10/1977*
Nunn Mrs JL, (was Darker), BA QTS MCLIP, Supply Teacher, Staffs.LEA. [0010932] *22/02/1967*
Nunn Ms RL, BA(Hons) MA MCLIP, Asst.Lib., Westminster Sch., London. [0056519] *03/08/1998*
Nunn Mrs RMJ, BA(Hons) MA, Inf.Researcher, Dept.of Trade & Ind., London. [0058489] *25/02/2000*
Nurcombe Miss LN, (was Weaver), BA(Hons) DipLib CMS MCLIP, Unemployed. [0044504] *17/10/1990*
Nurcombe Mrs VJ, (was Bradfield), BA MCLIP, freelance Inf.Consultant, Cheshire. [0001591] *18/09/1969*
Nurden Mrs J, (was Horseman), Asst.Dir., Royal Military Coll.of Sci., Cranfield Univ., Swindon. [0045965] *29/07/1991*
Nurse Mr EB, MA FSA MCLIP, Lib., Society of Antiquaries of London. [0010934] *19/01/1970*
Nurse Mr RA, BA MA MCLIP, Electronic Inf.Serv.Mgr., Barnet Cultural Serv. [0036443] *14/10/1983*
Nutkins Mrs GP, BA MA MCLIP, Lib., L.B.of Bromley. [0042615] *27/01/1989*
Nutsford Miss SG, BA PGCE DipLib MCLIP, Lib., Imperial Coll.of Sci.Tech.& Med., London. [0031401] *05/10/1979*
Nutt Mrs MC, (was Dryland), Lib., Abbey Sch., Reading. [0018648] *01/10/1972*
Nuttall Mr BS, BA MCLIP, Life Member, 10 Edgerton Court, Tadcaster, N.Yorks.,LS24 9NZ. [0010937] *01/10/1960*
Nuttall Mr CG, Stud., Manchester Metro.Univ. [0061833] *14/11/2002*
Nuttall Mrs JM, (was Burns), Unemployed. [0045776] *23/05/1991*
Nuttall Ms PA, BA MLS MCLIP, Catr., The Stationary Office, London. [0030783] *04/04/1979*
Nutton Miss A, BA(Hons) DipLib, Lib., Univ.of Notre Dame, London. [0055845] *25/11/1997*
Nwajei Mrs EF, BA MCLIP, Unemployed. [0015177] *01/01/1968*
Nwosu Miss GMI, Lib., Standards Org.of Nigeria. [0059760] *19/09/2001*
Nwude Mrs C, Head (L.& Inf.Serv.), Securities & Exchange Comm., Garki-Abuja. [0061500] *21/08/2002*
Nyawanda Miss P, BSc, Stud. [0061505] *02/09/2002*
Nye Mr DV, BA MCLIP, Arun Area Lib., Arun Grp., W.Sussex C.C.L.Serv. [0030499] *27/01/1979*

Nylinder Miss AM, BA MA, Customer Serv.Lib., L.B.of Brent. [0055411] 10/10/1997
Nzacahayo Mrs H, (was Ayinkamiye), Unemployed. [0056111] 20/02/1998
O Doibhlin Mr C, BA(Hons) MLib, Lib., Cardinal O Fiaich L.& Arch., Armagh. [0049286] 20/10/1993
O Doibhlin Mrs DL, (was McKeefry), BA(Hons) DipLIS, Asst.Lib., Dundalk Inst.of Tech., Co.Louth. [0051789] 01/07/1995
O'Beirne Mr R, BA(Hons), Sen.Inf.Offr., Shipley L., Bradford M.D.C. [0047150] 12/05/1992
O'Boyle Mr J, BSc MSc MCLIP, Employment not known. [0060618] 11/12/2001
O'Brien Miss AF, BA MCLIP ALIA, Retired, [0025619] 30/01/1976
O'Brien Miss BA, BA(Hons), Stud., Manchester Metro.Univ. [0061671] 16/10/2002
O'Brien Miss BM, BSc DipLIB MCLIP, p./t.Lib., Zurich Risk Serv., Birmingham. [0033735] 09/02/1981
O'Brien Mr C, MCLIP, Research Lib., BBC, Bristol. [0019835] 02/01/1973
O'Brien Miss CE, BA MSc, Dep.Lib., Masons, London. [0054571] 28/01/1997
O'Brien Mrs E, (was Plummer), BA MCLIP, Life Member. [0010952] 20/02/1960
O'Brien Miss F, BA HDE DLIS MCLIP, Reader Development, London Borough of Harringey. [0043339] 23/10/1989
O'Brien Ms FG, MA MCLIP, Project Mgr., BBC Factual & Learning, BBC/LA L.Project. [0036644] 27/10/1983
O'Brien Mrs HM, (was Blair), BA(Hons), Sen.L.Asst., Redcar & Cleveland Bor.Council, Brotton L. [0045719] 07/05/1991
O'Brien Mrs JA, (was Currie), BA MCLIP, Asst.Lib., Worcestershire C.C. [0039386] 21/01/1986
O'Brien Miss K, MA DipLib MCLIP, Employment not known. [0037722] 09/10/1984
O'Brien Miss MJ, MCLIP, Child.Co-ordinator, L.B.of Sutton. [0010954] 20/03/1970
O'Brien Mrs MPG, (was Pollock), MCLIP, Inf.Researcher, Halliburton (UK) Ltd., Leatherhead. [0011789] 07/11/1970
O'Brien Mrs P, (was Hodges), BA(Hons) MCLIP, Lend.Serv.Lib., Chichester L., W.Sussex. [0029905] 24/10/1978
O'Byrne Miss M, DIP LIP FLAI, Retired. [0017482] 01/01/1962
O'Byrne Ms S, (was Lefolii), MCLIP, Resident in Canada. [0060093] 07/12/2001
O'Callaghan Miss EM, BA DipLIB MCLIP, Sen.Lib., Kent C.C.Educ.& L., Cent.L., Maidstone. [0022944] 01/10/1974
O'Callaghan Ms EM, BA MCLIP, Site Lib., Chelsea Coll.of Art & Design, London Inst. [0029775] 01/10/1978
O'Callaghan Mrs MC, BSc PGCE MSc MCLIP, Field Co-Ordinator, Scholastic Ltd., Coventry. [0037468] 01/10/1984
O'Callaghan Mrs R, BPharm MScMRPharms MCLIP, Employment not known. [0060639] 11/12/2001
O'Callaghan Mrs SM, MCLIP, Lib., N.Warwickshire & Hinckley Coll., Hinckley, Leics. [0020121] 19/01/1973
O'Callaghan Mrs SP, (was Lamerton), BA MCLIP, Unemployed. [0033022] 13/10/1980
O'Carroll Miss A, BA DipILS, Unemployed. [0054846] 17/04/1997
O'Connell Miss CA, Inf.Offr., Charles Russell, London. [0041699] 18/02/1988
O'Connell Mr D, BA(Hons) MSc, Stud., Leeds Metro.Univ. [0061591] 02/10/2002
O'Connell Edwards Ms LA, BA MA MCLIP, Lib., Lend.& Inf.Serv., Bromsgrove L. [0042336] 12/10/1988
O'Connor Miss BA, (was Gilroy), BSc MCLIP, Unemployed. [0010961] 30/04/1964
O'Connor Ms E, DipLIS, Inf.Specialist, Yell Group Ltd., Reading. [0058815] 07/08/2000
O'Connor Mrs G, (was Veriod), BA MCLIP, Lib., Inf.Point, Neston Cheshire C.C. [0035919] 17/01/1983
O'Connor Miss J, MSc, Research Consultant, Off.of Govt.Comm., Norwich. [0057467] 29/03/1999
O'Connor Mr K, Inf.Specialist, NBS Serv., Newcastle upon Tyne. [0047784] 17/01/1992
O'Connor Ms LA, BA DipLIB MCLIP MA, Inst.Lib., Dundalk Inst.of Tech., Republic of Ireland. [0033761] 12/02/1981
O'Connor Ms MB, BA(Hons) DipLib PGCE MCLIP, Lib., Manchester L., Crumpsall L. [0052528] 01/01/1967
O'Connor Ms MG, Catg.Asst., John Rylands Univ.L., Manchester. [0052542] 06/11/1995
O'Connor Mrs MI, (was Absolon), BA(Hons) MCLIP, Unemployed, 37 Northiam, Woodside Park, London, N12 7ET. [0022705] 13/09/1974
O'Connor Mrs MJ, (was Lane), BA MCLIP, Class Teacher, Birmingham City Council. [0030324] 18/01/1979
O'Connor Ms MM, P./t.Stud./Sen.L.Asst., Univ.of Wales, Aberystwyth, Univ.of Limerick, Ireland, Malvern L. [0059736] 10/09/2001
O'Connor Mrs RM, (was Cooke), MCLIP, Tutor/Lib., (HMP Send), Surrey Co.L.(N.W.Area), Runnymead Cent., Addlestone. [0003083] 21/09/1970
O'Connor Mrs S, Lifelong Learning Offr., SCRAN, Edinburgh. [0061456] 01/08/2002 **AF**
O'Connor Mrs SA, (was Kemp), BA(Hons) DipIS MCLIP, Lib., Keighley & W.Area, Bradford Counc. [0056200] 01/04/1998
O'Dell Ms C, BSc(Hons) MSc MCLIP, Inf.Scientist, CERN, Geneva. [0052383] 30/10/1995
O'Dell Mrs TL, (was Gordon-Cumming), BA(Hons) MCLIP, Position Unknown, Worcs.C.C., Malvern L. [0042314] 21/10/1988
O'Deorain Mr FA, BSc DipLIB MCLIP, L.Inf.Serv.Offr., N.Western Health Board, Letterkenny, Co.Donegal. [0033235] 10/10/1980
O'Deorain Mrs S, (was Hodgson), B Lib MCLIP, Homemaker. [0034640] 19/01/1982
O'Doherty Ms EMG, BA(Hons) MA PGCE, p./t.Stud./Tutor, Manchester Met.Univ. [0059996] 16/11/2001

O'Doherty Mrs PA, (was Bell), MCLIP, Inf.Offr., Medway Council, Chatham L. [0001088] 10/01/1966
O'Donnell Miss CMA, L.Asst., Bovingdon L. [0059557] 16/05/2001 **AF**
O'Donnell Mrs ME, BA DipLib, Lib., W.Dunbartonshire Council, Educ.Dept. [0046280] 22/10/1991
O'Donnell Mrs ML, (was Killett), MCLIP, Lib., Thomas Bennett Comm.Coll., Crawley. [0019944] 15/01/1973
O'Donoghue Ms KM, BA DipLib MCLIP, p./t.Sch.Lib., Harrytown Catholic High Sch., Stockport. [0026000] 03/04/1976
O'Donohue Miss KJ, BA(Hons), Grad.Trainee, Exeter Univ. [0061113] 21/02/2002
O'Donovan Mrs K, (was Wood), BA MCLIP, Asst.Dir., Head of Div.of Inf.Serv.& Systems, Sheffield Univ.L. [0021191] 28/09/1973
O'Dornan Mrs PEM, (was Reilly), BA(Hons) DipLIS, Unemployed. [0052164] 10/10/1995
O'Driscoll Mrs CA, (was Archer), BA MCLIP, Sen.Researcher, S.G.Warburg, London. [0038040] 17/01/1985
O'Driscoll Ms G, BA DipLib, p./t.Lib., L.B.of Brent, Willesden Green L. [0037156] 15/01/1984
O'Dwyer Miss MM, Sub-Lib., Univ.Coll.,Dublin. [0027551] 01/05/1977
O'Flynn Miss HY, BA MCLIP, Lib., Dept.of Trade & Ind., London. [0041031] 03/10/1987
O'Grady Ms JMK, (was Hogan), BSc(Econ) MCLIP, Young Readers Lib., Jersey L., Jersey. [0053022] 06/02/1996
O'Hara Mrs A, MA, Stud., Thames Valley Univ., L.Asst., Cent.Milton Keynes L., Milton Keynes. [0058040] 20/10/1999
O'Hara Mr K, BA MCLIP, Retired. [0010981] 20/05/1963
O'Hara Mr R, MBE FCLIP, Retired. [0017499] 02/03/1963 **FE 19/05/1978**
O'Hara Mrs SH, BLib, Unemployed. [0058765] 10/07/2000
O'Hare Miss C, BA MCLIP, Sen Lecturer, Univ.of N.London. [0035394] 15/10/1982
O'Hare Mr LJ, BA(Hons) DipEd DipLIB MCLIP, L.Asst., Belfast Educ.& L.Board. [0039920] 02/10/1986
O'Hare Miss R, MA DipILS, Trainee Lib., Bell Coll., Hamilton. [0056787] 15/10/1999
O'Hare Mrs S, (was Eglintine), MCLIP, Reader Services(Job share), Sale L., Sale, Trafford. [0010982] 19/02/1963
O'Hare Ms UH, BA DipLib MCLIP, Unemployed. [0037557] 12/10/1984
O'Kane Mr Q, MA MCLIP, Ch.Lib., Bournemouth & Poole Coll.of F.E., Poole. [0029469] 22/08/1978
O'Kelly Ms JL, BA MCLIP, Sch.Lib., Sch.L.Serv., Bucks.Co.L. [0022651] 29/07/1974
O'Leary Mrs A, (was Savage), MCLIP, Lib., Special Serv., L.& Heritage, Derbys.C.C. [0061364] 01/01/1967
O'Leary Miss BH, BA(Hons), L.& Inf.Asst., Hammond Suddards Edge, London. [0057222] 20/11/1992 **AF**
O'Leary Miss R, BA(Hons) MSc MCLIP, Web Editor, NBS Serv., Newcastle-upon-Tyne. [0048271] 20/11/1992
O'Mahony Miss K, BA, Stud., Univ.of Wales, Aberystwyth [0061352] 11/06/2002
O'Mahony Ms M, BA MA HDipLIS, Asst.Lib., RTE Stills L., Dublin. [0061252] 25/04/2002
O'Mahony Mrs NM, (was McConkey), Catr., BBC Inf.& Arch. [0056290] 28/04/1998
O'Malley Miss SM, BSc, Inf.Offr.(Temp.), E.London Tower Hamlets NHS Trust, London. [0053163] 01/04/1996
O'Meara Ms M, MA, Electronic Inf.Offr., Research Council for Comp.Med., London. [0056693] 05/10/1998
O'Neil Ms JA, BA MCLIP, Lib., Brighton & Hove Council. [0044160] 14/06/1990
O'Neil Miss KJ, BA MCLIP, Princ.Lib.-Youth Serv., Bedford C.C. [0041726] 24/02/1988
O'Neill Ms A, BA MA, Inf.Offr., Eversheds, London. [0055698] 04/11/1997
O'Neill Ms C, BSc(Hons), Loans Lib., Scottish Parliament Inf.Cent., Edinburgh. [0059392] 27/02/2001
O'Neill Miss CJ, MCLIP, Life Member. [0011016] 18/03/1959
O'Neill Mr DJ, MCLIP, Head of Learning Res., Anglo European Coll.of Chiropractic, Bournemouth. [0027202] 14/01/1977
O'Neill Mr FJ, BA DipLIB MCLIP, Asst.Lib., Southern Educ.& L.Board, Armagh. [0031012] 28/06/1979
O'Neill Mrs GC, (was Bromiley), BA MCLIP, Unemployed. [0030116] 14/01/1979
O'Neill Ms HA, BA MSc, Asst.Lib., Barbican L., London. [0046456] 07/11/1991
O'Neill Mrs HG, (was Hayes), BA MCLIP, Retired. [0006595] 22/01/1969
O'Neill Miss JV, BLS MA MCLIP, Coll.Lib., Fermanagh Coll.of F.E., W.E.L.B., N.Ireland. [0027085] 01/01/1977
O'Neill Mr LM, BA(Hons) MA, Asst.Systems Lib., Univ.of Luton. [0054074] 24/10/1996
O'Neill Mr MS, BSc MCLIP, Employment unknown. [0060567] 11/12/2001
O'Neill Mrs N, Stud., Univ.of Brighton. [0057324] 09/02/1999
O'Neill Mrs P, BA DipLib MCLIP, Inf.Lib., London Guildhall Univ., London. [0039279] 08/01/1986
O'Neill Ms R, BA, Sen.L.Asst., Univ.of Wales Coll.Newport, Allt-Yr-Yn Campus. [0058631] 20/04/2000
O'Rafferty Mrs S, BA HDipEd DLIS, Lib., Royal Irish Academy, Dublin. [0052920] 09/01/1996
O'Regan Mr JA, BA MCLIP, Lib., City & Islington Coll., London. [0028353] 03/11/1977
O'Reilly Mr JC, MA ALAI MCLIP, Managing Dir., Aisling Inf.Systems Ltd., Ireland. [0060115] 07/12/2001
O'Rourke Mr DT, BSc MCLIP DipHSW, Retired. [0011038] 01/01/1953
O'Shaughnessy Mr PE, BA(Hons) DipLib, Asst.Lib., Univ.of the W.of England, Bristol. [0047447] 18/08/1992
O'Shea Miss LH, L.Asst., Barbican L., London. [0058201] 16/11/1999

Personal Members

O'Shea Miss NM, Pg Dip BA(Hons), Inf.Scientist, Inst.of Marine Engineers, London. [0052335]   30/10/1995
O'Sullivan Miss CA, BA MCLIP, IRC Systems Co-ordinator, St.Marys Coll., Twickenham. [0035507]   14/10/1982
O'Sullivan Mrs CL, (was Swain), BA(Hons) MA MCLIP, Unemployed. [0049174]   08/10/1993
O'Sullivan Mr KMC, BA(Hons) MA MSc(Econ) MCLIP, Asst.Lib./Lib.i/c., Wellcome Unit for the Hist.of Med., Univ.of Oxford. [0052814]   18/12/1995
O'Sullivan Mr NP, BA(Hons) MA MCLIP, Unemployed. [0054367] 25/11/1996
O'Sullivan Miss S, Revenue Asst., Inland Revenue, Liverpool. [0048096]   06/11/1992
O'Sullivan Ms S, BSc MA, Stud., City Univ. [0061315]   17/05/2002
O'Sullivan Mr TJ, BSc(Hons) MSc, Inf.Offr., Clifford Chance, LLP, London. [0056090]   06/02/1998
O'Toole Mrs CA, (was Hill), MCLIP, Lib., Notts C.C., Newark L. [0011071]   09/01/1967
O'Toole Miss PM, MCLIP, Lib., Cambs.L.& Inf., Co.L.H.Q. [0011073]   01/01/1970
Oades Miss C, MSc, Mgr. Business Inf. Serv., Institute of Directors, London. [0060983]   23/01/2002
Oakden Mr S, BA MCLIP DipHE, Learning Res.Cent.Mgr., York Coll. [0021755]   08/01/1974
Oakes Mr PB, BA, Stud./p./t.Inf.Asst., City Univ./CBA, London. [0061569]   02/10/2002
Oakes Ms RM, BSc MSc(Econ), Asst.Subject Lib., Oxford Brookes Univ., Headington. [0055374]   06/10/1997
Oakley Ms A, BA, Stud., Univ.Strathclyde. [0059702]   14/08/2001
Oakley Mrs AE, (was Cowan), BA DipLib MCLIP, p./t.Sch.Lib., Dame Allans Sch., Newcastle upon Tyne. [0030387]   08/02/1979
Oakley Ms HJ, BA(Hons) MA MCLIP, Team Leader - User Serv., Royal Inst.of Chartered Srveyors, London. [0044389]   03/10/1990
Oakley Mrs JE, (was Tompkins), BA MCLIP, Prin.Lib., Inf.Serv., W.Sussex C.C , Worthing. [0036278]   01/10/1983
Oakley Ms TC, BA MSt MA MCLIP, Research Stud., Dept.of Archaeology, Southampton Univ. [0049592]   19/11/1993
Oaten Mrs AM, (was Maxwell), MCLIP, Retired. [0010945]   06/03/1964
Oates Mrs CE, (was Bignell), BA(Hons), Data Inputter,(Temp.), CYREN, London. [0052262]   19/10/1995
Oates Miss JL, BA(Hons) MA MCLIP, Site Serv.Mgr., Taylor L., Univ.of Aberdeen. [0049233]   14/10/1993
Oates Ms LK, MA BSc DMS MCLIP AIL MILT, Head of Dept.of Learning Tech.Supp., Univ.of Gloucestershire. [0014810]   01/01/1969
Oates Mrs M, (was Lawson), MCLIP, Life Member. [0010946]   26/03/1944
Obasi Mrs IF, BA, Unemployed. [0058585] 04/04/2000
Obasi Mr JU, MA MCLIP, Unemployed. [0010950]   31/01/1962
Oberhauser Dr OC, FCLIP, Consortium Offr., Fed.Min.of Educ.,Sci.& Culture, The Austrian L.Network, Vienna. [0041161]   15/10/1987 FE 18/11/1998
Oberwarth Mr MA, BA, Inf.Offr., Nabarro Nathanson, London. [0058503]   08/03/2000
Obieze Ms B, BSc, Med.Records L.Clerk, Royal Brompton Hospital, London. [0052577]   08/11/1995
Ochia Dr BA, BSc PhD MSc CBiol MIBi MCLIP, Employment not known. [0060229]   10/12/2001
Ocock Mr KF, MCLIP, Comm.Ref.Lib., Fendalton, Christchurch City L., New Zealand. [0010960]   05/10/1970
Oda Mr M, BEd MA, Associate Prof., Aoyama Gakuin Univ., Tokyo, Japan. [0050501]   22/08/1994
Oddone Ms N, Asst.Prof., Inst.de Ciencia da Inf., Univ.Fed.da Bahia, Brazil. [0061539]   17/09/2002
Oddy Miss EJ, BA(Hons) MSc MCLIP, Hybrid Systems Mgr., Univ.of Wolverhampton. [0042270]   13/10/1988
Oddy Mrs JM, (was Owen), BA MCLIP, Life Member. [0011100]   24/03/1954
Oddy Mrs JME, (was Fitch), BA DipIS MCLIP, Lib., Bradford Council. [0048486]   22/01/1993
Odeinde Mrs WA, (was Fafunwa), MCLIP, Ch.Lib., Cent.L., Ebute-Metta, Lagos, Nigeria. [0022100]   19/03/1956
Odintsov Mr IN, Unemployed. [0043801] 15/01/1990
Offord Mrs JA, L.Manager/Open Learn.Co-Ordinator. [0059546] 04/05/2001 AF
Offord Mrs JD, (was Brown), BEd(Hons) DipLib MCLIP, Advisory Lib., Sch.L.Serv., Suffolk C.C. [0036744]   25/11/1983
Ogden Mr DB, MCLIP, Retired. [0010973] 02/03/1962
Ogden Mr DJ, LLB DipLib MCLIP, Unemployed. [0036745]   24/11/1983
Ogilvie Miss HD, MA DipLib MCLIP, Sen.Asst.Lib.,p./t., Harrow L. [0036507]   07/10/1983
Ogilvie Mrs KL, (was Welsby), BA MCLIP, Unemployed. [0030569]   15/01/1979
Ogleby Miss JA, P./t.Home-based Indexer, Transport Research Lab., Berks. [0037894]   23/10/1994
Ogundipe Mr OO, MA FCLIP, L.Consultant, Retired, London & Nigeria. [0017495]   20/02/1957   FE 01/01/1968
Ogunsola Dr BL, BA(Hons) MSc PhD MCLIP, Catr., Leics.L.& Inf.Servs., Glenfield. [0056060] 19/01/1998
Oji Mr CA, BSc BSc MEd, Learning Res.Asst., S.Bank Univ., Whipps Cross Hosp. [0056016]   19/01/1998
Okabe Mrs V, Stud., Liverpool John Moores. [0061652]   14/10/2002
Okello Mr F, Resource Asst., Lewisham Coll., London. [0056534] 10/08/1998
Okemadu Mrs TN, BA(Hons) MA MCLIP, Asst.Lib., M.O.D L., London. [0050607]   01/10/1994
Okewole Mrs FRA, MCLIP, Lib./Project Arch., American Baptist Churches USA. [0021297]   15/10/1973
Okoro Mr IO, MLS MCLIP, Unemployed. [0010987]   20/03/1963
Oktay Mrs SC, (was Connolly), BA(Hons) DipLib, Unemployed. [0047611]   06/10/1992

Okure Miss C, BLS MCLIP, p./t.Asst.Learning Cent.Co-ord., Hammersmith & W.London Coll. [0049925]   24/01/1994
Okwuonu Miss UA, BSc, Unemployed. [0058868]   15/09/2000
Oladjins Ms E, MA DipILS MCLIP, L.Asst., Aberdeenshire L.& Inf.Serv., Oldmeldrum. [0057098]   09/12/1998
Olafsson Mr S, MSc, Systems Lib., Nat.& Univ.L.of Iceland, Arngrimsgata. [0059026]   23/10/2000
Olamigoke Mrs OA, MA BLS, Poly.Lib., Federal Poly., Ilaro, Ogun State. [0043154]   16/08/1989
Old Ms SA, BA DipLib, L.Serv.Mgr., Oxon.Mental Healthcare NHS Trust, Oxford. [0035265]   05/10/1982
Oldcorn Mrs DS, (was Myles), BA(Hons) DipLib, Merchandiser. [0032448]   01/04/1980
Olden Dr EA, BA MLS PhD FCLIP, Sen.Lect., Thames Valley Univ. [0017512]   23/07/1972   FE 12/09/2001
Oldfield Mrs CA, (was Sullivan), BA(Hons) MCLIP, Unemployed. [0039190]   06/01/1986
Oldfield Mrs DM, (was Hudson), FCLIP, Life Member. [0007358]   08/03/1940 FE 01/01/1954
Oldfield Ms JM, BSc MCLIP MCLIP MA, Asst.Dir.-Inf.Serv., R.I.B.A., London. [0030859]   27/04/1979
Oldham Miss CA, BA MA DipLib MCLIP, Lib., Forestry Commission, Forest Research Station,Farnham,Sy. [0033330]   20/11/1980
Oldham Miss ME, BSc(Econ) MCLIP, Sch.Lib., Welshpool High School. [0010994]   26/09/1962
Oldman Mrs H, MA MA MCLIP, Head of Learning Res., Leeds Grammar Sch. [0053848]   04/10/1996
Oldridge Mrs RV, (was Berry), BA(Hons), Inf.Offr., Univ.of Herts., Hertford. [0057633]   03/06/1999
Oldroyd Mrs ME, (was Spencer), BA MLib MCLIP, Staff & Quality Devel.Mgr., De Montfort Univ., Leicester. [0013811]   01/10/1970
Oldroyd Mr P, MCLIP, Ch.Lib., Leics.C.C. [0010998]   13/10/1965
Oldroyd Miss RC, LIS Stud., Sheffield Univ. [0058371]   31/01/2000
Oldroyd Mr RE, BA MA DipLib FCLIP, Dir.of L.Serv., Univ.of Nottingham L. [0030344]   15/02/1968   FE 25/05/1994
Oledzka Miss EE, MA MA, Lib., The British Musuem, London. [0061598]   03/10/2002
Oliff Mrs L, Learning Cent.Facilitator, Southwark Coll., London. [0051608]   10/04/1995 AF
Oliff Ms WJ, BA, Journals Lib., Bucks.Chilterns Univ.Coll. [0043449]   26/10/1999
Olive Mr JM, MA MCLIP, Lect.(Local Hist.), Self-employed, Sheffield. [0011001]   29/10/1964
Oliver Mr A, Sales Consultant, epixtech Ltd. [0045264]   20/09/1990 AF
Oliver Mrs FME, (was Lougheed), BA(Hons) DipLib MCLIP, p./t.L.Asst., Univ.of Hull. [0021127]   01/01/1973
Oliver Miss GM, BA DipLib MCLIP, Comm.Lib.(Burton on Trent), Staffs.C.C. [0023104]   26/10/1974
Oliver Ms HL, BA MCLIP, Asst.Lib., Tavistock L., Tavistock & Portman, NHS Trust, London. [0038789]   08/10/1985
Oliver Mr IC, BA(Hons) DipInf/Lib, Help Desk Lib., Keele Univ.Inf.Serv., Staffs. [0042916]   14/10/1989
Oliver Mrs J, (was Crowther), Inf.Offr.-Purchasing, Univ.of Teesside, L.& Inf.Servs., Middlesbrough. [0047344] 17/07/1992 AF
Oliver Mrs JA, BA(Hons) MA MCLIP, Team Lib., Selly Oak Hosp., Birmingham. [0055779]   17/11/1997
Oliver Mrs JM, (was Gulliford), BSc(Hons) MCLIP, Serv.Devel.Lib., L.B.of Bexley, Thamesmead. [0049732]   25/11/1993
Oliver Miss JS, BA MCLIP, Lifelong Learning Lib., Bor.of Poole. [0011002]   17/03/1971
Oliver Miss KM, BA MCLIP, Retired. [0019055]   09/12/1963
Oliver Miss LS, MSc MA, Inf.& Training Offr., Ashridge. [0051385] 01/02/1995
Oliver Ms P, BA MCLIP, Unemployed. [0027119]   07/10/1970
Oliver Miss SM, BA(Hons), Unemployed. [0055789]   24/11/1997
Oliver Mr T, BA(Hons), Stud., Univ.of Strathclyde. [0061029]   07/02/2002
Oliver-Watts Mrs J, (was Harvey), BA(Hons) MCLIP, Inf.Offr., Univ.of Cent.Lancashire., Sumbria Campus L. [0020479]   03/04/1973
Olizar Ms EM, MCLIP, Employment unknown. [0060341]   01/01/2001
Ollerenshaw Mrs HE, BA(Hons) MSc DMS MCLIP, Patient Inf.Mgr., N.Bristol NHS Trust. [0056165]   01/04/1998
Ollerton Miss J, MCLIP MIMgt, Dir.of Communication, Construction Ltd. [0011008]   15/03/1963
Ollier Mrs AC, (was Purnell), MCLIP, Customer Care Mgr., Holt Jackson Book Co.Ltd., Lytham,Lancs. [0012051]   18/05/1970
Olliver Mrs AS, BA MCLIP, Community Lib., Stalybridge L., Tameside M.B.C. [0021919]   30/01/1974
Olney Ms SD, MA DipLib MCLIP, H.of Collection Storage, Brit.L., Scholarship & Collections. [0035220]   07/10/1982
Olsen Mr AJ, BA MCLIP, Arts L.& Mus.Mgr., Southwark Council. [0011009]   01/04/1970
Oluikpe Mr P, BLS, Stud., Loughborough Univ. [0060918]   10/01/2002
Omissi Mrs L, BA(Hons) MA MCLIP, Lend.Lib., Jersey L., St.Helier. [0055019]   01/07/1997
Omokaro Mr GN, BSc(Hons), Unemployed. [0059695]   08/08/2001
Omotayo Mrs M, BA(Hons) PGCert, p./t.Stud./Eurodirect Mgr., Univ.Coll.London, Med.Control Agency. [0061052]   01/02/2002
Onasanya Mr OO, BA MA, Inf.Offr., The Brit.L., Business Inf.Serv., London. [0057776]   02/08/1999
Oni Ms S, BA(Hons) MSc, Senior Libr.Asst., Woolwich, [0061840] 15/11/2002
Onyekpe Ms ON, BSc(Hons) MSc, Inf.Offr., Council for Environment, Reading. [0059884]   29/10/2001 AF
Ooi Mr KWT, BA(Hons) HND DipLib, Grad.Trainee., Tunbrige Wells L., Kent. [0059479]   05/04/2001
Oparinde Mr SA, BSc(Hons) MSc DipIM, Inf.Lib., Cent.L., L.B.of Enfield. [0047518]   22/09/1992

319

Oppenheim Prof C, BSc PhD FCLIP HonFCLIP, Dept.of Inf.Sci., Loughborough Univ., Leics. [0046639] 29/11/1991
FE 16/09/1992
Oram Mrs IL, (was Tocock), MCLIP, Computer Operator, Mendip Curriculum Serv.Ltd., Tiverton, Devon. [0011024] 03/03/1962
Oram Mrs MA, (was Hamer-Jones), MCLIP, Retired. [0006191] 31/01/1969
Ord Miss S, BA MCLIP, Unemployed. [0042169] 06/10/1988
Ordidge Mrs I, BSc DipLib MCLIP, Learning Cent.Mgr., Univ.of Wolverhampton. [0033648] 20/01/1981
Orford Mr JP, MCLIP, Employment not known. [0050658] 05/10/1994
Organ Mrs CH, (was Macpherson), MA DipLib MCLIP, L.Offr.-Inf., Co.Ref.& Inf.L., Cornwall C.C. [0036753] 21/11/1983
Organ Ms ML, Inf.Offr., Sheffield Healthline. [0055741] 11/11/1997
Orgill Mr AA, MA DipLib MCLIP, Sen.Lib., Royal Military Academy Sandhurst, Camberley. [0031409] 05/10/1979
Orme Mrs SP, (was Renn), MSc BSc MCLIP, Unemployed. [0047288] 03/07/1992
Ormiston Ms TM, BA MA MSc MCLIP, Employment not known. [0060507] 11/12/2001
Orna Ms E, MA DipLib PhD FCLIP, Employment unknown. [0060565] 11/12/2001 FE 01/04/2002
Orna Ms MM, (was Bell), MA MCLIP, Neigbourhood Lib., Bristol L.Serv. [0001086] 02/10/1971
Orpen Mrs A, (was Henwood), MCLIP BSc, Librarian, Gateway High School, Zimbabwe. [0020275] 21/02/1973
Orr Mr AJ, BMus, Stud., Univ.Aberystwyth. [0059970] 14/11/2001
Orr Miss L, MA(Hons), Stud., Univ.of Strathclyde. [0059959] 12/11/2001
Orr Mrs LM, (was Wright), MCLIP, Unemployed. [0016356] 05/12/1970
Orr Mrs P, (was White), BA(Hons) DipILS, Unemployed. [0046673] 06/12/1991
Orsborn Ms LEA, MA MCLIP, Dir. of Inf., Shell Int's Ltd., London. [0021657] 05/01/1974
Ortega Miss MS, BA (Hons) MLib MCLIP, Inf.Training Officer, Lincs.C.C., Lincoln. [0048093] 06/11/1992
Ortiz-Jimenez Mr L, DipLib, Customer Serv.Consultant, Sirsi Iberia S.L., Madrid, Spain. [0052719] 27/11/1995
Orton Mr GIJ, BA MSc DMA FRSA MILAM MIMgt MCLIP, Best Value Mgr., N.Herts Dist.Co. [0011046] 25/01/1968
Orton Mr R, MA(Hons) MSc, Sen.L.Asst.-Bibl.Serv., Homerton Coll., Cambridge. [0057216] 20/01/1999
Orton Ms VE, BA MCLIP, L.Projects Co-ordinator, Royal Coll.of Nursing, Leeds. [0041759] 18/03/1988
Orzechowska Ms J, MA DipLib, Catg. Team Super., Mann L., Univ. of Edinburgh. [0060959] 21/01/2002
Osafo Mrs L, BA MA, Stud., Univ.of Wales, Aberystwyth. [0061563] 02/10/2002
Osbeck Miss DS, BA, Asst.Lib., DNO Heather Ltd., Aberdeen. [0059861] 18/10/2001
Osborn Ms H, MLib MCLIP, Head of L.& Inf., Western Educ.& L.Board, N.Ireland. [0033497] 13/01/1981
Osborn Ms K, MA BA, Grad.Trainee, DTI. [0061632] 08/10/2002
Osborn Mr RM, BA AKC DipLib, Co-Ordinating Lib., W.London NHS Workforce Devel., Middlesex. [0037413] 30/08/1984
Osborn-Little Mrs J, BA(Hons), Unemployed. [0055255] 29/08/1997
Osborn Mr A, MSc DipLib MCLIP, Academic Lib., Univ.of Huddersfield. [0043481] 27/10/1989
Osborne Mrs AS, (was Kinnear), BSc DipLib MCLIP, Subject Lib., St.Marys Coll., Twickenham. [0030203] 11/01/1979
Osborne Mrs AV, (was Bateson), MCLIP, Learning Cent.Lib., Rhodesway Sch., Allerton, Bradford, W.Yorks. [0000927] 01/01/1969
Osborne Mr BD, BA MCLIP, Retired. [0011051] 08/02/1963
Osborne Ms ES, BA(Hons) PGCE MA, Inf.Devel.Offr., Health First, London. [0050803] 18/10/1994
Osborne Mrs JE, MA DipLib MCLIP, Life Member. [0030021] 05/11/1978
Osborne Mrs LM, (was Offord), BA MCLIP, Head of L.& Inf.Serv., Devon C.C., L.Dept.H.Q. [0010972] 26/07/1972
Osborne Ms SF, (was Drewery), BA MSc MCLIP, Sen.Inf.Off., Careers Partnership., Manchester. [0035309] 06/10/1994
Osborne Mrs SL, BA(Hons) MCLIP, Team Lib.-Inf., Northamptonshire L.& Inf.Serv. [0050882] 26/10/1994
Osbourn Mr MA, BA(Hons) MA, Asst.Lib., Min.of Defence. [0059108] 16/11/2000
Osgathorpe Miss E, BA MA, Stud., Loughborough Univ. [0059175] 05/12/2000
Osman Mr AM, MA, Unemployed. [0059668] 25/07/2001
Osman Ms SJ, MA MSc MCLIP, L.Serv.Mgr., Instant L.Ltd., London. [0042955] 03/05/1989
Osment Mrs ME, MCLIP, Employment not known. [0060480] 11/12/2001
Osterloh Miss KL, MA BA, Inf.Offr., Freshfields, London. [0050845] 21/10/1994
Ostler Mrs EK, (was Littlewood), BA(Hons) DipILS MCLIP, Lib., Fordingbridge/Ringwood L. [0048407] 06/01/1993
Osuntoki Mrs T, BSc DipIM, Asst.Lib., Office of Fair Trading. [0051618] 12/04/1995
Oswald Mr N, BA DipLib, Unemployed, 12 Richardson Street, Wallsend, Tyne & Wear, NE28 7PS. [0039016] 24/10/1985
Ott-Bissels Mrs SP, MA MA MCLIP, Catr., The London L., London. [0052723] 27/11/1995
Ottaway Ms J, BA MCLIP, Asst.Dist.Lib., Hazlemere, Bucks.C.C. [0036411] 06/10/1983
Ottley George , FCLIP, 12 Hendon Grange, 420 London Rd., Leicester, LE2 2PY, Tel.(0116) 2707650. [0011075] 29/04/1961 FE 01/01/1967
Ottley Mrs HE, (was Russell), BA(Hons) MCLIP, Inf.& L.Asst., Northbrook Coll.Sussex, Worthing. [0050905] 28/10/1994
Ottway Mr TW, MCLIP, Life Member. [0011077] 15/01/1934

Otty Miss P, L.& Inf.Mgr., Womens Tech.& Educ.Cent., Liverpool. [0052159] 09/10/1995
Outhwaite Miss HK, BA(Hons) MCLIP, L.& I.T.Serv.Co-ordinator, Marie Curie - Educ.Dept., Bradford. [0052602] 13/11/1995
Ovenden Mr D, BA DipLib MCLIP, Sen.Inf.Offr.(Acquisitions), Liverpool John Moores Univ. [0031410] 28/09/1979
Ovenden Miss E, BA(Hons) DipIM MCLIP, Inf.Team Lib., Chatham Ref.L., Kent. [0053580] 02/08/1996
Ovens Mr JP, BA(Hons) MCLIP, Dep.Lib., United Bristol Healthcare, NHS Trust, Bristol. [0049605] 19/11/1993
Overall Ms LA, BSc(Hons), Inf.Specialist (Nursing), Royal Coll.of Nursing, London. [0050517] 31/08/1994
Overin Mrs CA, (was Shaw), MCLIP, Sen.Lib.(Customer Serv.), Middlesbrough L.& Inf., Middlesbrough. [0013204] 25/01/1968
Overington Mr MA, MA PhD FCLIP, Life Member. [0017530] 19/09/1955
FE 01/01/1967
Overton Mrs LA, (was Gardner), BA MCLIP CIM, Child.Lib.(Job Share), L.B.Croydon, New Addington L. [0026963] 22/01/1977
Owen Mrs A, BA(Hons), Grad.Trainee L.Asst., Reading Univ. [0059903] 26/10/2001
Owen Mrs AJ, BA, Br.Lib., Wolverhampton City Council. [0054575] 23/01/1997
Owen Ms AJ, BA(Hons) ACIB MA, Asst.Lib., Charles Russell Solicitors, London. [0051643] 25/04/1995
Owen Miss B, Sch.Lib., William Farr (CE) Comp.Sch., Lincoln. [0059813] 10/10/2001 AF
Owen Ms C, PGDip BA(Hons), Exec.Dir., Performing Arts Data Serv., Glasgow. [0052411] 30/10/1995
Owen Mrs CA, (was Winter), BA MCLIP, Cent.Serv.Mgr., W.Berks.Council, Newbury. [0029112] 31/01/1978
Owen Mr D, OBE BA DipLib MCLIP, Dir., Share The Vision. [0011089] 10/10/1965
Owen Mr DIJ, BA(Hons), Lib., Halton Lea P.L., Halton Bor.Council. [0050217] 28/05/1988
Owen Mr DJ, Lib., Longford Sch., Middlesex. [0060885] 18/12/2001
Owen Miss F, MA DipLib MCLIP, Dir.of Learning Serv., Stanmore Coll.F.E.C., Middx. [0022780] 08/10/1974
Owen Mrs JD, (was Pickering), MCLIP, Retired. [0011099] 20/03/1941
Owen Ms K, BA MCLIP, Princ.Lib., Notts.C.C. [0033332] 03/11/1980
Owen Miss KA, BA(Hons) DipILS MCLIP, Inf.Serv.Lib., Vale of Glamorgan Pub.Ls., Barry. [0049302] 20/10/1993
Owen Mrs KA, (was Stephens), BA(Hons) MA, Asst.Lib., British Architectural L., R.I.B.A., London. [0054030] 21/10/1996
Owen Mrs LG, (was Ward), MCLIP, Prof.Relief Lib., Derby City Council. [0015355] 12/02/1969
Owen Mr M, BA MCLIP, Life Member. [0019234] 14/09/1956
Owen Mrs M, (was Jones), p./t.Stud./Asst.Lib., Univ.of Wales Aberystwyth, Coleg Menai, Bangor. [0045253] 06/09/1990
Owen Ms ME, BA(Hons) DipILS, Inf.Mgr., The Food & Drink Federation, London. [0047273] 01/07/1992
Owen Mrs MOW, (was Jones), MCLIP, p./t.Lib., Univ.of Wales, CAWCS, Aberystwyth. [0011101] 09/04/1965
Owen Mrs PJ, (was Lawrence), BA MCLIP, Learning Resources Offr., Harris CTC., London. [0019876] 01/01/1973
Owen Dr PS, BSc DPhil MSc, Employment not known. [0060421] 11/12/2001
Owen Ms RE, Stud., Univ.of Wales, Aberystwyth. [0058983] 16/10/2000
Owen Mrs S, (was Nunn-Price), BSc(Hons) MCLIP, Teacher Lib., L.B.of Hillingdon. [0045643] 12/02/1991
Owen Mrs SJ, (was Powell), BLib MCLIP MBA, Sen.Lib., Bolton Cent.L., Greater Manchester. [0039469] 05/02/1986
Owen Mrs SL, (was Fox), MCLIP, Community Lib.-P./t., Hanley L., Stoke-On-Trent. [0025278] 13/01/1976
Owen Mr TJK, BA DipLib MCLIP, Head of Mktg., CILIP., London. [0011110] 01/01/1972
Owen Mrs TR, BSc, L.Asst., Leicester Coll., Leicester. [0056046] 30/01/1998
Owen-McGee Mr DJ, BA(Hons), IT Advisor-Electronic Serv., Univ.of Derby. [0057670] 01/07/1999
Owens Mr AG, MA MCLIP, Sub-Lib.-Soc.Sci., Coventry Univ., Lanchester L. [0011112] 28/02/1972
Owens Miss J, BSc MCLIP, Employment not known. [0060219] 10/12/2001
Owens Mrs L, BEd DipLib MCLIP, Educ.Res.Offr., Educ.Res.Serv., E.Dunbartonshire. [0036510] 17/10/1983
Owens Mrs M, (was Bond), BA DipLib MCLIP, Learning Res.Mgr., Sutton Coldfield Coll.of F.E., W.Midlands. [0037573] 01/10/1984
Owens Mr NP, Lib., Home Office L., London. [0037305] 13/06/1984
Owston Ms FC, (was Page), BA MCLIP, Inf.Serv.Mgr., B.T.Labs., Ipswich. [0029782] 05/10/1978
Owston Mr JA, BA MCLIP, Lib., Oxford & Cambridge Club, London. [0021819] 19/09/1953
Owusu Mrs PA, (was Harrington), BA DipLib MCLIP, Unemployed. [0030986] 03/07/1979
Oxbrow Mr N, BSc MSc FCLIP, Position unknown, TFPL Ltd., London. [0055661] 11/12/2001 FE 01/04/2002
Oxford Ms LE, BSc(Hons), Stud., Strathclyde Univ. [0061778] 05/11/2002
Oxley Mrs C, (was Mitchell), Sen.Asst.Lib., Wirral Bor.Council, Bebington, Merseyside. [0049874] 20/01/1994
Oxley Mr JF, BA MCLIP, Inf.Lib., Salop.Co.L. [0011118] 30/08/1968
Oxley Mrs JN, BA DipLib MCLIP, Sch.Lib., Herts.& Essex High Sch., Bishops Stortford. [0019235] 10/08/1972
Oyebo Mrs YG, MCLIP, Corporate Lib., Shell Petrol.Devel.Co., Warri, Nigeria. [0057821] 24/08/1999
Oyelekan Mr GO, BLS MLS PhD, Resident in Nigeria. [0061192] 08/04/2002
Oyeoku Mr KK, BA MCLIP, Univ.Lib., Abia State Univ., Nigeria. [0018994] 12/01/1963
Oyston Mr E, BA MSc MCLIP, Head of Tech.Servs.& Devel., Learning Cent., Sheffield Hallam Univ. [0011121] 26/04/1971

Personal Members

Pace Mr CL, BA DipLib MCLIP, Unemployed. [0033666]   18/01/1981
Pacey Mrs GK, (was Terrill), BA DMS MCLIP, LLRC Mgr., Cardinal Newman Sixth Form Coll., Preston. [0011123] 14/10/1968
Pache Mr JE, BA FCLIP, Employment unknown. [0060568]   11/12/2001 **FE 01/04/2002**
Pachent Ms GJ, (was Morriss), BA DLIS MILAM MIMgt MCLIP, Asst.Dir.(L.& Heritage), Suffolk C.C. [0024770]   01/10/1975
Pack Mr PJ, BA MCLIP, Life Member. [0011125]   19/04/1951
Packard Mrs SA, BSc(Hons), p./t.Sen.L.Asst., Anglia Poly.Univ., Chelmsford. [0054740]   01/04/1997
Packman Mrs EM, (was Watson), Sch.L.Asst., The Cottesloe Sch., Wing,Leighton Buzzard. [0049109]   04/10/1993   **AF**
Packwood Mrs A, (was Hammond), BSc MSc, Unemployed. [0047018]   01/04/1992
Padden Mrs SCR, (was Bird), MA MCLIP, Educ.& Health Serv.Lib. &, Staff Training & Devel.Coordinator, Univ.of Manchester. [0035681]   01/01/1964
Paddock Mrs RE, (was Tipping-Alston), BA DipLib MCLIP, Div.Bibl.Serv.Lib., Hants.C.C. [0035813]   17/01/1983
Paddon Ms P, BA MCLIP, Lib., Cambs C.C., St Ives. [0040116]   15/10/1986
Paddon Ms TC, BSc(Hons) DipAppSc, Team Lib., Kettering P.L., Northants.C.C. [0057700]   01/07/1999
Paddy Mrs L, (was John), BA(Hons) DipLib MCLIP, Lib.-Inf.Mgmt., Dept.of Health-Corp.Inf.Mgmnt.Web., Elephant & Castle. [0037511] 03/10/1984
Padley Miss B, MCLIP, Retired. [0020083]   28/03/1955
Padmore Mrs JH, BA(Hons) MA MCLIP, L.Administrator/Lib., Freethcartwright Solicitors, Nottingham. [0037864]   22/10/1984
Padwick Mr EW, FCLIP, Life Member. [0011131]   09/02/1940 **FE 01/01/1950**
Padwick Miss VM, BA MCLIP, Area Mgr., L.B.of Barnet. [0024039]   10/03/1975
Pagan Mr RO, BSc MCLIP, Employment not known. [0060570]   11/12/2001
Page Ms AC, BA(Hons) MSc, Asst.Lib., St.Martin's Coll., Harold Bridges L., Lancaster. [0047916]   26/10/1992
Page Miss AK, MCLIP, Lib.-Inf.Serv.Team, Leamington L., Warwicks.Co.L. [0011134]   03/04/1967
Page Miss AM, BA DipLib MCLIP, Study Cent.Mgr., Surrey C.C. [0029280]   18/05/1978
Page Mr BF, FCLIP, Retired. [0011136]   17/01/1950   **FE 01/01/1968**
Page Mrs C, Inf.Offr., Dresdner Kleinwort Wasserstein, London. [0059169]   04/12/2000   **AF**
Page Mrs CL, (was Beyer), BA MCLIP, L.Mgr., Prettys Solicitors, Ipswich. [0030579]   14/02/1979
Page Miss EK, MA(Hons) MSc(Econ), L.Mgr., Widnes Sixth Form Coll. [0051197]   23/11/1994
Page Ms FA, BA(Hons) DipLib, Princ.Lib., L.B.Camden, Leisure & Comm. [0037855]   31/10/1994
Page Mrs HM, (was Croxford), MCLIP, Lib., Knutsford High Sch., Cheshire C.C. [0025025]   29/10/1975
Page Mrs I, (was Loe), MCLIP, Retired. [0011140]   20/02/1961
Page Mrs J, (was Webb), BA MSc, Learning Support Asst., Loughborough Coll. [0040124]   07/10/1986
Page Mr KJ, BA MSc, Employment not known. [0060351]   10/12/2001
Page Mrs MA, (was Whittington), MCLIP, Primary Advisory Lib., Sch.L.Serv., E.Sussex Co.L. [0020353]   12/03/1973
Page Mrs MC, BA MA DipLib MCLIP, Asst.Lib., Huddersfield Tech.Coll. [0029081]   20/02/1978
Page Mrs P, (was Johnson), MCLIP, Retired. [0011144]   24/03/1960
Page Miss RJ, BA, Stud., Univ.of Brighton. [0059078]   08/11/2000
Page Mrs SD, Inf.Lib., Univ.of Bath L. [0011149]   30/11/1999
Page Ms T, BA(Hons) MA MCLIP, L.& Key Skills Facilitator, Rhyl Coll., Denbighshire. [0053824]   09/11/1999
Page Mrs V, BA(Hons) MCLIP, Sen.Lib.(Inf.), N.Tyneside Cent.L., N.Shields. [0046566]   12/11/1991
Page Ms VM, MA(Hons) DipLib MCLIP, Cent.Lib., Jewel & Esk Valley Coll., Midlothian. [0024228]   28/04/1975
Page-Jones Mrs M, (was Henson), BA MCLIP, Asst.Lib., Inst.of Civil Engineers, London. [0006745]   12/08/1971
Paget-Woods Ms J, BA(Hons) DipLib MCLIP, Inf.& Learning Serv.Co-ordinator, Univ.of Plymouth. [0044436]   08/10/1990
Pagowska Miss HC, BA(Hons) PGCE, Supply Teacher, Staffs County Council. [0058682]   19/05/2000
Paice Mrs AS, (was Anderson), FCLIP, Retired. [0011150]   03/09/1946 **FE 01/01/1951**
Paige Mr M, BA(Hons) MA, Lib., BBC, London. [0055256]   03/09/1997
Pain Mrs CJ, (was Honnor), BSc MCLIP, I./c. Map Coll., Univ.of Greenwich., Medway Campus L. [0019917]   10/01/1973
Paine Mrs BJ, (was Wilkinson), BA MCLIP, Asst.Lib., Univ.of Portsmouth. [0011154]   17/09/1969
Paine Miss BMS, BA, L.Super., Bordon L., Forest Cent., Bordon, Hants. [0057797]   09/08/1999
Paine Miss JE, MCLIP, Sen.L.Asst., Univ.Coll.London. [0011157] 12/08/1968
Paine Ms KP, BA(Hons), Sen.L.Asst., Brit.L.of Political & Econ.Sci., London. [0054663]   12/02/1997
Paine Mrs R, ETD Facilitator, Eastbourne Downs PCT, Lewes, E.Sussex. [0058480]   29/02/2000
Painter Mrs MJ, (was Holden), BLib MCLIP, Asst.Lib., Darwen L., Lancs. [0033982]   30/06/1981
Painting Miss J, MCLIP, Cent.Serv.Lib., Portsmouth City Council. [0022805] 15/10/1974
Pak Mr KFJ, Photo Researcher, S.China Morning Post, L., Hong Kong. [0048309]   25/11/1992
Pakes Mrs UB, FIL MAG MA, Retired. [0040830]   08/07/1987
Palfrey Ms M, BA(Hons), Stud., Univ.of Sheffield. [0059992]   16/11/2001
Palk Mr JE, BSc, Unemployed. [0061622]   04/10/2002
Palka Mrs JB, (was Tuck), BA DipLib MCLIP, Stud. [0026587]   12/10/1976

Pallett Mrs HM, (was Roper), MCLIP, Sch.Lib., Big Wood Sch., Notts. [0011162]   19/07/1965
Pallister Mrs SM, (was Johnson), BA MCLIP, Unemployed. [0020530]   04/04/1973
Pallot Miss S, SRN MCLIP, L.Serv.Mgr., Heatherwood & Wexham Pk.Hosp.NHS, Trust, E.Berks. [0023943]   31/01/1975
Palmar Miss FJ, BSc(Hons), Stud., Univ.of Strathclyde. [0061768]   05/11/2002
Palmer Mrs AJ, (was Guy), BA MCLIP, Lib., The Firs Sch., Chester. [0011165]   07/08/1969
Palmer Miss BJ, B MUS DipLib MCLIP, Asst.Lib., Royal Academy of Music, London. [0029784]   06/10/1978
Palmer Mrs DM, MBE HonFCLIP, Freelance Consultant. [0011169]   06/02/1969   **FE 16/06/1978**
Palmer Mrs JF, (was Marshall), BA MCLIP, P./t.Lib., Waterlooville L., Hants. [0027279]   18/02/1977
Palmer Mrs JG, (was Frost), BA(Hons) DipLIS MCLIP, Team Lib.(Young People), KentC.C., Deal, Kent. [0023914]   07/01/1975
Palmer Dr JMP, BSc DipLib PhD MCLIP FCLIP, Keeper of Sci.Books, Radcliffe Sci.L., Univ.of Oxford. [0017540]   23/03/1972 **FE 21/05/1997**
Palmer Mrs JS, (was Adlington), BA MCLIP, Serv. Mgr., Saffron Walden P.L., Essex. [0025709]   29/02/1976
Palmer Miss KD, BA MCLIP, Sen.Inf.Offr., Simmons & Simmons, London. [0041739]   02/03/1988
Palmer Mr M, BA MBA MIMgt MCLIP, Res.& Reader Devel.Mgr., Essex C.C.Ls., Chelmsford. [0011181]   18/01/1971
Palmer Mrs M, MCLIP, Sen.Lib., Clitheroe, Lancs.C.C. [0026139] 21/06/1976
Palmer Mrs M, MLib MCLIP, Princ.Offr.L., Caerphilly Co.Bor. [0011180] 22/03/1967
Palmer Ms M, MCLIP, Employment not known. [0060446]   11/12/2001
Palmer Ms MA, BA, Sen.Knowledge Analyst, Management Horizons Europe. [0053309]   23/04/1996
Palmer Mr ME, MA(Cantab) MSc, Sci.Inf.Offr., CAB International, Wallingford, Oxon. [0051450]   15/02/1995
Palmer Ms ML, MA MCLIP, Maternity leave/Head of Inf.Mgmt., E.Sussex C.C. [0040795]   16/06/1987
Palmer Mr ND, BA MCLIP, Lib., Imperial Coll.at St.Mary's, London. [0011184]   14/10/1966
Palmer Mrs PM, (was Springall), MCLIP, P./t.Catr., L.B.of Harrow. [0011185] 25/03/1961
Palmer Ms PS, (was Dyer), DMS MIMgt MCLIP, Head of L.& Heritage, Wilts.C.C. [0023076]   31/01/1974
Palmer Mr RJ, PhD MCLIP, Lib.& Arch., Lambeth Palace L., London. [0011188]   10/07/1971
Palmer Ms S, BSc, Trainee L.Asst. [0061230]   18/04/2002
Palmer Mrs SH, BA, Researcher/Lib., Property Investment Res.Cent., City Univ.Business Sch., London. [0041905]   11/05/1988
Palmer Miss SL, BA(Hons) MA, Lib., Television Arch., BBC. [0052257] 18/10/1995
Palmer Mrs SP, DipInf, Asst.Lib., L., Oxford Brookes Univ. [0056027] 28/01/1998
Pamma Miss J, Asst.Lib./Trainer, Univ.Hosp.Birmingham., Birmingham. [0057351]   17/02/1999
Pamphilon Miss JM, BA MCLIP, Retired. [0011195]   11/03/1964
Pan Miss R, BA MLIB DipLR MCLIP, Sub.Lib., Durham Univ.Library. [0041536]   14/01/1988
Pandya Mr HU, Retired. [0017542]   01/01/1961
Pang Ms M, BA MLib FCLIP, Lib., Hong Kong P.L., Hong Kong. [0045642] 11/04/1971   **FE 18/11/1998**
Pang Mr SC, BSc DipLibInf, Mgr., Kinta Kellas Public Ltd.Co., Kuala Lumpur, Malaysia. [0024229]   09/05/1975
Pankhurst Miss JM, BA MCLIP, Team Lib.-Inf.Serv., Luton Cent.L., Luton Bor.Council. [0011201]   18/10/1971
Pankhurst Mrs RJ, MA FCLIP, Retired. [0017543]   03/06/1959 **FE 15/09/1993**
Pankiewicz Mrs SJ, (was Stannard), BA(Hons) MSc MCLIP, Mgr., Bus.Inf., Defence Evaluation & Research, Agency, Farnborough, Hants. [0039201]   01/01/1986
Pantin Mr AD, BA DipLib MSc, Unemployed. [0034590]   01/01/1982
Panton Miss S, BA MCLIP, Child.Lib., Portsmouth City Council, Hants. [0023851]   12/02/1975
Pantry Mrs S, (was Armitage), BA OBE FCLIP, Dir., Sheila Pantry Assoc.Ltd., (01909 771024, Fax 01909 772829). [0011204]   23/03/1953 **FE 18/01/1989**
Panzetta Mrs SJ, DipIM, L.& Inf.Cent.Mgr., Camden & Islington CHS NHS Trust, London. [0049734]   06/12/1993
Pao Mr G, HonFCLIP, Hon.Fellow. [0057253]   04/02/1999 **FE 01/01/1999**
Papantoniou Mrs F, BSc MSc, P./t.Stud./Lib., Univ.Aberystwyth, Dept.Anatomy, Cambridge Univ. [0059774]   02/10/2001
Papatriantafyllou Miss C, BA(Hons), Stud., Manchester Met.Univ. [0059987] 16/11/2001
Papi Miss CA, MA DipLIS MCLIP, L.Mgr., Berks.Shared Serv.Organisation, Chosley, Oxon. [0052166]   11/10/1995
Pappas Miss LC, Asst.Lib., Royal Soc. of Med., London. [0057483] 06/04/1999
Papps Mr TA, BA MCLIP, Systems Support Lib., Bournemouth Univ. [0022703]   18/09/1974
Parcell Ms EJ, MA, Asst.Lib., Univ.of Wales, Swansea., E: e.j.parcell@swan.ac.uk. [0038973]   24/10/1985
Pardoe Mrs A, (was Macfarlane), DipLib MCLIP, Learning Cent.Co-ordinator, Wolverhampton Coll. [0033315]   23/10/1980
Pardoe Mrs FH, (was Postlethwaite), BA DipLib MCLIP, Unemployed. [0034243]   17/10/1981
Parekh Miss H, MA MCS, Prof.of L.Sci.& Univ.Lib., S.N.D.T.Womens Univ., Mumbai, India. [0034030]   27/07/1981

321

Parfitt Mrs LD, (was Mason), BSc MCLIP, Unemployed. [0029521] 07/09/1978
Parfitt Mrs ST, (was Mawdsley), BSc MCLIP, Career Break. [0046003] 19/08/1991
Parfitt Mrs YJ, BSc MCLIP, Unemployed. [0024296] 28/05/1975
Pargeter Miss SM, MA MA CERT ED MCLIP, Service Support Lib., Devon L.& Inf.Serv. [0028113] 12/10/1977
Paris Mr KR, BA PGDipLib, Inf.Mgr., Pinsent Curtis Biddle, London. [0043217] 04/10/1989
Parish Mr C, FCLIP, Hon.Consultant Lib., The Lit.& Philosophical Soc., Newcastle-Upon-Tyne. [0011214] 07/05/2029 **FE 01/01/1964**
Parish Mr DR, BA MCLIP, Sen.Lib.-Stock, Bor.of Poole. [0021213]30/09/1973
Parish Mrs FL, (was Pitman), MCLIP, Lib.(Local Studies), Cambs.C.C. [0011727] 26/02/1969
Parish Mr R, BA MA MCLIP, Sen.Lib.Local Studies, Nottingham City L.Inf.& Mus.Serv. [0023557] 21/01/1975
Parish Mr RH, MCLIP, Retired. [0011216] 06/09/1956
Park Mrs AK, (was Lockwood), MCLIP, L.Asst., Suffolk C.C. [0021656] 05/01/1974
Park Mr DS, BA(Hons) MA MCLIP ILTA, Inf.Mgr., Sport England, Leeds. [0048711] 23/04/1993
Park Mrs GE, (was Hughes), BA DipLib MCLIP, p./t.Community Lib., Bolton Metro.Borough Council. [0041368] 10/11/1987
Park Ms MA, BA(Hons) MA, Stud., Leeds Met. [0060050] 06/12/2001
Park Mr RDM, MCLIP, Asst.Campus Lib., Bell.Coll.of Tech., Dumfries Campus. [0046551] 14/11/1991
Park Mr RM, MA MCLIP, Intermittent Temp. [0011219] 27/06/1964
Parkar Mr FA, BSc MCLIP, Position unknown, SmithKline Beecham, Harlow. [0060326] 10/12/2001
Parke Mr DA, BA(Hons) DipLib, Inf.Specialist, H.M.Customs & Excise, Salford. [0043809] 22/01/1990
Parke Mr JTE, BA(Hons) DipLib, Informatics Coordinator, MRC Dunn Human Nutrition Unit, Wellcome Trust, Cambridge. [0055363] 03/10/1997
Parker Ms A, BA DipLib MCLIP, Stock Unit Mgr., Blackburn with Darwen Cent.L. [0032144] 28/01/1980
Parker Mr AD, MA DipLib MCLIP, Higher L.Exec., House of Commons L., London. [0334473] 07/01/1981
Parker Mrs AM, MBE HonFCLIP, Life Member, 21 Woodlands Rd., Hertford, SG13 7JE. [0011222] 26/08/1949 **FE 01/01/1994**
Parker Miss BJ, BA(Hons) MCLIP DipEngLit, Life Member, 2 Plough Close, Wolvercote Grn., Oxford, OX2 8DE. [0019802] 03/10/1972
Parker Mrs C, (was Davies), BA(Hons), Asst.Lib., Worcester City L. [0035264] 05/10/1982
Parker Mr DF, MCMI FCLIP, Life Member, 11 Tormead Road, Guildford, GU1 2JA. [0019236] 28/02/1954 **FE 01/01/1959**
Parker Mr DS, BA(Hons) MA, L.Asst., Met.Bor.of Wirral, Moreton. [0057872] 22/09/1999
Parker Miss E, MCLIP, Sen.Inf.& Special Serv.Lib., Northumberland, Amenities Div. [0011229] 16/01/1970
Parker Ms EK, BA, Comm.Lib., Forres L. [0054284] 15/11/1996
Parker Mr FN, FCLIP, Life Member. [0011232] 10/09/1952 **FE 01/01/1966**
Parker Mrs GD, (was Hallybone), BA(Hons) MCLIP, Asst.Reader Serv.Lib., Univ.of Greenwich, Dartford Campus. [0022747] 06/09/1974
Parker Mr GR, MCLIP, Picture Researcher, BSkyB. [0045434] 01/02/1991
Parker Miss HM, BLib MCLIP, ICT & Special Systems Mgr., Oxon.C.C. [0038585] 01/07/1985
Parker Mrs J, (was Schofield), BA MA DipAdEd MCLIP, Self-employed free-lance. [0022884] 03/10/1974
Parker Mrs J, (was Redfern), MCLIP, Lib., Highfields Sch., Matlock, Derbys. [0011237] 27/02/1963
Parker Miss JE, MCLIP, Retired. [0011238] 15/01/1958
Parker Mrs JE, (was Bugby), MCLIP, Community Serv.Lib., Northants C.C., Wellingborough. [0027517] 14/05/1977
Parker Ms JE, BA(Hons) MA MCLIP, Inf.Literacy Unit Mgr., Open Univ. [0052062] 02/10/1995
Parker Mrs JH, (was Martindale), MA D PH I, Lib., Worcester Coll., Oxford. [0030480] 05/02/1979
Parker Mrs JJ, (was Lethbridge), BA MA MCLIP, Child.Lib., Amber Valley Dist., Derbys.C.C. [0029726] 07/10/1978
Parker Miss JM, BA(Hons), Network Analyst, CICT, L.B.of Newham. [0047776] 14/10/1992
Parker Mrs JM, (was Solloway), BA MCLIP, Learning Cent.Mgr., New College, Nottingham. [0028683] 13/01/1978
Parker Mr JS, FCLIP, Retired. [0019237] 26/09/1952 **FE 10/08/1978**
Parker Mr KT, BSc(Hons) MLib, Inf.Consultant. [0050401] 18/07/1994
Parker Mrs L, (was Wheatcroft), MCLIP, Unemployed. [0015659] 18/10/1969
Parker Mrs LA, BA DipLib MEd MCLIP, Asst.lib., Univ.of Sheffield. [0021249] 04/10/1973
Parker Mrs M, MCLIP, Sch.Lib., S.Lanarkshire Council, Hamilton. [0053052] 19/02/1996
Parker Mrs NJ, BA(Hons) MCLIP, Dist.L.Mgr., Manchester City L. [0036870] 12/01/1984
Parker Mr NM, BSc MCLIP, Inf.Res., Inst.of Management, Management Inf.Cent., Corby. [0035702] 17/01/1983
Parker Miss NS, BSc CBiol MIBiol MCLIP, Retired. [0060596] 11/12/2001
Parker Mrs P, (was McMullen), MCLIP, Employment not known. [0009532] 01/01/1970
Parker Mrs P, (was Linsdell), MCLIP, Retired. [0008961] 01/01/1968
Parker Mrs PC, (was Casimir-Mrowczynska), BA DipLib MCLIP, Unemployed. [0032891] 20/10/1980
Parker Miss PE, MCLIP, Local Studies Offr., Borough of Poole, Poole Local History Cent. [0011244] 10/10/1968
Parker Mr RJ, BSocSc, Position unknown, NHS, NBMHT, Birmingham. [0055099] 08/07/1997

Parker Miss RM, L.Asst., Beachcroft Wansbroughs, Bristol. [0058401] 28/01/2000
Parker Miss SA, BA MCLIP, L.Serv.Mgr., Surrey C.C., Mid Surrey. [0025386] 12/01/1976
Parker Miss SG, (was Briggs), BA MCLIP, Princ.Lib.:S.W., Staffs.C.C. [0037778] 09/10/1984
Parker Miss SM, BA DMS FCLIP, Retired. [0011251] 01/03/1962 **FE 25/01/1995**
Parker Mrs WM, BA MCLIP, Retired. [0011255] 20/04/1961
Parker-Dennison Mrs DC, DipLib, Lib., Chengelo Sch., Mkushi, Zambia. [0058632] 20/04/2000
Parker-Munn Mrs SA, (was Parker), BA(Hons) BScEcon(Hons), W/e Issue Desk Super., Hugh Owen L., Univ.of Wales, Aberystwyth. [0050198] 04/05/1994
Parkes Dr D, BA(Hons) MSc MA MCLIP, Ref.& Enquiry Lib., John Rylands Univ.L., Manchester. [0052897] 17/01/1996
Parkes Mr DJ, BA(Hons) DipLib MCLIP, Head of Operations & User Serv., Staffs.Univ., Thompson L., Stoke on Trent. [0046795] 28/01/1992
Parkes Mrs EC, BA(Hons), L.Asst., Sutton Child.L. [0059278] 25/01/2001
Parkes Ms GA, BA DipLib MCLIP, Employment not known. [0033856] 02/04/1981
Parkin Mrs BA, Asst.Lib., Scarborough Lib. [0061576] 02/10/2002
Parkin Miss ER, BA(Hons) DipIS MCLIP, Team Lib., Norfolk L., Kings Lynn. [0048903] 15/07/1993
Parkin Mrs H, L.Res.Co-ordinator, Mill Hill Sch., Ripley, Derbys. [0051792] 01/07/1995 **AF**
Parkin Mr M, BA(Hons) MA, Learning Cent.Mgr., Fir Vale Learning Cent., Fir Vale Sch., Sheffield. [0054988] 13/06/1997
Parkin Mrs SM, (was Woods), BA, Inf.Asst., Taylor L., Univ.of Aberdeen. [0045303] 04/10/1990 **AF**
Parkin Mr SNJ, Curator-Early Printed Collections, The British L., London. [0045999] 15/08/1991
Parkinson Mr A, BA, Unemployed. [0035868] 05/02/1983
Parkinson Mrs AL, (was Clark), MCLIP, Gift & Card Shop Owner, Bury, Lancs. [0002722] 06/10/1971
Parkinson Mrs F, (was Ure), BLS MCLIP, Knowledge Mgr., Law Society, London. [0028197] 13/10/1977
Parkinson Mrs J, (was Harrison), BA(Hons), Lib.-Reader Devel., City L.& Arts Cent., City of Sunderland. [0050508] 25/08/1994
Parkinson Mr JK, BA DipLib MCLIP, Lib., Home Off., Emergency Planning Coll., York. [0026502] 20/10/1976
Parkinson Ms L, BSc MCLIP, [0011271] 22/09/1965
Parkinson Mrs SA, (was Walters), MCLIP, Life Member. [0011273] 01/01/1957
Parkinson Mrs VA, (was Baker), MCLIP, Asst.Lib., Bucks.C.C., Beaconsfield. [0000649] 09/05/1968
Parkinson Miss WH, MCLIP, Retired. [0011276] 13/02/1947
Parks Mrs J, (was Pickering), MCLIP, Housewife. [0011660] 09/01/1964
Parks Miss SAI, BSc, Grad.Trainee, MacFarlanes, London. [0061751] 01/11/2002
Parlain Miss K, BA(Hons) MA MCLIP, Team Leader, Young people's Serv., Kent C.C. [0042695] 25/01/1989
Parlane Ms CM, CERT ED, Learning Resource Cent.Mgr., Sir George Monoux 6th Form Coll., London. [0043294] 16/10/1989
Parmar Mr S, BSc MCLIP, Employment not known. [0060788] 12/12/2001
Parmenter Ms JR, BA MCLIP, Readers Serv.Lib., Anglia Poly.Univ., Chelmsford. [0003441] 21/10/1967
Parmiter Mr TM, BA MCLIP, Outreach Serv.Mgr., City of Westminster, Church St.L. [0036918] 14/10/1983
Parnaby Ms BJ, BA DipIlS, Asst.Lib., Dept.of Health, London. [0061158] 21/03/2002
Parr Mrs BE, (was Matthews), BA DipLIS, Budget & Admin.Team Asst., Cambs.C.C., Cambridge. [0046295] 24/10/1991
Parr Mrs CM, (was Perrin), MA MCLIP, Asst.Dir.:Staff Devel., Campus Learning Res.Mgr., Univ.of Herts., Hatfield. [0011555] 01/07/1974
Parr Mrs IJ, (was Holmes), BA DipLib MCLIP, L.Mgr., Bolton 6th Form Coll. [0021879] 04/02/1974
Parr Mrs J, (was Tyzack), BA(Hons) MA MCLIP, Lib., Social Sciences Dept., Manchester Cent.L. [0038390] 16/04/1985
Parr Mrs LJ, BA MA DipLib MCLIP, Unemployed. [0026503] 06/10/1976
Parr Mr MW, MCLIP, Retired, Tel:0116 243 2301. [0011282] 26/09/1952
Parr Mrs NR, BA(Hons) DipILM MCLIP, Asst.Lib., Countryside Council for Wales L. [0055584] 21/11/1997
Parr Ms SC, (was Butlin), BA MCLIP MA MCLIP, Lib., Heathfield Sch., Pinner, Middlesex. [0035545] 01/11/1982
Parra Ms C, BA MILS, Unemployed. [0050199] 06/05/1994
Parratt Mrs JP, (was Sutton), BA MCLIP, User Serv.Lib., Univ.of Brighton, Queenwood L. [0040359] 21/01/1987
Parrett Mr AJ, BA DipLib MCLIP, L.Skills Training Facilitator, W.Suffolk Hosp.NHS Trust, Bury St.Edmunds. [0026504] 09/10/1976
Parris Ms HW, BA, Inf.Offr., Greater Manchester Probation, Manchester. [0043920] 20/02/1990
Parrish Ms LA, BSc MCLIP, Head of Inf.Serv., Esso UK Ltd., Leatherhead. [0034930] 24/05/1982
Parrott Mrs EK, (was Fair), BA MCLIP, Team Leader, Liverpool L.& Inf.Serv. [0018086] 01/10/1972
Parry Mr C, BA MCLIP, Asst.Lib., Nat.L.of Wales, Aberystwyth. [0011289] 22/10/1970
Parry Mrs CM, BA MA MCLIP, Systems Project Lib., City Univ., London. [0042346] 24/10/1988
Parry Mr D, BSc Econ, L.Asst., Halliwell Landau, Manchester. [0061672] 16/10/2002
Parry Mr D, BA MA MCLIP, Self-employed Consultant. [0034587] 04/01/1982
Parry Mr DE, MA DipLib MCLIP, Retired, Fax 01224 743 433. [0022665] 31/07/1974

Parry Mrs DE, (was Carter), BA MCLIP, Asst.Lib., Sutton Coldfield L., Birmingham L.Serv. [0022876]   09/10/1974
Parry Ms DO, (was Sharples), BA MCLIP, [0013194]   01/01/1965
Parry Ms E, MA(Hons) MA, Lib., Beeston P.L., Notts.C.C. [0055538] 20/10/1997
Parry Mr FP, MCLIP, Asst.Lib., Loughborough Univ., The L. [0030227] 12/01/1979
Parry Mrs GM, (was Foster), BA MCLIP, Foundation Lib., Kings Sch., Macclesfield, Cheshire. [0011295]   12/06/1966
Parry Miss J, BA(Hons) MLIS, Lib., Powys NHS Healthcare Trust. [0056441] 10/07/1998
Parry Mrs JD, (was Walker), MLib MCLIP, Head of L.I.S., Bath Spa Univ.Coll. [0015230]   15/04/1971
Parry Mrs JS, (was Wilkinson), BA MCLIP, Team Leader, Home Off., London. [0042183]   10/10/1988
Parry Miss MM, BA DipLib MCLIP, Asst.Lib.,Liverpool Cent.L., Liverpool City Council, Liverpool. [0028115]   05/10/1977
Parry Dr PM, (was Pinder), MA MSc PhD MCLIP, Unemployed. [0011705] 15/02/1971
Parry Mrs RC, (was Hewett), BA MLS MCLIP, Company Secretary, Bill Brookman Productions Ltd., Loughborough. [0006790]   10/10/1969
Parry Mrs SM, (was Watson), MA MCLIP, Educ.Lib., Northumberland Sch.L.Serv., Hexham L. [0026602]   01/10/1976
Parry Ms ST, BLib MCLIP, Dept.Lib., Civil Eng.Dept., Imperial Coll.,London. [0041756]   10/03/1988
Parry Mr VTH, MA(Oxon) FCLIP FRSA FRAS, Life Member. [0011302] 29/09/1950   **FE 01/01/1959**
Parsonage Miss AMG, MCLIP, Life Member. [0011304]   10/02/1961
Parsons Mr AJ, BA(Hons) MPhil MCLIP, Inf-Analyst. [0038310]   04/03/1985
Parsons Mrs C, (was Moore), B LIB MCLIP, Princ.Lib., Bracknell Forest Bor.Council, Berks. [0033075]   01/01/1980
Parsons Ms DJ, BA(Hons) MSc(Econ) MCLIP, Subject Support Lib., Bournemouth Univ. [0049826]   10/11/1993
Parsons Mr DST, DipLib MCLIP, Inf.Offr., Becta, Coventry. [0039927] 02/10/1986
Parsons Miss JE, MCLIP, Advisory Lib., Sch.L.Serv., E.Sussex C.C. [0011314] 09/02/1964
Parsons Miss LD, BSc MCLIP, Employment not known. [0060735] 12/12/2001
Parsons Mr MG, BSc(Hons) MA, Libr., Univ.of Newcastle Upon Tyne. [0057102]   14/12/1998
Parsons Mr NS, BA DipLib MCLIP, Dir. of Business & Devel., Hesstar Ltd, Essex. [0038060]   08/01/1985
Parsons Miss SC, BA MCLIP, Lib., Learning, Literacy & Child., Eastbourne Grp. [0027127]   09/01/1977
Parsons Mrs SM, (was Eden), MCLIP, Asst.to the Ed., Scientific Update, E.Sussex. [0024442] 29/07/1975
Partington Miss J, BA DipLib MCLIP, Sen.Asst.Lib., Goldsmiths Coll. [0033333]   07/11/1980
Parton Mrs G, (was Harp), BA(Hons) MCLIP, Lib., Northbrook Coll.Sussex, Worthing. [0049114] 06/10/1993
Parton Mr S, BA, Grad.Trainee. [0061024] 05/02/2002
Partridge Miss AH, BSc(Hons) MSc MCLIP, Systems Lib., Cranfield Univ., Kings Norton L. [0048139]   11/11/1992
Partridge Mr DA, FCLIP, Life Member, Tel.01708 768804, 11 Mashiters Walk, Romford, Essex, RM1 4DA. [0011320]   10/02/1950 **FE 01/01/1969**
Partridge Mr GA, BA(Hons), L.Systems Mgr., Allen & Overy, London. [0049845]   21/12/1993
Partridge Mr GF, BA DipLib MCLIP, Community Area Lib., Willenhall L., Coventry. [0019240] 26/08/1972
Partridge Mrs JD, (was Couchman), BA(Hons) MCLIP, Weekend Super., Univ. of Leeds, Health Sci.L. [0036680]   25/10/1983
Partridge Mrs JLM, (was Searle), MCLIP, L.Super., Milford-on-sea, Hants.C.C. [0023983]   24/01/1960
Partridge Miss SJ, BA, Employment not known. [0060510]   11/12/2001
Parvin Mrs JI, BA MCLIP, Retired. [0029785]   10/10/1978
Pasadas-Urena Mr C, Dir., Biblioteca Facultad de Psicologia, Univ.of Granada. [0043235] 09/10/1989
Paskin Ms KJ, BA(Hons) MA MCLIP, Lib., Manchester P.L., Cent.Dist. [0046682]   10/12/1991
Passmore Ms K, BA(Hons) DipInf, Lib., Penrith L., Cumbria. [0058617] 18/04/2000
Passmore Mrs RB, MA MSc MCLIP, Employment not known. [0060571] 11/12/2001
Patalong Mrs SL, BA MCLIP, Subject Lib., Computer Sci.& Electrical Eng., Coventry Univ. [0031034]   02/07/1979
Patchett Mrs GW, (was Crampin), MCLIP, Unemployed. [0003314] 26/08/1969
Patching Mrs L, DipInf, Inf.Offr., Legal Servs.Dept., Lloyds of London. [0053310]   23/04/1996
Pate Mrs HJ, (was Daniell), BA MCLIP, Sen.Lib., Manchester City Council, Longsight L. [0020001]   12/01/1973
Pate Mr T, BA(Hons), Stud., Univ.of Bristol, & Sub.Asst., Univ.of Wales Coll. Newport. [0058374] 28/01/2000
Patel Mrs BM, BA DipEd DipLIS MCLIP, Retired. [0024122]   01/04/1975
Patel Miss C, BSc, Inf.Asst., Cable & Wireless, London. [0061759]   15/10/2002 **AF**
Patel Mrs G, BA B LIB MCLIP, Teaching Asst.(Reading & English), Reddiford Sch., Pinner, Middx. [0030228]   09/01/1979
Patel Miss J, BSc MA, L.Exec., House of Commons, London. [0057581] 12/05/1999
Patel Mrs J, BSc, Lib., BSRIA, Bracknell. [0044042]   17/04/1990
Pateman Mrs JM, (was Middleton), BA(Hons) DipLib MCLIP, Team Lib., Ref.Inf.& Local Studies, Kent C.C., Maidstone. [0010118]   12/01/1972
Pateman Mr JP, BA DipLib MBA FCLIP, Head of L.& Heritage, Merton Council, London. [0032146]   01/02/1980 **FE 26/11/1997**

Paterson Miss A, BA DipILS, Learning Cent.Res.Worker, One Plus, Glasgow. [0058011]   12/10/1999
Paterson Mrs C, (was Mcewan), MCLIP, Sch.Lib., Clackmannanshire Council, Educ.& Comm.Serv. [0009355]   12/10/1970
Paterson Miss CE, BA, Stud. [0059496]   10/04/2001
Paterson Miss CLL, BA(Hons), Sch.Lib., Stewarts Melville Coll., Edinburgh. [0043163]   05/09/1989
Paterson Mrs DW, (was Laird), MA MCLIP, Housewife & Mother. [0042133] 05/10/1988
Paterson Mrs EA, (was Cleeve), MCLIP, Retired. [0011338]   02/03/1962
Paterson Ms EC, BA(Hons), Stud., Queen Margaret Univ.Coll. [0061819] 11/11/2002
Paterson Mrs GS, (was Lowe), MA DipLib MCLIP, Young People's Lib., Medway Council, Strood. [0026871] 14/12/1976
Paterson Mrs K, (was Kibbee), MCLIP, Faculty Team Mgr., Economics & Social Sci., Reading Univ.L. [0027691]   01/07/1977
Paterson Mrs MT, (was Fair), MA MCLIP, Bursar/Lib., W.Sussex C.C., Baldwins Hill C.P.Sch. [0011345]   01/01/1969
Paterson Mrs RG, (was Mays), BA(Hons) DipLib, Asst.Lib., GCHQ, Cheltenham. [0051162]   23/11/1994
Paterson Mrs SE, (was Roberts), MA DipLib, Curator F,Lib., Dept.of Printed Books, Imperial War Mus. [0038364] 01/04/1985
Paterson Mrs SM, (was Vassie), BA, MCLIP, Inf.Worker, Highland Carers Project. [0023248]   15/11/1974
Pathak Mrs P, Unemployed. [0059971]   14/11/2001
Paton Mr HCM, BA DipLib MCLIP, L.Devel.Mgr., L.B.of Bexley. [0030659] 21/02/1979
Paton Mr MW, FCLIP, Life Member. [0011348]   19/10/1940 **FE 01/01/1956**
Patrick Ms C, BA(Hons) DipILS MCLIP, Inf.Offr., Council for Voluntary Serv.Fife. [0055066] 03/07/1997
Patrick Mrs E, (was Patton), MCLIP, Lib., S.Lanarkshire Council, Rutherglen L. [0021229]   08/10/1973
Patrick Dr S, (was Cantaluppi), Inf.Sci., Roche Bioscience, Palo Alto, CA, U.S.A. [0035977]   11/02/1983
Pattanaik Mrs G, BA MA DipLib MCLIP, Sen.Lib., Corona P.L., U.S.A. [0038888]   14/10/1985
Patten Mrs AL, (was Houldsworth), MSc, Inf.Serv.Mgr(Know-How), Eversheds, Nottingham. [0048527]   05/02/1993
Patten Mr J, BA MA, L.Asst., N.Sheilds. [0058023]   14/10/1999
Patten Mrs J, p./t.L.Asst., N.E.E.& L.Board, Ballymena. [0056412] 06/07/1998
Patten Mr MN, FCLIP, Retired. [0011356] 24/09/1954 **FE 07/01/1982**
Patterson Mrs CM, p./t.Stud., Moray Coll. [0061137]   07/03/2002
Patterson Miss H, Stud., & Learning Cent.Coordinator, Learning Cent., North East Inst., Ballymena, Co Antrim. [0058683]   24/05/2000
Patterson Mr KR, BMus DipLib MCLIP, Team Lib., Cent.L., St.Helens M.B.C. [0033104]   21/10/1980
Patterson Ms LC, BA(Hons) MA MCLIP, Family Inf.Lib., Child.Serv., Queens Med.Cent., Nottingham. [0049595]   19/11/1993
Patterson Miss ME, BA DipLib MCLIP, Grade 2 Lib., Queens Univ.L., Belfast. [0026506]   01/10/1976
Patterson Mrs NJ, (was Blake), Unemployed. [0049596]   19/11/1993
Patterson Mr SJ, MVO MA MA MCLIP, Computer Systems Mgr., Royal Collection, Buckingham Palace. [0039374]   17/01/1986
Pattinson Mrs PM, (was Eagles), BSc MCLIP, Freelance Record Agent. [0011364]   08/11/1966
Pattison Ms HC, MA MA, Lib., Wolfson Coll., Cambridge. [0058351] 18/01/2000
Pau Miss AKP, BA(Hons) MA MCLIP, Asst.Lib., Hong Kong Univ.L., Hong Kong. [0039204]   06/01/1986
Paul Miss AE, BSc(Econ), Inf.Serv.Advisor, AXA Assistance UK Ltd., Redhill, Surrey. [0054644]   06/02/1997
Paul Mrs HE, (was Seeley), BA DipLib MCLIP, Systems Mgr., Guilles-Alles L., Guernsey. [0033226]   23/10/1980
Paul Mrs JE, (was Mackrell), MA MCLIP, Retired. [0011368]   01/01/1959
Paul Mr RM, BSc DipLIS MCLIP, Asst.Lib., Univ.of Southampton, Southampton. [0051204]   23/11/1994
Paulger Mr T, MA DMS MCLIP, Retired. [0011370]   03/09/1965
Paulin Miss LV, OBE MA HonFCLIP FCLIP, Life Member, 26 Church Road, Bengeo, Hertford, Herts., SG14 3DP, Tel:01992 584828. [0011371] 22/10/1935   **FE 01/01/1939**
Paulls Dr DA, BSc PhD, Head of Inf.Serv., Huntingdon Life Sciences, Cambs. [0060441]   11/12/2001
Pavey Mrs M, (was Richardson), BA MCLIP, Employment not known. [0010122]   01/01/1966
Pavey Mr MJ, BLib MCLIP, Area Lib., Southampton City Council. [0031682] 31/10/1979
Pavey Mrs SJ, BSc MSc MCLIP, Employment not known. [0060802] 12/12/2001
Pavlik Mrs D, FCLIP, Curator, Slavonic & E.European Coll., Brit.L., London. [0011376]   28/02/1971   **FE 29/10/1976**
Pawley Mrs EF, L.Asst., St Johns Theological Coll., Bramcote, Nottingham. [0057054]   25/11/1998   **AF**
Paxton Miss GC, MSc, Stud., Univ.of Wales Aberystwyth. [0061558] 01/10/2002
Pay Miss MA, MA DIP NZLS MCLIP, Management Systems Lib., Lincolnshire Co.L.H.Q. [0030927]   08/06/1979
Payn Mrs JS, Sch.Lib., Welling Sch., Kent. [0053481]   01/07/1996 **AF**
Payne Mrs CM, (was Williams), MCLIP, Asst Lib., Parsons Brinckerhoff, Bristol. [0015898]   02/06/1969
Payne Mr D, BA MLS, Pub.Serv.Lib., Free L.of Philadelphia, USA. [0041475] 01/01/1988
Payne Ms EA, BA DipLib MCLIP, Inf.Scientist, NCCHTA, Univ.of Southampton. [0044489]   15/10/1990

Payne Miss GF, BA(Hons) MSc MCLIP, Res.Asst.-OPAL Project, Open Univ., Milton Keynes. [0058718] 01/07/2000
Payne Mr GS, MCLIP, Retired. [0011388] 09/10/1958
Payne Miss HC, BA, Asst.Lib., New Coll., Oxford. [0052296] 23/10/1995
Payne Mrs HM, BA MA, L.Asst., Brighton, Hove & Sussex 6th Form, Coll. [0054006] 16/10/1996
Payne Mr IC, BA MA CertEd DipLib MCLIP, P./t.F.E.Coll.Lect., Leicester Coll. [0035732] 04/01/1983
Payne Mrs JBC, (was Leach), MCLIP, Retired. [0011389] 18/08/1939
Payne Mrs LME, (was Carson), MA MCLIP, Devel.Offr., Norfolk L.& Inf.Serv., Norwich. [0033212] 28/01/1980
Payne Mr M, BA DipLib MCLIP, Sen.Lib., Penarth L., Vale of Glamorgan. [0037794] 26/10/1984
Payne Mr MB, BA MCLIP, Asst.Princ.Lib., Brierley Hill Area L., Dudley Met.Bor. [0011393] 21/10/1970
Payne Ms N, (was Black), BA(Hons) MA, Asst.Lib., House of Lords. [0055697] 04/11/1997
Payne Miss NA, BA(Hons) DipISM, Asst.Lib., Law Soc., London. [0053091] 01/03/1996
Payne Mr PM, MCLIP, Head of Learning Support Serv., Leeds Metro.Univ., City Campus. [0011394] 20/01/1972
Payne Ms S, BA DipLib, Asst.Lib., Barlow Lyde & Gilbert, London. [0056803] 19/10/1998
Payne Ms SE, BA MA MCLIP, Position unknown, [0043541] 02/11/1989
Payne Miss VJ, BA MLIS DipLib MCLIP ALAI, Periodicals Lib., Nat.Univ.of Ireland, Maynooth. [0030784] 03/04/1979
Paynter Mrs DB, (was Thomas), BA(Hons) CertEd MCLIP, Lib., St Lawrence Coll., Ramsgate, Kent. [0014534] 29/09/1967
Paynter Mr DF, MCLIP, Head of Policy & Devel., Kent Arts & L. [0011398] 10/01/1968
Pazdzierski Mrs M, (was Kaye), BA(Hons) MCLIP, Weekend Super., Univ.of Sheffield. [0008183] 19/11/1964
Peabody Mr RI, MCLIP, Retired. [0011399] 03/09/1936
Peace Ms AM, L.&Inf.Services Mgr., Chartered Society of Physiotherapy, London. [0049616] 19/11/1993
Peace Miss S, BSc(Hons) MCLIP, Unemployed. [0043544] 06/11/1989
Peach Mrs SP, (was Lancaster), BA MCLIP, Local Studies Lib., Derbys.C.C. [0023395] 14/01/1975
Peacock Mr DM, BA(Hons) MSc DipLib MCLIP, Reg.Lib.(IM&T), NY Reg.L.Advisory Serv., Northumberland Health Auth. [0042652] 31/01/1989
Peacock Mrs J, (was Howes), MCLIP, Life Member, 4 Melrose Close, Heworth, York, YO31 0YA. [0024172] 27/10/1948
Peacock Mrs JA, (was Roberts), MCLIP, Tech.Serv.Lib., L.B.of Bexley. [0012486] 30/09/1968
Peacock Mrs MA, (was Yates), MA MCLIP, Comm.Lib., Lincs.C.C. [0023496] 01/01/1975
Peacock Miss MS, MCLIP, Life Member. [0011409] 05/04/1949
Peacock Miss RJ, BA(Hons) DipILM MCLIP, Project Offr., Gateshead Council., Cent.L. [0052850] 09/01/1996
Peacock Mrs SL, BA DipLib MCLIP, Trust Lib., Good Hope Hosp.NHS Trust, Sutton Coldfield. [0037847] 16/10/1984
Peacock Mr TE, BA MCLIP, Asst.Lib., Bolton Cent.L., Lancs. [0011410] 21/03/1971
Peacock Miss VA, BA(Hons) MA MCLIP, Head, Brit.L.Bus.Inf.Servs., London. [0039588] 07/03/1986
Peacocke Miss RE, BSc(Hons) MSc, Researcher, Ceridian Performance Partners Ltd., London. [0055622] 28/10/1997
Peaden Mrs AM, (was Storr), BA MCLIP, Asst.Lib., Kirklees Metro.Council, Huddersfield. [0033167] 07/10/1980
Peadon Miss F, BA MCLIP, Teaching Asst., Warwickshire C.C. [0023584] 21/01/1975
Peake Mrs HM, BSc(Hons), Asst.Lib., Cranfield Sch.of Mgmnt. [0055737] 10/11/1997
Peake Mr HS, BA MCLIP, Life Member, 0384 288571, 74 Court Cres., Kingswinford, W.Midlands, DY6 9RL. [0011412] 23/09/1954
Peake Miss ST, BA MCLIP, Sen.Lib., Educ.L.Serv., Berks. [0039392] 22/01/1986
Peake Mrs VE, BA(Hons), Unemployed. [0050412] 22/07/1994
Pearce Ms AI, (was Papakyriakou), BA(Hons) MCLIP, Asst.Lib., Coll.of Law, London, [0052992] 13/02/1996
Pearce Mr BL, MA FRSA FCLIP, Life Member, The Marish,72 Heathfield S., Twickenham,Middx,TW2 7SS. [0011414] 23/02/1950
FE 01/01/1961
Pearce Miss CM, BA MCLIP, Sen.Asst.Co.Bor.Lib.(Devel.), Neath Port Talbot, L.& Inf.Serv. [0011416] 03/10/1966
Pearce Mr CS, BA(Hons), Inf.Offr., London Chamber of Commerce. [0055873] 05/12/1997
Pearce Miss EH, BA MCLIP, Stud., Univ.Sheffield. [0059894] 30/10/2001
Pearce Mrs GL, BSc MCLIP, Employment not known. [0060747] 12/12/2001
Pearce Miss GM, BA MCLIP, Unemployed. [0032329] 27/02/1980
Pearce Mrs J, BA(Hons) MCLIP, Sen.L.Asst., Univ.of Liverpool, Sydney Jones L. [0049441] 27/10/1993
Pearce Ms J, BA, Freelance Indexer & Abstractor, Copy Editor, Proofreader, TEL: 01992 586267. [0036676] 04/11/1983
Pearce Mrs J, BA DipLib MCLIP, Database Co-ordinator, London Inst. [0022585] 06/07/1974
Pearce Mrs LA, BEd(Oxon), Open Learning Cent.Mgr., Gillotts Sch., Henley on Thames. [0057922] 05/10/1999
Pearce Mrs LM, (was Hallam), BSc MSc, Employment not known. [0060836] 12/12/2001
Pearce Mr MJ, BA(Hons) MA, Stud. [0055294] 18/09/1997
Pearce Mrs P, (was Cook), BA MCLIP, Team Lib., Cheltenham L., Glos.C.C. [0032033] 11/02/1980
Pearce Mrs PJ, (was Reynolds), BA MCLIP, Admin.Offr., Univ.of the W.of England, Bristol. [0012311] 27/01/1966

Pearce Mr R, BA MCLIP, Sen.Lib., Croydon P.L., Cent.L. [0038822] 10/10/1985
Pearce Miss SE, BA, Stud., Univ.of Sheffield. [0061588] 02/10/2002
Peare Mr JDT, MCLIP, Keeper (Systems), Trinity Coll.L., Dublin. [0018999] 02/10/1972
Pearl Mr CJ, BA MCLIP, Retired. [0011432] 25/05/1970
Pearless Mrs B, (was Gray), BA(Hons) DipLib, Promo.Lib.(p./t.), Arts & L.Offr., Kent Arts & L. [0037272] 23/05/1984
Pearlman Mrs DP, (was Cash), BA MCLIP, Lib., Freelance. [0020003] 12/01/1973
Pearman Mrs AR, BA(Hons), TEFL Teacher, Bell Sch.of English, Szczecin, Poland. [0057224] 20/01/1999
Pearman Mr MA, BA MCLIP, Retired. [0011433] 07/02/1969
Pears Mr RM, BA(Hons) DipILM MCLIP, Inf.Specialist, Learning Resources, City Campus L., Univ.of Northumbria at Newcastle. [0050811] 19/10/1994
Pears Mrs S, (was Kirk), BSc MSc MCLIP, Employment not known. [0060737] 12/12/2001
Pearse Mrs EM, (was Peckett), MCLIP, Life Member. [0011461] 19/09/1947
Pearson Miss A, BA MCLIP, Retired. [0011437] 01/01/1960
Pearson Miss A, BA(Hons) MA, Lib., CYPHER, Leeds. [0059152] 28/11/2000
Pearson Mr B, DMA MILAM FCLIP, Retired. [0011439] 06/02/1957
FE 13/06/1990
Pearson Ms CA, BA DipLib MCLIP, Lib.-Inf., Sherburn Grp., N.Yorks.Co.L. [0027704] 04/07/1977
Pearson Mr DRS, BA MA DipLib FCLIP, Lib., Wellcome L., London. [0033163] 01/10/1980 FE 25/07/2001
Pearson Mr DS, BA MCLIP, Stock Ed., Worcs.L.& Inf.Serv. [0034564] 13/01/1982
Pearson Mrs FE, (was Meikle), MCLIP, p./t.Lib., L.B.of Richmond. [0021335] 17/10/1973
Pearson Mrs GJ, BA(Hons) MA DipLib, Clinical Effectiveness Lib., Cardiothoracic Cent.NHS Trust, Liverpool. [0046841] 13/02/1992
Pearson Mrs J, (was Adams), MCLIP, Unemployed, Tel:01743 873984. [0011443] 30/01/1964
Pearson Mrs JM, (was Seeley), BA(Hons) MCLIP, Dep.H.of L.& Learning Resources, Walsall Coll.of Arts & Tech. [0045923] 17/07/1991
Pearson Ms JS, BA(Hons) MCLIP, Inf.Lib., Enfield L. [0048577] 22/02/1993
Pearson Mr JV, BA(Hons) MCLIP, B TECH DipLIB MCLIP, Asst.Lib., Syngenta Crop Protection Ag, Basel. [0011447] 25/04/1968
Pearson Miss KE, BA MSc, Inf.Offr., Freshfields, London. [0057095] 08/12/1998
Pearson Miss M, MCLIP, Life Member. [0011448] 08/03/1937
Pearson Mrs MF, BA DipLib, Sch.Lib., St.Edwards C.of E.Comp., Romford. [0058641] 25/04/2000
Pearson Mr MG, BA MA MSc MCLIP, Unemployed. [0028242] 24/10/1977
Pearson Mr PJ, BSc MA MCLIP, Dep.L.Mgr., ISLS.Univ.of Westminster. [0043273] 09/10/1989
Pearson Dr PM, BTh MTh PhD MA MCLIP, Dir.& Arch., Thomas Merton Cent., Bellarmine Univ., Louisville. [0052093] 03/10/1995
Pearson Mr RFM, MCMI MIMS MCLIP, Cent.L.Mgr., Sandwell M.B.C. [0011451] 05/02/1964
Pearson Miss RH, Stud., Manchester Met.Univ., &, Learn.Resources Asst., Univ.of Cent.Lancs., Preston. [0058932] 06/10/2000
Pearson Mr S, BA MLS CertED MCLIP, Dep.H., Tech.Serv., Brit.Film Inst.Nat.L., London. [0021845] 05/02/1974
Pearson Mrs SE, (was Wharton), BA MCLIP, Sch.Lib., Northants C.C., Pk.Junior Sch. [0031976] 14/01/1980
Pearson Mrs SER, (was Brookes), BA MCLIP, Unemployed. [0026226] 24/09/1976
Pearson Miss SJ, BA(Hons) MA, Subject Lib., Univ.of Plymouth, Exmouth. [0052339] 30/10/1995
Pearson Mr T, BA(Hons) DipILM, Asst.Lib., Univ.of Sunderland, St.Peters L. [0055101] 14/07/1997
Pearson Mrs T, BSc, L.Admin.Asst., L.Admin., Bridgwater. [0061607] 03/10/2002 AF
Pearson Mr W, MBE BSc HonMRTPI MCLIP, Life Member, Tel:01494 726114. [0011452] 01/01/1934
Pearson Mr WD, MCLIP, Retired. [0019244] 20/01/1965
Pearsons Miss DM, BA(Hons) MCLIP, Inf.Offr., Olswang, London. [0054265] 11/11/1996
Pease Ms CA, BA(Hons) DipIM MCLIP, Lib.Res.Mgr., The Law Soc., London. [0049645] 17/11/1993
Peasgood Mr AN, BA MCLIP, Retired. [0017550] 07/01/1961
Peasley Mr ME, MA(Oxon) DipLib MCLIP, County Ref.& Inf.Serv.Lib., Devon L.& Inf.Serv., Exeter. [0035633] 19/11/1982
Peat Mrs RA, (was Walsh), BA(Hons) MCLIP, Sch.Lib., Wick High Sch., Wick/Caithness. [0042613] 18/01/1989
Peat Mrs SA, BSc(Econ), Unemployed. [0057194] 12/01/1999
Peate Ms ACI, BA(Hons), Inf.Cent.Mgr., Philips Research Labs., Redhill. [0053509] 10/07/1996
Peattie Mr PR, MCLIP, Coll.Lib., Northern Ireland Civil Serv., Greenmount Coll.of Agric.& Hort. [0026648] 26/10/1976
Peaty Mr C, BA, Stud., John Moores Univ. [0061714] 24/10/2002
Peberdy Mrs RJ, BA MSc(Econ) MCLIP, Devel.Mgr., Derbyshire C.C. [0024782] 14/01/1975
Peck Mrs J, DipIS, Lib., Ipswich High Sch., Suffolk. [0050050] 01/03/1994
Peck Mrs JE, BA MCLIP, Lib., Cheshire C.C., Chester. [0022026] 01/01/1974
Peddlesden Ms KK, BA(Hons) MCLIP, CIRC Mgr., Edexcel, London. [0039752] 16/06/1986
Peden Miss AM, MCLIP, Support Serv.Mgr., Lincs.Co.L. [0011462] 01/08/1967
Peden Mrs JE, (was Boyd), BLib BA(Hons) MSc MCLIP, Asst.Lib., Univ.of Ulster, Coleraine Campus. [0044368] 01/10/1990
Peden Mrs RC, (was Beal), BLib MCLIP, LRC Mgr., The Bournemouth & Poole Coll., Bournemouth. [0026677] 09/11/1976

Pedersen Mr VB, BA(Hons) MA, Asst.Lib., Civil Aviation Auth., Gatwick. [0055744] *12/11/1997*
Pedley Mrs AJM, MA MCLIP, Lib.& Alumni Offr.& Arch., The Alcuin L., St.Peter's Sch., York. [0040402] *05/02/1987*
Pedley Rev CJ, BA(Econ) BA MTh ThM, Stud./L.Asst., Thames Valley Univ., Heythrop Coll. [0057993] *11/10/1999*
Pedley Mr D, BA, Learning Res.Mgr., Sion-Manning RC Girls Sch., R.B.Kensington & Chelsea. [0043516] *06/11/1989*
Pedley Mrs HM, MCLIP, Lib., Notts.C.C. [0039675] *06/05/1986*
Pedley Mrs KA, (was Hoad), MLib MCLIP, Serv.Delivery Mgr., L.B.Newham. [0006973] *11/10/1968*
Pedley Mr PD, MA MLib FCLIP, Head of Research, Economist Intelligence Unit, London. [0036884] *11/01/1984* **FE 18/11/1998**
Peebles Miss MA, MBE MCLIP, Retired. [0011467] *29/08/1955*
Peel Mrs JD, BSc MCLIP, Life Member. [0022576] *08/07/1974*
Peel Mrs LM, (was McHale), BA(Hons) DiplLS, Bus.Inf.Specialist, Welsh Devel.Agency, N.Div. [0049097] *01/01/1993*
Peel Yates Miss JS, BA MA MSc, Asst.Lib., DFES, Westminster. [0059398] *01/03/2001*
Peers Mrs OD, (was Robins), MCLIP, Inf.Mgr., L.B.of Sutton, Sutton. [0012549] *15/02/1971*
Peffer Ms ME, BA(Hons) PGDipLib, Lib., Dept.of Health, London. [0049554] *09/11/1993*
Pegg Miss KA, BA DipLib MCLIP, Sen.Asst.Lib., Sheffield City L., S.Yorks. [0027004] *06/01/1977*
Pegg Mr NA, MA MCLIP, Dir., D.S.Ltd., Nottingham, Notts. [0022765] *19/09/1974*
Pegg Mrs SA, (was Smart), BLib MCLIP, p./t.Lend.Lib., Fleet L., Hants.C.C. [0038196] *16/01/1985*
Pegrum Ms AF, BA MA MCLIP, Sen.Inf.Mgr., Corp.Knowledge Team, Cambs.C.C. [0033108] *20/10/1980*
Peill Mr JL, MCLIP, Neighbourhood Lib., Staffs Co.L., Stafford. [0011474] *17/07/1967*
Peisley Ms SL, (was Kemp), MCLIP, Sen.Lib., The Child.Soc., London. [0027767] *15/08/1977*
Pellegrino Mrs M, BA DipLib MCLIP, Lib., Philosophy L., Univ.of Cambridge. [0039886] *06/10/1986*
Pellett Mrs GR, p./t./ng Res.Asst., Univ.of Brighton, Eastbourne Coll. [0059298] *31/01/2001*
Pellow Mrs SJ, (was Rowe), BA(Hons) DipLib, Maternity Leave. [0047706] *19/10/1992*
Pelopida Mrs RC, (was Burton), BA MCLIP, Unemployed. [0038489] *02/05/1985*
Pelowski Mrs MM, MA, Asst.Lib., Univ.of Essex. [0038845] *14/10/1985*
Pelowski Mr P, MA MCLIP, Unemployed. [0041362] *08/11/1987*
Pemberton Mrs MM, (was Willoughby), MA BA(Hons) MCLIP, Neighbourhood Lib., Bristol City Council, Westbury. [0016022] *16/06/1971*
Pemberton Mrs S, Asst.Lib., Univ.of Cent.England, Newman Coll.of H.E. Birmingham. [0058811] *04/08/2000*
Pemberton Miss SJ, BA DipLib MCLIP, L.Trainer, L.Automation Serv., Oxford Univ. [0030025] *23/11/1978*
Pemble Mrs J, (was Hewins), BA(Hons), L.Asst., Anglia Polytech.Univ.-Cambridge. [0058639] *25/04/2000* **AF**
Pembridge Mrs MC, (was Porter), BA(Hons), Customer Serv.Mgr., M.O.D. Abbey Wood Inf.& L.Serv., Bristol. [0041623] *02/02/1988*
Pembroke Mrs SM, (was Hughes), BA DipLib MCLIP, Inf.Mgr., CFBT Advice & Guidance, Luton. [0009246] *01/01/1971*
Pendino Miss F, BA(Hons) MCLIP, Lib., Dewsbury Health Care NHS Trust, Dewsbury. [0048383] *16/12/1992*
Pendlebury Mrs B, (was Wilson), MCLIP, Life Member. [0011484] *30/03/1937*
Pendred Miss PL, BA(Hons) MCLIP, Lib.Mgr., E.Finchley L., L.B.of Barnet. [0038511] *20/05/1985*
Penfold Dr DW, PhD DIC BSc Arcs MCLIP, Postion unknown, Edgerton Publishing Serv., Hastings. [0060572] *11/12/2001*
Penfold Mr FA, BA MCLIP, Inf.Cent.Mgr., City of Edinburgh Council, Edinburgh. [0021132] *14/10/1973*
Penfold Mrs KA, BA MCLIP, Catr., Univ.of Edinburgh/New Coll.L., Edinburgh. [0018144] *07/10/1972*
Penfold Mrs PA, (was Brindle), MCLIP, Lib.Child.work, Hants C.C., Tadley L. [0024608] *10/10/1975*
Penin Mrs GM, (was Mallett), MCLIP, Learning Res.Mgr., Sir John Deanes Sixth Form Coll., Northwich, Cheshire. [0011492] *12/02/1962*
Penn Miss CE, BA MA DiplS, Documentalist, Amnesty Internat., London. [0051069] *10/11/1994*
Penn Ms EA, BA(Hons) MA MCLIP, Lib., Newark & Ollerton. [0051584] *03/04/1995*
Penn Mr MW, LLB(Hons) MCLIP, Retired. [0026507] *12/09/1976*
Penn Mrs SJ, (was Scorer), BEd DipLib MCLIP, Lib., Hewitson Becke & Shaw, Cambridge. [0031441] *27/09/1979*
Penn Mr SW, BA(Hons) DipLib MCLIP, Product Marketing Mgr., DS Ltd., Ferndown, Dorset. [0028355] *14/11/1977*
Pennells Mr JE, DMS MCLIP, Princ.Lib.-Lend.Serv., L.B.Harrow. [0011499] *21/02/1965*
Pennells Mrs LM, (was Schoon), MCLIP, Lib., N.London Collegiate Sch., Edgware. [0011500] *01/01/1965*
Pennells Mrs PL, BA(Hons) DiplLS MCLIP, Asst.Lib.-P./t., Manchester Met.Univ. [0050939] *02/11/1994*
Penney Mrs BM, (was Rudd), MCLIP, Life Member. [0028998] *23/08/1950*
Penney Miss CL, BA DipLib MCLIP, H.of Spec.Collections, Univ.of Birmingham L. [0011503] *01/01/1966*
Penney Miss VR, MCLIP, Life Member. [0011505] *10/01/1945*
Pennick Mr KP, (was Townsend), BA MA MCLIP, Asst.Lib., Univ.of Brighton. [0042205] *05/10/1988*

Pennie Mr DA, MA MCLIP, Asst.Lib., The Brynmor Jones L., Univ.of Hull. [0011507] *14/10/1970*
Pennington Ms JM, (was Doherty), BA(Hons) MA, Inf.Consultant, HM Customs & Excise. [0055315] *01/10/1997*
Penny Mr A, BA MCLIP, Customer Serv.Lib., Herts.C.C., Stevenage L. [0043454] *26/10/1989*
Penny Mrs JE, (was Mitchell), BLib MCLIP, Unemployed. [0026483] *12/10/1976*
Penny Mrs LS, BA MCLIP, Sch.Lib., Aberdeen City Council. [0041435] *07/12/1987*
Penny Mrs S, (was Thomson), MA DipLib MCLIP, Sch.Lib.,(Casual). [0043420] *26/10/1989*
Penny Miss SM, FCLIP, Retired. [0011511] *11/09/1954* **FE 01/01/1965**
Pentelow Mr DA, BLib MCLIP, Head of Inf.Mgmt., Defence Estates, Sutton Coldfield, W.Midlands. [0011513] *25/10/1971*
Pentelow Miss GM, MCLIP, Life Member. [0011514] *13/01/1955*
Pentney Mrs SJ, BSc(Econs), Professional Support Lib., City of Plymouth L.& Inf.Serv. [0055153] *24/07/1997*
Penycate Mrs MD, (was Liggett), MBE BA FCLIP, Life Member. [0011518] *27/03/1936* **FE 01/01/1944**
Peoples Miss MA, BA MCLIP DMS, Asst.Ch.Lib., N.E.Educ.& L.Bd., Ballymena, Co.Antrim. [0021175] *01/10/1973*
Pepin Mr AB, MA MCLIP, Retired. [0011519] *11/09/1951*
Percik Mr D, BA(Hons) MPhil, S.L.A.(Continuations), Inst.of Advanced Legal Studies. [0059221] *09/01/2001*
Percival Miss AMA, BA DipLib MCLIP, Res.Cent.Mgr., Brass Cent., Cardiff Univ., Dept.of City & Reg.Planning. [0040170] *06/11/1986*
Percival Mr D, BA, Asst.L.Super., Cosham L., Portsmouth. [0061420] *15/07/2002*
Percy Mrs BA, (was Morrison), BA MCLIP, Unemployed. [0011534] *14/02/1967*
Pereira Mrs CM, (was D'Lima), BSc DipLib MCLIP, Br.Lib., L.B.of Barking & Dagenham P.L. [0033378] *03/11/1980*
Pereira Miss IMC, DipLIS, L.Asst.,p./t., R.B.Kensington & Chelsea. [0056990] *24/11/1998*
Pereira Ms MJ, BA MCLIP, Consultant, Infoman Inc., Canada. [0026509] *21/10/1976*
Perera Mr H, MA, Asst.Dir., Brit.Council, Sri Lanka. [0061441] *23/07/2002*
Perera Mrs R, BA with QTS, Unemployed, [0060990] *25/01/2002*
Perfitt Ms MT, FCLIP, Life Member. [0011538] *01/01/1961* **FE 29/10/1976**
Perham Mrs L, (was Conroy), JP MP BA MCLIP, Member of Parliament. [0011539] *01/01/1969*
Periel Mrs A, BA (Hons), Graduate Trainee, Inst.of Classical Studies L. [0060933] *11/01/2002*
Perkin Miss JJ, Inf.Cent.Mgr., DLA, Leeds. [0049763] *06/12/1993*
Perkin Mr MR, MA MCLIP, Retired. [0011547] *06/10/1960*
Perkins Mr AB, B Tech M Inf Sc, Unemployed. [0035715] *15/01/1983*
Perkins Mrs AJ, BA, Inf.Lib., Sutton Cent.L., L.B.of Sutton. [0042802] *02/03/1989*
Perkins Miss C, BA(Hons) MCLIP, Team Lib.;CYPS, Luton Bor.Council. [0049364] *29/10/1993*
Perkins Mrs CM, (was D'Arcy), MCLIP, Contracts Asst., NEXUS, Newcastle upon Tyne. [0003600] *05/03/1972*
Perkins Mrs H, (was Wooding), BA MCLIP, Area Child. Co-ord., Nottingham City L. [0011542] *22/05/1964*
Perkins Miss HE, BA, Grad.Trainee, Bodeian L., Oxford. [0061595] *02/10/2002*
Perkins Mrs J, (was Rees), MCLIP, Unemployed. [0012243] *03/10/1970*
Perkins Miss JA, BA(Hons), Asst.Inf.Adviser, Univ.of Brighton. [0051632] *21/04/1995*
Perkins Mr MA, BA MLib MCLIP, Lib., Secretariat of the Pacific Comm., Noumea, New Caledonia. [0045004] *18/05/1990*
Perkins Mrs N, (was Jones), MCLIP, Child.Lib., Hants.C.C., Chineham L. [0008068] *22/09/1976*
Perkins Miss NJ, BA(Hons), Asst.Lib., Wyggeston & QEI Coll., Leicester. [0052322] *26/10/1995*
Perkins Miss VA, BA(Hons) MCLIP, Lib., Inf.Servs., Marylebone L., Westminster L.& Arch. [0011551] *13/09/1967*
Perks Mrs EA, (was Hookings), Asst.Lib., Hereford & Worcester C.C., Kidderminster. [0041804] *07/04/1988* **AF**
Perks Mrs JM, (was Edwards), MCLIP, Sen.Lib.-Community Inf., Shropshire C.C., Shrewsbury. [0021121] *10/10/1973*
Perrett Mrs CHJ, (was Tough), BA DipLib MCLIP, Catg.Co-ordinator, Middlesex Univ., London. [0036620] *24/10/1983*
Perrin Miss PM, FRSA BA MCLIP, Retired. [0011556] *17/02/1949*
Perris Miss KC, BA(Hons), Stud., London Metro.Univ. [0061730] *29/10/2002*
Perrott Mrs M, BA HDipEd MA MCLIP, Asst.Lib., Learner Support, Open Univ., Milton Keynes. [0047575] *02/10/1992*
Perrow Mr DE, MA MA(LIB) MCLIP, Dir.of Inf.Systems & Serv., Templeton Coll., Oxford. [0026510] *01/10/1976*
Perry Mrs A, (was McCormack), BSc DipLib MCLIP, Inf.Specialist, Unilever Research. [0042279] *13/10/1988*
Perry Mrs C, BA, Postgraduate Stud., Univ. of Brighton. [0058895] *02/10/2000*
Perry Mrs CA, (was Stroud), BA MCLIP, Head of Res.Mgmt., Birmingham City Council, Cent.L. [0027784] *15/07/1977*
Perry Ms CJ, Inf.Mgr., Ogier & Le Masurier, St.Helier, Jersey. [0061428] *18/07/2002*
Perry Mr DA, BA MCLIP, Lib., Nat.Radiological Protection Board, Oxon. [0022104] *20/02/1974*
Perry Ms EJ, (was Howe), BA(Hons), Unemployed. [0039194] *07/01/1986*
Perry Mrs FAS, (was Olver), BA DipLib MCLIP BA(OU), Inf.Offr., Inst.of Mining & Metallurgy, London. [0031764] *03/12/1979*
Perry Mrs GE, (was Parris), BA MCLIP, Unemployed. [0025804] *26/02/1976*
Perry Mrs H, BEd DipILM, Lib., Knutsford L., Cheshire C.C. [0054707] *06/03/1997*

325

Perry Mrs M, (was Lancaster), MCLIP, Trust Lib., E.Cheshire NHS Trust, Macclesfield. [0008607] 18/01/1970
Perry Mr MD, BA(Hons) DMS MCLIP, Princ.Lib., L.B.of Brent, Harlesden L. [0011562] 14/01/1969
Perry Mr P, MCLIP, Unemployed. [0011563] 07/02/1955
Perry Miss RK, BA MCLIP, Learning Res.Mgr., BCA. [0042596] 18/01/1989
Perry Ms SJ, BSc(Hons) MSc MCLIP, Unemployed. [0049000] 24/08/1993
Persaud Mr R, BSc(Hons), Asst.Subject Lib., Oxford Brookes Univ., Oxford. [0054394] 03/12/1996
Persey Miss VA, MCLIP, Lib., Guildford Sch.of Acting, Surrey. [0018105] 04/10/1972
Perthon Miss SF, BLS(Hons) MCLIP, Lib., Basildon & Thurrock NHS Trust, Basildon Hosp. [0058575] 04/04/2000
Pestell Mr R, BSc MSC ALAA FCLIP JP, Dir., P.L.Div., State L.of Queensland. [0019247] 01/01/1965 **FE 22/01/1997**
Pester Mr DR, BA DipLib MCLIP, Catr., London Guildhall Univ. [0037135] 20/02/1984
Peter Miss J, BA(Hons), L.Manager, Latham & Watkins, London. [0047486] 02/09/1992
Peters Mrs AE, (was Prideaux), MCLIP, Life Member. [0011569] 03/03/1960
Peters Miss AL, BA(Hons), Asst.Lib., Park Lane Coll., Leeds. [0058692] 06/06/2000
Peters Mrs C, (was Williams), BSc MCLIP, p./t.Inf.Lib., Surrey C.C., Guildford. [0033366] 26/10/1980
Peters Mrs EJ, (was Hunnisett), MCLIP, Lib., Steyning Grammar Sch., W.Sussex. [0026418] 01/10/1976
Peters Mrs JL, (was Meyer), MCLIP, Relief Asst.Lib., W.Sussex C.C. [0028241] 21/10/1977
Peters Mrs JM, (was Taylor), BA MLS MCLIP, Head of L.& Learning Resources, Univ.of Wales Coll., Newport. [0034208] 12/10/1981
Peters Mrs K, (was Pearson), MCLIP, Lib., The Royal Soc., London. [0026875] 01/01/1974
Peters Miss LJ, BSc(Hons) MSc(Econ), Project Mgr., Chester Coll.of H.E. [0053495] 04/07/1976
Peters Ms M, BA, Stud., Univ.of Brighton. [0059929] 06/11/2001
Peters Mrs NA, (was Higgs), BA MA MCLIP, p./t.Asst.Lib., Redditch L., Worcs.C.C. [0035301] 01/10/1982
Peters Miss SM, Lib., G.Maunsell & Partners, Witham. [0040391] 28/01/1987
Petersen Miss CL, BA(Hons), Lib.(Syp), Derbys.C.C., Bolsover Dist. [0051539] 01/04/1995
Petersen Mrs LA, p./t.Stud./Asst.Lib., Univ.of Cent.England, Birmingham, Lordswood Boys Sch.& 6th Form Cent. [0059021] 27/10/2000
Petherbridge Mrs JM, (was Doughty), MCLIP DMS MIMgt, L.& Mus.Mgr., N.Somerset Council. [0018643] 01/10/1972
Pethers Ms HJ, BA(Hons), L.& Inf.Asst., Nat.Maritime Mus., Greenwich. [0057577] 06/05/1999
Pethick Mrs SM, (was West), BA MCLIP, Unemployed. [0039307] 08/01/1986
Petit Mr GMJ, MA, Stud., Thames Valley Univ. [0061195] 08/04/2002
Peto Mrs GW, (was Cartwright), BA DipLib MCLIP, Lib., Nottingham Cent.L., Notts. [0026307] 01/10/1976
Petocz Mr L, MCLIP, Retired, Resident Australia. [0017558] 12/09/1966
Petrie Miss A, MA MCLIP, 2nd Sec.Commercial, Foreign & Commonwealth Off., London. [0011582] 25/09/1968
Petrie Mr JH, BSc MSc MCLIP, Resident in Germany. [0060056] 07/12/2001
Petrie Mrs JLB, (was Penman), MCLIP, Career Break. [0060573] 21/08/1970
Petrie Miss KM, MBE MCLIP, Life Member, Tel.01462 450447, 16 Wratten Road East, Hitchin, SG5 2AS. [0011583] 21/08/1942
Petrie Miss M, MA, Unemployed (Career Break). [0046012] 16/08/1991
Pettifer Miss LC, BA(Hons), Asst.Lib., Brit.Geological Survey, Keyworth. [0059337] 09/02/2001
Pettigrew Mrs DJ, (was Billingsley), MA MCLIP, Retired. [0001247] 13/01/1972
Pettit Mr CPC, MA MCLIP, Asst.Co.Lib., Oxon.C.C. [0026790] 27/10/1976
Pettit Mrs PR, (was Grimsey), BA MCLIP, P./t.L.Asst., Estover Comm.Coll., Plymouth. [0023028] 22/01/1974
Pettit Ms S, BSc MCLIP, Subject Lib., Wills L., Univ.of Bristol. [0024785] 06/10/1975
Pettitt Miss JM, MCLIP, Life Member. [0011586] 31/03/1938
Petts Ms CP, BA MA MSc MCLIP, Retired. [0060573] 11/12/2001
Petty Mr D, BA FCLIP, Assoc.Dir., Univ.of Georgia L., U.S.A. [0011590] 01/01/1957 **FE 01/01/1957**
Petty Mr MJ, MBE MA(Hons) MCLIP, Retired. [0011593] 01/01/1964
Petursdottir Mrs KH, (was Bokafulltrui), Dir., Public & Sch L., Iceland. [0017560] 22/03/1968
Pewtress Mrs JM, (was Anderson), BSc(Econ), Bus.Support Mgr., Surrey C.C., Leatherhead. [0046044] 06/09/1991 **AF**
Pfleger Ms AJ, (was Dolphin), Inf.Cent.Mgr., Nat.Audit Off., London. [0038033] 15/01/1985
Pflug Dr G, HonFCLIP, Hon.Fellow. [0046054] 11/09/1989 **FE 11/09/1989**
Phelan Mrs EA, (was Roberts), BA MCLIP, Dir.of L.and Theatres, Manchester Central L. [0020966] 23/08/1973
Phelps Mrs HJ, (was Leighton), MBA BA DipLib MCLIP, Writer. [0029725] 05/10/1974
Phelps Miss JM, MCLIP, Sen.Inf.Lib., Farnborough, Hants.C.C. [0011596] 06/10/1969
Phelps Mr M, MA MCLIP, Asst.Area Lib., Bradford Metro.Dist.L. [0024786] 01/01/1973
Phelps Mrs PJ, MCLIP, Princ.Lib.-N.E., Burton L., Staffs.C.C. [0011598] 17/01/1969
Phelps Mrs SH, MCLIP, Unemployed, Tel:0141 578 3039. [0031684] 05/11/1979
Phelpstead Mrs LJ, BA(Hons) MCLIP, Lib., Leics.L.& Inf.Serv., Syston L. [0054122] 31/10/1996
Phenix Mr AP, LLB(Hons), Inf.Specialist, Irwin Mitchell Solicitors, London. [0061078] 04/03/2002 **AF**

Philip Mrs HR, (was Farrell), BA MCLIP, Sch.Lib., Millburn Academy, Inverness. [0020945] 11/09/1973
Phillifent Mr R, BSc(Hons) MA PGCE, Dir./Lib., L.of Japanese Sci.& Tech., Whitley Bay. [0051268] 14/12/1994
Phillip Mrs ME, MA (Hons), Stud., Robert Gordon Univ. [0061007] 30/01/2002
Phillipps Mrs TL, (was Mingard), BA MCLIP, Unemployed. [0035983] 01/03/1983
Phillips Miss A, Sen.L.Offr., Home L.Serv., Stockport. [0059814] 10/10/2001 **AF**
Phillips Ms A, BA MA, Temp. Work, [0060951] 15/01/2002
Phillips Mr AB, BA MCLIP, Retired, 23 Meynell Rd., London E9 7AP. [0011607] 08/10/1967
Phillips Mr C, BA DipLib MCLIP, L.& Inf.Serv.Co-ordinator, Highland Council. [0029791] 08/10/1978
Phillips Mr CJ, BA DipLib MCLIP, L.Serv.Devel.Mgr., Surrey Co.L., Mid-Area, Ewell. [0025392] 09/01/1976
Phillips Mrs CK, (was Edwards), BA DipLib MCLIP, Yoga Teacher, Surrey C.C. [0026356] 03/10/1976
Phillips Miss CM, MA MCLIP, Lib., Brit.Antarctic Survey, Cambridge. [0011613] 12/10/1970
Phillips Ms CM, (was Coomer), MCLIP, p./t.Sch.Lib./L.Asst., Felsted Sch., Gt.Dunmow. [0011129] 09/02/1966
Phillips Mrs CP, (was Beckett), BA MCLIP, Mgr., Pyle Life Cent., Bridgend L.& Inf.Serv. [0001029] 01/10/1976
Phillips Mrs DJ, BA MCLIP, LSEIRC Project Mgr., Defence Diversification Agency, Farnborough, Hants. [0028118] 01/10/1977
Phillips Mrs E, (was Gray), BA DipLib MCLIP, Asst.Lib., Royal Coll.of Surgeons in Ireland, Dublin. [0011618] 18/10/1966
Phillips Mrs ER, (was Evans), BA MCLIP, Inf.Lib., Univ.of Glamorgan. [0011619] 11/10/1966
Phillips Mr GA, BA(Hons) DiplLM, Bus.Inf.Lib., Bury M.B.C. [0051664] 04/05/1995
Phillips Mrs HM, (was Burchell), MA MSc MCLIP, Asst.Lib., Oxford Brookes Univ.L. [0052548] 08/11/1995
Phillips Dr HP, (was May), BA MA DipLib MCLIP, Performance Mgr., Plymouth C.C. [0036145] 01/07/1983
Phillips Mrs JA, (was Garrett), BA MCLIP, Dep.Lib., Broadmoor Hosp.Auth., Berks. [0026726] 01/11/1976
Phillips Mrs JB, (was Nash), BLib MCLIP, Unemployed. [0025615] 24/01/1976
Phillips Mr JR, MCLIP, Cent.L., Sutton, Surrey. [0027006] 10/01/1977
Phillips Mr KC, BSc MSc, Self-employed, Sole Trader, Kindred UK., Newcastle Upon Tyne. [0056291] 28/04/1998
Phillips Ms KE, BA MCLIP, Stud. [0033743] 16/02/1981
Phillips Miss KL, BA(Hons) MCLIP, Asst.Lib., Dept.of Health, London. [0051864] 08/11/1995
Phillips Miss L, BA MCLIP, Inf.Off., Members Serv.Unit, Newcastle upon Tyne City Council. [0011625] 30/01/1968
Phillips Mr L, BA MCLIP, Leisure Dept.Lib., Cardiff Cent.L. [0020913] 18/08/1973
Phillips Mrs L, (was Smith), BA(Hons) MCLIP, p./t.Learning Adviser, Leeds Metro.Univ., W.Yorks. [0021045] 24/09/1973
Phillips Ms LA, BA(Hons), Unemployed. [0050824] 20/10/1994
Phillips Mrs LJ, (was Barford), MCLIP, Lib., Dartford Tech.Coll. [0000745] 16/10/1967
Phillips Ms LM, (was Sandy), BA DipEd, Classroom Asst., Cornwall C.C. [0036243] 19/08/1983
Phillips Mr ME, MA MA MCLIP, Asst.Lib., Christ Church L., Oxford. [0050672] 07/10/1994
Phillips Mrs ME, (was Davies), MCLIP, Asst.Lib., Carmarthensire C.C. [0021595] 16/10/1973
Phillips Miss MH, BA MCLIP, Asst.Lib., Nat.L.of Wales. [0011626] 08/02/1967
Phillips Mr MJ, MCLIP, Retired. [0011627] 02/10/1931
Phillips Mr MR, MCLIP, Lib., Edinburgh City L. [0011629] 23/09/1966
Phillips Mrs NJ, (was Atkins), BA(Hons) MA MCLIP, Industrial Design Subject Lib., Coventry Univ., Frederick Lanchester L. [0053795] 01/10/1996
Phillips Miss R, BA(Hons), Stud., Univ.of Sheffield. [0058877] 27/09/2000
Phillips Mr R, DipIM MCLIP, L.Serv.Mgr., L., Mayday Univ.Hosp., Croydon. [0056713] 07/10/1998
Phillips Mr R, MA FCLIP, Life Member. [0011631] 05/10/1960 **FE 01/01/1967**
Phillips Mrs RA, BA MCLIP, Employment not known. [0018217] 02/10/1972
Phillips Mr RD, BA MCLIP, Librarian., Brighton Library. [0033111] 02/10/1980
Phillips Miss RJ, BSc, Sconul Trainee, Nat. L. of Wales. [0060988] 25/01/2002
Phillips Mr S, BA DipLib MCLIP, Lib., Univ.Coll., Dublin, Eire. [0011636] 02/03/1965
Phillips Mrs S, (was Avery), BL FCLIP, Retired. [0017564] 22/01/1958 **FE 13/06/1990**
Phillips Miss SE, BA(Hons) MA, Sales Process Super., Talis Inf., Birmingham. [0047083] 22/04/1992
Phillips Mrs SE, (was Nettleton), BA CertEd MCLIP, Consultant Lib., Read Educ. Trust, South Africa. [0010738] 07/07/1971
Phillips Mr SF, BA MLib MCLIP, Head of Learning Support Serv., Norwich City Coll., Norfolk. [0024126] 06/04/1975
Phillips Mr SG, BA DipLib MCLIP, Sen.Lib., Aldershot L., Hants.Co.L. [0029792] 03/10/1978
Phillips Mr SJ, BLib MCLIP, Mgr., Morgan Stanley & Co.Internat.Ltd., London. [0040788] 06/06/1987
Phillips Ms SL, BA, Unemployed. [0035699] 17/01/1983
Phillips Mr WT, BA DipLib MCLIP, Area Lib., Carmarthenshire C.C., Ammanford. [0035191] 08/10/1981
Phillips-Morgan Ms SR, (was Phillips), BA DIP CCS MLib MCLIP, Unemployed. [0042428] 20/10/1988
Phillpot Mr C, FCLIP, Art L.Consultant. [0011644] 12/08/1960 **FE 12/12/1990**

Personal Members

Phillpotts Ms CE, BA (Hons) MA MCLIP, Lib., English Heritage, London. [0043276] 10/10/1989
Philpot Mrs S, (was Cook), BA(Hons) MCLIP, Sch.Lib., The Royal Grammar Sch., High Wycombe, Bucks. [0011647] 21/03/1966
Philpott Mr SJ, MCLIP, Inf./Res.Off., M.O.D., London. [0036222] 01/08/1983
Phipps Mr CA, BA(Hons) MA MA MCLIP, Asst.Lib.(Reader Serv.), The London L. [0049084] 04/10/1993
Phipps Mrs JC, BA MCLIP, Retired. [0029206] 31/03/1978
Phipps Ms JL, Sen.L.Asst., p./t.Stud., Cambridge Univ.L., Cambridge. [0059523] 24/04/2001
Phipps Mr JS, BSc MCLIP, Asst.Lib., Gateshead L.& Arts Dept., Cent.L. [0018215] 03/10/1972
Physick Mrs HM, BA MCLIP, Sen.Asst.Lib., L.B.of Harrow L. [0033956] 17/06/1981
Piasecki Miss R, BA, Stud./L.Clerk, Hammersmith Hosp.Health Records. [0061161] 20/03/2002
Pickard Mrs E, L.Asst., Cranbrook L., Kent. [0045849] 21/06/1991 **AF**
Pickaver Miss CE, BA MSc(Econ) MCLIP, User Serv.Mgr., Brunel Univ.L., Uxbridge. [0028878] 22/01/1978
Pickerill Miss S, BSc MCLIP, Employment unknown. [0060574] 11/12/2001
Pickering Mr HJ, BA MCLIP, Mgr.Dir., BiblioMondo GmbH, Germany. [0011659] 21/01/1963
Pickering Miss HV, BSc MCLIP, Copyright Offr., Heron, Univ.of Stirling. [0047188] 26/05/1992
Pickering Mrs JE, (was Gopsill), MCLIP, Child.Lib.-N., Nuneaton, Warks.Co.L. [0000505] 25/02/1970
Pickering Mrs OM, BA MA MPhil, Asst.Lib., Warneford Hosp., Oxford. [0057876] 20/09/1999
Pickering Miss PL, MCLIP, Life Member. [0011662] 31/03/1955
Pickersgill Mrs A, (was Cockshott), BA MCLIP GradIPD, Off.Mgr., BPP Manchester. [0023879] 07/02/1975
Pickett Mrs KP, (was George), BA(Hons) MCLIP, p./t.L.Asst., Powergen plc., Power Tech.Cent., Nottingham. [0042445] 09/11/1988
Pickett Miss SC, BA(Hons), Stud., Loughborough Univ. [0059816] 10/10/2001
Pickles Mr NG, BA(Hons) MSc PGCE MCLIP, Dir.of Learning Res.Serv., Somerset Coll.of Arts & Tech. [0054788] 04/04/1988
Pickstone Ms ME, BSc DipLib MCLIP, Site L.Mgr.,(Alsager), Manchester Metro.Univ., Crewe & Alsager Fac. [0034325] 23/10/1981
Pickup Mr PWH, FCLIP, Life Member, Tel.01380 830037, 11 Upper Garston Lane, Bratton, Westbury, Wilts., BA13 4SN. [0011672] 23/02/1950 **FE 01/01/1959**
Picton Mr HA, BA MCLIP, Dep.Mgr.-Inf.Cent., Bank of England, London. [0022940] 21/09/1974
Picton Miss SD, BA(Hons) DipIM MCLIP, Asst.Lib., Essex Rivers Healthcare NHS Trust, N.Essex Hosp. [0051975] 29/08/1995
Pierce Ms AM, BA DipLib MPhil MCLIP, Asst.Lib., Llyfrgell Genedlaethol Cymru, Aberystwyth. [0043490] 30/10/1989
Pierce Ms KF, MPhil BA(Hons), p./t.Stud./L.Asst., Univ.of Wales, Aberystwyth, Sir Herbert Duthie L., UWCM. [0061197] 08/04/2002
Pierce Moulton Mrs M, (was Pierce-Jones), BA MCLIP, Lib.& Gen.Mgr., Liverpool Med.Inst. [0011680] 28/01/1969
Piercy Mrs LI, BA MCLIP, Stock Co-ordinator, L.B.of Hillingdon. [0011681] 02/07/1972
Pieris Mrs KS, (was (Form.Jayakuru)), BA MCLIP, Retired. [0019947] 15/01/1973
Piggott Miss M, BA FCLIP, Life Member, 01394 384405, 11 Suffolk Pl., Limekiln Quay Rd., Woodbridge, Suffolk, IP12 1XB. [0011684] 16/10/1935 **FE 01/01/1936**
Piggott Mrs PA, MCLIP, Lib., The Windsor Boys' Sch., Windsor. [0022655] 24/07/1974
Piggott Mr RL, MCLIP, Corporate Lib., Wokingham Dist.Council, Berks. [0022654] 30/07/1974
Pigott Mrs FC, (was Gullick), BA(Hons), Customer Serv.Mgr.(p./t.), Sirsi Ltd., Potters Bar. [0043324] 19/10/1989
Pigott Mrs H, BTec BSc(Hons), Career Break. [0050319] 21/06/1994
Pigula Mrs ED, MA, Asst.Lib., The Coll.of Law, Guildford, Surrey. [0057379] 22/02/1999
Pike Miss EJ, MA MSc, Lib., Pembroke Coll.Univ.of Oxford. [0055790] 24/11/1997
Pike Mrs JA, (was Caunce), BA MCLIP, p./t.Sch.Lib., Newland House Sch., Twickenham. [0032892] 15/10/1980
Pike Miss LJ, BSc(Hons), Stud., City Univ. [0061737] 30/10/2002
Pike Mrs RA, (was Shooter), BA(Hons) DipLib MCLIP, Sch.Lib., Bishops Stortford Coll., Jnr.Sch. [0034418] 05/11/1981
Pilbeam Miss KN, BA MA, Asst.Lib., Macfarlanes, London. [0055427] 07/10/1997
Pilcher Mrs A, BA(Hons) DipIS MCLIP, Comm.Lib., Kent C.C. [0049105] 04/10/1993
Pilcher Mrs JA, L.Inf.Offr., Dewsbury Coll., W.Yorks. [0061610] 03/10/2002 **AF**
Pilgram Mr T, Resident in Sweden. [0061477] 09/08/2002
Pilkington Mrs CA, BA(Hons), L.Mgr., Brookway High Sch.& Sports Coll., Wythenshawe. [0053616] 12/08/1996
Pilkington Mrs GH, (was Anderson), BSc, Inf.Analyst, Info to Go Ltd., Cambridge. [0046516] 15/11/1991
Pilkington Mrs IMV, (was Hickie), MCLIP, L.Operations Mgr., R.B.of Kensington & Chelsea, Cent.L. [0022304] 16/04/1974
Pilkington Mrs P, (was Greenwood), MCLIP, Br.Lib., L.B.of Havering, Gidea Park L. [0011693] 26/02/1973
Pill Mr TJH, MA MLib MA, ICT Consultant, The Brit.Council, Hong Kong. [0047740] 16/10/1992
Pillans Mrs HA, (was Cumming), BA MCLIP, Sch.Lib., Barrhead High Sch., E.Renfrewshire. [0027604] 15/06/1977
Pillar Ms CM, BA DipLib MA, Intranet/Internet Website Devel.Off., N.Cumbria Acute NHS Trust, Cumbria. [0039255] 02/10/1986

Pillath Ms CA, BA DipLib MCLIP, [0031686] 18/10/1979
Pilling Ms CM, BA DipLib, Unemployed. [0025629] 18/01/1976
Pilling Mr JC, MA MCLIP, Sen.Lib., Abingdon L., Oxon.C.C. [0035556] 27/10/1982
Pilling Mrs S, (was Blacknell), BA MBA MIMgt MCLIP, Co-operation & Partnership Prog., Brit.L., Boston Spa. [0001350] 22/02/1969
Pilmer Mr AC, BA(Hons), Stud. [0058869] 14/09/2000
Pilmer Ms SJ, BSc MSc MCLIP, Systems Lib., NSPCC, London. [0048884] 12/07/1993
Pilott Mrs SA, p./t.Stud., Univ.of Brighton. [0061072] 11/02/2002
Pilsworth Mrs SF, MCLIP, Unemployed. [0022022] 15/01/1974
Pimlett Mr GR, MA MIMgt MCLIP, Unemployed. [0011697] 01/01/1967
Pimperton Mrs L, (was Milne), BA(Hons) MA DipIS MCLIP, Inf.Mgr., E.Lancashire Career Serv., Blackburn. [0044879] 08/01/1991
Pinder Mr CJ, BA MLib MCLIP, Dir.of Learning Inf.Serv., Napier Univ.Learning Inf.Serv., Edinburgh. [0022582] 24/09/1973
Pinder Mrs E, (was Sumner), MCLIP, Retired. [0009248] 25/03/1943
Pinder Mr FD, BA MCLIP, Princ.Lib., Cent.L.& Arts Cent., Rotherham. [0022829] 09/09/1974
Pinder Ms MJ, BA(Hons) MCLIP, Faculty Team Lib., Brotherton L., Leeds Univ. [0047928] 26/10/1992
Pine-Coffin Miss H, BA MA MCLIP, Inf.Specialist, GCHQ. [0055332] 01/10/1997
Pinel Mrs E, BSc, Position Unkown, Southwark Coll., Waterloo Learning Cent. [0059158] 01/12/2000 **AF**
Pinfield Mr SJ, MA MCLIP, Academic Serv.Lib., Univ.of Nottingham. [0044397] 04/10/1990
Pinfold Ms D, BA DipLib MCLIP, Lib., London Guildhall Univ., London. [0031924] 07/01/1980
Pinfold Ms J, BA DipLib, Reader Serv.Lib., Plant Sci.L., Oxford Univ.L.Serv. [0038051] 09/01/1985
Pinfold Mr RC, FCLIP, Retired. [0011710] 29/11/1934 **FE 01/01/1948**
Pinion Miss CF, BA FRSA HonFCLIP FCLIP, AV Consultant, 65 Ranmoor Cres., Sheffield, S10 3GW, Tel./Fax.01142 305714. [0011711] 12/03/1961 **FE 20/09/2000**
Pink Miss S, BA(Hons) MA MCLIP, Asst.Lib., Univ.of Westminster. [0055152] 23/07/1997
Pinkney Miss RM, Inf.Asst., Teesside Univ., L.& Inf.Cent., Middlesbrough. [0057839] 03/09/1999
Pinnegar Ms SV, BA DipLib MCLIP, L.Consultant, Univ.of La Verne, Kifissia, Greece. [0039322] 12/01/1986
Pinnell Mr MH, BA DipLib, Business Inf.Serv.Mgr., L.B.of Bromley, Kent. [0044542] 22/10/1990
Pinnington Mrs MJ, (was Priestley), BA MCLIP, Lib., Group 4 Securitas, HMP Altcourse, Liverpool. [0028129] 03/10/1977
Pinnock Mr AC, MA MCLIP, Serv.Support Offr., Leeds City Ls. [0019581] 16/11/1972
Pinnock Mrs S, L.Asst., Clevedon L., N.Somerset Dist.Council. [0058601] 11/04/2000 **AF**
Pinsent Miss PA, BA MCLIP, Asst.Lib.p./t., Bodleian Law L., Cranfield Coll. [0022538] 16/07/1974
Pintat Mr R, Lib., Univ.of Paris VIII, France. [0061085] 04/03/2002
Pinto Mr PJA, BA DipLib MCLIP, Lib., Commission for Racial Equality, London. [0043910] 16/02/1990
Piorowski Mr A, MCLIP, Princ.L.Offr.-Community Ls.Serv., Sandwell M.B.C., W.Bromwich. [0022148] 25/02/1974
Piotrowicz Mrs AM, (was Vermeulen), BA(Hons) ALCM PGDipILS LTCL, Unemployed. [0048645] 01/04/1993
Piotrowska Miss AC, BA MCLIP, Sen.Lib., Kensington Central L., London. [0030510] 31/01/1979
Pipe Mr WSA, BSc MCLIP, Employment not known. [0060819] 12/12/2001
Piper Miss C, BA(Hons) DipInf, Higher L.Exec., House of Commons L., London. [0047976] 29/10/1992
Piper Mrs PA, (was Trim), BA MCLIP, LRC Mgr., Richard Aldworth Comm.Sch., Hants. [0036077] 26/04/1983
Pirie Ms A, BSc(Hons), Child.Lib., Perth & Kinross Council, Perth. [0051144] 23/11/1994
Pirwitz Ms H, MA DipLib MCLIP, Ch.Catr., Ove Arup Partnership, London. [0030785] 20/01/1979
Pitcher Miss M, BA MCLIP, Sen.Lib. (Acquisitions), Lancs.L.H.Q., Preston. [0023785] 13/01/1975
Pitman Mr AJ, BSc MA DipLIM, Grp.Inf.Support Lib., Leeds City Council. [0051950] 17/08/1995
Pitman Mrs AJ, (was Hunter), BA MCLIP, Housewife. [0029181] 06/04/1978
Pitman Ms C, MA DipLib MCLIP, L.Mgr.(Devel.), L.B.of Tower Hamlets. [0034529] 02/12/1981
Pitman Miss NJ, BA MCLIP, Acting Lib., Wilts.C.C., Warminster L. [0043688] 28/11/1989
Pitman Miss RW, MA(Hons) MPhil, Stud., Strathclyde Univ. [0061760] 05/11/2002
Pitt Mrs CP, (was Schofield), MCLIP, Lib.i/c., Padiham Br.L. [0013013] 01/01/1967
Pitt Ms KA, MA DipLib MCLIP, p./t.German Translator, Welcome Cottage Holidays., Skipton. [0031418] 01/10/1979
Pitt Miss LE, BA, Stud., Manchester Met.Univ. [0060033] 29/11/2001
Pitt Mrs R, L.Serv.Team Leader, N.Staffs.Healthcare NHS Trust. [0058664] 10/05/2000
Pitts Mrs DML, (was Adams), MCLIP, Unemployed. [0000039] 01/01/1963
Pittwood Mr AR, BSc MA MSc CertEd MCLIP, Employment not known. [0060781] 12/12/2001
Piwowar Mrs J, BSc(Econ), Stud., Univ.of Wales, Aberystwyth, & Asst.Lib., King's Coll.Sch., Wimbledon, London. [0057701] 01/07/1999
Place Mrs EJ, (was Worsfold), BSc MA MCLIP, Project Mgr., I.L.R.T., Univ.of Bristol. [0049008] 26/08/1993
Place Mrs MG, (was Lillington), MA MCLIP, Lib./Teacher, St.Mary Sch., Ascot. [0019964] 11/01/1973

Plaice Ms CJ, BLib(Hons) DipMgmtS MCLIP, Knowledge Serv.Mgr., L.& Inf.Serv., N.Bristol NHS Trust, Southmead Hosp. [0034174] 07/10/1981
Plaister Miss JM, OBE BSc FCLIP, Life Member, Tel.(020)8444 8860, 3 St.Regis Close, London, N10 2DE. [0011732] 01/01/1947 FE 01/01/1955
Plane Miss JR, MA MCLIP, Arts Liaison Lib., Newcastle-upon-Tyne Univ. [0011733] 11/10/1969
Plank Ms KA, Asst.Br.Super., Royal Bor.of Windsor & Maidenhead, Maidenhead L. [0053315] 01/05/1996 **AF**
Plank Miss SA, BA(Hons) MA, Lib., Treasury & Cabinet Off.L., London. [0052040] 01/01/1995
Plant Miss J, BSc LRSC MCLIP, Retired. [0060575] 11/12/2001
Plant Mrs VJ, (was Briggs), BA MCLIP, Grp.Lib., Leics.L.& Inf.Serv. [0025492] 12/02/1976
Platon Mrs ES, MCLIP, Lib., Abingdon L., Oxon.C.C. [0011741] 01/01/1968
Platt Mrs AA, BPharm(Hons), L.Asst., Oxted L., Surrey. [0058605] 15/10/1998
Platt Ms EC, MA MCLIP, Inf.Offr., ENABLE, Glasgow. [0037465] 01/10/1984
Platt Ms GS, BA DipLib MCLIP, Sch.of Mod.Lang.& Ling.Subject, Spec., Univ.of Manchester. [0022707] 16/09/1974
Platt Mr MR, Sen.Inf.Offr., Simmons & Simmons, London. [0041450] 01/01/1988
Platt Dr P, MA PhD FCLIP, Retired. [0011743] 01/01/1957 FE 01/01/1966
Platt Mrs RA, BA(Hons), Lib., Warrington Bor.Council. [0054041] 22/10/1996
Platts Mrs HJ, (was Hawkins), BA DipLib MCLIP, Lib., Al Sahwa Sch., Muscat, Oman. [0031854] 09/01/1980
Playford Ms TJ, BA(Hons) MCLIP, Child.L., W.Sussex C.C., Worthing L. [0048251] 18/11/1992
Playforth Ms SA, MCLIP, Independent Consultant. [0015983] 01/01/1971
Playle Mrs ED, (was Driver), MCLIP, Retired. [0018145] 10/10/1972
Pledge Ms D, BA(Hons), Stud., City Univ. [0061734] 30/10/2002
Plenty Mrs AS, BA(Hons) PGDip, P./t.Lib., Blenheim High Sch., Epsom, Surrey. [0055092] 10/07/1997
Plews Mrs LD, (was Keevill), BLib MCLIP, Housewife/p./t.Waitress/Mother. [0027534] 24/05/1977
Plimmer Miss NJ, BA(Hons), Relief L.Asst., Rochdale L.Serv., Wheatsheaf L. [0058226] 19/11/1999
Plincke Miss EM, BA FCLIP, Life Member, Tel.01264 860371. [0011751] 05/04/1950 FE 01/01/1955
Plom Ms HL, BA, Stud., Loughborough Univ. [0058132] 04/11/1999
Plowman Mrs L, (was Cathcart), BA(Hons) DipLIS MCLIP, Team Lib., Beds.C.C., Dept.Educ.Arts & L., Leighton Buzzard L., LU7 8RX. [0045489] 14/02/1991
Plum Mrs SM, (was McGrath), BA MCLIP, p./t.L.Asst., Priory Sch.L., Hitchin. [0028630] 03/01/1978
Plumb Mr DW, BA MCLIP, Catr., Brit.L.:Oriental & India Off.Coll., London. [0011754] 30/01/1972
Plumb Mr PW, JP FCLIP, Retired, Past President L.Assoc. [0011756] 02/01/1942 FE 01/01/1955
Plumbe Mr WJ, FCLIP HonFNLA, Retired. [0017573] 06/03/1931 FE 01/01/1940
Pluse Mr JM, MA MIMgt FCLIP, Ch.Exec., Inf.Serv.NTO, Bradford. [0011765] 30/09/1955 FE 19/03/1997
Poad Mrs AED, BA(Hons) MSc MCLIP, Dep.Programme Mgr., Dept.for Internat.Devel., E.Kilbride. [0046824] 11/02/1992
Poad Mrs DM, MCLIP, p./t.Catr., Cornwall Co.L., Truro. [0011766] 01/01/1965
Poad Mrs JE, MA MCLIP, L.Serv.Mgr., Beds.C.C. [0024127] 13/03/1975
Podmore Mr WR, BA MA MCLIP, Ch.Lib., Brit.Sch.of Osteopathy, London. [0034152] 09/10/1981
Pointer Mrs CAM, (was Stubbings), MCLIP, Lib.(Hon.), The Compassionate Friends, Bristol. [0014171] 07/02/1963
Pointer Miss RJ, BA MCLIP, Sen.Grp.Lib., Leics.C.C., Melton Mowbray. [0031545] 23/11/1979 FE 01/04/2002
Pointon Mrs BA, BA, L.Asst., Comberton Village Coll., Comberton, Cambs. [0052694] 23/11/1995 **AF**
Poke Ms JA, BA, Unemployed. [0035789] 14/01/1983
Polanowski Mrs E, (was Cierniak), BSc(Hons) MSc, Deputy Inf.Mgr., Dibb Lupton Alsop, London. [0048835] 01/01/1993
Polchow Ms SU, BA MA MCLIP, Learning Res.ICT Advisor, Northants. [0044647] 14/11/1990
Polding Mrs GM, (was Brown), MCLIP, Operational Support Mgr., Univ.of Herts., Learning & Inf.Serv., Hatfield. [0021254] 17/10/1973
Polfreman Mr MJ, BA(Hons) PhD MA, Ch.Catr., Marx Memorial L., London. [0051061] 01/01/1987
Pollard Mr B, p./t.Stud./System Administrator, Univ.of Wales, Aberystwyth, Anglia Poly.Univ., Cambridge. [0061276] 09/05/2002
Pollard Mr G, BA MCLIP DipLib, Princ.Lib.-Outreach Serv., L.B.of Tower Hamlets. [0030235] 12/01/1979
Pollard Mrs JH, (was Barker), MCLIP, Unemployed. [0000760] 14/05/1963
Pollard Mrs JH, (was Moreton), BA DipLib MCLIP, Lib., Notts.City L.s, Clifton L. [0010377] 05/05/1967
Pollard Miss JM, BSc MCLIP, Retired. [0011781] 01/01/1967
Pollard Ms M, MA FCLIP, Life Member. [0017574] 24/02/1947 FE 01/01/1966
Pollard Mr NP, BA MCLIP, Head of L.& Media Serv., Kingston Univ. [0011783] 04/03/1968
Pollecutt Ms NA, BA MA MCLIP, Inf.Lib., The Womens L., London. [0055853] 02/12/1997
Polley Mrs CL, (was Martin), BA MCLIP, Acquisitions & Catg.Lib., Southampton Univ., Winchester. [0043421] 26/10/1989
Polley Mrs JA, MCLIP, Dep.Area Lib.-Bognor Area, W.Sussex Co.L., Bognor Regis L. [0011784] 27/09/1966
Pollitt Dr AS, BSc PhD FBCS CEng MCLIP, Employment not known. [0060597] 11/12/2001

Pollitt Mrs ME, (was Daw), BA MCLIP, Coll.Lib., Dukeries Comm.Coll., Ollerton. [0011375] 18/09/1969
Pollitt Miss ML, MCLIP, Unemployed, Meads 77 Church Hill,Loughton, Essex, IG10 1QP. [0011786] 14/02/1972
Pollitt Mrs PL, (was Jones), BSc DipLib MCLIP, Sen.Lib.-Child.Serv.(Job Share), Shropshire C.C., L.H.Q. [0028238] 20/10/1977
Pollock Mrs I, (was Moe), BA(Hons) MCLIP, Sch.Lib., Falkirk Council. [0047543] 01/10/1992
Polson Mr RG, MA DipLib MCLIP FSA(Scot) MSc(Econ), Asst.Inf.Offr., Univ.of Stirling, Highland Health Sci.L., Inverness. [0044133] 25/05/1990
Polydoratou Miss P, Stud., City Univ. [0058560] 01/04/2000
Pomeroy Miss KM, MCLIP, Community Lib., Whalebone Br., Barking P.L. [0011792] 02/09/1968
Pond Mrs CP, (was Copeman), MCLIP, Unemployed, Forest Villa, Staples Road, Loughton, Essex, IG10 1HP. [0003144] 12/06/1969
Pond Miss FM, BA DipLib MCLIP, Systems Mgr., Univ.of Surrey Roehampton. [0032610] 04/05/1980
Ponka Mrs JA, (was Kerner), BA MCLIP, Lib., Holy Cross 6th Form Coll., Bury,Lancs. [0023147] 31/10/1974
Ponniah Mrs GV, (was Rason), BA MCLIP, Data Protection Offr., Surrey C.C. [0040376] 23/01/1987
Pons Ms PAE, MSc MCLIP, Temp. [0055296] 19/09/1997
Ponsonby Miss SE, BA MCLIP, Researcher, ITN, London. [0031926] 09/01/1980
Pontello Miss L, BA(Hons), L.& Collections Asst., The Kennel Club, London. [0059206] 08/01/2001 **AF**
Ponter Mrs PE, (was Rudge), MCLIP, p./t.Comm.Team Lib., Glos.C.C. [0011794] 25/03/1959
Pontin Ms DM, MCLIP, Freelance Lib./L.Consultant, 72 Hamilton Park W., London, N5 1AB. [0011796] 17/10/1974
Ponting Mr M, MA(Hons) DipIM, L.R.C.Mgr., Bracknell Coll., Berks. [0056387] 01/07/1998
Ponton Miss BJ, MCLIP, Retired. [0011797] 02/07/1965
Pook Miss CJ, BA(Hons), p./t.Stud., City Univ., Freshfields Bruckhaus Deringer. [0059356] 14/02/2001
Pool Miss ER, Life Member, 4 Kiln Gardens, Hartley Wintney, Basingstoke, Hants., RG27 8RG. [0011799] 25/09/1948
Pool Mr M, MCLIP, Asst.Lib., Torquay Ref.L., Torbay L.Serv. [0011800] 03/12/1969
Poole Mr AJ, BA DipLib MCLIP FETC, Inf.Offr., Instant L.Ltd., Loughborough. [0038779] 08/10/1985
Poole Miss BM, BA MCLIP, Grp.Lib., N.Yorks.Co.L., Malton Grp. [0021392] 08/11/1973
Poole Mrs FAC, MCLIP, Unemployed. [0007134] 01/01/1971
Poole Mrs G, (was Dunbar), BA MCLIP, [0037590] 10/10/1984
Poole Miss JL, MCLIP, Inf.Mgr., Marks & Clerk, Manchester. [0019253] 03/02/1964
Poole Miss K, BA, Grad.Trainee, Inst.of Hist.Research L., Univ.of London. [0061106] 25/02/2002
Poole Mr K, BA MCLIP, Retired. [0011802] 12/02/1952
Poole Mrs LE, (was Tattersall), BA MCLIP, Life Member, 1 Dene Hse.,Green Pastures, Heaton Mersey,Stockport,SK4 3RB. [0011803] 16/01/1950
Poole Mrs VJ, (was Guest), BA MCLIP, Team Leader, Bolton Inst.of H.E. [0006038] 27/10/1971
Pooley Miss EG, MCLIP, Life Member. [0011805] 07/07/1931
Poolton Mrs KE, BA MCLIP, Dual-Use Lib., Birchwood L., Warrington Bor.Council. [0033888] 30/04/1981
Pope Mrs AJ, (was Stubbs), BA LLB DipLib MCLIP ILTM, Sen.Subject & Learning Support Lib., Staffs.Univ., Leek Road L., Stoke on Trent. [0035207] 05/10/1982
Pope Mr BM, BSc MCLIP, L.Consultant. [0011806] 01/01/1972
Pope Ms GR, Self-Employed Trainer. [0061127] 19/02/2002 **AF**
Pope Dr JM, BSc PhD FCLIP, Employment unknown. [0060576] 11/12/2001 FE 01/04/2002
Pope Miss SE, BA DipLib MCLIP, Self-employed. [0035692] 19/01/1983
Pope Ms VP, BSc MCLIP, Ch.Catr., Univ.of Westminster, New Cavendish St.L. [0011812] 09/02/1965
Popham Mrs RM, (was White), MCLIP, Retired. [0025546] 01/01/1959
Popp Miss G, Catg.& Systems Lib., Royal Botanic Gardens, Kew. [0044982] 24/01/1991
Poppleston Mr M, MCLIP, Retired, 2 Highcroft Drive, Nottingham, NG8 4DX. [0011817] 07/02/1961
Poppy Miss PA, MCLIP, Asst.Lib., Bournemouth Univ. [0011819] 03/01/1972
Porritt Ms F, BA(Hons) DipLib, Sen.Inf.Offr., Univ.of Teesside, Middlesbrough. [0046274] 24/02/1999
Portch Ms E, Inf.Offr., L.& Inf.Serv., Merck Sharp & Dohme Ltd., Herts. [0056659] 01/10/1998
Portch Mrs SK, (was Pawley), MCLIP, L.Serv.Mgr., Ashridge, Berkhamsted,Herts. [0011377] 19/10/1970
Porteous Miss LD, BA MA MCLIP, Inf.Lib.(Humanities), Kingston Univ. [0039978] 07/10/1986
Porter Mr A, BA BSc CertHSC OblOSB MCLIP, Unemployed. [0041504] 01/01/1988
Porter Mrs AK, (was Wellen), BA MCLIP, Lib., Hants.Co.L.Serv., Ringwood. [0020972] 31/08/1973
Porter Mrs C, BA MCLIP, Employment unknown. [0060360] 10/12/2001
Porter Miss CE, BA MLib MCLIP, Med.,Health & Life Serv., Univ.of Birmingham. [0040026] 14/10/1986
Porter Ms D, BA MCLIP, Grp.Lib., Leics C.C., Blaby L., Leics. [0041977] 04/07/1988
Porter Mr DJ, BA DipLib MCLIP BPS, [0027363] 25/01/1977
Porter Mr DW, BA, Teacher, Riverview Jun.Sch., Gravesend, Kent. [0040066] 25/10/1986
Porter Mrs EB, BA MCLIP, Ch.Lib., S.E.E.L.B., Co.Down. [0023273] 25/11/1974

Porter Ms G, (was Atlay), BA(Hons) MCLIP, Acting CALIM Sec., Consortium of Academic L., Manchester. [0038069] 10/01/1985
Porter Mr GJ, BA MA MCLIP, Grp.Mgr., Hastings L. [0040300] 18/01/1987
Porter Mr JB, BSc DipLIB MCLIP, Grp.Lib., N.E.Educ.& L.Board, Ballymena, Co.Antrim. [0036739] 25/11/1983
Porter Mrs JE, (was Short), BA(Hons) PGDipIS, Head of Order Magr., Via Networks UK Ltd., Staines, Middx. [0049065] 01/10/1993
Porter Mr K, MA MLib MCLIP, Princ.Lib., N.Ireland Civil Serv. [0033115] 01/10/1980
Porter Mrs L, BA DipLIS, Lib., Univ.of S.Europe, Monaco. [0042700] 06/02/1989
Porter Mrs P, BA MCLIP, Unemployed. [0032150] 15/02/1980
Porter Mr TG, BSc MCLIP, H.of Cultural Serv., Worcs.C.C. [0019254] 01/01/1965
Porter Miss YM, BA(Hons), L.Asst., Bishops High L., Chester. [0061667] 16/10/2002 **AF**
Portman Mrs JE, (was Blackford), MCLIP, P./t.Asst.Inf.Advisor, Univ. of Surrey,Roehampton, [0001342] 14/09/1967
Posaner Mrs RD, (was Woolf), BA(Hons) MA, Lib., Univ.of Birmingham, Health Serv.Mgmt.Cent. [0052886] 15/01/1996
Postlethwaite Mrs FD, (was Cleveland), BA MCLIP, Comm.Devel.Lib., City of York Council, York. [0031802] 06/12/1979
Poston Mrs HE, (was Timbrell), BA(Hons) DipIM, Team Lib.-Child., N.E.E.L.B., Ballycastle L., Co.Antrim. [0048997] 23/08/1993
Poston Mr TDV, BA(Hons) MSc MCLIP, Stud., Loughborough Univ. [0053896] 07/10/1996
Pote Miss GF, BA MA MCLIP, Br.Lib., L.B.of Redbridge. [0034028] 02/07/1981
Pothen Dr PN, MA DPhil MCLIP, Communications Manager, Kings College London. [0038784] 10/10/1985
Potten Mr EJ, BA MSc, Stud., Univ.Coll.London. [0058607] 12/04/2000
Potter Ms CM, BA(Hons) MLib, Sen.Lib., St Clare's, Oxford. [0047627] 08/10/1992
Potter Mr DC, MSc BA MCLIP, H.of Inf.& Publications, The Nat.Autistic Soc., London. [0019811] 01/12/1972
Potter Mr DJ, BA MCLIP, Head of Systems & Corp., Univ.of Derby. [0011839] 01/01/1970
Potter Mrs JC, (was Murray), BA(Hons) MCLIP, Specialist Serv.Mgr., Halton Bor.Council L., Runcorn. [0044617] 07/11/1990
Potter Mrs JH, BSc MCLIP, Employment unknown. [0060577] 11/12/2001
Potter Mr JM, BA MCLIP, Sen.Lect., Sch.of Inf.Mgmt., Univ.of Brighton. [0019535] 26/02/1959
Potter Miss KS, BA(Hons) MA, Inf.Offr., The Waste & Res.Action Prog., Bambury. [0055435] 13/10/1997
Potter Mrs LM, (was Bozovich), BA DipLib MCLIP, Lib.& Inf.Offr., Fennemores, Milton Keynes. [0031571] 04/11/1979
Potter Mrs SP, (was Clarke), BA DipLib MCLIP, p./t.Asst.Inf.Specialist, Nottingham Trent Univ., Nottingham. [0037515] 02/10/1984
Potton Mr DM, MA DipLib MCLIP, Asst.City Lib.-Operations, Derby City Council. [0029795] 22/10/1978
Potton Mrs JK, (was Bradshaw), BA MCLIP, Dist.Lib., Amber Valley, Derbys.C.C. [0032880] 09/10/1980
Potts Mr D, BA(Hons), Network Adviser, Resource, The Council for Mus.Arch.& L. [0046502] 14/11/1991
Potts Mrs I, (was Bloomfield), MCLIP, Learning Resource Facilitator, Hopwood Hall Coll., Middleton. [0011845] 11/04/1967
Potts Mrs JV, Super., Chatteris L., Chatteris, Cambs. [0058426] 14/02/2000 **AF**
Poulter Mr AJ, BA MA MSc MCLIP, Lect., Dept.of Comp.& Inf.Sci., Glasgow. [0033117] 20/10/1980
Poulter Mr BW, MCLIP, Sen.Inf.Offr., Leeds Metro.Univ., Beckett Park. [0011848] 13/03/1963
Poulton Miss AJ, BA(Hons) MA MCLIP, Inf.Specialist, Aston Univ., Birmingham. [0052236] 17/10/1995
Poulton Mrs M, BA DipLib MCLIP, Health Lib., Univ.of Wales, Bangor, Gwynedd. [0025630] 26/01/1976
Pover Mrs AE, (was Pomroy), BSc MCLIP, Lib.,p./t., Cheshire C.C., Northwich L. [0032760] 08/08/1980
Powell Miss AM, BA MLS, Princ.Lect., Harare Poly., Zimbabwe. [0056288] 28/04/1998
Powell Miss CD, BA MA MA(LIB) MCLIP, Asst.Team Lib., Gloucester Co.Council, Gloucester. [0038938] 16/10/1985
Powell Mrs CH, (was Hill), BA(Hons) DipLib, Resources Lib., N.Staffs Combined H/Care Trust, Bucknall Hospital. [0050396] 15/07/1994
Powell Mrs COJ, (was Nossent), BA BSc DipLib MCLIP, Lib., Instant L.Ltd., London. [0010920] 02/11/1971
Powell Mr CV, LLB DipLib, Inf.Offr., Health Educ.Board for Scotland, Edinburgh. [0035158] 12/09/1982
Powell Mr D, BA FCLIP, Life Member, Tel.0604 406639, 31 Bush Hill, Northampton, NN3 2PD. [0011857] 01/01/1952 **FE 01/01/1955**
Powell Miss EC, Head of Catg., The London L. [0035286] 09/10/1982
Powell Mrs ER, BA DipLib, p./t.Stud./Asst.Lib., Univ.of Cent.England, Birmingham, Droitwich L., Worcs. [0061020] 01/02/2002
Powell Miss G, BA MCLIP, Business Inf.Specialist, Management Inf.& Res.Cent., Cranfield Univ. [0037553] 05/10/1984
Powell Mr G, BA, Training & Res.Co-ordinator, Comm.Council Devon. [0049116] 06/10/1993
Powell Miss GM, FCLIP, Life Member, Tel.0929 462141, Byways, Baileys Drove, Wool, Wareham, Dorset, BH20 6EP. [0011862] 12/03/1930 **FE 01/01/1934**
Powell Mrs HD, (was Gonzales), BA MCLIP, Sch.Lib., Claremont High Sch., Kenton,Harrow. [0031298] 01/10/1979
Powell Miss HM, BA(Hons), Stud., Univ.of Sheffield. [0058975] 13/10/2000
Powell Mrs J, (was Dixon), BA MCLIP, Dep.Dist.Lib., High Peak, Derbys.C.C. [0028801] 02/02/1978

Powell Mr JC, FCLIP, Life member, Cyfarthfa, 3 Fontwell Close, Maidenhaed, SL6 5JX. [0011867] 01/01/1941 **FE 01/01/1954**
Powell Mrs JE, (was Morton), BA MCLIP, Inf.Mgr., Comm.Fin.Solutions, Univ.of Salford. [0011870] 13/01/1966
Powell Mr JR, (was Goodall), BA DipLib MCLIP, Inf.Offr., Foseco Inter.Ltd., Tamworth. [0043518] 31/10/1989
Powell Mr JS, BA MA MCLIP, L.Asst., Univ.of York, Seconded to York Minster L. [0030662] 27/02/1979
Powell Miss K, BA(Hons) DipIM MCLIP, Br.Lib., States of Jersey. [0052174] 26/09/1995
Powell Mrs K, (was Fairbrother), BA(Hons) DipLib MCLIP, Business Serv.Lib., Nat.Air Traffic Serv.Ltd., Bournemouth Airport, Dorset. [0038430] 01/05/1985
Powell Mr LB, BA M DIV MCLIP, Pastor, Covenant Baptist Church, Toronto, Ontario, Canada. [0017588] 18/09/1953
Powell Mr M, BA(Hons) MA MSc MCLIP, Inf.Specialist, GCHQ, Cheltenham. [0054875] 14/04/1997
Powell Mrs N, (was Woodford), MCLIP, P./t.L.Asst., S.Glos.Council. [0023092] 29/10/1974
Powell Miss NM, BSc(Hons) MSc MCLIP, Sen.Inf.Offr., Eversheds, Birmingham. [0055011] 24/06/1997
Powell Mr PE, MCLIP, Employment not known. [0060497] 11/12/2001
Powell Mrs RJ, (was Brown), BA MCLIP, Dep.Div.Lib., Hants.C.L. [0001925] 01/01/1970
Powell Mrs RM, (was Thomas), MCLIP, Sen.L.Asst., Shropshire C.C., Much Wenlock L. [0014583] 26/07/1966
Powell Mr SD, BA MCLIP, Child.Serv.Co-ordinator, Notts. [0042943] 28/04/1989
Powell Miss SE, BA(Hons), Reg.L.& Inf.Mgr., Enviroment Agency, Reading. [0052999] 14/02/1996
Power Mr AG, BA MCLIP, Dep.Ref.& Inf.Lib., Co.Ref.L., Bucks.Co.L., Aylesbury, Bucks. [0034398] 30/10/1981
Power Mr AJ, BA PGDip, Inf.Offr., Freshfield Bruckhaus Deringer, London. [0061115] 21/02/2002
Power Mr GN, BA DipLib MCLIP, Access Lib., Inst.of Advanced Legal Studies, London. [0043193] 01/10/1989
Power Miss K, MCLIP, Retired. [0011883] 10/10/1966
Power Mrs MBA, (was Beange), MA DipLib MCLIP, Network Lib., Aberdeenshire Council, Aboyne Academy. [0023207] 09/11/1974
Power Ms RT, BA(Hons) MA MCLIP, Unemployed (Maternity Leave). [0052825] 05/01/1996
Power Miss S, Inf.Offr., Hants.Co.L., Ref.L., Winchester. [0058743] 03/07/2000
Powers Miss JS, BA(Hons) MA MCLIP, Lib., Tobermory High Sch. [0055024] 01/07/1997
Powis Mr CM, BA MLib MCLIP ILTM, Learning Support Coordinator, Univ.Coll.Northampton. [0042381] 21/10/1988
Powis Miss EA, MA, [0036093] 12/05/1983
Powles Mrs JC, (was Huse), BA MCLIP, Lib., Spurgeons Coll., London. [0022916] 08/10/1974
Powles Mrs SM, (was Baldwin), MCLIP, Learning Res.Cent.Mgr., Bracknell & Wokingham Coll. [0011886] 23/09/1969
Pownall Mrs RL, BA MA, p./t.Stud./L.Asst., Royal Inst.of Brit.Architects, Robert Gordon Univ./London. [0059370] 19/02/2001
Powne Ms CCA, BMus MA MCLIP, Sub-Lib.-Strategy & Planning, Durham Univ., Main L. [0036400] 06/10/1983
Poyner Mrs AE, (was Jones), MCLIP, Project Offr., London L.& Inf.Devel.Unit, London P.G.Med.& Dental Educ. [0032831] 01/01/1963
Pracy Mr DJ, MA MCLIP, Project Co-ordinator, Middlesex Univ., London. [0011894] 28/10/1964
Prada Mrs JA, (was Grew), BSc MCLIP, Sen.Catr., S.Bank Univ. [0042727] 13/02/1989
Praill Mrs DK, (was Herd), BA MCLIP, 11 Saltash Close, Bedford, MK40 3DT. [0006762] 13/01/1967
Prangley Mr PJ, BSc MA, Unemployed. [0059714] 28/08/2001
Prangnell Mr RD, BSc MCLIP, Employment not known. [0060624] 11/12/2001
Prasher Ms N, MSc, Lib., Westminster City Council. [0040924] 25/08/1987
Pratt Mr AL, BA, Asst.Lib., Highways Agency, London. [0040214] 17/11/1986
Pratt Mrs CA, (was Rose), BA(Hons), Project Support Off., Dept.of L.& Heritage, Warwickshire C.C. [0047338] 15/07/1992
Pratt Mrs EM, (was Stokes), MCLIP, Materials Spec., Harford Co.Pub.L., Maryland, U.S.A. [0019782] 06/10/1972
Pratt Mrs FH, MA, Stud.p./t.Stock Mgmnt Asst., London Metro, L.B.Southwark. [0061572] 02/10/2002
Pratt Mrs J, (was Baker), BSc(Hons) DipIM, Collection Devel.Lib., Young Peoples L.Serv., L.B.of Richmond upon Thames. [0048626] 19/03/1993
Pratt Mr JA, MCLIP, Pub.Serv.Lib.(Inf.), Cent.L., Aberdeen City Council. [0011899] 21/10/1971
Pratt Mrs JE, (was Rollo), MA DipLib MCLIP, Operations Lib., Cent.Area L.H.Q., Fife Council. [0024800] 01/08/1975
Pratt Miss LA, BA, Q.A.Admin.Asst., Uni-Mill Engineering, Swindon, Wilts. [0058703] 09/06/2000
Pratt Ms LA, BA DipLib MCLIP, Project Offr., Surrey C.C., Kingston on Thames. [0024259] 23/05/1975
Pratt Mrs LE, (was Etherington), BA(Hons), Team Lib.-Ref.Inf.& Local Studies, Sheerness L., Kent Educ.& Ls. [0047151] 12/05/1992
Pratt Mr MJ, MA MA, Info.Mgr., Univ.of Boston. [0051218] 28/11/1994
Pratt Mrs PK, (was Meara), BA MCLIP, Retired. [0010030] 09/02/1953
Pratt Mrs SL, (was Batty), BA(Hons) MA, L.Asst., York City P.L. [0054551] 20/01/1997
Precious Ms AJ, BA, Inf.Specialist, ICL, London. [0041627] 05/02/1988
Precious Mrs H, Stud., City Univ. [0061736] 30/10/2002
Preddle Ms C, BSc(Hons), Stud., Manchester Met.Univ. &, Lib., Cent.L., Manchester. [0057965] 05/10/1999
Preddle Mr CC, BA MCLIP, Retired. [0011904] 27/07/1968

329

Preece Ms JA, BA DipLib MCLIP, Campus Lib., Univ.of E.London. [0028655] 11/01/1978
Preece Miss KJ, BA DipLib MCLIP, Asst.Lib., Univ.of the W.of England at Bristol, . [0036004] 11/04/1983
Preece Ms LF, (was Magee), MSc, Career Break. [0053101] 27/02/1996
Preece Ms LJ, BA NZLS MCLIP, Map Lib., The Geological Soc., London. [0059189] 12/12/2000
Preece Ms TJ, BA(Hons) MSc(Econ), Asst.Lib., House of Lords, London. [0053901] 10/10/1996
Preedy Mrs DL, BA MCLIP, L.Asst., Bewdley L., Worcs. [0021532] 15/10/1973
Preedy Mr NM, MCLIP BSc, Princ.Lib., Worcs.C.C. [0021533] 15/10/1973
Preest Miss KJ, BA(Hons) DipILM MCLIP, Asst.Lib., Univ.Coll.London. [0055049] 01/07/1997
Prempe Mr A, MLS DipLib MCLIP, Lib., Greenwich Ls. [0011909] 01/01/1972
Prentice Mrs KM, (was Ormrod), BLib MCLIP, Asst.Dist.Mgr., Essex C.C., Harlow & Epping Forest. [0039436] 22/01/1986
Prescott Mr AR, BA(Hons) DipILS, Asst.Lib., Aberdare Cent.L., Aberdare, Rhondda-Cynon-Taff. [0054761] 01/04/1997
Prescott Mr HA, MA FCLIP, Retired. [0011917] 31/03/1936 FE 01/01/1950
Presley Ms FE, MPhil DipLib, Policy Offr., Assoc.of Community Health Councils, London. [0032152] 06/02/1980
Pressler Mr C, BA(Hons) MA MSc MCLIP, Content Mgr., Kings Coll.London. [0055808] 25/11/1997
Pressley Mrs D, BA DipLib MCLIP, P./t. Lib.Asst., East Devon Coll., Tiverton. [0026518] 11/10/1976
Prestage Mrs LR, (was Church), MA BA MCLIP, Princ.Young Peoples Lib.& Learning, Res.Mgr., Kent Arts & L., W.Malling. [0041070] 01/10/1987
Preston Mrs C, (was Skelton), BA(Hons) MCLIP, Unemployed. [0040090] 27/10/1986
Preston Mr DWM, BA DipLib MCLIP, Div.Lib., W.E.L.B., Omagh. [0023113] 05/11/1974
Preston Mrs EA, (was Wall), BSc MCLIP, Asst.Lib., Open Univ.L., Milton Keynes. [0019377] 01/01/1972
Preston Mrs ES, MCLIP, L.Mgr.(Job Share), Solihull Hosp.L., Birmingham Heartland & Solihull NHS. [0023948] 01/03/1975
Preston Mr J, BA FSA MCLIP, Unwaged. [0011925] 30/06/1964
Preston Mr JD, BSc DipIS, L.Administrator, L.B.of Richmond upon Thames, E.Sheen Dist.L. [0046189] 14/10/1991
Preston Mr M, BA(Hons) MLib, Sen.L.Asst., Goldsmiths Coll., London. [0048592] 25/02/1993
Preston Miss NJ, BA(Hons), Stud., Liv.John Moores Univ. [0059862] 18/10/2001
Preston Dr RA, MA DPhil CertEd MCLIP, Editor, Hants.Bibl., Hants.Co.L. [0026867] 01/01/1977
Preston Mrs SE, (was Efford), BA(Hons) MCLIP, Asst.Lib., W.Sussex C.C. [0004464] 02/06/1970
Preston Mrs SM, (was Haskey), MCLIP, Inf.Lib., Leeds L.& Inf.Serv. [0007762] 10/02/1966
Preuss Mrs RJ, BA MCLIP, Child.Lib., W.Berks.Council, Newbury L. [0036908] 13/01/1984
Prevett Mrs HR, (was Bennett), BA MCLIP, Career Break. [0048201] 16/11/1992
Price Ms AM, BSc, p./t.Stud./Inf.Offr., City Univ., London, Univ.of Southampton, Wesses Inst. [0061102] 25/02/2002
Price Ms AN, BA(Hons) MCLIP, Lib., E.Lincolnshire PCT., Lincs.Knowledge & Resource Service. [0049967] 31/01/1994
Price Mrs B, BA(Hons) MCLIP, Tutor Lib., Leeds Metro.Univ. [0039961] 03/10/1986
Price Mr C, BSc MSc MCLIP, Employment not known. [0060754] 12/12/2001
Price Mrs CA, (was Ellsmore), BA MCLIP, Unemployed. [0033705] 09/02/1981
Price Mr CH, MCLIP, Asst.Lib., Area L., Brecon. [0011934] 08/08/1969
Price Mrs CJ, (was Goodey), BA MCLIP, The Old Coach House, Manor Close, Almeley, Herefordshire, HR3 6NF. [0005677] 01/10/1971
Price Mrs CL, (was Falconer), BA(Hons) MA MCLIP, Inf.Adviser(Electronic Res.), Univ.of Surrey Roehampton, London. [0051038] 09/11/1994
Price Mr D, BSc(Econ) MCLIP, Br.Lib., Treorchy, Rhondda Cynon Taff CBC., Treorchy, Mid Glamorgan. [0056367] 18/06/1998
Price Mr DJ, BSc DipEthnol MCLIP, Head, Systems & Electronic Res.Serv., Univ.of Oxford. [0060309] 10/12/2001
Price Mrs E, (was Hinds), MCLIP, Sen.L.Asst., Sch.L.Serv., King Richard Sch., Portsmouth. [0011938] 10/01/1965
Price Mr EV, MCLIP, Ref.Lib., United Nations (I.A.E.A.), Vienna. [0019261] 11/09/1972
Price Miss FEM, BA DipLib, Asst.Lib.(Arch.), Reuters/ITN, London. [0033823] 02/03/1981
Price Ms FJ, BA MCLIP, Asst.Lib., Birmingham L.Serv., Sutton Coldfield Music L. [0030031] 01/11/1978
Price Miss FM, MCLIP, p./t.Res.Offr., Crawley Coll. [0011939] 01/01/1972
Price Miss G, BA MA MCLIP, Stud.Serv.Lib., Inst.of Educ.L., London. [0040146] 06/10/1986
Price Mr GD, BA DipLib MCLIP, Tech.Serv.Mgr., B.L.P.E.S., (L.S.E.), London. [0032153] 30/01/1980
Price Mrs HJ, MCLIP, Sen.Lib., Vale of Glamorgan L. [0021504] 27/10/1973
Price Ms HJ, MSc BA MCLIP, Unemployed. [0036943] 06/02/1984
Price Mrs HM, (was Fell), BA MCLIP, Resource Cent.Mgr., Bishop Wordsworth's Boys Gram.Sch., Salisbury. [0048302] 25/11/1992
Price Mrs J, (was Roberson), MCLIP, Retired. [0011942] 24/01/1961
Price Mrs JD, (was Filipiuk), MCLIP, Positioin Unknown, St.Bonifac's Coll., Devon. [0004899] 27/01/1972
Price Mrs KM, (was Johnson), MCLIP, Life Member. [0011948] 14/02/1953
Price Mrs LJ, (was Whitaker), BLib, L.& Learning Res.Mgr., Bristol Cathedral Sch., Bristol. [0050419] 25/07/1994

Price Mr PJ, BSc DipLib MCLIP, System Management Lib., Univ.of Plymouth. [0011952] 14/01/1972
Price Mrs RE, (was Duxbury), BA(Hons) MCLIP, Learning Res.Offr., Hackney Comm.Coll., London. [0051843] 12/07/1995
Price Mr RJR, BA(Hons) DipIS MCLIP, L.& Inf.Offr., NSPCC, London. [0049470] 03/11/1993
Price Mr RM, MA MCLIP, Retired. [0011953] 08/05/1967
Price Mrs S, (was Pagett), BLS MPhil MCLIP, Sen.L.Asst.(Eng.), Pilkington L.,Loughborough, Loughborough Univ.of Tech. [0042008] 17/07/1988
Price Mrs SA, (was Holt), BA MCLIP, Lib., Aldenham Sch., Elstree. [0011955] 01/01/1965
Price Mrs SA, MSc, Lib., Exeter Sch., Devon. [0051484] 28/02/1995
Price Miss SD, BA BTEC, Princ.L.Asst., Birmingham Conservatoire. [0043373] 09/10/1989
Price Mrs SE, (was Hearder), BA MCLIP, Retired. [0006651] 11/10/1971
Price Dr SM, (was Bounds), MSc MA MCLIP PhD, L.Mgr., Cent.St.Martins Coll.of Art & Des., London. [0026177] 02/08/1976
Price Miss ST, Asst.Br.Lib., Powys C.C., Newtown L. [0057025] 26/11/1998
Price Mrs TA, (was Mather), BLS MCLIP, L.& Inf.Mgr., Nottingham City Primary Care, NHS Trust. [0033459] 01/12/1980
Price Mrs VR, (was Wormald), MSc, L.Asst. [0046918] 25/02/1992
Price Mr WA, BA FCLIP, H.of L.Serv., Dublin Inst.of Tech. [0011957] 26/07/1962 FE 01/01/1967
Prichard Miss CL, Stud., Loughborough Univ. [0058024] 14/10/1999
Prichard Mr JA, FCLIP, Life Member. [0011959] 15/02/1943 FE 01/01/1957
Priday Miss ME, MCLIP, Performance Co-ordinator. [0011965] 09/04/1968
Priddey Mrs EJ, (was Pattison), MCLIP. [0011367] 04/01/1972
Priddle Miss LJ, BA(Hons) MA, Asst.Lib., Solicitors Off., Inland Rev., London. [0056821] 23/10/1998
Pridgeon Ms CA, BA(Hons) MSc, Sch.Lib., Salford Sch.L.Serv. [0043899] 09/02/1990
Pridham Mrs H, (was Morley), BA DipILS MCLIP, Asst.Lib., Bridgend Co.Bor.Council. [0054648] 07/02/1997
Pridham Mrs JP, (was Reavil), MCLIP, Life Member. [0011966] 01/01/1954
Pridmore Miss JC, BA DipLib MCLIP, Lib., Geoffrey Walton Practice, Charlbury, Oxon. [0032154] 24/01/1980
Pridmore Mr P, BA MCLIP, Retired. [0017594] 29/09/1956
Prieg Ms NS, BA DipLib MCLIP, Asst.Director: operations Mgr., St.Marys Univ.Coll., Inf.& Resource Centre. [0029412] 10/07/1978
Priest Miss M, BA PhD, Retired. [0022068] 01/01/1974
Priestley Ms A, BA, Lib.& Inf.Asst., Planning & Research, Bernard Thorpe. [0039219] 01/01/1986
Priestley Mrs J, (was Skidmore), BA MCLIP, Lib., Glenrothes Coll., Fife. [0030791] 03/04/1979
Priestley-Eaton Mrs HC, BSc, L.Asst., Wilmslow L., Cheshire. [0061418] 15/07/2002 **AF**
Priestner Mr AJ, BA(Hons) MA MCLIP, Sen.Inf.Offr., Said Business Sch., Oxford Univ. [0051583] 03/04/1995
Primmer Mrs C, BA(Hons) DipLibCIM MCLIP, Cent.L.& Operational Support Lib., Plymouth City Council. [0033338] 13/11/1980
Primrose Mrs CM, MA FSA Scot MCLIP, Retired/Research Stud. [0011973] 19/10/1965
Prince Mrs AJ, (was Millar), MCLIP, Unemployed. [0010134] 13/10/1971
Prince Mr AJ, BA(Hons) MCLIP, Operations Lead:Comm.Serv., Stoke-on-Trent City Council. [0052545] 06/11/1995
Prince Ms HK, BA MA, Asst.Lib.-Electronic Resources, Princess Alexandra Hosp.NHS Trust, Harlow, Essex. [0057991] 08/10/1999
Prince Mr NA, MCLIP, Lib.-Inf.Serv., N.Yorks.C.C. [0043011] 12/06/1989
Prince Miss RJ, MA MCLIP, Bibl.Serv.Co-ordinator, S.Glos.L.Serv., Yate. [0041108] 12/10/1987
Prince Mr SJ, BSc DipLib MCLIP, Acquisitions Lib., Brit.Geological Survey, Nottingham. [0039988] 08/10/1986
Prince Mrs SM, (was Boraman), MCLIP, Res.Cent.Mgr., Thomas Peacocke C.Coll., Rye, E.Sussex C.C. [0001491] 01/01/1969
Prince Miss VJ, BA, Stud., Queen Margarets Univ.Coll., Edinburgh. [0061779] 07/11/2002
Pringle Miss LA, BA(Hons) DipInf, Sen.Asst.Lib., Wirral Bor.Co., W. Kirby L. [0044447] 09/10/1990
Pringle Mrs MC, MSc MCLIP, Freelance. [0037106] 09/02/1984
Pringle Mrs MJ, (was Horn), BA DipLib MCLIP, Special Collections Lib., Shakespeare Birthplace Trust, Stratford-upon-Avon. [0017051] 09/10/1969
Prior Miss HI, BA MCLIP, Child.Serv.Lib., L.B.of Harrow, Middlesex. [0032334] 06/03/1980
Prior Miss K, BA(Hons), Stud., Cambridge. [0059825] 10/10/2001
Prior Ms LV, BA, Inf.Offr., CMS Cameron McKenna, London. [0036057] 06/05/1983
Prior Mrs MR, (was Marshall), BA MA MCLIP, Retired. [0011986] 04/03/1954
Prior Mrs PK, DSc CertEd MA MCLIP, Reg.Lib., W.Mids.Reg.Off., Birmingham. [0032611] 12/05/1980
Prior Miss PM, MA MCLIP, Head, Records Mgmt., Foreign & Commonwealth Off. [0011987] 30/09/1969
Prior Ms SD, BA(Hons) MA MCLIP, Child.Lib., Bexley Council, Bexley Cent.L. [0048823] 09/06/1993
Pritchard Mr A, BA(Hons) MCLIP, Asst.Lib., Pontypridd L., Rhondda-Cynon-Taff Co.Bor.Council. [0044965] 28/01/1991
Pritchard Mr A, MPhil MBCS FCLIP, Self-employed, ALLM Sys.& Marketing, Bournemouth. [0011988] 17/01/1962 FE 01/02/1978
Pritchard Mr AW, BA MCLIP, Serv.Devel.Offr., Leeds L.& Inf.Serv. [0038012] 01/01/1985
Pritchard Mrs FC, (was Whittle), BA MCLIP AdvDipEd, L.Res.Cent.Co-ordinator, Wallace High Sch., Stirling Council. [0045274] 01/10/1990
Pritchard Miss HJ, BA MCLIP, Team Lib., Arts & L.Dept., Kent Co.Council. [0023629] 13/01/1975

Personal Members — Quayle

Pritchard Miss J, BA MCLIP, Abstractor, Self Employed, London. [0030513] 24/01/1979
Pritchard Miss JM, BA(Hons), Inf.Centre Mgr., Birmingham CHildrens Hosp. [0052734] 29/11/1995
Pritchard Miss K, BA(Hons), Unemployed, [0060936] 10/01/2002
Pritchard Mrs L, (was Holt), BA(Hons) DipILS MCLIP, Lend.Lib., Wrexham Co.Bor.Council, Wrexham L.& Arts Cent. [0046540] 19/11/1991
Pritchard Mrs LC, (was Kessell), MCLIP, L.& Inf.Serv., Univ.Coll.of Wales, Swansea. [0025060] 22/10/1975
Pritchard Mrs M, (was Mitchell), MCLIP, Co-ordinator of Learning Res., Leek High Sch., Staffs. [0011993] 12/03/1962
Pritchard Mrs ME, Sch.Lib., Archbishop Beck R.C.High/Upper Sch, Cedar Road, Liverpool. [0044714] 13/11/1990
Pritchard Mr OJ, BA(Hons) MA MCLIP AIMgt, Learning Cent.Mgr., Dudley Campus, Univ.of Wolverhampton. [0045562] 07/03/1991
Pritchard Mr R, BSc DipLib MCLIP, Mgr., TALNET. [0024232] 16/05/1975
Pritchard Mrs SE, (was Breese), BA DipLib MCLIP, Inf.Offr., Linklaters & Alliance, London. [0043751] 01/01/1990
Pritchatt Ms DJ, BLS(Hons) DipLib MCLIP, Res.Mgmt.Lib., Queen Elizabeth Hosp., Trust L., Birmingham. [0029797] 15/09/1978
Pritchett Mrs CM, (was Bown), BA MA, Univ.Teacher, Loughborough Univ. [0048334] 27/11/1992
Pritchett Mrs E, (was Bridge), BA, Mother. [0042334] 12/04/1966
Privetti Mrs PA, (was Allitt), BA(Hons) DipMus MCLIP, L.Mgr., City of Portsmouth Boys Sch. [0000231] 07/10/1968
Probert Mrs L, MA, Child.Lib., L.B.of Lewisham, Central L. [0044715] 29/11/1990
Probert Mrs MD, (was Whittall), BLib MCLIP, Childcare Inf.Mgr., Herefordshire Council, Hereford. [0034322] 20/10/1981
Procter Mr GR, BA DipLib MCLIP, Services Mgr., Clacton L., Clacton-On-Sea, Essex. [0037706] 16/10/1984
Procter Miss SJ, BA MCLIP, Asst.Div.Lib., E.Lancs.Div., Lancs.Co.L. [0032550] 09/05/1980
Proctor Mr JM, FCLIP, Retired. [0019263] 01/01/1949 FE 01/01/1968
Proctor Mrs JW, (was Withers), BA MCLIP, Lend.Lib., Torbay L.Serv., Torquay. [0034692] 27/01/1982
Proctor Ms R, Learning Res.Cent.Mgr., Sheffield Coll., Loxley Cent. [0048386] 17/12/1992
Proctor Mr RV, BA FCLIP, Lect., Dept.of Inf.Studs., Univ.of Sheffield. [0012008] 11/01/1964 FE 21/01/1999
Proctor Mrs S, (was Greathead), BA(Hons) MCLIP, Sch.Lib., N.Yorks.Co.L.Serv., Harrogate. [0046840] 13/02/1992
Proctor Mr WL, BA MA, Thesis Asst., Univ.of London. [0055025] 31/07/1997
Prosser Mrs C, (was Ellis), MCLIP, L.Mgr., Ineos Silicas, Warrington. [0012012] 03/10/1966
Prosser Miss CM, P./t.Stud./Pensions Secretary, Carillion PLC, Robert Gordon Univ. [0059745] 10/09/2001
Prosser Mrs J, MA MSc, P./t.Stud., Inf.Asst., London B.of Barnet, Thames Vall.Univ. [0059832] 15/10/2001
Prosser Mr RJ, BA(Hons) MCLIP, Inf.Lib., L.B.of Barnet, Golders Green L. [0043879] 07/02/1990
Prosser Ms S, BA DILS MCLIP, p./t.Sen.L.Asst., Univ.of Warwick. [0040538] 16/02/1987
Proud Mrs CC, (was Brown), BA MCLIP, Learning Res.Mgr., Middlesbrough Coll., Middlesbrough. [0038063] 14/01/1985
Proudfoot Mrs E, (was Hastings), MCLIP, Retired. [0012015] 01/01/2027
Proudfoot Mr O, Support Offr., Registers in Scotland. [0057528] 16/04/1999
Prout Miss RA, BSc DipLib, Asst.Lib., Bridgend Co.Bor.Council, Porthcawl L. [0029798] 24/10/1978
Prout Mr RS, BA DCG DipInfSci MCLIP, Employment not known. [0060726] 12/12/2001
Proven Mrs JE, BA(Hons), Stud., Strathclyde Univ. [0061763] 05/11/2002
Prowse Mrs KE, (was Alcott), BSc MSc, p./t.Asst.Lib., London Sch.of Economics. [0040807] 01/07/1987
Prue Mr AJ, BA(Hons) MA DipLib, Web Devel.Lib., Health L.Network, LISSU, Pembury Hosp., Kent. [0051629] 19/04/1995
Prunty Miss A, BA(Hons) MCLIP, Child.Serv.Offr., Redcar & Cleveland Bor.Council. [0047782] 14/10/1992
Pryce Mr FR, FCLIP, Life Member. [0012017] 05/03/1936 FE 01/01/1965
Pryce Mrs I, (was Powell), BA MCLIP, p./t.Map Lib., Keele Univ.L., Staffs. [0012018] 16/01/1968
Pryce-Jones Mrs EM, (was Mclennan), MA(Hons) DipLib MCLIP, Dep.Dir.L.Serv., Inf.Serv., Univ.of Cent.England, Birmingham. [0031901] 17/01/1980
Pryce-Jones Mrs JE, BSc MCLIP, Asst.Lib., S.Lanarkshire L., Bibl.Serv., Cent.L. [0020221] 31/10/1973
Pryer Mr PLA, MA MCLIP, Life Member, 15 Hampton Close, Church Crookham, Fleet, GU13 0LB, Tel:01252 622667. [0012019] 01/01/1957
Pryor Miss HE, MCLIP, Marketing Asst., City Coll.Manchester, W.Didsbury. [0019993] 11/01/1973
Pryor Mrs KA, (was Griffiths), BD DipLib, Asst.Lib., Norfolk Studies, Norfolk L.& Inf.Serv. [0048621] 16/03/1993
Prys Mr A, BA MPHIL DipLib, Asst.Lib., Jews'Coll., London. [0032155] 01/02/1980
Prytherch Mr RJ, MA MPhil MCLIP, Inf.Consultant, Willow Vale, Colton, Tadcaster, LS24 8EP. [0012021] 18/08/1966
Ptolomey Mr J, BSc DipLIS, Clinical Effectiveness Lib., N.Glasgow Univ., Glasgow. [0054080] 24/10/1996
Puah Mrs BN, DipLib MCLIP, Sen.Asst.Lib., Nanyang Tech.Univ., Singapore. [0032694] 03/07/1980
Publicover Mr JR, BEM MCLIP, Life Member. [0012022] 25/07/1938
Publicover Mrs M, BSc(Hons) DipLib MCLIP, Trust Lib., Birmingham Womens Hosp. [0034693] 12/01/1982
Publicover Mrs NC, (was Bates), MCLIP, Life Member. [0012023] 23/09/1941

Pudner Mr RJ, BA DipLib MCLIP, Service Devel.Lib., Somerset L.Arts.& Inf., Bridgwater L. [0032335] 05/03/1980
Pugh Miss HA, BA DipLib MCLIP, Position unknown, Dept.of Trans.Local Govt., and the Regions, London. [0012030] 20/09/1969
Pugh Miss HJ, BA(Hons) BA MCLIP, Sch.Lib., Kings Coll.Sch., London. [0028401] 22/11/1977
Pugh Mrs J, Lib., White & Case, London. [0053412] 14/06/1996
Pugh Mrs JP, (was Aldred), MCLIP, Retired. [0000146] 01/01/1966
Pugh Miss KE, BA(Hons) MCLIP, Customer Serv.Lib., Merthyr Tydfil L.Serv. [0046505] 14/11/1991
Pugh Mr LC, BA MA MPhil MCLIP, Retired. [0019265] 01/04/1967
Puhlmann Dr H, Professor. [0061247] 18/04/2002
Pulford Mr DJ, BA DipLib MCLIP, Site Lib., Barber Fine Art L., Univ.of Birmingham. [0041622] 02/02/1988
Puligari Mrs P, MLISc, Unemployed. [0059459] 30/03/2001
Pullan Mrs JS, (was Crosskey), BA DipLib MCLIP, Lib., E.Grp., Bromley L. [0032792] 29/08/1980
Pullen Mrs B, (was Keen), MA MCLIP, Child.Lib., Hants.C.C., Petersfield. [0037787] 16/10/1984
Pullen Mr CJ, MCLIP, Stock & Client Mgr., N.Div., Dorset Co.L. [0012039] 28/03/1969
Pullen Mrs LJ, (was Smith), BLib MCLIP, Project Offr., Poole L., Bor.of Poole. [0021637] 01/01/1973
Pumfrey Miss SM, BA(Hons) DipILS MCLIP, Trainer, I S Oxford, Littlemore. [0052513] 02/11/1995
Punnett Miss FJ, BA(Hons) MCLIP, Unemployed-Travelling. [0047883] 23/10/1992
Punter Miss CL, Sch.Lib./Stud., Sheldon Sch./Univ.of Bristol. [0061461] 12/08/2002
Purbrick Mrs GW, (was Adams), MCLIP, p./t.H.of Learning Res., Eltham Hill Sch., London. [0012045] 01/01/1956
Purcell Mrs CW, (was Turner), MTheol MA MCLIP, Campus Lib., Univ.of Durham, Stockton Campus. [0028383] 08/11/1977
Purcell Mr J, BA DipLib DMS MCLIP, Dep.Lib., Newcastle Univ.L. [0031092] 15/08/1979
Purcell Ms K, BA(Hons) MA MCLIP, Media Lib., London Sch.of Fashion. [0056400] 01/07/1998
Purcell Mr ME, MA, L.& Books Curator. [0050628] 01/10/1994
Purchase Mr SWF, BN(Hons), L.Asst., Univ.of Birmingham. [0056975] 17/11/1974
Purchon Mrs KM, (was Bromley), BA MA MCLIP, Career Break. [0035779] 24/01/1983
Purdey Mr BG, BA FRSA MCLIP, Retired. [0012048] 13/01/1965
Purdy Mr D, Employment not known. [0060613] 11/12/2001
Purdy Mrs DJ, (was Baldwin), BA DMS MCLIP, Inf.Serv.Team Mgr., Guideline Career Serv.Ltd., Nottingham. [0037460] 01/10/1984
Purkis Ms R, BA DipIS, Reveal Project Offr., Nat.L.for the Blind, Stockport. [0042687] 02/02/1989
Purser Mrs EC, (was Harrison), BA MCLIP, Employment not known. [0012052] 23/08/1968
Pursey Ms HM, (was Themis), BA CertEd MCLIP, Tutor-Lib., Fircroft Coll., Birmingham. [0014511] 29/12/1974
Purves Mrs SG, (was Whitlam), BSc CEng MICE FSA, Retired. [0049181] 11/10/1993
Purvis Mrs BA, BA(Hons) PGDipInfSt, Lib., Colchester P.L., Essex C.C. [0042697] 02/02/1989
Purvis Mr BS, BA MSc MCLIP, Local Studies Lib., Wilts.C.C.Educ.& Ls. [0012058] 05/02/1969
Purvis Mrs S, BA(Hons), Ref.Lib., Cent.L., S.Tyneside Metropolitan B.C. [0047787] 14/10/1992
Puscas Miss I, BLib MCLIP, Lib., Bro Taf Health Auth., Cardiff. [0022089] 22/01/1974
Pussegoda Ms TN, BA MA, Learning Resource Co-ordinator, City of Westminster Coll., London. [0053159] 18/03/1996
Pyant Mr AF, Dip MA MCMI MCLIP, Asst.Co.Lib., W.Sussex Co.Council. [0042611] 16/01/1989
Pybus Miss SM, Local Studies Lib., Sheffield Ls.Arch.& Inf. [0030345] 21/02/1963
Pycock Mr LR, BA(Hons), Asst.Lib., L.B.of Barnet, Hendon L. [0050788] 18/10/1994
Pycroft Mr CJ, MCLIP, Sch.Lib., Bramcote Hills Comp.Sch., Notts. [0012062] 22/10/1969
Pye Mrs LE, (was Thomas), Asst.Lib., Univ.of Bristol. [0044157] 11/06/1990
Pye Mrs LEZ, (was Grzechowiak), BSc(Hons) MA MCLIP, p./t.Lib., Child.& Special Serv., Leics.C.C. [0049625] 17/11/1993
Pye-Smith Ms HME, MA, Res.Cent.Mgr., Public Record Off., Kew. [0040191] 04/11/1986
Pygott Mr DW, MCLIP, Unemployed. [0023988] 13/03/1960
Pyle Mrs BD, (was Watkins), MCLIP, Life Member. [0012067] 16/10/1943
Pyle Mr JC, MA MCLIP, Head of Communications, Destination Sheffield Ltd. [0025398] 28/12/1975
Pym Ms A, BA(Hons) MA, Dep.Counter Serv.Supervisor, Kings Coll.London. [0055758] 17/11/1997
Pyves Mrs IH, (was Napier), MCLIP, Life Member. [0012070] 01/01/1955
Quan Mrs EM, (was Mondoa), BA(Hons) MSc, Ch.Lib.& Ch.of Serv., Soc.Affairs, Limbe Urban Council, Rep.of Cameroon. [0040606] 01/04/1987
Quantrill Mr TJ, BSc(Hons) MCLIP, Child.& Yth.Serv.Offr., Stockton Bor.Council. [0047596] 05/10/1992
Quare Miss DC, BA M LITT MCLIP, Lib., St.Hugh's Coll., Oxford. [0022661] 01/08/1974
Quarmby Lawrence Mrs EA, (was Quarmby), Self-employed & Student. [0040517] 23/02/1987
Quayle Mr DR, BA MCLIP, Sen.Lib.-Lending & Spec.Serv., Milton Keynes L., Milton Keynes Council. [0012074] 14/09/1970

Quayle Mr VJ, DMA FRSHFCIEH MCLIP, Employment not known. [0060329] 10/12/2001
Quemard Mrs SP, BA(Hons), p./t.Catr., Royal Jersey Agric.Soc., Trinity. [0058755] 06/07/2000
Quesnel Mrs V, Resident in Trinidad. [0058988] 16/10/2000
Quibell Mr JRC, BA MCLIP, Lib., HMS Sultan L., Gosport. [0019272] 02/10/1972
Quick Mrs A, MA(Oxon) MA PGCE, Sub.Lib., (Liaison), Faculty of Health & Excercise Sci., Peirson L., Univ.Coll.Worcester. [0055275] 12/09/1997
Quicke Mr AC, BA FCLIP, Sen.Asst.Lib., Univ.of Huddersfield L. [0020406] 15/03/1973 **FE 14/06/1982**
Quigg Mrs SM, (was Bates), BA DipLib MCLIP, Sch.Lib., St.John Fisher Comp.Sch., Peterborough. [0023627] 13/01/1975
Quiggin Mr MB, BTechSc, Lib., Bradford Res.Cent. [0044767] 14/11/1990
Quigley Mr D, BSc DipLib MCLIP, Asst.Lib., Durham City L. [0024233] 29/04/1975
Quigley Ms MB, BLS DIP HE MCLIP, Tuition Mgr., Belle Associates, Coventry. [0033465]01/01/1981
Quilty Ms L, L.Asst., Bristol Cent.Lend.L. [0059504] 18/04/2001
Quine Ms M, MA MCLIP, Documentor, Ulster Mus., Belfast. [0012084] 08/04/1971
Quinn Miss AM, BA MSc, Br.Lib., S.Educ.& L.Board, Armagh Br.L. [0052103] 02/10/1995
Quinn Mrs B, BA MCLIP, Sen.Lib.-Farnborough, Farnborough L., Hants. [0019273] 01/01/1963
Quinn Mr EG, BA MCLIP, Access Serv.Lib., Univ.of Sydney, Australia. [0019042] 01/01/1965
Quinn Mr GP, BA DipLib DMS, Business & Ref.Lib., W.E.L.B., Londonderry Cent.L. [0035437] 01/10/1982
Quinn Miss HF, BA DipLib MCLIP, Lib., Whitby Bird & Partners, London. [0037009] 14/01/1984
Quinn Miss K, BA(Hons), Bibl.Lib., Joint Serv.Cent.L., Ashton-u-Lyne. [0051478] 15/02/1995
Quinn Mrs KM, (was Baskerville), BLib MCLIP, Bibl.Serv.Lib., Cent.L., Rotherham M.B.C. [0030359] 26/01/1979
Quinn Ms PM, (was Mcauley), BA MCLIP, Unemployed. [0022083] 15/01/1974 **AF**
Quinney Mrs L, MA, Stud., Univ.Newcastle @ Northumbria. [0059800] 03/10/2001
Quinsee Mr AG, BA FRSA MCLIP, Retired. [0012089] 05/10/1955
Qureshi Mr N, BA(Hons), Unemployed. [0055514] 20/10/1997
Rabbitt Miss K, Stud., Leeds Met.Univ. [0059220] 09/01/2001
Rabbitt Mr P, BA LLB DipLib, Asst.Lib., Galway Co.L., Ireland. [0028132] 06/10/1977
Rabe Mrs R, (was Hill), MCLIP, Retired. [0012093] 15/10/1936
Rabinowitz Dr II, MSc MBA MCLIP, Employment not known. [0060625] 11/12/2001
Rabson Mr S, BA MCLIP, Historian & Arch., P.& O. Steam Navigation Co., London. [0012096] 22/09/1968
Raby Ms AS, (was Raby Thompson), BA(Hons), Lib., Whitcliffe Mount Sch., Cleckheaton. [0048239] 17/11/1992
Rackley Mrs AL, (was Scott), MCLIP, Sch.L.Serv.Mgr., Blackburn with Darwen Bor., Blackburn, Lancs. [0013034] 26/01/1972
Radanne Miss C, MA DipLib, Hogarth Project Catr., Warburg Inst. [0047503] 09/09/1992
Radbourne Mrs MA, (was Shaw), BA MCLIP, Sen.Lib., Leigh Park L., Hampshire Co.L. [0013221] 28/09/1969
Radburn Mrs J, BA PGCE MCLIP, Young Peoples L.Serv.Mgr., Herefordshire Council., (Maternity Leave). [0040612] 01/04/1987
Radcliffe Miss EB, BA(Hons), L.Asst., Univ.of Manchester, John Rylands Univ. [0055533] 20/10/1997
Radcliffe Mr IF, BSc DipLib MCLIP, Head of L.Serv., Hertford Reg.Coll., Ware Centre. [0031423] 10/10/1979
Raddon Mrs C, MCLIP, Retired. [0012105]01/01/1954
Raddon Miss DL, BLib MCLIP, Asst.IS & T Mgr., Essex C.C., Co.L.H.Q., Chelmsford. [0029343] 22/05/1978
Raddon Miss RA, DipEdTech MA MSc MCLIP, Freelance/Consultant/Counsellor.`, [0012106] 26/03/1956
Radford Mrs EA, (was Clift), MCLIP, Asst.Lib., L.B.of Lewisham. [0026323] 22/10/1976
Radford Ms K, MA MCLIP, Asst.Lib., Univ.of York. [0049227] 14/10/1993
Radford Mrs RM, (was Robertson), BA MCLIP, Princ.Lib.Stock Mgmnt.& Devel., Rotherham M.B.C. [0012111] 07/01/1970
Radford Mr RS, MCLIP, Customer Serv.Asst., L.B.of Sutton, Wallington. [0012112] 23/09/1967
Radmore Mrs S, MCLIP, Retired. [0012114] 06/09/1959
Rae Mrs B, (was McPhie), BA MCLIP, Unemployed. [0037679] 11/10/1984
Rae Mr C, MA DipLib MCLIP, Training, W.Dunbartonshire Council, L.H.Q. [0036759] 03/12/1983
Rae Mr EM, MA, Lib., Royal Geographical Soc., London. [0044184]01/07/1990
Rae Ms FM, Unemployed. [0048967] 06/08/1993
Rae Ms H, BA, Asst.Lib., Benenden Sch., Kent. [0057436] 01/04/1999 **AF**
Rae Miss MA, BA MCLIP, Comm.Lib., Glasgow City Co. L.I.A. [0030034] 20/10/1978
Rae Ms MC, MA, p./t.Teacher, Aireview Pupil Referral Unit, Bradford. [0053142] 13/11/1997
Rae Miss PA, BA MCLIP, L.Mgr., Royal Coll.of Art, Lodon. [0027207] 01/02/1977
Rae Mrs SB, (was Deans), MA MCLIP, Cent.Lib., Jewel & Esk Valley Coll., Edinburgh. [0031595] 12/11/1979
Raffan Miss AK, BA MCLIP, Sen.L.Asst., City Univ., St.Bartholomew Sch., of Nursing & Midwifery. [0035770] 12/01/1983
Rafferty Ms EPF, BA MSc MCLIP, Subject Lib., Queen Mary L., Univ.of London. [0026521] 16/09/1976

Rafter Mr D, BA(Hons), L.Asst., The British Library, London. [0059653] 13/07/2001 **AF**
Ragab Mrs LA, (was Foulsham), BA MCLIP, Lib., CAB Internat.Biosciences Inst., Egham, Surrey. [0030412] 25/01/1979
Raggett Mrs HJ, L.Mgr., Bournemouth Bor.Council, Kinson L. [0050019] 16/02/1994 **AF**
Raggett Mr PJE, BA(Hons) MA MCLIP, Lib., OECD., Paris, France. [0032157] 30/01/1980
Raheem Ms Y, BA MCLIP, Exec.Asst.to the Sec.General, The Colombo Plan Secretariat, Bank of Ceylon, Sri Lanka. [0020028] 08/01/1973
Raikes Miss EG, BA(Hons), Asst.L.Mgr., Surrey C.C., Staines L. [0058027] 19/10/1999
Rainbow Mrs L, BA MCLIP, Ref.Arch.& Local Studies Mgr., Arch.& Local Studies Cent., Medway Council. [0038556] 01/07/1985
Raine Miss D, BA, Lib., Henry Moore Foundation, Leeds. [0042333] 24/10/1988
Raine Mrs M, (was Mais), MCLIP, Lend.Serv.Lib., Darlington L. [0012118] 13/01/1956
Rainer Mrs JE, (was Fryer), BA DipLib MCLIP, Learning Res.Lib., Leicester Coll. [0036333] 01/10/1983
Rainey Miss M, BA(Hons) MA, Asst.Lib., Denton Wilde Sapte, London. [0057128] 17/12/1998
Rainey Ms M, BSc MSc MCLIP, Employment not known. [0060785] 12/12/2001
Raisin Mrs AS, BA DipLib MLib MCLIP, Inf.Mgr., Dept.Trade & Ind., London. [0025399] 05/01/1976
Raistrick Mr CJ, MCLIP, Business Intelligence Serv.Mgr., Procter & Gamble, Newcastle upon Tyne. [0038807] 10/10/1985
Raistrick Mr D, FCLIP, Head of Inf.Mgmt., The Court Serv., London. [0012121] 27/03/1962 **FE 08/03/1988**
Raitt Dr DI, FCLIP FRAS, Space Technologist, European Space Agency., The Netherlands. [0017607] 01/02/1965 **FE 24/05/1979**
Raja Mrs J, (was Satterthwaite), MCLIP, Unemployed. [0012957] 13/09/1967
Rajacic Ms V, BA(Hons) MSc, Grad.Trainee/Trainee L.Offr., Sch.Inf.& Media, Faculty of Management, Aberdeen. [0059385] 27/02/2001
Rajendra Mrs V, Catr., Mckinsey & Co., London. [0049336] 25/10/1993 **AF**
Rajendran Miss MY, BSc MLib DipEd, Knowledge Mgr., Health Insurance Commision, Australia. [0044492] 15/10/1990
Ralli Mr RA, BA MSc AALIA MCLIP, Retired. [0012124] 11/08/1967
Ralls Mrs MC, BD MSc MCLIP, Stud., Edinburgh Univ., Hist.Dept. [0012125] 25/04/1972
Ralph Mrs LC, (was Ayles), MCLIP, Dir., Arrivel Ltd., Hants. [0000548] 01/01/1972
Ralston Mrs LMA, (was Taboureau), MCLIP, Retired. [0002328] 10/11/1964
Ramage Mrs PAW, (was Mutua), Stud. [0054715] 03/03/1997
Ramalingam Ms R, LLB(Hons) MCLIP, Lib., Perbadanan Perpustakaan Awam, Selangor, Malaysia. [0017609] 14/08/1969
Ramdhian Miss SD, BA(Hons) MA MCLIP, Mgr.Inf.& Research Services, Chem Systems - IBM UK Ltd. [0049835] 20/12/1993
Ramm Mrs BL, (was Raley), BA, Retired. [0012131] 19/01/1949
Rampton Mrs AM, Sch.Lib., Rookwood Sch., Hampshire. [0060878] 18/12/2001 **AF**
Ramsay Mrs AP, (was Lord), BA PGCE DipLib, Team Lib., Wirral Bor.Council. [0041606] 07/10/1987
Ramsay Mrs EA, (was Kilby), FCLIP, Retired. [0008354] 23/09/1957 **FE 07/11/1974**
Ramsay Mrs KA, (was Boyd), BA MCLIP, Lib., Priory Sch., Southsea, Hampshire. [0026210] 24/08/1976
Ramsbotham Miss B, FCLIP, Life Member. [0012134] 11/10/1937 **FE 01/01/1949**
Ramsbottom Mr M, MA MCLIP MIMgt, Sen.Lib., Fylde, N.Lancs.Div., Lancs.L. [0024173] 15/01/1959
Ramsden Ms A, BSc MCLIP, Position unknown, Open Univ.L. [0060626] 11/12/2001
Ramsden Mrs JM, Events Co-ordinator, Nottingham CVS. [0044028] 04/04/1990 **AF**
Ramsden Mr MJ, BA MSOCSC FALIA FCLIP, Retired. [0017618] 10/03/1958 **FE 01/01/1971**
Ramsden Mr ML, BA(Hons) MCLIP, Readers Advisor Lib., Altrincham L. [0055330] 29/09/1997
Ramsden Miss P, Community Lib., Bolton P.Ls., Westhoughton, Bolton,Gr.Manchester. [0057427] 01/01/1961
Ramsden Mr PA, BA CertEd MCLIP, NVQ Trainer/Assessor. [0027210] 01/01/1977
Ramshaw Mrs K, Inf.Serv.Mgr., Medway Council, Chatham. [0055258] 29/08/1997
Ramwell Miss J, BA(Hons) DipILS, Rare Books Catr., Chetham's L., Manchester. [0052848] 08/01/1996
Ranade Dr SS, BSc(Hons) MCLIP, Stud., Univ.of Sheffield. [0047985] 30/10/1992
Rance Ms N, (was Gabbitas), MCLIP, Knowledge Mgr., Business Link Surrey, Woking. [0019689] 10/10/1966
Ranchhod Ms U, Sch.Lib., President Kennedy Sch., Coventry. [0054401] 03/12/1996
Randall Mrs AS, (was Barker), DipLib, Asst.Lib., Slaughter & May, London. [0045280] 01/10/1990
Randall Mrs EJ, (was Wright), BA MCLIP, Unemployed. [0027478]01/04/1977
Randall Mrs FL, (was Webb), Housewife. [0038594] 17/07/1985
Randall Mrs G, MCLIP, Asst.Lib., L.B.of Lewisham. [0018089] 01/10/1972
Randall Ms JI, (was Foster), MCLIP, Child.& Young Peoples Lib., Bristol City Council, Cheltenham Road L. [0012140] 17/01/1969
Randall Mrs JM, DipLib, Sen.L.Asst., Periodicals & Inter-L.Loans, Imperial Coll., Charing Cross. [0003236] 03/01/1972
Randall Miss NJ, BA(Hons) MSc, Asst.Lib., FCO, London. [0053537] 15/07/1996

Personal Members

Randall Mr POP, CertEd, Unemployed. [0053442] 01/07/1996
Randall Mrs SJ, (was Massie), MCLIP, Child.Lib.p./t., L.B.of Croydon. [0026471] 15/10/1976
Randall Miss T, BA(Hons) MSc, Project Offr., Univ. Birmingham, Birmingham. [0061375] 01/07/2002
Randell Mrs CM, (was Anstey), MCLIP, Bookshop Asst., Norfolk Child.Book Cent. [0000324] 01/01/1969
Randerson Mrs ME, (was Lloyd), MCLIP, Retired. [0012141] 26/09/1964
Ranger Miss NM, BA MCLIP, Campus Lib., Univ.of W.of England, Bristol, Swindon. [0020793] 03/07/1973
Rankin Mrs CEM, MA BSocSc DipLib MCLIP, Sen.Lecturer, Sch.Inf.Mgmt., Leeds Met.Univ. [0028661] 01/11/1977
Rankin Mrs RC, MA(Hons) PGDip, Stud., Univ.of Strathclyde. [0061027] 11/02/2002
Rankine Mrs B, (was Eccles), BA MCLIP, Team Lib., Glasgow City L. [0004377] 20/01/1972
Ransley Mrs N, BA(Hons), p./t/Stud./Learning Cent.Asst., City & Islington Coll., London. [0059882] 29/10/2001
Ransome Mr PJ, BA MCLIP, Team Lib.-Comm.Devel., Norfolk L.& Inf.Serv., Gt.Yarmouth L. [0040208] 11/11/1986
Ranson Miss L, (was Hamilton), BA MCLIP, Head of Inf.Serv., Stockport M.B.C. [0012151] 17/01/1972
Ranson Mr MC, MCLIP, Retired. [0012152] 15/02/1949
Raper Ms D, BSc MA MCLIP, Unemployed. [0023487] 01/01/1975
Rapley Mrs HF, (was Randall), BSc DipLib MCLIP, Lib.,South Ham, Hants.C.C., Basingstoke. [0044046] 12/04/1990
Rapps Miss J, MCLIP, Relief Lib., W. Berks Council, Newbury, Berks. [0024789] 08/10/1975
Rasdall Mr M, BA(Hons) MSc, Dir.of Inf.Systems, Inst.of Pract.in Advertising, London. [0048607] 11/03/1993
Raseroka Ms HK, BSc MA, Dir., Univ.of Botswana L., Gaborone. [0053168] 01/04/1996
Rashidah Begum Miss FM, BA MCLIP, Ch.Lib., Univ.Sains Malaysia, 11800 Minden,Penang. [0018908] 11/08/1972
Rashidi Mrs S, (was Zar), BA MCLIP, Career Break. [0037369] 23/07/1984
Rasmussen Ms H, BA, Lib., Visiontext Ltd., London. [0061548] 11/09/2002
Rastall Mrs DM, (was King), MCLIP, Life Member. [0012156] 01/01/1951
Rastan Ms JT, Lib., Lenkiewicz Foundation, Plymouth. [0059941] 08/11/2001
Rastrick Mrs EF, (was Taylor), MCLIP, Advisory Lib., Suffolk L.& Heritage, Ipswich. [0018180] 10/10/1972
Raszpla Mrs A, (was Bilous), LLB(Hons) MSc, Lib., RPS, Swindon. [0057230] 25/01/1999
Ratcliff Mrs CE, (was Lewis), [0049954] 20/01/1994
Ratcliff Mrs CM, (was Elsmore), BA(Hons) DipLib, Data Analyst, Suffolk Health Auth., Ipswich. [0039977] 01/10/1986
Ratcliff Dr FW, CBE JP HonFCLIP MA PhD, Life Member, Tel.01379 898232, Ridge Hse., Rickinghall Superior, Diss, Norfolk, IP22 1DY. [0012159] 12/03/1962 **FE 06/01/1987**
Ratcliffe Mr J, MCLIP, Retired. [0012161] 21/09/1960
Ratcliffe Mrs JE, (was Davies), MCLIP, Sen.L.Asst., Midlothian Council L., Bonny Rigg L. [0037071] 05/01/1970
Ratcliffe Miss JV, BA(Hons) MSc, Inf.Offr., Clifford Chance, London. [0054568] 21/01/1997
Ratcliffe Mrs RAM, (was Voyez), BA MCLIP, Lend.Lib., Hants.C.C. [0031030] 09/07/1979
Ratcliffe Miss SA, BA(Hons) DipIA, Resource Asst.-Elec.Journals, Univ.of Aberdeen. [0054623] 04/02/1997
Ratcliffe Mrs SJ, (was Ness), p./t.Lib.(Adult Serv.), N.Shields Cent.L., N.Tyneside L. [0050590] 26/09/1994
Rath Mr AA, MCLIP, Consultant, London. [0012156] 10/01/1964
Ratnasamy Miss T, BA MCLIP, Sen.Mgr., C J Koh Law L., Nat.Univ.of Singapore. [0034054] 01/08/1981
Rattle Miss S, MCLIP, Asst.Lib., Liverpool City L., Liverpool. [0012168] 27/03/1971
Rattu Mrs C, BScEcon DipLib, p./t.Stud./L.Mgr., Univ.Aberystwyth, Peartree L.,Derbyshire. [0059622] 03/07/2001
Rattue Miss KEW, MCLIP, Retired, Surrey. [0012170] 11/01/1949
Rauch Mrs D, (was Jones), BA MCLIP, LRC Mgr., Douay Martyrs Sch., Uxbridge. [0000918]01/01/1971
Ravasso Ms JE, MCLIP, Lib., Woolwich Ref.L., L.B.of Greenwich. [0012171] 19/05/1969
Raven Mrs C, BA(Hons) MA MCLIP, Comm.Inf.Devel.Worker, Manchester Comm.Inf.Network. [0055619] 27/10/1997
Raven Conn Mrs CM, (was Raven), BSc(Econ), L.Asst., Leisure L., Cent.L., Nottingham City Council. [0048726] 27/04/1993
Raw Mrs A, (was Micklethwaite), MCLIP, Unemployed. [0010112] 17/09/1969
Rawes Mrs PM, (was Murphy), BA(Hons) MCLIP, Sen.Inf.Asst., Univ.of Leicester. [0034997]08/06/1982
Rawle Mr PJ, BA(Hons) DipLib MCLIP, Lib., PG L., Princess of Wales Hosp., Bridgend, Mid-Glamorgan. [0037388] 02/08/1984
Rawley Mrs MJ, Asst.Lib., Dept.for Trans.,Local Govern., & The Regions, London. [0041349] 03/11/1987
Rawlings Mr JF, MCLIP, [0021706] 01/01/1974
Rawlings Mrs PS, (was Levy), BA MCLIP, Unemployed. [0023720]07/01/1975
Rawlings Miss SD, BLib MCLIP, Community Serv.Lib., N.E.Lincs. [0030517] 03/02/1979
Rawlings Mrs SJ, (was Bradford), BA MCLIP, Catr., Norfolk Co.L. [0001593] 10/01/1966
Rawlings Gavure Ms J, (was Gavhure), BEd(Hons) CertEd, Inf.Asst., Kings Coll.London, Inf.Serv.& Systems, Inf.Cent. [0057926] 05/10/1999 **AF**
Rawlins Mr PN, BA(Hons), Volunteer, Home Farm Trust, Macclesfield. [0049374] 11/11/1993
Rawlinson Miss KA, MCLIP, Catr., L.& Inf.Serv.of W.Australia, Perth. [0017624] 17/04/1962
Rawlinson Ms R, L.Mgr., Lovells, London. [0040189] 01/11/1986

Rawlinson Mr S, BSc MCLIP, Inf.Serv.Lib., Leics.Univ. [0012177] 15/08/1969
Rawson Miss JL, BA(Hons), Grad.Trainee, Taylor Inst.L., Oxford. [0061823] 12/11/2002
Rawson Mr NRW, DipLib BA MCLIP FInstSMM, Dir., L.Serv., OCLC PICA, Birmingham. [0030929] 16/06/1979
Rawson Mr SD, MCLIP MA, Sub-Lib., Queens Univ., Belfast. [0021384] 13/11/1973
Rawsthorn Mrs JM, MA MCLIP, Ref./Inf.Serv.Mgr., Warrington Bor.Council, Cheshire. [0002264] 14/10/1971
Rawsthorne Mr L, MLib FCLIP, Co.Lib., Flintshire C.C., Mold. [0025095] 05/11/1975 **FE 20/05/1998**
Ray Mrs A, MA DMS MCLIP, Learning Cent.Mgr., Ealing Tertiary Coll. [0027211] 03/02/1977
Ray Ms A, BA DipLib MA MCLIP, Head of L.& Inf.Serv., Scarborough Hosp.L., N.Yorks. [0034365] 25/10/1981
Ray Mr AK, MA MCLIP, Life Member. [0017626] 06/01/1956
Ray Mr CH, FCLIP, Life Member. [0012186] 10/03/1947 **FE 01/01/1955**
Ray Mrs ER, (was Saunders), MCLIP, Retired/Unemployed. [0012188] 13/09/1966
Ray Mrs JR, (was Walker), BA(Hons) DipIS, Resource Offr., N.Peterborough Primary Care Trust. [0049508] 09/11/1993
Ray Mrs LA, (was Owen), MCLIP, Mgmt.Serv.Lib., L.B.of Lewisham. [0022123] 19/02/1974
Ray Mrs SG, (was Bannister), BA MPhil HonFCLIP FCLIP, Life Member, Tany-Capel, Bont Dolgadfan, Llanbrynmair, Powys, SY19 7BB. [0012191] 21/09/1951 **FE 01/01/1959**
Raybould Mr DJ, L.Mgr., Cornwall C.C., Bodmin. [0057193] 08/01/1999 **AF**
Raybould Mrs WJ, (was Pope), MA MCLIP, Head of Learning Res., Weston Favell Upper Sch., Northampton. [0011813] 11/01/1967
Rayfield Mrs S, (was Pugh), MCLIP, Inf.Offr., ERA Tech.Ltd., Leatherhead. [0055188] 05/08/1997
Rayment Mr I, BA(Hons) MA, Subject Lib., Seale-Hayne L., Univ.of Plymouth. [0058901] 01/10/2000
Raymer Miss MM, BA FCLIP, Life Member. [0012194] 14/10/1935 **FE 01/01/1941**
Raymont Mr DM, BA, Asst.Lib./Arch., Inst.of Actuaries. [0041549]18/01/1988
Rayner Ms HE, BA(Hons) DipILS MCLIP, Campus Lib., (job-share), Bath Spa Univ.Coll., Bath. [0042187] 10/10/1988
Raynor Miss E, MLIS BA, Unemployed. [0061071] 08/02/2002
Raynor Mrs JM, (was Braunsberg), MCLIP, Not employed, Elmhurst,24 S.Downs Rd.,Hale, Cheshire,WA14 3HW. [0021004] 03/10/1973
Raynor Mr MJ, BSc (Hons), p./t.Stud. Lib.Asst., Dept.Inf. and Commerce Manchester., All Saints L. Manchester. [0057349] 06/02/1999
Raywood Mrs LA, BA(Hons) PGDipIM, Enquiry Desk Lib., Reading Cent.L. [0056115] 22/02/1998
Rea Ms HL, BA(Hons) DipLIS MCLIP, Asst.Lib., Crawley P.L. [0057621] 19/05/1999
Rea Mrs ME, BA MCLIP, Sch.Lib., Merchant Taylors'Boys'Sch., Liverpool. [0027031] 10/01/1977
Read Miss CA, MA MCLIP, Life Member. [0012200] 07/10/1971
Read Mrs CR, Resident in U.S.A. [0047373] 27/07/1992
Read Mrs EA, (was Cromwell), MA MCLIP, Retired. [0012203] 13/01/1965
Read Ms EA, BA MCLIP, Div.Bibl.Serv.Lib., Basingstoke, Hants.Co.L. [0012202] 08/10/1967
Read Miss EM, BA MCLIP, Life Member. [0012205] 07/09/1945
Read Mrs FMA, DipInf DipLeg LLB, Unemployed. [0061340] 31/05/2002
Read Mr G, BA DipLib, Acquisitions Lib., Nat.Art L., Victoria & Albert Mus. [0047502] 09/09/1992
Read Mrs J, (was Martin), MA MCLIP, Arch., Froebel Arch.for Childhood Studies, Univ.of Surrey, Roehampton. [0009839] 28/08/1969
Read Mrs JE, (was Higgens), BA MCLIP, Sen.Lib., Bridport L., Dorset Co.L. [0006855] 01/01/1970
Read Mrs JM, (was Walsh), BA PGCE DipLib MCLIP, Rare Books Catr., Univ.of Reading. [0044528] 22/10/1990
Read Ms KJ, BA MA MCLIP, Sen.L.Asst., Inst.of Advanced Legal Studies, Univ.of London. [0043599] 09/11/1989
Read Miss LA, MA BA MCLIP, Coll.Lib., Robinson Coll., Cambridge. [0025401] 18/01/1976
Read Ms M, MA, Self-employed, 126 Queen Margaret Drive, Glasgow,G20 8NY. [0043562] 08/11/1989
Read Mrs MA, Lib., Morrab L., Penzance, Cornwall. [0057105] 14/12/1998
Read Mrs NC, BA(Hons) MCLIP, Life Member, Tel.Bournemouth 557856, 21 E.Ave., Talbot Woods, BH3 7BS. [0012208] 11/06/1935
Read Miss SFB, FCLIP, Retired. [0012209] 21/09/1940 **FE 01/01/1953**
Reade Mrs JG, (was Alldread), BA MLS MCLIP, Retired.,Vol.in L., Halifax Citadel Nat.Hist.Site, Canada. [0012210] 01/01/1966
Reader Mr DK, MCLIP, Retired. [0012211]01/10/1971
Reader Mrs SV, (was Lambe), BA DipLib MCLIP, Lib. (Sundays), Colchester P.L., Essex C.C. [0042191] 12/10/1988
Reading Ms JA, BA(Hons) MA MCLIP, Lib., Univ.of Oxford, Dept.of Educ.Studies. [0043293] 16/10/1989
Readle Mrs MP, (was Surry), BLib MSc MCLIP, Lect.:I.T., Nelson & Colne Coll., Lancs. [0027849] 23/09/1977
Readman Mr JG, BA MA MCLIP, Head of L.Serv., L.B.of Brent. [0039889] 01/10/1986
Ready Ms KW, B ED DipLib MCLIP, Business,Managemt.& Law Subj.Lib., Anglia Poly.Univ., Cambridge. [0038557] 01/07/1985
Reardon Mr DF, BSc MISM MCLIP, Employment not known. [0060629] 11/12/2001
Reason Mrs C, DipLS, Floor Mgr., Frewen L., Univ.of Portsmouth, Portsmouth. [0036034] 19/04/1983
Reavey Mrs L, (was Orritt), BA MCLIP, Comm.Lib., Tameside L.& Heritage. [0018176] 06/10/1972

333

Rebbeck Ms J, BA(Hons) MCLIP, Inf.Mgr., LPC Centre for Risk Sciences., Watford. [0034743] 16/02/1982
Rebuffa Mrs CG, L.Asst., St.Pauls Sch., London. [0059373] 21/02/2001 AF
Reddan Mrs MP, DipLib MCLIP, Lib., Nat.Univ.of Ireland, Galway, James Hardiman L. [0032387] 01/01/1972
Redding Ms FA, BA(Hons) DipLIS MCLIP, Grp.Lib.-N.Area, Portsmouth City L.Serv. [0049292] 20/10/1993
Redfearn Mrs J, (was Rose), MCLIP, p./t.Prison Lib., Leyhill Open Prison, S.Glos.L. [0022879] 01/10/1974
Redfern Mr BL, FCLIP, Life Member, 0181 541 3911, 14 Osborne Road, Kingston upon Thames. [0012223] 20/11/1944 FE 01/01/1956
Redfern Mrs EA, (was Parkinson), BA DipLib, Head of Inf., Cushman & Wakefield Healey & Baker, London. [0040440] 02/02/1987
Redfern Ms FMM, (was Amor), MA MCLIP, Life Member. [0015788] 13/03/1952
Redhead Miss JV, BA M LITT MCLIP, Asst.Lib., Darlington Bor.Council. [0023634] 20/01/1975
Redhead Mrs JW, (was Cooper), MCLIP, Bibl.Serv.Offr., Trafford B.Council. [0003124] 17/09/1962
Redhead Mr MK, MA MCLIP, Serv.Mgr.(Res.& Devel.), Trafford M.B.C. [0020773] 02/07/1973
Redican Ms H, MA, Unemployed. [0042518] 21/11/1988
Redlich Ms W, MA MSc, Arch.Asst., Glasgow Univ. [0057985] 08/10/1999
Redman Mr GC, BA, p./t.Stud./L.Asst., Worthing L., W.Sussex. [0061037] 11/02/2002
Redman Ms J, BSc(Hons) MSc PGCE MCLIP, [0057093] 07/12/1998
Redman Miss P, BA(Hons) MCLIP, Inf.Consultant, Lifetime Careers, Barnsley, Doncaster & Rotherham. [0048739] 30/04/1993
Redmond Ms MC, BA(Hons) PGDip, Subject Lib., Univ.of N.London. [0054488] 06/01/1997
Rednall Mrs C, (was Ashley-Smith), Housewife/Mother. [0049591] 19/11/1993
Redrup Mrs RMJ, (was Foster), BA MLib MCLIP, Marketing Co-ordinator, Univ.of Reading, Reading Univ. L. [0040997] 02/10/1987
Redwood Mrs HM, (was Francis), B Lib MCLIP, Self Employed Architectural Lib. [0005172] 29/04/1971
Reece Mrs ML, (was Watton), MCLIP, Sch.Lib., Shenley Court Secondary Sch., Birmingham. [0015475] 20/01/1972
Reed Miss A, MSc MCLIP, Employment not known. [0060770] 12/12/2001
Reed Mrs C, (was Ryan), BA MCLIP, Princ.Lib.-N., Worcs.C.C. [0032697] 01/07/1980
Reed Mr DM, BA MCLIP, Div.Lib., Warwickshire C.C., Nuneaton & Bedworth. [0040484] 12/02/1987
Reed Miss J, (was Wilson), Employment not known. [0060442] 11/12/2001
Reed Mrs J, (was Griffiths), MCLIP, Sch.Lib., St.Josephs Sch., Launceston. [0041945] 01/01/1963
Reed Mrs JM, (was Smith), BA(Hons) MCLIP, Librarian, Fair Oak High School, Staffordshire. [0025419] 16/12/1975
Reed Mrs JM, (was Harper), MCLIP, Tech.Serv.Lib., Univ.Coll.Worcester. [0006375] 01/01/1970
Reed Mr MW, BA, Community Lib., Birmingham L.Serv., Hall Green L. [0046895] 28/02/1992
Reed Miss PA, BA MCLIP, Unemployed. [0012234] 16/10/1969
Reed Mr RA, LLB DipLib MCLIP, Asst.Lib., RIBA, London. [0043224] 05/10/1989
Reed Mrs S, (was Probert), BA MCLIP, Learning Resources Mgr., S.Downs Coll.of H.E., Waterlooville. [0028965] 06/02/1978
Reed Miss SE, BA(Hons), p./t.Stud./L.Asst., Univ.of N.London/Bibl.Serv., Royal Soc.of Med., London. [0056730] 07/10/1998
Reed Ms SP, BA MA MCLIP, Resident in Australia. [0038151] 22/01/1985
Reed Mrs YM, (was Earl), MCLIP, Inf.Management Consultant, Self-employed. [0004344] 26/08/1969
Reedie Mrs SP, (was Adler), BA MA DipLib MCLIP, Housewife. [0029557] 07/10/1978
Reedy Mrs KJ, (was Wright), BA MA MCLIP, Asst.Lib.-Learner Support, Open Univ.L., Milton Keynes. [0038724] 01/10/1985
Reekie Mrs CS, (was Pinhas), MSc(Econ) MCLIP, Federation Lib., Cambridge Theological Fed. [0022560] 01/07/1974
Reeks Mrs JM, (was Hopkins), MCLIP, Sch.Lib., Bucks.C.C. [0007175] 01/01/1972
Reen Miss J, MA, L.Asst., Farrer and Co., London. [0059712] 28/08/2001
Rees Mrs A, (was Waldron), BA(Hons) MSc MCLIP, Unemployed. [0052316] 26/10/1995
Rees Mr ADW, BA MCLIP, Lib., Coleg Menai, [0038022] 16/01/1985
Rees Mr AG, BSc MIBiol MCLIP, Retired. [0060627] 11/12/2001
Rees Mrs AH, (was Talbot), BLib MCLIP, Records Off.Lib., Shakespeare Birthplace Trust, Stratford-on-Avon, Warks. [0019837] 01/01/1973
Rees Mr D, BA(Hons) PGCE, p./t.Stud./L.Asst., The Wellcome Trust L., London. [0061039] 11/02/2002
Rees Mr DH, Asst., Pembs.Co.L. [0012239] 22/01/1966
Rees Ms ES, BA MPhil MA, Web Editor., Sch.of Advanced Study, London. [0057781] 02/08/1999
Rees Mrs FA, (was MacDonald), BLib(Hons) MCLIP, Lib., S.Staffs.Healthcare NHS Trust, Stafford. [0028864] 23/01/1978
Rees Ms HA, BA MEd MCLIP, Head of L.& Learning Res., Plymouth Coll.of F.E. [0017632] 29/09/1969
Rees Mrs JR, (was Jenkins), BA(Hons), Child.Serv.Lib., City & Co.of Swansea. [0007795] 02/11/1971
Rees Mrs JSP, (was Carlton), BA(Hons) DipLib MCLIP, Town Lib.Lichfield/Burntwood, Staffs.C.C., Lichfield. [0038969] 21/10/1985
Rees Mr MK, MA MSc MCLIP, Marketing Exec., The Patent Off., Newport. [0060697] 12/12/2001
Rees-Jones Mrs EA, (was Clapham), BA MCLIP, Princ.Lib.-S.E.Grp., Lichfield L., Staffs.C.C. [0026702] 29/10/1976
Rees-Jones Ms L, (was Vaughan-Prosser), BA MCLIP, Workplace & Solo Adviser, CILIP. [0026594] 26/10/1976

Reeve Mr CF, BA MCLIP MSc, Lib., Barnardos, Barkingside, Essex. [0023179] 31/10/1974
Reeve Mrs G, Inf.Co-ordinator, Design House N.W.Ltd., Manchester. [0053862] 07/10/1996
Reeves Miss CL, MSc, Business Inf.Offr., Inst.of Directors, London. [0053539] 15/07/1996
Reeves Miss K, BA(Hons) MA, Temp.Inf.Specialist, The Open Univ.L., Milton Keynes. [0061140] 08/03/2002
Reeves Ms ME, (was Corry), BSc MCLIP, Lib., L.B.Islington, Pentonville Prison. [0018580] 20/01/1964
Reeves Mrs S, (was Pierce), BA(Hons), Trainee Lib. [0049790] 08/11/1993
Reeves Miss TL, BA(Hons), Grad.Trainee, L.Dept.for Ed.and Skills, London. [0059978] 15/11/2001
Refson Mrs MM, (was Lamble), BA MCLIP, Retired. [0012261] 02/10/1948
Regan Mrs CA, (was Strickland), BA MCLIP, Lib., John O'Gaunt Sch., Hungerford, Berks. [0012264] 25/09/1968
Regan Mrs CAE, (was Jamison), BLS MCLIP, L.Asst., Taunton NHS Trust. [0030845] 09/05/1979
Regan Mrs EA, (was Drummond), MA DipLib MCLIP, P./t.Asst.Lib., Pwllheli L., Gwynedd. [0032926] 04/10/1980
Regan Mr FR, MA FRSA FCLIP, Retired. [0012265] 15/01/1948 FE 01/01/1956
Regan Mr T, BA(Hons) DipILS, Dep.Lib., Hawick L., Scottish Borders Council. [0051621] 18/04/1995
Regan Mrs Y, (was Warner), MCLIP, Sch.Lib., The Priory Sch., Hitchin. [0021910] 01/10/1968
Rehahn Ms AS, BA MSc MCLIP, Inf.Offr., R.N.I.B., London. [0012268] 01/01/1971
Reid Mr A, L.Serv.Mgr., Jones, Day, Reavis & Pogue, London. [0041223] 13/10/1987
Reid Mr A, MA MCLIP, L.Serv.Mgr., MidLothian Council, Dalkeith. [0022822] 04/10/1974
Reid Ms A, MA DipInfSc MCLIP, Position unknown, Brit.L., London. [0060650] 11/12/2001
Reid Mrs AJ, (was Bodie), Rec.Mgmnt.Co-ordinator, TotalFinaElf Exploration UK PLC., Aberdeen. [0046218] 15/10/1991
Reid Mr BJ, BA AALIA MCLIP, Retired. [0038965] 23/10/1985
Reid Mrs CA, (was Elliott), BSc(Hons) MSc MCLIP, Lib., Univ.of Cambridge, Lucy Cavendish Coll. [0047377] 28/07/1992
Reid Miss CD, BA MA FCLIP, Mgr.,Bus.Inf.Serv., Grad.Business Sch., Univ.of Strathclyde. [0012270] 01/07/1972 FE 01/04/2002
Reid Mrs CJ, (was Miles), BA MCLIP, Lib., Seacroft Hosp., Leeds Teaching Hosp.NHS Trust. [0017633] 07/05/1965
Reid Ms CJ, (was Jeffries), MA(Hons) DipLib MCLIP, Sch.Lib., E.Lothian Council, Haddington, E.Lothian. [0046302] 25/10/1991
Reid Ms DJ, MA DipLIS, p./t.Sch.Lib., Educ.Dept., City of Edinburgh. [0051114] 16/11/1994
Reid Mrs J, MCLIP, L.Asst., John Ruskin 6th Form Coll., Croydon. [0009837] 01/01/1971
Reid Mrs JEK, (was Bennett), BA MCLIP, Asst.Lib.-Ref.& Inf., Bucks.Co.L., Aylesbury. [0037025] 12/01/1984
Reid Mrs JJ, (was Mcvey), MA MCLIP, Subject Lib., NESCOT, Epsom. [0021172] 30/09/1973
Reid Miss JLH, BA MCLIP, Sch.Lib., Grange Acad., Kilmarnock, E.Ayrshire. [0037890] 11/10/1984
Reid Ms JM, BA MA MA MCLIP, Dep.Lib., Dept.for Educ.& Skills, Sheffield. [0032160] 22/01/1980
Reid Miss KE, BA(Hons) DipIM, Inf.Executive, Sport England, London. [0051082] 14/11/1994
Reid Ms LC, BA(Hons) MA, Clinical Lib., Barnet Primary Care NHS Trust. [0053760] 01/10/1996
Reid Ms LC, BA MCLIP, Br.Lib., Broxburn & W.Calder L., W.Lothian Council. [0033122] 01/10/1980
Reid Mrs LJ, (was Howard), BLS, Sen.L.Asst., Univ.of Ulster, Co.Antrim. [0041736] 29/02/1988
Reid Miss LY, Lib., Hanover Parish L., Jamaica. [0059642] 09/07/2001
Reid Miss M, BLib MCLIP, Asst.Lib., Cranfield Univ.L., Beds. [0012273] 17/10/1971
Reid Mrs M, (was McMillan), BA MCLIP, Asst.Lib., Paisley Cent.L., Renfrewshire Council. [0032445] 16/04/1980
Reid Mr MA, BSc(Hons) MA MA MCLIP, Deputy Lib., Bradford Hosp.NHS Trust, Med.& Healthcare L. [0052003] 06/09/1995
Reid Mrs NJ, (was Lewis), Asst.Lib., Hertford Coll.L., Oxford. [0053241] 19/04/1996 AF
Reid Dr PH, BA(Hons) PhD FSA(Scot), Lect., Sch.of Inf.& Media, Robert Gordon Univ., Aberdeen. [0048679] 13/04/1993
Reid Mrs S, BSc MA DipLib MCLIP, Sch.Lib., Bathgate Academy, W.Lothian. [0026527] 07/10/1976
Reid Miss SE, MA(Hons), Stud., Univ.of Strathclyde. [0061318] 17/05/2002
Reid Miss SJ, BA(Hons), Stud., Univ.of Wales, Aberystwyth & Lib., Peniel Col.of H.E., Brentwood, Essex. [0057918] 01/10/1999
Reid Mrs SM, (was Brown), MA MCLIP, Young Peoples Serv.Lib., Stirling Council L. [0005182] 16/10/1968
Reid-Franczak Mrs JE, (was Reid), BSc(Hons), Unemployed. [0061159] 07/03/2002
Reid-Smith Dr ER, BA MEd FCLIP MEdAdmin MBus DipAdEd PhD, PhD EdD FLA, Life Member, 2 Salmon St., Wagga Wagga, NSW 2650, Australia. [0012277] 01/01/1947 FE 01/01/1967
Reilly Miss A, MCLIP, Unemployed. [0012284] 06/10/1964
Reilly Miss AM, BA DipLIS, Asst.Lib., L., House of Lords, London. [0049135] 07/10/1993
Reilly Mr AM, BA MA DipILS, Asst.Lib., Caledonian Univ.L., Glasgow. [0059501] 05/04/2001
Reilly Mrs AM, (was Tyrrell), BA MCLIP, Team Lib., Educ.Resource Serv., N.Lanarkshire Council, Coatbridge. [0019545] 20/10/1969
Reilly Ms C, BA PGCE PDipLibInf, Unemployed. [0043027] 26/06/1989

Reilly Miss CW, MLITT FCLIP, Life Member. [0012285]   30/03/1942 FE 07/05/1973
Reilly Miss JA, Lib.Asst., Joseph Chamberlain Coll., Birmingham. [0057030] 26/11/1998
Reilly Mr LJ, BA DipLib MCLIP, Local Studies Lib., L.B.of Southwark. [0039084]   29/10/1985
Reilly Mr PM, BSc DipInfSc, I.T.Mgr., Crockers Oswald Hickson, London. [0035974]   09/02/1983
Reilly-Cooper Mrs P, (was Briscoe), BSc DipLib MCLIP, L.Serv.Mgr., Halton Borough Council. [0034607]   11/01/1982
Reimer Mr ARB, BSc MSc MCLIP, Employment not known. [0060630] 11/12/2001
Reiner Ms E, BA DipLib MCLIP, L.Inf.Offr., Amnesty Internat., Internat.Secretariat, London. [0044429]   09/10/1990
Relf Mrs K, (was Kirton), MCLIP, Asst.Lib., Kimberley L., De Montfort Univ.,Leicester. [0008447]   01/09/1968
Relph Mr TR, BA(Hons) MCLIP, Ref.Lib., Cent.L., S.Tyneside M.B.C. [0043721]   01/12/1989
Relves Miss VJ, BA(Hons) DipLib MCLIP, Lib., Arup, Solihull. [0044449] 09/10/1990
Ren Ms M, BA, System Consultant, Ex Libris (UK) Ltd., Middlesex. [0043107] 28/07/1989
Rench Mr SF, BA, Lib., Cent.for Oxfordshire Studies, Oxford. [0042879] 04/04/1989
Rendall Miss EL, MA, Life Member. [0012288]   01/01/1948
Rendle Miss AE, BSc MCLIP, Team Leader(Child.L.Serv.), Clackmannanshire Council, Alloa. [0026025]   07/10/1974
Renney Mr DA, BA(Hons) MA, Team Lib., Northants.C.C. [0058047] 14/10/1999
Rennie Mrs AD, MA DipLib MCLIP, Staff Devel.Offr., Leeds L.& Inf.Serv. [0027455]   16/03/1977
Rennie Ms AH, BA DipLib MCLIP, Lib.(Job Share), S.Gloucestershire C>, Kingswood. [0040412]   23/01/1987
Rennie Mr AJ, MCLIP, Network Devel.Lib., Aberdeen City L. [0012291] 01/01/1966
Rennie Mr C, MA(Hons) DipLib, System Support Lib., SOAS., Univ.of London. [0050187]   26/04/1994
Rennie Mrs CM, (was Mcgregor), MA MCLIP, L.Super., E.Renfrewshire Cultural Serv., Glasgow. [0012292]   02/09/1967
Rennie Miss IA, MA(Hons), Stud., Univ.of Strathclyde. [0061014]   01/02/2002
Rennie Mr MP, Reader & Electronic/Tech.Serv., Northern Ireland Assembly, Belfast. [0058761]   05/07/2000
Rennison Mrs S, (was Dobson), BA FCLIP, Life Member. [0004013] 19/03/1957   FE 29/09/1986
Renshaw Mrs LM, (was Ellis), MCLIP, p./t.Sch.Lib., Bedminster Down Sch., Bristol. [0004537]   05/01/1971
Renshaw Mrs NM, MCLIP, Comm.Lib., Central Lib., Stockport. [0022435] 23/04/1974
Renson Ms HA, BA DipLib MCLIP, Asst.Area Mgr., Hendon L., L.B.of Barnet. [0034424]   30/10/1981
Renstead Miss EA, (was Martin), BA(Hons), Lib., Eyemouth High School., Berwickshire. [0043859]   05/02/1990
Renton Miss AM, MCLIP, Lib., Notts.Co.L. [0012294]   15/03/1968
Renwick Ms FM, BA(Hons) MA MCLIP, Sen.Lib., Child.& Educ., Derby City L. [0036047]   28/04/1983
Repp Miss MC, BA, Catr., Oxford Early Printed Books Project. [0056348] 03/06/1998
Resteghini Mrs J, (was Housdon), MCLIP, Lib., Sacred Heart R.C.Sch., London. [0032428]   10/04/1980
Revesz Mrs M, Learning Cent.Lib., Westminster Kingsway Coll., London. [0041927]   31/05/1988
Revill Dr DH, PhD MA BSc(Econ) AdvDipEdTech FCLIP, Retired, 3 Sandhills, Hightown, Liverpool, L38 9EP, Tel.0151 929 2012. [0012299] 14/09/1954   FE 01/01/1961
Revill Mrs OJ, (was Williams), BA(Hons) MSc, Faculty Liaison Lib., St.George's L., London. [0052696]   23/11/1995
Rew Miss PL, BA DipLib MCLIP, L.& Serv.Mgr., Wimbledon L., Merton B. [0021182]   28/09/1973
Rex Mr SP, BLib(Hons), Inf.Serv.Mgr., Building Societies Assoc., London. [0055184]   04/08/1997
Rey Mrs PBL, (was White), BA MCLIP, L.Serv.Mgr., Queen Vic. Hosp. NHS Trust., E.Grinstead, W.Sussex. [0029351]   14/06/1978
Reyner Mr RJ, Inf.Asst., Allen & Overy, London. [0057112]   11/12/1998
Reynier Mrs S, (was Mann), BA(Hon) LIB MCLIP, Unemployed. [0009695] 06/01/1971
Reynolds Mrs AJ, (was Allcock), BA(Hons), Career Break. [0049192] 12/10/1993
Reynolds Mrs AM, (was Harrington), BA MA MCLIP, Portal Lib., Staffs.C.C., Staffs. [0032078]   30/01/1980
Reynolds Mr DSI, BA MCLIP, Asst.Lib., St.Davids Coll., Lampeter. [0012306] 09/03/1965
Reynolds Mr J, L.Offr., NHS Exec.L., Leeds. [0056179]   01/04/1998 AF
Reynolds Miss JA, BScEcon, Stud., Univ.Aberystwyth. [0059856]   17/10/2001
Reynolds Miss JE, BA MSc DipLib MCLIP, Med.Lib., W.Hertfordshire Hosp.NHS Trust, Watford Gen.Hosp. [0042372]   20/10/1988
Reynolds Mr JG, BA(Hons), L.Mgr., Paisner & Co., London. [0048581] 24/02/1993
Reynolds Mrs K, (was Hussey), BA(Hons) MCLIP, Princ.Lib.-Comm.Serv., Stoke-on-Trent City Council. [0036046]   28/04/1983
Reynolds Mr KJ, MCLIP, Lib., Staffordshire C.C. [0028134]   15/10/1977
Reynolds Mr L, (was Travis), L.Mgr., N.Tyneside Ls., Cent.L., Tyne & Wear. [0014843]   29/05/1970
Reynolds Ms L, BA(Hons) MCLIP, Research Lib., Capital Internat.Research Inc., London. [0052429]   01/11/1995

Reynolds Ms PA, BA, p./t.L.Asst., Public Record Off., Richmond. [0058563] 01/04/2000   AF
Reynolds Mr PC, BA DipLib MCLIP, Inf.Offr., Royal Inst.of Chartered Surveyors, London. [0035072]   01/07/1982
Reynolds Mr PD, BA MCLIP, Retired. [0020797]   05/07/1973
Reynolds Mr PR, MA MCLIP, Serv.Devel.Mgr., Loughborough Univ.L. [0041834]   14/04/1988
Reynolds Mrs SE, (was Garrard), BA MCLIP, Retired. [0012314]   01/01/1966
Rhee Mrs H, (was Lahovary), BA FCLIP, Retired. [0017635]   01/01/1949 FE 01/01/1954
Rhind Mrs M, (was Nealon), MCLIP, Comm.Lib., Fife Council, Dunfermline. [0010700]   01/01/1967
Rhodes Mrs CA, (was Horwood), BA MA MCLIP, Maternity leave. [0044917] 14/01/1991
Rhodes Ms HJ, (was Watts), BSc(Hons) MSc MCLIP, Civil Serv.Asst.Lib. [0053244]   19/04/1996
Rhodes Miss J, MCLIP, Life Member. [0012317]   24/11/1960
Rhodes Ms JBL, LLB DipLib MCLIP, Stock Serv.Lib., Leeds L.& Inf.Serv. [0025638]   21/01/1976
Rhodes Miss LA, BA DipLib MCLIP, Local Studies Lib., L.B.of Barking & Dagenham. [0033124]   09/10/1980
Rhodes Mr RG, MSc C ENG MIM MCLIP, Retired. [0012323]   12/11/1964
Rhodes Mrs S, (was Johnson), BLib(Hons), Admin.Offr.p./t., Bath County Court. [0038502]   15/05/1985
Rhodes Miss SA, BSc(Hons), Lib.Stud., Univ.of Sheffield, [0059681] 31/07/2001
Rhymes Ms S, BSc(Hons), L.Super., Hampshire C.C. [0046238]   16/01/1991
Rhys-Jones Miss RH, BSc MCLIP, H.E.Lib., Blackburn Coll. [0012327] 07/10/1970
Ricardson Mrs JC, Asst.Mgr., Colchester Lib., Colchester. [0061442] 18/07/2002   AF
Ricci Miss C, p./t.Stud.,Russian Catr., Univ.Coll.London, The London L. [0059383]   27/02/2001
Rice Mr ADR, Admin. Asst., Derby Evening Telegraph. [0060915]   10/01/2002
Rice Mrs B, (was Jones), BA, Head of Serv.Provision, Leeds City Council, Leeds Cent.L. [0047184]   26/05/1992
Rice Miss CS, MA MLib, Pals.Admin.Worker, S.Derby.Community & Mental Health, Serv.(NHS) Trust, Derby. [0049299]   20/10/1993
Rice Miss D, BA(Hons), Stud., Sheffield Univ. [0059222]   09/01/2001
Rice Ms G, MA(Hons) MA, L.Asst., Glasgow Univ.L. [0061612]   03/10/2002 AF
Rice Mrs JJ, (was Hayman), BA DipLib MCLIP, Unemployed. [0039853] 05/09/1986
Rice Mr ME, BSc(Soc) MCLIP HND, Unemployed. [0020866]   03/08/1973
Rice Mrs VJ, (was Tucknott), MCLIP, Inf.Mgr., Brit-American Tobacco Co.Ltd., Southampton. [0012331]   27/05/1969
Rich Mr DM, MA MLS MS MCLIP, Special Collections Catg., Brown Univ.L., Providence, Rhode Island, U.S.A. [0017636]   20/02/1957
Rich Mrs JD, LLB(Hons) DipInf MSc, Careers Inf. Co-ordinator, Guidance Enterprises Grp., York. [0047260]   29/06/1992
Rich Mrs LJ, (was Grove), BA MCLIP DMS MIMgt, Local Servs.Team Leader, Kent C.C. Educ.& L. [0022832]   09/10/1974
Richards Mr A, BSc FCA MCLIP, Employment not known. [0060687] 12/12/2001
Richards Mrs AC, MA DipLib MCLIP, p./t.Lib., M.D.A.Ltd., London. [0031428]   01/10/1979
Richards Miss AFM, BA(Hons) DipLib MCLIP, Indexing/Arch.Co-ordinator, Alden Multimedia, Northampton. [0048276]   25/09/1972
Richards Mrs AJ, Br.Lib., Bilston L., Wolverhampton M.B.C. [0056034] 28/01/1998
Richards Ms CL, BA MA, Asst.Educ.Lib., Sch.L.Serv., Northumberland. [0056779]   14/10/1998
Richards Mr DF, FCLIP, Life Member. [0012336]   23/09/1949 FE 01/01/1964
Richards Mr DP, MCLIP, Not Employed. [0032338]   07/03/1980
Richards Miss EJ, BA(Hons), Asst.Learning Resources Mgr., Hugh Baird Coll., Merseyside. [0052137]   05/10/1995
Richards Mr EL, MCLIP, Asst.Lib., Ceredigion Co.L. [0012338]   01/01/1970
Richards Mrs EP, (was Harmer), MCLIP, Unemployed. [0006366]   29/07/1966
Richards Mrs KP, (was Moore), BA MCLIP, Teaching Asst. [0035473] 14/10/1982
Richards Mrs L, (was Beagan), Inf.Offr., John Moores Univ., Liverpool. [0049840]   09/12/1993
Richards Mr LCI, MCLIP, App.Lib., Pembrokeshire Co.L., Haverfordwest. [0012345]   27/02/1969
Richards Miss MC, BA(Hons), p./t.Stud./Inf.Offr., Manchester Met.Univ., Eversheds, Manchester. [0061031]   01/02/2002
Richards Mr MJ, BA, Company Lib., Cosworth Tech.Ltd., Northampton. [0055998]   08/01/1998
Richards Mrs NM, BA MCLIP, Employment not known. [0060852] 12/12/2001
Richards Mrs PD, BSc MSc CPhys MInstP MCLIP, Employment not known. [0060628]   11/12/2001
Richards Miss SF, BA MCLIP, Retired. [0012350]   14/04/1969
Richards Miss TC, BA(Hons) MA, Sen.Lib.Asst., Nuffield College L.Oxford, [0053837]   03/10/1996
Richardson Miss A, BA(Hons) PGDipIS, Asst.Lib., Allen & Overy, London. [0051520]   03/11/1995
Richardson Mrs A, (was Turner), BA(Hons) MCLIP, Lib., Colstons Girls Sch., Bristol. [0014936]   01/01/1970
Richardson Mrs ABM, BA(Hons), Sch.Lib., St Swithun's Sch., Winchester, Hants. [0053278]   12/04/1996
Richardson Mr AG, MCLIP, Knowledge Serv.Mgr., Queen Elizabeth Hosp.NHS Trust., London. [0025402]   04/12/1975
Richardson Mr C, MCLIP, Head of L.& Cultural Serv., L.B.of Waltham Forest. [0012355]   05/02/1968

335

Richardson Mr CT, MCLIP, Retired. [0012357] 22/09/1964
Richardson Miss DME, BA MCLIP, Life Member, Tel.01708 224418. [0012358] 07/01/1952
Richardson Ms FB, BA MSc MCLIP, Sen.Inf.Offr., Said Bus.Sch., Univ.of Oxford, Oxford. [0001866] 14/01/1969
Richardson Mr FP, FCLIP, Life Member, Tel.01273 845455. [0012360] 24/01/1938 **FE 01/01/1968**
Richardson Miss G, MSc, Inf.Offr., Eversheds. [0059225] 09/01/2001
Richardson Miss GE, BA(Hons) MScEcon MCLIP, Inf.Offr., Univ.of Portsmouth. [0054098] 28/10/1996
Richardson Mr GM, MCLIP, Sen.Inf.Mgr., Royal Coll.of Gen.Practitioners, London. [0019282] 24/03/1965
Richardson Miss HR, MCLIP, Arch./Records Mgr., Sanofi Winthrop, Alnwick. [0050545] 12/09/1994
Richardson Miss J, Employment not known. [0060508] 11/12/2001
Richardson Mrs J, (was Cuthbert), MCLIP, Spec.Serv.Lib./Sen.Lib., Malton Grp., N.Yorks.Co.L.,Norton. [0003528] 13/08/1969
Richardson Mrs J, (was Sidebottom), BA MCLIP, Relief Asst.Lib., Kirklees Met.Council, Huddersfield. [0012363] 17/03/1963
Richardson Mrs J, (was Caligari), BA(Hons) MCLIP, Unemployed. [0047350] 20/07/1992
Richardson Mrs J, MA MCLIP, Lib., Sheffield Assay Off. [0012364] 17/09/1968
Richardson Ms J, BA, Stud., Univ.of Northumbria. [0061624] 04/10/2002
Richardson Miss JC, L.Asst., St.Matthias L., Univ.of the W.of England. [0058647] 28/04/2000 **AF**
Richardson Mrs JM, (was Corney), BLIB MCLIP, p./t.Sen.Lib., Durning L., L.B.of Lambeth. [0022689] 15/08/1974
Richardson Ms JM, BA MA, L.Asst., Southampton City Coll. [0061152] 15/03/2002
Richardson Ms KE, (was McPherson), BA MCLIP, Child.Lib., L.B.of Enfield L., Ordnance Road L. [0012368] 12/10/1970
Richardson Mr KF, BA(Hons) DipLib MCLIP, L.& Inf.Mgr., W.Berks., Newbury. [0029496] 12/10/1969
Richardson Miss KJ, Catr., Home Off./Prison Serv., London. [0054043] 22/10/1996
Richardson Mrs MH, (was Logan), MCLIP, Unemployed. [0012370] 26/09/1962
Richardson Ms MJ, BA(Hons) DipIM, Content Mgr.Website, Inst.of Directors, London. [0051973] 29/08/1995
Richardson Mrs ML, BA(Hons) DipInf, Lib.(P./t.), L.B.of Bromley. [0055155] 24/07/1997
Richardson Mr PD, MCLIP, Sen.Grp.Lib., Market Harborough L., Leics. [0012374] 12/03/1963
Richardson Mrs PE, (was Turner), BA DipLib MCLIP, Child.Lib., Cent.L., Hartlepool. [0041753] 01/03/1988
Richardson Ms PK, MSc MCLIP, Employment not known. [0060459] 11/12/2001
Richardson Ms R, Applications Support Consultant, DS, Newcastle upon Tyne. [0038128] 23/01/1985
Richardson Mrs RE, (was Wellstead), MCLIP CertHE, P./t.Freelance Researcher/Asst., Kirkley Hall Coll., Northumberland. [0015595] 18/02/1964
Richardson Ms S, BSc DipLib MCLIP, Inf.Worker/Administrator, Job Support Cent., Wokingham. [0027776] 22/07/1977
Richardson Mrs SJ, (was Homer), MCLIP, Area Child.& Learning Lib., Solihull M.B.C. [0019852] 01/01/1973
Richardson Mrs SJ, (was Cooke), MCLIP, Retired. [0003085] 21/01/1959
Richardson Ms VM, (was Hannon), BA DipLib MCLIP, Lib., Cambs.C.C., Huntingdon L. [0034939] 14/05/1982
Richardson Mr WB, MCLIP, Life Member. [0012367] 14/04/1937
Richens Ms H, BA(Hons) DipILM MCLIP, Princ.Lib.:Child.& Yth., L.B.of Barnet. [0052670] 20/11/1995
Riches Mr W, BA MA, Stud., City Univ. [0057777] 02/08/1999
Richmond Mrs SE, (was Dunderdale), BA DipLib MCLIP, Area Lib., Kingston upon Hull City Council, Bransholme L. [0031817] 02/01/1980
Richter Mr G, Employment not known. [0060424] 11/12/2001
Richter Ms K, MA MSc, Researcher, New Bridge Street Consultants, London. [0050048] 28/02/1994
Richter Miss R, Catr., Dept.for Work & Pensions, London. [0059405] 05/03/2001
Rickard Mrs A, BA MCLIP, Position unknown, Stiefel Labs (Ireland) Ltd., Maidenhead. [0060631] 11/12/2001
Rickard Mr MD, BA MA MA, Princ.L.Asst./Music Dept.Lib., Univ.of Exeter L. [0035540] 02/11/1982
Rickard Miss S, BA(Hons), Marketing Mgr., Library & Information Show. [0059231] 10/01/2001 **SP**
Rickards Mr CH, BA(Hons), Unemployed, 5 Sophie Rd., Nottingham NG7 6AA. [0048602] 05/03/1993
Rickards Miss SL, BA(Hons), Sen.L.Asst., Med.Faculty L., Univ.of Manchester. [0055865] 08/12/1997
Rickerby Ms OJ, BA(Hons) MSc MCLIP, Inf.Mgr., Osborne Clarke, London. [0051312] 11/01/1995
Rickers Mrs CM, (was Adams), MCLIP, Volunteer, Rural Housebound Serv., Warks.Co.L./Age Concern. [0000038] 01/01/1961
Ricketts Mr AN, MA MCLIP, Retired. [0012390] 08/07/1946
Ricketts Miss EA, BA DipLib MCLIP, Div.Child.Lib., N.Div., Basingstoke L., Hants.C.C. [0026795] 26/10/1976
Ricks Miss A, LLB MA, Dep.Lib., Ashurst Morris Crisp, London. [0052033] 02/10/1995
Ricks Miss AE, BA MCLIP, Team Lib., Sch.L.Serv., Hucclecote, Glos. [0012393] 12/07/1974
Rickwood Mrs SK, (was Webber), PGDip, Acquisitions Lib., City of Bristol Coll., Bristol. [0045251] 05/09/1990
Rico Mr M, MSc, Learning & Teach.Tech.Officer., Open University., Milton Keynes. [0059538] 01/05/2001
Riddell Mr GB, MA, Lib., Oxford Univ.Computing Lab. [0040954] 01/10/1987

Riddell Ms L, BA(Hons), L.Asst., I.C.A.I., Belfast. [0057104] 14/12/1998
Riddell Mrs LM, BA(Hons) DipILM, Asst.Lib., Ashington L., Ashington, Northumberland. [0058939] 09/10/2000
Ridgeon Miss AM, BA, Stud., Univ.of Bristol, Grad.Sch.of Educ. [0061533] 16/09/2002
Ridgeway Mrs CI, (was Salmon), MCLIP, p./t.L.Asst., Herts.C.C., Hemel Hempstead. [0018198] 06/10/1972
Riding Mrs PA, BA DipLib MCLIP, Asst.Ref.Lib., Halifax Cent.L. [0030245] 27/12/1978
Riding Miss RE, MCLIP, Life Member. [0012405] 18/03/1954
Ridout Miss G, BA(Hons), Inf.Offr., Linklaters, London. [0057196] 08/01/1999
Rieg Mr F, Trainee Lib.Asst., Farrer & Co., London. [0061393] 03/07/2002
Rigby Mrs KI, BA MSc, Acting L.& Inf.Services Mgr., Hinchingbrooke H.Carer NHS Trust, Cambridgeshire. [0060035] 29/11/2001
Rigby Mrs S, (was Matthews), BA MCLIP, Asst.Lib., York Cent.L., City of York Council. [0038145] 06/10/1967
Rigglesford Mr DN, BA FCLIP, Res.Lib., Employment Relations Ltd., Cambs. [0012416] 01/10/1964
Riggs Miss SV, BSc(Hons), Stud., Robert Gordon Univ., Aberdeen. [0061643] 10/10/2002
Rigny Miss SC, MA MCLIP, Lib.(Catr.), L.of Congress, Washington D.C. [0044834] 11/12/1990
Rikowski Mrs RL, (was Turney), BA DipLib MCLIP MSc, Lect./Review Editor, S.Bank Uni./Aslib, London. [0028194] 20/10/1977
Riley Mrs AJ, (was Broughton), BA MCLIP, Database Lib., Bolton L. [0024405] 11/08/1975
Riley Mrs CL, (was Rudd), BA(Hons) MCLIP, L.& LRC Mgr., BHRV Healthcare NHS Trust, Blackburn, Lancs. [0050539] 09/09/1994
Riley Mrs DM, (was Birkhead), MCLIP, Housewife. [0001296] 10/05/1972
Riley Mr DW, FCLIP, Life Member. [0012417] 01/09/1952 **FE 01/01/1963**
Riley Miss EA, BA DipLib MCLIP, Sen.Team Lib.-Readers Serv., Glos.C.C., Cheltenham L. [0034985] 26/05/1982
Riley Mrs EH, (was Leahy), MA MCLIP, Higher L.Exec., House of Commons L., London. [0030456] 25/01/1979
Riley Mrs EJ, Lib./Researcher, Hawkins & Assoc., Cambridge. [0056509] 30/07/1998
Riley Mr G, MCLIP, County Specialist: Stock & Promo., Staffs.C.C., Cannock L. [0027012] 18/01/1977
Riley Mrs H, (was Scott), BA DipLib MCLIP, Unemployed. [0030254] 09/01/1979
Riley Miss JA, BSc, Tech.Support Offr., Nottingham Health Informatics. [0061362] 26/06/2002
Riley Mrs JL, BA(Hons) DipLIS PGCE, P./t.Sen.L.& Inf.Asst., Staffs.Univ., Stoke-on-Trent. [0056438] 13/07/1998
Riley Ms KR, MA MCLIP, Lib., London Coll.of Fash., London. [0026796] 15/11/1976
Riley Mrs LE, (was Rabbage), BA(Hons) DipEd MA CBA MCLIP, Co.Specialist- Learning & Heritage, Staffs.C.C. (Job Share). [0046922] 24/02/1992
Riley Mr PD, BA(Hons), Head of L.Div., Univ.of Wales, Inst., Cardiff. [0048459] 14/01/1993
Riley Mr RB, MCLIP, Retired. [0012424] 15/01/1940
Riley Miss S, BA(Hons) MA MCLIP, Team Lib.-Child.& Young People, Northants.C.C. [0054273] 11/11/1996
Riley Miss SC, MLS MCLIP, Sch.Lib., Royal Bor.of Kensington & Chelsea. [0012426] 22/01/1971
Rillie Mrs CM, (was Clark), B.Lib (Hons) MCLIP, Unemployed. [0045728] 02/05/1991
Rimba Mr B, L.Asst., City & Islington Coll., London. [0050259] 24/05/1994 **AF**
Rimmer Miss C, BA DIP LIB MCLIP, Knowledge Mgr., Open Univ. L., Milton Keynes. [0029413] 01/07/1978
Rimmer Mrs JE, BLib MCLIP, Br.Lib., Powys C.C., Newtown, Powys. [0032965] 08/10/1980
Rimmington Miss PJ, BA(Hons), Stud., Loughborough Univ. [0059984] 15/11/2001
Rimmington Mrs SM, (was Davies), BSc MCLIP, Asst.Subject Advisor, Univ.of Derby. [0038949] 18/05/1982
Rinaldi Mrs AM, (was Nicol), MA(Hons) MSc, Lend.Lib., Dumfries & Galloway Council, Ewart L. [0058153] 08/11/1999
Ring Ms SM, MCLIP, Unemployed. [0021635] 21/11/1973
Ring Ms VJ, BA(Hons) DipIM MCLIP, Asst.Lib.-User Serv., Univ.of the W.of England, Bolland L. [0049894] 07/01/1994
Ringrose Miss JS, (was Cook), MA MCLIP, Under Lib., Univ.of Cambridge L. [0012431] 06/10/1967
Ripley Mrs DC, (was Whitehouse), BA DipLib, Unemployed. [0035304] 05/10/1982
Rippe Mrs EM, (was Haigh), BSc MCLIP, Asst.Lib., Gloscat, Cheltenham. [0012433] 19/09/1962
Rippingale Mr RT, MA MCLIP, City Lib., Derby City L. [0012434] 16/01/1972
Rippon Mr JSV, BA(Hons) DipILS MCLIP, Prison Lib., H.M.P.Acklington, Northumberland C.C. [0045586] 26/03/1991
Risbey Mrs CR, Catg.Asst., City of Westminster, Marylebone L. [0052676] 17/11/1995
Risdon Miss H, MA MCLIP, Career Break. [0043842] 05/02/1990
Riste Mr JR, BA(Hons) MCLIP, Asst.Lib., Med.L.-W.Middx.Hosp., Isleworth. [0044049] 10/04/1990
Ristic Mrs L, DipILS MCLIP, Inf.Specialist, Doncaster M.B.C. [0051848] 13/07/1995
Ristic Mrs N, Unemployed. [0061354] 20/06/2002
Ritchie Miss CM, MA DipLib MCLIP, Lib., University Coll., Oxford. [0033127] 02/10/1980
Ritchie Miss FE, MA(Hons), Stud., Strathclyde Univ. [0059075] 08/11/2000
Ritchie Ms J, BA DipLib MCLIP, Asst.Lib., Huddersfield Tech.Coll., Huddersfield. [0039679] 07/05/1986

Ritchie Mr JS, MCLIP, Employment unknown. [0060246] 10/12/2001
Ritchie Mrs M, (was Smith), MA MCLIP, Volunteer Lib., Citizens Advice., Scottish Poetry Library. [0013635] 22/02/1972
Ritchie Ms MP, BA, Life Member. [0012438] 17/02/1969
Ritchie Mrs SFC, MA DMS MIPD MCLIP, Self Employed, Management Skills Trainer, Huntingdon. [0012439] 01/01/1967
Ritson Miss D, Admin.Asst., Employment Serv. [0042389] 27/10/1988
Riva Miss VJ, BA MCLIP, Life Member. [0012441] 04/03/1948
Rivers-Latham Mrs MJ, (was Revill-Latham), BA(Hons) DipIS MCLIP, Asst.Lib., Univ.of Westminster. [0055474] 17/10/1997
Rivers-Moore Miss AR, BA DipLib, Resident in Canada. [0035035] 13/07/1982
Rivett Mr M, MSc MCLIP, Position unknown, Astra Zeneca, Loughborough. [0060599] 11/12/2001
Rix Mrs C, BA MCLIP, Sen.Lib., Lancs.C.C., Colne. [0042281] 12/10/1988
Rix Mr DW, MCLIP, Sch.Lib., Tideway Sch., Newhaven, E.Sussex. [0026240] 17/09/1976
Rix Mrs RS, (was White), MCLIP, Retired. [0012444] 02/04/1959
Rix Ms SE, BSc(Hons) MA, Asst.Lib., HM Treasury, London. [0061148] 21/03/2002
Rizvi Mrs IJ, BA(Hons) PGDipLib MCLIP, Sen.Lib.:Social Inclusion, Slough Cent.L., Berks. [0041980] 01/07/1988
Rizzo Mr AT, BA PhD MA, Lifelong Learning Mgr., Kingston Ls., Surrey. [0055627] 28/10/1997
Roach Mrs MF, (was Key), BA MCLIP, Not Working. [0026895] 05/01/1977
Roache Miss A, BA MA, Head of Inf.Serv., Weil, Gotshal & Manges, London. [0044475] 11/10/1990
Road Mr JR, Lib., Surrey C.C., Woking L. [0039990] 09/10/1986
Roads Mr J, BA(Hons) DipLib MCLIP, Head of L.& Inf.Serv., Shropshire C.C., Shrewsbury. [0027457] 01/04/1977
Robb Mr CI, BA(Hons) DipILS, Tech.Asst., Weatherford DIS Manufacturing, Arbroath. [0058740] 03/07/2000
Robb Mrs JM, (was Mills), BA DipLib MCLIP, Non LIS. [0034217] 12/10/1981
Robb Ms M, BS MLS MCLIP, Soc.Stud.Lib., Oxford Univ. [0049968] 31/01/1994
Robb Mrs T, BA, Learning Cent. Co-ordinator, Harrow College, Harrow Weald. [0061004] 29/01/2002
Robbins Mr AP, BA MSc MCLIP, Head of Admin.Learning Resources, Oxford Brookes Univ. [0026142] 01/07/1976
Robbins Miss FJ, BA, Sen.Arts & L.Asst., Sevenoaks L., Kent C.C. [0026798] 26/10/1976
Robbins Mrs M, (was Trabichet), DipIS MCLIP, Unemployed. [0052627] 14/11/1995
Robbins Mrs RM, (was Haggarty), BA, Career break. [0043289] 16/10/1989
Robbins Mrs SE, (was Shirley), BA MCLIP, Grp.Lib., Leics.L.& Inf.Serv. [0021186] 01/10/1973
Roberg Miss KC, BA(Hons), Lib., London Sch.of Jewish Stud., London. [0046155] 07/10/1991
Roberson Miss J, BA MCLIP, Team Lib., Northants.C.C., Northants.Cent.L. [0012455] 15/01/1970
Robert Mrs IE, (was Campbell), BA DipLib MCLIP, Confederation Lib., W.M.S.Confederation, Coventry. [0034019] 15/07/1981
Roberts Miss A, BA(Hons), P./t.Stud./Bookseller, Waterstones, Swindon. [0059703] 14/08/2001
Roberts Mrs AC, (was Smith), MCLIP, Lib., HM Prison, Long Lartin. [0012459]
Roberts Ms AC, BA MLS MCLIP, Sub-Lib.(Staff Mgmt.), Edinburgh Univ.L. [0032339] 14/03/1980
Roberts Mrs AD, (was Vincent), MCLIP, Sch.Lib., Dorset Co.L., Dorchester. [0039733] 31/03/1967
Roberts Miss AL, BA(Hons), Stud., Univ.of Strathclyde. [0061131] 07/03/2002
Roberts Mrs AL, (was Fullick), BA(Hons) MCLIP, Child.Lib., Thornton Heath L., Croydon. [0050812] 19/10/1994
Roberts Mrs AM, BSc(Hons), Stud., Manchester Metro.Uni. [0061766] 05/11/2002
Roberts Mrs AM, (was McLuckie), BLib MCLIP, Learning Res.Mgr., N.Leamington Sch., Leamington Spa. [0022007] 19/01/1974
Roberts Mr BF, CBE MA PhD HonFCLIP, Lib., Nat.L.of Wales, Aberystwyth. [0039278] 06/01/1986 **FE 01/01/1994**
Roberts Mrs BJ, MCLIP, L.Co-ordinator, Chichester Coll.of Art, W.Sussex. [0026900] 23/09/1976
Roberts Mrs C, L.Asst., Rhuthun L., Denbighshire. [0049087] 01/10/1993 **AF**
Roberts Mr C, MA(Hons), Stud., Univ.Aberystwyth. [0059818] 10/10/2001
Roberts Mrs C, (was Brogan), MA DipInfSc, Asst.Lib., Theodore Goddard, London. [0055240] 08/09/1997
Roberts Mr C, (was Everson), MCLIP, Br.Lib., Civic Cent., Merthyr Tydfil. [0004717] 03/03/1971
Roberts Mrs CAH, (was Jolly), BSc MCLIP, p./t.Lib., The Kings Sch./The Queen's Sch., Chester. [0017126] 04/04/1972
Roberts Mrs CI, (was Payne), MCLIP, Complex Mgr., Metro.Bor.of Wirral, Merseyside. [0012464] 04/02/1967
Roberts Mrs CL, (was Mitchell), MA DipLib MCLIP, Network Lib., Peterhead Academy. [0033069] 08/10/1980
Roberts Ms CM, (was Craib), BSc PGCE MCLIP, Lib., Mid-Essex Hosp.Trust, Chelmsford. [0023691] 01/01/1975
Roberts Miss CW, MCLIP, Yth.Serv.Lib., Rhondda-Cynon-Taff, Mountain Ash L. [0021989] 22/10/1973
Roberts Mr D, BA(Hons) MA, Trainee Lib., Rugby P.L. [0058006] 12/10/1999
Roberts Mr D, (was Gibson), BA MSc MCLIP, Unemployed. [0005472] 29/01/1968
Roberts Mrs D, (was Vercouttere), MCLIP, Lib., L.B.of Greenwich. [0015095] 29/03/1963
Roberts Ms D, BLib MCLIP, Health Knowledge Mgr., Dyfed Powys Health Auth., St.Davids Hosp., Carmarthen. [0027458] 01/04/1977

Roberts Mr DA, BSc MSc MBA MCLIP, Employment unknown. [0060308] 10/12/2001
Roberts Mr DG, BA MCLIP, Life Member. [0012468] 15/04/1961
Roberts Prof DHE, MA JP DipLib MCLIP, Professor, Dept.of Inf.& L.Studies, Univ.of Wales, Aberystwyth. [0012469] 04/03/1970
Roberts Mrs DM, (was Val Davies), MA MA MCLIP, Data Manage.Offr., William Howard Sch., Cumbria. [0021346] 16/10/1973
Roberts Miss E, BA, Stud., Sheffield Univ. [0059015] 25/10/2000
Roberts Mrs E, (was Jones), LL B MCLIP, Support Serv.Mgr., Caerphilly C.B.C. [0008007] 03/03/1970
Roberts Mrs EC, (was Graham), BA(Hons) MA, Inf.Offr., The L.Partnership, W.Midlands. [0050952] 31/10/1994
Roberts Ms EH, BSc, Sch.Lib., The Ravensbourne Sch., Bromley. [0049489] 05/11/1993
Roberts Mrs EJ, (was Leveridge), BSc(Hons) MA, Sen.L.Asst., Nuffield Coll.L., Oxford. [0055710] 06/11/1997
Roberts Miss EK, BA DipLib MCLIP, Comm.Team Lib., Glos.C.C., Hucclecote L. [0041713] 20/02/1988
Roberts Miss F, BA MCLIP, Asst.Lend.Serv.Mgr., S.Lanarkshire Council. [0035194] 04/10/1982
Roberts Mrs FW, (was Imrie), MA MSc MCLIP, Under Lib., Med.L., Cambridge Univ. [0025323] 05/01/1976
Roberts Miss GM, MCLIP, Asst.Ref.Lib., Salisbury L., Wiltshire. [0012481] 27/07/1966
Roberts Miss IMB, MCLIP, Asst., Edinburgh P.L. [0012483] 20/03/1964
Roberts Miss J, BA(Hons) MA DipILM, Sen.L.Asst./Sunday Lib., Humanities Ref.L., Liverpool Cent.L. [0012485] 07/03/2002
Roberts Mrs J, (was Skeats), Br.L.Mgr., Donaghadee L., SEELB., Co.Down. [0045349] 18/10/1990 **AF**
Roberts Ms J, BA(Hons) MCLIP, Arch./Lib., Ryder-Cheshire & Leonard Cheshire, Foundns.,Ashby de la Zouch. [0045791] 31/05/1991
Roberts Mrs JA, (was Meehan), BSc MCLIP, Educ.Support Lib., Falkirk Council. [0019786] 26/10/1972
Roberts Mrs JFE, (was Connor), MCLIP, Area Lib., W.Sussex Co.L.Serv., E.Grinstead L. [0012489] 20/01/1960
Roberts Mr JGW, MA DMS MCLIP, Asst.Dir.:Personal Devel., N.Lincs.Council-Educ. [0012490] 21/08/1967
Roberts Mr JK, MSc MCLIP, Dir.of Inf.Serv., Cardiff Univ. [0012491] 06/02/1963
Roberts Mr JL, MA DipLib MCLIP, Princ.L.Offr.(Arts), Cornwall C.C., Performing Arts L. [0023276] 05/11/1974
Roberts Ms JL, BA(Hons) DipIS, Sen.L.& Inf.Offr., Legal Serv., Leeds. [0055840] 21/11/1997
Roberts Miss K, BLib MCLIP, Inf.Mgr., Gerald Eve Chartered Surveyors, London. [0045881] 08/07/1991
Roberts Ms KJ, BA(Hons) MSt, Stud., Univ.of Sheffield. [0061546] 10/09/2002
Roberts Mrs L, (was Coles), MCLIP, Sch.Lib., Bournemouth Sch. [0002971] 29/01/1965
Roberts Miss LE, MCLIP, Manager, Croydon Cent.L., L.B.of Croydon. [0012493] 01/01/1970
Roberts Miss LJ, BA MCLIP, Sen.Grp.Lib.(S.), Sefton L.& Arts. [0012496] 05/07/1967
Roberts Mrs LM, BA MCLIP, Inf.Offr.(Job Share), Child.Inf.Bureau, Wrexham Co.Bor. [0028451] 04/11/1977
Roberts Mr M, MA MCLIP, Sen.Lib., Andersonian L., Univ.of Strathclyde. [0021828] 15/02/1974
Roberts Mrs MAF, (was Rollo), MCLIP, Life Member. [0012498] 01/01/1957
Roberts Miss ME, MCLIP, Retired. [0012500] 07/10/1947
Roberts Mr MJ, MCLIP, Dir., Infodoc Serv.Ltd., London. [0012502] 09/08/1970
Roberts Mr MO, BA, Stud./Sen.L.Offr., Manchester Met./Stockport Cent.L. [0060038] 03/12/2001
Roberts Mr MV, MA MCLIP, Retired. [0012505] 01/01/1964
Roberts Mr N, BA DipLib MCLIP, Enquiries Asst., Brit.Council Inf.Cent., Manchester. [0038922] 21/10/1985
Roberts Mr NR, BA(Hons), Comm.Lib., Caerphilly P.L.Serv., Pontllanfraith. [0054125] 30/10/1996
Roberts Miss NW, BA(Hons), Asst.Lib., Cairns L., Oxford. [0056867] 29/10/1998
Roberts Mr ODR, DMS MCLIP, L.Serv.Mgr., Met.Bor.of Wirral. [0012508] 21/09/1976
Roberts Mrs P, Stud., Inf Resource Offr., Univ. John Moores. [0060956] 18/01/2002
Roberts Mrs PJ, (was Maccaddon), BA MCLIP, Position Unknown, The Inf.Exchange, Cambs. [0026306] 01/10/1976
Roberts Mrs PJ, (was Coles), MCLIP, L.& Serv.Mgr., L.B.of Merton, Raynes Pk.L. [0012510] 01/01/1960
Roberts Mr PT, BSc, Employment unknown. [0060742] 12/12/2001
Roberts Mr R, (was Collins), BA(Hons) MCLIP, Learning Res.Offr., Wolverhampton Coll. [0043082] 25/07/1989
Roberts Mrs RE, BSc AdvDipEd MA, p./t.Stud./L.Asst., Univ.of Wales, Aberystwyth, Abergele L. [0061255] 29/04/2002
Roberts Mr RJ, MA FSA MCLIP, Retired. [0012513] 20/10/1953
Roberts Mrs RM, (was Freeman), M LIB, Inf.Promotion Mgr., Inf.Serv.Mgmt., The Brit.Council, Manchester. [0037943] 19/10/1984
Roberts Mrs S, (was Ashton), BA(Hons) MA, P./t. Stud./Community Lib., Stoke-on-Trent C.C., Hanley L. [0059635] 09/07/2001
Roberts Ms S, BA(Hons) DipLib MA MCLIP, Head of Inf.& Media Serv., Edge Hill, Ormskirk. [0047599] 05/10/1992
Roberts Miss SM, BA(Hons) DipILM, Lib., Northwich P.L., Cheshire C.C. [0055513] 16/10/1997
Roberts Mrs SM, Knowledge Cent.Advisor, HEFCE. [0051123] 17/11/1994
Roberts Mrs SM, (was Benson), BA, L.Serv.Mgr., Leeds Grammar Sch., W.Yorks. [0001159] 11/01/1972
Roberts Dr T, (was Rodriguez Ricard), PhD, Careers Inf.Offr., Univ.of Reading, Careers Advisory Serv. [0049652] 19/11/1993

337

Roberts Mr T, Inf.Offr., NHS Direct, Dudley, W.Mids. [0052399] 30/10/1995
Roberts Mrs VEM, (was Hiles), MCLIP, Retired. [0012520] 22/03/1962
Roberts Mr WD, MA MCLIP, Inf.Strategist., Nat'L.of New Zealand,., Wellington. [0020877] 28/08/1973
Roberts Mrs WJ, (was Tomlin), MCLIP, Lib., Croydon High Sch., Surrey. [0014774] 01/10/1968
Roberts Mr WRG, BA MCLIP, L.Mgr., Coulsdon L., Croydon L. [0020692] 08/06/1973
Roberts Cuffin Mrs TL, (was Roberts), BA(Hons), L.Mgr., Trafford Healthcare NHS Trust, Manchester. [0040664] 28/04/1987
Robertshaw Miss J, MA DipLib MCLIP, Sen.Asst.Lib., Dept.of Printed Books, Imperial War Museum, London. [0039378] 23/01/1986
Robertshaw Mrs JA, BSc(Hons), P./t.L.Asst., Clearwater Bay Sch., Kowloon, Hong Kong. [0058841] 29/08/2000
Robertson Mrs AC, (was Griffin), BA DipLib MAppSc(LIM), Asst.Lib.(Catr.), Univ.of Hong Kong, Hong Kong. [0035534] 21/10/1982
Robertson Miss AJ, BA(Hons) DipLib, Ass.Lib., Wick Public L., Caithness. [0041777] 08/04/1988
Robertson Mrs AM, BA(Hons) DipLib, Jnr.Asst.Lib., The London L. [0046284] 16/10/1991
Robertson Mr B, BA DipLib MCLIP, Subject Lib., NESCOT, Ewell, Surrey. [0029804] 16/10/1978
Robertson Mrs CA, (was Grimshaw), BA MCLIP, Freelance proofreader & Researcher. [0012527] 17/05/1965
Robertson Mr CL, FCLIP, Retired. [0026259] 28/10/1943
FE 04/06/1964
Robertson Mr CP, MCLIP, Life Member. [0012528] 22/03/1938
Robertson Mrs DK, (was Bowsher), FCLIP, Life Member. [0012529] 05/03/1940 **FE 01/01/1968**
Robertson Mrs DM, Retired. [0012531] 11/05/1954
Robertson Mrs E, (was Bruce), BA MCLIP, Network Lib., Fraserburgh Acad., Fraserburgh. [0028517] 01/01/1978
Robertson Mrs EM, (was Stewart), BSC INF SC MCLIP, Clinical Sci.Lib., Health Serv.L., Univ.of Southampton. [0014025] 18/06/1969
Robertson Miss F, BA DipLib, Sub-Lib., Brit.Med.Assoc., London. [0042163] 07/10/1978
Robertson Mrs FE, (was Smith), MA MCLIP, Team Leader, Comm.Inf.Team, Cent.L., Dundee City Council. [0021084] 04/10/1973
Robertson Ms FM, BA MCLIP, Unemployed. [0037829] 29/10/1984
Robertson Mr G, BA MCLIP, Mob.Lib., E.Dunbartonshire Council, William Patrick L. [0041205] 01/10/1980
Robertson Mrs HE, BA DipLib, Catrr., Kings Coll.London, Franklin-Wilkin Inf.Serv.Cent. [0032556] 23/04/1980
Robertson Mrs HJ, MCLIP, p./t.L.Asst.-Music & Drama L., Glos.C.C. [0031783] 21/01/1980
Robertson Miss IM, MCLIP, Life Member. [0012536] 06/09/1955
Robertson Mrs JA, MA(Hons) DipILS MCLIP, Mgr.-L.Serv.(Europe), Booz Allen & Hamilton, Strand. [0051067] 10/11/1994
Robertson Miss JM, BA MCLIP, Enquiries Lib., The Court Serv., London. [0042560] 03/01/1989
Robertson Mrs KM, (was Simpson), MA MCLIP, Community Lib., S.Lanarkshire Council, Carluke Community L. [0013398] 15/10/1970
Robertson Ms L, BA(Hons), Administrator, ADMS, The Surgery, Borth. [0056201] 01/04/1970
Robertson Ms LM, MSc, Asst.Lib., Maclay, Murray & Spens, Glasgow. [0049607] 19/11/1993
Robertson Mrs P, BA PgDip, Inf.Offr., Scottish L., Hamilton. [0057275] 26/01/1999
Robertson Mrs PAC, (was Lunn), BSc(Hons) DipILS MCLIP, Asst.Lib.- Learner Support, Open Univ., Milton Keynes. [0051747] 14/06/1995
Robertson Mr RM, Stud., Univ.of N.London. [0050586] 26/09/1994
Robertson Mrs RM, (was Beattie), MCLIP, Lib., Ellon Academy, Aberdeenshire. [0012546] 12/10/1966
Robertson Mr S, L.& Inf.Worker., Dundee City C., Dundee. [0055695] 10/11/1999
Robertson Mr SD, BA DipLib MCLIP, Retired. [0023855] 03/02/1975
Robertson Miss SE, BA(Hons) DipILS MCLIP, Sch.Lib., Calderdale High Sch., Airdrie. [0058116] 03/11/1999
Robertson Mrs SE, (was Whittaker), BLib MCLIP, Lib., St.Marys Sch., Wantage. [0034584] 01/01/1982
Robertson Prof SE, PhD MBCS FCLIP, Position unknown, Microsoft Research Ltd., Cambridge. [0060632] 11/12/2001
FE 01/04/2002
Robertson Miss SJ, MA MA MCLIP, Inf.Offr., Simmons & Simmons, London. [0055462] 13/10/1997
Robertson Mr SO, MA MEd DipLib MCLIP, H.of L.Serv., Univ.Coll.Chichester, W.Sussex. [0023243] 08/11/1974
Robertson Miss V, BA(Hons) MCLIP, Inter-loans Lib., St.Georges Hosp.Med.Sch., London. [0048299] 25/11/1992
Robertson Mrs VAA, (was Fletcher), BA MCLIP, L.& Inf.Serv.Cent.Mgr., Kings Coll.London, Chancery Lane. [0005007] 03/11/1971
Robertson Mrs VM, BA(Hons) BSc(Hons)(LIS), Knowledge Mgmt.Asst., Internat.Fund for Agric.Devel., Rome. [0059182] 08/12/2000
Robertson Mrs VR, (was Cuthell), MCLIP, P/t.Sen.L.Asst., Napier Univ., Edinburgh. [0022859] 03/10/1974
Robin Mrs CRW, (was Harding), MCLIP, Unemployed (Housewife). [0006298] 18/08/1971
Robins Mrs EM, (was Slaney), MCLIP, Partner-Engineering Consultancy, Dove Thermal Engineering Ltd., Uttoxeter, Staffs. [0012548] 01/01/1959
Robins Miss JE, BA(Hons), Asst.Lib., Freshwater Fisheries Lab., Pitlochry, Perthshire. [0045510] 26/02/1991
Robins Ms PH, BA MCLIP, Systems Lib., SSEES L., Univ.Coll.London. [0024265] 06/05/1975
Robinson Miss A, MCLIP, Learning Cent.Offr., City of Sunderland Coll. [0022013] 07/01/1974
Robinson Miss A, BA(Hons), Inf.Offr., RICS, London. [0050977] 04/11/1994

Robinson Mrs A, (was Mair), MCLIP, Comm.Lib., N.Lanarkshire Council, Lanarkshire. [0021293] 01/10/1973
Robinson Mr AE, MA MCLIP, Retired. [0060634] 11/12/2001
Robinson Miss AM, BA(Hons) DipILM, Lib., Chester L. [0056675] 01/10/1998
Robinson Mrs AR, (was Onians), BA MCLIP, Asst.Lib., Redditch L., Worcs. Co.L. [0020226] 13/02/1973
Robinson Mrs B, (was Dingwall), Ref.Serv.Offr., Redcar & Cleveland Bor.Council, Redcar. [0021381] 31/10/1973
Robinson Miss BE, MCLIP, Retired. [0012554] 08/10/1941
Robinson Miss C, BA MCLIP, Customer Serv.Mgr., Cambs.C.C. [0029805] 29/09/1978
Robinson Mrs CA, (was Dowler), MCLIP, Lib.:Lend.Serv., Herefordshire C.C. [0005978] 01/01/1970
Robinson Miss CM, BA(Hons), L.Asst., Brotherton L., Univ.of Leeds. [0058263] 30/11/1999 **AF**
Robinson Miss CT, BA(Hons), L.& Inf.Mgr., Greenwoods Solicitors, Peterborough. [0054509] 09/01/1997
Robinson Mrs D, (was Hawkey), BA DipLib MCLIP, Unemployed. [0038867] 16/10/1985
Robinson Mrs D, BA(Hons) MCLIP, Sch.Lib., Stamford High Sch., Tameside. [0052567] 06/11/1995
Robinson Mr DR, MCLIP, Sen.Lib., Leicester City Council. [0019154] 17/08/1972
Robinson Ms EB, MA MSc DipLib MCLIP, Learning Res.Co-ordinator, Keighley Coll. [0026054] 25/05/1976
Robinson Mrs EC, (was Holmes), BA MCLIP, Account Mgr., Fretwell- Downing Informatics, Sheffield, S.Yorks. [0041704] 03/02/1988
Robinson Mr EDG, JP DL MA FRSA MCLIP, Life Member, 25 Park Rd., Salford, M6 8JP. [0012562] 28/09/1950
Robinson Ms EJ, BSc MCLIP, Lib., Univ.of London L. [0030523] 01/02/1979
Robinson Mrs G, (was Pell), BA DipLib MCLIP, Unemployed. [0035308] 10/10/1982
Robinson Mrs G, (was Rhodes), BA DipLib MCLIP, Sch.Lib., Madeley High Sch., Staffs.C.C. [0033123] 01/01/1980
Robinson Mr GA, BA(Hons) DipLIS MCLIP, Inf.Systems Lib., Barnet & Chase Farm Hosp.NHS Trust, London. [0041260] 25/10/1987
Robinson Mrs GMA, BA(Hons), Project Admin.& Research Sec., Dept of Sociology, Univ.of York. [0058258] 30/11/1999
Robinson Ms H, LLB(Hons) DipILS, Asst.Lib., The Law Soc. [0053614] 12/08/1996
Robinson Mrs HJ, (was Crowther), BA(Hons) PGDipLib, Head of Inf.Serv., Bevan Ashford Solicitors, Bristol. [0041289] 30/10/1987
Robinson Mr IP, BSc, Unemployed. [0057069] 07/12/1998
Robinson Mrs J, (was Hutson), BLib MCLIP, Sen.Child.& Sch.Lib., Bolton Metro.Bor. [0007550] 01/05/1970
Robinson Ms J, BA(Hons), Asst.Lib., DfES, London. [0057716] 06/07/1999
Robinson Mr JEG, MA MCLIP, Br.Lib., Bridgend Co.Bor.Council., Bridgend Br.L. [0027623] 04/06/1977
Robinson Mrs JL, (was Frith), MCLIP, Retired. [0020365] 15/02/1973
Robinson Mrs JL, (was Lawson), CD MBE FCLIP LLD, Gen.Mgr., Jamaica Broadcasting Corp., Kingston, Jamaica. [0017659] 07/07/1950
FE 01/01/1959
Robinson Ms K, BA(Hons) MA, Stud., Univ.Coll.London. [0061586] 02/10/2002
Robinson Miss KA, BA MCLIP, Div.Inf.Lib.,S.Div., Winchester Ref.L., Hants.C.C. [0038176] 04/02/1995
Robinson Ms KM, BA MA MCLIP, Head of Readers Serv., Univ.of Bath. [0044072] 30/04/1990
Robinson Mrs L, BSc (Hons), Unemployed. [0061460] 14/08/2002
Robinson Ms L, BSc MSc MCLIP, Staff Tutor, The Open Univ., Milton Keynes. [0060194] 10/12/2001
Robinson Mr LH, BA MCLIP, Retired. [0012574] 05/03/1964
Robinson Dr M, BA DipLib PhD, Faculty Lib., Crewe & Alsager Faculty, Manchester Metro.Univ. [0034849] 16/03/1982
Robinson Mr M, BA MCLIP, Team Lib.-Inf.Direct, Northants.C.C. [0028888] 08/02/1978
Robinson Mrs MM, MCLIP, Team Lib., Suffolk C.C., Cent.L. [0012579] 24/02/1971
Robinson Mrs MR, (was Campbell), MCLIP, Learning Res.Asst., Hugh Baird Coll., Liverpool. [0002334] 27/08/1970
Robinson Mr N, BSc MSc OND, p./t.Stud./L.Asst., Edinburgh's Telford Coll., W.Norwich Hosp. [0061275] 05/05/2002
Robinson Mr NJ, BSc MCLIP, Employment not known. [0060189] 10/12/2001
Robinson Mr NK, DipLib, p./t.Temp.L.Asst., Greenfield Med.L., Nottingham. [0043085] 24/07/1989
Robinson Mr NR, BA(Hons) MA MCLIP, Sen.L.Asst., Fitzwilliam Mus., Cambridge. [0051512] 13/03/1995
Robinson Mrs P, (was Hawley), MCLIP, Employment not known. [0012583] 04/04/1965
Robinson Miss PA, MCLIP, Lib., Child.Serv., Hereford L. [0012584] 01/01/1971
Robinson Mrs PA, DipInf, Resucts Offr.p./t., Dorset Police, Bournemouth. [0054728] 13/03/1997
Robinson Mrs PA, MA DipLib MCLIP, Local Govt.Inf.Offr., Peterborough City Council. [0040717] 05/05/1987
Robinson Ms PA, (was Schrocksnadel), MCLIP, Coll.Lib., S.Tyneside Coll., Tyne & Wear. [0013023] 01/01/1960
Robinson Miss PS, MCLIP, Retired. [0012585] 07/01/1960
Robinson Miss RA, BA(Hons), Stud., Loughborough Univ. [0061772] 06/11/2002
Robinson Mrs RAM, (was Ellwood), BA PGCE MA MCLIP, Team Lib., Child.& Young People, N.Area, Northants. [0044701] 29/11/1990
Robinson Miss RC, BSc(Hons) MA, Asst.Lib., Kennedys, London. [0053734] 20/09/1996
Robinson Mrs RE, (was Rochford), MCLIP, Retired. [0012586] 01/01/1949

Robinson Miss RH, BA (Hons) MCLIP, Sub Lib., Univ.of Paisley. [0043343] 24/10/1989
Robinson Mr RJ, BA PGCE DipLIS, L.Asst., S.E.E.L.B., Comm.L., Lisburn. [0041425] 02/12/1987
Robinson Mrs RM, (was Bell), BA DipLib MCLIP, p./t.Lib., Conway J.I., Birmingham. [0035814] 17/01/1983
Robinson Mr SD, BA MCLIP, Sen.L.Asst., Univ.of Leeds L. [0042791] 02/03/1989
Robinson Mrs SF, (was Barker), BA(Hons), Asst.Lib., Hull Coll., Hull. [0049505] 08/11/1993
Robinson Mr SL, BA DipLib MCLIP, Lib.& Arch., MOD, Aldershot. [0038684] 01/10/1985
Robinson Mr SM, Inf.Offr., Nabarro Nathanson, London. [0048846] 01/07/1993
Robinson Ms SM, (was Boddy), BA MCLIP, Employment not known. [0028262] 26/10/1977
Robinson Mrs SR, BA(Hons) MA MCLIP, Training Offr., Health Inf.E.London. [0049167] 08/10/1993
Robinson Mrs T, (was Loveless), BA MCLIP, 5 Shouler Close, Shenley Church End, Milton Keynes, MK5 6DZ. [0031361] 03/10/1979
Robinson Mrs VA, (was James), Lib.(Job Share), N.Lincs.Council. [0047297] 06/07/1992
Robinson Ms VE, BA DLIS MCLIP, Dir.of Comm.& Educ., Nat.Auth.for OTC Safety & Health, Co.Kildare. [0033343] 18/11/1980
Robisson Mme J, (was Parrott), DipLib MCLIP, Unemployed. [0039066] 02/11/1985
Roblin Ms CE, Lib.-Support Serv., Oxfordshire C.C., Cultural Serv. [0040531] 01/03/1987
Robson Mr ACW, Stud., Univ.Coll.Wales. [0049363] 22/10/1993
Robson Mr AJ, MCLIP, Lib., Lasswade High Sch.Cent., Bonnyrigg, Midlothian. [0021450] 15/10/1973
Robson Mrs AJ, P./t.Lib., Newcastle Univ., Newcastle upon Tyne. [0047821] 14/10/1992
Robson Mrs AM, (was Rapinet), BA MCLIP, Lib.-Bibl.Serv., L.& Inf.Serv., Wokingham L. [0012592] 06/08/1965
Robson Mrs C, (was Haberfield), Learning Res.Asst., E.Riding Coll., Bridlington. [0045228] 20/08/1990 **AF**
Robson Mrs H, BA(Hons), Stud., Univ.of Northumbria at Newcastle. [0058049] 15/10/1999
Robson Ms JM, MCLIP, Serv.Mgr., Essex Co.L., Colchester. [0020637] 17/05/1973
Robson Miss LS, L.Asst., Gateshead Cent.L., Gateshead. [0054877] 28/04/1997
Robson Mrs LT, (was Till), L.Super., Dudley M.B.C. [0049419] 21/10/1993
Robson Mr MS, BA MCLIP, Asst.Lib., Materials Serv.Dept., Gateshead P.L. [0012599] 12/01/1965
Robson Mr ROA, BA PGCE MCLIP, Retired, 15 Ainsdale Drive, Marlborough Gr., SE1 5JY, Tel:0171 231 3762. [0012600] 13/04/1967
Roby Mrs TA, BA MCLIP, Lib., Angus Council, Cultural Serv., Arbroath. [0041110] 05/11/1986
Rocha Ms NN, Head of Div., Procuradoria-Geral Da Republica, R.Da Escola Politecnica,Portugal. [0043912] 21/02/1990
Roche Mrs CML, BA(Hons), Sch.Lib., The Maplesden Noakes Sch., Maidstone, Kent. [0056636] 24/09/1998
Roche Mr JP, BA MCLIP, Music Lib., Harrow L. [0012603] 24/04/1967
Roche Ms KC, BA MLib MCLIP, Media Lib., Richmond Coll., Middlesex. [0041129] 11/10/1987
Roche Mrs MC, (was Finlay), MCLIP, Retired. [0030406] 11/02/1979
Roche Ms MN, BA MA, Child.Lib., Royal Bor.of Kensington & Chelsea, Brompton L. [0043337] 23/10/1989
Rochell Mrs SJ, (was Nicholls), BA MCLIP, Area L.Mgr., S.Lakeland, Cumbria C.C. [0012604] 20/01/1967
Rochelle Miss SF, BA MCLIP, Lib., Telford & Wrekin Auth., Shropshire. [0039509] 11/02/1986
Rochester Ms EC, BSc(Hons) MSc MCLIP, Sen.Inf.Offr., Engineering Employers'Fed., London. [0047027] 02/04/1992
Rochester Ms MK, BA MLS PhD FCLIP, Retired. [0053599] 05/08/1996 **FE 23/07/1997**
Rochester Mrs WM, Lib., Ward Hadaway Solicitors, Newcastle upon Tyne. [0055869] 02/12/1997
Rochford Ms HT, BA, Intranet Mgr., Freshfields Bruckhaus Deringer, London. [0038804] 10/10/1985
Rock Ms CJW, (was Peck), BA MA MCLIP, Deputy Lib., Coventry Univ. [0040929] 05/08/1987
Rock Ms FI, BA(Hons) DipLib MCLIP, L.Devel.Offr.(Job Share), Birmingham C.C., Cent.L. [0038823] 15/10/1985
Rockett Ms GL, BA DipLib MCLIP, Lib., Spec.Serv., Richmond L., N.Yorks.C.C. [0039439] 14/01/1986
Roczniok Mrs JF, (was Budds), FCLIP ALAA, Retired. [0017662] 01/01/1934 **FE 01/01/1943**
Rodda Mrs SJM, BA, Stud., Aberystwyth. [0061440] 29/07/2002
Roddom Miss ZE, BA(Hons), Stud., Northumbria Univ. [0061688] 21/10/2002
Roddy Ms KM, BA, Consultant, K.Roddy Research & Consultancy, London. [0046076] 26/09/1991
Roden Mrs K, (was Horton), DipEd MCLIP, Life Member. [0012607] 12/01/1949
Rodenhurst Mrs FH, (was Davies), BLib MCLIP, p./t.Freelance Abstractor, & p./t.L.Asst., Ellesmere L. [0041545] 20/01/1988
Roderick Mrs K, (was Carter), BSc MCLIP, Hlth.point Inf.Offr./p./t.Lect., Poole Bor.Council, Bournemouth & Poole Coll.of F.E. [0036358] 07/10/1983
Rodger Miss DT, L.Serv.Mgr., SNBTS Protein Fractionation Cent., Edinburgh. [0040506] 23/02/1987
Rodger Mrs EA, MA MSc MCLIP, Lib.-IT & Systems (Educ.Resources), S.Lanarkshire Council, Hamilton. [0057455] 01/04/1999
Rodger Miss EM, BSc MCLIP, Life Member. [0012608] 12/07/1965

Rodger Mrs J, (was Mckinlay), MCLIP, Redundant. [0009473] 10/10/1963
Rodger Mrs JH, MA DipLib MCLIP, Unemployed. [0021318] 26/09/1973
Rodgers Mrs EG, (was Cockburn), BA DipLib MCLIP, p./t.Lib., Northumbria Probation Serv., Gateshead. [0030582] 15/02/1979
Rodgers Mr EJ, BA MA PhD, Prof.of Spanish, Univ.of Strathclyde, Dept.of Modern Languages. [0048695] 15/04/1993 **SP**
Rodgers Mr JM, Stud., Napier Univ. [0056926] 10/11/1998
Rodgers Mrs MP, (was Knott), BA MCLIP, Sen.Lib.(Bibl.Serv.), Blackpool Cent.L. [0008502] 14/01/1971
Rodgers Miss SJ, Stud., Univ.Central London. [0060015] 26/11/2001
Rodgers Miss WA, MA, p./t.Inf./General Lib., Chesterfield L./Derbyshire C.C. [0054433] 06/12/1996
Rodgerson Miss J, MCLIP, Lib., Durham Arts L.& Mus.Dept., Co.Hall, Durham. [0012615] 08/03/1966
Rodrick Mrs SE, (was Glasspoole), BA DipLib MCLIP, Sch.Lib., Lord Williams Sch., Thame, Oxon. [0032783] 27/08/1980
Rodriguez Miss GM, Dir. of L., Comfenalco Antioqua, Medellin, Colombia. [0041631] 05/02/1988
Rodway Mrs A, (was Logan), MCLIP, Lib., Clacton L., Essex C.C. [0009058] 14/10/1970
Rodway Ms JH, BA(Hons) MA, P./t.Asst.Lib., Guildford Sch.of Acting. [0052214] 09/10/1995
Roe Mr GF, BA BSc MCLIP, L.Database Mgr., Univ.of Sheffield L., S.Yorks. [0012620] 01/08/1968
Roe Mr J, MA FCLIP, Retired. [0012621] 05/09/1949 **FE 01/01/1958**
Roe Mr JW, MCLIP, Not known. [0024176] 02/03/1953
Roe Mr NW, BA MCLIP, Bibl.Serv.Offr., N.E.Wales Inst.of H.E., Wrexham. [0012625] 27/02/1972
Roe Miss R, BA(Hons), Stud., Univ.Sheffield. [0059897] 30/10/2001
Roe Mrs S, (was Hughes), BA DipLib MCLIP, Child.Lib., Bebington Cent.L., Met.Bor.of Wirral. [0031336] 15/10/1979
Rogan Miss JTF, BA(Hons), Stud./L.Asst., City Univ./Field Fisherwaterhouse, London. [0056852] 27/10/1998
Roger Miss JG, FCLIP, Retired. [0012630] 05/06/1930 **FE 01/01/1930**
Roger Mr JK, BA MSc, Employment not known. [0060426] 11/12/2001
Rogers Mrs AD, (was Henderson), MCLIP, Learn.Resource Asst., Gateshead Coll., Gateshead. [0006713] 10/03/1962
Rogers Mrs AK, (was Smith), BA MCLIP, Unemployed. [0016315] 14/04/1969
Rogers Miss AM, MCLIP, Retired. [0012633] 07/03/1933
Rogers Miss AN, BA MCLIP, Retired. [0012634] 27/09/1964
Rogers Mrs B, (was Gillespie), BA MCLIP, Sch.Lib., Notts.C.C., Notts. [0031835] 18/01/1980
Rogers Mr CD, BA(Hons) DipLib MCLIP, Lib., Barmulloch Campus L., N.Glasgow Coll. [0035034] 12/07/1982
Rogers Mrs CD, (was Orr), MCLIP PGDip, Head of L.Serv., Warrington Coll.Inst., Lancs. [0011041] 15/08/1971
Rogers Mr CE, MCLIP, Life Member, Tel.01760 722457, Wayside Hse., Whitsands Rd., Swaffham, Norfolk, PE37 7BY. [0012636] 16/07/1949
Rogers Mrs DA, (was Orchard), BA MA MCLIP, Lib., Knights Templar Sch., Baldock, Herts. [0042138] 07/10/1988
Rogers Mrs DC, BA MCLIP, Retired. [0012638] 04/08/1960
Rogers Ms EMB, MCLIP, Retired. [0012641] 01/01/1965
Rogers Mr FR, BA M PHIL FCLIP, Life Member, 32 St Dominic Rd., Colchester, Essex, CO4 4PX. [0012641] 12/09/1952 **FE 01/01/1968**
Rogers Miss GK, L.Admin.Asst., Alcan Internat.Ltd., Banbury. Oxon. [0058622] 19/04/2000 **AF**
Rogers Ms HMA, BA(Hons) MCLIP, Lib., Westminster Ls.& Arch. [0038268] 18/02/1985
Rogers Mr I, BA(Hons) MA, Inf.Specialist, Nottm.Trent Univ. [0043693] 30/11/1989
Rogers Mrs J, (was Long), BSc MCLIP, Sch.Lib., The King's Sch., Peterborough. [0009072] 09/11/1971
Rogers Mrs JA, (was Pearce), BA MA MCLIP, Employment not known. [0037814] 29/10/1984
Rogers Mr JD, BA FCLIP, Life Member, 136 Ennisdale Dr., W.Kirby, Wirral, L48 9UB. [0012646] 21/03/1949 **FE 01/01/1963**
Rogers Mrs JD, MCLIP, Retired. [0012647] 15/05/1966
Rogers Mrs LA, (was Nutbeam), MCLIP, Unemployed. [0010935] 21/01/1972
Rogers Mrs LE, (was Howlett), FCLIP, Retired. [0007327] 17/02/1936 **FE 01/01/1949**
Rogers Mrs M, BA DipLib MCLIP, Br.& Mob.Lib., L.b.of Wandsworth, Alvering L. [0031432] 01/10/1979
Rogers Mrs MA, (was Maclean), Employment not known. [0055385] 09/10/1997
Rogers Mr MD, BA FCLIP, Retired. [0012653] 01/01/1955 **FE 01/01/1963**
Rogers Miss ME, MCLIP, Lib.(Resources), Chelmsford Cent.L., Essex L. [0012652] 01/01/1947
Rogers Mrs MH, MA MCLIP, Retired. [0012654] 11/10/1960
Rogers Mrs NB, (was Bailey), BA(Hons) MCLIP, Community Lib., Lincolnshire C.C. [0049361] 28/10/1993
Rogers Mrs RA, (was Walters), DipLib MCLIP, Music Lib., Music L.(Central), Westminster City Council. [0036976] 25/01/1984
Rogers Mrs SE, (was Reason), MCLIP, Mgr., Sch.L.Serv., Birmingham City Council. [0012218] 18/01/1971
Rogers Mrs SJ, (was Vinsen), BA(Hons) MA MCLIP, Inf.Offr., Inst.of Mech.Engineers, London. [0052902] 22/01/1996
Rogers Mrs SM, BA MCLIP, p./t.Secretarial, Reed Connections plc., London. [0022299] 01/04/1974
Rogers Miss VG, MCLIP, Sen.Lib., Stubbington Grp.(S.Div.), Hants.C.C. [0012657] 01/01/1947
Rogerson Prof I, MLS PhD DLitt FCLIP, Hon.Vis.F., John Rylands Inst., Univ.of Manchester. [0012658] 13/03/1948 **FE 12/03/1982**
Rogerson Mrs LD, MCLIP, Life Member, Tel.01756 760346. [0012659] 01/01/1945

Rogerson Mrs M, (was Kershaw), BA MCLIP, Area Lib., Bradford M.D.C., Yorks. [0007184] *11/10/1964*
Rogerson Mr P, MCLIP, Lib., Warrington L., Warrington Bor.Council. [0012660] *02/07/1970*
Rogoz Mrs EL, (was Nettlefold), MSc BSc(Hons), Cataloguer, British Library, Boston Spa. [0055839] *21/11/1997*
Rogula Mrs EJ, (was Jones), BA MCLIP, Unemployed. [0032667] *01/07/1980*
Roker Mrs B, (was Osguthorpe), DipIM MCLIP, Faculty Lib., Bucks.Chilterns Univ.Coll., High Wycombe, Bucks. [0055909] *11/12/1997*
Roland Mr JB, BA DipLib MCLIP, Research L.Mgr., Royal Nat.Inst.for the Blind, London. [0039136] *12/11/1985*
Rolf Mrs DC, BA MCLIP, Head of Res./Careers, Freman Coll., Buntingford, Herts. [0022871] *14/10/1974*
Rolfe Miss EL, BA(Hons), Student. [0056637] *01/10/1998*
Rolfe Mrs MA, Mgr.,Learn.Res.Cent., St.Edmund's Chiltern Sch., Kent. [0047243] *19/06/1992*
Rolfe Mr PJ, BA MA CertEd DipLib MCLIP, Asst.Lib., Inf.Servs., Univ.of Wales, Bangor. [0028360] *20/10/1977*
Roll Mrs MJ, (was Sydenham), BA MCLIP, Music Lib., Bucks.Co.L., Aylesbury. [0014298] *07/01/1971*
Rollason Mrs LA, (was Watton), BLib MCLIP MA, Planning Support Mgr., Keele Univ., Staffs. [0021644] *12/12/1973*
Rollo Mr DAT, MCLIP, Retired. [0012667] *19/10/1971*
Rolls Dr JJ, BA MA PhD, Asst.Lib., The Warburg Inst., London. [0058408] *07/02/2000*
Rolph Ms AV, BA FCLIP, Dep.Subject Lib., Univ.of Wales Swansea. [0012664] *21/01/1964* **FE 18/09/1991**
Ronchetti Miss BJ, MA MCLIP, Retired. [0012671] *04/02/1956*
Rone-Clarke Mr D, LRIC MRSC MCLIP, Asst.Lib., Army Tech.Foundation Coll., Reading. [0012672] *01/04/1971*
Ronicle Ms AMF, BA, L.Super., Cannington Coll., Bridgwater, Somerset. [0033633] *05/01/1981*
Ronson Mrs AR, BA, Stud./L.Asst., Liverpool John Moores Univ., Crosby L, Liverpool. [0061774] *06/11/2002*
Rook Mrs M, MA BA(Hons), Asst.Lib., The L., Brooklands Coll., Weybridge. [0047084] *21/04/1992*
Rook Ms RA, BSc(Hons) DipIS MCLIP, Knowledge Mgr., E.Elmbridge & Mid.Surrey PCT. [0050963] *03/11/1994*
Rooke Mrs EA, (was Wakelin), BA DipLib MCLIP, Sen.Lib., Cent.L., Oxford. [0031969] *04/01/1980*
Roome Mrs NM, BA MCLIP, Lib., Rother Valley Coll., Dinnington. [0022870] *04/10/1974*
Rooms Mrs EP, (was Hoyles), MCLIP, Lib., Oundle Sch., Peterborough. [0012676] *26/03/1968*
Rooney Ms CM, BA, Unemployed. [0039598] *09/03/1986*
Rooney Ms EA, BA(Hons) MCLIP, Unemployed. [0051692] *15/05/1995*
Rooney Mr J, BA(Hons), Learning Res.Asst., Liverpool Comm.Coll. [0043469] *26/10/1989*
Rooney Mrs MK, (was Jones), BA MCLIP, Resources Mgr., Chepstow L., Monmouthshire C.C. [0012970] *01/01/1965*
Roos Mrs J, BA(Hons), Stud., & Sen.L.Asst., Newnham Coll.L., Cambridge. [0058330] *11/01/2000*
Rooth Mrs IC, MSc MCLIP, Vol.Serv.Co-ordinator, Royal W.Sussex Trust, St.Richards Hosp, Chichester. [0055119] *21/07/1997*
Roper Miss AL, BMus MMus AKC, Grad.Trainee, The London L., London. [0059785] *02/10/2001*
Roper Mrs SJ, MCLIP, Asst.Catr., Kent Arts & L., W.Malling. [0035547] *01/01/1966*
Roper Mr TC, BA DipLib MCLIP, Head of L.& Inf.Serv., Royal Coll.of Vet.Surgeons. [0031433] *15/10/1979*
Roper Mr VdP, BSc MA FCLIP, Life Member. [0012680] *25/09/1951* **FE 01/01/1965**
Ropra Ms SKS, (was Sirha), BA, Unemployed. [0037086] *16/01/1984*
Rose Mrs E, Stud., Univ.of Brighton. [0061427] *19/07/2002*
Rose Miss EH, BA(Hons) MA MCLIP, Child.Lib., Selsdon L. [0055706] *05/11/1997*
Rose Mrs G, L.Asst., Berkhamsted Collegiate, Herts. [0053671] *28/08/1996* **AF**
Rose Mr GBK, BLib MCLIP, Inf.Offr., CMS Cameron McKenna, London. [0041615] *05/02/1988*
Rose Miss GM, MLib FCLIP FETC, Stud., Royal Holloway Coll., London. [0012682] *06/02/1972* **FE 15/07/1981**
Rose Mrs J, (was Carswell), BA DipLib MCLIP, p./t.Ref.Lib., Huddersfield L., Kirklees M.B.C. [0035761] *18/01/1983*
Rose Mr JA, BA(Hons) MA PGDipIM PGCE, Asst.Lib., Natural Hist.Mus., London. [0048401] *04/01/1993*
Rose Mrs JE, (was Walker), MCLIP, L.Mgr., Random House Group, Rushden,Northants. [0015232] *06/11/1971*
Rose Mrs JP, (was Atha), ACIS MCLIP, Unemployed. [0000482] *01/01/1972*
Rose Mrs JP, BSc(Hons) DipLIS MCLIP, Comm.Team Lib., Gloucestershire Lib.Arts&Mus.Serv., Cinderford,Gloucester. [0044026] *02/04/1990*
Rose Mr KW, BSc MSc MCLIP, Lib., Dept.of Trade & Ind., London. [0042368] *25/10/1988*
Rose Mr M, BA MA, p./t.Asst.Lib., De Montfort Univ., Leicester. [0055528] *20/10/1997*
Rose Ms SA, MSc, Br.Lib., Llandrindod Wells. [0059081] *10/11/2000*
Rose Miss SJ, BA(Hons) MA MCLIP, Inf.Lib., Northamptonshire L.& Inf.Serv., Northamptonshire Cent.L. [0056864] *29/10/1998*
Rose Miss SL, BA (Hons), Stud., Univ.of Cent.England. [0061658] *14/10/2002*
Rose Mr TJ, BA MCLIP, Asst.Lib.(Saturdays), Evesham L., Evesham, Worcester. [0040178] *05/11/1986*
Rosen Miss JA, BA(Hons) DipLib, Lib., Soc.for Co-op.Russian/Soviet Study, [0059900] *30/10/2001*
Rosenberg Ms DB, (was Hodge), MBE MA HonFCLIP FCLIP, Life Member, Tel.01453 887214. [0012688] *06/10/1964* **FE 16/01/1986**

Rosenberg Mrs PM, BA(Hons) DipIS MCLIP, p./t.Asst.Lib., Univ.of the W.of England. [0052988] *13/02/1996*
Rosenberg Mr S, L.Asst., Lichfield L., Staffs. [0059368] *20/02/2001* **AF**
Rosenior Mr ID, BA(Hons) MCLIP, Asst.Br.Mgr., N.E.Br.L., Aventura, FL., U.S.A. [0033721] *12/02/1981*
Rosenvinge Mr PJL, MA DipLib, Asst.Inf.Offr., Slaughter and May, London. [0034073] *02/09/1981*
Rosie Miss AS, MCLIP, Requests Lib., Aberdeen City L. [0021313] *03/10/1973*
Ross Mrs A, (was Davey), BA MCLIP, Mgmt.Res.Offr., Lancs.C.C. [0027756] *08/08/1977*
Ross Mrs AM, MA MCLIP, P./t.L.Asst., Aberdeen City L. [0025645] *26/01/1976*
Ross Mr JD, BSc MPhil CEng, Position unknown, Infologistix Ltd., Nottingham. [0060765] *12/12/2001*
Ross Miss JF, MA(Hons) DipILS, Sen.Inf.Specialist, Univ.of Abertay Dundee. [0054646] *07/02/1997*
Ross Miss JM, Geophysical Data Technician, Total Fina Elf Exploration UK, Aberdeen. [0033133] *02/10/1980*
Ross Mr JM, BSc MSc MILog MCLIP, Employment not known. [0060633] *11/12/2001*
Ross Miss JN, MA DipLib PGCE MCLIP, Dep.Dir.(Inf.Serv.), Bristol Univ.Careers Advisory Serv., Tel:0117 928 8232. [0035318] *05/10/1982*
Ross Mrs K, (was Thompson), BA MCLIP, Job-share Asst.Sch.Resources Offr., Cleveland Co.L., Redcar & Cleveland Bor. [0033176] *24/10/1980*
Ross Mrs KA, (was Moore), BA MBA MCLIP, LRC Mgr., Cwmcarn High Sch., Cwmcarn. [0035646] *18/11/1982*
Ross Mrs M, BA(Hons) MCLIP, Life Member. [0012702] *01/01/1941*
Ross Miss MJ, BA(Hons) MCLIP, Serv.Mgr.-Cult.Serv., L.B.of Barnet. [0012704] *22/07/1972*
Ross Miss MM, BA MCLIP, Retired. [0012705] *15/05/1967*
Ross Mrs N, BA(Hons) PGCE, L.Asst., Heathfield Comm.Sch., Somerset. [0059815] *10/10/2001* **AF**
Ross Mr NG, BA(Hons), IRC Mgr., Adventis, London. [0055000] *19/06/1997*
Ross Mr NJ, BA(Hons) DipIS MCLIP, Sub.Lib., Kent Inst.of Art & Design, Maidstone. [0053745] *07/12/1995*
Ross Mr PC, BA MA DipLib MCLIP, Asst.Lib., Printed Books, Guildhall L. [0041413] *27/11/1987*
Ross Mrs SH, (was Allan), BA MCLIP, N.Area Sales Mgr., Chivers Press Ltd., Bath. [0000175] *01/01/1972*
Ross Mrs VA, (was Metcalfe), BA MCLIP, Child.& Lifelong Learn.Coordinator, City of Westminster Ls. [0010100] *07/05/1970*
Ross Mrs VJ, (was Atkins), MCLIP, L.Asst., Belper Sch., Belper, Derbys. [0021266] *15/10/1973*
Ross-Parker Mrs MM, (was Williams), BA MCLIP, Unemployed. [0030697] *09/03/1979*
Rossall Mr D, BSc CPhys MInstP MCLIP, Employment not known. [0060688] *12/12/2001*
Rossall-Boyle Ms HC, (was Rossall), BA(Hons) MCLIP, Knowledge Mgr., Airedale Gen.Hosp., Keighley, W.Yorks. [0052307] *25/10/1995*
Rossell Mrs DJ, (was Matthews), BA(Hons) MA MCLIP, Learning Cent.Mgr., Stephenson Coll.L., Coalville. [0049102] *01/10/1993*
Rosser Miss EJ, MCLIP, Support Serv.Lib., Fife Council, E.Area L.H.Q. [0018238] *01/10/1972*
Rosser Mrs PE, (was Platts), BA MCLIP, Community Lib., Sheffield P.L. [0011746] *01/01/1966*
Rosset Mr RW, BA DipLib MCLIP, Solo Lib., ASLIB, London. [0037687] *17/10/1984*
Rossi Ms MS, BA(Hons), Asst.L., N.W.London Hosp.Trust, Avery Jones PGMC L. [0057915] *01/10/1999*
Rossiter Mrs SM, (was Hart), BA MCLIP, Lend.Lib., Weston-super-mare L., N.Somerset. [0012711] *23/03/1965*
Rosthorn Ms N, BA(Hons) MSc MCLIP, Librarian, Tameside College, Cheshire. [0055521] *20/10/1997*
Roszkowski Ms J, BA(Hons) DipIS MCLIP, Lib., Cambs.L's., Cambs.C.C. [0042561] *03/01/1989*
Roth Mrs KM, (was Cameron), BA MCLIP, Lib., King James's Sch., Knaresborough. [0027263] *15/02/1977*
Rothera Ms HM, BA(Hons) MA MCLIP, Subject Lib., Health Care, Oxford Brookes Univ. [0052424] *30/10/1995*
Rothwell Mrs J, (was Newton), BA DipLib MCLIP, Career Break. [0032135] *21/01/1980*
Roulinson Mrs PTM, BA, Retired. [0035992] *01/01/1965*
Roulston Ms DP, BA(Hons), Dep.L.Serv.Mgr., Waltham Forest Coll. [0041007] *02/10/1987*
Roulstone Mrs AS, BA, p./t.Learning Res.Administrator, Loughborough Coll. [0058735] *01/07/2000*
Roulstone . LH, (was Dunford), MCLIP, L.Advisor, Educ.L.Serv., L.B.of Southwark. [0020169] *29/01/1973*
Round Mrs UM, (was Drzewicka), MCLIP, Inf.Adviser (P./t.), Surrey Univ., Roehampton. [0029028] *26/03/1978*
Rouse Mrs JA, (was Price), MCLIP, Off.Mgr., Ekins & Co.(Chartered Accountants), Swindon, Wilts. [0012725] *09/09/1964*
Rouse Ms RC, BA MCLIP, Tech.Editor/Inf.Consultant, RUDI Ltd., Oxford Brookes Univ. [0027624] *30/05/1977*
Route Mrs N, (was Osborne), FCLIP, Retired. [0007234] *01/01/1931* **FE 01/01/1933**
Rowan Ms B, BA DipLib MCLIP, Princ.L.Offr.-Youth Serv., Edinburgh City L. [0029345] *05/06/1978*
Rowan Miss EIS, MCLIP, Retired. [0012729] *28/08/1953*
Rowan Mrs ER, (was Argustus), MSc, Employment not known. [0060138] *10/12/2001*
Rowan Ms ES, MSc, Head of L., Nat.Mus.of Scotland, Edinburgh. [0040671] *30/04/1987*
Rowan Dr ND, BSc PhD, Employment unknown. [0060260] *10/12/2001*

Personal Members

Rowbottom Mr T, BSc(Hons) CertEd MCLIP, Dep.Dir.(Learning Res.), Knowsley Comm.Coll., Merseyside. [0012732]   27/02/1966
Rowbury Mrs SA, (was Manton), BA(Hons), Catr., Public Record Off., Kew. [0052963]   31/01/1996   AF
Rowe Ms AKM, BA DipLib, Careers Adviser (Job Share), Univ.of Ulster, Coleraine. [0037301]   21/06/1984
Rowe Ms BM, BA DipLIS MCLIP, Area Sch.Lib., Hants.C.C., Winchester. [0044733]   27/11/1990
Rowe Mr CE, BA MA MCLIP, Lib., Partnership House Mission Studs.L., London. [0012733]   11/09/1963
Rowe Mrs FC, LLB(Hons), Stud. [0057461] 01/04/1999
Rowe Mrs FJ, BA(Hons) MCLIP, p./t.Lib., L.B.of Croydon. [0034035]   01/08/1981
Rowe Mrs I, (was Brooks), BSc, L.Mgr., Astrazeneca UK Ltd., Herts. [0046099]   22/10/1991
Rowe Mr JD, BA MCLIP, Artist, Lamberhust, Kent. [0012736]   04/01/1971
Rowe Mr JE, BSc(Hons), L.Exec., House of Commons, London. [0050945]   03/11/1994
Rowe Miss LD, BA, Unemployed. [0041703]   24/02/1988
Rowe Mr MW, BA(Hons), Med.Lib., Royal Hosp.Haslar, Min.of Defence, Hants. [0026242]   06/09/1976
Rowe Mr NC, MCLIP, Sch.Lib., Somerset C.C., Bridgwater. [0021837]   11/02/1974
Rowe Mr NR, Lib., Cheshire C.C., Ellesmere Port L. [0058982]   16/10/2000
Rowe Mrs OF, (was Williams), FCLIP, Retired, Jamaica. [0016605] 01/01/1956 FE 01/01/1966
Rowe Miss RM, MA MCLIP, Smuts Lib., S.Asian & Comm.Studies, Univ.of Cambridge. [0037628]   09/10/1984
Rowe Miss SG, BA MCLIP, Princ.L.Asst., Univ.of St.Andrews, Fife. [0021342]   16/10/1973
Rowell Ms G, BA(Hons) MA, Team Lib., Univ.of Northumbria at Newcastle. [0054040]   22/10/1996
Rowland Mr AP, Stud., Univ. Central England. [0060962]   18/01/2002
Rowland Ms DE, BLib MSc MCLIP, Lib., Dept.of Trade & Ind., London. [0025101]   01/11/1975
Rowland Mrs H, (was Fisher), BA MCLIP, Life Member, 2 Riversdene, Tarrant Keyneston, Blandford Forum, Dorset, DT11 9JF. [0012740]   22/02/1952
Rowland Miss HL, BA MCLIP, Lib., Religious Soc.of Friends (Quakers), London. [0034102]   01/10/1981
Rowland Ms JAB, BSc(Hons) MA, E-Journals Asst., Imperial Coll., London. [0055391]   01/10/1997
Rowland Dr JFB, MA FCLIP, Position unknown, Loughborough Univ. [0060600]   11/12/2001   FE 01/04/2002
Rowland Mr JS, BSc, Position unknown, Lafarge Roofing Tech.Cent., Crawley. [0052379]   30/10/1995
Rowland Mrs S, BA DipLib MCLIP, Retired, Cllr., Basingstoke & Deane Bor.Council. [0036289]   01/10/1983
Rowland Ms V, (was Lewington), MA BA(Hons) DipLib MCLIP, Retired. [0045192]   06/08/1990
Rowlands Mrs AM, (was Burton), DipInfMan, Learning Resources Mgr., Barnet Coll. [0050473]   11/08/1994
Rowlands Mr BW, BA BSc MSc BBibl, Unemployed. [0044176]   01/07/1990
Rowlands Mrs CM, (was Hill), MCLIP, Unemployed. [0012745]   05/02/1964
Rowlands Mrs DL, (was Russell), BA MCLIP, Unemployed. [0036353]   06/10/1983
Rowlands Miss EA, BSc, Stud., Univ.of Wales, Aberystwyth. [0061351]   12/06/2002
Rowlands Mrs JL, (was Barton), BA DipLib MCLIP, Head of L.Devel., Brit.Medical Assoc., London. [0043078]   04/07/1988
Rowlands Mrs PA, Team Leader, Scunthorpe Cent.L. [0039811]   27/07/1986
Rowlatt Mrs EJ, (was Cooke), MCLIP, Teaching Asst., All Saints Montacute Sch., Somerset. [0003078]   19/01/1971
Rowlatt Ms ME, (was Hughes), BA MSC MCLIP, Comm.Inf.Network Coordinator, Essex Cou. [0023708]   08/01/1975
Rowlett Ms EJ, BA MSc, Inf.Resources Worker, Stiirling Health &Well-Being, Edinburgh. [0059549]   10/05/2001
Rowley Mrs AB, BA MCLIP, Stock Lib., Bexhill, E.Sussex C.C. [0019163]   01/01/1966
Rowley Mrs AM, BSc MA MCLIP, Team Leader,/Site Lib., Worcs.Acute Hosp.NHS Trust, Worcester. [0012750]   01/01/1968
Rowley Mrs J, (was Ball), BA(Hons) MCLIP, Learning Res.Mgr., Tamworth & Lichfield Coll. [0047105]   30/04/1992
Rowley Dr JE, BA MSc FCLIP CEng MInstM, Head of Sch.-Mgmt.& Soc.Sci., Edge Hill Coll., Ormskirk. [0032458] 01/04/1980   FE 18/01/1989
Rowley Mr PB, MA MCLIP, Life Member. [0012752]   27/06/1963
Rowlinson Mrs CAG, (was Jamie), MA DipLibStud, Assoc.Dir., Inf.Serv., Univ.of Stirling. [0048674]   05/02/1968
Rowntree Mr ME, BA(Hons) MA MCLIP, Unemployed. [0049014] 31/08/1993
Rowson Miss AJ, BA(Hons) MA MCLIP, Team Leader Community Serv., E.Renfrewshire. [0037127]   23/02/1984
Roy Miss EA, Stud., Merton Coll., Oxford. [0059947]   09/11/2001
Roy Mr JV, BA DipEdTech MCLIP, Production Editor, Technical Indexes Ltd., Berkshire. [0032165]   17/01/1980
Roy Chowdhury Mrs K, (was Mukherjee), PGDipLIS BA, L.Systems Administrator, Brit.L.of Political & Econ.Sci., London. [0049210]   11/10/1993
Royan Prof B, BA MBA FIMgt FCLIP FSA(Scot), Ch.Exec., Scot.Cultural Res.Access Network, Edinburgh. [0029808]   02/10/1978 FE 22/05/1996
Royce Mr JR, BA MLib MCLIP, L.Dir., Robert Coll., Istanbul, Turkey. [0029216]   13/04/1978
Royds Mr J, BA MCLIP, Team Lib., Southwark P.L. [0027290]   14/02/1977
Ruba Mr RS, Freelance, p./t.Romanian Assoc.of the Blind, Bucuresti. [0061170]   19/03/2002

Ruberry Ms CS, (was Russell), BA MA, Lib., Forsters (Solicitors), London. [0047682]   13/10/1992
Rubidge Mr HE, MCLIP, Retired. [0012761]   20/09/1949
Rubidge Mrs J, (was Oliver), MCLIP, Employment not known. [0025620]   13/01/1976
Rubra Mrs EV, (was Loney), FCLIP, Life Member, Greensleeves, H.H.A., Box Hill, KT20 7LL. [0012762]   09/09/1948   FE 01/01/1964
Ruck Mrs RA, (was Chambers), BEd MCLIP, Sch.Lib., Col.Frank Seely Sch., Calverton, Notts. [0002559]   01/01/1966
Rudall Ms R, BA(Hons), Team Lib., L.B.of Tower Hamlets. [0045121]   13/07/1990   AF
Rudd Mrs J, (was Little), MCLIP, Sen.Community Lib., Bolton Ls. [0008983]   13/01/1972
Rudd Mrs S, BA, Stud./Vol.Worker, Rudd Engineering. [0061485]   19/08/2002
Rudd Mrs S, (was Cocker), BA MCLIP, p./t.L.Mgr., Wrightington L., Wigan & Leigh NHS Trust. [0019167]   07/02/1964
Rudd-Clarke Mrs AB, BA AIL DIP LIS MCLIP, Lib., Concord Coll., Shrewsbury. [0038360]   31/03/1985
Ruddom Mr DA, MCLIP, Life Member. [0012767]   20/09/1955
Rudjord Ms A, Dep.Lib., Literary & Philosophical Soc., Newcastle upon Tyne. [0048852]   02/07/1993
Rudkin Miss A, BA(Hons), Records Controller, HJ Banks & Co.Ltd., Durham. [0054150]   07/11/1996
Rudolph Mrs J, (was Walker), MCLIP, Team Lib.(E.), Kent Arts & L. [0012769]   11/11/1968
Rudwick Mrs C, (was Hope), BA MCLIP, Sessional L.Adviser, L.B.of Newham. [0029042] 28/02/1978
Ruehl Mann Ms A, MA, Stud., Univ Coll.London. [0061750]   01/11/2002
Ruff Mrs B, (was Smith (form Fabian)), HonFCLIP, Retired. [0017678]   22/02/1944   FE 11/10/1988
Rugg Miss SM, BA DipLib MCLIP, Counter Serv.Team Leader, Inf.Cent., Kings Coll.London. [0021883]   05/02/1974
Rughoo Mrs SD, (was Khemnah), BLib MCLIP, Sen.Lib., Municipality of Vacoas-Phoenix, Mauritius. [0032103]   22/01/1980
Ruhlmann Miss DE, MA, Sen.L.Asst., Cambridge Univ., Faculty of Oriental Studies. [0046137]   07/10/1991
Ruhnke Mr MG, MA, Lib., Steglitz-Zehlendorf P.L., Berlin. [0056193]   01/04/1998
Rule Dr JS, DPhil BA(Hons) DipILS, L.& Inf.Serv.Mgr., Nottingham City Hosp.NHS Trust. [0056832]   21/10/1998
Rule Mrs RM, (was Negus), BA MCLIP, Subject Lib.p./t.(Applied Sci.), Anglia Poly.Univ., Cambridge. [0010716]   08/05/1970
Rumball Mrs FM, (was Thompson), MCLIP, L.Mgr., Castle Bromwich L., Solihull M.B.C. [0014610]   15/01/1971
Rumble Mrs JD, (was Carter), BEd MCLIP, Sch.Lib., St.Joseph's Academy, Ayrshire. [0059679]   01/01/1968
Rumsey Mr DJ, BA MCLIP, Head of L.Serv., Royal United Hosp.NHS Trust, Bath, Banes. [0022779]   15/10/1974
Runciman Miss RJ, MCLIP, Arch., Cameron Mackintosh, London. [0028994]   22/02/1978
Rundell Mr KJ, MCLIP, Sen.Lib., Kent Arts & L., Maidstone. [0020021]   01/01/1969
Rundle Miss JL, BSc, Sen.Inf.Asst., St Marys Coll., Twickenham. [0059655]   13/07/2001
Rundle Mrs JM, (was Key), MCLIP, L.& Res.Mgr., L.B.Hounslow. [0012778]   17/01/1961
Ruse Mr DJ, MILAM MCLIP, Asst.Dir.(Lifelong Learning), Westminster City Council. [0012780]   01/01/1970
Rush Mrs CS, (was Claxton), BSc DipLib MCLIP, Sixth Form Ref.Lib., St. Peters High Sch., Gloucester. [0027927]   10/10/1977
Rush Mr MJ, MA MCLIP, Retired. [0012783]   28/10/1969
Rush Mr NP, LLB(Hons), Lib., Leicestershire C.C., Leicester. [0059410]   06/03/2001
Rushbrook Mrs AJ, BA(Hons) MA, Higher L.Exec., House of Commons L., POLIS, London. [0058390]   28/01/2000
Rushton Mrs DS, (was Kenyon), MCLIP, Local Stud.Mgr., Blackburn with Darwen Bor.Council, Lanc. [0028612]   17/01/1978
Rushton Mr JD, BA DipLib MCLIP, H.of L.Serv., Scottish TV., Glasgow. [0029810]   05/10/1978
Rushton Mr RJ, MCLIP, Br.Lib., Lancashire C.C. [0027018]   18/01/1977
Rushworth Miss AJ, BSc(Econ)(Hons), Intranet Content Developer, Freshfields Bruckhaus Deringer, London. [0056324]   18/05/1998
Russell Mrs A, (was Pugh), MCLIP, Retired. [0019168]   14/02/1961
Russell Mr AD, BA DipLib MCLIP, Asst.Curator Special Collections, Nat.Art L., Victoria & Albert Mus. [0034441] 06/11/1981
Russell Mrs CE, MCLIP, Lib., Newcastle Gen.Hosp., Teaching Cent.L. [0032166]   21/02/1980
Russell Mr DC, BA(Hons) MA, Employment not known. [0047803]   19/10/1992   AF
Russell Miss EK, BA(Hons), Elect.Records Project Support Offr., Public records Off., Surrey. [0057916]   01/10/1999
Russell Mrs EM, BA MCLIP, Sen.Ref.Lib., Southampton City Council. [0006568]   01/01/1962
Russell Mrs EM, (was Lang), MA MCLIP, Retired. [0012790]   12/10/1964
Russell Mr FG, BA BLS, Database Production Co-ordinator, Euromonitor plc., London. [0054300]   20/11/1996
Russell Ms HB, BA MCLIP, Inf.Lib., Barnet L. [0023763]   28/01/1975
Russell Mrs HD, BSc MCLIP, Self-employed Indexer. [0031094]   14/07/1979
Russell Miss HM, HNC, L.Asst., Dunfermline Carnegie L., Fife. [0061514]   24/08/2002   AF
Russell Mrs JA, MA DipLib MCLIP, Health & Welfare Lib., N.E.E.L.B., Ballymena. [0029812]   10/10/1978
Russell Mrs JM, BA MCLIP, Inf.Mgr., Linklaters, London. [0029532]   29/08/1978
Russell Dr MA, BSc MSc PhD MCLIP, Unemployed. [0060307]   10/12/2001

Russell Mr MR, BA(Hons) DipILS MCLIP, Sch.Lib., Kirkland High Sch.& Comm.Coll., Methil. [0055887] 16/12/1997
Russell Mrs RE, (was George), MCLIP, Lib., Manchester High Sch.for Girls, Rusholme. [0026665] 04/01/1967
Russell Miss RM, BA MCLIP, Project Lib., Nat.Grid, Wokingham. [0038809] 09/10/1985
Russell Mrs SM, MA MPhil DipLib MCLIP, Coll.Lib., The Queens Foundation, Birmingham. [0039564] 03/03/1986
Russell de Galina Dr JM, BSc MSc PhD MCLIP, Resident in Mexico. [0060097] 07/12/2001
Russell-Edu Mr SW, BSc DipLib MCLIP, Lib., Euro.Inst.of Oncology, Milan, Italy. [0039319] 06/01/1978
Russon Mr D, BSc FCLIP, Retired. [0044350] 01/10/1990 **FE 01/04/2002**
Ruston Miss L, BA(Hons), Resident in Bangladesh. [0050711] 12/10/1994
Ruston Mrs SEL, (was Anderson), BA MCLIP, Sen.L.Asst., St.Martins College, Cumbria. [0039544] 20/02/1986
Rutherford Mr AGM, BA(Hons) DipLib, Deputy Head QWS, DLO, Andover. [0042781] 28/02/1989
Rutherford Miss M, BSc, Position unknown, GlaxoSmithKline. [0060415] 11/12/2001
Rutland Mrs JD, (was Buckland), BSc DipLib MCLIP, Lib., W.Kent Health Auth., Aylesford. [0032885] 17/10/1980
Rutledge Dr HR, BA(Hons) DipLib MCLIP MA PhD, Reading Devel.Lib.(Job Share), Richmond Lend.L. [0040668] 14/04/1987
Rutstein Mrs A, (was Hyams), BA(Hons), Business Inf. Offr., Inst. of Dirs., London. [0047431] 12/08/1992
Rutt Ms JC, (was Shepherd), BA MCLIP, Lib., Sheffield Health. [0036879] 12/01/1984
Rutt Mrs JM, BA DipLib MCLIP, Coll.Lib., Queen Mary's Coll., Basingstoke. [0031017] 04/07/1979
Rutt Miss SE, MCLIP, Unemployed. [0012812] 18/02/1972
Rutter Ms A, BSc PhD, L.Asst., S.Ayrshire Council. [0058655] 08/05/2000
Rutter Mrs IF, (was Stevens), BA MCLIP, L.Mgr., Cornwall C.C. [0030682] 24/01/1979
Rutter Mrs MRJ, BSc, Sch.Lib., Northumberland Educ.Auth. [0053355] 23/05/1996
Ruzic Ms CY, BEd MBA Dip, Learning Cent.Mgr., Isle of Wight Coll. [0061166] 15/03/2002
Ryan Ms BM, BA(Hons) MCLIP, Lib., Caerphilly Sch.L.Serv. [0049421] 21/10/1999
Ryan Mr CS, BA DipLib MCLIP, L.Serv.Mgr., York Coll.of F.& H.E. [0033618] 29/01/1981
Ryan Mr D, BA(Hons) MSc(Econ), Lib., Harper Adams Univ.Coll., Newport. [0058723] 01/07/2000
Ryan Ms DC, BA MCLIP, Co.Sec., NWRLS, Manchester. [0035560] 26/10/1982
Ryan Mr EJ, MA MCLIP, City Bibl.Lib., Portsmouth City Council, Portsmouth. [0012815] 27/01/1969
Ryan Mr GM, MA(Hons) DipILS, Asst.Lib., (Law L.), Univ.of Strathclyde, Glasgow. [0058092] 27/10/1999
Ryan Mrs I, CertEd BA, Teacher i/c.L., White Hart Lane Sch., London. [0051551] 01/04/1995 **AF**
Ryan Ms IE, (was Parks), BA MCLIP AALIA, Lib. Ref.Serv., Queensland Univ.of Tech., Brisbane. [0020536] 02/04/1973
Ryan Mrs JH, (was Warren), BA DipLib MCLIP, L.Mgr., Royal Australian Coll.of G.P.s, Melbourne, Australia. [0032213] 08/02/1980
Ryan Ms KA, BA DipLIS MSc, Sch.Lib., Mount Saint Agnes Academy, Bermuda. [0042065] 21/04/1988
Ryan Mrs KC, (was Smith), BA MBA FCLIP, Ch.Lib., S.E.& L.Board. [0012820] 14/02/1963 **FE 26/01/1994**
Ryan Mr MA, BA MCLIP, Princ.Learning Support Offr., Bucks.C.C.L.Serv., Aylesbury. [0012821] 13/10/1970
Ryan Mr ML, BA MCLIP, Retired. [0012822] 25/09/1967
Ryan Mr PA, MBA BA MCLIP, Ch.Lib., D.f.E.S., London. [0030670] 19/01/1979
Ryan Mr PJ, BA(Hons) MCLIP, Asst.Dir.L.Serv., Christ Church Univ., Canterbury. [0038410] 20/04/1985
Ryan Ms S, BSc BA MLIS, Inf.Mgr., NM Rothschild & Sons(Hong Kong)Ltd, Hong Kong. [0057507] 14/04/1999
Ryder Mr DWH, MCLIP, Sen.Inf.Lib., Guildford Br.L., Surrey Co.L. [0012828] 15/03/1960
Ryder Mrs E, (was Mayhew), MCLIP, Sen.Lib.(Adult Serv.), Kingston-upon-Thames P.L. [0009996] 10/02/1965
Ryder Mrs EH, BA MCLIP, Retired. [0012829] 01/01/1939
Ryder Mrs JA, (was Salinger), MCLIP, Div.Inf.Lib., West Hampshire County L. [0012872] 06/03/1971
Ryder Mrs JC, (was Pickford), BA MCLIP, Freelance Consultant, L.& Inf.Serv.for people with, Disabilities and Housebound. [0012830] 01/10/1965
Rye Miss EJ, BA(Hons) MCLIP, Dep.Lib., Radley Coll., Abingdon. [0046988] 20/03/1992
Rye Mr GP, FCLIP, Life Member. [0012833] 30/10/1933 **FE 01/01/1951**
Ryland Mrs JA, (was Lawrence), BA MA MSc MCLIP, Lib., Bournemouth Univ. [0044908] 15/01/1991
Sabel Mr D, BA(Hons), L.Asst., Delhert, London. [0058998] 18/10/2000
Sabin Miss A, BA MCLIP, Princ.Asst.Lib., Sch.of Oriental & African Studies. [0012835] 17/01/1968
Sabin Mr JH, BA DipLib Dip MCLIP, Retired. [0026005] 25/04/1976
Sabovic Ms Z, BA, H.of Coll.Mgmt., The Wellcome L., London. [0046640] 02/12/1991
Sach Mrs VW, (was Ould), MA MCLIP, Life Member. [0012836] 24/01/1954
Sachs Miss MAP, MCLIP, Team Lib., Oxford Cent., Oxon.C.C. [0022934] 19/09/1974
Sackett Mr EJC, MA MCLIP, Retired. [0012840] 17/09/1955

Sacre Mr JF, MCMI MCLIP, L.Liaison Offr., Ulverscroft MagnaLarge Print Bks. [0012842] 19/03/1968
Sadden Mr JP, BEd(Hons) DipIS MCLIP, Ref.Lib., Hampshire C.C., Petersfield L. [0051366] 31/01/1995
Saddington Mr GH, DMA FCLIP ACIS MIMgt, Retired. [0012843] 28/02/1958 **FE 09/03/1982**
Saddleton Mrs HA, (was Payne), Comm.Serv.Bus.Mgr., Surrey C.C. [0045038] 01/07/1990 **AF**
Sadek Mrs OM, PhD, H.of Librarianship Dept., Menoufia Univ., Cairo, Egypt. [0035632] 29/10/1982
Sadler Ms C, MA, Inf.Resource Offr., Tate Liverpool. [0054218] 05/11/1996
Sadler Mr GW, MCLIP, Asst.Lib., Local Studies, Derbys.C.C. [0012846] 07/02/1963
Sadler Mrs RK, (was Southgate), BA(Hons) MA MCLIP, [0048202] 16/11/1992
Sadler Mrs WM, Distance Learning Stud., U.W.A., Aberystwyth, & Employee, W.Sussex, Health Auth., Worthing. [0054944] 22/05/1997
Sage Mrs EA, (was Bolan), MA MCLIP, Br.Lib.(Job-share), Perth & Kinross Council. [0012852] 14/10/1968
Sage Mr PR, MCLIP, Lib.-Stock Serv., E.Sussex Co., Eastbourne. [0012855] 01/01/1964
Sahadeo Mrs LA, (was Wessels), BA DipLIS, L.Offr., Queensmead Sch., Middx. [0047880] 23/10/1992
Sahlke Mrs EM, (was Winter), BA DipLib MCLIP, Dep.Br.Lib.(Job Share), L.B.of Redbridge. [0021071] 01/10/1973
Saich Mrs BP, (was Powney), BA MCLIP, Life Member. [0012861] 01/01/1954
Saich Mr MJ, FCLIP, Life Member. [0012862] 18/03/1950 **FE 01/01/1964**
Sainsbury Mrs AC, (was Beckett), BA MCLIP, Campus L.Mgr., Univ.of Westminster, Cavendish. [0012865] 01/01/1966
Sainsbury Mrs AJ, (was Grant), MCLIP, Asst.Lib., Notts.Co.L. [0005803] 04/01/1977
Sainsbury Mr IM, BA MCLIP, Liaison Lib., Univ.of Reading L. [0012868] 04/12/1967
Sainsbury Mrs WV, (was Skelton), BLib MCLIP, p./t.Asst.Lib., Home Off., Prison Serv.H.Q.L., Westminster. [0020065] 18/01/1973
Sakarya Mrs B, BA MA, Basic Skills Lib., Basic Skills Agency & Inst.of Educ., London. [0048462] 15/01/1993
Saker Miss JE, BA ALAA MCLIP, Lend.Lib., Weston Cent.L., N.Somerset Dist.Council. [0012869] 13/07/1965
Saklatvala Mrs MJ, p./t.Lib., Home Off., London. [0061150] 21/03/2002
Saksida Mr M, HonFCLIP, Hon Fellow. [0060751] 12/12/2001 **FE 01/04/2002**
Salbashian Mrs RM, MA DipLib, Librarian/Website Mgr., DEFRA, London. [0040868] 23/07/1987
Sale Miss A, BA(Hons) MSc, Electronic Inf.Serv.Administrator, Anglo Poly.Univ., Chelmsford. [0057097] 09/12/1998
Sale Mr R, BA DipLib MCLIP, Team Lib., Kent Arts & L., Tonbridge. [0041439] 01/10/1988
Salem Dr S, FCLIP, Resident in Egypt. [0060078] 07/12/2001 **FE 01/04/2002**
Saletes Mrs DL, (was Towers), BA DipLib MCLIP, Lib.(Child.Work), Watford Cent.L. [0032471] 01/04/1980
Salgado Mr MGH, DipLIS, Independent Consultant, Sri Lanka. [0048493] 26/01/1993
Salimon Mr O, HNC BTEC HDip, Stud., Thames Valley Uni. [0060948] 15/01/2002
Salinie Mrs F, (was Shealy), MBE HonFCLIP, Asst.Dir.-France, Global Business Mgr., Brit.L.Serv., Paris. [0041993] 01/07/1988 **FE 12/01/1993**
Salisbury Ms CE, BA(Hons), p./t.L.Asst., Allestree L., Derby. [0060028] 27/11/2001 **AF**
Salisbury Miss JP, BLib(Hons) MCLIP, Customer Serv.Mgr., Cambridge Cent.L., Cambs.C.C. [0031095] 14/08/1979
Salisbury Mrs RM, (was Wright), DipLib MCLIP, Database Lib., Beds.C.C. [0029876] 16/10/1978
Salkeld Mrs DA, (was Corkhill), BA(Hons)DipLib MCLIP, Independent Consultant. [0028765] 28/09/1957
Salkin Ms H, BA(Hons) DipLib, Knowledge Mgr., Allen & Overy, London. [0056735] 12/10/1998
Salmon Miss AA, MSc BA, Inf.Offr.& Lib., Nat.Childbirth Trust, London. [0043999] 01/04/1990
Salmon Mrs B, (was Perkins), BA DipLib MCLIP, Head of L.& Inf.Serv., C.I.P.D., London. [0031151] 30/08/1979
Salmon Mrs CA, BA(Econ) PGCE, Sch.Lib., St Margarets Sch., Watford, Herts. [0056838] 27/10/1998 **AF**
Salmon Mrs CE, (was Feast), BA MCLIP, L.Devel.Mgr., Holy Cross Coll., Bury. [0012878] 22/02/1972
Salmon Miss HC, (was Pickford), BA MCLIP MBS MCLIP, Univ.Lib., Univ.of Tech., Kingston, Jamaica. [0012879] 26/09/1966
Salmon Mr JMM, BA MCLIP, Unemployed. [0012881] 05/01/1970
Salt Mr DP, BSc FCLIP, Serials Lib.-Catg.Dept., Univ.of Saskatchewan, Saskatoon, Canada. [0012885] 03/05/1967 **FE 25/01/1995**
Salter Miss AJ, BA MCLIP, Humanities Lib., St.Matthias Campus, Univ.of the W.of England, Bristol. [0031694] 02/10/1979
Salter Mr CJM, BSc(Hons) MA, Team Lib., Coventry Cent.L., Coventry. [0052831] 23/01/1996
Salter Ms E, BA DipLib MLib MCLIP, Lib.Mgr., Univ.of Westminster. [0035225] 07/10/1982
Salter Mr GW, MCLIP, Dep.Div.Lib., Cent.Div., Hants.Co.L. [0012889] 01/01/1964
Salter Mrs H, (was Judd), MCLIP, Unemployed, 2 Abington Place, Haverhill, Suffolk, CB9 0AE. [0036829] 01/01/1957
Salter Mrs HM, (was Stapleton), MA MCLIP, Learning Res.Mgr., Aldercar Sch., Derbys. [0022562] 30/06/1974
Salter Mrs MCR, (was Dewing), BA MCLIP, Unemployed. [0039520] 11/02/1986

Personal Members

Salter Mrs NE, (was Teevan), BSc PGCE DipILM, Team Lib., Northants.c.c., Wellingborough L. [0053903] *09/10/1996*
Salvadori Mrs A, MA mclip, Retired. [0022708] *14/09/1974*
Salvage Miss DEC, MCLIP, Retired. [0012892] *29/08/1944*
Samara Miss P, Inf.Asst., HCIMA, London. [0059687] *23/07/2001*
Sambridge Mrs M, (was Harrington), MCLIP, P/t.L.Asst., E.Grinstead L. [0012896] *06/01/1964*
Sambrook Miss CJ, BA(Hons) MA MA MCLIP, Special Collections Lib., Kings Coll., Univ.of London. [0047042] *06/04/1992*
Sambrook Miss J, Inf.Offr., SJ Berwin & Co. [0055386] *09/10/1997*
Samkin Mrs ERC, BA(Hons), p./t.Stud./Lib., Stradbroke High Sch., Suffolk C.C. [0058685] *25/05/2000*
Samman Miss MJ, BA MCLIP, Asst.Lib., Kings Coll.London, Strand. [0012898] *10/10/1966*
Sampson Mr AA, NDD ATD ACP FRSA MCLIP, Life Member. [0012899] *02/01/1965*
Sampson Mrs F, MCLIP, Retired. [0032487] *01/01/1963*
Sampson Ms J, BA MCLIP, Asst.L.Mgr.: Med./Nursing,Serv., Med.& Prof.L., Doncaster Royal Infirmary. [0050354] *04/07/1994*
Sampson Mrs MM, BA, Asst.Lib., Varndean Coll., Brighton. [0040774] *03/06/1987*
Sampson Ms R, BA(Hons) DAA, Asst.Lib., City Coll., Coventry. [0061392] *03/07/2002*
Samson Mrs JM, (was Hood), BA MCLIP, Unemployed (Career Break). [0031642] *22/10/1979*
Samson Mrs SM, (was Tumber), BA DLIS MCLIP, Team Lib.RILS, Sittingbourne L., Kent C.C. [0022400] *01/05/1974*
Samuels Miss JE, BA MCLIP, Sen.Lib., Hammersmith, L.B.Hammersmith & Fulham. [0018220] *05/10/1972*
Samuels Ms KL, Research Specialist, Pricewaterhouse Coopers, Toronto. [0045944] *25/07/1991*
Sandell Ms JE, MA DipLib MCLIP, Lib.-L.Support, Falkirk Council. [0043338] *23/10/1989*
Sandeman Mr AG, BA MCLIP, Best Value Offr., City of Edinburgh Council, Edinburgh. [0012906] *22/08/1967*
Sander Ms LV, MCLIP, Inf./Research Offr., UWCM, Duthrie L., Cardiff. [0050968] *03/11/1994*
Sanders Mrs KJ, (was Martin), BA MCLIP, L.& Inf.Systems Mgr., The Brit.Inst.of Radiology, London. [0031896] *15/01/1980*
Sanders Miss MH, MPhil BA MCLIP, Retired. [0012911] *03/02/1957*
Sanderson Miss C, BSc, Stud., Univ.Newcastle @ Northumbria. [0059803] *03/10/2001*
Sanderson Mrs CA, (was Wood), MCLIP, Unemployed. [0012914] *01/01/1962*
Sanderson Mr DM, BSc(Hons) MSc, Inf.Specialist, GCHQ Inf.Serv., Cheltenham. [0055216] *22/08/1997*
Sanderson Mrs GA, BSc(Hons) MSc, Inf.Mgr., Southern Derbyshire Chamber. [0051002] *08/11/1994*
Sanderson Mr IJS, MCLIP, Retired. [0012918] *19/09/1960*
Sanderson Mrs J, BA DipLib MCLIP, County Specialist - Heritage, Lichfield, Staffs.C.C. [0034500] *18/11/1981*
Sanderson Miss JB, BA MCLIP, Lib., Theological Coll.of Cent.Africa, Ndola, Zambia. [0029282] *25/04/1978*
Sanderson Mr JP, BA BSc(Hons) MLib PGCE MCLIP, Inf.Serv.Co-ordinator, Worle Sch., Weston-super-Mare. [0027708] *01/07/1977*
Sanderson Mrs S, Lib., Ryde High Sch., Isle of Wight. [0056995] *19/11/1998 AF*
Sandford Mr AM, MCLIP, Asst.Lib., Bury Metro.P.L. [0023869] *10/02/1975*
Sandford Miss ML, BA(Hons) MA, Unemployed. [0051688] *12/05/1995*
Sandham Mr A, DIP AD MCLIP, Delivered Serv./Educ.Support Lib., Middlesbrough Bor.Council, Middlesbrough. [0023815] *13/01/1975*
Sandhu Mrs GK, (was Randhawa), BSc MSc MCLIP, Systems Mgr., Univ.of Salford, Manchester. [0047994] *30/10/1992*
Sandhu Miss K, BA, Stud., Univ.of Cent.England. [0046190] *14/10/1991*
Sandiford Mrs PJ, (was Hardman), MCLIP, Temp.Business Inf., Newcastle P.L. [0012919] *25/02/1967*
Sandiford Mrs YKT, MEd BEd, Learning Resources Asst., Univ.Coll.Northampton, Park Campus L. [0059074] *08/11/2000*
Sandison Mr PEC, MA DipLib MCLIP, Mgr.L.Serv.& Inf.Systems, Scottish Borders Campus, Heriot-Watt Univ., Galashiels. [0035317] *01/10/1982*
Sandison Mrs SMI, (was Brown), MA MCLIP, Sch.Lib.(Job Share), Galashiels Academy, Selkirkshire. [0035756] *10/01/1983*
Sandles Miss B, MCLIP, Br.Lib., Roseberry L., Stockton-on-Tees. [0012926] *10/02/1967*
Sands Mrs AW, (was Nibloe), MCLIP, Sch.Lib., Queen Margaret Academy, Ayr. [0012928] *11/10/1963*
Sands Miss GM, BA MSc MCLIP, Sen.L.Asst., Inst.of Advanced Legal Studies, London. [0053913] *10/10/1996*
Sands Miss LC, BA(Hons) MCLIP, Unemployed. [0056068] *06/02/1998*
Sands Mr LP, BA(Hons) MA, Records Exec. [0055591] *22/10/1997*
Sands Mrs P, (was Masters), BA(Hons), Asst.Lib., Royal W.Sussex Trust, Chichester, W.Sussex. [0047324] *26/10/1992*
Sandys Mrs J, (was Shepherd), HonFCLIP, Life Member. [0013272] *31/01/1952* **FE 01/01/1996**
Sanger Miss BM, MCLIP, Lib., Nat.Physical Lab., Middx. [0012930] *30/10/1971*
Sanger Mr SAC, (was Peters), MCLIP, Asst.Lib., Dept.of Trade & Ind., Kingsgate House, London. [0011577] *19/08/1969*
Sangha Mrs H, (was Sorrell), BA(Hons) DipLIS MCLIP, Comm.L.Mgr., Sandwell M.B.C. [0047650] *09/10/1997*
Sankey Miss CA, BA MCLIP, Inf.Lib., E.Finchley L., L.B.of Barnet. [0046585] *20/11/1991*
Sansby Miss EJ, BA(Hons) MA MCLIP, Learning Resouces Mgr., Stamford Coll.of F.E., Stamford, Lincs. [0050268] *26/05/1994*
Sansom Miss AJC, BA FCLIP, Retired. [0012935] *07/03/1950* **FE 01/01/1966**
Sansom Mrs S, (was White), BA(Hons) MA, Unemployed. [0055356] *03/10/1997*
Sansom Mrs SE, BA MCLIP, Lib., Edgbaston High Sch., Birmingham. [0039508] *30/01/1986*
Sant Mr D, BA DipLib MCLIP, L.Asst., DSLC, Foreign & Commonwealth Off., London. [0030248] *07/12/1978*
Santer Mrs MA, (was Clayton), MCLIP, P./t.L.Asst., Devon C.C. [0024200] *23/04/1975*
Sants Miss BHJ, FCLIP, Life Member. [0012939] *07/03/1940* **FE 01/01/1948**
Sardena Mrs SA, BSc, Med.Lib., Gibraltar Health Auth., Sch.of Health Studies. [0052275] *20/10/1995*
Sargant Mr MJ, MA DipLib MCLIP, Local Hist.Lib., Crosby L., Sefton M.B.C. [0027709] *06/07/1977*
Sargeant Mr B, MCLIP, Retired. [0017691] *01/01/1955*
Sargeant Mrs CD, BSc MA DipLib MCLIP, Lend.& Inf.Lib. - Eastleigh, Hants.Co.Ls. [0029817] *02/10/1978*
Sargeant Mr MR, MCLIP, Retired. [0012947] *24/09/1964*
Sargeant Mrs R, (was Hammond), BLib DMS MCLIP, Lifelong Learning Project Offf., Shropshire Co.L. [0038559] *01/07/1985*
Sargent Mrs B, MCLIP, Retired. [0012948] *08/09/1958*
Sargent Mrs CD, (was Scanes), MA MCLIP, Sen.Mgr., Radley Coll., Sch.L., Abingdon, Oxon. [0040507] *26/02/1987*
Sargent Mrs KH, (was Zaturska), BSc, Lib., Davenport Lyons, London. [0012949] *01/01/1969*
Sargent Mrs L, (was Ervine), BA DipLib MCLIP, H.of Sch., Learning Serv., City of Westminster Coll., London. [0028555] *09/01/1978*
Sarif Mrs EB, (was Beder), Lib., Australian Inst.of Company Dir., Sydney. [0031123] *14/09/1979*
Sarjeant Mrs AM, (was Crowe), BA MCLIP, Inf.Serv.Lib., Saskatoon P.L., Canada, S7N 0J2. [0017692] *18/09/1964*
Sarkar Mr PK, BA MCLIP, Retired. [0017693] *04/10/1940*
Sarosi Mrs MA, (was McCreadie), BA HDipLib, Lib., Keble Coll., Oxford. [0045724] *07/05/1991*
Sartin Mrs CI, (was Clarkson), MCLIP, LRC Asst., Gryphon Sch., Sherborne. [0006194] *01/01/1964*
Sarvilahti Miss HM, BA(Hons), Univ.of Tampere, Finland. [0057664] *01/07/1999*
Sato Mr T, MA, Stud.(PhD in Educ.), Faculty of Educ., Univ.of Manchester. [0058776] *17/07/2000*
Sauer Ms CD, DipLib, Dir.& Head, Gen.Inf.Dept., Zentral-und Landesbibliothek,Haus, Amerika-Gedenkbibliothek, Berlin. [0042901] *12/04/1989*
Sauer Mr R, APMI MCLIP, Team Mgr., William M Mercer, Croydon. [0012958] *05/12/1967*
Saulsbury Ms D, MA MCLIP, L.Serv.Mgr.-S., De Montfort Univ., Bedford. [0027463] *13/04/1977*
Saunders Mrs A, (was Mccoull), BA MCLIP, Dir.of Community & Leisure, E.Renfrewshire Council. [0009293] *20/01/1972*
Saunders Mrs CM, (was Whittle), BA MCLIP, p./t.L.Asst./N.T.A., Longcar J.& I.Sch., Barnsley. [0023685] *06/01/1975*
Saunders Mrs DL, (was Sage), BA MCLIP, Sen.Local Studies Lib., Cent.for Kentish Studies, Maidstone, Kent Arts & L. [0033984] *23/06/1981*
Saunders Mrs EA, (was Giles), BA DipLib MCLIP, L.Inf.& Knowledge Skills Trainer, Worcestershire Health. [0030168] *08/01/1979*
Saunders Mrs HC, (was Price), MA DipLib MCLIP, Sen.Br.Lib., Cardiff C.C. [0036405] *05/10/1983*
Saunders Mr HF, BA MCLIP, Mgr., Highlands & Abbottsfield Br., Edmonton P.L., Alberta, Canada. [0017695] *04/02/1964*
Saunders Mr JC, BA MCLIP, Head of Serv., Educ.L.Serv., Berks.Joint Auth. [0021975] *17/01/1974*
Saunders Mrs JM, (was Woodhouse), MCLIP, Asst.Lib., Redditch L., Redditch, Worcs. [0016241] *24/02/1958*
Saunders Mrs KI, BA DipInfLib, Lib., Kingswood Coll.at Scarisbrick Hall, Ormskirk, Lancs. [0046433] *04/11/1991*
Saunders Mrs LJ, BA DipLib MCLIP, Devel.Mgr., Lib. Partnership - W.Mids., Birmingham. [0032460] *14/04/1980*
Saunders Mr MD, BSc DipLib MCLIP, Asst.Lib., Pinderfields Hosp., Wakefield. [0032817] *16/09/1980*
Saunders Miss O, MCLIP, Retired. [0012972] *21/01/1946*
Saunders Mrs PE, (was Hines), BSc MA MCLIP, Inf.Offr., Surrey C.C. [0042367] *24/10/1988*
Saunders Mrs S, (was Fawkes), DMS BA MCLIP, Sen.L.Mgr.- Y.& Educ., L.B.of Greenwich, Plumstead L. [0028557] *12/01/1978*
Saunders Ms S, BA(Hons) DipILS MSc(Econ), L.Asst., Univ.of Wales, Aberystwyth. [0053823] *03/10/1996*
Saunders Mr SG, FCLIP, Life Member, Tel:0181 902 8663. [0012973] *18/08/1931* **FE 01/01/1937**
Saunders Prof WL, CBE MA LittD FCP FCLIP HonFCLIP, Retired. [0012974] *01/01/1936* **FE 01/01/1952**
Savage Mrs CL, (was Robinson), BA(Hons) DipILM, Inf.& Policy Asst., Yorkshire Mus.Council. [0054220] *05/11/1996*
Savage Mrs DRL, (was French), F./T.Mother/Housewife. [0039368] *16/01/1986*
Savage Miss EM, MLS MCLIP, Life Member. [0012978] *24/08/1957*
Savage Mr JG, BA MCLIP, Asst.Lib., Upper Norwood P.L. [0025811] *14/03/1976*
Savage Miss JM, BA(Hons), Inf.Asst., Univ.of Salford. [0051787] *01/07/1995*
Savage Mrs RA, (was Dudley), BA(Hons) DipIM MCLIP, Child.Lib., L.B.of Croydon, Coulsdon. [0052547] *08/11/1995*
Savage-Jones Ms M, (was Nitsch), BSc MSc DIS MIIS MCLIP, L.Systems Administrator, Wellcome Trust, London. [0041990] *08/07/1988*
Savidge Ms JC, MA MCLIP, Faculty Librarian, Kingston University, Surrey. [0034521] *06/10/1981*
Saville Miss AJ, MA MCLIP, Lib., The Queens Coll., Oxford. [0038907] *18/10/1985*

343

Savin Mr JA, MA(Oxon) DipLib, Employment Unknown. [0040950] 01/10/1987
Savitch Ms NM, BSc MSc MCLIP, Employment not known. [0060825] 12/12/2001
Savory Mrs AE, (was Rogan), BSc(Hons) MA MCLIP, Resident in Canada. [0049836] 17/12/1993
Sawalhi Mrs AL, (was Poole), BA MCLIP, Inf.Offr., S.Cambs.D.C., Cambridge. [0033336] 25/11/1980
Sawbridge Mrs JA, (was Perry), BA MSc MCLIP, Inf.Off., Nat.Probation Serv., W.Midlands, Birmingham. [0031013] 02/07/1979
Sawbridge Mrs L, (was Gardner), BA MCLIP, Princ.Lib.-Comm.Serv., L.B.of Bexley. [0005358] 09/11/1971
Sawers Mrs CGL, (was Richards), MSc FCLIP, Acting Head of S Thames L., London Univ., Royal Surrey Co.Hosp. [0012986] 07/01/1955 **FE 26/05/1993**
Sawers Mr CJ, BA(Hons), p./t.Lib., Nottinghamshire C.C., W.Bridgford L. [0053551] 16/07/1996
Sawhney Mr SC, MA MCLIP, Life Member. [0012987] 14/02/1968
Sawyer Mr A, BA MCLIP, Records Offr., Powys C.C., Llandrindod Wells. [0042680] 31/01/1989
Sawyer Mrs AE, BA(Hons), Stud., Aberystwyth. [0061409] 10/07/2002
Sawyer Ms TG, BA(Hons) PGDipIM, Subject Lib., Thames Valley Univ. [0054318] 20/11/1996
Sawyer Mrs VB, (was Jones), BLS MCLIP, Sen.Lib., Educ.Lib.Serv., Notts.C.C. [0033464] 01/01/1981
Saxby Ms D, BSocSc(Hons), Asst.Lib., Internat.Sch.of Amsterdam, Nederland. [0050786] 18/10/1994
Saxby Miss HJ, BLS MCLIP, Asst.Catr., Glos.C.C., Co.L.,Arts, & Museums, Glos. [0030250] 05/12/1978
Saxon Miss DG, MCLIP, Life Member. [0012990] 07/10/1971
Saxton Mr PB, BA(Hons) PGDip, Catr., L.B.of Richmond. [0054428] 06/12/1996
Say Mrs CA, (was Stott), BA DipLib MCLIP, Unemployed. [0031950] 07/01/1980
Sayed Mrs S, (was Colle), FCLIP, Life Member. [0012993] 17/03/1950 **FE 01/01/1958**
Sayer Mr AM, BA(Hons), Head of Inf.Serv., Owen Williams Consulting Eng., Birmingham. [0052423] 30/10/1995
Sayer Mrs PM, (was Taylor), MCLIP, Unemployed. [0014448] 27/04/1964
Sayers Miss KA, BA(Hons) MA MSc MCLIP, Catr., Brit.L., Boston Spa. [0054138] 01/11/1996
Sayers Ms MK, BSc MSc, Employment not known. [0060803] 12/12/2001
Sayers Miss TM, Stud., City Univ. [0059121] 20/11/2000
Saynor Miss SJ, BA, Child.Lib., L.B.Bexley. [0057129] 18/12/1998
Saywood Miss W, BSc MCLIP, Inf.Sci., Organon Labs.Ltd., Newhouse. [0042443] 10/11/1988
Scaife Mr AM, BA M ED MCLIP, Curriculum Devel., Park Lane Coll., Leeds. [0013001] 11/01/1968
Scaife Mr BM, BA(Hons) MCLIP, L.Systems Offr., Christ Church Univ.Coll., Canterbury. [0055557] 21/10/1997
Scales Mr RP, BA DipLib MCLIP, Faculty Lib., Bucks.Chilterns Univ.Coll., Chalfont St.Giles. [0032725] 23/07/1980
Scally Dr JJ, BA(Hons) PhD,Deputy Head (Coll.), Rare Books Div., Nat.L.of Scotland, Edinburgh. [0056518] 03/08/1998
Scalpello Mrs M, (was Hoggan), DipLib MA MCLIP, Lib., Glasgow Coll.of Nautical Studies. [0038726] 01/10/1985
Scandrett Mrs EJ, (was Lunn), BA(Hons) DipIM MCLIP, Mgr.CIS, Southampton L.Serv. [0049771] 26/12/1979
Scanlon Mr MJ, BA MCLIP, Asst.Lib., DEFRA, London. [0034052] 13/08/1981
Scantlebury Mrs NL, (was Morgan), BA DipLib MCLIP, Site/Team Lib., De Montfort Univ., Milton Keynes. [0034801] 04/02/1982
Scarborough Mrs DM, (was Oakes), BA MCLIP, Unemployed. [0038125] 12/01/1985
Scarbro Mrs LA, (was Elwick), MCLIP, Grp.Lib., Durahm City Br.L., Durham Co.Council. [0021917] 01/02/1974
Scarlett Mrs CAE, (was Nicklin), BA FCLIP, Life Member. [0010828] 17/01/1960 **FE 01/01/1964**
Scarlett Mrs SM, DipLib MCLIP, L.Asst., Lisburn Br.L. [0031695] 04/11/1979
Scarpa Mrs GJM, (was Hepworth), BA MLS MCLIP, Housewife. [0025048] 10/11/1975
Scarrott Mr M, BA DipLib MCLIP ILTM, Academic Serv.Mgr., St.Mary's Coll., Twickenham. [0041247] 13/10/1987
Scarsbrook Mrs PE, BMus MA MCLIP, Asst.Dir.(Inf.Serv.), Univ.of Surrey Roehampton, London. [0022770] 12/10/1974
Scatchard Mrs B, (was Marsden), MCLIP, Special Serv.Adviser, N.Yorks.Co.L., Northallerton. [0009767] 17/05/1967
Schaefers Ms SM, MSc(Econ), Academic Lib., German Cent.L.for Economics, Kiel, Germany. [0056431] 02/07/1998
Schafer Miss RJ, BA(Hons), Stud., Univ.of N.London, &, Admin.Offr., Brit.L., London. [0058473] 03/03/2000
Scharlau Mrs F, (was Carnegie), MCLIP, Local Studies Lib./Arch., Angus Council-Cultural Serv., Montrose L. [0037681] 15/10/1984
Scherr Miss JMS, BA MCLIP, Asst.Dir., Public Servs., Univ.of Bristol Inf.Serv. [0013008] 25/09/1968
Schidlof Ms L, BSc DipLib MCLIP, Unemployed. [0041843] 24/04/1988
Schlenther Mrs EC, DipLib MCLIP, Retired, Hillview Croft, Tyllwyd Lane, Llanfarian, Aberystwyth SY23 4UJ. [0035852] 01/02/1983
Schlesinger Mr JT, BA(Hons) DipLIS MCLIP, Professional Lib., Univ.of Birmingham. [0044815] 03/12/1990
Schlicke Ms PA, BA DipLib MCLIP, Freelance. [0023955] 25/02/1975
Schofield Miss AJ, Sen.L.Asst., Advocates L., Edinburgh. [0059554] 16/05/2001 **AF**
Schofield Miss AM, BLib, Slide Lib./Subject Inf.Offr., Aldham Roberts L.R.C., Liverpool John Moores Univ. [0047926] 26/10/1992
Schofield Ms C, BA, Unemployed. [0042557] 05/01/1989
Schofield Mrs DJ, (was Shilliday), BA MCLIP, L.Asst., Accrington Ref.L., Lancs.C.C. [0030536] 20/01/1979

Schofield Miss F, MA(Hons), Stud., Univ.of Strathclyde. [0061026] 01/02/2002
Schofield Mrs FA, BSc MCLIP, Team Lib., E.Sussex L., Inf.& Arts, Peacehaven L. [0018157] 10/10/1972
Schofield Ms H, BSc DipLib FCLIP, Clerical Asst., Corrosion & Protection Cent., Industrial Serv. [0033707] 15/01/1981 **FE 01/04/2002**
Schofield Mrs HL, MA(Hons) DipIS MCLIP, Government Publications Lib., Croydon Cent.L., Croydon. [0045986] 08/08/1991
Schofield Mrs IM, (was Booth), MCLIP, Ref.& Inf., Kirklees Cultural Serv., Huddersfield. [0013022] 01/01/1966
Schofield Mrs JA, (was Walder), BA DipLib MCLIP, L.& Inf.Mgr., Thomas Eggar Church Adams, Chichester, W.Sussex. [0030565] 25/01/1979
Schofield Mrs ME, (was Knowles), MCLIP, Spec.Serv.Lib., N.Yorks.Co.L., Harrogate Grp. [0013015] 19/08/1966
Scholes Mr B, MCLIP, Employment not known. [0013016] 15/10/1967
Scholes Mrs JA, (was Rivers), MCLIP, p/t.Sch.Lib., Henry Fanshawe Sch., Dronfield, Derbys. [0013018] 22/01/1968
Schopflin Ms K, MA(Hons) MA MCLIP, Sen.Inf.Researcher, BBC Inf.& Arch., London. [0056760] 09/10/1998
Schots Miss S, L.& Doc.Specialist, UNESCO-UNEVOC Cent., Germany. [0051709] 01/07/1995
Schulenburg Mrs DA, BA(Hons) PGDip MPhil, Unemployed. [0057323] 09/02/1999
Schulte-Nahring Mr S, (was Schulte Gen Naehring), DipLib MCLIP, Inf.Offr., Drugscope, London. [0050034] 22/02/1994
Schultz Mr RJ, L.Asst., Harris L., Preston. [0047645] 09/10/1992 **AF**
Schwier Miss JA, Student. [0059468] 04/04/2001
Sciberras Ms L, MA AIL FCLIP, Sen.Lect.in L.Stud., Univ.of Malta. [0017701] 21/09/1967 **FE 23/07/1997**
Scicinska Mrs I, BA, Stud., Thames Valley Univ. [0053802] 02/10/1996
Scoales Mr RA, MA MCLIP, Retired. [0013027] 05/01/1961
Scobbie Mr AA, BA MCLIP, Jun.Mobile Lib., The Midlothian Council. [0024803] 22/09/1975
Scolari Mr A, PhD, Dir., Univ.of Genova-Engineer L., Italy. [0045938] 26/07/1991
Scoones Miss J, BA DipLib MCLIP, L.Serv.Mgr., Trowers & Hamlins, London. [0036451] 06/10/1983
Scoones Mr MA, BSc MPhil FCLIP, Life Member, Tel.01895 672203, 69 Herlwyn Ave., Ruislip, Middx., HA4 6HE. [0013031] 28/08/1952 **FE 01/01/1957**
Scorah Mrs VE, Unemployed. [0039612] 01/04/1986
Scorey Ms SA, (was Cave), BA PGCE MCLIP, Head of Inf., Coll.of Law, London. [0040953] 01/10/1987
Scorgie Mrs J, (was Burton-Scorgie), Unemployed. [0044273] 07/08/1990
Scothern Miss C, BA(Hons) MA, Asst.Lib., Derbys.C.C. [0056899] 02/11/1998
Scothern Ms EM, BA MCLIP, Unemployed. [0030251] 08/01/1979
Scotney Miss LH, MSc MCLIP, Head L.Serv., Army L.Serv., L.H.Q., Cyprus. [0031939] 01/01/1980
Scotney Miss RE, MA, Unemployed. [0059346] 12/02/2001
Scott Mrs A, (was Reynolds), DipLib MCLIP, Princ.Offr., Comm.L.& Lifelong Learning, City of Sunderland. [0033832] 01/01/1971
Scott Ms A, BA DipLib MCLIP, Asst.Dir.-L., L.B.of Croydon, Cent.L. [0031940] 10/01/1980
Scott Dr AD, MA FSAILIS, Retired. [0013032] 02/04/1963
Scott Mrs B, (was Pugh), BLib MCLIP, Lib., Penrith L., Cumbria. [0029529] 22/09/1978
Scott Mr C, BA MCLIP, Strategic Mgr., Coventry City L. [0029819] 30/09/1978
Scott Mr C, Stud., Univ.of Aberystwyth. [0059647] 10/07/2001
Scott Mrs C, BA, p./t.Stud./L.Asst., Bristol Univ., Porthcawl L. [0061018] 01/02/2002
Scott Dr CF, MA MCLIP, Life Member. [0013040] 05/01/1961
Scott Mrs CL, (was Agnew), BA(Hons) MA MCLIP, Head of Collection Mgmt.Section, Main.L., Univ.of Sheffield. [0046582] 20/11/1991
Scott Mrs CS, (was Watson), BA MCLIP, Freelance Indexer. [0022483] 12/06/1974
Scott Miss DS, BA(Hons), L.Asst., Periodicals, The L., Anglia Poly.Univ. [0058419] 04/02/2000 **AF**
Scott Miss ES, BA FCLIP, Sch.Lib., Dundee City Council Educ.Dept. [0013047] 04/01/1972 **FE 15/10/2002**
Scott Miss EW, MCLIP, Research Support Offr., Learning Skills Council, Truro, Cornwall. [0028673] 17/01/1978
Scott Miss FA, MCLIP, Life Member. [0013048] 12/02/1951
Scott Mrs FJ, (was Buxton), BA MCLIP, Community Inf.Worker, Cent.L., Dundee. [0027916] 09/10/1977
Scott Mr G, MA BA MCLIP, Asst.Area Lib., Bolton P.L. [0013051] 04/02/1965
Scott Ms HV, BA(Hons) MSc MCLIP, Subject Specialist, Univ.of E.London Learning Res. [0051415] 10/02/1995
Scott Ms IMM, MA(Hons) DipEd DipLib MCLIP, Serv.Devel.Lib., Curriculum Res.& Inf.Serv., Aberdeen. [0032818] 02/09/1980
Scott Mrs J, (was Budge), BA MA MCLIP, Lib.-Inf.& Bibl.Serv., Derbys.C.C., Dronfield. [0046786] 23/01/1992
Scott Miss JA, BA(Hons) DipLib MCLIP, Lib., The Upper Bann Inst.of F.& H.E., Portadown Campus. [0033145] 02/10/1980
Scott Ms JM, BA DipLib, Site Lib., Barnes L., Med.Sch., Univ.of Birmingham. [0035903] 24/01/1983
Scott Mrs KM, (was Stanfield), MCLIP, Legal L.Consultant, Self-Employed, Kingston, Surrey. [0013882] 18/02/1972
Scott Mrs LB, (was Hacker), BA MCLIP, Team Lib., Norfolk C.C. [0006076] 18/01/1971
Scott Mrs LC, MCLIP, Unemployed. [0025652] 26/01/1976
Scott Miss LV, MCLIP, Sen.Lib., Min.of Defence, London. [0013061] 21/10/1974
Scott Mrs LV, (was Cooper), BA(Hons) MSc(Econ) MCLIP, Local Studies Lib., Sch.L.Serv., Powys [0056322] 14/05/1998

Scott Mrs M, (was Blitz), MCLIP, Asst.Lib., Bancrofts Sch., Essex. [0001394] 01/02/1970
Scott Ms M, MCLIP, Sen.Lib., N.Ayrshire Council, Irvine L. [0013063] 06/01/1972
Scott Mrs MA, (was Bryan), BLIB MCLIP, P/t.Asst.Lib., L.& Mus.Dept., Cheshire Co.Council. [0013062] 24/02/1970
Scott Mr MC, MA MCLIP, Sen.Lib., Corporation of London, London Metropolitan Arch. [0013064] 15/01/1970
Scott Miss ML, MCLIP, Unemployed. [0028900] 30/01/1978
Scott Ms NR, BA DipLib MCLIP, Dep.Learning Centre Mgr., Hackney Comm.Coll., Shoreditch Campus Learning Centre. [0031696] 02/11/1979
Scott Miss OD, FCLIP, Life Member, 51 Bank St., Glasgow, G12 8NF. [0013066] 11/10/1944 **FE 01/01/1961**
Scott Mr P, BA DipLib MCLIP, I.T.Mgr., Wirral P.L. [0031772] 12/12/1979
Scott Mrs PA, MCLIP, Asst.Team Lib., Suffolk C.C., Cent.L., Bury St.Edmunds. [0029497] 01/01/1968
Scott Mr PJ, BLS(Hons) MCLIP, Inf./Special Serv.Lib., Derbys.C.C., Chesterfield. [0036795] 01/01/1984
Scott Miss PK, BA MCLIP, Serv.Serv.Lib., Army L.Serv., MOD., Upavon, Wilts. [0033558] 19/01/1981
Scott Mrs PM, (was Bramley), Retired. [0049965] 01/02/1994
Scott Mr PR, BA MA PGCE MCLIP, Campus Lib., Schiller Internat.Univ., London. [0023828] 18/12/1963
Scott Mr RS, BSc MBA MCLIP, Employment not known. [0060637] 11/12/2001
Scott Mrs S, (was Young), MA MCLIP, Asst.Lib., Robert Gordon Univ. [0018262] 03/10/1972
Scott Mr SA, BA(Hons) MCLIP, Asst.Lib., Kidderminster L., Worcs. [0043406] 18/10/1989
Scott Mrs SA, Stud., Univ.of Northumbria at, Newcastle, & P./t.L.Asst., Br.L., Darlington. [0058554] 01/04/2000
Scott Mr SGM, BA DipLib MCLIP, L.Online Editor, Univ.of Edinburgh, Edinburgh. [0026548] 01/10/1976
Scott Miss V, BA(Hons), Learning Asst., Peoples Coll., Nottingham. [0057547] 28/04/1919 **AF**
Scott Ms VC, MA MCLIP, Pub.Inf.Offr., Tameside M.B.C., Audenshaw. [0042356] 17/10/1988
Scott Cree Mr JA, MA FCLIP, Sen.Lib., Dept.of Health, London. [0035101] 03/09/1982 **FE 23/09/1998**
Scott-Denness Miss H, BSc(Hons) MCLIP, Asst.Mgr., Inf.Centre, Knight Frank, London. [0048872] 07/07/1993
Scott-Picton Miss LS, BA(Hons) MLib MCLIP, Tech.Servs.Lib., Plymouth Coll.of F.E. [0044404] 05/10/1990
Scotting Mrs R, (was Lines), BLib MCLIP, Lib.:Young Peoples Serv., N.Lincs.C., Riddings L. [0034694] 30/01/1968
Scougal Mrs VJ, BSc(Hons)CertEd DipIM, Client Product Adviser, Limes Softward Ltd., London. [0048277] 20/11/1992
Scoular Miss LM, MA DipLib MCLIP, Retired. [0028674] 01/01/1978
Scourfield Mrs KJ, (was Keen), BA(Hons) MCLIP, [0040207] 08/11/1986
Scown Mr JM, BA MCLIP, Team Lib.:Lend., Somerset Co.L., Taunton. [0037566] 02/10/1984
Scragg Mr ADR, MA LLB DipHE MCLIP, Princ.L.Offr., Wolverhampton MBC. [0030255] 06/12/1978
Scragg Mrs B, (was Knowles), MCLIP, Retired, (2001 Fellow of the John Rylands, Research Inst.) [0008504] 11/01/1957
Scragg Mrs S, (was Street), BA MCLIP, Grp.Lib., Northwich, Cheshire C.C. [0024988] 22/03/1963
Scragg Mrs TM, (was Cleary), MA BLS(Hons) MCLIP, Head of Child.& Sch.Serv., Solihull M.B.C. [0027928] 17/10/1977
Scragg Mr TW, BA MA BPhil SSC FCLIP FRGS, Retired. [0021760] 14/01/1974 **FE 27/02/1991**
Scriven Miss AJ, Child.& Young Peoples Lib., Weston Pavell L. [0059179] 07/12/2000
Scriven Mrs DA, (was Helliar), BLib MCLIP, Lib.:Local Stud., Wakefield Met.Dist.L. [0006693] 02/02/1972
Scrivens Miss BN, MCLIP, Life Member. [0013075] 12/09/1942
Scrogham Mr MA, BA(Hons), Stud., Northumbria Univ. [0061687] 21/10/2002
Scruby Mr JD, FCLIP, Life Member. [0013076] 18/01/1939 **FE 01/01/1955**
Scruton Miss CK, BA MCLIP, Asst.Lib., Mitchell L., Glasgow Dist.L. [0028675] 08/01/1978
Scull Mrs N, Knowledge Offr., Andersen, London. [0053431] 19/06/1996
Scully Mr ER, BA MCLIP, Lib., Medicines Control Agency, London. [0035628] 09/11/1982
Scully Mrs N, (was Bullard), BA DipLib MCLIP, Asst.Lib. p./t., Weymouth L., Dorset. [0041718] 22/02/1988
Scurfield Miss JG, FCLIP, Retired. [0013077] 20/01/1936 **FE 01/01/1943**
Scutchings Ms L, BA(Hons) MSc, Sen.L.Asst., Edward Boyle L., Univ.of Leeds. [0053959] 16/01/1996
Scutt Mrs CE, BA MCLIP, Inf.Consultant/Freelance Lib., Self-employed, Loughborough,Leics. [0025185] 23/11/1975
Scutt Ms CS, BA(Hons), Stud. [0058314] 10/01/2000
Scutt Ms EM, (was Baker), BA DipLib CertEd MCLIP, Head of L.Serv., W.Kent Coll., Tonbridge. [0025208] 05/01/1976
Sdunnus Ms U, MA, p./t.Stud., Univ.Coll.London, Univ.of London, Warburg Inst. [0061046] 05/02/2002
Seabourne Miss J, BA(Hons) DipLIS MCLIP, Site Lib., Surrey Inst.of Art & Design, Epsom. [0043260] 12/10/1989
Seabridge Mrs CB, (was Allen), MCLIP, Research Lib., OCE (UK) Ltd, Rolls-Royce, Bristol. [0003165] 15/02/1970
Seabrook Mrs EC, (was Farrell), BMUS MSC MCLIP, Indexer. [0029959] 26/10/1978

Seager Mrs HJ, MA, Dep.Inf.Mgr., Univ.of Manchester & UMIST Careers, Manchester. [0057947] 04/10/1999
Seager Miss LR, MA(Hons) MLib MCLIP, Asst.Lib., The London L. [0049273] 20/10/1993
Seagrave Mr DJ, BA(Hons) DipILM, Unemployed. [0055605] 24/10/1997
Seagroatt Mr EH, FCLIP, Life Member, Athenaeum L., Church Alley, Liverpool, L1 3DD. [0013082] 30/03/1938 **FE 01/01/1946**
Seale Miss LJ, BA, Grad.Trainee, The London L. [0061458] 02/08/2002
Sealey Miss MMT, MCLIP, Life Member. [0013087] 13/01/1947
Sealy Miss AM, MCLIP, L.Asst., L.B.of Lewisham. [0020127] 14/02/1973
Seaman Miss JM, BA MCLIP, Lib., TICRE, MOD, Beeston, Nottingham. [0013090] 03/01/1970
Seaman Miss ML, BA MSc MCLIP, Head of Knowledge Mgmt., Higher Educ.Funding Council for, England (HEFCE), Bristol. [0041008] 01/10/1987
Seaman Mr P, BA(Hons), Principal Inf.Asst., Univ.of Salford. [0051233] 01/02/1994
Seamens Mrs MM, (was Reid), MCLIP, Lib.(Job Share), Bannockburn Community L., Stirling Council. [0012276] 10/10/1971
Sear Miss NJ, Stud., Univ.of Brighton. [0061293] 14/05/2002
Searl Mrs M, (was Brown), MCLIP, [0001903] 04/04/1962
Searle Mrs JS, (was Pickett), BEd(Hons), Inf.Specialist, L.& Inf.Cent., Qinetiq, Farnborough. [0056354] 08/06/1998
Searle Mr M, MA MCLIP, H.of Collection Serv., Radcliffe Sci.L., Oxford. [0028902] 31/01/1978
Searson Mrs KP, (was Gardner), B LIB MCLIP, Learning Resources Mgr., The Brunts Sch., Mansfield, Notts. [0027977] 07/10/1977
Seaton Miss J, B SOC SC FCLIP, Head of Research & Inf.Serv., Scottish Parliament. [0020265] 21/02/1973 **FE 18/03/1985**
Seaton Miss JG, BA DipLib MCLIP, Catg.Ed./Quality Controller, Univ.of N.London. [0013097] 01/10/1969
Seaton Mrs SM, BA DipLib MCLIP, p./t.Lib., Leigh Park L., Hants.C.C. [0032169] 12/02/1980
Seaword Miss LF, Unemployed. [0041233] 21/10/1987
Sebamalai Miss AP, ASLLA DipLib, L.Asst., Blackheath L., L.B.of Greenwich. [0039779] 01/07/1986
Sebury Mr PL, BA(Hons) DipLib, Asst.Lib., Wales Youth Agency. [0042382] 26/10/1988
Seddon Ms JA, MCLIP DipLib, p./t.Inf.Mgmt.Systems Consultant, Fretwell-Downing, Sheffield. [0037101] 21/02/1984
Seddon Mrs L, (was Baker), BA(Hons) DipLib MCLIP, Reports Lib., Royal Military Coll.of Sci., Shrivenham,Wilts. [0039985] 13/10/1986
Sedgley Mrs FMM, (was Wilson), BA DipLib, Inf.Asst., St.Michael's Hosp., S.Staffs.Healthcare NHS Trust. [0034264] 14/10/1981
Seedhouse Mrs EP, (was Hart), MCLIP, Sen.Asst.Lib., Dudley M.B.C. [0006466] 01/11/1970
Seeley Mr J, B ED MCLIP, Lib.:Res., Doncaster M.B.C., Carcroft L.H.Q. [0038610] 19/07/1985
Seeney Mr RWL, BA(Hons) MA MSc, Dept.Lib., Univ.of Leeds, Sch.of English. [0058756] 06/07/2000
Seffen Mrs LG, MA, Asst.Lib., Faculty of Educ., Univ.of Cambridge. [0057979] 08/10/1999
Sefton Ms A, (was Holland), Inf.Specialist, Cent.Sci.Lab., York. [0046398] 01/11/1991
Segal Mr K, BA, Subject Lib.(Computing), Middlesex Univ., London. [0038072] 17/01/1985
Segbert Mrs M, DipBibl MBE HonFCLIP, Head,Inf.& Books, The Brit.Council, Germany. [0044286] 13/08/1990 **FE 10/10/1995**
Segel Mrs SE, BA(Hons), Lib., L.B.of Haringey, Hornsey L. [0061713] 24/10/2002
Sekioka Miss T, MSc(Econ), Sch.Lib., Japanishe Internat.Schule, e.v in Dusseldorf. [0056914] 04/11/1998
Selby Mrs CG, (was Nutt), MSc(Econ) MCLIP, Princ.Lib., Sch.L.Serv., Caerphilly Bor. [0020514] 01/03/1973
Selby Mr GA, FCLIP, Life Member. [0013106] 10/04/1930 **FE 01/01/1940**
Selby Miss J, BSc, Sen.L.Asst., Univ.of Wales, Swansea. [0028152] 06/11/1977 **AF**
Selby Miss JF, MCLIP, Sen.Lib., Hants.Co.L., Winchester Lend. [0022496] 04/06/1974
Selby Miss JR, FCLIP, Retired. [0013107] 12/11/1943 **FE 01/01/1955**
Selby Mrs N, (was McSorley), MA DipLib MCLIP, Asst.Support Serv.Mgr., Hants.C.C., Winchester. [0037485] 04/10/1984
Self Mrs D, (was Bodsworth), MCLIP, Retired. [0013108] 08/02/1957
Sellar Mrs LD, (was Pickering), BA DipLib MCLIP, Subject Lib., Oxford Brookes Univ. [0022851] 03/10/1974
Sellars Mr JP, B LIB MCLIP, Sen.Lib.(Inf.Tech.), Nottingham City L. [0024805] 05/10/1975
Sellars Mrs VA, (was Chidwick), B LIB MCLIP, Sen.Lib., Arts L., Nottingham Cent.L. [0025727] 27/02/1976
Selleck Mrs A, City Child.Lib., Plymouth City Council. [0056507] 04/08/1998 **AF**
Sellers Rev JM, BA MCLIP, Methodist Minister. [0013112] 24/08/1968
Selley Miss MGL, BA(Hons), Sch.Lib., Putteridge High Sch., Luton. [0049115] 06/10/1993
Sellwood Mrs KJ, p./t.Stud./Sen.L.Asst., Uni.Wales Aberystwyth, Cent.L., Merthyr Tydfil. [0061370] 01/07/2002
Selman Mr D, BA(Hons) MA, ILS Serv.Mgr., Ministry of Defence Inf., London. [0054057] 24/10/1996
Selwood Miss AM, BA MPhil MCLIP, Asst.Lib., Nat.L.of Wales, Aberystwyth. [0019185] 07/08/1972
Selwyn Mrs PM, (was Black), BA MCLIP, Asst.Lib., Univ.of Wales, Lampeter, Lampeter, Dyfed. [0001332] 24/07/1961
Sembhi Ms JL, BA(Hons) MA MCLIP, Asst.Lib., D.J.Freeman, London. [0053633] 19/08/1996

345

Semmens Mr J, BA(Hons), Lib., Lenkiewicz Foundation, Plymouth. [0059943] *08/11/2001*
Semple Mrs G, Programme Mgr., BSI DISC, London. [0022894] *01/10/1974*
Semple Mrs H, (was Cameron), BLib MCLIP, Lib., Law Soc.of N.Ireland, Belfast. [0043638] *13/11/1989*
Semple Miss ME, MCLIP, Retired. [0017712] *11/07/1946*
Semple Mr PS, BA DipLib MCLIP FRSA, Subject Lib.(Art), London Guildhall Univ. [0029416] *14/07/1978*
Sen Mrs BA, (was Foster), BA(Hons) MA MCLIP, Lect., Liverpool John Moores Univ., Liverpool Business Sch. [0046578] *19/11/1991*
Sen Mrs JC, (was Morgan), BA MCLIP, Head of Collections Mgmt., John Rylands Univ.L., Univ.of Manchester. [0013123] *18/09/1967*
Sen Miss L, MA(Hons) MSc, L.Asst., Clydebank Coll.L., Clydebank. [0061397] *20/06/2002*
Senadeera Mr NTSA, BA MCLIP, Lib., Univ.of Peradeniya, Sri Lanka. [0017713] *10/10/1967*
Senadhira Dr MAP, FCLIP PhD, Life Member. [0017714] *04/10/1963* **FE 01/01/1974**
Senior Mrs C, (was Lockwood), BA, Sen.L.Asst., Univ.of Northumbria, Newcastle upon Tyne. [0036962] *18/01/1984*
Senior Mr CM, BA DipLib MCLIP ILTM, Faculty Team Leader, Brotherton L., Univ.of Leeds. [0041974] *01/07/1988*
Senior Miss K, BA(Hons) DipILS MCLIP, Reader Devel.Offr., Blackburn L., Blackburn with Darwen Bor.Council. [0040258] *11/11/1986*
Senior Mrs KW, (was Little), BA MCLIP MLib, Learn.Supp.Serv.Mgr., Bolton Inst.of H.E. [0013129] *03/10/1968*
Sennitt Ms JC, BA(Hons) MA MCLIP, Lib., L.Serv.for Educ., Leics.C.C. [0054172] *04/11/1996*
Sentongo Miss DNM, DipLib, Catrr., Makerere Univ., Uganda. [0035383] *04/10/1982*
Sephton Mr RS, BA FCLIP LTCL CertEd, Life Member, Tel.01865 730627, 33 Colley Wood, Kennington, Oxford, OX1 5NF. [0013133] *03/04/1945* **FE 01/01/1965**
Serebriakoff Ms EM, BSc, Stud., City Univ., London &, Inf.Asst., St Thomas' Med.L., St Thomas' Hosp., London. [0058994] *17/10/2000*
Sergeant Mrs CA, (was Goddard), BA MCLIP, Sch.Lib., Falkirk Council, Falkirk. [0028571] *10/01/1978*
Sergeant Miss V, BA(Hons), Position unknown, Health & Safety Exec. [0058907] *03/10/2000*
Serjeant Mr FP, BA DipLib, Local Hist.Lib., L.B.Hammersmith & Fulham. [0033880] *05/04/1981*
Serjeant Mrs ME, (was Beresford), BA DipLib MCLIP, F./t.Lib., Kingston Grammar Sch., Surrey. [0023757] *22/01/1975*
Serjeantson Mr M, BA DipLib MCLIP, Resident in New Zealand. [0023749] *02/02/1975*
Sermon Mrs KM, (was Warr), BA MSc MCLIP, Mother. [0042980] *15/05/1989*
Service Mr DJ, MA(Hons) DipLIS MCLIP, Inf.Serv.Offr., Scottish Intercollegiate, Royal Coll.of Physicians. [0049190] *12/10/1993*
Service Ms FM, BA MCLIP, Learning & Inf.Serv.Devel.Offr., N.E.Lincs Council, Grimsby. [0043761] *01/01/1990*
Setterfield Ms GJ, BA(Hons) MA, Asst.Lib., London Inst., Dept of Learning Resources. [0056149] *16/03/1998*
Setterfield Miss PJ, BSc, Stud., Univ.of Wales, Aberystwyth. [0061488] *19/08/2002*
Severino Miss A, BA(Hons), Stud. [0059226] *09/01/2001*
Sevier Miss AH, Asst.Lib., RAF Alconbury Base L., Cambs. [0043894] *12/02/1990*
Sewell Mrs AM, (was Dixon), MA FCLIP, Retired. [0007070] *25/09/1953* **FE 01/01/1966**
Sewell Mrs JA, (was Hardwicke), Asst.Lib., Bushey Hall Sch., Herts. [0049241] *18/10/1993* **AF**
Sewell Ms W, BSc MS DSC, Self-employed Consultant, USA. [0034432] *10/11/1981*
Sewerniak Ms AT, BSc(Hons) DipLIS MCLIP, Sen.Inf.Offr., The Chartered Soc.of Physiotherapy, London. [0043321] *19/10/1989*
Seyfried Mrs M, (was Cooksey), L.Operations Mgr., Allen & Overy, London. [0050541] *08/09/1994*
Seymour Mr AJ, BA(Hons), Grad.Trainee-Asst.Inf.Researcher, Dept.Trade & Industry. [0059693] *08/08/2001*
Seymour Mrs SM, BA DipLib MCLIP MPHIL, Lib., Arnewood Sch., New Milton, Hants. [0027368] *20/02/1977*
Seymour Ms VA, BA MCLIP, Sub-Lib., Nat.Univ.of Ireland Maynooth, Co.Kildare, Ireland. [0022109] *31/01/1974*
Sfrijan Mrs SM, (was Richardson), MCLIP, Princ.Lib., Rochdale M.B.C. [0012376] *23/10/1964*
Sfther Ms R, (was Ragnhild Saether), Lib., Bergen Offentlige Bibliotek, Bergen. [0052743] *01/12/1995*
Shackle Mr RWS, MCLIP, Lib., Colchester L., Essex. [0013154] *11/02/1967*
Shackleton Mr AJ, BA DipLib MCLIP, Translator & Book Editor, Self-employed. [0030535] *03/02/1979*
Shackleton Mrs JL, (was Pope), MCLIP, Requests Lib., Hampshire Co.L., Alton L. [0011810] *01/01/1969*
Shackleton Miss KE, BA MCLIP, Lib., Kent C.C. [0035830] *28/01/1983*
Shackleton Mr P, MA Dip LS, Asst.Lib., Camberwell Coll.of Arts, London. [0047202] *02/01/1997*
Shackleton Mrs SM, (was Richardson), MCLIP, Life Member. [0013158] *05/09/1951*
Shadbolt Mrs J, BA MCLIP, Sen.Lib., Cent.Dist., Longsight L., Manchester City Council. [0031942] *08/01/1980*
Shadbolt Miss VVM, BA MCLIP, Sen.Lib., Arup Group, London. [0022293] *01/04/1974*
Shafe Mr M, BSc MCLIP, Life Member. [0013160] *02/06/1959*
Shafee Rev KH, CertTh MCLIP, Life Member. [0013161] *20/01/1961*
Shah Ms HC, BA(Hons) DipILM MCLIP, Database Lib., Trafford M.B.C., Manchester. [0050759] *18/10/1994*

Shah Miss MK, BA MCLIP, Lib., WJB Chiltern plc., London. [0035606] *07/11/1982*
Shah Mr PR, BSc MCLIP, Retired. [0017719] *24/05/1954*
Shahtahmasebi Mrs BE, (was Cassidy), BA(Hons), Resident in New Zealand. [0037254] *14/05/1984*
Shaikh Miss H, BA(Hons) MCLIP, Inf.Scientist, Royal Coll.of Physicons of L., London. [0044695] *28/11/1990*
Shaikh Mrs LM, (was Gamage), BA (Hons), Asst.Lib., Linklaters & Paines, London. [0037562] *01/10/1984*
Shakeshaft Miss GC, BA MA, Asst.Lib., The Cheltenham Ladies Coll., Glos. [0050647] *06/10/1994*
Shakespeare Mr AD, BSc, Temp.Asst.Lib., DWP Legal L., London. [0055886] *09/12/1997*
Shakespeare Mrs EJ, Learning Res.Cent.Mgr., John Mason Sch., Abingdon, Oxon. [0056374] *01/07/1998* **AF**
Shakespeare Mrs HN, (was Mount), BA(Hons), Learning Res.Co-ordinator, New Coll.of F.E., Redditch, Worcs. [0056213] *07/04/1998*
Shakespeare Ms K, BA(Hons) MA MCLIP, Asst.Lib.(Loans), Frewen L., Univ.of Portsmouth. [0048178] *11/11/1992*
Shallcross Mrs E, BSc(Hons) DipILS, L.Asst., Queen Mother L.,(Taylor L.), Old Aberdeen, Univ.of Aberdeen. [0053114] *13/03/1996*
Shallcross Ms GM, BSc(Hons), L.Asst., Univ.of Derby. [0059125] *21/11/2000*
Shanks Miss JE, BA(Hons), Resident in Australia. [0049648] *18/11/1993*
Shannon Ms CS, (was Smyth), BA(Hons) DipLib, Lib., Grad.Sch. of Educ., Queen's Univ.Belfast. [0044608] *05/11/1990*
Shannon Miss ML, BA MA MCLIP, Sen.Lib., Research L., Cheshire C.C. [0037850] *06/11/1984*
Shannon Miss RM, Project Mgr., Brit.Standards Inst., London. [0042349] *12/10/1988*
Shannon Ms VE, BA MCLIP, Div.Inf.Specialist, Chester L., Cheshire C.C. [0030339] *01/01/1970*
Shaper Mrs SA, (was Smith), DipLib MA(Ed) MCLIP, Dir.of L.Res., The Broxbourne Sch., Herts. [0023706] *01/01/1975*
Shapiro Mrs CM, (was Dresback), MA, Unemployed. [0057939] *01/10/1999*
Shapland Mrs J, (was Clinton), MCLIP, p./t.Sch.Lib., Birkdale Sch., Sheffield. [0002860] *01/01/1968*
Shapley Mr DA, Tech.Indexer/Abstractor, 6 Cranley Place, London SW7 3AB. [0013168] *22/07/1971*
Sharkey Ms P, BA(Hons) MCLIP, Child.Lib., N.Tyneside Council. [0048669] *08/04/1993*
Sharma Miss N, BA, Inf.Asst., City Univ., London. [0058453] *22/02/2000*
Sharma Mr ND, BSc MCLIP, Employment not known. [0060487] *11/12/2001*
Sharman Miss AJ, BSc MCLIP, Learning Advisor, Univ.of Lincs.& Humberside. [0042157] *06/10/1988*
Sharman Mrs GS, (was Tricker), BA MCLIP, Market Intelligence Mgr., NHS purchasing supply agency., Berkshire. [0034140] *05/10/1981*
Sharman Ms GSP, BSc(Hons), Stud., Strathclyde Univ. [0058085] *25/10/1999*
Sharman Miss J, MCLIP, Retired. [0013175] *07/02/1953*
Sharman Mr M, (was Bartlett), MCLIP, Lib., St.Martins Hosp., Canterbury. [0000874] *07/10/1964*
Sharp Ms A, BLS(Hons), Lib., Nottingham City Council, Leisure & Comm.Serv. [0036113] *07/02/1983*
Sharp Dr B, BSc MPhil PhD MBCS MCLIP, Position unknown, Staffordshire Univ. [0060612] *11/12/2001*
Sharp Ms C, (was Davidson), BSc(Hons) MSc MCLIP, Sch.Lib., Springbank Academy, Glasgow Council. [0056810] *23/10/1998*
Sharp Mrs CA, (was Head), MSc MCLIP, Catg.Super., Royal Horticultural Soc., London. [0013179] *05/02/1968*
Sharp Miss CB, BA MA, L.Asst., Balne Lane L., Wakefield. [0059358] *14/02/2001*
Sharp Mrs CH, (was Morris), BA MCLIP, Lib., Kirriemuir L. [0027836] *30/08/1977*
Sharp Ms DC, (was Ross), BA MSc MCLIP, Workplace Travel Plan Offr., W.Yorkshire P.T.E., Leeds. [0025646] *27/01/1976*
Sharp Mr DG, Inf.Offr., N.Lanarkshire Council. [0024235] *29/04/1975*
Sharp Mr DK, BA MCLIP, Deputy Head - (User Serv.), BFI Nat.L., London. [0013180] *01/01/1970*
Sharp Mrs J, L.Asst., Stockport M.B.C. [0057207] *15/01/1999*
Sharp Ms JM, (was Bennett), BA DipLib MCLIP, Princ.Offr.:N.Dist., Manchester P.L. [0034831] *01/03/1982*
Sharp Mr JR, FCLIP, Retired. [0013187] *23/02/1939* **FE 01/01/1952**
Sharp Miss LJ, B LIB MCLIP, Team Lib., Greasby L., Met.Boro.of Wirral. [0027710] *13/07/1977*
Sharp Miss LM, BA(Hons) MA, Grad.Trainee, Surrey Univ.L. [0061677] *17/10/2002*
Sharp Mrs REA, (was Wallis), BA MCLIP, Unemployed. [0041518] *11/01/1988*
Sharp Mrs SJ, (was Patton), BA MCLIP, IT Devel.Mgr., Leeds L.& Inf.Serv. [0044931] *21/01/1991*
Sharp Mr SL, BA(Hons) MCLIP, Saber Team Leader, Brotherton L., Univ.of Leeds. [0039009] *25/10/1985*
Sharp Mr SP, BA(Hons) MSc(Econ) MCLIP, Electronic Inf.Lib., N.Staffs.Med.Inst.L. [0054250] *13/11/1996*
Sharpe Ms AV, BA DipLib MCLIP, Sen.Specialist:Adult Serv., S.Dist., Leics.L.& Inf.Serv. [0029346] *05/06/1978*
Sharpe Mr D, BA MA MCLIP, Staff Development Offr., City L.& Arts Cent., Sunderland. [0031120] *29/08/1979*
Sharpe Mrs G, (was Bracewell), BA MCLIP, Hosp Lib., Notts. C.C., Rampton Hosp. [0033275] *18/11/1980*
Sharpin Mr CE, BSc MSc, Asst.Lib., Royal Coll.of Surgeons, London. [0052775] *11/12/1995*
Sharples Mr C, BA(Hons), Stud., Loughborough Univ. [0059983] *15/11/2001*
Sharples Mrs P, (was Linsley), BA(Hons) MCLIP, Lib., Park View Community Sch., Durham. [0046688] *11/11/1991*
Sharr Mrs F, (was Mckeand), MCLIP ALAA, Life Member, 58 The Ave., Nedlands, Western Australia 6009. [0017724] *14/03/1938*

Sharr Mr FA, OBE BA FCLIP FLAA ARPS DLitt, Life Member, 58 The Avenue, Nedlands, Western Australia 6009. [0020090] 15/10/1935 **FE 01/01/1939**
Sharrock Mrs HM, Sensory Impairment Info.Asst., Bury MBC. [0056874] 27/10/1998
Sharrock Mrs MI, (was Ashworth), BA MCLIP, Sch.Lib., Kimberley Sch., Nottingham. [0038547] 18/06/1985
Sharrock Mr RA, BA MCLIP, Lib., SATIC, Ministry of Defence, Nottingham. [0033148] 06/10/1980
Sharrocks Miss H, MCLIP, Life Member. [0013198] 18/03/1939
Sharwood Miss R, BLib MCLIP, Asst.Lib., Sidley Austin Brown & Wood, London. [0047007] 01/04/1992
Shaughnessy Miss EM, BA(Hons) DipILM, L.Mgr., Morley Coll., London. [0047236] 16/06/1992
Shaughnessy Miss M, BA DipLib MCLIP, Asst.Lib., Dept.of Health, Catg.& data Quality Unit. [0033698] 12/01/1981
Shaw Mrs AE, (was Cutler), MCLIP, Team Leader, GMOCN, Manchester. [0018082] 01/10/1972
Shaw Mrs B, (was Bruce), MA DipLib MCLIP, Lib., E.Renfrewshire, Carolside Primary Sch. [0034359] 21/10/1981
Shaw Mr BA, BA CertEd, Unemployed. [0043843] 06/02/1990 **AF**
Shaw Mrs C, BA MCLIP, Stock Offr., Bristol Cent.L., Bristol City Council. [0018188] 10/10/1972
Shaw Mrs CJ, (was Clark), BA MCLIP, Head of Team - L.& Res., The Magnus Church of England Sch., Newark, Notts. [0013206] 16/10/1967
Shaw Mrs CM, (was Quaile), MA MCLIP, Marketing Media Offr., A-Z Supplies Ltd., Essex. [0013207] 09/01/1970
Shaw Mr D, MA MCLIP, Retired. [0013208] 24/10/1966
Shaw Mrs DA, (was Davies), BA(Hons) PGCE MCLIP, Career Break. [0036632] 30/10/1983
Shaw Mr DE, Position unknown, MOD, Swindon. [0054746] 01/04/1997
Shaw Mr DN, BA DipEdTech MCLIP DMS, Inf.Offr., N.Lanarkshire Council. [0013209] 14/02/1970
Shaw Miss GE, BA MCLIP, Admin., Hammersmith & Fulham Soc.Serv., London. [0013212] 08/11/1966
Shaw Mrs HA, BA(Hons) DipILS, Inf.Asst., Liverpool John Moores Univ. [0049440] 27/10/1993
Shaw Mrs HR, MCLIP, Team Leader, Business Inf.Serv., Birmingham L. [0025413] 06/12/1975
Shaw Mrs IA, (was Presanis), BSc MPhil MCLIP, Dep-Lib., Univ.of London, Goldsmiths Coll. [0011914] 20/10/1967
Shaw Mrs IW, BSc MCLIP, Employment unknown. [0060332] 10/12/2001
Shaw Mrs J, (was Shaw-Brookman), BA DipLib MCLIP, Sen.Asst.Br.Lib., L.B.of Harrow, Pinner L. [0008724] 01/01/1969
Shaw Miss JE, MA BEd MCLIP, H.of L.Systems Div., Univ.of Strathclyde, Glasgow. [0024807] 01/10/1975
Shaw Mrs JG, BSc M PHIL, Retired. [0033149] 01/10/1980
Shaw Mrs JJ, BSc MSc MCLIP, Inf.Sci., Glaxo Holdings. [0034541] 12/12/1981
Shaw Mr JT, MCLIP, Life Member, Tel:0191 528 5374. [0013217] 04/03/1932
Shaw Mrs LE, (was Roberts), MCLIP, Learning Res.Cent.Mgr., Nelson & Colne Coll., Lancs. [0022305] 21/02/1974
Shaw Mrs M, (was Ellis), MCLIP, Sch.Lib., N.E.Lincolnshire. [0004538] 08/11/1970
Shaw Mr MA, BA DipLib MCLIP, Comm.L.Mgr., Nottingham City L's. [0031943] 21/01/1980
Shaw Miss ML, BA MCSP MCLIP, Life Member. [0013223] 14/11/1971
Shaw Mrs PA, MA BA(Hons), p./t.Asst.Inf.Adviser, Aldrich L., Univ.of Brighton. [0061224] 15/04/2002
Shaw Miss RJ, Info.Sci.Team Leader, Unilever R&D Port Sunlight, Wirral. [0061716] 25/10/2002
Shaw Mr SR, MA MSc DipEdTech MCLIP, User Serv.Lib., Univ.of Plymouth. [0013227] 26/06/1972
Shawcross Miss J, Stud., Manchester Metro. [0061703] 22/10/2002
Shawyer Mrs CT, (was Parsons), BA MCLIP, P/t.Inf.Lib., Staines L., Surrey Co.Council. [0011308] 17/10/1969
Sheard Dr JP, BSc PhD MCLIP, Position unknown, Grifols (UK) Ltd., Cambridge. [0060827] 12/12/2001
Sheard Mrs K, (was Mellor), MCLIP, Info & Res.Mgr, Kirklees Sch.Effectiveness Serv., Huddersfield. [0013237] 25/03/1969
Shearer Mrs CM, (was Munro), BA MCLIP, Mother. [0031672] 16/10/1979
Shearer Ms JLC, MA DipLib, Inf.Offr., Essentia Group, Glasgow. [0043581] 09/11/1989
Shearer Mr JR, MA DipLib MCLIP, Inf.Consultant, 12 The Rowans, Cholsey, Oxon., OX10 9LN. [0013239] 12/10/1971
Shearman Mr AP, BA FCLIP, Life Member. [0013240] 10/03/1950 **FE 01/01/1963**
Shearman Mrs CA, (was Hawkins), BA MCLIP, Heritage Serv.Mgr., Herts.Arch.& Local Studies, Herts.C.C. [0039298] 30/01/1986
Shearring Mrs JA, (was Newman), BA MCLIP, Sen.Lib., Orpington L., L.B.of Bromley. [0010762] 01/01/1970
Shears Mrs NMC, BA(Hons) Lib., Trinity Sch., Teignmouth. [0061357] 24/06/2002
Sheasby Mr AE, MCLIP, Retired. [0013244] 06/02/1950
Shedwick Ms LA, BA(Hons) DipLib, Community Lib., Northfield & W.Heath Ls., Birmingham L.Serv. [0031446] 01/10/1979
Sheehan Mrs CB, (was Hewitt), MCLIP, Readers Serv.Lib., Farnborough Coll.of Tech., Hants. [0013245] 08/10/1963
Sheehan Mr JF, BA DipLIS, L.Mgr., United Bristol Healthcare Trust, Bristol Royal Infirmary. [0057689] 02/07/1999
Sheen Ms JH, BA(Hons) DipILS, Water Resources Asst., Environment Agency, Exminster, Devon. [0050166] 20/04/1994
Sheen Mr PA, BA, Research Offr., Learning Skills Council, Bristol. [0052906] 17/01/1996 **AF**
Sheerin Mrs CE, BA DipLib MCLIP, Sch.Lib., MOD. [0034272] 21/10/1981

Sheerin Miss R, BA(Hons) MCLIP, L.Mgr., Cheshire C.C., Chester. [0051717] 25/05/1995
Sheffield Mrs VC, (was Davis), BA MCLIP, Unemployed. [0031250] 09/10/1979
Sheikh Miss A, MSc MCLIP, Employment unknown. [0060340] 10/12/2001
Sheikh Mrs C, (was Polhill), MCLIP, Child.Lib., Hampshire Co.Council, Winchester. [0011775] 01/01/1970
Sheldon Mr MB, BA MCLIP, Br.Lib., Penylan L., Cardiff Co.L.Serv. [0023528] 09/01/1975
Shelley Miss J, BSc(Hons) MA MCLIP, Subj.Lib.(Nurse Educ.), Anglia Poly.Univ., Chelmsford,Essex. [0048152] 11/11/1992
Shelley Mr KM, BA(Hons), Catr., Courtauld Inst.of Art, London. [0055929] 11/12/1997
Shelton Ms A, BA(Hons), Stud., UCL., London. [0058766] 13/07/2000
Shelton Mrs MM, (was Whittle), MCLIP, L.Mgr.(P./t.), W.Lothian Co., Blackburn. [0015786] 01/01/1968
Shemilt Miss CL, BA(Hons) MSc(Econ) MCLIP, L.Network Co-ordinator, BaSE Consortium, Birmingham. [0051186] 23/11/1994
Shemndolwa Mr TR, Resident in Tanzania. [0047601] 05/10/1992
Shenton Mr AK, Research Stud., Sch.Inf.Studies., Univ.of Northumbria. [0043657] 20/11/1989
Shenton Mrs DB, (was Hiden), MCLIP, Rural Serv.Lib., Warwickshire C.C. [0013255] 22/03/1960
Shenton Mr DE, FCLIP, Retired, 31 Kipling Rd.,Stratford upon Avon, CV37 7JY. [0013256] 10/02/1958 **FE 06/10/1977**
Shenton Miss SK, BA(Hons) MA, Trainee Liaison Lib., Univ.of Reading. [0056725] 17/03/1998
Shepherd Mr A, BA DMS MIMgt MCLIP, Learning Res.Mgr., John Kelly Girls Tech.Coll., London. [0013262] 01/10/1965
Shepherd Mr A, MCLIP, Lib.Catr., Norfolk C.C., Norwich. [0013263] 19/02/1965
Shepherd Miss BM, FCLIP, Life Member. [0013266] 08/10/1940 **FE 01/01/1952**
Shepherd Ms FM, DipAD DipLS MCLIP, Records Mgr., The Hay Grp.Mgmnt.Ltd., London. [0025414] 31/12/1975
Shepherd Mrs H, (was Askew), MCLIP, Asst.Lib., Dept.of Trans.Local Govt.and the, Regions, London. [0019901] 01/01/1973
Shepherd Ms JL, BA MCLIP, Lib., Wellington Coll., Crowthorne, Berks. [0024963] 20/10/1975
Shepherd Ms K, (was Woollen), BA MCLIP, Info Co-ordinator, Cambridgeshire ACRE. [0041979] 01/07/1988
Shepherd Mrs NM, (was Morris), BA MCLIP, Sen.Young Person's Lib.(Job Share), Reading Bor.Council. [0013276] 12/10/1970
Shepherd Mr RC, BA DipLib MCLIP, Campus L.Mgr., Anglia Poly.Univ., Cambridge. [0029822] 01/10/1978
Shepherd Mr TD, MA, Stud., Strathclyde Univ. [0060980] 23/01/2002
Shepherd Ms TE, BSc MSC MCLIP, p./t.Teacher, Primary Sch., Notts. [0039550] 01/02/1986
Sheppard Mr C, MSc, Intranet Lib., Dept.for Work & Pensions, London. [0054399] 03/12/1996
Sheppard Mrs DJ, (was Thrall), MCLIP, Sen.Lib. Child.& Young People, Nottingham City Council. [0015215] 20/01/1970
Sheppard Miss J, BA MCLIP, Life Member. [0019540] 07/11/1960
Sheppard Miss SE, BSc(Hons) MCLIP, Stud. [0054454] 09/12/1996
Sheppard Ms SL, BA DipLib MCLIP, Unemployed. [0043042] 01/07/1989
Shercliff Mr WH, MA FCLIP DipArchAdmin CertEd, Life Member. [0013289] 29/04/1948 **FE 01/01/1955**
Sheridan Revd DJ, BA MCLIP, Chaplain, St Giles Hospice, Lichfield, Staffs. [0018312] 01/10/1972
Sheridan Miss J, BA(Hons), Site Lib., Bournemouth & Poole Coll., Dorset. [0059103] 15/11/2000
Sheridan Mrs SA, (was Vessey), BA MA MCLIP, Team Lib.-Ref.Inf.& Local Studies, Kent Arts & L., Ashford. [0040248] 19/11/1986
Sheridan Mr WP, BSc DMC MCLIP, Retired. [0060640] 11/12/2001
Sheriff Mr IP, BSc(Hons) MSc, Inf.Sci., Det Norske Veritas BV, London. [0054529] 14/01/1997
Sherington Ms JO, MA DipLib MCLIP, Ref.Lib., Cent.L., Stirling. [0040243] 10/11/1986
Sherley Mrs HJ, (was Loader), BLib MCLIP, Reader Serv.Lib., Peterborough City Council., Peterborough Cent.L. [0040582] 03/04/1987
Sherlock Mr CJA, BA(Hons), Lib., Lovells, London. [0049177] 08/10/1993
Sherlock Mr CS, Inf.Serv.Mgr., Spectrum Strategy Consultants, London. [0052112] 04/10/1995
Sherlock Miss PM, MCLIP, Lib., Solicitors Indemnity Fund, London. [0013291] 02/11/1962
Sherman Mrs G, (was Wilcox), BSc(Open) MCLIP, p./t.Lib., Wilts.C.C., Calne L. [0013293] 25/03/1968
Sherratt Miss AB, MCLIP, Life Member. [0013294] 15/01/1951
Sherriffs Mr GIF, MA(Hons) DipILS MCLIP, Acquisitions Lib., Royal Bot.Garden, Edinburgh. [0053776] 01/10/1996
Sherrin Miss PA, MCLIP, Life Member. [0013295] 29/02/1960
Sherrington Ms JD, BA(Hons) DipILM MCLIP, Subject Lib., Bradford Coll., Bradford. [0054734] 11/03/1997
Sherrington Miss RJ, BA(Hons), p./t.Stud./Coll.Lib., Univ.of Wales, Aberystwyth, Lipson Comm.Coll. [0057895] 01/10/1999
Sherwell Mr JR, MLib FCLIP MRSC, Digital L.Specialist, GlaxoSmithKline Plc., Harlow. [0018193] 02/10/1972 **FE 18/04/1989**
Sherwin Miss K, BA(Hons), Stud., Sheffield Univ. [0058792] 26/07/2000
Sherwood Mrs DM, (was Blake), MScEcon.DipLib MCLIP, L.Serv.Devel.Mgr., L.B.Wandsworth. [0010097] 23/01/1972
Shetye Mr HS, BA(Econ) BLibSc, Lib., India Inst.local Gov., India. [0061381] 21/06/2002
Shewring Mr PC, MCLIP, Inf.Lib., Univ.of Glamorgan, Pontypridd. [0013300] 14/01/1970
Shibuya Mr Y, Prof.on Lib.Sci., Sagami Women's Univ., Japan. [0027412] 22/03/1977

Shieh Miss LY, BA DipLib MA MCLIP, Asst.Lib., Univ.of Hong Kong Ls., Pokfulam, Hong Kong. [0041006] 02/10/1987
Shiel Ms KA, BSc(Hons) CertEd DipILM, Catg.Lib., Hartelpool Bor. L., Hartlepool. [0046036] 04/09/1991
Shields Miss E, BA(Hons) MSc, Community L.Offr., Stockton Borough Council. [0057225] 22/01/1999
Shields Ms ER, BA(Hons) DipLIS MCLIP, Asst.Lib., Granada, Manchester. [0058625] 18/04/2000
Shiell Ms LM, BA(Hons) MCLIP, Indexer, British Film Inst., London. [0041899] 15/05/1988
Shiels Mrs EC, (was Hunter), MCLIP, Lib., Wilmslow High Sch., Cheshire. [0013302] 31/07/1962
Shiels Ms LM, BSc(Hons) MSc, Inf.Systems Support Analyst, Freshfields Bruckhaus Deringer, London. [0055422] 09/10/1997
Shiels Mr SM, BSc(Hons), Stud., Strathclyde Univ. [0061304] 20/05/2002
Shier Mrs JL, BSc, Stud./Univ.Lib., Leeds Metro.Univ./Univ of Leeds. [0061773] 06/11/2002
Shillcock Miss LE, BA(Hons) DipILM MCLIP, Br.Lib., Wirral Bor.Council. [0053927] 11/10/1996
Shimmon Mr RM, OBE HonFCLIP FCLIP, Secretary General, IFLA, The Hague, The Netherlands. [0013305] 14/04/1961 FE 29/11/1972
Shine Mrs CR, (was Johnson), BA DipLib, L.Asst., Reading B.C. [0040049] 08/10/1986
Shiner Mrs E, BA MCLIP, p./t.Lect., Sandwell Coll., W.Bromwich Campus, W.Midlands. [0013307] 01/01/1964
Shipley Mrs M, Dist.Mgr., Essex C.C.Ls., Chelmsford. [0051081] 14/11/1994 AF
Shipley Mrs M, (was Shakespeare), BA MCLIP, Unemployed. [0042818] 01/03/1989
Shipman Ms CA, p./t.Stud./Sen.L.Asst., Univ.Aberystwyth, Univ.Warwick L. [0059626] 04/07/2001
Shippey Miss IJ, BA(Hons), TalkingBook Title Administrator, R.N.I.B., Peterborough. [0042579] 10/01/1989
Shipsey Ms FM, Serials Lib., Brit.L. of Political & Econ.Sci., London. [0039937] 06/10/1961
Shipton Miss RC, BA DipLib MSc MCLIP, Lib., Imperial Coll.Sch.Sci.Tech.& Med., Royal Brompton Campus, London. [0030537] 08/02/1979
Shire Mrs SA, (was Cammidge), MCLIP B SC, Lib., Bristol Baptist Coll., Bristol. [0021248] 06/10/1973
Shiri Mr AA, BA MSc, Stud., Univ.of Strathclyde. [0061329] 27/05/2002
Shirley Ms PE, BA DipLib, Photographic Lib., Ove Arup & Partners, London. [0033676] 06/02/1981
Shirt Mr JLI, MCLIP, Life Member. [0013315] 30/07/1947
Shoemark Mr HK, BSc MCLIP, Inf.Off., L.& Inf.Dept., Bnf.Metals Tech.Cent. [0022685] 12/08/1974
Shoemark Mrs ML, (was Harrison), BA MCLIP, Literacy Support Asst., City of York Council. [0023715] 17/01/1975
Shoesmith Miss CB, MCLIP, Lib.-Stock Serv., Hastings Grp., E.Sussex Co.L. [0019199] 01/10/1972
Shone Miss CT, L.Asst., L.B.of Bexley, Cent.Admin.Off. [0013317] 20/01/1963 AF
Shone Mr SA, BA(Hons) MA, Unemployed. [0058407] 07/02/2000
Shone Mrs SE, (was Connell), MCLIP, Unemployment Unknown. [0003036] 16/01/1968
Shoolbred Mr MA, BA MPhil MCLIP MIPD, Sen.Academic, Sch.of Inf.Studies, Univ.of Cent.England in Birmingham. [0019200] 01/10/1972
Shorley Mrs DC, BA MCLIP, Univ.Lib., Univ.of Sussex, Falmer, Brighton. [0027711] 01/07/1977
Short Ms CT, BA CertEd MCLIP, p./t.Teacher, Coventry City Council. [0013321] 18/10/1966
Short Ms JA, BA DipILM, Head Volunteer/Adviser, St.Johns Ambulance L.Serv., CAB, Gt.Yarmouth. [0052091] 02/10/1995
Short Miss MG, BA(Hons), Stud., London Metro. [0061582] 02/10/2002
Short Mr PJ, BA MCLIP, Retired. [0013325] 26/07/1967
Short Mrs PM, (was Brunton), Deputy Learning Cent.Offr., City of Sunderland Coll., Bede Cent. [0050181] 25/04/1994 AF
Shortreed Ms J, BA MSc, Inf.Offr., Univ.of Abertay Dundee. [0059469] 04/04/2001
Shovlin Mrs CL, (was Unsworth), BA DipLib, Sch.Lib., Barnard Castle School, Barnard Castle, Co. Durham. [0048236] 16/11/1992
Showell Mrs C, (was Preston), BA DipLib MCLIP, Lib., Brit.Trust for Ornithology, Thetford. [0030030] 13/11/1978
Showell Mrs I, Unemployed. [0013328] 01/01/1970
Shread Mrs J, (was Elwell), MCLIP, Sch.Lib., Sandwell Educ.Dept., W.Bromwich. [0004559] 18/02/1967
Shrigley Mr RM, BA MCLIP MIMgt, Retired. [0013330] 03/10/1966
Shrigley Mrs SM, (was Rudd), FCLIP, Lib., Inst.for Animal Health, Pirbright Lab., Woking. [0013331] 11/10/1966 FE 05/07/1988
Shrimpton Ms JM, BA MCLIP, Inf.Asst., Sci.Mus.L., S.Kensington. [0020374] 12/02/1973
Shrive Mr MA, BA MCLIP, Lib., Off.of Fair Trading, London. [0045437] 06/02/1991
Shrives Ms SJ, BSc DipLib MCLIP, Researcher. [0035949] 11/03/1983
Shrubshall Ms M, BA DipLib MCLIP, Asst.Lib., Univ.of the W.of England, Bristol. [0026652] 22/10/1976
Shute Miss AJ, BA MCLIP, Retired. [0013336] 26/01/1961
Shute Miss LJ, Inf.Asst./Junior Lib., CMS Cameron McKenna, London. [0059359] 14/02/2001 AF
Shuttleworth Mrs D, BA(Hons), Sen.Inf.Asst., Univ.of Salford. [0048227] 16/11/1992
Shuttleworth Mr DH, BLib MA MCLIP, Sen.Lib.(Ref.), Cent.Div., Lancs L. [0020554] 03/04/1973
Sibbet Mrs FH, BA(Hons) DipILS MCLIP, Asst.Lib., Univ.of Strathclyde, Glasgow. [0052192] 12/01/1995
Sibson Miss JM, Stud., Loughborough Univ. [0058306] 06/01/2000

Sibson Mr MFD, LLB(Hons) BA(Hons) MCLIP, Med.Lib., Eastbourne Dist.Gen.Hosp., E.Sussex. [0036182] 04/07/1983
Siddall Miss J, BA MCLIP, Retired. [0013342] 01/01/1959
Siddall Ms PM, MSc MCLIP, Inf.Serv.Mgr., ROSPA, Birmingham. [0013344] 16/03/1972
Siddiqi Mrs T, BA(Hons) DipLib, Sen.Lib., Corp.of London, City of London Freemans Sch. [0040451] 25/01/1987
Siddiqui Mr AR, BA LLB MCLIP, Retired. [0013345] 20/03/1964
Siddons-Smith Mr C, MCLIP, Retired. [0013346] 16/02/1972
Siddons-Smith Mrs MA, (was King), MCLIP, L.& Inf.Mgr., Hill Dickinson Solicitors, Liverpool. [0013347] 12/09/1967
Sidebottom Miss M, MCLIP, Retired. [0013348] 30/09/1942
Sidell Mrs M, BA(Hons) MSc, Healthcare Lib., H.E.R.C.H., Bridlington. [0056945] 13/11/1998
Sidgreaves Mr ID, BA DipEd DipLib FCLIP, Pro-Vice Chancellor, Univ.of Plymouth. [0013349] 03/10/1966 FE 23/07/1997
Sidwell Ms CA, BSc(Hons) MSc MCLIP, Asst.Lib., Cranfield Univ. [0054182] 08/11/1996
Siemaszko Ms AM, BA DipLib MCLIP, Lib., Summertown L., Oxon.C.C. [0034032] 25/05/1978
Siemaszko Mrs WM, (was Pollard), MA DipLib MCLIP, L.Offr., Wimbledon L., L.B.of Merton. [0029341] 25/05/1978
Siemsen Ms AMA, BA DipLib MCLIP, Project Coordinator, Haus der Kulturen der Welt, Berlin, Germany. [0018152] 11/10/1972
Siess Ms J, BA MA MLIS, Pres., Info.Bridges Internat.Inc., Cleveland, Ohio, USA. [0058322] 04/01/2000
Sig Ms H, Unemployed. [0061325] 22/05/2002
Siggery Mr P, Inf.Consultant, 28 Rosedene Gdns., Ilford, Essex, IG2 6YE. [0054902] 06/05/1997
Sigurdsson Mr E, Lib., The Nat.& Univ.L.of Iceland, Reykjavik. [0017733] 12/09/1966
Silburn Mrs RE, P./t.Stud./Enquiry Offr., Univ.Aberystwyth, Ipswich County Ref.L. [0059685] 31/07/2001
Silcocks Mrs SJ, (was Guise), BA DipLib MCLIP, Inf., N.Derbys.Chamber of Commerce &, Industry, Chesterfield. [0031307] 29/09/1979
Silcox Miss M, BA(Hons) PGDip, Stud./Inf.Offr., City Univ./Univ.of Herts., Watford. [0057764] 20/07/1999
Sillifant Ms KC, BLib MCLIP, Team Lib., Young Peoples Serv.-Thanet, Margate L. [0032176] 29/01/1980
Sillitto Mr DW, MA MCLIP, Catr., Holborn L., L.B.of Camden. [0023201] 30/10/1974
Silman Mrs RG, p./t.Lib.-John Ryland Univ.L., Manchester Univ. [0033152] 01/10/1980
Silmon Mrs VM, BSc, Stud.,L.Asst., Bristol Univ., Wells L. [0061749] 01/11/2002
Silva Mrs K, BSc MCLIP, Employment not known. [0060506] 11/12/2001
Silver Mrs HL, (was Cubbon), BLib MCLIP, Asst.Lib., De Montfort Univ.L., Leicester. [0021337] 17/10/1973
Silver Mrs MV, (was Nicholls), BA(Hons) DipIM MCLIP, Systems/IT Lib., Mid-Kent Coll., Chatham. [0052441] 31/10/1995
Silverman Mrs GA, (was Pollard), BA(Hons), Media & Inf.Mgr., Tobacco Manufacturers'Assoc., London. [0047955] 27/10/1992
Silverside Mrs CE, (was Fryer), BA(Hons) MSc MCLIP, Sen.Inf.Specialist, A.T. Kearney Ltd., London. [0049196] 12/09/1993
Silvester Mrs SC, (was Brittain), BA MCLIP, Sub-Lib.Art & Design, Coventry Univ. [0013356] 27/10/1966
Silvester Mrs SM, (was Heginbotham), BSc BA MCLIP, Sch.L.Advisor, Scarborough Cent.L., N.Yorks.C.C. [0033785] 02/03/1981
Sim Mrs JR, (was Harrhy), BSc MCLIP, Head of Tech.Serv., Univ.of Wales Coll., Newport. [0021877] 15/01/1974
Sim Mrs LA, (was Crowthers), BA MCLIP, Head of Serv.to Child.&, Young People, W.Sussex C.C. [0052087] 05/10/1977
Simcox Mr JL, BSc(Hons) PGDipILM, Inf.Specialist, Towers Perrin, London. [0052113] 04/10/1995
Sime Mrs AJ, (was Ross), BA MCLIP, Sch.Lib., Fife Reg.Council, Glenrothes. [0029531] 02/08/1978
Sime Mr WC, BSc(Econ) MCLIP, Knowledge & L.Serv.Mgr., Kettering Gen.Hosp.NHS Trust, Northants. [0053224] 04/04/1996
Simensky Mrs C, (was Leigh), MCLIP, Borough Lib., Tameside M.B.C., Ashton-under-Lyne. [0013361] 02/01/1969
Siminson Miss NJ, BA(Hons) MA MCLIP, Inf.Specialist-Art & Design, Nottingham Trent Univ., Boots L. [0049067] 27/09/1993
Simkin Mrs HM, (was Pryer), MCLIP, Asst.Lib., Brighton Coll.of Tech. [0023710] 15/01/1975
Simkins Mrs K, BA(Hons), Researcher, Walker Morris Solicitors, Leeds. [0058159] 09/11/1999
Simm Miss CA, BA MCLIP, Lib.i/c., Bo'ness L., Falkirk Dist.Council. [0027092] 24/01/1977
Simm Mrs JR, (was Budgen), BA MCLIP, Asst.Lib.(Job Share), Sunderland City L. [0037339] 04/07/1984
Simm Miss L, BA MCLIP, Lib., Hartford High Sch. [0013364] 07/01/1965
Simmonds Mr A, BA(Hons) MA MCLIP, Lib., The Coll.of Law, York. [0051229] 30/11/1994
Simmonds Mr CA, MA MCLIP, Under Lib., Cambridge Univ.L. [0030674] 07/03/1979
Simmonds Mr G, BSc MA, Stud./Enquiry Asst., Southend L. Essex, Univ. Brighton. [0059624] 03/07/2001
Simmonds Mrs JM, MCLIP, Life member, 21 D'Urberville Close, Dorchester, Dorset, DT1 2JT, Tel:01305 264742. [0013365] 18/03/1941
Simmonds Ms PA, BA DipLib AMIPD MCLIP, Head of Training & Devel., CILIP, London. [0034897] 15/04/1982
Simmons Ms AL, BA(Hons), Stud., Univ. of Wales, Aberystwyth. [0058865] 18/09/2000
Simmons Mrs CD, (was Spurgeon), BA(Hons), Unemployed (f./t.Mother). [0037774] 26/10/1984

Personal Members

Simmons Mrs F, MA(Cantab) MALib, Lib., The Japan Foundation, London. [0053750] 01/10/1996
Simmons Mrs G, (was Whitefoot), BA(Hons) MCLIP, Unemployed. [0029108] 23/02/1978
Simmons Mr JD, MCLIP MILAM, Operations Mgr., L.B.Lewisham. [0013372] 14/11/1968
Simmons Mr JSG, OBE MA FSA FCLIP HonDLitt(Birm), Emeritus Fellow, (Lib.1970-82), All Souls Coll., Oxford. [0013373] 12/11/1932 FE 12/11/1973
Simmons Miss MC, BA MCLIP, Coll.Lib., Duncan of Jordanstone Coll., Dundee. [0030538] 13/02/1979
Simmons Mrs MM, (was O'Connor), MCLIP, Freelance Indexer. [0013374] 18/01/1961
Simmons Mr NA, MA MA(LIB) MCLIP DMS, Prison L.& Resources Mgr., Cambs.Co.Ls. [0013375] 02/04/1972
Simmons Mrs S, (was Mansfield), MCLIP, Lib./L.Super., Huntingdon/Sawtry L., Cambs.C.C. [0009706] 29/06/1970
Simmons Ms S, BA DipSoc MCLIP, Freelance Researcher. [0055004] 12/06/1997
Simon Ms A, BA(Hons), Research Stud., Salford Univ. [0055859] 04/12/1997
Simon Mrs C, (was Francis), BA(Hons) MSc(Econ) MCLIP, Team Lib., (Young Peoples Serv.), Medway Council. [0055344] 02/10/1997
Simon Ms E, HonFCLIP, Hon.Fellow. [0054738] 01/01/1997 FE 01/01/1997
Simon Mrs HA, (was Cohen), MCLIP, Volunteer Lib., Citizens Advice Line for London, Ilford. [0031588] 08/11/1979
Simon Mrs JA, (was Bolton), MCLIP, Community Lib., Denton Br., Tameside L.& Heritage. [0001441] 12/04/1967
Simon Mrs KJ, (was Pycock), BA MCLIP, Learning Res.Cent.Mgr., W.Yorkshire Police, Wakefield. [0023631] 22/01/1975
Simon Miss LH, BA(Hons) MA MCLIP, Inf.Offr., The Wellcome Trust, London. [0043230] 01/10/1989
Simon-Norris Mrs FM, (was Gardiner), BA MCLIP, Br.Organiser, Volunteer Reading Help, Banbury. [0027161] 30/01/1977
Simons Ms DM, (was Bale), BA MCLIP, Family L.Link Lib., Portsmouth City Council, Hants. [0020193] 01/01/1973
Simons Mr G, BA(Hons), Stud.(non-LIS), Coll.of F.E., Cardigan, Ceredigion. [0057921] 05/10/1999
Simons Mr JC, MCLIP, [0013381] 11/08/1968
Simons Miss JDH, MCLIP, Life Member. [0013382] 01/11/1937
Simons Ms JM, (was Milne), MCLIP, Employment status unknown. [0029914] 09/09/1978
Simons Mrs LA, (was Lee), MCLIP, Sen.Lib., Cheshire C.C., Educ.Res.L. [0020038] 16/01/1973
Simons Mrs MB, (was Mccaig), BA MCLIP, Lib., St.George's Coll., Addlestone, Surrey. [0013383] 30/09/1968
Simons Ms PA, BA DipLib MCLIP, Training Assoc., Carter-Small Partnership, Wincanton. [0029477] 20/08/1978
Simpkin Mrs EG, (was Meakin), FCLIP, Life Member, 3 Anthonys Av., Poole, Dorset, BH14 8JQ, Tel:01202 700968. [0013385] 18/02/1935 FE 01/01/1963
Simpkin Ms L, BA, Unemployed. [0046654] 02/12/1991
Simpson Mr A, DipILS, Sen.L.Asst., S.Glasgow NHS Trust, Cent.L., S.Gen.Hosp. [0057713] 09/07/1999
Simpson Mr AE, MA MS PhD, Prof., L., John Jay Coll.of Criminal Justice, New York, NY 10019, USA. [0020137] 24/01/1973
Simpson Mr AG, Sch.Lib., Medway Council, Strood. [0053064] 21/02/1996
Simpson Mr AJ, BSc(Hons) MSc(Econ) MCLIP, Lib., Cent.Washington Univ., U.S.A. [0054146] 07/11/1996
Simpson Miss AM, BA MCLIP, Team.Lib., N.Yorkshire Co.L. [0024236] 06/05/1975
Simpson Ms C, BA MCLIP, Neighbourhood Lib., Bristol City Council. [0041700] 22/02/1988
Simpson Mrs CJ, (was Pritchard), BA MCLIP, Inf. Offr., Wolstenholme Int. Ltd., Lancs. [0028881] 01/01/1978
Simpson Mrs CM, (was Clark), MCLIP, Unemployed. [0013389] 01/01/1963
Simpson Miss DEB, MCLIP, Life Member, 01298 814963. [0013391] 11/10/1944
Simpson Mr DH, OBE MA FCLIP, Hon.Arch., The Royal Commonwealth Soc., London, WC2N 4BJ. [0013392] 16/03/1939 FE 01/01/1946
Simpson Mr DJ, BSc (ECON) FCLIP, Life Member, Tel.01908 373378. [0013393] 22/03/1946 FE 01/01/1954
Simpson Mr DM, MCLIP, Sec.Sch.Lib., Belfast Educ.& L.Board. [0013394] 05/04/1971
Simpson Ms EA, BA(Hons) DipLIS MCLIP, Inf.Lib., Royal Coll.of Physicians of, Edinburgh. [0050154] 13/04/1994
Simpson Mrs EJ, (was Smith), MCLIP, Team Lib - Child.Serv., Norfolk C.C., Norfolk & Norwich Millennium L. [0019982] 01/01/1973
Simpson Mr EWM, DipEdTech MCLIP, H.of Multimedia, Educ.Training &, Resource Opportunities, Anniesland Coll., Glasgow. [0019205] 26/02/1964
Simpson Mrs G, (was Cooper), BA MCLIP, Unemployed. [0003115] 12/01/1970
Simpson Mrs GA, (was Harries), BA MCLIP, Lib., Palmers Coll., Essex. [0006385] 26/10/1971
Simpson Mrs H, BA(Hons) MA, Housing Offr., Sheffield City Council. [0056904] 02/11/1998
Simpson Ms HT, (was Retallick), BA DipILM, Asst.Lib., Middx.Univ., Hendon. [0047156] 13/05/1992
Simpson Mrs J, (was Yates), JP BA MCLIP, Princ.Lib., Hanley, Stoke on Trent City Council. [0042000] 14/07/1988
Simpson Mrs J, (was Gray), BA MCLIP, Housewife. [0005831] 30/11/1967
Simpson Mrs JE, (was Elischer), Asst.Inf. Offr., Arts Council of England, London. [0048776] 20/05/1993
Simpson Mrs JE, BA(Hons) DipArchAdmin, L.Asst., St Brendan's Sixth Form Coll., Brislington, Bristol. [0054992] 13/06/1997 AF

Simpson Mrs JM, (was Ratcliff), BA MCLIP, Unwaged. [0023250] 13/11/1974
Simpson Mrs JV, (was Smith), MA(Hons) DipILS, Lib.(Electronic Support & Devel.), Georgina Scott Sutherland L., Robert Gordon Univ. [0052552] 08/11/1995
Simpson Miss LA, BA MCLIP, Bor.Lib., Community Initiative Partnership, Hounslow. [0019206] 23/08/1972
Simpson Ms LE, (was Errington), Inf.Skills Coordinator, Univ.of Newcastle. [0046571] 12/11/1991
Simpson Dr MCT, MA MA PhD MCLIP, Dir.of Spec.Collections, Nat.L.of Scotland, Edinburgh. [0021538] 29/10/1973
Simpson Mrs ME, (was Allington), MCLIP, Housewife. [0000227] 01/01/1969
Simpson Mrs MI, (was Edgar), MCLIP, Life Member. [0013404] 01/01/1940
Simpson Mr NA, MCLIP, Life Member. [0013406] 25/01/1963
Simpson Mrs P, (was Yates), BA MCLIP, Head of Inf.Serv., Southampton Oceanography Cent., Hants. [0013407] 28/03/1961
Simpson Mrs PD, BA MCLIP, Stud., Cambridge. [0022317] 01/04/1974
Simpson Miss PH, MCLIP, Retired. [0013408] 06/01/1968
Simpson Mrs PM, (was Mander), MCLIP, Lib., King Edward VI Coll., Nuneaton, Warwick. [0024466] 16/09/1963
Simpson Mrs R, Stud., City Univ. [0058355] 19/01/2000
Simpson Mrs S, BA DipLib MCLIP, Arch.Asst., Angus Council, Montrose. [0033154] 07/10/1980
Simpson Mr SA, BA PGDipIT MCLIP, Systems Lib., Cultural Serv., E.Renfrewshire. [0044136] 29/05/1990
Simpson Mr SM, MA, Retired. [0013412] 08/07/1959
Simpson Mrs SM, (was Kendal), BSc MCLIP, Website Mgr., Dept.for Work & Pensions, Sheffield. [0034998] 08/06/1982
Sims Mrs AM, (was Braunton), BA MCLIP, Lib., Uxbridge High Sch., Middx. [0001651] 12/01/1972
Sims Mrs GD, BA MCLIP, p./t.Inf.Lib., Kingston Univ.L., Surrey. [0022903] 07/10/1974
Sims Mrs IA, (was Wilson), MCLIP, Acting Head of L.& Media Serv., Bucks.Chilterns Univ.Coll., High Wycombe. [0019208] 20/03/1963
Sims Mrs KJ, (was Stokes), BA MCLIP, Sch.Lib., Plume Sch., Maldon, Essex. [0023663] 17/01/1975
Sims Mr PS, MCLIP, Employment unknown. [0060354] 10/12/2001
Sims Mrs SE, BA(Hons) MA PGCE PGDipILM, p./t.Hosp./Prison Lib., Stockton Bor.Council Educ.Leisure, & Cult.Serv., Stockton on Tees. [0051490] 03/03/1995
Simsova Mrs S, M PHIL FCLIP, Inf.Systems Consultant, Data Help, London. [0013418] 07/03/1952 FE 01/01/1957
Sinagoga Miss MC, BA(Hons) MA, Inf.Offr., Univ.of Herts., Watford Campus LRC. [0058741] 01/07/2000
Sinai Mr A, BA DLS MCLIP, Retired. [0017735] 28/08/1963
Sinar Mr GT, BLib MCLIP, Systems Lib., Lancs.Co.L. [0022492] 10/06/1974
Sinclair Mr CA, BA MCLIP, Head of Bibl.Serv., Univ.of Stirling. [0038530] 05/06/1985
Sinclair Miss EJ, BA, Research Lib., BBC., Bristol. [0037406] 20/08/1984
Sinclair Mrs F, (was Mullineux), BA MCLIP, Sch.Lib., Orkney Islands Council, Stromness Academy. [0041102] 05/10/1987
Sinclair Miss HA, BA(Hons) MA MCLIP, Reader Development Lib., Herts.C.C., Watford. [0053809] 02/10/1996
Sinclair Miss L, Sen.Learning Res.Asst., Franklin Coll., Grimsby. [0058562] 01/04/2000 AF
Sinclair Mrs SJ, (was Turkington), MA DipLib MCLIP, Lib., Dunblane High Sch., Stirling Council. [0029854] 09/10/1978
Sinclair Miss SK, L.Mgr., Pangbourne Coll., Berkshire. [0059719] 05/09/2001
Sinclair Ms VA, BA(Hons), p./t.Stud., Regional Dev.Worker, Gingerbread, UWE. [0059896] 30/10/2001
Sinclair Miss VM, BA DipInf, Acq.Lib., Wellcome L., London. [0056950] 13/11/1998
Sinden Miss JM, Asst.i./c., Ore L., E.Sussex C.C. [0057544] 28/04/1999 AF
Sinden Mrs MA, (was Loftus), BSc MCLIP, Asst.Lib., Ministry of Defence, London. [0025591] 28/01/1976
Sinden-Evans Ms R, (was Evans), BA MA BMus MMus MCLIP, Sen.Subject Lib., Music & Performing Arts, Middx.Univ., Trent Park L. [0035660] 13/11/1982
Sinfield Mrs EAJ, (was May), BA(Hons) MCLIP, Comm.Access Lib., Northants.C.C., Daventry L. [0013425] 12/10/1964
Singer Ms HJ, BA(Hons) MA MCLIP, Inf.Consultant, Univ.of Herts., St.Albans. [0052818] 19/12/1995
Singh Mr CJ, HND AMIRSH MCLIP, Retired. [0060739] 12/12/2001
Singh Miss ML, BA(Hons), Records & Inf.Offr., London L.& Inf.Devel.Unit, London. [0061517] 29/08/2002
Singleton Mrs AL, (was Taylor), MCLIP, L.Serv.for Sch.Mgr., Cumbria C.C. [0014373] 04/10/1970
Singleton Mr D, BSc(Hons)DipLib MA MCLIP, Campus Lib., Univ.of Cent.Lancs., Cumbria Campus. [0021190] 24/09/1973
Singleton Mr MJ, BA MLS MCLIP, Community Hist.Lib., L.& Inf., Middlesbrough. [0013428] 01/01/1969
Sinker Mrs R, (was Daunton-Fear), BA MCLIP, Housewife/Self-employed. [0003621] 07/12/1971
Sinkinson Mr JV, BA MCLIP, Civil Servant. [0024139] 04/04/1975
Sinnatamby Miss A, Lib., Nat.L.Bd., Singapore. [0022160] 30/01/1974
Sinnock Mrs VA, Retired. [0045990] 12/08/1991 AF
Sippings Mrs GM, (was Hughes), MLib FCLIP, Dir.of Inf.Resources, Inland Revenue, London. [0024895] 14/10/1975 FE 01/04/2002
Sirdi Mr N, BA MA DipLib MCLIP, Lib., Greenwich L. [0039329] 15/01/1986
Siriwardene Miss S, BA, p./t.Stud./Ch.L.Asst., Univ.coll.London, Univ.of Cambridge. [0061363] 21/06/2002
Sirkar Ms S, BA, Snr.L.Asst., Aberdeen Univ.L., Scotland. [0027406] 25/03/1977
Sirr Mrs RM, (was Tonks), MCLIP, Team Lib., Slough Cent.L., Berks. [0013430] 01/12/1966
Sisson Miss F, BA(Hons) MA, Dep.Lib., Merton Coll. [0051461] 24/02/1995

349

Sisson Miss RE, BA(Hons), Stud., Loughborough Univ. [0059981] 15/11/2001
Sissons Miss JT, BA(Hons) MA MCLIP, Learning Res.Lib., Worcester Coll.of Tech. [0053559] 22/07/1996
Sisterson Miss J, BA MCLIP, Retired. [0013433] 18/09/1962
Siswell Miss A, BA DipLib MCLIP, H.of L.Systems, Bath Spa Univ.Coll. [0028162] 11/10/1977
Sivajnanam Ms C, MCLIP, Lib., Sedgehill Sch., L.B.of Lewisham. [0013434] 13/01/1972
Sivakumaran Mrs K, (was Chelliah), BA, Child.Lib., Kingston L. [0042406] 01/11/1988
Siwek Mrs GR, (was Devlin), MA DipLib MCLIP, Sch.Lib., Portree High Sch., Isle of Skye. [0032918] 08/10/1980
Sizer Mrs CA, BA DipLib MCLIP, p/t Libr., London College of Fashion, London. [0030930] 18/06/1979
Sjolund Ms M, BA, Unemployed & p./t. Stu., Coll. of Boras, Sweden. [0060953] 18/01/2002
Skakle Mrs SM, (was McLeod), MA(Hons) MLib, Bibl.Serv.Lib., Scottish Parliament Inf.Cent., Edinburgh. [0047746] 16/10/1992
Skander Mrs JR, (was Griffin), Sen.L.Asst., Cheshire C.C., Hurdsfield L., Macclesfield. [0021674] 03/01/1974
Skea Mrs JR, MCLIP, Retired. [0013437] 07/03/1934
Skea Miss RMM, MA MCLIP, DipLIS, Sch.Lib., E.Dunbartonshire Council. [0048339] 27/11/1992
Skeates Mrs CA, (was Bell), BA DipLib MCLIP MBA, Inspector, Best Value Insp.Serv. [0040334] 09/01/1987
Skedgell Miss EP, BA (Hons), Asst.Lib., Rose Bruford Coll., Sidcup. [0043564] 08/11/1989
Skee Mrs CM, (was Allan), MA MCLIP, Retired. [0000165] 01/01/1969
Skeen Miss NK, BA(Hons), Employment not known. [0057724] 08/07/1999
Skelly Rev ODG, BA MCLIP STB, Catholic Curate, Diocese of Meath, Ireland. [0026557] 12/10/1976
Skelton Mrs A, (was Dennis), MCLIP, Lib.Aide, St Francis Xavier Sch., Brisbane, Australia. [0013442] 17/10/1965
Skelton Ms HC, Unemployed. [0041498] 04/01/1988
Skelton Miss SA, BA(Hons), Grad.Trainee L.Asst., Manchester Met.Univ., Hollings L. [0061613] 03/10/2002
Skelton Ms SA, BA(Hons), L.Mgr., D.F.I.D., London. [0049622] 18/11/1993
Skene Mrs SP, (was Lee), BA MCLIP, L.Asst., Homerton Coll., Sch.of Health Studies, Cambridge. [0030461] 02/02/1979
Skerrow Mr CJD, MA(Hons) DipLib, Circulation Offr., Univ.of Lincs., Hull. [0048055] 03/11/1992
Skiffington Mrs M, (was Vidler), BA MCLIP, Life Member. [0017739] 01/01/1954
Skillen Mr BS, MLITT BA DipLib MCLIP, Asst.Lib., The Mitchell L., Glasgow. [0031451] 01/10/1979
Skillern Mrs IH, FCLIP, Retired. [0013452] 06/06/1932 **FE 01/01/1936**
Skinn Mr EH, MCLIP, Retired. [0013456] 01/01/1940
Skinner Mrs APM, (was Lunn), BSc(Hons) MCLIP, L.Mgr., L.& Inf.Serv., Northants.Health Auth.Cripps L. [0013459] 01/01/1969
Skinner Mr BJ, BSc(Hons), Inf.Offr., Univ.of Salford. [0056486] 21/07/1998
Skinner Mrs BM, (was Medlock), MCLIP, Asst.p/t.Lincoln Div., Lincs Co.L. [0013460] 13/02/1955
Skinner Mrs CH, ASCOT MCLIP, Retired. [0032764] 07/08/1980
Skinner Mr EH, DipEdTech MCLIP, Resources & Devel.Mgr., Cheshire C.C. [0013462] 03/03/1966
Skinner Mr I, MCLIP, Subject Lib., Lanchester L., Coventry Univ. [0013463] 04/01/1971
Skinner Miss JB, BLib MCLIP, Lib., Valuation Off.Agency, London. [0021406] 06/11/1973
Skinner Mr JI, BA MCLIP, p./t.Lib., E.Devon Primary Care Trust, Exeter. [0030931] 18/06/1979
Skinner Mrs PA, (was Taylor), BA MCLIP, Sch.Lib., Whitburn Academy, W.Lothian Council. [0040111] 21/10/1986
Skinner Mrs PJ, (was Lawton), MA, Princ.L.Asst., Bodleian L., Oxford. [0030639] 02/03/1979
Skinner Mr RC, MCLIP, Comm.L.Mgr., Monmouthshire C.C. [0013466] 01/01/1966
Skinner Miss SJE, BA(Hons) MA, Stud., Loughborough Univ. [0059778] 02/10/2001
Skinner Mrs SM, (was Smith), BA MCLIP, Accessions Lib., Aberdeenshire L.& Inf.Serv. [0038981] 24/10/1985
Skipp Miss M, MCLIP, Life Member. [0013468] 16/02/1956
Skirrow Mrs IH, MSc Econ ILS, Lib.Co-ordinator, Vienna Internat.Sch., Austria. [0059569] 26/06/2001
Skirving Miss SM, BA MCLIP, Grp.Lib., Easington Colliery, Durham C.C. [0022773] 12/10/1974
Skwirzynska Mrs HMA, (was Drysdale), BA MCLIP, L. - L.R. Co-ordinator, Stratford Coll., Warwickshire. [0041822] 18/04/1988
Slack Mrs A, (was Lysandrides), MCLIP, Sen.Lib., Adult & Community Servs., Beds.C.C. [0009220] 03/11/1965
Slack Miss EM, BA MCLIP, Life Member. [0013471] 28/01/1960
Slade Mrs WM, BA(Hons), Stud./Learning Resources Asst., Bristol Univ../Weston Coll. [0061666] 16/10/2002
Slaney Mr RW, MCLIP, Tech.Leader, Qinetiq Ltd., Farnborough. [0027299] 16/11/1965
Slapp Mrs DE, (was Bailey), BA MCLIP, Inf.Serv.Mgr., Lincs.C.C., S.Area H.Q., Boston. [0038024] 18/07/1985
Slark Mrs AM, (was Woolley), MCLIP, Sen.Lib.:Community Link Serv., Bedford Cent.L. [0013480] 03/07/1965
Slark Mrs SL, (was Grainger), MCLIP, Lib., Chestnut Grove Sch., Wandsworth L.E.A. [0005800] 26/05/1971
Slasor Miss A, BA MA MCLIP, Unemployed. [0027022] 12/01/1977
Slater Mrs BG, (was Rhodes), BA MCLIP, Comm.Lib., Nottingham City Council. [0020156] 27/01/1973
Slater Miss G, BA(Hons) MSc MCLIP, Learning Resources Adviser (ILT), Thomas Danby Coll., Leeds. [0053448] 01/07/1996

Slater Miss J, MA MCLIP, Lib., Soc.of Analytical Psychology, London. [0013481] 31/01/1964
Slater Ms J, BA(Hons) MA, Project Offr., Learning Teaching Support Network., Engineering Subject Centre, LGU. [0058080] 25/10/1999
Slater Mrs JA, (was Entwistle), BA MCLIP, p./t.Inf.Offr., MS Accountancy & Taxation Serv., Dunfermline. [0020620] 03/05/1973
Slater Mrs JA, MA(Hons), p./t.Learning Res.Mgr., Army Foundation Coll., Harrogate. [0051971] 24/08/1995
Slater Miss K, BA MCLIP, Community Lib., Tameside M.B.C. [0034642] 20/01/1982
Slater Mrs M, BEd(Hons) PGC, Learning Resource Asst., Perth Grammar Sch., Tayside. [0061446] 18/07/2002
Slater Mr MK, BA MCLIP, L.Res.Lib., Limehouse L., L.B.of Tower Hamlets. [0035384] 19/10/1982
Slator Mr CH, MSc(Econ) MCLIP, Learning & Media Mgr., Colchester Inst., Essex. [0013485] 01/01/1969
Slator Mrs MD, (was Hill), MCLIP, Business Lib., Essex C.C., Chelmsford L. [0006890] 19/04/1971
Slaughter Miss KP, BA(Hons) MCLIP, ICT Lib., LBN P.L., E.Ham. [0055413] 08/10/1997
Slaughter Mr RM, BA DipLib MCLIP, Inf.Offr., Birmingham City L. [0034508] 19/11/1981
Slavic Ms A, BA BA BSc MSc, Researcher, LITC/PhD Stud., South Bank Univ./Univ.Coll.London. [0057683] 01/07/1999
Sleap Miss SE, BA DipLib MCLIP, Life Member. [0031155] 07/09/1979
Sleat Mr AJF, BA(Hons) DipLib MCLIP, Asst.Lib., Univ.of the W.of England, Bristol. [0036821] 01/01/1984
Sleath Mr CV, BA MCLIP, Retired. [0013489] 09/10/1962
Sleep Mrs ME, (was Frost), MCLIP, Community Lib., Plymouth City Council, Estover Community Coll. [0013491] 13/01/1964
Sleight Mr A, MCLIP, Sen.Lib., N.District, Lancs Co. [0013492] 21/02/1969
Sliney Miss MT, MSocSci DipLib MCLIP ALAI, Sen.Lib., Fingal C.C., Ireland. [0033347] 16/11/1980
Slingsby Miss CP, BA MCLIP, Resident in Colombia. [0017740] 15/01/1971
Slingsby Mrs TA, (was Spencer), BA(Hons) MCLIP PGCE, Self-employed, St.Edmundsbury Tutorial Coll., Ripon. [0041477] 07/01/1988
Sloan Miss J, Sch.Lib., W.Denton High Sch., Newcastle upon Tyne. [0059530] 26/04/2001
Sloan Mrs MG, (was Adams), BA MCLIP, Operational Unit Mgr., (Child.& Young Peoples Serv.), S.E.E.L.B., Ballynahinch. [0023506] 20/11/1974
Sloss Ms K, BA(Hons) DipLIS MCLIP, Inf.Serv.Mgr., London Sch.of Economics. [0041147] 12/10/1987
Slough Mr NSJ, BA(Hons) MA MCLIIP, Asst.Lib., Corp.of London, Guildhall L. [0044467] 10/10/1990
Sloyan Mrs GJ, BA(Hons), Lib., City Discovery Cent., Bradwell Abbey, Milton Keynes. [0052145] 06/10/1995
Sly Miss AG, BA(Open) FCLIP, Retired. [0013500] 27/02/1934 **FE 01/01/1946**
Slythe Mrs RM, (was Fone), MA PGCE FCLIP, Hon.Fundraiser, Faversham Soc., Kent. [0013501] 12/10/1949 **FE 01/01/1967**
Smailes Mr PJ, BSc, Employment not known. [0060209] 10/12/2001
Smakowska Ms CJ, BSc DipLib MCLIP, Resident in Germany. [0013502] 01/10/1971
Smales Mrs J, BA(Hons) PGCE, Pupil Res.Mgr., Norton Coll., Malton. [0059423] 12/03/2001
Smales Mrs LA, (was Guthrie), L.&Inf.Worker, Dundee City Council. [0056966] 11/11/1998
Small Mr GS, BA(Hons) DipLib MCLIP, Freelance Advisor, Consultancy & Training. [0036830] 01/01/1984
Small Miss SA, MA(Hons) MSc, Unemployed. [0048090] 05/11/1992
Small Mrs SS, BA MCLIP, China Studies Lib., S.O.A.S., London. [0026684] 03/11/1976
Smallwood Miss AE, BA(Hons) MCLIP, Res.Cent.Co-ordinator, Withins Sch., Bolton. [0054884] 29/04/1997
Smallwood Ms C, BA(Hons) DipILM MCLIP, Unemployed. [0056209] 03/04/1998
Smallwood Ms E, BEd(Hons) MA PGDip(IM), L.& Serv.Mgr., L.B.of Merton, Morden. [0057972] 07/10/1999
Smart Miss AE, BA MA MCLIP, Lib., Royal Northern Coll.of Music, Manchester. [0031452] 07/10/1979
Smart Ms CA, MA MCLIP, Sen.L.Asst., Univ.of Leicester. [0048582] 01/03/1993
Smart Miss CR, BA MCLIP, Retired. [0013507] 23/03/1952
Smart Mrs HM, BA MCLIP, Inf.Off., Univ.of Strathclyde, Glasgow. [0029418] 30/06/1978
Smart Mr J, BA DipLib MCLIP, Coordinator - Bus., Univ.of Plymouth. [0032465] 02/03/1980
Smart Mrs M, (was Howat), BA(Hons) MCLIP, Inf.Offr., Univ.of Salford. [0043128] 08/08/1989
Smart Miss PA, BA MPhil, Stud., Sch.of Lib.& Inf.Studies, N.London Poly. [0034274] 13/10/1981
Smart Mrs T, BA(Hons) MA, Unemployed. [0058121] 03/11/1999
Smeaton Miss M, Life Member. [0020529] 22/01/1973
Smeaton Mrs PD, Child.Serv.Super., St.Andrews P.L., Fife. [0059409] 28/03/2001 **AF**
Smedley Miss A, BA(Hons), Grad.Trainee, Lytham L., Lancs. [0056804] 19/10/1998
Smethurst Mrs BS, (was Cook), MCLIP, Sch.Lib.(Job-Share), Shavington High Sch., Crewe. [0013514] 01/01/1968
Smethurst Miss J, BA MCLIP, Lib., Med.L., Pontefract Gen.Infirmary. [0026143] 01/07/1976
Smethurst Dr JM, CBE BA MCLIP, Retired, 72 Grove Road, Tring, Herts. [0013516] 14/01/1964
Smith Miss A, BA MCLIP, Learning Resources Mgr., Tower Hamlets Coll., London. [0029226] 18/04/1978

Personal Members — Smith

Smith Mr A, BSc DIP LIB MCLIP, Lib., Chemical Info.Serv., Dept.of the Environment. [0023159]   11/11/1974
Smith Mr A, BSc AIMgt MCLIP, Faculty Team Lib., Edward Boyle L., Univ.of Leeds. [0013522]   19/10/1966
Smith Mrs A, BA MCLIP, Sen.Lib., Trafford M.B.S., Sale, Gtr.Manchester. [0040057]   15/10/1986
Smith Ms AA, BA(Hons) CertEd DipLIS, Lib., Chichester High Sch.for Girls. [0048471]   18/01/1993
Smith Mr AE, MPP BA(Hons) ALIANZA, Univ.Lib., Victoria Univ.of Wellington, New Zealand. [0019892]   13/07/1970
Smith Mrs AH, (was Christie), MA MCLIP, Sch.Lib., Lochend Comm.High Sch., Glasgow. [0013527]   01/10/1969
Smith Mrs AH, (was Robertson), BA MCLIP, Mother/housewife. [0035772]   10/01/1983
Smith Ms AH, (was Adams), BA DipLib MCLIP, Child.Lib., L.B.of Harrow. [0041418]   09/12/1987
Smith Miss AK, BA(Hons) MCLIP, Lib., Worcester L., Worcs.C.C. [0030043]   14/11/1978
Smith Mrs AM, BTh DipLib MCLIP, Employment unknown. [0060251]   10/12/2001
Smith Mrs AM, (was Gillett), BA MCLIP, Sch.Mob.Lib., Midlothian Council, Loanhead. [0036191]   01/07/1983
Smith Ms AMH, BA(Hons) DipILS MCLIP, Resident in Canada. [0048781]   21/05/1993
Smith Mr AP, BSc(Hons) PGCE DipIM MCLIP, Lib., Chartered Inst.of Building, Ascot. [0052197]   12/10/1995
Smith Mr AR, MCLIP, Life Member, 48 Neston Dr., Chester, CH2 2HR. [0013530]   29/06/1948
Smith Mrs AV, (was Latham), MCLIP, Team Lib.(Job Share), L.B.of Ealing, L.Support Cent. [0013532]   26/11/1964
Smith Mr AW, BLib MCLIP ARCM, Head, Special Acquisitors, Brit.L.Doc.Supply Cent.,Boston Spa. [0013533]   20/10/1971
Smith Mr BB, DMS MIMgt MCLIP, Retired. [0013537]   13/01/1954
Smith Miss BE, BSc ALAA MCLIP, Dep.Lib., Queen Margaret Univ.Coll., Edinburgh. [0021014]   02/10/1973
Smith Mrs BG, (was Pope), BA MCLIP, Lib.-Grade D, London Inst., London Coll.of Fashion. [0013538]   09/08/1968
Smith Mr BJ, MA MCLIP, Bibl.Serv.Lib., Western Isles L., Stornoway. [0023307]   25/11/1974
Smith Mrs BL, (was Jackson), BA, Life Member. [0013541]   05/09/1942
Smith Mrs BM, (was Pask), BA MCLIP, Inf.Cent.Mgr., Spelthorne Coll., Ashford, Middx. [0031681]   15/10/1979
Smith Miss C, BLib MCLIP, Collectioin Devel.Mgr., Bolton Inst. [0030792]   08/04/1979
Smith Mr C, MA FCLIP, Life Member. [0013543]   08/02/1938   FE 01/01/1955
Smith Mr C, MCLIP, Retired. [0019067]   28/09/1950
Smith Mr C, (was Lewis), MCLIP, Sen.Ed.Lib., N.E.Wales Sch.L.Serv. [0008865]   27/01/1970
Smith Mrs C, (was Barnes), MCLIP, Lib.& Res.Mgr., St.Marys Coll., Middlesbrough. [0031183]   20/10/1979
Smith Mrs C, Inf.Analyst, Smithkline Beecham Pharmaceuticals, Harlow, Essex. [0053167]   20/03/1996   AF
Smith Mr CA, MA DipLib MCLIP, Sch.Lib., Hillhead High Sch., Glasgow. [0043534]   06/11/1989
Smith Mr CA, BA MCLIP, Unemployed. [0035367]   11/10/1982
Smith Mrs CA, (was Dundas), BA(Hons), Inf.Offr.-(Pub.Health), Fife NHS Board, Fife. [0049685]   25/11/1993
Smith Ms CA, BA(Hons), New Media Arch., BBC., London. [0053971]   15/10/1996
Smith Miss CB, MA(Hons), L. & Inf. Serv. Mgr., Guild Academic L., Royal Preston Hosp. [0047122]   05/05/1992
Smith Mrs CE, (was Fielding), Bsc DipLib MCLIP, Community Lib., Hyde Library, Cheshire. [0030161]   01/01/1979
Smith Mrs CE, (was Whimster), DipLib MA MCLIP, Housewife. [0036453]   05/10/1983
Smith Mrs CE, BA DipLIS, p./t.Lib., Nursing & Midwifery Educ., Beeches Mgmt.Cent., Belfast. [0053378]   29/05/1996
Smith Mr CJ, BSc PGDipLib MCLIP, Facilities Mgr., Univ.L., Univ.of Surrey, Guildford. [0026217]   24/08/1976
Smith Mr CJ, MCLIP, Retired, Park House, 7 Kerry Lane, Eccleshall, Stafford, ST21 6EJ. [0013548]   08/01/1958
Smith Mrs CL, (was Pike), MCLIP, Lib., Lees Brook Comm.Sports Coll., Lees Brook Comm.Sch. [0020253]   27/01/1973
Smith Mr CM, MIPD MCLIP, Personnel & Training Consultant, Self-employed, Seaford, Sussex. [0013549]   07/01/1965
Smith Mrs CM, (was Crocker), BA MCLIP, Position Unknown, Premier Prisons Serv.Ltd., Uttoxeter. [0053378]   26/09/1969
Smith Mrs CM, (was Cameron), MA DipLib MCLIP, H.of L.& Inf.Serv., NHS Exec.Northern & Yorks., Durham. [0027918]   01/10/1977
Smith Ms CM, Informatics L.Trainer, S.Humber Health Auth., Brigg. [0052665]   17/11/1995
Smith Miss CMW, MA MCLIP, Retired. [0013533]   22/09/1967
Smith Mrs CP, (was Dickerson), BLib MCLIP, Lib., The Royal Sch.of Signals, Blandford, Dorset. [0039472]   30/01/1986
Smith Miss CR, BA MCLIP, Lib., DEFRE, London. [0024814]   02/10/1975
Smith Mrs CRH, (was Mcbrien), BA DipLib MCLIP, Employment not known. [0026775]   22/11/1976
Smith Miss CS, BA MA, Stud., Loughborough Univ. [0058948]   10/10/2000
Smith Miss D, Customer Serv.Mgr., Essex C.C., Chelmsford. [0059476]   04/04/2001   AF
Smith Mr D, BA MCLIP, Team Lib., The Mitchell L., Glasgow. [0033156]   01/10/1980
Smith Mrs D, Learning Res.Cent.Mgr., Marden High Sch., N.Shields. [0052559]   07/11/1995

Smith Ms D, (was Lightowler), BA MCLIP, Employment not known. [0060335]   10/12/2001
Smith Ms D, Unemployed. [0061233]   17/04/2002
Smith Mr DA, MA MCLIP, Sect.Head, Corp.Inf.Mgmt.& Web Devel., Dept.of Health, London. [0034206]   13/10/1981
Smith Dr DF, MA DPhil MCLIP, Lib., St Annes Coll.L., Oxford. [0033427]   30/11/1980
Smith Mr DH, MCLIP, Dir., Crofthouse Books Ltd., Addlestone, Surrey. [0023174]   30/10/1974
Smith Mr DJ, BA(Hons) DMS MCLIP MIMgt, Corp.Inf.Lib., Conwy Co.Bor.Council, L.Inf.& Arch.HQ. [0041578]   20/01/1988
Smith Mrs DM, (was Hiscox), BSc MCLIP, Lib., Anglia Poly.Univ. [0041705]   15/02/1988
Smith Mr DP, MLS, Br.Mgr., Columbia Br.L., The New York Pub.L., USA. [0057805]   10/08/1999
Smith Mr DRM, MA DipLib MCLIP, Lect., Robert Gordon Univ., Aberdeen. [0038998]   23/10/1985
Smith Mr E, MCLIP, Sen.Super., Cent.Ref.L., Doncaster M.B.C. [0013563]   08/01/1967
Smith Mr E, BA(Hons) MCLIP MIMgt, Business & Tech.Lib., Aberdeen City Council. [0045495]   20/02/1991
Smith Mrs E, (was Mcneill), MCLIP, Lib., Royal High Sch., Edinburgh. [0023932]   24/02/1975
Smith Miss EA, BA(Hons) MCLIP, Sen.L.Asst., Imperial Coll.of Sci.Tech.& Med., London. [0039404]   27/01/1986
Smith Mrs EA, (was Hannah), BA (Hons) DipILM MCLIP, Sch.Lib., Pembroke Sch., Wales. [0043633]   13/11/1989
Smith Mrs EB, (was Barker), MCLIP, Lib., City of Edinburgh Council. [0000754]   18/01/1972
Smith Mrs ELM, (was Morland), BA MCLIP, Unemployed. [0033079]   09/10/1980
Smith Mrs EM, (was Barnett), BA MCLIP, Sen.Lib., Conwy & Denbighshire NHS Trust, Glan Clwyd Hosp., Bodelwyddan. [0031782]   11/12/1979
Smith Mrs F, (was Laverty), MA MCLIP, Acting Ch.Lib., Glasgow Caledonian Univ. [0008689]   24/10/1969
Smith Mr FJL, BSc PGDipILS, Unemployed. [0057866]   16/09/1999
Smith Ms FMM, BEd DipLIS MCLIP, Sch.Lib., Loudoun Academy, E.Ayrshire Council. [0051573]   03/04/1995
Smith Mr G, BA DipLib FCLIP, Dir.-Cooperation Programme, Brit.L., London. [0026560]   03/10/1976   FE 20/09/2000
Smith Mrs G, (was Bryant), MCLIP, Unemployed, (0121) 550 6166. [0001984]   07/01/1970
Smith Mrs G, MA, Stud., Manchester Met.Univ. [0059976]   14/11/2001
Smith Mr GE, OBE FCLIP, Consultant/Life Member, 16 Soar Rd., Quorn, Loughborough, Leics., LE12 8BW. [0013579]   11/01/1948   FE 01/01/1956
Smith Miss GF, BA(Hons) MSc(Econ) MCLIP, Health Sci.Lib., Coventry Univ. [0052531]   06/11/1995
Smith Mr GHR, MCLIP, Lib.,Sally Howell L., Epsom Gen.Hosp., Surrey. [0013581]   23/02/1966
Smith Mr H, MA FCLIP, Life Member. [0013585]   31/03/1945   FE 01/01/1954
Smith Mrs H, (was Eddon), BA MCLIP, Sen.Lib., Skipton Group, N.Yorks Co.L. [0040512]   24/02/1987
Smith Mrs H, (was Dobson), BA DMS MCLIP, Resident in U.S.A. [0039617]   01/04/1986
Smith Mrs HA, (was Cotter), BA(Hons) DipILS, Sen.Learning Cent.Asst., Glos.Coll.of Arts & Tech., Gloucester. [0052313]   25/10/1995
Smith Miss HE, BA MCLIP, Social Inclusion Lib., Bor.of Poole. [0037882]   01/11/1984
Smith Mrs HIL, (was Robinson), MA DipLib MCLIP, Unemployed. [0013590]   21/10/1968
Smith Mrs HM, (was Harris), BA DipLib MCLIP, Dep.Grp.Leader, Neath Port Talbot CBC., Port Talbot L. [0023353]   20/11/1974
Smith Mrs HM, (was Lawrence), BA MCLIP, L.Asst., Northants.C.C. [0024516]   11/09/1975
Smith Miss HR, MSc MCLIP, L.Mgr., Kennedys, London. [0039825]   09/08/1986
Smith Ms HS, Head Lib., Ashurst Morris Crisp, London. [0049581]   19/11/1993
Smith Mr HSA, MA FCLIP, Life Member. [0013594]   06/10/1934   FE 01/01/1939
Smith Mrs IA, BA MA FCLIP, Lect., Dept.of Inf.Sci., Loughborough Univ. [0030718]   01/01/1971   FE 22/03/1995
Smith Mr IM, BA DipLib MCLIP, Inf.Serv.Mgr., CAFOD, London. [0035204]   05/10/1982
Smith Mr IR, BSc, Partner, House of Images, Blackburn. [0056777]   12/10/1998   SP
Smith Miss J, Stud., Univ.of Cent.England, Birmingham. [0059038]   31/10/2000
Smith Mr J, MA MCLIP, Cent.Lend.Lib., Cent.L., Aberdeen. [0030262]   06/12/1978
Smith Mr J, FCLIP, Retired. [0013600]   05/10/1948   FE 01/01/1956
Smith Mrs J, BA MA, E & W Inf.Desk Supervisor, University L., Univ.of Surrey. [0059986]   15/11/2001
Smith Miss JA, MA BA(Hons) MCLIP, Stock Lib., Suffolk C.C., Ipswich. [0013603]   24/09/1962
Smith Mr JA, BSc LRAMARCM MCLIP, Employment not known. [0060643]   11/12/2001
Smith Mrs JA, MA MCLIP, Relief Lib., Bournemouth L. [0025665]   21/01/1976
Smith Ms JA, (was Dobson), BA(Hons), Lib., Boyes, Turner, Reading. [0040561]   07/03/1987
Smith Miss JC, BSc DipLib MCLIP, Coll.Lib., Soundwell Coll., Bristol. [0047472]   26/08/1992
Smith Mrs JC, Learning Res.Mgr., Beaminster Sch., Dorset. [0052079]   02/10/1995
Smith Ms JD, BA MCLIP, Retired. [0025112]   01/01/1975

351

Smith Mrs JE, BA(Hons), L.Asst., Corporation of London. [0056850] 27/10/1998
Smith Ms JE, (was Nixon), Asst.Lib., Glasgow Caledonian Univ., Glasgow. [0044601] 05/11/1990
Smith Ms JE, Dep.Lib., British Med.Assoc., London. [0039592] 14/03/1986
Smith Ms JE, BA MCLIP, Child.Spec., Ilkeston L., Derbys. [0031156] 16/09/1979
Smith Miss JH, (was Hurst), BLS(Hons), Catr., Univ.of Warwick, Coventry. [0033462] 01/01/1981
Smith Miss JH, BSc(Hons), Stud., Robert Gordons Univ. [0059090] 13/11/2000
Smith Mr JH, BA, Dir., L.& Inf.Serv., The Brit.Council, Islamabad, Pakistan. [0044149] 06/06/1990
Smith Mrs JI, (was Watts), BA MCLIP, Unemployed. [0021784] 15/01/1974
Smith Dr JM, BA PhD DipLib MCLIP, Haldane Lib., Imperial Coll., London. [0013616] 05/10/1971
Smith Miss JM, BA(Hons), Asst.Lib., Law & Tax, Andersen. [0058452] 11/02/2000
Smith Miss JM, BA MCLIP, Inf.Serv.Mgr., Scottish Parliament Inf.Cent., Edinburgh. [0013615] 01/04/1970
Smith Miss JM, MCLIP, Retired. [0013611] 01/01/1965
Smith Mrs JM, (was Shepherd), MCLIP, Learning Res.Cent.Mgr., Duchy Coll., Cornwall. [0013610] 01/03/1963
Smith Mrs JM, (was Lawrence), MCLIP, L.Exec., Dept.of the L., House of Commons. [0013609] 09/11/1966
Smith Mrs JM, (was Thorman), MCLIP, Unemployed. [0025418] 06/01/1976
Smith Ms JM, BA(Hons) MCLIP, Subject Lib., Grove L., Bradford Coll. [0043593] 09/11/1989
Smith Mr JP, BA DipLib MCLIP, Sen.L.Asst., Plymouth NHS Trust. [0025420] 09/01/1976
Smith Ms JS, BA DMS MCLIP, Account Mgr., DS Group, c/o Roswell, Glasgow. [0040289] 07/01/1987
Smith Revd. JS, MA FCLIP, Retired. [0013619] 12/03/1954 FE 01/01/1968
Smith Mr JWT, BA MSc MCLIP, Employment not known. [0029828] 04/10/1978
Smith Mr K, BA(Hons) MCLIP, Mgr, Inclusive & Devel.Serv., Rotherham MBC, Maltby L.HQ. [0022172] 01/03/1974
Smith Mrs K, (was Lindley), MCLIP, Educ.Lib., Canterbury Christ Church Univ.Coll. [0013623] 13/10/1965
Smith Ms K, (was Connelly), BA MCLIP, w/e Lib., Sheffield Hallam Univ. [0003038] 16/09/1971
Smith Mrs KA, (was Foley), BA MCLIP, Sen.Lib., Sch.L.Serv., Wakefield M.D.C. [0013625] 10/01/1970
Smith Mrs KB, BA MCLIP, p./t.L.Asst., Chester Coll.(H.E.), Chester. [0033962] 18/06/1981
Smith Miss KL, BA DipLib MCLIP, Sen.Lib.:Sch.L.Offr., Shropshire Sch.L.Serv. [0031157] 23/09/1979
Smith Mrs KL, MA(Ord) PGDip, Trainee Lib., Glasgow City Council, Cultural & Leisure Serv. [0059104] 15/11/2000
Smith Mrs KL, (was Day), BA MCLIP, L.Asst., Brockenhurst Coll., Brocknhurst, Hants. [0018275] 10/10/1972
Smith Mrs KS, P./t. Stud./Study Cent.Asst., Univ.Aberystwyth, Edinburgh Telford Coll. [0059633] 09/07/2001
Smith Mrs L, BA(Hons), L.Asst., Hempsons Solicitors, Manchester. [0059567] 30/05/2001 AF
Smith Mrs L, DipLib MCLIP, Asst.Lib., Middx.Univ. [0030263] 12/01/1979
Smith Mrs L, BEd DipLib, W/E.Lib., St.Helens Coll.L., Merseyside. [0056074] 06/02/1998
Smith Mrs L, BA MCLIP, Child.Lib., Kirklees M.B.C., Huddersfield. [0013629] 02/04/1971
Smith Mrs L, BSc DipLib MCLIP, Employment unknown. [0060302] 10/12/2001
Smith Miss LA, MCLIP, Inf.Tech.Lib., City Business L., Corporation of London. [0023094] 28/10/1974
Smith Mrs LC, (was Gilbert), MCLIP, Team Lib., Kent.C.C., Folkestone. [0005497] 01/11/1970
Smith Ms LC, BA(Hons), Careers Inf.Offr., Univ.of Brighton. [0058618] 14/04/2000
Smith Mrs LE, (was Burt), BA MA(Hons), Stud./Unemployed. [0061404] 09/07/2002
Smith Ms LJ, (was Whitehead), MA MA, Careers Inf.Mgr., Univ.of Essex, Colchester. [0043039] 10/07/1989
Smith Miss LM, MCLIP, Publications Mgr., Nottingham Trent Univ.L. [0013631] 01/10/1971
Smith Mrs LM, (was Jones), MCLIP, Sch.Lib., Ecclesbourne Sch., Derbys. [0008049] 02/01/1970
Smith Ms LM, (was Carbett), BA MCLIP, ICT/Knowledge Team Leader, Staffs.C.C., Cannock L. [0043655] 21/09/1989
Smith Miss LMR, MCLIP, Life Member. [0013632] 01/01/1955
Smith Mrs M, (was Kybett), Asst.Lib., Univ.of Portsmouth. [0049215] 13/10/1993
Smith Mrs M, Sen.Offr.Comm.Services, Rotherham Borough Council. [0059720] 05/09/2001 AF
Smith Mrs M, BSc(Hons) MCLIP, Lib., Higher Coll.of Tech., U.A.E. [0046940] 04/03/1992
Smith Mrs M, (was Walker), MCLIP, Team Lib., Torry Br.L., Aberdeen City Council. [0015241] 01/10/1971
Smith Ms M, (was MacVicar), MCLIP, Coll.Lib., Royal Coll.of Surgeons, Edinburgh. [0013642] 21/09/1967
Smith Ms M, (was Chubb), MCLIP, Sch.Lib., Thirsk Sch., N.Yorks C.C. [0013640] 29/09/1970
Smith Mr MA, MA MCLIP, Retired. [0013643] 27/02/1959
Smith Mrs MA, (was Garson), MCLIP, Unemployed. [0005385] 09/09/1965
Smith Mrs MA, (was Galpin), MCLIP, Sch.Lib., City of London Sch.for Girls, London. [0005320] 13/01/1966

Smith Ms MC, BA (Hons), Head Cent.Inf.Services, Linklaters, London. [0028367] 07/11/1977
Smith Mr MD, BA FCLIP DipM MCIM, Employment not known. [0013645] 09/01/1969 FE 27/02/1991
Smith Mrs MD, (was Lawson), MCLIP, Self-employed. [0013646] 23/01/1961
Smith Mrs MD, (was Grey), BA MCLIP, Lib.& Inf.Offr., Newcastle City L. [0015047] 01/01/1972
Smith Mr MGR, BA MA MCLIP, Planning & Admin.Mgr., Inf.Serv.Dir., Univ.of Nottingham. [0013650] 31/10/1967
Smith Mr MJ, BA(Hons), Inf.Specialist, NBS Serv., Newcastle upon Tyne. [0054683] 19/02/1997
Smith Mrs MJ, (was Posluschny), BA MLS MA MCLIP, Head Cat.& Presentation Prog., Univ.of San Diego, California, USA. [0041478] 01/01/1988
Smith Ms MJ, MCLIP, Lib., Cambridge Cent.L., Cambs.C.C. [0026195] 18/08/1976
Smith Mrs MM, (was Ralston), BSc PG DipLib MCLIP, Access Serv.Lib., Perth & Kinross Council. [0013654] 25/10/1969
Smith Miss MMA, Sen.Inf.Mgr., Borders Primary Care Trust, Melrose. [0045669] 19/04/1991
Smith Mrs MR, (was Wensley), BA MCLIP, Med.Lib., Devon Partnership Trust, Exeter, Devon. [0034554] 01/01/1982
Smith Mr MS, BA(Hons), Stud., Loughborough Univ. [0059951] 09/11/2001
Smith Mr MS, (was Macartney), FCLIP, Retired. [0013656] 15/09/1950 FE 01/01/1968
Smith Mr MT, BA(Hons) DipILM, Lib., Cheshire C.C., Ellesmere Port L. [0058266] 03/12/1999
Smith Mrs MY, (was Mirfield), BA MCLIP, Lib., Sch.of Linguistics & Applied, Language Stud., Univ.of Reading. [0022479] 11/06/1974
Smith Mr NA, MA MCLIP, Under-Lib., Cambridge Univ.L. [0013658] 06/11/1965
Smith Mr ND, BA(Hons), Stud., UCE Birmingham. [0061670] 16/10/2002
Smith Miss NE, MA MCLIP, Life Member. [0013661] 31/05/1946
Smith Mr NG, BA(Hons) MA, Inf.Spec., Nottingham Trent Univ., Clifton Campus L. [0055638] 30/10/1997
Smith Ms NL, MA MSc MCLIP, Principal Lect., Univ.of Brighton., Brighton, E.Sussex. [0033159] 01/10/1980
Smith Mrs NN, (was Archibald), MA DipLib MCLIP, Dept.Mgr., Schroder Salomon Smith Barney, London. [0029437] 18/08/1978
Smith Dr NR, MSc MCLIP, Position unknown, Aston Univ., Birmingham. [0060644] 11/12/2001
Smith Mr P, BA DipLib MCLIP DMS, Research, Projects & Mktg.Offr., Somerset C.C. [0026806] 05/11/1976
Smith Mrs PCA, BA MCLIP, Sen.Subject Lib., Manchester Metro.Univ.L. [0013667] 01/01/1967
Smith Miss PL, BA MLS MCLIP, Retired. [0017747] 16/01/1950
Smith Miss PM, BA AKC MCLIP, Lib., Paul Hamlyn L., Brit.Museum, London. [0023080] 25/10/1974
Smith Mr PM, BA(Hons) MSc(Econ), Learning Res.Adviser, Colchester Institute. [0059573] 04/06/2001
Smith Mrs PM, BA MCLIP, Sch.Lib., Runcorn St.Chads High Sch., Halton Bor.Council. [0022221] 25/02/1974
Smith Mrs PME, (was Archer), MCLIP, p./t.Educ.Support Asst., Northants.C.C. [0013674] 01/01/1962
Smith Mr PR, BScEcon(Hons) PGCE MPhil, L.Asst., Univ.of Cent.England, Birmingham. [0061608] 03/10/2002 AF
Smith Mr PT, BLib MCLIP, Team Leader: ICT, Newcastle L., Staffs. [0033546] 17/01/1981
Smith Ms R, (was Hartnett), MSc DIC MCLIP, Reader Serv.Lib., Sci.Mus.L., London. [0006494] 25/09/1964
Smith Mr RA, BA MCLIP, Resident in U.S.A. [0032180] 28/01/1980
Smith Mr RC, MCLIP, Lib., European Sch.of Osteopathy, Maidstone, Kent. [0013677] 24/06/1969
Smith Mr REG, FCLIP, Retired, [0013678] 09/10/1930 FE 01/01/1951
Smith Mr RF, MCLIP, Life Member, Tel.0226 791206, 18 Hall Royd Walk, Silkstone Comm., Barnsley, S75 4QA. [0013680] 03/05/1937
Smith Mr RG, MCLIP, Retired. [0013682] 10/01/1964
Smith Ms RJ, BA(Hons) DipIS, Asst.Lib., Univ.of Westminster, London. [0052196] 12/10/1995
Smith Mr RWC, Inf.Offr., Astrazeneca, Loughborough. [0055910] 11/12/1997 AF
Smith Mr S, BA(Hons) MA MCLIP, Learning Adviser, Learning Support Serv., Leeds Metro.Univ. [0028970] 14/02/1978
Smith Mrs S, BA PGCE MCLIP, Lib.-Child.Serv., Loughton L., Essex. [0013690] 08/10/1969
Smith Mrs S, L.Supervisor, Wiltshire C.C., Malmesbury Pub.L. [0056556] 24/08/1998 AF
Smith Miss SA, BA(Hons) MSc, Lib.(Ref.& Inf.), Gosport L., Hampshire. [0057179] 07/01/1999
Smith Mrs SA, (was Rider), BSc, Unemployed. [0060719] 12/12/2001
Smith Miss SE, BA MLS MCLIP, Asst.Lib., Imperial College, Sch.of Med., London. [0033160] 04/10/1980
Smith Mrs SE, BSc MCLIP, Retired. [0060738] 12/12/2001
Smith Mrs SE, (was Kirk), BA(Hons) DipILM MCLIP, Lib., Cricklade Coll., Andover. [0047822] 14/10/1992
Smith Mrs SG, MSc BA(Hons) PGDip, Business Inf.Exec., Small Business Gateway, Aberdeen. [0061054] 19/02/2002
Smith Mr SJ, BA(Hons) MCLIP, Lib.(Lending), Reading Bor.Council. [0053720] 16/09/1996
Smith Mrs SJ, (was Balls), BA MCLIP, Lib., Watford Cent.L., Herts.C.C. [0041725] 22/02/1988
Smith Miss SKH, MA, P./t.Stud.,Inf.Asst., Kings Coll.London., Univ.N.London. [0059810] 10/10/2001
Smith Mrs SL, (was Kemp), BA MCLIP, Asst.Area Lib., Telford L., Shropshire. [0025579] 22/01/1976
Smith Miss SM, BA MCLIP, Retired. [0013699] 01/01/1967

Smith Ms SM, BSc(Hons) MA MCLIP, L.Supervisor, Sefton Council. [0004750] 01/01/1971
Smith Mr SP, BSc DipLib MCLIP, Inst.Lib., Inst.of Grassland & Environ.Res., Aberystwyth. [0030266] 30/12/1978
Smith Miss SRR, BSc MA MCLIP, Sch.L.Serv.Lib., L.B.of Enfield Leisure Servs. [0042989] 26/05/1989
Smith Mr TAD, BA FCLIP, Life Member, 311 Brincliffe Edge Rd., Sheffield, S11 9DE. [0013702] 05/02/1949 FE 01/01/1961
Smith Ms TL, BA(Hons) MA DipLIS MCLIP, Unemployed. [0044322] 06/09/1990
Smith Mrs V, (was Levett), BSc(Econ) MCLIP, Lib.Offr., City of Edinburgh L.Serv., Westerhailes L. [0050983] 07/11/1994
Smith Mrs VA, (was Sage), MCLIP, Unemployed. [0012857] 14/09/1965
Smith Mrs WJ, (was Benns), FCLIP, Life Member. [0001149] 22/02/1937 FE 01/01/1948
Smith Mrs WJ, (was Harris), BA(Hons) MA MCLIP, Inf.Adviser, Univ.of Wales Inst., Cardiff. [0046382] 30/10/1991
Smith Mrs Y, (was Hayes), BSc MCLIP, Prison Lib., H.M.P.Leeds. [0006599] 05/11/1970
Smith Mrs Y, Learning Cent.Supervisor, Univ.of Derby. [0059972] 14/11/2001 AF
Smith-Burnett Mr GCK, MA MCLIP, Retired. [0013576] 01/01/1966
Smith-Haddon Mr BA, Stud., Univ.of Aberystwyth, [0060031] 28/11/2001
Smith-Haye Mrs MG, MCLIP, Head of Bibl.Serv., ProBiblio, Zuid, Netherlands. [0020129] 16/02/1973
Smitherman Mrs FPM, BA, L.Asst., Southampton Univ.Hosp.NHS Trust, Hants. [0040390] 30/01/1987
Smithson Mrs D, (was Birkin), MCLIP, Staff L., Weston-super-mare Gen.Hosp., Weston Area Health Trust. [0013711] 23/08/1968
Smithson Mr DPR, BA(Hons) MSc, Inf.Advisor, Kingston Coll.F.E., Kingston-upon-Thames. [0056627] 23/09/1998
Smithson Ms H, BA(Hons), P./t.Stud./L.Asst., The Royal Society, London. [0059606] 27/06/2001
Smithurst Dr DLS, (was Brown), BSc MSc PhD MCLIP, Employment not known. [0060523] 11/12/2001
Smits Ms ID, BA DipLib, Community Lib., L.B.of Camden. [0037856] 31/10/1994
Smitton Mr S, MCLIP, Mob.& Support Serv.Mgr., Walsal M.B.C., Mob.L.Unit, Bloxwich. [0028895] 14/02/1978
Smout Mrs A-M, MA DipIT MCLIP, Retired. [0028168] 01/10/1977
Smullen Ms EL, BA(Hons) MSc, Asst.Lib., Newman Coll.of H.E., Birmingham. [0058722] 01/07/2000
Smyth Mr AL, MBE FCLIP, Life Member, 21 Westmorland Rd., Urmston, Manchester, M41 9HJ. [0013719] 24/03/1936 FE 01/01/1946
Smyth Mrs AV, BA MLS MCLIP, Life Member. [0013720] 01/01/1970
Smyth Ms DM, (was Coles), BA MCLIP CMS CertEd, Retired. [0013721] 03/10/1967
Smyth Mrs GE, (was Humphreys), BA(Hons) MCLIP, Health Inf.Adviser, NHS Direct Anglia, Riverside Clinic, Ipswich. [0007453] 01/10/1968
Smyth Mrs JE, (was Watson), BSc PhD MSC, Career Break. [0039782] 17/07/1986
Smyth Miss MM, BA MCLIP, Sen.L.Mgr., Belfast P.L. [0023300] 15/11/1974
Smyth Mr NT, BA MSc(Econ), Asst.Inf.Systems.Lib., Univ.of Wales Swansea. [0056472] 23/07/1998
Snape Mr CH, BA(Hons) MA, Seeking work. [0058873] 20/09/2000
Snape Mr FR, BA, Lib.(p/t.), Cox, Hallett & Wilkinson, Hamilton,Bermuda. [0036066] 10/05/1983
Snape Mr T, MCLIP, Group.Lib., Sefton.Met.Dist.L. [0013730] 24/09/1966
Snape Mr WH, DPA FCLIP, Retired. [0013731] 03/10/1933 FE 24/09/1948
Snazell Ms E, MA(Hons), p./t.Stud., City Univ., London, Freshfields. [0061116] 21/02/2002
Sneddon Mr CH, MCLIP, Retired. [0019075] 01/01/1951
Sneddon Mrs JJ, BA(Hons), Study Support Network Mgr., Barnsley Met.Bor.Council., Barnsley. [0057363] 23/02/1999
Sneesby Miss MA, BA MCLIP, Bibl.Serv.Lib., Cent.Div., Hants.C.C. [0020699] 29/05/1973
Snell Miss AC, Asst.Lib., Wimbledon Lawn Tennis Museum, & Kenneth Ritchie Wimbledon L. [0058524] 06/03/2000 AF
Snell Mrs C, BSc, Employment not known. [0040701] 05/05/1987
Snell Mr MJ, BSc MSc MCLIP, Position unknown, Univ.of Stirling. [0060230] 10/12/2001
Snelling Mrs CA, (was Isaac), BA DMS MCLIP, Br.Mgr., Blackburn with Darwen B.C., Lancs. [0034629] 19/01/1982
Snelling Mrs HR, (was Vogwell), BSc MCLIP, Sen.Lib., Local Govt.Inf.Serv., Cambs.Co.Council. [0031479] 12/10/1979
Snelling Ms JR, BA(Hons) MA MCLIP, Lib.i/c., Corpus Christi Coll., Oxford. [0050138] 08/04/1994
Snelling Mr MW, BA DMS MCLIP, Subject Lib., UMIST, Manchester. [0034563] 13/01/1982
Snelling Mrs SM, (was Barker), BSc DipLib MCLIP, p./t.Inf.Lib., Kingston Univ., Kingston Hill L. [0025210] 02/01/1976
Sng Mrs S, (was Liu), BA, Child.& Young Adults Lib., Holroyd City Council, NSW., Australia. [0013740] 06/10/1970
Snook Miss LM, LLB MSc MCLIP, Asst.Lib., Univ.of Exeter, Devon. [0052227] 16/10/1995
Snook Ms M, BLib MCLIP, H.of Community Serv., L.B.Greenwich. [0031703] 19/11/1979
Snow Mrs C, BSc MSc DipAdminStud MCLIP, Employment not known. [0060646] 11/12/2001
Snow Mrs DL, (was Lees), BA(Hons) MSc MCLIP, Sen.Inf.Offr., Osborne Clarke, Bristol. [0054870] 24/04/1997
Snow Miss K, BA, Stud., Univ.of Cent.England, Birmingham. [0058810] 04/08/2000 AF
Snowden Mr A, BSc MSc MCLIP, Employment not known. [0060647] 11/12/2001

Snowden Mr CW, MCLIP, Life Member, Tel.0482 706302, 169 Holmgarth Dr., Bellfield Ave., Hull, N.Humberside, HU8 9DX. [0013746] 18/03/1946
Snowden Ms JE, BA MCLIP, Research Mgr. [0021756] 11/01/1974
Snowden Mr SM, BA(Hons) DipLib, Unemployed. [0032700] 07/06/1980
Snowdon Ms KA, BA MSc MCLIP, Position unknown, Glos.L.Serv. [0056175] 01/04/1998
Snowdon Mrs L, BA MCLIP, Lib., Co.Durham Health Auth., Durham. [0021111] 08/10/1973
Snowdon Mrs MA, (was Smithells), BA DipLib MCLIP, F./t.Lib., Study Cent.L., Friarage Hosp., Northallerton. [0018056] 13/10/1972
Snowley Mr IR, BA MBA MCLIP MIMgt, Dir.of Inf.Serv., Royal Soc.of Med., London. [0035753] 11/01/1983
Soames Miss NA, BA DipLib MCLIP, Secretary-Family Team, Amphlett Lissimore, London. [0032181] 23/01/1980
Soames Mrs Y, (was White), BA MCLIP, Child.Lib., Wirral Bor.Council. [0026606] 01/10/1976
Soar Mr GDE, BA MCLIP, Hon.Research Lib., Univ.Coll.London L. [0013750] 04/06/1955
Soare Miss M, L.Keeper, P.L.for the Visually Disabled, Bucharest, Romania. [0060965] 21/01/2002
Softley Ms K, BA MCLIP, Team Leader, Edinburgh City L. [0033838] 14/03/1981
Soley Barton Mrs CF, (was Soley), MSc, Exec.Offr., Dept.of Trans.Local Govt.and the Regions, London. [0037319] 02/07/1984
Solomon Mrs CM, LLB, Asst.Lib., C.ofLondon Freemens Sch., Surrey. [0059834] 16/10/2001
Solomons Mrs HC, (was Johnson), BA(Hons) MA, Lib., Lovells. [0054126] 31/10/1996
Solomonsz Ms FT, BA MCLIP, Retired. [0013755] 28/08/1961
Somervell Ms JEM, MA PGCE, Stud., Univ.of Central England. [0060039] 03/12/2001
Somerville Mr JHB, BA MA MCLIP, Unemployed. [0040051] 16/10/1986
Somerville Mrs MP, (was Lloyd), BA MCLIP, Retired. [0013759] 16/03/1955
Somovilla Miss CL, MA, Research & Inf.Offr., Financial Ombudsman Serv., London. [0056756] 08/10/1998
Sonley Mrs V, (was Gray), BA MCLIP, Sen.Inf.Offr., Teesside Univ.L., Cleveland. [0027990] 16/10/1977
Sonpal Mrs JM, (was Hemming), BSc DipLIS MCLIP, Princ.Lib.-E., Northants.L.& Inf.Serv., Wellingborough. [0047030] 01/04/1992
Soogali Mr AF, ACIS MLib, Sen.Lib., Ministry of Educ., Port Louis, Mauritius. [0050880] 25/10/1994
Soons Mr ANJ, Unemployed. [0054208] 04/11/1996
Sopher Mr AJ, MA FCLIP, Life Member. [0013762] 03/10/1957 FE 01/01/1962
Sorby Mrs BJ, (was Green), BA MCLIP, Lib.(Job-share), Sheffield L.& Inf.Serv., Sch.L.Serv., Bannerdale Educ.Cent. [0031042] 24/01/1964
Sore Mrs LA, BA DipLib MCLIP, Team Lib., Child.& Young People, Northants.C.C.-Educ.& L. [0028170] 17/10/1977
Soremekun Mrs MO, BLS MA MLS DipLib, Stud., Univ.of N.Carolina at Greensboro, U.S.A. [0061088] 04/03/2002
Sorrigan Mrs D, (was Clempner), BA MCLIP, Princ.Lib., Bury Cent.L., Bury MBC. [0002842] 28/07/1972
Sotheran Ms SC, MCLIP, Sen.Asst.Lib., Barbican L., Barbican Cent.Corp.of, London. [0013766] 24/01/1969
Soto Ms S, Lib., Univ.Abierta Inter-emericema, Argentina. [0026563] 11/10/1976
Soukup Mrs D, Inf.Asst., Kings Coll.London. [0059525] 25/04/2001 AF
Souter Mrs FE, PGDipIS, Unemployed. [0058404] 02/02/2000
Souter Ms LJ, BA(Hons) MA, Subject Lib., Univ.of Huddersfield. [0055518] 16/10/1997
South Mrs AJ, (was Ormerod), BSc DipLib, Young People's Serv.Lib., Herts.C.C., Hertsmere District. [0042373] 24/10/1988
South Ms HL, BSc DipLib MCLIP, Asst.Lib., Univ.of Bath. [0047594] 05/10/1992
South Mrs S, (was Collins), BA DipLib, Head of L., Bradford Grammar Sch. [0040796] 15/06/1987
Southall Mrs HV, (was Warner), BA MCLIP, Positioin Unknown, Sanctuary Houseing Assoc. [0032212] 25/01/1980
Southan Mrs BM, (was French), BA MCLIP, Retired. [0013770] 10/09/1964
Southby Miss GJ, BA(Hons) PGDipILS, Child.Lib., Stanmore L., London. [0055765] 14/11/1997
Southcombe Ms D, (was Portingale), BA MCLIP, Sen.Lib., Sch.L.Serv., Bristol City Council. [0011835] 17/05/1966
Southern Miss P, BA(Hons) MA MPhil MCLIP, Local Studies Lib., Trafford M.B.C. [0013773] 04/03/1969
Southgate Mrs DA, (was Smith), DipHE BA MCLIP, Inf.Serv.Mgr., Chartered Inst.of Marketing, Maidenhead. [0039247] 01/01/1986
Southon Miss RA, BA(Hons), Outreach Lib., N.Hampshire Hosp. [0057284] 27/01/1999
Southworth Mrs V, (was Entwistle), MCLIP, P/t.Sen.Asst.Lib., Hyndburn Dist.L., Lancs.Co.Council. [0013704] 23/03/1962
Soutter Mrs P, (was Fernyhough), MCLIP, Life Member, Tel:01277 899423. [0013778] 06/03/1957
Sowerbutts Mr DL, BA MCLIP, Asst.Lib., Durham Univ.L. [0013780] 14/01/1963
Sowman Ms S, (was Gramopadhye), BA MCLIP, Content Mgmnt.Lib., Chartered Inst.of Personnel & Devel, London SW19. [0028573] 13/01/1978
Sowry Mrs PA, (was Turner), BA DipEd MCLIP ILT, Campus Lib., Kent Inst.of Art & Design, Rochester. [0026265] 14/10/1969
Spacey Ms RE, BA(Hons) MA, Stud., Loughborough Univ. [0059230] 09/01/2001
Spackman Mrs KM, (was Birkhead), BLib MCLIP, Co.Ref.& Inf.Lib., Oxon.C.C. [0037187] 22/02/1984

Spain *(was Roe)*, MCLIP, Employment not known. [0013782] 15/01/1969
Spalding Mrs CJ, (was Philpott), BA(Hons) MCLIP, Lib., Redland High Sch., Bristol. [0028119] 04/10/1977
Spalding Mr DD, MCLIP, Area Lib.(S.), Kirkcaldy Dist.Council. [0019076] 25/03/1964
Spalding Mrs MA, (was Gossman), BSc MCLIP, Sch.Lib., Tomlinscote Sch., Frimley. [0038224] 04/02/1985
Spalding Ms MP, BA(Hons) DipLib, Asst.Lib.,Catg., Dept.of Health, Skipton House, London. [0044409] 05/10/1990
Spalton Mrs BA, (was Morley), MCLIP, Retired. [0013784] 24/04/1935
Sparham Mrs SE, (was Annis), BA(Hons) MCLIP, Lib., Mark Rutherford Upper Sch., Bedford. [0050148] 11/04/1994
Sparkes Miss EKJ, BA MA MCLIP, Lifelong Learning Lib., Warwickshire C.C., Rugby. [0051680] 09/05/1995
Sparkes Ms RAM, BA(Hons), Sen.Sib.Asst., Radcliffe Sci.L., Oxford. [0058340] 17/01/2000
Sparks Miss HT, BA MCLIP, Dep.Lib., Inst.of Elect.Eng.L., London. [0033162] 08/10/1980
Sparks Mrs J, BA DipLib MCLIP, Sen.Asst.Lib., Sci.Res.Cent., Univ.Wales Cardiff. [0023305] 12/11/1974
Sparks Mrs MA, (was Joy), BA MCLIP, Unemployed. [0027689] 03/07/1977
Sparks Mr MD, BSc MSc DipLib MCLIP, Media Serv.Mgr., Univ.of Glamorgan, Pontypridd. [0023351] 11/11/1974
Sparks Mrs S, (was Steed), MCLIP, Area Serv.Mgr., Kent C.C. [0022799] 16/10/1974
Sparrow Mr DA, MA MCLIP, Inf.Offr., Disability Rights Comm., Manchester. [0038924] 18/10/1995
Sparrow Miss DEM, FCLIP, Life Member, Tel.0983 753924, The Deyne, Afton Rd., Freshwater, I.O.W. [0013788] 29/09/1931 **FE 01/01/1938**
Sparrow Mrs GM, BA MCLIP, P./t.Team Member, Child., L.B.of Enfield. [0037939] 16/11/1984
Sparrow Mr KT, BA DipLib MCLIP, L.Asst., Sch.of Oriental & African Studies, Univ.of London. [0034788] 16/02/1984
Sparrowhawk Ms AM, BA(Hons), L.Asst., London Borough of Enfield. [0059717] 05/09/2001 **AF**
Sparrowhawk Mrs D, (was Honnor), BA(Hons) DipLib, Child.Offr., Hartlepool Bor.L., Hartlepool. [0041607] 26/01/1988
Speak Ms MA, BA(Hons) MCLIP, Comm.Access Offr., Leicester City L., Leics. [0027466] 19/04/1977
Speake Mrs A, BSc (Hons), L.Asst./Stud., Prudhoe.Comm.High Sch., Univ.Of Northumbria at Newcastle. [0061336] 29/05/2002
Speake Ms RA, BA(Hons) DipLIS MCLIP, Area Lib.: I.T.& Inf., Doncaster M.B.C., Bentley L. [0049560] 12/11/1993
Speakman Mrs HC, (was Davies), MCLIP, Med.Sec. [0025741] 22/03/1976
Spear Mrs KJ, (was Whitton), BA MA MCLIP, Asst.Lib., Warren Memorial L., USA. [0043396] 19/10/1989
Speare Mrs CD, BA DipLib DHSA MCLIP, Subject Lib., Bradford Coll., W.Yorks. [0041709] 19/02/1988
Spears Mr KG, OBE BSc MBA MCLIP, Lib., Millfield Sch., Street, Somerset. [0013790] 08/05/1965
Speed Mrs JA, BA(Hons), Legislation Project Mgr., Lawtel, London. [0045732] 07/05/1991
Speed Ms JL, BA MCLIP, Peoples Network Project Asst., Cheshire C.C., Northwich. [0038147] 23/01/1985
Speed Mrs LM, (was Shipton), BA MCLIP AALIA, Regional Coordinator, Manukau City Council, New Zealand. [0017761] 29/01/1962
Speeding Mrs T, (was Freeland), BA(Hons), Asst.Inf.Offr., Univ.of Northumbria, Career Serv., City Campus. [0050091] 14/03/1994
Speight Mr AE, BA MCLIP, p./t.Asst.Lib., Dept.for Educ.& Skills, Sheffield L. [0013791] 29/02/1960
Speight Mr SG, BA(Hons) MA MCLIP, Dep.L.Serv.Mgr., Elizabeth Gaskell L., Manchester Met.Univ. [0048451] 13/01/1993
Speight Mr TD, MA(Oxon) MSc(Econ) MCLIP, Research Lib., Baker & Mckenzie, London. [0052497] 02/11/1995
Spellman Miss JF, BA MCLIP, Lib., Queen Elizabeth Sixth Form Coll., Darlington. [0035032] 02/07/1982
Spells Mrs LK, (was Robertson), BSc DipLib MCLIP, Div.Lib., Edinburgh City L. [0034455] 10/11/1981
Spells Miss SJ, LLB(Hons), Stud. [0061504] 02/09/2002
Spence Mrs G, (was Westmoreland), BA MCLIP, Comm.Lib., Wilts.Co.Educ.& L., Chippenham L. [0023396] 08/01/1975
Spence Mrs GM, (was Lambirth), BA DipLib, Lib.i/c., Sidmouth, Devon. [0044593] 01/11/1990
Spence Ms HP, BEd(Hons) MA MCLIP, L.& Intelligence Offr., Enfield & Haringey Health Auth. [0047578] 02/10/1992
Spence Mr I, BA DMS MCLIP, Sen.Lib.(Bibl.& Support Serv.), N.Lancs.Div., Lancs. [0030542] 17/01/1979
Spence Miss JB, MCLIP, Lib., Aloha Coll., Spain. [0025424] 16/01/1976
Spence Mrs K, (was Wallington), BA(Hons) MSc, Lib., Edwards Geldard, Cardiff. [0054425] 09/12/1996
Spence Mrs SA, (was Richardson), BA(Hons) MCLIP, L.&Inf.Service Mgr., Swinton L. [0029083] 06/03/1978
Spencer Mr BC, BA MCLIP, Lib., Duncan Macmillan House, Nottingham. [0013799] 28/09/1964
Spencer Mr C, BA(Hons) PGDipLib, Lib., Transport I., Univ.Newcastle Upon Tyne. [0056666] 24/07/2001
Spencer Mr C, BSc DipLib MCLIP, L.Procurement & Systems Devel.Mgr., Bournemouth Univ., Poole. [0031458] 16/10/1979
Spencer Mr DR, BA MCLIP, Retired. [0021439] 31/10/1975
Spencer Miss GD, BSc DipInf, Unemployed. [0052576] 06/11/1995
Spencer Miss GL, BA(Hons) DipILM MCLIP, Asst.Lib., Hollings L., Manchester Met.Univ. [0057710] 09/07/1999
Spencer Ms H, BA(Hons) DipILS MCLIP, Sen.Lib., Music & Recorded Sound, Burnley Cent.L., Lancs.C.C. [0056245] 17/04/1998

Spencer Mrs J, (was Higham), MBE BA MCLIP, Reg.Co-ordinator, Everybodys Reading Project, Bolton M.B.C. [0028237] 03/10/1977
Spencer Ms KE, DipIS MA MCLIP, Learning Res.Adviser, Cambridge Reg.Coll., Cambridge. [0050749] 17/10/1994
Spencer Mr KJ, FCLIP, Life Member, 6 Moffats Lane, Brookmans Park, Hatfield, Herts., AL9 7RU. [0013807] 08/09/1948 **FE 01/01/1964**
Spencer Miss LA, BA DipLib MCLIP DMS MIMgt, Ref.Inf.& Local Studs.Team Leader, Kent C.C.Arts & L., Tonbridge L. [0028174] 18/10/1977
Spencer Ms LO, (was Wilmot), MCLIP, Deputy Co.Lib., Staffs.L.& Inf.Serv., Stafford. [0016038] 19/02/1970
Spencer Mrs MM, (was Harding), MCLIP, Arts & L.Offr., Kent C.C. [0026026] 04/10/1966
Spencer Revd NR, BA(Hons) MCLIP DipAppTheol, Grp.Lib., Hereford L. [0010526] 07/01/1972
Spencer Mr PG, BA MCLIP, Team Lib., Norfolk C.C., Dereham. [0013812] 23/10/1970
Spencer Mr PJ, BA DipLib MCLIP, Teacher/IT Coordinator, Eltham Coll.Jnr.Sch., London. [0028173] 06/10/1977
Spencer Mr RCH, MA MCLIP, Retired. [0060603] 11/12/2001
Spencer Mr V, Asst.Lib., Westwood Coll., Kent. [0061391] 03/07/2002 **AF**
Spencer Mrs VF, Bibl.Asst., John Rylands Univ.L., Manchester. [0039309] 07/01/1986
Sperling Mrs SVD, BA MA MCLIP, Principal Lib.-Young Peoples Serv., Kent Arts & L., Herne Bay L. [0023063] 26/10/1974
Spiby Mr DR, MA FCLIP, Retired, 2 Montgomery Rd., Barnard Castle, Co.Durham, DL12 8AS. [0017763] 11/07/1951 **FE 01/01/1960**
Spiby Mrs JN, MA DipLib MCLIP, Lib., Stuartholme Sch., Australia. [0029462] 14/07/1978
Spice Mr CG, MBCS MCLIP, Employment not known. [0060412] 11/12/2001
Spickernell Mrs MP, (was Woodhams), MCLIP, Retired. [0016235] 05/02/1949
Spiers Ms ALT, BA MSc, Inf.Offr., Inst.of Mech.Engineers, London. [0052592] 10/11/1995
Spiers Mr DL, MCLIP, Unemployed. [0023161] 07/11/1974
Spiller Miss DH, BA, L.Asst., Univ.of Strathclyde Law L., Glasgow. [0054675] 21/02/1997
Spiller Mr DJ, OBE MLS MCLIP, Retired. [0017765] 27/03/1960
Spink Mr PJ, BA MCLIP, Head of Inf.Serv., Advertising Assoc., London. [0021958] 22/01/1974
Spink Mrs S, (was Davies), MSc BA MCLIP, Dept.Inf.and L.Studies, Univ.of Wales, Aberystwyth. [0003746] 23/01/1968
Spink Mrs WT, (was Spinks), BA MCLIP, Asst.Lib., Epsom Coll., Surrey. [0013829] 06/10/1971
Spires-Lane Mrs VMC, (was Spires), BSc(Hons) MCLIP, Med.Inf.Specialist, Inf.Inspires, Loughton. [0024451] 05/07/1975
Spiteri Mr JP, MCLIP, Retired. [0017766] 01/06/1967
Spittal Mrs AK, (was Rach), BA MCLIP, Learning Cent.Mgr., Westminster Kingsway Coll., London. [0013830] 18/02/1965
Spittal Mr CJ, MCLIP, Life Member. [0013831] 02/07/1945
Splaine Mrs J, Lib., Manchester City Council, Manchester Cent.L. [0055534] 20/10/1997
Spooner Mrs GF, (was Harvey), BSc MCLIP, ICT Support, Ashlyns Sch., Herts. [0030839] 07/05/1979
Spooner Mr MP, B ED MCLIP, Self-Employed. [0020881] 14/08/1973
Spooner Mr PV, MCLIP, Life Member, Tel.020 8693 3697, 76 Homestall Rd., London, SE22 OSB. [0013834] 11/07/1938
Sprague Ms MA, BA(Hons) DipILS MCLIP, Unemployed. [0043893] 13/02/1990
Sprague Ms NR, MLS, Physical Sci.Lib., Univ.of Edinburgh L., Edinburgh. [0057905] 01/10/1999
Spratt Ms VS, BA(Hons), Resources Mgr., Scottish Parliament Inf.Cent., Edinburgh. [0040308] 06/01/1987
Sprawling Mrs JE, (was Hoare), BA MCLIP, Sch.Lib.& Inf.Offr., Salendine Nook, Kirklees. [0035007] 15/06/1982
Spreadbury Ms HE, BSc(Hons), Inf.Offr., Weil, Gotshal & Manges, London. [0054154] 07/11/1996
Spreckley Mr AW, MA MCLIP, Stud.Adviser, Blackpool & the Fylde Coll., Lancs. [0024380] 01/07/1975
Sprevak Mrs MY, (was Derby), BA DipLib MCLIP, Asst.Lib., Queens Univ.of Belfast. [0013835] 05/10/1967
Spriggs Mrs KA, (was Perkins), BA MCLIP, Sen.Lib., (Serv.to Child.& Young People), Chesterfield Cent.L. [0011545] 08/09/1966
Spriggs Mrs SM, (was Reddaway), BSc MCLIP, Toxicology Lib., Leicester Univ. [0013836] 17/01/1972
Spring Mr PN, MSc BA DipLib FCLIP, Product Design Mgr., SilverPlatter Inf.Ltd., London. [0028175] 12/10/1977 **FE 25/05/1994**
Springbett Mrs SR, (was Martin), BA MCLIP, p./t.L.Mgr., L.B.of Croydon, Sanderstead. [0022386] 01/04/1974
Springer Mrs JM, (was Butterworth), BA DipLib MCLIP, Asst.Lib., Southampton Univ. [0027914] 12/10/1977
Springham Miss SA, BLib MCLIP, Dep.H.of L.Serv., Brighton & Sussex Univ.Hosp., NHS Trust, E.Sussex. [0041603] 26/01/1988
Sproat Miss AE, BA(Hons) MA DipLib MCLIP, Spec.Collections Lib., Book L., Courtauld Inst.of Art, London. [0047995] 30/10/1992
Sproat Miss K, BA(Hons) MSc, Business Lib., ESCP-EAP European Sch.of Mgmt., Oxford. [0055792] 24/11/1997
Sproston Mr GF, BA MCLIP, Retired. [0013839] 14/02/1967
Sproston Mrs LAC, (was Munford), BA MCLIP, Eccles Lib., British Museum. [0013840] 10/01/1968
Spruce Ms CA, BA MA MCLIP, Lib., Warwicks.C.C., Rugby L. [0044851] 18/12/1990
Spruce Mrs JE, (was Smithson), MCLIP, p./t.Sch.Lib., Ashcroft High Sch., Luton. [0013841] 16/03/1965
Spruce Mrs WJ, (was Clark), BA MCLIP, Retired. [0013842] 28/01/1957

Personal Members — Stead

Spry Miss ER, BA MCLIP, Lib.Team Leader, Norfolk Co.L., Plumstead Road L. [0013843] 20/10/1967
Spry-Leverton Capt HHS, Lib., Uppingham Sch. [0037326] 01/07/1984
Spurgin Miss CB, MA(Hons), Sch.Lib., Kilgraston Sch., Bridge of Earn, Perth. [0052050] 02/10/1995
Spurrier Miss HL, MCLIP, Lib., Swindon & Marlborough NHS Trust, Wilts. [0013847] 13/10/1961
Squire Miss GM, BA, Sen.L.Asst., SSEES L., Univ.Coll.London. [0052265] 20/10/1995
Squire Mrs SC, BA, P./T.Stud., P./t.L.Technician, St.Pauls C of E Junior Sch., Univ.Coll. London. [0059795] 03/10/2001
Squires Miss CA, BD MA, L.Asst., Goldsmiths Coll., London. [0057791] 06/08/1999 **AF**
Squires Mrs LA, (was Manley), BLib MCLIP, Sen.Lib.-Child.& Learning, Glos.C.C. [0041308] 01/11/1987
Squirrell Miss A, BA(Hons) PGCE, Res.Mgr., Bell Language Sch., Saffron Walden. [0061262] 10/05/2002
St Aubyn Miss PM, MCLIP, Lib., Scottish Police Coll., Kincardine, Fife. [0029832] 02/10/1978
St Clair Ms SJ, DipEd DipHistArt MCLIP, Self Employed. [0022962] 01/10/1974
St John Ms RV, BA DipLib MCLIP, Retired. [0025117] 15/11/1975
St John Mrs SA, (was Davies), BA MA MCLIP, Maternity leave. [0044941] 23/01/1991
St.John-Coleman Mrs MA, (was Sweeting), BSc MCLIP, Housewife. [0014285] 14/10/1971
Stables Mrs B, DipIM, p./t.Lib., Royal Bournemouth Hosp., Dorset. [0052662] 16/11/1995
Stacey Ms A, BA DipLib MCLIP, Team Leader, Talis Inf.Ltd., Birmingham. [0038129] 21/01/1985
Stacey Mrs EA, (was Hanger), Asst.Lib., De Montfort Univ., Leicester. [0037266] 14/05/1984
Stacey Miss KD, (was Cottingham), DipLIS, Unemployed. [0041540] 19/01/1988
Stacey Mrs MC, (was Granville), BA MCLIP, Retired, 1 Arnesby Rd., Nottingham, NG7 2EA. [0013854] 02/10/1964
Stacey Mr MJ, MA MCLIP, Lib., Business L., Nottingham City L. [0013855] 22/04/1964
Stacey Mr RW, FCLIP, Life Member. [0017771] 12/02/1952 **FE 01/01/1959**
Stack Mrs A, (was Goldsbrough), MCLIP, p./t.Child.Lib., N.Finchley L., L.B.of Barnet. [0005645] 01/01/1971
Stadler Mrs DE, (was Rawkins), MCLIP, Life Member. [0013857] 16/03/1941
Staff Mrs DK, Resource Offr, Substance Misuse, HIV Partnerships Local Health NHS, Bury St.Edmunds. [0053707] 10/09/1996 **AF**
Stafford Mr CJ, MCLIP, p./t.L.Asst., N.E.Wales Inst., Wrexham. [0013858] 04/11/1965
Stafford Mr GA, MA ALAA FCLIP, Life Member. [0017772] 10/03/1953 **FE 01/01/1960**
Stafford Miss HM, BA(Hons) PGDip, Inf.Specialist, GCHQ L.Serv., Cheltenham. [0053568] 24/07/1996
Stafford Mr JAT, BA MCLIP, Sen.Lib., Worcester L., Worcs.C.C. [0013860] 28/05/1965
Stafford Mr JB, MCLIP, Area Sales Mgr., Demco Interiors. [0013861] 01/02/1960
Stafford Mrs JC, BA MCLIP, L.& Inf.Mgr., N.Tyneside Bor.Council. [0029348] 09/06/1978
Stafford Mrs SM, (was Orton), MCLIP, L.& Inf.Serv.Mgr., Health Sci.L., PG Educ.Cent., Ashford & St.Peters Hosp.NHS Trst. [0017773] 07/04/1964
Stagg Mrs SN, DipEdTech MCLIP, Retired. [0009282] 01/01/1953
Staig Mr MI, LLB MCLIP, Sen.Asst.Lib., Goldsmiths Coll., London. [0013865] 12/05/1967
Stainer Miss A, BA(Hons), Legal Inf.Offr., Scottish Exec., Edinburgh. [0058882] 01/10/2000
Stainer Ms C, BA(Hons) MA, Music Catr., Royal Coll.of Music, London. [0053861] 08/10/1996
Staines Mrs FE, Serv.Mgr., Loughton L., Essex. [0061065] 01/02/2002 **AF**
Stainton Mrs E, BA(Hons), Inf.Offr., Eversheds Solicitors, Cardiff. [0058379] 24/01/2000
Staley Mrs SA, Head of Learning Res.Cent., The Warren Comp.Sch., Essex. [0059589] 11/06/2001
Stalker Miss MM, FCLIP, Retired. [0013870] 27/08/1945 **FE 01/01/1965**
Stalker-Booth Mrs CS, (was Saunders), BAS(Info) DipLit, Lib., Highlands Sch., London. [0056051] 20/01/1998
Stallard Ms VM, BMus(Hons) MA, Asst.Lib., Cardiff Univ., Cardiff. [0059082] 09/11/2000
Stamenkovic Ms JM, (was Cooper), MA PGDip MCLIP, Asst.Lib.(Academic Liaison), Frewen L., Univ.of Portsmouth. [0029618] 16/09/1978
Stamp Mr AD, MCLIP, Sen.Lib., Adult Lend.L., Wolverhampton Cent.L. [0025426] 08/01/1976
Stanbury Mrs FED, (was Newton), MCLIP, Princ.Lib., L.B.of Hounslow. [0010780] 29/09/1970
Stanbury Mrs SC, (was Smith), BA MA MCLIP, Unemployed. [0035088] 26/07/1982
Stancombe Mrs S, (was Gerrard), BA MCLIP, Housewife & Mother. [0035928] 14/02/1983
Standen Miss L, BA(Hons) MA, Inf.Offr., Healey & Baker, London. [0057006] 20/11/1998
Standen Miss PM, MCLIP, Educ.Liaison Offr., E.Ayrshire Council. [0022611] 01/10/1974
Standish Mrs H, (was Thorpe), BSc(Hons), Asst.Lib., Manchester Met.Univ. [0048489] 26/01/1993

Stanford Mrs AM, (was Dunn), BA DipLib MCLIP, Acquisitions & Data Base Mgr., Bibl.Serv.Div., Birmingham L.Serv. [0033628] 26/01/1981
Stanford-Harris Mrs PJ, MA, Unemployed. [0052042] 02/10/1995
Stanforth Miss JM, MCLIP, Div.Young Peoples Lib., N.Div., Lancs.C.C. [0020302] 05/02/1973
Stanforth Mrs SM, MA MCLIP, Volunteer Catr., York Minster L., Univ.of York. [0018071] 02/10/1972
Stanier Mrs E, (was Johnstone), MA DipLib MCLIP, Team Lib., Mitchell L., Glasgow. [0028033] 19/10/1977
Staniforth Mrs ME, (was Harrison), BA MA MCLIP, Inf.Librarian, Derbyshire C.Council. [0034542] 15/12/1981
Staniland Mrs AC, (was Bown), MCLIP, Sen.Lib., Sheffield City L., S.Yorks. [0013884] 01/01/1958
Stanistreet Mrs JE, (was Einchcomb), MA MCLIP, Princ.L.Serv.Offr.(N.), Sefton M.B.C., Southport. [0013885] 25/11/1968
Stanisz Miss JV, BA(Hons), Team Leader - Learning Resources, S.Trafford Coll., Altrincham, Cheshire. [0049324] 22/10/1993
Stanley Mrs BTM, Interpreter, IND, Croydon. [0041734] 01/03/1988
Stanley Ms J, BA(Hons) DipLib MCLIP, p./t. Comm.Librarian, Stoke-on-Trent L. [0037690] 02/10/1984
Stanley Mrs RE, Sen.Inf.Offr., J.P.Kenny Ltd., Staines. [0036162] 09/07/1983
Stanley Mrs SA, (was Mearns), MCLIP, Consultant, Todays Off., Bishops Stortford, Herts. [0010031] 14/10/1970
Stanley Ms TS, BA(Hons) MSc, Head of E-Strategy, Brotherton L., Univ.of Leeds. [0050481] 18/08/1994
Stanley Mrs W, (was Griffiths), BA DipEd, Sch.Lib., Marlborough Sch., St.Albans. [0043237] 13/10/1989
Stannard Mrs A, (was Yates), MCLIP, P/t.L.Asst., Bolton Metro.Bor. [0016408] 11/09/1971
Stannard Mrs JM, (was Howe), MCLIP, Ashdown House L.& Inf.Cent.Mgr., Dept.of Trans.Local Govt.and the, Regions, London. [0007296] 30/08/1971
Stannard Mr P, BA(Hons) MCLIP, Sch.Lib., Nottingham City Council. [0054510] 09/01/1997
Stannett Dr A, (was Jacoby), Retired. [0013894] 01/01/1955
Stansbury Ms CT, BLib MCLIP, Legal Lib., Mundays Solicitors, Esher. [0038554] 01/07/1985
Stansfield Mrs CA, (was Curley), BA MCLIP, Catr., Univ.of Warwick. [0031244] 11/10/1979
Stansfield Mrs EF, BA MCLIP, Asst.Lib., G.C.H.Q., Cheltenham. [0032282] 25/02/1980
Stansfield Mrs MF, (was Harrington), BA(Hons) MCLIP, Inf.Analyst, Wincanton plc, Somerset. [0049818] 15/12/1993
Stanton Mrs C, (was Bell), MCLIP, Retired. [0027246] 01/01/1968
Stanton Mrs JR, (was Holmes), MCLIP, Reviewer., Whitakers Good Book Guide. [0020552] 04/04/1973
Stanton Mrs KA, (was Prestwood), BA DipLib, Dir.-Inf.Servs., Univ.of Nottingham. [0037091] 07/02/1984
Stanton Mr TM, BA(Hons) MA, Asst.Lib., W.Sussex Co.L.Serv., Worthing L. [0055268] 11/09/1997
Stanton Mrs WJ, (was Watts), BA MCLIP, Med.Lib., Univ.of Nottingham, Queens Med.Cent., Notts. [0023718] 01/01/1975
Staples Mr FD, MCLIP, Retired. [0013900] 09/02/1954
Staples Mrs LM, (was Thompson), MCLIP, Life Member. [0013902] 26/09/1949
Stapleton Ms C, MCLIP, Mgr., Ergonomics Inf.Analysis Cent., Birmingham. [0013903] 09/01/1966
Stapleton Mrs JA, (was Reedman), MCLIP, Music Lib., Birmingham P.L. [0012237] 23/02/1970
Stapley Mrs GE, (was Baxter), MCLIP, Training Adviser, Independent. [0027304] 25/03/1977
Starbuck Mrs FA, BA DipLib MCLIP, Knowledge Content Developer, Brit.Council, Manchester. [0040447] 31/01/1987
Starbuck Mr JE, BA MCLIP, Princ.Corp.Projects Mgr., Wakefield M.D.C., W.Yorks. [0013906] 06/01/1970
Starbuck Mrs SR, (was Clark), LLB DipLib MA MCLIP, Employment not known. [0039912] 01/10/1986
Stares Mrs EAL, MA, Asst.Lib., Gonville & Caius Coll., Cambridge. [0057029] 26/11/1998
Stark Miss KL, BA(Hons), Stud., Loughborough Univ. [0059974] 14/11/2001
Stark Mrs LA, (was Dale), BA DipLib MCLIP, Sen.Asst.Lib., Harrow Pub.L., Middlesex. [0025518] 21/01/1976
Stark Mrs R, (was Workman), MCLIP, L.B.of Lewisham, Lewisham Ref.L. [0016302] 01/01/1966
Stark Mrs RM, (was Suff), BA(Hons) DipLib, L.& Inf.Serv.Mgr., Norfolk Health Auth., Norwich. [0044383] 04/10/1990
Starkey Miss GM, BA MCLIP, Child.& Young Peoples Lib., Northumberland Co.L., Morpeth. [0026565] 01/10/1976
Starkey Mr PB, BA(Hons), Business Inf.Offr., Rhyl L., Denbighshire C.C. [0054513] 15/01/1997
Starling Miss L, BA(Hons), Stud. [0056483] 21/07/1998
Starrs Mrs JM, BA(Hons) DipIM, Sch.Lib., Ballymena Academy. [0053864] 07/10/1996
Statham Mr MHW, MA FCLIP, Life Member. [0013912] 01/01/1953 **FE 01/01/1959**
Statham Mr MS, BA(Hons) MA MCLIP, Sub-Lib., Gonville & Caius Coll., Cambridge. [0049164] 08/10/1993
Stauch Mrs JP, MCLIP, Coll.Lib., Richmond-u-Thames Tertiary Coll., Twickenham. [0013914] 01/01/1972
Staughton Mr DJ, BSc, Knowledge Mgmnt., Schlumberger, Crawley. [0058348] 17/01/2000
Staunton Ms MT, BA DipLib MCLIP, Dist.Lib., Rickmansworth L., Herts. Co. Council. [0039605] 01/04/1986
Stead Mrs CE, BA(Hons) MA MCLIP, Lib., Doncaster Col., Doncaster, S Yorks. [0059672] 25/07/2001

Stead Mr M, BA(Hons), Grad.Trainee, JB Priestly L., Univ.of Bradford. [0059776] 02/10/2001
Stead Ms M, BA(Hons) DipLIS, Asst.Lib., Nat.Art L., London. [0050624] 01/10/1994
Stead Miss ZE, BA(Hons) MA, Unemployed. [0055274] 12/09/1997
Stearn Miss AL, BA(Hons) MA MCLIP, L.Asst., Univ.Coll.Oxford. [0056765] 08/10/1998
Stearn Mrs CG, (was Hales), BA, Asst.Lib., Dewsbury L., Kirklees M.C. [0040613] 03/04/1987
Stearn Mr RR, BA MCLIP, Child.Serv.Lib.-Special Serv., Wheatsheaf L., Rochdale M.B.C. [0030878] 22/05/1979
Stebbing Ms DJ, (was Orry), BLib MCLIP, Subject Lib. Business and Law, A.P.U.L., Chelmsford, Essex. [0026137] 01/07/1976
Stebbings Mrs AC, (was Tucker), BA MLib MCLIP, Sen.Lib., L.B.of Barnet, Chipping Barnet L. [0045445] 06/02/1991
Stedman Mr R, FCLIP, Life Member, Tel:01493 731987). [0013923] 05/02/1956 **FE 01/01/1971**
Stedman Mrs R, (was Sutherland), MA(Hons) DipILS, Enquiry Serv.Mgr., Health & Safety Exec., Bootle. [0052842] 04/01/1996
Steed Mrs AM, MA DipLib MCLIP, Inf.Asst., Univ.of Aberdeen, Taylor L.& EDC. [0029835] 26/09/1978
Steedman Miss T, MA DipILS MCLIP, Asst.Customer Serv.Lib., Carnegie L., Dunfermline. [0054597] 30/01/1997
Steel Mrs AJ, (was Evans), MCLIP, Asst.Lib., Southend Bor.L., Essex. [0021164] 02/10/1973
Steel Mrs BA, (was Johns), Sen.L.Asst., Univ.of Sheffield. [0045085] 06/07/1990 **AF**
Steel Mrs EZM, (was Rzeznik), BLib PGCE, Childrens Lib., Northampton Cent.L. [0028667] 12/01/1978
Steel Miss LE, BA (Hons), Inf.Offr., PA Consulting Group. [0059341] 12/02/2001
Steel Mrs P, BSc MSc MCLIP, Nkowledge Serv.Mgr., WS Atkins Plc., Epsom, Surrey. [0052256] 18/07/1995
Steele Mr CR, MA FALIA FCLIP, Univ.Lib., Australian Nat.Univ.L., Canberra. [0013925] 14/01/1966 **FE 22/07/1998**
Steele Mr HF, BA FCLIP, Life Member, 711 Scottsdale Drive, Guelph, Ontario N1G 3P3, Canada. [0017777] 21/10/1944 **FE 01/01/1951**
Steele Mrs JA, BSc MCLIP, Employment not known. [0060648] 11/12/2001
Steele Mrs JEA, (was Waight), BA DipLib MCLIP, Retired. [0042348] 10/10/1988
Steele Mrs JP, (was Richmond), MCLIP, Ch.Asst., Cambridge Univ.Med.L., Addenbrookes Hosp. [0013929] 01/01/1962
Steele Ms ME, BA MCLIP, Sch.Serv.Lib., L.B.of Harrow. [0021074] 03/10/1973
Steele Mr P, BSc DipInfSc MCLIP MRSC, Position unknown, Current Patents Ltd., London. [0060645] 11/12/2001
Steele Miss UM, p./t.L.Asst., New Coll., Oxford. [0057139] 21/12/1998 **AF**
Steele Miss V, BSc(Econ)(Hons), Stud., Univ.of Wales, Aberystwyth, & Asst.Ch.Lib., Cent.Mus.L., Royal Marines Band Serv. [0055987] 08/01/1998
Steele-Morgan Miss S, B Ed DipLib MCLIP, Sen.Asst.Lib., Neath Port Talbot Co.Bor., Port Talbot. [0043621] 17/10/1983
Steemson Mr MJ, Resident in New Zealand. [0060100] 07/12/2001
Steer Mr AC, BA MCLIP, Film Researcher, Border TV., Carlisle. [0042731] 14/02/1989
Steer Miss CM, BA MCLIP, Life Member. [0013932] 07/01/1952
Steer Mrs MJ, (was Elliott), BA(Hons) DipLIS MCLIP, Inf.Mgr., Osborne Clarke, Bristol. [0046498] 12/11/1991
Steer Mrs RA, (was Rogers), BA MBA DAA, Mid.Suffolk Locality Mgr., Lowestoft L., Suffolk C.C. [0053283] 23/04/1996
Steere Mrs AM, (was Baker), BA(Hons) MCLIP, p./t.L.Super., Hants.C.C., Winchester. [0026625] 27/10/1976
Stein Mrs AM, (was Thomson), MA(Hons) DipLIS MCLIP, Asst.Lib., Lothian NHS Board, Edinburgh. [0049832] 16/12/1993
Stein Mr J, BSc DipLib MSc, Inf.Specialist, Cent.Sci.Lab., York. [0046726] 02/01/1992
Stein Mr R, BSc MSc, Employment not known. [0060452] 11/12/2001
Steiner Mrs BK, (was Smith), BA FCLIP, Life Member. [0013936] 19/08/1947 **FE 25/11/1975**
Steiner Mrs S, (was Reeves), BA MA MCLIP, Unemployed. [0045610] 01/04/1991
Steiner Mr WAF, LLM MA FCLIP, Life Member. [0013937] 01/07/1946 **FE 16/03/1981**
Steinhaus Mrs ER, (was Levy), BA DipLib MCLIP, p./t.Sch.Lib., Menorah Prim.Sch., Barnet L.E.A. [0028055] 06/10/1977
Steinle Mrs J, (was Narey), BA MCLIP, Sch.Clerical Asst./Auxiliary, Highland Reg.Council, Inverness. [0020660] 14/05/1973
Stekis Miss SJ, MCLIP, Life Member. [0017781] 22/02/1954
Stelling Mrs CR, (was Selkirk), BA MCLIP, Sen.Lib.-Tadley Grp., Hants.C.C. [0028364] 04/11/1977
Stelling Mr DE, BA MCLIP, Inf.Lib., Hants.Co.L., Farnborough. [0025427] 06/01/1976
Stemp Miss AJ, BA, Lib., Yale Coll., Wrexham. [0027467] 04/04/1977
Stemp Miss LM, Reader Serv.Lib., Home Off., London. [0052388] 26/10/1995
Stennett Ms RE, MA DipInf, Asst.Bibl.Serv.Lib., Canterbury Christ Church Univ.Coll. [0047600] 05/10/1992
Stenning Mr CM, BA DipLib MCLIP, Intranet Systems Administrator, Bracknell Forest Bor.Council. [0036590] 16/10/1983
Stenson Ms R, BA DipEd, Bibl.Serv.Mgr., Glasgow Univ.L. [0045321] 08/10/1990
Stenson Miss SM, MCLIP, L.Super., Maghull L., Sefton L.& Arts Serv. [0013939] 17/04/1968
Stenzel Miss DJ, BSc(Hons), Stud., Univ.of N.London. [0059041] 31/10/2000

Stepan Mrs SM, (was Sanderson), BA, Sen.L.Asst., Cent.L., Leeds City Council. [0041738] 28/02/1988
Stephanou Ms M, Principal libr., L.B.of Haringey L.Servs., Hornsey L. [0049565] 11/11/1993
Stephany Miss JR, BA(Hons) MA MHSM DipHSM MIMC CMC, Self Employed. [0054217] 05/11/1996 **SP**
Stephen Miss AE, B ED MCLIP, Child.Servs.Lib., Aberdeen City L. [0025114] 17/10/1975
Stephen Mr DWR, BA MCLIP, Dep. Lib., Heriot-Watt Univ., Edinburgh. [0013943] 08/10/1971
Stephen Ms HE, MSc MCLIP, Inf.Lib.(Eves.)/Sunday Super., London Guildhall Univ., Goldsmiths Coll. [0044030] 03/04/1990
Stephen Miss JM, MCLIP, Retired. [0013944] 15/03/1965
Stephen Mrs RAR, (was Reid), MA DipLib MCLIP, Career Break. [0036357] 01/10/1983
Stephens Mrs AJ, (was Kennard), MCLIP, Lib., Ashford High Sch., Middx. [0013948] 25/02/1965
Stephens Mrs C, (was Verity), BA MCLIP, [0013949] 20/07/1965
Stephens Mr DJ, BA DipEd MCLIP, Retired. [0013950] 01/10/1969
Stephens Mrs GJ, (was Vaughan), MCLIP, Unemployed. [0015084] 12/01/1972
Stephens Mr J, BA(Hons) MCLIP, Head of New Initiatives, Cornwall C.C., Truro. [0013953] 01/10/1971
Stephens Mr JM, BA MCLIP, Stock Res.Mgr., Devon C.C. [0013955] 01/01/1972
Stephens Mrs JM, (was Davys), MBE MCLIP, Retired. [0013954] 01/01/1938
Stephens Miss ME, BLib MCLIP LMusTCL LTCL, Lib.Music & AV/Lend., Hammersmith N., L.B.of Hammersmith & Fulham. [0027628] 24/05/1977
Stephens Ms SE, (was Ormerod), BSc MA MCLIP, Lib., Scottish Crop Research Inst., Dundee. [0013959] 22/10/1970
Stephens Miss SV, BA, Lib., Lane & Partners, London. [0037404] 20/08/1984
Stephens Mr TJ, Resource Asst., Queenwood Lib., Univ. of Brighton. [0059209] 08/01/2001
Stephens Mrs V, (was Harper), MCLIP, Unemployed. [0020359] 06/03/1973
Stephenson Ms A, BA(Hons) PgD, L.& Inf.Offr., Newcastle L.& Inf.Serv. [0053299] 26/04/1996
Stephenson Miss B, MCLIP, Stock Serv.Mgr., Newcastle upon Tyne L.& Inf. [0013962] 14/03/1967
Stephenson Mrs J, (was Nicholas), BLib MCLIP, Health Serv.L.Mgr., Univ.of Southampton, Southampton. [0029769] 09/10/1978
Stephenson Mrs JT, BA(Hons) MCLIP, Project Offr.-Integrated Access, Durham C.C., Dept.of Arts L.& Mus., Co.Durham. [0051346] 25/01/1995
Stephenson Mrs KD, BA, Inf.Mgr., Univ.of Southampton. [0046250] 18/10/1991
Stephenson Mrs MS, (was Hilton), BA MCLIP, Sch.Lib., St.Thomas More School, London. [0013971] 11/01/1966
Stephenson Mr RB, BA MCLIP, Loc.Stud.Lib., Bedford Cent.L., Beds.C.C. [0013972] 15/03/1963
Stephenson Mrs S, (was Lawrence), MCLIP, Unemployed. [0008715] 16/01/1968
Sterling Mrs LJ, (was Dye), BA MCLIP, Bibl.Serv.Mgr., Met.Boro.of Wirral, Cent.L. [0004321] 05/03/1969
Stern Mr JA, BA MA, Legal Inf.Offr., The Environment Agency, Bristol. [0057316] 10/02/1999
Sterry Miss SH, BA(Hons) MScILM, Stud., Univ.of Central England, &, L.Asst., LRC., Univ.of the West, of England. [0058583] 04/04/2000
Stevart Mrs A, BA MCLIP, Lib., Havering Coll. of F.&H.E., Hornchurch,Essex. [0008472] 05/02/1968
Steven Mrs EJ, BEng, Grad.Trainee, Manchester Met.Univ. [0061609] 03/10/2002
Stevens Mr AD, MA DipLib MCLIP, Lib., Saffron Walden L., Essex. [0041688] 11/02/1988
Stevens Mrs AE, BA MCLIP, Br.Lib., Blackpool Bor.Council. [0038544] 25/06/1985
Stevens Ms AH, (was Cunningham), BA MCLIP, Child.Lib., Chandlers Ford L., Hants. [0034125] 26/09/1981
Stevens Mr AJ, BA MCLIP, Westminster L.Mgr., City of Westminster, London. [0036565] 04/10/1983
Stevens Ms AJ, BA MCLIP, Asst.Bibl.& Support Serv.Lib., Bolton L. [0035771] 19/01/1983
Stevens Miss BES, BA MCLIP, Retired. [0013980] 01/04/1957
Stevens Mrs DL, (was Hulbert), BLib MCLIP, Serv.Devel.Lib., Yeovil L., Somerset L.Arts & Inf.Serv. [0036948] 18/01/1984
Stevens Miss E, BA(Hons) PGCE, Sch.Lib., Beaumont Sch., St.Albans. [0056445] 10/07/1998
Stevens Mrs EA, MCLIP, Inf.Res.Exec., Bristol-Myers Squibb Pharmaceutical, Hounslow. [0043014] 12/06/1989
Stevens Mrs HM, (was Rees), BA DipLib MCLIP, Resident in Canada. [0042249] 13/10/1988
Stevens Mrs J, (was Mason), BA(Hons), Prison Lib., HM Prison Manchester. [0049686] 25/11/1993
Stevens Mrs J, L.Systems Admin., W.Berks.Council Ls., Inf.&, Communication, Newbury. [0058292] 15/12/1999 **AF**
Stevens Mrs JF, BA MCLIP, Lib.-Stock Serv., Warwickshire L., Warwick. [0026567] 07/10/1976
Stevens Mrs JF, (was Town), MCLIP, Housewife. [0013986] 23/03/1960
Stevens Mrs JL, (was Hall), BSc(Hons) MCLIP, Dep.Inf.Mgr., Societe Generale, London. [0047137] 06/05/1992
Stevens Miss KE, BA(Hons), Lib.Offr., Morden L., L.B.of Merton. [0044228] 18/07/1990
Stevens Mr KR, BSc MA MSc FRSA FCLIP, Dir., ACT Ltd., Herts. [0020592] 04/05/1973 **FE 27/02/1991**

Stevens Miss LA, Sen.L.Asst., Princess Royal Hosp.NHS Trust, Telford, Shropshire. [0058383] 24/01/2000 **AF**
Stevens Mrs MA, (was Blaze), BA MCLIP, Child.Lib., Barbican L., Corporation of London. [0013988] 01/01/1969
Stevens Mrs ME, (was Evans), MCLIP, Lib., Cent.L., Swindon Borough Council. [0004686] 30/10/1969
Stevens Mr PA, BSc, p./t.Enquiries Desk Lib., St.Georges Hosp.Med.Sch., London. [0056250] 17/04/1998 **AF**
Stevens Mrs PE, (was Clifford), BA MCLIP, Co.Local Studies Lib., Hampshire Co.L. [0013990] 06/02/1963
Stevens Miss PM, MCLIP, Retired. [0013991] 04/09/1964
Stevens Ms SA, BScEcon(Hons) MLib, Electronic Inf.Res.Team Leader &, Asst.Systems Lib., Cardiff Univ. [0044809] 04/12/1990
Stevens Ms SC, BA(Hons) PGDipLib, Learning Adviser, Univ.of Birmingham, Orchard Learning Res.Cent. [0045387] 22/11/1990
Stevens Miss SJ, MCLIP, Child.Lib., Purley L., Croydon. [0022860] 08/10/1974
Stevens Ms SJ, DipIM, Inf.Offr., Bank of England, London. [0052717] 24/11/1995
Stevens Mrs SL, (was Wadsworth), BA DipLib MCLIP, Sen.Asst.Lib., Univ.of Huddersfield. [0040825] 01/01/1970
Stevens Mrs SM, (was Owen), MA BA(Hons) DipLib MCLIP, Asst.Lib., Staff L., Grantham & Dist.Hosp., NHS Trust, Lincs.C.C. [0022911] 03/10/1974
Stevens Miss WD, FCLIP, Retired. [0013996] 29/09/1944 **FE 01/01/1957**
Stevenson Mrs AJ, (was Whyte), MCLIP, Unemployed. [0015793] 19/04/1968
Stevenson Mr AW, MCLIP, Co.Local Studies Lib., Leics.Mus.Arts & Recs.Serv., Leicester. [0013999] 01/01/1970
Stevenson Mr BG, BA DMS MCLIP AMITD, Lead Inspector, Audit Commission, Leeds. [0014001] 02/04/1966
Stevenson Mrs C, Distance Services Coordinator, Univ.Sunderland, Tyne & Wear. [0054978] 05/06/1997 **AF**
Stevenson Mr CC, MCLIP, Head of Loans Dept., The London L., St.James's Sq. [0014004] 01/01/1958
Stevenson Mr DJ, BA MCLIP, Sen.Area Lib.(W.), Midlothian Dist.L., Bonnyrigg L. [0030546] 09/02/1979
Stevenson Ms DJ, BA(Hons) DipLib, Sen. L. Asst., Nuffield Coll. L., Oxford. [0056669] 01/10/1998
Stevenson Mr DT, Records Clerk, Fife Council, Kirkcaldy Town House. [0032347] 07/03/1980
Stevenson Ms E, (was Dodds), MCLIP, [0039488] 05/02/1986
Stevenson Mrs EJ, BA MCLIP, Asst.Lib., Edinburgh Univ.L., Lan & Europa L. [0032185] 11/01/1980
Stevenson Mrs EM, (was Wood), MCLIP, Community Lib., Liverpool City L. [0014395] 08/03/1965
Stevenson Miss EP, BSc MCLIP, Unemployed. [0035105] 03/09/1982
Stevenson Miss FMJ, BA MCLIP, Sch.Lib., Bannerman High Sch., Baillieston. [0023693] 13/01/1975
Stevenson Mrs GM, (was Pead), MCLIP, Filing/Admin.Clerk, Paull & Williamson, Aberdeen. [0002694] 01/01/1960
Stevenson Ms HA, BLib MCLIP, Area Lib., Adur Grp., W.Sussex Co.L.Serv. [0021925] 01/02/1974
Stevenson Mrs JA, BA(Hons) PGDipILS, Sen.L.Asst., Kemnay L., Aberdeenshire. [0061042] 05/02/2002
Stevenson Ms K, Unemployed. [0057559] 04/05/1999 **AF**
Stevenson Ms L, MA(Hons)PGDipLib MCLIP, Unemployed. [0024547] 21/08/1975
Stevenson Mr MA, BA MCLIP, Life Member, 11 Gills Cliff Road, Ventnor, IOW, PO38 1LH. [0014009] 09/09/1957
Stevenson Dr MB, BSc PhD MA, Retired. [0045871] 01/07/1991
Stevenson Mr MD, Employment not known. [0060206] 10/12/2001
Stevenson Mrs MJ, MA(Hons) DipLib MCLIP, L.Mgr., Scotsman Publications L., Edinburgh. [0019963] 10/01/1973
Stevenson Mrs P, BA(Hons) MCLIP, Sch.Lib., Hartshead High Sch., Ashton-under-Lyne. [0055569] 21/10/1997
Stevenson Mrs SV, (was Lemon), BA MCLIP, Coll.Lib., Highbury Coll., Portsmouth. [0026641] 26/10/1976
Stevenson Mrs TC, BA, Stud. [0061495] 21/08/2002
Stevenson Mrs TM, OHN Website Advisor, Health Devel.Agency, London. [0058521] 17/03/2000 **AF**
Steventon Mrs MF, BTech MCLIP, Position unknown, Du Pont (UK) Ltd., Brockworth. [0060705] 12/12/2001
Steward Mrs JC, BA MA MCLIP, Dir.of L.& Learning Res., Univ.of E.Anglia L. [0021018] 01/10/1973
Steward Mr RD, BA DAA MCLIP, Arch., Highland Council, Inverness. [0014015] 16/10/1965
Steward Mrs SA, (was Lett), BA DipLib MCLIP, Career Break. [0031355] 15/10/1979
Steward Mrs YF, BA MSc, Lib., Highgate Sch., London N6. [0043013] 12/06/1989
Stewart Mrs A, (was Robinson), MCLIP, Br.Lib., Guisborough Br.L. [0019836] 01/01/1973
Stewart Mrs A, (was Porter), BA(Hons), System Support Lib., Aberdeenshire L.& Inf.Serv., Oldmeldrum. [0048028] 04/11/1992
Stewart Mrs AEM, (was Thornton), BA MCLIP, Site Lib., Univ.of Luton. [0014016] 26/09/1968
Stewart Miss AJ, MA(Hons) DipILS, Sch.Lib., Shawlands Academy, Glasgow. [0059883] 29/10/2001
Stewart Mrs C, (was Mccraken), BA MCLIP, Head of Knowledge Serv., Defence Sci.& Tech.Lab., Farnborough, Hants. [0009297] 04/07/1972
Stewart Mrs CA, (was Manson), MCLIP, Learn.Res.Cent.Co-ordinator, St.Modan's High Sch., Stirling. [0014022] 01/01/1963
Stewart Ms CH, BA(Hons) MA MCLIP, Cent.Mgr., Reading Coll.& Sch.of Arts & Design, [0053833] 03/10/1996

Stewart Mr DC, BA DipLib MCLIP, Reg.Dir.of L.& Inf.Serv., N.W. NHS Reg. [0033528] 14/01/1981
Stewart Miss DJ, MCLIP, Team Lib., Mitchell L., Glasgow. [0020376] 28/02/1973
Stewart Mrs DV, (was Collins), BA(Hons) MA, Asst.Lib., Off.for Nat.Statistics, London. [0055696] 04/11/1997
Stewart Miss H, Unemployed. [0058130] 04/11/1999
Stewart Mrs HC, (was Walkiden), MA MCLIP, Inf.Offr., Regeneration & Partnership, Sheffield City Council. [0038879] 17/10/1985
Stewart Miss HR, BSc(Hons) MSc, L.Asst., Imperial Coll., London. [0054418] 05/12/1996
Stewart Mrs J, (was Rodger), Prof.Lib., Argyll & Bute Hosp. [0042873] 05/04/1989
Stewart Mrs JA, (was Napier), BA MCLIP, Comm.Lib., Fife Council. [0039419] 19/01/1986
Stewart Ms JE, DipLib MCLIP, Sen.Lib.(Pub.Serv.), Cent.L., Belfast. [0014031] 08/10/1969
Stewart Mrs JED, BLib MA, Learning Res.Cent.Mgr., Yale Coll., Wrexham. [0042997] 31/05/1989
Stewart Mr JL, Dip, Stud., Univ.of Strathclyde, Glasgow. [0061544] 10/09/2002
Stewart Mr JM, BA(Hons) DipIS, Asst.Lib., Home Off., London. [0046317] 24/10/1991
Stewart Ms LA, MCLIP, Customer Serv.Mgr., DS, Nottingham. [0023146] 04/11/1974
Stewart Mrs LM, (was Macdonald), BA MCLIP, Team Lib., Aberdeen. [0040201] 06/11/1996
Stewart Mrs M, (was Hulbert), BSc(Hons)Econ, Asst.Lib., Barton Peveril Coll., Hants. [0049195] 11/10/1993
Stewart Miss MA, MA, Asst.Lib., Univ.of Paisley, Ayr Campus. [0044238] 23/07/1990
Stewart Mrs MC, (was Jones), BA MCLIP, Lib., Rydens Sch., Surrey. [0024715] 03/10/1975
Stewart Miss MJ, MCLIP, Sch.Lib., Gourock High Sch., Strathclyde Region. [0028686] 27/11/1977
Stewart Mrs MK, PGCE, Lib., Dover Grammar Sch.for Girls, Kent. [0056665] 01/10/1998 **AF**
Stewart Mrs O, (was Arrowsmith), MCLIP, Life Member. [0014036] 22/02/1962
Stewart Mrs P, (was Carr Woods), MA MCLIP, Retired. [0002403] 29/09/1969
Stewart Mr PN, MA MCLIP, Inf.Adviser, Collegiate Learning Cent., Sheffield Hallam Univ. [0022664] 30/07/1974
Stewart Miss RM, BA MCLIP, Lib., N.Lanarkshire Council, Cumbernauld. [0031160] 28/08/1979
Stewart Mrs SM, MA(Hons) PhD, Res.Stud./L.Asst., Balerno Community High Sch./, St.Bernards Educ.Cent. [0060866] 13/12/2001
Stewart Mrs VMK, (was Mcivor), MCLIP, Retired. [0014040] 24/09/1968
Stewart Mr WJ, BA MA, Stud. [0056353] 08/06/1998
Stidworthy Mrs SE, BA MCLIP, Employment not known. [0060651] 11/12/2001
Stiemens Ms VM, BA DipLib MSc MCLIP, Lib., Policy Studies Inst., London. [0032228] 15/02/1980
Stiles Mr DE, MCLIP, Retired. [0017790] 19/10/1942
Stiles Mr WG, BA(Hons) FCLIP, Life Member. [0017791] 01/01/1950 **FE 01/01/1959**
Still Miss BM, FCLIP, Retired. [0014049] 15/01/1941 **FE 01/01/1956**
Still Mr JG, MA FCLIP, Life Member. [0014050] 16/10/1947 **FE 01/01/1965**
Still Mrs L, (was Rice), BA MCLIP, Asst. Lib., Tormead Sch., Guildford. [0028135] 10/10/1977
Still Mr TS, BA(Hons), Lib., Instant L.Ltd., Aberdeen. [0055130] 16/07/1997
Stillone Ms P, BA DipInfSc, L.Asst., Univ.Coll.London. [0052987] 13/02/1996
Stirling Ms IE, BA MCLIP, Lib., Strathclyde Univ., Faculty of Educ., Glasgow. [0019554] 20/11/1972
Stirling Miss JA, BA, Stud., Leeds Met.Univ. [0061289] 02/05/2002
Stirrup Mrs AC, (was Smith), MCLIP, Unemployed. [0014054] 23/03/1966
Stirrup Ms AJ, (was Hill), BA(Hons) MCLIP, L.Devel.Mgr., Hammersmith & Fulham Ls., London. [0034952] 14/05/1982
Stirrup Mrs TA, (was Chadwick), BA(Hons), Child.Lib.(Job Share), Leigh L., Lancs. [0040528] 27/02/1987
Stirton Mrs BJ, (was Walker), BA MCLIP, Club Mgr., The Royal Crescent Hotel, Bath. [0039412] 24/01/1986
Stitson Mrs CA, BA DipLib MCLIP, Lib., Henley-on-Thames/Didcot P.L., Oxon.C.C. [0038891] 15/10/1985
Stitt Ms DE, BA, p./t.Stud./Inf.Offr., City Univ., London. [0061117] 21/02/2002
Stitt Mrs EM, (was Heyworth), BA(Hons) MA MCLIP, L.Serv.Mgr., Calderstones NHS Trust, Clitheroe. [0050053] 02/03/1994
Stoakley Mr RJ, FCLIP, Retired. [0014056] 14/03/1956 **FE 01/01/1966**
Stock Ms EJ, Comm.Lib., Tameside Met.Bor., Hyde L. [0047567] 02/10/1992
Stock Mr JH, MCLIP, Retired. [0014062] 10/02/1953
Stock Miss KM, BA(Hons) MSc(Econ), Asst.Lib., The Nat.Assembly for Wales, Members L., Cardiff Bay. [0051156] 23/11/1994
Stock Mr NM, LLB MCLIP, Asst.Lib., Supreme Court L., The Court Serv., London. [0040005] 09/10/1986
Stock Mrs SJ, BA DipLib MCLIP, Employment not known. [0060484] 11/12/2001
Stockbridge Mrs HD, (was Clampin), MCLIP, [0020130] 23/01/1973
Stockbridge Bland Mrs SC, (was Stockbridge), BA MA MCLIP, 18 Hall Green Lane, Hutton,Brentwood,Essex,CM13 2QX. [0014063] 01/01/1970
Stockdale Miss JH, MCLIP, Citizens Inf.Lib., Kirklees Metro.Council, Huddersfield. [0014064] 24/01/1969
Stocken Mrs JM, (was Jones), BA(Hons) MBA MCLIP, H.of Research, Egon Zehnder Internat., London. [0021823] 07/02/1974

357

Stocker Mrs FM, (was Bassett), BA DipLib MCLIP, Strategic Devel.Mgr., Vaughan P.L., Ontario. [0031185] 03/10/1979
Stockley Mrs CR, BSc (Hons), Sen.Inf.Analyst, ICT Serv., Portsmouth. [0061455] 01/08/2002
Stockley Ms LJ, BA(Hons) MA, Asst.Lib., Inst.Electrical Engineers. [0053854] 07/10/1996
Stocks Miss MY, MCLIP CertEd, Life Member. [0014071] 17/03/1941
Stocks Miss SC, BA MCLIP, Inf.Lib., Pickering L., N.Yorks. [0033630] 27/01/1981
Stockton Earl, Hon.Vice President. [0046051] 11/09/1991
Stockton Mrs C, BA MBA MCLIP, Dir.of Learning Res., Chester Coll.of H.E. [0014072] 23/01/1969
Stockton Mr NJ, MA, p./t.Stud./Sen.L.Asst., Univ.Central England, Solihull College L. [0060026]27/11/2001
Stockwell Mrs AP, (was Harrington), MCLIP, Lib., St.Augustines Sch., Redditch. [0032742] 01/08/1980
Stockwell Miss CA, (was Le Ray), BA MCLIP, Sch.Lib., The Ladies Coll., St.Peter Port, Guernsey. [0018316] 07/10/1984
Stoddard Mrs G, (was Mumford), Unemployed. [0044135] 29/05/1990
Stoddart Miss A, BA DipLib MCLIP, Employment not known. [0036564] 21/10/1983
Stokell Mr AJ, BA MRes MCLIP PGCRM, Faculty Team Support Lib., Univ.of Leeds, Bretton Hall Campus. [0041245] 15/10/1987
Stoker Mrs AH, (was Morris), BA MCLIP, Comm.Serv Lib., Hants.Co.L., Basingstoke. [0018325] 01/01/1972
Stokes Mrs A, Sch.Lib., St John's Sch.& Community Coll., Marlborough. [0056381] 01/07/1998 **AF**
Stokes Ms AJ, (was Randle), BA(Hons), Mob.Lib., Mob.L.Serv., Tyseley, Birmingham. [0037593] 05/10/1984
Stokes Mrs CE, (was Rosette), BA(Hons) MCLIP, Unemployed. [0052722] 27/11/1995
Stokes Mrs GB, (was Lemon), MCLIP, Lib., Inst.L.Ltd., Loughborough, Leics. [0023780] 27/01/1975
Stokes Mr SM, BA(Hons) MCLIP, Team Lib., Medway Educ.& Leisure, Strood L. [0043472] 26/10/1989
Stokes Ms HJ, BA(Hons) MCLIP, Asst.Lib., Huddersfield K., Kirklees Met.Council. [0052460] 02/11/1995
Stokes Ms HM, (was Ward), BA, Child.Lib., Telford L. [0041383] 17/11/1987
Stokes Ms IA, BA DipLib PGCE, p./t.Inf./Ref.Team Lib., Hornsey L., L.B.of Haringey. [0040857] 09/07/1987
Stokes Mrs LC, (was Wood), BA(Hons) MCLIP, Unemployed. [0033202] 18/10/1979
Stokes Mrs M, FCLIP, Life Member. [0017793] 12/04/1937 **FE 01/01/1951**
Stokes Mrs OR, FCLIP, Life Member. [0014080] 12/10/1931 **FE 01/01/1954**
Stokes Mr PJ, BA(Hons) BSc(Open) MCLIP, Asst.Lib., Homerton Coll, Sch.of Hlth.Stud., Educ.Cent.L.,Peterborough Dist.Hosp. [0057178] 04/01/1979
Stokes Mrs SM, (was Shilliday), BA MCLIP, Sen.Educ.Lib., S.E.Educ.& L.Board. [0022040] 15/01/1974
Stokes Ms SM, BA MA DipLib MCLIP, Consultant., New Zealand. [0031461] 08/10/1979
Stokoe Miss S, BA(Hons), p./t.Stud., Sen.L.Asst., Kingston Univ.L., Surrey. [0059837] 16/10/2001
Stone Mrs AF, (was Plenty), MCLIP, Unemployed. [0019575] 14/11/1972
Stone Mrs B, MCLIP, Sub.Lib., Health & Soc.Care, & Engineering, Univ.of Wales, Newport. [0030730] 27/03/1979
Stone Mr ER, FCLIP, Life Member, Tel.01483-563491. [0014087] 29/01/1934 **FE 01/01/1948**
Stone Mr G, BSc DipILS MCLIP, Serials & Electronic Devel.Mgr., Bolton Inst., Bolton. [0049528] 10/11/1993
Stone Ms G, (was Shaffer), BA MLS, L.S.A., Western Primary Sch., Hants.C.C. [0038652] 02/09/1985
Stone Mr HL, BA MCLIP, Learning Cent.Co-ordinator, E.Berkshire Coll., Berkshire. [0037594] 03/10/1984
Stone Mr JA, BA, L.Asst., Univ.of N.London. [0056085] 06/02/1998 **AF**
Stone Ms JMC, (was Colley), BA MCLIP, Sen.Asst.Lib., Collections & Tech.Serv., Imperial Coll.Sch.of Med. [0030381] 02/02/1979
Stone Mr KG, Bus.Inf.Mgr., Suffolk Chamber of Commerce, Ipswich. [0054797] 01/04/1997 **AF**
Stone Mrs LR, (was Holman), FCLIP, Retired. [0017798] 20/08/1931 **FE 01/01/1931**
Stone Mr MB, DipLib MCLIP, Grp.L.Mgr., L.B.of Greenwich. [0030549] 31/01/1979
Stone Mr MP, BA MCLIP HonFCLIP, Asst.Ch.Leisure Serv.Offr., Calderdale Council, Halifax, W.Yorks. [0027371] 18/03/1977 **FE 24/10/2002**
Stone Mr NHF, MCLIP, Retired. [0014091] 24/01/1952
Stone Mr PT, BA MCLIP, Retired. [0014093] 09/01/1968
Stone Mr RN, BA MArAd MCLIP, Employment not known. [0060430] 11/12/2001
Stone Mrs RS, (was Cossar), BA MLib MCLIP, Inf.Resources Mgr., Univ.of Herts., Hatfield Campus. [0041728] 24/02/1988
Stone Mr RW, MCLIP, Life Member. [0014094] 01/01/1933
Stone Miss S, BA MCLIP, Area L.Mgr., Knowsley Borough Council, Merseyside. [0028371] 18/10/1977
Stone Mr TP, MA DipLib CertEd MCLIP, Dir.Learning Resources, Univ.of Luton, Luton. [0032189] 11/01/1980
Stonebanks Mrs J, (was Stansfield), BA(Hons) MCLIP, Sen.Lib.(IT & Inf.), Eccles L., Eccles. [0028685] 06/01/1978
Stoneham Mr GCJ, MA FCLIP, Life Member. [0014100] 01/01/1938 **FE 01/01/1950**
Stoner Mrs ME, (was Haynes), BA, L.Asst., Banchory L., Kincardineshire. [0047707] 19/10/1992

Stones Miss BJ, BA(Hons) DipInfMgmt, Unemployed. [0050915] 31/10/1994
Stoney Mr JB, Stud., Univ.of Canberra. [0056210] 31/03/1998
Stoney Ms L, BA MCLIP, Unemployed/Travelling abroad. [0022226] 17/02/1974
Stoney Mrs VM, (was Mundella), MCLIP, Lib.(Job Share), Brit Sch., Croydon. [0014102] 24/01/1967
Stoppani Miss JM, BA(Hon), Lib., Mid Kent Coll., Chatham,Kent. [0050124] 05/03/1994
Stopper Miss J, BA(Hons) MCLIP, Sen.Lib., N.Lincs.L., Scunthorpe Cent.L. [0032613] 29/05/1980
Storah Mrs C, (was Manning), BA DipLib MCLIP, P./t.Inf.Lib., Essex Ls., Chelmsford. [0027539] 02/05/1977
Storer Miss RM, Stud./L.Asst., Brooksby Melton Coll., Melton Mowbray. [0058345] 10/01/2000
Stores Mr M, BA DipLib MCLIP, Head of Inf.Serv., LGS, Manchester. [0058346] 30/08/1988
Storey Mrs AV, (was West), BA MCLIP, Research Lib., Baker & Mckenzie, London. [0058316] 13/10/1972
Storey Dr C, BA MPhil PhD FCLIP, Univ.L., The Chinese Univ.of Hong Kong, Shatin. [0014105] 29/09/1971 **FE 25/09/1996**
Storey Ms INJ, BSc MSc MCLIP, Higher Sci.Offr., Food Standards Agency, London. [0032705] 01/07/1980
Storey Mrs J, (was Laws), BA MCLIP ACIM DipMkt, Sen.Lib., Univ.of Northumbria at Newcastle. [0025581] 28/01/1976
Storey Mrs J, MCLIP, Asst.Catr., London L. [0014107] 17/08/1960
Storey Mr L, MCLIP, Grp.Mgr., Stanley Grp., Durham C.C. [0014110] 24/03/1969
Storey Mrs M, BA, Unemployed. [0060982] 23/01/2002
Storey Mrs M, Sen.L.Asst., Huntingdon L., Cambs. [0052582] 09/11/1995 **AF**
Storey Mrs SC, (was Sturman), MSc MCLIP, Unemployed. [0049901] 10/01/1994
Storey Mr SM, BSc DipLib, Lib., Univ.of Wales, Swansea, Swansea. [0033654] 03/02/1981
Storie Ms C, BA MCLIP, Comm.Lib., Gallowhill Comm.Lib., Renfrewshire. [0032191] 06/02/1980
Stormer Mrs MM, (was Kirwin), BA(Hons) MCLIP, Inf.Lib., E.Barnet L., L.B.of Barnet. [0041590] 25/01/1988
Story Mrs BA, BSc MCLIP, Relief Lib. [0020931] 17/09/1973
Stothard Mrs J, (was Milburn), BA(Hons) DipEd DipLib DILM, Lib., St.Bedes R.C.Comp.Sch., Lanchester. [0046973] 19/03/1963
Stott Mrs F, (was Leach), MA BA MCLIP, Sen.Community Lib., Oldham M.B.C., Oldham L. [0008749] 01/01/1971
Stott Mrs PM, BA DipLib MCLIP, Learning Resources Mgr., Morcambe High Sch. [0030545] 09/01/1979
Stout Ms HL, BA(Hons) PG DipLib, Unemployed. [0050876] 25/10/1994
Stout Mr RW, BA MCLIP, Lib., Soro P.L., Denmark. [0017800] 23/10/1953
Stovin Mrs KA, (was Lancaster), BA DipLib MCLIP, p./t.Sch.Lib., Priory Sch., Hitchin, Herts. [0033609] 22/01/1981
Stow Miss EA, MA MCLIP, Retired. [0010484] 27/09/1954
Stoyle Mrs J, (was Wood), LRC Mgr., Bishop Foxs Comm.Sch., Taunton, Somerset. [0050472] 05/04/1994 **AF**
Strachan Mr AD, MA(Hons) DipLib, Intranet Mgr., Brit.Trade Internat., London. [0042219] 11/10/1988
Strachan Mrs E, L.Inf.Offr., William Harvey Hosp., Ashford. [0058819] 09/08/2000 **AF**
Strachan Mrs GE, (was Phillips), MCLIP, Unemployed. [0014123] 01/10/1964
Strachan Mr GP, BA(Hons) MA, Inf.Spec., Hewitt Assoc., St Albans. [0052072] 02/10/1995
Strachan Mr IS, MCLIP, Unemployed. [0014125] 25/09/1967
Strachan Mrs M, (was Evans), BA MCLIP, Writer, Self Employed. [0028459] 15/01/1969
Strachan Mrs ME, FCLIP, Life Member., Supreme Courts, Edinburgh. [0026808] 04/11/1976 **FE 07/04/1986**
Strachan Mrs MJ, (was Ferguson), MCLIP, Unemployed. [0020783] 01/07/1973
Stradling Mr B, MBE FCLIP LRPS FRSA, Life Member, Tel.01242 516167, Beechcroft, Kenelm Dr., Cheltenham, GL53 0JR. [0014129] 17/02/1947 **FE 01/01/1966**
Stradling Ms J, (was Byard), BA(Hons) DipLib MCLIP, Lending Lib., Southampton Cent.L. [0049329] 22/10/1993
Strafford Miss L, (was Wormald), BA, Employment not known. [0060471] 11/12/2001
Strain Mrs HC, BSc(Hons) MSc, Career Break. [0050998] 08/11/1994
Strain Mrs MH, (was Preece), BA MCLIP, Life Member. [0039541] 29/09/1954
Strain Miss TS, BSc(Hons) DipInf MCLIP, Inf.Sci., DERA, Pyestock Inf.Cent., Farnborough, Hants. [0057578] 11/05/1999
Strain Mr WM, MA FCLIP, Life Member. [0014131] 22/03/1958 **FE 01/01/1968**
Stranders Mrs AE, (was Eldridge), BA(Hons) MA MCLIP, Learning Resources Mgr., Havering Coll. of F. & H.E., Hornchurch, Essex. [0043668] 21/11/1989
Strang Mr WC, BA MCLIP, Lib., James Young High Sch., Livingston. [0014134] 11/02/1968
Stranger Mrs S, (was Brown), BA MCLIP, Position unknown, St.Peter's Catholic Comp.Sch., Guildford. [0022936] 01/10/1974
Strasburger Mrs HA, (was Allan), BA DipLib MCLIP, Area Co-ordinator, Bingham Area, Notts.C.C. [0036495] 12/10/1983
Stratford Mrs DM, BA MCLIP ILTM, Asst.Lib., Univ.of Southampton New Coll., Southampton. [0014899] 01/01/1967
Stratford Mr GR, BA MCLIP, Subject Lib., Coventry Univ. [0027292] 10/02/1977
Stratton Ms BA, BA DipLib MSc MCLIP, Adviser-Copyright & Inf.Devel., CILIP, London. [0030274] 17/01/1979

Stratton Mrs JL, (was Terry), MCLIP, Reg.PR & Communications Mgr., Environment Agency, Solihull, W.Mids. [0021723] 01/01/1964
Stratton Ms S, BA(Hons) DipLib, Lib., Herts.C.C., Tech.Support Serv. [0036205] 17/07/1983
Strauss Mrs SM, (was Kelly), BA FCLIP, Life Member. [0014140] 09/03/1965 FE 01/01/1966
Strawbridge Miss J, Stud., Univ.Central England. [0060018] 26/11/2001
Streatfield Mr DR, MA MCLIP, Princ., Inf.Management Assoc., Twickenham. [0014142] 06/02/1962
Streather Miss SK, BA DipLib MCLIP, Asst.Lib., Liverpool John Moores Univ., Merseyside. [0029840] 09/10/1978
Street Mrs EN, (was Pass), MCLIP, Lib., Cheshire C.C. [0014143] 17/01/1970
Street Dr KJ, BSc MA MCLIP, Subject Inf.Specialist, The Open Univ., Milton Keynes. [0044096] 03/05/1990
Street Ms KR, BA(Hons), Stud., UWE. [0054562] 24/01/1997
Street Miss KRA, BA(Hons) MA, Learning Adviser, Leeds Metro.Univ. [0056040] 21/01/1998
Street Mrs MS, (was Rowley), BSc MA MCLIP, Young Peoples Lib., Dacorum Dist., Herts.L.Serv. [0043196] 02/10/1989
Street Mrs VH, (was Gillanders), BA(Hons) MCLIP, Unemployed. [0005540] 08/03/1966
Streeter Miss HJ, BLS, Arts & L.Offr.(Mobile), W.Malling, Kent, & Team Lib., Local Stud., Cent.for Kentish Stud., Maidstone. [0036793] 01/01/1984
Streets Mr CJ, BA(Hons), Stud., City Univ., London. [0057481] 06/04/1999
Stretton Mr CJ, BA(Hons) MA MCLIP, Project Offr., Technical Services, Liv.J.M.Univ. [0053274] 11/04/1996
Strickland-Hodge Dr B, MSc PhD MRPharmS MCLIP, Employment unknown. [0060587] 11/12/2001
Stringer Mrs GR, BA(Hons) DipLIS MCLIP, Sen.Lib., L.B.of Croydon. [0039827] 10/08/1986
Stringer Mr IM, MCLIP, Support Serv.Offr., Barnsley M.B.C., & Ed.-"Service Point". [0014150] 01/02/1968
Stringer Ms J, BA DipLib MCLIP BSc DipPollCon, Team Lib., Norfolk L.Serv. [0035833] 18/01/1983
Stringer Miss JE, BA(Hons) MSc(Econ) MCLIP, Inf.Specialist, Govt.Comm.H.Q., Cheltenham. [0054780] 01/04/1997
Stringer Mrs LH, (was Steel), BA MCLIP, Lib., Chelmsford L., Essex C.C. [0039265] 07/01/1986
Stringer Mr MJ, BA(Hons), Grad.Trainee, Imperial Cancer Research Fund, London. [0058481] 29/02/2000
Stringer Mr RD, BA DipLib MBA MCLIP, Managing Dir., Textpertise (PVT) Ltd., Harare, Zimbabwe. [0019094] 24/09/1972
Strivens Mrs RA, BA(Hons), L.Asst., Imperial War Mus., Dept.Printed Books, London. [0058148] 05/11/1999
Stromberg Mrs D, (was Cains), MCLIP, Sch.Lib., Beds.C.C., Kempston. [0007169] 13/01/1966
Strong Mr RT, BA DipLib MCLIP, Head of L.& Heritage, Bucks.C.C., Aylesbury. [0014157] 04/01/1971
Strong Ms SL, Local Land Search Asst., Brighton & Hove Council, Environ.& Housing Serv. [0053011] 14/02/1996
Stroud Miss J, MCLIP, Team Lib., Ealing Cent.L., L.B.of Ealing. [0023272] 20/11/1974
Strudwick Ms CJC, BA MCLIP, L.& Learning Cent.Mgr., Solihull Coll. [0025818] 13/03/1976
Strugnell Mr M, BA DipLib, Learning Resources Co-ordinator, Reading Coll. [0033801] 30/01/1981
Strutt Miss KA, BA MCLIP, Bibl.Servs.Lib., Argyll & Bute Council, Dunoon, Argyll. [0023252] 14/11/1974
Strutt Mrs SE, (was Graves), MA, Project Mgr., The Brit.L., London. [0036439] 10/10/1983
Stuart Mrs CA, (was Newman), MCLIP, Off.Support Asst., New Life Christian Fellowship, Kent. [0030018] 01/11/1978
Stuart Mr CJ, BA(Hons) MSc MCLIP, L.& Inf.Serv.Co-ordinator, Solihull. [0051939] 14/08/1979
Stuart Mrs CL, (was Rothwell), BA DipLib MCLIP, Readers Serv.Lib., Urmston L., Manchester. [0026193] 09/08/1976
Stuart Mrs EEJ, (was Owen), MA MA, Asst.Bibl., Royal Collection Trust, Windsor. [0046140] 07/10/1991
Stuart Mr IM, BSc MSc AIInfSc MCLIP, Asst.Lib., Lancaster Univ.L. [0014164] 01/01/1965
Stuart Mr JH, MA PGCE DipILS, Unemployed. [0058700] 09/06/2000
Stuart-Jones Mr EAL, MCLIP MA, Retired. [0014169] 29/07/1966
Stubbings Ms RE, BA, Acad.Serv.Mgr., Loughborough Univ. [0040462] 12/02/1987
Stubbington Miss Y, BA(Hons) MCLIP, Comm.Devel.Lib., Weston Favell L., Northampton. [0049306] 20/10/1993
Stubbs Mr EA, Lib., Federacion Bioquimica Prov., Buenos Aires, Argentina. [0058638] 25/04/2000
Stubbs Mrs LJH, (was Joseph Henry), BA(Hons), Company Lib., Celltech R.& D.Ltd., Cambridge. [0052360] 26/10/1995
Stubbs Mr MF, BTH DipLib MCLIP, Community L., Cent.L., Luton. [0041480] 11/01/1988
Stubbs Miss MJ, BSc(Hons), Stud. [0058936] 09/10/2000
Stubbs Mrs ND, (was Walls), Sen.L.Asst., Malton L., N.Yorks. [0048526] 04/02/1993 AF
Stuckey Mrs GV, MCLIP, Stock Lib., Slough L., Berks. [0014181] 25/03/1971
Studd Miss JL, BA(Hons), Lib., Morgan Cole, Oxford. [0014183] 28/08/1991
Stump Mrs C, Sen.L.Asst., Soc.Inclusion Dept., Cult.Serv.H.Q., Huddersfield. [0061287] 02/05/2002 AF
Sturdy Miss GM, MCLIP, Inf.Lib., Church End L., L.B.of Barnet. [0014184] 24/02/1969
Sturdy Mr W, CChem MRSC MCLIP, Employment not known. [0060604] 11/12/2001
Sturdy-Morton Miss AH, LLB MCLIP FRSA, Freelance Law Lib. [0014186] 02/11/1971
Sturges Dr RP, MA PhD FCLIP, Reader in L.in Social Devel., Dept.of Inf.Sci., Loughborough Univ. [0014191] 24/11/1966 FE 27/03/1991

Sturgess Mrs SA, (was Welch), MCLIP, Asst.Housebound Serv.Lib., L.B.of Harrow. [0015573] 11/03/1969
Sturrock Mrs SM, MA (Hons), Retired. [0059224] 09/01/2001
Sturt Mrs F, (was Page), FCLIP, Life Member, Tel:01245 268648. [0014193] 16/01/1952 FE 01/01/1960
Sturt Mr NF, BA(Hons) MCLIP, Site Lib., Highbury Coll., Portsmouth. [0041254] 24/10/1987
Sturt Mr RE, MBE MA FCLIP, Life Member, Tel:01245 268648. [0014194] 27/10/1947 FE 01/01/1960
Stuttard Mrs B, (was Guest), MCLIP, Sch.Lib., Staindrop Comprehensive, Co.Durham. [0021211] 29/09/1973
Stych Mr FS, PH D MA FCLIP, Bagno Alla Villa, Bagni Di Lucca Villa, Italy. [0014195] 08/08/1933 FE 01/01/1960
Styles Mr BR, MCLIP, Retired. [0014197] 17/12/1968
Styles Miss C, BA(Hons) MSc(Econ) MCLIP, Strategy, Comm.& Devel.Offr., L., L.B.of Southwark. [0051152] 23/11/1994
Styles Mrs SA, (was Morgan), BLib MCLIP, Asst.Lib.-Catg., Oxfordshire C.C., Cultural Serv. [0010417] 12/06/1972
Styles Ms WN, MCLIP, Unemployed. [0014199] 30/03/1963
Subocz Ms T, BA(Hons) MA, Dep.Head Inf.Serv. [0054407] 05/12/1996
Subrahmanyan Mrs M, (was Sastry), MBE FCLIP BA BEd, Retired. [0017804] 28/10/1953 FE 01/01/1967
Suddaby Miss KM, MCLIP, Life Member. [0014200] 25/02/1955
Suddell Mrs GU, BSc, p./t.Stud./Sen.L.Asst., Bristol Univ., Bristol Cent.L. [0061151] 15/03/2002
Sudell Mr PD, BSc MSc DipLib, L.Systems Mgr., King's Coll.London. [0060649] 11/12/2001
Sudworth Mrs RA, (was Guilfoyle), BA MCLIP, Sen.Lib.-Operations & Lend., Lancs C.C., Accrington. [0031845] 10/01/1980
Suga Ms C, BA MA, Lect., Keio Univ. [0061478] 14/08/2002
Sugden Mrs C, (was Hardaker), BA MCLIP, Lib., Med.PG.Cent.L., Nobles Hosp., Douglas. [0029673] 17/10/1978
Sugden Mr PV, MA DipLib MCLIP, Area Lib., Horsham L., W.Sussex C.C. [0032467] 17/04/1980
Suggitt Mrs AM, Sen.L.Asst.& p./t.Stud., Bath Cent.L. [0055260] 08/09/1997 AF
Sulch Mrs KJ, (was Eggleton), MCLIP, Sch.Lib., Thomas Alleyne Sch., Stevenage, Herts. [0021807] 04/02/1974
Sulistyo-Basuki Mr L, PhD, Head, Dept.of L.Sci.Sch.of Grad.Studies, Univ.of Indonesia. [0049213] 13/10/1993
Sullivan Mrs FDE, BA DipLib MCLIP, Inst.Lib., Inst.for Devel.Policy & Management, Univ.of Manchester. [0037212] 10/04/1984
Sullivan Mrs FM, (was Goodwin), BA DipLib, P./t.Asst.Lib., Kirklees MC., Huddersfield. [0041836] 18/04/1988
Sullivan Ms J, BA(Hons) MCLIP, Dep.Lib., Dr.J.H.Burgoyne & Partners, London. [0046950] 09/03/1992
Sullivan Mrs JJ, (was Dunkley), MCLIP, Prison Lib., Verne Prison, Dorset C.C., Dorchester, Dorset. [0004268] 05/01/1968
Sullivan Ms S, Dep.Inf.Mgr., Rouse & Co.International, London. [0057673] 01/07/1999
Sulston Mrs DE, MA, Applied Maths Dept.L., Univ.of Cambridge. [0050288] 01/06/1994
Sultan Mr M, Lib., Birmingham L.Serv., Music L. [0053456] 01/07/1996 AF
Sultana Miss S, BA(Hons), Unemployed, [0059625] 04/07/2001
Summerfield Mrs SA, (was Fletcher), BA MCLIP, Inf.Res.Mgr., Min.of Defence, Cambs. [0019984] 12/01/1973
Summers Miss CL, Inf.Offr.-Ref.Serv., Wolverhampton P.L. [0041678] 07/02/1988
Summers Mr D, BA(Hons) MA MCLIP, Dep.Lib., Lancaster Univ.L. [0034123] 06/10/1981
Summers Miss PA, BA DipLIS MCLIP, L.Offr., Edinburgh City L.& Inf.Serv. [0053324] 07/05/1996
Summers Ms S, BA, Unemployed. [0043800] 16/01/1990
Summerscales Mrs J, P./t.Stud., Leeds Met.Univ., &, Sen.Inf.& L.Offr., Dewsbury Coll.L. [0027221] 08/02/1977
Summerscales Mrs S, (was Badham), BA MCLIP, Learning Resources Mgr., Bolton Coll.L., Lancs. [0000564] 01/01/1979
Summerton Miss SC, BSc(Hons), Grad.Trainee, Manchester Met.Univ. [0059821] 10/08/2001
Summit Dr RK, HonFCLIP, Hon Fellow. [0060083] 07/12/2001 FE 01/04/2002
Sumner Mr I, BA MCLIP, Hon.Lib., Flag Inst., Hull. [0022046] 01/01/1974
Sumner Mrs J, (was Branch), BA DipLib MCLIP, p./t.L.Asst., Gravesend Grammar Sch.for Girls, Kent. [0031574] 25/10/1979
Sumner Mrs JP, BA(Hons) DipLIS MCLIP, Comm.Lib., Mob.L.Serv., Staffs.C.C. [0050865] 24/10/1994
Sumpter Mrs SL, (was Willoughby), BA(Hons) MCLIP, Educ.Offr., BECTA, Coventry. [0046480] 12/11/1991
Sumsion Mr JW, OBE HonFCLIP, Sen.Hon.Fellow, Dept.of Inf.& L.Studies, Univ.of Loughborough. [0046810] 30/09/1990 FE 30/09/1990
Sunderland Mr D, BA FRSA MCLIP, Med.Lib., Sheffield Teaching Hosp.Trust, Weston Park Hosp. [0014223] 18/01/1963
Sunderland Mr N, BA, Stud., Univ.of Brighton. [0061283] 08/05/2002
Sunley Mr JW, MCLIP, Life Member. [0014226] 10/08/1950
Surendra Mrs SDP, MA BA DipLib MCLIP, Periodicals Mgr - Job Share, L.Coll.of Printing, London. [0034521] 21/11/1981
Suriyanarayanan Mrs T, BSc, Sch.Lib., N.Westminster Community Sch., London. [0053314] 10/01/1996
Surrey Mrs SE, (was Wright), MCLIP, Unemployed. [0016380] 30/01/1970
Surridge Mr RG, MA FRSA HonFCLIP FCLIP, Freelance Consultant, 3 Dower Ave., Wallington, Surrey, SM6 0RG, Tel.020 8647 2003. [0014232] 10/03/1947 FE 01/01/1953
Surtees Miss J, Stud., Manchester Metro.Univ. [0061830] 14/11/2002
Surzyn Miss AJM, BLS MCLIP, Lib.:Bibl.Serv., Leics.C.C. [0030275] 08/12/1978

Sutcliffe Mr GS, MPhil MCLIP, Freelance Indexer. [0014238]   19/07/1972
Sutcliffe Miss JD, BA MCLIP, Learning Res.Mgr., The Peoples Coll., Nottingham. [0014240]   08/10/1968
Sutcliffe Mrs M, (was Bell), MCLIP, Sch.Lib., The Longfield High Sch., Melton Mowbray, Leics. [0014241]   07/01/1965
Suter Mrs AJ, (was Griffith), BA DipLib MCLIP, Lib.(Ref.), Lewisham P.L. [0041557]   21/01/1988
Suter Mr M, BA, Asst.Lib., Kingston Coll., Kingston upon Thames. [0035641]   25/11/1982
Sutherland Mr A, FCLIP, Life Member, Tel. 01202 395834, 12 Glencoe Rd., Bournemouth, BH7 7BE. [0014244]   31/01/1941   **FE 01/01/1949**
Sutherland Miss AJ, BA(Hons) MCLIP, Lifelong Learning Mgr., Glasgow City Council, Glasgow. [0043620]   14/11/1989
Sutherland Miss AM, MA DipLib, Catr., Brit.L., Collection Mgmt., Boston Spa. [0034328]   23/10/1981
Sutherland Miss AM, MCLIP, Life Member. [0026076]   23/01/1962
Sutherland Mr AP, BA MCLIP, Asst.Lib., City of Sunderland Educ.& Community, Serv., Sunderland, Tyne & Wear. [0025119]   13/10/1975
Sutherland Mrs FA, (was Cameron), BA DMS MCLIP MIMgt, Asst.Lib., Cent.for Ecology & Hypology, Wallingford. [0036502]   17/10/1983
Sutherland Mr FM, MA FCLIP, Life Member. [0014249]   09/10/1947   **FE 01/01/1953**
Sutherland Miss J, BA(Hons), L.Asst., St.Bernards Educ.Cent., Edinburgh. [0061383]   08/07/2002
Sutherland Mr JG, BA MCLIP, Unemployed. [0028692]   13/01/1978
Sutherland Miss JRE, MCLIP, Retired. [0014252]   15/10/1968
Sutherland Miss LAR, p./t.Stud/Inf.Analyst, Tayside Univ.Hosp.Trust, Perth Royal Infirmary. [0051654]   01/05/1995
Sutherland Miss LM, MA DipLib MCLIP, Freelance Lib.& Indexer. [0026247]   02/09/1976
Sutherland Ms MC, BA, L.Asst., Stirling Council L., Bridge of Allan L. [0042889]   07/04/1989   **AF**
Sutherland Mrs MR, (was Langham-Hobart), BA MCLIP, Retired. [0014255]   04/10/1947
Sutherland Ms NM, BA(Hons) DipInf, Exec.Offr., House of Commons L., London. [0058387]   31/01/2000
Sutherland Mrs RE, MCLIP, Retired. [0017847]   01/01/1951
Sutherland Mrs SA, (was Cunningham), BSc DipLib MCLIP, p./t.Lib., Queen Margaret Univ.Coll., Edinburgh. [0036749]   22/11/1983
Suto Mrs JC, (was Baker), MCLIP ALAA, Retired. [0017848]   29/09/1943
Sutton Miss A, BA, Stud., City University London. [0061789]   07/11/2002
Sutton Miss AJ, BA(Hons), Research Asst., Univ.of Sheffield. [0059010]   24/10/2000
Sutton Mrs AM, BA MA DipLib MCLIP, Lib., Dept.of Meteorology, Univ.of Reading. [0041140]   13/10/1987
Sutton Ms CM, BA(Hons), Asst. Lib., Lancashire Co. Council, Preston. [0058649]   02/05/2000
Sutton Dr DC, MA AM PhD, Dir.of Research Projects, The L., Univ.of Reading. [0024549]   07/09/1975
Sutton Mrs DE, BSc(Hons) MA, Sch.Lib., Stockport Grammar Sch. [0055103]   14/07/1997
Sutton Miss E, FCLIP, Life Member. [0014257]   21/03/1941   **FE 01/01/1951**
Sutton Mrs GD, L.Super., Worcs.C.C., Pershore, Worcs. [0045408]   01/01/1991   **AF**
Sutton Mr IW, BA MCLIP, Inf.& Devel.Mgr., Blackburn with Darwen Council. [0029097]   16/01/1978
Sutton Mrs J, BSc MSc DMS MCLIP, Employment not known. [0060695]   12/12/2001
Sutton Miss JE, MCLIP, Local Studies Lib., (Nuneaton & Bedworth Div.), Warwickshire C.C. [0027248]   25/02/1965
Sutton Mr JH, Reading Room Mgr., Brit.L., Oriental & Ind.Off.Collec, London. [0031709]   13/11/1979
Sutton Mrs JP, (was Hayward), MCLIP, p./t.Asst.Sch.Lib., Haberdashers Aske's Boys Sch., Borehamwood, Herts. [0006613]   11/09/1971
Sutton Mrs K, (was Foster), BA MCLIP, Lend.Serv.Mgr., Blackburn with Darwen Bor.Council, Lancs. [0028813]   18/01/1978
Sutton Mr L, BA MCLIP, Sen.Lib., Thamesmead Cent., Bexley L.B. [0022877]   01/10/1974
Sutton Ms SA, (was Thomas), BA MBA MCLIP, L.Serv.Mgr., Leicester Coll., Leicester. [0026577]   05/10/1976
Sutton Mr TJ, MCLIP, Sen.Lib., Sheffield L.& Inf.Serv. [0028693]   17/01/1978
Sutton Mrs WS, Dep.Mgr., Dudley Citizens Advice Bureau, W.Midlands. [0014260]   01/01/1960
Sutton Mrs YA, (was Clements), BA DLS MCLIP, Unemployed. [0002840]   13/10/1970
Suzuki Mr H, Life Member. [0017849]   01/01/1970
Svoboda Mr E, BA MA DLIS MCLIP, Lib., Internat.Study Cent., Queens Univ.Canada, Herstmonleux Castle, E.Sussex. [0032348]   26/02/1980
Swain Ms B, BSc DipInfSc MCLIP, Employment not known. [0060654]   11/12/2001
Swain Ms E, MA MSc, Inf.Specialist, Cardiff Univ. [0058680]   18/05/2000
Swain Miss M, BA, Retired. [0014262]   04/02/1952
Swain Ms M, (was Nix), MA MCLIP, Contract Catr. [0019217]   01/10/1972
Swain Mrs RL, (was Graham), BA DipLib MCLIP, Resource Lib., Sch.L.Serv., Herts.C.C. [0045628]   02/04/1991
Swainson Miss NJ, BA DipLib MCLIP, Coll.Lib., Sparsholt Coll.Hampshire, Winchester. [0033168]   11/10/1980
Swainston Ms S, MA MPhil, Knowledge Agent, DSTL Knowledge Serv., Farnborough. [0061554]   18/09/2002
Swales Mrs BJ, (was Ridley), BA MCLIP MSc, Lib., Warwickshire C.C. [0034891]   15/04/1982
Swales Ms GE, BA DipLib MCLIP, Section Lib., Serv.to Young People & Sch., Dumfries & Galloway C. [0029287]   23/04/1978
Swallow Mrs C, (was Farrar), MSc, Catr., Brit.L.(N.) [0044899]   10/01/1991

Swamy-Russell Mrs JA, (was Swamy), MLib, Learning Serv.Co-ordinator, City of Westminster F.E.Coll., London. [0045893]   10/07/1991
Swan Mr RP, MCLIP, Educ.Lib.Consultant. [0014272]   01/01/1968
Swanick Mrs VP, (was Nash), MCLIP, Retired. [0020861]   26/02/1959
Swann Miss KL, BA(Hons) MA MCLIP, Curatorial Asst., Nat.Art L., Victoria & Albert Mus. [0054634]   27/01/1997
Swann Mrs MJ, (was Bailey), BA MCLIP, Unemployed, [0000590]   16/03/1965
Swann Mr RG, MA MCLIP, Retired. [0014275]   02/10/1953
Swann Ms SE, BA(Hons) MCLIP, Lib., St.Pauls Girls Sch., Hammersmith. [0033170]   26/09/1980
Swann Mrs VR, (was Holley), MCLIP, Inf.Offr.(Gridwatch), Brit.Educ.Comm.& Tech.Agency, (Becta), Coventry. [0014276]   12/01/1969
Swann-Price Mrs JMB, BA(Hons) MSc, Lib., Devizes L., Wilts.C.C. [0055994]   13/01/1998
Swanson Mrs CA, (was Jones), BA(Hons) MA MCLIP, Inf.Serv.Co-ordinator, Gen.Teaching Council, London. [0052713]   24/11/1995
Swanson Mr E, MA, Mgr., Contract Catg.Program, MINITEX L.Inf.Network, U.S.A. [0045568]   18/03/1991
Swarbrick Miss MJ, BA MCLIP, Life Member. [0014280]   09/10/1958
Swash Mrs GD, MCLIP, Knowledge & L.Project Mgr., S.Cheshire Health Auth., Chester. [0023070]   30/10/1974
Sweek Mrs CC, (was Newman), BA(Hons) MA, Inf.Offr., Royal Inst.of Chartered Surveyors, London. [0050741]   13/10/1994
Sweeney Mrs CH, (was Blain), Exec.Offr./Lib., E.Antrim Coll.of F.& H.E., Newtownabbey, Co Antrim. [0050197]   04/03/1994
Sweeney Mr GP, FCLIP, Resident in Ireland. [0017850]   19/02/1949   **FE 01/07/1989**
Sweeney Mr JM, MSc MCLIP, Position unknown, Brit.L., London. [0060653]   11/12/2001
Sweeney Mrs LJ, MA PGCE DipLibMan, Info.Offr., Liverpool John Moores Univ. [0052219]   17/10/1995
Sweeney Miss ME, BA MSc(Econ), Resident in Ireland. [0052494]   02/11/1995
Sweeney Mr R, BA FCLIP, Retired. [0014284]   01/01/1950   **FE 01/01/1964**
Sweet Mrs KL, BSc MCLIP, Employment not known. [0060800]   12/12/2001
Sweet Miss LJ, MLS MCLIP, Customer Serv.Adviser, Virgin Mobile, Trowbridge. [0033658]   20/01/1981
Sweetland Ms JM, (was Edge), BA(Hons) MSc MCLIP, Neurosciences Lib., N.Bristol NHS Trust, Frenchay Hosp. [0029323]   17/06/1978
Sweetman Ms J, (was Burnie), BA DipLib, Manager, CIKM, Cent.for Inf.& Knowledge Mgmt., Essex C.C. [0032401]   01/04/1980
Sweetman Mr PB, BA MCLIP, Consultant, Rewell Knowledge Serv., Arundel. [0022970]   24/09/1974
Sweetman Mrs S, MCLIP, Sen.Asst.Lib., Cent.Div., Lancs.L. [0023416]   06/01/1975
Swift Ms AJ, BA(Hons) MCLIP, Area Support Lib., Powys C.C., Co.L.H.Q., Llandrindod Wells,Powys. [0037251]   11/05/1984
Swift Miss CA, Sch.Lib., Waverley Sch., Birmingham. [0051609]   10/04/1995
Swift Ms HA, BA(Hons) DipILS MCLIP, European Union Lib., The Law Soc., London. [0051164]   23/11/1994
Swift Mr MJ, Life Member, Tel:0181 656 5649. [0014293]   01/01/1947
Swift Mr RA, BA DipLib MCLIP, Sen.Inf.Adviser, Sheffield Hallam Univ.L. [0034678]   01/02/1982
Swindells Mr RJ, MCLIP, Head of Bibl.& Tech.Serv., R.B.of Kensington & Chelsea. [0014295]   24/05/1965
Swinyard Miss JKF, MCLIP, Area Lib., Wells Area, Somerset Co.L. [0014296]   25/03/1958
Swyny Ms LF, BA(Hons) MA, Asst.Lib., HM Treasury & Cabinet Off., London. [0055408]   08/10/1997
Sydenham Mrs A, (was McElroy), BA(Hons) PGDipLib, Team Lib., City Campus L., Univ.of Northumbria at Newcastle. [0036359]   07/10/1983
Sydenham Mrs RE, (was Gibbs), MCLIP, Unemployed - bringing up family. [0037610]   09/10/1984
Syder Mrs CHM, (was Perkins), BA DipLib MCLIP, Young Peoples Serv.Mgr., Warrington L., Cheshire. [0029789]   05/10/1978
Sykes Mr AR, BA MCLIP, Sen.Lib., L.B.Richmond upon Thames, Cent.Ref.L. [0030551]   30/01/1979
Sykes Mrs E, (was Smith), Sib., The Hulme Grammar Schs., Oldham. [0046775]   22/01/1992
Sykes Mr HG, BA MCLIP, Ref.Serv.Lib., Bristol Ref.L. [0027373]   07/03/1977
Sykes Mrs HM, (was Davis), MCLIP, Grp.Mgr., Eastbourne, E.Sussex.Co.L. [0026343]   01/10/1976
Sykes Mr J, MA FCLIP, Dept.Lib., Art., Bradford P.L. [0014301]   01/01/1949   **FE 01/01/1965**
Sykes Mrs JM, MA DipLib MCLIP, Lib. & Dir.(Inf.Serv.), L., London Sch.of Econ. [0021020]   03/10/1973
Sykes Mrs PA, (was Kemp), BA(Hons) MCLIP, Lib., G.C.H.Q., Cheltenham. [0049577]   19/11/1993
Sykes Miss RA, BA(Hons) DipILM, Faculty Liaison Lib.(Ed.), Canterbury Christ Church Univ.Coll. [0047788]   14/10/1992
Sylph Ms EA, BSc MSc MCLIP, Lib.(Maternity Leave), Zoological Soc.of London. [0060691]   12/12/2001
Sylvester Miss K, MA, Learning Resource Lib., Leicester Coll. [0059734]   10/09/2001
Sylvester Miss RC, BA(Hons) MA, Bus.Inf.Spec., London Business Sch. [0054031]   21/10/1996
Syme Mrs J, (was Robson), BA MA MCLIP, Career Break. [0041304]   01/11/1987
Syme Mr WS, BA MCLIP, Lib.i/c.-Br.L., Cent. L., Dundee. [0028377]   05/11/1977
Symes Miss CE, BA MCLIP, L.Mgr., Univ.of Westminster. [0030548]   28/01/1979
Symes Mrs MR, (was Noak), BA MCLIP, p./t.Asst.Lib., Univ.of Brighton. [0042663]   07/02/1989

Symmons Mrs B, (was Beasley), MCLIP, Retired, Australia. [0017851] 17/09/1931
Symonds Mr KM, p./t.Stud., Univ.of Wales, Aberystwyth. [0051198] 23/11/1994
Symonds Miss RE, BA(Hons) MCLIP, Comm.Lib., Tameside M.B.C., Ashton-under-Lyne. [0055556] 21/10/1997
Symons Mrs AC, (was Baird), DipLIS MCLIP, Res.Cent.Mgr., Sch.L., Shaftesbury Sch., Dorset. [0045347] 19/10/1990
Symons Mr HJM, MA MCLIP, Curator, (Early Printed Books), Wellcome L. [0014310] 17/01/1968
Symons Miss PA, MCLIP, Retired. [0014311] 01/01/1958
Symons Mr RJ, BA(Hons) DipLib MA, Asst.Lib., Imperial War Mus., London. [0050587] 26/09/1994
Syrotiuk Mr N, MLIS BA BSc, Employed outside LIS, [0060943] 14/01/2002
Sytsema Dr J, PhD, Unemployed, [0060987] 25/01/2002
Sze Miss MWM, BSc, Stud., UCL. [0061640] 09/10/2002
Szenes Mrs A, Retired. [0014316] 01/01/1971
Szotkowski Ms HE, BSc MA MCLIP, Career Break. [0043911] 16/02/1990
Szpera Miss J, MCLIP, L.Offr., City of Edinburgh Council. [0022050] 16/01/1974
Szpytman Miss TM, BSc MSC MCLIP, Career break. [0041397] 20/11/1987
Szurko Mrs MM, BA DipLib MRes MCLIP, Lib., Oriel Coll., Oxford Univ. [0031955] 21/01/1980
Szwann Ms AJ, p./t.Stud./L.Asst., Univ.N.London, The Tavistock L. [0059526] 25/04/2001
Ta-Min Mrs AJS, BSc DipLib MCLIP, Lib., Queen Elizabeth Girls Sch., Barnet. [0026147] 25/07/1976
Taal Ms M, B.SocSci(Hons) BA, Unemployed. [0059738] 10/09/2001 **AF**
Taberner Mrs LK, (was Bishop), BA(Hons) MCLIP, Asst.Lib., Lancs.Co.L.Serv., Preston. [0048225] 16/11/1992
Taborn Ms MR, BA MLS, Learning Res.Mgr., N.Devon Coll., Barnstaple. [0029229] 19/04/1978
Taft Mr DC, BA DipLib MCLIP, Asst.Lib., Health & Safety Exec., London. [0035130] 26/08/1982
Tagg Mrs EJ, BA(Hons) FCLIP, Life Member, Tel.01705 837828, 25 Park House, 1 Clarence Parade, Southsea, Hants., PO5 3RJ. [0014321] 01/01/1941 **FE 01/01/1951**
Taggart Mrs C, (was Barnes), MCLIP, Serv.Review Support Offr., Leics.L.& Inf.Serv. [0014323] 22/08/1967
Tahan Mrs IA, MPhil, Curator, Brit.L., OIOC, London. [0039440] 28/01/1986
Tahir Mrs E, BPharm(Hons), Bilingual Nursery Nurse/Pharmacist. [0058255] 30/11/1999
Tai Miss S, BA(Hons), Stud., Northumbria Univ. [0061691] 21/10/2002
Tailby Mrs AP, BA(Hons), Inf.Serv.Mgr., Dept.Social Security, London. [0041301] 01/11/1987
Tailby Miss SJ, BA, L.Asst., Southampton City Coll. [0057206] 15/01/1999
Tait Mr DR, MA DipLib MCLIP, Asst.Lib., Univ.of Glasgow. [0032564] 06/05/1980
Tait Ms FI, MCLIP, Reg.Inf.Coordinator, Brit.Council, London. [0014325] 19/03/1963
Tait Mrs HFC, (was Henderson), MCLIP, Retired, 34 Quadrant Rd., Glasgow, G43 2QR. [0014326] 12/02/1949
Tait Mrs JM, MA MCLIP, Lib., The Tank Mus., Dorset. [0028697] 12/01/1978
Tak Mr AJ, (was Birchall), BA MSc, Asst.Systems Lib., Middx.Univ. [0042067] 21/09/1988
Takawashi Mr T, B ED, Prof., Tokyo Gakugei Univ., Japan. [0024452] 24/07/1975
Takhar Mr S, Adult Lib., Royal Bor.Windsor & Maidenhead, Maidenhead. [0057623] 27/05/1999
Talbi Mr MH, BA MA LIS, Dir.of L., Univ.of Bahrain. [0042012] 14/07/1988
Talbot Miss BG, BLib MCLIP, Sch.Lib., Queen Elizabeths Upper Sch., Mansfield, Notts. [0026809] 23/10/1976
Talbot Mrs DL, (was Harrington), BA DipLIS, Lib., GCHQ, Cheltenham. [0049642] 16/11/1993
Talbot Mrs HD, MCLIP, Life Member. [0014333] 01/01/1957
Talbot Mrs HM, (was Slora), MCLIP, Sch.Lib., Bromsgrove Sch., Bromsgrove, Worcs. [0018358] 13/10/1972
Talbot Mr RG, Inf.Asst., QINETIQ Ltd., Dorchester, Dorset. [0054585] 11/02/1997 **AF**
Talboys Mr A, MCLIP, Partner, Kingsley & Talboys, London. [0060652] 11/12/2001
Tales Mrs A, (was Owen), BA MCLIP, Unemployed, [0020410] 03/03/1973
Tallach Mr S, Inf.Cent.Asst., Scottish Parliament. [0058609] 30/03/2000 **AF**
Tam Ms DC, MApplSc BA DipLib, Lend.Serv.Lib., Hong Kong Inst.of Educ., Hong Kong. [0057618] 18/05/1999
Tamblyn Mrs KL, (was Bartlett), BA DipLib MCLIP, Land Charges Asst., Tunbridge Wells Bor.Council. [0044440] 08/10/1990
Tamby Miss Z, B EC MCLIP, Sen.Asst.Lib., Inst.of S.E.Asian Studies, Singapore. [0022156] 13/10/1975
Tan Miss CH, MCLIP, Asst.Lib., Ngee Ann Poly., Singapore. [0022462] 09/05/1974
Tancock Miss JA, MCLIP, Lib., Morecambe Bay Hosp.NHS Trust, Barrow-in-Furness. [0027223] 14/02/1977
Tandoh Miss K, Stud., Thames Valley Univ. [0058243] 24/11/1999
Tanfield Miss JB, BSc, Retired. [0048960] 04/08/1993
Tanner Mrs AJ, Co-ordinator of L.& Flexible Learn., Serv., Coll.L., N.Lincs.Coll., Lincoln. [0053541] 15/07/1996 **AF**
Tanner Mr DA, BA MCLIP, Grp.Lib.-Sherburn, N.Yorks.Co.L. [0019671] 26/10/1972
Tanner Mr ME, BA DipLib MCLIP, Sen.Lib., Torfaen Ls., Pontypool. [0039168] 04/11/1985
Tanner Mr SG, BA MCLIP, Digitisation Consultant, H.E.Digitisation Cent., Univ.of Herts. [0039395] 13/01/1986

Tanner Miss W, BA(Hons), p./t.Stud./Inf.Offr., City Univ./I.P.A., London. [0058677] 16/05/2000
Tansley Mr IP, MCLIP, Grp.Lib., N.W.Devon, Devon L.& Inf.Serv. [0014343] 11/03/1968
Tanti Mrs C, (was Lee), BA(Hons) DipLib, Asst.Lib., Northants.Cent.L., Northampton. [0041920] 20/05/1988
Taplin Mr BK, BA(Hons) DipIM MCLIP, Asst.Lib., The Brit.Mus., Dept.of Ethnography, London. [0051013] 09/11/1994
Taplin Mrs MS, (was David), MCLIP, Lib., Macfarlanes, London. [0003631] 01/01/1972
Tapril Mr S, BA, Stud., Oxford Univ. [0061745] 30/10/2002
Tarbox Mrs S, (was Fletcher), MCLIP, L.Consultant, Bromley NHS Trust, W.Kent P.G.Med.Cent. [0014346] 20/10/1965
Targett Ms K, BA(Hons), Inf.Serv.Mgr., Plunkett Foundation, Long Hanborough, Oxon. [0054691] 21/02/1997 **AF**
Tarling Mr MR, MCLIP, Community Team Lib., Glos.C.C. [0014348] 01/08/1971
Tarn Miss FJ, BSc DipInf MCLIP, Lib., Croydon Council, Croydon Cent.L. [0046142] 07/10/1991
Tarrant Mrs M, (was Murphy), MCLIP, Child.Learners Serv.Mgr., Essex C.C.L. [0014350] 01/04/1971
Tarrant Mrs SE, (was Abbott), BA MCLIP, Subject Lib.(Psychology), Univ.of London L. [0014352] 12/01/1967
Tarron Mrs MP, BA DipIS, Learning Resource Mgr., St Peters Catholic Comp.Sch., Guildford, Surrey. [0055472] 14/10/1997
Tarter Mrs A, (was Adams), BA MS MCLIP, Sch.Lib., Ripon Grammar Sch., N.Yorks. [0044316] 29/08/1990
Tasker Mrs J, (was Harris), MCLIP, Retired. [0014355] 05/03/1964
Tasker Miss MJ, Employment not known. [0041716] 17/02/1988
Tassoni Ms L, BA MA MSc, Inf.Advisor., Sheffield Hallam Univ. [0057062] 02/12/1998
Tate Mr GJ, BA DipLib MCLIP, H.of Knowledge Serv., GCHQ, Cheltenham. [0040951] 01/10/1987
Tate Mrs JM, (was Kennell), BA(Hons) MSc(Econ), Asst.Lib., Cranfield Univ. [0058318] 07/01/2000
Tate Mrs P, (was Shallcross), BA MA, L.Mgr., Coudert Brothers, London. [0050110] 05/04/1994
Tatem Ms S, MCLIP, Retired. [0014359] 01/10/1971
Tatham Ms VJ, LLB PGDipInf MA, Asst.Lib., Liverpool Inst.of H.E., Beck L.,Christs & Notre Dame Coll. [0044048] 10/04/1990
Tatler Mrs VA, MA, PBJ Select Exec., PJB Publications Lt., Surrey. [0050671] 07/10/1994
Tatlow Mrs J, (was Bowles), Employment not known. [0036069] 09/05/1983
Tattersall Mrs E, (was French), MCLIP, Unemployed. [0018125] 03/10/1972
Tattersall Mr S, MSc MCLIP, Mgr.Informatics, Hewlett Packard Ltd., Bristol. [0029536] 18/09/1978
Tatum Mrs SJ, (was Pope), MCLIP, Lib., Animal Health Trust, Newmarket. [0014362] 01/10/1965
Taubinger Mrs SL, (was Loughlin), BA(Hons) MCLIP, Asst.Lib., Cheshire C.C., Northwich L. [0046525] 18/11/1991
Tavendale Mrs DBL, (was Lovell), BA(Hons) MCLIP, Unemployed. [0014363]
Taverner Mrs HF, (was Tolhurst), BA DipLib MCLIP, Quality Assurance Mgr., Shepherd Design, York. [0036325] 01/10/1983
Tavner Mrs EH, (was Moore), MA MCLIP, Lib.Team Leader, Norfolk LIS., Great Yarmouth L. [0014364] 06/10/1969
Tawalama Mr B, MA BLibSc PGDipLIS, Lib., London Buddhist Vihara. [0040820] 03/07/1987
Tawn Mrs HV, (was Blakey), BA(Hons) DipLib MCLIP, Unemployed, The Rectory, Low Mill Lane, Addingham, Ilkley, LS29 0QP. [0044343] 01/10/1990
Tayler Mrs J, (was Humphreys), BA DipLib MCLIP, Unemployed(Career Break), Newman Coll., Bartley Green, Birmingham. [0044611] 06/11/1990
Tayler Mrs M, (was Coelho), MCLIP, Inf.Lib.(Job Share), Chipping Barnet L., L.B.of Barnet. [0018346] 13/10/1972
Taylor Miss A, BA, Child.Lib., Cent.L., L.B.of Barking & Dagenham. [0035514] 21/10/1982
Taylor Ms AA, BA DipLib MCLIP, Div.Lib., Cheshire C.C., Macclesfield. [0031768] 07/12/1979
Taylor Mrs AB, (was Grief), BA DipLib MCLIP, Head of L.Serv., Univ.of the W.of England, Bristol. [0033527] 14/01/1981
Taylor Mrs AE, (was Van Hien), MCLIP, [0015066] 01/01/1968
Taylor Ms AE, BSc MCLIP, Inf.Worker, Vol.Serv.Aberdeen, Aberdeen. [0030868] 29/04/1979
Taylor Mrs AM, (was Digby (Form.Durrant)), MCLIP, Retired. [0004304] 11/02/1963
Taylor Miss AP, BA MA MCLIP, Team Lib., Somerset C.C. [0043653] 16/11/1989
Taylor Miss BJ, DipILS, Housing Asst., Manchester Housing. [0051364] 30/01/1995
Taylor Mrs BJ, (was Kelly), MA MCLIP PGCE, LRC Mgr., Macclesfield Coll., Cheshire. [0020959] 06/09/1973
Taylor Mr BL, BA(Hons) MA, Services Mgr., Basildon L., Essex C.C. [0059649] 11/07/2001 **AF**
Taylor Miss BR, MCLIP, Retired. [0014380] 01/01/1966
Taylor Miss C, BSc, Stud., City University London. [0061803] 12/11/2002
Taylor Ms C, BSc(Hons) MA MCLIP, Asst.Lib., Field Fisher Waterhouse, London. [0052951] 26/01/1996
Taylor Mrs CA, (was Binks), BSc MCLIP, Sen.Child.Ref.Lib., Natal Soc.L., Pietermaritzburg, S.Africa. [0021697] 01/01/1974
Taylor Ms CJ, BA DipLib MCLIP, Lifelong Learning Devel.Mgr., Westminster City Council. [0034727] 05/02/1982
Taylor Miss CL, BSc(Hons), Stud./Inf.Asst., City Univ., The Maughan L.& Inf.Serv. [0061300] 16/05/2002

Taylor Miss CM, MA MCLIP, Asst.Ref./Local Studies Lib., Aberdeen City.L. [0021038] 02/10/1973
Taylor Ms CM, (was Aitken), MA DipLib MCLIP, Lib., Inverness Royal Academy, Highland Reg.Council. [0036292] 01/10/1983
Taylor Mr CV, BA(Hons) MA MCLIP, Cur.E - Collection Dept., Nat.L.of Scotland, Edinburgh. [0047731] 15/10/1992
Taylor Mr D, MA MCLIP, L.Asst., Birmingham L.Serv., Cent.L. [0014384] 07/05/1968
Taylor Mrs D, (was Musgrove), BA MCLIP, Sch.Lib., Strathclyde Reg.Council, Dunbarton. [0014383] 17/01/1970
Taylor Mr DA, BA MLS MCLIP, Customer Support Mgr., Fretwell-Downing Informatics, Sheffield. [0014387] 14/08/1970
Taylor Mrs DA, (was Thomas), BA(Hons), Child.Lib., Brierley Hill Area, Dudley M.B.C. [0040781] 06/06/1987
Taylor Miss DE, MSc MCLIP M I BIOL, Stud., Teeside Univ. [0025120] 15/11/1975
Taylor Mrs DJ, Lib., Hull City Council. [0055132] 16/07/1997
Taylor Mrs DK, (was Bowden), BA MCLIP, Unemployed. [0001533] 01/01/1967
Taylor Mrs DM, (was Hunter), MCLIP, Lib., N.Dist., Manchester P.L. [0007491] 25/09/1968
Taylor Mr DN, BA MCLIP, Intranet Cont./Inf.Asset Reg.Mgr., Dept.for Work & Pensions, Quarry Hill, Leeds. [0034643] 30/01/1982
Taylor Mrs DR, (was Morgan), Retired. [0014389] 01/10/1947
Taylor Miss E, BLib MCLIP, Chartered Lib.-Stock Mgmt., Bibl.Serv.Dept., Edinburgh City L. [0027026] 11/01/1977
Taylor Miss E, BA(Hons) MA MCLIP, Asst.Lib., Lincolns Inn L. [0055683] 04/11/1997
Taylor Mrs E, (was Scurr), BA(Hons) MA MCLIP, Inf.Specialist, GCHQ. [0050115] 05/04/1994
Taylor Mrs EE, MCLIP, Life Member. [0014392] 01/01/1936
Taylor Mrs EG, (was Haslam), BSc DipLib MCLIP, Asst.Area Sch.Lib., Hants.Sch.L.Serv. [0032081] 06/02/1980
Taylor Miss EJ, BA MA MCLIP, Lib.-Support Serv., Lincs.C.C. [0043392] 19/10/1989
Taylor Mrs EL, BA, p./t.Stud., Learning Asst., Univ.Bristol, Bolland L. [0059266] 23/01/2001
Taylor Miss FKM, MA DipLib MCLIP, Lib., Fife Council. [0031524] 12/10/1979
Taylor Mrs G, (was Walker), BA MCLIP, Stock Co-ordinator, Stoke-on-Trent Ls., Hanley, Stoke -on-Trent. [0028248] 25/10/1977
Taylor Mrs G, BSc(Hons), Lib., N.Tyneside Central L., Tyne & Wear. [0059671] 25/07/2001
Taylor Mr GA, BA(Hons) MA, Inf.Editor, W.Yorks.Passenger Trans.Exec., Metro, Leeds. [0058321] 05/01/2000
Taylor Mr GG, MSc MCLIP, Asst.Lib., E.Kilbride Cent.L., S.Lanarkshire Council. [0043792] 18/01/1990
Taylor Mrs GS, (was Tonkinson), MCLIP, H.of Learning Res.Cent., Shrewsbury Coll.of Arts & Tech., Shropshire. [0014789] 14/01/1971
Taylor Mrs H, (was Legge), MCLIP, Family Serv.Co-ordinator, W.Sussex C.C., Chichester. [0008814] 06/11/1971
Taylor Ms H, BA MLS MCLIP, Position unknown, Gale Group, London. [0028184] 14/10/1977
Taylor Miss HE, BA DipLib MCLIP, Retired. [0020704] 06/06/1973
Taylor Miss HJ, (was Tomlinson), BA(Hon), Sch.Lib., Our Lady's Convent Sch., Loughborough, Leics. [0050208] 04/05/1994
Taylor Miss HK, BSc MCLIP, Teacher/Sch.Lib., Swaffham V.C. First Sch., Norfolk. [0043090] 20/07/1989
Taylor Mrs HM, (was Chicken), MA MCLIP, Learning Cent.Mgr., Winchcombe Sch., Glos. [0026700] 27/10/1976
Taylor Miss IJ, BA(Hons) DipILM, Inf.Serv.Admin., PB Group Serv.Ltd., Newcastle upon Tyne. [0052026] 18/09/1995
Taylor Miss J, BA, Stud. [0059452] 30/03/2001
Taylor Mrs J, MCLIP, Sen.Lib., Christchurch L., Dorset C.C. [0014410] 19/09/1968
Taylor Mrs J, (was Roberts), BLib MCLIP, Unemployed. [0028136] 12/10/1977
Taylor Ms J, BEd, Lib.(Temporary), Gateshead Met.Bor.Council. [0046595] 21/11/1991
Taylor Mr JA, BA(Hons) DipIS, Customer Serv.Lib., Herts.C.C., Three Rivers Dist. [0050974] 04/11/1994
Taylor Mrs JA, (was Crum), MLS MCLIP, Retired. [0003440] 16/10/1969
Taylor Mrs JE, MA BA DipLib MCLIP, Inf.Mgr., Communication Workers Union, Wimbledon. [0039363] 16/01/1986
Taylor Mrs JKK, (was Lim), BA BSc MCLIP, Lib., Leics.L.& Inf.Serv., Coalville. [0020317] 05/02/1973
Taylor Mrs JL, (was Williams), CertEd DipLib MCLIP, Lib., Halton Unitary Council, Inf.& Leisure Serv. [0043301] 17/10/1989
Taylor Miss JM, MCLIP, Unemployed, 4 South Street, Ventnor, Isle of Wight, PO38 ING. [0014418] 26/04/1967
Taylor Mr JW, BA MCLIP, Retired. [0019110] 20/03/1957
Taylor Mr JWH, MCLIP, 112,Slewins Lane, Hornchurch, Essex. [0014423] 01/03/1940
Taylor Ms KH, (was Power), BA(Hons), p./t.Stud./Flexible Learning Offr., RMCS Cranfield Univ., Swindon. [0055269] 11/09/1997
Taylor Miss KJ, BA(Hons) MCLIP, Inf.Specialist, GCHQ, Cheltenham. [0045458] 11/02/1991
Taylor Miss KJ, BA DipLib MCLIP, [0038956] 24/10/1985
Taylor Mrs L, (was Sinha), MA, Sen.L.Asst.(Catg.), Kings Coll.London L., London. [0040947] 25/09/1987
Taylor Mrs L, (was King), BLib MCLIP MSc(Econ), Learning Res.Mgr., Norwood Sch., London. [0026434] 06/10/1976
Taylor Ms L, BSc, Employment not known. [0060198] 10/12/2001
Taylor Mrs LA, (was Malcolm), BA, Unwaged. [0038737] 01/10/1985
Taylor Mr LJ, BA FCLIP, Retired, Tamarisk Books, Hastings, E.Sussex. [0014426] 28/08/1958 FE 14/11/1991
Taylor Mrs LJ, (was Bell), MEd BA MCLIP, Dir.of Learning Res., Liverpool Hope. [0029145] 16/04/1978

Taylor Mrs LM, (was Johnson), Lib., Health Educ.Res.Cent., Birmingham. [0042233] 14/10/1988
Taylor Mrs LV, (was Williams), BA MCLIP, Housewife. [0027594] 26/05/1977
Taylor Mr M, BA MCLIP, Employment not known. [0060214] 10/12/2001
Taylor Mr M, BA MCLIP, L.& Inf.Serv.Mgr., Royal Bor.of Windsor & Maidenhead, Maidenhead. [0029842] 03/10/1978
Taylor Mrs M, BSc (Hons) MSc, L. Asst., Nat. Museum & Gallery, Cardiff. [0060961] 21/01/2002
Taylor Ms M-T, (was Paisley), MA(Hons) DipILS MCLIP, Sch.Lib./Inf.Cent.Mgr., Fife Council Educ.Dept. [0052947] 26/01/1996
Taylor Miss MC, BA(Hons), Asst.Inf.Offr., TPAS, Salford. [0053629] 19/08/1996
Taylor Miss MJ, MCLIP, Retired. [0014436] 01/01/1941
Taylor Mr MJ, BA MCLIP, Retired. [0014435] 07/08/1957
Taylor Mr MR, BA MCLIP, Research Asst., Brent,Kensington, Chelsea &, Westminster Mental Health Trust. [0039246] 01/01/1986
Taylor Mr MR, BA(Hons), Stud., Manchester Met Univ. [0061307] 20/05/2002
Taylor Mr MS, BEd CertEd MA, Lib., Faber Maunsell, Birmingham. [0052329] 30/10/1995
Taylor Miss NE, MA FCLIP, Life Member, Tel.0181 455 4121, 2 Phildor Crt., Princes Pk.Av., Golders Grn., London, NW11 9QA. [0014441] 17/10/1935 FE 01/01/1939
Taylor Mrs NME, Grad.Trainee L.Asst., Chester Coll.Higher Ed. [0059737] 10/09/2001
Taylor Mrs NR, (was Stedman), MCLIP, Asst.Area Sch.Lib., Hants.C.C., Farnborough. [0014442] 01/01/1967
Taylor Mr P, BSc(Hons) MCLIP, Area Lib., Peebles Area L., Scottish Borders. [0014444] 10/03/1971
Taylor Mrs P, (was Heywood), BSc MCLIP, Area L.Mgr., Knowsley M.B.C. [0006813] 30/10/1971
Taylor Miss PA, BA MCLIP, Public Serv.Mgr., Suffolk C.C., Ipswich. [0030554] 08/02/1979
Taylor Mrs PF, BLib MCLIP, Sen.Lib., Sheffield L.Arch.& Inf.Serv. [0027602] 27/05/1977
Taylor Mr PG, MA DMS FCLIP, Unemployed. [0014446] 08/01/1968 FE 21/11/1983
Taylor Mrs PM, (was Hudson), MCLIP, Retired. [0014443] 01/01/1949
Taylor Mrs R, MA MPHIL MCLIP, Life Member. [0014451] 09/01/1958
Taylor Mrs RA, (was Whitley), BA(Hons) MCLIP, Sch.Lib., Crossley Heath Sch., Halifax. [0024385] 08/07/1975
Taylor Ms RC, BA MA, Business Consultant, Ramesys Ltd., Stoke on Trent. [0042263] 13/10/1988
Taylor Mr RD, BA MCLIP, Performing Arts Lib., Somerset L.,Arts & Inf., Yeovil. [0014454] 06/07/1971
Taylor Mrs RG, (was Baker), MCLIP, User Serv.Lib., Dunstable Coll.Corporation, Beds. [0022035] 21/02/1974
Taylor Mr RH, MCLIP MA, Retired. [0014455] 12/06/1962
Taylor Miss RL, BA(Hons), Inf.Offr., Linklaters & Alliance, London. [0049571] 19/11/1993
Taylor Mr RS, BA(Hons) DipILM MCLIP, Dep.Lib., Dartington Coll.of Arts, Devon. [0046820] 11/02/1992
Taylor Mrs S, (was Semple), MA DipLib DMS MCLIP, Res.& Documentation Asst., Potteries Mus.& Art Assoc.Gallery., Stoke-on-Trent. [0025672] 28/01/1976
Taylor Mrs S, BA(Hons), Stud., Robert Gordon Univ. [0061619] 04/10/2002
Taylor Mrs S, (was Lake), BA(Hons) MSc, Sen.Lib.Asst., Univ.Sheffield. [0054235] 11/11/1996
Taylor Mrs S, (was Quinn), BSc MCLIP, Employment not known. [0012087] 08/07/1968
Taylor Mrs S, (was Smith), MCLIP, Life Member. [0014461] 01/02/1955
Taylor Ms S, BA(Hons) MCLIP, Asst.Lib., St.Martins Coll., Lancaster. [0044756] 15/11/1990
Taylor Mr SC, BA, Bookshop Asst.(p/t.), Wells,Somerset. [0024966] 13/10/1975
Taylor Miss SE, BA(Hons) MSc, Inf.Serv.Mgr., Arjo Wiggins Fine Papers Ltd., Beaconsfield. [0047569] 02/10/1992
Taylor Miss SE, BA MCLIP, Lib.Erlestoke Prison p./t., Wilts.L.& Heritage, Trowbridge. [0014464] 14/07/1972
Taylor Mrs SEC, MA(Hons) DipILS MCLIP, Lifelong Learning Project Offr., Glasgow City Council. [0053974] 15/10/1996
Taylor Mrs SH, BA(Hons) MA MCLIP, Inf.& Records Controller, H.J.Banks & Co.Ltd., Durham. [0056311] 01/05/1998
Taylor Mr SJ, BA MCLIP, Comm.Lib., Louth, Lincs.C.C. [0041577] 28/01/1988
Taylor Mrs SJ, (was Goodman), BSc(SocSci), L.Asst., John Ruskin Coll., S.Croydon. [0049804] 13/12/1993 AF
Taylor Miss SM, BSc(Hons) DipLIM, Sen.Learning Res.Asst., Exeter Coll.of F.E. [0060735] 01/02/1995
Taylor Mrs SM, BA(Hons), Stud., Univ.of N.London. [0059923] 02/11/2001
Taylor Mrs SMC, FCLIP, Retired. [0014466] 17/08/1941 FE 01/01/1951
Taylor Mr T, BA DipILS MCLIP, Inf.Offr., Univ.of Salford, Manchester. [0048125] 10/11/1992
Taylor Mr TM, Chairman, DEMCO Worldwide Ltd., Wellingborough. [0041917] 20/05/1988
Taylor Mrs VL, (was Edwards), MSc BA MILAM MCLIP, Retired. [0001229] 07/10/1965
Taylor Roome Mrs D, (was Taylor), BSc MCLIP AdvDipEd, Retired - Voluntary Steward, Redbourn Vill.Mus., Herts. [0014470] 24/01/1962
Taylor-Durant Mr CC, BSc MCLIP, Employment not known. [0060801] 12/12/2001
Taylor-Reid Mrs JP, (was Taylor), Lib., Freshfields Bruckhaus Deringer, London. [0044788] 15/11/1990
Taylor-Roe Mrs JL, (was Taylor), MA MCLIP, Sub-Lib., Liaison & Acad.Serv.&Special Col., Newcastle Univ.L. [0035137] 13/09/1982

Personal Members

Taylorson Mrs EM, (was Cooke), BA(Hons) MA, L.Asst., Durham Univ.L. [0051042] 09/11/1994
Teague Mr SJ, BSc(Econ) FCLIP FRSA, Retired. [0014474] 02/01/1940 FE 01/01/1950
Teal Miss KM, MA(Hons) PGDip, Sen.Research Advisor, Inf.Serv., Business Link Herts., St.Albans. [0050251] 17/05/1994
Tearle Miss BM, (was Wells), LLB MSt MCLIP, Law Lib., Bodleian L., Oxford. [0015583] 18/02/1967
Teasdale Mrs FS, BSc(Hons) DipIS MCLIP, Acquisitons Lib., Surrey Inst.of Art & Design, Farnham. [0051892] 31/07/1995
Teather Miss JK, BA MCLIP, Saturday Serv.Super., City Univ. [0035872] 31/01/1983
Tedd Mrs L, BSc MCLIP, Employment not known. [0060656] 11/12/2001
Teeger Mrs BS, BA MCLIP, Enquiries Serv., Dept.of Transport (DTLR) L., London. [0030048] 10/11/1978
Teijken Ms A, (was Teijken Harrison), BA(Hons), p./t.Asst.Inf.Offr., Gtr.Manchester Probation Serv. [0045914] 19/07/1991
Teiser Miss E, BLib MCLIP, Lib., Ross on Wye L., Herefordshire Council. [0019843] 01/01/1973
Telfer Mrs DD, BBibl, Asst.Lib., Worcs.C.C., City L. [0051339] 23/01/1995
Telfer Mrs JE, (was Thompson), BA MCLIP, Asst.Lib., Barnsley M.B.C., Cent.L. [0021847] 03/02/1974
Telfer Mrs RA, (was Bower), BA(Hons) DipLib MCLIP, Grp.Mgr., Sheffield L.Arch.& Inf. [0024164] 17/02/1961
Telfer Miss SE, BA MCLIP, Retired. [0014484] 18/10/1968
Telford Ms NT, MA DipLib MCLIP, Joint Head Lib., Wyggeston & Queen Elizabeth I, 6th Form Coll., Leicester. [0023641] 06/01/1975
Telling Mrs REA, (was Palfree), BA MCLIP, Lib.,(job Share), Big Wood Sch., Nottingham City Council. [0038657] 01/01/1961
Tempest Ms PM, (was Cropper), MA BA MCLIP, Area Serv.Mgr.-E.Kent, Kent C.C.-Arts & L. [0021687] 09/01/1974
Templar Mrs A, p./t.Stud./L.Asst., Univ.of Cent.England, Birmingham, Lye L., Stourbridge. [0061545] 10/09/2002
Temple Ms E, MSc MCLIP, Employment not known. [0060856] 12/12/2001
Temple Mrs J, (was Keighley), MCLIP, Lib.-Job Share, Wythall L., Birmingham. [0008216] 01/10/1969
Temple Mrs SE, (was Ferguson), MCLIP, Sch.Lib.(P/T), Trinity Sch., Carlisle. [0004859] 01/01/1965
Templeman Mr SRJ, BA(Hons) DipInf, Unemployed. [0047989] 30/10/1992
Templer Mrs CM, (was Tomkins), MCLIP, L.Offr., Catholic Educ.Office, Canberra, ACT. [0017866] 07/09/1967
Templeton Mrs E, BSc DipLib, Inf.Offr., Building Design Partnership, Manchester. [0022500] 03/06/1974
Templeton Ms E, BA(Hons) DipILS MCLIP, Online Course Devel.Advisor, Robert Gordon Univ., Aberdeen. [0045616] 04/02/1997
Templeton Mr RTEP, BA MCLIP FRSA, Head of BFI Nat.L., Brit.Film Inst., London. [0024528] 07/10/1975
Tennis Mrs D, (was Moore), JP BA DLS DGC MCLIP, Nat.Secretary, The Girls Brigade, N.Ireland. [0019347] 01/10/1972
Terrett Mrs LD, (was Fletcher), BA MCLIP, Unemployed. [0035217] 05/10/1982
Terrey Mrs MD, (was Bull), MCLIP, Resident Overseas. [0014494]01/01/1960
Terris Mr GK, BSc MCLIP, Inf.Sci., Kodak Ltd., R&D., Harrow, Middx. [0021611] 24/11/1973
Terry Mrs CP, MCLIP, Employment not known. [0060655] 11/12/2001
Terry Ms JV, BA DipLib MCLIP, Unemployed. [0021301] 11/10/1973
Teteris Mrs R, MCLIP, Retired. [0014501] 25/03/1971
Tetley Mrs MC, P/t.Catrr., Dean & Chapter, Lichfield Cathedral, Staffs. [0030280] 11/12/1978
Tew Mr CS, B ED, Lib., Bishop David Brown Sch., Woking. [0041454] 01/01/1988
Thacker Mrs P, BA(HonsO PGCE, Stud.,Study Cent.Mgr., Robert Gordon,S.E.Essex Coll. [0061663] 14/10/2002
Thacker Mrs SE, (was Dancy), BA(Hons), Stud., Hon.Sec., Tel.01925 755175, 10 Richmond Close, Lymm, Cheshire, WA13 9HF. [0014503] 16/07/1941
Thacker Mrs SJ, (was Winkley), MCLIP, Asst.Lib.(Catg.), Havering P.L., Essex. [0016127] 08/02/1967
Thain Ms AE, BA MCLIP, Lib., Beastson Oncology Cent., Western Infirmary, Glasgow. [0025431] 18/12/1975
Thatcher Mr BF, MCLIP, Retired. [0014506] 28/01/1952
Thatcher Mr MJ, ARCM ABSM, Community Lib., Luton Bor.Council. [0040768] 29/05/1987
Theaker Mrs MH, BSc MCLIP, Unemployed. [0037892] 08/11/1984
Theakston Mr C, BA DipLib PGCE MPhil MCLIP, Departmental Lib., Business Sch., Univ.of Durham. [0045611] 01/04/1989
Thebridge Mrs SW, (was Pearcey), BA DipLib MCLIP, p./t.Research Fellow, Univ.of Cent.England, Birmingham. [0029788] 01/01/1978
Theis Ms KM, BSc DipLib MCLIP, Inf.Consultant, Freelance. [0029422] 01/07/1978
Thelwall Dr MA, BSc PhD, Employment not known. [0060503] 11/12/2001
Thickins Mr JOT, BA(Hons) MA, Electronic Inf.Offr., Coll.of N.E.London, Centenary Learning Cent. [0057966] 06/10/1999
Thies Ms AM, BA MLib MCLIP, Princ.Lib.-Cultural Serv., Co.L.H.Q., Lancs.C.C. [0039981] 03/12/1986
Thimann Ms CF, MCLIP, Not known. [0028933] 29/08/1967
Thirsk Mr JW, FCLIP, Life Member, 1 Hadlow Castle, Hadlow, Tonbridge, Kent, TN11 0EG, Tel:01723 850708. [0014515] 20/06/1933 FE 01/01/1947
Thistlethwaite Ms LE, (was Perrins), MCLIP, Sen.Asst.Lib.(Readers Adviser), Bolton Cent.L., Lancs. [0011558] 11/09/1971
Thistlethwaite Mr R, BA(Hons) DipLIS MCLIP, Unemployed. [0032468] 01/04/1980
Thoburn Ms J, BA DipLib MCLIP DMS, Bibl.Serv.Offr., Univ.of Northumbria at Newcastle. [0031711] 05/11/1979

Thom Mrs M, BA DipLib, Inf.Offr., Scottish Council for Vol.Org., Edinburgh. [0039837] 26/08/1986
Thom Mrs TL, BA MA MCLIP, Lib., The Hon.Soc.of Grays Inn L., London. [0026576] 07/10/1976
Thomas Mrs A, (was Wood), BLib MCLIP N.Dip.M, Grp.Lib.N., The Co.L., Haverfordwest, Pembrokeshire C.C. [0035343] 09/10/1982
Thomas Ms A, BA(Hons) MCLIP, Asst.Lib., Conwy Co.Bor.Council. [0029099] 27/02/1978
Thomas Mrs AA, (was Primrose), BA DipLib MCLIP, Lib., Harrow High Sch., Middx. [0025632] 17/01/1976
Thomas Mrs AC, BA DipLIS MCLIP, L.Mgr., Suffolk C.C. [0047369] 24/07/1992
Thomas Mr AD, MCLIP, Retired. [0014522] 11/01/1935
Thomas Mrs AE, (was Lane), BSc MCLIP, L.Asst., Monmouth C.C. [0018869] 01/01/1971
Thomas Mrs AE, BA MA MCLIP, Sen.Team Leader, Warks.C.C. [0041179] 14/10/1987
Thomas Miss AJ, BA(Hons), Asst.Lib., Birmingham Post & Mail. [0058403] 26/01/2000
Thomas Mrs AJ, (was Honeyman), FCLIP, Life Member, Tel.020 8769 5106. [0007145] 26/09/1950 FE 13/12/1979
Thomas Ms AJ, BA DipILM MSc MCLIP, Campus Lib., Univ.of Wales Inst., Cardiff. [0046570] 12/11/1991
Thomas Miss AP, MCLIP, Mgr.Botley L., Oxfordshire C.C., Oxfordshire. [0014524] 12/09/1963
Thomas Mr AR, MA FCLIP, Life Member. [0014525] 01/07/1947 FE 01/01/1958
Thomas Mr B, MCLIP, Retired. [0014526] 01/03/1949
Thomas Mr B, BA(Hons), Legal Inf.Mgr., Fox Williams, London. [0047895] 22/10/1992
Thomas Miss BM, BSc(Hons), Inf.Sci., Cent.for Inf.on Beverage Alcohol, London. [0058696] 02/06/2000
Thomas Mrs C, (was Miller), BSc(Hons) MSc DipLIS MCLIP, Serv.Devel.Lib., Walsall Hosp.NHS Trust, Walsall. [0046445] 06/11/1991
Thomas Mrs CE, BSc MRPharmS, Sen.L.Asst., Bournemouth Univ.L. [0061740] 01/11/2002
Thomas Mr CJ, BA, Sen.Inf.Offr., Bank of England Inf.Cent., London. [0039303] 09/01/1986
Thomas Mrs CK, (was Davies), BLib MCLIP, p./t.Curriculum Support Lib., Powys Co.L.Serv., Llandrindod Wells. [0031248] 07/10/1979
Thomas Miss CM, BA(Hons) DipLib MCLIP, Inf.Offr., Linklaters, London. [0031163] 12/09/1979
Thomas Miss CM, MCLIP, Sch.Lib., Southampton City Council. [0014532] 05/10/1971
Thomas Mr DB, BA DipLib MCLIP, Unemployed. [0030557] 16/02/1979
Thomas Ms DE, BSc DipInfSc MCLIP, Asst.Lib.(Job Share), English Heritage, Swindon. [0040549] 06/03/1987
Thomas Ms DG, BSc(Hons) MCLIP, Higher L.Exec., House of Commons, London. [0054088] 25/10/1996
Thomas Mr DJ, MCLIP, Retired. [0014536]31/01/1941
Thomas Mr DP, BA DipLib MCLIP, Reg.Lib.(Carmarthen), Carmarthenshire C.C. [0030938] 08/06/1979
Thomas Mr DR, MA DipLib MCLIP, Product Mgr., SIRSI Ltd., Potters Bar. [0024837] 01/10/1975
Thomas Mrs E, (was Pieri), MCLIP, Life Member, The Annexe, Cwmassie House, Redstone Rd., Narbeth, SA67 7ES. [0014541] 28/02/1939
Thomas Mrs E, (was Williams), MCLIP, Community Lib., Gwynedd Council, Caernarfon L. [0029234] 10/04/1978
Thomas Miss EJ, BA MCLIP, Loc.Stud.Lib., Wrexham Co.Bor.Council. [0025124] 14/11/1975
Thomas Miss EL, BA MCLIP, Projects Mgmt.Lib., Hampshire C.C., Winchester, Hants. [0026810] 24/11/1976
Thomas Mrs F, (was Godfrey), MCLIP, Retired. [0014547] 01/01/1939
Thomas Mr G, BA(Hons), Stud., Northumbria Univ. [0061690] 21/10/2002
Thomas Mr G, BA FCLIP, Life Member. [0014548] 21/09/1951 FE 01/01/1961
Thomas Mr GCG, BA MA MCLIP, Sen.Asst.Arch., Dept.of Manuscripts, Nat.L.of Wales. [0014551] 05/04/1971
Thomas Miss GL, PGCE BA, Sch.Lib., Blue Coat Sch., Nottingham. [0059329] 07/02/2001
Thomas Mrs GL, (was Hill), BA(Hons) MCLIP, Dir.Library & Learning Res., Wiltshire Coll., Wiltshire. [0024347] 18/07/1975
Thomas Mrs GN, (was Eisenegger), BA DipIS MCLIP, Sen.Lib.-Community Outreach, L.B.of Barking & Dagenham, Cent.L. [0044109] 16/05/1990
Thomas Mr H, BMus DipRCM DipLIS, Lib., City of Westminster. [0049366] 29/10/1993
Thomas Mrs H, (was Simpson), MCLIP, Retired. [0014552] 24/07/1967
Thomas Ms A, MCLIP, Univ.of Sheffield. [0059954] 09/11/2001
Thomas Miss HC, BA(Hons) Msc(Econ) MCLIP, Asst.Lib.-Linguistics, Univ.of Oxford, Taylor Inst.L. [0051184] 23/11/1994
Thomas Mr HC, BSc DipLib MCLIP, Retired. [0024146] 01/04/1975
Thomas Miss HI, MA MCLIP, Lend.Serv.Lib., Royal Coll.of Nursing, London. [0032196] 11/02/1980
Thomas Mr HR, BA MA MCLIP, Marshall Lib., The Marshall L., Cambridge. [0023325] 05/12/1974
Thomas Ms J, BA MCLIP, L.Serv.Devel.Mgr., Redhill L., Surrey C.C. [0033173] 08/10/1980
Thomas Dr JA, MA DipLib DipLA MCLIP PhD, Unemployed. [0022938] 01/01/1974
Thomas Ms JA, BSc MLIS, Lib., Freshfields Bruckhams Deringer, London. [0059394] 28/02/2001
Thomas Mr JE, BA MCLIP, Sen.Asst.Lib., Wrexham Co.Bor.C. [0029423] 10/07/1978
Thomas Mrs JE, BA(Hons) MLitt, Asst.Lib., Moray Council. [0057900] 01/10/1999

363

Thomas Ms JF, BA(Hons) MSc MCLIP, L.Supervisor, Surrey Inst.of Art & Design. [0041192] 08/10/1987
Thomas Mrs JH, BA MCLIP, Sch.Lib., St.Bartholomews Sch., Newbury. [0014562] 29/04/1972
Thomas Miss JL, BA MCLIP, Stock Devel.Lib., Bexley Council. [0029846] 02/10/1978
Thomas Miss JM, BA DipLib MCLIP, Unemployed. [0014563] 13/10/1970
Thomas Mrs JM, BSc(Hons) MA MCLIP, Subject Inf.Specialist for Sci., Health & Soc.Welfare, Open Univ.L., Milton Keynes. [0056818] 23/10/1998
Thomas Mr JR, BSc DipLib MCLIP, Head of Serv., Leisure & Heritage, Ynys Mon. [0037926] 21/11/1984
Thomas Mrs KE, (was Punt), BA(Hons) PGCE, P./t.Lib., Lymington Co.L., Hants. [0018030] 07/10/1972
Thomas Mrs KM, (was Thomson), BA MCLIP, Sch.Lib., Thomas Muir High Sch., Glasgow. [0036860] 10/01/1984
Thomas Miss L, BA(Hons) DipLIS MCLIP, Asst.Lib., Learning Res.Cent., Univ.of Glamorgan. [0044321] 07/09/1990
Thomas Miss M, BA DipLib MCLIP, Sen.Asst.Lib., Swansea Inst.of H.E. [0038236] 04/02/1985
Thomas Miss M, BA MCLIP, Hosp.Lib., Rampton Hosp., Notts. [0024832] 06/10/1975
Thomas Miss M, BA(Hons), Stud., Univ.of Wales, Aberystwyth. [0061299] 16/05/2002
Thomas Mr M, BSc(Econ) DipLib MCLIP, Sen.Comm.Lib., Conwy Co.Bor.Council, Colwyn Bay. [0033825] 16/03/1981
Thomas Mrs M, (was Fareneau), BA DipLib MCLIP, Asst.Sen.Lib., Stony Stratford L., Milton Keynes Council. [0044229] 18/07/1990
Thomas Mr M, (was Sankey), MCLIP, Community Lib., Wrexham Co.Bor.Council. [0021536] 11/10/1973
Thomas Mrs MB, (was Grew), BA DipLib MBA MCLIP, Systems & Tech.Serv.Lib., De Montfort Univ., Bedford. [0021128] 08/10/1973
Thomas Mrs MBB, BSc MCLIP, Life Member. [0060795] 12/12/2001
Thomas Mrs MG, (was Williams), BA MCLIP, Retired. [0014570] 10/08/1954
Thomas Mr MH, BA DipLib MCLIP, Non-LIS, Govt.of the Hong Kong S.A.R., Hong Kong. [0014571] 10/09/1971
Thomas Mr MJ, BA DIP ARCH, Retired. [0040631] 01/04/1987
Thomas Mrs MJ, (was McVeagh), BA(Hons) DipLIS, Learning Resources Mgr., Farnham Coll., Surrey. [0046727] 03/01/1992
Thomas Miss NJ, BA(Hons) MA MCLIP, Asst.Lib., Solihull M.B.C. [0050921] 01/11/1994
Thomas Mr NR, BLib(Hons) MCLIP, Dist.Lib., Leics.C.C., Hinckley. [0030689] 28/02/1979
Thomas Mr OC, BA(Hons) DipIS, Asst.Inf.Offr., De Montfort Univ., Bedford. [0050214] 05/04/1994
Thomas Mrs P, (was Warner), MCLIP, Lib., The Magna Carta Sch., Staines. [0015385] 21/09/1969
Thomas Mrs PA, BSc(Hons), p./t.Stud./Branch Supervisor., THames Valley Univ., Cookham L. Berkshire. [0059201] 19/12/2000
Thomas Miss PC, BA MCLIP, Unemployed. [0037790] 26/07/1993
Thomas Mr PD, ACIB MCLIP, Retired, 25 Bromford Gardens,Westfield Road, Edgbaston, Birmingham, B15 3XD. [0023968] 25/02/1975
Thomas Mrs RA, BA MCLIP, Advice Session Super., Burntwood Citizens Advice Bureau. [0014580] 03/01/1972
Thomas Mr RE, BA MCLIP, Asst.Lib., Inst.of Civil Engineers, London. [0039500] 07/02/1986
Thomas Mrs RH, BA DipLib MCLIP, L.Serv.Mgr., Reading Bor.Council, Reading L. [0041357] 11/11/1987
Thomas Mrs S, (was Londt), BA Sch.Lib., Eton Coll., Windsor, Berks. [0043782] 11/01/1990
Thomas Mrs S, (was Harris), BA MCLIP, Lib., City of Salford, Educ.& Leisure Dept. [0033685] 05/02/1981
Thomas Mrs SA, (was Eltoft), BA MCLIP, p./t.Lib., Leeds Coll.of Building. [0025746] 23/02/1976
Thomas Mrs SJ, (was Loker), Sch.Lib., Sir William Romney Sch., Tetbury,Glos. [0048930] 26/07/1993
Thomas Ms SJ, BA DipLib MCLIP, Health Promotion L., Nat.Assembly for Wales, Cardiff. [0033845] 01/04/1981
Thomas Ms SJ, BA(Hons), Inf.Serv.Co-ordinator, Birmingham Voluntary Serv.Council. [0050799] 18/10/1994
Thomas Mrs SM, Inf.Offr., Cent.for Local Econ.Strategies, Manchester. [0058689] 31/05/2000
Thomas Mrs SM, BAMWeldI MCLIP, Employment not known. [0060657] 11/12/2001
Thomas Mrs SR, (was Gaunt), BA MCLIP, Inf.Consultant, Univ.of Herts., Hatfield Campus. [0005404] 11/10/1971
Thomas Mrs SS, (was Davies), MCLIP, Sen.Asst.Lib., Lancs.Co.L., Sch.L.Serv. [0003753] 01/01/1967
Thomas Mrs TC, BA(Hons) MA, Unemployed. [0058976] 13/10/2000
Thomas Mrs V, MCLIP, Community L.Mgr., Monmouthshire C.C. [0008597] 01/01/1970
Thomas Mrs V, (was Mainwaring), MCLIP, L.Offr., Morden L., L.B.of Merton. [0009632] 03/03/1970
Thomas Mrs V, BA(Hons) MCLIP, Stud. [0042031] 11/07/1988
Thomas Mr VEO, BA MCLIP, Unemployed. [0033174] 01/10/1980
Thomas Dr WT, MSc PhD, Sen.Lib., St.Christophers Sch., Bahrain. [0061384] 05/07/2002
Thomason Ms BJ, BA DipLib MCLIP, L.Mgr., Theodore Goddard, London. [0036158] 01/07/1983
Thompson Mrs A, (was Sawers), MCLIP, Life Member. [0019177] 01/01/1958
Thompson Mrs AB, (was Clarke), BA MA DipLib MCLIP, Sen.Lib., L.B.Waltham Forest, Arts & Lesiure Serv., Cent.L., Founder African-Caribbean L.Assoc. [0021503] 23/10/1973
Thompson Mrs AD, (was Saunders), BA MCLIP, Asst.Lib., Hull Coll. [0014592] 08/08/1966
Thompson Mrs AE, BSc (Hons), Stud., Liverpool John Moores Univ. [0059426] 12/03/2001

Thompson Dr AH, MA FCLIP, Self-employed Consultant, Ed.Multimedia Inf.& Tech., E:anthonyhugh.thompson@btinternet. [0014593] 26/02/1957 FE 01/01/1962
Thompson Mrs AM, BSc, P./t.Stud./Lib., Univ.Aberystwyth, Notre Dame Prep.Sch.Surrey. [0059906] 01/11/2001
Thompson Mrs AS, BA BSc MCLIP, Employment not known. [0060605] 11/12/2001
Thompson Mr B, BSc MCLIP, Retired. [0023543] 01/01/1975
Thompson Mrs BA, BA BSc DipLib MCLIP, Consultant Inf.Mgmnt., Brunel Univ., Middx. [0014595] 01/01/1969
Thompson Mrs CA, (was Burgess), MCLIP, Sch.L.& Resource Serv.Mgr., L.B.of Richmond upon Thames. [0018282] 03/10/1972
Thompson Mrs CAP, BA MCLIP, Coll.Lib., Coombeshead Coll., Newton Abbot. [0028188] 12/10/1977
Thompson Mrs D, (was Bean), BA MCLIP, Lib., Attleborough High Sch., Norfolk. [0000980] 03/11/1971
Thompson Mrs D, (was Stewart), MCLIP, Sen.Asst., Bebington L., Wirral P.L. [0014601] 19/03/1965
Thompson Mrs DC, BA(Hons) MCLIP, Inf.Lib., Surrey Co.L., Staines L. [0019659] 10/10/1972
Thompson Mr DG, BA MCLIP, Corp.Inf.Mgr., Leics.C.C., Glenfield. [0022503] 04/06/1974
Thompson Ms DM, (was Ward), MCLIP, Sch.Lib., Belle Vue Boys Sch., Bradford. [0015344] 27/10/1971
Thompson Miss EH, BA, Stud., Liverpool John Moores Univ. [0059155] 30/11/2000
Thompson Mrs EP, BA LLB MCLIP, Editor, Sweet & Maxwell, Mytholmroyd, W.Yorks. [0026580] 18/10/1976
Thompson Mrs FF, (was Davis), L.Technician, Glebelands Sch., Cranleigh, Surrey. [0048731] 28/04/1993 AF
Thompson Mr G, MA FSA FRSA FCLIP, Life Member, Tel.01483 810382. [0014611] 01/01/1938 FE 01/01/1950
Thompson Mrs G, (was Gratton), BA MCLIP, Lib., Royal Photographic Soc., Bath. [0018406] 25/10/1972
Thompson Ms G, BA DipLib MCLIP, Unemployed. [0033357] 06/11/1980
Thompson Mr GB, MCLIP, Asst.Area Lib., Shipley/Bradford W., Bradford L. [0014613] 26/10/1968
Thompson Mr GE, FCLIP, Life Member, 34 Downfield lidge, Downfield Rd., Clifton, Bristol, BS8 2TQ. [0014614] 03/05/1934 FE 01/01/1950
Thompson Mrs GM, (was Norman), MCLIP, Analyst Programmer, Cheshire. [0010891] 10/02/1972
Thompson Mr H, FCLIP, Retired. [0014616] 05/10/1936 FE 01/01/1951
Thompson Mrs H, (was Robson), BA(Hons), Special Serv.Lib., Darlington Bor.Council. [0046310] 28/10/1991
Thompson Mrs HC, (was Murray), BA DipLib MCLIP, Mgr.,Local Gateway, Business Link Berks & Wilts., Swindon. [0041731] 22/02/1988
Thompson Miss HJ, BA(Hons) MSc MCLIP, Lib., Leeds Health Auth. [0049746] 29/11/1993
Thompson Mrs HM, (was Korinkova), MSc MCLIP, Lib., Tring Sch., Herts. [0044416] 05/10/1990
Thompson Mrs ID, BA(Hons), L.Serv.Mgr., E.Riding & Hull Health Auth., E.Yorks. [0039482] 01/02/1986
Thompson Ms IJR, MA DipLib MCLIP, Standards Policy Adviser, Resource. [0025433] 05/01/1976
Thompson Miss J, BA, Employment not known. [0060491] 11/12/2001
Thompson Mr J, BA FCLIP, Life Member. [0014618] 18/02/1949 FE 01/01/1963
Thompson Mrs J, (was Cooper), BA MCLIP, Princ.Lib., City of York L., York. [0028794] 26/01/1978
Thompson Mrs J, Inf.Specialist, 3289 Granville Ave., Los Angeles, CA 90066, USA. [0033863] 08/04/1981
Thompson Mrs J, (was Kirk), BA MCLIP, Unemployed, 9 Welburn Ave., W.Park,Leeds,LS16 5HJ. [0008432] 06/10/1966
Thompson Mrs JA, (was English), BSc(Hons) MA MCLIP, Team Lib., Kingston L., Royal Bor.of Kingston Upon Thames. [0047264] 01/07/1992
Thompson Mrs JA, (was Crooks), Admin.Offr., Staffordshire Probation Serv. [0059162] 04/12/2000 AF
Thompson Mr JE, BA DipLib MCLIP, Div.Lib., Edinburgh City L. [0033383] 21/11/1980
Thompson Mrs JM, (was Hembrow), MCLIP, L.Operations Mgr., Somerset Co.L., Bridgwater. [0041505] 01/01/1966
Thompson Ms JM, MCLIP, Lib./Res.Cent.Mgr., Plashet School, L.B.of Newham. [0014620] 05/01/1968
Thompson Mrs JW, (was Collins), BA MCLIP, Team Lib., S.E.E.L.B., Castlereagh Grp., Co.Down. [0037223] 16/04/1984
Thompson Miss K, BSc MA, Unemployed. [0057208] 18/01/1999
Thompson Ms KE, BA(Hons), User Services Lib., Archway Healthcare L., London. [0055907] 12/12/1997
Thompson Mrs LA, MA(Hons) MLIS, Lib., John Wheatley Coll., Glasgow. [0054775] 01/04/1997
Thompson Mrs LM, (was Hoggarth), BA(Hons), Learning Advisor, Univ.of Lincs. [0052652] 16/11/1995
Thompson Mrs LS, L.Asst., Leics.C.C., Birstall L. [0056011] 19/01/1998 AF
Thompson Mrs M, Business Intelligence Adviser, Bus.Link.Surrey, Woking. [0052427] 26/10/1995 AF
Thompson Mrs ME, (was Wood), BA MCLIP, Unemployed. [0026616] 19/10/1976
Thompson Mrs MKN, (was Nowell), MCLIP, Life Member. [0014626] 01/01/1940
Thompson Mrs ML, (was Wilson), BA(Hons) BEd MA, Lib., St.Vincent & the Grenadines Comm., Coll., The L. [0041535] 19/01/1988
Thompson Mrs P, BA(Hons) MA, Business Support Offr., Hartlepool Borough Council, [0054760] 01/04/1997

Thompson Mr PS, BA(Hons) MCLIP, Child.& Sch.L.Serv.Mgr., Walsall M.B.C., Educ.Devel.Cent. [0020218] 26/01/1973
Thompson Ms REA, (was Weir), Inf.Mgr., Univ.of Strathclyde, Careers Serv. [0039132] 10/11/1985
Thompson Mr RH, FSA MCLIP, Lib., Homerton L., L.B.of Hackney. [0014630] 03/02/1963
Thompson Mr RM, BA MA DipLib MCLIP, Head of Learning Res., Bexley Coll., Belvedere. [0028381] 08/11/1977
Thompson Miss S, Unemployed. [0048801] 01/06/1993
Thompson Mrs SA, BA(Hons), Asst.Lib., CIP, Hounslow L.Serv., Chiswick L. [0051011] 09/11/1994
Thompson Mrs SJ, MA, Acquisitions Lib., Univ.of York L., York. [0051030] 09/11/1994
Thompson Mrs SL, (was Hollaway), BA(Hons) MSc MCLIP, L.Serv.Mgr., Frimley Park Hosp., Surrey. [0049617] 19/11/1993
Thompson Mrs SL, (was Mills), BA(Hons) MA, Resident in Japan. [0054546] 17/01/1997
Thompson Mrs SM, (was Hammond), BA MCLIP, Retired. [0032386] 01/01/1956
Thompson Mr SR, BSc MCLIP, Personnel Mgr., Halcrow Grp., London. [0014637] 16/02/1966
Thompson Mrs VE, (was Beeley), BA MCLIP, Chartered Lib., Scott Wilson Kirkpatrick, Chesterfield. [0014640] 17/03/1967
Thompson Mrs WJ, (was Atkinson), BA DipLib MCLIP, Researcher, Corporate Finance, Warburg Dillon Read, London. [0043557] 07/11/1989
Thomson Mrs A, (was Cleworth), MCLIP, Lib., Woolwich Poly.Sec.Boys Sch., London. [0014641] 27/09/1961
Thomson Ms AJ, BA MCLIP, p./t.Catr., Soc. of Genealogists, London. [0018212] 05/10/1972
Thomson Mrs B, (was Bills), MA DipLib MCLIP, Liaison Lib., Sch.of Construction & Engineering, City Coll., Norwich. [0014643] 20/05/1966
Thomson Mrs CC, (was Mowatt), MA DipLib MCLIP, Acq.Lib., Middlesbrough Council, Middlesbrough. [0014644] 17/07/1970
Thomson Mrs CL, (was Betts), MSc, Research Exec., Appleby Spurling & Kempe, Bermuda. [0052353] 30/10/1995
Thomson Mrs DM, (was Gray), MCLIP, Adult Non-fiction Lib., Aberdeenshire L.& Inf.Serv., Aberdeenshire. [0021016] 01/10/1973
Thomson Ms EH, BSc MSc MCLIP, Employment not known. [0060702] 12/12/2001
Thomson Mrs EM, (was Beber), BA MCLIP, Br.Lib., E.Lothian Council. [0028224] 26/10/1977
Thomson Mrs I, Sen.L.Asst., Manchester Met.Univ. [0061243] 01/04/2002
Thomson Mrs JMM, (was Greenall), MCLIP, p./t., M.O.D., Scotland. [0014650] 01/01/1956
Thomson Miss KS, BSc(Hons), Stud., Robert Gordon Univ. [0058925] 05/10/2000
Thomson Mrs L, MA(Hons), Position Unknown, Dept.of Work and Pensions. [0059110] 16/11/2000
Thomson Mrs LI, Lib., Scottish Borders Council, Melrose. [0061394] 01/07/2002
Thomson Ms LM, L.Asst., Angus Council, Forfar. [0057319] 10/02/1999
Thomson Mrs M, (was Alexander), MA MCLIP, Lib., Surrey Coll., Guildford. [0014653] 01/01/1967
Thomson Mrs MM, BA MCLIP, Unemployed. [0030050] 26/10/1978
Thomson Mrs MR, (was Strutt), MCLIP, Life Member. [0014161] 01/01/1956
Thomson Mrs PE, (was Davies), BLib MCLIP, Team Lib.- Local Studies, Thanet Dist., Kent C.C. [0039563] 03/03/1986
Thomson Mr RJ, MA(Hons) DipLIS MCLIP, Catr., Univ.of Edinburgh, Reid Music L. [0050290] 31/05/1994
Thomson Ms SE, BA(Hons), Lib., Pimlico Sch., London. [0048272] 20/11/1992
Thomson Miss SM, L.Asst., Cent.L., Redbridge Essex. [0050071] 05/04/1994 AF
Thomson Mrs SM, (was Fowlie), MA DipLib MCLIP, Careers Advisory Off., Univ.of Aberdeen. [0030907] 30/05/1979
Thomson Mr WD, BA MCLIP, Retired. [0029349] 05/06/1978
Thorbinson Mrs AE, (was Shaw), BA(Hons) MCLIP, Res.Lib., City of Ely Comm.Coll., Cambs. [0035624] 16/11/1982
Thorburn Mr D, BA(Hons) MA, Inf.Offr., Royal Inst.of Chartered Surveyors, London. [0051460] 27/02/1995
Thorburn Ms EI, BA, Prof.Dev.Asst., Healthcare L.Unit. [0048221] 16/11/1992
Thorn Mrs L, BSc MCLIP, Employment not known. [0060474] 11/12/2001
Thornborow Mr P, MA BA DipLib MCLIP, L.Resources Mgr., Univ.Coll.Northampton, Northampton. [0029851] 02/10/1978
Thorne Miss AM, BLib MCLIP, Team Lib., Norfolk C.C., Hunstanton L. [0041604] 26/01/1988
Thorne Mrs CVE, (was Cutler), BA FCLIP, Retired. [0006356] 03/11/1954 FE 01/01/1955
Thorne Mr JD, BSc MSc MCLIP, Asst.Lib., Imperial Coll., London. [0057539] 21/04/1999
Thorne Mrs MC, MA DipLit, Sch.Lib., Kirk Hallam Community Tech.Coll., Derbys. [0014668] 01/01/1968
Thorne Mrs SM, BA MCLIP, Unemployed. [0033178] 06/10/1980
Thorne Miss VM, BA MCLIP, Sen.Lib., Young People & Sch., L.B.of Barking & Dagenham. [0040350] 21/01/1987
Thorne Miss WK, FCLIP, Life Member. [0014669] 01/01/2029 FE 01/01/2029
Thorner Miss J, BA MA MCLIP, Sen.Inf.Asst., King's Coll.London. [0029852] 11/10/1978
Thornes Mrs SL, BSc(Hons), Stud., Univ.Newcaslte @ Northumbria. [0059801] 03/10/2001
Thorneycroft Miss SA, BA MCLIP, Res.& Inf.Offr., N.Cornwall Dist.C., Cornwall. [0035963] 01/03/1983

Thornhill Ms BJ, (was Corbett), JP DipSoc DipPsych MCLIP, Life Member, Tel.0181 883 2879, 4 Trinity Ave., London, N2 0LX. [0014670] 27/09/1952
Thornhill Mr JM, BA MCLIP, L.& Inf.Consultant, Herts. [0014671] 07/12/1963
Thornhill Mrs MA, (was Brebner), MPhil FCLIP, Life Member, Tel.0131 452 8744, 27 Mount Grange, Strathearn Rd., Edinburgh, EH9 2QX. [0017859] 12/02/1941 FE 01/01/1954
Thornhill Mrs PM, (was Hand), MCLIP, Sch.Lib., Hitchin Boys Sch., Herts. [0014672] 02/01/1965
Thorning Ms SA, BSc GradDip DipILS Lib., Withers, London. [0058870] 14/09/2000
Thornley Mrs AL, (was Lewis), BSc(Econ)(Hons) MCLIP, Electronic Devel.Lib., N.Staffs.Med.Inst.L. [0055746] 12/11/1997
Thornley Mrs CM, (was Bennett), BSc(Hons) MSc, Weekend Inf.Advisor, Sheffield Hallam Univ. [0052285] 23/10/1995
Thornley Miss L, BA(Hons) MCLIP, Inf.Offr., (Health), Univ.of Cent.Lancs., Preston. [0043863] 05/02/1990
Thornley Mrs LA, BA(Hons) MA MCLIP, Team Lib., Kingston L., Surrey. [0055532] 20/10/1997
Thornley Ms ME, BSc(Hons) MSc, NLIS Mgr.-S.W.Reg., Environment Agency, Exeter. [0052913] 02/01/1996
Thornton Mrs CA, (was Davies), BA MCLIP, Asst.Learning Res.Mgr., Shrewsbury Coll.of Arts & Tech. [0034674] 01/02/1982
Thornton Mrs CS, (was Llewellyn), BEd(Hons) MA MCLIP, Sen.Trust Lib./L.Serv.Mgr., Cent.Manchester Healthcare NHS Tr., Manchester. [0046055] 17/09/1991
Thornton Mrs CVSL, (was Lightfoot), BA DipILS MCLIP, Inf.Offr., Linklaters, London. [0055775] 18/11/1997
Thornton Mrs D, (was Whittle), Lib., Cent.Manchester & Manchester Child., Univ.Hosp.Trust, L., St.Marys Hosp. [0033702] 06/02/1981
Thornton Ms DK, (was Clayton), BA(Hons) MCLIP, Spec.Serv.Lib., Knaresborough L., Yorks. [0034737] 03/02/1982
Thornton Miss E, MCLIP, Retired. [0014680] 08/03/1960
Thornton Mrs EJ, (was Wheelband), MCLIP, Team Lib., Sch.L.Serv., Beds.C.C. [0015665] 05/09/1967
Thornton Ms I, BA, Comm.Lib., Aston L., Birmingham. [0038053] 17/01/1985
Thornton Mrs JW, (was Johnson), BA MCLIP, Retired. [0007893] 16/10/1967
Thornton Miss KIM, MCLIP, Life Member. [0014686] 27/01/1949
Thornton Mr M, MA(Hons) DipLIS, L.Serv.Consultant, OCLC PICA, Birmingham. [0050697] 12/10/1994
Thornton Mrs M, BA(Hons) PGDipLib MA, Unemployed. [0053483] 01/07/1996
Thornton Mrs RM, BA MSc(Econ) DipILS, Asst.Lib., Cardiff Univ. [0052386] 30/10/1995
Thorp Dr RG, MA MSc DPhilCChem MCLIP, Retired. [0060616] 11/12/2001
Thorpe Ms CM, BSc(Hons) MSc MCLIP, Inf.Adviser, Sheffield Hallam Univ.Learn.Cent. [0033424] 27/11/1980
Thorpe Ms HM, MCLIP, Stud., Nottingham Univ. [0030723] 01/01/1973
Thorpe Mrs IA, BA MPhil MCLIP, Retired. [0027472] 06/04/1977
Thorpe Mrs JM, (was Hall), MCLIP, L.Serv.Mgr., Mid Sussex NHS Trust, Haywards Heath, W.Sussex. [0014692] 16/01/1961
Thorpe Mrs MMM, (was Allard), MCLIP, Learning Resources Admin., Loughborough Coll. [0000177] 01/01/1967
Thorpe Mr P, BSc FCLIP, Sci.Info., Royal Tropical Inst., Amsterdam. [0014694] 13/01/1969 FE 01/04/2002
Thow Mrs JA, (was Fearnley), MCLIP, Retired. [0022392] 12/03/1951
Thresh Mrs PA, (was Webb), BA(Hons) MCLIP, Learning Support Lib., Leeds L.& Inf.Serv., W.Grp.- Holt Park L. [0030061] 06/11/1978
Thrift Mrs HJ, (was Clark), BMus MA MCLIP, Head of User Serv., Univ.of Sheffield. [0039021] 18/01/1985
Throssell Mrs M, (was Hutchison), MCLIP, Retired. [0014704] 23/10/1942
Thulbon Mrs V, (was Walker), BA(Hons) MA, Asst.Lib. [0058633] 20/04/2000
Thurgood Mr V, BA(Hons) ma lis, L.Asst., Univ.Coll London L. [0056583] 04/09/1998
Thurley Miss MJ, MCLIP, Retired. [0017860] 26/10/1942
Thurley Mr NM, BA(Hons) MA, Asst.Lib., Univ.of Oxford. [0054461] 16/12/1996
Thurlow Miss SF, MCLIP, Lib., Min.of Defence L., London. [0014708] 24/03/1963
Thursfield Mrs J, (was Hobson), MCLIP, Prin.Lib.; Cent.& Support, Stoke on Trent L.I.A. [0022980] 01/10/1974
Thursfield Mrs J, (was Dunn), MCLIP, Semi-Voluntary, 59 Tennyson Avenue, Swadlincote,Derbys,DE11 0DT. [0004278] 21/03/1970
Thurston Mr JW, Unemployed. [0060924] 11/02/2002
Thwaite Ms N, MA, Under-Lib., Cambridge Univ.L. [0042136] 07/10/1988
Thwaites Ms ME, BA(Hons) DipILS MCLIP, Lib., Nottinghamshire C.C., Arnold L. [0046584] 22/11/1991
Thwaites Mr RH, BA MCLIP, Asst.Lib., Warrington P.L., Cheshire Co.L. [0014712] 14/10/1970
Tibbetts Mrs WA, (was Cosnett), MCLIP, Lib., Sandwell P.L. [0020671] 01/01/1973
Tibbitt Mrs MD, Asst.Lib., Sherborne Sch for Girls, Dorset. [0053209] 02/04/1996 AF
Tibbitts Mrs GM, (was Jones), MCLIP, P./t.Team Lib., L.B.Tower Hamlets, Lansbury L. [0031118] 20/08/1979
Ticehurst Mrs SE, (was Burgess), BA MCLIP, Resource Asst., Falmer L., Univ.of Brighton. [0025154] 15/12/1975
Tidman Mrs CF, (was Foster), BA, Lib./Res.Cent.Mgr., L.B.of Merton, Wimbledon. [0023443] 01/01/1975
Tidy Mrs PC, (was Brookes), BSc MCLIP, Unemployed. [0001805] 07/10/1970
Tiernan Mrs D, (was Knowles), MCLIP, Retired. [0008506] 26/02/1963
Tiernan Mr JJ, MA FCLIP, Retired. [0019810] 01/12/1972 FE 14/08/1991
Tierney Ms A, BA DipLIS, Reg.L.Ser.Mgr., S.E.Health Bd., Kilkenny, Ireland. [0057145] 23/12/1998
Tighe Mr CO, BA MCLIP, Unemployed. [0014717] 12/01/1967

Tighe Ms JAR, (was Richards), BA(Hons) MA, Unemployed. [0037749] 15/10/1984
Tihhomirova Mrs L, Unemployed. [0059284] 29/01/2001
Tiksmann Miss MA, BA DipLib MCLIP, Asst.Lib., L.B.of Ealing, Acton L. [0038110] 23/01/1985
Tilbury Mrs ME, (was Hammond), MCLIP, Dep.Area Lib., Southampton City L. [0014719] 21/11/1968
Tiley Mr SD, BA(Hons) MA DipLIM MCLIP, Rare Books Catr., St.John's Coll., Cambridge. [0055578] 21/10/1997
Tilke Mr A, BA MEd FRSA FCLIP ATCL, Head Lib., Yokohama Internat.Sch., Japan. [0026582] 23/10/1976 **FE 24/09/1997**
Till Ms JL, BA(Hons) DipLS MCLIP, Sen.Inf.Adviser, Univ.of Gloucestershire. [0034878] 26/03/1982
Till Mrs M, (was Appleby), BA MCLIP, Sch.Lib., Parklands Girls High Sch., Leeds. [0042732] 01/01/1957
Tiller Mrs MH, L.Mgr., Leigh-on-sea L., Essex. [0047998] 28/10/1992 **AF**
Tilley Miss BJ, BA MCLIP, Lib.,Child.Serv., Worcs.Co.Ls., Kidderminster L. [0030558] 10/02/1979
Tilley Mrs BJ, (was Lintorn), MCLIP, Life Member. [0014721] 01/01/1948
Tilley Mrs EA, MA PGCE, Stud., Univ.of Wales, Aberystwyth, & Asst.Lib., Dept.of Earth Sci., Univ.of Cambridge. [0058942] 05/10/2000
Tilley Ms J, Stud., Univ.of Northumbria at Newcastle. [0055536] 20/10/1997
Tilley Ms JE, BA MA DipLaw, Libra Team Leader, Herbert Smith. [0041076] 02/10/1987
Tilley Mr NV, MCLIP, Retired. [0019117] 10/03/1951
Tilly Mr NJ, MCLIP, Life Member, Tel.01983 293684, Holly Bank 24 Albert Rd., Gurnard, Cowes, I.O.W., PO31 8JU. [0014726] 14/03/1954
Tillyard Mr S, MA MCLIP, Retired. [0014727] 03/02/1955
Tilsed Mr IJ, BA MCLIP, Computing Devel.Offr., Univ.of Exeter L.& Inf.Serv., Exeter. [0060361] 10/12/2001
Tim Mr YF, BA MCLIP, Head, Ref.& Inf.Serv., Nat.Univ.of Singapore L. [0035103] 25/08/1982
Timbers Mrs VJ, (was Foster), MCLIP, Unemployed. [0005122] 15/02/1967
Timbrell Miss M, BA(Hons) DipILM, Sen.Lib., Derby City Ls. [0054600] 27/01/1997
Timmins Miss GFM, BA(Hons) MCLIP, Asst.Lib., Ferndown, Dorset. [0050816] 19/10/1994
Timmons Mr A, BA(Hons) DipLIS MCLIP, Inf.Researcher, Dept.Environ.Trans.& the Regions, London. [0049995] 07/02/1994
Timms Mr DB, MCLIP, Retired. [0014730] 17/03/1953
Timms Mrs JA, (was Sutton), BA MCLIP, Catr., Derbys.L.& Heritage, Matlock. [0028908] 18/01/1978
Timms Mr MG, BA MCLIP, Ch.Lib., L.B.of Redbridge. [0018448] 23/10/1972
Timms Mrs MJ, (was Warden), BA MCLIP, Br.Lib., Kenton L., L.B.of Harrow. [0022006] 12/12/1973
Timms Mrs SM, (was Scarlett), BA MCLIP MCMI, Freelance Writer/Comm.Consultant. [0019179] 31/08/1972
Timothy Mrs W, (was Forbes), BA MLib MCLIP, Sen.Lib.:Mgmnt.Inf., Staffs.C.C. [0043896] 13/02/1990
Timson Mrs J, (was Marsden), MCLIP, Lib., Coalville L., Leics.L.& Inf.Serv. [0020058] 10/01/1973
Timsonne Ms J, Relief L.Asst., New Mills L., High Peak, Derbys. [0058922] 04/10/2000 **AF**
Tinant Ms DS, BA MCLIP, Sen.Lib., The Child.Soc., London. [0037076] 07/02/1984
Tindale Mr JW, BA(Hons) MA MCLIP, Inf.Mgr., Dept.for Work & Pensions, London. [0054990] 12/06/1997
Tindall Mrs J, (was Elliott), BA MCLIP, [0009704] 16/01/1969
Tiney Mrs PC, (was Elliott), DipLib MCLIP, Catr., The Brit.L., Boston Spa. [0029955] 23/11/1978
Tingey Mr PC, MA, Unemployed, 17 Hassendean Rd., Blackheath, London, SE3 8TR. [0047831] 19/10/1992
Tinker Ms AJ, MSc BA(Hons) MCLIP, p./t.Research Asst./Sen.Asst.Lib., Dept.of Computing & Mathematics, Univ.of Huddersfield. [0053582] 01/08/1996
Tinker Miss EO, BA MCLIP, Asst-Lib., Sunderland.P.L. [0014739] 01/01/1971
Tinker Mr ME, BA(Hons) MCLIP, Asst.Lib.:Local Hist.(N.), Sefton L., Southport. [0041440] 05/12/1987
Tinkham Mrs JM, (was Robbins), MCLIP, Ptnr./Florist, Forget-me-not Florist, Banbury. [0027014] 13/01/1977
Tipler Mrs LJ, (was Sanderson), MCLIP, Res.Asst. (p./t.), Univ. of Brighton, Queenwood L., Eastbourne, Sussex. [0019173] 05/08/1972
Tipler Mrs PA, BA MCLIP, Cent.Music Lib., Cent.L., Oxon.C.C. [0032616] 06/06/1980
Tipple Mrs L, (was Duignan), MA DipLib ALAI, Sub.Lib.-Bibl.Serv., Main L., Univ.Coll., Dublin. [0024369] 01/07/1975
Tipple Mr WR, Learning Support Offr., Canterbury Coll. [0046845] 13/02/1992
Tirimanne Mrs GS, (was Raymond), DipLib MCLIP, Tech.Serv.Lib., Kangan Inst.of TAFE, Broadmeadows, Australia. [0027010] 10/01/1977
Titchmarsh Mrs JE, BA PGCE MCLIP, Lib., Gtr.Manchester Police, Training Sch., Prestwich. [0040773] 02/06/1987
Titcombe Mrs JM, (was Crewdson), MPhil FCLIP, Head Bus. Planning Unit, Brit.Trade Internat., London. [0003367] 25/09/1968 **FE 18/07/1990**
Titcombe Ms SC, BLib MEd DMS AIMgt MCLIP, Business Devel.Mgr., Caerphilly Co.Bor.Council. [0034435] 06/11/1981
Tite Ms C, DipLib MCLIP, Lib.(Job Share), N.S.P.C.C., London. [0033501] 15/01/1981
Tither Mrs JM, (was Grant), BA MCLIP, Lib., English Nature, Peterborough. [0005810] 05/01/1971
Titley Mr GDC, BA MCLIP, Lib., The Bateman Cent., Birch Hill Hosp. [0034141] 05/10/1981
Titley Mr SD, Unemployed. [0058965] 11/10/2000

Tittensor Ms J, BA(Hons) MSc(Econ), Learning Cent.Super. [0055109] 15/07/1997
Titterington Mrs SF, (was Allan), MCLIP, Grp.Mgr., Leeds L.& Inf.Serv. [0036619] 24/10/1983
Titterton Miss GR, BEd(Hons) DipLib MSc MCLIP, Catr., Manchester Cent.L. [0031964] 06/01/1980
Tivey Ms GP, (was Conn), BA MA MCLIP, Ref.Lib., Doriot L., Insead Business Sch., France. [0036723] 04/11/1983
To Mr PK, Lib., Hong Kong Govt., City Hall P.L. [0050503] 23/08/1994
To Miss VMY, BA(Hons) LLB MCLIP, Resident in Hong Kong. [0039356] 10/01/1986
Toase Mr CA, HonFCLIP, Ref.Bks.Consultant, 6 Watery Lane, London SW20 9AA. [0014747] 09/02/1946 **FE 12/01/1993**
Toase Miss S, p./t.Stud./L.Asst., Univ.of Bristol, Patchway L., S.Glos.Council. [0061547] 11/09/2002
Toase Mrs SA, (was Dinning), BA MCLIP, Lend.Lib., Oxford Cent.L., Oxfordshire C.C. [0033779] 06/02/1981
Tobin Mrs CM, MA, Sch.Lib., Portland Sch., Worksop. [0052078] 02/10/1995
Todd Dr B, BSc PhD, Inf.Sci., Techfill Ltd., Dewsbury. [0056429] 08/07/1998
Todd Mrs CF, (was Bell), MCLIP, Hosp.Lib., Royal Infirmary of Edinburgh. [0001061] 01/01/1968
Todd Mr JKP, BA(Hons) MCLIP, Ch.Lib., Sothebys, London. [0031965] 11/01/1980
Todd Ms JM, BA MCLIP, Unwaged. [0022442] 10/05/1974
Todd Mrs ME, BSc(Econ) MCLIP, Business & Learning Gateway Lib., Belfast Educ.& L.Board. [0054494] 02/01/1997
Todd Miss RE, BA(Hons) MA, Unemployed. [0057482] 06/04/1999
Todd Mrs S, (was Bishop), BA MA(Ed) MCLIP, Lib., St.Johns Sch., Leatherhead. [0001310] 21/09/1970
Todd Mrs SC, (was Wood), BSc MCLIP, Ref.Lib., Royal Bor.of Windsor & Maidenhead, Maidenhead. [0036444] 13/10/1983
Todd-Jones Mr MJ, MCLIP, Asst.Lib., Univ.of Cambridge, Dept.of Chemis. [0028705] 17/01/1978
Tokwe Mr H, Lib./Dep.Lib., Mkoba Teachers Coll., Zimbabwe. [0061664] 14/10/2002
Toland Miss DJ, Stud., Univ.of Wales, Aberystwyth. [0061061] 15/02/2002
Tolley Dr PL, BA MCLIP, Unemployed. [0033252] 08/02/1981
Tolley Mrs SJ, (was Murrell-Orgill), BA, Unemployed. [0046164] 07/10/1991
Tollington Ms JE, MCLIP, Team Lib.(Child.), Taunton L., Somerset. [0014759] 01/07/1972
Tomalin Ms AL, MA BA MCLIP, Sen.Specialist Lib., Child.& Young People, Leics.L.& Inf.Serv. [0034145] 05/10/1981
Tomblin Mrs JM, MA MCLIP, Life Member. [0017865] 22/03/1966
Tomeny Mr AP, BA(Hons) BSc(Hons) MCLIP, Co-ordinator for Inf.& Bus.Serv., Mitchell L., Glasgow. [0014767] 07/10/1971
Tomes Mrs J, (was Gardner), FCLIP, Life Member. [0014768] 10/04/1953 **FE 01/01/1964**
Tomkins Mr AP, BA(Hons), Stud., Thames Valley Univ. [0060010] 22/11/2001
Tomkins Miss SR, MCLIP, Learning Cent.Mgr., Eastleigh Coll., Hants.C.C. [0014772] 18/08/1966
Tomkinson Miss A, BA MCLIP, Asst.Dist.Mgr., Colchester, Essex Co.L. [0020750] 25/06/1973
Tomkinson Ms GM, MA, Broadcast Asst., BBC Nottingham. [0038659] 17/09/1985
Tomkys Mr A, BA(Hons), Stud., Univ.of Cent.England, &, Employee, Cent.L., Wolverhampton. [0058217] 18/11/1999
Tomlin Mrs B, Sen.Inf.Offr., Learning Resource Cent., Univ.of Hertfordshire, St Albans. [0057803] 04/08/1999 **AF**
Tomlinson Ms DM, BA MCLIP, Competitive Intell.Mgr., Siemens Building Tech., Zug, Switzerland. [0024243] 13/05/1975
Tomlinson Miss JA, BA MA MCLIP, Asst.Lib., Inst.of Adv.Legal Studies, London. [0034485] 12/11/1981
Tomlinson Ms JM, BA(Hons) MCLIP, Stud., Sheffield Univ. [0045855] 02/07/1991
Tomlinson Miss JV, BA DipLib MCLIP, Unwaged. [0035361] 14/10/1982
Tomlinson Mrs KS, (was Lopaty), BA MLS MCLIP, Acq.Lib., Rutherford Appleton Lab., Chilton, Didcot, Oxon. [0043194] 02/10/1989
Tomlinson Mrs R, (was Knight), MCLIP, P/t.Sch.Lib., Sir Frank Markham Sch., Milton Keynes. [0014783] 22/02/1967
Tomney Ms HM, BA(Hons) Msc, Lib., Hutchesons Grammar Sch., Glasgow. [0051126] 17/11/1994
Tompkinson Mr A, BA(Hons) MLib MPhil, Princ.L.Asst., The L., Keele Inf.Serv., Univ.of Keele. [0047015] 01/04/1992
Toms Miss AL, BA(Hons), Sen.L.Asst., Manchester Metro Univ. [0058874] 20/09/2000
Toms Mrs SJ, (was Hopkins), Dist.L.Super., Willenhall P.L., W.Midlands. [0046764] 16/01/1992 **AF**
Tomson Mrs G, CertEd, Learning Res.Co-ordinator, Weston Coll., N.Somerset. [0058558] 01/07/2000
Toney Miss KA, BSc(Hons) MA MCLIP, Asst.Lib.-Electronic Resources, Pfizer, Global R.& D., Cambridge. [0052636] 15/11/1995
Tong Miss L, MA MCLIP, [0042283] 19/10/1988
Tong-Choi Mrs MML, (was Tong), BA MCLIP, Retired. [0017868] 11/03/1972
Tonkiss Mr HF, BA, Systems Lib., Carshalton Coll., Surrey. [0053799] 01/10/1996
Tonkiss Cameron Mrs R, BA(Hons) MA MCLIP, Resident in U.S.A. [0022081] 01/01/1974
Tonks Mr JDM, BA DipLib MCLIP, Inf.Lib., Northants.L.& Inf.Serv., Wellingborough L. [0038333] 15/03/1985
Tonner Mrs NC, (was Montgomery), BA(Hons) DipLib MCLIP, Team Leader, Edinburgh City L. [0048976] 12/08/1993
Toogood Mrs L, (was Yeadell), MCLIP, Unemployed. [0012420] 19/02/1963
Tooke Miss J, MCLIP, Princ.Lib.-Reader Serv., Wokingham Dist.Council. [0024837] 06/10/1975
Tooley Mr JFB, HonFCLIP, Retired. [0014796] 10/01/1955 **FE 01/01/1965**

Personal Members — Troake

Toomey Miss MC, MCLIP, Lib., Tech.Inf., Castrol Ltd., Pangbourne. [0030693] *15/01/1979*
Tooms Miss AE, BA DipLib MCLIP, Head of L.Serv., Allen & Overy, London. [0037775] *25/10/1984*
Toon Mr JE, MCLIP MA, Life Member. [0014797] *29/08/1957*
Toon Mrs R, (was Chapman), BLib MCLIP, Self-employed, Hitchin, Herts. [0027803] *17/09/1977*
Toop Mr S, BSc(Hons) MCLIP, Inf.Specialist, Connexions, Shropshire. [0047123] *05/05/1992*
Tooth Mrs GM, (was Smith), MCLIP, Retired. [0014802] *06/02/1961*
Topham Miss EM, MCLIP, Retired. [0017871] *14/10/1937*
Topp Mrs HMC, (was Richards), CERT ED MCLIP, Lib.-Ripon, L., Harrogate Grp. [0019761] *01/01/1970*
Toppin Mrs MJ, (was Sked), BA MCLIP, Retired. [0019210] *25/09/1954*
Topping Mr D, BA(Hons), Stud., Univ.of Wales, Aberystwyth, & L.Asst., Local Stud.Dept., Belfast Cent.L. [0058066] *22/10/1999*
Topping Mrs D, (was Matrunola), BLib MCLIP, Asst.Lib.(p./t.), De Montfort Univ., Leicester. [0034995] *08/06/1982*
Topping Mrs KJ, (was Willis), BA DipLib MCLIP, p./t.Asst.Lib., Health & Safety Exec. [0039676] *07/05/1986*
Topping Mrs PR, BA(Hons) BEd MEd, Lib., Kingussie High Sch., Inverness-shire. [0057761] *28/07/1999*
Torbet Mr DM, FCLIP, Retired. [0014806] *01/01/1934* **FE 01/01/1953**
Torley Mr A, BA(Hons) DipLIS MCLIP, Sen.Lib., Northbrook Coll., W.Sussex. [0043571] *09/11/1989*
Torley Mr G, BA MSc MCLIP, Lib., The Mitchell L., Glasgow. [0034815] *12/03/1982*
Torrens Mr WM, MA DipLib MCLIP, Local Studies Lib., Bucks.C.C., Aylesbury. [0050738] *13/10/1994*
Torrero Mr CL, BA MCLIP, Editor/Inf.Scientist, Pira Internat., Leatherhead. [0053600] *06/08/1996*
Toscani Mrs D, p./t.Stud./Lib., Thames Valley Univ., L.B.of Haringey. [0061248] *22/04/2002*
Totham Mrs P, (was Shields), BA(Hons) MCLIP, Self-employed, Snodland, Kent. [0026554] *01/10/1976*
Totten Mrs J, Stud., Aberystwyth Univ. [0061741] *31/10/2002*
Totterdell Mrs AC, (was Ward), BA(Hons) MCLIP, p./t.L.Educ.Tutor, Somerset Coll.of Arts & Tech., Taunton. [0042935] *01/01/1954*
Totterdell Mr BDC, FCLIP, Retired. [0014812] *02/02/1954* **FE 01/01/1968**
Totterdell Mrs AM, (was Downes), MCLIP, Retired. [0005218] *16/02/1965*
Totty Miss JT, BA(Hons) MA, Asst.Prison Serv.Lib., HMP Low Newton, Durham C.C. [0056081] *12/02/1998*
Tough Mrs B, (was McKenna), MA(Hons) MA MCLIP, Sen.Asst.Lib., Garretts. [0052130] *05/10/1995*
Tough Miss DS, BA(Hons) MCLIP, Catr., Natural Hist.Mus., S.Kensington [0014814] *18/01/1972*
Touhey Mrs C, MCLIP, Resident in Ireland. [0060118] *10/12/2001*
Toulmin Mrs PB, (was Preece), MLib MCLIP, Serv.Devel.Lib., Northants.L.& Inf.Serv. [0011907] *01/04/1971*
Tourtel Ms AJ, BA(Hons) MCLIP, Lib., L.B.of Greenwich. [0042644] *30/01/1989*
Tovey Mrs HG, (was Hathorn), MCLIP, Retired. [0006544] *13/01/1950*
Towers Mrs GM, (was Vose), BA MCLIP, Housewife. [0015147] *05/09/1968*
Towers Mrs H, (was Tebay), BA MCLIP, Area Lib.:Young Peoples L.Serv., Cumbria C.C. [0036334] *04/10/1983*
Towers Mrs HS, MA, Team Lib., Northamptonshire C.C.L& Inf.Serv., Daventry L. [0058439] *14/02/2000*
Towle Ms D, BA(Hons) MLib MCLIP, PG Cent.Lib., George Eliot Hosp.NHS Trust, Nuneaton. [0043447] *26/10/1989*
Towle Ms SJ, BSc MA, Resident in Australia. [0058000] *11/10/1999*
Towler Mr JW, MA MCLIP, Retired, (Member, Sydenham Soc.). [0014820] *07/09/1964*
Towlson Mrs J, MCLIP, Retired. [0020465] *01/01/1962*
Towlson Ms KB, (was Smith), BSc(Hons) MA MCLIP, Sen.Asst.Lib., DeMontfort Univ., Leicester. [0041078] *08/10/1987*
Town Mr JS, MA DipLib FCLIP, Dir.of Inf.Serv./Dep.Lib., Royal Military Coll.of Sci., Cranfield Univ.,Swindon. [0029350] *02/06/1978* **FE 22/05/1991**
Towner Mr S, MCLIP, Retired. [0014821] *01/01/1949*
Townsend Miss AC, BA MA MCLIP, Site Mgr., Morden L., L.B.of Merton. [0044112] *18/05/1990*
Townsend Mrs AL, (was Brett), MCLIP, p./t.Sch.Lib., Wisbech Grammar Sch., Cambs. [0018175] *08/10/1972*
Townsend Mrs AM, BSc(Hons) MSc, Spec.Collections Lib., Plant Sci.L., Oxford Univ.L.Serv. [0056769] *08/10/1998*
Townsend Mr LP, FCLIP, Life Member. [0014826] *27/10/1944* **FE 01/01/1957**
Townsend Mr MR, BA(Hons), Re-Classification Offr., Inst.of Historical Research, London. [0058707] *01/07/2000*
Townsend Mr PR, MCLIP, ICT & Training Co-ordinator, S.Glos.Council:L.& Inf.Serv. [0021257] *18/10/1973*
Townson Mrs A, (was Hellenburgh), BA(Hons) MCLIP, Inf.Offr., Bristows, London. [0055161] *28/07/1997*
Townson Ms E, L.Mgr., King George V Internat.Sch., Kowloon, Hong Kong. [0038240] *07/02/1985*
Townson Miss ESL, BA(Hons) MA DipLIM MCLIP, Reader Research & Devel.Offr., Blackburn with Darwen L., Blackburn Cent.L. [0058035] *18/10/1999*
Towsey Mr MA, MCLIP, Lib., L.B.of Lambeth. [0023652] *20/01/1975*
Toy Mrs L, (was Renwick), BA MCLIP, L.& Inf.Offr., Newcastle upon Tyne City Council, City L. [0035738] *21/01/1983*
Toyne Miss J, L.Asst., Hoddesdon L., Herts. [0054393] *02/12/1996* **AF**
Toyne Ms JM, BA(Hons) MA, Researcher, Univ.of Lincs., Lincoln. [0053637] *19/08/1996*

Tozer Mrs AE, (was Cooper), BSc DipLib MCLIP, Childs.& Sch.Section Sen.Lib., Hants.C.C., Winchester. [0027938] *01/10/1977*
Tozer-Hotchkiss Dr G, (was Tozer), MA PhD, Employment not known. [0060717] *12/12/2001*
Tracey Ms CC, BA(Hons) DipInf, Inf.Mgr., Oliver, Wyman & Co., London. [0049130] *07/10/1993*
Tracey Ms FM, BA(Hons) MA MCLIP, Unemployed. [0038613] *16/07/1985*
Trahearn Mrs J, (was McKenzie), MCLIP, Communications Mgr., Lincs.L., Lincoln. [0009455] *06/07/1995*
Train Ms BK, BA(Hons) MA, Research Fellow, Dept.of Inf.Studies, Univ.of Sheffield. [0051811] *06/07/1995*
Tran Ms A, BA(Hons) MSc, L.Inf.Serv.Mgr., NHS London Reg.Off., London. [0058231] *22/11/1999*
Tran Miss KH, BA(Hons), Asst.Lib., Lovells, London. [0052978] *07/02/1996*
Tranmer Ms C, MLS MCLIP, Editorial Director, RUDI Ltd., Oxford Brookes Univ. [0014836] *01/01/1967*
Tranmer Mrs JM, (was Whitmore), MCLIP, Catr., Brit.L.Oriental & India Off.Coll., London. [0015772] *01/01/1970*
Tranter Mrs K, (was Fortune), BA(Hons), Area Mgr., Owton Manor L., Hartlepool. [0037267] *19/05/1984*
Travers Mr J, BA(Hons), Sen.L.Asst., N.Kensington L., R.B.of Kensington & Chelsea. [0058540] *01/04/2000*
Travers Miss KS, BA(Hons), p./t.Stud., Inf Offr., Kings Coll. London. [0059537] *01/05/2001*
Travis Ms C, (was Scott), BA MCLIP, Unemployed. [0019762] *16/11/1967*
Travis Mrs CM, (was Phipps), MCLIP, Speech Therapy Asst., N.H.S., Crawley/Horesham, W.Sussex. [0021341] *10/10/1973*
Travis Mr R, BA(Hons) MCLIP, Acting Mgr.Community L., Liverpool L.& Inf.Serv. [0014844] *10/02/1970*
Trayhurn Mr RJ, MCLIP, Ref.Lib., Swindon Bor.L. [0014846] *01/01/1970*
Traynor Miss EM, BA DipLib MCLIP, Lib., Agricultural & Food Sci., Queens Univ.Belfast. [0037494] *01/10/1984*
Treacy Mr N, BSc DipLib MCLIP, L.Inf.Offr., Amnesty Internat., London. [0024838] *06/10/1975*
Treadgold Mrs KE, (was Vacchina-Vack), MCLIP, Lib., Banbury L., Oxon.C.C. [0031968] *05/01/1980*
Treadwell Mr MR, BSc(Hons) MA, Asst.Lib.(Reader Serv.), The Coll.of St.Mark & St.John, Plymouth. [0057435] *01/04/1999*
Treagus Mrs KG, (was Jordan), MCLIP, Unemployed. [0014850] *01/01/1964*
Treasure Mrs M, (was Bates), MCLIP, Unemployed. [0000923] *01/01/1968*
Trebi-Ollennu Ms RA, Employment not known. [0044938] *23/01/1991*
Tredinnick Mr LM, Systems Lib., Intranet Content Co-ordinator, Baker Tilly, London. [0058432] *11/02/2000*
Tree Mr KS, Lib., The Law Comm., London. [0035988] *17/03/1983*
Tree Mrs L, (was Dodd), BA MCLIP, Team Lib.-N.W., Norfolk L.& Inf.Serv. [0025160] *11/12/1975*
Treen Ms EH, Sen.L.Asst.:Catr., Inst.of Educ., London. [0061288] *02/05/2002* **AF**
Tregear Mrs ME, FCLIP, Retired. [0003203] *28/02/1940* **FE 01/01/1950**
Treglohan-Chisholm Mr AC, BA(Hons) MA MCLIP, Open Govt.Adviser, D.T.I., London. [0053870] *07/10/1996*
Treherne Ms JJ, BA(Hons), Pub.Serv.& Systems Mgr., Univ.of Surrey, Guildford. [0045779] *28/05/1991*
Trenaman Mrs P, MA MCLIP, Retired. [0014855] *01/01/1953*
Trench Mrs SG, (was McGarr), MCLIP, Sen.Vice President, Corporate Research & Devel., American Internat.Companies. [0023500] *06/01/1975*
Trenchard Mrs SM, MCLIP, Sch.Lib., Roundwood Park Sch., Herts.C.C. [0000491] *04/10/1967*
Trevelyan Miss AM, MA MSc MCLIP, Clerical Asst., L.B.of Sutton, Wallington. [0014860] *01/01/1972*
Trevelyan Miss L, BA (Hons) MA, Issue Desk Super., Economics L., Oxford. [0060913] *10/02/2002*
Trevett Ms PA, BA FCLIP, Freelance Ed. [0014861] *01/01/1956* **FE 01/01/1964**
Trevett Mr PW, MCLIP, Knowledge Agent, Defence Sci.& Tech.Lab., Malvern, Worcs. [0014862] *01/01/1965*
Trevor Mrs RW, (was Jones), BA(Hons) MCLIP, P./t.Lib., Sir John Lawes Sch., Herts. [0032101] *05/02/1980*
Tribe Mrs CD, (was Apted), BA DipLib MCLIP, Lib., L.B.Islington., Archway L. [0027870] *10/10/1977*
Tricker Mr KF, BA MCLIP, Retired. [0028405] *01/11/1977*
Trickey Mr KV, BA MA FCLIP, p./t.Sen.Lect.&Training Consultant, Liverpool Bus.Sch., Liverpool John Moores Univ. [0021882] *28/01/1974* **FE 23/09/1998**
Tricklebank Mrs SA, BA DipLib MCLIP, Subj.Spec.Lib., Cent.L., Northants.C.C. [0027095] *18/01/1977*
Triffitt Mrs JH, (was Unwin), BA MCLIP, Area Lib., Bradford Met.Dist.Co., Cent.L. [0025922] *30/04/1976*
Triffitt Mr JS, MCLIP, Princ.Offr.- L., Cent.L., Bradford Metro.Council. [0014865] *01/01/1966*
Trigg Ms N, BA MCLIP, dep.Lib.Mgr., Univ.Westminster. [0038552] *01/07/1985*
Triggol Mr GJ, MCLIP, Retired. [0014866] *01/01/1966*
Trinder Miss VM, BEd CertEd FCLIP LTCL, Asst.Head of Div., Dept.of Health S.W.Reg.Off., Frenchay Hosp., Bristol. [0031100] *13/08/1979* **FE 20/05/1998**
Tring Mr TJ, BA MSc, Lib., Broxtowe Coll., Nottingham. [0061015] *01/02/2002*
Tripathi Mrs U, (was Pathak), MA MCLIP, Retired, 31 Ambleside Dr., London, Ontario, N6G 4C4, Canada. [0014870] *11/09/1962*
Tripp Miss LJ, BA(Hons), Sen.L.Asst., Lancaster Univ. [0052468] *02/11/1995*
Trivedi Mrs SJ, MCLIP, Sen.Asst.Lib., L.B.of Harrow. [0022458] *01/01/1970*
Troake Mr J, MCLIP, Retired. [0014876] *01/01/1948*

Trodd / **Trott** / **Tucker** / **Tudor** / **Turner**

Trodd Miss JE, (was Stamper), MA, Lib., Instant L.Ltd., London. [0049928] 24/01/1994
Tromans Ms EHC, BA(Hons), Sen.Asst.Lib., Dudley Coll., W.Midlands. [0049694] 25/11/1993
Trompiz Mrs MMT, BA DipLib MCLIP, Sen.Lib., Croydon Cent.L. [0043748] 01/01/1990
Troon Mr M, Reg.LIS Liaison Offr., Reg.L.& Inf.Serv., The Court Serv., Birmingham. [0059023] 27/10/2000 **AF**
Trott Mrs A, BA DipLib MCLIP, Inf.Spec.(L.), Kings Coll., Univ.of London. [0034660] 18/01/1982
Trott Mrs CL, BA(Hons), L.Asst., Sch.of Pharmacy, Univ.of London. [0056089] 10/02/1998 **AF**
Trott Mrs FJ, (was Maynard), BA MCLIP, Inf.Consultant, BCIS Associates, East Bergholt. [0027078] 26/01/1977
Trotter Mr RR, BA FCLIP, Retired. [0014882] 01/01/1966 FE 24/09/1997
Troughton Mrs HC, (was Hansford), MCLIP, p./t.Lib., Mildmay Hosp.UK, London. [0014883] 01/01/1964
Trout Mr EAR, BA DipLib MCLIP, Mgr.-Cent.for Concrete Inf., Brit.Cement Assoc., Crowthorne, Berks. [0038385] 03/04/1985
Truebridge Ms JE, Self Employed, J.E.T Enterprises. [0039645] 21/04/1986
Truelove Ms M, MCLIP, Sen.Bibl.Offr.(HQ Stock& Requests), Bucks.C.C., Aylesbury. [0028707] 13/01/1978
Trueman Mrs GR, (was Greensmith), MA MCLIP, Unemployed. [0041939] 22/05/1998
Truen Mrs G, MEd MCLIP, Head of Learning Cent., Penair Sch./Cornwall C.C., Truro. [0056254] 17/04/1998
Trugeon-Smith Mr EO, Stud. [0061507] 29/08/2002
Trumble Mrs SA, (was Dean), MPhil DipLIS, Music Lib., Chetham`s Sch. of Music, Manchester. [0043918] 20/02/1990
Trumper Miss MC, BLS MCLIP, Comm.lib., Sevenoaks L., Kent. [0031966] 10/01/1980
Truran Mrs JE, BA, Sch.Lib., Francis Coombes Sch., Watford. [0059051] 06/11/2000 **AF**
Truscott Miss CL, BA, Research Asst., Working Links, Plymouth, Devon. [0059056] 01/11/2000
Truslove Mrs CL, (was Pennell), BA(Hons) DipIM MCLIP, Business Link Lib., Reading Bor.Council. [0046724] 02/01/1992
Truslove Mrs EJ, (was Wilton), BSc(Hons) MA, Reader Devel.Lib., Northampton.C.C., Wellingborough L. [0057040] 27/11/1998
Tsang Ms PKY, Sen.Tech., Map L., Dept.of Geography, Univ.of Hong Kong. [0052782] 12/12/1995
Tsang Miss TKL, BA MA, Stud., Univ.Coll.London. [0061575] 02/10/2002
Tsang Mr YS, MSc, Resident in Hong Kong. [0060104] 07/12/2001
Tsang Sik Yan Miss S, (was Tsang), BA MLib MCLIP, Section Head-Inf.Serv., Hong Kong Poly.Univ.L. [0039932] 03/10/1986
Tse Miss S, Asst.Lib., Lazard, London. [0055301] 23/09/1997
Tse Miss TLP, BA(Hons) MA, Inf.Offr., Simmons & Simmons, London. [0052950] 26/01/1996
Tse Mr WT, MLib MCLIP, Sen.Lib.-Leisure & Cult.Serv.Dept., Tuen Mun Pub.L., Hong Kong, China. [0017878] 01/01/1969
Tse Miss YYF, MA, L.Asst., Chinese Univ.of Hong Kong, Hong Kong. [0048336] 27/11/1992
Tsegaye Mr K, BA MSc, Employment not known. [0060749] 12/12/2001
Tseng Mrs C, (was Wu), Freelance Lib., Tel:01895 256328. [0047660] 12/01/1992
Tseng Mrs GM, (was Cheetham), MSc MCLIP, Lect., Dept.of L.& Inf.Studies, Loughborough Univ.of Tech. [0025017] 31/10/1975
Tsirtou Mr B, CertEd BMus DipIS, Learning Support Lib., Westminster City Council, Victoria L. [0044543] 23/10/1990
Tubb Mr R, BA(Hons) MCLIP, Unemployed. [0024554] 17/09/1975
Tubby-Hille Ms ME, Unemployed. [0043500] 31/10/1989
Tuck Mr JP, MA MCLIP, Dep.to the Dir.of Univ.L.Serv., Univ.of Oxford. [0030799] 10/04/1979
Tuck Miss N, MCLIP, Retired. [0014897] 01/01/1948
Tucker Mr AFD, MCLIP AInstAM, Unemployed. [0014898] 01/01/1959
Tucker Mr BS, BA LiB MSc MCLIP, L.Tech., Univ.of Dist.of Columbia, Washington DC. [0021852] 15/02/1974
Tucker Mrs CAN, (was Lewis), BA(Hons) MCLIP, Corporate Communication Mgr., MOD, Whitehall L. [0052239] 01/01/1995
Tucker Mrs CL, BA DLS, Learning Res.Lib., Leicester Coll. [0034386] 21/10/1981
Tucker Mrs CM, BA(Hons) MA, Teaching Materials Offr., The Open University. [0059623] 03/07/2001 **AF**
Tucker Ms E, BA DipIS MCLIP, Research Lib., Research Cent., B.B.C., Bristol. [0047922] 26/10/1992
Tucker Mrs HJ, Sch.Lib., St.Edwards Sch., Cheltenham. [0055734] 10/11/1997
Tucker Miss JL, L.Asst., Barnet L., Childs Hill L. [0059584] 01/01/1969 **AF**
Tucker Mrs JM, (was Brown), BEd MA MCLIP, Sch.Lib.(P./t.), Fearnhill Sch., Letchworth. [0046138] 07/10/1991
Tucker Miss LK, BA, L.Asst., Cranfield Univ., Swindon. [0061415] 01/07/2002 **AF**
Tucker Mrs LR, BSc, Clinical & Res.Gov.Support Lib., Med.L., Royal Free Hosp., London. [0058472] 01/03/2000
Tucker Mrs ME, (was Hepworth), BA MLib MCLIP, Grp.Lib., Stroud, Glos.Co.L. [0006753] 10/01/1968
Tucker Mrs MC, Knowledge Systems Mgr., UK Nirex Ltd., Didcot. [0061202] 08/04/2002
Tucker Miss SJF, MCLIP, L.Asst., S.Glos.L. [0014906] 01/01/1964
Tucker M/s SMG, MA BBS DipLib MCLIP, Asst.Lib., Trinity Coll. [0027033] 12/01/1977
Tuckey Mr DL, BA(Hons) MCLIP, Unemployed. [0024555] 23/09/1975
Tuckwell Mr GC, BA MCLIP, Lib., N.Somerset Dist.Council, Clevedon. [0028709] 11/01/1978
Tudge Mrs H, (was Bradley), MA, Career Break. [0041118] 07/10/1987

Tudor Mr JA, MBA MCLIP, Subject Lib., Bournemouth Univ., Poole. [0014909] 01/01/1965
Tuey Ms SC, BEd(Hons) DipInf, Lib., Mount Carmel Girls' Sch., Islington, London. [0050269] 26/05/1994
Tugwell Mr AC, BPharm MSc MPS MCLIP, Employment not known. [0060736] 12/12/2001
Tulasiewicz Mr E, BA, Stud., Univ.Coll.London. [0061193] 08/04/2002
Tulip Ms JL, BA, Inf.Mgr., IPC Media, London. [0043626] 13/11/1989
Tull Mrs VM, (was Parry), BA(Hons) DipIM, MCLIP, Adult Lend.Lib., W.Berks.Council, Newbury L. [0051497] 16/03/1995
Tulloch Mrs LM, (was Gulland), MA DipLib MCLIP, Study Support Asst., Hull City Council, Cent.L. [0035239] 07/10/1982
Tulloch Mrs N, BSc, Off.Serv.Mgr., Ward Hadaway, Newcastle upon Tyne. [0056620] 22/09/1998
Tulloch Ms P, MA MBA DipLib MCLIP, Comm.Ls.Network Mgr., Glasgow City Council. [0037670] 17/10/1984
Tully Mr RIJ, MSc FCLIP, Life Member, Tel.01248 364538, 5 Glantraeth, Bangor, Gwynedd, LL57 1HQ. [0014915] 01/01/1931 FE 01/01/1937
Tully Mrs SJ, (was Poynton), MCLIP, Retired. [0014916] 01/01/1953
Tumilty Miss AM, MCLIP, Unemployed. [0014917] 01/01/1964
Tunesi of Liongam Mrs JEM, (was Nickels), BA MCLIP, Asst.Lib., The Coll.of Arms, London. [0038329] 20/03/1985
Tunks Mrs DC, (was Rutherford), BA DipLib MCLIP, Unemployed. [0042365] 24/10/1988
Tunley Mr MF, MA FCLIP, Life Member. [0014920] 01/01/1954 FE 01/01/1963
Tunley Mrs SAV, (was Smith), FCLIP, Retired. [0014921] 26/03/1957 FE 01/01/1965
Tunnicliffe Mrs AE, (was Emmerson), MSc MCLIP, Planning & LMS Mgr., Cheshire C.C., Chester. [0020934] 12/09/1973
Tunnicliffe Mr NW, BSc MCLIP, Retired. [0014923] 01/01/1967
Tunstill Mrs CA, BA DipLib MCLIP, Inf.& Learning Resources Mgr., Lowestoft Coll. [0042115] 04/10/1988
Tupling Mr AM, MA FCLIP, Life Member. [0014924] 01/01/1951 FE 01/01/1959
Turfan Mrs RB, (was Jefferies), BA MA DipLib MCLIP, Lib.-African Studies Sect., Sch.of Oriental & African Studies, Univ.of London L. [0026424] 01/01/1976
Turker Ms G, BA, Learning Res.Cent.Mgr., Friern Barnet Sch., London. [0037029] 01/02/1984
Turland Mrs S, (was May), BA MCLIP, Lib., Havant Grove L., Hants.Co.L. [0014931] 12/01/1965
Turley Mrs PJ, (was Brown), BSc(Econ)(Hons), L.Exec., House of Commons L., London. [0045157] 27/07/1990
Turnbull Miss AL, Stud., Uni. of Aberystwyth, [0060947] 15/01/2002
Turnbull Mr GT, BA MCLIP, Sen.Lib., Wythenshawe Cent.L., Manchester. [0014932] 01/01/1968
Turnbull Mrs JA, (was Lindsey), BA DipLib MCLIP, p./t.L.Asst., St.Helen's Sch., Northwood. [0044952] 22/01/1991
Turnbull Ms L, Asst.Lib., Latymer Upper Sch., Hammersmith. [0050919] 28/10/1994
Turnbull Ms SE, BLib MCLIP, Internat.Tax Inf.Mgr., PricewaterhouseCoopers, London. [0024840] 01/10/1975
Turnbull Mrs V, BA PGDip, Sch.Lib., Trinity Coll., Carlisle. [0058749] 05/07/2000
Turner Dr AF, BSc DPhil, Systems Lib., Royal Soc.of Medicine, London. [0040974] 01/10/1987
Turner Mrs AH, BA MCLIP, Asst.Lib., Harris L., Lancs.Co. [0037867] 08/11/1984
Turner Mrs AJ, (was Hicks), BA(Hons) MLib MCLIP, Inf.Mgr., NHS Inf.Auth., Birmingham. [0047757] 16/10/1992
Turner Mrs AL, BSc, Career Team Lib., Metro.Bor.of Wigan. [0055182] 04/08/1997
Turner Mr AR, BA MCLIP, Learning Res.Mgr., Reading Coll.& Sch.of Arts & Design, Berks. [0035987] 17/03/1983
Turner Mrs BE, (was Walker), BA MCLIP, Team Lib., Young Peoples Serv., Sittingbourne L. [0052239] 05/01/1971
Turner Mrs BM, (was Dean), Sen.L.Asst., South Thames Coll., London. [0045144] 24/07/1990 **AF**
Turner Mrs C, (was Smeaton), BA MCLIP, N.Area Child.& Learn.Lib., Solihull M.B.C. [0013512] 01/01/1967
Turner Mrs CA, BA, Sen.L.Asst., Newbold Coll., Binfield, Berks. [0056335] 26/05/1998
Turner Ms CA, (was Bunter), MSc, Applications Support Consultant, DS Ltd., Ferndown, Dorset. [0029899] 19/10/1978
Turner Mrs CE, (was Dupre), MA MCLIP, Lib., Anna Freud Cent., Hampstead. [0041594] 28/01/1988
Turner Mr CM, BA MA DipLib MCLIP, Unemployed. [0022414] 07/05/1974
Turner Mrs D, (was Jackson), BA(Hons) MCLIP, Sen.Inf.Offr.(Job Share), Univ.of Teesside, Middlesbrough. [0033690] 06/02/1981
Turner Ms DE, BA(Hons) MSc, Web Ed., WS Atkins, Epsom, Surrey. [0058474] 03/03/2000
Turner Mrs DF, (was Thornton), BA MCLIP, Learning Cent.Super., Reading Coll.& Sch.of Arts & Design, Berks. [0014943] 01/01/1956
Turner Mrs EJ, (was Nicholls), BA(Hons) MA MCLIP, Asst.Lib.(Aerospace, Eng.& Envir.), Cranfield Univ. [0049480] 26/10/1993
Turner Mrs ER, BA, L.Asst., Oxford Brookes Univ. [0057705] 05/07/1999
Turner Ms GC, MA MCLIP, Acq.Support Lib., Spanish Acq.L., The London L. [0049957] 31/01/1994
Turner Miss GM, BSc MCLIP, Life Member. [0014949] 01/01/1952
Turner Mrs HM, (was Game), C BIOL M I BIOL MCLIP, Lib.:S.Dir., Manchester L.& Theatres, Cent.L. [0025283] 13/01/1976
Turner Mrs I, MA DipLib MCLIP, Network Lib., Aberdeenshire Council, Banff Academy. [0022653] 01/06/1974

Personal Members

Turner Mr IJ, BA(Hons) PGDipLIS MCLIP, Lib., Nat.Assembly for Wales, Cardiff. [0039393]   21/01/1986
Turner Mrs J, (was Coles), MCLIP, Community Lib., Birmingham L.Serv. [0002968]   01/01/1968
Turner Mrs J, (was Nichol), MA BA MCLIP, Reader Devel.Co-ordinator, Essex L. [0028347]   01/11/1977
Turner Ms JA, BA MCLIP, Lib., Hants Co.L., Gosport. [0026149]   08/07/1976
Turner Ms JA, BA DipLib MCLIP, Team Lib.Comm.Devel., Northants L.& Inf.Serv. [0036285]   03/10/1983
Turner Miss JC, BA(HONS), Dep.Lib., Royal Geographical Soc.L., London. [0040547]   18/03/1987
Turner Ms JF, BA(Hons) DipLIS MCLIP, Trust Lib., E.Sussex Hosp.NHS Trust, St.Leonards on Sea. [0041780]   08/04/1988
Turner Mrs JK, (was Ashley), MCLIP, Lib.-Rosemount H.S./Tech.Cent., English Montreal Sch.Board, Montreal, Canada. [0014956]   26/09/1964
Turner Mr JP, BA MCLIP, Serv.Mgr., Cent.L., Nottingham City Council. [0014960]   01/01/1970
Turner Miss JS, MCLIP, Cent.L.Mgr., Oxon.C.C., Cultural Serv. [0014961]   01/01/1969
Turner Mr JW, BA(Hons), Asst.Lib., Chichester Coll., W.Sussex. [0048179]   11/11/1992
Turner Mr JWS, MA MCLIP, Life Member. [0014962]   01/01/1960
Turner Miss K, MA(Hons) MA MCLIP, Lib., Cheshire C.C. [0055409]   08/10/1997
Turner Mrs KE, BEng, Stud., Univ.of Wales, Aberystwyth. [0058979]   16/10/2000
Turner Mr KF, BSc DipLib MCLIP, Local Government Inf.Lib., Leics.C.C. [0035934]   19/02/1983
Turner Mr KG, MCLIP, Retired. [0014963] 01/01/1954
Turner Mrs KJ, (was Ostler), BA DipLib MCLIP, Asst.Lib., Cent.L., Bexley L.B. [0041441]   06/01/1988
Turner Mrs KL, BA(hons), p./t.Stud./Sci.Inf.Asst., Univ.of Cent.England, Birmingham, Warwick. [0053877]   07/10/1996
Turner Mrs KL, BSc, Stud., Loughborough Univ. [0061728]   29/10/2002
Turner Mrs LJ, (was Hill), BSc MCLIP, Area Co-ordinator, Notts.Co.L., Mansfield. [0036702] 07/11/1983
Turner Mrs LJ, (was Willett), MCLIP, Learner Serv.Mgr., Stafford Coll. [0015881]   01/01/1971
Turner Mrs LM, (was Rigarlsford), BA MCLIP, Princ.Lib.-N.Notts.Grp., Notts.L.,Arch.& Inf.Serv., Retford, Notts. [0020983]   22/07/1973
Turner Mrs M, BA(Hons) MCLIP, Unemployed. [0035581]   06/10/1982
Turner Mr NDW, BA(Hons) MA MCLIP, Subject Lib., Kent Inst.of Art & Design, Maidstone. [0054580]   27/01/1997
Turner Mr NW, LLB FCMI MCLIP FSA Scot, Dir.of Leisure Serv., L.B.of Newham. [0014969] 01/01/1968
Turner Mrs P, (was Radley), BA MCLIP, Special Needs Support Asst., Calderdale M.B.C., Halifax. [0023402]   14/01/1975
Turner Mrs P, (was Rodzik), IAG Inf.Devel.Offr., Herts.Careers Serv.Ltd., Hertford. [0047609] 05/10/1992
Turner Mrs PM, (was Stone), MCLIP, Inf.Specialist, QINETIQ, Farnborough, Hants. [0014974]   01/01/1969
Turner Mr PN, FCLIP, Life Member. [0014975]   01/01/1952
FE 01/01/1961
Turner Mrs R, (was Harvey), BA DipLib MCLIP, Tutor Lib., Barnfield Coll., Luton, Beds. [0029276]   10/05/1978
Turner Mr RG, BA DipLib MCLIP, Lend.Lib., Co.Br.L., Winchester,Hants. [0026590]   06/10/1976
Turner Mr RJ, BA DipLib MA MCLIP, Head of Learning Res., Mount St.Marys Coll., Derbys. [0041947]   08/06/1988
Turner Mr RJ, MA DipLib MCLIP, Head of Business Devel., Blackwell's UK., Oxford. [0025921]   01/04/1976
Turner Mrs S, BLib MCLIP, Sen.Inf.Adviser, Univ.of Gloucestershire. [0044597]   02/11/1990
Turner Mrs S, (was Doyle), BA MCLIP, Lib., Glasgow Dist.L. [0004156]   13/10/1971
Turner Mrs SE, (was Overfield), BA MCLIP, Sen.Lib., Scarborough Grp., N.Yorks.C.C. [0020562]   05/04/1973
Turner Mrs SJ, (was Venn), MCLIP, Unemployed. [0014976]   26/03/1966
Turney Mr AG, FCLIP, Life Member, Tel.0115 9612708, 35 Chatsworth Ave., Carlton, Notts., NG4 3JL. [0014982] 01/01/1940   FE 01/01/1959
Turpie Mrs GS, BSc(Hons) MCLIP, Publishing Consultant. [0029856]   03/10/1978
Turpin Mrs AE, (was Gosden), BA DipLIS MCLIP, Lib., Cambs.C.C., Cambridge. [0048038]   04/11/1992
Turpin Ms CM, MA(Oxon) MA MCLIP, Lib., Essex Health Auth., Brentwood. [0041121]   02/10/1987
Turpin Ms L, BA MA MCLIP, Inf.Serv. Mgr. (Moulsecoomb), Univ.of Brighton, E.Sussex. [0020904] 24/08/1973
Turrell Miss A, MCLIP, Princ.L.Asst., Keele Univ.L. [0014985]   01/01/1969
Turrell Mrs KH, BA, Employment not known. [0060760]   12/12/2001
Turrell Mrs SA, (was Travis), BA DipLib MCLIP, Sch.Lib., Clarendon House Grammar Sch., Ramsgate. [0035497] 25/10/1982
Turriff Mrs A, (was Yate), BA MEd FCLIP, Princ.Offr., Aberdeen City Council, Curriculum Resources & Inf.Serv. [0024388]   04/07/1975
FE 22/05/1996
Turtell Miss A, BSc MCLIP, Employment not known. [0060692]   12/12/2001
Turtle Mrs KM, (was May), BA MCLIP, Lib.-P.G.Educ.Cent., Chorley & S.Ribble NHS Trust, Lancs. [0022132]   15/02/1974
Turton Mrs CS, (was Walker), BA MCLIP, Team Lib.Local Studies, Gloucester L., Glos.L.Serv. [0030566]   09/02/1979
Turton Mrs M, (was Jones), MCLIP, P/t.Asst.Lib.(Catg.), Shakespeare Birthplace Trust, Stratford upon Avon. [0014988]   01/01/1968
Tutin Mr J, L.Asst., Leeds City Council. [0054152]   07/11/1996
Tutin Miss PD, MA MCLIP, Life Member. [0014991]   01/01/1954
Tuttiett Ms PJ, BA MCLIP, Area L.Mgr., Palmers Green L., L.B.of Enfield. [0028973]   17/01/1978

Tutton Mrs RM, (was Mcguire), BA MCLIP, Sen.Lib., Urmston, Trafford Lifelong Learning. [0025782]   19/02/1976
Tutty Mrs JL, (was Gagg), MCLIP, Stud., Open Univ. [0005288]   01/01/1967
Tuxford Mr D, BA MCLIP DMS MIMgt, Social Sci.Lib., City of Manchester L., & Theatres Dept., Cent.L. [0014992] 01/01/1967
Twaddle Mr G, MA(Hons) MSc, Lib., Strathaven Academy, Lanarkshire. [0052962]   01/02/1996
Twamley Mrs D, (was Jolly), BA(Hons), Lib., Royal Grammar Sch., Newcastle upon Tyne. [0046762]   01/01/1963
Tweed Mrs JE, (was Boyd), BLib MCLIP, p./t.L.Asst., North Eastern Educ.and L.B. [0025953]   09/05/1976
Tweed Mrs LM, (was Milligan), BLS MCLIP, Temp.p./t.Asst.Lib./L.Asst., Univ.of Ulster, Co.Londonderry, Cloughmills Br.L., N.E.E.L.B. [0032127]   11/02/1980
Tweedie Mr GL, MCLIP, Retired. [0023204]   26/10/1974
Tweedie Mrs JR, (was Williams), MCLIP, Unemployed. [0022963]   24/09/1974
Tweedie Mrs UEE, Local L.Mgr., Gloucestershire C.C. [0057679]   01/07/1999
AF
Tweedy Miss JA, BA MCLIP, Sen.Lib.-ICT/Devel., Middlesbrough Bor.Council. [0038228]   09/02/1985
Twelves Mrs S, (was Hunt), Retired. [0014999]   01/01/1945
Twiddy Mr P, BA DipLib MCLIP, Lib.&Inf.Serv.Co-ordinator, Leeds Teaching Hosp.NHS Trust. [0034706]   02/02/1982
Twigg Mr EG, FCLIP, Life Member, Tel.01904 424676, 20 Oakland Ave., Stockton Lane, York, YO3 0BY. [0015001]   01/01/1932
FE 01/01/1948
Twigg Mrs SA, (was Welton), MCLIP, Comm.Lib.(Job Share), Staffs.C.C., Newcastle. [0015603]   18/01/1968
Twine Mr TJ, BA DipLib, Managing Dir., EOS Internat., London. [0038929]   21/10/1985
Twining Ms EJ, MA MCLIP, Publicity Offr., Calibre Cassette L., Aylesbury, Bucks. [0015005]   01/01/1986
Twinn Ms RDT, BA, P/t.Lib., BBC Film & VT L., Plymouth,Devon. [0039335]   16/01/1986
Twiss Miss R, BEd MA MCLIP, Subject Lib., Univ.Coll.Chichester. [0047034]   06/04/1992
Twist Mrs AM, (was Patrick), BA(Hons) DipLib, Asst.Lib., Commando Training Cent., Royal Marines, Lympstone. [0040280]   16/01/1987
Twist Mrs M, (was Kurkiewicz), BA MCLIP, Lib., Loc.Stud.& Hist.Serv., Birmingham Cent.L. [0008534]   01/04/1967
Twite Mrs VJ, (was Marshall), MCLIP, Learning Resource Cent.Mgr., Lymm High Sch., Lymm, Cheshire. [0015007]   29/08/1964
Twomey Mrs CEJ, BSc(Hons) MA PhD MCLIP, Electronic Projects Lib., London L.& Inf.Devel.Unit, Univ.of London. [0055171]   29/07/1997
Twomey Miss RE, BA MA, Stud., Sheffield Univ. [0061787]   07/11/2002
Twose Mrs MJ, MCLIP, Area Comm.Liaison Offr., W.Cornwall, Redruth L., Cornwall C.C. [0029103]   15/03/1978
Tye Miss MM, MCLIP BA, Life Member, Tel.01925 819182. [0015008]   01/01/1951
Tyerman Mrs DM, (was Livesey), MCLIP, Inf.& Comm.Devel.Offr., Cult.Serv., Durham. [0015009]   08/03/1966
Tyerman Ms K, DipLib BA MCLIP, Asst.Dir., L.& Lifelong Learning, L.B.of Brent. [0034498]   11/11/1981
Tyers Mrs MK, BA, p./t.Stud./L.Asst., Harold Bridges L., Lancaster. [0059570]   04/06/2001
Tylee Ms C, BA(Hons) MA MCLIP, Campus Lib., Bath Spa Univ.Coll. [0050793]   18/10/1994
Tyler Mrs AM, (was Evans), MCLIP, Resident in Norway, Hildertunet 11, 1341 Slependen, Norway. [0015012] 07/08/1963
Tyler . GS, BA(Hons) MA, Reader's Adviser, House of Commons L. [0049891]   07/01/1994
Tyler Miss KA, BA(Hons) MA MCLIP, Child.Lib., Gosport L., Hants. [0057261]   02/02/1999
Tyler Mrs LJ, (was Bass), MSc BSc, Unemployed, [0046605]   20/11/1991
Tyler Mr SC, MA, Stud., Northumbria Univ. [0061708]   23/10/2002
Tyler Prof WE, MA FCLIP, Retired. [0015018]   01/01/1938
FE 01/01/1950
Tyrer Mrs JA, (was Leach), BA DipLib MCLIP, Lib.-Database Mgr., N.Yorks C.C., Northallerton. [0042836]   28/03/1989
Tyrrell Ms F, BA(Hons) MCLIP, Circulation Mgr., St.Marys Univ.Coll., Twickenham. [0043799]   15/01/1990
Tyrrell Mrs MA, (was Murphy), MA MCLIP, Self-employed. [0015027]   01/01/1969
Tyrrell Miss SJ, BA (Hons), L.& Collections Mgr., The Kennel Club, London. [0057213]   18/01/1999
Tyson Mrs KE, BA MCLIP, Lib., The Blandford Sch., Dorset. [0028196]   29/07/1977
Tzopa Mr R, BA DipLIS MCLIP, Sch.Lib., Corpus Christi Sch., Ottawa. [0048943]   30/07/1993
Udensi Mrs ME, BSc(Hons) DipMRS, Unemployed. [0057329]   12/02/1999
Udogaranya Mrs IO, BA, Unemployed. [0052900]   22/01/1996
Uekawa Mr C, BA(Hons) MPhil, Inf.Adviser, Watson Wyatt Partners, Reigate. [0057257]   01/02/1999
Ugonna Mrs JA, (was Corran), MA DipLib MCLIP, Knowledge & Learning Cent.Proj.Mgr., Brit.Council, Manchester. [0017888]   30/05/1969
Ugwu Mrs CC, BSc(Hons) DipLib MCLIP, Learning Res.Cent.Mgr., Whitefield Sch., Barnet, London. [0039148]   11/11/1985
Ulas Ms EM, MA(Hons) DipLib MBA MCLIP, Sub-Lib., Reader Serv., Strathclyde Univ.,Glasgow. [0025675]   03/02/1976
Ullersperger Miss KA, BA(Hons) DipLIS MCLIP, Lib., Cent.L., Royal Bor.of Kensington & Chelsea. [0047956]   27/10/1992
Umbima Mrs P, (was Warren), CertEd MCLIP, Life Member. [0017889]   15/03/1948
Umbima Mr WE, BA MA MCLIP, Head Lib., ICRAF, Nairobi, Kenya. [0017890]   05/06/1968

369

Underhill   *CILIP*

Underhill Mrs AC, MCLIP ALAA, Sch.Lib., Redborne Sch., Ampthill, Beds. [0017892]   01/01/1964
Underwood Mrs AF, MA DipLib MCLIP, Lib., St.Gregorys High Sch., L.B.of Brent. [0027036]   26/01/1977
Underwood Mrs AM, (was Max), CertEd BA DipLib MCLIP, Position unknown, Societe Jersiaise, St.Helier. [0047745]   16/10/1992
Underwood Miss CI, BA MA(Dist), Sen.L.Asst., Univ.of Nottingham. [0058118]   03/11/1999
Underwood Mr GM, BA MCLIP, Retired. [0015037]   21/08/1958
Underwood Mrs JI, (was Scanes), BA MCLIP MLib, Subject Lib., Hiddingh Hall L., Univ.of Cape Town. [0042328]   14/10/1988
Underwood Miss L, BA DipLib MCLIP, Sch.Lib., Langdon Park Sch., L.B.of Tower Hamlets. [0026592]   14/10/1976
Underwood Prof PG, MBA MIIS FCLIP, Dir.-Cent.for Inf.Literacy, Univ.of Cape Town, R.S.A., e-mail:pgu@education.uct.ac.za. [0019134] 15/10/1966   **FE 11/07/1977**
Underwood Mr RJ, BA(Hons), Learning Resources Mgr., Kensington & Chelsea Coll., London. [0058334]   12/01/2000
Uniechowski Mrs KJ, FCLIP, Retired. [0017893]   01/01/1930 **FE 01/01/1945**
Unsworth Miss EA, Stud., Manchester Met.Univ. [0059989]   16/11/2001
Unter Ms ED, L.Asst., Canterbury Christ Church Univ.Coll., Kent. [0056424]   03/07/1998
Unwin Mrs KE, (was Wragg), BA MCLIP, Career Break. [0030304]   15/01/1979
Unwin Miss L, BA(Hons), P.Grad.L.Asst., Denton Wilde Sapte, London. [0061811]   12/11/2002
Upchurch Miss FAM, BA MCLIP, Sen.Lib.Asst., Univ.of Sheffield L. [0015041]   08/05/1963
Uppal Dr M, BSc PhD MCLIP, Resident in India. [0060086]   07/12/2001
Upson Mrs EA, BA MCLIP, Head of L.& Inf.Serv., New Coll., Univ.of Southampton. [0019135]   01/01/1960
Upton Mrs C, MusB, Stud./Lib in Charge, Oxford/Oxford Union. [0061798]   13/11/2002
Upton Mr JC, Bibl.Serv.Mgr., Univ.of Edinburgh, Main L. [0039888]   03/10/1986
Upton Miss NR, BA(Hons), L.Asst., Newcastle City L., Newcastle upon Tyne. [0059311]   02/02/2001
Urch Miss ME, MCLIP, Life Member, Earlfield Lodge, 29 Trewartha Pk., Weston-super-mare, BS23 2RR. [0015044]   04/11/1932
Ure Mr AM, BA MA DipLib MCLIP, Lib., Chelmsford L., Essex C.C. [0038238]   04/02/1985
Ure Miss CM, MA(Hons) PGDip, L.Asst.,p./t., Heriot-Watt Univ., Edinburgh. [0056023]   28/01/1998
Ure Miss LJ, BA(Hons), Inf.Cent.Admin., Nabarro Nathanson, London. [0058571]   04/04/2000
Uren Miss AC, BA MCLIP, Br.Lib., Pencoed L., Bridgend Co.Bor.L. [0031967]   18/01/1980
Uren Dr VS, MSc MCLIP, Employment not known. [0060794]   12/12/2001
Urquhart Dr CJ, (was Simpson), BSc MSc MCLIP PGCE, Lect., Dept.of Inf.& L.Studies, Univ.of Wales, Aberystwyth. [0051129]   23/11/1994
Urquhart Mrs ED, (was Gold), BA DipLib MCLIP, Lib., Auchenharvie Acad., N.Ayrshire Council, Stevenston, Ayrshire. [0030420]   29/01/1979
Urquhart Mrs EE, MA DipLib MCLIP, Employment not known. [0060107]   07/12/2001
Urquhart Mr JCC, BA MA, Lib.Serv.Offr., Age Concern Scotland, Edinburgh. [0045482]   19/02/1991
Urwin Mrs D, (was Agnew), BA MCLIP, Asst.Lib.p/t., S.Cheshire Coll., Crewe. [0000091]   01/01/1971
Urwin Ms JP, BA, Sen.Lect., Univ.of Northumbria at Newcastle. [0034928]   19/04/1982
Urwin Miss LM, BSc, Freelance Law Lib., Genealogical Research. [0042807]   01/03/1989
Usher Mr JA, BSc DipLib, ICT Devel.Mgr., Islington Council L.& Inf.Serv., London. [0039462]   01/02/1986
Usher Miss JE, BA, Stud., Univ.of Strathclyde. [0061162]   18/03/2002
Usher Mrs JM, (was Howes), BA MCLIP, Princ.Lib., Inf.Serv., W.Sussex C.C. [0040543]   03/03/1987
Usher Mrs KPH, (was Smith), MCLIP, Lib., S.Hunsley Sch., N.Ferriby. [0013628]   12/10/1971
Usher Mrs PJ, (was Simpkin), BA DMS MCLIP, Head of Cult.Serv., L.B.of Barnet. [0031450]   12/10/1979
Usher Ms SE, BA(Hons)DipLib MCLIP, Lib., English Faculty L., Oxford Univ.L.Serv. [0024383]   01/07/1975
Usherwood Mrs H, (was Quick), BA PGCE MA, Sen.L.Asst., Sheffield Univ., Crookesmoor L. [0044111]   01/01/1956
Usherwood Prof RC, BA PhD HonFCLIP FCLIP, Reader in L.& Inf.Studies, Univ.of Sheffield. [0015049]   19/02/1962   **FE 01/01/1968**
Uta Dr JJ, MLS PhD FCLIP, Univ.Lib., Mzuzu Univ., Mzuzu, Malawi. [0017894]   24/08/1967   **FE 17/11/1999**
Utting Mrs SJ, (was Buckwell), MCLIP, Life Member. [0016665]   06/03/1953
Uttley Mr PD, DipM, Stud., Univ.of Cent.England, Birmingham. [0059077]   08/11/2000
Uwah Mr K, MA MCLIP, Lib., The American Inter-Continental Univ, London. [0046156]   02/10/1991
Vacher Ms M, Strategic Devel.Dir., Random House Child.Books, London. [0061540]   10/09/2002   **SP**
Vadi Wala Mr K, MLIS, Research Lib., Industrial Bank of Kuwait, Kuwait. [0061424]   12/07/2002
Vain Mrs SM, (was Donohue), MCLIP, Mgr.-L.& Learning Res., Wilts.Coll.Lackham, Chippenham. [0015052]   10/03/1957
Vaisey Mr CR, BSc DipLib MCLIP, Freelance Consultant, Self-employed. [0026593]   07/10/1976
Vale Mrs G, (was Gauntlett), Sen.L.Asst., Wantage L., Oxfordshire C.C. [0045270]   01/10/1990   **AF**

Valencia Ms MA, MA(Hons) MA, Performing Arts Lib., Herts.C.C., Cent.Res.L. [0058213]   18/11/1999
Valentine Ms AB, BA MCLIP, Lib., N.Lanarkshire Council. [0023199]   19/10/1974
Valentine Mrs KA, BA DipLib, Sch.Lib., Stowmarket High Sch., Suffolk. [0035138]   10/09/1982
Valentine Mrs M, (was McIlwain), MCLIP, Trust Lib., Freeman Hosp., Newcastle-upon-Tyne Hosp.NHS Trust. [0009413]   09/01/1968
Valentine Mr P, BA MCLIP, L.Serv.Mgr., W.London Mental Health NHS Trust, Southall, Middx. [0015055]   25/09/1970
Valentine Mrs P, (was Gornall), MBE BA FCLIP, Ch.Lib., N.E.Educ.& L.Board, L.H.Q., Ballymena. [0015056]   22/03/1963 **FE 15/03/1989**
Valentine Ms S, BA MCLIP, E Business Devel.Mgr., Health & Safety Exec., New Media Section. [0038197]   17/01/1985
Valentine Mrs SA, (was Nelson), BA MCLIP, Stock Mgr., Herts.C.C., Hatfield. [0027840]   15/09/1977
Valiant Mrs FE, (was Jones), MA MLib PGCE MCLIP, Lib., Wycombe Abbey Sch. [0045826]   14/06/1991
Vallance Miss DM, BA(Hons) PGLIS MCLIP, Inf.Offr., The Dick Inst., Kilmarnock. [0050457]   04/08/1994
Vallis Mrs L, Sch.Lib., King Arthur's Community Sch., Wincanton, Somerset C.C. [0056427]   02/07/1998
Van Arkadie Mr IP, BA DipLib DipMgt MCLIP, Strategy & Serv.Devel.Mgr., Stoke on Trent L. [0014175]   17/10/1987
Van Den Bergh Mrs E, (was Kerouac), MA, Maternity Leave. [0050896]   28/10/1994
van der Hoff Miss F, MA, Research Skills Trainer, Freshfields Bruckhaus Deringer, London. [0057722]   09/07/1999
Van Der Laan Mrs PA, Lib.Asst., Hilton L., Aberdeen. [0061434]   24/07/2002
Van Der Linde Mrs SL, DipLib, Asst.Learning Res.Cent.Mgr., City of Bristol Coll., Bristol. [0058384]   24/01/2000
Van Der Meer Dr K, PhD MCLIP, Resident in The Netherlands. [0060057]   07/12/2001
Van Der Walt Miss A, BLib MCLIP, Asst.Lib., American Intercontinental Univ., London. [0057616]   18/05/1999
Van Der Wateren Mr JF, MA FCLIP, Retired. [0015064]   25/04/1967 **FE 22/11/1995**
Van Dort Mr C, BSc(Hons) MSc, Lib., DEFRA, London. [0057263]   02/02/1999
Van Halm Mr J, MCLIP, Resident in the Netherlands. [0060062]   07/12/2001
van Hengel Mrs JFA, (was Worby), BSc DipLib MSc, Sen.Documentalist, European Space Agency-ESTEC, The Netherlands. [0046526]   18/11/1991
Van Holby Mrs B, Employment not known. [0060481]   11/12/2001
Van Loo Mr JR, BA DMS MCLIP, Health Sci.Lib., Univ.of Sheffield, Royal Hallamshire Hosp. [0020661]   15/05/1973
van Loo Mrs NS, (was Ormerod), MA BA MCLIP, Lib., New Coll., Oxford. [0020738]   16/06/1973
Van Mellaerts Mrs MH, (was Chad), MA MCLIP, Interlend.Mgr., Essex C.C., Co.L.H.Q., Chelmsford. [0021608]   27/11/1973
Van Niekerk Dr RV, BSc HDipLib MBibl DPhil, Asst.City Admin., Msuwduzi Municipality, Republic of South Africa. [0061641]   08/10/2002
van Noorden Mr A, BSc(ECON) MA MCLIP, Life Member. [0015068]   29/03/1962
Van Rooyen Mrs JM, (was Stocker), MCLIP, p./t.Asst.Lib., Bishop Grosseteste Coll., Lincoln. [0014066]   13/10/1970
Van Tol Mrs L, (was Porter), BA MCLIP, Co-ordinator Bus.Inf.Cent., Posford Haskoning, Peterborough. [0023240]   08/11/1974
Van Zetten Mrs FS, (was Bruce), MCLIP, Asst.Lib., Guildford Coll.of F.E., Surrey. [0030894]   11/06/1979
van Zon Mrs K, (was Danskin), LLB(Hons) DipILS MCLIP, Lib., Glenwood High Sch., Fife. [0055613]   28/10/1997
Vane Mrs GM, (was Humphries), MCLIP, Lib., Hants.Co.L., Bishops Waltham. [0007461]   14/10/1968
Vanes Miss SI, BA(Hons) DipLib MCLIP, Asst.Database Lib.p./t., Trafford L., Bibl.Serv., Davyshulme L.Site. [0046543]   19/11/1991
Vanlaecken Ms MM, Catr.& Antiquarian Bookseller, Christian F Verbeke Law Books, Belgium. [0056641]   01/10/1998
Varathungarajan Mrs ME, (was Tranter), MCLIP, Tech.Editor, Bayer Corp., Hudson, OH, USA. [0014837]   01/01/1972
Vardy Miss A, MA, Stud., The Robert Gordon Univ., Aberdeen. [0061058]   14/02/2002
Varga Mrs SL, (was Lyle), MA BSc(Econ)(Hons), Lib., Western Gen.Hosp., Edinburgh. [0050445]   09/08/1994
Vargues Miss MM, Lib., Universidade do Algarve, Faro, Portugal. [0040811]   30/06/1987
Varilly Mrs S, (was Howells), MCLIP, Lib., Havant Coll., Hants. [0000516]   17/01/1968
Varley Mr A, FCLIP, Life Member, Tel.01705 864093, 170 Moorings Way, Milton, Southsea, PO4 8YN. [0015071]   18/02/1950 **FE 01/01/1968**
Varley Mrs DL, (was West), DipRSA, Learning Res.Mgr., Sponne Sch., Towcester. [0059074]   01/01/1967
Varley Mrs SB, BA, Lib., Clydach L., City & County of Swansea. [0015074]   01/10/1967
Varnes Mr AJ, BA(Hons), Grad.Trainee, Christ Church, Oxford. [0059844]   16/10/2001
Varney Mrs JM, (was King), MCLIP, Head of Support Serv., Bucks.Co.L.H.Q. [0015076]   10/01/1967
Varty Miss EJ, BA DipLib MCLIP, Acquisitions Lib., Dept.for Work & Pensions, London. [0034601]   17/01/1982
Varty Miss J, MCLIP, Life Member. [0015078]   15/03/1956
Vasbenter Mrs MD, (was Howard), MCLIP, Life Member, 8 Upper Chyngton Gdns., Seaford, Sussex, BN25 3SA, 0323 891951. [0015079]   11/10/1946
Vasey Mrs EP, Customer Liaison Offr., Nettleham L., Lincoln. [0059948]   09/11/2001   **AF**

Vasishta Mrs R, BSc MA, Community Lib., Cliftor L., Nottingham. [0054837] 14/04/1997
Vassie Dr R, BA MA PhD, Unemployed. [0061577] 02/10/2002
Vaughan Mr A, DipLIS, Co.Lib., Mayo Co.L., Eire. [0055013] 25/06/1997
Vaughan Mr AH, MA MCLIP, Hon.Member, Univ.of N.London. [0015081] 09/03/1963
Vaughan Mrs AM, (was Smith), Sch.Lib., Solihull Sch. [0046080] 01/10/1991
Vaughan Mrs B, (was Molloy), MCLIP, Retired. [0015082] 18/02/1952
Vaughan Miss BJ, BA(Hons), Stud., Univ.of Wales, Aberystwyth, & Learning Adviser, Isle of Wight Coll. [0058225] 19/11/1999
Vaughan Miss EK, BA(Hons) DipIS MCLIP, Higher L.Exec., House of Commons L., London. [0052132] 05/10/1995
Vaughan Mr GA, BA, Catr., The Stationery Off., London. [0041729] 26/02/1988
Vaughan Mrs J, BA(Hons) DipLIS, Ref.Lib., Altrincham L., Cheshire. [0058237] 24/11/1999
Vaughan Mr JE, MA FSA FRSA, Retired. [0015086] 18/02/1964
Vaughan Mrs M, (was McDonald), MA(Hons) DipILS MCLIP, Unemployed. [0051723] 30/05/1995
Vaughan Mr PR, BA(Hons) MA MCLIP, Unemployed. [0045769] 22/05/1991
Vaughan Mr SM, BA(Hons) DipLib MBA, Sen.Reader Adviser, Nat.L.for the Blind, Stockport. [0031714] 13/11/1979
Vaughan-Spickers Dr N, MSc PhD, Employment not known. [0060513] 11/12/2001
Veal Dr DC, BSc PhD FRSC HonFCLIP, Hon Fellow. [0060660] 11/12/2001 **FE 01/04/2002**
Veevers Mrs C, (was Sutcliffe), BA MCLIP, Casual L.Asst., Trafford M.B.C., Altrincham. [0029910] 13/10/1978
Velluet Mrs E, (was Lee), BA MCLIP, Asst.Lib., Cent.L., Imperial Coll., London, SW7 2AZ. [0000842] 08/10/1966
Venables Mrs KL, (was Fullwood), BMus, Learning Res.Co-ordinator, Coventry Tech.Coll. [0044621] 08/11/1990
Veness Mrs VM, BSc, Inf.Asst., Entomology L., The Nat.Hist.Mus., London. [0057994] 12/10/1999
Vennall Mrs JC, (was Barrowcliffe), BSc MCLIP, Sch.Lib., Sch.L.Serv., W.Lothian Council. [0036731] 14/11/1983
Venner Ms JC, (was Grosvenor), BA MSc, Asst.Inf.Offr., Univ.of Hull, The Language Inst. [0043779] 11/01/1990
Venning Ms EJ, Stud., Univ.of Wales, Aberystwyth. [0061060] 15/02/2002
Verik Mrs PK, (was Sindhu), BA(Hons), Resident in Sweden. [0036999] 17/01/1984
Vernon Miss EA, MA(Hons) DipLib, Employment not known. [0056716] 07/10/1998
Vernon Ms JTM, BA MA, Curator, The Brit.L., London. [0041122] 08/10/1987
Vernon-Gill Mrs MS, (was Thomas), B LIB MCLIP, Lib.Asst., Rosewell Library, St.Leonard on Sea. [0021968] 25/01/1974
Verran Ms L, MCLIP, Employment not known. [0060449] 11/12/2001
Verrier Mrs S, (was Gosling), BA MCLIP, Unemployed. [0018170] 06/11/1972
Verschuere Mrs JA, BA(Hons) MCLIP, L.Serv.Mgr., Glenfield Hosp.UHL NHS Trust, Leics. [0054511] 09/01/1997
Verth Ms M, BA MCLIP, EMEA KM CRM Mgr., PricewaterhouseCoopers, Edinburgh. [0039255] 13/01/1986
Veryard Mrs CM, (was Sladdin), BA MCLIP, L.Operations Mgr., Yeovil L., Somerset Co. [0013476] 05/01/1970
Vezza Miss CA, BA MCLIP, Young Peoples Lib., Glasgow City L., The Mitchell L. [0035643] 22/11/1982
Vick Mrs E, BA MCLIP, Asst.Lib., Rother Valley Coll., Dinnington. [0022000] 14/01/1974
Vick Mrs G, BA MCLIP, Sen.Lib., Falkirk S. [0020718] 24/03/1973
Vickerman Mrs HJ, (was Turner), BA MCLIP, Princ.L.Offr.(Cent.L.), Sandwell M.B.C., W.Bromwich,W.Mids. [0030694] 22/02/1979
Vickers Miss EPD, MCLIP, Ethnic Minorities Lib., Kent Arts & L. [0015112] 24/07/1961
Vickers Mr PH, MCLIP, Lib., Prince Consort's L., Aldershot, Hants. [0020555] 03/04/1973
Vickers Mrs PM, (was Lawman), BA MCLIP, Princ.Lib.(Tech.Serv.), L.B.of Havering, Cent.L., Romford. [0015115] 12/01/1967
Vickery Prof BC, MA HonFCLIP, Hon Fellow. [0019141] 14/03/1950 **FE 01/04/2002**
Vickery Mr JE, MA FCLIP, Head of Acquisitions, The Brit.L., Boston Spa. [0015118] 01/03/1972 **FE 20/05/1998**
Vickery Miss SJ, BA(Hons) MSc Econ, Qual.& Curriculum Auth., London. [0058458] 22/02/2000
Victor Mr LM, BA, Sch.Lib.Administrator, Hatch End High Sch., Harrow, Middx. [0034598] 01/01/1982
Vidana Ms M, BA MA MCLIP, Web Lib., Richmond Bor.L., London. [0056137] 05/03/1998
Vidanapathirana Mr P, BA MLS DipLib FCLIP, Lib., Univ.of Sri Jayawardenepura, Nugegoda, Sri Lanka. [0027651] 16/09/1971 **FE 17/03/1999**
Vidgen Mr GA, BLib MCLIP, Tutor/Liaison Offr., D.I.L.S., Aberystwyth. [0040917] 20/08/1987
Vidler Mrs SJ, P./t.Stud.,Ward Sister, Manchester Met.Univ., Manchester Royal Infirmary. [0060019] 26/11/2001
Viejo Lopez De Roda Miss B, BA(Hons), Sen.L.Asst., SOAS., London. [0058762] 07/07/2000
Vignoli Ms NA, Inf.Offr., Clyde & Co., London. [0057747] 16/07/1999
Vigor Mrs WA, (was Baggot), BSc MCLIP, Lib., Huntingdonshire Reg.Coll., Cambs. [0018192] 01/10/1972
Vigurs Mrs M, (was Davies), MCLIP, Res.Cent.Offr., Soc.Serv.Dept., Civic Cent., Stoke-on-Trent. [0000908] 09/03/1967
Vile Mrs MA, BA MCLIP, Catr. [0056655] 01/10/1998
Viles Mr JF, MCLIP, Independent Consultant, The Curatage, Pulham Market, Nr.Diss, Norfolk, IP21 4SR. [0015122] 16/02/1951
Villa Mrs DJ, (was Davis), BA MCLIP, Frenchay L.Mgr., N.Bristol NHS Trust, Bristol. [0003767] 27/10/1970

Villa Mr PJ, MLib MCLIP, LIS Consultant. [0015125] 15/10/1965
Village Mrs P, MSc MCLIP, Employment not known. [0060458] 11/12/2001
Vince Miss J, MCLIP, Business Lib., Portsmouth City Council. [0015126] 08/10/1968
Vince Mrs MA, Asst.Lib., Prestwich L., Bury M.B.C. [0040964] 01/10/1987
Vince Mrs SR, (was Wheeler), BA DipLib MCLIP, Princ.Lib., Kent Arts & L. [0027040] 14/01/1977
Vincent Mr GD, BSc MCLIP, Employment not known. [0060659] 11/12/2001
Vincent Ms HR, BA(Hons), p./t.Stud./Inf.Asst., Wellcome Trust, London. [0061040] 11/02/2002
Vincent Mr IW, BA MCLIP, Retired. [0015130] 17/03/1963
Vincent Mr JC, MCLIP, Networker, Social Exclusion Action Planning, Network. [0015131] 10/10/1966
Vincent Mrs SJ, (was Duerden), BSc MSc MCLIP, Sen.Inf.Specialist, Clinical Evidence, BMJ Publishing Grp., BMA., London. [0043781] 11/01/1990
Vincett Mr PJ, BSc(Hons) PGDip, Unemployed. [0035030] 01/07/1982
Vine Miss AL, BA(Hons) DipLib, Career Break. [0046518] 15/11/1991
Viner Mr D, BA(Hons), Stud., Univ.of Cent.England, Birmingham. [0061284] 08/05/2002
Viner Miss JS, BSc MSc MCLIP, Position unknown, Medicine Control Agency, London. [0060826] 12/12/2001
Viner Mr MCJ, BA(Hons), L.Asst., Lytchett Minster Sch., Poole. [0061611] 03/10/2002 **AF**
Viner Mr RF, MA BSc(Hons), Inf.Offr., Royal Inst.of Chartered Surveyors, London. [0056761] 08/10/1998
Vingoe Mrs GR, (was Cameron), L.Asst., Cathays Br.L., Cardiff. [0045277] 01/10/1990 **AF**
Vinnicombe Mr RAJ, DMA MCLIP, Princ.Lib., Eastern Grp., Notts.Co.L. [0015139] 10/09/1964
Vinson Mr AA, MA MCLIP, Employment not known. [0060658] 11/12/2001
Vint Mrs M, (was Bailey), MCLIP, Area Offr.(L.Operations), L.H.Q., N.Ayrshire Council. [0000589] 01/01/1971
Violet Mr RJC, MCLIP, Community Lib., Wiltshire C.C., Warminster L. [0020212] 01/01/1973
Virdee Mrs KK, BSc DipInfSc MCLIP, Position unknown, Thames Valley Univ. [0060709] 12/12/2001
Virgo Mrs PJ, (was Broughall), BA MCLIP, Sen.Asst.Lib., Garstang, Lancs. [0001827] 01/01/1971
Virnes Mrs H, MSc, Internet Catr., Inst.for Learning & Res.Tech., Univ.of Bristol. [0058363] 26/01/2000
Virone Mrs JA, BSc(Hons), Asst.Lib., Manchester Met.Univ. [0058968] 11/10/2000
Visram Mrs TA, (was Warne), MCLIP, Asst.Lib., L.& Inf.Serv., Newham Healthcare NHS Trust. [0015381] 01/01/1968
Visschedijk Miss AEM, MSc MCLIP, Stud., Dept.of Inf.Sci., Univ.of Strathclyde. [0045498] 21/02/1991
Vitai Mrs JGT, (was Hooper), FCLIP, Life Member, 604 Ross St., London, Ont.N5Y 3V7, Canada. [0017911] 26/05/1952 **FE 01/01/1963**
Vizard Mr RW, MCLIP, Retired. [0015143] 20/09/1957
Vizosomandrak Ms A, Stud., London Metro. [0061583] 02/10/2002
Voaden Ms SL, (was Taylor), MCLIP, Sen.Lib., Ely L., Cambs.Co.L.Serv. [0002833] 01/01/1968
Vodden Ms GJ, BSc(Hons) DipIS, Asst.Lib., Field Fisher Waterhouse, London. [0046334] 28/10/1991
Voisey Miss AR, MCLIP, Asst.Lib., Lewisham L. [0015144] 01/01/1963
Voisey Mrs GA, BA DipInfSc MCLIP, European Mgr.Know.& Learn.Prog., Factiva, London. [0030870] 23/04/1979
Von Bulow Miss BK, [0061400] 04/07/2002
Vowles Mr PJ, MLS MA MCLIP, ICT Sector Leader., Weymouth Coll., Dorset. [0015149] 03/02/1971
Voy Mr E, MCLIP, Life Member. [0015150] 01/01/1954
Voyce Mr PD, BA MCLIP, Community Lib., Wednesbury L.& Hill Top L., Sandwell M.B.C. [0035649] 01/12/1982
Voysey Miss JP, MCLIP, Life Member. [0015152] 02/09/1949
Voysey Ms VN, MA, Maternity Career Break. [0052381] 26/10/1995
Vuolo Ms DG, BA MA MCLIP, Sen.Lib.:Inf.Serv., Beds.C.C. [0031480] 01/10/1979
Vuong Ms DN, PGDip ILS, Resource Cent.Mgr., Univ.of Birmingham. [0054173] 07/11/1996
Vyskocil Mr AJ, BA(Hons) DipILM, Lib., Liverpool Hope Univ., Sheppard Worlock L. [0056692] 05/10/1998
Wace Mrs CF, (was Ritter), BA(Hons) MCLIP, Career Break. [0036553] 20/10/1983
Waddilove Miss K, BA MCLIP, Tutor Lib., Westfield Sch, Watford, Herts. [0015155] 13/02/1970
Waddington Mrs MA, (was Stylianides), BA(Hons) DipIM MCLIP, Asst.Lib., Inst.ofChild.Health, London. [0053856] 01/10/1996
Wade Eva, BA DipLib MCLIP, Unemployed, Hylands, Sewardstone Rd., N.Chingford, London, E4 7RG. [0037483] 01/10/1984
Wade Mr AJ, MA FCLIP, Retired. [0015159] 24/06/1951 **FE 01/01/1962**
Wade Ms EC, (was Nuttall), BA(Hons) MA MCLIP, Career Break. [0049598] 19/11/1993
Wade Miss J, BA(Hons), Asst.Faculty Lib., Univ.Coll.Northampton. [0054390] 04/12/1996
Wade Mrs J, (was Stewart), MA MCLIP, L.Asst., Beds.C.C. [0035155] 01/10/1982
Wade Mrs MA, (was Gann), Sen.L.Asst., Clifton Coll.Prep.Sch., Bristol. [0057881] 01/10/1999 **AF**
Wade Mr MJ, BA MLib MCLIP, Head of L.Inf.& Arch., Glasgow City Council. [0023782] 01/01/1975
Wadey Mrs CA, (was Mitten), BA MCLIP, Relief Lib., Horsham L., W.Sussex C.C. [0031666] 01/11/1979
Wadge Mrs PM, (was Thompson), MA, L.Asst., Wantage L., Oxfordshire C.C. [0049805] 13/12/1993 **AF**

Wadkin Mrs HJ, (was Stone), MCLIP, Inf.Serv.Mgr., ADAS, Wolverhampton. [0014088] 03/01/1972
Wadsworth Mrs C, (was Hodgetts), MCLIP, Sen.Lib., Wakefield Metro.Dist.L.& Inf.Serv., L.H.Q. [0016751] 18/02/1974
Wadsworth Mrs JM, (was Wilson), BLib MCLIP, Jnr.L.Asst.(Maternity Leave), Univ.of Cambridge, Board of Cont.Ed. [0041325] 04/11/1987
Wadsworth Miss JR, MCLIP, Employed outside LIS. [0022052] 15/01/1974
Wafer Mr RA, MCLIP, Life Member, Rhynwick Hill Rd., Reydon, Southwold, Suffolk, IP18 6NL. [0019374] 10/03/1947
Wager Ms JE, (was Hitchins), MCLIP, Lib., Essex Ls., Braintree, Essex. [0006970] 07/03/1971
Wagstaff Mr DJ, BA MMus DipLib MCLIP, Lib., Music Fac., Oxford Univ. [0044195] 04/07/1990
Wagstaff Miss HC, BSc(Hons), Lib., Deloitte & Touche, London. [0057870] 23/09/1999
Wainwright Mr EJ, MCLIP MA, Pro-Vice-Chancellor, Inf.Serv.& Tech., James Cook Univ., Cairns. [0017916] 07/02/1968
Wainwright Mrs JM, BA FCLIP, Retired. [0060661] 11/12/2001 **FE 01/04/2002**
Wait Mrs C, (was Salkeld), MCLIP, Retired. [0012874] 01/10/1970
Waite Miss ER, BA(Hons) MSc MCLIP, Lib., Lovells, London. [0055407] 10/10/1997
Waite Mrs JA, (was Lawson), MCLIP, Inst.Lib., Arts Inst.at Bournemouth, Dorset. [0015178] 18/06/1969
Waite Mrs JA, BA BSc(Hons), Lib./Data Mgr., General Dynamics UK Ltd., St Leonards on Sea, E.Sussex. [0057228] 25/01/1999
Waite Mrs M, (was Bancroft), BA MCLIP, p./t.Comm.Lib.-Child., Stoke-on-Trent City Council, Hanley L. [0047036] 06/04/1992
Waite Mrs MH, (was Watson), MCLIP, Prison Lib., H.M.P.Wealston (closed), Leeds. [0015458] 21/01/1969
Wake Mrs MC, (was Wood), BA(Hons) MA MCLIP, Dep.Lib., The Sch.of Pharmacy, Univ.of London. [0046254] 21/10/1991
Wake Mr RL, MA MA MCLIP, Dep.Lib., Univ.of Southampton. [0032353] 20/02/1980
Wake Mrs S, (was Whittaker), BA MCLIP, L.Inf.Cent.Mgr., Ansford Community Sch., Castle Cary, Somerset. [0023696] 05/01/1975
Wake Mrs VS, (was Green), BSc MCLIP, [0030421] 05/02/1979
Wakefield Miss JD, BA MCLIP, Area Co-ordinator, Worksop, Notts.C.C. [0033181] 21/10/1980
Wakefield Miss KH, BSc, L.Asst., Berkhamsted L., Herts. [0045240] 28/08/1990 **AF**
Wakefield Ms N, BA(Hons) MSc, Asst.Lib., Manchester Met.Univ.L., Hollings L. [0058343] 14/01/2000
Wakefield Mr PW, LLB LLM DipLib MCLIP, Head of L., Broxtowe Coll., Nottingham. [0030564] 12/01/1979
Wakeford Dr R, BSc MSc MCLIP, Employment not known. [0060662] 11/12/2001
Wakeham Mr MW, MA DipLib MCLIP, Acad.Liaison Lib., Health & Soc.Care, Anglia Poly.Univ. [0039820] 30/07/1986
Wakeling Mrs M, (was Smyth), BA(Hons) DipLib MCLIP, Inf.Offr., Bristol Univ.Careers Serv., Bristol. [0029829] 23/10/1978
Wakeman Mrs IJ, (was Dawson), BA MCLIP, Sch.Lib., Chosen Hill Sch., Gloucester. [0015190] 17/01/1969
Wakerley Mr K, BA DipLib MCLIP, Learning Cent.Coordinator, S.E.Derbys.Coll., Ilkeston. [0041275] 20/10/1987
Walaitis Miss CJ, B LIB MCLIP, Lib., Cathkin L., Glasgow. [0030289] 09/01/1979
Walden Mr NR, BSc MCLIP, Employment not known. [0060410] 11/12/2001
Waldhelm Mr RJ, BA DipLib MCLIP, Lib., GLSS, Scottish Executive, Edinburgh. [0029859] 10/10/1978
Wale Mr AC, BA MCLIP, Dir.of L.Serv., Univ.Of Glasgow. [0017920] 01/01/1966
Wale Ms DA, BA MCLIP, Lib., L.B.of Hammersmith & Fulham. [0033182] 06/10/1980
Wales Dr A, BSc PhD DipLib MCLIP, L.Coordinator, Glasgow Royal Infirmary. [0048046] 06/11/1992
Wales Mrs CM, (was Thomson), BA MCLIP, Lend.Serv.Mgr., N.Lanarkshire Council. [0031472] 16/10/1979
Wales Mrs GC, (was Croxon), MCLIP, Sen.L.Asst., N.W.London Hosp.NHS Trust, John Squire L., Harrow. [0015196] 08/05/1965
Wales Mr JG, MCLIP, L.Serv.Devel.Mgr.-Spec.Serv., Tooting L., L.B.of Wandsworth. [0015197] 06/10/1970
Wales Mr TB, BA(Hons) MSc MCLIP, Asst.Lib., Open Univ.L., Milton Keynes. [0055082] 09/07/1997
Walford Mrs JE, (was Binder), FCLIP, Retired. [0015199] 19/11/1942 **FE 01/01/1954**
Walgrave Miss BJ, MCLIP, Life Member. [0015200] 27/08/1941
Walke Mrs V, (was Holt), BA MCLIP, Tuition Mgr., Belle Assoc.Ltd., Coventry. [0043326] 19/10/1989
Walker Mrs A, (was Willetts), BA(Hons) MCLIP, Asst.Lib., Health & Safety Exec., Sheffield. [0043389] 06/10/1989
Walker Mrs A, (was Kelly), MCLIP, Unemployed. [0015204] 25/02/1960
Walker Miss AC, BSc(Hons), Sen.Inf.Asst., Wellcome Trust, London. [0054800] 03/03/1997 **AF**
Walker Mrs AD, (was Crook), BA(Hons) MCLIP, Res.Lib., Bury Coll. [0048442] 11/01/1993
Walker Mrs AF, (was Steinberg), BA MCLIP, Sch.Lib., Lealands High Sch., Luton Bor.Council. [0026010] 04/05/1976
Walker Mr AJ, BA MCLIP, Support Serv.Lib., Isle of Wight Council. [0036587] 21/10/1983
Walker Mrs AL, (was Rawlinson), BA MA MCLIP, Dep.Head L.Serv., Suffolk Coll. [0031425] 03/10/1979
Walker Mr ALN, MA CEng MIEE ACMA, Stud., Univ.of Wales at Aberystwyth. [0016719] 29/10/2002
Walker Miss AM, MA DipLib MCLIP, Princ.Asst.Lib., L.B.of Havering, Cent.L. [0038723] 01/10/1985

Walker Ms AR, BA MCLIP, Lib., Signet L., Edinburgh. [0038057] 10/01/1985
Walker Miss C, BA (Hons), Asst. Lib., Freshfields Bruckhaus Deringer, London. [0061000] 29/01/2002
Walker Miss C, MCLIP, Head,Inf.& Registry Serv., NATO C3 Agency, The Hague. [0022948] 26/09/1974
Walker Mrs C, (was Brown), BA MA MCLIP, Learning Cent.Mgr., Napier Univ., Edinburgh. [0045875] 03/07/1991
Walker Mrs CA, BA(Hons) MCLIP, Project Devel.Mgr., Leeds City Council. [0027038] 13/01/1977
Walker Ms CE, BA MCLIP, Retired. [0015210] 24/02/1960
Walker Mr CG, BA(Hons) MA MCLIP, Lib.&Inf.Programme Support Offr., Leeds Teaching Hosp. Trust, Leeds. [0047929] 26/10/1992
Walker Revd CJ, DipTh MCLIP, Rector, Church Commissioners, S.Moreton. [0015211] 04/10/1971
Walker Mr D, BSc MCLIP, Sen.Lib., Chelsea L., Royal Bor.of Kensington & Chelsea. [0038649] 23/08/1985
Walker Mrs DD, (was Knapp), Retired. [0045062] 03/07/1990 **AF**
Walker Mrs F, (was Moore), BA MCLIP, L.& Inf.Services Coordinator, NHS Primary Care Trust, Glasgow. [0029759] 01/10/1978
Walker Mrs FM, (was Hatfield), MEd FSA(S) MCLIP, Princ.Res.Devel.Offr., Glasgow City Council, Educ.Dept. [0006538] 17/03/1969
Walker Dr GPM, MA PhD FCLIP, Head of Collection Devel., Bodleian L., Oxford. [0015220] 30/06/1964 **FE 24/12/1980**
Walker Mrs HS, (was Hamilton), MCLIP, Retired. [0015221] 01/09/1950
Walker Mr IC, BA MCLIP, Area Lib.-EYP, Doncaster M.B.C. [0015222] 26/08/1969
Walker Miss IRY, MCLIP, L.Co-ordinator, Hamilton, S.Lanarkshire L. [0015224] 04/04/1965
Walker Ms J, BA MCLIP, Unemployed. [0003181] 01/01/1962
Walker Miss JA, BSc MCLIP, Employment not known. [0060715] 12/12/2001
Walker Mr JG, BA(Hons) PGDip, Clearing House Website Offr., NSPCC, London. [0056718] 07/10/1998
Walker Mr JRA, FCLIP, Retired, 8 Heath Croft Rd.,Sutton Coldfield, B75 6RA, 0121 308 4493. [0015235] 25/10/1946 **FE 04/06/1965**
Walker Miss K, BA(Hons) MCLIP, Stud., UCE, Birmingham. [0061432] 24/07/2002
Walker Mr K, MA(Hons) DipILS, L.Offr., City of Edinburgh Council. [0057033] 27/11/1998
Walker Mr K, BA MCLIP, Research & Tech.Mgr., Intelli Corp.Finance, Edinburgh. [0060248] 10/12/2001
Walker Mrs K, BA MBA, Unemployed., Seeking work. [0060909] 10/10/2001
Walker Mr KC, BA FCLIP, Life Member, 0208 449 2262. [0015237] 06/10/1949 **FE 01/01/1962**
Walker Miss KE, BA(Hons) MA MCLIP, Lib., Reading Bor.Council. [0056868] 29/10/1998
Walker Mrs KE, (was Profittlich), BA DipLib MCLIP, Sen.Analyst, GEAC Software Solutions Ltd., Bristol. [0039107] 04/11/1985
Walker Mrs KJ, (was Lane), BA MCLIP, Principal Lib.,Inf.Serv., Worthing L., W.Sussex L.Serv. [0033564] 17/01/1981
Walker Miss KMB, BA MCLIP, Customer Serv.Mgr., L.B.of Newham, E.Ham L. [0015238] 15/01/1968
Walker Miss LAW, BA MCLIP, Lib./Supported Study Offr., E.Renfrewshire (Comm.Res.), Barrhead. [0023361] 11/12/1974
Walker Mrs LE, MA BA(Hons) BSc, Asst.Lib., Hertford Coll., Oxford. [0058072] 25/10/1999
Walker Mr M, BA(Hons) MSc, Inf.Offr., Linklaters & Alliance, London. [0052937] 29/01/1996
Walker Mr M, MCLIP, Lib., Derby Cent.L. [0022229] 25/02/1974
Walker Mr M, BA FCLIP, Retired. [0015240] 16/09/1969 **FE 12/12/1991**
Walker Mrs M, L.Asst., Broadstone L., Dorset. [0061704] 22/10/2002 **AF**
Walker Mrs ME, (was Monk), BA MCLIP, Retired. [0010297] 29/03/1956
Walker Mrs ML, (was Peters), MCLIP, Retired. [0015245] 24/01/1969
Walker Ms N, BA DipLIS, Sen.L.Asst., Fingal Co.L., Ireland. [0061349] 17/06/2002
Walker Mr NL, DipLib MCLIP, Lib., Nat.Mus.of Wales, Cardiff. [0027227] 07/02/1977
Walker Miss O, BA(Hons) MSc, Asst.Prof.Support Lib., Baker & Mckenzie, London. [0054075] 24/10/1996
Walker Miss P, BA MCLIP, Unemployed. [0029861] 10/10/1978
Walker Mrs PH, (was Malvern), BA MCLIP, Lib., Burges Salmon,Solicitors, Bristol. [0015251] 01/01/1966
Walker Mrs PV, (was Holloway), MCLIP, Retired. [0015253] 19/01/1948
Walker Mr RA, MCLIP, Stock Devel./Galaxy Offr., The Mitchell L., Glasgow. [0031121] 28/08/1979
Walker Mrs RM, BSc, Sen.Researcher, Credit Suisse First Boston, London. [0044686] 26/11/1990
Walker Mrs RM, BA(Hons) BSc(Hons) MCLIP, Knowledge Cent.Team Leader, Logica UK, Nottingham. [0048147] 11/11/1992
Walker Mr RP, MA(Oxon) DipLib MCLIP, Learning Resources Mgr., Chichester Coll.of Arts,Sci.& Tech, W.Sussex. [0042795] 06/03/1989
Walker Mrs S, L.Mgr., CEFAS, Weymouth, Dorset. [0052102] 02/10/1995
Walker Ms S, BA DipLib MCLIP, Lib., Min.of Defence L., London. [0022059] 16/01/1974
Walker Mr SB, BA MA, Med.Lib., MOD. [0055838] 21/11/1997
Walker Miss SE, BA MCLIP, Sch.Lib., St.Marys Sch., Shaftesbury. [0023449] 06/01/1975
Walker Mr SJ, BA MSc, Employment not known. [0060457] 11/12/2001
Walker Mrs SM, HNC MCLIP, Employment not known. [0060831] 12/12/2001
Walker Mrs SM, (was Shephard), BSc MCLIP, Knowledge Systems Lib., Surrey & Sussex Healthcare, NHS Trust, Surrey. [0013260] 09/10/1968
Walker Ms SM, (was Allcott), BLib MCLIP, Team Lib., Kent C.C., Gravesend. [0021557] 01/10/1973

Personal Members

Walker Mr TC, BA(Hons) MCLIP, Regional Mgr, Small Business Serv., Manchester. [0043400] 18/10/1989
Walker Miss V, MTheol(Hons) MSc MCLIP, Inf.Serv.Assoc., Marchfirst, London. [0050600] 29/09/1994
Walker Mrs VL, (was Pryce), MCLIP, Lib., Maidenhill Sch., Stonehouse,Glos. [0019967] 09/01/1973
Walker Ms VM, MCLIP, Serv.Lib., City of Edinburgh Council, Sch.L.Serv. [0010583] 01/01/1967
Walker Mr WS, BA MCLIP, L.Servs.Mgr., W.Lothian Council. [0019376] 29/06/1961
Walkers Mrs CM, (was Jansen), MCLIP, Ancillary Asst., St.Norberts Sch., Spalding. [0019440] 01/01/1971
Walkey Miss EL, BA(Hons) MA MCLIP, Asst.Lib.(Humanities), Albert Sloman L., Univ.of Essex, Colchester. [0058235] 23/11/1999
Walkington Ms E, BA DipLib MCLIP, Unemployed. [0044435] 08/10/1990
Walkington Mrs NJ, (was Davies), BA MA, Housewife/Mother. [0043983] 21/03/1990
Walkins Mr PS, DFC MCLIP, Life Member, Tel.0202 684427, 27 Homedene Hse., Seldown Rd., Poole, Dorset, BH15 1UJ. [0015262] 28/01/1938
Walkinshaw Mr BR, BA MCLIP, Chief Lib., L.B.of Bromley. [0015263] 10/02/1965
Walkinshaw Mrs HA, MA DipLib MCLIP, Unemployed. [0027228] 10/01/1977
Wall Mrs AV, (was Haggett), BA(Hons) DipLib MCLIP, P./t.Lib., St.Albans Girls Sch., St.Albans. [0026397] 01/10/1976
Wall Mr CJ, MCLIP, Knowledge Specialist, Andersen Consulting, London. [0042387] 27/10/1988
Wall Ms CP, (was Chandler), MCLIP, Lib., Tuxford Comp.Sch., Newark, Notts. [0002571] 01/04/1968
Wall Ms G, BSc MSc, Employment not known. [0060208] 10/12/2001
Wall Mr MD, BSc DipLib MCLIP, Asst.Lib., Univ. of Bristol. [0039970] 07/10/1986
Wall Mrs MM, BA DipLib MCLIP, Team Lib.-Inf.& Ref., Banbridge Br.L., S.E.L.B. [0032712] 01/07/1980
Wall Ms MR, (was Hosey), BA DMS MCLIP, Princ.L.Serv.Offr., Sefton M.B.C. Leisure Serv., Merseyside. [0028021] 11/07/1977
Wall Dr RA, PhD FCLIP HonFCLIP, Life Member. [0015266] 24/01/1942 FE 01/01/1950
Wall Mrs RE, (was Matthews), MCLIP, Learning Res.Cent.Mgr., Cheltenham Kingsmead Sch., Cheltenham. [0009950] 02/02/1964
Wallace Miss A, BA MCLIP, Learning Res.Offr., Buxton Comm.Sch., Derbys.C.C. [0036588] 26/10/1983
Wallace Mr A, FCLIP DMA, Life Member. [0015269] 11/03/1936 FE 01/01/1951
Wallace Ms AME, BEd(Hons) DipIS MCLIP, Sch.Lib., Burntwood Sch., Wandsworth. [0050272] 25/04/1994
Wallace Mrs CA, (was Mayou), MCLIP, Sen.Asst.Lib., Business Insight, Birmingham Cent.L. [0031370] 19/10/1979
Wallace Mr DA, MCLIP, Life Member. [0015270] 17/03/1950
Wallace Miss EH, BA MCLIP, Inf.Offr., Euro-Inf.Cent.E.Anglia, Norwich. [0029862] 10/10/1978
Wallace Mrs EN, (was Hart), Scone Br.Lib., Perth & Kinross Council, Perth. [0048020] 02/11/1992
Wallace Mr EW, BSc(Hons) MA, Health Inf.Lib., NHS Direct S.E.London. [0054065] 22/10/1996
Wallace Ms GL, BA(Hons) DipILM, Higher L.Exec., House of Commons L., London. [0055598] 24/10/1997
Wallace Miss J, (was meiklejohn), MA DipLib MCLIP, Lect., Glasgow Coll.of Bldg.& Printing. [0030057] 09/11/1978
Wallace Mrs KM, (was Lamb), BA MCLIP, Area Lib., Chichester Grp., W.Sussex C.C. [0035316] 11/10/1982
Wallace Miss M, MCLIP, Lib., Warrington P.L. [0015274] 04/02/1971
Wallace Mrs M, MCLIP, Retired. [0015275] 08/03/1964
Wallace Mrs M, Sen.L.Super., Renfrewshire Council, Paisley. [0045535] 28/02/1991 AF
Wallace Mrs MG, (was Stephen), BA MCLIP DPA, Casual Lib., Falkirk Council L. [0023590] 21/01/1975
Wallace Mr PJ, BA MSc, Employment not known. [0060454] 11/12/2001
Wallace Mr PR, BA MCLIP, Sen.Comm.Lib., Allerton Community L., Liverpool. [0015277] 20/01/1972
Wallace Miss SA, BSc MCLIP, Sch.Lib., Brannock High.Sch., Motherwell. [0022840] 01/10/1974
Wallace Mrs SJ, Sch.L.Mgr., Redruth Sch., Cornwall. [0059417] 07/03/2001 AF
Wallace Mrs SM, BSc(Econ), Asst.Lib., Hartley L., Univ.of Southampton. [0061064] 01/02/2002
Wallace Mrs SM, (was Thorne), BLib PGCE MCLIP, Career Break. [0037194] 01/04/1984
Wallace Mrs TR, (was Gauld), DipLib MA MCLIP, Sen.Inf.Offr., Learning & Teaching Scotland, Dundee. [0032956] 03/10/1980
Wallace Mr W, MA MCLIP, Cent.L.& Inf.Serv.Mgr., Edinburgh City L. [0021896] 17/02/1974
Wallbank Mrs MM, (was Eaton), MCLIP, p./t.Community Lib., Flintshire C.C., Holywell. [0015324] 19/09/1970
Wallbank Mrs SP, (was Fairlamb), MCLIP, L.Asst., Monmouthshire C.C. [0020400] 23/02/1973
Waller Mrs A, (was Dobson), MCLIP, L.& Info.Offr., Newcastle City L., Cent.L. [0004003] 21/02/1972
Waller Miss AV, MCLIP, Life Member. [0015280] 12/09/1951
Waller Miss EL, BA(Hons) DipLib MCLIP, Br.Serv.Lib., Trafford M.B.C. [0036765] 14/12/1983
Waller Miss JC, BA(Hons) MA, Learning Resource C.Mgr., The Sheffield College. [0055364] 03/10/1997
Waller Mr RM, BD MCLIP, Support & Devel.Offr., Wigan Met.Bor. [0022509] 01/04/1974

Waller Mrs S, (was Meadows), MCLIP, L.Res.Mgr., Kent Coll., Pembury, Kent. [0022196] 18/02/1974
Waller Mrs SA, (was Meacock), BA MCLIP, Sch.Lib., Marlwood Sch., S.Glos. [0010012] 15/02/1972
Waller Mrs SM, (was Hines), FCLIP, Life Member, 33 Witheby, Cotmaton Rd, Sidmouth, EX10 8SR. [0015284] 01/01/1933 FE 01/01/1939
Wallis Miss CK, BSc(Hons) PgDLIS, Inf.Offr., The Environment Agency, Warrington. [0054161] 06/11/1996
Wallis Mrs JM, (was Sturdy), BA DipLib MCLIP, Lib., Norton Radstock Coll., Radstock. [0014185] 08/10/1968
Wallis Ms K, BA MCLIP, Grp.Lib., Oadby L., Leics.C.C. [0037358] 10/07/1984
Wallis Mrs KM, BA(Hons) MA, p./t.Stud./L.Asst., Loughborough Univ., Peterborough. [0059043] 07/11/2000
Wallis Ms MK, BA DipLib MCLIP, Head, Inf.Strategy Research Unit, Univ.of Brighton. [0020602] 24/04/1973
Wallis Miss SE, BA(Hons) MA, ICT Offr., Hants.L.Serv. [0056377] 01/07/1998
Wallis Mrs SM, (was George), MCLIP, Stock Lib., Lincs.Co.L., Lincs.C.C. [0015292] 17/04/1966
Wallner Mr RJG, BA BA MCLIP, Lib., Inchbald Sch.of Design, London. [0024191] 15/02/1975
Walls Miss PJ, MCLIP, Music Lib., Warwickshire C.C., Nuneaton, Warwickshire. [0015295] 17/02/1960
Walls Mr R, MA DipLib MCLIP, Asst.Lib., Harrogate Cent.L., N.Yorks.C.C. [0032210] 28/01/1980
Walmer Mr MH, BA, Bookseller, Waterstones. [0059869] 18/10/2001
Walmsley Mr AJ, BA MA DipLib MCLIP, Sen.Lib., Lancs.C.C., Harris L., Preston. [0042197] 10/10/1988
Walmsley Mrs CE, (was Perris), BA Joint Hons, Asst.Lib., S.Tyneside Coll., S.Shields. [0051473] 20/02/1995
Walmsley Mrs JB, (was Smith), BA MCLIP, Retired. [0013604] 09/01/1951
Walmsley Ms SJ, BA(Hons), Stud., Univ.Coll.London. [0059806] 03/10/2001
Walne Mrs LR, (was Knight), BA MCLIP, Retired. [0015300] 08/02/1952
Walne Mr MJ, BA(Hons), Asst.Lib., W.Middx.Univ.Hosp.NHS Trust, Isleworth. [0058872] 20/09/2000
Walpole Mr JM, BA MCLIP AIL, Life Member. [0017926] 29/10/1948
Walpole Miss L, BSc(Econ), Inf.Adviser, Havering Primary Care Trust, Harold Wood Hosp. [0059043] 12/01/1995
Walsgrove Ms SM, Sen.Learning Cent.Asst., Wolverhampton Coll., W.Midlands. [0045417] 21/01/1991 AF
Walsh Miss A, BA, Asst.Lib., Trinity Coll., Dublin. [0041352] 02/11/1987
Walsh Mrs AM, (was Kilgannon), BLib MCLIP, Asst.Dir., Academic & User Serv., Chester Coll. [0029994] 27/10/1978
Walsh Mrs DC, BA DipLib, Lib., City of Birmingham Educ.Dept. [0035014] 29/06/1982
Walsh Mr DM, p./t.Stud./L.Asst., Manchester Met.Univ., Bury L., Ref.& Inf.Serv. [0061163] 18/03/2002
Walsh Miss HM, MCLIP, Retired. [0015305] 19/10/1945
Walsh Mrs JA, (was Holmes), BA MCLIP, Lib. Bibl. Support. (Jobshare), N.Yorks. Co. L. H.Q., Northallerton. [0029396] 18/06/1978
Walsh Mrs JA, BA(Hons) MA, Sen.L.Asst., Univ.of Nottingham. [0054392] 02/12/1996
Walsh Mrs MJ, (was Walker), MCLIP, Asst.Area Lib., (Br.), Bolton P.L. [0015311] 02/02/1965
Walsh Mr PJ, M SC B ED MCLIP, Mgr.-Inf.Serv.Cent., King's Coll.London. [0020564] 18/04/1973
Walsh Mr PVN, MSc MCLIP, Inf.Sci., Credit Suisse Boston, London. [0060437] 11/12/2001
Walsh Miss RL, MSc, Inf.Offr., Linklaters & Paines, London. [0049199] 12/10/1993
Walsh Ms RM, p./t.Stud./Sen.L.Asst., Manchester Met.Univ., Millom L. [0061358] 24/06/2002
Walsh Mrs S, (was Whittle), BA DipLib MCLIP, Co-ordinator of L.Serv., to Young People, Plymouth City Council. [0035454] 05/10/1982
Walsh Mrs S, (was Shuttleworth), MCLIP, Young Peoples Serv.Lib.N.Herts., Herts.C.C., Baldock, Herts. [0023077] 29/10/1974
Walsh Mrs SA, (was Andrew), BSc HDLS MCLIP, Inf.Serv.Mgr., Dr J H Burgoyne & Partners, London. [0048350] 01/12/1992
Walter Mr MA, BA MCLIP, Peoples Network Off., Northants.L.& Inf.Serv., Northampton. [0018273] 03/10/1972
Walters Miss CE, BA(Hons) MA MCLIP, Lib., Kensington & Chelsea P.L. [0054815] 08/04/1997
Walters Mrs EB, BA MLib MCLIP, Br.Lib., Wandsworth Bor.Council, Balham L. [0038679] 01/10/1985
Walters Mrs FC, BA(Hons), Sen.L.Asst., Bristol Univ., Nuffield Coll.L. [0059308] 01/02/2001
Walters Mr J, BA MCLIP, Retired. [0015322] 23/02/1954
Walters Mrs KO, (was Lewis), BA DipLib MCLIP, Asst.Lib., The Athenaeum, London. [0033678] 09/02/1981
Walters Mr L, BSc MSc, Position unknown, McKinsey & Co. [0060482] 11/12/2001
Walters Miss MA, BA(Hons) MSc(Econ), Asst.Lib., Powys C.C., Newtown Area L. [0054621] 04/02/1997
Walters Mr RE, BA MCLIP, Princ.Lib. [Support], Bradford Council, Cent.L. [0015323] 12/09/1968
Walters Mr RJ, MA B PHIL MCLIP, Lib., Dept.for Educ.& Skills, London. [0018228] 06/10/1972
Walton Mrs A, BLib DMS MCLIP, L.Mgr., Environment Agency, Warrington. [0030611] 23/02/1979
Walton Mr AD, MCLIP, Life Member. [0015326] 01/01/1939
Walton Ms AL, BA(Hons) MLib MCLIP, Asst.Faculty Lib., Univ.Coll.Northampton. [0047949] 07/10/1991
Walton Mr GL, BA(Hons) MA MCLIP, p./t.Subject & Learning Supp.Lib., Staffs.Univ., Thompson L., Stoke-on-Trent. [0047672] 13/10/1992
Walton Miss HL, BLS MCLIP, Reader Serv.Mgr., Peterborough City Council, Cent.L. [0047213] 08/06/1992

373

Walton Mrs HM, (was Briercliffe), BA MCLIP, Advisory Lib., Sch.L.Serv., Suffolk C.C. [0038037] 08/01/1985
Walton Mrs IC, (was Purnell), BA(Hon)MA DipINF, Unemployed. [0049996] 07/02/1994
Walton Miss J, BA MCLIP MCIPD, Dir., Yorks.Mus.Council, Leeds. [0034683] 26/01/1982
Walton Mr JG, BSc MA MBA FETC MCLIP, Faculty Lib., Univ.of Northumbria at Newcastle. [0026599] 01/10/1992
Walton Ms JM, BA MPhil, Clinical Effectiveness Co-ord., E.Surrey P.C.G. [0059527] 25/04/2001 **AF**
Walton Ms N, BSc, Stud., Univ.Newcastle @ Northumbria. [0059799] 03/10/2001
Walton Ms RR, BA BSc MCLIP, Inf.Serv.Mgr./Ch.Lib., Inst.of Food Research, Colney, Norwich. [0060431] 11/12/2001
Walworth Dr JC, BA PhD, Fellow Lib., Merton Coll., Oxford. [0047108] 01/05/1992
Wan Miss LT, BSc MCLIP, Head, Acq., Singapore Poly. [0022159] 25/01/1974
Wan Dr YC, BA MPhil PhD MCLIP FHKLA, Sen.Sub.Lib., Univ.of Hong Kong L. [0041864] 26/04/1988
Wan Cheung Mrs MYA, Sen.Lib., Hong Kong P.L. [0041865] 26/04/1988
Wan Kee Cheung Miss CK, BSc(Hons) MA MCLIP, Enquiries & Comm.Offr., Comm.Fund, Leeds. [0054087] 24/10/1996
Wan-Yeoh Mrs SK, (was Yeoh), MLib BA, Asst.Dir./Tech.Serv., Temasek Poly.L., Singapore. [0046385] 01/11/1991
Wand Mr FR, MA MCLIP MRSA, Head of Lifelong Learning, Lancs.C.C. [0015334] 07/09/1967
Wands Miss J, BSc(Hons) DipLIS MCLIP, Inf.Sci., DSTL Knowledge Serv., Glasgow. [0051112] 16/11/1994
Wands Miss MC, MA DipLib, Asst.Lib., Aberdeen City Council, Aberdeen. [0037172] 20/03/1984
Wang Ms M, Assoc.Prof., Hsuan Chuang Univ., Dept.of L.& Inf.Sci., Taiwan. [0052083] 22/09/1995
Wang Mr RZ, BSc MSc, Employment not known. [0060814] 12/12/2001
Wanless Miss GE, BA MCLIP, Retired. [0015335] 03/01/1966
Wann Miss LS, BA(Hons) MCLIP, Asst.Lib., W.Middx.Univ.Hosp., Isleworth. [0056744] 08/10/1998
Wannop Miss S, BA DipLib MCLIP, Employment not known. [0042601] 17/01/1989
Want Mr CJ, MSc MCLIP, Unemployed. [0025678] 05/02/1976
Want Miss CVR, BA(Hons) MA, Asst.Inf.Mgr., Dept.of Trade & Industry, London. [0055353] 02/10/1997
Want Miss PC, MCLIP, Lib., Royal Coll.of Obstetricians &, Gynaecologists, London. [0015338] 10/11/1966
Warburton Mr JF, PGDip, Inf. Offr., Environment Agency, Bristol. [0061376] 01/07/2002
Warburton Mr RD, BA MCLIP, Asst.Head of Cult. Serv.(L.& Inf.), Kirklees Metro.Council. [0015339] 15/10/1968
Warburton Mrs SA, (was Edwards), MCLIP, Asst.Lib.,Local Studies, Rochdale MBC., Rochdale. [0004459] 06/01/1969
Warburton Mr SR, PGDipLS, Inf.Offr., Inf.Serv., Wellcome Trust, London. [0048767] 17/05/1993
Ward Mrs A, (was Hatfield), BA MA MCLIP, Inf.Spec., Sheffield Hallam Univ. [0029675] 02/10/1978
Ward Ms AD, BA(Hons), p./t.Stud./Learning Res.Mgr., Univ.of Brighton, Loxford Sch.of Sci.& Tech., Ilford. [0057769] 29/07/1999
Ward Mrs AE, (was Johnston), MA DipLib FCLIP, Inf.& L.Serv.Mgr., Learning & Skills Council, Coventry. [0034318] 11/10/1981 **FE 16/11/1994**
Ward Mr AJ, BA MCLIP, Reader Devel.Lib., Northampton Area. [0019934] 16/01/1973
Ward Mrs BJ, Learning Serv.Co-ordinator, The Study Cent., Yeovil Coll. [0061084] 01/03/2002 **AF**
Ward Mr C, LLB(Hons) MA, Asst.Lib., Field Fisher Waterhouse, London. [0056988] 18/11/1998
Ward Mrs CA, (was Lawrence), BA DipLib MCLIP, Full-time mother. [0042709] 10/02/1989
Ward Miss CD, Co.Lib., Faber Maunsell, St.Albans. [0054005] 17/10/1996 **AF**
Ward Miss CE, Inf.Lib., Chelmsford L., Essex. [0035486] 19/10/1982
Ward Mrs DM, (was Powell), MCLIP, Princ.Lib., Sch.L.& Inf.Serv., Dudley M.B.C. [0011858] 26/09/1969
Ward Mr DP, BA(Hons) DipLib MCLIP, Academic Serv.Mgr., Royal Holloway, Univ.of London, Egham. [0015345] 01/01/1970
Ward Mrs EF, BA(Hons) MA MCLIP, Team Lib., Norfolk C.C. [0050632] 01/10/1994
Ward Mrs FM, BLib, Lib., House of Commons L. [0059322] 07/02/2001
Ward Mrs G, (was Metcalf), p./t.Br.Lib., Lancs.C.C., E.Lancs.Div. [0039420] 23/01/1986
Ward Mr GBJ, BA(Hons) PGCE MEd MSc, Sen.L.Asst., Univ.of Sheffield. [0057644] 09/06/1999
Ward Miss H, BA MCLIP, Mgr.-Update Standards, B.S.I., Chiswick, London. [0019908] 08/01/1973
Ward Mrs HJ, (was Clayton), BA MSc, Asst.Lib., Chartered Inst.of Marketing, Cookham. [0053989] 14/10/1996
Ward Mrs J, (was Leary), BA MCLIP, Sch.Teacher, Bucks.C.C., Amersham. [0025583] 29/01/1976
Ward Ms JL, BA, Lib., London Underground., London. [0056696] 05/10/1998
Ward Mrs JM, (was Silvester), FCLIP, Retired. [0015353] 18/09/1940 **FE 01/01/1946**
Ward Mrs KE, (was Taylor), BA MCLIP, Sen.L.Asst., Univ.of Sheffield L. [0038271] 11/02/1985
Ward Mrs KM, (was Wood), BA MCLIP, Lib., Thompsons Solicitors, Manchester. [0016205] 25/04/1969
Ward Mrs LJ, (was Kerfoot), BA MCLIP, Knowledge Co-ordinator, Inf.Devel.Dept., CSU Ltd., Manchester. [0041819] 21/04/1988

Ward Mrs LM, BSc(Hons) MSc MCLIP, Clinical Lib., Univ.Hosp.of Leicester NHS Trust, Leicester Gen.Hosp. [0052672] 17/11/1995
Ward Mrs M, BA MCLIP, Res.Cent.Mgr., Glasgow City Council. [0036613] 10/10/1983
Ward Mr ML, MLIB MCLIP, Inf.Specialist, Ricardo Consulting Engineers, Shoreham-by-Sea, W.Sussex. [0015359] 22/04/1970
Ward Mr MS, Curatorial Asst., Nat.Art L., Victoria & Albert Mus. [0047313] 10/07/1992
Ward Mr NJ, BA MA DMS MCLIP, Head of L.& Arts, Solihull M.B.C. [0028201] 04/10/1977
Ward Ms NR, Stud., Univ.of Brighton. [0061261] 10/05/2002
Ward Mrs P, (was Coyle), BLS MCLIP, Sen.Lib., Cent.L., Londonderry. [0034740] 20/01/1982
Ward Mr PEM, MA MA DipLib PhD, Higher L.Exec., Research Serv., House of Commons L. [0038926] 21/10/1985
Ward Miss PL, BA DipLib MCLIP, Sen.Asst.L., House of Lords L. [0036545] 21/10/1983
Ward Mrs PM, (was Elgey), BA ATCL MCLIP MLib, Lib., St.Marys Coll., Blackburn. [0018203] 05/10/1972
Ward Mr R, BA MCLIP FBIS, Asst.Lib., Dept.of Health L., London. [0015363] 01/01/1965
Ward Mrs RA, MCLIP, Child.Co-Ord., Cent.Grp., Notts Co.L. [0001700] 28/09/1962
Ward Mrs RH, (was Naylor), BA MCLIP, Principal Lib., Northants.C.C., Weston Favell L. [0026491] 06/10/1976
Ward Mr RJ, MLib MCLIP, Head of Arts & L., Kent C.C. [0015364] 30/05/1968
Ward Mr RM, Inf.Asst., Univ.of Salford, Academic Inf.Serv. [0049599] 19/11/1993
Ward Miss S, BA(Hons), Stud. [0061752] 01/11/2002
Ward Mrs S, (was Chivers), MA CertEd MCLIP, Subject Lib., Bolton Inst.of H.E., Lancs. [0021938] 01/02/1974
Ward Mrs S, (was Muirhead), MCLIP, Sch.Lib., Arnold Hill Sch., Nottingham. [0010555] 17/02/1969
Ward Mrs SA, BA, Asst.Catr., Mountbatten L., Southampton. [0059565] 30/05/2001 **AF**
Ward Dr SE, BSc PhD CertEd FCLIP HonFCLIP, Hon.Fellow. [0060663] 11/12/2001 **FE 01/04/2002**
Ward Miss SF, MSc, Inf.Specialist, Sheffield Hallam Univ. [0034240] 16/10/1981
Ward Mrs SM, (was Boothroyd), BA MA MCLIP, Asst.Child.Lib., Chesterfield L., Derbys.C.C. [0029898] 23/10/1978
Ward Mr T, BLib MCLIP, Head of L.Serv., Prince Consort's L., Aldershot. [0024306] 07/06/1975
Warden Miss JA, MCLIP, Lib., Cheshire C.C., Northwich L. [0015368] 11/10/1966
Warden Mrs JA, (was Burrows), MCLIP, Unemployed. [0002145] 14/10/1971
Wardlaw Ms JE, BA(Hons) MA MCLIP, Asst.Lib., Dept for Educ.& Skills, London. [0051301] 01/01/1995
Wardle Mrs KA, MA MCLIP, Employment not known. [0060763] 12/12/2001
Wardle Mr RJ, BA DipLib MCLIP, Asst.Lib., Britannia Royal Naval Coll. [0036364] 05/10/1983
Wardle Mrs WA, (was Eades), BA MCLIP, Head of Learning Resources, Woodway Pk.Sch., Coventry. [0031259] 10/10/1979
Wardrope Miss A, L.& Study Cent.Mgr., Stevenson Coll., Edinburgh. [0035750] 14/01/1983
Ware Ms CH, (was Wood), BA BLS MIIS, Team Leader, Enquiry & Market Intelligence, Business Link London W. [0042007] 18/07/1988
Ware Mr PT, BA MCLIP, Comm.Liaison Lib., Thamesmead L., L.B.of Bexley. [0023105] 08/10/1974
Wareham Mrs AD, MCLIP, Lib.& H.of Inf.Servs., Royal Naval Mus., Portsmouth. [0037825] 06/11/1984
Wareing Ms G, BA(Hons) DipLib, Sen.Inf.Offr., SHS International Ltd., Liverpool. [0049070] 01/10/1993
Wares Mr C, BA(Hons) MA MCLIP, Dir.of Inf.Serv., BPP Law Sch., London. [0052029] 02/10/1995
Warhurst Mrs CM, (was Fountain), BA MCLIP, Lib., L.B.of Greenwich. [0025276] 05/01/1976
Warhurst Ms S, (was McKnight), BScEcon(Hons), Tech.Analyst & Bus.Inf.Consultant, London. [0043070] 11/07/1989 **AF**
Waring Ms H, BA MCLIP, p./t.Lib., Business L., Nottingham. [0015378] 29/09/1970
Waring Mr JG, Area Mgr., Coutts L.Serv.(UK), Ringwood. [0050925] 17/10/1990 **SP**
Wark Mr PP, MCLIP, Princ.Lib., Midlothian Council, Loanhead. [0021511] 22/10/1973
Warmington Mr J, MA DipLib MCLIP, Civil Servant, Dept.for Work & Pensions. [0015379] 07/09/1966
Warmoth Mrs KM, (was Stalker), BA DipLib, Lib., Fladgate Fielder., London. [0041141] 08/10/1987
Warne Mr P, MA MCLIP, Life Member. [0015380] 13/02/1960
Warneford Mrs CM, (was Peskett), MCLIP, Asst.Lib., Malvern L., Worcs.C.C. [0011568] 01/01/1965
Warner Mr AD, BA(Hons) MCLIP, Sch.Lib., Guiseley Sch., Leeds [0053914] 10/10/1996
Warner Mr AM, BA, Head of DISC, DG Inf., Swindon. [0033442] 05/01/1981
Warner Miss AR, BA MCLIP, Asst.Lib., DTLR L., London. [0023535] 05/01/1975
Warner Miss CS, BA(Hons) MA, Asst.Lib., Gateshead L., Co.Durham. [0056621] 21/09/1998
Warner Mrs FM, BA DipLib MCLIP, Comm.Lib.(Job Share), Bishopbriggs L., E.Dunbartonshire Council. [0035307] 10/10/1982
Warner Miss HC, BA(Hons) MA, Lib., Rochester Grammar Sch.for Girls, Kent. [0058491] 23/02/2000

Warner Mrs J, (was Booth), MCLIP, L.Serv.Mgr., Park Lane Coll., Leeds. [0001481]   03/10/1969
Warner Mrs JA, (was Williams), MCLIP, Inf.Asst., Sports Council, Birmingham. [0023281]   18/11/1974
Warner Dr JC, BA MA MA(Lib) DPhil MCLIP, Lect., Sch.of Mgmt.& Economics, The Queens Univ.of Belfast. [0036650]   31/10/1983
Warner Mrs JM, (was Beard), BSc(Hons), p./t.Stud./L.Asst., Brookland Coll., Weybridge, Surrey. [0058392]   20/01/2000
Warner Miss S, BA(Hons) MSc MCLIP, Princ.Inf.Offr., Consumers Assoc., London. [0049202]   12/10/1993
Warner Ms SL, MCLIP, Employment not known. [0060490]   11/12/2001
Warner Miss SM, BA(Hons) PGCert InfMgt, ICT Lib., Newham L.Serv., London. [0051793]   01/07/1996
Warner Mr T, BA MA MCLIP, Lib., Notts.C.C. [0040326]   21/01/1987
Warnock Mr AP, MA DipLib, Unemployed. [0029865]   19/10/1978
Warr Dr WA, MA DPhilCChem FRSC FCLIP, Position unknown, Wendy Warr & Assoc., Crewe. [0060615]   11/12/2001   FE 01/04/2002
Warren Mrs AS, (was Carter), MA MCLIP, Asst.Lib., Milton Keynes L., Bucks. Co.Council. [0015391]   27/11/1967
Warren Miss BM, MCLIP, Life Member. [0015392]   14/03/1952
Warren Mrs CM, (was Woolston), MCLIP, Brit.Embassy. [0017935]   01/09/1959
Warren Ms D, (was Headley), PGDipLib, Lib., Bevan Ashford, Bristol. [0041779]   08/04/1988
Warren Mrs DM, (was Clarke), MCLIP, Sch.Lib., Biddenham Upper Sch., Beds.C.C. [0002760]   25/01/1969
Warren Mr GR, BA MCLIP, Dir., The L.Partnership, W.Midlands. [0019389]   01/10/1972
Warren Mrs H, (was Marjoram), BA MCLIP, Sch.Lib., Amberfield Sch., Ipswich. [0005599]   29/09/1971
Warren Mrs I, BA(Hons), L.Asst., E.Sussex Co.L.Serv., Lewes. [0049376]   01/11/1993
Warren Mrs J, (was Vaughton), BA MCLIP, L.Asst., Hillel Day Sch., Farmington Hills, USA. [0015088]   17/11/1971
Warren Ms K, BA DipInf, Sen.Researcher, KPMG., London. [0053690]   06/09/1996
Warren Mrs MD, (was Brice), BSc MCLIP, Retired. [0001697]   27/01/1959
Warren Mr PJ, BA ALCM MCLIP, Course.Res Off., Univ.of Brighton. [0015395]   01/10/1965
Warren Mr PJR, BA MCLIP, Life Member. [0015396]   19/09/1952
Warren Mrs RA, (was Buckett), BA MCLIP, p./t.Asst.Lib., St.Loye's Sch.of Health Studies, Exeter. [0015397]   18/10/1967
Warren Ms S, (was Ainscough), BA MCLIP, Dir.of Inf.Serv., Halliwell Landau, Manchester. [0041531]   14/01/1988
Warren Mrs SP, (was Powell), BA DipLib MCLIP, Unemployed. [0022997]   02/10/1974
Warren Mrs VM, (was Hurrey), BA MCLIP, Head of Lifelong Learning, & Soc.Inclusion, L.Inf.& Arts, E.Sussex C.C., Lewes. [0015398] 16/10/1969
Warren Mrs YE, (was Taylor), BA MCLIP, Cent.L.Mgr., Doncaster M.B.C., Cent.L. [0029288]   15/05/1978
Warren-Morgan Miss K, MCLIP, Sen.Lib.-Ref./Local Hist., Rhondda-Cynon-Taff Co.Bor.Council, Aberdare L. [0015399]   23/01/1961
Warrilow Mr RJ, BSc MCLIP, Resident in Australia. [0060080]   07/12/2001
Warrington Mr B, BA MCLIP, Retired. [0015404]   12/01/1951
Warrington Mrs SR, (was Cayton), MCLIP, Semi-retired., NVQ Assessor, City Coll.Manchester. [0042839]   01/01/1952
Warwick Mrs J, (was Fairhurst), MCLIP, Sen.Lib.(Child),p./t., Wokingham Unitary Auth. [0010818]   15/10/1966
Warwick Mrs LJ, (was Stratton), BA(Hons) MCLIP, Employment not known. [0014138]   07/02/1969
Washington Mr B, BA(Hons) MSc MCLIP, Inf.Serv.Mgr., Sports Marketing Surveys Ltd., Wisley. [0042947]   27/04/1989
Washington Dr L, BA MA MCLIP, Lib., Seeley L., Cambridge. [0042571]   03/01/1989
Wass Mrs HM, (was Easton), DipHE MCLIP, P./t.Sch.Lib., Peterborough City Council, Peterborough. [0026681]   14/10/1976
Waterhouse Mr I, Stud., Brighton Univ. [0059839]   16/10/2001
Waterhouse Mrs LJ, (was Ratcliffe), MCLIP, Ref.Lib., Rawtenstall L., Lancs.Co.L. [0012162]   21/09/1971
Waterhouse Mr N, BA(Hons), Stud., Sheffield Univ. [0059838]   16/10/2001
Waters Miss CJ, BA MA, Inf.Specialist, QinetiQ. [0046649]   02/12/1991
Waters Mrs G, (was Fargher), MCLIP, Asst.Lib., L.B.of Bromley. [0015419]   15/01/1967
Waters Mrs J, (was Killingbeck), BSc MCLIP, Inf.Consultant, Univ.of Herts., Hatfield. [0015422]   09/09/1968
Waters Mrs JA, (was Darlington), DipLib MCLIP MA(Ed), Sch.Lib., Weydon Sch.(Surrey C.C.), Farnham, Surrey. [0044305]   22/08/1990
Waters Mrs JS, BA, User Serv.Lib., Totton Coll., Southampton. [0036049]   01/05/1983
Waters Mrs MJ, (was Breen), Lib.(Job Share), Derbys.C.C., Matlock. [0029369]   01/07/1978
Waters Mr PJ, BA DipLIS MCLIP, Inf.Specialist., GCHQ. [0043355]   25/10/1989
Waterson Mr ES, MA FCLIP, Life Member. [0015424]   06/10/1949   FE 01/01/1958
Waterson Ms S, BA MCLIP, Resident in U.S.A. [0021258]   14/10/1973
Waterston Mr DT, PGDipLIS, p./t.Asst.Lib., E.Kilbride Cent.L. [0057361]   19/02/1999
Waterton Mr MJ, Cashier, Wickes Home Improvement Cent., Hemel Hempstead, Herts. [0057004]   23/11/1998
Watford Mrs SMM, (was Gaw), BA MCLIP, Unemployed. [0038940]   18/10/1985
Wathern Ms AK, BA(Hons) DipLib, Maternity Leave. [0046957]   11/03/1992
Watkin Mr A, BA DipLib FCLIP MIMgt FRSA, Ch.Offr.-L.,Leisure & Culture., Co.Bor.of Wrexham, Wrexham. [0023110]   24/10/1974   FE 19/08/1992

Watkin Ms RM, BA(Hons), Asst.Lib., Swansea Inst.of H.E. [0047204]   02/06/1992
Watkins Mrs AE, (was Curtis), MA MCLIP, Arts & L.Offr., Kent C.C., Dartford Cent.L.,Dartford, Kent. [0015427]   19/09/1967
Watkins Ms CA, BA MCLIP, Inf.Res.Mgr., Simmons & Simmons, London. [0015431]   21/01/1971
Watkins Mrs CJH, (was Hurley), BA(Hons) MCLIP, Team Lib.-Electronic Inf., Glos.C.C., L.Arts & Mus.Serv. [0046493]   13/11/1991
Watkins Mr DT, BA(Hons) DipLib, Principal Inf.Serv.Lib., L.B.Waltham Forest, London. [0036136]   13/06/1983
Watkins Mrs FR, (was Norman), MCLIP, Volunteer Lib., RHS Wisley, Surrey. [0024120]   08/04/1975
Watkins Mrs H, (was McIntyre), BA(Hons), Product Specialist, Epixtech Ltd. [0035668]   05/01/1983   AF
Watkins Ms HM, BA MA MCLIP, Subject Advisor (Art & Design), Univ.of Derby. [0042099]   01/10/1988
Watkins Mr IA, BSc(Hons) DipLib, Ass.Lib., City Business Library., London. [0051836]   11/07/1995
Watkins Mrs JM, (was Hosford), BA MCLIP, Asst.Catr., Thames Valley Univ. [0015434]   18/10/1966
Watkins Mrs MA, (was Camps), BA MCLIP, Sen.Lib.-Sch.L.Serv., Birmingham L.Serv., Cent.L. [0025235]   05/01/1976
Watkins Miss TJ, BA DipLib MCLIP, Sch.Lib., King Edward VI Five Ways Sch., Birmingham. [0041224]   16/10/1987
Watkins Mrs VE, (was Graham), BA(Hons) DipIT MCLIP, Sch.Lib., Belfast Royal Acad. [0019973]   04/01/1973
Watkinson Ms AH, BA(Hons), Sen.L.Asst., Health Sci.L., Univ.of Sheffield. [0051317]   10/01/1995
Watkinson Mrs J, (was Webber), BA MCLIP, Grp.Lib.,E.Calderdale, Calderdale L., Halifax. [0035539]   29/10/1982
Watkinson Mrs JM, MA MCLIP, LRC Asst., Belmont Comp.Sch., Durham. [0015440]   01/01/1967
Watkinson Ms NJ, BSc MCLIP, Acad.Liaison Co-ordinator, NEWI., Wrexham. [0058588]   06/04/2000
Watkinson Mrs PM, (was Russell), BA MCLIP, p./t.Asst.Lend.Lib., Salisbury, Wilts.Co.L. [0020004]   08/01/1973
Watkis Mrs MJ, (was Thornhill), MCLIP, Lib., Glos.Co.L. [0019116]   31/08/1972
Watkiss Miss BM, BSc(Hons), Box Office/Admin.Asst., British Film Inst., London. [0059352]   13/02/2001
Watkiss Mrs EL, (was Baker), BA(Hons) MCLIP, Research Mgr., Ernst & Young, Birmingham. [0043566]   08/11/1989
Watkiss Mrs JM, BA(Hons) DipILM, L.Super., Prestwich L., Bury MBC. [0055090]   08/07/1997
Watkiss Mrs ST, (was Burman), BA MCLIP, Unemployed. [0030819]   03/05/1979
Watling Mrs PC, (was Dawson), MCLIP, Retired. [0031043]   01/01/1957
Watmough Miss DJ, MCLIP, Site Mgr., Health L., S.Bank Univ., Harold Wood Hosp., London. [0021609]   27/11/1973
Watson Mr A, BTech MCLIP, Employment not known. [0060199] 10/12/2001
Watson Mrs A, LLB DipILM, p./t.Lib.Asst., Northumberland L.E.A. [0052983]   12/02/1996
Watson Mr AJ, (was Hulme), MSc MCLIP, p./t.Home Literature Searcher, Royal Coll.of Nursing, London. [0037755]   23/10/1984
Watson Mrs C, BA MCLIP, Plymouth L.Mgr., Univ.of Plymouth. [0015459]   01/01/1969
Watson Mr CCW, BA MCLIP, Sen.Lib., Defence Procurement Agency, Bristol. [0024844]   01/10/1975
Watson Miss CM, MA PGDip, On-Line Website Editor, The Herald, Glasgow. [0056827]   19/10/1998
Watson Mrs DAH, (was Greaves), MCLIP, Unemployed. [0005852]   04/01/1971
Watson Mr DJ, BA MCLIP, Med.Lib., Southern Derbyshire Acute Hosp., NHS Trust. [0040937]   05/09/1987
Watson Mr DT, MA DipLib MCLIP, Network Lib., The Gordon Schools, Aberdeenshire. [0041761]   07/03/1988
Watson Mr DV, BA MCLIP, Lib., Cunninghame Dist.L., N.Ayrshire L. [0028387]   11/11/1977
Watson Miss EA, BSc(Hons) MSc, Med.Inf.Resources Mgr., Schering Health Care Ltd., Burgess Hill. [0049247]   18/10/1993
Watson Ms EA, BA DipLib MCLIP, Res.Lib., Wolverhampton Univ., Burton on Trent. [0033616]   27/01/1981
Watson Ms EF, MLS BA FCLIP, Lib., Learning Res.Cent., Univ.of The W.I. [0024569]   16/02/1970   FE 21/03/2001
Watson Mrs GF, (was Taylor), BA MCLIP, Acquisitions Lib., Queens Univ.Belfast. [0019642]   26/10/1972
Watson Ms H, BA(Hons) MA MCLIP, Asst.Lib., Bevan Ashford, Exeter. [0048829]   16/06/1993
Watson Mrs HK, BA, Curator F, Nat.Galleries of Scotland, Edinburgh. [0048431]   06/01/1993
Watson Mrs HM, (was Bravington), MCLIP, Retired. [0015450]   19/01/1940
Watson Mr I, BA MCLIP, Head of Lib.Arch.& Inf., City of Bradford Met.Dist.Council. [0035028]   04/07/1982
Watson Mr I, MA MCLIP, Position unknown, Scottish Media Newspapers, Glasgow. [0061328] 29/05/2002
Watson Miss J, BA(Hons), Clinical Inf.Analyst, ATTRACT, Gwent Health Auth. [0051236]   01/12/1994
Watson Miss J, BEng(Hons) MA, Inf.Spec., (Physical Sci.& Engineering), Kings College London. [0057852]   10/09/1999
Watson Miss J, B LIB MCLIP, Asst.Customer Serv.Lib., Fife Council, Kirkcaldy Cent.L. [0023074]   21/10/1974
Watson Mr J, DMS MCLIP, Sen.Mgr., Local Hist.L., Greenwich L. [0015451]   28/04/1967
Watson Mrs J, (was Hampton), BA MCLIP, p./t.Lib., Essex C.C., Colchester Cent.L. [0034689]   29/01/1982

375

Watson Mrs JE, (was Ashcroft), BA(Hons), Lib., L.Associates, Beverly Hills, California. [0050899] 28/10/1994
Watson Mrs JL, (was Mason), BA(Hons) MCLIP MTh(Oxon), Asst.Lib.(Systems/IT), Fire Serv.Coll.L., Moreton in Marsh, Glos. [0049936] 01/01/1963
Watson Mr JW, Journals Asst., ICAEW, London. [0058078] 25/10/1999
Watson Ms JY, MA(Hons) DipLIS, Head of Requests/Res.Offr., W.Lothian Council L., L.H.Q., Blackburn. [0048052] 03/11/1992
Watson Mrs LC, MA BPHIL ED MCLIP, Dep.Lib., Exeter Coll. [0040118] 16/10/1986
Watson Miss LJ, BA(Hons) DipILM MCLIP, Lib., Leics.C.C. [0052015] 12/09/1995
Watson Mrs LS, (was Gray), MCLIP, L.Asst., Herts.C.C., St.Albans. [0018110] 04/10/1972
Watson Mr M, BA MCLIP, Asst.Dir.(Support Servs.), Gateshead P.L. [0015455] 19/05/1967
Watson Mrs M, (was Maguire), BSc MCLIP, Lib., N.N.C.Ltd., Knutsford, Cheshire. [0009616] 01/01/1964
Watson Mrs MA, (was Leggett), BA MA MCLIP, Principal Lecturer, Univ.of Northumbria at Newcastle. [0015456] 21/09/1966
Watson Mr MJ, BA(Hons) DipILM MCLIP, Asst.Subject Lib., Oxford Brookes Univ. [0057428] 01/04/1999
Watson Miss MM, MA DipLib MCLIP, Asst.Lib., Bodleian L., Oxford. [0035181] 06/10/1982
Watson Miss MS, MA DipLib MCLIP, Lib./Legal Dept., BAA Plc., London. [0027727] 01/01/1960
Watson Mr N, BA(Hons) MSc, Inf.Lib., Univ.of Bath, L.& Learning Cent. [0058822] 14/08/2000
Watson Mr PJ, BA(Hons) PGDip, p./t.Stud./Inf.Asst., Manchester Met.Univ., Liverpool John Moores Univ. [0059086] 13/11/2000
Watson Mr RDJ, MA(Oxon) PgDipILS PGCE, Unemployed. [0054291] 13/11/1996
Watson Mr RF, FCLIP, Retired. [0015462] 19/10/1936 **FE 01/01/1949**
Watson Mr RP, BSc MCLIP, Customer Consultant, Talis Inf.Ltd., Inst.of Research & Devel. [0015463] 15/02/1971
Watson Miss S, BA(Hons) MA MCLIP, Quality Assurance Mgr., Whitaker Inf.Serv., Stevenage, Herts. [0050625] 01/10/1994
Watson Miss S, BA(Hons), Careers Lib., Univ.Coll.London. [0055552] 20/10/1997
Watson Miss SD, Retired. [0015465] 03/02/1956
Watson Mrs SE, (was Forman), MCLIP, p./t.Lib., Nottingham City Council. [0022583] 11/07/1974
Watson Mrs SJ, (was Slack), BA MCLIP, Project Lib.-Books for Babies, Derbys.C.c. [0034774] 12/02/1982
Watson Miss SM, BA MCLIP, Reader Serv.Lib., Stretford L., Trafford Educ., Arts & Leisure. [0028717] 09/01/1978
Watson Mr T, BA(Hons), Inf.Offr., Alzheimers Soc., Newcastle upon Tyne. [0061348] 07/06/2002
Watson Mrs V, (was Wofford), BA MCLIP, Self-employed. [0032618] 13/06/1980
Watson Mr WH, BA MCLIP, Team Lib., Glasgow District L. [0026655] 27/10/1976
Watson Mr WJH, BA(Hons) FCLIP, Retired. [0015467] 25/03/1951 **FE 30/08/1972**
Watson Mr WM, DAES FCLIP, Life Member. [0015468] 09/08/1950 **FE 01/01/1958**
Watson-Bore Mrs J, (was Watson), BA CertEd MCLIP, Dir.of L., Ashford Sch., Kent. [0027230] 04/02/1977
Watt Mrs AJ, (was Thomas), BA MCLIP, Young Person's Offr., Halton Bor.Council, Runcorn, Cheshire. [0039597] 14/03/1986
Watt Ms DM, BSc, Stud., UCL. [0061629] 09/10/2002
Watt Mr I, MCLIP, Head of Serv., Parliamentary Doc.Cent., European Parliament, Bruxelles. [0035873] 04/02/1983
Watt Mrs JM, (was Smart), MA(Hons) MSc, Inf.Mgr., UK Transplant, Stoke Gifford, Bristol. [0047193] 28/05/1992
Watt Mr RW, BA(Hons) DipLib, Document Delivery Serv.Team Leader, London Univ., Kings Coll.London. [0043307] 17/10/1989
Watt Ms SC, DipLib MCLIP, Employment not known. [0060822] 12/12/2001
Watt Mrs SJ, (was Gillespie), BA MCLIP, Unemployed. [0042671] 07/02/1989
Watt Mrs SM, (was Gill), BA MCLIP, Team Lib., (Job-share), Newcastle City L. [0033295] 16/10/1980
Watt Mrs VAC, (was Cumming), MA(Hons) MA, Faculty Team Lib., Univ.of Leeds. [0054711] 06/03/1997
Watt Mr WJ, MCLIP, Glasgow L.& Arch. [0022085] 25/01/1974
Wattam Mrs YJ, (was Harvey), BA MSc, Asst.Lib., Record Off.(Arch.), Leicester. [0056917] 04/11/1998
Watters Mr JWH, MCLIP, Life Member. [0015472] 27/01/1952
Watthews Miss EM, BA MCLIP, Life Member. [0015474] 12/01/1954
Watts Ms AE, BSc MSc MCLIP, Inf.Cent.Mgr., PJB Publications Ltd. [0033186] 15/09/1980
Watts Miss G, MCLIP, Retired. [0015481] 04/02/1935
Watts Miss GL, BA (Hons), Sales Specialist., Clarks Ltd., Manchester. [0060124] 10/12/2001
Watts Miss H, Stud., Sheffield Univ. [0061793] 08/11/2002
Watts Mr J, Stud., Univ.of North London. [0060921] 10/01/2002
Watts Miss NJ, BSc MSc MCLIP, Employment not known. [0060706] 12/12/2001
Watts Mrs NJ, BA(Hons), Child.Inf.Serv.Offr., Brighton & Hove Council. [0052674] 17/11/1995
Watts Mrs PE, (was Dowling), MCLIP, Unemployed. [0004128] 23/01/1967
Watts Mr SD, MCLIP, Inf.Lib., Mid Sussex Grp., W.Sussex Co.L. [0015484] 01/01/1966
Watts Mr SG, BA CChem MRSC MCLIP, Position unknown, Brit.L., London. [0060744] 12/12/2001
Watts Mr SL, BA DipLib, Retired. [0030060] 26/10/1978

Waudby Mr AD, MCLIP, Life Member, 35 Grigor Drive, Inverness, IV2 4LS. [0017938] 01/01/1939
Waugh Mrs JD, BA DipLib MCLIP, Marketing & Res.Co-ordinator, Essex C.C., L., Chelmsford. [0033502] 12/01/1981
Waugh Mrs ME, (was Fawcett), BSc DipLib MCLIP, Learning Res.Mgr.(Job Share), KGV Coll., Southport. [0028952] 13/02/1978
Waugh Mrs S, (was Carr), MCLIP, Unemployed. [0023697] 13/01/1975
Way Mr DJ, MA FCLIP, Life Member. [0015492] 24/01/1951 **FE 01/01/1958**
Wayne Mrs L, (was Goldberg), BA MCLIP, Lib., John Smeaton Community High Sch., Leeds. [0021931] 24/01/1974
Wayte Miss AC, MCLIP, L.Mgr., Southwark P.L. [0015494] 12/01/1965
Weal Mrs PBM, Retired. [0045526] 26/02/1991 **AF**
Weare Mrs J, (was Dowsett), MA BA MCLIP, Hist.Researcher. [0015496] 13/03/1964
Wearing Mrs C, (was Legumi), BA MCLIP, Lib.Serv.Mgr., Medway Hosp.NHS Trust, Gillingham. [0035001] 08/06/1982
Weatherall Mrs JIJ, MA DipLib, Sch.Lib., Friends Sch., Saffron Walden, Essex. [0034960] 14/05/1982
Weatherall Mr P, BSc MCLIP, Learning Res.Mgr., Isle of Man Internat.Bus.Sch., Douglas. [0015498] 01/01/1970
Weatherhead Ms SJ, MA MCLIP, Sen.Lib., Cent.for Oxfordshire Studies, Cent.L. [0029433] 18/07/1978
Weatherley Mrs S, (was Bowler), MCLIP, Res.Mgr., Derbys.L.& Heritage Dept. [0018514] 25/01/1968
Weatherly Mr H, FCLIP, Life Member. [0015500] 01/01/1953 **FE 01/01/1968**
Weatherly Miss K, MCLIP, L.Serv.Devel.Mgr., N.W.Surrey L., Surrey C.C. [0015501] 13/01/1967
Weaver Mrs EA, (was Lett), BA MCLIP, Stud. [0038058] 08/01/1985
Weaver Ms HJ, Admin.Offr., Police Training Cent.Force L., Braintree. [0061319] 17/05/2002 **AF**
Weaver Mrs M, BA, Shaftesbury Assoc., Toronto. [0054996] 12/06/1997
Weaver Mrs ML, (was Castle), BA MCLIP MSc, Head of User Support, Univ.of Cent.Lancs. [0044022] 05/04/1990
Weavers Ms SP, (was Bevan), BA MCLIP, Reg.Sales Mgr., Ingenta, Oxford. [0025318] 15/01/1976
Weaving Mrs BV, (was Tombs), MCLIP, Retired. [0015506] 08/07/1946
Webb Ms AE, MBA DipIM, Self-employed. [0059704] 14/08/2001
Webb Ms CA, BA(Hons), Stud., Loughborough Univ. [0061063] 14/02/2002
Webb Miss CJM, BA MA MCLIP, Sch.Lib., Forest Hill Sch., London. [0037905] 07/11/1984
Webb Mr DR, BA FCLIP, Life Member. [0015513] 10/03/1962 **FE 28/01/1975**
Webb Ms ER, BA(Hons) MA MCLIP, Periodicals Lib., Univ. of Sunderland., Tyne & Wear. [0031491] 08/10/1979
Webb Mrs GJ, BA MCLIP, Area Lib., So'ton City Council, E.L. [0015516] 03/01/1972
Webb Miss GM, BA MCLIP, Team Lib.-Local Servs., Kent Co.Arts & L., Dartford L. [0022766] 20/09/1974
Webb Mrs GM, MCLIP, Retired. [0013332] 01/01/1965
Webb Miss HS, MA, Bibl.Serv.L., Royal Coll.of Surgeons, London. [0055897] 15/12/1997
Webb Ms J, BA MSc DipLib MCLIP, p./t.Asst.Lib., Univ.of the W.of England, Bristol. [0037043] 26/01/1984
Webb Ms JM, MA MLib MBA ILTM MCLIP, Academic Lib., De Montfort Univ., Leicester. [0042399] 27/10/1988
Webb Miss LA, BSc(Hons) DipILS, Lib., Newbury Coll., Berks. [0053126] 07/03/1996
Webb Mrs LM, MCLIP, L.Serv.Mgr., Norwich City Coll. [0015521] 19/09/1968
Webb Mrs M, (was Millicheap), BA(Hons) DipILM, Asst.Lib./Catr., R.N.I.B., Peterborough. [0054084] 24/10/1996
Webb Mrs MI, (was Cox), MCLIP, Life Member, 020 8858 1876, 36 Kidbrooke Gdns., Blackheath, London, SE3 0PD. [0015525] 01/01/1939
Webb Mrs SM, (was Bell), BA MCLIP, Inf.Developer, Peregrine Systems., Mountain View, U.S.A. [0001096] 24/02/1966
Webb Mrs SP, (was Cutler), BA FCLIP, Independent Consultant, Northenhay, Droridge Lane, Totnes, Devon, TQ9 6JG. [0009175] 30/01/1957 **FE 22/05/1987**
Webb Mrs TA, (was Northwood), BA(Hons) DipIS MCLIP, Asst.Lib., Winchester Sch.of Art, Hants. [0048430] 06/01/1993
Webb Mr W, BA MCLIP, Retired. [0015529] 25/06/1969
Webb Ms Y, BSc(Hons), Lib., L.B.of Islington. [0055209] 15/08/1997
Webber Mrs E, (was Rata), MCLIP, Dep.Lib., Harrow Sch., Middlesex. [0012158] 07/10/1963
Webber Mrs H, (was Szysz), BA(Hons)DipLib MCLIP, P./t.Asst.Lib., Batley L., Kirklees Met.Council Cult.Serv. [0032194] 18/01/1980
Webber Mrs JC, DipLib MCLIP, Resident Rwanda. [0015533] 12/10/1971
Webber Mr JH, BA BTH MCLIP GradDipLib, Unemployed. [0021864] 26/02/1974
Webber Mrs L, (was Marriott), BA MCLIP, Sch.Lib., Q.E.Cambria Sch., Carmarthen. [0027540] 26/04/1977
Webber Dr NA, MA PhD FCLIP, Life Member. [0015535] 27/07/1950 **FE 01/01/1962**
Webber Mr PN, MCLIP, Operations Mgr., N.Div., Dorset, Blandford. [0015537] 21/01/1970
Webber Mrs SAE, BA FCLIP, Manager, Blaise Link, Brit.L. [0028718] 16/01/1978 **FE 01/04/2002**
Webber Mrs WS, MA, Stud., Univ.of Brighton. [0060868] 13/12/2001
Webby Mrs KA, (was Turner), BA, Sen.Lib., G.C.H.Q., Cheltenham. [0040098] 22/10/1986
Weber Mrs LDR, (was Riddle), BA MLS MCLIP, Contract Catr., Self-employed. [0042141] 06/10/1988
Webster Miss C, BSc MCLIP, Employment not known. [0060722] 12/12/2001
Webster Mrs CM, (was Smith), MCLIP, City Stock Mgr., Derby City Council. [0015539] 07/10/1968

Personal Members — West

Webster Ms DCF, (was Smith), MA MCLIP, Head of Map L., Nat.L.of Scotland,(Map L.), Edinburgh. [0019068] 19/09/1972
Webster Miss EZ, BA(Hons), Lib., NHS Direct, Avon Ambulance NHS Trust. [0055067] 03/07/1997
Webster Mr GJ, BSc DipLib FCLIP, Asst.Dir.,D.Inf.Exp., M.O.D., London. [0027039] 17/12/1976 **FE 22/05/1987**
Webster Mrs HL, Unemployed. [0015540] 01/07/1971
Webster Mr HTI, Life Member. [0015541] 23/02/1953
Webster Mr I, MCLIP, Retired. [0015542] 19/02/1964
Webster Mrs J, BSc(Hons) MA, Lib., Leics.C.C., Leics. [0039968] 07/10/1986
Webster Mr JM, LLB(Hons), Stud., Loughborough Univ. [0059966] 13/11/2001
Webster Ms JM, BA, Stud., Univ.of Wales, Aberystwyth. [0061560] 02/10/2002
Webster Mr JR, BSc MLib AIMgt MCLIP FCLIP HonFCLIP, Lib.& Dir.of Inf.Serv., SOAS, Univ.of London. [0036428] 06/10/1983 **FE 01/04/2002**
Webster Mrs L, (was Crook), BA MCLIP, Princ.L.Offr.-Young People, Cornwall L., Truro. [0005700] 23/03/1972
Webster Ms LJ, BA(Hons) DipLIS, Customer Serv.Advisor, IKEA, Croydon. [0020633] 04/05/1973
Webster Mrs M, (was Beattie), LLB BA MCLIP, L.& Inf.Serv.Mgr., Browne Jacobson, Nottingham. [0049750] 01/12/1993
Webster Mrs M, BA(Hons) MCLIP, p./t.L.& Learning Res.Cent.Offr., Blackburn, Hyndburn & Ribble, Valley Healthcare NHS Trust. [0039133] 10/11/1985
Webster Miss MO, FCLIP, Life Member, 20 Sycamore Drive, Swanley, Kent, BR8 7AY, Tel:01322 663339. [0015550] 21/09/1937 **FE 01/01/1949**
Webster Mr P, MA MCLIP, Force Lib., Thames Valley Police, Reading. [0037008] 31/01/1984
Webster Mr PH, MCLIP, Sen.Inf.Offr., Liverpool P.L. [0023644] 23/01/1975
Webster Ms RG, BA DipLib, p./t.Stud./Researcher, City Univ./Lehman Brothers, London. [0052922] 11/01/1996
Webster Mr SAH, MA MCLIP MSc, Inf.Offr., MS Trust, Letchworth. [0041027] 01/10/1987
Webster Miss SCM, BSc(Hons) MA, Asst.Lib., Lovells, London. [0054038] 22/10/1996
Weddell Mrs RD, Inf.Offr., United Buscuits, High Wycombe. [0061510] 27/08/2002 **AF**
Wedlake Mrs CK, (was Avery), BSc, Grad.Trainee, The Bramham Inst., Cambridge. [0059891] 29/10/2001
Wedmore Miss A, BA DipLib MCLIP, Career Break. [0042659] 09/02/1989
Weeden Miss BJ, BA DipLib, Catr./Periodicals Lib., Heythrop Coll., London. [0036480] 17/10/1983
Weedon Mrs CG, BA(Hons), Unemployed. [0056286] 28/04/1998
Weedon Mr RL, BA MA, Internet Copyright Offr., Cent.for Educ.Systems, Glasgow. [0060305] 10/12/2001
Weeks Miss CM, MCLIP, Lib.i/c., Paignton Br.L., Torbay L.Serv. [0015557] 25/09/1967
Weeks Mrs EM, (was Hulme), MCLIP, Acquisitions Serv.Lib., Univ.W.of England, Bristol. [0007432] 09/10/1968
Weeks Mrs LB, Resource Cent.Super., Res.Cent., Cent.for Investigative Skills, Kent Co.Constabulary, Maidstone. [0054594] 31/01/1997
Weeks Ms MP, BA, Community Lib., Vale of Glamorgan Council, Dinas Powys L. [0045190] 06/08/1990
Weetman Ms JD, BA DipLib MCLIP, Academic Lib., De Montfort Univ., Leicester. [0037022] 30/01/1984
Weighell Mrs EA, (was Kirby), BA MCLIP, Div.Child.Lib., Cent.Div., Hants.C.C. [0039163] 25/11/1985
Weighell Mrs JE, (was Dixon), MCLIP, Inf.Serv.& Local Studies Lib., Durham C.C. [0003984] 28/02/1972
Weightman Dr AL, BSc PhD DipLib, Dep.Dir.of L.Serv., Division of Inf.Serv., Univ.of Wales Coll.of Med.,Cardiff. [0048543] 11/02/1993
Weightman Ms KE, BA(Hons), Sen.L.Asst., Cumbria Coll.of Art & Design, Carlisle. [0044671] 22/11/1990
Weir Mrs ALC, MA, Graduate Trainee, East Surrey Coll. [0060977] 23/01/2002
Weir Ms EA, BA DipLib MCLIP, Story Teller/Child.L.Consultant. [0018309] 12/10/1972
Weir Mrs HE, BSc DipLib, Asst.Lib., Leeds Coll.of Building. [0043754] 01/01/1990
Weir Mrs HW, BA MCLIP, Life member. [0033428] 17/10/1980
Weir Mrs JH, (was Morton), BA MCLIP, L.Devel.Offr., E.Renfrewshire Council. [0029764] 10/10/1978
Weir Mrs KG, (was Morton), L.Offr., Morden L., Surrey. [0056575] 01/09/1998 **AF**
Weir Miss LJ, BSc(Hons) MSc MCLIP, Inf.Offr., MWH Ltd., High Wycombe. [0056350] 04/06/1998
Weist Ms AH, (was Fitzgerald), BA(Hons) MSc MCLIP, Lib./N.E.London Mgr./Coord.Lib., N.E.London W.D.C., London. [0042214] 10/10/1988
Welbourn Mr RW, BA MA MCLIP, Retired. [0015567] 28/01/1967
Welby Mrs JP, (was Evans), MCLIP, Lib., Shebbear Coll., Shebbear, Devon. [0022749] 04/09/1974
Welch Ms CA, MCLIP, Chartered Lib., Bramcote Park Sch., Nottingham. [0038274] 03/02/1985
Welch Ms CM, MCLIP, Unemployed. [0015569] 22/02/1962
Welch Mrs DE, (was Tarran), MCLIP, Life Member, Tel.01892 539326, 13 College Dr., Tunbridge Wells, Kent, TN2 3PN. [0015570] 12/03/1947
Welch Mr DH, FCLIP, Life Member. [0015571] 22/03/1956 **FE 01/01/1964**
Welch Mr GJ, Unemployed. [0038371] 01/04/1985
Welch Mrs JM, BA(Hons), P./t.Stud./L.Asst., Robert Gordon Univ., Bracknell Forest C.C. [0059752] 17/09/2001
Welch Miss MJ, BSc(Hons) MA MCLIP, Asst.Lib., Manchester Met.Univ. [0055052] 02/07/1997

Welchman Mrs KP, Sen.L.Asst., Glos.C.C. [0053019] 31/01/1996 **AF**
Welding Mr JD, MA MCLIP, Tech.Serv.Lib., Univ.of Leicester. [0015575] 16/01/1966
Welford Mr JG, BA MLib DipLib MCLIP, L.Serv.Mgr., Marconi Communications, Coventry. [0025924] 03/04/1976
Wellard Ms EK, BA(Hons) DipILS MCLIP, User Serv.Team Leader, Univ.of the W.of England, Bristol. [0052560] 07/11/1995
Wellbelove Miss FB, BA(Hons), Inf.Offr., Landwell, London. [0054720] 17/03/1997
Wellburn Mr P, BA MCLIP, Head of Official Publications, Nat.L.of Scotland, Edinburgh. [0017942] 21/09/1965
Wellen Ms D, BA MCLIP, Asst.Systems Offr., Notts.Co.L. [0033701] 06/02/1981
Weller Miss AL, MCLIP, Child.L.Co-ordinator, L.B.of Sutton. [0022710] 16/09/1974
Weller Ms JC, (was Sayle), BA(Hons) DipLib MCLIP, Princ.Lib.-Inf.Serv., Hampshire Co.L., H.Q.L., Winchester. [0023340] 20/11/1974
Weller Mrs JS, (was Store), L.Asst., Wolfson Sch.L., Sch.of Hlth.Sci., Thames Valley Univ., Reading. [0045326] 10/10/1990 **AF**
Weller Miss KJ, Inf.Asst., Sainsbury L., Univ.of Oxford. [0060867] 13/12/2001
Wellesley-Smith Mr HN, MA MCLIP, Retired. [0015579] 10/01/1969
Wellings Mrs KM, (was Smith), MCLIP, Sen.Product Analyst, TALIS Inf.Ltd., Birmingham Inst.of Research& Devel. [0030032] 24/11/1978
Wellington Ms V, BA(Hons) DipLib DipIM MCLIP, Special Serv.Mgr., Lincs.C.C. [0030063] 28/10/1978
Wellman Mrs RM, (was Scott), MCLIP, Unemployed, Lea Riggs House, Crook of Devon, Kinross, KY13 0UL. [0032461] 01/04/1980
Wells Mrs A, (was Smith), MA, Unemployed. [0040292] 15/01/1987
Wells Mrs AM, (was Taylor), BA MCLIP, Lib., Withington Girls Sch., Fallowfield,Manchester. [0021678] 03/01/1974
Wells Mr C, BSc MSc MCLIP, Employment not known. [0060769] 12/12/2001
Wells Ms EA, BSc DipLIS, Inf.Cent.Mgr., The Financial Serv.Auth., London. [0040344] 25/01/1988
Wells Dr EMP, MA DipLib DPhil, p./t.L.Asst., Tech.Serv., Bodleian Law L. [0039887] 06/10/1986
Wells Mrs HJ, (was Perrins), BSc MSc MCLIP, Learning Res.Cent.Mgr., Greenwich Comm.Coll., Charlton. [0029367] 10/07/1978
Wells Mrs JA, BA(Hons) DipLit, p./t.Stud./Business Inf.Admin., Univ.of Brighton. [0059914] 30/10/2001
Wells Miss JM, MCLIP, Life Member. [0015588] 25/07/1949
Wells Miss JM, BA MCLIP, Reader Serv.Lib., Anglia Poly.Univ. [0042126] 03/10/1988
Wells Miss JT, BA DipLib MCLIP, Community Lib., Kent Arts & L., Springfield, Maidstone. [0033606] 24/01/1981
Wells Mrs N, (was Mace), MCLIP, Asst.Lib., Univ.of Wales, Aberystwyth. [0019027] 11/03/1954
Wells Mr NP, Asst.Stock Mover, The Brit.L., London. [0061257] 30/04/2002 **AF**
Wells Mrs SE, BS M ED, Inf.Offr., Tillinghost-Towers Perrin, London. [0041445] 01/01/1988
Wells Mrs SE, (was Jowett), BSc MCLIP, Sch.Lib., St.John Houghton Sch., Derbys. [0015592] 22/04/1971
Wells Mr SLM, BA MCLIP, Position unknown, Dept.of Health, London. [0060423] 11/12/2001
Wells Ms VM, MA(Hons) DipLib MCLIP, Faculty Lib., Univ.of Stirling. [0036649] 09/10/1983
Wellsted Mrs JL, (was Farrington), BA DipLib MCLIP, Legal Lib., Esso Petroleum Co.Ltd., Leatherhead. [0034938] 22/04/1982
Welsh Ms A, (was Robertson), MA DipLib MCLIP, Career Break. [0037528] 03/10/1984
Welsh Mrs BJ, (was Whitford), BA DipLIS MCLIP, Lend.Lib., Hants.C.C., Farnborough P.L. [0049630] 15/11/1993
Welsh Miss JM, BA(Hons) MBA MCLIP, Campus Lib., Univ.of Wales Inst., Cardiff. [0042762] 07/02/1989
Welsh Miss SM, PhD DipLib MCLIP, Sen.Catr., Liverpool John Moores Univ.L.Serv. [0030293] 12/01/1979
Welsher Miss AD, MCLIP, Comm.Lib., Southbourne Br., Bournemouth Bor.Council. [0015602] 15/09/1967
Welton Mr JA, BA MCLIP, Lib.Serv.Mgr., Cumbria C.C., Carlisle, Cumbria. [0018421] 14/10/1972
Wemyss Mrs EM, (was Robson), BSc DipLib MCLIP, Asst.Lib., Ref./Local Stud.Dept., Aberdeen City L. [0028137] 08/10/1977
Wenban-Smith Ms A, BA(Hons), Electronic Inf.Mgr., London Inst. [0047738] 16/10/1992
Wendl Mrs ME, (was Wilkinson), BA MCLIP, Coll.Lib., Stoke on Trent 6th Form Coll. [0021667] 28/12/1973
Wendon Mr DW, BA MCLIP MIMgt FRSA, Life Member. [0015605] 29/10/1955
Wenham Mrs JMM, (was Blois), FCLIP, P/t Lib., Bournemouth Sch.for Girls. [0015606] 01/01/1952 **FE 01/01/1959**
Wenham Miss RC, BSc DipLib MCLIP, Asst.Lib., Nat.Inst.for Med.Research, London. [0023292] 18/11/1974
Wentworth Ms SF, BA DipLib MCLIP, Bus.Inf.Lib., Cultural Serv., Oxfordshire C.C. [0032767] 12/08/1980
Wesencraft Mr AH, DipLib FCLIP, Life Member, Consultant: Harry Price L., Univ.of London. [0015609] 13/10/1931 **FE 01/01/1936**
Wess Ms BA, MCLIP, L.Devel.Mgr., L.B.of Waltham Forest, Leytonstone. [0026893] 05/01/1977
West Miss A, BA DipLib MCLIP, Lib., Royal Coll.of Nursing, Inf.& Advice, Serv., Cardiff. [0042819] 08/03/1989
West Mrs AJ, (was Chamberlain), BA(Hons) MCLIP, Unemployed. [0041521] 18/01/1988
West Ms AM, (was Crichton), FCLIP MLitStud PhD, Resident Overseas. [0017947] 01/01/1940 **FE 01/01/1942**

377

West Mr AP, Sector Specialist-Consumer, Fidelity Investments, London. [0044182]   01/07/1990
West Mrs BM, (was Egerton), MCLIP, Grp.Lib., Cheshire C.C.L.& Culture, Wilmslow. [0030725]   01/03/1965
West Mrs CA, (was Green), BA(Hons) MA MCLIP, Learning Res.Devl.Mgr., City Coll., Birmingham. [0041218]   12/10/1987
West Mr CB, BA DipLib MCLIP, Retired. [0015612]   04/10/1962
West Mrs CC, (was Thomas), MCLIP, Retired. [0014531]   18/03/1967
West Mr CM, MA BA DipLib MCLIP, Dir.of L.& Inf.Serv., Univ.of Wales, Swansea. [0025132]   27/10/1975
West Ms E, BA MCLIP, Sen.Offr., Elec.L.Project, Univ.of Northumbria at Newcastle, Newcastle upon Tyne. [0039948]   06/10/1986
West Ms EA, BEd DipLib MCLIP, Br.Lib., L.B.Wandsworth. [0042142]   03/10/1988
West Miss H, BA, Asst.Faculty Lib., UCN. [0059111]   17/11/2000
West Mr J, BA DipLib MCLIP, Unemployed. [0044166]   18/06/1990
West Ms JH, (was Wardman), MCLIP, 6th Form Lib., Holland Pk.Sch., London. [0015614]   06/01/1959
West Mr LE, BSc MCLIP, Employment not known. [0060666]   11/12/2001
West Miss M, L.Asst., Cent.L., Birmingham. [0059283]   08/05/2001 AF
West Mrs MJ, (was Hipkin), BA DipLib MCLIP, Unemployed. [0041582]   21/01/1988
West ML, BA DipLib MCLIP, Child.Lib., Exeter, Devon C.C. [0040742]   23/05/1987
West Miss NH, BA(Hons), Inf.Offr., Brit.Dental Assoc., London. [0056892]   02/11/1998
West Mr NJM, BA(Hons) DipLIS MCLIP, Sessional Lib., L.B.of Camden. [0043018]   23/06/1989
West Mrs PP, MCLIP, Stock Lib., Kent C.C., Kings Hill. [0015617]   05/09/1968
West Mr RWC, MCLIP, Life Member. [0015618]   14/01/1963
West Mrs S, (was Kitchin), BA AKC DipLib MCLIP, Team Lib.-Local Serv., Kent C.C. [0008454]27/07/1972
West Miss TA, MA(Hons) MSc, Inf.Asst., Univ.of Aberdeen [0059718]   05/09/2001
West Mr TRJ, MA BD MCLIP, Retired. [0015619]   31/07/1966
West Ms V, Lib., Sandbach Sch.Foundation, Sandbach, Cheshire. [0055659]   01/01/1969
Westall Mrs GM, (was Fleming), BA MCLIP, Head of Inf.Cent., Jones Lang Wootton, London. [0014835]   22/01/1969
Westall Mrs JA, (was Fairclough), MCLIP, Retired. [0015622]   01/08/1956
Westaway Miss CA, B LIB MCLIP, p./t.Catr., Royal Horticultural Soc., London. [0021638]   20/11/1973
Westaway Dr JH, MA PhD, Electronic Resources Admin., Edgehill Coll., Info & Media Serv., Lancashire. [0056695]   05/10/1998
Westbrook Mrs KB, (was Brown), BA MCLIP, Web Mgr., Sch.of Engineering, Napier Univ., Edinburgh. [0027794]   05/11/1965
Westcott Mrs DM, (was Moore), BA DipLib MCLIP, Team Lib., L.B.of Southwark. [0033076]   03/10/1980
Westcott Miss EL, BA MCLIP, Life Member. [0015624]   01/01/1958
Westcott Ms JC, (was Phillips), BLib MCLIP, Asst.Lib.(Res.& Planning & Mgmt.), Open Univ.L., Milton Keynes. [0038999]   24/10/1985
Westcott Mrs K, (was Jones), BA DipILS MCLIP, Career Break. [0043262]   11/10/1989
Westcott Miss MR, MA MCLIP, Life Member. [0015625]   19/09/1958
Westcott Ms S, MA DipLib MCLIP, Sen.Lib., Dept.of the Env.,Trans.& the Reg., London. [0043264]   10/10/1989
Westcott Ms SA, BA(Hons), L.Asst., Exeter Coll. [0056121]   03/03/1998 AF
Westgate Miss JM, MCLIP, Child.Serv.Lib., W.Sussex C.C.L.Serv. [0034595]   01/01/1982
Westgate Mrs S, Sen.L.& Inf.Asst., Arthurstone L., Dundee. [0057509]   14/04/1999   AF
Westhead Miss D, MCLIP, Retired. [0015627]   01/11/1938
Westmancoat Mrs HT, (was March), MCLIP, Princ.Asst.Lib., York St.John Coll., York. [0009719]   19/10/1971
Westmorland Ms L, BA(Hons) MA MCLIP, Reader Devel.Co-ordinator, Wokingham L., Berks. [0049012]   31/08/1993
Weston Mr CGH, B ENG AMIEE MCLIP, Lect., Sch.of Inf.& Media, The Robert Gordon Univ. [0015630]   05/10/1969
Weston Ms K, Acting Lib., North Derbyshire Tertiary Coll. [0061817]   11/11/2002   AF
Weston Ms LM, BA(Hons) MA MA, Asst.Lib., Royal Acad.of Arts L., London. [0057931]   04/10/1999
Weston Mr MK, BA MCLIP, Inf.Offr., URS Corp.Ltd., London. [0024851]   17/10/1975
Weston Mr N, BA MA MCLIP, Lib.i/c., S.Glos.Council, Yate,nr.Bristol. [0043849]   31/01/1990
Weston Mr PC, BSc CChem FRSC MCLIP, Employment not known. [0060664]   11/12/2001
Weston Mrs RE, (was Boustead), BLib MCLIP, Volunteer Lib., SILUK, High Wycombe. [0026685]   26/10/1976
Weston Mrs V, (was Hogan), MCLIP, Sch.Lib., Harlington Upper Sch., Harlington, Beds. [0015637]   27/11/1964
Weston Mrs VE, (was Noone), BA MCLIP, Learning Lib., Rayleigh Area L., Essex Co.L. [0010882]   20/10/1971
Weston-Smith Ms SJ, (was Weston), BA(Hons) MA, Book Acquisitions, Inst.of Advanced Legal Studies, London. [0056853]   27/10/1998
Westwood Mr DG, L.Offr., Hackney Council. [0045467]   14/02/1991
Westwood Miss HM, BA(Hons), p./t. Asst.Lib., Univ.of Brighton, Eastbourne. [0059493]   09/04/2001
Westwood Miss J, BSc(Econ) MCLIP, Asst.Lib., Royal Hosp.Haslar, Gosport. [0055636]   30/10/1997
Westwood Miss R, BA(Hons), p./t.Stud./L.Asst., Newman Coll., Birmingham. [0061303]   16/05/2002

Westwood Mrs SC, (was Claridge), BA MCLIP, Sen.Team Lib., Stroud L., Glos.C.C. [0027431]02/04/1977
Westwood Ms SE, Asst.Lib., Univ.of Brighton, Brighton. [0057034]   27/11/1998
Wetenhall Mrs MC, MLib BA DipLib MCLIP, Retired.   , [0036776]   08/09/1967
Wetherell Mrs FD, MCLIP, p./t.Catr., Trinity College, Cambridge. [0015642]   26/10/1971
Wetherill Mrs HC, (was Chew), BA(Hons) MA MCLIP, Unemployed. [0042670]   07/02/1989
Wetherill Mr J, BA MA MCLIP, Inf.Res.Mgr., Understanding & Solutions, Dunstable. [0042495]   23/11/1988
Weyman Mr KS, MCLIP, Retired. [0015644]   22/09/1957
Weyman Miss M, BA MCLIP, Life Member. [0015645]   26/09/1957
Whale Mrs HA, (was Carlin), MCLIP, Inf.& Educ.Co-ordinator, S.Tyneside M.B.C. [0002373]   08/02/1966
Whale Mrs J, (was Orme), BA Area L.Mgr., Bentley, Doncaster M.B.C. [0011033]   01/01/1968
Whalley Mr JH, BLib MCLIP, Sen.Asst.Lib., Manchester Metro.Univ., Cheshire. [0030570]   28/01/1978
Whapham Miss EBG, MCLIP, Life Member. [0015650]   27/02/1940
Wharam Ms HM, BSc MCLIP, Employment unknown. [0060348]   10/12/2001
Wharrad Mr AJ, MSc PGDip MCLIP, Knowledge Agent, QinetiQ, Malvern. [0054270]   12/11/1996
Wharton Mrs AE, (was Carr), BA MCLIP, Unemployed - Housewife. [0031584]   10/11/1979
Wharton Miss JC, BA DipLib PhD MCLIP, Asst.Lib., Univ.of Nottingham L. [0040010]   14/10/1986
Wharton Mrs SB, (was Neal), BA MCLIP, Dep.Lib., N.E.R.C.(C.E.H.), Wallingford, Oxon. [0010695]   02/12/1968
Whatley Mr HA, MA FCLIP, Life Member, Tel.01270 623360, 16 Newbold Way, Nantwich, CW5 7AX. [0015654]   02/03/1931   FE 01/01/1937
Whatmore Mrs IA, (was Garselis), BLib MCLIP, Dep.Learning Res.Cent.Mgr., Farnham Coll., Surrey. [0025035]   31/10/1975
Wheatcroft Mrs AV, BSc MA DMS MCLIP, Website Co-ordinator, Inst.of Occupational Safety &, Health. [0047560]   01/10/1992
Wheater Mrs EA, (was Bamford), BEd DipLib MCLIP, Retired. [0042290]   12/10/1988
Wheatley Mr GWJ, FCLIP DipFE, Life Member, 16 Maplehurst Rd., Chichester, W.Sussex, PO19 4QL. [0015661]   22/03/1943   FE 01/01/1966
Wheatley Mrs JF, (was Stoneman), FCLIP, Life Member. [0015662]   10/03/1941   FE 01/01/1950
Wheatley Ms KA, BA(Hons) MA PGCE MCLIP, p./t.Inf.Adviser, Sheffield Hallam Univ. [0041901]   24/04/1988
Wheatley Mr SR, BA MCLIP, Sen.L.Asst.(ICT), Sandwell M.B.C. [0035740]   17/01/1983
Wheatman Mrs HE, (was Owen), MCLIP, Lib., Manor Comp.Sch., Mansfield Woodhouse. [0011097]   12/03/1971
Wheeldon Mrs C, (was Waudby), MCLIP, Company Sec., ERW Consulting Ltd., Bedfordshire. [0015486]   06/02/1969
Wheeler Ms A, BA(Hons) MCLIP, Inf.Mgr., Rouse & Co.Internat., London. [0049160]   08/10/1993
Wheeler Mrs AR, (was Wotherspoon-Stewart), MCLIP, Reg.Lib., Cent.L., Ipswich. [0028393]   25/10/1977
Wheeler Miss BJ, MCLIP, Unemployed. [0028997]   03/02/1978
Wheeler Mrs CD, BA DipLib MCLIP, Dep.Lib., Guildford Coll., Guildford,Surrey. [0040996]   01/10/1987
Wheeler Miss HA, BA(Hons) MCLIP MA, Dep.Learning Resources Mgr., Vauxhall Cent., Lambeth Coll. [0015666]   01/01/1971
Wheeler Miss HE, BA DipLib MCLIP, Sen.Lib., Lymington L. [0037552]   02/10/1984
Wheeler Mrs M, (was Williams), BLib MCLIP, Unemployed. [0015951]   11/10/1971
Wheeler Mr MD, BA, Lib., Cent.Off.of Inf., London. [0038258]   18/02/1985
Wheeler Miss PC, MCLIP BA, Retired. [0015668]   29/01/1962
Wheeler Mr WG, MA DipLib FCLIP ALAI, Life Member, Tel.01396 613586, 27 English St., Downpatrick,Co.Down,BT30 6AB. [0015669]   29/10/1954   FE 01/01/1960
Wheelton Mrs JH, (was Unsworth), MCLIP, Sen.Lib., Banbury L., Oxon. [0013472]   03/01/1970
Whelan Mr DA, Stud., Manchester Met.Univ. [0058197]   16/11/1999
Whelan Mrs V, L. Devel. Support Offr., Shropshire Co.L, [0060991]   25/01/2002
Whelehan Mr BM, BA(Hons) MCLIP, Sen.L.Asst., Inter-L.Loans, Cent.L., Imperial Coll., London. [0046450]   07/11/1991
Whelehan Mr TD, BA MA, Asst.Lib., Dept.for Educ.& Skills, London. [0052587]   09/11/1995
Whellams Mrs IM, MCLIP, Lib., Planning Inspectorate, Bristol. [0019407]   16/08/1972
Whetham Miss SA, MCLIP, Freelance Abstractor &, Casual L.Asst., Wilts.C.C. [0024852]   03/10/1975
Wetherly Mrs JM, (was Woodcock), BA MCIPD MCLIP CertCC, Facilitator, Devel.& Training, Consultant, St.Albans. [0015671]   17/09/1965
Whibley Mr SG, BA(Hons), Catr., Brit.L., Boston Spa. [0047285]   03/07/1992
Whibley Mr V, MA FRSA MIMgt FCLIP, Serv.Devel.Team Lib., L.B.of Lewisham P.L. [0015672]   21/09/1959   FE 01/07/1972
Whincup Mrs PE, (was Lewis), MCLIP, Retired. [0015677]   08/09/1955
Whinnerah Miss CA, L.Asst./Asst.i/c., Glossop Dist.L./Hayfield L., Derbys. [0045048]   07/01/1990   AF
Whitaker Mr DH, OBE BA, Chairman, J.Whitaker & Sons, London. [0040257]   11/11/1986
Whitaker Mr GH, MA FCLIP, Sen.Asst.Lib./Research Fellow, Univ.of Glasgow. [0022480]   10/06/1974   FE 18/03/1985

Whitaker Miss HD, BA MSc MCLIP, Asst.Faculty Lib., Univ.Coll.Northampton. [0056343] 01/06/1998
Whitaker Mr R, BA MA, Planning Asst., L.B.of Hounslow, Hounslow, Middlesex. [0052599] 10/11/1995 SP
Whitby Mrs EJ, (was Ravenscroft), BSc(Hons) DipILS, Tech.Lib., FLS Aerospace, Altrincham, Cheshire. [0050241] 12/05/1994
Whitby Miss SE, BA(Hons) MA, Inf.& Stud.Serv.Asst., N.E.Wales Inst.of H.E., Plas Coch Campus, Wrexham. [0056313] 29/04/1998
Whitcombe Mrs AC, MSc MCLIP, Employment unknown. [0060231] 10/12/2001
Whitcombe Ms NE, Sen.L.Asst., Univ.of Wales, Swansea. [0052908] 22/01/1996 AF
White Mrs AA, MCLIP, Comm.Lib., Linwood L., Renfrewshire Council. [0018078] 03/10/1972
White Mr AC, MA CChemMRSC MCLIP, Retired. [0060671] 11/12/2001
White Mr AGD, FCLIP, Life Member, 39 Gilmour Road, Edinburgh, EH16 5NS. [0015688] 30/03/1957 FE 15/03/1975
White Mr AJ, BSc DipLIB MCLIP, Mgr., Risley Inf.Cent., AEA Tech. [0046361] 30/10/1991
White Miss AM, BEd(Hons) DipLIS MCLIP, Team Lib., Oxon.C.C. [0045730] 03/05/1991
White Mrs ASM, (was Cocks), BA(Hons) MCLIP, Career Break. [0040089] 21/10/1986
White Mr AV, BA MCLIP, Sen.Lib., (Euro.Inf.), Woking L., Surrey Co.L. [0015689] 17/02/1965
White Mrs B, (was Newton), HonFCLIP, Retired. [0015691] 29/08/1955 FE 19/01/1982
White Miss CE, BA MCLIP, Sch.L.Advisor, Sch.L.Support Serv., Walsall. [0022301] 21/02/1974
White Miss CE, BA(Hons) MA, Business Inf.Offr., Inst.of Directors. [0056409] 01/07/1998
White Mrs CL, H.of L.Learning Resources, Holyrood Community Sch., Chard, Somerset. [0051842] 12/07/1995
White Mrs E, Self-employed, Surrey. [0054839] 07/04/1997 AF
White Miss ED, BA(Hons) MSc(Econ) MCLIP, Herefordshire Coll.of Tech., Learning Res.Cent. [0052505] 02/11/1995
White Mrs G, (was Brown), BA MCLIP, MCLIP. [0027515] 13/05/1977
White Ms GM, BA(Hons)PG DipLIB, Ch.Catr., Nat.Art L., Victoria & Albert Mus. [0034653] 19/01/1982
White Mr H, MCLIP, Retired. [0015703] 20/02/1950
White Mrs HA, (was Colledge), BSc MSc MCLIP, Stud. [0038911] 21/10/1985
White Miss IO, (was Stockton), BA MCLIP, Sen.L.Exec., House of Commons L., London. [0031488] 01/10/1979
White Mrs J, (was Aspin), MCLIP, Lib., The Winton Sch., Andover. [0000471] 01/01/1971
White Mrs J, (was Oakley), MA MBA MCLIP, p./t.External Support Advisor, Napier Univ.L., Edinburgh. [0010943] 21/10/1969
White Mrs JA, (was Lawry), MA MCLIP, [0028848] 23/01/1978
White Mrs JA, BA(Hons) MA, Sen.Inf.Asst.(Enquiries), Royal Holloway Coll. [0057615] 28/05/1999
White Mrs JC, (was Lumley), BA MCLIP, Asst.Lib., Children & Young Peoples Team, Northumb.County L. [0035754] 10/01/1983
White Miss JD, MA (Hons), Stud., Strathclyde Univ. [0061006] 30/01/2002
White Mrs JF, MBE MCLIP, Retired. [0015705] 01/01/1953
White Miss JM, BA(Hons) MCLIP, Comm.Librarian, Tameside M.B.C. [0045768] 22/05/1991
White Mr JM, BA, Learning Cent.Asst., Sandwell Coll., Smethwick. [0057476] 01/04/1999
White Mrs JME, (was Murray), MSc MCLIP, Sch.Lib., Fife Council, Buckhaven High Sch. [0010612] 02/10/1968
White Mrs JMO, (was Williams), MLib AMus TCL MCLIP, Relief Lib., Norfolk C.C., Norwich. [0025824] 01/03/1976
White Mr JT, FCLIP, Flat 15 The Gables, 290 Heston Rd., Heston, Hounslow, Middx., TW5 0RP,Tel:020 8574 7491. [0015710] 17/10/1935 FE 01/01/1951
White Mrs K, (was Walker), MCLIP, Retired. [0015236] 31/08/1961
White Mrs K, (was Montacute), BA MCLIP, Corp.Intelligence & L.Serv.Mgr., Bradford Health Auth. [0035430] 04/10/1982
White Miss L, BScHons), L.& Inf.Mgr., Thomson Legal & Regulatory, Europe, London. [0053684] 05/09/1996
White Mr L, FCLIP, Life Member. [0015714] 28/09/1950 FE 01/01/1968
White Mr L, FCLIP, Life Member, Ty Gwyn, Llvest, Llanbadarn Fawr, Aberystwyth, Dyfed, Tel: 01970. [0015713] 24/05/1932 FE 01/01/1934
White Ms LE, MA MSc DipLIB MCLIP, Inf.& Systems Offr., Royal Bor.Kensington & Chelsea, London. [0030064] 01/11/1978
White Mrs M, (was Timms), MCLIP, Asst.Lib., Darlington Bor.Council. [0019410] 06/02/1960
White Mr MS, BSc FRSA FCLIP, Hon Fellow. [0060667] 11/12/2001 FE 01/04/2002
White Mrs N, (was Edmonds), BA MCLIP, Unemployed. [0004403] 18/01/1967
White Mrs PA, (was Rooke), MCLIP, Asst.Lib., Dept.for Educ.& Skills, Sheffield. [0048509] 01/01/1961
White Mrs PV, (was Dear), MCLIP, Casual Lib., Leics.C.C. [0015724] 13/03/1964
White Miss RK, BSc(Hons), Sen.L.Asst., Imperial Coll., Nat.Heart & Lung Inst. [0056879] 29/10/1998
White Mrs RK, (was Moore), BA MA MCLIP, Youth Serv.Lib.-Job Share, Bexley Leisure Serv.Directorate, Kent. [0031388] 08/10/1979
White Mr RLW, Lib.& Curator, Berks Masonic Cent., Sindlesham, Berks. [0058999] 18/10/2000
White Miss RM, MCLIP, Prison & Asian Language Lib., Hants.Co.L. [0024853] 10/10/1975

White Miss RMH, MA BSc DipLib, Retired. [0017953] 01/01/1965
White Mrs RO, (was Burgess), BA DIP HE MCLIP, Resource Cent.Mgr., City of York Council, York. [0026297] 21/10/1976
White Mrs S, BSc MSc, Sen.Inf.Asst., Leicester Univ. [0052435] 01/11/1995
White Mrs SA, MSc MCLIP, Research Co-ordinator, Queen Mary, Univ.of London. [0024384] 02/07/1975
White Mrs SA, (was Pearey), BA DipLib MCLIP, Asst.Dir.L.Serv., Univ.of Huddersfield. [0032693] 11/07/1980
White Mr SD, BA DipLIB MCLIP, Serv.Lib., Herts.Sch.L.Serv., New Barnfield,Hatfield. [0038449] 25/04/1985
White Mrs SE, (was Cook), DipLIB MCLIP, Lib.(Leicester S.), Leics.Co.C. [0038112] 18/01/1985
White Mrs SE, BA MLib MCLIP, Equal Access Lib., Shropshire L., Shrewsbury. [0041284] 15/10/1987
White Mrs SK, (was Hughes), BLib MCLIP, Learning Serv.Mgr., Hextable Sch., Kent. [0042745] 21/02/1989
White Mrs SM, (was Jordan), MCLIP, Sen.Lib., Co.Bor.of Blaenau Gwent. [0022224] 01/03/1974
White Mrs T, BA, p./t.Stud./Princ.L.Asst., Univ.of Cent.England, Birmingham, Rothemere American Inst., Oxford. [0061146] 13/03/2002
White Miss VJ, BSc(Hons) MSc, Inf.Offr., Instant L.Ltd., Loughborough, Leics. [0055714] 06/11/1997
White Ms WH, BA(Hons) MA DipLib MCLIP, Asst.Lib., Univ.of Southampton. [0051201] 23/11/1994
White Mrs WJ, (was Perry), BA DipLib MCLIP, Asst.Lib.-p./t., London Guildhall Univ., London. [0039489] 08/02/1986
Whitehead Mr DW, MCLIP, Life Member. [0015736] 22/02/1955
Whitehead Mrs P, (was Dean), FCLIP, Life Member. [0015741] 02/09/1942 FE 01/01/1949
Whitehead Ms P, BA DipLIB MCLIP, Community Serv.Devel.Lib., Herfordshire L.Serv. [0028390] 24/10/1977
Whitehead Ms S, L.Asst., Hayle L., Cornwall. [0059431] 14/03/2001 AF
Whitehead Mrs V, (was Shackleton), BA FCLIP CTextFTI, Retired. [0006496] 14/02/1968 FE 24/05/1995
Whitehead Mrs VE, BA MCLIP, Lib., Gordons Sch., Woking, Surrey. [0027636] 27/06/1977
Whitehouse Mrs EM, (was Edwards), BA(Hons) MCLIP, Asst.Lib., Worcs.Comm.& Mental Health NHS, Newtown Hosp. [0004425] 23/01/1970
Whitehouse Mrs HD, (was Poole), BSc DipInfSc, Team Leader, L.& Inf.Serv., Aston Univ., Birmingham. [0040940] 08/09/1987
Whitehouse Mrs HS, (was Green), MCLIP, Sen.Lib., Haringey P.L. [0020009] 08/01/1973
Whitehouse Mrs L, BA(Hons), Lib., High-Point Rendel, Birmingham. [0053998] 17/10/1996
Whitehouse Mr SC, BA(Hons) PGDip MPhil, L.Asst., Codsall L., S.Staffs.Dist.Council. [0061295] 14/05/2002 AF
Whitehouse Mrs SE, (was Willetts), BA MCLIP, Group Lib., Kingswinford Pub.Library. [0033196] 02/10/1980
Whitehurst Mr AJ, MA PGCE, p./t.Stud./L.Asst., Univ.Coll.London, Templeman L., Univ.of Kent. [0061165] 15/03/2002
Whiteley Mrs A, (was Barham), MCLIP, Catr., Rochdale P.L. [0000746] 23/03/1964
Whiteley Mrs N, BA (Hons), Stud., City Univ., Admin. Asst. [0060976] 22/01/2002
Whiteley Mrs SE, (was Jaques), MCLIP, Asst.Lib., Milton Keynes Gen.NHS Trust, Bucks. [0007739] 27/10/1966
Whitelock Dr J, MA MPhil PhD MA MCLIP, Lib., Univ.of Cambridge, Whipple L. [0055976] 07/01/1998
Whiteman Mrs CJ, (was Broom), BA DipLib MCLIP, Filton Br.Lib., S.Glos. [0040965] 01/10/1987
Whiteman Mrs GA, (was Holliday), MCLIP, Lib., London Probation Area. [0007086] 13/09/1965
Whiteman Mr PM, MA FCLIP, 15 Blackpot Lane, Oundle, Peterborough, PE8 4AT. [0015756] 18/09/1942 FE 14/12/1951
Whiteside Miss JM, MA MCLIP, Lib., Lancaster Univ. [0021898] 24/01/1974
Whiteside Mrs JR, Lib., St.Elphin School., Derbyshire. [0059146] 28/11/2000 AF
Whiteside Mrs SC, (was Smith), BA MCLIP, Coll.Lib., S.Cheshire Coll., Crewe. [0021929] 28/01/1974
Whitethread Mrs EA, (was Makin), BSc(Hons) MA MCLIP, Asst.Lib., Richards Butler, London. [0051217] 28/11/1994
Whiteway Mrs CE, (was Fox), MA MCLIP, Unemployed. [0015758] 05/01/1968
Whitfield Mrs JE, (was Ashworth), BA(Hons) MCLIP PGCE, Lib., Leicester City Council. [0042159] 07/10/1988
Whitfield Mr P, BLib, Asst.Lib., National Assembly for Wales. [0039405] 27/01/1986
Whitham Mr D, BSc MCLIP, Div.Lib., Lancs.Co.Ls., Lancs. [0022062] 17/01/1974
Whitham Mrs LA, (was Reid), MA MCLIP, P/t.Lib., E.Renfrewshire Council, Glasgow. [0022591] 05/07/1974
Whitham Mrs MA, (was Thompson), MCLIP, Sch.Lib., Bolsover Sch., Derby. [0015761] 09/02/1966
Whiting Mr AD, BA MCLIP, Life Member. [0019412] 06/01/1958
Whiting Mr DJ, Inf.& Res.Mgr., Kensington & Chelsea & Westminster, Health Auth., London. [0051721] 26/05/1995
Whiting Mrs JB, (was Senior), BA DipInf MCLIP, Inf.Specialist, NCU, Ipswich. [0042514] 23/11/1988
Whiting Mrs SA, (was Hoy), BA MCLIP, Inf.Offr., Nabarro Nathanson, London. [0032480] 03/04/1980
Whitington Ms MT, MA DLIS MCLIP, Lib., Cent.Catholic L., Dublin. [0042763] 20/02/1989
Whitlam Mr SJ, BA(Hons) MSc(Econ), Knowledge Mgr., NHS London Reg.Off., London. [0051191] 23/11/1994

Whitlock Mrs C, (was Semple Piggot), BSc MRPharmS MCLIP, Employment not known. [0060750] *12/12/2001*
Whitlock Mrs LJ, (was Dungey), BA(Hons) MA, Company Sec., Small Private Co., Southampton. [0047299] *07/07/1992*
Whitmarsh Miss S, Sch.Lib., Brownhills High Sch., Stoke on Trent. [0057212] *18/01/1999*
Whitmill Mrs HJ, (was Smith), BA DipLib MCLIP, Unemployed. [0034704] *11/01/1982*
Whitmore Miss JM, BA MCLIP, Life Member, 90 Greenhill Rd., Leicester, LE2 3DL. [0015771] *26/09/1962*
Whitmore Miss KB, MCLIP, Retired. [0015773] *06/02/1953*
Whitney Miss JE, BA MCLIP, Subject Classifier, Whitaker Inf.Serv., Herts. [0035763] *19/01/1983*
Whitrow Mrs AM, (was Mostel), BA MCLIP, Retired. [0015776] *27/08/1945*
Whitsed Mrs NJ, (was Barnby), MSc FCLIP, Dir., L.Serv., Open Univ., Milton Keynes. [0000786] *14/09/1970* **FE 16/09/1992**
Whitson Mrs M, (was McIntosh), MA MCLIP, Sen.L.Asst., Napier Univ., Edinburgh. [0009422] *07/01/1971*
Whittaker Miss BA, BA MA, Relief L.Asst., Lincoln Cent.L., Lincoln. [0043398] *19/10/1989*
Whittaker Mrs C, (was Bardsley), BA MCLIP, Learning Res.Cent.Mgr., E.Riding Coll.at Beverley. [0022138] *29/01/1974*
Whittaker Mrs DB, (was Geddes), BA MCLIP, Retired, Resident France. [0017955] *19/03/1969*
Whittaker Mrs DC, (was Hill), MLib MCLIP, Sales Territory Mgr., DS Ltd., Nottingham. [0028013] *10/10/1977*
Whittaker Miss FL, BA MA, Employment Unknown. [0060475] *11/12/2001*
Whittaker Ms HK, BA DipLib MCLIP, Subject Lib.-Soc.Sci.& Law, Oxford Brookes Univ. [0043654] *16/11/1989*
Whittaker Ms JC, MA MCLIP, Stud., Birmingham Poly. [0044486] *12/10/1990*
Whittaker Mr KA, MA FCLIP, Life Member. [0015779] *20/02/1950* **FE 01/01/1957**
Whittaker Ms SP, BA(Hons) MA MCLIP, Sen.Asst.Lib.-Systems, Nat.Foundation for Educ.Research. [0053944] *14/10/1996*
Whittaker Ms SR, BMus(Hons) MA, Sen.Inf.Asst., Univ.of Leicester. [0056715] *07/10/1994*
Whittaker Mrs VI, (was Quirk), BA MCLIP, Spec.Servs.Lib., Selby, N.Yorks.Co.L. [0039556] *28/02/1986*
Whittall Mrs SJ, (was Gaworska), BSc MSc MCLIP, Position unknown, GlaxoSmithKline, Harlow. [0060286] *10/12/2001*
Whittingham Miss CF, BA DipLib MCLIP, Lib./Learning Res.Mgr., Walford & N.Shropshire Coll., Oswestry. [0038569] *05/07/1985*
Whittingham Mrs CM, (was Vaughan), BSc MCLIP, Receptionist/Clerk (p./t.), Shropshire & Mid Wales Hospice, Telford. [0015784] *08/10/1968*
Whittingham Mr W, BSc MCLIP, Employment unknown. [0060339] *10/12/2001*
Whittle Mr MA, BA MA MLib, Acting Lib., L., Defence Estates, Sutton Coldfield. [0043756] *01/01/1970*
Whittlestone Miss RA, BA MSc(Econ) MCLIP, Training Co-ordinator, Reg.L.Unit of the West Midlands, Birmingham. [0052644] *15/11/1995*
Whittock Mrs SR, (was George), Yth.Serv.Lib., Gateshead M.B.C. [0038444] *18/04/1985*
Whitton Mr JB, MA MCLIP, DGI Educ., Youth Cult., AV., Council of Ministers, 00DH17, Brussels. [0015789] *16/08/1967*
Whitton Mr MJ, MA MChem, Asst.Lib., Criddale Coll., Andover. [0059148] *28/11/2000*
Whitwell Mrs LMK, BA DipLib, Retired, 19 Blomfield St., Bury St Edmunds, Suffolk. [0040786] *12/06/1987*
Whitworth Mrs JM, (was Smith), BA MCLIP, Sen.Learning Resources Lib., Worcester Coll.of Tech. [0020160] *01/04/1973*
Whorwood Miss M, BA(Hons), L.Asst., Poole Hosp.NHS Trust, Dorset. [0053220] *01/04/1996* **AF**
Whybrow Mrs KM, (was Morris), MCLIP, Life Member. [0015790] *01/01/1948*
Whyte Mr A, BSc MSc PhD, Employment unknown. [0060247] *10/12/2001*
Whyte Ms LC, BA MCLIP, Managing Dir., Bibliographic Data Serv.Ltd. [0034150] *08/10/1981*
Wibrow Mrs JM, (was Bristow), BA DipLIS, Team Lib., Slough Bor.Council. [0047443] *17/08/1992*
Wickenden Mrs J, (was Dixon), MA MCLIP, [0046130] *07/10/1991*
Wickenden Mr JA, MCLIP, Biomedical Inf.Sci., Eli Lilly & Co.Ltd., Windlesham, Surrey. [0015795] *01/01/1971*
Wickenden Mrs JVS, MA(Oxon) DipLib, Historic Collections Lib., Inst.of Naval Medicine., Hants. [0060886] *19/12/2001*
Wickens Mr SC, BA (Hons), Stud., Univ.of Brighton. [0060872] *18/12/2001*
Wickham Mrs AJ, L.Mgr., Corp.L.& Inf.Cent., Kent C.C. [0056930] *10/11/1998*
Wickham Mrs JE, DipILS, Asst.Lib., W.Pennine Health Auth., Oldham, Lancs. [0057282] *02/02/1999*
Wickramasinghe Miss BC, BA MCLIP, L.Offr., Nadesan Cent.L., Colombo, Sri Lanka. [0017959] *06/11/1969*
Wicks Mrs AF, (was Holmes), MCLIP, Sales Asst., Sevenoaks Bookshop. [0007106] *05/10/1971*
Wicks Miss C, MCLIP, Lib., Brighton & Hove L. [0021090] *08/10/1973*
Wicks Mrs G, (was Jones), BA MCLIP, Comm.Lib., Atherstone L., Nuneaton L. [0008019] *08/02/1968*
Wicks Mr JD, BEd(Hons) MA MCLIP, Asst.Access Serv.Mgr., Essex C.C., Chelmsford, Essex. [0047830] *15/10/1992*
Widdows Mr AP, Unemployed. [0036301] *01/01/1983*
Widdows Miss JC, BSc(Hons) MA, Electronic L.Serv.Offr., Nat.L.for the Blind, Stockport. [0055587] *22/01/1998*
Widdows Doughty Mrs CD, (was Widdows), PGCE BSc(Hons), L.Asst., Berkhamsted L., Herts. [0048584] *22/02/1993* **AF**
Wieczorek Mrs JA, (was Stanbury), MCLIP, Casual Lib./Relief, Cambs.Co.L., Cambridge & Huntingdon. [0019079] *02/10/1972*

Wiener Miss S, L. & Inf Serv. Asst., Central Sch. of Speech and Drama, London. [0060993] *28/01/2002*
Wiggans Mrs EL, MCLIP, Life Member. [0022599] *03/07/1974*
Wiggett Miss JA, MCLIP, Sen.Lib., W.Grp., Notts.C.C. [0015807] *21/03/1968*
Wiggins Miss L, BA (Hons), Stud. [0061466] *08/08/2002*
Wiggins Mr RE, BSc FCLIP, Managing Dir., Cura Consortium Ltd., W.Sussex. [0060674] *11/12/2001* **FE 01/04/2002**
Wigglesworth Ms GS, BA MCLIP, Lib., Bingley Grammar Sch. [0031979] *04/01/1980*
Wigglesworth Miss JA, PG DipLIS, Market Data Mgr., Perot Systems Europe, London. [0040875] *22/07/1987*
Wigglesworth Ms JS, BA(Hons), Asst.Inf.Offr., Clifford Chance, London. [0058773] *17/07/2000* **AF**
Wigley Mrs JE, (was Alcock), BLib MCLIP, Unemployed. [0039145] *12/11/1985*
Wigley Mrs VR, BA(Hons) PGDip, p./t.Neighbourhood Lib., Codsall L., Staffs. [0052108] *03/10/1995*
Wignall Mrs GA, (was Cartwright), BA MCLIP, Lib., John Leggott Sixth Form Coll., Scunthorpe. [0002465] *27/01/1971*
Wignall Mr JR, BA MCLIP MSc, Lib., Swindon Cent.L. [0021345] *15/10/1973*
Wignall Dr MB, PhD MIMgt DipTA MCLIP, Retired. [0060780] *12/12/2001*
Wijetunge Mrs GCW, BLib MCLIP, Formerly Site Lib., Newham Community Coll., W.Ham. [0029133] *14/11/1972*
Wijetunge Mrs P, (was Perera), BA(Hons) DipLIS MLib ASLA MCLIP, Dir., Nat.Inst.of L.&Inf.Sci., Sri Lanka. [0043631] *13/11/1989*
Wijnstroom Ms M, FCLIP, Retired. [0041389] *06/01/1987* **FE 06/01/1987**
Wilcock Mrs JP, BSc MSc MCLIP, Employment not known. [0060703] *12/12/2001*
Wilcox Mrs CA, (was Shoreman), BA MCLIP, Keeper of the L., S.S.C.Soc., Edinburgh. [0034699] *18/01/1982*
Wilcox Mr SB, BA(Hons), Stud. [0039252] *01/01/2000*
Wilcox-Jay Ms K, (was Wilcox), BA(Hons) MSc, Research Asst., City Univ. [0057749] *21/07/1999*
Wild Mrs DM, MA MCLIP, Lib./Field Offr., City of Edinburgh Council (Educ.), Edinburgh. [0032215] *21/01/1980*
Wild Miss EJ, BA, Learning Serv.Co-ordinator, Yeovil Coll. [0059574] *04/06/2001*
Wilde Mrs LJ, Cent.Lib.(p./t.), Ealing,Hammersmith & W.London Coll. [0026817] *02/11/1976*
Wilde Miss M, BA(Hons), Stud., Manchester Met.Univ. [0059994] *16/11/2001*
Wilde Mr NC, BA MCLIP, p./t.Asst.Lib., De Montfort Univ., Bedford. [0015822] *28/09/1962*
Wilder Miss HJ, MA MLIS, Knowledge Offr., Univ.of Oxford, Dept.of Psychiatry. [0061207] *08/04/2002*
Wildgoose Ms E, BA(Hons), Stud., Manchester Met.Univ. [0057754] *23/07/1999*
Wilding Miss H, BSc DipLib, Asst.Lib., Crewe L., Manchester Metro.Univ. [0043286] *16/10/1989*
Wilding Miss JM, (was Meager), BA DipLib MCLIP, Data Auditor, Chartered Inst.of Management, Accountants, London. [0025682] *28/01/1976*
Wildridge Mr CD, MCLIP, Inf.& Admin.Mgr., Wilts.L.Mus.& Arts, Trowbridge. [0019768] *01/01/1968*
Wildsmith Ms SM, (was Dowse), MCLIP, Sen.Lib., Vale of Glamorgan Council, Barry. [0004149] *14/02/1969*
Wileman Mr D, MA MCLIP, Retired. [0015829] *05/11/1966*
Wilhelm Miss M, Document Mgmnt.Offr., L.B.of Enfield Legal Dept., Middlesex. [0058791] *24/07/2000* **AF**
Wilkes Mrs FE, (was Knight), BA(Hons) MA DipLib MCLIP, Asst.Lib., Merton Coll., Oxford. [0044967] *28/01/1991*
Wilkes Miss MB, MCLIP, Retired. [0015839] *02/09/1937*
Wilkes Mr RE, BEd FCLIP, Princ.Educ.Lib., Educ.L.Serv., SERCO. [0015840] *18/07/1957* **FE 01/01/1965**
Wilkes Mrs RJ, BSc MA MCLIP, Child.Lib., Orange Co.P.L., U.S.A. [0046594] *21/11/1991*
Wilkes Mrs S, (was Marfell), MCLIP, Retired. [0009731] *08/02/1965*
Wilkey Ms GM, (was Haslam), BA MCLIP, Dep.Lib., Surrey Inst.of Art & Design, Farnham. [0021233] *10/10/1973*
Wilkie Miss DC, p./t.Asst.Educ.Lib.(Maternity), Sch.L.Serv., Northumberland C.C. [0044558] *26/10/1990*
Wilkie Mrs EA, L.Asst., Gosport Library, Hampshire. [0056371] *22/06/1998* **AF**
Wilkie Mrs SJ, (was Hill), BLib MCLIP, Lifelong Learning Mgr., City of Westminster. [0026263] *24/09/1976*
Wilkins Mr DA, BA DipLib MCLIP, Asst.Lib., Univ.of Bristol L. [0034277] *21/10/1981*
Wilkins Mrs FM, (was Holt), BA MCLIP, L.Res.Mgr., Swanmore Secondary Sch., Hants. [0021210] *29/09/1973*
Wilkins Mr J, BSc MCLIP, Area Mgr.(Cent.), L.B.of Bromley. [0023417] *07/01/1975*
Wilkins Mrs JA, BA MCLIP, Support Serv.Mgr., Wakefield Coll., W.Yorks. [0033623] *30/01/1981*
Wilkins Mrs JA, BA MCLIP, Resident U.S.A. [0028210] *01/10/1977*
Wilkins Mrs JI, (was Spencer), BA MCLIP, Grp.Lib., Birmingham L. [0033529] *13/01/1981*
Wilkins Ms LA, BA MCLIP, L.Mgr., Croydon L., Surrey. [0041560] *28/01/1988*
Wilkins Mrs RG, MCLIP, Retired. [0015848] *02/02/1961*
Wilkins Mrs RJR, (was Macpherson), MA DipLib MCLIP, Position unknown, Moray House L., Univ.of Edinburgh. [0036460] *11/10/1983*
Wilkins-Jones Dr C, BA MCLIP, Team Lib., Norfolk & Norwich Millennium L. [0007971] *01/01/1970*
Wilkinson Miss AJ, BA, Grad.Trainee, Univ.of Sheffield L. [0061550] *11/09/2002*
Wilkinson Mr D, BA MCLIP, Operations Mgr.-S.Div., Dorset Co.L., Dorchester. [0015852] *02/08/1965*

Wilkinson Mrs D, (was Nutter), BA MCLIP, Life Member. [0010940] 12/03/1963
Wilkinson Mr DJ, MA MCLIP, Business Inf.& Res.Offr., Business Link, Cheshire & Warrington. [0015853] 04/02/1970
Wilkinson Mrs DK, (was Harper), BA(Hons) PgD, Second Lib., Merchant Taylors Sch., Northwood. [0052524] 03/11/1995
Wilkinson Miss DL, MA(Hons), Inf.Specialist, GCHQ, Cheltenham. [0058531] 21/03/2000
Wilkinson Mrs EC, (was Hime), BA MCLIP, L.Team Leader, R.N.I.B., Peterborough. [0046187] 14/10/1991
Wilkinson Miss EE, BA, Stud., Loughborough Univ. [0058837] 25/08/2000
Wilkinson Mrs EMH, (was Wilkins), MCLIP, Mother. [0029501] 10/01/1974
Wilkinson Mrs GA, (was Bateson), BA DipLib, Indexer/Abstractor, Self Employed-Wetherby. [0041851] 25/04/1988
Wilkinson Ms H, BA(Hons) MA, Asst.Lib., Beachcroft Wansbroughs, Leeds. [0051708] 23/05/1995
Wilkinson Mrs J, (was Marker), BA MCLIP, L.Asst., Anglo-Euro.Sch., Ingatestone. [0009734] 07/10/1971
Wilkinson Ms J, BA DipLib DMS FCLIP FRSA, Univ.Lib.& Keeper,Brotherton Colle., Univ.of Leeds. [0034794] 20/01/1982 **FE 24/09/1997**
Wilkinson Mrs JA, (was Thorp), MA DipLib MCLIP, Area Mgr., S., Warwickshire C.C. [0027029] 10/01/1977
Wilkinson Mrs K, (was Johnson), BA MCLIP, Sch.Lib., St.George's Brit.Internat.Sch., Rome, Italy. [0025570] 16/01/1976
Wilkinson Mrs LE, (was Carpenter), BA MCLIP, Sen.Lib., Orpington L., L.B.of Bromley. [0002390] 09/10/1968
Wilkinson Mrs LM, (was Davenport), MCLIP, Lib., Cheshire C.C., Ellesmere Port. [0021394] 05/11/1973
Wilkinson Mrs MA, (was Simpson), BA MCLIP, Unemployed. [0018124] 02/10/1972
Wilkinson Miss ME, FCLIP, Life Member. [0015863] 14/09/1943
FE 01/01/1957
Wilkinson Ms NAJ, BA MCLIP MLib, Lib., RAF Cent.of Aviation, Henlow. [0015868] 06/10/1970
Wilkinson Miss R, BA(Hons), Lib., Cumbria C.C., Whitehaven. [0052637] 15/11/1995
Wilkinson Mrs RE, (was Andrews), BA MCLIP, Site Serv.Lib., Oxford Brookes Univ., Oxford. [0028479] 18/01/1978
Wilkinson Mrs S, (was Bailie), BA(Hons), Business Inf.Exec., Small Business Gateway, Aberdeen. [0059721] 05/09/2001
Wilkinson Ms SA, BA DipLib MCLIP AIL, Dep.Lib.:Systems, Trinity Coll., Carmarthen. [0039059] 28/10/1985
Wilkinson Mrs SJ, (was Williams), Inf.Offr., Isaac Newton Inst.for Math.Sci., Univ.of Cambridge. [0051650] 27/04/1995 **AF**
Wilkinson Mrs SL, (was Scott), BA(Hons) DipLIS MCLIP, Lib., Beachcroft Wansbroughs, Bristol. [0040879] 14/07/1987
Wilkinson Mrs SM, (was Jobling), MCLIP, Housewife. [0007844] 08/06/1968
Wilkinson Mrs SM, (was Dennick), MCLIP, Prison L.Mgr., HM Prison Birmingham. [0020273] 12/02/1973
Wilkinson Mr T, BA MCLIP, Comm.Lib.(Lifelong Learning), Lincs.C.C., Cent.L. [0036083] 22/04/1983
Wilkinson Mr T, BSc MCLIP, Employment not known. [0060672] 11/12/2001
Wilkinson-Graham Mrs VL, (was Wilkinson), MA, Asst.Lib., Lewis Silkin, London. [0056451] 14/07/1998
Wilks Mrs C, (was Walmsley), BA DipLib MCLIP, Deeds Offr., Blackpool Bor.Council. [0038198] 18/01/1985
Wilks Mr JEG, IEng AMIERE MIMgt MCLIP, Retired. [0060675] 12/12/2001
Wilks Mrs LJ, (was Brigden), BA MA MCLIP, Inf.Mgr., Open Univ., Milton Keynes. [0034220] 11/10/1981
Wilks Mrs V, (was Holmes), MCLIP, Unemployed. [0015872] 05/08/1965
Will Dr CD, PhD BA MCLIP, Planning Offr., Royal Botanic Gardens, Edinburgh. [0015873] 16/01/1964
Will Mrs EJ, BA(Hons), Learning Res.Co-ordinator, Fife Constabulary, Police H.Q., Glenrothes. [0051611] 11/04/1995
Will Dr LD, BSc PhD MCLIP, Inf.Mgmt.Consultant, Willpower Inf., Enfield,Middx. [0024855] 26/09/1975
Willans Mrs SJ, (was Thomas), MCLIP, p./t.Lib., L.B.of Bromley. [0014585] 01/01/1972
Willars Mrs G, (was Hewes), MA MCLIP, Head of L.Serv.for Educ., Leics.L.& Inf.Serv. [0006788] 01/01/1971
Willats Mr EA, FCLIP, Retired. [0015877] 29/07/1936 **FE 01/01/1944**
Willatts Ms EM, MCLIP BA, Asst.Lib., Watson Farley & Williams, London. [0021995] 19/01/1974
Willers Ms JM, BA MA MSc MCLIP, Retired. [0018204] 01/10/1972
Willett Ms MF, Unemployed. [0046157] 02/01/1991
Willett Mrs MT, BSc(Hons) MSc, Counter Super./Sen.L.Asst., Univ.of Sheffield L. [0059860] 18/10/2001
Willett Prof P, MA MSc PhD DSc FCLIP, Employment not known. [0060606] 11/12/2001 **FE 01/04/2002**
Willetts Mrs L, (was Peacock), BA DipLib MCLIP, Sen.Lib., Northallerton Grp., N.Yorks.C.C. [0031415] 01/10/1979
Willetts Ms SJ, MSc BA DipLib MCLIP, Sen.L.Asst., Inst.of Classical Studies, Hellenic & Roman Soc., London. [0033371] 27/11/1980
William-Powlett Mrs TE, (was Pearce), BA MCLIP, Lib., More Fisher Brown, London. [0045788] 30/05/1991
Williams Miss A, BA(Hons) MA, Team Lib., Luton Cent.L. [0059251] 17/01/2001
Williams Ms AE, Mother. [0042352] 26/10/1988
Williams Mr AF, BA, Builders Labourer, Jonathan Hornbrook. [0055990] 12/01/1998
Williams Mr AH, BA DipLib MCLIP, Sen.Lib., Gwynedd L.Serv., Caernarfon L. [0027379] 09/03/1977
Williams Mrs AI, Lib., Rainhill High Sch., Prescot. [0058199] 16/11/1999
Williams Miss AJ, BEd DipLib MCLIP, L.& Serv.Mgr.(Lifelong Learning), L.B.of Merton. [0038731] 01/10/1985

Williams Miss AJ, BA(Hons) MCLIP, Sen.Asst.Lib., Swansea Inst.of H.E. [0051824] 07/07/1995
Williams Mr AJ, MCLIP, Retired. [0015884] 22/03/1963
Williams Mr AJ, MCLIP, L.Super., GlaxoSmithKline, London. [0058809] 04/08/2000 **AF**
Williams Mr AJ, BA DipLib MCLIP, Principal Lib., Bridgnorth L., Shropshire. [0026609] 11/10/1976
Williams Mr AJ, BA, Stud., Univ.of Northumbria. [0061330] 27/05/2002
Williams Mr AJ, (was Disbury), BA DipLib MCLIP, Subject Lib.-Educ., Chester Coll. [0037631] 09/10/1984
Williams Mrs AJA, BA MCLIP, Freelance, Tel:H:(01274) 496306, Mob:(07977)590189. [0015885] 20/10/1967
Williams Mrs AM, MSc(Econ), p./t.Stud./L.Asst., Univ.Aberystwyth, St.Michaels Coll., Cardiff. [0059629] 05/07/2001
Williams Mr AP, BA MCLIP, Sen.Res.Offr., Cannock Chase Tech.Coll., Staffs. [0034631] 16/01/1982
Williams Ms B, BA DipLIS MCLIP MA, Mgr.L.R.C., Leek Coll.Further Ed., Staffs. [0048367] 08/12/1992
Williams Mrs BC, BA, Inf.& Research Adviser, Sanderson Townend & Gilbert, Newcastle upon Tyne. [0038309] 26/02/1985
Williams Mr BJS, MA HonFCLIP FCLIP, Life Member, BJSW Ed.Options, 16 Stag Green Av., Hatfield, Herts., AL9 5DZ, Tel/Fax:01707 264453. [0015891] 10/10/1991 **FE 01/01/1969**
Williams Ms BM, BA MCLIP, Unemployed. [0035858] 24/01/1983
Williams Mr C, MCLIP, Ref.Lib., Bridgend L.& Inf.Serv., Bridgend Co.Bor. [0023375] 10/12/1974
Williams Miss CA, BA DipLib MCLIP, L.Serv.Mgr., Manchester Met.Univ. [0044372] 02/10/1990
Williams Mrs CA, (was Blyghton), BA(Hons) MSc(Econ) MCLIP, Lib., Bucks.& Chilterns Univ.Coll. [0051206] 23/11/1994
Williams Mrs CA, (was Roberts), BA MCLIP, Community Lib.(Job Share), Conwy Co.Bor.Council, Abergele. [0015895] 15/03/1961
Williams Ms CA, BA DipLib MCLIP, Sch.Lib., Fernwood Comp.Sch., Nottingham. [0029869] 02/10/1978
Williams Mr CC, DMA MCLIP, Retired. [0015896] 03/06/1961
Williams Miss CFH, BA MLib MCLIP, Inf.Specialist, Schlumberger Cambridge Research, Cambridge. [0042342] 10/10/1988
Williams Ms CJ, BA DipTefla, Stud., Univ.of Brighton. [0059940] 08/11/2001
Williams Mr CM, Unemployed. [0034729] 02/02/1982
Williams Mrs CR, BA FCLIP, Life Member. [0015899] 24/09/1958
FE 01/01/1965
Williams Mr CRG, Unemployed, 128 Brookwood Rd., London SW18. [0048924] 23/07/1993
Williams Mrs CS, BA(Hons) MSc(Econ) MCLIP, Inf.Offr., Pinsent Curtis Biddle, Leeds. [0052110] 04/10/1995
Williams Mrs CV, BA(Hons) MA, L.Exec., House of Commons L., London. [0056489] 27/07/1998
Williams Prof DA, BSc PhD DipLib, Reader, The Robert Gordon Univ., Aberdeen. [0035321] 11/10/1982
Williams Mrs DE, (was Shippey), BA MCLIP, p./t.Lib., Hipperholme Grammar Sch., Halifax. [0041211] 15/10/1987
Williams Mr DG, BA(Hons) PGDipIM, Knowledge Systems Mgr., Kensington, Chelsea & Westminster, Health Auth., London. [0050653] 03/10/1994
Williams Miss DM, BA(Hons), Stud., Univ.of Brighton. [0061145] 11/03/2002
Williams Mrs DR, Project Co-ordinator, Stories from the Web, Birmingham L. [0052551] 08/04/2002
Williams Miss E, BA(Hons) DipLIM, Inf.Serv.Asst., Main L., Univ.Coll.Wales, Bangor, Gwynedd. [0057969] 06/10/1999
Williams Mrs E, BChD DipLib MCLIP, Faculty Lib., Bristol Business School, Univ.West England. [0045196] 08/08/1990
Williams Mrs EA, (was Stone), BA MCLIP, Retired. [0015912] 28/01/1957
Williams Mrs EA, (was Pedley), BA MCLIP, Educ.& Communications Exec., BSI, London. [0023510] 01/01/1975
Williams Mrs EE, BA(Hons), p./t.Stud./PA/Training Co-ord., Manchester Met.Univ., KPMG, Manchester. [0061188] 08/04/2002
Williams Miss EL, Stud., Loughborough Univ. [0058131] 04/11/1999
Williams Miss EM, BA MCLIP, Asst.Lib., World Mission Assoc., Ptnrshp.House L., London. [0048304] 18/02/1982
Williams Mr EM, BSc MCLIP, Sen.Res.Offr., Battersea Dist.L., L.B.of Wandsworth. [0025190] 02/05/1976
Williams Mrs EP, BA DipLib MCLIP, Lib., Robert Gordon Univ., Aberdeen. [0026610] 04/09/1976
Williams Miss F, BA(Hons) MA MCLIP, Sen.Lib., Bracknell Forest L. [0046094] 01/10/1991
Williams Mrs FC, BA DipLib MCLIP, Strategic Devel.Mgr., Bor.of Poole. [0041685] 15/02/1988
Williams Miss FHB, MA DipLib MCLIP, Retired. [0024178] 04/10/1950
Williams Mrs FHM, BA(Hons), Lib., Bishops Stortford Coll., Herts. [0056086] 04/02/1998
Williams Mrs G, (was Lee), BA DipLib MCLIP, Educ.Lib., Llyfrgell Llangefni, Ynys Mon. [0026763] 10/11/1976
Williams Miss GA, BA(Hons), Sch.L.Serv.Mgr., Knowsley Council, Merseyside. [0038071] 11/01/1985
Williams Mr GA, BA(Hons), Sen.Lib.Asst., Inst.of Advanced Legal Studies, London. [0059482] 09/04/2001
Williams Mr GD, MCLIP, Retired. [0015930] 08/11/1940
Williams Mr GH, MA DAA, Asst.Dir.:Culture, Dept.of Educ.Culture & Leisure, Cyngor Gwynedd Council. [0053208] 02/04/1996 **SP**
Williams Mr GL, BA Lib MCLIP, Mgr.:Inf.Resource Serv., Derby Coll., Wilmorton. [0019423] 01/01/1972
Williams Ms HAK, MSc MCLIP, Legal Lib.(Temp.)/Lib., Infomatch/DFES/Bindman & Ptnrs., London. [0031497] 07/10/1979
Williams Mrs HE, MCLIP, Lib., Wilts C.C., Devizes L., Wilts. [0015907] 01/01/1970

Williams Mrs HEM, (was Dawson), BA MCLIP, p./t.Lib., Hants.C.,C., New Milton Br. [0029631] 17/10/1978
Williams Miss HKR, Stud., Univ.Coll.London. [0059494] 09/04/2001
Williams Mrs HL, (was Broad), BA(Hons) PGDipIM, Unemployed. [0058157] 09/11/1999
Williams Miss HM, BA(Hons), L.Asst., Univ.Coll.London. [0058964] 11/10/2000
Williams Mrs HM, (was Scott), BA(Hons) MSc MCLIP, [0046086] 01/10/1991
Williams Mrs HM, (was Willis), BA MCLIP, Housewife/Mother, 12 Woodloes Ave.S., Woodloes Pk., Warwick, CV34 5TF, (01926)491452. [0023977] 27/02/1975
Williams HS, (was Pierce), MA MPhil MCLIP, Res.Asst., Napier Univ., Edinburgh. [0034110] 30/09/1981
Williams Dr IA, MA PhD CChem FRSC MCLIP, Retired. [0060676] 12/12/2001
Williams Dr J, BSc (Hons) PhD, Inf.Devel.Serv., Imperial Tobacco Ltd., Bristol. [0061452] 31/07/2002
Williams Miss J, BA(Hons) DipILM, Lib., Macclesfield L., Cheshire C.C. [0055441] 13/10/1979
Williams Miss J, BA MPhil MCLIP, Lib., Hereford Cathedral L. [0018187] 04/10/1972
Williams Mrs J, (was Mathias), ALCM MCLIP, Ref.& Inf.Lib.(S.), Crosby L., Sefton M.B.C. [0009926] 03/03/1967
Williams Mrs J, (was Crowther), MCLIP, Retired. [0017967] 28/01/1961
Williams Ms J, BA DipLib MCLIP, Team Lib., Greenford L. [0035358] 11/10/1982
Williams Mrs JA, BA DipLib MCLIP, Lib., WS Atkins, Epsom. [0000202] 01/01/1969
Williams Mrs JE, (was Chambers), BA DipLib MCLIP, Lib., Shropshire C.C., Shrewsbury. [0027265] 12/02/1977
Williams Mr JH, BA DipLib MCLIP, Head of Learning Cent., City Literary Inst., London. [0025452] 07/01/1976
Williams M/s JL, (was Brocklesby), MCLIP, Retired. [0015941] 01/02/1965
Williams Mrs JM, (was Sugg), BA MCLIP, Head Lib., Royal Bolton NHS Trust, Bolton. [0045500] 21/02/1991
Williams Mrs JM, (was Wood), MCLIP, Team Leader, Stock & Promotion, Staffs.C.C., Tamworth. [0015943] 22/02/1962
Williams Mr JT, MIPP BA MCLIP, Tech.Serv.Lib., Johns Hopkins Univ., Bologna, Italy. [0030874] 03/05/1979
Williams Mrs JV, BSc(Hons) MSc, Inf.Offr., Environment Agency, Wales, Cardiff. [0053038] 16/02/1996
Williams Mrs KM, MCLIP, Sen.Lib., Birmingham L.Serv., Business Inf. [0029540] 30/08/1978
Williams Ms KY, (was Leung), BA CertEd MA MCLIP, Unemployed. [0044415] 05/10/1990
Williams Mrs L, (was Askew), BA(Hons) DipLIS MCLIP, Asst.Lib., Univ.of the W.of England, Bristol. [0049348] 26/10/1993
Williams Mrs LE, (was Woodward), BA MCLIP, Inf.Lib., Denbighshire L.& Inf.Serv., Rhuthun. [0023731] 27/01/1975
Williams Miss LEM, BA MCLIP FRSA, Retired. [0015947] 09/08/1961
Williams Mrs LM, (was Evans), MCLIP, Sen.Br.Lib., Cardiff L.Serv., Cardiff. [0004681] 10/03/1970
Williams Miss M, MCLIP, Retired. [0015952] 23/01/1951
Williams Mr M, BLib MCLIP MA, Electronic Res.Lib., Univ.of Wolverhampton. [0038510] 30/05/1985
Williams Mr M, p./t.Stud./Dep.Mgr., Trade Partners UK, London. [0060042] 03/12/2001
Williams Mrs M, BA MCLIP, Inf.Serv.Mgr., Kimberlin L., De Montfort Univ. [0015954] 15/09/1969
Williams Mrs M, (was Pigg), BA MCLIP, Learning Res.Mgr., W.Herts.Coll., Cassio Campus. [0015955] 01/01/1965
Williams Prof M, BA MA HonFCLIP, Hon Fellow. [0060087] 07/12/2001 FE 01/04/2002
Williams Mr MA, BSc, L.Asst., The Queens Coll., Oxford. [0059072] 07/11/2000
Williams Mrs MA, BA(Hons) MCLIP, Sen.Lib.-Child.Serv.,(Job-share), Shropshire Co.L.H.Q. [0035189] 30/09/1982
Williams Mrs MA, (was Izatt), MCLIP, Unemployed. [0015957] 21/07/1952
Williams Mrs MAM, (was Rees), BA DipLib MCLIP, L.Asst., Newport Cent.L., Newport Co.Bor.Council. [0034594] 01/01/1982
Williams Miss ME, Comm.Lib., Caerphilly Co.Bor. [0035647] 18/11/1982
Williams Mrs ME, (was Brinkley), BA(Hons), Retired. [0045748] 14/05/1991
Williams Mrs MG, BA FCLIP, Retired. [0015958] 17/09/1953 FE 01/01/1963
Williams Mr MHM, (was Steven), MA DipLib MCLIP, Head of L.Support Serv., Staffs.L.& Inf.Serv., Stafford. [0029419] 12/08/1978
Williams Mrs MM, BA MSc, Lib., Goethe Inst., Romania. [0051758] 01/07/1975
Williams Mrs NMJ, (was Davies), BA DipLib MCLIP, Sen.Inf.Adviser, Univ.of Gloucestershire. [0041675] 10/02/1988
Williams Ms NP, BA DipLib, Local Hist.L.Asst. & Indexer, L.B.of Ealing,Cent.L., London. W5. [0043786] 11/01/1990
Williams Mr NR, BA MCLIP, Lib.Computer Serv.Mgr., Inst.of Chartered Accountants in, England & Wales,London. [0021571] 30/10/1973
Williams Mr P, DipTS MCLIP, Position unknown, Beds.Health Auth. [0060677] 12/12/2001
Williams Mrs P, BA, Inf.Offr., Knowsley Comm.Coll. [0049433] 27/10/1993
Williams Mrs P, BA(Hons) MCLIP, Acq.Lib., Liverpool Hope Univ.Coll. [0049434] 27/10/1993
Williams Miss PC, MCLIP, Retired. [0015970] 08/03/1961
Williams Mrs PC, (was Freck), BA DipLib MCLIP, Lib., Birmingham P.L. [0005205] 07/08/1967
Williams Mrs PC, (was Burke), MCLIP, Sch.Lib., Howell's Sch., Cardiff. [0015969] 19/01/1964
Williams Mr PF, BA MA MCLIP, Asst.Dir.of Learning Res., Chester Coll.of H.E., Cheshire. [0015971] 25/07/1966

Williams Miss PJ, BA, Lib., St Deiniols L., Flintshire. [0039987] 08/10/1986
Williams Mr PJ, BA MA MCLIP, Asst.Lib., L.Serv., Univ.Coll.London. [0054951] 29/05/1997
Williams Mrs PL, (was Mathews), BA(Hons) MA MCLIP, Lib., S.Staffs.Health Auth., Stafford. [0052168] 11/10/1995
Williams Mrs PM, (was Carroll), B Lib MCLIP, Lib., Morgan Cole, Cardiff. [0002414] 18/01/1972
Williams Mrs PS, (was Dryburgh), BSc DipLib MCLIP, Career Break. [0043642] 15/11/1989
Williams Miss R, (was Marshall), L.Asst., Sefton M.B.C., Southport. [0058120] 03/11/1999
Williams Mr R, BA MCLIP, Sen.Br.Lib., Cardiff C.C. [0033974] 30/06/1981
Williams Mrs R, (was Hughes), MSc MCLIP, Area Lib., N., Rhondda Cynon Taff Co.Bor.L., Aberdare. [0024034] 07/03/1975
Williams Mr RFS, BA MCLIP, Dir.of Inf.Systems & Serv., Univ.of N.London. [0015976] 01/07/1972
Williams Dr RG, MA MPhil PhD MCLIP, Inf.Tech.Trainer/Lib./Arch., London & Quadrant Housing Trust, Mapledurham & Hendred House. [0015978] 27/01/1968
Williams Mr RG, BA(Hons) MCLIP, Ref.& Inf.Specialist, Cheshire L.& Cult., E.Div., Macclesfield Area. [0015977] 22/02/1962
Williams Mrs RhG, BA DipLib MCLIP, Princ.Lib., Conwy Co.Bor.Council, Conwy L.,Inf.& Arch.Serv. [0028211] 26/09/1977
Williams Mrs RL, (was Crawford), BA(Hons) MA, Asst.Lib., Airedale Gen.Hosp. [0058833] 23/08/2000
Williams Mrs RM, (was Harte), BA DipLib MCLIP, Unemployed. [0031318] 16/10/1979
Williams Mr RN, BA(Hons) MA MCLIP, Libr.Mgr., Bloomsbury Healthcare Lib., London. [0055071] 02/10/1995
Williams Mr RT, MILAM FCLIP, Retired. [0015980] 08/10/1965 FE 27/11/1996
Williams Mr RV, BA(Hons), Unemployed. [0060049] 06/12/2001
Williams Miss S, BA(Hons) MSc, Asst.Lib., Middlesex Univ., Art & Design L. [0058711] 01/07/2000
Williams Mrs S, (was Judson), BA MCLIP, Retired. [0004545] 06/10/1961
Williams Mrs SA, (was Clough), BA DipLib MCLIP, Asst.Lib., Birkenhead Cent.L., Wirral Bor.Council. [0029615] 24/10/1978
Williams Mrs SB, (was Wright), BA(Hons) MCLIP, Sch.Lib., Hammond Sch., Chester. [0033901] 01/05/1981
Williams Miss SC, BA MCLIP, Sen.Lib., Lend.Serv. Cent.L., Bradford Metro.Dist. [0015984] 03/03/1972
Williams Mrs SC, MSc MLS MCLIP, Retired. [0019034] 07/11/1966
Williams Mrs SE, (was Davies), BA(Hons) DipLib, Unemployed. [0044005] 04/04/1990
Williams Miss SF, BSc(Hons) MCLIP, Lib., S.Wales Miners' L., Univ.of Wales, Swansea, Swansea. [0045623] 04/04/1991
Williams Mrs SJ, BA MCLIP, Sen.Inf.Offr., Research L., Gtr.London Auth. [0029426] 01/07/1978
Williams Miss SL, MCLIP, Database Mgr., L.B.of Richmond. [0015986] 04/03/1971
Williams Mrs SM, (was Wildblood), BA MCLIP, Learning Res.Cent.Mgr., Dr.Challoners High Sch., Little Chalfont, Bucks. [0026607] 17/10/1976
Williams Ms SR, BSc(Hons) DipLib MCLIP, Relief Asst.Lib. [0046728] 02/01/1992
Williams Miss T, Employment not known. [0037394] 08/08/1984
Williams Mrs TD, BA MCLIP, Local Studies Lib., Wolverhampton Arch.& Local Studies. [0036567] 20/10/1983
Williams Mr TD, B.th(Hons), Resource Mgr., Croydon R.E.Cent., London. [0059480] 09/04/2001
Williams Mr TG, PGDipLib, Lib./Inf.Offr., Roskill Inf.Serv., London. [0037900] 20/10/1984
Williams Miss TL, BA(Hons), Stud., Univ.of Wales, Aberystwyth. [0059205] 08/01/2001
Williams Mrs VK, (was Broster), BSc(Hons) CertEd MSc MCLIP, Lib., The Leeds Teaching Hosp.NHS Trust, Otley. [0050127] 17/03/1994
Williams Mrs WF, (was Boast), MCLIP, Unemployed. [0001425] 25/09/1969
Williams Mr WG, OBE HonFCLIP MInstAM FRSA, Head of Cultural Serv., Denbighshire C.C. [0015993] 12/06/1964 FE 12/01/1993
Williamson Mr AR, BA MA, Music Lib., Bor.of S.Tyneside, Cent.L. [0042185] 11/10/1988
Williamson Mrs E, (was Marcinowicz), BA MCLIP, Sch.Lib.(Ancillary), N.W.Essex Educ.Dept., Essex C.C. [0009726] 23/10/1970
Williamson Mrs G, (was Smith), BA MCLIP, Resource Lib., Univ.of Wolverhampton, W.Midlands. [0046471] 13/01/1966
Williamson Miss H, Project Offr., The L.Partnership - W.Mids. [0052336] 30/10/1995
Williamson Mrs HMF, (was Strachan), MA MCLIP, Princ.L.Offr., Fine Art Dept., Edinburgh City L. [0022656] 01/08/1974
Williamson Miss J, MCLIP MPhil, Lib.& Res.Mgr., Bloomsbury Healthcare L., London. [0022182] 28/02/1974
Williamson Mrs JB, (was Clouston), MLib MCLIP, Retired. [0017969] 25/02/1962
Williamson Mrs JM, (was Bull), BA PGDipLib MCLIP, Asst.Lib., Bucks.C.C., Amersham L. [0044235] 19/07/1990
Williamson Miss KA, MA, Local Studies Lib.(Job Share), Darlington Bor.Council. [0051230] 30/11/1994
Williamson Mr MC, BA MA MCLIP, Sch.Lib., Milton Keynes Unitary Auth., M.Keynes. [0038343] 19/03/1985
Williamson Mr ME, BA MCLIP, Bookseller p./t., Waterstones, Manchester. [0038491] 17/05/1985
Williamson Mr MG, MCLIP, Retired. [0015999] 03/02/1962
Williamson Mr MJ, BA(Hons) PhD, Lect.-Media & Inf.Stud., Sch.of Inf.Mgmt., Univ.of Brighton. [0047920] 26/10/1992
Williamson Mrs MJ, (was Exton), BA MCLIP, L.Asst., Acquisition, CCLRC, Rutherford Appleton Lab., Oxon. [0020652] 20/05/1973

Personal Members / Wilson

Williamson Ms R, BA, Stud., Univ.of N.London, &, L.Asst., Kings Coll.London. [0058949] 10/10/2000
Williamson Mrs SA, (was Yelton), BA MCLIP, Lib.(Lend.& Inf.), Evesham P.L., Worcs. [0031508] 01/10/1979
Williamson Ms SA, BA(Hons) MCLIP, Editorial Mgr., NBS Serv., Newcastle-upon-Tyne. [0044752] 19/11/1990
Williamson Mrs YC, Lib., Wilson Carlile Coll.of Evangelism, Sheffield. [0061308] 20/05/2002 **AF**
Willimott Mrs PM, BA(Hons) MCLIP, Learning Cent.Mgr., Barnsley Coll., S.Yorks. [0020467] 01/01/1969
Willimott Mr TS, BA AIL MCLIP, Catr., Brit.L. [0034553] 11/01/1982
Willing Ms JA, BA MCLIP, Sen.Lib., Glasgow Dist.L. [0016004] 24/10/1969
Willingham Miss AE, BA MSc(Econ) MCLIP, Asst.Lib., Milton Keynes Cent.L. [0055399] 09/10/1997
Willis Mrs AJ, (was Platts), BA(Hons) MCLIP, Sen.L.Asst., St.James's Univ.Hosp.Med.L. [0052687] 20/11/1995
Willis Miss AL, MCLIP, Unemployed. [0016007] 10/09/1968
Willis Miss AM, L.Super., Crosby L., Met.Bor.of Sefton. [0046273] 22/01/1991
Willis Mrs CA, BA DipLib, Med.Lib., Wits L.of Mgmt., S.Africa. [0059320] 07/02/2001
Willis Mrs DM, Sen.L.Asst., Business L., Nottingham City L. [0046206] 02/10/1991 **AF**
Willis Mrs G, (was Hutchinson), BA, Sen.Learning Cent.Asst., Sandwell Coll., Wednesbury. [0035292] 12/10/1982
Willis Miss HG, MCLIP, Retired. [0017971] 29/01/1957
Willis Mr PJ, MCLIP, Life Member. [0016013] 01/01/1957
Willis Mrs S, MCLIP, Inf.Serv.Asst., Mishon De Reya, London. [0056132] 03/03/1998
Willis Mr ST, BA DipLib MCLIP, Princ.Offr.:S.Dist., Manchester P.L. [0025136] 06/11/1975
Willis-Fear Mrs RM, BA MCLIP, Ref.Lib., Ilford Cent.L. [0033818] 21/02/1981
Willison Mr IR, HonFCLIP, Hon.Fellow. [0044039] 30/09/1988 **FE 30/09/1988**
Willison Ms MC, MA MSc MCLIP, Head of Enquiry Serv., Glasgow Univ.L. [0041307] 02/11/1987
Willmot Mrs DM, (was Russell), MCLIP, Unemployed, 53 Pier Ave., Whitstable,Kent,CT5 2HJ. [0012788]08/02/1972
Willmott Miss EM, MCLIP, Life Member. [0016018] 14/03/1959
Willoughby Mrs AM, (was Mitchell), BA, Unemployed. [0041579] 21/01/1988
Willoughby Mrs CB, (was Hawdon), BA DipLib DMS MCLIP, Asst.Dir.-Learning Resources, Univ.of Northumbria at Newcastle. [0023387] 01/01/1975
Willows Ms J, BA(Hons), p./t.Stud./Princ.Inf.Asst., Manchester Met.Univ., Univ.of Salford. [0061056] 14/02/2002
Willox Miss NP, MA MCLIP, Life Member. [0016024] 27/09/1953
Wills Mr A, BA MCLIP, L.Network Mgr., Leics.City Ls. [0019926] 16/01/1973
Wills Mr AL, MCLIP, Hon.Ed."Northern Lib.", 7 Wansfell Dr., Kendal, LA9 7JF, Tel.01539 726264. [0016025] 03/03/1951
Wills Mr DF, MA DipLib MCLIP, Lib., Squire Law L., Univ.of Cambridge. [0043159] 31/08/1989
Wills Ms HJ, BLib MCLIP, Idea Stores Programme Dir., L.B.of Tower Hamlets. [0040832] 01/07/1987
Wills Mrs J, BA(Hons), Sch.Lib., Sir Joseph Williamson's Math.Sch., Rochester. [0054344] 27/11/1996
Wills Mrs JJ, (was Karle), BA DipLib MCLIP, p./t.L.Asst., Warwickshire Coll., Royal Leamington Spa. [0039737] 02/06/1986
Wills Miss JM, BA MCLIP, Retired. [0017972] 22/09/1962
Wills Miss SM, MCLIP, Team Lib., Enfield P.L. [0016032] 19/11/1967
Willsher Mr MJD, BSc DipLib MCLIP, Data Res.& Systems Asst., Croydon L. [0016033] 20/10/1964
Willson Mr AEG, Mgr., L.& Inf.Serv., Atomic Weapons Establishment, Reading, Berks. [0016034] 01/01/1978
Willson Miss EJ, FCLIP, Retired. [0017973] 17/03/1936 **FE 01/01/1946**
Willson Mr JP, BA MA, Princ.Lect., Dept.of Inf.& Communications, Manchester Metro.Univ. [0034222] 12/10/1981
Wilman Mrs HE, M(Hons), P./t.Stud., Lib., Thames Valley Univ., Easthampstead Park Sch., Berks. [0059789] 03/10/2001
Wilman Mrs L, MCLIP, Ref.& Local Studies Lib., Lancs.L., Morecambe L. [0024458] 21/07/1975
Wilmot Ms C, MA(Hons), Stud., Newcastle Univ. [0059803] 10/11/2000
Wilmot Mrs F, (was Headford), MCLIP, Inf.Offr., Warks.Assoc.for the Blind, Warwick. [0006637] 06/02/1962
Wilmot Mr RS, BA DipLib, Lib., Rowley Regis Cent.of Dudley Coll., W.Midlands. [0042165] 11/10/1988
Wilsher Mrs JC, (was Simpson), BA MCLIP, Unemployed. [0038398] 16/04/1985
Wilsher Mr RF, MA DipLib, Lib., ACAS, London. [0037074] 23/01/1984
Wilson Miss AD, MA MCLIP, Retired. [0017973] 01/01/1964
Wilson Mrs AE, (was Kemble), BSc(Hons), Trainee Lib., Market Harborough L. [0058573] 03/04/2000
Wilson Mr AJ, P./t.Stud./L.Asst., Spellow L., Liverpool John Moores Univ. [0053563] 24/07/1996
Wilson Miss AM, Finance & Inf.Offr., Historic Scotland, Edinburgh. [0055818] 26/11/1997
Wilson Mrs AM, MA, Dep.Lib., Bromley Coll.of F.& H.E., Kent. [0023595] 22/01/1975
Wilson Ms AM, (was Gomm), MA MSc DipLib MCLIP, Inf.Consultant, Inside Information, Cambridge. [0035682] 26/09/1966
Wilson Mr AR, BA, Stud., Robert Gordon Univ., Aberdeen. [0061057] 14/02/2002
Wilson Mr BAH, MA(Hons) BD, High Sch.Lib., Woodstock Sch., Mussoorie, India. [0050712] 12/10/1994
Wilson Miss BI, BA MCLIP, Area Co-ordinator, E.Grp., Notts. [0016048] 09/10/1968
Wilson Miss CA, MA MCLIP, Retired. [0016050] 20/02/1959

Wilson Mrs CA, (was Brown), MCLIP, Serv.Co-ordinator(Kent & Sussex), Reg.L.& Inf.Unit, Royal Surrey Hosp. [0016051] 03/10/1962
Wilson Miss CE, BA(Hons) PGCE MA MCLIP, Deputy L.Serv.Mgr., Manchester Metro.Univ.L. [0048881] 09/07/1993
Wilson Miss CH, BA MCLIP, Lib., Strathclyde Police, Force Training Cent., Glasgow. [0034470] 16/11/1981
Wilson Mr CJ, BA(Hons) DipLib MA MCLIP, Sen.Asst.Lib.-Inf.Servs., London Sch.of Economics. [0048289] 24/11/1992
Wilson Mrs CS, BA(Hons) MCLIP, Asst.Lib., Bromsgrove L., Worcs.C.C. [0043387] 13/10/1989
Wilson Mr CWJ, FCLIP, Life member. [0016055] 01/01/1941 **FE 01/01/1950**
Wilson Mrs CWL, MA(Hons) MCLIP, Stud., Dept.of Inf.Sci., Univ.of Strathclyde. [0046556] 14/11/1991
Wilson Mrs D, BA MCLIP, Employment not known. [0060205] 10/12/2001
Wilson Miss DA, BA(Hons), Stud., Manchester Metropolitan Univ. [0059238] 12/01/2001
Wilson Miss DA, MA(Hons) MLitt MCLIP, Inf.Offr., Fife Adult Guidance & Educ.Serv. [0055959] 22/12/1997
Wilson Mr DAG, MA MCLIP, Retired., 27,Lower Stoke, Limpley Stoke. [0016056] 15/09/1948
Wilson Mr DR, BA LIB MCLIP, Asst.Lib., Bradford Cent.L., Lend.Dept. [0019658] 31/10/1972
Wilson Mr DV, FCLIP, Retired. [0016058] 04/09/1952 **FE 01/01/1964**
Wilson Miss EF, MCLIP, Sen.L.Asst., Sheffield Univ., Main L. [0030300] 02/01/1979
Wilson Ms EJ, BA Hons, Stud., Strathclyde Uni. [0060946] 15/01/2002
Wilson Miss EKM, BA MA, Princ.L.Asst., Sch.of Oriental & African Studies, The L., London. [0057090] 04/12/1998
Wilson Miss EM, MCLIP, Team Lib., Met.Bor.Stockport. [0016062] 01/01/1967
Wilson Mrs EM, (was Miles), MCLIP, Unemployed. [0016063] 30/01/1964
Wilson Miss EM, Stud., Univ.of Wales, Aberystwyth. [0061561] 02/10/2002
Wilson Miss FM, BSc(Hons) MSc, Trainee Lib., Reading Bor.Council. [0057219] 20/01/1999
Wilson Miss G, MCLIP, Asst.Lib., Darlington Ref., Darlington Bor.Council. [0022049] 08/01/1974
Wilson Mrs GM, (was Slater), BA DipLib MCLIP, Reader Devel.Offr., Blackburn with Darwen Bor., Blackburn Cent.L. [0024237] 01/05/1975
Wilson Mrs HM, (was Ogle), BA(Hons) MA MCLIP, Unemployed. [0049251] 18/10/1993
Wilson Mrs HV, BSc MA MCLIP, Inf.Mgr., Lloyds TSB., Bristol. [0044015] 06/04/1990
Wilson Mr IL, BA MCLIP, Adult Lend.Serv.Offr., Redcar & Cleveland Bor.C. [0016072] 04/01/1971
Wilson Ms IL, BA(Hons) MA MCLIP, Faculty Lib., Univ.of Cent.England, Birmingham. [0051077] 14/11/1994
Wilson Mrs J, BA MCLIP, Sch.Lib., Marshalls Park Sch. [0033198] 01/10/1980
Wilson Mrs J, (was McSkimming), BA MCLIP, Inf.Sci., DNV, Aberdeen. [0039859] 19/09/1986
Wilson Miss JE, BA(Hons) DipIS, L.Exec., House of Commons L., London. [0057024] 26/11/1998
Wilson Mrs JE, (was Lawson), BA MCLIP, Career Break. [0040866] 23/07/1987
Wilson Mrs JES, (was Shipp), BA MCLIP, Freelance indexer. [0025105] 28/10/1975
Wilson Mr JM, BSc DipLib MCLIP, Employment not known. [0060808] 12/12/2001
Wilson Mrs JM, (was Young), MCLIP, Head of L.(Job Share), Wyggeston & Queen Elizabeth I, 6th Form Coll., Leicester. [0017976] 14/09/1964
Wilson Miss K, BSc(Hons) MSc DipLIS MCLIP, Inf.Offr., BAAF Adoption & Fostering, London. [0053796] 01/10/1996
Wilson Miss KC, MA(Hons) MLitt, Stud., Strathclyde Univ. [0061761] 06/11/2002
Wilson Miss KE, BA(Hons), Community Lib., Kent C.C. [0055786] 17/11/1997
Wilson Mr KM, BA(Hons) MCLIP, Inf.Serv.Dir., Nat.Building Specification, Newcastle upon Tyne. [0016078] 19/01/1972
Wilson Mrs KM, BA(Hons), Sen. Learning Res. Asst., Leeds Met. Univ. [0060925] 10/01/2002 **AF**
Wilson Mrs L, (was Bell), BA(Hons), Lib., Pinderfields & Pontefract Hosp., NHS Turst. [0050691] 12/10/1994
Wilson Mrs L, (was Montgomery), BA DipLib MCLIP, p./t.Team Lib., Univ.of Northumbria at Newcastle. [0028088] 13/10/1977
Wilson Mrs LC, (was Whiting), MLS MCLIP, Lib., Leics.L.& Inf.Serv., Hinckley. [0015765] 01/01/1971
Wilson Mrs LC, (was White), BA(Hons) MCLIP, Co-ordinating Lib., W.Dunbartonshire Council, Alexandria L. [0047919] 26/10/1992
Wilson Miss LM, MA(Hons) DipLib MCLIP, Princ.Lib., Educ.Res.Serv., N.Lanarkshire Council. [0035484] 21/10/1982
Wilson Ms LS, BSc(Hons) MSc, Faculty Lib., Univ.of Durham. [0047065] 21/04/1992
Wilson Miss M, BEd DipLib MCLIP DMS, Br.Serv.Lib., Aberdeen City L. [0024837] 27/09/1975
Wilson Miss MA, MCLIP, Stock Team Lib., Nuneaton & Bedworth Div., Warks.C.C. [0018063] 04/10/1972
Wilson Mrs MA, (was Marshall), DipLib, Child.Lib., Glossop L., Derbys. [0009801] 15/01/1969
Wilson Mrs MB, (was Quin), MCLIP, Retired. [0012082] 26/09/1958
Wilson Miss ME, MA(Hons) PgDip, Trainee Lib., Falkirk Council L.Serv. [0061526] 13/09/2002
Wilson Miss MH, OBE MSc MCLIP, Life Member. [0016086] 08/03/1963
Wilson Dr MI, BA PhD MCLIP, Retired. [0039627] 16/04/1986
Wilson Mrs MK, BA(Hons) MCLIP, Asst.Lib., Christchurch L., Dorset C.C. [0055665] 07/11/1997
Wilson Mrs MMM, (was Spielberg), MCLIP, Prof.Lib.-Enquiry Serv., Inf.Serv., Univ.of Birmingham. [0013821] 01/01/1970

Wilson Mr MP, BA(Hons) MA, p./t.Asst.Lib., Selwyn Coll., Cambridge. [0054332] 21/11/1996
Wilson Miss MR, MCLIP, Life Member. [0016088] 31/10/1949
Wilson Mr P, MA DLIS MCLIP, Learning Res.Mgr., S.Nottingham Coll., W.Bridgford. [0020968] 24/08/1973
Wilson Mrs PA, (was Roe), MCLIP, Asst.Bibl.Offr., The Royal Bor.of, Kensington & Chelsea L.& Arts Serv. [0029308] 01/01/1967
Wilson Mrs PA, (was Moore), MCLIP, Priority Serv.Offr., Stockton Bor.Council, Billingham L. [0010354] 01/01/1970
Wilson Ms PJ, BA(Hons), Coll.Lib., Leics.City Council, Leicester, Leics. [0033199] 08/10/1980
Wilson Mr PR, BA, Stud. [0061453] 01/08/2002
Wilson Mr RBH, BSc(Econ) MCLIP, Grp.Lib., Barnsley Met.Dist.Council, Royston Br.L. [0016094] 09/04/1969
Wilson Mrs RD, (was Allum), BA MCLIP, Sen.Lib., Nat.L.of Australia, Canberra. [0017978] 01/01/1955
Wilson Mr RG, BA(Hons) DipIS, Inf.Offr., MIDIRS., Bristol. [0048503] 28/01/1993
Wilson Miss RJ, BA MCLIP, Economics Lib., DEFRA, London. [0032360] 02/02/1980
Wilson Mr RM, MSc, Unemployed. [0060934] 10/01/2002
Wilson Mrs RS, BA DipLib MCLIP, Educ.Support Lib., Middlesbrough Bor.C., Middlesbrough. [0033742] 08/02/1981
Wilson Mr RTM, MA DipLib CertEd MCLIP, Retired. [0016095] 23/09/1957
Wilson Mr S, BA(Hons) DipLib MCLIP, Business Inf.Offr., Business Link Cheshire & Warrington, Cheshire. [0043885] 08/02/1990
Wilson Miss SA, MCLIP, Life Member. [0016098] 28/02/1950
Wilson Mrs SE, MCLIP, Indexer, SPICE., Scottish Parliament HQ., Edinburgh. [0028978] 04/02/1978
Wilson Mr SJ, BA(Hons) DipLib MCLIP, Inf.Sci., DePuy Internat.Ltd., Leeds. [0053783] 01/01/1996
Wilson Mrs SJ, (was Hawthorne), BA DipLib MCLIP, p./t.Inf.Offr./Lib., Scottish Motor Neurone Disease Ass., Glasgow. [0032973] 01/10/1980
Wilson Mrs SJ, (was Mole), Lib., Nat.Assembly of Wales, Cardiff. [0039763] 01/07/1986
Wilson Ms SJ, BA(Hons) DipIS, Unemployed. [0052689] 17/11/1995
Wilson Miss SK, BSc(Hons) DipLIS MCLIP, Inf.Mgr., Business Link Lincs.& Rutland, Lincoln. [0044578] 30/10/1990
Wilson Mrs SL, (was Howden), BA(Hons) MSc, Career Break. [0045690] 24/04/1991
Wilson Mrs SM, (was Rabson), BA DipLib MCLIP, p./t.Asst.Lib., Royal Soc.of Med., London. [0027009] 07/01/1977
Wilson Ms SM, DipInf, Policy Adviser, D.T.I., Consumer Affairs, London. [0052934] 30/01/1986
Wilson Dr TD, BSc FCLIP HonFCLIP, Retired. [0016101] 24/01/1952 FE 01/01/1961
Wilson Mrs W, (was Garrett), BA MCLIP, Lib., Scottish Baptist Coll., Univ.of Paisley. [0005383] 09/01/1970
Wilson Mr WP, BA, Lay Staff, Collegiate Church of St.Peter, Westminster. [0054849] 17/04/1997
Wilson Miss Y, BA MCLIP, Child.Lib., Wigan Child.L., Met.Wigan. [0024043] 14/03/1975
Wilson Miss ZC, BSc MSc, Info.Sci., HMC & E., London. [0055436] 13/10/1997
Wilton Mrs SE, MA, Unemployed. [0059212] 08/01/2001
Wiltshire Miss E, BA DipLib MCLIP CertMgt, Area Mgr., N.Tyneside Council. [0032218] 05/02/1980
Winch Mr SJ, BA(Hons), Digitisation Researcher, E.Dunvartonshire Council. [0059446] 30/03/2001
Winchester Ms K, BA, Inf.Offr., Social Care Inst.for Excellence, London. [0044219] 12/07/1990
Winchester Mrs S, (was Tookey), MCLIP, Sch.Lib., Mount Grace Sch., Potters Bar. [0014795] 26/01/1967
Winchester Miss SJ, MCLIP AALIA, Lib., Melbourne Museum, Victoria, Australia. [0016114] 10/01/1972
Windaybank Mrs EMA, (was Mockett), MCLIP, YPLS Reading Devel.Lib., L.B.Richmond. [0010268] 01/01/1969
Winder Ms JR, BA(Hons) DipILS MCLIP, Sen.L.Asst., Special Collections, Leeds Univ.L. [0054136] 01/11/1996
Winder Miss NA, MCLIP, Life Member, Tel.01565 653264. [0016117] 04/10/1938
Windle Miss L, BA, Learning Res.Cent.Mgr., The Sheffield Coll., Peaks Learning Res.Cent. [0042693] 02/02/1989
Windsor Mrs RJ, (was Lumb), BA MCLIP, Retired. [0016122] 25/01/1953
Winfield Mrs JA, (was Willcox), BA MCLIP, Lib.;Child. & Young people, Derby City L. [0033670] 04/02/1981
Wing Mr HJR, MA MCLIP, Retired. [0016125] 01/01/1957
Wingate-Martin Ms DE, (was Walker), BA MCLIP, Dir.of Learning & Inf.Serv., Univ.of Herts. [0015214] 09/01/1970
Winkworth Mrs LT, (was Johnson), Sch.Lib., Headington Sch., Oxford. [0045405] 03/01/1991 AF
Winkworth Miss RA, BA MCLIP, Inf.Mgr., SG Asset Mgmt., London. [0022561] 06/06/1974
Winlo Mrs REM, (was Newell), MA MCLIP, Unemployed. [0028871] 01/02/1978
Winn Miss JT, BA(Hons), Inf.Cent.Asst., The Scout Assoc., London. [0049431] 27/10/1993
Winn Miss VA, MA FCLIP, Retired. [0016132] 16/03/1957 FE 01/01/1966
Winning Mrs E, BA DipLib MCLIP DPs MSc, p./t.Temp.Lib., IACR-Rothamsted, Herts. [0041686] 12/02/1998
Winning Miss MA, BSc(Hons) MSc, Inf.Offr., Scharr, Univ.of Sheffield. [0057058] 02/12/1998
Winser Miss AJ, BA MCLIP, Retired/L.Volunteer, Sussex Archaeological Soc., Lewes. [0016134] 21/03/1958

Winship Mr IR, BA MA MCLIP, Mgr.-Elec.Serv., Univ.of Northumbria at Newcastle. [0016135] 03/04/1968
Winsor Mrs AN, (was Messenger), MCLIP, Health Inf.Super., NHS Direct, Milton Keynes. [0028343] 18/10/1977
Winstanley Mrs JV, (was Mansell), BA MCLIP, L.Asst., Beech Green Primary Sch., Gloucester. [0023563] 21/01/1975
Winter Ms CA, BA DipLib MCLIP, Child.Lib., Bristol City Council. [0041548] 18/01/1988
Winter Mrs DT, (was Churchill), BA(Hons), L.Specialist Support Mgr., Sandwell Comm.L.Serv. [0049412] 21/10/1993
Winter Mr DW, BA(Hons), Lib., City of Manchester L., Manchester. [0044745] 15/11/1990
Winter Mr EC, BA MCLIP FCLIP HonFCLIP, Exec.Sec., L.Serv.Ltd., London. [0019435] 10/03/1953 FE 01/01/1957
Winter Miss JK, BA(Hons) MCLIP, Grp.Mgr., Arts L.& Mus.Dept., Durham C.C. [0040435] 03/02/1987
Winter Mrs SE, BA(Hons) MA, Asst.Lib.& Training Co-ordinator, Denton Wilde Sapte, London. [0053887] 01/10/1996
Winterbotham Miss D, MBE FCLIP, Life Member, Tel:01204 707885. [0019436] 23/03/1953 FE 01/01/1963
Winterbottom Mrs G, Lib./Res.Mgr., Alderman Callow S.& C.C., Coventry. [0061049] 05/02/2002 AF
Winterbottom Mr PL, BA(Hons) MCLIP DMS, Inf.Systems Lib., Wakefield Met.Dist.Council, W.Yorks. [0041367] 10/11/1987
Winterburn Miss SJ, BA MCLIP, Retired. [0016139] 10/09/1954
Winterman Dr V, BSc MSc PhD MCLIP, Employment not known. [0040330] 08/01/1987
Winters Mr M, BA, PG Stud., Univ.of Wales, Aberystywth. [0056103] 17/02/1998
Winters Mrs MR, (was McAllister), BA MCLIP, Comm.Lib., Glenburn L., Renfrewshire Council. [0032751] 12/08/1980
Wintersgill Mr I, BA DipLib MCLIP, Record Off.Super., Berks.Record Off., Reading Bor.Council. [0016140] 25/01/1972
Winterton Mr JR, BA DipLib LLB MCLIP, Lib., Inst.of Adv.Legal Stud., Univ.of London. [0027384] 11/01/1977
Wintle Mrs EM, (was Wardall), LLB DipLib MCLIP, Lib.& Editor, Brit.Inst.of Internat.& Comp.Law, London. [0027376] 24/02/1977
Wintle Miss KE, BA DipLib, Unemployed., 33 Fontwell Drive, Downend, Bristol. BS16 6RR. [0043791] 09/01/1990
Winton Mrs LA, BA MCLIP, Tech.& Systems Lib., Croydon Coll., Surrey. [0016141] 01/10/1969
Winton Mr SR, BA DipLib MCLIP, Sen.Lib.-Inf.& Systems Support, Midlothian Council L. [0033430] 29/11/1980
Wintour Mr BJC, MA MCLIP, Life Member. [0016142] 28/04/1954
Wintrip Mr JA, BA MSc MCLIP, Applied Sci.Lib., Univ.of the W.of England, Bristol. [0022919] 05/10/1974
Wiper Mr CK, BA(Hons) DipLib MCLIP, Sen.Inf.Offr., Cent.for Local Economic Strategies, Manchester. [0031984] 07/01/1980
Wisdom Mr JJ, MA MCLIP, Asst.Lib./Lib., Guildhall L./St.Paul's Cathedral. [0030302] 11/12/1978
Wisdom Miss S, PhD Stud. [0054489] 08/01/1997
Wise Mr AP, BA MCLIP, Authorised Interviewer, Off.for Nat.Statistics, London. [0016144] 03/09/1966
Wise Mrs CM, (was Mathewson), BA MA DipLib MCLIP, Head of Historic Collections, Univ.of London L. [0036234] 09/08/1983
Wise Mrs JD, MCLIP, Retired. [0029250] 01/01/1952
Wiseman Miss HM, BSc MSc, Employment not known. [0060682] 12/12/2001
Wiseman Mrs LK, (was Snowdon), BA DipLib MLIB MCLIP, Lib., Herts.L., Bishops Stortford. [0039956] 09/10/1986
Wishart Mrs D, Sen.L.Asst., Southport Pub.L. [0055180] 01/08/1997 AF
Wishart Mrs L, (was Lagden), BSc MA DipLib MCLIP, Head of Inf.Mgmnt., Dept.of Health, London. [0008553] 02/01/1972
Wishart Mrs RI, MA DipEd MCLIP, Lib., Queen Marys L., St.Leonards Sch., Fife. [0027477] 01/04/1977
Witcombe Mrs V, (was Craigie), MA DipLib, Learning Support Asst., Abbotswood Sch., Totton. [0029621] 08/10/1978
Witham Miss SJ, MCLIP, Team Lib.-N.Norfolk, Norfolk L.& Inf.Serv. [0016155] 01/04/1971
Witham Mrs SM, (was Monk), MCLIP, Young People's Lib.(Job-share), Dartford L. [0021220] 04/10/1973
Withecombe Miss LM, BA(Hons) MSc(Econ) MCLIP, Br.Lib., Coll.of Law, Birmingham. [0052504] 02/11/1995
Witherden Miss DM, MCLIP, Inf.Offr., Audit Commission, Bristol. [0044912] 14/01/1991
Withers Mrs SD, (was Neal), BA MCLIP, Retired. [0010696] 20/02/1964
Withington Miss CJ, BA(Hons), Stud., City Univ., London. [0059140] 28/11/2000
Withington Miss LM, BA MCLIP, Area Lib.- Bognor Regis, W.Sussex L.Serv. [0029873] 12/08/1978
Withnall Miss JC, BA(Hons) MA MCLIP, Sen.Inf.Offr., Osborne Clarke, London. [0053894] 09/10/1996
Witkowski Mr SF, MCLIP, Lib./Inf.Offr., City Arch.L., Manchester. [0036700] 14/11/1983
Witter Mrs JB, (was Byron), BA MCLIP, Full-time Mother-Career break. [0027917] 15/10/1977
Witton-Davies Mrs M, (was Lloyd-Hewitt), BA MCLIP, Retired. [0009241] 01/01/1968
Witts Mrs C, BA(Hons) DipLib MCLIP, Lib., Hillview Sch.for Girls, Tonbridge. [0033200] 06/10/1980
Wo Miss KLO, Stud., Univ.of Northumbria, Newcastle. [0061019] 01/02/2002
Wolf Ms CA, (was Pringle), MA(Hons) MA, Lib., HM Treasury, London. [0053780] 01/01/1996
Wolf Ms DC, BA MLS, Cyber Cent.Lib., Queens Bor.P.L., New York, USA. [0054785] 01/04/1997

Wolf Mr MJ, BA(Hons) MA, Asst.Inf.Specialist, Cardiff Univ., Inf.Serv. [0058442] 16/02/2002
Wolfe Mrs RJ, Inf.Mgr., Careers Cent., Univ.of Leeds. [0056741] 12/10/1998 **AF**
Wolff Miss ME, DipLib MCLIP, Community Lib., Selly Oak & Stirchley L., Birmingham. [0028725] 07/01/1978
Wolffsohn Miss PJ, BA(Hons) MCLIP, Lib., Morgan Cole, London. [0046520] 15/11/1991
Wolpert Prof L, DIC PhD FRS HonFCLIP, Hon Fellow. [0060743] 12/12/2001 **FE 01/04/2002**
Wolsey Mrs C, (was Davies), B LIB MCLIP, Learning Support Asst., Studley High Sch., Warks. [0028799] 30/01/1978
Wolsoncroft Mrs FF, (was Sim), MCLIP, Subject Classifier, Whitaker Inf.Serv., Herts. [0016164] 23/09/1964
Wolstenholme Mrs JL, (was Campbell), MCLIP, Mgr.-Young Peoples Serv., Lancs.Co.L. [0016165] 16/02/1964
Wolstenholme Miss S, MCLIP, Cent.Lend.Lib., Cent.L., L.B.of Havering. [0016167] 23/01/1963
Wolverson Miss A, Med.L.Asst., L.& Knowledge Serv., Derby City Gen.Hosp. [0061129] 19/02/2002 **AF**
Womersley Miss PA, BA MCLIP, Area Resources Mgr., E.Surrey, Community Serv., Surrey C.C., Redhill L. [0025456] 12/01/1976
Wong Miss APW, MA(Hons) MScIS, Hosp.Lib., Tuen Mun Hosp.L., Hong Kong. [0051732] 01/06/1995
Wong Mr B, BSc(Hons), Unemployed. [0061439] 29/07/2002
Wong Miss CLM, Lib., Theological Coll., Malaysia. [0058959] 11/10/2000
Wong Miss KL, MCLIP, Retired. [0017989] 24/09/1958
Wong Mr PK, BA, Lib., Hong-Kong P.L. [0050156] 13/04/1994
Wong Miss PYG, BLib(Hons) AALIA MLib MCLIP, Asst.Lib.-Inf.Serv., Hong Kong Poly.Univ.L., Hong Kong. [0046376] 30/10/1991
Wong Miss R, LLB MSc LLM, Stud., Sheffield Univ. [0056649] 01/10/1998
Wong Mrs R, (was Lawton), BA MCLIP, Database Lib., Beds.C.C. [0022802] 11/10/1974
Wong Ms WM, MCLIP, Lib., The Open Univ.of Hong Kong. [0036446] 10/10/1993
Wong Tape Miss YWR, BA MCLIP, Res.Cent.Inf.Offr., Ontario Min.of Labour, Toronto, Canada. [0017996] 29/09/1970
Wontner Miss EMJ, BA(Hons) MSc, Intranet Administrator, Brit.Trade Internat., London. [0056723] 07/10/1998
Woo Mr TYL, BSocSc DipLib MCLIP, Asst.Lib., Univ.of Otago, Dunedin,New Zealand. [0031725] 02/11/1979
Wood Miss A, MA(Hons), Catr., Brit.L., Boston Spa. [0048111] 09/11/1992
Wood Miss A, BA MCLIP, Asst.Lib., Dept.for Educ.& Skills, London. [0016171] 02/01/1969
Wood Mrs A, L.Mgr., Comm.Care, Walsall M.B.C. [0056035] 28/01/1998
Wood Mr AF, BA MCLIP, Life Member. [0016172] 21/08/1960
Wood Mr AG, B LIB MCLIP, Sen.Inf.Sci., GlaxoSmithKline PLC, Ware, Herts. [0027637] 01/06/1977
Wood Mr AG, FCLIP, Retired. [0016173] 09/01/1931 **FE 01/01/1933**
Wood Miss AJ, MA BA MCLIP AssocCIPD MITOL, Training & Devel.Co-ordinator, London P.G.Med.& Dental Educ., London. [0021783] 04/02/1974
Wood Mr AJ, MSc FCLIP, Retired. [0016174] 01/01/1952 **FE 01/01/1958**
Wood Ms AJ, BA(Hons) DipLIS, Sen.Asst.Lib.-Local Studies, L.B.of Harrow. [0049393] 21/10/1993
Wood Miss AKA, (was Hall), MSc BSc(Hons), Unemployed. [0045714] 01/05/1991
Wood Miss AM, BA, Lib., Campden & Chorleywood Food Res., Assoc., Chipping Campden. [0035823] 21/01/1983
Wood Mrs B, (was Tallentire), BA MCLIP, Yth.Serv.Mgr., Gateshead L.& Arts Serv. [0014336] 04/03/1972
Wood Mrs CA, BA MCLIP, Lib., Rothesay Acad., Isle of Bute. [0058671] 16/05/2000
Wood EmLibn CG, MA MLitt FCLIP, Retired. [0016176] 09/03/1937 **FE 01/01/1952**
Wood Mrs CL, (was Gill), MCLIP, Bookbus Lib., Stockton Bor.Council, Stockton on Tees. [0005528] 24/01/1972
Wood Mrs D, (was Whittaker), MCLIP, Retired. [0016178] 01/01/1959
Wood Mr DF, BA MCLIP, Stock Ed.& Requests Lib., Croydon P.L. [0016180] 15/06/1965
Wood Ms EA, BLIB MCLIP, Mgr., Sch.L.Serv., Worcs. [0030699] 14/03/1979
Wood Miss ED, BA(Hons), Published Inf.Asst., Merck Sharp & Dohme, Harlow, Essex. [0052321] 26/10/1999
Wood Mrs EM, (was Spencer), MCLIP, Sch.Lib., S.Wilts.Grammar Sch., Salisbury. [0013802] 01/01/1969
Wood Mrs GWE, BA(Hons) DipLib MCLIP, Head of L.Serv., Herts.C.C., Co.Hall, Hertford. [0038172] 09/01/1985
Wood Ms HE, DipLib CertEd, Lib., Huish Episcopi Sch., Somerset. [0040848] 12/07/1987
Wood Miss HF, BA(Hons) DiplLM MCLIP, Project Offr., L.B.of Hillingdon. [0050645] 06/10/1994
Wood Miss HJ, BA (Hons) MCLIP, Inf.Adivser, Watson Wyatt Worldwide, Reigate. [0046609] 25/11/1991
Wood Miss HMR, MA MCLIP, p./t.Lib., Richmond Coll., London, Thomas More Chambers, London. [0016190] 10/05/1965
Wood Mrs IF, (was Slade), MCLIP, Br.Lib.(Job Share), Cardiff C.C., Rhiwbina Br.L. [0013477] 26/02/1965
Wood Mr IJ, Stud., Univ.of Northumbria, Newcastle. [0059958] 12/11/2001
Wood Mrs JE, (was Mallows), MCLIP, Unemployed. [0016196] 14/10/1964
Wood Miss JG, Trainee Asst.Lib., Elgin Pub.L., Moray Council. [0054931] 14/05/1997 **AF**
Wood Mrs JH, (was Cowham), MA(Cantab) DipLIS, p./t.w/e.L.Super., Univ.of Reading, Whiteknights. [0040001] 06/10/1986
Wood Mrs JI, Stud., Univ of Wales Aberystwyth. [0061580] 02/10/2002
Wood Mr JM, MA FCLIP, Retired, 34a Eleanor Cres., Newcastle,Staffs.,ST5 3SA. [0016199] 07/08/1957 **FE 01/01/1961**

Wood Mrs JM, (was Hayes), MCLIP, Retired. [0017997] 01/01/1946
Wood Mrs JO, (was Ogley), BSc MCLIP, Serv.Devel.Mgr., Canning Town L., L.B.of Newham. [0046687] 11/12/1991
Wood Mr JR, FCLIP, Life Member, Tel.01242 235944, 25 Boulton Rd., Cheltenham, Glos., GL50 4RZ. [0016201] 01/01/1945 **FE 01/01/1965**
Wood Mrs JVB, (was Bailes), BA MCLIP, Sen.Lib.-Young Peoples Serv., Lancs.C.C., Preston. [0000579] 16/01/1970
Wood Ms K, HonFCLIP MA FCLIP, Retired. [0016217] 01/01/1959 **FE 21/03/2001**
Wood Mrs L, (was Woodall), MCLIP, Sen.Lib., E.Lancs.Div., Lancs.C.C. [0016223] 08/10/1971
Wood Ms L, MLS FCLIP, Training Consultant, Self-employed, Manchester. [0000654] 01/01/1971 **FE 24/07/1996**
Wood Miss LGC, BA MCLIP, Catg.Asst., Admin.Centre Devon L. Serv., Exeter. [0016208] 05/10/1970
Wood Mr M, MCLIP, Retired. [0016212] 28/09/1971
Wood Mrs M, MA, Stud., Univ.Newcastle @ Northumbria. [0059798] 03/10/2001
Wood Mrs MB, (was Robertson), L.Asst., Portknockie L., Banffshire. [0045582] 18/03/1991 **AF**
Wood Mrs ME, (was Davis), BA(Hons) MSc, Inf.Researcher, Inst.of Mgmt., Corby, Northants. [0049806] 13/12/1993
Wood Mrs ME, (was MacArthur-Moir), MCLIP, Relief Sch.Lib.Res.Cent.Co-ord., Aberdeen City Council. [0009236] 01/01/1969
Wood Miss N, BA(Hons) MCLIP, Asst.Lib.-Bibl.Serv., Royal Soc.of Med.L., London. [0041506] 13/01/1988
Wood Mrs NA, BA MCLIP, Unemployed. [0025929] 01/04/1976
Wood Mr NV, AIL MCLIP, Retired. [0016215] 08/02/1964
Wood Ms P, (was Maguire), DipLib MCLIP, Comm.Serv.Lib., Hants.Co.Council, Winchester. [0033439] 15/01/1981
Wood Mrs R, (was Thompson), BA(Hons) MCLIP, P./t.Sch.Lib., AlderleyEdge Sch.for Girls, AlderleyEdge, Cheshire. [0035555] 24/09/1982
Wood Ms RI, (was Adamson), BA MCLIP, L.& Inf. ICT Offr., B.S.U., Stockport. [0025943] 07/05/1976
Wood Mr RJM, B PHIL MA DipLib, Asst.Lib., Brit.L of Political & Econ Sci. [0028215] 11/10/1977
Wood Mrs S, BA MCLIP, Sch.Lib., Weaverham High Sch., Cheshire C.C. [0033203] 13/10/1980
Wood Mrs SD, L.Asst., Regent's Pk.Coll., Oxford. [0054955] 28/05/1997 **AF**
Wood Mr SM, BA(Hons), Lect., IM Grp., Liverpool Business Sch., Liverpool John Moores Univ. [0055264] 29/08/1997
Wood Mrs SM, (was Pegg), BA MCLIP, Retail Sales Marketing Mgr., Books for Students Ltd., Warwick. [0024297] 20/05/1975
Wood Ms SP, BA MCLIP, Electronic Inf.Mgr., Thames Valley Univ., Ealing. [0032769] 08/08/1980
Wood Miss SS, BA DipLib MCLIP, Metadata Co-ordinator/Liaison Lib., Univ.of Reading. [0038934] 01/10/1985
Wood Miss ZA, BSc(Hons), Child.Lib., Leicester City Council, Fosse Cent.L. [0052389] 26/10/1995
Wood-Lamont Mrs SM, (was Lamont), MBE FCLIP, L.Consultant, Univ.Med.& Pharmacy, Cluj-Napoca, Romania. [0021777] 04/01/1974 **FE 25/09/1996**
Woodard Mrs HJ, BA MA MCLIP, Lib.Gov.& Ecclesiastical, Hon.Soc.of the Middle Temple, London. [0034556] 11/01/1982
Woodason Mrs E, (was Harvey), BA(Hons) MSc, Inf.Sci., Nat.Marine Biological L., Plymouth. [0054165] 06/11/1996
Woodbridge Ms S, (was Dormer), MA MCLIP, Campus Lib., Bucks.Chilterns Univ.Coll., High Wycombe. [0044420] 08/10/1990
Woodburn Miss SM, BA(Hons) MA MCLIP, Asst.Lib., Inst.of Child Health, London. [0053871] 07/10/1996
Woodburne Miss EP, Operator, Manpower@firstinfo., Plymouth. [0054042] 22/10/1996
Woodcock Ms EJ, BA ALA, Asst.Head of Libs., Dudley MBC, Dudley L. [0001946] 01/01/1968
Woodcock Ms L, BA(Hons) MA MCLIP, Liaison Lib., Univ.of Birmingham. [0055785] 11/10/1977
Woodcock Mrs RE, (was Hart), BSc(Hons) DipLib, Catr., Doncaster M.B.C., Carcroft L.H.Q. [0028004] 11/10/1977
Woodforde Mr CH, BA DipLib MCLIP, Area Sales Mgr., Scotland & N.England, Riley Dunn & Wilson Ltd. [0026151] 04/07/1976
Woodforde Mrs SE, MCLIP, Joint Librarian in charge, Grangemouth Library, Falkirk. [0023211] 14/11/1974
Woodhams Mrs GC, (was Butler), BA DipLib MCLIP, L.Inf.& Mus.Serv.Mgr., Medway Council, Chatham L. [0034415] 05/11/1981
Woodhead Mrs MS, (was Stabb), MCLIP, Child.& Young Peoples Res.Offr., Kirklees M.C., Huddersfield. [0013851] 01/01/1969
Woodhead Mr PA, MCLIP BA MLS, Freelance Editorial Work. [0016238] 22/02/1968
Woodhouse Mrs A, MA MCLIP, Retired. [0021146] 06/10/1973
Woodhouse Mr BW, MA DipLib MCLIP, Sch.Lib., Smithycroft Sch., Glasgow C.Co.Educ.Dept. [0043134] 10/08/1989
Woodhouse Mrs DE, (was Whitfield), MCLIP, Retired. [0007988] 18/03/1948
Woodhouse Mr JS, BA DipLIS MA, L.Exec., House of Commons L., London. [0052211] 13/10/1995
Woodhouse Miss M, MCLIP, Sen.Subject Lib., Middx.Univ. [0016242] 16/01/1968
Woodhouse Mr RG, BA MA PGCE MCLIP, Life Member. [0016245] 20/07/1974
Woodhouse Mrs S, (was White), MA DipLib MCLIP, Sen.Network Advisor, Resource:the Council for Mus.,Arch., & L., London. [0022830] 09/10/1974
Woodland Mr AN, MCLIP, 11737 Carr St., Maple Ridge, BC, V2X 5N1, Canada, Tel.604 463 9207. [0018000] 23/01/1948

Woodland Mrs JK, (was Hobbs), BA(Hons) MCLIP, Editor, Whitaker Bibl.Serv. [0049572] 19/11/1993
Woodland Mrs MHJ, (was James), MCLIP, Retired. [0018001] 21/09/1967
Woodland Miss RE, BA(Hons) MSc, Sen.Inf.Offr., St.Marys Coll., Twickenham. [0057110] 11/12/1998
Woodley Mrs HJ, (was Drage), CertEd BEd(Hons) MSc, Lib., McTimoney Coll.of Chiropractic, Abingdon. [0048150] 11/11/1992
Woodley Mr TN, MCLIP, Lib., L.B.of Hammersmith & Fulham. [0016247] 16/01/1970
Woodley Ms Z, BA(Hons) MCLIP, Inf.Mgr., L.& Inf.Serv., Ove Arup & Partners. [0052809] 01/12/1995
Woodman Ms G, BA(Hons) MCLIP, Sen.L.Asst., Leeds Univ. [0046275] 22/10/1974
Woodman Mr GD, BA DipLib MCLIP, Lib.(Readers Serv.), N.Ireland Assembly L., Belfast. [0024861] 07/10/1975
Woodman Mrs RM, BA MLS, Sen.Lib., Educ.L.Res.Cent., Reading. [0033431] 01/11/1980
Woodman Miss SM, BA MCLIP, Lib., Building Res.Establishment, Watford. [0036012] 08/04/1983
Woodroffe Ms JE, (was Gleeson), BA MCLIP, Early Retirement. [0035996] 01/01/1964
Woodroofe Mr SR, BA(Hons) PGDipInfMgt, Asst.Prison Lib., HM Prison Pentonville, Islington. [0049380] 01/11/1993
Woodrow Mrs EM, (was Mellor), BA MCLIP, Unemployed. [0016251] 08/01/1969
Woodrow Miss GL, BA(Hons) MCLIP, Asst.Lib., Thomas Eggar Church Adams, Chichester, W.Sussex. [0042666] 06/02/1989
Woodrow Ms L, MCLIP, Lib., Cheshire L., Poynton. [0016252] 01/01/1966
Woodrow Miss NBM, Lib., Lowestoft Coll., Suffolk. [0047533] 01/10/1992
Woodrow Mrs SM, L.Asst., Weston Central L. [0059575] 04/06/2001
AF
Woodruff Mrs ETC, (was Masterman), BSc MIIS MCLIP, Retired. [0033802] 11/03/1981
Woods Mrs AF, (was Moore), MCLIP, Lib., W.Grp., L.B.of Bromley. [0026859] 01/01/1969
Woods Mrs BL, (was Jensen), Employment not known. [0039792] 17/06/1986
Woods Miss BM, MA MCLIP, L.Offr., Edinburgh City L., Cent.L. [0024862] 03/10/1975
Woods Mrs CM, (was O'Rourke), BSc, Higher Clerical Offr., Merseyside Police, Liverpool. [0044126] 23/05/1990
Woods Mrs D, (was Smith), BA MCLIP, Mgr.:SLS, Sch.L.Serv., Worcs.C.C. [0031947] 05/01/1980
Woods Miss DM, FCLIP, Life Member. [0016257] 28/01/1951
FE 01/01/1963
Woods Mr DN, BA MCLIP, Retired. [0020035] 15/01/1973
Woods Mrs GA, (was Dyer), BA, Dep.Lib., Council of Europe, Human Rights L., Strasbourg. [0035174] 06/10/1982
Woods Ms HE, (was Buckley), BA(Hons) MSc, Asst.Inf.Offr., Barnsley M.B.C. [0056481] 22/07/1998
Woods Mr LD, BA MCLIP, Support Lib., L.B.of Newham. [0025137] 18/11/1975
Woods Mrs MJ, (was Simpson), BA MCLIP, p./t.Sen.Lib., Wokingham Dist.Council., Woodley L., Reading. [0029826] 20/10/1978
Woods Mrs N, (was Benfold), MCLIP, Sen.Lib., Lancs.Co.L.,Sch.L.Serv., Thornton L.,Thornton Cleveleys. [0001119] 01/07/1971
Woods Mr PG, MA DipLib MCLIP, Sen.Lib., HM Board of Inland Revenue L., London. [0041938] 31/05/1988
Woods Mrs RE, (was Solway), BA(Hons), Sen.Inf.Offr., Cent.for Inf.& Knowledge Mgmt., Essex C.C. [0045749] 14/05/1991
Woods Mr RG, MA DipLib MCLIP, Life Member. [0016264] 01/10/1951
Woods Miss RM, BA DipLib, Lib., N.Lanarkshire Council, Motherwell. [0044134] 25/05/1990
Woods Mr SR, MCLIP, Grp.L.Mgr., L.B.of Greenwich. [0022704] 17/09/1974
Woods Mr ST, BA(Hons), Unemployed. [0050863] 24/10/1994
Woods Mrs VL, (was Holt), BA MCLIP, Unemployed. [0033682] 16/01/1981
Woods Mr WTW, JP FCLIP, Life Member, 14 Windsor Road, Brentwood, Esse., CM15 9LB., Tel:0277 225263. [0016266] 02/01/1949
FE 01/01/1957
Woodward Mr AW, MA MCLIP, Sen.Lib., Northampton Cent.L., Northants.C.C. [0016267] 24/09/1966
Woodward Mrs CA, (was Mills), BA MCLIP, Comm.Serv.Lib., South Ham L., Hants.C.C. [0021792] 18/01/1974
Woodward Dr HM, (was Jefferson), BA PhD MCLIP, Univ.Lib., Cranfield Univ. [0007765] 10/11/1969
Woodward Ms J, BA(Hons) DipInf MSc MCLIP, Resource Cent.Mgr., Shipley Coll., Shipley. [0057655] 17/06/1999
Woodward Mrs JH, (was Seddon), BA(Hons) MCLIP, Lib., The N.of England Zoological Soc., Chester. [0032172] 22/01/1980
Woodward Mrs JL, BS(Hons), Inf.Mgr., Perkins Engine Co. Ltd., Peterborough. [0059199] 19/12/2000 **AF**
Woodward Mrs KS, (was Barlow), BA MCLIP, Sen.Lib., Market Drayton L., Shropshire C.C. [0032860] 06/10/1980
Woodward Mr RJ, BA MCLIP, Acquisitions Lib., Shropshire L.H.Q., Shrewsbury. [0040526] 20/02/1987
Wooff Miss IK, BA DipLib, Unemployed. [0042062] 03/09/1988
Woolf Mr J, MA BA, Sen.L.Asst., Wanstead L., London. [0039890] 06/10/1986
Woolford Ms JW, FCLIP, Life Member. [0016279] 01/01/1939
FE 01/01/1951
Woolfrey Miss CG, BA MCLIP, Unemployed. [0037052] 03/02/1984
Woolfson Mrs MA, (was McCullough), BLS MCLIP, Asst.Lib., The Cedars Upper Sch., Leighton Buzzard. [0032120] 01/02/1980
Woolgar Mr T, MCLIP, Area Mgr., L.B.of Bromley. [0032476] 01/04/1980
Woollacott Mrs K, (was Goodwin), MCLIP, L.Serv.Mgr.-Adult Lend., Medway Council, Strood L. [0009302] 18/09/1968
Woollard Mr SJ, MCLIP, L.Res.Mgr., L.B.of Southwark. [0016284] 04/01/1972
Woollatt Miss HJ, MCLIP, Retired. [0016285] 11/07/1961

Woolley Mrs CA, (was Hunter), B Lib MCLIP, Stourport Lib.(Job Share), Worcestershire C.C., Stourport on Severn. [0036978] 24/01/1984
Woolley Mr M, BA MCLIP, Dep.Lib., Univ.of Luton. [0035837] 14/01/1983
Woolley Mrs SE, (was Ellis), BA MPhil MCIT MCLIP, Sch.Lib., Roade Sch., Northampton. [0031819] 18/01/1980
Woolley Mrs SE, (was Harris), BA(Hons) DipLIS MCLIP, Br.Lib., Acklam, Middlesbrough Bor.Council. [0049415] 21/10/1993
Woolridge Mrs EA, BA MCLIP, Sen.Lib., Carlisle L., Cumbria L.Serv. [0021771] 07/01/1974
Woolven Ms GB, BA MCLIP, Retired from post at, Assoc.of Commonwealth Univ., London. [0016290] 01/01/1959
Woolvin Mr RT, MCLIP, L.Asst., Univ.Coll.L., London. [0016291] 01/07/1970
Woore Miss RL, BA(Hons) DipLIS MCLIP, Learning Res.Co-ordinator, Univ.Coll.London, Dept.of Geography. [0046326] 28/10/1991
Wootton Ms AM, BA(Hons) DipLIB MCLIP, Sen.Asst.Lib., Dept.of Printed Books, Imperial War Museum. [0016295] 08/01/1971
Wootton Mrs CB, BEd, p./t.Stud./Sen.L.Asst., Leeds Metro.Univ., Cent.Jnr.L., Doncaster. [0059065] 01/11/2000
Wootton Dr G, BSc PhD MSc, Employment not known. [0060310] 10/12/2001
Wootton Mrs JA, P./t.L.Asst., Kingsbridge L., Devon. [0057767] 29/07/1999
AF
Worcester Mr RK, MA DipLib MCLIP, Borough Lib., L.B.of Havering, Romford Cent.L. [0024864] 01/10/1975
Worden Ms AE, MA MCLIP, (Subject Lib.) Languages Lib., Univ.of Portsmouth. [0042203] 11/10/1988
Worden Miss KE, BA(Hons) MA MCLIP, Faculty Liaison Lib., Canterbury Christ Church Univ.Coll. [0043353] 25/10/1989
Workman Miss D, BA(Hons), Subject Lib., Univ.of Exeter. [0051537] 01/04/1995
Workman Dr HM, BSc MA PhD MCLIP, Dir.of Learning Res./Univ.Lib., Oxford Brookes Univ. [0028216] 12/10/1977
Workman Mrs M, p./t.Stud./L.Super., Univ.of Wales, Aberystwyth, The Open Learning Unit. [0061531] 16/09/2002
Workman Mrs MJ, (was Williams), MCLIP, Lib., Birkett,Stevens,Colman & Ptnr., Leeds. [0012503] 17/01/1970
Workman Ms MM, (was Bradford), BA MCLIP MIIS MIED, Digital Champion, Scottish Enterprise, Dundee. [0016300] 14/10/1965
Workman Mr R, MCLIP, Lib., Northumbrian Water Auth. [0016301] 20/04/1967
Workman Ms V, p./t.Stud./Br.Lib., Univ.of Wales, Aberystwyth, Hay-on-Wye L., Powys. [0061196] 08/04/2002
Worley Miss C, BA(Hons), Inf.Cent.CO-ordinator, Panne Sanders and Sidney, London. [0059739] 10/09/2001
Worley Mr JR, MCLIP, Serv.Support Lib., Northants.L.& Inf.Serv., L.H.Q. [0016303] 20/10/1969
Worley Ms LM, BA MCLIP, Head of L.& Inf.Serv., Richards Butler, London. [0027100] 24/01/1977
Worley-Gibbons Ms SL, BA(Hons) PGCert, Asst.Lib., Worcestershire C.C., Worc.City L. [0058234] 19/11/1999
Wormald Mr JH, ISO BSc(Econ) MCLIP, Life Member. [0016305] 12/09/1951
Worman Ms CA, BA(Hons) MCLIP, Stud., Sheffield Hallam Univ. [0034367] 06/10/1981
Worrall Mrs CBE, (was Naylor), BA MCLIP, Admin.Offr., DLO Caversfield, Bicester. [0035433] 01/10/1982
Worrall Mrs JR, (was Foster), BLib MCLIP, p./t.Lib., City Discovery Cent., Bradwell Abbey. [0005106] 04/10/1971
Worrall Mrs K, BSc, Jnr.Asst.Lib., Macfarlanes, London. [0061083] 01/03/2002
Worrall Miss S, BA(Hons) MCLIP, Asst.Lib., W.Sussex C.C., Crawley. [0054169] 04/11/1996
Worron Mr AJ, BA(Hons) DipInf, Asst.Lib., Nat.Statistics, London. [0046669] 15/11/1991
Worth Mrs AM, (was Sawyer), BA(Hons) MCLIP, Super., Sefton Council, Merseyside. [0056527] 10/08/1998
Worth Ms CS, BA(Hons), Stud., Univ.Coll.London. [0059099] 14/11/2000
Worth Mrs EJ, BA DipLib, Quality & Performance Offr., L.B.of Haringey. [0037177] 15/03/1984
Worthington Mrs GRA, BSc(Econ), Lib., Cambs.Ls.& Inf.Serv., Cambridge. [0054692] 05/03/1997
Worthington Miss ME, BA(Hons) DipLIS, Asst.Lib., Preservation & Stack Mgmt., The London L. [0037387] 14/01/1980
Worthington Ms RM, BA(Hons) MSc, Sen.Inf.Offr., Irwin Mitchell Solicitors, Sheffield. [0056174] 01/04/1998
Worthy Miss AM, BA(Hons) MSc MCLIP, Asst.Lib., Univ.Westminster, Harrow Campus. [0054244] 14/11/1996
Worthy Miss M, MSc MCLIP, Employment not known. [0060203] 10/12/2001
Wortley Mrs HV, (was Ironside), BA(Hons) DipLib MCLIP, P./t.Self-employed. [0018803] 01/10/1972
Wortley Miss PJ, BSc DipLib CIBiol MIBiol MCLIP, Retired. [0060683] 12/12/2001
Wotherspoon Mrs GC, BA(Hons) MSc MCLIP, Sen.L.Asst., Univ.of Cambridge, Dept.of Physics. [0049250] 18/10/1993
Wragg Mrs PRD, (was Allen), BA MCLIP, Housewife. [0020072] 18/01/1973
Wragge-Morley Miss JC, BLib MA MCLIP, Inf.Offr., Literature Dept., The Brit.Council. [0031988] 22/01/1990
Wraight Mr AW, BA MCLIP, Acting Head of Serv., Newcastle L.& Inf.Serv., Newcastle upon Tyne. [0016322] 15/03/1967
Wraight Mrs SML, (was Mills), BSc(Hons), Inf.Asst., Nokia UK Ltd. [0056971] 16/11/1998
Wrathall Mrs C, BA(Hons), Learning Res.Mgr., Herefordshire Coll.of Tech., Hereford. [0052486] 02/11/1995
Wrathmell Ms SP, (was Claxton), BA(Hons) MA MCLIP, Self-emp.Consultant, Historic Buildings. [0002804] 23/09/1968
Wray Mrs B, (was Smith), MCLIP, Princ.Lib., Walsgrave Hosp., Coventry City L. [0016323] 01/01/1957

Personal Members

Wray Miss DC, BA MCLIP, Membership Offr., Pensions Mgmt.Inst., London. [0030305]   02/01/1979
Wray Mrs SJ, (was Staal), BA MCLIP, Unemployed. [0034215]   07/10/1981
Wray Mrs SJ, (was Kite), BA MCLIP, Asst.Lib., Royal United Hosp.NHS Trust, Bath. [0032106]   28/01/1980
Wren Mrs DJ, (was MacRae), BA MCLIP, Sch.Lib., Beeslack High Sch., MidLothian. [0038664]   14/09/1985
Wressell Ms P, (was Stitt), BA, Freelance Editor, 37 Moor Crt., Westfield, Newcastle upon Tyne, NE3 4YD. [0044110]   01/01/1963
Wride Mrs PL, (was Faris), BA MCLIP, Sen.L.Asst.(Job Share), Housebound Readers Serv., S.Tyneside M.B.C. [0031609]   17/10/1979
Wright Miss A, B LIB MCLIP, L.Offr., Edinburgh City L. [0029542] 24/08/1978
Wright Mrs A, (was King), MCLIP, Sec., Trinity Sch., Carlisle. [0008363]   22/01/1969
Wright Mr AC, BMus(Hons) DipLib, Lib., Wakefield M.D.C., Drury Lane L. [0054843]   14/04/1997
Wright Mrs AC, (was Montgomery), BSc(Hons) MCLIP, Lib., S.Glos.Council, Hanham/Cadbury Heath L. [0046352]   30/10/1991
Wright Miss AJ, Tech.Lib.Trainee, Brit.Standards Inst.L., London. [0060941]   14/01/2002   AF
Wright Mrs AM, BA(Hons) PGCE, p./t.Stud./Res.Cent.Asst., Univ.of Wales, Aberystwyth, Long Road Sixth Form Coll., Cambs. [0061267]   13/05/2002
Wright Miss BA, MVO MA DipLib MCLIP, Bibl., Royal L., Windsor Castle, Berks. [0026619]   11/10/1976
Wright Mrs C, (was Elliott), MCLIP, Community Lib., Renfrewshire L. [0032054]   12/02/1980
Wright Mrs C, BA, Lib., N.Lanark Council, St.Ambrose High Sch. [0058281]   07/12/1999
Wright Mrs CA, Sch.Lib., Mostyn House Sch., S.Wirral. [0057755] 23/07/1999
Wright Mrs CD, BA(Hons) PGCE MCLIP, Sen.Lib.:Bibl.Serv., Staffs.L. [0023415]   06/01/1975
Wright Miss CEG, MCLIP, Life Member. [0016333]   16/05/1955
Wright Mrs CM, (was Sculthorpe), BA(Hons) MCLIP, Sch.Lib.& Learning Res.Mgr., RNIB New Coll., Worcester. [0033955]   17/06/1981
Wright Mr D, MA MCLIP, Asst.Lib., Health Mgmt., Univ.Southampton. [0045566]   15/03/1991
Wright Miss DJ, BA(Hons), Sales Asst./p./t.Stud., W.H.Smith., Univ.Northumbria. [0059349]   13/02/2001
Wright Mr DJ, BA(Hons) MCLIP, Sch.Lib., St.Columba's High Sch., Dunfermline. [0055670]   07/11/1997
Wright Mrs DJ, (was Hannant), BA MCLIP, Unemployed. [0006274]   04/10/1971
Wright Mrs DJ, (was Maddison), BA DipLib MCLIP, Child.Lib., Rutland C.C., Oakham. [0036242] 01/08/1983
Wright Mr DRD, MCLIP, Retired, 199,St.Margaret's Road, Lowestoft. [0016338]   25/03/1965
Wright Ms DT, BA DipLib, Trust L.Serv.Mgr., S.Manchester Univ.Hosp.NHS Trust, Manchester. [0041074]   05/10/1987
Wright Ms DW, BA MCLIP, Asst.Lib., Northumberland Co.L., Alnwick L. [0038438]   16/04/1985
Wright Mrs EA, BA MA, Unemployed. [0059350]   13/02/2001
Wright Mrs EA, (was Reeve), MA MCLIP, Mgr., Sheffield L.,Arch.& Inf. [0021890]   23/01/1978
Wright Miss EJ, BA(Hons) MCLIP, Marketing Adviser, Linklaters & Alliance, Bangkok, Thailand. [0046915]   25/02/1992
Wright Mrs EM, (was Pye), MCLIP, Unemployed. [0012063]   18/01/1968
Wright Mr EW, MA B SOC B PHIL MCLIP, Co.L.& Inf.Offr., Northants C.C. [0025191]   15/12/1975
Wright Mrs FJ, (was Briggs), MCLIP, Life Member. [0016342]   01/01/1945
Wright Mr GA, MLS MCLIP, Register Lib., Leics.Ls.& Inf.Serv. [0016343]   23/08/1969
Wright Mr GH, FIRT MCLIP, Retired. [0018005]   02/01/1940
Wright Mrs GJ, (was (Form Hibbert)), MCLIP, Lib./p./t.MA Stud., E.Grp., Orpington L., L.B.of Bromley. [0006819]   10/01/1966
Wright Ms HC, MA(Hons), Clerical Offr., EDINA, Univ.of Edinburgh. [0057080]   04/12/1998
Wright Miss HM, BA DipLib MCLIP, Knowledge Training Offr., Singleton Hosp., Swansea. [0031727]   22/11/1979
Wright Miss HM, MA MCLIP, Retired. [0016346]   24/11/1965
Wright Miss J, BA(Hons) MCLIP, Town Lib., Staffs.C.C. [0046977] 17/03/1992
Wright Miss J, BA MCLIP, Career Break. [0041957]   01/07/1988
Wright Mr J, BA(Hons) DipILM, Asst.Lib., Univ.of Glamorgan. [0056752]   08/10/1998
Wright Ms J, BA(Hons), Inf.Offr., Freshfields Bruckhaus Deringer, London. [0061118]   21/02/2002
Wright Mrs JM, (was Williams), BA MCLIP, P./t.Lib., Pub.Serv., L.B.of Greenwich, Acquisitions Dept. [0029340]   04/10/1979
Wright Mrs JM, (was Loveridge), BA(Hons) MSc MCLIP, Freelance, Website Abstractor & Indexer, ALACRA, Leeds. [0041706]   23/05/1995
Wright Mrs JWM, BA PGCE DipLib, Asst.Lib., Richmond Adult & Community Coll., Twickenham. [0037645]   02/10/1984
Wright Mrs L, (was Hull), BA LIB MCLIP, Lib., Leics.L.& Inf.Serv. [0036237]   19/10/1983
Wright Miss LA, BA(Hons), Inf.Asst., Kings Coll.London, Guys Campus. [0055265]   28/08/1997
Wright Mrs LE, BA MCLIP, Team Lib., Somerset C.C. [0016354]   17/07/1972
Wright Miss LJ, BA(Hons), Project Catr., Worcs.Comm.& Mental Hlth.NHS Trust. [0051883]   25/07/1995
Wright Mr LR, BSc(Econ), Asst.Lib., GAIA Energy Cent., N.Cornwall. [0057001]   19/11/1998
Wright Mrs M, (was Dolan), BA(Hons) MCLIP, Projects Admin., Argyll & The Islands Enterprise, Lochgilphead. [0035371]   14/10/1982
Wright Mrs MA, (was Tester), MCLIP, Asst.Lib., Open Univ.L., Milton Keynes. [0016360]   25/10/1966

Wright Ms MA, (was Gardner), MCLIP, Employment not known. [0016359]   11/02/1965
Wright Mrs MC, (was Sheffield), FCLIP, Retired. [0016362]   03/04/2029   FE 01/01/1932
Wright Mr MD, MSC MCLIP, Life Member. [0016363]   01/01/1963
Wright Mr MGH, MA FCLIP, Life Member, Calliope, Parkstone Dr., Camberley, Surrey, GU15 2PA. [0016365]   23/03/1953   FE 01/01/1967
Wright Mrs MH, L.Serv.Mgr., Inverclyde Royal Hosp., Greenock. [0045542]   28/02/1991
Wright Miss N, MCLIP, Life Member, Tel.0161 962 5330. [0016367]   17/09/1948
Wright Mrs P, BA(Hons) MA MCLIP, Sub.Lib., Hants.C.C. [0055651]   31/10/1997
Wright Mrs P, BA(Hons) MSc, Learning Resource Cent.Advisor, W.Notts.Coll., Mansfield. [0052830] 11/01/1996
Wright Mrs PA, BA DipLib MCLIP, Unemployed. [0026620]   04/10/1976
Wright Mr PKJ, BA FCLIP, Life Member. [0016372]   10/06/1949   FE 01/01/1958
Wright Mr R, FCLIP, Retired. [0016374]   29/10/1941   FE 01/01/1962
Wright Ms RE, BA MCLIP, L.& Inf.Offr., Inst.of Personnel & Devel., Wimbledon. [0016376]   28/08/1970
Wright Mrs RJ, (was Leslie), BA MCLIP, Sen.L.Asst., Royal Conrwall Hosp. [0040578]   02/04/1987
Wright Ms RJ, (was Robson), BLS MCLIP, Yth.Team Lib., Tullycarnet L., S.E.Educ.& L.Board. [0030789]   04/04/1979
Wright Miss S, Local Enquiry Offr., Business Link, Tees Valley Business Cent. [0039424]   01/01/1986
Wright Mrs SE, (was Hannam), Keyworker, Ecclesall Pre-Sch., Sheffield. [0038748]   01/01/1985
Wright Mrs SJ, (was Omer), MCLIP, Inf.Offr., Brit.Cement Assoc., Crowthorne, Berks. [0028643]   23/01/1978
Wright Miss SM, Asst.Br.Administrator, L.B.of Barnet, E.Barnet L. [0045074]   05/07/1990   AF
Wright Miss SM, BA(Hons) MCLIP, Asst.Lib., N.Staffs.Med.Inst.L., Stoke-on-Trent. [0042953]   08/05/1989
Wright Mr TC, BA(Hons) DipLIS MCLIP, Associate, McKinsey & Company, London. [0046577]   13/11/1991
Wright Ms TM, BA(Hons) DipLib, Curator, Brit.L. [0040183]   24/10/1986
Wright Mrs V, (was Dowling), BA DipLib, Sen.Lib., Co.Cent.L., Kent C.C. [0035076]   08/07/1982
Wright Mr VJ, BA MCLIP, Retired. [0016383]   23/01/1969
Wright Ms WR, BA B ED BLS MCLIP, P./t.Lib., Diocese of Truro, Cornwall. [0030574]   26/01/1979
Wright Ms Z, MA, Inf.Cent.Mgr., Dibb Lupton Alsop, Solicitors, Manchester. [0053928]   11/10/1996
Wrighting Mr AM, BA MCLIP, L.Mgr., Popperfoto, Northampton. [0035345]   14/10/1982
Wrighton Miss SM, MCLIP, Sch.Lib., S.Wolds Comp.Sch., Nottingham. [0016385]   02/06/1970
Wrightson Mrs C, (was Glasby), BA MCLIP, Sen.Inf.Adviser, Univ.of Gloucestershire, Cheltenham. [0025874]   26/03/1976
Wrightson Miss S, BSc(Hons), Stud., Manchester Metro.Univ. [0061769]   05/11/2002
Wrigley Mrs GJ, Lib., Thompsons Solicitors, Newcastle upon Tyne. [0044966]   28/01/1991
Wrigley Mrs SM, (was Fenlon), BA MCLIP, Catr., Dudley Grp.of Hosp.NHS Trust. [0023534]   02/01/1975
Wrigley Mr TC, BA MCLIP, Retired. [0060685]   12/12/2001
Wroe Mrs JL, (was Airey), MCLIP, Bibl.Serv.Mgr., Kirklees Cult.Servs., Huddersfield. [0027255]   10/02/1977
Wrynn Miss SE, BA, Resident in Ireland. [0058897]   02/10/2000
Wurcbacher Miss CA, BSc MSc, Survey Mgr., Merseyside Inf.Serv., Liverpool. [0056948]   09/11/1998
Wurzal Miss LJ, BA(Hons), Employment not known. [0046263]   21/10/1991
Wyatt Ms CA, BA DipLib MCLIP, Head -Vriefing Database, Dept.of Health Skipton Hse., London. [0028729]   16/01/1978
Wyatt Miss GM, BA MCLIP, Retired. [0016390]   14/09/1959
Wyatt Mrs LM, L.Mgr., Surrey Comm.Serv., Dorking L. [0053790] 01/01/1996   AF
Wyatt Mrs M, BA MCLIP, Welfare Benefits Adviser, Shirley Citizens Advice Bureau, Solihull. [0009041]   01/01/1967
Wyatt Mr MA, BA MCLIP, Serv.Mgr., Cambridge City, Cambs.C.C. [0025460]   13/01/1976
Wyatt Mrs MA, BA DipLib MCLIP, Unemployed. [0039824]   10/08/1986
Wyatt Miss MM, BA(hons) DipHE, Unemployed. [0058715]   01/07/2000
Wyatt Mr NJ, BA, Collections Serv.Lib., Sci.Mus.L., London. [0034978]   24/05/1982
Wyatt Miss PM, MCLIP, Retired. [0016394]   04/02/1952
Wyburn Mr RM, BSc DipLib MCLIP, Catr.(Temp.), Wellcome Trust, London. [0025930]   01/04/1976
Wyeth Mrs N, (was Marckwald), MA, Computing & systems Consultant, Univ.of Herts., Learning Resource Cent. [0043873]   30/01/1990
Wygard Mrs SJ, BA(Hons), Asst.Lib., Anglia Support Partnership., Doddington. [0058938]   09/10/2000
Wykes Mr HJF, BSc MCLIP, Employment not known. [0060686]   12/12/2001
Wykes Miss JPL, BA(Hons), p./t.Stud./L.Asst., Loughborough Univ., Univ.of Nottingham. [0061368]   01/07/2002
Wylde Miss V, BA(Hons), Asst.Lib., King Alfred's Coll., Winchester, Hants. [0056721]   07/10/1998
Wylie Miss K, RGN, Sen.Inf.Offr., Manchester Royal Infirmary. [0044764]   14/11/1990
Wylie Mrs SE, (was Price), BA(Hons), Unemployed. [0047874]   22/10/1992
Wylie Ms SJ, BTh(Oxon), Unemployed. [0051707]   23/05/1995
Wyllie Mrs MC, BA BSc, Life Member. [0016398]   18/06/1951

Wyman Mrs RE, (was Ward), MCLIP, Sch.Lib., Montsaye Sch., Rothwell. [0018126] 03/10/1972
Wymer Mrs CJ, (was Stockings), MCLIP, Sen.Lib., Norfolk County L.& Inf.Serv., Norfolk & Norwich Millennium L. [0019088] 02/10/1972
Wyness Mrs EA, (was Wykes), BA(Hons) MA, Asst.Lib.(ILT Devel.), Wyggeston & Queen Elizabeth I Coll., Leicester. [0057083] 04/12/1998
Wynn Mr GA, BSc DIP TCHG MCLIP, Catr., Reading Borough. [0043543] 06/11/1989
Wynn Mr V, (was Pemberton), MCLIP, p./t.L.Asst., St.Josephs R.C.High Sch., Wrexham. [0023547] 06/01/1975
Wynne Mr BBL, BA DipLIB MCLIP DMS, Sub-Lib.(Electronic Serv.), Univ.Coll.Dublin Main L., Ireland. [0039475] 01/02/1986
Wynne Mr G, BA(Hons) DipILM MA PGCE, Asst.Locality Mgr., Suffolk L.& Heritage, Ipswich. [0048737] 30/04/1993
Wynne Miss L, BA DipLIS, User Serv.Lib., Middx.Univ., Hendon. [0059020] 27/10/2000
Wynne Mr PM, BA MLitt DipLib MCLIP, Docusend Project Mgr., Kings Coll.London, Manchester Metro.Univ. [0038121] 21/01/1985
Wynton-Doig Mrs ST, (was Wynton), BA MCLIP, Unwaged. [0032718] 01/07/1980
Wyspianska Mrs PM, (was Bullock), BA MCLIP, Sch.Lib., Stratford upon Avon High Sch., Warwickshire. [0002049] 01/10/1969
Wythers Ms HM, BA(Hons), p./t.Stud./Literacy Asst., Univ.of Wales, Aberystwyth, Linden Lodge Sch., London. [0061271] 09/05/2002
Wythes Mrs JA, (was Kisby), MA MCLIP, Unemployed. [0033799] 03/03/1981
Wyver Mrs GKL, (was Dennis), BA(Hons) MA MCLIP, Subject Lib.-Fashion & Clothing, Kent Inst.of Art & Design, Rochester. [0043060] 01/07/1989
Yamin Mrs N, LLB DipIS, Lib., Lovells, London. [0050913] 31/10/1994
Yan Mrs ASW, BA MLS MCLIP, Resident in U.S.A. [0060099] 07/12/2001
Yandle Miss AC, BA(Hons) PGDipPhil, Trainee Teacher, Castledown Sch., Andover. [0049126] 06/10/1993
Yang Ms D, BA, Stud., Univ.of Wales. [0059024] 25/10/2000
Yapp Mrs J, BEd, L.Asst., Clinical L., Sandwell Gen.Hosp. [0055819] 26/11/1997
Yaqoob Miss A, BSc, Unemployed. [0061182] 03/04/2002
Yarde Ms M, BA DipLib MCLIP, Asst.Grp.Lib., L.B.of Lewisham. [0033673] 05/02/1981
Yardley Mr AK, BA MCLIP, Music Lib., Guildhall Sch.of Music & Drama, London. [0022795] 15/10/1974
Yardley Ms CA, BA(Hons) DipILS MCLIP, Database Mgr., Stoke-on-Trent Ls., Inf.& Arch. [0049678] 25/11/1993
Yardley Mr RJE, MA MSc MCLIP, Lib., Enquiry Team, Cambridgeshire C.C. [0022847] 02/10/1974
Yardley Mrs S, (was Wright), Line Mgr.- Sch.L., Alderman Callow Sch.& Comm. Coll., Warwickshire. [0047501] 08/09/1992 **AF**
Yardley Jones Miss A, BLib MCLIP, Unemployed. [0039879] 01/10/1986
Yarker Mr JM, BSc(ECON) MCLIP, Retired. [0016407] 25/09/1936
Yarr Mrs AH, BA, [0049889] 11/01/1994
Yarrow Mrs AV, B ED DipLib MCLIP, p./t.Teacher/Librarian, Marches Sch., Shropshire. [0024044] 12/02/1975
Yarwood Mrs KJ, (was Brook), BA MCLIP, Community Lib., Salford City L. [0001788] 06/10/1969
Yasemela Ms A, BA(Hons) MA, Asst.Lib., Goldsmiths Coll., London. [0056732] 07/10/1998
Yashina-Thomas Mrs N, Coll.Lib., Aberdare Coll.of F.E. [0061412] 16/07/2002
Yates Mrs CA, BA(Hons) MCLIP, Inf.& Lifelong Learning Lib., Bolton Cent.L. [0053628] 19/08/1996
Yates Mrs CE, (was Biltcliffe), BA MCLIP, Dir., Roy Yates Books, Horsham, W.Sussex. [0016411] 16/03/1962
Yates Miss CJ, BLib MCLIP, Local Studies Lib., Walsall M.B.C. [0036179] 05/07/1983
Yates Mr CP, MA MCLIP, Asst.Lib., Westminster Kingsway Coll., London. [0016412] 12/09/1969
Yates Mrs ES, (was Stewart), BA(Hons) DipLib MCLIP, Subject & Learning Support Llb., Staffs.Univ.L. [0048204] 16/11/1992
Yates Mrs J, (was Kemball-Cook), MA MCLIP, Lib., Sch.of St.David & St.Katharine, London. [0008249] 04/01/1971
Yates Mrs JM, (was Wilding), DiplM, Dep.Learning Res.Cent.Mgr., Basingstoke Coll.of Tech., Hants. [0056004] 19/01/1998
Yates Mrs ME, (was Stevens), BSc(Hons) DipLib, Resource Cent.Mgr., B.S.I., London. [0045691] 24/04/1991
Yates Mrs MMM, BA MLS, Unemployed. [0040963] 01/10/1987
Yates Mrs PJ, (was Davis), BA MCLIP, Sch.Lib., Vandyke Upper Sch., Leighton Buzzard, Beds. [0032040] 07/02/1980
Yates Mrs PM, (was Matthews), BA MCLIP, Lib., Wakefield Drury Lane L., Wakefield. [0016417] 30/01/1964
Yates Mr SG, BA(Hons), L.Asst., Sandwell Clinical L., P.Grad.Med.Centre, W.Mids. [0057120] 15/12/1998
Yates Mrs SJ, (was Ashmore), BA MCLIP, Life Member. [0016419] 01/01/1951
Yates-Mercer Dr PA, BSc MSc PhD FCLIP, Employment not known. [0060806] 12/12/2001 **FE 01/04/2002**
Yeadon Mrs JE, (was Dutnall), MSc MCLIP, Sub-Lib.:Coll.& Inf.Resources, Imperial Coll.Cent.L., London. [0016422] 08/11/1963
Yeadon Mrs L, BA DLIS MCLIP, p./t.Sen.L.Asst., Loughborough Univ., Leics. [0034058] 24/08/1981
Yeadon Ms VJ, BSc MSc PGDipIS, Web Site Co-ordinator, S.Bank Univ.L. [0049493] 05/11/1993
Yeates Mr AR, BA MA MCLIP, Asst.Dir.-LITC, S.Bank Univ., London. [0026657] 25/10/1976
Yeats Mrs FJ, (was Pilditch), BA MCLIP, Grp.Lib., Shropshire C.C., Bishops Castle. [0023679] 13/01/1975
Yelland Mr M, BA MCLIP, Life Member, Ambleside, 4 32 Winchelsea Lane, Hastings, E.Sussex, TN35 4LG. [0016429] 27/09/1951

Yelland Mrs SC, (was Tonge), L.& Inf.Mgr., Landwell, London. [0050901] 28/10/1994
Yendall Mr DJ, BLib DipEd MCLIP, Sch.L.Serv.Mgr., Isle of Wight Council. [0032362] 08/03/1980
Yenn Mrs JM, (was Daniels), MCLIP, Unemployed. [0016430] 01/01/1964
Yeoh Dr JM, (was Stott), BA MEd PhD MCLIP, Inf.Serv.Mgr., Kings Coll.London. [0019809] 01/01/1972
Yeoh Miss MM, Med.Inf.Specialist. [0059109] 22/03/2001
Yeoman Mrs FA, (was Rumble), MA MCLIP, Lend.Lib., Fareham L., Hants. [0042252] 13/10/1988
Yeoman Ms KR, MA DipLib MCLIP, Sch.Lib., Aberdeen City Council, Dyce Academy. [0042236] 18/10/1988
Yeomans Mrs KH, (was Evans), BA(Hons) MCLIP, Customer Serv. Team Leader, Staffs.C.C. [0044748] 15/11/1990
Yeomans Mrs TI, (was Hartill), MCLIP, Retired. [0016434] 23/01/1935
Yerbury Ms H, BA DipLib MA MLib, Resident in Australia. [0060089] 07/12/2001
Yescombe Mr ER, MBE FIM FCLIP, Life Member, Tel.01234 391 531, 60 Kilpin Grn., N.Crawley, Newport Pagnell, MK16 9LY. [0016435] 06/01/1933 **FE 01/01/1950**
Yeung Miss CS, BSc IS MAppSc, Asst.Dir., LIS, The Brit.Council L., Hong Kong. [0042052] 02/08/1988
Yewdall Mrs AJ, (was Page), BA(Hons) MA MCLIP, Inf.Specialist, HSE, Sheffield. [0047576] 02/10/1992
Yip Ms CC, BA MCLIP, Dep.Lib., Nanyang Tech.Univ., Singapore. [0018245] 06/10/1972
Yip Ms SY, BA(Hons), Stud., The Robert Gordon Univ. [0061781] 05/11/2002
Yirrell Ms LE, BSc(Hons) MA MCLIP, Academic Serv.Lib., St.Johns Coll., Cambridge. [0052390] 26/10/1995
Yockney Mrs SAJ, BA DipLib MCLIP, Sch.Lib., Educ.Resource Cent., Dorset C.C. [0027102] 26/01/1977
York Mrs JA, (was Hazlehurst), MCLIP, Grp.Lib., Birmingham L.Serv. [0006534] 01/01/1971
York Ms JM, BA MCLIP, Comm.Serv.Mgr., Bristol S.E., Cent.L., Bristol City Council Leisure Serv. [0035178] 05/01/1982
York Mrs LCE, (was Richards), Tech.& Systems Team Leader, Croydon Coll. [0043868] 02/02/1990
Youd Mrs AM, (was Barr), BSSc MCLIP, Advocacy Worker, E.Ayrshire Advocacy Serv., Kilmarnock. [0022675] 05/10/1976
Youens Mrs AM, (was Graham), MCLIP, Learning Cent.Mgr., Harrow Coll., Harrow Weald, Middx. [0005773] 01/01/1969
Young Miss A, MCLIP, Employee, John Rylands Univ., Manchester. [0022679] 24/07/1974
Young Miss AJ, LLB MSc, Lib., BBC-Scotland, Glasgow. [0056087] 12/02/1998
Young Mr BC, MCLIP, Poet - Self-employed. [0020135] 29/01/1973
Young Miss BJ, MCLIP, Unemployed. [0016441] 01/01/1967
Young Mrs C, (was Herbert), MCLIP, NTA Secondary Sch., Maidenhead. [0023126] 06/11/1974
Young Miss CS, MCLIP, Retired. [0016446] 02/03/1964
Young Mrs D, (was Mckellar), MCLIP, Life Member. [0009443] 01/03/1964
Young Ms E, Asst.Lib., Dundee City Council, Blackness L. [0042344] 23/01/1988
Young Mr G, FCLIP, Retired. [0016452] 23/04/1949 **FE 01/01/1957**
Young Mr GF, Retired Translator. [0059438] 23/03/2001
Young Mrs GR, (was Cope), BA(Hons) DipLIS MCLIP, CALIM Support Offr., Manchester Met.Univ. [0050008] 18/02/1994
Young Mrs H, (was Johnson), MCLIP, Sch.Lib., Sharnbrook Upper Sch., Beds. [0016454] 23/09/1961
Young Ms H, BA(Hons) PGCE MA, L.Asst., S.London & Maudsley NHS Trust. [0059531] 26/04/2001
Young Mrs HB, BA(Hons) DipIM MCLIP, L.Offr.:Child.& Learning, Bournemouth Bor.Council, Lansdowne L. [0051318] 10/01/1995
Young Mrs HM, (was Browning), BA(Hons) MA MCLIP, Inf.Lib., (Law & Official Pubs.), Univ.of Leicester. [0050771] 18/10/1994
Young Mr IA, BA DipLib MCLIP, Faculty Team Leader, Edward Boyle L., Univ.of Leeds. [0041791] 05/04/1988
Young Mrs J, (was Tadd), MCLIP, Sen.Lib., Cambs.C.C., Huntingdon L. [0022953] 22/09/1974
Young Ms J, BA MCLIP, Tech.Lib., Metropolitan Police, London. [0022557] 01/07/1974
Young Miss JA, BSc DipILS MCLIP, Trainee Lib., Falkirk Council L.Serv., Falkirk. [0053963] 16/10/1996
Young Mrs JC, (was Rowles), MBE FCLIP, Retired. [0012749] 14/03/1956 **FE 15/03/1982**
Young Mr JD, BSc(Econ) FCLIP, Life Member, Kennet Beeches, 54 George Lane, Marlborough, Wilts., SN8 4BY. [0016460] 27/04/1943 **FE 01/01/1970**
Young Miss JE, MCLIP, Life Member. [0016461] 05/09/1942
Young Ms JE, (was Bridge), BA MCLIP, Special Serv.Lib., Stockport M.B.C. [0039187] 01/01/1964
Young Mrs LA, (was Alexander), BEd DipLib MCLIP, Asst.Lib., Warwickshire C.C. [0041621] 02/02/1988
Young Ms LA, BA DipLib MCLIP, Asst.Lib., Inst.of Advanced Legal Studies. [0036171] 11/07/1983
Young Miss MA, BA MCLIP, Team Leader, Edinburgh City L.& Inf.Serv., Newington L. [0028220] 08/11/1977
Young Mrs ME, BA MCLIP, Lect., Edinburgh's Telford Coll., Edinburgh. [0016470] 11/03/1970
Young Mr ML, BA MCLIP, p./t.Lib./L.Asst., Univ.of Northumbria, City of Newcastle City L. [0019459] 31/01/1962
Young Mr MR, BA(Hons) PGDipLib MCLIP, Inf.Unit Mgr., Hewitson Becke & Shaw, Cambridge. [0025139] 25/10/1975
Young Mrs PA, BA(Hons), Circulation Team Leader, Univ.of Lincs., Lincoln. [0058775] 18/07/2000 **AF**
Young Mrs PM, (was Kelly), BA MCLIP, Maternity Leave. [0042353] 25/10/1988

Young Mrs PO, (was Swann), MCLIP, Retired. [0016472] 17/10/1944
Young Ms RE, BA DipLIB MCLIP, Comm.& Yth.Serv.Lib., Kensal L. [0040313] 09/01/1987
Young Mr RJ, MCLIP, Br.Lib., Stanmore, L.B.of Harrow. [0016474] 17/08/1971
Young Mrs RS, (was Temple), MCLIP, User Educ.Lib., The Open Poly.of New Zealand, Lower Hutt. [0036732] 16/11/1983
Young Miss S, Stud., Queen Margaret Univ.Coll., Edinburgh. [0057125] 14/12/1998
Young Ms SL, (was Ledamun), BA, Unemployed. [0041442] 01/01/1988
Young Mrs SS, (was McCaskill), BA(Hons), Asst.Ref./Local Stud.Lib., Aberdeen City Council. [0048305] 25/11/1992
Young Kim Fat Miss M, Acting Sen.Lib., Municipality of Quatre-Bornes, Mauritius. [0052392] 31/10/1995
Younger Mrs LA, (was Gordon), BA MCLIP, Sen.Catr., Univ.of Northumbria, Newcastle-upon-Tyne. [0016476] 18/01/1972
Younger Miss MC, BLib MCLIP, Lib., Lord Chancellor's Dept., London. [0026154] 01/07/1976
Younger Ms PM, BA(Hons) PGCE MA MCLIP, Med.Lib., Defence Med.Training L. [0052680] 20/11/1995
Youngman Ms F, BSc MSc MCLIP, Employment not known. [0060728] 12/12/2001
Youngman Mrs G, (was Heelis), BA DipLib MCLIP, Inf.Services.Mgr., Redhill L. [0035071] 02/07/1982
Youngs Mrs EM, (was Turley), MCLIP, Asst., Long Ashton L., N.Somerset. [0018023] 01/01/1966
Youngson Miss LC, MA DipLib MCLIP, p./t.Catr., Univ.of Stirling L., Stirling. [0016477] 01/01/1970
Younie Ms KA, (was Wallace), MA DipILS, Inf.Asst., Aberdeen Coll. [0054620] 04/02/1997
Youthed Mrs C, (was Quinlan), MCLIP, Tech.Lib., Planning, Highways & Design, L.B.of Barnet. [0054515] 01/01/1997
Yu Dr L, PhD, Assoc.Prof., Dept.of Inf.Mgmt., Nankai Univ., Tianjin, China. [0058561] 01/04/2000
Yu Ms MCM, BA MLib MCLIP, Asst.Lib., Pamela Youde Nethersole E.Hosp., Hong Kong. [0046796] 28/01/1997
Yu Miss YNR, BEd(Hons) MA MCLIP, Asst.Lib., Bibl.Control Section, Hong Kong.Poly.Univ. [0054577] 14/01/1997
Yuen Miss LW, MLib, Asst.Lib., Hong Kong Govt. [0058537] 01/04/2000
Yuen Mr TK, MCLIP, Inf.Res.Offr., Hong Kong Consumer Council L. [0019867] 01/01/1973
Yuile Mr DM, BA MCLIP, Prin.Lib., Shropshire C.C. [0016478] 04/10/1971
Yung Miss KC, BA(Hons), Sen.Asst.Lib., Vocational Training Council, Hong Kong. [0047555] 01/10/1992
Zado Dr VY, BSc MSc MPhil PhD, Employment not known. [0036000] 15/04/1983 **AF**
Zaghini Mr EO, PGDipLib MCLIP, Child.L.& Inf.Offr., Book Trust, London. [0045983] 08/08/1991
Zakiewicz Mrs AE, (was Greenaway), MCLIP, p./t.Lib., Charles Edward Brooke Sch., Dennen L.-London. [0016482] 28/02/1962
Zalin Mrs RA, (was Mould), BA MCLIP, Retired. [0017414] 08/01/1968
Zammit Mrs BE, (was Trusler), MCLIP, Life Member. [0016483] 01/01/1947
Zandonade Mr T, MA, Asst.Lec., Univ.of Brasilia, Brasilia, DF (Brazil). [0024308] 30/05/1975
Zanelli Mr P, BA(Hons), Team Lib., Enfield Council. [0057371] 26/02/1999
Zarach Ms VR, BA(Hons), Stud., Univ.of Brighton. [0059229] 09/01/2001
Zarywacz Mrs SG, (was Castle), BA MCLIP, Lib., Steel Construction Inst. [0038876] 14/10/1985
Zehtabi Mr AF, Stud., Univ.of Bristol, &, Learning Resource Asst., Acq.Unit, City of Bristol Coll. [0058958] 10/10/2000
Zelinger Mr AJ, BA(Hons) DipIM, Asst.Lib., House of Lords, London. [0055928] 11/12/1997
Zeller Dr G, PhD, Specialist, Special Area Collection, Univ.L., Tuebingen, Germany. [0046837] 14/02/1992
Zellweger Mrs EC, (was Lawrence), BA MCLIP, Res.Serv.Offr., Redcar & Cleveland Bor.Council. [0008700] 24/01/1972
Zenobi-Bird Mrs L, (was Zenobi), BA MA MA MCLIP, Customer Serv.Consultant, SIRSI Ltd., Potters Bar. [0053853] 07/10/1996
Zhaodong Mr LIU, HonFCLIP, Hon Fellow. [0060088] 07/12/2001 **FE 07/12/2001**
Zhou Mrs K, MA, Filing Clerk, Consignia Ltd., Sheffield. [0044779] 17/11/1990
Zhou Mrs Y, BA MSc MCLIP, Asst.Community Serv.Lib., Southampton City L., Southampton. [0050679] 11/10/1994
Zicari Ms J, (was Holliday), MCLIP, Retired. [0028771] 01/01/1960
Zielstra Ms JR, BA(Hons) MSc MCLIP, [0046096] 01/01/1991
Ziomek Miss JA, BA(Hons) MCLIP, Br.Lib., Rhondda-Cynon-Taff, Mountain Ash. [0049308] 20/10/1993
Zissimos Mr D, BA, L.Asst., Honourable Soc.of Grays Inn, London. [0058701] 09/06/2000
Zolynski Miss BA, BA DipECLaw DipLib MCLIP, Head LIS, City Univ., London. [0028731] 01/01/1978
Zolynski Miss RH, BA DipLib MCLIP, Asst.Head of ILS, Dept.of Trade & Ind., London. [0033205] 03/10/1980
Zorba Miss I, BA, Lib., Univ.of Thessely, Volos, Greece. [0058621] 19/04/2000
Zumpe Mr M, BA MA, Trainee Lib., W.Sussex Co.L., Chichester. [0059665] 24/07/2001
Zylstra Mrs C, BSc DipInfSc MCLIP, Customer Serv.Mgr., Essex C.C., Saffron Walden. [0031547] 20/10/1979

CILIP

Institutional Members

Institutional Members

Name	Date	Number
Aberdeen Council, Aberdeen.	01/01/1890	8000840
Aberdeen University, Aberdeen.	01/01/2028	8000004
Aberdeenshire Council, Aberdeenshire.	01/01/2027	8000002
ADT College, London.	13/08/2001	8001419
Alcan International Ltd, Banbury.	08/09/1997	8001316
Alzheimers Society, London.	31/03/2000	8001376
American Community School Ltd, The, Cobham.	21/09/1998	8001339
American International University in London, Richmond.	02/07/2001	8001414
Amnesty International, London.	18/05/1995	8001235
Angus Council, Forfar.	01/01/1930	8000014
Aquinas College, Stockport.	15/11/2002	8001447
Argyll & Bute Council, Dunoon.	01/01/1946	8000017
Arts Institute at Bournemouth Ltd, The, Poole.	03/06/1999	8001361
Astrazeneca, Macclesfield.	12/09/2002	8001443
B.B.C. Information & Archives, London.	21/06/1985	8001021
B.B.C. Scotland, Information & Archives, Glasgow.	07/11/1996	8001289
Bacon & Woodrow, Epsom.	28/02/1992	8001138
BAE Systems Electronics Ltd, Waterlooville.	30/04/2002	8001434
Barnet College, London.	06/04/1998	8001329
Barnfield Technology Centre, Luton.	31/03/2000	8001375
Barnsley Metropolitan Borough Council, Barnsley.	01/01/2009	8000035
Barton Court Grammar School, Canterbury.	20/07/1999	8001363
Bath College, City of, Bath.	18/11/1987	8001049
Bath, University of, Bath.	21/04/1983	8000042
BECTA, Coventry.	27/03/1998	8001327
Bedfordshire County Council, Bedford.	27/06/1989	8001074
Bexley, London Borough of, Thamesmead.	01/01/1959	8000056
Birkbeck College Library, London.	09/08/1996	8001277
Birmingham Metropolitan District Council, Birmingham.	01/01/1887	8000067
Birmingham, University of, Birmingham.	11/01/2003	8000069
Birmingham, University of Central England in, Birmingham.	30/11/1976	8000065
Bishopsgate Institute, London.	01/01/1952	8000432
Blessed John Roche School, London.	19/05/1999	8001358
BLPES - London Sch of Economics & Political Sci, London.	25/03/1999	8001349
Bolton College, Bolton.	01/01/1952	8000082
Bolton Metropolitan District Council, Bolton.	01/01/1886	8000081
Bournemouth School, Bournemouth.	30/04/1991	8001120
Bradford Metropolitan Council, City of, Bradford.	01/01/1964	8000092
Bradford Metropolitan Council, City of, Bradford.	01/01/1964	8000091
Brent, London Borough of, Brent.	01/01/1965	8000098
Bridgend Library & Information Service, Bridgend.	01/01/2029	8000286
Brighton & Hove Council, Brighton.	17/06/1997	8001308
Brighton, University of, Brighton.	01/01/1962	8000104
Bristol, University of, Bristol.	01/01/1930	8000114
Bristol, University of the West of England, Bristol.	03/04/1987	8001042
British Council, Manchester.	11/05/1976	8000935
British Golf Museum, St.Andrews.	10/06/1994	8001200
British Library, Boston Spa.	01/01/1966	8000088
British Library, London.	18/09/2000	8001386
British Library, Boston Spa.	09/12/1998	8001344
British Library, Boston Spa.	25/06/1975	8000908
British Library, Chief Executive, London.	29/07/1983	8001003
British Library, National Preservation Office, London.	14/05/1990	8001103
British Library, Public Affairs, London.	01/08/1997	8001313
British Museum, London.	23/05/2001	8001412
Britten-Pears Library, Aldeburgh.	03/03/1999	8001348
Bromley, London Borough of, Bromley.	01/01/1965	8000115
Brunel University, Uxbridge.	01/01/1961	8000759
Buckinghamshire County Council, Buckinghamshire.	18/07/1975	8000913
Burnley College, Burnley.	25/05/1995	8001239
Bury Metropolitan District Council, Bury.	01/01/1901	8000121
Cadbury Sixth Form College, Birmingham.	04/01/1993	8001164
Calderdale Metropolitan District Council, Halifax.	20/05/2007	8000862
Cambridge, University of, Cambridge.	01/01/1968	8000132
Cambridgeshire County Council, Huntingdon.	01/01/1933	8000350
Cambridgeshire County Council, Cambridge.	01/01/1946	8000623
Cambridgeshire County Council, Huntingdon.	14/10/1976	8000943
Cambridgeshire County Council, Cambridge.	31/03/1992	8001139
Cambridgeshire County Council, Huntingdon.	14/10/1976	8000942
Camden, London Borough of, Camden.	01/01/1967	8000135
Canterbury College, Canterbury.	26/04/1999	8001353
Carlisle College-Learning Resource Centre, Carlisle.	01/01/1959	8000147
Carmel College, St.Helens.	15/10/1998	8001340
Central St Martins College of Art & Design, London.	30/06/1993	8001179
Ceredigion County Library, Aberystwyth.	01/01/2025	8000146
Charity Commission, The, Taunton.	29/01/2002	8001429
Cheshire County Council, Cheshire.	01/01/2025	8000163
City & Islington College, London.	24/12/1998	8001345
City Hospital NHS Trust, Birmingham.	18/05/1999	8001357
City University, London.	01/01/1966	8000444
CNBC, London.	23/02/2001	8001406
College of Optometrists, London.	25/10/2002	8001446
Corporation of London, London.	01/01/1978	8000453
County Durham Careers Service, Durham.	18/10/1996	8001286
Courtauld Institute of Art, London.	01/12/1996	8001290
Coventry Metropolitan District Council, Coventry.	01/01/1969	8000187
Cumbria County Council, Cumbria.	01/01/1950	8000193
Cystic Fibrosis Trust, Bromley.	17/06/1999	8001359
Dartington College of Arts Ltd, Totnes.	06/10/1981	8000993
Davies Wallis Foyster, Manchester.	12/08/1997	8001315
Dawson Books, Rushden.	04/10/2002	8001444
De Montfort University, Leicester.	01/01/1970	8000400
Department of Culture, Media & Sport, London.	01/01/1960	8000447
Derby City Council, Derby.	18/07/1997	8001310
Derbyshire County Council, Matlock.	01/01/1898	8000204
Derry Paper & Book Conservation Ltd, Nottingham.	02/07/1986	8001033
Devon & Cornwall Workforce Development Confed, Exeter.	15/10/2002	8001445
Devon County Council, Exeter.	01/01/2027	8000205
Dick Institute, The, Kilmarnock.	01/01/1968	8000963
Doncaster Metropolitan District Council, Doncaster.	01/01/1952	8000209
Doncaster Metropolitan District Council, Doncaster.	01/01/2007	8000210
Dorset County Council, Dorchester.	01/01/1930	8000211
Douglas Public Library, Douglas.	01/01/1932	8000881
Dr Williams's Library & Trust, London.	01/01/1897	8000448
Driffield School, Driffield.	21/10/1992	8001159
Dudley Metropolitan Borough Council, Dudley.	01/01/1930	8000216
Dumfries & Galloway Council, Dumfries.	02/05/1979	8000977
Dunbartonshire Council, East, Glasgow.	11/01/1944	8000381
Dunbartonshire Council, West, Dumbarton.	01/01/1944	8000220
Dundee Council, City of, Dundee.	01/01/1883	8000223
Dundee University, Dundee.	01/01/1946	8000224
Durham County Council, Durham.	01/01/1930	8000226
Ealing, London Borough of, Ealing.	01/01/1930	8000230
East Anglia, University of, Norwich.	01/01/2001	8000591
East Lothian Council, Haddington.	01/01/1951	8000234
East Riding of Yorkshire, Beverley.	01/01/2026	8000235
East Sussex County Council, Lewes.	01/01/2026	8000237
Edge Hill University College, Ormskirk.	16/03/1998	8001328
Edinburgh College of Art, Edinburgh.	14/04/1993	8001174
Edinburgh Council, City of, Edinburgh.	01/01/2029	8000244
Edinburgh Council, City of, Edinburgh.	01/01/2022	8000243
Education for Change Ltd, London.	10/12/1990	8001112
Education Library Service, London.	03/11/2000	8001395
Electricity Association, London.	13/10/2000	8001390
ENDS (Environmental Data Services) Ltd, London.	07/12/2000	8001400
Enfield College, Enfield.	25/03/1997	8001299
Enfield, London Borough of, Enfield.	01/01/2021	8000254
English Speaking Union, London.	19/03/1993	8001171
Epsom & Ewell High School, W.Ewell.	09/06/1993	8001177
Epsom College, Epsom.	22/09/1995	8001246
Esher College, Thames Ditton.	14/02/2002	8001427
Essex County Council, Chelmsford.	01/01/1930	8000260
European School of Osteopathy, Boxley.	25/04/1985	8001016
Evansville, University of, Grantham.	27/06/1989	8001073
Exeter, University of, Exeter.	01/01/2029	8000262
Family Planning Association, London.	12/10/1990	8001108
Farnham Heath End School, Farnham.	18/11/1992	8001162
Food Standards Agency, London.	11/01/2002	8001423
Foreign & Commonwealth Office, London.	01/01/1952	8000449
Forensic Science Service, London.	24/01/2002	8001425
Fountain Court Chambers, London.	07/05/2002	8001435
Frances Perry Library, Enfield.	16/01/1995	8001230
Gatehouse Publishing Charity Ltd, Manchester.	10/04/2001	8001408
Gateshead College, Gateshead.	27/03/1995	8001231
Gateshead Metropolitan Borough Council, Gateshead.	01/01/1959	8000285
Gateshead Metropolitan Borough Council, Gateshead.	19/03/1975	8000899
Geological Society, The, London.	03/11/1998	8001341
Glasgow Council, City of, Glasgow.	01/01/1893	8000289
Glasgow University, Glasgow.	01/01/1870	8000291
Glasgow Womens Library, Glasgow.	04/10/1999	8001364
Glen Recruitment, London.	20/05/1996	8001266
Gloucestershire County Council, Gloucester.	01/01/1931	8000293
Godalming College, Godalming.	20/02/2001	8001404
Goethe-Institut London, London.	19/02/1973	8000829
Goldsmiths College, University of London, London.	01/01/1962	8000451
Government Actuarys Department, London.	12/06/2002	8001437
Greenwich, London Borough of, Greenwich.	01/01/1966	8000302
Guille-Allès Library, Guernsey.	22/04/1987	8001043
Gyosei International College in the UK, Reading.	16/02/1993	8001167
Hacker Young, London.	14/04/1999	8001351
Hackney, London Borough of, Hackney.	01/01/2029	8000306
Haggerston School, London.	27/09/1996	8001283
Hampshire County Council, Winchester.	01/01/1930	8000315
Haringey, London Borough of, Haringey.	17/03/1986	8001029
Harrow, London Borough of, Harrow.	01/01/1965	8000321
Hartlepool Borough Council, Hartlepool.	28/05/1996	8001268
Hartlepool Borough Council, Hartlepool.	01/01/1906	8000323

393

Organisation	Date	Number
Haseltine Lake & Co, London.	01/01/1973	8000826
Havering, London Borough of, Havering.	01/01/1969	8000327
Hay Group, London.	15/04/2002	8001433
Haydon School, Pinner.	31/03/1998	8001330
Hayes School, Bromley.	23/06/1992	8001150
Haywards Heath College, Haywards Heath.	14/02/2002	8001426
Help for Health Trust, Winchester.	25/02/2000	8001371
Herefordshire Libraries & Information Service, Hereford.	20/07/1999	8001362
Hertfordshire County Council, Hertford.	01/01/1930	8000333
Hillingdon, London Borough of, Uxbridge.	01/01/1965	8000338
Hispanic & Luso-Brazilian Council, London.	21/07/1978	8000974
House of Commons, London.	01/01/1963	8000455
House of Lords, London.	29/02/1996	8001263
Huddersfield, University of, Huddersfield.	01/01/1952	8000345
Imperial College, London.	14/12/2000	8001401
Imperial War Museum, London.	01/01/1949	8000458
Infologistix Ltd, Nottingham.	31/01/1990	8001097
Information Commissioner, Wilmslow.	07/08/2002	8001442
Information North, Newcastle-upon-Tyne.	31/01/1990	8001098
Inner Temple Library, London.	19/02/1996	8001261
Inns of Court School of Law, London.	20/10/1997	8001318
Institut Francais, London.	31/05/1996	8001269
Institute of Biomedical Science, London.	01/01/1963	8000464
Institute of Commonwealth Studies, London.	10/10/2000	8001388
Institute of Commonwealth Studies, Oxford.	01/01/1961	8000609
Institute of Development Studies, Brighton.	09/05/1995	8001232
Institute of Education University of London, London.	01/01/1960	8000511
Islington, London Borough of, Islington.	01/01/2005	8000363
Itchen College, Southampton.	01/04/1996	8001264
Jewish Chronicle Library, London.	13/07/2000	8001383
John Innes Centre, Norwich.	01/07/1994	8001205
Kensington & Chelsea, Royal Borough of, Kensington & Chelsea.	01/01/1965	8000369
Kent County Council, Maidstone.	01/01/2026	8000371
King Edward VI High School for Girls, Birmingham.	15/01/2001	8001403
King Edward's School, Birmingham.	30/05/2002	8001438
Kings College London Library, London.	27/07/1992	8001151
Kings Fund, London.	28/02/1991	8001116
Kingston College, Kingston upon Thames.	17/02/1998	8001323
Kingston University, Kingston upon Thames.	01/01/1962	8000377
Kingston upon Hull City Council, Hull.	01/01/1930	8000349
Kirklees Metropolitan District Council, Kirklees.	01/01/1898	8000346
Knitting & Crochet Guild, Whitland.	21/02/2000	8001370
Knowsley Community College, Roby.	01/07/1991	8001128
The Lakes College-West Cumbria, Workington.	01/01/1962	8000817
Lancashire County Council, Preston.	01/01/2029	8000387
Learning Centre Health First, London.	20/02/2002	8001431
Leeds City Council, Leeds.	01/01/1966	8000392
Leeds Metropolitan University, Calverey Street, Leeds.	01/01/1960	8000395
Leeds, University of, Leeds.	01/01/1930	8000398
Leicestershire County Council, Leicester.	04/02/1982	8000994
Leicestershire County Council, Leicester.	01/01/1930	8000401
Leicestershire County Council, Leicester.	28/05/1974	8000864
Lewisham College, Lewisham.	08/06/1998	8001335
Lincoln's Inn Library, London.	01/01/1974	8000849
Lincolnshire County Council, Lincoln.	01/01/1930	8000415
Listening Books, London.	05/09/1996	8001279
Literary & Philosophical Society, Newcastle-Upon-Tyne.	01/01/1947	8000569
Liverpool Institute for Performing Arts, Liverpool.	11/12/1995	8001253
Liverpool Libraries & Information Services, Liverpool.	01/01/1884	8000417
Liverpool-Sydney Jones Library, University of, Liverpool.	01/01/2029	8000423
London Guildhall University, London.	01/01/1961	8000443
London Institute, The, London.	24/07/2000	8001384
London Metropolitan Archives, London.	01/01/1949	8000452
London Voluntary Service Council, London.	01/02/2000	8001369
Loretto School, Musselburgh.	30/04/2000	8001378
Loughborough University, Loughborough.	01/01/1965	8000524
Luton Borough Council, Luton.	19/12/1997	8001321
Macmillan Cancer Relief, London.	24/01/2000	8001368
Magna Print Books Ltd, Long Preston.	25/01/1978	8000967
Malvern College Library, Malvern.	26/05/2000	8001380
Manchester City Council, Manchester.	01/01/2021	8000541
Manchester Metropolitan University, Manchester.	16/05/1997	8001303
Manchester Metropolitan University, Manchester.	01/01/1963	8000539
Medway Council, Strood.	20/07/1998	8001336
Merseyside Maritime Museum, Liverpool.	16/10/2000	8001389
Merton College, Morden.	01/06/1993	8001175
Middlesbrough Borough Council, Middlesbrough.	26/06/1996	8001272
Milton Keynes Council, Milton Keynes.	30/04/1997	8001301
Multiple Sclerosis Society, The, London.	06/03/2000	8001373
Napier University Learning Information Services, Edinburgh.	01/03/1976	8000930
National Art Library, Victoria & Albert Museum, London.	31/07/1986	8001035
National Inst for Biological Standards & Control, London.	20/03/1987	8001040
National Institute of Adult Continuing Education, Leicester.	18/07/1996	8001274
National Institute of Economic & Social Research, London.	26/07/1993	8001181
National Library for the Blind, Stockport.	01/01/2008	8000483
National Library of Scotland, Edinburgh.	01/01/1930	8000248
National Library of Wales, Aberystwyth.	01/01/2021	8000005
Neath Port Talbot Library & Information Services, Port Talbot.	01/07/1974	8000872
New College Durham, Framwellgate Moor.	24/10/1996	8001287
Newcastle upon Tyne City Council, Newcastle-upon-Tyne.	01/03/1985	8001013
Newham 6th Form College, London.	08/10/1992	8001157
Newport County Borough Council, Newport.	31/01/1990	8001090
Newquay Tretherras School, Newquay.	29/01/1996	8001256
NHS Direct Online, Southampton.	07/05/2002	8001436
North Devon College Library, Barnstaple.	01/07/1991	8001125
North Down & Ards Institute, Bangor.	25/02/2000	8001372
North East Lincolnshire Council, Grimsby.	17/02/1975	8000894
North Essex Health Authority, Witham.	02/11/1998	8001342
North Lincolnshire Council, Scunthorpe.	01/01/1935	8000690
North London, University of, London.	01/01/1961	8000870
North Tyneside College, Wallsend.	27/09/1991	8001131
North Tyneside Metropolitan District Council, North Shields.	01/01/1968	8000756
North West Kent PG Medical Library, Dartford.	17/08/1990	8001106
North Yorkshire County Council, Northallerton.	24/06/1974	8000869
Northamptonshire Library & Information Service, Northampton.	01/01/2027	8000583
Northern Ireland Assembly Library, Belfast.	20/09/2001	8001420
Northgate Hospital, Morpeth.	22/01/2002	8001424
Northumberland County Council, Morpeth.	01/01/1930	8000586
Northumbria at Newcastle, University of, Newcastle-upon-Tyne.	01/01/1948	8000563
Northumbria, University of, Newcastle-upon-Tyne.	22/11/1999	8001366
Norwich Institute of Art & Design, Norwich.	22/04/1986	8001030
Nottingham City Council, Nottingham.	04/03/1975	8000898
Nottingham Health Trust, Nottingham.	08/03/2002	8001430
Nottingham Trent University, Nottingham.	16/02/1993	8001166
Nuffield Orthopaedic Centre, Oxford.	01/01/1969	8000329
Oldham Metropolitan District Council, Oldham.	01/01/1931	8000604
Onchan Public Library, Onchan.	01/12/1997	8001320
Open University, Milton Keynes.	01/01/1970	8000077
Orpington College, Kent.	23/02/2001	8001405
Oxford Brookes University, Headington.	03/03/1995	8001229
Oxford High School, Oxford.	19/03/1993	8001173
Oxford-Faculty of Music, University of, Oxford.	01/01/1958	8000612
Oxfordshire County Council, Oxford.	01/01/2029	8000613
Paisley, University of, Paisley.	25/03/1976	8000933
Patients Library, Whitechapel.	01/10/1989	8001084
Pembrokeshire County Council, Haverfordwest.	19/07/1976	8000939
Perth & Kinross Council, Perth.	01/01/2026	8000621
Pimlico School, London.	16/03/2002	8001432
Plymouth, University of, Plymouth.	01/01/1972	8000626
Poetry Library, London.	17/08/1989	8001078
Portsmouth Central Library, Portsmouth.	15/08/1997	8001314
Portsmouth, University of, Portsmouth.	01/01/1956	8000639
Public Record Office, Kew.	16/02/1977	8000952
Queen Margaret University College, Edinburgh.	04/01/1993	8001163
Reading, University of, Reading.	01/01/2029	8000652
Redbridge College, Romford.	23/01/1997	8001295
Redbridge, London Borough of, Ilford.	01/01/1965	8000653
Redbridge, London Borough of, Ilford.	14/02/2002	8001428
Redcar & Cleveland Borough Council, Middlesbrough.	24/05/1996	8001267
Regent's College Library, Head Lib..	25/07/1986	8001036
Reid Kerr College, Paisley.	08/11/1995	8001251
Remploy Library Services, Leicester.	01/01/1962	8000497
Resource, London.	30/09/1995	8001243
Rhondda College, Tonypandy.	29/11/1989	8001089
Robert Gordon University, The, Aberdeen.	01/01/1960	8000003
Rotherham Metropolitan Borough Council, Rotherham.	01/01/1890	8000667
Rowecom UK Ltd, Oxford.	31/01/1992	8001134
Royal Academy of Dance, London.	08/06/1995	8001240
Royal Commission on Ancient & Hist Monuments, Aberystwyth.	31/01/1996	8001259
Royal Pharmaceutical Society, Edinburgh.	01/01/1968	8000242
Royal South Hampshire Hospital, Southampton.	21/05/1992	8001144
Ruskin College, Oxford.	10/10/1991	8001132
Salford, University of, Salford.	01/01/1957	8000686
Sandwell Metropolitan Borough Council, West Bromwich.	01/01/1937	8000781
School of Oriental & African Studies, London.	05/02/1997	8001297
Science Museum Library, London.	01/01/1971	8000506
Scottish Agricultural College, Edinburgh.	01/01/1965	8000247
Scottish Borders Council, Selkirk.	01/05/1976	8000937
Seaham Comprehensive School, Co.Durham.	07/10/1996	8001284
Sheffield College, The, Sheffield.	31/07/1994	8001209
Sheffield Hallam University, Sheffield.	01/10/1989	8001082
Sheffield Metropolitan District Council, Sheffield.	27/10/1983	8001006
Sheffield Metropolitan District Council, Sheffield.	01/01/2022	8000696
Sheffield-Library, University of, Sheffield.	01/01/1939	8000699
Shepherd Design & Build, York.	05/03/1997	8001298

Institutional Members

Name	Date	ID
Smithkline Beecham Consumer Healthcare, Weybridge.	01/01/1954	8000054
Solihull Metropolitan Borough Council, Solihull.	01/01/1947	8000707
South Bank University, London.	18/09/1989	8001075
South East Museums Agency, Winchester.	08/08/2001	8001418
South East Museums Agency, Chatham.	08/08/2001	8001416
South Eastern Education & Library Board, Ballynahinch.	01/01/1940	8000215
South Thames College, London.	01/01/1966	8000772
South West Museums Council, Ch. Exec..	08/10/2001	8001421
Southampton, University of, Southampton.	03/07/1988	8001062
Southern Education & Library Board, Armagh.	23/04/1974	8000855
Southern Water Technology Group, Crawley.	30/10/1995	8001249
Southwark College, London.	30/04/2001	8001410
Southwark, London Borough of, Southwark.	01/01/1972	8000715
St Cleres School, Stanford Le Hope.	10/05/1995	8001234
St Francis Xavier College, London.	18/03/1999	8001350
St Georges Hospital Medical School Library, Tooting.	17/07/2002	8001440
St Helens, Metropolitan Borough of, St.Helens.	01/01/1950	8000679
St Thomas More High School, Westcliff-on-Sea.	07/10/1996	8001282
Stafford College of Further Education, Stafford.	01/01/1969	8000719
Staffordshire County Council, Stafford.	01/01/2027	8000721
Stirling Council Library Service, Stirling.	01/01/1931	8000724
Stirling, University of, Stirling.	01/01/1967	8000725
Stockport Metropolitan Borough Council, Stockport.	01/01/2009	8000727
Stockton on Tees Borough Libraries, Middlesbrough.	01/01/2026	8000746
Stoke-on-Trent City Council, Stoke-on-Trent.	10/05/1999	8001355
Stranmillis College, Belfast.	01/01/1966	8000052
Strathclyde Hospital, Motherwell.	10/02/1997	8001296
Strathclyde, University of, Glasgow.	01/01/1953	8000287
Sunderland College, City of, Sunderland.	27/06/2000	8001381
Surrey County Council, Dorking.	01/01/1965	8000733
Surrey History Centre, Woking.	01/01/1999	8001346
Surrey, University of, Guildford.	01/01/1963	8000305
Sussex, University of, Brighton.	22/03/1999	8001352
Swansea, City & County of, Swansea.	01/07/1997	8001309
TalkingTech.com Ltd, Manchester.	09/11/2001	8001422
Talkingtech.com Ltd, Kineton.	10/02/1999	8001398
Tameside Metropolitan District Council, Ashton under Lyne.	07/08/1974	8000873
Telford College of Arts & Technology, Wellington.	11/06/1998	8001334
Thames Valley University, London.	01/01/1955	8000233
Thomas Rotherham College, Rotherham.	08/08/2001	8001417
Trading Standards Institute, Hadleigh.	03/06/1993	8001176
Trafford Metropolitan Borough Council, Trafford.	14/08/1975	8000914
Trinity & All Saints College, Horsforth.	01/01/1966	8000342
Trinity College, Bristol.	30/06/1980	8000989
Ulster at Coleraine, University of, Coleraine.	01/01/1968	8000830
UMIST Library & Information Service, Manchester.	01/01/2017	8000543
United States Information Service, London.	30/08/1985	8001022
University College, University of London, London.	01/01/1930	8000513
Wakefield Metropolitan District Council, City of, Wakefield.	02/08/1974	8000877
Wakefield Metropolitan District Council, City of, Wakefield.	11/09/2000	8001385
Wales College of Medicine, University of, Cardiff.	30/04/1991	8001119
Wales Institute, Cardiff, University of, Cardiff.	24/04/1996	8001265
Wales, Aberystwyth, University of, Aberystwyth.	01/01/1965	8000007
Wales, Bangor, University of, Bangor.	01/01/1937	8000029
Walsall Metropolitan Borough Council, Walsall.	01/01/1893	8000766
Waltham Forest, London Borough of, Waltham Forest.	01/01/1965	8000768
Wandsworth, London Borough of, Wandsworth.	01/01/1965	8000771
Warwickshire County Council, Warwick.	01/01/2020	8000777
West Thames College, Isleworth.	01/01/1962	8000361
Western Education & Library Board, Omagh.	01/01/1930	8000757
Western Education & Library Board, Enniskillen.	01/01/1955	8000519
Western Isles Islands Council, Stornoway.	21/05/1975	8000904
Weston College, Weston Super Mare.	17/02/1983	8000999
Wigan & Leigh College, Wigan.	30/04/2000	8001379
Wigan Metropolitan Borough Council, Wigan.	01/01/2019	8000802
Wigan Metropolitan Borough Council, Wigan.	19/06/1975	8000907
Wiltshire County Council, Wiltshire..	01/01/1931	8000803
Wirral, Metropolitan Borough of, Birkenhead L., Wirral.	01/01/1898	8000060
Wolverhampton Borough Council, Wolverhampton.	01/01/1888	8000810
Wolverhampton, University of, Wolverhampton.	17/03/2000	8001374
Worcester County Council, Worcester.	01/01/1930	8000815
Worcester, University College, Worcester.	30/03/1994	8001194
Worshipful Company of Goldsmiths, London.	01/01/1948	8000518
Wragge & Co, Birmingham.	06/08/2002	8001441
XREFER, London.	17/06/2002	8001439
York, University of, Heslington.	01/01/1962	8000823

Overseas Institutional Members

Overseas Institutional Members

Austria
Graz, Universitatsbibliothek, Graz. — 01/07/1991 — 9000709

Australia
Armadale Libraries, City of, Armadale. — 05/11/2001 — 9000751
Hurstville Library Service, New South Wales. — 16/01/1975 — 9000501
Library Board of Western Australia, Perth. — 01/01/1953 — 9000030
Macquarie University, North Ryde. — 01/01/1966 — 9000028
Monash University, Clayton. — 01/01/1967 — 9000020
National Library of Australia, Canberra. — 01/01/1965 — 9000439
New South Wales, University, Sydney. — 31/01/2000 — 9000740
Queensland, University of, Brisbane. — 01/01/1966 — 9000012
South Australia, State Library of, Adelaide. — 01/01/1969 — 9000000
Sydney Institute of Technology, Ultimo. — 01/01/1963 — 9000035
Sydney, University of, Sydney. — 01/01/1966 — 9000034
Tasmania, State Library of, Hobart. — 14/08/1974 — 9000492
Victoria, State Library of, Melbourne. — 01/01/1966 — 9000038

Barbados
Central Bank of Barbados, Bridgetown. — 19/06/1978 — 9000590
West Indies, University of the, Bridgetown. — 01/01/1971 — 9000412

Belgium
Universiteitsbibliotheek K U L, Leuven. — 29/04/1974 — 9000484
Vlaamse Vereniging Voor Bibliotheek, Antwerpen. — 03/03/1988 — 9000678

Cameroon
British Council, Bamenda. — 01/01/1996 — 9000731

Canada
Alberta, University of, Edmonton. — 01/01/1967 — 9000053
British Columbia, University of, Vancouver. — 01/01/1962 — 9000082
Carr McLean Ltd, Toronto. — 10/01/1990 — 9000693
McGill University, Montreal. — 01/01/1956 — 9000061
National Library of Canada, Ottawa. — 01/01/1963 — 9000070
Toronto, University of, Ontario. — 01/01/1972 — 9000078

British West Indies
Cayman Islands National Archives & Records Cent, George Town. — 31/01/1990 — 9000695

Croatia
National & University Library, Zagreb. — 25/08/1999 — 9000737

Cyprus
British Council, Nicosia. — 01/01/1961 — 9000094
Cyprus, University of, Nicosia. — 31/03/1992 — 9000712

Denmark
Danish National Library Authority, Copenhagen. — 01/09/1973 — 9000467
Roskilde Bibliotek, Roskilde. — 01/01/1954 — 9000102
Royal School of Library and Information Science, Copenhagen. — 01/01/1959 — 9000100
Statsbiblioteket, Arhus. — 01/01/1970 — 9000098

Ethiopia
British Council, Addis Ababa. — 02/04/1975 — 9000514

Fiji
South Pacific, The University of the, Suva. — 01/01/1969 — 9000123

Finland
Helsinki University, Helsinki. — 01/01/1961 — 9000124
Tampere University, Tampere. — 01/11/1990 — 9000702

France
British Council, Paris. — 01/01/1963 — 9000125

Germany
Giessen, Universitatsbibliothek, Giessen. — 01/02/1973 — 9000448
IFLA UBCIM Programme, Frankfurt. — 04/07/1991 — 9000708
Niedersachsische Staats-u Universitatsbibliothek, Gottingen. — 29/10/2001 — 9000750

Hong Kong
Hong Kong Polytechnic University, Kowloon. — 01/08/1973 — 9000465
Hong Kong Public Libraries, Hong Kong. — 01/01/1960 — 9000140
Hong Kong, University of, Hong Kong. — 01/01/1955 — 9000141

Hungary
Pecs University, Pecs. — 13/07/2000 — 9000743

India
British Council, Bangalore. — 01/01/1961 — 9000143
British Council, Bombay. — 01/01/1952 — 9000146
British Council, Madras. — 01/01/1952 — 9000155
British Council, Maharashtra. — 01/01/1960 — 9000162
British Council, New Delhi. — 01/01/1956 — 9000158
British Council, Oxford. — 16/08/2002 — 9000755
British Council, Oxford. — 16/08/2002 — 9000756
British Council, Trivandrum. — 01/01/1965 — 9000165
Mumbai, University of, Bombay. — 01/01/1936 — 9000542
National Science Library, New Delhi. — 05/04/1974 — 9000481

Ireland
Carlow County Library, Carlow. — 19/03/1981 — 9000634
Carlow Institute of Technology, Carlow. — 11/03/1998 — 9000733
Clare County Library HQ, Ennis. — 28/02/1977 — 9000555
Cork Corporation, Cork. — 01/01/1956 — 9000106
Cork County Library, Cork. — 31/05/1983 — 9000623
Cork, University College, Cork. — 19/07/1985 — 9000667
Donegal County Library, Letterkenny. — 16/02/1996 — 9000701
Dublin City University, Dublin. — 16/10/2000 — 9000744
Dublin Corporation Public Libraries, Dublin. — 01/01/1935 — 9000112
Dublin Institute of Technology, Dublin. — 05/09/1989 — 9000689
Dublin Public Libraries, Dublin. — 01/01/1964 — 9000108
Dublin, University College, Dublin. — 17/01/1977 — 9000556
Dun Laoghaire-Rathdown County Library Service, Co.Dublin. — 01/01/1936 — 9000116
Galway, University College, Galway. — 01/01/1971 — 9000117
Library Council, Dublin. — 01/01/1968 — 9000109
Limerick, University of, Limerick. — 01/01/1978 — 9000588
Longford County Library, Longford. — 17/02/1989 — 9000683
National Library of Ireland, Dublin. — 01/01/1958 — 9000111
Roscommon County Library, Roscommon. — 28/04/1976 — 9000529
Trinity College, Dublin. — 01/01/1959 — 9000115
Wexford County Council, Wexford. — 10/07/2002 — 9000754
Wicklow County Library, Greystones. — 14/05/1993 — 9000722

Israel
Bar Ilan University, Ramat.Gan. — 23/03/1981 — 9000635
Jewish National & University Library, Jerusalem. — 01/01/1966 — 9000171

Italy
Biblioteca Serv Beni Librari, Firenze. — 30/11/1977 — 9000575
British Council, Milan. — 13/03/1978 — 9000581

Jamaica
Jamaica Library Service, Kingston. — 01/01/1950 — 9000416

Japan
Jippro Research Library, Tokyo. — 01/01/1971 — 9000178
Keio University, Tokyo. — 01/01/1986 — 9000668

Mauritius
Municipality of Quatre Bornes, Quatre-Bornes. — 07/08/1979 — 9000609
Port-Louis City Library, Port-Louis. — 14/05/1998 — 9000734

Malaysia
International Islamic Univ Malaysia, Kuala Lumpur. — 07/02/2001 — 9000745
Kebangsaan, University of, Selangor. — 01/01/1970 — 9000193
Penang Public Library, Penang. — 01/01/1963 — 9000195

Netherlands
Bibliotheek Vrije Universiteit, Amsterdam. — 07/04/1975 — 9000512
NBLC, The Hague. — 01/01/1958 — 9000207
Org for the Prohibition of Chemical Weapons, The Hague. — 16/02/2000 — 9000741

New Zealand
Auckland Public Library, Auckland. — 01/01/2022 — 9000213
Auckland, University of, Auckland. — 01/01/1971 — 9000214
Canterbury, University of, Christchurch. — 01/09/1974 — 9000494
Christchurch City Libraries, Christchurch. — 12/06/1991 — 9000707
Christchurch City Libraries, Christchurch. — 01/01/1935 — 9000215
Dunedin Public Library, Dunedin. — 01/01/1934 — 9000218
Massey University, Palmerston North. — 31/01/1990 — 9000696
Wanganui District Library, Wanganui. — 26/08/1983 — 9000658
Wellington Library, Wellington. — 01/01/1930 — 9000226

Norway
Universitetsbibl I Trondheim, Trondheim. — 01/01/1970 — 9000245

Peru
Pontificia University Catolica Peru, Lima. — 01/01/1986 — 9000669

Poland
Warsaw University, Warsaw Univ. — 30/04/1991 — 9000704

Portugal
Fundacao Calouste Gulbenkian, Lisboa Codex. — 10/10/1989 — 9000690

Puerto Rico
Bib Ciencias Bibliotecarias, San Juan. — 24/09/1976 — 9000509

Saudi Arabia
King Fahd National Library, Riyadh. — 28/11/1991 — 9000710

Sierra Leone
British Council, Freetown. — 12/01/1979 — 9000598

Republic of Singapore
National Library Board, Singapore. — 01/01/1966 — 9000259
National University of Singapore, Singapore. — 01/01/1951 — 9000261
Temasek Polytechnic, Singapore. — 19/03/1993 — 9000720

Republic of South Africa
Cape Town City Libraries, Cape Town. — 01/01/1958 — 9000265
Johannesburg Public Library, Johannesburg. — 01/01/1957 — 9000271
Potchefstroom University, Potchefstroom. — 25/11/1974 — 9000498
Stellenbosch, University of, Stellenbosch. — 01/01/1972 — 9000280

Spain

Barcelona, Universitat de, Barcelona.	30/07/1987	9000673
Diputacio de Barcelona, Barcelona.	01/11/1999	9000739

Sri Lanka
National Library of Sri Lanka, Colombo.	01/01/1972	9000089

Sudan
Khartoum, University of, Khartoum.	10/03/1989	9000684

Sweden
Lund, University Library of, Lund.	01/01/1931	9000287
Malmo Stadsbibliotek, Malmo.	18/05/1992	9000714
Malmo Stadsbibliotek, Malmo.	01/01/1967	9000288
Stockholms Stadsbibliotek, Stockholm.	21/03/1983	9000651

Switzerland
International Labour Office, Geneva.	02/09/1992	9000715

Thailand
Mahidol University, Nakornpathom.	16/12/1988	9000682

Trinidad & Tobago
West Indies, University of the, St. Augustine.	01/01/1948	9000495

Turkey
Bilkent University, Ankara.	30/04/1991	9000705

USA
American Library Association, Chicago.	01/01/1966	9000319
Arizona, University of, Tucson.	17/07/1974	9000490
Boston Public Libraries, Boston.	11/08/1976	9000540
California, University of, Berkeley.	01/01/1971	9000305
Detroit Public Library, Detroit.	01/01/2029	9000334
East Carolina University, Greenville.	14/02/2002	9000753
Emporia State University, Kansas.	01/01/1958	9000337
Georgia, University of, Athens.	01/01/1951	9000301
Hawaii University, Honolulu.	01/01/1965	9000345
Iowa, State University of, Iowa City.	01/01/1935	9000349
Long Island University, New York.	01/01/1971	9000344
Louisiana State University, Baton Rouge.	01/01/1952	9000304
Maryland, University of, College Park.	01/01/1968	9000327
Michigan, University of, Ann Arbor.	01/01/1935	9000299
Missouri, University of, Columbia.	01/01/1944	9000329
New York, State University of, Binghampton.	01/01/1971	9000308
North Carolina, University of, Greensboro.	01/01/1965	9000343
Northwestern University, Illinois.	01/01/2029	9000339
OCLC Information Center, Dublin.	17/10/2001	9000752
Ohio, State Library of, Columbus.	01/11/1999	9000738
Oregon, University of, Eugene.	01/01/1965	9000338
Pittsburgh University, Pittsburgh.	01/01/1968	9000382
Princeton University, New Jersey.	01/01/1962	9000386
Purdue University, West Lafayette.	01/01/1973	9000545
Rhode Island, University of, Kingston.	01/01/1972	9000354
Rock Crusher Elementary School, Homosassa.	12/09/2002	9000757
San Francisco Public Library, California.	31/01/1990	9000697
South Carolina, University of, Columbia.	01/01/1995	9000729
Stanford University Library, California.	01/01/1971	9000397
Tennessee, University of, Knoxville.	01/01/1971	9000403
Texas at Austin, University of, Austin.	01/01/1935	9000303
Wisconsin, University of, Madison.	01/01/1969	9000364
Yale University, Connecticut.	11/08/1976	9000534

Part 5
HISTORICAL INFORMATION

A short history of the Institute of Information Scientists

The Institute of Information Scientists (IIS) was born in response to rapid advances in science and technology. Fittingly, it was thanks to convergence in technology, and increasingly generalised access to the applications of some of the technology, that IIS has joined forces with the library community once more, after a schism lasting more than 40 years.

Although it was not set up until 1958, the IIS can trace its history back to 1923. In that year a meeting was organised by Professor Hutton of Oxford University and Ben Fullman of the British Non-Ferrous Metals Research Association to discuss issues arising from the rapid growth of scientific research and publication after WW1. The Library Association declined to take part in that meeting, and as a result the Association of Special Libraries and Information Bureaux was set up in 1924. Jumping forward to 1948 Fullman presented proposals to the Aslib Annual Conference for a syllabus for the education of information professionals to cope with the even more rapid growth of science after the Second World War. This visionary approach was not adopted, and for the next few years progress towards professional education and standards for information work (rather than librarianship) was minimal.

The final straw for scientific information officers was the defeat of some revised proposals at the Aslib Conference in 1957 and on 23 January 1958 a meeting was held at the IEE to discuss proposals for a new professional association. The meeting was chaired by Dr G. Malcolm Dyson. Jason Farradane and Chris Hanson made the opening speeches to a motion: 'that a professional body be, and is hereby set up, to promote and maintain high standards in scientific and technical information work and to establish qualifications for those engaged in the profession'. There were 125 people at this first meeting. At a subsequent meeting on 23 May 1958 at the Royal Society of Arts the Constitution of the Institute of Information Scientists was approved. Dr Dyson was elected as President, Chris Hanson as Vice President, Gordon Foster as Hon. Treasurer and Jason Farradane as Hon. Secretary. By the end of the year around 100 Members had joined the Institute.

The first issue of the *Bulletin* was written by Farradane and published in April 1959. Although slightly outside the scope of a history of the IIS it is important to record the establishment in 1963 of the first full-time post-graduate course in information science at what was then the Northampton College of Advanced Technology (now City University). In 1964 the IIS held its first conference at Merton College, Oxford, at which there were 60 delegates. A notable event in 1965 was the first Salary Survey, developed by Dr Malcolm Campbell.

The first issue of *The Information Scientist*, the direct forerunner of the *Journal of Information Science*, was published in 1967. Peter Vickers and John Williams were the initial Editors, until Alan Gilchrist took over in the mid-1970s, continuing as Editor of *JIS* until 2002.

Widening the scope

As the Institute grew in size in the late 1960s and early 1970s it became clear that the use of the phrase 'scientific and technical information work' was too limiting. At the 1972 AGM there was a motion to widen the scope, but there was also concern that this would mean rewriting the Memorandum of Association, so the proposals were withdrawn. Subsequently Council found that there was no need to change the Memorandum, and they could construe the phrase as they wished, which they then proceeded to do.

Inform was launched in 1975 to complement *The Information Scientist*. Also in 1975 another major change in the structure of the IIS took place. At the AGM Martin White, together with Charles Oppenheim, decided that it was time that Associate Members were represented on Council, rather than just Members and Fellows. To the surprise of Council the motion was passed.

In 1978 the publishing activities of the Institute expanded further with the publication of the first of the celebrated Monograph series of books on information science, managed by John Campbell. The year was also notable for a very lively discussion at the Annual Conference about the future of the Institute as it neared its 21st Anniversary with around 1400 Members. This was to a significant extent the result of an informal meeting of the STIR group of younger members (the Steering Team for Institute Reform). That year had already marked the creation of Special Interest Groups which could accept non-Members of the IIS. The first to be set up was the Online User Group (now UKOLUG), followed soon after by the Patent and Trade Marks Group.

1979 was quite a year, and not only because the IIS office moved out to Reading. For the first time the Annual Conference was held at

A short history of the Institute of Information Scientists

a hotel, the Imperial Hotel, Torquay, and ended up making a very substantial profit for the Institute in its 21st year. Discussions were also taking place to heal the differences between the IIS, The Library Association and Aslib through the creation of the first Tripartite Conference, to be held in Sheffield in 1980. Further cooperation with The Library Association resulted in the first combined Salary Survey.

By 1980 Council had approved a radical reshaping of the membership and committee decision-making structures of the Institute. This made it much more welcoming and open to younger people and to those from outside traditional scientific and technical information backgrounds. New entrants to the profession could now participate fully in the activities and governance of the Institute, and make their voices heard.

A sign that the Institute had become much more open and informal was its launch of the Infotainers. There were four major shows in 1980, 1983, 1985 and 1990, and several smaller ones, all in the best tradition of satirical review.

Acquiring a secretariat

The Silver Jubilee Conference took place in 1983 at St Catherine's College, Oxford, though Council were not exactly concentrating on the papers as there was a very real chance that the IIS had fallen foul of VAT legislation over its charitable/educational status. Luckily the danger passed. The problems did highlight the need for a full-time employee running the IIS office, and the IIS was very fortunate to be able to appoint Sarah Carter, a Member of the Institute, to the post of Executive Secretary in 1984, by which time the membership had reached almost 2000.

From 1985 the IIS had a central focus for its activities with a central London base. Its administrative structure was developed, but it continued to be very dependent on its Members for organising events and conferences, drafting and agreeing professional standards, and accreditation activities in universities and colleges offering courses in information science. Lobbying and advocacy, and all the Branch and Special Interest Group activities, also depended on volunteers from the membership. In addition to UKOLUG and PATMG, the IIS set up the City Information Group, the Computerised Information Management Special Interest Group (it was later disbanded), the Small Business Group for consultants et al. (which lasted into the early 1990s), and ALGIS (the Affiliation of Local Government Information

Specialists). At least three of these groups became significant organisations within their own specialisations, due entirely to the hard work and enthusiasm of their members.

During this period the Branch structure was revised, and the Midlands Branch disappeared, mainly because the road and public transport links did not make it easy for members from both East and West Midlands to attend any meeting. There were also Local Groups in Reading, Oxford and elsewhere that thrived for a time. The number of branches was a tribute to the energy of Members, given the comparatively small size of the IIS as a whole.

Significant activities organised and developed by members for members included the very successful series of annual Text Retrieval Conferences, and the IIS Evening Events. These were short, affordable professional development workshops and seminars conceived by Martin White when he was IIS President. They attracted many younger members. They came to learn from eminent senior members who were generous in offering their time for professional development opportunities.

The second tripartite conference was held in 1985, as a five-way multipartite event in Bournemouth. The third and final multipartite conference was held in 1990, also in Bournemouth.

1990 was a momentous year for the Institute. After a series of exploratory discussions with the Charity Commissioners, the Institute was granted charitable status. This conferred considerable tax advantages, and enabled the IIS to make the best use of a generous bequest from an early member, John Campbell. Part of the bequest was used to set up the John Campbell Trust, which was to be used for the provision of scholarships, prizes, travel grants or research fellowships. Its work continues today.

1990 also marked the first serious effort by The Library Association, Aslib and the IIS to move closer together with a view to merger. Although support for the merger was not strong enough for formal moves to be made, the discussions (marked by the Saunders Report), and a second series of discussions (the Tripartite discussions) did result in some fundamental reviews of the similarities and differences between the organisations.

For the Institute, the 1990s were dominated by two significant factors:

- Changes in work, cultures and attitudes, that resulted in members having much less time to devote to running the Institute and its activities.

- Increasing use of electronic sources of information, increased availability and ease of use of information resources by non-specialists, and from 1995 onwards, the development of the world wide web and its prospects of freely available information.

These developments led to uncertainties about the long-term future of the Institute, its role, its name and who should form its core membership – their background, qualifications, and what the criteria for Information Science should be. Until then, the IIS had been a group of specialists with fairly clearly defined skills. Once the specialist focus had been lost, it became harder to sustain the IIS network. It was at this point that I succeeded Sarah Carter with a much wider brief: to represent and promote the IIS externally.

By this time, the opportunities for information professionals to attract publicity were enormous. But so was the logic of increased collaboration. The IIS, working with The Library Association and supported by the Association for Geographic Information, launched the Coalition for Public Information. This was a broad-based, cross-sectoral body of organisations with an interest in 'public information' – information generated by government in the course of conducting its business. With some success, CoPI lobbied the government on issues associated with 'the information society' – a term then only beginning to find common currency.

It was not only on grounds of a shared platform for advocacy that the IIS was moving closer to The Library Association. Advances in technology and much more generalised use of electronic resources, together with much more widespread adoption of information management techniques in industry and the public sector, was making it increasingly difficult to distinguish between those who were clearly information scientists, and librarians who used the techniques of information science.

Informal talks on greater collaboration, and a proposal by Dr Ray Lester at the IIS's AGM in 1996 suggesting more of the same, led to more formal talks, and, eventually to unification in April 2002.

In the meantime, and without prejudice to attempts at unification, a joint working party of senior Library Association and IIS members (led by Kate Wood, and Professor Peter Enser) aligned the criteria of both organisations for accrediting academic courses in information science and library management. And IIS celebrated its 40th anniversary with its Ruby Conference in Sheffield in 1998.

In its heyday the IIS's membership reached nearly 2750 members.

In proportion to its size, its profile was high, thanks to the personal commitment and direct involvement of many eminent senior members. In the end, the logic of convergence (in academic criteria and technologies and the practice of both professional bodies) on the one hand, and of the need for advocacy from a shared platform on the other, made unification the only logical option.

Compiled with information from and the generous help of a number of IIS members, including most notably Martin White, Sarah Carter, Diana Clegg and Charles Oppenheim.

Elspeth Hyams
Editor, *Library & Information Update*

The Library Association 1877–2002

'We have only to hope that the Library Association of the United Kingdom will flourish and that it will justify itself in public estimation by assisting libraries to become what they ought to be, efficient instruments of national education.' With these words, *The Athenaeum* welcomed the newly established association in 1877.

Foundation

The Association was founded at an international conference held at the London Institution, attended by over 200 delegates from Australia, Belgium, Denmark, France, Germany, Greece, Italy and the USA, in addition to those from the UK. Melvil Dewey, later to become famous as the author of the Decimal Classification, was there as Secretary of the American Library Association, founded the previous year. Some of the topics discussed at the conference sound familiar 125 years later: Sunday opening, the application of the latest technology (in the shape of the telephone) and salaries of librarians were among them. The organiser of the conference, Edward Nicholson, librarian of the host institution, was moved to describe the salaries then on offer as an 'insult to the liberality and intelligence of our great towns.'

Purpose

The Association was born in the great Victorian tradition of mutual self-improvement, with the intention of promoting the role of libraries and librarians by the exchange of information on good practice, visits to interesting libraries, publishing a journal and manuals, the holding of conferences and, in due course, the running of training courses and holding examinations. Its original object was to 'unite all persons engaged or interested in library work, for the purpose of promoting the best possible administration of existing libraries and the formation of new ones...'

Advocacy

The first President was John Winter Jones, Principal Librarian of the British Museum. Most of those closely involved in the early development of the association were librarians of university and research libraries. However, the fledgling Association devoted a great deal of time and effort in campaigning for the abolition of the restrictions on the amount local councils could spend on their public libraries (they were prevented at that time from spending more than the product of a penny rate on the value of property in their areas) and in persuading councils to establish such libraries under the legislation, which was enabling rather than compulsory. Thus began a long tradition of working to influence public policy, which would be described these days as advocacy and lobbying. Because so much of this has to be conducted behind closed doors and because the final decisions cannot usually be firmly attributed to the Association's efforts, its Members have probably given it less credit for success in this activity than it has deserved. The Association continued its interest in the relationship between local government and public libraries until the present day. After the First World War, the association worked with the Carnegie United Kingdom Trust (CUKT) to persuade the Government finally to lift the restrictions on the amount councils were permitted to spend on public libraries. This resulted in legislation in 1919, which not only did that, but also allowed county councils to provide public libraries for the first time. A large network in rural areas of branch and mobile libraries and collections in village halls and similar locations gradually emerged as a result. At about same time, the Association proposed the establishment of a national library of science and technology, as part of a plan to establish technical and commercial services in public libraries, and pleaded for greater cooperation between public libraries and specialised libraries. After the Second World War, the Association also actively encouraged the development of regional technical and commercial library services by cooperation between different kinds of libraries and Government agencies. It was not until the successful Russian space shot in the sixties prompted greater investment in scientific research that the Government set up the National Lending Library of Science and Technology (NLLST) in Boston Spa, Yorkshire, which eventually became the Document Supply Centre of the British Library.

Public Policy

The Association gave firm evidence to the Dainton Committee in 1968, stressing the need for a UK national library. The Committee's findings led directly to the formation of the British Library, by bringing together the National Central Library, the NLLST, the British Museum Library, the National Reference Library of Science and Invention and the British National Bibliography (BNB). The latter had been established by cooperation between a number of groups representing libraries and the book trade, with an initial financial guarantee by the Association.

Another area of public policy that the Association can be fairly said to have influenced is the allocation of public library responsibilities to local councils. Since the publication in 1942 of its own radical report on the subject, prepared by Lionel McColvin, it fairly consistently supported larger authorities, as more able to provide comprehensive services. This approach inevitably led to great controversy within the profession and the establishment from time to time of breakaway groups representing those working in smaller councils.

The Association also took a great interest in copyright legislation, both within the UK and the European Union, undoubtedly influencing the 1988 Copyright, Designs and Patents Act, especially the inclusion of the concept of fair dealing exceptions for libraries and for the purposes of research and private study. The fight still goes on to ensure that the implementation of the European Directive does not abolish this provision in the UK.

Among the many areas of public policy which have engaged the attention of the Association were postage rates for materials for the visually impaired, public lending right, taxes on publications, the national school curricula, freedom of information legislation, and the provision of libraries in prisons, hospitals and other institutions.

A recent success story, which the Association initiated, is the People's Network, linking every public library to the internet and providing electronic content and training for public library staff. Although it was a report by the former Library and Information Commission (LIC) that persuaded the government to adopt the idea, it was the Association's earlier bid for National Lottery funding which established the desirability of such a project. The Library Association campaigned, with several other organisations, for a government advisory body on library and information matters, which finally came into existence as the LIC. The Commission recently merged with a similar body for museums to become Resource: the Council for Museums, Archives and Libraries.

The Association developed its contacts with politicians and civil servants over the years and was instrumental in the establishment of the All-Party Parliamentary Group on Libraries, which ensures that a wide range of library and information issues are drawn to the attention of MPs and peers.

The Library Association 1877–2002

Education and Training

The education and training of library staff was a constant concern of the Association. Its first move, in 1885, was to hold examinations leading to certificates in English and European literature, classification and cataloguing and library administration. Few sat these tests and fewer passed. But summer schools began in 1894. The first lasted three days attracting 45 students. The summer schools increased in length and attendance, the examinations broadened in scope, eventually leading to formal qualifications and Fellowship of the Association. Correspondence courses were set up, to be handed over later to the once independent Association of Assistant Librarians (AAL), after it came within The Library Association's fold as a specialist section. The first full-time library school was established in 1919, at University College London, with the help of the CUKT. In the interwar period many part-time day and evening classes developed to prepare candidates for the Association's examinations held at several centres around the country. After World War Two, education and training of returning servicemen became a priority for the Government. A number of full-time library schools were set up in colleges of technology under this programme, as the result of negotiations by The Library Association. They were intended to be temporary arrangements, but demand was such that the schools developed along with their institutions, which later became polytechnics and eventually universities. New schools were also set up in the 1960s in a few universities and one, the College of Librarianship Wales, Aberystwyth, was established as a separate institution, only becoming a part of the University of Wales much later. These schools gradually developed systems of internal examining, followed by their own syllabuses, recognised by the Association and, in the case of those in polytechnics, validated by the former Council for National and Academic Awards (CNAA). These developments, not without controversy, eventually led to an all-graduate entry to the profession, and a great variety of courses at undergraduate, post-graduate and master's levels. The Association gave up its own examinations in the 1970s, in favour of accrediting courses, latterly often as a joint exercise with the Institute of information Scientists (IIS).

The Royal Charter

The Association acquired a Royal Charter in 1898, with revised objects. At the same time, its name became simply The Library

Association, which it retained, despite some attempts in the 1980s to change it to include 'information', until unification with the IIS under the title Chartered Institute of Library and Information Professionals (CILIP). The professional register was introduced after the Second World War. Those who completed the newly introduced registration examination, followed by a period of approved employment in a library, could describe themselves as 'Chartered Librarians'. They were also entitled to use the post nominal letters 'ALA' (Associate of the Library Association). After a further period of employment, they could progress, by means of a final examination, to become Fellows (FLA). When the undergraduate and postgraduate courses replaced the registration examination, Fellowship could be obtained by means of a thesis, later replaced by a variety of routes, leading to proof of attainment of a high standard of professional achievement. Discussions took place over a long period on the possibilities for introducing a system of validating continuing professional development. A voluntary scheme was introduced in the 1990s. The possibility of developing in due course a compulsory 're-licensing' requirement, similar to those coming into vogue in other professions was discussed, but never agreed. The possession of the Royal Charter gave the Association status comparable to professional bodies in other spheres, and was the source of much pride. The centenary of the granting of the Charter by Queen Victoria was celebrated in style at the new British Library building at St Pancras in 1998, in the presence of the Princess Royal and the Secretary of State for Culture, Chris Smith. The Princess presented centenary medals to one hundred Library Association Members representing the thousands who had worked for the profession over the century.

Awards

One way to encourage high standards in any field is to present awards. The Library Association's first initiative in this area was the Carnegie Medal for the best children's book. Awarded for the first time in 1937 to Arthur Ransome for *Pigeon Post* and occasionally not awarded at all for a lack, in the opinion of the judges, of a suitable winner, it has become established as a coveted honour. It was joined in 1955 by the Kate Greenaway Medal for the best illustrated children's book. The Youth Libraries Group judges the nominations for both medals, which have attracted significant sponsorship in recent years and increasing publicity in the national press, aided by a 'shadow' judging process organised in schools. Other awards introduced over the years recognise excellence in published indexes (jointly with the Society of Indexers), bibliographies and reference works, as well as best practice in publicity and public relations.

Publications

The publication of a journal is a basic function of most professional bodies. The Library Association's first initiative in this area was to decide at its inaugural meeting to adopt the *American Library Journal* as its official organ (without the first word in its title). This had obvious drawbacks, exacerbated when Melvil Dewey became its editor and introduced his simplified spelling. In 1880, *Monthly Notes of the Library Association of the United Kingdom*, published commercially on behalf of the Association, took over the role. It was itself succeeded by *The Library Chronicle* in 1884 and *The Library* in 1888. The latter was the personal property of John MacAlister, at that time Honorary Secretary of the Association, an unsatisfactory arrangement. Ten years later *The Library Association Record* was established as the official organ of the Association, the property of the Association and 'under the control of Council'. It continued until 2002, celebrating its centenary in 1998. For most of that time it was edited by a series of Honorary Editors, until the appointment in 1976 of the first full-time professional Editor, Roger Walter. One of the first publications of the Association in book form was the *Yearbook*, first published in 1891, which, despite its title, did not become a regular annual, until 1932. For many years the financing of publications caused concern to the Association's Council. Various arrangements were made for the sale and distribution of a growing range of titles, including manuals, textbooks and guidelines to standards of service. At first contracts were made with commercial publishers, at other times the responsibilities were carried out in-house and, for a while in the 1970s and 80s, a wholly-owned company was responsible. Eventually all the business units of the Association (Library Association Publishing; INFOmatch, the recruitment agency; the *Record* and conferences and continuing education) were brought together under the title Library Association Enterprises. At the time of unification, approximately 30 new titles were published a year, with a backlist of over 200.

Branches

In common with many membership organisations in the UK, the

Association exhibited tensions between those based in London and those elsewhere in the country. This tension was emphasised by the fact that, in the public library sphere at least, development was much slower in London in the early days than in other major cities. It was also not helped by the fact that most of the early meetings were held in London. Long working hours and poor salaries combined to prevent many from outside the capital taking part in the affairs of the Association. This led to the establishment of several independent regional Associations, for example the Birmingham and District and the North Midlands Library Associations. They amalgamated with The Library Association in 1928-9. The Scottish Library Association, formed in 1908, also affiliated under special conditions in 1931 and new Branches were formed to cover Wales and Monmouthshire and Northern Ireland. However, complete coverage of the UK by a network of Branches was not achieved until after the Second World War.

Sections and Groups

A characteristic of most professional bodies is the need to cater for specialisms within the overall discipline. It was gradually recognised that The Library Association had to cater for different types of library, or client groups, and specialist materials and skills. In 1932, two sections were established to reflect the interests of those working in county libraries and those in university and research libraries. The union with the independent AAL, which had taken place in 1930, provided a section designed to provide for those at an early stage in their careers. It was to prove a useful training ground for future leaders of the profession. Sections, later renamed 'Groups', were gradually added to reflect such diverse interests as prison libraries, information technology and library history.

Headquarters

As early as 1888, the Association identified the need for permanent premises. Its first home was in Hanover Square in London, which it rented from 1890 to 1898. This was followed by a series of other rented premises, one shared with the trade union NALGO, another with Association of Special Libraries and Information Bureaux (Aslib) and the CUKT. Eventually the CUKT provided a more permanent solution with the offer of a derelict property in what was to become Malet Place. Opened in 1933 by Lord Irwin, deputising for the then Prime Minister, Stanley Baldwin, it was named Chaucer House. The refurbished building provided offices, a members' room and a council chamber, with spare floors which were rented to other organisations. One of the initial tenants was the Museums Association. Chaucer House served until 1965, when the present purpose-built headquarters in Ridgmount Street was completed. The Association was fortunate in that the University of London offered to build the Ridgmount Street building in exchange for the acquisition of Chaucer House, which it required to cater for the needs of the rapidly expanding institution. The new building was considerably larger and contained many highly desirable new facilities. From time to time there were discussions on the desirability of moving the headquarters to a location outside London. During the 1980s the most concrete proposal, to move to the University of Liverpool campus, was considered and rejected. The transport routes of the UK, which radiate from London, rendered such proposals unviable. The Ridgmount Street building was recently refurbished and extended.

International developments

Given that the Association was born at an international conference, it is not surprising that it has often been involved in international developments. At its fiftieth anniversary Conference, held in Edinburgh in 1927, a resolution, which led to the establishment of the International Federation of Library Associations and Institutions (IFLA), was adopted. K. C. Harrison was inaugurated as the first President of the Commonwealth Library Association (COMLA) at its formation in Lagos, Nigeria, in 1972. He became Library Association President in the same year. During the 1987 IFLA Conference in Brighton talks were started in London, which led to the formation of the European Bureau of Library, Information and Documentation Associations (EBLIDA) in The Hague in 1992. George Cunningham, Chief Executive of The Library Association from 1984 to 1992, played a leading role in identifying the need for such a body to ensure that the profession's views were heard the European Union's institutions. Ross Shimmon, Library Association Chief Executive from 1992 to 1999, was its founder President.

Unification

The Association was, at times with some justification, more recently with none, criticised for being primarily a public library association. Received wisdom suggests that it was this bias that led to the establishment of the Aslib to cater for those working in specialist libraries in industry. W. A. Munford, the Association's official historian for its first century, argued that the Library Association Council 'could hardly have done more to make [such a move] unnecessary.' Nevertheless, Aslib was established in 1926. After the Second World War, alleged lack of flexibility on the part of the Association is said to have led to the establishment of the Institute of Information Scientists in 1958. The existence of several bodies representing different elements of the profession was thought by many to be unhelpful in the task of influencing government and other decision makers. Various moves were made to try to bring the organisations together, including the organisation of joint conferences. The Library Association Council, on behalf of all three organisations, commissioned Professor Wilfred Saunders, a former president of both the Association and the Institute, to write a pamphlet exploring the pros and cons of unification. In the pamphlet, published in 1989, he recommended the establishment of a new organisation, representing the broad spectrum of library and information professionals. The Association's Council approved the proposal in principle. But Aslib pulled out of the subsequent talks and the IIS soon followed suit. However, his efforts proved not to have been entirely in vain. Informal talks between representatives of the Association and the Institute began in 1998, which eventually led to the unification of the two bodies to form CILIP in 2002. This satisfactorily closed an era in professional history which had lasted exactly 125 years.

The main sources used in the preparation of this article were:

Munford, W. A. (1977) *A History of The Library Association 1877-1977*, London, The Library Association.
Plumb, Philip (1977) *Libraries by Association: The Library Association's first century*, London, The Library Association.

Ross Shimmon
Secretary General,
International Federation of Library Associations and Institutions

Presidents of the Institute of Information Scientists

2001–02	P. Enser	
2000–01	P. Enser	Director, M. Shearer (started)
1999–2000	B. Clifford	
1998–99	P. Brophy	
1997–98	S. E. Ward	
1996–97	B. Hatvany	
1995–96	M. F. Lynch	
1994–95	C. Oppenheim	Director, E. Hyams (started)
1993–94	B. A. Lang	
1992–93	M. White	
1991–92	M. Saksida	
1990–91	B. White	
1989–90	P. Laister	
1988–89	K. Cooper	
1987–88	T. Aitchison	
1986–87	Prof. L. Wolpert	
1985–86	Sir R. Clayton	
1984–85	M. Aldrich	Director, S. A. Carter (started)
1983–84	A. R. Haygarth Jackson	
1982–83	J. Dukes	
1981–82	R. K. Appleyard	
1980–81	C. W. Cleverdon	
1979–80	M. Hyams	
1978–79	J. W. Barrett	
1977–78	Dr J. W. Barrett	
1975–76	H. T. Hookway	
1974–75	H. T. Hookway	
1973–74	H. T. Hookway	
1972–73	Sir James Tait	
1968–69	Prof. Sir H. Thompson	
1960–61	Dr M. Dyson	
1958–59	Dr M. Dyson	

Presidents of The Library Association

2001	Mr B. Naylor
2000	Rev. G. P. Cornish
1999	Mrs V. Taylor
1998	Prof. R. C. Usherwood
1997	Mr J. D. Hendry
1996	Ms S. M. Parker
1995	Mr M. P. K. Barnes OBE
1994	Dr G. A. Burrington OBE
1993	Mr R. G. Astbury
1992	Mr P. W. Plumb
1991	Mr T. M. Featherstone
1990	Prof. M. B. Line
1989	Mr A. G. D. White
1988	Miss Jean M. Plaister OBE
1987	Mr E. M. Broome OBE
1986	Mr A. Wilson CBE
1985	Sir Harry Hookway Kt
1984	Mr R. G. Surridge
1983	Dr N. Higham OBE
1982	Mr K. A. Stockham
1981	Mr A. Longworth OBE
1980	Prof. W. L. Saunders CBE
1979	Mr W. A. G. Alison
1978	Mr G. Thompson
1977	The Lord Dainton
1976	Mr D. J. Foskett OBE
1975	Mr E. V. Corbett
1974	Mr E. A. Clough
1973	Mr K. C. Harrison OBE
1972	Dr Donald J. Urquhart
1971	Mr G. Chandler
1970	Mr D. T. Richnell CBE
1969	Prof. W. Ashworth
1968	Mr T. E. Callander
1967	Mr F. G. B. Hutchings OBE
1966	Miss Lorna V. Paulin OBE
1965	Sir Frank Francis KCB

Presidents of The Library Association

1964	Mr F. M. Gardner CBE
1963	Mr J. N. L. Myres OBE
1962	Prof. W. B. Paton OBE
1961	Sir Charles Snow CBE
1960	Dr B. S. Page
1959	The Rt Hon. The Earl Attlee KG PC OM CH
1958	Prof. Raymond Irwin
1957	Dr J. Bronowski
1956	Mr E. Sydney MC
1955	Sir Philip Morris KCMG Kt CBE
1954	Mr C. B. Oldman CB CVO
1953	Sir Sidney C. Roberts Kt
1952	Mr L. R. McColvin CBE
1951	Mr J. Wilkie MC
1950	His Royal Highness The Prince Philip, Duke of Edinburgh Kg Kt Com GBE PC
1949	Sir Ronald Forbes Adam Bt KCE GCB CB DSO OBE
1948	Mr C. Nowell
1947	Mr R. J. Gordon
1946	Mr H. M. Cashmore MBE
1939-45	Mr A. Esdaile CBE
1938	Mr W. C. Berwick Sayers
1937	The Most Rev. & Hon. Wm. Temple
1936	Mr E. A. Savage
1935	Mr E. S. Davies CBE
1934	Mr S. A. Pitt
1932-3	Sir Henry A. Miers Kt DSC
1931	Lt Col J. M. Mitchell OBE MC
1930	Mr L. Stanley Jast
1929	The Lord Balniel MP
1928	Mr A. D. Lindsay CBE
1927	The Rt Hon. The Earl of Elgin and Kincardine Kt CMG
1926	Mr H. Guppy CBE
1925	Sir Charles Grant Robertson Kt CVO
1924	Sir Robert Sangster Rait Kt CBE
1923	The Most Honourable The Marquis of Hartington MP MBE
1922	Sir John Ballinger KBE
1921	Alderman T. C. Abbott JP
1920	The Rt Hon. Sir John H. Lewis PC GBE
1919	Mr G. F. Barwick

Presidents of The Library Association

1915-18	Sir J. Y. W. MacAlister
1914	Mr F. Madan
1913	The Rt Hon. The Earl of Malmesbury
1912	Mr F. J. Leslie CC
1911	Sir John A. Dewar Bt MP
1910	Sir Frederic G. Kenyon
1909	Alderman W. H. Brittain JP Chairman, Sheffield Public Libraries Committee
1908	Sir C. Thomas-Standford
1907	Mr F. T. Barrett
1906	Sir William H. Bailey
1905	Mr F. J. Jenkinson
1904	Dr T. Hodgkin
1902-3	Prof. W. Macneile Dixon
1901	Mr G. K. Fortescue
1900	The Rt Hon. Sir Edward Fry PC
1899	Sir James W. Southern JP
1898	The Rt Hon. The Earl of Crawford Kt
1897	Mr H. R. Tedder
1896	Alderman H. Rawson
1895	The Lord Windsor
1894	The Most Honourable the Marquess of Dufferin and Ava KP GCB
1893	Mr R. Garnett
1892	Mr A. Beljame
1891	Mr R. Harrison
1890	Sir E. Maunde Thompson
1889	Mr R. Copley Christie
1888	Prof. W. P. Dickson
1887	Mr G. J. Johnson
1886	Sir Edward A. Bond KCB
1885	Mr E. James
1884	Prof. J. K. Ingram
1883	Sir James Picton
1882	Mr Henry Bradshaw
1881	His Honour Judge Russell
1879-80	Mr H. O. Coxe
1877-78	Mr J. Winter Jones

Honorary Secretaries of the Institute of Information Scientists

2001–02	K. G. Webster
2000–01	K. G. Webster
1999–2000	K. G. Webster
1998–99	K. G. Webster
1997–98	K. G. Webster
1996–97	K. G. Webster
1995–96	K. G. Webster
1994–95	K. G. Webster
1993–94	A. J. Wood
1992–93	P. Griffiths
1991–92	D. Clegg
1990–91	D. Clegg
1989–90	D. Clegg
1988–89	D. Edmonds
1987–88	D. Edmonds
1986–87	D. Edmonds
1985–86	P. Brown
1984–85	P. Brown
1983–84	P. J. Brown
1982–83	J. M. Pope
1981–82	J. M. Pope
1980–81	J. M. Pope
1979–80	Mrs S. A. Carter
1978–79	Mrs S. A. Carter
1977–78	M G. Howes,
1975–76	Mrs M. Siddiqui,
1974–75	Mrs M. Siddiqui
1973–74	Mrs M. Siddiqui
1972–73	S. P. Cooper
1970–71	R. W. Prior
1968–69	J. Farradane
1960–61	J. Farradane
1958–59	J. Farradane

Secretaries of The Library Association

1999–2002	Dr R. McKee
1992–99	Mr R. Shimmon
1984–92	Mr G. Cunningham
1978–84	Mr K. Lawrey
1974–78	Mr R. P. Hilliard
1959–74	Mr H. D. Barry
1931–59	Mr P. S. J. Welsford
1928–31	Mr G. Keeling

Honorary Secretaries of The Library Association

1961	Honorary Secretary appointments discontinued
1955–61	Mr W. B. Paton
1952–55	Dr W. A. Munford
1934–51	Mr L. R. McColvin
1933–34	Mr E. A. Savage and Mr L. R. McColvin
1928–33	Mr E. Savage
1919–28	Mr F. Pacy
1918–19	Mr F. Pacy and Mr G. F. Barwick
1915–18	Mr F. Pacy (Acting Secretary)
1905–15	Mr L. S. Jast
1902–05	Mr L. Inkster (Mr L. S. Jast, Acting Secretary 1904–1905)
1902	Mr B. Soulsby
1898–1901	Mr F. Pacy
1892–98	Sir J. Y. W. MacAlister
1887–90	Sir J. Y. W. MacAlister and Mr T. Mason
1882–87	Mr E. C. Thomas and Mr J. Y. W. MacAlister
1880–82	Mr E. C. Thomas and Mr C. Welch
1878–80	Mr H. R. Tedder and Mr E. C. Thomas
1877–78	Mr E. B. Nicholson and Mr H. R. Tedder

Library Association honorary awards

Dates given below apply to the year award was made.

Honorary Vice-Presidents

1995	Prof. J. Meadows
1993	Dame E. Esteve-Coll
1991	Dr H.-P. Geh
1990	Baroness David of Romsey
	Mr D. Whitaker
1988	Alexander Macmillan, The Earl of Stockton
1987	Miss M. Wijnstroom
1973	Mr H. Liebaers
	Mrs J. L. Robinson
1969	Mr Bengt Hjelmqvist
1967	Miss M. O'Byrne

Honorary Fellows

2001	Dr M. Clanchy
2000	Miss M. E. Going
	Mr E. Moon
	Miss C. F. Pinion
	Mr R. Shimmon
1999	Mr R. Collis
	Mr C. Earl
	Mr M. Evans
	Mr G. Pau
1998	Mr C. Batt
	Mr B. C. Bloomfield
	Mr P. R. Craddock
	Ms M. Hoffman
	Dr N. Horrocks
1997	Sir Brian Follett
	Ms S. Hughes
	Dr B. Lang
	Ms E. Simon

Year	Recipients
1996	Ms L. A. Colaianni
	Cllr F. Emery-Wallis
	Mr D. Jones
	Miss J. Shepherd
1995	Mr E. M. Broome
	Mr P. A. Hoare
	Ms M. Segbert
	Mr E. C. Winter
1994	Mr P. Blunt
	Prof. R. Bowden
	Mr M. Bragg
	Miss A. M. Parker
	Mr B. Roberts
1993	Dame C. A. Cookson
	Dr I. Lovecy
	Ms F. Salinie
	Mr C. A. Toase
	Mr W. G. Williams
1992	Mr P. Bryant
	Mr G. Cunningham
	Mr J. Gattegno
	Mr W. D. Linton
	Dr R. C. Usherwood
1991	Mr T. Dickinson
	Mr P. H. Mann
	Ms D. B. Rosenberg
	Mr B. J. S. Williams
1990	Prof. G. W. A. Dick
	Prof. A. J. Evans
	Mrs S. G. Ray
	Mr J. W. Sumsion
	Mr A. L. van Wesemael
1989	Mr W. R. H. Carson
	Mr E. Dudley
	Mr P. R. Lewis
	Dr G. Pflug
1988	Mr D. Harrison
	Mrs B. Ruff
	Mr R. G. Surridge
	Mr I. R. Willison

Library Association honorary awards

1987	Mr D. Mason
	Prof. M. B. Line
	Dr F. W. Ratcliffe
1986	Prof. R. C. Alston
	Mr C. H. Bingley
	The Lord Dainton
	Prof. P. Havard-Williams
1985	Mrs H. Anuar
	Mrs E. Granheim
	Dr H. Wallis
1984	Mrs D. Anderson
	Mr D. K. Devnally
	Mr M. C. Fessey
	Mr T. Kaung
	Mr A. Wilson
1983	Mr L. J. Anthony
	Mr L. A. Gilbert
1982	Mr H. Faulkner Brown
	Sir Harry Hookway
	Mr P. E. Morris
	Mr C. L. J. O'Connell
1981	Mr R. Brown
	Mr J. C. Downing
	Mr A. C. Jones
1980	Prof R. C. Benge
	Miss L. V. Paulin
	Mr K. W. Humphreys
	Mr P. A. Larkin
1979	Mr R. Buchanan
	Mr E. Coates
	Mr R. P Hilliard
	Mr D. T Richnell
1978	Mrs D. M. Palmer
	Mr H. Holdsworth
1977	Mr P. Kirkegaard
	Sir Robin Mackworth Young
	Dr W. A. Munford
	Mr P. H. Sewell
1976	Prof J. D. Pearson
1975	Mr E. A. Clough
	Mr S. W. Hockey

Library Association honorary awards

1974	Mr D. J. Foskett
	Mr F. W. Jessup
	Mr T. Kelly
	Mr B. I. Palmer
1973	Mr H. D. Barry
	Mr A. D. Jones
	Mr W. B. Paton
1972	Mr H. Coblans
	Dr A. J. Walford
	Mr A. J. Wells
1971	Miss E. H. Colwell
	Mr W. S. Haugh
	Mr S. H. Horrocks
1970	Mr A. H. Chaplin
	Miss A. S. Cooke
	Mr W. R. LeFanu
	Mr R. D. Macleod
	Mr W. Tynemouth
1969	Mr T. Besterman
	F. N. Withers
1968	Mr S. W. Martin
	Mr E. F. Patterson
	Mr N. F. Sharp
1966	Mr E. Austin Hinton
	Miss F. E. Cook
	Mr F. M. Gardner
1965	Miss E. J. A. Evans
	Mr W. J. Harris
1964	Sir Sydney Roberts
	Mr E. Sydney
1963	Mr R. Irwin
	Mr C. B. Oldman
1962	Mr E. J. Carter
	Sir Frank Francis
1961	Mr L. R. McColvin
	Mr B. S. Page
1959	Mr J. D. Stewart
	Mr P. S. J. Welsford
1948	Mr R. J. Gordon
1947	Mr W. C. Berwick Sayers
	Mr H. M. Cashmore

Library Association honorary awards

1946	Mr Arundell Esdaile
	Mr Albert Mansbridge
1938	Mr Wilson Benson Thorne
1935	Mr H. Tapley-Soper
1933	Rt Hon. Stanley Baldwin
	Mr Ernest A. Savage
1932	Rt Hon. Earl of Elgin and Kincardine
	Mr J. M. Mitchell
1931	Mr W. W. Bishop
	Mr George H. Locke
1929	Sir John Ballinger
1924	Mr A. W. Pollard
	Mr W. E. Doubleday
1915	Mr L. S. Jast
1914	Mr J. Potter Briscoe
	Mr R. K. Dent
1913	Mr James Duff Brown
1909	Mr T. C. Abbott
	Mr H. W. Fovargue
1908	Mr J. J. Ogle
1907	Rt Hon. Earl of Plymouth
1906	Mr Henry D. Roberts
1905	Mr Lawrence Inkster
1903	Mr Henry Guppy
1902	Mr W. Macneile Dixon
	Mr Frank Pacy
1901	Mr Thomas Greenwood
1899	Rt Hon. Lord Avebury
	Marquess of Dufferin and Ava
	Mr Samuel Timmins
	Rt Hon. Lord Windsor
1898	Mr J. Y. W. MacAlister
1896	Mr James Bain
	Conte Ugo Balzani
	Prof. Alexander Beljame
	Mr J. S. Billings
	Mr R. R. Bowker
	Mr C. W. Bruun
	Mr Andrew Carnegie
	Mr C. A. Cutter
	Mr Leopold Delisle

Mr Melvil Dewey
Sir George Grey
Mr Justin Winsor
Mr C. Dziatzko
Mr J. Passmore Edwards
Mr S. S. Green
Mr P. G. Horsen
Rt Hon. Sir John Lubbock
Sir Henry Tate
Baron O. de Watteville

Certificates of Merit

2001	Mr R. S. Eagle
	Ms A. Edmunds
	Dr J. Harvey
2000	Mrs V. Nurcombe
1999	Mr M. Stacey
1998	none
1997	Mr I. M. Jamieson
	Mrs J. Machell
1996	Dr H. Fuchs
	Ms F. M. M. Redfern
1995	Miss V. A. Fea
	Mr R. Sweeney
1994	Mr F. Chambers
	Mrs L. Elliott
	Mrs S. Harrity
	Mr J. Pyle
	Mr J. Merriman
1993	Mr A. Chadwick
	Mr D. F. Keeling
1992	Mr P. Thomas
1991	Mr R. Phillips
1990	Mr T. C. Farries
1989	Mr E. Frow
	Mrs R. Frow
1985	Dr F. A. Thorpe

Institute of Information Scientists Award winners

Jason Farradane Award winners

- 2001   Professor Bruce Royan for SCRAN
- 2000   Jill Foster for her pioneering work in establishing the Mailbase discussion and distribution list
- 1999   Michael Keen for his Lifetime's Work in Information Retrieval
- 1998   Norman Wood and the EIRO Team of the European Foundation for the Improvement of Living and Working Conditions Dublin, for their outstanding and original work on the European Industrial Relations Observatory (EIRO)
- 1997   Newcastle University Library for the Development and Administration of the Newcastle Electronic Reference Desk - NERD
- 1996   The Higher Education Funding Council's Electronic Libraries Programme for innovation in the exploitation of IT in Higher Education Libraries
- 1995   Dennis Nicholson and the BUBL team for the development of the Bulletin Board for libraries
- 1994   Rita Marcella and colleagues at the School of Librarianship and Information Studies at Robert Gordon University for the development of their innovative Postgraduate Course in Information Analysis
- 1993   Peter Ingwersen in recognition of his services to Information Science
- 1992   European Foundation for the Improvement of Living and Working conditions, Dublin, for developing the series of European and Industrial Relations Glossaries
- 1991   Arnold Myers, Information Scientist, for contribution to information services with the international oil and gas industry
- 1990   Scottish Science Library, setting up of an important new library for Scotland
- 1989   Patricia Baird, Blaise Cronin, Noreen MacMarrow, academics, University of Strathclyde, work in the field of hypertext on producing an electronic conspectus on the life and times of the City of Glasgow

1988 No award – no nomination received before closing date
1987 Sandra Ward, Information Scientist, work in raising the profile of industrial information services
1986 Phil Williams, academic and businessman, contributions to making online searching more readily accessible to users
1985 Phil Holmes, achievements in applying technological advances to library development especially in the development of BLAISE (British Library), and PEARL (Blackwell Technical Services)
1984 Jacqueline Welch, librarian at Wessex Medical Library, contributed to promotion of information science particularly within the field of medical information
1983 Karen Sparck-Jones, academic, information science research, eg automation classification and indexing, methods of testing and evaluation, weighting and relevance feedback
1982 Monty Hyams, businessman, Derwent Publictaion Ltd. Developed Central Patents Index for patent searching
1981 William Wisswesser (USA), work with chemical notation, giving his name to Wisswesser line notation (WLN)
1980 Michael Lynch, academic, Sheffield University, expert in chemical structure handling
1979 Jason Farradane, founder of the IIS and a cornerstone of information science teaching and research

Tony Kent Strix Award winners

2002 Malcolm Jones
2001 Professor Peter Willett.
2000 Dr Martin Porter
1999 Dr Donna Harman
1998 Professor Stephen Robertson

Library Association Medal and Award winners

Carnegie Medal winners

Please note that the year refers to when the book was published rather than when the medal was awarded i.e. the 2001 winner was announced and the medal presented in July 2002.

2000	Beverley Naidoo, *The Other Side of Truth*, Puffin
1999	Aidan Chambers, *Postcards From No Man's Land*, Bodley Head
1998	David Almond, *Skellig*, Hodder Children's Books
1997	Tim Bowler, *River Boy*, OUP
1996	Melvin Burgess, *Junk*, Andersen Press
1995	Philip Pullman, His Dark Materials: Book 1 *Northern Lights*, Scholastic
1994	Theresa Breslin, *Whispers in the Graveyard*, Methuen
1993	Robert Swindells, *Stone Cold*, H Hamilton
1992	Anne Fine, *Flour Babies*, H Hamilton
1991	Berlie Doherty, *Dear Nobody*, H Hamilton
1990	Gillian Cross, *Wolf*, OUP
1989	Anne Fine, *Goggle-eyes*, H Hamilton
1988	Geraldine McCaughrean, *A Pack of Lies*, OUP
1987	Susan Price, *The Ghost Drum*, Faber
1986	Berlie Doherty, *Granny was a Buffer Girl*, Methuen
1985	Kevin Crossley-Holland, *Storm*, Heinemann
1984	Margaret Mahy, *The Changeover*, Dent
1983	Jan Mark, *Handles*, Kestrel
1982	Margaret Mahy, *The Haunting*, Dent
1981	Robert Westall, *The Scarecrows*, Chatto & Windus
1980	Peter Dickinson, *City of Gold*, Gollancz
1979	Peter Dickinson, *Tulku*, Gollancz
1978	David Rees, *The Exeter Blitz*, H Hamilton
1977	Gene Kemp, *The Turbulent Term of Tyke Tiler*, Faber
1976	Jan Mark, *Thunder and Lightnings*, Kestrel
1975	Robert Westall, *The Machine Gunners*, Macmillan
1974	Mollie Hunter, *The Stronghold*, H Hamilton
1973	Penelope Lively, *The Ghost of Thomas Kempe*, Heinemann
1972	Richard Adams, *Watership Down*, Rex Collings

LA Medal and Award winners

1971 Ivan Southall, *Josh*, Angus & Robertson
1970 Leon Garfield & Edward Blishen, *The God Beneath the Sea*, Longman
1969 Kathleen Peyton, *The Edge of the Cloud*, OUP
1968 Rosemary Harris, *The Moon in the Cloud*, Faber
1967 Alan Garner, *The Owl Service*, Collins
1966 Prize withheld as no book considered suitable
1965 Philip Turner, *The Grange at High Force*, OUP
1964 Sheena Porter, *Nordy Bank*, OUP
1963 Hester Burton, *Time of Trial*, OUP
1962 Pauline Clarke, *The Twelve and the Genii*, Faber
1961 Lucy M. Boston, *A Stranger at Green Knowe*, Faber
1960 Dr I. W. Cornwall, *The Making of Man*, Phoenix House
1959 Rosemary Sutcliff, *The Lantern Bearers*, OUP
1958 Philipa Pearce, *Tom's Midnight Garden*, OUP
1957 William Mayne, *A Grass Rope*, OUP
1956 C. S. Lewis, *The Last Battle*, Bodley Head
1955 Eleanor Farjeon, *The Little Bookroom*, OUP
1954 Ronald Welch (Felton Ronald Oliver), *Knight Crusader*, OUP
1953 Edward Osmond, *A Valley Grows Up*
1952 Mary Norton, *The Borrowers*, Dent
1951 Cynthia Harnett, *The Woolpack*, Methuen
1950 Elfrida Vipont Foulds, *The Lark on the Wing*, OUP
1949 Agnes Allen, *The Story of Your Home*, Faber
1948 Richard Armstrong, *Sea Change*, Dent
1947 Walter De La Mare, *Collected Stories for Children*
1946 Elizabeth Goudge, *The Little White Horse*, University of London Press
1945 Prize withheld as no book considered suitable
1944 Eric Linklater, *The Wind on the Moon*, Macmillan
1943 Prize withheld as no book considered suitable
1942 'BB' (D. J. Watkins-Pitchford), *The Little Grey Men*, Eyre & Spottiswoode
1941 Mary Treadgold, *We Couldn't Leave Dinah*, Cape
1940 Kitty Barne, *Visitors from London*, Dent
1939 Eleanor Doorly, *Radium Woman*, Heinemann
1938 Noel Streatfield, *The Circus is Coming*, Dent
1937 Eve Garnett, *The Family from One End Street*, Muller
1936 Arthur Ransome, *Pigeon Post*, Cape

LA Medal and Award winners

Kate Greenaway Medal winners

Please note that the year refers to when the book was published rather than when the medal was awarded i.e. the 2000 winner was announced and the medal presented in July 2001.

2000	Lauren Child, *I Will Not Ever Never Eat a Tomato*, Orchard Books
1999	Helen Oxenbury, *Alice's Adventures in Wonderland*, Walker Books
1998	Helen Cooper, *Pumpkin Soup*, Doubleday
1997	P. J. Lynch, *When Jessie Came Across the Sea*, Walker Books
1996	Helen Cooper, *The Baby Who Wouldn't Go To Bed*, Doubleday
1995	P. J. Lynch, *The Christmas Miracle of Jonathan Toomey*, Walker Books
1994	Gregory Rogers, *Way Home*, Andersen Press
1993	Alan Lee, *Black Ships Before Troy*, Frances Lincoln
1992	Anthony Browne, *Zoo*, Julia MacRae
1991	Janet Ahlberg, *The Jolly Christmas Postman*, Heinemann
1990	Gary Blythe, *The Whales' Song*, Hutchinson
1989	Michael Foreman, *War Boy: a Country Childhood*, Pavilion
1988	Barbara Firth, *Can't You Sleep Little Bear?*, Walker Books
1987	Adrienne Kennaway, *Crafty Chameleon*, Hodder & Stoughton
1986	Fiona French, *Snow White in New York*, OUP
1985	Juan Wijngaard, *Sir Gawain and the Loathly Lady*, Walker Books
1984	Errol Le Cain, *Hiawatha's Childhood*, Faber
1983	Anthony Browne, *Gorilla*, Julia MacRae
1982	Michael Foreman, *Long Neck and Thunder Foot* and *Sleeping Beauty and Other Favourite Fairy Tales*, Kestrel and Gollancz
1981	Charles Keeping, *The Highwayman*, OUP
1980	Quentin Blake, *Mr Magnolia*, Cape
1979	Jan Pienkowski, *The Haunted House*, Heinemann
1978	Janet Ahlberg, *Each Peach Pear Plum*, Kestrel
1977	Shirley Hughes, *Dogger*, Bodley Head
1976	Gail E. Haley, *The Post Office Cat*, Bodley Head
1975	Victor Ambrus, *Horses in Battle and Mishka*, OUP
1974	Pat Hutchins, *The Wind Blew*, Bodley head
1973	Raymond Briggs, *Father Christmas*, H Hamilton
1972	Krystyna Turska, *The Woodcutter's Duck*, H Hamilton
1971	Jan Pienkowski, *The Kingdom under the Sea*, Cape
1970	John Burningham, *Mr Gumpy's Outing*, Cape

LA Medal and Award winners

1969 Helen Oxenbury, *The Quangle Wangle's hat* and *The Dragon of an Ordinary Family*, Heinemann
1968 Pauline Baynes, *Dictionary of Chivalry*, Longman
1967 Charles Keeping, *Charlotte and the Golden Canary*, OUP
1966 Raymond Briggs, *Mother Goose Treasury*, H Hamilton
1965 Victor Ambrus, *The Three Poor Tailors*, OUP
1964 C. W. Hodges, *Shakespeare's Theatre*, OUP
1963 John Burningham, *Borka: the Adventures of a Goose with No Feathers*, Cape
1962 Brian Wildsmith, *A.B.C.*, OUP
1961 Antony Maitland, *Mrs. Cockle's Cat*, Constable
1960 Gerald Rose, *Old Winkle and the Seagulls*, Faber
1959 William Stobbs, *Kashtanka* and *A Bundle of Ballads*, OUP
1958 Prize withheld as no book considered suitable
1957 V. H. Drummond, *Mrs Easter and the Storks*, Faber
1956 Edward Ardizzone, *Tim All Alone*, OUP
1955 Prize withheld as no book considered suitable

Libraries Change Lives Award winners

2001 Merton Libraries Refugee Resources Collection and Service
2000 Kensal Library's Community Action Initiative
1999 The Ad Lib Project, Sheffield
1998 Pontefract's Readers Group
1997 Horley's Local History Centre
1996 Liverpool 8 Law Centre
1995 Sunderland Libraries Bookstart Project
1994 Petersburn Community Library and Teenage Drop in Centre
1993 Wandsworth Prison and Springfield Psychiatric Hospital
1992 Annex Community Centre, Hartlepool

Public Relations and Publicity Awards: Personal PR Achievement winners

2001 June Turner, Essex Libraries
2000 Jim Jackson, Library Association Affilaited Members National Committee
1999 Desmond Heaps, Warwickshire County Council Libraries and Heritage
1997 The Awards programme for 1997-8 did not run
1996 Dominic Bean, Southwark Library and Information Service
1995 Annie Everall, Centre for the Child, Birmingham City Library

LA Medal and Award winners

1994	Maggie Goodbarn, Gateshead Libraries and Arts Service
1993	John Stafford, Northamptonshire Libraries and Information Service
1992	Gill Whitehead, Brent Department of Education, Arts and Libraries
1991	Ann-Marie Parker, Hertfordshire Libraries, Arts and Information Service
1990	Max Broome, Library Association President 1987
1989	Peter Grant, City Librarian, Aberdeen
1987	Sue Broughton, Hungerford Branch Library, Berkshire County Libraries
1986	Liz Weir, Belfast Education and Library Board
1985	Joe Hendry, Renfrew District Libraries
1984	Ron Surridge, Library Association President 1984

Reference Award winners

The Library Association Reference Awards comprised the Besterman/McColvin Medals, the Walford Award and the Wheatley Medal.

Besterman/McColvin Medal winners
Electronic category

2001	*The World Shakespeare Bibliography Online* by James L. Harner. The Folger Shakespeare Library www-english.tamu.edu/wsb/
1999/2000	*The British 1881 Census Index on CDROM*. Church of Jesus Christ of the Latter Day Saints

Printed category

2001	*The Encyclopedia of Ephemera* by Maurice Rickards / Michael Twyman (Ed.). The British Library
1999/2000	*The Oxford Companion to Food* by Alan Davidson. OUP

Previously, a Besterman Medal was awarded for bibliography and a McColvin Medal for an outstanding reference work – hence the two lists below.

Besterman Medal winners

1998	*The Victoria and Albert Museum – a Bibliography and Exhibition Chronology 1852-1996* by Elizabeth James. Fitzroy Dearborn
1997	*Handbook for British and Irish Archaeology* by Cherry Lavell. Edinburgh University Press

LA Medal and Award winners

1996 — *The World Shakespeare Bibliography 1990-1993 on CD/ROM* by Professor James L. Harner. Cambridge University Press

1995 — *A Football Compendium: a comprehensive guide to the literature of Association Football* by Peter J. Seddon. The British Library

1994 — *Bibliography of Printed Works on London History to 1939* by Heather Creaton. Library Association Publishing

1993 — *Africa: A Guide to Reference Material* by John McIlwaine. Hans Zell

1992 — Award witheld.

1991 — *A Short-title Catalogue of Books Printed in England, Scotland, Ireland and English Books Printed Abroad 1475-1640... volume 3* by Katherine Pantzer. Oxford University Press/The Bibliographical Society

1990 — *British Architectural Books and Writers 1556-1785* by Eileen Harris and Nicholas Savage. Cambridge University Press

1989 — *Bibliography and Index of English Verse Printed 1476-1558* by William Ringler Jnr. Mansell

1988 — *T E Lawrence: a bibliography* by Philip O'Brien. St Paul's Bibliographies

1987 — *Dickens Dramatized* by Philip H. Bolton. Mansell

1986 — *English Poetry of the Second World War: a bibliography* by Catherine W. Reilly. Mansell

1985 — *Employee Relations Bibliography and Abstracts* by Arthur Marsh. Employee relations bibliography and abstracts

1984 — *A Bibliography of the Kelmscott Press* by William S. Peterson. Clarendon Press

1983 — *London Illustrated, 1604-1851: a survey and index to topographical books and their plates* by Bernard Adams. Library Association Publishing

and *Ted Hughes: a bibliography, 1946-1980* by Keith Sagar and Stephen Tabor. Mansell

1982 — *Walford's Guide to Reference Material* 4th edition. Vol. 2: *Social and Historical Sciences, Philosophy and Religion* edited by A. J. Walford. Library Association Publishing

1981 — *British and Irish Architectural History: a bibliography and guide to sources of information* by Ruth H. Kamen. Architectural Press

1980 — *Alchemy: a bibliography of English-language writings*, by Alan Pritchard. Routledge and Kegan Paul jointly with The Library Association

1979 — *Knowhow: a guide to information, training and campaigning materials for information and advice workers* compiled by G. Morby, edited by E. Kempson. Community Information project and

South Asian Bibliography: a handbook and guide compiled by the South East Asia Library Group, general editor J. D. Pearson. Harvester Press

1978 Award withheld.
1997 *A Bibliography of Cricket* compiled by E. W. Padwick. Library Association Publishing for the Cricket Society
1976 *Guide to Official Statistics, No 1, 1976* by Central Statistical Office. HMSO
1975 *Printed Maps of Victorian London* by Ralph Hyde. Dawson
1974 *Agriculture: a bibliographical guide* by E. A. R. Bush. Macdonald and Jane's
1973 Award withheld.
1972 *A Bibliography of British and Irish Municipal History* Vol. 1: *General Works.* by Dr G. H. Martin and Sylvia McIntyre. Leicester University Press
1971 *Sourcebook of Planning Information: a discussion of sources of information for use in urban and regional planning; and in allied fields* by Brenda White. Bingley
1970 *English Theatrical Literature 1559-1900* by J. F. Arnott and J. W. Robinson. Society for Theatre Research

McColvin Medal winners

1998 *Parrots* by Tony Juniper and Mike Par. Pica Press
1997 *Ancestral Trails* by Mark D. Herber. Sutton Publishing/ Society of Genealogists
1996 *Who's Who 1897-1996 on CD/ROM* by Christine Ruge-Cope and Roger Tritton. A & C Black and Oxford University Press.
1995 *The Tithe Maps of England and Wales* by Roger Kain and Richard Oliver. Cambridge University Press
1994 *Dictionary of British and Irish Botanists and Horticulturists* by Ray Desmond. Taylor and Francis
1993 *History of Canal and River Navigation* edited by Edward Paget-Tomlinson. Sheffield Academic Press
1992 *The New Grove Dictionary of Opera* edited by Stanley Sadie. Macmillan
1991 *The Cambridge Encyclopedia of Ornithology* by Michael Brooke and Tim Birkhead. Cambridge University Press
1990 *William Walton: a catalogue* by Stewart Craggs. 2nd edition. Oxford University Press.

1989	*The Oxford English Dictionary* 2nd edition edited by John Simpson and Edmund Weiner. Oxford University Press
1988	*The Encyclopaedia of Oxford* edited by Christopher Hibbert. Macmillan
1987	*Fermented Foods of the World: a dictionary and guide* by Geoffrey Campbell- Platt. Butterworths
1986	*The British Musical Theatre* by Kurt Ganzl. Vol 1: 1865-1914; Vol 2: 1915-1984. Macmillan
1985	*The Artist's Craft: a history of tools, techniques and material* by James Ayres. Phaidon
1984	*The History of Glass* general editors Dan Klein and Ward Lloyd. Orbis
1983	*Dictionary of British Book Illustrators: the twentieth century* by Brigid Peppin and Lucy Micklewait. Murray
1982	*The Dictionary of Blue and White Printed Pottery, 1780-1880* by A. W. Coysh and R. K. Henrywood. Antique Collectors' Club
1981	*The New Grove Dictionary of Music and Musicians* edited by Stanley Sadie. Macmillan
1980	*Guide to the Local Administrative Units of England*, Volume 1: *Southern England* by Frederic A. Youngs Jr. Royal Historical Society
1979	Award withheld.
1978	Award withheld.
1977	Award withheld.
1976	*A manual of European languages for librarians* by C. G. Allen. Bowker
1975	*Folksongs of Britain and Ireland* by Peter Kennedy. Cassell
1974	*Reviews of United Kingdom Statistical Sources* Volumes 1 to 3. edited by W. F. Maunder, Heinemann Educational Books published for the Royal Statistical Society and the Social Science Research Council
1973	Award withheld.
1972	*Music Yearbook 1972/3* edited by Arthur Jacobs. Macmillan
1971	*Shepherd's glossary of graphic signs and symbols* by Walter Shepherd. Dent
1970	*Councils, Committees and Boards: a handbook of advisory, consultative, executive and similar bodies in British political life.* CBD

Walford Award winners

2001	Professor John McIlwaine
1999/2000	Charles Toase HonFLA

LA Medal and Award winners

1998	George Ottley FLA
1997	Barry Bloomfield MA FLA HonFLA
1996	Professor Ian Rogerson MLS PhD Dlitt FLA
1995	Magda Whitrow BA ALA
1994	Professor S W Wells
1993	Professor D F McKenzie
1992	Professor Robin C Alston OBE MA PhD FSA HonFLA FLA
1991	Professor James Douglas Pearson MA HonFLA

Wheatley Medal winners

2001	Crystal, David and Crystal, Hilary for index to *Words on Words*. Penguin Books
1999	Hird, Barbara for index to *The Cambridge History of Medieval English 2000 Literature*. Cambridge University Press
1998	Sheard, Caroline, for the index to *Textbook of Dermatology*. 6th ed. 4 vols. Blackwell Science
1997	Ross, Jan, for the index to *Rheumatology*. Mosby International
1996	Levitt, Ruth and Northcott, Gillian, for the index to *Dictionary of Art*. Macmillan
1995	Richardson, Ruth and Thorne, Robert, *The Builder Illustrations Index*. Hutton and Rostron
1994	Matthew, Professor H G C, for the index to *The Gladstone Diaries*. Clarenden Press
1993	Merrall Ross, Janine, for the index to *Encyclopedia of Food Science, Food Technology and Nutrition*. Academic Press
1992	Nash, Paul, for the index to *The World Environment 1972-1992*. London, Chapman and Hall (on behalf of the United Nations Environment Programme)
1991	Moys, Elizabeth, for the index to British tax encyclopedia. Sweet and Maxell
1990	Award withheld as no index considered suitable.
1989	Raper, Richard, for the index to *The Works of Charles Darwin*. Pickering and Chatto
1988	Burke, Bobby, for the index to *Halsbury's Laws of England*. 4th edition. Butterworths
1987	Fisk, Neil R., for the index to *A Short History of Wilson's School*. 3rd edition. Wilson's School Charitable Trust
1986	Award withheld as no index considered suitable.
1985	Gibson, John, for the index to *Brain's Diseases of the Nervous System*. 9th edition. Oxford University Press

LA Medal and Award winners

1984   Award withheld as no index considered suitable.

1983   Hewitt, A. R., for the index to *The Laws of Trinidad and Tobago*. Government of Trinidad and Tobago
and Latham, Robert, for the index to *The Diary of Samuel Pepys*. Bell and Hyman

1982   Blayney, Peter W. M., for the index to *The Texts of King Lear and their Origins*. Volume 1: *Nicholas Okes and the First Quarto*. Cambridge University Press

1981   Holmstrom, J. Edwin. *Analytical Index to the Publications of the Institution of Civil Engineers. January 1975-1979*. Institution of Civil Engineers

1980   Taylor, Laurie J., for the index to *The Librarian's Handbook*. Vol. 2. Library Association Publishing

1979   Bakewell, K. G. B., for the index to *Anglo-American Cataloguing Rules*. 2nd edition. Library Association Publishing
and
Surrey, A., for the index to *Circulation of the Blood*. Pitman Medical

1978   Prize withheld as no index considered suitable.

1977   Pavel, T. Rowland, for the index to *Archaeologia Cambrensis 1901-60*. Cambrian Archaeological Association

1976   Vickers, John A., for the index to Vol 11 of *The Works of John Wesley: the appeals to men of reason and religion and certain related open letter*. Oxford, Clarendon Press

1975   Anderson, M. D., for the index to *Copy-editing*. Cambridge University Press.

1974   Banwell, C. C., for the index to *Encyclopaedia of Forms and Precedents*. 4th ed. Butterworths

1973   Boodson, K., for the index to *Non-ferrous Metals*. Macdonald Technical and Scientific
and
Harrod, L. M. *Index to History of King's Works*. Vol. 6. HMSO

1972   Prize withheld as no index considered suitable.

1971   Prize withheld as no index considered suitable.

1970   Mullins, E.L.C., for the index to *A Guide to the Historical and Archaeological Publications of Societies in England and Wales, 1901-1933*. Athlone Press

1969   Thornton, James, for the index to *The Letters of Charles Dickens*. Vol 2. Oxford, Clarendon Press

1968   Blake, Doreen and Bowden, Ruth E. M. for the index to the *Journal of Anatomy, first 100 years, 1866-1966*. Cambridge

LA Medal and Award winners

	University Press
1967	Knight, G. Norman, for the index to *Winston S. Churchill*. Vol. 2. Heinemann
1966	Prize withheld as no index considered suitable.
1965	Quinn, Alison, for the index to *The Principall Navigation Voyages and Discoveries of the English Nation* by R. Hakluyt. Cambridge University Press, for the Hakluyt Society and Peabody Museum of Salem
1964	Parsloe, Guy, the index to *The Warden's Accounts of the Worshipful Company of Founders of the City of London*, 1497–1681. Athlone Press
1963	Dickie, J. M. for the index to *How to Catch Trout*. 3rd ed. W & R Chambers
1962	Maclagan, Michael, for the index to *Clemency Canning*. Macmillan

Robinson Medal winners

1999	Margie Mason for *Battling with books*, a guide for new library staff.
1997	Janet Audain for the design, development and delivery of library services to users with disabilities.
1995	(Award re-launched) Beverley Britton for online submission of off-print database for a reading list database.
1994	Award withheld
1992	Award withheld
1990	JANET Users Group for Libraries for their work in promoting the Joint Academic Network, and plescon limited for the development of the DISCOSAFE and VIDEO TAG electronic security devices.
1988	Award withheld
1986	Prof Nick Moore for the production of guidelines for conducting library and information manpower surveys.
1984	Renfrew district libraries for the inauguration of the Johnstone Information and Leisure Library (JILL).
1982	Award withheld
1980	London Borough of Sutton for innovation in library marketing.
1978	Award withheld
1976	Award withheld
1974	Award withheld
1972	University of Lancaster library research for the development

of simulation games in education for library management.
1970   Mr Frank Gurney, of Automated Library Systems Limited for book-charging.
1968   Mansell Information Publishing Limited, of London, for their development of an automatic abstracting camera for use in producing book catalogues from library cards or other sequential material.

Index

Advertising and *Library and Information Appointments* 8
Advisory team 7
Affiliated Members National Committees 109
Affiliated Members Regulations 101
African Caribbean Library Association (ACLA) 154
Agency Information Group (AIG) 154
Archives 166
Arts Libraries Society of the United Kingdom and Ireland (ARLIS/UK and Ireland) 155
Asian Librarians and Advisors Group (ALAG) 155
Association for the Education and Training of Library Technicians and Assistants 155
Association of British Theological and Philosophical Libraries 155
Association of Land-based Librarians in Colleges and Universities (ALLCU) 156
Auditors 4

Bankers 4
Benevolent Fund 110
Berkshire, Buckinghamshire and Oxfordshire Branch 112
Besterman/McColvin Medal 152
Bliss Classification Association 156
Branch and Mobile Libraries Group (BMLG) 125
Branch Councillors 14
Branches 111ff
Bye-laws 26

Career Development Group (CDG) 126
Carnegie and Kate Greenaway Medals 149, 432
Cataloguing and Indexing Group (CIG) 127
Certificates of Merit 122
Chair of Council 12
Chief Executive's Directorate 6

Children's Book History Society 156
CILIP Benevolent Fund 110
CILIP Carnegie and Kate Greenaway Medals 149
CILIP Consultancy services 8
CILIP Cymru 3, 10, 114
CILIP Enterprises 8
CILIP in Ireland 4, 10, 115
CILIP in Scotland 3, 10, 113
CILIP Jason Farradane Award 150
CILIP Members 171
CILIP offices 3
CILIP representatives on other bodies 161
CILIP Robinson Medal 151
CILIP Royal Charter 18
CILIP Wales/CILIP Cymru 3, 10, 114
CILIP/Emerald Public Relations and Publicity Awards 151
CILIP/Library + information Show Libraries Change Lives Award 150
CILIP/Nielsen BookData Reference Awards 152
Code of Conduct 88
Colleges of Further and Higher Education Group (CoFHE) 128
Committees and Panels 16
Community Care Network 156
Community Services Group (CSG) 129
Conferences 8
Construction Industry Information Group 156
Consumer Health Information Consortium (CHIC) 157
Council 12
Council for Learning Resources in Colleges (CoLRIC) 157

Disciplinary Committee 16
Disciplinary Proceedings 88

East Midlands Branch 116
Eastern Branch 117
Education Librarians Group (ELG) 130
Enterprise Board (EB) 16
Ewart Room 165

Index

Executive Board (EB) 16
External Relations and Marketing 6

Facet Publishing 9
Finance 6
Foreword xi

General regulations 48
Governance 11
Government Libraries Group (GLG) 131
Group Councillors 14

HE Colleges Learning Resources Group 157
Health Libraries Group (HLG) 132
Historic Libraries Forum 157
Historical information 401
History of the Institute of Information Scientists 403
Honorary Fellows 118
Honorary Officers 12
Honorary Secretaries of the Institute of Information Scientists 422
Honorary Treasurer 12

ICT 6
Immediate Past Presidents 12
Independent Library Learner Award 134
Industrial and Commercial Libraries Group (ICLG) 133
INFOmatch 9
Information and Advice 166
Information Centre 166
Information Focus for Allied Health 158
Information for Social Change 158
Information Services Group (ISG) 134
Institutional Members 391
Institute of Information Scientists Award winners 430
International Association of Music Libraries, Archives and Documentation Centres (United Kingdom Branch) (IAML UK) 158
International Library and Information Group (ILIG) 135
International Relations and Information Services 7
Introduction vii

Jason Farradane Award 150, 430

Librarians' Christian Fellowship 157
Libraries Change Lives Award 150, 435
Library and Information Appointments 8
Library and Information Research Group (LIRG) 158
Library and Information Update 9
Library Association 1877–2002 409
Library Association honorary awards 424
Library Association Medal and Award winners 432
Library History Group (LHG) 136
Library Services Trust Awards 142
LINK: a Network for North-South Library Development 159
List of Members as at 18 November 2002 171
Local Studies Group (LSG) 137
London and Home Counties Branch 118

Map Curators Group of the British Cartographic Society 159
Medals and Awards 149ff
Membership List as at 18 November 2002 171
Membership Services Directorate 7
Membership, Careers and Qualifications 7
Mission ix
Multimedia Information and Technology Group (MmIT) 138

National Councillors 12
North West Branch 119
Northern Branch 120

Offices 3
Organisations in Liaison with CILIP 154
Overseas Institutional Members 397

Patent of Trademark Group 139
Personnel and Administration 6
Personnel, Training and Education Group (PTEG) 140
Policy and Advice 7
Policy Development Committee (PolDC) 15
President ii, 12
President-Elect 12

Index

Presidents of the Institute of Information Scientists 418
Presidents of The Library Association 419
Prison Libraries Group (PRLG) 141
Private Libraries Association 159
Professional Development Committee (PDC) 17
Professional Practice Committee (PPC) 17
Professional Qualifications Regulations 70-87
Public Libraries Group (PLG) 142
Public Relations and Publicity Awards 151
Publicity and Public Relations Group (PPRG) 143

Rare Books Group (RBG) 144
Reference Awards 152, 436
Registered Charity Number 4
Regulations 2002 48
Regulations 2002: Code of Conduct of Disciplinary Proceedings 88
Regulations 2002: Retired Members' Guild 96
Regulations for Affiliated Members 101
Regulations for Professional Qualifications 70
Regulations index 48
Regulations, general 49
Retired Members Guild 164
Retired Members' Guild: Regulations 96
Ridgmount Street facilities 165
Robinson Medal for Innovation in Library Administration 151, 442
Royal Charter 18

School Libraries Group (SLG) 145
Secretaries of The Library Association 423
Sexuality in Libraries Group (SILG) 159
Society of Indexers 159
Solicitors 4
South Western Branch 121
Special Interest Groups 124ff
SPRIG 160
Statutory information 4
Structure 6
Subject index for CILIP Charter, Bye-laws and Regulations 105
Subscriptions 168

Suppliers Network 170

Tony Kent Strix Award 153, 431
Trade Union Information Group 160
Training and Development 9

UKOLUG: the UK Online User Group 146
University, College and Research Group (UCRG) 147

VAT Number 4

Walford Award 152, 439
Website 5
West Midland Branch 122
Wheatley Medal 153, 440

Yorkshire and Humberside Branch 123
Youth Libraries Group (YLG) 148